Also by Robert M. Parker, Jr.:

BORDEAUX: THE DEFINITIVE GUIDE
FOR THE WINES PRODUCED SINCE
1961

THE WINES OF THE RHÔNE VALLEY
AND PROVENCE

PARKER'S WINE BUYER'S GUIDE
1987–1988

PARKER'S WINE BUYER'S GUIDE
1989–1990

BURGUNDY: A COMPREHENSIVE GUIDE
TO THE PRODUCERS, APPELLATIONS,
AND WINES

BORDEAUX: A COMPREHENSIVE GUIDE
TO THE WINES PRODUCED FROM
1961–1990

PARKER'S WINE BUYER'S GUIDE
1993–1994

PARKER'S
WINE BUYER'S
GUIDE Fourth Edition

ROBERT M. PARKER, JR.

A Fireside Book
Published by
Simon & Schuster

NEW YORK   LONDON   TORONTO   SYDNEY   TOKYO   SINGAPORE

SIMON & SCHUSTER/FIRESIDE

Rockefeller Center
1230 Avenue of the Americas
New York, NY 10020

Portions of this book were previously published in the
author's bimonthly newsletter, *The Wine Advocate*.

Designed by Levavi & Levavi, Inc.
Maps by Jeanyee Wong
Drawings by Christopher Wormell
Manufactured in the United States of America

1 3 5 7 9 10 8 6 4 2
1 3 5 7 9 10 8 6 4 2 (Pbk)

Library of Congress Cataloging-in-Publication Data
Parker, Robert M.
[Wine buyer's guide]
Parker's wine buyer's guide / Robert M. Parker, Jr. — 4th ed.
p. cm.
"A Fireside book."
Includes index.
1. Wine and wine making. I. Title.
TP548.P287 1995
641.2'2—dc20   95-23983
CIP

ISBN 0-684-80282-1
ISBN 0-684-80283-X (Pbk)

ACKNOWLEDGMENTS

I would like to thank the following for their support and encouragement: Eric Agostini, Hanna Agostini, Jean-Michel Arcaute, Jim Arsenault, Bruce Bassin, Ruth Bassin, Jean-Claude Berrouet, Michel Bettane, Bill Blatch, Jean-Eugene Borie, Monique Borie, Gail Bradney, Christopher Cannan, Dick Carretta, Bob Cline, Annette Corkey, Jean Delmas, Michael Dresser, Stanley Dry, Leslie Ellen, Michael Etzel, Paul Evans, Terry Faughey, Joel Fleischman, Bernard Godec, Dan Green, Philip Guyonnet-Duperat, Josué Harari, Alexandra Harding, Brenda Hayes, Tom Hurst, Barbara G. and Steve R. R. Jacoby, Jean-Paul Jauffret, Nathaniel Johnston, Archie Johnston, Denis Johnston, J. P. Jones, Ed Jonna, Allen Krasner, Dominique Lafon, Bob Lescher, Susan Lescher, Eve Metz, Frank Metz, Jay Miller, François Mitterrand, Gilbert Mitterrand, Kishin Moorjani, Christian Moueix, Jean-François Moueix, Jean-Pierre Moueix, Mitchell Nathanson, Bernard Nicolas, Jill Norman, Les Oenarchs-Bordeaux Chapter, Les Oenarchs-Baltimore Chapter, Daniel Oliveros, Bob Orenstein, Joan Passman, Allen Peacock, Frank Polk, Bruno Prats, Nicholas De Rabaudy, Martha Reddington, Dominique Renard, Dr. Alain Raynaud, Michel Rolland, Dany Rolland, Tom Ryder, Ed Sands, Bob Schindler, Jay Schweitzer, Ernie Singer, Jeff Sokolin, Elliott Staren, Peter Vezan, Jean-Claude Vrinat, Karen Weinstock, Joseph Weinstock, Jeanyee Wong, Robin Zarensky, and Murray Zeligman.

To my Pat, Maia, Mother, and Father

"Sans la liberté de blâmer, il n'est point d'éloge
flatteur."
—Beaumarchais

CONTENTS

INTRODUCTION

HOW TO USE THIS GUIDE

This book is both an educational and a buying manual; it is not an encyclopedic listing of wine producers and growers. It is intended to make you a more formidable, more confident wine buyer by providing you with sufficient insider's information to permit the wisest possible choice when you make a wine-buying decision. The finest producers as well as the best known (not necessarily a guarantee of quality) from the world's greatest viticultural regions are evaluated, as well as many of the current and upcoming releases available in the marketplace. If readers cannot find a specific vintage of a highly regarded wine, they still have at their fingertips a wealth of information and evaluations concerning the best producers for each viticultural area. Readers should be confident in knowing that they will rarely make a mistake (unless, of course, the vintage is absolutely dreadful) with a producer rated "outstanding" or "excellent" in this buying manual. These producers are the finest and most consistent in the world. Taste is obviously subjective, but I have done my best to provide an impartial and comprehensive consumer's guide, whose heart, soul, and value is the evaluations (star ratings) of the world's finest producers.

ORGANIZATION

Each section on a specific viticultural region covered in this manual is generally organized as follows:
1. An overview of the viticultural region
2. A buying strategy for 1995–1996
3. A summary of the quality of recent vintages for the area
4. A quick reference chart to that area's best producers/growers
5. Tasting commentaries, a specific numerical rating for the wine, and a general retail price range for a 750-ml bottle of wine. (See the Wine Price Guide on page 15, which explains the coding system.)

VITICULTURAL AREAS COVERED

This guide covers the world's major viticultural regions. In Western Europe, France and Italy receive the most detailed coverage, followed by Spain, Portugal, and Germany. In North America, California receives significant coverage, reflecting its dominance in the marketplace. The wine regions that are represented most significantly in wine shops are given much more detailed coverage than minor areas whose wines are rarely seen in or exported to the United States. Consequently, the sections dealing with Bordeaux, Burgundy, Champagne, Alsace, and the Rhône Valley in France; Piedmont and Tuscany in Italy; and California receive priority in terms of amount of coverage because those regions produce the world's greatest wines. In each section there is a thorough analysis of the region's producers, its overachievers and underachievers, as well as the region's greatest wine values.

RATING THE PRODUCERS AND GROWERS

Who's who in the world of wine becomes readily apparent after years of tasting the wines and visiting the vineyards and wine cellars of the world's producers and growers. Great producers are, unfortunately, still quite rare, but certainly more growers and producers today are making better wine, with better technology and more knowledge. The charts that follow rate the best producers on a five-star system, awarding five stars and an "outstanding" to those producers deemed to be the very best, four stars to those producers who are "excellent," three stars to "good" producers, and two stars to those producers rated "average." Since the aim of this book is to provide you with the names of the very best producers, its overall content is dominated by the top producers rather than the less successful ones.

Those few growers/producers who have received five-star ratings are those who make the world's finest wines, and have been selected for this rating because of the following two reasons: (1) They make the greatest wine of their particular viticultural region, and (2) they are remarkably consistent and reliable even in mediocre and poor vintages. Ratings, whether they be numerical ratings of individual wines or classifications of growers, are always likely to create controversy among not only the growers but wine tasters themselves. But if done impartially, with a global viewpoint and firsthand, on-the-premises *("sur place")* knowledge of the wines, the producers, and the type and quality of the winemaking, such ratings can be reliable and powerfully informative. The important thing for readers to remember is that those growers/producers who received either a four-star or five-star rating are producers to search out; I suspect few consumers will ever be disappointed with one of their wines. The three-star-rated growers/producers are less consistent but can be expected to make average to above-average wines in the very good to excellent vintages. Their weaknesses can be either from the fact that their vineyards are not as strategically placed, or because for financial or other reasons they are unable to make the severe selections necessary to make only the finest-quality wine.

The rating of the growers/producers of the world's major viticultural regions is perhaps the most important point to this book. Years of wine tasting have taught me many things, but the more one tastes and assimilates the knowledge of the world's regions, the more one begins to isolate the handful of truly world-class growers and producers who seem to rise above the crowd in great as well as mediocre vintages. I always admonish consumers against blind faith in one grower or producer, or in one specific vintage. But the producers and growers rated "outstanding" and "excellent" are as close to a guarantee of high quality as you are likely to find.

VINTAGE SUMMARIES

Although wine advertisements proclaiming "a great vintage" abound, I have never known more than several viticultural areas of the world to have a great vintage in the same year. The chances of a uniformly great vintage are extremely remote, simply because of significantly different microclimates, soils, and so on in every wine-producing region. It is easy to fall into the trap of thinking that because Bordeaux had great vintages in 1982, 1989, and 1990, every place else in Europe did too. Certainly in 1982 nothing could have been further from the truth. Nevertheless, a Bordeaux vintage's reputation unfortunately seems to dictate what the world thinks about many other wine-producing areas. This obviously creates many problems, since in poor Bordeaux vintages the Rhône or Alsace or Champagne could have an excellent vintage, and in great Bordeaux vintages those same areas could have bad years because of poor climate conditions. For California, many casual observers seem to think every year is a top year, and this image is, of course, promoted by that state's publicity-conscious Wine Institute. It may be true that California rarely has a disastrous vintage, but tasting certainly proves that 1988 and 1989 are different in style and more irregular in quality than either 1984, 1985, 1986, or 1987. Yet no other viticultural area in the world has enjoyed as many consecutive great vintages as California has in the nineties; 1990, 1991, 1992, 1993, and 1994 have all been terrific years for California. Wow! In this guide, there are vintage summaries for each viticultural area because the vintages are so very different in both quantity and quality. Never make the mistake of assuming that one particular year is great everywhere or poor everywhere. I know of no year when that has happened.

TASTING NOTES AND RATINGS

When possible, all of my tastings are done in peer-group, single-blind conditions; in other words, the same type of wines are tasted against each other, and the producers' names are not known. The ratings reflect an independent, critical look at the wines. Neither price nor the reputation of the grower/producer affects the rating in any manner. I spend three months of every year tasting in vineyards. During the other nine months of the year, I devote six- and sometimes seven-day workweeks solely to tasting and writing. I do not participate in wine judgings or trade tastings for many reasons, but principal among these are the following: (1) I prefer to taste from an entire bottle of wine, (2) I find it essential to have properly sized and cleaned professional tasting glasses, (3) the temperatures of the wine must be correct, and (4) I prefer to determine the amount of time allocated for the number of wines I will critique.

The numerical rating given is a guide to what I think of the wine vis-à-vis its peer group. Certainly, wines rated above 85 are good to excellent, and any wine rated 90 or above will be outstanding for its particular type. While some would suggest that scoring is not well suited to a beverage that has been romantically extolled for centuries, wine is no different from any consumer product. There are specific standards of quality that full-time wine professionals recognize, and there are benchmark wines against which all others can be judged. I know of no one with three or four different glasses of wine in front of him or her, regardless of how good or bad the wines might be, who cannot say "I prefer this one to that one." Scoring wines is simply taking a professional's opinion and applying a numerical system to it on a consistent basis. Moreover, scoring permits rapid communication of information to expert and novice alike.

The score given for a specific wine reflects the quality of the wine at its best. I often tell people that evaluating a wine and assigning a score to a beverage that will change and evolve in many cases for up to ten or more years is analogous to taking a photograph of a marathon runner. Much can be ascertained, but, like a picture of a moving object, the wine will also evolve and change. I try to retaste wines from obviously badly corked or defective bottles, since a wine from such a single bad bottle does not indicate an entirely spoiled batch. If retasting is not possible, I will reserve judgment on that wine. Many of the wines reviewed have been tasted several times, and the score represents a cumulative average of the wine's performance in tastings to date. Scores do not reveal the most important facts about a wine. The written commentary (tasting notes) that accompanies the ratings is a better source of information regarding the wine's style and personality, its relative quality level vis-à-vis its peers, and its relative value and aging potential than any score could ever indicate.

Here, then, is a general guide to interpreting the numerical ratings:

90–100 is equivalent to an A and is given for an outstanding or a special effort. Wines in this category are the very best produced for their type. There is a big difference between a 90 and a 99, but both are top marks. Few wines actually make it into this top category, simply because there are not that many truly great wines.

80–89 is equivalent to a B in school, and such a wine, particularly in the 85–89 range, is very good. Many of the wines that fall into this range are often great values as well. I have many of these wines in my personal cellar.

70–79 represents a C, or an average mark, but obviously 79 is a much more desirable rating than 70. Wines that receive scores between 75 and 79 are generally pleasant, straightforward wines that lack complexity, character, or depth. If inexpensive, they may be ideal for uncritical quaffing.

Below 70 is a D or an F, depending on where you went to school. It is a sign of an unbalanced, flawed, or terribly dull or diluted wine that is of little interest to the discriminating consumer.

In terms of awarding points, my scoring system gives a wine 50 points to start with. The wine's general color and appearance merit up to 5 points. Since most wines today have been well made thanks to modern technology and the increased use of professional oenologists, most tend to receive at least 4, often 5 points. The aroma and bouquet merit up to 15 points, depending on the intensity level and dimension of the aroma and bouquet, as well as the wine's cleanliness. The flavor and finish merit up to 20 points, and again, intensity of flavor, balance, cleanliness, and depth and length on the palate are all important considerations when giving out points. Finally, the overall quality level or potential for further evolution and improvement—aging—merits up to 10 points.

Scores are important for the reader to gauge a professional critic's overall qualitative placement of a wine vis-à-vis its peers. However, it is also vital to consider the description of the wine's style, personality, and potential. No scoring system is perfect, but a system that provides for flexibility in scores, if applied by the same experienced taster without prejudice, (1) can quantify different levels of wine quality, and (2) can be a responsible, reliable, uncensored, and highly informative account that provides the reader with one professional's judgment. However, there can never be any substitute for your own palate nor any better education than tasting the wine yourself.

QUOTED PRICES

For a number of reasons, no one suggested retail price for a particular wine is valid throughout the country. Take Bordeaux as an example. Bordeaux is often sold as "wine futures" 2 full years before the wine is bottled and shipped to America. This opening or base price can often be the lowest price one will encounter for a Bordeaux wine, particularly if there is a great demand for the wines because the vintage is reputed to be excellent or outstanding. Prices will always vary for Bordeaux, as well as for other imported wines, according to the quality of the vintage, the exchange rate of the dollar against foreign currencies, and the time of purchase by the retailer, wholesaler, or importer. Was the Bordeaux wine purchased at a low futures price in the spring following the vintage, or was the wine purchased when it had peaked in price and was very expensive?

Another consideration in pricing is that, in many states, wine retailers can directly import the wines they sell and can thereby bypass middlemen, such as wholesalers, who usually tack on a 25% markup of their own. The bottom line in all of this is that in any given vintage for Bordeaux, or for any imported wine, there is no standard suggested retail price. Prices can differ by as much as 50% for the same wine in the same city. However, in cities where there is tremendous competition among wine shops, the markup for wines can be as low as 10% or even 5%; this is significantly less than the normal 50%–55% markup. In cities where there is little competition, the prices charged are often full retail price. I always recommend that consumers pay close attention to the wine shop advertisements in major newspapers and wine publications. For example, *The New York Times*'s Living Section and *The Wine Spectator* are filled with wine advertisements that are a barometer for the market price of a given wine. Readers should remember, however, that prices differ considerably, not only within the same state, but also within the same city. The approximate price range that is used reflects the suggested retail price that includes a 40%–60% markup by the retailer in most major metropolitan areas. Therefore, in many states in the Midwest and in other less populated areas where there is little competition among wine merchants, the price may be higher. In major competitive marketplaces where there are frequent discount wars, such as Washington, D.C., New York, San Francisco, Boston, Los Angeles, Chicago, and Dallas, prices are often lower. The key for you as the reader and consumer is to follow the advertisements in a major newspaper and to shop around. Most major wine retailers feature sales in the fall and spring; summer is the slow season and generally the most expensive time to buy wine.

Following is the price guide I have used throughout the book.

WINE PRICE GUIDE

CODE
A: Inexpensive/less than $10
B: Moderate/between $10 and $15
C: Expensive/between $15 and $25
D: Very expensive/between $25 and $50
E: Luxury/between $50 and $75
EE: Super luxury/between $75 and $125
EEE: Over $125

THE ROLE OF A WINE CRITIC

"A man must serve his time to every trade save censure—critics all are ready made." Thus wrote Lord Byron.

It has been said often enough that anyone with a pen, notebook, and a few bottles of wine can become a wine critic. And that is exactly the way I started when, in late summer 1978, I sent out a complimentary issue of what was then called the *Baltimore/Washington Wine Advocate*.

There were two principal forces that shaped my view of a wine critic's responsibilities. I was then, and remain today, significantly influenced by the independent philosophy of consumer advocate Ralph Nader. Moreover, I was marked by the indelible impression left by my law school professors, who pounded into their students' heads in the post-Watergate era a broad definition of conflict of interest. These two forces have governed the purpose and soul of my newsletter, *The Wine Advocate*, and my books.

In short, the role of the critic is to render judgments that are reliable. They should be based on extensive experience and on a trained sensibility for whatever is being reviewed. In practical terms, this means the critic should be blessed with the following attributes:

Independence   It is imperative for a wine critic to pay his own way. Gratuitous hospitality in the form of airline tickets, hotel rooms, guest houses, etc., should never be accepted either abroad or in this country. And what about wine samples? I purchase over 75% of the wines I taste, and while I have never requested samples, I do not feel it is unethical to accept unsolicited samples that are shipped to my office. Many wine writers claim that these favors do not influence their opinions. Yet how many people in any profession are prepared to bite the hand that feeds them? Irrefutably, the target audience is the wine consumer, not the wine trade. While it is important to maintain a professional relationship with the trade, I believe the independent stance required of a consumer advocate often, not surprisingly, results in an adversarial relationship with the wine trade. It can be no other way. In order to effectively pursue this independence, it is imperative to keep one's distance from the trade. While this can be misinterpreted as aloofness, such independence guarantees hard-hitting, candid, and uninfluenced commentary.

Courage   Courage manifests itself in what I call the "democratic tasting." Judgments ought to be made solely on the basis of the product in the bottle, and not the pedigree, the price, the rarity, or one's like or dislike of the producer. The wine critic who is totally candid may be considered dangerous by the trade, but an uncensored, independent point of view is of paramount importance to the consumer. A judgment of wine quality must be based on what is in the bottle. This is wine criticism at its purest, most meaningful. In a tasting, a $10 bottle of petit château Pauillac should have as much of a chance as a $75 bottle of Lafite-Rothschild or Latour. Overachievers should be spotted, praised, and their names highlighted and shared with the consuming public. Underachievers should be singled out for criticism and called to account for their mediocrities. Few friends from the wine commerce are likely to be earned for such outspoken and irreverent commentary, but wine buyers are entitled to such information. When a critic bases his or her judgment on what others think, or on the wine's pedigree, price, or perceived potential, then wine criticism is nothing more than a sham.

Experience   It is essential to taste extensively across the field of play to identify the benchmark reference points and to learn winemaking standards throughout the world. This is the most time-consuming and expensive aspect of wine criticism, as well as the most fulfilling for the critic; yet it is rarely followed. Lamentably, what so often transpires is that a tasting of ten or twelve wines from a specific region or vintage will be held. The writer will then issue a definitive judgment on the vintage based on a microscopic proportion of the wines. This is as irresponsible as it is appalling. It is essential for a wine critic to taste as comprehensibly as is physically possible. This means tasting every significant wine produced in a region or vintage before reaching qualitative conclusions. Wine criticism, if it is ever to be regarded as a serious profession, must be a full-time endeavor, not the habitat of part-timers dabbling in a field that is so complex and requires such time commitment. Wine and vintages, like everything in life, cannot be reduced to black and white answers.

It is also essential to establish memory reference points for the world's greatest wines. There is such a diversity of wine and multitude of styles that this may seem impossible. But tasting as many wines as one possibly can in each vintage, and from all of the classic wine regions, helps one memorize benchmark characteristics that form the basis for making comparative judgments between vintages, wine producers, and wine regions.

Individual Accountability   While I have never found anyone's wine-tasting notes compelling reading, notes issued by consensus of a committee are the most insipid, and often the most misleading. Judgments by committees tend to sum up a group's personal preferences. But how do they take into consideration the possibility that each individual may have reached his or her decision using totally different criteria? Did one judge adore the wine because of its typicity while another decried it for such, or was the wine's individuality given greater merit? It is impossible to know. That is never in doubt when an individual authors a tasting critique.

Committees rarely recognize wines of great individuality. A look at the results of tasting competitions sadly reveals that well-made mediocrities garner the top prizes. The misleading consequence is that blandness is elevated to the status of being a virtue. Wines with great individuality and character will never win a committee tasting because at least one taster will find something objectionable about the wine.

I have always sensed that individual tasters, because they are unable to hide behind the collective voice of a committee, hold themselves to a greater degree of accountability. The opinion of a reasonably informed and comprehensive individual taster, despite the taster's prejudices and predilections, is always a far greater guide to the ultimate quality of the wine than the consensus of a committee. At least the reader knows where the individual stands, whereas with a committee, one is never quite sure.

Emphasis on Pleasure and Value Too much wine writing focuses on glamour French wine regions such as Burgundy, Bordeaux, and on California Cabernet Sauvignon and Chardonnay. These are important, and they make up the backbone of most serious wine enthusiasts' cellars. But value and diversity in wine types must always be stressed. The unhealthy legacy of the English wine-writing establishment that a wine has to taste bad young to be great old should be thrown out. Wines that taste great young, such as Chenin Blanc, Dolcetto, Beaujolais, Côtes du Rhône, Merlot, and Zinfandel, are no less serious or compelling because they must be drunk within a few years rather than be cellared for a decade or more before consumption. Wine is, in the final analysis, a beverage of pleasure, and intelligent wine criticism should be a blend of both hedonistic and analytical schools of thought—to the exclusion of neither.

The Focus on Qualitative Issues It is an inescapable fact that too many of the world's renowned growers/producers have intentionally permitted production levels to soar to such extraordinary heights that many wines' personalities, concentration, and character are in jeopardy. While there remain a handful of fanatics who continue, at some financial sacrifice, to reject significant proportions of their harvest to ensure that only the finest-quality wine is sold under their name, they are dwindling in number. For much of the last decade production yields throughout the world have broken records, almost with each new vintage. The results are wines that increasingly lack character, concentration, and staying power. The argument that more carefully and competently managed vineyards result in larger crops is nonsense.

In addition to high yields, advances in technology have provided the savoir faire to produce more correct wines, but the abuse of practices such as acidification and excessive fining and filtration have compromised the final product. These problems are rarely and inadequately addressed by the wine-writing community. Wine prices have never been higher, but is the consumer always getting a better wine? The wine writer has the responsibility to give broad qualitative issues high priority.

Candor No one argues with the incontestable fact that tasting is a subjective endeavor. The measure of an effective wine critic should be his or her timely and useful rendering of an intelligent laundry list of good examples of different styles of winemaking in various price categories. Articulating in an understandable fashion why the critic finds the wines enthralling or objectionable is manifestly important both to the reader and to the producer. The critic must always seek to educate, to provide meaningful guidelines, never failing to emphasize that there can never be any substitute for the consumer's palate, nor any better education than the reader's own tasting of the wine. The critic has the advantage of having access to the world's wine production and must try to minimize bias. Yet the critic should always share with the reader his or her reasoning for bad reviews. For example, I will never be able to overcome my dislike for vegetal-tasting new world Cabernets, overtly herbaceous red Loire Valley wines, or excessively acidified new world whites.

My ultimate goal in writing about wines is to seek out the world's greatest wines and greatest wine values. But in the process of ferreting out those wines, I feel the critic should never shy away from criticizing those producers whose wines are found lacking. Given the fact that the consumer is the true taster of record, the "taste no evil" approach to wine writing serves no one but the wine trade. Constructive and competent criticism has proven that it can benefit producers as well as consumers, since it forces underachievers to improve the quality of their fare, and by lauding overachievers, it encourages them to maintain high standards to the benefit of all who enjoy and appreciate good wine.

About Wine

HOW TO BUY WINE

On the surface, having made your choices in advance, buying wine seems simple enough— you go to your favorite wine merchant and purchase a few bottles. However, there are some subtleties to buying wine that one must be aware of in order to ensure that the wine is in healthy condition and is unspoiled.

To begin with, take a look at the bottle of wine you are about to buy. Wine abuse is revealed by the condition of the bottle in your hand. First of all, if the cork has popped above the rim of the bottle and is pushed out on the lead or plastic capsule that covers the top of the bottle, then look for another bottle to buy. Wines that have been exposed to very high temperatures expand in the bottle, thereby putting pressure on the cork and pushing it upward against the capsule. And it is the highest-quality wines, those that have not been overly filtered or pasteurized, that are the most vulnerable to the ill effects of abusive transportation or storage. A wine that has been frozen in transit or storage will likewise push the cork out, and while the freezing of a wine is less damaging than the heating of it, both are hazardous to its health. Any cork that is protruding above the rim of the bottle is a bad sign, and the bottle should be returned to the shelf and never, ever purchased.

Finally, there is a sign indicating poor storage conditions that can generally be determined only after the wine has been decanted, though sometimes it can be spotted in the neck of the bottle. Wines that have been exposed to very high temperatures, particularly deep, rich, intense, red wines, will often form a heavy coat or film of coloring material on the inside of the glass. With a Bordeaux that is less than 3 years old, a coating such as this generally indicates that the wine has been subjected to very high temperatures and has undoubtedly been damaged. However, one must be careful here, because this type of sediment does not always indicate a poor bottle of wine; vintage port regularly throws it as do the huge, rich Rhône and Piedmontese wines.

On the other hand, there are two conditions consumers frequently think are signs of a flawed wine when nothing could be further from the truth. Many consumers return bottles of wine for the very worst reason—because of a small deposit of sediment in the bottom of the bottle. Ironically, this is actually the healthiest sign one could find in most bottles of wine. However, keep in mind that white wines rarely throw a deposit, and it is rare to see a deposit in young wines under 2 to 3 years of age. However, the tiny particles of sandlike sediment that precipitate to the bottom of a bottle simply indicate that the wine has been naturally made and has not been subjected to a flavor- and character-eviscerating traumatic filtration. Such wine is truly alive and is usually full of all its natural flavors.

Another reason why wine consumers erroneously return bottles to retailers is because of the presence of small crystals called tartrate precipitates. These crystals are found in all types of wines but appear most commonly in white wines from Germany and Alsace. They often shine and resemble little slivers of cut glass, but in fact they are simply indicative of a wine that somewhere along its journey was exposed to temperatures below 40 degrees F in shipment, and the cold has caused some tartaric crystals to precipitate. These are harmless, tasteless, and totally natural in many bottles of wine. They have no effect on the quality and they normally signify that the wine has not been subjected to an abusive, sometimes damaging, cold stabilization treatment by the winery for cosmetic purposes only.

Fortunately, most of the better wine merchants, wholesalers, and importers are more cognizant today of the damage that can be done by shipping wine in unrefrigerated containers, especially in the middle of summer. However, far too many wines are still tragically damaged by poor transportation and storage, and it is the consumer who suffers. A general rule is that heat is much more damaging to fine wines than cold. Remember, there are still plenty of wine merchants, wholesalers, and importers who treat wine no differently than they treat beer or liquor, and the wine buyer must therefore be armed with a bit of knowledge before he or she buys a bottle of wine.

HOW TO STORE WINE

Wine has to be stored properly if it is to be served in a healthy condition. All wine enthusiasts know that subterranean wine cellars that are vibration-free, dark, damp, and kept at a constant 55 degrees F are considered perfect for wine. However, few of us have our own castles and such perfect accommodations for our beloved wines. While such conditions are ideal, most wines will thrive and develop well under other circumstances. I have tasted many old Bordeaux wines from closets and basements that have reached 65–70 degrees F in summer, and the wines have been perfect. In cellaring wine keep the following rules in mind and you will not be disappointed with a wine that has gone over the hill prematurely.

First of all, in order to safely cellar wines for 10 years or more keep them at 65 degrees F, perhaps 68, but no higher. If the temperature rises to 70 degrees F, be prepared to drink your red wines within 10 years. Under no circumstances should you store and cellar white wines more than 1 to 2 years at temperatures above 70 degrees F. Wines kept at temperatures above 65 degrees F will age faster, but unless the temperature exceeds 70 degrees F, will not age badly. If you can somehow get the temperature down to 65 degrees F or below, you will never have to worry about the condition of your wines. At 55 degrees F, the ideal temperature according to the textbooks, the wines actually evolve so slowly that your grandchildren are likely to benefit from the wines more than you. Constancy in temperature is most essential, and any changes in temperature should occur slowly. White wines are much more fragile and much more sensitive to temperature changes and higher temperatures than red wines. Therefore, if you do not have ideal storage conditions, buy only enough white wine to drink over a 1- to 2-year period.

Second, be sure that your storage area is odor-free, vibration-free, and dark. A humidity level above 50% is essential; 70%–75% is ideal. The problem with a humidity level over 75% is that the labels become moldy and deteriorate. A humidity level below 40% will keep the labels in great shape, but will cause the corks to become very dry, possibly shortening the potential life expectancy of your wine. Low humidity is believed to be nearly as great a threat to a wine's health as high temperature. There has been no research to prove this, and limited studies I have done are far from conclusive.

Third, always bear in mind that wines from vintages that have produced powerful, rich, concentrated, full-bodied wines travel and age significantly better than wines from vintages that have produced lighter-weight wines. It is often traumatic for a fragile, lighter-styled wine from either Europe or California to be transported transatlantic or cross country, whereas the richer, more intense, bigger wines from the better vintages seem much less travel-worn after their journey.

Fourth, in buying and storing wine I always recommend buying a wine as soon as it appears on the market, assuming of course that you have tasted the wine and like it. The reason for this is that there are still too many American wine merchants, importers, wholesalers, and distributors who are indifferent to the way wine is stored. This attitude still persists, though things have improved dramatically over the last decade. The important thing for you as a consumer to remember, after inspecting the bottle to make sure it appears healthy, is to stock up on wines as quickly as they come on the market and to approach older vintages with a great deal of caution and hesitation unless you have absolute faith in the merchant from whom you bought the wine. Furthermore, you should be confident your merchant will stand behind the wine in the event it is flawed from poor storage.

THE QUESTION OF HOW MUCH AGING

The majority of wines made in the world taste best when they are just released or consumed within 1 to 2 years of the vintage. Many wines are drinkable at 5, 10, or even 15 years of age, but based on my experience only a small percentage are more interesting and more enjoyable after extended cellaring than they were when originally released.

It is important to have a working definition of what the aging of wine actually means. I define the process as nothing more than the ability of a wine, over time, (1) to develop more pleasurable nuances, (2) to expand and soften in texture, and in the case of red wines, to exhibit an additional melting away of tannins, and (3) to reveal a more compelling aromatic and flavor profile. In short, the wine must deliver additional complexity, increased pleasure, and more interest as an older wine than it did when released. Only such a performance can justify the purchase of a wine in its youth for the purpose of cellaring it for future drinking. Unfortunately, just a tiny percentage of the world's wines fall within this definition of aging.

It is fundamentally false to believe that a wine cannot be serious or profound if it is drunk young. In France, the finest Bordeaux, the northern Rhône Valley wines (particularly Hermitage and Côte Rôtie), a few red burgundies, some Châteauneuf du Papes, and, surprisingly, many of the sweet white Alsace wines and sweet Loire Valley wines do indeed age well and are frequently much more enjoyable and complex when drunk 5, 10, or even 15 years after the vintage. But virtually all other French wines, from Champagne to Côtes du Rhône, from Beaujolais to the petits châteaux of Bordeaux, to even the vast majority of red and white burgundies, are better in their youth.

The French have long adhered to the wine-drinking strategy that younger is better. Centuries of wine consumption, not to mention gastronomic indulgences, have taught the French something that Americans and Englishmen have failed to grasp: Most wines are more pleasurable and friendly when young than old.

The French know that the aging and cellaring of wines, even those of high pedigree, are often fraught with more disappointments than successes. Nowhere is this more in evidence than in French restaurants, especially in Bordeaux, the region that boasts what the world considers the longest-lived dry red wines. A top vintage of Bordeaux can last for 20 to 30 years, sometimes 40 or more, but look at the wine lists of Bordeaux's best restaurants. The great 1982s have long disappeared down the throats of French men and women. Even the tannic, young, yet potentially very promising 1986s, which Americans have squirreled away for drinking in the next century, are now hard to find. Why? Because they have already been consumed. Many of the deluxe restaurants, particularly in Paris, have wine lists of historic vintages, but these are largely for rich tourists.

This phenomenon is not limited to France. Similar drinking habits prevail in the restaurants of Florence, Rome, Madrid, and Barcelona. Italians and Spaniards also enjoy their wines young. This is not to suggest that Italy does not make some wines that improve in the bottle. In Tuscany, for example, a handful of Chiantis and some of the finest new-breed Tuscan red wines (e.g., the famed Cabernet Sauvignon called Sassicaia) will handsomely repay extended cellaring, but most never get the opportunity. In the Piedmont section of northern Italy, no one will deny that a fine Barbaresco or Barolo improves after a decade in the bottle. But by and large, all of Italy's other wines are meant to be drunk young, a fact that Italians have long known and that you should observe as well.

With respect to Spain, there is little difference, although a Spaniard's tastes differ considerably from the average Italian's or Frenchman's. In Spain, the intense aroma of smoky vanillin new oak is prized. As a result, the top Spanish wine producers from the most renowned wine region, Rioja, and other viticultural regions as well tend to age their wines in oak barrels so that they can develop this particular aroma. Additionally, unlike French and Italian wine producers, or even their new world counterparts, Spanish wineries are reluctant to release their wines until they are fully mature. As a result, most Spanish wines are smooth and mellow when they arrive on the market. While they may keep for 5 to 10 years, they generally do not improve. This is especially true with Spain's most expensive wines, the Reservas and Gran Reservas from Rioja, which are usually not released until 5 to 8 years after the vintage. The one exception may be the wine long considered Spain's greatest red, the Vega Sicilia Unico. This powerful wine, frequently released when it is already 10 or 20 years old (the immortal 1970 was released in 1995), does appear capable of lasting for 20–35 years after its release. Yet I wonder how much it improves.

All of this impacts on the following notion: Unlike any other wine consumers in the world, most American wine enthusiasts, as well as many English consumers, fret over the perfect moment to drink a wine. There is none. Most modern-day vintages, even age-worthy Bordeaux or Rhône Valley wines, can be drunk when released. Some of them will improve, but many will not. If you enjoy drinking a 1989 Bordeaux now, then who could be so foolish as to suggest that you are making an error because the wine will be appreciably better in 5 to 10 years?

In America and Australia, winemaking is much more dominated by technology. While a handful of producers still adhere to the artisanal, traditional way of making wine as done in Europe, most treat the vineyard as a factory and the winemaking as a manufacturing process. As a result, such techniques as excessive acidification, brutally traumatic centrifugation, and eviscerating sterile filtration are routinely utilized to produce squeaky clean, simplistic, sediment-free, spit-polished, totally stable yet innocuous wines with statistical profiles that fit neatly within strict technical parameters. Yet it is these same techniques that denude wines of their flavors, aromas, and pleasure-giving qualities. Moreover, they reveal a profound lack of respect for the vineyard, the varietal, the vintage, and the wine consumer, who, after all, is seeking pleasure, not blandness.

In both Australia and California, the alarming tendency of most Sauvignon Blancs and Chardonnays to collapse in the bottle and to drop their fruit within 2 to 3 years of the vintage has been well documented. Yet some of California's and Australia's most vocal advocates continue to advise wine consumers to cellar and invest (a deplorable word when it comes to wine) in Chardonnays and Sauvignon Blancs. It is a stupid policy. If the aging of wine is indeed the ability of a wine to become more interesting and pleasurable with time, then the rule of thumb to be applied to American and Australian Sauvignon Blancs and Chardonnays is that they must be drunk within 12 months of their release unless the consumer has an eccentric fetish for fruitless wines with blistering acidity and scorchingly noticeable alcohol levels. Examples of producers whose Chardonnays and Sauvignon Blancs can last for 5 to 10 years and improve during that period can be found, but they are distressingly few.

With respect to red wines, a slightly different picture emerges. Take, for example, the increasingly fashionable wines made from the Pinot Noir grape. No one doubts the immense progress made in both California and Oregon in turning out fragrant, supple Pinot Noirs that are delicious upon release. But I do not know of any American producer who is making Pinot Noir that can actually improve beyond 10 to 12 years in the bottle. Under no circumstances is this a criticism.

Even in Burgundy there are probably no more than a dozen producers who make their wines in such a manner that they improve and last for more than a decade. Many of these wines can withstand the test of time in the sense of being survivors, but they are far less interesting and pleasurable at age 10 than when they were 2 or 3 years old. Of course the producers and retailers who specialize in these wines will argue otherwise, but they are in the business of selling. Do not be bamboozled by the public relations arm of the wine industry or the fallacious notion that red wines all improve with age. If you enjoy them young, and most likely you will, then buy only the quantities needed for near-term consumption.

America's most famous dry red wine, however, is not Pinot Noir but Cabernet Sauvignon, particularly that grown in California and to a lesser extent in Washington State. The idea that most California Cabernet Sauvignons improve in the bottle is a myth. Nonetheless, the belief that all California Cabernet Sauvignons are incapable of lasting in the bottle is equally unfounded. Today no one would be foolish enough to argue that the best California Cabernets cannot tolerate 15 or 20, even 25 or 30 years of cellaring.

I frequently have the opportunity to taste 20- to 30-year-old California Cabernet Sauvignons, and they are delicious. But have they significantly improved because of the aging process? A few of them have, though most still tend to be relatively grapy, somewhat monolithic, earthy, and tannic at age 20. Has the consumer's patience in cellaring these wines for all those years justified both the expense and the wait? Lamentably, the answer will usually be no. Most of these wines are no more complex or mellow than they were when young.

Because these wines will not crack up and fall apart, there is little risk associated with stashing the best of them away, but I am afraid the consumer who patiently waits for the proverbial "miracle in the bottle" will find that wine cellaring can all too frequently be an expensive exercise in futility.

If you think it over, the most important issue is why so many of today's wines exhibit scant improvement in the aging process. While most have always been meant to be drunk when young, I am convinced that much of the current winemaking philosophy has led to numerous compromises in the winemaking process. The advent of micropore sterile filters, so much in evidence at every modern winery, may admirably stabilize a wine, but, regrettably, these filters also destroy the potential of a wine to develop a complex aromatic profile. When they are utilized by wine producers who routinely fertilize their vineyards excessively, thus overcropping, the results are wines that reveal an appalling lack of bouquet and flavor.

The prevailing winemaking obsession is to stabilize wine so it can be shipped to the far corners of the world 12 months a year, stand upright in overheated stores indefinitely, and never change or spoil if exposed to extremes of heat and cold, or unfriendly storage conditions. For all intents and purposes, the wine is no longer alive. This is fine, even essential, for inexpensive jug wines, but for the fine-wine market, where consumers are asked to pay $20 or more for a bottle of wine, it is a winemaking tragedy. These stabilization and production techniques thus impact on the aging of wine because they preclude the development of the wine's ability to evolve and to become a more complex, tasty, profound, and enjoyable beverage.

HOW TO SERVE WINE

There are really no secrets for proper wine service—all one needs is a good corkscrew, clean, odor-free glasses, a sense of order as to how wines should be served, and whether a wine needs to be aired or allowed to breathe. The major mistakes that most Americans, as well as most restaurants, make are (1) fine white wines are served entirely too cold, (2) fine red wines are served entirely too warm, and (3) too little attention is given to the glass into which the wine is poured. (It might contain a soapy residue or stale aromas picked up in a closed china closet or cardboard box.) All of these things can do much more to damage the impact of a fine wine and its subtle aromas than you might imagine. Most people tend to think that the wine must be opened and allowed to "breathe" well in advance of serving. Some even think a wine must be decanted, a rather elaborate procedure, but only essential if sediment is present in the bottle and the wine to be poured carefully off. With respect to breathing or airing wine, I am not sure anyone has all the answers. Certainly, no white wine requires any advance opening and pouring. With red wines, 15–30 minutes of being opened and poured into a clean, odor- and soap-free wine decanter is really all that is necessary. There are of course examples that can always be cited where the wine improves for 7 to 8 hours, but these are quite rare.

Although these topics seem to dominate much of the discussion in wine circles, a much more critical aspect for me is the appropriate temperature of the wine and of the glass in which it is to be served. The temperature of red wines is very important, and in America's generously heated dining rooms, temperatures are often 75–80 degrees F, higher than is good for fine red wine. A red wine served at such a temperature will taste flat and flabby, with its bouquet diffuse and unfocused. The alcohol content will also seem higher than it should be. The ideal temperature for most red wines is 62–67 degrees F; light red wine such as Beaujolais should be chilled to 55 degrees F. For white wines, 55–60 degrees F is perfect, since most will show all their complexity and intensity at this temperature, whereas if they are chilled to below 45 degrees F, it will be difficult to tell, for instance, whether the wine is a Riesling or a Chardonnay.

In addition, there is the all-important issue of the glasses in which the wine is to be served. An all-purpose, tulip-shaped glass of 8 to 12 ounces is a good start for just about any type of wine, but think the subject over carefully. If you go to the trouble and expense of finding and storing wine properly, shouldn't you treat the wine to a good glass? The finest glasses for both technical and hedonistic purposes are those made by the Riedel Company of Austria. I have to admit that I was at first skeptical about these glasses. George Riedel, the head of his family's crystal business, claims to have created these glasses specifically to guide (by specially designed rims) the wine to a designated section of the palate. These rims, combined with the general shape of the glass, emphasize and promote the different flavors and aromas of a given varietal.

Over the last six months, I have tasted an assortment of wines in his glasses, including a Riesling glass, Chardonnay glass, Pinot Noir glass, and Cabernet Sauvignon glass, all part of his Sommelier Series. For comparative purposes, I then tasted the same wines in the Impitoyables glass, the INAO tasting glass, and the conventional tulip-shaped glass. The results were consistently in favor of the Riedel glasses. American Pinot Noirs and red burgundies performed far better in his huge 37-ounce, 9½-inch-high Burgundy goblet (model number 400/16) than in the other stemware. Nor could any of the other glassware compete when I was drinking Cabernet and Merlot-based wines from his Bordeaux goblet (model number 400/00), a 32-ounce, 10½-inch-high, magnificently shaped glass. His Chardonnay glass was a less convincing performer, but I was astounded by how well the Riesling glass (model number 400/1), an 8-ounce glass that is 7¾ inches high, seemed to highlight the personality characteristics of Riesling.

George Riedel realizes that wine enthusiasts go to great lengths to buy wine in sound condition, to store it properly, and to serve it at the correct temperature. But how many connoisseurs invest enough time exploring the perfect glasses for their Pichon-Lalande, Méo-Camuzet, Clos Vougeot, or Maximin-Grunhaus Riesling Kabinett? His mission, he says, is to provide the "finest tools," enabling the taster to capture the full potential of a particular varietal. His glasses have convincingly proven his case time and time again in my tastings. I know of no finer tasting or drinking glasses than the Sommelier Series glasses from Riedel.

I have always found it amazing that most of my wine-loving friends tend to ignore the fact that top stemware is just as important as making the right choice in wine. When using the Riedel glasses, one must keep in mind that every one of these glasses has been engineered to enhance the best characteristic of a particular grape varietal. Riedel believes that regardless of the size of the glass, they work best when they are filled to no more than one-quarter of their capacity. If I were going to buy these glasses (the Sommelier Series tends to run $40–$70 a glass), I would unhesitatingly purchase both the Bordeaux and Burgundy glasses. They outperformed every other glass by a wide margin. The magnificent 37-ounce Burgundy glass, with a slightly flared lip, directs the flow of a burgundy to the tip and the center of the tongue, thus avoiding contact with the sides of the tongue, which deemphasizes the acidity, making the burgundy taste rounder and more supple. This is not just trade puffery on Riedel's part. I have done it enough times to realize these glasses do indeed control the flow, and by doing so, enhance the character of the wine. The large 32-ounce Bordeaux glass, which is nearly the same size at the Burgundy glass, is more conical, and the lip serves to direct the wine toward the tip of the tongue, where the taste sensors are more acutely aware of sweetness. This enhances the rich fruit in a Cabernet/Merlot-based wine before the wine spreads out to the sides and back of the palate, which picks up the more acidic, tannic elements.

All of this may sound absurdly highbrow or esoteric, but the effect of these glasses on fine wine is profound. I cannot emphasize enough what a difference they make.

If the Sommelier Series sounds too expensive, Riedel does make less expensive lines that are machine-made rather than hand-blown. The most popular are the Vinum glasses, which sell for about $20 per glass. The Bordeaux Vinum glass is a personal favorite as well as a spectacular glass for not only Bordeaux, but for Rhône wines and white burgundies. There are also numerous other glasses designed for Nebbiolo-based wines, rosé wines, old white wines, and port wines, as well as a specially designed glass for sweet Sauternes-type wines.

For more complete information about prices and models, readers can get in touch with Riedel Crystal of America, P.O. Box 446, 24 Aero Road, Bohemia, NY 11716; telephone number (516) 567–7575. For residents of or visitors to New York City, Riedel has a showroom at 41 Madison Avenue (at Twenty-sixth Street).

Two other good sources for fine wineglasses include St. George Crystal in Jeannette, PA, at (412) 523-6501, and the all-purpose Cristal d'Arques Oenologist glass. I have found the latter glass to work exceptionally well with white wines such as Sauvignon, Chardonnay, Riesling, and Marsanne, and red wines such as Cabernet Sauvignon, Merlot, Malbec, Syrah, Zinfandel, Gamay, Mourvèdre, and Sangiovese. For very fragrant red wines such as those produced from Pinot Noir, Nebbiolo, and Grenache, this glass is acceptable, but I prefer other stemware. Designed by Dany Rolland, the gifted oenologist/wife/partner of Libourne's Michel Rolland, the dimensions are: height 8 inches (4½ inches of that is the stem); circumference 10 inches at the base of the tulip-shaped bowl, narrowing to 8 inches at the rim; capacity 12 ounces, or a half bottle of wine. The cost is $10–$12, depending on the quantity purchased. For more information, readers should contact either Grand Cru Imports, Souderton, PA, at (215) 723–2033, or Portside, Inc., Alexandria, VA, at (703) 683–6220.

And last but not least, remember: No matter how clean the glass appears to be, be sure to rinse the glass or decanter with unchlorinated well or mineral water just before it is used. A decanter or wine glass left sitting for any time is a wonderful trap for room and kitchen odors that are undetectable until the wine is poured and they yield their off-putting smells. That, and soapy residues left in the glasses, has ruined more wines than any defective cork or, I suspect, poor storage from an importer, wholesaler, or retailer. I myself put considerable stress on one friendship simply because I continued to complain at every dinner party about the soapy glasses that interfered with the enjoyment of the wonderful Bordeaux wines being served.

FOOD AND WINE MATCHUPS

The art of serving the right bottle of wine with a specific course or type of food has become one of the most overly legislated areas, all to the detriment of the enjoyment of both wine and food. Newspaper and magazine columns, even books, are filled with precise rules that seemingly make it a sin to be guilty of not having chosen the perfect wine to accompany the meal. The results have been predictable. Instead of enjoying a dining experience, most hosts and hostesses fret, usually needlessly, over their choice of which wine to serve with the meal.

The basic rules of the wine/food matchup game are not difficult to master. These are the tried-and-true, allegedly cardinal principles such as young wines before old wines, dry wines before sweet wines, white wines before red wines, red wines with meat and white wines with fish. However, these general principles are filled with exceptions, and your choices are a great deal broader than you have been led to expect. One of France's greatest restaurant proprietors once told me that if people would simply pick their favorite wines to go along with their favorite dishes, they would be a great deal happier. Furthermore, he would be pleased not to have to witness so much nervous anxiety and apprehension on their faces. I'm not sure I can go that far, but given my gut feeling that there are more combinations of wine and food that work reasonably well than there are those that do not, let me share some of my basic observations about this whole field. There are several important questions you should consider:

Does the food offer simple or complex flavors? America's, and I suppose the wine world's, two favorite grapes, Chardonnay and Cabernet Sauvignon, can produce majestic wines of exceptional complexity and flavor depth. However, as food wines, they are remarkably one-dimensional. As complex and rewarding as they can be, they work well only with dishes with relatively straightforward and simple flavors. Cabernet Sauvignon marries beautifully with basic meat and potato dishes, filet mignon, lamb filets, steaks, etc. Furthermore, as Cabernet Sauvignon– and Merlot-based wines get older and more complex, they require simpler and simpler dishes to complement their complex flavors. Chardonnay goes beautifully with most fish courses, but when one adds different aromas and scents to a straightforward fish dish, from either grilling, or from ingredients in an accompanying sauce, Chardonnays are often competitive rather than complementary wines to serve. The basic rule, then, is simple, uncomplex wines with complex dishes, and complex wines with simple dishes.

What are the primary flavors in both the wine and food? A complementary wine choice can often be made if one knows what to expect from the primary flavors in the food to be eaten. The reason that creamy and buttery sauces with fish, lobster, even chicken or veal, work well with Chardonnay or white burgundies is because of the buttery, vanillin aromas in the fuller, richer, lustier styles of Chardonnay. On the other hand, a mixed salad with an herb dressing and pieces of grilled fish or shellfish beg for an herbaceous, smoky, Sauvignon Blanc or French Sancerre or Pouilly Fumé from the Loire Valley. For the same reason, a steak au poivre in a creamy brown sauce with its intense, pungent aromas and complex flavors requires a big, rich, peppery Rhône wine such as a Châteauneuf du Pape or Gigondas.

Is the texture and flavor intensity of the wine proportional to the texture and flavor intensity of the food?   Did you ever wonder why fresh, briny, sea-scented oysters that are light and zesty taste so good with a Muscadet from France or a lighter-styled California Sauvignon Blanc or Italian Pinot Grigio? It is because these wines have the same weight and light texture as the oysters. Why is it that the smoky, sweet, oaky, tangy flavors of a grilled steak or loin of lamb work best with a Zinfandel or Rhône Valley red wine? First, the full-bodied, supple, chewy flavors of these wines complement a steak or loin of lamb cooked over a wood fire. Sauté the same steak or lamb in butter or bake it in the oven and the flavors are less complex; then a well-aged Cabernet Sauvignon– or Merlot-based wine from California, Bordeaux, or Australia is required. Another poignant example of the importance of matching the texture and flavor intensity of the wine with the food is the type of fish you have chosen to eat. Salmon, lobster, shad, and bluefish have intense flavors and a fatty texture, and therefore require a similarly styled, lusty, oaky, buttery Chardonnay to complement them. On the other hand, trout, sole, turbot, and shrimp are leaner, more delicately flavored fish and therefore mandate lighter, less intense wines such as nonoaked examples of Chardonnay from France's Mâconnais region, or Italy's Friuli-Venezia-Guilia area. In addition, a lighter-styled Champagne or German Riesling (a dry Kabinett works ideally) goes extremely well with trout, sole, or turbot, but falls on its face if matched against salmon, shad, or lobster. One further example of texture and flavor matchups is the classic example of drinking a heavy, unctuous, rich, sweet Sauternes with foie gras. The extravagantly rich and flavorful foie gras cannot be served with any other type of wine, as it would overpower a dry red or white wine. The fact that both the Sauternes and the foie gras have intense, concentrated flavors and similar textures is the exact reason why this combination is so decadently delicious.

What is the style of wine produced in the vintage that you have chosen?   Several of France's greatest chefs have told me they prefer off years of Bordeaux and Burgundy to great years, and have instructed their sommeliers to buy the wines for the restaurant accordingly. Can this be true? From the chef's perspective, the food should be the focal point of the meal, not the wine. They fear that a great vintage of Burgundy or Bordeaux with wines that are exceptionally rich, powerful, and concentrated not only takes attention away from their cuisine, but makes matching a wine with the food much more troublesome. Thus, chefs prefer a 1987 Bordeaux on the table with their food as opposed to a superconcentrated 1982 or 1990. For the same reasons, they prefer a 1989 red burgundy over a 1990. Thus, the great vintages, while being marvelous wines, are not always the best vintages to choose if the ultimate matchup with food is desired. Lighter-weight yet tasty wines from so-so years can complement delicate and understated cuisine considerably better than the great vintages, which should be reserved for very simple courses of food.

Is the food to be served in a sauce?   Fifteen years ago when eating at Michel Guerard's restaurant in Eugénie Les Bains, I ordered a course where the fish was served in a red wine sauce. Guerard recommended a red Graves wine from Bordeaux, since the sauce was made from a reduction of fish stock and a red Graves. The combination was successful and opened my eyes for the first time to the possibilities of fish with red wine. Since then I have had tuna with a green peppercorn sauce with California Cabernet Sauvignon (the matchup was great), and salmon sautéed in a red wine sauce that did justice to a young vintage of red Bordeaux. A white wine with any of these courses would not have worked. For the very same reason I have enjoyed veal in a creamy morel sauce with a Tokay from Alsace. A corollary to this principle of letting the sauce dictate the type of wine you order is where the actual food is prepared with a specific type of wine. For example, Coq au Vin, an exquisite peasant dish, can be cooked and served in either a white wine or red wine sauce. I have found when

I had Coq au Vin au Riesling the choice of a dry Alsace Riesling to go with it is simply extraordinary. In Burgundy I have often had Coq au Vin in a red wine sauce consisting of a reduced burgundy wine and the choice of a red burgundy makes the dish even more special. *When you travel, do you drink locally produced wines with the local cuisine?* It is no coincidence that the regional cuisines of Bordeaux, Burgundy, Provence, and Alsace in France, and Tuscany and Piedmont in Italy seem to enhance and complement the local wines. In fact, most restaurants in these areas rarely offer wines from outside the local region, thus mandating the drinking of the locally produced wines. One always wonders what came first, the cuisine or the wine? Certainly, America is beginning to develop its own regional cuisine, but except for California and the Pacific Northwest few areas promote the local wines as appropriate matchups with the local cuisine. For example, in my backyard a number of small wineries make an excellent white wine called Seyval Blanc that is the perfect foil for both the oysters and blue channel crabs from the Chesapeake Bay. Yet few restaurants in the Baltimore-Washington area promote these local wines, which is a shame. Regional wines with regional foods should not only be a top priority when traveling in Europe, but also in America's viticultural areas.

Have you learned the best and worst wine and food matchups? If this entire area of wine and food combinations still seems too cumbersome, then your best strategy is to simply learn some of the greatest combinations as well as some of the worst. I can also add a few pointers I have learned through my own experiences, usually bad ones. Certain wine and food relationships of contrasting flavors can be sublime. Perhaps the best example is a sweet, creamy-textured Sauternes wine with a salty, aged Stilton or Roquefort cheese. The combination of having two opposite sets of flavors and textures is sensational in this particular instance. Another great combination is Alsace Gewürztraminers and Rieslings with ethnic cuisine such as Indian and Chinese. The juxtaposition of sweet and sour combinations in Oriental cuisine and the spiciness of both cuisines seems to work beautifully with these two types of wine from Alsace.

One of the great myths about wine and food matchups is that red wines work well with cheese. The truth of the matter is that they rarely ever work well with cheese. Most cheeses, especially favorite wine cheeses such as Brie and double and triple creams, have such a high fat content that most red wines suffer incredibly when drunk with them. If you want to shock your guests but also enjoy wine with cheese, it should not be a red wine you serve, but rather a white wine made from the Sauvignon Blanc grape such as a Sancerre or Pouilly Fumé from France. The dynamic personalities of these two wines and their tangy, zesty acidity stand up well to virtually all types of cheese, but they especially go well with fresh goat cheeses.

Another myth is that dessert wines go best with desserts. Most people seem to like Champagne or a sweet Riesling, sweet Chenin Blanc, or a Sauternes with dessert. Besides the fact that chocolate-based desserts are always in conflict with any type of wine, I find dessert wines to be best served *as* the dessert or *after* the dessert. Whether it be cake, fruit tarts, ice cream, or candy, I've always enjoyed dessert wines more when they are the centerpiece of attention than when they are accompanying a sweet dessert.

If wine and food matchups still seem too complicated for you, remember that in the final analysis a good wine served with a good dish to good company is always in good taste. *À votre santé!*

WHAT'S BEEN ADDED TO YOUR WINE?

Over the last decade people have become much more sensitive to what they put in their bodies. The hazards of excessive smoking, fat consumption, and high blood pressure are taken seriously by increasing numbers of people, not just in America but in Europe as well.

While this movement is to be applauded, an extremist group, labeled by observers as "neo-prohibitionists" or "new drys," have tried to exploit an individual's interest in good health by promoting the image that the consumption of any alcoholic beverage is an inherently dangerous abuse that undermines society and family. These extremist groups do not care about moderation; they want the total elimination of wine (one of alcohol's evil spirits) from the marketplace. To do so, they have misrepresented wine and have consistently ignored specific data that demonstrates that moderate wine-drinking is more beneficial than harmful to individuals. Unfortunately, the law prohibits the wine industry from promoting the proven health benefits of wine.

Wine is the most natural of all beverages, but it is true that additives can be included in a wine (the neo-prohibitionists are taking aim at these as being potentially lethal). Following are those items that can be added to wine.

Acids Most cool-climate vineyards never have the need to add acidity to wine, but in California and Australia acidity is often added to give balance to the wines, as grapes from these hot-climate areas often lack enough natural acidity. Most serious wineries add tartaric acid, which is the same type of acidity found naturally in wine. Less quality-oriented wineries dump in pure citric acid, which results in wine that tastes like a lemon/lime sorbet.

Clarification Agents A list of items that are dumped into wine to cause suspended particles to coagulate includes morbid names such as dried oxblood, isinglass, casein (milk powder), kaolin (clay), bentonite (powdered clay), and the traditional egg whites. These fining agents are designed to make the wine brilliant and particle free; they are harmless, and top wineries either don't use them or use them minimally.

Oak Many top-quality red and white wines spend most of their lives aging in oak barrels. It is expected that wine stored in wood will take on some of the toasty, smoky, vanillin flavors of wood. These aromas and flavors, if not overdone, add flavor complexity to a wine. Cheap wine can also be marginally enhanced by the addition of oak chips that provide a more aggressive, raw flavor of wood.

Sugar In most of the viticultural regions of Europe except for southern France, Portugal, and Spain, the law permits the addition of sugar to the fermenting grape juice in order to raise the alcohol levels. This practice, called *chaptalisation,* is done in cool years where the grapes do not attain sufficient ripeness. It is never done in the hot climate of California or in most of Australia where low natural acidity, not low sugars, is the problem. Judicious *chaptalisation* raises the alcohol level by 1%–2%.

Sulfites All wines must now carry a label indicating that the wine contains sulfites. Sulfites (also referred to as SO_2 or sulfur dioxide) are preservatives used to kill bacteria and microorganisms. They are sprayed on virtually all fresh vegetables and fruits, but a tiny percentage of the population is allergic to SO_2, especially asthmatics. The fermentation of wine produces some sulfur dioxide naturally, but it is also added to oak barrels by burning a sulfur stick inside the barrel in order to kill any bacteria; it is added again at bottling to prevent the wine from oxidizing. Quality wines should never smell of sulfur (a burning match smell) because serious winemakers keep the sulfur level very low. Some wineries do not employ sulfites. When used properly, sulfites impart no smell or taste to the wine, and except for those who have a known allergy to them, are harmless to the general population. Used excessively, sulfites impart the aforementioned unpleasant smell and a prickly taste sensation. Obviously, people who are allergic to sulfites should not drink wine, just as people who are allergic to fish roe should not eat caviar.

Tannin Tannin occurs naturally in the skins and stems of grapes, and the content from the crushing of the grape skins and subsequent maceration of the skins and juice is usually more than adequate to provide sufficient natural tannin. Tannin gives a red wine grip and backbone, as well as acting as a preservative. However, on rare occasions tannin is added to a spineless wine.

Yeasts While many winemakers rely on the indigenous wild yeasts in the vineyard to start the fermentation, it is becoming more common to employ cultured yeasts for this procedure. There is no health hazard here, but the increasing reliance on the same type of yeast for wines from all over the world leads to wines with similar bouquets and flavors.

ORGANIC WINES

Organic wines, those that are produced without fungicides, pesticides, or chemical fertilizers, with no additives or preservatives, continue to gain considerable consumer support. In principle, organic wines should be as excellent as nonorganic. Because most organic-wine producers tend to do less manipulation and processing of their wines, the consumer receives a product that is far more natural than those wines that have been manufactured and processed to death.

There is tremendous potential for huge quantities of organic wines, particularly from those viticultural areas that enjoy copious quantities of sunshine and wind, the so-called Mediterranean climate. In France, the Languedoc-Roussillon region, Provence, and the Rhône Valley have the potential to produce organic wines if their proprietors desire. Much of California could do so as well. Parts of Australia and Italy also have weather conditions that encourage the possibility of developing organic vineyards.

THE DARK SIDE OF WINE

The Growing International Neutralization of Wine Styles
Although technology allows winemakers to produce better and better quality wine, the continuing obsession with technically perfect wines is unfortunately stripping wines of their identifiable and distinctive character. Whether it is the excessive filtration of wines or the excessive emulation of winemaking styles, it seems to be the tragedy of modern winemaking that it is now increasingly difficult to tell an Italian Chardonnay from one made in France or California or Australia. When the corporate winemakers of the world begin to make wines all in the same way, designing them to offend the least number of people, wine will no doubt lose its fascinating appeal and individualism to become no better than most brands of whiskey, gin, scotch, or vodka. One must not forget that the great appeal of wine is that it is a unique, distinctive, fascinating beverage and different every time one drinks it. Winemakers and the owners of wineries, particularly in America, must learn to take more risks so as to preserve the individual character of their wines, even at the risk that some consumers may find them bizarre or unusual. It is this distinctive quality of wine that will ensure its future.

Destroying the Joy of Wine by Excessive Acidification, Fining, and Filtration
Since the beginning of my career as a professional wine critic, I have tried to present a strong case against the excessive manipulation of wine. One look at the world's greatest producers and their wines will irrefutably reveal that the following characteristics are shared by all of them—whether they be California, France, Italy, Spain, or Germany. (1) They are driven to preserve the integrity of the vineyard's character, the varietal's identity, and the vintage's personality. (2) They believe in low crop yields. (3) Weather permitting, they harvest only physiologically mature (versus analytically ripe) fruit. (4) Their winemaking and cellar techniques are simplistic in the sense that they are minimal interventionists, preferring to permit the wine to make itself. (5) While they are not opposed to fining or filtration if the wine is unstable or unclear, if the wine is made from healthy, ripe grapes,

and is stable and clear, they will absolutely refuse to strip it by excessive fining and filtration at bottling.

Producers who only care about making wine as fast as possible and about collecting their accounts receivable quickly also have many things in common. While they turn out neutral, vapid, mediocre wines, they are also believers in huge crop yields, with considerable fertilization to promote massive crops, as large as the vineyard can render (6 or more tons per acre, compared with modest yields of 3 tons per acre). Their philosophy is that the vineyard is a manufacturing plant, and cost efficiency dictates that production be maximized. They rush their wine into bottle as quickly as possible in order to get paid. They believe in processing wine, such as centrifuging it initially, then practicing multiple fining and filtration procedures, particularly a denuding sterile filtration. This guarantees that the wine is lifeless but stable, a goal where the ability to withstand temperature extremes and stand upright on a grocery store's shelf is given priority over giving the consumer a beverage of pleasure. These wineries harvest earlier than anybody else because they are unwilling to take any risk, delegating all questions regarding wine to their oenologists, who they know have as their objectives security and stability, which is at conflict with the consumer's goal of finding joy in wine.

The effect of excessive manipulation of wine, particularly overly aggressive fining and filtration, is dramatic. It destroys a wine's bouquet as well as its ability to express its *terroir* and varietal character. It also mutes the vintage's character. Fining and filtration can be lightly done, causing only minor damage, but most wines produced in the new world (California, Australia, and South America in particular), and most bulk wines produced in Europe, are sterile-filtered. This procedure requires numerous prefiltrations to get the wines clean enough to pass through a micropore membrane filter. This system of wine stability and clarification strips, eviscerates, and denudes a wine of much of its character.

Some wines can suffer such abuse with less damage. Thick, tannic, concentrated, Syrah- and Cabernet Sauvignon–based wines may even survive these wine lobotomies, diminished in aromatic and flavor dimension, but still alive. Wines such as Pinot Noir and Chardonnay are destroyed in the process.

Thanks to a new generation of producers, particularly in France, aided by a number of specialist importers from America, there has been a movement against unnecessary fining and filtration. One only has to look at the extraordinary success enjoyed by such American importers as Kermit Lynch and Robert Kacher to realize how much consumer demand exists for producers to bottle a natural, unfiltered, uncompromised wine that is a faithful representation of its vineyard and vintage. Most serious wine consumers do not mind not being able to drink the last half ounce of wines because of sediment. They know this sediment means they are getting a flavorful, authentic, unprocessed wine that is much more representative than one stripped at bottling.

Other small importers who have followed the leads of Lynch and Kacher include Peter Weygandt of Weygandt-Metzler, Unionville, PA; Neal Rosenthal Select Vineyards, New York, NY; Eric Solomon of European Cellars, New York, NY; Robert Haas of Vineyard Brands, Chester, VT; Don Quattlebaum of New Castle Imports, Myrtle Beach, SC; Fran Kysela of Kysela Père et Fils of Winchester, VA; Martine Saunier of Martine's Wines, San Rafael, CA; and North Berkeley Imports, Berkeley, CA, to name some of the best known. They often insist that their producers not filter those wines shipped to the United States, resulting in a richer, more age-worthy wine being sold in America than elsewhere in the world. Even some of our country's largest importers, most notably Kobrand, Inc., in New York City, are encouraging producers to move toward more gentle and natural bottling techniques.

I am certain there would have been an even more powerful movement to bottle wines naturally with minimal clarification if the world's wine press had examined the effect of excessive fining and filtration. I find it difficult to criticize many American wine writers since the vast majority of them are part-timers. Few have either the time or resources to taste the same wines before and after bottling. Yet I remain disappointed that many of our most influential writers and publications have remained strangely silent, particularly in view of the profound negative impact filtration can have on the quality of fine wine. The English wine-writing corps, which includes many veteran, full-time wine writers, has an appalling record on this issue, especially in view of the fact that many of them make it a practice to taste before and after bottling. For those who care about the quality of wine, and the preservation of the character of the vineyard, vintage, and varietal, the reluctance of so many writers to criticize the wine industry undermines the entire notion of wine appreciation.

Even a wine writer of the stature of Hugh Johnson comes out strongly on the side of processed, neutral wines that can be safely shipped 12 months of the year. Readers may want to consider Johnson's, and his coauthor, James Halliday's, comments in their book, *The Vintner's Art—How Great Wines Are Made.* Halliday is an Australian wine-writer and winery owner and Hugh Johnson may be this century's most widely read wine author. In their book they chastise the American importer, Kermit Lynch, for his "romantic ideals," which they describe as "increasingly impractical." Johnson and Halliday assert that "the truth is that a good fifty percent of those artisan burgundies and Rhônes are bacterial time bombs." Their plea for compromised and standardized wines is supported by the following observation: "The hard reality is that many restaurants and many consumers simply will not accept sediment." This may have been partially true in America twenty years ago, but today the consumer not only wants, but demands a natural wine. Moreover, the wine consumer understands that sediment in a bottle of fine wine is a healthy sign. The fact that both writers argue that modern-day winemaking and commercial necessity require that wines be shipped 12 months a year, and be durable enough to withstand months on retailers' shelves in both cold and hot temperature conditions, is highly debatable. America now has increasing numbers of responsible merchants, importers, and restaurant sommeliers who go to great lengths to guarantee the client a healthy bottle of wine that has not been abused. Astonishingly, Johnson and Halliday conclude that consumers cannot tell whether a wine has been filtered or not! In summarizing their position, they state, "but leave the wine for 1, 2, or 3 months (one cannot tell how long the recovery process will take), and it is usually impossible to tell the filtered from the non-filtered wine, provided the filtration at bottling was skillfully carried out." After 14 years of conducting such tastings, I find this statement not only unbelievable, but insupportable! Am I to conclude that all of the wonderful wines I have tasted from cask that were subsequently damaged by vigorous fining and filtration were bottled by incompetent people who did not know how to filter? Am I to think that the results of the extensive comparative tastings (usually blind) that I have done of the same wine, filtered versus unfiltered, were bogus? Are the enormous aromatic, flavor, textural, and qualitative differences that are the result of vigorous clarification techniques figments of my imagination? Astoundingly, the wine industry's reluctance to accept responsibility for preserving all that the best vineyards and vintages can achieve is excused rather than condemned.

If excessive fining and filtration are not bad enough, consider the overzealous additions of citric and tartaric acids employed by Australian and California oenologists to perk up their wines. You know the feeling—you open a bottle of Australian or California Chardonnay and not only is there no bouquet (because it was sterile-filtered), but tasting the wine is like biting into a fresh lemon or lime. It is not enjoyable. What you are experiencing is the result of the misguided philosophy among new world winemakers to add too much acidity as a cheap but fatal life insurance policy for their wines. Because they are unwilling to reduce their yields, because they are unwilling to assume any risk, and because they see winemaking as nothing more than a processing technique, acidity is generously added. It does serve as an antibacterial, antioxidant agent, thus helping to keep the wine fresh. But those who acidify the most are usually those who harvest appallingly high crop yields. Thus, there is little flavor to protect! After 6–12 months of bottle age what little fruit is present fades, and the consumer is left with a skeleton of sharp, shrill acid levels, alcohol, wood (if utilized), and no fruit—an utterly reprehensible way of making wine.

I do not object to the use of these techniques for bulk and jug wines, which the consumer is buying for value, or because of brand-name recognition. But for any producer to sell a wine as a hand-crafted, artisan product at $20 or more a bottle, the adherence to such philosophies as excessive acidification, fining, and filtration is shameful. Anyone who tells you that excessive acidification, fining, and filtration does not damage a wine is either a fool or a liar.

The Inflated Wine Pricing of Restaurants

Given the vast sums of American discretionary income that is being spent eating at restaurants, a strong argument could be made that the cornerstone to increased wine consumption and awareness would be the consumption of wine at restaurants. However, most restaurants treat wine as a luxury item, marking it up an exorbitant 200%–500%, thereby effectively discouraging the consumption of wine. This practice of offering wines at huge markups also serves to reinforce the mistaken notion that wine is only for the elite and the superrich.

The wine industry does little about this practice, being content merely to see its wines placed on a restaurant's list. But the consumer should revolt and avoid those restaurants that charge exorbitant wine prices, no matter how sublime the cuisine. The Inn at Little Washington, Virginia, considered by many food critics to be this country's finest eating establishment, displays appalling markups of 400%–500%. This is nothing more than legitimized mugging of the consumer.

Fortunately, things are slightly better today than they were a decade ago, as some restaurant owners are now regarding wine as an integral part of the meal, and not merely a device to increase the bill.

Collectors versus Consumers

I have reluctantly come to believe that many of France's greatest wine treasures—the first growths of Bordeaux, including the famous sweet nectar made at Château Yquem; Burgundy's most profound red wines from the Domaine de la Romanée-Conti; and virtually all of the wines from the tiny white wine appellation of Montrachet—are never drunk, or should I say swallowed. Most of us who purchase or cellar wine do so on the theory that eventually every one of our splendid bottles will be swirled, sloshed, sniffed, sipped, and yes, guzzled with friends. That, of course, is one of the joys of wine, and those of you who partake of this pleasure are true wine lovers. There are, however, other types of wine collectors—the collector-investor, the collector-spitter, and even the nondrinking collector. Needless to say, these people are not avid consumers.

Several years ago I remember being deluged with telephone calls from a man wanting me to have dinner with him and to tour his private cellar. After several months of resisting, I finally succumbed. A very prominent businessman, he had constructed an impressive cellar beneath his sprawling home. It was enormous and immaculately kept, with state-of-the-art humidity and temperature controls. I suspect it contained in excess of 10,000 bottles. While there were cases of such thoroughbreds as Pétrus, Lafite-Rothschild, Mouton-Rothschild, and rare vintages of the great red burgundies such as Romanée-Conti and La Tache, to my astonishment there were also hundreds of cases of 10- and 15-year-old Beaujolais, Pouilly-Fuissé, Dolcetto, and California Chardonnays—all wines that should have been drunk during their first 4 or 5 years of life. I diplomatically suggested that he should inventory his cellar, as there seemed to be a number of wines that mandated immediate consumption.

About the time I spotted the fifth or sixth case of what was clearly 10-year-old Beaujolais vinegar, I began to doubt the sincerity of my host's enthusiasm for wine. These unthinkable doubts (I was much more naïve then than I am now) were amplified at dinner. As we entered the sprawling kitchen and dining room complex, he proudly announced that neither he nor his wife actually drank wine, and then asked if I would care for a glass of mineral water, ice tea, or, if I preferred, a bottle of wine. On my sorrow-filled drive home that evening, I lamented the fact that I had not opted for the mineral water. For when I made the mistake of requesting wine with the meal, my host proceeded to grab a bottle of wine that one of his friends suggested should be consumed immediately. It was a brown-colored, utterly repugnant, senile Bordeaux from perhaps the worst vintage in the last thirty-five years, 1969. Furthermore, the château chosen was a notorious underachiever from the famous commune of Pauillac. Normally the wine he chose does not merit buying in a good vintage, much less a pathetic one. I shall never forget my host opening the bottle and saying, "Well, Bob, this wine sure smells good."

Regrettably, this nondrinking collector continues to buy large quantities of wine, not for investment, and obviously not for drinking. The local wine merchants tell me his type is not rare. To him, a collection of wine is like a collection of crystal, art, sculpture, or china, something to be admired, to be shown off, but never, ever to be consumed.

More ostentatious by far is the collector-spitter, who thrives on gigantic tastings where 50, 60, sometimes even 70 or 80 vintages of great wines, often from the same châteaux, can be "tasted." Important members of the wine press are invited (no charge, of course) in the hope that this wine happening will receive a major article in *The New York Times* or *Los Angeles Times*, and the collector's name will become recognized and revered in the land of winedom. These collector-spitters relish rubbing elbows with famous proprietors, and telling their friends, "Oh, I'll be at Château Lafite-Rothschild next week to taste all of the château's wines between 1870 and 1987. Sorry you can't be there." I have, I confess, participated in several of these events, and have learned from the exercise of trying to understand them that their primary purpose is to feed the sponsor's enormous ego, and often the château proprietor's ego as well.

I am not against academic tastings where a limited number of serious wine enthusiasts sit down to taste twenty or thirty different wines (usually young ones), because that is a manageable number that both neophytes and connoisseurs can generally grasp. But to taste 60 or more rare and monumental vintages at an 8- or 12-hour tasting marathon is carrying excess to its extreme. Most simply, what seems to happen at these tastings is that much of the world's greatest, rarest, and most expensive wines are spit out. No wine taster I have ever met could conceivably remain sober, even if only the greatest wines were swallowed. I can assure you, there is only remorse in spitting out 1929 or 1945 Mouton-Rothschild.

Other recollections of these events have also long troubled me. I vividly remember one tasting held at a very famous restaurant in Los Angeles, where a number of compelling bottles from one of France's greatest estates were opened. Many of the wines were exhilarating. Yet, whether it was the otherworldly 1961 or the opulent 1947, the reactions I saw on the faces of those 40 or so people, who had each paid several thousand dollars to attend, made me wonder whether it was 50 different vintages of France's greatest wines we were tasting, or 50 bottles of Pepto-Bismol. Fortunately, the organizer did appear to enjoy the gathering and appreciate the wines, but among the guests I never once saw a smile or any enthusiasm or happiness in the course of this extraordinary 12-hour tasting.

I remember another marathon tasting held in France by one of Europe's leading collector-spitters, which lasted all day and much of the night. There were over 90 legendary wines served, and midway through the afternoon I was reasonably certain there was not a sober individual remaining, except for the chef and his staff. By the time the magnum of 1929 Mouton-Rothschild was served (one of the century's greatest wines), I do not think there was a guest left who was competent enough to know whether he or she was drinking claret or Beaujolais, myself included.

I have also noticed at these tastings that many collector-spitters did not even know that a bottle was corked (had the smell of moldy cardboard and was defective), or that a bottle was oxidized and undrinkable, adding truth to the old saying that money does not always buy good taste. Of course, most of these tastings are media happenings designed to stroke the host's vanity. All too frequently they undermine the principle that wine is a beverage of pleasure, and that is my basic regret.

The third type of collector, the investor, is motivated by the possibility of reselling the wines for profit. Eventually, most or all of these wines return to the marketplace, and much of it wends its way into the hands of serious consumers, who share it with their spouses or good friends. Of course they often must pay dearly for the privilege, but wine is not the only product that falls prey to such manipulation. I hate to think of wine being thought of primarily as an investment, but the world's finest wines do appreciate significantly in value, and it would be foolish to ignore the fact that more and more shrewd investors are looking at wine as a way of making money.

Unspeakable Practices

It is a frightening thought, but I have no doubt that a sizable percentage (between 10% and 25%) of the wines sold in America has been damaged because of exposure to extremes of temperature. Smart consumers have long been aware of the signs of poor storage. They have only to look at the bottle. The first sign that a bottle has been poorly stored is when a cork is popped above the rim and is pushed out against the lead or plastic capsule that covers the top of the bottle. Wines that have been exposed to very high temperatures expand, which puts pressure on the cork and pushes it upward against the capsule. It is the highest-quality wines, those that have not been overly filtered or pasteurized in order to stabilize them, that are most susceptible to poor transportation or storage conditions, and most likely to show the effect of heat damage. A wine that has been frozen while in transit or storage will also push the cork out. The freezing of wine is less damaging than the heating of it, but both are hazardous to its health. Any cork protruding above the rim of the bottle is a bad sign, indicating you should return that bottle to the shelf and look for another one.

Another sign indicating the wine has been poorly stored is the presence of seepage, or "legs," down the rim of the bottle. This is the sometimes sticky, dry residue of a wine that has expanded, seeped around the cork, and dripped onto the rim. Cases of this are almost always due to excessively high temperatures in transit or storage. Few merchants take the trouble to wipe the legs off, and they can often be spotted on wines that are shipped during the heat of the summer, or that are brought into the United States through the Panama Canal in unair-conditioned containers. Consumers should avoid buying wines that show dried seepage legs originating under the capsule and trickling down the side of the bottle.

You should also be alert for young wines (those less than 4 years old) that have more than one-half inch of air space, or ullage, between the cork and the liquid level in the bottle. Modern bottling operations generally fill bottles within one-eighth inch of the cork, so more than one-half inch of air space should arouse your suspicion.

The problem, of course, is that too few people in the wine trade take the necessary steps to assure that the wine is not ruined in shipment or storage. The wine business has become so commercial that wines, whether from California, Italy, or France, are shipped 12 months of the year, regardless of weather conditions. Traditionally, wines from Europe were shipped only in the spring or fall when the temperatures encountered in shipment would be moderate, assuming they were not shipped by way of the Panama Canal. The cost of renting an air-conditioned or heated container for shipping wines adds anywhere from 20 to 40 cents to the wholesale cost of the bottle, but when buying wines that cost over $200 a case, I doubt the purchaser would mind paying the extra premium knowing that the wine will not smell or taste cooked when opened.

Many importers claim to ship in reefers (the trade jargon for temperature-controlled containers), but only a handful actually do. America's largest importer of high-quality Bordeaux wine rarely, if ever, uses reefers, and claims to have had no problems with their shipments. Perhaps they would change their minds if they had witnessed the cases of 1986 Rausan-Ségla, 1986 Talbot, 1986 Gruaud-Larose, and 1986 Château Margaux that arrived in the Maryland–Washington, D.C., market with stained labels and pushed-out corks. Somewhere between Bordeaux and Washington, D.C., these wines had been exposed to torridly high temperatures. It may not have been the fault of the importer, as the wine passed through a number of intermediaries before reaching its final destination. But pity the poor consumers who buy this wine, put it in their cellars, and open it 10 or 15 years in the future. Who will grieve for them?

The problem with temperature extremes is that the naturally made, minimally processed, hand-produced wines are the most vulnerable to this kind of abuse. Therefore, many importers, not wanting to assume any risks, have gone back to their suppliers and demanded "more stable" wines. Translated into real terms this means the wine trade prefers to ship not living wines, but vapid, denuded wines that have been "stabilized," subjected to a manufacturing process, and either pasteurized or sterile-filtered so they can be shipped 12 months a year. While their corks may still pop out if subjected to enough heat, their taste will not change, because for all intents and purposes these wines are already dead when they are put in the bottle. Unfortunately, only a small segment of the wine trade seems to care.

While there are some wine merchants, wholesalers, and importers who are cognizant of the damage that can be done when wines are not protected, and who take great pride in representing hand-made, quality products, the majority of the wine trade continues to ignore the risks. They would prefer that the wine be denuded by pasteurization, cold stabilization, or a sterile filtration. Only then can they be shipped safely under any weather conditions.

Wine Producers' Greed

Are today's wine consumers being hoodwinked by the world's wine producers? Most growers and/or producers have intentionally permitted production yields to soar to such extraordinary levels that the concentration and character of their wines are in jeopardy. There remain a handful of fanatics who continue, at some financial sacrifice, to reject a significant proportion of their harvest so as to ensure that only the finest quality wine is sold under their name. However, they are dwindling in number. Fewer producers are prepared to go into the vineyard and cut bunches of grapes to reduce the yields. Fewer still are willing to cut back prudently on fertilizers. For much of the last decade production yields throughout the world continued to break records with each new vintage. The results are wines that increasingly lack character, concentration, and staying power. In Europe, the most flagrant abuses of overproduction occur in Germany and Burgundy, where yields today are three to almost five times what they were in the fifties. The argument that the vineyards are more carefully and competently managed, and that this results in larger crops, is misleading. Off the record, many a seriously committed wine producer will tell you that "the smaller the yield, the better the wine."

If one wonders why the Domaine Leroy's burgundies taste richer than those from other domaines, it is due not only to quality winemaking, but to the fact that their yields are one-third those of other Burgundy producers. If one asks why the best Châteauneuf du Papes are generally Rayas, Pegau, Bonneau, and Beaucastel, it is because their yields are one-half those of other producers of the appellation. The same assertion applies to J. J. Prum and Muller-Cattoir in Germany. Not surprisingly, they have conservative crop yields that produce one-third the amount of wine of their neighbors.

While I do not want to suggest there are no longer any great wines, and that most of the wines now produced are no better than the plonk peasants drank in the nineteenth century, the point is that overfertilization, modern sprays that prevent rot, the development of highly prolific clonal selections, and the failure to keep production levels modest have all resulted in yields that may well be combining to destroy the reputations of many of the most famous wine regions of the world. Trying to find a flavorful Chardonnay from California today is not much easier than finding a concentrated red burgundy that can age gracefully beyond ten years. The production yields of Chardonnay in California have often resulted in wines that have only a faint character of the grape, and seem almost entirely dominated by acidity and/ or the smell of oak barrels. What is appalling is that there is so little intrinsic flavor. Yet Chardonnays remain the most popular white wine in this country, so what incentive is there to lower yields?

Of course, if the public, encouraged by a noncritical, indifferent wine media, is willing to pay top dollar for mediocrity, then little is likely to change. On the other hand, if consumers start insisting that $15 or $20 should at the very minimum fetch a wine that provides far more pleasure, perhaps that message will gradually work its way back to the producers.

Wine Writers' Ethics and Competence

The problems just described have only occasionally been acknowledged by the wine media, which generally has a collective mind-set of never having met a wine it didn't like.

Wine writing in America has rarely been a profitable or promising full-time occupation. Historically, the most interesting work was always done by those people who sold wine. There's no doubting the influence or importance of the books written by Alexis Lichine and Frank Schoonmaker. But both men made their fortunes by selling, rather than by writing about, wine, yet both managed to write about wine objectively, despite their ties to the trade.

There are probably not more than a dozen or so independent wine experts in this country who support themselves entirely by writing. Great Britain has long championed the cause of wine writers and looked upon them as true professionals. But even there, with all their experience and access to the finest European vineyards, most of the successful wine writers have been involved in the sale and distribution of wine. Can anyone name an English wine-writer who criticized the performance of Lafite-Rothschild between 1961 and 1974, or Margaux between 1964 and 1977 (periods of time when the consumer was getting screwed)?

It is probably unrealistic to expect writers to develop a professional expertise with wine without access and support from the trade, but such support can compromise their findings. If they are beholden to wine producers for the wines they taste, they are not likely to fault them. If the trips they make to vineyards are the result of the winemaker's largesse, they are unlikely to criticize what they have seen. If they are lodged at the châteaux and their trunks are filled with cases of wine (as, sadly, is often the case), can a consumer expect them to be critical, or even objective?

Putting aside the foolish notion that a wine writer is going to bite the hand that feeds him, there is the problem that many wine writers are lacking the global experience essential to properly evaluate wine. Consequently, what has emerged from such inexperience is a school of wine-writing that is primarily geared toward looking at the wine's structure and acid levels, and it is this philosophy that is too frequently in evidence when judging wines. The level of pleasure that a wine provides, or is capable of providing in the future, would appear to be irrelevant. The results are wine evaluations that read as though one were measuring the industrial strength of different grades of cardboard rather than a beverage that many consider nature's greatest gift to mankind. Balance is everything in wine, and wines that taste too tart or tannic rarely ever age into flavorful, distinctive, charming beverages. While winemaking and wine technology are indeed better, and some of the most compelling wines ever made are being produced today, there are far too many mediocre wines sitting on the shelves that hardly deserve their high praise.

There are, however, some interesting trends. The growth of *The Wine Spectator*, with its staff of full-time writers obligated to follow a strict code against conflict of interest, has resulted in better and more professional journalism. It also cannot be discounted that this flashy magazine appears twice a month. This is good news for the wine industry, frequently under siege by the antialcohol extremists. Some may protest the inflated ratings that *The Wine Spectator*'s tasting panel tends to bestow, but tasting is, as we all should know, subjective. The only criticism some might have is that their wine evaluations are the result of a committee's vote. Wines of great individuality and character rarely win a committee tasting because there is going to be at least one taster who will find something objectionable about the wines. Therefore, tasting panels, where all grades are averaged, frequently appear to find wines of great individuality unusual. The wines that too often score the highest are those that are technically correct and designed to please the greatest number of people. Wouldn't most Americans prefer a hamburger from McDonald's than seared salmon served over a bed of lentils at New York City's famed Le Montrachet restaurant? To *The Wine Spectator*'s credit, more of their tasting reports are authored by one or two people, not an anonymous, secretive committee. The results of the numerous California wine judgings support the same conclusion—that many a truly great, individualistic, and original wine has no chance. The winners are too often fail-safe, technically correct, spit-polished, and clean examples of winemaking. In short, wines for fans of Velveeta cheese, Muzak, and frozen dinners. The opinion of a reasonably informed and comprehensive individual taster, despite that taster's prejudices and predilections, is always a far greater guide to the ultimate quality of the wine than that of a committee. At least the reader knows where the individual stands; whereas with a committee, one is never quite sure.

Given the vitality of *The Wine Spectator* and a few other wine guides, it is unlikely that wine writers will have less influence in the future. The thousands and thousands of wines that come on the market, many of them overpriced and vapid, require consumer-oriented reviews from the wine writing community. But until a greater degree of professionalism is attained, until more experience is evidenced by wine writers, until their misinformed emphasis on a wine's high acidity and structure is forever discredited, until most of the English wine media begin to understand and adhere to the basic rules of conflict of interest, until we all remember that this is only a beverage of pleasure, to be seriously consumed but not taken too seriously, then and only then will the quality of wine writing and the wines we drink improve. Perhaps all of this will happen, or perhaps we will be reminded of these words of Marcel Proust:

> We do not succeed in changing things according to our desire, but gradually our desire changes. The situation that we hope to change because it was intolerable becomes unimportant. We have not managed to surmount the obstacle as we are absolutely determined to do, but life has taken us round to it, let us pass it, and then if we turn round to gaze at the road past, we can barely catch sight of it, so imperceptible has it become.

WINE TRENDS IN THE MARKETPLACE

Some General Observations about American Wine

1. California will continue to dominate the marketplace as that beautiful state has had 5 consecutive, extremely high quality vintages. The only downside to California's recent success is that the strong demand for these wines means that prices are likely to rise.
2. While wine writers continue to lament the popularity of Chardonnay, it shows no signs of losing the support of its most important followers—wine consumers. Thankfully, the sterile, high-acid, hollow Chardonnays of the past are less noticeable because of the high-quality vintages of the nineties as well as a movement among California's better wine producers to intervene less in the winemaking process. The result is an abundance of rich, fruity, sumptuous Chardonnays. Consequently, the strength of this varietal will continue to soar.
3. Zinfandel, the red, full-blooded type, which I predicted in 1993 to be California's hottest wine, continues to be so. Prices per ton of Zinfandel have soared, so it is just a matter of time before that gorgeous $12 Zinfandel becomes significantly more expensive. Its easy-to-drink, in-your-face, berry, peppery, spicy personality is the style of dry red wine consumers love. Moreover, while prices are rising, most Zinfandels can still be purchased for $15–$20.
4. For 15 years I have been an outspoken critic of the vegetal, often eviscerated, funky Pinot Noirs made in California. However, that has all changed in the nineties, with more and more wineries turning out velvety-textured, rich, berry-scented, voluptuous Pinot Noirs that are proving an embarrassment to many Burgundy producers, as well as to the importers who represent those wines. There are over two dozen California producers making gorgeous Pinot Noir that is ready to drink when bottled. These wines are being poured down the throats of eager wine enthusiasts at an unparalleled rate. Look for the emergence of more specific regional Pinot Noir identities to develop—especially from the Sonoma Coast, Carneros, Santa Barbara, and Mendocino.

Some General Observations about European Wines

1. The golden decade of the century, the eighties, with its abundant number of very good to great vintages, is a distant memory. Although 1990 was a uniformly exceptional vintage throughout Europe, 1991, 1992, 1993, and 1994 were plagued by rain. Europe, especially France and Italy, desperately need a great vintage to resurrect the excitement that seemed routine during much of the eighties, culminating with the exceptional years of 1989 and 1990. However, readers should remember that even in such rain-plagued vintages as 1991, 1992, 1993, and 1994 there are areas of undeniable success in France, Italy, Spain, and Germany. Even in the worst-hit viticultural regions there are winemakers who heroically triumphed over the unfavorable climatic conditions hurled at them by Mother Nature.
2. Even more troublesome for most European wineries than Mother Nature is the continued weakness of the American dollar. As of the time of writing it continues to perform like a third world currency against the French franc, German mark, Swiss franc, and Spanish peso. As long as the dollar remains weak, Americans will pay shockingly high prices for imported goods, whether it is cheese, perfume, cars, or wine. An inescapable fact of the mid-nineties is the dollar's amazingly poor purchasing power.
3. The days of buying Burgundy or Bordeaux wine futures 1 to 2 years before these wines are bottled and released is a thing of the past. Scandals following the nondelivery of the 1990 Bordeaux by several major retailers, as well as the ascendancy of California wine, dictates strongly against a reasonable person risking his or her money to purchase wine futures for most European wines.

4. Look for Italy's red wines, particularly from Tuscany and Piedmont, as well as Spain's new-style red wines to garner a larger share of the American marketplace.
5. Europe's best red wine bargains will continue to emerge from the Montepulciano d'Abruzzo section of Italy, France's Languedoc-Roussillon region, and just about everywhere in Spain save for the two most renowned viticultural areas, Rioja and Ribero del Duero.
6. Expect more and more famous estates in France, and to a lesser extent in Italy, to be sold to large corporations (often insurance companies or foreign consortiums).
7. The importance of small specialty importers that select and/or demand unprocessed, authentic, unfined, and unfiltered wines will continue to grow and will have a significant impact on the imported fine-wine market. These importers also fill the needs of small, specialized retailers for high-quality, naturally made wines, for which consumers will pay a premium.

Some General Observations about the Wines of the Southern Hemisphere

1. After permitting wine quality to drop (because of frightfully high yields), Chile's better producers are once again turning out finer wines while keeping prices stable.
2. Look for more $20–$25 luxury cuvées from top Chilean and Argentinean producers.
3. The significant influence of foreign oenologists, particularly Michel Rolland from France and Paul Hobbs from California, has resulted in an increasing number of stunning red and white wines from both Chile and Argentina. Such Argentinean wineries as Catena, Weinert, and Etchart, and Chile's Casa Lapostolle are making superb wines at bargain prices. I expect this trend to continue.
4. Australia will continue to find a ready market for its inexpensive wines, but quality is extremely erratic. Moreover, too many wines are still damaged in transport to the United States. Australia's neighbor, New Zealand, continues to fashion some delicious Sauvignon Blancs, but the red wines are grotesquely vegetal and frightfully overpriced.

RECOMMENDED READING

Following is a personal list of publications and books I have found to offer authoritative information and reliable opinion on the world's wines.

Journals and Magazines

La Revue du Vin de France, 10 rue Guynemer, 92136 Issy-Les-Moulineaux Cedex, France; fax (1) 40 95 18 99. France's leading wine magazine is only available in the French language, but if you are bilingual and are a French-wine enthusiast, this is a must-read. Europe's finest taster, Michel Bettane, has left the teaching profession to write full-time for this magazine, only enhancing its value. In addition to Bettane, a group of highly respected tasters contribute extremely well-written articles on French vineyards and producers. The magazine does accept advertising.

Stephen Tanzer's International Wine Cellar, P.O. Box 20021, Cherokee Station, New York, NY 10021; $48.00 for six bimonthly issues, written by Stephen Tanzer. For 10 years Stephen Tanzer has published the *International Wine Cellar,* which is my favorite wine publication. Tanzer is a terrific taster, excellent writer, and his publication, which accepts no advertising, is extremely reliable for both European and American wines. If you are seriously interested in the upscale wine market, this is an essential publication.

The Veronelli News, 44 Via Sudorno, 24100 Vergno, Italy; $25.00 for six bimonthly issues. The first Italian wine newsletter, this publication has been in existence for 4 years. It offers terrific commentary, as well as superb, reliable reviews on Italian wines and from time to time on top French wines. If you love Italian wines and want authoritative tasting notes and candid, authoritative opinions from the two most renowned specialists on Italian wine, Daniel Thomases and Luigi Veronelli, this is an outstanding publication. It accepts no advertising.

The Wine Advocate, P.O. Box 311, Monkton, MD 21111; $40.00 for six bimonthly issues, written by a guy named Robert M. Parker, Jr. Much of this book is based on articles and tasting notes that have appeared in my journal, aimed at the serious wine enthusiast. The publication accepts no advertising.

The Wine Enthusiast, P.O. Box 392, Pleasantville, NY 10570; $24.00 for twelve monthly issues. Publisher, Adam Strum, created this magazine to offer an alternative to *The Wine Spectator*. It is neither as comprehensive, as thorough, nor as valuable as the *Spectator*, but it is still in its infancy. Such fine wine writers as Edward McCarthy and his wife Mary Mulligan, M.W., and Alexis Bespaloff have been brought in for commentaries. This publication appears to stress American wines. It does accept advertising.

The Wine Spectator, P.O. Box 1960, Marion, OH 43305-1960; $40.00 for 22 issues per year. This is the world's best and most widely read wine magazine. Publisher Marvin Shanken continues to fine-tune and improve an already strong magazine devoted to covering the wines of the world. No one does a better job in keeping its readers abreast of current events in the wine world. Mixing restaurant pieces with extensive wine ratings, as well as highly laudable articles on traveling in various wine regions, food and wine matchups, interesting recipes, and profiles of leading wine personalities, publisher Shanken has built this onetime obscure newsletter into a serious publication read around the world. This magazine is required reading for wine enthusiasts. It does accept advertising.

Books

Burton Anderson—*Vino*, published by Alfred A. Knopf, and *The Wine Atlas of Italy*, published by Simon & Schuster, New York. *Vino* was a breakthrough book on the importance and potential of Italian wine. *The Wine Atlas of Italy* is a very good reference book for the wine regions of that beautiful country.

Alexis Bespaloff—*Frank Schoonmaker's Encyclopedia*, published by William Morrow, New York. This dry but well-researched reference should be a part of all wine enthusiasts' libraries.

Michael Broadbent—*The Great Vintage Wine Book, editions I and II*, published by Mitchell Beazley, London. Broadbent was the first writer to make an art out of exceptionally descriptive and meaningful tasting notes. Moreover, he is a gifted taster whose experience in classic, older Bordeaux vintages is unmatched.

Oz Clarke—*Essential Wine Book, Annual Wine Guide*, and *Regional Wine Guides*, published by Simon & Schuster, New York. These lively, informative, well-written books from this multitalented English wine-writer offer un-Brit-like candor and lively prose more typical of the American wine-writing style than that of an Englishman. The witty Oz Clarke is also a terrific taster.

William H. Edgerton—*Wine Price File*, self-published by Mr. Edgerton, P.O. Box 1007, Darien, CT. For purchasing information, call (203) 655-2448. Given the increasing number of states that are permitting private collectors to sell their wines through authorized wine auctions, as well as the number of consumers seeking the most current prices on their wines, this is an indispensable guide. Published twice a year, it is the only independent source of pricing information available to consumers.

James M. Gabler—*Wine into Words—A History and Bibliography of Wine Books in the English Language*, published by Bacchus Press Ltd., Baltimore. This superbly organized, comprehensive book needs to be updated, but it is an essential contribution to the history of wine writing, as well as a much-needed reference work.

James Halliday—*The Wine Atlas of Australia and New Zealand* and *The Wine Atlas of California*, published by Viking Press, New York. These two extraordinary books are classics that are unequaled in their scope and quality, as well as impressive guides on two important wine regions. While the atlas on Australia and New Zealand is impressive, Halliday's tome on California is a tour de force, offering the finest perspective of California wine yet authored. It is destined to be a reference guide for years to come.

Hugh Johnson—*Modern Encyclopedia of Wine, World Atlas of Wine*, and *Vintage: The History of Wine*, published by Simon & Schuster, New York. These classic reference books written by the world's best-selling wine writer should be part of every wine lover's library.

Matt Kramer—*Making Sense of Wine, Making Sense of California*, and *Making Sense of Burgundy*, published by William Morrow, New York. Whether you agree or disagree with winedom's most articulate *terroirist*, Kramer's provocative books offer riveting, aggravating, as well as controversial insights and perspectives that are required reading.

John Livingstone-Learmonth—*The Wines of the Rhône Valley*, published by Faber and Faber, London. The most comprehensive book on the great wines of the Rhône Valley, this reliable guide is a must-purchase for partisans of the wines from this great winemaking region.

Robert M. Parker, Jr.—*Bordeaux, Burgundy*, and *The Wines of the Rhône Valley and Provence*, published by Simon & Schuster, New York. All three books are comprehensive consumer guides offering passionate but critical, independent, and uncensored views of three important winemaking regions.

Edmund Penning-Rowsell—*The Wines of Bordeaux*, published by Penguin Books, London. This is a classic reference for the history of Bordeaux, its most renowned proprietors, and their châteaux.

Jancis Robinson—*Vines, Grapes, and Wines*, published by Alfred A. Knopf, New York; *Vintage Time Charts*, published by Weidenfeld & Nicholson, New York; and *The Oxford Companion to Wine*, published by the Oxford University Press, Oxford, England. Perhaps the most talented of the world's wine writers, Robinson's three classics are authoritative evidence of this woman's seemingly infinite ability to fashion informative, accurate books that are essential reading.

Norman S. Roby and Charles E. Olken—*The New Connoisseurs' Handbook of California Wines*, published by Alfred A. Knopf, New York. This mini A-to-Z reference on West Coast wines is dry and unenthusiastically written, but it does provide valuable thumbnail sketches of virtually all Oregon, Washington, and California wineries.

Andrew Sharp—*Wine Taster's Secrets—A Step-by-Step Guide to the Art of Wine Tasting*, published by Warwick, Toronto. This is an extremely well written book with the most informative and perceptive chapters on wine tasting I have read. This is the finest book for both beginners and serious wine collectors about the actual tasting process—lively, definitive, and candid.

Steven Spurrier and Michel Dovaz—*Academié du Vin Introductory Course to Wine*, published by Willow Books, London. Along with Kevin Zraley's book, this is one of the finest guides to winedom for beginners.

Tom Stevenson—*The Wines of Alsace*, published by Faber and Faber, London. This is the definitive work on the underrated wines of Alsace. Extremely thorough, accurate, and erudite, this is a must-purchase for enthusiasts of these wines.

James Suckling—*Vintage Port*, published by The Wine Spectator Press, New York. This is the only reliable, comprehensive consumer's guide to vintage port that has been written. Suckling's exceptionally well-done book merits considerable attention from port enthusiasts.

Sheldon and Pauline Wasserman—*Italy's Noble Reds*, published by New Century, Piscataway, N.J. This book's organization seems consciously designed to give readers a migraine.

Nevertheless, it is a significant book crammed full of valuable information on Italy's great red wines.

Alan Young—*Making Sense of Wine Tasting*, published by Lennard, Sydney, Australia. An underrated book from an Australian who has clearly given an exceptional amount of thought to the process of tasting wine, this classic has remained undiscovered by much of the world's wine press.

Kevin Zraley—*Windows on the World Wine Course*, published by Sterling Press, New York. This is one of the two finest introductory guides to wine. I highly recommend it to readers who are trying to get a handle on the complicated world of vino.

THE TOP FIFTEEN BIGGEST LIES

Readers should keep in mind the fifteen biggest lies in the wine world.

15. The reason the price is so high is the wine is rare and great.
14. You probably had a "corked" bottle.
13. It is going through a dumb period.
12. We ship and store all our wines in temperature-controlled containers.
11. You didn't let it breathe long enough.
10. You let it breathe too long.
 9. Sediment is a sign of a badly made wine.
 8. Boy, are you lucky . . . this is my last bottle (case).
 7. Just give it a few years.
 6. We picked before the rains.
 5. The rain was highly localized; we were lucky it missed our vineyard.
 4. There's a lot more to the wine business than just moving boxes.
 3. Parker or *The Wine Spectator* is going to give it a 94 in the next issue.
 2. This is the greatest wine we have ever made, and, coincidentally, it is the only wine we now have to sell.
 1. It's supposed to smell and taste like that.

THE WINES OF WESTERN EUROPE

France
Alsace
Bordeaux
Burgundy and Beaujolais
Champagne
The Loire Valley
Languedoc-Roussillon
Provence
The Rhône Valley
Bergerac and the Southwest

Italy
Piedmont
Tuscany

Germany

Portugal

Spain

1. FRANCE

ALSACE

True connoisseurs of wine must find it appalling that so many importers trip over each other trying to find yet another excessively priced, overcropped, generally insipid Italian Chardonnay or French red burgundy that provides little joy, while ignoring the treasures of this fairy-tale viticultural area in the most beautiful wine-producing region of France. Every time I serve a dry Riesling, Gewürztraminer, Pinot Blanc, or Tokay-Pinot Gris blind to my guests, they are ecstatic about its quality. Why then have these wines failed to earn the popularity they so richly deserve?

For consumers who love wine with food, Alsace produces a bevy of dry, surprisingly flavorful, personality-filled wines that generally offer superb value for the dollar. Alsace also makes it easy for the consumer to understand its wines. As is done in California, the wines are named after the grape varietal used to make them. Additionally, one of Alsace's fifty-one grand cru vineyards can be annexed to the name of the varietal. When that occurs, it usually means the wine sells at a price two to three times higher than wines that do not come from grand cru vineyards.

Another remarkable aspect of Alsace wines is how long-lived a top Riesling, Gewürztraminer, and Tokay-Pinot Gris can be. Ten to twenty years of longevity is not out of the question for the totally dry, regular cuvées and grands crus, while the rich, opulent Vendange Tardive and the supersweet, luxuriously priced dessert wines called Sélection de Grains Nobles can survive and benefit from even longer bottle age.

To help readers' appreciation and understanding of Alsace, I have briefly profiled the region's grape varieties, and have included some comments about the more expensive and rarer Vendange Tardive and Sélection de Grains Nobles. I have also provided a brief overview of the grands crus of Alsace.

The Grapes and Flavors of Alsace

Sylvaner   This is my least favorite grape of Alsace. The wines often lack an interesting bouquet, tending to be neutral, even vegetal to smell. Because of its high acidity, Sylvaner should frequently be employed as a blending grape rather than be permitted to stand by itself. Aging potential: 1–5 years.

Pinot Blanc   Looking for a crisp, dry, flavorful, complex white wine for less than $15? Pinot Blanc has always represented an excellent value. In Alsace, the finest examples have an engaging bouquet of honeyed, stony, apple- and orange-scented fruit, as well as stylishly elegant, applelike flavors. While several producers have begun to barrel-ferment this wine,

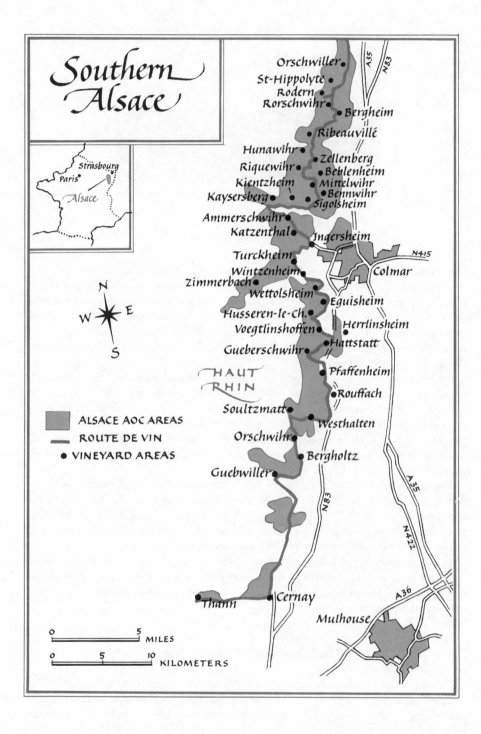

Southern Alsace

Orschwiller
St-Hippolyte
Rodern
Rorschwihr
Bergheim
Ribeauvillé
Hunawihr
Zellenberg
Riquewihr
Beblenheim
Kientzheim
Mittelwihr
Kaysersberg
Bennwihr
Sigolsheim
Ammerschwihr
Katzenthal
Ingersheim
Colmar
Turckheim
Wintzenheim
Zimmerbach
Wettolsheim
Eguisheim
Husseren-le-Ch.
Herrlinsheim
Voegtlinshoffen
Hattstatt
Gueberschwihr
Pfaffenheim
Rouffach
Soultzmatt
Westhalten
Orschwihr
Bergholtz
Guebwiller
Thann
Cernay
Mulhouse

Strasbourg
Paris
Alsace

HAUT
RHIN

N W E S

ALSACE AOC AREAS
ROUTE DE VIN
VINEYARD AREAS

0 5 MILES
0 5 10 KILOMETERS

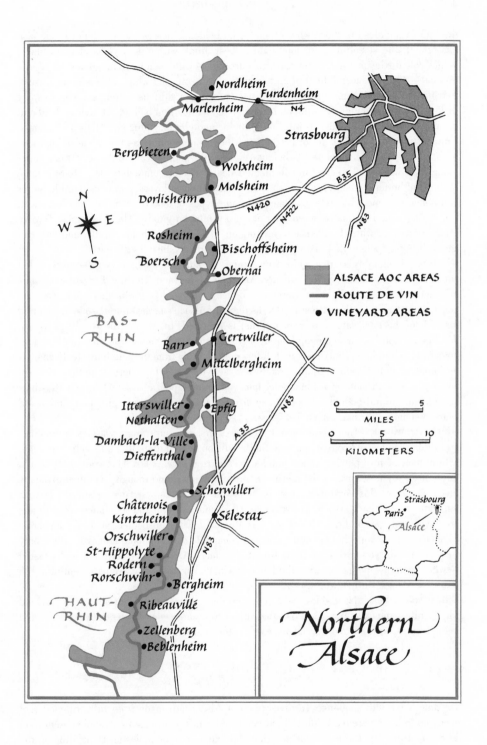

Nordheim
Furdenheim
Marlenheim
N4
Strasbourg
Bergbieten
Wolxheim
Molsheim
Dorlisheim
N420
N422
B35
N63
Rosheim
Bischoffsheim
Boersch
Obernai

ALSACE AOC AREAS
ROUTE DE VIN
VINEYARD AREAS

BAS-
RHIN

Barr
Gertwiller
Mittelbergheim

Itterswiller
Epfig
N83
Nothalten
Dambach-la-Ville
Dieffenthal
A35

0   5
MILES
0   5   10
KILOMETERS

Scherwiller

Châtenois
Kintzheim
Sélestat
Orschwiller
N83
St-Hippolyte
Rodern
Rorschwihr
Bergheim
HAUT-
RHIN
Ribeauvillé
Zellenberg
Beblenheim

Strasbourg
Paris
Alsace

Northern
Alsace

the finest examples are those where there is no evidence of wood aging. Pinot Blanc also has remarkable versatility with food, and is best drunk within 4–5 years of the vintage. Wines called Klevener and Pinot Auxerrois are Pinots with even more breed and finesse.

Muscat   Alsace's most delightful and seductively fragrant dry white table wine is Muscat. Terribly underrated, even ignored, this dry wine makes a glorious accompaniment to spicy dishes, and in particular, Oriental and Indian cuisine. Medium bodied yet vividly floral and perfumed, dry Alsatian Muscats offer pure finesse and charm. Aging potential: 3–5 years.

Tokay-Pinot Gris   Capable of producing wines as compelling as the greatest Chardonnays, Tokay-Pinot Gris reaches its height as a dry, full-bodied wine in Alsace. It is a super grape that, when picked late and fermented nearly dry or completely dry, offers a huge perfume of buttery, creamy, smoky fruit, unctuous, intense flavors, and considerable power and palate presence. Its style mandates the same types of food (rich fish dishes, etc.) with which one would normally serve a grand cru white burgundy. The Vendange Tardive Tokay-Pinot Gris wines from Alsace can contain 14%–15% alcohol naturally, and they can age well. Aging potential: 4–10 years; Vendange Tardive wines: 5–20 years.

Riesling   Irrefutably a great white wine grape, Riesling produces very differently styled wines in Alsace than it does in Germany. Alsatians prefer their Riesling dry, with considerably more body than do most German producers. It would appear that some German consumers also prefer their Riesling dry, as they are Alsace's largest purchasers, accounting for 57% of the total volume of Riesling that is exported. In Alsace, the Rieslings have a floral component, but also a deep *goût de pétrol* that is nearly impossible to articulate. It is an earthy, minerallike, flinty taste that differs considerably from the slatelike, steely character found in many Rieslings from Germany's Mosel vineyards. Less floral than their German counterparts, with more of a pineapple, honeyed, orange peel character, Alsace Rieslings are medium- to full-bodied wines that can also age remarkably well. Aging potential: 3–15 years; Vendange Tardive wines: 5–25 years.

Gewürztraminer   There is no doubt that one's first exposure to a great Gewürztraminer seems to cause one of two reactions—either revulsion or adoration. It is intensely perfumed, with aromas of rose petals, lychee nuts, and superripe pineapples. The word *subtleness* is rarely used when discussing the merits of Gewürztraminer, and though I am unequivocally in the corner of this controversial grape, it is best drunk by itself as an aperitif or with pungent fish and pork dishes. In France, great restaurants applaud its choice when diners are having foie gras or a rich cheese such as Muenster. This full-bodied, generally alcoholic wine (13.5%–14% alcohol is not uncommon) is capable of exceptional longevity. If the only Gewürztraminer you have tasted was from California or Oregon, you have not really tasted Gewürztraminer—no matter what the label or winemaker might say. Aging potential: 5–15 years; Vendange Tardive wines: 8–25 years.

Pinot Noir   Yes, Alsace does make red wine, but I have never been able to understand why. While some exceptions do exist, their Pinot Noirs are generally expensive, feeble, and insipid wines, with washed-out flavors, even in the best vintages.

A NOTE ABOUT VENDANGE TARDIVE AND SÉLECTION DE GRAINS NOBLES WINES

The late-harvested Vendange Tardive wines of Alsace are made from fully ripened (not overripe) fruit, and are powerful, rich, large-scaled wines that range in alcohol content from 14.3% to 16%. The levels of concentration and extract can be majestic. Depending on the wine producer, a Vendange Tardive wine can be fermented completely dry or left with a slight degree of residual sugar. The best of these wines are superlative expressions of winemaking and can provide thrilling as well as provocative drinking. They also age extremely well. A little-known fact is that these wines frequently age longer and more gracefully than France's premier and grand cru white burgundies. Any late-harvested wine will have the designation "Vendange Tardive" on the label.

The wines called Sélection de Grains Nobles represent the sweet, nectarlike, albeit rare and luxury-priced segment of the Alsatian wine hierarchy. They are often riveting wines because their sumptuous levels of fruit extract are unencumbered by aromas of new oak. Alsatian winemakers, as a general rule, eschew new wood casks. A Sélection de Grains Nobles can easily last 15–30 years. Many of these wines now cost over $100—for a half bottle!

RECENT VINTAGES

1994—This is destined to be a year with an extraordinary range in quality. Many of the low-lying vineyards that were encouraged to bear heavy crops have made light, diluted wines. However, the finest hillside vineyards, as well as those controlled by growers who crop-thinned and kept yields small, produced massive, extremely concentrated wines. Additionally, while September's weather was fitful, those producers who harvested late were rewarded with an extraordinarily sunny and warm October. Unlike 1993, 1992, and 1991, there will be abundant quantities of high-octane, rich, full-bodied Vendange Tardive wines, particularly from the finest vineyards and producers. At the top level, this is a great year.

1993—The 1993s have turned out well, as Alsace escaped the bad weather that battered much of France. The wines are lighter than the 1992s, with better acidity and more structure, as well as clean, ripe fruit. They will not be long-lived. Most 1993s will require consumption in their youth. Very little Vendage Tardive, or the sweet nectar, Sélection de Grains Nobles, was produced in this vintage.

1992—Alsace fared far better than most of southern France in this vintage. The harvest was the earliest since 1976, and the producers reported very high yields, with a lot of ripeness and richness, but wines that are extremely low in acidity. There are a lot of near-term drinking wines that are forward, juicy, and user-friendly.

1991—This is Alsace's toughest vintage since 1987. Nevertheless, some producers, such as Domaine Weinbach and Zind-Humbrecht, made wines that it is hard to believe came from a mediocre to below-average quality year. Most wines are relatively light, overly acidic, and slightly green, in complete contrast to the soft, fruity 1992s.

1990—Amazingly, this vintage is even more consistent in quality than 1989. There were fewer Vendange Tardive and Sélection de Grains Nobles wines produced, which should be good news for consumers looking for the drier Alsatian wines. I was impressed with the quality of all the varietals, but top marks must go to the glorious Rieslings, which are even superior to the 1989s. The Gewürztraminers, which were so stunningly perfumed and rich in 1989, are slightly less intense in 1990, but perhaps better balanced and less overwhelming. All things considered, this is a top-notch vintage that looks to be every bit as good as such previous great vintages as 1989, 1985, and 1983.

1989—Nineteen eighty-nine most resembles 1983 in that the wines are superripe, strong, forceful, and heady, with exceptional perfume, and at times, mind-boggling richness. The vintage produced amazing quantities of Vendange Tardive and Sélection de Grains Nobles wines. In fact, at the sweeter end of the spectrum, 1989 is probably unequaled by any recent Alsace vintage. Even the totally dry wines tend to be massive. There is plenty of great wine from which to pick, although most wines' aging potential will have to be monitored, given the relatively low acidity.

1988—This is a very good vintage that suffers only when compared with 1989 and 1990. The very dry, stylish wines may lack the concentration and sheer drama of the 1989s and 1990s; they are, nevertheless, elegant, suave, and graceful. Most of the top Rieslings, Gewürztraminers, and grands crus will easily last for a decade or more.

1987—This vintage is surprisingly good, particularly in view of its so-so reputation. Some producers, such as Domaine Zind-Humbrecht, made superb wines in 1987. Overall, the quality is at least good, and in many cases excellent. Hardly any Vendange Tardive or Sélection de Grains Nobles were made in this vintage because of fall rains.

1986—A patchy vintage, but Zind-Humbrecht and Domaine Weinbach made many glorious wines in 1986.

Older Vintages

To the extent one can still find any of the 1985s, it is one of the four or five best vintages for Alsace in the last 15 years. The wines are rich, with decent acidity, and are evolving gracefully in the bottle. They should provide delicious drinking and, in the case of the better Tokay-Pinot Gris, Rieslings, and Gewürztraminers, are capable of lasting for at least another decade. The 1984 and 1982 vintages get my vote as the two worst of the decade, and are of no interest. However, 1983 was another great vintage for Alsace. I bought nearly twenty cases of the 1983s and have drunk them with immense pleasure since their release. Despite their low acidity and relatively intense, concentrated style, they have displayed no signs of cracking up. Many of the bigger-styled Rieslings and Gewürztraminers are still improving.

To the extent that anyone is lucky enough to find well-stored bottles of 1976s, 1971s, or 1967s, these wines can provide remarkable evidence of the aging potential of Alsace's top wines. I suspect the only places they may appear are at auctions, and probably at alluring prices.

THE SIGNIFICANCE OF ALSACE'S GRAND CRU SYSTEM

Alsace, like Burgundy, has developed a complicated grand cru system that is still the subject of considerable controversy. There is no doubt that many of the best hillside vineyards in Alsace have been included in the grand cru classification. However, there is no qualitative justification for excluding the *monopole* (single-proprietor) vineyards from being considered grands crus. For this reason, irrefutably superb sites such as the Clos Sainte Hune, Clos Windsbuhl, and Clos des Capucins are deprived of such status. Moreover, some of the region's top producers—Hugel, Beyer, and Trimbach—have refused to indicate any grand cru designation on their top cuvées of wine, despite the fact that the bulk of their réserve wines are made from grand cru vineyards. Add to these problems the fact that the politicians of each wine village in Alsace have effectively persuaded authorities to give them their "own" grand cru. The political concessions have already resulted in over 50 grands crus, which is nearly 20 more than what is permitted in Burgundy's Côte d'Or. Moreover, some of these vineyards have not yet had their boundaries defined by the authorities.

In spite of its weaknesses, the grand cru system is an incentive for producers to achieve the best from the most privileged hillside vineyards. Because so few Alsace producers use new oak, one can also argue that these vineyards do indeed have their own special *terroir* character that is strongly reflected in the wine. My experience has been that the *terroir* character of a number of the grands crus is more forcefully expressed in Alsace's wines than in the grands crus of Burgundy, where the signature of the winemaker usually takes priority.

To help readers understand the grands crus, which will, for better or worse, become of increasing significance, I have listed the major grands crus in alphabetical order, along with the best producers from each grand cru. Additionally, I have attempted to summarize some of the more relevant characteristics of each vineyard from information provided to me by the Alsace Wine Information Bureau.

THE PRINCIPAL GRANDS CRUS OF ALSACE

Altenberg de Bergbieten SIZE: 67.3 acres; RELEVANT FACTS: hillside vineyard with a full southeast exposure and gypsum, clay, and gravelly soils; PRIVILEGED VARIETALS: Riesling and Gewürztraminer are considered superb, but Tokay-Pinot Gris and Muscat are also grown on these slopes; BEST PRODUCER: Frédérick Mochel

Altenberg de Bergheim SIZE: 80.6 acres; RELEVANT FACTS: limestone and marl dominate the soil of this hillside vineyard, which is renowned for its superb Riesling, and to a lesser extent, for its Gewürztraminer; PRIVILEGED VARIETALS: Riesling and Gewürztraminer; BEST PRODUCERS: Marcel Deiss, Charles Koehly, Gustave Lorentz

Brand SIZE: 140 acres; RELEVANT FACTS: This gorgeous hillside vineyard behind the village of Turckheim has a south-southeast exposure. The soil is deep granite, laced with black mica. PRIVILEGED VARIETALS: Riesling, Tokay-Pinot Gris, and Gewürztraminer; BEST PRODUCERS: Zind-Humbrecht, Dopff "Au Moulin," Pierre Sparr, Albert Boxler

Eichberg SIZE: 142.3 acres; RELEVANT FACTS: Not far from Colmar, Eichberg is renowned for its Gewürztraminers, followed by Tokay-Pinot Gris and Riesling. With its limestone/marl soil and gentle southeast slope, this area can produce powerful wines in hot, sunny years. PRIVILEGED VARIETALS: Gewürztraminer, Riesling, and Tokay-Pinot Gris; BEST PRODUCERS: Leon Beyer's Comtes d'Eguisheim (100% from the Eichberg vineyard), Kuentz-Bas Gewürztraminer

Engelberg SIZE: 27 acres; RELEVANT FACTS: a limestone/marl soil that drains exceptionally well; PRIVILEGED VARIETALS: Gewürztraminer and Riesling

Florimont SIZE: 27 acres; RELEVANT FACTS: This steep, south-and-east-facing, limestone vineyard is located outside the village of Ingersheim. PRIVILEGED VARIETAL: Gewürztraminer

Frankstein SIZE: 131 acres; RELEVANT FACTS: Actually four separate parcels, this is a steep, southeast-facing vineyard with superb drainage. PRIVILEGED VARIETALS: Riesling and Gewürztraminer; BEST PRODUCERS: Louis Gisselbrecht, Willi Gisselbrecht

Froehn SIZE: 32 acres; RELEVANT FACTS: Located outside the village of Zellenberg, this small grand cru has a reputation for long-lived wines. PRIVILEGED VARIETALS: Gewürztraminer, Tokay-Pinot Gris, and Muscat; BEST PRODUCER: Jean Becker

Furstenturm SIZE: 68 acres; RELEVANT FACTS: This superbly situated, steep, hillside vineyard not far from Kaysersberg has a warm microclimate, producing full-bodied, rich wines. PRIVILEGED VARIETALS: Gewürztraminer, Riesling, and Tokay-Pinot Gris; BEST PRODUCERS: Domaine Weinbach, Paul Blanck

Geisberg SIZE: 21 acres; RELEVANT FACTS: A steep, terraced vineyard overlooking the charming village of Ribeauvillé, Geisberg is known for its very gravelly and limestone-mixed soils, and its powerful, elegant wines. PRIVILEGED VARIETAL: Riesling; BEST PRODUCER: Trimbach (Cuvée Frédéric Emile)

Gloeckelberg SIZE: 57.8 acres; RELEVANT FACTS: Located near the villages of Saint-Hippolyte and Rodern, this moderate-sized vineyard has a south and southeast exposure with round, relatively acidic soil composed of sand, gypsum, and gravel. PRIVILEGED VARIETALS: Tokay-Pinot Gris, followed by Gewürztraminer; BEST PRODUCER: Charles Koehly

Goldert SIZE: 111.9 acres; RELEVANT FACTS: One of the more striking vineyards in Alsace, located north of the village of Gueberschwihr, Goldert is situated at a relatively high altitude with deep calcareous soil and an east-southeasterly exposure. It is particularly renowned for its well-drained soils that produce superb Gewürztraminer and Muscat. PRIVILEGED VARIETALS: Gewürztraminer, followed by Muscat; BEST PRODUCERS: Ernest Burn, Zind-Humbrecht

Hatschbourg SIZE: 116.8 acres; RELEVANT FACTS: Located south of Colmar, near the village of Voegtlinshoffen, this hillside vineyard has a calcareous, marllike soil that provides excellent drainage, and a south-southeast exposure. PRIVILEGED VARIETALS: Gewürztraminer, followed by Tokay-Pinot Gris and Riesling; BEST PRODUCERS: Joseph Cattin, Gerard Hartmann

Hengst SIZE: 187.2 acres; RELEVANT FACTS: This relatively large vineyard, south of the village of Wintzenheim, has a south-southeast exposure. The combined calcareous and marl soils tend to produce rich, full-bodied wines. PRIVILEGED VARIETALS: Gewürztraminer, followed by Tokay-Pinot Gris and Riesling; BEST PRODUCERS: Josmeyer, Zind-Humbrecht, Albert Mann, Barmes-Bucher

Kanzlerberg SIZE: 8.1 acres; RELEVANT FACTS: This tiny vineyard near the village of Bergheim, just west of the grand cru Altenberg, has a very heavy clay/limestone soil intermixed with gypsum and marl. Powerful wines emerge from this gem of a vineyard. PRIVILEGED VARIETALS: Tokay-Pinot Gris and Gewürztraminer; BEST PRODUCER: Gustave Lorentz

Kastelberg SIZE: 14.3 acres; RELEVANT FACTS: This steeply terraced vineyard in the very northern part of Alsace's viticultural region, near Andlau, is composed of deep layers of schist and quartz, the perfect soil base for Riesling. PRIVILEGED VARIETAL: Riesling; BEST PRODUCERS: Marc Kreydenweiss, Klipfel

Kessler SIZE: 70.4 acres; RELEVANT FACTS: Steep, terraced vineyards composed of red sandstone, clay, and sand are situated in the very southern part of Alsace's viticultural region, with a stunning southeast exposure. PRIVILEGED VARIETALS: Gewürztraminer and Tokay-Pinot Gris, followed by Riesling; BEST PRODUCERS: Schlumberger, Dirler

Kirchberg de Barr SIZE: 92 acres; RELEVANT FACTS: Located in the northern section of Alsace's viticultural region, behind the village of Barr, this vineyard has a southeast exposure and a soil base of calcareous marl with underlying beds of limestone and gravel. PRIVILEGED VARIETALS: Gewürztraminer, Riesling, and Tokay-Pinot Gris; BEST PRODUCERS: Emile Boeckel, A. Willm

Kirchberg de Ribeauvillé SIZE: 28.2 acres; RELEVANT FACTS: The stony, claylike soil, with a south-southwest exposure, produces relatively full-bodied wines that require some time in the bottle to develop their bouquets. PRIVILEGED VARIETALS: Riesling and Muscat, followed by Gewürztraminer; BEST PRODUCER: Trimbach

Kitterlé SIZE: 63.7 acres; RELEVANT FACTS: Perhaps the most striking terraced vineyard in Alsace, Kitterlé, which sits on the photogenic, steep slopes overlooking the town of Guebwiller, has three different exposures: south, southeast, and southwest. The soils consist of red sandstone, with plenty of quartz intermixed with lighter, sandier, gravelly soil that produces wines of extraordinary richness and aging potential. PRIVILEGED VARIETALS: Gewürztraminer, Riesling, and Tokay-Pinot Gris; BEST PRODUCER: Schlumberger (astonishing wines from this vineyard)

Mambourg SIZE: 161 acres; RELEVANT FACTS: Mambourg, a hillside vineyard overlooking the village of Sigolsheim, has a calcareous and marllike soil that produces very low yields. This heavy soil base is ideal for Gewürztraminer. PRIVILEGED VARIETALS: Gewürztraminer, followed by Tokay-Pinot Gris, Muscat, and Riesling; BEST PRODUCER: Sparr

Mandelberg SIZE: 29.7 acres; RELEVANT FACTS: Located near the village of Mittelwihr, this hillside vineyard has a marl and limestone soil base. PRIVILEGED VARIETALS: Gewürztraminer, followed by Riesling

Marckrain SIZE: 111.7 acres; RELEVANT FACTS: Calcareous marl soil with clay makes up this vineyard, located just south of the village of Bennwihr. The heavy soil produces relatively rich, fragrant, full-bodied wines. PRIVILEGED VARIETALS: Gewürztraminer and Tokay-Pinot Gris

Moenchberg SIZE: 29.5 acres; RELEVANT FACTS: Light, red sandstone intermixed with limestone makes up the soil of this hillside vineyard in northern Alsace, between the villages of Andlau and Eichhoffen. PRIVILEGED VARIETAL: Riesling; BEST PRODUCERS: Ostertag, Kreydenweiss

Muenchberg SIZE: 62 acres; RELEVANT FACTS: Light gravelly, sandy, nutrient-poor soil is ideal for producing closed but highly concentrated wines. PRIVILEGED VARIETAL: Riesling; BEST PRODUCERS: Julien Meyer, André Gresser

Ollwiller SIZE: 86.5 acres; RELEVANT FACTS: Located in the most southern sector of Alsace's viticultural region, near the village of Wuenheim (situated midway between Guebwiller and Thann), this hillside vineyard with a southeast exposure has soils made up of red sandstone and clay. PRIVILEGED VARIETALS: Riesling and Gewürztraminer

Osterberg SIZE: 59.3 acres; RELEVANT FACTS: With stony, claylike soils, the Osterberg vineyard is located near the village of Ribeauvillé. PRIVILEGED VARIETALS: Riesling, Gewürztraminer, and Tokay-Pinot Gris; BEST PRODUCER: Trimbach

Pfersigberg SIZE: 138 acres; RELEVANT FACTS: Gravelly soils with rich deposits of magnesium make up this vineyard, located near the village of Eguisheim within view of the three ruined towers that dominate the hillside above Huseren-les-Châteaux. PRIVILEGED VARIETALS: Gewürztraminer, Tokay-Pinot Gris, Riesling, and Muscat; BEST PRODUCERS: Kuentz-Bas, Scherer

Pfingstberg SIZE: 69 acres; RELEVANT FACTS: With its southeast exposure and location in the southern part of Alsace's viticultural region, just to the north of Guebwiller, the red sandstone– and mica-based soils produce classic, long-lived wines. PRIVILEGED VARIETALS: Gewürztraminer, Tokay-Pinot Gris, and Riesling; BEST PRODUCER: Albrecht

Praelatenberg SIZE: 29.6 acres; RELEVANT FACTS: This hillside vineyard, located beneath the formidable mountaintop château of Haut-Koenigsbourg, possesses a heavy but well-drained soil consisting of gravel and quartz. PRIVILEGED VARIETALS: Riesling, followed by Gewürztraminer and Muscat

Rangen SIZE: 46.4 acres; RELEVANT FACTS: One of the greatest of the grands crus, this vineyard, located at the very southern end of the viticultural region of Alsace, on steeply terraced hillsides with a full southerly exposure, has a soil base composed of volcanic rocks, schist, and numerous outcroppings of rocks. PRIVILEGED VARIETALS: Tokay-Pinot Gris, Gewürztraminer, and Riesling; BEST PRODUCERS: Zind-Humbrecht, Bernard Schoffit, Bruno Hertz, Meyer-Fonne

Rosacker SIZE: 67.2 acres; RELEVANT FACTS: Located north of the village of Hunawihr, near two of the greatest enclosed vineyards (called "clos"), the Clos Windsbuhl and Clos Sainte Hune, this hillside vineyard with its east-southeast exposure is planted on calcareous, magnesium-enriched, heavy soil, with some sandstone. PRIVILEGED VARIETALS: Riesling, followed by Gewürztraminer; BEST PRODUCER: Mittnacht-Klack

Saering SIZE: 66 acres; RELEVANT FACTS: The Saering vineyards, with their east-southeasterly exposure, form part of the same striking hillside that contains the famous Kitterlé vineyard. Both overlook the bustling town of Guebwiller. The soil at Saering is heavy, sandy, mixed gravel and chalk, which is perfect for Riesling. PRIVILEGED VARIETAL: Riesling; BEST PRODUCERS: Schlumberger, Jean-Pierre Dirler

Schlossberg SIZE: 197 acres; RELEVANT FACTS: Steep, terraced, sandy, gravelly, mineral-rich soils dominate this vineyard, located behind the charming village of Kaysersberg in the direction of Kientzheim. This is one of the largest grands crus, so quality varies enormously. PRIVILEGED VARIETAL: Riesling; BEST PRODUCERS: Domaine Weinbach, Pierre Sparr, Albert Mann

Schoenenbourg SIZE: 99 acres; RELEVANT FACTS: This outstanding, as well as scenically beautiful, steep vineyard behind the walled village of Riquewihr is rich in marl, gypsum, sandstone, and fine gravelly soil. PRIVILEGED VARIETALS: Riesling, followed by Muscat and some Tokay-Pinot Gris; BEST PRODUCERS: Hugel (their top cuvées usually contain high percentages of Riesling from the Schoenenbourg vineyard), Deiss, Beyer, Mittnacht-Klack

Sommerberg SIZE: 66.7 acres; RELEVANT FACTS: One of the steepest hillside vineyards in Alsace, Sommerberg is composed of hard granite and black mica, and has a full southerly orientation. The vineyard is located behind the village of Niedermorschwihr. PRIVILEGED VARIETAL: Riesling; BEST PRODUCERS: Albert Boxler, Jean Geiler

Sonnenglanz SIZE: 81.5 acres; RELEVANT FACTS: The southeasterly exposure and sloping hillside location, with vines planted on relatively heavy soil in a particularly dry microclimate, make Sonnenglanz one of the most favorable vineyard sites for Tokay-Pinot Gris and Gewürztraminer. PRIVILEGED VARIETALS: Tokay-Pinot Gris and Gewürztraminer; BEST PRODUCER: Bott-Geyl

Spiegel SIZE: 45.2 acres; RELEVANT FACTS: Located between Guebwiller and Bergholtz in the southern area of Alsace, the Spiegel vineyards are on sandy soils with a full easterly exposure. PRIVILEGED VARIETALS: Tokay-Pinot Gris and Gewürztraminer; BEST PRODUCER: Dirler

Sporen SIZE: 54.3 acres; RELEVANT FACTS: This great vineyard for Gewürztraminer, planted on deep, rich soils with a great deal of phosphoric acid, overlooks the splendid, pretty-as-a-postcard village of Riquewihr. The wines that emerge are among the richest and longest-lived in the region, although they need time in the bottle to develop. PRIVILEGED VARIETALS: Gewürztraminer, followed by Tokay-Pinot Gris; BEST PRODUCERS: Hugel (their top cuvées of Gewürztraminer are almost entirely made from the Sporen vineyard), Mittnacht-Klack, Dopff "Au Moulin"

Steinert SIZE: 93.8 acres; RELEVANT FACTS: The stony limestone soils of this vineyard, located on a sloping hillside in a particularly dry area of Alsace, produce very aromatic wines. PRIVILEGED VARIETALS: Gewürztraminer, followed by Tokay-Pinot Gris and Riesling

Steingrubler SIZE: 47 acres; RELEVANT FACTS: Another hillside vineyard with a sandy soil at the top slopes, and richer, less well drained soils at the bottom of the slopes, Steingrubler has a reputation for producing wines of great longevity. PRIVILEGED VARIETALS: Riesling and Gewürztraminer

Steinklotz SIZE: 59.3 acres; RELEVANT FACTS: This most northerly grand cru Alsace vineyard, located near the village of Marlenheim, has a south-southeasterly orientation and very gravelly calcareous soils. PRIVILEGED VARIETALS: Tokay-Pinot Gris, followed by Riesling and Gewürztraminer

Vorbourg SIZE: 178 acres; RELEVANT FACTS: This vineyard, located near the village of Rouffach in the southern sector of Alsace's viticultural region, is composed of limestone- and marl-enriched soils spread over the hillside, with a south-southeast exposure. Ideal ripening conditions exist in this relatively hot, dry microclimate. PRIVILEGED VARIETALS: Riesling, Gewürztraminer, Tokay-Pinot Gris, and Muscat; BEST PRODUCER: Muré

Wiebelsberg SIZE: 25.5 acres; RELEVANT FACTS: This spectacularly situated hillside vineyard, overlooking the village of Andlau, is planted on well-drained sandstone, sandy soils. PRIVILEGED VARIETAL: Riesling; BEST PRODUCERS: Marc Kreydenweiss, Boeckel

Wineck-Schlossberg SIZE: 59.2 acres; RELEVANT FACTS: Located west of the city of Colmar in the foothills of the Vosges Mountains, near the village of Katzenthal, this relatively obscure grand cru vineyard is planted on deep granite soils, producing very long lived, subtle wines. PRIVILEGED VARIETALS: Riesling, followed by Gewürztraminer

Winzenberg SIZE: 123 acres; RELEVANT FACTS: Located in the northern Bas-Rhin sector of Alsace, with a south-southeast exposure, and a granite, mica-infused soil base, Winzenberg is one of the least known Alsace grands crus. PRIVILEGED VARIETALS: Riesling, followed by Gewürztraminer

Zinnkoepflé SIZE: 153 acres; RELEVANT FACTS: This stunningly beautiful, steep, hillside vineyard, oriented toward the south-southeast, and planted on deep beds of sandstone in the southern part of Alsace's viticultural region near Soultzmatt, produces very powerful, spicy, rich wines. PRIVILEGED VARIETALS: Gewürztraminer, followed by Riesling and Tokay-Pinot Gris

Zotzenberg SIZE: 84 acres; RELEVANT FACTS: This vineyard, located north of Epfig just

south of Barr, has an easterly and southerly exposure, and is planted on marl- and limestone-based soils. The gradual sloping hillside is best known for its Gewürztraminer and Riesling.
PRIVILEGED VARIETALS: Gewürztraminer and Riesling

THE MOST FAMOUS CLOS OF ALSACE

Some of Alsace's greatest wines come not from grand cru vineyards, but from vineyards entitled to be called "clos" (meaning enclosed or walled vineyards). The most famous of these clos include the spectacular Clos des Capucins (12.6 acres), just outside the village of Kaysersberg, that is owned by the remarkable Madame Faller of Domaine Weinbach. Extraordinary Riesling, Gewürztraminer, and Tokay-Pinot Gris that are often far superior to most grands crus emerge from this vineyard. The Clos Gaensbroennel (14.8 acres), located near the northerly village of Barr, has provided me with some of the most remarkable and long-lived Gewürztraminers I have had the pleasure to taste. Clos Gaensbroennel is owned by Willm. Perhaps the best-known clos in all of Alsace is Clos Sainte Hune (3.08 acres), which is owned by the famous firm of Trimbach in Ribeauvillé. It is planted entirely with Riesling. Rieslings that emerge from this vineyard, often referred to as the Romanée-Conti of Alsace, can easily last and evolve in a graceful manner for 15–20 or more years.

Other exceptional clos include the Clos Saint Imer (12.5 acres), owned by Ernest Burn. As the tasting notes evidence, the Riesling, Gewürztraminer, and Tokay-Pinot Gris that come from this spectacularly placed clos near the village of Gueberschwihr rank among the very finest in all of Alsace.

Near Rouffach is one of the largest enclosed Alsace vineyards, the Clos Saint Landelin (39.5 acres), owned by the firm of Muré. Rich, full-bodied, opulent Gewürztraminer, Riesling, Tokay-Pinot Gris, and even a splendid dry Muscat are made from this enclosed hillside vineyard's grapes.

The Domaine Zind-Humbrecht also owns and/or controls the production of two well-known vineyards entitled to the designation clos. Their most famous, which they also own, is the Clos Saint Urbain (12.5 acres). This sensationally located, steeply terraced vineyard, planted on granite soils, with a full southeasterly exposure near the village of Thann, makes astonishingly rich, long-lived Gewürztraminer, Riesling, and Tokay-Pinot Gris. The latter wine, for my money, is the Montrachet of Alsace. The other great clos that is farmed by Zind-Humbrecht (they do not own it) is the Clos du Windsbuhl (11.1 acres). Located on a steep hillside behind the magnificent church of Hunawihr, and adjacent to the renowned Trimbach vineyard of Clos Sainte Hune, Clos du Windsbuhl is planted on a limestone and stony soil, with an east-southeast exposure. Majestic Gewürztraminer is produced, as well as small quantities of Tokay-Pinot Gris and Riesling.

Though I am less familiar with the following vineyards, I have been impressed with the Clos Zisser (12.5 acres), owned by the Domaine Klipfel and planted entirely with Gewürztraminer. Other well-known clos with which I have less experience include proprietor Jean Sipp's Clos du Schlossberg (3 acres) outside the village of Ribeauvillé. Lastly, Marc Kreydenweiss has consistently made some of the finest dry Muscat from the Clos Rebgarten (0.5 acre), which is planted on sandy, gravelly soil just outside the village of Andlau.

The wines from these clos are every bit as sensational as, and in many cases greatly superior to, many of the grands crus. *In vino politiques?*

BUYING STRATEGY

Alsace's wines do not move briskly through the marketplace, so stocks of great 1990s can be found in some top wine shops. Be sure they have been well stored. The 1991s, 1992s, and 1993s must be chosen with care (stick with the four- and five-star producers), as they will not be as rich as the 1989s and 1990s, but they will be less expensive. Wines from the top producers will drink well between now and 2000.

IN SEARCH OF THE BEST
(A personal perspective of the single greatest wines of Alsace)

J. B. Adam Gewürztraminer Kaefferkopf

Lucien Albrecht Gewürztraminer Cuvée Martine

Lucien Albrecht Tokay-Pinot Gris Pfingstberg

Barmes-Buecher Gewürztraminer Steingrubler

Domaine J. M. Baumann Gewürztraminer Sporen

Domaine J. M. Baumann Riesling Schoenenbourg

Jean-Claude Beck Gewürztraminer Fronholtz Vieilles Vignes

Jean-Pierre Becker Gewürztraminer Froehn

Leon Beyer Gewürztraminer Cuvée des Comtes d'Eguisheim

Bott-Geyl Gewürztraminer Schoesselreben Vieilles Vignes

Bott-Geyl Gewürztraminer Sonnenglanz Vieilles Vignes

Bott-Geyl Muscat Schoenenbourg

Bott-Geyl Tokay-Pinot Gris Sonnenglanz

Albert Boxler Gewürztraminer Brand

Albert Boxler Riesling Brand

Albert Boxler Riesling Sommerberg

Albert Boxler Tokay-Pinot Gris Brand

Albert Boxler Tokay-Pinot Gris Sommerberg

Ernest or J. et F. Burn Gewürztraminer Clos Saint Imer Goldert

Ernest or J. et F. Burn Gewürztraminer Clos Saint Imer Goldert Cuvée La Chapelle

Ernest or J. et F. Burn Riesling Clos Saint Imer Goldert

Ernest or J. et F. Burn Tokay-Pinot Gris Clos Saint Imer Goldert

Ernest or J. et F. Burn Tokay-Pinot Gris Clos Saint Imer Goldert La Chapelle

Marcel Deiss Gewürztraminer Altenberg

Marcel Deiss Riesling Altenberg

Marcel Deiss Riesling Burg

Marcel Deiss Riesling Engelgarten Vieilles Vignes

Marcel Deiss Riesling Grasberg

Marcel Deiss Riesling Schoenenbourg

Jean-Pierre Dirler Gewürztraminer Spiegel

Jean-Pierre Dirler Muscat Saering

Jean-Pierre Dirler Riesling Kessler

Dopff "Au Moulin" Gewürztraminer Brand

Dopff "Au Moulin" Gewürztraminer Sporen

Dopff "Au Moulin" Riesling Schoenenbourg

Sick Dreyer Riesling Kaefferkopf Cuvée J. Dreyer

Robert Faller et Fils Riesling Geisberg

Pierre Frick Gewürztraminer Steinert

Jean Geiler Gewürztraminer Florimont

Gérard et Serge Hartmann Gewürztraminer Hatschbourg

Gérard et Serge Hartmann Tokay-Pinot Gris Hatschbourg

Hugel Gewürztraminer Cuvée Jubilee

Hugel Riesling Cuvée Jubilee

Hugel Tokay-Pinot Gris Cuvée Jubilee

Josmeyer-Joseph Meyer Gewürztraminer Cuvée de Folastries

Josmeyer-Joseph Meyer Gewürztraminer Hengst

Josmeyer-Joseph Meyer Pinot Auxerrois "H" Vieilles Vignes

Josmeyer-Joseph Meyer Riesling Hengst Cuvée de la Sainte Martine

Josmeyer-Joseph Meyer Tokay-Pinot Gris Cuvée du Centenaire

Charles Koehly et Fils Riesling Altenberg

Charles Koehly et Fils Tokay-Pinot Gris Altenberg

Marc Kreydenweiss Gewürztraminer Kritt

Marc Kreydenweiss Klevner Kritt

Marc Kreydenweiss Riesling Kastelberg

Marc Kreydenweiss Riesling Wiebelsberg

Marc Kreydenweiss Tokay-Pinot Gris
  Moenchberg
Kuehn Gewürztraminer Cuvée Saint
  Hubert
Kuentz-Bas Gewürztraminer Eichberg
Kuentz-Bas Gewürztraminer Pfersigberg
Kuentz-Bas Riesling Pfersigberg
Kuentz-Bas Tokay-Pinot Gris Réserve
  Personnelle Cuvée Caroline
Gustave Lorentz Gewürztraminer
  Altenberg
Albert Mann Gewürztraminer Furstentum
Albert Mann Gewürztraminer Hengst
Albert Mann Gewürztraminer Steingrubler
Albert Mann Riesling Pfleck
Albert Mann Riesling Schlossberg
Albert Mann Tokay-Pinot Gris Hengst
Julien Meyer Riesling Muenchberg
Meyer-Fonne Gewürztraminer Schlossberg
Meyer-Fonne Riesling Kaefferkopf
Mittnacht-Klack Gewürztraminer Rosacker
Mittnacht-Klack Gewürztraminer Sporen
Mittnacht-Klack Riesling Rosacker
Mittnacht-Klack Riesling Schoenenbourg
  Vieilles Vignes
Muré-Clos Saint Landelin Gewürztraminer
  Vorbourg
Muré-Clos Saint Landelin Muscat
  Vorbourg
Muré-Clos Saint Landelin Riesling
  Vorbourg
Muré-Clos Saint Landelin Tokay-Pinot
  Gris Vorbourg
Domaine Ostertag Gewürztraminer
  Fronholtz
Domaine Ostertag Muscat Fronholtz
Domaine Ostertag Riesling Fronholtz
Domaine Ostertag Riesling Heissenberg
Domaine Ostertag Riesling Muenchberg
Rolly-Gassmann Gewürztraminer
  Kappelweg
Rolly-Gassmann Muscat Moenchreben
Rolly-Gassmann Pinot Blanc Auxerrois
  Moenchreben
Rolly-Gassmann Riesling Kappelweg
Jean Schaetzel Gewürztraminer
  Kaefferkopf Cuvée Catherine
Jean Schaetzel Riesling Kaefferkopf Cuvée
  Nicolas
André Scherer Gewürztraminer Eichberg
André Scherer Gewürztraminer Pfersigberg

Charles Schleret Gewürztraminer Cuvée
  Exceptionnelle
Charles Schleret Gewürztraminer
  Herrenweg
Charles Schleret Pinot Blanc Herrenweg
Charles Schleret Tokay-Pinot Gris Cuvée
  Exceptionnelle
Charles Schleret Tokay-Pinot Gris
  Herrenweg
Schlumberger Gewürztraminer Cuvée
  Anne
Schlumberger Gewürztraminer Cuvée
  Christine
Schlumberger Gewürztraminer Kessler
Schlumberger Gewürztraminer Kitterlé
Schlumberger Riesling Kitterlé
Schlumberger Riesling Saering
Schlumberger Tokay-Pinot Gris Cuvée
  Clarisse Schlumberger
Schlumberger Tokay-Pinot Gris Kitterlé
Domaine Schoffit Chasselas Vieilles
  Vignes
Domaine Schoffit Gewürztraminer Rangen
  Clos Saint Théobald
Domaine Schoffit Riesling Rangen Clos
  Saint Théobald
Domaine Schoffit Tokay-Pinot Gris Rangen
  Clos Saint Théobald
Pierre Sparr Gewürztraminer Brand
Pierre Sparr Gewürztraminer Mambourg
Pierre Sparr Riesling Schlossberg
Domaine Trimbach Gewürztraminer
  Seigneurs de Ribeaupierre
Domaine Trimbach Riesling Clos Sainte
  Hune
Domaine Trimbach Riesling Cuvée
  Frédéric Emile
Domaine Weinbach Gewürztraminer Cuvée
  Laurence
Domaine Weinbach Gewürztraminer Cuvée
  Laurence Altenbourg
Domaine Weinbach Gewürztraminer Cuvée
  Laurence Furstentum
Domaine Weinbach Gewürztraminer Cuvée
  Théo
Domaine Weinbach Gewürztraminer
  Réserve Personnelle
Domaine Weinbach Riesling Cuvée Théo
Domaine Weinbach Riesling Schlossberg
Domaine Weinbach Tokay-Pinot Gris
  Sainte Catherine

Willm Gewürztraminer Clos
  Gaensbroennel
Zind-Humbrecht Gewürztraminer Clos
  Windsbuhl
Zind-Humbrecht Gewürztraminer Goldert
Zind-Humbrecht Gewürztraminer
  Heimbourg
Zind-Humbrecht Gewürztraminer Hengst
Zind-Humbrecht Gewürztraminer Rangen
Zind-Humbrecht Gewürztraminer Rangen
  Clos Saint Urbain
Zind-Humbrecht Gewürztraminer
  Wintzenheim
Zind-Humbrecht Riesling Brand

Zind-Humbrecht Riesling Clos Hauserer
Zind-Humbrecht Riesling Clos Windsbuhl
Zind-Humbrecht Riesling Gueberschwihr
Zind-Humbrecht Riesling Herrenweg
Zind-Humbrecht Riesling Rangen Clos
  Saint Urbain
Zind-Humbrecht Riesling Turckheim
Zind-Humbrecht Riesling Wintzenheim
Zind-Humbrecht Tokay-Pinot Gris Clos
  Jebsal
Zind-Humbrecht Tokay-Pinot Gris
  Heimbourg
Zind-Humbrecht Tokay-Pinot Gris Vieilles
  Vignes

RATING ALSACE'S BEST PRODUCERS

* * * * * (OUTSTANDING)

Albert Boxler
Ernest and J. et F. Burn
Marcel Deiss
Jean-Pierre Dirler
Hugel (Cuvée Jubilee)
Josmeyer (single-vineyard cuvées)
Marc Kreydenweiss

Albert Mann
Mittnacht-Klack
Charles Schleret
Bernard and Robert Schoffit
Domaine Trimbach (top cuvées)
Domaine Weinbach
Zind-Humbrecht

* * * * (EXCELLENT)

J. B. Adam
Lucien Albrecht
Bott-Geyl
Dopff "Au Moulin" (single-vineyard
  cuvées)
Sick Dreyer
Pierre Frick
Hugel (Cuvée Tradition)
Josmeyer (regular cuvées)
Kuehn

Kuentz-Bas
Julien Meyer
Meyer-Fonne
Muré-Clos Saint Landelin
Domaine Ostertag
Rolly-Gassmann
Jean Schaetzel
Schlumberger
Pierre Sparr (single-vineyard cuvées)
Jeane-Martin Spielmann

* * * (GOOD)

Barmes-Buecher
J. M. Baumann
Jean-Claude Beck
Jean-Pierre Becker
Leon Beyer
Emile Boeckel
Bott Frères
Joseph Cattin
Cave de Pfaffenheim
Cave Vinicole Turckheim
Dopff "Au Moulin" (regular cuvées)
Dopff et Irion

Jean Geiler
Gérard et Serge Hartmann
Charles Koehly et Fils
Seppi Landmann
Gustave Lorentz
Muré-Clos Saint Landelin (regular cuvées)
Preiss-Henny
André Scherer
Maurice Schoech
Pierre Sparr (regular cuvées)
Domaine Trimbach (regular cuvées)
Willm

* * (AVERAGE PRODUCERS)

Cave Vinicole de Bennwihr	Jean-Pierre Klein
Cave Vinicole de Hunawihr	Preiss Zimmer
Cave Vinicole Kientzheim	Albert Seltz
Cave Vinicole d'Obernai	Louis Sipp
Robert Faller	Bernard Weber
Hubert Hartmann	Wolfberger
Bruno Hertz	Wunsch et Mann

J. B. ADAM (AMMERSCHWIHR)* * * *

1992 Pinot Blanc	A	87

J. B. Adam has fashioned an excellent 1992 Pinot Blanc. It possesses a bouquet redolent with scents of honeyed oranges, as well as medium body, excellent richness, generous fruit, and a dry, rich finish. Drink it over the next 2–3 years. This estate also produced a nonvintage Edelzwicker that should sell for well under $10 for a liter bottle. It is a very good, fruity, dry white wine. At the time of writing, Adam's importer was not sure if it would be sold in America, given the difficult marketplace for most Alsace wines. Do not hesitate to buy a bottle if you see it on retailers' shelves.

BOTT-GEYL (BEBLENHEIM)* * * *

1993 Gewürztraminer Schoesselreben Vieilles Vignes	C	91
1993 Gewürztraminer Sonnenglanz Vieilles Vignes	C	93
1993 Muscat Schoenenbourg	C	89
1993 Riesling Grafenreben	C	87
1993 Riesling Mandelberg	C	88
1992 Tokay-Pinot Gris Réserve	C	89
1993 Tokay-Pinot Gris Sonnenglanz	C	90

Now that the young Jean-Christophe Bott-Geyl has begun to take more risks in producing his wines (harvesting later, bottling with minimal clarification), the quality of the wines of Domaine Bott-Geyl, situated in the Alsatian village of Beblenheim, has soared. This is an impressive group of dry Alsatian white wines.

The 1993 Riesling Grafenreben offers a pretty bouquet of flowers, peaches, and honey. This is a dry, light- to medium-bodied, stylish, crisp wine with a long finish. It should drink well for 3–4 years. The 1993 Riesling Mandelberg reveals more opulence, as well as an underlying sense of elegance and a strong mineral character, with less of the honeyed fruit character found in the Grafenreben. It is a more focused, richer, medium-bodied, dry Riesling. I am a pushover for a glass of great, dry Alsatian Muscat, and Bott-Geyl's 1993 Muscat Schoenenbourg is a real turn-on. These wines must be drunk within a year or two of bottling, as much of their appeal is the delicacy and intensity of their huge, perfumed, fragrant noses. This wine offers up a smorgasbord of tropical fruits combined with spring flower-garden scents. It is dry, elegant, and ripe, with gorgeous balance and freshness. Drink it over the next several years.

The only 1992 I tasted from Bott-Geyl is the Tokay-Pinot Gris Réserve, a honeyed, waxy, rich, medium-bodied wine that avoids the heaviness that some Tokays possess. This chunky wine is loaded with intensity. It is a candidate for 5–8 years of cellaring. The superb 1993 Tokay-Pinot Gris Sonnenglanz reveals an intriguing honeyed, nutty, flowery, tropical fruit–scented nose, long, rich, medium- to full-bodied flavors, and a dry, multidimensional, wonderfully textured finish. It should drink well for a decade.

Bott-Geyl's two 1993 Gewürztraminers are both knockouts. The Schoesselreben Vieilles Vignes possesses a huge, intense nose of rose petals and honeyed fruit. It is intense and full bodied, with gorgeously well-delineated flavors and a superb mineral character that gives it finesse, while avoiding the heavy-handedness offered by some powerhouse Gewürztraminers. Even more remarkable is the Sonnenglanz Vieilles Vignes. It has a textbook nose of lychee nuts, roses, and honeyed cherries and pineapples that is a knockout. This huge wine displays masses of concentrated, rich fruit buttressed by decent acidity, superb purity, full body, and a wonderfully long, crisp finish. Both of these Gewürztraminers should drink well for a decade.

MARCEL DEISS (BERGHEIM)* * * * *

1991 Gewürztraminer Altenberg Vendange Tardive	D	90
1992 Pinot Blanc Bergheim	B	87
1991 Pinot Blanc Bergheim	B	86
1991 Riesling Altenberg	C	89
1991 Riesling Burg	C	87

Marcel Deiss is a producer who believes that vineyard character is everything. His Pinot Blancs, which are among the most elegant yet flavorful of the region, are pure Auxerrois. They offer wonderfully fresh, mineral and orangelike flavors presented in a light- to medium-bodied format. The 1991 Pinot Blanc exhibits lovely crispness, plenty of fruit, and excellent purity. Although the 1992 Pinot Blanc is softer, riper, and richer, it is well balanced by fine acidity. Both of these wines will drink well for 2–3 years.

The 1991 Riesling Burg reveals an enticing bouquet of tangerines and peaches, ripe, botrytised fruit, crisp acidity, and a long, rich, intense finish. This dry wine should age well for a decade. The 1991 Riesling Altenberg exhibits an apple-, mineral-, and orange-scented nose, excellent richness and definition, superb density and balance, and a long, dry, complex finish. Drink it over the next 10 years. Lastly, Deiss's 1991 Gewürztraminer Altenberg Vendange Tardive is a rich, full-bodied, honey-, flower-, and grapefruit-scented wine, with superb depth, medium to full body, and excellent definition. Although it is not as flamboyant or ostentatious as Zind-Humbrecht's and Domaine Weinbach's Gewürztraminers, it is an authoritatively rich wine for drinking over the next decade.

JOSMEYER-JOSEPH MEYER (WINTZENHEIM)
SINGLE-VINEYARD CUVÉES * * * * * REGULAR CUVÉES * * * *

1992 Gewürztraminer Folastries	B	86
1992 Pinot Gris Le Fromenteau	B	87
1992 Riesling Le Kottabe	B	86

If you are looking for the power and the blockbuster, chewy richness of an Alsace offering from the Domaine Zind-Humbrecht or Domaine Weinbach, these understated, elegant, crisp, dry, Alsatian white wines are not for you. Josmeyer's style, particularly at this level in his quality hierarchy, is to produce wines that possess excellent varietal character, but delicate personalities. The 1992 Riesling Le Kottabe exhibits a wonderful bouquet scented with apples, wet stone, and flowers, admirable crisp, dry, medium-bodied flavors, and a pure finish. Drink it over the next 2–3 years. The 1992 Pinot Gris Le Fromenteau is a more polite, subtle wine than one expects from this varietal, which normally produces rich, intense, massive wines. Dry and medium bodied, it offers attractive buttery fruit, and a spicy, crisp finish. Drink it over the next 2–4 years. The 1992 Gewürztraminer Folastries also displays Josmeyer's enticingly subtle style. The wine reveals fine ripeness, body, and viscosity, an exotic pineapple/lychee nut–scented nose, and a dry, refreshing finish. Drink it over the next 2–3 years.

ALBERT MANN (WETTOLSHEIM)* * * * *

1993 Gewürztraminer Altenbourg	C	92
1993 Gewürztraminer Steingrubler	C	94
1991 Gewürztraminer Steingrubler	C	88
1993 Pinot Auxerrois Vieilles Vignes	B	88
1992 Pinot Auxerrois Vieilles Vignes	A	87
1993 Riesling Rosenberg	C	92
1991 Riesling Rosenberg Cuvée Pauline	D	87
1993 Riesling Schlossberg	C	90
1993 Tokay-Pinot Gris Furstentum	C	92
1991 Tokay-Pinot Gris Furstentum	C	90
1993 Tokay-Pinot Gris Hengst	C	92+
1993 Tokay-Pinot Gris Vieilles Vignes	C	90

Proprietors Maurice and Jacky Barthelme of the Domaine Albert Mann have made so many great wines over the last few years that they are not far from challenging the supremacy of such great Alsace domaines as Zind-Humbrecht and Domaine Weinbach for top place in this fairy-tale wine region. Domaine Mann produces wines of uncompromising richness and intensity, generally from extremely small yields and old vines.

The 1993 Pinot Auxerrois Vieilles Vignes (from 60-year-old vines adjoining the grand cru Hengst Vineyard) is a dry, ripe, concentrated wine with medium to full body and an intense bouquet of oranges and other honeyed fruits. Rich, fresh, and exuberant, it is ideal for drinking over the next 3–4 years.

The two Rieslings are both outstanding efforts. The 1993 Riesling Schlossberg (from a vineyard planted on granite soil) exhibits a floral, earthy, applelike nose and intense, beautifully ripe flavors buttressed by zesty acidity. The finish is dazzlingly long, ripe, and crisp. This is a lovely, dry, intense Riesling for drinking over the next 10+ years. Even more profound is the 1993 Riesling Rosenberg. It reveals a pronounced, intense bouquet that is almost the essence of flowers, minerals, and honeyed applelike fruit. Dry and full bodied, with extraordinary focus and delineation, this marvelously concentrated, intense wine remains lively and exuberant. Drink this superb Riesling over the next 10–15 years.

The three Tokay offerings are outstanding wines that vary in intensity and power. The 1993 Tokay-Pinot Gris Vieilles Vignes (from the grand cru vineyard Pfersigberg's 50-year-old vines) possesses extremely high extract and nearly 13.5% natural alcohol. The wine is exceptionally full bodied, with a buttery, smoky, nutty nose, intense, dry, concentrated flavors, excellent acidity, and a long, expansive, chewy finish. It should drink well for at least a decade. The 1993 Tokay-Pinot Gris Furstentum offers a huge, powerful, buttery, waxy, fruity nose, chewy, dense, massive flavors, adequate acidity, and a heady, lush finish. It is nearly too much of a good thing, but lovers of white Alsatian wines, particularly Tokay, will admire its large proportions and creamy, bold, slam-dunk style. It should drink well for 10–15 years. The extremely unevolved 1993 Tokay-Pinot Gris Hengst is so backward it almost tastes as if it were a barrel sample. Although big, deep, honeyed, and off-dry, it is unformed and in need of 3–4 years of cellaring. The wine is clearly outstanding, with superb concentration and length, but patience is a necessity.

The 1993 Gewürztraminer, primarily from the vineyard of Altenbourg, exhibits that varietal's telltale, intense, lychee nut, rose petal, and honeyed grapefruitlike fragrance. Dry, full bodied, and rich, with superb purity and ripeness, it should drink well for at least 7–8 years. Unfortunately, there are less than 50 cases of the 1993 Gewürztraminer Steingrubler allocated to the United States. This wine is well structured, with amazing richness and ripeness. It offers a huge rose- and lychee nut–scented nose, massive body, and flavors that make the taster think he or she is drinking liquified rose petals. The wine's huge finish is dry and lively. This is a monster Gewürztraminer for drinking over the next 10–15 years.

Made from a parcel of 60-year-old vines of Pinot Auxerrois, situated next to the Hengst, one of Alsace's most famous grands crus vineyards, the light, straw-colored 1992 Pinot Auxerrois Vieilles Vignes exhibits a perfumed bouquet offering scents of ripe oranges, honey, and flowers. Rich and medium bodied with enough acidity for balance, and gobs of fruit, the wine finishes with a heady lustiness. Although unlikely to age given its roundness, it is delicious for drinking before the end of 1995.

The 1991 Tokay-Pinot Gris Furstentum reveals a classic Tokay nose of honeyed sweet corn and rich, buttery fruit. Full bodied, with fleshy, chewy flavors that display impressive fruit extraction, this wine has a touch of the famous flinty, earthy character found in Alsace's best vineyards planted on rocky soils, as well as a long, deep, heady finish. Treat this wine as you would a big white burgundy grand cru. The light- to medium-bodied 1991 Riesling Rosenberg Cuvée Pauline exhibits a high-strung personality. Vague scents of flint, oranges, and apples are followed by a medium-bodied wine with fine acidity and ripeness, as well as a tight, compact personality. More flamboyant is the 1991 Gewürztraminer Steingrubler. This big, bold, ostentatious wine offers a lusty nose of rose petals, lychee nuts, and honeyed fruit. Unctuously textured, with rich flavors and full body, this soft, well-balanced wine is opulent and long. All of these offerings should be drunk over the next 7–8 years.

DOMAINE OSTERTAG (EPFIG)* * * *

1992 Gewürztraminer Epfig	C	89
1992 Gewürztraminer Fronholtz Vieilles Vignes	C	91
1992 Muscat du Fronholtz	C	87
1992 Pinot Gris Muenchberg Vieilles Vignes	C	89+
1992 Pinot Gris Zelberg	C	87

After tasting through the lineup of Ostertag's 1992 white wines, the following were my favorites. All of these bone-dry wines were bottled without filtration. Longtime readers know I love Muscat from Alsace. The 1992 Muscat du Fronholtz (bottled without fining or filtration) exhibits a big, floral, fruit cocktail–scented nose, excellent richness, a dry, austere finish, super purity, and lovely balance. While all of Alsace's white wines are terribly underrated by American wine drinkers, Alsace Muscat is appallingly underesteemed by wine consumers. Drink this lovely Muscat over the next year.

Although Ostertag's 1992 Pinot Gris Zelberg is aged in 50% new oak casks, the oak is hardly noticeable. This is a dry, spicy, buttery wine, with elegant mineral scents, excellent definition, and a long, crisp finish. The 1992 Pinot Gris Muenchberg Vieilles Vignes reveals a honeyed, spicy, buttery note to its bouquet, a rich, medium- to full-bodied palate, and a long, dry finish. It has the potential to improve for at least 10–12 years, and it may ultimately justify an even higher score.

Ostertag made two superrich, dry Gewürztraminers in 1992. The bone-dry 1992 Gewürztraminer Epfig reveals a big, exotic bouquet of ripe fruit, earth, and spice. Long and rich, with layers of flavor, this is a beautiful expression of this varietal made in an intense yet elegant style. Drink it over the next 7–8 years. The 1992 Gewürztraminer Fronholtz Vieilles

Vignes is a knockout example of a full-bodied, dry Gewürztraminer. Superintense, with a huge bouquet and long, well-delineated, pure flavors that go on and on, this dry wine should be drunk over the next 10–12 years.

CHARLES SCHLERET (TURCKHEIM)* * * * *

1992 Gewürztraminer Herrenweg	C	92
1990 Gewürztraminer Vendange Tardive Herrenweg	D	96
1992 Muscat Herrenweg	C	88
1993 Pinot Blanc Herrenweg	B	90
1993 Riesling Herrenweg	C	90
1992 Riesling Herrenweg	C	86
1992 Tokay-Pinot Gris Herrenweg	C	89
1992 Tokay-Pinot Gris Herrenweg Vendange Tardive	E	92

It continues to be a source of personal frustration that the great white wines of Alsace are largely ignored by American wine consumers. I have frequently served these wines blind to discerning guests, and the oohs and aahs would suggest that they would be rushing off to buy these wines by the case. But once the identity is revealed, Alsace's lack of "prestige value" compels these people to throw away their money on something else.

Charles Schleret may not be as well known as Zind-Humbrecht or Domaine Weinbach, but like several other low-profile, great Alsatian wine producers (Bernard Schoffit, Albert Mann, Marcel Deiss, Albert Boxler, and E. Burn, to name a few), Schleret consistently produces brilliant wines. Unfortunately, only 75 cases of the 1993 Pinot Blanc Herrenweg made it into the United States. This wine is an extraordinary value, as well as a knockout example of just what heights Alsatian Pinot Blanc can attain. From its dazzling nose of honeyed, buttery, Mandarin orange–like fruit, this pure, ripe, clean, medium- to full-bodied wine is loaded with oodles of fruit. There is admirable freshness, vibrancy, and mouth-filling seductiveness to this Pinot Blanc. Drink it over the next 2–3 years. In total contrast is the 1993 Riesling Herrenweg. Precision, minerals, and exquisite delineation are displayed in this dry Riesling that offers a beautifully scented, mineral, apple, and floral nose, medium body, and subtle but powerful flavors. This glorious Riesling should drink well for up to a decade. Few readers are likely to shell out $50+ for Schleret's 1992 Tokay-Pinot Gris Herrenweg Vendange Tardive. But if you are looking for a Montrachet-styled, dry white wine with awesome depth, outstanding balance, and extraction of flavor that puts most white burgundies to shame, this is the wine. Still monolithic in terms of its aromatic development (typical for most young Tokay-Pinot Gris), it requires 5–6 years of cellaring. It is extremely rich and buttery, with the essence of honeyed hazelnuts and lush fruit to its personality. The wine's length pushes the stopwatch to nearly a minute. This off-dry, classic, late-harvest Tokay-Pinot Gris is best consumed by itself or with foie gras.

One would not expect such richness and intensity from the 1992 vintage, but Schleret has performed admirably. The 1992 Riesling Herrenweg displays a white pepper–like, spicy nose, crisp, tasty, stony, tart flavors, medium body, and a dry, austere finish. A bone-dry, steely Riesling with considerable character, it should drink well for 7–8 years. The 1992 Muscat Herrenweg exhibits this varietal's delicate, flowery perfume, as well as beautifully dry, crisp, medium-bodied flavors, and an impressive sense of elegance. Drink it over the next year. The 1992 Tokay-Pinot Gris Herrenweg is not made in the typical blockbuster, unctuously textured, chewy, thick style so common among top producers of Alsatian Tokay. It reveals a roasted nut–scented, buttery, rich, fragrant bouquet, and crisp, medium-bodied, concentrated, stylish flavors. Long in the mouth, with wonderful vibrancy and uplift, as well as noteworthy delineation, this dry, medium-bodied wine should drink well for a decade. If you like an intense bouquet of rose petals and honeyed fruits, check out Schleret's 1992 Gewürztraminer Herrenweg. It contains all the spice one could want from this varietal, as well as impressive extraction and precision, yet it comes across as medium bodied and surprisingly fresh and lively for a Gewürztraminer of such intensity. It should drink well for a decade.

The blockbuster wine in Schleret's current offerings is the late-released 1990 Gewürztraminer Vendange Tardive Herrenweg, a huge, ripe wine oozing with honeyed lychee nut and spicy fruit aromas and flavors. Full bodied, slightly sweet, and phenomenally rich, this layered, viscous wine manages to provide buoyancy in the mouth because of its crisp underlying acidity. An immense wine, it would be best drunk by itself or served with superrich foie gras.

DOMAINE SCHOFFIT (COLMAR)* * * * *

1992	Gewürztraminer Harth Cuvée Caroline	C	93
1991	Gewürztraminer Rangen Clos Saint Théobald	D	92
1990	Gewürztraminer Rangen Clos Saint Théobald Vendange Tardive	D	93
1992	Gewürztraminer Rangen de Thann Clos Saint Théobald	D	96
1991	Muscat Rangen Clos Saint Théobald	D	91
1992	Pinot Blanc Cuvée Caroline	B	90
1991	Pinot Blanc Cuvée Caroline	B	89
1992	Riesling Harth	C	92
1991	Riesling Harth Cuvée Prestige	B	87
1991	Riesling Rangen Clos Saint Théobald	D	95
1992	Riesling Rangen de Thann	D	93
1991	Tokay-Pinot Gris Rangen Clos Saint Théobald	D	93
1992	Tokay-Pinot Gris Rangen de Thann Clos Saint Théobald	D	91+

Bernard Schoffit, whose cellars are in the southeast sector of the beautiful town of Colmar, is now at the pinnacle of Alsatian winemakers committed to making wines of the highest quality. His wines, which offer extraordinary elegance combined with remarkable power and concentration, are all highly recommended. If you are looking for a great bargain in dry white wine, don't miss Schoffit's 1992 Pinot Blanc Cuvée Caroline. His best cuvée (named after his daughter), it is made from 30-year-old vines. It exhibits a provocative bouquet of minerals and oranges, followed by superb, honeyed, ripe, medium-bodied flavors with wonderful, juicy, succulent fruit, good acidity, and a long finish. This is a super Pinot Blanc for drinking over the next 4–5 years. I tasted two wonderful 1992 Riesling cuvées. The 1992 Riesling Harth is a wine of spectacular richness and precision. Its huge, stony, citrusy, apple-scented nose is followed by a wine with exceptional fruit extraction, as well as wonderful definition. Full bodied and concentrated, it retains a sense of lightness and elegance despite its admirable concentration and power. I advise drinking it in its first 3–5 years because of the soft nature of the 1992 vintage, but I suspect it will last for a decade. In comparison to Schoffit's 1992 Riesling Rangen de Thann (from that frightfully steep, sun-drenched vineyard in southern Alsace), the Harth is a more delicate wine. The Rangen de Thann displays a mind-boggling, exotic nose of honeyed peaches and apples intermingled with scents of spring flowers. Full bodied and fabulously concentrated, this magnificent expression of Alsace Riesling should drink well for more than a decade. It was made from less than 2 tons of grapes per acre—and keep in mind, that is from a tightly spaced vineyard!

Readers know that I am a pushover for personality-filled wines with decadent levels of fruit and exotic bouquets. The value-priced 1992 Gewürztraminer Harth Cuvée Caroline is a wine with 14% natural alcohol and thrilling levels of fruit extraction that accompany a bold, flamboyant personality. The ultrahoneyed, spicy, lychee nut–scented nose is followed by an extraordinarily rich wine oozing with flavor, crisp acidity, and a powerful, heady, dry finish. Drink it over the next decade. Made in a sweeter style, the awesome 1992 Gewürztraminer Rangen de Thann Clos Saint Théobald reveals an exquisite nose of honeyed tropical fruits and cherries, and unctuously thick, rich, powerful flavors that avoid heaviness. That is remarkable given the natural alcohol of nearly 14% and the slight degree of residual sugar. This wine should last for 15 or more years.

Lastly, I am convinced that Schoffit's 1992 Tokay-Pinot Gris Rangen de Thann Clos Saint Théobald will turn out to be extraordinary. However, Tokay requires 7–8 years of bottle age to reveal its bouquet. Although this example is closed, the wine resembles a cavalry charge, roaring across the palate with huge, massive, botrytised flavors buttressed by acidity. This wine should be served with dishes such as sautéed foie gras or by itself.

While it is tempting to measure a winemaker's genius by superb vintages such as 1989 and 1990, it is a vintage such as 1992 that reveals who's who in winemaking. Bernard Schoffit has proven that he deserves to be compared with Alsace's greatest domaines, such as Zind-Humbrecht and Domaine Weinbach.

Schoffit's performance in 1991 comes close to rivaling that of Alsace's legendary Domaine Zind-Humbrecht. His 1991s are remarkably rich, well-balanced, complex wines that taste as if they came from an excellent to outstanding vintage, not a year that, on paper, is of average quality. For example, the 1991 Riesling Harth Cuvée Prestige exhibits stony, crisp, apple, and floral scents, excellent, deep, dry, medium-bodied flavors, lovely purity to its fruit, and a fresh, minerallike finish. Drink it over the next 5–6 years. The 1991 Riesling Clos Saint Théobald from the exceptional Rangen vineyard is spectacular. Although the price may appear high, this is an uncompromising wine of remarkable brilliance and intensity. The huge nose of honeyed oranges, apples, and acacia flowers is followed by a stunningly rich, well-proportioned, dry wine that is oozing with fruit. Its personality is one of razor-sharp precision, elegance, and phenomenal depth and length. Drink this beautiful wine over the next decade.

Given its richness and perfume, one would think the stunning 1991 Pinot Blanc Cuvée Caroline was from a great vintage. The huge aromas of oranges, honeyed apples, and flowers are superb. The wine has tremendous precision to its rich, medium-bodied flavors, excellent length, good acidity, and exceptionally high extract. Made from old vines of the low-yielding Pinot Auxerrois clone, this cuvée is a sensational bargain. Drink it over the next 1–3 years.

Schoffit's 1991 Muscat Rangen Clos Saint Théobald is made from exceptionally old vines and yields of under 2 tons an acre. It possesses a spectacular, perfumed, showy nose of apricots, peaches, and flowers. Very dry, with deep, unctuous, superconcentrated flavors, it tastes more like a 1989 or 1990 Alsace wine than a 1991. Because of the fragility of Muscat's perfume, this is a wine to consume early—over the next 1–2 years. The 1991 Gewürztraminer Rangen Clos Saint Théobald was harvested at very high sugar levels from yields that were also under 2 tons an acre. It reveals a huge, spicy bouquet of lychee nuts and rose scents, unctuous, thick, spectacularly rich flavors, and a dry, full-bodied, powerful finish. It should last for up to a decade. The 1991 Tokay-Pinot Gris Clos Saint Théobald from the Rangen vineyard, also made from tiny yields, is slightly off-dry, with a huge, honeysuckle- and butterscotch-scented, creamy nose, and massively rich, full-bodied flavors allied to fine underlying acidity. This makes for a huge, nearly monstrous mouthful of Tokay that is best drunk with superrich pâtés and foie gras. It should last for up to 15 years.

The superexpensive 1990 Gewürztraminer Rangen Vendange Tardive from Schoffit's *monopole* vineyard, Clos Saint Théobald, is an amazingly rich, honeyed wine with medium sweetness, and spectacular perfume and density. Given its overwhelming size, it is not particularly food-friendly, but it is a brilliant winemaking effort.

PIERRE SPARR (SIGOLSHEIM)
SINGLE-VINEYARD CUVÉES * * * * REGULAR CUVÉES * * *

1992	Chasselas Vieilles Vignes	A	86
1991	Chasselas Vieilles Vignes	A	84
1991	Crémant Dynastie	B	87
1992	Gewürztraminer Carte d'Or	A	87
1991	Gewürztraminer Mambourg	C	90
1992	Gewürztraminer Réserve	B	88
1992	Pinot Blanc Réserve	A	85
1991	Pinot Blanc Réserve	A	86
1992	Pinot Blanc Vieilles Vignes	B	86
1993	Pinot Gris Carte d'Or	A	85
1992	Pinot Gris Carte d'Or	A	87
1991	Pinot Gris Carte d'Or	A	86
1992	Pinot Gris Réserve	B	87
1992	Riesling Carte d'Or	A	86
1991	Riesling Carte d'Or	A	85
1990	Riesling Mambourg	C	90
1992	Riesling Réserve	B	87

While Sparr's wines are rarely capable of hitting the peaks reached by the likes of Alsace's Domaine Weinbach, Zind-Humbrecht, Albert Mann, or Bernard Schoffit, they are consistently reliable as well as fairly priced. All of these offerings are attractive, up-front, delicious, dry whites for drinking over the next 2–10 years, depending on the cuvée.

The light-bodied 1993 Pinot Gris Carte d'Or is elegant, tasty, and fresh, with loads of fruit. It offers considerable flexibility with an assortment of food. Drink it over the next 1–2 years.

For over a decade, shrewd wine buyers have been seeking out Alsace Pinot Blanc as an attractive, tasty, medium-bodied, dry white wine that can age, as well as offer value. Sparr's 1992 Pinot Blanc Réserve reveals copious amounts of ripe apple/tangerinelike fruit, fine freshness, and a crisp, low-acid finish. Drink it over the next 2 years. Sparr's 1992 Chasselas Vieilles Vignes exhibits an attractive, crisp, buttery, floral-scented nose, tasty, fresh, medium-bodied flavors, and good ripeness, length, and precision. An excellent bargain, it should drink well for 1–2 years.

Consumers looking for medium- to full-bodied, ripe, concentrated, dry white wines with considerable character should check out Sparr's 1992 Pinot Gris Carte d'Or, 1992 Gewürztraminer Carte d'Or, and 1992 Riesling Carte d'Or. The 1992 Riesling Carte d'Or is the most fragrant, perfumed, and lightest of this trio. Forward and elegant, it offers a mineral-, apple-, and floral-scented nose, crisp, tasty, ripe flavors, medium body, and a dry finish. The 1992 Pinot Gris Carte d'Or reveals a big, spicy, buttery, opulent bouquet, and rich, medium-bodied, heady flavors with low acid and plenty of alcohol. It is a powerhouse wine, as well as a marvelous bargain. It will last for 4–5 years. The 1992 Gewürztraminer Carte d'Or is another super bargain. The kinky nose of pineapples, lychee nuts, and rose petals is followed by gobs of ripe fruit presented in a full-bodied, lush style, with plenty of alcohol, glycerin, and fruit in the finish. Gewürztraminer can never be accused of being subtle, so expect an ostentatious, in-your-face wine that should drink well for 5–6 years. For $10, it is nearly impossible to find a Gewürztraminer of this quality level.

Several other Sparr 1992s that are priced in the $12.50–$14.00 range are noteworthy wines. Consumers should be on the lookout for the 1992 Pinot Blanc Vieilles Vignes (rated 86); the 1992 Riesling Réserve (87; wonderful mineral/orangelike flavors in a dry, medium-bodied format); 1992 Pinot Gris Réserve (87; spicy, oily, buttery, and chewy); and the 1992 Gewürztraminer Réserve (88; textbook rose petal/grapefruit flavors in a full-bodied, dry format).

Low yields resulted in a ripe, viscous, rich, well-structured 1991 Gewürztraminer Mambourg with layers of ripe fruit, medium to full body, and a heady, long finish with plenty of acidity for aging. This is a top-notch Gewürztraminer! Sparr's 1990 Riesling Mambourg, from a super vintage, exhibits lemony, gunflint, petrollike scents in its bouquet. Dry, rich, and medium to full bodied, with excellent depth and precision, this is the first Riesling Sparr has made from the grand cru Mambourg vineyard. While drinkable now, this wine should last for a decade.

The 1991 Chasselas Vieilles Vignes is an elegant, fresh, lively wine with tart acidity and a vibrant personality. Drink it over the next year. The 1991 Pinot Blanc Réserve offers up an enticing orange peel– and floral-scented bouquet, lovely fruit flavors, medium body, and a fresh, lively finish. It is a delicious white wine for drinking as an aperitif or with simple fish and fowl dishes.

The 1991 Pinot Gris Carte d'Or exhibits the waxy, honeyed Pinot Gris style, an admirable ripe, medium-bodied taste, and a fine finish. The 1991 Riesling Carte d'Or reveals a lemony, tart, green apple–scented nose, tasty, surprisingly long flavors, and a dry, pure, stony finish. All of these completely dry offerings should be consumed over the next 1–2 years.

Lastly, Sparr consistently makes one of the best sparkling wine values in France. The 1991 Crémant Dynastie is made from 50% Pinot Blanc, with the remainder Pinot Gris and other Alsace varietals. Sparr's top sparkling wine cuvée, it is a light-bodied, rich, creamy-textured, frothy sparkling wine with lovely fruit and ripeness—all presented in a dry, crisp format. Drink it over the next 12 months.

DOMAINE TRIMBACH (RIBEAUVILLÉ)
TOP CUVÉES * * * * * REGULAR CUVÉES * * *

1990 Gewürztraminer Réserve	C	87
1989 Gewürztraminer Réserve	C	86
1990 Gewürztraminer Seigneurs de Ribeaupierre	C	90
1989 Gewürztraminer Seigneurs de Ribeaupierre	C	90
1989 Gewürztraminer Sélection de Grains Nobles	E	88
1989 Gewürztraminer Sélection de Grains Nobles Hors Choix	E	97
1990 Gewürztraminer Vendange Tardive	D	91
1989 Gewürztraminer Vendange Tardive	D	87
1990 Riesling	B	84
1990 Riesling Clos Sainte Hune	D	92

1989 Riesling Clos Sainte Hune Vendange Tardive	E	96
1989 Riesling Clos Sainte Hune Vendange Tardive Hors Choix	EE	99
1990 Riesling Cuvée Frédéric Emile	C	91
1989 Riesling Cuvée Frédéric Emile	C	90
1988 Riesling Cuvée Frédéric Emile	C	89
1990 Riesling Cuvée Frédéric Emile Sélection de Grains Nobles	E	93
1989 Riesling Cuvée Frédéric Emile Sélection de Grains Nobles	E	96
1990 Riesling Cuvée Frédéric Emile Vendange Tardive	D	92
1989 Riesling Cuvée Frédéric Emile Vendange Tardive	D	94
1990 Riesling Réserve	B	86
1989 Riesling Réserve	B	87
1990 Tokay-Pinot Gris Réserve	B	86
1989 Tokay-Pinot Gris Réserve	B	87
1989 Tokay-Pinot Gris Sélection de Grains Nobles Hors Choix	E	95

The wines of the Trimbach family, along with those of their neighbors in Riquewihr, the Hugels, are the best-known Alsace wines in the American marketplace, and probably the world. The Trimbachs, who can trace their origins as a winemaking family to 1626, are today both vineyard owners and *négociants*, producing a range of wines that are the most elegant and restrained of the region. For that reason, and the fact that most of their top cuvées need 3–5 years to develop, this is not a firm that rushes to release its wines. The quality is consistently very fine, although the wines rarely have the sheer drama and concentration of those from Zind-Humbrecht or Domaine Weinbach. Hubert Trimbach states that he wants all of the estate wines from the firm's 53 acres of vineyards, as well as those wines made from grapes they buy, "to have vitality, long life, and finesse."

Wines that have the word "Réserve" or "Sélection" on the label tend to be cuvées that are meant to be slightly richer and longer lived than the standard offerings named after the varietal. I thought Trimbach's 1989 and 1990 Riesling Réserves were both high-class wines with flinty, floral, apricot, and apple noses, medium body, plenty of lively acidity, and excellent concentration. The 1990 was slightly more austere and more closed, whereas the 1989 appeared softer and more obvious. Both should drink well for 7–8 years. One of the classic dry Alsace Rieslings is Trimbach's Riesling Cuvée Frédéric Emile. The average yearly production is only 3,000 cases, but it is one of the firmest and longest-lived Rieslings made, often needing 3–4 years after the vintage to reveal its floral, herbal aromas and honeyed richness. I did a minivertical back to 1983, and found the 1983 to be still amazingly rich, incredibly young, bone dry, and just beginning to evolve. Among the more recent vintages, there is a superb 1985 that may be still languishing on retailers' shelves, a good 1986, and three excellent to outstanding wines in 1988, 1989, and 1990. The 1988 Riesling Cuvée Frédéric Emile was extremely understated and backward, almost steely in a dramatic sense, but dry, with wonderful purity of fruit, and apple, orange, citrusy flavors. It should drink well for the next decade. The 1989 Riesling Cuvée Frédéric Emile, which is also bone dry, has more depth to it, as well as some evidence of botrytis in the apricot/peach fruitiness that I detected in both the nose and taste. It is more austere at the moment than the 1988, but full of charm, and long, with an inner core of highly extracted fruit. Perhaps the best example of this wine since the glorious 1983 is the 1990 Riesling Cuvée Frédéric Emile. It is a richer, bigger, more complete wine than the 1989 or 1988, with super-extraction of fruit and a very dry, crisp finish. Most impressively, it blossoms and opens considerably in the glass after thirty minutes of airing. This is a superb, penetrating, brilliantly focused Riesling for drinking over the next 10–15 years.

I have never thought of Trimbach as being one of Alsace's leading specialists in Tokay-Pinot Gris, but their 1989 and 1990 Tokay-Pinot Gris Réserves were stylish, elegant, graceful wines, with a creamy, buttery texture and smoky fruit allied with relatively high acidity, medium body, and an understated personality. Both should be drunk over the next 5–7 years. I had a slight preference for the richer, more opulent 1989.

The style of Gewürztraminer sought by Trimbach is, not surprisingly, one of elegance rather than pure muscle and blockbuster opulence. Both the 1989 and 1990 Gewürztraminer Réserves were beautifully poised, smoke-scented wines hinting at more grapefruit than lychee nut, with medium body, crisp acidity, and plenty of fruit in their dry, medium-bodied formats. The lighter 1990 had more elegance, whereas the 1989 was riper, displayed some evidence of botrytis, and finished with more glycerin and alcohol. Trimbach's top-of-the-line, dry Gewürztraminer is the Seigneurs de Ribeaupierre. Both the 1989 and 1990 are outstanding, with the 1990 exhibiting exceptional elegance, a rich, superbly concentrated feel on the palate, crisp acidity, wonderful purity of flavors, and a medium-bodied, authoritative finish. The 1989 Gewürztraminer Seigneurs de Ribeaupierre displayed more of a lychee nut, smoky character to go along with its intense grapefruity character. It is a medium- to full-bodied, larger-scaled wine than Trimbach normally produces. More up-front, more obvious, and more flattering to taste than the 1990, it should therefore be drunk over the next 6–8 years.

The Trimbach family turns out what many people consider to be the greatest expression of dry Riesling in France. It emerges from a tiny 3.06-acre vineyard called the Clos Sainte Hune. This vineyard, which is solely owned by the Trimbachs and therefore not entitled to grand cru status, is situated in the middle of the Rosacker grand cru vineyard. The clay and limestone-based soil produces Rieslings of extraordinary perfume and unbelievable aging potential. The Trimbachs generously put on a vertical tasting of this Riesling (only 500–600 cases are produced each year) back to 1964. Yes, the greatest wines of the tasting were the 1967 and 1964, which are just becoming drinkable—after more than 20 years of cellaring! I have mixed feelings about extolling such a wine, because it is almost impossible to find in the marketplace. But for those lucky enough to visit Alsace, or to find it on a wine list, it is probably best cellared, even in the lighter-weight vintages, for it appears to require at least 10 years before it begins to evolve. Of the recent vintages, the 1990 Riesling Clos Sainte Hune was very closed, but one could sense its superextraction of fruit, long, dry, tightly knit flavors, and medium-bodied, austere finish. It had a very strong mineral character. The 1989 Riesling Clos Sainte Hune Vendange Tardive was essentially a dry wine, but was powerful, with extraordinary richness and a pronounced essence of mineral taste combined with scents of apples and apricots. There is even a strong smell of paraffin in the nose that makes this wine more intriguing still. The Trimbachs also produced a 1989 Riesling Clos Sainte Hune Vendange Tardive Hors Choix. The grapes were picked at almost Sélection de Grains Nobles ripeness, but vinified dry. This is an amazingly rich, ripe, yet dry wine with extraordinary intensity and length, as well as a finish that must last up to several minutes. Neither the 1990 nor the 1989s will be released for several more years. The current release of this wine is the 1985, which is more evolved, marvelously rich, and scented with apples, flint, and petrol, with superb acidity, wonderful ripeness and purity, and a terrifically long, dry finish. It should drink well for at least 20 years. Should you happen to be lucky enough to find any Clos Sainte Hune being offered at auction, or languishing on some obscure retailers' shelves, the other great vintages for this phenomenal Riesling are 1983 (rated 94), 1976 (rated 93), the famed 1967 (rated 96), and 1964 (rated 93).

When Trimbach makes Vendange Tardive Rieslings, they can be some of the greatest in Alsace. For example, who can forget the riveting 1983 Riesling Cuvée Frédéric Emile Vendange Tardive? It would appear that Trimbach has again hit the jackpot with two compelling late-harvest Rieslings in 1989 and 1990. The 1989 and 1990 Riesling Cuvée Frédéric Emile Vendange Tardive are both sensational, rich, concentrated, slightly off-dry, intense wines, with exotic ripeness, superb firmness and length, and exceptional extract, aromatic purity, and complexity. These will both be great, long-lived, late-harvest Rieslings that will prove amazingly flexible with food given their near dryness. On the downside, the small quantities produced will not be released for several years, and if you have to make the difficult choice between the two, the 1990 has more of the highly desirable mineral, or petrollike character, intertwined with wonderfully intense aromas and flavors of apricots, whereas the 1989 is richer, fuller, and dazzling from beginning to end. Both should last for at least 10–15 years.

Another great late-harvest wine was the 1990 Gewürztraminer Vendange Tardive. Trimbach thinks it is their finest since the 1971. What is so impressive with this wine, in addition to its purity, is the impeccable balance it exhibits despite its power, high extraction, and massive, smoky, meaty, apricot and peachlike flavors. This superb Gewürztraminer, ideal for drinking with richly sauced fish dishes, should drink well for at least 15 or more years. On the other hand, the 1989 Gewürztraminer Vendange Tardive was cloying, flat, and flabby, without enough balancing acidity.

I tasted six Sélection de Grains Nobles (S.D.G.N.) offerings from Trimbach, four of which were extraordinary. The only less-than-profound wine was the 1989 Gewürztraminer S.D.G.N., which was supersweet, huge, and fat in the mouth, with opulence, but perhaps not enough acidity to give the wine the desired clarity and structure I had hoped to find. Nevertheless, it is still an excellent wine. Both the 1989 and 1990 Riesling Cuvée Frédéric Emile S.D.G.N. should prove to be monumental efforts. The 1990, with its 80 grams per liter of residual sugar, is a lighter wine, but with superripeness, medium sweetness, and a near essence of apricot flavor. The 1989, with 110 grams per liter of residual sugar, is a titan of a wine, with a smashingly intense nose of apples, minerals, and peaches, extraordinary richness and fullness, an off-dry to medium-sweet taste, and great acidity and clarity to its immense flavors. Three hundred bottles were produced of a 1989 Gewürztraminer S.D.G.N. Hors Choix. This is a nearly perfect wine, with a nectarlike richness, superb poise and balance, and a bouquet that soars from the glass. Its penetrating acidity and massive fruit flavors come together to make this a dazzling example of sweet Gewürztraminer that is fabulous and exciting to taste. Nearly as good is the 1989 Tokay-Pinot Gris S.D.G.N. Hors Choix. With an astounding 200 grams of residual sugar per liter, this thick, honeyed, extraordinary, rich wine would seemingly appear to be too heavy and cloying. But fine acidity balances everything. I would not be surprised to see this compelling sweet wine drink well for 25–30 years.

DOMAINE WEINBACH (KAYSERBERG)* * * * *

1993 Gewürztraminer Cuvée Laurence Altenbourg	D	92
1993 Gewürztraminer Cuvée Laurence Furstentum	D	91
1992 Gewürztraminer Cuvée Laurence Furstentum	D	94
1993 Gewürztraminer Cuvée Théo	C	90
1992 Gewürztraminer Cuvée Théo	C	93
1993 Gewürztraminer Réserve Personnelle	C	88
1992 Gewürztraminer Réserve Personnelle	C	90

1993	Muscat Réserve Personnelle	C	87
1992	Muscat Réserve Personnelle	C	89
1993	Pinot Réserve	C	90
1992	Pinot Réserve	B	88
1993	Riesling Cuvée Sainte Catherine	D	90
1992	Riesling Cuvée Sainte Catherine	D	90
1993	Riesling Cuvée Théo	C	90
1992	Riesling Cuvée Théo	C	91
1993	Riesling Réserve Personnelle	C	89
1992	Riesling Réserve Personnelle	B	87
1993	Riesling Schlossberg	C	92
1992	Riesling Schlossberg	D	90
1993	Riesling Schlossberg Cuvée Sainte Catherine	D	94
1992	Riesling Schlossberg Cuvée Sainte Catherine	D	93
1992	Sylvaner Réserve	B	87
1993	Tokay-Pinot Gris Cuvée Sainte Catherine	D	90

Laurence, one of Colette Faller's two daughters, is now in full control of the Domaine Weinbach, and the 1993 vintage showcases her talent. She has moved the domaine to an even higher quality level, fashioning fuller-bodied, drier wines with slightly higher alcohol levels. Domaine Weinbach's small 1993 crop is evident in the following wines—all impressively rich, fragrant, and—most important—delicious.

This estate often makes gorgeous Pinot Blanc and the 1993 Pinot Réserve exhibits a knockout nose of honeyed, mandarin oranges, and buttery, apple fruit. It is rich, medium to full bodied, with excellent purity, and plenty of length. Moreover, there is no evidence of oak to interfere with the wine's flexibility with food. I cannot think of many Pinot Blancs this delicious.

There are six 1993 dry Riesling cuvées, each with its own personality. The intensity level, amount of body, and concentration varies in each wine. The 1993 Riesling Réserve Personnelle is the lightest, but it is still rich, medium to full bodied, and concentrated. Its bouquet of crisp apples and citrusy fruits is followed by a wine with good depth and length, as well as fine overall harmony. Drink this elegant, stylish, dry Riesling over the next 5–7 years. The 1993 Riesling Cuvée Théo possesses greater precision, and a more intriguing aromatic display of minerals combined with ripe apples and flowers. It is a rich, crisp, dry, beautifully balanced wine that can be drunk now or cellared for a decade. The 1993 Riesling Schlossberg is an outstanding example of the type of rich, full-bodied, powerful Riesling that can only be made in Alsace. This dry, full-bodied, fruit-filled Riesling reveals gobs of tropical fruit in its intense, ostentatious bouquet, as well as superb depth and intensity. Drink it over the next decade. At present, the 1993 Riesling Cuvée Sainte Catherine is dominated by a strong mineral *terroir* character, resulting in a wine of considerable stature and finely knit character. Less showy than Domaine Weinbach's other cuvées, it is a dry, medium- to full-bodied, tightly constructed wine with huge reserves of fruit. In complete contrast is the property's top Riesling cuvée, the decadent, awesomely rich, full-bodied, dry 1993 Riesling Schlossberg Cuvée Sainte Catherine. Fanatics of dry, full-throttle Riesling should make an effort to latch on to a bottle of this massively rich, yet refreshingly light, dry Riesling. The bouquet of tropical fruits, apples, and minerals is followed by layers of concentrated fruit. This wine is the essence of extremely ripe Riesling fruit grown in stony, mineral-filled soils. The finish lasts for nearly a minute. Despite all its intensity, power, and extract, the wine is not heavy or flabby.

Although the perfumed, light-bodied 1993 Muscat Réserve Personnelle is delicious, tasty, and dry, it is less impressive than Domaine Weinbach's other cuvées. The outstanding 1993 Tokay-Pinot Gris Cuvée Sainte Catherine possesses an undeveloped, buttery, hazelnut, honeyed nose, a plush, chewy texture, highly extracted flavors exhibiting great fruit and ripeness, and a long, spicy, dry finish. This wine will continue to develop more aromatic dimension over the next 5–10 years.

Domaine Weinbach's Gewürztraminers are always among the finest made in the world. The 1993 Gewürztraminer Réserve Personnelle exhibits a textbook nose of roses, honey, and smoky nuts, deep, cherrylike flavors, great fruit, and an off-dry, full-bodied, powerful finish. Although it is a heavyweight Gewürztraminer, it manages to avoid the oiliness that sometimes detracts from this varietal's pleasure. More exotic and compelling is the 1993 Gewürztraminer Cuvée Théo. Its exotic, intense, smoky, honeyed, cherry- and lychee nut–scented nose is powerful and dramatic. The wine is full bodied, with great fruit, plenty of spice, and a dry, crisp, rich finish. It should drink well for at least a decade. As good as the Cuvée Théo is, it takes a backseat to the 1993 Gewürztraminer Cuvée Laurence Altenbourg. This is a Gewürztraminer of immense stature, full body, amazing richness, and a dry, long, remarkably well-balanced, heady finish. Given its blast of intense Gewürztraminer perfume, fruit, and body, it will not be everybody's favorite choice. But, wow, what a mouthful of wine! Over the next 10–12 years, it will be delicious with rich, creamy Muenster cheese or Asian dishes. The 1993 Gewürztraminer Cuvée Laurence Furstentum is a full-bodied, rich, more oily, off-dry Gewürztraminer. While it lacks the precision of the Altenbourg and Cuvée Théo, it offers considerable power and intensity. It should drink well for at least a decade. Once again, Domaine Weinbach has produced some of Alsace's finest white wines.

The problem in Alsace in 1992 was not one of ripeness but, rather, of too large a crop. Domaine Weinbach was one of a handful of estates that employed serious crop thinning. The results of their efforts are admirably displayed in these concentrated wines.

I am not a fan of the normally neutral-tasting Sylvaner, but Weinbach's elegant 1992 Sylvaner Réserve reveals excellent fruit, fine ripeness, and attractive body. Drink it over the next several years. This estate always turns out beautiful Pinot Blanc and their 1992 Pinot Réserve exhibits a lovely nose of ripe tangerines, excellent depth and richness, surprising power and length, and a long, dry, subtle finish. This is a super Pinot Blanc for drinking over the next 2–4 years.

There are five Riesling cuvées in 1992, all of which merit serious attention. All are dry, medium to full bodied, and intensely concentrated. Although the 1992 Riesling Réserve Personnelle possesses the lowest extract, it is loaded with fruit, as well as excellent crispness and delicacy. It should drink well for at least 4–6 years. Displaying a flinty richness to its fruit, the 1992 Riesling Cuvée Théo is full bodied, with stunning intensity and impressive length. A lovely, intense Riesling, it admirably combines power with grace. The dry, mineral-, apple-, and floral-scented 1992 Riesling Cuvée Sainte Catherine offers rich, finely focused flavors and plenty of extract, as well as higher acidity and a more tightly structured feel than the Riesling Cuvée Théo. There are two offerings from the grand cru Schlossberg Vineyard. The 1992 Riesling Schlossberg exhibits a stony, flowery-scented nose, copious amounts of mineral-flavored fruit, and crisp acidity. With a tight, backward feel, it is not as flattering or as easy to taste as the other Rieslings. The 1992 Riesling Schlossberg Cuvée Sainte Catherine was made from Riesling grapes harvested on November 23, 1992. It was fermented dry and is a majestically rich, impeccably balanced, full-bodied Riesling with a huge bouquet of flowers, peaches, apples, and honey. Superbly extracted, with loads of fruit, this formidable wine should drink well for 10–15 years.

Do not make the mistake of ignoring Domaine Weinbach's 1992 Muscat Réserve Personnelle. This decadent, dry wine offers a superb bouquet with aromas of ripe fruits. The intense perfume and gorgeously crisp, fresh flavors beg for this wine to be consumed over the next 1–2 years. It will make an ideal aperitif wine.

This firm fashions full-throttle, intensely concentrated, full-bodied Gewürztraminers that are loaded with aromas and flavors of grapefruit, roses, and lychee nuts. The 1992 Gewürztraminer Réserve Personnelle is a fat, rich, full-bodied wine with gobs of fruit, an exotic, chewy texture, and a long, heady finish. Drink it over the next 5–6 years. The 1992 Gewürztraminer Cuvée Théo exhibits that unmistakable scent of roses combined with ripe grapefruit and lanolin aromas. The wine possesses great richness, full body, and layers of fruit buttressed nicely by zesty acidity. There has been a succession of terrific Cuvée Théo Gewürztraminers from Domaine Weinbach over the last decade, and the 1992 offering is among the best. If you want an outrageously rich, full-bodied, big, ripe wine, check out Weinbach's 1992 Gewürztraminer Cuvée Laurence Furstentum. It is almost too rich and intense for drinking with food, but if foie gras is part of your diet, this is the perfect accompaniment. It would also work well with superrich, fat cheeses. In Alsace, a Gewürztraminer of this stature, intensity, and slight sweetness is often served with Muenster cheese. It should drink well for another 8–10 years.

Among the most successful wines of the vintage in Alsace, Domaine Weinbach's 1992s compete favorably with the great wines produced at this estate in 1990 and 1989. Moreover, the international recession and a slightly stronger dollar have resulted in the lowest prices in the last decade.

ZIND-HUMBRECHT (WINTZENHEIM)* * * * *

1992	Gewürztraminer Clos Windsbuhl	D	94
1991	Gewürztraminer Clos Windsbuhl	D	95
1992	Gewürztraminer Goldert	D	92
1991	Gewürztraminer Goldert	D	93
1990	Gewürztraminer Goldert Vendange Tardive	D	97
1992	Gewürztraminer Gueberschwihr	C	87+
1992	Gewürztraminer Heimbourg	D	95
1991	Gewürztraminer Heimbourg	D	93
1990	Gewürztraminer Heimbourg Vendange Tardive	E	100
1992	Gewürztraminer Hengst	D	92
1991	Gewürztraminer Hengst	D	91
1990	Gewürztraminer Hengst Vendange Tardive	D	96
1992	Gewürztraminer Herrenweg Turckheim	C	93
1991	Gewürztraminer Herrenweg Turckheim	C	90
1992	Gewürztraminer Rangen Clos Saint Urbain	D	93+
1992	Gewürztraminer Turckheim	C	90
1992	Gewürztraminer Wintzenheim	C	91

1992	Muscat d'Alsace	C	89
1991	Muscat d'Alsace	C	90
1992	Muscat Goldert	C	89+
1991	Muscat Goldert	D	88+
1992	Pinot d'Alsace	C	89
1991	Pinot d'Alsace/Pinot Blanc	C	90
1992	Riesling Brand	D	88
1991	Riesling Brand	D	93
1990	Riesling Brand Vendange Tardive	E	98
1992	Riesling Clos Hauserer	C	88
1991	Riesling Clos Hauserer	D	92
1990	Riesling Clos Hauserer Vendange Tardive	D	92
1992	Riesling Clos Windsbuhl	C	93
1990	Riesling Clos Windsbuhl Vendange Tardive	D	96
1992	Riesling Gueberschwihr	C	89
1992	Riesling Heimbourg	D	93
1991	Riesling Herrenweg Turckheim	C	89
1990	Riesling Herrenweg Turckheim Vendange Tardive	D	96
1992	Riesling Herrenweg Turckheim Vieilles Vignes	C	89
1992	Riesling Rangen Clos Saint Urbain	D	96
1991	Riesling Rangen Clos Saint Urbain	D	92
1992	Riesling Thann	C	89
1992	Riesling Turckheim	C	87
1991	Riesling Turckheim	C	89
1992	Riesling Wintzenheim	C	86
1992	Sylvaner	B	85
1991	Sylvaner	C	86
1990	Tokay-Pinot Gris Clos Jebsal Vendange Tardive	E	96
1992	Tokay-Pinot Gris Clos Windsbuhl	D	95
1990	Tokay-Pinot Gris Clos Windsbuhl Vendange Tardive	E	100
1992	Tokay-Pinot Gris Heimbourg	D	90
1990	Tokay-Pinot Gris Heimbourg Vendange Tardive	E	98
1992	Tokay-Pinot Gris Rangen Clos Saint Urbain	D	95
1991	Tokay-Pinot Gris Rangen Clos Saint Urbain	E	96
1992	Tokay-Pinot Gris Vieilles Vignes	D	92
1991	Tokay-Pinot Gris Vieilles Vignes	C	90

There are few winemaking firms in the world that produce such sublime wines in great years. There are even fewer that can turn out exceptional-quality wines in difficult vintages. Zind-Humbrecht's 1992s, from an excessively abundant vintage, are super wines. They reveal why the young, thirty-something Olivier Humbrecht is, along with the even younger twenty-something Michel Chapoutier, one of the two most prodigiously talented winemakers in France.

Consumers who love Alsace wines will be glad to know that because of the stronger dollar, prices for 1992s are lower. Virtually all of the Zind-Humbrecht 1992s are dry, as no Vendange Tardive (late harvest) or Sélection de Grains Nobles (decadently rich, sweet wine) were produced. This is a domaine that defines the widely used concept of *terroir*, that fuzzy notion that the vineyard's soil plays a determining factor in a wine's personality. I have some misgivings about applying the concept of *terroir* to Burgundy, despite the overwhelming Burgundian discipline that would have everyone believe no other place on earth can equal the quality of the Pinot Noir grown on the limestone slopes of the Côte d'Or. However, I would be willing to take up the cause of the *terroir*ists with respect to Zind-Humbrecht. The Humbrechts do everything possible to emphasize the differences in their vineyard holdings. No new oak is used in the vinification or aging of their dry wines; only wild yeasts indigenous to the vineyard are utilized in the wines' fermentation; and there is an extensively long lees contact, giving the wines an identifiable character that differs significantly from one vineyard to another. Moreover, and perhaps most important, these wines are made from the smallest yields in Alsace, resulting in levels of concentration and intensity that accentuate, or, I should say, exaggerate, the vineyard character.

With respect to the 1992 vintage, yields for the Zind-Humbrecht wines ranged from under 2 tons to slightly above 2 tons per acre—about one-fourth that of many other Alsace vineyards. Moreover, the best Zind-Humbrecht vineyards are on hillsides. Because of the potential for a troublesome crop size, the Humbrechts crop-thinned many of their vineyards by 30%–40%. The results are superb wines. Although they do not possess the power and concentration of such Zind-Humbrecht vintages as 1989 and 1990, nor are they as structured and potentially long-lived as the 1991s, the 1992s will have more mass appeal given their excellent concentration and softer, more flattering style.

I am not a fan of the Sylvaner grape, which produces monochromatic, herbal wines, but Zind-Humbrecht's 1992 is an excellent example. Light bodied and fresh, with good fruit and balance, this dry wine should be drunk over the next 1–2 years. This estate does a superb job with Pinot d'Alsace, which is always put through a malolactic fermentation and is one of the best values in their portfolio. It compares favorably with a big, rich, boldly flavored white burgundy. The 1992 offers a marvelous orange peel and honeyed-apple bouquet, medium body, excellent ripeness, wonderfully crisp, vibrant fruit, and a zesty, long finish. Drink it over the next 3–4 years. The two Muscats differ only in structure. The enthralling 1992 Muscat d'Alsace is a perfumed, medium-bodied, sexy, dry white Alsace. Made from 80% Muscat Ottonel from 30-year-old vines, it is a knockout, dry Muscat for drinking over the next 2–3 years. Made from a limestone-based vineyard, the 1992 Muscat Goldert is more reserved, backward, and tighter, as well as richer, fuller, and in need of another 4–6 months of bottle age. Given the delicacy and fragility of Muscat's perfume, neither is a wine I would cellar for more than 1–2 years.

There were ten dry Rieslings produced by Zind-Humbrecht in 1992. The medium-bodied, tight 1992 Riesling Wintzenheim exhibits tangy, citrusy, applelike fruit, and a crisp, fresh, dry finish. Made from grapes grown on limestone soil, the 1992 Riesling Gueberschwihr reveals a richer, honeyed, fragrant character with medium body, excellent depth, a stony, honeyed, floral, applelike personality, and a long, rich, medium-bodied, dry finish. The 1992 Riesling Herrenweg Turckheim Vieilles Vignes is a classic example of the taste of *terroir*. This wine, from a vineyard planted on granite soil, exhibits a distinctive flinty character to its nose. It admirably displays the fine extract Humbrecht achieved in 1992, as well as layers of rich fruit, medium body, and a dry, crisp, long finish. The 1992 Riesling Turckheim displays a more obvious tropical fruit–scented nose, elegant, light- to medium-bodied flavors, and excellent depth and precision. The 1992 Riesling Thann (from a vineyard planted on volcanic soil) offers an exceptionally fragrant bouquet of spring flowers and exotic, honeyed tropical fruit scents. Medium to full bodied, with stunning length and depth, this wine should drink well for 3–7 years. The backward, steely 1992 Riesling Clos Hauserer is reminiscent of a bigger-styled, dry German Riesling. It is stylish and concentrated, but reserved and understated.

I am a great fan of the fabulous Clos Windsbuhl vineyard, which is planted primarily on limestone soils. The 1992 Riesling Clos Windsbuhl possesses surprisingly high acidity, superb richness and density, medium to full body, and a huge finish. This is a wine of remarkable length and a sense of nearly perfect harmony. It should drink well for 10+ years. The 1992 Riesling Rangen Clos Saint Urbain offers superbly etched apple, mineral, smoky, exotic aromas, combined with fabulous richness, medium to full body, great clarity, and a long, dry, zesty, impeccably pure finish. A spectacular effort, it should age well for 10+ years. The 1992 Riesling Brand is the only off-dry wine among these offerings. Its huge, honeyed, exotic nose suggests that some botrytis was present. The wine is rich and full bodied, with excellent depth, and a long finish. The 1992 Riesling Heimbourg's intense nose of exotic tropical fruit, minerals, and citrus notes is followed by incredibly extracted, rich layers of fruit buttressed by excellent acidity. A large, broad-shouldered Riesling with a pronounced honeysuckle character, it promises to drink well for two decades.

In the hands of the top Alsatian producers, Tokay-Pinot Gris is a dry, full-bodied wine, offering a huge perfume of buttery, creamy, smoky fruit, unctuous, intense flavors, and awesome power and palate presence. It is generally a richer, fuller wine than even the largest-scaled grand cru white burgundies. It gets my nod as the Montrachet of Alsace. When made by a producer who emphasizes unmanipulative winemaking and extremely low yields, Tokay-Pinot Gris can reach unprecedented heights of richness and complexity. I tasted four dry Tokay-Pinot Gris wines from Zind-Humbrecht in 1992. The 1992 Tokay-Pinot Gris Vieilles Vignes exhibits a polite, medium straw color, and a lavish nose of buttered nuts, honey, and waxy scents. Superrich, with an unctuous thickness that suggests low yields, the wine is full bodied, dry, and capable of lasting for at least a decade. The 1992 Tokay-Pinot Gris Heimbourg is more exotic, with evidence of botrytis in the citrusy, buttery nose. Although the wine possesses rich, smoky, spicy, deep, full-bodied flavors, it does not appear to have the complexity and length of the Vieilles Vignes. The 1992 Tokay-Pinot Gris Clos Windsbuhl (which took 11 months to ferment dry) is a wine of magnificent power and gracefulness. Packed with glycerin and rich, concentrated flavors, it displays a full-bodied, decadent, superbly well-balanced finish. An infant in terms of its evolution, this wine requires 3–4 years of cellaring; it will drink well for over a decade. This is a richer, fuller, more complex wine than most Montrachets! The reticent bouquet of the 1992 Tokay-Pinot Gris Rangen Clos Saint Urbain offers huge, honeyed, cherry, smoky, nutty, buttery aromas that are just beginning to blossom. Superbly rich, with a chewy, full-bodied texture, this nearly viscous, superconcentrated wine should drink well for 10–15 years.

A wine enthusiast's first exposure to a great Gewürztraminer seems to elicit one of two reactions—revulsion or admiration. Because of its intensely perfumed, flamboyant bouquet of rose petals, lychee nuts, and superripe pineapples, it will never impress those looking for understatement and subtlety. However, I am unequivocally in the corner of this controversial wine, as I find it to be remarkably flexible with food. Moreover, its longevity exceeds most dry white wines produced in nearby Burgundy. As the following notes attest, Zind-Humbrecht does a spectacular job with Gewürztraminer. The 1992 Gewürztraminer Turckheim exhibits an exotic, spicy, grapefruit-scented nose intermingled with telltale aromas of what the Alsatians call "petrol." Medium bodied, with great fruit and a dry finish, this is a superb medium-weight Gewürztraminer for drinking over the next 5–7 years. Made from vines averaging 46 years, the 1992 Gewürztraminer Wintzenheim is a more restrained, as well as a more complex, wine that relies on a multitude of aromas and flavors to carry its rich, medium- to full-bodied personality. The 1992 Gewürztraminer Herrenweg Turckheim originates from deep, gravelly soil and vines averaging 25 years. I thought its exotic nose of lychee nuts and cherries, oily flavor richness, and fine underlying acidity made for a mouth-filling, full-bodied, ostentatious Gewürztraminer that will be adored by fans of this varietal. Drink it over the next decade.

The 1992 Gewürztraminer Gueberschwihr (from limestone soil) is more closed, with reticent but promising aromas of minerals, petrol, and delicate pineapple-scented fruit. This medium-bodied, backward wine is in need of another year of bottle age. The 1992 Gewürztraminer Goldert achieved 14% alcohol naturally. It is a dry, full-bodied, honeyed wine that offers copious quantities of lavishly rich, ripe fruit. Its bacon fat–scented, smoky, honeyed aromas jump from the glass. It will drink beautifully with foie gras or Muenster cheese. The 1992 Gewürztraminer Hengst combines elegance (a word not often applied to Gewürztraminer) with considerable power and richness. There is an exotic side to its mineral- and cold steel–scented bouquet, fine underlying acidity, rich, full-bodied, dry flavors, and its superb finish. The compelling, full-bodied, dry 1992 Gewürztraminer Clos Windsbuhl exhibits exceptional concentration, as well as amazing finesse and harmony. There are layers of flavor, and the dry, long finish lasts for a minute. It is a wine of great vibrancy, brilliant focus, and spectacular, spicy, smoky, mineral, floral, honeyed-pineapple richness. Drink it over the next 10–12 years. The 1992 Gewürztraminer Heimbourg is an awesomely powerful, superconcentrated, staggering example of Gewürztraminer at its most dramatic. It slams the taster in the face with a barrage of intense, exotic, perfumed aromas of lychee nuts, roses, and ripe fruit. Extremely full bodied and spectacularly concentrated, this dry Gewürztraminer should drink well for 10–15 years. Lamentably, most readers will not have the good fortune to latch on to any of the microquantities of the 1992 Gewürztraminer Rangen Clos Saint Urbain. This is the only off-dry, medium-sweet Gewürztraminer in the 1992 Zind-Humbrecht portfolio. It tasted more like a Vendange Tardive wine than a drier-styled Gewürztraminer. The exotic, honeyed bouquet and full-bodied, slightly sweet flavors offer spectacular concentration, as well as refreshing underlying acidity. It is a wine of remarkable length and nearly perfect harmony that should drink well for 15+ years.

Although quantities are limited, these four great 1990 Vendange Tardive Rieslings are must purchases if you are a Riesling lover. The 1990 Riesling Herrenweg Turckheim Vendange Tardive offers a spectacular nose of steely, apple-, and floral-scented fruit, and superrich, authoritative, dry flavors that are remarkably elegant for their size and depth. This crisp, fresh, penetratingly rich Riesling should drink well for 10–15 years. The 1990 Riesling Clos Hauserer Vendange Tardive displays a cherry- and wet stone–scented nose, and exceptionally high acidity that masks some of the wine's huge, rich fruit. Its razor-sharp focus, fabulous depth, and long finish are admirable. The most backward of this quartet of Vendange Tardive Rieslings, it should last for up to two decades. The 1990 Riesling Clos Windsbuhl's compelling fragrance of slate and honeyed oranges, the deep, multidimensional, layered flavors suggestive of tropical fruits, cherries, and apples, and the spicy, magnificently long, crisp finish are exquisite. This profound, superconcentrated, dry Riesling will last for 15 or more years. Lastly, the 1990 Riesling Brand Vendange Tardive may turn out to be a perfect wine in 4–5 years. Its tropical fruit–scented nose exhibits the most botrytis in its scents of apricots, peaches, and, remarkably, roses (an aroma found most frequently in Barolo and Gewürztraminer). A full-bodied, huge, massively concentrated, off-dry wine, crammed with the essence of the Riesling grape, it offers a remarkable wine-tasting experience. It will improve in the bottle for 7–10 years and will last for up to two decades.

What Leonard Humbrecht's son, Olivier, has achieved in 1991 must go down as one of the most remarkable performances in French winemaking. On paper, 1991 is a so-so year. In my writings I seek to identify the top producers for every significant wine region in the world. The finest producers frequently turn out better wine in mediocre years than average-quality producers do in great years. The production of the Zind-Humbrecht vineyards in 1991 was tiny, between 20 and 35 hectoliters per hectare. This is undoubtedly the secret to their success. Additionally, only two of these wines had to undergo *chaptalisation*, the process of adding sugar to the must before fermentation, so the ripeness they attained was natural. The key, as Olivier Humbrecht says, is that 80% or more of his time is spent in the vineyard. Moreover, his father spends 100% of his time working in their vineyards. As Olivier states, "Winemaking is simple if the grapes are fully ripe and healthy, and the yields are tiny."

As extraordinary as the 1989 and 1990 Zind-Humbrecht wines are, these 1991s, largely because of the difficulties presented by the vintage, are even more amazing. Readers must keep in mind that for the top Alsatian producers the situation is much like that in Burgundy —only tiny quantities of wine are available. Between 50 and 150 cases of each wine is the entire allocation for the American market.

With respect to the dry wines, Zind-Humbrecht, along with Domaine Weinbach, makes one of the best Sylvaners. Humbrecht's is from exceptionally old vines in two vineyards, Herrenweg and Rottenberg. The 1991 Sylvaner possesses personality and character, a rarity for this varietal. There is excellent fruit and plenty of ripeness. Drink it over the next several years. The 1991 Pinot d'Alsace is super! In 1991 Zind-Humbrecht harvested their Pinot Blanc at even higher ripeness levels than in 1989 and 1990, two torridly hot, drought years. This wine is bursting with fruit and aromas of oranges and ripe apples. It is medium to full bodied, with gorgeous levels of rich fruit, crisp acidity, and a terrific finish. It is a shame more readers do not know what a dazzling wine Pinot Blanc can be. It is one of the most delicious, food-friendly white wines in the world.

The five dry Riesling offerings are all remarkable wines. The lightest is the 1991 Riesling Turckheim. It offers a complex, apple, lemon, gunflintlike nose, lovely ripe, light-bodied flavors, and a dry, exceptionally well-delineated finish. It is a gorgeous Riesling for drinking over the next 3–5 years. The 1991 Riesling Herrenweg Turckheim exhibits a taut, mineral, fragrant nose, serious richness, and that wonderful interplay of Riesling flavors, such as apples, citrus, and stones. There is excellent richness, medium body, and a long, dry finish. It should drink well for at least 4–6 years. The powerful 1991 Riesling Rangen Clos Saint Urbain displays a huge, fragrant, flinty, cold steel, slatelike nose, full-bodied, crisp, deep, dry flavors, sensational focus and definition, and a long, rich finish. It should last for up to a decade. The 1991 Riesling Brand exhibits some evidence of botrytis in its mélange of apricot, peach, and apple blossom aromas. It is a deep, highly extracted, spectacularly rich, dry Riesling with medium body and a super finish. Drink it over the next 7–10 years. The Riesling Clos Hauserer is usually a wine that needs some time in the cellar. The 1991 is the most opulent example I have tasted from this vineyard, located at the bottom of the famed Hengst vineyard. It is rich, with more opulence and alcohol than usual. Olivier Humbrecht stated it was produced from microscopic yields of 20 hectoliters per hectare. This big, forceful Riesling should drink well for another decade.

I hope consumers have begun to discover the extraordinary dry Muscats of Alsace. They are unlike any other wines in the world. A good introduction is Zind-Humbrecht's 1991 Muscat d'Alsace, a wine made from yields of only 35 hectoliters per hectare. A fruit cocktail–scented nose, interspersed with scents of flowers, soars from the glass. There are unbelievable quantities of fruit in this dry, medium-bodied wine, as well as plenty of richness and a heady, alcoholic (14%) finish. Unfortunately, only 40 cases were allocated to the United States, which is 260 less than usual—giving you an idea of just how small Humbrecht's 1991 crop was. The 1991 Muscat Goldert is made from 50- to 60-year-old vines. Backward, with considerable finesse and elegance, the wine is tight and dry, and in need of at least 2–3 years of cellaring. It is far less flattering than Zind-Humbrecht's regular cuvée.

Zind-Humbrecht is synonymous with fabulous Tokay. It reaches Montrachet-like dimensions of power, texture, and aromatic as well as flavor intensity when made by this estate. The 1991 Tokay-Pinot Gris Vieilles Vignes exhibits powerful scents of butter and ripe fruit, as well as staggeringly rich, concentrated flavors buttressed by crisp acidity. This powerhouse is less open than either the 1989 or 1990, but it may prove to be even more concentrated and longer lived. It is an amazing wine! If you can latch on to any of the handful of bottles that make it into the United States, do not miss the chance to try the 1991 Tokay-Pinot Gris Rangen Clos Saint Urbain, made from one of the most extraordinary white wine vineyards in the world. The steep slopes, composed of volcanic soil, serve as home to old vines that produce an unctuously textured, unbelievably rich Tokay with a huge nose of honeyed fruit. There is layer upon layer of rich fruit, crisp acidity, and fabulous density, definition, and length. This wine was made of yields of only 20 hectoliters per hectare, which is about one-fourth to one-fifth of what many growers in Puligny-Montrachet and Chassagne-Montrachet obtain! If past efforts are indicative, this wine will need 3–5 years to open; it has the potential to last for up to 20.

The Gewürztraminers are also stunning in 1991. The 1991 Gewürztraminer Herrenweg Turckheim is a classic. A huge nose of spices, roses, and cherries, and deep, heady, intoxicating flavors coat the palate with that viscous, exotic Gewürztraminer character. Made from yields of only 25 hectoliters per hectare, it is the most forward of these 1991s. It should drink well for at least a decade. The 1991 Gewürztraminer Goldert, made from 60-year-old vines, offers an exquisite, superfragrant nose of roses, buttered lychee nuts, and fruit. The flavors are exquisitely well balanced, full bodied, authoritative, and superbly balanced by crisp acidity. This big-styled Gewürztraminer should drink well for another 10–12 years. As in most vintages, the 1991 Gewürztraminer Clos Windsbuhl possesses the highest acidity. It is also the most unctuous, richest, and highest in extract. Because of the acidity, it is the least flattering to taste. It is a profound example of how great Gewürztraminer can be when made from exceptionally low yields by a prodigious winemaker. The nose of minerals, roses, and spices is followed by a massively endowed, rich, stunningly proportioned wine that should be at its best between 1995 and 2005. Both the 1991 Gewürztraminer Heimbourg and 1991 Gewürztraminer Hengst display evidence of botrytis. They also share the unctuousness and richness of the other Zind-Humbrecht 1991 Gewürztraminers. Each is spectacular, with full-bodied flavors, and perfumed, intense aromas. All of these wines will keep easily for a decade, but only the Clos Windsbuhl requires cellaring. Only 70 cases of the 1991 Gewürztraminer Rangen were produced. It possesses a degree of residual sweetness. It is another powerful, boldly styled, dramatic wine that will drink well for at least 10 or more years.

I do not ever remember a producer in a so-so year making such magnificent wines! Bravo to Olivier and Leonard Humbrecht.

Given the sheer power and nectarlike qualities of the 1990 late-harvest wines of Alsace, readers will be amazed by their riveting aromatic and flavor intensity. They are massive yet extraordinarily well balanced. A question I am frequently asked is how does one serve a Vendange Tardive wine? They are best served prior to a meal as an aperitif, or at the end of a meal—alone! Of the three Tokays, the easiest to find will be the 1990 Tokay-Pinot Gris Clos Jebsal Vendange Tardive, of which 350 cases were produced. This is a stunningly balanced, spectacular, rich, honeyed wine with moderate sweetness. Its superhigh acidity makes the wine taste dry. Its presence and finish make for an unforgettable wine-tasting experience. It should drink well for 15–25 years. I thought the 1990 Tokay-Pinot Gris Clos Windsbuhl Vendange Tardive was perfect. The awesome nose of minerals, honeyed fruits, and exotic spices is followed by a wine with unbelievable masses of fruit intertwined with crisp acidity, full body, huge quantities of glycerin, and a spectacularly long, zesty finish that lasts for over a minute. It should keep for at least two decades. The limited-production 1990 Tokay-Pinot Gris Heimbourg Vendange Tardive (50 cases) is going to be impossible to find, but it is a huge, super wine with spectacular concentration, unctuous texture, and fascinating concentration.

The Gewürztraminer Vendange Tardive selections range from compelling to otherworldly. The 1990 Gewürztraminer Hengst Vendange Tardive is great stuff, with spectacular cherry, lychee nut, and rose scents, viscous, rich, chewy flavors that go on and on, and a huge, explosive finish. This giant of a wine is tied together with searingly high acidity. Even more aromatic and developed, the 1990 Gewürztraminer Goldert Vendange Tardive displays a nose that offers up scents of lychee nuts, cherries, and apricots. The wine has fabulous concentration, and a decadently long finish. The 1990 Gewürztraminer Heimbourg Vendange Tardive is as compelling as the 1989, with huge aromas of cherries and honeyed fruits, and remarkable freshness and length. In fact, it is the freshness, zesty acidity, and sheer definition and focus of these massive wines that make them such remarkable achievements.

Although it has not yet been released, I tasted a 1990 Sélection de Grains Nobles Tokay-Pinot Gris Clos Jebsal, to which I also bestowed a perfect rating. I was told it was made from 3 hectoliters per hectare, which is essentially a half glass of wine per vine. Keep in mind that Château d'Yquem is proud (and justifiably so) of the fact that they produce one glass of wine per vine. This offering will not be released for several years, and I am sure the price will be outrageous. It is among the most unforgettable nectars I have ever tasted. Those consumers searching for the rare Zind-Humbrecht Sélection de Grains Nobles offerings are advised to ask their retailers about the half-bottles of this firm's 1986s that were recently released. This vintage turned out to be a stunning year for Alsace's late-harvest wines, and the 1986 S.D.G.N.s from Humbrecht are spectacular.

BORDEAUX

The Basics

TYPES OF WINE

Bordeaux is the world's largest supplier of high-quality, age-worthy table wine, from properties usually called châteaux. The production in the eighties and the nineties has varied between 25 and 60 million cases of wine a year, of which 75% is red.

Red Wine Much of Bordeaux's fame rests on its production of dry red table wine, yet only a tiny percentage of Bordeaux's most prestigious wine comes from famous appellations such as Margaux, St.-Julien, Pauillac, and St.-Estèphe, all located in an area called the Médoc, and Graves, Pomerol, and St.-Émilion. From these areas the wine is expensive yet consistently high in quality.

White Wine Bordeaux produces sweet, rich, honeyed wines from two famous areas called Sauternes and Barsac. An ocean of dry white wine is made, most of it insipid and neutral in character, except for the excellent dry white wines made in the Graves area.

GRAPE VARIETIES

Following are the most important types of grapes used in the red and white wines of Bordeaux.

RED WINE VARIETIES

For red wines, three major grape varieties are planted in Bordeaux, as well as two minor varieties, one of which—Petit Verdot—will be discussed below. The type of grape used has a profound influence on the style of wine that is ultimately produced.

Cabernet Sauvignon A grape that is highly pigmented, very astringent, and tannic, and that provides the framework, strength, dark color, character, and longevity for the wines in a majority of the vineyards in the Médoc. It ripens late, is resistant to rot because of its thick skin, and has a pronounced black currant aroma, which is sometimes intermingled with subtle herbaceous scents that take on the smell of cedar wood with aging. Virtually all Bordeaux châteaux blend Cabernet Sauvignon with other red grape varieties. In the Médoc, the average percentage of Cabernet Sauvignon in the blend ranges from 40% to 85%; in Graves, 40% to 60%; in St.-Émilion, 10% to 50%; and in Pomerol, 0% to 20%.

Merlot Utilized by virtually every wine château in Bordeaux because of its ability to provide a round, generous, fleshy, supple, alcoholic wine, Merlot ripens, on an average, one to two weeks earlier than Cabernet Sauvignon. In the Médoc this grape reaches its zenith, and several Médoc châteaux use high percentages of it (Palmer, Cos d'Estournel, Haut-Marbuzet, and Pichon Lalande), but its fame is in the wines it renders in Pomerol, where it is used profusely. In the Médoc the average percentage of Merlot in the blend ranges from 5% to 45%; in Graves, from 20% to 40%; in St.-Émilion, 25% to 60%; and in Pomerol, 35% to 98%. Merlot produces wines lower in acidity and tannin than Cabernet Sauvignon, and as a general rule wines with a high percentage of Merlot are drinkable much earlier than wines with a high percentage of Cabernet Sauvignon, but frequently age just as well.

Cabernet Franc A relative of Cabernet Sauvignon that ripens slightly earlier, Cabernet Franc (called Bouchet in St.-Émilion and Pomerol) is used in small to modest proportions in order to add complexity and bouquet to a wine. Cabernet Franc has a pungent, often very spicy, sometimes weedy, olivelike aroma. It does not have the fleshy, supple character of Merlot, nor the astringence, power, and color of Cabernet Sauvignon. In the Médoc the average percentage of Cabernet Franc used in the blend is 0% to 30%; in Graves, 5% to 25%; in St.-Émilion, 25% to 66%; in Pomerol, 5% to 50%.

Petit Verdot A useful but generally difficult red grape because of its very late ripening characteristics, Petite Verdot provides intense color, mouth-gripping tannins, and high sugar and thus high alcohol when it ripens fully, as it did in 1982 and 1983 in Bordeaux. When unripe it provides a nasty, sharp, acidic character. In the Médoc few châteaux use more than 5% in the blend, and those that do are generally properties like Palmer and Pichon Lalande that use high percentages of Merlot.

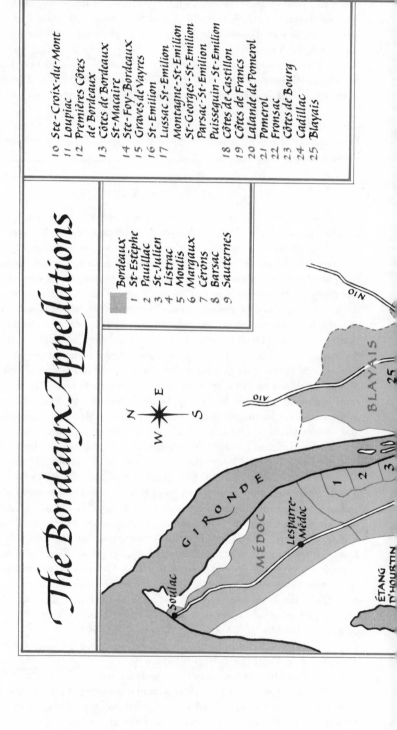

The Bordeaux Appellations

Bordeaux

1 St-Estèphe
2 Pauillac
3 St-Julien
4 Listrac
5 Moulis
6 Margaux
7 Cérons
8 Barsac
9 Sauternes

10 Ste-Croix-du-Mont
11 Loupiac
12 Premières Côtes
   de Bordeaux
13 Côtes de Bordeaux
14 St-Macaire
15 Ste-Foy-Bordeaux
16 Graves de Vayres
   St-Emilion
17 Lussac St-Emilion
   Montagne-St-Emilion
   St-Georges-St-Emilion
   Parsac-St-Emilion
   Puisseguin-St-Emilion
18 Côtes de Castillon
19 Côtes de Francs
20 Lalande de Pomerol
21 Pomerol
22 Fronsac
23 Côtes de Bourg
24 Cadillac
25 Blayais

GIRONDE

MÉDOC

Soulac

Lesparre-Médoc

ÉTANG D'HOURTIN

BLAYAIS

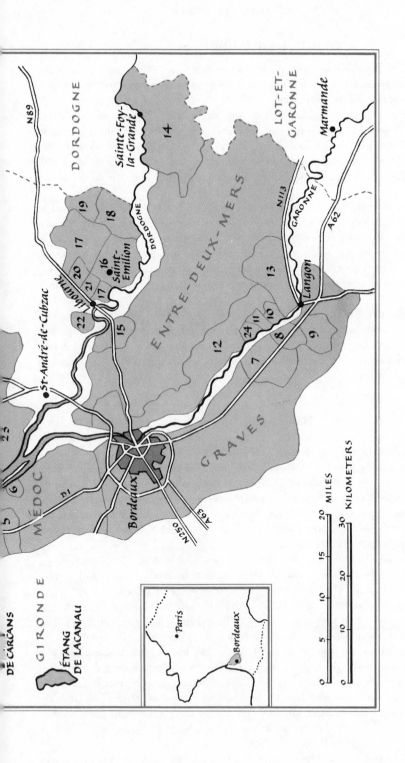

DE CARÇANS

GIRONDE

ÉTANG DE LACANAU

DORDOGNE

N89

Sainte-Foy-la-Grande

LOT-ET-GARONNE

Marmande

14

19
18
17
16
Saint-Émilion
20
21
17

Libourne

22

15

ENTRE-DEUX-MERS

DORDOGNE

N113

GARONNE

A62

Langon

13

12

24 11
10
8
9

7

St-André-de-Cubzac

23

MÉDOC

5 6

D1

GRAVES

Bordeaux

N250
A63

Paris

Bordeaux

0   5   10   15   20 MILES
0   10   20   30 KILOMETERS

WHITE WINE VARIETIES

Bordeaux produces both dry and sweet white wine. There are usually only three grape varieties used: Sauvignon Blanc and Semillon, for dry and sweet wine, and Muscadelle, which is used sparingly for the sweet wines.

Sauvignon Blanc   Used for making both the dry white wines of Graves and the sweet white wines of the Barsac/Sauternes region, Sauvignon Blanc renders a very distinctive wine with a pungent, somewhat herbaceous aroma, and crisp, austere flavors. Among the dry white Graves, a few châteaux employ 100% Sauvignon Blanc, but most blend it with Semillon. Less Sauvignon Blanc is used in the winemaking blends in the Sauternes region than in Graves.

Semillon   Very susceptible to the famous noble rot called botrytis, which is essential to the production of excellent, sweet wines, Semillon is used to provide a rich, creamy, intense texture to both the dry wines of Graves and the rich, sweet wines of Sauternes. Semillon is quite fruity when young, and wines with a high percentage of Semillon seem to take on weight and viscosity as they age. For these reasons, higher percentages of Semillon are used in making the sweet wines of the Barsac/Sauternes region than in producing the white wines of Graves.

Muscadelle   The rarest of the white wine grapes planted in Bordeaux, Muscadelle is a very fragile grape that is quite susceptible to disease, but when healthy and mature, produces a wine with an intense flowery, perfumed character. It is used only in tiny proportions by châteaux in the Barsac/Sauternes region. It is not used at all by the white wine producers of Graves.

Major Appellations

Following are the general flavor characteristics of Bordeaux's most notable types of wines.

St.-Estèphe   While the wines of St.-Estèphe are known for their hardness because of the heavier, thicker soil in this area, the châteaux have more Merlot planted in their vineyards than elsewhere in the Médoc. Although generalizations can be dangerous, most St.-Estèphe wines possess less expressive and flattering bouquets, have a tougher character, and are more stern, tannic wines than those found elsewhere in the Médoc. They are usually full bodied, with considerable aging potential.

Pauillac   A classic Pauillac seems to define what most people think of as Bordeaux—a rich black currant, cedary bouquet, followed by medium- to full-bodied flavors with a great deal of richness and tannin. The fame of this area equates with high prices.

St.-Julien   St.-Juliens are frequently indistinguishable from the wines of Pauillac. The wines of St.-Julien are filled with rich curranty fruit, and smell of cedar and spices. The overall quality of this appellation's winemaking is superb, so consumers take note!

Margaux   Margaux are the lightest wines of the Médoc, but in great vintages they are perhaps the most seductive. Although the overall quality of the winemaking in this appellation is lower than any other appellation in the Médoc, in a top vintage a great Margaux has an undeniable floral, berry-scented bouquet backed up by the smell of new oak. In body and tannin, Margaux wines, despite elevated percentages of Cabernet Sauvignon, tend to mature more quickly than a St.-Julien, Pauillac, or St.-Estèphe. For bouquet lovers, the best wines of Margaux can be compelling.

Graves Red   Textbook Graves wines are the easiest of all Bordeaux wines to pick out in blind tastings, as they have a distinctive mineral smell as well as the scent and taste of tobacco and cedar. Graves are generally the lightest wines made in Bordeaux.

St.-Émilion   It is difficult to generalize about the taste of St.-Émilions, given the divergent styles, but most St.-Émilions tend to be softer and fleshier wines than Médocs, but not as succulent and lush as Pomerols. Because of the elevated percentages of Cabernet Franc planted in this appellation, St.-Émilions often have a distinctive herbaceous, cedary bouquet.

Pomerol   Pomerols are often called the burgundies of Bordeaux because of their rich, supple, more monolithic personalities, but they age extremely well and are undeniable choices for hedonists, as they provide oodles of rich black currant, black cherry, sometimes blackberry fruit. In the great vintages one can find an exquisite opulence in these wines.

Graves White   The top-notch white Graves are aged in oak and made from the Sauvignon Blanc and Semillon grapes. They start off life often excessively oaky, but fill out beautifully with age and develop creamy, rich flavors that marry beautifully with the oak. Other white wines of Bordeaux are often totally neutral and insipid in character and simply taste of acidity and water.

Barsac/Sauternes   Depending on the vintage and the degree of the noble rot (botrytis) that affects the grapes, the wines can either taste fat, ripe, and characterless in those years when there is little botrytis, or wonderfully exotic with a bouquet of honeyed tropical fruits, buttered nuts, and crème brûlée in those great vintages where there has been plenty of the noble rot.

Satellite Appellations   There are very large quantities of wine produced in a bevy of other lesser-known appellations of Bordeaux. Most of these wines are widely commercialized in France, but have met with little success in America because of this country's obsession with luxury names and prestigious appellations. For the true connoisseur, the wines of Bordeaux's satellite appellations can in fact represent outstanding bargains, particularly in top vintages such as 1982, 1985, 1989, and 1990 where excellent climatic conditions and the improved use of modern technology by many of these estates resulted in a vast selection of fine wines at modest prices. Following are the most important satellite appellations.

Fronsac and Canon-Fronsac—In the eighteenth and nineteenth centuries the vineyards sprinkled over the hillsides and hollows of Fronsac and Canon-Fronsac—only several miles west of Libourne—were better known than the wines of Pomerol and sold for higher prices than the wines of St.-Émilion. But because access to Pomerol was easier and because most of the brokers had their offices in Libourne, the vineyards of Pomerol and St.-Émilion were exploited more than those of Fronsac and Canon-Fronsac. Consequently, this area fell into a long period of obscurity from which it has just recently begun to rebound.

Lalande-de-Pomerol—Lalande-de-Pomerol is a satellite commune of nearly 2,250 acres of vineyards located just north of Pomerol and Néac. The vineyards, which produce only red wine, are planted on relatively light, gravelly, sandy soils with the meandering river, Barbanne, as the appellation's northern boundary. The very top level of good Lalande-de-Pomerol is easily the equivalent of a mid-level Pomerol, with certain wines, such as Belles-Graves, La Croix-St.-André, and du Chapelain, very good, even by Pomerol's standards. The only downside to the wines of Lalande-de-Pomerol is that they generally need to be consumed within 5–6 years of the vintage. Sadly, the only recent vintage that can be recommended is 1990.

Côtes de Bourg—The Côtes de Bourg, a surprisingly vast appellation of nearly 10,000 acres, is located on the right bank of the Gironde River, just a five-minute boat ride from the more famous appellation of Margaux. The vineyards here are actually older than those in the Médoc, as this attractively hilly area was once the center of the strategic forts built during the Plantagenet period of France's history. The views from the hillside vineyards adjacent to the river are magnificent. The local chamber of commerce has attempted to draw the public's attention to this area by calling Bourg "the Switzerland of the Gironde." They should instead stress the appeal of the best wines from the Côtes de Bourg, which are made in an uncomplicated but fruity, round, appealing style, and talk up the lovely port village of the area, the ancient hillside town of Bourg-Sur-Gironde.

Blaye—There are just over 6,700 acres of vines in the Blaye region, located directly north of Bourg. The best vineyard areas are entitled to the appellation called Premières Côtes de Blaye. While there are quantities of white wine produced in the Blaye region, most of the Premières Côtes de Blaye are dedicated to the production of red wine, which is very similar to the red wine of Bourg. At its best, it is forward, round, richly fruity, soft, and immensely satisfying in a low-key manner.

Loupiac and Ste.-Croix-de-Mont—With the wine prices of Barsac and Sauternes soaring, I predict a more important role for the producers of the sweet white wines of Loupiac and Ste.-Croix-du-Mont. These two appellations, twenty-four miles south of Bordeaux on the right bank of the Garonne, facing Barsac and Sauternes across the river, have an ideal southern exposure. These areas received appellation status in 1930, and many observers believe the excellent exposure of the top vineyards and the clay/limestone soil base is favorable for producing sweet wines, particularly in view of the fact that the morning mists —so essential for the formation of the noble rot, *Botrytis cinerea*—are a common occurrence in this area. The entire appellation of Loupiac consists of 1,359 acres. Although the sweet wines are receiving increasing attention from wine lovers, dry white wines, as well as a moderate quantity of dry red wines, are also produced.

AGING POTENTIAL

St.-Estèphe: 8–35 years

Pauillac: 8–40 years

St.-Julien: 8–35 years

Margaux: 8–30 years

Graves Red: 8–30 years

St.-Émilion: 8–25 years

Pomerol: 5–30 years

Graves White: 5–20 years

Barsac/Sauternes: 10–50+ years

Fronsac/Canon-Fronsac: 5–20 years

Lalande-de-Pomerol: 3–6 years

Bourg: 3–10 years

Blaye: 2–4 years

Loupiac: 5–15 years

Ste.-Croix-de Mont: 4–12 years

OVERALL QUALITY LEVEL

Of all the great viticultural regions of the world, Bordeaux consistently produces wine of the highest level of quality. Although one-dimensional, innocuous wines can be found, bad wine is rare. For the world's top producers of Cabernet Sauvignon, Merlot, and Cabernet Franc, Bordeaux remains the point of reference.

THE MOST IMPORTANT INFORMATION TO LEARN

For the wine consumer trying to develop a degree of expertise when buying the wines of Bordeaux, the most important information to learn is which wine-producing estates (called châteaux) are producing the best wines today. A review of the top categories of châteaux in Bordeaux is a quick way to learn of those producers with high commitments to quality. However, consumers should also familiarize themselves generally with the styles of the wines from the different appellations. Some tasters will prefer the austere, sterner style of Bordeaux represented by St.-Estèphe or Pauillac, whereas others will love the lavish lushness and opulence of a Pomerol. It has been my experience that the Graves wines with their distinctive mineral scent and tobacco bouquet are often the least-favored wines for neophytes, but with more experience this character becomes one that is admired by connoisseurs. As far as the famous official classifications of wine quality in Bordeaux, they are all out of date and should only be of academic interest to the consumer. These historic classifications of wine quality were employed both to promote more wines and to establish well-delineated, quality benchmarks. But because of negligence, incompetence, or just plain greed, some of these châteaux produce mediocre and poor wines that hardly reflect their placement in these classifications. A more valid guideline to the quality of Bordeaux wines is the rating of producers starting on page 179; these ratings reflect the overall quality of the wines produced rather than their historical pedigree.

BUYING STRATEGY

Virtually all of the top 1989s and 1990s have either disappeared from the marketplace or are priced so high as to make them affordable only by the superrich. Buyers searching for Bordeaux are advised to be extremely selective when looking at discounted 1991s, 1992s, and 1993s. It may be wiser to seek out the burgeoning auction market (particularly active now in New York, Illinois, and California) and to search for stars from well-stored, underpriced 1986s, 1985s, and 1983s. The year 1982 is the only great Bordeaux vintage where limited quantities can still be found in the marketplace. However, staggeringly high prices and the usual worries about how the wine may have been stored appear to have had little impact on the buying frenzy for these wines.

There will unquestionably be a futures campaign for the 1994s. It is doubtful that many Americans will take the bait, even though many American merchants who sell Bordeaux have little stock. The 1994 vintage, which could have been a great one, was adversely affected by rain. It is safe to say that Pomerol, Graves, and St.-Émilion fared better than the Médoc. Cuvées of Merlot tasted in Pomerol and St.-Émilion looked remarkably rich and intense, suggesting that some top wines will emerge from these right bank appellations. Depending on the varietal composition, as well as the selection procedure of a château, it should be at least a good to very good vintage with some stars emerging, particularly from Pomerol and St.-Émilion.

Today's Marketplace

With the ongoing collapse of the American dollar against the German mark, French franc, and Japanese yen, imported goods from those countries have jumped in price by 10%–20% in only the last 6 months. I have made a strong case, both in previous editions of *Wine Buyer's Guide* and in my *Bordeaux* books, about the perils and pitfalls of buying wine futures. I believe the prices asked for Bordeaux wines are actually reasonable, but the problem is the American distribution system, which creates a triple-tiered, multilayered, Jurassic system of wine delivery where Bordeaux wines are marked up in price by no less than the broker, importer, wholesaler, and retailer. At the importer, wholesaler, and retailer stops, significant margins, from 20%–50% at each stop, are tacked on, thus beating up the consumer and making a wine that was sold by the château for $20 cost $40–$60 by the time the wine drinker has an opportunity to purchase it. It is a cruel irony of the production of fine wine that the people who take the least amount of risk, do virtually no work on behalf of the wine, and in the process often abuse and destroy the wine by appalling storage conditions, take a more significant markup than the estate that produced the wine! For most Americans, there is no alternative but to purchase Bordeaux from this archaic distribution system, but there are some top-quality wines in 1994 that merit interest. The American and world marketplace are no longer saturated with large quantities of high-quality Bordeaux. A look at the recent auction sales figures from Christie's and Sotheby's in New York reveal significant price escalation (and I fear speculation) in the 1990 and 1982 vintages. The glut of fine Bordeaux wine that existed a mere 3 years ago is ancient history, thus increasing the interest in a very good vintage such as 1994. Yet given the economic conditions in spring 1995, it seems prudent, except for potential buyers of the limited-production Pomerols (the strength of this particular vintage), in addition to the finest first-growths and superseconds, to adopt a "wait and see" attitude. At the time of writing, it was not known what the results of the French elections (to be held in late April) would be, but it was no secret that Monsieur Chirac (ahead in the opinion polls in mid-April) would devalue the French franc if he were elected. The dollar should regain some of its strength this year, and each upward movement may make the prices of the 1994s look more attractive. Will there be significant futures buying in the 1994 vintage? No doubt wine enthusiasts from countries with stronger currencies will exhibit considerable interest in this vintage, as it is the finest Bordeaux vintage since 1990, and one that is not that far off the lofty peaks of quality established in such stellar years as 1982 and 1990. But in America, the futures market is likely to be quiet— at least until the dollar regains some buying clout vis-à-vis the franc.

VINTAGE SUMMARIES

1994 Bordeaux Vintage Summary

After spending two weeks in Bordeaux tasting the young 1994s, I reached the following conclusions:

1. *Nineteen ninety-four is an excellent vintage.* To put it in perspective, I designed a chart that provides a candid and thorough look at where 1994 stands in relationship to the finest Bordeaux vintages of the last 25 years. For example, among more recent vintages, 1994 is superior to both 1983 and 1988, and possibly equal to, if not better than, 1985, although many 1994s will not have the early charm of the 1985s.

2. *The best wines of all appellations exhibit no evidence of dilution.* This is remarkable given the fact that between September 7 and September 29, 11 days of significant rain fell before anyone had begun to harvest the red grapes. The only explanation (and one that explains why the 1993 red burgundies, also harvested under and after torrential rains, have turned out so well) is that during the month of September, the temperature never rose above 55 degrees. In what was an atypically cool month for Bordeaux, the thermometer remained in the mid to upper forties. It is speculated by viticulturists that since it was so cool, the vines resisted the temptation to pump moisture into the grapes, thus bloating them, and seriously diluting the end product. Tasting the finest wines of 1994 confirms this, as no one would think there had been significant rainfall during this harvest. Almost all the Merlot was harvested between September 12 and 23. Most of the Cabernet Sauvignon was picked between September 22 and October 8. The last significant rainfall was on September 27, with intermittent showers for several days, followed by gorgeous sunny weather the entire month of October. The temperatures remained relatively low, between the mid-40s and mid-50s.

3. *The vintage is at its finest in Pomerol,* where the majority of wines are excellent, with a number of outstanding efforts. Only a handful exhibit any evidence of dilution. The reason for this is simple. Although the Merlot was picked during the rain, it was physiologically mature, and yields were modest. In addition, given the small size of most estates, the harvest was over in 1 to 4 days.

4. In the other major red wine appellations, *those estates that were willing to make a strict selection and declassify 30%–55% of their harvest have turned out rich, ripe, concentrated wines with high tannin levels.* Those properties that could not afford such a brutal selection process, or did not have sufficient high-quality Merlot to give the wines fat and flesh, made tannic, hollow wines that are likely to be unbalanced.

5. With respect to the white wines, most of the Pessac-Léognan vineyards were harvested between August 31 and September 18. *The quality of many of these dry white Graves is*

outstanding, with many rich, concentrated, low-acid wines that are soft, forward, and impressively endowed. In contrast, heavy September rains presented numerous problems for the sweet white wine producers, but October was nearly rain-free, and it was late in this month that some of the great estates harvested, i.e., Yquem. I have not included reviews of the 1994 sweet white Bordeaux wines because it is so early, and sweet wines are much more difficult to assess when young. I did do extensive tastings of them, and at this point, 1994 appears to be a correct, average-quality year for Barsac and Sauternes, with the superb exceptions of those estates that waited until mid-October or later to pick.

6. It is always difficult to make comparisons of one vintage with another, but given the obvious success of the Merlot grape, the obvious consistency of the Pomerols, and the high tannin content in most Médocs, *it appears that 1994 may well represent the modern-day clone of 1970.* While the weather pattern of 1970 does not resemble 1994 (weather-wise, 1994 resembles—up to a point—1959), the style of the 1994s recalls 1970. There will be enough exceptional wine to create excitement, but there will be disappointments, as some renowned wines will lack fat and fruit, and be too austere and tannic.

In summary, the 1994 vintage, which might well have been the proverbial vintage of the century if it had not rained, exceeds expectations given the gloomy September weather that caused such premature pessimism. The lack of dilution in the finest 1994s and their quality has had me pondering over the same question: What would this vintage have been had it not rained?

A quick summary of the weather follows to give readers an idea of how this vintage was shaped by weather conditions. (I am indebted to Bill Blatch of Vintex for providing me with superbly detailed weather data for each day of the harvest.) When I visited Piedmont and the Rhône Valley in March 1994, it was clearly the hottest weather I had ever experienced in Europe during that month. The unusual March heat wave created an early bud break, leading growers to fear that a cold spell in April could wreak colossal frost damage, as occurred in 1991. The spring frosts never materialized, and the flowering began on May 23, 10 days ahead of the average year, in addition to being the seventh earliest flowering period in the post–World War II era (in order of earliest to latest, the others were 1990, 1952, 1989, 1982, and 1961). Many of the greatest vintages of this century have been a result of an early bud break and early flowering, for the simple reason that the earlier the bud break and flowering, the earlier the harvest, thus reducing the enormous risk of rains that tend to strike Bordeaux around the fall solstice, or harvest moon, as it is often called.

The remainder of the summer was hot. June was slightly above average in temperature, but July was torrid, with 24 days where the temperature was over 25 degrees centigrade (12 of those exceeded a sultry 30 degrees). July averaged 16 days over 25 degrees centigrade and 4 days over 30 degrees centigrade. The heat, accompanied by intermittent violent storms, continued through August, providing the vineyards with sufficient rainfall and preventing the droughtlike conditions that occurred in 1989 and 1990.

By the end of August, the grapes' sugar readings were so impressive that many producers were beginning to believe that a magnificent vintage, only several weeks away, was within their grasp. Sugar readings taken at the end of August revealed grapes with sugar levels that were higher than in 1982, and equal to those of 1990. More important, the grapes were healthy, and yields were well below those in 1990.

The white wine harvest began at Haut-Brion and Carbonnieux with great excitement on August 31. The red wine harvest was expected to begin exceptionally early, around September 12, putting it in the company of such great vintages as 1921 (September 15), 1945 (September 13), 1982 (September 13), and 1990 (September 12). Just as sentiment was building for an extraordinary harvest, the long-range weather reports became increasingly ominous, predicting a series of low depressions in the Atlantic that computers indicated would begin striking the Bordeaux region as early as September 9. Lamentably, the weather service computers proved to be far too accurate, as light but persistent rains arrived early on the 9th, followed by heavier rainfall that evening. The weather then cleared for several days, and the first of the early pickers, especially those in the Merlot vineyards, began. Light rain fell on September 12 and 13, but that was followed by very cool, overcast conditions. Significant rain fell on September 14, 15, and 16. When the rain stopped on the 17th, massive harvesting began in all appellations. The weather remained cool and reasonably dry between September 17 and 25, and most of the red grapes were harvested during this period, although some Médoc châteaux waited, and were rewarded with a fine period of weather that began on September 22 and continued until the 25th. Other châteaux, relying on the weather computers, which called for a week of "exceptionally fine" weather starting September 26, decided to wait in the hope of obtaining extra maturity in the Cabernet Sauvignon and Petit Verdot. In this instance, the weather computers were off the mark, as heavy rain fell on September 26 and 27. The pattern of damp weather broke on September 28, as mostly dry and sunny days were the rule for the next month. A handful of Bordeaux châteaux finished harvesting their Cabernet Sauvignon, which had not rotted, during the first 10 days of October.

In addition to the abnormally cool weather during September, the other principal reason why so many estates turned out deeply colored, big, tannic, structured red wines, with the best of them also possessing copious quantities of ripe fruit, is that the yields were much lower. Most top châteaux averaged yields between 40 and 55 hectoliters per hectare, which is far below the yields in top vintages such as 1990, 1989, 1986, and 1985. Lastly, the use of revolutionary techniques for removing water and for concentrating the wine cannot be discounted. While the process of bleeding the *cuves (saigner)* has been used for decades, the use of new high-tech machines that extract water from the grape by the principle of reverse osmosis cannot be minimized in turning potentially average-quality wines into wines with more intensity and character. Whether such techniques produce wines that age gracefully, with the same complexity as wine made from low-yielding vineyards and/or undiluted grapes, remains to be answered.

As the following tasting notes demonstrate, selection is critical in the 1994 vintage. Almost all of the top wines are made from estates that declassified a minimum of 30%–35% to as much as 55% of the harvest in order to produce cuvées with impressive concentration and richness. Moreover, most top wines (there are a handful of exceptions) possess a higher percentage of Merlot in the final blend than normal. Merlot was unquestionably successful except in those vineyards with poorly drained, low-lying soils (primarily in the Margaux communes of Assac and Cantenac), where the Merlot was excessively productive and soaked up too much moisture. This explains the great success in Pomerol, the success of some of the most quality-conscious St.-Émilion estates, as well as some of the Médocs, particularly Pontet-Canet and Latour, two châteaux that used historically high proportions of Merlot in the final blend in order to achieve as much richness and complexity as possible.

While the Pomerols are unquestionably rich, succulent, and voluptuous, they also contain considerable tannin, which in many cases is nearly masked by the abundant richness and ripeness of the wine's fruit. On the other hand, even the top Médocs possess considerable tannin. The torrid heat of July and August can be detected in the finest wines, which taste ripe and undiluted, and fall just short of being truly exceptional.

To reiterate, 1994 is an excellent vintage, but extremely inconsistent. It is comparable (in a modern-day context) to 1970, because the excellent Merlot crop caused Pomerol to be the most successful appellation. Elsewhere the wines range from outstanding to excessively tannic, austere, and astringent—precisely what occurred in 1970. Of course, winemaking has been significantly improved over the last 25 years. In addition, billions of francs have been invested in both the vineyards and cellars. For these reasons, the 1995s exhibit more purity and have far deeper colors than just about anything produced in 1970. Factoring in the brutal selection process employed by the most serious estates, the result is a 1994 vintage that will turn out a surprising number of top wines, and in time, this vintage may ultimately produce more top wines than 1985, as well as 1988, 1983, 1981, 1979, 1978, 1976, 1975, 1971, and, of course, 1970.

1993—A Quick Study (9-25-93)†

St.-Estèphe **	Graves Red ***/****
Pauillac ***	Graves White ****
St.-Julien ***	Pomerol ***/****
Margaux **	St.-Émilion ***
Médoc/Haut-Médoc Crus Bourgeois **	Barsac/Sauternes 0

Size: A moderately large crop, although not as abundant as 1992.

Important Information: In complete contrast to the soft 1992s, the 1993s, especially from the Médoc, possess relatively high tannin levels and are austere and backward. Like 1992, it was important for a high percentage of Merlot to be part of the blend for most wines to have turned out successfully. However, some of the big Médoc châteaux were so severe in their selection process that they produced very good wines that are mostly all Cabernet Sauvignon.

Maturity Status: It is hard to project, but most 1993s will not be approachable young. It will be a race between how fast the fruit fades versus how quickly the tannin melts away that determines when these wines will, if ever, achieve complete balance. The most-concentrated and best-balanced 1993s will have 15–20+ years of longevity.

Price: Most Bordeaux châteaux raised prices by 20% over 1992s, marking the beginning of an upward spiral in Bordeaux prices.

In many respects, the 1993 Bordeaux had no legitimate reason to turn out well. Given the enormous quantities of rain that fell on the vineyards in September, this appeared to be a disastrous year. The year 1993 set a record for the highest amount of precipitation for the month of September in the last thirty years, exceeding the average September rainfall by an astonishing 303%. Under such conditions it would be easy to conclude that it was impossible to make a good wine in 1993. However, as the following tasting notes indicate, not only were many satisfactory wines made, but there are a surprising number of wines with the potential to be outstanding—rather mind-boggling given September's appalling weather conditions. How could this have happened?

The spring of 1993 began under deplorable conditions, with heavy rains in both April and June. The flowering was mixed, with the crop size far below the abundant 1992 vintage. In late June and July, the weather was slightly warmer than average. August was both sunny and at times torrid, causing producers' optimism to rise. When I was in France in early September, I remember talking with a number of producers who were beginning to think the potential existed for a very good to excellent vintage. But, as in 1992, the weather deteriorated, with a series of low depressions and storms beginning on September 6 that savaged the region. For the subsequent five weeks, the weather was unstable, with episodes of rain-drenching storms, followed by a handful of dry, sunny days. In most vintages producers boast that they picked either "before" or "after" the rains, but in 1993, producers harvested their red wine grapes between or during the rainstorms. The red wine grape harvest terminated by mid-October, with the Bordelais as pessimistic as I have ever witnessed.

When I visited Bordeaux in November to taste the 1992s after one year in cask and the

† Dates in parentheses denote actual day on which the Bordeaux harvest began, according to the French Ministry of Agriculture.

1991s from bottle, producers revealed their surprise and shock at how much color the 1993s exhibited, as well as the fact that the wines appeared richer and healthier than anyone had reason to expect.

After having spent two weeks in Bordeaux in November 1994 (this was not a vintage for consumers to buy as a future), it can be stated that the 1993 vintage has turned out to be a good year, close in overall quality (should readers want to make a comparison) to the 1988 vintage. While there are many diluted wines, the real downside for many 1993s is the level of hard tannin these wines possess. Because so much underripe Cabernet Sauvignon was harvested before it rotted on the vine, the hallmark of 1993 is a leanness and tannic ferocity reminiscent of vintages such as 1975, 1966, and 1952.

In order to have made a balanced and fine wine in 1993, it was essential to have included a high percentage of Merlot in the blend. For that reason, Pomerol (also the most favored region in 1992) and Graves (healthy percentages of Merlot, plus exceptionally well drained soils) were the two most favored appellations. In the Médoc and St.-Émilion, it was a question of how much of the harvest producers were willing to eliminate in order to produce the best possible cuvée. For the first-growths and the usual overachievers among the superseconds, where 50% or more of the crop was eliminated, the quality of the final wine is frequently excellent, sometimes even outstanding.

The real qualitative test for the 1993s will take place after bottling. Because of the high tannin level in these wines, there will be a tendency to excessively fine and filter the wines, hoping to soften the tannin. No doubt that will work, but it will also remove fruit and body, something many of the 1993s cannot afford to lose. It will require a delicate hand to gently push these wines through the bottling process, retaining the fruit and substance the best of the 1993s possess, trying at the same time to soften the tannin level. Nevertheless, 1993 is a vintage that in many respects is a modern-day equivalent of tannic, austere years such as 1975 and 1966. To put the vintage in another context, there are few 1993s that are sumptuously rich, thick, big, blockbuster, flamboyant wines such as were produced in 1990, 1989, and 1982.

TOP WINES FOR 1993

St.-Estèphe: Cos d'Estournel, Montrose

Pauillac: Grand-Puy-Lacoste, Lafite-Rothschild, Latour, Mouton-Rothschild, Pichon-Longueville Baron

St.-Julien: Ducru-Beaucaillou, Gruaud-Larose, Lagrange, Léoville-Barton, Léoville-Las Cases

Margaux: Château Margaux, Prieuré-Lichine, Rausan-Ségla

Médoc/Haut-Médoc/Moulis/Listrac Crus Bourgeois: None

Graves Red: Haut-Bailly, Haut-Brion, La Louvière, La Mission-Haut-Brion, Pape-Clément

Graves White: Couhins-Lurton, de Fieuzal, Haut-Brion, Laville-Haut-Brion, La Louvière, Pape-Clément, Smith-Haut-Lafitte

Pomerol: Clinet, Lafleur, Pétrus, Trotanoy

Fronsac/Canon-Fronsac: None

St.-Émilion: L'Angélus, Beauséjour-Duffau, Canon-La-Gaffelière, Ferrand-Lartigue, Pavie-Macquin, Le Tertre-Roteboeuf, Troplong-Mondot

Barsac/Sauternes: None

1992—A Quick Study (9-21-92)

St.-Estèphe **	Graves Red **/***
Pauillac **	Graves White ***/****
St.-Julien **	Pomerol ***

Margaux*   St.-Émilion**
Médoc/Haut-Médoc Crus Bourgeois 0   Barsac/Sauternes*

Size: A gigantic crop.

Important Information: Because rain diluted so much of 1992's potential, successes emerged from extremely well drained vineyards (Graves), and where a high proportion of Merlot (less adversely impacted by the rain) is grown (Pomerol and St.-Émilion).

Maturity Status: Low-acid, light-bodied, soft wines are ideal for restaurants and consumers looking for easygoing claret that needs to be consumed before the turn of the century.

Price: The lowest prices asked in nearly a decade, and the end of the slump in Bordeaux wine pricing.

The year 1992 was not marked by a tragic frost, but rather by excessive rainfall at the worst possible time. Following a precocious spring, with an abundance of humidity and warm weather, the flowering of the vines occurred eight days earlier than the 30-year average, raising hopes of an early harvest. The summer was exceptionally hot, with June wet and warm, July slightly above normal in temperature, and August well above normal. However, unlike such classic hot, dry years as 1982, 1989, and 1990, there was significant rainfall (more than three times the normal amount) in August. For example, 193 millimeters of rain were reported in the Bordeaux area in August 1992 (most of it falling during several violent storms the last two days of the month) compared with 22 millimeters in 1990 and 63 millimeters in 1989.

By mid-August, it was evident that the harvest would be enormous. For the serious estates, it was imperative that crop thinning be employed to reduce the crop size. Properties that crop-thinned produced wines with more richness than the light, diluted offerings of those that did not.

The first two weeks of September were dry, although abnormally cool. During this period the Sauvignon and Semillon were harvested under ideal conditions, which explains the excellent and sometimes outstanding success (despite high yields) of the 1992 white Graves.

From September 20 through most of October the weather was unfavorable, with considerable rain interspersed with short periods of clear weather. The harvest for the majority of estates took place over a long period of time, although most of the Merlot crop from both sides of the Gironde was harvested during three days of clear, dry weather on September 29, 30, and October 1. Between October 2 and October 6, more violent rainstorms lashed the region, and the châteaux, realizing nothing could be gained from waiting, harvested under miserable weather conditions. To make good wine it was essential to handpick the grapes, leaving the damaged, diseased fruit on the vine. An even stricter selection was necessary in the cellars.

Overall, 1992 is a more successful vintage than 1991 because no appellation produced a high percentage of poor wines, such as occurred in Pomerol and St.-Émilion in 1991. Readers may recall that many top Pomerol and St.-Émilion estates declassified their entire 1991 crop. The 1992s are the modern-day equivalents of the 1973s. But with better vinification techniques, stricter selection, better equipment, and more attention to yields, the top properties produced 1992s that are more concentrated, richer, and overall better wines than the best 1973s, or, for that matter, the 1987s. The best 1992s tend to be soft, fruity, and low in acidity, with moderate tannin levels and moderate to good concentration. But far too many wines reflect the difficult harvest conditions, exhibiting diluted, compact personalities, a lack of ripe fruit, and aggressively high tannin.

The appellations that have fared best are Graves and Pomerol. The Graves region, because of the excellent drainage potential of that appellation's deep, stony soils, and Pomerol, because the earlier-harvested Merlot grape was less seriously damaged (particularly where the estates crop-thinned and had modest yields), consistently produced the vintage's finest wines.

Elsewhere, properties that practiced brutal selections enjoyed some success. In the Médoc, Léoville-Las Cases, Margaux, Lafite-Rothschild, Rausan-Ségla, Latour, Pichon-Baron, and Cos d'Estournel stand out in quality because at most of these estates less than 50% of the crop was used for the grand vin. Yet in most appellations the number of average-to below-average-quality wines is proportionally far higher than the successes. Those properties that were attentive to the enormous crop size and thus crop-thinned, those lucky enough to complete part of their harvest before the deluge of October 2–6, and those that possessed the financial ability to discard any questionable grapes or cuvées, have turned out fruity, soft, charming wines that will have to be drunk young.

Will these wines find a favorable reception in the American marketplace? I cannot see this vintage selling well unless the wines are modestly priced. Certainly the Bordeaux proprietors and *négociants* worked hard to keep the prices low for this average- to below-average-quality vintage. If the best second- through fifth-growths are available at prices of $15–$20 a bottle, the finest examples will find an audience looking for ready-to-drink, reasonably priced claret. If the first-growths are discounted under $45, they may also enjoy a limited audience for curiosity seekers wanting to see what a first-growth tastes like. Certainly all of the Médoc first-growths, plus Haut-Brion and Pétrus on the right bank, have made very fine wines that reflect the personalities and *terroir* of these estates. However, it will be difficult to muster much enthusiasm for wines priced higher than $45 a bottle.

Many Bordeaux insiders now realize that the 1992 vintage was so fragile that it would have been wise to have bottled the wines without much clarification. The fact that most Bordeaux châteaux routinely fine and filter their wines at bottling worked against the light, soft fruit the 1992s possessed. Those properties that fined less and utilized more porous filter pads have produced the most charming, fruity wines. Estates that did not take into account the lightness and fragility of the 1992's fruit eviscerated the wines at bottling. Given the massive amount of state-of-the-art technology and the talent pool of highly trained Bordeaux oenologists, I find it amazing that so many of these technicians continue to exhibit an inflexibility and an appalling lack of concern about the dangers of excessive fining and filtration.

TOP WINES FOR 1992

St.-Estèphe: Cos d'Estournel
Pauillac: Lafite-Rothschild, Latour
St.-Julien: Ducru-Beaucaillou, Léoville-Barton, Léoville-Las Cases
Margaux: Margaux, Rausan-Ségla
Médoc/Haut-Médoc/Moulis/Listrac Crus Bourgeois: None
Graves Red: Haut-Bailly, Haut-Brion, La Mission-Haut-Brion
Graves White: Domaine de Chevalier, Haut-Brion, Laville-Haut-Brion, La Louvière
Pomerol: Clinet, Lafleur, Pétrus, Trotanoy
Fronsac/Canon-Fronsac: None
St.-Émilion: L'Angélus, L'Arrosée, Beauséjour-Duffau, Canon-La-Gaffelière,
   Troplong-Mondot
Barsac/Sauternes: Nnone

1991—A Quick Study (9-19-91)

St.-Estèphe**	Graves Red***
Pauillac**	Graves White*
St.-Julien**	Pomerol 0
Margaux*	St.-Émilion 0
Médoc/Haut-Médoc Crus Bourgeois 0	Barsac/Sauternes 0

Size: A tiny crop with most of the right-bank appellations such as Pomerol and St.-Émilion producing even smaller quantities of wine.

Important Information: The worst in Pomerol and St.-Émilion since 1972, 1977, and 1984. Many top properties in these two appellations refused to produce a wine under the château's label. Some surprisingly good efforts emerged from Graves and the Médoc, mainly because the top estates declassified 50% or more of their production. The further north one went in the Médoc, the better the wines became, with St.-Julien, Pauillac, and St.-Estèphe more successful than Margaux.

Maturity Status: The wines should drink well for 10–15 years but will not be long-lived.

Price: Prices dropped significantly, marking the second year in a row where the Bordeaux châteaux realized the marketplace was saturated and would not support high prices for, at best, a mediocre vintage.

Nineteen ninety-one was the year of the big freeze. During the weekend of April 20–21, temperatures dropped as low as −9 degrees centigrade, destroying most vineyards' first-generation buds. The worst destruction occurred in Pomerol and St.-Émilion, east of the Gironde. Less damage occurred in the northern Médoc, especially in the northeastern sector of Pauillac and the southern half of St.-Estèphe. The spring that followed the devastating freeze did see the development of new buds, called second-generation fruit by viticulturists.

Because the crop size was expected to be small, optimists began to suggest that 1991 could resemble 1961 (a great year shaped by a spring killer frost that reduced the crop size). Of course, all of this hope was based on the assumption that the weather would remain sunny and dry during the growing season. By the time September arrived, most estates realized that the Merlot harvest could not begin until late September and the Cabernet Sauvignon harvest, in mid-October. The second-generation fruit had retarded most vineyards' harvest schedules, yet sunny skies in late September gave hope for another 1978-ish "miracle year." Then, on September 25, an Atlantic storm dumped 116 millimeters of rain, precisely twice the average rainfall for the entire month!

Between September 30 and October 12 the weather was generally dry. Most of the Merlot vineyards on the right bank (Pomerol and St.-Émilion) were harvested as quickly as possible during this period. In Pomerol and St.-Émilion there was significant dilution, some rot, and unripe grapes. In the Médoc much of the Cabernet Sauvignon was not yet fully ripe, but many estates recognized that it was too risky to wait any longer. Those estates that harvested between October 13 and 19, before the outbreak of six consecutive days of heavy rain (another 120 millimeters), picked unripe but surprisingly healthy and low-acid Cabernet Sauvignon. Those properties that had not harvested by the time the second deluge arrived were unable to make quality wine.

The 1991 vintage is a poor, frequently disastrous year for most estates in Pomerol and St.-Émilion. I find it inferior to 1984, making it the worst vintage for these two appellations since the appalling 1969s. Many well-known estates in Pomerol and St.-Émilion completely declassified their wines, including such renowned St.-Émilion estates as L'Arrosée, Ausone, Canon, Cheval Blanc, La Dominique, and Magdelaine. In Pomerol, several good wines were somehow made, but overall it was a catastrophe for this tiny appellation. The following Pomerol châteaux are among the better-known properties that declassified their entire crop: Beauregard, Bon Pasteur, L'Évangile, Le Gay, La Grave Trigant de Boisset, Lafleur, Latour à Pomerol, Pétrus, Trotanoy, and Vieux Château Certan.

Despite all this bad news, some soft, pleasant, light- to medium-bodied wines did emerge from Graves and those Médoc vineyards adjacent to the Gironde. Consumers will be surprised by the quality of many of these wines, particularly from St.-Julien, Pauillac, and St.-Estèphe. In these northern Médoc appellations, especially those vineyards adjacent to the Gironde, much of the first-generation fruit was not destroyed by the frost, resulting in diluted but physiologically riper fruit than second-generation fruit produced. However, the good wines must be priced low or no consumer interest will be justified.

The appellations that stand out for consistently good wines in 1991 are St.-Julien, Pauillac, and St.-Estèphe. These areas suffered less frost damage to the first-generation grapes. Virtually all of the better-run estates in these appellations made above-average-quality, sometimes excellent wine.

Because the intelligent properties in the Médoc utilized more Merlot in the blend rather than the unripe Cabernet Sauvignon, the 1991s are soft, forward wines that will need to be drunk in their first decade of life.

TOP WINES FOR 1991

St.-Estèphe: Cos d'Estournel, Montrose
Pauillac: Latour, Pichon-Longueville–Comtesse de Lalande
St.-Julien: Léoville-Barton, Léoville-Las Cases
Margaux: Château Margaux, Palmer, Rausan-Ségla
Médoc/Haut-Médoc/Moulis/Listrac Crus Bourgeois: None
Graves Red: Domaine de Chevalier, La Mission-Haut-Brion, Pape-Clément
Graves White: None
Pomerol: None
Fronsac/Canon-Fronsac: None
St.-Émilion: L'Angélus
Barsac/Sauternes: None

1990—A Quick Study (9-12-90)

St.-Estèphe *****   Graves Red ****
Pauillac *****   Graves White ***
St.-Julien *****   Pomerol *****
Margaux ***   St.-Émilion *****
Médoc/Haut-Médoc Crus Bourgeois ****   Barsac/Sauternes *****

Size: Enormous

Important Information: The hottest year since 1947, the sunniest year since 1949—a great vintage!

Maturity Status: Very rich yet approachable wines are full of extract, ripeness, and tannin. Accessible, but full maturity will occur after 2000.

Price: Offered at prices 15%–20% below the 1989s' opening prices, 1990 has begun to behave like 1982; it has become increasingly apparent that 1990, along with 1989 and 1982, is one of the three finest vintages since 1961.

Most of the great Bordeaux vintages of this century are the result of relatively hot, dry years. For that reason alone, 1990 should elicit considerable attention. The most revealing fact about the 1990 vintage is that it is the second-hottest vintage of the century, barely surpassed by 1947. It is also the second-sunniest vintage, eclipsed only by 1949 in the post–World War II era. The amount of sunshine and the extraordinarily hot summers Bordeaux enjoyed during the decade of the eighties is frequently attributed to the so-called greenhouse effect and the consequent global warming, about which such ominous warnings have been issued by the scientific community. Yet consider the Bordeaux weather for the period between 1945 and 1949. Amazingly, that era was even more torrid than 1989–1990. One might wonder if there was concern then about the glaciers of the north and south poles melting.

The weather of 1990 was auspicious because of its potential to produce great wines, but weather is only one part of the equation. The summer months of July and August were the driest since 1961, and August was the hottest since 1928, the year records were first kept. September (the month that most producers claim "makes the quality") was not, weather-wise, a particularly exceptional month. Nineteen ninety was the second-wettest year among the great hot-year vintages, surpassed only by 1989. As in 1989, the rain fell at periods that should give rise for concern. For example, on September 15 a particularly violent series of thunderstorms swung across Bordeaux, inundating much of the Graves region. On September 22–23 there was modest rainfall over the entire region. On October 7 and October 15 light showers were reported throughout the region. Most producers have been quick to state that the rain in September was beneficial. They argue that the Cabernet Sauvignon grapes were still too small and their skins too thick. Many Cabernet vines had shut down and the grapes refused to mature because of the excessive heat and drought. The rain, the producers suggest, promoted further ripening and alleviated the blocked state of maturity. This is an appealing argument that has some merit, but unfortunately, too many châteaux panicked and harvested too soon after these rainstorms.

When tasting the wines from 1990, the most striking characteristic is their roasted quality, no doubt the result of the extremely, perhaps excessively hot summer. The September rains may have partially alleviated the stress from which those vineyards planted with Cabernet in the lighter, better drained soils were suffering, but they also swelled many of the grape bunches and no doubt contributed to another prolifically abundant crop size. There is also the question of balance. Bordeaux has always possessed a marginal climate, and its wines are considered to gain their complexity from long, less-extreme ripening conditions. Yet there is no doubt that the great vintages have all been relatively hot, dry years. Were the yields so high that in spite of the exceptional weather there were just too many grapes to make profound wines? These early doubts have been erased by the performance of the wines in the bottle. One of the keys to understanding this vintage is that the best wines of 1990 have often emerged from those vineyards planted on the heavier, less well drained soils. For example, in my tasting notes, heavier soils from such appellations as St.-Estèphe, Fronsac, and the hillside and plateau vineyards of St.-Émilion produced richer, more concentrated, and more complete wines than many of the top vineyards planted on the fine, well-drained, gravel-based soils of Margaux and Graves.

The crop size was enormous in 1990, approximately equivalent to the quantity of wine produced in 1989. In reality, more wine was actually made, but because the French authori-ties intervened and required significant declassifications, the actual declared limit matches 1989, which means that for both vintages the production is 30% more than in 1982. Officially, however, many châteaux made even stricter selections in 1990 than in 1989 and the actual quantity of wine declared by many producers under the grand vin label is less than in 1989.

Across almost every appellation, the overall impression one gets of the dry red wines is one of extremely low acidity (as low as and in some cases even lower than in 1989), high tannins (in most cases higher than in 1989), but an overall impression of softness and forward, precocious, extremely ripe, sometimes roasted flavors. Because the tannins are so soft (as in 1982, 1985, and 1989), it is very likely that these wines will provide considerable enjoyment when they are young.

The unprecedented second consecutive year of great heat, sunshine, and drought appar-ently caused even more stress for those vineyards planted in light, gravelly soil than in 1989. Many proprietors in the Graves and Margaux regions suggested that they were almost forced to harvest their Cabernet too soon because it was drying up on the vine. This, combined with extremely high yields, no doubt explains why the Graves and Margaux appellations, much as in 1989 and 1982 (two other hot, dry years), were less successful.

Some surprising strengths in this vintage include all four of the Médoc first-growths.

Astoundingly, it can be safely said that they have made slightly richer, fuller, more complete wines in 1990 than in 1989. Elsewhere in the Médoc, particularly in St.-Julien and Pauillac, a bevy of relatively soft, round, forward, fruity, large-scale wines with high alcohol, high, soft tannin, and extremely low acidity have been made. There is no doubting that the strongest left-bank appellation in 1990 is St.-Estèphe, followed closely by Pauillac and St.-Julien. Sensational in quality, many wines are superior to their 1989 counterparts.

On the right bank, Pomerol enjoyed as successful a vintage as it did in 1989. In short, it is another great vintage for Pomerol. St.-Émilion, never a consistent appellation, has produced perhaps its most homogeneous and greatest vintage of this century.

The 1990 vintage is forward and charming, with most wines (except, of course, the first-growths) having an aging potential of 15–25 years. Nevertheless, the irony is that the St.-Émilions, normally the most inconsistent wines of Bordeaux, will probably prove, along with the St.-Estèphes, first-growths, and superseconds, the longest-lived wines in this vintage.

The dry white wines of Graves, as well as generic white Bordeaux, have enjoyed an excellent vintage that is superior to 1989. Poor judgment in picking the 1989s too soon was not repeated with the 1990s, which have more richness and depth than most 1989s. Two notable exceptions are Haut-Brion and Laville-Haut-Brion.

As for the sweet white wines of the Barsac/Sauternes region, this vintage will be historic in the sense that most of the white wine producers finished their harvest before the red wine producers, something that has not happened since 1949. With considerable power and a sweet, sugary style, as well as emerging complexity and focus, these wines continue to grow in stature in the bottle.

TOP WINES FOR 1990

St.-Estèphe: Calon-Ségur, Cos d'Estournel, Haut-Marbuzet, Montrose
Pauillac: Les Forts de Latour, Grand-Puy-Lacoste, Lafite-Rothschild, Latour, Lynch-Bages, Pichon-Longueville Baron
St.-Julien: Lagrange, Léoville-Barton, Léoville-Las Cases, Léoville-Poyferré, St.-Pierre
Margaux: Château Margaux, Rausan-Ségla
Médoc/Haut-Médoc/Moulis/Listrac Crus Bourgeois: Sociando-Mallet
Graves Red: Domaine de Chevalier, Haut-Bailly, Haut-Brion, La Mission-Haut-Brion, Pape-Clément
Graves White: None
Pomerol: Bon Pasteur, Certan de May, Clinet, La Conseillante, L'Église-Clinet, L'Évangile, Gazin, Lafleur, Petit-Village, Pétrus, Le Pin, Vieux Château Certan
Fronsac/Canon-Fronsac: None
St.-Émilion: L'Angélus, L'Arrosée, Ausone, Beauséjour-Duffau, Canon-La-Gaffelière, Cheval Blanc, Clos Fourtet, La Dominique, Figeac, La Gaffelière, Grand-Mayne, Larcis-Ducasse, Magdelaine, Pavie, Pavie-Decesse, Pavie-Macquin, Le Tertre-Roteboeuf, Troplong-Mondot
Barsac/Sauternes: Climens, Clos Haut-Peraguey, Coutet-Cuvée Madame, Doisy-Daëne, Doisy-Daëne l'Extravagance, Filhot, Guiraud, Lamothe-Guignard, de Malle, Rabaud-Promis, Rieussec, Suduiraut, La Tour Blanche

1989—A Quick Study (8-31-89)

St.-Estèphe ****	Graves Red ***
Pauillac *****	Graves White **
St.-Julien ****	Pomerol *****

Margaux ***   St.-Émilion ****
Médoc/Haut-Médoc Crus Bourgeois ****   Barsac/Sauternes ****

Size: Mammoth; along with 1990 and 1986, the largest declared crop in the history of Bordeaux.

Important Information: Excessively hyped vintage by virtually everyone but the Bordeaux proprietors. American, French, even English writers were all set to declare it the vintage of the century until serious tasters began to question the extract levels, phenomenally low acid levels, and the puzzling quality of some wines. However, plenty of rich, dramatic, fleshy wines have been produced that should age reasonably well.

Maturity Status: High tannins and extremely low acidity, much like 1990, suggest early drinkability, with only the most concentrated wines capable of lasting 20–30 or more years.

Price: The most expensive opening prices of any vintage.

The general news media, primarily ABC television and *The New York Times,* first carried the news that several châteaux began their harvest during the last days of August, making 1989 the earliest vintage since 1893. An early harvest generally signifies a torrid growing season and below-average rainfall—almost always evidence that a top-notch vintage is achievable. In his annual *Vintage and Market Report,* Peter Sichel reported that between 1893 and 1989 only 1947, 1949, 1970, and 1982 were years with a similar weather pattern, but none of these years were as hot as 1989.

Perhaps the most revealing and critical decision (at least from a qualitative perspective) was the choice of picking dates. Never has Bordeaux enjoyed such a vast span of time (August 28–October 15) over which to complete the harvest. Some châteaux, most notably Haut-Brion and the Christian Moueix–managed properties in Pomerol and St.-Émilion, harvested during the first week of September. Other estates waited and did not finish their harvesting until mid-October. During the second week of September, one major problem developed. Much of the Cabernet Sauvignon, while analytically mature and having enough sugar to potentially produce wines with 13% alcohol, was actually not ripe physiologically. Many châteaux, never having experienced such growing conditions, became indecisive. Far too many deferred to their oenologists, who saw technically mature grapes that were quickly losing acidity. The oenologists, never ones to take risks, advised immediate picking. As more than one proprietor and *négociant* said, by harvesting the Cabernet too early, a number of châteaux lost their chance to produce one of the greatest wines of a lifetime. This, plus the enormously large crop size, probably explains the good yet uninspired performance of so many wines from the Graves and Margaux appellations.

There was clearly no problem with the early-picked Merlot as much of it came in between 13.5% and a whopping 15% alcohol level—unprecedented in Bordeaux. Those properties who crop-thinned—Pétrus, La Fleur Pétrus, and Haut-Brion—had yields of 45–55 hectoliters per hectare, and superconcentration. Those who did not crop-thin had yields as preposterously high as 80 hectoliters per hectare.

Contrary to the reports of a totally "dry harvest," there were rain showers on the 10th, 13th, 18th, and 22nd of September that did little damage unless the property panicked and harvested the day after the rain. Some of the lighter-styled wines may very well be the result of jittery châteaux owners who unwisely picked after the showers.

The overall production was, once again, staggeringly high.

While the enormous hype from spectators outside of Bordeaux bordered on irresponsible, the Bordelais had a far more conservative view of the 1989 vintage. Consider the following. Before it went bankrupt, England's Hungerford Wine Company, once run with great flair by Nicholas Davies, sent out a questionnaire to 200 of the major Bordeaux proprietors. Their comments were fascinating. When asked to compare the 1989 vintage to another vintage, the most popular comparison (25% of those polled) was to 1982. Fourteen percent compared it to 1985, 10% to 1986, 8% to 1988, 7% to 1961, and 6% to 1947. Only Peter Sichel, the president of Bordeaux's prestigious Union des Grands Crus (who appears far too young to remember) compared it to 1893. In this same intriguing survey, the proprietors, when asked for a general qualitative assessment, responded in the following manner. Sixty-four percent rated it excellent, 17% rated it very good, 4% said it was the vintage of the century, and 10% rated it superb (meaning, I suppose, better than excellent, but not vintage-of-the-century material). The other 5% were unsure of what they had produced.

In general, the wines are the most alcoholic Bordeaux I have ever tasted, ranging from 12.8% to over 14.5% for many Pomerols. Acidities are extremely low and tannin levels surprisingly high. Consequently, in looking at the structural profile of the 1989s, one sees wines 1% to 2% higher in alcohol than the 1982s or 1961s; with much lower acidity levels than the 1982s, 1961s, and 1959s, yet high tannin levels. Fortunately, the tannins are generally ripe and soft, à la 1982, rather than dry and astringent as in 1988. This gives the wines a big, rich fleshy feel in the mouth similar to the 1982s. The top 1989s have very high glycerin levels, but are they as concentrated as the finest 1982s and 1986s? In Margaux the answer is a resounding "no" as this is clearly the least-favored appellation, much as it was in 1982. In Graves, except for Haut-Brion, La Mission-Haut-Brion, Haut-Bailly, and de Fieuzal, the wines are relatively light and undistinguished. In St.-Émilion, the 1982s are more consistent as well as more deeply concentrated. Some marvelously rich, enormously fruity, fat wines were made in St.-Émilion in 1989, but there is wide irregularity in quality. However, in the northern Médoc, primarily St.-Julien, Pauillac, and St.-Estèphe, as well as in Pomerol, many exciting, full-bodied, very alcoholic, and tannic wines have been made. The best of these seem to combine the splendidly rich, opulent, fleshy texture of the finest 1982s with the power and tannin of the 1986s.

However, the softness of the tannins, very high pHs (3.7–4.0 is the norm in this vintage), and low acidity, characteristics that caused a number of American critics to malign and erroneously dismiss the 1982s, are even more evident in the 1989s. Furthermore, the 1989s were made from much higher yields (20%–40% more wine per acre) than the 1982s. This has caused more than one *négociant* to suggest, in a pejorative sense, that the best 1989 red Bordeaux have more in common with Côte-Rôtie or California than classic claret. Such statements are pure nonsense. The best of these wines are powerful, authoritative examples of their types; they do not taste like Côte-Rôtie or California Cabernet. However, because these wines are so individualistic as well as forward, I expect the vintage, much like 1982, to be controversial.

As with the 1982s, this is a vintage that will probably be enjoyable to drink over a broad span of years. Despite the high tannin levels, the low acidities combined with the high glycerine and alcohol levels give the wines a fascinatingly fleshy, full-bodied texture. While there is considerable variation in quality, the finest 1989s from Pomerol, St.-Julien, Pauillac, and St.-Estèphe will, in specific cases, rival some of the greatest wines in 1982 and 1986.

TOP WINES FOR 1989

St.-Estèphe: Cos d'Estournel, Haut-Marbuzet, Meyney, Montrose

Pauillac: Clerc-Milon, Grand-Puy-Lacoste, Lafite-Rothschild, Lynch-Bages, Mouton-Rothschild, Pichon-Longueville Baron, Pichon-Longueville–Comtesse de Lalande

St.-Julien: Beychevelle, Branaire-Ducru, Ducru-Beaucaillou, Léoville-Barton, Léoville-Las Cases, Talbot

Margaux: Cantemerle, Margaux, Monbrison, Palmer, Rausan-Ségla

Médoc/Haut-Médoc/Moulis Listrac Crus Bourgeois: Beaumont, Le Boscq, Chasse-Spleen, Gressier Grand-Poujeaux, Lanessan, Maucaillou, Moulin-Rouge, Potensac, Poujeaux, Sociando-Mallet, La Tour de By, Tour Haut-Caussan, Tour du Haut-Moulin, La Tour St.-Bonnet, Vieux-Robin

Graves Red: Bahans-Haut-Brion, Haut-Bailly, Haut-Brion, La Mission-Haut-Brion

Graves White: Clos Floridene, Haut-Brion, Laville-Haut-Brion

Pomerol: Bon Pasteur, Clinet, La Conseillante, Domaine de L'Église, L'Évangile, La Fleur Pétrus, Le Gay, Gombaude-Guillot, Lafleur, Lafleur de Gay, Les Pensées de Lafleur, Pétrus, Le Pin, Trotanoy, Vieux Château Certan

Fronsac/Canon-Fronsac: Canon, Canon-de-Brem, Canon-Moueix, Cassagne-Haut-Canon-La-Truffière, Dalem, La Dauphine, Fontenil, Mazeris, Moulin-Haut-Laroque, Moulin-Pey-Labrie

St.-Émilion: L'Angélus, Ausone, Cheval Blanc, La Dominique, La Gaffelière, Grand-Mayne, Magdelaine, Pavie-Macquin, Soutard, Le Tertre-Roteboeuf, Trottevieille

Barsac/Sauternes: Climens, Coutet, Coutet-Cuvée Madame, Doisy-Védrines, Guiraud, Lafaurie-Peyraguey, Rabaud-Promis, Raymond-Lafon, Rieussec, Suduiraut, Suduiraut-Cuvée Madame, La Tour Blanche

1988—A Quick Study (9-20-88)

St.-Estèphe***	Graves Red****
Pauillac***	Graves White***
St.-Julien***	Pomerol****
Margaux***	St.-Émilion***
Médoc/Haut-Médoc Crus Bourgeois**	Barsac/Sauternes*****

Size: A large crop equivalent in size to 1982, meaning 30% less wine than was produced in 1989 and 1990.

Important Information: Fearing a repeat of the rains that destroyed the potential for a great year in 1987, many producers once again pulled the trigger on their harvesting teams too soon. Unfortunately, copious quantities of Médoc Cabernet Sauvignon were picked too early.

Maturity Status: Because of good acid levels and relatively high, more astringent tannins, there is no denying the potential of the 1988s to last for 20 or 30 years. How many of these wines will retain enough fruit to stand up to the tannin remains to be seen.

Price: Prices range 20%–40% below the 1989s, so the best wines offer considerable value.

The year 1988 is a good but rarely thrilling vintage of red wines, and one of the greatest vintages of this century for the sweet wines of Barsac and Sauternes.

The problem with the red wines is that there is a lack of superstar performances on the part of the top châteaux. This will no doubt ensure that 1988 will always be regarded as a good rather than excellent year. While the 1988 crop size was large, it was exceeded in size by the two vintages that followed it, 1989 and 1990. The average yield in 1988 was between 45 and 50 hectoliters per hectare, which was approximately equivalent to the quantity of wine produced in 1982. The wines tend to be well colored, extremely tannic, and firmly structured, but also too often they exhibit a slight lack of depth, and finish short, with noticeably green, astringent tannins.

These characteristics are especially evident in the Médoc where it was all too apparent that many châteaux, apprehensive about the onset of rot and further rain (as in 1987) panicked and harvested their Cabernet Sauvignon too early. Consequently, they brought in Cabernet that often achieved only 8%–9% sugar readings. Those properties that waited (too few indeed) made the best wines.

In Pomerol and St.-Émilion the Merlot was harvested under ripe conditions, but because of the severe drought in 1988 the skins of the grapes were thicker and the resulting wines were surprisingly tannic and hard.

In St.-Émilion many properties reported bringing in Cabernet Franc at full maturity and obtaining sugar levels that were reportedly higher than ever before. However, despite such optimistic reports much of the Cabernet Franc tasted fluid and diluted in quality. Therefore, St.-Émilion, despite reports of a very successful harvest, exhibits great irregularity in quality.

The appellation of Graves probably produced the best red wines of Bordeaux in 1988.

While there is no doubt that the richer, more dramatic, fleshier 1989s have taken much of the public's attention away from the 1988s, an objective look at the 1988 vintage will reveal some surprisingly strong performances in appellations such as Margaux, Pomerol, and Graves, and in properties in the northern Médoc that eliminated their early-picked Cabernet Sauvignon, or harvested much later. The year 1988 is not a particularly good one for the Crus Bourgeois because many harvested too soon. The lower prices they receive for their wines do not permit the Crus Bourgeois producers to make the strict selection that is necessary in years such as 1988.

The one appellation that did have a superstar vintage was Barsac and Sauternes. With a harvest that lasted until the end of November and textbook weather conditions for the formation of the noble rot, *Botrytis cinerea*, 1988 is already considered by European authorities to be the finest vintage since 1937. Almost across the board, including the smaller estates, the wines have an intense smell of honey, coconut, oranges, and other tropical fruits. It is a remarkably rich vintage with wines of extraordinary levels of botrytis, great concentration of flavor; yet the rich, unctuous, opulent textures are balanced beautifully by zesty, crisp acidity. It is this latter component that makes these wines so special and the reason why they have an edge over the 1989s.

One must also remember that the 1988 Bordeaux vintage offers wines that, in general, are priced 25%–40% below the same wines in 1989. It is a vintage where the best wines will be ready to drink in 4–5 years, but will last for up to 15–25 years. For the sweet wines of Barsac/Sauternes, 30–40 more years of aging potential is not unrealistic.

TOP WINES FOR 1988

St.-Estèphe: Calon-Ségur, Haut-Marbuzet, Meyney, Phélan-Ségur

Pauillac: Clerc-Milon, Lafite-Rothschild, Latour, Lynch-Bages, Mouton-Rothschild, Pichon-Longueville Baron, Pichon-Longueville–Comtesse de Lalande

St.-Julien: Gruaud-Larose, Léoville-Barton, Léoville-Las Cases, Talbot

Margaux: Monbrison, Rausan-Ségla

Médoc/Haut-Médoc/Moulis/Listrac Crus Bourgeois: Fourcas-Loubaney, Gressier Grand-Poujeaux, Poujeaux, Sociando-Mallet, Tour du Haut-Moulin

Graves Red: Les Carmes Haut-Brion, Domaine de Chevalier, Haut-Bailly, Haut-Brion, La Louvière, La Mission-Haut-Brion, Pape-Clément

Graves White: Domaine de Chevalier, Clos Floridene, Couhins-Lurton, de Fieuzal, Laville-Haut-Brion, La Louvière, La Tour-Martillac

Pomerol: Bon Pasteur, Certan de May, Clinet, L'Eglise-Clinet, La Fleur de Gay, Gombaude-Guillot-Cuvée Speciale, Lafleur, Petit-Village, Pétrus, Le Pin, Vieux Château Certan

St.-Émilion: L'Angélus, Ausone, Canon-La-Gaffelière, Clos des Jacobins, Larmande, Le Tertre-Roteboeuf, Troplong-Mondot

Barsac/Sauternes: d'Arche, Broustet, Climens, Coutet, Coutet-Cuvée Madame, Doisy-Daëne, Doisy-Dubroca, Guiraud, Lafaurie-Peyraguey, Lamothe-Guignard, Rabaud-Promis, Rayne-Vigneau, Rieussec, Sigalas Rabaud, Suduiraut, La Tour Blanche

1987—A Quick Study (10-3-87)

St.-Estèphe **   Graves Red ***
Pauillac **   Graves White ****
St.-Julien **   Pomerol ***
Margaux **   St.-Émilion **
Médoc/Haut-Médoc Crus Bourgeois *   Barsac/Sauternes *

Size: A moderately sized crop that looks almost tiny in the scheme of the gigantic yields during the decade of the eighties.

Important Information: The most underrated vintage of the decade of the eighties, producing a surprising number of ripe, round, tasty wines, particularly from Pomerol, Graves, and the most seriously run estates in the northern Médoc.

Maturity Status: The best examples are deliciously drinkable and should be consumed now.

Price: Low prices are the rule rather than the exception for this attractive, undervalued vintage.

More than one Bordelais has said that if the rain had not arrived during the first two weeks of October 1987 ravaging the quality of the unharvested Cabernet Sauvignon and Petit Verdot, then 1987—not 1989 or 1982—would be the most extraordinary vintage of the decade of the eighties. Wasn't it true that August and September had been the hottest two months in Bordeaux since 1976? But, the rain did fall, plenty of it, and it dashed the hopes for a top vintage. Yet much of the Merlot was primarily harvested before the rain. The early-picked Cabernet Sauvignon was adequate, but that picked after the rains began was in very poor condition. Thanks in part to the two gigantic-sized crops of 1985 and 1986, both record years at the time, most Bordeaux châteaux had full cellars, and were mentally prepared to eliminate the vats of watery Cabernet Sauvignon harvested in the rains that fell for 14 straight days in October. The results for the top estates are wines that are light to medium bodied, ripe, fruity, round, even fat, with low tannins, low acidity, and lush, captivating, charming personalities.

While there is a tendency to look at 1987 as a poor year and to compare it with such other recent uninspiring vintages as 1977, 1980, and 1984, the truth is that the wines could not be more different. In the 1977, 1980, and 1984 vintages, the problem was immaturity because of cold, wet weather leading up to the harvest. In 1987, the problem was not a lack of maturity, as the Merlot and Cabernet were ripe. In 1987, the rains diluted fully mature, ripe grapes.

The year 1987 is the most underrated vintage of the decade for those estates where a strict selection was made and/or the Merlot was harvested in sound condition. The wines are deliciously fruity, forward, clean, fat, and soft, without any degree of rot. Prices remain a bargain even though the quantities produced were relatively small. This is a vintage that I search out on restaurant wine lists. I have bought a number of the wines for my cellar because I regard 1987, much like 1976, as a very soft, forward vintage that produced wines for drinking in their first decade of life.

TOP WINES FOR 1987

St.-Estèphe: Cos d'Estournel
Pauillac: Lafite-Rothschild, Latour, Mouton-Rothschild, Pichon-Longueville Baron, Pichon-Longueville–Comtesse de Lalande
St.-Julien: Gruaud-Larose, Léoville-Barton, Léoville-Las Cases, Talbot
Margaux: d'Angludet, Margaux, Palmer
Médoc/Haut-Médoc/Moulis/Listrac Crus Bourgeois: None
Graves Red: Bahans-Haut-Brion, Domaine de Chevalier, Haut-Brion, La Mission-Haut-Brion, Pape-Clément

Graves White: Domaine de Chevalier, Couhins-Lurton, de Fieuzal, Laville-Haut-Brion, La
   Tour-Martillac
Pomerol: Certan de May, Clinet, La Conseillante, L'Evangile, La Fleur de Gay,
   Petit-Village, Pétrus, Le Pin
St.-Émilion: Ausone, Cheval Blanc, Clos des Jacobins, Clos Saint-Martin, Grand-Mayne,
   Magdelaine, Le Tertre-Roteboeuf, Trottevieille
Barsac/Sauternes: Coutet, Lafaurie-Peyraguey

1986—A Quick Study (9-23-86)

St.-Estèphe****	Graves Red***
Pauillac*****	Graves White**
St.-Julien*****	Pomerol***
Margaux****	St.-Émilion***
Médoc/Haut-Médoc Crus Bourgeois***	Barsac/Sauternes*****

Size: Colossal; along with 1989 and 1990 one of the largest crops produced in Bordeaux.

Important Information: An irrefutably great year for the Cabernet Sauvignon grape in the northern Médoc, St.-Julien, Pauillac, and St.-Estèphe. The top 1986s beg for 10–15 more years of cellaring, and one wonders how many purchasers of these wines will lose their patience before the wines have reached full maturity.

Maturity Status: The wines from the Crus Bourgeois, Graves, and the right bank can be drunk now, but the impeccably structured Médocs need at least 10–15 more years.

Price: Still realistic, except for a handful of the superstar wines, but I expect this vintage to begin to soar in price when the wines are about 10–12 years of age.

   The year 1986 is without doubt a great vintage for the northern Médoc, particularly for St.-Julien, Pauillac, and St.-Estèphe, where many châteaux produced wines that are their deepest and most concentrated since 1982, and with 20–30 plus years of longevity. Yet it should be made very clear to readers that unlike the great vintage of 1982, or very good vintages of 1983 and 1985, the 1986s are not flattering wines to drink young. Most of the top wines of the Médoc will require a minimum of a decade of cellaring to shed their tannins, which are the highest ever measured for a Bordeaux vintage. If you are not prepared to wait for the 1986s to mature, this is not a vintage that makes sense to buy. If you can defer your gratification, then many wines will prove to be the most exhilarating Bordeaux wines produced since 1982.

   Why did 1986 turn out to be such an exceptional year for many Médocs, as well as Graves wines, and produce Cabernet Sauvignon grapes of uncommon richness and power? The weather during the summer of 1986 was very dry and hot. In fact, by the beginning of September, Bordeaux was in the midst of a severe drought that began to threaten the final maturity process of the grapes. Rain did come, first on September 14 and 15, which enhanced the maturity process and mitigated the drought conditions. This rain was welcome, but on September 23, a ferocious, quick-moving storm thrashed the city of Bordeaux, the Graves region, and the major right bank appellations of Pomerol and St.-Émilion.

   The curious aspect of this major storm, which caused widespread flooding in Bordeaux, was that it barely sideswiped the northern Médoc appellations of St.-Julien, Pauillac, and St.-Estèphe. Those pickers who started their harvest around the end of September found bloated Merlot grapes and unripe Cabernets. Consequently, the top wines of 1986 came from those châteaux that (1) did most of their harvesting after October 5, or (2) eliminated from their final blend the early-picked Merlot, as well as the Cabernet Franc and Cabernet Sauvignon harvested between September 23 and October 4. After September 23 there were an extraordinary 23 days of hot, windy, sunny weather that turned the vintage into an exceptional one for those who delayed picking. It is, therefore, no surprise that the late-harvested Cabernet Sauvignon in the northern Médoc that was picked after October 6, but primarily between October 9 and 16, produced wines of extraordinary intensity and depth. To no one's surprise, Château Margaux and Château Mouton-Rothschild, which produced the vintage's two greatest wines, took in the great majority of their Cabernet Sauvignon between October 11 and 16.

In Pomerol and St.-Émilion, those châteaux that harvested soon after the September 23 deluge got predictably much less intense wines. Those that waited (e.g., Vieux Château Certan, Lafleur, Le Pin) made much more concentrated, complete wines. As in most vintages, the harvest date in 1986 was critical, and without question the late pickers made the finest wines. Perhaps the most perplexing paradox to emerge from the 1986 vintage is the generally high quality of the Graves wines, particularly in spite of the fact that this area was ravaged by the September 23 rainstorm. The answer in part may be that the top Graves châteaux eliminated more Merlot from the final blend than usual, therefore producing wines with a much higher percentage of Cabernet Sauvignon.

Lastly, the size of the 1986 crop established another record, as the harvest exceeded the bumper crop of 1985 by 15%, and was 30% larger than the 1982 harvest. This overall production figure, equaled in both 1989 and 1990, is somewhat deceiving, as most of the classified Médoc châteaux made significantly less wine in 1986 than in 1985. It is for that reason, as well as the super maturity and tannin levels of the Cabernet Sauvignon grape, that most Médocs are noticeably more concentrated, more powerful, and more tannic in 1986 than they were in 1985.

All things considered, 1986 offers numerous exciting as well as exhilarating wines of profound depth and exceptional potential for longevity. Yet I continue to ask myself, how many readers are willing to defer their gratification until the turn of the century when these wines will be ready to drink?

TOP WINES FOR 1986

St.-Estèphe: Cos d'Estournel, Montrose
Pauillac: Clerc-Milon, Grand-Puy-Lacoste, Haut-Bages-Libéral, Lafite-Rothschild, Latour, Lynch-Bages, Mouton-Rothschild, Pichon-Longueville Baron, Pichon-Longueville–Comtesse de Lalande
St.-Julien: Beychevelle, Ducru-Beaucaillou, Gruaud-Larose, Lagrange, Léoville-Barton, Léoville-Las Cases, Talbot
Margaux: Margaux, Palmer, Rausan-Ségla
Médoc/Haut-Médoc-Moulis Listrac Crus Bourgeois: Chasse-Spleen, Fourcas-Loubaney, Gressier Grand-Poujeaux, Lanessan, Maucaillou, Poujeaux, Sociando-Mallet
Graves Red: Domaine de Chevalier, Haut-Brion, La Mission-Haut-Brion, Pape-Clément
Graves White: None
Pomerol: Certan de May, Clinet, L'Église-Clinet, La Fleur de Gay, Lafleur, Pétrus, Le Pin, Vieux Château Certan
St.-Émilion: L'Arrosée, Canon, Cheval Blanc, Figeac, Pavie, Le Tertre-Roteboeuf
Barsac/Sauternes: Climens, Coutet-Cuvée Madame, de Fargues, Guiraud, Lafaurie-Peyraguey, Raymond-Lafon, Rieussec, Yquem

1985—A Quick Study (9-29-85)

St.-Estèphe***	Graves Red****
Pauillac****	Graves White****
St.-Julien****	Pomerol****
Margaux***	St.-Émilion***
Médoc/Haut-Médoc Crus Bourgeois***	Barsac/Sauternes**

Size: A very large crop (a record at the time) that was subsequently surpassed by harvest sizes in 1986, 1989, and 1990.

Important Information: The top Médocs may turn out to represent clones of the gorgeously seductive, charming 1953 vintage. Most of the top wines are suprisingly well developed, displaying fine richness, a round, feminine character, and exceptional aromatic purity and complexity.

Maturity Status: Seemingly drinkable from their release, the 1985s continue to develop quickly, yet should last in the top cases for 20–25 years. The top Crus Bourgeois are delicious and should be consumed before the mid-nineties.

Price: Released at outrageously high prices, the 1985s have not appreciated in value to the extent of other top vintages. Prices in 1995 now look more attractive, particularly in view of the delicious drinking these wines now offer.

Any vintage, whether in Bordeaux or elsewhere, is shaped by the weather pattern. The 1985 Bordeaux vintage was conceived in a period of apprehension. January 1985 was the coldest since 1956. (I was there on January 16 when the temperature hit a record low 14.5 degrees centigrade.) However, fear of damage to the vineyard was greatly exaggerated by the Bordelais. One wonders about the sincerity of such fears and whether they were designed to push up prices for the 1983s and create some demand for the overpriced 1984s. In any event, the spring and early summer were normal, if somewhat more rainy and cooler than usual in April, May, and June. July was slightly hotter and wetter than normal; August was colder than normal but extremely dry. The September weather set a meteorological record —it was the sunniest, hottest, and driest September ever measured. The three most recent top vintages—1961, 1982, and 1989—could not claim such phenomenal weather conditions in September.

The harvest commenced at the end of September and three things became very apparent in that period between September 23 and September 30. First, the Merlot was fully mature and excellent in quality. Second, the Cabernet Sauvignon grapes were not as ripe as expected, and barely reached 11% natural alcohol. Third, the enormous size of the crop caught everyone off guard. The drought of August and September had overly stressed the many Cabernet vineyards planted in gravelly soil, and actually retarded the ripening process. The smart growers stopped picking Cabernet, risking foul weather, but hoping for higher sugar levels. The less adventurous settled for good rather than very good Cabernet Sauvignon. The pickers who waited and picked their Cabernet Sauvignon in mid-October clearly made the best wines as the weather held up throughout the month of October. Because of the drought, there was little botrytis in the Barsac and Sauternes regions. Those wines have turned out to be monolithic, straightforward, and fruity, but in general, lacking complexity and depth.

In general, 1985 is an immensely seductive and attractive vintage that has produced numerous well-balanced, rich, very perfumed yet tender wines. The 1985s are destined to be consumed over the next 15 years while waiting for the tannins of the 1986s to melt away and for richer, fuller, more massive wines from vintages such as 1982 and 1989 to reach full maturity. The year 1985 was a year of great sunshine, heat, and drought, so much so that many of the vineyards planted on lighter, more gravelly soil were stressed.

In the Médoc, 1985 produced an enormous crop. Where the châteaux made a strict selection, the results are undeniably charming, round, precocious, opulent wines with low acidity, and an overall elegant, almost feminine quality. The tannins are soft and mellow.

Interestingly, in the Médoc it is one of those years, much like 1989, where the so-called superseconds, such as Cos d'Estournel, Lynch-Bages, Léoville-Las Cases, Ducru-Beaucaillou, Pichon-Longueville–Comtesse de Lalande, and Léoville-Barton, made wines that rival and in some cases even surpass the more illustrious first-growths. In many vintages

(1986 for example) the first-growths soar qualitatively above the rest. That is not the case in 1985.

In the best-case scenario, the top 1985s may well evolve along the lines of the beautiful, charming 1953 vintage.

Most of the Médoc growers, who were glowing in their opinion of the 1985s, called the vintage a blend in style between 1982 and 1983. Others compared the 1985s to the 1976s. Both of these positions seem far off the mark. The 1985s are certainly lighter, without nearly the texture, weight, or concentration of the finest 1982s or 1986s, but at the same time most 1985s are far richer and fuller than the 1976s.

On Bordeaux's right bank, in Pomerol and St.-Émilion, the Merlot was brought in at excellent maturity levels, although many châteaux had a tendency to pick too soon (e.g., Pétrus and Trotanoy). While the vintage is not another 1982 or 1989, it certainly is a fine year in Pomerol. It is less consistent in St.-Émilion because too many producers harvested their Cabernet before it was physiologically fully mature. Interestingly, many of the Libourneais producers compared 1985 stylistically to 1971.

The vintage, which is one of seductive appeal, was priced almost too high when first released. The wines have not appreciated to the extent that many deserve and now look more reasonably priced than at any time in the past.

TOP WINES FOR 1985

St.-Estèphe: Cos d'Estournel, Haut-Marbuzet

Pauillac: Lafite-Rothschild, Lynch-Bages, Mouton-Rothschild, Pichon-Longueville–Comtesse de Lalande

St.-Julien: Ducru-Beaucaillou, Gruaud-Larose, Léoville-Barton, Léoville-Las Cases, Talbot

Margaux: d'Angludet, Lascombes, Margaux, Palmer, Rausan-Ségla

Médoc/Haut-Médoc/Moulis/Listrac Crus Bourgeois: None

Graves Red: Haut-Brion, La Mission-Haut-Brion

Graves White: Domaine de Chevalier, Haut-Brion, Laville-Haut-Brion

Pomerol: Certan de May, La Conseillante, L'Église-Clinet, L'Évangile, Lafleur, Pétrus, Le Pin

St.-Émilion: Canon, Cheval Blanc, de Ferrand, Soutard, Le Tertre-Roteboeuf

Barsac/Sauternes: Yquem

1984—A Quick Study (10-5-84)

St.-Estèphe*	Graves Red**
Pauillac**	Graves White*
St.-Julien**	Pomerol**
Margaux*	St.-Émilion*
Médoc/Haut-Médoc Crus Bourgeois*	Barsac/Sauternes*

Size: A small- to medium-sized crop of primarily Cabernet-based wine.

Important Information: The least attractive current vintage for drinking today, the 1984s, because of the failure of the Merlot crop, are essentially Cabernet-based wines that remain well colored, but compact, stern, and forbiddingly backward and tannic. The best examples may prove surprisingly good, but they need at least another 5–7 years.

Maturity Status: Will they be worth the wait?

Price: Virtually any 1984 can be had for a song as most retailers who bought this vintage are stuck with the wines.

The wine press is a curious thing to behold. Many wine writers, most of whom should have known better, maliciously condemned the 1984 vintage as a wash-out during the summer, a good 2 months before the harvest began. Then when the wines were released, the same critics were urging buyers to "purchase these lovely miracle" wines. As usual, the truth lies somewhere in between.

After three abundant vintages, 1981, 1982, and 1983, the climatic conditions during the summer and autumn of 1984 hardly caused euphoria among the Bordelais. First, the vegetative cycle began rapidly, thanks to a magnificently hot, sunny April. However, that was followed by a relatively cool and wet May, which created havoc in the flowering of the quick-to-bud Merlot grape. The result was that much of the 1984 Merlot crop was destroyed long before the summer weather actually arrived. The terrible late spring and early summer conditions made headlines in much of the world's press, which began to paint the vintage as an impending disaster. However, July was dry and hot, and by the end of August, some overly enthusiastic producers were talking about the potential for superripe, tiny quantities of Cabernet Sauvignon. There were even several reporters who were calling 1984 similar to the 1961 vintage. Their intentions could only be considered sinister as 1984 could never be justly compared to 1961.

Following the relatively decent beginning in September, the period between September 21 and October 4 was one of unexpected weather difficulties climaxed by the first cyclone (named Hortense) ever to hit the area, tearing roofs off buildings and giving nervous jitters to winemakers. However, after October 4 the weather cleared up and producers began to harvest their Cabernet Sauvignon. Those who waited picked relatively ripe Cabernet in good condition, although the Cabernet's skin was somewhat thick and the acid levels extremely high, particularly by the standards of more recent vintages.

The problem that existed early on with the 1984s and that continues to present difficulties today is that the wines lack an important percentage of Merlot to counterbalance their narrow, compact, high-acid character. Consequently, there is a lack of fat and charm, but the wines are deep in color, as they are made from Cabernet Sauvignon.

Unquestionably the late pickers made the best wines and most of the top wines have emerged from the Médoc and Graves. They will be longer lived, but probably less enjoyable than the wines from the other difficult vintage of that decade, 1980.

In St.-Émilion and Pomerol, the vintage, if not quite the unqualified disaster painted by the wine press, is, nevertheless, disappointing. Many top properties—Ausone, Canon, Magdelaine, Belair, La Dominique, Couvent-des-Jacobins, and Tertre-Daugay—declassified their entire crop. It was the first vintage since 1968 or 1972 where many of these estates made no wine under their label. Even at Pétrus only 800 cases were made, as opposed to the 4,500 cases produced in both 1985 and 1986.

Eleven years after the vintage, the top 1984s remain relatively narrowly constructed, tightly knit wines still displaying a healthy color, but lacking depth, flesh, ampleness, and charm. While there is no doubt that the best examples of the 1984 vintage will keep for some time to come, don't expect them to ever blossom.

TOP WINES FOR 1984

St.-Estèphe: Cos d'Estournel
Pauillac: Latour, Lynch-Bages, Mouton-Rothschild, Pichon-Longueville–Comtesse de Lalande
St.-Julien: Gruaud-Larose, Léoville-Las Cases
Margaux: Margaux
Médoc/Haut-Médoc/Moulis/Listrac Crus Bourgeois: None
Graves Red: Domaine de Chevalier, Haut-Brion, La Mission-Haut-Brion
Graves White: None

Pomerol: Pétrus, Trotanoy
St.-Émilion: Figeac
Barsac/Sauternes: Yquem

1983—A Quick Study (9-26-83)

St.-Estèphe**	Graves Red****
Pauillac***	Graves White****
St.-Julien***	Pomerol***
Margaux*****	St.-Émilion****
Médoc/Haut-Médoc Crus Bourgeois**	Barsac/Sauternes****

Size: A large crop, with overall production slightly inferior to 1982, but in the Médoc, most properties produced more wine than they did in 1982.

Important Information: Bordeaux, as well as all of France, suffered from an atypically tropical heat and humidity attack during the month of August. This caused considerable overripening, as well as the advent of rot in certain *terroirs*, particularly in St.-Estèphe, Pauillac, Pomerol, and the sandier plateau sections of St.-Émilion.

Maturity Status: At first the vintage was called more classic (or typical) than 1982, with greater aging potential. Twelve years later, the 1983s are far more evolved and closer to maturity than the 1982s. In fact, this is a vintage that is approaching full maturity at an accelerated pace.

Price: Prices for the top 1983s remain reasonable because virtually everyone who admires great claret bought heavily in 1982. The only exceptions are the 1983 Margauxs, which are irrefutably superior to their 1982 counterparts.

The year 1983 was one of the most bizarre growing seasons in recent years. The flowering in June went well for the third straight year, ensuring a large crop. The weather in July was so torrid that it turned out to be the hottest July on record. August was extremely hot, rainy, and humid, and as a result, many vineyards began to have significant problems with mildew and rot. It was essential to spray almost weekly in August of 1983 to protect the vineyards. Those properties that did not spray diligently had serious problems with mildew-infected grapes. By the end of August, a dreadful month climatically, many pessimistic producers were apprehensively talking about a disastrous vintage like 1968 or 1965. September brought dry weather, plenty of heat, and no excessive rain. October provided exceptional weather as well, so the grapes harvested late were able to attain maximum ripeness under sunny, dry skies. Not since 1961 had the entire Bordeaux crop, white grapes and red grapes, been harvested in completely dry, fair weather.

The successes that have emerged from 1983 are first and foremost from the appellation of Margaux, which enjoyed its greatest vintage of the decade. In fact, this perennial under-achieving appellation produced many top wines, with magnificent efforts from Margaux, Palmer, and Rausan-Ségla (the vintage of resurrection for this famous name), as well as d'Issan and Brane-Cantenac. These wines remain some of the best-kept secrets of the decade.

The other appellations had numerous difficulties, and the wines have not matured as evenly or as gracefully as some prognosticators had suggested. The northern Médoc, particularly the St.-Estèphes, are disappointing. The Pauillacs range from relatively light, overly oaky, roasted wines that are hollow in the middle, to some exceptional successes, most notably from Pichon-Longueville–Comtesse de Lalande, Mouton-Rothschild, and Lafite-Rothschild.

The St.-Juliens will not be remembered for their greatness, with the exception of a superb Léoville-Poyferré. In 1983 Léoville-Poyferré is amazingly as good as the other two Léovilles, Léoville-Las Cases and Léoville-Barton. During the eighties, there is not another vintage where such a statement could be made. The Cordier siblings, Gruaud-Larose and Talbot, made good wines, but overall, 1983 is not a memorable year for St.-Julien.

In Graves, the irregularity continues, with wonderful wines from those Graves châteaux in the Pessac-Léognan area (Haut-Brion, La Mission-Haut-Brion, Haut-Bailly, Domaine de Chevalier, and de Fieuzal), but with disappointments elsewhere in the appellation.

On the right bank, in Pomerol and St.-Émilion, inconsistency is again the rule of thumb. Most of the hillside vineyards in St.-Émilion performed well, but the vintage was mixed on the plateau and in the sandier soils, although Cheval Blanc made one of its greatest wines of the decade. In Pomerol, it is hard to say who made the best wine, but the house of Jean-Pierre Moueix did not fare well in this vintage. Other top properties, such as La Conseillante, L'Évangile, Lafleur, Certan de May, and Le Pin, all made wines that are not far off the quality of their great 1982s.

Even the top wines continue to mature at an accelerated pace and are far more developed from both an aromatic and palate perspective than their 1982 peers.

TOP WINES FOR 1983

St.-Estèphe: None
Pauillac: Lafite-Rothschild, Mouton-Rothschild, Pichon-Longueville–Comtesse de Lalande
St.-Julien: Gruaud-Larose, Léoville-Las Cases, Léoville-Poyferré, Talbot
Margaux: d'Angludet, Brane-Cantenac, Cantemerle (southern Médoc), d'Issan, Margaux, Palmer, Prieuré-Lichine, Rausan-Ségla
Médoc/Haut-Médoc/Moulis/Listrac Crus Bourgeois: None
Graves Red: Domaine de Chevalier, Haut-Bailly, Haut-Brion, La Louvière, La Mission-Haut-Brion
Graves White: Domaine de Chevalier, Laville-Haut-Brion
Pomerol: Certan de May, L'Évangile, Lafleur, Pétrus, Le Pin
St.-Émilion: L'Arrosée, Ausone, Belair, Canon, Cheval Blanc, Figeac, Larmande
Barsac/Sauternes: Climens, Doisy-Daëne, de Fargues, Guiraud, Lafaurie-Peyraguey, Raymond-Lafon, Rieussec, Yquem

1982—A Quick Study (9-13-82)

St.-Estèphe *****	Graves Red ***
Pauillac *****	Graves White **
St.-Julien *****	Pomerol *****
Margaux ***	St.-Émilion *****
Médoc/Haut-Médoc Crus Bourgeois ****	Barsac/Sauternes ***

Size: An extremely abundant crop, which at the time was a record year, but has since been equaled in size by 1988, and surpassed in volume by 1985, 1986, 1989, and 1990.

Important Information: The most concentrated and potentially complex and profound wines since 1961 were produced in virtually every appellation except for Graves and Margaux.

Maturity Status: Most Crus Bourgeois should have been drunk by 1990 and the lesser wines in St.-Émilion, Pomerol, Graves, and Margaux are close to full maturity. For the bigger-styled Pomerols, St.-Émilions, and the northern Médocs—St.-Julien, Pauillac, and St.-Estèphe—the wines are evolving at a glacial pace. They have lost much of their baby fat and have gone into a much more tightly knit, massive yet much more structured, tannic state.

Price: No modern-day Bordeaux vintage since 1961 has accelerated as much in price and yet continues to appreciate in value. Prices are now so frightfully high consumers who did not purchase these wines as futures can only look back with envy at those who bought the 1982s when they were first offered as futures at what now appear to be bargain-basement prices. Who can remember a great vintage being sold at opening prices of: Pichon-Lalande

($110), Léoville-Las Cases ($160), Ducru-Beaucaillou ($150), Pétrus ($600), Cheval Blanc ($550), Margaux ($550), Certan de May ($180), La Lagune ($75), Grand-Puy-Lacoste ($85), Cos d'Estournel ($145), and Canon ($105)? These were the average prices for which the 1982s were sold during the spring, summer, and fall of 1983!

France's most respected wine publication, *Revue du Vin de France*, and Europe's most skilled and authoritative wine commentator, Michel Bettane, were the first to announce that the 1982 vintage was one of exceptional richness, ripeness, and concentration. Bettane called 1982 the greatest Bordeaux vintage since 1929.

When I issued my report on the 1982 vintage in the April 1983 *Wine Advocate*, I remember feeling that I had never tasted richer, more concentrated, more promising wines than the 1982s. Twelve years later, despite some wonderfully successful years such as 1985, 1986, 1989, and 1990, 1982 remains the modern-day point of reference for the greatness Bordeaux can achieve.

The finest wines of the vintage have emerged from the northern Médoc appellations of St.-Julien, Pauillac, and St.-Estèphe, as well as Pomerol and St.-Émilion. They have hardly changed since their early days in barrel, and while displaying a degree of richness, opulence, and intensity I have rarely seen, as they approach their thirteenth birthdays, most remain relatively unevolved and backward wines.

The wines from other appellations have matured much more quickly, particularly those from Graves and Margaux, and the lighter, lesser wines from Pomerol, St.-Émilion, and the Crus Bourgeois.

Today, no one could intelligently deny the greatness of the 1982 vintage. However, in 1983 this vintage was received among America's wine press with a great deal of skepticism. There was no shortage of outcries about these wines' lack of acidity and "California" style after the vintage's conception. It was suggested by some writers that 1981 and 1979 were "finer vintages," and that the 1982s, "fully mature," should have been "consumed by 1990." Curiously, these writers fail to include specific tasting notes. Of course, wine tasting is subjective, but such statements are nonsense, and it is impossible to justify such criticism of this vintage, particularly in view of how well the top 1982s taste in 1995, and how richly as well as slowly the first-growths, superseconds, and big wines of the northern Médoc, Pomerol, and St.-Émilion are evolving. Even in Bordeaux the 1982s are now placed on a pedestal and spoken of in the same terms as 1961, 1949, 1945, and 1929. Moreover, the marketplace and auction rooms, perhaps the only true measure of a vintage's value, continue to push prices for the top 1982s to stratospheric levels. Pierre Coste, one of Bordeaux's most astute tasters and writers, and someone who also feels 1982 is the greatest Bordeaux vintage since 1929, contends that the consistent criticism of the 1982s by certain Americans has nothing to do with the vintage's quality. Could it be that these writers, having failed to inform their readers of the vintage's greatness, could only protect their standing by criticizing it and/or trying to instill doubt about the merits of having purchased it? *In vino veritas* becomes *in vino politique.*

The reason why so many 1982s were so remarkable was that the weather conditions were outstanding. The flowering occurred in hot, sunny, dry, ideal June weather that served to ensure a large crop. July was extremely hot and August slightly cooler than normal. By the beginning of September the Bordeaux producers were expecting a large crop of excellent quality. However, a September burst of intense heat that lasted for nearly 3 weeks sent the grape sugars soaring, and what was considered originally to be a very good to excellent vintage was transformed into a great vintage for every appellation except Margaux and Graves, whose very thin, light, gravelly soils suffered during the torrid September heat. For the first time many producers had to vinify their wines under unusually hot conditions. Many lessons were learned that were employed again in subsequent hot vinification years such as 1985, 1989, and 1990. Rumors of disasters from overheated or stuck fermentations proved to be without validity, as were reports that rain showers near the end of the harvest caught some properties with Cabernet Sauvignon still on the vine.

When analyzed, the 1982s are the most concentrated, high-extract wines since 1961, with acid levels that while low, are no lower than in years of exceptional ripeness such as 1949, 1953, 1959, 1961, and, surprisingly, 1975. Though some skeptics pointed to the low acidity, many of those same skeptics fell in love with the 1985s, 1989s, and 1990s, all Bordeaux vintages that produced wines with significantly lower acids and higher pH's than the 1982s. Tannin levels were extremely high, but subsequent vintages, particularly 1986, 1988, 1989, and 1990, produced wines with even higher tannin levels than the 1982s.

Recent tastings of the 1982s continue to suggest that the top wines of the northern Médoc need another 10–15 years of cellaring. Most of the best wines seem largely unevolved since their early days in cask. They have fully recovered from the bottling and display the extraordinary expansive, rich, glycerin- and extract-laden palates that should serve these wines well over the next 15–20 years. If the 1982 vintage remains sensational for the majority of St.-Émilions, Pomerols, St.-Juliens, Pauillacs, and St.-Estèphes, the weakness of the vintage becomes increasingly more apparent with the Margaux and Graves wines. Only Château Margaux seems to have survived the problems of overproduction, loosely knit, flabby Cabernet Sauvignon wines, from which so many other Margaux properties suffered. The same can be said for the Graves, which are light and disjointed when compared to the lovely 1983s Graves produced. Only La Mission-Haut-Brion and Haut-Brion produced better 1982s than 1983s.

On the negative side are the prices one must now pay for a top wine from the 1982 vintage. Is this a reason why the vintage still receives cheap shots from a handful of American writers? Those who bought them as futures made the wine buys of the century. But those who did not and still want to drink the wines of this vintage are faced with the prospect of paying prices that are often higher than what one would pay for a fine 1970 claret. That may make no sense, but for today's generation of wine enthusiasts 1982 is what 1945, 1947, and 1949 were for an earlier generation of wine lovers.

Lastly, the sweet wines of Barsac and Sauternes in 1982, while maligned originally for their lack of botrytis and richness, are not that bad. In fact, Yquem and the Cuvée Madame of Château Suduiraut are two remarkably powerful, rich wines that can stand up to the best of the 1983s, 1986s, and 1988s.

TOP WINES FOR 1982

St.-Estèphe: Calon-Ségur, Cos d'Estournel, Haut-Marbuzet, Montrose

Pauillac: Les Forts de Latour, Grand-Puy-Lacoste, Haut-Batailley, Lafite-Rothschild, Latour, Lynch-Bages, Mouton-Rothschild, Pichon-Longueville Baron, Pichon-Longeville–Comtesse de Lalande

St.-Julien: Beychevelle, Branaire-Ducru, Ducru-Beaucaillou, Gruaud-Larose, Léoville-Barton, Léoville-Las Cases, Léoville-Poyferré, Talbot

Margaux: Margaux, La Lagune (southern Médoc)

Médoc/Haut-Médoc/Moulis/Listrac Crus Bourgeois: Maucaillou, Potensac, Poujeaux, Sociando-Mallet, Tour Haut-Caussan, La Tour St.-Bonnet

Graves Red: Haut-Brion, La Mission-Haut-Brion, La Tour-Haut-Brion

Graves White: None

Pomerol: Bon Pasteur, Certan de May, La Conseillante, L'Enclos, L'Évangile, Le Gay, Lafleur, Latour à Pomerol, Petit-Village, Pétrus, Le Pin, Trotanoy, Vieux Château Certan

St.-Émilion: L'Arrosée, Ausone, Canon, Cheval Blanc, La Dominique, Figeac, Pavie

Barsac/Sauternes: Raymond-Lafon, Suduiraut-Cuvée Madame, Yquem

1981—A Quick Study (9-28-81)

St.-Estèphe **	Graves Red **
Pauillac ***	Graves White **
St.-Julien ***	Pomerol ***
Margaux **	St.-Émilion **
Médoc/Haut-Médoc Crus Bourgeois *	Barsac/Sauternes *

Size: The moderately large crop that in retrospect now looks modest.

Important Information: The first vintage in a succession of hot, dry years that would continue nearly uninterrupted through 1990. The year 1981 would have been a top vintage had the rain not fallen immediately prior to the harvest.

Maturity Status: Most 1981s are close to full maturity, yet the best examples are capable of lasting for at least another decade.

Price: A largely ignored and overlooked vintage, 1981 remains underpriced and a reasonably good value.

This vintage has been labeled more "classic" than either 1983 or 1982. What classic means to those who call 1981 a classic vintage is that this year is a typically good Bordeaux vintage of medium-weight, well-balanced, graceful wines. Despite a dozen or so excellent wines, 1981 is in reality only a good vintage, surpassed in quality by both 1982 and 1983, and also by 1978 and 1979.

The year 1981 could have been an outstanding vintage had it not been for the heavy rains that fell just as the harvest was about to start. There was a dilution of the intensity of flavor in the grapes as heavy rains drenched the vineyards between October 1 and 5, and again between October 9 and 15. Until then, the summer had been perfect. The flowering occurred under excellent conditions; July was cool, but August and September hot and dry. One can only speculate, that had it not rained, 1981 might well have also turned out to be one of the greatest vintages in the post–World War II era.

The year 1981 did produce a large crop of generally well-colored wines of medium weight and moderate tannin. The dry white wines have turned out well, but should have been consumed by now. Both Barsac and Sauternes suffered as a result of the rains and no truly compelling wines have emerged from these appellations.

There are a number of successful wines in 1981, particularly from such appellations as Pomerol, St.-Julien, and Pauillac. Fourteen years after the vintage, the 1981s have generally reached their plateau of maturity, and only the best will keep for another 10–15 years. The wines' shortcomings are their lack of the richness, flesh, and intensity that more recent vintages have possessed. Most red wine producers had to *chaptalise* significantly because the Cabernets were harvested under 11% natural alcohol, and the Merlot under 12%, no doubt because of the rain.

TOP WINES FOR 1981

St.-Estèphe: None

Pauillac: Lafite-Rothschild, Latour, Pichon-Longueville–Comtesse de Lalande

St.-Julien: Ducru-Beaucaillou, Gruaud-Larose, Léoville-Las Cases, St.-Pierre

Margaux: Giscours, Margaux

Médoc/Haut-Médoc/Moulis/Listrac Crus Bourgeois: None

Graves Red: La Mission-Haut-Brion

Graves White: None

Pomerol: Certan de May, La Conseillante, Pétrus, Le Pin, Vieux Château Certan

St.-Émilion: Cheval Blanc

Barsac/Sauternes: Climens, de Fargues, Yquem

1980—A Quick Study (10-14-80)

St.-Estèphe*	Graves Red**
Pauillac**	Graves White*
St.-Julien**	Pomerol**
Margaux**	St.-Émilion*
Médoc/Haut-Médoc Crus Bourgeois*	Barsac/Sauternes****

Size: A moderately sized crop was harvested.

Important Information: Nothing very noteworthy can be said about this mediocre vintage.

Maturity Status: With the exception of Château Margaux and Pétrus, virtually every 1980 should be consumed over the next several years.

Price: Low.

For a decade that became known as the golden age of Bordeaux, or the decade of the century, the eighties certainly did not begin in an auspicious fashion. The summer of 1980 was cool and wet, the flowering was unexciting because of a disappointing June, and by early September the producers were looking at a return of the two most dreadful vintages of the last 30 years, 1963 and 1968. However, modern-day antirot sprays did a great deal to protect the grapes from the dreaded *pourriture.* For that reason, the growers were able to delay their harvest until the weather began to improve at the end of September. The weather in early October was favorable until rains began in the middle of the month, just as many producers began to harvest. The results have been light, diluted, frequently disappointing wines that have an unmistakable vegetal and herbaceous taste and are often marred by excessive acidity as well as tannin. Those producers who made a strict selection and who picked exceptionally late, such as the Mentzelopoulos family at Château Margaux (the wine of the vintage), made softer, rounder, more interesting wines that began to drink well in the late eighties and should continue to drink well until the turn of the century. However, the number of properties that could be said to have made wines of good quality are few.

As always in wet, cool years, those vineyards planted on lighter, gravelly, well-drained soils, such as some of the Margaux and Graves properties, tend to get better maturity and ripeness. Not surprisingly, the top successes generally come from these areas, although several Pauillacs, because of a very strict selection, also have turned out well.

As disappointing as the 1980 vintage was for the red wine producers, it was an excellent year for the producers of Barsac and Sauternes. The ripening and harvesting continued into late November, generally under ideal conditions. This permitted some rich, intense, high-class Barsac and Sauternes to be produced. Unfortunately, their commercial viability suffered from the reputation of the red wine vintage. Anyone who comes across a bottle of 1980 Climens, Yquem, or Raymond-Lafon will immediately realize that this is an astonishingly good year.

TOP WINES FOR 1980

St.-Estèphe: None
Pauillac: Latour, Pichon-Longueville–Comtesse de Lalande
St.-Julien: Talbot
Margaux: Margaux
Médoc/Haut-Médoc/Moulis/Listrac Crus Bourgeois: None
Graves Red: Domaine de Chevalier, La Mission-Haut-Brion
Graves White: None
Pomerol: Certan de May, Pétrus
St.-Émilion: Cheval Blanc
Barsac/Sauternes: Climens, de Fargues, Raymond-Lafon, Yquem

1979—A Quick Study (10-3-79)

St.-Estèphe **   Graves Red ****
Pauillac ***   Graves White **
St.-Julien ***   Pomerol ***
Margaux ****   St.-Émilion **
Médoc/Haut-Médoc Crus Bourgeois **   Barsac/Sauternes *

Size: A huge crop that established a record at that time.

Important Information: In the last 2 decades this is one of the only cool years that turned out to be a reasonably good vintage.

Maturity Status: Contrary to earlier reports, the 1979s have matured very slowly, largely because the wines have relatively hard tannins and good acidity, two characteristics that most of the top vintages during the decade of the eighties have not possessed.

Price: Because of the lack of demand, and the vintage's average-to-good reputation, prices remain low except for a handful of the limited production, glamour wines of Pomerol.

The year 1979 has become the forgotten vintage in Bordeaux. A record-setting crop that produced relatively healthy, medium-bodied wines that displayed firm tannins and good acidity closed out the decade of the seventies. Over the next decade this vintage was rarely mentioned in the wine press. No doubt most of the wines were consumed long before they reached their respective apogees. Considered inferior to 1978 when conceived, the 1979 vintage will prove superior—at least in terms of aging potential. Yet aging potential alone is hardly sufficient to evaluate a vintage, and many 1979s remain relatively skinny, malnourished, lean, compact wines that naïve commentators have called classic rather than thin.

Despite the inconsistency from appellation to appellation, a number of strikingly good, surprisingly flavorful, rich wines have emerged from appellations such as Margaux, Graves, and Pomerol.

With few exceptions, there is no hurry to drink the top 1979s since their relatively high acid levels (compared to more recent hot year vintages) and good tannin levels, as well as sturdy framework, should ensure that the top 1979s age well for at least another 10–15 years.

This was not a good vintage for the dry white wines or sweet white wines of Barsac and Sauternes. The dry whites did not achieve full maturity and there was never enough botrytis for the Barsac and Sauternes to give the wines that honeyed complexity that is fundamental to their success.

Prices for 1979s, where they can still be found, are the lowest of any good recent Bordeaux vintage, reflecting the general lack of excitement for most 1979s.

TOP WINES FOR 1979

St.-Estèphe: Cos d'Estournel
Pauillac: Lafite-Rothschild, Latour, Pichon-Longueville–Comtesse de Lalande
St.-Julien: Gruaud-Larose, Léoville-Las Cases
Margaux: Giscours, Margaux, Palmer, du Tertre
Médoc/Haut-Médoc/Moulis/Listrac Crus Bourgeois: None
Graves Red: Les Carmes Haut-Brion, Domaine de Chevalier, Haut-Bailly, Haut-Brion,
    La Mission-Haut-Brion
Graves White: None
Pomerol: Certan de May, L'Enclos, L'Évangile, Lafleur, Pétrus
St.-Émilion: Ausone
Barsac/Sauternes: None

1978—A Quick Study (10-7-78)

St.-Estèphe **   Graves Red *****
Pauillac ***   Graves White ****
St.-Julien ****   Pomerol **
Margaux ****   St.-Émilion ***
Médoc/Haut-Médoc Crus Bourgeois **   Barsac/Sauternes **

Size: A moderately sized crop was harvested.

Important Information: The year Harry Waugh, England's gentlemanly wine commentator, dubbed, "the miracle year."

Maturity Status: Most wines are fully mature.

Price: High.

The year 1978 turned out to be an outstanding vintage for the red wines of Graves and a good vintage for the red wines from the Médoc, Pomerol, and St.-Émilion. There was a lack of botrytis for the sweet white wines of Barsac and Sauternes and the results were monolithic, straightforward wines of no great character. The dry white Graves, much like the red wines of that appellation, turned out exceedingly well.

The weather profile for 1978 was hardly encouraging. The spring was cold and wet, and poor weather continued to plague the region through June, July, and early August, causing many growers to begin thinking of such dreadful years as 1963, 1965, 1968, and 1977. However, in mid-August a huge anticyclone, high-pressure system settled over southwestern France and northern Spain and for the next nine weeks the weather was sunny, hot, and dry, except for an occasional light rain shower that had negligible effects.

Because the grapes were so behind in their maturation (contrast that scenario with the more recent advanced maturity years such as 1989 and 1990), the harvest began extremely late on October 7. It continued under excellent weather conditions, which seemed, as Harry Waugh put it, miraculous, in view of the miserable weather throughout much of the spring and summer.

The general view of this vintage is that it is a very good to excellent year. The two best appellations are Graves and Margaux, which have the lighter, better-drained soils that support cooler weather years. In fact, Graves (except for the disappointing Pape-Clément) probably enjoyed its greatest vintage after 1961. The wines, which at first appeared intensely fruity, deeply colored, moderately tannic, and medium bodied, have aged much faster than the higher acid, more firmly tannic 1979s, which were the product of an even cooler, drier year. Most 1978s had reached full maturity twelve years after the vintage and some commentators were expressing their disappointment that the wines were not better than they had believed.

The problem is that, much like in 1979, 1981, and 1988, there is a shortage of truly superstar wines. There are a number of very good wines, but the lack of excitement in the majority of wines has tempered the postvintage enthusiasm. Moreover, the lesser wines in 1978 have an annoyingly vegetal, herbaceous taste because those vineyards not planted on the best soils never fully ripened despite the impressively hot, dry, *"fin de saison."* Another important consideration is that the selection process, so much a fundamental principle in the decade of the eighties, was employed less during the seventies as many properties simply bottled everything under the grand vin label. In talking with proprietors today, many feel that 1978 could have lived up to its early promise had a stricter selection been in effect when the wines were made.

This was a very difficult vintage for properties in the Barsac/Sauternes region because very little botrytis formed due to the hot, dry autumn. The wines, much like the 1979s, are chunky, full of glycerin and sugar, but lack grip, focus, and complexity.

TOP WINES FOR 1978

St.-Estèphe: None

Pauillac: Les Forts de Latour, Grand-Puy-Lacoste, Latour, Pichon-Longueville–Comtesse de Lalande

St.-Julien: Ducru-Beaucaillou, Gruaud-Larose, Léoville-Las Cases, Talbot

Margaux: Giscours, La Lagune (southern Médoc), Margaux, Palmer, Prieuré-Lichine, du Tertre

Médoc/Haut-Médoc/Moulis/Listrac Crus Bourgeois: None

Graves Red: Les Carmes Haut-Brion, Domaine de Chevalier, Haut-Bailly, Haut-Brion, La Mission-Haut-Brion, La Tour-Haut-Brion

Graves White: Domaine de Chevalier, Haut-Brion, Laville-Haut-Brion

Pomerol: Lafleur

St.-Émilion: L'Arrosée, Cheval Blanc

Barsac/Sauternes: None

1977—A Quick Study (10-3-77)

St.-Estèphe*	Graves Red*
Pauillac*	Graves White*
St.-Julien*	Pomerol 0
Margaux*	St.-Émilion 0
Médoc/Haut-Médoc Crus Bourgeois*	Barsac/Sauternes*

Size: A small crop was produced.

Important Information: A dreadful vintage, clearly the worst of the decade; it remains, in a pejorative sense, unequaled since.

Maturity Status: The wines, even the handful that were drinkable, should have been consumed by the mid-eighties.

Price: Despite distress sale prices, there are no values to be found.

This is the worst vintage for Bordeaux during the decade of the seventies. Even the two mediocre years of the eighties, 1980 and 1984, are far superior to 1977. Much of the Merlot crop was devastated by a late spring frost. The summer was cold and wet. When warm, dry weather finally arrived just prior to the harvest, there was just too little time left to save the vintage. The harvest resulted in grapes that were both analytically and physiologically immature and far from ripe.

The wines, which were relatively acidic and overtly herbaceous to the point of being vegetal, should have been consumed years ago. Some of the more successful wines included a decent Figeac, Giscours, Gruaud-Larose, Pichon Lalande, Latour, and the three Graves estates of Haut-Brion, La Mission-Haut-Brion, and Domaine de Chevalier. However, I have never been able to recommend any of these wines. They have no value from either a monetary or pleasure standpoint.

1976—A Quick Study (9-13-76)

St.-Estèphe***	Graves Red*
Pauillac***	Graves White***
St.-Julien***	Pomerol***
Margaux**	St.-Émilion***
Médoc/Haut-Médoc Crus Bourgeois*	Barsac/Sauternes****

Size: A huge crop, the second largest of the decade, was harvested.

Important Information: This hot, droughtlike vintage could have proved to be the vintage of the decade had it not been for preharvest rains.

Maturity Status: The 1976s tasted fully mature and delicious when released in 1979. Yet the best examples continue to offer delightful, sometimes even sumptuous drinking. It is one of a handful of vintages where the wines have never closed up and been unappealing.
Price: The 1976s have always been reasonably priced because they have never received accolades from the wine pundits.

A very highly publicized vintage, 1976 has never quite lived up to its reputation. All the ingredients were present for a superb vintage. The harvest date of September 13 was the earliest harvest since 1945. The weather during the summer had been torridly hot, with the average temperatures for the months of June through September exceeded only by the hot summers of 1949 and 1947. However, with many vignerons predicting a "vintage of the century," very heavy rains fell between September 11 and 15, bloating the grapes.

The crop that was harvested was large, the grapes were ripe, and while the wines had good tannin levels, the acidity levels were low and their pH's dangerously high. The top wines of 1976 have offered wonderfully soft, supple, deliciously fruity drinking since they were released in 1979. I had fully expected that these wines would have to be consumed before the end of the decade of the eighties. However, the top 1976s appear to have stayed at their peak of maturity without fading or losing their fruit. I wish I had bought more of this vintage given how delicious the best wines have been over such an extended period of time. They will not make "old bones," and one must be very careful with the weaker 1976s, which have lacked intensity and depth from the beginning. These wines were extremely fragile and have increasingly taken on a brown cast to their color as well as losing their fruit. Nevertheless, the top wines continue to offer delicious drinking and persuasive evidence that even in a relatively diluted, extremely soft-styled vintage, with dangerously low acid levels, Bordeaux wines, where well stored, can easily last 15 or more years.

The 1976 vintage was at its strongest in the northern Médoc appellations of St.-Julien, Pauillac, and St.-Estèphe, weakest in Graves and Margaux, and mixed in the Libournais appellations of Pomerol and St.-Émilion.

For those who admire decadently rich, honeyed, sweet wines, this is one of the two best vintages of the seventies, given the abundant quantities of botrytis that formed in the vineyards and the lavish richness and opulent style of the wines of Barsac/Sauternes.

TOP WINES FOR 1976

St.-Estèphe: Cos d'Estournel, Montrose
Pauillac: Haut-Bages-Libéral, Lafite-Rothschild, Pichon-Longueville–Comtesse
  de Lalande
St.-Julien: Beychevelle, Branaire-Ducru, Ducru-Beaucaillou, Léoville-Las Cases, Talbot
Margaux: Giscours, La Lagune (southern Médoc)
Médoc/Haut-Médoc/Moulis/Listrac Crus Bourgeois: Sociando-Mallet
Graves Red: Haut-Brion
Graves White: Domaine de Chevalier, Laville-Haut-Brion
Pomerol: Pétrus
St.-Émilion: Ausone, Cheval Blanc, Figeac
Barsac/Sauternes: Climens, Coutet, de Fargues, Guiraud, Rieussec, Suduiraut, Yquem

1975—A Quick Study (9-22-75)

St.-Estèphe **	Graves Red **
Pauillac ****	Graves White ***
St.-Julien ****	Pomerol *****

Margaux **   St.-Émilion ***
Médoc/Haut-Médoc Crus Bourgeois ***   Barsac/Sauternes ****

Size: After the abundant vintages of 1973 and 1974, 1975 was a moderately sized crop.

Important Information: After three consecutive poor-to-mediocre years, the Bordelais were ready to praise to the heavens the 1975 vintage.

Maturity Status: The slowest-evolving vintage in the last thirty years.

Price: Trade and consumer uneasiness concerning the falling reputation of this vintage, as well as the style of even the top wines that remain hard, closed, and nearly impenetrable, makes this an attractively priced year for those with patience.

Is this the year of the great deception, or the year where some irrefutably classic wines were produced? Along with 1964 and 1983, this is perhaps the most tricky vintage with which to come to grips. There are some undeniably great wines in the 1975 vintage, but the overall quality level is distressingly uneven, and the number of failures is too numerous to ignore.

Because of the three previous large crops and the international financial crisis brought on by high oil prices, the producers, knowing that their 1972, 1973, and 1974 vintages were already backed up in the marketplace, pruned their vineyards to guard against a large crop. The weather cooperated; July, August, and September were all hot months. However, in August and September several large thunderstorms dumped enormous quantities of rain on the area. It was localized, and most of it did little damage except to frazzle the nerves of winemakers. However, several hailstorms did ravage the central Médoc communes, particularly Moulis, Lamarque, and Arcins, and some isolated hailstorms damaged the southern Léognan-Pessac region.

The harvest began during the third week of September and continued under generally good weather conditions through mid-October. Immediately after the harvest, the producers were talking of a top-notch vintage, perhaps the best since 1961. So what happened?

Looking back after having had numerous opportunities to taste and discuss the style of this vintage with many proprietors and winemakers, it is apparent that the majority of growers should have harvested their Cabernet Sauvignon later. Many feel it was picked too soon, and the fact that at that time many were not totally destemming only served to exacerbate the relatively hard, astringent tannins in the 1975s.

This is one of the first vintages I tasted (although on a much more limited basis) from cask, visiting Bordeaux as a tourist rather than a professional. In 1975, many of the young wines exhibited great color, intensely ripe, fragrant noses, and immense potential. Other wines appeared to have an excess of tannin. The wines immediately closed up 2–3 years after bottling, and in most cases still remain stubbornly hard and backward. There are a number of badly made, excessively tannic wines where the fruit has already dried out and the color has become brown. Many of them were aged in old oak barrels (new oak was not nearly as prevalent as it is now), and the sanitary conditions in many cellars were less than ideal. However, even allowing for these variations, I have always been struck by the tremendous difference in the quality of wines in this vintage. To this day the wide swings in quality remain far greater than in any other recent year. For example, how could La Mission-Haut-Brion, Pétrus, L'Évangile, and Lafleur produce such profoundly great wines yet many of their neighbors fail completely? This remains one of the vintage's mysteries.

This is a vintage for true Bordeaux connoisseurs who have the patience to wait the wines out. The top examples, which usually come from Pomerol, St.-Julien, and Pauillac (the extraordinary success of La Mission-Haut-Brion and La Tour-Haut-Brion, and to a lesser extent, Haut-Brion, is an exception to the sad level of quality in Graves), are wines that have still not reached their apogees. Could the great 1975s turn out to resemble wines from a vintage such as 1928 that took 30-plus years to reach full maturity? The great successes of this vintage are capable of lasting and lasting because they have the richness and concentration of ripe fruit to balance out their tannins. However, there are many wines that are too dry, too astringent, or too tannic to develop gracefully.

I purchased this vintage as futures, and I remember thinking I secured great deals on the first-growths at $350 a case. But I have invested in nearly 20 years of patience, and the wait for the top wines will be at least another 10 years. Waiting 25–30 years for a wine to mature can painfully push one's discipline to the limit. This is the vintage for delayed gratification.

TOP WINES FOR 1975

St.-Estèphe: Haut-Marbuzet, Meyney, Montrose

Pauillac: Lafite-Rothschild, Latour, Mouton-Rothschild, Pichon-Longueville–Comtesse de Lalande

St.-Julien: Branaire-Ducru, Gloria, Gruaud-Larose, Léoville-Barton, Léoville-Las Cases

Margaux: Giscours, Palmer

Médoc/Haut-Médoc/Moulis/Listrac Crus Bourgeois: Greysac, Sociando-Mallet, La Tour St.-Bonnet

Graves Red: Haut-Brion, La Mission-Haut-Brion, Pape-Clément, La Tour-Haut-Brion

Graves White: Domaine de Chevalier, Haut-Brion, Laville-Haut-Brion

Pomerol: L'Enclos, L'Évangile, La Fleur Pétrus, Le Gay, Lafleur, Nenin, Pétrus, Trotanoy, Vieux Château Certan

St.-Émilion: Cheval Blanc, Figeac, Magdelaine, Soutard

Barsac/Sauternes: Climens, Coutet, de Fargues, Raymond-Lafon, Rieussec, Yquem

1974—A Quick Study (9-20-74)

St.-Estèphe*	Graves Red**
Pauillac*	Graves White*
St.-Julien*	Pomerol**
Margaux*	St.-Émilion*
Médoc/Haut-Médoc Crus Bourgeois*	Barsac/Sauternes*

Size: An enormous crop was harvested.

Important Information: Should you still have stocks of the 1974s, it is best to consume them over the next several years, or donate them to charity.

Maturity Status: A handful of the top wines of the vintage are still alive and well, but aging them any further will prove fruitless.

Price: These wines were always inexpensive and I can never imagine them fetching a decent price unless you find someone in need of this year to celebrate a birthday.

As a result of a good flowering and a dry, sunny May and June, the crop size was large in 1974. The weather from mid-August through October was cold, windy, and rainy. Despite the persistent soggy conditions, the appellation of choice in 1974 turned out to be Graves. While most 1974s remain hard, tannic, hollow wines lacking ripeness, flesh, and character, a number of the Graves estates did produce surprisingly spicy, interesting wines. Though somewhat compact and attenuated, they are still enjoyable to drink 21 years after the vintage. The two stars are La Mission-Haut-Brion and Domaine de Chevalier, followed by Latour in Pauillac and Trotanoy in Pomerol. Should you have remaining stocks of these wines in your cellar, it would be foolish to push your luck. In spite of their well-preserved status, my instincts suggest drinking them soon.

The vintage was equally bad in the Barsac/Sauternes region. I have never seen a bottle to taste.

It is debatable as to which was the worst vintage during the decade of the seventies— 1972, 1974, or 1977.

1973—A Quick Study (9-20-73)

St.-Estèphe**	Graves Red*
Pauillac*	Graves White**
St.-Julien**	Pomerol**
Margaux*	St.-Émilion*
Médoc/Haut-Médoc Crus Bourgeois*	Barsac/Sauternes*

Size: Enormous; one of the largest crops of the seventies.

Important Information: A sadly rain-bloated, swollen crop of grapes in poor-to-mediocre condition was harvested.

Maturity Status: The odds are stacked against finding a 1973 that is still in good condition, at least from a regular-size bottle.

Price: Distress sale prices, even for those born in this year.

In the mid-seventies, the best 1973s had some value as agreeably light, round, soft, somewhat diluted yet pleasant Bordeaux wines. With the exception of Domaine de Chevalier, Pétrus, and the great sweet classic, Yquem, all of the 1973s have faded into oblivion.

So often the Bordelais are on the verge of a top-notch vintage when the rains arrive. The rains that came during the harvest bloated what would have been a healthy, enormous grape crop. Modern-day sprays and techniques such as *saigner* were inadequately utilized in the early seventies, and the result in 1973 was a group of wines that lacked color, extract, acidity, and backbone. The wines were totally drinkable when released in 1976. By the beginning of the eighties, they were in complete decline, save Pétrus.

TOP WINES FOR 1973[†]

St.-Estèphe: de Pez
Pauillac: Latour
St.-Julien: Ducru-Beaucaillou
Margaux: None
Médoc/Haut-Médoc/Moulis/Listrac Crus Bourgeois: None
Graves Red: Domaine de Chevalier, La Tour-Haut-Brion
Graves White: None
Pomerol: Pétrus
St.-Émilion: None
Barsac/Sauternes: Yquem

1972—A Quick Study (10-7-72)

St.-Estèphe 0	Graves Red*
Pauillac 0	Graves White 0
St.-Julien 0	Pomerol 0
Margaux*	St.-Émilion*
Médoc/Haut-Médoc Crus Bourgeois 0	Barsac/Sauternes 0

Size: A moderately sized crop was harvested.

Important Information: The worst vintage of the decade.

Maturity Status: Most wines have long been over the hill.

Price: Extremely low.

The weather pattern of 1972 was one of unusually cool, cloudy summer months with an abnormally rainy month of August. While September brought dry, warm weather, it was too late to save the crop. The 1972 wines turned out to be the worst of the decade—acidic,

† This list is for informational purposes only as I suspect all of the above wines, with the possible exception of Pétrus, are in serious decline unless found in larger-format bottlings that have been perfectly stored.

green, raw, and vegetal tasting. The high acidity did manage to keep many of them alive for 10–15 years, but their deficiencies in fruit, charm, and flavor concentration were far too great for even age to overcome.

As in any poor vintage, some châteaux managed to produce decent wines, with the well-drained soils of Margaux and Graves turning out slightly better wines than elsewhere.

There are no longer any wines from 1972 that would be of any interest to consumers.

TOP WINES FOR 1972†

St.-Estèphe: None
Pauillac: Latour
St.-Julien: Branaire-Ducru, Léoville-Las Cases
Margaux: Giscours, Rausan-Ségla
Médoc/Haut-Médoc/Moulis/Listrac Crus Bourgeois: None
Graves Red: La Mission-Haut-Brion, La Tour-Haut-Brion
Graves White: None
Pomerol: Trotanoy
St.-Émilion: Cheval Blanc, Figeac
Barsac/Sauternes: Climens

1971—A Quick Study (9-25-71)

St.-Estèphe**	Graves Red***
Pauillac***	Graves White**
St.-Julien***	Pomerol****
Margaux***	St.-Émilion***
Médoc/Haut-Médoc Crus Bourgeois**	Barsac/Sauternes****

Size: Small to moderate crop size.

Important Information: A good to very good, stylish vintage with the strongest efforts emerging from Pomerol and the sweet wines of Barsac/Sauternes.

Maturity Status: Every 1971 has been fully mature for nearly a decade, with the best cuvées capable of lasting another decade.

Price: The small crop size kept prices high, but most 1971s, compared to other good vintages of the last 35 years, are slightly undervalued.

Unlike 1970, 1971 was a small vintage because of a poor flowering in June that caused a significant reduction in the Merlot crop. By the end of the harvest, the crop size was a good 40% less than the huge crop of 1970.

Early reports of the vintage have proven to be overly enthusiastic. Some experts (particularly Bordeaux's Peter Sichel), relying on the small production yields when compared to 1970, even claimed that the vintage was better than 1970. This has proved to be totally false. Certainly the 1971s were forward and delicious, as were the 1970s when first released, but unlike the 1970s, the 1971s lacked the great depth of color, concentration, and tannic backbone. The vintage was mixed in the Médoc, but it was a fine year for Pomerol, St.-Émilion, and Graves.

Buying 1971s now could prove dangerous unless the wines have been exceptionally well stored. Twenty-four years after the vintage there are a handful of wines that have just reached full maturity—Pétrus, Latour, Trotanoy, La Mission-Haut-Brion. Well-stored examples of these wines will continue to drink well for at least another 10–15 years. Elsewhere, storage is everything. This could be a vintage at which to take a serious look provided one can find reasonably priced, well-preserved bottles.

† This list is for informational purposes only as I suspect all of the above wines are in serious decline unless found in larger-format bottlings that have been perfectly stored.

The sweet wines of Barsac and Sauternes were successful and are in full maturity. The best of them have at least 1–2 decades of aging potential and will certainly outlive all of the red wines produced in 1971.

TOP WINES FOR 1971

St.-Estèphe: Montrose
Pauillac: Latour, Mouton-Rothschild
St.-Julien: Beychevelle, Gloria, Gruaud-Larose, Talbot
Margaux: Palmer
Médoc/Haut-Médoc/Moulis Listrac Crus Bourgeois: None
Graves Red: Haut-Brion, La Mission-Haut-Brion, La Tour-Haut-Brion
Graves White: None
Pomerol: Petit-Village, Pétrus, Trotanoy
St.-Émilion: Cheval Blanc, La Dominique
Barsac/Sauternes: Climens, Coutet, de Fargues, Yquem

1970—A Quick Study (9-27-70)

St.-Estèphe ****	Graves Red ****
Pauillac ****	Graves White ***
St.-Julien ****	Pomerol ****
Margaux ***	St.-Émilion ***
Médoc/Haut-Médoc Crus Bourgeois ***	Barsac/Sauternes ***

Size: An enormous crop that was a record setter at the time.

Important Information: The first modern-day abundant crop that combined high quality with large quantity.

Maturity Status: Initially, the 1970s were called precocious and early maturing. Most of the big 1970s have aged very slowly and are now in full maturity, with only a handful of exceptions. The smaller wines, Crus Bourgeois, and lighter-weight Pomerols and St.-Émilions should have been drunk by 1980.

Price: Expensive, no doubt because this is the most popular vintage between 1961 and 1982.

Between the two great vintages 1961 and 1982, 1970 has proved to be the best year, producing wines that were attractively rich, and full of charm and complexity. They have aged more gracefully than many of the austere 1966s and seem fuller, richer, more evenly balanced and consistent than the hard, tannic, large-framed but often hollow and tough 1975s. The year 1970 proved to be the first modern-day vintage that combined high production with impeccable quality. Moreover, it was a splendidly uniform and consistent vintage throughout Bordeaux, with every appellation able to claim its share of top-quality wines.

The weather conditions during the summer and early fall were perfect. There was no hail, no weeks of drenching downpours, no frost, and no spirit-crushing inundation at harvest time. It was one of those rare vintages where everything went well and the Bordelais harvested one of the largest and healthiest crops they had ever seen.

The year 1970 was the first vintage that I tasted out of cask, visiting a number of châteaux with my wife as tourists on my way to the cheap beaches of Spain and north Africa during summer vacations in 1971 and 1972. Even from their early days I remember the wines exhibiting great color, an intense richness of fruit, fragrant, ripe perfume, full body, and plenty of tannin. However, it seems inevitable that when wines taste good young, certain writers falsely assume they will not last. Terry Robards, then the wine reporter for *The New York Times*, even went so far as to call the wines the product of a "nouvelle" vinification, claiming many of them would not last until 1980. It is an irony that almost all of Bordeaux's greatest vintages—1900, 1929, 1947, 1949, 1953, 1961, and most recently, 1982, and perhaps 1989—have all been produced from superripe grapes where the wines tasted extremely good when young, causing a certain degree of controversy with respect to their perceived aging potential. Keeping in mind that even lightweight Bordeaux vintages such as 1976 can last up to 15 or more years when well stored, it is not surprising that most top 1970s, 25 years after the vintage, are just reaching their plateau of maturity. Certain wines, for example, Latour, Pétrus, Gruaud-Larose, Mouton-Rothschild, and Montrose, are still not close to maturity.

Perhaps the most phenomenal characteristic of the 1970s is the overall balance and consistency of the wines. I long ago consumed all my Cru Bourgeois and smaller-scaled wines, as it was the first vintage where buying from lesser appellations paid off handsomely.

As for the sweet wines, they have had to take a back seat to the 1971s because there was less botrytis. Although the wines are impressively big and full, they lack the complexity, delicacy, and finesse of the best 1971s.

In conclusion, 1970 will no doubt continue to sell at high prices for decades to come, because this is the most consistently excellent, and in some cases outstanding, vintage between 1961 and 1982.

TOP WINES FOR 1970

St.-Estèphe: Cos d'Estournel, Haut-Marbuzet, Lafon-Rochet, Montrose, Les-Ormes-de-Pez, de Pez
Pauillac: Grand-Puy-Lacoste, Haut-Batailley, Latour, Lynch-Bages, Mouton-Rothschild, Pichon-Longueville–Comtesse de Lalande
St.-Julien: Ducru-Beaucaillou, Gloria, Gruaud-Larose, Léoville-Barton, St.-Pierre
Margaux: Giscours, Lascombes, Palmer
Médoc/Haut-Médoc/Moulis/Listrac Crus Bourgeois: Sociando-Mallet
Graves Red: Domaine de Chevalier, de Fieuzal, Haut-Bailly, La Mission-Haut-Brion, La Tour-Haut-Brion
Graves White: Domaine de Chevalier, Laville-Haut-Brion
Pomerol: La Conseillante, La Fleur Pétrus, Lafleur, Latour à Pomerol, Pétrus, Trotanoy
St.-Émilion: L'Arrosée, Cheval Blanc, La Dominique, Figeac, Magdelaine
Barsac/Sauternes: Yquem

1969—A Quick Study (10-6-69)

St.-Estèphe 0	Graves Red*
Pauillac 0	Graves White 0
St.-Julien 0	Pomerol*
Margaux 0	St.-Émilion 0
Médoc/Haut-Médoc Crus Bourgeois 0	Barsac/Sauternes*

Size: Small.

Important Information: My candidate for the most undesirable wines produced in Bordeaux in the last 30 years.

Maturity Status: I never tasted a 1969, except for Pétrus, that could have been said to have had any richness or fruit. I have not seen any of these wines except for Pétrus for a number of years, but they must be unpalatable.

Price: Amazingly, the vintage was offered at a relatively high price, but almost all the wines except for a handful of the big names are totally worthless.

Whenever Bordeaux has suffered through a disastrous vintage (like that of 1968) there has always been a tendency to lavish false praise on the following year. No doubt Bordeaux, after their horrible experience in 1968, badly wanted a fine vintage in 1969, but despite some overly optimistic proclamations by some leading Bordeaux experts at the time of the vintage, 1969 has turned out to be one of the least attractive vintages for Bordeaux wines in the last two decades.

The crop was small, and while the summer was sufficiently hot and dry to ensure a decent maturity, torrential September rains dashed everyone's hopes for a good vintage, except some investors who irrationally moved in to buy these insipid, nasty, acidic, sharp wines. Consequently, the 1969s, along with being extremely unattractive wines, were quite expensive when they first appeared on the market.

I can honestly say I have never tasted a red wine in 1969 I did not dislike. The only exception would be a relatively decent bottle of Pétrus (rated in the upper seventies) that I had twenty years after the vintage. Most wines are harsh and hollow, with no flesh, fruit, or charm, and it is hard to imagine that any of these wines are today any more palatable than they were during the seventies.

In the Barsac and Sauternes region, a few proprietors managed to produce acceptable wines, particularly d'Arche.

1968—A Quick Study (9-20-68)

St.-Estèphe 0	Graves Red*
Pauillac 0	Graves White 0
St.-Julien 0	Pomerol 0
Margaux 0	St.-Émilion 0
Médoc/Haut-Médoc Crus Bourgeois 0	Barsac/Sauternes 0

Size: A small, disastrous crop in terms of both quality and quantity.

Important Information: A great year for California Cabernet Sauvignon, but not for Bordeaux.

Maturity Status: All of these wines must be passé.

Price: Another worthless vintage.

The year 1968 was another of the very poor vintages the Bordelais had to suffer through in the sixties. The culprit, as usual, was heavy rain (it was the wettest year since 1951) that bloated the grapes. However, there have been some 1968s that I found much better than anything produced in 1969, a vintage with a "better" (I am not sure that is the right word to use) reputation.

At one time wines such as Figeac, Gruaud-Larose, Cantemerle, La Mission-Haut-Brion, Haut-Brion, and Latour were palatable. Should anyone run across these wines today, the rule of caveat emptor would seemingly be applicable, as I doubt that any of them would have much left to enjoy.

1967—A Quick Study (9-25-67)

St.-Estèphe**	Graves Red***
Pauillac**	Graves White**
St.-Julien**	Pomerol***
Margaux**	St.-Émilion***
Médoc/Haut-Médoc Crus Bourgeois*	Barsac/Sauternes****

Size: An abundant crop was harvested.

Important Information: A Graves, Pomerol, St.-Émilion year that favored the early-harvested Merlot.

Maturity Status: Most 1967s were drinkable when released in 1970 and should have been consumed by 1980. The top wines, where well stored, will keep for another few years but are unlikely to improve.

Price: Moderate.

The year 1967 was a large, useful vintage in the sense that it produced an abundant quantity of round, quick-maturing wines. Most should have been drunk before 1980, but a handful of wines continue to display remarkable staying power and are still in the full bloom of their maturity. This is a vintage that clearly favored Pomerol, and to a lesser extent Graves. Holding on to these wines any longer seems foolish, but I have no doubt that some of the biggest wines, such as Latour, Pétrus, Trotanoy, and perhaps even Palmer, will last until the turn of the century. Should one find any of the top wines listed below in a large-format bottle (magnums, double magnums, etc.) at a reasonable price, my advice would be to take the gamble.

As unexciting as most red wines turned out in 1967, the sweet wines of Barsac and Sauternes were rich and honeyed, with gobs of botrytis present. However, readers must remember that only a handful of estates were truly up to the challenge of making great wines during this very depressed period for the wine production of Barsac/Sauternes.

TOP WINES FOR 1967

St.-Estèphe: Calon-Ségur, Montrose
Pauillac: Latour
St.-Julien: None
Margaux: Giscours, La Lagune (southern Médoc), Palmer
Médoc/Haut-Médoc/Moulis/Listrac Crus Bourgeois: None
Graves Red: Haut-Brion, La Mission-Haut-Brion
Graves White: None
Pomerol: Pétrus, Trotanoy, La Violette
St.-Émilion: Cheval Blanc, Magdelaine, Pavie
Barsac/Sauternes: Suduiraut, Yquem

1966—A Quick Study (9-26-66)

St.-Estèphe ***	Graves Red ****
Pauillac ***	Graves White ***
St.-Julien ***	Pomerol ***
Margaux ***	St.-Émilion **
Médoc/Haut-Médoc Crus Bourgeois **	Barsac/Sauternes **

Size: An abundant crop was harvested.
Important Information: The most overrated "top" vintage of the last 30 years.
Maturity Status: The best wines are in their prime, but most wines are losing their fruit before their tannins.
Price: Expensive and overpriced.

While the majority opinion is that 1966 is the best vintage of the decade after 1961, I would certainly argue that for Graves, Pomerol, and St.-Émilion, 1964 is clearly the second-best vintage of the decade. And I am beginning to think that even 1962, that grossly underrated vintage, is, on overall merit, a better year than 1966. Conceived in somewhat the same spirit as 1975 (overhyped after several unexciting years, particularly in the Médoc), 1966 never developed as well as many of its proponents would have liked. The wines, now 29 years of age, for the most part have remained austere, lean, unyielding, tannic wines that are losing their fruit before their tannin melts away. Some notable exceptions do exist. Who could deny the exceptional wine made at Latour (the wine of the vintage) or the great Palmer?

All the disappointments that emerged from this vintage were unexpected in view of the early reports that the wines were relatively precocious, charming, and early maturing. If the vintage is not as consistent as first believed, there are an adequate number of medium-weight, classically styled wines. However, they are all overpriced as this vintage has always been fashionable and it has had no shortage of supporters, particularly from the English wine-writing community.

The sweet wines of Barsac and Sauternes are also mediocre. Favorable conditions for the development of the noble rot, *Botrytis cinerea,* never occurred.

The climatic conditions that shaped this vintage started with a slow flowering in June, intermittently hot and cold weather in July and August, and a dry and sunny September. The crop size was large, and the vintage was harvested under sound weather conditions.

I would be skeptical about buying most 1966s except for one of the unqualified successes of the vintage.

TOP WINES FOR 1966

St.-Estèphe: None

Pauillac: Grand-Puy-Lacoste, Latour, Mouton-Rothschild, Pichon-Longueville–Comtesse de Lalande

St.-Julien: Branaire-Ducru, Ducru-Beaucaillou, Gruaud-Larose, Léoville-Las Cases

Margaux: Lascombes, Palmer

Médoc/Haut-Médoc/Moulis/Listrac Crus Bourgeois: None

Graves Red: Haut-Brion, La Mission-Haut-Brion, Pape-Clément

Graves White: Domaine de Chevalier, Haut-Brion, Laville-Haut-Brion

Pomerol: Lafleur, Trotanoy

St.-Émilion: Canon

Barsac/Sauternes: None

1965—A Quick Study (10-2-65)

St.-Estèphe 0	Graves Red 0
Pauillac 0	Graves White 0
St.-Julien 0	Pomerol 0
Margaux 0	St.-Émilion 0
Médoc/Haut-Médoc Crus Bourgeois 0	Barsac/Sauternes 0

Size: A tiny vintage.

Important Information: The quintessential vintage of rot and rain.

Maturity Status: The wines tasted terrible from the start and must be totally reprehensible today.

Price: Worthless.

The vintage of rot and rain. I have had little experience tasting the 1965s. It is considered by most experts to be one of the worst vintages in the post–World War II era. A wet summer was bad enough, but the undoing of this vintage was an incredibly wet and humid September that caused rot to voraciously devour the vineyards. Antirot sprays had not yet been developed. It should be obvious that these wines are to be avoided.

1964—A Quick Study (9-22-64)

St.-Estèphe ***	Graves Red *****
Pauillac *	Graves White ***
St.-Julien *	Pomerol *****
Margaux **	St.-Émilion ****
Médoc/Haut-Médoc Crus Bourgeois *	Barsac/Sauternes *

Size: A large crop was harvested.

Important Information: The classic examples of a vintage where the early-picked Merlot and Cabernet Franc produced great wine, and the late-harvested Cabernet Sauvignon, particularly in the Médoc, was inundated. The results included numerous big name failures in the Médoc.

Maturity Status: The Médocs are past their prime, but the larger-scaled wines of Graves, Pomerol, and St.-Émilion can last for another 10 years.

Price: Smart Bordeaux enthusiasts have always recognized the greatness of this vintage in Graves, Pomerol, and St.-Émilion, and consequently prices have remained high. Nevertheless, compared to such glamour years as 1959 and 1961, the top right-bank and Graves 1964s are not only underrated, but in some cases underpriced as well.

One of the most intriguing vintages of Bordeaux, 1964 produced a number of splendid, generally underrated and underpriced wines in Pomerol, St.-Émilion, and Graves where many proprietors had the good fortune to have harvested their crops before the rainy deluge began on October 8. Because of this downpour, which caught many Médoc châteaux with unharvested vineyards, 1964 has never been regarded as a top Bordeaux vintage. While the vintage can be notoriously bad for some of the properties of the Médoc and the late-harvesting Barsac and Sauternes estates, it is excellent to outstanding for the three appellations of Pomerol, St.-Émilion, and Graves.

The summer had been so hot and dry that the French minister of agriculture announced at the beginning of September that the "vintage of the century was about to commence." Since the Merlot grape ripens first, the harvest began in the areas where it is planted in abundance. St.-Émilion and Pomerol harvested at the end of September and finished their picking before the inundation began on October 8. Most of the Graves properties had also finished harvesting. When the rains came, most of the Médoc estates had just begun to harvest their Cabernet Sauvignon and were unable to successfully complete the harvest because of torrential rainfall. It was a Médoc vintage noted for some extraordinary and famous failures. Pity the buyer who purchased Lafite-Rothschild, Mouton-Rothschild, Lynch-Bages, Calon-Ségur, or Margaux! Yet not everyone made disappointing wine. Montrose in St.-Estèphe and Latour in Pauillac made the two greatest wines of the Médoc.

Because of the very damaging reports about the rainfall, many wine enthusiasts approached the 1964 vintage with a great deal of apprehension.

The top wines from Graves, St.-Émilion, and Pomerol are exceptionally rich, full-bodied, opulent, and concentrated wines with high alcohol, an opaque color, super length, and unbridled power. Amazingly, they are far richer, more interesting and complete wines than the 1966s, and in many cases, compete with the finest wines of the 1961 vintage. Because of low acidity, all of the wines reached full maturity by the mid-eighties. The best examples exhibit no sign of decline and can easily last for another 10–15 or more years.

TOP WINES FOR 1964

St.-Estèphe: Montrose
Pauillac: Latour
St.-Julien: Gruaud-Larose
Margaux: None
Médoc/Haut-Médoc/Moulis/Listrac Crus Bourgeois: None
Graves Red: Domaine de Chevalier, Haut-Bailly, Haut-Brion, La Mission-Haut-Brion
Graves White: None
Pomerol: La Conseillante, La Fleur Pétrus, Lafleur, Pétrus, Trotanoy, Vieux Château
   Certan

St.-Émilion: L'Arrosée, Cheval Blanc, Figeac, Soutard
Barsac/Sauternes: None

1963—A Quick Study (10-7-63)

St.-Estèphe 0	Graves Red 0
Pauillac 0	Graves White 0
St.-Julien 0	Pomerol 0
Margaux 0	St.-Émilion 0
Médoc/Haut-Médoc Crus Bourgeois 0	Barsac/Sauternes 0

Size: A small to moderate-sized crop was harvested.

Important Information: A dreadfully poor year that rivals 1965 for the feebleness of its wines.

Maturity Status: The wines must now be awful.

Price: Worthless.

The Bordelais have never been able to decide whether 1963 or 1965 was the worst vintage of the sixties. Rain and rot, as in 1965, were the ruination of this vintage. I have not seen a bottle of 1963 for over 20 years.

1962—A Quick Study (10-1-62)

St.-Estèphe ****	Graves Red ***
Pauillac ****	Graves White ****
St.-Julien ****	Pomerol ***
Margaux ***	St.-Émilion ***
Médoc/Haut-Médoc Crus Bourgeois ***	Barsac/Sauternes ****

Size: An abundant crop size, in fact, one of the largest of the decade of the sixties.

Important Information: A terribly underrated vintage that had the misfortune of following one of the greatest vintages of the century.

Maturity Status: The Bordeaux old-timers claim the 1962s drank beautifully by the late sixties, and continued to fill out and display considerable character, fruit, and charm in the seventies. At the midpoint of this decade, the top 1962s are still lovely, rich, round wines full of finesse and elegance.

Price: Undervalued, particularly when one considers the prices of its predecessor, 1961, and the overpriced 1966s.

Coming after the great vintage of 1961, it was not totally unexpected that 1962 would be underestimated. This vintage appears to be the most undervalued year for Bordeaux in the post–World War II era. Elegant, supple, very fruity, round, and charming wines that were neither too tannic nor too massive were produced in virtually every appellation. Because of their precociousness, many assumed the wines would not last, but they have kept longer than anyone would have ever imagined. Most 1962s do require consumption, but they continue to surprise me, and well-preserved examples of the vintage can easily be kept through the turn of the century.

The weather was acceptable but not stunning. There was a good flowering because of a sunny, dry May, a relatively hot summer with some impressive thunderstorms, and a good, as the French say, *fin de saison,* with a hot, sunny September. The harvest was not rain-free, but the inundations that could have created serious problems never occurred.

Not only was the vintage very successful in most appellations, but it was a top year for the dry white wines of Graves as well as the sweet nectars from Barsac/Sauternes.

TOP WINES FOR 1962

St.-Estèphe: Cos d'Estournel, Montrose
Pauillac: Batailley, Lafite-Rothschild, Latour, Lynch-Bages, Mouton-Rothschild,
    Pichon-Longueville–Comtesse de Lalande
St.-Julien: Ducru-Beaucaillou, Gruaud-Larose
Margaux: Margaux, Palmer
Médoc/Haut-Médoc/Moulis/Listrac Crus Bourgeois: None
Graves Red: Haut-Brion, Pape-Clément
Graves White: Domaine de Chevalier, Laville-Haut-Brion
Pomerol: Lafleur, Pétrus, Trotanoy, La Violette
St.-Émilion: Magdelaine
Barsac/Sauternes: Yquem

1961—A Quick Study (9-22-61)

St.-Estèphe *****	Graves Red *****
Pauillac *****	Graves White ***
St.-Julien *****	Pomerol *****
Margaux *****	St.-Émilion ***
Médoc/Haut-Médoc Crus Bourgeois ***	Barsac/Sauternes **

Size: An exceptionally tiny crop was produced: In fact, this is the last vintage where a minuscule crop resulted in high quality.

Important Information: One of the legendary vintages of the century.

Maturity Status: The wines, drinkable young, have, with only a handful of exceptions, reached maturity and are all at their apogee in 1995. Most of the best examples will keep for at least another 10–15 years.

Price: The tiny quantities plus exceptional quality have made the 1961s the most dearly priced, mature vintage of great Bordeaux in the marketplace. Moreover, prices will only increase, given the microscopic quantities that remain—an auctioneer's dream vintage, but the prices of the 1990s and 1982s are quickly catching up.

The year 1961 is one of nine great vintages produced in the post–World War II era. The others—1945, 1947, 1949, 1953, 1959, 1982, 1989, and 1990—all have their proponents, but none is as revered as 1961. The wines have always been prized for their sensational concentration and magnificent penetrating bouquets of superripe fruit and rich, deep, sumptuous flavors. Delicious when young, these wines, which have all reached full maturity except for a handful of the most intensely concentrated examples, are marvelous to drink. However, I see no problem in holding the best-stored bottles for at least another 10 years.

The weather pattern was nearly perfect in 1961, with spring frosts reducing the crop size and then sunny, hot weather throughout the summer and the harvest, resulting in splendid maturity levels. The small harvest guaranteed high prices for these wines, and today's prices for 1961s make them the equivalent of liquid gold.

The vintage was excellent throughout all appellations of Bordeaux except for the Barsac/Sauternes. This region benefited greatly from the vintage's reputation, but a tasting of the 1961 sweet wines will reveal that even Yquem is mediocre. The incredibly dry weather conditions resulted in very little botrytis, and the results are large-scaled but essentially monolithic sweet wines that have never merited the interest they have enjoyed. The only other appellation that did not appear to be up to the overall level of quality was St.-Émilion, where many vineyards had still not fully recovered from the killer freeze of 1956.

In tasting the 1961s, the only two vintages that are somewhat similar in richness and style are 1959 and 1982. The 1959s tend to be lower in acidity, but have actually aged more slowly than the 1961s, whereas the 1982s would appear to have the same physical profile of the 1961s, but less tannin.

TOP WINES FOR 1961

St.-Estèphe: Cos d'Estournel, Haut-Marbuzet, Montrose

Pauillac: Latour, Lynch-Bages, Mouton-Rothschild, Pichon-Longueville–Comtesse de Lalande, Pontet-Canet

St.-Julien: Beychevelle, Ducru-Beaucaillou, Gruaud-Larose, Léoville-Barton

Margaux: Malescot St.-Exupéry, Margaux, Palmer

Médoc/Haut-Médoc/Moulis/Listrac Crus Bourgeois: None

Graves Red: Haut-Bailly, Haut-Brion, La Mission-Haut-Brion, Pape-Clément, La Tour-Haut-Brion

Graves White: Domaine de Chevalier, Laville-Haut-Brion

Pomerol: L'Évangile, Latour à Pomerol, Pétrus, Trotanoy

St.-Émilion: L'Arrosée, Canon, Cheval Blanc, Figeac, Magdelaine

Barsac/Sauternes: None

1960—A Quick Study (9-9-60)

St.-Estèphe**	Graves Red**
Pauillac**	Graves White*
St.-Julien**	Pomerol*
Margaux*	St.-Émilion*
Médoc/Haut-Médoc Crus Bourgeois 0	Barsac/Sauternes*

Size: A copious crop was harvested.

Important Information: The two rainy months of August and September were this vintage's undoing.

Maturity Status: Most 1960s should have been consumed within their first 10–15 years of life.

Price: Low.

I remember drinking several delicious magnums of 1960 Latour, as well as having found good examples of 1960 Montrose, La Mission-Haut-Brion, and Gruaud-Larose in Bordeaux. However, the last 1960 I consumed, a magnum of Latour, was drunk over 20 years ago. I would guess that even that wine, which was the most concentrated wine of the vintage according to the Bordeaux cognoscenti, is now in decline.

1959—A Quick Study (9-20-59)

St.-Estèphe*****	Graves Red*****
Pauillac*****	Graves White****
St.-Julien****	Pomerol***
Margaux****	St.-Émilion**
Médoc/Haut-Médoc Crus Bourgeois***	Barsac/Sauternes*****

Size: Average.

Important Information: The first of the modern-day years to be designated "vintage of the century."

Maturity Status: The wines, maligned in their early years for having low acidity and lacking backbone (reminiscent of the 1982s), have aged more slowly than the more highly touted 1961s. In fact, comparisons between the top wines of the two vintages often reveal the 1959s to be less evolved, with deeper color, and more richness and aging potential.

Price: Never inexpensive, the 1959s have become increasingly more expensive as serious connoisseurs have begun to realize that this vintage not only rivals 1961, but in specific cases, surpasses it.

This is an irrefutably great vintage that inexplicably was criticized at its inception, no doubt because of all the hype and praise it received from its conception. The wines, which are especially strong in the northern Médoc and Graves, and less so on the right bank (Pomerol and St.-Émilion were still recovering from the devastating deep freeze of 1956), are among the most massive and richest wines ever made in Bordeaux. In fact, the two modern-day vintages that are frequently compared to 1959 are the 1982 and 1990. Those comparisons may have merit.

The 1959s have evolved at a glacial pace, and are often in better condition (especially the first-growths Lafite-Rothschild and Mouton-Rothschild) than their 1961 counterparts, which are even more highly touted. The wines do display the effects of having been made in a classic, hot, dry year, with just enough rain to keep the vineyards from being stressed. They are full bodied, extremely alcoholic and opulent, with high degrees of tannin and extract. Their colors have remained impressively opaque and dark, and display less brown and orange than the 1961s. If there is one nagging doubt about many of the 1959s, it is whether they will ever develop the sensational perfume and fragrance that is so much a part of the greatest Bordeaux vintages. Perhaps the great heat during the summer of 1959 did compromise this aspect of the wines, but it is still too soon to know.

TOP WINES FOR 1959

St.-Estèphe: Cos d'Estournel, Montrose, Les-Ormes-de-Pez
Pauillac: Lafite-Rothschild, Latour, Lynch-Bages, Mouton-Rothschild,
    Pichon-Longueville–Comtesse de Lalande, Pichon-Longueville Baron
St.-Julien: Ducru-Beaucaillou, Langoa-Barton, Léoville-Barton, Léoville-Las Cases
Margaux: Lascombes, Malescot St.-Exupéry, Margaux, Palmer
Médoc/Haut-Médoc/Moulis/Listrac Crus Bourgeois: None
Graves Red: Haut-Brion, La Mission-Haut-Brion, Pape-Clément, La Tour-Haut-Brion
Graves White: Laville-Haut-Brion
Pomerol: La Conseillante, L'Évangile, Lafleur, Latour à Pomerol, Pétrus, Trotanoy, Vieux
    Château Certan
St.-Émilion: Cheval Blanc, Figeac
Barsac/Sauternes: Climens, Suduiraut, Yquem

1958—A Quick Study (10-7-58)

St.-Estèphe*	Graves Red***
Pauillac*	Graves White**
St.-Julien*	Pomerol*
Margaux*	St.-Émilion**
Médoc/Haut-Médoc Crus Bourgeois*	Barsac/Sauternes*

Size: A small crop was harvested.
Important Information: An unfairly maligned vintage.
Maturity Status: The wines are now fading badly. The best examples almost always emerge from the Graves appellation.
Price: Inexpensive.

I have less than two dozen tasting notes of 1958s, but several that do stand out are all from the Graves appellation. Haut-Brion, La Mission-Haut-Brion, and Pape-Clément all made very good wines. They probably would have provided excellent drinking if consumed during the sixties or early seventies. I most recently had the 1958 Haut-Brion in April 1991. It was still a relatively tasty, round, soft, fleshy, tobacco- and mineral-scented and -flavored wine, but one could see that it would have been much better if it had been consumed 10–15 years ago. Even richer was the 1958 La Mission-Haut-Brion, which should still be excellent if well-preserved bottles can be found.

1957—A Quick Study (10-4-57)

St.-Estèphe **	Graves Red ***
Pauillac ***	Graves White **
St.-Julien **	Pomerol *
Margaux *	St.-Émilion *
Médoc/Haut-Médoc Crus Bourgeois *	Barsac/Sauternes ***

Size: A small crop.

Important Information: A brutally cold, wet summer.

Maturity Status: Because the summer was so cool, the red wines were extremely high in acidity, which has helped them stand the test of time. Where well-kept examples of 1957 can be found, this could be a vintage to purchase, provided the price is right.

Price: The wines should be realistically and inexpensively priced given the fact that 1957 does not enjoy a good reputation.

For a vintage that has never been received very favorably, I have been surprised by how many respectable and enjoyable wines I have tasted, particularly from Pauillac and Graves. In fact, I would be pleased to serve my most finicky friends the 1957 La Mission-Haut-Brion or 1957 Haut-Brion. And I would certainly be pleased to drink the 1957 Lafite-Rothschild. I had two excellent bottles of Lafite in the early eighties, but have not seen the wine since.

It was an extremely difficult year weather-wise, with very wet periods from April through August that delayed the harvest until early October. The wines had good acidity, and in the better-drained soils there was surprising ripeness given the lack of sunshine and excessive moisture. The 1957 Bordeaux, much like their Burgundy counterparts, have held up relatively well given the high acid and green tannins these wines have always possessed.

1956—A Quick Study (10-14-56)

St.-Estèphe 0	Graves Red 0
Pauillac 0	Graves White 0
St.-Julien 0	Pomerol 0
Margaux 0	St.-Émilion 0
Médoc/Haut-Médoc Crus Bourgeois 0	Barsac/Sauternes 0

Size: Minuscule quantities of pathetically weak wine were produced.

Important Information: The coldest winter in Bordeaux since 1709 did unprecedented damage to the vineyards, particularly those in Pomerol and St.-Émilion.

Maturity Status: I have not seen a 1956 in over 20 years, and only have a total of five notes on wines from this vintage.

Price: A worthless vintage produced worthless wines.

The year 1956 stands out as the worst vintage in modern-day Bordeaux, even surpassing such unspeakably bad years as 1963, 1965, 1968, 1969, and 1972. The winter and unbelievably cold months of February and March killed many of the vines in Pomerol and St.-Émilion, and retarded the budding of those in the Médoc. The harvest was late, the crop was small, and the wines were virtually undrinkable.

1955—A Quick Study (9-21-55)

St.-Estèphe ****	Graves Red ****
Pauillac ***	Graves White ***
St.-Julien ***	Pomerol ***
Margaux ***	St.-Émilion ****
Médoc/Haut-Médoc Crus Bourgeois **	Barsac/Sauternes ****

Size: A large, healthy crop was harvested.

Important Information: For a vintage that is now almost 40 years old, this tends to be an underrated, undervalued year, although it is not comparable to 1953 or 1959. Yet the wines have generally held up and are firmer and more solidly made than the once-glorious 1953s.

Maturity Status: After a long period of sleep, the top wines appear to finally be fully mature. They exhibit no signs of decline.

Price: Undervalued, except for La Mission-Haut-Brion, the wine of the vintage, if not the decade.

For the most part, the 1955s have always come across as relatively stern, slightly tough textured, yet impressively deep, full wines with fine color, and excellent aging potential. What they lack, as a general rule, is fat, charm, and opulence.

The weather conditions were generally ideal, with hot, sunny days in June, July, and August. Although some rain fell in September, its effect was positive rather than negative.

For whatever reason, the relatively large 1955 crop has never generated the excitement that other vintages in the fifties, such as 1953 and 1959, elicited. Perhaps it was the lack of many superstar wines that kept enthusiasm muted. Among more recent years, could 1988 be a rerun of 1955?

TOP WINES FOR 1955

St.-Estèphe: Calon-Ségur, Cos d'Estournel, Montrose, Les-Ormes-de-Pez
Pauillac: Latour, Lynch-Bages, Mouton-Rothschild
St.-Julien: Léoville-Las Cases, Talbot
Margaux: Palmer
Médoc/Haut-Médoc/Moulis/Listrac Crus Bourgeois: None
Graves Red: Haut-Brion, La Mission-Haut-Brion, Pape-Clément
Graves White: None
Pomerol: L'Évangile, Lafleur, Latour à Pomerol, Pétrus, Vieux Château Certan
St.-Émilion: Cheval Blanc, La Dominique, Soutard
Barsac/Sauternes: Yquem

1954—A Quick Study (10-10-54)

St.-Estèphe 0	Graves Red *
Pauillac *	Graves White 0
St.-Julien *	Pomerol 0
Margaux 0	St.-Émilion 0
Médoc/Haut-Médoc Crus Bourgeois 0	Barsac/Sauternes 0

Size: A small crop was harvested.

Important Information: A terrible late-harvest vintage conducted under appalling weather conditions.

Maturity Status: It is hard to believe anything from this vintage would still be worth drinking.

Price: The wines have no value.

The year 1954 was a miserable vintage throughout France, but especially in Bordeaux where the producers continued to wait for full maturity after an exceptionally cool, wet August. While the weather did improve in September, the skies opened toward the end of the month and for nearly four weeks one low-pressure system after another passed through the area, dumping enormous quantities of water that served to destroy any chance for a moderately successful vintage.

It is highly unlikely any wine from this vintage could still be drinkable today.

1953—A Quick Study (9-28-53)

St.-Estèphe*****	Graves Red****
Pauillac*****	Graves White***
St.-Julien*****	Pomerol***
Margaux****	St.-Émilion***
Médoc/Haut-Médoc Crus Bourgeois***	Barsac/Sauternes***

Size: An average-sized crop was harvested.

Important Information: One of the most seductive and hedonistic Bordeaux vintages ever produced.

Maturity Status: According to Bordeaux old-timers, the wines were absolutely delicious during the fifties, even more glorious in the sixties, and sublime during the seventies. Charm, roundness, fragrance, and a velvety texture were the hallmarks of this vintage, which now must be approached with some degree of caution unless the wines have been impeccably stored and/or the wines are available in larger-format bottlings.

Price: No vintage with such appeal will ever sell at a reasonable price. Consequently, the 1953s remain luxury-priced wines.

The year 1953 must be the only Bordeaux vintage where it is impossible to find a dissenting voice about the quality of the wines. Bordeaux old-timers and some of our senior wine commentators (particularly Edmund Penning-Rowsell and Michael Broadbent) talk of 1953 with adulation. Apparently the vintage never went through an unflattering stage. The wines were delicious from cask, and even more so from bottle. For that reason, much of the vintage was consumed before its tenth birthday. Those who waited have seen the wines develop even greater character during the sixties and seventies. Many wines, especially on this side of the Atlantic, began displaying signs of age (brown color, dried-out fruit flavors) during the eighties. In Bordeaux, when a château pulls out a 1953 it is usually in mint condition, and it is one of the most beautifully sumptuous, rich, charming clarets anyone could ever desire. A more modern-day reference point for 1953 may be the very best 1985s, perhaps even some of the lighter 1982s, although my instincts tell me the 1982s are more alcoholic, richer, fuller, heavier wines.

If you have the discretionary income necessary to buy this highly prized vintage, prudence should dictate that the wines be from cold cellars, and/or in larger-format bottles.

TOP WINES FOR 1953

St.-Estèphe: Calon-Ségur, Cos d'Estournel, Montrose

Pauillac: Grand-Puy-Lacoste, Lafite-Rothschild, Lynch-Bages, Mouton-Rothschild

St.-Julien: Beychevelle, Ducru-Beaucaillou, Gruaud-Larose, Langoa-Barton, Léoville-Barton, Léoville-Las Cases, Talbot

Margaux: Cantemerle (southern Médoc), Margaux, Palmer

Médoc/Haut-Médoc/Moulis/Listrac Crus Bourgeois: None

Graves Red: Haut-Brion, La Mission-Haut-Brion

Graves White: None

Pomerol: La Conseillante

St.-Émilion: Cheval Blanc, Figeac, Magdelaine, Pavie
Barsac/Sauternes: Climens, Yquem

1952—A Quick Study (9-17-52)

St.-Estèphe **	Graves Red ***
Pauillac ***	Graves White ***
St.-Julien ***	Pomerol ****
Margaux **	St.-Émilion ***
Médoc/Haut-Médoc Crus Bourgeois **	Barsac/Sauternes **

Size: A small crop was harvested.

Important Information: The 1952 vintage was at its best in Pomerol, which largely completed its harvest prior to the rains.

Maturity Status: Most wines have always tasted hard and too astringent, and lacked fat, charm, and ripeness. The best bottles could provide surprises.

Price: Expensive, but well-chosen Pomerols may represent relative values.

An excellent spring and summer of relatively hot, dry weather with just enough rain was spoiled by stormy, unstable, cold weather before and during the harvest. Much of the Merlot and some of the Cabernet Franc in Pomerol and St.-Émilion was harvested before the weather turned foul, and consequently, the best wines tended to come from these appellations. The Graves can also be successful because of the superb drainage of the soil in that appellation, particularly in the Pessac/Léognan area. The Médocs have always tended to be relatively hard and disappointing, even the first-growths.

TOP WINES FOR 1952

St.-Estèphe: Calon-Ségur, Montrose
Pauillac: Latour, Lynch-Bages
St.-Julien: None
Margaux: Margaux, Palmer
Médoc/Haut-Médoc/Moulis/Listrac Crus Bourgeois: None
Graves Red: Haut-Brion, La Mission-Haut-Brion, Pape-Clément
Graves White: None
Pomerol: La Fleur Pétrus, Lafleur, Pétrus, Trotanoy, Vieux Château Certan
St.-Émilion: Cheval Blanc, Magdelaine
Barsac/Sauternes: None

1951—A Quick Study (10-9-51)

St.-Estèphe 0	Graves Red 0
Pauillac 0	Graves White 0
St.-Julien 0	Pomerol 0
Margaux 0	St.-Émilion 0
Médoc/Haut-Médoc Crus Bourgeois 0	Barsac/Sauternes 0

Size: A tiny crop was harvested.

Important Information: Even today, 1951 is considered one of the all-time worst vintages for dry white, dry red, and sweet wines from Bordeaux.

Maturity Status: Undrinkable young. Undrinkable old.

Price: Another worthless vintage.

Frightfully bad weather in the spring, summer, and both before and during the harvest (rain and unseasonably cold temperatures) was the complete undoing of this vintage, which has the ignominious pleasure of having one of the worst reputations of any vintage in the post–World War II era.

1950—A Quick Study (9-17-50)

St.-Estèphe**	Graves Red***
Pauillac***	Graves White***
St.-Julien***	Pomerol*****
Margaux***	St.-Émilion****
Médoc/Haut-Médoc Crus Bourgeois*	Barsac/Sauternes****

Size: An abundant crop was harvested.

Important Information: Many of the Pomerols are great, yet they have been totally ignored by the chroniclers of the Bordeaux region.

Maturity Status: Most Médocs and Graves are now in decline. The top heavyweight Pomerols can be splendid with years of life still left.

Price: The quality of the Pomerols has remained largely a secret and the wines are, consequently, undervalued.

The year 1950 is another example where the Médoc formed the general impression of the Bordeaux vintage. This relatively abundant year was the result of good flowering, a hot, dry summer, and a difficult early September complicated by large amounts of rain.

The Médocs, all of which are in decline, were soft, forward, medium-bodied wines that probably had a kinship to more recent vintages such as 1971 and 1981. The Graves were slightly better, but even they are probably passé. The two best appellations were St.-Émilion, which produced a number of rich, full, intense wines that aged quickly, and Pomerol, which had its fourth superb vintage in succession—unprecedented in the history of that area. The wines are unbelievably rich, unctuous, and concentrated, and in many cases are capable of rivaling the greatest Pomerols of such more highly renowned vintages as 1947 and 1949.

The other appellation that prospered in 1950 was Barsac/Sauternes. Fanciers of these wines still claim 1950 is one of the greatest of the post–World War II vintages for sweet wines.

TOP WINES FOR 1950

St.-Estèphe: None
Pauillac: Latour
St.-Julien: None
Margaux: Margaux
Médoc/Haut-Médoc/Moulis/Listrac Crus Bourgeois: None
Graves Red: Haut-Brion, La Mission-Haut-Brion
Graves White: None
Pomerol: L'Évangile, La Fleur Pétrus, Le Gay, Lafleur, Pétrus, Vieux Château Certan
St.-Émilion: Cheval Blanc, Figeac, Soutard
Barsac/Sauternes: Climens, Coutet, Suduiraut, Yquem

1949—A Quick Study (9-27-49)

St.-Estèphe*****	Graves Red*****
Pauillac*****	Graves White***
St.-Julien*****	Pomerol****
Margaux****	St.-Émilion****
Médoc/Haut-Médoc Crus Bourgeois***	Barsac/Sauternes*****

Size: A small crop was harvested.

Important Information: The driest and sunniest vintage since 1893, and rivaled (weather-wise not qualitatively) in more recent years only by 1990.

Maturity Status: The best wines are still in full blossom, displaying remarkable richness and concentration.

Price: Frightfully expensive.

Among the four extraordinary vintages of the late forties—1945, 1947, 1948, and 1949 —this has always been my favorite. The wines, slightly less massive and alcoholic than the 1947s, also appear to possess greater balance, harmony, and fruit than the 1945s and more complexity than the 1948s. In short, the top wines are magnificent. The year 1949 is certainly one of the most exceptional vintages of this century. Only the right-bank wines (except for Cheval Blanc) appear inferior to the quality of their 1947s. In the Médoc and Graves it is a terrific vintage, with nearly everyone making wines of astounding ripeness, richness, opulence, power, and length.

The vintage was marked by the extraordinary heat and sunny conditions that Bordeaux enjoyed throughout the summer. Those consumers who have been worried that 1989 and 1990 were too hot to make great wine only need to look at the weather statistics for 1949. It was one of the two hottest vintages (the other being 1947) since 1893, as well as the sunniest vintage since 1893. It was not a totally dry harvest, but the amount of rainfall was virtually identical to that in a year such as 1982. Some of the rain fell before the harvest, which, given the dry, parched condition of the soil, was actually beneficial.

Even the sweet wines of Barsac and Sauternes were exciting. Buying 1949s today will cost an arm and a leg as these are among the most expensive and sought-after wines of the twentieth century.

TOP WINES FOR 1949

St.-Estèphe: Calon-Ségur, Cos d'Estournel
Pauillac: Grand-Puy-Lacoste, Latour, Mouton-Rothschild
St.-Julien: Gruaud-Larose, Léoville-Barton, Talbot
Margaux: Palmer
Médoc/Haut-Médoc/Moulis/Listrac Crus Bourgeois: None
Graves Red: Haut-Brion, Latour-Haut-Brion, La Mission-Haut-Brion, Pape-Clément
Graves White: Laville-Haut-Brion
Pomerol: La Conseillante, L'Évangile, Lafleur, Pétrus, Trotanoy, Vieux Château Certan
St.-Émilion: Cheval Blanc
Barsac/Sauternes: Climens, Coutet, Yquem

1948—A Quick Study (9-22-48)

St.-Estèphe ***	Graves Red ****
Pauillac ****	Graves White ***
St.-Julien ****	Pomerol ***
Margaux ****	St.-Émilion ***
Médoc/Haut-Médoc Crus Bourgeois ***	Barsac/Sauternes **

Size: An average to below-average crop size was harvested.

Important Information: A largely ignored, but good-to-excellent vintage overshadowed by both its predecessor and successor.

Maturity Status: The hard and backward characteristics of these wines have served them well during their evolution. Most of the larger, more concentrated 1948s are still attractive wines.

Price: Undervalued given their age and quality.

When Bordeaux has three top vintages in a row it is often the case that one is totally forgotten, and that has certainly proven correct with respect to 1948. It was a very good year that had the misfortune to fall between two legendary vintages.

Because of a difficult flowering due to wet, windy, cool weather in June, the crop size was smaller than in 1947 and 1949. However, July and August were fine months weather-wise, with September exceptionally warm and dry.

Despite the high quality of the wines, they never caught on with claret enthusiasts. And who can fault the wine buyers? The 1947s were more flashy, opulent, alcoholic, and fuller bodied, and the 1949s more precocious and richer than the harder, tougher, more tannic, and unforthcoming 1948s.

In 1995, this is a vintage that in many cases has matured more gracefully than the massive 1947s. The top wines tend to still be in excellent condition. Prices remain reasonable, if only in comparison to what one has to pay for 1947 and 1949.

TOP WINES FOR 1948

St.-Estèphe: Cos d'Estournel, Montrose
Pauillac: Grand-Puy-Lacoste, Latour, Lynch-Bages, Mouton-Rothschild
St.-Julien: Langoa-Barton, Léoville-Barton (the wine of the Médoc)
Margaux: Cantemerle (southern Médoc), Margaux, Palmer
Médoc/Haut-Médoc/Moulis/Listrac Crus Bourgeois: None
Graves Red: La Mission-Haut-Brion, Pape-Clément
Graves White: None
Pomerol: Latour à Pomerol, Petit-Village, Pétrus, Vieux Château Certan
St.-Émilion: Cheval Blanc
Barsac/Sauternes: None

1947–A Quick Study (9-15-47)

St.-Estèphe ****	Graves Red ****
Pauillac ****	Graves White ***
St.-Julien ****	Pomerol *****
Margaux ***	St.-Émilion *****
Médoc/Haut-Médoc Crus Bourgeois *	Barsac/Sauternes ***

Size: An abundant crop was harvested.

Important Information: A year of extraordinary extremes in quality with some of the most portlike, concentrated wines ever produced in Bordeaux. This is also a vintage of unexpected failures (e.g., Lafite-Rothschild).

Maturity Status: Except for the most concentrated and powerful Pomerols and St.-Émilions, this is a vintage that requires immediate consumption as many wines have gone over the top and are now exhibiting excessive volatile acidity and dried-out fruit.

Price: Preposterously high given the fact that this was another "vintage of the century."

This quintessentially hot-year vintage produced many wines that are among the most enormously concentrated, portlike, intense wines I have ever tasted. Most of the real heavy-weights in this vintage have emerged from Pomerol and St.-Émilion. In the Médoc, it was a vintage of remarkable irregularity. Properties such as Calon-Ségur, Mouton-Rothschild, and Margaux made great wines, but certain top growths, such as Lafite-Rothschild and Latour, as well as superseconds such as Léoville-Barton, produced wines with excessive acidity.

The top wines are something to behold if only because of their excessively rich, sweet style that comes closest, in modern-day terms, to 1982. Yet I know of no 1982 that has the level of extract and intensity of the greatest 1947s.

The reasons for such intensity were the exceptionally hot months of July and August, which were followed (much like in 1982, 1989, and 1990) by a torridly hot, almost tropical heat wave in mid-September just as the harvest began. Those properties that were unable to control the temperatures of hot grapes had stuck fermentations, residual sugar in the wines, and in many cases, levels of volatile acidity that would horrify modern-day oenologists. Those who were able to master the tricky vinification made the richest, most opulent red wines Bordeaux has produced during the twentieth century.

TOP WINES FOR 1947

St.-Estèphe: Calon-Ségur
Pauillac: Grand-Puy-Lacoste, Mouton-Rothschild
St.-Julien: Ducru-Beaucaillou, Léoville-Las Cases
Margaux: Margaux, Palmer
Médoc/Haut-Médoc/Moulis/Listrac Crus Bourgeois: None
Graves Red: Haut-Brion, La Mission-Haut-Brion, La Tour-Haut-Brion
Graves White: Laville-Haut-Brion
Pomerol: Clinet, Clos René, La Conseillante, L'Enclos, L'Évangile, La Fleur Pétrus,
    Lafleur, Latour à Pomerol, Nenin, Pétrus, Rouget, Vieux Château Certan
St.-Émilion: Canon, Cheval Blanc, Figeac, La Gaffelière-Naudes
Barsac/Sauternes: Climens, Suduiraut

1946—A Quick Study (9-30-46)

St.-Estèphe **	Graves Red *
Pauillac **	Graves White 0
St.-Julien **	Pomerol 0
Margaux *	St.-Émilion 0
Médoc/Haut-Médoc Crus Bourgeois 0	Barsac/Sauternes 0

Size: A small crop was harvested.
Important Information: The only year in the post–World War II era where the Bordeaux vineyards were invaded by locusts.
Maturity Status: The wines must certainly be over the hill.
Price: Except for the rare bottle of Mouton-Rothschild (needed by billionaires to complete their collections), most of these wines have little value.

A fine, hot summer, particularly in July and August, was spoiled by an unusually wet, windy, cold September that delayed the harvest and caused rampant rot in the vineyards. The 1946s are rarely seen in the marketplace. I have only eleven tasting notes for the entire vintage.

I do not know of any top wines, although Edmund Penning-Rowsell claims the 1946 Latour was excellent. I have never seen a bottle.

1945—A Quick Study (9-13-45)

St.-Estèphe ****	Graves Red *****
Pauillac *****	Graves White *****
St.-Julien *****	Pomerol *****
Margaux ****	St.-Émilion *****
Médoc/Haut-Médoc Crus Bourgeois ****	Barsac/Sauternes *****

Size: A tiny crop was harvested.
Important Information: The most acclaimed vintage of the century.

Maturity Status: Certain wines from this vintage (only those that have been stored impeccably) are still not fully mature.

Price: The most expensive clarets of the century.

No vintage in the post–World War II era, not even 1989, 1982, 1961, 1959, or 1953, enjoys the reputation that the 1945 vintage does. The celebration of the end of an appallingly destructive war, combined with the fact that the weather was remarkable, produced one of the smallest, most concentrated crops of grapes ever seen. I have been fortunate to have had the first-growths on three separate occasions, and there seems to be no doubt that this is indeed a remarkable vintage that has taken almost 45 years to reach its peak. The great wines, and they are numerous, could well last for another 20–30 years, making a mockery of most of the more recent great vintages that must be consumed within 25–30 years of the vintage.

The vintage is not without critics, some of whom have said that the wines are excessively tannic and many are drying out. There are wines that match these descriptions, but if one judges a vintage on the performance of the top properties, such as the first-growths, super-seconds, and leading domaines in Pomerol and St.-Émilion, 1945 remains in a class by itself.

The reason for the tiny crop was the notoriously frigid spell during the month of May *(la gelée noire)* that was followed by a summer of exceptional heat and drought. An early harvest began on September 13, the same day that the harvest began in both 1976 and 1982.

TOP WINES FOR 1945

St.-Estèphe: Calon-Ségur, Montrose, Les-Ormes-de-Pez

Pauillac: Latour, Mouton-Rothschild, Pichon-Longueville–Comtesse de Lalande, Pontet-Canet

St.-Julien: Gruaud-Larose, Léoville-Barton, Talbot

Margaux: Margaux, Palmer

Médoc/Haut-Médoc/Moulis/Listrac Crus Bourgeois: Chasse-Spleen, Lanessan, Poujeaux

Graves Red: Haut-Brion, La Mission-Haut-Brion, La Tour-Haut-Brion

Graves White: Laville-Haut-Brion

Pomerol: La Fleur Pétrus, Gazin, Latour à Pomerol, Pétrus, Rouget, Trotanoy, Vieux Château Certan

St.-Émilion: Canon, Cheval Blanc, Figeac, La Gaffelière-Naudes, Larcis-Ducasse, Magdelaine

Barsac/Sauternes: Suduiraut, Yquem

THIS CENTURY'S GREATEST RED BORDEAUX WINES

Over the last several years I have benefited enormously from the generosity of others who have permitted me to participate in some extraordinary tastings. It has been a longtime objective to taste well-stored bottles of every so-called great Bordeaux of this century. For nearly all of the finest châteaux I have achieved this goal. Nevertheless, I remain convinced that specific wines in certain vintages from obscure and/or minuscule estates—for example, Pomerols from the 1948, 1949, and 1950 vintages—would also qualify among the century's most profound winemaking efforts. Such wines tend to emerge from areas such as Pomerol, because that appellation's wines are made in tiny quantities and the châteaux have never been classified. Moreover, for most of this century the appellation has been ignored by the British press, who found the Médoc and Graves regions more hospitable and easier to comprehend. Furthermore, the châteaux were already classified in a rigid hierarchy of quality.

The notes on the wines that follow constitute my short list of (1) the greatest wines Bordeaux has produced this century, and (2) wines that still provide compelling drinking in the mid-nineties. All of these wines have been tasted (frequently more than once) since 1992. My who's who does not include those legendary wines that, while selling for stratospheric prices at wine auctions such as Christy's or Sotheby's, are, if the truth be known, in serious decline, representing the world's most expensive undrinkables.

While finally putting this entire subject in perspective, readers should realize the importance of several things. First, for wines older than 25 years, the expression "there are no great wines, only great bottles" has some legitimacy. Second, my tasting notes have come largely from bottles that spent most of their lives in the cold, humid private cellars of northern Europe. Younger Bordeaux vintages from the decades of the seventies and eighties have usually come from my underground cellar, where temperatures hover around 55–58 degrees Fahrenheit and the humidity is a damp 78%.

There are some noteworthy vintage omissions from what are deemed to be renowned châteaux (e.g., Lafite's 1945, 1949, and 1961), as well as surprises, which, if the wines can still be found, can undoubtedly be purchased for a song. It is evident from a cursory review of the following notes that Bordeaux's first-growths frequently merit their hallowed standing. But there are extraordinary wines produced by tiny, unclassified, obscure properties as well. It is also interesting to note that such ancient vintages as 1900, 1920, 1921, 1928, and 1929 produced many extraordinary wines, but tasting many of these legends today reinforces the words of the English poet, James Bramston, "What's not destroyed by Time's devouring hand?" Save for the remarkably vibrant 1928s, the aforementioned vintages are largely of historical rather than of hedonistic significance. These wines may still sell at appallingly high prices, but only a handful (e.g., the 1929 La Mission-Haut-Brion and 1900 Château Margaux) merit buying.

Among the pre–World War II vintages, 1928 is the vintage of choice. The top wines from 1945, 1947, 1948, and 1949, and a handful of 1950 Pomerols, can be, and in fact often are, spectacular wines. The following reviews also confirm what many insiders have long thought: There were as many great wines produced in 1959 as in 1961.

As this century inevitably marches to its end, 1966 and 1970, the two vintages of reference for me during my "formulative period," increasingly suffer in comparison with the greatness of more recent years such as 1982, 1985, 1986, 1989, and 1990. The glorious decade of the eighties is well represented. And it should be, as no other decade this century produced so many great wines and superb vintages. With the lamentable news of two weeks of cold weather and rain destroying the opportunity for Bordeaux to have an exceptional year in 1994, what do readers make of the fact that this extraordinary wine region has had four consecutive vintages—1991, 1992, 1993, and 1994—adversely affected by September rains? My longtime readers should be delirious with joy, assuming they realized that the eighties were the decade of the century and purchased intelligently, because despite the greatness of 1990, it is doubtful that Bordeaux has produced any truly profound wines for the fourth straight year.

For an overview of this century's most superb vintages, readers should consider the following thumbnail sketch of the century and the characteristics of the specific vintages, reviewed in the context of each decade.

AN IMPORTANT NOTE ON PRICING

The letter code for price designation has been abandoned given the fact that these wines sell for such lavishly high prices and the limited quantities available insure that prices will only soar over years to come.

L'ANGÉLUS

1990 TASTED 8 TIMES SINCE BOTTLING, WITH CONSISTENT MID-90–POINT SCORES ($45.00–$60.00) **96**

This moderately sized 62-acre vineyard planted with 50% Cabernet Franc, 45% Merlot, and 5% Cabernet Sauvignon emerged as a legitimate superstar in the late eighties. This is attributable to the dedicated, energetic, young proprietor, Hubert de Bouard de Laforest. L'Angélus is the classic example of an overachieving estate. Amazingly, the 1989 appeared to be the best L'Angélus could achieve, but the 1990 has proven even more extraordinary.

The 1990 has a saturated purple color and a textural appearance akin to port. Even more exotic, concentrated, and voluptuous than the 1989, it exhibits terrific concentration, as well as a dazzling bouquet of coffee, mocha, herbs, black fruits, oak, and smoke. In the mouth, there is layer upon layer of extract, and perhaps slightly more tannin than the 1989. This massive wine was bottled unfiltered, a rarity in Bordeaux. A monumental effort! **A.M.: Now–2008.**

Other possible candidates: 1989, consistently rated between 91 and 94

AUSONE

1990 TASTED 3 TIMES SINCE BOTTLING, WITH CONSISTENT NOTES ($135.00–$150.00) **94+**
1983 TASTED 7 TIMES SINCE BOTTLING, WITH CONSISTENT NOTES ($75.00–$100.00) **94**
1982 TASTED 6 TIMES SINCE BOTTLING, WITH VERY INCONSISTENT NOTES ($100.00–$150.00) **95**
1976 TASTED 11 TIMES SINCE BOTTLING, WITH RATINGS IN THE LOW TO MID-90S ($75.00–$100.00) **94**
1929 TASTED ONLY ONCE ($400.00–$500.00) **96**
1900 TASTED ONLY ONCE ($300.00–$350.00) **94**

This historic property is a must-visit for any readers who make the thirty-minute trek from downtown Bordeaux to the charming walled town of St.-Émilion. Ausone enjoys an extraordinary reputation, but to my taste rarely merits all the accolades. A tiny vineyard planted with 50% Merlot and 50% Cabernet Franc, it rarely produces more than 2,000 cases from its nearly 20 acres of hillside vineyards. Perhaps the wine is just too cerebral and intellectual for my taste. While I often find Ausone intriguing aromatically, its penchant for excessively compact, austere wines lacking a midpalate is distressing. Certainly there have been some great wines with Ausone's renaissance occurring with the 1976, a wine that looks more and more like a candidate to surpass the great Lafite-Rothschild and to become the wine of the vintage. It possesses the requisite stuffing and strength to be the longest-lived wine of that year.

I predict that over the next 25 years the 1990 will develop into the best Ausone since the 1982 and 1983. It has a deep ruby color, excellent richness, an exotic, kinky, Oriental spice component, and a rich, minerallike, tightly knit, backward character, as well as admirable concentration and length. I prefer it to the impressive 1989. It should only be purchased for your children. **A.M.: 2005–2040.**

Ausone's 1983 is a powerful, rich, full-bodied wine with a higher alcohol content than normal. Medium ruby, rich, and jammy, with low acidity but great concentration as well as that glorious perfume of minerals and Asian spices, this wine should last 15–20 years, but should provide fine drinking early on—a rarity for Ausone. **A.M.: Now–2010.** Finally, there are signs that the 1982 Ausone is beginning to live up to the extraordinary potential it revealed out of cask, when many (including yours truly) felt it had the potential to become the wine of the vintage. It is still a broodingly dark-ruby-colored, tightly strung wine that with airing offers far less aromatic dimension than the more supple and showy 1983. But what does come forth reveals rich scents and intense concentration. Tannic, larger scaled, and more massive than most Ausones, the monolithic dumbness this wine had revealed since it was bottled is finally a thing of the past. Patience here will still be a valuable commodity as it could prove to be one of the all-time great Ausones, but it will not be ready to drink for at least 10–15 more years.

The finest Ausone of the seventies, and along with Lafite-Rothschild of Pauillac, one of the two outstandingly great wines of this vintage, the 1976 Ausone is indeed a profound wine. Surprisingly dark colored for the vintage, with a voluptuous, intense, complex bouquet of minerals, licorice, truffles, and ripe, spicy black currant fruit, this full-bodied, powerful, large-scaled Ausone has remarkable size given the vintage. Amazingly, it is a bigger wine than more recent Ausones such as the 1978, 1979, 1985, and 1986. It is a winemaking triumph for this difficult vintage. **A.M.: Now–2010.**

The first comment in my notes on the 1929 was "cedar city." Although lightly colored, with a rusty tint to the entire wine, the 1929 Ausone exhibits a fabulous bouquet of spices, cedar, and sweet, jammy fruit. It displays wonderful ripeness, as well as the telltale austerity and dry finish that often characterize Ausone. The wine remains rich, medium bodied, and intact, but I would not gamble on holding it any longer. However, it possesses more fruit, richness, and complexity than the shallow color suggests. My notes indicate that the 1900 Ausone had a 90-point nose and 99-point flavors. Most Ausones are big on bouquet but short on flavor. It is unbelievable that a 94-year-old wine could have had this much richness and flavor. The huge nose of roasted cloves, coffee, and honeyed red fruits is followed by a wine with supersweetness, big, jammy, alcoholic, ripe flavors, and remarkable length with elevated alcohol. The light color is akin to a rusty-colored white Zinfandel. The extreme sweetness makes me think the fermentation halted and the wine has some residual sugar. This stunning wine remains fresh and lively.

Other possible candidates: 1989; this is an outstanding but amazingly variable wine

BEAUSÉJOUR-DUFFAU

1990 TASTED 7 TIMES SINCE BOTTLING, WITH REMARKABLY SIMILAR SCORES OF 97–100! ($60.00–$75.00) **100**

This microscopic estate of 17 acres planted with 55% Merlot, 25% Cabernet Franc, and 20% Cabernet Sauvignon has made terrific wines since the 1988 vintage. The 1990 is one of those extraordinary efforts from an estate that is usually not expected to produce one of the century's legends.

The blockbuster 1990, a superstar of the vintage, is unquestionably the finest wine I have ever tasted from Beauséjour-Duffau. An opaque black/ruby color is followed by a bouquet that offers up intense, lingering aromas of herb-scented cassis, licorice, minerals, sweet plums, and new oak. In the mouth, there is outstanding extraction of fruit, superlative depth and power, a formidable unctuosity and density, as well as an overall sense of elegance and finesse—an exceedingly difficult combination to produce in a wine. This profound St.-Émilion is a must-buy, but move quickly, as the production of 3,000 cases is among the smallest of the St.-Émilion premiers and grands crus. **A.M.: Now–2008.**

BON PASTEUR

1982 TASTED 15 TIMES FROM 375 ML, 750 ML, AND MAGNUM, WITH CONSISTENTLY EUPHORIC NOTES ($50.00) **97**

Behind the talented ownership of Dany and Michel Rolland, Bon Pasteur has made many friends for its rich, complex, supple style of Pomerol. In the process, Michel Rolland has become a world-famous oenologist/consultant to many of the finest winemaking estates in France, Italy, Argentina, and California. The small vineyard (17 acres) has produced one wine of extraordinary dimensions. The 1982 Bon Pasteur continues to remind me of a 1947 Pomerol, given its viscosity and opulent, flamboyant, exaggerated style. Unquestionably, it is the finest Bon Pasteur made to date. The black/purple color reveals only slight amber at the edge. The nose offers up huge, jammy aromas of black fruits, roasted nuts, and sweet oak. There is extraordinary richness and concentration, as well as a nectarlike essence. Although fully mature, this wine displays no signs of losing any of its lavish fruit. Drink it over the next 10–15 years.

CALON SÉGUR

1982 TASTED 12 TIMES SINCE BOTTLING, WITH INCONSISTENT NOTES ($50.00) **94+**
1953 TASTED 3 TIMES, WITH CONSISTENT NOTES ($150.00–$175.00) **96**
1949 TASTED 5 TIMES, WITH INCONSISTENT NOTES ($250.00) **93**
1947 TASTED 7 TIMES, WITH REMARKABLY CONSISTENT AND ECSTATIC NOTES ($250.00–$300.00) **97**
1926 TASTED ONCE ($125.00–$150.00) **94**

This estate of 123 acres producing approximately 20,000 cases from a blend of 65% Cabernet Sauvignon, 25% Merlot, and 10% Cabernet Franc is one of the more perplexing estates to follow. The wines make no concession to modern-day tasters, preferring supple, up-front, flattering wines dominated by toasty vanillin scents. In fact, Calon-Ségur, which can be impressive from barrel, often descends into a backward, withdrawn state for years after bottling (e.g., the 1982). Yet there is no doubt about the heights Calon-Ségur can achieve. From the mid-forties through the mid-fifties Calon-Ségur was one of the most brilliantly made wines in Bordeaux. It also enjoyed a great decade in the twenties.

Proprietor Gasqueton has never wavered in his belief that the 1982 is the finest Calon-Ségur the property has made since the legendary 1947. The 1982 was extraordinary from cask, but its early years in the bottle were dominated by its tannin, giving the wine an astringent, hard, forbidding personality. The wine tasted impenetrable, backward, and completely closed. Recent tastings, all from half-bottles, are the first authoritative evidence I have seen since the wine was in barrel that this is unquestionably a great Calon-Ségur. It is made in a traditional style, so do not expect to get turned on by lavish quantities of vanillin-scented, toasty new oak, and sweet, jammy fruit. Although massive, with incredible richness and plenty of fruit, this wine is dominated by its black currant, mineral, cedar character. The copious tannins are still present, but they are integrated with the wine's other components. This classic Calon-Ségur is built to stand the test of time. From a half-bottle it should reach full maturity by the turn of the century and last for at least 20–30 years. This is a remarkable wine that should find many admirers among true connoisseurs. Among the high-priced 1982s, it remains undervalued, no doubt because it suffered in early tastings against more flashy wines.

I have heard that the 1953 was sumptuous even before it reached 10 years of age. When drunk recently from magnum, the wine was a classic example of the glorious fragrance and velvety richness this vintage achieved. While most Calon-Ségurs possess a hefty degree of tannin, this wine offers a glorious concoction of cedar, sweet jammy fruit, full body, and remarkable intensity without the husky roughness Calon-Ségur can display. Although the color exhibits noticeable amber at the edge, this wine remains in magnificent condition.

Made during a period when Calon-Ségur was one of Bordeaux's top producers, the superb 1949 boasts glorious opulence and balance, wonderfully sweet, rich, cedary, black cherry fruit intermingled with gobs of leather and meaty notes, and a long, full-bodied, superrich finish. The color reveals moderate amber. With no hard edges, low acidity, and tremendous reserves of fruit, this fully mature wine should drink well for another decade. The 1947 has been a personal favorite since the first time I had it at the estate over a decade ago. It is one of the great Médoc success stories, rivaling the extraordinary Mouton-Rothschild for one of the few stars of Bordeaux's left bank in this vintage known for the decadently rich Pomerols and St.-Émilions produced. Made in a blockbuster, high-alcohol, full-throttle style, the wine exhibits some amber at the edge, but remains totally intact. I consumed this wine during the summer of 1994, once from a regular bottle and twice from magnums (to celebrate my 47th birthday). This is clearly the most opulent and voluptuous Calon-Ségur produced this century.

The 1926 is not a wine for modern-day oenologists. The color is mainly orange/rust with some ruby remaining. Noticeable volatile acidity blows off within several minutes. The sweet, plummy, cedary, roasted nut– and clove-scented nose is followed by a surprisingly sweet wine, with fine ripeness, and chewy glycerin. The well-balanced finish is long, authoritative, and generous. Although the feeble color suggests a degree of decrepitude, such is not the case.

Other possible candidates: 1928

CANON

1982 TASTED 9 TIMES SINCE BOTTLING, WITH CONSISTENT NOTES ($65.00–$70.00) **96**
1959 TASTED 2 TIMES, WITH CONSISTENT NOTES ($100.00) **95**

This property was one of Bordeaux's hot estates during the eighties, but some of the vintages from the forties have withstood the test of time, although they do not qualify as wines of the century. Canon's style exhibits a Médoc-like austerity, although in very ripe years this 44-acre vineyard planted with 55% Merlot and 45% Cabernet Franc produces wines with fleshy, chewy characters.

I do not believe I have ever tasted a greater Canon than the 1982, although old-timers claim 1928 and 1929 were of this stature. Like so many 1982s, this wine was dramatic, even flamboyant, for several years after bottling, but is now a broodingly backward, large-scaled massive wine with tremendous levels of fruit extraction, glycerin, body, and tannin. It still displays a dark, saturated purple color, a nose that reluctantly offers up scents of black currants, toasty new oak, and wet stones and minerals. Full bodied, powerful, and tannic, this 1982 needs another 5–6 years of cellaring; it should keep for another 20–25 years. This is a sensational Canon made in a classic, nearly Médoc-like style.

Due to the fact that the 1959 was undoubtedly made from relatively young vines (the 1956 freeze caused a significant loss of vines at Canon), this bottle performed spectacularly. The sweet, chocolatey, jammy, black cherry–scented nose and opaque garnet color revealed few signs of age. The wine exhibited an underlying herbaceous quality (young vines?), but its superb richness and chewy, viscous, thick flavors were sensational. There is enough richness and tannin for the wine to evolve for another 15–20 years. It is a magnificent example of Canon!

Other possible candidates: Both the 1948 and 1947 are still 90- to 93-point wines; the 1947 is richer and more alcoholic, and the 1948 is more structured as well as denser and more tannic.

CERTAN DE MAY

1982 TASTED 9 TIMES SINCE BOTTLING, WITH CONSISTENT NOTES ($125.00–$150.00) **98+**
1945 TASTED ONCE ($250.00–$300.00) **96**

Made from a tiny vineyard of 12+ acres situated on the high ground of Pomerol between Vieux Château Certan and Pétrus, Certan de May is one of the most difficult wines to find. This estate's renaissance began in the late seventies (with exceptional efforts in 1979 and 1981) and has continued throughout the eighties, although I have occasionally been alarmed by the aggressively herbaceous character in certain vintages (e.g., 1983 and 1989). Older vintages are virtually impossible to find, although I was able to taste the 1945 and found it to be extraordinary. This is one estate that may have made great wines in 1947, 1948, 1949, and 1950, but I have never seen a bottle.

Consistently one of the most remarkable wines of this great vintage, the 1982 Certan de May has tightened up. It gets my nod as the most backward wine among the 1982 Pomerols, as it is even more tannic than Pétrus. The impressive saturated dark purple/garnet color suggests super flavor extraction. The nose offers scents of Asian spices, cedar, black fruits, truffles, and new oak. It is full bodied and massive, with exceptional concentration to accompany the boatload of tannins. The wine's thick viscosity and huge, unctuous texture are mouth filling. It remains broodingly backward and little evolved since its early days in the barrel. Even half-bottles are youthful. The 1982 Certan de May should easily turn out to be one of the great wines of the vintage. It will come close to perfection. Do not drink it until the end of this century; it will keep easily through the first two decades of the next millennium. After blind tasting the 1945 Certan de May I was convinced it was either Pétrus or a great vintage of Trotanoy. It exhibits an opaque garnet color, and a huge nose of sweet plums, black raspberries, thyme, and grilled meats. Spectacular in the mouth, with a wonderful, sweet, inner core of fruit and an unctuously textured, glycerin-imbued, heady, alcoholic finish, with enough concentration to conceal most of its tannin, this massive wine should drink well for 20 more years.

Other possible candidates: 1988 and 1985 may develop into mid-90-point efforts.

CHEVAL BLANC

1990 TASTED 7 TIMES SINCE BOTTLING, WITH CONSISTENT NOTES ($80.00–$100.00) **95**
1983 TASTED 14 TIMES SINCE BOTTLING, WITH CONSISTENT NOTES ($75.00–$95.00) **95**
1982 TASTED 9 TIMES SINCE BOTTLING, WITH CONSISTENT NOTES ($175.00–$200.00) **100**
1964 TASTED 6 TIMES, WITH CONSISTENT NOTES ($150.00–$225.00) **95**
1949 TASTED 5 TIMES, WITH CONSISTENT NOTES ($500.00–$650.00) **100**
1948 TASTED 3 TIMES, WITH CONSISTENT NOTES ($125.00–$175.00) **96**
1947 TASTED 11 TIMES, WITH REMARKABLY CONSISTENT NOTES EXCEPT FOR ONE BAD
DOUBLE MAGNUM ($950.00–$1,000.00) **100**

One of the most extraordinary and distinctive wines of Bordeaux, Cheval Blanc is well represented in this list of the twentieth century's greatest Bordeaux wines. This property of nearly 89 acres produces over 15,000 cases from an unusual blend of 66% Cabernet Franc, 33% Merlot, and 1% Malbec. Cheval Blanc produced an extraordinary string of wines in the late forties, and has rebounded from a difficult, uninspiring decade of the seventies. The 1981 marked the estate's return to form, where it has remained.

Will the 1990 turn out to be a replay of Cheval Blanc's glorious 1983? It appears to be the most complete Cheval produced since their historic duo of 1982 and 1983. Richer and longer in the mouth than the lightish 1988, and significantly deeper and more complete than the 1989, the 1990 exhibits deeper color than recent vintages of Cheval, as well as a profound menthol aroma intermingled with scents of truffles, mocha, toast, and sweet black fruits. This expansive, typical, exotic example of Cheval Blanc is captivating because of its opulence and rich, velvety finish. It already provides immense pleasure. An attention grabber! **A.M.: Now–2010.**

A classic example of Cheval Blanc's style, the 1983 continues to put on weight and to develop favorably in the bottle. A saturated dark ruby color with some faint lightening at the edges exhibits less age than most right-bank 1983s. The huge nose of mint, jammy black fruits, chocolate, and coffee is sensational, as well as surprisingly well developed. The wine offers lusty, rich, unctuous fruit presented in a medium- to full-bodied, low-acid, concentrated, rather hedonistic style. There are no hard edges to be found, but there is plenty of tannin in the lush finish. Gorgeous for drinking now, this is a great Cheval Blanc that should continue to drink well, and will possibly improve for another 20 years. The 1983 is far superior to anything (except the 1990) Cheval Blanc has subsequently produced. It remains somewhat undervalued for its quality. For me, the 1982 remains the greatest Cheval Blanc produced after the 1949 and 1947. It is no longer as dramatic as it was during its first 4 years after bottling. Between 1985 and 1989, the 1982 Cheval Blanc and 1982 Pichon-Lalande were the favorites to win any blind tasting of this vintage. It has closed and is displaying considerable structure and potential for extended longevity. The dense, saturated, nearly opaque dark ruby/garnet color reveals no lightening at the edges. The wine has a thick portlike viscosity to its texture. The nose is more subdued, yet still offers those fragrant aromas of vanillin and lavishly sweet berry fruit intermingled with aromas of roasted meats, soy, and herbs. For the first time, this wine's high level of tannin is noticeable. This full-bodied, superrich, brilliantly rendered wine still has as its hallmark layer upon layer of creamy fruit that offers a compelling glassful of wine. It appears to be at least 3–5 years from blossoming once again, although I cannot argue with anyone consuming it now. If you did not catch it in its youthful glory between 1984 and 1989, I would advise sitting on it until the late nineties and enjoying it over the following 20 years.

The 1964 is a wonderfully rich, thick, powerful, and concentrated wine that is the most authoritative Cheval Blanc produced since the monumental wines made by this château in 1947, 1948, and 1949. Opaque dark ruby, with only some amber, and a powerful yet restrained bouquet of roasted ripe fruit, cedar, herbs, and gravelly, mineral scents, the wine remains amazingly young and tannic, with layer upon layer of ripe fruit. This is a heavy-weight, old-style Cheval Blanc that should be pure nectar for at least another 10–15 years. It continues to evolve at a snail's pace. **A.M.: Now–2010.**

Although the extraordinary 1949 does not have the portlike unctuosity and heaviness of the 1947, it is an enormously rich, concentrated wine. It is better balanced than the heavyweight 1947, yet every bit as complex and extraordinary, both from an aromatic and a flavor perspective. The wine exhibits a phenomenally fragrant bouquet of overripe red and black fruits, cedar, Asian spices, and minerals. Decadently rich and jammy, it has an amazing plum/garnet color with very little amber or rust at the edge. It may outlive the heavier, thicker, more exotic 1947. The 1948 is the most backward Cheval Blanc among vintages of the forties. The wine retains an opaque plum/licorice-like color. A huge, earthy, soy, cedar, roasted herb nose is followed by a wine of immense power, body, intensity, and structure. It will easily last for another 20+ years. Having a 1947 Cheval Blanc served out of an impeccably stored magnum twice in three months during the summer of 1994, and on another occasion, from an extraordinary jeroboam, made me once again realize what a great job I have. The only recent Bordeaux vintage that comes even remotely close to the richness, texture, and viscosity of so many of these right-bank 1947s is 1982. What can I say about this mammoth wine that is more like port than dry red table wine? The 1947 Cheval Blanc exhibits such a thick texture it could double as motor oil. The huge nose of fruitcake, chocolate, leather, coffee, and Asian spices is mind-boggling. The unctuous texture and richness of sweet fruit are amazing. Consider the fact that this wine is, technically, appallingly deficient in acidity and excessively high in alcohol. Moreover, its volatile acidity levels would be considered intolerable by modern-day oenologists. Yet how can they explain that after 47 years the wine was still remarkably fresh, phenomenally concentrated, and profoundly complex? It has to make you wonder about the direction of modern-day winemaking. Except for one dismal, murky, troubled, volatile double magnum, this wine has been either perfect or nearly perfect every time I have had it.

Other possible candidates: 1961, 1953 (can be sublime but all recent tastings have suggested the wine is fading), and 1945 (outstanding, but so rustic and tough). The 1929 (rated 90) was still holding on to life when drunk in the summer of 1994.

CLINET

1989 TASTED 5 TIMES SINCE BOTTLING, WITH CONSISTENTLY EXCEPTIONAL NOTES ($65.00–
$90.00) **99**

It will be interesting to note whether Clinet ever produces another wine as remarkable as
their 1989. Certainly the 1988 and 1990 are noteworthy efforts from this estate, which
emerged from the doldrums in the late eighties to become one of Pomerol's bright shining
stars.

The black/purple-colored 1989 Clinet is one of the blockbusters of the vintage. The
bouquet gushes with aromas of black raspberries, licorice, chocolate, and minerals. In the
mouth, the weight, concentration, and highly extracted style have resulted in a massive wine
with a whopping finish. **A.M.: Now–2015.**

CLOS RENÉ

1947 TASTED ONCE ($125.00–$250.00) **95**

It is a tribute to the 1947 vintage that Clos René, a mid-80-point performer in most top
years, could have produced such a phenomenal wine. For those lucky enough to run across
a bottle at auction, it will undoubtedly sell at well below its true value. An underrated
property, Clos René produced a 1947 that exhibited the viscosity possessed by many of the
great Pomerols of this vintage. The thick-looking garnet color is followed by scents of
apricots, coffee, and jammy black cherries. Full bodied, with layers of chewy fruit, this fully
mature yet remarkably healthy, macho wine will continue to offer decadent drinking for
another 10–15 years.

LA CONSEILLANTE

1990 TASTED 8 TIMES SINCE BOTTLING, WITH CONSISTENT NOTES ($50.00–$90.00) **98**
1989 TASTED 14 TIMES SINCE BOTTLING, WITH CONSISTENT NOTES ($65.00–$90.00) **97**
1959 TASTED ONCE ($250.00–$325.00) **95**
1949 TASTED 6 TIMES, WITH CONSISTENT NOTES ($300.00–$350.00) **97**

Perhaps the most Burgundian-like wine from Pomerol, this extremely fragrant, medium-
weight wine rarely possesses the body or concentration of its peers (Pétrus, Lafleur, L'Évangile, and Certan de May), but for complexity, finesse, and lush, silky fruit that boasts
exceptional ripeness and flavors of black raspberries, cherries, and currants, La Conseillante
has few rivals. This 32-acre vineyard is planted with 45% Merlot, 45% Cabernet Franc, and
10% Malbec. The property, off form for much of the sixties and seventies (save for the
outstanding 1970), has made terrific wines since 1981.

How much fun millionaires will have debating the virtues of the 1989 versus the 1990 La
Conseillante. The latter is deep ruby/purple, with a sexy nose of exotic spices, sweet black
fruits, and new oak. It displays La Conseillante's creamy/velvety texture, gobs of rich
raspberry fruit, exceptional concentration, and a suave, superb finish that goes on and on. It
will provide memorable drinking young, yet should age beautifully for 20 or more years.
A.M.: Now–2012. The 1989 boasts an awesome bouquet of plums, exotic spices, and
vanillin. A wine of brilliant definition, and a remarkable marriage of power and elegance,
this fabulously long wine has a sweet finish, with abundant tannin. **A.M.: 1996–2010.**

I must confess I never dreamed so many 1959 Pomerols would turn out so rich and
concentrated. La Conseillante's 1959 exhibits a fragrant bouquet of flowers, black raspberries, and smoke, medium to full body, soft tannin, and wonderful, pure, sweet, expansive
fruit. It is a classic example of La Conseillante's ability to produce authoritatively rich wines
of extraordinary elegance and complexity.

It has been several years since I had the 1949, but having gone through a half case I
purchased in outstanding condition, I must say that every bottle was exceptional, with a

gorgeously ripe, jammy nose of black fruits, sweet, expansive, medium-bodied flavors, and a silky texture. It is interesting that La Conseillante, never the most tannic, muscular, or powerful wine, appears to be drinkable at a remarkably young age yet holds its fruit for decades. The proprietor, a friend of the Nicolas family, told me he consumed several cases of the 1949 in the early fifties because it was so tasty—further proof that balance, not tannin, is often the key to a graceful evolution. I have high hopes that the 1989 and 1990 will prove to be as awesome and ageworthy as the 1949.

Other possible candidates: 1985, 1982, 1970

COS D'ESTOURNEL

1986 TASTED 7 TIMES SINCE BOTTLING, WITH CONSISTENT NOTES ($45.00–$50.00) **95**
1985 TASTED 8 TIMES SINCE BOTTLING, WITH CONSISTENT NOTES ($45.00–$60.00) **95**
1982 TASTED 10 TIMES SINCE BOTTLING, WITH CONSISTENT NOTES ($75.00–$90.00) **97**
1953 TASTED 4 TIMES, WITH VIRTUALLY IDENTICAL NOTES ($250.00–$300.00) **93**

Cos d'Estournel, off form for much of the sixties and seventies, began to show signs of improved quality with the 1976 vintage. In 1982 a complete turnabout in the quality of this estate's wines was complete. Since then Cos d'Estournel has been a sterling example of complex, rich St.-Estèphe with two to three decades of aging potential.

The 1986 is a highly extracted wine, with a black/ruby color and plenty of toasty, smoky notes in its bouquet that suggest ripe plums and licorice. Evolving at a glacial pace, it exhibits massive, huge, ripe, extremely concentrated flavors with impressive depth and richness. It possesses more power, weight, and tannin than the more opulent and currently more charming 1985. **A.M.: 1996–2010.** The 1985 is cast from the same mold as the 1982 and 1953 vintages. Forward, with a fabulously scented bouquet of toasty new oak and concentrated red and black fruits (especially black cherries), it is rich, lush, long, and full bodied. Already delicious, it should age beautifully for 12–18 years. **A.M.: Now–2010.** A monumental wine, the 1982 exhibited gobs of explosive black currant fruit from the very first cask samples tasted at the château in March 1983. Unctuous, massive, rich, full bodied, and loaded with extract and tannin, this remains one of the greatest Cos d'Estournels I have ever tasted. It is still youthful and firm, with huge reserves of fruit. **A.M.: Now–2015.**

The 1953, most recently drunk from magnums in 1994, 1993, and 1989, is a classic example of the vintage, displaying a huge, fragrant, flowery, berry-scented nose. From a regular bottle I suspect this wine could be on the downside, but from pristinely kept magnums this fully mature wine is a terrific example of the vintage, and certainly one of the greatest wines of the century.

Other possible candidates: 1928 (once sublime, but now fading from 750-ml bottles)

DUCRU-BEAUCAILLOU

1982 TASTED 11 TIMES SINCE BOTTLING, WITH CONSISTENT NOTES ($50.00–$60.00) **96**
1961 TASTED 6 TIMES, WITH CONSISTENT NOTES ($275.00–$350.00) **96**

This property, known for some of the most elegant wines of Bordeaux, has gained its reputation largely since the decade of the sixties. One of the most consistent properties during the so-so decade of the sixties, Ducru-Beaucaillou continued throughout the seventies and eighties to produce high-class wines. The estate has been called, with considerable justification, the Lafite-Rothschild of St.-Julien because the wines exhibit such symmetry, balance, breeding, class, and distinction. Located on the well-drained banks of the Gironde River, the vineyards are planted with 65% Cabernet Sauvignon, 25% Merlot, 5% Cabernet Franc, and 5% Petit Verdot.

Just beginning to blossom and open, the 1982 Ducru-Beaucaillou is unquestionably the finest wine made at this estate since 1961. The concentrated, viscous, dark ruby/purple color is followed by explosive aromas of spring flowers, black currants, minerals, and toast. It is fuller bodied than normal, with remarkable delineation, great richness, and that wonderful sweetness that is a hallmark of this vintage. This long, exceptionally well focused, classic Ducru should reach its peak in 3–5 years and last through the first two or three decades of the next century.

Fully mature, yet continuing to exhibit gobs of rich, lush, expansive fruit, the dark ruby 1961 has amber/orange edges, and possesses an exotic bouquet of ripe fruit, vanillin, caramel, mint, and cedar. Fat, rich, and loaded with sweet, highly extracted fruit, this velvety, beautifully crafted wine has a 60- to 75-second finish. It is a brilliant wine that should hold up nicely for up to a decade. **A.M.: Now–2005.**

Other possible candidates: 1985, 1953

L'ÉVANGILE

1990 TASTED 10 TIMES SINCE BOTTLING, WITH CONSISTENT NOTES ($70.00–$85.00) **96**
1985 TASTED 8 TIMES SINCE BOTTLING, WITH INCONSISTENT NOTES ($70.00–$85.00) **95**
1982 TASTED 15 TIMES SINCE BOTTLING, WITH CONSISTENT NOTES ($80.00–$100.00) **97**
1975 TASTED 8 TIMES SINCE BOTTLING, WITH INCONSISTENT NOTES ($150.00–$175.00) **95**
1961 TASTED 5 TIMES, WITH INCONSISTENT NOTES ($175.00–$250.00) **99–100**
1947 TASTED 5 TIMES, WITH CONSISTENT NOTES ($300.00–$400.00) **100**

One of the great ladies of France, Madame Ducasse, continues to oversee virtually every aspect of this tiny 35-acre vineyard sandwiched between Pétrus, La Conseillante, Vieux Château Certan, and the great St.-Émilion, Cheval Blanc. The vineyard is planted with 75% Merlot and 25% Cabernet Franc. The property often produces wines of first-growth quality. Consequently, it has a number of wines that are among my legends of this century. The top vintages of L'Évangile are extremely difficult to find because of the fanatical support this wine has in European (mostly Belgium and Switzerland) wine circles. In the top years it is a lavish, rich (with plums, cassis, and black cherries galore) wine with an unctuous, dense personality.

The 1990 could prove to be one of the finest L'Évangiles in the post–World War II era, competing with the superb wines this renowned estate produced in 1947, 1950, 1975, 1982, and 1985. This is a blockbuster, black/ruby/purple-colored wine, with a restrained but promising nose of black fruits, toffee, new oak, and minerals. It offers exceptional richness, full body, an unctuous, nearly portlike texture, and great length and depth. The fruit's massive richness nearly obscures a considerable amount of tannin. Yet this is one of the most tannic and large scaled Pomerols of the vintage. This riveting wine resembles in weight and force the pre-1976 vintages of its neighbor, Pétrus. **A.M.: 1997–2015.**

L'Évangile's 1985 remains relatively unevolved and youthful. The dark ruby color exhibits no signs of age, and the hugely complex, multidimensional bouquet of black currants, raspberries, exotic spices, and oak requires coaxing from the glass. Rich, medium to full bodied, superconcentrated, well balanced, and tannic, this wine continues to evolve more slowly than other 1985s. **A.M.: Now–2015.** From its early days L'Évangile's 1982 has been a knockout. It has demonstrated no signs over the last decade of closing up and going into that so-called dumb stage. The color is a dense, nearly opaque dark garnet/purple. The bouquet offers oodles of jammy black currants and raspberries, intermingled with scents of tea, smoked duck, *sauce périgourdine,* and licorice. The lavish, multidimensional bouquet is followed by a thick, unctuous, superconcentrated wine with low acidity, huge, massive quantities of fruit, and a spectacularly long finish. The 1982 is one of this century's greatest L'Évangiles, clearly rivaling what this magnificent estate produced in 1947, 1950, and 1990. Drink it over the next 15–20 years.

The 1975 has been inconsistent, especially early in its life, but over the last 5 years at every tasting it has revealed an extraordinary, rich, profound character. Unlike most 1975s, it has reached full maturity, exhibiting a huge, nearly overripe nose of prunes, cedar, sweet jammy plums, spices, and caramel. Rich and full bodied, with surprisingly sweet tannin for the vintage, this exotic, voluptuously textured wine should continue to drink well for 15+ more years.

The 1961 possesses a huge nose of coffee, sweet, jammy, black fruits, buttered nuts, and truffles. The syrupy texture and fabulous concentration, viscosity, and richness were unbelievable. Given its portlike richness, this full-bodied, massively endowed, fully mature wine is reminiscent of the great 1947. Interestingly, Madame Ducasse told me that two-thirds of the vineyard was replanted in 1957, so 66% of the blend is from 3-year-old vines! Readers who are fortunate enough to have bottles of this nectar should plan on drinking it over the next 10–15 years. Tasted three times over the last year, the monumental 1947 is a great example of the thick, viscous, chewy, superconcentrated wines that were produced in Pomerol in that vintage. The color is opaque garnet. The nose explodes from the glass, offering sweet, mocha, chocolate, black cherry, anise, and smoky scents. Fabulously concentrated, with a nectarlike unctuosity, this incredible wine is still young and amazingly rich and well balanced for its massive size. Wines such as this can bring tears to your eyes!

Other possible candidates: 1964, 1950, 1949 (never tasted but reports from knowledgeable tasters suggest it is a superb wine)

FIGEAC

1990 TASTED 6 TIMES SINCE BOTTLING, WITH CONSISTENT NOTES ($50.00–$65.00) **94**
1982 TASTED 9 TIMES SINCE BOTTLING, WITH CONSISTENT NOTES ($60.00–$75.00) **94**
1964 TASTED 8 TIMES, WITH CONSISTENTLY BRILLIANT NOTES ($75.00–$85.00) **94**
1955 TASTED ONCE ($75.00–$100.00) **95**
1953 TASTED 2 TIMES, WITH CONSISTENT NOTES ($150.00–$250.00) **93**

This distinctively styled wine is known more for its penetrating fragrance and elegance than for its depth, power, or muscle. Made from a blend of nearly equal portions of Cabernet Sauvignon, Cabernet Franc, and Merlot, it is a wine that drinks remarkably well young, yet possesses the uncanny ability to put on considerable weight and character as it ages. Consequently, I have shown a strong predilection to underestimate Figeac. That being said, the wine is distressingly irregular in quality, and often too light in highly successful years (e.g., 1985, 1986, and 1989).

The exceptional 1990 is the first authoritative Figeac since their splendid 1982. The huge nose of new saddle-leather, herbs, black fruits, and smoke is followed by a wine with exceptional concentration, excellent balance and depth, and a smooth-as-silk finish. Ripe tannin and sweet fruit combine to produce a splendidly opulent, rich Figeac that should drink well for two decades. This is undoubtedly one of the most impressive notes I have ever given an infant vintage of Figeac. The wine bears more than a casual resemblance to its renowned neighbor, Cheval Blanc. **A.M.: Now–2010.**

The 1982 appears to get fuller and fuller each time I go back to it. I have already said I have had a tendency to underestimate Figeac young, when it seemed to lack concentration and structure. I have frequently regretted those early low marks, as the wine has an uncanny ability to fill out and display more richness and structure than it initially suggests. The 1982 is turning out to be the best Figeac made at this property since their glorious 1964. It reveals gobs of Cabernet fruit in its herbaceous, cedary, olivelike bouquet, but there is plenty of berry fruit behind it to balance out the herbaceousness. On the palate, the wine is dense and rich, has great extract and length, and is supple and precocious, but the wine has increasingly become more and more structured as it has aged. **A.M.: Now–2010.**

After having gone through numerous regular-sized bottles and a case of magnums, I can unequivocally say that the 1964 is one of the two or three greatest Figeacs I have ever tasted. It has drunk fabulously well since the early seventies and is the type of wine that offers persuasive evidence that Figeac has one of the broadest windows of drinkability of any Bordeaux wine. The wine is still a great example of the 1964 vintage—opulent, with an intense, deep, rich fruitiness, a velvety texture, and a sensational bouquet of cedar, chestnuts, plums, herbs, and smoke. Extremely smooth and ripe, it continues to defy the laws of aging. **A.M.: Now–2000.**

The 1955 is one of those brilliant, unknown great wines of the century that no doubt appears from time to time at auction and is undoubtedly sold for a song, given the fact that it has received so little press. From a château that tends to produce quickly maturing wines, this offering is more backward than the fully mature 1964, and even richer than the 1982 and 1990 (at least as they appear today). The 1955 offers an extraordinary fragrance of ripe plums, cassis, mint, herbs, smoke, and spices. Dense and concentrated for a Figeac, with some tannin yet to melt away, this wine is a candidate for a half century of aging. Purchasing the 1953 can be a risky business if the bottle has not been stored impeccably. At its best, this wine exhibits a huge nose of smoke, earth, herbs, minerals, fruit, and menthol, soft, velvety, medium-bodied flavors, no noticeable tannin, and heady alcohol in the finish. It has been fully mature for at least two decades, so it is unlikely to get any better.

Other possible candidates: 1970, 1947

LA FLEUR DE GAY

1989 TASTED 5 TIMES SINCE BOTTLING, WITH CONSISTENT NOTES ($65.00–$80.00) **95**

This luxury cuvée of 1,000–1,500 cases from a 5-acre vineyard planted with 100% Merlot is the product of the larger vineyard of La Croix de Gay. The first vintage was 1982. The 1989 La Fleur de Gay offers a veritable smorgasbord of aromas. The dark ruby/purple color is opaque, suggesting low yields and superconcentration. The wine is amazingly concentrated, structured, and tannic, with a chewy texture and layers of fruit. Despite the low acidity, the tannins tend to keep the level of enjoyment down. Nevertheless, it is so crammed with ripe fruit and glycerin that I suspect many consumers will not be able to resist it. It will be a legend. **A.M.: Now–2008.**

GRAND-PUY-LACOSTE

1982 TASTED 14 TIMES SINCE BOTTLING, WITH CONSISTENT NOTES ($50.00–$60.00) **95**
1949 TASTED ONCE ($225.00–$350.00) **96**

This has always been somewhat of an insider's wine that rarely gets the attention it deserves. Moreover, it tends to sell at a significantly lower price than most other top Pauillacs. The 111-acre vineyard, planted with 70% Cabernet Sauvignon, 25% Merlot, and 5% Cabernet Franc, is run by Xavier Borie, the son of Jean-Eugene Borie, the proprietor of Ducru-Beaucaillou. Grand-Puy-Lacoste's style is one of considerable richness, fruit, body, and tannin—in short, a classic Pauillac.

Certainly the best Grand-Puy-Lacoste since the remarkable 1949, the 1982 has first-growth qualities. Still an opaque purple color with no signs of lightening, with a huge, superpure nose of black currants, minerals, and spicy oak reminiscent of an exceptionally young wine, and layer upon layer of black currant fruit allied to gobs of glycerin, high but sweet tannins, and full body, this large-scaled, impeccably well-balanced wine should reach full maturity by the late nineties and should easily last through the first 15 years of the next century. This is a colossal effort from this underrated Pauillac fifth-growth!

The 1949 exhibits a fragrant nose of cedar, black currants, and woodsy, trufflelike aromas.

Gorgeously opulent and full bodied, it is a superconcentrated, velvety-textured, fully mature wine.

Other possible candidates: 1961, 1947

GRUAUD-LAROSE

1982 TASTED 11 TIMES SINCE BOTTLING, WITH CONSISTENT NOTES ($40.00–$55.00) **96+**
1961 TASTED 7 TIMES, WITH CONSISTENT NOTES ($145.00–$175.00) **96**
1945 TASTED 5 TIMES, WITH INCONSISTENT NOTES ($200.00–$225.00) **96+**
1928 TASTED 2 TIMES, WITH CONSISTENT NOTES ($350.00–$400.00) **97**

Gruaud-Larose, situated inland from the Gironde, has produced some of St.-Julien's most massive and tannic wines. Despite the estate's enormous production, Gruaud-Larose has consistently demonstrated high quality, especially during the period from the late seventies through the late eighties. In some vintages, this property can produce wines of first-growth quality. The finest vintages generally require 10–15 years of bottle age. In their youth they have a tendency to taste overly chunky, rustic, and excruciatingly tannic.

Probably the most massive, concentrated Gruaud-Larose produced in the post–World War II era, the densely colored 1982 displays a tight but highly promising bouquet of jammy black plums, Asian spices, truffles, and licorice. This huge wine is massively rich and incredibly well endowed with layer upon layer of juicy, thick, unctuous fruit flavors buttressed by frightfully high tannin levels and plenty of alcohol, glycerin, and body. It needs at least 5–7 more years to reach its plateau of maturity. The 1982 boasts remarkable concentration, and should drink well through the first two decades of the next century. The 1961 is among the greatest mature wines of Gruaud-Larose I have drunk. This powerful, rich, densely concentrated wine remains young, fresh, and vigorous, with a full decade of life ahead. It continues to exhibit a dark garnet color with some amber, a wonderfully fragrant quality (plus minerals, tar, cedar, soy sauce, and licorice), a viscous texture, sensational depth of fruit, and a fabulous albeit alcoholic finish. This is claret at its most decadent. **A.M.: Now–2015.**

The 1945 is a remarkably young, backward, massive Gruaud-Larose, similar in style to the 1961, 1975, 1982, and 1986. Still opaque, garnet/black-colored, with a tight but promising nose of licorice, black fruits, and herbs, this full-bodied, meaty, chewy wine exhibits huge reserves of fruit, as well as a spicy, powerful, tannic finish. While it can be drunk now (I would suggest decanting of at least an hour), it is another immortal 1945 that will last for 20–30 more years. The 1928 Gruaud-Larose is an amazingly intact wine as it approaches 70 years of age. It exhibits huge, sweet aromas of earth, truffles, cedar, and spices, huge body, noticeably high tannin, and stunning concentration. A slight austerity creeps in at the finish. The dark garnet color with only light amber is remarkable given the wine's age.

Other possible candidates: 1986 (still too young to be sure) and 1953 (probably in decline)

HAUT-BRION

1989 TASTED 10 TIMES SINCE BOTTLING, WITH CONSISTENT NOTES ($135.00–$150.00) **100**
1961 TASTED 13 TIMES, WITH CONSISTENT NOTES ($550.00) **97**
1959 TASTED 9 TIMES, WITH CONSISTENT NOTES ($500.00) **98**
1955 TASTED 4 TIMES, WITH CONSISTENT NOTES ($450.00) **97**
1953 TASTED 4 TIMES, WITH CONSISTENT NOTES ($450.00) **95**
1949 TASTED 3 TIMES, WITH CONSISTENT NOTES ($400.00–$450.00) **98**
1945 TASTED 5 TIMES, WITH CONSISTENT NOTES ($1,000.00) **100**
1928 TASTED 4 TIMES, WITH INCONSISTENT NOTES ($550.00–$650.00) **97**
1926 TASTED 3 TIMES, WITH INCONSISTENT NOTES ($450.00–$600.00) **97**

As I have matured, I have developed an insatiable desire to drink as much Haut-Brion as I can afford. In my opinion, it is the most distinctive, complex, and compelling of the Bordeaux first-growths. While it lacks the flamboyance and ostentatious boldness of Mouton-Rothschild, the massive, extraordinary concentration of a great Latour, and the delicate perfume of a top Lafite (but great vintages of that estate are few and far between), Haut-Brion possesses, along with Cheval Blanc, the most penetrating, intense, complex aromatic profile of the first-growths. Its flavors build intensity and layers with aging. I have often noticed that the wine can taste deceptively light and uninspiring young, only to fatten up and expand with bottle age, often making early assessments look ridiculous. The property, 113 acres located in the bustling commercial suburb of Pessac, produces between 12,000 and 18,000 cases of wine that is made from a blend of 55% Cabernet Sauvignon, 25% Merlot, and 20% Cabernet Franc. Along with Château Margaux, Haut-Brion was the most consistently successful first-growth in the decade of the eighties.

The 1989 is the most profound young Haut-Brion I have ever tasted. While most producers made considerably more wine in 1989 than in 1988, administrator Jean Delmas made 30% less. Significantly concentrated, with a huge perfume, this is a monumental wine that may be a modern-day clone of the heroic 1959. Deep ruby/purple, with a roasted tobacco, cassis, smoky aroma, the 1989 has enormous depth, an opulent texture suggestive of the richest 1982s, great length, and a lavish, multilayered feel. Charged with fruit and tannin, it seems destined to drink sublimely for the next 20–30 years. An awesome wine! **A.M.: Now–2015.**

Although the 1961 is a great Haut-Brion, it is eclipsed in my view by its predecessor, the 1959, and more recently by the monumental 1989. Not as darkly colored as many 1961s, with surprisingly more amber/brown at the edge, this rich, luxurious wine has an intense, earthy, ripe, cedary, spicy bouquet crammed with sweet fruit. On the palate, the wine has fabulous intensity of fruit, a long, rich, alcoholic finish, and a chewy texture. The 1961 has been fully mature for the last decade, but it does not reveal any signs of decline. This is Haut-Brion at its most sumptuous and hedonistic. **A.M.: Now–2000.**

The 1959, which is certainly less evolved than the 1961, gets my nod as slightly superior to the full-blown, mature 1961. The 1959 offers a spectacular, rich, garnet/plummy color, a magnificent bouquet of roasted chestnuts, sweet, jammy black cherry and raspberry fruit, and an intense, mineral, chocolate, coffee aroma. Superconcentrated, with layer upon layer of fat, supple, jammy fruit, a voluptuous texture, and a sweet, long, heady finish, this magnificent Haut-Brion has reached its plateau of maturity, where it should remain for 10–15 years. A dark-ruby-colored wine with noticeable amber/rust, the 1955 Haut-Brion offers a huge, fragrant bouquet of walnuts, tobacco, wet stones, and smoky, cassislike fruit. Medium bodied, with extraordinary elegance and sweetness, this rich, concentrated wine exhibits no hard edges. Remarkably youthful, as well as concentrated and impeccably well balanced, it is capable of lasting for another 10–20 years. Haut-Brion's 1953 is best purchased today in magnums or larger-format bottles. Although it has been fully mature since its release, it has retained the hallmark singed-leather, tobacco-leaf, superripe fragrance that makes Haut-Brion so distinctive. The wine is extremely soft, revealing considerable amber and rust at the edge, but it still possesses rich, creamy fruit and medium to full body. It does require drinking, so be very careful with regular-sized bottles.

The 1949 is a blockbuster wine with an opaque garnet color, and a huge nose of smoked duck, soy sauce, minerals, truffles, and overripe jammy fruit. Rich, thick, chewy, and intense, with huge body, and a portlike quality, this wine should continue to drink well for another decade. The 1945 Haut-Brion is profound. It demonstrates the essence of Haut-Brion's style. The color remains a healthy, opaque garnet with only slight amber at the edge. A huge, penetrating bouquet of sweet black fruits, smoked nuts, tobacco, and tar soars from the glass. The wine possesses extraordinary density and extraction of fruit, massive, full-bodied, unctuously textured flavors that reveal little tannin, and copious quantities of glycerin and alcohol. It is a fabulously rich, monumental example of a fully mature Haut-Brion that exhibits no signs of decline. Awesome!

I had mixed tasting notes on the 1928. At its best, it is the most concentrated, portlike wine I have ever tasted from Haut-Brion. Its huge, meaty, tar, caramel, and jammy black fruit character is unctuously textured. The wine oozes out of the glass and over the palate. In some tastings it has been overripe yet healthy and intact, but nearly bizarre because of its exaggerated style. There is a timeless aspect to it. The 1926 vintage, one of the best years in the decade of the twenties, has always been overlooked in favor of the 1921, 1928, and 1929. Reputed to be one of the great wines of the vintage, the 1926 Haut-Brion is unusual in its roasted, chocolatey, sweet, dense, thick style. It reveals an impressive deep color with some orange at the edge and a huge nose of tobacco, mint, chocolate, grilled nuts, and smoked duck. Full bodied and powerful, with amazing thickness and unctuosity, but extremely tannic and rustic, this atypical Haut-Brion will last for another 20–30 years.

Other possible candidates: 1988, 1986, 1985, 1982

LAFITE-ROTHSCHILD

1990   TASTED 3 TIMES SINCE BOTTLING, WITH CONSISTENT NOTES ($65.00–$80.00) **94+**
1988   TASTED 7 TIMES SINCE BOTTLING, WITH CONSISTENT NOTES ($50.00–$80.00) **94**
1986   TASTED 4 TIMES SINCE BOTTLING, WITH CONSISTENT NOTES ($75.00–$95.00) **99**
1982   TASTED 8 TIMES SINCE BOTTLING, WITH INCONSISTENT NOTES ($125.00–$175.00) **98+**
1959   TASTED 9 TIMES, WITH CONSISTENT NOTES EXCEPT FOR ONE CORKED MAGNUM
        ($500.00) **99**
1953   TASTED 5 TIMES, WITH CONSISTENT NOTES ($385.00–$485.00) **99**

The most famous wine of Bordeaux, Lafite-Rothschild is known for its elegant style. However, my scorecard for Lafite is sprinkled with far more disappointments than successes. When Lafite does get it right, it is the quintessential example of elegance and delicacy.

The 1990 Lafite appears to be a synthesis in style of the backward, tannic 1988 and the more forward, softer 1989. The nose is not yet as seductive as the 1989's, but the wine exhibits a deeper, thicker, ruby/purple color, and cuts a fuller, more complete profile on the palate. It not only rivals the seductiveness of the 1989, but it is also a far richer and more tannic wine. Although it needs at least a decade of cellaring, it should last for 30 or more years. An impressive wine, the 1990 Lafite is this estate's finest wine since the 1982 and 1986. **A.M.: 2000–2025.**

Broodingly backward and in need of considerable bottle age, the 1988 is a classic expression of Lafite. This deeply colored wine exhibits the telltale Lafite bouquet of cedar, subtle herbs, dried pit fruits, minerals, and cassis. Extremely concentrated, with brilliantly focused flavors and huge tannins, this backward yet impressively endowed Lafite-Rothschild may well turn out to be the wine of the vintage! **A.M.: 2000–2035.** The 1986 possesses outstanding richness, a deep color, medium body, a graceful, harmonious texture, and superb length. The penetrating fragrance of cedar, chestnuts, minerals, and rich fruit is a hallmark of this wine. Powerful, dense, rich, and tannic, as well as medium to full bodied, with awesome extraction of fruit, this Lafite has immense potential. Patience is required. **A.M.: 2000–2030.** I have rated the 1982 Lafite-Rothschild as high as 100 and as low as 95, but it remains a strong candidate for perfection. The wine closed down completely after bottling, opening in the mid- to late eighties to reveal phenomenal richness and the essence of the Lafite-Rothschild style. It has recently shut down again and appears to need another 10–15 years of cellaring. The color is among the most saturated and opaque of any Lafite-Rothschild I have seen. The bouquet, explosive several years ago, now appears to be tight, with only hints of the lead pencil and mineral Lafite fragrance. The superrich, cedary, berry-scented fruit is noticeable. Full bodied, with more unctuosity than normal, as well as high tannins, this extraordinary Lafite should develop along the lines of the great 1959. In size it resembles that vintage more than any other. Do not touch a bottle before the turn of the century; it should last for 40–50 years into the next millennium. The 1959 is unquestionably the greatest Lafite-Rothschild that has approached full maturity. It remains to be seen whether vintages such as 1982, 1986, and 1990 will reach a similar height. The superaromatic bouquet of flowers, black truffles, cedar, lead pencil, and red fruits is followed by one of the most powerful and concentrated Lafites I have tasted. Medium to full bodied, velvety-textured, rich, and pure, it is a testament to what this great estate can achieve when it hits the mark. This youthful wine will last for another 30 or more years. On two occasions I rated the 1953 100, and on another occasion, nearly perfect. According to some old-timers, the wine has been fully mature for almost 30 years. It possesses that extraordinary Lafite fragrance of minerals, lead pencil, cedar, and spice. It is velvety-textured, wonderfully round, and sweet, but so well delineated and balanced. It is best purchased today in magnum and larger formats, unless you can be assured that the wine came from a cold cellar and has not been traded frequently.

Other possible candidates: Only once out of ten bottles has the 1961 merited an outstanding rating.

LAFLEUR

1990 TASTED 4 TIMES SINCE BOTTLING, WITH CONSISTENT NOTES ($150.00–$200.00) **98**
1989 TASTED 3 TIMES SINCE BOTTLING, WITH CONSISTENT NOTES ($125.00–$175.00) **96**
1982 TASTED 12 TIMES SINCE BOTTLING, WITH CONSISTENT NOTES ($250.00–$400.00) **96**
1979 TASTED 10 TIMES, WITH CONSISTENT NOTES ($250.00) **98+**
1975 TASTED 13 TIMES, WITH CONSISTENTLY IMPROVING AND REMARKABLE NOTES
          ($500.00) **100**
1966 TASTED 7 TIMES, WITH CONSISTENT NOTES ($500.00) **96**
1961 TASTED 5 TIMES, WITH VERY INCONSISTENT NOTES ($1,500.00) **100**
1950 TASTED 3 TIMES, WITH CONSISTENT NOTES ($1,500.00) **100**
1949 TASTED ONCE ($2,000.00) **96+**
1947 (ESTATE BOTTLING) TASTED 4 TIMES, WITH CONSISTENT NOTES ($2,500.00) **100**
1945 TASTED ONCE ($3,500.00) **100**

This tiny gem of 11 acres, located on the Pomerol plateau adjacent to Pétrus, Certan de May, and Vieux Château Certan, produces only 1,000 cases from a blend of 50% Merlot and 50% Cabernet Franc. Along with Pétrus, it is the most backward and ageworthy Pomerol, often requiring 10–15 years to open up. Vintages such as 1975 and 1979 seemingly require another two or three decades of bottle age before they reach maturity.

The thick purple color of the 1990 Lafleur is accompanied by a bouquet that offers up aromas of minerals, licorice, flowers, overripe black and red fruits (especially cherries), and prunes. The wine possesses gobs of tannin and glycerin, as well as superconcentration and richness. More viscous and weighty than the phenomenal 1989, the 1990 appears destined for three decades of life. Of the many great wines made at this estate, the 1990 has the potential to rival the 1979, 1975, 1950, and 1947. **A.M.: 2000–2020.**

The 1989 Lafleur is super, but the exotic, dense, kinky style that Lafleur usually exhibits is more refined. Dark ruby/purple in color, superconcentrated, and closed, it has a great deal of tannin and alcohol in the finish. This is a wine to be drinking between the turn of the century and the first two and a half decades of the next millennium. **A.M.: 2000– 2030.** The backward 1982 boasts a saturated color and enormous layers of superripe plummy/pruny fruit. An unctuous, thick, rich wine that has consistently drunk well since being bottled, it exhibits little sign of full maturity, giving me reason to believe that it will have a life of at least 20 or more years. Full bodied, alcoholic, and intense, with a spectacularly pure and penetrating nose of black fruits (overripe black cherries), truffles, and spices, it is an enormously rich wine that can be drunk now because of its velvety texture. It will be interesting to see if this great Lafleur holds its own against the phenomenal 1989 and 1990.

In the early nineties I began to think that the 1979 Lafleur would be the wine of the vintage, particularly for serious collectors who judge a wine's quality not only by its potential for longevity, but by its extraction of flavor and complexity. This wine, so atypical for the vintage, is phenomenally concentrated and thick, as well as massively full bodied and tannic. It is a different style of Lafleur than what emanated from this château in the early and mid-eighties. The 1979 is backward, with a reticent but promising bouquet of minerals, damp earth (truffles?), and supersweet, rich blackberries and plums. One has to taste it to believe that in this vintage such awesome flavor, body, and lavish quantities of glycerin could be obtained. It remains the only great, potentially legendary wine from this vintage. Do not touch a bottle before the end of the decade. It should age effortlessly through the first three decades of the next millennium. The 1975 Lafleur is a monster wine. While it is fashionable to criticize the 1975 vintage, it is a spectacular year for many Pomerols. There are some terrific successes that may prove to be the modern-day equivalents of the 1928 vintage (e.g., La Mission-Haut-Brion, Léoville-Las Cases, Léoville-Barton, Pétrus, L'Évangile, Le Gay, Trotanoy, and Latour). The 1975 Lafleur needs, and I underscore the word *needs,* another 20 years of cellaring. It reveals a dark purple/garnet color, with no amber at the edge. The nose reluctantly offers up aromas of minerals, flowers, licorice, coffee, and cassis. There is awesome concentration, as well as a frightfully high tannin level. I have enjoyed it when it has been decanted for 2–3 hours before serving. The wine exhibits sweet fruit, and it has the potential to achieve perfection around 2010. This should prove to be the most enormous, concentrated, and backward wine of the 1975 vintage, with perhaps 70–100 years of longevity. It is a monumental effort.

Along with Palmer and Latour, Lafleur is consistently one of the finest wines of the vintage. This 1966 magnum displays a deep-ruby/purple color with slight amber at the rim. It offers the essence of black cherry flavors intertwined with wet stone and cold steel notes, full body, superconcentration, admirable structure, magnificent depth and delineation, massive reserves of fruit, and an amazingly long finish. It is approaching full maturity and should last for 20–25 more years. After encountering so many disappointing bottles of the 1961 Lafleur (it was bottled barrel by barrel), I am delighted to report that it can be stupendous. Still an opaque black/garnet/plum color, this dense, deep, rich wine possesses remarkably sweet fruit, and flavors so expansive they must be tasted to be believed. The spicy nose of licorice, smoked nuts, cinnamon, and jammy plums lingers and lingers. Fabulously rich and concentrated, this full-bodied, remarkably young, viscous wine is capable of lasting another 20 years.

Perhaps the greatest-kept secret in all of Bordeaux is how spectacular the 1950 vintage was in Pomerol. The 1950 Lafleur could easily pass for a 1947 or 1945 wine given its extraordinary level of concentration. The color remains black/purple, and the bouquet offers aromas of cedar, spices, and black fruits. The wine is unbelievably concentrated, massively full, and rich, with sweet tannin in the finish. With a viscous, chewy texture, this pure wine could easily last for another 15–20 years. The 1949 Lafleur's saturated purple/garnet color is followed by a reluctant nose that with coaxing reveals intense, pure, cherry, jammy aromas intermingled with scents of minerals and licorice. Sensationally concentrated, with layers of thick, rich fruit and high tannin, this sweet, remarkably youthful wine is still not fully mature! It will last for another 20–30 years. There are many 1947s that were bottled in Belgium. I have had the 1947 Lafleur Belgian bottling, which ranges from very good to occasionally outstanding. As good as it is, the château bottling, from which this tasting note emanates, can leave you speechless. This is an extraordinarily profound wine that surpasses Pétrus and Cheval Blanc in this vintage, even though they can all be perfect wines. The 1947 Lafleur is more developed and forward than the 1949 and 1945. It reveals a thick, portlike color with slight amber at the edge. The nose offers a smorgasbord of aromas, ranging from caramel, to jammy black raspberries and cherries, to honeyed nuts, to chocolate and truffles. The wine's unctuosity and viscosity are unequaled in any other dry wine I have tasted. There is neither volatile acidity nor residual sugar present, something that many of the greatest 1947s possess. This wine's richness and freshness are unbelievable. The finish, which lasts more than a minute, coats the mouth with layers of concentrated fruit. There have been many great Lafleurs, but the 1947 is the quintessential expression of this tiny yet marvelous vineyard, which was ignored by wine critics for most of this century. Similar to the 1947 Lafleur in aromatic complexity and flavor, richness, and textural thickness, the 1945 is blacker in color, is less evolved, and possesses a more classic structural profile than the portlike 1947. The 1945 tastes young, yet astonishingly unctuous, rich, and powerful. It will easily last for another 40–50 years. Will the 1975 turn out to be this memorable?

LATOUR

1990 TASTED 6 TIMES SINCE BOTTLING, WITH CONSISTENT NOTES ($85.00–$125.00) **98+**

1982 TASTED 9 TIMES SINCE BOTTLING, WITH CONSISTENT NOTES ($150.00) **99**

1970 TASTED 13 TIMES, WITH CONSISTENT NOTES ($200.00) **98**

1966 TASTED 11 TIMES, WITH CONSISTENT NOTES ($165.00–$175.00) **96**

1961 TASTED 8 TIMES, WITH CONSISTENT NOTES ($750.00) **100**

1949 TASTED 4 TIMES, WITH CONSISTENT NOTES ($695.00) **100**

1948 TASTED 3 TIMES, WITH INCONSISTENT NOTES ($450.00) **94**

1945 TASTED 8 TIMES, WITH INCONSISTENT NOTES ($1,200.00) **99**

1928 TASTED 5 TIMES, WITH 4 IDENTICAL NOTES AND 1 OFF BOTTLE ($1,500.00) **100**

1926 TASTED 2 TIMES, WITH CONSISTENT NOTES ($550.00–$750.00) **93**

1924 TASTED 2 TIMES, WITH INCONSISTENT NOTES ($550.00–$750.00) **94**

Along with La Mission-Haut-Brion, this 148-acre vineyard planted with 80% Cabernet Sauvignon, 10% Merlot, and 10% Cabernet Franc has been the twentieth century's most consistent wine. It is the most backward of the Médocs, with a superconcentrated, firm, classic, ageless character. It can possess such extraordinary intensity and opulence of fruit that in vintages such as 1961 I have mistaken it for Pétrus, as strange as that may sound.

Unquestionably the 1990 is the finest, most archetypal Latour since the 1982 and 1970. This monumental wine signals a return to the more forceful, opaquely colored, powerful, brutelike-strength style for which Latour was famous during most of this century. The flirtation, intentional or otherwise, with a lighter style of wine is not apparent in this blockbuster. The 1990 exhibits tight but highly promising aromas of minerals, roasted nuts, and superripe, rich cassis fruit. It is an exceptionally powerful wine, with massive intensity, plenty of glycerin, as well as extraordinary extract and mouth-searing tannins that explode on the palate. Along with Margaux and Pétrus, Latour is a strong favorite for the wine of the vintage! A triumph! **A.M.: 2000–2035.** One of the ironies of the 1982 vintage is that among the Médoc first-growths, the 1982 Latour is the most delicious and flattering to drink as 1995 comes to a close. Its supersaturated, opaque purple/garnet color is followed by a huge bouquet that gushes from the glass, offering aromas of walnuts, minerals, and sweet jammy cassis. The wine is awesomely concentrated and full bodied, with a roasted, meaty character to its flavors. Although softer and more fleshy, it is reminiscent of the great 1970. As rich and concentrated as it is, it does not taste much different than it did from barrel, except that it is fuller and weightier. Approachable now, it will be even better with 4–5 more years of cellaring; it should last for 30 years.

The 1970 Latour is made in a more robust, less silky style than more recent vintages, but there is no doubting its extraordinary concentration. The more I taste this wine, the more I am convinced that it, along with Pétrus, is the finest wine of the vintage. Although it has taken on some amber, there is tremendous saturation and thickness to the deep ruby/garnet color. The nose offers a fragrant concoction of cedar, sweet red and black fruits, herbs, wood, and roasted nuts. In the mouth, this is a formidably concentrated, powerful wine that has shed much of its tannins, but is still extremely dense, massive, and rich. This great example of Latour is just beginning to reach full maturity. It should last for another 20–30 years.

The 1966 Latour is the wine of the vintage! Very dark ruby colored with an amber edge, the wine boasts a top-notch bouquet of leather, spices, tobacco, and ripe fruit. Quite concentrated, rich, and powerful, it has shed much of its ferocious tannin and is easily the best wine produced by Latour in the sixties, omitting, of course, the monumental 1961. **A.M.: Now–2008.** This is the first tasting where I had the 1961 from magnum and, not surprisingly, it was remarkably unevolved and backward, although no one at the tasting could ignore the lavish quantities of sweet, jammy fruit. There is great density and concentration to the wine. The bouquet was less evolved, but the presence of copious quantities of rich black fruits, damp earth, leather, and spicy wood did not go unnoticed. This full-bodied, monumental wine tastes like syrup of Cabernet. The portlike, unctuous, chewy finish is to die for. If you are fortunate enough to have magnums stashed away, no matter what your age, this wine will undoubtedly outlive you. **A.M.: Now–2040+.**

The 1949 Latour is one of those wines that can take a taster's breath away. It is a wine of extraordinary richness, yet it is perfectly balanced. It has remarkable extraction of flavor, perfect balance, layers of flavor, and a finish that is both supple and authoritative. Drink it over the next 25 years. The 1948 boasts a forceful, exotic nose of mint, cassis, walnuts, and leather that jumps from the glass. The wine exhibits impressive richness, density, and body, as well as a long, soft finish. Fully mature, it is capable of lasting another 15–25 years. Two other bottles revealed a more inky color and greater flavor depth and richness. I once had a 1945 Latour that was volatile, fading, and disappointing. Several other bottles tasted excessively tannic and ungenerous, although admirable, if only because of their size and massiveness. All other bottles have exhibited a dense, impressive garnet color with hues of purple, and no trace of amber. The bouquet revealed penetratingly rich aromas of walnuts, cassis, cedar, and herbs. In the mouth, the wine has enormous muscle and exceptional richness. While the hard, formidable tannins of the 1945 vintage were present, the lavish quantities of sweet fruit necessary for balance dominated. The best bottles of this classic wine can easily last for another 50 years.

Purchased from the Nicolas cellars, this bottle of 1928 Latour was absolute perfection. The wine exhibited an astonishing bouquet of hickory wood, smoke, walnuts, and gobs of sweet black truffle and raspberry-scented fruit. Full bodied, with layers of sweet, expansive fruit, with no hard edges, this large-scaled wine still possesses phenomenal flavor concentration, as well as marvelous aromatic and flavor dimension. One of the great wines of the century, it is a winemaking tour de force! It revealed little tannin and appeared completely mature. I found it to be in superb condition at 65 years of age, so who among us would argue that it will not last another 20–25 years? This bottle of 1926 Latour, which clearly demonstrates the fact that there are no great wines, just great bottles, was in far better shape than the 1929, and was vastly superior to a 1926 Latour I tasted in Bordeaux in March 1991. At first the aromas were muddled, but with breathing they offered up the classic Latour scents of walnuts, black fruits, herbs, and oak. Surprisingly, in the mouth the wine was muscular and rustic, with considerable tannin, plenty of richness, and amazing freshness. Fully mature, with some amber and brown hues in its color, as well as acidity in the finish, this wine should be consumed over the near term. My first experience with the

1924 Latour came at a blind tasting held several years ago in Bordeaux. The wine had been purchased by my host's father, and although cellared impeccably, it was astringent and disappointing. This example was profound, with a sensational fragrance of leafy tobacco, damp earth, cedar, and fruit. Intensely spicy for a Latour, this wine displayed crisp acidity, but little tannin and only medium body. Most of the wine's complexity and character emanated from its fragrant bouquet, which did not fade with airing. Quite impressive!

Other possible candidates: 1959, 1929 (in large formats only), 1900 (somewhat tired but still impressive in 1994)

LATOUR À POMEROL

1961 TASTED 8 TIMES, WITH CONSISTENT PERFECT RATINGS ($2,200.00) **100**
1959 TASTED 4 TIMES, WITH CONSISTENT RATINGS ($450.00) **98**
1950 TASTED 2 TIMES, WITH CONSISTENT RATINGS ($2,200.00) **96**
1948 TASTED ONCE ($2,200.00) **100**
1947 TASTED 3 TIMES, WITH INCONSISTENT RATINGS ($2,500.00) **100**

This estate of nearly 20 acres planted with 90% Merlot and 10% Cabernet Franc produced some of this century's greatest wines in 1947, 1959, and 1961. Since that time it has been content to make very good wines rather than anything profound, although readers should be aware that the 1970 and 1982 are also special.

Although the 1947 Cheval Blanc is widely considered to be the wine of the century among collectors, the 1961 Latour à Pomerol also merits a share of the title. Giving points to a wine such as this makes one think of Shakespeare's reflection that "comparisons are odious." To put it mildly, this wine is "off the charts." If I had only one Bordeaux to drink, the 1961 Latour à Pomerol would have to be at the top of my list. Given its phenomenal richness and amazing precision and balance, it can bring tears to one's eyes. Still a saturated dark-purple color with no signs of amber, orange, or rust, the nose offers extraordinarily rich, intense aromas of jammy plums, black currants, licorice, and truffles. Portlike, with remarkable viscosity and thickness, as well as a finish that lasts for more than a minute, this wine is in a class by itself. Even greater than the 1961 Pétrus and 1961 Latour (two perfect wines), it is phenomenal. Given its youthfulness (it is the least evolved wine of the vintage), it has the potential to last for another 20–30 years. The 1959 is a worthy rival to the incredible 1961 Latour à Pomerol. Although the 1959 does not possess the 1961's viscosity and unreal concentration, it does exhibit a huge nose of black truffles and sweet, jammy red and black fruits. Fully mature, full bodied, with layers of concentration, this sweet, expansive wine reveals considerable amber at the edge. It should drink well for another decade. Latour à Pomerol's 1950 is another example of an extraordinarily rich, powerful, concentrated wine. As with many of the great 1950 Pomerols, it escaped coverage by wine writers for decades. An almost youthful, opaque, garnet/purple color suggests a wine of extraordinary ripeness and extraction. The wine offers a huge, intense fragrance of overripe red and black fruits, licorice, spices, and truffles. Extremely full bodied, with an unctuously thick, rich texture (yet not heavy), this superrich, youthful wine is reminiscent of some of the right-bank 1947s. It will drink well for at least 25 more years.

Following all the accolades bestowed upon 1945, 1947, and 1949, 1948 has been a forgotten vintage. However, some great 1948s were produced, and Latour à Pomerol may be the wine of the vintage, although Pétrus, Cheval Blanc, La Mission-Haut-Brion, Latour, and Mouton-Rothschild are worthy competitors. When tasted in November 1994, Latour à Pomerol's 1948 still retained the color of a barrel sample. The wine's dark-purple color is followed by a huge nose of jammy blackberries and raspberries intertwined with scents of herbs and spice. Extremely full bodied, with remarkable concentration and a portlike texture (reminiscent of the 1961), this blockbuster wine tasted as if it were only 4–5 years old. Amazing as well as awesome! At the tasting where I had the 1947 someone said to me, "If you think the 1961 is 100 points, what do you rate the 1947?" It is every bit as rich as the 1961, and still remarkably well preserved, showing no signs of losing its fruit. Think of a wine with layer upon layer of jammy, exotic, red and black fruits intermingled with flavors of coffee, chocolate, cedar, and spices. Phenomenally opulent and chewy, with a finish that must last for 2 minutes, this powerful, unbelievably extracted wine is a worthy rival to the 1961.

LÉOVILLE-BARTON

1990 TASTED 5 TIMES SINCE BOTTLING, WITH CONSISTENT NOTES ($32.00–$40.00) **95**
1982 TASTED 8 TIMES SINCE BOTTLING, WITH CONSISTENT NOTES ($45.00–$60.00) **94**
1959 TASTED 3 TIMES, WITH CONSISTENT NOTES ($45.00–$75.00) **94**
1953 TASTED 4 TIMES, WITH CONSISTENT NOTES ($125.00–$200.00) **95**
1949 TASTED ONCE ($150.00–$305.00) **95**
1948 TASTED 3 TIMES, WITH CONSISTENT NOTES ($150.00–$300.00) **96**
1945 TASTED ONCE ($125.00) **98**

For whatever reason, Léoville-Barton rarely receives the attention it merits. Given the number of great wines that have emerged from this estate since World War II, it is a terribly underrated château. Moreover, since Anthony Barton assumed control of the property in the mid-eighties, prices have continued to be among the most sensitive and pro-consumer of any Bordeaux estate. Léoville-Barton is a wine that seems to synthesize the cedary, black curranty, full-bodied richness of Pauillac with the finesse and elegance of St.-Julien.

The 1990 is a dense, full-bodied, tannic, and concentrated wine with significant potential. It should turn out to be among the richest and most complex St.-Juliens proprietor Anthony Barton has yet fashioned. For comparative purposes, it is sweeter and more unctuous than the 1986, and more concentrated than the 1985, two other admirable vintages. A classic wine, as well as a notable bargain, it will age effortlessly. **A.M.: 1996–2020.**

The 1982 may prove to be the best Léoville-Barton made in the last 30 years. It is very concentrated as well as extremely backward and tannic. Given the wine's massive concentration, power, and body, it will not be ready to drink until the end of this decade. It has beautifully balanced oak, acidity, tannin, and ripe, red currant fruit. The bouquet is starting to emerge, but this wine remains a closed blockbuster example of the vintage. The late Ronald Barton claimed this was the greatest wine he made—what praise! **A.M.: 1998–2015.**

Léoville-Barton had a strong decade from the late forties through the fifties. The power-house 1959 is fully mature, but exhibits no signs of fading. It is large-scaled and muscular, with a huge, cedary, earthy, black fruit–scented nose, gobs of glycerin and alcohol, and a heady, spicy finish with some noticeable tannin. Will the 1982 be its contemporary counter-part? The 1953 is a seductive, voluptuously textured, gloriously fragrant and fruity claret that has admirably stood the test of time. Undoubtedly fragile from a regular bottling (as most 1953s tend to be), purchasers should consider larger-format bottles, as I am sure it would be superb.

The 1949, 1948, and 1945 Léoville-Bartons are all great efforts. The 1949 is made in the mold of the 1953, although it is a more forceful, bare-boned wine with more muscle, tannin, and body. The 1948 is an extraordinary wine from an underrated vintage. It is still extremely powerful and young, offering a classic cedary, tobacco, curranty, full-bodied richness that suggests extremely low yields and ripe fruit. The blockbuster 1945 is one of the great wines of the vintage. It possesses extraordinarily thick, massive fruit and body that stand up to the formidable tannin level. These three wines will last for two more decades.

LÉOVILLE-LAS CASES

1986 TASTED 8 TIMES SINCE BOTTLING, WITH CONSISTENT NOTES ($60.00–$75.00) **97**
1982 TASTED 14 TIMES SINCE BOTTLING, WITH CONSISTENT NOTES ($120.00–$145.00) **100**

For such a large property (209 acres) and for an estate that has made so many high-class wines since the mid-seventies, it is surprising that Léoville-Las Cases has only two entries in this list of the century's greatest Bordeaux wines. While there has been no shortage of successful vintages produced by Léoville-Las Cases, the estate was surprisingly inconsistent prior to 1975.

Michel Delon, the formidable administrator of Léoville-Las Cases, likens his 1986 to his 1966 and 1961. Having had both of those wines, I have to say the 1986 vintage is far superior. From the dense, virtually opaque, ruby/black/purple color, which offers up aromas of intense black currants and black cherries, as well as a hefty dose of toasty new oak, this beautifully crafted, full-bodied wine shows extraordinary extract, near-perfect balance, and remarkable length and persistence on the palate. With as much tannin as in any recent Léoville-Las Cases, this wine is certainly going to need a minimum of 10–15 years of cellaring. **A.M.: 1998–2030.**

The 1982 is unquestionably the greatest Léoville-Las Cases I have tasted. As fine as the 1986, 1988, 1989, and 1990 are, this is the wine to own. The color has moved from a dark, opaque ruby/purple, to a more garnet tone. The nose offers huge, still immature aromas of cassis and minerals, and that elusive lead-pencil smell that is associated more with Pauillac than with St.-Julien. There is a roasted richness to the wine, as well as tremendous viscosity and unctuosity to the chewy, superconcentrated flavors. Full bodied, and not as classically austere as purists might wish, this multidimensional, profound wine is loaded with flavor, and has a phenomenal finish. It is the essence of Léoville-Las Cases. Like many 1982s, the sweetness that resulted from such ripe grapes is displayed throughout the aromas and flavors. While drinkable now, it is still youthful and at least 4–5 years away from full maturity. It should last for 35 years.

Other possible candidates: 1953, 1900

LYNCH-BAGES

1989 TASTED 7 TIMES SINCE BOTTLING, WITH CONSISTENT NOTES ($45.00–$55.00) **96**
1970 TASTED 14 TIMES, WITH CONSISTENT NOTES ($75.00–$90.00) **95**

One of the most popular wines in Bordeaux, Lynch-Bages produces a fat, ripe, rich, easy-to-understand and -consume Pauillac that is crammed with cassis/cedary-scented fruit presented in a muscular, full-bodied format. The estate has a large vineyard of 188 acres planted with 70% Cabernet Sauvignon, 15% Merlot, 10% Cabernet Franc, and 5% Petit Verdot. Inconsistent for most of the seventies, Lynch-Bages has been particularly brilliant since 1982.

The 1989 is the finest Lynch-Bages I have tasted. Its opaque, black/purple color suggests a level of concentration one rarely sees in Bordeaux. It is a wine with extraordinary flavor extraction, huge body, high glycerin and tannin levels, and a viscous, powerful finish. The wine, which was overwhelmingly ostentatious after bottling, has closed down. This super wine needs another 3–4 years of bottle age. **A.M.: 1996–2015.**

The 1970 Lynch-Bages remains a massive, inky-colored wine with gobs of black currant, cedary, ground beef, leathery flavors and aromas. This huge, ponderous wine is still youthfully powerful, but the ferocious tannins are melting away. Although it lacks finesse and elegance, it offers an immensely enjoyable, robust, generous mouthful of hedonistic claret that will last for at least another decade. **A.M.: Now–2008.**

Other possible candidates: 1990, 1961, 1955, 1953

CHÂTEAU MARGAUX

1990 TASTED 7 TIMES SINCE BOTTLING, WITH CONSISTENT NOTES ($90.00–$120.00) **100**
1986 TASTED 12 TIMES SINCE BOTTLING, WITH CONSISTENT NOTES ($75.00–$90.00) **96+**
1985 TASTED 8 TIMES SINCE BOTTLING, WITH INCONSISTENT NOTES ($75.00–$100.00) **95**
1983 TASTED 14 TIMES SINCE BOTTLING, WITH CONSISTENT NOTES ($75.00–$85.00) **96**
1982 TASTED 20 TIMES SINCE BOTTLING, WITH CONSISTENT NOTES ($120.00–$150.00) **99**
1953 TASTED 6 TIMES, WITH CONSISTENT NOTES ($500.00) **98**
1928 TASTED 3 TIMES, WITH CONSISTENT NOTES ($1,200.00) **98**
1900 TASTED 2 TIMES, WITH CONSISTENT NOTES ($3,000.00) **100**

Off form in the decade of the sixties and seventies, Château Margaux has been one of Bordeaux's bright shining success stories of the eighties. Moreover, some of its legendary older vintages are a tribute to how long-lived a great Bordeaux can be. It can be a wine of extraordinary aromatic and flavor dimension. The large vineyard of 210 acres is planted with a high percentage of Cabernet Sauvignon (75%), followed by 20% Merlot and 5% Cabernet Franc.

More than any other recent vintage, the 1990 reminds me of what Château Margaux's classic 1953 might have tasted like at age three. Not a heavyweight in the style of their 1982, the 1990 exhibits an ethereal bouquet of flowers, cassis, smoke, new oak, and Oriental spices. The tannins are significant but tender, and the wine is expansive, with remarkable finesse, richness, and a smooth-as-silk finish. The wine's exceptional richness and harmony are hallmarks. This vintage gets my nod as the most classic example of Margaux made under the Menzelopoulos administration. Nineteen ninety is a majestic vintage for Château Margaux, as well as one of the greatest wines of this superb vintage. **A.M.: 1997–2020.**

The 1986 Margaux continues to be the most powerful, tannic, and muscular Margaux made in decades. One wonders if the 1928 or 1945 had as much power and depth as the 1986. The black/ruby/purple color reveals no sign of age. The reluctant nose offers up aromas of smoky, toasty new oak and black currants, as well as a few flowers. The wine is mammoth, with extraordinary extract, superb balance, and a frightfully tannic finish. A Margaux of immense stature, it is made in a masculine, full-bodied style that is in complete contrast to the 1990. It should prove nearly immortal in terms of aging potential, but will it have the awesome potential I first predicted? **A.M.: 2000–2050.** Every time I retaste the 1985 Margaux my evaluation becomes more enthusiastic and the point score continues to creep upward. Yes, I do believe I underestimated this wine when it was young. It continues putting on weight, displaying more richness and completeness, as well as developing that extraordinary perfume a top Margaux can achieve. The color is a healthy dark-ruby/purple, and the nose offers up scents of spring flowers, cassis, and new oak. The wine is opulent and rich, but not heavy. Given its silky texture, the 1985 Margaux is approachable, but it will not hit its plateau of maturity for another 5–6 years. As with the 1990, it may turn out to be a modern-day clone of the 1953. **A.M.: 2002–2030.** The 1983 Margaux is a breathtaking wine. The Cabernet Sauvignon grapes achieved perfect maturity in 1983, and the result is an astonishingly rich, concentrated, atypically powerful and tannic Margaux. The color is dark ruby, the aromas exude ripe cassis fruit, violets, and vanillin oakiness, and the flavors are extremely deep and long on the palate with a clean, incredibly long finish. This will certainly be a monumental wine, but it remains stubbornly backward and at least a decade away from maturity. **A.M.: 2000–2030.** The 1982 is Château Margaux at its most opulent and decadent. The opaque purple/garnet color is followed by a bouquet that soars from the glass, offering scents of roasted black currants, herbs (thyme), licorice, and spring flowers. Magnificently concentrated and expansive on the palate, this volup-tuously styled, huge, lavishly rich, overwhelming style of Château Margaux is almost too much of a good thing. Its low acidity and huge tannins in the finish make it approachable, so I would not quibble with anyone who wants to drink it. But do not forget that this wine should have at least 25–35 years of evolution. If indeed it turns out to be a clone of this estate's legendary 1900, it may have 3 to 4 times the longevity I have suggested.

The 1953 Margaux has been delicious for most of its life. Bottles from the cold, damp Paris cellars of the French wine merchant, Nicolas, have exhibited an impressively dark-ruby/purple color with only slight lightening at the edge. Its huge nose possesses rich scents of violets, sweet cassis fruit, and spices. Round and opulent, with a velvety texture and gobs of sweet, jammy fruit, this is Château Margaux at its most seductive.

Atypically powerful and masculine for a wine from this property, the deep-garnet-colored 1928 Margaux offers a floral, perfumed bouquet, superrich, muscular, tannic flavors, and great presence and length in the mouth. It is amazing how much tannin was still left after 66 years of aging. The 1928 Margaux will last for a century. The 1900 Margaux is one of this century's most renowned wines. Interestingly, it was originally thought to lack aging potential because it was so drinkable by the time it was 10 or 12 years old. The production of 1900 Margaux was in excess of 30,000 cases, which is nearly identical to what was produced in 1982, a wine with shockingly similar acidity, alcohol, and extraction levels. Will the 1982 last 100 years? The 1900 Margaux is an immortal wine largely because it is still so young and fresh, with all the nuances and complexities that wine enthusiasts hope will develop. Splendidly rich, with a perfume that must fill a room, unbelievably unctuous, opulent, and well focused, this is a winemaking tour de force. The fact that it manages to balance power and high extraction of flavor with both finesse and elegance makes it stand out as one of the most extraordinary wines I have ever tasted. Not only will this wine live for another decade, I suspect it has the potential to last for 20–30 years into the next century. A breathtaking wine!

LA MISSION-HAUT-BRION

1989 TASTED 9 TIMES SINCE BOTTLING, WITH CONSISTENT NOTES ($65.00–$90.00) **99**
1982 TASTED 14 TIMES SINCE BOTTLING, WITH CONSISTENT NOTES ($125.00–$165.00) **95**
1975 TASTED 11 TIMES, WITH CONSISTENT NOTES ($275.00–$350.00) **100**
1961 TASTED 7 TIMES, WITH CONSISTENT NOTES ($600.00) **100**
1959 TASTED 11 TIMES, WITH CONSISTENT NOTES ($475.00) **100**
1955 TASTED 13 TIMES, WITH CONSISTENT NOTES ($550.00) **100**
1953 TASTED 6 TIMES, WITH CONSISTENT NOTES ($500.00) **93**
1950 TASTED ONCE ($275.00) **95**
1949 TASTED 7 TIMES, WITH CONSISTENT NOTES ($975.00) **100**
1948 TASTED 3 TIMES, WITH CONSISTENT NOTES ($500.00) **93**
1947 TASTED 5 TIMES, WITH CONSISTENT NOTES ($975.00) **95**
1945 TASTED 7 TIMES, WITH INCONSISTENT NOTES ($1,000.00) **94**
1929 TASTED 2 TIMES, WITH CONSISTENT NOTES ($1,200.00) **97**

For much of this century La Mission-Haut-Brion produced Bordeaux's most consistently great wine. Even in off years (e.g., 1957 and 1958) this estate made amazingly fine wines. This tiny vineyard of nearly 50 acres planted with 50% Cabernet Sauvignon, 40% Merlot, and 10% Cabernet Franc, situated next to several congested apartment complexes and facing its longtime rival, Haut-Brion, produces wines of extraordinary density, richness, power, fruit, and muscle. If La Mission were to be criticized, it would be because commentators in favor of a more-polished, elegant style felt La Mission was often excessively rich and full bodied.

The 1989 La Mission-Haut-Brion is irrefutably the finest wine made at this château since 1975. Certainly it is much more "user-friendly" than the 1975. It is a thick, muscular, sensationally concentrated wine that is even bigger than its nearby sibling, Haut-Brion.

Once past the roasted cassis and smoky nose, the wine is superbly extracted with plum and tarlike flavors framed with generous quantities of new oak (100% was used). While there is a tendency to compare the 1989 with the unctuous 1982, the 1989 is even more concentrated and offers greater structure and grip. Nevertheless, it should drink well given its heady alcohol content and soft tannins. It is a formidable, probably legendary La Mission that will last for at least several decades. If you can still find it (and afford it), this is a must-purchase. **A.M.: 1998–2020.** Among this estate's wines of the last 25 years, the 1982 is the most opulent and fleshiest. Deep, dark-ruby/purple with a ripe bouquet of cassis fruit, the 1982 has finally begun to develop cedary, tobacco, leather, and cassis nuances. On the palate, the wine is crammed with rich, unctuous, berry fruit, is showing a great deal more tannin than it did several years ago, and is very full bodied and concentrated. At this stage, it looks to be in need of 2–4 more years of bottle age, but should last for at least 20–30 years. **A.M.: 1996–2010.**

The 1975 continues to demonstrate that it is one of the most extraordinary wines made at La Mission-Haut-Brion in the post–World War II era. It has a fabulous perfume of cassis fruit, minerals, licorice, truffles, and spicy oak. Unbelievably concentrated, full bodied, and powerful with no sign of age in the very dark ruby color, this massive La Mission remains extremely tannic and far from maturity. The finish must be experienced to be believed, as it must last 90 seconds or more. This is one of the most concentrated and highly extracted La Missions made in the last 20 years, and I cannot see it ever being ready to drink before the year 2000. It is a monumental effort and certainly the wine of the vintage. In terms of aging potential, it may be the wine of the decade. **A.M.: 2005–2050.**

One of the greatest 1961s, La Mission-Haut-Brion has been fabulous to drink for the last 5–10 years. Where well stored, this wine will continue to drink well for 10–20 years. More developed and drinkable than the 1959, it remains a thick, rich, superaromatic wine with a textbook Graves bouquet of tobacco, barbecued meats, minerals, spices, and sweet red and black fruits. Dense, full bodied, alcoholic, and superrich, this soft, opulently textured wine makes for a fabulous drink.

It is interesting to note that many 1959s, much like the 1982s, were maligned for lacking both acidity and aging potential. How does one explain the fact that many 1959s are less evolved, as well as richer, fresher, and more complete, than many 1961s? For example, as great as the 1961 La Mission is, the 1959 is a richer, deeper-colored, more concentrated and powerful wine. It needs at least 3–5 more years of cellaring to reach its plateau of maturity. Spicy and superconcentrated, with a dense, plummy/purple color, this young, broodingly backward, formidably endowed wine should be at its best before the end of the century and drink well for the first 20–25 years of the next millennium. Even allowing for the greatness of Haut-Brion and Mouton-Rothschild, the 1955 La Mission is the wine of the vintage. It possesses sweet aromas of cedar, cloves, smoke, and black raspberry, and rich, full-bodied, remarkably harmonious flavors that ooze with ripe fruit, glycerin, and heady alcohol. The tannin has totally melted away, and the wine reveals considerable rust at the edge, so it is unlikely that the 1955 will improve with further cellaring. There is no indication of any fragility or decline, so this wine can be safely drunk for 10–15 more years. It is an amazing, complex, superbly well-balanced La Mission-Haut-Brion! I have been told by a number of people who have followed the 1953 vintage from its youth that it drank exceptionally well in the late fifties. Apparently, it has lost none of its hedonistic, supple, explosive fruit. It will not get any better, so consumption is recommended now. It offers a delicious, smoky, berry fragrance, a silky, creamy texture, and a long, heady finish. The low acidity provides vibrance, and the tannins have melted away. Should you be fortunate enough to have the beauty cellared, drink it over the next several years. The 1950 possesses a huge nose of freshly brewed coffee, hickory wood, cedar, and chocolate. Superrich and dense, with little evidence of its age (the color is still an opaque dark garnet color), this full-bodied, concentrated wine is at its apogee. It should continue to drink well for another 15–20 years.

The 1949 exhibits an intense, singed nose of roasted herbs, smoky black currant fruit, and grilled meat aromas. Enormously rich yet sweet, soft, fat, and opulent, the fully mature 1949 La Mission is awesomely intense and long. It is a magnificent bottle of wine from the most harmonious Bordeaux vintage of the century. The 1948 offers up a powerful, roasted, rich bouquet of tobacco, ripe currancy fruit, and smoky chestnuts. It reveals no amber or brown, and has concentrated, highly extracted fruit, full body, and plenty of alcohol and tannin in the finish. The wine is clearly at its plateau of maturity and shows no signs of losing its fruit. It should last for another 10–20 years. A huge, portlike bouquet of choco-latey, cedary, earthy, plummy fruit demonstrates the extraordinary ripeness that was achieved in the 1947 vintage. Very alcoholic, powerful, and rich, but at the same time velvety and sweet, this wine was probably as close to a late-harvest La Mission-Haut-Brion as one is likely to experience. It is an exceptional wine with great flavor dimension and length. The 1945 La Mission is certainly a great wine with fabulous concentration, but also a leathery, tough, hard texture. It is very powerful, broodingly rich, and opaque, but the tannin is extremely elevated and one wonders what is going to fall away first—the fruit or the tannin? This wine still has the potential to last for another 20–25 years, and therein lies much of the mystique of this vintage.

The extraordinary 1929 vintage, which may well have been the vintage of the century, with a style that old-timers compare to modern-day 1982s, or more recently, the 1990s, produced wines that were wonderfully opulent and unctuous. Henri Woltner wrote that the 1929 La Mission drank fabulously well in 1933, yet he doubted its ability to age well. How wrong he was! Still deep garnet in color with only a trace of amber at the edge, this wine exhibits a fabulously exotic, sensual bouquet filled with aromas of tobacco, black currants, cedar, and leather. On the palate it reveals high alcohol, as well as the remarkably sweet, rich, expansive, staggering concentration of fruit necessary to stand up to the alcohol. This is a velvety, lush, full-bodied wine that is an incredible privilege to drink.

Other possible candidates: 1986, 1985, 1978, 1964

MONTROSE

1990 TASTED 8 TIMES SINCE BOTTLING, WITH CONSISTENT NOTES ($70.00–$125.00) **100**
1989 TASTED 7 TIMES SINCE BOTTLING, WITH CONSISTENT NOTES ($40.00–$50.00) **95**
1961 TASTED 4 TIMES, WITH CONSISTENT NOTES ($175.00–$225.00) **95**
1959 TASTED 3 TIMES, WITH CONSISTENT NOTES ($150.00–$200.00) **95**

There is no question that Montrose can fashion one of Bordeaux's longest-lived wines. It has a track record of producing top-notch wines in ripe vintage years such as 1959 and 1961. The fact that Montrose is so often frightfully backward and in need of 20 years of cellaring has always made it a favorite among true connoisseurs.

The 1990 Montrose is one of this century's monumental efforts. Dense black/purple-colored, with a tight yet potentially sensational bouquet of new saddle-leather, black fruits, Oriental spices, new oak, and minerals, the 1990 exhibits profound concentration of fruit, a spectacularly intense mid-palate, and massive power. One of the superstars of this superb vintage, Montrose is also one of the most concentrated, forceful, and monumental wines made in Bordeaux over recent decades. **A.M.: 2000–2045.** Save for the 1990, the 1989 is the finest Montrose since the colossal 1970. Dark ruby/purple with an intense aroma of crushed raspberries and minerals, the 1989 has a full-bodied, highly extracted feel on the palate, plus gobs of soft tannin, low acidity, and high alcohol in the long finish. Much like the 1990, there are layers of fruit and body to this multidimensional wine. **A.M.: 1998–2025.**

A stunning wine from a superb vintage, the 1961 Montrose is still in need of another 10 years of cellaring. The deep, opaque, dark ruby color, the huge bouquet of ripe cassis fruit and mineral scents, the full-bodied, dense, compelling richness and length, plus gobs of tannin, all point to a monumental bottle of wine for drinking during the first 20–30 years of the next century. **A.M.: 2000–2030.** The 1959 is a surprising clone of the 1961, with sweeter fruit, a more rustic, tannic personality, and the same enormous weight, richness, and distinctively old style found in both the 1959 and 1961. The 1959 is just reaching full maturity; it will last another 20–30 years!

Other possible candidates: 1964, 1955, and 1953 are all outstanding low- to mid-90-point wines.

MOUTON-ROTHSCHILD

1986 TASTED 9 TIMES SINCE BOTTLING, WITH CONSISTENT NOTES ($130.00–$175.00) **100**
1982 TASTED 14 TIMES SINCE BOTTLING, WITH CONSISTENT NOTES ($135.00–$175.00) **100**
1961 TASTED 8 TIMES, WITH INCONSISTENT NOTES ($750.00) **98**
1959 TASTED 11 TIMES, WITH CONSISTENT NOTES ($650.00) **100**
1955 TASTED 3 TIMES, WITH CONSISTENT NOTES ($500.00) **97**
1953 TASTED 7 TIMES, WITH INCONSISTENT NOTES ($650.00) **95**
1949 TASTED 3 TIMES, WITH INCONSISTENT NOTES ($1,500.00) **94**
1947 TASTED 9 TIMES, WITH CONSISTENT NOTES ($1,500.00) **97**
1945 TASTED 5 TIMES, WITH ONE INCONSISTENT NOTE ($2,500.00) **100**

Mouton-Rothschild can often be the most dramatic and flamboyant wine of the Médoc. The heavy reliance on Cabernet Sauvignon (85%) with tiny quantities of Merlot (8%) and Cabernet Franc (7%) in the 185-acre vineyard tends to produce powerful, nearly opaque purple wines that taste remarkably well young but close up quickly, with the wine's tannin dominating the fruit for 10–15 or more years. Examples such as the 1970 and 1982 are cases in point. The 1986 is just now beginning to shut down.

In 1986, Mouton-Rothschild produced the most profound wine of a great northern Médoc vintage. The sensational opaque black/ruby color may be even denser than that of the 1982. It requires coaxing and extended airing to bring forth the subdued bouquet of minerals, celestial black currants, smoky new oak, and spices. The wine possesses incredible concentration, full body, and fabulous length, and is—well—perfect. At present, this exemplary effort is a huge, monolithic, totally unevolved wine. **A.M.: 2005–2050.** Mouton-Rothschild's 1982, which has always been the star among the Médoc first-growths in early tastings of the vintage, is totally closed and nearly impenetrable. Still an opaque dark-purple color with no lightening at the edges, the 1982 Mouton exhibits a tight but promising bouquet of superripe black currants, minerals, roasted nuts, licorice, and spices. It needs considerable coaxing to reveal its nuances. This wine may now be one of the most backward 1982s. Enormous in the mouth, with mouth-drying tannins, and layer upon layer of sweet, superconcentrated fruit, it represents the essence of the Mouton style. This enormous wine is at least 10–15 years away from hitting its plateau of maturity. The finish is all youthful power and tannin. It remains one of the most remarkable young wines I have ever tasted, but I am beginning to think I will be an old man before it is fully ready to drink. It should last for at least 50 years. Could this be another 1945?

I have found the 1961 Mouton-Rothschild to be distressingly variable in quality, much like the consistently inconsistent 1970. At its best the wine is a great Mouton. Huge, cedary, cassis, lead pencil, menthollike aromas soared from the glass. The black/purple color revealed no signs of lightening or amber at the edge. Full bodied, rich, and superintense, this was a profound bottle of 1961 Mouton that would have stood up against the compelling 1959. I am always blown away by the 1959 Mouton, one of the three greatest Moutons made in the last 36 years (1982 and 1986 being the others). Every time I have this wine it is undeniable that Mouton made a richer, more persuasive wine in 1959 than in 1961. Astonishingly young and unevolved, with a black/purple color, the wine exhibits a youthful nose of cassis, minerals, and new oak. Exceptionally powerful and superextracted, with the fruit supported by high levels of tannin and some lusty quantities of alcohol, this mammoth, full-bodied Mouton-Rothschild should continue to evolve for another 20–30 years. It may well be a 100-year wine!

The 1955 should be a vintage to buy at auction, as I suspect the price is more reasonable than what such acclaimed vintages as 1959 and 1961 fetch. The color reveals no amber or rust, only a slight lightening of intensity at the edge. The nose offers up that explosive Mouton perfume of mint, leather, cassis, black olives, and lead pencil. In the mouth, there is stunning concentration, magnificent extraction of fruit, and plenty of tannin in the long finish. The wine still tastes remarkably young and could easily last another 20–30 years. Amazing! I remember a friend of mine decanting a magnum of the 1953 and sticking it under my nose to share with me the incredible bouquet. In addition to the exotic aromas of soy sauce, new saddle leather, cassis, herbs, and spices, the 1953 offers a deep ruby color with some amber at the edge. Sweet and fat, with voluptuously textured fruit, this low-acid wine has no noticeable tannin. While it may be living dangerously, it is a decadent treat if it is drunk immediately after decanting.

Nineteen forty-nine was always considered to be the late baron's favorite vintage. While I find it a formidable Mouton, I have a preference for the 1945, 1947, 1959, 1982, and 1986. The bouquet offers copious amounts of sweet, ripe cassis fruit, herbs, spicy oak, and a touch of coffee and cinnamon. Medium bodied, with moderate tannin still noticeable, this compact, dark garnet, opaquely colored wine possesses superb concentration and a remarkably long finish. It appears to be fully mature, yet the balance, length, and tannin level suggest this wine could last for another 20 years. Most 1947 Médocs have a tendency to be attenuated, with excessive volatile acidity. Many have long ago dropped their fruit. Most knowledgeable observers agree that the greatest success in the Médoc was the Mouton-Rothschild. The wine reveals a spectacularly opaque, garnet color, and thick-looking, fruity flavors that display coffee, chocolate, mint, and black currant notes. Amazingly full bodied, with a fleshy, high-alcohol finish, this decadent, succulent Mouton-Rothschild is one of the most powerful wines I have ever tasted. It should continue to drink well for another 10–15 years. The 1945 Mouton has always had a special place in the hearts of those who have tasted a well-stored bottle. I remember first having it in 1985 at a friend's birthday celebration. At that time, I gave it a perfect score. Several times since it has performed less spectacularly. In two recent tastings the wine displayed a huge, flamboyant, in-your-face bouquet of mint, Asian spices, ginger, and gobs of sweet black fruits. It was like eating chocolate-covered raspberries and raisins. Supersweet, unbelievably rich, and less structured and tannic than I remember, this gloriously opulent wine could easily have been a Pomerol except for its haunting bouquet.

Other possible candidates: 1929 (once sublime, now faded in the standard bottle size)

PALMER

1989 TASTED 6 TIMES SINCE BOTTLING, WITH CONSISTENT NOTES ($50.00–$75.00) **96**
1983 TASTED 14 TIMES SINCE BOTTLING, WITH CONSISTENT NOTES ($70.00–$90.00) **97**
1966 TASTED 12 TIMES, WITH CONSISTENT NOTES ($275.00–$325.00) **96**
1961 TASTED 9 TIMES, WITH CONSISTENT NOTES ($350.00–$450.00) **99**
1945 TASTED 2 TIMES, WITH CONSISTENT NOTES ($500.00–$625.00) **97**
1928 TASTED 3 TIMES, WITH INCONSISTENT NOTES ($500.00–$600.00) **96**

This 111-acre vineyard planted with 55% Cabernet Sauvignon, a whopping 40% Merlot (atypically high for a Médoc estate and the key to Palmer's succulence), and 5% Cabernet Franc produces 12,000–13,000 cases of wine. It has always been one of the most popular wines of Bordeaux as well as an insider's wine. Why? Palmer often performs at a supersecond or first-growth level, making wines of extraordinary fragrance and opulent richness that recalls the finest wines of St.-Émilion and Pomerol. No doubt the huge percentage of Merlot utilized in the blend contributes to the precociousness and immense fragrance of this wine.

Palmer has done a magnificent job with their 1989, which continues to be a wine of immense seduction. The expansive, rich, fat texture owes its opulence to the high percentage of Merlot used by this property. Opaque deep ruby/purple, this full-bodied, satiny wine has considerable alcoholic clout, is low in acidity, but is splendidly concentrated and abundantly full of velvety tannins. It will be fascinating to see if this wine ultimately rivals the great Palmers made in 1983, 1970, 1966, and 1961. This is a thrilling 1989! **A.M.: Now– 2012.** One of the superb wines of the vintage, the 1983 Palmer continues to display a saturated purple/garnet color, and an intense perfume of jammy black fruits, smoked meats, flowers, cedar, and Asian spices. Superconcentrated, powerful, and full bodied, this huge, unctuously textured wine is approaching its plateau of maturity. Because of the high Merlot content it can easily be drunk now, yet promises to last for another 20–25 years. I remain convinced that the 1983 will be the finest Palmer since the great 1961.

The 1966 continues to be one of the greatest examples of Palmer I have ever tasted. It is almost atypical for the 1966 vintage, which produced so many austere, angular wines. Not only rich and full, it is also delicate and loaded with complexity and finesse. This wine gets my nod as one of the best of the vintage, rivaled only by Latour and Lafleur. The haunting bouquet is similar to the 1961's. It reveals a plummy, mulberrylike fruitiness, exotic spices, licorice, and a hint of truffles. Medium bodied, with a velvety richness, it has a long, ripe, lush finish, and enough grip and focus to continue to drink well for another decade. **A.M.: Now–2000.** The 1961 Palmer has long been considered a legend from this vintage, and its reputation is well deserved. The wine is at its apogee and has an extraordinary, sweet, complex nose with aromas of flowers, cassis, toast, and minerals. It is intensely concentrated, offering a cascade of lavishly ripe, full-bodied, opulent fruit, soft tannins, and a voluptuous finish. This is a decadent Palmer, unparalleled in quality with the exception of Palmer's 1983 and 1989.

Palmer's 1945 (never tasted stateside) is one of the few 1945s that can be called exceptionally opulent, superrich, and fat in its chewy, nearly overripe fruit. It is a rich, succulent, decadently fruity, alcoholic wine that remains in top condition. The 1928 is another extraordinary wine from that vintage that has taken 50+ years to reach its plateau of maturity. Pity the consumers who purchased a wine from this vintage in the thirties thinking they would drink it within their lifetime! The wine exhibits considerable rust and amber at the edge, as well as an intensely fragrant fruitcake, cedar, gingery nose, remarkably chewy, ripe flavors, and some of the vintage's renowned austerity and tannic bite. Where it has been well stored, it remains a terrific example of the vintage.

Other possible candidates: 1970, 1959, 1949, 1948

PÉTRUS

1990 TASTED 2 TIMES SINCE BOTTLING, WITH CONSISTENT NOTES ($300.00–$350.00) **100**
1989 TASTED 2 TIMES SINCE BOTTLING, WITH CONSISTENT NOTES ($350.00–$400.00) **98**
1982 TASTED 10 TIMES SINCE BOTTLING, WITH INCONSISTENT NOTES ($475.00–$625.00) **97**
1975 TASTED 9 TIMES, WITH CONSISTENT NOTES ($420.00–$600.00) **98**
1970 TASTED 13 TIMES, WITH INCONSISTENT NOTES ($700.00–$750.00) **99+**
1964 TASTED 8 TIMES, WITH CONSISTENT NOTES ($800.00–$900.00) **97**
1961 TASTED 12 TIMES, WITH CONSISTENT NOTES ($2,500.00) **100**

1950 TASTED 3 TIMES, WITH CONSISTENT NOTES ($2,200.00) **100**
1949 TASTED 3 TIMES, WITH INCONSISTENT NOTES ($2,400.00) **95**
1948 TASTED ONCE ($1,200.00) **95**
1947 TASTED 11 TIMES, WITH CONSISTENT NOTES ($3,500.00) **100**
1945 TASTED 2 TIMES, WITH CONSISTENT NOTES ($3,500.00) **98+**

This small 20-acre vineyard produces 4,000 cases of what can often be one of the richest, most unctuously textured wines of Bordeaux. Made from over 95% Merlot and aged in 100% new oak, it is Bordeaux's most expensive red wine. Pétrus has turned out numerous legendary vintages, all of them in the post–World War II era. It should be noted that Pétrus made only one great wine during the decade of the fifties (1950). While the estate appeared to have lightened its style in the late seventies and the decade of the eighties, the 1989 and 1990 are reassuringly blockbuster wines.

The 1990 is a majestic return to the massive, unctuous, viscous, profoundly concentrated style of vintages such as 1947, 1948, 1950, 1961, 1970, 1971, and 1975. The 1990 is a remarkably dense, rich, concentrated wine with tons of tannin, gobs of glycerin, and exotic flavors and scents of coffee, tobacco, herbs, and superripe berries. It is the most powerful, intense, and concentrated Pétrus to emerge from this estate since 1961. I could not bring myself to spit this one out. Another legend! **A.M.: 2000–2025.**

By cutting off nearly half the crop in July and August, by deciding to pick early (September 5 and 6, and the balance on September 14), and by eliminating anything less than perfect from the final blend, Christian Moueix authoritatively demonstrated that Pétrus would spare no expense to produce a profound wine in 1989. A compelling wine, it resembles the 1982 in many respects, but is more concentrated. Moueix thinks it is the finest Pétrus since the 1947 (I say the 1990 is). Black/purple, with the intense, dramatic bouquet of superconcentrated black currants and plums, this wine makes an unforgettable palate impression. It possesses extraordinary extraction of fruit, a dense, huge, massive texture, and a fabulous black fruit–scented nose that is gently touched by aromas of new oak, mocha, and spice. Almost thick, this wine is also extremely tannic. My guess is that despite its high alcohol and low acidity, it will need at least 10 years after bottling to fully reveal its considerable potential. If you have not realized it by now, Pétrus is making a wine to drink later and last longer than any of the first-growths in the Médoc. **A.M.: 2000–2035.** So hauntingly perfect and phenomenally concentrated from cask, only to taste awkward and funky during its first 5–6 years in the bottle, the 1982 Pétrus is showing signs of living up to the uncontrolled hype I heaped on it. At least 7–10 years from its apogee, the wine's dense, saturated ruby/purple color displays no signs of amber. The nose is beginning to offer up intense aromas of ripe black fruits, smoked nuts, coffee, and vanilla. Layers of thick, viscous fruit are buttressed by huge amounts of body, glycerin, and tannin. Despite its size, the wine has a certain polished elegance that partisans of the Médoc will find admirable. This large-scaled, rich, highly structured Pétrus is made for the long haul. Lamentably, as marvelous as it is, I doubt it will live up to the perfect rating I bestowed upon it in my early reviews, but my optimism for it is returning.

One of the best wines of the vintage as well as the most concentrated and tannic Pétrus of the seventies, the 1975 is a blockbuster wine, opulently rich, still broodingly dark in color, and massive. This wine has layers of sweet, ripe black currant fruit, awesome extract, huge tannins, and an explosive finish—all suggesting decades of life. It is a monumental Pétrus that will keep for 50+ years. **A.M.: 2000–2050.** For much of the last two decades the 1971 Pétrus outshined the 1970. The former wine was more flattering, whereas the 1970 was a behemoth—huge, phenomenally extracted, but tight and impenetrable. Over the last 5 years the greatness of the 1970 Pétrus has become more apparent. In fact, with a few more years of cellaring it will undoubtedly achieve perfection. The opaque dark-ruby/garnet color is followed by a nose revealing huge, sweet scents of truffles, licorice, black fruits, and smoky oak. Phenomenally concentrated and remarkably fresh and young, this massively endowed wine is oozing with extract and potential. It promises to last for another 30 years. This is a legendary Pétrus in the making! Deep, dark ruby/garnet-colored, with a hint of orange and rust at the edge, the 1964 Pétrus offers a huge, smoky, roasted bouquet of jammy fruit, coffee, and mocha. This huge, massively endowed wine is packed with alcohol, glycerin, and high tannin. There is stupendous extraction of fruit and amazing length. The only criticism is that it is perhaps too big and robust for its own good. Lucky owners of well-stored bottles are advised to cellar it for a few more years. As they say, it's a tough job, but someone's got to do it! The 1961 Pétrus is consistently a perfect wine. Fully mature, and more evolved than several of its neighbors (e.g., the 1961 Latour à Pomerol), it offers a huge, sweet nose of ginger, mint, exotic spices, and gobs of jammy black fruits. Its extraordinary viscosity, sweetness of fruit, and heady alcohol level, as well as its remarkable extract, make for one of the most sumptuous, hedonistic bottles of wine anybody could ever consume. The color is revealing noticeable amber/rust, and the tannin has melted away. This decadent bottle of Pomerol is at its peak of maturity; drink it over the next 10–15 years.

It was the extraordinary 1950 Pétrus, along with the 1950 Lafleur, first served to me years ago by Jean-Pierre Moueix, that made me realize how spectacular this vintage must have been in Pomerol. The wine is still a young, mammothly constituted Pétrus that is less evolved than more-recent knockout vintages such as 1961. Massive and rich, with spectacular color saturation and the sweet, unctuous texture Pétrus obtains in ripe years, this wine will last for another 20–30 years.

While variable, the 1949 has always been a huge, thick, chewy, immense wine without the unctuosity and portlike quality of the 1947 or 1950. The first time I tasted it a decade ago it seemed to be chunky and one-dimensional, but enormously rich. Since then the wine has begun to display the huge, exotic fleshiness of Pétrus, as well as marvelously pure plum and black cherry fruit flavored with mocha and coffee. It is developing well and remains remarkably youthful for a 46-year-old wine. Nineteen forty-eight is another one of those vintages that was largely ignored by the press. Shrewd consumers would be smart to take a look at well-stored bottles of 1948s that might appear in the marketplace. In the past I have reported on some of the other great 1948s, such as Vieux Château Certan, La Mission-Haut-Brion, and Cheval Blanc, but the 1948 Pétrus has fooled me completely in blind tastings. The nose of cedar, leather, herbs, and cassis suggested to me that this was a first-growth Pauillac. The color is still dense, with only a moderate orange hue at the edge. The wine is rich, more austere and lineal than usual, but full bodied, with considerable flavor, and a spicy, moderately tannic finish. It has peaked, but is clearly capable of lasting another 10–15 years. The 1947 Pétrus is the most decadent wine of the century. While not as portlike as the 1947 Cheval Blanc, it is a massive, unctuously textured, viscous wine with amazing power, richness, and sweet fruit. The nose explodes from the glass, offering jammy fruit, smoke, and buttery caramel scents. The wine's viscosity is reminiscent of 10-W-40 motor oil. It is so sweet, thick, and rich one suspects a spoon could stand upright. The wine is loaded with dreamlike quantities of fruit, as well as high alcohol, but there is no noticeable tannin. While drinkable now, given its amazing fruit extract and high levels of glycerin and alcohol, it is capable of lasting two more decades. While the 1947 Pétrus is a big, juicy, succulent, fruity wine, the 1945 remains a backward, tannic colossus needing another 5–10 years of cellaring. The color reveals more purple hues than the 1947, and the nose offers aromas of black fruits, licorice, truffles, and smoked meat. Massively constituted, with formidably high tannin and extract levels, this sleeping giant may evolve into another perfect example of Pétrus.

Other possible candidates: 1971

PICHON-LONGUEVILLE–COMTESSE DE LALANDE

1986 TASTED 7 TIMES SINCE BOTTLING, WITH CONSISTENT NOTES ($40.00–$60.00) **96**
1982 TASTED 25 TIMES SINCE BOTTLING, WITH CONSISTENT NOTES ($110.00–$165.00) **99– 100**

One of the most consistent wines made in Bordeaux since the late seventies, Pichon-Longueville–Comtesse de Lalande (called Pichon-Lalande by its admirers) is unquestionably one of France's most popular wines. It combines wonderful finesse, complexity, and supple richness with adequate availability and early drinkability. Although it only has two candidates among this century's greatest Bordeaux wines, the estate has produced a bevy of delicious, well-made wines. Pichon-Lalande produces approximately 25,000 cases of wine from its 150-acre vineyard planted with 50% Cabernet Sauvignon, 35% Merlot, 8% Petite Verdot, and 7% Cabernet Franc.

The 1986 is the most tannic as well as the largest-framed Pichon-Lalande in over three decades. Whether it will ultimately eclipse the 1982 is doubtful, but it will be longer-lived. Dark ruby/purple, with a tight yet profound bouquet of cedar, black currants, spicy oak, and minerals, this full-bodied, deeply concentrated, exceptionally well balanced wine is, atypically, too brawny and big to drink young. **A.M.: Now–2015.** I have drunk the 1982 Pichon-Lalande as often as any 1982 Bordeaux. With over two dozen tasting notes since its bottling, it is amazing that my scores have always been in the upper 90s. In short, Pichon-Lalande (or any Pauillac) could not be much better than this full-bodied, unctuous, super-complex, concentrated wine. From its explosive bouquet of cedar, black currants, herbs, and spices, to its layer upon layer of rich fruit that coats the mouth, this is an awesome bottle of wine. It has been sensational since it was bottled. Will it ever close up or begin to lose some fruit? There is some lightening at the edge (something that is not apparent in other 1982 Pauillacs), but keep in mind that this is the only Pauillac with significant quantities (about 40%) of Merlot, which accounts for the faint amber edge. This wine should continue to drink well for at least 10–15 more years. Although astronomically expensive and virtually impossible to find, this is what great Bordeaux is all about! The $110-a-case future price sure looks great today!

Other possible candidates: 1989 and 1983 are strong candidates, but 1961, 1959, 1953, and 1945 are now in decline.

LE PIN

1990 TASTED 4 TIMES SINCE BOTTLING, WITH CONSISTENT NOTES ($125.00–$180.00) **95**
1983 TASTED 9 TIMES SINCE BOTTLING, WITH CONSISTENT NOTES ($200.00–$300.00) **98**
1982 TASTED 7 TIMES SINCE BOTTLING, WITH CONSISTENT NOTES ($200.00–$350.00) **99**

The Thienpont family, owners of the well-known Pomerol estate, Vieux Château Certan, have created a minitreasure with this 3-acre vineyard planted with 88% Merlot and 12% Cabernet Franc that only produces a microscopic 500–700 cases of wine. They are obviously attempting to fashion a wine with Pétrus-like richness and intensity. Their debut release, the 1979, as well as subsequent vintages, has been admired by lovers of lavishly rich, intensely oaky, unctuously textured wines. Le Pin is a candidate for the most exotic and decadent wine of Bordeaux.

The 1990 Le Pin is a well-focused, richly extracted wine, with impressive persistence and depth. It also exhibits a flamboyant nose of exotic spices, black fruits, and smoky new oak. The voluptuous texture that has turned this wine into a cult item is present, along with a smashingly intense, opulent finish with enough tannin to suggest that 10–15 years of aging is possible. But who can resist it now? This is the finest Le Pin since the 1982 and 1983.

And remember, I have a tendency to underestimate this wine when it is young! **A.M.: Now–2005.**

The 1983 Le Pin offers a huge, soaring bouquet of smoky oak, spices, and sweet fruits. This splendidly opulent, voluptuously textured wine reveals the gorgeous sweetness and ripeness of fruit so much a hallmark of this estate. The 1983 Le Pin has low acidity, gobs of glycerin, superb extraction of fruit, and a sensational finish. It appeared lighter in its youth, with less aromatic and flavor dimension. Now that it has reached its plateau of maturity, it is one of my two or three favorite examples of this exotically styled, kinky wine. Drink it over the next 7–8 years. The 1982 is an example of the weight and richness Le Pin can gain with aging. While never a light wine in its youth, it now exhibits a portlike quality. Bordeaux vintages such as 1961, 1959, and 1947 offer the same sort of viscous, thick texture and lavish quantities of sweet fruit. The bouquet has moved from pure sweet black fruits and toasty new oak, to a complex set of aromas ranging from coffee, mocha, and chocolate, to herbs and blackberries. In the mouth, there is extraordinary depth of fruit, unbelievable viscosity and richness, and an amazingly sweet, opulent finish. Wow! This is an extraordinary 1982 for drinking now. It should continue to drink well for at least 7–8 more years.

TROPLONG-MONDOT

1990   TASTED 4 TIMES SINCE BOTTLING, WITH CONSISTENT NOTES ($25.00–$35.00) **94**

I hope those who followed my advice on the 1990 Troplong-Mondot realize it is a candidate for one of the best wines of the century. Troplong-Mondot is one of St.-Émilion's hot properties, having made terrific wines since 1988. Madame Fabre-Valette fashions an atypically rich, concentrated yet strikingly elegant, complex wine from her 75-acre vineyard planted with 65% Merlot, 15% Cabernet Sauvignon, 10% Cabernet Franc, and 10% Malbec. Among all the potential candidates for the century's greatest wine, the 1990 remains one of the best values—assuming it can still be found in the marketplace.

The awesome 1990 Troplong-Mondot exhibits an impressively opaque dark-ruby/purple color and a rich, penetrating bouquet of minerals, herbs, anise, spicy new oak, and black fruits. Fabulously concentrated, there is a lovely combination of power, finesse, and graceful, medium- to full-bodied, lavishly endowed, chewy, focused flavors. The acidity is sound and the wine reveals moderate, sweet tannins. It is considerably richer and more tannic than the outstanding 1989. Drink it over the next 10–20 years.

TROTANOY

1982   TASTED 10 TIMES SINCE BOTTLING, WITH CONSISTENT NOTES ($175.00–$225.00) **96**
1975   TASTED 13 TIMES, WITH CONSISTENT NOTES ($95.00–$125.00) **94**
1970   TASTED 9 TIMES, WITH CONSISTENT NOTES ($125.00–$250.00) **96**
1961   TASTED 7 TIMES, WITH CONSISTENT NOTES ($650.00) **98**
1945   TASTED 4 TIMES, WITH INCONSISTENT NOTES ($650.00–$900.00) **95**

This tiny 21-acre vineyard planted with 90% Merlot and 10% Cabernet Franc produces just over 3,500 cases. It remains to be seen whether Trotanoy will reach the heights and consistency it did during the decades of the forties, fifties, sixties, and seventies, as the 1982 appears to be the last great Trotanoy. Trotanoy can easily be confused with Pétrus, although over the last 10–15 years the strength and richness of Pétrus have eclipsed Trotanoy.

The 1982, which is just reaching full maturity, exhibits a dense, saturated ruby/purple color, and a huge bouquet filled with aromas of jammy, curranty fruit, spicy oak, chocolate, coffee, and herbs. Massive yet unctuous and velvety-textured, this superconcentrated, precociously styled Trotanoy is a thrilling wine. It should last for at least another 15–20 years.

What a shame that it represents the last of the great Trotanoys. Perhaps when the average age of the vineyard increases (Trotanoy had significant replanting in the early and mid-seventies), the wine's richness will increase.

The 1975 Trotanoy is a great success. It is very concentrated with broad, deep, rich, long, ripe fruity flavors, and a bouquet that combines scents of tobacco, toffee, leather, and mulberries to reveal sensationally complex aromas. Fleshy, full bodied, and velvety, this is an excellent Trotanoy for drinking over the next decade. **A.M.: Now–2005.** When I first had the 1970 Trotanoy at Bordeaux tastings in the mid-seventies, it was often ranked first, largely because of its massive power, richness, and ferocious tannin level. The wine has barely changed. Although the tannin remains high, the fruit is as rich, highly extracted, and impressive as it was 20 years ago. Displaying a youthful, opaque, garnet/plum color, and a moderately intense nose of truffles, minerals, earth, sweet cassis, and caramel, this wine is full bodied, dense, and rich, with massive extract. Consumers with well-stored bottles are advised to wait 2–3 more years before opening a bottle; it will last for another 25–30 years.

The 1961, which I have consistently rated between 96 and 100, is unquestionably the greatest Trotanoy in the post–World War II era. The wine's saturated, thick, inky, plummy color reveals slight amber at the edge. The magnificent bouquet of jammy black raspberries, smoke, cloves, tar, and caramel is a knockout. With dense, unctuous, thick, sweet, rich flavors loaded with glycerin and extract, this massive, full-bodied, stunningly rich, fully mature wine is capable of lasting for another 10–20 years.

Nearly black in color, the 1945 Trotanoy offers a reticent but emerging nose of minerals, licorice, and jammy plums. The wine is nearly impenetrable as well as frightfully tannic. With such amazing concentration and extract levels, there still remains the possibility that everything will weld together. If so, this wine could easily live for 100 years. It is not yet ready for prime-time drinking! People fortunate enough to own well-stored bottles should either decant it 7–8 hours before drinking, wait another 15–20 years, or enroll their children in a wine-appreciation course. Amazing!

Other possible candidates: 1971

VIEUX CHÂTEAU CERTAN

1990	TASTED 4 TIMES SINCE BOTTLING, WITH CONSISTENT NOTES ($45.00–$60.00)	**94**
1952	TASTED 3 TIMES SINCE BOTTLING, WITH CONSISTENT NOTES ($125.00–$175.00)	**94**
1950	TASTED 5 TIMES, WITH CONSISTENT NOTES ($175.00–$200.00)	**97**
1948	TASTED 8 TIMES, WITH CONSISTENT NOTES ($175.00–$250.00)	**98**
1947	TASTED 7 TIMES, WITH CONSISTENT NOTES ($275.00–$400.00)	**97**
1945	TASTED 2 TIMES, WITH CONSISTENT NOTES ($300.00–$450.00)	**98–100**
1928	TASTED ONCE ($350.00–$425.00)	**96**

From the end of World War II until the early fifties, Vieux Château Certan was producing wines of extraordinary quality, surpassed in consistency, richness, and complexity by only a handful of Bordeaux estates. The property slumped in the late sixties and seventies, but rebounded (although they are not making the huge, massive wines of the past) in the early eighties. Situated next to Pétrus on the Pomerol plateau, this 34-acre vineyard is planted with an unusually high percentage of Cabernet Sauvignon (20%), with 5% Malbec, 25% Cabernet Franc, and 50% Merlot (atypically low for most Pomerols). This is one of the great wines to look for at auction in the following vintages.

Deeply colored, with a marvelously fragrant nose of herbs, berry fruit, oak, and exotic spices, the compelling 1990 Vieux Château Certan displays surprising opulence and ripeness, more unctuosity than usual, as well as admirable structure and definition. The acid is lower, yet the extract level much higher in the 1990 than in the 1989. This is a superlative, medium- to full-bodied, multidimensional wine. **A.M.: Now–2010.**

The 1952 Vieux Château Certan is in extraordinary condition. The wine, a sleeper, was sweet and cedary, with a huge, almost hickory, roasted, smoky nose that was reminiscent of a top Graves. Full bodied, with glorious concentration and richness, this wine still possesses plenty of tannin and youthfulness. It will easily keep for another 10–20 years. The 1950 is a remarkably rich, still youthful wine from this fabulous vintage in Pomerol. The color remains an amazing garnet/purple, and the nose offers sensationally ripe, chocolatey, cassis aromas intertwined with herbs, licorice, Asian spices, and coffee. Extremely full bodied with portlike viscosity similar to the 1947, this blockbuster wine must be one of the least-known profound wines of the century.

The 1948 Vieux Château Certan is another profoundly great wine from the forgotten vintage of the forties. I have tasted this wine four times in the last year and it was exceptional in each tasting. The opaque dark-purple/garnet color is followed by a huge, exotic nose of caramel, sweet cassis, soy sauce, walnuts, and coffee. Thick, chewy, fabulously concentrated flavors with low acidity and high tannin coat the palate. There is amazing glycerin and an elevated alcohol level to this superconcentrated wine. Although fully mature, it exhibits no signs of decline and will easily last for 15–20 more years. Remarkable! A dazzling wine, which I have tasted a number of times over the years, the 1947 Vieux Château Certan is typical of so many 1947 Pomerols. Its thick, viscous, portlike style and texture are the hallmarks of this vintage. More advanced than the 1948, it reveals smoky, meaty, truffle, and black currant aromas, as well as massive, chewy flavors loaded with glycerin, extract, and alcohol. It exhibits more amber at the edge than the 1948, but—wow—what a mouthful of wine! Like many 1947 Pomerols, its unctuosity and thickness make me wonder if a spoon would stand up in the glass without any support. Drink it over the next 10–12 years. Tasted twice and rated highly each time, the 1945 is an exceptional winemaking effort in what can be a frightfully tannic vintage. It exhibits a dark, murky, plum color with little garnet at the edge. It also possesses a huge nose of smoked meats, black raspberries, plums, licorice, and tar. Dense, chewy, and powerful, with gobs of tannin and amazing fruit extraction, this full-throttle wine must be at its plateau of maturity, yet I see no reason why it cannot last for two more decades.

Dark garnet, with noticeable rust/amber at the edge, the 1928 Vieux Château Certan offers up spicy, peppery, herbaceous, sweet, caramel, and black fruit aromas, and possesses huge, chewy flavors, copious quantities of tannin, full body, and a rustic, astringent finish. Still in superb condition, it is capable of lasting 10–20 more years.

Other possible candidates: 1959

MISCELLANEOUS OTHER CANDIDATES

There are at least a dozen other wines that should be considered for inclusion in this list of the century's greatest red Bordeaux. Half of the wines come from the tiny property of Latour-Haut-Brion, which for some time has been the second wine of La Mission-Haut-Brion. Anyone who has tasted the 1982 (rated 94), 1975 (97), 1961 (95), 1959 (97), 1955 (94), 1949 (98), and the inconsistent but potentially superb 1947 (94) recognizes that this estate, now largely forgotten by the Bordeaux cognoscenti, has produced some extraordinarily rich, beefy, full-bodied, powerhouse wines that have admirably stood the test of time. Moreover, since Latour-Haut-Brion has always been eclipsed by the justifiable prestige accorded to its neighbors, La Mission-Haut-Brion and Haut-Brion, it can be purchased for a reasonable price at auction.

Another estate relegated to the background given how many excellent Pauillacs are produced each year is Château Pontet-Canet. Since the Tesseron family acquired this vast estate situated adjacent to Mouton-Rothschild, the quality has increased, particularly since the late eighties. Pontet-Canet unquestionably produced three of the greatest wines of the century. The 1961 remains an extraordinary wine. The 1945 is a classic example of both the vintage and Pauillac. The 1929, although now beginning to fade, was for many years a decadently sweet, opulent Pauillac. If readers have the opportunity to purchase any of these older vintages (provided they have emerged from cold, damp cellars), I am sure they can be bought for reasonable prices given the status of this château today.

A Bordeaux estate that is beginning to enjoy a renaissance is Château Cantemerle. The high quality of recent vintages such as 1983 and 1989 has provided considerable excitement. The largely forgotten 1953 and 1949 Cantemerles are two of Bordeaux's greatest efforts. It has been many years since I have tasted these wines. I suspect the 1953 is in decline, at least in regular bottles, but well-stored magnums and larger formats probably remain riveting. The 1949 is also an extraordinary wine. I suspect well-stored examples are as hauntingly perfumed and as suave, velvety, and rich as they were 20 years ago.

A relative newcomer to Bordeaux's scene, Le Tertre-Roteboeuf has made two of this century's greatest wines. This tiny 11-acre estate, run by one of the most obsessive proprietors in Bordeaux, is aiming for a style of wine that can match the extract and intensity of such great right-bank wines as Pétrus, Lafleur, L'Évangile, and Certan de May. Both the 1989 (rated 94) and 1990 (96) are extraordinary wines, but Bordeaux traditionalists are reluctant to give this property the credit it deserves.

THE CENTURY'S GREATEST VINTAGES

1900—A huge crop of overripe, low-acid, opulent, full-bodied wines that were considered high in alcohol and extremely fruity, rich, and precocious.

1910–1919—no candidates

1920—A small crop of concentrated, moderately tannic wines that I have tasted only rarely over recent years. The wines are nearly impossible to find.

1921—A classic, hot, dry year with the wines having opulent, roasted personalities, much like modern-day vintages such as 1959, 1982, 1989, and 1990. Of all the famous 1921s I have not found any that have stood the test of time and merit purchasing, although I suspect large-format bottles of Cheval Blanc could prove interesting.

1926—A sleeper vintage that clearly has held up far better than the more highly praised 1921s and 1929s. Recent tastings of top châteaux have revealed intense, tannic, concentrated, powerful wines.

1928—The slowest-evolving vintage of the century, even more so than 1945 and 1975, the top 1928s can be glorious today. Remarkably, it is difficult to find a wine that is past its prime—just wines that still taste excessively tannic!

1929—Splendidly opulent, rich, velvety-textured wines thought to be too tasty when young to last. Old-timers who remember them remain astonished that they held their spectacular fruit and intensity for nearly 50 years. This may well have been the most seductive vintage of the century, but it is hard to find bottles that are still intact, although if I had the financial inclination to do so, I would always put my money on the 1929 La Mission-Haut-Brion, Latour, and Mouton-Rothschild—three candidates for the wine of the century.

1930–1939—no candidates

1945—A historical year for many reasons, but certainly for the Bordelais. While the vintage did produce examples of excessively tannic, harsh, frightfully hard wines that remain so today, there are enough monumental efforts in 1945 that this vintage remains one of the century's hallmarks.

1947—An extremely hot year and harvest created enough problems to spell disaster for a number of properties, particularly in the Médoc. Nevertheless, even the Médoc produced some extraordinary 1947s, notably Mouton-Rothschild and Calon-Ségur. In Pomerol and St.-Émilion it was an extraordinary vintage, with such wines as Cheval Blanc, Pétrus,

Lafleur, and L'Evangile among the most concentrated and portlike examples I have ever tasted. They remain extraordinary, with a sweetness and opulence of fruit to their personalities that is unrivaled by any other vintage this century. In Graves, La Mission-Haut-Brion is fabulous.

1948—Largely forgotten in the late forties, sandwiched between so many other more dramatic vintages, 1948 has matured surely and slowly. There are enough profound wines —Latour, Mouton-Rothschild, Cheval Blanc, Pétrus, Vieux Château Certan, La Mission-Haut-Brion, and Léoville-Barton—for 1948 to qualify as the most underrated and undervalued great vintage of the century.

1949—For my palate, 1949 produced the most harmonious and classic Bordeaux wines of the century. There are some disappointments—Lafite-Rothschild and Ausone lead the list of underachievers—but wines such as Latour, Mouton-Rothschild, La Mission-Haut-Brion, Haut-Brion, Cheval Blanc, and La Conseillante can be awesome.

1950 (Pomerol only)—An absolutely extraordinary vintage in Pomerol that I began bringing to consumers' attention in *The Wine Advocate* and in my books on Bordeaux. The quality of wines such as Lafleur, Pétrus, Vieux Château Certan, and Latour à Pomerol suggest that it was a year of extremely low yields and abundant sunshine. Given the extraordinary ripeness, intensity, and greatness of Pomerol's wines, how could this vintage be ignored? The Pomerols from this vintage remain in splendid condition. If any can be found, this is a vintage to purchase.

1953—Undoubtedly a great vintage, but one that turned out to be a sprinter rather than a marathon runner. According to the old-timers, the wines were delicious, complex, and full of charm when young. Today, buying them is fraught with risk unless readers purchase the larger-format bottles, preferably procured from the original purchaser who stored them in a damp, cold cellar. From regular bottles, most 1953s reveal considerable fragility. Out of magnums, this remains one of the most elegant, complex, and fragrant vintages of the century. The wines are not muscular, large-scaled, blockbuster heavyweights, such as 1945 or 1959; rather, they represent the quintessentially elegant style.

1955 (Graves and Pauillac only)—In this vintage the wines of Graves and Pauillac have proven to be superb. Much like 1948 and 1950 (only in Pomerol), this is an underrated, underpriced vintage.

1959—Like 1929, 1961, 1982, and 1990, 1959 has been criticized by technocrats for producing wines that were too ostentatious, too low in acidity, with too much flavor. All of these charges are true, and as a result, 1959 has turned out to be one of the great vintages of the century, especially in the Médoc and Graves. Pomerol and St.-Émilion (less obviously great in this year) were still recovering from the devastating freeze of 1956.

1961—An unqualified great vintage that turned out consistently spectacular wines. The finest wines possess extraordinary intensity, opulently rich, sweet fruit, and awesome concentration. Yet the 1961s have aged moderately fast, save for the monumental Latour. Ironically, 1961 has evolved more quickly than 1959, which is interesting because authorities initially maligned 1959 for being the faster-maturing vintage.

1964 (Pomerol, St.-Émilion, and Graves only)—When the skies opened and the rains inundated Bordeaux, virtually the entire havest had been completed in Pomerol, St.-Émilion, and Graves under textbook conditions. The Médoc had just begun to harvest, and this potentially great vintage was spoiled in that sector. Spectacular 1964s from Pomerol, St.-Émilion, and Graves, but disappointing wines from the Médoc are the rule of thumb. Since the Médoc tends to set the reputation for a given vintage in Bordeaux, 1964 has always been relegated to a second-class status—making some wines fine values.

1970–1979—no candidates

Note: Yes, 1970 has always been considered a reference-point year, and 1975 continues to be a perplexing, stubbornly tannic vintage with a number of great wines. As good as 1971,

1976, 1978, and 1979 can be, there is no vintage in this decade that has produced enough great wines to get my vote, although 1975 may ultimately prove to be a great vintage for Pomerol.

1982—Forgetting the soft, sometimes flabby wines of the Margaux appellation (except for the monumental Château Margaux, a present-day clone of the immortal 1900), only a fool could deny the greatness of this vintage. Extremely rich, full-bodied wines that continue to reveal increasing levels of tannin (to even *my* surprise) were uniformly produced in this abundant year. After having risen in price by 300%–500%, they are now the most expensive wines produced in Bordeaux since the legendary 1961s. Stylistically they represent a hypothetical blend of 1959 and 1947—thick, rich, blockbuster wines that in Graves, Pomerol, and St.-Émilion can now be drunk with exceptional pleasure. In the northern Médoc, the wines remain immense and massive as well as backward and dense. This vintage will only become rarer and more expensive.

1985—A consistently top-notch vintage of gorgeously seductive, charming wines that appear to be developing quickly. They exhibit all of the characteristics necessary to provide elegant and balanced drinking for several more decades. Is 1985 the modern-day equivalent of 1953?

1986—In total contrast to the soft, plush, user-friendly 1985s, 1986 is a vintage shaped by the strength and ripeness of the Cabernet Sauvignon. Great, potentially very long-lived wines were made in the Médoc and its four principal communes of Margaux, St.-Julien, Pauillac, and St.-Estèphe. The wines are backward but rich and concentrated, with only a handful appearing ready to drink prior to the end of this century.

1989—At first, 1989 looked to be a replay of 1982, but few of the wines possess that vintage's concentration and extract. The wines are ostentatious, fat, and ripe. They already show signs of closing down and revealing more structure and aging potential. It was a vintage shaped by extreme drought and heat. While none of the Médoc's first-growths produced wines that live up to their lofty reputations, Haut-Brion and La Mission-Haut-Brion turned in two of the century's most profound performances! It is a superb year for Pomerol.

1990—A blockbuster vintage that increasingly appears to be a rival to 1982's position as the finest vintage subsequent to 1959 and 1961. The 1990s are richer, fuller, denser, more structured and tannic wines than the 1989s. Yet they share with that vintage an extraordinary sweetness and ripeness of fruit. Knowledgeable insiders and Bordeaux speculators have been stockpiling 1990s in preference to 1989s. In 1994/1995, this is the vintage to purchase, but stocks are already depleted.

RATING BORDEAUX'S BEST PRODUCERS OF DRY RED WINES

Note: Where a producer has been assigned a range of stars, * * */* * * * for example, the lower rating has been used for placement in this hierarchy.

* * * * * (OUTSTANDING)

L'Angélus (St.-Émilion)

Beauséjour-Duffau (St.-Émilion)

Canon-La-Gaffelière (St.-Émilion)

Cheval Blanc (St.-Émilion)

Clinet (Pomerol)

La Conseillante (Pomerol)

Cos d'Estournel (St.-Estèphe)

Ducru-Beaucaillou (St.-Julien)

L'Évangile (Pomerol)

La Fleur de Gay (Pomerol)

Haut-Brion (Graves)

Lafite-Rothschild (Pauillac)

Lafleur (Pomerol)

Latour (Pauillac)

Léoville-Las Cases (St.-Julien)

Lynch-Bages (Pauillac)

Château Margaux (Margaux)

La Mission-Haut-Brion (Graves)

Mouton-Rothschild (Pauillac)
Palmer (Margaux)
Pétrus (Pomerol)
Pichon-Longueville Baron (Pauillac)
Pichon-Longueville–Comtesse de Lalande
   (Pauillac)

Le Pin (Pomerol)
Le Tertre-Roteboeuf (St.-Émilion)
Troplong-Mondot (St.-Émilion)

* * * * (EXCELLENT)

L'Arrosée (St.-Émilion)
Ausone (St.-Émilion)
Bon Pasteur (Pomerol)
Canon (St.-Émilion)
Certan de May (Pomerol)
Domaine de Chevalier (Graves)
Clerc-Milon (Pauillac)
La Dominique (St.-Émilion)
Duhart-Milon-Rothschild (Pauillac)
L'Église-Clinet (Pomerol)
Ferrand-Lartique (St.-Émilion)
de Fieuzal (Graves)
Figeac (St.-Émilion)
La Fleur Pétrus (Pomerol)
Gazin (Pomerol)
Grand-Mayne (St.-Émilion)
Grand-Puy-Lacoste (Pauillac)
Gruaud-Larose (St.-Julien)****/*****
Haut-Bailly (Graves)

Haut-Marbuzet (St.-Estèphe)****/*****
Lagrange (St.-Julien)****/*****
La Lagune (Ludon)
Latour à Pomerol (Pomerol)
Léoville-Barton (St. Julien)****/*****
La Louvière (Graves)
Montrose (St.-Estèphe)****/*****
Pape-Clément (Graves)
Pavie-Macquin (St.-Émilion)
Petit-Village (Pomerol)
Phélan-Ségur (St.-Estèphe)
Prieuré-Lichine (Margaux)
Rausan-Ségla (Margaux)****/*****
Sociando-Mallet (Haut-Médoc)
Talbot (St.-Julien)
Trotanoy (Pomerol)
Valandraud (St.-Émilion)
Vieux Château Certan (Pomerol)

* * * (GOOD PRODUCERS)

d'Angludet (Margaux)
d'Armailhac (Pauillac)
L'Arrivet-Haut-Brion (Graves)
Bahans Haut-Brion (Graves)
Balestard-La-Tonnelle (St.-Émilion)
Batailley (Pauillac)
Beau Séjour-Bécot (St.-Émilion)
Beauregard (Pomerol)
Bel-Air (Lalande-de-Pomerol)
Belles-Graves (Lalande-de-Pomerol)
Bertineau St.-Vincent
   (Lalande-de-Pomerol)
Beychevelle (St.-Julien)
Bonalgue (Pomerol)
Le Boscq (Médoc)
Branaire-Ducru (St.-Julien)
Cadet-Piola (St.-Émilion)
Calon-Ségur (St.-Estèphe)
Canon (Canon-Fronsac)
Canon de Brem (Canon-Fronsac)
Canon-Moueix (Canon-Fronsac)

Cantemerle (Macau)
Cantenac-Brown (Margaux)
Cap de Mourlin (St.-Émilion)
Carbonnieux (Graves)
de Carles (Fronsac)
Les Carmes-Haut-Brion (Graves)
Cassagne-Haut-Canon-La Truffière
   (Canon-Fronsac)
Certan-Giraud (Pomerol)
Chantegrive (Graves)
La Chapelle de la Mission (Graves)
Chasse-Spleen (Moulis)***/****
Chauvin (St.-Émilion)
Citran (Haut-Médoc)
Clos du Clocher (Pomerol)
Clos Fourtet (St.-Émilion)
Clos des Jacobins (St.-Émilion)
Clos du Marquis (St.-Julien)
Clos de L'Oratoire (St.-Émilion)
Clos René (Pomerol)
Clos St.-Martin (St.-Émilion)

La Clotte (St.-Émilion)
Corbin (St.-Emilion)
Corbin-Michotte (St.-Émilion)
Cormeil-Figeac (St.-Émilion)
Cos Labory (St.-Estèphe)
Coufran (Haut-Médoc)
Château Courrière Rongieras
     (Lussac-St.-Émilion)
La Couspade (St.-Émilion)
Coutelin-Merville (St.-Estèphe)
Couvent des Jacobins (St.-Émilion)
La Croix du Casse (Pomerol)
La Croix de Gay (Pomerol)
Croque Michotte (St.-Émilion)
Dalem (Fronsac)
La Dame de Montrose (St.-Estèphe)
Dassault (St.-Émilion)
Daugay (St.-Émilion)
La Dauphine (Fronsac)
Domaine de L'Église (Pomerol)
L'Enclos (Pomerol)
de Ferrand (St.-Émilion)
Fongaban (Puisseguin-St.-Émilion)
Fonplégade (St.-Émilion)
Fontenil (Fronsac)
Les Forts de Latour (Pauillac)
Fourcas-Loubaney (Listrac)
La Gaffelière (St.-Émilion)
La Garde Réserve du Château (Graves)
Le Gay (Pomerol)
Giscours (Margaux) ***/****
Gloria (St.-Julien)
Gombaude-Guillot (Pomerol)
Grand-Corbin (St.-Émilion)
Grand-Pontet (St.-Émilion)
Grand-Puy-Ducasse (Pauillac)
Les Grandes Chênes (Médoc)
La Grave à Pomerol (Trigant de Boisset)
     (Pomerol)
Guillot-Clauzel (Pomerol)
La Gurgue (Margaux)
Haut-Bages-Libéral (Pauillac)
Haut-Batailley (Pauillac)
Haut-Corbin (St.-Émilion)
Haut-Faugères (St.-Émilion)
Haut-Sociondo (Blaye)
Hortevie (St.-Julien)
Château Hostens-Picant (Sainte-Foy)
Jonqueyrès (Bordeaux Supérieur)
Kirwan (Margaux)
Labégorce-Zédé (Margaux)

Lafon-Rochet (St.-Estèphe)
Lalande-Borie (St.-Julien)
Lanessan (Haut-Médoc)
Langoa-Barton (St.-Julien)
Larmande (St.-Émilion)
Lascombes (Margaux)
Léoville-Poyferré (St.-Julien)
Magdelaine (St.-Émilion)
Magneau (Graves)
Marquis de Terme (Margaux)
Maucaillou (Moulis)
Mazeris (Canon-Fronsac)
Meyney (St.-Estèphe)
Monbrison (Margaux)
Moulin-Haut-Laroque (Fronsac)
Moulin-Pey-Labrie
     (Canon-Fronsac) ***/****
Moulin Rouge (Haut-Médoc)
Les Ormes de Pez (St.-Estèphe)
Les Ormes-Sorbet (Médoc)
Parenchère (Bordeaux Supérieur)
Pauillac (Pauillac)
Pavie (St.-Émilion)
Pavie-Decesse (St.-Émilion)
du Pavillon (Canon-Fronsac)
Pavillon Rouge de Margaux (Margaux)
Les Pensées de Lafleur (Pomerol)
Pey Labrie (Canon-Fronsac)
Peyredon-Lagravette (Listrac)
de Pez (St.-Estèphe)
Picque-Caillou (Graves)
de Pitray (Côtes de Castignon)
Plaisance (Premières Côtes de Bordeaux)
Pontet-Canet (Pauillac)
Potensac (Médoc)
Poujeaux (Moulis)
Roc des Cambes (Côtes de Bourg)
Rouet (Fronsac)
St.-Pierre (St.-Julien)
La Serre (St.-Émilion)
Siran (Margaux)
Smith-Haut-Lafitte (Graves) ***/****
Soudars (Haut-Médoc)
Soutard (St.-Émilion)
Tayac (Côtes de Bourg)
Tertre-Daugay (St.-Émilion)
La Tonnelle (Blaye)
La Tour de By (Médoc)
La Tour-Haut-Brion (Graves)
Tour Haut-Caussan (Médoc)
Tour du Haut-Moulin (Haut-Médoc)

La Tour du Pin Figeac Moueix
   (St.-Émilion)
La Tour-St.-Bonnet (Médoc)
La Tour Seguy (Bourg)

La Tourelles de Longueville (Pauillac)
Trotte Vieille (St.-Émilion)
La Vieille-Cure (Fronsac)
La Violette (Pomerol)

* * (AVERAGE)

L'Arrivet-Haut-Brion (Graves)**/***
Beaumont (Haut-Médoc)
Belair (St.-Émilion)
Belgrave (Haut-Médoc)
Bellegrave (Pomerol)
Bourgneuf-Vayron (Pomerol)
Boyd-Cantenac (Margaux)
Brane-Cantenac (Margaux)
La Cabanne (Pomerol)
Cadet-Bon (St.-Émilion)
Carruades de Lafite (Pauillac)
Chambert-Marbuzet (St.-Estèphe)
Clarke (Listrac)
Clos L'Église (Pomerol)
Clos La Madeleine (St.-Émilion)
La Clusière (St.-Émilion)
Cordeillan-Bages (Pauillac)
La Croix (Pomerol)
Croizet-Bages (Pauillac)
Curé-Bon (St.-Émilion)
Dauzac (Margaux)
Destieux (St.-Émilion)
Durfort-Vivens (Margaux)
Faurie de Souchard (St.-Émilion)
Ferrière (Margaux)
Feytit-Clinet (Pomerol)
La Fleur (St.-Émilion)
La Fleur Gazin (Pomerol)
La Fleur Pourret (St.-Émilion)
La Fleur St.-Georges (Lalande-de-Pomerol)
Fonbadet (Pauillac)
Fonreaud (Listrac)
Fonroque (St.-Émilion)
Fourcas-Dupré (Listrac)
Fourcas-Hosten (Listrac)
Franc-Mayne (St.-Émilion)
de France (Graves)
Château Gassies (Premières Côtes de
   Bordeaux)
Gressier Grand Poujeaux (Moulis)
Haut-Bages-Averous (Pauillac)
Haut-Bergey (Graves)

Haut-Sarpe (St.-Émilion)
d'Issan (Margaux)
Le Jurat (St.-Émilion)
Lagrange (Pomerol)
Lamarque (Haut-Médoc)
Larcis-Ducasse (St.-Émilion)
Larose-Trintaudon (Haut-Médoc)
Laroze (St.-Émilion)
Larruau (Margaux)
Liversan (Haut-Médoc)
Malartic-Lagravière (Graves)
Malescasse (Haut-Médoc)
Malescot-St.-Exupéry (Margaux)
Marbuzet (St.-Estèphe)**/***
Marjosse (Bordeaux)**/***
Martinens (Margaux)
Mazeyres (Pomerol)
Montviel (Pomerol)
Moulin du Cadet (St.-Émilion)
Nenin (Pomerol)
Olivier (Graves)
Patache d'Aux (Medoc)**/***
Pedesclaux (Pauillac)
Petit-Faurie-Soutard (St.-Émilion)
Petit-Figeac (St.-Émilion)
Pibran (Pauillac)
Plince (Pomerol)
Pouget (Margaux)
Puy-Blanquet (St.-Émilion)
Rahoul (Graves)
Rauzan-Gassies (Margaux)
Réserve de la Comtesse (Pauillac)
Rocher-Bellevue-Figeac (St.-Émilion)
Rolland-Maillet (St.-Émilion)
de Sales (Pomerol)
Taillefer (Pomerol)
La Tour-Martillac (Graves)
La Tour de Mons (Margaux)
Vieux Clos St.-Émilion
   (St.-Émilion)**/***
Villemaurine (St.-Émilion)

RATING BORDEAUX'S BEST PRODUCERS OF DRY WHITE WINES

* * * * * (OUTSTANDING)

Domaine de Chevalier (Graves)
de Fieuzal (Graves)
Haut-Brion (Graves)

Laville-Haut-Brion (Graves)
La Louvière (Graves)

* * * * (EXCELLENT)

Carbonnieux (Graves)
Clos Floridene (Graves)
Couhins-Lurton (Graves)
Pape-Clément (Graves)

Pavillon Blanc de Château Margaux
  (Bordeaux)
Smith-Haut-Lafitte (Graves)
La Tour-Martillac (Graves)

* * * (GOOD)

d'Archambeau (Graves)
L'Arrivet-Haut-Brion (Graves)
Bauduc Les Trois Hectares (Bordeaux)
Blanc de Lynch-Bages (Pauillac)
Bouscaut (Graves)
Caillou Blanc de Talbot (Bordeaux)
Carsin (Bordeaux)
Domaine Challon (Bordeaux)
Chantegrive (Graves)
La Closière (Bordeaux)
Château Coucheroy (Pessac-Léognan)
Doisy-Daëne (Bordeaux)
Château Ferbos (Graves)
Ferrande (Graves)
G de Château Guiraud (Bordeaux)
La Garde-Réserve du Château (Graves)
Château Graville-Lacoste (Graves)

Haut-Gardère (Graves)
Loudenne (Bordeaux)
Malartic-Lagravière (Graves)
Château de Malle (Graves)
Château Millet (Graves)
Numéro 1 (Bordeaux)
Pirou (Graves)
Plaisance (Bordeaux)
Pontac Monplaisir (Graves)
R de Rieussec (Graves)
Rahoul (Graves)
Respide (Graves)
Reynon (Bordeaux)***/****
Château de Rochemorin (Pessac-Léognan)
Roquefort (Bordeaux)
Thieuley (Bordeaux)

* * (AVERAGE)

Aile d'Argent (Bordeaux)
de France (Graves)

Olivier (Graves)

RATING BORDEAUX'S BEST PRODUCERS OF BARSACS/SAUTERNES

* * * * * (OUTSTANDING)

Climens (Barsac)
Coutet-Cuvée Madame (Barsac)
Fargues (Sauternes)
Raymond-Lafon (Sauternes)

Rieussec (Sauternes)
Suduiraut-Cuvée Madame (Sauternes)
d'Yquem (Sauternes)

* * * * (EXCELLENT)

Coutet (regular cuvée) (Barsac)
Doisy-Daëne L'Extravagance (Barsac)
Doisy-Dubroca (Barsac)
Gilette (Sauternes)
Guiraud (Sauternes)

Lafaurie-Peyraguey
  (Sauternes)****/*****
Rabaud-Promis (Sauternes)
Suduiraut-Crème de Tête (Sauternes)
La Tour Blanche (Sauternes)

*** *** *** *(GOOD)*

d'Arche (Sauternes)
Bastor-Lamontagne (Sauternes)
Caillou (Barsac)
Clos Haut-Peyraguey (Sauternes)
Doisy-Daëne (Barsac)
Doisy-Védrines (Barsac)

Filhot (Sauternes)
Lamothe-Despujols (Sauternes)
Lamothe-Guignard (Sauternes)***/****
de Malle (Sauternes)
Rayne-Vigneau (Sauternes)
Sigalas Rabaud (Sauternes)

*** *** *(AVERAGE)*

Romer du Hayot (Sauternes)   Suau (Barsac)

GETTING A HANDLE ON SECONDARY LABELS

Secondary wines with secondary labels are not a recent development. Léoville-Las Cases first made a second wine (Clos du Marquis) in 1904, and in 1908 Château Margaux produced its first Le Pavillon Rouge du Château Margaux.

Yet a decade ago, about the only second labels most Bordeaux wine enthusiasts encountered were those from Latour (Les Forts de Latour), Margaux (Le Pavillon Rouge du Château Margaux), and perhaps that of Lafite-Rothschild (Moulin des Carruades). Today, virtually every classified growth, as well as many Crus Bourgeois and numerous estates in Pomerol and St.-Émilion, has second labels for those batches of wine deemed not sufficiently rich, concentrated, or complete enough to go into their top wine, or grand vin. This has been one of the major developments of the eighties, fostered no doubt by the enormous crop sizes in most of the vintages. A handful of cynics have claimed it is largely done to keep prices high, but such charges are nonsense. The result has generally been far higher quality for a château's best wine. It allows a château to declassify the production from young vines, from vines that overproduce, and from parcels harvested too soon or too late, into a second, or perhaps even a third wine that still has some of the quality and character of the château's grand vin.

The gentleman who encouraged most châteaux to develop second wines was the famed oenologist, Professor Emile Peynaud. Over the last decade, the number of second wines has increased more than tenfold. Some properties, such as Léoville-Las Cases, have even begun to utilize a third label for wines deemed not good enough for the second label!

Of course all this complicates buying decisions for consumers. The wine trade has exacerbated matters by seizing on the opportunity to advertise wine that "tastes like the grand vin" for one-half to one-third the price. In most cases, there is little truth to such proclamations. I find that most second wines have only a vague resemblance to their more esteemed siblings. Most are the product of throwing everything that would normally have been discarded into another label for commercial purposes. Some second wines, such as those of the first-growths, particularly Les Forts de Latour and Bahans-Haut-Brion, are indeed excellent, occasionally outstanding (taste the 1982 Les Forts de Latour or 1989 Bahans-Haut-Brion), and can even resemble the style and character of the grand vin. But the words *caveat emptor* should be etched strongly in the minds of consumers who routinely purchase the second labels of Bordeaux châteaux thinking they are getting something reminiscent of the property's top wine.

In an effort to clarify the situation of second labels, the following chart rates the secondary wines on a 1- to 5-star basis. While I think it is important to underscore the significance that the stricter the selection, the better the top wine, it is also important to remember that most second wines are rarely worth the price asked.

Note: Where a second wine merits purchasing, the vintage is listed.

*****—The finest second wines
****—Very good second wines
***—Pleasant second wines
**—Average-quality second wines
*—Of little interest

SECONDARY LABELS

GRAND VIN	SECOND VIN
Andron-Blanquet	St.-Roch**
L'Angélus	Carillon de L'Angélus**
d'Angludet	Domaine Baury**
d'Arche	d'Arche-Lafaurie**
L'Arrosée	Les Côteaux du Château L'Arrosée**
Balestard-La-Tonnelle	Les Tourelles de Balestard**
Bastor-Lamontagne	Les Remparts du Bastor**
Beau Séjour-Bécot	Tournelle des Moines**
Beaumont	Moulin-d'Arvigny*
Beauséjour-Duffau	La Croix de Mazerat**
Belair	Roc-Blanquant*
Beychevelle	Amiral de Beychevelle***
	Réserve de L'Amiral***
Bonalgue	Burgrave*
Bouscaut	Valoux**
Branaire-Ducru	Duluc**
Brane-Cantenac	Château Notton**
	Domaine de Fontarney**
Broustet	Château de Ségur**
La Cabanne	Compostelle**
Cadet-Piola	Chevaliers de Malta**
Caillou	Petit-Mayne*
Calon-Ségur	Marquis de Ségur**
Canon	Clos J. Kanon**
Canon-La-Gaffelière	Côte Migon-La-Gaffelière**
Cantemerle	Villeneuve de Cantemerle**
Cantenac-Brown	Canuet**
	Lamartine**
Carbonnieux	La Tour-Léognan**
Certan-Giraud	Clos du Roy**
Chambert-Marbuzet	MacCarthy**
Chasse-Spleen	L'Ermitage de Chasse-Spleen**
Chauvin	Chauvin Variation*
Cheval Blanc	Le Petit Cheval**
Climens	Les Cyprès de Climens**
Clos Fourtet	Domaine de Martialis**
Clos Haut-Peyraguey	Haut-Bommes**
Clos René	Moulinet-Lasserre**
Columbier-Monpelou	Grand Canyon**
Corbin-Michotte	Les Abeilles**
Cos d'Estournel	Pagodes de Cos***
Couvent-des-Jacobins	Beau-Mayne***

GRAND VIN	SECOND VIN
La Croix	Le Gabachot **
Croizet-Bages	Enclos de Moncabon *
Dauzac	Laborde **
Doisy-Védrines	La Tour-Védrines **
La Dominique	Saint-Paul de la Dominique **
Ducru-Beaucaillou	La Croix **
Duhart-Milon-Rothschild	Moulin de Duhart **
Durfort-Vivens	Domaine de Curé-Bourse *
L'Église-Clinet	La Petite L'Église **
de Fieuzal	L'Abeille de Fieuzal **
Figeac	Grangeneuve **
Fonplégade	Château Côtes Trois Moulins **
La Gaffelière	Clos la Gaffelière **
	Château de Roquefort **
Giscours	Cantelaude **
Gloria	Haut-Beychevelle Gloria **
	Peymartin **
Grand-Mayne	Les Plantes du Mayne **
Grand-Puy-Ducasse	Artigues-Arnaud **
Grand-Puy-Lacoste	Lacoste-Borie **
Gruaud-Larose	Sarget de Gruaud-Larose ***
Guiraud	Le Dauphin **
Haut-Bailly	La Parde de Haut-Bailly ***
Haut-Batailley	La Tour d'Aspic **
Haut-Brion	Bahans Haut-Brion ***** (1989, 1988, 1987)
Haut-Marbuzet	Tour de Marbuzet **
d'Issan	Candel **
Labegorcé-Zédé	Château de L'Amiral **
Lafite-Rothschild	Carruades de Lafite **** (1989)
Lafleur	Les Pensées de Lafleur ***** (1990, 1989, 1988)
Lafon-Rochet	Le Numero 2 de Lafon-Rochet ***
Lagrange	Les Fiefs de Lagrange ***
La Lagune	Ludon-Pomiès-Agassac **
Lanessan	Domaine de Sainte-Gemme **
Langoa-Barton	Lady Langoa **** (1989)
Larmande	Château des Templiers **
Lascombes	Segonnes **
	La Gombaude **
Latour	Les Forts de Latour ***** (1989, 1982, 1978)
Léoville-Barton	Lady Langoa **** (1989)
Léoville-Las Cases	Clos du Marquis ***** (1990, 1989, 1988, 1986, 1982)
	Grand Parc ***
Léoville-Poyferré	Moulin-Riche **
La Louvière	L de Louvière **** (1989)
	Coucheray **
	Clos du Roi **
Lynch-Bages	Haut-Bages-Averous **** (1989)
Malescot St.-Exupéry	de Loyac *
	Domaine du Balardin *

GRAND VIN	SECOND VIN
de Malle	Château de Sainte-Hélène **
Château Margaux	Pavillon Rouge du Château Margaux ***
Marquis de Terme	Domaine des Gondats **
Maucaillou	Cap de Haut **
	Franc-Caillou **
Meyney	Prieuré de Meyney ***
Monbrison	Cordat ***
Montrose	La Dame de Montrose ***
Palmer	Réserve du Général ***
Pape-Clément	Le Clémentin du Pape-Clément ***
Phélan-Ségur	Franck Phélan ***
Pichon-Longueville Baron	Les Tourelles de Pichon ***
Pichon-Longueville–Comtesse de Lalande	Réserve de la Comtesse ***
Pontet-Canet	Les Hauts de Pontet **
Potensac	Gallais-Bellevue **
	Lassalle **
	Goudy-la-Cardonne **
Poujeaux	La Salle de Poujeaux **
Le Prieuré	Château L'Olivier **
Prieuré-Lichine	Clairefont **
Rabaud-Promis	Domaine de L'Estremade **
Rahoul	Petit Rahoul **
Rausan-Ségla	Lamouroux **
Rieussec	Clos Labère ***
St.-Pierre	Clos de Uza **
	St.-Louis-le-Bosq **
de Sales	Chantalouette **
Siran	Bellegarde **
	St.-Jacques **
Smith-Haut-Lafitte	Les Hauts de Smith-Haut-Lafitte *
Sociando-Mallet	Lartigue de Brochon **
Soutard	Clos de la Tonnelle **
Talbot	Connétable de Talbot ***
Tertre-Daugay	Château de Roquefort ***
La Tour-Blanche	Mademoiselle de Saint-Marc ***
La Tour de By	Moulin de la Roque *
	La Roque de By *
Tour Haut-Caussan	La Landotte **
La Tour-Martillac	La Grave-Martillac **
Troplong-Mondot	Mondot ***
Valandraud	Virginie de Valandraud ***
Vieux Château Certan	Clos de la Gravette ***

THE BEST WINE VALUES IN BORDEAUX
(The top estates for under $20 a bottle)

St-Estèphe   Marbuzet, Meyney, Les-Ormes-de-Pez, Phélan-Ségur, Tronquoy-Lalande

Pauillac   Fonbadet, Grand-Puy-Ducasse, Pibran

St.-Julien   Clos du Marquis, Gloria, Hortevie

Margaux and the Southern Médoc   d'Angludet, La Gurgue, Labégorcé-Zédé

Graves   Bahans Haut-Brion, La Louvière, Picque-Caillou

Moulis and Listrac   Fourcas-Loubaney, Gressier Grand Poujeaux, Maucaillou, Poujeaux

Médoc and Haut-Médoc   Beaumont, Le Boscq, Lanessan, Latour St.-Bonnet, Moulin-Rouge, Potensac, Sociando-Mallet, La Tour de By, Tour Haut-Caussan, Tour du Haut-Moulin, Vieux-Robin

Pomerol   Bonalgue, L'Enclos

St.-Émilion   Grand-Mayne, Grand-Pontet, Haut-Corbin, Pavie-Macquin

Fronsac and Canon-Fronsac   Canon de Brem, Canon-Moueix, Cassagne-Haut-Canon-La Truffière, Dalem, La Dauphine, Fontenil, La Grave, Mazeris, Moulin-Haut-Laroque, Moulin-Pey-Labrie, du Pavillon, Pez-Labrie, Rouet, La Vieille-Cure

Lalande-de-Pomerol   Bel-Air, Bertineau-St.-Vincent, du Chapelain, Grand-Ormeau, Les Hauts-Conseillants, Siaurac

Côtes de Bourg   Brûléscailles, Guerry, Haut-Maco, Mercier, Roc des Cambes, Tayac-Cuvée Prestige

Côtes de Blaye   Bertinerie, Pérenne, La Rose-Bellevue, La Tonnelle

Bordeaux Premières Côtes and Supérieurs   La Croix de Roche, Dudon-Cuvée Jean-Baptiste, Fontenil, Haux Frère, Jonqueyrès, Plaisance, de Plassan, Prieuré-Ste.-Anne, Recougne, Reynon

Côtes de Castillon   Pitray

Barsac/Sauternes   Bastor-Lamontagne, Doisy-Dubroca, Haut-Claverie, de Malle

Loupiac   Bourdon-Loupiac, Clos-Jean, Loupiac-Gaudiet, Ricaud

Entre-Deux-Mers (dry white wines)   Bonnet, Bonnet-Cuvée Réserve, Tertre-Launay, Turcaud

Bordeaux Premières Côtes and Generic Bordeaux (dry white wines)   Alpha, Bauduc-Les Trois-Hectares, Blanc de Lynch-Bages, Caillou Blanc de Talbot, Cayla-Le Grand Vent, Clos-Jean, De La Cloisère du Carpia, Numéro 1-Dourthe, Reynon-Vieilles Vignes, Roquefort-Cuvée Spéciale, Sec de Doisy-Daëne, Thieuley

Buying Bordeaux Wine Futures: The Pitfalls and Pleasures

The purchase of wine, already fraught with plenty of pitfalls for consumers, becomes immensely more complex and risky when one enters the wine futures sweepstakes.

On the surface, buying wine futures is nothing more than investing money in a case or cases of wine at a predetermined "future price" long before the wine is bottled and shipped to this country. You invest your money in wine futures on the assumption that the wine will appreciate significantly in price between the time you purchase the future and the time the wine has been bottled and imported to America. Purchasing the right wine, from the right vintage, in the right international financial climate, can represent significant savings. On the other hand, it can be quite disappointing to invest heavily in a wine future only to witness the wine's arrival 12 to 18 months later at a price equal to or below the future price and to discover that the wine is inferior in quality as well.

For years, future offerings have been largely limited to Bordeaux wines, although they are seen occasionally from other regions. In Bordeaux, during the spring following the harvest, the estates or châteaux offer for sale a portion of their crops. The first offering, or *première tranche*, usually offers a good indication of the trade's enthusiasm for the new wine, the prevailing market conditions, and the ultimate price the public will have to spend.

Those brokers and *négociants* who take an early position on a vintage frequently offer portions of their purchases to importers/wholesalers/ retailers to make available publicly as a "wine future." These offerings are usually made to the retail shopper during the first spring after the vintage. For example, the 1990 Bordeaux vintage was being offered for sale as a wine future in April 1991. Purchasing wine at this time is not without numerous risks. While 90% of the quality of the wine and the style of the vintage can be ascertained by professionals tasting the wine in its infancy, the increased interest in buying Bordeaux wine futures has led to a soaring number of journalists, some qualified, some not, to judge young Bordeaux wines. The results have been predictable. Many writers serve no purpose other than to hype the vintage as great, and have written more glowing accounts of a vintage than the publicity firms doing promotion for the Bordeaux wine industry. Consumers should read numerous points of view from trusted professionals and ask the following questions: (1) Is the professional taster experienced in tasting young as well as old Bordeaux vintages? (2) How much time does the taster actually spend tasting Bordeaux during the year, visiting the properties, and thinking about the vintage? (3) Does the professional taster express his or her viewpoint in an independent, unbiased form, free of trade advertising? (4) Has the professional looked deeply at the weather conditions, harvesting conditions, grape-variety-ripening profiles, and soil types that respond differently depending on the weather scenario?

When wine futures are offered for sale there is generally a great deal of enthusiasm for the newest vintage from both the proprietors and the wine trade. The saying in France that "the greatest wines ever made are the ones that are available for sale" are the words many wine producers and merchants live by. The business of the wine trade is to sell wine, and consumers should be aware that they will no doubt be inundated with claims of "great wines from a great vintage at great prices." This has been used time and time again for good vintages and, in essence, has undermined the credibility of many otherwise responsible retailers, as well as a number of journalists. In contrast, those writers who fail to admit or to recognize greatness where warranted are no less inept and irresponsible.

In short, there are only four valid reasons to buy Bordeaux wine futures.

1. Are you buying top-quality, preferably superb wine from an excellent, or better yet, a great vintage?

No vintage can be reviewed in black-and-white terms. Even in the greatest vintages there are disappointing appellations, as well as mediocre wines. At the same time, vintages that are merely good to very good can produce some superb wines. Knowing who are the underachievers and overachievers is paramount in making a good buying decision. Certainly in looking at the last 20 years the only irrefutably great vintages have been 1982 for Pomerol, St.-Émilion, St.-Julien, Pauillac, and St.-Estèphe; 1983 for selected St.-Émilions and Pomerols, as well as the wines from Margaux; 1985 for the wines of Graves; 1986 for the northern Médocs from St.-Julien, Pauillac, St.-Estèphe, and the sweet wines from Barsac/Sauternes; 1989 for selected Pomerols, St.-Émilions, St.-Juliens, Pauillacs, and St.-Estèphes; and 1990 for the first-growths and a handful of Pomerols and St.-Émilions. There is no reason to buy wines as futures except for the top performers in a given vintage, because prices generally will not appreciate in the period between the release of the future prices and when the wines are bottled. The exceptions are always the same—top wines and great vintages. If the financial climate is such that the wine will not be at least 25% to 30% more expensive when it arrives in the marketplace, then most purchasers are better off investing their money elsewhere.

Recent history of the 1975 and 1978 Bordeaux future offerings provides a revealing prospectus to futures buyers. Purchasers of 1975 futures have done extremely well. When offered in 1977, the 1975 future prices included $140 to $160 per case for such illustrious wines as Lafite-Rothschild and Latour, and $64 to $80 for second-growths, including such proven thoroughbreds as Léoville-Las Cases, La Lagune, and Ducru-Beaucaillou. By the time these wines had arrived on the market in 1978, the vintage's outstanding and potentially classic quality was an accepted fact, and the first-growths were retailing for $325 to $375 per case; the lesser growths, $112 to $150 per case. Buyers of 1975 futures have continued to prosper, as this vintage is now very scarce and its prices have continued to escalate from $900 to $1,200 a case for first-growths, and $350 to $550 for second- through fifth-growths. In 1995, the 1975 prices have come to a standstill because of doubts about how gracefully many of the wines are evolving. I would not be surprised to see some prices even drop—another pitfall that must always be considered.

The 1978 Bordeaux futures, offered in 1980, present a different picture; 1978 was another very good vintage year, with wines similar in style but perhaps less intense than the excellent 1970 vintage. Opening prices for the 1978 Bordeaux were very high, and were inflated because of a weak dollar abroad and an excessive demand for the finest French wines. Prices for first-growths were offered at $429 to $499, prices for second- through fifth-growths at $165 to $230. Consumers who invested heavily in Bordeaux have purchased good wine, but when the wines arrived on the market in spring 1981, the retail prices for these wines were virtually the same as future price offerings. Thus, consumers who purchased 1978 futures and invested their money to the tune of 100% of the case price could have easily obtained a better return by simply investing in any interest-bearing account.

With respect to the vintages 1979, 1980, 1981, 1982, 1983, and 1985, the only year that has represented a great buy from a futures perspective was 1982. Nineteen eighty was not offered to the consumer as a wine future because it was of mediocre quality. As for the 1979 and 1981, the enthusiast who purchased these wines on a future basis no doubt was able, within 2 years after putting his or her money up, to buy the wines when they arrived in America at approximately the same price. While this was not true for some of the highly rated 1981s, it was true for the 1979s. As for the 1982s, they have jumped in price at an unbelievable pace, outdistancing any vintage in the last 20 years. The first-growths of 1982 were offered to consumers in late spring 1983 at prices of $350 to $450 for wines like Lafite-Rothschild, Latour, Mouton-Rothschild, Haut-Brion, and Cheval Blanc. By March 1985, the Cheval Blanc had jumped to $650–$800, the Mouton to $800–$1,000, and the rest to $700. Today, prices for 1982 first-growths range from a low of $2,000 a case for Haut-Brion to $3,000–$5,000 a case for any of the three Pauillac first-growths. This is a significant price increase for wines so young, but it reflects the insatiable worldwide demand for a great vintage. Rare, limited-production wines like the Pomerols have skyrocketed in price. Pétrus has clearly been the top performer in terms of increasing in price; it jumped from an April 1983 future price of $600 to a 1991 price of $7,500. This is absurd given the fact that the wines will not be close to maturity for a decade. Other top 1982 Pomerols such as Trotanoy, Certan de May, and L'Évangile have quadrupled in price. Trotanoy, originally available for $280, now sells (when you can find it) for at least $2,500. Certan de May has jumped from $180 to $1,000, and L'Évangile from $180 to $1,000.

The huge demand for 1982 Bordeaux futures and the tremendous publicity surrounding this vintage have led many to assume that subsequent years would similarly escalate in price. That has not happened, largely because Bordeaux has had too many high-quality, abundant vintages in the decade of the eighties. The only exceptions have been the 1986 first-growths that continue to accelerate because it is a great, long-lived, so-called classic year.

2. Do the prices you must pay look good enough that you will ultimately save money by paying less for the wine as a future than for the wine when it is released in 2–3 years?

Many factors must be taken into consideration to make this determination. In certain years, Bordeaux may release its wines at lower prices than it did the previous year (the most recent examples are 1986 and 1990). There is also the question of the international marketplace. In 1995 the American dollar is weak. Other significant Bordeaux-buying countries, such as England, have unsettled and troublesome financial problems as well. France's economy is stable but fragile. Newer marketplaces, such as Japan, are experiencing financial apprehension and increasing banking problems. Even Germany, which has become such a major Bordeaux player, has experienced an economic downspin because of the financial ramifications of trying to revitalize the moribund economy of East Germany. Three countries that appear to have sound economies and are in a healthy enough economic position to afford top-class Bordeaux are Belgium, Denmark, and Switzerland. These factors change, but the international marketplace, the perceived reputation of a given vintage, and the rarity of a particular estate all must be considered in determining whether the wine will become much more expensive when released than its price when offered as a wine future. There are not likely to be many American wine buyers of 1994 Bordeaux futures, even though this is a successful year.

3. Do you want to be guaranteed of getting top, hard-to-find wine from a producer with a great reputation who makes only small quantities of wine?

Even if the vintage is not irrefutably great, or you cannot be assured that prices will increase, there are always a handful of small estates, particularly in Pomerol and St.-Émilion, that produce such limited quantities of wine, and who have worldwide followers, that their wines warrant buying as a future if only to reserve your case from an estate whose wines have pleased you in the past. In Pomerol, limited-production wines such as Le Pin, Clinet, La Conseillante, L'Évangile, Le Fleur de Gay, Lafleur, Gombaud-Guillot, and Bon Pasteur have produced many popular wines during the decade of the eighties, yet are very hard to find in the marketplace. In St.-Émilion, some of the less-renowned yet modestly sized estates such as L'Angélus, L'Arrosée, Canon, Grand-Mayne, Pavie-Macquin, La Dominique, Le Tertre-Roteboeuf, and Troplong-Mondot produce wines that are not easy to find after bottling. Consequently, their admirers throughout the world frequently reserve and pay for these wines as futures. Limited-production wines from high-quality estates merit buying futures even in good to very good years.

4. Do you want to buy wine in half-bottles, magnums, double magnums, jeroboams, or imperials?

Frequently overlooked as one of the advantages of buying wine futures is the fact that you can request that your merchant have the wines bottled to your specifications. There is always a surcharge for such bottlings, but if you have children born in a certain year, or you want the luxury of buying half-bottles (a size that makes sense for daily drinking), the only time to do this is when buying the wine as a future.

Lastly, should you decide to enter the futures market, be sure you know the other risks involved. The merchant you deal with could go bankrupt, and your unsecured sales slip would make you one of probably hundreds of unsecured creditors of the bankrupt wine merchant hoping for a few cents on your investment. Another risk is that the supplier the merchant deals with could go bankrupt or be fraudulent. You may get a refund from the wine merchant, but you will not get your wine. Therefore, be sure to deal only with a wine merchant who has dealt in selling wine futures before and one who is financially solvent. And finally, buy wine futures only from a wine merchant who has received confirmed commitments as to the quantities of wine he or she will receive. Some merchants sell Bordeaux futures to consumers before they have received commitments from suppliers. Be sure to ask for proof of the merchant's allocations. If you do not, then the words *caveat emptor* could have special significance to you.

For many Bordeaux wine enthusiasts, buying wine futures of the right wine, in the right vintage, at the right time guarantees that they have liquid gems worth four or five times the price they paid for the wine. However, as history has proven, only a handful of vintages over the last 20 years have appreciated that significantly in their first 2 or 3 years (e.g., 1982, 1989, and 1990). The fact that Bordeaux has had four consecutive vintages that have been plagued by rain at the harvest (1991, 1992, 1993, and 1994) for the first time since the early seventies has eliminated the need to buy wine futures, although the finest 1994 merit interest. The 1990s merited considerable attention from serious Bordeaux collectors, since many of the wines are extraordinary. However, prices for the top wines had more than doubled at the time of writing in summer 1995, with demand seemingly insatiable.

For the next several years consumers should be looking back to bargains that exist from inventories of already bottled Bordeaux, rather than investing their money in wine futures, which, at the time of writing, makes no sense except for a rare case where a parent may desire to buy a child's birth-year wine in large-format bottles such as magnums or double magnums.

The Dry Red Wines of Bordeaux

L'ANGÉLUS (ST.-ÉMILION)* * * * *

1993	C	91
1992	C	89
1991	C	87

Since 1988 L'Angélus has represented a blue-chip investment, as the quality of this estate's wines has been nothing less than sensational, not only in great years, such as 1989 and 1990, but also in less than stellar vintages such as 1992 and 1993. In 1993, L'Angélus has produced an exceptional wine, with an opaque purple/black color, and a huge, smoky nose of tobacco, chocolate, herbs, licorice, and cassis. There is a roasted ripeness to the wine, as well as full body, great concentration and purity, and a long, rich, superbly delineated personality. The wine's moderate tannin is nearly concealed by lavish quantities of ripe fruit. This blockbuster 1993 will be bottled without fining or filtration—a tribute to the proprietor's commitment to excellence. Drink it between 1998 and 2012. Bravo!

In what can be a light-bodied, sometimes dilute year, L'Angélus has turned out one of the vintage's stars. The 1992 exhibits a dark-ruby/purple color, a big, smoky, licorice-, and herb-scented nose, and gobs of ripe, chocolatey, cassis fruit. It finishes with sweet tannin and no evidence of dilution. Charm, fatness, depth, purity, and suppleness are present in this impressive wine. **A.M.: Now–2004.** Bravo again!

One of the few successful wines of the vintage in St.-Émilion, the 1991 reveals a complex bouquet of chocolate, coffee, toasty new oak, herbs, and jammy red fruits. Lusciously ripe fruit is presented in a medium-bodied, sweet, round format that offers immediate gratification. It should drink well for another 5–6 years. Given how difficult the 1991 vintage was, this effort is noteworthy.

Past Glories: 1990 (96), 1989 (95), 1986 (89)

Past Mediocrities . . . or Worse: Just about anything made in the sixties or seventies

D'ANGLUDET (MARGAUX)* * *

1993	B	84
1992	B	73
1991	B	74

D'Angludet's 1993 appears to be far superior to this estate's diluted 1992. The wine reveals a pretty bouquet of ripe berry fruit intermingled with scents of earth, herbs, and wood. It is medium bodied, compact, and small-framed, as well as soft, accessible, and capable of 6–8 years of drinkability.

Much of the 1992's herb-tinged fruit did not survive the fining, filtering, and bottling process. Light ruby with a washed-out hollowness, this is a surprisingly feeble effort from this estate. Drink it over the next 3–4 years.

D'Angludet's excessively weedy, light-bodied, shallow 1991 needs more stuffing and character. Drink it over the next 4–5 years.

Past Glories: 1983 (89)

D'ARMAILHAC (PAUILLAC)* * *
Note: Formerly called Mouton-Baron-Philippe

1993	C	85
1992	C	86
1991	C	74

It is rare to find a soft, supple, deliciously fruity, seductive, ready-to-drink Médoc in the 1993 vintage. D'Armailhac's 1993 is an intelligently made wine from this vintage. Producers had two choices in 1993—to go for low yields, knowing that extended maceration would produce a formidably tannic, backward wine, or to attempt to produce a lighter, more supple wine, hoping purchasers would recognize its charm and finesse. D'Armailhac is undeniably seductive, juicy, and fruity, with enough Pauillac character and breed to carry it through 7–10 years of cellaring. Although there is some tannin, this wine is best drunk early on. Restaurants take note!

D'Armailhac's 1992 is a charming, straightforward, richly fruity wine with moderate- to dark-ruby color, and a spicy nose of roasted nuts and jammy black currants. The attack offers lush, velvety-textured fruit that fades quickly. Nevertheless, this is a pure, attractive, elegant wine for drinking over the next 5–6 years.

The 1991 exhibits superficial appeal in its lavishly oaky, sweet nose, but once past the makeup, the wine is thin and angular, with little depth, and a short, tannic, tough finish. It will get more attenuated with age. Drink it before the end of the century.

L'ARRIVET-HAUT-BRION (GRAVES)* */* * *

1992	C	85

An attractive, dark-plum-colored wine with a moderately intense nose of jammy black cherries and spicy fruitcake aromas, this soft, round, light- to medium-bodied wine possesses pretty fruit, admirable purity, and a velvety finish. This light yet flavorful wine is ideal for drinking over the next 3–5 years.

L'ARROSÉE (ST.-ÉMILION)* * * *

1993	C	89
1992	C	87

NOTE: No 1991 was produced under the L'Arrosée label.

L'Arrosée produced one of the most seductive 1992s and has once again turned in an excellent effort with an even richer and more expansively flavored 1993. The wine's deep ruby color is followed by a fragrant, sweet, jammy, black cherry nose, intertwined with lavish quantities of toasty, smoky new oak. Seductive and round, with a velvety texture and excellent concentration, this voluptuously rich, soft St.-Émilion should be drunk over the next 10–12 years.

Only 36 hectoliters per hectare were produced by L'Arrosée in the abundant 1992 vintage. The results are one of the more hedonistic wines of the vintage. True to the L'Arrosée style, this wine offers generous amounts of smoky, toasty new oak and jammy black cherries and raspberries in both its aromatic and flavor profiles. Succulent, expansive, ripe, and smooth as silk, this is a delicious, up-front wine for drinking over the next 5–7 years. The Richebourg of St.-Émilion?

Past Glories: 1990 (92), 1986 (93), 1985 (92), 1983 (88), 1982 (93), 1961 (94)

AUSONE (ST.-ÉMILION)* * * *

1993	E	88?
1992	E	80?

NOTE: No 1991 was produced under the Ausone label.

Purchasers of Ausone's 1993 will not be able to enjoy it for at least 15–25 years. It may be more of a gamble than the following tasting notes suggest. This medium- to dark-ruby-colored 1993 possesses Ausone's telltale austerity, and an elusive perfume of minerals and spices. The attack offers up ripe fruit that is quickly buried under a cascade of tannin and acidity. Spicy and hard, but intriguing, it is typically Ausone-like—admirable, but painful to taste. If it does not dry out, it could turn out to be an excellent, possibly outstanding Ausone.

Ausone's firmly structured, tannic 1992 reluctantly reveals a nose of dusty, flowery red fruits, wood, and minerals. Light bodied and shallow, with cherry fruit flavors intermingled with the taste of herbs, this wine appears to lack a finish, depth, and intensity. Too tannic and sinewy to enjoy over the near term, Ausone's 1992 is a likely candidate to dry out before its tannins ever melt away.

Past Glories: 1990 (94+), 1989 (92), 1983 (94), 1982 (95), 1976 (94), 1929 (96), 1900 (94)

Past Mediocrities . . . or Worse: 1971 (78), 1970 (69), 1961 (74)

BAHANS HAUT-BRION (GRAVES)* * *

1993	C	86
1992	C	85
1991	B	76

I continue to consume my 1989 Bahans Haut-Brion with enormous pleasure. It is one of the two greatest second wines (the 1982 Les Forts de Latour is a noteworthy rival) that I have known. That being said, the 1991 is short, diluted, light bodied, and lacking color and fruit. Medium-dark ruby with a currant/herbal bouquet, the 1992 is supple, medium bodied, charming, and harmonious. It should drink well for 4–6 years.

The 1993 Bahans Haut-Brion exhibits excellent, sweet black cherry fruit in a medium-bodied format. The wine is low in acidity, contains a considerable amount of Merlot and Cabernet Franc, and displays good ripeness as well as an easygoing, round, gentle personality. Drink it over the next 5–7 years.

BALESTARD-LA-TONNELLE (ST.-ÉMILION)* * *

1992	B	75

NOTE: No 1991 was produced under the Balestard-La Tonnelle label.

This light-ruby-colored 1992 exhibits a spicy, dull nose, tannic, medium-bodied flavors, and a lean, tough finish. Readers can expect it to become even more attenuated with cellaring.

BATAILLEY (PAUILLAC)* * *

1992	C	77

This estate has a tendency to turn out tough-textured, hard, ageworthy wines. While that may be a worthy goal in many vintages, it was not a desirable agenda for producing an attractive 1992. This medium-bodied wine is loaded down with an excessive amount of tannin for its fragile fruit constitution. The result is a tough, hard, sharply tannic wine that will dry out long before its tannin melts away.

BEAU SÉJOUR-BÉCOT (ST.-ÉMILION)* * *

1993	C	87
1992	C	86

NOTE: No 1991 was produced under the Beau Séjour-Bécot label.

It is ironic that this estate, demoted in the 1985 classification of St.-Émilion, has been completely reenergized by the Bécot family, and is now making wines that are better than some of the premiers grands crus classés. The results of the 1995 reclassification of St.-Émilion's wines (to be published within a year) will be interesting. Beau Séjour-Bécot's 1993 may turn out to be an outstanding effort in this vintage. Although the wine possesses a bit too much new oak, that trait can be overlooked in view of the high extraction and flavor purity the estate has achieved. This sweet, full-bodied, ripe wine possesses gorgeous richness, as well as length and intensity. The elevated tannin is sweet, rather than hard and astringent. This wine should drink well between 1998 and 2010.

A solid, ripe, concentrated 1992, this deeply colored, oaky wine reveals a sweet, ripe, red- and black-fruit component, dramatic, spicy, lavishly oaked flavors, low acidity, fine richness, and a medium-bodied, heady finish. It is smooth enough to be drunk now, and should last for 6–7 years. This St.-Émilion estate is on its way up the quality scale.

BEAUREGARD (POMEROL)* * *

1993	C	87
1992	C	88

NOTE: No 1991 was produced under the Beauregard label.

This property is on the rebound and merits readers' attention. The 1992 is the best Beauregard in years. It offers a dark-ruby color, an intensely spicy, fragrant, richly fruity nose, soft, fleshy flavors, medium to full body, and a round, gentle finish. Drink it over the next 5–7 years. This is a surprisingly extracted and powerful 1992. Kudos to Beauregard!

This property has followed their successful 1992 with a powerful, concentrated, medium- to full-bodied, tannic, well-made 1993. Offering plenty of mocha-tinged, black cherry fruit, the 1993 is pure, rich, dense, and ideal for drinking between 1998 and 2010.

BEAUSÉJOUR-DUFFAU (ST.-ÉMILION)* * * * *

1993	D	89?
1992	D	87+

NOTE: No 1991 was produced under the Beauséjour-Duffau label.

As evidenced by their excellent 1988, 1989, and blockbuster, rich, monumental 1990, this château is on a hot streak. In many ways the 1993 is a perfect example of both the attributes and liabilities of the finest 1993 Bordeaux. The color is an opaque purple, and the nose offers up sweet, ripe, black currilanty aromas intermingled with scents of dusty earth and toasty new oak. Extremely powerful and concentrated, but with abrasive tannin that assaults the palate, this is a backward, broodingly rich, formidable wine that requires 10–15, perhaps even 20, years of cellaring. The sweetness of fruit and high extraction suggest it will have the requisite concentration to balance out the tannin. Could this wine turn out similar to the 1975 Lafleur or 1975 La Mission, where the phenomenal flavor extraction continues to outweigh the high tannin level? Do not touch a bottle before 2005; it may be a 30+ year wine.

This microestate's (less than 2,000 cases) 1992 is a standout effort among an undistinguished group of St.-Émilion premiers grands crus classés. The wine exhibits a deep, dark, opaque ruby/purple color, and a heady bouquet of ripe black cherry fruit intermingled with scents of minerals, flowers, earth, and new oak. Surprisingly dense, medium to full bodied, concentrated, and noticeably tannic, this is a powerful, rich, ageworthy 1992 that needs 3–4 years to shed its tannin. It will last for 10–15 years. It is one of the most backward wines of the 1992 vintage, offering further evidence that Beauséjour-Duffau is producing one of Bordeaux's finest wines.

As a postscript, I recently tasted the 1990 Beauséjour-Duffau on three separate occasions, and once again in a blind tasting of 1990s sponsored by Executive Wine Seminars in New York City with 150 tasters in attendance. The 1990 Beauséjour-Duffau came in first, crushing such awesome competition as Château Margaux, Lafite-Rothschild, Latour, Pétrus, and even Montrose. I also served it to guests who are serious Bordeaux enthusiasts, but who had not purchased the property's 1990 (not prestigious enough, I suppose). I am beginning to think this wine is a modern-day legend and a candidate for perfection in 10–15 years—it is that awesomely concentrated and rich. This mind-blowing effort will be very difficult to find, as this property is tiny. According to advertisements I have seen, the price has jumped over 100%, with the wine currently retailing for $900 a case. It is worth it!

Past Glories: 1990 (100), 1989 (90)

BELAIR (ST.-ÉMILION)* *

1993	C	79
1992	C	74?

NOTE: No 1991 was produced under the Belair label.

Belair's muscular, hard-bodied 1993 is all skeleton and framework, without sufficient underlying fruit or charm to offset the wine's formidable tannin level. There may be some tasters who can muster enthusiasm for such a style, but I am not one.

The 1992's light, washed-out color and weak, muted nose is followed by a wine lacking fruit, depth, and grip. There is little finish in this shallow, diluted wine. Three cask notes revealed similar results. The wine was not offered for tasting following its bottling—not an encouraging sign.

BELGRAVE (HAUT-MÉDOC)* *

1993	C	79

A lean, tough-textured, hollow wine, the 1993 Belgrave reveals good color, but not enough fruit to balance out the wine's structural components.

BELLEGRAVE (POMEROL)* *

1993	C	81
1992	C	85

NOTE: No 1991 Bellegrave was offered for tasting.

This up-and-coming property has recently begun fashioning better wine. The 1992 displays attractive black raspberry/plumlike fruit, toasty new oak, and a touch of herbal tea in its bouquet and flavors. Medium bodied, with sufficient depth and a soft, easygoing finish, it should be drunk over the next 5–6 years. The 1993 Bellegrave is a pleasant, monolithic, fruity Pomerol with light tannin, fine body, and a solid but uninspiring finish. Drink it over the next 5–7 years.

BELLES-GRAVES (LALANDE-DE-POMEROL)* * *

1993	B	85

A fine effort from this meticulously run Lalande-de-Pomerol château, the 1993 Belles-Graves offers more sweetness and opulence than many of its more famous, as well as more expensive, Bordeaux peers. The wine exhibits very good concentration, plump, black cherry flavors, low acidity, and a chewy, clean finish. Drink it over the next 4–5 years.

BEYCHEVELLE (ST.-JULIEN)* * *

1993	C	77?
1992	C	81
1991	C	85

The 1993 Beychevelle tasted lean, compact, excessively tannic, and frightfully austere. This is a sobering example of Beychevelle that will remain hard and sinewy.

The 1991 has outperformed the 1992. The 1991 offers an attractive, curranty, sweet, oaky nose, soft, round, elegant flavors, admirable ripeness, low acidity, and a plush finish. Although not a big wine, it is graceful, fruity, and tasty. Drink it over the next 5–6 years. The herb-tinged 1992 is a straightforward, compact wine with its tannin dominating its fruit. Light bodied and angular, but attractively supple with low acidity, the 1992 Beychevelle needs to be drunk over the next 3–4 years.

Past Glories: 1989 (91), 1986 (92), 1982 (92)

BON PASTEUR (POMEROL)* * * *

1993	C	88
1992	C	86

NOTE: No 1991 was produced under the Bon Pasteur label.

Bon Pasteur is a perennial overachiever, so it is not surprising that the husband and wife oenology team of Dany and Michel Rolland have crafted a wine far better than this estate's *terroir* warrants. The 1993 Bon Pasteur boasts a saturated dark-ruby color, and a spicy, moderately intense nose of vanillin, roasted nuts, black fruits, and chocolate-covered caramels. Rich, medium to full bodied, with an intriguing texture, as well as admirable chewiness and purity, this luscious, ripe wine will drink well for 10–15 years. The lovely deep-ruby-colored 1992 exhibits a smoky, mocha/chocolate/black cherry–scented nose, ripe fruit, medium body, a tannic backbone, satisfying depth, and more structure and length than many 1992s. It will drink well for 5–7 years, possibly longer.

Past Glories: 1990 (92), 1982 (97)

BONALGUE (POMEROL)* * *

1993	C	85

This small estate consistently fashions medium-bodied, flavorful, solidly made, and well-endowed Pomerols. Although they lack complexity, they offer plenty of sweet, ripe, tasty, black cherry fruit. With fine concentration and moderate tannin, the 1993 is ideal for drinking over the next 5–7 years—uncomplicated, but satisfying.

LE BOSCQ (MÉDOC)* * *

1993 Vieilles Vignes	B	85

This property often makes good wine in top years, so it was unexpected that in a more difficult vintage, Le Boscq turned out a spicy, sweet, ripe, one-dimensional but fleshy 1993 that will drink well for 5–6 years.

BOURGNEUF-VAYRON (POMEROL)* *

1993	C	68
1992	C	74

NOTE: No 1991 was produced under the Bourgneuf-Vayron label.

Appallingly vegetal, hollow, and ferociously tannic, the densely colored 1993 looks good, but tastes bad. Avoid. With its medium-ruby color and light-intensity bouquet consisting primarily of underripe fruit, the straightforward, one-dimensional 1992 suffers from excessive tannin as well as a green, vegetal character. Unimpressive. It should be drunk over the next 4–5 years.

BRANAIRE-DUCRU (ST.-JULIEN)* * *

1993	C	87
1992	C	82
1991	C	85

I admire the charm, elegance, and sweet ripe fruit of Branaire's 1991. It is an elegant, stylish wine with adequate ripeness, medium body, a soft, velvety texture, and fine balance. Already delicious, it will drink well for 4–5 years. With respect to the 1992, a spicy, light, vaguely fruity nose is followed by some evidence of ripe fruit, medium body, and low tannin. The wine delivers some oak-tinged, ripe berry/curranty fruit in a soft, easygoing style. Drink it during its first 4–6 years of life as a picnic or luncheon wine. Branaire's 1993 reveals the classy, suave, elegant style perfected by this estate. Made from 70% Cabernet Sauvignon and 30% Merlot, and aged in 50% new oak casks, the wine boasts a healthy dark-ruby/purple color, sweet ripe fruit, medium body, and moderately hard tannin in the finish. The 1993 Branaire may turn out to be the modern-day equivalent of this property's 1966. The 1993 should drink well between 1998 and 2015.
Past Glories: 1989 (91), 1982 (91), 1975 (92)

BRANE-CANTENAC (MARGAUX)* *

1993	C	72

I rarely have the opportunity to taste Brane-Cantenac before it is bottled. The 1993 cask sample revealed a high-acid, hollow, diluted wine with herb-tinged, washed-out fruit, and a medium-bodied, extremely tannic style.

LA CABANNE (POMEROL)* *

1993	C	76
1992	B	80

NOTE: No 1991 La Cabanne was offered for tasting.
La Cabanne's 1992 is typical of many wines from the vintage. It offers an uncomplicated but attractively fruity, ripe nose, light to medium body, soft tannin, and low acidity. It will last for 4–6 years. The 1993's good, clean, spicy, light-intensity fruit is followed by a lean, tough-textured, tannic wine lacking depth and ripeness. Drink it over the next 7–8 years.

CADET-BON (ST.-ÉMILION)* *

1993	C	77
1992	C	74

The vegetal, underripe 1992 Cadet-Bon offers a sound color and some roundness and fruit, but it is oh so herbaceous, and not my style. Drink it over the next 4–5 years. Medium ruby with a nondescript nose of herbs, damp earth, and old wood, the medium-bodied, compact, tough-textured 1993 is lean and lacking ripeness, extract, and body. Drink it over the next 7–8 years.

CADET-PIOLA (ST.-ÉMILION)* * *

1993	C	85
1992	C	72

NOTE: No 1991 was produced under the Cadet-Piola label.

Given the 1993 vintage's potential for tough, hard, tannic wines, and Cadet-Piola's tendency to produce rustic, dense, tough wines, one would have expected a wine that would melt a tooth's enamel. Not so. This estate has produced a soft, fleshy, medium-bodied, supple, easygoing 1993 that will offer pleasant drinking over the next 5–7 years. The compact 1992 Cadet-Piola displays a medium-ruby color, an unimpressive, watery bouquet, and short, soft, ripe, but insubstantial flavors dominated by an astringent, dry, tannic taste. The wine will dry out in 4–6 years, so drink it young.

CALON-SÉGUR (ST.-ESTÈPHE)* * *

1992	C	74?
1991	C	84

The deep-ruby-colored 1991 exhibits a tight, old-fashioned, rustic bouquet of leather, cedar, tea, and ripe berry fruit, adequate body, a tight structure, and fine depth. I would not be surprised to see it improve with 3–4 years of cellaring. It should keep for 10–15 years. Cask samples of the 1992 were all disappointingly light and soft. Although fruity, the wine tastes thin, with little grip or concentration. It was not presented for tasting after bottling.
Past Glories: 1988 (91), 1986 (89), 1982 (94+), 1953 (96), 1949 (93), 1947 (97), 1945 (92), 1928 (94), 1926 (92), 1900 (90)
Past Mediocrities . . . or Worse: 1970 (80), 1964 (75), 1961 (83)

CANON (CANON-FRONSAC)* * *

1993	C	85
1992	C	78

NOTE: No 1991 Canon will be offered for sale in the United States.

One of the more impressive wines from the Canon-Fronsac region, the 1993 Canon exhibits expansive, sweet fruit that more than compensates for the moderate tannin level. This well-made, medium-bodied, lean wine is an ideal candidate for cellaring or drinking over the next 10–15 years. The 1992 is a pleasant, straightforward, fruity, monochromatic, tasty wine with fine ripeness, a lean texture, low acidity, and an austere finish. Drink it over the next 5–6 years. This is another 1992 that revealed more fruit before bottling.

CANON (ST.-ÉMILION)* * * *

1993	C	86?
1992	C	83?

NOTE: No 1991 was produced under the Canon label.

Canon's 1993 is perplexing as well as difficult to assess. It possesses several positive attributes—a saturated dark-ruby color, an attractive, sweet, ripe attack, and plenty of power. On the downside, the frightfully high tannin level dominates the wine's personality, making it taste compact and raising doubts about its balance. Optimistically, the tannin may subside before the fruit fades, but that rarely happens during the evolution of most wines. This offering will develop an intriguing bouquet, but the astringency of tannin is a legitimate concern. Certainly the 1993 Canon is capable of lasting 20–25 years, but it may turn out like the 1978 and 1979 Canons—impressive in a dry, austere style, rather than enjoyable in a hedonistic sense.

From cask, I had thought the 1992 Canon to be one of St.-Émilion's most successful wines. Like many 1992s, the wine's fragile fruit appears to have suffered from the fining and filtering that the Bordelais routinely do at bottling. The results offer a perplexingly ripe but hard, tough, sculptured wine that appears slightly eviscerated. The color is sound, the fruit and attack begin well, but there is not much depth or length—just tannin, alcohol, acidity, and wood. Is this wine closed, or merely empty and hollow? The dark-ruby color is followed by a spicy bouquet of new oak, sweet cassis fruit, melon, and earth. The wine exhibits good depth, medium body, a supple texture, and a round, generous finish. Drink it over the next 7–8 years.

Past Glories: 1989 (92), 1986 (91), 1985 (90), 1983 (89), 1982 (96), 1961 (88), 1959 (95), 1955 (88), 1948 (89), 1947 (93)

Past Mediocrities . . . or Worse: 1975 (65), 1970 (84)

CANON DE BREM (CANON-FRONSAC)* * *

1993	C	82?
1992	C	80

NOTE: No 1991 Canon de Brem will be offered for sale in the United States.

While the rustic, extremely tannic 1993 displays some attractive cherrylike fruit, most of its charm is blasted away by the astringent, green tannin in the wine's flavors and finish. It will be interesting to see how this wine tastes after bottling, as this is one of the finest vineyards of the appellation. The light-bodied, stern, ready-to-drink 1992 exhibits hard tannin and a rustic personality. Simple, lean, and likely to dry out, it should be drunk over the next 4–5 years.

CANON-LA-GAFFELIÈRE (ST.-ÉMILION)* * * * *

1993	C	90
1992	C	87

One of the bright, shining stars of Bordeaux's right-bank appellation of St.-Émilion, this impeccably run estate has produced an atypically rich, concentrated, delicious 1992. Very dark ruby, with a spicy, toasty, black currant–scented bouquet, ripe, medium- to full-bodied flavors, and excellent richness, this fine 1992 should spark considerable consumer interest. Drink it over the next 7–8 years.

The great success this property has enjoyed continues with a sterling effort in 1993. The 1993 boasts a saturated, opaque, plum/purple color, and a knockout bouquet of jammy black currants, licorice, smoke, and flowers. Full bodied and highly extracted, with a sweet, expansive chewiness, this superconcentrated, moderately tannic wine will drink well young and age gracefully for 15 or more years. This is an outstanding, impressively endowed 1993.

Past Glories: 1990 (93), 1989 (89), 1988 (90)

CANON-MOUEIX (CANON-FRONSAC)* * *

1993	C	83?
1992	C	83

NOTE: No 1991 was produced under the Canon-Moueix label.

Although the 1993 Canon-Moueix is an extremely tannic, backward wine, it does possess good concentration. The raw materials are weighed down by considerable tannin. The medium- to deep-ruby-colored 1992 reveals a sweet nose of earth, red and black fruits, and spice. Round, well-endowed flavors are presented in a medium-bodied, supple-textured format that is marred only by obtrusively aggressive tannin in the wine's rough finish. Drink it over the next 4–5 years.

CANTEMERLE (MACAU)* * *

1993	C	86
1992	C	86
1991	B	76

Cantemerle's innocuous 1991 is disappointingly weedy, light bodied, and short in the finish. It exhibits some soft fruit flavors, but lacks substance. The deeply colored 1992 offers spicy, ripe fruit and olive aromas, a supple, ripe, smooth-as-silk palate, and plenty of juicy, uncomplicated fruit in the finish. An elegant wine, it should be drunk over the next 4–6 years. The 1993 reveals a deep-ruby/purple color, more new oak than Cantemerle generally possesses, admirable quantities of rich cassis fruit backing up considerable tannin and structure, and an inner core of sweetness and ripeness. This is an elegant, slightly austere 1993 for drinking between 2000 and 2010.

Past Glories: 1989 (91), 1983 (91), 1961 (90), 1959 (89), 1953 (94), 1949 (90)

Past Mediocrities . . . or Worse: 1986 (82), 1975 (84)

CANTENAC-BROWN (MARGAUX)* * *

1993	C	82
1992	C	78
1991	C	74

Cantenac-Brown's 1991 is typical for this property—a hard, austere, tough-textured, mean wine that will have a tendency to dry out before the tannins soften. In spite of its impressive color, it is a hollow wine lacking charm and finesse. The dark-ruby-colored, lean 1992 exhibits adequate concentration and length, but the austere, forbiddingly tannic and astringent style assaults the palate. I cannot imagine this wine ever achieving a balance between fruit and structure. Drink it over the next 4–5 years. A backward, densely colored, compact, tannic wine, the 1993 Cantenac-Brown lacks ripe fruit. The high tannin level gives the wine a structured, austere, lean personality. Masochists who want to take a chance on it should give it at least 4–5 years of cellaring; it will keep 15–20 or more years.

CAP DE MOURLIN (ST.-ÉMILION)* * *

1992	B	76

NOTE: No 1991 was produced under the Cap de Mourlin label.

An element of menthol and jam in this wine's bouquet offers pleasure. The wine reveals a medium-ruby color, light tannin, and a compact, muscular yet soft feel. There is an absence of depth and length. Drink it over the next 5–6 years.

CARBONNIEUX (GRAVES)* * *

1993	C	87
1992	C	86
1991	C	86

More renowned for its classy, stylish dry white wines, this estate has made considerable improvement in its red wine program, fashioning richer, more concentrated, yet undeniably elegant wines that are classic examples of the appellation. The 1991 is one of the most seductive and graceful wines of the vintage. The medium-ruby color is followed by a bouquet that soars from the glass, offering copious scents of tobacco, herbs, black fruits, and sweet oak. Medium bodied, with gobs of rich, creamy-textured fruit, this elegant, well-balanced, smooth-edged wine reveals soft tannin and a lush finish. Drink it over the next 7–8 years.

It is a terrific choice for restaurants. The deeply colored 1992 exhibits an attractive bouquet of tobacco, toast, and black fruits. There is fine ripeness, solid body, light tannin, and an expansive, lush, silky personality. This is a delicious, pure, elegant 1992 that will provide plenty of joy over the next decade.

The 1993 exhibits a medium- to dark-ruby color, a big, smoky, tobacco, earthy nose, vanillin-tinged, sweet, jammy, berry flavors, medium body, and a smooth-as-silk finish. It is a seductive (not an adjective commonly used to describe the 1993 clarets) wine that can be drunk when released or cellared for 12–15 years.

DE CARLES (FRONSAC)* * *

1993	B	83
1992	B	81

NOTE: No 1991 de Carles will be offered for sale in the United States.

The 1993 de Carles exhibits ripe fruit, some fat, and a supple personality—an especially noteworthy and laudable characteristic in what can be a frightfully hard vintage for many Fronsacs and Canon-Fronsacs. Drink it over the next 5–6 years. This well-run estate has turned out a ripe, medium-ruby-colored 1992 with admirable fruit and depth, low acidity, and a lean but pleasant finish. Drink it over the next 7–8 years.

LES CARMES-HAUT-BRION (GRAVES)* * *

1993	C	85

A major improvement over the light, diluted 1992, Les Carmes-Haut-Brion's 1993 offers a medium-dark-ruby color, a spicy, earthy, berry-scented nose, soft, ripe flavors exhibiting fine concentration, medium body, and a round finish. As with many 1993 Graves, the tannin level is less severe than that found in many Médocs. I admired this wine's soft fruit and forward, precocious personality. Drink it over the next 5–7 years.

CARRUADES DE LAFITE (PAUILLAC)* *

1993	C	85
1992	C	82
1991	C	84

Lafite-Rothschild's second wine in 1991 exhibits a light to medium body, spicy, tobacco, and tealike flavors, adequate ripeness, and a soft, concentrated finish. It should drink well for 7–8 years. The 1992 Carruades de Lafite reveals light body, adequate ripeness, a soft, smooth texture, and a clean, spicy finish. Drink it over the next 4–5 years. Of the 64% of Lafite-Rothschild's harvest eliminated from the grand vin, only 40% made it into the 1993 Carruades de Lafite. It displays a character similar to Lafite's in its elegance and finesse, as well as fine ripeness, and tasty, curranty fruit wrapped in a medium-bodied, supple framework. A noteworthy introduction to Lafite-Rothschild's elegant style, it should drink well for 5–6 years.

CASSAGNE-HAUT-CANON-LA TRUFFIÈRE (CANON-FRONSAC)* * *

1992	B	81

NOTE: No 1991 was produced under the Cassagne-Haut-Canon-La Truffière label.

Readers may remember how splendid this property's 1989 turned out. While the 1992 is no 1989, it does offer a deep-ruby/purple color, a ripe nose, attractive, medium-bodied flavors with sufficient concentration, and a spicy, moderately tannic finish. This austere wine will keep for up to a decade.

CERTAN-GIRAUD (POMEROL)* * *

1993	C 85

This property tends to fashion plump, slightly unfocused, but lusciously fruity, occasionally fat, juicy wines that are best drunk in their first 6–10 years of life. Although monolithic, the mouth-filling, pure 1993 has good fruit and is not burdened by excessive tannin. Drink it over the next 6–8 years.

CERTAN DE MAY (POMEROL)* * * *

1993	D ?
1992	D 87?

NOTE: No 1991 was produced under the Certan de May label.

First the good news. Certan de May's 1992 is obviously a powerful, concentrated wine, with the intensely herbaceous side of Certan de May fortunately subdued. The result is a wine with a forcefully rich, black currant nose combined with scents of smoky new oak, tobacco, and herbs, medium to full body, a soft, silky texture, excellent concentration, low acidity, and soft tannin. It should be drinkable when released and age well for 10–12 years. The bad news is that some bottles reveal a damp, musty, cardboard character in the bouquet but not in the flavors. If it is not a cork problem, might this musty element relate to the use of steam in the fabrication or cleaning of the barrels, with the steam's moisture trapped in the wood's interior, giving off unclean aromas of wood? I would welcome readers' thoughts on this wine.

Unfortunately, samples of the 1993 displayed a musty, damp-cellar, old, funky wood character that dominated the wine's aromatic personality. Lamentable, because otherwise, Certan de May's 1993 possesses considerable color pigmentation, a ripe, full-bodied, powerful constitution, and moderate tannin in a long, forceful, authoritatively flavored finish. I will be anxious to retaste this wine after bottling. Judgment reserved.

Past Glories: 1990 (92), 1988 (93), 1986 (92), 1985 (94), 1982 (98+), 1981 (90), 1979 (92), 1945 (96)

CHAMBERT-MARBUZET (ST.-ESTÈPHE)* *

1993	B 74
1992	B 76

NOTE: No 1991 Chambert-Marbuzet was offered for tasting.

The 1992 Chambert-Marbuzet has not handled its bottling too well, as this wine has lost considerable fruit. Although lighter than usual, this spicy, minty, watery wine possesses medium body, decent concentration, and a short, attenuated finish. Drink it over the next 2–3 years. As for the 1993, a minty, spicy, soft, fruity nose fades quickly, as do the wine's flavors once they touch the palate. This offering is diluted, too earthy and woody, and short in the finish.

CHANTEGRIVE (GRAVES)* * *

1993	B 81

This light- to medium-ruby-colored 1993 displays a surprisingly advanced, nearly mature nose of soft cherry and cassis fruit, some oak, low acidity, and a spicy, round finish. Drink it over the next 4–5 years.

LA CHAPELLE DE LA MISSION (GRAVES)* * *

1993	C 85
1992	C 86

This is the new second wine of La Mission-Haut-Brion. The 1992 is a soft, fruity, attractively made, medium-bodied wine with a pure, ripe black cherry fruit and smoky tobacco character. Drink it over the next 3–4 years. Approximately 1,000 cases of 1993 were made. Not surprisingly, it is a tasty, rich, medium-bodied, soft wine that is ideal for drinking over the next 7–8 years. The elimination of 18%–20% of the harvest is undoubtedly the reason both this wine and La Mission-Haut-Brion are superb in 1993.

CHASSE-SPLEEN (MOULIS)* * */* * * *

1993	C	86
1992	C	85

Light, with an atypically herbaceous character, the 1992 offers good ripeness, a chunky, medium-bodied personality, excellent color saturation, and light tannin in the attractive, firmly structured finish. It should drink well for 7–8 years. This estate has produced a good, impressively colored, medium-bodied 1993 with the vintage's telltale, firm, tannic structure, as well as enough fruit and fat for balance. The wine reveals fine ripeness, extraction, and purity, along with the black-fruit character Chasse-Spleen routinely achieves. It should drink well between 1998 and 2010.

Past Glories: 1990 (88), 1989 (91), 1986 (90), 1985 (90), 1975 (90), 1970 (90), 1949 (92)

CHAUVIN (ST.-ÉMILION)* * *

1993	C	82
1992	C	79

NOTE: No 1991 was produced under the Chauvin label.

The ruby-colored 1993 Chauvin is a light-bodied, fruity, soft-styled St.-Émilion with attractive herb-tinged, cherry, curranty fruit, light tannin, fine purity, and a short finish. Medium-ruby-colored, with light intensity and charming fruit in the nose, the moderately tannic 1992 lacks depth. The wine's ripeness and decent fruit will provide uncritical, light drinking for 4–5 years.

CHEVAL BLANC (ST.-ÉMILION)* * * * *

1993	D	86?
1992	D	77

NOTE: No 1991 was produced under the Cheval Blanc label.

Medium to dark ruby colored, with sweet scents of cassis, mulberries, menthol, and smoky new oak, Cheval Blanc's medium-bodied 1993 reveals fine concentration, as well as elevated tannin in the finish. The tannin gives the wine a dry, angular, compact personality. It will be interesting to see how this wine behaves after bottling. Will fining bring everything into balance, at the same time cutting the intrusive tannin level? A light-bodied, shallow wine for this great estate, the 1992 Cheval Blanc displays a vanillin-dominated nose with berry, jammy, herb, and coffee notes. There is not much depth, body, or length. Drink it over the next 4–5 years, as the hard tannin in the finish suggests that this wine will dry out quickly.

Past Glories: 1990 (95), 1986 (93), 1985 (94), 1983 (95), 1982 (100), 1981 (89), 1975 (90), 1964 (95), 1961 (93), 1955 (90), 1953 (94), 1949 (100), 1948 (96), 1947 (100), 1945 (91)

Past Mediocrities . . . or Worse: 1971 (84), 1970 (85), 1966 (85)

DOMAINE DE CHEVALIER (GRAVES)* * *

1993	C	86?
1992	C	85
1991	C	87

Domaine de Chevalier often makes attractive wines in off years and the 1991 is no exception. The wine reveals a deep-ruby color, a spicy, oaky nose, admirable structure, dense, ripe, sweet fruit, medium body, and a long, tannic finish. It will benefit from 2–3 years of cellaring. The 1992 offers toasty vanillin notes in its fruity nose, as well as a fine dark-ruby color. While lighter and more one-dimensional than usual, it is concentrated, soft, and oaky. It should drink well for 7–8 years. This 1993's impressive attack falls off in the mouth. With a saturated dark-ruby color and an attractive nose of ripe fruit and new oak, Domaine de Chevalier's 1993 exhibits fine ripeness and medium body, but the fruit, glycerin, and extract fade quickly as the tannin becomes more pronounced at the back of the mouth. If the wine fills out and/or gains weight, a very good to excellent score is possible. It will require 3–4 years of cellaring after its release. It will keep for 12–15 years.

Past Glories: 1990 (90), 1989 (91), 1988 (90), 1986 (90), 1983 (90), 1978 (92), 1970 (89), 1964 (90), 1959 (89), 1953 (92)

Past Mediocrities . . . or Worse: 1982 (67?), 1975 (68), 1971 (67)

CITRAN (HAUT-MÉDOC)* * *

1993	B	84?
1992	C	82
1991	B	86

For the last 7 or 8 years this estate has been making excellent wines characterized by dark, opaque colors and lavish quantities of smoky new oak in their aromas and ripe, concentrated flavors. The 1991 offers a bouquet of grilled nuts, new oak, and black currants. Spicy and ripe, this medium-bodied, soft, concentrated wine is a notable success. It will offer delicious drinking for at least 4–5 years. The impressive black/purple-colored 1992 exhibits a tight and overtly woody nose. Spicy, with medium body, moderate tannin, and some length, this is an atypically pigmented, tannic, and woody 1992. If more fruit emerges, the wine will merit a higher score. It will keep for a decade. I tasted the 1993 Citran on four separate occasions. Although my notes were variable, there is no question that the wine is a densely colored purple/black, with lavish quantities of toasty new oak. My only reservation is whether the wine will fill out, or whether the tannin will get the upper hand and dominate the wine's personality. There is some good red fruit, but is it enough to stand up to the tannic bite?

CLARKE (LISTRAC)* *

1993	B	80

Despite its toughness, the 1993 Clarke possesses some depth, a spicy, curranty nose and flavors, medium body, and moderate length. It should be drinkable in 2–3 years and last for a decade or more.

CLERC-MILON (PAUILLAC)* * * *

1993	C	88
1992	C	87
1991	C	79

Clerc-Milon normally produces a soft, round, easy-to-understand and -consume style of Pauillac. The 1991 is atypically hard and tough-textured, with a ruby color, some intriguing spicy, cinnamon, and cassis aromas, and an angular, short finish. A little more flesh on the bones would have added to its appeal. Drink it over the next 7–8 years. This lush, sexy 1992 is a meritorious effort in this irregular vintage. The wine possesses a moderately dark ruby color, and an up-front fragrance of *pain grillé,* roasted nuts, and cassis. Supple, with jammy black currant fruit, this silky, medium-bodied wine is ideal for drinking over the next 7–8 years.

A potentially outstanding wine, Clerc-Milon's 1993 is undeniably a success for the vintage. One of the keys to producing a successful 1993 was to include enough Merlot in the blend to cut the potential astringency and underripeness of the Cabernet Sauvignon. Clerc-Milon's 1993 blend of 40% Merlot, 55% Cabernet Sauvignon, and 5% Cabernet Franc has resulted in one of the most opulent Médocs of the vintage. The color is a healthy dark-ruby/purple, and the nose offers up flamboyant aromas of roasted herbs, jammy cassis, and lavish quantities of smoky, toasty new oak. The wine is soft and round, with low acidity and light tannin in the finish. It will offer irresistible drinking over the next decade.

Past Glories: 1989 (90)

CLINET (POMEROL)* * * * *

1993	D	91
1992	D	88+
1991	D	87

This property has been one of Bordeaux's superstars since 1988. I recently had the 1989 Clinet in a blind tasting, side by side with the 1989 Pétrus. Of the twenty-two tasters, the majority preferred the Clinet, although it was a tight race, as both wines were blockbuster examples of this outstanding vintage. An excellent wine in what was a disastrous year for most Pomerol estates, Clinet's 1991 may turn out to be the best wine of the appellation! Its surprisingly deep ruby/purple color does not suggest the horrendous conditions under which the grapes were harvested. The bouquet of pure, rich, black raspberry fruit and subtle oak is followed by a medium-bodied wine with surprising ripeness, richness, and an especially long finish. It is difficult to imagine the effort that went into producing a wine this seductive and rich in 1991. Clinet's 1991 should drink well for 7–10 years. The backward, dense, opaque purple-colored 1992 is an impressive, albeit backward wine for the vintage. In terms of body, extract, and ripeness, it is as well endowed as any 1992. Medium to full bodied, with superb purity and richness, an overall sense of balance, fine length, and low acidity, it is a candidate for an outstanding score in 3–4 years. It should drink well for 10–15 or more years. A very impressive 1992!

The 1993 Clinet should rival the 1993 Pétrus (perhaps the strongest candidate for the wine of the vintage). Given its black/purple color and huge, ripe, pure nose of black raspberries, licorice, vanillin, and sweet truffle scents, Clinet is one of the most concentrated wines of the vintage, with an inner core of sweet, expansive, intense fruit, medium to full body, noticeable, firm tannin, and a long, closed but rich finish. It will require 4–5 years of cellaring and should age for 20+ years. Readers should think of it as a modern-day version of a top-notch 1975 Pomerol—a powerful wine with ferocious tannin backed up by huge reserves of richness and fruit was typical of most 1975 Pomerols, although Clinet was a disappointment in that vintage.

Past Glories: 1990 (92), 1989 (99), 1988 (90)

Past Mediocrities . . . or Worse: Anything prior to 1985 should be approached with considerable caution.

CLOS DU CLOCHER (POMEROL)* * *

1993	C	80?
1992	C	85?

NOTE: No 1991 Clos du Clocher was offered for tasting.

Medium ruby, with spicy, washed-out, fruity scents, the medium-dark-colored 1993 is dominated by its tannin and body rather than by ripeness and fruit extraction. It is a likely candidate to dry out before any charm emerges. A successful wine for the vintage, with plenty of sweet, ripe, mocha/cassis fruit, the medium-bodied, chewy, fleshy 1992 exhibits fine ripeness and a sense of elegance, but the astringent tannin in the finish gives cause for concern. I suggest drinking it over the near term, say the next 4–5 years.

CLOS L'ÉGLISE (POMEROL)* *

1992	C	78

NOTE: No 1991 Clos L'Église will be offered for sale in the United States.

Moderately intense aromas of oak and herbaceously scented, curranty fruit are presented in a light-bodied, moderately tannic format. Drink the 1992 Clos L'Église over the next 4–5 years, as it does not possess the depth of fruit necessary to outlast the tannin.

CLOS FOURTET (ST.-ÉMILION)* * *

1993	D	86
1992	C	86

NOTE: No 1991 was produced under the Clos Fourtet label.

This is a property to watch, as it is now under the direction of André Lurton. The rise in quality is noticeable. The saturated, dark-ruby-colored 1993 displays plenty of toasty new oak, a backward, tannic, medium- to full-bodied personality, and a tough but spicy finish. There is an inner core of sweet, ripe fruit; therefore, it may just be a question of waiting 4–5 years for some tannin to melt away. It should last for 15–20 years. Exhibiting far more fruit, ripeness, depth, and length than I had previously thought, Clos Fourtet's 1992 offers a dark-ruby color, a pleasing jammy nose of black fruits and toast, medium body, sweet, expansive fruit, and a velvety texture. A fine effort, it should be consumed over the next 6–7 years.

CLOS DES JACOBINS (ST.-ÉMILION)* * *

1993	C	83

The well-colored, moderately tannic, one-dimensional 1993 Clos des Jacobins lacks the fat and charm this wine usually possesses. It is a candidate for up to 10 years of cellaring.

CLOS DU MARQUIS (ST.-JULIEN)* * *

1993	C	87
1992	C	86+
1991	B	85

Restaurants looking for an inexpensive, classy 1991 St.-Julien should check out the second wine from Léoville-Las Cases, Clos du Marquis. It displays fine ripeness, soft, round, complex fruit flavors, medium body, and a surprisingly long, soft finish. Drink it over the next 7–8 years. An impressive 1992, Clos du Marquis exhibits excellent ripeness, medium body, and plenty of richness in a soft, forward style. The finish boasts impressive depth and persistence, with no harshness. This is a noteworthy effort that should drink well for 7–10 years. It looks like a sure bet to be the best *deuxième* wine of the vintage. The 1993 is a surprisingly concentrated, powerful wine, revealing plenty of curranty fruit, attractive spice, a clean, well-focused winemaking style, and a long, rich, medium-bodied finish. There is enough tannin for this wine to last 12–15 years. In just about every vintage since 1982, Clos du Marquis has made wines of classified-growth quality.

CLOS DE L'ORATOIRE (ST. ÉMILION)* * *

1993	C 86

This well-situated St.-Émilion vineyard (next to Figeac) has produced an interesting 1993. The saturated dark-ruby color and the ripe, moderately intense bouquet of black cherries, herbs, spicy oak, and earth are laudable. Medium to full bodied, with an expansive, sweet, concentrated palate and light tannin, this well-made claret should drink well for 5–7 years.

CLOS RENÉ (POMEROL)* * *

1992	C 75
1991	C 78

For drinking over the next 3–4 years, the smoked herb– and tea-scented nose of the seemingly mature, shockingly evolved 1991 Clos René offers some attraction. Although the wine displays ripeness and substance, it finishes short. Overall, it is an acceptable effort for a right-bank 1991. The 1992 is soft and watery, with ripe berry fruit and a strong note of roasted peanuts. Supple, even diffuse, this is a wine to drink over the next 2–4 years.
Past Glories: 1947 (95)

CLOS ST.-MARTIN (ST.-ÉMILION)* * *

1993	C 85
1992	C 83

The 1993 Clos St.-Martin possesses a burgundian-like sweetness and expansiveness, as well as good ripeness, a round, fat, plump personality, and low acidity. Drink it over the next 5–6 years. The soft, round, richly fruity, smooth 1992 reveals an amiable personality. Drink it over the next 3–4 years.

LA CLOTTE (ST.-ÉMILION)* * *

1993	C 85
1992	C 85

This estate's wines are largely sold in Europe. The style offers enticingly ripe, jammy fruit in a supple format. The medium-bodied 1992 is fruity, soft, and jammy. Drink it over the next 4–5 years. The 1993 exhibits medium body, good fruit and ripeness, light tannin, low acidity, and a smooth-as-silk finish. Drink it over the next 7–8 years.

LA CLUSIÈRE (ST.-ÉMILION)* *

1992	C 76

NOTE: No 1991 was produced under the La Clusière label.
An earthy, herbal nose and moderately endowed, tight flavors display medium body and muscle, but little charm or fruit. This austere, ferociously tannic wine will undoubtedly dry out before any real grace or elegance emerges.

LA CONSEILLANTE (POMEROL)* * * * *

1993	D 86
1992	D 79
1991	D 83

La Conseillante's silky, soft, graceful style can be found in the light-bodied, delicate 1991. The medium-ruby color is followed by a perfumed nose of toasty, smoky, new oak and raspberry fruit. Although the finish is short, there is some lovely fruit in the middle. Drink it over the next 4–5 years. The 1992 displays light to medium body, an attractive but diluted raspberry- and vanillin-scented nose, a supple texture, and a short, shallow, woody finish. Given the wine's lack of concentration, it should be drunk over the next 3–4 years. For one of the most elegant and stylish Bordeaux wines (as well as a personal favorite), the 1992 is a disappointment. Medium-ruby-colored, with La Conseillante's attractive, moderately intense, sweet, raspberry and curranty fruit scents intertwined with toasty vanillin notes, the clean, well-made, light- to medium-bodied 1993 offers low acidity and light tannin in the finish. Reminiscent of this estate's delicious, charming 1987, it is a supple, charming, precocious Pomerol that requires consumption during its first 5–7 years of life.

Past Glories: 1990 (98), 1989 (97), 1986 (89), 1985 (94), 1983 (88), 1982 (91), 1981 (91), 1970 (92), 1959 (95), 1953 (90), 1949 (97), 1947 (91)

Past Mediocrities . . . or Worse: 1978 (75), 1976 (72), 1975 (83)

CORBIN (ST.-ÉMILION)* * *

1993	C	80

A correct, fruity, medium-bodied St.-Émilion, the 1993 Corbin reveals straightforward, tasty, curranty fruit, and spicy notes, but it lacks complexity and concentration. It should drink well for 5–6 years.

CORDEILLAN-BAGES (PAUILLAC)* *

1992	C	78
1991	C	77

This vineyard adjacent to the luxury hotel of the same name on the plateau of Bages continues to display a New World–like, tart acidic character that destroys the wine's charm. The 1991 reveals an impressively deep color, but little bouquet. The wine's high acidity and compressed personality make for an angular impression. Although there is some spicy, cassis fruit, the wine lacks depth to its understated, shallow format. Drink it over the next 5–7 years. The 1992 possesses good color but meagerly endowed fruit. Excessive acidity and a compact personality are its undoing. Drink it over the next 3–4 years.

COS D'ESTOURNEL (ST.-ESTÈPHE)* * * * *

1993	C	89
1992	C	88
1991	C	87

Cos d'Estournel's 1991 (about 50% of the harvest was declassified) is one of the wines to buy, given its relatively low price and fine quality. It displays a dark-ruby color, and a big, rich nose of cassis fruit married intelligently with spicy new oak. Offering surprising fatness and fleshiness, fine length, and a sweet, creamy texture, it should drink well for at least a decade. One of the stars of the vintage, the 1992 Cos d'Estournel exhibits a deep-ruby/purple color, medium to full body, scents of smoky oak, and copious amounts of black currant fruit. Velvety textured and medium to full bodied, this is an atypically ripe, concentrated, impressively endowed wine that should drink well for 6–10 years. It is a 1992 that merits considerable interest!

The 1993 Cos d'Estournel should turn out to be one of the most successful wines of the vintage. The saturated ruby/purple color is followed by a pure, sweet nose of black fruits (cherries and cassis), abundant notes of smoky new oak, and an intriguing floral component. There is excellent concentration, fine density, and an expansive, medium- to full-bodied palate, with a surprising degree of fleshiness and suppleness. Although moderately tannic, this is one 1993 Médoc where the wine's flesh, chewy texture, and flavor extraction dominate the tannin. No doubt Cos d'Estournel's high Merlot content (40%) has given this wine more fat than many of its peers. Look for the 1993 Cos to be drinkable within 4–5 years of its release, and to last for 15–20 years. Readers should also note that beginning with the 1994 vintage, Cos d'Estournel's second wine will no longer be Marbuzet. It will be called Pagodes de Cos.

Past Glories: 1990 (92), 1989 (89), 1986 (95), 1985 (95), 1982 (97), 1961 (92), 1959 (92), 1953 (93), 1928 (97)

Past Mediocrities . . . or Worse: 1975 (77), 1966 (85), 1964 (72)

COS LABORY (ST.-ESTÈPHE)* * *

1993	C	82
1992	C	82?
1991	C	86

This is another estate that has performed well in the tough years of 1991, 1992, and 1993. The 1991 exhibits a surprisingly saturated color, and a tight but promising nose of peppery, black currant, and smoky new oak scents. Medium bodied and tannic, with good depth, this wine will benefit from 4–5 years of cellaring; it should last for 15 or more years. This soft 1992 is well made, with moderate depth, medium body, fine ripeness, and adequate length. The high tannin in the finish suggests it should be cellared for at least 3–4 years, although I wonder if the modest level of fruit extraction will dry out before the tannin melts away. As with many 1993s, Cos Labory's color is a dark, saturated purple. The wine displays medium body, a compact, stern, tough-textured personality, and some spicy notes. I wonder if the fruit will last during the 10–15 years of cellaring this wine requires.

Past Glories: 1990 (89), 1989 (89)

COURRIÈRE RONGIERAS (LUSSAC-ST.-ÉMILION)* * *

1990	A	86

1990 was a fabulous vintage for St.-Émilion, and this wine from one of St.-Émilion's satellite appellations reveals the high quality of the vintage. Forward, with a complex, ripe cherry and spicy nose, this deeply colored wine offers chunky, fleshy, corpulent flavors, medium body, soft tannin, low acidity, and a lush, heady, fruity finish. Drink it over the next 3–4 years.

LA COUSPADE (ST.-ÉMILION)* * *

1993	C	86
1992	C	85

This 18-acre estate bears watching, as the Aubert brothers are intent on pushing La Couspade's quality to a higher level. The brilliant Libourne oenologist, Michel Rolland, has been brought in as a consultant, and the producers have begun to practice partial malolactic fermentation in new oak. With low yields and later harvesting, this is an estate to follow. The 1992 has turned out to be a respectable effort in a tough year. The wine's dark-ruby color is followed by an attractive, ripe nose of black cherries and smoky oak. Medium bodied, soft, and velvety, with fine purity and ripeness, this wine should be drunk over the next 3–4 years. The 1993's only weakness is a slight green pepper quality to its fruit. Otherwise, it is a darkly colored, dense, concentrated, impressively endowed wine with fine purity, ripeness, a natural, chewy texture, and a long finish. It should drink well for 10–12 years.

COUTELIN-MERVILLE (ST.-ESTÈPHE)* * *

1993	C	86

The samples I saw of this wine were indeed impressive, displaying excellent color, fine richness, medium to full body, firm but ripe tannin, and a long, pure, clean finish. This attractive wine may be one of the sleepers of the vintage. It should drink well for 10–15 years.

COUVENT DES JACOBINS (ST.-ÉMILION)* * *

1992	C 85

NOTE: No 1991 was produced under the Couvent des Jacobins label.

This has always been one of my favorite St.-Émilions. The 1992 is a seductive, elegant wine with good ripeness, and attractive new oak judiciously infused with sweet, herbal, black cherry, and curranty flavors. The wine possesses a supple texture and a moderately long finish. It should be drunk up over the next 5–6 years.

LA CROIX (POMEROL)* *

1993	C 78

This medium-bodied, straightforward, one-dimensional Pomerol reveals some earthy, herbal-tinged, berry fruit, some spice, and a moderately tannic finish. Drink it during its first decade of life.

LA CROIX DU CASSE (POMEROL)* * *

1993	C 87
1992	C 86

NOTE: No 1991 La Croix du Casse was offered for tasting.

Managed impeccably by Jean-Michel Arcaute, La Croix du Casse has produced exceptionally well made wines over recent years. The ruby/purple-colored 1992 reveals a moderately intense bouquet of sweet black cherries and toasty new oak, fine extraction of flavor, medium body, low acidity, and moderate tannin in the finish. Drink it over the next 5–8 years. This estate's 1993 is a firmly structured, densely colored, rich, medium-bodied wine with plenty of sweet fruit hidden beneath the formidable levels of tannin and structure. The wine displays very good to excellent concentration and ripeness, fine balance, and an attractive, berry, olive, spice, and toasty new-oak-scented nose. It should drink well for 10–12 years.

LA CROIX DE GAY (POMEROL)* * *

1992	C 86
1991	C 82

The light 1991 reveals sweet fruit in the nose, toasty new oak, and a light-bodied, easygoing finish. Drink it over the next 4–5 years. The round, charming, seductive 1992 possesses sweet black currant fruit married intelligently with toasty oak. An elegant wine with fine depth, low acidity, and light tannin in the finish, this light- to medium-bodied 1992 is ideal for drinking over the next 5–6 years.

CROIZET-BAGES (PAUILLAC)* *

1993	C 78

Given the frightening number of dismal past performances by Croizet-Bages, the 1993 is a surprisingly pleasant effort. There is good color, some ripeness and supple fruit, and a general sense of balance in this light-bodied wine. To its credit, it has managed to avoid the vintage's ferocious tannin. Drink it over the next 7–8 years.

CURÉ-BON (ST.-ÉMILION)* *

1993	C	75
1992	B	76

Although inconsistent, this St.-Émilion estate is capable of turning out fine wines. Unfortunately, neither the 1993 nor 1992 will be counted among its top successes. The 1993 possesses excessively hard, tough-textured tannin, green, underripe fruit, and a muscular personality lacking finesse and charm. Too much tannin is the undoing of the herbal, medium-bodied, tough-minded, charmless, fruitless 1992. It will dry out over the next 4–5 years.

DALEM (FRONSAC)* * *

1993	C	85

Proprietor Roullier has once again turned in a well-made, concentrated, spicy Fronsac with curranty, cherrylike fruit, medium body, light tannin, and a generous finish. It should drink well for 6–7 years.

LA DAME DE MONTROSE (ST.-ESTÈPHE)* * *

1992	B	86
1991	B	85

With the surge in quality at Montrose, it is not surprising to see similar improvements in the second wine. The 1991 La Dame de Montrose exhibits a deeply saturated color, and a big, spicy, ripe nose of dusty black fruits and minerals. The wine is deep, with medium body, moderate tannin, and excellent ripeness and concentration. It should drink well for 5–7 years. The softer, less concentrated 1992 possesses an excellent ruby/purple color, an attractive floral, black currant–scented bouquet, medium body, low acidity, noticeable alcohol, and a plump, fresh finish. It should drink well for 7–8 years.
Past Glories: 1990 (90)

DASSAULT (ST.-ÉMILION)* * *

1993	C	84

This soft, richly fruity wine exhibits some tannin, but it can be enjoyed for its up-front fruit and spicy, easygoing personality. Drink it over the next 3–6 years.

DAUGAY (ST.-ÉMILION)* * *

1993	C	87

Made by Hubert Brouard (the brother of L'Angélus's proprietor), the 1993 Daugay has been cloned from the image of L'Angélus. The saturated, dark-ruby/purple color is accompanied by a big, expansive nose of sweet, jammy black fruits, herbs, chocolate, and vanilla. This medium to full-bodied, luscious, ripe wine, from a little-known estate, should prove to be a sleeper of the vintage.

LA DAUPHINE (FRONSAC)* * *

1993	B	81
1992	B	77

NOTE: No 1991 was produced under the La Dauphine label.
La Dauphine's 1992 is made in a soft, supple, fruity, earthy style. The wine exhibits average ripeness and an austere, lean, compact personality. Drink it over the next 3–4 years. The light-bodied, pleasant, moderately tannic, essentially one-dimensional 1993 is best consumed over the next 4–5 years.

DAUZAC (MARGAUX)* *

1993	C	88
1992	C	74
1991	C	72

Readers can expect greatly improved wines from this perennial underachiever now that André Lurton (of La Louvière in Graves) is responsible for all critical decisions regarding harvesting, winemaking, and bottling. The 1993 is the finest Dauzac I have tasted, with an almost black color, and a sweet, rich nose of cassis, licorice, and toasty oak. The wine is pure, impressively extracted, medium bodied, and moderately tannic, and has excellent balance. This should be one 1993 that ages well for 20 years, but has the requisite depth and ripeness of fruit to balance out the wine's structure. My instincts suggest this wine will be at its best between 2002 and 2020. Most readers will also admire the attractive new label.

The 1991 Dauzac is empty and hollow, with one-dimensional fruit flavors and no finish. Drink it over the next 3–4 years. The thin, disjointed 1992 is, to be diplomatic, uninteresting.

DESTIEUX (ST.-ÉMILION)* *

1993	C	80

Destieux's wines always possess plenty of color, muscle, body, and tannin. What they lack is charm and finesse. The 1993 is typical in its hardness, excessive tannin, and stern, chewy, essentially charmless style. Although the wine will last 10–15 years, how much joy it is capable of providing is debatable.

LA DOMINIQUE (ST.-ÉMILION)* * * *

1993	C	87
1992	C	79

NOTE: No 1991 was produced under the La Dominique label.

After a disappointing 1992, La Dominique's 1993 is a reassuringly fine effort. The wine exhibits a dark-ruby/purple color, big, smoky, toasty oak and black cherry scents, medium-bodied flavors with fine intensity, adequate acidity, and a moderately tannic finish. It represents a chewy, mouth-filling St.-Émilion for drinking between 1997 and 2008. The 1992's ripe nose of herbs, cassis, and vanillin is fleeting but attractive. This medium-bodied wine offers straightforward cassis fruit, but the finish is short, compact, and moderately tannic. It is vaguely reminiscent of this property's 1981 and 1979, but lighter and more austere.

Past Glories: 1990 (93), 1989 (94), 1986 (90), 1982 (91), 1971 (90), 1970 (88), 1955 (89)
Past Mediocrities . . . or Worse: 1985 (74), 1975 (79)

DUCRU-BEAUCAILLOU (ST.-JULIEN)* * * * *

1993	D	91
1992	C	87+
1991	C	86+

Despite the obvious difficulties posed by the 1991, 1992, and 1993 vintages, Ducru-Beaucaillou's proprietor, Jean-Eugène Borie, has turned in three highly laudable performances. Strict selection and fine winemaking have once again resulted in a classic 1993 Ducru-Beaucaillou, with a dark-ruby/purple color, and a moderately intense nose of black and red fruits, minerals, vanilla, and lead pencil. The wine possesses outstanding flavor intensity, medium body, a sweet inner core of fruit, and a long, dry, moderately tannic finish. The 1993 is reminiscent of this property's outstanding 1988. Give it at least 5–7 years of cellaring (Ducru-Beaucaillou is normally one of the most reticent and least flattering wines to taste during its first decade of life), and expect it to age gracefully for 20–25 years.

At present, the concentrated, promising 1991 is a backward, tannic, young wine, a textbook Ducru in that sense. It will benefit from 4–5 years of cellaring and will last for 15 years. It has plenty of depth, and with time, Ducru's elegance and complexity are sure bets to emerge. An excellent 1992 that reveals impressive concentration, this vintage of Ducru boasts fine structure, as well as an attractive berry-scented, floral nose. Rich and authoritative, with firm tannin, medium body, and a spicy, long finish, this impressive wine begs for 2–3 years of cellaring. It is a candidate for 10–15 years of positive evolution. This is one of the most complete wines of the vintage.

Past Glories: 1986 (94), 1985 (91), 1982 (96), 1981 (90), 1978 (90), 1970 (91), 1961 (96)

DUHART-MILON-ROTHSCHILD (PAUILLAC)* * * *

1993	C	88
1992	C	85
1991	C	84

Readers should keep an eye on Duhart-Milon, as the Rothschilds are clearly attempting to upgrade the quality as well as the image of this Pauillac. For example, 57% of the harvest was eliminated from Duhart's 1993 and no Merlot made it into the final blend. The result is a strong Cabernet Sauvignon–dominated wine with a textbook lead-pencil, herb, cedar, and cassis nose. With excellent ripeness, richness, and definition, this medium-bodied wine reveals well-integrated tannin that is neither astringent nor vegetal. This impressive, classically rendered Pauillac should age well for 15+ years. It may merit a higher rating with additional bottle age.

Duhart's 1991 possesses more depth, ripeness, and potential complexity than the soft, light, one-dimensional 1992. Although the 1991 exhibits deep color, attractive, spicy, grilled nut, cassis, and weedy aromas, and fine depth, it reveals astringent tannin. This medium-bodied wine should be drinkable within 2–3 years and last for 10–12. This soft, currant- and oak-scented 1992 is revealing more depth and ripeness than it did from cask. Medium bodied, spicy, ripe, and moderately rich, this supple wine should drink well for 5–7 years.

Past Glories: 1982 (92)
Past Mediocrities . . . or Worse: 1975 (75), 1970 (70)

L'ÉGLISE-CLINET (POMEROL)* * * *

1993	D	88
1992	C	85
1991	C	84

This well-run estate turned out successful wines in 1991, 1992, and 1993. The 1991 is among only a handful of Pomerols that are supple, ripe, and drinkable. It offers an enticing bouquet of red and black fruits, tobacco, tea, and chocolate. Spicy, soft, and round, this medium-bodied wine is well endowed for a 1991 Pomerol. Drink it over the next 4–5 years. Deep ruby colored, concentrated, with a spicy, ripe, black cherry– and smoky oak–scented nose, and ripe, medium-bodied flavors, L'Église-Clinet's 1992 reveals admirable intensity, and a spicy, rich, fleshy finish. It should provide uncomplicated, delicious drinking for 5–7 years.

A textbook wine from this consistently fine, underrated producer, the dark-ruby/purple-colored 1993 L'Église-Clinet displays a nose of admirably extracted, black cherry and raspberry fruit wrapped with smoky oak scents. The wine exhibits admirable intensity, low acidity, and moderate tannin, resulting in a generous, well-delineated, structured feel. It will be approachable young and last for 10–12 years. It is an excellent effort from proprietor Denis Durantou.

Past Glories: 1986 (92), 1985 (95)

L'ENCLOS (POMEROL)* * *

1992	C	74
1991	C	72

One of my favorite Pomerol estates has turned in two disappointing efforts. The simple, diluted 1991 is lacking in fruit and personality. Dilution and possibly a less than strict selection have resulted in an uncharacteristically poor performance. The 1992 L'Enclos is light, thin, and compact. Drink it up.

L'ÉVANGILE (POMEROL)* * * * *

1993	D	89?
1992	D	78

NOTE: No 1991 was produced under the L'Évangile label.

Far more impressive prior to bottling, L'Évangile's 1992 has turned out to be a fruity, medium-bodied, soft, shallow wine that exhibits light body, hard tannin, and an obvious deficiency of both fruit and depth. Given the fine potential this wine displayed in cask, I wonder whether this is one more 1992 that was eviscerated at bottling. It is disappointing in the context of the vineyard and the proprietor's commitment to excellence.

A number of responsible tasters I know have judged L'Évangile's 1993 to be among the finest wines of the vintage. It is unquestionably excellent, possibly outstanding. The color is dark ruby and the nose offers L'Évangile's bewitching blend of violets, truffles, and black raspberries. Medium bodied, ripe, pure, and well balanced, with moderate to high tannin in the finish, its austerity and high tannin level may make an outstanding rating after bottling questionable. This wine requires 3–4 years of cellaring and should age well for 15+ years. A 1979 with more color, oak, and tannin?

Past Glories: 1990 (96), 1985 (95), 1983 (92), 1982 (97), 1975 (97), 1961 (99–100), 1950 (92), 1947 (100)

Past Mediocrities . . . or Worse: 1981 (73), 1970 (84)

FAURIE DE SOUCHARD (ST.-ÉMILION)* *

1993	C	81

Despite the hard, forbidding, tannic style of this wine, there is some admirable fruit and concentration behind its framework. Nevertheless, its dusty, tannic, coarse personality does not offer hope for a positive evolution. Although it possesses more fruit than many of its peers, it will dry out quickly.

DE FERRAND (ST.-ÉMILION)* * *

1993	C	87

In the past, this impeccably run estate (owned by the late Baron Bich of ballpoint pen fame) has made some delicious wines. The 1993 appears to be a very successful example. The color is a dark, deep ruby, and the nose offers up ripe, juicy aromas of red and black fruits, earth, and toasty oak. Opulent, with excellent concentration, fine purity, low acidity, and moderate tannin, this will be a plump, succulently styled St.-Émilion for drinking over the next 7–10 years.

FERRAND-LARTIQUE (ST.-ÉMILION)* * * *
1993   D 89

The 1993 is the debut release of this property owned by Monsieur Ferrand, a man in love with the wines of Bordeaux's right bank who is also dedicated to making a rich, unfiltered, artisanal wine from extremely low yields. An example of Ferrand's dedication is his decision before the picking of the 1994 vintage to employ ten people to harvest the 5-acre vineyard grape by grape, rather than bunch by bunch! Only Château d'Yquem and a handful of other Barsac/Sauternes estates utilize such expensive, labor-intensive techniques. The vineyard, located at the bottom of the southern hills of St.-Émilion, near the commune of Les Bigaroux, has produced approximately 800 cases of wine. This tiny estate is bent on producing a luxury cuvée in the style of the famed mini-Pomerol estate of Le Pin. Aged in 100% new oak and made from 100% Merlot, the impressive 1993 possesses an exotic, flamboyant character more akin to a 1989 or 1990 than to a 1993 claret. It exhibits a saturated dark-ruby/purple color, an exotic nose of smoky oak, jammy black currant fruit, and cherries intertwined with scents of mocha, and a medium- to full-bodied, lush palate with gobs of fruit, glycerin, and smoky wood. This decadently styled, rich, lusty wine should drink well for 10–15 years. Look for this estate's prices to jump quickly once the world's rich Bordeaux enthusiasts learn of Ferrand-Lartique.

FERRIÈRE (MARGAUX)* *
1992   B 74

This thin, hard, light-ruby-colored wine possesses an excess of tannin, giving it a compact, dry, harsh personality.

FEYTIT-CLINET (POMEROL)* *
1993   C 75
1992   C 76

NOTE: No 1991 was produced under the Feytit-Clinet label.
The lush, ripe fruit of this estate's 1992 cask samples has been replaced by a green, hard, tannic wine with an absence of charm. What happened? Although the 1993 possesses excellent color, a vegetal, underripe fruit character in both its aromatics and flavors renders it a weak effort. Moreover, the dry, astringent finish suggests a problematic evolution.

DE FIEUZAL (GRAVES)* * * *
1993   C 87
1992   C 86
1991   C 82

Characteristic of the vintage, the 1991 is compressed and compact, but it possesses an excellent dark-ruby color, a monolithic, spicy, toasty, earthy nose, fine depth and ripeness, and a one-dimensional personality. Drink it over the next decade. This deep-ruby/purple-colored 1992 exhibits ripe, sweet fruit and fine depth. The wine is medium bodied, with plenty of juicy black fruit flavors wrapped in smoky oak. This stylish, tasty, elegant, and flavorful Graves will benefit from 2–3 years of cellaring and last for a decade.

De Fieuzal's 1993 is a noteworthy success. It represents the second year in a row that this estate has turned out a fine effort under less than ideal vintage conditions. A blend of 60% Cabernet Sauvignon, 30% Merlot, and the remainder Petit Verdot and Cabernet Franc, the 1993 reveals a saturated dark-ruby/purple color, and a tight but promising nose of underbrush, black fruits, and smoky oak. The wine possesses good spiciness, medium body, a hard tannic edge to the finish, but fine ripeness and depth. If it retains its fruit and depth after bottling, this wine will be capable of 15 or more years of cellaring. It requires 4–5 years to shed its tannin.

Past Glories: 1990 (88), 1988 (89), 1970 (90)

FIGEAC (ST.-ÉMILION)* * * *

1993	D	75?

Following this estate's profound 1990, only unexciting wines have emanated from Figeac. The light-bodied 1993 exhibits a vegetal, herbaceous, dusty component to its straightforward, cherry-scented nose. The wine tails off in the mouth, and lacks concentration and length. Hopefully, Figeac's 1993 will put on some weight. It is clearly an improvement over the diluted 1992.

Past Glories: 1990 (94), 1986 (90), 1983 (87), 1982 (94), 1970 (90), 1964 (94), 1961 (89), 1959 (91), 1955 (95), 1953 (93)

Past Mediocrities . . . or Worse: 1988 (83), 1979 (83), 1966 (85)

LA FLEUR (ST.-ÉMILION)* *

1993	C	85?
1992	C	86

NOTE: No 1991 was produced under the La Fleur label.

This estate has been producing better wines recently, so it is not surprising that the deliciously opulent 1992 has been followed by a more tannic and structured, but still concentrated and promising, 1993. The wine may possess too much tannin, but there is good depth and ripeness. After fining, it may be more approachable and supple. An estate to watch. There is no need to defer your gratification with this plump, succulent, fat and juicy 1992 La Fleur. Bursting with jammy fruit and toasty oak, it is a lush, in-your-face claret that should drink well for 4–6 years.

LA FLEUR DE GAY (POMEROL)* * * * *

1993	D	88
1992	D	87
1991	D	85

While La Fleur de Gay did make a 1991, at the time of this report it was uncertain as to whether it would be released in the American market. The wine has turned out well for the vintage, displaying a solid medium-ruby color, and a spicy, ripe, black currant–scented nose infused judiciously with smoky new oak. Medium bodied, with low acidity, this pleasant, straightforward wine will drink well for 4–7 years. This 1992 exhibits one of the most saturated purple colors of a wine from this vintage. With its ripe, black raspberry– and plum-scented, toasty nose, excellent concentration, medium to full body, moderate to high tannin level, low acidity, and excellent length, this is a broodingly backward and structured 1992. It should drink well for 10–15 years. Bravo!

The 1993's beautiful, healthy, black/purple color suggests fine ripeness and flavor intensity. The bouquet of pure black cherries, black currants, vanilla, and truffles is followed by a medium- to full-bodied, tannic, austere wine that should handsomely repay 4–5 years of cellaring. It appears the wine possesses the requisite concentration of fruit to stand up to its structure and muscular style. I find the 1993 to be a downsized, leaner and meaner version of the 1988. Drink it between 2000 and 2012.

Past Glories: 1990 (89), 1989 (95), 1988 (93), 1987 (90), 1986 (90)
Past Mediocrities . . . or Worse: 1982 (83)

LA FLEUR GAZIN (POMEROL)* *

1993	C	74
1992	C	72

NOTE: No 1991 was produced under the La Fleur Gazin label.

Impressively colored but closed, hard, and austere, this 1992 displayed far more fruit, body, and quality prior to bottling. The wine tastes gutted out, hollow, and tough. The 1993's medium-dark ruby color is followed by a green, herbal-scented wine with hard, austere, compact flavors, and a lack of fruit, charm, and finesse.

LA FLEUR PÉTRUS (POMEROL)* * * *

1993	D	88
1992	D	87

NOTE: No 1991 was produced under the La Fleur Pétrus label.

It is no secret that the Moueix family has been attempting to elevate the quality of the wine produced at this vineyard that bears the name of two of Pomerol's greatest wines—Lafleur and Pétrus. A new cellar has been built, crop thinning is routinely employed, and the age of the vines has become more respectable. Perhaps La Fleur Pétrus will begin to live up to its grandiose name. The excellent 1992 offers a deep-ruby/purple color, and a big, sweet, jammy nose of black fruits, caramel, and vanillin. Ripe, rich, and medium bodied, with excellent density, this concentrated, elegant yet powerful wine should drink exceptionally well during its first 8–15 years of life.

The 1993 is a noteworthy success, displaying a saturated dark-ruby/purple color, and a moderately intense nose of jammy black cherries, earth, spices, and vanilla. Dense and powerful, yet elegant, this medium-bodied, concentrated, ripe 1993 possesses enough tannin (backed up by sufficient fruit) to age well for 15 or more years. Don't think about pulling a cork before the turn of the century.

Past Glories: 1982 (90), 1975 (90), 1970 (88), 1952 (91), 1950 (95), 1947 (96)

LA FLEUR POURRET (ST.-ÉMILION)* *

1992	B	79
1991	B	64

Although not all properties can afford to completely declassify their production in a disastrous vintage, the decision to bottle the 1991 La Fleur Pourret was a mistake. The wine is frightfully acidic, vegetal, austere, and pleasureless. On the other hand, the 1992 reveals plenty of soft, ripe, gentle, red fruit flavors, light body, and a soft, straightforward finish. It should drink adequately for 4–5 years.

LA FLEUR ST.-GEORGES (LALANDE-DE-POMEROL)* *

1993	B	84

A solidly made, fruity, straightforward, generously endowed wine, with surprising fat and ripeness, the 1993 La Fleur St.-Georges should drink well for 5–6 years.

FONGABAN (PUISSEGUIN-ST.-ÉMILION)* * *

1993	B	86

Depending on what emerges from the bottle, the 1993 Fongaban may turn out to be one of the sleepers of the vintage. The samples I tasted exhibited an impressively saturated, black/

ruby/purple color, a big, spicy, black cherry, licorice, subtlely herbaceous nose, medium to full body, surprising suppleness, and light tannin in the finish. It will be interesting to taste this wine after bottling.

FONPLÉGADE (ST.-ÉMILION)* * *

1993	C 75
1992	C 80

NOTE: No 1991 Fonplégade was available for tasting.

Medium ruby/purple colored, with a spicy nose intermingled with scents of jammy cherries, the medium-bodied 1992 offers some tannin, low acidity, and average concentration. It makes for a pleasant, albeit uninteresting glass of wine. Drink it over the next 5–6 years. Too much tannin and too little fruit sum up the deficiencies in Fonplégade's tough, hard, malnourished 1993. It will undoubtedly dry out within 2–3 years.

FONREAUD (LISTRAC)* *

1993	C 74

Listrac's propensity to turn out hard wines, even in ripe, sunny, hot, dry years, was not helped in a vintage where much of the Cabernet Sauvignon had not ripened when the deluge of rain began. Consequently, Fonreaud's 1993 is too hard, tough, lean, and undernourished to offer a satisfying glass of wine.

FONROQUE (ST.-ÉMILION)* *

1993	C 84?
1992	C 74?

NOTE: No 1991 was produced under the Fonroque label.

From cask, I thought Fonroque produced an excellent wine in 1992, with a deep-ruby color, a big, spicy, earthy, meaty, roasted nose, and ripe, medium-bodied flavors. Now that the wine has been bottled, it is savagely tannic, already devoid of fruit, and a sure bet to dry out over the next 3–4 years. A charmless wine, it is all muscle and no brains. Pass it by. Fonroque's 1993 displays plenty of fatness, sweetness, and an opulent, Merlot-dominated personality. However, readers should remember that the 1992, so impressive from cask, turned out to be tannic, severe, and hollow, so who knows how much fining and filtering are being practiced at this estate. Certainly cask samples reveal good ripeness, a fleshy, medium-bodied personality, and plenty of charm and appeal.

FONTENIL (FRONSAC)* * *

1993	B 85

The high tannin level is worrisome in this otherwise medium-bodied, muscular, structured 1993. There is good ripeness and rich chewiness beneath the tannic framework. If the fruit does not fade and the tannin melts away, this wine will deserve a very good rating. It should drink well for up to a decade.

LES FORTS DE LATOUR (PAUILLAC)* * *

1993	C 86
1992	C 85
1991	C 86

In keeping with the high quality of Latour's 1991, the property's second wine is a graceful, elegant, medium-weight wine with moderate tannin, a spicy, berry-scented nose, fine length, and enough tannin to give it grip and structure. Drink it over the next 7–8 years. The 1992 Les Forts de Latour is supple and fruity, with fine color and low acidity. Although surprisingly light and easygoing, this classy wine will offer ideal drinking over the next decade.

Given the 1993 Latour's exceptional quality, it is not surprising to see how well made the 1993 Les Forts de Latour has turned out. It displays a deep-ruby color, and a spicy nose of wood, herbs, nuts, and red and black fruits. More supple than its brawnier big brother, this wine possesses moderate tannin, as well as a medium-bodied, slightly austere personality. This classically rendered Pauillac should drink well for 10–15 years.

Past Glories: 1982 (92)

FOURCAS-DUPRÉ (LISTRAC)* *

1993	B	71?

It was painfully frustrating trying to find any fruit, charm, or finesse in this small-scaled, compact, attenuated wine. The tannin is just too excessive for the wine's fruit.

FOURCAS-HOSTEN (LISTRAC)* *

1993	B	72

This is a harsh, astringent, diluted wine that assaults the palate without enough fruit and glycerin for balance.

FRANC-MAYNE (ST.-ÉMILION)* *

1993	C	76
1992	C	76
1991	C	73

The 1991's aggressive, herbaceous nose reveals a lack of fruit and too much greenness. Some diluted, soft fruit flavors can be found, but this is a thin, undistinguished effort. The dark-ruby-colored 1992 reveals a pronounced herbal, vegetal component to its bouquet, light to medium body, hollow, shallow flavors, and excessive tannin in the finish. This is not my style. Franc-Mayne always possesses an impressively saturated dark-ruby/purple color, but the 1993's blatantly herbaceous, vegetal nose and hollow flavors dominated by tannin, wood, and structure present a problem. This wine needs more fruit, glycerin, and extract. It will require drinking over the near term, as it will dry out quickly.

DE FRANCE (GRAVES)* *

1993	C	72

This medium-ruby-colored wine possesses a monolithic, straightforward nose of earth and old wood. The wine is sharp and lean, with high acidity, hard tannin, and little substance or fruit in the flavors or finish. It will only become more astringent as it ages.

LA GAFFELIÈRE (ST.-ÉMILION)* * *

1993	C	84
1992	C	85
1991	C	78

With its medium-ruby color and its tightly knit, light-bodied, elegant style, it is easy to pass over La Gaffelière in favor of some of the more forceful, powerful St.-Émilion offerings. That would be a mistake, as this property can turn out exceptionally elegant wines. I am not convinced 1993 will be one of those wines, although it reveals moderate quantities of curranty and cherry fruit accompanied by a touch of smoky new oak. However, the tannin is noticeably hard and dominates the wine's flavor and finish. Time will tell. It will be interesting to see how this wine tastes after it has been fined and/or filtered.

The 1991 La Gaffelière possesses the hollowness typical of right-bank 1991s. Yet there is a sense of elegance, some ripeness, light to medium body, and a spicy finish. Drink it over the next 4–5 years. The 1992 reveals good fruit and toasty new oak presented in a light- to medium-bodied, soft, supple-textured format. Round and graceful, it is ideal for drinking over the next 5–6 years. It is a success for the vintage, particularly for its seductive, smooth, refined style.

Past Glories: 1982 (87), 1953 (89), 1947 (88)

Past Mediocrities . . . or Worse: 1981 (72), 1978 (67), 1975 (79), 1971 (68), 1966 (78)

LA GARDE RÉSERVE DU CHÂTEAU (GRAVES)* * *

1993	C 86

Significant investments have been made in this Pessac-Léognan vineyard, resulting in increasingly impressive wines—both white and red. The 1993 La Garde Réserve du Château exhibits well-integrated new oak, a moderately intense, pure nose of ripe cassis, a medium-bodied, elegant personality, and authoritative flavors. The wine's tannin is neither aggressive nor astringent. This offering should be drinkable when released and should last for a decade.

CHÂTEAU GASSIES (PREMIÈRES CÔTES DE BORDEAUX)* *

1990	B 85

This medium-weight, pleasantly scented wine exhibits attractive, nearly overripe flavors of Bing cherries, medium body, succulence, a certain elegance despite the ripe style, and a medium-bodied, soft finish. Drink it over the next 2–3 years.

LE GAY (POMEROL)* * *

1992	C 78

NOTE: No 1991 was produced under the Le Gay label.

An atypically light, diluted style for Le Gay without the robustness and savage intensity generally found in this wine, the medium-ruby-colored 1992 is short, lean, and tannic. Drink it over the next 4–5 years.

Past Glories: 1989 (92), 1975 (90)

GAZIN (POMEROL)* * * *

1993	D 88?
1992	D 89

NOTE: No 1991 Gazin was produced.

A property on the rebound, Gazin has produced strong efforts over recent vintages. Located adjacent to Pétrus, Gazin's vineyard is capable of producing wines with a few Pétrus-like qualities, particularly in the wine's aromatics. But Gazin will never possess Pétrus's intensity, power, or tannic backbone. The 1993 Gazin is an unqualified success for the vintage. I tasted the wine four times and on two occasions felt it had the potential to be outstanding. It exhibits a dense, ruby/purple color, and a moderately intense, sweet, smoky, clean nose of black cherries, currants, and toasty oak. The sweet, expansive, medium- to full-bodied flavors reveal fine ripeness, moderate tannin, a touch of austerity, but overall top-notch balance and well-integrated acid and tannin. This wine requires 2–3 years of cellaring and will last for 12–15 years.

Gazin's 1992 is one of the vintage's most noteworthy wines. It displays an opaque deep-ruby/purple color and a bold, penetrating, sweet nose of caramel, black cherries, vanillin, and smoke. With ripe, medium- to full-bodied, rich, concentrated flavors and a succulent texture, this is an impeccably well-made wine! Approachable now, it should improve for 3–4 years and last for a decade or more. Gazin has been making a strong comeback over recent years—readers take note. Bravo!

Past Glories: 1990 (90), 1989 (88)

GISCOURS (MARGAUX)* * */* * * *

1993	C	85
1992	C	86
1991	C	87

Giscours used to be one of the Médoc's most consistent properties in off years. The estate's shaky performances in the eighties (in both good and bad vintages) left me looking elsewhere for overachievers in mediocre years. Yet Giscours has turned in two fine performances in 1991 and 1992. The deeply colored 1991 offers an exotic nose of black cherries, coffee, chocolate, and cinnamon, fine depth, and a chewy, cassis richness to its fruit. Supple, with low acidity, and a plump, fleshy feel, this medium-bodied, attractively made, well-endowed wine should drink well for 7–8 years. The 1992 is noteworthy for its saturated dark-ruby/purple color, big, plummy, licorice, Asian spice–scented nose, round, concentrated, chewy flavors, medium body, and heady, alcoholic finish. It is a plump, rich, concentrated wine for a 1992. Drink it over the next 7–8 years.

The 1993's plump, corpulent style is typical for Giscours. Possessing more fat than most wines of the vintage, this chunky, straightforward, mouth-filling claret reveals moderate tannin, as well as fine ripeness, body, and fruit. It should drink well over the next 7–10 years.

Past Glories: 1979 (88), 1978 (90), 1975 (91)

GRAND-CORBIN (ST.-ÉMILION)* * *

1993	C	86

This full-bodied, opulently styled 1993 exhibits good color, a plump, roasted herb, coffee, black cherry, Merlot-like character, plenty of juicy fruit, low acidity, and heady alcohol in the finish. It is a beefy, mouth-filling St.-Émilion for drinking during its first 7–8 years of life.

GRAND-MAYNE (ST.-ÉMILION)* * * *

1993	C	88
1992	C	86

Grand-Mayne, along with such other illustrious St.-Émilion grand cru estates as L'Angélus, Troplong-Mondot, Canon-La-Gaffelière, and Beau Séjour-Bécot, is producing a wine that is better than many of its more prestigious and highly elevated siblings, St.-Émilion's premiers grands crus classés. In 1995, St.-Émilion will update its classification of estates. It will be interesting to see if the politicians who compose the tasting jury will have the courage to promote the aforementioned estates, at the same time demoting some of the more notorious underachievers.

Grand-Mayne's 1992 has turned out to be a very good wine for the vintage, with an attractive dark-ruby color, a big, spicy, black currant– and cherry-scented nose, medium body, excellent ripeness, light tannin, and a lush, heady, succulent finish. Drink it over the next 5–6 years. The 1993 is unquestionably one of the most successful wines of the St.-Émilion appellation. It exhibits an impressively saturated dark-ruby/purple/black color, and a bold, rich nose of jammy black cherries, minerals, spring flowers, and licorice. The wine is intensely concentrated and medium to full bodied, with highly extracted flavors that possess a sweetness and expansiveness not found in most 1993 clarets. Although there is plenty of tannin in the finish, this wine's balance is not in question. Drink it between 1997 and 2010.

Past Glories: 1990 (89), 1989 (91)

GRAND-PONTET (ST.-ÉMILION)* * *

1993	C	86
1992	C	82

NOTE: No 1991 was produced under the Grand-Pontet label.

Grand-Pontet is an up-and-coming St.-Émilion estate. My only reservation is the blatant and possibly excessive use of new oak. There is no doubting that Grand-Pontet's wines have become more concentrated and are examples of the full-bodied, highly extracted, muscular-styled school of St.-Émilions. The 1993 is a successful wine for the vintage. It offers an impressive dark-ruby/purple color, a lavish, toasty, oaky nose, medium- to full-bodied, highly extracted, concentrated flavors, supple, sweet tannin, and a long, heady, alcoholic finish. While it is not the most elegant wine, it is mouth filling, satisfying, and obviously designed to grab the taster's attention. It should drink well for 10–12 years.

The 1992's heady nose with noticeable alcohol, aggressive oak (too much?), and ripe fruit, is followed by a light-bodied wine with a soft, chunky personality. This fleshy, obvious style of St.-Émilion will offer an uncomplicated mouth-filling glass of wine over the next 3–5 years.

GRAND-PUY-DUCASSE (PAUILLAC)* * *

1992	C	86

A saturated dark-ruby color with hints of purple is impressive, particularly for the 1992 vintage. Soft, ripe, cassis aromas drift from the glass. The 1992's attack offers plenty of sweet fruit, low tannin, and gentleness. The wine is medium bodied, soft, and a success for the vintage. Drink it now and over the next 6–7 years.

GRAND-PUY-LACOSTE (PAUILLAC)* * * *

1993	C	88
1992	C	86
1991	C	87

Unquestionably a star of the vintage, Grand-Puy-Lacoste's 1991 reveals a deep-ruby color, a lovely perfumed nose of black fruits, cedar, and herbs, medium body, soft, ripe, fleshy flavors, and surprising length. It should drink well for at least 10–15 years. It is an excellent effort for the vintage. A success for the vintage, Grand-Puy-Lacoste's ruby-colored 1992 offers sweet, ripe, up-front cassis fruit, as well as some fat and softness. Although it lacks the depth, focus, and concentration of the 1991 and 1993, it is a charming, velvety-textured wine for drinking over the next 5–6 years.

The 1993 Grand-Puy-Lacoste is a potentially outstanding wine. Proprietor Xavier Borie has fashioned a classic Pauillac, with a saturated dark-ruby/purple color, a sweet nose of cassis fruit and spice, full body, superb concentration, and moderate tannin in the heady finish. This large-scaled 1993 avoids the tannin and austerity of many of its peers. Drink it between 2000 and 2015. Bravo!

Past Glories: 1990 (90), 1989 (89), 1986 (90), 1982 (95), 1970 (90), 1949 (96)

LES GRANDES CHÊNES (MÉDOC)* * *
1993 Cuvée Prestige   C   86

A potential sleeper of the vintage, this small, 17-acre estate near the northern Médoc village of St.-Christoly has fashioned a good regular cuvée (potential rating of 82–85), but a more interesting Cuvée Prestige. The latter wine exhibits a deep-ruby color, an intense, pure, ripe, curranty nose, and spicy, medium-bodied, concentrated flavors with well-integrated tannin and attractive flesh and ripeness. It should drink well for 7–8 years, possibly longer.

LA GRAVE À POMEROL (TRIGANT DE BOISSET) (POMEROL)* * *
1992   C   85

NOTE: No 1991 was produced under the La Grave Trigant de Boisset label.

This soft, medium-bodied wine possesses some attractively sweet cherry, herbal, and currant fruit in the nose, as well as roasted nut and berry flavors on the palate. Supple, with good concentration, no hard edges, and a sense of elegance and grace, it should be drunk over the next 4–5 years. Readers should note the new name, now shortened to La Grave à Pomerol.

GRUAUD-LAROSE (ST.-JULIEN)* * * */* * * * *

1993	C	89
1992	C	86
1991	C	85?

Gruaud-Larose, on a hot streak from the late forties to the mid-eighties, appeared to shift gears to a delicate, lighter style in such blockbuster vintages as 1989 and 1990. It is too soon to know if that is a permanent change in their winemaking direction, but the 1991, with its dark color and leathery, smoked-meat, tar, and licorice scents, is a return to the estate's bold, intense style. Spicy, with sweet fruit, low acidity, and a soft, plump texture, it is already drinking well and will last for another 8–10 years. If in fact the 1989 and 1990 were intentionally made in a lighter style, the black/purple-colored 1992 gives evidence that Gruaud-Larose may have returned to the forceful, robust, muscular style that made the estate famous. In general, the 1992 vintage did not produce big, rich wines, but this effort from Gruaud-Larose is a reassuringly large-scaled, dense, powerful, rich, thick wine. The 1992 is more cleanly made than the leathery, *bret*-tinged 1991, exhibits gobs of earthy, rich, peppery, black currant, and herbal fruit flavors, low acidity, and a thick, chewy, lush finish. The wine's tannin is noticeable, but well integrated, making this wine appealing today, yet capable of 8–10 years of evolution.

What is impressive about Gruaud-Larose's 1993 is its superb richness and wild blackberry, cassis character that resembles a blockbuster Syrah from the Hermitage hillsides. Certainly the samples I tasted were massive, full-bodied wines that will no doubt become more civilized with cellaring. One of the more burly wines of 1993, it will need to be cellared for 5–10 years. This bruiser is capable of lasting for 20–25 years.

Past Glories: 1986 (95), 1985 (90), 1983 (90), 1982 (96+), 1961 (96), 1953 (90), 1949 (93), 1945 (96+), 1928 (97)

GUILLOT-CLAUZEL (POMEROL)* * *
1993   C   86

Proprietor Clauzel, who is rebuilding the fortunes of nearby Château Beauregard, owns this tiny Pomerol vineyard. The 1993 Guillot-Clauzel is an impressive effort, offering a saturated dark-ruby/purple color, evidence of new oak in the smoky, vanillin scents, and a rich, medium-bodied, concentrated, soft, velvety-textured personality. It should be delicious when released later this year, and age well for up to a decade.

HAUT-BAGES-AVEROUS (PAUILLAC)* *

1993	C	80
1992	B	75
1991	B	74

Haut-Bages-Averous, the second wine of Lynch-Bages, is light and thin in 1991, with an angular, acidic personality, and a short finish. The dark-ruby-colored 1992 Haut-Bages-Averous offers a lean, compact, somewhat dilute character. Moreover, I was not fond of the peppery, herbaceous bouquet. The 1993 possesses an impressively saturated dark-ruby color. The wine's aromas include attractive peppery, herb, and cassis notes. While there is adequate concentration and moderate tannin in the finish, the wine tails off quickly after it hits the palate. It will need to be drunk within 5–8 years of the vintage.

HAUT-BAGES-LIBÉRAL (PAUILLAC)* * *

1993	C	85
1992	C	76

The 1992 Haut-Bages-Libéral is a light-bodied, tough-textured, tannic, insubstantial wine that is too astringent and hard. Drink it over the next 3–4 years before it loses any more fruit. Far more interesting, the corpulent, dark-ruby/purple-colored 1993 offers an initial gush of cassis fruit intermixed with scents of underbrush, damp earth, and spices. Although not complex, it is medium bodied, tannic, dense, and chewy in a husky, monolithic sense. This mouth-filling 1993 may merit a higher rating if the tannin becomes more integrated and if the wine begins to display more complexity.

Past Glories: 1986 (90), 1985 (89), 1982 (92), 1975 (88)

HAUT-BAILLY (GRAVES)* * * *

1993	C	88
1992	C	87

NOTE: No 1991 was produced under the Haut-Bailly label.

This estate has been coming on strong of late, with wines of undeniable finesse that are produced in an uncompromising fashion. The 1992 Haut-Bailly displays a penetrating, elegant, smoky, cherry-scented nose, ripe, round, generous, plump, fruity flavors (suggesting a high percentage of Merlot), and a soft, velvety-textured, graceful finish. Haut-Bailly's classic elegance, combined with admirable ripeness, flavor extraction, and depth, is well displayed. The 1992 should drink well for 7–10 years. An impressive 1992!

This estate's 1993 is also much better than most of its peers. The saturated dark-ruby/ purple color is accompanied by an enticingly intense, jammy nose of black fruits, smoke, and vanillin. On the palate, the wine reveals richness that could have come only from old vines and conservative yields. There is an inner core of sweet, ripe fruit, an elegant personality, and a persuasively long, rich, beautifully balanced finish with unobtrusive tannin. This wine will be surprisingly delicious young, but look for it to put on even more weight and richness as it ages gracefully over the next 15 or more years. Impressive!

Past Glories: 1990 (91), 1989 (90), 1988 (89), 1983 (87), 1979 (87), 1964 (88), 1961 (93), 1928 (90), 1900 (90)

Past Mediocrities . . . or Worse: 1982 (?), 1975 (67), 1971 (75)

HAUT-BATAILLEY (PAUILLAC)* * *

1993	C	85
1992	C	81
1991	C	84

Haut-Batailley's 1991 exhibits attractive berry fruit aromas, good ripeness, medium body, and moderate tannin in the finish. The only danger is that the fruit may dry out before the tannin melts away. Drink it over the next 5–7 years. Haut-Batailley's 1992 has put on weight since bottling, revealing more fruit in its light- to medium-bodied, supple, up-front style. Low in acidity with some oak apparent, this wine should be drunk over the next 3–6 years.

Haut-Batailley tends to resemble a St.-Julien more than a Pauillac, so I am never surprised by its elegant, stylish personality. The 1993 offers sweet fruit, but the tannin level may be too excessive. Nevertheless, there is charm, elegance, and ripeness to this light- to medium-bodied wine. It will require drinking during its first decade of life.

HAUT-BERGEY (GRAVES)* *

1993	B	80
1992	B	74
1991	B	78

The light-ruby color of the 1991 is deceptive in view of the moderately intense bouquet of herbs, damp earth, tea, and cherry fruit. Soft, with light body and little grip or tannin, this pleasant, straightforward wine should be drunk over the next several years. The high acidity in this 1992 suggests underripeness. The wine exhibits spice and greenness to its bouquet. Although it offers some fruit, the taste fades quickly, leaving a hollow, sharp finish.

A soft, medium-bodied, oaky wine with good ripeness and a forward, precocious personality, the 1993 Haut-Bergey possesses a herbaceous, vegetal component, but the overall impression is one of forward, supple fruit. It should be drunk in its first 5–7 years of life.

HAUT-BRION (GRAVES)* * * * *

1993	D	92
1992	D	90
1991	D	86

Haut-Brion's 1991 is austere, tannic, and closed. However, the wine does exhibit good dark-ruby color, and a tight but promising nose of black fruits, minerals, and vanillin. It is spicy, with good depth and excellent definition. Will this wine emerge from its shell to reveal more charm and finesse? If not, it may dry out before the tannin subsides. **A.M.: 1997–2008.** Forty percent of the 1992 harvest was eliminated from Haut-Brion's final blend. The result is a stylish yet authoritatively flavored wine that reminds me of a slightly downsized version of the superb 1985. A beautiful deep-ruby color is followed by a penetrating bouquet of black fruits, smoke, and minerals. Fine ripeness and outstanding richness allied to medium body, an elegant personality, and a supple, moderately tannic finish suggest this wine will be mature in 4–5 years and last for 15–20. A terrific success in 1992!

One of the stars of the vintage, the 1993 Haut-Brion is richer as well as more concentrated, powerful, and tannic than the outstanding 1992. It may even turn out to be better than Haut-Brion's 1990! The 1993 displays an attractive, saturated dark-ruby color, and a reticent but emerging bouquet of red and black fruits, minerals, vanillin, and spice. With Haut-Brion's characteristically intense, earthy, tobacco flavors well displayed in this wine's medium-bodied format, this is once again one of Bordeaux's greatest examples of outstanding concentration and flavor intensity combined with finesse and elegance. There is moderate tannin, but like most Haut-Brions it will be delicious at a young age. It will undoubtedly put on weight and richness as it ages over the next 25 years. Very impressive!

Past Glories: 1990 (94), 1989 (100), 1988 (91), 1986 (92), 1985 (93), 1983 (90), 1982 (93), 1979 (93), 1978 (92), 1975 (90), 1964 (90), 1961 (97), 1959 (98), 1955 (97), 1953 (95), 1949 (98), 1945 (100), 1928 (97), 1926 (97)

Past Mediocrities . . . or Worse: 1970 (84), 1966 (86), 1948 (76), 1947 (81)

HAUT-FAUGÈRES (ST.-ÉMILION)* * *

1993	Cap de Faugères	A	84
1992	Cap de Faugères	A	84
1992	Haut-Faugères	B	85

These two estates are reviewed together, since they are both under the ownership of Corinne and Péby Guisez. The 1992 Cap de Faugères offers soft, ripe fruit, an attractive, medium-bodied personality, and a pleasing finish. Drink it over the next several years. The 1993 Cap de Faugères is one of the more attractive wines from Bordeaux's satellite appellations. It offers good color, fine ripeness, medium body, and an attractive, pure, black cherry, subtlty oaky personality. It should drink well for 5–6 years.

The 1992 Haut-Faugères reveals more oak, spice, herbs, and tannin, as well as ripe fruit presented in an easy-to-understand, medium-bodied format. It will drink well for 4–5 years.

HAUT-MARBUZET (ST.-ESTÈPHE)* * */* * * * *

1993	C	82
1992	C	82

NOTE: No 1991 Haut-Marbuzet was offered for tasting.

Long one of my favorite Bordeaux wines, I had the opportunity to drink the extraordinary 1982 Haut-Marbuzet twice during the recent holidays. Wow, what a sumptuous, rich, complex wine! I would have liked to find the 1993 more impressive, but it is austere, extremely tough and tannic, and atypically hard for Haut-Marbuzet. Close scrutiny does reveal some spicy, ripe cassis fruit, but there is not enough to balance out the wine's stern, hollow personality. Is my rating too generous? Haut-Marbuzet's penchant for using 100% new oak works great in top years such as 1990, 1989, and 1982, but in 1992 the wood dominates the wine. The excessively oaky 1992 displays a deep, concentrated ruby color, a spicy, plummy, oaky bouquet, medium-bodied, soft flavors, above-average depth, low acidity, and a supple finish. Precocious and ostentatious to an extreme in this vintage, it is best consumed in its first 6–7 years of life.

Past Glories: 1990 (94), 1989 (89), 1988 (88), 1986 (90), 1985 (88), 1983 (88), 1982 (94), 1975 (90)

HAUT-SARPE (ST.-ÉMILION)* *

1993	C	73
1992	B	72

NOTE: No 1991 was produced under the Haut-Sarpe label.

Ruby colored, with a closed, monolithic nose of damp earth and spices, the one-dimensional, compact 1992 possesses excessive tannin. Without enough fruit to cover the wine's skeleton, it is all tough, hard tannin and alcohol. The ferociously tannic, tough, hard-as-nails 1993 left me reaching for a glass of mineral water.

CHÂTEAU HOSTENS-PICANT (SAINTE-FOY)* * *
1992 Cuvée des Demoiselles   A   86

This tasty, supple wine offers copious quantities of red fruit and a velvety-textured personality. Drink it over the next 1–2 years.

D'ISSAN (MARGAUX)* */* * *
1993   C   73

This light-bodied, vegetal, one-dimensional wine lacks concentration and is devoid of fruit and charm in the finish.

JONQUEYRÈS (BORDEAUX SUPÉRIEUR)* * *
1993   A   85
1992   A   85

NOTE: No 1991 Jonqueyrès was produced.

The home estate of Jean-Michel Arcaute (of Clinet fame) is known for its high-quality wines that can compete with many famous estates. The 1992 Jonqueyrès is a tasty, ripe, well-made wine with good concentration, an attractive berry-scented nose, medium body, and a soft finish. It should drink well for 2–3 years. Also a noteworthy effort, the 1993 offers a dark-ruby/purple color, a moderately intense nose of cassis, and soft, nicely concentrated flavors with light tannin in the finish. It should drink well for 5–6 years.

KIRWAN (MARGAUX)* * *
1993   C   85
1992   C   85
1991   C   77

Kirwan is a Margaux classified growth that is making noticeable improvement. The 1993 possesses a dense, ruby/purple color, and straightforward, clean, ripe aromas of black fruits, herbs, and new oak. With medium body and above-average ripeness and concentration, this moderately tannic, well-made wine requires 5–6 years of cellaring; it will age well for 15+ years.

The light-bodied, medium-ruby-colored 1991 exhibits a bouquet reminiscent of herbal tea. Its fragile constitution, low acidity, and disjointed feel suggest it should be drunk over the next 3–4 years. The 1992 Kirwan is a good effort from this perennial underachiever. The color is a dark ruby/purple. The nose offers up plenty of toasty new oak and black cherries. With some fatness, low acidity, and ripe fruit, this medium-bodied wine may be the best Kirwan in years.

LABÉGORCE-ZÉDÉ (MARGAUX)* * *
1993   C   73
1992   B   75
1991   B   70

The rusty, rosé color of the 1991 Labégorce immediately raises suspicions about its quality. A weedy, vegetal, tealike nose confirms the lackluster quality of this thin, short, malnourished wine. The 1992 exhibits too little ripeness and fruit to support its ferociously tannic personality. It will dry out within 4–5 years. A tough, hard-textured, skinny wine, without enough flesh to cover its bones, the 1993 is sure to dry out over the next 4–5 years.

LAFITE-ROTHSCHILD (PAUILLAC)* * * * *

1993	E	91
1992	E	89
1991	E	86?

Lafite's light-bodied 1991 possesses moderate ruby color, a solid inner core of fruit, as well as potentially excessive tannin for its size and constitution. The wine exhibits Lafite's subtle personality with a leafy, tobacco, lead-pencil nose intertwined with sweet aromas of cassis. Dry, austere, and lacking length, it should turn out to be a good representation of Lafite-Rothschild in this so-so year. In 1992 only 36% of the harvest was utilized, resulting in a deeply colored wine with a nearly exceptional cedary, chocolatey, cassis character, medium body, surprisingly concentrated flavors, as well as the classic Lafite aromatic profile. If discounted, readers should take the opportunity to experience Lafite's finesse in a softer, more precocious vintage. The 1992 Lafite should drink well in 2–3 years and should last for 12–20 more.

Sixty-four percent of Lafite's 1993 crop was eliminated from the final blend. The 1993 Lafite contains an atypically high percentage of Cabernet Sauvignon (92%, plus 8% Merlot). Unlike in Graves, St.-Émilion, and Pomerol, the Merlot harvest was considered disappointing at Lafite. This wine reveals none of the hardness or tough-textured personality of the 1993 vintage. It offers Lafite's classic, intense, subtle perfume, great intensity and purity in the mouth, medium body, and a sweet, generous, authoritative yet elegant personality. The wine exhibits fine ripeness, wonderful richness, and a layered character. It is a terrific success for the vintage.

Past Glories: 1990 (94+), 1989 (92), 1988 (94), 1986 (94), 1983 (92), 1982 (98+), 1981 (93), 1976 (96), 1975 (92?), 1959 (99), 1953 (99), 1899 (96)

Past Mediocrities . . . or Worse: 1971 (60), 1970 (79), 1966 (84), 1961 (84?), 1955 (84), 1949 (86), 1945 (77), 1929 (62), 1928 (60)

LAFLEUR (POMEROL)* * * * *

1993	EE	90?
1992	E	91

NOTE: No 1991 was produced under the Lafleur label.

Lafleur has fashioned a blockbuster wine in 1992 that must be tasted to be believed. After seeing so many diluted, light, soft wines, it is hard to believe the level of concentration Lafleur achieved. Lafleur's color is an impressively saturated dark-purple/black. The tight nose offers up sweet cassis and jammy black cherry scents, intertwined with aromas of Asian spices and minerals. The wine possesses great richness, medium to full body, admirable density, layers of ripe fruit that linger on the palate, considerable tannin, and remarkable length. This would be a great wine in any vintage, but in 1992 it is a remarkable achievement. An amazing wine for the year! **A.M.: 2000–2015.**

The most tannic, backward, closed wine of the vintage is unquestionably Lafleur's 1993. The wine's color is an opaque purple/black, and the nose reluctantly offers up scents of Asian spices, licorice, and black fruits. Full bodied, as well as ferociously tannic and hard, with considerable weight, this painfully astringent yet awesomely extracted wine demands 10–15 years of cellaring. Perhaps a downsized version of the blockbuster, still frightfully tannic and backward yet mind-boggling 1975, the 1993 is a candidate for 30+ years of longevity—but only the wealthiest, healthiest, and most patient readers will have the fortitude to wait it out. Drink it after 2010!

Past Glories: 1990 (98), 1989 (96), 1988 (93), 1986 (95), 1985 (96), 1983 (94), 1982 (96),

1979 (98+), 1978 (90), 1975 (100), 1966 (96), 1962 (95), 1961 (100?), 1955 (92), 1950 (100), 1949 (96+), 1947 (100), 1945 (100)

Past Mediocrities . . . or Worse: 1981 (?), 1976 (78), 1971 (83)

LAFON-ROCHET (ST.-ESTÈPHE)* * *

1993	C	86
1992	C	85?
1991	B	85

Lafon-Rochet remains an obscure, underpriced, and underrated St.-Estèphe. This property has a tendency to turn out powerful, tannic wines, so it is not surprising that the 1993 is even more tannic and tougher than usual. Nevertheless, there is plenty of extracted ripe fruit, a chunky personality, and fine depth, as well as some toughness in the finish.

Although compact, the 1991 is a good wine. The color is dark ruby and the nose offers ripe black cherries, herbs, and spicy scents. Despite some compression, the wine offers sweet, fat fruit flavors, medium body, and fine depth. A softening of the tannin may provide even greater richness over the next 10–12 years. The 1992 appears to possess adequate rich, ripe fruit. While not a blockbuster wine, it is tannic and possibly ageworthy. It should drink well in 3–4 years and last for 12 or more—if the fruit holds. It may be a gamble, but Lafon-Rochet remains an obscure, underpriced, and underrated St.-Estèphe.

LAGRANGE (POMEROL)* *

1993	C	77
1992	C	84+

NOTE: No 1991 was produced under the Lagrange label.

Dark ruby colored, with a spicy, tightly knit nose, Lagrange's 1992 suffers from a compact personality and considerable tannic toughness. There is good underlying fruit, resulting in a chunky, robust, coarsely styled wine that should be cellared for another 2–3 years. It should keep for a decade, assuming it does not dry out. The 1993's medium- to dark-ruby color is followed by spicy, damp, earthy notes in its nose and tough, medium-bodied, lean flavors. With cellaring, the high tannin level will dominate the wine's fruit.

LAGRANGE (ST.-JULIEN)* * * */* * * * *

1993	C	88
1992	C	87

This property is fashioning reasonably priced, rich, concentrated, lavishly oaked wines. The 1992 is one of the top successes for the vintage. The color is an impressive dark ruby, and the nose offers up scents of smoky, toasty new oak accompanied by surprisingly rich, black currant fruit scents. Medium bodied, concentrated, and soft, with a mid-palate of ripe fruit, this sweet, sexy example of the vintage should drink well for 7–10 years. Readers who enjoy lavishly oaked, intense, ostentatious, smoky, richly fruity wines will love the 1993 Lagrange. It is opulent for the vintage, as well as medium to full bodied, with excellent, perhaps outstanding concentration, low acidity, and moderate tannin in the finish. It can be drunk young or cellared for 15 or more years.

Past Glories: 1990 (93), 1989 (89), 1986 (92), 1985 (89)

Past Mediocrities . . . or Worse: 1978 (80), 1975 (70), 1971 (65), 1970 (84)

LA LAGUNE (LUDON)* * * *

1993	C	86
1992	C	85
1991	C	81

La Lagune's 1991 is a firm, compact wine with a deep-ruby/purple color, toasty, black cherry aromas, and an austere, compact flavor profile. Although it should last for 10–15 years, it is unlikely to develop much charm. From both cask and bottle, the 1992 La Lagune has revealed a charming, soft, round, medium-bodied personality, some attractive herb, vanillin, and berry scents, and no hard tannin. The wine's weakness is its shortness. For drinking over the next 6–7 years, this is a fruity, charming style of wine.

The 1993 La Lagune possesses a sweetness and suppleness of fruit rarely found in 1993 Médocs. There is a layered density and ripeness, an attractive plum, cherry, and oaky nose, and a soft, rich, tannic finish. This medium-bodied wine should prove to be a charming, generous, and elegant La Lagune for drinking over the next 10–15 years.

Past Glories: 1990 (89), 1989 (90), 1986 (90), 1982 (93), 1978 (88), 1976 (88)

Past Mediocrities . . . or Worse: 1966 (84), 1961 (60)

LALANDE-BORIE (ST.-JULIEN)* * *

1993	C	85

This dark-ruby-colored wine exhibits attractive, chocolatey, sweet, currANTY fruit, fine ripeness, medium body, and a sense of elegance and grace. It is a 1993 that has managed to keep the tannin level well integrated and unobtrusive. Drink it over the next decade.

LANESSAN (HAUT-MÉDOC)* * *

1993	C	86
1992	B	83

NOTE: No 1991 Lanessan was offered for tasting.

Another well-run cru bourgeois that has managed to tame the ferocious tannin of the 1993 vintage, Lanessan has produced a plump, tasty, supple wine with a forward nose of cassis, cedar, and herbs, excellent ripeness, medium body, and a round, generous finish. It should drink well for 10–12 years. The medium-ruby-colored 1992 offers an attractive herbal-scented nose of dusty red and black fruits and earthy wood. This soft, medium-bodied, low-acid wine reveals some tannin in the finish. Drink it over the next 4–5 years before it drys out.

LANGOA-BARTON (ST.-JULIEN)* * *

1993	C	86
1992	C	83
1991	C	86

Another successful 1991, Langoa-Barton's effort in this vintage produced a deeply colored wine with an attractive nose offering up cedary, cassis, and leather scents, medium body, firm flavors, admirable richness and depth, and a spicy, masculine finish. While drinkable now, it should last for a decade. In 1992, both Barton estates turned out pleasant wines, although Langoa clearly does not possess the intensity of its sibling, Léoville-Barton. However, it is an attractively fruity, soft, charming, traditionally styled wine with some achingly painful tannin in the finish. The wine does not possess the fruit or depth to balance out its structure. Nevertheless, this is a cedary, herb- and currANTY-flavored wine for drinking over the next 5–7 years.

The 1993 is a medium-weight, classically styled, austere St.-Julien with good spice, some earthiness, ripe fruit, medium body, firm tannin, and excellent concentration. Although lighter and less well endowed than its sibling, Léoville-Barton, it should drink well for 12–15 years.

LARCIS-DUCASSE (ST.-ÉMILION)* *

1993	C	74
1992	C	76
1991	C	76

The 1991 and 1992 are pleasant, soft, light-bodied wines meant to be consumed over the next 4–6 years. The 1991 is clean, soft, and herbaceous. The 1992's light- to medium-ruby color lacks depth. The vegetal, herbaceous nose and hard, tannic, medium-bodied, fruitless flavors give further evidence of a problematical vintage for this well-placed hillside St.-Émilion vineyard. This wine will undoubtedly drop what little fruit it possesses over the next 3–4 years. As impressively colored as the 1993 is, its vegetal, hollow, hard personality made it impossible to bestow a good rating. The 1993 will undoubtedly dry out before it ever sheds enough tannin to come into balance.

LARMANDE (ST.-ÉMILION)* * *

1993	C	86
1992	C	85

NOTE: No 1991 was produced under the Larmande label.

This well-run property has fashioned a 1992 with a California Cabernet Sauvignon–like mintiness, and soft, ripe, pure, black currant fruit. Medium bodied and round, with attractive new oak and tough tannin in the finish, it can be drunk now as well as over the next 5–7 years. The attractive, rich, dark-ruby-colored 1993 exhibits a sweet, jammy, roasted nut, herb, and black cherry nose, medium body, admirable flavor concentration, and moderate tannin. Some roughness in the finish held my score down. When all the component parts come into focus, this will be a very good example of the vintage. Drink it during its first 10–12 years of life.

Past Glories: 1990 (89), 1989 (88), 1988 (90)

LAROSE-TRINTAUDON (HAUT-MÉDOC)* *

1993	B	85

I have been a longtime critic of this estate's wines, which have had a tendency to possess musty aromatics. However, over recent vintages that problem appears to have been solved. The 1993 Larose-Trintaudon is an attractive, all-purpose claret for drinking in its first 5–7 years of life. The wine possesses good spice, clean, ripe, currant fruit, medium body, and a well-balanced, elegant personality. It is a good, inexpensive choice for restaurants.

LAROZE (ST.-ÉMILION)* *

1993	C	73
1992	C	74

NOTE: No 1991 Laroze will be offered for sale in the United States.

The lean, herbaceous, light-bodied 1992 reveals some engaging cigarlike and watery black cherry fruit in the nose, but there is little more than acidity, alcohol, tannin, and wood in the mouth. The 1993's thin, diluted, hard flavors are accompanied by excessive tannin and too little fruit and ripeness.

LASCOMBES (MARGAUX)* * *

1992	C	82
1991	C	82

This property has begun turning out better wines, as both of these examples attest. The light-bodied 1991 is well made, given the vintage's limitations. The color is a sound medium ruby, and the nose offers up attractive spicy, vanillin, berrylike aromas. The wine possesses good body, as well as an attractive ripe fruitiness and suppleness. Drink it over the next 4–5 years. This 1992's medium-ruby color and ripe curranty fruit intertwined with scents of cedar are initially pleasing, but the dilution is apparent in the mouth, where the tannin and wood dominate the wine's meager fruit. Perhaps more depth will emerge with aging, but it appears this wine should be drunk over the next 4–5 years.

Past Glories: 1966 (88), 1959 (90)

Past Mediocrities . . . or Worse: 1981 (72), 1979 (76), 1978 (76)

LATOUR (PAUILLAC)* * * * *

1993	E	91
1992	E	88+
1991	D	89

After Latour's exquisite performance in 1990, the 1991 is somewhat of a letdown. Nevertheless, it is a candidate for the wine of the vintage because of its concentration and class. After a strict selection, only 11,500 cases were made. The wine offers a dense, dark-ruby color, and a reticent but promising bouquet of black cherries, cassis, minerals, roasted nuts, spices, and subtle herbs. Medium bodied, with excellent richness, fine glycerin, and aggressive tannin, this ripe, muscular, beefy 1991 needs 5–6 years to shed its tannin; it should last for 15 or more years. Only 50% of the 1992 harvest went into the grand vin. The result is a sweet, expansive, rich, medium-bodied, surprisingly supple Latour with the telltale English walnut, black currant, and mineral scents, very good to excellent flavor concentration, low acidity, and moderate tannin in the finish. This is an extremely well made, approachable style of Latour that should age well for 10–15 years. It may develop even further, thus justifying an even higher score.

Latour's 1993 is a top success for the vintage, but it will not be ready to drink for at least 8–10 years. Approximately 50% of the harvest was eliminated from the final blend. In stylistic terms, the 1993 is similar to this property's 1966 and 1971—both among the finest efforts for these vintages. The dense, medium- to full-bodied 1993 exhibits layers of richness, plenty of dry, hard tannin, and enough sweet fruit, glycerin, and extraction to balance out the wine's tough personality. This muscular, dense wine requires 10 years of cellaring; consume it over the subsequent 15–20 years.

Past Glories: 1990 (98+), 1989 (90), 1988 (89), 1986 (91), 1982 (99), 1978 (92), 1975 (92), 1971 (91), 1970 (98), 1966 (96+), 1964 (90), 1962 (93), 1961 (100), 1959 (95), 1949 (100), 1948 (94), 1945 (99), 1928 (100), 1926 (93), 1924 (94), 1900 (89), 1899 (93), 1870 (90)

Past Mediocrities . . . or Worse: Virtually none in top vintages, although the 1985, 1983, 1979, and 1976 are below the château's extraordinarily high standards.

LATOUR À POMEROL (POMEROL)* * * *

1993	D	86
1992	D	86

NOTE: No 1991 was produced under the Latour à Pomerol label.

Latour à Pomerol continues to make lighter, more supple and fruity wines that remain stylistically different from the legendary efforts this vineyard turned out in 1947, 1948,

1950, 1959, and 1961. The 1993 is a medium-bodied, round wine with moderate tannin, fine ripeness, a nose that offers up spicy, coffee, black cherry scents with a touch of toasty new oak, and a moderately long finish. Cellar it for 2–5 years and drink it over the subsequent 12–15.

Latour à Pomerol's 1992 is a good example of what a conscientious winemaker should have been attempting to do in a lighter-styled vintage like 1992. Rather than aim for power, intensity, structure, and ageability, it seems to me that the best strategy was to try and capture the charm and fruit of the vintage. Latour à Pomerol has done that and the result is a seductive, easy-to-drink, pleasantly fruity, soft wine with a berry-, herb-, and coffee-scented nose, good ripeness, an attractive mid-palate, and a supple finish. Drink it over the next 4–6 years.

Past Glories: 1983 (88), 1982 (93), 1970 (90), 1961 (100), 1959 (98), 1950 (96), 1948 (100), 1947 (100)

Past Mediocrities . . . or Worse: 1978 (83), 1975 (67), 1971 (82)

LÉOVILLE-BARTON (ST.-JULIEN)* * * */* * * * *

1993	C	89
1992	C	87
1991	C	87

Without much fanfare, Léoville-Barton continues to turn out textbook Médocs of great style, aging potential, and richness. Of utmost interest, these wines are priced among the most sensible of all the finest classified growths. No doubt the proprietor, Anthony Barton, has a healthy ego, but it is not reflected in his pro-consumer pricing policy. In the last three difficult vintages, Léoville-Barton has produced one of the most successful 1991s, a delicious 1992, and an authoritatively flavored, powerful yet elegant 1993. The latter wine is potentially the best Léoville-Barton of the last 3 years. Medium to full bodied, with excellent purity, a classic nose of cedar, cassis, spice, and oak, and admirable concentration, this beautifully balanced, rich, stylish wine requires 4–6 years of cellaring; it will keep for two decades. Impressive!

If you are looking for a terrific value from a so-called off year, check out Léoville-Barton's 1991! It possesses a deep-ruby color, a big, cedary, black currant– and herb-scented nose, and ripe, rich, medium-bodied flavors that offer impressive concentration, moderate tannin, and admirable length. This impressive Léoville-Barton is significantly better than vintages such as 1981 and 1979. It should drink well for 10–15 years. The 1992, which was impressive from cask, continues to prove that it is one of the finest wines of the vintage. It exhibits a dark-ruby color, a spicy, cedary, black cherry– and curranty-scented nose, rich, medium-bodied flavors with excellent ripeness, a sense of elegance, and a succulent, juicy personality. The wine reveals no signs of dilution, and the tannin is sweet rather than hard and astringent. Drink this noteworthy 1992 over the next 10–12 years.

Past Glories: 1990 (95), 1989 (88), 1988 (88), 1986 (92), 1985 (92), 1982 (94), 1975 (90), 1961 (92), 1959 (94), 1953 (95), 1949 (95), 1948 (96), 1945 (98)

Past Mediocrities . . . or Worse: 1979 (75), 1971 (70), 1966 (84)

LÉOVILLE-LAS CASES (ST.-JULIEN)* * * * *

1993	D	92
1992	D	90
1991	D	87

In 1993, this great estate, straddling the border of Pauillac, adjacent to Latour, once again produced an exceptional wine that is clearly one of the superstars of the vintage. Proprietor

Michel Delon eliminated 55% of the 1993 harvest. The wine boasts a saturated ruby/purple color, and a textbook nose of superdelineated, ripe, black cherry and cassis fruit subtly touched by toasty oak and minerals. In the mouth it is reminiscent of this property's top-notch 1988—a rich, stunningly proportioned, medium- to full-bodied wine, with great purity, focus, and vibrancy. While there is plenty of tannin, it is not excessive, especially when compared with the wine's exceptional concentration. This wine requires 4–8 years of cellaring; it should age gracefully for at least 20–25 years.

In 1991, 50% of Léoville-Las Cases's production was eliminated from the final blend. The 1991 exhibits a textbook Pauillac/St.-Julien lead-pencil nose intertwined with scents of ripe cassis. The style of the wine is one of elegance, fine ripeness and body, and powerful tannin. Some austerity keeps the score from going even higher. Stylistically the wine is similar to the 1987, although more tannic and potentially longer-lived. While it has the potential to last for 10–15 years, it will remain an austerely styled wine, much like the 1970. In the bottle, the 1992 Léoville-Las Cases confirms the outstanding quality of the cask samples I tasted with Michel Delon. Only 45% of the harvest made it into this wine. The result is another classic Léoville-Las Cases with a sweet black currant— and toasty mineral-scented nose, bold, medium- to full-bodied flavors with excellent richness (there are layers of fruit in this 1992), and a long, tannic finish. The wine can be drunk now or cellared for 12–15 years. It is an outstanding success for the vintage, revealing Léoville-Las Cases's classic style. With elegance and a flattering precociousness, it is more charming at a younger age than Las Cases is from blockbuster vintages such as 1990, 1989, 1986, 1985, and 1982. This is one of the top stars of the vintage!

Past Glories: 1990 (96), 1989 (95), 1988 (92), 1986 (97), 1985 (92), 1983 (90), 1982 (100), 1981 (88), 1978 (92), 1975 (92), 1966 (90)

Past Mediocrities . . . or Worse: 1971 (73), 1970 (77), 1961 (84)

LÉOVILLE-POYFERRÉ (ST.-JULIEN)* * *

1993	C	81
1992	C	79
1991	C	84

Léoville-Poyferré turned in a solidly made, muscular 1991 with good color, ripe fruit, plenty of tannin, and noticeable oak. The wine lacks charm and finesse, but should last for 12 or more years. It will benefit from 2–3 years of cellaring. Medium ruby colored, with an oak overlay, the 1992 lacks fruit and tastes monolithic, tannic, angular, and compact. It may improve with 2–3 years of cellaring, but my instincts suggest it will dry out long before the tannin fades. The 1993's ruby color is followed by a wine with a light-intensity nose of earth, fruit, and wood. With tough tannin and a one-dimensional personality, this lean wine may turn out to be above average in quality, but the low extraction level is worrisome.

Past Glories: 1983 (90), 1982 (92)

Past Mediocrities . . . or Worse: 1976 (75), 1975 (?), 1970 (65), 1962 (67)

LA LOUVIÈRE (GRAVES)* * * *

1993	C	87
1992	C	87

Anyone who follows Bordeaux knows that La Louvière is on a hot streak. Moreover, their wines remain underpriced, so jump on the bandwagon before there is a 20%–30% rise in price. The 1993 exhibits a saturated dark-ruby/purple color, and a tight but excellent nose of ripe, black cherry and cassis fruit, minerals, and toasty new oak. The wine possesses excellent flavor concentration and fatness (not a trait of many 1993 clarets), a ripe, chewy texture, and a long, heady, rich, moderately tannic finish. The fruit and tannin suggest it should be drunk early; it should last for 10–15 years.

The 1992 is another fine La Louvière. It offers a dark, saturated, ruby/purple color, a big nose of spicy, sweet, cassis, herb, and tobacco scents, and smoky, black curranty flavors touched intelligently with oak for structure and sweetness. This lush, delicious, already complex, medium- to full-bodied wine should drink well for 7–10 years.

Past Glories: 1990 (89), 1989 (88), 1988 (90)

LYNCH-BAGES (PAUILLAC)* * * * *

1993	C	87
1992	C	86
1991	C	86

Lynch-Bages has fashioned an attractive, medium-bodied, soft wine in 1991. It would make a noteworthy bargain if it were selling for under $18 a bottle. The color is dense, and the nose offers up bold cassis aromas intertwined with earth and new oak. The wine is moderately deep, reveals some tannin, but finishes quickly. It is a good, ripe, light- to medium-weight Lynch-Bages that is best drunk over the next 7–8 years. Lynch-Bages has produced an impressively colored 1992. The wine has not begun to display much complexity in its cassis-, damp earth–, and spicy-scented nose. There is fine fatness and ripeness, medium body, and light tannin in the finish. This is a very good, spicy, cedary Lynch-Bages for drinking over the next 6–8 years.

Wow! Lynch-Bages's 1993 reveals a thick, opaque purple color. The initial subdued aromas of earth, subtle red and black fruits, and oak require coaxing to unleash. The wine's attack begins well, with a first impression of muscle, richness, body, and intensity, but a weakness in the mid-palate and a tannic ferocity quickly suggest the wine's extraction of fruit may not be sufficient. If this wine fills out, it will merit a rating in the upper eighties. If it does not, look for this to be a chunky, husky, frightfully tannic and tough wine that may evolve along the lines of this property's very good but austere 1966. The 1993 needs 4–6 years of cellaring; it will last for 15+ years.

Past Glories: 1990 (93), 1989 (96), 1986 (92), 1985 (93), 1983 (88), 1982 (93), 1970 (95), 1962 (89), 1961 (94), 1959 (94), 1957 (88), 1955 (92), 1953 (90), 1952 (91)

Past Mediocrities . . . or Worse: 1979 (79), 1978 (82), 1976 (72), 1975 (79), 1971 (58), 1966 (84)

MAGDELAINE (ST.-ÉMILION)* * *

1993	D	87
1992	D	86

NOTE: No 1991 was produced under the Magdelaine label.

Dark ruby colored, with a spicy, black cherry, oaky nose with a tealike character, the medium-bodied, moderately tannic 1992 exhibits more depth and ripeness than most premier grand cru classé St.-Émilions. There is moderate length and a modest amount of black cherry fruit in this classy, elegant St.-Émilion. It will keep well for 10–12 years.

In 1993 it was usually imperative either to include a high percentage of Merlot or to eliminate a significant percentage of Cabernet to produce a top-notch wine. This atypical St.-Émilion has always relied far more on Merlot than on Cabernet Franc or Cabernet Sauvignon. Magdelaine's 1993 is a dense, powerful, tannic claret with excellent concentration, plenty of rich, sweet fruit, and an austere, dry, structured, yet well-delineated finish. This should turn out to be a long-lived Magdelaine with 10–20 years of aging potential.

Past Glories: 1982 (90), 1961 (91)

Past Mediocrities . . . or Worse: 1986 (?), 1985 (82), 1981 (80), 1979 (84)

MAGNEAU (GRAVES)* * *

1993		B	85

An obscure Graves estate, Magneau turns out pretty, elegant, stylish, soft wines that are ready to drink when released. The 1993 exhibits fine sweetness, a ripe, tobacco, cedar, and currant nose, no bitterness or astringency to its tannin, and a velvety finish. Drink it over the next 5–6 years.

MALARTIC-LAGRAVIÈRE (GRAVES)* *

1993		C	72
1992		C	71
1991		C	72

This property consistently fashioned austere, green, thin wines up until 1994. Since 1994, the quality of the wines has increased due to the investments of the vineyard's puchaser, the Laurent-Perrier group. The 1991 exhibits a weak, watery color, and a soft, vague bouquet of earthy red fruits and spice. There is little depth and only tannin and acidity in the finish. Medium ruby colored, with a closed, nearly nonexistent bouquet that reluctantly offers up a few scents of dried, stale herbs and new wood, this compact, stern, charmless 1992 reveals excruciatingly hard tannin, little fruit, and no redeeming characteristics. The 1993 reveals a healthy dark-ruby/purple color, but a green, vegetal nose, light body, angular, narrowly constructed flavors, and an excess of hard tannin in the finish. It will only become more astringent with cellaring.

MALESCASSE (HAUT-MÉDOC)* *

1993		C	86

Pichon-Lalande's former cellar-master, Monsieur Godin, has taken up residence at Malescasse. Not surprisingly, this property's predilection for turning out angular, tough-textured wines has diminished under Godin's magical hands. In what is undeniably a stern vintage, he has fashioned a round, generous, expansively flavored wine with an obvious ripe, sweet, black currant fruitiness, and soft tannin in the finish. It should drink well for 6–8 years.

MALESCOT-ST.-EXUPÉRY (MARGAUX)* *

1992		C	82
1991		C	84

This property has gotten more serious over recent years. Their 1991 is a stylish, herbaceous, moderately endowed wine with round, fruity flavors, a sense of elegance, and an immediate appeal. It should be drunk over the next 5–6 years. What it lacks in weight, power, and concentration it makes up for with its finesse. The light- to medium-bodied 1992 Malescot-St.-Exupéry exhibits herbaceous, curranty fruit, and oak scents in its bouquet, as well as rough tannin in the finish. The wine's graceful, fruity character suggests it should be consumed over the next 4–5 years.

Past Glories: 1961 (92), 1959 (90)

Past Mediocrities . . . or Worse: 1986 (82), 1985 (74), 1983 (83), 1981 (78), 1978 (78), 1975 (76), 1966 (67)

MARBUZET (ST.-ESTÈPHE)* */* * *

1992		B	81
1991		B	84

Cos d'Estournel's second wine, the 1991 Marbuzet is a pleasant, herbaceous, peppery, soft, fruity wine with no tannin evident. Its velvety-textured, ripe, light- to medium-bodied style is ideal for drinking over the next 2–3 years. Also soft and pleasant, the 1992 is less concentrated, with a short finish. Nevertheless, it will provide competent drinking over the next 4–5 years.

CHÂTEAU MARGAUX (MARGAUX)* * * * *

1993	D	92
1992	D	89
1991	D	88

Margaux's 1991 is a candidate for wine of the vintage. It reveals a deep-ruby color, and a tight but promising nose of rich cassis, licorice, and toasty new oak. Dense, medium to full bodied, with plenty of depth, it possesses moderate tannin and a long, rich finish. **A.M.: Now–2007.** A bigger, more powerful wine than Margaux's 1987, it is close in quality to the estate's 1988. The 1992 Margaux displays an impressively saturated, dark-ruby/purple color, and a fragrant bouquet of cassis, vanillin, and floral scents. The wine is smooth, supple, wonderfully ripe, and seductive, with medium body, low acidity, and light tannin in the finish. It is drinking extremely well. Some tasters will no doubt rate it even higher than I have, given its elegance and layers of ripe, generous fruit that are presented in a medium-bodied format. This impressive wine should drink well for 10–15 years.

Less than 50% of Margaux's 1993 harvest made the grade for the estate's grand vin. A blend of 72% Cabernet Sauvignon, 20% Merlot, 6% Petit Verdot, and 2% Cabernet Franc, Margaux's 1993 is atypically supple and seductive. It offers an impressively saturated ruby/purple color, an intense fragrance of red and black fruits, toast, and spring flowers, and a voluptuously textured, multilayered personality, with expansive, sweet, ripe fruit. It is surprisingly forward, without the mouth-aching tannin possessed by many 1993s. The wine is medium to full bodied, beautifully pure, and reminiscent of this property's splendid 1985. Capable of lasting for 20–25 years, it should turn out to be one of the most seductive and popular 1993 clarets. Very impressive!

Past Glories: 1990 (100), 1989 (90), 1986 (96+), 1985 (95), 1983 (96), 1982 (99), 1981 (90), 1979 (92), 1978 (94), 1961 (93), 1953 (98), 1947 (92), 1945 (94), 1928 (98), 1900 (100)

Past Mediocrities . . . or Worse: 1976 (70), 1975 (68), 1971 (70), 1970 (76), 1966 (83), 1964 (78)

MARJOSSE (BORDEAUX)* */* * *

1992	A	85

This inexpensive generic Bordeaux made from nearly 100% Merlot is one of the sleepers of this modest vintage. The wine is ripe, fruity, and supple, with admirable purity and plenty of delicious, creamy-textured fruit. Drink it over the next 2–3 years.

MARQUIS DE TERME (MARGAUX)* * *

1993	C	81
1992	C	76
1991	C	74

From time to time this property turns out surprisingly strong efforts. However, the 1991 and 1992 are not among them. The light-bodied, short, compact, uninteresting 1991 reveals considerable dilution. Medium ruby colored, with a bouquet of wood, dusty earth, and herbs, this light-bodied, soft, insubstantial wine should be drunk over the next 4–5 years.

The 1993 Marquis de Terme is a dark-colored, medium-bodied, concentrated wine. However, it did not escape the 1993 vintage's downside—compact flavors and an excess of tannin. Some positive components—ripeness, extract, and purity—suggest this wine will last for 10 or more years.

MARTINENS (MARGAUX)* *

| 1993 | | B | 75 |

This shallowly constructed wine reveals a medium-ruby color, light body, soft, berry fruit, excessive tannin, and an underlying herbaceous streak. Drink it over the next 7–8 years.

MAZERIS (CANON-FRONSAC)* * *

| 1993 | | B | 85 |
| 1992 | | B | 82 |

NOTE: No 1991 Mazeris will be offered for sale in the United States.

The 1992 Mazeris offers a dark-ruby color, and a tight but pleasant nose of wet stones, herbs, and berry fruit. Firm and tannic, with a Médoc-like personality, as well as good underlying fruit and sweetness, this wine will undoubtedly become more attenuated as it ages. For drinking over the near term, it is a pleasant, although tightly knit offering. Mazeris's 1993 is a tannic but sweet, ripe wine with medium body, some concentration, a compact, austere personality, and fine purity and complexity. It should drink well within 2–3 years of its release and last for 10 or more years.

MAZEYRES (POMEROL)* *

| 1993 | | B | 79 |

This is normally a light-bodied, easygoing wine meant to be consumed in its first 4–5 years of life. The soft, fruity 1993 will need to be drunk before the end of the century.

MEYNEY (ST.-ESTÈPHE)* * *

| 1993 | | B | 77 |
| 1992 | | B | 81 |

In 1992 Meyney is a dark-ruby-colored claret with medium body, adequate acidity, and excessive tannin and toughness in the finish. While it is better than many 1992s, its excess of tannin will result in an ungracious evolution. This perennially overachieving, consumer favorite has turned in a mediocre performance in 1993. The color is dark ruby, but the wine is hard with an excess of tannin for its meager fruit. The result is a wine that tastes compact and attenuated, and lacks charm and ripeness.

Past Glories: 1986 (91), 1982 (90), 1975 (90)

LA MISSION-HAUT-BRION (GRAVES)* * * * *

1993		D	91
1992		D	89
1991		D	87

La Mission enjoyed considerable success in the 1991 vintage. This deep-ruby-colored wine boasts a fragrant, smoky, mineral- and berry-scented nose. Suave, elegant, and rich, with noticeable fatness to its harmonious flavors, good balance, and a long, medium-bodied finish, the wine exhibits fine ripeness, and a tasty, aromatic personality. This precocious La Mission should drink well for the next 6–10 years. An excellent wine for the vintage, La Mission-Haut-Brion's 1992 exhibits a dark-ruby color, an intense, black currant-, mineral-, and floral-scented nose, and supple, medium-bodied flavors that cascade over the palate. The wine is soft and opulent, with plenty of glycerin and lusty alcohol in the gorgeous finish.

Drink it over the next 10–12 years. Don't be surprised if this wine turns out to merit an even higher rating in a few years.

A terrific example of the vintage, La Mission's 1993 exhibits a saturated dark-ruby/purple color, a thick texture, and a promising bouquet of jammy cassis, lead pencil, smoke, and spices. Surprisingly voluptuous, this medium- to full-bodied, admirably concentrated wine's great ripeness and fruit conceals moderate tannin in the finish. La Mission-Haut-Brion's 1993 may turn out to be as good as the estate's 1990! While it will drink well young, it possesses the necessary backbone and depth to age for 20+ years.

Past Glories: 1990 (92), 1989 (99), 1988 (90), 1986 (90), 1985 (94), 1983 (90), 1982 (95), 1981 (90), 1979 (91), 1978 (94), 1975 (100), 1970 (94?), 1966 (89), 1964 (91), 1961 (100), 1959 (100), 1958 (94), 1957 (93), 1955 (100), 1953 (93), 1952 (93), 1950 (95), 1949 (100), 1948 (93), 1947 (95), 1946 (90), 1945 (94), 1937 (88), 1929 (97), 1928 (98)

Past Mediocrities . . . or Worse: Virtually none, although the 1976 is somewhat of a disappointment, and, of course, many bottles of the 1970 are plagued by excessive volatile acidity.

MONBRISON (MARGAUX)* * *

1993	C	80?
1992	C	74
1991	C	85

Monbrison's 1991, a success for the vintage, displays spicy, toasty new oak, solid color, ripe fruit, medium body, and a compact yet flavorful finish. It should drink well for 4–5 years. The 1992 is the most disappointing wine made at this estate in over a decade. Lean, short, and woody, with excessive tannin and oak, and lacking concentration, it will only become more extreme in style and is thus best consumed over the next several years.

Several tastings of the 1993 left me unpersuaded. All my tasting notes contained such damning descriptions as "too oaky," "too tannic," and "too hollow." Monbrison has been one of the bright shining stars of Margaux, so perhaps I saw the wine at an unflattering stage of its development.

MONTROSE (ST.-ESTÈPHE)* * * */* * * * *

1993	C	87
1992	C	87
1991	C	88

St.-Estèphe enjoyed more success in 1991 than any other Bordeaux appellation, largely because the damaging frost caused little damage to the first-generation fruit in the northern Médoc. Consequently Montrose's production was close to normal and the wine is one of the stars of the vintage. That being said, it is not close to the wondrous quality of the 1989 and 1990, but it is superior to this property's 1988. It reveals a dark, saturated color (one of the most opaque wines of the vintage), and a tight but promising nose of sweet, jammy, black raspberry fruit, minerals, and subtle new oak. With a medium- to full-bodied personality boasting considerable tannin, admirable ripeness, and layers of fruit, this excellent wine should reach full maturity in 7–8 years and last for nearly two decades. Dark ruby colored, with a tight but promising nose of licorice, black currants, and minerals, the medium-bodied 1992 possesses attractively sweet, rich, cassis fruit and moderate tannin. The wine reveals fine concentration and ripeness, but it requires 2–4 years of cellaring; it should last for 12–14 years. It appears to be one of the few 1992s with sufficient fruit to balance out the tannin.

Montrose's 1993 possesses an impressive dark-ruby/purple color, a tight but promising nose of sweet black fruits, smoke, herbs, and minerals, admirable concentration and ripeness, as well as pronounced, hard tannin. This wine lacks the expansiveness and huge fat and richness of the 1989, 1990, and even the 1991. While it is capable of lasting 20–25 years, it is likely to be an austerely styled wine.

Past Glories: 1990 (100), 1989 (95), 1986 (91), 1982 (89), 1970 (94), 1964 (92), 1961 (95), 1959 (95), 1955 (90), 1953 (93)

Past Mediocrities . . . or Worse: 1988 (83), 1985 (85), 1983 (83), 1981 (84), 1979 (82), 1978 (84)

MONTVIEL (POMEROL)* *

1993	B	81

This is a soft, straightforward, pleasant wine with attractive berry fruit, spice, light to medium body, and a compact finish. Drink it over the next 4–5 years.

MOULIN DU CADET (ST.-ÉMILION)* *

1993	C	86

Looking for a 1993 that is all chewy, fleshy, succulent fruit presented in an opulent, voluptuously textured style? Check out Moulin du Cadet's 1993 offering. This ripe, fruity, low-acid, medium-bodied wine is ideal for readers who are unable to defer their gratification.

MOULIN-PEY-LABRIE (CANON-FRONSAC)* * */* * * *

1993	B	85
1992	B	85

NOTE: No 1991 was offered for tasting.

Moulin-Pey-Labrie is one of the best-run estates in Canon-Fronsac, so it is not surprising that they have fashioned a soft, nicely extracted, fruity 1992 with good color, medium body, and a charming, straightforward style offering ripeness and finesse. Drink it over the next 5–6 years. The 1993 Moulin-Pey-Labrie should turn out to be one of the top wines from the Canon-Fronsac/Fronsac region. Unlike many of its peers from this beautiful, pastoral wine region located outside Libourne, this offering reveals sweet, curranty fruit, fine concentration, medium body, and firm but unaggressive tannin. It should drink well for 10–12 years.

MOUTON-ROTHSCHILD (PAUILLAC)* * * *

1993	E	91
1992	E	88
1991	E	86+

The 1991 exhibits a moderately dark ruby/purple color, as well as a promising and complex nose of such classic Pauillac aromas as lead pencil, roasted nuts, and ripe cassis. The initial richness is quickly obliterated by frightful levels of tannin, and a tough, hard finish. Although there is an interesting and alluring dimension to this wine, the tannin level is excessively high and the wine is likely to dry out after 10–15 years of cellaring. Readers who admire austere, fruitless wines will rate it higher. In 1992, Mouton has fashioned a flattering, soft, opulently styled wine with medium body, a healthy dark-ruby/purple color, and a big, fragrant nose of jammy cassis, smoky oak, and roasted herbs and nuts. The wine offers a sweet, expansive mid-palate and a lush, velvety-textured finish. It is an ostentatious, flashy Mouton for drinking over the next 10–12 years.

Mouton's 1993 has turned out exceptionally well. The color is a healthy, brilliant purple, and the wine's aromatic personality borders on ostentatious, with its display of cassis fruit, minerals, lead pencil, Asian spices, caramel, vanilla, and toasty oak. Spicy, with great purity of fruit, this medium-bodied wine exhibits fine density, an attractive inner core of ripeness and extraction, and a moderately tannic, surprisingly long finish. Tasted side by side against the tannic, stern, tough-as-nails 1990, I thought this to be the better wine, although Mouton's raw materials in 1990 must have been significantly superior to those in 1993. Given the high percentage of Cabernet Sauvignon (84%), the 1993 will firm up and close, but there is plenty of sweet fruit in this unquestionably successful wine. Drink it over the next 15–20 years.

Past Glories: 1986 (100), 1985 (91), 1983 (90), 1982 (100), 1970 (92?), 1966 (90), 1962 (92), 1961 (98), 1959 (100), 1955 (97), 1953 (95), 1952 (87), 1949 (94), 1947 (97), 1945 (100)

Past Mediocrities . . . or Worse: 1981 (83), 1979 (84), 1978 (86)—Note: The jury is still out on the very good but less-than-spectacular Moutons made in 1990, 1989, and 1988.

NENIN (POMEROL)* */* * *

1993	C	86?

After a long-term stay in the qualitative doldrums, this estate is beginning to turn out better wines. The 1993 Nenin displays a healthy dark-ruby/purple color, a sweet nose of black raspberry and cherry fruit, medium body, and firm tannin in the finish. One sample I tasted displayed an element of musty wood, but the other examples were pure, healthy, ripe, and potentially very good. As with many 1993s, the Nenin will benefit from several years of cellaring and will age for 10–15 years. Look for confirmed improvements at Nenin as evidenced by a very fine 1994.

OLIVIER (GRAVES)* *

1993	C	79
1992	C	75
1991	C	85

This estate tends to produce densely colored, blatantly smoky wines that possess too much new oak for their meager flavor concentration. The 1993 adds some vegetal, herbal notes to the mélange and the result is a lean, superficial wine without substance and length.

Olivier has turned in a meritorious performance in the tough 1991 vintage. The deep-ruby color is followed by a weedy, tobacco-scented, spicy, curranty, open, and easy-to-appreciate nose. Lavish quantities of new oak give the wine a forward, sexy, cosmetic appeal. Once past all the oak, attractive ripe fruit is presented in a soft, velvety-textured, medium-bodied format. Drink this charming wine over the next 4–5 years. Although the 1992 offers impressive deep color and spicy notes in its oaky bouquet, it lacks the fruit, concentration, and length of the 1991. A shallowness becomes increasingly apparent as the wine rests on the palate. This is a wine that must be drunk in its first 2–3 years of life.

LES ORMES DE PEZ (ST.-ESTÈPHE)* * *

1993	B	86
1992	B	85
1991	B	81

Savvy consumers should realize this bargain-priced wine is often a fine value. The deeply colored 1993 is soft and more velvety textured than many of its peers, with admirable concentration, light to moderate tannin, and fine length and extract. Drink it over the next 5–10 years.

The 1991 exhibits spicy, herbaceous fruit, above-average depth for the vintage, adequate tannin, and a clean, one-dimensional finish. It should drink well for 5–8 years. Given the fact that this wine rarely sells for more than $15, the 1992 is a good bargain. The wine displays a dark-ruby color, excellent ripe berry fruit, some tannin in the finish, a lush, medium-bodied, chewy style, and fine fruit and suppleness. It should drink well for at least 7–8 years. I may have underrated this wine.

LES ORMES-SORBET (MÉDOC)* * *

1993	B	85
1992	B	85
1991	B	75

In years such as 1991, 1992, and 1993, the less prestigious Bordeaux châteaux classified as cru bourgeois cannot demand high enough prices for their wines that would permit them to make the severe selections necessary to produce a good wine. While this makes these vintages difficult for the less-renowned estates, there are always pleasant surprises. In 1992 Les Ormes-Sorbet is one. This Médoc estate has been fashioning very good wines recently, and in 1992 they have turned out a soft, spicy, vanillin- and black currant–scented wine with medium body, attractive fruit, and 3–5 years of drinkability. Given the many disappointing, watery, and/or excessively tannic 1992 cru bourgeois offerings, this is one wine that stands out for value and quality.

The 1991 is straightforward, austere, and lacking fruit, although not new wood. The 1993 should prove that even in a tough year the property is capable of making a strict enough selection to turn out a fine cuvée. Toasty oak and ripe black cherry scents are followed by a wine with some opulence (a rarity in a 1993), light tannin, and a soft finish. It should drink well for 5–6 years.

PALMER (MARGAUX)* * * * *

1993	C	87
1992	C	84?
1991	C	87

Palmer's 1991 is a noteworthy effort. The deep-ruby/purple color is followed by aromas of ripe black fruits and new oak. There is excellent definition, a sweet, creamy, medium- to full-bodied texture, noticeable fatness, and a lush, concentrated, rich finish. This seductive, hedonistic 1991 should drink well for 7–10 years. Palmer's 1992 revealed good ripeness and more concentration from cask samples. Now that it has been bottled, it is clear that the fining/filtration done at bottling has removed some of the delicately constructed fruit and finesse. The color is a medium ruby and the nose offers up aggressive aromas of toasty new oak, black cherries, and black currant fruit. So far so good, but once past the charming, light- to medium-intensity bouquet, the wine's most obvious characteristics are its lightness, dilution of fruit, and lack of concentration. This medium-bodied, light wine possesses an extremely short finish. Drink it over the next 4–5 years.

Palmer's 1993 is significantly richer and more concentrated than the light-bodied, diluted 1992. The 1993 exhibits an excellent dark-ruby color, and an attractive, precociously developed bouquet of smoky scents, black fruits (cherries galore!), damp earth, and spices. The wine is medium bodied, with enough ripe fruit and succulence to be considered nearly opulent. Low acidity, moderate tannin, and fine concentration have rendered this a very successful 1993. It should last for 10–15 years.

Past Glories: 1989 (96), 1986 (90), 1983 (97), 1979 (91), 1978 (91), 1975 (90), 1970 (96), 1966 (96), 1961 (99), 1959 (93), 1949 (93), 1945 (97), 1928 (96)

Past Mediocrities . . . or Worse: 1981 (81)

PAPE-CLÉMENT (GRAVES)* * * *

1993	C	89
1992	C	83
1991	C	87

Since 1986 Pape-Clément has been producing some of the most elegant and aromatically complex wines in Bordeaux. I am delighted to report the estate did not stumble in 1991, 1992, or 1993. The excellent 1991 offers an intensely fragrant bouquet of cedar, tobacco, smoke, and black fruits. Medium bodied, with fine depth, sweet, jammy fruit, wonderful elegance, and a soft, satiny-textured finish, this admirably long wine is already delicious; it should last for 7–8 years. Impressive! Although the 1992's light- to medium-ruby color suggests dilution, Pape-Clément's characteristically complex bouquet reveals aromas of tobacco, herbs, cedar, and sweet red and black fruits. Light bodied, with low acidity, this pleasant but short wine lacks concentration. It does possess enough of this well-run estate's character to merit some attention. Drink it over the next 2–4 years.

After the disappointing 1992, Pape-Clément rebounded with an exceptionally strong effort in 1993. In fact, this wine appears to be one of the best of the vintage and comes close to rivaling what Pape-Clément achieved in 1990. It reveals a deep-ruby/purple color, an intense fragrance of roasted herbs, smoky oak, and sweet black cherries and cassis, a layered, medium-bodied feel, outstanding richness, and considerable tannin in the finish. It behaves like a close relative of the exceptional 1986—the finest Pape-Clément in the last 30 years! The 1993 will be drinkable by the end of the century and will last for 15–20 years thereafter. This is a powerful yet elegant, pure, stylish example of Pape-Clément.

Past Glories: 1990 (93), 1988 (92), 1986 (91), 1961 (93), 1959 (90), 1955 (89)

Past Mediocrities . . . or Worse: 1982 (59), 1981 (65), 1978 (72), 1976 (62)

PATACHE D'AUX (MÉDOC)* */* * *

1993	A	85

This curranty-scented, medium-bodied, fruity, clean wine is ideal for drinking over the next 4–6 years.

PAUILLAC (PAUILLAC)* * *

1993	C	85

For several years, Château Latour has been producing this third wine with the generic name, Pauillac. A medium- to dark-ruby-colored, supple offering, it is ideal for drinking over the next 6–7 years. Although none of Latour's personality is expressed in the wine, it is representative of a good, easygoing Pauillac. To the wine's credit, it has managed to avoid the harsh tannin of the 1993 vintage.

PAVIE (ST.-ÉMILION)* * *

1993	C	83
1992	C	78
1991	C	82

Pavie is one of a handful of St.-Émilion premiers grands crus classés to produce a 1991. While it is hardly a stellar effort, the wine does offer medium-ruby color, a spicy, attractive, Bing cherry– and vanillin-scented nose, ripe, medium-bodied flavors, light tannin, and adequate depth. Drink it over the next 7–8 years. In 1992 Pavie produced a light-bodied, compact, structured wine with an excess of tannin that gives the wine an excessively tough texture and rough finish. There is not enough fruit to balance out the structure; thus, the end result is a wine that may keep for 10 or more years but will become more attenuated, with the fruit drying out over the next 4–5 years.

Three separate tastings of the 1993 all revealed a severe, austere wine with a high tannin level, noticeable sweet, toasty new oak, and attractive spicy, berry fruit. The overall impression suggests this backward wine will need at least 7–8 years to soften. It is a wine to respect, rather than to enjoy.

Past Glories: 1986 (90), 1983 (88), 1982 (92)

Past Mediocrities . . . or Worse: 1975 (72), 1970 (83)

PAVIE-DECESSE (ST.-ÉMILION)* * *

1993	C	83?
1992	C	84
1991	C	78

Although light, the 1991 Pavie-Decesse displays attractive ripeness, decent body, soft, moderately endowed flavors, and a quick finish. Drink it over the next 3–4 years. Cask samples and two tastings following bottling offer convincing evidence that in 1992, Pavie-Decesse, the less expensive sibling of Pavie, produced the better wine. The dark-ruby color is followed by some spicy, earthy fruit in the nose to go along with subtle wood and herbaceous notes. Spicy in the mouth, this medium-bodied, narrowly constructed, austere, muscular St.-Émilion will benefit from 1–2 years of aging and last for 5–6 years.

This 1993's medium-dark-ruby color is typical of the vintage. The tight, reticent bouquet is followed by a severely styled wine with high tannin, an attenuated character, lean, compact flavors, and an astringent finish. It requires more fruit and concentration to stand up to its tannic ferocity.

PAVIE-MACQUIN (ST.-ÉMILION)* * * *

1993	C	89?
1992	B	84

NOTE: No 1991 was produced under the Pavie-Macquin label.

Pavie-Macquin had the smallest yields of any Bordeaux estate in 1993. The organically farmed vineyard produced less than 1,000 cases of wine, so finding a bottle of this supercon-centrated, savagely rich, tannic, black/purple-colored wine will not be easy. The wine reveals plenty of new oak and is remarkably concentrated. It is so rich and intense that it is almost overwhelming. The presence of coarse tannin kept me from bestowing an unqualified 90-point potential rating. If the tannin softens, this could be one of the sleepers of the vintage. I recommend cellaring the wine for 5–6 years and drinking it over the subsequent 15 years.

The soft, tasty, elegant 1992 is light to medium bodied, with fine ripeness and balance, and a pleasing, gentle finish. Drink it over the next 4–5 years.

Past Glories: 1990 (90), 1989 (90)

PEDESCLAUX (PAUILLAC)* *

1993	C	74

I continue to hear about the improvements being made at this perennially underachieving fifth-growth Médoc. The 1993 displays some vague ripeness, but the wine's high tannin and acidity levels make it unpleasant to taste. Its future is dubious.

LES PENSÉES DE LAFLEUR (POMEROL)* * *

1993	D	86
1992	D	86
1991	D	74

There was no Lafleur produced in 1991. Much of the production was declassified into this second wine, Les Pensées de Lafleur. It is easy to understand why. The only positive thing the light, diluted, short, compact 1991 exhibits is some decent cherry fruit. Drink it over the next 4–5 years. The 1992 is dark ruby colored, with a sweet nose of black cherries, minerals, and earth. Although the wine is tannic, it exhibits sweet, jammy fruit beneath its structure and toughness. After it sheds some tannin, it should be a good example of this vintage. I find it remarkable as well as admirable that an estate with a production of only 1,500 cases is willing to declassify 500 cases into its second wine to ensure that Lafleur is exceptional. Now that is a commitment to excellence!

It appears that the 1993 (500 cases produced) was fashioned from this microestate's softer, more supple cuvées. The 1993 Les Pensées de Lafleur exhibits impressive color, good ripeness, the exotic, jammy black cherry component found in top vintages of Lafleur, and moderate tannin. It is far more accessible than its bigger sister. This wine can be drunk in 2–3 years and should keep for 10–15.

PETIT-FAURIE-SOUTARD (ST.-ÉMILION)* *

1992	B	79

NOTE: No 1991 was produced under the Petit-Faurie-Soutard label.
This light- to medium-ruby-colored wine reveals a pleasant but uninspiring nose of red fruits, herbs, and damp earth. Light to medium bodied, with adequate depth but excessive tannin as well as high acidity, this lean, sinewy, compact wine should be drunk over the next 3–4 years.

PETIT-FIGEAC (ST.-ÉMILION)* *

1992	B	77
1991	B	72

The 1991 is thin, light, and watery. Light ruby colored, with a soft, vegetal nose of dusty earth and cherries, the light-bodied 1992 should be drunk over the next 2–3 years.

PETIT-VILLAGE (POMEROL)* * * *

1993	C	88
1992	C	79
1991	C	74

When this property gets everything right it produces a decadent, exotic, smoky, supersoft Pomerol that is delicious young and capable of lasting for up to a decade. For example, the 1982, one of the best Petit-Villages I have ever tasted, has been drinkable since its release. The 1993, a tannic vintage for many Bordeaux wines, is atypically soft, generous, ripe, and fruity, with a smooth-as-silk texture, a deep, saturated, ruby/purple color, and gobs of mocha-tinged, chocolatey, black cherry fruit intertwined with lavish quantities of smoky new oak. If you are looking for a Pomerol at its most seductive and sensual, this wine will provide delicious drinking over the next 7–10 years.

The light-ruby-colored 1991 offers a muted bouquet of herbal notes intertwined with scents of coffee, new oak, and berries. The wine has a decent attack, but the primary impression is one of softness and herbal fruit. The flavors evaporate quickly, revealing a thin, short finish. Drink it over the next several years. The medium-ruby-colored 1992 reveals a soft, herbal, slightly oaky nose that lacks fruit. Some black cherry flavors are apparent in the mouth, but the wine's overall character is of straightforward, simple fruit wrapped in a medium-bodied, unfocused format. It should be drunk over the next 2–3 years.

Past Glories: 1990 (90), 1989 (88), 1988 (92), 1985 (89), 1982 (93), 1948 (93)

PÉTRUS (POMEROL)* * * * *

1993	EEE	93
1992	EEE	90+

NOTE: No 1991 was produced under the Pétrus label.

Pétrus is unquestionably one of the strongest, richest, fullest, most powerful wines of the 1993 vintage. When Pétrus enjoys an abundant, healthy crop, production averages between 4,000 and 4,500 cases. In 1993, only 2,000 cases were produced. The result may be the wine of the vintage. The color is rich black/purple. The nose offers up powerful scents of vanilla, Asian spices, black cherries, and other sweet black fruits. Full-bodied, extremely concentrated, unctuous, and powerful, this massive, chewy, backward Pétrus will need 10 years of cellaring and last for 25–35 years. It is revealing better sweetness and expansiveness of fruit on the mid-palate than its neighbor and rival, Lafleur. Hence, the slightly higher numerical rating. Don't anticipate full enjoyment of the 1993 Pétrus before 2005.

The 1992 Pétrus is clearly one of the two candidates for wine of the vintage. The normal production of 4,500 cases was severely reduced to only 2,600 cases, resulting in an atypically concentrated, powerful, rich wine with a dark, saturated ruby/purple color, a tight but promising nose of sweet black cherry fruit, vanillin, caramel, and herb-tinged mocha notes. Concentrated and powerful, with superb density of fruit and richness, as well as wonderful sweetness to its tannin, this is a brilliant effort for the vintage. The wine requires 3–5 years of cellaring and should keep for 15–20+.

Interestingly, the Pétrus vineyard, along with that of its sibling, Trotanoy, was covered with black plastic in early September 1992 to trap most of the rain rather than allowing it to saturate the vineyard's soil and dilute the grapes. It was a strategy that obviously paid off.

Past Glories: 1990 (100), 1989 (100), 1988 (94), 1986 (89), 1985 (89), 1982 (99), 1979 (89), 1975 (98), 1971 (95), 1970 (99+), 1967 (92), 1964 (97), 1961 (100), 1950 (100), 1949 (95), 1948 (95), 1947 (100), 1945 (98+)

Past Mediocrities . . . or Worse: Virtually none, although the 1983, 1981, and 1978 have not lived up to my initial expectations.

PHÉLAN-SÉGUR (ST.-ESTÈPHE)* * * *

1993	C	86
1992	C	86
1991	C	86

One of the best-run estates of the St.-Estèphe appellation, Phélan-Ségur made good wines in 1991, 1992, and 1993. This property has been on a qualitative hot streak since the mid-eighties, with top-notch efforts in 1988, 1989, and 1990. The prices make these wines undervalued. The 1991 is a deeply colored, soft wine with a moderately intense nose of black fruits, minerals, and oak. Medium bodied and soft, with fine concentration and a smooth, tannic finish, it should drink well for 7–10 years. The 1992 exhibits a dark-ruby color, a sweet nose of black currants, oak, and spices, tasty, medium-bodied flavors with good ripeness, extract, and suppleness, and a chewy, smooth finish. It is a noteworthy effort for the vintage. Drink it over the next 3–4 years.

Phélan-Ségur turned in an even better performance in 1993. It is a black/ruby/purple-colored wine with pure, sweet black currant fruit and mineral scents in its aromatic profile. While there is firm tannin in the mouth, the wine is medium to full bodied, rich, concentrated, and capable of lasting 10–15 years.

Past Glories: 1990 (89+), 1989 (88+)

PIBRAN (PAUILLAC)* *

1992	C	74
1991	B	76

The straightforward, deep-ruby-colored 1991 exhibits little bouquet, as well as hard tannin in its tough-textured, medium-bodied finish. It will no doubt dry out before any real charm emerges. Pibran's 1992 offers an impressively saturated color, but little else. The acidity is too high, the tannin too noticeable, and the absence of fruit too glaring. The result is a hollow, tough-textured wine with no charm.

PICHON-LONGUEVILLE BARON (PAUILLAC)* * * * *

1993	D	89
1992	C	89
1991	C	86+

This property, which made brilliant wines in 1988, 1989, and 1990, fashioned respectable wines in 1991, 1992, and 1993. How many Bordeaux estates, at any time this century, can boast that their vineyard produced a wine that was among the top dozen of the region in six consecutive vintages?

The 1991 exhibits a formidable, opaque, dark-purple color, and a tight but promising nose of licorice, minerals, and black currants. The attack offers wonderfully ripe fruit in a medium-bodied format, but the finish is dominated by hard, tough tannin. Is there sufficient fruit? I think so. It is one of the most promising wines of the vintage, but backward. This wine needs a good 2–3 years of cellaring; it should last for 15 or more years. The 1992 Pichon-Baron is one of the legitimate stars of the vintage. The wine exhibits a saturated dark-ruby/purple color, and a big, flashy, bold bouquet of jammy black currants, cedar, and smoky oak. Medium to full bodied, with wonderful sweet, rich, concentrated fruit and moderate tannin, this highly extracted, gorgeously made wine is low enough in acidity to be drunk now, yet promises to evolve gracefully for 12–15 years. It is a terrific effort for the vintage!

The 1993 Pichon-Baron displays an impressive, nearly opaque dark-ruby/purple color. The pure, sweet nose of smoky wood, combined with ripe cassis fruit and spices, is moderately intense. Like most 1993s containing a large percentage of Cabernet Sauvignon, Pichon-Baron is formidably tannic and structured, but also impressively extracted and rich. While it will not possess the pure sweetness of fruit and awesome concentration of the 1989 and 1990, it is a noteworthy success for the vintage. It will require 6–7 years of cellaring and will last for 20 years.

Past Glories: 1990 (96), 1989 (96+), 1988 (90), 1986 (90), 1982 (90), 1959 (89), 1953 (89)
Past Mediocrities . . . or Worse: 1981 (83), 1978 (82), 1975 (64), 1970 (73), 1966 (82)

PICHON-LONGUEVILLE–COMTESSE DE LALANDE (PAUILLAC)* * * * *

1993	D	89
1992	C	79
1991	C	89

Pichon-Lalande's 1991 is among only a handful of 1991s worthy of being the wine of the vintage. Only 30% of the harvest went into the final wine, resulting in a deeper-colored, richer, more concentrated and complex wine than the 1990, which was atypically light—even for the elegant Pichon-Lalande style. The 1991, which possesses plenty of tannin, displays an opaque, deep-ruby/purple color, and a sweet nose of chocolate, cedar, and ripe, plummy, black currant fruit. Round, medium to full bodied, and opulent (atypical for a 1991), this wine finishes with considerable length and authority. Drink it over the next 10–15 years. The 1991 Pichon-Lalande is one of the stars of the vintage!

The 1992 is the most disappointing wine made at this estate in nearly a decade. The wine reveals medium-ruby color, a disjointed, awkward personality with compact, attenuated flavors, a stewed, tannic character, and harsh tannin in the short finish. The color is sound, but there is no charm or ripe fruit, resulting in a wine that is all structure, tannin, and alcohol. Three tastings after bottling, with nearly identical notes to those from cask tastings, confirm this wine's performance.

The 1993 is a significant improvement over the disjointed 1992. Atypically for Pichon, the 1993 does not exhibit any of the fat, fleshy, succulent Merlot character normally found in this wine's personality. The wine appears to be dominated more by Cabernet Sauvignon than by Merlot. Have the vintage's characteristics made the Merlot component less noticeable? Pichon-Lalande, traditionally among the softest, most seductive, and hedonistic wines from St.-Julien, St.-Estèphe, and Pauillac, has taken on more structure, as well as a more classic Pauillac aromatic and flavor profile. I hope it is not trying to emulate the style of its across-the-street neighbor and rival, Pichon-Longueville Baron. The 1993 Pichon-Lalande is a high-class, rich, medium- to full-bodied Pauillac with firm structure and a well-delineated personality. It should age well for 12–15+ years.

Past Glories: 1989 (95), 1988 (90), 1986 (96), 1985 (90), 1983 (96), 1982 (99–100), 1981 (89), 1979 (92), 1978 (93), 1975 (90), 1961 (95?), 1945 (96)

PICQUE-CAILLOU (GRAVES)* * *

1993	B	?

The only tasting I did of this offering revealed a strangely vegetal and underripe wine.

LE PIN (POMEROL)* * * * *

1993	EE	88?
1992	D	82?

The 1992 unquestionably possesses an excessive amount of toasty new oak for its fragile, delicate constitution. The wine displays medium- to dark-ruby color, an aggressively woody, slightly smoky, herb-scented nose, and medium-bodied, black cherry–like flavors that are insufficient to stand up to the veneer of wood. Low in acidity, slightly diluted, and full of cosmetic smoke, vanillin, and wood, it should be consumed over the next 5–6 years. Given the frightfully high price asked for the 500+ cases of Le Pin (usually an exotic as well as brilliant wine), this is a vintage for which the proprietor should have declassified the wine.

The 1993 Le Pin is a significant improvement over the frightfully oaky, light-bodied 1992. While the wine's aggressive smoky, toasty new oak component is nearly excessive, there is plenty of sweet, ripe, jammy fruit, an attractive nose of smoke, herbs, mocha, and coffee, and lush, ripe, exotic flavors exhibiting moderate tannin, medium body, and admirable sweetness and concentration. If the wine fills out and the tannin and oak both become less intrusive, the 1993 Le Pin has the potential to be an outstanding wine. At present, it appears to be an excellent rather than a profound effort.

Past Glories: 1990 (95), 1989 (91), 1988 (90), 1987 (89), 1986 (90), 1985 (94), 1983 (98), 1982 (99), 1981 (93), 1980 (89), 1979 (93)

DE PITRAY (CÔTES DE CASTILLON)* * *

1992	A	75
1991	A	74

This wine is often an insider's favorite because of its noteworthy value, but the tough, hollow, light-bodied, diluted 1991 is no bargain. The 1992 Pitray reveals all the problems of the vintage—dilution, lightness, thin flavors, and a weedy fruitiness.

PLAISANCE (PREMIÈRES CÔTES DE BORDEAUX)* * *

1993 Cuvée Tradition	B	85

From one of the best-run estates in the Premières Côtes de Bordeaux, this unfiltered offering is a spicy, black cherry–scented wine with good fruit, medium body, fine purity and elegance, and a soft finish. It should drink well for 5–6 years.

PLINCE (POMEROL)* *

1993	C	79
1992	C	76

NOTE: No 1991 was produced under the Plince label.

I appreciated the uncomplicated robustness of the 1992 Plince from cask, but now that it has been bottled it has lost much of its charm and fruit. The wine is dry, hard, and lean, with tough tannin and an old, stale, herb/black cherry–scented nose. Drink it over the next 2–4 years. The 1993 displays good color and density, but the tannin level dominates the fruit. The wine's overall personality is one-dimensional and chunky. It should last for 6–7 years.

PONTET-CANET (PAUILLAC)* * *

1993	C	87
1992	C	85?
1991	B	84

Pontet-Canet is a sleeping giant that is largely ignored by many Pauillac enthusiasts. I believe a slightly stricter selection and the harvesting of physiologically riper fruit would propel Pontet-Canet into the top echelon of Bordeaux wines. The wines have been very good over the last decade, as well as reasonably priced. The 1993 is a robust, dense, chewy Pauillac with gobs of cassis fruit and tannin, medium body, and the potential to develop well over 15–20 years. The wine's downside is the vintage's telltale austerity, combined with a hard, tannic edge in the finish. Don't touch a bottle before the turn of the century.

The light-bodied, fruity, soft, decently colored 1991 Pontet-Canet offers gentle, cedary, cassis fruit, a sense of elegance, and a velvety finish. Drink it over the next 5–6 years. The 1992 exhibited very good ripe cassis fruit and a round, medium-bodied, soft, juicy personality on two occasions, and a lighter-bodied, more simplistic, tannic character at two other tastings. It is a large estate, so perhaps there is some unexpected bottle variation, but this wine can be a reasonably good value and an attractive 1992 for drinking over the next 5–6 years. The question mark signifies the confusing array of evaluations I experienced.

Past Glories: 1986 (88), 1982 (87), 1961 (95), 1945 (96), 1929 (92?)

Past Mediocrities . . . or Worse: 1979 (80), 1978 (82), 1971 (81), 1970 (82), 1966 (77)

POTENSAC (MÉDOC)* * *

1992	A	75
1991	A	74

Potensac's 1991 is a lean, hollow, hard-styled wine with little fruit. Its astringence has the upper hand, so look for the 1991 to become more out of balance as it ages. The 1992 is a lean, vegetal, medium-bodied wine with hard tannin, but with some ripe fruit beneath the wine's structure. Drink this undistinguished wine over the next 3–4 years.

POUJEAUX (MOULIS)* * *

1993	C	84

Poujeaux's 1993 exhibits a healthy dark-ruby color, some ripeness in the dusty, earthy, curranty nose, moderate depth, medium body, and a walloping tannin level in the finish. Although this is one of my favorite estates in the central Médoc, this wine will undoubtedly dry out after 5–7 years of cellaring.

PRIEURÉ-LICHINE (MARGAUX)* * * *

1993	C	88
1992	C	87
1991	B	84

With a stricter selection, a later harvest, and the assistance of Libourne oenologist, Michel Rolland, Prieuré-Lichine has begun to produce richer, more complete and complex wines. The 1993 is unquestionably a success for the vintage, as well as one of the few southern Médocs with enough fruit, ripeness, and extract to stand up to the tannin and structure. This dark-ruby/purple-colored wine offers up an enticing, floral, black currant– and toasty-scented nose, round, supple, medium-bodied flavors with fine depth, and a firm, juicy, deliciously long finish. It should drink well when released later this year and last for 12–14 years.

Consumers should be on the lookout for the 1991 Prieuré-Lichine, which may be discounted to sell for as low as $10–$12 a bottle. It offers solid color, medium body, soft, ripe, cedary, cassis, fruity flavors, and a spicy, supple finish. It should drink well for at least 5–6 years. It is better than many of the lightweight efforts Prieuré produced between 1979 and 1985. An unqualified success for the vintage, Prieuré-Lichine's 1992 exhibits a saturated dark-ruby color, and a seductive bouquet of creamy black currant fruit intertwined with aromas of smoky, vanillin-scented new oak. The wine is supple, velvety textured, and surprisingly concentrated, with medium body, and an authoritatively long, extracted, rich finish.

Past Glories: 1986 (88)

Past Mediocrities . . . or Worse: 1981 (75)

PUY-BLANQUET (ST.-ÉMILION)* *

1993	C	75
1992	B	75

NOTE: No 1991 was produced under the Puy-Blanquet label.

I found some charming fruit and style in this 1992 from cask, but now that it is in the bottle it appears to be dried out, with an excess of tannin and acidity. Why did all that finesse and charm disappear? The 1993's tannic, hard, tough flavors are typical for a mediocre wine from this vintage. This wine will dry out before it ever develops any charm.

RAHOUL (GRAVES)* *

1993	C	85
1992	B	85
1991	B	83

Rahoul has fashioned an attractive 1991. The medium-ruby color is followed by a sweet, ripe nose of cassis, tobacco, and spice. Soft, round, and elegant, this well-made 1991 should drink well for 3–4 years. The 1992 Rahoul has turned out much better than I would have thought. Graves was a consistently successful appellation in 1992, and this wine possesses a medium- to dark-ruby color, and an attractive nose of black cherries, tobacco, and smoky new oak. It is straightforward, medium bodied, soft, and ideal for drinking over the next 4–5 years.

The 1993 Rahoul reveals a healthy dark-ruby/purple color, and a smoky, jammy, rich, black cherry– and toasty-scented nose. Although the dense, powerful, concentrated flavors may lack complexity, that deficiency is compensated for by considerable intensity and power, as well as a supple, lightly tannic finish. If it is not overly processed at bottling, this medium-bodied, concentrated Graves could merit a score in the upper eighties. It should drink well for a decade.

RAUSAN-SÉGLA (MARGAUX)* * * */* * * * *

1993	C	90
1992	C	88
1991	C	87

Only 40% of the harvest was included in the 1993 grand vin. Another 40% went into the property's second wine, Ségla, and 20% was sold in bulk. The result is an uncommonly powerful, rich, black/purple-colored 1993 Rausan-Ségla that reveals intoxicating aromas of jammy black fruits, licorice, and Asian spices. The wine is full bodied, fleshy, and rich, with considerable structure, and the vintage's formidable tannin level. There is more than enough extract and flesh to stand up to the wine's structure. This will be a long-lived, backward Rausan-Ségla built along the lines of the 1986. Give it at least 5–8 years of cellaring; it should age well for 20+ years.

The 1991 is one of the vintage's stars. The saturated dark-ruby color is followed by a bouquet of spicy fruitcake, cedar, cassis, and floral scents. Sweet and round, with excellent definition, layers of richness, and a long, supple finish, this well-endowed, concentrated, impeccably balanced wine should drink well for 10–15 years. Also one of the stars of the vintage, Rausan-Ségla's 1992 is an uncommonly rich, opulent wine with an impressively saturated dark-ruby/purple color, and a forceful, penetrating fragrance of black cherries, currants, spicy oak, smoke, and flowers. The wine is medium to full bodied, with gorgeously sweet, rich layers of fruit, ripe tannin, and a long, heady, voluptuously textured finish. Only 50% of the production went into the 1992 Rausan-Ségla, resulting in a brilliant wine for this tough vintage. Drink it over the next decade.

As a postscript, the acquisition of Rausan-Ségla by the French house of Chanel in May 1994, and the subsequent hiring of Château Latour's resurrectionists, David Orr and John Kolasa, suggest to me that this property is going to build on the splendid success it has enjoyed since 1983, vying with Palmer and Château Margaux for top honors in this appellation. Keep an eye on Rausan-Ségla.

Past Glories: 1990 (92), 1989 (90), 1988 (92), 1986 (96), 1983 (92)

Past Mediocrities . . . or Worse: 1981 (65), 1979 (72), 1978 (74), 1975 (75)

RAUZAN-GASSIES (MARGAUX)* *

1993	C	67
1992	B	71

Life is far too short to spend time drinking wines such as these. Rauzan-Gassies has hired a new vineyard manager who is responsible for the 1994 vintage, so perhaps someone's wake-up call finally got through. The lean 1993 is bitterly tannic and devoid of charm and personality. The 1992's harsh, vegetal, light-bodied flavors accompanied by frightfully hard tannin are unappealing.

RÉSERVE DE LA COMTESSE (PAUILLAC)* *

1992	?	76
1991	B	85

A noteworthy second wine from Pichon-Lalande, the 1991 Réserve de la Comtesse reveals lovely ripe, plummy, and cassis fruit kissed gently by toasty new oak. It is a soft, medium-bodied wine with some corpulence and excellent ripeness. Drink it over the next 4–6 years. The 1992 did not show well when I tasted it, revealing a stemmy, intensely herbal nose, light-bodied, peppery flavors, and a soft, disjointed finish. Further time in cask and the addition of some press wine might help bolster it.

ROC DES CAMBES (CÔTES DE BOURG)* * *

1993	B	86
1992	A	84
1991	A	82

The delicious, value-packed 1993 from Le Tertre-Roteboeuf's proprietor, François Matja-vile, offers an impressive dark-ruby/purple color, a big, smoky, chocolatey, berry-scented nose, dense, opulent flavors, medium body, and a supple finish. Drink it over the next 5–7 years. It is a terrific restaurant selection.

Two moderately successful wines were produced by Roc des Combes in 1991 and 1992. The 1991 exhibits a medium-ruby color, ripe, berry aromas, light to medium body, soft tannin, and a smooth finish. Drink it over the next 3–4 years. The 1992 Roc des Combes has turned out well, with attractive, spicy aromas of coffee, tobacco, and sweet cherries, and round, gentle, velvety-textured flavors. Medium bodied and soft, it is ideal for uncomplicated drinking over the next 3–4 years.

ROUET (FRONSAC)* * *

1993	B	85

Proprietor Patrick Danglade admirably declassified Rouet's entire harvest in 1991 and 1992, so the 1993 is the first Rouet produced since 1990. It is one of the most successful wines of Fronsac, with a ripe, moderately intense bouquet of minerals and red and black fruits. Elegant, medium-bodied flavors also reveal an attractive extract level, sweet tannin, and no harshness or vegetal aspects. Drink this lovely wine over the next 5–7 years.

DE SALES (POMEROL)* *

1993	C	?

Both the 1992 and 1993 de Sales have exhibited the same problem—odd, musty, damp wood/wet dog–like aromas. Judgment reserved.

LA SERRE (ST.-ÉMILION)* * *

1993	C 87
1992	B 85

This property, long in the doldrums, has fashioned an attractive, sweet, cherry-scented, soft, tasty, velvety-textured 1992. The wine is delicious for drinking now and over the next 3–4 years. Readers will appreciate its red fruit component and easygoing personality. I was seduced by the 1993's chocolatey, black cherry, fragrant bouquet, and medium- to full-bodied, expansively rich, well-delineated, concentrated flavors. Offering a brilliant marriage of power and finesse, the wine is soft enough to be drunk when released later this year. A vibrant, pure, authoritatively flavored St.-Émilion, it should have broad crowd appeal. It will last for 12 or more years.

SIRAN (MARGAUX)* * *

1993	C 85

A perennial overachiever, Siran has a fine track record for producing long-lived, rich, structured wines. With its highly extracted, tannic style, the 1993 will unquestionably be an ageworthy effort. The color is an impressive ruby/purple. Although not complex, the wine has medium body, excellent concentration, high extract, and a beefy, chewy, muscular personality. It will require 5–7 years of cellaring and should drink well for 15–20 years.

SMITH-HAUT-LAFITTE (GRAVES)* * */* * * *

1993	C 86
1992	C 86
1991	C 85

A new, enthusiastic, quality-oriented ownership has committed millions of dollars to resurrecting this property. Progress is already evident. For example, consider the fact that in the proprietors' first two vintages, 1991 and 1992, they were able to produce better wines in these frightfully difficult years than their predecessors did in the potentially great years of 1989 and 1990! I assume that when Bordeaux has another top vintage, Smith-Haut-Lafitte may fashion something sublime. Readers may want to stash this information away for future use. As for the 1991, it reveals a dark-ruby color, an attractive perfume of cassis, tobacco, herbs, and spices, excellent balance, considerable finesse, medium body, admirable ripeness, and light tannin in the finish. A good effort for the vintage, it should drink well for 7–8 years. The 1992 is unquestionably a successful wine for this vintage. It exhibits elegant, spicy, mineral- and black cherry–scented notes in its smoky bouquet, medium body, fine ripeness and extraction, a velvety texture, and light tannin in the finish. Drink it over the next 7–8 years.

The 1993 is a classic example of an elegant, finesse-styled Graves. The healthy dark-ruby color is followed by a bouquet offering spicy, smoky aromas of moderately intense cassis, tobacco, and vanillin. Medium bodied, with ripe fruit to balance out the moderate tannin level, this is a stylish, understated, flavorful wine. It is a 1993 where patience will not be essential; it should drink well within 3–4 years and last for 10–15 or more.

SOCIANDO-MALLET (HAUT-MÉDOC)* * *

1993	C 87
1992	C 87

This exceptionally well run estate has turned out a very fine 1992. The color is an opaque ruby/purple and the nose offers up sweet, ripe, black currants intertwined with scents of minerals and wood. Medium bodied and moderately tannic, with fine purity and sweetness, this is a firm, well-built wine. It should be cellared for 3–4 years and drunk over the subsequent 10–15. Sociando-Mallet has turned out an enormously extracted, opaque purple-colored wine, which is extremely powerful and muscular, but oh so tannic and backward. Sociando-Mallet is not known for making wimpish, light, easily accessible wines, so in a vintage such as 1993, readers can imagine how much tannin this wine possesses. Although the high quality of the fruit, flavor extraction, and purity all bode well for the 1993 Sociando-Mallet's future development, some risk remains. Given the massive tannin level, this wine could turn out to be too austere and lean; but the wine's balance appears to be fine. Don't dare touch a bottle before the middle of the next decade. It should drink well through 2020+.

Past Glories: 1990 (90), 1986 (90), 1985 (90), 1982 (92), 1975 (90)

SOUDARS (HAUT-MÉDOC)* * *

1993		B	85

Soudars achieved a degree of plumpness and suppleness in its earthy, black curranty–scented and –flavored 1993, as well as fine purity and ripeness. It is ideal for drinking over the next 4–5 years.

SOUTARD (ST.-ÉMILION)* * *

1993	C	87
1992	C	77
1991	C	64

Soutard should have second thoughts about placing its 1991 on the market. This hollow, light, disappointing, vapid, vegetal offering is nearly undrinkable. Soutard's 1992 displays a medium-ruby color, weedy, smoky, berry fruit in the nose, modest proportions in the mouth, and hard tannin in the finish. It should be drunk over the next 4–5 years before the tannin begins to dominate the fragile fruit.

I tasted impressive barrel samples of Soutard's 1993. This estate, which tends to march to the beat of a different drummer when it comes to bottling (later than most) and selling (much is sold directly to consumers rather than through a *négociant*), has fashioned a full-bodied, concentrated, ripe 1993 with surprising suppleness, good underlying structure, and moderate tannin. It offers plenty of juicy Merlot fruit and a jammy personality. More tannin and delineation should emerge with age. This big, beefy, mouth-filling wine appears to be an excellent example of the vintage; it is capable of 10–15 years of cellaring.

Past Glories: 1990 (89+), 1985 (90), 1982 (88), 1964 (90), 1955 (88)

TAILLEFER (POMEROL)* *

1992		B	77

NOTE: No 1991 was offered for tasting.
Taillefer's 1992 is a light-bodied, straightforward Pomerol with a soft, albeit diluted finish. It should be drunk over the next 3–4 years.

TALBOT (ST.-JULIEN)* * * *

1993	C	86
1992	C	86
1991	B	72

Talbot, which produced so many terrific wines in the early 1980s (a splendid 1982, superb 1983, delicious 1985, and a blockbuster 1986), has exhibited signs of slumping in quality since the late eighties. The property's disappointing 1991 is an appallingly weak effort for this estate. The diluted medium-ruby color is suspicious, and the weedy, vegetal, washed-out herbal nose and flavors are lamentable. In the mouth the wine is odd, disjointed, and soft. I found the 1992 lacking fruit and tasting sinewy and tannic from cask, but I am delighted to say it is performing well from bottle. It will be a noteworthy wine to purchase if it is discounted as much as I suspect it will be. Talbot's 1992 reveals an exotic nose of jammy black cherries, truffles, licorice, and smoky, herbal scents. Following the extroverted bouquet, the wine offers a medium-bodied, supple, juicy, succulent style with low acidity and plenty of ripe fruit. This delicious wine promises to drink well for 6–7 years.

Talbot's 1993 should be popular with consumers. It has avoided the tough texture and hard tannin of the vintage. The result is a deep-ruby-colored supple wine with gobs of herb and chocolatey-scented and -flavored cassis fruit presented in a medium-bodied, expansively flavored style with good purity. The acidity is low and the wine is already delicious and seductive. Drink it over the next decade.

Past Glories: 1988 (89), 1986 (96), 1985 (89), 1983 (91), 1982 (95), 1953 (90), 1949 (90), 1945 (94)

Past Mediocrities . . . or Worse: 1975 (84), 1970 (78), 1966 (77)

TAYAC (CÔTES DE BOURG)* * *

1993 Clos du Pin de Sucre	A	85
1993 Cuvée Réservée	B	86
1993 Rubis du Prince Noir	A	85

For most Americans, Château Tayac is the best-known wine from the Côtes de Bourg appellation. The estate's operation is similar to many California wineries, offering different cuvées, beginning with the basic Clos du Pin de Sucre, and moving up in both intensity and aging potential, as well as price, to the Rubis du Prince Noir and their top wine, the Cuvée Réservée. In exceptional vintages (e.g., 1985 and 1989), the best barrels are used to produce a Cuvée Prestige offering. Tayac's 1993 Clos du Pin de Sucre has already been bottled. It exhibits a dark-ruby color, a solidly knit framework of ripe fruit, some roundness, and a tart, clean, moderately long finish. It should drink well for 4–5 years. The 1993 Rubis du Prince Noir is more austere and tannic, with more body and concentration. It will be interesting to see how it reacts to bottling. It could turn out to be drier and more astringent than the less expensive Clos du Pin de Sucre. Lastly, the 1993 Cuvée Réservée exhibits an impressive dark-ruby color, denser, richer, more powerful flavors, as well as more tannin. Medium bodied, with crisp acidity, it should turn out to be the finest of these three cuvées.

TERTRE-DAUGAY (ST.-ÉMILION)* * *

1993	C	75

Although this property has made major improvements, the 1993 is a light-bodied, undernourished wine with excessive tannin and little ripe fruit in evidence.

LE TERTRE-ROTEBOEUF (ST.-ÉMILION)* * * * *

1993	D	91
1992	C	77
1991	C	83

Ironically, the 1991 reveals more depth, ripeness, and fruit than the excessively woody, diluted, light-bodied 1992. The soft, berry, oaky, medium-bodied 1991 will provide pleasant drinking for 4–5 years. I am an enthusiastic fan of the wines of Le Tertre-Roteboeuf, but even this fanatically run property failed to triumph over the unkind hand dealt by Mother Nature in September 1992. This light-bodied, soft, spicy, weedy, diluted wine should be drunk up over the next 2–3 years. It is low in acidity and lacking depth. Le Tertre-Roteboeuf fans will be delighted to hear that the exceptional 1993 is a return to the glorious style evidenced by this estate in 1988, 1989, and 1990.

The 1993 boasts a nearly opaque purple/black color, and a huge, exotic nose of ripe black fruits intertwined with scents of licorice, smoke, herbs, and truffles. There is great intensity to this full-bodied, concentrated, impeccably well-balanced wine that offers both harmony and high flavor extraction. The wine's sweetness and ripeness are lovely to experience, particularly in a vintage such as 1993. It should drink well for 10–15 years.

Past Glories: 1990 (96), 1989 (94), 1988 (91)

LA TOUR-HAUT-BRION (GRAVES)* * *

1993	C	87
1992	C	87
1991	C	85

The 1991 displays a deep-ruby/purple color, a sweet, spicy, mineral- and tobacco-scented nose, excellent attack and richness, but some shortness in the finish. This attractive, up-front wine should be consumed over the next 4–5 years. The 1992 is a successful wine for the vintage. It offers a healthy, medium-dark ruby color, a pungent, smoky, earthy, tobacco-, sweet plum–, and cherry-scented nose, attractive, supple flavors with fine concentration, and a sweet, elegant, ripe, expansive finish. Drink it over the next 5–6 years.

This excellent 1993 Graves exhibits a healthy plum/dark-ruby color, an intensely spicy, open-knit, hickory smoke/black currant/mineral–scented nose, and surprisingly supple, rich, medium-bodied flavors that possess elegance and intensity. The wine's velvety texture is a rarity in 1993 clarets. It can be drunk or cellared for 10–15 years.

Past Glories: 1988 (89), 1982 (94), 1978 (93), 1975 (97), 1970 (87), 1966 (88), 1961 (95), 1959 (97), 1955 (94), 1953 (96), 1949 (98), 1947 (95)

Past Mediocrities . . . or Worse: 1986 (82), 1983 (84)

LA TOUR-MARTILLAC (GRAVES)* *

1993	C	83
1992	C	75
1991	C	76

The light-bodied, aggressively herbal (nearly vegetal) 1991 needs to be drunk over the next 4–5 years. There is no denying the 1992's impressive dark-ruby, saturated color, but once past the color, the absence of any bouquet other than vague, earthy, weedy notes is cause for concern. On the palate the wine offers a blast of tannin, wood, and earth, but little fruit, ripeness, or charm. It should be drunk up over the next 4–5 years before it becomes even more out of balance.

The elegant, medium-bodied 1993 exhibits a solid ruby color, a pleasant but uninspiring nose of berry fruit, new oak, and spice, soft, light-bodied flavors, low acidity, some tannin, and a short finish. Drink it over the next 7–8 years.

LA TOUR DE MONS (MARGAUX)* *

1992	B	72

NOTE: No 1991 La Tour de Mons was offered for tasting.

The cask samples I saw of this wine were far superior to what turned up in the bottle. The bottling process must certainly have eviscerated what fruit the wine possessed, as this offering is thin, light bodied, sharp, tannic, and out of balance.

LA TOURELLES DE LONGUEVILLE (PAUILLAC)* * *

1993	C	82
1992	B	75
1991	B	79

In 1991, Pichon-Baron's second wine is a correct effort that offers modest quantities of weedy, cassis fruit. Although the wine reveals some dilution, it offers a dark-ruby color, and up-front berry fruit intertwined with spice. Drink this soft claret over the next 3–4 years. The 1992 is attractively colored, medium bodied, lean, and muscular with its structure dominating the fragile fruit. It should be drunk over the next 4–5 years.

The 1993 offers an impressive color and ripe aromas in the bouquet, but excessive tannin gives it a lean, austere style. This pleasant, correct, compact wine will last for a decade.

TROPLONG-MONDOT (ST.-ÉMILION)* * * * *

1993	C	91
1992	C	89+
1991	C	85

There will be a reclassification of St.-Émilion wines in 1995 and four or five estates deserve serious consideration for elevation to premier grand cru status. Most of the support will be for Troplong-Mondot, L'Angélus, and Canon-La-Gaffelière, but Grand-Mayne and Pavie-Macquin should also be considered. Troplong-Mondot has been on a headlong charge to higher and higher quality since 1988. Their 1993 is a black/purple-colored wine with gorgeous purity, ripeness, and extract, aligned to a wine with considerable elegance, finesse, and personality. It offers superb richness, medium body, layers of beautifully delineated black cherry and cassis fruit, fine acidity, and ripe tannin. A stunning example of the vintage, it is ideal for drinking between 2000 and 2020.

It is because of vintages such as 1991 and 1992 that Christine Fabré-Valette was one of my "winemakers of the year" in 1993. In both of these tough years, Troplong-Mondot has produced a successful wine. In a disastrous vintage for Pomerol and St.-Émilion, the 1991 Troplong-Mondot stands out for its medium- to dark-ruby color, and spicy, ripe nose of cassis, vanillin, licorice, and toast. With elegant, medium-bodied, attractive, rich flavors, this supple, well-endowed wine should drink well for 4–6 years. At three separate bottle tastings, Troplong-Mondot's 1992 blew away much of the other St.-Émilion competition, and embarrassed many of the premiers grands crus classés. The wine boasts a saturated black/purple color, and a huge, sweet, ripe nose of black currant fruit intermingled with scents of toasty new oak, herbs, and licorice. It is amazingly concentrated for the vintage, with superb denseness and ripeness of fruit, moderate tannin, and a long, pure, beautifully proportioned finish. It will benefit from 2–3 years of cellaring and last for 15 years. Once it has more bottle age, it may merit an outstanding score.

Past Glories: 1990 (94), 1989 (91), 1988 (89)

TROTANOY (POMEROL)* * * *

1993	E	91
1992	D	88

NOTE: No 1991 was produced under the Trotanoy label.

I have often acknowledged the greatness of Trotanoy in the forties, fifties, sixties, and early seventies. Yet I also voiced my concerns between 1976 and the late eighties when Trotanoy produced wines far below what its fans had come to expect (save for the superb 1982). Much of the vineyard had been replanted and the style undoubtedly lightened. All of that appears to be changing, as Trotanoy is clearly on the rebound with a very strong effort in 1992 and a superb performance in 1993. The 1993 is unquestionably the finest wine Trotanoy has produced since 1982 and 1975. With its dark, saturated, purple/black color and huge nose of jammy cherry fruit intertwined with scents of roasted nuts, herbs, coffee, and new oak, this powerful, dense, full-bodied Trotanoy reveals impressively extracted flavors, high tannin, and a muscular, chewy, concentrated finish. As with many 1993s, it possesses ferocious tannin levels, but they are backed up by huge reserves of rich, concentrated fruit. It should be at its best between 2005 and 2020.

The 1992 offers a dense, saturated dark-ruby color, an excellent nose scented with sweet black cherries, mocha, minerals, and vanillin, medium-bodied, concentrated flavors, a wonderful succulence and suppleness to its fruit, and a long, heady, tannic, rich finish. This is an expansively flavored, moderately tannic Trotanoy that will benefit from another 2–3 years of cellaring, and will keep for 12–15 years.

How reassuring it is to see this estate, which made so many of the greatest wines in the forties, fifties, sixties, and early seventies, return to form.

Past Glories: 1982 (96), 1975 (94), 1971 (93), 1970 (96+), 1967 (91), 1964 (90), 1961 (98), 1959 (92), 1945 (95)

Past Mediocrities . . . or Worse: 1983 (81)

TROTTE VIEILLE (ST.-ÉMILION)* * *

1993	C	75?
1992	C	78
1991	C	72

This property is high on its 1991, but I cannot understand why. It is diluted and thin, with some vegetal fruitiness, but little grip or concentration. The light-bodied, soft 1992 avoids the harsh tannin and vegetal character of so many 1992s, but it offers no real density or depth. Nevertheless, there is some pleasant, straightforward charm in the wine's berry fruit and gentle, easygoing, diluted, Burgundian-like character. Drink it over the next 4–5 years.

More toasty, vanillin-scented new oak aromas than fruit aromas are present in the 1993's bouquet. In the mouth this medium-bodied wine offers some ripeness, which is quickly obliterated by the wood and astringent tannin. Sharp and compact, it appears to be already drying out.

VALANDRAUD (ST.-ÉMILION)* * * *

1993	E	89
1992	D	88
1991	E	83

In France, Bordeaux wine enthusiasts are already calling this miniestate, dedicated to handcrafted, unfiltered, superconcentrated wines, the second coming of Le Pin. Unfortunately, Valandraud's first two efforts are from tough vintages; thus, it is difficult to know just how special this wine might be. The 1991 is exceptionally oaky, with the wood dominating the moderate quantities of sweet ripe fruit. Although it is a good wine, it is preposterously overpriced vis-à-vis its quality. The 1992 reveals a saturated, opaque dark-ruby/purple color, and a rich nose of sweet oak backed by gobs of jammy black currants and cherries. The wine possesses excellent richness, medium to full body, surprising opulence and chewiness (a rarity in the 1992 vintage), and a long, lusty, low-acid, concentrated finish. It should drink well for 7–10 years. Bravo!

The outstanding 1993 is superrich and opulent, with lavish quantities of toasty new oak and concentrated, jammy, cassis and black cherry fruit. This full-bodied, unctuously textured, thick, rich, moderately tannic wine will drink well for 10–15 years.

LA VIEILLE-CURE (FRONSAC)* * *

1993	B	85
1992	B	85

The American consortium that owns La Vieille-Cure recognized the need to augment Merlot in the soils of Fronsac. The results are encouraging, as La Vieille-Cure continues to turn out some of the most balanced and charming wines of the appellation. The 1992 exhibits an attractive ruby color, a sweet, moderately intense nose of spice, black cherries, and herbs, fine ripeness and roundness, low acidity, and a soft, generous finish. Drink it over the next 4–5 years.

One of the most successful 1993 Fronsacs, the deep-ruby-colored La Vieille-Cure exhibits a ripe, red and black fruit–scented nose with subtle hints of wood and herbs. The wine is medium bodied, concentrated, and rich, with well-integrated tannin. A fine effort from this Fronsac estate, it should be approachable when released and age well for 10–12 years.

VIEUX CHÂTEAU CERTAN (POMEROL)* * * *

1993	D	87
1992	C	78

Medium ruby with a light-intensity bouquet of herbaceous cherry fruit, the spicy, compact, medium-bodied 1992 reveals some tannin, but its finish is short and insubstantial. Drink it over the next 4–5 years.

The 1993 Vieux Château Certan reveals an impressive dark-ruby color, a nose of herbs, licorice, black currants, and earthy scents, sweet, forward, well-concentrated flavors, medium body, light tannin, and an expansive, succulent, fleshy finish. More tannin and structure will undoubtedly emerge, but this is a good to excellent effort for the vintage. It should drink well for 12–15 years.

Past Glories: 1990 (94), 1988 (91), 1986 (93), 1983 (88), 1982 (91), 1964 (90), 1959 (93), 1952 (94), 1950 (97), 1948 (98+), 1947 (97), 1945 (98–100), 1928 (96)

Past Mediocrities . . . or Worse: 1971 (74), 1970 (80), 1966 (74)

VIEUX CLOS ST.-ÉMILION (ST.-ÉMILION)* */* * *

1992	B	77
1991	B	70

As disappointingly austere, light, and diluted as the 1991 is, the soft, ripe, weedy, but charming 1992 exhibits light body, attractive berry fruit flavors, and a short, soft finish. Drink it over the next 3–4 years.

VILLEMAURINE (ST.-ÉMILION)* *

1993	C	74

Copious aromas of new oak obliterate what little fruit this wine possesses. The combination of light body and high tannin does not result in a delicious wine. The 1993 Villemaurine will dry out quickly.

The Dry White Wines of Bordeaux

AILE D'ARGENT (BORDEAUX)* * *

1993	E	89
1992	E	87
1991	E	74

Mouton-Rothschild's 1991 debut release of this luxury-priced dry white wine is an unequivocal failure. The wine has already lost whatever fruit it may have possessed, is excessively woody, and has virtually no length. The 1992 and 1993 are much more noteworthy, displaying plenty of rich honeyed fruit.

D'ARCHAMBEAU (GRAVES)* * *

1993	C	87

This excellent, soft, opulently rich, honeyed, crisp, dry white Graves possesses plenty of ripe fruit. It will provide ideal drinking over the next 1–2 years.

L'ARRIVET-HAUT-BRION (GRAVES)* * *

1993	C	75
1992	C	88

The 1992 is an excellent effort from L'Arrivet-Haut-Brion. A big, honeyed, ripe nose soars from the glass, offering up waxy, mineral, toasty scents suggestive of Semillon. Rich and full bodied, with layers of fruit infused with considerable glycerin, this dry, corpulent, rich, full-throttle, delicious white Graves should be drunk in its first 5–7 years of life. With respect to the 1993 L'Arrivet-Haut-Brion, flat, soft, low-acid flavors are diffuse and lack concentration. The wine tails off on the palate with significant dilution.

BAUDUC LES TROIS HECTARES (BORDEAUX)* * *

1993	B	85
1992	A	85

The 1992's attractive perfume of fruit, some tart, mineral, fruity flavors, light to medium body, and an austere finish make for a pleasant glass of crisp, dry white wine. Drink it over the next year. The fruity, heady, herb- and spice–scented 1993 exhibits medium body, excellent purity and liveliness, and a dry, refreshing finish. Drink it over the next year.

BLANC DE LYNCH-BAGES (PAUILLAC)* * *

1993	D	89
1992	D	87
1991	D	70

Jean-Michel Cazes continues to do a super job with this dry white wine made just outside the Pauillac appellation. The 1991 may already be beginning to drop its fruit, so the lesson with these Médoc whites (except for Pavillon Blanc de Margaux) may be to drink them as early as possible. The 1991 is developing an austere nose and its attractive fruit has become more muted. I would pass it up in favor of the riper, aromatic 1992. It displays a floral, tropical fruit–scented nose with subtle toasty components. Medium bodied, crisp, and exhibiting loads of fruit, it is a stylish, exuberant dry white, which, although delicious, is overpriced. The 1993's admirable qualities include a fragrant, floral, tropical fruit–scented nose, crisp, medium-bodied, vivacious flavors, well-integrated oak, and a wonderfully fresh, dry finish. The overall impression is one of lightness yet admirable fruit intensity. Drink it over the next 2–3 years.

CARBONNIEUX (GRAVES)* * * *

1993	C	89
1992	C	88

One of the benchmark producers for crisp, elegant, dry, white Graves, Carbonnieux's recent efforts have displayed more richness and weight without sacrificing any of their ethereal elegance and style. The 1992 exhibits a spicy, rich, honeyed nose, medium-bodied flavors, with excellent ripeness and enough crisp acidity and toasty oak to support this pure wine's richness. Carbonnieux's exuberant, fresh style makes it one of the most popular dry white Bordeaux. It should drink well for 10 or more years. The 1993 is a rich, honeyed wine with fine purity and attractive smoky oak that adds to the complexity of the wine's otherwise waxy, melony, herb, and smoky fruit character. Drink it over the next 10–15 years.

CARSIN (BORDEAUX)* * *

1993	A	85
1992	A	85

Run by Australians, this estate is making delicious, dry, fruity white wines that are meant to be drunk in their first year of life. They also produced a 1993 Cuvée Prestige that was aged in new oak. It is one of those generic white Bordeaux that has good integration of oak as opposed to allowing the oak to obliterate the wine's elegance and fruit. It is a wine I have rated 85 points, but it costs several dollars more than the regular cuvée. The 1992 exhibits a lemon/limelike nose, crisp, fruity, light-bodied flavors, and a dry, austere finish. It would make a delightful aperitif wine, or one to drink with shellfish.

CHANTEGRIVE (GRAVES)* * *

1992	B	85
1993 Cuvée Caroline	C	87
1992 Cuvée Caroline	C	87

This well-known Graves property can produce delicious, reasonably priced red and white wines. The 1992 regular cuvée exhibits a honeyed, herb, melony nose, light to medium body, fine flavor definition, and a dry, crisp finish. Drink it over the next 1–2 years. The 1992 Cuvée Caroline displays more toasty new oak, more honey and exotic fruits, and a medium-bodied, spicy finish. Greater body and flavor suggest it should be matched with richer foods.

The honeyed, richly fruity, medium-bodied 1993 Cuvée Caroline reveals wonderful purity, loads of zesty, ripe fruit, and a dry, crisp finish. Like many wines from this vintage, it is soft and ideal for drinking over the next 1–2 years.

DOMAINE DE CHEVALIER (GRAVES)* * * * *

1993	D	89
1992	D	93
1991	D	89

One of three terrific efforts from the Domaine de Chevalier, the 1991 reveals excellent fruit, an intense, mineral, oaky fruitiness, medium body, and tremendous length. The wine, which is already beginning to close up, explodes on the back of the palate, so this is one white wine that will keep for several decades. Even in light vintages, Domaine de Chevalier's white wines can last for 15–20 years. The 1992 exhibits a tight but promising nose of rich, melony, waxy, honeyed fruit complemented nicely by smoky new oak. Well structured and concentrated, with layers of fruit and an inner core of mineral, steely fruit, this formidably endowed, backward wine will need 7–12 years to open; it should last 25 or more years. Impressive!

Domaine de Chevalier's 1993 does not yet reveal the chewy, rich, fat, muscular character of the outstanding 1992. The unformed, citrusy 1993 is backward and unevolved with abundant quantities of crisp, tart fruit complemented by lavish quantities of toasty new oak.

Although the wine is tightly knit, firm, and certainly very good, my instincts suggest it is not as rich and complete as the 1992. It will last for 15–20+ years.
Past Glories: 1985 (93), 1983 (93), 1970 (93), 1962 (93)

CLOS FLORIDENE (GRAVES)* * * *

1993	C	89

One of several estates owned by Denis Dubourdieu, Clos Floridene produces an insider's wine. Why? It is far less expensive than most of the more prestigious, well-known Graves wines. A blend of 70% Semillon and 30% Sauvignon Blanc from vines planted on limestone soil, this is a wonderfully rich, hedonistic style of white Graves that is loaded with fruit. It is best drunk within its first 3–4 years of life. The 1993 is a plump, delicious white Graves that readers will admire for its purity, fragrance, and rich fruit.

LA CLOSIÈRE (BORDEAUX)* * *

1992	A	86

Intense herb and melon aromas jump from the glass of this excellent dry white wine that exhibits fine ripeness, purity, and finesse. Drink it over the next year.

CHÂTEAU COUCHEROY (PESSAC-LÉOGNAN)* * *

1992 Graves	A	86

This is a textbook, stylish, mineral- and herb-scented wine with good fruit, medium body, and a soft finish. Drink it over the next 1–2 years.

COUHINS-LURTON (GRAVES)* * * *

1993	D	91

It is a shame so little of this wine is produced, as it is one of my favorite dry white Graves. Made from 100% Sauvignon Blanc, it possesses an intensity and a richness that suggest there is Semillon in the blend, but such is not the case. The 1993 is a classic, textbook white Graves with wonderful mineral, smoky, intense, honeyed flavors, medium to full body, great purity and vibrancy, and wonderful focus in the long finish. It should drink well for at least a decade. By the way, the 1992 Couhins-Lurton is also outstanding, and a wine that I have consistently rated 90 points. With a more expansive, softer, chewier palate, it does not possess the vibrancy and exceptional finesse of the 1993.

DOISY-DAËNE (BORDEAUX)* * *

1993 Blanc Sec	A	86

A juicy, lively, richly fruity wine, the 1993 Doisy-Daëne Blanc Sec is dry, well made, and fresh. Drink it over the next year.

CHÂTEAU FERBOS (GRAVES)* * *

1990	A	86

This is a rich, medium- to full-bodied, surprisingly concentrated, creamy-textured wine for near-term consumption. I especially admired its marriage of mineral/melony/honey flavors.

DE FIEUZAL (GRAVES)* * * * *

1993	D	92
1992	D	91
1991	D	86

Since 1985 Fieuzal has been producing gorgeous dry Graves. The 1985 Fieuzal remains one of the most sensational white wines this property has yet made. It was followed by terrific efforts in 1988 and 1989, and very strong offerings in both 1992 and 1993. The 1991 has turned out well in what was a tough year. Although understated, it possesses a sense of elegance, crisp, lemony/honeyed flavors, light to medium body, toasty new oak, and a tasty, dry finish. Drink it over the next 5–6 years. The 1992 exhibits a big, creamy, rich nose of smoky new oak and ripe fruit, medium to full body, excellent concentration, and a chewy finish. While it is not as well delineated as some vintages, it offers a lusty mouthful of Fieuzal. Drink it over the next 7–8 years.

The rich, powerful 1993 offers authoritative flavors presented in a full-bodied style that is crammed with honeyed, waxy, melony fruit and spicy new oak. The wine possesses a chewy, thick texture, and a long, crisp finish. Fieuzal's white wines are made of 50% Semillon and 50% Sauvignon Blanc and are vinified and aged in 100% new oak. This offering should last for at least 10–15 years.

Past Glories: 1989 (90), 1988 (90+), 1985 (94)

DE FRANCE (GRAVES)* *

1993	C	74
1992	C	86

This stylish, understated 1992 dry white wine possesses crisp fruitiness, medium body, toasty oak, and a dry finish. It should drink well for 3–4 years. The 1993's green, light-bodied, diluted flavors are disappointing and of little interest.

G DE CHÂTEAU GUIRAUD (BORDEAUX)* * *

1993	B	85
1992	B	86

Guiraud has had considerable success with this dry, reasonably priced white wine from their vineyard in Sauternes. The 1992 reveals a big, spicy, honeyed nose, ripe, rich, medium-bodied flavors, fine length, and a robust, heady finish. This forceful, dry white should drink well for 1–2 years. A tart, crisp, refreshing wine with lively fruit, light body, and a dry finish, the 1993 "G" is ideal for drinking over the next year.

LA GARDE-RÉSERVE DU CHÂTEAU (GRAVES)* * *

1993	C	89

Significant investments have been made in this Pessac-Léognan vineyard, resulting in increasingly impressive wines—both white and red. I thought the 1993 La Garde-Réserve du Château white wine to be a highly successful, rich white Graves with plenty of honeyed fruit and a crisp, clean, pure finish.

CHÂTEAU GRAVILLE-LACOSTE (GRAVES)* * *

1992	A	86

In 1992, most Bordeaux vineyards planted with white wine varietals were harvested before any significant rain fell. That is obvious when tasting this delicious, dry white Graves. It reveals plenty of crisp, mineral, fig/melony fruit, medium body, good crisp acidity, and a fresh, long, dry finish. This personality-filled, fairly priced wine should be drunk over the next 2–4 years.

HAUT-BRION (GRAVES)* * * * *

1993	E	94
1992	E	93

NOTE: No 1991 was produced under the Haut-Brion-Blanc label.

The 1992 is another blockbuster Haut-Brion-Blanc, with a big, ostentatious bouquet of sweet, honeyed fruit. Full bodied, with layers of richness, this creamy-textured, fleshy wine is at present more evolved and dramatic than its sibling, the 1992 Laville. The wine possesses fine acidity and an explosively long, dry finish. This dazzling Haut-Brion-Blanc should drink well for 30+ years. Slightly superior to the 1992, the 1993 exhibits a flattering nose of oily, mineral-scented, ripe, honeyed fruit, full-bodied, superconcentrated flavors, admirable acidity, great vibrancy and delineation, and a rich, long, dry, refreshing finish. It is a rich Haut-Brion-Blanc with more aromatic complexity than the muscular and chewy 1992. These wines are almost ageless. Like its older sibling, the 1993 will age effortlessly for 20–30 years.

Past Glories: 1989 (98), 1985 (97)

LAVILLE-HAUT-BRION (GRAVES)* * * * *

1993	E	90
1992	E	91

NOTE: No 1991 was produced under the Laville-Haut-Brion label.

Laville's 1992 was the most backward, dry white Graves I tasted. It possesses a medium-straw color, a tight but promising nose of sweet waxy fruit, long, rich, full-bodied flavors, adequate acidity, an opulent, chewy richness, and tremendous length. Although not as monumental as the 1989, this is a top-class Laville-Haut-Brion that should drink well for 20–30 years. While the 1993 Laville-Haut-Brion should rival the 1992 after a few more years of cellaring, at present it is tight and lighter bodied than the fat, robust 1992. This stylish, backward yet finesse-styled Laville-Haut-Brion exhibits aromas of spicy, honeyed fruit and toasty new oak, crisp acidity, and a rich, firmly structured personality.

Past Glories: 1989 (98+), 1985 (93), 1983 (90), 1975 (90), 1966 (92), 1962 (88), 1947 (93), 1945 (96)

LA LOUVIÈRE (GRAVES)* * * * *

1993	C	90

This estate is making superlative red and white wines. It is, therefore, not surprising that the 1993 is a superb, medium- to full-bodied, smoky, honeyed wine with layers of flavor, excellent purity, and the potential to last for up to a decade. By the way, if you run across any of the rich 1992s, it is also a knockout example of dry white Graves that is bursting with a nose of melons, honey, smoke, and herb-scented fruit. It does not possess the complexity or length of the 1993, but it is a wine I have consistently rated between 87 and 89.

MALARTIC-LAGRAVIÈRE (GRAVES)* * *

1993	C	72
1992	C	76

If you like the aroma of mashed green peas and unripe limes you will admire Malartic-Lagravière's 1992 more than I did. While sharp and angular on the palate, its purity, lightness, and superausterity may offer some interest to masochists. It's not my style. The 1993 is extremely thin, watery, and light bodied, with green, overtly herbaceous flavors.

OLIVIER (GRAVES)* *

1993	C	81
1992	C	84
1991	C	76

None of these dry whites provides distinguished drinking. The diluted 1991 exhibits a sugary, cloying finish. The delicate 1992 displays a citrusy, stony-scented nose, medium-bodied, pleasant flavors, and a compact finish. The monolithic 1993 offers some toasty new oak in a light- to medium-bodied format. This simplistic, dry white wine should be drunk over the next year.

PAPE-CLÉMENT (GRAVES)* * * *

1993	D 90

Pape-Clément owns only 6.5 acres of vines dedicated to white grape varietals. The blend utilized is 45% Semillon, 45% Sauvignon Blanc, and 10% Muscadelle. The wines are vinified and aged in new oak. The 1993 is the best white wine Pape-Clément has yet made, exhibiting a fragrant, wonderfully ripe nose of spicy fruit and well-integrated oak, rich, medium- to full-bodied, crisp flavors of minerals, honey, and melons, and a lively, refreshing finish. It should drink well for 10–15 years.

PLAISANCE (BORDEAUX)* * *

1993 Cuvée Tradition	B 86

Made from 100% Semillon, this 1993 offers a honeyed, spicy, oaky nose, rich, medium-bodied flavors exhibiting good concentration, and a fine finish. It should be drunk over the next year.

R DE RIEUSSEC (GRAVES)* * *

1993	C 87

Made from equal proportions of Sauvignon Blanc and Semillon, this wine is made in an elegant style that is easy to drink and understand. The 1993 is a classic example of a dry, richly fruity white Bordeaux. Offering an attractive, melony/pineapplelike fruitiness, it is ideal for drinking over the next 1–2 years.

RAHOUL (GRAVES)* * *

1993	C 85

The 1993 Rahoul displays attractive, fat, ripe, pineapple fruit, medium body, and a juicy, lively, dry finish. It should drink well for 3–4 years.

REYNON (BORDEAUX)* * */* * * *

1992	B 87
1993 Vieilles Vignes	B 87

Bordeaux's "Mr. White Wine," Denis Dubourdieu, owns this estate that consistently turns out one of the finest dry whites. A fragrant bouquet of fruit, honey, and spice jumps from the glass in this rich, medium-bodied 1992. The wine possesses loads of luscious fruit, low acidity, and a long, rich, dry, lusty finish. A superb value, this wine merits purchasing by the case. Drink it now.

Reynon's 1993 exhibits smoky, herb, honeyed, melony scents, wonderfully rich, exuberant fruit, medium body, and lively freshness and crispness. Drink it over the next 2–3 years.

CHÂTEAU DE ROCHEMORIN (PESSAC-LÉOGNAN)* * *

1992 Graves	B 86

One of the André Lurton Bordeaux estates, this well-run property has produced an attractively clean, medium-bodied, fruity, nicely concentrated white wine for drinking over the next 1–2 years. Tasters will appreciate the fleshy, citrusy, fig, and melonlike flavors.

ROQUEFORT (BORDEAUX)* * *

1993	A	86
1992	A	85

Thanks to the talented oenological team of Denis Dubourdieu and his assistant, Christophe Olivier, Roquefort is generally one of the most interesting generic white Bordeaux. The 1993 reveals wonderfully ripe, melony, honeyed fruit, medium body, good purity, and excellent richness. The aromatic, dry 1992 offers an herb- and melon-scented nose, excellent fruit, medium body, and a dry finish. Drink it over the next year.

SMITH-HAUT-LAFITTE (GRAVES)* * * *

1993	C	89
1992	C	87
1991	C	84

This property is pushing quality higher and higher and the estate's white wines are among the finest being produced in Graves. The 1993, made from 100% Sauvignon Blanc, offers a rich, honeyed, melony-scented nose with attractive notes of toasty new oak. The wine is fat and rich, with good underlying acidity and plenty of freshness and vibrancy. It should drink well for 3–4 years. The 1991 is a light bodied, melony, crisp, citrusy, dry, 100% Sauvignon with medium body and admirable purity, but its finish is too short to merit higher marks. The excellent 1992 combines all the herbaceous, melony, citrusy components of the 1991 with a touch of honey and smoky oak. The result is a rich, concentrated, medium-bodied wine with brilliant definition, gobs of fruit, and a crisp, long finish. Delicious now, it promises to last for 10 or more years.

THIEULEY (BORDEAUX)* * *

1993	A	86

One of the best-run Bordeaux estates, Château Thieuley has fashioned a deliciously dry, crisp, 1993 white wine with gobs of fruit and a medium-bodied, zesty finish. In 1993, all of the dry white Bordeaux grapes were harvested before the rains.

LA TOUR-MARTILLAC (GRAVES)* * * *

1993	C	89
1992	C	90
1991	C	86

This property has been fashioning marvelous dry white wines over the last few years. Even their 1991 exhibits lovely fruit, presented in a light- to medium-bodied, elegant format. A stylish, light Graves, with a moderately intense nose, fine depth, and a lovely crisp finish, it should be drunk over the next 5–6 years. The 1992 displays the big, rich, smoky, honeyed nose that is the result of reasonable yields and barrel fermentation. This medium-bodied wine is loaded with rich, chewy fruit, wonderful purity and definition, and an excellent dry finish; it should drink well for another 7–9 years. The 1993 boasts gobs of rich, concentrated fruit, medium body, wonderful purity, fine underlying acidity, and a long, smoky, honeyed finish. Drink it over the next 10–12 years.

The Sweet White Wines of Bordeaux
1988, 1989, 1990 Barsac/Sauternes

The most difficult tastings I do are those involving sweet wines. Because of high alcohol combined with various degrees of residual sugar, and the fact that sweet wines tend to evolve at a slower pace than dry red wines, judging young vintages of Barsac and Sauternes is extremely difficult.

That being stated, the Barsac/Sauternes region enjoyed an unprecedented period of three consecutive high-quality vintages—1988, 1989, and 1990. Each vintage has its share of supporters, with the majority of nectar addicts split over the question of whether 1988 or 1990 is the greatest of this historic trilogy. Many châteaux also produced outstanding wine in 1989, making the debate even more interesting.

I decided to retaste all of these wines, doing the tasting blind with a single estate's 1988, 1989, and 1990 arbitrarily presented. After methodically tasting these three vintages of each estate, I could compare the top wines from each vintage. As the following tasting notes indicate, 1988 and 1990 clearly revealed their potential for greatness. Only a handful of 1989s demonstrated as much character and complexity as the finest 1988s and 1990s. Yet all three vintages are exceptional, the first time this has occurred this century.

Nineteen eighty-eight remains the most elegant vintage, combining attractive botrytis levels with underlying crisp acidity and well-balanced, harmonious sweetness and richness; 1989 is more overblown, leaning toward heaviness and high residual sugar levels; 1990 is a big, weighty, blockbuster vintage. Yet despite the massive size of these wines, they have managed to remain well balanced, with enough acidity to provide delineation and focus. My instincts suggest the 1990s will last as long as the 1988s, but they will show well at an earlier age. If stylistic comparisons are made, I believe 1988 is similar to 1975, 1971, and 1962. The 1990 vintage begs for comparison with 1976, 1959, and 1949, and 1989 could well be the modern-day clone of 1967.

In addition to the blind tastings conducted in Bordeaux, tastings of some of the luxury cuvées and a handful of the other wines were held in America.

D'ARCHE (SAUTERNES)* * *

1990	C	87?
1989	C	86

The 1990 d'Arche may be overripe and too alcoholic. It is quite powerful, but its lack of acidity may prove to be its undoing. If the wine pulls itself together, it will turn out to be a good to very good, muscular Sauternes that will offer big, thick, chewy fruit in a high-alcohol, fiery format. It will hopefully evolve for another decade. The 1989, which seemed heavy-handed and out of focus in both barrel and bottle, appears to have come together (a hopeful sign for the 1990), displaying straightforward, ripe, chewy, muscular fruit in a low-acid, moderately sweet style. It should drink well for 7–8 years.

CAILLOU (BARSAC)* * *

1990	C	88
1989	C	84
1988	C	87

Caillou tends to produce compact, richly fruity, moderately sweet wines that rarely have the complexity found in the better Barsac/Sauternes estates. The 1990 displays a honeyed, ripe cherry/apricot/orange–scented nose, surprisingly good acidity, and a medium- to full-bodied, thick, chewy finish. About as impressive as Caillou can be, it will last for 10–15 years. The 1989 is a fat, sweet, chunky wine without much complexity or delineation. I liked previous examples more, but the wine's low acidity is causing it to taste more diffuse as it ages. The 1988 is thick, ripe, and rich, with attractive honeyed pineapplelike fruitiness, medium to full body, and a more elegant personality than its two siblings. It should drink well for another decade.

CLIMENS (BARSAC)* * * * *

1990	D	95
1989	D	90
1988	D	96

The 1988 reveals layer upon layer of honeyed pineapple– and orange-scented and -flavored fruit, vibrant acidity, high levels of botrytis, and a fabulously long yet well-focused finish. It is a great wine. **A.M.: 1998–2015.** For whatever reason, the 1989 is merely outstanding rather than dazzling. Although it lacks the complexity of the 1988, it is a plump, muscular, rich, intense, full-bodied, and sweeter-than-usual Climens. For a 1989, it possesses good acidity. If more complexity and grip develop, my rating may look stingy. **A.M.: Now– 2010.** The 1990 continues to develop exceptionally well (better than I thought), and now looks to be a worthy rival of the dazzling 1988. The superb aromatics (pineapple, acacia, vanilla, and honey) are followed by a rich, full-bodied, atypically powerful Climens that possesses adequate acidity, high alcohol, and even higher levels of extract and fruit. **A.M.: 2000–2030.**

Past Glories: 1986 (96), 1983 (93), 1980 (90), 1975 (89), 1971 (96), 1959 (92), 1949 (96), 1947 (94?), 1937 (92), 1929 (90)

CLOS HAUT-PEYRAGUEY (SAUTERNES)* * *

1990	C	90
1989	C	86
1988	C	89

All three of these wines merit higher scores than I had initially bestowed. The finest bouquet and aromatics are found in the 1988, which exhibits a striking nose of honeysuckle, sweet peaches, apricots, and pineapples. The award for the richest, most full-bodied, and unctuously textured and powerful wine goes to the 1990. Again, the 1988's medium- to full-bodied, elegant style contrasts with the blockbuster, dramatic, ostentatious, powerful 1990. The 1988 has a full degree less alcohol than the 1990.

The 1989 suffers in comparison with the other two vintages, largely because it is drier, with a waxy, Tokay-Pinot Gris–like personality. Although it shows well, it appears smaller-scaled than the fragrant 1988 and superrich 1990. I have not had much experience with the aging capabilities of Clos Haut-Peyraguey, but the 1990 unquestionably has 20 years of evolution ahead, and the 1988, 15 or more years. Even the 1989 will last that long, but it does not have the same level of fruit extraction; once it begins to dry out, it will be less interesting.

COUTET (BARSAC)* * * */* * * * *

1990	D	88
1989	D	90
1988	D	89+
1990 Cuvée Madame	E	98
1989 Cuvée Madame	E	95
1988 Cuvée Madame	E	99

This was one of the few wines where the 1989 was the superior offering. The richest, sweetest, and fattest, it offers a pure nose of pineapples, full body, and excellent concentration. The lighter-bodied, drier 1988 is less weighty, with attractive, spicy, vanillin, citrus scents, medium body, and an earthy note that kept my score from going higher. The full-bodied 1990 is sweet, rich, and honeyed, but it lacks the clarity and complexity of the 1989.

Tiny quantities are made of Coutet's Cuvée Madame, a spectacularly rich Barsac that, along with Yquem, is the quintessential example of what heights a great sweet wine can achieve. All three of these Cuvée Madame vintages are nearly perfect wines. The 1990 is the richest and most powerful, but the 1988's extraordinary perfume is otherworldly. All three wines offer a profound bouquet of smoky, toasty new oak combined with honeyed peaches and apricots, as well as coconuts and a touch of crème brûlée. With extraordinarily rich, full-bodied, marvelously extracted personalities, as well as wonderful underlying acidity, these are spectacular wines.

As a postscript, many readers may not realize that Coutet's Cuvée Madame is only released in great vintages. It is produced from the oldest vines and most botrytised grapes. The first vintage produced was 1943, followed by 1949, 1950, 1959, 1971, 1975, 1981, 1986, and the three vintages reviewed above.

Past Glories: Cuvée Madame—1986 (96), 1981 (96), 1975 (94), 1971 (98)

DOISY-DAËNE (BARSAC)* * *

1990	C	91
1989	C	89
1988	C	89
1990 L'Extravagance	E	95

In 1990 Doisy-Daëne produced 100 cases of a sensational luxury cuvée called L'Extravagance. It possesses considerable botrytis, awesome extract levels and intensity, and despite massive power, remarkable balance. Readers are unlikely to find any of this wine (bottled in a heavy 375-ml bottle) outside Bordeaux. Its medium-gold color and extraordinary richness and power suggest it will age effortlessly for another 20+ years. The 1990 regular cuvée is revealing far more complexity and richness than it did in the past. It is a bold, opulent, exquisite example of Barsac, with more richness and intensity than I have encountered in previous vintages of Doisy-Daëne. Light to medium gold colored, with a honeyed, botrytised nose, huge amounts of alcohol and power, and a heady finish, the wine possesses just enough acidity to balance out its bold flavors and forcefulness. Drink it over the next 15+ years. The 1989 also performed better than in previous tastings, exhibiting plenty of honeyed ripe fruit, a more elegant personality, fine richness, chunkiness, and depth, full body, and low acidity. It does not reveal the botrytis found in the 1990 or 1988. The 1988 is the lightest of these wines, with medium body, and a fragrant pineapple-, peach-, and apple-scented nose, with a honeysuckle component that adds complexity. The wine is crisp, dry, and ideal for drinking now and over the next 10 years.

DOISY-VÉDRINES (BARSAC)* * *

1990	C	84
1989	C	88
1988	C	86

My ratings in this tasting mirrored earlier ratings from both barrel and bottle. The 1989 is clearly the richest wine. While it possesses more honeyed fruit and fuller body, it appears to lack botrytis. Nevertheless, it offers a rich, interesting mouthful of sweet Bordeaux. The

1988 possesses better acidity and more focus. It would make an excellent choice with foie gras or such rich fish dishes as lobster with melted butter. The very sweet 1990 is simple, dull, and rustic. All three of these wines should be drunk over the next 10–15 years.

FILHOT (SAUTERNES)* * *

1990	C	90
1989	C	86
1988	C	88

Filhot, which prefers to tank rather than to barrel ferment its wines, produced a 1990 that is clearly the best wine I have tasted from this estate. It exhibits gorgeously ripe, honeyed tropical fruit, an intense, medium- to full-bodied personality, wonderful purity, fine acidity, plenty of botrytis, and a long, zesty finish. What makes this wine so appealing is its combination of richness, crisp acidity, liveliness, and zestiness. The thick, very sweet, slightly heavy 1989 appears to be maturing at a fast pace. If drunk over the next 5–8 years, it will provide an uncomplicated mouthful of sweet, candied fruit. The 1988 showed far better than in previous tastings. It displayed a wonderfully pure, honeyed pineapple–scented nose, rich, medium- to full-bodied flavors, fine underlying acidity, an earthiness that added to the wine's complexity, and a clean, rich, crisp finish. Drinkable now, it should continue to evolve graciously for 10–15 years.

GUIRAUD (SAUTERNES)* * * *

1990	D	91
1989	D	86
1988	D	89+

In the past, I preferred the 1988 Guiraud, followed by the 1989, and lastly, the 1990. In recent tastings the 1990 has taken first prize with its showy display of power, highly extracted, smoky, buttery, pineapple- and orange-scented fruit, lavish quantities of toasty new oak, and unctuously thick, massive flavors and texture. This huge wine avoids being overbearing because of its adequate acidity. The 1989 is extremely disjointed. Although big and rich, it tastes like a glob of sugar, alcohol, and wood. This was a disappointing showing for the 1989. More tight and backward than I remembered it, the 1988 exhibits a stylish, spicy nose of ripe fruit, some botrytis, medium- to full-bodied flavors with well-integrated oak, an attractive, smoky, honeyed fruit character, and a lively finish. It is more shy and reticent than usual. Look for the 1990 to evolve well for another 15–20 years, the 1989 hopefully to gain focus and return to the form predicted for it when it was in barrel, and the 1988 to last for 20–30 years. It represents a more understated style of wine than the more ostentatious 1990.

LAFAURIE-PEYRAGUEY (SAUTERNES)* * * */* * * * *

1990	D	89
1989	D	88+
1988	D	95

Previously I rated the 1988 the highest of these three vintages, and I did not feel the 1989 was not significantly inferior. However, at this tasting, the 1988 towered qualitatively over the other two vintages. The massively rich, yet fresh, lively 1988 offers a compelling, flowery, honeyed bouquet of vanilla, and buttery orange/apricot scents. The wine's wonderful, zesty acidity brings everything into extraordinary clarity. It is a full-bodied, superconcentrated, fascinating, precocious Sauternes that will age beautifully for 25–30 years.

Both the 1989 and 1990 are more one-dimensional. The 1990 is thick, chewy, alcoholic, and diffuse. The backward 1989 is Barsac-like in its crispness and less weighty style. These wines may just be closed. I remember after the 1988 was bottled it appeared to be far tighter and more restrained than it now tastes.

Past Glories: 1986 (92), 1983 (92)

LAMOTHE-DESPUJOLS (SAUTERNES)* * *

1990	C	88
1989	C	87

Unfortunately, I have been unable to locate a 1988 Lamothe-Despujols to retaste, but three past tastings revealed it to be a very disappointing effort in what was unquestionably a top-notch vintage. As for the 1990, it performed far better. It reveals an oily personality, big, ripe, honeyed fruit flavors, low acidity, plenty of intensity, and a full-bodied, chewy style that suggests it should be drunk over the next 10 years. Although similarly styled, the 1989 is displaying far greater richness, intensity, and cleanliness than previous examples revealed. The 1989 exhibited good fatness, an unctuous texture, low acidity, and lovely rich, intense, tropical fruit. It should drink well for 7–8 years. These two vintages garnered significantly higher ratings than previous bottles merited.

LAMOTHE-GUIGNARD (SAUTERNES)* * */* * * *

1990	C	91
1989	C	91
1988	C	89+

It is a shame that this estate is not more well known, as the proprietor, the Guignard family, has made considerable improvements at this underrated property. The 1990 is a forceful, unctuous, thick, chewy Sauternes with plenty of heady alcohol, gobs of fruit, and an exuberant personality. It reveals greater aromatics, complexity, dimension, and delineation than it did several years ago. It should age well and evolve for 15–20 more years. The 1989 also displays more personality and complexity. Although it possesses very high alcohol (nearly 15%), it is a massive, highly extracted, extremely rich, impressively endowed wine that is oozing with honeyed, buttery, apricot, orange, pineapple, and lemony fruit. Noticeable acidity gives uplift and vibrance to this huge wine. Lamothe-Guignard's 1989 has turned out to be a sleeper of the vintage and should be available at a reasonable price. The 1988 is the most backward and streamlined of these three vintages. It possesses a waxy, honeyed, Tokay-Pinot Gris–like fragrance, and rich, full-bodied flavors that appear reticent and restrained because of the wine's good acidity. A shy example of this estate's wine, it is not nearly as ostentatious or muscular as the 1989 or 1990. All three of these sweet Bordeaux should last for 20–25 years, which is far longer than I would have guessed several years ago.

DE MALLE (SAUTERNES)* * *

1990	C	90
1989	C	87
1988	C	91

The results of this tasting were extremely interesting, as I and most Bordeaux brokers and enthusiasts believed that Château de Malle's 1990 was the finest sweet wine the estate had made in decades. Certainly it is an outstanding effort, and given the reasonable price, it is a noteworthy purchase. However, the 1988 was singing at the top of its lungs in a recent tasting. Closer to maturity than the 1990, the 1988's heavenly bouquet of cherries and coconuts, as well as its ostentatious display of honeyed pineapples and toasty oak, are noteworthy. Medium to full bodied, with excellent purity, freshness, and ripeness, it is an ideal candidate for drinking or cellaring over the next 10–12 years. The 1989 performed well, although it appeared to be somewhat simple compared with its two siblings. It is medium to full bodied, with ripe, rich fruit, enough acidity to provide uplift, and a fleshy finish. It should drink well for another decade. The 1990 is full bodied, with excellent sweetness, fine purity, and plenty of rich, honeyed fruit buttressed by noticeable new oak. It has not yet developed the complexity and aromatics displayed by the 1988, but the 1990 is clearly an outstanding effort for the vintage. It should evolve gracefully for 10–15 years.

RABAUD-PROMIS (SAUTERNES)* * * *

1990	C	89
1989	D	92
1988	D	93

At one time, Rabaud-Promis was among the most notorious underachievers of Barsac/ Sauternes. That all changed in 1986. These three vintages offer formidable evidence that Rabaud-Promis is exhibiting more consistency in quality than many of its more renowned neighbors. The 1990 is the least impressive of this trio, but it is nevertheless an outstanding wine. It reveals plenty of honeyed richness, a full-blown, heavyweight style, and considerable spice. While there is a slight lack of acidity, it is a huge, full-bodied wine for drinking over the next 15 or so years. The 1989 is richer and more complex aromatically, as well as huge and massive. It exhibits greater delineation, with enough freshness and vibrancy to make a strong case for this estate's 1989. It should age well for 20–25 years. The 1988 remains the most classic of these three vintages. It possesses great richness, sweetness, and unctuous texture, as well as higher acidity, plenty of botrytis, a wonderful, rich nose of honeyed pineapple, coconut, and orange, gobs of rich fruit, and excellent delineation. Approachable now, it promises to age effortlessly for 25–30 years.

RAYMOND-LAFON (SAUTERNES)* * * * *

1990	E	95
1989	E	91+
1988	E	92+

This small estate continues to turn out remarkably rich, unctuously textured, thick, powerful wines that brilliantly balance power and intensity with elegance and finesse. Now that these three vintages have had some time in the bottle, it appears that the 1990 may be the most complete and botrytised among this trio of exceptional wines from Raymond-Lafon. All the wines possess a light- to medium-gold color, with the 1989 revealing a more evolved color. The 1989 exhibits aromas of honeyed pineapple/tropical fruit and toasty new oak, as well as an exotic, flashy perfume that is not as pronounced in either the 1990 or the 1988. The 1989 exhibits less botrytis than the other two vintages. All three wines share opulent, full-bodied, exotic, lavishly rich personalities, moderate sweetness (the 1990 is the sweetest), and huge quantities of extract, glycerin, and alcohol in their finishes. All three wines are also extremely young and unevolved. The 1990 appears to be the richest. The 1988 offers the most refined aromatic profile and the tightest structure, and the 1989 tastes the most restrained. All of these wines can be drunk now, but purchasers are advised to wait until the turn of the century and enjoy them over the following two decades.

Past Glories: 1986 (92), 1983 (93), 1980 (90), 1975 (90)

RAYNE-VIGNEAU (SAUTERNES)* * *

1990	D	85
1988	D	89

Previously I have been disappointed with this estate's 1989. The 1988 is much finer than the monolithic, thick, juicy, succulent 1990. The 1988's flowery, peach- and honey-scented nose and medium- to full-bodied, complex, finesse style is more refreshing than the in-your-face, sweet, low-acid 1990. Neither of these wines will make old bones. Drink this commercially styled Sauternes over the next decade.

RIEUSSEC (SAUTERNES)* * * * *

1990	D	90
1989	D	92?
1988	D	93+

Aside from the odd 1989 that appeared disjointed and out of character (other tastings have shown this to be a very rich, alcoholic, fat, blockbuster wine), the other two vintages of Rieussec confirmed their superb quality. Although the 1988 received the highest marks, it remains a very backward wine. Full bodied and powerful, extremely rich and dense, it may be the least evolved 1988. The nose offers enticing coconut, orange, vanilla, and honeyed scents. The flavors are highly extracted. The wine's acidity and youthfulness suggest this wine needs another 5–10 years of cellaring. It should keep for 30 years. The 1990 was more precocious and flattering, with its tropical fruit–scented nose, big, spicy, rich, high-alcohol flavors, and a fine underpinning of acidity, giving everything clarity and crispness. The 1990 will be drinkable at an earlier age than the 1989, but it will last just as long.

ROMER DU HAYOT (SAUTERNES)* *

1990	B	86
1989	B	85?
1988	B	?

The 1990 Romer du Hayot exhibits a moderately intense, pineapple-scented nose, medium-bodied, ripe, sweet flavors, and a clean, fresh finish. It is an uncomplicated, easygoing wine for drinking over the next 7–8 years. The 1989 revealed excessive sulfur in the nose, combined with a pronounced pungent, dirty earthiness in the mouth. Behind the annoying off components is a simple, medium-bodied, moderately sweet wine. The 1988, pulled from inventory, and a wine I have noted as possessing off aromas in the past, has gotten worse rather than better. Although there is good ripeness and concentration, the wine's skunky aromas are unpleasant.

SUAU (BARSAC)* *

1990	C	89
1989	C	87
1988	C	78

Given the fact that I have never had a high opinion of the 1988, I was not surprised by its mediocre showing. On the other hand, I was pleasantly surprised to see how well the 1989 and 1990 are developing. The 1989 exhibits elegance combined with medium body, which is atypical for this fat, heavyweight vintage. The wine possesses considerable finesse, a lovely apricot/pineapplelike fruitiness, and a crisp, fresh personality. It is not a wine for aging, but rather one for drinking over the next 5–7 years. The 1990 is the most opulent, concentrated, and powerful Suau I have ever tasted. Big and full bodied, the wine's original monolithic personality appears to have been replaced by greater precision and complexity in its nose. A fine example of Suau, it should age well for 7–8 years.

SIGALAS RABAUD (SAUTERNES)* * *

1990	D	89
1989	C	86
1988	D	84

In previous tastings I have preferred the 1988 Sigalas Rabaud, but in this tasting it appeared simple, sugary, medium bodied, and lacking botrytis, concentration, and personality. The 1989 was not much better, exhibiting an advanced medium-gold color, some bitterness in the finish, but good ripe fruit. The most complete wine was the 1990. It displayed a rich, honeyed, peachlike fruitiness, spicy oak, medium to full body, and a chewy, alcoholic finish. None of these wines possessed a great deal of complexity or intensity. They should be drunk over the next 10–15 years.

SUDUIRAUT (SAUTERNES)* * * */* * * * *

1990	D	88
1989	D	89
1988	D	88?

Suduiraut can make powerful, rich wines that are often rustic and excessively alcoholic and hot when young. I am told they become more civilized with age, and certainly older, classic Suduiraut vintages have proven that to be true. I feel this estate's propensity to produce a luxury cuvée (Cuvée Madame) in vintages such as 1989 tends to have a negative impact on the regular cuvée.

All three of these wines exhibit close to 15% alcohol, with the 1989 tasting very hot, and the 1988 and 1990 revealing bitterness as well as fiery alcohol in the finish. The evolved, medium-gold color of the 1990 is prematurely advanced, raising questions about future longevity. The 1990 possesses plenty of intensity, and an unctuous, thick, juicy style, but high alcohol and coarseness kept my rating down. The 1988 reveals a textbook, light-gold color with a slight greenish hue. Although it does not display the weight of the 1990 or 1989, it has better acidity, high alcohol, and considerable sweetness. It is somewhat disjointed, needing time to knit together. It is impressive if its components are evaluated separately, but it is less noteworthy when reviewed from an overall perspective.

The 1989 is the most well-balanced wine of this trio, but its fruit does not appear to be sufficient to stand up to the wine's high alcohol and aggressive style. None of these wines offers much delineation, so cellaring should prove beneficial, as they do have admirable levels of extract.

LA TOUR BLANCHE (SAUTERNES)* * * *

1990	D	92
1989	D	90
1988	D	92

The 1988 exhibits superb richness, plenty of botrytis, creamy, honeyed, tropical fruit (pineapples galore), wonderfully integrated, toasty oak, crisp acidity, and a rich, full-bodied, long finish. The wine is just beginning to evolve and it is clearly capable of lasting for 25–35 years. The 1990 is less aromatic, but richer and fuller bodied. It has not lost any of its elegant, honeyed, botrytised style. Interestingly, at bottling the 1988 contained 13.5% alcohol and the 1990, 13.2%. The 1990 comes across as slightly fatter and richer. Both wines are classic Sauternes that remain underpriced, given the resurgence of this well-known estate. Both will keep for three decades or more.

The 1989 is the most loosely structured, but it reveals plenty of intense, honeyed fruit in a rich, authoritative, full-bodied format. A big, powerhouse, sweet, heavy wine with a penetrating fragrance of honey and flowers, this generously endowed 1989 already drinks well, but can easily last for 15–20 years.

D'YQUEM (SAUTERNES)* * * * *

1989	E	97+
1988	E	99

The favorite sweet wine of millionaires, Château d'Yquem has, not unexpectedly, turned in a brilliant effort with their newly released 1989. It is a large-scaled, massively rich, unctuously textured wine that should evolve effortlessly for a half century or more. It does not reveal the compelling finesse and complexity of the 1988 or 1986, but it is a far heavier, richer wine than either of those vintages. It is reminiscent of the 1976, with additional fat and glycerin. The wine is extremely alcoholic and rich, with a huge nose of smoky, honey-covered coconuts and overripe pineapples and apricots. As with most young vintages of Yquem, the wine's structure is barely noticeable. These wines are so highly extracted and rich, yet approachable young, it is difficult to believe they will last for 50 or more years. The 1989 is the richest Yquem made in the eighties, and it has an edge in complexity over the powerhouse 1983. It remains to be seen whether this wine will develop the extraordinary aromatic complexity possessed by the promising 1988 and 1986 Yquems.

As for the 1988, it is a more backward-styled Yquem, built along the lines of the extraordinary 1975. With a honeyed, smoky, orange/coconut/pineapple-scented nose, this powerful wine possesses full body, layers of highly concentrated, extracted flavors, considerable botrytis, and a sensational finish.

Unfortunately, I have not yet tasted the 1990 Yquem. Given the vintage, it will undoubtedly be an extremely powerful wine.

Past Glories: 1983 (96), 1982 (92), 1981 (90), 1980 (93), 1976 (96), 1975 (99), 1971 (92), 1967 (96), 1962 (90), 1959 (96), 1949 (95), 1948 (91), 1947 (98?), 1945 (98), 1937 (99), 1921 (100)

Note: If you are not among the rich and famous who can afford Yquem, consider Château de Fargues. It often tastes as good as Yquem when young, and it also keeps for 15–25 years. It is owned by the same family that produces Yquem, and is made in exactly the same manner. The top vintages include 1986 (93), 1983 (92), 1980 (91), 1976 (90), and 1975 (91).

BURGUNDY AND BEAUJOLAIS

The Côte d'Or Minefield

Even the most enthusiastic burgundy connoisseurs admit that the wines of Burgundy are too expensive, too variable in quality, and too quick to fall apart, as well as too difficult and troublesome to find. Why, then, are they so cherished?

While it is tempting for those who have neither the financial resources nor the enthusiasm for these wines to conclude that burgundies are purchased only by wealthy masochists, the point is that burgundy at its best is the world's most majestic, glorious, and hedonistic Pinot Noir and Chardonnay. Burgundy has somehow defied definition, systemization, or even standardization. No matter how much research and money is spent trying to taste and understand the complexity of the wines of Burgundy and Burgundy's myriad vineyards, to a large extent they remain a mystery.

Perhaps this is best shown in the analogy between several famous Bordeaux vineyards and a handful of renowned Burgundy vineyards. Take the famous St.-Julien vineyard of Ducru-Beaucaillou in the heart of the Médoc. It is 124 acres in size. Compare it with its famous neighbor about 10 miles to the south, Château Palmer in Margaux, with a vineyard of 111 acres in size. Any consumer who buys a bottle of a specific vintage of Ducru-Beaucaillou or Palmer will be getting exactly the same wine. Of course it may have been handled differently or subjected to abuse in transportation or storage, but the wine that left the property was made by one winemaking team, from one blend, and the taste, texture, and aromatic profile of a specific vintage should not be any different whether drunk in Paris, Vienna, Tokyo, New York, or Los Angeles.

Compare that situation with the famous grand cru from Burgundy's Côte de Nuits, Clos de Vougeot. Clos de Vougeot has 124 acres, making it approximately the same size as Ducru-Beaucaillou. Yet while there is only one proprietor of the latter vineyard, Clos de Vougeot is divided among 77 different proprietors. Many of these proprietors sell their production to *négociants,* but in any given vintage there are at least three dozen or more Clos de Vougeots in the marketplace. All of them are entitled to grand cru status, they vary in price from $50 to $200+ a bottle, but less than a half dozen are likely to be compelling wines. The remainder range in quality from very good to dismal and insipid. Clos de Vougeot is the most cited as a microcosm of Burgundy—infinitely confusing, distressingly frustrating. Yet majestic wines do indeed come out of Clos de Vougeot from a few top producers.

Also consider the most renowned Burgundy vineyard—Chambertin. This 32-acre vineyard is 3 acres larger than Château Pétrus, maker of Bordeaux's most expensive red wine. Pétrus has only one producer, and there is only one wine from a given vintage, all of which has been blended prior to bottling, and all of it equal in quality. But among Chambertin's 32 acres, there are 23 different proprietors, with only a handful of them committed to

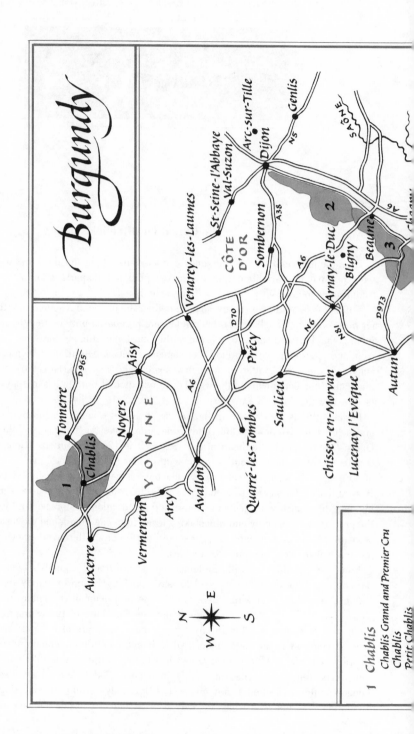

Burgundy

Tonnerre
D965
Chablis
1
Noyers
Aisy
D965
Auxerre
Vermenton
Arcy
Avallon
Y O N N E
A6
Quarré-les-Tombes
Précy
D70
Venarey-les-Laumes
CÔTE D'OR
Sombernon
A38
St-Seine-l'Abbaye
Val-Suzon
Arc-sur-Tille
Dijon
N5
Genlis
SAÔNE
A6
Saulieu
N6
Arnay-le-Duc
Bligny
A6
Chissey-en-Morvan
Lucenay l'Evêque
N81
Autun
D973
Beaune
2
3
A6

N W E S

Chablis

1 Chablis
   Chablis Grand and Premier Cru
   Chablis
   Petit Chablis

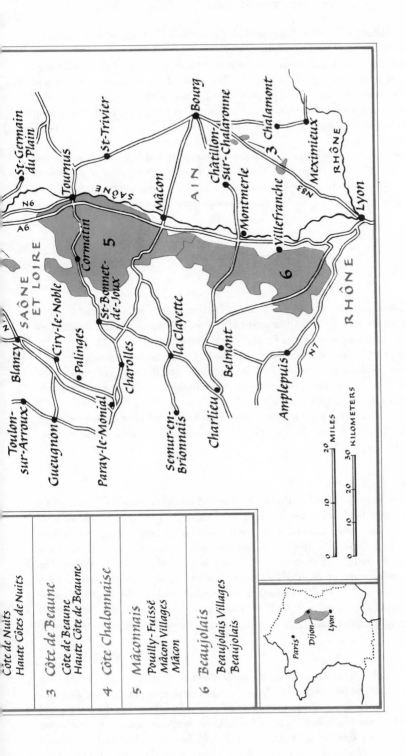

Côte de Nuits
Haute Côtes de Nuits

3 Côte de Beaune
Côte de Beaune
Haute Côte de Beaune

4 Côte Chalonnaise

5 Mâconnais
Pouilly-Fuissé
Mâcon Villages
Mâcon

6 Beaujolais
Beaujolais Villages
Beaujolais

MILES

KILOMETERS

Paris
Dijon
Lyon

producing extraordinary wine. Most Chambertins sell for well in excess of $150 a bottle. Most of them are thin, watery, and a complete rip-off.

The situation is the same among the rest of the greatest Burgundy vineyards. The 24-acre Musigny vineyard is split among 17 proprietors. The famed Richebourg vineyard of just under 20 acres is divided among *only* 12 proprietors (a low number by Burgundy standards). Even Burgundy's greatest white wine vineyard, Le Montrachet (20 acres), is divided among 15 producers. Only 5 or 6 of these proprietors are making outstanding wines, yet all of them fetch $200–$300 a bottle.

Any consumer still driven to make some sense of Burgundy will have to learn who are the best producers in each of Burgundy's appellations, for while the quality of a vineyard and the vintage are certainly important, nothing is of more paramount significance in Burgundy than the commitment to quality and the competence of the grower/wine producer.

The Basics—Burgundy

TYPES OF WINE

This modestly sized viticultural area in France's heartland, three hours by car south of Paris, produces on the average 22 million cases of dry red and white wine as well as tiny quantities of rosé. This represents 3% of France's total wine production.

Red Wine   Burgundy's dry red wines come from the Côte d'Or, which is divided into two distinct areas: the northern half, called the Côte de Nuits, and the southern portion, the Côte de Beaune. A bit farther south, red wines are made in the Côte Chalonnaise and even farther south in Beaujolais and Mâconnais.

White Wine   Dry white wine is made everywhere in Burgundy, but most of the production is centered in the Côte de Beaune, in the Côte Chalonnaise, in Mâconnais, and in Burgundy's most northern area, Chablis.

GRAPE VARIETIES

There are three major grapes used in Burgundy. The red burgundies are made from Pinot Noir, the world's most fickle and troublesome grape. Although it is an extremely difficult grape to make into wine, when handled with care it produces the great, sumptuous, velvety red burgundies of the Côte d'Or. The Gamay, another widely planted grape, offers up the succulent, effusively fruity, easy-to-drink and easy-to-understand wine of Beaujolais. The Chardonnay, the other major grape, produces the great white wines of Chablis and the Côte de Beaune. Grapes grown in smaller quantities in Burgundy include the Aligoté grape— planted in less hospitable sites—and the Pinot Blanc and Pinot Beurrot, also called Pinot Gris (planted in minute quantities).

FLAVORS

When it is great, Pinot Noir produces the most complex, hedonistic, and remarkably thrilling red wine in the world, but the problem is that only a tiny percentage of Burgundy's wines attain this level. At its best, the bouquet is one filled with red fruits and exotic spices, and the taste is broad, expansive, round, lush, and soft. Great burgundy always tastes sweeter than Bordeaux and has a significantly lighter color. Rarely does young burgundy have more than a medium cherry color. Gamay is not drunk for its complexity but rather for its heady, direct, ripe, soft, fleshy, exuberant fruitiness and easygoing texture. Chardonnay can range from stony and mineral-scented with high acidity in Chablis, to buttery, smoky, creamy, decadently rich and tasting of sautéed almonds and hazelnuts in a great Côte de Beaune white burgundy, to refreshingly light, lemony, floral, and thirst-quenching in the wines of Mâconnais.

AGING POTENTIAL
RED WINES
Côte de Nuits: 2–15 years
Côte de Beaune: 2–15 years
Beaujolais: 1–5 years
WHITE WINES
Chablis: 1–10 years
Côte de Beaune: 4–10 years
Mâconnais: 1–4 years

OVERALL QUALITY LEVEL
No matter which appellation one looks at in Burgundy, the range in quality from watery, poorly made, incompetent wines to majestic wines of great flavor and dimension is enormous. Burgundy is filled with precarious pitfalls for the uninformed consumer, as the number of poor and mediocre wines, while significantly less than in years past, still greatly outnumbers the amount of fine wines made.

THE MOST IMPORTANT INFORMATION TO LEARN
Consult the guide to Burgundy's best producers on pages 286–291 to avoid buying poor and mediocre wine. There are many pitfalls awaiting uninformed consumers who are seeking out the wines of Burgundy.

IMPROVEMENTS IN QUALITY

More top estates and increasing numbers of *négociants* are bottling their wines without fining and/or filtration. For the last 15 years, this issue, as well as that of overcropping, has been at the top of my Burgundy agenda. Consumers spending frightfully high sums of money for top burgundies have all too frequently been victimized by producers who have been petrified that consumers would return bottles of wine with sediment. Encouraged by their principal buyers, especially the English wine trade and European restaurateurs (astonishingly, France's sommeliers are among the worst offenders), many growers eviscerated what were majestic wines at the time of bottling by overzealous fining and filtration. This tragic, inexcusable trend has been reversed, and it is Americans who can take credit for it.

American consumers should be especially proud of the activist role small specialty burgundy importers in this country have played. Special recognition should be given to Robert Kacher Selections, David Hinkle (North Berkeley Wines), Kobrand, Inc., Louis/Dressner, Kermit Lynch Wine Merchant, Martine's Wines (Martine Saunier), Select Vineyards (Neal Rosenthal), Peter Vezan Selections (a Paris broker), Vineyard Brands (Robert Haas), and Weygandt-Metzler (Peter Weygandt). All of these importers have aggressively persuaded their growers to halt unnecessary fining and filtration if the wines are otherwise stable and clear. For many wines, Americans are getting far better burgundy cuvées than any other consumers in the world because some growers only bottle unfined and unfiltered wines for sale in America. These American specialists have seen what damage can be done to wines by excessive crop yields, overmanipulation, and aggressive fining and filtration. I still find it appalling that so many of my colleagues continue to defend the status quo, and those underachieving producers who compromise and process their wines, demonstrating little respect for the consumer. Thankfully, the tide has turned. The above-mentioned importers deserve considerable credit for insisting that the wines be bottled naturally. All of us who love wines that reflect the integrity of the varietal, vineyard, and vintage are the beneficiaries of this strong trend favoring pure, unmanipulated wine. I have no doubts that the reason so many 1991s, 1992s, and 1993s have turned out far better than most observers originally thought is that fewer wines were tampered with and/or gutted at bottling.

RECENT VINTAGES

1994—This was the fourth consecutive vintage where rain fell immediately before and during the harvest. Much of the Chardonnay crop was brought in with minimal dilution, and early reports suggest this will be a vintage of relatively low-acid, rich, high-alcohol, ripe wines that consumers will adore—somewhere between the fat rich wines of 1992 and the high-acid, somewhat hollow wines of 1993. As for the red wines, the Pinot Noir vineyards were hit hard by the heavy rains Mother Nature hurled at France during September. The wines are not expected to have the color, body, or intensity of the very good 1993s. They are optimistically reported to be somewhere between the 1992s and 1991s.

1993—Almost the exact opposite of 1994, the 1993 Chardonnay crop was abundant and sadly diluted by heavy rain immediately prior to the harvest. Many of the white wines are monolithic, lack interior flavor, and are simply shells of acidity and alcohol with light fruit and concentration. Those growers/producers who crop-thinned and had very low yields have produced wines with more depth and concentration, but overall this is an average-quality year for white burgundy. The 1993 vintage will have to be carried by the reputation of the very good reds. The red wines are unbelievably dark-colored, rich, and tannic, rather astonishing given the heavy rainstorms that pummeled the Côte d'Or in early September. The crop size was not large, and the Pinot skins were surprisingly resistant to the formation of rot as the temperatures remained cool during the harvest. While there is impressive color (as deep in most cases as the 1990s), the wines do not reveal the fat and richness possessed by the finest 1990s. There is plenty of tannin and the wines have fine structure. The 1993 burgundies will be more appreciated by readers with a Bordeaux mind-set than by those who prefer the traditional style of succulent, expansively rich, velvety-textured red burgundies. The 1993s will require patience, but the top wines should turn out to be very good, with some exceptional, because of tiny yields and highly concentrated and extracted flavors. The 1993 vintage is unlikely to be one of precocious wines, but rather, one where some aging will be required.

1992—A glorious year of big, ripe, juicy, succulent white burgundies, and, at the top quality level, remarkably charming, round, delicious, low-acid, moderately concentrated red burgundies. The white wines have moved through to the marketplace with considerable speed, not withstanding what are frightfully high prices. The red wines have been bashed by many wine-writing professionals, but the fact remains that there are plenty of top-quality, supple red wines from both the Côte de Beaune and Côte de Nuits that have been offered at the lowest prices consumers have seen in more than a decade. Careful selection of the best wines is imperative, but treasures can be found in this vintage. The 1992s need to be consumed over the next 5–8 years.

1991—The stars of this vintage are usually from the Côte de Nuits. Because of abnormally low yields (15–35 hectoliters per hectare) the top wines display excellent concentration and richness. The stars of the 1991 vintage are closer in quality to the 1990s than I would have ever believed, and are richer, fuller, more complete wines than the finest 1988s, 1987s, and 1986s. These wines, which are often priced 25%–40% below the 1990s, are worthy additions to any burgundy connoisseur's cellar. Because the yields were so low, quantities of the top wines are small. Many producers made 50% less wine than they turned out in 1990.

If the vintage has a dark side, it is the tannin level in many wines. Consumers must be careful, because balance is everything. Many 1991s possess tannin levels that may never melt away. My most enthusiastic notes and highest scores went to those wines that display rich levels of fruit to balance out the tannins. Moreover, I look for sweet, ripe tannins (always a sign of late physiological grape maturity) and I tend to be critical of wines with hard, astringent, and green (vegetal) tannin.

In the Côte de Beaune the vintage is much more difficult to peg, but there are numerous disappointments—wines that are excessively light and/or frightfully tannic and out of balance.

1990—This is a very good vintage for white burgundies, but only a handful of producers achieved greatness, because the yields were entirely too high to obtain the requisite concentration. Those growers who meticulously pruned back to restrict their yields and who picked physiologically mature fruit have made stunning wines. There are some high-class wines in Chablis, above-average-quality wines in Meursault, and good to excellent wines in Puligny-Montrachet and Chassagne-Montrachet. One appellation that enjoyed considerable success is Corton-Charlemagne, where the wines are superior to the 1989s! At the top levels, the red wines are the finest red burgundies I have ever tasted. I have never seen a vintage that is as darkly colored, with such sumptuous, rich, thick fruit. Moreover, many of the wines possess excellent structure and moderate levels of sweet tannins. The 1990 vintage is one of those rare red burgundy vintages that will offer an exceptionally broad window of drinkability. Qualitatively, it towers above such vintages as 1988 and 1985.

1989—It is a spectacular vintage for white burgundy that may ultimately prove to be the best year for the white wines of Corton-Charlemagne, Meursault, Puligny-Montrachet, and Chassagne-Montrachet in more than 20 years. The 1989 red burgundies are delicious, forward, ripe wines that are flattering at present, and in many cases better balanced and more complex than the 1988s. Not surprisingly, most growers prefer their 1989s to the 1988s. I would opt for drinking them sooner (over the next 6–9 years) than later.

1988—The question about this vintage is why so many wine writers, above all the English press (who judge burgundy as if it is Bordeaux), rated this vintage so highly. A handful of great wines have been produced that can be compared with the superb red burgundies of 1969. But what about the high yields and astringent level of tannins of the 1988s? It will be an aging race between the fruit and the tannin. In Pinot Noir, highly tannic wines usually age poorly. Burgundy enthusiasts who have stashed away quantities of 1988s are likely to be more disappointed than pleased by what they find in 5–6 years. Most Burgundy growers have already begun to express concerns about the high level of tannins, which are astringent, green, and dry, rather than soft, sweet, and mature, as in 1985 and 1990. Recent tastings of the 1988s have shown many to be excessively austere and hard. The lean, austere 1988 white burgundies recall the 1981s. If they develop along similar lines, they will be more acidic and alcoholic than fruity in 5–6 years.

1987—From the top estates, delicious, supple red wines were made, which is amazing given the fact that most producers had to harvest under heavy rain. While there are some good buys to be found, consumers remain apprehensive about the vintage's reputation. This is a mediocre year for white wines.

1986—1986 is a great year for white burgundy and an unexciting one for red burgundy. Most of the red wines possess structure and tannin, but are hollow on the mid-palate. Their lack of succulence and chewiness found in top years such as 1985 and 1990 makes them dubious choices. While the wines have held up reasonably well, I have noticed a number of examples that appear to have dropped their tannin in the last 1–2 years and are now taking on amber at the edge. I would steer clear of the 1986 red burgundies unless you have access to the few gems of this vintage.

1985—Initially proclaimed as Burgundy's vintage of the century, the white wines continue to merit the accolades they received, providing rich, sumptuous drinking. The top whites should last for another 5–7 years. Today, the red wines present a mixed bag of impressions. Some of the larger-scaled red wines appear muted, monolithic, and one-dimensional. The best of them continue to exhibit a healthy deep ruby color and good depth and weight. The lighter reds have taken on some amber at the edge, are soft and fruity, but have not developed the aromatic complexity I would have thought. The 1985 vintage has produced some outstanding wines, but as the 1985s have matured, the overall quality is mixed.

1984—All of us remember 1984. This year, like 1980, was declared by several wine writers to be a major catastrophe long before they ever tasted the wines. In 1980, the source for information was the *négociant*, Louis Latour, who had all sorts of problems with the vintage, and indeed made poor wine that year. As all burgundy lovers know, 1980 has turned out some of the most delicious and best balanced wines of the last 7–8 years, and some of the wines from the Côte de Nuits are superb. Well, 1984 is not likely to be as good as 1980, but many of the good growers have made wines that I predict will be better balanced and richer than the 1982s. The vintage was late, and everyone had to employ *chaptalisation* because the natural alcohol levels were only 9%–10%. However, the resulting red wines are often quite elegant, very cleanly made, fruity, soft, and agreeable. The yields were low because of a poor flowering. There is the normal irregularity, but the wines of the Côte de Nuits are better colored and richer than those of the Côte de Beaune. The good 1984s should have been consumed. They were not long-lived, and are dubious choices today.

1983—At the time of harvest, before any wine could be tasted, a number of critics were calling this vintage one of the greatest ever, solely on the basis of some astonishing levels of sugars in the very ripe grapes. Others based their praise on actual tasting notes. After a comprehensive tasting of the wines, one of England's most experienced burgundy writers, Clive Coates, said, "This is the sort of Burgundy vintage the world has been anxiously waiting for. They have a concentration of ripe fruit which is exhilarating. These are wines of depth, character, complexity and length." For about 5% of the red burgundies, the latter assessment was correct, but as I had advised readers of *The Wine Advocate* in August 1984, over three-fourths of the red burgundies I tasted in 1984 and again in 1985 were flawed either from the rampant rot that plagued the grapes, or by the hailstorm that wreaked havoc on some of the Côte d'Or's most famous vineyards. Twelve years after the vintage it is safe to say that 1983 is largely a failure as a red wine vintage. Far too many wines smell and taste of rot and/or are unbelievably tannic and astringent. However, this being said, the great 1983s, from producers such as Roumier, the Domaine de la Romanée-Conti, Henri Jayer, Hubert Lignier, Mongeard-Mugneret, and Ponsot, should provide some of the longest-lived wines of the last three decades. Yet this is a vintage to approach with the greatest of caution.

BURGUNDY'S GREATEST RED WINES

Bertrand Ambroise Corton Les Rognets

Bertrand Ambroise Nuits St.-Georges Les
   Vaucrains

Robert Arnoux Vosne-Romanée Les
   Suchots

Fougeray de Beauclair Bonnes Mares

Bourée Père et Fils Charmes-Chambertin

Bourée Père et Fils Clos de la Roche

Jean Chauvenet Nuits St.-Georges Les
   Vaucrains

Chopin-Groffier Clos de Vougeot

J. J. Confuron Romanée St.-Vivant

J. Confuron-Cotetidot Clos de Vougeot

J. Confuron-Cotetidot Echézeaux

Claude et Maurice Dugat
   Charmes-Chambertin

Claude et Maurice Dugat
   Gevrey-Chambertin Lavaux St.-Jacques

Claude et Maurice Dugat
   Griottes-Chambertin

Dujac Bonnes Mares

Dujac Clos de la Roche

Dujac Clos St.-Denis

Michel Esmonin Gevrey-Chambertin Clos St.-Jacques

Jean Grivot Clos de Vougeot

A.-F. Gros Echézeaux

A.-F. Gros Richebourg

Anne et François Gros Clos de Vougeot Le Grand Maupertius

Anne et François Gros Richebourg

Jean Gros Clos de Vougeot

Jean Gros Richebourg

Gros Frère et Soeur Clos de Vougeot de Musigny

Gros Frère et Soeur Richebourg

Haegelen-Jayer Clos de Vougeot

† Hospices de Beaune Beaune Nicolas Rollin

† Hospices de Beaune Corton Charlotte Dumay

† Hospices de Beaune Mazis-Chambertin

† Hospices de Beaune Pommard Dames de la Charité

† Hospices de Beaune Savigny-Les-Beaune Arthur Girard

† Hospices de Beaune Volnay Santenots Jehan de Massol

Louis Jadot Beaune Clos des Ursules

Louis Jadot Bonnes Mares

Louis Jadot Corton-Pougets

Louis Jadot Gevrey-Chambertin Clos St.-Jacques

Henri Jayer Richebourg

Henri Jayer Vosne-Romanée Les Brûlées

Henri Jayer Vosne-Romanée Cros Parantoux

Jayer-Gilles Echézeaux

Jayer-Gilles Nuits St.-Georges Les Damodes

Jayer-Gilles Nuits St.-Georges Les Hauts Poirets

Michel Lafarge Volnay Les Chênes

Michel Lafarge Volnay Clos du Château des Ducs

Comte Lafon Volnay Champans

Comte Lafon Volnay Santenots

Domaine Lecheneaut Clos de la Roche

Domaine Lecheneaut Nuits St.-Georges Les Cailles

Domaine Lecheneaut Nuits St.-Georges Les Damodes

Philippe Leclerc Gevrey-Chambertin Les Cazetiers

Philippe Leclerc Gevrey-Chambertin Combe aux Moines

Domaine Lejeune Pommard Les Rugiens

Leroy Chambertin

Leroy Clos de la Roche

Leroy Clos de Vougeot

Leroy Corton Les Rénardes

Leroy Latricières-Chambertin

Leroy Mazis-Chambertin

Leroy Nuits St.-Georges Les Boudots

Leroy Richebourg

Leroy Romanée St.-Vivant

Leroy Savigny-Les-Beaune Les Narbantons

Leroy Volnay Santenots

Leroy Vosne-Romanée Les Beaux Monts

Leroy Vosne-Romanée Les Brûlées

Hubert Lignier Charmes-Chambertin

Hubert Lignier Clos de la Roche

Domaine Jean Méo-Camuzet Clos de Vougeot

Domaine Jean Méo-Camuzet Richebourg

Domaine Jean Méo-Camuzet Vosne-Romanée Les Brûlées

Domaine Jean Méo-Camuzet Vosne-Romanée Cros Parantoux

Mongeard-Mugneret Richebourg

Jacques-Frédéric Mugnier Bonnes Mares

Jacques-Frédéric Mugnier Musigny

A. Mussy Pommard Epenots

Ponsot Chambertin

Ponsot Clos de la Roche Vieilles Vignes

Ponsot Clos St.-Denis Vieilles Vignes

Ponsot Griottes-Chambertin

Pothier-Rieusset Pommard Rugiens

Pousse d'Or Volnay La Bousse d'Or

Domaine de la Romanée-Conti Grands Echézeaux

Domaine de la Romanée-Conti Romanée-Conti

---

† The Hospices de Beaune wines are sold in cask to different buyers. Between 1978 and 1987 the quality of the Hospices' wines was superb, but between 1988 and 1994, the wines have lacked richness, structure, and concentration. The talented André Porcheret was rehired (he resigned from the Domaine Leroy in 1993) and was responsible for the 1994 vintage at the Hospices.

Domaine de la Romanée-Conti La Tâche
Joseph Roty Charmes-Chambertin
Joseph Roty Mazis-Chambertin
Emmanuel Rouget Echézeaux
Emmanuel Rouget Vosne-Romanée Cros
  Parantoux
Georges et Christophe Roumier Bonnes
  Mares
Georges et Christophe Roumier
  Chambolle-Musigny Les Amoureuses
Georges et Christophe Roumier
  Ruchottes-Chambertin
Armand Rousseau Chambertin

Armand Rousseau Chambertin Clos de
  Bèze
Armand Rousseau Gevrey-Chambertin
  Clos St.-Jacques
Christian Serafin Charmes-Chambertin
Christian Serafin Gevrey-Chambertin Les
  Cazetiers
Château de la Tour Clos de Vougeot
  Vieilles Vignes
Truchot-Martin Charmes-Chambertin
  Vieilles Vignes
Comte de Vogüé Musigny Vieilles Vignes
  (prior to 1973 and after 1989)

RATING THE RED BURGUNDY GROWERS, PRODUCERS, AND *NÉGOCIANTS*

No one will ever have a great deal of success selecting a burgundy without a thorough knowledge of the finest growers and *négociants*. The most meticulous producers often make better wine in mediocre vintages than many less dedicated growers and producers make in great vintages. Knowing the finest producers in Burgundy is unquestionably the most important factor in your success in finding the best wines.

The following is a guide to the best red and white burgundy producers. Consistency from year to year and among the producers' total range of wines were the most important considerations. One should be cognizant of the fact that many lower-rated producers may make specific wines that are qualitatively above their placement.

Note: Where a producer has been assigned a range of stars, ***/**** for example, the lower rating has been used for placement in this hierarchy.

RATING BURGUNDY'S RED WINE PRODUCERS

* * * * * *(OUTSTANDING)*

Jean-Jacques Confuron
  (Prémeaux)
Domaine Daniel Chopin-Groffier
  (Prémeaux)
Domaine Claude et Maurice Dugat
  (Gevrey-Chambertin)
Domaine Henri Jayer (Vosne-Romanée)
Domaine Robert Jayer-Gilles
  (Magny-Les-Villers)
Domaine Comte Lafon (Meursault)

Domaine Leroy (Vosne-Romanée)
Domaine Hubert Lignier (Morey St.-Denis)
Domaine Jean Méo-Camuzet
  (Vosne-Romanée)
Domaine Ponsot (Morey St.-Denis)
Domaine de la Romanée-Conti
  (Vosne-Romanée)
Domaine Comte de Vogüé
  (Chambolle-Musigny) (before 1973 and
  after 1989)

* * * * *(EXCELLENT)*

Domaine Bertrand Ambroise
  (Prémeaux)
Amiot-Servelle (Chambolle-Musigny)
Domaine Marquis d'Angerville (Volnay)
Domaine de l'Arlot (Prémeaux)
Domaine Robert Arnoux (Vosne-Romanée)

Domaine Barthod-Noëllat
  (Chambolle-Musigny)
Domaine Bourée Père et Fils
  (Gevrey-Chambertin)
Domaine Jacques Cacheux-Blée et Fils
  (Vosne-Romanée)

Château de Chambolle-Musigny
(Chambolle-Musigny)

Domaine Jean Chauvenet (Nuits
St.-Georges)

Chézeaux (Morey St.-Denis)

Domaine Georges Chicotot (Nuits
St.-Georges)

Domaine J. Confuron-Cotetidot
(Vosne-Romanée)

Domaine Dujac (Morey St.-Denis)

Domaine Maurice Ecard et Fils
(Savigny-Les-Beaune)

Domaine René Engel (Vosne-Romanée)

Domaine Michel Esmonin et Fille
(Gevrey-Chambertin)

Domaine Jean Faurois (Vosne-Romanée)

Domaine Michel Gaunoux (Pommard)

Domaine Pierre Gelin (Fixin)

Domaine Armand Girardin (Pommard)

Machard de Gramont (Nuits St.-Georges)

Domaine Jean Grivot (Vosne-Romanée)

Domaine Haegelen-Jayer (Vosne-
Romanée)****/*****

Hospices de Beaune (Beaune)

Hospices de Nuits (Nuits St.-Georges)

Domaine Alain Hudelot-Noëllat (Vougeot)

Louis Jadot (Beaune)****/*****

Domaine Joblot (Givry)

Domaine Michel Lafarge
(Volnay)****/*****

Domaine Dominique Laurent (Nuits
St.-Georges)****/*****

Domaine Lecheneaut
(Nuits St.-Georges)****/*****

Domaine Philippe Leclerc
(Gevrey-Chambertin)****/*****

René Leclerc (Gevrey-Chambertin)

Domaine Lejeune (Pommard)****/*****

Domaine Meix Foulot (Mercurey)

Domaine Prince Florent de Mérode
(Ladoix-Serrigny)

Domaine Mongeard-Mugneret
(Vosne-Romanée)****/*****

Domaine Albert Morot (Beaune)

Domaine Mugneret-Gibourg
(Vosne-Romanée)

Domaine André Mussy
(Pommard)****/*****

Domaine Pernin-Rossin (Vosne-Romanée)

Domaine Les Perrières
(Gevrey-Chambertin)

Domaine Pothier-Rieusset (Pommard)

Domaine Michel Prunier (Auxey-
Duresses)

Domaine Daniel Rion (Nuits St.-Georges)

Domaine Joseph Roty
(Gevrey-Chambertin)****/*****

Domaine Emanuel Rouget (Nuits
St.-Georges)****/*****

Domaine Georges et Christophe Roumier
(Chambolle-Musigny)

Domaine Armand Rousseau
(Gevrey-Chambertin)

Domaine Christian Serafin
(Gevrey-Chambertin)****/*****

Château de la Tour (Vougeot)****

Domaine J. Truchot-Martin (Morey
St.-Denis)

*** *** *(GOOD)*

Bernard Amiot (Chambolle-
Musigny)

Domaine Comte Armand (Pommard)

Domaine Ballot-Millot (Meursault)

Fougeray de Beauclair (Marsannay)

Château de Beauregard (Fuissé)

Domaine Joseph Belland (Santenay)

Domaine Pierre Bertheau
(Chambolle-Musigny)***/****

Besancenot-Mathouillet (Beaune)

Domaine Bitouzet-Prieur (Volnay)

Domaine Simon Bize et Fils
(Savigny-Les-Beaune)***

Domaine Marcel Bocquenet (Nuits
St.-Georges)

Domaine Henri Boillot (Pommard)

Domaine Jean Boillot (Volnay)

Domaine Jean-Marc Boillot (Pommard)

Domaine Pierre Boillot (Meursault)

Domaine Bonnot-Lamblot
(Savigny-Les-Beaune)

Domaine Bordeaux-Montrieux (Mercurey)

Domaine Bouchard Père et Fils (Beaune)

Domaine Jean-Marc Bouley (Volnay)

Domaine Denis Boussey (Monthelie)

Domaine Jean-Claude Brelière (Rully)

Georges Bryczek (Morey St.-Denis)

Alain Burguet (Gevrey-Chambertin)

Domaine Guy Castagnier (Morey
St.-Denis)***/****

Domaine Cathiard-Molinier
(Vosne-Romanée)

Domaine Ceci (Vougeot)

Domaine Émile Chandesais (Fontaines)

Domaine Chandon de Briailles
(Savigny-Les-Beaune)

Domaine Chanson Père et Fils (Beaune)

Domaine Maurice Chapuis (Aloxe-Corton)

Domaine Philippe Charlopin-Parizot
(Marsannay)

Domaine Jean Chartron
(Puligny-Montrachet)

Georges et Michel Chevillon (Nuits
St.-Georges)

Robert Chevillon (Nuits St.-Georges)

Domaine Bruno Clair (Marsannay)

Domaine Michel Clair (Santenay)

Domaine Michel Clerget (Vougeot)

Domaine Coche-Bizouard (Meursault)

Domaine J. F. Coche-Dury
(Meursault) ***/****

Domaine Les Colombiers (Saint-Véran)

Domaine Edmond Cornu (Ladoix-Serrigny)

Domaine Coron Père et Fils (Beaune)

Domaine Coste-Caumartin (Pommard)

Domaine de Madame de Courcel
(Pommard)

Domaine Pierre Damoy
(Gevrey-Chambertin) ***/**** (since
1993)

Domaine Marius Delarche
(Pernand-Vergelesses) ***/****

Domaine Jean-Pierre Diconne
(Auxey-Duresses)

Domaine Joseph Drouhin
(Beaune) ***/****

Domaine Drouhin-Larose
(Gevrey-Chambertin)

Jean-Luc Dubois (Savigny-Les-Beaune)

Domaine P. Dubreuil-Fontaine et Fils
(Pernand-Vergelesses)

Domaine Duchet (Beaune)

Domaine Pierre Dugat
(Gevrey-Chambertin)

Domaine M. Frederic Esmonin
(Gevrey-Chambertin)

Faiveley (Nuits St.-Georges)

Domaine Bernard Fèvre (Saint-Romain)

Domaine Fichet (Volnay)

Domaine René Fleurot-Larose (Santenay)

Domaine de la Folie (Rully)

Domaine Jean Garaudet
(Pommard) ***/****

Domaine du Gardin-Clos Salomon (Givry)

Philippe Gavignat (Nuits St-Georges)

Geantet-Pansiot (Gevrey-
Chambertin) ****

Domaine Lucien Geoffroy
(Gevrey-Chambertin)

Domaine François Gerbet
(Vosne-Romanée)

Domaine Jacques Germain
(Chorey-Les-Beaune)

Domaine Jacques Girardin (Santenay)

Domaine Bernard Glantenay (Volnay)

Domaine Michel Goubard (Saint-Desert)

Domaine Bertrand de Gramont (Nuits
St.-Georges)

Domaine Alain Gras (Saint-Romain)

Domaine Robert Groffier (Morey St.-Denis)

Domaine A.-F.Gros (Pommard)

Domaine Anne et François Gros
(Vosne-Romané)

Domaine Jean Gros (Vosne-
Romanée) ***/****

Domaine Gros Frère et Soeur
(Vosne-Romanée) ***/****

Domaine Pierre Guillemot
(Savigny-Les-Beaune)

Domaine Heresztyn (Gevrey-Chambertin)

Domaine Alain Hudelot-Noëllat
(Vougeot) ***/****

Paul et Henri Jacqueson (Rully) ***/****

Domaine Georges Jayer (Vosne-Romanée)

Domaine Jacqueline Jayer
(Vosne-Romanée)

Domaine Lucien Jayer (Vosne-Romanée)

Domaine Jeannin-Naltet Père et Fils
(Mercurey)

Domaine Philippe Joliet (Fixin)

Domaine Jean-Luc Joillot-Porcheray
(Pommard)

Domaine Michel Juillot (Mercurey)

Domaine François Labet (Vougeot)

Domaine Labouré-Roi (Nuits
St.-Georges)

Domaine Lafouge (Auxey-Duresses)

Domaine Laleure-Piot Père et Fils
(Pernand-Vergelesses)

Domaine Lamarche (Vosne-Romanée)

Domaine Hubert Lamy (Saint-Aubin)

Domaine Louis Latour (Beaune)

Olivier Leflaive Frères
(Puligny-Montrachet)

Domaine François Legros (Nuits
St.-Georges)

Domaine Lequin-Roussot (Santenay)

Domaine Thierry Lespinasse (Givry)

Domaine Georges Lignier (Morey
St.-Denis)

Loron et Fils (Pontanevaux)

Château de la Maltroye
(Chassagne-Montrachet)

Domaine Manière-Noirot (Vosne-Romanée)

Tim Marshall (Nuits St.-Georges)

Domaine Joseph Matrot (Meursault)

Domaine Maume (Gevrey-
Chambertin) ***/****

Domaine Michel (Vosne-Romanée)

Domaine Alain Michelot (Nuits
St.-Georges)

Domaine Jean Michelot (Pommard)

Michael Modot (Chambolle-Musigny)

Domaine Daniel Moine-Hudelot
(Chambolle-Musigny)

Domaine de la Monette (Mercurey)

Domaine Bernard Morey
(Chassagne-Montrachet)

Domaine Denis Mortet
(Gevrey-Chambertin)

Domaine Gérard et René Mugneret
(Vosne-Romanée)

Philippe Naddef (Couchey) ***/****

Domaine André Nudant et Fils
(Ladoix-Serigny)

Domaine Parent (Pommard)

Domaine Parigot Père et Fils (Meloisey)

Domaine Pavelot-Glantenay
(Savigny-Les-Beaune)

Domaine des Perdrix (Prémeaux-Prissey)

Domaine des Pierres Blanches (Beaune)

Domaine de la Pousse d'Or
(Volnay) ***/****

Domaine Jacques Prieur (Meursault)
/* (since 1990)

Domaine Prieur-Brunet (Santenay)

Domaine Henri Prudhon (Saint-Aubin)

Domaine Ramonet (Chassagne-Montrachet)

Remoissenet Père et Fils (Beaune)

Domaine Henri Remoriquet
(Nuits St.-Georges)

Domaine Arnelle et Bernard Rion
(Vosne-Romanée)

Antonin Rodet (Mercurey) ***/**** (since
1990)

Domaine Michel Rossignol (Volnay)

Domaine Philippe Rossignol
(Gevrey-Chambertin)

Domaine Régis Rossignol-Changarnier
(Volnay)

Domaine Rossignol-Trapet
(Gevrey-Chambertin)

Domaine Rougeot (Meursault)

Domaine Roux Père et Fils (Saint-Aubin)

Château de Rully (Rully)

Domaine Daniel Senard (Aloxe-Corton)

Domaine Bernard Serveau (Morey
St.-Denis) ***/****

Domaine Servelle-Tachot
(Chambolle-Musigny)

Domaine Robert Sirugue
(Vosne-Romanée)

Domaine Jean Tardy (Vosne-Romanée)

Domaine Thevenot-Le-Brun et Fils
(Marey-Les-Fussey)

Domaine Gérard Thomas (Saint-Aubin)

Domaine Tollot-Beaut et Fils
(Chorey-Les-Beaune) ***/****

Domaine Jean et J. L. Trapet
(Gevrey-Chambertin)

Domaine Michel Voarick (Aloxe-Corton)

Domaine Joseph Voillot (Volnay)

Domaine Leni Volpato
(Chambolle-Musigny)

* * (AVERAGE)

Pierre Amiot et Fils
(Morey St.-Denis) **/***

Domaine Pierre André (Aloxe-Corton)

Domaine Arlaud Père et Fils (Nuits
St.-Georges)

Domaine Arnoux Père et Fils
(Chorey-Les-Beaune)

Domaine Denis Bachelet
(Gevrey-Chambertin) **/***

Domaine André Bart (Marsannay)

Domaine Philippe Batacchi
(Gevrey-Chambertin)

Domaine Adrien Belland
(Santenay) **/***

Domaine Bertagna (Vougeot)

Domaine Denis Berthaut (Fixin)

Domaine Albert Bichot (Beaune)*/****

Domaine Billard-Gonnet (Pommard)

Domaine Pierre Bitouzet
    (Savigny-Les-Beaune)

Domaine de Blagny (Blagny)

Domaine Lucien Boillot et Fils
    (Gevrey-Chambertin)

Domaine Jean-Claude Boisset (Nuits
    St.-Georges))*/**

Domaine Bouchard-Ainé et Fils
    (Beaune)

Domaine Michel Briday (Rully)

Domaine Marc Brocot (Marsannay)

Domaine Camus (Gevrey-Chambertin)

Domaine Luc Camus
    (Savigny-Les-Beaune)

Domaine Lucien Camus-Bauchon
    (Savigny-Les-Beaune)

Domaine Capitain-bagnerot
    (Ladoix-Serrigny)

Domaine Capron-Manieux
    (Savigny-Les-Beaune)

Domaine Chanzy Frères-Domaine de
    l'Hermitage (Bouzeron)

F. Chauvenet (Nuits St.-Georges)

Bruno Clavelier-Brosson (Vosne-Romanée)

Domaine Georges Clerget (Vougeot)

Domaine Yvon Clerget (Volnay)

Domaine Clos Frantin-Bichot
    (Vosne-Romanée)**/*****

Domaine Clos des Lambrays
    (Morey St.-Denis)

Domaine Michel Clunny et Fils (Brochon)

Domaine Coquard-Loison-Fleurot
    (Flagey-Echézeaux)**/***

Domaine Claude Cornu
    (Magny-Les-Villers)

Domaine Gérard Creusefond
    (Auxey-Duresses)

Domaine David et Foillard
    (St.-Georges-de-Reneins)

Domaine Denis Père et Fils
    (Pernand-Vergelesses)

Domaine Doudet-Naudin
    (Savigny-Les-Beaune)

Dufouleur Père et Fils (Nuits St.-Georges)

Domaine Dupont-Tisserandot
    (Gevrey-Chambertin)

Domaine René Durand (Comblanchien)

Domaine Jacques Durand-Roblot
    (Fixin)

Domaine Dureuil-Janthial (Rully)

Domaine Forey Père et Fils
    (Vosne-Romanée)

Dedier Fournerol (Nuits St.-Georges)

Domaine Jean-Claude Fourrier
    (Gevrey-Chambertin)

Domaine Gay Père et Fils
    (Chorey-Les-Beaune)

Domaine Geisweiler et Fils (Nuits
    St.-Georges)

Domaine Maurice et Jean-Michel Giboulot
    (Savigny-Les-Beaune)

Domaine Girard-Vollot et Fils
    (Savigny-Les-Beaune)

Domaine Henri Gouges (Nuits St.-Georges)

Domaine Jean Guitton
    (Bligny-Les-Beaune)

Domaine Antonin Guyon
    (Savigny-Les-Beaune)

Domaine Hubert Guyot-Verpiot (Rully)

Château Philippe Le Hardi (Santenay)

Domaine des Hautes-Cornières (Santenay)

Domaine André l'Heritier (Chagny)

Domaine Huguenot Père et Fils
    (Marsannay)

Domaine Frederick Humbert
    (Gevrey-Chambertin)

Domaine Lucien Jacob (Echevronne)

Jaffelin (Beaune)

Domaine Jessiaume Père et Fils
    (Santenay)

Domaine Henri Lafarge (Bray)

Domaine Lahaye Père et Fils (Pommard)

René Lamy-Pillot (Santenay)

Domaine Henri Latour (Auxey-Duresses)

Domaine Lumpp Frères (Givry)

Domaine Lupé-Cholet (Nuits St.-Georges)

Lycée Agricole et Viticole (Beaune)

Domaine Henri Magnien
    (Gevrey-Chambertin)

Domaine Michel Magnien (Morey
    St.-Denis)

Domaine Maillard Père et Fils
    (Chorey-Les-Beaune)

Domaine Maldant (Chorey-Les-Beaune)

Domaine Michel Mallard et Fils
    (Ladoix-Serigny)

Domaine Yves Marceau-Domaine de la
    Croix Gault (Mercurey)

Domaine Marchand-Grillot et Fils
(Gevrey-Chambertin)
P. de Marcilly Frères (Beaune)
Domaine Jean Marechal (Mercurey)
Domaine Mazilly Père et Fils (Meloisey)
Domaine Louis Menand Père et Fils
(Mercurey)
Domaine Mestre Père et Fils (Santenay)
Alain Michelot (Nuits St.-Georges) **/***
Domaine Pierre Millot-Battault (Meursault)
P. Misserey (Nuits St.-Georges)
Moillard (Nuits St.-Georges) **/****
Château de Monthélie (Monthélie)
Domaine Monthélie-Douhairet (Monthélie)
Domaine Hubert de Montille
(Volnay) **/***
Domaine Jean Moreau (Santenay)
Frédéric Mugneret (Château
Chambolle-Musigny)
(Chambolle-Musigny)
Domaine Gabriel Muskovac
(Pernand-Vergelesses)
Domaine Newman (Morey St.-Denis)
Domaine Patriarche Père et Fils (Beaune)
Domaine Pavelot (Pernand-Vergelesses)
Domaine Paul Pernot
(Puligny-Montrachet)
Domaine Henri Perrot-Minot
(Morey St.-Denis)
Château de Pommard (Pommard) **/***
Domaine de la Poulette (Corgoloin)
Domaine du Prieuré (Rully)
Domaine du Prieuré (Savigny-Les-Beaune)
Prosper-Maufoux (Santenay)
Domaine Maurice Protheau et Fils
(Mercurey)
Domaine Roger Prunier (Auxey-Duresses)
Max Quenot Fils et Meuneveaux
(Aloxe-Corton)

Domaine Charles Quillardet
(Gevrey-Chambertin)
Domaine Gaston et Pierre Ravaut
(Ladoix-Serigny)
Domaine Rebougeon-Mure (Pommard)
Domaine Henri Rebourseau
(Gevrey-Chambertin)
La Reine Pedauque (Aloxe-Corton)
Domaine Louis Remy (Gevrey-Chambertin)
Domaine Henri Richard
(Gevrey-Chambertin)
Domaine Maurice Rollin Père et Fils
(Pernand-Vergelesses)
Domaine Hervé Roumier
(Chambolle-Musigny)
Domaine Roy Frères (Auxey-Duresses)
Domaine Roy Père et Fils
(Gevrey-Chambertin)
Domaine Fabian et Louis Saier (Mercurey)
Domaine Maurice et Hervé Sigaut
(Chambolle-Musigny)
Domaine Suremain (Mercurey)
Domaine Taupenot Père et Fils
(Saint-Romain)
Domaine Tortochot (Gevrey-Chambertin)
Domaine Louis Trapet
(Gevrey-Chambertin)
Domaine G. Vachet-Rousseau
(Gevrey-Chambertin)
Domaine des Varoilles
(Gevrey-Chambertin) **/***
Domaine Henri de Villamont
(Savigny-Les-Beaune)
Domaine Emile Voarick
(Saint-Martin-Sous-Montaigu)
Domaine Alain Voegeli
(Gevrey-Chambertin)
Domaine André Ziltener Père et Fils
(Gevrey-Chambertin)

Where Are Burgundy's Red Wine Values?

The glamour appellations of the Côte de Nuits and the Côte de Beaune offer exorbitant prices as well as irregular quality. If values are to be found, consumers must look beyond the most prestigious names and most renowned appellations, searching out some of the less highly acclaimed appellations. Following are some producers to check out in the Côte de Nuits, Côte de Beaune, and possibly the best source of red and white burgundies, the Côte Chalonnaise, located just south of the Côte d'Or.

Marsannay Appellation (Côte de Nuits) You are not likely to find great wines from this appellation, but good producers can make wines that are far above the normal quality level, which means something better than the compact, straightforward, hard, charmless Pinot Noirs that often emanate from Marsannay. Look for the following Marsannays that can still be purchased for under $20 a bottle.

The best producers include Regis Bouvier—Marsannay Clos du Roy, Marsannay Vieilles Vignes; Marc Brocot—Marsannay; Bruno Clair—Marsannay, Marsannay Les Longerois, Marsannay Vaudenelles; Jean-Pierre Guyard—Marsannay Les Recilles; Louis Jadot—Marsannay; Philippe Naddef—Marsannay.

Fixin Appellation (Côte de Nuits)   It may be situated next to the famed appellation Gevrey-Chambertin, but Fixin has never overcome its reputation of producing exceptionally robust, sturdy, muscular wines that are short on finesse. However, some producers excel in producing wines with serious flavor and balance.

The best producers include André Bart—Fixin Les Hervelets; Denis Berthaut—Fixin Les Arvelets, Fixin Les Clos, Fixin Les Crais; Bruno Clair—Fixin; Faiveley—Fixin; Pierre Gelin—Fixin Clos du Chapitre, Fixin Clos Napoleon, Fixin Les Hervelets; Philippe Joliet —Fixin Clos de la Perrière; Mongeard-Mugneret—Fixin.

Ladoix Appellation (Côte de Beaune)   Ladoix is Burgundy's least-known appellation, making it one of the more attractive places to shop, but you must know the right addresses. Amazingly, the best Pinot Noirs here cost less than Pinot Noirs from California and Oregon. This is not an appellation to buy blindly, as the wines can be dusty and earthy, with too little fruit.

The best producers include Capitain-Gagnerot—Ladoix, Ladoix Les Micaudes; Chevalier Père et Fils—Ladoix Premier Cru; Edmond Cornu—Ladoix, Ladoix Premier Cru; Michel Mallard—Ladoix Les Joyeuses; André Nudant—Ladoix Premier Cru; Gaston et Pierre Ravaut—Ladoix Les Corvées.

Savigny-Les-Beaune (Côte de Beaune)   Savigny-Les-Beaune has a good reputation for light, berry-scented (primarily cherry) wines that at their worst can have an overwhelming rusty, earthy undertone. The vineyards on the northern hillsides overlooking the Rhoin River, which cuts this appellation in half, produce the finest wine. Most sell for prices between $18 and $25 a bottle. They are not as inexpensive as Marsannay or Ladoix, but at their best they exhibit considerably more complexity as well as a compelling Pinot Noir perfume.

The best producers include Simon Bize—Savigny-Les-Beaune Les Guettes, Savigny-Les-Beaune Premier Cru, Savigny-Les-Beaune aux Vergelesses; Bonnot-Lamblot—Savigny-Les-Beaune Les Dominaudes; Capron-Manieux—Savigny-Les-Beaune Les Lavières; Chandon de Briailles—Savigny-Les-Beaune Les Lavières; Chanson—Savigny-Les-Beaune Les Dominaudes; Bruno Clair—Savigny-Les-Beaune Les Dominaudes; Doudet-Naudin—Savigny-Les-Beaune Les Guettes; Joseph Drouhin—Savigny-Les-Beaune Premier Cru; Maurice Ecard—Savigny-Les-Beaune Les Narbantons, Savigny-Les-Beaune Les Serpentières; J. M. Giboulot—Savigny-Les-Beaune Les Serpentières; Machard de Gramont—Savigny-Les-Beaune Les Guettes; Pierre Guillemot— Savigny-Les-Beaune Les Jarrons, Savigny-Les-Beaune Les Serpentières; Hospices de Beaune—Savigny-Les-Beaune Cuvée Forneret, Savigny-Les-Beaune Cuvée Fouquerand, Savigny-Les-Beaune Cuvée Arthur Girard; Louis Jadot—Savigny-Les-Beaune Les Dominaudes; Albert Morot—Savigny-Les-Beaune Les Vergelesses Clos la Bataillère; Pavelot-Glantenay—Savigny-Les-Beaune Les Dominaudes, Savigny-Les-Beaune Beaune Les Guettes; Jean Pichenot—Savigny-Les-Beaune; Tollot-Beaut—Savigny-Les-Beaune Les Lavières.

Monthélie Appellation (Côte de Beaune)   The vineyards of Monthélie are adjacent to Volnay, yet the wines could not be more different. The old-style Monthélies are plagued by excessive tannin and body, but a younger generation of winemakers is bringing out the wines' fruit and character, hoping that consumers will make the 1- to 2-minute trek from the neighboring villages of Volnay and Pommard to take a look at this hilltop village where most red burgundies can still be bought for under $20–$25 a bottle.

The best producers include Eric Boussey—Monthélie; J. F. Coche-Dury—Monthélie; Louis Deschamps—Monthélie Les Mandenes; Gérard Doreau—Monthélie Les Champs Fulliot; Jean Garaudet—Monthélie; Hospices de Beaune—Monthélie Cuvée Lebelin; Louis Jadot—Monthélie; Jehan-Changarnier—Monthélie; Comte Lafon—Monthélie; Pernin-Rossin—Monthélie; Henri Potinet-Ampeau—Monthélie; Eric de Suremain—Monthélie Château de Monthélie, Monthélie Sur La Velle.

Auxey-Duresses (Côte de Beaune)   Auxey-Duresses has often been described as the poor person's Volnay. Such comments are pejorative and tend to irritate the local vignerons, who are proud of their spicy, robust, black cherry–scented and –flavored wine that often possesses surprising aging potential. The key is ripe fruit. If the fruit is not ripe when picked, the tannins tend to be green and the acids can reach shrill levels.

The best producers include Robert Ampeau—Auxey-Duresses Ecussaux; Jean-Pierre Diconne—Auxey-Duresses; Hospices de Beaune—Auxey-Duresses Cuvée Boillot; Domaine Jessiaume—Auxey-Duresses Ecussaux; Domaine Lafouge—Auxey-Duresses La Chapelle; Leroy—Auxey-Duresses; Duc de Magenta (Jadot)—Auxey-Duresses; Maroslavic-Leger—Auxey-Duresses Les Bréterins; Pernin-Rossin—Auxey-Duresses; Michel Prunier—Auxey-Duresses Clos du Val; Roy Frères—Auxey-Duresses Le Val; René Thevenin—Auxey-Duresses Clos du Moulin aux Moines.

Chassagne-Montrachet (Côte de Beaune)   The downside to Chassagne-Montrachet's fame as one of Burgundy's great white wine villages is that few people pay attention to the tasty red wines with their Bing cherry, almond, earthy fruitiness. There are premiers crus that can be bought for $25 a bottle, making this an interesting market. Most red Chassagnes also have the virtue of lasting for 10 years in a top vintage.

The best producers include Jean-Noël Gagnard—Chassagne-Montrachet Clos de la Maltroie, Chassagne-Montrachet Clos St.-Jean; Duc de Magenta (Louis Jadot)—Chassagne-Montrachet Clos de la Chapelle; Château de la Maltroye—Chassagne-Montrachet Clos de la Boudriotte, Chassagne-Montrachet Clos du Château, Chassagne-Montrachet Clos St.-Jean; Paul Pillot—Chassagne-Montrachet Clos St.-Jean; Domaine Ramonet—Chassagne-Montrachet Clos de la Boudriotte; Domaine Roux—Chassagne-Montrachet Clos St.-Jean.

Saint-Romain Appellation (Côte de Beaune)   Although this quaint village is off the beaten track, it is only a 10-minute drive from either Meursault or Volnay. It is worth the extra effort to visit, as some tasty, bargain-priced burgundies can be found, white burgundy being Saint-Romain's claim to fame—today.

The best producers include Bernard Fèvre—Saint-Romain; Alain Gras—Saint-Romain; Taupenot Père et Fils—Saint-Romain; René Thévenin—Monthélie Saint-Romain.

Saint-Aubin Appellation (Côte de Beaune)   Saint-Aubin is a true burgundy lover's paradise. Filled with young, talented, ambitious growers, it produces a number of wines that sell for well under $25 a bottle. The red wines can be surprisingly robust, full, concentrated, and chewy.

The best producers include Jean-Claude Bachelet—Saint-Aubin Derrière la Tour; Raoul Clerget—Saint-Aubin Les Frionnes; Marc Colin—Saint-Aubin; Lamy-Pillot—Saint-Aubin; Langoureau (Gilles Bouton)—Saint-Aubin en Remilly; Henri Prudhon—Saint-Aubin Les Frionnes, Saint-Aubin Sentiers de Clou; Domaine Roux Père et Fils—Saint-Aubin; Gérard Thomas—Saint-Aubin Les Frionnes.

Rully (Côte Chalonnaise)   As with any appellation, one has to be well informed, but the spicy, cherry, strawberry, dusty aromas and flavors of a good Rully can be purchased for prices in the mid-teens.

The best producers include Michel Briday—Rully; Domaine de la Folie—Rully Clos de

Bellecroix; Jacqueson—Rully Les Chaponnières, Rully Les Cloux; Domaine de la Rénarde —Rully Premier Cru; Antonin Rodet—Rully; Château de Rully—Rully; Domaine de Rully St.-Michel—Rully Les Champs Cloux, Rully Clos de Pelleret.

Mercurey (Côte Chalonnaise)   Mercurey prices have risen to $25 a bottle as the world has begun to discover the progress Mercurey producers have made. This is an up-and-coming source of good wines.

The best producers include Château de Chamirey—Mercurey; Charton et Trébuchet—Mercurey Clos des Hayes; Faiveley—Mercurey Clos des Myglands, Mercurey Clos du Roi, Mercurey La Croix Jacquelet, Mercurey La Framboisière, Mercurey Les Mauvarennes; Michel Juillot—Mercurey Clos des Barraults, Mercurey Clos Tonnerre; Domaine de Meix Foulot—Mercurey Clos du Château de Montaigu, Mercurey Les Veleys; Domaine de la Monette—Mercurey; Domaine de Suremain—Mercurey Clos L'Eveque, Mercurey Clos Voyen.

Givry Appellation (Côte Chalonnaise)   Givry has two of the finest winemakers in all of Burgundy, Monsieur Joblot and Monsieur Lespinasse. Both are making wines that compete with some of the finest of the Côte d'Or. They have caused a popular boom in this backwater appellation.

The best producers include Jean Chofflet—Givry; Domaine Joblot—Givry Clos du Bois Chevaux, Givry Clos du Cellier aux Moines, Givry Clos de la Servoisine; Louis Latour —Givry; Thierry Lespinasse—Givry en Choué; Gérard Mouton—Givry; Domaine Veuve Steinmaier—Givry Clos de la Baraude; Domaine Thenard—Givry Cellier aux Moines, Givry Clos Saint-Pierre, Givry Les Bois Chevaux.

Santenay Appellation (Côte de Beaune)   It is amazing that Santenay continues to have problems overcoming its image as the last of the Côte d'Or appellations. Over 99% of its wine is red, all of it made from the Pinot Noir grape. The wine trade still bristles when reminded of a quotation from one of Britain's leading wine merchants who said, "Life is too short to drink Santenay." That has not been the case for some time, but Santenay remains unfashionable. That is a boon for thrifty consumers looking for a solid, frequently delicious bottle of Pinot Noir for $15–$25 a bottle. While many Santenays can be excessively tannic, hollow, and pleasureless, the good producers make a wine that is medium weight by Burgundy standards, with a pronounced bouquet of strawberry and cherry fruit allied to a mineral, almost almondlike smell.

The best producers include Bernard Bachelet—Santenay; Adrien Belland—Santenay Clos des Gravières, Santenay La Comme; Marc Colin—Santenay; Joseph Douhin—Santenay; Jean-Noël Gagnard—Santenay Clos de Tavannes; Jessiaume Père–Santenay Gravières; Lequin-Roussot—Santenay Premier Cru; Château de la Maltroye—Santenay La Comme, Santenay Les Gravières; Bernard Morey—Santenay Grand Clos Rousseau; Jean-Marc Morey—Santenay Grand Clos Rousseau; Domaine de la Pousse d'Or—Santenay Clos Tavannes; Prieur-Brunet—Santenay La Comme, Santenay La Maladière; Remoissenet—Santenay Les Gravières.

Beaujolais

What is the most successful and lucrative wine produced in Burgundy? The answer is Beaujolais. This wine is made from vineyards strung across a number of enchanted mountainsides that mark the beginning of what is known as France's "Massif Central." The region of Beaujolais is 34 miles long from north to south, and 7 to 9 miles wide. The granite mountainsides range in height from 2,300 feet to more than 3,400 feet, and provide a backdrop for what is one of France's two most beautiful viticultural regions (the other being Alsace). There are nearly 4,000 growers making a living in this idyllic area. Some of them sell tiny portions of their crops locally, but most prefer to sell to one of the large firms that dominate the business.

The only grape permitted by law to be used in making Beaujolais is the Gamay, or Gamay Noir à jus Blanc, its official name. It seems to thrive in the stony, schistous soils of the region. Most red wine grapes have trouble producing high-quality crops in granite-based soils, but Gamay seems to be a natural. The compelling characteristic of Gamay is its youthful, fresh, exuberant, crunchy fruit, which the vignerons of Beaujolais have learned to maximize by producing it in an unusual method called carbonic maceration. In this style of vinification, the grapes are not pressed, but are simply dumped unceremoniously into a vat in full bunches. Grapes at the very bottom of the vat burst because of the weight on top of them. That juice begins to ferment, warming up the vat and causing fermentation in the unbroken grapes to actually begin inside their skins. The advantage of this technique is that a wine's perfume and fruity intensity is largely related to what is inside the grape skin. The acid and tannin are largely extracted from the breaking and pressing of the skins.

This interesting fermentation method results in fruity, exuberant, intensely perfumed wines that are ideal when chilled and drunk in the so-called nouveau style. Today this nouveau style is a phenomenon in the export markets, but it only started in the late seventies. Nouveau Beaujolais, which can only be released on the third Thursday in November, accounts for nearly half of the enormous production of this region. It is one of France's most successful export items, since the insatiable thirst for this wine results in hundreds of thousands of cases being air-freighted to such far-flung locations as Sydney, Tokyo, Hong Kong, Seoul, San Francisco, New York, Stockholm, London, and, of course, Paris.

The Nouveau hysteria and incredible profits taken by the wine trade from the sales of Nouveau have resulted in a school of thought that has attempted to disparage not only the wine, but those who consume it. This is all nonsense, because there is no doubting that in vintages such as 1994, delicious, zesty, exuberant, fresh, vibrantly fruity Beaujolais Nouveau is made. The only limitation is that it should be drunk within 3–4 months of its release. Beaujolais Nouveau has become a useful wine for introducing people to the glories of red wine. It has also weaned people off some of the sugary, sweet, white Zinfandels and cloying Liebfraumilchs that dominate the marketplace. A few arrogant wine snobs would have you believe it is not fashionable, but that is ludicrous.

However, to think of Beaujolais only in terms of Beaujolais Nouveau is to do this fascinating region a great injustice. In addition to Beaujolais Nouveau, there is Beaujolais Supérieur, which generally comes on the market about a month after Beaujolais Nouveau. There is also Beaujolais-Villages, which is an appellation unto itself, spread out over most of the entire Beaujolais appellation, where 39 communes have been selected by the legislature for producing some of the better wines of the region. Many of the top producers produce a Beaujolais-Villages Nouveau because it has a firmer, more robust character and can last 3 to 4 months longer than the straight Beaujolais Nouveau. If you are drinking Nouveau for its up-front, exuberant, fresh, unabashed fruitiness, then a good Beaujolais Nouveau will often be more pleasing than a Beaujolais-Villages Nouveau.

The glories of Beaujolais, aside from its narrow, winding roads, sleepy valleys, photogenic hillsides, and quaint, old villages, are the 10 Beaujolais crus. These wines all come from a village or group of villages in the northern end of the Beaujolais region; each cru is believed to have its own individual style.

RATING BEAUJOLAIS'S BEST PRODUCERS

***** *(OUTSTANDING)*

Domaine Bachelard—Georges Duboeuf (Fleurie)

Domaine René Berrod (Moulin à Vent)

Domaine René Berrod—Les Roches du Vivier (Fleurie)

Domaine Guy Braillon (Chénas)

Domaine des Brureaux (Chénas)

Manoir du Carra—Sambardier (Beaujolais-Villages)

Domaine des Champs Grilles— J. G. Revillon (Saint-Amour)

Domaine Chauvet—Georges Duboeuf (Moulin à Vent)

Michel Chignard Les Moriers (Fleurie)

Clos de la Roilette—F. Coudert (Fleurie)

Domaine de la Combe-Remont—Georges Duboeuf (Chénas)

Château des Deduits—Georges Duboeuf (Fleurie)

Domaine Jean Descombes—Georges Duboeuf (Morgon)

Domaine Diochon (Moulin à Vent)

Domaine des Grandes Vignes— J. C. Nesme (Brouilly)

Domaine du Granit—A. Bertolla (Moulin à Vent)

Domaine des Héritiers-Tagent—Georges Duboeuf (Moulin à Vent)

Domaine Jacky Janodet (Moulin à Vent)

Domaine de la Madone—J. Bererd (Beaujolais)

Château Moulin à Vent—Jean-Pierre Bloud (Moulin à Vent)

Domaine des Terres Dorées—J. P. Brun (Beaujolais-Villages)

Domaine de la Tour du Bief—Georges Duboeuf (Moulin à Vent)

Domaine Jacques Trichard (Morgon)

**** *(EXCELLENT)*

L. Bassy (Côte de Brouilly)

Alain Bernillon (Côte de Brouilly)

Domaine Bouillard (Chiroubles)

Georges Boulon (Chiroubles)

Georges Brun (Morgon)

Domaine de la Bruyère (Moulin à Vent)

Domaine Louis Champagnon (Chénas)

Domaine Cheysson (Chiroubles)

Guy Cotton (Côte de Brouilly)

Domaine des Darroux—Georges Duboeuf (Chénas)

Guy Depardon (Fleurie)

Domaine Desmeures—Georges Duboeuf (Chiroubles)

Georges Duboeuf (Régnié)

Jean Durand (Régnié)

Château de Grand Pré—Pierre Ferraud (Fleurie)

Domaine du Granite Bleu—Georges Duboeuf (Beaujolais-Villages)

Château des Jacques (Moulin à Vent)

Domaine Janin (Saint-Amour)

Château de Javernand—Georges Duboeuf (Chiroubles)

Hubert Lapierre (Chénas)

Manoir des Journets—Georges Duboeuf (Chénas)

Domaine des Mouilles—Georges Duboeuf (Juliénas)

Château de Nervers—Georges Duboeuf (Brouilly)

J. C. Nesme (Côte de Brouilly)

Domaine des Nugues—Gérard-Gelin (Beaujolais-Villages)

Georges Passot (Chiroubles)

Domaine André Pelletier (Juliénas)

Domaine Pirolette—Georges Duboeuf (Saint-Amour)

Domaine Ponchon—J. Durand (Régnié)

Domaine du Potet—Georges Duboeuf (Régnié)

Domaine de la Princess Lieven—Georges Duboeuf (Morgon)

Domaine des Quartre Vents—Georges Duboeuf (Fleurie)

Joel Rochette (Régnié)

Jean-Paul Ruet (Brouilly)

Jean-Paul Ruet (Régnié)

Jean-Louis Santé (Chénas)

Domaine de la Seigneurie de Juliénas— Georges Duboeuf (Juliénas)

Domaine de la Sorbière—J. C. Pivot
   (Beaujolais-Villages)
Domaine de la Teppe—Chanut Frères
   (Moulin à Vent)
Trenel (certain cuvées may be five-star
   quality, but the overall level is at least
   four-star)

Georges Trichard (Saint-Amour)
Domaine Vatoux—Georges Duboeuf
   (Morgon)
Château des Vierres—Georges Duboeuf
   (Beaujolais-Villages)
Château des Vignes—Georges Duboeuf
   (Juliénas)

* * * *(GOOD)*

M. Gabriel Aligne (Moulin à Vent)
M. Gabriel Aligne (Régnié)
Ernest Aujas (Juliénas)
Paul Beaudet (virtually all of their
   cuvées)
Antoine Beroujon (Brouilly)
Château de Bluizard—Georges Duboeuf
   (Brouilly)
Domaine de Boischampt (Juliénas)
Domaine de la Boittière (Juliénas)
Château Bonnet (Chénas)
Domaine des Caves—Georges Duboeuf
   (Moulin à Vent)
Château de la Chaize (Brouilly)
Domaine Louis Champagnon (Moulin à
   Vent)
Domaine de la Chanaise (Morgon)
Château des Chénas (Chénas)
Paul Cinquin (Régnié)
Domaine du Clos du Fief (Juliénas)
Domaine du Clos du Fief (Saint-Amour)
Robert Condemine (Brouilly)
Pierre Cotton (Brouilly)
Deplace Frères-Domaine du Cret des
   Bruyères (Régnié)
Claude Desvignes (Morgon)
Joseph Drouhin (virtually all of their
   cuvées)
Domaine des Ducs (Saint-Amour)
Pierre Ferraud (Régnié)
Pierre Ferraud (other cuvées)
Sylvain Fessy Cuvée André Gauthier
   (Morgon)
Domaine de la Gerarde (Régnié)
Domaine Gonan (Juliénas)
Domaine de la Grand Cour (Brouilly)
Domaine de la Grand Cour (Fleurie)
Domaine de la Grand Cru (Fleurie)
Domaine de Grande Grange—Georges
   Duboeuf (Beaujolais-Villages)
Claude et Michel Joubert (Juliénas)
Marcel Joubert (Brouilly)

Château de Juliénas (Juliénas)
Château des Labourons (Fleurie)
Domaine André Large (Côte
   de Brouilly)
Domaine de Lavant (Brouilly)
Domaine Lémonon—Loron et Fils (Moulin
   à Vent)
Bernard Meziat (Chiroubles)
Giles Meziat (Chiroubles)
Domaine du Paradis—Georges Duboeuf
   (Saint-Amour)
Georges Passot (Morgon)
Domaine Jean Patissier (Saint-Amour)
Domaine Pavillon de Chavannes (Côte de
   Brouilly)
Domaine du Petit Pressoir (Côte de
   Brouilly)
Alain Pierre (Régnié)
Domaine des Pillets (Morgon)
Domaine des Pins (Saint-Amour)
Domaine de Pizay (Morgon)
Domaine du Prieuré—Georges Duboeuf
   (Brouilly)
Château de Raousset (Chiroubles)
Michel et Jean-Paul Rampon (Régnié)
Domaine Remont—Pierre Ferraud
   (Chénas)
Domaine de la Roche—Georges Duboeuf
   (Brouilly)
Domaine André Ronzière (Brouilly)
Claude et Bernard Roux (Régnié)
Francis Saillant (Saint-Amour)
René Savoye (Chiroubles)
Domaine Savoye (Morgon)
Domaine de la Source (Chiroubles)
Château Thivin (Côte de Brouilly)
Michel Tribolet (Fleurie)
Château des Tours (Brouilly)
René et Bernard Vassot (Régnié)
Lucien et Robert Verger (Côte de Brouilly)
Domaine des Versaudes—Georges
   Duboeuf (Morgon)

* * (AVERAGE)

Château de la Chaize	Robert Pain
Château de Corcelles	Pasquier-Desvigne
Jaffelin	Piat
Loron	Roger Rocassel
Moillard	Paul Spain
Mommessin	Louis Tête

A NOTE ON RECENT VINTAGES AND GENERAL CHARACTERISTICS OF THE 10 BEAUJOLAIS CRUS

While examples of old bottles of Beaujolais that have retained their fruit can be found (in 1991 I drank a bottle of 1929 Moulin à Vent at New York's superb restaurant, Le Montrachet, with its sommelier, Daniel Johnnes, that was marvelously intact), most Beaujolais should be consumed within several years of the vintage. If you are going to take a gamble on aging Beaujolais, it should be Moulin à Vent. It comes down to a matter of personal taste, but if you are buying these wines for their vibrant, up-front, exuberant, unabashed fruitiness, then drink them young!

With respect to a quick overview of the different crus and what you might expect, the top Beaujolais crus, from north to south, begin with Saint-Amour.

Saint-Amour is a wine known for its good color, but it is often lacking in body and length, as the vineyards often fail to achieve maximum ripeness except in exceptionally hot, dry years such as 1989. When good, the wines exhibit a blackberry, raspberry fruitiness, medium body, and soft textures.

Juliénas is one of the larger appellations for top Beaujolais. There are many fine producers from Juliénas, so the competition for top-quality wine is intense. The finest examples display the exuberant, rich, fresh fruitiness of Beaujolais, backed up by plenty of body, intensity, and relatively high alcohol.

The smallest Beaujolais cru, Chénas, produces wines with a kinship to the full-bodied wines of its neighbor, Moulin à Vent. A top Chénas displays a deep, robust, intense color and a muscular, rich, concentrated style. It is a fuller, more chunky style of Beaujolais that occasionally lacks perfume and elegance. Given its rusticity, many wines of Chénas can age for 4–5 years.

Moulin à Vent is often referred to as the King of Beaujolais, and it is certainly the most expensive. Moulin à Vent costs $3–$5 more than other Beaujolais. Moulin à Vent produces the most powerful, concentrated, and age-worthy Beaujolais. While it is highly prized, in many ways it is atypical, resembling a medium-weight red burgundy from the Côte d'Or rather than an effusively fruity Beaujolais. The wines can easily last for more than 10 years, particularly those from the best producers.

The same people who call Moulin à Vent King of Beaujolais refer to Fleurie as its Queen. With one of the bigger vineyard acreages, Fleurie may be the quintessential example of Beaujolais—heady, perfumed, and rich, without the weight, body, or tannin of the bigger wines from Moulin à Vent or Chénas. At its best it is a pure, lush, silky, fruity wine that is undeniably seductive and disarming.

Chiroubles's vineyards sit at the highest altitude of Beaujolais. The wines are considered the most ethereal and fragrant of all the Beaujolais cru. Chirouble derives much of its character from its penetrating, pervasive fragrance. The downside is that it can lack body, can mature very quickly, and almost always must be drunk within 1–2 years of the vintage for its freshness.

Morgon has a reputation of being among the more robust and age-worthy of the Beaujolais crus. There is considerable variation in style, given the large size of this cru. Many wines are quite full and rich, while others are dull and hollow. A great Morgon will have exotic flavors of overripe cherries, peaches, and apricots as well as a taste of kirsch.

The newest of the Beaujolais crus, Régnié offers many different styles. Most of the local cognoscenti claim a classic Régnié possesses an intense smell of cassis and raspberries. It is a relatively light- to medium-bodied wine that needs to be drunk within 3 years of the vintage.

Brouilly, another large Beaujolais cru, produces relatively light, aromatic, fruity wines that are often no better than a Beaujolais-Villages. However, in the hands of the best producers, the wines have an additional degree of charm and fruit, making them ideal Beaujolais.

In contrast, the Côte de Brouilly is composed of vineyards on better-drained and -exposed slopes. The wines tend to be more alcoholic than those from Brouilly, with more body and glycerin.

As for the generic Beaujolais and Beaujolais-Villages, again, the producer is most important. One of the best values in the marketplace is a top-quality Beaujolais or Beaujolais-Villages.

With respect to vintages, in 1994 most Beaujolais producers were able to harvest before the deluge that hit France during the middle two weeks of September. The 1994s reflect the torridly hot months of July and August. At their best, usually in Régnié, Moulin à Vent, Juliénas, Morgon, and Fleurie, the wines are deeply colored, fat, heady, very ripe, and loaded with fruit. Most of them should be consumed between now and 2000.

THE "REAL" REALITIES OF BURGUNDY

What is the most important information to know in order to purchase top-quality red and white burgundy? The French frequently utilize the following expression when they discuss Burgundy, *"l'homme qui fait la différence,"* meaning, it is the man who makes the difference. This simplistic and male-chauvinistic viewpoint (it is a woman, Lalou Bize-Leroy, who produces Burgundy's greatest wines) reflects the cardinal rule when it comes to buying red or white burgundy. While the quality of the vintage is an important fact to know when buying burgundy, it is essential to recognize the quality of the producer. This is important because a superb grower or *négociant* will make a better wine in an off year than a mediocre or incompetent producer or *négociant* will make in a great year. If readers desire to have the odds in their favor when purchasing burgundy, it is imperative that they learn the names of the finest producers for each of the Burgundy appellations. Of course, their styles of wine may not always be to your liking, but at least you should be aware of the names of the most committed and highly motivated winemakers. Simply memorizing a top vintage year in Burgundy and then buying blindly is a practice fraught with the potential for disaster.

What's all the hoopla over the concept of "terroir"? The following Asian proverb sums up this issue quite well: "Knowing in part may make a fine tale, but wisdom comes from seeing the whole."

And so it is with the concept of *terroir*, that hazy, intellectually appealing notion that a plot of soil plays the determining factor in a wine's character. The French are the world's most obsessed people regarding the issue of *terroir*. And why not? Many of that country's most renowned vineyards are part of an elaborate hierarchy of quality based on their soil and exposition. And the French would have everyone believe that no one on planet Earth can match the quality of their Pinot Noir, Chardonnay, Cabernet, Syrah, etc., because their privileged *terroir* is unequaled. One of France's most celebrated wine regions, Burgundy is often cited as the best place to search for the fullest expression of *terroir*. Followers of *terroir* (the *terroir*-ists) argue that a particular piece of ground and its contribution to what is grown there give its product a character that is distinctive and apart from that same product grown on different soils and slopes. Burgundy, with its classifications of grand cru and premier cru vineyards, village vineyards and generic viticultural areas, is the *terroir*-ists raison d'être.

Lamentably, *terroir* has become such a politically correct buzzword that in some circles it is an egregious error not to utter some profound comments about finding "a sense of somewhereness" when tasting a Vosne-Romanée Les Malconsorts or a Latricières-Chambertin. Leading *terroir*-ists include the wine producer Lalou Bize-Leroy, Burgundy wine broker Becky Wasserman, and author Matt Kramer. It is Kramer who makes the most persuasive and eloquent case about the necessity of finding, as he puts it, "the true voice of the land" in order for a wine to be legitimized.

Yet like so many things about wine, especially tasting it, there is no scientific basis for anything Bize, Wasserman, or Kramer propose. What they argue is what most Burgundians and owners of France's finest vineyards give lip service to—that for a wine to be authentic and noble it must speak of its *terroir*.

On the other side of this issue are the "realists," or should I call them modernists. They suggest that *terroir* is merely one of many factors that influence the style of a wine. The realists argue that a multitude of factors determine a wine's style, quality, and character. Soil, exposition, and microclimate *(terroir)* most certainly impart an influence, but so do the following:

1. rootstock—Is it designed to produce prolific or small crop levels?

2. yeasts—Does the winemaker use the vineyard's wild yeasts or are commercial yeasts employed? Every yeast, wild or commercial, will give a wine a different set of aromatics, flavor, and texture.

3. yields and vine age—High yields from perennial overcroppers result in diluted wine. Low yields, usually less than 2 tons per acre or 35–40 hectoliters per hectare, result in wines with much more concentration and personality. Additionally, young vines have a tendency to overproduce, whereas old vines produce small berries and less wine. Crop-thinning is often employed with younger vineyards to increase the level of concentration.

4. harvest philosophy—Is the fruit picked underripe to preserve more acidity, or fully ripe to emphasize the lushness and opulence of a given varietal?

5. vinification techniques and equipment—There are an amazing number of techniques that can change the wine's aromas and flavors. Moreover, equipment choice (different presses, destemmers, etc.) can have a profound influence on the final wine.

6. *élevage* (or the wine's upbringing)—Is the wine brought up in oak barrels, concrete vats, stainless steel, or large oak vats (which the French call *foudres*)? What is the percentage of new oak? All of these elements exert a strong influence on the wine's character. Additionally, transferring wine (racking) from one container to another has an immense impact on a wine's bouquet and flavor. Is the wine allowed to remain in long contact with its lees (believed to give the wine more aromatic complexity and fullness)? Or is it racked frequently for fear of picking up an undesirable lees smell?

7. fining and filtration—Even the most concentrated and profound wines that *terroir*-ists consider quintessential examples of the soil can be eviscerated and stripped of their personality and richness by excessive fining and filtering. Does the winemaker treat the wine with kid gloves, or is the winemaker a manufacturer/processor bent on sculpturing the wine?

8. bottling date—Does the winemaker bottle early to preserve as much fruit as possible, or does he or she bottle later to give the wine a more mellow, aged character? Undoubtedly, the philosophy of when to bottle can radically alter the character of a wine.

9. cellar temperature and sanitary conditions—Some wine cellars are cold and others are warm. Different wines emerge from cold cellars (development is slower and the wines are less prone to oxidation) than from warm cellars (the maturation of aromas and flavors is more rapid and the wines are quicker to oxidize). Additionally, are the wine cellars clean or dirty?

These are just a handful of factors that can have extraordinary impact on the style, quality, and personality of a wine. As the modernists claim, the choices that man himself makes, even when they are unquestionably in pursuit of the highest quality, can contribute far more to a wine's character than the vineyard's *terroir*.

If one listens to Robert Kacher, a realist, or to Matt Kramer, a *terroir*-ist, it is easy to conclude that they inhabit different worlds. But the irony is that in most cases, they tend to agree as to the Burgundy producers making the finest wines.

If you are wondering where I stand on *terroir*, I do believe it is an important component in the production of fine wine. However, I would argue that the most persuasive examples of *terroir* do not arise from Burgundy, but rather, from Alsace. If one is going to argue *terroir*, the wine has to be made from exceptionally low yields, fermented with only the wild yeasts that inhabit the vineyard, brought up in a neutral medium, such as old barrels, cement tanks, or stainless steel, given minimal cellar treatment, and bottled with little or no fining or filtration.

For example, if I were to take up the cause of the *terroir*-ists, I would use one of Alsace's greatest domaines, that of Leonard and Olivier Humbrecht, to make a modest case for *terroir*. The Humbrechts do everything to emphasize the differences in their vineyard holdings. Yet in a blind tasting, why is it so easy to identify the wines of Zind-Humbrecht? Certainly their Hengst-Riesling tastes different from their Riesling from Clos St.-Urbain. The question is, is one tasting the *terroir* or the winemaker's signature? Zind-Humbrecht's wines, when matched against other Alsatian wines, are more powerful, richer, and intense. Zind-Humbrecht's yields are lower and they do not filter the wine at bottling. Yet this is a case where the wines not only possess an identifiable winemaker's signature, but also a distinctive vineyard character.

Lalou Bize-Leroy of the Domaine Leroy is often cited as the preeminent *terroir*-ist. She is a persuasive woman and talks a mighty game when it comes to how her vineyard parcels impart specific characteristics to her wines. But when Bize's wines are evaluated in blind tastings, the obvious conclusion is that she fashions more concentrated and age-worthy red burgundies than her peers. Once a taster is familiar with the style of her wines (there are subtle differences), I believe Leroy's wines can be easily identified in a blind tasting because of their power, purity, richness, and exceptional intensity rather than by any pervasive or dramatic *terroir* characteristic. The same can be said for many of Burgundy's finest producers. Anyone who is familiar with the style of the Domaine de la Romanée-Conti can usually pick a DRC wine out of a blind tasting because of the singular style of its winemaking. Winemaker Jacques Seysses, a producer who receives a four-star rating in my book on Burgundy, and someone I admire, runs up the *terroir* flag as fast as any Frenchman, saying, "Man can destroy, not create." Seysses, who utilizes 100% new oak for all of his grands crus, produces wines of extraordinary finesse and elegance. However, when tasted, his wines are dominated by his own winemaking autograph and can be picked out, not because they emanate from vineyards such as Clos de la Roche, Clos St.-Denis, or Bonnes Mares, but because of his distinctive style.

Terroir, as used by many of its proponents, is often a convenient excuse for upholding the status quo. If one accepts the fact that *terroir* is everything, and is essential to legitimize a wine, how should consumers evaluate the wines from Burgundy's most famous grand cru vineyard, Chambertin? This 32-acre vineyard boasts 23 different proprietors. But only a handful of them appear committed to producing an extraordinary wine. Everyone agrees this is a hallowed piece of ground, but I can think of only a few producers—Domaine Leroy, Domaine Ponsot, Domaine Rousseau, Domaine des Chézeaux (Ponsot makes the wine for Chézeaux)—that produce wines that merit the stratospheric reputation of this vineyard. Yet the Chambertins of three of these producers, Leroy, Ponsot, and Rousseau, are completely different in style. The Ponsot wine is the most elegant, supple, and round, Leroy's is the most tannic, backward, concentrated, and meaty, and Rousseau's is the darkest-colored, most dominated by new oak, and most modern in style, taste, and texture. Among the other 18 or 20 producers (and I am not even thinking about the various *négociant* offerings) what Burgundy wine enthusiasts are likely to encounter on retailers' shelves ranges from mediocre to appallingly thin and insipid. What wine, may I ask, speaks for the soil of Chambertin? Is it the wine of Leroy, the wine of Ponsot, the wine of Rousseau?

Arguments such as this can be made with virtually any significant Burgundy vineyard. Consider Corton-Charlemagne and the products of four of its most celebrated producers. The firm of Faiveley may own the most prized parcel atop this famous hill, and they make an elegant Corton-Charlemagne. Stylistically, it is the antithesis of the superconcentrated, lavishly oaky, broadly flavored, alcoholic Corton-Charlemagne made by Louis Latour. Again, Domaine Leroy makes a backward, hard, tough Corton-Charlemagne that resembles a tannic red more than a white wine. Domaine Coche-Dury makes a wine with extraordinary mineral components, as well as remarkable richness, unctuosity, and opulence where the oak takes a backseat to the wine's fruit and texture. Which of these Corton-Charlemagnes has that notion of "somewhereness" that is raised by the *terroir*-ists to validate the quality of a vineyard?

Are *terroir*-ists sophomoric intellectuals who should be doing more tasting and less talking? Of course not. But they can be accused of naïvely swallowing the tallest tale in Burgundy. On the other hand, the realists should recognize that no matter how intense and concentrated a wine can be from a modest vineyard in Savigny-Les-Beaune, it will never have the sheer complexity and class of a Vosne-Romanée grand cru from a conscientious producer.

In conclusion, think of *terroir* as you do salt, pepper, and garlic. In many dishes they can represent an invaluable component, imparting wonderful aromas and flavors. But if consumed alone, they are usually difficult to swallow. Moreover, all the hyperventilation over *terroir* obscures the most important issue of all—identifying and discovering those producers who make wines worth drinking and savoring!

Are the wines of Burgundy as good today as they were 20 or 40 years ago? The wines of Burgundy are better today than they were in the past. First, there is no longer any evidence of adulterating red burgundies. The illegal practice of blending inferior, more alcoholic, and more deeply colored wine from southern France and northern Africa, a wide practice until the early seventies, appears to have been discontinued.

Second, many producers recognized the folly of planting clones of Pinot Noir (such as the Pinot Droit, which emphasized prolific yields rather than quality), and have begun, encouraged and supported by the oenology departments of the leading universities, to replant with lower-yielding Pinot Noir clones, such as the Pinot Fin called 115.

A third, and possibly even more important, quality factor has been the strong movement, started in the mid-eighties, to move away from the excessive fining and filtration of Pinot Noir and Chardonnay for fear of eviscerating the wine and removing its flavor. With the advent of modern technology, many growers learned how to bottle their wines as quickly as possible, aided immeasurably by German micropore filters and centrifuges that could clarify (and eviscerate) a wine with a push of a button. This eliminated the need for the cumbersome and labor-intensive racking. It also allowed the growers to be paid for their wines more quickly, since the wines could be rushed into the bottle. The results, all too often, were wonderfully brilliant, polished, attractive-looking wines that had little character or flavor. The excessive fining and filtration of wines continues to be a major problem in Burgundy. Yet more and more producers are assessing the need to fine on a vintage-by-vintage basis and have stopped filtering in response to increasing demands from some of America's finest Burgundy importers for natural, unprocessed, and unmanipulated wines. Even Professor Feuillat, the head of the Department of Oenology at the University of Dijon, has recommended not filtering premiers crus and grands crus of Burgundy if the wine was otherwise biologically stable and clear. However, too many of those brokers and importers responsible for purchasing burgundy have encouraged their producers to excessively fine and filter, rather than to assume responsibility for shipping the wine in temperature-controlled containers, and guaranteeing that the wine be distributed in a healthy condition. The growing number of American burgundy importers who not only insist that their wines be minimally fined and filtered, but who also ship their wines in temperature-controlled containers is to be applauded. Martine Saunier of Martine's Wines in San Rafael, CA; Neal Rosenthal in Shekomeko, NY; Robert Kacher of Robert Kacher Selections in Washington, D.C.; Kermit Lynch in Berkeley, CA; Joe Dressner of Louis/Dressner Selections in New York City; Peter Weygandt of Weygandt-Metzler in Uniontown, PA; David Hinkle of North Berkeley Wines in Berkeley, CA; Fran Kysela of Kysela Père et Fils in Winchester, VA; Daniel Johnnes of Jeroboam Imports in New York City, and the transplanted American, Peter Vezan, who has immersed himself in Burgundy in search of natural unmanipulated wines, are the most prominent importers of high-quality burgundy who do indeed care.

These factors, combined with lower yields, the use of higher-quality barrels, and improved sanitary conditions in the cellars, have resulted in more complete and aromatically complex as well as more flavorful wines. In addition, there is a new generation of highly motivated winemakers who are taking quality more seriously than ever. Such people as André Porcheret, Lalou Bize-Leroy, Dominique Laurent, Jean Méo, Christophe Roumier, Dominique Lafon, Jean-François Coche-Dury, Laurent Ponsot, Jacques Lardière, and Jean-Pierre De Smet are pushing themselves as well as their peers to produce the highest-quality burgundies possible.

In addition, more and more producers and *négociants* are branding the corks used in the bottle with both the vintage and the vineyard name, packaging the wines in wooden cases, and using heavier and better bottles for their wines. In the last decade, the use of excessive fertilization and other chemical soil enhancers, as well as herbicides, fungicides, and pesticides has continued to be a dangerous practice, but some producers, such as Lalou-Bize at her Domaine Leroy, have decided to produce wines under the severe organic doctrine known as biodynamic farming.

Despite all the positive trends, I do not want to suggest that all is well. There remain many underachievers, some with historically revered names, who are turning out wines that are thin, vapid, denuded, and pleasureless. There remain too many producers who present buyers and writers with barrel samples of wine that are not representative of what later appears in the bottle—misrepresentation at the minimum, fraud at the worst.

Finally, there have been too many Burgundy vintages, praised by me as well as others, that have not lived up to their reputations and have evolved at a frighteningly quick pace.

What are the significant differences in the wines of the Côte de Beaune and Côte de Nuits? The Côte d'Or, or Burgundy's Golden Slope, as it is sometimes called, is where the most profound wines from all of Burgundy are produced. However, there are significant differences between the two hillsides that make up the Côte d'Or. The Côte de Nuits, which starts just south of Dijon and runs south of Nuits St.-Georges, produces essentially all red wine, while the Côte de Beaune, which starts just north of Beaune and extends to Santenay south of Beaune, produces both superlative red and white wines.

The red wines of the Côte de Nuits tend to be fuller and slightly more tannic, and are characterized by a more earthy, black fruit (black currants, black cherries, and plums), and exotic character than those from the Côte de Beaune. Of course, these are generalizations, but the red wines from the Côte de Beaune tend to offer slightly less body, as well as less tannin (Pommards being a notable exception), and seem to be filled with aromas and flavors of red fruits (strawberries, cherries, and red currants). In addition, they seem less earthy, less exotic, and in most cases less age-worthy, although there are exceptions. One might also argue that a big, rich, generous, virile Pommard from the Côte de Beaune is a larger-scaled, fuller wine than anything produced from Chambolle-Musigny in the Côte de Nuits.

While the Côte de Nuits produces only a handful of white wines, of which a few are superlative, the Côte de Beaune produces the world's greatest white wines from the Chardonnay grape. Whether it is the extraordinarily long-lived, rich, precisely defined white wines of Corton-Charlemagne; the nutty, luscious, lusty, easy-to-drink Meursaults; the elegant, steely Puligny-Montrachets; or the opulent, fleshy Chassagne-Montrachets, the Côte de Beaune is known for both elegant, stylish reds, and extraordinary whites.

Does burgundy have to be handled or served differently from Bordeaux? The most striking thing to anyone who has eaten in a restaurant in Burgundy, or in the home of a Burgundy producer, is the revelation that rarely does a Burgundian decant a bottle of red burgundy, even an old one with a great deal of sediment. In contrast to Bordeaux, where even young vintages are routinely decanted, the practice in Burgundy is simply to pull the cork and serve the wine directly from the bottle. This has intrigued me for a number of years, and I have often wondered why there was such a dramatic difference in wine service between these two regions. Was it based on the fact that Bordeaux actually improved with decantation and burgundy did not? Or were there other reasons, based more on history?

Some Burgundians have suggested that Burgundy, being principally a land of farmers and small growers, never tolerated the sort of haute service and rigidity experienced in Bordeaux, which for centuries was dominated by the British, long known for their emphasis on formality. This is apparent in the way of life of both these regions today. It is quite unusual to find anyone in the wine trade or any professional taster traveling around Bordeaux without a suit and tie. On the other hand, I do not think I have ever seen a grower in Burgundy in a suit and tie. Casual dress is not only tolerated, but it is accepted form when visiting the growers. Does this extend also to the table where a decanter clearly seems to imply a more pompous sort of service? Certainly the large English glassworks built in the eighteenth and nineteenth centuries promoted the use of decanters for claret, which has always seemed to have a heavier sediment than the lighter, finer sediment often found in burgundies. Is this why it became routine to decant Bordeaux and not burgundy? Perhaps, but many growers in Burgundy have told me that decanters were looked upon as an extravagance and were therefore to be eschewed.

It has been my experience that much of a great burgundy's character comes from its immense aromatic complexity. Bottle bouquet, particularly a highly nuanced one, can be very ephemeral and begin to break apart if exposed to air. Decanting a tight, young, austere Bordeaux can often make it seem more open after 5 or 10 minutes in a decanter. However, I have found, with only a handful of exceptions, that excessive airing of burgundy by decanting often causes it to totally lose its bouquet and become flaccid and formless. No doubt there are exceptions. Many of the *négociants* who have old stocks claim that certain ancient wines require a good one to two hours of breathing as well as decantation prior to being consumed. My feelings on this matter are at odds with this position. It seems that most of the old burgundies I have tasted were at their very best when the cork was pulled and they were poured, regardless of how much sediment was at the bottom of the bottle. I say all this because I personally never decant red burgundy, although I have on occasion decanted some of the great white burgundies, simply because I think they look attractive in a decanter. I have noticed that wines such as the Meursaults of the Comte Lafon, and the Chassagne-Montrachets and Montrachets of the Domaine Ramonet often improve significantly with 15–20 minutes of airing. Superrich Montrachets from producers such as Ramonet or the Domaine de la Romanée-Conti are best served at room temperature and decanted, as aeration of 10–20 minutes tends to enhance these particular wines.

Another major difference between Burgundy and Bordeaux is the stemware in which burgundy is often served. In Bordeaux, the standard tulip-shaped glass or the famous INAO glass is preferred. In Burgundy, a balloon-shaped, cognac-styled, fat, squat glass with a short stem can be found not only in the growers' cellars and *négociants'* offices, but even in Burgundy's restaurants. It is believed that these broader glasses tend to accentuate the intense, heady burgundian perfume. Some restaurants carry this to the extreme and offer their clients an oversized, 24-ounce glass. This glass is so large the wine can actually get lost, and the bouquet disappears so quickly the patron never has a chance to smell it. The small balloon-shaped, cognac-styled glasses are excellent for burgundy, but the INAO and tulip-shaped glasses should be used only for Bordeaux.

It is extremely important that red burgundy be served cooler than Bordeaux, preferably at 58–62 degrees Fahrenheit, no warmer. Red burgundy, given its relatively high alcohol content and perfume, is best served at a slightly chilled temperature where the precision of its flavors and the purity and delineation of all the complex nuances in its bouquet can be deciphered. To prove my point, all you have to do is serve the same wine at 65–70 degrees and see how soupy, muddled, and alcoholic the wine tastes. Beaujolais should be served even colder, 53–56 degrees Fahrenheit, and good white burgundy at 58–60 degrees Fahrenheit. A great Montrachet or Meursault should be served slightly warmer, at 60–65 degrees Fahrenheit, or at room temperature, assuming it is not over 68 degrees. It is foolish to spend the money for a compelling, complex white burgundy and then overchill it, ushering its bouquet and flavors into hibernation.

In conclusion, there are two things to remember when serving and handling burgundy as opposed to Bordeaux. First, burgundy can be damaged severely by excessive aeration, whereas Bordeaux is rarely hurt, although it is debatable as to how much it improves with decanting. Secondly, burgundy must be served slightly chilled to be at its very best, but Bordeaux can be served at 64–66 degrees Fahrenheit, a good 4 to 6 degrees warmer than burgundy.

What is the optimum age at which to drink red and white burgundy? To try and predict when most burgundies will reach maturity is a particularly dangerous game to play, given the variation in winemaking techniques and philosophies employed by the growers and *négociants* in Burgundy.

However, the majority of the wines of Chablis should be consumed in their first 5 or 6 years of life, as only a handful of Chablis producers (e.g., Raveneau) make wines that last or improve after 6 years in the bottle.

In terms of the wines of Beaujolais and Mâconnais, while one can always point to a 10-year-old Beaujolais or an extraordinary Pouilly-Fuissé that lasted 10 or 20 years, these are indeed rare wines. Ninety-five percent of the wines of Beaujolais and Mâconnais should be drunk before they attain 3 years of age. Once past 3 years the odds are stacked against the consumer.

As for the big red and white wines of Burgundy's Côte d'Or, while it is a matter of taste, if readers are buying burgundy and not drinking it within its first 10 years of life, I am convinced that they will be disappointed by most bottles opened after that time. Even the most rugged, concentrated, intense red and white burgundies seem to shed their tannins surprisingly fast and reach a plateau of maturity 5 to 6 years after the vintage. At that point they begin to lose their freshness, and decay sets in after 10 to 12 years. Obviously the vintage itself can make a great deal of difference. Those who purchased 1982 red burgundies should have consumed them well before they reached the age of 10. Those who purchased 1983s and felt that time would only make these brawny, tannic, often rot-afflicted, controversial wines better are going to be disappointed. The once sensational 1985 red burgundies are fully mature and excellent wines in 1995, but few have gained in stature and hedonistic pleasure over the last few years. More alarming, many 1985s have begun to drop their fruit and taste dried out. A good rule of thumb is to drink your red burgundy within 10 years of the vintage, realizing there are certain vintages, such as 1993, 1990, 1988, 1978, 1976, and

1972 for red burgundy, which may, for a handful of the finest examples, take more than 10 years to reach full maturity. But these are the exceptions, even for wines from those vintages.

The window of opportunity for drinking red and white burgundy is also one of the smallest of any great wine in the world. One of the great attributes of Bordeaux, and a reason, no doubt, why it commands the prices and international following it does, is the broad span of years over which it can be drunk. When a bottle of Bordeaux reaches its plateau of maturity, it can frequently remain there for 10, 15, sometimes 20 years before it begins a very slow process of decline. I have seen burgundies reach their plateau of maturity in 5 years and unceremoniously begin to fade after another 6 or 7 months. The optimum drinking window for most red and white burgundies is small, and closes quickly. This is not an unusual phenomenon. Collectors who have cellared and drunk burgundy relate similar experiences, many of them sad. While Bordeaux has a broad, generous period over which it can be consumed, connoisseurs of burgundy should pay fastidious attention to the development of their burgundies, or suffer the unsavory consequences. Most burgundies can literally peak and begin their decline, which is often frightfully rapid, within 6 to 9 months after having attained full maturity. This is distressing, but it is a reality of buying and cellaring both red and white burgundies. Put another way, a reliable tasting evaluation of a top Bordeaux can be accurate for a 10- to 15-year period. A tasting note on a top burgundy may only have meaning and reliability for 6 months or less. Consequently, readers should attach significantly less importance to burgundy tasting notes and devote more attention to the producer, the quality of his or her wines, and the producer's finest vineyards or offerings.

What should a great red burgundy taste like when fully mature? It is easier to agree upon those key factors that frequently result in great red burgundy. In order of importance they are (1) the soil and exposition of the vineyard, (2) low yields, (3) physiologically ripe grapes, and (4) superior winemaking, which includes exacting sanitary conditions as well as vigilant concern over the wine's upbringing, with minimal intervention save for the occasional racking (transfer of the wine from one barrel to another barrel). All the greatest red burgundies, at the very least, are the product of these factors. But red burgundy at its most sublime is the most difficult wine to describe, as it matures quickly, goes through numerous stages of evolution, and can fade at an alarming pace. Truly profound red burgundy is rarely encountered, because the Pinot Noir grape possesses an unfathomable mystery that yields no telltale, discernible signature such as Cabernet Sauvignon or Chardonnay.

The greatest examples of mature red burgundy I have ever tasted, whether it was the 1959, 1962, 1978, 1980, or 1990 La Tâche; the 1966 or 1978 Richebourg (all from the Domaine de la Romanée-Conti); the 1949 Pommard-Rugiens from Pothier-Rieusset; the 1945 or 1947 Clos des Lambrays; the 1949 or 1955 Chambertin from the Maison Leroy; the 1969 Chambertin from Armand Rousseau; the 1947 or 1980 Ponsot Clos de la Roche; the 1964 Domaine de la Pousse d'Or's Volnay La Bousse d'Or; the 1969 and 1988 Roumier Bonnes Mares; or the 1947, 1969, or 1972 Comte de Vogüé's Musigny Vieilles Vignes, all shared in common the following characteristics. First, they had penetrating and compelling bouquets that exhibited a decadent, even raunchy, almost decaying or aged-beef sort of smell, combined with an intense and exhilarating aroma of Asian spices and dried herbs. Second, they had layers and layers of black and red fruits that virtually exploded on the palate with a cascade of increasingly expanding textural sensations. They were relatively high in alcohol, possessed adequate acidity rather than tannin for structural delineation, and texturally finished with a lusciousness and a silky quality that lasted several minutes. Drinking these wines was an experience akin to eating candy because of the extraordinary sweetness they conveyed.

Are these the characteristics of great red burgundy? I am not certain, but all these wines, coming from different vineyards, vintages, and winemakers, possessed these same intrinsic qualities.

What constitutes the aromatic and flavor profiles of great white burgundy? Everyone who drinks wine no doubt has a strong idea of what the finest Chardonnays, particularly those from the new world, offer in terms of smell and taste. But how many of you have drunk truly profound white burgundy? Certainly the frightfully high prices of $75–$150+ a bottle for grands crus limits their market to less than 1% of the wine-consuming public. Actually, comparing a great white burgundy with a new world Chardonnay is almost unfair. The preponderant number of new world Chardonnays must be consumed within 2–3 years after the vintage. As enjoyable as they are, they often have all their components playing against one another rather than in complete harmony. Perhaps because most new world Chardonnays must be acidified, when one tastes them, the overall perception is one of separate but equal building blocks of acid, structure, fruit, and wood. On the other hand, great white burgundies incorporate all these components, resulting in a blend where no one element has the upper hand. The greatest examples combine an extraordinary perfume of apples, honey, vanilla, wet stones, and sometimes oranges, lemons, and tangerines with flavors that range from a smoky, buttery, and nutty taste to occasionally peaches, and in the more opulent, ripe examples, to tropical fruits such as bananas, mangos, and pineapples. Of course, what makes them so compelling is their precision and balance, with all of these marvelously complex components unfolding in the glass and on the palate. I should also note that some white burgundies have the added advantage that in certain vintages a small percentage can last for as many as 10 to 20 years in the bottle, improving and developing more nuances as they age, but the number of them that truly improve beyond 7–8 years is minuscule.

The greatest producers of white burgundy, such as Domaine Niellon, Colin-Deleger, Amiot-Bonfils, and Ramonet in Chassagne-Montrachet; Sauzet and Leflaive in Puligny-Montrachet; Jean-Marie Raveneau in Chablis; Château Fuissé and Ferret in Pouilly-Fuissé; the fabled Domaine de la Romanée-Conti Montrachet; the exquisite Corton-Charlemagnes of the Maison Louis Latour and Louis Jadot in Corton-Charlemagne; and the unfiltered, compelling Meursaults of Patrick Javillier, Jean-François Coche-Dury, and Comte Lafon, all seem to share these characteristics in various proportions, depending on the quality of the vintage.

Is burgundy as good a candidate for cellaring and aging as a top Bordeaux, Hermitage, California Cabernet, or Italian Barolo or Barbaresco? The answer to this question is a resounding "no." While some old-timers lament that burgundy is not made the way it once was, they seem to have forgotten that most burgundy has never aged extremely well. There is no doubt that one can point to a handful of rare examples of truly exciting burgundies that lasted two, three, sometimes four or more decades, retaining their fruit and developing greater nuances and subtleties, but those cases are a distinct minority. This applies equally to both red and white burgundy.

It is an uncontestable truism that anyone who advises readers to lay away burgundies for a decade clearly does not have the consumer's best interests at heart. To reiterate once more, most modern-day red burgundies, even from the finest vintages (e.g., 1990), should be consumed within 10–12 years of the vintage. This rule is even more restrictive for white burgundies. The window of drinking opportunity is normally within 7–8 years of the vintage for white burgundies.

The reasons for this are simple. Red burgundies, made from the Pinot Noir grape, simply do not have the tannin level or extraction of flavor to sustain them for more than 10–12 years. Additionally, the Pinot Noir grape's most distinct pleasures are its bouquet and its sweet, ripe, velvety fruitiness, both of which tend to be the first characteristics of a Pinot Noir to crack up and dissipate. Even the finest red burgundies, while they may last two or more decades, are generally more enjoyable to drink in their first decade of life. Even the rare, long-lived, powerful vintages such as 1959, 1964, 1969, and 1978 were best drunk during their first 10–15 years of life, although the finest examples of the top producers can still be wondrous today. Anyone who loves great red burgundy should only buy enough to drink within the immediate future. Red burgundy's suspect aging capabilities have always been a problem and are not due to any modern-day winemaking techniques, although high yields and addictive reliance on chemical fertilizers as well as fungicides, herbicides, and pesticides have further exacerbated red burgundy's ability to age gracefully beyond a decade.

I have come to the realization that if you are buying burgundy for drinking in 15 or 20 years, you should be restricting your purchases to the wines from no more than a half-dozen or so producers. In particular, the Maison Leroy, the Gevrey-Chambertin *négociant*, Bourée, and small producers such as Comte Lafon still produce wines that are compelling and sumptuous at 10 years of age, and in some cases, 20 years. Even Burgundy's most expensive and frequently greatest wines, those of such superlative producers as the Domaine de la Romanée-Conti, Domaine Méo-Camuzet, Henri Jayer, Domaine Dujac, Philippe Leclerc, and Jean Gros, are usually at their best between 8 and 15 years of age, rarely improving or holding well beyond that.

Are the best wines of Burgundy viable candidates for investment? While investment in wine has become more popular given the luxury prices demanded for the top châteaux of Bordeaux, Burgundy has never represented as good an investment as Bordeaux. I abhor the practice of investing in wine for financial profit. It is done regularly, at least with the first-growths and supersecond châteaux of Bordeaux, as well as a handful of the limited-production Pomerols and St.-Émilions. But there is a great deal of difference between buying Bordeaux and buying burgundy. For starters, in the spring following the vintage, Bordeaux is offered as a wine future at what is called an "opening" or entry-level price. If the vintage is widely acclaimed and of great quality, the price is propelled in only one direction—upward. For example, the 1982 Bordeaux prices have escalated by 400%–600% over the last decade. Prices for the top dozen or so 1990s, potentially an overall greater vintage than either 1961 or 1982 (more châteaux made finer wines in the latter years), have risen 100%–300% in less than 5 years. Burgundy is not sold as a wine future, although specialist merchants (regrettably in my view) offer to sell burgundy to their customers on a "prearrival" basis. This often requires the consumer to put up considerable monetary sums 6–12 months prior to arrival. In essence, consumers are financing the merchant's burgundy purchases. Today, most burgundies from current vintages sell at prices higher than do the older vintages of the same wine. A review of any of the auction results from Christie's, Sotheby's, the Chicago Wine Company, or the numerous New York and California auctions illustrates this. Some of the greatest burgundies from vintages from the forties, fifties, and sixties sell at prices that are significantly less than those from 1990 and 1993, the two most recent highly regarded vintages. The reasons for this are (1) consumers lack confidence in burgundy, (2) smart buyers recognize burgundy's fragility and dubious aging potential, and (3) merchants ask and receive astronomical prices for the wines upon their release because of the microscopic production of the finest wines. But rarely do these same wines appreciate in value after release. In fact, in most cases their value collapses. There are exceptions, such as some limited-production Montrachets and Romanée-Conti and La Tâche of the Domaine de la Romanée-Conti. All in all, burgundy is a notoriously bad investment.

Why are the best burgundies so expensive? The pricing of burgundy can be explained entirely by the rules of supply and demand. Historically, Burgundy has had the unique and enviable situation of having far more admirers and prospective purchasers than available wine. This is particularly true at the premier and grand cru levels, which are usually the only burgundies that merit purchasing, given the feeble qualities of most village and generic burgundies. In addition, great burgundy alone among the finest French wines has no competition from within the borders of France, or in most of the wine world. The problem at the premier cru and grand cru levels is exacerbated by the truly microscopic quantities of wine offered by the best producers. Some specific case production figures demonstrate the point dramatically. For example, the most expensive red burgundies are those of the Domaine de la Romanée-Conti. In an abundant year, the production of their Romanée-Conti ranges from 300 to 500 cases. Their exclusively owned *monopole* vineyard, La Tâche, produces between 900 and 1,800 cases a year. One of Burgundy's most sought-after wine-makers, Henri Jayer, usually produces, in a prolific year, 50 cases of Richebourg and 125 cases of Echézeaux. Lalou Bize-Leroy, whose Domaine Leroy in Vosne-Romanée since 1988 has consistently produced Burgundy's most sublime and age-worthy wines, usually makes only 25 cases of her two grands crus of Musigny and Chambertin. The Domaine Roumier is one of the most revered names in Burgundy, and their Bonnes Mares Cuvée Vieilles Vignes is considered to be a heroic wine, but only 100 cases were made in the plentiful vintage of 1988. Everyone who loves great burgundy considers Hubert Lignier's Clos de la Roche to be one of the top dozen or so red wines made in Burgundy, yet he rarely makes more than 300 cases.

By no means are these isolated examples. Louis Jadot's production of the excellent Beaune-Clos des Ursules is considered massive by Burgundy standards, but only 1,100 cases are made in a hugely abundant year, about one-fourth the amount of a very-limited-production Pomerol such as Pétrus! Jadot sells his wines to every civilized country in the world. How much of this lovely wine will make it to the shelves of the finest wine merchants in Omaha, Nebraska, or Edinborough, Scotland? Perhaps a case or two? In Bordeaux a production of 1,000 cases is considered minuscule. A favorite Bordeaux of wine consumers' is the muscular and flavorful Lynch-Bages, and a popular California Cabernet Sauvignon is Robert Mondavi's exquisite Reserve. There are 35,000–45,000 cases of Lynch-Bages and 15,000–20,000 cases of Mondavi Reserve Cabernet produced!

This frustrating situation (at least for buyers) is similar for white burgundies. There are usually no more than 50 cases made of J. F. Coche-Dury's ethereal Corton-Charlemagne. Louis Jadot, who makes sublime Corton-Charlemagne, can, in an abundant year, produce 1,200 cases, but that must be spread around not only to the restaurants of France, but to Jadot's clients throughout the world. Even worse is the situation with the Domaine Ramonet's celestial Montrachet. A whopping 50 cases are made in an abundant vintage!

Most of the finest grand cru and premier cru red and white burgundies could be sold exclusively to a few of Europe's top restaurants, should the producers so desire. Of course, that is not their intention, and they try to ensure an equitable distribution to their suppliers throughout the world. But it is because of these tiny quantities that the prices for burgundy are so astronomically high. As more and more wine connoisseurs from a growing number of countries demand fine wine, the pressure on suppliers will only create more and more exorbitant prices for the new vintages.

Why are the finest burgundies so difficult to find in the American marketplace? The answer again relates to the tiny quantities of top wines that are produced. America has been an extremely important purchaser of top-quality burgundies, particularly white burgundies. Once the small quantities sold to the best producers' importers are allocated to the ten or twelve best wine markets in the United States, however, a top merchant may only end up with a case or two of Leflaive Chevalier-Montrachet, and six bottles of a Domaine de la Romanée-Conti Montrachet. This situation is no different in the United States than it is in Switzerland, the United Kingdom, Belgium, or Japan. It is immensely frustrating for buyers to learn of a superb producer, and then discover that only 10 or 15 cases will be allocated to the American market. These are the realities when dealing with burgundy, and seemingly only add to its mystique. More worrisome in 1995 is the continued weakness of the American dollar. At the time of writing it is undervalued and behaving like a third-world currency vis-à-vis its value against the French franc. All this does is make burgundy sold in dollars to Americans even more outrageously expensive.

Are estate-bottled burgundies superior to those from the négociants? *Négociant* is the French word for a wine broker. *Négociants* include firms that do not own any vineyards. They rely totally on purchases of finished wines from growers, which they then sell under their own names. *Négociants* can also be firms that own vineyards. Several, for example, Faiveley and Bouchard Père et Fils, are among the largest vineyard owners in Burgundy. *Négociants* have long controlled the Burgundy wine business, as the movement of growers to estate-bottle their wines has been a relatively recent phenomenon. The fact that many of the most insipid and vapid burgundies have consistently been produced by several of the largest and most prominent *négociants* has been the principal reason for the negative image many consumers have of a Burgundy *négociant*. *Négociants* have also been maligned by growers and importers, who argue that the most authentic and individualistic burgundies can only emerge from individual domaines. The better *négociants* have responded in a positive manner to this criticism. Since the mid-eighties, Louis Jadot has been a reference point for high-quality *négociant* wine, as has Louis Latour for their white wines. Other firms, particularly Bouchard Père et Fils, have significantly upgraded the quality of their wines.

The trend of estate-bottled burgundies, started by the late founder of the *Revue du Vin de France,* Raymond Baudoin, and subsequently encouraged by the American importer, the late Frank Schoonmaker, has still not reached its zenith. The *négociants,* faced with losing many of their sources for wine thanks to growers who decided to become freelancers and to estate-bottle their own production, not only tried to sign up certain growers to exclusivity contracts, but recognized the need to improve the quality of their wines.

There are, however, *négociants* that continue to lag behind in quality. Among the most notable of these is the huge firm of Jean-Claude Boisset, the firms of Patriarche, Albert Bichot (except for their exquisite wines from the Domaine de Clos Frantin and Domaine Long-Depaquit), and the highly promoted wines of La Reine-Pedauque. Today, you are not likely to get a bad wine from these firms, but rather a sound, commercial one with no soul or personality. Admittedly, there must be a vast market for such wines, as these firms are among the wealthiest and most successful in France.

One argument frequently offered is that the wines of the *négociants* have the same taste. To me that seems irrelevant. The top *négociants,* while they respect the individual vineyard's *terroir,* obviously employ the same philosophy in making all of their wines, and try to keep the identity of the vineyard and appellation unto itself. The wines of Louis Jadot or Bourée all share a similar signature, but then so do the wines of domaines such as Roumier, Ponsot, Roty, Jean Gros, or the Domaine de la Romanée-Conti. At the most meticulously run estate-bottled operation the same philosophy is employed for making each wine. The wines from the well-known domaine of Armand Rousseau in Gevrey-Chambertin will have a certain similarity because the winemaking, the *élevage,* and the overall philosophy is precisely the same for each wine. Nevertheless, Rousseau's Chambertin will taste different from a Gevrey-Chambertin Clos St.-Jacques or Clos de la Roche from neighboring Morey St.-Denis. The signature is just as prominent in a grower's cellar as it is in a *négociant*'s.

How is great red burgundy made? Most burgundy growers will only tell you so much, but from what I have been able to glean after years of research, the three most important components that contribute to great red burgundy are (1) the excellence of the vineyard, (2) low yields, and (3) the competence of the winemaker. If all three of these exist, the end result is likely to be quite compelling and exciting.

How all the different growers and *négociants* vinify and handle their wines differs far more in Burgundy than it does in Bordeaux. In Bordeaux, the basic winemaking and upbringing of the wine are essentially the same at all the major properties. In Burgundy, there are many different ways of making top-class red wine.

One of the most popular techniques today at the top level is partial or total destemming of the grapes. Destemming is the process whereby the stems are removed from the grape bunches. Many producers feel the stems impart a vegetal flavor to the wine and decrease the color, as well as add astringent tannin. For these reasons, many producers routinely destem 100% of the grapes. Other producers believe a certain percentage of stems adds structure and more character to the wine. Most of the finest producers tend to use between 50% and 100% new oak for their top premiers and grands crus. Many burgundies taste excessively woody, but new oak is ideal for Pinot Noir and is the most sanitary vessel in which to make wine. However, high yields combined with the lavish use of new oak is a formula for thin, woody wines. As the controversial Belgian, Jean-Marie Guffens-Heynen (a proponent of new oak), says, "No wine is overoaked, merely underwined."

Today, many Burgundy producers follow the methods of Burgundy's most influential winemaker, Henri Jayer, who employs a 5- to 7-day cold prefermentation maceration of his Pinot Noir. Proponents of this practice believe this "cold soak" adds color, richness, aromatics, and fat to a wine.

But even these talented winemakers disagree on certain principles. Henri Jayer, the Domaine de la Romanée-Conti, and the Domaine Ponsot believe that 90% of the wine is made in the vineyard and that "winemaking" in the cellars can destroy, but cannot contribute more than another 10% to, the final quality. They feel the search for high quality obligates the grower to prune back the vineyard, if conditions warrant, by cutting off grape bunches—in essence doing a "green harvest" in summer to reduce yields. To these producers, high yields are the undoing of the wine, regardless of how talented the winemaker is, or what wizardry can be accomplished within the cellar. On the other hand, some producers, most notably Jacques Seysses, argue that large yields are acceptable, and that concentration can still be obtained by the process of bleeding off the excess juice (which the French call *saigner*). This technique increases the proportion of skins and stems to the remaining juice and therefore, according to its proponents, increases the concentration. Henri Jayer claims this is nothing but a gimmick whose shortcomings become apparent after the wine spends 5 or 6 years in the bottle. I'll stick with Henri Jayer on this issue.

Another area where these irrefutably great winemakers disagree concerns the percentage of new oak used. Henri Jayer believes in 100% new oak, the firms of Bourée and Jadot significantly less, and the Domaine Ponsot abhors it altogether. However, it should be noted that the trend for premiers and grands crus in Burgundy is toward increased percentages of new oak. Great wines have emerged more from an elevated use of new oak than the absence of it.

Another school of winemaking embraces an extremely long period of cold maceration prior to fermentation, a technique that lasts well beyond the 5–7 days employed by the Jayerists. It is practiced by a group of winemakers who have employed the controversial Nuits St.-Georges oenologist, Guy Accad, to look after their winemaking. This practice has been condemned by many in Burgundy for producing wines that have more in common with Côte Rôtie than Pinot Noir. However, it is still too early to know whether Accad's extreme techniques will stand the test of time. They do indeed produce irrefutably impressive, almost black-colored wines that are explosively rich and aromatic when young. But do they reflect their appellations as well as some of the less-extreme methods of fermentation? No one yet knows, but everyone has a definitive opinion on the subject. Accad does not believe in destemming, and allows the grape bunches to macerate chilled for 10 days or more before any fermentation starts. To his credit, he does not believe in rushing anything into the bottle. He counsels his clients against fining and filtration, and advises them not to bottle their wines until they are fully ready. Former clients, such as Jacky Confuron in Vosne-Romanée, Étienne Grivot in Vosne-Romanée, Georges Chicotot in Nuits St.-Georges, Daniel Senard in Aloxe-Corton, and the Château de la Clos Vougeot in Vougeot, to name a few of the most prominent, all seem to produce intensely colored, rich, aromatic, concentrated wines that are impressive young. Unfortunately, I do not know how well these wines stand the test of time. It is doubtful that Accad is Burgundy's new winemaking wizard, but much of the criticism aimed at Accad and his clients has bordered on the paranoid, and may be the result of jealousy and envy rather than anything scientifically based—at least for now.

The other schools of thought for making top-quality red burgundy basically eschew any of the cold maceration prior to fermentation. They believe in crushing and fermenting at warm temperatures in order to extract color, body, and tannin via a more traditional method. They disagree with those who argue that great aromatic Pinot Noir can only be obtained by a cool fermentation or cold maceration prior to fermentation. Some of the best examples of this school of thought include the Maison Louis Jadot and Bourée Père et Fils, whose red wines are macerated for a long time, fermented at extremely high temperatures, yet still retain their aromatic purity and last and last in the bottle. Philippe Leclerc, the Domaine Ponsot, and the Domaine Georges Mugneret are three other superlative producers who think cold maceration prior to fermentation is nonsense.

Of course, the big question is what does the Domaine Leroy do? Unquestionably, these are the most consistently brilliant, as well as among the most expensive, wines of Burgundy. Leroy's yields are half, sometimes one-third, that of the other domaines. That in itself is probably the reason why these wines attain such great concentration. The Domaine Leroy averages 20–25 hectoliters per hectare as opposed to the 55–65 obtained elsewhere. There is usually no destemming. A cold maceration of 5–6 days prior to fermentation, a long fermentation, and maceration using only wild yeasts are employed. The wines spend 15–18 months in 100% new Allier oak casks and are bottled unfined and unfiltered.

As all of this indicates, there are a multitude of methods employed that can result in great wines. All of the producers I have mentioned are capable of producing some of the finest wines in Burgundy. Those people who tend to turn out neutral, vapid, mediocre red burgundies seem to also possess the following things in common: (1) Their crop sizes are excessive; (2) they bottle either too early or too late; (3) they are processors and manufacturers of wine, practicing traumatic fining and filtering; and (4) they take no risks, as their goal is complete stability and/or sterility of the product. As a result, most of the wines are pale imitations of what red burgundy should be.

I am more convinced than ever that overproduction and excessive fining and/or filtration are the undoing of most Pinot Noirs.

How is great white burgundy made? White burgundy seems remarkably easy to produce and the techniques relatively similar when compared with the numerous variations used to make red burgundy.

While most generic white burgundies, and wines from the Mâconnais and Chalonnais regions, ferment in stainless steel and are bottled early, the great white burgundies of the Côte d'Or are all barrel-fermented, generally kept in contact with their lees for 10–12 months, and racked as little as possible. At the same time, it should be pointed out that those producers who keep their yields under control produce white burgundies with the greatest levels of concentration and depth. I am speaking of producers such as the Comte Lafon, Jean-François Coche-Dury, Domaine Leflaive, Domaine Ramonet, and Domaine Michel Niellon. While there are others, these producers all have low yields, long lees contact, and a reluctance to intervene or interfere with the natural evolution of the wine in the cask unless there is an emergency. For the Comte Lafon and Coche-Dury there is the almost unheard of idea of bottling their white wines without filtration, a particularly risky and dangerous operation, because if there is any bacteria or yeast left in the wine, exposure of the bottle to heat could trigger a secondary fermentation. However, the Comte Lafon's cellars are so cold and the wines kept in cask so long that their wines are totally stable by the time they are bottled. The techniques employed by Jean-François Coche-Dury are similar, but he bottles much sooner than Comte Lafon.

As great as these wines are, this is not to say that filtration, if done lightly, harms white burgundy. Anyone who has tasted the wines of Domaine Leflaive or Domaine Ramonet knows how extraordinary white burgundy can be, and yet these wines are lightly filtered.

Today, most white burgundies at the premier cru and grand cru levels see about 50% to 100% new oak casks, usually Allier, but it can be a blend of different oaks. They are normally bottled after 12 to 14 months. But again, the vineyard site, the competence of the winemaking, and the attention to keeping yields conservative are the three major factors that result in great white burgundies.

Will the prices for burgundy wines ever moderate? Unfortunately, the answer to this question is no. There is always the chance that an international financial crisis could precipitate a worldwide depression that would affect a luxury item such as fine wine. For example, prices for 1991 and 1992 red burgundies dropped by 35%–50% compared with the prices of 1989s and 1990s. But prices for 1993s and 1994s are soaring, the result of small crops and, for Americans, our weak currency. However, given the international demand for the top-quality wines of this region, the general trend for prices in Burgundy can only be upward. While the huge quantities of wines produced in Mâconnais, Beaujolais, and Chablis may show more variation in prices, the economic prognosis for the premiers and grands crus from Burgundy's famed Côte d'Or is for frighteningly higher prices. When one considers the fact that there are only 30 grands crus, producing barely 1% of the total wine of Burgundy, the unmistakable message conveyed is that prices can only escalate. Given the tiny quantity of potentially great burgundy and the growing number of purchasers, it is not unlikely that by the turn of the century prices for grands crus will be double what they are today. Presently, there are more purchasers of fine wine than ever before.

The wine market has become even more competitive in the last 5 years with the aggressive purchasing by the Swiss, Germans, and Pacific Rim countries, especially Singapore. Their strong currency and yearning thirst to discover what the best French wine is all about has created an entirely new pricing structure for premier cru and grand cru burgundies. History has proven that it is the wealthiest countries that drink the world's finest wines. If the emerging Asian countries are prepared to pay the premium prices, why shouldn't they enjoy the best?

The same can be said for the awakening interest in great wines in France itself. While France has traditionally consumed oceans of wine, it has never developed much of an appreciation for its own great wines. Increasing interest from Switzerland, Germany, Belgium, Sweden, and Denmark, all with strong economies and a thirst for fine wine, has further strained the supplies of good burgundies. The traditional markets of England and America will have to adjust to higher and higher prices or be isolated from the Burgundy marketplace. Eastern Europe, now that the walls of communism have been torn down, offers an entirely new market. Its countries have rich traditions that frequently involve the consumption of fine wine. For nearly four decades their hedonistic desires have been suppressed. When their economies strengthen and a middle class arises, what additional pressures will they put on the available supplies of red and white burgundy?

As for the generic appellation wines, they certainly will not appreciate to the extent that the premiers crus and grands crus will. However, Burgundy, much like Bordeaux, has become somewhat of a caste system for wine producers. The greatest wines from the greatest producers are able to fetch astronomical prices because there is no shortage of wealthy clients prepared to buy them. While the prices exclude most consumers and students of wine, it does encourage them to look for values in the more obscure appellations, such as Saint-Aubin, Saint-Romain, and, of course, the up-and-coming appellations of the Côte Chalonnaise. While none of these wines will ever approach the magnificent qualities of a grand cru such as Musigny or Chambertin Clos de Bèze, they still have enough burgundy character to satisfy a great majority of even the most demanding palates.

The situation with the great white burgundies is even more exacerbated by excessive demand. When one considers that such great grands crus as Montrachet and Chevalier-Montrachet consist of only 19.7 and 18.1 acres respectively, it seems inevitable that prices will double or even triple over the next decade.

Today's connoisseur of burgundy must be prepared either to pay a high price, or to search elsewhere for great Pinot Noir and Chardonnay.

The growth of estate-bottled burgundies is a relatively recent phenomenon. Who was responsible for that development? Raymond Baudoin was the man responsible for encouraging some of Burgundy's best small growers, such as Ponsot in Morey St.-Denis, Rousseau in Gevrey-Chambertin, Roumier in Chambolle-Musigny, Gouges in Nuits St.-Georges, and d'Angerville in Volnay, to estate-bottle their wines. In the 1920s Baudoin founded *Revue du Vin de France*, which to this day remains the leading French wine publication. Baudoin had lamented the fact that the great burgundies of the Côte d'Or would be sold to *négociants*, and then would lose their individual identities by being blended with a large quantity of inferior wine. He began to purchase barrels of wine directly from the growers, who would estate-bottle them for him. In turn, he would sell them privately to clients and restaurants in Paris. Baudoin, who died in 1953, is the father of the estate-bottling movement in Burgundy.

However, it was Frank Schoonmaker, the American importer, who deserves the recognition for being the first to see the potential and quality of these estate-bottled burgundies, and to expose the American market to them. Frank Schoonmaker died in 1976, and most wine neophytes, unfortunately, are probably not familiar with the significance of his contributions. For these wine consumers, I highly recommend *The Frank Schoonmaker Encyclopedia of Wine*, a classic that was first published in 1964 and most recently updated by the well-known New York wine writer, Alex Bespaloff, in 1988. This encyclopedia is only one of the legacies Frank Schoonmaker left wine enthusiasts. Schoonmaker, a Renaissance man born in the town of Spearfish, South Dakota, came from a family that stressed education and enlightenment. His father taught at Columbia University and his mother was a leading feminist of her time. After graduating from college in the mid-twenties, Schoonmaker went to Europe. There he had his first exposure to wine. In 1927, at age 21, he authored the book, *Through Europe on $2 a Day*. Although it appeared just before the Depression, the book was a success, and led to Schoonmaker's collaboration with Lowell Thomas on two additional travel books: *Come with Me through France* and *Come with Me through Spain*. These in turn resulted in several magazine articles about wine in *The New Yorker*, commissioned by shrewd editors who realized the potential for interest in wine when Prohibition ended in 1933.

In 1935 Schoonmaker and some other investors formed the importing firm of Bates and Schoonmaker. At the same time men like Freddy Wildman and Julian Street were starting merchant businesses dedicated to the sale of fine French wine and estate-bottled burgundies. The Marquis d'Angerville shared with me a copy of his first wine order from Bates and Schoonmaker. It came on April 30, 1935, when Schoonmaker ordered 10 cases of Volnay Clos des Fremiets 1929, costing a total of 1,680 francs. Other producers, such as the Tollots in Chorey-Les-Beaune as well as Rousseau and Gouges, remember selling wine directly to Schoonmaker's firm in New York City at about the same time.

Schoonmaker's heir apparents include Robert Haas, who founded one of America's leading companies dedicated to estate-bottled burgundies, and the late Alexis Lichine, who in the 1960s developed the idea of purchasing wine directly from the growers, commercializing it under his own name, but also indicating the name of the grower on the label.

These gentlemen were the cornerstones of the estate-bottled burgundy movement. The Schoonmaker selections are represented today by Châteaux and Estates. Frederick Wildman and Company is still an import firm in New York City, as is Vineyard Brands, the company started by Robert Haas in Chester, Vermont. Alexis Lichine sold his wine company to the English firm of Bass-Charrington and concentrated on his beloved Château Prieuré-Lichine, which he purchased in 1951.

As more and more growers begin to domaine-bottle their wines, the recognition and promotion of estate-bottled burgundies has never been stronger. In addition to Châteaux and Estates, Frederick Wildman and Company, and Robert Haas, the American importers of estate-bottled burgundy include the idiosyncratic, outspoken Berkeley importer, Kermit Lynch; Neal Rosenthal of Select Vineyards in Shekomeko, NY; Robert Kacher Selections in Washington, D.C.; Martine Saunier Selections in San Rafael, CA; Kysela Père et Fils in Winchester, VA; North Berkeley Wines in Berkeley, CA; Louis/Dressner Selection in New York, NY; Weygandt-Metzler in Uniontown, PA; Kobrand, Inc., a leading importer that also owns the excellent house of Louis Jadot; and a handful of American and French specialists living and working in France. These include the Paris-based Peter Vezan, a transplanted American who is one of the most knowledgeable people I have ever talked to about Burgundy. Patrick Lesec is another broker in search of handcrafted great burgundies. He has ferreted out many top growers, whose wine he sells to importers in America, the United Kingdom, and Europe.

Red Burgundy

THE INSIDE SCOOP

A CONSUMER'S PROFILE OF THE BEST-KNOWN BURGUNDY PRODUCERS

DOMAINE BERTRAND AMBROISE (PRÉMEAUX)* * * *

Ambroise, a youthful, robust, exuberant individual, makes wines similar to his own physical profile. These are powerful, muscular, full-bodied, highly concentrated burgundies. They often require aging, as they are among the more backward, concentrated, tannic red burgundies being made in Nuits St.-Georges. Ambroise has been successful in so-called off vintages such as 1991 and 1992.

Best Wines: Corton Les Rognets, Nuits St.-Georges Rue du Chaux, Nuits St.-Georges Les Vaucrains

BERNARD AMIOT (CHAMBOLLE-MUSIGNY)* * *

Until 1991, I was unmoved by Amiot's light, fragile, diluted style of winemaking, but since the 1991 vintage Amiot has produced wines of charm and finesse from Chambolle-Musigny, with more depth and intensity.

Best Wine: Chambolle-Musigny Les Charmes

PIERRE AMIOT ET FILS (MOREY ST.-DENIS)* */* * *

Relatively light, insubstantial burgundies emerged from Amiot's impressive holdings spread out over some of the best sites of Morey St.-Denis and Chambolle-Musigny. The wines frequently turn out light and do not hold up to cellaring longer than 8–10 years.

Best Wines: Clos de la Roche, Clos St.-Denis, Gevrey-Chambertin Les Combottes

DOMAINE MARQUIS D'ANGERVILLE (VOLNAY)* * * *

I have to admit I have consistently underrated the wines of d'Angerville, no doubt because of poor examples I tasted stateside that in retrospect were probably not handled properly in the distribution chain. However, vintages since 1989 have impressed me for their silky richness, firm structure, and pure, concentrated Pinot Noir fruit. I have come to believe that d'Angerville's reputation is largely justified by his wines. In such top vintages as 1990 and 1993, these are wines to drink over 12–15 years.

Best Wines: Volnay Les Caillerets, Volnay Champans, Volnay Clos des Ducs, Volnay Taillepieds

DOMAINE ARLAUD PÈRE ET FILS (NUITS ST.-GEORGES)* *

I have had relatively sweet, sugary, fat wines from Arlaud that seemed monolithic, highly commercial, and enjoyable, but lacking typicity and complexity. Arlaud's wines are meant to be drunk within the first 5 years after their release.

Best Wines: Bonnes Mares, Charmes-Chambertin, Clos de la Roche, Clos St.-Denis

DOMAINE DE L'ARLOT (PRÉMEAUX)* * * *

Jean-Pierre de Smet, a former apprentice of Jacques Seysses of the Domaine Dujac, fashions wines in the image of Domaine Dujac. I adore the elegant, sweet, juicy, pure fruit Smet obtains in his Pinot Noir. If readers want to see how much flavor can be crammed into a light ruby-colored wine, they should take a look at this estate's wines. Smet has been especially consistent, even in tough years such as 1991 and 1992. The wines are aged in oak casks, at least half of which are new, and there is no question that the smoky, vanillin character adds considerable seductiveness to the sweet berry fruit. These are wines to drink within their first 5–7 years of life.

Best Wines: Nuits St.-Georges Clos de l'Arlot, Nuits St.-Georges Clos des Forêts St.-Georges, and in the future, Vosne-Romanée Les Suchots (a parcel recently purchased by this estate)

DOMAINE COMTE ARMAND (POMMARD)* * *

As I look back on my tasting notes, I have always admired the manner in which these wines are produced and the way they perform when young. I have not yet seen a mature example, and even in the more precocious vintages such as 1985 and 1987, the only wine then produced at this estate, Pommard Clos des Epeneaux, has reached full maturity yet still tastes rustic, coarse, and incapable of fulfilling my earlier expectations. I still have high hopes that the 1990 will turn out to be the real thing, but are these wines too tannic, burly, and rustic to ever develop into harmonious examples of Pinot Noir?

Best Wine: Pommard Clos des Epeneaux

DOMAINE ROBERT ARNOUX (VOSNE-ROMANÉE)* * * *

I first fell in love with the wines of Robert Arnoux when I tasted his 1978s and 1980s. Both vintages are now exhibiting some wear and tear, but if stored in cold cellars, they can still be thrilling but fully mature red burgundies. Interestingly, after 1980, Arnoux did not have a great vintage until 1991. A large estate by Burgundy standards, it has a tendency to opt for high yields, resulting in diffuse, loosely knit wines lacking delineation and concentration. If Mother Nature intervenes to keep Arnoux's yields down (e.g., 1991), the wines can be complex, rich, textbook Pinots that can possess an aromatic kinship with the Domaine de la Romanée-Conti wines. With the exception of vintages such as 1978 and 1980, these are wines to be drunk in the first decade of life.

Best Wines: Clos de la Vougeot, Nuits St.-Georges Les Procès, Romanée St.-Vivant, Vosne-Romanée Les Chaumes, Vosne-Romanée Les Suchots

DOMAINE DENIS BACHELET (GEVREY-CHAMBERTIN)* */* * *

This tiny domaine can hit some home runs, but it happens too infrequently. Tiny quantities of Charmes-Chambertin and Gevrey-Chambertin Vieilles Vignes in vintages such as 1990 are worth pursuing. However, Bachelet's performance in off years is not likely to ensure a great degree of loyalty from shrewd consumers.

Best Wine: Charmes-Chambertin

DOMAINE BARTHOD-NOËLLAT (CHAMBOLLE-MUSIGNY)* * * *

Ghislaine Barthod, the daughter of Gaston Barthod, now manages the cellar of this impeccably run, underrated Chambolle-Musigny producer. Firm but elegant wines are produced.
Although never the richest or flashiest, they are consistently stylish and age-worthy. There
is not much difference between the bevy of premiers crus offered, but Les Charmes is
generally the most precocious and elegant. Despite their lack of muscle, these wines have
the uncanny ability to age well for 10–12 years.

Best Wines: Chambolle-Musigny Les Beaux Bruns, Chambolle-Musigny Les Charmes,
Chambolle-Musigny Les Cras, Chambolle-Musigny Les Varoilles

DOMAINE PHILIPPE BATACCHI (GEVREY-CHAMBERTIN)* *

I have yet to understand the wines of this Gevrey-Chambertin producer. They are darkly
colored, big, and muscular, as well as tannic, hard, and rough around the edges. They are
reminiscent of the coarse style of the Domaine Maume with more color and tannin. It
appears that Batacchi would make better wines in Bordeaux than in Burgundy.

Best Wine: Clos de la Roche

DOMAINE ADRIEN BELLAND (SANTENAY)* */* * *

The vast array of wines produced in Belland's cellars are all average to slightly above
average in quality. The wines are firm, rustic, and age-worthy, but unexciting.

Best Wines: Santenay Clos des Gravières, Santenay La Comme

DOMAINE BERTAGNA (VOUGEOT)* *

This good-sized domaine, situated just off the main road through the Côte d'Or in the village
of Vougeot, continues to produce a perplexing array of average to slightly above-average
wines. They are light, compact, attenuated, and bland. Improvements are said to be forthcoming, but I have yet to see them.

Best Wines: Clos de Vougeot, Vosne-Romanée Les Beaux Monts

DOMAINE PIERRE BERTHEAU (CHAMBOLLE-MUSIGNY)* * */* * * *

Traditionally made, old-style, rustic burgundies are the rule of thumb from Pierre Bertheau.
Some vintages reveal funky aromas (brett galore) because of the ancient barrels that are
utilized. Nevertheless, Bertheau is capable of turning out blockbuster, rich, mouth-filling,
savory burgundies that can last over a decade. This domaine has never received as much
praise as it deserves.

Best Wines: Bonnes Mares, Chambolle-Musigny Les Amoureuses, Chambolle-Musigny Les
Charmes

DOMAINE ALBERT BICHOT (BEAUNE)*/* * * *

There are a multitude of wines produced under this firm's private labels, but the wines from
Bichot's own estates, particularly those from Clos Frantin in Vosne-Romanée and the
Domaine Long Depaquit in Chablis, can be superb. The Clos Frantin wines can be variable,
as there is a tendency to process the wines too much, but there have been enough rich and
compelling wines from Clos Frantin (the 1985s, for example) for this estate to merit serious
consideration.

Best Wines: Chambertin, Clos de Vougeot, Grands-Echézeaux, Vosne-Romanée Les Malconsorts

DOMAINE BILLARD-GONNET (POMMARD)* *

Coarse, hard Pinots emerge from Billard-Gonnet. They are reputed to be age-worthy wines,
but those I have purchased and cellared have lost their fruit and died long before the tannin
melted away.

Best Wines: Pommard Clos des Vergers, Pommard Les Pézerolles, Pommard Les Rugiens

DOMAINE BITOUZET-PRIEUR (VOLNAY)* * *

Bitouzet is better known for his white than red wines, but the reds, especially the Volnay Clos des Chênes, Volnay Pitures, and Volnay Taillepieds, are attractive, well-made wines. They rarely hit the highest peaks, but they are consistently authentic examples of Volnay. They can last for 5–10 years.

Best Wines: Volnay Clos des Chênes, Volnay Pitures, Volnay Taillepieds

DOMAINE SIMON BIZE ET FILS (SAVIGNY-LES-BEAUNE)* * *

One of the few Burgundian winemakers I have never met, Simon Bize is a man whose wines I have admired for some time. They are classic, light- to medium-bodied wines from the unheralded appellations of Savigny-Les-Beaune. They are clean, moderately fruity, and surprisingly age-worthy. Moreover, this is one Burgundy producer where there is a good quality/price rapport.

Best Wines: Savigny-Les-Beaune Les Forneau, Savigny-Les-Beaune aux Guettes, Savigny-Les-Beaune Les Marconnets, Savigny-Les-Beaune Les Vergelesses

DOMAINE JEAN-MARC BOILLOT (POMMARD)* * *

This producer's domaine has grown in both quantity and quality. The white wines possess more life than the rather processed reds, but Boillot is using a more cautious hand in terms of interventionist techniques that can rob Pinot Noir of its subtleness. Will he exploit the existing potential?

Best Wines: Beaune Les Montrevenots, Pommard Jarolières

DOMAINE LUCIEN BOILLOT ET FILS (GEVREY-CHAMBERTIN)* *

I have had good wines from Lucien Boillot, but he is too inconsistent, failing in difficult years such as 1986, 1987, 1991, and 1992. Although he has fashioned some fine wines, there is considerable potential for improvement.

Best Wines: Nuits St.-Georges Les Pruliers, Volnay Les Angles

DOMAINE JEAN-CLAUDE BOISSET (NUITS ST.-GEORGES)*/* *

This huge *négociant* may be the most successful and wealthiest firm in Burgundy, which tells readers all they need to know about Burgundy. The firm includes a number of other Burgundy houses such as Charles Vienot, Lionel J. Bruck, and Thomas-Bassot. The Boisset wines are not made for connoisseurs in search of hand-crafted, estate-bottled wines, but rather for the mass market that desires burgundies from a prestigious appellation. As Serena Sutcliffe stated in her *Guide to White Burgundy,* "I am afraid these burgundies give me absolutely no lift at all."

DOMAINE BOUCHARD PÈRE ET FILS (BEAUNE)* * *

This firm has significantly increased the quality of its wines since the late eighties. Bouchard's estate-bottled wines from vintages such as 1989 and 1990 are good enough to compete with the finest wines of Burgundy. This is encouraging news for burgundy lovers, because Bouchard, along with the Faiveley firm, possesses the largest and most impressive vineyard holdings in the entire Côte d'Or. The red wines are now handled more gently in their state-of-the-art facilities in Beaune. There are a number of luscious, rich, impressively endowed reds emerging from Bouchard Père et Fils. Their unequivocal successes in 1990 were followed by good but uninspiring 1991s, and very attractive, soft, forward 1992s that were well above the standard level of quality for the vintage.

Best Wines: Beaune Les Grèves Vignes de L'Enfant Jésus, Beaune-Marconnets, Chambertin Clos de Bèze, Le Corton, Echézeaux, La Romanée, Volnay Les Caillerets Cuvée Carnot

DOMAINE JEAN-MARC BOULEY (VOLNAY)* * *

I have been more impressed with Bouley's wines in the past. This is an important estate with many fine vineyards, but often the wines taste overly oaked or underwined, depending on your point of view. There have been some successful vintages, but it appears Bouley should be lowering his crop yields and going for more concentration, especially in view of his love of lavish doses of toasty oak.

Best Wines: Pommard Les Pézerolles, Pommard Les Rugiens, Volnay Clos des Chênes

DOMAINE BOURÉE PÈRE ET FILS (GEVREY-CHAMBERTIN)* * * *

This unheralded, low-profile enterprise, located on Route National 74 in the middle of Gevrey-Chambertin, is run by the highly capable Monsieur Vallet. This is not a high-tech cellar with rows of sparkling clean, stainless steel tanks and stacks of brand-new oak barrels. Rather, the cellar is dingy, the barrels are old, but the wines are rich, concentrated, and bottled naturally without filtration, barrel by barrel. The wines are also bottled much later than most (something I do not always agree with), but there is no doubting many rich, occasionally rustic, concentrated, age-worthy red burgundies emerge from these cellars. In most vintages, Bourée's wines need 5–8 years to open; they can last for 20 or more years— a rarity in present-day Burgundy. The firm owns only small parcels of Charmes-Chambertin and Beaune Les Epenottes. Bourée produces the only top-flight wine from the Clos de la Justice vineyard situated east of Route N 74.

Best Wines: Beaune Les Epenottes, Bonnes Mares, Chambertin, Charmes-Chambertin, Clos de la Roche, Gevrey-Chambertin Clos de la Justice

ALAIN BURGUET (GEVREY-CHAMBERTIN)* * *

Perhaps it is because of the tough vintages of the nineties, but I sense Burguet's finest efforts in the eighties outdistance what he has accomplished in 1991 and 1992. This tiny, seriously run domaine owns a bevy of vineyard parcels in Gevrey. Recent vintages have revealed a lack of depth, but perhaps with such a tiny estate it is impossible to make a strict selection.

Best Wine: Gevrey-Chambertin Vieilles Vignes

DOMAINE JACQUES CACHEUX-BLÉE ET FILS (VOSNE-ROMANÉE)* * * *

Beautifully rendered burgundies that are rich, elegant, and aromatically compelling are the rule of thumb from this underrated Vosne-Romanée estate. Moreover, the Cacheux's wines age well for 12–15 years. Cacheux produced brilliant wines in 1985, 1987, 1988, 1989, 1990, and 1992.

Best Wines: Echézeaux, Vosne-Romanée Les Suchots

DOMAINE CAMUS (GEVREY-CHAMBERTIN)* *

This well-endowed estate continues to putter along, keeping its wines entirely too long in cask, resulting in wines that seem advanced and frequently already dried out by the time they make the transatlantic journey to the United States. A handful of 1985s initially looked good, but they have now fallen apart. Recent vintages such as 1987 and 1988 were frightfully tannic, hard wines that lacked charm and flesh. With some of the finest plots of Chambertin, Charmes-Chambertin, Latricières-Chambertin, and Mazis-Chambertin, this estate has the potential *terroirs* to produce superb wines.

Best Wines: Chambertin, Charmes-Chambertin, Mazis-Chambertin

DOMAINE GUY CASTAGNIER (MOREY ST.-DENIS)* * */* * * *

These wines, which also appear under the label of Vadey-Castagnier, are supple, ripe, attractive red burgundies for drinking during their first 7–8 years of life. The style in recent vintages has been for oaky, fragrant, pure, elegant, supple, user-friendly Pinot Noirs.

Best Wines: Bonnes Mares, Clos de la Roche, Clos St.-Denis, Latricières-Chambertin

DOMAINE CATHIARD-MOLINIER (VOSNE-ROMANÉE)* * *

This tiny estate was once the favorite of such renowned European restaurants as Taillevent in Paris and Florence's l'Enoteca Pinchiorri. I have not seen a Cathiard-Molinier wine in years, but they were traditionally made, full-bodied red burgundies that admirably stood the test of time.

Best Wines: Clos de Vougeot, Nuits St.-Georges Les Murgers, Romanée St.-Vivant, Vosne-Romanée Les Malconsorts

CHÂTEAU DE CHAMBOLLE-MUSIGNY (DOMAINE JEAN FRÉDÉRIC MUGNIER) (CHAMBOLLE-MUSIGNY)* * * *

Since the debut vintage in 1978, this domaine has displayed considerable potential. If the yields were lower, Mugnier would undoubtedly deserve five stars. The wines are marked by generous amounts of new oak as well as wonderfully ripe, pure, red and black fruit presented in a supple, velvety-textured style. Surprisingly, the 1989s were more muscular than the 1988s. All of Mugnier's recent vintages have demonstrated why top-notch red burgundy is so alluring—they are wines with fragrant, intense personalities loaded with gobs of sweet fruit marked by noticeable but not intrusive toasty new oak. The only downside is that these wines lack staying power. Even the 1985s are beginning to tire.

Best Wines: Bonnes Mares, Chambolle-Musigny Les Amoureuses

DOMAINE CHANDON DE BRIAILLES (SAVIGNY-LES-BEAUNE)* * *

This is a frustrating estate to follow. It is a beautifully run domaine with impeccable cellars and excellent vineyard holdings, but the wines are entirely too manipulated and processed. The excellent raw materials present in cask often taste light and fragile after bottling. Multiple filtrations and too much fining are the culprits. Nevertheless, if someone could persuade the proprietor, the Comte Aymard-Claude de Nicolay, to at least abandon their Kisselguhr filtration system and fine less, this would be a domaine to take note of.

Best Wines: Corton Clos du Roi, Corton Les Maréchaudes

DOMAINE PHILIPPE CHARLOPIN-PARIZOT (MARSANNAY)* * *

In many ways this domaine symbolizes the problems that must be overcome if burgundy wines are to justify the astronomically high prices they fetch. In the early 1980s, when American importer Neal Rosenthal began representing Charlopin-Parizot, I remember giving this estate's wines superb scores, especially an extraordinary 1980 Charmes-Chambertin. I first had the wine in a tasting with some of the 1980s from the Domaine de la Romanée-Conti (my favorite burgundies from the entire decade of the eighties), and Charlopin's 1980 Charmes-Chambertin came out first. Neal Rosenthal discontinued representing Charlopin (justifiably) as the subsequent wines were bland, dilute, and highly processed. When I last visited Charlopin, I felt the wines were good, but I asked him why he was doing so much filtering when the 1980 was bottled completely unfiltered. He denied that there had ever been an unfiltered wine cuvée, so I simply said that when I returned to the United States I would send his broker a bottle for him to taste. I did, and the results of the tasting (as reported to me) proved that the 1980 unfiltered Charmes was superior to the filtered cuvée of the same wine sold in Europe. Nevertheless, Charlopin continues to filter his wines. These are good, fruity, ripe, medium-bodied Pinot Noirs, but given his terrific vineyards, much more could be achieved.

Best Wines: Charmes-Chambertin, Clos St.-Denis

F. CHAUVENET (NUITS ST.-GEORGES)* *

This *négociant* fashions pleasant, straightforward, commercial-style burgundies that are clean, fruity, and generously oaked. Although not complex, they are ideal for drinking in their first 5–6 years of life.

DOMAINE JEAN CHAUVENET (NUITS ST.-GEORGES)* * * *

This underrated producer makes pure, well-delineated Pinot Noirs from fine holdings in Nuits St.-Georges. While approachable in their youth, these wines age beautifully. Chauvenet's 1985s, which are just now reaching full maturity, are sumptuous examples of that very good vintage. Chauvenet neither fines nor filters his wines, resulting in Pinot Noirs in the top vintages that are loaded with copious quantities of red and black fruits.

Best Wines: Nuits St.-Georges Les Bousselots, Nuits St.-Georges Les Perrières, Nuits St.-Georges Les Vaucrains

ROBERT CHEVILLON (NUITS ST.-GEORGES)* * *

I have lost some of my enthusiasm for Chevillon's wines, partly because the wines from the eighties have not lived up to expectations. The 1985s never seemed to develop, the 1986s are bland and monolithic, and the 1988s hard and hollow. Nevertheless, Chevillon does produce darkly colored, spicy, tough wines that are flattering to taste from cask, but take on a toughness with age and never fully blossom. There may be exceptions; I hope his 1989s are the real thing.

Best Wines: Nuits St.-Georges Les Cailles, Nuits St.-Georges Les Roncières, Nuits St.-Georges Les St.-Georges, Nuits St.-Georges Les Vaucrains

DOMAINE GEORGES CHICOTOT (NUITS ST.-GEORGES)* * * *

This obnoxiously aggressive, self-proclaimed Communist has long been a disciple of the controversial oenologist, Guy Accad. His wines are powerful, densely colored, full-bodied examples of Nuits St.-Georges that could be even better if he bottled them sooner. Nevertheless, readers in search of intense, muscular, powerful Nuits St.-Georges should remember that Chicotot delivers the goods.

Best Wines: Nuits St.-Georges Les Pruliers, Nuits St.-Georges Les St.-Georges, Nuits St.-Georges Les Vaucrains

DOMAINE DANIEL CHOPIN-GROFFIER (PRÉMEAUX)* * * * *

More and more I am convinced that Daniel Chopin is the true heir apparent to the great Henri Jayer. Chopin's wines exhibit extraordinary purity, flavor, ripeness, and richly fragrant personalities. It is a shame Chopin-Groffier does not have a large domaine or more great vineyards. Even his lower-level wines can be remarkably seductive red burgundies. The wines are also consistent. For example, few Burgundians made better wines than Chopin-Groffier in 1991 and 1992. The downside is that Chopin-Groffier's wines require drinking early—in their first 10–12 years of life.

Best Wines: Chambolle-Musigny, Clos de Vougeot, Nuits St.-Georges Les Chaignots, Vougeot

DOMAINE BRUNO CLAIR (MARSANNAY)* * *

I have always had high hopes for this estate, but Clair has never delivered the quality I had anticipated. Certainly he says all the right things during an interview, and he has the correct answers regarding *terroir*, vinification, and *élevage*. But the proof is always in the bottle, and too many of Clair's wines taste stripped, compact, and lean, and lack intensity and personality. The 1991s were extremely disappointing, and vintages such as 1990, 1988, and, shame on me, 1983 (I rated them very highly) have not stood the test of time. This is all unfortunate given Clair's fine holdings. On a positive note, Clair's 1992s did turn out well.

Best Wines: Chambertin Clos de Bèze, Gevrey-Chambertin Les Cazetiers, Gevrey-Chambertin Clos St.-Jacques, Savigny-Les-Beaune Les Dominaudes

DOMAINE GEORGES CLERGET (VOUGEOT)* *

I have never tasted an inspirational wine from Georges Clerget, and recent efforts suggest a continuance of the status quo. The wines lack color, are frightfully inconsistent, and are not nearly as concentrated as they should be. An annoying earthiness in some cuvées suggests the lack of proper cooperage. The 1991s and 1992s were disappointing, but rumors continue that it is just a matter of time before someone steps in and provides some much-needed investment capital.

Best Wines: Chambolle-Musigny Les Charmes, Echézeaux

DOMAINE CLOS DES LAMBRAYS (MOREY ST.-DENIS)* *

This estate continues to struggle, which is unfortunate given the fact that this historic vineyard can trace its existence to 1365. It was elevated to grand cru status in 1981, presumably because of its superb *terroir* rather than because of the quality of the wines. The dismal track record of disappointing vintages includes a terrible 1983, a now-senile 1985, a frightfully light, diluted 1986, 1987, and 1988, and a fruitier but undistinctive 1990 and 1991. This remains one of the most notable underachievers in the Côte d'Or. When asked what they do, everything seems to sound right, with all the proper acknowledgments to vineyard management, small crops, noninterventionist winemaking policies, healthy amounts of new oak, and little manipulation of the wine. So what's the problem?

DOMAINE JEAN-JACQUES CONFURON (PRÉMEAUX)* * * * *

A potential superstar may be emerging. It is no secret why this estate's wines have become superb as opposed to merely good. The domaine now practices extensive crop-thinning, with average yields of under 30 hectoliters per hectare, even in abundant vintages such as 1992. These are powerful, rich wines that are bottled early to protect their rich, concentrated fruit. Confuron enjoyed stunning success in 1991 and 1992, and early reports indicate that the 1993s are off the charts! The old days of musty, vegetal, overcropped wines are a thing of the past. The daughter of the late Jean-Jacques Confuron, Sophie Meunier, deserves many kudos for this estate's renaissance.

Best Wines: Clos de Vougeot, Nuits St.-Georges Les Boudots, Nuits St.-Georges Les Chaboeufs, Romanée St.-Vivant, Vosne-Romanée Les Beaux Monts

DOMAINE J. CONFURON-COTETIDOT (VOSNE-ROMANÉE)* * * *

The stocky, bulldoglike Jacky Confuron is not an easy guy to either talk to or taste with. However, he makes rich, muscular, full-bodied red burgundies from extremely low yields. Eschewing new oak, Confuron bottles very late and rarely touches or manipulates his wines from barrel to bottle. Quality can be superb, but he is inconsistent and tends to bottle too late. The assortment of musty old barrels he utilizes adds little to his beefy, husky red burgundies.

Best Wines: Clos de Vougeot, Echézeaux, Nuits St.-Georges Premier Cru, Vosne-Romanée Les Suchots

DOMAINE COQUARD-LOISON-FLEUROT (FLAGEY-ECHÉZEAUX)* */* * *

These wines are erratic, which is a shame given the fact that the Coquard family have impressively situated parcels in such esteemed grands crus as Clos St.-Denis, Grands Echézeaux, and Charmes-Chambertin. Occasionally big, thick, rich, full-bodied Pinot Noir emerges, but in most cases the wines are a bit dull, heavy, formless, and uninspiring.

Best Wines: Charmes-Chambertin Clos de la Roche, Clos St.-Denis, Clos de Vougeot, Grands Echézeaux

DOMAINE EDMOND CORNU (LADOIX-SERRIGNY)* * *

Except for Cornu's Corton Les Bressandes, his vineyard holdings are in modest appellations. Nevertheless, he turns out better and better wines by keeping yields moderate and by not overly processing the wines. Recent vintages have included strong efforts in 1989 and 1990.

I should also note that Cornu's 1985 Corton Les Bressandes is living up to my high expectations.

Best Wines: Aloxe-Corton Les Moutottes, Corton Les Bressandes

DOMAINE DE MADAME DE COURCEL (POMMARD)* * * ?
This important Pommard estate has provided me with some thrilling wines, particularly from the 1962, 1964, 1966, 1971, and 1978 vintages. Since then I have often wondered if I have not been overrating Courcel's wines. They are always solidly colored with plenty of body, but vintages since 1985 have tasted lighter, without the concentration that I have come to expect. I was shocked to read in Englishman Remington Norman's *Great Domaines of Burgundy* that the wines are subjected to a "very light, flat filtration, above all for the USA." It is hard to believe that serious burgundy importers would request highly processed and manipulated Pinot Noir cuvées, but that may explain the so-so performance of these wines over recent vintages. This property produced disappointing 1991s, adequate 1992s, good rather than spectacular 1990s, pleasant 1989s, and hard, astringent, charmless 1988s.

Best Wines: Pommard Grands Clos des Epenots, Pommard Les Rugiens

DOMAINE PIERRE DAMOY (GEVREY-CHAMBERTIN)* * */* * * *
With its prestigious holdings of Chambertin Clos de Bèze (13+ acres) and the 1.25-acre parcel of Chambertin, this is an estate with extraordinary potential. Damoy has turned things around with their 1993s, the best wines made at the estate in decades.

Best Wines: Chambertin, Chambertin Clos de Bèze, Chapelle-Chambertin

DOMAINE MARIUS DELARCHE (PERNAND-VERGELESSES)* * */* * * *
Delarche is one of the Côte de Beaune's up-and-coming producers. When I first visited this estate over a decade ago the quality level was only average, but since the mid-eighties they have lowered crop yields and are taking more risks during the harvest and winemaking, resulting in far more interesting wines. Delarche makes impressive wines in top years and came on particularly strong with the 1992 vintage.

Best Wine: Corton Les Rénardes

DOMAINE JOSEPH DROUHIN (BEAUNE)* * */* * * *
Fifty-one percent of this well-known producer was sold in 1995 to a Japanese firm, although Robert Drouhin will remain in charge of this enterprise. Drouhin's red wines rarely inspire excitement, although they are consistently well-made, fruity, light- to medium-bodied, accessible, and highly commercial products. In many respects they are ideal for beginners who are looking for the most flattering style. I have always felt that if they had slightly more concentration and depth they would rival the wines of several top *négociants,* such as Louis Jadot. Andrew Barr, in his book, *Pinot Noir,* quoted Drouhin when asked why consumers pay high prices for burgundies. Drouhin stated, "We're not selling wine, we're selling luxury. We're selling an image. . . ." With more and more knowledgeable consumers, I wonder if Drouhin would say that today. The best bet with Drouhin is always the estate wine, Beaune Clos des Mouches, but top vintages can provide very rewarding examples of this firm's Grands Echézeaux, Musigny, Volnay Clos des Chênes, Chambolle-Musigny Les Amoureuses, and Bonnes Mares. Whether it be a grand or premier cru, Drouhin's reds need to be drunk before the age of 10.

Best Wines: Bonnes Mares, Chambolle-Musigny Les Amoureuses, Grands Echézeaux, Musigny, Volnay Clos des Chênes

DOMAINE DROUHIN-LAROSE (GEVREY-CHAMBERTIN)* * *
This impeccably run domaine boasts some of the best-placed vineyards in Gevrey-Chambertin. Moreover, I have had many memorable bottles from top vintages between 1959 and 1980. Sadly, recent vintages have turned out much lighter wines, without the intensity

and concentration found in the older Drouhin-Larose vintages. Highly fined and filtered examples of Pinot Noir must be hugely successful for this firm! This change of style, while undoubtedly profitable, is hardly encouraging for serious burgundy enthusiasts.

Best Wines: Bonnes Mares, Chambertin Clos de Bèze, Chapelle-Chambertin, Clos de Vougeot, Latricières-Chambertin, Mazis-Chambertin

DOMAINE P. DUBREUIL-FONTAINE ET FILS
(PERNAND-VERGELESSES)* * *

Elegant, light- to medium-bodied red wines are the rule of thumb from Bernard Dubreuil. They are characterized by stylish, pure cherry fruit and supple textures; these wines can age for up to a decade.

Best Wines: Corton Les Bressandes, Corton Clos du Roi, Corton Les Perrièrers

DOMAINE CLAUDE ET MAURICE DUGAT
(GEVREY-CHAMBERTIN)* * * * *

One of Burgundy's greatest wine producers, this estate is making sensationally sumptuous and age-worthy wines. Tiny yields, physiologically ripe grapes, and a noninterventionist winemaking philosophy (there is rarely any fining or filtering done) result in enormously rich, aromatically complex, spectacular wines. Even in difficult vintages such as 1991 and 1992, Claude and Maurice Dugat produced superb wines, proving once again that the producer makes all the difference. Lamentably, this is a tiny estate, as evidenced by the fact that only 5–10 cases of Griottes- or Charmes-Chambertin make it to the United States —another reason why burgundy remains so frustrating, even for those wine enthusiasts who can afford it!

Best Wines: Charmes-Chambertin, Gevrey-Chambertin Lavaux St.-Jacques, Gevrey-Chambertin Premier Cru, Griottes-Chambertin

DOMAINE PIERRE DUGAT (GEVREY-CHAMBERTIN)* * *

After selling much of his production to *négociants,* Pierre Dugat is now estate-bottling his wines. They are rich, solidly made, occasionally massive, and capable of a decade or more of aging.

Best Wine: Gevrey-Chambertin Vieilles Vignes

DOMAINE DUJAC (MOREY ST.-DENIS)* * * *

This is an extremely well run estate managed with an intelligent, open-minded view of winemaking by proprietor Jacques Seysses. Seysses is a member of the new generation of Burgundy winemakers who have traveled extensively and who recognize that if Burgundy is going to make a viable product, it must be devoted to producing extremely high quality wines that justify the astronomical prices asked, as well as the high expectations of consumers. The style of wine Seysses aims for is one of elegant, soft, sweet, fragrant, velvety-textured Pinot fruit. The wines are light colored and aromatically superb, with rarely more than medium body, and earthy, juicy, Pinot flavors. My confidence in their ability to age has been shaken by the disappointingly rapid evolution of the 1982s, 1983s, 1986s, 1987s, 1988s, and to some extent the estate's excellent 1985s. It seems to me that Jacques Seysses's greatest vintages, 1969 and 1978 (both of which are still superb), possess a measure of concentration and intensity that he does not achieve today. Even the 1990 Dujac wines, which were delicious young, are on the fast evolutionary track and are thus best consumed in their first 7–8 years of life. While Jacques Seysses does no filtering, perhaps there is too much fining. Additionally, are the yields of his relatively young vineyard too high?

Best Wines: Bonnes Mares, Charmes-Chambertin, Clos de la Roche, Clos St.-Denis

DOMAINE MAURICE ECARD ET FILS (SAVIGNY-LES-BEAUNE)* * * *

It is a shame there are not more red burgundies like Ecard's premiers crus from Savigny-Les-Beaune. His wines go from strength to strength, offering vivid, ripe, elegant Pinot Noirs that are full of fruit, wonderfully pure, representative of their different *terroirs*, and sold at modest prices. Ecard's wines drink well young, yet can age for 10–12 years. This is an estate to seek out for modestly priced Pinot Noir that delivers the goods.

Best Wines: Savigny-Les-Beaune Les Narbantons, Savigny-Les-Beaune Les Peuillats, Savigny-Les-Beaune Les Serpentières

DOMAINE RENÉ ENGEL (VOSNE-ROMANÉE)* * * *

The young Philippe Engel produces wines that continue to exhibit his strengths as a winemaker. The first vintages I tasted were above average, but hardly inspiring. Today, his wines are close to five-star quality. Engel owns some wonderful vineyards, including a plot of Clos de Vougeot composed mostly of vines planted in 1922. The wines are authoritatively rich, well-colored, medium- to full-bodied red burgundies with well-integrated tannin, as well as excellent purity, richness, and complexity. Just about everything produced by Engel is noteworthy. The wines can be drunk young or cellared for 10–15 years. Engel has enjoyed considerable success both in top years and in off years such as 1991.

Best Wines: Clos de Vougeot, Echézeaux, Grands Echézeaux, Vosne-Romanée Les Brûlées

DOMAINE M. FREDERIC ESMONIN (GEVREY-CHAMBERTIN)* * *

This is a typical burgundy estate. Although it is loaded with fine vineyards, much of the estate's considerable potential is not exploited. Too much fining and filtering often result in dried-out, compact wines that are much smaller-scaled after bottling than when tasted from cask. As long as consumers are willing to pay high prices for stripped red burgundies, there is no reason why any of these growers should change their methods. Nevertheless, Esmonin is an estate to follow closely, as he does everything right in the cellars—up to bottling.

Best Wines: Gevrey-Chambertin Lavaux St.-Jacques, Griotte-Chambertin, Mazis-Chambertin

DOMAINE MICHEL ESMONIN ET FILLE (GEVREY-CHAMBERTIN)* * * *

Unfortunately, only one premier cru (insiders argue that Gevrey-Chambertin Clos St.-Jacques should be a grand cru) is produced here. Michel Esmonin is now in quasi-retirement and his attractive daughter, Sylvie, is handling the winemaking responsibilities. Esmonin's wines are bottled naturally and are among the finest of the village. This is a relatively young domaine, having sold virtually all of its production to *négociants* prior to 1985. Vintages from 1988 through 1992 are immensely impressive. They require 4–5 years of cellaring and have the potential to last for 10–15 years.

Best Wine: Gevrey-Chambertin Clos St.-Jacques

FAIVELEY (NUITS ST.-GEORGES)* * *

As longtime readers know, I have been a supporter of the Faiveley burgundies, giving them very high praise over a number of vintages. Faiveley now claims to be the largest landholder in the Côte d'Or, with significant holdings also in the Côte Chalonnais. François Faiveley, who took over from his father, Guy, in 1976, appears to do everything correctly, emphasizing the finest clones in the vineyard, bleeding the cuve to increase the wine's concentration in abundant years such as 1982 and 1986, and bottling most of the grands crus as well as some of the premiers crus by hand, without filtration. While I have been impressed with the Faiveley wines when tasted in Europe, other burgundy critics have been unmoved by the Faiveley style. American wine writer, Matt Kramer, in his book, *Making Sense of Burgundy*, states that the Faiveley wines are "tough, rather dried out" and "the winemaking is old-fashioned in the less attractive sense of the term." Andrew Barr, the controversial English writer, in his book, *Pinot Noir*, claims to "find them too earthy and too coarse." I have come to the conclusion that Barr and Kramer are more correct than I have been, particularly given the tastings of Faiveley wines after they have had several years of bottle age. Too many wines lack rich, concentrated fruit, and are relatively hard, compact, tannic, and austere. They are potentially long-lived wines, but very tough and blunt. This is a huge firm, and the grands and premiers crus are among the most expensive red burgundies produced by any *négociant*. Yet good values can be found among Faiveley's Côte de Chalonnais wines, particularly from the bevy of wines made from vineyard sites in Mercurey, such as Clos de Myglands, Clos de Roy, Domaine de la Croix-Jacquet, and La Framboisière, as well as the firm's very good generic Bourgogne Rouge.

Best Wines: Chambertin Clos de Bèze, Charmes-Chambertin, Corton Clos des Cortons, Nuits St.-Georges Les St.-Georges

DOMAINE JEAN-CLAUDE FOURRIER (GEVREY-CHAMBERTIN)* *

I cut my teeth on some great wines from this estate when it was called Pernot-Fourrier. The 1966, 1969, and 1971 vintages produced excellent wines. But that is ancient history. Although this estate possesses some gorgeous vineyards, they are turning out light-bodied, fruity, soft wines that lack concentration and authority.

Best Wines: Gevrey-Chambertin Clos St.-Jacques, Gevrey-Chambertin Combe aux Moines, Griotte-Chambertin

DOMAINE JEAN GARAUDET (POMMARD)* * */* * * *

This is a reliable source for attractively rich, medium- to full-bodied red burgundies. Garaudet's Pommard Les Charmots from a vineyard planted in 1902 is a five-star wine in top vintages. My only reservation concerning Garaudet's red wines is that they are sometimes monolithic. However, they are cleanly made, rich, and satisfying, with Les Charmots a cut above the rest.

Best Wines: Beaune Clos des Mouches, Pommard Les Charmots

DOMAINE MICHEL GAUNOUX (POMMARD)* * * *

This well-run estate occasionally produces Pommards of five-star quality. I have had some remarkable older vintages from Gaunoux, particularly 1962, 1964, and 1966. While recent vintages are lighter, they remain impressively endowed, rich, full-bodied wines. Madame Gaunoux has run this estate since her husband died in 1984 and she plays it close to the vest in terms of how the wines are sold. Most vintages are held back for several years (for example, the 1990s were sold in 1994), and she has exhibited the courage to declassify her entire crop (1986). This is an estate with a very high average of old vines. Readers looking for a bottle of Gaunoux wine are best advised to seek out some of France's most luxurious restaurants, since many sommeliers are enchanted with the Gaunoux wines. It is a shame these Pommards are not better known in the United States as this is a seriously run estate. Cuvées of Madame Gaunoux's wines tasted in Europe are richer than the same wines tasted in America. Is the American importer requesting fined and filtered cuvées, or are the wines not traveling well?

Best Wines: Beaune Les Boucherottes, Beaune Les Epenottes, Corton Les Rénardes, Pommard Les Charmots, Pommard Les Grands Epenots, Pommard Les Rugiens

DOMAINE PIERRE GELIN (FIXIN)* * * *

For whatever reason, this domaine, run by Stephen Gelin, has never received the accolades it deserves. The wines are not made in the up-front, fruity, commercial style favored by many Burgundy producers. These are large-scaled, muscular, powerful red burgundies that often require 4–5 years of cellaring. There is an admirable leathery component to many of the wines that may be annoying to technocrats, but these are wines of unmistakable personality and distinction. There are also some top-notch values made by Gelin from their

holdings in the relatively unknown Côte d'Or appellation of Fixin. Gelin made very fine 1990s, but all of them require cellaring.
Best Wines: Chambertin Clos de Bèze, Fixin Clos de Chapitre, Fixin Clos Napoleon, Mazis-Chambertin

DOMAINE LUCIEN GEOFFROY (GEVREY-CHAMBERTIN)* * *

As I said in my book, *Burgundy,* I am not sure I am capable of appreciating the blatantly oaky style of wine produced by Geoffroy. Although these large-scaled wines exhibit fine color, they possess an excess of wood and tannin.
Best Wines: Gevrey-Chambertin Les Champeaux, Gevrey-Chambertin Clos Prieur, Mazis-Chambertin

DOMAINE JACQUES GERMAIN (CHOREY-LES-BEAUNE)* * *

Readers who prefer light-bodied, elegant, silky, fruity red burgundies generously touched by toasty new oak will find Germain's bevy of wines to be good to very good examples. While rarely superb, they are consistently well made and ideal for drinking in the first decade of life.
Best Wines: Beaune Les Boucherottes, Beaune Les Cent Vignes, Beaune Les Teurons, Beaune Les Vignes-Franches

DOMAINE ARMAND GIRARDIN (POMMARD)* * * *

Americans receive a special cuvée of Girardin's wines that is not available elsewhere in the world. My European readers have complained about the wines they purchase, which they claim are musty and oxidized. Girardin's American importer insists on 100% new oak and that the wines be bottled unfined and unfiltered. In most vintages they look almost like barrel samples with their dark purple colors. They are thick, rich, and in some vintages (1989 and 1990) among the richest, most powerful, and most muscular Pommards produced. These massive, old-style, chewy, highly extracted Pommards are not for drinking in their youth.
Best Wines: Beaune Clos des Mouches, Pommard Les Charmots, Pommard Les Epenots, Pommard Les Rugiens

DOMAINE HENRI GOUGES (NUITS ST.-GEORGES)* *

In his book, *Making Sense of Burgundy,* American wine writer, Matt Kramer, wrote, "It is time to take the gloves off: the wines of Domaine Henri Gouges are second rate and have been for years. No domaine in Burgundy has coasted longer on a once-lustrous reputation than this one." In 1975, I paid my first visit to Domaine Gouges, tasting an array of remarkable burgundies from the 1969, 1966, and 1964 vintages. Then I returned home, purchased the 1971s, and was horrified to find them watery and light. Two and a half decades since, only slight improvements have been made at this famous estate. The wines of the nineties possess better color than those produced between 1970 amd 1989, but they remain hard, austere, small-scaled Pinot Noirs without impressive depth or intensity. And that's the way it is.
Best Wines: Nuits St.-Georges Les St.-Georges, Nuits St.-Georges Les Vaucrains

MACHARD DE GRAMONT (NUITS ST.-GEORGES)* * * *

This is a large, 50-acre estate with vineyards dotted throughout the Côte d'Or landscape in 19 different appellations. I have always enjoyed the rich, structured, concentrated style that proprietor Arnaud Gramont produces. Moreover, he remains one of the most open and candid Burgundy producers and is quick to castigate vintages such as 1987 and 1986, and to justifiably praise 1990. These are not wines to drink young, but rather, they usually require 3–4 years of cellaring. Gramont is one of the few Burgundians to question the adverse affect fining can have on Pinot Noir in some vintages. A light filtration is utilized at

Gramont, although he is generally against the use of interventionist techniques. Lastly, Gramont's wines remain reasonably priced. These are no-nonsense, substantial wines.

Best Wines: Beaune Les Chouacheux, Beaune Les Epenottes, Nuits St.-Georges Les Damodes, Nuits St.-Georges Les Hauts Poirets, Pommard Le Clos Blanc

DOMAINE JEAN GRIVOT (VOSNE-ROMANÉE)* * * *

Much has been made of the fact that Grivot is a follower of Guy Accad. Because of that he has, in my opinion, been unfairly criticized. While Accad does not make the wine, he does offer advice, some of which is followed by his clients. Grivot's wines tend to be robust, rich, and generally age-worthy. That being said, except for the most concentrated vintages I would opt for drinking his wines within 10–12 years of the vintage. Certainly there is no lack of extract or color at this domaine, and the wines consistently perform well in vintages such as 1987 and 1991.

Best Wines: Clos de Vougeot, Echézeaux, Nuits St.-Georges Les Boudots, Nuits St.-Georges Les Pruliers, Richebourg, Vosne-Romanée Les Brûlées, Vosne-Romanée Les Suchots

DOMAINE ROBERT GROFFIER (MOREY ST.-DENIS)* * *

This domaine's irritating inconsistency is largely a result of overcropping. Just when I had given up on Groffier after frightfully light wines in 1985, he turned around and produced good wines in 1986. The disappointing 1990s were followed by very good 1991s. Groffier's wines are extremely expensive, but when he gets it right (and that seems to be when Mother Nature intervenes to cut back the crop size), they offer plenty of succulent, opulent, ripe fruit intertwined with lavish quantities of smoky, toasty new oak. Groffier's wines can represent red burgundy's most precocious, decadent, up-front style, but interested parties will pay dearly.

Best Wines: Bonnes Mares, Chambertin Clos de Bèze, Chambolle-Musigny Les Amoureuses

DOMAINE A.-F. GROS (POMMARD)* * *

The high hopes I initially had for this domaine with the magical family name have largely not materialized, although this estate has turned out a few vintages of impressive Richebourg. One of numerous Burgundy estates bearing the Gros name, it typifies Burgundy's fragmented and confusing vineyard ownership. This Gros domaine (in Pommard) was formed by the marriage of Jean Gros's daughter, Anne-Françoise, to François Parent, of Domaine Parent. If you can find and afford the Richebourg in the very finest years, it merits purchasing.

Best Wine: Richebourg

DOMAINE ANNE ET FRANÇOIS GROS (VOSNE-ROMANÉE)* * *

This domaine also makes very fine Richebourg, but it has had a shaky track record with its other wines. At best, the Richebourg is a wonderfully black fruit– and floral-scented wine with an exotic opulence and richness. However, it must be drunk within its first 10–12 years of life.

Best Wine: Richebourg

DOMAINE JEAN GROS (VOSNE-ROMANÉE)* * */* * * *

The quality here has been shockingly spotty over recent vintages with only the Richebourg hitting the high notes from the 30+ acres of vineyards run by Madame Jean Gros and her son, Michel. Madame Gros, the longtime mayor of Vosne-Romanée, appears to be forcing the bulk of her Bourgogne Hautes Côtes de Nuits on any importer trying to get a few cases of Richebourg. It's a bad deal, as the expensive Hautes Côtes de Nuits is rarely exciting. The once superb Vosne-Romanée Clos des Réas also seems to have lightened up over recent years. It can be a profound example of red burgundy in top vintages. Recently replanted, their parcel of Clos de Vougeot is just returning to production. This plot is situated in one of the most prized locations on the upper slope of the Clos de Vougeot vineyard.

Best Wines: Clos de Vougeot, Richebourg, Vosne-Romanée Clos des Réas

DOMAINE GROS FRÈRE ET SOEUR (VOSNE-ROMANÉE)* * */* * * *

This estate, run by the enigmatic Bernard Gros, another son of Madame Gros, possesses a great wealth of vineyards and is capable of producing extraordinarily rich, opulent, decadent Pinot Noir that is sweet, jammy, and intoxicating. As I stated in my book, *Burgundy,* incredible bouquets of oranges, raspberries, and apricots have emerged from bottles of Clos de Vougeot, Grands Echézeaux, and Richebourg from Bernard Gros. Of all the Gros domaines, this one appears to be producing the most interesting wines in 1995, but they are frightfully expensive.

Best Wines: Clos de Vougeot, Grands Echézeaux, Richebourg

DOMAINE HAEGELEN-JAYER (VOSNE-ROMANÉE)* * * */* * * * *

I lament the fact that so little wine is produced at this microsized estate. Haegelen, a cousin of Henri Jayer, has the magic touch, much like the great Jayer himself. Although I have seen only a handful of vintages from this estate, the Clos de Vougeot and Echézeaux can be superb, even in off vintages. These are meaty, rich, concentrated, old-style burgundies.

Best Wines: Clos de Vougeot, Echézeaux

DOMAINE ALAIN HUDELOT-NOËLLAT (VOUGEOT)* * * *

The 1991s from Alain Hudelot-Noëllat were so impressive it makes me wonder if his excessive filtration techniques are a thing of the past. These are seductive, rich, medium- to full-bodied wines with excellent fruit and that expansive, velvety texture that makes top-notch red burgundy so wonderful. The grands crus also see plenty of new oak, so do not be surprised to find some smoky new oak notes in these wines. They are best drunk in their first 10–12 years of life.

Best Wines: Chambolle-Musigny Les Charmes, Clos de Vougeot, Richebourg, Romanée St.-Vivant, Vosne-Romanée Les Malconsorts, Vosne-Romanée Les Suchots

PAUL ET HENRI JACQUESON (RULLY)* * * */* * * *

Few American consumers make a special effort to search out the wines of Rully, but Jacqueson's red wines would please even the most snobbish connoisseur of burgundy. These fruit-filled, rich, pure wines are the darlings of many of France's top restaurants. Delicious when young, they are capable of lasting for up to a decade.

Best Wines: Mercurey Les Naugues, Rully Les Cloux, Rully Les Chaponnières

LOUIS JADOT (BEAUNE)* * * */* * * * *

This firm, a *négociant* as well as a vineyard owner, remains the reference point for how a Burgundy *négociant* should make wine. Run for years by one of Burgundy's great gentlemen, André Gagey, this estate is now being run by André's son, Pierre-André. He is supported by one of the Côte d'Or's finest oenologist/winemakers, Jacques Lardière. Just about everything produced by Jadot, from their generic Bourgogne Rouge, to their top-of-the-line Chambertin Clos de Bèze or Bonnes Mares, is of high, often superb quality. But insiders know Jadot's real bargains are the bevy of gorgeously made, rich, seductive, fruity Beaune premiers crus. These wines range from the Beaune Clos des Ursules to their supremely luscious premiers crus, Beaune Les Avaux, Beaune Les Boucherottes, Beaune Les Bressandes, Beaune Les Chouacheux, Beaune Les Couchereux, Beaune Les Grèves, Beaune Les Teurons, and Beaune Les Touissant (all splendid in years such as 1989 and 1990). The most underrated red wine of the Jadot portfolio is the Corton-Pougets, an especially long-lived red. In general, the 1991s from the Côte de Beaune were not as successful as I would have hoped, and their 1986s were relatively tough and hard, but this is one producer who came through the eighties with fine 1983s, rich, firmly structured 1985s, very good 1987s, excellent 1988s and 1989s, dazzling 1990s, and gorgeous 1992s. There is no house style, save for rich, well-delineated, structured wines that stand the test of time. In 1988, all the grands crus were bottled without filtration. That vintage was followed in 1990 with all the premiers and grands crus bottled without filtration.

Best Wines: In addition to the Beaune cuvées listed above and the Corton-Pougets, Chambolle-Musigny Les Amoureuses, Chapelle-Chambertin, Clos de Vougeot, Gevrey-Chambertin Clos St.-Jacques, Nuits St.-Georges Clos des Thorey, Romanée St.-Vivant, Ruchottes-Chambertin

JAFFELIN (BEAUNE)* *

This négociant firm was sold by Robert Drouhin. While I have not tasted the wines made under the new owner, Jean-Claude Boisset, the Jaffelin offerings have tended to be well-made, straightforward, clean, commercial wines designed for uncritical consumers looking for user-friendly, uncomplicated, fruity red burgundies.

DOMAINE HENRI JAYER (VOSNE-ROMANÉE)* * * * *

So much has been written about Henri Jayer, it seems pointless to add to the justifiable praise and accolades this great Burgundy producer merits. He has been a fountain of wisdom for this writer, and tasting in his cellars has been an extraordinary experience that I have always cherished. Jayer, who radiates warmth and confidence, has made many legendary wines. While tiny quantities of Echézeaux, Vosne-Romanée Cros Parantoux, and Vosne-Romanée Les Beaux Monts emerge, they are almost impossible to find given the insatiable worldwide demand. Jayer has never been secretive about why his red burgundies are so fragrant, rich, expressive, and satisfying. Hard work in the vineyard and keeping crop yields under 30 hectoliters per hectare are the secrets to his success. Simplistically, he believes that the vineyard makes the wine. All his wines are kept in 100% new oak, racked as few times as possible, and bottled without filtration. The results speak for themselves. His 1978s, 1980s, and 1985s all stand as monuments to how red burgundy should taste, but rarely does. Fortunately, Jayer's nephew, Emmanuel Rouget, continues to make wines à la Henri Jayer.

Best Wines: Echézeaux, Richebourg, Vosne-Romanée Les Beaux Monts, Vosne-Romanée Cros Parantoux

DOMAINE ROBERT JAYER-GILLES (MAGNY-LES-VILLERS)* * * * *

Although the handsome Robert Jayer, a cousin of Henri Jayer, has always made excellent wines, recent vintages have exhibited even more perfume and richness. All the wines are aged in 100% new oak in one of the most beautiful cellars in Burgundy. Jayer practiced a light Kisselguhr filtration in the past, but he has come to realize that even the lightest filtration affects the wines' aromas and their capacity to age. He produces seductive, rich wines that are capable of lasting for 10–15 years. The best value in Jayer-Gilles's portfolio is the Côte de Nuits-Villages, which is often better than many producers' premiers or grands crus. His best-kept secret is the exquisite Nuits St.-Georges Les Damodes. Recently, Jayer-Gilles has added a small parcel of Nuits St.-Georges Les Hautes Poirets. Jayer-Gilles has been especially consistent in years such as 1987 and 1992.

Best Wines: Côte de Nuits-Villages, Echézeaux, Nuits St.-Georges Les Damodes, Nuits St.-Georges Les Hautes Poirets

DOMAINE JOBLOT (GIVRY)* * * *

It is a shame there are not more producers as dedicated and talented as Jean-Marc Joblot. Working in one of the lesser-known appellations, Givry, he continues to fashion rich, concentrated, chewy, pure red burgundies that can be drunk young, yet are capable of lasting over a decade. They embarrass many premiers and grands crus from the more prestigious Côte d'Or. Burgundy fanatics have been gobbling up Joblot's wines since he burst on the scene with gorgeous 1985s. His wines have continued to demonstrate a progression in quality.

Best Wines: Givry Clos du Cellier aux Moines, Givry Clos de la Servoisine

DOMAINE MICHEL JUILLOT (MERCUREY)* * *

I have had mixed results with Juillot's wines. In good vintages such as 1990, he turns out very fine, rich, medium- to full-bodied Pinot Noirs, but he has stumbled badly in years such as 1991 and 1992.

Best Wines: Mercurey Les Champs, Mercurey Clos des Barraults, Mercurey Clos Tonnerre

DOMAINE LABOURÉ-ROI (NUITS ST.-GEORGES)* * *

This *négociant* firm is a source of sturdy, rustic, but pleasant red burgundies that are good, but unexciting.

Best Wines: As with any *négociant,* there is a broad range of quality, but the finest examples tend to come from the Domaine Chantal Lescure and from Nuits St.-Georges vineyards such as Les Damodes.

DOMAINE MICHEL LAFARGE (VOLNAY)* * * */* * * * *

As I have gotten older and, hopefully, wiser, I have come to develop a greater appreciation for Lafarge's wines than I had in my formative days. Perhaps the wines have also gotten better. I find Lafarge's Volnays as seductive and classic as any made in the village. Moreover, they have been extremely consistent, even in tough years such as 1981. In top years Lafarge is capable of hitting home runs, particularly with his top cuvées. These are rich, concentrated, seductive, elegant, yet authoritatively flavored Volnays that can age well for 10–15 years.

Best Wines: Volnay Clos des Chênes, Volnay Clos du Château des Ducs

DOMAINE COMTE LAFON (MEURSAULT)* * * * *

This producer is renowned the world over for its spectacular white burgundies. Proprietor Dominique Lafon makes equally riveting red wines. Since quantities are so tiny, the extraordinary quality of these red wines goes largely unnoticed. Lafon's Volnay Champans, Volnay Clos des Chênes, and Volnay Santenots are the finest wines of the Volnay appellation. Rich, extremely concentrated, gorgeously pure, yet never heavy or tannic, these are wines that can last and evolve for decades, even in years such as 1987. Unfortunately, they are extremely difficult to find.

Best Wines: Volnay Champans, Volnay Clos des Chênes, Volnay Santenots

DOMAINE LAMARCHE (VOSNE-ROMANÉE)* * *

This domaine is typical of some of Burgundy's historic estates. Great wines were often the rule of thumb following World War II, but the quality declined in the seventies and early eighties. When Henri Lamarche passed away in 1985, his son, François, began to slowly take stock of how far this estate (which owns a treasure trove of great vineyards) had slipped. Since 1989 a cold maceration has been utilized and there is clearly an effort to obtain more color and depth in the wines. The results have been an improvement over Henri's last vintages, but Domaine Lamarche is still producing wines far below the level readers would expect, given the acclaim of the vineyard holdings and the formidable prices. Lamarche needs to throw away his filters and have an open mind with respect to fining. His defenders argue that the light, delicate style is intentional, but this is a euphemism for a lack of concentration.

Best Wines: Clos de Vougeot, Echézeaux, La Grande Rue, Grands Echézeaux

DOMAINE LOUIS LATOUR (BEAUNE)* * *

Much has been made of the flash pasteurization process that Louis Latour utilizes for this firm's red wines. Opinion is divided as to whether it is significant. Latour maintains that the wines require less processing and the procedure is less brutal than sterile filtration. This firm is, justifiably, widely renowned for their bevy of rich, full-bodied white wines. While there is a tendency for the lower-level red wines to taste alike, this is a good source for sturdy, full-bodied, tannic Cortons. Latour is the largest owner of Corton, and the firm's flagship wine, Corton-Grancey, is a macho, beefy, muscular red wine that can stand up to 20+ years of cellaring. Although it will never be the most aromatic or complex wine, it is mouth-filling and satisfying in the finest vintages. Other red wines, especially the selections from Beaune, Pernand-Vergelesses, and Savigny can be meager.

Best Wines: Corton Clos de la Vigne au Saint, Corton-Grancey, Romanée St.-Vivant

DOMAINE DOMINIQUE LAURENT (NUITS ST.-GEORGES)* * * */* * * * *

Laurent, an ex–pastry chef, launched his wine career with the 1989 vintage. I have not tasted any of his 1989s, 1990s, or 1991s, but Laurent, who purchases the wines from growers, ages them in 100% new oak, and bottles them without fining or filtration, hit the bull's-eye with spectacular 1992s. They are among the most seductive, sumptuous wines of the vintage. Given the vintage's softness and precociousness they need to be drunk young, but Dominique Laurent appears serious about establishing himself as one of the few guardians of rich, traditionally made, high-quality burgundies. This is a name to follow.

Best Wines: There are sure to be variations, depending on what Laurent is able to purchase. To date, his Bonnes Mares, Charmes-Chambertin, and Clos de la Roche have been stunning.

DOMAINE LECHENEAUT (NUITS ST.-GEORGES)* * * */* * * * *

The wines of Domaine Lecheneaut were discovered by France's leading wine publication, *Revue du Vin de France.* Based on what Lecheneaut has achieved in 1990, 1991, and 1992, it is easy to conclude that this must be the new superstar of Nuits St.-Georges. Philippe and Vincent Lecheneaut are making far greater wines than some of the village's more illustrious *négociants* and growers. Their successes in tough years such as 1991 and 1992 suggest this could be a five-star producer. The wines are deeply colored, rich, framed by significant toasty new oak, succulent, expansive, structured, and well balanced. This is a fabulous new source for great red burgundies that drink well young, yet possess the requisite harmony to age for 10–15 years.

Best Wines: Clos de la Roche, Nuits St.-Georges Les Cailles, Nuits St.-Georges Les Damodes

DOMAINE PHILIPPE LECLERC (GEVREY-CHAMBERTIN)* * * */* * * * *

Much has been written about this distinct individual whose looks and style of dress would qualify him as a member of the notorious Hell's Angels motorcycle gang. Leclerc finds focus, and I suspect redemption, in his cellars, where he produces red burgundies unlike any others made in the Côte d'Or. His wines spend over 3 years in 100% new oak barrels, and are bottled without fining or filtration. In light vintages the wines can taste too oaky, but Leclerc rarely produces wimpish wines. His muscular, highly concentrated winemaking style is actually enhanced by the lavish oak. Leclerc, whose wines are made to last 15–20 years, is an outspoken critic of modern-day, commercially styled burgundies that drink well young. He has produced some extraordinary wines, particularly from his two top vineyard sites, Combe aux Moines and Les Cazetiers. The wines often need 5–7 years to open up. Over the last few years Leclerc changed the bottle and label design, with his new Armageddon-inspired label poignantly revealing Leclerc's complicated personality.

Best Wines: Chambolle-Musigny Babillaires, Gevrey-Chambertin Les Cazetiers, Gevrey-Chambertin Combe aux Moines

RENÉ LECLERC (GEVREY-CHAMBERTIN)* * * *

Gevrey-Chambertin is full of interesting families. René Leclerc is the brother of Philippe Leclerc, whom he worked with until his brother's mystical personality led René to decide that he'd better have his own cellar. Their mother owns and manages Gevrey's Hôtel Les Terroirs. René's performance over the last few years has been more mixed than his brother's. Although he makes a different style of wine, his wines possess considerable concentration, high extraction, and a full-bodied personality with plenty of intensity. They are also bottled after considerable cask aging and, like those of Philippe, are never filtered. In the late eighties, the wines appeared to take on more character both aromatically and on the palate. I was extremely impressed with René's 1991s. Given the long cask aging in a small percentage of new oak (in complete contrast to Philippe), René's wines can be drunk when released, but have the capacity to age well for more than 10 years in top vintages.

Best Wines: Gevrey-Chambertin Clos Prieur, Gevrey-Chambertin Combe aux Moines, Gevrey-Chambertin Lavaux St.-Jacques

DOMAINE LEJEUNE (POMMARD)* * * */* * * * *

I underestimated this estate in my book, *Burgundy*. The 1988, 1989, and 1990 Lejeune Pommards were about as rich, concentrated, and flashy Pinot Noirs as readers are likely to encounter. The 1991s were less successful, but the property bounced back in 1992. These are superrich, concentrated wines, but only tiny quantities of Lejeune's finest wines are produced, most of which remain in France. Filled with opulence and richness, they can be drunk young yet will last for a decade.

Best Wines: Pommard Les Argillières, Pommard Les Poutures, Pommard Les Rugiens

DOMAINE LEROY (VOSNE-ROMANÉE)* * * * *

I have said it so many times that it may seem redundant, but if readers bypassed purchasing my heavyweight 1990 tome, *Burgundy*, let me repeat it—Lalou Bize-Leroy stands alone at the top of Burgundy's quality hierarchy. Because she is a perfectionist, and because she has had the courage to produce wines from low yields and to bottle them naturally, without fining or filtration, she has been scorned by many Burgundy *négociants*, and even by the proprietors of other top domaines. Not only is the level of their envy and jealousy appalling, but they are frightened of Bize-Leroy, because they fear there will be increasing pressure for lower yields and biodynamic farming. Anyone who loves great burgundy must realize that her wines embarrass much of what is produced in Burgundy.

Since she launched her wines from the Domaine Leroy (formerly the Noëllat estate), Lalou Bize-Leroy has made the highest percentage of Burgundy's greatest wines. She made the finest 1988s, 1989s, 1990s, 1991s, and 1992s. The 1993s are her greatest vintage to date. Just about everything in Leroy's portfolio is profound, as well as—to understate it— expensive. Moreover, these wines are a sure bet when it comes to buying red burgundy for aging more than 15–20 years. The wines often need 5–10 years just to open. Leroy offers an education in what great burgundy is all about.

Best Wines: Chambertin, Chambolle-Musigny Les Charmes, Clos de la Roche, Clos de Vougeot, Gevrey-Chambertin Les Combottes, Latricières-Chambertin, Musigny, Nuits St.-Georges Les Boudots, Nuits St.-Georges Les Vignes Rondes, Pommard Les Vignots, Richebourg, Romanée St.-Vivant, Savigny-Les-Beaune Les Narbantons, Volnay Santenots, Vosne-Romanée Les Beaux Monts, Vosne-Romanée Les Brûlées

DOMAINE GEORGES LIGNIER (MOREY ST.-DENIS)* * *

Georges Lignier's wines are mystifying. Lignier is young and enthusiastic, and possesses great vineyards, yet often the wines turn out light and diluted. I have often tasted spectacular barrel samples of his grands crus, only to find the bottled wines significantly lighter, as if they were excessively fined and/or filtered. Opinions are divided as to how good Lignier's wines are, but the English wine press, notably Norman Remington in his Burgundy book, says, "Georges Lignier . . . knows as well as anyone how to make red wine." American wine writer Matt Kramer came to the conclusion that Lignier's wines "lack the essential element of *terroir*." It seems to me that if Lignier lowered his yields and threw away his filter, and perhaps bottled his wines before they went through a second winter in cask, he would be a consistent five-star producer. At present, his wines rarely stand above the crowd.

Best Wines: Clos de la Roche, Clos St.-Denis, Gevrey-Chambertin Les Combottes, Morey St.-Denis Clos des Ormes

DOMAINE HUBERT LIGNIER (MOREY ST.-DENIS)* * * * *

The fact that Hubert Lignier is a source for fabulous wines has remained a well-kept secret. The estate is not nearly as large as that of Georges Lignier, and Hubert has not received much attention from the European wine press, leaving it to me and New York's fine wine-writer/taster, Stephen Tanzer, to spread the news about the greatness of Hubert Lignier's wines. For example, British wine merchant/author, Anthony Hanson, in his book *Burgundy*, says "Not so sure a touch here, I feel, as at Georges Lignier." What Hanson does not reveal is the fact that he sells the wines of Georges Lignier in England! This is burgundy at its finest—rich, aromatic, medium to full bodied, concentrated, and velvety-textured, with a stunning bouquet of black raspberries and black cherries intertwined with scents of new oak. The wines also age well, as a taste of Lignier's 1978s will prove. Magnificent wines emerge from his holdings in Clos de la Roche and Charmes-Chambertin.

Best Wines: Chambolle-Musigny Premier Cru, Charmes-Chambertin, Clos de la Roche, Morey St.-Denis Premier Cru

CHÂTEAU DE LA MALTROYE (CHASSAGNE-MONTRACHET)* * *

This gorgeous Chassagne-Montrachet estate turns out spicy, rustic, medium-bodied red wines that offer reasonably good value. They are a good introduction to the underrated, modestly priced red wines of Chassagne-Montrachet.

Best Wine: Chassagne-Montrachet Clos St.-Jean

DOMAINE MARCHAND-GRILLOT ET FILS (GEVREY-CHAMBERTIN)* *

I had high hopes for this estate when the American importer succeeded in getting the proprietor to reduce yields and bottle the wines naturally. However, the huge demand for wines from top Gevrey-Chambertin vineyards has resulted in uninspiring wines made from high yields that are commercial, straightforward, and made to be drunk in their first 5–7 years of life.

Best Wines: Gevrey-Chambertin Petite Chapelle, Ruchottes-Chambertin

DOMAINE MAUME (GEVREY-CHAMBERTIN)* * */* * * *

Many years ago these were the types of burgundies that inspired me—densely colored, rustic wines with savage intensity and dark, opaque colors that were bottled unfiltered. An investment in numerous vintages of the wines of Bernard Maume has left me with increasing reservations about just how many of these wines ever develop into harmonious beverages of pleasure. There is no question that Maume's Mazis-Chambertin can be among the richest and longest-lived wines of any vintage, but just as frequently they can be astringent, too tannic, and out of balance. The other wines are even less predictable. If you are an optimist, purchase Maume's wines from years of high heat and abundant sunshine so the tannin will be sweet and ripe rather than green and vegetal. For all my reservations, Maume has made gorgeous Mazis-Chambertin and top-notch Charmes-Chambertin in vintages such as 1982, 1985, and 1990.

Best Wines: Charmes-Chambertin, Mazis-Chambertin

DOMAINE MEIX FOULOT (MERCUREY)* * * *

Proprietor Yves de Launay continues to exhibit a fine touch with his bevy of rich, age-worthy, concentrated Pinot Noirs from Mercurey. Old vines and good, traditional winemaking result in wines that can age for 10–15 years.

Best Wines: Mercurey Clos de Château Montaigu, Mercurey Cuvée Spéciale, Mercurey Meix Foulot

DOMAINE JEAN MÉO-CAMUZET (VOSNE-ROMANÉE)* * * * *

This superb domaine, which only began estate-bottling in 1983, is clearly on top of their game. Henri Jayer was initially consulted to provide his philosophy of winemaking, *élevage,* and bottling until the two talented, brilliant young men who are responsible for the superb wines emanating from this estate, Jean-Nicolas Méo and Christian Faurois, assumed complete responsibility. One might argue that Henri Jayer's legacy is evident in all of the wines that emerge from this impeccably run estate. It is a pleasure to write about a producer whose wines actually live up to their vineyards' potential. These thrilling red burgundies are made from yields of under 30 hectoliters per hectare, aged in primarily new oak casks, and bottled without filtration and in some cases without fining. There are riveting expressions both aromatically and on the palate—rich, authoritative, velvety-textured, and concentrated, as well as complex, elegant, and exceptionally well balanced. This is one of the great domaines of the future. Méo-Camuzet has been successful not only in years such as 1990, but also in more troublesome vintages such as 1991 and 1992.

Best Wines: Clos de Vougeot, Corton, Nuits St.-Georges Les Boudots, Nuits St.-Georges aux Murgers, Richebourg, Vosne-Romanée Les Brûlées, Vosne-Romanée Cros Parantoux

DOMAINE PRINCE FLORENT DE MÉRODE (LADOIX-SERRIGNY)* * * *

Since the 1989 vintage, Prince Florent de Mérode has returned to the form that made this estate so famous in the fifties and sixties. The wines are being bottled without fining or filtration, resulting in wines with sweeter, richer, creamier textures, and far more aromatic intensity and development potential. Mérode's 1992s, which were richly fruity but light, and neither tannic nor powerful in cask, have been transformed into delicious wines from bottle —in large part because the wines were bottled naturally.

This historic domaine, owned by the Mérode family since the mid-seventeenth century, is a treasure trove of top vineyards. The estate's return to an emphasis on low yields and natural bottling is to be applauded by all who adore red burgundy.

Best Wines: Corton Les Bressandes, Corton Clos du Roi, Corton Les Maréchaudes, Corton Les Rénardes, Pommard Clos de la Platière

Note: Mérode's Ladoix Les Chaillots is one of the few bargains in Burgundy.

DOMAINE ALAIN MICHELOT (NUITS ST.-GEORGES)* * *

There is a lot to like about Alain Michelot, a large, playful man who owns some of the top vineyards in Nuits St.-Georges. His wines are always good, but, sadly, lighter and less age-worthy than they should be. Michelot's winemaking techniques are sound, but yields of 50+ hectoliters per hectare are high. While I am not certain what type of filtration system he utilizes, the wines lose more than an insignificant amount of aromatics, fruit, and body after going through the bottling process. Nevertheless, they are among the most seductive wines from Nuits St.-Georges, an appellation that often produces hard, tough Pinot Noir. To Michelot's credit, he was one of the first Burgundy producers to brand all his bottles with both the vineyard name and vintage, a practice now routinely employed by all the better producers.

Best Wines: Nuits St.-Georges Les Champs Perdrix, Nuits St.-Georges La Richemone, Nuits St.-Georges Les Vaucrains

MOILLARD (NUITS ST.-GEORGES)* */* * * *

This large *négociant* makes a huge array of wines of different quality levels. The best wines (their domaine wines) tend to be highly extracted, deeply colored, rich, full bodied, and age-worthy. While they never hit the peaks of aromatic complexity or finesse, they offer a rich, chewy, concentrated style that can age for 15–20 years. Matt Kramer, in his book, *Making Sense of Burgundy,* may have said it best when he stated, "Moillard's wines seem to attract those who want their burgundies to resemble Cabernets, only inky dark, powerful, fruity, and fairly tannic. Distinctions of *terroir* take a backseat, if they are admitted at all."
Best Wines: Wines labeled Domaine Thomas-Moillard are usually the best, including the Beaune Les Grèves, Bonnes Mares, Corton Clos du Roi, Nuits St.-Georges Clos de Torey, Nuits St.-Georges La Richemone, Vosne-Romanée Les Beaux Monts, Vosne-Romanée Les Malconsorts.

DOMAINE MONGEARD-MUGNERET (VOSNE-ROMANÉE)* * * */* * * * *

Jean Mongeard has made many superb burgundies. The quality may have dipped slightly in the late eighties, but Mongeard made gorgeous 1990s and 1991s. A large, playful man with an impish smile, Mongeard has a large domaine with vineyards spread throughout the Côte d'Or. His grands crus possess the most class, but for value, his Savigny-Les-Beaune Les Narbantons and two premiers crus, Vosne-Romanée Les Orveaux and Nuits St.-Georges Les Boudots, pack the most juice for the money. These expansive, pure, rich, succulent wines are deceptively easy to drink young. While not the most age-worthy wines, they will provide satisfaction if drunk in their first 10–12 years of life.
Best Wines: Clos de Vougeot, Echézeaux Vieilles Vignes, Grands Echézeaux, Nuits St.-Georges Les Boudots, Richebourg, Savigny-Les-Beaune Les Narbantons, Vosne-Romanée Les Orveaux, Vosne-Romanée Les Suchots

DOMAINE MONTHÉLIE-DOUHAIRET (MONTHÉLIE)* *

I remember with fondness a meeting with the elderly Madame Douhairet in the late eighties, but I must confess I have never found her wines to my liking. They are too earthy, musty, and rustic. These wines can be full bodied, but odd, funky aromas reminiscent of damp, moldy chestnuts and stale mushrooms are off-putting. The fact that winemaking guru André Porcheret is a consultant should translate into higher quality, but that has yet to happen.
Best Wines: Monthélie-Premier Cru, Volnay Les Champans

DOMAINE HUBERT DE MONTILLE (VOLNAY)* */* * * *

I am in the minority on the subject of Montille's wines. Just about every burgundy wine writer writes about these classic *vins de garde* as authoritatively rich, pure examples of Pommard and Volnay. Having purchased, cellared, and opened many Montille Pommards and Volnays from the seventies and eighties, I note that far too many have been disappointing, appallingly high in acidity, astringently tannic, and while enticingly perfumed, lacking fruit and balance. Occasionally (in 1971 and 1978, for example), the Pommard Les Rugiens can be stunning. Other vintages (1976, 1979, 1980, and 1985) have been disappointing. I am not sure things have improved, as recent vintages of the wines (which are never meant to be flattering in their youth) have seemed abnormally hard and abrasive. Perhaps miracles will occur after two decades of life in the bottle—but don't bet on it.
Best Wines: Pommard Les Epenots, Pommard Les Pezerolles, Pommard Les Rugiens, Volnay Champans, Volnay Taillepieds

DOMAINE ALBERT MOROT (BEAUNE)* * * *

Albert Morot, both a *négociant* and a vineyard owner, has always fashioned classic wines from his Côte de Beaune holdings. However, in the early nineties, Mademoiselle Choppin began to do severe crop thinnings, and increased the percentage of new oak casks to 60%.

Perhaps even more important, she returned to bottling all of her wines without fining or filtration. The results have been beautiful expressions of savory, succulent, yet structured Pinot Noir that are both modestly priced and age-worthy. Most of her top Beaune premiers crus sell for under $25 a bottle, making them extremely attractive wines.

Best Wines: Beaune Les Bressandes, Beaune Les Cent Vignes, Beaune Les Teurons, Beaune Les Toussaints, Savigny Vergelesses Clos la Bataillère

DOMAINE DENIS MORTET (GEVREY-CHAMBERTIN)* * *

I have always enjoyed Mortet's elegant, finesse style of red burgundy and thought he had the potential to be one of the stars of Gevrey-Chambertin. Since I published my book on Burgundy in 1990, I have to say that the quality appears to have stagnated at a pleasant but uninspiring level. As do many Burgundy growers, Mortet relies on the Kisselguhr system of filtration, despite the request of his American importer to abandon the practice. Is this what precludes his wines from achieving higher accolades? These are wines to drink in their first 5–8 years of life.

Best Wines: Chambertin, Chambolle-Musigny Les Beaux Bruns, Gevrey-Chambertin Les Champeaux

DOMAINE MUGNERET-GIBOURG (VOSNE-ROMANÉE)* * * *

This estate, which often turns out five-star wines, particularly its Ruchottes-Chambertin, Clos de Vougeot, and Echézeaux, is now run by the late Dr. Georges Mugneret's widow, daughter, and niece. These traditionally made burgundies are meant to develop and last in the bottle. Great wines made in years such as 1953, 1959, and 1966 remain among the reference-point wines for burgundy. In the eighties, the wines' concentration levels may not have been as impressive as those of the past, but the tannin level and youthful toughness remain. These are high-quality, high-class, excellent to outstanding red burgundies that generally require 5–6 years to display their full potential. Having said that, I have to admit that the 1983s and 1985s to which I initially gave superlative reviews have not developed as well as I would have liked. The 1983s are dry and hard, and the 1985s are somewhat monolithic and dull. The 1988s may still be too young to judge, but they are frightfully astringent.

Best Wines: Chambolle-Musigny Les Feusselottes, Clos de Vougeot, Echézeaux, Nuits St.-Georges Les Chaignots, Ruchottes-Chambertin

DOMAINE ANDRÉ MUSSY (POMMARD)* * * */* * * * *

The youthful 81-year-old André Mussy continues to produce wines that are among the reference points for great burgundy, particularly his rich, expansive, powerful Beaunes and Pommards. Mussy remains an open-minded, extremely flexible winemaker who adjusts his harvest dates and winemaking style to the conditions presented by each vintage. Mussy has produced many sensational wines, especially the Pommard Les Epenots and Beaune Les Montrevenots. His wines drink well young, but age well for 10–15 years. In many respects, Mussy is the quintessential Burgundy winemaker, born and raised in the vineyard and cellars. He is the twelfth generation of the Mussy family to make wines in Pommard.

Best Wines: Beaune Les Epenottes, Beaune Les Montrevenots, Pommard Les Epenots

PHILIPPE NADDEF (COUCHEY)* * */* * * *

Naddef's Mazis-Chambertin and Gevrey-Chambertin Les Cazetiers can be stunning, especially in top vintages. Unfortunately, there is not much of it. The other wines are less enticing, but they are always soundly made. My experience indicates the Mazis is a 10- to 15-year wine in top years, and Les Cazetiers can age gracefully for nearly as long. Naddef is close to entering the top hierarchy of Burgundy wine producers.

Best Wines: Gevrey-Chambertin Les Cazetiers, Mazis-Chambertin

DOMAINE PARENT (POMMARD)* * *

I may sound a bit ancient, but my introduction to the Pommards of Domaine Parent was some extraordinarily full-bodied, beefy, mouth-filling 1964s, 1966s, and 1969s. They were splendid wines that threw huge sediments and possessed a chewiness and richness that are sadly missing in today's burgundies. Domaine Parent continues to make tasty, heady wines from its considerable holdings in Pommard, but the wines appear more processed and cleaned up, no doubt because many of Parent's customers do not want to deal with sediment or a slightly hazy wine. That's a shame, because the great aromatic profiles and extraordinary flavor dimensions I remember from the sixties are not to be found in any wines I have tasted from the eighties and nineties. Most Domaine Parent wines should be drunk in their first 8–10 years of life.

Best Wines: Pommard Les Epenots, Pommard Les Rugiens

DOMAINE PERNIN-ROSSIN (VOSNE-ROMANÉE)* * * *

André Pernin suffered unjustified criticism because he employed the controversial Lebanese oenologist, Guy Accad. While it is true that some of Pernin's wines did fall apart quickly (not an unusual occurrence for most burgundies), his vintages from the late eighties and his 1990 are splendid. Pernin's winemaking style results in deeply colored, pure, rich, perfumed (black fruits) wines that are capable of lasting for 10–12 years. I have not had a chance to see what Pernin achieved in the tough years of 1991 and 1992, but this is clearly a four-star domaine that occasionally hits the five-star level.

Best Wines: Clos de la Roche, Morey St.-Denis Les Mont Luisants, Nuits St.-Georges La Richemone, Vosne-Romanée Les Beaux Monts

DOMAINE PAUL PERNOT (PULIGNY-MONTRACHET)* *

I am not a fan of Pernot's light, woody, herbaceous red wines. They are ready to drink when released and possess 3–4 years of aging potential.

Best Wine: Beaune Les Teurons

DOMAINE LES PERRIÈRES (GEVREY-CHAMBERTIN)* * * *

I do not often see this estate's wines, but I have fond recollections of the 1978s, 1980s, and 1985s. They are beefy, muscular, concentrated wines with Gevrey-Chambertin's earthy, leathery, meaty character well displayed. They are also capable of aging 12–15 years, a relatively long time for most modern-day burgundies.

Best Wine: Gevrey-Chambertin Petite Chapelle

CHÂTEAU DE POMMARD (POMMARD)* */* * *

These beautifully packaged, chunky, deeply colored, tannic wines are representative of their appellation. These Pommards tend to be big, husky, hard, and tannic wines. While I have not cellared any of proprietor Dr. Laplanche's Pommards, it appears they are tannic and firm enough to last for a decade or more. But, there is not enough fruit for my tastes.

Best Wine: Pommard

DOMAINE PONSOT (MOREY ST.-DENIS)* * * * *

In vintages such as 1947, 1949, 1972, 1980, 1985, 1990, 1991, and 1993, this fascinating domaine produced some of the greatest wines of Burgundy. However, there has also been a frustrating lack of consistency, with deplorable wines being produced in 1984, 1986, and 1987, and less than thrilling 1988s and 1989s. Jean-Marie Ponsot and his son, Laurent, are notoriously late harvesters and utilize traditional winemaking methods. No new oak is employed, and the wines are fined with egg whites, but never filtered. Moreover, no sulfur dioxide is used in the winemaking—a rarity in winedom. At their finest, Ponsot's wines are classic examples of great red burgundy. While rich and accessible enough to be drunk young, they are capable of lasting 20–30 years, making Ponsot one of a handful of Burgundy growers (the other most notable being Madame Leroy) committed to making long-lived wines.

Best Wines: Chambolle-Musigny Les Charmes, Clos de la Roche Vieilles Vignes, Clos St.-Denis, Griottes-Chambertin, Latricières-Chambertin

Note: Occasionally, Ponsot produces tiny quantities of Chambertin and Chapelle-Chambertin. Ponsot also makes and bottles wines for the Domaine Chézeaux.

DOMAINE POTHIER-RIEUSSET (POMMARD)* * * *

This traditionally run estate makes long-lived, rich, concentrated wines that, while inconsistent, can be superb in top years. Some of the lighter years in the seventies were top notch, but Pothier's success with off years in the eighties was not as evident, as the 1984s, 1986s, and 1987s are mediocre. Pothier made successful wines in 1985, 1988, 1989, and 1990. In some years the wines need 5–10 years of cellaring and can last for 20–30 years. To date, two of the greatest red burgundies I have ever tasted were Pothier's 1947 and 1949 Pommard Les Rugiens.

Best Wines: Beaune Les Boucherottes, Pommard Les Charmots, Pommard Clos de Vergers, Pommard Les Epenots, Pommard Les Rugiens

DOMAINE DE LA POUSSE D'OR (VOLNAY)* * */* * * *

This estate used to be one of my reference points for great burgundy. Their 1964s, 1966s, and 1978s were classic examples of elegant, seductive, richly fruity, complex red burgundies. Even the 1976s were superb in what could have been an irregular vintage. During the decade of the eighties, Pousse d'Or produced more sculptured wines that taste lighter in extraction and possess less aging potential. The 1985s, which were striking from barrel, have turned out to be very good rather than stunning. The 1986s and 1987s were disappointing, yet the 1989s and 1990s have turned out well. This remains an excellent source of top-class Volnay and Pommard, but could the wines be even better?

Best Wines: Pommard Les Jarolières, Volnay Les Caillerets, Volnay Les Caillerets Clos des 60 Ouvrées, Volnay Clos de la Bousse d'Or

DOMAINE JACQUES PRIEUR (MEURSAULT)* * */* * * *

Since this property was acquired by the firm of Antonin Rodet the quality has increased significantly. The best wines come from the estate vineyards, which include impressive parcels in renowned grands and premiers crus. Since the Rodet regime began in 1989, the wines have been large-sized, lavishly oaked, solidly colored red burgundies that are capable of 10–15 years of aging. The firm's 1990s are successful, the 1991s and 1992s less so.

Best Wines: Beaune Clos de la Féguine, Chambertin Clos de Bèze, Clos de Vougeot, Meursault Clos de Mazeray Rouge, Musigny, Volnay-Champans, Volnay Clos des Santenots

DOMAINE MICHEL PRUNIER (AUXEY-DURESSES)* * * *

This little gem works from relatively low-prestige vineyards, although Prunier does have a small parcel of Volnay Les Caillerets. The wines are richly fruity, medium to full bodied, made from ripe grapes, and bottled without excessive intervention. They are expressive, reasonably priced, and capable of lasting a decade. If you are searching for attractive, seductive, modestly priced red burgundies, remember the name Michel Prunier.

Best Wines: Auxey-Duresses Clos du Val, Beaune Les Sizies, Volnay Les Caillerets

REMOISSENET PÈRE ET FILS (BEAUNE)* * *

This wealthy *négociant* produces a huge range of wines. They tend to release most top vintages (Remoissenet often avoids off years) much later than other firms. While the wines are not the most complex, Remoissenet does produce fleshy, rich, medium- to full-bodied wines that have the potential to age well. The firm often releases small stocks of red burgundies from great years such as 1949 and 1959. I had always wondered why wines so old never contain any sediment and have fills to the cork. Apparently the sediment is siphoned off and the bottles are reconditioned prior to shipment to the export markets. Although Remoissenet may be criticized for the fact that their wines all possess a certain similarity, that can be said about most estate-bottled wines where the grower's personality and winemaking style can present a strong signature.

Best Wines: Beaune Les Grèves, Beaune Les Marconnets, Beaune Les Toussaints, Grands Echézeaux, Pommard Les Epenots, Richebourg, Santenay Clos de Tavennes, Santenay La Comme, Santenay Les Gravières, Savigny-Les-Beaune Les Serpentières

DOMAINE HENRI REMORIQUET (NUITS ST.-GEORGES)* * *

This modestly sized estate tends to produce chunky, darkly colored, hard, husky red burgundies that, to me, lack complexity and finesse. Nevertheless, this style is appreciated by many consumers, and Remoriquet's best premiers crus from Nuits St.-Georges can age for 10–15 years.

Best Wines: Nuits St.-Georges Les Bousselots, Nuits St.-Georges Les Damodes, Nuits St.-Georges Rue de Chaux, Nuits St.-Georges Les St.-Georges

DOMAINE DANIEL RION (NUITS ST.-GEORGES)* * * *

This is one of the few Burgundy domaines from the Côte de Nuits that has a popular following in the United States. Made in a forward, seductive, easy-to-understand style, these wines exhibit ripe fruit and the generous use of toasty new oak. Excellent vintages include 1986, 1988, 1989, and 1990; 1991 and 1992 were less successful. If there is a downside to Rion's forward, fruity style of red burgundy, it is that the wines are usually at their peak by age 5 or 6 and begin to decline by age 7 or 8.

Best Wines: Chambolle-Musigny Les Beaux Bruns, Clos de Vougeot, Nuits St.-Georges Les Hauts Pruliers, Nuits St.-Georges Les Vignes Rondes, Vosne-Romanée Les Beaux Monts, Vosne-Romanée Les Chaumes

ANTONIN RODET (MERCUREY)* * */* * * *

I have been increasingly impressed by the quality of Rodet's red wines from his vineyards in the Côte Chalonnaise. The 1990s were attractive and noteworthy bargains. These soft, fruity, fleshy, nicely oaked Pinot Noirs are worth searching out for their good quality/price rapport. This is one firm that seems to recognize the potential for quality and value present in Mercurey.

Best Wines: Château de Chamirey Mercureys, Château de Rully

DOMAINE DE LA ROMANÉE-CONTI (VOSNE-ROMANÉE)* * * *

The most famous estate in Burgundy, if not in all of France, the DRC went through a period of turmoil in the early nineties with the dispute with and ultimate dismissal of comanager Lalou Bize-Leroy. _The Wine Spectator_'s long, narrative account by Per-Henrik Mansson of the internal squabbles and discharge of Bize-Leroy makes for terrific reading. The DRC has always been a target for criticism given their exquisite _monopole_ vineyards of La Tâche and Romanée-Conti, and the staggeringly high prices fetched for these wines. While there have been some disappointments, there have been enough great wines, particularly in 1978, 1980, and 1990, to keep the domaine's mythical reputation intact. Small yields and late harvests result in some of the most fragrant and opulent wines of Burgundy. All the wines are aged in 100% new oak, and, according to the domaine, the wines are fined but never filtered.

In 1980 the wines were neither fined nor filtered, which may explain why the 1980s, now fully mature, remain my favorite DRC wines from the decade of the eighties. Although criticized by many, some stunning 1983s were produced, but there is unquestionably bottle variation with many of the wines. The 1984s were good for the vintage, but they are now in serious decline. The 1985s are somewhat perplexing and at present do not appear to be living up to my high expectations. The 1986s and 1987s are good wines; the 1988s are dull, tannic, and monolithic at present. Their future seems far less certain than I would have thought possible 3–4 years ago. Every time I taste the extraordinary 1990s I am convinced that this is one of the greatest vintages for the DRC. The last few times I have tasted La Tâche it has been perfect. The 1991s are also well made, but the 1992s, which I have tasted twice from bottle, are the most disappointing wines the domaine has produced in the last 15 years. They are peppery, vegetal, and herbaceous, and lack depth and fruit. The DRC did not produce a Le Montrachet in 1992, an outstanding vintage for white burgundy.

It will be interesting to follow this property now that the brilliant Lalou Bize-Leroy is no longer involved in the decision making and wine production. Her last vintage at the DRC was 1991.

Best Wines: Grands Echézeaux, Richebourg, Romanée-Conti, Romanée St.-Vivant, La Tâche

DOMAINE ROSSIGNOL-TRAPET (GEVREY-CHAMBERTIN)* * *
This relatively new domaine acquired half of the vineyards formerly owned by Domaine Trapet in Gevrey-Chambertin, largely because Trapet's daughter married a Rossignol. There are now 27 acres spread out over 17 appellations. The proprietor apparently believes in too much racking, too much fining, too much filtration, and as early bottling as possible. The wines are predictably light, fruity, supple, and ideal for drinking in their first 5–6 years of life.

Best Wines: Chambertin, Chambertin Vieilles Vignes, Latricières-Chambertin

DOMAINE JOSEPH ROTY (GEVREY-CHAMBERTIN)* * * */* * * * *
This idiosyncratic domaine, run by the loquacious, chain-smoking Roty, has made extraordinary wines in a number of vintages, particularly 1978, 1980, 1985, 1988, and 1990. In less concentrated years the wines can turn out frightfully woody and out of balance. The finest vintages reveal wines crammed with concentrated, ripe fruit and tannin. These are forceful, rich, lavishly oaked wines that require 5–7 years of cellaring. Roty is one of the few burgundy producers who produced 1985s that are still not ready to drink. His 1988s and 1989s require another decade of cellaring. Roty is capable of producing five-star red burgundies, but the inconsistency in years such as 1983, 1986, 1987, and 1992 remains a problem.

Best Wines: Charmes-Chambertin, Gevrey-Chambertin Les Fontenys, Mazis-Chambertin, Vosne-Romanée Cros Parantoux

DOMAINE EMANUEL ROUGET (NUITS ST.-GEORGES)* * * */* * * * *
The young nephew of Henri Jayer, Emanuel Rouget, continues to turn out classy, rich, Jayeresque wines that are well colored, with sweet aromatic profiles and wonderfully ripe, opulent, medium- to full-bodied personalities. Not to denigrate Rouget's talents, but it is obvious that Uncle Henri is looking over his shoulder. And aren't we all thrilled about that?

Best Wines: Echézeaux, Vosne-Romanée Les Beaux Monts

DOMAINE GEORGES ET CHRISTOPHE ROUMIER (CHAMBOLLE-MUSIGNY)* * * *
Many great wines have emerged from this 40-acre domaine. The late American importer, Frank Schoonmaker, discovered these wines, which were estate-bottled long before that was a common practice in Burgundy. Now run by Christophe and Jean-Marie Roumier, this estate has been remarkably consistent in light years such as 1986 and 1982. They slipped a bit in 1985 and 1991, but they produced some of the finest 1988s and demonstrated a strong effort in 1990. Roumier's offerings remain among the few great wines of the perplexing, frustrating, rot-laden 1983 vintage. They follow traditional winemaking techniques

and bottle their wines with a light fining and no filtration. Their Bonnes Mares, Musigny, and Chambolle-Musigny Les Amoureuses are reference points for these renowned vineyards. Their unheralded Morey St.-Denis Clos de la Bussière can also be a terrific wine, as well as one of the better values in the Roumier portfolio. For whatever reason, the Charmes-Chambertin lacks the spark, vibrance, and concentration of the other wines. Roumier's wines can age well for 20 years.

Best Wines: Bonnes Mares, Chambolle-Musigny Les Amoureuses, Morey St.-Denis Clos de la Bussière, Musigny

DOMAINE ARMAND ROUSSEAU (GEVREY-CHAMBERTIN)* * * *

This historic estate, which began to estate-bottle in the thirties, could easily be a five-star producer if Charles Rousseau would junk his filters. There are spectacular raw materials in his cellars, particularly Rousseau's Chambertin, Chambertin Clos de Bèze, and Gevrey-Chambertin Clos St.-Jacques. While those wines often turn out superbly, Rousseau's insistence on utilizing the Kisselguhr filtration system does strip some of the wine's potential for aromatic and flavor development. Rousseau needs to remember why his 1969s remain some of the most magical wines ever made in Burgundy—they were not filtered! Rousseau went through a slump in quality in the late seventies, but the top-notch 1980s were followed by very good but tannic 1983s, somewhat light 1985s, powerful 1988s, and excellent 1989s, 1990s, and 1991s. In top vintages, his finest grands crus age well for 15 years. For whatever reason, Rousseau's other wines, Gevrey-Chambertin Les Cazetieres, Mazis-Chambertin, Clos de la Roche, and Charmes-Chambertin, are surprisingly less interesting and compelling. I wonder why?

Best Wines: Chambertin, Chambertin Clos de Bèze, Gevrey-Chambertin Clos St.-Jacques, Ruchottes-Chambertin Clos des Ruchottes

DOMAINE CHRISTIAN SERAFIN (GEVREY-CHAMBERTIN)* * * */* * * * *

In a village populated by many underachievers, Christian Serafin stands out as one of its sure-handed winemakers. His wines have been remarkably consistent since I first visited him in the mid-eighties. The wines continue to go from strength to strength, with Serafin now bottling with no fining or filtration. He is a perfectionist in the vineyards and the cellars, taking great care to not manipulate his wines. They are rich and medium to full bodied, with considerable complexity and aging potential. To date, his top two wines, Gevrey-Chambertin Les Cazetieres and Charmes-Chambertin, are capable of lasting 10–15+ years.

Best Wines: Charmes-Chambertin, Gevrey-Chambertin Les Cazetieres, Gevrey-Chambertin Le Fonteny, Gevrey-Chambertin Vieilles Vignes

DOMAINE BERNARD SERVEAU (MOREY ST.-DENIS)* * * */* * * *

When Serveau gets it right his wines are among the most stylish, elegant expressions of Pinot Noir from the Côte d'Or. But he often misses the mark, turning out thin, light wines that lack depth. Serveau hit the bull's-eye in 1985, 1987, and 1988. Although never deeply colored or blockbuster wines, they are gracious Pinot Noirs with considerable elegance and finesse.

Best Wines: Chambolle-Musigny Les Amoureuses, Chambolle-Musigny Les Chabiots, Morey St.-Denis Les Sorbès

DOMAINE JEAN TARDY (VOSNE-ROMANÉE)* * *

Tardy is capable of producing four- or five-star-quality wines, particularly from his small holdings in Clos de Vougeot and Nuits St.-Georges Les Boudots. Vintages from the late eighties and early nineties were overoaked and did not possess the concentration evident in the mid-eighties. Nevertheless, this is a producer who can fashion top-notch wines, as evidenced by the fact that he often sells part of his production to top *négociants* such as Louis Jadot.

Best Wines: Clos de Vougeot, Nuits St.-Georges Les Boudots

DOMAINE TOLLOT-BEAUT ET FILS (CHOREY-LES-BEAUNE)* * */* * * *

Although this historic estate should also throw away its filters, their top wines (e.g., Corton Les Bressandes, Corton, and Beaune Clos du Roi) are filled with black cherry fruit judiciously touched by toasty oak. However, as delicious as they are young, many wines are tired by the age of 10. The 1978 and 1985 Corton Les Bressandes were brilliant during their first 5–8 years of life, but they began to tire as they approached a decade of life. Nevertheless, this is a good source of well-made red burgundies.

Best Wines: Beaune Clos du Roi, Beaune Les Grèves, Corton, Corton Les Bressandes

CHÂTEAU DE LA TOUR (VOUGEOT)* * * *

Proprietor François Labet completely resurrected this estate's image in the late eighties. Prior to 1986 Château de la Tour was one of Burgundy's most notorious underachievers. Since the late eighties their Clos de Vougeot cuvée has been consistently excellent, and the Clos de Vougeot Vieilles Vignes has been superb, yet expensive and rare. In vintages such as 1988, 1989, 1990, and 1991 it is worth the effort to find, assuming you have the riches of a movie star or superstar athlete. The current style of wines (Guy Accad is this property's oenologist) are deeply colored, rich, full-bodied, lavishly oaked wines that are capable of lasting for 10–15 years.

Best Wines: Clos de Vougeot, Clos de Vougeot Vieilles Vignes

DOMAINE LOUIS TRAPET (GEVREY-CHAMBERTIN)* *

Jean Trapet's son, Jean-Louis, has taken over the responsibility for this domaine and has begun to make some significant changes in its operation. Yields have been curtailed and a cold maceration prior to vinification has been instituted in order to improve the color and aromatic complexity of the wines. Cask aging remains the same, but both the fining and filtration are being studied to see if they can be diminished or completely eliminated. The wines made by Jean-Louis's father in the seventies and eighties were disappointing, with a number of poor efforts, including the estate's $150-a-bottle Chambertin, which often displayed a tealike color and was completely dead by age 5 or 6. Those disasters are past history, as the wines since the early nineties have been soundly made, albeit uninspiring. Stylistically, the fruity, soft, forward wines that have emerged under Jean-Louis are best consumed within their first 5–8 years of life.

Best Wines: Chambertin, Chambertin Vieilles Vignes, Latricières-Chambertin

DOMAINE J. TRUCHOT-MARTIN (MOREY ST.-DENIS)* * * *

Jacky Truchot is a relatively obscure but serious producer making highly traditional, sometimes tantalizing Pinot Noirs. If you are looking for wines with saturated colors, do not seek out Truchot's offerings, as they are traditionally among the lightest-hued in Burgundy, although I noticed that his 1990s and 1991s possessed deeper colors. His wines are compelling in their stunning fragrances and remarkable richness that seems crammed into such light, medium-bodied wines. These are seductive wines for drinking within their first 7–10 years of life.

Best Wines: Charmes-Chambertin Vieilles Vignes, Clos de la Roche, Morey St.-Denis Les Sorbès

DOMAINE DES VAROILLES (GEVREY-CHAMBERTIN)* */* * *

I purchased and cellared the 1976, 1978, and 1980 Domaine des Varoilles wines and found the young wines to be impressively extracted, big, beefy, tannic, and in need of considerable aging. However, by the time the tannin had subsided, the fruit was nearly gone. More recently, the 1986s and 1987s were hard, tannic, and thin. This estate owns important Gevrey-Chambertin holdings and the wines have a reputation for being long-lived, lean, and firm. But isn't wine also meant to be a beverage of pleasure? I find little enjoyment in these masochistic offerings. Proprietor Jean-Pierre Naigeon continues to believe in this firm, backward, tough style of wine.

Best Wines: Clos de Vougeot, Gevrey-Chambertin Clos du Meix des Ouches, Gevrey-Chambertin Clos des Varoilles, Gevrey-Chambertin La Romanée

DOMAINE COMTE DE VOGÜÉ (CHAMBOLLE-MUSIGNY)* * * * *

This is Chambolle-Musigny's most significant and famous estate, largely because it owns 18 acres, or 70%, of the grand cru, Musigny. It also has important holdings in Bonnes Mares and Chambolle-Musigny Les Amoureuses. In the forties, fifties, and sixties it was hard to find a greater Burgundy than this estate's Musigny Vieilles Vignes. I have fond memories of the 1945, 1947, 1966, 1969, and 1972. Between 1973 and 1988 the quality slipped badly. Since then, the young oenologist, Monsieur Millet, has resurrected the quality of this estate. Comte de Vogüé has produced splendidly rich, impressively concentrated, full-bodied, powerful wines in 1990 and 1991, and very good wines in 1992. These wines are now among the most concentrated, deeply colored, and respected burgundies. Moreover, they possess the requisite richness and intensity to age well for 20–30 years. The Domaine Comte de Vogüé is back on track—fantastic news for burgundy connoisseurs.

Best Wines: Bonnes Mares, Musigny Vieilles Vignes

SELECTED TASTING NOTES

BERTRAND AMBROISE (PRÉMEAUX)* * * *

1992	Corton Les Rognets	E	91+
1991	Corton Les Rognets	E	90
1991	Côte de Nuits-Villages	C	87+
1991	Nuits St.-Georges	D	83
1992	Nuits St.-Georges Rue de Chaux	D	90+
1991	Nuits St.-Georges Rue de Chaux	D	87
1992	Nuits St.-Georges Les Vaucrains	D	90+
1991	Nuits St.-Georges Les Vaucrains	D	87+

If you like unfined, unfiltered, lusty, full-bodied, muscular Pinot Noirs from the Côte de Nuits, Ambroise is your man. I discovered this producer while researching my Burgundy book and I am delighted to see how successful he has become, not only in America, but also in the burgundy circles of Europe. Ambroise makes some of the most extracted, deeply colored wines of Burgundy, but they are not meant to be sipped while sitting poolside. These are superendowed, tannic *vins de garde* that will repay cellaring. Year in and year out Ambroise makes one of the best Côte de Nuits-Villages wines, and the 1991 possesses a dense ruby/purple color, a spicy, vanillin- and berry-scented nose, big, medium- to full-bodied, tannic flavors, and a long finish. This is a Côte de Nuits to buy and cellar for the next 10–12 years. The 1991 Nuits St.-Georges is less well endowed, and a bit tough, hard, and astringent.

The 1991 Nuits St.-Georges Les Vaucrains offers a fragrant, spicy, herbal, earthy, peppery, black fruit–scented nose, deep, medium- to full-bodied, muscular flavors, and considerable tannin in the finish. Backward and in need of at least 4–5 years of cellaring, the underlying depth for balance is present. Drink it between 1998 and 2009. Slightly softer and more elegant, the 1991 Nuits St.-Georges Rue de Chaux is more precocious than Les Vaucrains. Deep ruby/purple colored, with a moderately intense bouquet of black fruits and flowers, this supple, graceful wine will provide a delicious, expansive mouthful of Pinot Noir over the next 10–12 years. Ambroise's 1991 Corton Les Rognets is also less robust and forceful than his Nuits St.-Georges Les Vaucrains or Côte de Nuits Villages. Densely colored, with a spicy, berry- and vanillin-scented nose, medium- to full-bodied, sweet, expansive flavors, excellent concentration, and an overall sense of elegance, this is an exceptionally well-made, impressively endowed wine for drinking between 1996 and 2008.

All of the 1992 offerings from young Bertrand Ambroise are atypically masculine, big, forceful, dense, tannic wines that behave more like 1990s than the soft 1992s. None is ready for prime-time drinking, as they all require cellaring of several years. The impressive ruby/purple color of the 1992 Nuits St.-Georges Les Vaucrains is followed by a tight, spicy, earthy, licorice- and black cherry–scented nose, dense, full-bodied, moderately tannic, impressively concentrated flavors, and a firm, structured finish. Drink it between 1998 and 2010. The 1992 Nuits St.-Georges Rue de Chaux is the most forward of this trio, exhibiting a terrific bouquet of roasted meats, black raspberries, and truffles. With plenty of spicy oak, sweet, jammy black cherry fruit, gobs of glycerin, and considerable tannin, this ripe, dense, chunky, brawny, brooding wine is drinkable now, but ideally needs another 2–3 years of cellaring. It will keep for 10–15 years. The dark ruby/purple-colored 1992 Corton Les Rognets offers up a gorgeous nose of herbs, smoke, black cherries, and underbrush. Full bodied and well structured, with massive layers of fruit, tannin, and glycerin, it requires 4–5 years of cellaring; it is one of the handful of 1992 red burgundies that will last for 20 years.

BERNARD AMIOT (CHAMBOLLE-MUSIGNY)* * *

1991 Chambolle-Musigny	D	86
1991 Chambolle-Musigny Les Charmes	D	89
1991 Chambolle-Musigny Les Chatelots	D	87
1991 Chambolle-Musigny Premier Cru	D	86

Amiot's wines tend to be light, so I was pleasantly surprised (shocked) to find the 1991s so concentrated and rich. Yields were low, thanks to Mother Nature, but also Amiot finally was persuaded by his American importer to put the wines in the bottle without resorting to a filter. These wines are full of charm, finesse, and wonderfully sweet, succulent Pinot fruit. The medium-bodied 1991 Chambolle-Musigny displays fine ruby color, a ripe, fragrant nose, and round, generous, graceful flavors. Drink it over the next 5–6 years. The 1991 Chambolle-Musigny Premier Cru is also medium bodied, with admirable deep, ripe fruit, more floral elements in the bouquet, and a lovely sweet, succulent, juicy, velvety texture. It, too, should be consumed over the next 5–6 years. Slightly richer, more expansive, and perfumed is the 1991 Chambolle-Musigny Les Chatelots. This lovely wine is exceptionally elegant. Drink it over the next 7–8 years. Amiot's best 1991 is the beautiful Chambolle-Musigny Les Charmes. Rich, with gobs of black cherry fruit and floral scents in the intense bouquet, this medium-bodied wine possesses superb ripeness, impeccable balance, and a long, satiny smooth finish. It is a classic example of the finesse allied with richness provided by a top Chambolle-Musigny. Drink it over the next 7–8 years.

AMIOT-SERVELLE (CHAMBOLLE-MUSIGNY)* * * *

1992 Chambolle-Musigny Les Amoureuses	E	87
1991 Chambolle-Musigny Les Amoureuses	E	89

1991	Chambolle-Musigny Les Charmes	D	87
1992	Chambolle-Musigny Derrière La Grange	D	88
1991	Chambolle-Musigny Derrière La Grange	D	88
1991	Clos de Vougeot	E	91

Of the two 1992 offerings, the Chambolle-Musigny Derrière La Grange is more concentrated and complete, although I am splitting hairs at this quality level. The wine exhibits a dark ruby color, a beautiful, seductive nose of ripe berry fruit, toasty vanillin, new oak, and floral scents, excellent concentration, low acidity, and surprising length for a 1992. Sweet, expansive, and already precocious, this charming, well-extracted wine should drink well for 5–6 years. The lighter, more elegant 1992 Chambolle-Musigny Les Amoureuses exhibits a fragrant, intense perfume of vanilla and jammy cherries, a round, velvety texture, and attractive ripeness. There is no evidence of dilution or astringent tannin. Drink this wine over the next 4–5 years.

Daniel Servelle irrefutably made better 1991s than 1990s. Low yields and the fact that the wines are now going into the bottle unfiltered have made a difference. These are wines of unmistakable charm and elegance, yet they are imbued with plenty of rich, sweet fruit. The silky 1991 Chambolle-Musigny Les Charmes is a pure delicacy. The ripe berry–scented nose, and supple, impeccably balanced flavors reveal excellent richness, sweet, soft tannins, and a long finish. Delicious now, it should improve and last for 7–10 years. The 1991 Chambolle-Musigny Derrière La Grange is slightly bigger and denser, with deeper, saturated color, an excellent bouquet of black cherries, herbs, and spicy, vanillin new oak, and a rich, expansive, long finish. It admirably combines power and finesse.

Servelle's superb 1991 Clos de Vougeot exhibits a dark ruby/purple color and an explosive nose of jammy black and red fruits and toasty new oak. Rich, unctuous, and opulent, it possesses layers of flavor without the harsh tannins that afflict many 1991s. The finish is persuasively long and well balanced. Drink it over the next 10–12 years. Lastly, the 1991 Chambolle-Musigny Les Amoureuses is a textbook example of how rich, intense, and flavorful Pinot Noir can be in what is a light, elegant style. The wine displays a velvety-textured, sweet, classic nose of red and black fruits, flowers, and herbs, medium body, and a finish that is all glycerin, smooth tannins, and moderate alcohol. Drink it over the next decade. These immensely impressive 1991s are the best wines I have tasted from this up-and-coming domaine.

DOMAINE ARLAUD PÈRE ET FILS (NUITS ST.-GEORGES)* *

1991	Clos de la Roche	E	86
1991	Clos St.-Denis	E	88
1991	Gevrey-Chambertin	D	86
1991	Gevrey-Chambertin Les Combottes	D	85

If you like your red burgundy slightly overripe, rich, round, sweet, and deliciously up-front, this is a producer to take note of. Arlaud has a tendency to overcrop and to resort to a heavy-handed use of sugar to add body and flavor. But there is no doubting that in a low-yield year such as 1991 everything in the wine is natural. These four offerings avoid the hard, green, astringent, sharp tannins that plague many 1991s. All are wines to be consumed in their first 5–7 years of life.

The 1991 Gevrey-Chambertin displays an excellent deep color, a lovely nose of black fruits, meats, and herbs, and a ripe, round, medium-bodied, lush finish. It is pure seduction. The 1991 Gevrey-Chambertin Les Combottes should be a more complex wine, but that is not the case. Although more elegant and slightly lighter than the Gevrey, it shares the same sweet, round, ripe flavors, and juicy, succulent texture. Both wines should be consumed over the near term. The 1991 Clos de la Roche offers a more earthy, herbal, sweet black cherry–scented nose, and ripe, medium-bodied flavors with gobs of glycerin, alcohol, and lushness. This is an up-front, in-your-face style of red burgundy for consuming over the next 5–6 years. The richest and most complete of Arlaud's 1991s is the 1991 Clos St.-Denis. The deep ruby color and rich, sweet nose of cassis fruit, roasted nuts, and toast are turn-ons. Rich and medium to full bodied, with admirable extraction, and a juicy, 1990-like opulence and voluptuousness to its flavors and texture, this heady, expansively flavored wine is delicious. It promises to last for at least 6–8 years.

DOMAINE DE L'ARLOT (PRÉMEAUX)* * * *

1991	Côte de Nuits-Villages Clos du Chapeau	C	87
1992	Côte de Nuits-Villages Clos du Chapitre	C	86
1991	Nuits St.-Georges	C	86
1992	Nuits St.-Georges Clos de l'Arlot	D	89
1991	Nuits St.-Georges Clos de l'Arlot	D	88
1991	Nuits St.-Georges Clos des Forêts St.-Georges	D	89
1992	Nuits St.-Georges Clos des Forêts St.-Georges	D	91
1992	Vosne-Romanée Premier Cru	D	87

The 1992 red burgundy vintage may justifiably be considered mediocre when looked at from an overall perspective, but now that the wines have been bottled, it is easy to identify who has produced the finest wines—all of which tend to share a rich, velvety texture, and gorgeous suppleness and richness. I have been an admirer of the delicious wines produced by Jean-Pierre de Smet since his debut 1987 vintage. The 1992s are all that red burgundies should be—expansive, pure, rich, deliciously supple, and ideal for drinking over the next 5–6 years. The 1992 Côte de Nuits-Villages Clos du Chapitre offers a medium ruby color, a wonderfully expressive, precocious, perfumed nose of sweet black fruits, earth, and vanilla, and round, generous, supple flavors. Drink it over the next 2–3 years. The 1992 Vosne-Romanée Premier Cru (all from the excellent Les Suchots vineyard) reveals copious quantities of sweet toasty oak combined with rich, smoky, black cherry fruit. Ripe, with low acidity and no hard edges or detectable tannin, this attractive, fruity, and seductive wine should drink well for 3–4 more years.

The two top wines from Domaine de l'Arlot are the 1992 Nuits St.-Georges Clos de l'Arlot and the 1992 Nuits St.-Georges Clos des Forêts St.-Georges. The medium ruby-colored 1992 Clos de l'Arlot offers outstanding aromatics (gobs of jammy black cherries, smoke, spice, new oak, and herbs), medium body, silky flavors, admirable fatness, and juicy, succulent Pinot fruit that caresses the palate. It is low in acidity, with no rough edges, so there is no reason to delay your gratification. Consume it over the next 3–5 years for its considerable charms. The 1992 Clos des Forêts St.-Georges is more structured, as well as the richest, longest, most complete Domaine de l'Arlot. It reveals a terrific nose of sweet, smoky, black cherry– and floral-scented fruit, expansive, medium- to full-bodied flavors, light tannin, low acidity, and layers of rich, creamy-textured fruit. This is a fleshy, generous 1992 for drinking over the next 7–8 years.

Influenced by Jacques Seysses of the Domaine Dujac, winemaker Jean-Pierre de Smet fashions silky-textured wines of extraordinary finesse and elegance. The successful 1991s are gorgeous to drink, and will hold nicely for another 5–6 years. The 1991 Côte de Nuits-Villages Clos du Châpeau is a terrific bargain. It offers wonderful aromas of sweet raspberry fruit, a velvety-textured palate, excellent concentration, and a lovely, satiny smooth finish. Drink it over the next 4–5 years. I prefer it to the 1991 Nuits St.-Georges. The latter wine displays deep color, toasty new oak, and medium body. There is some slight astringency from the vintage's coarse tannins. This is a wine to drink in its first 6–7 years of life.

Two efforts that may merit outstanding scores with another year of bottle age are the 1991 Nuits St.-Georges Clos de l'Arlot and 1991 Nuits St.-Georges Clos des Forêts St.-Georges. The former wine displays a deep ruby color (more color than this estate normally achieves), and a big, sweet, perfumed nose of vanillin, raspberries, cherries, and spices. Deep, rich, and succulent, with gobs of velvety, fat fruit, this wine possesses richness and elegance. Drink it over the next 7–8 years. The Clos des Forêts St.-Georges also exhibits an intensely perfumed, sweet nose of red and black fruits and toasty new oak. Ripe and opulent, with layers of fruit, this medium- to full-bodied, expansively flavored, supple wine should be drunk over the next 7–8 years. It is slightly deeper than the Clos de l'Arlot.

Readers who admire the wines of this estate will be delighted to know that Domaine de l'Arlot purchased a parcel of vines in one of the finest Vosne-Romanée premiers crus, Les Suchots.

ROBERT ARNOUX (VOSNE-ROMANÉE)* * * *

1991	Bourgogne Pinot Noir	C	87
1991	Clos de Vougeot	D	89
1991	Nuits St.-Georges Les Corvées Pagets	D	86
1991	Nuits St.-Georges Les Poisets	D	89
1991	Romanée St.-Vivant	EEE	90
1991	Vosne-Romanée Les Hautes Mazières	D	86
1991	Vosne-Romanée Les Suchots	E	92

Arnoux, the perennial overcropper, saw nature cut back his yields to under 35 hectoliters per hectare, his smallest yields since 1978. The results are wines that are as stunning and opulent as his fine 1990s. These 1991s must be tasted to be believed. Do not avoid them because you lack confidence in the vintage. These are seductive, complex red burgundies.

For starters, there is a lovely generic 1991 Bourgogne Pinot Noir with a deep color, a big, juicy, ripe, black cherry–scented nose, sweet, velvety-textured flavors, soft tannins, and a heady, surprisingly rich, concentrated finish. Drink it over the next 3–4 years. Generic burgundy does not get much better. It is even better than the smooth, ripe, rich, supple 1991 Vosne-Romanée Les Hautes Mazières. One of the sleepers in Arnoux's portfolio is the Nuits St.-Georges Les Poisets. The 1991 rivals the superb 1990. The deep ruby color and big, explosive nose of black fruits, earth, toast, and flowers are knockouts. Ripe, with layers of sweet, jammy fruit, low acidity, and moderate tannins in the finish, this wine is gorgeous now and promises to last 7–8 years. The deep ruby-colored 1991 Nuits St.-Georges Les Corvées Pagets is a leaner, more tightly knit wine. Although the tannins are noticeable, the excellent ripeness and sweet fruit achieved by Arnoux in this vintage are present. Nearly outstanding is the deep ruby-colored 1991 Clos de Vougeot. The big, perfumed nose of ripe cassis, vanillin, and smoke is followed by a lush, satiny-textured, voluptuously rich wine with gobs of jammy fruit, soft tannin, and a dazzling finish. It may merit an outstanding score after another 6 months in the bottle.

Arnoux's two finest wines in 1991 should surprise no one who has followed this domaine's wines over the last decade. The deep color of the Vosne-Romanée Les Suchots suggests superb extraction and concentration. The nose offers expansive, sweet aromas of roasted nuts, herbs, and toast, accompanied by lavish quantities of jammy black cherry and black raspberry fruit. A rich, full-bodied, remarkably concentrated wine, it exhibits surprisingly sweet, soft tannin. In a blind tasting one would think this is a great 1990, not a 1991. Delicious now, and already revealing considerable complexity, this wine should continue to drink well for another decade. The 1991 Romanée St.-Vivant displays that elusive, Domaine de la Romanée-Conti, decadent, meaty, overripe, black cherry– and plum-scented bouquet intertwined with aromas of Asian spices and smoked game. Deep, fat, and rich, with layers of flavor, this magnificent wine can be drunk now, yet it will keep for up to a decade. Arnoux's 1991s are among the superstars of the vintage.

BARTHOD-NOËLLAT (CHAMBOLLE-MUSIGNY)* * * *

1991 Bourgogne	C	87
1991 Chambolle-Musigny	D	87
1991 Chambolle-Musigny Les Baudes	D	88
1991 Chambolle-Musigny Les Beaux Bruns	D	87
1991 Chambolle-Musigny Les Charmes	D	89
1991 Chambolle-Musigny Les Cras	D	88+
1991 Chambolle-Musigny Les Varoilles	D	86+

NOTE: Some of these wines also appear under the Ghislaine Barthod label.

This well-run estate continues to make better and better wines. The 1991s are equal to their 1990s. Consumers looking for a top bargain should seek out the 1991 Bourgogne, a wine with considerable fruit, wonderful ripeness, and a supple, smooth texture. It should drink well for the next 3–4 years. The 1991 Chambolle-Musigny offers a sweet, late-harvest, apricot- and jammy, black cherry–scented nose, round, low-acid flavors, and a lush finish. It makes for a joyous mouthful of decadent burgundy. Drink it over the next 5–6 years.

Many of Barthod's 1991 premiers crus have an element of what the French call *sur-maturité*. The fruit is so ripe it adds to the wines' character. What one gets are wonderfully expansive, sweet black cherry aromas and flavors. There is a fatness to these 1991s that has more in common with many 1990s. The most forward and delicious for drinking over the next 7–8 years are the 1991 Chambolle-Musigny Les Varoilles and Chambolle-Musigny Les Baudes. The 1991 Chambolle-Musigny Les Beaux Bruns is soft, but slightly more structured, as is the 1991 Chambolle-Musigny Les Cras, easily the most backward and tannic of the Barthod premier cru Chambolle-Musignys. The 1991 Chambolle-Musigny Les Charmes falls between the tannic, muscular style of Les Cras and the open-knit, ripe, fat, fleshy style of Les Baudes. These are rich, well-balanced, gloriously fruity, and complex red burgundies that will make excellent drinking over the next decade.

PHILIPPE BATACCHI (GEVREY-CHAMBERTIN)* *

1991 Clos de la Roche	E	?
1991 Côte de Nuits	C	?
1991 Gevrey-Chambertin Evocelles	D	78
1991 Gevrey-Chambertin Jeunes Rois	D	78
1991 Morey St.-Denis	D	?

This young producer does a lot of things right (e.g., low yields, negligible fining, and no filtration). However, these 1991s were a troublesome group of wines to taste. The 1991 Côte de Nuits is hard, tannic, tough, and charmless. The 1991 Gevrey-Chambertin Evocelles is lean, malnourished, and frightfully short. Although the 1991 Gevrey-Chambertin Jeunes Rois is closed, there is enough evidence of astringent green tannins not to recommend it. The 1991 Morey St.-Denis and the grand cru Clos de la Roche exhibit impressive deep, saturated colors, but both possess unclean lees aromas, as well as mercaptans, suggesting these wines should have been racked or adjusted with higher levels of SO_2. They may clean up, but they are impossible to judge.

PIERRE BERTHEAU (CHAMBOLLE-MUSIGNY)* * */* * * *

1991	Bonnes Mares	E	89?
1991	Chambolle-Musigny	D	87
1991	Chambolle-Musigny Les Amoureuses	D	88
1991	Chambolle-Musigny Les Charmes	D	?
1991	Chambolle-Musigny Premier Cru	D	86

The wines of Bertheau are consistently among the most traditionally made, rustic red burgundies from the Côte de Nuits. Never filtered, they tend to throw a heavy sediment, and thus will annoy technocrats. Bertheau's wines possess high quantities of the brett yeast, which gives a leathery, meaty, sometimes funky character to a wine. However, there is no evidence of sweaty leather or aged beef smells in the beautiful, medium ruby-colored 1991 Chambolle-Musigny. Supple, with ripe fruit and an opulent texture, this is a gorgeously rich, low-acid wine for drinking over the next 7–8 years. I thought it to be richer and more complex than the 1991 Chambolle-Musigny Premier Cru. The latter is a medium-bodied, elegant, light wine. When tasted side by side with the village cuvée it appears less deep.

A huge nose of black cherries, roasted herbs, earth, and vanillin jumps from the glass of the 1991 Chambolle-Musigny Les Amoureuses. Rich and fat, gushing with flavor, and loaded with glycerin and alcohol, this is a luscious, decadently styled red burgundy for drinking over the next 8–9 years. The antibrett crowd will no doubt go ballistic when they put their noses into a glass of Bertheau's 1991 Bonnes Mares. It exhibits an intense smell of jammy black cherries intermingled with sweaty saddle leather and roasted meat. Deeply colored, and clearly the richest, most concentrated, broadest flavored of all of Bertheau's 1991s, this decadent, controversial wine is loaded. But be forewarned—it is not for everybody. It should drink well for 10–15 years.

LUCIEN BOILLOT ET FILS (GEVREY-CHAMBERTIN)* *

1991	Bourgogne	C	84
1991	Gevrey-Chambertin Les Cherbaudes	D	84
1991	Nuits St.-Georges Les Pruliers	D	85

Boillot produced good but uninspiring efforts in 1991. The best value is the pleasant, ripe, round, easy-to-drink 1991 Bourgogne. It should be consumed over the next several years. The 1991 Nuits St.-Georges Les Pruliers (from 72-year-old vines) displays an excellent deep ruby color, a spicy, damp, earthy-scented nose, medium body, spicy, ripe, medium-bodied flavors, and moderate tannins in the finish. Drink it between 1996 and 2003. The lighter 1991 Gevrey-Chambertin Les Cherbaudes would provide adequate drinking for calorie watchers, but I am looking for more flavor and depth. Tough tannins in the finish made me gasp for my glass of mineral water. While it is a good wine, it is unexciting, and is a candidate for drying out before the tannins melt away.

BOUCHARD PÈRE ET FILS (BEAUNE)* * *

1990 Aloxe Corton	D	85
1990 Beaune Les Grèves Vignes de l'Enfant Jésus Estate	E	90
1990 Beaune-Marconnets Estate	D	87
1990 Le Corton Estate	E	90+
1990 Echézeaux	E	87
1990 Nuits St.-Georges Clos St.-Marc Estate	D	87
1990 La Romanée	EEE	94
1990 Volnay Les Caillerets Ancienne Cuvée Carnot Estate	E	88
1990 Volnay Taillepieds Estate	E	85+
1990 Vosne-Romanée aux Reignots Estate	E	86

There has been a total reversal of the winemaking philosophy at Bouchard Père et Fils. This is one of the wealthiest firms in France, as well as the largest landowner of premiers and grands crus in Burgundy. For years their wines, while commercially acceptable, were uninspiring. Yields were not limited, excessive amounts of SO_2 were employed, the wines were processed and racked excessively, and, most damaging, they were aggressively filtered, often with sterile micropore filters. Inspired by the exceptional success enjoyed by such *négociant* firms as Faiveley and Louis Jadot (they had stopped filtering all of their premiers and grands crus by 1988, opting for a minimal interventionist process in their winemaking), Paul Bouchard and his son Jean-François have begun to turn out their finest wines since the forties and fifties. The wines are deeper-colored and noticeably more concentrated. All the premiers and grands crus are bottled with minimal additions of SO_2, and are not filtered. Consequently, as the notes and scores reveal, there has been a significant leap in quality.

For starters, there is an attractive, earthy, spicy, ripe, nicely extracted 1990 Aloxe Corton. It possesses fine ripeness to hold up to the tough tannins in the finish, and should last for at least 10–12 years. The 1990 Beaune-Marconnets offers deep ruby color, a sweet nose of jammy black cherries and spices, and persuasive medium- to full-bodied flavors with low acidity, excellent richness, and a long, lush finish. The superb 1990 Beaune Les Grèves Vignes de l'Enfant Jésus is the best wine to come from this famous vineyard in over 25 years. The dense, dark ruby/purple color is followed by gorgeously sweet aromas of roasted herbs, sweet black cherries, raspberries, and toasty vanillin. Rich and full bodied, with an opulent, voluptuous texture, and superb depth, focus, and finish, this is a thrilling wine to drink over the next 10–15 years. Bravo! The 1990 Volnay Taillepieds exhibits a saturated, impressive color, although it is closed, with a Bordeaux-like austerity. There are impressive levels of fruit, as well as copious amounts of tannin in the tight finish. It does not possess the supple, rich, velvety texture of many 1990s. This wine needs at least 4–5 years in the cellar. The 1990 Volnay Les Caillerets Ancienne Cuvée Carnot is made in a different style. From its huge bouquet of sweet black fruits, spices, and herbs, to its excellent medium- to full-bodied richness, layers of fruit, and deeply etched flavors, this rich, powerful, concentrated wine begs for attention. The amount of fruit hides lofty tannin levels. This wine can be drunk now or cellared for 10–15 years.

Another outstanding wine that needs 4–5 years of cellaring is the 1990 Le Corton. Deeply colored, it offers up spicy, rich aromas of cassis, minerals, and dusty, earthy notes. Powerful and tannic, with superb richness and an expansive, sweet mid-palate, this long, structured, *vin de garde* should be at its best between 1998 and 2012.

From the Côte de Nuits, the 1990 Nuits St.-Georges Clos St.-Marc is a powerful, tannic, backward wine that needs 4–5 years of cellaring; it should keep for 12–15 years. Darkly colored, and closed from an aromatic point of view, the wine is long, rich, full, and promising. Patience is required. The light-colored 1990 Vosne-Romanée aux Reignots is tannic in the finish without the apparent depth and richness of the other wines. While good, it is slightly awkward and disjointed. The deep, richly colored 1990 Echézeaux is full-bodied, with a masculine personality, and gobs of tannin and depth in the long, formidable finish. This backward, unevolved wine needs at least 5–6 years of cellaring; it should keep for 12–15 years.

There can be little doubt that Bouchard's finest wine is La Romanée, a wine with an extraordinary fragrance reminiscent of the Domaine de la Romanée-Conti's La Tâche or Romanée-Conti. The 1990 offers aromas of smoked game and Asian spices, combined with lavish quantities of sweet, jammy black fruits and new oak. There is spectacular depth and richness. Moderate tannins are present, but this wine is irresistible because of abundant sweet, opulent, rich fruit, full body, and its velvety texture. If you can find a few bottles of this treasure, cellar them for 3–4 years. It should drink well for the next 15 years. Kudos to Bouchard Père et Fils for recognizing that improvements had to be made, and for having the courage to implement them.

BOURÉE PÈRE ET FILS (GEVREY-CHAMBERTIN)* * * *

1990	Beaune Les Epenottes	D	87
1990	Bonnes Mares	E	94
1990	Bourgogne	C	86
1990	Chambertin	EE	90
1990	Chambolle-Musigny	D	75
1990	Chambolle-Musigny Les Amoureuses	E	88
1990	Chambolle-Musigny Les Charmes	E	86
1990	Chapelle-Chambertin	D	89
1990	Charmes-Chambertin	E	90
1990	Corton	E	90
1990	Côte de Nuits-Villages	C	87
1990	Gevrey-Chambertin	D	87
1990	Gevrey-Chambertin Les Cazetiers	D	87+
1990	Gevrey-Chambertin Clos de la Justice	D	90
1990	Gevrey-Chambertin Clos St.-Jacques	E	88+
1990	Gevrey-Chambertin Lavaux St.-Jacques	E	90
1990	Mazis-Chambertin	E	90
1990	Pernand-Vergelesses Les Vergelesses	D	85
1990	Pommard Epenots	D	90
1990	Savigny-Les-Beaune Les Guettes	C	86
1990	Volnay Santenots	D	88

All of Bourées' selections from the Côte de Beaune are well-made wines. The elegant, ripe, tasty, broad, surprisingly full-bodied 1990 Bourgogne offers current drinkability, and should keep for another 3–4 years. I have never been a fan of Pernand-Vergelesses, but the 1990

Pernand-Vergelesses Les Vergelesses exhibits attractive cherry notes to accompany its intense earthiness and spiciness. It is a good, solid wine with firmness and tannin. The underrated 1990 Savigny-Les-Beaune Les Guettes offers value. The nose of Bing cherry fruit and herbs is followed by a medium-bodied, solidly made, natural-tasting wine with fine length and tannin. It should drink well for a decade. The 1990 Beaune Les Epenottes (from the firm's own vineyard) displays a voluptuously scented nose of decadently rich, jammy black cherries and sweet oak. The medium ruby color belies superb flavor extraction and moderate tannins. This opulent, chewy, elegant premier cru should be drunk over the next decade. Bourée's 1990 Volnay-Santenots is a powerful, dense, tannic, rich, full-bodied wine loaded with extraction. Deeply colored, with tremendous reserves of fruit, glycerin, body, and tannin, it is capable of at least 15 years of longevity. If you have patience and a cold cellar, it will be an exceptional wine in 5–6 years. The massive, powerful 1990 Pommard Epenots possesses the body of a big, rich Rhône. Formidable on the palate, and oozing with earthy, spicy, black cherry and cassis fruit, it is thick and big, with considerable power, alcohol, and tannin. Drink it between 1996 and 2010. The 1990 Corton is another superbly rendered wine, with full body, plenty of rich, juicy fruit, and a bouquet of flowers, black cherries, spices, and minerals. Dense and concentrated, with layers of fruit, this wine is surprisingly firm and unevolved for a 1990. It should ideally be given 2–3 more years of cellaring and should keep through the first 10–15 years of the next century.

One of the sleeper wines of the entire Bourée portfolio is their Côte de Nuits-Villages. The 1990 is bursting with aromas of licorice, minerals, and black raspberries. Rich and medium bodied, with a lovely, succulent, fleshy texture, and a long finish, this is a budget pleaser. The 1990 Gevrey-Chambertin is excellent, with a sweet, black curranty nose, ripe, earthy flavors, and a lovely, medium-bodied, elegant finish. Drink it over the next 5–6 years.

Bourée's Gevrey-Chambertin Clos de la Justice is one of Burgundy's perennial over-achievers. The soil is not the best, but because of old vines and low yields, the wine approaches and even surpasses the quality of many premiers and grands crus. The terrific 1990 offers up a huge, meaty, smoky, black and red fruit–scented nose, and deep, full-bodied, rich, expansive flavors that exhibit copious levels of glycerin, alcohol, and tannin. This muscular, rich, opulently textured wine should drink well for the next 12–15 years. The short, thin, angular 1990 Chambolle-Musigny is disappointing. The 1990 Chambolle-Musigny Les Charmes is surprisingly tannic and hard for a 1990. While it exhibits good spice and ripeness, the tannins dominate. Similar criticism is unjustified for the 1990 Chambolle-Musigny Les Amoureuses. Deep ruby color and wonderfully fragrant, sweet black cherry fruit intertwined with aromas of roasted nuts, flowers, and herbs, are followed by a medium-bodied, moderately tannic wine with gobs of sweet fruit, admirable purity and focus, and a rich, long finish. Drink it between 1996 and 2006.

This firm has few weaknesses, and their premiers and grands crus from Gevrey-Chambertin are top notch. The 1990 Gevrey-Chambertin Lavaux St.-Jacques is an exceptional wine, with gobs of sweet fruit in its exotic bouquet. Flamboyant and jammy, this rich, chewy, medium-bodied, deep wine offers delicious drinking; it will age well for 10–12 years. The 1990 Gevrey-Chambertin Les Cazetiers is a backward, rustic, deeply colored wine with a boatload of tannin, as well as plenty of underlying depth and ripeness. Do not touch a bottle before the turn of the century, and then enjoy it through the first decade of the next century. The dark ruby-colored 1990 Gevrey-Chambertin Clos St.-Jacques displays an unevolved, tight, closed nose, offering hints of ripe black cherry fruit, minerals, and smoked meats. Rich and full bodied, as well as tough, hard, and austere, this is a wine to lay away for at least 7–8 years. **A.M.: 2000–2012.** The 1990 Charmes-Chambertin could not be more different. With a medium to dark ruby color and an expansive, sweet, evolved nose of roasted herbs, nuts, and red and black fruits, this satiny-textured, rich, opulent red burgundy makes for a decadent glass of high-class wine. Velvety and easy to drink, it should be enjoyed over the next 10–12 years. The 1990 Mazis-Chambertin is an intense, powerful, muscular wine with an expressive nose of jammy black raspberries, minerals, and flowers. It is deep, full bodied, massive, and backward; considerable patience is necessary in order to enjoy this wine at its peak of maturity. Drink it between 2000 and 2015.

While you are waiting for the Mazys-Chambertin to mature, enjoy the gloriously fat, ripe, chewy, powerful 1990 Chapelle-Chambertin. It is a burgundy that admirably marries elegance and finesse with considerable richness, resulting in a wine that makes an intense impression, yet does not taste heavy or overly extracted. Although soft, there is plenty of tannin in the finish, as well as the juicy, sweet fruit that is characteristic of the best 1990s. Drink it over the next 10–12 years. The 1990 Chambertin is an authentic product of this grand cru vineyard that frequently turns out appallingly overpriced, hollow, thin wines. Deeply colored, rich, full bodied, and highly extracted, this concentrated, muscular wine needs another 8–10 years of cellaring; it should last a quarter of a century. As compelling as Bourée's Chambertin is (there are only 125 cases for the world), the best 1990 I tasted from this firm is Bonnes Mares. It is a spectacular wine, with a huge nose of minerals, black fruits, spices, and grilled meats. This opulent, viscous, well-endowed wine possesses superconcentration, full body, low acidity, and plenty of tannin in the finish. Broad-shouldered and mouth-filling, this wine exhibits admirable glycerin, alcohol, and extract. Drink it between 1996 and 2012. Only 75 cases were produced.

ALAIN BURGUET (GEVREY-CHAMBERTIN)* * *

1991 Bourgogne	C	85
1991 Gevrey-Chambertin	D	76
1991 Gevrey-Chambertin Vieilles Vignes	D	83

Burguet's 1991 Bourgogne is elegant, with ripe, spicy, cherry fruit, a soft texture, and a round, medium-bodied, surprisingly long finish. Drink it over the next 3–4 years. The regular cuvée of 1991 Gevrey-Chambertin is light bodied, with a tart, austere, compact style, and plenty of hard tannins in the lean finish. The fruit will not outlast the high tannins. The 1991 Gevrey-Chambertin Vieilles Vignes is marginally better, with more fruit, and slightly more body and glycerin. Again, abrasively high, hard tannins in the finish dominate the wine's personality.

JACQUES CACHEUX-BLÉE ET FILS (VOSNE-ROMANÉE)* * * *

1992 Echézeaux	E	90
1991 Echézeaux	E	93
1991 Vosne-Romanée	D	87
1991 Vosne-Romanée La Croix Rameau	D	89
1991 Vosne-Romanée Les Suchots	D	89

I have been an admirer of Cacheux's wines since I first visited him in 1985 while doing research for my book on Burgundy. This estate has never filtered its wines, and in 1991 they made the decision not to fine. What the consumer gets in the bottle is an uncompromised product that reflects what was in the barrel.

This underrated Vosne-Romanée producer has fashioned a terrific 1992 Echézeaux. It is a rich, sweet, expansively flavored, smoky, jammy, black cherry– and raspberry-scented wine oozing with fruit, glycerin, and personality, with medium to full body, excellent concentration, and a long, heady finish. It hits the palate with a blast of velvety-textured fruit. This seductive wine is developing quickly, so don't let the rapture pass you by. Drink it over the next 3–5 years.

Few village Vosne-Romanées are likely to be as exciting as Cacheux's 1991. It exhibits a saturated deep ruby/purple color, and superripe, expansive, chewy, black cherry flavors that offer fine ripeness, glycerin, body, and satisfaction. Soft for a 1991, with sweet tannins in the finish, this wine should drink well for another 7–8 years. I may be conservative with my ratings of the 1991 Vosne-Romanée La Croix Rameau and 1991 Vosne-Romanée Les Suchots. La Croix Rameau offers an immensely impressive saturated, dark ruby/purple color, followed by a sweet, toasty, vanillin-scented (plenty of new oak!) nose, intermingled with aromas of jammy black raspberries. Exquisite, rich, and lusty, this exotic, flattering style of 1991 is loaded with extract, sweet tannin, and abundant fruit. Enjoy it over the next decade. Les Suchots is impressively colored, although it is not as saturated as La Croix Rameau. It has a terrific nose of flowers, black fruits, and spices. Given its opulence and chewy, fleshy texture, this rich, medium-bodied, elegant wine should drink well for 7–8 years.

Lastly, the huge framboise-scented bouquet of the 1991 Echézeaux is an attention-grabber. The wine possesses great richness, wonderful precision, and a spectacular, multidimensional personality with layers of flavor and a velvety-textured, ripe, long, concentrated finish. The low yields provided by nature, Cacheux's noninterventionist policy of no fining or filtering, and the slight increase of new oak have resulted in wines that are among the best this fine domaine has produced. Stylistically, they resemble those of the excellent Domaine Méo-Camuzet.

PHILIPPE CHARLOPIN-PARIZOT (MARSANNAY)* * *

1991 Chambertin	EE	87
1991 Charmes-Chambertin	E	86
1991 Gevrey-Chambertin Vieilles Vignes	D	86

Charlopin continues to practice a whoppingly long 10-day cold maceration. This has resulted in deeply colored 1991s. These three offerings are solid, concentrated, well-made wines, but they lack the complexity and intensity to warrant outstanding ratings. The 1991 Gevrey-Chambertin Vieilles Vignes offers up a sweet, chocolatey, currZanty nose, ripe, rich, chunky flavors, low acid, and moderate tannins in the finish. Drink it over the next 7–8 years. The 1991 Charmes-Chambertin is similarly styled, with slightly more tannin in the finish. Monolithic, but impressively colored, rich, and chewy, it too should be drunk over the next 7–8 years. The most backward wine of this trio is the 1991 Chambertin, which reveals a tight but promising nose of coffee, herbs, cedar, and black fruits. Medium bodied, with excellent ripeness and richness, it is unevolved and in need of at least 3–4 years of cellaring. Drink it over the next 12–15 years.

JEAN CHAUVENET (NUITS ST.-GEORGES)* * * *

1991 Nuits St.-Georges	D	86
1991 Nuits St.-Georges Les Bousselots	D	90
1991 Nuits St.-Georges Les Vaucrains	D	88+

Jean Chauvenet remains one of the best kept secrets of the Côte d'Or. His consistency is admirable. His 1991s are rich and intense, but not excessively tannic. The dark ruby color of the 1991 Nuits St.-Georges suggests fine extraction. The wine possesses an elegant nose of black fruits, sweet, well-focused flavors, medium body, and a soft, well-delineated finish. Drink it over the next 4–5 years. The superb 1991 Nuits St.-Georges Les Bousselots reveals an opaque purple color, a super nose of black currants, minerals, and floral scents, and rich, velvety-textured, highly extracted flavors presented in a medium-bodied, smooth-as-silk format. Drink this seductive, beautifully graceful wine over the next decade. The 1991 Nuits St.-Georges Les Vaucrains is a bigger-framed, more alcoholic and massive wine with considerably more tannin in the finish. It packs power and punch, as well as gobs of deep black cherry and currFrancy fruit. Larger-scaled than the Bousselots, but also less charming and graceful, Les Vaucrains may merit an outstanding rating after 4–5 years of cellaring. It should keep for 12 years. Since the mid-eighties, all of Chauvenet's wines have been bottled unfined and unfiltered.

ROBERT CHEVILLON (NUITS ST.-GEORGES)* * *

1991	Bourgogne	C	85
1991	Nuits St.-Georges	D	77
1991	Nuits St.-Georges Les Cailles	D	87
1991	Nuits St.-Georges Les Chaignots	D	85
1991	Nuits St.-Georges Les Perrières	D	86
1991	Nuits St.-Georges Les Pruliers	D	86
1991	Nuits St.-Georges Les Roncières	D	84?
1991	Nuits St.-Georges Les St.-Georges	D	89
1991	Nuits St.-Georges Les Vaucrains	D	87

As the scores and tasting notes attest, Chevillon was successful in 1991. I am delighted that in this vintage all filtration was halted, something that can only be considered a positive development. All of these offerings are well colored and tannic. There may be a slight gamble with a handful of these selections, but in most cases I feel Chevillon's 1991s possess the requisite depth of fruit to balance out the tannin. One exception is the earthy, hard, short, compact 1991 Nuits St.-Georges. It is a much lighter, more attenuated wine than Chevillon's excellent 1991 Bourgogne, which offers plenty of charm, sweet, ripe fruit, medium body, and soft tannin.

Among the premiers crus, the 1991 Nuits St.-Georges Les Chaignots is the lightest. It should be consumed over the next 5–6 years. The 1991 Nuits St.-Georges Les Pruliers is the most earthy and spicy wine, with medium weight, ripe fruit, and light tannins in the finish. The closed 1991 Nuits St.-Georges Les Roncières exhibits considerable tannin, and is in need of 3–4 years of cellaring. It is a chancy choice, as it may dry out before the tannins melt away. The 1991 Nuits St.-Georges Les Perrières is similarly styled, but with more underlying fruit and personality than Les Roncières. As with most of these wines, it possesses deep ruby color, a chewy density to its fruit, and some spice and toughness in the finish.

The best of these offerings include the Nuits St.-Georges Les Vaucrains (from 75-year-old vines), Nuits St.-Georges Les Cailles (the most underrated premier cru vineyard in the appellation), and Nuits St.-Georges Les St.-Georges (the strongest candidate for elevation to grand cru status). The 1991 Les Vaucrains displays a sweet, peppery, earthy-scented nose, rich, long, medium- to full-bodied flavors, moderate tannins, and excellent length. Drink it between 1996 and 2006. The 1991 Nuits St.-Georges Les Cailles possesses elegant, rich, black cherry fruit, medium body, an excellent layered texture, soft, moderate tannins, and a fine, rich, vibrant finish. The richest, fullest, deepest, most concentrated 1991 is the Nuits

St.-Georges Les St.-Georges. It exhibits moderate tannin, but the overall impression is one of excellent depth, ripeness, admirable purity, and a medium- to full-bodied feel in the mouth. Cellar it for 3–4 years and enjoy it for 15 or more.

CHÉZEAUX (MOREY ST.-DENIS)* * * *

1991 Chambolle-Musigny Les Charmes	D	89
1991 Clos St.-Denis Vieilles Vignes	EE	96
1991 Gevrey-Chambertin	D	87
1991 Griottes-Chambertin	EE	91

On my recent visit to Burgundy I learned something I had not known about this estate. As many readers who follow the wines of Domaine de Chézeaux know, the Griottes-Chambertin, Chambertin, and Chambolle-Musigny Les Charmes, as well as part of the Clos St.-Denis, are made by Ponsot. In principle it is the identical wine produced by Ponsot (who leases the vineyards from the Domaine de Chézeaux and in return makes the wines). However, some wines, including the Clos St.-Denis, are made by the Domaine Denis Berthaut in Fixin. The wines that are made by Domaine Berthaut are completely different in style and character from those made at Ponsot. How do consumers know what they are getting from Domaine de Chézeaux? According to Laurent Ponsot, the labels are the same except for three letters. If the label reads SNV—Domaine de Chézeaux, the wine has been made at Domaine Berthaut. If the label reads JFA—Domaine de Chézeaux, the wine has been made at Ponsot. This may account for the totally different style of wine appearing under the same vineyard and producer name. Who said Burgundy was complicated? The tasting notes that follow are from those wines made at the Domaine Ponsot.

For the tasting notes on Chézeaux's 1991 Chambolle-Musigny Les Charmes, 1991 Griottes-Chambertin, and 1991 Clos St.-Denis Vieilles Vignes, refer to my notes for Domaine Ponsot on page 392. The 1991 Gevrey-Chambertin is rich and sweet, with fine concentration, medium body, and some tannin. Drink it over the next 5–7 years.

DANIEL CHOPIN-GROFFIER (PRÉMEAUX)* * * * *

1992 Clos de Vougeot	E	95
1991 Clos de Vougeot	E	90
1991 Nuits St.-Georges	D	86
1992 Nuits St.-Georges Les Chaignots	D	92
1991 Nuits St.-Georges Les Chaignots	D	88
1992 Vougeot	D	92
1991 Vougeot	D	87

If you love the Henri Jayer style of red burgundy but have not been able to find his wines (now virtually impossible because he has taken full retirement and only makes several barrels), then try the wines of Chopin-Groffier. They are made in that wonderfully pure, sensual style of the great master. Chopin-Groffier is an amazingly consistent winemaker regardless of vintage conditions. The 1991s are successful, which is not surprising since Chopin-Groffier made delicious wines in vintages such as 1987 and 1986.

The 1991 Nuits St.-Georges reveals Chopin's telltale medium dark ruby color, and ripe, sweet nose of raspberries intermingled with earthy aromas. Delicate and elegant, this beauty should be drunk over the next 5–6 years. The 1991 Vougeot is slightly sweeter, with more jammy fruit, wonderful purity and precision to its flavors, medium body, and a lovely, glycerin-infused, round, generous finish. It should drink well for the next 7–8 years. The 1991 Nuits St.-Georges Les Chaignots exhibits the spicy, trufflelike scent of a top-notch Nuits St.-Georges, medium body, rich, ripe berry fruit, and a medium-bodied, soft, lush finish with light tannin.

There is no question that Chopin owns one of the best parcels of Clos de Vougeot (adjacent to the château). The 1991 Clos de Vougeot is a great wine. Deep, dark ruby colored, with an explosive nose of black cherries, vanillin, and flowers, this gorgeously textured, voluptuously styled, succulent wine has more in common with the 1990s than the firmer-structured 1991 red burgundies. Drink it over the next decade.

Chopin was exceptionally successful in 1992, which is not surprising as he rarely makes a mistake, even in Burgundy's most difficult vintages. These offerings are all decadent, opulent wines that are best drunk in their first 5–7 years of life, although I am sure the Clos de Vougeot will last longer.

The medium dark ruby-colored 1992 Vougeot exhibits a sweet, expansive, fragrant nose of nearly overripe red and black fruits and toasty oak, wonderful succulence and lushness, and fat, chewy, low-acid, gorgeously pure, fruity flavors. It is a super red burgundy for drinking over the next 4–5 years. The 1992 Nuits St.-Georges Les Chaignots offers a deeper ruby/purple color, and an earthy, trufflelike, licorice scent that combines nicely with the abundant red and black cherry aromas. The wine explodes on the mid-palate with sweet red and black fruits, considerable glycerin, and noticeable tannin and structure in the finish. Delicious now, this wine should improve for 7–8 years. Chopin's 1992 Clos de Vougeot is a winemaking tour de force! It is everything great burgundy should be, but so rarely is— decadent, voluptuous, opulent, seductive, and charming. It displays a stunning bouquet, fabulously rich, ripe flavors, and a huge finish loaded with fruit, glycerin, and alcohol. I wish there were unlimited cases of this wine so all readers could have the opportunity to see just how great burgundy can be. Drink it over the next decade.

BRUNO CLAIR (MARSANNAY)* * *

1991	Chambertin Clos de Bèze	E	76
1991	Gevrey-Chambertin Les Cazetiers	E	72
1991	Gevrey-Chambertin Clos du Fonteny	D	76
1991	Gevrey-Chambertin Clos St.-Jacques	E	74
1991	Marsannay Les Crasses Tête	D	77
1991	Marsannay Les Longeroies	D	79
1991	Morey St.-Denis en la Rue de Vergy	D	72
1991	Savigny-Les-Beaune Les Dominaudes	D	76
1991	Vosne-Romanée Les Champs Perdrix	D	74

For one of the more enthusiastically run Burgundy domaines, Bruno Clair's 1991s are a major disappointment. They lack color, concentration, and richness, and are dominated by excessively high tannins that make all of these wines, save for the soft, light-bodied 1991 Marsannay Les Longeroies, hollow, harsh, tough, and devoid of charm and finesse. One can only speculate on how the 1991 harvest was handled by Bruno Clair, but he is far more talented and conscientious than these wines suggest. Even allowing for the fact that they may have been tasted at an ungraceful period of development, their light ruby colors and the severity of their tannins are unfortunate.

BRUNO CLAVELIER-BROSSON (VOSNE-ROMANÉE)* *

1991 Vosne-Romanée Les Beaux Monts Vieilles Vignes	D	86
1991 Vosne-Romanée Les Brûlées Vieilles Vignes	D	85

Both of these wines were made from low yields of 30–35 hectoliters per hectare and bottled with neither fining nor filtration. Made in a soft, supple, up-front style, neither wine displays the hard tannins that plague some 1991s. The soft 1991 Vosne-Romanée Les Brûlées Vieilles Vignes exhibits a sweet cherry– and herb-scented nose, elegant, medium-bodied flavors, and a velvety-textured, lush finish. Drink it over the next 5–6 years. The 1991 Vosne-Romanée Les Beaux Monts Vieilles Vignes is similarly styled, only slightly more perfumed, with a longer finish. Both are elegant, delicious Pinot Noirs for drinking over the near term.

JEAN-JACQUES CONFURON (PRÉMEAUX)* * * * *

1991 Chambolle-Musigny Premier Cru	D	89
1992 Clos de Vougeot	E	93
1991 Clos de Vougeot	E	90+
1992 Nuits St.-Georges Les Boudots	D	92
1992 Nuits St.-Georges Les Chaboeufs	D	90
1991 Nuits St.-Georges Les Chaboeufs	D	86
1992 Romanée St.-Vivant	EE	94
1991 Romanée St.-Vivant	EE	92
1992 Vosne-Romanée Les Beaux Monts	D	88?
1991 Vosne-Romanée Les Beaux Monts	D	87

Americans should be grateful that the Jean-Jacques Confuron wines sold in this country are produced from 100% new oak casks and bottled without fining or filtration, and in the case of the 1992s, not racked until just prior to bottling. Compared with the wines sold in Europe, America is receiving far richer and significantly more complex and compelling wines. Do not believe any of the nonsense from some of importer Robert Kacher's critics that these wines are overoaked. The well-known, supertalented white wine–maker Jean-Marie Guffens-Heynen has often succinctly stated everything readers need to know about the use of new oak—"No wine is overoaked, just underwined." Those who complain about too much new oak are usually those who cannot afford it. If yields are low and the wines have the power and extract such as Confuron has achieved, new oak is the perfect vessel, as it is sanitary and it actually enhances the quality of the fruit and the *terroir*. Because of his commitment to crop-thinning and extremely low yields (an average of 28–30 hectoliters per hectare in 1992), Confuron has made even greater wines in 1992 than he did in 1990.

With the exception of the 1992 Vosne-Romanée Les Beaux Monts, which may turn out better than my rating, all of these offerings are sure bets for super drinking. The closed and backward 1992 Vosne-Romanée Les Beaux Monts is dominated by its oak, with the fruit taking a backseat and the tannin extremely elevated. The wine is rich, powerful, and long, but unevolved—tasting more like a barrel sample.

The 1992 Nuits St.-Georges Les Chaboeufs offers up a huge nose of black plums and cherries. It is superripe and full bodied, with a moderately tannic, rich palate, and a long, spicy, smoky, earthy finish. For a 1992 from the Côte de Nuits, it possesses a surprisingly saturated dark ruby color. Approachable now, this wine should be even better in 1–2 years and last for 12 or more. The sexy 1992 Nuits St.-Georges Les Boudots exhibits a dark ruby/

purple color, and an explosive nose of fresh pepper, black cherries, raspberries, smoke, and vanillin. The wine is enormously concentrated, surprisingly supple, and velvety-textured, with gobs of fruit and glycerin, and heady alcohol in the lusty finish. This is a decadent, superrich burgundy for drinking over the next decade.

Among the grands crus, the 1992 Clos de Vougeot (made from vines planted in 1932) reveals a dark ruby/purple color and a huge, fragrant nose of toasty vanillin, plums, and black cherries. The wine is fat and rich, with layers of jammy fruit oozing from its full-bodied personality. This knockout wine can be drunk now or cellared for 10 years. Confuron's 1992 Romanée St.-Vivant (from vines planted in 1920) exhibits that profound burgundian perfume of smoked duck, Asian spices, and black cherries and raspberries. It is awesomely concentrated, with profound fruit that unquestionably came from extremely low yields. Made in a generous, highly extracted style, the wine possesses layers of fruit, gobs of glycerin, and sweet tannin. It is beautifully balanced, with well-integrated wood, and a velvety, glycerin-, fruit-, and alcohol-imbued finish. Drink it over the next 10–15 years.

The 1991 Nuits St.-Georges Les Chaboeufs (25 hectoliters per hectare) exhibits an impressive dark ruby/purple color and an admirable nose of black fruits, earth, and spices. Tannic and backward, with fine depth of fruit and extraction, this firm, balanced 1991 should be at its best from the late nineties through the first decade of the next century. Confuron's black/purple-colored 1991 Chambolle-Musigny Premier Cru is a beautiful wine. Dense, concentrated flavors offer sweet aromas of black cherries, roasted nuts, and new oak. Ripe, rich, and long, with considerable tannin in the finish, this backward, well-built, concentrated wine should be drunk between 1998 and 2010. The same can be said for the 1991 Vosne-Romanée Les Beaux Monts, an austere, well-built, highly structured, big, chewy wine with plenty of extract and moderate tannins in the long finish. Do not touch a bottle before the end of this century.

Confuron's two grands crus are stunning wines that are among the stars of the vintage. The 1991 Clos de Vougeot offers a beautiful nose of sweet black fruits, minerals, and roasted nuts. Sensationally concentrated, with layers of flavor, this rich, powerful, full-bodied wine is loaded with fruit, and buttressed nicely by firm tannins. Drink it between 1997 and 2010. The dark ruby/purple-colored 1991 Romanée St.-Vivant is sweeter in the mouth, with more perfume and a magnificent, full-bodied, voluptuous finish that nearly conceals the hefty tannin levels. A gorgeously balanced and structured wine, with layers of ripe fruit, this wine must have been made from astonishingly low yields. Drink it over the next 15 or more years.

J. CONFURON-COTETIDOT (VOSNE-ROMANÉE)* * * *

1991 Clos de Vougeot	E	89
1991 Echézeaux	E	87
1991 Nuits St.-Georges Premier Cru	D	87

Jackie Confuron produced fine 1991s. The wines exhibit deep color and plenty of muscle and extraction of fruit, and should have 10 or more years of longevity. The 1991 Nuits St.-Georges Premier Cru offers a deep ruby/purple color, a ripe, spicy, earthy-scented nose (truffles?), and tannic, medium- to full-bodied flavors, with excellent richness and a long finish. The wine's power and muscle suggest 2–3 years in the cellar is necessary; it should last at least 10 years. The 1991 Echézeaux reveals a deep ruby/purple color, a more fragrant, up-front bouquet of sweet raspberry and black cherry fruit, soft, medium-bodied, rich flavors, low acidity, and moderate yet ripe tannins in the finish. It is the most evolved and seductive of the 1991 Confurons. Drink it over the next decade. The richest and deepest of this trio is the 1991 Clos de Vougeot. With a saturated deep ruby color, this large-scaled wine offers plenty of vanillin, cassis, herbs, and cedar in the bouquet. Medium to full bodied, with ripe, concentrated fruit, a layered, multidimensional appeal, and long, glycerin-dominated, alcoholic flavors, this big, lusty red burgundy should drink well for 10–12 years.

MARIUS DELARCHE (PERNAND-VERGELESSES)* * */* * * *

1992 Corton Les Rénardes	D	91+

There is really no secret to making great red burgundy, so it is remarkable how many terrific wines tasted in barrel are destroyed at bottling by overzealous fining and filtering, not to mention the adding of excessive levels of fruit-killing sulfur dioxide. This 1992 Corton Les Rénardes, bottled without fining or filtration, and made from yields of only 25 hectoliters per hectare, is what great red burgundy is all about. It has more in common with a terrific, blockbuster 1990 than the more loosely knit, softer 1992s. The wine reveals an opaque ruby/purple color, and a huge, sweet, jammy nose of black plums, cherries, spicy new oak, and minerals. Full bodied, rich, and moderately tannic, it possesses gobs of concentration as well as a wonderfully sweet mid-palate. It requires 3–4 years of cellaring and should age well for 15 years.

JOSEPH DROUHIN (BEAUNE)* * */* * * *

1991 Chambolle-Musigny Les Amoureuses	E	87
1991 Clos de Vougeot	E	86
1991 Echézeaux	D	86
1991 Gevrey-Chambertin	C	84
1991 Musigny	EE	87

This selection of Drouhin's 1991s from the Côte de Nuits were all good to excellent wines. The meaty, spicy, gamey, medium-bodied, ripe, soft 1991 Gevrey-Chambertin should be drunk over the next 3–4 years. The light ruby-colored 1991 Echézeaux offers up a lovely nose of raspberries, spices, and spring flowers. Although there is some tannin in the finish, it is made in an up-front, forward, elegant, medium-bodied, soft style for drinking over the next 5–6 years. The richest of the 1991 Drouhin selections I tasted is the 1991 Chambolle-Musigny Les Amoureuses. The deep ruby color and excellent bouquet of toasty new oak, black raspberries, and spice are followed by a medium-bodied wine with moderate tannins and a long finish. The wine will benefit from another 6–12 months in the bottle; it should keep for 5–8 years. The 1991 Clos de Vougeot boasts an attractive deep ruby color, a ripe nose of rich cassis and black cherries, medium to full body, and some spicy tannin in the finish. The deep ruby-colored 1991 Musigny exhibits new oak in the nose, plenty of ripe raspberry and cherry fruit, supple flavors, good depth, and overall balance. Both should drink well over the next 7–8 years.

JEAN-LUC DUBOIS (SAVIGNY-LES-BEAUNE)* * *

1993 Chorey Les Beaune	C	86
1993 Savigny-Les-Beaune	C	88

Fortunately for American wine consumers, particularly those on the West Coast, who are looking for high-quality, reasonably priced red burgundy, the North Berkeley Import Co. in

Berkeley, California, convinced Dubois to bottle these two offerings without filtration. Here are two totally natural, rich, concentrated wines that are super bargains. The 1993 Chorey Les Beaune exhibits wonderfully ripe black cherry fruit and spice in the nose, medium-bodied, fleshy fruit flavors, a natural texture, and a lush, firm finish. Drink it over the next 4–5 years. Even more impressive is the 1993 Savigny-Les-Beaune. Made from 45-year-old vines, it offers a saturated dark ruby/purple color, an explosive nose of black cherry fruit, spices, and sweet oak, medium body, loads of concentration, and a clean, pure, lively, tannic finish. It should drink well for 6–7 years.

CLAUDE ET MAURICE DUGAT (GEVREY-CHAMBERTIN)* * * * *

1992 Charmes-Chambertin	E	94
1991 Charmes-Chambertin	E	92
1992 Gevrey-Chambertin Lavaux St.-Jacques	D	89
1991 Gevrey-Chambertin Lavaux St.-Jacques	D	86
1992 Gevrey-Chambertin Premier Cru	D	90
1991 Gevrey-Chambertin Premier Cru	D	88
1992 Griottes-Chambertin	E	93
1991 Griottes-Chambertin	EE	91

This producer makes microscopic quantities of wines that have long been the backbone for some of the best cuvées from *négociants* who used to buy regularly from Dugat. Dugat now estate-bottles nearly all of his production, so consumers can see just how talented he is. There is no secret to making fine wine—low yields, old vineyards, sanitary cellars, and noninterventionist winemaking do indeed work wonders. Claude and Maurice Dugat produced highly successful 1991s. The gorgeous 1991 Gevrey-Chambertin Premier Cru offers a remarkably deep, dark ruby/purple color, a sweet, seductive nose of black fruits and flowers, and layers of ripe, supple, voluptuously textured Pinot Noir fruit and flavors. This satiny-textured, seductive wine should drink well for the next 10–12 years. The 1991 Gevrey-Chambertin Lavaux St.-Jacques shares the same sweetness and excellent color, but it does not possess the aromatic or flavor dimensions of the Gevrey-Chambertin Premier Cru.

The Dugats make spectacular Griottes and Charmes-Chambertin. Their 1991s will make believers of anyone who doubts what heights this vintage was capable of achieving. The opaque dark ruby color of the 1991 Griottes-Chambertin is followed by a dazzling bouquet of roasted herbs, smoky oak, and black cherries. *Sumptuous* is the only word necessary to describe the palate impression. Sweet, expansive, and loaded with flavor and extraction, this decadent, superrich red burgundy should drink well for at least another decade. Combine the character of the Griottes with aromas of black truffles and smoked meats and nuts, add some additional length and richness, and you have Dugat's 1991 Charmes-Chambertin. It is another hedonistic, rich, magnificent wine that must be tasted to be believed. It should drink well for at least 10 more years.

The 1992 Gevrey-Chambertin Lavaux St.-Jacques (from 30-year-old vines) is a rich, sweet, expansive wine with the essence of black and red fruits gently infused with smoky, toasty new oak. It should provide wonderful drinking over the next 7–8 years. I am not sure it doesn't deserve an outstanding rating. The 1992 Gevrey-Chambertin Premier Cru is a dark ruby/purple-colored wine with dense, black cherry fruit, toasty new oak, and meaty aromas. It offers more cassis than normally found in burgundies, great fruit, ripeness, full body, and a long, rich, multilayered finish. It should drink well for a decade.

The two grand cru offerings are both profound examples of red burgundy. Robert Kacher, among all of our specialty importers, is breaking new ground with the intense pressure he has put on burgundy growers to crop-thin, to do little or no racking, and to bottle with minimal levels of sulfur and no fining or filtration. Every bit of the essence of the wine that comes from the vineyards is presented in the bottle in as natural a way as possible. There is no better evidence of his success in what can be a diluted vintage than these two great, concentrated wines from Dugat. The 1992 Griottes-Chambertin displays a deep, saturated ruby/purple color, a huge, stunning bouquet of black fruits, and spicy, toasty new oak. With rich, full-bodied, wonderfully expansive, pure flavors, superb harmony, and well-integrated acidity and tannin, this spectacularly endowed, rich, lusty red burgundy should drink well for 10–12+ years. The 1992 Charmes-Chambertin is a candidate for the wine of the vintage. A superb expression of red burgundy, it possesses a huge, forceful, sweet, jammy nose of black and red fruits, smoke, and oak. Full bodied, with layers of ripe fruit that cascade across the palate, this sensational, marvelously rich, well-delineated red burgundy is a marvel to smell and taste. These are winemaking gems, particularly in view of the difficulties encountered by so many other Côte d'Or producers in 1992.

DOMAINE DUJAC (MOREY ST.-DENIS)* * * *

1991 Chambolle-Musigny Premier Cru	E	89
1991 Charmes-Chambertin	E	87
1991 Clos de la Roche	E	89
1991 Clos St.-Denis	E	86?
1991 Echézeaux	E	86?
1991 Gevrey-Chambertin Les Combottes	E	86
1991 Morey St.-Denis	D	76

Jacques Seysses tried to modify his vinification style to avoid the hard tannins that were a potential negative characteristic of 1991. As the following notes attest, he had some success, although these offerings are more structured and austere than most vintages of Domaine Dujac. The 1991 Morey St.-Denis is compact and hollow, as well as excessively tannic. The medium ruby-colored 1991 Gevrey-Chambertin Les Combottes offers attractive sweet, earthy, meaty, berry fruit in the nose, medium body, and high tannin. Although it exhibits complexity and charm, I wonder how long the fruit will hold. The 1991 Charmes-Chambertin displays fine focus and precision, excellent medium to dark ruby color, and round, ripe, herbal, berry flavors intertwined with toasty new oak. The finish is dominated by hard tannin. My instincts suggest drinking this wine between 1996 and 2003.

In 1991, the Clos St.-Denis, normally one of the stars of the Dujac portfolio, is lean and austere, with abrasive tannin in evidence. It needs at least 3–4 years of cellaring and will last for 12 or more, but I wonder if the fruit will hold. If the tannins melt away, its score will soar, but don't bet on that happening. The same can be said for the 1991 Echézeaux. More closed than the Clos St.-Denis, it possesses a lean, tough character despite some attractive notes in its bouquet and ripe fruit on the palate. A wine that appears to have an excellent chance of maturing gracefully is the 1991 Clos de la Roche. Deep and rich, with a meaty, mineral- and black fruit–scented nose, medium to full body, and spicy, sweet, expansive fruit, this wine displays plenty of tannin, suggesting it should be cellared for 3–4 years; but it should age gracefully for 12–15 years.

Jacques Seysses did not produce any Bonnes Mares in 1991 because hail destroyed nearly half his crop. What he did harvest was declassified and blended with the 1991 Chambolle-Musigny Premier Cru. That wine is the sleeper pick of the Dujac portfolio. It reveals the deepest color, the richest, ripest fruit, and a wonderful multidimensional, chewy, rich texture, with plenty of sweet, berry fruit. The complex, smoky, vanillin component and a long, luscious, rich, slightly tannic finish are impressive. It may merit an outstanding rating with another 6–12 months in the bottle. Drink it over the next 10–12 years.

DOMAINE RENÉ ENGEL (VOSNE-ROMANÉE)* * * *

1991 Clos de Vougeot	E	87
1991 Echézeaux	E	87
1991 Grands Echézeaux	E	90
1991 Vosne-Romanée	C	85
1991 Vosne-Romanée Les Brûlées	D	86

In 1991, young Philippe Engel decided to utilize a higher percentage of new oak, to extend his cold maceration prior to fermentation to 4–5 days, and to put his wines in the bottle without filtration. The results are wines that rival his 1990s. For starters, there is an excellent 1991 Vosne-Romanée with an attractive, black cherry–scented nose, soft, velvety-textured, ripe flavors, and a smooth finish. Drink it over the next 4–5 years. The 1991 Vosne-Romanée Les Brûlées exhibits a smoky, roasted nose, admirable sweet black fruit, and an overall sense of elegance and precision. It is a soft, pleasant, ripe wine without excessive tannin.

The well-colored, stylish 1991 Echézeaux offers a sweet, perfumed, floral, red and black fruit–scented nose, rich, medium-bodied flavors with good balance, ripe tannins, and a moderately long finish. Delicious now, it should continue to drink well for 7–8 years. The Echézeaux sweetness is a characteristic of the Clos de Vougeot and Grands Echézeaux. The 1991 Clos de Vougeot reveals a ripe cassis component, as well as a chunky, rich, fleshy texture. The tannins do not dominate either the Clos de Vougeot or Grands Echézeaux. Rather, the wines are characterized by their perfumed personalities, expansive, rich, supple flavors, and velvety textures. Both are exceptionally well made 1991s. The Grands Echézeaux displays more dimension to its bouquet and flavors. Both wines should drink well for a decade.

MICHEL ESMONIN ET FILLE (GEVREY-CHAMBERTIN)* * * *

1992 Gevrey-Chambertin Clos St.-Jacques	E	87

Michel Esmonin's attractive daughter has taken over the winemaking responsibilities at this estate. The 1992 Gevrey-Chambertin Clos St.-Jacques offers aromas of smoked duck, sweet cherries, and spice, rich, medium-bodied, ripe flavors, light tannin, and a generously rich, fruity finish. Drinkable now yet structured and deep enough to age for 5–6 years, this is a classic example of the 1992 vintage.

FAIVELEY (NUITS ST.-GEORGES)* * *

1991 Chambertin Clos de Bèze	EE	93
1991 Chambolle-Musigny La Combe d'Orveau	E	88
1991 Chambolle-Musigny Les Fuées	E	89
1991 Charmes-Chambertin	EE	92
1991 Clos de Vougeot	EE	90
1991 Echézeaux	EE	88
1991 Gevrey-Chambertin	D	86
1991 Gevrey-Chambertin Les Cazetiers	E	79?

1991 Gevrey-Chambertin La Combe aux Moines	E	76
1991 Latricières-Chambertin	EE	92
1991 Mazis-Chambertin	EE	93
1991 Morey St.-Denis Clos des Ormes	E	77
1991 Nuits St.-Georges Clos de la Maréchale	D	88
1991 Nuits St.-Georges Les Damodes	D	87+
1991 Nuits St.-Georges Les Lavières	D	88
1991 Nuits St.-Georges Les Porets St.-Georges	D	83?
1991 Nuits St.-Georges Les St.-Georges	D	90
1991 Vosne-Romanée Les Chaumes	D	89

Faiveley enjoyed success in 1991, producing deeply colored, powerful, noticeably tannic wines. These are not wines to consume early, but rather to cellar for several years while the tannins melt away. I do not foresee any difficulty with most of these wines drying out because of excessive tannin, as they possess the concentration of fruit necessary to support the tannin.

The 1991 Nuits St.-Georges Les Lavières exhibits an impressively dark color, a medium-to full-bodied personality, a tight but promising bouquet of minerals and black fruits, and an excellent, moderately tannic, long finish. Drink it between 1996 and 2008. The backward, tannic 1991 Nuits St.-Georges Les Damodes displays a broad, large-scaled structure, impressively deep color, and excellent density and richness. Although the nose is closed and the finish is austere and tannic, there is fine weight and ripeness. Give it at least 4–5 years of cellaring; it should keep for at least 15 years.

Faiveley's other premiers crus from Nuits St.-Georges are also impressive. The 1991 Nuits St.-Georges Clos de la Maréchale is one of the best wines Faiveley has made from this vineyard. It reveals a sweet, seductive, ripe plum-scented nose, smooth, velvety-textured, rich, concentrated flavors, and a long, lusty finish. It is one 1991 Faiveley that can be drunk now; it promises to keep for a decade. The 1991 Nuits St.-Georges Les Porets St.-Georges may be the only Nuits St.-Georges premier cru that is a gamble. It possesses huge quantities of tannin, austerity and compactness, excellent color, and admirable weight and ripeness. Nevertheless, the tannins dominate the wine; thus I have more reservations about it. Do not touch it for at least 3–4 years. The 1991 Nuits St.-Georges Les St.-Georges is a classic example of this vineyard. The dark ruby/purple color is followed by aromas of anise, black fruits, new oak, and flowers. Deep, rich, full bodied, and moderately tannic, with superb depth, this is an impressively endowed, broad-shouldered wine for drinking between 1996 and 2008.

The hollow, excessively tannic, light and skinny 1991 Morey St.-Denis Clos des Ormes offers some strawberry and cherry aromas, but not enough flesh to cover the tannin. It is likely to dry out over the next 4–5 years.

Faiveley receives worldwide attention for its excellent wines from Nuits St.-Georges and Gevrey-Chambertin. Overlooked is the firm's fine premiers crus from Chambolle-Musigny and Vosne-Romanée. All of these wines are now bottled unfiltered, giving them even more flavor dimension and aromatic complexity. The 1991 Vosne-Romanée Les Chaumes matches up nicely with some of the best premiers crus of the vintage. It exhibits a sweet, creamy, cassis- and vanillin-scented nose, and deep, supple, rich flavors that effectively conceal most of the wine's tannin. It is a full-bodied, ripe, luscious 1991 that should be drunk over the next 8–12 years. The less muscular 1991 Chambolle-Musigny La Combe d'Orveau is elegant, soft, and ripe, with gobs of sweet red and black fruits in its bouquet, and velvety-textured, fleshy, graceful flavors and finish. Drink it over the next 8–9 years. The huge nose of framboise and spring flowers, as well as toasty new oak, make for a dramatic introduction to the 1991 Chambolle-Musigny Les Fuées. Deep and supple, with an impressive color, long, luscious fruit flavors, enough acidity for balance, and round tannin in the finish, this quintessentially elegant wine should drink well for at least a decade. Interestingly, I preferred these premiers crus to the two from Gevrey-Chambertin. I found both the 1991 Gevrey-Chambertin Les Cazetiers and the 1991 Gevrey-Chambertin La Combe aux Moines to be average-quality wines, severe, with hard tannins, and in the case of La Combe aux Moines, to have a closed, tough, sharp, angular style. It is likely to lose its fruit long before its abrasive tannins. Les Cazetiers reveals better fruit and depth, as well as a broader, richer palate, with fine sweetness behind the huge wall of tannin. A big wine, it is a gamble given its tannic clout. Cellar it for at least 3–4 years; it should last for 12–15 years, but I am not sure how harmonious it will become.

All of Faiveley's 1991 grands crus were aged in 50% new oak and bottled by hand, without filtration. The lightest, the 1991 Echézeaux exhibits attractive toasty, vanillin oak notes, along with weedy black raspberry and black cherry fruit. Medium bodied, with lovely ripeness and moderately sweet tannins, this elegant, stylish Echézeaux should be drunk in its first 10–11 years of life. Faiveley's 1991 Clos de Vougeot is a larger-scaled, more tightly knit wine with plenty of oak in its forceful, ripe, black cherry aromas and flavors. It is well proportioned, with copious quantities of tannin, and fine depth and balance. Still unevolved, it should not be drunk for 4–5 years; it should keep for 15 or more years.

All of Faiveley's grands crus from Gevrey-Chambertin are outstanding wines and far superior to what he produced in 1986, 1987, 1989, and probably even 1988. They were made from very low yields, and the balance between the tannin and fruit favors the latter.

The 1991 Mazis-Chambertin, Chambertin Clos de Bèze, Charmes-Chambertin, and Latricières-Chambertin are among the top wines of the vintage. The flamboyant 1991 Mazis-Chambertin is more accessible than most wines from this grand cru vineyard. The color is dark ruby/purple and the nose offers up huge scents of jammy plums, black cherries, a roasted element, and attractive toasty new oak. Lush and unctuously rich, this big, deep, full-bodied wine is loaded with extract. Already approachable, it will be at its best between now and 2010. The 1991 Latricières-Chambertin is also opulent, with a gorgeously scented, evolved nose of smoky black cherries, herbs, and Asian spices. There is even a scent of Peking duck. Rich, supple, and with a sweet mid-palate that comes from low yields rather than residual sugar, this wine can be enjoyed now as well as over the next 12–15 years. In most vintages Charmes-Chambertin is a much softer wine than either Mazis or Latricières. Faiveley's 1991 is a big, masculine style of Charmes, with plenty of tannin in the finish. This is one grand cru that begs for 4–5 years of cellaring. It should last for at least 12–15 years. The wine is deep, rich, full bodied, tightly knit, and impressively endowed. One of Faiveley's flagship wines, the 1991 Chambertin Clos de Bèze displays an opaque dark ruby/ purple color, and a superb yet tight bouquet of black fruits, minerals, licorice, and herbs. Rich, with firm tannins buttressing sweet, highly concentrated fruit, this big, chewy wine should be at its best between 1997 and 2012.

JEAN FAUROIS (VOSNE-ROMANÉE)* * * *

1991 Vosne-Romanée Les Chaumes   D 89

Faurois continues to exhibit a firm hand in his winemaking. His magnificent Clos de Vougeot is no longer being made, as he had rented part of that vineyard from Méo-Camuzet. This is the only wine he now makes, and the unfined and unfiltered 1991 Vosne-Romanée Les Chaumes possesses a beautiful, sweet, fragrant nose, ripe, intense flavors that suggest low yields and old vines, and a soft, velvety-textured finish. Drink this beauty over the next 7–8 years.

DOMAINE FOREY PÈRE ET FILS (VOSNE-ROMANÉE)* *

1991 Echézeaux	D	86
1991 Nuits St.-Georges Les Perrières	D	79
1991 Vosne-Romanée	D	76

Forey's 1991 Vosne-Romanée and Nuits St.-Georges Les Perrières were subdued when I tasted them, with high levels of astringent, tough tannins, and hard, lean personalities. Am I being unfair in judging them so soon after bottling? The 1991 Echézeaux displays more sweet fruit and balance, with a spicy, elegant, floral-scented nose, light to medium body, and an absence of the harsh tannins that plague Forey's other wines. Drink it over the next 5–6 years.

FOUGERAY (MARSANNY)* *

1991 Bonnes Mares	E	87
1991 Marsannay St.-Jacques	C	85

The 1991 Marsannay St.-Jacques reveals a soft, easy, ripe style, and fine color. It is an attractive wine for drinking over the next 4–5 years. The 1991 Bonnes Mares exhibits a deep ruby color, spicy new oak aromas, medium to full body, a spicy, ripe, black cherry, and mineral richness, and a soft yet firm finish. It will benefit from another 12 months in the bottle. Drink it over the next 7–8 years.

DIDIER FOURNEROL (NUITS ST.-GEORGES)* *

1991 Côte de Nuits-Villages	C	87
1990 Côte de Nuits-Villages	C	86

This young producer works for the Domaine l'Arlot. He has turned out two rich, elegant, fruity wines that should be drunk over the next 5–6 years. They are both notable values. The 1991 possesses more concentration, glycerin, and intensity than the lovely 1990. Both are supple, with the 1991 exhibiting slightly darker, more saturated color, and a richer, smoother finish. The attractive 1990 offers a raspberry-scented nose and fat, juicy flavors.

GEANTET-PANSIOT (GEVREY-CHAMBERTIN)* * * *

1991 Bourgogne Pinot Noir	B	82
1991 Charmes-Chambertin	D	90
1991 Gevrey-Chambertin Vieilles Vignes	D	87
1991 Marsannay Champ Perdrix	C	86

A member of the younger generation has taken over the direction of this estate, and he is producing better wines. The 1991 Bourgogne Pinot Noir is light, tasty, pure, and elegant. Drink it over the next 2–3 years. The 1991 Marsannay Champ Perdrix exhibits more depth, medium body, and admirable ripe raspberry fruit allied to attractive scents of underbrush and earth. Spicy, with fine depth and light tannins, this offering should drink well for another 5–6 years. The gorgeously pure bouquet of ripe raspberries jumps from the glass of the 1991 Gevrey-Chambertin Vieilles Vignes. Medium bodied, with excellent concentration and ripeness, as well as soft tannins, this graceful, stylish wine should be drunk over the next 5–6 years.

The superb 1991 Charmes-Chambertin reveals an attractively intense bouquet of spicy new oak, black raspberries, cherries, and licorice. Dense, rich, and medium to full bodied, with outstanding concentration, this wine offers fine richness, a supple texture, and sweet tannin in the long finish. Drink it over the next 7–8 years. Geantet made superb 1993s.

DOMAINE HENRI GOUGES (NUITS ST.-GEORGES)* *

1991 Nuits St.-Georges	D	83
1991 Nuits St.-Georges Clos des Porrets	D	86
1991 Nuits St.-Georges Les Pruliers	D	87
1991 Nuits St.-Georges Les St.-Georges	D	86?
1991 Nuits St.-Georges Les Vaucrains	D	87

These wines may turn out to be the most complete Gouges wines in over two decades. Although not exceptional, they display more color, bouquet, richness, and length than any vintage since Gouges's marvelous 1969s. The 1991 Nuits St.-Georges offers deep color, an attractive, earthy, plum-scented nose, and ripe, medium-bodied, spicy flavors with moderate tannins in the finish. While somewhat compact, it is successful for its appellation. Drink it over the next 7–8 years. The 1991 Nuits St.-Georges Clos des Porrets exhibits a deep ruby color, a spicy, tight, reticent bouquet, and rich, well-focused structure and flavors. There is plenty of tannin in the finish, but the balance is not suspect. It needs 4–5 years of cellaring, so drink it between 1998 and 2007. The 1991 Nuits St.-Georges Les Pruliers is a much denser wine, with adequate depth to balance out the noticeably high tannin. Medium to full bodied, with excellent depth and precision, it offers an earthy, sweet, cassis-scented nose and long, ripe flavors. It will reward cellaring of 4–5 years and will drink well for at least 12. The 1991 Nuits St.-Georges Les Vaucrains (from 45-year-old vines) possesses a big, spicy, earthy, licorice- and black cherry–scented nose, tannic, muscular, powerful flavors, excellent depth, and an austere, backward, youthful finish. It too needs 4–5 years of cellaring and should keep for 15. The similarly colored 1991 Nuits St.-Georges Les St.-Georges is more closed, with a tough, almost Bordeaux-like austerity to its flavors and personality. There appears to be sweet fruit and fine depth to this medium-bodied wine, but it is somewhat of a gamble given the fact that the tannins are more astringent than in the other Gouges wines. I would not touch a bottle of it for at least 5–6 years.

MACHARD DE GRAMONT (NUITS ST.-GEORGES)* * * *

1991 Chambolle-Musigny Les Nazoires	D	85
1991 Nuits St.-Georges Les Damodes	D	85
1991 Nuits St.-Georges Les Hauts Poirets	D	81
1991 Nuits St.-Georges Les Hauts Pruliers	D	85

I am a big fan of Gramont's red burgundies. Although he did not fall on his face in 1991, his wines possess less flavor dimension and richness than I prefer. The three 1991 Nuits St.-Georges premiers crus range from an elegant, soft, round, supple, medium-bodied, ready-to-drink Les Hauts Pruliers, to the lighter, less concentrated Les Hauts Poirets, and the medium-bodied, satiny-textured, spicy, earthy, richly fruity Les Damodes. Gramont obviously tried to produce wines without harsh tannins. These forward, soft wines should be drunk over the next 4–5 years.

The similarly styled 1991 Chambolle-Musigny Les Nazoires possesses more interesting scents in its curranty, spicy, floral bouquet. In addition, there are elegant, medium-bodied, soft, red fruit flavors and a smooth finish. It too should be consumed over the near term.

ROBERT GROFFIER (MOREY ST.-DENIS)* * *

1991 Bonnes Mares	EE	88
1991 Chambertin Clos de Bèze	EE	87+

1991 **Chambolle-Musigny Les Amoureuses**	E	88
1991 **Chambolle-Musigny Les Hauts Doix**	D	87
1991 **Chambolle-Musigny Les Sentiers**	D	84?

Groffier is a consistently inconsistent wine producer. His 1991s are significantly richer, more complete, and more complex wines than his 1989s and 1990s. If you find that hard to figure out, remember that he also made superlative 1986s and mediocre 1985s. Groffier, never one to worry about excessive crop levels, let Mother Nature prune his vineyards in 1991. That, plus the fact that the 1991s were put in the bottle without filtration, resulted in promising wines that are certainly the best he has made since 1986.

The 1991 Chambolle-Musigny Les Hauts Doix offers a deep, dark ruby color, a rich, spicy, black cherry– and herb-scented nose, ripe, medium-bodied flavors, admirable extraction of flavor, and an overall sense of balance and finesse. Drink this sweet, expansively flavored wine over the next 6–7 years. The impressively colored 1991 Chambolle-Musigny Les Sentiers is deep and rich, as well as hard, tannic, and closed. It is one 1991 that is difficult to judge, but my instincts suggest the fruit is likely to fade before the tannins. That is not a problem with the 1991 Chambolle-Musigny Les Amoureuses or Bonnes Mares. Both are wonderfully rich, medium- to full-bodied wines with superb extraction of flavor, and plenty of ripe, rich, black cherry fruit intertwined with lavish amounts of toasty, vanillin new oak. Les Amoureuses is soft and succulent, with gobs of fruit and a wonderfully layered, voluptuous texture. Drink it over the next 7–8 years. The Bonnes Mares is slightly deeper in color, with more noticeable tannins in the finish. Big and well balanced, it possesses more of that underlying, mineral, stony character in its flavors than Les Amoureuses. Approachable now, it should be drunk over the next 8–10 years.

The 1991 Chambertin Clos de Bèze is the most subdued and restrained of Groffier's 1991s. Rich, medium to full bodied, with excellent color, definition, and flavor extraction, it needs at least 3–4 years in the cellar; it should keep for 10–12 years. How great it is to see Groffier come through with such high-quality wines in 1991.

A.-F. GROS (POMMARD)* * *

1991 **Bourgogne Hautes Côtes de Nuits**	C	75
1991 **Echézeaux**	EE	84
1991 **Richebourg**	EEE	90
1991 **Vosne-Romanée Mazières**	D	83
1991 **Vosne-Romanée aux Réas**	D	81

This vintage unquestionably produced mixed performances by this member of the Gros family. The Bourgogne Hautes Côtes de Nuits, Vosne-Romanée Mazières, Vosne-Romanée aux Réas, and even the grand cru Echézeaux (allegedly made from 70-year-old vines) reveal the worst side of the 1991 vintage. The wines are lean, austere, and compact, with excessive tannin overwhelming the meager fruit. The only successful wine is the superb 1991 Richebourg. Its deep ruby/purple color is followed by a sweet nose of black raspberries and flowers, and rich, concentrated flavors that linger on the palate. It is an example of how red burgundy can be both light and elegant yet persuasively rich and compelling. Drink it over the next 7–8 years.

Note: Everyone claims the Gros family divides their allocations of Richebourg after it is bottled, but after tasting the 1991 Richebourgs of Jean Gros, A.-F. Gros, and Anne and François Gros side by side I was left with the impression that despite what the three domaines claim, there are differences among the wines.

ANNE ET FRANÇOIS GROS (VOSNE-ROMANÉE)* * *

1991 Clos de Vougeot	E	86
1991 Richebourg	EEE	88+
1991 Vosne-Romanée	D	85

This estate produced a better village Vosne-Romanée in 1991 than other family members. Deeply colored, with an excellent cherry- and raspberry-scented nose, medium body, and soft flavors, it is a wine to drink over the next 3–4 years. Only slightly better, the 1991 Clos de Vougeot offers medium dark ruby color and a ripe, elegant nose. An aggressive, tannic bite in the finish kept my score from being higher. This wine may merit a higher score if the fruit holds and the tannin fades. It is best drunk after 1996. The 1991 Richebourg is the leanest, most tannic of the three Gros Richebourgs I tasted side by side. It possesses excellent ripeness and a fine sense of elegance and balance, but not the suppleness or richness of the 1991 Richebourgs from Jean Gros and A. F. Gros. Everyone, including the estates, says this is the same wine as the other two Richebourgs, but it did not taste similar to them when I sampled them side by side.

DOMAINE JEAN GROS (VOSNE-ROMANÉE)* * */* * * *

1991 Bourgogne	C	65
1991 Bourgogne Hautes Côtes de Nuits	C	62
1991 Richebourg	EEE	91
1991 Vosne-Romanée	D	70
1991 Vosne-Romanée Clos des Réas	D	86

At the lower level, Jean Gros's 1991s were disappointing—from the oxidized generic Bourgogne, to a sour, harsh, astringent Bourgogne Hautes Côtes de Nuits, and a lean, tart, tannic village Vosne-Romanée. Even the 1991 Vosne-Romanée Clos des Réas, while elegant and ripe, with moderate toasty new oak and black cherry scents and flavors, left me wanting more concentration and length. Certainly the 1991 Richebourg, which is alleged to be the same wine as that of A.-F. Gros and that of Anne and François Gros, is superb. Its deep ruby/purple color is followed by a marvelous nose of cassis, flowers, and sweet, toasty new oak. Rich, velvety, and voluptuous, this expansive, medium- to full-bodied wine makes for a gorgeously opulent, seductive mouthful of red burgundy.

ALAIN HUDELOT-NOËLLAT (VOUGEOT)* * * *

1991 Chambolle-Musigny Les Charmes	D	90
1991 Clos de Vougeot	E	88
1991 Nuits St.-Georges Les Murgers	D	88
1991 Richebourg	EE	90
1991 Romanée St.-Vivant	EE	87
1991 Vosne-Romanée Les Beaumonts	D	87
1991 Vosne-Romanée Les Suchots	D	88
1991 Vougeot Les Petits Vougeot	D	87

Potentially, this is a spectacular domaine, but it has been a perennial underachiever for years. Hudelot appears to have begun to recognize that ferocious competition in the marketplace requires high quality. His 1991s are the finest wines I have tasted from this estate. Low yields, along with Hudelot's junking his mobile bottler, who often stripped the wines by excessive filtration, have worked wonders regarding the final product. All of these offerings taste like fat, voluptuous, opulent 1990s. Gobs of sweet ripe fruit can be found in every wine, and this makes for luscious, decadent mouthfuls of red burgundy. All the wines are recommended, but several possess more complexity and aromatic dimension.

The 1991 Nuits St.-Georges Les Murgers is a powerful, rich, supple wine with considerable density of fruit, and a big, spicy, earthy, black fruit–scented nose. The emphasis is on fruit and full body, without a heavy overlay of new oak. Drink it over the next decade. Some new oak was detectable in the 1991 Chambolle-Musigny Les Charmes, but the overall impression is of a wine of exceptional ripeness and richness, with beautiful balance, low acidity, and a soft, sumptuous finish. Perfumed and rich, it is ideal for drinking over the next 7–8 years. The 1991 Vougeot Les Petits Vougeot offers an attractive cherry-scented nose, fine ripeness and richness, medium body, and a heady, alcoholic finish. It lacks the complexity of the Chambolle-Musigny Les Charmes, and the power and earthy spiciness of the Nuits St.-Georges Les Murgers.

Both Vosne-Romanée premiers crus are top notch. The 1991 Vosne-Romanée Les Beaumonts is supple, soft, and ready for prime-time drinking. Its low acidity and luscious style suggest it should be consumed over the next 5–6 years. The 1991 Vosne-Romanée Les Suchots exhibits a deep ruby color and a more fragrant nose of black fruits, herbs, and sweet oak. More opulent, richer, and fuller bodied than Les Beaumonts, this is a beautiful wine for drinking over the next 7–8 years.

The grands crus range from very good in the case of the 1991 Romanée St.-Vivant, which is fat and seductive but lacking the complexity one expects in a grand cru, to excellent in the case of the oaky, cassis-scented, rich, chunky yet concentrated and powerful 1991 Clos de Vougeot. The best grand cru is the 1991 Richebourg, a wine with a huge bouquet of spring flowers, black currants, and black raspberries complemented judiciously by spicy new oak. Full bodied, deep, and surprisingly soft and accessible, this luscious wine should be drunk over the next 7–8 years.

LOUIS JADOT (BEAUNE)* * * */* * * * *

1991 Bonnes Mares	E	86
1991 Chambertin	E	86+
1991 Chambertin Clos de Bèze	E	89
1991 Chambolle-Musigny Les Amoureuses	D	87
1991 Chambolle-Musigny Les Feusselottes	D	87
1991 Chapelle-Chambertin	D	87
1991 Clos de Vougeot	D	87
1991 Gevrey-Chambertin Estournelles St.-Jacques	D	86
1991 Gevrey-Chambertin Clos St.-Jacques	D	87
1991 Gevrey-Chambertin Lavaux St.-Jacques	D	87
1991 Musigny	EEE	86
1991 Nuits St.-Georges Les Boudots	D	86
1991 Nuits St.-Georges Les Corvées	D	85+
1991 Romanée St.-Vivant	E	90
1991 Vosne-Romanée Les Beaux Monts	D	86
1991 Vosne-Romanée Les Suchots	D	87

The 1991 Nuits St.-Georges Les Corvées exhibits deep ruby color, fine underlying depth, and Bordeaux-like structure, as well as tough, dry, austere tannins in the finish. Cellar this wine for at least 2–3 years and drink it over the following decade. More seductive than Les Corvées, the 1991 Nuits St.-Georges Les Boudots is a solidly made, medium-bodied, ripe wine with tough tannins, but fine fruit, depth, and chewiness.

The 1991 Chambolle-Musigny Les Feusselottes offers considerable charm. Deeply colored, with a nose of floral, berry, herb, and earth scents, this medium-bodied, attractively textured, and concentrated wine possesses the requisite fruit to balance the tannins. The finish is long and convincing. Drink it over the next decade. The deep ruby color of the 1991 Vosne-Romanée Les Beaux Monts is followed by a tight but promising bouquet of berries, spices, and vanillin. While some tannins are evident, the wine possesses good depth, ripeness, and a medium-bodied personality. Drink it between 1996 and 2003. Slightly richer, more expansive, sweeter, and more perfumed is the deep ruby-colored 1991 Vosne-Romanée Les Suchots. Les Suchots is one of the finest premiers crus of Vosne-Romanée and this wine offers a rich, expansive, luscious mouthful. Equal to the 1990 from this vineyard, it already exhibits more complexity than many 1991s.

Jadot's premiers crus from the village of Gevrey-Chambertin are all well-made, solidly constructed wines exhibiting the compactness and tannins of the 1991 vintage, as well as excellent color and the potential for longevity. Will the fruit outlive the tannin? The 1991 Gevrey-Chambertin Estournelles St.-Jacques exhibits an attractive, spicy, meaty, earthy nose, medium-bodied flavors with good extraction and concentration, and a spicy, long finish with soft tannin. Drink this seductive 1991 over the next decade. The 1991 Gevrey-Chambertin Lavaux St.-Jacques offers sweeter fruit, with a spicy, meaty richness, chewy, well-endowed flavors, attractive glycerin levels, and moderate tannin in the firm finish. It should drink well for the next 10–12 years. The closed, lean, austere 1991 Gevrey-Chambertin Clos St.-Jacques reveals a Bordeaux-like character. Usually one of the best wines in the Jadot portfolio, I may have caught it during an unflattering stage of development. Although the wine possesses good weight and some ripe aromas, the finish is tough, and the tannins appear excessive.

The 1991 Chambolle-Musigny Les Amoureuses is made from exceptionally low yields because of the hail that hit Chambolle. This deep ruby-colored wine offers an excellent nose of red and black fruits and vanillin, a tasty, rich, well-knit, medium-bodied personality, fine depth and ripeness, and a moderately tannic finish. It should drink well for at least a decade.

Among the grands crus, the elegant 1991 Chapelle-Chambertin is well colored, with black cherry fruit and multidimensional characteristics to its flavors, as well as a spicy, solid finish. The tannins are noticeable, but not excessive. The 1991 Chambertin Clos de Bèze should turn out to be among Jadot's finest wines of the vintage. With a saturated, deep ruby color, and a tight but promising nose of roasted herbs, black fruits, and vanillin, this long, rich, medium- to full-bodied, concentrated, powerful wine reveals moderate tannins in the finish, as well as plenty of depth. Drink it between 1996 and 2005. In contrast, the 1991 Chambertin reveals a less impressive color. Although there are some attractive ripe, black cherry flavors, and a chewy, spicy finish, the heavy load of tannin makes the wine taste austere and hard. It is a gamble. Similar objections can be raised concerning the tough, hard, compact 1991 Bonnes Mares and 1991 Musigny. Both reveal deep ruby colors and are solidly built with good depth, medium body, and spicy, ripe fruit, but their tannin tends to possess an astringency that I find troubling. They both need at least 4–5 years of cellaring. If the fruit holds up, my judgments will look not only conservative, but off-base.

The 1991 Clos de Vougeot is more complete than most of the other Jadot grands crus. Deep ruby-colored, with a forceful nose of cassis and plummy fruit, this medium- to full-bodied, spicy, dense, chewy wine lacks complexity, but offers a big, juicy, firm, tannic mouthful of burgundy that should age well for 10–15 years. My highest rating is bestowed on Jadot's 1991 Romanée St.-Vivant (only 50 cases were produced). The deep ruby color is followed by a nose of sweet black cherry fruit, Asian spices, herbs, and floral scents. Rich and expansive, with a gorgeously voluptuous texture supported by fine acidity and tannin, this exceptionally rich, concentrated wine possesses brilliant balance, and a long, lusty, moderately tannic finish. It should drink well for at least 10–15 years.

DOMAINE ROBERT JAYER-GILLES (MAGNY-LES-VILLERS)* * * * *

1991 Côte de Nuits	D	83
1991 Echézeaux	EE	87
1991 Hautes Côtes de Nuits	C	82
1991 Nuits St.-Georges Les Damodes	E	87+
1991 Nuits St.-Georges Les Hauts Poirets	D	86

Robert Jayer is one of the surest-handed winemakers in the Côte de Nuits, and the reviews that follow are somewhat disappointing in light of what he has accomplished over the last decade. Some of the difficulties of the 1991 vintage—high, hard tannin levels and a deficiency of sweet, ripe fruit—are evident in the 1991 Hautes Côtes de Nuits and 1991 Côte de Nuits. Both wines exhibit fine color, but the tannins have the upper hand. Certainly the 1991 Nuits St.-Georges Les Hauts Poirets and 1991 Nuits St.-Georges Les Damodes reveal better overall balance and more ripeness and richness to balance out their noticeable tannin level. Both wines are at least 3–4 years away from full maturity. If the fruit becomes more evident and the tannin dissipates without any reduction in fruit, my ratings will seem ungenerous. The 1991 Echézeaux is light bodied for a Jayer wine, as well as more compact and austere. The wine offers an attractive floral, berry-scented nose, spicy, medium-bodied, moderately concentrated flavors, and noticeably hard, astringent tannin in the finish. These five 1991 offerings are not the sure bet Jayer's wines have been in the past.

LAMARCHE (VOSNE-ROMANÉE)* * *

1991 Bourgogne Passetoutegrain	B	85
1991 Clos de Vougeot	E	87
1991 Grands Echézeaux	E	86+
1991 Vosne-Romanée Les Charmes	D	81+
1991 Vosne-Romanée La Grande Rue	E	86
1991 Vosne-Romanée Les Malconsorts	D	?

These are among the most deeply colored wines I have tasted from François Lamarche. I was delighted to learn that in 1991 he stopped filtering, one more encouraging sign that many of the top burgundy producers are beginning to return to the traditional methods used by their fathers and grandfathers in the forties and fifties. Lamarche fashioned an excellent 1991 Bourgogne Passetoutegrain. It reveals ripe, strawberry and cherry fruit in the nose, sweet, jammy fruit on the palate, and a round, low-acid finish. Drink it over the next several years. The 1991 Vosne-Romanée Les Charmes and 1991 Vosne-Romanée Les Malconsorts exhibit deep color, but both are tannic, hard, firm, austere wines with adequate depth yet questionable balance given the high level of astringent tannin. I have rated them conservatively rather than give them the benefit of the doubt. If readers have not realized it, Pinot Noir loses its fruit more quickly than its tannin.

The 1991 Clos de Vougeot is a bigger, richer wine, with plenty of deep black cherry and cassis fruit, admirable body, glycerin, and extraction, and a long, moderately tannic finish.

The tannins are supported by the requisite depth of fruit to provide balance. Drink this wine between 1997 and 2008. The impressively colored 1991 Grands Echézeaux reveals a muted, nondescript nose. Tough, hard tannins make this a gamble in terms of its ability to develop harmony among its components. Although there is underlying fruit, the tannin is severe and compact. Do not plan on drinking it before the end of the decade. If it fattens out, the wine will merit a higher score. It should easily keep for 12–15 years. The 1991 Vosne-Romanée La Grande Rue possesses excellent color, as well as a wonderfully complex nose of violets, red and black fruits, and spicy new oak. The entry and attack start off well, with plenty of richness and sweet fruit, but the hard, astringent tannins take over and dominate the finish. I am impressed with the direction Lamarche's wines are taking. This could become a fabulous domaine given its superlative vineyards.

DOMINIQUE LAURENT (NUITS ST.-GEORGES)* * * */* * * * *

1992 Bonnes Mares	EE	90
1992 Charmes-Chambertin	E	90
1992 Clos de la Roche	E	87

Laurent, an ex–pastry chef, launched his wine career with the 1989 vintage. I have not tasted any of the earlier vintages, but certainly Laurent, who purchases the wines from growers, ages them in 100% new oak, and bottles them without fining or filtration, has hit the bull's-eye with some gorgeous 1992s. They are among the most seductive, sumptuous wines of the vintage. The three grands crus I tasted, obviously expensive, do indeed exhibit far more richness, complexity, and style than most wines from Laurent's peers.

The dark ruby-colored 1992 Clos de la Roche offers up plenty of smoky, earthy, gamelike aromas with a touch of Asian spices, good structure, wonderfully sweet fruit, moderate tannin, and a long finish. It should be consumed over the next 6–7 years. The 1992 Bonnes Mares reveals a medium ruby color, a big, dramatic nose of sweet, jammy, black cherry fruit, herb, and coffee scents, as well as lavish quantities of toasty new oak. While the wine is aggressively oaky, there is plenty of juicy, succulent, berry fruit to accompany the wood. It reveals medium to full body, a satiny smooth texture, and plenty of heady alcohol in the soft finish. Drink it over the next 6–7 years. The 1992 Charmes-Chambertin is a terrific wine from what is generally acknowledged to be a mediocre vintage for red wine. It boasts big, rich, sweet, jammy, black cherry fruit backed up by hefty notes of smoky, toasty, new oak. Sweet, chewy, and concentrated, with soft tannin and full body, this lush, thick, sumptuous 1992 should be drunk over the next 7–8 years. These immensely impressive wines merit burgundy enthusiasts' attention.

DOMAINE LECHENEAUT (NUITS ST.-GEORGES)* * * */* * * * *

1992 Clos de la Roche	E	90+
1991 Clos de la Roche	E	87
1992 Nuits St.-Georges Les Cailles	D	91
1991 Nuits St.-Georges Les Cailles	D	89+
1992 Nuits St.-Georges Les Damodes	D	92
1991 Nuits St.-Georges Les Damodes	D	87

I cannot claim to have discovered the wines of Philippe and Vincent Lecheneaut, but they are certainly among the stars of Nuits St.-Georges. Domaine Lecheneaut is making far greater wines than some of that village's more illustrious and renowned *négociants* and growers. For example, Lecheneaut's 1992 Nuits St.-Georges Les Damodes was terrific from the cask, but unlike many of the wines from its neighbors, it also tastes terrific from bottle.

The wine reminds me of an Henri Jayer Richebourg—and that's saying something! Its tremendous deep ruby/purple color is followed by a huge, provocative, fragrant bouquet of black fruits, flowers, and toasty oak. There is superrichness, full body, a succulent, decadent personality, and gobs of fruit, glycerin, and alcohol in the long, lusty finish. It should drink well for at least a decade. The dark ruby-colored 1992 Nuits St.-Georges Les Cailles exhibits more new oak in the nose, with copious quantities of blackberries and cherries. The wine is stunningly rich and seductive, with lavish quantities of fruit, all presented in a full-bodied, supple, velvety-textured style. It is a generous, mouth-filling, knockout wine that will prove immensely pleasing to burgundy wine enthusiasts.

The 1992 Clos de la Roche is not as fat, jammy, or voluptuous as the two premiers crus from Nuits St.-Georges. It reveals a dark ruby color, a mineral, earthy, blackberry-scented nose, outstanding concentration, plenty of new oak, and more tannin and structure. As befits a grand cru, it is approachable, but it is questionable whether it will ever develop the pure, decadent, nearly overripe qualities and succulence of the two premier cru offerings.

The 1991s are very good wines, led by a Nuits St.-Georges Les Cailles. Deep ruby-colored, with a fragrant bouquet of red and black fruits, herbs, and minerals, this rich, concentrated wine exhibits brilliant winemaking, with wonderful flesh and extraction, as well as admirable firmness and structure. Drink it over the next 10–12 years. The berry-scented, medium-bodied, round, smooth 1991 Nuits St.-Georges Les Damodes also exhibits fine concentration, good overall balance, and a personality that suggests it is best drunk over the next 7–8 years.

I thought Lecheneaut's 1991 Clos de la Roche (mind-boggling and magnificent in both 1990 and 1992) to be less impressive and more narrowly constructed than either of the premiers crus from Nuits St.-Georges. How can I be right? Keep in mind that I say that, even though I believe that Clos de la Roche, along with Clos St.-Denis and Bonnes Mares, are Burgundy's three most underrated grand cru vineyards. Nevertheless, while Lecheneaut's Clos de la Roche reveals good elegance, and spicy, ripe fruitiness, it lacks the depth and concentration of his Nuits St.-Georges Les Cailles. I would opt for drinking it over the next 7–8 years.

PHILIPPE LECLERC (GEVREY-CHAMBERTIN)* * * */* * * * *

1991	Bourgogne Les Bons Batons	C	?
1991	Chambolle-Musigny Les Babillaires	E	90
1991	Gevrey-Chambertin Les Cazetiers	E	91
1991	Gevrey-Chambertin Les Champeaux	E	88
1991	Gevrey-Chambertin Les Champs	D	86
1991	Gevrey-Chambertin Combe aux Moines	EE	92
1991	Gevrey-Chambertin Les Platières	D	85?

As anyone who has met him recognizes immediately, Philippe Leclerc marches to the beat of a different drummer. His love of new oak is legendary. While it often appears excessive when his wines are tasted from barrel and during their first several years of life, based on how his 1979s, 1980s, 1982s, and 1983s are evolving, they quickly absorb the oak after 3–4 years of bottle age. Having said that, I must admonish readers that Leclerc's 1991s are at the limit of being too woody. These 1991 offerings are all immense, even massive, red burgundies, which, because of the abnormally low yields, are loaded with flavor. However, they also reveal aggressive wood levels—too much in the 1991 Bourgogne Les Bons Batons. There is plenty of fruit, but there is a sawdustlike flavor to the wine, and the oak is annoyingly high.

The 1991 Gevrey-Chambertin Les Platières exhibits a chocolatey, herbal, black fruit character intermingled with lavish quantities of toasty new oak. But the wood appears to have the upper hand, and it is hard to believe it will become integrated. The 1991 Gevrey-Chambertin Les Champs possesses a chocolatey, jammy, black fruit character, remarkable density, and an unctuous quality. In spite of the high levels of wood, it appears to have the requisite concentration to soak up the vanillin and toast. The 1991 Gevrey-Chambertin Les Champeaux is superconcentrated, with layers of flavor and plenty of toasty new oak, but also gobs of glycerin, alcohol, and sweet tannin. It is a big, blockbuster, rustic wine that should age well for 10–15 years.

Leclerc now owns a plot of 40-year-old vines in Chambolle-Musigny, and his 1991 Chambolle-Musigny Les Babillaires reveals that he can lighten up on the oak when he moves to an appellation known for finesse-styled wines. This offering exhibits a sweet nose of black fruits, flowers, and minerals, with the oak playing a more subtle role. The result is a terrifically concentrated, rich, expansive, opulent wine that should drink well for 12–15 years. It is the sleeper wine, as well as the best bargain among the Leclerc offerings. Leclerc always fashions a powerful, tannic, blockbuster Gevrey-Chambertin Les Cazetiers, and the 1991 is textbook Leclerc. Frightfully oaky, loaded with power, muscle, and layers of fruit, it is as impressive and concentrated as the 1990. Based on longevity, potential richness, and complexity, Leclerc's finest wine is the Gevrey-Chambertin Combe aux Moines, made from vines that are 80+ years old. The 1991 reveals huge density and a magnificent perfume of black fruits, truffles, herbs, and smoked game. While the ubiquitous new oak is present, it is less pronounced than in Leclerc's other wines. There is huge richness, and full-bodied, powerful flavors oozing with extract, glycerin, and tannin. Like Les Cazetiers, it is best drunk from the late nineties through the first 10–15 years of the next century.

Leclerc's wines are undoubtedly controversial, but one has to admire their rugged, individualistic style. Based on their track record, they possess impeccable aging credentials, with the oak becoming more refined and subtle as the wines evolve in the bottle.

RENÉ LECLERC (GEVREY-CHAMBERTIN)* * * *

1991 Gevrey-Chambertin	D	86
1991 Gevrey-Chambertin Combe aux Moines	D	90
1991 Gevrey-Chambertin Lavaux St.-Jacques	D	87

René Leclerc is making excellent wines, and his 1991s are capable of rivaling his superb 1990s. The 1991 Gevrey-Chambertin displays deep color, a sweet, smoky, animallike, meaty nose, and ripe, unctuous, thick flavors. Although lacking complexity, it offers a big, chewy mouthful of intense Pinot Noir. Drink it over the next 6–7 years. The 1991 Gevrey-Chambertin Lavaux St.-Jacques is also superripe and highly extracted. The deep purple color and smoky, chocolatey, cassis-scented nose are followed by a supple, fat, ripe, lusty wine with plenty of alcohol, soft tannins, and low acidity. Drink it over the next 8–9 years. The superb 1991 Gevrey-Chambertin Combe aux Moines exhibits a huge nose of prunes, black fruits, herbs, minerals, and soy sauce. Spectacularly concentrated, deep, and expansive, with a wonderful inner core of sweet, jammy fruit, this low-acid yet massively concentrated, powerful wine reveals moderate tannins in the finish. Its principal attribute is the sheer essence of fruit it possesses. It should drink well for at least 10–12 years.

FRANÇOIS LEGROS (NUITS ST.-GEORGES)* * *

1991 Bourgogne	C	83
1991 Chambolle-Musigny	D	83
1991 Chambolle-Musigny Les Noirots	D	84

1991	Morey St.-Denis Les Sorbès	D	78
1991	Nuits St.-Georges Les Bousselots	D	78
1991	Nuits St.-Georges Les Perrières	D	85
1991	Nuits St.-Georges Les Roncières	D	85
1991	Nuits St.-Georges Les Rue de Chaux	D	79
1991	Vougeot Les Cras	D	82

This young, enthusiastic grower/winemaker has fashioned light, occasionally elegant, but frequently rough, hard 1991s. With the exception of the Nuits St.-Georges Les Roncières and Nuits St.-Georges Les Perrières, the wines are either too light or too astringent. Les Roncières and Les Perrières both possess more depth and richness. Les Perrières is a medium-bodied, spicy, concentrated wine with some muscle and well-integrated tannins. Les Roncières is slightly richer, as well as more tannic. It reveals good underlying ripeness and concentration to stand up to the tannins. I found the 1991 Nuits St.-Georges Les Rue de Chaux too hard-edged and tough for its light body and suspect concentration. The same can be said about the light 1991 Nuits St.-Georges Les Bousselots and the hard, astringent, ungenerous, skinny 1991 Morey St.-Denis Les Sorbès. The 1991 Vougeot Les Cras is soft, round, ripe, and ready to drink. It should be consumed over the next 3–4 years. While the 1991 Chambolle-Musigny Les Noirots exhibits some elegance, it finishes with the worst attributes of the 1991 vintage—leanness, hard tannins, and a compact, angular shortness. The other wines range from a light, well-balanced, but one-dimensional 1991 Chambolle-Musigny, to a fruity, sweet, round, generic 1991 Bourgogne.

LEROY (VOSNE-ROMANÉE)* * * * *

1991	Chambertin	EEE	95+
1992	Chambolle-Musigny Les Charmes	EE	92
1992	Chambolle-Musigny Les Fremières	E	89
1991	Chambolle-Musigny Les Fremières	E	90
1992	Clos de la Roche	EEE	94
1991	Clos de la Roche	EEE	95
1992	Clos de Vougeot	EE	90
1991	Clos de Vougeot	EE	92
1992	Corton Les Rénardes	EE	93
1992	Gevrey-Chambertin Les Combottes	EE	88
1991	Gevrey-Chambertin Les Combottes	EE	92
1992	Latricières-Chambertin	E	90
1991	Latricières-Chambertin	EEE	96
1991	Musigny	EEE	96+
1992	Nuits St.-Georges Les Allots	E	87
1991	Nuits St.-Georges Les Allots	E	90
1992	Nuits St.-Georges aux Bas de Combe	E	89
1991	Nuits St.-Georges aux Bas de Combe	E	88

1992	Nuits St.-Georges Les Boudots	E	91
1991	Nuits St.-Georges Les Boudots	EE	93
1992	Nuits St.-Georges Les Lavières	E	86
1991	Nuits St.-Georges Les Lavières	E	92
1992	Nuits St.-Georges Les Vignes Rondes	EE	92
1991	Nuits St.-Georges Les Vignes Rondes	EE	91
1992	Pommard Les Trois Follots	E	87
1992	Pommard Les Vignots	E	90
1992	Richebourg	EEE	91+
1991	Richebourg	EEE	95
1992	Romanée St.-Vivant	EEE	94+
1991	Romanée St.-Vivant	EEE	96
1992	Savigny-Les-Beaune Les Narbantons	D	88+
1992	Volnay Santenots	D	93
1992	Vosne-Romanée Les Beaux Monts	EE	92
1991	Vosne-Romanée Les Beaux Monts	EE	93
1992	Vosne-Romanée Les Brûlées	EE	90
1992	Vosne-Romanée Les Genevrières	E	86
1991	Vosne-Romanée Les Genevrières	E	91

Once again, the remarkable Lalou Bize-Leroy and her gifted winemaker, André Porcheret, have made the wines of the vintage. Of course, Ponsot's Chambertin, Clos St.-Denis, and Clos de la Roche offer worthy competition, but considering the numerous vineyards she possesses, and the remarkable success she has enjoyed with all of them, she gets the gold medal in 1991. These are spectacularly rich, concentrated, compelling red burgundies that are significantly less expensive than her magnificent 1990s, yet very close in quality to those wines. And the 1990s were among the finest Pinot Noirs I have ever tasted. Lalou, with her characteristic bravado, compares 1991 with 1959. Her average yields were under 15 hectoliters per hectare, ranging from a low of 9 hectoliters per hectare to the highest, 18 hectoliters per hectare. Translated into production per vine, keeping in mind that Burgundy's vineyards have from 8,000 to 10,000 vines per hectare compared with about 1,200 vines per hectare in California and Oregon, there are astonishingly low yields.

Because of the minuscule quantities produced and their high prices, the saddest thing about the Domaine Leroy's red burgundies is that few people have a chance to taste them. To taste the wines of Leroy is to know what heights Pinot Noir can attain. After tasting the 1991s from barrel last year, I thought she had fashioned the top wines of the vintage. Now that they are in the bottle, they are even more impressive. Prices are significantly lower (down by 25%–30%), but quantities are tiny.

Among the Côte de Nuits selections is a top-flight village wine, the 1991 Nuits St.-Georges aux Bas de Combe. With its dark, dense, ruby color and rich nose of ripe black fruits, this medium- to full-bodied, supple wine is better than most premiers crus. Low yields and impeccable winemaking have elevated its quality to an amazingly high level. Smooth enough to be approached now, this wine should continue to age well for another 10–15 or more years. The 1991 Nuits St.-Georges Les Allots exhibits a deep ruby color, a sweet nose of ripe fruit, medium body, excellent structure, moderate tannin, and that inner richness and mid-palate so often missing in modern-day red burgundy. The overall impression is of a supple-textured, ripe, concentrated, impressive wine with at least 12–15 years of cellaring potential.

Three outstanding premiers crus include the Nuits St.-Georges Les Lavières, Nuits St.-Georges Les Vignes Rondes, and Nuits St.-Georges Les Boudots. Picking a favorite is akin to splitting hairs, as they are all superrich, densely colored, broadly built, expansive, full-bodied Pinot Noirs with superb complexity and richness. Perhaps the most elegant marriage of both power and finesse is found in the Nuits St.-Georges Les Lavières. This forceful, powerful, superconcentrated wine is one of the best buys of the 1991 Leroy portfolio. Drink it between 1996 and 2010. The 1991 Nuits St.-Georges Les Vignes Rondes possesses a wonderful purity of character in its gorgeously ripe, expansive, perfumed nose of black cherries and other black fruits such as plums. Decadently rich, generous, and well endowed, this medium- to full-bodied wine reveals deep layers of flavor, soft tannins, low acidity, and a finish that lasts for more than 30 seconds. It can be drunk now, but will easily keep for two decades. The most opulent, hedonistic, and decadent of this trio of premiers crus is the 1991 Nuits St.-Georges Les Boudots. Its huge, exotic nose of smoke, ripe cassis fruit, herbs, minerals, and roasted nuts is a turn-on. Low in acid, this blockbuster, massively concentrated, voluptuously textured wine is a knockout. Drink it over the next 15–18 years.

Leroy's estate on the back streets of Vosne-Romanée is called Les Genevrières, after a parcel of very old vines that is not entitled to premier cru status. It makes the finest Vosne-Romanée, a wine that is better than most producers' grands crus. The 1991 Vosne-Romanée Les Genevrières displays a wonderfully pure, vivid, vibrant, black fruit–scented nose, ripe, generous, sweet, medium- to full-bodied flavors, superb length, and a fleshy, velvety-textured finish. Drink it over the next 10–12 years. The gorgeous 1991 Vosne-Romanée Les Beaux Monts is deeper and more saturated in color than Les Genevrières. The sweet fragrance of chocolate, black fruits, herbs, and toasty vanillin is followed by a long, unctuously textured, layered wine with magnificent concentration, soft acid, and moderate ripe tannin in the finish. Drink it between 1996 and 2010.

The portfolio of superb premiers crus does not stop in Vosne-Romanée. The 1991 Chambolle-Musigny Les Fremières reveals an opaque ruby/purple color. A moderately intense bouquet of red fruits, flowers, and vanillin is followed by rich, medium-bodied, silky-textured flavors that are brilliantly well defined and long. One of the smoothest, most seductive 1991s, it should be drunk over the next 12–15 years, although I suspect Leroy would consider that infanticide. The other outstanding premier cru is the 1991 Gevrey-Chambertin Les Combottes. This magnificent vineyard, sandwiched between such revered grands crus as Clos de la Roche and Latricières-Chambertin, reaches heights in Leroy's cellars that do not exist elsewhere. It offers a decadent nose of smoked duck, grilled meats, black fruits, spices, and trufflelike smells. Superb black cherry fruit flavors are loaded with glycerin and extract. This unctuously textured, hedonistic wine is remarkably long, sweet, and velvety. Tasting more like an unevolved barrel sample than a finished wine, it should be drunk between 1996 and 2012.

Leroy's grands crus are both reference points for their appellations, as well as for the majestic aromatic and flavor dimensions Pinot Noir can attain. They are all spectacular wines that rival the 1990s, and in some cases may turn out to be even better, at prices 30% below that heralded vintage. Those lucky enough to find a bottle of both the Romanée St.-Vivant and the Richebourg will enjoy debating which wine is better. It is not easy to pick a favorite, but no one produces Romanée St.-Vivant such as that from Domaine Leroy. The 1991 is quintessential burgundy in the sense that it represents a perfect alliance between power, high extraction, intensity, and an almost surreal elegance, finesse, and complexity. It makes a great impression on the palate, yet never tastes heavy, thick, or tiring. Don't get me wrong—this is a big, rich, powerful wine, but to combine this much power and finesse is a winemaking tour de force. The finish lasts for up to a minute. This spectacularly perfumed, rich, opulent wine should drink well young, and last for up to 20 years. What a wine! The 1991 Richebourg relies more on its pure force and unbelievable extraction of fruit. The gloriously scented nose of black raspberries and toasty vanillin oak soars from the glass. Dense, opulent, and voluptuous, this rich, multidimensional, profound wine will drink well for the next 20 years. Will it display the sheer complexity and attention-getting presence of the Romanée St.-Vivant? The 1991 Clos de Vougeot is the most austere, monolithic, and massive of Leroy's 1991s. It is big, dense, chunky, thick, rich, and loaded, but it does not exhibit the complexity and sublime characteristics flaunted by the other grands crus. Like the Chambertin, Leroy's 1991 Musigny is a definitive wine reference. I cannot imagine who could make a greater wine from this vineyard than Leroy. It is the most closed, backward, and tannic of all the domaine's 1991s, but unlike other wines of this vintage, there is no problem with the depth of fruit being insufficient to match the ferocity of its tannin. An enormously concentrated, provocatively elegant wine, it reluctantly offers up a black cherry– and floral-scented bouquet. Enormously rich, with a layered texture, this closed wine needs to be cellared for a decade. It should be at its best between 2002 and 2025.

Leroy produced another spectacular Clos de la Roche in 1991. A deep, dark ruby/purple-colored wine, it is bursting with fruit and complexity. There are powerful tannins in the finish, but don't worry; this superbly concentrated, muscular, rich wine with its mineral and Grave-like scents and flavors possesses a magnificently chewy texture and high extraction. It rivals the otherworldly 1990 that Leroy produced. Perhaps the most surprising wine in 1991 is the Latricières-Chambertin. I call this wine the "Musigny among Gevrey's grands crus." A hauntingly intense, fragrant bouquet sets it apart. Latricières is compellingly complex, with a spicy, sweet black fruit, smoked duck–like bouquet, astonishing concentration, deep, rich, full-bodied flavors, and a fabulous, exotic, opulent finish. I was hardpressed to spit this one out. There is considerable tannin lurking behind the fruit. While it may be tempting to say it should be drunk over the next 10–15 years, my instincts suggest cellaring it for 3–4 years and enjoying it over the subsequent two decades.

The 1991 Chambertin is nearly as backward as the Musigny. Nearly opaque in color, it displays spectacular, deep, rich, earthy, roasted cassis flavors, superb definition, huge tannin, and magnificent concentration. Drink it between 2001 and 2030. Produced according to the rigid organic farming disciplines of biodynamics, Lalou Bize-Leroy's 1991s are extraordinary.

For the fifth consecutive vintage since she launched her wines from the Domaine Leroy (formerly the Noëllat estate), Lalou Bize-Leroy has made the highest percentage of Burgundy's greatest wines. Although not as phenomenally concentrated and extracted as her 1991s and 1990s, the 1992s are more closely aligned to her sumptuous 1989s. The best value in Domaine Leroy's portfolio comes from the Côte de Beaune. The 1992 Savigny-Les-Beaune Les Narbantons reveals a dark, saturated ruby color, a tight but promising nose of spice, black cherries, and earth, and medium- to full-bodied, concentrated flavors. It can be drunk now, but it promises to be better in 1–2 years and will last for 15 or more. The 1992 Pommard Les Vignots would embarrass many of the sloppily made, overcropped Pommards from supposedly top-notch domaines. It is a big, rich, tannic, muscular wine with significant body and a backward personality. Do not touch a bottle for 3–4 years; it is a 15- to 20-year wine.

Two exceptionally great wines produced by Bize-Leroy in 1992 are the Volnay Santenots and Corton Les Rénardes. Having tasted it several times from cask and twice from bottle, I can unequivocally state that the 1992 Volnay Santenots is a blockbuster, superrich, authoritatively flavored yet wonderfully harmonious, elegant example of Volnay. The color is a saturated dark ruby and the nose offers up superintense, jammy scents of sweet black cherry fruit intertwined with oak and floral notes. It is a wine of extraordinary intensity, power, richness, and overall grace and harmony. This is another winemaking tour de force! Moreover, this must be the "bargain" wine of her portfolio. It should drink well between 1998 and 2015. The 1992 Corton Les Rénardes is extremely backward and tannic, but, oh so promising. It possesses a huge, ripe bouquet, great color saturation, magnificent intensity and full body, and moderate tannin in the long finish that lasts for nearly a minute. Don't touch a bottle before the end of the decade; it should last through the first few decades of the twenty-first century.

Turning to the bevy of selections from Nuits St.-Georges, the 1992 Nuits St.-Georges aux Bas de Combe is one of the softer, more opulent, and more fleshy wines of Lalou Bize-Leroy. It displays a dark ruby color, a big, earthy nose of licorice, truffle, and black cherry scents, ripe, medium- to full-bodied flavors, and a soft, velvety-textured finish. It should drink well for 15+ years. The 1992 Nuits St.-Georges Les Allots is less impressive than several of the other Leroy offerings. It reveals an herbaceous, green pepper–scented nose (extremely rare in a Bize-Leroy wine), some scents of black cherries, full body, excellent ripeness, and a long, moderately tannic finish. If the greenness works its way out and the mineral character becomes more dominant, this wine will deserve a higher rating. The 1992 Nuits St.-Georges Les Lavières possesses a leesy nose, with a leafy, green, vegetal character. Lean and densely concentrated, this is not one of Lalou Bize-Leroy's successes. The same cannot be said for the exceptional 1992 Nuits St.-Georges Les Vignes Rondes and the 1992 Nuits St.-Georges Les Boudots. Both are terrific wines bursting with concentrated, jammy red and black fruits, and succulent, lavishly rich, opulent characters. The deep ruby/purple-colored 1992 Vignes Rondes exhibits a sweet, smashingly intense, fragrant bouquet, superb concentration, full body, wonderful suppleness, and a sweet, expansive, opulent palate. It is a seductive yet structured wine for drinking over the next 15+ years. The 1992 Les Boudots is another decadent red burgundy, with a sweet, toasty, vanillin nose complemented by generous quantities of jammy black cherry and flower scents. The wine displays great fruit, wonderful purity, a vibrant, full-bodied personality, and layers of rich fruit that fill the mouth. This wine exhibits more tannin in the finish, and thus will be even better after 2–3 years of cellaring. It is clearly a 20-year wine.

The 1992 Vosne-Romanée Les Genevrières offers an herbaceous, peppery nose, excellent ripeness and richness, fine depth, and moderate tannin in the finish. It should be cellared for 1–2 years and drunk over the following 15+ years. With respect to the two premiers crus, readers will find the 1992 Vosne-Romanée Les Brûlées to be lighter than the Vosne-Romanée Les Beaux Monts, but it is wonderfully spicy, with a sweet, smoky, black cherry– and raspberry-scented nose, a touch of toasty new oak, excellent ripeness, and a chewy, fleshy finish. It is a delicious, precocious wine that can be drunk now and over the next 10–15 years. The sensational 1992 Vosne-Romanée Les Beaux Monts offers up a staggering bouquet of violets, cassis, black cherries, and smoky, toasty new oak. The wine possesses great richness, full body, and layers of opulent fruit. This terrific wine is one of Domaine Leroy's top successes. It should drink well for 15–20 years.

Lalou Bize-Leroy is assuming a stronger position in the village of Chambolle-Musigny, and she has turned out a very fine 1992 Chambolle-Musigny Les Fremières. The wine boasts an elegant, floral, vanillin- and cherry-scented nose, medium-bodied, concentrated flavors, a supple, velvety texture, and an easygoing, graceful, complex finish. It should drink well for 12–15 years. Possessing an extra measure of concentration, the superb 1992 Chambolle-Musigny Les Charmes is a classic example of a top-notch wine from Chambolle-Musigny. It combines rich, harmonious, ripe black and red fruits with a super elegance and

finesse. Supple, full bodied, never heavy or tannic, this smooth-as-silk wine is so concentrated that some powerful tannin is nearly hidden by the wine's gorgeous richness.
It can be drunk now, but 2–3 years of cellaring is recommended. It should keep for 20+
years.

I found the 1992 Gevrey-Chambertin Les Combottes to be spicy and tannic, with fine
richness, but some leanness and herbaceous toughness in the flavors and finish kept my
score short of exceptional. It possesses fine depth as well as a meaty, smoky character, but
the wine's vegetal aspect is off-putting. The outstanding 1992 Latricières-Chambertin exhibits a medium deep ruby color, a tremendously fragrant, sweet nose of spicy red and black
fruits, earth, smoked meats, and herbs. This ripe, seductive, voluptuously textured, rich,
copiously fruity, full-bodied wine should drink well for 15 or more years.

The other grands crus I tasted included the outstanding 1992 Clos de Vougeot. While it
lacks the sheer magnificence and compelling bouquet of some of the other Domaine Leroy
wines, it possesses a rich, monolithic, superconcentrated, sweet black fruit character, full
body, excellent purity, and a round, generous, long finish. It should drink well for 15–20
years, but it will never reach the heights of complexity some of Bize-Leroy's other wines
have achieved. The Clos de la Roche, so fabulous in 1991, is again a superb wine in 1992.
A sweet, spicy, toasty oak nose is complemented with lavish quantities of black cherry fruit.
Full bodied, with a floral element that develops with airing, the wine is made in a layered,
concentrated, muscular yet elegant style with admirable richness, and a finish that lasts for
nearly a minute. It is a great example of the vintage, as well as a candidate for 20+ years of
aging. The 1992 Romanée St.-Vivant is the kind of wine that must make Lalou Bize-Leroy's
former employer, Domaine de la Romanée-Conti, extremely nervous. This great wine boasts
layers of rich red and black fruits and is multidimensional, sweet, expansive, and superconcentrated, with a spectacularly long, powerful finish. It is a wine of exceptional depth,
harmony, and balance, with moderate tannin. The wine requires 2–3 years of cellaring and
should last for 20–25 years. Millionaire, make that billionaire, collectors who have the
opportunity to compare Domaine Leroy's 1990, 1991, and 1992 Romanée St.-Vivant with
those of the DRC will understand why Lalou Bize-Leroy is *persona non grata* at Burgundy's
most famous estate. Lastly, the supple, forward 1992 Richebourg is showing extremely well.
It displays a dark ruby/purple color, and wonderfully expansive, chewy, black cherry flavors
complemented by floral and spicy new oak scents. Deep, rich, and layered, it is filled with
purity and grace.

I have not tasted from the bottle the Musigny and Chambertin, but several cask tastings
(she does not fine or filter) revealed that the 1992 Musigny looked to be the best wine in her
entire portfolio. It possessed that extra dimension of finesse as well as sensational concentration and a velvety-textured, sweet, ripe palate. The 1992 Chambertin was also terrific, but
perhaps less complex and impressive when compared with the Musigny.

GEORGES LIGNIER (MOREY ST.-DENIS)* * *

1991	Bonnes Mares	EE	82
1991	Chambolle-Musigny	D	77
1991	Charmes-Chambertin	E	86
1991	Clos de la Roche	E	83
1991	Clos St.-Denis	E	82
1991	Gevrey-Chambertin	D	82
1991	Gevrey-Chambertin Les Combottes	D	84

1991 Morey St.-Denis	D	72
1991 Morey St.-Denis Clos des Ormes	D	81

Lignier owns one of the most potentially promising domaines in the Côte de Nuits, and I am delighted to report that his American importer convinced him to stop filtering in 1991. While the yields were low (15–30 hectoliters per hectare), I was uninspired by his 1991s. All of them taste light, and some, such as the Morey St.-Denis, Morey St.-Denis Clos des Ormes, and Clos St.-Denis, are compact and hard, with excessive tannin, light body, and insufficient depth of fruit. Even the Clos de la Roche, while pleasant, reveals a shockingly short finish. The Bonnes Mares is lean and diluted. The light ruby color exhibited by all these offerings suggests a lack of intensity and flavor extraction. Only the Charmes-Chambertin displays ripe, supple fruit in the mid-palate, and enough concentration to balance out the tannins. The wines had only been in bottle one month when I tasted them, so they may improve slightly, but it appears this is not a vintage where Georges Lignier has excelled.

DOMAINE HUBERT LIGNIER (MOREY ST.-DENIS)* * * * *

1991 Bourgogne	C	86
1991 Chambolle-Musigny	D	87
1991 Chambolle-Musigny Premier Cru Vieilles Vignes	D	90
1991 Charmes-Chambertin	EE	92
1991 Clos de la Roche	EE	96
1991 Gevrey-Chambertin Les Combottes	D	91
1991 Morey St.-Denis	D	87

One of the superstars of Burgundy, Hubert Lignier's stunning 1991s are even better than his 1990s (which were amazing wines). All the 1991s were bottled unfined and unfiltered. The elegant 1991 Bourgogne exhibits good ripeness, copious quantities of spicy, black cherry fruit, round, generous flavors, and a smooth finish. Drink it over the next 2–3 years. The 1991 Morey St.-Denis resembles the 1990 with its sweet, fragrant perfume, and round, supple, low-acid flavors. A rich, complete wine with tons of fruit, it should drink well for at least 7–8 years. The 1991 Chambolle-Musigny is also beautifully supple and stout, with gobs of black cherry fruit, an opulent texture, and long, deep, generous flavors. Delicious now, it promises to last for 5–6 years.

Lignier's 1991 Chambolle-Musigny Premier Cru Vieilles Vignes is a sensational wine. A terrific nose of black fruits, toasty new oak, and minerals is followed by a rich, beautifully concentrated and focused wine with medium body and soft tannin. This terrific wine reveals a voluptuous texture and tremendous quantities of jammy fruit buttressed nicely by adequate tannin and new oak. The 1991 Charmes-Chambertin is as riveting as the 1990. Like all the Lignier offerings, it exhibits a dense ruby/purple color, and a huge, fragrant bouquet of black fruits, new oak, and floral scents. Deep, unctuous, and rich, this full-bodied wine displays tremendous concentration and a long, lusty finish. The tannin is concealed by the wine's remarkable richness. Lignier's 1991 Gevrey-Chambertin Les Combottes (only 15 cases will be available in the United States) is also a great wine, offering up an exotic bouquet of jammy red and black fruits intermingled with scents of Asian spices, herbs, and sweet oak. Round, luscious, and concentrated, there are no hard edges to this hedonistic Pinot Noir. Drink it over the next 8–10 years.

The remarkable 1991 Clos de la Roche is even more concentrated and powerful than Lignier's 1990. Opaquely colored with a promising but unformed bouquet of minerals, black fruits, and toasty new oak, there is significant tannin in this powerful wine. It displays magnificent concentration, sweetness, and definition, as well as that unctuous, thick, rich mid-palate and length that suggest exceptionally low yields and old vines. One of the superstars of the vintage, it should be drunk between 1996 and 2012.

MANIÈRE-NOIROT (VOSNE-ROMANÉE)* * *

1991 Echézeaux		D	84
1991 Nuits St.-Georges Les Boudots		D	86
1991 Nuits St.-Georges Les Damodes		D	86
1991 Vosne-Romanée Les Suchots		D	86

Reliable 1991s were produced by this estate. Although the 1991 Vosne-Romanée Les Suchots is tannic, it also reveals fine oak, fruit, and depth. The wine comes across as muscular and stern, but I enjoy the component parts, as well as its level of ripeness and depth. Give it several years in the cellar and drink it over the following 7–8 years. Both the 1991 Nuits St.-Georges Les Boudots and the 1991 Nuits St.-Georges Les Damodes are softer wines, with plenty of toasty new oak, ripe, rich fruit, and long finishes. Les Boudots reveals slightly more elegance, whereas Les Damodes offers more power and extraction. Both are medium-bodied, moderately concentrated wines that should provide good to very good drinking over the next 7–8 years. All of the above-mentioned wines possess more stuffing and potential richness and complexity than the light, understated 1991 Echézeaux. A medium ruby color is followed by pleasant, strawberry and floral scents, but the wine offers only straightforward, fruity flavors and finishes short. Drink it over the next 4–5 years.

DOMAINE MAUME (GEVREY-CHAMBERTIN)* * */* * * *

1991 Gevrey-Chambertin		D	83
1991 Gevrey-Chambertin Lavaux St.-Jacques		D	80?
1991 Gevrey-Chambertin en Pallud		D	84?
1991 Gevrey-Chambertin Premier Cru		D	78?
1991 Mazis-Chambertin		E	86?

Longtime readers know I am a fan of the rustic, long-lived, powerful wines made by Maume. Old vines, a noninterventionist policy, and bottling without fining or filtering result in superconcentrated wines that age effortlessly. This is one domaine where the 1982s (most red burgundies from this vintage are falling apart) are just beginning to reach their plateau of maturity, and are among the candidates for the finest wines of the vintage.

All that being said, Maume obtained ferociously high tannin levels in 1991. With every wine I wondered where the ripe fruit had gone. All of these offerings are big, back-strapping, dark-colored wines. They remind me of an elderly man who still has a large frame, but no muscle tone. The wines are frightfully tough and hard, and I just do not see enough fruit to ever balance out the tannins. I hope I'm wrong. If you are a Maume fan, and you want to take what appears to be a dangerous gamble, buy the 1991 Mazis-Chambertin, which appears to have the most depth. However, its mouth-searing tannins could represent a problem. None of these wines will be close to maturity for at least 7–10 years.

DOMAINE JEAN MÉO-CAMUZET (VOSNE-ROMANÉE)* * * * *

1991 Bourgogne		C	82
1991 Clos de Vougeot		E	88

1992 Corton	E	87
1991 Corton Clos Rognet	E	89
1991 Nuits St.-Georges	D	86
1991 Nuits St.-Georges Les Boudots	E	88
1992 Nuits St.-Georges aux Murgers	E	87
1991 Nuits St.-Georges aux Murgers	E	90
1992 Richebourg	EEE	87
1991 Richebourg	EEE	90
1991 Vosne-Romanée	D	86
1992 Vosne-Romanée Les Brûlées	E	88
1991 Vosne-Romanée Les Brûlées	E	92
1991 Vosne-Romanée Les Chaumes	D	85
1992 Vosne-Romanée Cros Parantoux	E	89
1991 Vosne-Romanée Cros Parantoux	E	91

This outstanding domaine continues to prove that it is one of the superstar estates of Burgundy. The wines, which are remarkably pure, rich, and supple, have gone from strength to strength since the 1988 vintage. The influence of Burgundy's great master, Henri Jayer, on the young M. Méo and his enthusiastic assistant, M. Faurois, cannot be underestimated. This team is intent on making exceptional wine. Filtration was stopped in 1988, and in 1991 several cuvées were put in the bottle with no fining.

Méo-Camuzet held its 1992 yields to a conservative 25–30 hectoliters per hectare, resulting in generally sound wines that have been bottled without filtration. Méo-Camuzet's finest 1992 offerings include the Nuits St.-Georges aux Murgers (from 30-year-old vines), which displays a solid, dark ruby color, and a big, spicy nose of smoky new oak, black fruits, and herbs. Thick, soft, round, and generous, with no hard edges, plenty of smoky, rich fruit, and a long, lush finish, it should be drunk over the next 4–5 years. Readers should note that I thought the 1992 Nuits St.-Georges Les Boudots (from 50-year-old vines) was also an excellent wine, but the only bottle I tasted was musty and undoubtedly off form.

The 1992 Vosne-Romanée Les Brûlées offers a smoky, roasted nose of herbs, black fruits, and toasty new oak. Sweet, round, and creamy-textured, with wonderfully ripe fruit, and a seductive, silky finish, it should be drunk over the next 5–6 years. The 1992 Vosne-Romanée Cros Parantoux is richer and more structured, with greater fruit and ripeness. Although it is capable of lasting for 5–7 years, few readers will be able to resist its flashy display of charm and seductive Pinot power.

Among the two grands crus, the 1992 Corton displays gobs of sweet oak (perhaps excessive), good ripeness, and a more cassis-dominated character, as well as a compact, moderately tannic personality. My rating may turn out to be conservative. Presently, the wine lacks the charm, sweetness, and flavor expansion of the other cuvées. Although light bodied, the 1992 Richebourg possesses a fragrant perfume of black fruits, oak, and flowers. Round and medium bodied, with a gentle softness and grace, it should be consumed over the next 4–5 years.

There is an attractive, light, fruity, soft 1991 Bourgogne that should be consumed over the next 3–4 years. The 1991 Vosne-Romanée is a delicious village wine, with wonderful sweet, pure, black cherry fruit kissed gently by toasty new oak. Ripe and medium bodied, with a smooth texture and a long, lush finish, it should be drunk over the next 5–6 years.

While equally seductive, the 1991 Nuits St.-Georges displays firmer tannins in the finish, as well as a distinctive, earthy/truffle/mushroomy component to its bouquet. An authoritatively flavored village wine, it should drink well for another 5–6 years.

Among the premiers crus are some delicious wines. The lightest is the 1991 Vosne-Romanée Les Chaumes. It exhibits a medium ruby color, a fine, moderately scented bouquet of cherries, herbs, and toast, and moderate tannins in the finish. The overall level of concentration is good rather than spectacular. The spicy, compact finish suggests it is best drunk young, before the fruit fades. The deep ruby-colored 1991 Nuits St.-Georges Les Boudots offers up a perfumed nose of sweet red and black fruits, smoke, herbs, and toast. Rich, round, and succulent, with medium to full body, low acidity, and moderately soft tannins, this beauty should be consumed over the next 7–8 years. Méo's 1991 Nuits St.-Georges aux Murgers is stunning, even better than the super 1990. With a deep, saturated, ruby/purple color, and a fragrant, perfumed nose of sweet black fruits, herbs, licorice, and flowers, this deep, medium- to full-bodied, rich, sweet, expansively flavored wine possesses enough structure to warrant leaving a few bottles in the cellar for the next 3 years; drink it between 1996 and 2006. It is an exceptionally fine burgundy, as well as another example of a 1991 that turned out richer and more complete than the 1990.

This firm does a spectacular job with its two premiers crus from Vosne-Romanée. While the Vosne-Romanée Les Brûlées (yields of only 15–20 hectoliters per hectare) and the Vosne-Romanée Cros Parantoux (a Richebourg look-alike) may be premiers crus in name and price, they are grands crus in quality. Both are must-purchases in 1991 if you are a burgundy fanatic. The 1991 Vosne-Romanée Les Brûlées, from some of Méo's oldest vines, exhibits a superb, saturated, deep purple color, and a fragrant, stunningly gorgeous nose of black fruits, smoked meats, herbs, and toasty new oak. Deep, with a voluptuous texture, this full-bodied wine possesses stunning richness, a high glycerin level, and sweet, soft tannins in the finish. Drink this lusty, full-throttle red burgundy over the next decade. The 1991 Vosne-Romanée Cros Parantoux is more tannic and structured than Les Brûlées. Deep ruby/purple-colored, yet more closed from an aromatic standpoint, it is rich and full, with exceptional concentration, and a ripe, long, moderately tannic finish. Approachable now, I would suggest 3–4 years of cellaring and an optimum drinking window of 1997–2008.

Méo's grands crus include the 1991 Corton Clos Rognet, a sweet, ripe, and medium-bodied wine, with excellent jammy, cherry fruitiness, and soft tannins. Although it is a top success for the Côte de Beaune in 1991, it is not as profound as their wines from the Côte de Nuits. Drink it over the next 7–8 years. The 1991 Clos de Vougeot offers a medium ruby color, and a sweet nose of raspberries and currants. Medium bodied, elegant rather than powerful and concentrated, it is destined to be drunk in its first 7–8 years of life. For a grand cru, it appears less complex and complete than the Nuits St.-Georges aux Murgers, Vosne-Romanée Les Brûlées, and Vosne-Romanée Cros Parantoux. Lastly, the 1991 Richebourg is all silky suppleness, with a supersweet perfume of black fruits, toasty new oak, roasted herbs, and flowers. Medium bodied, with gorgeous concentration and a terrific, even explosively long, velvety-textured finish, this is an elegant wine for drinking over the next 7–8 years.

PRINCE FLORENT DE MÉRODE (LADOIX-SERRIGNY)* * * *

1992	Corton Les Bressandes	D	88
1992	Corton Clos du Roi	D	88
1992	Corton Les Maréchaudes	D	86
1992	Corton Les Rénardes	D	87

1992 Ladoix Les Chaillots	C	86
1992 Pommard Clos de la Platière	D	86+?

Since the 1989 vintage, Prince Florent de Mérode has returned to the form that made this estate so famous in the fifties and sixties. The wines are being bottled without fining or filtration, resulting in wines with sweeter, richer, creamier textures, and far more aromatic intensity and development potential. Mérode's 1992s, which were richly fruity, but light and neither tannic nor powerful in cask, have been transformed into delicious wines from bottle —in large part because the wines were bottled naturally. Consumers who claim it is hard to find a delicious red burgundy for under $20 (it is) will be delighted by the 1992 Ladoix Les Chaillots. It is a sweet, berry-scented, attractively ripe, medium-bodied wine with consider- able grace and elegance, a supple texture, ripe fruit, and gobs of black cherries and earthy notes. It is an ideal wine for drinking over the next 4–5 years. The 1992 Pommard Clos de la Platière offers a sweet, burgundian nose, expansive yet elegant, ripe, spicy flavors exhib- iting toasty new oak and black cherry fruit, and light to moderate tannin in the finish. It may improve over the next 1–2 years; drink it over the next 5–6 years.

There are four Cortons in the Mérode portfolio. The least concentrated is the Corton Les Maréchaudes. Although the 1992 exhibits a trifle too much new oak, it offers a sexy bouquet of jammy black cherry fruit, smoke, and vanilla, as well as medium-bodied, ripe, chewy flavors that hit the palate with authority, but tail off quickly (a characteristic of the 1992 red burgundy vintage). Even though the finish may be shorter than desired, there is still plenty of appeal to this attractive, precocious-tasting wine that is best consumed over the next 4–6 years.

The other three Cortons exhibit slightly more depth and length. For example, the 1992 Corton Les Rénardes reveals a darker, more saturated ruby color, an enticing nose of sweet oak, jammy black cherry fruit, and flowers, low acidity, and a soft, fat, chewy, hedonistic texture and finish. This is a delicious, user-friendly burgundy for drinking over the next 5– 6 years. Both the 1992 Corton Les Bressandes and 1992 Corton Clos du Roi are richer than the Corton Les Rénardes. They offer deep, dark ruby colors, and plenty of lavish, smoky, toasty new oak aromas balanced by gobs of pure, ripe, black cherry fruit. The Corton Les Bressandes possesses more alcohol, glycerin, and fatness in its medium- to full-bodied, expansively flavored personality. The Corton Clos du Roi is more delineated and structured, with the potential to age and improve for 8–10 years. The overwhelming characteristics exhibited by all of Mérode's 1992s are their natural feel on the palate, their clean red and black fruit–scented noses, and their lush, velvety-textured palates. Moreover, these seduc- tive, delicious 1992s are reasonably priced.

ALAIN MICHELOT (NUITS ST.-GEORGES)* * *

1991 Nuits St.-Georges	D	75
1991 Nuits St.-Georges Les Cailles	D	82
1991 Nuits St.-Georges Les Chaignots	D	85
1991 Nuits St.-Georges Les Porets St.-Georges	E	83
1991 Nuits St.-Georges Les St.-Georges	E	79
1991 Nuits St.-Georges Les Vaucrains	E	85

This is a potentially outstanding domaine, but high crop yields (not a problem in low- yielding vintages such as 1991) and the producer's excessive fining and filtration result in spit-polished wines that are wonderful to taste from cask, but are stripped at bottling. They are a lesson in what damage can be done to beautiful raw materials. As long as uncritical European and English wine-drinkers line up to buy Michelot's wines based on his reputation and wealth of top vineyards, he is not likely to change. All of these offerings started life with excellent raw materials, but are now light bodied, superbrilliant (in terms of color and clarity), moderately concentrated wines that exhibit some ripe fruit and muted, innocuous bouquets. The best of the group includes the 1991 Nuits St.-Georges Les Chaignots, which possesses sweet, complex aromas, and a light- to medium-bodied, lovely suppleness. The 1991 Nuits St.-Georges Les Vaucrains is slightly deeper, as well as more spicy and earthy. It exhibits good richness and follow-through. The 1991 Nuits St.-Georges Les St.-Georges is hard, lean, stripped, tough, and tannic. The light ruby-colored 1991 Nuits St.-Georges Les Porets St.-Georges is light and shallow, with a hollow finish. The same can be said for the 1991 Nuits St.-Georges Les Cailles and the disappointing, mediocre, eviscerated 1991 Nuits St.-Georges. Consumers who are willing to accept this level of mediocrity deserve what they get.

MONGEARD-MUGNERET (VOSNE-ROMANÉE)* * * */* * * * *

1991	Bourgogne	B	83
1991	Bourgogne Hautes Côtes de Nuits	B	84
1991	Clos de Vougeot	D	92
1991	Echézeaux Vieilles Vignes	E	90
1991	Fixin	C	85
1991	Grands Echézeaux	E	92
1991	Nuits St.-Georges Les Boudots	D	89
1991	Richebourg	EE	93
1991	Vosne-Romanée	D	86
1991	Vosne-Romanée Les Orveaux	D	89

One of my favorite producers, Mongeard-Mugneret has rebounded strongly in 1991 with far superior wines than those he made in 1989 and 1990. Why? Not only did nature keep yields under 30 hectoliters per hectare (less than 2 tons per acre), but in 1991 Mongeard's son persuaded his father to return to the traditional method of bottling—meaning no fining or filtration. The results are wines with more expansive, rich mid-palates and that enticing, seductive, sweet burgundy perfume that has not been obliterated by excessive fining or filtration.

There are some attractive wines at the lower level, including a solid, elegant, ripe, supple 1991 Bourgogne, and a tasty, smooth, velvety-textured 1991 Bourgogne Hautes Côtes de Nuits. Even Mongeard's 1991 Fixin reveals none of the toughness or hardness that so many wines from that appellation possess. It reveals a deep ruby color, a round, ripe, berry-scented nose, and a juicy, smooth finish. All three of these wines should be consumed over the next 3–4 years.

It is hard to find good village Vosne-Romanée, but Mongeard's 1991 is excellent. A sweet, expansive nose of ripe fruit and toast is followed by a medium-bodied, deliciously ripe, well-balanced, satiny-textured wine with fine concentration and a lush finish. Drink it over the next 4–5 years.

The two premiers crus, Vosne-Romanée Les Orveaux and Nuits St.-Georges Les Boudots, may well merit outstanding ratings with additional bottle age. Both possess deep, saturated ruby colors, sweet, perfumed bouquets, and opulent, voluptuously rich, medium- to full-bodied flavors. The Vosne-Romanée Les Orveaux offers more cassis fruit in its concentrated, silky style, whereas the Nuits St.-Georges Les Boudots possesses a licorice and/or fennel component to accompany its opulent black fruit flavors and lusty personality. Both wines have beautiful balance. They can be consumed now or over the next decade.

The 1991 Echézeaux Vieilles Vignes exhibits toasty new oak, as well as gobs of rich black currants and black cherries. There is a wonderful purity and persuasive mid-palate to this supple yet rich, authoritatively flavored wine that displays no hard edges. One of the finest Echézeauxs of the vintage, it can be drunk now and over the next 10–12 years. The 1991 Clos de Vougeot displays a sumptuous quality to its rich, expansive, sweet, jammy fruit. It exhibits a deep, saturated, dark ruby/purple color, and a magnificent yet unformed nose of red and black fruits, vanillin, and spices. Large-scaled and muscular, with superb extraction of fruit and a long finish, it is soft enough to drink now, but it will improve over the next 5–6 years and last for 12–15.

Mongeard's brilliance in 1991 continues with his two flagship wines—the Grands Echézeaux and Richebourg. Both are terrific, certainly the best wines he has produced over recent years. The Grands Echézeaux offers a stunning nose of black fruits, flowers, new oak, and minerals. Expansive, with gorgeously rich flavors, a voluptuous texture, and brilliant clarity and precision to its components, this full-bodied, decadently styled grand cru will provide riveting drinking over the next 10–12 years. The Richebourg is equally sublime. Slightly sweeter and fatter, with layers of rich black fruits, this unctuous, thick, rich burgundy is bursting with flavor. It possesses enough balance, power, alcohol, and tannin to continue to drink well for at least 10–12 years. These are super efforts from Mongeard-Mugneret and should not be missed. Bravo!

ALBERT MOROT (BEAUNE)* * * *

1992	Beaune Les Bressandes	C	91
1992	Beaune Les Cent Vignes	C	91
1992	Beaune Les Teurons	C	90+
1992	Beaune Les Toussaints	C	88
1992	Savigny Vergelesses Clos La Bataillère	C	89

Wines such as these from Mademoiselle Choppin are of such high quality and reasonable prices that one's faith in Burgundy is restored. For the first time, Mademoiselle Choppin did a severe crop thinning. In addition, she increased the percentage of new oak casks to 60% and, most important, bottled all of her wines without fining or filtration. The results are beautiful expressions of her glorious vineyards. These 1992s are the best wines Mademoiselle Choppin has ever made, including her 1990s. For that reason, I do not think they will last long on retailers' shelves. They all possess 10–15 years of aging potential, as well as the richest, most complete flavors I have tasted from Côte de Beaune wines.

For starters, there is a nearly exceptional 1992 Savigny Vergelesses Clos La Bataillère. It reveals deep, dark ruby color, a big, spicy, beautiful black cherry– and toasty-scented nose, rich, sweet, expansive flavors, and considerable finesse to accompany its wonderful length and suppleness. It should drink well for at least 10+ years. It is an exceptional bargain—perhaps the best value in Pinot Noir in the market!

The succulent 1992 Beaune Les Cent Vignes is filled with charm and suppleness. The toasty vanillin, jammy black cherry, and floral scents leap from the glass, enveloping the olfactory senses. The wine possesses great fruit, beautiful texture, and a layered, concentrated, marvelously pure personality. It is soft enough to be drunk, but should age well for 10–15 years. Quite mouth-filling, this is a terrific example of a Beaune premier cru. The 1992 Beaune Les Toussaints is one of the two most closed wines from the Morot portfolio. The nose reluctantly offers up sweet, earthy, black fruit and spice aromas. The wine exhibits fine sweetness, as well as tougher tannin and more austerity in the finish. There is plenty of weight and richness evident, but it is a question of waiting 2–3 years before drinking this 15- to 20-year wine. The 1992 Beaune Les Bressandes is a knockout wine for drinking over the next 10–12 years. Its huge, saturated, dark ruby/purple color is followed by a sweet, fragrant bouquet of black and red fruits, vanillin, smoke, herbs, and flowers. Expansive and full bodied, with gobs of black cherry and black raspberry–like flavors, this wine's finish lasts for nearly a minute. A stunning, well-structured, authoritatively flavored and precocious-tasting Beaune, it should evolve effortlessly for a decade or more. Lastly, the 1992 Beaune Les Teurons is the most tannic, as well as the most concentrated, of the Morot wines. It requires 4–5 years of cellaring and is capable of lasting for two decades—an amazingly long time for a modern-day burgundy. The wine exhibits a saturated dark ruby color, an earthy, spicy, black cherry–scented nose, massive fruit flavors, adequate acidity, moderate tannin, and a whoppingly long finish. These terrific wines are the best I have tasted from Mademoiselle Choppin.

DENIS MORTET (GEVREY-CHAMBERTIN)* * *

1991	Bourgogne	C	85
1991	Chambertin	EE	84
1991	Chambolle-Musigny Les Beaux Bruns	D	87
1991	Clos de Vougeot	E	82
1991	Gevrey-Chambertin	D	84
1991	Gevrey-Chambertin Les Champeaux	D	88
1991	Gevrey-Chambertin Clos Prieur	D	86

Denis Mortet continues to improve. Save for the grands crus, his 1991s are wonderfully elegant, supple, tasty wines with good clarity and balance. The attractive 1991 Bourgogne offers ripe fruit, medium body, and soft tannins. The 1991 Gevrey-Chambertin is light but spicy, with meaty red fruit scents in the bouquet, and a short finish.

The best wines include the violet-, raspberry-, spice-, and vanillin-scented 1991 Gevrey-Chambertin Clos Prieur. This wine exhibits good ripeness, medium body, excellent harmony, and a soft finish. It should drink well for the next 5–6 years. The 1991 Chambolle-Musigny Les Beaux Bruns is a stylish, graceful wine, with supple, ripe fruit, moderately intense flavors, fine ripeness, and a crisp, medium-bodied finish. It is also best drunk over the next 5–6 years. The 1991 Gevrey-Chambertin Les Champeaux is the sweetest, richest, most concentrated of the Mortet 1991s, with an excellent deep ruby color, a lovely bouquet of flowers, red and black fruits, and subtle new oak. Long, ripe, and luscious, this elegant, flavorful wine should be drunk over the next 7 years.

The two 1991 grands crus, Clos de Vougeot and Chambertin, are not as impressive as their prices and pedigree would suggest. The 1991 Clos de Vougeot is soft, light bodied, and finishes quickly. Although the 1991 Chambertin exhibits some spicy, leathery, raspberry fruit in the nose, it is medium bodied, compact, and short. Once again, Chambertin fails to live up to its mythical reputation.

FRÉDÉRIC MUGNERET (CHÂTEAU CHAMBOLLE-MUSIGNY)
(CHAMBOLLE-MUSIGNY)* * * *

1991	Bonnes Mares	EE	85
1991	Chambolle-Musigny	D	77
1991	Chambolle-Musigny Les Amoureuses	E	82

1991 Chambolle-Musigny Les Fuées	E	81
1991 Musigny	EE	81

This firm can fashion immensely seductive, supple red burgundies that reveal copious quantities of oak and sweet, ripe fruit. Mugneret's 1991s are surprisingly light, to the point of being diluted. The 1991 Chambolle-Musigny is pleasant, but thin. The 1991 Chambolle-Musigny Les Fuées is also pleasant, but light bodied and soft. It requires consumption over the next several years. Sadly, the 1991 Chambolle-Musigny Les Amoureuses suffers from the same problems, as does the great grand cru Musigny. Both reveal inadequate concentration, feeble color, and nonexistent finishes. Where are the finesse and flavor? The only wine with adequate concentration and enough ripeness to provide some pleasure is the 1991 Bonnes Mares, but it needs to be consumed over the next 3–4 years.

MUGNERET-GIBOURG (VOSNE-ROMANÉE)* * * *

1991 Bourgogne	C	86
1991 Clos de Vougeot	E	88
1991 Echézeaux	EE	90
1991 Nuits St.-Georges Les Chaignots	D	87
1991 Vosne-Romanée	D	79

The daughters of the late Georges Mugneret appear to have made better 1991s than 1990s. The colors are deeper, and the wines' richness and concentration of fruit are more evident, no doubt because of the tiny yields. As shrewd followers of the Burgundy scene have long known, the Domaine Mugneret-Gibourg has routinely fashioned a fine generic Bourgogne. The 1991 Bourgogne reveals an excellent deep ruby color, followed by spicy vanillin and ripe cherry aromas. It is a rich, medium-bodied wine with admirable texture and a soft finish. It should drink well for another 4–5 years. I found the 1991 Vosne-Romanée lean, malnourished, and hard. The 1991 Nuits St.-Georges Les Chaignots offers an excellent nose of earth, truffles, and peppery black fruit. Sweet, long, and well endowed, this rich, concentrated red burgundy possesses enough tannin to support a decade of aging. It may merit a higher score as additional complexity emerges. Impressive!

The top-notch, deep ruby-colored 1991 Echézeaux displays a spicy nose of cloves, cherries, vanillin, and herb scents, lovely rich, supple, medium-bodied flavors, excellent concentration and precision, and a spicy, moderately tannic, sweet finish. It should be at its best in several years and last for over a decade. Mugneret-Gibourg's 1991 Clos de Vougeot is monolithic, but impressive in its chunky, fleshy, rich, full-bodied style, with plenty of sweet black fruits. Little complexity has emerged, but the excellent depth and spicy, medium-bodied, moderately tannic finish suggest it should keep for 10–15 years.

PHILIPPE NADDEF (COUCHEY)* * */* * * *

1991 Fixin	C	80
1991 Gevrey-Chambertin	D	82
1991 Gevrey-Chambertin Les Cazetiers	D	85
1991 Gevrey-Chambertin Les Champeaux	D	84
1991 Marsannay	C	72
1991 Mazis-Chambertin	E	86

This young, talented producer has made competent, but generally unexciting 1991s. The lower-level wines such as the Marsannay, Fixin, and Gevrey-Chambertin should be consumed over the next 2–3 years, and the Gevrey-Chambertin Les Champeaux and Gevrey-Chambertin Les Cazetiers, over the next 5–6 years. The only wines with meritorious levels of fruit and balance are the 1991 Gevrey-Chambertin Les Cazetiers, which possesses excellent color, lavish quantities of toasty new oak, fine depth and ripeness, and a medium-bodied, soft, supple style that avoids the harsh tannins so obvious in Les Champeaux, Fixin, and Marsannay, and should be consumed over the next 5–6 years. The 1991 Mazis-Chambertin is a lighter wine than Naddef normally produces. However, it reveals an admirable deep ruby color, some spicy, toasty new oak, and smooth, velvety-textured, ripe, moderately concentrated flavors. It should drink well for at least 6–7 years.

PONSOT (MOREY ST.-DENIS)* * * * *

1991	Chambertin	EE	94
1991	Chambolle-Musigny Les Charmes	E	89
1991	Chapelle-Chambertin	EE	88
1991	Clos de la Roche Vieilles Vignes	EE	95
1991	Clos St.-Denis Vieilles Vignes	EE	95
1991	Gevrey-Chambertin Cuvée L'Abeille	D	86
1991	Griottes-Chambertin	EE	90
1991	Latricières-Chambertin	EE	90
1991	Morey St.-Denis Cuvée des Grives	D	86

The perennially inconsistent Domaine Ponsot has, along with the Domaine Leroy, turned in the vintage's most extraordinary performances. This domaine made mind-boggling 1990s, but a strong case can be built that Laurent Ponsot and his father have fashioned 1991s that are as rich and profound as their 1990s. Certainly their yields were significantly lower. In fact, only Domaine Leroy had yields as low as Ponsot's average of 16 hectoliters per hectare (less than 1 ton per acre). Keep in mind that 1 ton per acre on 8,000–10,000 vines per hectare is considerably different from 1 ton per acre from new-world vineyards that have 1,200 vines per hectare. In the top grands crus, such as Chambertin, Clos St.-Denis, and Clos de la Roche, Ponsot's yields were between 9 and 13 hectoliters per hectare—and from exceptionally old vines. This domaine abhors new oak, uses no SO_2, and bottles its wines with no fining or filtration, utilizing only nitrogen gas to protect the wine as it is moved from cask to bottle.

At the lower level there are deliciously supple, round, fruity wines such as the 1991 Morey St.-Denis Cuvée des Grives and Gevrey-Chambertin Cuvée L'Abeille. Both are medium ruby-colored wines with fragrant bouquets, sweet, round, opulent palates, excellent ripeness, and low acidity. Both should be consumed over the next 5–6 years. The outstanding 1991 Chambolle-Musigny Les Charmes exhibits a huge bouquet of raspberries and flowers. Splendidly rich and medium to full bodied, with exceptional elegance and richness, this brilliant wine should drink well for at least a decade.

Both the 1991 Chapelle-Chambertin and 1991 Latricières-Chambertin are opulent, beautifully concentrated, perfumed wines with lavish quantities of sweet fruit. Both are soft and velvety-textured with wonderful mid-palates and length. Their tremendous richness explodes at the back of the palate. However, the low acidity and sweet tannins already make these wines delicious. Each should drink well for another 10–12 years.

The hugely seductive, harmonious, flamboyant, head-turning 1991 Griottes-Chambertin is full bodied, with a deep ruby color, gobs of sweet black cherry fruit, enough glycerin to make the wine chewy and unctuous, and a whoppingly long, splendidly rich finish.

No matter how many wines I taste, or how long the days can be in damp, dingy cellars, it is hard to spit out wines such as Ponsot's Chambertin, Clos St.-Denis, and Clos de la Roche. The 1991 Chambertin is one of the rare wines from this grand cru vineyard that justifies the price and mythical reputation. It is a great wine, with deep ruby color, and a splendid perfume of smoked meats, jammy black and red fruits, and Asian spices. Layers of supple, juicy, succulent fruit filled with glycerin, sweet tannin, and high alcohol make for a hedonistic, decadent mouthful of wine. It should drink well for at least 10–15 years. As compelling as the Chambertin is, Ponsot's 1991 Clos St.-Denis Vieilles Vignes (from 60-year-old vines cropped at just over ½ ton per hectare!) and 1991 Clos de la Roche Vieilles Vignes (55-year-old vines that also produced ½ ton per hectare) are mind-boggling wines that rival virtually anything produced in Burgundy over the last several decades. The sad news is that only 5–10 cases of the Clos St.-Denis were imported to the United States. The color is saturated ruby/purple, and the huge nose of cassis, smoke, minerals, and spices is mindblowing. An unctuous texture and phenomenal richness are evident in this wine that is held together by moderate tannin and relatively low acidity. This is a huge, massively extracted, amazingly well defined, impeccably balanced wine for drinking over the next 15 or more years. It is reminiscent of the great Ponsot 1980 Clos de la Roche Vieilles Vignes, but more concentrated. The 1991 Clos de la Roche Vieilles Vignes offers an amazingly sweet bouquet redolent of crushed black raspberries, and black cherries, with underlying earthy, trufflelike notes. Awesomely rich, dense, and full bodied, this spectacular low-acid, multidimensional wine has a blockbuster finish. While drinkable now, it should age effortlessly for 15–20 or more years. Bravo to the Ponsots for making some of the greatest red burgundies I have ever tasted—and they have done it in back-to-back vintages!

JACQUES PRIEUR (MEURSAULT)* * */* * * *

1991 Clos de Vougeot Estate	E	86
1991 Musigny Estate	EE	87

If you have not yet discovered them, Jacques Prieur's wines are improving significantly in quality and merit more attention. The two selections from their estate vineyards in the Côte de Nuits include a soft, rich, fragrant, expansively flavored, luscious 1991 Musigny. Although it lacks complexity and concentration, it is ripe, fragrant, and delicious for drinking over the next 7–8 years. The 1991 Clos de Vougeot exhibits a deep ruby color, spicy, vanillin, new oak, and round, attractive flavors presented in a medium-bodied, easy-to-understand format. It should be drunk over the next 6–7 years.

ARNELLE ET BERNARD RION (VOSNE-ROMANÉE)* * *

1991 Chambolle-Musigny Les Echézeaux	D	84
1991 Nuits St.-Georges Les Lavières	D	82
1991 Nuits St.-Georges aux Murgers	D	84
1991 Vosne-Romanée	D	79

Rion's 1991s are correct and competent wines, but unexciting. The pleasant, compact 1991 Vosne-Romanée and 1991 Nuits St.-Georges Les Lavières offer attractive spicy, cherry fruit, medium body, and some of the 1991 vintage's austerity. They should be drunk over the next 4–5 years. The 1991 Nuits St.-Georges aux Murgers exhibits more power, flavor dimension, and length, as well as more tannin. It should be drunk young, before the fruit dries out and the tannin takes over. The deepest-colored and densest wine is the 1991 Chambolle-Musigny Les Echézeaux. It reveals a broader palate, more stuffing, concentration, and length, and hard tannin in the finish. How it will evolve is somewhat of a gamble.

DANIEL RION (NUITS ST.-GEORGES)* * * *

1991 Chambolle-Musigny Les Beaux Bruns	E	87
1991 Chambolle-Musigny Les Charmes	E	87
1991 Clos de Vougeot	EE	87
1991 Nuits St.-Georges Clos des Argillières	E	85
1991 Nuits St.-Georges Les Hauts Pruliers	E	75
1991 Nuits St.-Georges Les Lavières	D	85
1991 Nuits St.-Georges Les Vignes Rondes	E	87
1991 Vosne-Romanée	D	81
1991 Vosne-Romanée Les Beaux Monts	E	86
1991 Vosne-Romanée Les Chaumes	E	85

Rion produces some of the most elegant, modern-styled red burgundies from the Côte de Nuits. He did not have the success in 1991 that he enjoyed in 1990, but his 1991s range from good to very good. This is a firm with four Nuits St.-Georges premiers crus. My favorite is the succulent, rich, seductive, deeply colored, expansively flavored, concentrated 1991 Nuits St.-Georges Les Vignes Rondes. It exhibits the most depth, intensity, and balance of his premiers crus. The leanest, most tannic, and most suspect is the 1991 Nuits St.-Georges Les Lavières. While the nose offers up some ripe plums and earthy fruit, the tannin is hard in this rustic, lean wine that is a candidate to dry out before the tannin fades. The 1991 Nuits St.-Georges Clos des Argillières is a firmly structured, medium-bodied wine with good color, depth, and ripeness. However, it is essentially one-dimensional. The same thing can be said about the soft, medium- to full-bodied, round, moderately concentrated, earthy, fragrant 1991 Nuits St.-Georges Les Hauts Pruliers. Both Les Hauts Pruliers and Clos des Argillières should be consumed over the next 6–7 years.

Among the three selections from Vosne-Romanée, the 1991 Vosne-Romanée is tannic, spicy, and lean, with only adequate concentration, and a stemmy, hard finish. The 1991 Vosne-Romanée Les Beaux Monts offers ripe berry fruit and spicy new oak in the nose. Medium bodied, with excellent length and richness, this wine will merit a score several points higher if the tannins melt away, as I suspect they will. Drink it between now and 2002. The 1991 Vosne-Romanée Les Chaumes is the most supple of this trio, as well as the lightest. Moreover, it reveals some dilution in the mid-palate and finish. Drink it over the next several years.

The three best wines from this producer in 1991 include the two excellent premiers crus from Chambolle-Musigny. Both Les Beaux Bruns and Les Charmes reveal impressively saturated, deep ruby/purple colors, fragrant, spicy, cassis- and floral-scented noses, medium-bodied, concentrated flavors, wonderful elegance and focus, and moderately tannic, long finishes. There is an admirable sweetness and richness of fruit to these wines, and their tannin is soft rather than astringent and green. Both wines should drink well for the next decade. The 1991 Clos de Vougeot exhibits more spicy new oak in its nose, offers plenty of ripe curranty fruit, depth, and richness, and has a medium- to full-bodied, long finish. Drink it over the next 7–8 years.

ANTONIN RODET (MERCUREY)* * */* * * *

1990 Bourgogne Vieilles Vignes	A	86

This serious, complex, rich wine offers excellent value; it could easily be mistaken for many premiers crus from the Côte d'Or. The deep ruby color is followed by wonderfully pure, rich black cherry scents backed up by spicy vanillin. Medium bodied, with excellent ripeness, this classic, stylish wine can be drunk now or cellared for 2–3 years. Given how disappointing so many high-priced burgundies can be, this is a rare find for under $10 a bottle.

DOMAINE DE LA ROMANÉE-CONTI (VOSNE-ROMANÉE)* * * * *

1992 Echézeaux	EE	78
1991 Echézeaux	EE	92
1992 Grands Echézeaux	EEE	82
1991 Grands Echézeaux	EEE	93
1992 Richebourg	EEE	78
1991 Richebourg	EEE	89
1992 Romanée Conti	EEE	86+
1991 Romanée Conti	EEE	91+
1992 Romanée St.-Vivant	EEE	78
1991 Romanée St.-Vivant	EEE	88
1992 La Tâche	EEE	85
1991 La Tâche	EEE	93

The 1992s from this hallowed domaine are the least impressive wines produced in several decades. All of these offerings, which are very light, with stemmy, green peppery, herbaceous personalities, and black fruit concentration, taste hollow, as if there is just not enough extract and concentration to stand up to the wine's framework. The light ruby-colored 1992 Echézeaux exhibits herbal aromas, light body, and harsh tannin in the finish. The 1992 Grands Echézeaux is even more peppery and vegetal, with a stemmy, spicy nose, medium body, some fruit, and harsh, astringent tannin. The thin, dusty 1992 Romanée St.-Vivant is overtly spicy, earthy, light to medium bodied, and lacking concentration. The 1992 Richebourg is disjointed, light, and out of balance with excessive tannin and acidity for the amount of fruit it possesses. The green, vegetal peppery bouquet is very unbecoming.

Both the 1992 La Tâche and 1992 Romanée-Conti exhibit more stuffing. The La Tâche is the beefiest and more muscular, but it does not have enough fruit to cover its framework. The Romanée-Conti reveals leathery, spicy, herbal aromas, and a dry, austere personality, with high tannin and little fruit. Both of these wines will undoubtedly develop pleasing aromatic profiles, but they are bony wines without much charm. These wines were tasted from cask and twice from bottle with similar impressions.

As did most Burgundy domaines, the DRC had exceptionally low yields in 1991, ranging from under 20 hectoliters per hectare to a high of 26 hectoliters per hectare for the Grands Echézeaux. Unquestionably, all of these wines are successful and should age for two decades. The Echézeaux is usually their lightest wine. The 1991 displays a deep ruby color, a tight but promising bouquet of smoky oak and rich red and black fruits, and moderate tannin in the finish. More backward and dense than normal, it should be at its best between 1996 and 2008. It is no secret among DRC aficionados that the "best buy" is the exceptional Grands Echézeaux. The 1991, along with La Tâche, gets my vote (currently) as the most complex and rich wine the DRC produced. In 20 years the Romanée-Conti may display its magical perfume that is unrivaled in Burgundy. The Grands Echézeaux exhibits a deep ruby/purple color, gorgeous as well as copious quantities of sweet, jammy, cassis fruit, and smoky, toasty new oak. Powerful, rich, medium to full bodied, with exceptional concentration, this complex wine should be at its best between 1998 and 2012.

I found the Romanée St.-Vivant to be softer and lighter than the other 1991s from the DRC. It offers distinctive aromas of cloves, cinnamon, and earthy black fruits. Medium bodied and supple, with light tannins, this is one 1991 that can be drunk now or over the next 12–15 years. The 1991 Richebourg is dominated by sweet vanillin and toasty new oak scents intermingled with aromas of cassis. Medium bodied, with excellent richness and a long, moderately tannic finish, this wine (as virtually all the DRC wines do) will put on considerable weight as it ages. Drink it between 1998 and 2012. As usual, La Tâche is compelling. It possesses the deepest color of any of the 1991s, as well as a telltale, decadent bouquet of smoked meats, jammy black fruits, and Asian spices. Expansive, full bodied, and oozing with rich, sweet fruit, this example of La Tâche, despite its flamboyance, is structured, tannic, and in need of at least 3–4 more years of cellaring. It should last for up to 20 years. The 1991 Romanée-Conti reveals a deep color, but there is less color saturation than that possessed by La Tâche or Grands Echézeaux. Backward and medium to full bodied, this is the most closed and impenetrable of all the 1991 DRC wines. No doubt its pedigree and breeding will emerge, but for now, I must rate the Grands Echézeaux and La Tâche higher.

ROSSIGNOL-TRAPET (GEVREY-CHAMBERTIN)* * *

1991 Chambertin	EE	79
1991 Chapelle-Chambertin	EE	85
1991 Gevrey-Chambertin	D	73
1991 Gevrey-Chambertin Petite Chapelle	D	77
1991 Latricières-Chambertin	EE	85

This domaine, which has considerable resources, continues to provide a lamentable level of mediocrity. The filter pad nose of the 1991 Gevrey-Chambertin could only be loved by a cardboard box manufacturer. The flavors are washed out, and the finish is short and bitter. The 1991 Gevrey-Chambertin Petite Chapelle is made in a narrow, lean, compact, hard, tannic style that represents the darker side of the 1991 vintage. Thankfully, the 1991 Chapelle-Chambertin reveals some elegance, as well as modest amounts of sweet berry fruit intertwined with aromas of spicy new oak and roasted nuts. Medium bodied and spicy, this attractive yet restrained style of wine should be drunk over the next 4–5 years. The 1991 Latricières-Chambertin tasted identical (so much for *terroir*). With the same spicy new oak, elegant berry, roasted fruit, and vanillin bouquet, fresh acidity, and a short, medium-bodied, pleasant finish, it should be drunk over the next 5–6 years. The light, insipid, innocuous 1991 Chambertin is another insult to a wine consumer's intelligence. I can think of a dozen or so generic 1991 Bourgognes that are superior to this washed-out, hollow wine. What a travesty!

GEORGES ET CHRISTOPHE ROUMIER (CHAMBOLLE-MUSIGNY)* * * *

1991 Bonnes Mares	E	86
1991 Chambolle-Musigny	D	81
1991 Chambolle-Musigny Les Amoureuses	D	77
1991 Clos de Vougeot	D	85
1991 Morey St.-Denis Clos de la Bussière	D	86
1991 Musigny	EE	86
1991 Ruchottes-Chambertin	E	86+

Although this is one of Burgundy's finest domaines, and a reference point for quality in most vintages, Roumier's 1991s are less successful than other top Côte de Nuits producers'. The yields were minuscule, ranging from 8–10 hectoliters per hectare, to 16–20 hectoliters per hectare for several of the grands crus. Though well-colored, the wines tend to be hard, tannic, and lacking the intensity of fruit necessary to match the tannin. Like some other 1991s, the balance between tannin and fruit is questionable. My experience has shown that the fruit usually fades more quickly than the tannin.

The 1991 Chambolle-Musigny reveals a deep ruby color, a spicy, earthy, closed nose, and firm, hard tannins in the medium-bodied, moderately concentrated flavors. Two to three years of cellaring is required, but I wonder if the fruit will hold. The 1991 Morey St.-Denis Clos de la Bussière exhibits a more expressive bouquet of spicy, earthy, berry fruit, herbs, and meaty aromas, and medium-bodied, powerful flavors with significant tannin in the finish. It requires 4–5 years of cellaring. Although there is more intensity of fruit than in the other Roumier wines, the tannins dominate the wine's personality. The 1991 Chambolle-Musigny Les Amoureuses is too tough, hard, and tannic. It possesses medium to dark ruby color and a closed nose, but its roughness and astringent, green tannins are troublesome. Despite the use of 6 egg whites per barrel to try and soften the tannin, the wine is still frightfully hard. Readers who play for high stakes may want to gamble.

The 1991 Clos de Vougeot displays a healthy ruby color, and a muted nose of cassis fruit, spice, herbs, and vanillin. Moderate tannins are a prominent feature in this medium-bodied, well-structured, but compact and austerely styled Clos de Vougeot. It should last for a decade. The 1991 Ruchottes-Chambertin displays the meaty, spicy, animal side of Pinot Noir, deep ruby color, fine richness, power, and intensity, yet plenty of tannin in the finish. The tannins are less dry and astringent than in the other Roumier offerings, so this wine may evolve gracefully for 10–12 years. Lastly, the 1991 Bonnes Mares and 1991 Musigny are both dominated by their tannin. Both have good color and vague scents of ripe cherry fruit, but their toughness and ferocious tannin kept my scores conservative.

In summary, the 1991 Roumiers all possess very good to excellent color and muted but ripe noses, but they are all dominated by their tannin. Those readers with faith that the tannin will melt away before the fruit fades will enjoy these wines more than I did.

DOMAINE ARMAND ROUSSEAU (GEVREY-CHAMBERTIN)* * * *

1991 Chambertin	EE	96
1991 Chambertin Clos de Bèze	EE	94
1991 Charmes-Chambertin	E	88
1991 Clos de la Roche	E	85?
1991 Clos des Ruchottes-Chambertin	E	90
1991 Gevrey-Chambertin	D	86
1991 Gevrey-Chambertin Les Cazetieres	D	86+
1991 Gevrey-Chambertin Clos St.-Jacques	EE	90
1991 Mazis-Chambertin	E	88

Rousseau, one of the reference points for great burgundy, appears to have made 1991s that are even richer and more profound than his 1990s. His production was one-half of normal, so these wines will be difficult to find. Rousseau normally excels with his three top cuvées —Gevrey-Chambertin Clos St.-Jacques, Chambertin Clos de Bèze, and Chambertin, but the lower-level wines often lack concentration and intensity. That is not the case in 1991. Even the village Gevrey-Chambertin offers a deep, saturated, dark ruby color, a big, spicy, meaty, black fruit–scented nose, ripe, medium-bodied flavors, excellent richness, and admirable definition and length. It should drink well for at least a decade. The 1991 Gevrey-Chambertin Les Cazetieres will certainly evolve into a good wine, but at present it is only slightly better than the village Gevrey. It is closed because of its high tannin and backward, almost impenetrable style. While there is underlying fat and good length, it is a hard, tough-styled 1991. My judgment may be conservative.

The 1991 Charmes-Chambertin is the best I have tasted from Rousseau in over 15 years. A deep, saturated, ruby/purple color is followed by a splendidly ripe, glorious nose of smoke, roasted black cherries, herbs, and animal fat. Long, luscious, and rich, with sweet tannin in the finish, this concentrated, chewy, wine should drink beautifully for another 10–12 years. The 1991 Mazis-Chambertin is more tannic, but the race between the fruit and tannin favors the fruit. The wine is deep ruby/purple-colored, with excellent ripeness, a rich, layered feel, chewy texture, and sweet, ripe, cassis fruit in the finish. The tannins suggest 2–4 years of cellaring are warranted for this civilized, refined Mazis. It should age well for up to 15 years. Rousseau's 1991 Clos de la Roche is the toughest and most problematic wine to evaluate. Unquestionably, it possesses power and body, but it is closed, and the tannins taste astringent. For now, I have given this wine the benefit of the doubt, but it requires monitoring for the next 3–4 years.

I adored Rousseau's 1991 Clos des Ruchottes-Chambertin. It is another example of a 1991 that is richer and more flavorful and complex than its 1990 counterpart. The color is deep ruby/purple. The bouquet soars from the glass, offering scents of smoked meats, black and red fruits, herbs, and toasty oak. Rich and full bodied, with exceptional concentration and focus, this beautifully made, pure, well-structured red burgundy should be at its best between 1996 and 2008. The 1991 Gevrey-Chambertin Clos St.-Jacques exhibits an impressively saturated, deep ruby/purple color, and a tight but promising bouquet of cassis fruit, new oak, and flowers. Concentrated and rich, with medium to full body, and high tannins, this powerful yet backward wine needs at least 5–6 years of cellaring. It should last for 15 or more years.

Rousseau's two finest wines should come as no surprise. The 1991 Chambertin Clos de Bèze (from yields of only 22 hectoliters per hectare) reveals a black/purple color. The nose offers a dazzling display of black raspberries and black cherries intermingled with scents of minerals, flowers, and toasty new oak. The wine possesses great intensity and richness, full body, a magnificent layered texture, and oodles of sweet, ripe fruit in the long, moderately tannic finish. Drink it between 1997 and 2015. The darker-colored 1991 Chambertin is almost black. After Comte de Vogüé's Musigny Vieilles Vignes, it is the darkest-colored grand cru red burgundy of the vintage. It displays a lead pencil, Mouton-like element in the bouquet, gobs of rich, sweet, black raspberry fruit, plenty of smoky, toasty new oak, and remarkable concentration and length. A quintessential Chambertin, it makes a mockery of all the watery, vapid wines priced at over $100 a bottle that emerge from this grand cru vineyard. Superrich, yet young and unevolved, this is a Chambertin to drink from the turn of the century through the first two decades of the next millennium. Kudos to Rousseau for producing his finest portfolio of wines in over two decades!

CHRISTIAN SERAFIN (GEVREY-CHAMBERTIN)* * * */* * * * *

1992	Charmes-Chambertin	D	92
1991	Charmes-Chambertin	E	85
1992	Gevrey-Chambertin Les Cazetiers	D	90+
1991	Gevrey-Chambertin Les Cazetiers	D	85+
1991	Gevrey-Chambertin Les Corbeaux	D	82
1992	Gevrey-Chambertin Le Fonteny	D	88
1991	Gevrey-Chambertin Le Fonteny	D	83

1992 Gevrey-Chambertin Vieilles Vignes	D	86
1991 Gevrey-Chambertin Vieilles Vignes	D	82

I am one of Christian Serafin's biggest admirers. It is no secret that he is considered one of the finest viticulturists and winemakers in Gevrey-Chambertin. That being said, my instincts suggest that I tasted his 1991s at an awkward period in their development, as these are the most conservative scores I have given his wines. Yet my notes from the barrel were nearly identical. His yields were certainly low in 1991, but the common themes throughout these offerings are austere, lean personalities, tough, hard, astringent tannins, and closed, ungenerous palates. They had not been in the bottle very long, and some wines, because of a high dosage of SO_2 or their reaction from going from wood to glass, shut down completely. For whatever reason, these wines were not impressive. The 1991 Gevrey-Chambertin Les Cazetiers and Charmes-Chambertin had more to them, but even they appear to be structured, compact, austere wines without the sweet richness of fruit one expects from Serafin.

These wines will require another look in the near future. It is hard to believe they do not possess more fruit than they exhibited when I tasted them just after bottling.

The 1992 Gevrey-Chambertin Vieilles Vignes is a pretty, delicate wine with good color, attractive berry- and herb-scented fruit, medium body, and a compact personality. This spicy, ripe wine is ideal for drinking over the next 5–6 years. Richer, with more length and sweetness, as well as fine structure, is the 1992 Gevrey-Chambertin Le Fonteny. Made from a vineyard abutting two of the village's grands crus, Mazis-Chambertin and Ruchottes-Chambertin, this spicy wine displays excellent ripeness and concentration, medium body, and a sweet, forward, moderately tannic finish. It should be at its best in 1–2 years and last for up to 12. Serafin always produces one of the finest wines from the hillside vineyard, Les Cazetiers. His 1992 Gevrey-Chambertin Les Cazetiers is of grand cru quality. The wine exhibits a dark ruby color, and a whopping bouquet of black fruits, herbs, earth, and toasty new oak. Rich and backward, with noticeable tannin and structure, it offers outstanding concentration and length. Ideally, it should be drunk between 1998 and 2008.

Lastly, the 1992 Charmes-Chambertin is atypically muscular, dense, and concentrated for a wine from this grand cru vineyard. Its saturated ruby/purple color is followed by intense, sweet fruit flavors presented in a full-bodied, ripe, well-structured, heady format. This is a terrific 1992 from the Côte de Nuits. It should drink well for 15+ years.

BERNARD SERVEAU (MOREY ST.-DENIS)* * */* * * *

1991 Bourgogne	C	82
1991 Chambolle-Musigny Les Amoureuses	D	74
1991 Chambolle-Musigny Les Chabiots	D	86
1991 Chambolle-Musigny Les Sentiers	D	86
1991 Morey St.-Denis Les Sorbès	D	83
1991 Nuits St.-Georges Les Chaines Carteaux	D	77

Serveau is known for his light, delicate, lacy style of Pinot Noir. In 1991, his wines range from merely competent, to two very good premiers crus from Chambolle-Musigny. The ruby-colored 1991 Bourgogne displays fine ripeness and a pleasant, straightforward style. It warrants consumption over the next several years. The 1991 Morey St.-Denis Les Sorbès reveals a medium ruby color, an earthy, damp, foresty, currant-scented nose, medium-bodied, moderately concentrated flavors, and firm, hard tannin in the finish. It will benefit from 1–2 years in the cellar. The 1991 Nuits St.-Georges Les Chaines Carteaux has problematically high tannin levels, a hard, tight-fisted style, lean, austere structure, and seemingly insufficient fruit to hold up and balance out the wine's astringency. It is a long shot at best. Another surprising disappointment from Serveau is the 1991 Chambolle-Musigny Les Amoureuses. Year in and year out this is the pick of the Serveau portfolio, but the 1991 tastes uncommonly light, even by Serveau's delicate stylistic standards, with hard tannin and a compact, short, malnourished finish. There is just not enough fruit and depth to balance out the wine's harshness.

Two fine examples are the 1991 Chambolle-Musigny Les Sentiers and 1991 Chambolle-Musigny Les Chabiots. Both exhibit healthy, medium ruby colors, and sweet, ripe, fragrant bouquets, with Les Sentiers displaying more spice and Les Chabiots more vanillin and pure, sweet, jammy fruit. Both possess medium body, fine balance, moderate tannin, and admirable concentration, as well as a sense of grace and elegance. Although each can be drunk now, they will both keep for at least a decade.

JEAN TARDY (VOSNE-ROMANÉE)* * *

1991 Chambolle-Musigny Les Athets	D	83
1991 Clos de Vougeot	E	74
1991 Nuits St.-Georges aux Bas de Combe	D	78
1991 Nuits St.-Georges Les Boudots	E	84
1991 Vosne-Romanée Les Chaumes	D	80

These are all light-flavored, medium-bodied, tannic wines. I expected more depth and intensity given Tardy's track record. Although the tannic, austere 1991 Clos de Vougeot is a disappointment, the other offerings exhibit various degrees of light cherry fruit, spice, and new oak, but little depth.

CHÂTEAU DE LA TOUR (VOUGEOT)* * * *

1991 Clos de Vougeot	E	87
1991 Clos de Vougeot Vieilles Vignes	EE	89+

This property has been making superlative wines since the late eighties, and their 1991s are successful. The most commonly encountered cuvée is the regular bottling of their Clos de Vougeot. Deep ruby/purple in color, with a big, sweet nose of toasty new oak, cassis fruit, and spices, this rich, medium- to full-bodied wine displays low acidity, admirable ripeness, a fleshy, nearly unctuous texture, and a heady, alcoholic, soft, moderately tannic finish. Approachable now, it will be even better after 1–2 years in the cellar; it should last for 8–10 years. The 1991 Clos de Vougeot Vieilles Vignes (extremely limited in availability) is similarly styled, with as much new oak in evidence, but even richer, more jammy fruit, and a long, superconcentrated, thick, rich palate. Made from the estate's oldest vines, it exhibits plenty of fat and intensity. The finish is long, moderately tannic, and filled with chewy levels of glycerin, plenty of alcohol, and sweet tannins. It should easily merit an outstanding score with 2 more years of bottle age; it should keep for 10–15 years.

DOMAINE LOUIS TRAPET (GEVREY-CHAMBERTIN)* *

1991 Chambertin	EE	82
1991 Chapelle-Chambertin	E	83
1991 Gevrey-Chambertin	D	74
1991 Gevrey-Chambertin Petite Chapelle	D	81
1991 Latricières-Chambertin	E	85

I am still holding out hope that the young son of Jean Trapet, Jean-Louis, will get this domaine back on the right track. However, the 1991s are unexciting wines. The 1991

Gevrey-Chambertin exhibits good color (as do virtually all of the Côte de Nuits' 1991s), but the tough, hard, excessive tannins and a hollow personality are disappointments. The 1991 Gevrey-Chambertin Petite Chapelle offers more bouquet, with elements of smoky new oak and herb-scented cherry fruit. There is noticeable oak in the flavors, as well as hard, astringent tannins. The wine exhibits some depth, but not enough to balance out the tannins. The 1991 Chapelle-Chambertin is also exceptionally tannic, as well as hollow, compact, and short, with an attractive loamy, underbrush, aged-beef sort of aroma. Despite that appealing characteristic, it is hard to get excited by this wine's harshness and rough tannin. The top choice from Trapet's portfolio is their 1991 Latricières-Chambertin. It exhibits some leanness, but it reveals a deeper, more saturated color, some attractive sweet, smoky, roasted berry fruit, a spicy component, and ripe, medium-bodied flavors that display plenty of tannin. Unlike the other 1991 offerings from Trapet, Latricières possesses sweet fruit as well as sufficient depth to hold its own against the tannin level.

There are no thrills to be found in the luxury-priced bottle of 1991 Chambertin. This is a wine that will dry out in 7–8 years. The fruit is completely overwhelmed by the harsh, astringent, abrasive tannin. The wine is medium bodied, not very concentrated, and somewhat hollow. How many pitiful examples of Chambertin must the consumer endure?

DOMAINE J. TRUCHOT-MARTIN (MOREY ST.-DENIS)* * * *

1992 Bourgogne	C	86
1992 Charmes-Chambertin Vieilles Vignes	E	91
1992 Gevrey-Chambertin Les Combottes	D	87
1992 Morey St.-Denis Les Blanchards	D	87

Truchot produces a seductive style of burgundy that is often deceptively light in color, but as readers should know, color is not nearly as significant a factor with Pinot Noir as it is with other varietals, particularly Cabernet Sauvignon and Syrah. Take the 1992 Bourgogne as an example. The wine's color is a light rosé, but the wonderful bouquet of rich, jammy strawberries and flowers jumps from the glass. The wine is supple, with lovely ripe fruit, and a round, generous, soft finish. Drink this fragile wine over the next 1–2 years. The 1992 Morey St.-Denis Les Blanchards offers a medium ruby color, sweet berry fruit aromas, and medium- to full-bodied, concentrated flavors with light tannin. It is ideal for drinking now and over the next 3–5 years. The 1992 Gevrey-Chambertin Les Combottes (made from 55-year-old vines) reveals a darker ruby/purple color, a superripe nose of red and black fruits, chewy, black cherry fruit, a seductive, medium-bodied personality, and a low-acid, lush finish. It should be drunk over the next 4–5 years. While I found the 1992 Clos de la Roche from Jacky Truchot to be tannic, light, backward, and not impressive enough to recommend, the 1992 Charmes-Chambertin Vieilles Vignes is a superb example of this grand cru vineyard known to produce elegant, finesse-filled wines. Made from 73-year-old vines and aged in 100% new oak (only 25 cases are available for the United States), this wine exhibits a gorgeously decadent nose of jammy red and black fruits, flowers, and toasty, smoky new oak. Rich, yet velvety smooth and supple, it is hard to resist drinking it immediately. Given its succulent, juicy, lush style, this decadent red burgundy is best drunk over the next 4–5 years. All of Jacky Truchot's wines are bottled without fining or filtration.

COMTE DE VOGÜÉ (CHAMBOLLE-MUSIGNY)* * * * *

1991 Bonnes Mares	EE	91+
1991 Chambolle-Musigny	D	87
1991 Chambolle-Musigny Les Amoureuses	E	90
1991 Musigny Vieilles Vignes	EE	93+

By any standards these are impressive wines. They reveal the deepest colors of any red burgundies I tasted from the 1991 vintage. In fact, their deep purple, saturated colors are reminiscent of barrel samples of Cabernet Sauvignon or Syrah. Made in a Bordeaux-like style, they are tannic, exceptionally well structured, and loaded with flavor and muscle. Are they the most elegant and personality-filled red burgundies? Only time will tell, as all these wines need at least 5–6 years of cellaring. One cannot ask for a more impressive, at least for now, Chambolle-Musigny. The Comte de Vogüé's 1991 offers a deep, saturated purple color, and a reticent but promising nose of cassis, vanillin, minerals, and flowers. Tannic and muscular, this big, boldly styled wine should be at its best between 1997 and 2010. The 1991 Chambolle-Musigny Les Amoureuses is nearly black in color, with huge amounts of fruit, glycerin, and body supported by equally massive amounts of tannin. This is one 1991 where the tannins appear excessive—until you taste the sweetness and rich, concentrated fruit. It is a wine for drinking between 2000 and 2015.

The 1991 Bonnes Mares enjoys a similar dark purple/black color, and huge, dense, concentrated fruit flavors tightly bound by structure, tannin, and acidity. Clean, yet impressively rich and full, it should also be at its best between 2000 and 2015. Wealthy collectors should not miss the opportunity to see whether the 1991 equals or surpasses the 1990 Musigny Vieilles Vignes made at the Comte de Vogüé. The saturated, dense purple color is magnificent. The big, yet unformed bouquet of framboise, cassis, vanillin, and minerals suggests the wine is loaded. It is. Powerful, rich, concentrated, and marvelously clean and pure, this irrefutably impressively endowed, large-scaled red burgundy exhibits a Médoc-like austerity and structure, as well as a squeaky-clean, international style. It will be interesting to see what develops over the next 15–20 years. Do not drink it before the turn of the century; it should last an uncommonly long time for modern-day burgundy. Very impressive!

White Burgundy

RECENT VINTAGES

1994—More successful than the red wines, the 1994 white burgundies are, at the top levels, fleshy, fruity, low-acid wines. They are lightweight versions of the 1992 white burgundies, which is not bad given the significant rainfall before and during the 1994 harvest. Consumers desiring supple, fruity, easy-to-understand white burgundies will adore these wines. They will need to be drunk early on, within 5–6 years of the vintage.

1993—The weather in June and July was unfriendly to the growers, with cold, windy rainstorms and hail wreaking havoc. The Meursault premiers crus, particularly Les Genevrières, Les Charmes, and Les Perrières, were virtually wiped out by hail. August was superb—hot and dry. The first 7 days of September put Burgundy on schedule to begin an early harvest of modest quantity, but potentially high quality. However, a violent storm struck in the early morning hours of September 8, causing considerable flooding. While a small amount of rain was desirable, the storm of September 8 could not have been beneficial. September 9 was a cold but rain-free day; on the 10th it rained most of the day, and showers continued to fall off and on on the 11th. What may prove the undoing of this vintage is the five inches of rain that fell throughout Burgundy on the 12th. On Monday the 13th, the weather remained overcast and misty, but on the 14th the storms blew to the east and the weather improved. Between Wednesday the 15th and early Tuesday the 21st, there was considerable sunshine and heat. However, heavy rains, more than two inches in some areas, hit Burgundy again on September 22 and 23. With over 7 full days of rain during 18 of the most critical days prior to the harvest, the prospects for anything higher than average quality are doubtful. Yet the finest producers who kept crop levels low and have well-drained soils have produced some good wines. Qualitatively, this is a vintage of foursquare, high-acid, somewhat green and hollow wines. The farther south one goes, the better the wines become.

1992—This vintage has turned out to be a top-flight year for white burgundy. Rain did catch some of the harvesters, but the weather cleared, and those who waited saw the acidity and sugars rebound. Crop size was moderately large, but not excessive. The wines are fat, ripe, rich, and flattering. The acidity is low, but high acidity is noticeable in those white wines that were acidified or had their malolactic fermentation blocked. Nineteen ninety-two is the most exciting white burgundy vintage since 1989, comparable to such top years as 1985, 1986, and 1989. Most 1992 white burgundies will have to be drunk young (within 10–12 years of the vintage) as they are ripe, alcoholic, rich, and low in acidity.

1991—On paper this is a below-average to mediocre year for Burgundy's white wines. Most lack weight and generosity because the harvest took place under atrocious weather conditions. However, some surprisingly good wines were made by those who picked very late and/or had exceptionally low yields. For example, anyone who tasted the 1991 whites from Comte Lafon would think these wines emerged from a great year.

1990—This is a very good vintage for white burgundy, but only a handful of wines are exceptional. The yields were phenomenally high, and many wines lack concentration. Once past the cosmetic window-dressing provided by copious quantities of new oak, there is a lack of richness and intensity. Appellations that enjoyed considerable success include Corton-Charlemagne, where the 1990s may turn out to be greater than the 1989s. Some Montrachets also turned out to be as spectacular and rich as their 1989 counterparts. There is also the potential for high-class wines from Chablis. Most wines from Meursault and Puligny-Montrachet are light and fluid. Nevertheless, this is a good to very good white burgundy vintage, with some superb wines.

1989—Among more recent vintages, this is a stunning year for white burgundy, with exceptional quality in all appellations—from Corton-Charlemagne south through Chassagne-Montrachet and the Côte Chalonnais. The wines are rich and intense, and are now exhibiting much more structure than many initially believed possible.

Top Older Vintages—While 1988 is average in quality and 1987 below average, 1986 and 1985 are terrific white burgundy years. Arguments will continue for years as to which is superior. Certainly there was more botrytis in 1986, and as a result, the wines display an apricot, peachy character. In 1985 many growers considered the grapes too healthy and clean. Consequently, the 1985s are often purer and cleaner, but sometimes less interesting, than the more flamboyant 1986s. Nevertheless, both vintages produced many exceptional wines. Finding them is virtually impossible.

BURGUNDY'S GREATEST WHITE WINES

Amiot-Bonfils Chassagne-Montrachet Les Caillerets
Amiot-Bonfils Le Montrachet
Amiot-Bonfils Puligny-Montrachet Les Demoiselles
Domaine Bessin Chablis Valmur
Jean-Marc Boillot Bâtard-Montrachet
Jean-Marc Boillot Puligny-Montrachet Les Combettes
Jean-Marc Boillot Puligny-Montrachet La Truffière

Domaine de la Bongrand (Jean Thevenet) Mâcon-Clessé
Domaine J. F. Coche-Dury Corton-Charlemagne
Domaine J. F. Coche-Dury Meursault Les Perrières
Domaine J. F. Coche-Dury Meursault Rougeot
Domaine Marc Colin Le Montrachet
Domaine Colin-Déléger Chassagne-Montrachet Les Chaumes

Domaine Colin-Déléger
Chassagne-Montrachet Les Chevenottes
Domaine Colin-Déléger
Chevalier-Montrachet
Domaine Colin-Déléger
Puligny-Montrachet Les Demoiselles
Domaine Jean Collet Chablis Vaillons
Domaine Jean Dauvissat Chablis Les
Preuses
Domaine Jean Dauvissat Chablis Les
Vaillons Vieilles Vignes
Domaine René et Vincent Dauvissat
Chablis Les Clos
Domaine Marius Delarche
Corton-Charlemagne
Joseph Drouhin Beaune Clos des
Mouches
Joseph Drouhin Montrachet Marquis de
Laguiche
Gérard Duplessis Chablis Les Clos
Domaine J. A. Ferret Pouilly-Fuissé Hors
Classe Cuvées
Fontaine-Gagnard Bâtard-Montrachet
Château Fuissé Pouilly-Fuissé Vieilles
Vignes
Domaine Jean-Noël Gagnard
Bâtard-Montrachet
Domaine Jean-Noël Gagnard
Chassagne-Montrachet Les Caillerets
Domaine Guffens-Heynen Pouilly-Fuissé
Clos des Petits Croux
Domaine Guffens-Heynen Pouilly-Fuissé
Les Croux
Domaine Guffens-Heynen Pouilly-Fuissé
La Roche
Hospices de Beaune Corton-Charlemagne
Cuvée Françoise de Salins
Hospices de Beaune Meursault Les
Charmes Cuvée Albert Grivault
Hospices de Beaune Meursault Cuvée
Goureau
Hospices de Beaune Meursault Cuvée
Loppin
Hospices de Beaune Meursault Les
Genevrières Cuvée Baudot
Hospices de Beaune Meursault Les
Genevrières Cuvée Philippe Le Bon
Louis Jadot Chevalier-Montrachet Les
Demoiselles
Louis Jadot Corton-Charlemagne
Louis Jadot Le Montrachet

Domaine Patrick Javillier Meursault Les
Casse Tête
Domaine Patrick Javillier Meursault Les
Narvaux
Domaine François Jobard Meursault Les
Genevrières
Domaine Comte Lafon Meursault Les
Charmes
Domaine Comte Lafon Meursault Les
Perrières
Domaine Comte Lafon Le Montrachet
Domaine René Lamy-Pillot Le Montrachet
Louis Latour Bâtard-Montrachet
Louis Latour Chevalier-Montrachet Les
Demoiselles
Louis Latour Corton-Charlemagne
Domaine Leflaive Bâtard-Montrachet
Domaine Leflaive Chevalier-Montrachet
Domaine Leflaive Le Montrachet
Domaine Leflaive Puligny-Montrachet Les
Combettes
Domaine Leflaive Puligny-Montrachet Les
Folatières
Domaine Leflaive Puligny-Montrachet Les
Pucelles
Leroy Chevalier-Montrachet
Leroy Corton-Charlemagne
Leroy Meursault Les Narvaux
Leroy Puligny-Montrachet Les
Folatières
Domaine A. Long-Depaquit Chablis Les
Clos
Domaine A. Long-Depaquit Chablis Les
Preuses
Domaine A. Long-Depaquit Chablis
Valmur
Domaine Louis Michel et Fils Chablis Les
Clos
Domaine Louis Michel et Fils Chablis
Vaudesir
Domaine Bernard Morey
Chassagne-Montrachet Les Caillerets
Domaine Bernard Morey
Chassagne-Montrachet Les Embrazées
Domaine Michel Niellon
Bâtard-Montrachet
Domaine Michel Niellon
Chassagne-Montrachet Les Champs
Gains
Domaine Michel Niellon
Chassagne-Montrachet Clos St.-Jean

Domaine Michel Niellon
  Chassagne-Montrachet Les Vergers
Domaine Michel Niellon
  Chevalier-Montrachet
Domaine Ramonet Bâtard-Montrachet
Domaine Ramonet Chassagne-Montrachet
  Les Caillerets
Domaine Ramonet Chassagne-Montrachet
  Les Ruchottes
Domaine Ramonet Le Montrachet
Domaine François et Jean-Marie Raveneau
  Chablis Les Blanchots

Domaine François et Jean-Marie Raveneau
  Chablis Les Clos
Domaine François et Jean-Marie Raveneau
  Chablis Montée de Tonnerre
Domaine François et Jean-Marie Raveneau
  Chablis Valmur
Remoissenet Père et Fils
  Corton-Charlemagne Diamond Jubilee
Domaine de la Romanée-Conti Le
  Montrachet
Domaine Étienne Sauzet
  Bâtard-Montrachet

RATING BURGUNDY'S WHITE WINE PRODUCERS

(excluding Mâconnais wine producers)

* * * * *(OUTSTANDING)

J. F. Coche-Dury (Meursault)
Colin-Déléger (Chassagne-Montrachet)
Domaine René et Vincent Dauvissat
  (Chablis)
Domaine Comte Lafon (Meursault)
Domaine Leflaive (Puligny-Montrachet)
Leroy and Domaine d'Auvenay
  (Vosne-Romanée)

Domaine Michel Niellon
  (Chassagne-Montrachet)
Domaine Ramonet (Chassagne-Montrachet)
François et Jean-Marie Raveneau (Chablis)
Domaine de la Romanée-Conti
  (Vosne-Romanée)
Étienne Sauzet (Puligny-Montrachet)
Verget (Vergisson)

* * * *(EXCELLENT)

Amiot-Bonfils (Chassagne-Montrachet)
Domaine de l'Arlot (Prémeaux)
Francine Bachelier (Chablis)
Charles et Paul Bavard
  (Puligny-Montrachet)
Domaine Bessin (Chablis)
Pierre Bitouzet (Savigny-Les-Beaune)
Blain-Gagnard (Chassagne-Montrachet)
Jean-Marc Boillot (Pommard)
Pierre Boillot (Meursault)
Marc Colin (Chassagne-Montrachet)
Jean Collet (Chablis)
Darnat (Meursault)
Domaine Jean Dauvissat (Chablis)
Jean Defaix (Chablis)
Georges Déléger (Chassagne-Montrachet)
Joseph Drouhin (Beaune)
Domaine Gérard Duplessis (Chablis)
Domaine Fontaine-Gagnard
  (Chassagne-Montrachet)
Jean-Noël Gagnard
  (Chassagne-Montrachet)

Château Grenouille (Chablis)
Albert Grivault (Meursault)
Louis Jadot (Beaune)
Domaine Patrick Javillier
  (Meursault)****/*****
Domaine François Jobard (Meursault)
Hubert Lamy (Saint-Aubin)
P. Lamy (Charraque)
Roger Lassaret (Vergisson)
Louis Latour (Beaune)
A. Long-Depaquit (Chablis)
Domaine du Duc de Magenta
  (Chassagne-Montrachet)
Manciat-Poncet (Charnay-Les-Mâcon)
Château de Meursault (Meursault)
Domaine Louis Michel et Fils/Domaine de
  la Tour Vaubourg (Chablis)
Michelot-Buisson (Meursault)
Domaine Bernard Morey
  (Chassagne-Montrachet)
Jean-Marc Morey (Chassagne-Montrachet)
Marc Morey (Chassagne-Montrachet)

Remoissenet Père et Fils (Beaune)
Guy Robin (Chablis)
Guy Roulot (Meursault)

Château de la Saule (Montagny)
Philippe Testut (Chablis)

* * *(GOOD)

Robert Ampeau (Meursault)
Château Bader-Mimeur
  (Chassagne-Montrachet)
Ballot-Millot et Fils (Meursault)
Billaud-Simon (Chablis)***/****
Bitouzet-Prieur (Volnay)
Domaine Henri Boillot (Pommard)
Bonneau du Martray
  (Pernand-Vergelesses)
Bouchard Père et Fils (Beaune)
Domaine Michel Bouzereau (Meursault)
A. Buisson-Battault (Meursault)
Roger Caillot et Fils (Meursault)
Domaine Louis Carillon
  (Puligny-Montrachet)
La Chablisienne (Chablis)
Jean Chartron (Puligny-Montrachet)
Chartron et Trébuchet
  (Puligny-Montrachet)
Anne-Marie Chavy (Puligny-Montrachet)
Chavy-Chouet (Puligny-Montrachet)
Julien Coche-Debord (Meursault)
Cooperative La Chablisienne (Chablis)
Jean Defaix (Milly)
Jean-Paul Droin (Chablis)
Paul Droin (Chablis)
Druid Wines (Morey St.-Denis)
P. Dubreuil-Fontaine et Fils
  (Pernand-Vergelesses)
Domaine de l'Eglantière (Maligny)
Faiveley (Nuits St.-Georges)
William Fèvre/Domaine de la Maladière/
  Ancien Domaine Auffray (Chablis)
René Fleurot-Larose (Santenay)
Domaine de la Folie (Rully)
Gagnard-Delagrange
  (Chassagne-Montrachet)
Domaine Michel Gaunoux (Pommard)
Château Génot Boulanger (Meursault)
Domaine Henri Germain (Meursault)
Maison Jean Germain (Meursault)

Jean-Paul Jauffroy (Meursault)
Domaine Michel Juillot
  (Mercurey)***/****
Lafouge (Auxey-Duresses)
Domaine Laleure-Piot
  (Pernand-Vergelesses)***/****
René Lamy-Pillot (Santenay)
Laroche (Chablis)
Latour-Giraud (Meursault)
Olivier Leflaive Frères
  (Puligny-Montrachet)***/****
Lequin-Roussot (Santenay)
Château de la Maltroye
  (Chassagne-Montrachet)
Domaine Joseph Matrot (Meursault)
Michelot-Buisson (Meursault)***/****
Domaine Pierre Millot-Battault (Meursault)
J. Moreau et Fils (Chablis)
Domaine P. N.
  Ninot-Cellier-Meix-Guillaume (Rully)
Domaine Paul Pernot (Puligny-Montrachet)
Perrin-Ponsot (Meursault)
Paul Pillot (Chassagne-Montrachet)
Louis Pinson (Chablis)
Jacques Prieur (Meursault)
Prieur-Brunet (Santenay)
Domaine Henri Prudhon (Saint-Aubin)
Château de Puligny-Montrachet
  (Puligny-Montrachet)
Rapet Père et Fils (Pernand-Vergelesses)
Antonin Rodet (Mercurey)
Ropiteau Frères (Meursault)
Roux Père et Fils (Saint-Aubin)
Château de Rully (Rully)
Domaine de Rully St.-Michel (Rully)
Gérard Thomas (Saint-Aubin)
Jean Vachet (Saint-Vallerin)
Domaine de Vauroux (Chablis)
A. P. de Villaine (Bouzeron)
Robert Vocoret et Fils (Chablis)

* *(AVERAGE)

Bachelet-Ramonet (Chassagne-Montrachet)
Blondeau-Danne (Meursault)
Guy Bocard (Meursault)

Boisson-Vadot (Meursault)
Boyer-Martenot (Meursault)
Bressand (Pouilly-Fuissé)

Xavier Bouzerand (Monthélie)
Hubert Bouzereau-Gruère (Meursault)
Chanzy Frères-Domaine de l'Hermitage
   (Bouzeron)
Chevalier Père et Fils (Buisson)
Chouet-Clivet (Meursault)
Henri Clerc et Fils (Puligny-Montrachet)
Michel Dupont-Fahn (Meursault)
Gabriel Fournier (Meursault)
Domaine l'Heritier-Guyot (Dijon)
Lamblin et Fils (Maligny)
Domaine des Malandes (Chablis)
Maroslavac-Léger (Chassagne-Montrachet)
M. Millet (Montagny)
Raymond Millot et Fils (Meursault)
René Monnier (Meursault)
Henri Morconi (Puligny-Montrachet)

Bernard Moreau
   (Chassagne-Montrachet)
Domaine Pierre Morey (Meursault)
Mosnier-Sylvain (Chablis)
Jean Pascal et Fils (Puligny-Montrachet)
Baron Patrick (Chablis)
Michel Pouhin-Seurre (Meursault)
Prosper Maufoux (Santenay)
A. Regnard et Fils (Chablis)
La Reine Pedauque (Aloxe-Corton)
Riger-Briset (Puligny-Montrachet)
Domaine Maurice Rollin Père et Fils
   (Pernand-Vergelesses)
Simonnet-Febvre et Fils (Chablis)
Jacques Thevenet-Machal
   (Puligny-Montrachet)
Domaine Tribut (Chablis)

WHERE ARE BURGUNDY'S WHITE WINE VALUES?

Jean-Claude Bachelet Saint-Aubin Les
   Champlots
Michel Briday Rully-Grésigny
Château de Chamirey Mercurey
Charton et Trébuchet Rully Chaume
Charton et Trébuchet Saint-Aubin
Charton et Trébuchet Saint-Aubin La
   Chatenière
Raoul Clerget Saint-Aubin
   Le Charmois
Marc Colin Saint-Aubin La Chatenière
Joseph Drouhin Mâcon La Forêt
Joseph Drouhin Rully
Faiveley Bourgogne
Faiveley Mercurey Clos Rochette
Domaine de la Folie Rully Clos de
   Bellecroix
Domaine de la Folie Rully Clos
   St.-Jacques
Jean Germain St.-Romaine Clos Sous Le
   Château
Alain Gras St.-Romaine
Jacqueson Rully-Grésigny
Louis Jadot Bourgogne Blanc
Robert Jayer-Gilles Bourgogne Hautes
   Côtes de Beaune

Robert Jayer-Gilles Bourgogne Hautes
   Côtes de Nuits
Michel Juillot Mercurey
Louis Latour Mâcon Lugny
Louis Latour Montagny
Louis Latour Saint-Véran
Lequin-Roussot Santenay Premier Cru
Moillard Montagny Premier Cru
Bernard Morey Saint-Aubin
Jean-Marc Morey Saint-Aubin Le
   Charmois
Prieur-Brunet Santenay-Clos Rousseau
Henri Prudhon Saint-Aubin
Antonin Rodet Bourgogne Blanc
Antonin Rodet Montagny
Château de Rully Rully
Domaine de Rully St.-Michel Rully Les
   Cloux
Domaine de Rully St.-Michel Rully
   Rabourcé
Château de la Saule Montagny
Gérard Thomas Saint-Aubin Murgers des
   Dents de Chien
Jean Vachet Montagny Les Coeres
Aubert de Villaine Bourgogne Aligoté
Aubert de Villaine Bourgogne Le Clous

AND DON'T FORGET . . .
Virtually all of the best producers of inexpensive Chardonnay from the vast region known
as the Mâconnais are rated in subsequent pages, but the wines that come from this huge

region, particularly the Mâcon-Villages wines (made from Chardonnay), can be super bargains. At their best they offer wonderfully fresh aromas and flavors of apples and lemony fruit.

RATING THE MÂCONNAIS WHITE WINE PRODUCERS

(Mâcon-Villages, Saint-Véran, Pouilly-Fuissé, Pouilly-Loché, and Beaujolais Blanc)

* * * * *(OUTSTANDING)

Domaine de la Bongrand (Jean Thevenet) Mâcon-Clessé

André Bonhomme Mâcon-Villages

Domaine J. A. Ferret Pouilly-Fuissé

Château Fuissé Pouilly-Fuissé Cuvée Vieilles Vignes

Emilian Gillet Mâcon-Viré

Guffens-Heynen Pouilly-Fuissé Clos des Petits Croux

Guffens-Heynen Pouilly-Fuissé Les Croux

Guffens-Heynen Pouilly-Fuissé La Roche

Olivier Merlin Mâcon La Roche

Jean-Claude Thevenet Saint-Véran Clos de l'Hermitage

Domaine Valette Mâcon-Chaintré Vieilles Vignes

Domaine Valette Pouilly-Fuissé Clos Reyssié

Verget—*négociant* brand for Guffens-Heynen (Vergisson)

Domaine du Vieux St.-Sorlin Mâcon La Roche Vineuse

* * * *(EXCELLENT)

Auvigue-Burrier-Revel Mâcon-Villages

Auvigue-Burrier-Revel Pouilly-Fuissé Vieilles Vignes

Daniel Barraud Mâcon-Vergisson La Roche

Daniel Barraud Pouilly-Fuissé Cuvée Vieilles Vignes

Daniel Barraud Pouilly-Fuissé La Verchère

Château de Beauregard Pouilly-Fuissé

Domaine de Chazelle Viré

Domaine Chenevière Mâcon-Villages

Domaine Corsin Pouilly-Fuissé

André Forest Pouilly-Fuissé Cuvée Vieilles Vignes

Château Fuissé Pouilly-Fuissé

Domaine des Granges (J. F. Cognard) Mâcon-Villages

Château de la Greffière Mâcon La Roche Vineuse Vieilles Vignes

Thierry Guérin Pouilly-Fuissé Clos de France

Guffens-Heynen Mâcon-Villages

Louis Jadot Mâcon-Villages

Domaine Henri Lafarge Mâcon-Bray

Roger Lasserat Pouilly-Fuissé

Roger Lasserat Pouilly-Fuissé Clos de France

Roger Lasserat Pouilly-Fuissé Cuvée Prestige

Roger Lasserat Saint-Véran Cuvée Prestige

Roger Lasserat Saint-Véran Fournaise

Louis Latour Mâcon-Lugny Les Genevrières

Château de Leynes Saint-Véran

Manciat-Poncet Mâcon-Villages

Manciat-Poncet Pouilly-Fuissé

René Michel Mâcon-Villages

Gilles Noblet Pouilly-Fuissé

Domaine de Roally Mâcon-Viré

Robert-Denogent Pouilly-Fuissé Cuvées

Domaine Talmard Mâcon-Villages

Domaine des Vieilles Pierres Mâcon-Vergisson

* * *(GOOD)

Château de Beauregard Saint-Véran

André Besson Saint-Véran

Domaine de Chervin (Albert Goyard) Mâcon-Villages

Cooperative Clessé Mâcon-Clessé

Cooperative Igé Mâcon-Igé

Cooperative Lugny Mâcon-Lugny

Cooperative Prissé Mâcon-Prissé

Cooperative Viré Mâcon-Viré

Alain Corcia Collection

Corsin Pouilly-Fuissé

Corsin Saint-Véran

Louis Curvieux Pouilly-Fuissé

Joseph Drouhin Mâcon-Villages La Forêt

Georges Duboeuf Beaujolais Blanc

Georges Duboeuf Mâcon-Villages

Georges Duboeuf Saint-Véran

Château Fuissé Saint-Véran

Domaine de la Greffière (Henri Greuzard)
   Mâcon-Villages

Henry-Lucius Grégoire Saint-Véran

Thierry Guérin Saint-Véran

Louis Jadot Beaujolais Blanc

Louis Jadot Pouilly-Fuissé

Edmond Laneyrie Pouilly-Fuissé

Louis Latour Pouilly-Fuissé

Bernard Léger-Plumet Pouilly-Fuissé

Bernard Léger-Plumet Saint-Véran

Jean-Jacques Litaud Pouilly-Fuissé

Loron et Fils Mâcon-Villages

Roger Luquet Pouilly-Fuissé

Roger Luquet Saint-Véran

Domaine de la Maison (Georges Chagny)
   Saint-Véran

Jean Manciat Mâcon-Villages

Maurice Martin Saint-Véran

Mathias Pouilly-Fuissé

Domaine de Montbellet Mâcon-Villages

Perrusset Mâcon-Farges

Domaine des Pierres Rouge Saint-Véran

Domaine du Prieuré (Pierre Janny)
   Mâcon-Villages

Domaine Saint-Martine Saint-Véran

Domaine Seve Pouilly-Fuissé

Jacques Sumaize Saint-Véran

Roger Sumaize Pouilly-Fuissé

Trenel Fils Mâcon-Villages

Trenel Fils Pouilly-Fuissé

AMIOT-BONFILS (CHASSAGNE-MONTRACHET)* * * *

1992 **Bourgogne Blanc Chardonnay**	C	87
1992 **Chassagne-Montrachet Les Caillerets**	E	93
1992 **Chassagne-Montrachet Clos St.-Jean**	E	92
1992 **Chassagne-Montrachet Les Vergers**	E	90
1992 **Le Montrachet**	EEE	98
1992 **Puligny-Montrachet Les Demoiselles**	E	93

Since 1989 the Domaine Amiot-Bonfils has catapulted to the top echelon of quality. This estate produced excellent, even stunning 1989s, excellent 1990s, and sensational 1992s.

Amiot has fashioned an attractive, medium- to full-bodied, ripe, fruity, mouth-filling 1992 Bourgogne Blanc Chardonnay. Drink it over the next 1–2 years. The 1992 Chassagne-Montrachet Les Vergers is the most tightly knit and backward of Amiot's three premier cru Chassagnes. It possesses higher acidity than the other two wines, but shares with them the same power, richness, and intensity. It needs another year in the bottle, after which it should keep for 7–10 more. While impressively endowed, it is not as flattering and dramatic as the Clos St.-Jean and Les Caillerets. Both the 1992 Chassagne-Montrachet Clos St.-Jean and the 1992 Chassagne-Montrachet Les Caillerets are superrich, blockbuster white burgundies. The Clos St.-Jean is more elegant, with a mineral-scented component to its tropical fruit–scented richness. Full bodied, with low acidity and layers of flavor, this compelling wine should reach maturity in 1–2 years and last for up to a decade. Les Caillerets is an exceptional wine in every respect. From its perfume of smoky, toasty new oak and honeyed melons and pineapples, to its lavishly rich flavors with explosive ripeness and extraction, this deep, full-bodied, majestic white burgundy should be at its best between 1994 and 2003. It is a remarkably rich and well-defined wine.

In 1992, Amiot bottled his Puligny-Montrachet Les Demoiselles and Le Montrachet without filtration. To bottle a white burgundy without filtration means that the malolactic must be completely finished, and there must be no residual sugar in the wine. It is commendable to see increasing numbers of Burgundy producers returning to their grandfathers' style of winemaking. By so doing, they are not cheating the consumer of any of the vineyard's flavors. The exquisite 1992 Puligny-Montrachet Les Demoiselles does not possess the power and unctuosity of the Chassagne-Montrachet Clos St.-Jean or Les Caillerets, but it does offer extraordinary finesse allied with considerable richness. The profound bouquet of oranges, coconuts, flowers, lemons, and minerals is superb. There is exquisite richness, impeccable balance, and harmony. This dazzling 1992 white burgundy exhibits low acidity, as well as magnificent flavor definition and length. Drink it over the next 10 years. The 1992 Le Montrachet is one of the candidates for the best Le Montrachet of the vintage. Also bottled unfiltered, it is more open-knit and flattering to taste than many Le Montrachets are at such a young age. But wow, what extraordinary power, richness, unctuosity, and length! Honeyed, wheat cracker, apple blossom, and mineral scents are followed by exceptionally deep, precise flavors. This mammoth yet astonishingly well-balanced wine should drink well for the next 15 or more years.

AUVIGUE-BURRIER-REVEL (POUILLY)* * * *

1992 Pouilly-Fuissé Vieilles Vignes	C	88

This top cuvée of unfined, unfiltered, barrel-fermented Pouilly-Fuissé is made from low-yielding, old vines. It exhibits a rich, intense bouquet of ripe apple fruit and flowers. Full bodied, with excellent purity and richness, as well as a lively, zesty feel in the mouth, this attractive, multidimensional Pouilly-Fuissé should drink well over the next 1–2 years.

FRANCINE BACHELIER (CHABLIS)* * * *

1992 Chablis Vieilles Vignes	C	90

If memory serves, I do not think I have given a regular cuvée of Chablis as high a score as this offering from Francine Bachelier. This young producer, who ferments half her wine in new oak and the other half in stainless steel, has fashioned a Chablis of extraordinary precision, great focus and concentration, and superb richness and character. This is what great Chablis should taste like, but so rarely does, as most producers aim for a muscular style, trying to emulate a big premier or grand cru from the Côte d'Or. This Chablis possesses exceptional flavor, intensity, and power, yet it is crisp, light, and fresh, making it one delicious glass of wine to savor. Drink it over the next several years.

BALLOT-MILLOT ET FILS (MEURSAULT)* * *

1991 Meursault	D	78
1992 Meursault Les Genevrières	D	75

Neither of these wines performed well, being uncommonly light and high in acidity. Are they the products of overcropping? Perhaps there is more than my notes suggest, but I could not find much depth no matter how hard I looked.

DANIEL BARRAUD (POUILLY-FUISSÉ)* * * *

1993 Pouilly-Fuissé La Roche	D	90
1992 Pouilly-Fuissé La Roche	D	87
1993 Pouilly-Fuissé La Verchère	C	90
1992 Pouilly-Fuissé La Verchère	D	86
1993 Pouilly-Fuissé Vieilles Vignes	D	90
1992 Pouilly-Fuissé Vieilles Vignes	D	89
1991 Pouilly-Fuissé Vieilles Vignes	D	90
1993 Saint-Véran en Crèches	B	87

One of the up-and-coming producers in the Mâconnais, Daniel Barraud is a member of the younger generation committed to quality, and in 1992 he decided to bottle all of his white wines unfiltered. The above scores may be conservative, since the 1992s had just been bottled. The 1992 Pouilly-Fuissé La Verchère displays excellent richness, crisp, underlying tartness that gives the wine definition, and rich, buttery, ripe applelike fruit. It should drink well for another 4–5 years. The slightly longer, richer, more backward 1992 Pouilly-Fuissé La Roche is in need of 4–6 months of bottle age. This impressively pure, well-structured wine should last for 4–8 years. The 1992 Pouilly-Fuissé Vieilles Vignes exhibits huge body, stunning depth, a honeyed, apple butter–scented nose, rich, medium- to full-bodied flavors that display a judicious use of toasty new oak, adequate acidity, and a lusty finish.

The 1991 Pouilly-Fuissé Vieilles Vignes is drinking beautifully, with superb extraction of flavor, an excellent nose of butter, honey, and grilled nuts, superb stuffing, low acidity, and a lusciously rich, intense finish. Drink it over the next 2–3 years.

As readers will discover while tasting through the 1993 white burgundies, especially those from the renowned Côte d'Or, it is largely a mediocre vintage with surprisingly hollow, high-acid wines. But the finest producers should not be judged by vintage assessments.

For value, the 1993 St.-Véran en Crèches offers plenty of substance, an excellent, citrusy, fruity nose, medium body, fine ripeness, and a crisp, fresh, lively finish. Drink it over the next 1–3 years.

The three Pouilly-Fuissé cuvées are outstanding wines. The full-bodied 1993 Pouilly-Fuissé La Verchère offers great fruit and purity, wonderful ripeness, and a multidimensional personality. The 1993 Pouilly-Fuissé La Roche is more tightly structured and reserved, but its finish is even longer. My instincts suggest it is also more intense. As expected, the 1993 Pouilly-Fuissé Vieilles Vignes exhibits the most honeyed, concentrated, old-vine character. A luxury cuvée fashioned from the best barrels of the two single-vineyard Pouilly-Fuissés, it is the most tightly knit and promising of these three offerings. All of these wines should be drunk in their first 5–6 years of life.

DOMAINE BESSIN (CHABLIS)* * * *

1992 Chablis	C	88
1992 Chablis Fourchaume	C	90
1992 Chablis Valmur	D	92

How delightful it is to see Chablis of this quality. Even the generic 1992 Chablis is excellent. It represents exactly what Chablis is all about—a wine with refreshing acidity, wonderful steely, mineral-dominated, crisp fruit, fine precision, and a long, zesty, tangy finish. Drink it over the next 1–2 years. The premier cru, the 1992 Chablis Fourchaume, exhibits superb fruit and purity, medium to full body, an underlying mineral, flinty component, and outstanding concentration. The same can be said for the grand cru, the 1992 Chablis Valmur. This wine combines exceptional opulence and rich, full-bodied concentration with a profound sense of the gunflint, earthy, stony character that sets Chablis apart from the wines produced further south in the Côte d'Or. This terrific grand cru Chablis should drink well for 5–6 years. These are all reassuringly top-notch Chablis that are faithful to their viticultural region and, thankfully, have not been overly oaked.

BILLAUD-SIMON (CHABLIS)* * */* * * *

1992 Chablis Les Clos	D	90
1992 Chablis Mont de Milieu	D	90
1992 Chablis Mont de Milieu Vieilles Vignes	D	92
1992 Chablis Montée de Tonnerre	D	89

These are terrific offerings from Billaud-Simon. The tank-fermented 1992 Chablis Montée de Tonnerre displays wonderful, vibrant Chardonnay fruit intertwined with scents of minerals and apple blossoms. With superb ripeness and purity, this excellent, rich, medium-bodied wine is an example of Chablis at its best. Drink it over the next 5–7 years. The 1992 Chablis Mont de Milieu's citrusy, pineapple-scented nose is followed by a lively, pure wine with layers of fruit. Ripe, long, crisp, and refreshing, this is an intensely flavored yet vivacious Chablis for drinking over the next 7–8 years.

The 1992 Chablis Mont de Milieu Vieilles Vignes reveals evidence of toasty new oak aging as a vanillin component makes its presence known in the sweet, expansive, ripe nose. The wine possesses outstanding ripeness, the sweetness that comes from low yields rather than from sugar, and a long, full-bodied, lovely finish. This superb Chablis should drink well for 7–8 years. Lastly, the full-bodied, muscular 1992 Chablis Les Clos exhibits a pronounced earthy, mineral component, as well as fine ripeness, and plenty of depth and power. It is the most backward and unevolved of these offerings. These are impressive wines from an outstanding vintage for white burgundy.

PIERRE BITOUZET (SAVIGNY-LES-BEAUNE)* * * *

1992 Corton-Charlemagne	E	89
1992 Savigny-Les-Beaune Les Goudelettes	D	87

One of the sleeper wine bargains among high-quality white burgundies is Bitouzet's consistently fine Savigny-Les-Beaune Les Goudelettes. The 1992 displays excellent richness, toasty, vanillin oak, admirable definition, and rich, medium- to full-bodied flavors. For a Savigny it is uncommonly big, bold, and dramatic. Drink it over the next 3–4 years. While the 1992 Corton-Charlemagne is rich and medium to full bodied, it is softer than normal. It offers fine richness and body, as well as a sweet, round finish. Drink it over the next 6–7 years.

BITOUZET-PRIEUR (VOLNAY)* * *

1992 Meursault Clos du Cromin	D	88
1992 Meursault Les Corbins	D	85
1992 Meursault Les Perrières	D	87+
1992 Meursault Les Santenots	D	88

Although Bitouzet's wines start off life slowly, they have proven to be age-worthy. The tight 1992s reveal elegance, rich, ripe fruit, and crisp acidity. The 1992 Meursault Les Corbins is the lightest and most delicate. The richest are the 1992 Meursault Clos du Cromin and 1992 Meursault Les Santenots. The Clos du Cromin exhibits an attractive, mineral nose scented with hazelnuts and tropical fruit, fine definition, medium to full body, and long, rich flavors that possess crisp acidity. Les Santenots displays more spice and earthiness, as well as a heavy, dense, concentrated feel and fine underlying acidity. The 1992 Meursault Les Perrières is the most backward wine in this quartet. Made from the youngest vines, it possesses the highest acidity, some leanness, and plenty of underlying fruit, body, and character. All of these wines will benefit from another 1–2 years of bottle age; they should last for 7–8 years.

DOMAINE HENRI BOILLOT (POMMARD)* * *

1992 Meursault Les Genevrières	E	87
1992 Puligny-Montrachet	D	84
1992 Puligny-Montrachet Clos de la Mouchere	E	85
1992 Puligny-Montrachet Les Pucelles	E	85

Jean Boillot believes in relatively early harvesting, aiming for crisp, elegant, fruity wines. Consequently, these wines do not possess the depth and intensity of most 1992s. They are stylish, light- to medium-bodied white burgundies, with fine purity and freshness. The richest of this quartet is the 1992 Meursault Les Genevrières. They should all be drunk over the next 4–5 years.

JEAN-MARC BOILLOT (POMMARD)* * * *

1992 Bâtard-Montrachet	EE	93
1992 Puligny-Montrachet	D	85
1992 Puligny-Montrachet Les Champs Canets	D	91
1992 Puligny-Montrachet Les Combettes	E	91
1992 Puligny-Montrachet Les Referts	D	88
1992 Puligny-Montrachet La Truffière	D	89

Jean-Marc Boillot has become an important domaine for white-burgundy enthusiasts as the vineyards formerly leased to Domaine Sauzet have reverted back to Boillot's control. The 1992s are the best wines I have tasted from Jean-Marc—rich, authoritatively flavored, luscious white burgundies for drinking over the next 5–6 years.

The 1992 Puligny-Montrachet exhibits gobs of tropical fruit (pineapples, tangerines) in its nose, rich, soft, medium-bodied flavors, and a ripe, pure, long finish. Drink it over the next 3 years. The 1992 Puligny-Montrachet Les Referts displays mineral, floral, and honeysuckle scents, rich, medium-bodied, fleshy, low-acid flavors, and copious amounts of alcohol and fruit in the finish. It should be consumed over the next 3 years. The superb 1992 Puligny-Montrachet Les Champs Canets reveals great fruit in a bouquet that zooms from the glass, offering ripe aromas of cherries, oranges, and honey. Opulent and full bodied, with layers of fruit and good acidity for focus, this is a powerful, lusty Puligny for drinking over the next 4–5 years. The same can be said for the 1992 Puligny-Montrachet La Truffière. It boasts a honeyed character in its bouquet, medium body, excellent extraction of fruit, soft, low acidity, and plenty of powerful alcohol and extract in the finish. Drink this decadent white burgundy over the next 4–5 years. The 1992 Puligny-Montrachet Les Combettes is a wine for hedonists. The huge nose of butter-coated nuts, honeyed melons, oranges, apples, and new oak is dramatic. The wine reveals an unctuous texture, low acidity, fat, ripe, superconcentrated flavors, and an explosively long finish. Its low acidity suggests it should be drunk over the next 5 years.

Boillot's 1992 Bâtard-Montrachet exhibits a huge nose of honeyed fruit and a long, glycerin-dominated, alcoholic yet superrich finish. With sensational depth, as well as tremendously fat, thick, ripe flavors, and low acidity, tasting it is like tasting a big, juicy, buttery piece of candy. It should keep for 4–5 years.

ANDRÉ BONHOMME (MÂCON)* * * * *

1992 Mâcon-Viré Cuvée Spéciale	C	89

Shrewd consumers should be scarfing up top Mâcons from the likes of Jean Thevenet (Domaine de Bongrand and Emilian Gillet), Jean-Claude Thevenet (Domaine du Vieux St.-Sorlin), Guffens-Heynen, and, of course, this Mâcon superstar, André Bonhomme. I realize these wines do not possess the weight of a Louis Latour Bâtard-Montrachet or the extraordinary richness of a Coche-Dury Corton-Charlemagne, but for less than $20 a bottle, the wines from the aforementioned Mâcon producers are knockout values in Chardonnay that rival all but a handful of the Côte d'Or's greatest producers. André Bonhomme's 1992 Mâcon-Viré Cuvée Spéciale is an explosively rich, ripe, fruity wine. Although 20%–25% of the wine was aged in small oak barrels, it reveals no evidence of wood because of its opulent, honeyed fruitiness. Wonderfully pure, vibrant, and exuberant, this Chardonnay goes down the gullet far too easily for its hefty alcohol level. Drink it over the next 2–3 years.

BOUCHARD PÈRE ET FILS (BEAUNE)* * *

1992	Bâtard-Montrachet	E	90
1992	Beaune Clos St.-Landry	D	87
1992	Bourgogne-Chardonnay La Vignée	C	86
1992	Chevalier-Montrachet	EE	90+
1992	Corton-Charlemagne	EE	87
1992	Meursault	D	83
1992	Meursault Blagny Sous Le Dos D'Ane	D	88
1992	Meursault Les Genevrières	D	88
1992	Le Montrachet	EEE	94
1992	Puligny-Montrachet Les Chalumeaux	D	86
1992	Puligny-Montrachet Les Champs Gains	E	85
1992	Puligny-Montrachet Les Folatières	E	87
1992	Puligny-Montrachet Les Pucelles	E	86

The Bouchards have made significant changes in their white wine–making philosophy. Since 1989 the white wines have been put through malolactic fermentation and been vinified in barrels, of which 15% are new. More extensive lees contact, lower vineyard yields, and less traumatic clarification and filtration techniques have resulted in the best group of white wines Bouchard has produced in over two decades.

The overall quality level in 1992 is good to very good. The excellent 1992 Bourgogne-Chardonnay La Vignée exhibits ripe fruit, fine suppleness, and an easygoing personality. The elegant 1992 Meursault is less fruity, but well made and crisp in an understated style. The excellent 1992 Beaune Clos St.-Landry offers a rich, honeysuckle-scented nose, lovely ripe apple and buttery flavors with fine acidity, and a rich, medium-bodied finish. The 1992 Meursault Les Genevrières is fatter, but not overbearing, with excellent ripeness and acidity, as well as a long, lusty, full-bodied finish. It admirably combines power with finesse. The similarly styled 1992 Meursault Blagny Sous Le Dos d'Ane displays wonderful sweetness and ripeness, and a multidimensional personality. Although fat, it is buttressed by adequate acidity.

The 1992 Puligny-Montrachet Les Chalumeaux is medium weight, soft, ripe, and elegant. It lacks the intensity and flavor depth of the two Meursaults. While good, the 1992 Puligny-Montrachet Les Champs Gains is restrained and terribly polite and subtle. Nevertheless, it reveals good fruit and balance. Much better is the 1992 Puligny-Montrachet Les Folatières. It is a rich, ripe, medium- to full-bodied wine with excellent depth of fruit and a crisp finish. The 1992 Puligny-Montrachet Les Pucelles falls between the understated, restrained style of Les Champs Gains and the extroverted, fatter, richer style of Les Folatières. Like all of these premiers crus, as well as the Bourgogne-Chardonnay and village Meursault, Les Pucelles should be drunk over the next 6–8 years.

Bouchard's grands crus include a ripe, medium- to full-bodied, soft 1992 Corton-Charlemagne. While fragrant, it lacks the depth and intensity of a grand cru. No such complaints can be lodged against the 1992 Bâtard-Montrachet or the 1992 Chevalier-Montrachet. Unfortunately, only 35 cases of the 1992 Bâtard-Montrachet were produced. It is a rich, deep, unctuously textured, full-bodied wine with excellent purity, superb richness of fruit, and deep, full-bodied flavors. Drink it over the next decade. The 1992 Chevalier-Montrachet is backward, dense, unevolved, and needing at least 3–4 years of bottle age; it should keep for at least a decade. Bouchard's 1992 Le Montrachet is the finest wine the Bouchards have produced from this vineyard in over 20 years. They crop-thinned to keep yields down and the result is a superb, rich, full-bodied, intense wine displaying an under-current of minerals and flint. There is magnificent richness to the wine's fruit, a voluptuous texture, decent acidity, and a blockbuster finish. Drink it between 1996 and 2010.

DOMAINE MICHEL BOUZEREAU (MEURSAULT)* * *

1992 Bourgogne-Chardonnay	C	85
1992 Meursault Les Genevrières	D	88
1992 Puligny-Montrachet Les Champs Gains	D	88

This producer has made noteworthy strides in quality as evidenced by the three 1992s I was able to taste. A solid, chunky, fleshy, medium-bodied 1992 Bourgogne-Chardonnay should be drunk over the next year. There is a beautifully elegant, rich, medium- to full-bodied, expansively flavored, supple, chewy 1992 Meursault Les Genevrières, and an oaky, buttery, honey-scented, dense, full-bodied 1992 Puligny-Montrachet Les Champs Gains. The acids are sound and the concentration excellent in these wines. They should have no problem lasting, perhaps even improving, for the next 5–7 years.

BOYER-MARTENOT (MEURSAULT)* *

1991 Meursault Les Narvaux	D	85
1991 Meursault l'Ormeau	D	87
1991 Meursault Les Perrières	E	82

I have been unimpressed with these wines in the past, but Boyer has lowered his yields, put most of the wines in the bottle unfiltered, and increased the amount of new oak used to one-third. The best of this group is the least expensive wine, the 1991 Meursault l'Ormeau, made from grapes harvested before the rainy deluge of 1991. It is a big, rich wine, with a nose of toasty, ripe, pineapple, and buttery fruit, medium body, impressive richness, and a lovely, long, well-defined finish. Drink it over the next 3–4 years. The lighter 1991 Meursault Les Narvaux is elegant, ripe, and pleasant. The 1991 Meursault Les Perrières is reserved and tightly knit, with promising aromas in the bouquet, but not enough stuffing and richness in the flavors or finish. Drink it over the next 3–4 years.

DOMAINE LOUIS CARILLON (PULIGNY-MONTRACHET)* * *

1992 Bienvenue-Bâtard-Montrachet	EE	91
1992 Puligny-Montrachet	D	88
1992 Puligny-Montrachet Les Champs Canets	D	90
1992 Puligny-Montrachet Les Perrières	D	91

In 1992, Jacques and François Carillon have fashioned the finest white wines I have tasted from this domaine. While there has been an upward progression in quality since the mid-eighties, the 1992s exceed anything the Carillons have produced in over 20 years. The 1992 Puligny-Montrachet is a knockout wine for its appellation. Its wonderfully sweet, honeyed perfume is followed by an unctuous, thick, rich, medium- to full-bodied wine with loads of fruit, and enough acidity for focus and uplift. Drink it over the next 3–4 years.

The other three offerings are all outstanding. The buttery, fragrant, richly fruity, medium- to full-bodied, soft, luscious 1992 Puligny-Montrachet Les Champs Canets is not to be missed. It offers a seductive, rich mouthful of Chardonnay for drinking over the next 4–5 years. If you are looking for more mineral scents, a flinty, cold steel–like bouquet, and more structure, check out Carillon's 1992 Puligny-Montrachet Les Perrières. Rich, full bodied, and deep, with layers of flavor, as well as more precision and finesse, this superb white burgundy could easily pass for a grand cru. It should drink well for the next 7–9 years. I am often underwhelmed by the wines from the grand cru Bienvenue-Bâtard-Montrachet. While they are a grand cru in price, they rarely rival a great Bâtard-Montrachet or Chevalier-Montrachet. Carillon's 1992 is the real thing. The wine exhibits a huge nose of coconuts, orange marmalade, sweet toasty new oak, and butter. Rich and full bodied, with tremendous precision, this backward, exceptionally well balanced wine offers fine integrated acidity for the vintage. Approachable now, it promises to improve for at least 2–3 more years and last for a decade.

CHARTRON ET TRÉBUCHET (PULIGNY-MONTRACHET)* * *

1992	Chassagne-Montrachet Les Morgeot	D	84
1992	Meursault	C	77
1992	Pernand-Vergelesses	C	82
1992	Pouilly-Fuissé	C	81
1992	Puligny-Montrachet	D	86
1992	Puligny-Montrachet Clos du Cailleret	D	86
1992	Puligny-Montrachet Clos des Pucelles	D	?
1992	Saint-Aubin La Chatenière	C	87
1992	Saint-Romain	C	86

In nearly every vintage, Chartron et Trébuchet's Saint-Aubin La Chatenière is better than most of the other wines. The 1992 is the pick of this generally uninspiring lineup of *négociant* wines. La Chatenière is not only a great bargain, but a wonderfully rich, medium- to full-bodied wine loaded with mineral-tinged, honeyed, applelike fruit, lusciously rich, chewy flavors, and a long finish. Another good value is the 1992 Saint-Romain, a stony, mineral-scented, medium-bodied wine with fine character and ripe fruit. Both the Saint-Romain and the Saint-Aubin should be drunk over the next 2–3 years.

The 1992 Pouilly-Fuissé is light and diluted; the 1992 Pernand-Vergelesses is chunky and straightforward; the 1992 Meursault is short, watery, and inexcusably thin; and the 1992 Chassagne-Montrachet Les Morgeot is diluted. I did like the well-made, ripe, rich, creamy-textured 1992 Puligny-Montrachet. I am sure I had a bad bottle of the 1992 Puligny-Montrachet Clos des Pucelles, as it was oxidized and undrinkable. Judgment reserved. The 1992 Puligny-Montrachet Clos du Cailleret is good, but given how well Jean Chartron's neighbors did with this great vineyard, it should have been superb. On a positive note, prices are as low as I have seen them from this firm.

CHAVY-CHOUET (PULIGNY-MONTRACHET)* * *

1992	Bourgogne Blanc	C	81
1992	Meursault Les Casse Tête Vieilles Vignes	D	86
1992	Meursault Les Grands Charrons Vieilles Vignes	D	88
1992	Meursault Les Narvaux Vieilles Vignes	D	86
1992	Puligny-Montrachet Les Enseigneres	D	87

These barrel-fermented 1992s are all good, if unexciting. Proprietor Hubert Chavy is beginning to lower his yields and augment the percentage of new oak. Although short, the 1992 Bourgogne Blanc is light, crisp, medium bodied, and pleasant. The 1992 Puligny-Montrachet Les Enseigneres offers a sweet, smoky vanillin scent, ripe, round, generous flavors, low acidity, and a plump, heady, alcoholic finish. Drink it over the next 4–5 years.

The 1992 Meursault Les Narvaux Vieilles Vignes exhibits fine underlying acidity, a moderately intense, buttery, nutty-scented nose, medium body, good ripeness, fine definition, but only average length. Drink it over the next 3–4 years. The 1992 Meursault Les Casse Tête Vieilles Vignes possesses high acidity, as well as fine richness, medium to full body, a buttery, toasty-scented nose, and a shorter finish than I would have hoped. The best of the Chavy-Chouet wines is the 1992 Meursault Les Grands Charrons Vieilles Vignes. It offers an alluring nose of sweet, creamy, buttery apples and toasty, smoky new oak. Rich, ripe, medium to full bodied, with excellent extraction of fruit, decent acidity, and a spicy, long finish, it should be drunk over the next 4–5 years.

J. F. COCHE-DURY (MEURSAULT)* * * * *

1992	Bourgogne Blanc	C	87
1992	Corton-Charlemagne	EEE	95
1991	Corton-Charlemagne	EEE	90
1991	Meursault	D	86
1992	Meursault Les Chevalières	E	88
1992	Meursault Les Luchets	E	88
1992	Meursault Les Narvaux	E	87
1992	Meursault Les Perrières	E	92
1991	Meursault Les Perrières	E	90
1992	Meursault Rougeot	E	91
1991	Meursault Rougeot	E	89
1992	Meursault Les Vireuils	E	88

Coche-Dury continues to be one of our planet's finest winemakers. It is hard to believe that his first vintage was 1976 and he now has 18 years of experience. There has been a succession of mind-boggling wines from this domaine and the microquantities available are difficult to find. Coche, the ultimate no-nonsense producer, smiles when the visitor's appointment is over. This is a man who subscribes to the theory that 90 percent of the quality of the wine is determined in the vineyard, and that is the place he prefers to be.

Although Coche admits to harvesting too late in 1991, his wines are excellent, with several exceptions. The 1991 Meursault possesses plenty of fat and ripeness, as well as the lovely mineral, smoky, nutty, creamy fruit Coche routinely obtains. Its low acidity makes it a wine to drink over the next several years. The 1991 Meursault Rougeot is deep and rich, with a sweet, creamy mid-palate, and long, lusty, low-acid, thick, unctuous flavors. It is fragile and thus should be consumed over the next 2–3 years. The exceptional 1991 Meursault Les Perrières, which Coche feels is too supple, offers a nose of buttery overtones intermixed with aromas of vanillin, smoked nuts, and coconut. Rich and medium to full bodied, with gobs of juicy, succulent, lush fruit, this precocious Les Perrières should be consumed over the next 3–4 years.

The 1991 Corton-Charlemagne is fat, opulent, and full bodied, with laudable intensity, low acid, and copious amounts of glycerin and fruit. While Coche may lament the fact that these wines do not possess structure and acidity for longevity, they are decadent, rich, lusty white burgundies.

In 1992, Coche's yields were higher than he would have liked. For value-conscious consumers, there is an attractive mineral- and floral-scented, ripe, medium- to full-bodied 1992 Bourgogne Blanc that should drink well for another 3–4 years.

For the first time Coche will be offering some of his Meursaults with their vineyard name, rather than blending them together into a village Meursault. There are six separate single-vineyard Meursault cuvées. The lightest are the 1992 Meursault Les Luchets and 1992 Meursault Les Vireuils. Both are rich, stylish, medium- to full-bodied wines, with gorgeous aromas of tropical fruits, spicy new oak, and nuts. Les Luchets is more stylish, elegant, and lighter, and Les Vireuils is deeper, more powerful, unctuous, and thick. Coche's 1992 Meursault Les Narvaux offers an interesting contrast with his Meursault Les Chevalières and Meursault Rougeot. Les Narvaux is elegant and streamlined by Coche's standards, with higher acidity, and a crisp, medium-bodied finish. It is one of the most restrained and understated wines I have ever tasted from Coche. Both the 1992 Meursault Les Chevalières and 1992 Meursault Rougeot are forceful, dramatic, flamboyant wines loaded with honeyed, hazelnut-scented fruit, full body, unctuously thick, rich textures, low acidity, and plenty of power, alcohol, glycerin, and fruit. I gave Rougeot a slightly higher rating because it is more expansive and longer. The world will have 350 cases of the 1992 Meursault Les Perrières to fight over. The battle will be worth it. It offers a compelling bouquet of steel, minerals, ripe honeyed apple fruit, and floral aromas. The long, full-bodied, rich, multidimensional, chewy flavors are decadent. The acid is low, but that will only serve to guarantee that this wine is guzzled down in its first 5–6 years of life. It is a magnificent Meursault Les Perrières.

The 1992 Corton-Charlemagne reveals a huge, spicy nose scented with vanillin, butter, coconut, and tropical fruit, astonishingly rich, unctuously-textured flavors that linger on the palate, and enough glycerin, extract, and alcohol to satisfy the most demanding hedonist. It is softer than the exceptional Corton-Charlemagnes made in 1990 and 1989.

COLIN-DÉLÉGER (CHASSAGNE-MONTRACHET)* * * * *

1992	Chassagne-Montrachet Les Chaumées Clos St.-Abdon	D	93
1992	Chassagne-Montrachet Les Chenevottes	D	93
1992	Chassagne-Montrachet Clos Devant	D	87
1992	Chassagne-Montrachet Maltroie	D	90
1992	Chassagne-Montrachet Morgeot	D	90
1992	Chassagne-Montrachet Remilly	D	90+
1992	Chassagne-Montrachet Les Vergers	D	90+
1992	Chevalier-Montrachet	EE	94
1992	Puligny-Montrachet Les Demoiselles	E	92+
1992	Saint-Aubin Les Combes	C	88

Colin, who has become one of the top stars of white burgundy, excelled in 1989, made very fine wines in 1990, and produced competent and above-average-quality 1991s. The 1992s are the strongest lineup I have yet to taste from him. They should be sought out by lovers of white burgundy. One will not find a better Saint-Aubin than Colin's 1992 Saint-Aubin Les Combes. An excellent wine, with admirable richness, a big, mineral-, apple blossom–, and orange-scented nose, heady, lusty, powerful flavors, and low acidity, it should be drunk over the next 2–3 years. Although the lush, round, supple, medium- to full-bodied 1992

Chassagne-Montrachet Clos Devant exhibits less precision, it offers a sumptuous mouthful of Chardonnay, provided it is drunk over the next several years.

The concentration, distinction, and complexity of Colin's 1992s jump in quality with the 1992 Chassagne-Montrachet Maltroie. It reveals an attractive bouquet of spicy new oak and ripe pineapples, intertwined with floral scents. Deep, with impressive purity, this medium- to full-bodied, rich wine should drink well for 5–6 years. The 1992 Chassagne-Montrachet Morgeot offers a compelling nose of wet stones and ripe fruit. More restrained and well structured, this medium- to full-bodied, well-knit, elegant, powerful wine is loaded. Give it another 12 months in the bottle and drink it over the subsequent 7–8 years. If you are looking for lavish richness combined with superb definition in a full-bodied, flashy style, check out the 1992 Chassagne-Montrachet Les Chenevottes. Reminiscent of a grand cru, with its huge, multidimensional bouquet of honeyed fruit, coconuts, oranges, and smoke, ripe and full bodied, with decadent levels of fruit extraction, this wine offers immense richness and a long finish. Dazzling! Drink it over the next 5–7 years. The 1992 Chassagne-Montrachet Remilly is a more tightly knit wine, with intriguing honeyed apple, cherry, and floral aromas. Full bodied and admirably marrying elegance with power, it possesses better acidity and less power. Among the tightest and most backward of the 1992s is the Chassagne-Montrachet Les Vergers. It exhibits adequate acidity, but the nose requires some coaxing. The wine is rich, full bodied, and well proportioned. Put it away for at least a year; it should last until the end of the century.

The magnificent 1992 Puligny-Montrachet Les Demoiselles boasts fine structure, stunning richness, and a promising bouquet of ripe honeyed fruit, flowers, and smoky new oak. Long yet well defined, this expansive, full-throttle white burgundy should be at its best between now and 2002. The 1992 Chassagne-Montrachet Les Chaumées Clos St.-Abdon seems unevolved, but wow, what intensity and unctuous richness to its fruit! It offers subtlety combined with massive levels of fruit, glycerin, and 14+% alcohol. What marvelous intensity and richness this wine possesses! I could not get over the superb buttery, tropical fruit, glycerin-dominated, heady finish. Drink it over the next decade. There were 75 cases made (15 cases will be brought into the United States) of the 1992 Chevalier-Montrachet. It is a phenomenal wine that will undoubtedly merit a score in the upper nineties when it is fully mature in 1–3 years. Its massive intensity and thick, buttery, blockbuster nose scented with honey, flowers, and tropical fruits are backed up by spicy, smoky new oak. With great fruit, and oodles of apple, butter, orangelike flavors, this huge, thick wine should be at its best by 1996–1997 and last for at least a decade. Colin-Déléger is one of the superstars of the 1992 white burgundy vintage.

ALAIN CORCIA COLLECTION (BEAUNE)* * *

1992 Bourgogne Blanc	B	86
1992 Mâcon-Clessé	B	82
1992 Mâcon-Villages Vieilles Vignes	B	86
1992 Pouilly-Fuissé	B	77
1992 Pouilly-Fuissé Vieilles Vignes	C	85
1992 Saint-Véran Domaine Jobert	B	79
1992 Saint-Véran Vieilles Vignes	B	86

A number of these selections from the Beaune *négociant* Alain Corcia offer good value. The top picks include a rich, medium- to full-bodied, luscious 1992 Bourgogne Blanc; a concentrated, medium-bodied 1992 Mâcon-Villages Vieilles Vignes; a honeyed apple, buttery, fruity 1992 Saint-Véran Vieilles Vignes; and an oaky, rich, ripe 1992 Pouilly-Fuissé

Vieilles Vignes. All of these wines are soft, with low acidity, and up-front fruit. They should be consumed over the next 1–2 years.

The other selections range from adequate to barely above average. Although they are not listed, I tasted the domaine wines from Domaine Pinson in Chassagne-Montrachet, and Domaine Jean-Paul Gauffroy in Meursault. I found them to be no better than above-average quality.

DOMAINE JEAN DAUVISSAT (CHABLIS)* * * *

1992 Chablis	C	86
1992 Chablis Les Montmains	D	88
1992 Chablis Les Preuses	D	92
1992 Chablis Les Vaillons	D	90
1992 Chablis Les Vaillons Vieilles Vignes	D	91

This is an exceptional range of Chablis from Jean Dauvissat. Even the 1992 Chablis offers fine ripeness, wonderful definition, and copious amounts of crisp, clean, lovely fruit. The other wines are superbly concentrated, with brilliant focus and considerable complexity. The 1992 Chablis Les Vaillons exhibits a fascinating flinty, mineral-scented nose with wonderful ripe fruit. Rich and medium bodied, with elegance and power, admirable purity of fruit, and wonderful concentration, it should be drunk over the next 5–7 years. The 1992 Chablis Les Montmains reveals some toasty, vanillin-scented new oak, an intense, earthy, flinty nose, and rich, ripe, medium- to full-bodied flavors. It too should drink well for the next 5–7 years. The 1992 Chablis Les Vaillons Vieilles Vignes offers up a gorgeous nose of lemony/apple blossom–scented fruit and minerals. It is full bodied, with superb extraction, and zesty, crisp acidity that gives this large-scaled wine precision and clarity. It is a deep, rich, multidimensional Chablis for drinking over the next 7–8 years. Dauvissat's 1992 Chablis Les Preuses is also a winemaking tour de force, with fabulous fruit, a riper, tropical fruit–scented nose, and honeyed, rich, full-bodied flavors. Atypically powerful for a Chablis, this wine's unctuously thick, rich fruit and full-bodied, macho style make for a terrific glass of wine. Drink it over the next 5–6 years.

DOMAINE RENÉ ET VINCENT DAUVISSAT (CHABLIS)* * * * *

1992 Chablis	C	88
1992 Chablis Les Clos	D	91
1992 Chablis Le Forêt	D	88
1992 Chablis Les Preuses	D	91
1992 Chablis Sechet	D	88
1992 Chablis Vaillons	D	88

There are no secrets in the winemaking at Dauvissat; impeccable viticultural techniques, modest yields, and barrel fermentation, with 10 months' aging in cask, produce lusty, rich, spicy wines. Dauvissat's 1992s look to be as exciting as his 1989s and 1986s.

The 1992 Chablis is a terrific bargain. An excellent nose of vanillin and honeyed apples, and long, rich, fat flavors make for a plump mouthful of wine. Drink it over the next 1–2 years. The 1992 Chablis Sechet is a juicy, fruity wine, with medium weight and some elegance. It relies on copious amounts of buttery, superripe, low-acid fruit to give it a big, fleshy mouth-feel. Displaying more typical Chablis charm and aromatic complexity is the

1992 Chablis Vaillons. Whiffs of wet stones and cold steel are intermingled with ripe pineapple and apple fruit. Sweet tasting because of its richness and ripeness, this medium-bodied, attractive, delicious Chablis should be drunk over the next 2–3 years. The 1992 Chablis Le Forêt exhibits more structure and acidity than other premiers crus, as well as rich fruit presented in a medium- to full-bodied format, with crisp acidity (a rarity for a 1992), admirable perfume, and a long, powerful, concentrated finish. It should last for 5–6 years. The 1992 Chablis Les Preuses is the most powerful wine in the Dauvissat portfolio. It reveals a huge nose of ripe apples, minerals, and honeyed fruits. Multidimensional, with gorgeous levels of extract, this full-bodied, authoritatively flavored wine possesses adequate acidity and a huge finish. Purists may feel it is too overwhelming to be classic, but it is an impressive wine. If you want more focus and delineation, and less power without sacrificing the opulence and chewy, fleshy character of this vintage, check out the 1992 Chablis Les Clos. Although low in acidity, it is long and rich, with an explosive finish. It displays a penetrating bouquet of minerals combined with citrus aromas, and apple/orangelike fruit. Full bodied, rich, and more structured than any of the other grands crus from Dauvissat, this is a full-throttle Chablis for drinking over the next 7–8 years.

JOSEPH DROUHIN (BEAUNE)* * * *

1992	Beaune Clos des Mouches	E	90
1992	Chablis Valdon	C	87
1992	Chablis Vaudesir	C	86
1992	Chassagne-Montrachet	C	86
1992	Chassagne-Montrachet Marquis de Laguiche	D	87
1992	Meursault	D	81
1991	Montrachet Marquis de Laguiche	EEE	87
1992	Puligny-Montrachet	D	86
1992	Puligny-Montrachet Les Folatières	D	88
1992	Rully	C	86

Drouhin's 1992s are similar in style to the excellent 1989s. The wines are fat, ripe, tasty, and ideal for drinking over the near term because of their low acidity and their fleshy, open-knit style. For value, consumers should seek out the 1992 Rully, an excellent wine with good body, length, richness, and fruitiness. The 1992 Chablis Valdon, a crisp, elegant wine with fine depth, medium body, freshness, and zest, is also a noteworthy bargain. I preferred it to the 1992 Chablis Vaudesir, a subtle, less intense, restrained, understated wine.

The 1992 Chassagne-Montrachet is fat, ripe, and round, with some attractive orange fruit, and plenty of glycerin and alcohol in the finish. The 1992 Chassagne-Montrachet Marquis de Laguiche exhibits a creamier, richer, broader palate, fat, ripe, long, lusty flavors, and low acidity. Both wines should be drunk over the next 5–6 years. I found the 1992 Meursault to be crisp, light bodied, and innocuous, with little definition or depth. The 1992 Puligny-Montrachet is tasty, elegant, and medium bodied.

The 1992 Puligny-Montrachet Les Folatières is nearly outstanding, with a formidable, buttery, spicy, rich nose, full body, surprising power for a Drouhin white wine, and an unctuous, layered, lusty finish. It may merit an outstanding rating with another 6 months of bottle age. It should drink well for at least 5–6 years. In top vintages Drouhin always does a superb job with Beaune Clos des Mouches. The 1992 is a full-bodied, rich, complex wine with mineral, floral, buttery fruit, medium to full body, excellent ripeness, and a long, layered finish. Drink it over the next 5–7 years.

The fine 1991 Montrachet Marquis de Laguiche offers aromas of toasty oak, medium body, fine depth and balance, and low acidity in the finish. Drink it over the next 5–7 years.

DRUID WINES (MOREY ST.-DENIS)* * *

1991 Meursault Les Clous	D 86
1991 Meursault Limozin	D 87
1991 Morey St.-Denis	D 85
1991 Puligny-Montrachet	D 86

Druid's wines are made by Jacques Seysses of the Domaine Dujac. The best vintages to date have been the 1989 and 1990. However, very good 1991s have been produced. They are soft, rich, ripe, and ideal for drinking over the next 2–3 years. The attractive 1991 Meursault Les Clous offers fine ripeness and depth, as well as a big, spicy, oaky nose. It is a big-boned wine with the requisite flesh to cover its framework. The 1991 Meursault Limozin exhibits more depth, a honeyed, oaky, hazelnut-scented bouquet, medium- to full-bodied flavors, decent acidity, and a long finish. The 1991 Puligny-Montrachet is ripe and elegant, with crisp fruit, medium body, and a graceful finish. The 1991 Morey St.-Denis is a tougher, harder wine with more earthiness, medium body, and decent acidity.

DOMAINE GÉRARD DUPLESSIS (CHABLIS)* * * *

1990 Chablis Les Clos	D 92+
1990 Chablis Montée de Tonnerre	C 89

These two 1990s are just being released by Duplessis, who must be the last vigneron in Chablis to bottle his wines. The 1990 Chablis Montée de Tonnerre, which may be an outstanding wine after 6–12 months in the bottle, is capable of lasting 10 or more years. A classic example of a nonoaked style of Chablis, it offers superb fruit, admirable precision, purity, and ripeness, and plenty of rich, deep, layered fruit flavors. Although medium to full bodied, with outstanding depth, yet still young and unevolved, it cannot match the explosive richness, great precision, and huge depth of fruit found in the 1990 Chablis Les Clos. The latter wine (125 cases—for the world) is a backward, massive Chablis in need of 3–4 years of cellaring. Those lucky enough to have purchased the 1989 Les Clos know what spectacular concentration Duplessis can obtain. However, the 1989 is more forward than the 1990. For those who love classic, old-style Chablis, made from low yields and handled gently during its upbringing, the 1990 is a must-purchase. It should last for 10 years.

DOMAINE J. A. FERRET (POUILLY-FUISSÉ)* * * * *

1992 Pouilly-Fuissé Les Clos	D 93
1992 Pouilly-Fuissé Les Menestrières	D 93
1990 Pouilly-Fuissé Les Menestrières	D 92
1992 Pouilly-Fuissé La Perrière	D 92
1992 Pouilly-Fuissé Les Reiss Hors Classe	D 92
1993 Pouilly-Fuissé Réserve Les Scelles	C 90
1993 Pouilly-Fuissé Réserve Les Vernays	C 92
1992 Pouilly-Fuissé Tête de Cru Les Pelloux	D 90
1990 Pouilly-Fuissé Tournant de Pouilly	D 92

Among the saddest news I've received recently was of the death of Madame Jeanne Ferret. A remarkably active and forceful personality well into her eighties, she made some of France's most magnificent white burgundies. Fortunately, her daughter Colette has assumed control of the estate with the same enthusiasm and commitment to quality as her mother. Colette's first wines, the 1992s, easily compete with the finest grands crus of the Côte d'Or. The same can be said for the 1990s. Pouilly-Fuissés from Ferret, as well as those from her friendly rival, Monsieur Vincent's Château Fuissé, are the most expensive of the appellation. But keep in mind that at $35 a bottle, they are equivalent in quality to grands crus selling at $65–$100 a bottle. All of the Ferret Pouilly-Fuissé vineyards are located on the steep slopes near the village of Pouilly, rather than the four neighboring villages of Vergisson, Fuissé, Chaintré, and Solutré. Madame Ferret believed that Pouilly-Fuissé was authentic only if it came from Pouilly. Many disagree, and there are some outstanding winemakers, such as the Belgian Guffens-Heynen, who vociferously take exception to this.

Having tasted so many disappointing 1993 white burgundies from the Côte d'Or, one can only imagine what low yields and ripeness Colette Ferret must have achieved in 1993 in order to make such intense wines. The 1993 Pouilly-Fuissé Réserve Les Scelles exhibits full-bodied richness, a honeyed, ripe apricot/tangerine– and mineral-scented nose, great fruit and purity, and a long, intense, dry, powerful finish. It should drink well for 5–7 years. More concentrated and more dominated by the stony, mineral, earthy soil is the 1993 Pouilly-Fuissé Réserve Les Vernays. It reveals a pure, crisp nose of ripe cherries, oranges, minerals, and flowers. Heady, alcoholic, ripe, and full bodied, with an unctuous texture, this 1993 tastes more like a 1992!

The superb 1992 Pouilly-Fuissé Tête de Cru Les Pelloux offers great fruit, that honeyed, unctuous thickness of the 1992 vintage, superb ripeness, and a chewy, full-bodied, alcoholic finish. It is a wine to drink over the next 5–8 years. Even classier, the 1992 Pouilly-Fuissé Les Reiss Hors Classe is a wine of great richness and complexity, with curranty, cherry fruit flavors combined with hints of overripe tangerines along with a strong mineral component. Full bodied, powerful, and rich, it is capable of lasting for 10–15+ years. Like her late mother, Colette Ferret will use the designation "Hors Classe" for those vineyard bottlings considered to be the estate's very best. The words "Tête de Cru" signify the finest pickings from a selected vineyard. It has been my experience that while there has not been a great deal of *qualitative* difference between the crus, the estate's Hors Classe bottlings tend to be slightly fatter and richer. However, all of these offerings are intriguing wines of great personality and quality. The 1992 Pouilly-Fuissé La Perrière is a fabulous, rich, full-bodied wine with gobs of fruit, massive structure and intensity, and an opulent, strikingly long finish. It has at least a decade of aging potential. The 1992 Pouilly-Fuissé Les Clos is a beautifully built, big, rich, muscular and concentrated wine, with a mineral undertone to its fruit. It will also last for a decade. The most enormously concentrated wine of this trio is the 1992 Pouilly-Fuissé Les Menestrières. Reminiscent of a Zind-Humbrecht Vendange Tardive Tokay-Pinot Gris, it offers an incredible buttery, waxy, roasted nut–scented bouquet. Phenomenally concentrated and unctuous, this mammoth wine represents a spectacular glass of decadently hedonistic Chardonnay! Although its alcohol must be close to 14.5%, the wine possesses decent acidity, as well as wonderful purity and overall balance. It should drink well for 10–15 years. You can be sure that I will be on the lookout for Colette Ferret's 1992 Pouilly-Fuissés when they are released next year.

The 1990 Pouilly-Fuissé Tournant de Pouilly is a sensational wine with nearly 14% alcohol. With a light golden color, a stunning nose of honeyed pineapple, peach, and applelike fruit, it offers gobs of extract, a thick, rich, unctuously textured palate, and a stunningly long, full-throttle finish. Despite its richness and massiveness it is an amazingly well-balanced, youthful wine that should drink well for another 5–10 years. The 1990 Les Menestrières offers a bouquet of cherries, apricots, smoked hazelnuts, and rich pineapple and apple fruit. Massively full bodied, yet beautifully balanced by crisp acidity, this huge, rich, deep, lavishly endowed wine should drink well for at least a decade.

DOMAINE FONTAINE-GAGNARD (CHASSAGNE-MONTRACHET)* * * *

1992 Bâtard-Montrachet	EE	93
1992 Chassagne-Montrachet	D	87
1992 Chassagne-Montrachet Les Caillerets	D	91
1992 Chassagne-Montrachet Les Chenevottes	D	90
1992 Chassagne-Montrachet La Grande Montagne	D	88
1992 Chassagne-Montrachet La Maltroie	D	90
1992 Chassagne-Montrachet Morgeot	D	90
1992 Chassagne-Montrachet Les Vergers	D	90
1992 Criots-Bâtard-Montrachet	E	89

In the confusing world of Burgundy's domaine names, there are many with the family name Gagnard (e.g., Gagnard-Delagrange, Blaine-Gagnard). This estate, owned by Richard Fontaine, is considered the finest of the Gagnard-named domaines. These 1992s are knock-out white burgundies.

The 1992 Chassagne-Montrachet is a honeyed, medium- to full-bodied, ripe wine with fine fruit and a long, lusty finish. It should be drunk over the next 3–4 years. Even richer, the 1992 Chassagne-Montrachet Morgeot offers copious amounts of honeyed, vanillin-scented, applelike fruit, wonderful fatness, and steely acidity in the full-bodied finish. Drink it over the next 6–7 years. The 1992 Chassagne-Montrachet La Maltroie is more ostentatious, with a heady, intoxicating nose of cherries, oranges, apples, and butter. Alcoholic and fat, this low-acid wine should be drunk over the next 3–4 years. The 1992 Chassagne-Montrachet Les Chenevottes exhibits outstanding depth and superb definition. It is a rich, gorgeously well-built and -proportioned wine, with full body, decent acidity, and a long, intense finish. Although more closed than the other wines, it may turn out to be as profound as Fontaine's 1992 Bâtard-Montrachet.

As for the other premiers crus, the rich 1992 Chassagne-Montrachet La Grande Montagne is oily and fat. Not exhibiting the complexity and definition of the other premiers crus, it is a lusty, alcoholic, voluptuously textured mouthful of Chardonnay. If it does not begin to reveal more structure, I would opt for drinking it over the near term. The superb 1992 Chassagne-Montrachet Les Caillerets is a huge, buttery, spicy wine, with a cinnamon-, baked apple–scented nose, deep, rich, honeyed flavors, full body, admirable structure, and gobs of fat, fruit, glycerin, and alcohol. Drink it over the next 7–8 years. The similarly styled 1992 Chassagne-Montrachet Les Vergers offers a bigger lemony/steely-scented nose, rich, superbly extracted flavors, full body, and fine intensity in the finish.

I was surprised that the 1992 Criots-Bâtard-Montrachet did not perform as well as Fontaine's top premiers crus from Chassagne. Although an excellent wine, it is monolithic, full bodied, dense, and chunky, without as much expression. The knockout 1992 Bâtard-Montrachet is oozing with fruit. It reveals a huge, massive bouquet of apple blossoms, honeysuckle, and buttery, peachlike fruit. Full bodied, deep, and chewy, this low-acid, blockbuster wine should offer superb drinking over the next 8–10 years.

DOMAINE MICHEL GAUNOUX (POMMARD)* * *

1992 Meursault Goutte d'Or	D	86
1992 Meursault Les Perrières	D	88

While this firm is better known for their red wines, these crisp, elegant, stylish whites exhibit fine body, plenty of ripe, luscious fruit, and a delicate touch of new oak. Both should be drunk over the next 3–4 years.

DOMAINE HENRI GERMAIN (MEURSAULT)* * *

1991 Chassagne-Montrachet Morgeot	D	86
1991 Meursault	D	86
1991 Meursault Les Charmes	D	86
1991 Meursault Limozin	D	86

It is interesting to see that while all of these wines are different, they merited identical scores. Attractive and successful wines for the vintage, they offer an elegant, light- to medium-bodied style, and good ripeness, purity, and freshness. The oak is kept to a minimum, and the result is vivacious wines that are easy to consume and appreciate. Drink all of them over the next 2–3 years.

MAISON JEAN GERMAIN (MEURSAULT)* * *

1992 Bourgogne Chardonnay	B	83
1992 Mâcon-Clessé Chardonnay	B	85
1992 Meursault Bouchères	D	86
1992 Meursault Goutte d'Or	D	85
1992 Puligny-Montrachet Les Champs Gains	D	87
1992 Saint-Aubin Premier Cru	C	86

This producer's stylish, crisp, tasty white burgundies are made in a medium-bodied, elegant style. For value, it is hard to beat his 1992 Mâcon-Clessé Chardonnay, with light to medium body, zesty acidity, and pleasing applelike fruit. It should be drunk over the next 1–2 years. The lighter 1992 Bourgogne Chardonnay is well made and pleasant, as is the 1992 Meursault Bouchères. Because of Germain's high yields and tendency to aim for a delicate style, the 1992 Meursault Goutte d'Or did not exhibit much intensity or richness. Both the Bouchères and Goutte d'Or should be drunk over the next 4–5 years. The 1992 Saint-Aubin Premier Cru and 1992 Puligny-Montrachet Les Champs Gains are richer, more obvious white burgundies, with medium body and flavor intensity. The low acidity and moderately concentrated style of these wines suggest they should be consumed over the next 3–4 years.

CHÂTEAU DE LA GREFFIÈRE (MÂCON)* * * *

1992 Mâcon La Roche Vineuse Vieilles Vignes	A	87

Made from a cuvée of 80% 50-year-old vines and 20% 30-year-old vines, this is a knockout Chardonnay from the Mâconnais area. It is full bodied and powerful, with intensely rich, honeyed, buttery fruit, long, opulent flavors, and superb purity and crispness. A percentage of this wine saw some small-oak-cask aging, but the real pleasure is the vivid, rich, concentrated fruitiness presented in a medium-bodied, intensely flavored, crisp format. Drink it over the next year.

THIERRY GUÉRIN (MÂCON)* * * *

1992 Pouilly-Fuissé Clos de France	C	90
1992 Pouilly-Fuissé La Roche	C	86
1992 Pouilly-Fuissé La Roche Vieilles Vignes	C	88

Thierry Guérin is another up-and-coming star in the Mâconnais. He has made gorgeous 1992s. Although the 1992 Pouilly-Fuissé La Roche does not exhibit the complexity of his other offerings, it is a rich, long, opulent, deep, full-bodied, lusciously fruity wine. Drink it over the next 3–4 years. The 1992 Pouilly-Fuissé La Roche Vieilles Vignes displays evidence of toasty new oak in its honeyed apple– and spring flower–scented bouquet, full-bodied, concentrated flavors, and its long, low-acid, authoritative finish. Drink it over the next 4–5 years. The voluptuous 1992 Pouilly-Fuissé Clos de France reveals a huge nose of buttery fruit and honeysuckle, laced with subtle toasty new oak. Expansive and dense, with gobs of sweet fruit, this large-scaled, concentrated wine could pass for a grand cru. A superb effort! Drink it over the next 5–7 years.

DOMAINE GUFFENS-HEYNEN (MÂCON)* * * *

1992 Mâcon Pierreclos en Chavigne Vieilles Vignes	C	90
1991 Mâcon Pierreclos en Chavigne Vieilles Vignes	C	87
1992 Pouilly-Fuissé Clos des Petits Croux	E	92+
1992 Pouilly-Fuissé La Roche	D	93
1991 Pouilly-Fuissé La Roche	D	88

There are at least a half-dozen superb Mâconnais estates making wines that rival and often surpass many Côte d'Or premiers and grands crus. The young Belgian, Jean-Marie Guffens-Heynen, is one of them. His 1991s include a fresh, mineral- and apple-scented 1991 Mâcon Pierreclos en Chavigne Vieilles Vignes. With medium body, excellent freshness, and a long, zesty finish, it should drink well for at least 2–3 years. The deeper 1991 Pouilly-Fuissé La Roche exhibits a provocative bouquet of wet stones, and rich, medium- to full-bodied, applelike flavors. Drink it over the next 3–4 years.

The riper, richer 1992 vintage, combined with Guffens's notoriously low yields, has resulted in super wines. Readers will find the 1992 Mâcon Pierreclos en Chavigne Vieilles Vignes to be an outstanding wine. Rich and lusty, with deep, layered, full-bodied flavors, excellent balance, and admirable complexity, this knockout Mâcon should be drunk over the next 5–6 years. The spectacular 1992 Pouilly-Fuissé La Roche offers up a huge, mineral-, orange-, and buttery apple–scented nose, deep, rich, full-bodied flavors with formidable intensity, and wonderful structure. This stunning, well-delineated wine is unevolved, yet promises to age for 7–8 years or more. The 60 or so cases of the 1992 Pouilly-Fuissé Clos des Petits Croux are largely of academic interest. It is a backward, majestic Pouilly-Fuissé, with intense aromas of ripe apples and wet stones. Deep, spicy, rich, and tight, it requires at least 2–3 years of cellaring. Based on other vintages, it should keep for 10–12 years.

LOUIS JADOT (BEAUNE)* * * *

1992 Auxey-Duresses Duc de Magenta	C	86
1992 Bâtard-Montrachet	EE	91
1992 Beaune Les Grèves	D	89
1992 Bienvenue Bâtard-Montrachet	EE	90
1992 Bourgogne Blanc	B	85
1992 Chassagne-Montrachet	C	84
1992 Chassagne-Montrachet Morgeot Duc de Magenta	D	87

1992 Chevalier-Montrachet Les Demoiselles	EE	91+
1992 Corton-Charlemagne	EE	89
1992 Meursault	C	83
1992 Meursault Les Charmes	D	86
1992 Meursault Les Perrières	E	87
1992 Le Montrachet	EEE	93
1992 Pernand-Vergelesses	C	85
1992 Pouilly-Fuissé Cuvée Spéciale	C	87
1992 Puligny-Montrachet	D	86
1992 Puligny-Montrachet Les Caillerets	E	87
1992 Puligny-Montrachet Les Champs Gains	E	87
1992 Puligny-Montrachet Clos de la Garenne	E	87
1992 Puligny-Montrachet Les Folatières	E	90
1992 Puligny-Montrachet Les Referts	E	88
1992 Saint-Aubin	C	82
1992 Savigny-Les-Beaune	C	77

The Gageys make no bones about rating 1989, 1985, and 1986 as significantly richer, more complex vintages for white burgundy than 1992. Their 1992s are successful, but based on my impressions of the 1992s vis-à-vis the 1989s, 1986s, and 1985s, I would agree with their assessment.

The white wine–making philosophy in low-acid years such as 1992 is to only do a partial malolactic fermentation in order to preserve the natural acidity. This has proven to be a highly successful policy, resulting in some of the longest-lived white burgundies of the region. Jadot's Bourgogne Blanc continues to be an excellent introductory wine to their style. It is clean and pure, with attractive, subtle, buttery, applelike fruit, decent acidity, and a lovely medium-bodied, fresh taste. Drink it over the next 3–4 years. The 1992 Pouilly-Fuissé Cuvée Spéciale exhibits a light golden color, an excellent bouquet of buttery apples, and delicious, medium- to full-bodied, luscious fruit. It should drink well for 7–8 years. The steely, mineral-scented nose of the 1992 Auxey-Duresses Duc de Magenta is followed by a medium-bodied, zesty wine with lovely fruit, considerable elegance and finesse, and a refreshing finish. It should drink well for 4–6 years. Although not complex, the fat, monolithic 1992 Pernand-Vergelesses offers an uncomplicated mouthful of chunky Chardonnay fruit. Jadot's 1992 Savigny-Les-Beaune (made from 60% Pinot Blanc and 40% Chardonnay) is acidic, lean, and austere. The straightforward 1992 Saint-Aubin displays good fruit as well as a softer style. Like the Savigny-Les-Beaune, it should be drunk earlier rather than later.

The village wines from Meursault and Chassagne-Montrachet are competent, correct, light wines that are solidly made with good, ripe fruit, but little complexity. The 1992 Puligny-Montrachet exhibits more character, along with a mineral, steely component.

Among the premiers crus, the 1992 Chassagne-Montrachet Morgeot from the Duc de Magenta offers an excellent nose of buttery popcorn, ripe apples, and flowers. Medium to full bodied, with fine richness, as well as a sense of grace and style, this lovely wine should drink well for another 7–8 years. The 1992 Meursault Les Charmes possesses lusty, buttery, hazelnut-flavored fruit, a soft, fat texture, fine density, and a chunky, alcoholic finish. It should be drunk over the next 4–5 years. The 1992 Meursault Les Perrières reveals more power, the steely, mineral aroma that comes from this stony vineyard, and admirable definition and length.

Jadot's five Puligny-Montrachet premiers crus are all impressive. The 1992 Puligny-Montrachet Les Champs Gains is the most understated and elegant, with crisp acidity, medium body, plenty of freshness, and lovely mineral fruit. The 1992 Puligny-Montrachet Les Referts offers more stuffing and intensity, as well as a more forceful nose of oranges, minerals, steel, and butter, medium to full body, and a long, rich finish. The 1992 Puligny-Montrachet Clos de la Garenne is ripe and rich. Despite its intensity, it maintains considerable elegance. Slightly deeper in color, the 1992 Puligny-Montrachet Les Caillerets displays honeyed apple and buttery aromas and flavors, decent acidity, and a broader, richer, more alcoholic finish. The best of this group is the 1992 Puligny-Montrachet Les Folatières. A gorgeous nose of honeysuckle, oranges, and buttered apples is a turn-on. Medium to full bodied, with excellent acidity, plenty of concentration, and a rich, long finish, this wine should drink well for at least a decade. The other 1992 premiers crus from Puligny-Montrachet are best consumed within their first 8 years of life.

The 1992 Beaune Les Grèves blanc is the best wine I have tasted from this small vineyard that is better known for its red wines. It possesses surprising intensity and ripeness, with an earthy, lemony, buttery nose, medium body, and crisp acidity to buttress the richness and heady finish. Drink it over the next 7–8 years.

The impressive grands crus include an excellent, lusty, rich, full-bodied 1992 Bienvenue Bâtard-Montrachet, and a dense yet elegant, hazelnut- and honey-scented 1992 Bâtard-Montrachet. The latter wine exhibits richer, denser, more unctuously textured fruit than the Bienvenue Bâtard-Montrachet. One of the specialties of Jadot is the Chevalier-Montrachet Les Demoiselles. Made from vines planted in 1955, this is the most backward wine of the Jadot stable. Although completely closed, the 1992 reveals high acidity and a rich, full-bodied, intense, and powerful personality. While the wine's length and weight are impressive, it will not be close to maturity for 7–8 years; it should keep for up to 20 years, an uncommonly long time for a 1992.

The 1992 Corton-Charlemagne is not as impressively endowed as I expected. Nevertheless, it is an excellent wine, with a big, ripe, spicy, vanillin-scented nose, medium body, and fine richness and ripeness. The finish does lack length. The 1992 Le Montrachet exhibits a huge nose of minerals, cherries, oranges, and honeysuckle. Full bodied, ripe, and long, with fine underlying acidity, and plenty of weight and richness in the finish, this tightly knit wine should be at its best for 5–6 years and keep for 15.

DOMAINE PATRICK JAVILLIER (MEURSAULT)* * * */* * * * *

1991 Bourgogne Cuvée des Forgets	D	87
1992 Meursault Les Casse Têtes	D	90
1991 Meursault Les Casse Têtes	D	90
1992 Meursault Les Cloux	D	89
1991 Meursault Les Cloux	D	87
1992 Meursault Les Narvaux	D	91
1991 Meursault Les Narvaux	D	90
1991 Meursault Les Tillets Vieilles Vignes	D	87

For a considerable time the Javillier family was content to act as grape and juice brokers, selling their purchases to major *négociants* such as Chartron et Trébuchet and Drouhin. After Patrick Javillier became enamored with the wines of such highly talented winemakers as Guffens-Heynen and Coche-Dury, he overhauled the estate's winemaking philosophy. Readers who have tasted this property's insipid, watery, thin, sterile wines of the past are in for a shock when they taste the 1991s and 1992s. In contrast to what I wrote in my book *Burgundy*, the wines are now 100% barrel-fermented. Moreover, there is considerable lees contact and yields have been restricted. Following in the footsteps of Coche-Dury and Comte Lafon, the whites are bottled unfiltered.

The generic 1991 Bourgogne Cuvée des Forgets is a rich, medium- to full-bodied wine with nicely integrated new oak, and big, buttery, honeyed flavors. Drink it over the next several years. All of the 1991 Meursaults reveal considerable richness, a soft, low-acid, plump style, excellent depth, subtle oak, and in the case of Les Casse Têtes and Les Narvaux, deep, concentrated finishes. They are excellent 1991s, with chewy mid-palates, and sweet, honeyed Chardonnay fruit, suggesting low yields and noninterventionist winemaking. They should be drunk over the next 2–3 years.

The 1992s are less evolved aromatically, but with 6 more months in the bottle, they may merit higher scores. They all possess superb depth, admirable clarity and richness, adequate acidity, and superb, rich, well-balanced, lusty finishes. The most developed and precocious is the 1992 Meursault Les Cloux. It boasts sweet, unctuously textured fruit, fine balance, and a nutty, honeyed nose. The 1992 Meursault Les Casse Têtes and 1992 Meursault Les Narvaux are richer, with Les Casse Têtes displaying greater precision and elegance allied to considerable power and intensity. The classic Meursault Les Narvaux exhibits a nose of grilled hazelnuts, honeyed tropical fruits, and attractive vanillin. Rich, full bodied, and thick, this superb Meursault should be drunk over the next 4–5 years.

DOMAINE FRANÇOIS JOBARD (MEURSAULT)* * * *

1992 Meursault	D	86
1992 Meursault Blagny	D	86
1992 Meursault Les Genevrières	D	87+
1992 Meursault Le Poruzot	D	86

Anyone who has followed Jobard's wines knows they resemble the man—lean, stern, and needing time to express their personalities. That being said, I thought the 1992s were atypically austere and light. They were not as rich as Jobard's exceptional 1989s or fine 1990s. The 1992 Meursault offers elegant, flowery scents, mineral flavors, medium body, and crisp acidity. The similarly styled, medium-weight, elegant 1992 Meursault Blagny reveals a cold steely feel. The 1992 Meursault Le Poruzot is atypically backward, high in acidity, and austere. However, it displays adequate weight, and my instincts suggest there may be more to it than what I tasted. The most impressive wine of this quartet is the 1992 Meursault Les Genevrières. While it is an austere, tightly knit wine, it is also richer, with attractive lemony, applelike fruit allied to scents of wet stones. Stylish yet restrained, it should be long-lived for a 1992.

DOMAINE MICHEL JUILLOT (MERCUREY)* * */* * * *

1992 Bourgogne Blanc	B	85
1992 Corton-Charlemagne	EE	87
1992 Mercurey Blanc	C	79
1992 Mercurey Les Champs Martins	D	87

Juillot fashioned soft, ripe, medium-bodied 1992s. They do not appear to be as successful as his blockbuster 1990s or 1989s. The 1992 Bourgogne Blanc is soft, ripe, and ideal for drinking over the next year. The 1992 Mercurey Blanc is light bodied, with attractive ripeness and an abrupt finish. The most interesting wines include the excellent 1992

Mercurey Les Champs Martins, an opulent, rich, honeyed white burgundy with medium to full body, fine depth, and a soft finish. Drink it over the next 3–4 years. Juillot's Corton-Charlemagne can be stunning. The 1992 is certainly good, yet it is less powerful and not as concentrated as I expected. It reveals noticeable evidence of spicy new oak, ripe aromas of honeyed pineapple and buttery, apple fruit, and a medium-bodied, oaky finish. Drink it over the next 4–5 years.

DOMAINE HENRI LAFARGE (MÂCON)* * * *

1992 Mâcon Bray	B	88

I am increasingly impressed by the super quality coming from the top small estates in the Mâconnais region. The 1992 Domaine Lafarge Mâcon Bray is a fat, sumptuously rich, chewy wine loaded with honeyed pineapple and buttery, applelike fruit. It possesses excellent definition, medium to full body, and loads of heady alcohol in the bold, rich finish. This is a delicious, fuller style of Mâcon for drinking over the next year.

DOMAINE COMTE LAFON (MEURSAULT)* * * * *

1992 Meursault	D	86
1991 Meursault	D	87
1992 Meursault Les Charmes	E	92
1991 Meursault Les Charmes	E	93
1992 Meursault Clos de la Barre	E	90
1991 Meursault Clos de la Barre	E	91
1992 Meursault Les Desirées	E	89
1991 Meursault Les Desirées	E	89
1992 Meursault Les Genevrières	E	94
1991 Meursault Les Genevrières	E	89
1992 Meursault Les Perrières	E	92
1991 Meursault Les Perrières	E	93
1992 Le Montrachet	EEE	96
1991 Le Montrachet	EEE	92?

What Lafon achieved in 1991 is extraordinary. His wines are the greatest wines of the vintage. Lafon rarely filters his wines. In 1991 he put most of the cuvées of white wine in the bottle with neither fining nor filtration.

All of Lafon's 1992s are ripe, rich, precocious wines that will not have the aging potential of the superb 1989s and excellent 1990s. Lafon, who sells only 10% of his production to the United States, believes his 1992s are similar to the 1982s (probably the best wines of the vintage), but with more intensity and purity. The 1992 Meursault exhibits attractive ripe, honeyed flavors, medium body, and a long finish. The lighter-bodied 1992 Meursault Les Desirées is elegant and full of finesse. Tasters will notice a jump in intensity and concentration with the 1992 Meursault Clos de la Barre. The wine reveals a flowery, honey-, nut-, and butter-scented bouquet and flavors. The 1992 Meursault Les Charmes reveals more sweetness to its fruit and more elegance. It does not possess the overwhelming intensity and extraction noticeable in vintages such as 1989. Among the 1992 premiers crus, the top wine is the exquisite, awesome 1992 Meursault Les Genevrières. It is a huge wine, with extraordinary richness, broad, intense flavors, magnificent length, and uncanny precision.

This full-bodied, dazzling Meursault should turn out to be fabulous. The tight 1992 Meursault Les Perrières is a more backward wine, with a steely, mineral-scented nose, superb length, and ripe, long, powerful flavors that are supported by crisp acidity. It will be the slowest 1992 to evolve. There are 100 cases of the 1992 Le Montrachet. It will rival the great 1992 Le Montrachets produced by Domaine Leflaive, Amiot-Bonfils, and Ramonet. It possesses fabulous richness and a huge, massive feel. Impeccably well balanced, with a sense of elegance and precision, this wine must be tasted to be believed. Given the wine's size and profound concentration, it will need 5–10 years of cellaring. It has the potential to last for 25–30 years.

Lafon's 1991s are the wines of the vintage. Modestly, Lafon says he took some unnecessary gambles by waiting out the rains and picking late, harvesting fruit that was not diluted. The results are splendidly rich, full-bodied wines with amazing intensity. They are as exceptional as the 1990s, and superior to Lafon's 1988s, 1987s, and 1986s. Average yields were 25 hectoliters per hectare, compared with 55–70 at other domaines. The 1991 offerings include a rich, round, deep, fruity 1991 Meursault, and an unfined/unfiltered, opulent, superrich 1991 Meursault Les Desirées. The latter wine tends to be among the fruitiest and most obvious of Lafon's wines, but in 1991 it possesses a level of extract and complexity that I have rarely detected in the past. This long, full-bodied wine will be among the shortest lived of the vineyard-designated Meursaults.

Three of the four single-vineyard Meursaults were outstanding. The superb 1991 Meursault Clos de la Barre is as compelling as the magnificent 1989. It was put in the bottle unfined and unfiltered, so do not be surprised by any sediment that forms within the next 6–12 months. The wine offers up a magnificent nose of minerals, buttery apples, and spring flowers. Honeyed, rich, and full bodied, this deep, layered wine exhibits low acidity, as well as sensational balance and depth. Drink it over the next 10–15 years. The 1991 Meursault Les Charmes displays incredible extract, remarkable power, fabulous richness, and a multidimensional personality. This superb wine is oozing with minerallike, buttery, popcorn- and apple blossom–scented fruit. Long, unctuous, and chewy, this formidably endowed wine should drink beautifully for another 10–15 years. The closed 1991 Meursault Les Genevrières does not reveal the power, richness, and complexity of the Clos de la Barre, Les Charmes, or Les Perrières. Nevertheless, I was impressed with its lemon/apple blossom–scented nose, rich, medium-bodied flavors, and crisp acidity (a rarity for a 1991). I intend to retaste the wine in a year to see if it has opened. The backward 1991 Meursault Les Perrières needs time, but it exhibits that extraordinary rich, mineral-scented nose with an element of earthy flint and slate one associates with certain Sauvignons from Pouilly-Fumé. Magnificently rich, with a phenomenally long finish, this dense, full-bodied, admirably concentrated wine should drink well for 15 or more years.

The 1991 Le Montrachet is not an easy wine to evaluate. The color is significantly deeper than that of the Meursaults. There are scents of overripe apricots and oranges, in addition to minerals and honey. Full bodied, high in acidity, with massive weight, but a disjointed personality, this wine looks to be magnificent, but idiosyncratic. An immensely impressive wine, it will be controversial. I would not touch a bottle for at least 5–6 more years; it will easily keep for 20–25 years.

DOMAINE LALEURE-PIOT (PERNAND-VERGELESSES)* * */* * * *

1992 Corton-Charlemagne	EE	92
1992 Pernand-Vergelesses Premier Cru	D	86

These are two fine efforts from Laleure-Piot. The 1992 Pernand-Vergelesses Premier Cru exhibits wonderful richness and ripeness, medium to full body, and none of the earthiness or high acidity that often plagues wines from this appellation. It should drink well for 4–6 years. The sensational, elegant 1992 Corton-Charlemagne is immensely rich and concentrated, with impeccable balance, a spicy bouquet of ripe apples, cinnamon, and orange scents, medium body, and superb extraction of flavor. Its acidity suggests it is one 1992 burgundy that can be kept for 7–8 years.

LOUIS LATOUR (BEAUNE)* * * *

1992	Bâtard-Montrachet	EE	92
1992	Beaune Blanc	D	86
1992	Bienvenue Bâtard-Montrachet	EE	89
1992	Chardonnay Ardeche	A	85
1992	Chassagne-Montrachet	C	86
1991	Chassagne-Montrachet	C	78
1992	Chassagne-Montrachet Premier Cru	D	87
1992	Chevalier-Montrachet	EE	89+
1992	Corton-Charlemagne	EE	93
1991	Corton-Charlemagne	EE	89
1992	Mâcon Lugny Les Genievres	B	87
1992	Meursault	C	87
1991	Meursault	C	85
1992	Meursault Château de Blagny	D	90
1991	Meursault Château de Blagny	D	86
1992	Meursault Les Genevrières	D	86
1992	Meursault Les Perrières	D	87
1991	Montagny Premier Cru	C	87
1992	Le Montrachet	EEE	88+
1992	Pouilly-Fuissé	C	86
1992	Puligny-Montrachet	D	77
1991	Puligny-Montrachet	D	74
1992	Puligny-Montrachet Les Folatières	D	88
1992	Puligny-Montrachet Premier Cru	D	86
1992	Puligny-Montrachet Les Referts	D	91
1992	Saint-Véran	C	86

This famous *négociant*/vineyard owner, founded in 1797, has made very fine 1992s. The big wines, such as the top premiers crus and grands crus, spend a year in 100% new oak and have considerable lees contact for the first 7–8 months, although there is no stirring, or so-called *bâtonage*, practiced.

Although not located in Burgundy, one of the excellent bargains from Latour is their Chardonnay from Ardeche. The 1992 is a crisp, elegant, tasty, light- to medium-bodied wine with fine purity and ripeness. It is a wine to drink within 1–2 years of the vintage. One of the best choices for quality and value is always Latour's Mâcon Lugny Les Genievres, a rich, medium- to full-bodied, surprisingly intense Mâcon with gobs of buttery, honeyed fruit.

The 1992 is a top success that should be drunk within its first 3 years of life. I also enjoyed the 1992 Saint-Véran, although it did not have the depth, fat, and fleshy character of the Mâcon Lugny. The 1992 Pouilly-Fuissé is tasty, elegant, and ripe, with good body and an alcoholic finish. Slightly richer, fuller, and nuttier, with low acidity and high alcohol, the 1992 Meursault should be drunk over the next 3–4 years. Latour's 1992 Puligny-Montrachet is light and lean. In terms of richness and body, it is overwhelmed by the 1992 Chassagne-Montrachet. The latter wine is chunky, fleshy, and well made.

White wines from the appellation of Beaune are rare. Latour's 1992 Beaune Blanc exhibits a floral, honeysuckle-scented fruitiness, medium body, excellent ripeness, low acidity, and a fleshy, heady finish. Drink it over the next 4–5 years. The 1992 Chassagne-Montrachet Premier Cru is buttery and smoky, with rich, medium-bodied flavors. Nearly all of the grapes for this wine come from the excellent premier cru vineyard Chevenottes. The steely, mineral, stony, restrained, yet forceful 1992 Meursault Les Perrières should have 7–8 years of longevity. It displays fine concentration, medium to full body, and higher acidity than most 1992s. In contrast, the 1992 Meursault Les Genevrières is leaner, with a spicy, toasty new oak component to accompany its buttered hazelnut flavors.

Among the three premiers crus from Puligny-Montrachet, the 1992 Puligny-Montrachet Premier Cru is elegant, tasty, and attractive in a straightforward, satisfying fashion. The 1992 Puligny-Montrachet Les Folatières is full bodied, with an expansive nose of butter, minerals, spicy oak, and floral scents. Excellent richness allied with considerable body and depth make for a mouth-filling wine that should drink well for 4–6 years. The superb 1992 Puligny-Montrachet Les Referts possesses a bacon fat, smoky, oaky nose intertwined with sweet, perfumed aromas of honeyed apples, melons, and oranges. The wine reveals great richness and intensity, as well as full body, superb extraction and glycerin, and a long, rich finish. However, its low acidity suggests it should be drunk during its first 5–6 years of life.

Latour's terrific 1992 Corton-Charlemagne is a worthy rival to the firm's great 1990, 1989, and 1986. It is the most powerful, richest, and deepest wine in Latour's portfolio. There is plenty of smoky, toasty new oak, a forceful, earthy nose of peaches, melons, oranges, and buttery apple scents, deep flavors that cut a bold, dramatic swath, and a long finish with crisp acidity. It should drink well for 10–15 years. The rich and full 1992 Bienvenue Bâtard-Montrachet is monolithic, but exhibits considerable depth, muscle, and alcohol. It should last for 7–8 years. More impressive is the richer 1992 Bâtard-Montrachet. This highly extracted, unctuously textured, succulent wine is loaded with fruit, glycerin, alcohol, and body. It is a large-framed wine for drinking over the next decade. The closed, tightly knit 1992 Chevalier-Montrachet boasts spicy new oak and good weight and length, but remains completely unevolved; it should keep for at least a decade. Latour's 1992 Le Montrachet is impressively rich and well balanced, but it needs 2–3 years of cellaring. Although it is not one of the stars of the vintage, it should keep for over a decade.

I tasted only six 1991 white burgundies from Latour. The excellent 1991 Montagny Premier Cru is a bargain, given the lowly reputation of this vintage. The 1991 Meursault is pleasant and elegant, with some ripe fruit. The lean 1991 Puligny-Montrachet and 1991 Chassagne-Montrachet are diluted, but the 1991 Meursault Château de Blagny is ripe, rich, and intense, with nutty, buttery fruit, medium to full body, and low acid in the soft finish. It should be drunk over the next 1–2 years. The Corton-Charlemagne is the finest 1991 Latour I saw. Although it does not possess the power and intensity of the 1992, 1990, or 1989, it is a complex, muscular, rich, medium- to full-bodied wine with low acidity, yet fine depth and intensity. A top success for the vintage, it should drink well for the next 5–6 years.

DOMAINE LEFLAIVE (PULIGNY-MONTRACHET)* * * * *

1992 Bâtard-Montrachet	EE	97
1992 Bienvenue Bâtard-Montrachet	EE	94
1992 Bourgogne Blanc	C	89
1992 Chevalier-Montrachet	EEE	97
1992 Le Montrachet	EEE	99
1992 Puligny-Montrachet	C	89
1992 Puligny-Montrachet Clavoillon	E	92
1992 Puligny-Montrachet Les Combettes	E	94
1992 Puligny-Montrachet Les Folatières	E	93
1992 Puligny-Montrachet Les Pucelles	E	96

The Domaine Leflaive has enjoyed many successful vintages over the years—1979, 1985, 1986, and 1989 come to mind immediately—but the 1992s are the finest young wines this domaine has produced. Yields averaged 45 hectoliters per hectare, far below most recent vintages. The wines are renowned for their purity and elegance, but the 1992s also display a special level of richness and intensity.

Even the 1992 Bourgogne Blanc is a gorgeously made wine, with a wonderful buttery, mineral, steely nose, rich, medium-bodied, crisp flavors, and a long, authoritative finish. Drink it over the next 3–4 years. The 1992 Puligny-Montrachet exhibits a deep, apple/buttery/lemony-scented nose, great fruit and finesse, medium body, a honeyed richness, and lively acidity. It should drink well for 6–7 years. I cannot remember tasting a better Puligny-Montrachet Clavoillon from Leflaive. The 1992 offers a vibrant, beautifully focused nose of oranges, apples, and wet stones. It is a surprisingly full-bodied, silky, chewy wine, with gobs of intensity and flavor extraction. Drink it over the next 10 years. Leflaive owns a tiny parcel of Les Folatières and the 1992 is marvelous. Its honeysuckle-scented, buttery nose and rich, creamy flavors are admirable. Rich and medium to full bodied, with excellent definition and superb intensity, this wine should drink well for at least a decade. Followers of the Domaine Leflaive know that for the money, the estate's Puligny-Montrachet Les Combettes is the wine to buy. This vineyard, situated next to the great Meursault vineyard Les Charmes, is as much of a Meursault as it is a Puligny-Montrachet. The wine's formidable nose of grilled hazelnuts, butter, steel, and flowers is mind blowing. Huge, unctuous, thick, chewy flavors exhibit magnificent extraction of flavor. There is enough acidity to provide definition to this wine's sizable components. The finish is rich, long, and mouth filling. It should drink gorgeously for the next decade. Les Combettes represents the more lusty, hedonistic side of the Leflaive portfolio. In terms of marrying power with finesse, the Puligny-Montrachet Les Pucelles is a classic. The 1992 is richer and more unctuous than usual. It possesses fabulous clarity and definition, a great bouquet of oranges/tangerines combined with toasty vanillin, buttered popcorn, and apple scents. Sensationally concentrated, with layers of flavor beautifully buttressed by vibrant acidity, this is a magnificent wine.

The dense 1992 Bienvenue Bâtard-Montrachet displays a cherry/orange/ripe apple–scented nose, powerful, thick, rich flavors, fine acidity, and a long, lusty, alcoholic finish. It is a big wine for drinking over the next 7–8 years. Millionaires should have fun debating whether the Bâtard-Montrachet or the Chevalier-Montrachet is superior. The Bâtard is the more evolved and precocious of the two, and the Chevalier appears to be holding more in reserve. Both are beautifully well-knit, expansively flavored, full-bodied, superconcentrated white burgundies that display honeyed, orange, roasted nut, overripe apple scents, buttery, creamy textures, super extraction of flavor, and long finishes. The Bâtard exhibits more mineral scents in its nose and flavors, and is more up-front, whereas the Chevalier explodes on the back of the palate and looks to have greater longevity.

Lastly, Leflaive's 1992 Le Montrachet (only their second vintage) is a candidate for the Montrachet of the vintage. Only 25 cases were produced. The quintessential Chardonnay, it is an awesomely rich, highly extracted wine oozing with flavor, yet it is marvelously precise and focused. A mammoth-sized wine, it should drink well for 15 or more years.

OLIVIER LEFLAIVE FRÈRES (PULIGNY-MONTRACHET)* * */* * * *

1992	Bâtard-Montrachet	EEE	91
1992	Bienvenue Bâtard-Montrachet	EE	90
1992	Bourgogne Les Setilles	B	86
1992	Chassagne-Montrachet	D	85
1992	Chevalier-Montrachet	EE	92
1992	Corton-Charlemagne	E	90
1992	Criots Bâtard-Montrachet	EE	93
1992	Mercurey Blanc	C	86
1992	Meursault	D	82
1992	Meursault Les Perrières	D	89
1992	Meursault Poruzot	D	88
1992	Montagny Premier Cru	C	86
1992	Le Montrachet	EEE	90
1992	Puligny-Montrachet	D	86
1992	Puligny-Montrachet Les Champs Gains	D	87
1992	Puligny-Montrachet Les Folatières	D	88
1992	Rully Premier Cru	C	86
1992	Saint-Aubin Remilly	C	86

This firm has dramatically improved the quality of its winemaking. Olivier Leflaive brought in the talented Frank Greux, and the quality of their wine since 1989 has gone from one strength to another. In 1992 several of the wines will be bottled unfiltered. With three consecutive good vintages, Olivier Leflaive is now a name to be considered seriously.

The attractive 1992 Bourgogne Les Setilles comes from a vineyard adjacent to Puligny-Montrachet. It offers crisp acidity, tasty, ripe, lemon/applelike, fleshy fruit, fine definition, and power in the finish. Drink it over the next 4–5 years. The 1992 Montagny Premier Cru displays an attractive floral, mineral, lemony-scented nose, medium-bodied, elegant flavors, adequate acidity, and a fat finish. It should be drunk over the next 3–4 years. The 1992 Rully Premier Cru exhibits crisp acidity, a steely, more earthy-scented nose, excellent ripe fruit, medium body, good balance, and a pleasant finish. I also enjoyed the medium-bodied 1992 Mercurey Blanc for its bouquet of steel, herbs, and crisp apple aromas, pure fruit, and fine finish.

I found the 1992 Saint-Aubin Remilly, 1992 Puligny-Montrachet, and 1992 Chassagne-Montrachet to be good, lower-level white burgundies. Each possesses crisp acidity, elegant flavors, moderate intensity, and definition and character. All should be consumed over the next 3–4 years. The 1992 Meursault appears to have less intensity than Leflaive's other

1992s. It is a straightforward, chunky wine revealing some dilution. That is not the case with either the 1992 Meursault Poruzot or 1992 Meursault Les Perrières. The Poruzot exhibits a ripe, honeyed, apple butter–scented nose, tasty, medium- to full-bodied flavors, excellent depth and precision, and a lusty, heady finish. Les Perrières possesses that telltale steely, mineral, crisp bouquet, rich, honeyed, apple and tangerine fruit, medium to full body, and admirable acidity. Both of these wines should drink well over the next 5–6 years.

The exceptionally elegant, buttery 1992 Puligny-Montrachet Les Champs Gains offers attractive floral-scented fruit, good acidity, and a medium-bodied finish. It is more subtle and restrained than the 1992 Puligny-Montrachet Les Folatières, which is a bigger, thicker, richer wine, with a citrusy, apple-, honey-scented nose, and excellent richness and defini-tion. Its long finish displays adequate acidity and plenty of glycerin, fruit, and alcohol.

Among the grands crus, the 1992 Corton-Charlemagne boasts a big, ripe, pineapple-, mineral-scented nose, long, rich, fabulous fruit, and a full-bodied, muscular, tight finish. This is one 1992 that will easily last for a decade. The thick, buttery, unctuously textured, fat, lush 1992 Bienvenue Bâtard-Montrachet is more developed. It should be drunk over the next 7 years. The 1992 Bâtard-Montrachet exhibits a light golden color, a huge, honeyed, apple butter–scented bouquet, rich, ripe flavors, low acidity, and gobs of fruit, alcohol, and glycerin in the long, heady finish. This flamboyant wine should be drunk over the next 6–7 years. Equally impressive is the 1992 Criots Bâtard-Montrachet. It displays a bouquet of overripe cherries, oranges, and buttery popcorn intertwined with aromas of sweet, smoky new oak. Rich and full bodied, with layers of flavor, this superb wine is thick, heavy, and rich. It possesses enough acidity to provide freshness. Drink it over the next 7–9 years. The backward 1992 Chevalier-Montrachet is made in a chewy, thick style, with great flavor concentration, admirable acidity, and well-integrated, toasty new oak. More forward than the Chevalier-Montrachet made at Domaine Leflaive, it is broad shouldered, long, and impressive. It should drink well for 10–12 years. The 1992 Le Montrachet does not have the depth of the Criots Bâtard or Chevalier-Montrachet. Its mineral, orange, and honey-suckle scents, medium to full body, crisp acidity, and tightly knit framework make it an outstanding wine, but it is eclipsed in richness, power, intensity, and complexity by the Chevalier-Montrachet, Criots Bâtard-Montrachet, Bâtard-Montrachet, and Corton-Charlemagne.

LEROY AND DOMAINE D'AUVENAY (VOSNE-ROMANÉE)* * * * *

1991	Auxey-Duresses	D	87
1990	Auxey-Duresses	D	86
1990	Bourgogne Blanc	C	84
1991	Corton-Charlemagne	?	90+
1990	Corton-Charlemagne	?	91
1991	Meursault Les Narvaux	E	92
1990	Meursault Les Narvaux	E	88
1991	Puligny-Montrachet Les Folatières	EE	92+
1990	Puligny-Montrachet Les Folatières	EE	90

Some remarkable 1991 white burgundies were produced by Lalou Bize-Leroy. Yields aver-aged only 9 hectoliters per hectare in her Chardonnay vineyards, and alcohol levels averaged 13.5%. These wines will be the longest-lived whites of the 1991 vintage. Even the 1991 Auxey-Duresses displays uncommon power for a wine from this appellation. It is slightly richer than the 1990, with excellent definition, a big, floral, honeysuckle-scented nose, and rich, medium- to full-bodied, elegant flavors. Drink it over the next decade. The 1991

Meursault Les Narvaux is reminiscent of Chardonnay nectar. The amazingly intense nose of grilled hazelnuts, honeyed apples, and oranges is followed by an unctuously textured, superbly defined, rich, highly concentrated wine with exquisite balance and amazing richness and power. Tasted blind, most would think this is from a top white burgundy vintage such as 1989 or 1986. Equally impressive is the 1991 Puligny-Montrachet Les Folatières, which I am sure Leroy will feel I have underrated, as she feels it is the finest white wine she has made since her 1969 Meursault Les Perrières. The 1991 Les Folatières exhibits unbelievable richness, unctuous texture, admirable definition and focus, and a huge, flowery nose of butter, ripe apples, and tangerine scents. The flavors go on and on. Although low, the acidity is adequate to give the wine lift and balance. It is one of the few 1991 white burgundies that should not be consumed for 4–5 years; drink it over the subsequent 20 years.

The 1991 Corton-Charlemagne from Domaine Leroy needs at least 10 years of cellaring. It is a candidate for 25–30 years of aging. Huge and massive, with great density, it is totally unevolved, with a reticent bouquet. The power, weight, and density are something to behold, but this is an infantile, backward wine that should be purchased only by consumers with cold cellars and plenty of patience. If you had a child born in 1991 and want a Chardonnay grand cru for his or her twenty-first birthday, this would be a great choice.

Although none of the 1990s are as concentrated as the 1991s, they are still fine wines. The rich 1990 Auxey-Duresses offers oak-tinged, flowery, buttery fruit. It should drink well for 6–7 years. The 1990 Meursault Les Narvaux exhibits more mineral scents and flavors in its medium-bodied, elegant style. It is lighter than the 1989 and significantly less concentrated than the 1990. The 1990 Puligny-Montrachet Les Folatières is also made in an elegant, ripe, stylish manner, with excellent fruit and definition and a long finish. It gets my nod as the most concentrated of the 1990 Leroy white burgundies, save for the 1990 Corton-Charlemagne.

With respect to Leroy's 1990 Corton-Charlemagne, it is an oaky, bold, dramatic wine, with huge quantities of fruit, glycerin, and what appears to be tannin. Long, dense, and ripe, this wine needs at least 10 years of cellaring; it should keep for 25 years.

Admirers of Lalou Bize-Leroy's uncompromising style of highly concentrated, age-worthy white burgundy will be delighted to hear that she has acquired a parcel of vines in both Chevalier-Montrachet and Criots Bâtard-Montrachet. One can only imagine what levels of majesty these wines will reveal under the skills of Lalou and Bize-Leroy.

CHÂTEAU DE LEYNES (SAINT-VÉRAN)* * * *

1992 Saint-Véran Vieilles Vignes	B	87

Saint-Véran gets my nod as the most underrated white wine–producing village of Burgundy. This deep, honeyed, unctuously textured yet fresh and lively wine is loaded with fruit. Drink it over the next 4–5 years.

CHÂTEAU DE LA MALTROYE (CHASSAGNE-MONTRACHET)* * *

1992 Bâtard-Montrachet	E	93
1992 Chassagne-Montrachet Clos du Château de Maltroye	D	87
1992 Santenay La Comme	D	86

A new generation has taken control of de la Maltroye and the appallingly high levels of sulfur dioxide utilized in the past have been cut to a minimum. This is an estate on the verge of fully exploiting its potential. The excellent 1992 Santenay La Comme is a ripe, tasty wine with medium to full body, gobs of mineral, earthy, fleshy fruit, low acidity, and a precocious personality. Drink it over the next 1–2 years. The 1992 Chassagne-Montrachet

Clos du Château de Maltroye is richer and fuller, with spicy new oak, deep, fleshy flavors, medium to full body, and a soft, luscious finish. It should be drunk over the near term. The fabulous 1992 Bâtard-Montrachet offers a huge nose of spring flowers, honeysuckle, melted butter, and toast. The stupendous concentration, unctuous texture, and fleshy, full-bodied, low-acid, superbly concentrated flavors combine to provide a huge, massive mouthful of Chardonnay fruit. This terrific wine should age well for at least 5–7 years.

JEAN MANCIAT (MÂCON)* * *

1993 Mâcon-Villages Franlieu	B	87
1992 Mâcon-Villages Franlieu	B	86
1992 Mâcon-Villages Vieilles Vignes	B	86

Jean Manciat's 1993 Mâcon-Villages Franlieu is a floral-scented, pretty wine with crisp, tangy, delicious apple/buttery fruit, medium body, superb purity and delineation, and a dry finish. Drink it over the next 2–3 years.

Manciat has produced two competent Mâcons in 1992. Both exhibit fresh, spring flower blossom, lemony, apple-scented bouquets, and rich, medium-bodied flavors with adequate acidity. I did not detect any significant difference in concentration between the Vieilles Vignes and the Franlieu cuvées. Both display plenty of intensity, purity, and character. Drink them over the next 2–3 years.

DOMAINE JOSEPH MATROT (MEURSAULT)* * *

1992 Bourgogne Blanc Chardonnay	B	85
1992 Meursault	B	86
1992 Meursault Blagny	D	85
1992 Meursault Les Charmes	D	88
1992 Meursault Les Chevaliers	D	83
1992 Puligny-Montrachet Les Chalumeaux	D	86

Matrot's white wines tend to be austere and lean, but in a ripe vintage of thick, juicy wines such as 1992, his wines exhibit more flesh and up-front charm. This is another domaine that has made an attractive 1992 Bourgogne Blanc Chardonnay. Elegant, with crisp, steely fruit, medium body, and fine freshness, this is a wine to drink over the next year.

The 1992 Meursault is understated, subtle, refreshing, and pleasant. The monolithic 1992 Meursault Les Chevaliers is pleasant in a straightforward manner. The 1992 Meursault Blagny is crisp and elegant, as well as richer and more complete than the Meursault and Les Chevaliers. The top wine of this quartet is the 1992 Meursault Les Charmes. It is a powerful, rich wine with light golden color, a big, spicy, oaky, smoked nut–scented bouquet, luscious, fat, unctuous flavors, full body, and a long, low-acid, powerful, alcoholic finish. Drink it over the next 5–6 years.

The 1992 Puligny-Montrachet Les Chalumeaux is also monolithic and foursquare. It offers chunky fruit, but lacks finesse and elegance. It will make a fine mouthful of wine for drinking over the next 4–5 years.

OLIVIER MERLIN (MÂCON)* * * * *

1993 Mâcon La Roche Vieilles Vignes	B	88
1993 Mâcon La Roche Vineuse	B	87

One of a handful of bright, shining stars from Mâcon, Olivier Merlin's 1993 Mâcon La Roche Vineuse possesses the crisp, vibrant, rich fruit found in a top-notch Mâcon, unencumbered by any wood notes. Its purity, flowery, apple/orangelike fruitiness, excellent delineation, and uplifting finish are all a Mâcon should be. Drink it over the next several years with seafood or fowl dishes. The 1993 Mâcon La Roche Vieilles Vignes includes the same fruit character, as well as more ripeness, depth, and body, in addition to some smoky, toasty new oak in the fragrant bouquet. A bigger, more alcoholic Mâcon, it should last for 3–4 years.

DOMAINE LOUIS MICHEL ET FILS (CHABLIS)* * * *

1992 Chablis	C	86
1992 Chablis Les Clos	D	90
1992 Chablis Grenouilles	D	89
1992 Chablis Montée de Tonnerre	C	89
1992 Chablis Montmains	C	89
1992 Chablis Vaillons	C	90
1992 Chablis Vaudesir	D	90

Jean-Luc Michel's Chablis is fermented and aged in stainless steel. His wines possess extraordinary purity and precision. While there is no question that I love the barrel-fermented Chablis of Dauvissat and Raveneau, I admire these wines equally. With their extraordinary amount of fruit- and mineral-scented austerity and clarity, these 1992s are the finest overall group of wines made by Michel in years.

The 1992 Chablis is crisp and fresh, with lovely mineral-scented, applelike fruit, and a ripe, surprisingly rich finish. Drink it over the next 2–3 years. The cold steel–, wet stone–scented personality of the 1992 Chablis Montmains is classic. The wine possesses ripe, rich fruit, medium to full body, lovely purity and balance, and impeccable focus. Big, elegant, and fresh, it should be drunk over the next 5–6 years. The superb 1992 Chablis Vaillons reveals lower acidity and an opulent, rich, multidimensional character. Drink it over the next 4–5 years.

Michel's excellent 1992 Chablis Montée de Tonnerre is supple and fatter than the other wines, with less definition. This weighty wine should be consumed over the next 3–4 years. The 1992 Chablis Vaudesir is full bodied and rich, with a superb bouquet of spring flowers, lemons, buttered apples, and minerals. Marvelously rich and full, with superb clarity and low acidity, this large-scaled Chablis should drink well for another 5–7 years. The 1992 Chablis Grenouilles exhibits an intense, penetrating nose of honeyed fruit, wet stones, and flowers. The acid is low, and the wine is rich, full, and more powerful than Michel's other 1992s. It makes for a mouthful of decadent Chardonnay fruit; I would opt for drinking it over the next 3–4 years. A formidable nose of honey, spring flowers, butter, and steel soars from the glass of the 1992 Chablis Les Clos. Ripe, fat, and full bodied, with gobs of fruit, excellent purity, and a blockbuster finish, this is a great Chablis for drinking over the next 4–5 years.

DOMAINE PIERRE MILLOT-BATTAULT (MEURSAULT)* * *

1992 Meursault	D	75
1992 Meursault Les Charmes	D	85

Attractive, light, pleasant wines were made by this estate in 1992. The 1992 Meursault Les Charmes is fashioned in a lighter, more delicate style.

DOMAINE BERNARD MOREY (CHASSAGNE-MONTRACHET)* * * *

1992 Bâtard-Montrachet	EE	90
1992 Bourgogne Blanc Chardonnay	B	85

1992	Chassagne-Montrachet Les Baudines	D	87
1992	Chassagne-Montrachet Les Caillerets	D	92
1992	Chassagne-Montrachet Les Embrazées	D	90
1992	Chassagne-Montrachet Morgeot	D	90
1992	Chassagne-Montrachet Vieilles Vignes	D	87
1992	Saint-Aubin Les Charmots	C	87

It continues to be rare to find anything less than exciting from Bernard Morey, a red-cheeked vigneron with a fifties pompadour haircut. His wines are delicious in off years, so it is not surprising he has hit the bull's-eye with the 1992s. Although these offerings had just been bottled when I tasted them, they were still immensely impressive wines.

The 1992 Bourgogne Blanc Chardonnay is a ripe, tasty, mouth-filling, fruity wine. Slightly better and more elegant, without sacrificing any of the vintage's fat and flesh, is Morey's 1992 Saint-Aubin Les Charmots. It offers excellent richness, a big, floral, buttery nose, medium to full body, and a long, lusty, heady finish. Drink it over the next 3–4 years.

The fat, unctuously textured, chewy 1992 Chassagne-Montrachet Vieilles Vignes exhibits gobs of fruit and plenty of alcohol in the finish. It is not for the shy. For drinking over the next 3–4 years it provides a sumptuous glass of uncomplicated, rich white burgundy. The 1992 Chassagne-Montrachet Les Baudines displays an attractive bouquet of buttery apples, floral scents, and toasty, smoky new oak. Rich, with medium to full body, less alcoholic punch, and a crisp, elegant finish, it is more subtle. The 1992 Chassagne-Montrachet Les Embrazées is a full-throttle, in-your-face style of white burgundy with a huge nose of candied oranges, honeyed nuts, and buttery popcorn. Thick, unctuous, and rich, this thoroughly seductive, decadent wine possesses low acidity, as well as gobs of fruit, glycerin, and alcohol. Drink it over the next 4–5 years. The 1992 Chassagne-Montrachet Les Caillerets boasts all of the flamboyance, drama, and heady richness of Les Embrazées, but it reveals even more impressive extraction of flavor, not to mention an amazingly long finish. The wine provides a huge, massive mouthful of voluptuously textured Chardonnay fruit wrapped in smoky new oak. Although it possesses more structure than Les Embrazées, my instincts suggest it should be drunk over the next 4–6 years. Consumers looking for less drama, some subtlety, and more focus should try the 1992 Chassagne-Montrachet Morgeot. A rich, buttery, floral, mineral-scented nose is followed by a wine with medium to full body, higher acidity than Morey's other offerings, and plenty of power, alcohol, and glycerin in the finish. It may not last any longer than the other 1992s, but it is more structured.

Less evolved, the 1992 Bâtard-Montrachet reveals mammoth richness, a thick, chewy, powerful, full-bodied texture, and gobs of fruit. It is still a large-scaled, monolithic wine. A wine of power and immense stature, it relies more on its superconcentrated, thick juicy fruitiness than on its elegance for its appeal. Drink it between now and 2000.

DOMAINE PIERRE MOREY (MEURSAULT)* *

1991	Bâtard-Montrachet	D	85
1991	Bourgogne Aligoté	B	84
1991	Bourgogne Chardonnay	C	84
1991	Meursault Les Charmes	D	84
1991	Meursault Les Genevrières	D	84
1991	Meursault Les Narvaux	D	83

1991 Meursault Les Perrières	E	82
1991 Meursault Les Tessons	D	78

Pierre Morey is capable of making super wines, but his 1991s all reveal the effects of dilution caused by the heavy rains that plagued the harvest. Two of the less expensive wines merit attention. Morey has turned out a fine 1991 Bourgogne Aligoté. It is crisp, light, elegant, and ideal for drinking over the next year. The same can be said for the 1991 Bourgogne Chardonnay.

As for the other wines, the 1991 Meursault Les Tessons is lean, tart, and one-dimensional. The 1991 Meursault Les Narvaux is elegant and medium bodied, but short. The 1991 Meursault Les Charmes is riper and richer, but small-scaled and abrupt. The tight 1991 Meursault Les Genevrières exhibits crisp acidity, and a pleasant, straightforward finish. The 1991 Bâtard-Montrachet is the most ambitious of these offerings. It is an understated, subtle wine with some elegance, but it is dominated by oak. Drink it over the next several years.

I did not have a chance to taste Morey's 1992s, lamentably, in view of the fact that they are highly regarded by a number of my Burgundy friends.

DOMAINE MICHEL NIELLON (CHASSAGNE-MONTRACHET)* * * * *

1992 Bâtard-Montrachet	EE	93
1991 Bâtard-Montrachet	EE	93
1992 Chassagne-Montrachet	D	88
1991 Chassagne-Montrachet	D	87
1992 Chassagne-Montrachet Les Champs Gains	D	91
1991 Chassagne-Montrachet Les Champs Gains	D	87
1992 Chassagne-Montrachet Clos St.-Jean	D	93
1992 Chassagne-Montrachet La Maltroie	D	89
1991 Chassagne-Montrachet La Maltroie	D	89
1992 Chassagne-Montrachet Les Vergers	D	90+
1991 Chassagne-Montrachet Les Vergers	D	90
1992 Chevalier-Montrachet	EEE	90+
1991 Chevalier-Montrachet	EEE	91

Michel Niellon is among the top-half dozen white-burgundy producers. He consistently turns out brilliant, frequently awesome wines from his tiny domaine of 12.5 acres. In terms of decadence and complexity, Niellon is at the top of my personal shopping list. He fashioned terrific 1992s and 1991s.

The 1992s were bottled a month before I saw them, and despite Niellon's belief that they were subdued, I was blown away by most of them. Niellon's perennially low yields are reflected in his wines. Even in lighter years, they possess a superb mid-palate and that unctuous, rich, chewy personality that can only emanate from low-yielding Chardonnay vines. The 1992s are all fat, ripe, concentrated wines. It would be hard to find a better Chassagne-Montrachet than Niellon's 1992. It is a hefty, ripe, full-bodied wine with an opulent palate, gobs of fruit, and enough acidity to hold everything together. Drink it over the next 4–5 years. The 1992 Chassagne-Montrachet Les Champs Gains also displays great extraction of fruit, as well as a superb smorgasbord of tropical fruit aromas married with butter and toasty new oak. It is a powerful wine, with fascinating richness that is the essence of Chardonnay's character. Drink this decadent Chassagne over the next 7–8 years. The sensational 1992 Chassagne-Montrachet Clos St.-Jean is fatter, richer, and longer. From both an aromatic and flavor perspective, it is even more compelling than Les Champs Gains. The Clos St.-Jean exhibits fabulous richness, unbelievable quantities of glycerin and fruit extraction, and lusty alcohol levels. Drink this decadent, blockbuster white burgundy over the next 6–7 years. The 1992 Chassagne-Montrachet La Maltroie is restrained, with slightly less fat and unctuosity than Niellon's other 1992s. Still voluptuous, superrich, deep, and full bodied, it should be drunk in its first decade of life.

The tightest wines among the 1992s are the Chassagne-Montrachet Les Vergers and Chevalier-Montrachet. The Chassagne-Montrachet Les Vergers is of grand cru quality, and the 1992 is the wine highest in acidity and firmest in structure. Large-scaled, with an inner core of sweet, ripe, unctuous fruit, it is unevolved and tight. Cellar it for 2–3 years and drink it over the following decade. The 1992 Chevalier-Montrachet displays similar attributes. Although it is the most expensive wine from the Niellon portfolio, it is not as intense as several of his premiers crus, and never as rich as the Bâtard-Montrachet. It is an outstanding, elegantly styled 1992.

If you have the requisite money and contacts, the wine to buy is Niellon's Bâtard-Montrachet, made from a vineyard planted in 1927. It is one of the great white wines of Burgundy. The 1992 is no exception, offering a huge nose and mouth-feel of massively extracted Chardonnay fruit. There is a mélange of aromas and flavors, ranging from oranges, apples, and coconuts, to buttered vanilla cookies and honey. Huge and superrich, it is capable of another 10–15 years of cellaring. Absolutely magnificent!

Niellon's 1991s are special wines. He makes no bones about saying that much of his low-yielding vineyards were harvested before the rains. The yields in 1991 were a minuscule 20–25 hectoliters per hectare. The 1991 Chassagne-Montrachet is a lovely, fat, fruity wine with plenty of glycerin and alcohol, low acidity, and a lush finish. Drink it over the next 3–4 years. The 1991 Chassagne-Montrachet Les Champs Gains, from some of the youngest vines, displays a lovely, honeyed, apple blossom–scented nose, ripe, medium- to full-bodied flavors, a juicy, succulent texture, and a soft, smooth finish. It should be drunk over the next 3–4 years. The 1991 Chassagne-Montrachet La Maltroie (unfortunately, all of it is sold in Japan and England) offers a stunning nose of spring flowers, honeyed melons, and apples. Superrich, with low acidity, and a fat, forward, blockbuster personality, this wine should be drunk over the next 3–4 years. The 1991 Chassagne-Montrachet Les Vergers exhibits superb fruit, an unctuous, thick, full-bodied texture, low acidity, wonderful ripeness, and magnificent length. Niellon's yields were 22 hectoliters per hectare. For drinking over the next 5–6 years this wine offers a decadent glass of complex, rich Chardonnay fruit.

The 1991 Chevalier-Montrachet (100 cases produced) appears to be richer, deeper, and more alcoholic and powerful than the 1992. There is gobs of sweet fruit, as well as a tremendous, almost oily thickness to it. This beautiful Chardonnay is reminiscent of the remarkable 1980 and 1981 from Chalone. Drink it over the next 5–6 years. While Niellon's 1991s are superb, they are not long-term wines because of low acidity. The top wine in 1991 is no surprise. It is the Bâtard-Montrachet (only 3 barrels, or 75 cases, were produced). It is the fattest and richest wine with the longest finish. Large-scaled, alcoholic, and sensationally perfumed, it is loaded with extraction. Drink it over the next 7–8 years.

DOMAINE P. N. NINOT-CELLIER-MEIX-GUILLAUME (RULLY)* * *
1991 Rully Gresigny   C   88

Ninot is one of those hot vignerons whose wines can be found on many French two- and three-star restaurant's wine lists. This offering, of which two-thirds is barrel-fermented, is unquestionably one of the finest Rullys I have tasted. Anyone who has read my book on Burgundy, or the chapter on that region in my 1993 *Wine Buyer's Guide*, knows that Rully, an overachieving appellation in the Côte Chalonnaise, is a terrific source for reasonably priced white burgundy. This rich, deep, concentrated wine exhibits superb fruit, loads of flavor, a touch of mint that adds to the complexity, and a long, zesty, wonderfully clean and well-delineated finish. Drink it over the next 3–4 years.

DOMAINE PAUL PERNOT (PULIGNY-MONTRACHET)* * *

1992	Bâtard-Montrachet	EE	89
1992	Bienvenue Bâtard-Montrachet	E	87
1992	Bourgogne Chardonnay Champerrier	C	82
1992	Puligny-Montrachet	C	82
1992	Puligny-Montrachet Les Folatières	D	87
1991	Puligny-Montrachet Les Folatières	D	91
1992	Puligny-Montrachet Les Pucelles	D	86

Pernot is capable of producing some of the greatest white burgundies, but his recent fame (unfortunately augmented by my ecstatic reviews of him in my *Burgundy* book) may be having some undesirable ramifications. Yields have become too high, and Pernot, a conservative man not given to taking many risks, clearly pulled the trigger and harvested too early in 1992. These are among the most acidic wines of the vintage. The acidity along with abundant yields has resulted in Pernot turning out less successful wines in 1992 than in 1991 or 1990.

The straightforward 1992 Bourgogne Chardonnay Champerrier is crisp and tart. The 1992 Puligny-Montrachet is acidic and light, but pleasant. The 1992 Puligny-Montrachet Les Folatières and 1992 Puligny-Montrachet Les Pucelles are competent, elegant wines, with high acidity, fine fruit, and pleasant, straightforward personalities. While they are attractive, well-made wines, they are disappointing in the context of Pernot's vineyards and the vintage. The 1992 Bienvenue Bâtard-Montrachet is bigger and richer, with some spicy fruit, as well as annoyingly high acidity.

The only wine that has pretensions of being something grand is the 1992 Bâtard-Montrachet. It is deeper and riper, with tart acidity, good, rich, fleshy fruit, and full body.

After years of anonymity, Paul Pernot has begun to enjoy the success he worked so hard to obtain. However, his 1992s are not that impressive.

If you are looking for a top-notch Pernot wine that has probably been ignored because of the vintage's lousy reputation, check out Pernot's superb 1991 Puligny-Montrachet Les Folatières. It is an opulent, rich, full-bodied wine with more concentration than any of Pernot's 1992s. Because of its low acidity, it should be drunk over the next 3–4 years.

PERRUSSET (MÂCON)* * *

1992	Mâcon-Farges	C	86
1992	Mâcon-Farges Futs de Chêne	C	84

These are two well-made 1992s from the Mâconnais. The nonoak-aged Mâcon-Farges was bottled unfiltered. It reveals a good, floral, fruity nose, medium-bodied flavors with excellent purity and definition, and a rich, medium-bodied finish. Drink it over the next 1–2 years. The oaked cuvée, Mâcon-Farges Futs de Chêne, is plump and ripe, but heavier, and not as fresh. Both are good, but the nonoaked cuvée offers more flexibility with food.

DOMAINE HENRI PRUDHON (SAINT-AUBIN)* * *

1992	Chassagne-Montrachet Les Chenevottes	D	90
1992	Saint-Aubin	C	82
1992	Saint-Aubin Les Perrières	C	86

Prudhon is one of the stars of the village of Saint-Aubin. His 1992 Saint-Aubin village wine is pleasant, crisp, and lively. It should be drunk over the next 1–2 years. More interesting is the richer, more concentrated, perfumed 1992 Saint-Aubin Les Perrières. The unfiltered 1992 Chassagne-Montrachet Les Chenevottes makes for a sumptuous glass of Chardonnay. The huge nose of smoky bacon fat, buttered popcorn, and apple blossoms is a turn-on. This rich, deep, multidimensional, chewy, fleshy, full-bodied wine will provide stunning drinking for 5–6 years.

DOMAINE RAMONET (CHASSAGNE-MONTRACHET)* * * * *

1992 Bâtard-Montrachet	EEE	93
1991 Bâtard-Montrachet	EEE	90+
1992 Bienvenue Bâtard-Montrachet	EEE	90
1991 Bienvenue Bâtard-Montrachet	EEE	89
1992 Bourgogne Aligoté	B	86
1992 Chassagne-Montrachet Les Boudriottes	D	87
1992 Chassagne-Montrachet Les Caillerets	E	92
1991 Chassagne-Montrachet Les Caillerets	E	87
1992 Chassagne-Montrachet Les Chaumées	D	90
1992 Chassagne-Montrachet Morgeot	D	87
1991 Chassagne-Montrachet Morgeot	D	84
1992 Chassagne-Montrachet Les Ruchottes	E	93
1991 Chassagne-Montrachet Les Ruchottes	E	89
1991 Chassagne-Montrachet Les Vergers	E	86
1992 Le Montrachet	EEE	96
1991 Le Montrachet	EEE	90+
1991 Saint-Aubin Le Charmois	C	84

Because the Domaine Ramonet enjoys a mythical status it is fashionable to criticize the wines as not being as exceptional as they used to be. Don't fall for this line of thinking. This domaine produces some of the finest Chardonnays in the world. While other domaines have begun making superb wines over recent years (e.g., Amiot-Bonfils and Colin-Déléger), and others have always made wines as profound as Ramonet, in particular Michel Niellon, the name Ramonet still carries with it a magical significance. If there is any criticism to be leveled, it is that vintages in the late eighties and early nineties appear to possess high acidity. The domaine adamantly denies doing any acidification. Ramonet made excellent 1992s, and very good 1991s that are worthy of serious buyers' interest.

A good introduction to the Ramonet style of white burgundy is their fine Bourgogne Aligoté. Made in a ripe style, the 1992 offers the scent of ripe peaches, round, rich flavors, and a lush finish. It should be drunk over its first 2–3 years of life.

There are five premier cru white wines from the village of Chassagne-Montrachet. The 1992 Chassagne-Montrachet Morgeot is the lightest and leanest, with the most obvious minerallike character. It may be the most intellectual of these offerings, but it is also the least opulent. The 1992 Chassagne-Montrachet Les Boudriottes (usually a red wine vineyard) is round, ripe, and easy to understand and to drink and savor. It will not last, but it is tasty. The 1992 Chassagne-Montrachet Les Chaumées is soft, fat, and opulent, with deep flavors of honeyed nuts, pineapples, and apples. Medium to full bodied, with decent acidity, it is a wine to drink in its first decade of life. The 1992 Chassagne-Montrachet Les Caillerets offers a smoky, earthy, tropical fruit–scented nose, full body, power, and intensity, and crisp acidity in the finish. It is a large-scaled wine that approaches grand cru quality. The Chassagne-Montrachet Les Ruchottes (referred to as "the little Montrachet" by the Ramonets) is the wine to buy. It is powerful and alcoholic, with great fruit and structure, as well as remarkable density and intensity. The 1992 is all of those things, with fabulous quantities of fruit and an explosively long, crisp finish. It is one 1992 that requires 3–4 years of cellaring; it should keep for 12–15 years.

The tightly knit, high-acid 1992 Bienvenue Bâtard-Montrachet makes one wonder if some acid adjustments were made. Ripe, tart, tightly knit, and big, it needs another 2–3 years of cellaring; it should keep for 10–12 years. Even richer, the 1992 Bâtard-Montrachet exhibits some mouth-searing, crisp acidity that is not yet integrated. Deep, rich, and full bodied, it offers buttery tropical fruit aromas intermingled with scents of smoke, earth, and vanillin. It will benefit from 4–5 years in the cellar; it will keep for 12–15 years.

There are four barrels of the 1992 Le Montrachet, but according to Noël Ramonet, "two will be declassified." Wouldn't you like to be the lucky recipient of some of that wine? The two barrels that will be estate-bottled come from 70-year-old vines. It is an awesomely rich, full-bodied, massive wine oozing with fruit and that distinctive steely, minerallike Montrachet character. As usual, the price will be astronomical. This magnificent Montrachet will drink well for 15–20 years.

The 1991 Ramonet offerings are crisp, lean, elegant, and tightly knit. Again, high acidity is a hallmark in what was a notoriously low-acid year. The 1991 Chassagne-Montrachet is less acidic than the 1992, as well as well made and light bodied, with ripe fruit, and an interesting touch of mint in the nose. The attractive 1991 Saint-Aubin Le Charmois is elegant, crisp, fruity, and medium bodied. The austere 1991 Chassagne-Montrachet Morgeot is tight, hard, and backward, with high acidity. It may improve with another 1–2 years in the bottle. The lightweight 1991 Chassagne-Montrachet Les Vergers offers good ripeness, medium body, and attractive buttery, popcornlike fruit presented in a compact format.

The quality takes a significant leap with the 1991 Chassagne-Montrachet Les Caillerets. It offers whiffs of wonderfully ripe, rich tropical fruits intertwined with lavish quantities of toasty, smoky oak. The wine is full bodied, rich, and dense, as well as concentrated and powerful, with good acidity. Drink it over the next decade. The closed 1991 Chassagne-Montrachet Les Ruchottes exhibits surprising structure for a 1991, impressive power, admirable richness, and fine depth. Unlike most top 1991s, this is a wine to cellar for 2–3 years; it should last through most of the first decade of the next century.

The elegant, understated, ripe, crisp, acidic 1991 Bienvenue Bâtard-Montrachet possesses fine flavor and length, wonderful purity, and a fascinating steely, apple blossom–scented bouquet. The acidity appears to be suppressing much of its charm and fatness. The two best wines from the Ramonet stable in 1991 are the Bâtard-Montrachet and the Le Montrachet. Although closed, the 1991 Bâtard offers light-intensity aromas of honey, butter, and sweet, smoked apples, medium to full body, and excellent precision and depth. This wine needs at least 4–5 years in the cellar; it should keep for over a decade. The medium-weight 1991 Le Montrachet reveals copious amounts of fruit and depth. A lovely bouquet of buttered apples, spring flowers, and honey is followed by a medium-bodied wine with layers of rich, sweet fruit. Drink this outstanding wine over the next 10–12 years.

As a sidelight, while discussing Noël Ramonet's favorite Le Montrachets, he proceeded to open the 1978, the only vintage of Ramonet's Le Montrachet that I had never tasted. The wine exhibits a deep golden color, but is extremely austere and backward. It appears capable of lasting another 15–20 years. It is one of those wines that is impressive more for its structure and potential longevity than for its depth of fruit or hedonistic virtues. The 1990 and 1983 Le Montrachets are Noel's favorites. He feels the 1982 should be consumed (I agree). Moreover, he thinks 1982 and 1989 are better than 1986 (I disagree).

REMOISSENET PÈRE ET FILS (BEAUNE)* * * *

1992	Bâtard-Montrachet	E	90
1992	Bienvenue Bâtard-Montrachet	E	90
1992	Bourgogne Blanc Posanges	B	84
1992	Chassagne-Montrachet Les Caillerets	D	88
1992	Corton-Charlemagne Diamond Jubilee	D	91
1992	Meursault	C	84
1992	Meursault Les Charmes	D	87
1992	Meursault Les Genevrières	D	87
1992	Le Montrachet Baron Thenard	EEE	89
1992	Puligny-Montrachet	D	85
1992	Puligny-Montrachet Les Combettes	D	90
1992	Puligny Montrachet Les Folatières	D	89

Remoissenet enjoys a well-deserved reputation for his white wines. There is a tendency at this estate to block the malolactic fermentation, to keep the wines off their lees, to rack them frequently, and to bottle them after a relatively vigorous filtration. The fact that so much remains in the wines makes one wonder what they would be like if they were not manipulated so much.

The 1992s all reveal ripe fruit, higher acidity than most white burgundies (remember, the malolactic fermentation was blocked), and laudable purity. The generic wines, including the 1992 Bourgogne Blanc Posanges, the 1992 Meursault, and the 1992 Puligny-Montrachet, are pleasant, straightforward wines. Somewhat light for the vintage, they are attractive and cleanly made. The 1992 Meursault Les Charmes and 1992 Meursault Les Genevrières are understated, restrained wines, with crisp fruit, moderately high acidity, admirable purity, and considerable elegance. Both wines should drink well for 10–12 years.

The quality jumps with the excellent 1992 Puligny-Montrachet Les Folatières, a deep, luscious, medium- to full-bodied wine with loads of fruit, a lovely mineral-, floral-, and honey-scented nose, and excellent length. It should drink well for 10–12 years. The 1992 Puligny-Montrachet Les Combettes is denser, riper, and fuller, with a smoky, buttery, hazelnut-scented nose. Rich, full, and long, it should last for a decade.

Among the grands crus, the 1992 Bienvenue Bâtard-Montrachet exhibits considerable richness, density, and body, as well as a nice touch of toasty new oak and heady, alcoholic, ripe, concentrated fruit in the finish. It should drink well for 10–12 years. Even richer, the 1992 Bâtard-Montrachet is dense and unctuous, with fine acidity, powerful, authoritative flavors, and whoppingly long length. The finest wine in Remoissenet's 1992 portfolio is the Corton-Charlemagne Diamond Jubilee. The complex orange, mineral, smoky, buttery, apple aromas are combined with full body, superb concentration, and crisp acidity. It should be at its best between now and 2007. The 1992 Le Montrachet from Baron Thenard is impressive, but shy and understated when compared with Remoissenet's Corton-Charlemagne and Bâtard-Montrachet. It possesses the component parts to last for 10–15 or more years.

DOMAINE DE ROALLY (MÂCON)* * * *

1993 Mâcon-Viré (André Goyard)	C	87
1992 Mâcon-Viré	B	89

The 1993 is a dense, buttery, medium-bodied Mâcon with considerable character, gobs of fruit, and an overall sense of elegance and grace. There is even a mineral *terroir* character —unusual for a wine from the Mâconnais region. Drink this stylish, crisp, deliciously fruity wine over the next 1–2 years. The 1992 Mâcon-Viré is superserious, medium to fullbodied and loaded with concentrated fruit. Drink this rich, well-balanced Chardonnay over the next 4–5 years.

ROBERT-DENOGENT (MÂCON)* * * *

1992 Mâcon-Villages Clos des Bertillonnes	C	86
1992 Pouilly-Fuissé La Croix Vieilles Vignes	D	88
1992 Pouilly-Fuissé Les Reisses Vieilles Vignes	D	89

This is a highly respected estate in the Mâconnais, with yields that did not exceed 30 hectoliters per hectare in the abundant 1992 vintage. The attractive 1992 Mâcon-Villages Clos des Bertillonnes offers a pure, floral-scented nose, crisp, tart, elegant, medium-bodied flavors, and a zesty, lively finish. Drink it over the next year. The 1992 Pouilly-Fuissé La Croix Vieilles Vignes exhibits a big, honeyed, apricot- and buttery-scented nose, rich, deep, fat flavors with gobs of extract and richness, and a plush, lavishly fat, ripe finish. Drink it over the next 2–3 years. The 1992 Pouilly-Fuissé Les Reisses Vieilles Vignes is produced from one of the finest vineyards in Pouilly-Fuissé. The wine is as rich as La Croix, with greater body and more flavor, as well as an attractive mineral component. Possessing fine structure and definition, it is an impressively deep, multidimensional Pouilly-Fuissé for drinking over the next 4–5 years.

DOMAINE MAURICE ROLLIN PÈRE ET FILS (PERNAND-VERGELESSES)* *

1992 Corton-Charlemagne	E	90
1992 Pernand-Vergelesses	C	84

While Rollin's 1992 Pernand-Vergelesses is a chunky, crisp, straightforward wine, the 1992 Corton-Charlemagne (made from yields of 40 hectoliters per hectare) is the best I have tasted from this estate. Rich, with wonderful, sweet, unctuously textured fruit, this lavishly rich wine exhibits enough acidity to provide 10 years of cellaring potential.

DOMAINE DE LA ROMANÉE-CONTI (VOSNE-ROMANÉE)* * * * *

1991 Le Montrachet	EEE	90
1990 Le Montrachet	EEE	92

The DRC was unhappy with their 1992 and did not produce any Le Montrachet in that vintage. Those millionaires lucky enough to have access to this rarity, frequently the most concentrated Chardonnay made in the world, should be pleased with the 1991 and 1990. The 1991 Le Montrachet is a fat, unctuously styled wine made from yields of only 32 hectoliters per hectare. Although rich, it does not have the depth and power of vintages such as 1990, 1989, and 1986. Soft and precocious because of low acidity, it should be drunk over the next decade. The 1990 Le Montrachet exhibits considerable opulence, as well as a telltale nose of coconut, buttered apples, and smoky, toasty new oak. Magnificently deep, expansive, and rich, with moderate acidity, it should prove to be a sensational DRC Le Montrachet. It is capable of lasting 15–20 years, but readers should note that on two occasions the 1990 was oxidized, once from a rare magnum that had been stored perfectly!

Note: I recently had the good fortune to taste all the DRC Le Montrachets from 1979 through 1989. The 1986, followed by 1983, 1979, and 1989, were show-stoppers. The 1989 has the potential to be another 1986. The 1983 is phenomenally powerful and intense. I also enjoyed the 1982 and 1985, although the latter wine is backward, with high acidity and a monolithic personality. It will be interesting to see how much complexity develops. If you are a multimillionaire and feel compelled to taste the most lavish Chardonnays in the world, these wines are obligatory purchases.

GUY ROULOT (MEURSAULT)* * * *

1992 Bourgogne Blanc	C	84
1992 Meursault Les Charmes	D	88
1991 Meursault Les Charmes	D	88
1992 Meursault Les Luchets	D	86
1992 Meursault Les Meix Chavaux	D	86
1991 Meursault Les Meix Chavaux	D	86
1992 Meursault Les Perrières	D	89
1992 Meursault Les Tessons	D	87
1991 Meursault Les Tessons	D	87
1992 Meursault Les Tillets	D	87
1992 Meursault Les Vireuils	D	85

Guy Roulot's wines are made in an elegant style. The young Roulot feels his best vintage over recent years has been 1990, followed by 1992. As the following notes reflect, the 1991s were also successful. The 1992s are slightly lighter than other producers', yet they are graceful wines. All of the 1992s had just been bottled when I tasted them, so they may have been somewhat subdued.

The 1992 Bourgogne Blanc is crisp, light, refreshing, and fruity. Drink it over the next 1–2 years. The single-vineyard Meursaults, such as the 1992 Les Vireuils, are light and flowery, with medium body, fine balance, and freshness. The 1992 Les Meix Chavaux exhibits more richness and ripeness than Les Vireuils, as well as a broader palate. Both wines should be consumed over the next 5–6 years. The 1992 Meursault Les Tillets offers crisp acidity, good ripeness, and complex nutty, lemon/apple-scented aromas and flavors. It is well balanced, with admirable depth and richness. Although the soft, peachy, nut-scented 1992 Meursault Les Luchets may be too obvious, it is round, generous, and attractive.

The three best Meursaults from Roulot are generally Les Tessons, Les Charmes, and Les Perrières. Roulot's father Guy always adored Les Tessons, stating on the label, the Clos de Mon Plaisir. This wine is usually an opulent, medium- to full-bodied, classic example of the appellation. The 1992 Meursault Les Tessons represents an elegant, understated style. It exhibits a buttery, applelike richness, fine depth, and excellent balance. Like most of Roulot's single-vineyard Meursaults, it should be consumed over the next 5–7 years. The 1992 Meursault Les Charmes is the fattest, richest, most powerful of these offerings. With a honeyed, nutty, apple butter–scented nose, medium to full body, crisp acidity, and a fine finish, it should drink well for 6–7 years. The 1992 Meursault Les Perrières possesses that exquisite steely, mineral-scented nose combined with aromas of apple blossoms, ripe fruit, and medium to full body. There is zesty acidity, and plenty of richness and length.

Roulot's surprisingly intense 1991 Meursault Les Charmes exhibits a delectable orange/honey-scented nose, and ripe, lush, fat flavors. It should be consumed over the next 2–3 years.

CHÂTEAU DE LA SAULE (MONTAGNY)* * * *
1992 Montagny Les Burnins   C 87

This has always been one of my favorite Montagny estates. The well-built 1992 offers sweet, cherry and apple–like fruit, medium to full body, purity, and a lush finish. Drink it over the next 1–2 years.

DOMAINE SEVE (POUILLY)* * *
1991 Pouilly-Fuissé   C 87

The excellent wines from this tiny Pouilly estate (17.5 acres) are made from a high percentage of old vines. The 1991 Pouilly-Fuissé possesses an excellent nose of honeyed apple fruit, rich, medium-bodied flavors with that inner core of fruit that suggests old vines, and a long, ripe, tangy aftertaste with well-integrated acidity. It is a beautifully pure, well-made Pouilly-Fuissé for drinking over the next 2–4 years.

DOMAINE TALMARD (UCHIZY)* * * *
1992 Mâcon-Chardonnay   A 87

Proprietors Paul and Philibert Talmard have fashioned a rich, medium- to full-bodied Chardonnay with copious quantities of tropical fruit, as well as fine depth, focus, and purity. An excellent value, this delicious wine should be drunk over the next year.

DOMAINE JEAN THEVENET/DOMAINE DE LA BONGRAND (MÂCON)* * * * *
1992 Mâcon Clessé   C 92

1990 Mâcon-Clessé Cuvée Tradition   C 90

1989 Mâcon-Clessé Cuvée Tradition   C 91

1992 Mâcon-Viré Emilian Gillet   C 90

Mâconnais is a largely undiscovered, fertile source for producers committed to making wines that qualitatively compare with their more prestigious and expensive siblings from the Côte d'Or. In my opinion, the finest Mâconnais producer is Jean Thevenet. It is no secret why he does so well. Exceptionally low yields, physiologically ripe fruit, and respect for the noninterventionist philosophy of wine production give Thevenet's Mâcon-Clessé and the Emilian Gillet Mâcon-Viré an intensity and opulence that have more in common with a great wine from Meursault or Chassagne-Montrachet than other Mâcons. I told Thevenet his wines were great if drunk in the first 5–6 years of life and he responded by presenting me with some older bottles that blew me away. The 1962 and 1971 were still remarkable wines when drunk in 1993. Thevenet has been on a roll with terrific wines in 1988, 1989, and 1990, surprisingly good 1991s, and exceptional 1992s.

The 1992 Mâcon-Clessé reveals a light gold color, and an extraordinary perfume of honeyed, buttery, apple fruit, flowers, and an underlying mineral scent. Full bodied, with layers of chewy, rich, glycerin-endowed, highly concentrated Chardonnay flavors, this splendid, complex, profound white burgundy should drink well for 10+ years. If you think $22 for a Mâcon is too high, consider how much a grand cru white burgundy of this quality would cost! This wine is a steal! Thevenet's 1992 Mâcon-Viré (sold under the name Emilian Gillet) is slightly lighter, with more emphasis on the lemony/floral side of Chardonnay. Good underlying acidity gives vibrancy and zest to the rich, medium- to full-bodied, mineral-laden flavors. Although this wine will not last as long as the Domaine de la Bongrand's Mâcon-Clessé, it is capable of evolving nicely for 4–5 years.

The 1989 Mâcon-Clessé Cuvée Tradition reveals a huge nose of smoked nuts, pineapples, and apples. There is superb acidity, great richness and precision to its full-bodied flavors, and a whoppingly long, intense finish. The 1990 is similarly styled, but crisper acids and less fat make for an authoritative and slightly more elegant wine.

JEAN-CLAUDE THEVENET (MÂCON)* * * * *

1993 Mâcon Pierre Clos	B	86
1993 Saint-Véran Clos de l'Hermitage Vieilles Vignes	C	88
1992 Saint-Véran Clos de l'Hermitage Vieilles Vignes	C	90

Jean-Claude Thevenet is one of Mâcon's up-and-coming stars, producing moderately priced wines that are capable of challenging some of the best white burgundies from the Côte d'Or's more prestigious and expensive appellations. The 1993 Mâcon Pierre Clos offers more ripeness and intensity than many 1993 Côte d'Or white wines. The nose of tangerines and buttery apple fruit is followed by a round, medium-bodied wine with good concentration and purity, and crisp, underlying acidity. It is a delicious, uncomplicated, generously endowed wine for drinking over the next 3–4 years. The 1993 Saint-Véran Vieilles Vignes Clos de l'Hermitage would have been outstanding had not the toasty new oak been a trifle too aggressive in the wine's aromatic profile. Hopefully, the oak will be absorbed with more bottle age. This wine possesses fatness, a rich, honeyed quality to the fruit, admirable purity, and a sexy personality. Medium to full bodied and loaded with fruit, it should drink well for 3–4 years.

The 1992 Saint-Véran Clos de l'Hermitage Vieilles Vignes is made from 65-year-old vines. Loaded with honeyed pineapple and applelike fruit, it is an exuberant, rich, medium-to full-bodied wine that nobly expresses what heights the Chardonnay grape can reach when handled with care from low-yielding old vines. It is a super bargain as well. A wine to buy by the case!

DOMAINE TRIBUT (CHABLIS)* *

1992 Chablis	C	82
1992 Chablis Beauroy	D	84

These offerings are straightforward, fruity, pleasant, round, and clean. The light-bodied, pleasant 1992 Chablis is best drunk over the next year. The 1992 Chablis Beauroy possesses a tropical fruit–scented nose, adequate depth, and a one-dimensional character.

DOMAINE VALETTE (MÂCON)* * * *

1992 Mâcon-Chaintré Vieilles Vignes	A	88

Only 823 cases were produced of this superlative Mâcon. Made from 40- to 50-year-old vines and barrel-fermented in 15% new oak, the wine's concentration and character are impressive. A compellingly sweet, ripe nose of buttery, mineral-scented fruit is followed by a rich, expansive, medium-bodied wine exhibiting a lovely balanced, authoritatively flavored personality. This is an explosively ripe, rich Mâcon for drinking over the next 1–2 years.

VERGET (MÂCON)* * * * *

1992 Bâtard-Montrachet	EE	97
1992 Chassagne-Montrachet Les Champs Gains	D	89
1992 Chassagne-Montrachet Morgeot	D	90
1991 Chassagne-Montrachet Morgeot	D	89
1992 Chassagne-Montrachet La Romanée	D	92
1992 Chevalier-Montrachet	EE	93
1993 Mâcon-Villages	B	86

1992	Mâcon-Villages Tête de Cuvée	B	87
1992	Meursault Les Genevrières	D	94
1992	Meursault Les Narvaux	D	90
1992	Meursault Les Poruzot	D	94
1992	Le Montrachet	EEE	94
1991	Le Montrachet	EEE	92
1992	Pouilly-Fuissé	C	89
1991	Pouilly-Fuissé	C	87
1992	Puligny-Montrachet Les Enseignères	D	93
1991	Puligny-Montrachet Les Enseignères	D	90
1992	Puligny-Montrachet Les Pucelles	D	92
1992	Puligny-Montrachet Sous Le Puits	D	87
1992	Saint-Aubin Premier Cru	C	84
1993	Saint-Véran	B	87
1992	Saint-Véran	B	89
1991	Saint-Véran	B	87

In the 1990 edition of my book on Burgundy I profiled the exuberant young Belgian producer Guffens-Heynen, saying "the quality is superb" and the wines "absolutely brilliant." Those statements referred to the estate-bottled wines from Guffens's small vineyard near the village of Vergisson. Since then, Guffens has begun a *négociant* business. Buying grapes rather than juice, Guffens works closely with his growers, encouraging them to limit their yields and to harvest only physiologically ripe fruit. As the following notes attest, Guffens is one of France's greatest white wine–makers. The quality of his wines in so-so years such as 1991 shames many famous names. In 1992 the overall quality level is extraordinary.

Most wine enthusiasts continue to labor under the myth that if you are going to buy great white burgundies you must pay the price for a top grand cru from the Côte d'Or. A half-dozen or so Mâconnais producers fashion extraordinary wines that frequently approach premier and grand cru quality. These wines sell at one-sixth to one-tenth the price of a Bâtard-Montrachet, Bienvenue Bâtard-Montrachet, or Chevalier-Montrachet. Is anyone listening? Have readers tasted the Chardonnays produced by Jean Thevenet's Domaine Bongrand, Domaine Ferret, André Bonhomme, Château Fuissé, Domaine de Vieux St.-Sorlin, and Jean-Claude Thevenet's Clos de l'Hermitage? The quality of their wines is among the most riveting in Burgundy. Moreover, their wines sell for $15-$20 a bottle.

Fifty percent of Verget's production is in Mâcon-Villages, Saint-Véran, and Pouilly-Fuissé, all of which can be superb wines. Verget's Mâcon-Villages and Saint-Véran sell at low prices and their quality competes with the aforementioned producers!

The most remarkable aspect of Guffens's wines is the extraordinary purity, richness, and definition. Writers frequently utilize the words *clarity, focus,* and *precision,* but I do not know of any producer who obtains so much definition without sacrificing Chardonnay's richness and intensity. All of these white wines are put in the bottle with minimal intervention. Some cuvées are lightly fined and bottled unfiltered, whereas others receive no fining and minimal filtration.

Guffens's 1991s are immensely successful wines. His 1991 Saint-Véran offers crisp acidity, a beautiful nose of lemon/buttery/applelike fruit and minerals, crisp, medium-bodied flavors, good balance, and a lovely fresh finish. Drink it over the next 3–4 years. The 1991 Pouilly-Fuissé is an impeccably well-balanced, rich, medium-bodied wine with more acidity than most 1991s, as well as excellent depth and ripeness. Drink it over the next 3–4 years.

Among the Côte d'Or offerings, the 1991 Puligny-Montrachet Les Enseignères is light golden colored, with a super, well-focused bouquet of honeyed melons, apples, and floral scents, rich, medium- to full-bodied flavors, and a long, crisp, zesty finish. It is a classically made, textbook Puligny-Montrachet that should drink well for the next 5–6 years. Verget's 1991 Chassagne-Montrachet Morgeot shares the same freshness, in addition to gorgeous structure, vivid clarity, a long, rich, buttery, apple blossom–scented nose, and steely, rich flavors. It should drink well for 4–5 years. The only other 1991 I tasted (most cuvées had already sold out) was the 1991 Le Montrachet. A big wine, with a smoky, bacon fat–, vanillin-scented bouquet, this dense, rich Le Montrachet offers oodles of glycerin and intensity, full body, and wonderful richness. It should drink well for 10–15 years.

Verget's excellent 1992 selections from Mâconnais surpass many premiers and grands crus from the Côte d'Or. The 1992 Mâcon-Villages Tête de Cuvée is a rich, ripe, classic Mâcon with a spring flower garden– and buttery apple–scented nose, rich, admirably extracted flavors, medium body, fine underlying acidity, and a well-focused finish. It should drink well for 4–5 years—an uncommonly long time for a Mâcon. The 1992 Saint-Véran offers superb fruit, a big, lusty, honeyed, buttery nose, and intense, ripe, medium- to full-bodied flavors allied with crisp acidity. The impression is one of power and finesse. This is a complex, beautifully proportioned Saint-Véran for drinking over the next 4–5 years. Verget's 1992 Pouilly-Fuissé exhibits rich, buttery, apricotlike fruit, underlying mineral scents and flavors, medium to full body, and excellent depth and finish. It reveals more oak than the Saint-Véran, but not as much up-front, rich fruit. It should drink well for another 4–5 years.

Verget's 1992 premiers crus are marvelous wines. The lightest cuvée is the 1992 Saint-Aubin Premier Cru. Although it is lively and elegant, it does not possess the richness or complexity of the other wines. The 1992 Puligny-Montrachet Sous Le Puits reveals a mineral-scented, gunflintlike, Chablis bouquet, medium body, and fine ripeness. A stylish, graceful wine, it should drink well for the next 7–8 years. The quality jumps considerably with the 1992 Chassagne-Montrachet Les Champs Gains. This is a powerful, yet remarkably graceful, stylish wine with an intense nose of buttered apples and apricots. Concentrated, with admirable ripeness, zesty underlying acidity, and a long finish, it is a wine to drink over the next 7–8 years. The outstanding 1992 Meursault Les Narvaux represents a lusty, decadent style of burgundy. It exhibits brilliant clarity and precision. Concentrated, with layers of fruit and fine acidity, this is a marvelous, superconcentrated Meursault for drinking over the next 5–6 years. Even more profound is the 1992 Meursault Les Genevrières. It reveals a huge, hazelnut, buttery, applelike, flinty-scented nose, full-bodied, fabulously concentrated flavors, fine acidity, and a blockbuster finish. There is also an indescribable mineral character. Les Genevrières should drink well for up to a decade. Another spectacular wine is the 1992 Meursault Les Poruzot. As with most of Verget's 1992 selections, Guffens encouraged his growers to keep yields to 25–30 hectoliters per hectare, resulting in a Les Poruzot with fabulous richness, density, and length. A smoky, honeyed nose of hazelnuts, flowers, and buttery fruit is followed by a wine with great richness, full body, fabulous freshness and liveliness, and an authoritative finish. This riveting Meursault must be tasted to be believed.

The good news does not end with Verget's Meursaults. The mineral-scented, stony, floral 1992 Chassagne-Montrachet Morgeot is a brilliantly made wine, relying more on subtlety than on power and muscle. There is gobs of rich, intense fruit, medium body, and a long finish. It should drink well for at least a decade. The 1992 Chassagne-Montrachet La

Romanée is a more flamboyant white burgundy, with a dramatic, honeyed, oaky, smoky, buttery-scented nose, and luscious rich, thick, glycerin-dominated flavors that ooze from the glass. Despite its size and intensity, the wine's crisp acidity holds everything in focus. Drink this large-scaled, full-throttle wine over the next 7–8 years.

The two premier cru Puligny-Montrachets include an elegant, classy, floral-scented, subtle, medium-bodied 1992 Puligny-Montrachet Les Pucelles, and a spectacularly rich, layered, full-bodied, deep, intense, blockbuster 1992 Puligny-Montrachet Les Enseignères. If you prefer restraint and finesse, buy Les Pucelles, because Les Enseignères is decadent.

The three grands crus include the superb, full-bodied, powerful, intense, backward 1992 Chevalier-Montrachet. Cellar it for 2–3 years and drink it over the next 12–15. Verget's 1992 Le Montrachet is also superb, with layers of rich fruit, a compelling mineral and wet stone fragrance allied with smoky, toasty new oak, and tons of fruit. Drink this full-bodied, rich wine over the next 12–15 years. Interestingly, this is one of the few wines made by Guffens from purchased juice, not grapes. I will not reveal the name of the *négociant* that sold Guffens this batch of Le Montrachet, but it is ironic that Verget's 1992 Le Montrachet is significantly better than the same wine from the *négociant*. Why? The *négociant* blocks the malolactic fermentation, does no lees contact, racks the wine three times, and then sterile-filters it prior to bottling. Guffens asked that all the lees be given to him, and was able to complete the malolactic fermentation. He kept the wine in contact with the lees, did not fine it, racked it only once, and bottled it with a rough filter designed only to extract fruit flies.

Verget's Le Montrachet is a great wine, but it is not the best wine he made. Those well-heeled readers should check out the 1992 Bâtard-Montrachet, a wine of enormous power (14.5% natural alcohol) and superrich, dense flavors that linger on the palate. It is a wine with extraordinary flavor dimension and body, as well as a finish that lasts over a minute. I have to rate this magnificent Bâtard-Montrachet with the dazzling Bâtards made by Michel Niellon. A winemaking tour de force!

The two least expensive wines in the Verget portfolio are the excellent Mâcon-Villages and Saint-Véran. Both 1993s exhibit wonderfully pure, citrusy, mineral- and apple-scented fruit, medium body, admirable focus, and plenty of length and ripeness. The 1993 Saint-Véran possesses a more honeyed character, as well as more body. Both offerings are delicious, fresh, lively Mâconnais wines that should drink well for several years.

These are truly the wines of a genius. I suspect their quality is so high it will shake up a lot of white-burgundy producers who have been resting on their historical reputations for far too long. The wines of Guffens are proof of the great quality that can be achieved without compromise. For that, consumers who care should be thankful. Bravo to Jean-Marie Guffens-Heynen!

DOMAINE DES VIEILLES PIERRES (MÂCON)* * * *
1992 Mâcon-Vergisson   B   87

An excellent Mâcon from proprietor Jean-Jacques Litaud, this medium to full-bodied, fleshy wine reveals plenty of fresh, mineral-scented, citrusy fruit, admirable body, surprising depth, and a long, lusty finish. It is a delicious Mâcon for drinking over the next 1–2 years.

DOMAINE DU VIEUX ST.-SORLIN (MÂCON)* * * * *
1992 Mâcon La Roche Vineuse   C   90

One of the great young producers in the Mâconnais area, M. Meurlin has fashioned a phenomenal wine bargain. This 1992 exhibits tons of rich, honeyed, orange and applelike fruit, a tremendously rich, medium- to full-bodied palate, and a long, crisp, zesty finish. Made from vines averaging 50–60 years in age, this is a sensational Chardonnay for drinking over the next 3–4 years. It is worth buying by the case—don't miss it!

CHAMPAGNE

Not so long ago champagne buyers never had it so good. The strong dollar, bumper crops of solid-quality wine in Champagne, and intense price competition by importers, wholesalers, and retailers all combined to drive prices down. It was a wonderful buyer's market. A small, mediocre crop in 1984, a top-quality but tiny crop in 1985, and a sagging American dollar caused champagne prices to soar. This was evident in the nineties as prices rose 30%–75%. But the international recession, the downsizing of the consumer's appetite for expensive products, including champagne, and a bevy of abundant crops have caused most champagne houses to slice prices, except for their luxury cuvées. Nevertheless, champagne remains the quintessential luxury product—expensive.

The Basics

TYPES OF WINE

Only sparkling wine (about 200 million bottles a year) is produced in Champagne, a viticultural area 90 miles northeast of Paris. Champagne is usually made from a blend of three grapes—Chardonnay, Pinot Noir, and Pinot Meunier. A champagne called Blanc de Blancs must be 100% Chardonnay. Blanc de Noirs means that the wine has been made from red wine grapes, and the term *crémant* signifies that the wine has slightly less effervescence than typical champagne.

GRAPE VARIETIES

Chardonnay   Surprisingly, only 25% of Champagne's vineyards are planted in Chardonnay.
Pinot Meunier   The most popular grape in Champagne, Pinot Meunier accounts for 40% of the appellation's vineyards.
Pinot Noir   This grape accounts for 35% of the vineyard acreage in Champagne.

FLAVORS

Most people drink champagne young, often within hours of purchasing it. However, some observers would argue that high-quality, vintage champagne should not be drunk until it is at least 10 years old. French law requires that nonvintage champagne be aged at least 1 year in the bottle before it is released, and vintage champagne 3 years. As a general rule, most top producers are just releasing their 1988s, 1989s, and 1990s in 1995/1996. The reason for this is that good champagne not only should taste fresh, but should also have flavors akin to buttered wheat toast, ripe apples, and fresh biscuits. When champagne is badly made it tastes sour, green, and musty. If it has been abused in shipment or storage, it will taste flat and fruitless. A Blanc de Blancs is a more delicate, refined, lighter wine than those champagnes that have a hefty percentage of Pinot Noir and Pinot Meunier, the two red grapes utilized.

AGING POTENTIAL

Champagne from the most illustrious houses such as Krug, Bollinger, and Pol Roger can age for 25–30 years, losing much of its effervescence and taking on a creamy, lush, buttery richness not too different from a top white burgundy. Moët & Chandon's Dom Pérignon 1947, 1964, 1969, and 1971 were gorgeous when tasted in 1994. Also, Krug's 1947, 1961, 1962, 1964, and 1971; and Bollinger's 1966, 1969, and 1975 R.D. were exquisite when drunk in 1994, as were Pol Roger's 1928 and 1929 when drunk in 1992. These were profound examples of how wonderful champagne can be with age. But readers should realize that each champagne house has its own style, and the aging potential depends on the style preferred by that producer. Below are some aging estimates for a number of the best-known brands currently available in the market. The starting point for measuring the aging potential is 1995/1996, not the vintage mentioned.

1975 Bollinger R.D.: now plus 6 years

1979 Bollinger R.D.: now plus 5 years

1982 Bollinger R.D.: now plus 10 years

1985 Bollinger Grande Année: now plus 15 years

1982 Bollinger Vieilles Vignes: now plus 5–20 years

1985 Bollinger Vieilles Vignes: now plus 5–25 years

1985 Gosset Grand Millésime: now plus 8 years

1979 Krug: now plus 15 years

1981 Krug: now plus 15 years

1982 Krug: now plus 5–30 years

1985 Krug: now plus 5–30 years

1982 Krug Clos du Mesnil: now plus 12 years

1985 Laurent-Perrier Grand Siècle: now plus 10 years

1982 Dom Pérignon: now plus 10 years

1985 Dom Pérignon: now plus 12 years

1988 Dom Pérignon: now plus 15 years

1982 Pol Roger Blanc de Chardonnay: now plus 8 years

1985 Pol Roger Brut: now plus 12 years

1979 Pol Roger Cuvée Winston Churchill: now plus 8 years

1982 Pol Roger Cuvée Winston Churchill: now plus 20 years

1985 Pol Roger Cuvée Winston Churchill: now plus 15 years

1985 Louis Roederer Cristal: now plus 8 years

1986 Louis Roederer Cristal: now plus 6 years

1988 Louis Roederer Cristal: now plus 10 years

1982 Salon: now plus 15 years

1985 Taittinger Comtes de Champagne: now plus 15 years

1988 Taittinger Comtes de Champagne: now plus 15 years

1985 Veuve Clicquot La Grande Dame: 5 plus 20 years

1988 Veuve Clicquot La Grande Dame: now plus 10 years

OVERALL QUALITY LEVEL

French champagne is irrefutably the finest sparkling wine in the world. Despite the hoopla and vast sums of money invested in California, there is no competition from any other wine-producing region if quality is the primary consideration. Nevertheless, the extraordinary financial success enjoyed by many of the big champagne houses has led, I believe, to a lowering of standards. Commercial greed has resulted in most firms' calling nearly every harvest a vintage year. For example, in the fifties there were four vintage years, 1952, 1953, 1955, and 1959, and in the sixties there were five, 1961, 1962, 1964, 1966, and 1969. This increased to eight vintage years in the seventies (only 1972 and 1977 were excluded). In the decade of the eighties, eight vintages were again declared, the exceptions being 1984 and 1987. A number of the top champagne houses need to toughen their standards when it comes to vintage champagne.

In addition to too many vintage years, the quality of the nonvintage brut cuvées has deteriorated. The wines, which are supposed to be released when they are showing some

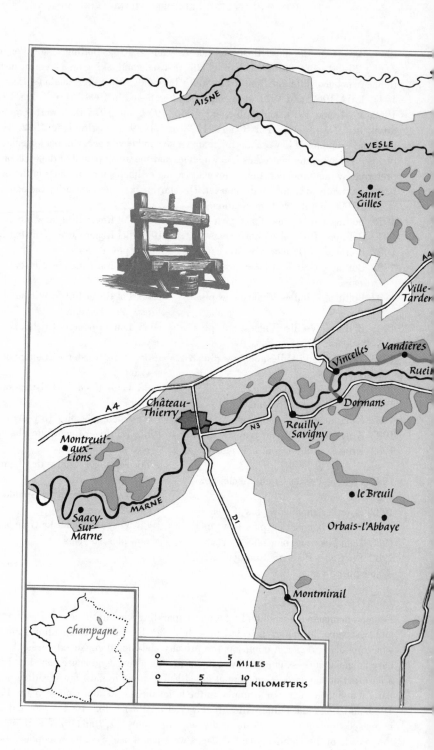

AISNE

VESLE

Saint-Gilles

Ville-Tarden

Vincelles   Vandières

Rueil

Château-Thierry

A4

Dormans

N3

Reuilly-Savigny

Montreuil-aux-Lions

le Breuil

MARNE

Orbais-l'Abbaye

D1

Saacy-sur-Marne

Montmirail

Champagne

0   5   MILES
0   5   10   KILOMETERS

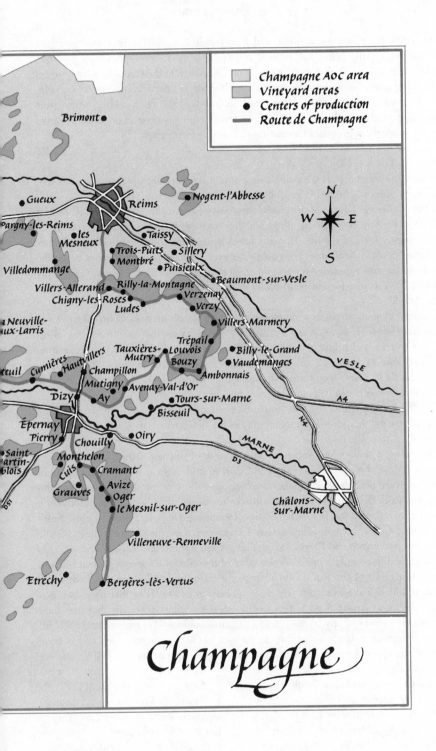

Champagne

Brimont●

Gueux●   ●Reims   ●Nogent-l'Abbesse

Pargny-les-Reims

●les
Mesneux   ●Taissy

Villedommange   ●Trois-Puits   ●Sillery
●Montbré
●Puisieulx

Villers-Allerand   ●Rilly-la-Montagne   ●Beaumont-sur-Vesle
Chigny-les-Roses   Verzenay●
Ludes●   Verzy●

La Neuville-
aux-Larris   ●Villers-Marmery

●Trépail
Tauxières-   Louvois●   ●Billy-le-Grand
Mutry   Bouzy●   ●Vaudemanges
euil   Cumières   Hautvillers
●Champillon   ●Ambonnais
Mutigny●   ●Avenay-Val-d'Or
Dizy●   ●Ay   ●Tours-sur-Marne
●Bisseuil
Épernay●
Pierry●   ●Chouilly   ●Oiry
●Saint-
Martin-   ●Monthelon
blois   Cuis●   ●Cramant
Grauves●   ●Avize
●Oger
●le Mesnil-sur-Oger

Châlons-
sur-Marne

●Villeneuve-Renneville

Étrechy●   ●Bergères-lès-Vertus

VESLE
A4
N4
MARNE
D3
D51

signs of maturity, have become greener and more acidic, suggesting that producers not only have lowered quality standards, but are releasing their wines as quickly as possible. Unfortunately, the sad fact is that there is really no alternative to the complexity and finesse of French champagne. There are less-expensive alternatives, particularly sparkling Loire Valley wines, some *crémants* from Alsace and Burgundy, and the sparkling wines from California, Spain, and Italy. However, save for a few exceptions, none of the bubblies from these sources remotely approaches the quality of French champagne.

MOST IMPORTANT INFORMATION TO KNOW

First, you have to do some serious tasting to see which styles of champagne appeal to you. Additionally, consider the following guidelines:

1. The luxury or prestige cuvées of the champagne houses are always overpriced (all sell for $75–$150 a bottle). The pricing plays on the consumer's belief that a lavish price signifies a higher level of quality. In many cases it does not. Moreover, too many luxury cuvées have become pawns in an ego contest between Champagne's top houses as to who can produce the most expensive wine in the most outrageous, dramatic bottle. Consumers often pay $20–$30 just for the hand-blown bottle and expensive, hand-painted, labor-intensive label.

2. Purchase your champagne from a merchant who has a quick turnover in inventory. More than any other wine, champagne is a fragile, very delicate wine that is extremely vulnerable to poor storage and bright shop lighting. Buying bottles that have been languishing on retailers' shelves for 6–12 months can indeed be a risky business. If your just-purchased bottle of champagne tastes flat, has a deep golden color, and few bubbles, it is either too old, or dead from bad storage.

3. Don't hesitate to try some of the best nonvintage champagnes I have recommended. The best of them are not that far behind the quality of the best luxury cuvées, yet they sell for a quarter to a fifth of the price.

4. There has been a tremendous influx of high-quality champagnes from small firms in Champagne. Most of these wines may be difficult to find outside of major metropolitan markets, but some of these small houses produce splendid wine worthy of a search of the marketplace. Look for some of the estate-bottled champagne from the following producers: Baptiste-Pertois, Paul Bara, Bonnaire, Cattier, Delamotte, Drappier, Duvay-Leroy, Egly-Ouriet, Michel Gonet, Lancelot-Royer, Guy Larmandier, Lassalle, Legras, Mailly, Serge Mathieu, Joseph Perrier, and Ployez-Jacquemart, Alain Robert, and Tarlant.

5. Several technical terms that appear on the label of a producer's champagne can tell you additional things about the wine. Brut champagnes are dry but legally can have up to 0.2% sugar added (called dosage). Extra-dry champagnes are those that have between 1.2% and 2% sugar added. Most tasters would call these champagnes dry, but they tend to be rounder and seemingly fruitier than brut champagnes. The term *ultra brut, brut absolu,* or *dosage zéro* signifies that the champagne has had no sugar added and is bone dry. These champagnes are rarely seen, but can be quite impressive as well as austere and lean tasting.

6. Below is a guide to champagne bottle sizes:

Nebuchadnezzar = 20 bottles = 16 liters	Jeroboam = 4 bottles = 3.2 liters
Balthazar = 16 bottles = 12.8 liters	Magnum = 2 bottles = 1.6 liters
Salmanazar = 12 bottles = 9.6 liters	Bottle = 75 centiliters
Methuselah = 8 bottles = 6.4 liters	Half-bottle = 37.5 centiliters
Rehoboam = 6 bottles = 4.8 liters	Quarter-bottle = 20 centiliters

Prices have fallen a bit for the nonvintage cuvées and some vintage champagne, but the luxury cuvées remain appallingly expensive. The 1982 and 1985 vintages were both stunning, but the wines have largely disappeared from the marketplace. The current vintages— 1986 and 1988—are very good. The 1989 vintage looks to be superb, but most top wines will not appear in the marketplace before 1996. The vintage of choice remains the magnificent 1985. If you love the sublime fizz offered by champagne, 1985 is a mandatory purchase. Keep in mind that it is often smart to seek out some of the smaller producers who do not have national importers, which often means that prices are more reasonable.

VINTAGE GUIDE

1994—Very difficult weather conditions (considerable rain fell between August 20 and September 14) have resulted in a small crop of average quality. Because of this, pressure to increase prices significantly is likely.

1993—With a large crop of mostly average-quality juice, 1993 is unlikely to be a highly desirable vintage year.

1992—This hugely abundant yet potentially good-quality vintage escaped most of the bad weather that plagued the southern half of France. If the quality is as high and the quantity as enormous as reported, this could provide price stability—a good sign. Possibly a vintage year.

1991—1991 is a small, exceptionally difficult vintage that is unlikely to be declared a vintage year except by the greediest of producers. It rivals 1987 and 1984 as one of the three worst vintages for champagne in the last 15 years.

1990—A huge crop of ripe fruit was harvested. The 1990 vintage has all the earmarks for the best champagne vintage since 1985. The wines will be full, rich, aromatic, and destined to be drunk early because of low acidity. Such a large, high-quality crop will also keep prices stable.

1989—Another high-quality, abundant year should produce wines similar to the ripe, rich, creamy style of the 1982 champagnes, with a very ripe, fat style of fizz.

1988—Not much champagne was made because of the small harvest, but this is undoubtedly a vintage year. The 1988s are leaner, more austere, and higher in acidity than the flamboyant 1989s and 1990s.

1987—A terrible year, the worst of the decade, 1987 is not a vintage year.

1986—This is a vintage year, producing an abundant quantity of soft, ripe, fruity wines.

1985—Along with 1982, 1985 is the finest vintage of the eighties thanks to excellent ripeness and a good-sized crop. A superb champagne vintage!

1984—A lousy year, but there were vintage champagnes from 1984 in the market. Remember what P. T. Barnum once said?

1983—A gigantic crop of good-quality champagne was produced. Although the wines may lack the opulence and creamy richness of the 1982s, they are hardly undersized wines. Most 1983s have matured quickly and are delicious now. They should be drunk up.

1982—A great vintage of ripe, rich, creamy, intense wines. If they were to be criticized, it would be for their very forward, lower than normal acids that suggest they will age quickly. No one should miss the top champagnes from 1982; they are marvelously rounded, ripe, generously flavored wines.

1981—The champagnes from 1981 are rather lean and austere, but that has not prevented many top houses from declaring this a vintage year.

OLDER VINTAGES

The 1980 vintage is mediocre; 1979 is excellent; 1978 is tiring; 1976, once top-notch, is now fading; 1975 is superb, as are well-cellared examples of 1971, 1969, and 1964. When buying champagne, whether it is 3 years old or 20, pay the utmost care to the manner in which it was treated before you bought it. Champagne is the most fragile wine in the marketplace, and it cannot tolerate poor storage.

RATING CHAMPAGNE'S BEST PRODUCERS

* * * * *(OUTSTANDING)

Bollinger (full bodied)
Egly-Ouriet (full bodied)
Gosset (full bodied)
Henriot (full bodied)
Krug (full bodied)
J. Lassalle (light bodied)
Laurent-Perrier (medium bodied)

Alain Robert (full bodied)
Pol Roger (medium bodied)
Louis Roederer (full bodied)
Salon (medium bodied)
Taittinger (light bodied)
Veuve Clicquot (full bodied)

* * * *(EXCELLENT)

Baptiste-Pertois (light bodied)
Paul Bara (full bodied)
Billecart-Salmon (light bodied)
Bonnaire (light bodied)
de Castellane (light bodied)
Cattier (light bodied)
Charbaut (light bodied)
Delamotte (medium bodied)
Diebolt-Vallois (medium bodied)
Drappier (medium bodied), since 1985
Alfred Gratien (full bodied)
Grimonnet (medium bodied)
Heidsieck Monopole (medium bodied)
Jacquart (medium bodied)
Jacquesson (light bodied)
Lancelot-Royer (medium bodied)

Guy Larmandier (full bodied)
Lechère (light bodied)
R. & L. Legras (light bodied)
Mailly (medium bodied)
Serge Mathieu (medium bodied)
Moët & Chandon (medium bodied)
****/*****
Bruno Paillard (light bodied)
Joseph Perrier (medium bodied)
Perrier-Jouët (light bodied)
Ployez-Jacquemart (medium bodied)
Dom Ruinart (light bodied)
Jacques Selosse (light bodied)
Taillevent (medium bodied)
Tarlant ****/*****

* * *(GOOD)

Ayala (medium bodied)
Barancourt (full bodied)
Bricout (light bodied)
Canard Duchêne (medium bodied)
Deutz (medium bodied)
Duval-Leroy (medium bodied)
H. Germain (light bodied)
Michel Gonet (medium bodied)
Georges Goulet (medium bodied)

Charles Heidsieck (medium bodied)
Lanson (light bodied)
Launois Père (light bodied)
Mercier (medium bodied)
Mumm (medium bodied)
Philipponnat (medium bodied)
Piper Heidsieck (light bodied)
Pommery and Greno (light bodied)

* *(AVERAGE)

Beaumet-Chaurey (light bodied)
Besserat de Bellefon (light bodied)

Boizel (light bodied)
Nicolas Feuillatte (light bodied)

Goldschmidt-Rothschild (light bodied)   Rapeneau (medium bodied)
Jestin (light bodied)   Alfred Rothschild (light bodied)
Oudinot (medium bodied)   Marie Stuart (light bodied)

FINDING THE BEST CHAMPAGNE

THE BEST PRODUCERS OF NONVINTAGE BRUT

Billecart-Salmon   Larmandier
Bollinger Special Cuvée   Lechère Orient Express
Cattier   Bruno Paillard Première Cuvée
Charbaut   Perrier-Jouët
Delamotte   Ployez-Jacquemart
Drappier Maurice Chevalier   Pol Roger
Gosset Grand Réserve   Louis Roederer Brut Premier
Krug   Tarlant Cuvée Louis
                                    Veuve Clicquot Yellow Label

THE BEST PRODUCERS OF ROSÉ CHAMPAGNE

Billecart-Salmon N.V.   Moët & Chandon Dom Pérignon 1980,
Bollinger Grande Année 1985, 1988   1982, 1985
Delamotte   Perrier-Jouët Blason de France N.V.
Egly-Ouriet   Perrier-Jouët Fleur de Champagne 1986,
Gosset 1985, 1988   1988
Heidsieck Monopole Diamant Bleu 1985,   Pol Roger 1985, 1986, 1988
  1988   Dom Ruinart 1985, 1988
Krug N.V.   Taittinger Comtes de Champagne 1985,
Laurent-Perrier Grand Siècle Cuvée   1988
  Alexander 1985, 1988   Veuve Clicquot 1985, 1988
Moët & Chandon Brut Imperial 1988,
  1989

THE BEST PRODUCERS OF 100% CHARDONNAY BLANC DE BLANCS

Ayala 1988   Lancelot-Royer
Baptiste-Pertois Cuvée Réservée N.V.   R. & L. Legras
Charbaut N.V.   Bruno Paillard
Delamotte 1985, 1988   Joseph Perrier Cuvée Royale
Jacquart 1988   Alain Robert
Jacquart Cuvée Spéciale   Pol Roger Blancs de Chardonnay 1985,
Jacquesson 1990   1986, 1988
Krug Clos de Mesnil 1983, 1985   Salon 1982, 1983
Lassalle 1985   Taittinger Comtes de Champagne

THE BEST PRODUCERS OF LUXURY CUVÉES

Bollinger R.D. 1975, 1982   Krug 1982, 1985
Bollinger Grande Année 1985, 1988   Lassalle Cuvée Angeline 1985
Bollinger Vieilles Vignes 1985   Laurent-Perrier Grand Siècle 1985,
Cattier Clos du Moulin 1985   1988
Drappier Grand Sendrée 1985   Moët & Chandon Dom Pérignon 1982,
Heidsieck Monopole Diamant Bleu 1985,   1985, 1988
  1988   Mumm René Lalou 1985
Henriot Cuvée des Enchanteleurs 1985   Joseph Perrier Cuvée Josephine 1985

Alain Robert Le Mesnil Séléction 1979
Pol Roger Cuvée Winston Churchill 1985,
   1988
Louis Roederer Cristal 1985, 1988
Jacques Selosse Origine N.V.

Taittinger Comtes de Champagne 1985,
   1988
Veuve Clicquot La Grande Dame 1985,
   1988

THE LOIRE VALLEY

The Basics

TYPES OF WINE

Most wine drinkers can name more historic Loire Valley châteaux than Loire Valley wines. That is a pity, because the Loire Valley wine-producing areas offer France's most remarkable array of wines. The region stretches along one-third of the meandering 635-mile Loire River, and the astonishing diversity of grapes planted in the valley is far greater than that in the better-known wine-growing regions of Burgundy and Bordeaux.

With 60 wine appellations and *vin délimité de qualité supérieure* (VDQS) areas, the vastness and complexity of the Loire Valley as a winemaking area are obvious. Dry white table wines dominate the production as do the three major white wine grapes found in the Loire. The Sauvignon Blanc is at its best in Sancerre and Pouilly-Fumé. The Chenin Blanc produces dry, sweet, and sparkling white wines. It reaches its zenith in Vouvray, Savennières, Bonnezeaux, Coteaux du Layon, and Quarts de Chaume. Lastly, there is the Muscadet grape (its true name is Melon de Bourgogne), from which Muscadet wines are made. There is plenty of light, frank, fruity, herbaceous red wine made from Gamay, Cabernet Franc, and Cabernet Sauvignon grapes in appellations with names such as Bourgueil, Chinon, St.-Nicolas-de-Bourgueil, Touraine, and Anjou. Rosés, which can be delicious but are frightfully irregular in quality, tend to emerge from Anjou, Sancerre, Chinon, and Reuilly.

GRAPE VARIETIES

Chenin Blanc, Sauvignon Blanc, Muscadet, and Gros Plant are the four dominant white wine grapes, but Chardonnay, especially in the VDQS region called Haut-Poitou, is frequently seen. For red wines, Gamay and Pinot Noir are seen in the VDQS vineyards, but in the top red wine Loire appellations it is virtually all Cabernet Sauvignon and Cabernet Franc.

A QUICK GUIDE TO THE DIVERSITY OF THE LOIRE VALLEY

Anjou   This large appellation is acclaimed for its rosé wines, which can range from dry to medium sweet. In the eighties, red wine grapes such as Cabernet Sauvignon, Cabernet

Franc, and Gamay began to receive considerable attention from bargain hunters looking for inexpensive, light-bodied, fruity red wines. In particular, Gamay has done well in Anjou, producing richly fruity wines. Cabernet Franc and Cabernet Sauvignon, while admired by many, are too vegetal for my taste.

With respect to white wines, Chenin Blanc, Chardonnay, and Sauvignon Blanc made with modern vinification methods can result in fragrant, fruity, light wines that are adored by consumers. There is even some sparkling wine called Anjou Mousseux. Its principal virtue is its price of $12.

ANJOU PRODUCERS OF MERIT

Ackerman-Laurence (sparkling wines) **	Colombier **
Château de Chamboureau **	Fougeraies **
Clos de Coulaine **	Richou Rochettes ****

Bonnezeaux   There is only one grape grown in this appellation, Chenin Blanc, which reaches extraordinary heights of richness, complexity, and aging ability in Bonnezeaux. This is a decadently rich, sweet wine that demonstrates what pinnacles Chenin Blanc can reach. These wines can live for decades. This grand cru appellation, technically within the larger Coteaux du Layon, made phenomenally rich, long-lived wines in 1989 and 1990. Recent vintages such as 1991, 1992, and 1993 were troublesome, but 1994 should turn out to be very good.

BONNEZEAUX PRODUCERS OF MERIT

Domaine de la Croix des Loges (Christian Bonnin) ****	Domaine des Gagneries ****
	Domaine Ogoreau ***
Château de Fesles (this estate is in a class of its own) *****	Domaine du Petit Val **/***
	Domaine de Terrebrune (René Renou) ****

Bourgueil   If you ask a Parisian about Bourgueil, chances are it is one of his or her favorites. More popular in France than in America, Bourgueil makes a fruity, raspberry-scented and -flavored wine that should be drunk in its first 5–6 years of life. The problem is that unless the vintage is exceptionally ripe, as it was in 1989 and 1990, these wines are strikingly vegetal. The 1994 vintage is the best one since 1990.

BOURGUEIL PRODUCERS OF MERIT

Caslot-Galbrun ***	Lamé-Delille-Boucard ***
Christophe Chasle ***	Domaine des Mailloches ****
Pierre-Jacques Druet ****	Domaine des Ouches ****
Domaine des Forges ***/****	

Cabernet d'Anjou   The name suggests a red wine, but in essence this is a rosé that tends to be herbaceous and sweet. I am not an admirer of these wines, but should you want to take the plunge, check out one of the following producers.

CABERNET D'ANJOU PRODUCERS OF MERIT

Bertrand **	Château de Tigné **
Poupard **	Verdier **

Châteaumeillant   This little-known wine region near Sancerre does not have appellation status, but rather, VDQS. Gamay and small amounts of Pinot Noir are the grape varieties

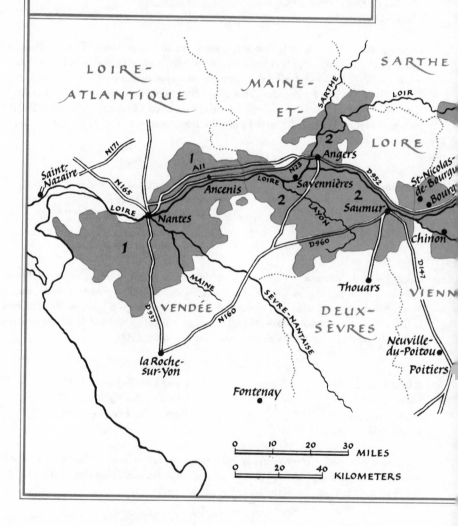

The Loire Valley and Central France

N
W ✳ E
S

LOIRE-
ATLANTIQUE

MAINE-
ET-

SARTHE

SARTHE

LOIR

LOIRE

N171

1
Ail

N23

2
Angers

Saint-
Nazaire

N165

LOIRE

Ancenis

LOIRE

Savennières

D952

St-Nicolas-
de-Bourgu

LOIRE

Nantes

2

LAYON

2
Saumur

Bourg

1

D960

Chinon

D147

MAINE

D937

VENDÉE

N160

SÈVRE-NANTAISE

Thouars

DEUX-
SÈVRES

VIENN

la Roche-
sur-Yon

Neuville-
du-Poitou

Poitiers

Fontenay

0   10   20   30 MILES

0   20   40 KILOMETERS

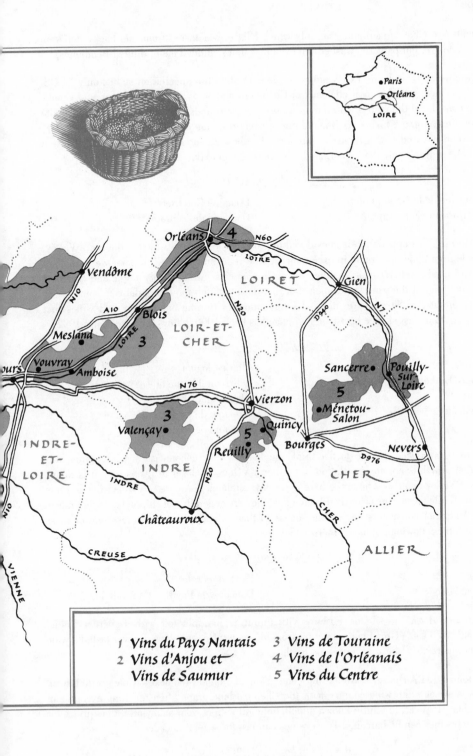

Paris
Orléans
LOIRE

Orléans 4 N60
Vendôme
LOIRET
Gien
Blois
LOIR-ET-
CHER
Mesland 3
Vouvray
Amboise
Sancerre
Pouilly-
sur-
Loire
5
N76
Vierzon
Ménetou-
Salon
Valençay 3
Quincy
INDRE-
ET-
LOIRE
5
Reuilly
Bourges
Nevers
INDRE
D976
CHER
Châteauroux
CHER
CREUSE
ALLIER
VIENNE

1 Vins du Pays Nantais   3 Vins de Touraine
2 Vins d'Anjou et   4 Vins de l'Orléanais
  Vins de Saumur   5 Vins du Centre

planted in Châteaumeillant. The only wines I have ever tasted from this backwater were inexpensive, but pathetic, washed-out examples that reminded me of diluted Beaujolais.

Cheverny   This Loire Valley subregion is not entitled to appellation status, only VDQS. It is located near the great châteaux of Chambord and Blois. Sauvignon Blanc and Gamay are considered the grapes with the most potential. This area does make a dry, acidic, white wine from a grape known as Romorantin (a trivia test candidate). Most of these wines are inexpensive, and few of them are bargains. The best recent vintages have been 1994 and 1990, but drink only the former, as these wines age quickly.

CHEVERNY PRODUCERS OF MERIT

Domaine de la Gaudronnière   Domaine Gendrier***
   (Dorléans-Ferrand)****   Domaine de Veilloux***

Chinon   This appellation is considered to produce the best red wines of the Loire Valley. Made from Cabernet Franc, in exceptionally ripe years such as 1990 it possesses abundant herb-tinged raspberry fruit. In other years, Chinon wines are intensely acidic and vegetal. I am not fond of the wines of Chinon, but that does not stop me from admiring some of the best producers. Several are minimal interventionists turning out handcrafted wines that deserve to be tasted. The best recent vintage has been 1990, followed by 1989 and 1992.

CHINON PRODUCERS OF MERIT

Baudry***   Charles Joguet
Couly-Dutheil***   (irrefutably the finest)****/*****
Duret***   Olga Raffault****
Château de la Grille***   Domaine de la Roche-Honneur**
                           Domaine de Roncée***

Côte Roannaise   If you do not think the Loire Valley encompasses a huge area, this region, which is not an appellation but rather a VDQS, is closer to Lyons than it is to any Loire Valley château. The grape here is Gamay, although there are tiny quantities of Pinot Noir. While these wines can rival Beaujolais, they are generally not shipped outside France, so American consumers have little access to them. Should you run across one of these wines, the following producers merit a look.

CÔTE ROANNAISE PRODUCERS OF MERIT

Chargros**   Lapandéry**/***
Chaucesse**/***   Domaine de Pavillon (Maurice Lutz)***

Coteaux d'Ancenis   This obscure viticultural region, planted with Cabernet Franc, Gamay, and some Gros Plant, is not far from Muscadet. Not only have I never tasted a wine from this region, I have never seen a bottle.

Coteaux de l'Aubance   An up-and-coming appellation located next to Coteaux du Layon, this is sweet white wine country with the Chenin Blanc grape often reaching exceptional heights. However, this little-known appellation still suffers from anonymity, thus prices for the top wines can be bargains. These wines can last for several decades.

COTEAUX DE L'AUBANCE PRODUCERS OF MERIT

Bablut***   their Cuvée Les Trois
Domaine de Haute-Perche (Papin)***   Demoiselles)****
Domaine Didier Richou (particularly   Domaine des Rochettes (Chauvin)****

Coteaux du Giennois This appellation just north of Sancerre should be an excellent region for good values, but to date, the quality has been average. The best producer is Balland-Chapuis.

Coteaux du Layon One of the Loire Valley's most renowned appellations, Coteaux du Layon produces decadently sweet wines from Chenin Blanc grapes that have been attacked by the same noble rot that is famous for the wines of Barsac and Sauternes in Bordeaux, and the Sélection des Grains Nobles in Alsace. The spectacular vintages of 1989 and 1990, considered by most growers to be the finest since 1959 and 1947, caused much of the world to take notice of the excellent quality that often emerges from this region—at modest prices. Readers should be aware that some labels say Coteaux du Layon Villages, which reflects the fact that the French government has allowed seven villages in Coteaux du Layon to affix their names to the wine. A top Coteaux du Layon can be drunk as an aperitif for its opulent peach and apricot fruitiness, but I feel it is best consumed after a meal by itself. The best vintages are 1990, 1989, and if you can still find any, 1986 and 1983.

COTEAUX DU LAYON PRODUCERS OF MERIT

Alfred Bidet***
Domaine de Brizé****
Domaine Cady Valette***
Clos de la Ste.-Catherine (Baumard)*****
Jean-Louis Foucher***
Domaine Gaudard***
Guimonière***/****
Domaine des Hauts Perrays***/****
Jolivet***/****
Domaine des Maurières (Fernand Moron)****
Château Montenault (Clos de la Hersé)****

La Motte (André Sorin)***
Moulin-Touchais (a producer with an enormous array of vintages going back to the late forties that can still be purchased)***
Domaine Ogereau***
Château de Passavant (Jean David)***
Domaine de la Pierre Blanche (Vincent Lecointre)***
Domaine de la Pierre Saint-Maurille***
Château des Rochettes****
Pierre-Yves Tijou (La Soucherie)****
Domaine de Villeneuve***

Coteaux du Vendômois Some pretty wretched red wines made from Pinot Noir, Gamay, and an oddity called Pineau d'Aunis, as well as some meager white wines from Chardonnay and Chenin Blanc emerge from this VDQS region situated north of Tours. I cannot see any reason to get excited about this area.

Côtes d'Auvergne This is another red wine VDQS making strawberry- and cherry-flavored, light, insipid wines from Gamay. Some Pinot Noir is also made, the best of which comes from Michel Bellard (***). Bellard makes not only a good red wine, but also a crisp, scented rosé.

Crémant de Loire This is the Loire Valley's best appellation for both pink and white sparkling wine. If the American importers do a good job of getting the wines into the country without abusing them in transport, readers will enjoy these tasty, light, inexpensive sparkling wines. Many of these wines are nonvintage, so it is important to buy only the freshest stock, which is often impossible to know until you pull the cork. Sparkling Loire wines have to be drunk within 1–2 years of their bottling.

CRÉMANT DE LOIRE PRODUCERS OF MERIT

Ackerman-Laurence***
Domaine Gabillière***

Gratien and Meyer***

Gros Plant du Pays Nantais This region, entitled only to a VDQS, is planted with one of the meanest, nastiest white wine grapes in the world, the Gros Plant. It goes by different names in other parts of France, such as Picpoul and Folle Blanche. Normally only used as a blending agent to buttress other varietals that produce richer, low-acid wines, unripe Gros Plant can shatter your teeth with its acidity and greenness. The best advice is to stay away from it despite what appear to be superlow prices. Some of the big Muscadet producers (e.g., Métaireau and Sauvion) have begun to tame some of Gros Plant's acidity, but you are much better off spending another dollar for Muscadet, unless you are a masochist.

Haut-Poitou   The production of this region, which is VDQS rather than an appellation, is dominated by the huge cooperative at Neuville. Thus, anyone can buy a cuvée, slap whatever name they want on it, and simply call it "Mr. Smith's Haut-Poitou." Nevertheless, the white wines, such as Sauvignon Blanc and Chardonnay, are light, fresh, floral, and tasty, which is surprising when you consider that this is a very inexpensive wine. The bad news is that the red wines, made from Cabernet Sauvignon, Cabernet Franc, and Gamay, are nasty, raw, lip-stinging wines with little flavor, but plenty of acidity and vegetal characteristics. The cooperative is the only producer in this region of which I am aware.

Jasnières   This 47-acre appellation just north of Tours produces very dry, often excellent white wines from Chenin Blanc. They are not easy to find, but if you come across any, you are well advised to try them for their delicacy, as well as rarity.

JASNIÈRES PRODUCERS OF MERIT

Gaston Cartereau****   J. B. Pinon***
Domaine de la Chanière****

Ménétou-Salon   Ménétou-Salon, a relatively small appellation of 250 acres, produces excellent white wines from Sauvignon Blanc and some herbal, spicy, light-bodied rosé and red wines from Pinot Noir. In my opinion, the wines to buy are the Sauvignons, which exhibit a pungent, herbaceous, earthy, curranty nose, and crisp, rich, grassy flavors. The best recent vintage has been 1990, followed by 1982 and 1989.

MÉNÉTOU-SALON PRODUCERS OF MERIT

Domaine de Chatenoy***   Marc Lebrun***
Domaine Chavet**** (many think he   Henri Pellé**** (his Clos des Blanchais
   makes one of the greatest dry rosés from   gets 5 stars)
   Pinot Noir in France)   Jean Teiller***
Cuvée Pierre-Alexandre****

Montlouis   Montlouis is often regarded as the stepchild of its more famous southern neighbor, Vouvray. It is a good source for sparkling wines made from Chenin Blanc that can range from bone dry to honeyed, sweet, sticky examples. They are less expensive than those from Vouvray. The white wines also range from dry to medium sweet. Quality from the top producers is generally good.

MONTLOUIS PRODUCERS OF MERIT

Domaine Berger***   Domaine de Labarre***
Domaine Délétang*****   Claude Levasseur***/****
Domaine de l'Entre-Coeurs***   Pierre Mignot***

Muscadet   This vast area is known for making inexpensive, fresh wines that must be consumed within several years of the vintage. There is generic Muscadet, but even better is the Muscadet de Sèvre et Maine, which is bottled *sur-lie* by the best producers. Muscadet, which possesses an enthralling crispness and freshness, works wonders with fresh shellfish.

This vast area offers a tremendous range in quality, from insipid, vapid, hollow wines, to wines with considerable personality. Readers should note the following chart to see who is producing the best Muscadet. Keep in mind that Muscadet is made from a grape called Melon de Bourgogne, which is also found in America from the likes of the Beaulieu winery in the Napa Valley and the Panther Creek winery in Oregon. The best recent vintages for Muscadet have been 1994 and 1990, the latter being risky now because Muscadet is best consumed within 2–3 years of the vintage.

RATING MUSCADET'S BEST PRODUCERS

* * * *(EXCELLENT)

Michel Bahuaud
Domaine de la Borne
André-Michel Brégeon
Château de Chasseloir
Chéreau-Carré
Joseph Drouard
Domaine de l'Ecu
Domaine du Fief Guérin
Marquis de Goulaine
Domaine Les Hautes Noëlles
Château de la Mercredière

Louis Métaireau
Domaine de la Mortaine
Domaine des Mortiers-Gobin
Château La Noë
Domaine La Quilla
Sauvion Cardinal Richard
Domaine Le Rossignol
Sauvion Château de Cléray
Domaine des Sensonnières
Domaine de la Vrillonnière

* * *(GOOD)

Serge Bâtard
Domaine de la Botinière
Château de la Bretesche
La Chambaudière
Domaine des Dorices
Domaine de la Fevrie
Le Fief du Breil
Domaine de la Fruitière
Domaine de la Grange

Domaine de la Guitonnière
Domaine des Herbauges
Domaine de l'Hyvernière
Château de la Jannière
Château l'Oiselinière
Château de la Preuille
Château de la Ragotière
Sauvion (other cuvées)

Pouilly-Fumé Pouilly is the name of the village and *fumé* means smoke. This appellation, renowned the world over for its richly scented, flinty (some say smoky), earthy, herbaceous, melony white wines that can range from medium bodied to full and intense, does indeed produce some of the world's most exciting wines from Sauvignon. The downside of this fame is the high prices fetched by the region's top producers of Pouilly-Fumé. Is a superb Pouilly-Fumé worth $40? Readers should also realize that most producers make numerous cuvées and often offer a luxury cuvée at prices of $25–$40 a bottle, which exceeds the limit I will pay. The best recent vintages include excellent 1989s that should be drunk up, spectacular 1990s that should drink well until the end of the century, and the 1992s. The following chart comprehensively covers the finest producers. By the way, a food that is heavenly with Pouilly-Fumé is goat cheese.

RATING POUILLY-FUMÉ'S BEST PRODUCERS

* * * * *(OUTSTANDING)

Domaine Cailbourdin
J. C. Chatelain

Didier Dagueneau (Clos des Chailloux)
Didier Dagueneau (Cuvée Silex)

Serge Dagueneau
Château du Nozet-Ladoucette (Baron de L
  Pouilly-Fumé)

Michel Redde (Cuvée Majorum)

* * * *(EXCELLENT)

Marc Deschamps
Masson-Blondelet-Les Angelots
Masson-Blondelet-Villa Paulus

Didier Pabiot
Tinel-Blondelet****/*****
Château de Tracy

* * *(GOOD)

Henri Beurdin (Reuilly)
Gérard Cordier (Reuilly)
Henri Pellé (Ménétou-Salon)
Raymond Pipet (Quincy)

Michel Redde
Guy Saget
Jean Teiller (Ménétou-Salon)

Pouilly-sur-Loire This interesting appellation relies on the Chasselas grape, a lowly regarded varietal that can make fruity, soft wines when yields are restricted. Wines from this appellation should be inexpensive and consumed within 1 year of the vintage.

Quarts de Chaume This appellation produces what may be France's least-known great sweet wine. One hundred acres, planted entirely with Chenin Blanc, produce crisp, backward wines that are almost impenetrable when young. They gradually open to reveal a honeyed, splendid, floral, apricot, peachy richness that lingers and lingers. Quarts de Chaume is not only one of the greatest sweet wines in France, but in the world. Insiders have tended to keep its magical qualities a secret. The noble rot, which is the key to the compelling bouquet of sweet wine, frequently attacks the Chenin Blanc grown on the slopes of the Quarts de Chaume appellation. The yields, limited to 22 hectoliters per hectare, are the lowest permitted in France. What does that tell you? Unlike Barsac and Sauternes, Quarts de Chaume is not aged in new oak casks. Consequently, the full expression of Chenin Blanc, not influenced by oak, is vividly on display. There is not much of this wine produced, but, fortunately, a number of American importers have been selling the wines from this underrated appellation for years.

QUARTS DE CHAUME PRODUCERS OF MERIT

Domaine des Baumard*****
Domaine Belle Rive****
Domaine l'Echarderie***/****
Domaine du Petit-Metris***/****

Château Pierre Bise***/****
Domaine de la Roche-Moreau***/****
Domaine Suronde****

Quincy Another appellation dedicated to Sauvignon Blanc, Quincy, which is near the historic city of Bourges, takes Sauvignon to its most herbaceous, some would say vegetal, limit. This can be an almost appallingly asparagus-scented and -flavored wine in underripe years, but in top years, such as 1990, that character is subdued. Quincy wines are bone dry and can last for 5–6 years.

QUINCY PRODUCERS OF MERIT

Domaine Jérôme de la Chaise***
Claude Houssier (Domaine du Pressoir)
  ***
Domaine Jaumier***

Domaine Mardon*****
Raymond Pipet***
Alain Thirot-Duc de Berri (a co-op wine)
  ***

St.-Nicolas-de-Bourgueil If I had to pick a favorite red-wine-producing region of Loire it would be this charming area. The red wines, which are all drinkable when released, are light, with intense perfumes of raspberry and curranty fruit flavors, followed by a soft, round, supple texture. They are currently in fashion in Paris, and prices are rising for wines that should never sell for more than $8–$10 a bottle. The red wine grapes utilized are Cabernet Franc and Cabernet Sauvignon. There are also small quantities of rosé produced.

ST.-NICOLAS-DE-BOURGUEIL PRODUCERS OF MERIT

Max Cognard*** Domaine de la Rodaie****
J. P. Mabileau*** Joel Taluau***
Domaine des Ouches***

Sancerre Sancerre and Vouvray are probably the best-known appellations of the vast Loire Valley viticultural region. A highly fashionable wine for over two decades, its success is based on its crisp acidity allied with rich, zesty, Sauvignon fruitiness. A small amount of red wine, which I find disappointing, is made from Pinot Noir. It, too, is called Sancerre. Sancerre's success is justifiable in view of the number of high-quality producers in this region. The only legitimate concern about Sancerre is the high price this wine fetches. The steep slopes of chalk and flint that surround Sancerre's best villages—Bué, Chavignon, and Verdigny—are undoubtedly responsible for the flinty, subtle, earthy character evident in so many of the top wines. There is no shortage of superlative Sancerre producers as evidenced by the following chart. The finest recent vintages have been 1990, 1989, and 1982. White Sancerre and the limited quantities of rosés should be drunk within 2–3 years of the vintage, although some can last longer. Sancerre Pinot Noir can last for 4–5 years.

RATING SANCERRE'S BEST PRODUCERS

* * * * *(OUTSTANDING)

Bailly-Reverdy Edmond Vatan
Paul Cotat (all three cuvées)
Château du Nozet-Ladoucette (Comte
   Lafond Sancerre)

* * * *(EXCELLENT)

Lucien Crochet Vincent Pinard (all cuvées)
Christian Dauny H. Reverdy
Jean Delaporte Jean Reverdy (Domaine de Villots)
Gitton Père et Fils Jean-Max Roger
Paul Millerioux Claude Thomas
Domaine de la Moussière-Cuvée Edmond Lucien Thomas
André Neveu (all cuvées) Domaine Vacheron

* * *(GOOD)

Pierre Archambault Château de Maimbray
Bernard Balland Domaine de la Moussière (other cuvées)
Henri Bourgeois Roger Neveu
Clos de la Poussie (Cordier) Domaine du Nozay
Pascal Jolivet

Saumur White, red, and rosé wines all emerge from this Loire Valley appellation. Two related appellations are Saumur-Champigny, which many feel produces good fresh red wines —although I do not agree—and Saumur-Mousseux, an underrated area for producing fresh, lively, inexpensive sparkling wines. Consumers should be able to find some good values from this latter appellation. Look for the sparkling wine cuvées from such producers as Ackerman-Laurence (**/***), Bouvet-Ladubay (**/***), Gratien and Meyer (**/****), Langlois and Château (***), and De Neuville (***). Unfortunately, many of these sparkling wine cuvées are beat up in transit to America, so what consumers encounter are oxidized, flat wines unlike what is seen in France. Delicious, dry white wines (from Chenin Blanc) and some reliable reds are made by Château de Hureau.

Savennières Savennières, the Montrachet of the Loire Valley, produces dry Chenin Blanc that can age for 15–20 years and can possess an intensity, richness, and complexity that one has to taste to believe. There are only 150 acres, but the production is limited to 30 hectoliters per hectare, and the minimum alcohol level is 12 percent. The results are sensationally rich, intense wines that develop a honeyed complexity and a huge, floral, mineral bouquet after 7–8 years of cellaring. The wines start life relatively backward and tart, but if you are looking for a great dry white wine that can out-age most Chardonnays, check out a Savennières. The best recent vintages have been 1990 (one of the three greatest years since World War II), 1989, and 1983.

RATING SAVENNIÈRES'S BEST PRODUCERS

* * * * *(OUTSTANDING)
Domaine des Baumard (Clos du Papillon)   Clos de la Coulée de Sérrant (N. Joly)
Domaine des Baumard (Trie Spéciale)   Domaine du Closel (Clos du Papillon)

* * * *(EXCELLENT)
Domaine des Baumard (regular cuvée)   Roche aux Moines (Pierre and Yves
Domaine des Baumard (Clos de St.-Yves)   Soulez)
Château de Chamboureau (Y. Soulez)   Roche aux Moines Clos de la Bergerie
Château d'Epiré   (Pierre and Yves Soulez)
Domaine Laffourcade   Pierre-Yves Tijou Clos des Perrières

* * *(GOOD)
Château de la Bizolière   Château de Plaisance
Clos de Coulaine (F. Roussier)

Touraine This general appellation covers considerable acreage, so it is important to know who are the best producers, as generalizations about the wines cannot be made. Certainly the Sauvignon Blanc and Chenin Blanc range from plonk to delicious fruity, vibrant wines. The red wines can also range from disgustingly vegetal, to richly fruity, aromatic offerings. One constant is that any Touraine white or red wine should be consumed within 2–3 years of the vintage. The best recent vintage has been 1990, followed by 1992.

TOURAINE PRODUCERS OF MERIT (WHITE WINES)

Domaine de Charmoise ****   Domaine des Corbillières ***
Domaine de Charmoise M   Domaine Délétang *****
   de Marionet *****

Vouvray Vouvray vies with Sancerre for the best-known appellation of the Loire Valley. Unlike Sancerre, no rosé or red wine is produced in Vouvray. It is all white and all from the Chenin Blanc grape, which can reach shrill acidity levels in the limestone and chalky/clay soils of these charming vineyards located east of Tours. A huge appellation (over 3,800 acres), Vouvray produces tasty, sparkling wines, wonderfully crisp, delicious, bone-dry wines, and some of the most spectacularly honeyed sweet wines one will ever taste. The sweet wines, indicated by the word *moelleux* on the label, are the result of the noble rot and can last for 40–50 or more years. The 1990 vintage was the greatest one for Vouvray sweet wines since 1959 or 1947; 1989 is a close second. Consumers who adore these wines should not wait too long to stock up. The following chart lists the top producers, but several deserve special mention, including Gaston Huet, whose three vineyard-designated sweet wines called Le Haut-Lieu, Le Mont, and Le Clos du Bourg are riveting examples of Vouvray. Another up-and-coming Vouvray superstar is Philippe Foreau, who makes wines from his estate called Clos Naudin. Like most producers in this area he fashions numerous cuvées, but the quality in vintages such as 1989 and 1990 has been extraordinary. Domaine Bourillon-Dorléans is another emerging superstar, especially for their decadently rich cuvées called Moelleux and Coulée d'Or.

RATING VOUVRAY'S BEST PRODUCERS

*****(OUTSTANDING)

Domaine Bourillon-Dorléans	Gaston Huet
Philippe Foreau Clos Naudin	

****(EXCELLENT)

Domaine de la Charmoise	Château Moncontour

***(GOOD)

Marc Brédif	J. M. Monmousseau
Jean-Pierre Freslier	D. Moyer
Sylvain Gaudron	Prince Poniatowski Le Clos Baudin

FLAVORS

There is an unbelievable variety in flavors and textures to the wines of the Loire Valley. Below is a quick summary of the flavors of the major wines.

DRY WHITE WINES

Muscadet-sur-Lie   A classic Muscadet, sur-Lie has light body, tart, dry, fresh, stony, and delicate flavors with refreshing acidity.

Savennières   A good Savennières is marked by a stony, lemon and lime–like bouquet with dry, austere yet floral, deep flavors and medium body.

Vouvray   Dry, very flowery, and fruity with crisp acidity for balance, a Vouvray is delightful as an aperitif wine.

Sancerre   Assertive aromas of fresh herbs, recently cut grass, wet stones, and currants dominate this crisp, intense, and flavorful wine.

Pouilly-Fumé   Pouilly-Fumé is very similar in aromatic character to Sancerre, but on the palate it is a fuller, more opulent and alcoholic wine.

DRY RED WINES

Bourgueil   Bourgueils are prized for their herb-tinged strawberry and cherry fruit in a light, soft, compact format.

Chinon   Aggressively herbaceous aromas and cherry fruit age nicely into a cedary/curranty wine of character in a good Chinon.

Touraine   Most wines of Touraine are light, soft, and fruity, and dominated by herbaceous or vegetal bouquets.

SWEET WHITE WINES

Vouvray Buttery, overripe tropical fruit, honey, and flowers are the aromas and tastes in a sweet Vouvray. Crisp acidity gives a vibrance and a well-delineated character to these wines.

Coteaux du Layon, Quarts de Chaume, Bonnezeaux While undistinguished when young, in great years these sweet wines age into honeypots filled with rich, ripe, decadent levels of fruit. They are probably the world's most undervalued great sweet wines.

AGING POTENTIAL

Dry White Wines
Muscadet: 1–3 years
Pouilly-Fumé: 3–5 years
Sancerre: 3–5 years
Savennières: 3–12 years
Vouvray: 2–6 years
Dry Red Wines
Bourgueil: 3–7 years

Chinon: 3–10 years
Touraine: 3–6 years
Sweet White Wines
Bonnezeaux: 5–20 years
Coteaux du Layon: 5–20 years
Quarts de Chaume: 5–20 years
Vouvray: 10–30 years

OVERALL QUALITY LEVEL

Poor to superb. The Loire Valley, with thousands of growers, is a minefield for the consumer who is not armed with the names of a few good producers. The best producers charts above list the top proprietors. Avoid anything labeled Rosé d'Anjou.

MOST IMPORTANT INFORMATION TO KNOW

Learn the multitude of appellations and the different types of wines produced, and memorize a few of the top producers. Then and only then will you be able to navigate the turbulent waters of the Loire.

1995–1996 BUYING STRATEGY

To the extent you can still find any of the great 1989s and 1990s from Vouvray, Savennières, Bonnezeaux, Coteaux du Layon, and Quarts de Chaume, you should move quickly to purchase them. Most insiders have long known that 1990, for both Savennières and the sweet wines of Loire, is one of the three or four greatest vintages in the post–World War II era. The 1991 vintage is a disappointing one and 1992, an excessively abundant, average-quality vintage; 1993 is a good year, and 1994 is irregular, but undoubtedly the best of the last four rain-plagued vintages for dry Sauvignon. If you wish to drink the lighter wines from the Loire, look for the 1994s and 1993s from Muscadet. Avoid anything older.

VINTAGE GUIDE

1994—A stormy, hot summer had most producers hoping for a repeat of 1989 and 1990. September's three weeks of intermittent rain and storms prevented 1994 from being a great vintage. Nevertheless, the top producers have fashioned very good dry white wines, if the rot-tinged grapes were left in the vineyard. Production is smaller than normal for the finest estates that practiced serious selection. Consequently, pressure to raise prices is a strong possibility. Sauvignon Blanc is the most successful varietal in 1994. With respect to the red wine grapes, Gamay was the least affected by the rains. The tastings I have completed for the first-released 1994 whites revealed surprisingly rich, full-bodied, low-acid Sauvignons. The Chenin Blancs were more mixed.

1993—Another rain-plagued harvest, 1993 has turned out to be a good to very good vintage for the dry whites, an average-quality vintage for the reds, and an irregular vintage for the sweet white wines. The 1993 dry Sauvignons are crisp, lively, medium-bodied wines, with more pleasing aromas than the soft, diffuse 1992s or the lean, high-acid 1991s. All things considered, 1993 is a far more successful vintage than was expected following the miserable, wet, cold month of September.

1992—The Loire Valley escaped most of the horrific downpours that plagued southern France, but the crop size was appallingly large. Reports of excessive yields from virtually every appellation were numerous. Growers had a chance to pick relatively ripe fruit that produced a good vintage, but only those who kept their yields low produced good wines. This is a vintage of pleasant, straightforward, fruity, soft wines that should be drunk up by 1996. The most successful appellations for white wines are Muscadet, Sancerre, and Pouilly-Fumé. Chinon was the most successful for red wines.

1991—This is a difficult vintage throughout the Loire Valley, with relatively acidic, lean, light-bodied wines that lack ripeness and flavor authority. Successes can be found, but overall, a small crop combined with inadequate ripeness produced ungenerous wines lacking fruit and charm.

1990—This is one of the all-time greatest vintages for just about every region of the Loire Valley, especially the sweet wine appellations and the great dry white wines of Savennières, Pouilly-Fumé, and Sancerre. The levels of richness and intensity of the 1990s are mind-boggling. Consumers lucky enough to be able to find and afford the top cuvées of the decadently sweet wines from Bonnezeaux, Coteaux du Layon, Quarts de Chaume, and Vouvray, as well as some of the spectacularly full-bodied, awesomely rich, dry Savennières, will have treasures that will last in their cellars for 25–30 or more years. Most Muscadet should have been drunk by the beginning of 1993, but the top cuvées of dry Sancerre and Pouilly-Fumé will last (where well stored) through 1996.

The red wines are also surprisingly good (I have a strong bias against most of them because of their overt vegetal character), but because of the drought and superripeness they are less herbaceous than usual and offer copious quantities of red and black fruits.

1989—Somewhat similar to 1990, although yields were higher and there was less botrytis in the sweet wine vineyards, 1989 is an excellent, in many cases a superb, vintage for Vouvray, Quarts de Chaume, Coteaux du Layon, and Bonnezeaux. It is also a super vintage for Savennières. All the drier wines from Sancerre, Pouilly-Fumé, Touraine, and Muscadet should have been consumed by now, as they were exceptionally low in acidity.

1988—A good but unexciting vintage produced pleasant, textbook wines that admirably represent their appellation or region, but lack the huge perfumes, richness, and depth of the finest 1989s and 1990s.

1987—A mediocre to poor year.

OLDER VINTAGES

The decadently rich dessert wines of the Coteaux du Layon, Bonnezeaux, Quarts de Chaume, and Vouvray from 1983, 1976, 1971, 1962, 1959, 1949, and 1947 can be spectacular wines. These wines are still modestly priced and are undoubtedly the greatest bargains in rich dessert-wines in the world. While it is not easy to find these older vintages, consumers should put this information to good use by stocking up on the 1989s and 1990s.

Savennières is probably the world's greatest buy in dry, full-bodied white wines. Older Savennières vintages to look for are 1986, 1985, 1978, 1976, 1971, 1969, 1962, and 1959. Occasionally, small quantities of these wines come up for auction. They are well worth the low prices being asked.

Gaston Huet's sweet Vouvrays from 1959 and 1962 remain in superb condition. Why don't more people realize just how fine these wines are? For red wines Charles Joguet's best

LANGUEDOC-ROUSSILLON

Great Wine Values for Tough Economic Times

Among all the French viticultural regions, none has made more progress than the vast region referred to as the Languedoc-Roussillon area. Bounded on the northeast by the Rhône Valley, on the east by the Mediterranean Sea, on the west by the hilly terrain known as the "massif central," and on the south by the Pyrenees Mountains of Spain, this sun-drenched region produces more than half of France's red table wine. Once known for its barely palatable, acidic, thick, alcoholic wines from huge industrial-oriented cooperatives that placed quantity before quality, the Languedoc-Roussillon region has undergone an amazing transformation since the mid-eighties. Moreover, some of America's most innovative importers are flocking to the region in search of delicious, bargain-priced white, red, and rosé wines.

There is no shortage of wine from which to choose, because the Languedoc-Roussillon area, with its 72,000 acres of vines, annually produces an ocean of 310 million cases. The finest vineyard sites generally tend to be planted on hillsides, with heavy soils that provide outstanding drainage. Excluding Corsica, Languedoc-Roussillon is the hottest viticultural region of France. Torrential rainstorms are common during the summer, but the amount of rainfall is small and the area, much like the southern Rhône, is buffeted by winds from both inland and the Mediterranean, thus creating an ideal climate for the sanitary cultivation of vineyards, with minimal need for fungicides, herbicides, and insecticides.

Most of the progress that has been made is attributable to two major developments. The advent of temperature-controlled stainless steel fermentation tanks (an absolute necessity in this torridly hot region) has greatly enhanced the aromatic purity and fruit in the wines. Even more important, many of the indigenous grape varieties of this area, Carignan, Cinsault, and Terret Noir for red and rosé wines, and Clairette, Ugni Blanc, Picpoul, and Maccabeo for white wines, are used decreasingly in favor of widely renowned, superstar grapes such as Syrah, Mourvèdre, Cabernet Sauvignon, Merlot, and Grenache. White wine varietals making significant inroads include Chardonnay, Sauvignon Blanc, and Chenin Blanc. Since the mid-eighties, thousands of acres of these varietals have been planted.

Across this vast area, stretching from southwest of Avignon, where the appellations of Châteauneuf du Pape and Tavel end, to the Spanish border, are well over 20 different viticultural regions producing an enormous array of dry white, rosé, and red table wine, as well as the famed *vins doux naturels*, those sweet dessert wines that are slightly fortified. Much of the wine from the region has either just recently achieved *appellation contrôlée* status, or remains entitled to VDQS status, or nothing more than a *vin de pays* designation. As the following tasting notes indicate, some of the very finest wines can legally be called only *vins de pays*.

Following is a quick rundown of the major viticultural areas.

Costières de Nîmes   This area, which received *appellation contrôlée* status in 1986, produces white, red, and rosé wines. The area takes its name from the extraordinary Roman city of Nîmes. The vineyard area consists of a group of pebble-strewn slopes and a plateau region that lie in the Rhône delta. Seventy-five percent of the production is in red wine, 20% in rosé, and the remainder in white. The two best estates are, irrefutably, Château de la Tuilerie and Château de Campuget. Other interesting domaines include the Domaine Saint-Louis-La-Perdrix and Château Belle-Coste. The red wines are permitted to be made from a maximum of 50% Carignan. Other allowable grape varieties include Cinsault, Counoise Grenache, Mourvèdre, Syrah, Terret Noir, and two obscure red varietals called Aspiran Noir and Oeillade. White varietals are dominated by Clairette and Grenache Blanc, with small amounts of Picpoul, Roussanne, Terret Blanc, Ugni Blanc, Malvoisie, Marsanne, and Maccabeo also present.

Coteaux du Languedoc   This vast area (given *appellation contrôlée* status in 1985) includes vineyards in three French departments, Aude, Garde, and Herault. It runs from Nîmes in the north to Narbonne in the south. Consumers will find wines labeled merely with the appellation of Coteaux du Languedoc, as well as those where the individual village names are affixed. Two of the finest villages, Saint-Chinian and Faugères, were elevated to their own *appellation contrôlée* status in 1982. The grape varieties are essentially the same as in the Costières de Nîmes, although the more serious estates use higher percentages of Syrah, Mourvèdre, Grenache, and Counoise in their red wines, generally at the expense of Carignan and Cinsault. The best wines of Faugères have consistently come from Haut-Fabrègues and Gilbert Alquier. Among the best wines of Saint-Chinian are those from Domaine des Jougla and Cazal Viel. Perhaps the greatest wine of the entire appellation of Coteaux du Languedoc (as well as the most expensive) is the Prieuré de St.-Jean-de-Bebian. This wine, and the Mas-de-Daumas Gassac, a *vin de pays*, are irrefutably the two reference-point red wines of the Languedoc-Roussillon region.

Minervois   Minervois may have the best long-range potential of the appellations in the Languedoc-Roussillon area. To say that there are still many underachievers would not be unjust. This area of nearly 14,000 acres of vineyards is bounded on the west by the extraordinary fortified fortress city of Carcassonne and on the east by Saint-Chinian. Minervois flourished under Roman rule, but never recovered from the phylloxera epidemic that devastated France's vineyards in the late nineteenth century. The vineyards, the best of which tend to be located on gently sloping, south-facing, limestone hillsides sheltered from the cold north winds, endure the hottest microclimate of the region. Virtually all of the wine production is red, although it is not surprising to see microquantities of a surprisingly tasty rosé emerge. The amount of white wine produced makes up less than 2% of the total production. Some of the best estates represented in America include Château de Paraza, Château de Gourgazaud, Daniel Domergue, Tour-Saint-Martin, and Domaine Sainte-Eulalie.

Corbières   Corbières, which is located further down the coast, south of Minervois, was recently elevated to *appellation contrôlée* status. It boasts the largest production area (over 57,000 acres) of the entire Languedoc-Roussillon region. Red wine accounts for 90% of the production, and the predominant varietal is the omnipresent Carignan, although the more serious estates have begun to employ increasing percentages of Syrah and Mourvèdre. The outstanding estates in Corbières include the brilliant Château Le Palais, Château Etang des

Colombes, Domaine Saint-Paul, Domaine de Villemajou, and the Guy Chevalier wines produced at a cooperative called Les Vignerons d'Octaviana.

Fitou   Fitou, the oldest of the *appellation contrôlée* regions of the Languedoc-Roussillon area (its *appellation contrôlée* status was bestowed in 1948), represents two separate areas bounded on the north by Corbières. One region, representing low-lying vineyards near the coast, is planted on shallow, gravelly soil atop limestone beds. No one I have ever talked with believes top-quality wines can emerge from this particular sector. On the hillsides further inland, the best vineyards are planted on sloping, well-drained, sandstone-and-limestone-mixed soils. The ripest, fattest, fruitiest wines from Fitou generally emanate from this area. The grape varieties for Fitou are the same as for the other regions of Languedoc, with Carignan once again the dominant varietal, but the more serious producers are utilizing more Mourvèdre, Syrah, and Grenache. Some rosé wines are made in Fitou, but I have never seen a bottle of white. I do not believe any is permitted under the *appellation contrôlée* laws.

Côtes de Roussillon and Côtes de Roussillon-Villages   The Roussillon vineyards, all of which run from the Mediterranean Sea inland, surrounding Perpignan, France's last urban bastion before the Spanish border, are known to have produced wines since the seventh century B.C. There is immense potential, not only for dry red table wines, but for the sweet, fortified wines that often excel in this windy, sun-drenched region. The best vineyards, which are entitled to the Côtes de Roussillon or Côtes de Roussillon-Villages appellation, stretch out over a semicircle of hills facing the Mediterranean Sea. These hillside vineyards, planted on expanses of limestone and granite, enjoy a phenomenally sunny, hot summer. Virtually all of the rainfall results from thunderstorms. It has always amazed me that these wines are still so reasonably priced given the amount of labor necessary to cultivate so many of the terraced vineyards of this region. The tiny amount of white wine produced is generally from such obscure varietals as Malvoise de Roussillon and Maccabeo. The red wines are generally produced from the ubiquitous Carignan, as well as Grenache, Syrah, and Mourvèdre. These are full-bodied, relatively rich wines, with a big, fleshy, peppery character. Despite their softness and easy drinkability when young, several properties make wines that can last for up to a decade. The best estates in the Côtes de Roussillon and Côtes de Roussillon-Villages are Pierre d'Aspres, Cazes Frères, Château de Jau, Domaine Sarda-Malet, Domaine Salvat, and Domaine Saint-Luc. There are also a bevy of cooperatives, none of which I have visited, but several have received high praise, particularly the cooperative of Maury.

Collioure   This tiny appellation, the smallest in the Languedoc-Roussillon region for dry red wine, is located just to the south of the Côtes de Roussillon on an expanse of terraced, hillside vineyards called the Côtes Vermeille. Virtually all of the Collioure vineyards are located on these steeply terraced slopes, and the red wine is produced largely from a blend of Grenache, Carignan, Mourvèdre, Syrah, and Cinsault. Tiny yields are commonplace in Collioure, and as a result the wines tend to be relatively rich and full. They have never been discovered by American wine enthusiasts. The best Collioures come from the great Domaine du Mas Blanc of Dr. Parcé, also renowned for his fabulous fortified, portlike Banyuls. There are generally two cuvées of Collioure, one called Les Piloums, and the other, Cosprons Levants. Other interesting producers include Thierry Parcé at the Domaine de la Rictorie, and the Celliers des Templiers.

Vins Doux Naturels   The Languedoc-Roussillon area abounds with some of the greatest values in sweet and fortified sweet dessert wines in Europe. The most famous are those from Banyul (located on the coastline south of Perpignan) and Maury (located in the hillsides north of Perpignan). Both appellations require that these decadently rich, fortified wines be made from at least 50% Grenache. In the case of those wines entitled to the Banyul Grand Cru designation, they must be composed of at least 75% Grenache.

Other areas producing sweet wines include Muscat de Rivesaltes, Muscat de Lunel,

Muscat de Frontignan, and the two smaller appellations of Muscat de Mireval and Saint-Jean-de-Minervois. Both the Muscat de Frontignan and Muscat de Mireval are located near Herault. Muscat de Lunel is produced east of Nimes in the northern sector of the Languedoc-Roussillon.

The most famous of these wines are the great Banyuls from Dr. Parcé. They have a legendary reputation in France, but remain, to my surprise, largely unknown in the United States.

Almost all of these wines can handle considerable aging and are remarkable for their value, particularly when compared with the soaring prices for vintage and tawny ports.

The Basics

TYPES OF WINE

The appellations, the wines, the estates, and the areas here are not well known to wine consumers; consequently there are some great wine values. The range in wines is enormous. There is sound sparkling wine such as Blanquette de Limoux; gorgeously fragrant, sweet muscats like Muscat de Frontignan; oceans of soft, fruity red wines, the best of which are from Minervois, Faugères, Côtes du Roussillon, Costières du Gard, and Corbières; and even France's version of vintage port, Banyuls. These areas have not yet proven the ability to make interesting white wines, except for sweet muscats.

GRAPE VARIETIES

Grenache, Carignan, Cinsault, Mourvèdre, and Syrah are the major red wine grapes planted in this hot region. Small vineyards of Cabernet Sauvignon and Merlot are becoming more common.

With respect to white wine varietals, Chardonnay, Sauvignon Blanc, and Chenin Blanc can now be found in this area, but the older white wine vineyards generally consist of such workhorse varietals as Ugni Blanc, Picpoul, Maccabeo, and two of the better traditional varietals, Marsanne and Roussanne.

FLAVORS

Until the late eighties, this hot, frequently torrid part of France produced wines that never lacked ripeness, but rather suffered from overripeness. However, the advent of a new generation of young, enthusiastic, and better-equipped winemakers, significant investment in temperature-controlled stainless steel fermentation tanks, and more attention to harvesting the fruit before it becomes raisiny have resulted in soaring quantities of inexpensive, gorgeously ripe, perfumed, fruity wines. There are remarkable variations in style—from serious, relatively long-lived reds, to those made by the carbonic maceration method and designed to be drunk within several years of the vintage. Top producers have begun to offer luxury cuvées (for now, still modestly priced) that have been aged in new oak barrels. Some of these cuvées are highly successful, while others are overwhelmingly oaky.

AGING POTENTIAL

The dry red wines of Mas de Daumas Gassac, St.-Jean de Bebian, and a few other top producers can age for 10–15 years. The longest-lived wines of the region are the portlike wines of Banyuls, which can last for up to 30 years when made by a great producer such as Dr. Parcé. Other red wines should be drunk within 5–7 years of the vintage.

The white wines should be drunk within several years of the vintage.

Long known for monotonous mediocrity, quality levels have increased significantly as wine market insiders have realized the potential for well-made, inexpensive wines from this area. America's small specialist importers now make annual pilgrimages to this area looking for up-and-coming producers.

MOST IMPORTANT INFORMATION TO KNOW
Most consumers, as well as retailers, probably cannot name more than two or three Languedoc-Roussillon producers. However, if you are going to take advantage of some of the best-made wines that sell at low prices, it is important to learn the names of the finest producers, as well as their American importers.

1995–1996 BUYING STRATEGY
With the exception of Mas de Daumas Gassac, St.-Jean de Bebian, and Dr. Parcé's wines from Banyuls, do not buy anything older than 1990, unless it is one of the luxury cuvées. With the aforementioned producers, you can go back 10 years and feel confident you have bought a wine in good condition. For all other producers, the vintages of choice, 1994, 1990, and 1991, are excellent.

SUPER SPARKLING WINE VALUES

It is probably the least-known, well-made sparkling wine of France, at least to the Anglo-Saxon world. From an appellation called Blanquette de Limoux, hidden in the Languedoc-Roussillon area just north of Spain's border, comes France's oldest sparkling wine, made a century before a monk named Dom Pérignon was credited with discovering the process of producing champagne. Made primarily from the Chardonnay, Chenin Blanc, and Mauzac grapes, the wines are qualitatively close to a high-quality, nonvintage champagne at one-third the price—most dry brut vintage sparkling wines from this appellation retail for $10 a bottle. The best are the Saint-Hilaire Blanc de Blancs, the Maison Guinot, and the two top wines from the Cooperative Aiméry, the Cuvée Alderic and Cuvée Sieur d'Arques.

THE WORLD'S GREATEST WINES WITH CHOCOLATE

Some of the most unique wines in the world are the late-harvested wines from Banyuls made by Dr. Parcé at his Domaine du Mas Blanc. One Banyuls labeled *dry* is an explosively rich, full-bodied, Grenache-based wine that should be drunk with hearty fare on cool fall and winter evenings. Another, a dry red wine called Collioure, is a complex table wine, impeccably made from a blend of 40% Syrah, 40% Mourvèdre, and 20% Grenache. And then there are Dr. Parcé's famous portlike sweet Banyuls made from very ripe Grenache. Complex, decadent, and the only wine I have found to work well with chocolate desserts, this is a spectacular wine that can age well for 20–25 years. The alcohol content averages 16%–18%. Parcé also makes a special cuvée of Vieilles Vignes (old vines) that is even more stunning. Dr. Parcé's sweet Banyuls usually sell for under $25 a bottle, making them a moderately priced alternative to vintage port. The other decadent wine to serve with chocolate is from the Domaine Mas Amiel, a superlative producer from the obscure appellation of Maury. The French equivalent of a vintage port, Mas Amiel's wines are stunning in quality, and remarkably low in price. Don't miss them.

MARVELOUS MUSCATS

Looking for a sweet, ripe, honeyed, aromatic, reasonably priced wine to serve with fresh fruit or fruit tarts? Then be sure to try the Muscat de Frontignan from the Château de la

Peyrade or the Muscat de Lunel from Clos Bellevue, both sell for about $15 a bottle. They represent a heady drink, but the Muscat's seductive charm and power is very evident in this excellent wine. Another terrific sweet wine comes from Domaine Cazes. They produce a splendid Muscat de Rivesaltes that sells for about $20.

RECENT VINTAGES

Heat and sun are constants in this region. Vintages are incredibly consistent, and the quality of most wines has more to do with the availability of modern technology to keep the grapes and grape juice from overheating in the frightfully hot temperatures. Nevertheless, recent vintages that stand out are 1994 and 1991 (one of the most successful regions in France), 1990, and 1989. The 1992s and 1993s are mixed because of harvest rains, but most of the white wine varietals were harvested prior to the deluge. Moreover, the rains were highly localized, with some vineyards being inundated, while others remained untouched. Vintages are significantly less important in an area such as Languedoc-Roussillon than in others because ripeness is rarely ever a problem. With each vintage since 1987 there has been a significant leap in quality.

FINDING THE WINES OF LANGUEDOC-ROUSSILLON

Unlike most other wines, the wines of Languedoc-Roussillon remain a specialized item. It will assist readers to list the importers who have done most of the exploration of this area. Some of these importers are regional, and others are national. These include:

Arborway Imports, Lexington, MA; (617) 863-1753 (a regional importer dealing primarily in Massachusetts)

European Cellars, New York, NY; (212) 924-4949 (the enthusiastic Eric Solomon, a top specialist for the wines of southern France, sells his wines nationally)

Hand Picked Selections, Warrenton, VA; (703) 347-3471 (perhaps the top importer in the country for specializing in wines that sell for under $10, owner Dan Kravitz represents a considerable number of wines from this region)

Ideal Wines, Medford, MA; (617) 395-3300

Robert Kacher Selections, Washington, D.C.; (202) 832-9083 (one of the first to exploit this region's potential, Robert Kacher brings in some of the finest wines from the Languedoc-Roussillon region)

Langdon-Shiverick, Chagrin Falls, OH; (216) 247-6868

Kermit Lynch Selections, Berkeley, CA; (510) 524-1524 (this trailblazer, who has long represented many of France's small artisan producers, has plunged into Languedoc-Roussillon with considerable enthusiasm)

Wines of France, Mountainside, NJ; (908) 654-6173 (Frenchman Alain Junguenet, the first to see Languedoc-Roussillon's potential, has the most extensive portfolio of wines from this region, as well as some of its top estates)

RATING LANGUEDOC-ROUSSILLON'S BEST PRODUCERS

* * * *(EXCELLENT)

Domaine l'Aiguelière-Montpeyroux (Coteaux du Languedoc)

Gilbert Alquier-Cuvée Les Bastides (Faugères)

Domaine d'Aupilhac (Vin de Pays)

Château La Baronne (Corbières)

Château Bastide-Durand (Corbières)

Domaine Bois Monsieur (Coteaux du Languedoc)

Château de Calage (Coteaux du Languedoc)

Château de Campuget Cuvée Prestige (Costières de Nimes)

Domaine Capion (Vin de Pays)

Domaine Capion Merlot (Vin de Pays)

Château de Casenove (Côtes du Roussillon)

Les Chemins de Bassac Pierre Elie (Vin de Pays)

Domaine La Colombette (Vin de Pays)

Daniel Domergue (Minervois)

Château Donjon Cuvée Prestige (Minervois)

Château des Estanilles (Faugères)

Château des Estanilles Cuvée Syrah (Faugères)

La Grange des Peres ****/***** (Vin de Pays-Herault)

Château Hélène Cuvée Hélène de Troie (Vin de Pays)

Domaine de l'Hortus (Coteaux du Languedoc)****/*****

Château des Lanes (Corbières)

Domaine Maris (Minervois)

Mas Amiel (Maury)

Mas des Bressades Cabernet Sauvignon

Mas des Bressades Syrah

Mas de Daumas Gassac (L'Hérault) ****/*****

Mas Jullien Les Cailloutis (Coteaux du Languedoc)

Mas Jullien Les Dedierre (Coteaux du Languedoc)

Château d'Oupia Cuvée des Barons (Minervois)

Château Les Palais (Corbières)

Château Les Palais Cuvée Randolin (Corbières)

Château de Paraza Cuvée Speciale (Minervois)

Dr. Parcé Mas Blanc (Banyuls)****/*****

Domaine Peyre Rose Clos des Sistes (Coteaux du Languedoc)****/*****

Domaine Peyre Rose Clos Syrah (Coteaux du Languedoc)****/*****

Château Routas Agrippa (Coteaux Varois)

Château Routas Infernet (Coteaux Varois)

Château Routas Truffière (Coteaux Varois)

Prieuré de St.-Jean de Bebian (Vin de Pays)

Catherine de Saint-Juery (Coteaux du Languedoc)

Château La Sauvagéonne (Coteaux du Languedoc)

Château Le Thou (Vin de Pays d'Oc)

Domaine La Tour Boisée Cuvée Marie-Claude (Minervois)

* * *(GOOD)

Abbaye de Valmagne (Coteaux du Languedoc)

Gilbert Alquier (Faugères)

Domaine de L'Arjolle (Côtes de Thongue)

Pierre d'Aspres (Côtes du Roussillon)

Domaine des Astruc (Vin de Pays)

Château Belle-Coste (Vin de Pays)

Château de Blomac Cuvée Tradition (Minervois)

Château du Campuget (Costières de Nimes)

Domaine Capion Syrah (L'Hérault)

Château Capitoul (Coteaux de Languedoc)

Cazal-Viel (Saint-Chinian)

Cazal-Viel Cuvée Georges A. Aoust (Saint-Chinian)

Cazes Frères (Côtes du Roussillon)

Celliers des Tempières (Vin de Pays)

Guy Chevalier La Coste (Corbières)

Guy Chevalier La Coste-Cabernet/Syrah (L'Aude)

Guy Chevalier L'Église-Grenache Noir (Corbières)

Guy Chevalier Le Texas-Syrah (Corbières)

Domaine Dona Baissas (Côtes du Roussillon)

Château Etang des Colombes Cuvée du Bicentenaire (Corbières)

Château Fabas Cuvée Alexandre (Minervois)

Domaine des Gautier (Fitou)

Château de Gourgazaud (Minervois)

Domaine de Gournier (Vin de Pays)

Château Haut-Fabrègues (Faugères) ***/****

Le Jaja de Jau (Vin de Pays)

Les Jamelles (Vin de Pays)

Château de Jau (Côtes du Roussillon)

Domaine Lalande (Vin de Pays d'Oc)

Laville-Bertrou (Minervois)

Château de Luc (Corbières)

Mas Champart (Coteaux du Languedoc)

Mas Jullien Les Vignes Oubliés (Coteaux du Languedoc)

Mas de Ray Cuvée Caladoc (Bouches du Rhône)

Mas de Ray Cuvée Camargue (Bouches du Rhône)

Château Maurel Fonsalade (Saint-Chinian)

Domaine La Noble (Vin de Pays)

Château d'Oupia (Minervois)

Prieuré Château Les Palais (Corbières)

Dr. Parcé Mas Blanc Collioure-Cosprons Levants (Banyuls)

Dr. Parcé Mas Blanc Collioure-Les Piloums (Banyuls)

Château de Pena Côtes du Roussillon-Villages (Côtes du Roussillon)

Château de la Peyrade (Muscat-Frontignan)

Domaine Piccinini (Minervois)

Domaine de Pilou (Fitou)

Domaine de Pomaredes Merlot (Vin de Pays)

Château La Roque (Coteaux du Languedoc)

Château Rouquette sur Mer (Coteaux du Languedoc)

Château Routas Traditionnel (Coteaux Varois)

Domaine du Sacre Coeur (Saint-Chinian)

Domaine Salvat (Côtes du Roussillon)

Domaine Sarda-Malet Black Label (Côtes du Roussillon)

Tour St.-Martin (Minervois)

Château de la Tuilerie (Costières de Nimes)

Bernard-Claude Vidal (Faugères)

Les Vignerons d'Octaviana Grand Chariot (Corbières)

* *(AVERAGE)*

Domaine des Bories (Corbières)

Domaine du Bosc (L'Hérault)

Domaine du Bosccaute (L'Hérault)

Château de Cabriac (Corbières)

Domaine de Capion (L'Hérault)

Domaine de Coujan (Vin de Pays)

Château L'Espigne (Fitou)

Château Etang des Colombes Cuvée Tradition (Corbières)

Domaine de Fontsainte (Corbières)

Château de Grezan (Faugères)

Château Hélène (Vin de Pays)

Domaine des Jougla Cuvée Tradition (Saint-Chinian)

Domaine des Jougla Cuvée White Label (Saint-Chinian)

Château de Lascaux (Coteaux du Languedoc)

Domaine de la Lecugne (Minervois)

Domaine de Mayranne (Minervois)

Château Milhau-Lacugue (Saint-Chinian)

Château La Mission Le Vignon (Côtes du Roussillon)

Caves de Mont Tauch (Fitou)

Domaine de Montmarin (Côtes de Thongue)

Château de Nouvelles (Fitou)

Château de Paraza (Minervois)

Cuvée Claude Parmentier (Fitou)

Château Pech-Rédon (Coteaux du Languedoc)

Domaine Perrière-Les Amandiers (Corbières)

Qrmand de Villeneuve (Côtes du Roussillon)

Château de Queribus (Corbières)

Domaine de la Rictorie (Banyuls)

Domaine de la Roque (Coteaux du Languedoc)

Château de Roquecourbe (Minervois)

Saint-André (L'Hérault)

Château Saint-Auriol (Corbières)

Château Saint-Laurent (Corbières)

Domaine Sainte-Eulalie (Minervois)

Sarda-Malet (Côtes du Roussillon)

Domaine du Tauch (Fitou)

Domaine de Villemajou (Corbières)

Château de Villerambert-Julien (Minervois)

Caves de Vins de Roquebrun (Saint-Chinian)

PROVENCE

It is easy to regard Provence as just the dramatic playground for the world's rich and famous, for few wine lovers seem to realize that this vast viticultural region in southern France is at least 2,600 years old. For centuries, tourists traveling through Provence have been seduced by the aromatic and flavorful thirst-quenching rosés that seem to complement the distinctive cuisine of the region so well. Yet today, Provence is an exciting and diverse viticultural region that is turning out not only extremely satisfying rosés but immensely promising red wines and a few encouraging whites. However, it remains largely uncharted territory for wine consumers.

Provence is a mammoth-sized region that has seven specific viticultural areas. The best way to get a grasp on the region is to learn what each of these viticultural areas has to offer, and which properties constitute the leading wine-producing estates. While Provence is blessed with ideal weather for grape growing, not all the vintages are of equal merit. Certainly for the white and rosé wines of Provence, which require consumption in their youth, only 1994 and 1993 ought to be drunk today. Nineteen ninety, 1989, and 1985 are the super vintages for all of Provence, followed by 1983 and 1982. As a general rule, the top red wines of Provence can handle aging for up to a decade in the aforementioned vintages.

Following is a brief synopsis of the seven major wine-producing areas in Provence, along with a list of the top wines from each area that merit trying. While the wines of Provence are not overpriced, the recent collapse of the American dollar against the French franc has made these wines less attractively priced than they were several years ago. Yet when the top wines are compared with wines of similar quality from France's more famous areas such as Burgundy and Bordeaux, their relative value as French wines is obvious.

Bandol In France, Bandol is often called the most privileged appellation of France. Certainly, the scenic beauty of this storybook area offers unsurpassed views of the azure-colored Mediterranean Sea with the vineyards spread out over the hillsides overlooking the water. Bandol produces red, rosé, and white wines. It is most famous for its rosé wine, which some people consider the best made in France, and its long-lived, intense, tannic red wine, which is unique in France in that it is made from at least 50% of the little-known Mourvèdre grape. If anyone has any doubts about the quality of Mourvèdre, Pradeaux's 1989 and 1990 Mourvèdre Vieilles Vignes are monumental wines. Prices for Bandol have never been cheap, largely because of the never-ending flow of tourists to the area who buy up most of the wine made by the local producers.

There seems to be no doubt among connoisseurs that the best red wines come from such producers as the Domaine Pradeaux, Domaine Tempier, Domaine de Pibarnon, Ott's Château Romassan, Château Vannières, and two properties called Moulin des Coste and Mas des Rouvière. While most of these producers also make a white wine, it is not a wine I can recommend with a great deal of enthusiasm, as it seems to always taste dull and heavy. However, the red wines as well as the fresh, personality-filled rosés from these estates are well worth seeking out and are available in most of the major markets in America. Prices for the rosés now average $15–$20 a bottle with the red wines costing $20–$30 a bottle. While I have had the good fortune to taste red wines of Bandol as old as 15–20 years, most of the wines seem to hit their peak after 6–10 years in the bottle. Bandol, one of the most strictly regulated appellations in France, is certainly the leading candidate of all the Provence appellations for producer of the longest-lived and best-known red wines.

Bellet   Like all of the Provence appellations, the tiny appellation of Bellet, tucked in the hillside behind the international seaside resort of Nice, produces red, white, and rosé wines. The history of Bellet is rich, as its vineyards were originally cultivated by the Phoenician Greeks in 500 B.C. But unless one actually spends time on the Riviera, one is unlikely to ever know how a fine Bellet tastes. Most of the wine produced in this microappellation of only 100-plus acres never makes it outside of France, as the local restaurant demand is insatiable.

There are only a handful of producers making wine here, and the very best is the Château de Crémat, owned by the Bagnis family, a splendid estate of 50 acres that produces nearly 6,000 cases of wine. It is imported to the United States, but its high price of $20–$25 a bottle has ensured that few consumers know how it really tastes. Château de Crémat is a unique estate in Provence in that the white wine is of extremely high quality, and the local connoisseurs claim the rosé and red wines are the best made in this part of the French Riviera. The best recent vintages have been the 1994, 1990, 1989, and 1988, but I have tasted the red wines from Château de Crémat back through 1978, and they have shown no signs of decline. However, the wines of Bellet remain esoteric, enjoyed only by a handful of people, with prices that seem steep for the quality.

Cassis   The tiny village of Cassis, located on the western end of France's famous Côte d'Azur, is one of the most charming fishing villages on the Riviera. Located on a secluded bay, it is dwarfed by the surrounding steep limestone cliffs. The hordes of tourists that frequent the area ensure that most of the wine made here is consumed at the local bistros along with the area's ubiquitous *soupe de poisson.* While this appellation makes red wine as well as rosé, it is white wine that has made Cassis famous. The red wine tends to be heavy and uninteresting, and while the rosé can be good, it never seems to approach the quality level of its nearby neighbor Bandol. The white wine, which is often a blend of little-known grapes such as Ugni Blanc, Clairette, and Bourboulenc, is a spicy, fleshy wine that often seems unattractive by itself, but when served with the rich, aromatic seafood dishes of the region, it takes on a character of its own. The estates of Cassis producing the best white wines include Clos Ste.-Magdelaine, La Ferme Blanche, and Domaine du Bagnol. Prices average $15–$20 for these white wines, which, in 1995, make them bad values. They have a distinct character that requires fairly rich, spicy fish courses to complement their unique personality.

Coteaux d'Aix-en-Provence   This gigantic viticultural region, which extends primarily north and west of Aix-en-Provence, has numerous small estates making acceptable but generally overpriced wines that require drinking within the first 7–8 years of their lives. However, two of the very finest red wines produced in Provence are produced here: Domaine Trevallon and the better-known Château Vignelaure. Both producers specialize in red wine, capable of aging 15–20 years, made from a blend of two great red wine grapes, the Cabernet Sauvignon and the Syrah. Other estates have tried to imitate the wines made by Trevallon and Vignelaure, and a handful are worth watching.

The Domaine Trevallon is owned by the ruggedly handsome Eloi Durrbach, who carved his vineyard out of the forbidding and lunarlike landscape near the medieval ghost town of Les Baux. Its first vintage was only in 1978, but that vintage has been followed by other successful vintages that have produced wines that are compellingly rich and intense with

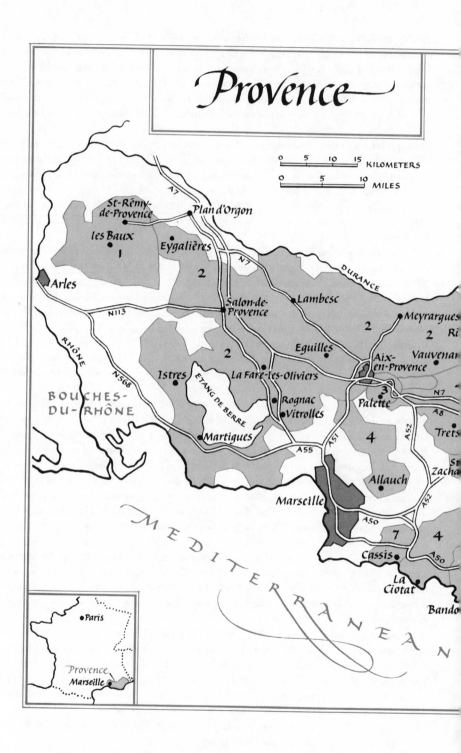

Provence

KILOMETERS
0 5 10 15

MILES
0 5 10

A7

St-Rémy-de-Provence

Plan d'Orgon

les Baux

1

Eygalières

2

N7

Arles

DURANCE

Salon-de-Provence

Lambesc

2

Meyrargues

N113

2

Ri

RHÔNE

2

Eguilles

Aix-en-Provence

Vauvenar

2

N7

N568

Istres

La Fare-les-Oliviers

Palette

A8

BOUCHES-DU-RHÔNE

ÉTANG DE BERRE

Rognac

3

Trets

Vitrolles

4

A52

St-Zacha

Martigues

A55

A57

Allauch

A50

Marseille

7

4

A50

Cassis

La Ciotat

Bando

MEDITERRANEAN

Paris

Provence
Marseille

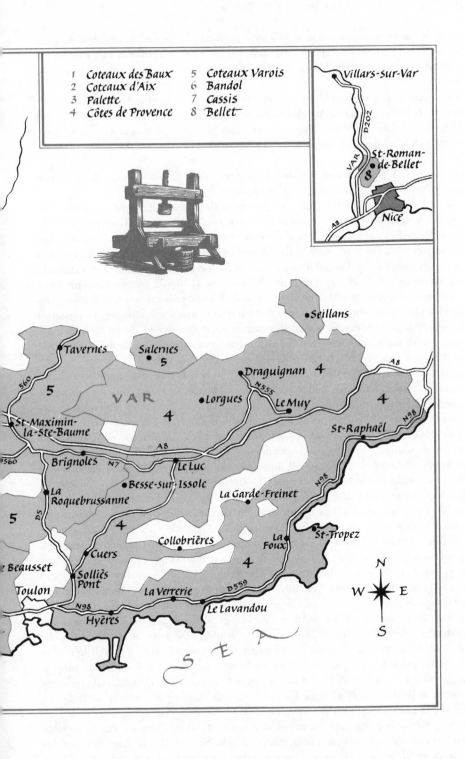

1 Coteaux des Baux   5 Coteaux Varois
2 Coteaux d'Aix   6 Bandol
3 Palette   7 Cassis
4 Côtes de Provence   8 Bellet

Villars-sur-Var

St-Roman-
de-Bellet
8

VAR

Nice

D202

A8

Seillans

Tavernes   Salernes
                  5

VAR

560

5

St-Maximin-
la-Ste-Baume

Draguignan   4

N555

Lorgues   Le Muy

4

A8

4

N98

St-Raphaël

N560

Brignoles   N7

A8

Le Luc

Besse-sur-Issole

La
Roquebrussanne

D5

5

4

La Garde-Freinet

N98

La Garde-Freinet

Collobrières

La
Foux   St-Tropez

Cuers

e Beausset

Solliès
Pont

4

La Verrerie   D559

N

Toulon

N98

Hyères

Le Lavandou

W   E

S

E   A

S

enormously complex bouquets and significant concentration, as well as tremendous aging potential. The most recent successes have included the 1990, a fabulously rich wine with a cascade of silky, concentrated cassis and blackberry fruit intermingled with scents of wild thyme.

Not surprisingly, proprietor Durrbach apprenticed at Château Vignelaure, another well-known estate in the Coteaux d'Aix-en-Provence. Vignelaure's wines, while not as bold and striking as Trevallon's, are still elegant expressions of Provençal winemaking at its best. They are widely available in America, and the best recent vintages are the 1990, 1989, and 1985.

The wines of Vignelaure and Trevallon both retail in the $20–$25 range, making them modest values for their quality level and aging potential.

Côtes du Lubéron   Virtually all the wine made in the Côtes du Lubéron is produced by one of the many cooperatives that dominate this region's production. However, this area, which is located in the northern area of Provence near the villages of Apt and Pertuis, has immense potential. The best estate in the Côtes du Lubéron is the Château Mille, run with great meticulousness by Conrad Pinatel. However, there is also a new and extremely promising estate called Château Val-Joanis, launched in 1978 with an initial investment of $6 million to construct a 494-acre vineyard and château near the town of Pertuis. The Chancel family, great believers in the idea that top-quality wines will ultimately be produced from the Côtes du Lubéron, is behind this extraordinary investment. At present, they are making a good, fresh white wine, a delicious, fragrant rosé, and an increasingly serious red wine. All sell for under $12 a bottle, making them outstanding values.

Côtes de Provence   The Côtes de Provence is the best-known and largest viticultural region of Provence, with just under 50,000 acres planted in vines. This appellation is famous for the oceans of dry, flavorful rosé wine that tourists gulp down with great thirst-quenching pleasure. There are many fine producers of Côtes de Provence wines, but the best include the very famous Domaines Ott, which is available on virtually every restaurant wine list in southern France, the Domaine Gavoty, the Domaine Richeaume, and the Domaine Saint-André de Figuière. All these estates, with the exception of the Domaine Richeaume, produce outstanding rosé wine. The Domaine Richeaume specializes in intense, rich, complex red wines that are surpassed only by the aforementioned wines from the Domaine Trevallon and Château Vignelaure. In addition, one of the best white wines produced in Provence is made by the Domaine Saint-André de Figuière. All these wines are currently available in most of the major metropolitan markets in the United States, but they are not inexpensive. The Ott wines, no doubt due to their fame in France, sell for fairly hefty prices, but I have never heard anyone complain regarding the quality of their superb rosés and underrated red wines. Certainly, the white wine made by Saint-André de Figuière is not overpriced, and is an especially fine representative example of just how good a white wine from Provence can be. Saint-André de Figuière also makes a delicious, supple red wine that is well worth trying. Should you find a bottle of the Domaine Richeaume's red wine, made by a fanatical German by the name of Henning Hoesch, it is well worth the $15-a-bottle price to taste one of Provence's finest examples of red wine. His serious, densely colored red wines are loaded with heaps of fruit, power, and tannin, and give every indication of being capable of aging for over a decade, as they are usually made from a blend of Cabernet Sauvignon and Syrah with some Grenache added at times.

Palette   Palette is a tiny appellation just to the east of Aix-en-Provence that in actuality consists of only one serious winemaking estate, Château Simone. Run by René Rougier, this tiny estate of 37 acres produces a surprisingly long-lived and complex red wine, a fairly oaky, old-style rosé wine, and a muscular, full-bodied white wine that behaves as if it were from the northern Rhône Valley. Simone's wines are not inexpensive, but they do age extremely well, and have always had a loyal following in France.

The Basics

TYPES OF WINE

A huge quantity of bone-dry, fragrant, crisp rosés is made as well as rather neutral but fleshy white wines, and higher-and-higher-quality red wines.

GRAPE VARIETIES

For red wines, the traditional grape varieties have always been Grenache, Carignan, Syrah, Mourvèdre, and Cinsault. Recently, however, a great deal of Cabernet Sauvignon has been planted in the Côtes de Provence and Coteaux d'Aix-en-Provence. The most interesting red wines are generally those with elevated levels of either Syrah, Mourvèdre, or Cabernet Sauvignon. For white wines, Ugni Blanc, Clairette, Marsanne, Bourboulenc, and to a lesser extent Semillon, Sauvignon Blanc, and Chardonnay are used.

FLAVORS

There is immense variation due to the number of microclimates and different grapes used. Most red wines have vivid red fruit bouquets that are more intense in the Coteaux des Baux than elsewhere. In Bandol the smells of tree bark, leather, and currants dominate. The white wines seem neutral and clumsy when served without food, but when drunk with the spicy Provençal cuisine, they take on life.

AGING POTENTIAL

Rosés: 1–3 years
White wines: 1–3 years, except for that of Château Simone, which can last for 5–10 years
Red wines: 5–12 years, often longer for the red wines of Bandol and specific wines such as
   Domaine Trevallon that can age well for 15+ years

OVERALL QUALITY LEVEL

The level of quality has increased and in general is well above average, but consumers must remember to buy and drink the rosé and white wines only when they are less than 3 years old.

MOST IMPORTANT INFORMATION TO KNOW

Master the types of wine of each appellation of Provence, as well as the names of the top producers.

1995–1996 BUYING STRATEGY

There is a bevy of top vintages from which to choose, but the problem in America is finding these wines. Except for some of the Côtes du Ventoux wines, most wholesalers and retailers find that the wines have to be hand-sold and therefore, incredibly, are reluctant to stock them. Vintages of choice are 1989 and 1990. The 1991, 1992, and 1993 are spotty, except for the rosés. As for 1994, it looks to be another difficult year, especially in Bandol.

RATING PROVENCE'S BEST PRODUCERS

* * * * *(OUTSTANDING)

Luigi-Clos Nicrosi (Corsica)
Château Pradeaux (Bandol)
Château Pradeaux Mourvèdre Vieilles
   Vignes (Bandol)
Domaine Tempier Cabasseau (Bandol)

Domaine Tempier Cuvée Spéciale (Bandol)
Domaine Tempier La Migoua (Bandol)
Domaine Tempier La Tourtine (Bandol)
Domaine de Trevallon (Coteaux d'Aix-en
   Provence-Les Baux)

* * * *(EXCELLENT)

Domaine Canorgue (Côtes du Lubéron)

Domaine Champagna (Côtes du Ventoux)

Commanderie de Bargemone (Côtes de
Provence)

Commanderie de Peyrassol (Côtes de
Provence)

Château de Crémat (Bellet)

Domaine de Féraud (Côtes de Provence)

Domaine Le Gallantin (Bandol)

Domaine de la Garnaude Cuvée Santane
(Côtes de Provence)

Domaines Gavoty (Côtes de Provence)

Domaine Hauvette (Coteaux des Baux)

Domaine de l'Hermitage (Bandol)

Mas de la Dame (Coteaux
d'Aix-en-Provence-Les Baux)

Mas de Gourgonnier (Coteaux
d'Aix-en-Provence-Les Baux)

Mas de la Rouvière (Bandol)

Château de Mille (Côtes du Lubéron)

Moulin des Costes (Bandol)

Domaines Ott—all cuvées (Bandol and
Côtes de Provence)

Domaine de Pibarnon (Bandol)

Domaine Richeaume (Côtes de Provence)

Domaine de Rimauresq (Côtes de Provence)

Saint-André de Figuière (Côtes de
Provence)

Domaine Saint-Jean de Villecroze
(Coteaux Varois)

Domaine Tempier Rosé (Bandol)

Château Val-Joanis (Côtes du Lubéron)

Château Val-Joanis Cuvée Les Griottes
(Côtes du Lubéron)

Château Vannières (Bandol)

La Vieille Ferme (Côtes du Lubéron)

* * *(GOOD)

Domaine du Bagnol (Cassis)

Château Barbeyrolles (Côtes de Provence)

Château Bas (Coteaux d'Aix-en-Provence)

La Bastide Blanche (Bandol)

Domaine de Beaupré (Coteaux
d'Aix-en-Provence)

Domaine La Bernarde (Côtes de Provence)

Domaine Caguelouf (Bandol)

Château de Calissanne (Coteaux
d'Aix-en-Provence)

Castel Roubine (Côtes de Provence)

Cave Cooperative d'Aleria Réserve du
Président (Corsica)

Clos Catitoro (Corsica)

Clos Ste.-Magdelaine (Cassis)

Domaine de Curebreasse (Côtes de
Provence)

Château Ferry-Lacombe (Côtes de
Provence)

Domaine Fiumicicoli (Corsica)

Château de Fonscolombe (Coteaux
d'Aix-en-Provence)

Domaine du Fontenille (Côtes du
Lubéron)***/****

Domaine Frégate (Bandol)

Hervé Goudard (Côtes de Provence)

Château de l'Isolette (Côtes du Lubéron)

Domaine de Lafran-Veyrolles (Bandol)

Domaine La Laidière (Bandol)

Domaine Lecci (Corsica)

Domaine du Loou (Coteaux Varois)

Château Maravenne (Côtes de Provence)

Mas de Cadenet (Côtes de Provence)

Mas Sainte-Berthe (Coteaux
d'Aix-en-Provence)

Domaine de la Noblesse (Bandol)

Domaine Orenga (Corsica)

Domaine de Paradis (Coteaux
d'Aix-en-Provence)

Domaine Peraldi (Corsica)

Château de Rasque (Côtes de Provence)

Domaine Ray-Jane (Bandol)

Château Real-Martin (Côtes de Provence)

Château Saint-Esteve (Côtes de Provence)

Château Saint-Jean Cuvée Natasha (Côtes
de Provence)

Château Sainte-Anne (Bandol)

Château Sainte-Roseline (Côtes de
Provence)

Domaine des Salettes (Bandol)

Domaine de la Sanglière (Côtes de
Provence)

Château Simone (Palette)

Domaine de Terrebrune (Bandol)

Domaine de Torraccia (Corsica)

Toussaint Luigi-Muscatella (Corsica)

Domaine de la Vallongue (Coteaux des
Baux)

Château Vignelaure (Coteaux
d'Aix-en-Provence-Les Baux)

THE RHÔNE VALLEY

The Basics

TYPES OF WINE

In actuality, the Rhône Valley has two halves. The wines of the northern Rhône Valley, from famous appellations such as Côte Rôtie, Hermitage, and Cornas, are age-worthy, rich, full-bodied red wines from the noble Syrah grape. Minuscule quantities of fragrant and delicious white wine are made at Condrieu. White wine is also made at Hermitage and both good, but not great, red and white wine is made in the appellations of Crozes-Hermitage and St.-Joseph.

The southern Rhône, with its Mediterranean climate, primarily produces lusty, full-bodied, heady red wines, but some very fragrant underrated rosés are made, as well as better and better white wines. In the appellation of Muscat des Beaumes de Venise, a honeyed, perfumed, sweet white wine is made, and in Tavel, France's most famous rosé wine is produced.

GRAPE VARIETIES

RED WINE VARIETALS

Cinsault All the growers seem to use a small amount of Cinsault. It ripens very early, gives good yields, and produces wines that offer a great deal of fruit. It seems to offset the high alcohol of the Grenache and the tannins of the Syrah and Mourvèdre. Despite its value, it seems to have lost some appeal in favor of Syrah or Mourvèdre, but it is a valuable asset to the blend of a southern Rhône wine.

Counoise Very little of this grape exists in the south because of its capricious growing habits. However, I have tasted it separately at Château Beaucastel in Châteauneuf du Pape, where the Perrin family is augmenting its use. It had great finesse and seemed to provide deep, richly fruity flavors and a complex perfume of smoked meat, flowers, and berry fruit. The Perrins feel Counoise has as much potential as Mourvèdre, a high-quality ingredient in their blend.

Grenache A classic hot-climate grape varietal, Grenache is, for better or worse, the dominant grape of the southern Rhone. The quality of the wines it produces ranges from hot, alcoholic, unbalanced, coarse wines to rich, majestic, very long-lived, sumptuous wines. The differences are largely caused by the yield of juice per vine. Where Grenache is pruned back and not overly fertilized, it can do wondrous things. The sensational Châteauneuf du Pape, Château Rayas, is one of the most poignant examples of what majestic heights Grenache can achieve. At its best, it offers aromas of kirsch, black currants, pepper, licorice, and roasted peanuts.

Mourvèdre Everyone seems to agree on the virtues of the Mourvèdre, but few people want to take the risk and grow it. It flourishes in the Mediterranean appellation of Bandol,

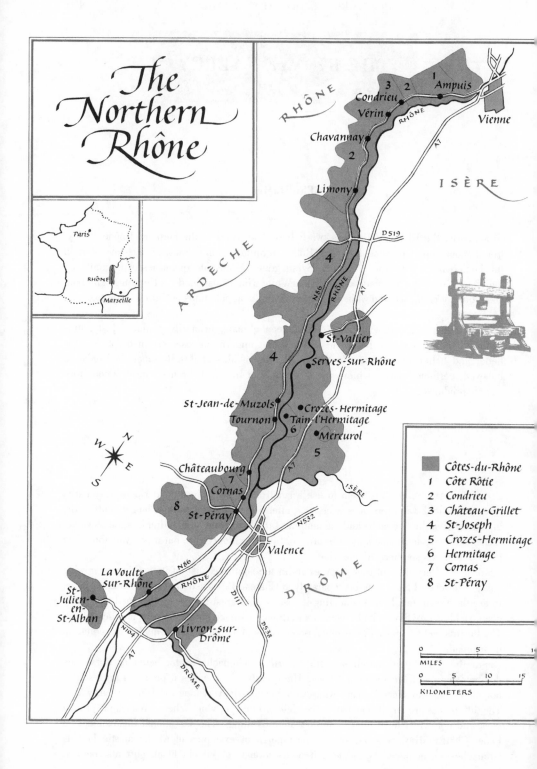

The
Northern
Rhône

RHÔNE

3
2
1 Ampuis
Condrieu
Vérin
2
RHÔNE
Vienne
Chavannay

ISÈRE

2

Limony

D519

A7

ARDÈCHE

N86

4

RHÔNE

A7

Paris

RHÔNE

Marseille

4

St-Vallier

Serves-sur-Rhône

St-Jean-de-Muzols
Tournon
Crozes-Hermitage
Tain-l'Hermitage
6
Mercurol
5

N
W   E
S

Châteaubourg
7
Cornas
8
St-Péray

A7

ISÈRE

N532

Valence

DRÔME

La Voulte-
sur-Rhône
St-
Julien-
en-
St-Alban
N86
RHÔNE
D111
D538

N104
A7
Livron-sur-
Drôme
DRÔME

	Côtes-du-Rhône
1	Côte Rôtie
2	Condrieu
3	Château-Grillet
4	St-Joseph
5	Crozes-Hermitage
6	Hermitage
7	Cornas
8	St-Péray

0   5   10
MILES

0   5   10   15
KILOMETERS

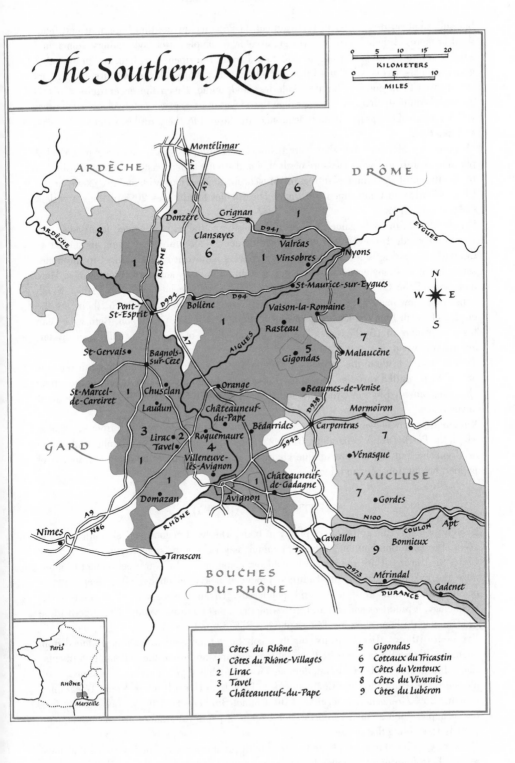

The Southern Rhône

KILOMETERS
0 5 10 15 20

MILES
0 5 10

ARDÈCHE

DRÔME

Montélimar

Donzère
Grignan

Clansayes

6

Valréas
Vinsobres

Nyons

St-Maurice-sur-Eygues

Pont-
St-Esprit

Bollène

Vaison-la-Romaine

Rasteau

St-Gervais

Bagnols-
sur-Cèze

Gigondas
5

Malaucène

7

St-Marcel-
de-Careiret

Chusclan

Orange

Beaumes-de-Venise

Mormoiron

Laudun

Châteauneuf-
du-Pape

Bédarrides

Carpentras

7

GARD

Lirac
Tavel

Roquemaure

Vénasque

Villeneuve-
lès-Avignon

Châteauneuf-
de-Gadagne

VAUCLUSE

Domazan

Avignon

Gordes

Nîmes

COULON
Apt

Cavaillon

Bonnieux

Tarascon

BOUCHES
DU-RHÔNE

Mérindal

Cadenet

DURANCE

Paris

RHÔNE

Marseille

	Côtes du Rhône	5	Gigondas
1	Côtes du Rhône-Villages	6	Coteaux du Tricastin
2	Lirac	7	Côtes du Ventoux
3	Tavel	8	Côtes du Vivarais
4	Châteauneuf-du-Pape	9	Côtes du Lubéron

but only Château Beaucastel in Châteauneuf du Pape has made it an important part (one-third or more) of their blend. It gives great color, a complex, woodsy, leathery aroma, and superb structure, and is resistant to oxidation. However, it ripens very late, and unlike other grape varietals, has no value until it is perfectly mature. When it lacks maturity, the growers say it gives them nothing, for it is colorless and acidic. Given the eccentricities of this grape, it is unlikely that anyone other than the adventurous or passionately obsessed growers will make use of this grape. Its telltale aromas are those of leather, truffles, fresh mushrooms, and tree bark.

Muscardin   More common than Terret Noir, Muscardin provides wine with a great deal of perfume as well as a solid measure of alcohol and strength. Beaucastel uses Muscardin, but by far the most important plantings of Muscardin at a serious winemaking estate are at Chante Perdrix in Châteauneuf du Pape. The Nicolet family uses 20% in their excellent Châteauneuf du Pape.

Syrah   Syrah, the only game in town in the northern Rhône, is relegated to an accessory role in the south. However, its role in providing needed structure, backbone, and tannin to the fleshy Grenache is incontestable. Some growers believe it ripens too fast in the hotter south, but it is, in my opinion, a very strong addition to many southern Rhône wines. More and more of the Côtes du Rhône estates are producing special bottlings of 100% Syrah wines that show immense potential. The finest Syrahs made in the southern Rhône are the cuvées of Syrah from the Château de Fonsalette and Domaine Gramenon. Both wines can last and evolve for 15–25 years. Their aromas are those of berry fruit, coffee, smoky tar, and hickory wood.

Terret Noir   Little of this grape is now found in the southern Rhône, although it remains one of the permitted varieties. It was used to give acidity to a wine and to mollify the strong character provided by the Grenache and Syrah. None of the best estates care to employ it anymore.

Vaccarese   It was again at Beaucastel where I tasted the wine produced from this grape, which the Perrins vinify separately. It is not as powerful and deep as Syrah, nor as alcoholic as Grenache, but has its own unique character that I would describe as giving aromas of pepper, hot tar, tobacco, and licorice.

WHITE WINE VARIETALS

Bourboulenc   This grape offers plenty of body. The local cognoscenti also attribute the scent of roses to Bourboulenc, although I cannot as yet claim the same experience.

Clairette Blanc   Until the advent of cold fermentations and modern equipment to minimize the risk of oxidation, the Clairette produced heavy, alcoholic, often deep yellow–colored wines that were thick and ponderous. Given the benefit of state-of-the-art technology, it produces soft, floral, fruity wine that must be drunk young. The superb white Châteauneuf du Pape of Vieux Télégraphe has 35% Clairette in it.

Grenache Blanc   Deeply fruity, highly alcoholic yet low-acid wines are produced from Grenache Blanc. When fermented at cool temperatures and when the malolactic fermentation is blocked, it can be a vibrant, delicious wine capable of providing wonderful near-term pleasure. The exquisite white Châteauneuf du Pape from Henri Brunier, Vieux Télégraphe, contains 25% Grenache Blanc; that of the Gonnet Brothers' Font de Michelle, 50%. In a few examples such as this, I find the floral scent of paperwhite narcissus and a character vaguely resembling that of Condrieu.

Marsanne   The Marsanne planted in the south produces rather chunky wines that must receive help from other varieties because they cannot stand alone. Jancis Robinson often claims it smells "not unpleasantly reminiscent of glue."

Picardin This grape has fallen out of favor, largely because the growers felt it added nothing to their blends. Apparently, its neutral character was its undoing.

Picpoul Frankly, I have no idea what this grape tastes like. I have never seen it isolated or represented in such a hefty percentage as to be identifiable. Today, it is seen very rarely in the southern Rhône.

Roussanne For centuries, this grape was the essence of white Hermitage in the northern Rhône, but its small yields and proclivity to disease saw it largely replaced by Marsanne. Making somewhat of a comeback in the southern Rhône, it has the most character of any of the white wine varietals—aromas of honey, coffee, flowers, and nuts—and produces a wine that can be very long-lived, an anomaly for a white wine in the southern Rhône. The famous Châteauneuf du Pape estate, Beaucastel, uses 80% Roussanne in their white wine, which, not surprisingly, is the longest-lived white wine of the appellation. Since 1986, they have also produced a 100% old-vine Roussanne that can be profound.

Viognier Viognier produces a great and unique white wine that is synonymous with Condrieu and Château Grillet, both in the northern Rhône. In the south, there is little of it, but the experimental plantings that have been made have exhibited immense potential. The finest example in the southern Rhône is the Domaine Ste.-Anne in the Côtes du Rhône village of Gervais. Saint-Estève is another domaine in the Côtes du Rhône that produces a good Viognier. Beaucastel began to utilize it in their white Coudoulet in 1991. Unfortunately, Viognier is not a permitted varietal in Châteauneuf du Pape, where it could immensely enhance the neutral character of so many of that village's white wines. Viognier is increasingly an important component of white Côtes du Rhône and in large measure, the most significant reason why these wines have increased in quality.

APPELLATIONS

NORTHERN RHÔNE

Condrieu This exotic, often overwhelmingly fragrant wine is low in acidity and must be drunk young, but offers hedonistic aromas and flavors of peaches, apricots, and honey, and an unbelievably decadent, opulent finish.

Cornas The impenetrable black/ruby color, the brutal, even savage tannins in its youth, the massive structure, and the muddy sediment in the bottle are all characteristics of a wine that tastes as if it were made in the nineteenth century. But Cornas wines are among the most virile, robust wines in the world, with a powerful aroma of cassis and raspberries that develops into chestnuts, truffles, licorice, and black currants as it ages. These wines are among the most underrated great red wines of the world, but one must have patience with them.

Côte Rôtie This is an immense, fleshy, rich, fragrant, smoky, full-bodied, stunning wine with gobs of cassis fruit frequently intertwined with the smell of frying bacon. It is one of France's greatest wines and can last for up to 25 years where well stored.

Crozes-Hermitage Despite this appellation's proximity to the more famous appellation of Hermitage, the red wines tend to be soft, spicy, fruity, chunky, vegetal, and rather one-dimensional, instead of distinguished. The white wines vary enormously in quality and can be pleasant, but are often mediocre and too acidic.

Hermitage At its best, Hermitage is a rich, almost portlike, viscous, very full-bodied, tannic red wine that can seemingly last forever. It is characterized by intense, even pungent smells of pepper and cassis, intertwined at times with aromas of Provençal herbs. The white Hermitage can be neutral, but the finest examples display a bouquet of herbs, minerals, nuts, acacia flowers, peaches, and a stony, wet slate–like component.

St.-Joseph This is the northern Rhône's most underrated appellation for red and white wine. The reds and whites are juicy and best drunk young.

St.-Péray Tiny quantities of still and sparkling white wines are made from this forgotten appellation of the Rhône Valley. Neither merits consumer interest, as the wines often are dull, heavy, and diffuse.

SOUTHERN RHÔNE

Châteauneuf du Pape There is an enormous diversity in the styles of Châteauneuf du Pape produced. It can be made to resemble a Beaujolais, in which case it offers jammy, soft, fruity flavors and must be drunk quite young. If the wine is vinified in a classic manner, it can be very dense in color, quite rich, and full bodied, and can last 15–20 years. It is often characterized by the smell of saddle leather, fennel, licorice, black truffles, pepper, nutmeg, and smoked meats. Wines made by both these methods and then blended together, and dominated by the Grenache grape, often smell of roasted peanuts and overripe Bing cherries. White Châteauneuf du Papes are usually neutral and uninteresting, but a few examples have a floral- and tropical fruit–scented bouquet. However, they must be drunk extremely young.

Côtes du Rhône The best Côtes du Rhônes offer uncomplicated but deliciously succulent, crunchy, peppery, blackberry and raspberry fruit in a supple, full-bodied style that is meant to be consumed within 5–6 years of the vintage.

Gigondas Gigondas offers up a robust, chewy, full-bodied, rich, generous red wine that has a heady bouquet and supple, rich, spicy flavors. A tiny quantity of a very underrated rosé wine is often made and should be tried by consumers looking for something special.

Muscat de Beaumes de Venise This sweet, alcoholic, but extraordinarily perfumed, exotic wine offers up smells of peaches, apricots, coconut, and lychee nuts. It must be drunk in its youth to be fully appreciated.

AGING POTENTIAL

NORTHERN RHÔNE	SOUTHERN RHÔNE
Condrieu: 2–5 years	Châteauneuf du Pape (red): 5–20 years
Cornas: 5–15 years	Châteauneuf du Pape (white): 1–2 years
Côte Rôtie: 5–25 years	Côtes du Rhône: 4–8 years
Crozes-Hermitage: 3–8 years	Gigondas: 5–12 years
Hermitage (red): 5–30 years	Muscat de Beaumes de Venise: 1–3 years
Hermitage (white): 3–15 years	Tavel: 1–2 years
St.-Joseph: 3–8 years	

OVERALL QUALITY LEVEL

In the northern Rhône appellations of Côte Rôtie, Hermitage, Condrieu, and Cornas, the general level of winemaking is excellent. In the other appellations, it is irregular. In the southern Rhône, Châteauneuf du Pape has the broadest range in quality, from superb to irresponsible and inept producers. Gigondas has the highest level of quality winemakers.

NORTHERN RHÔNE

Côte Rôtie—An Overview

Type of wine produced: Red wine only

Grape varieties planted: Syrah and a tiny quantity of Viognier (up to 20% can be added)

Acres currently under vine: 395

Quality level: Exceptional; among the finest red wines in the world

Aging potential: 5–30 years

General characteristics: Fleshy, rich, very fragrant, smoky, full-bodied, stunning wines

Greatest recent vintages: 1991, 1989, 1988, 1985, 1983, 1978, 1976, 1969

Price range: $25–$55, except for the single-vineyard wines of Guigal, which retail, if one can find them, for $150. Beware of speculators, particularly the English wine trade, which often asks $250–$350 a bottle.

RATING THE CÔTE RÔTIE PRODUCERS

* * * * *(OUTSTANDING)

Chapoutier Cuvée Mordorée
Clusel-Roch Les Grandes Places
Marius Gentaz-Dervieux †
Guigal La Landonne
Guigal La Mouline
Guigal La Turque

Jean-Paul and Jean-Luc Jamet
René Rostaing Côte Blonde
René Rostaing Côte Brune La Landonne
René Rostaing Côte Brune La Viaillère
   (since 1991)
L. de Vallouit Les Roziers

* * * *(EXCELLENT)

Gilles Barge
Pierre Barge
Bernard Burgaud
Clusel-Roch (other cuvées)
Henri Gallet ****/*****
Vincent Gasse ****/*****
J. M. Gérin Les Grandes Places

Guigal Côtes Blonde et Brune
Michel Ogier
René Rostaing (regular cuvée)
Lyliane Saugère
L. de Vallouit Vagonier
Vidal-Fleury La Chatillonne Côte Blonde
Vidal-Fleury Côtes Blonde et Brune

* * *(GOOD)

Guy Bernard
Domaine de Bonserine
Émile Champet
Joël Champet La Viaillère
Chapoutier (regular cuvée)
Clusel-Roch (regular cuvée)
Delas Frères Seigneur de Maugiron

Albert Dervieux-Thaize ‡
Georges Duboeuf Domaine Ile Rousse
Pierre Gaillard
J. M. Gérin Champin de Seigneur
Paul Jaboulet-Ainé Les Jumelles
Robert Jasmin

† Gentaz retired following the 1992 vintage and his vineyard holdings are now farmed by René Rostaing, a 5-star producer.
‡ Dervieux-Thaize has been retired since 1991 and the wines from his vineyards are now made by René Rostaing.

Condrieu—An Overview

Type of wine produced:	White wine only
Grape varieties planted:	Viognier
Acres currently under vine:	197, plus 9.4 acres of Château Grillet
Quality level:	Exceptional; one of the rarest and most unique wines in the world
Aging potential:	1–4 years
General characteristics:	An exotic, often overwhelming tropical fruit fragrance intertwined with floral aspects; a low-acid, very rich wine that is usually short-lived
Greatest recent vintages:	1994, 1993, 1991, 1990 (only for the sweeter Vendange Tardive wines), 1989 (they may already be getting old)
Price range:	$30–$60

RATING THE CONDRIEU PRODUCERS

* * * * *(OUTSTANDING)

Yves Cuilleron Les Chaillets

Yves Cuilleron Les Eguets

Pierre Dumazet

Guigal

Guigal-Doriane

Antoine Montez-Domaine du Monteillet

André Perret Coteau du Chery

Philippe Pichon

Georges Vernay Coteaux du Vernon

* * * *(EXCELLENT)

Gilles Barge

Patrick et Christophe Bonnefond

Chapoutier

J. L. Chave

Delas Frères

Robert Niero

Christophe Pichon

Hervé Richard

Georges Vernay (regular cuvée)

François Villand

Gérard Villano

* * *(GOOD)

Domaine du Chêne-M. and D. Rouvière

Louis Cheze

Domaine Farjon

Pierre Gaillard

J. M. Gérin

Grillet †

Paul Jaboulet-Ainé

Nero-Pinchon

Patrice Porte

Du Rozay

Vidal-Fleury

Hermitage—An Overview

Type of wine produced:	Red and white wine
Grape varieties planted:	Syrah for the red wine; primarily Marsanne and some Roussanne for the white wine
Acres currently under vine:	331
Quality level:	Exceptional for the red wines, good to exceptional for the white wines
Aging potential:	Red wine: 5–25 years
	White wine: 3–15 years

† Prior to 1979, *****; since 1979, ***. Château Grillet is entitled to its own appellation—a very unusual situation in France.

General characteristics: Rich, portlike, viscous, chunky, full-bodied, tannic red wines; full-bodied white wines with a unique scent of herbs, minerals, and peaches

Greatest recent vintages: 1991, 1990, 1989, 1978, 1972, 1970, 1966, 1961, 1959

Price range: $35–$75

RATING THE RED HERMITAGE PRODUCERS

* * * * *(OUTSTANDING)

Chapoutier Le Pavillon
J. L. Chave
J. L. Chave Cathiard Red Label Cuvée

Paul Jaboulet-Ainé La Chapelle
Henri Sorrel Le Gréal

* * * *(EXCELLENT)

Albert Belle
Chapoutier La Sizeranne (since 1989)
Delas Frères Les Bessards
Bernard Faurie

Ferraton Père et Fils Cuvée des Miaux
Lyliane Saugere
Henri Sorrel (regular cuvée)
L. de Vallouit Greffières

* * *(GOOD)

Dard et Ribo
Delas Frères Marquise de la Tourette
Desmeure
Jules Fayolle et Fils

Alain Graillot
J. L. Grippat
Jean-Marc Sorrel
Vidal-Fleury

RATING THE WHITE HERMITAGE PRODUCERS

* * * * *(OUTSTANDING)

Chapoutier Cuvée de l'Orvée   J. L. Chave

* * * *(EXCELLENT)

J. L. Grippat
Guigal

Paul Jaboulet-Ainé Chevalier de
Stérimberg (since 1989)
Henri Sorrel Les Rocoules

Crozes-Hermitage—An Overview

Type of wine produced: Red and white wine

Grape varieties planted: Marsanne and Roussanne for the white wine; Syrah for the red wine

Acres currently under vine: 2,840

Quality level: Mediocre to very good

Aging potential: Red wine: 3–10 years
White wine: 1–4 years

General characteristics: Tremendous variability in the red wines; white wines are fleshy, chunky, solid, and rather undistinguished

Greatest recent vintages: 1991, 1990, 1989, 1988, 1985, 1978

Price range: $20–$25

RATING THE CROZES-HERMITAGE PRODUCERS

*****(OUTSTANDING)

Albert Belle Cuvée Louis Belle   Paul Jaboulet-Ainé Thalabert
Alain Graillot La Guiraude

****(EXCELLENT)

Albert Belle   Domaine du Pavillon-Mercurol
Alain Graillot (regular cuvée)   L. de Vallouit L'Arnage
Paul Jaboulet-Ainé

***(GOOD)

Chapoutier Les Meysonniers   Delas Frères Marquise de la Tourette
Curson-Étienne Pochon   Ferraton Père et Fils
Dard et Ribo

St.-Joseph—An Overview

Type of wine produced:	Red and white wine
Grape varieties planted:	Marsanne and Roussanne for the white wine; Syrah for the red wine
Acres currently under vine:	1,580
Quality level:	Average to very good
Aging potential:	Red wine: 1–6 years; the *vieilles vignes* (old vine) and prestige cuvées can last for a decade or more White wine: 1–5 years
General characteristics:	The red wines are the lightest, fruitiest, and most feminine of the northern Rhône. The white wines are perfumed and fleshy with scents of apricots and pears.
Greatest recent vintages:	1991, 1990, 1989, 1988, 1985, 1983, 1978
Price range:	$12–$20

RATING THE ST.-JOSEPH PRODUCERS

*****(OUTSTANDING)

J. L. Chave   Paul Jaboulet-Ainé Le Grande Pompée
Domaine du Chêne Anais   Antoine Montez-Domaine du Monteillet
Yves Cuilleron Cuvée Prestige   André Perret Les Grisières
Domaine de Gachon-Pascal Perrier   Raymond Trollat
J. L. Grippat Cuvée des Hospices   L. de Vallouit Les Anges

****(EXCELLENT)

Chapoutier Deschants   Alain Graillot
Domaine du Chêne-M. and D. Rouvière   André Perret (regular cuvée)
Bernard Faurie   Pascal Perrier
Domaine du Fauterie   Hervé Richard

***(GOOD)

Louis Chèze ***/****   Yves Cuilleron
Pierre Coursodon   Dard et Ribo

Pierre Gaillard   Saint-Desirat Cave Co-op
J. L. Grippat (regular cuvée)

Cornas—An Overview

Type of wine produced:	Red wine only
Grape varieties planted:	Syrah
Acres currently under vine:	240
Quality level:	Good to exceptional
Aging potential:	5–15 years
General characteristics:	Black/ruby in color, tannic, full-bodied, virile, robust wines with a powerful aroma
Greatest recent vintages:	1991, 1990, 1988, 1985, 1983, 1979, 1978, 1976, 1972
Price range:	$25–$30

RATING THE CORNAS PRODUCERS

* * * * *(OUTSTANDING)

Auguste Clape   Noël Verset
Jean-Luc Colombo Les Ruchets   Alain Voge Cuvée Vieilles Vignes

* * * *(EXCELLENT)

Thierry Allemand   Jacques Lemencier
Chapoutier   Robert Michel Le Geynale
Dumien-Serette   Alain Voge
Marcel Juge Cuvée C

* * *(GOOD)

René Balthazar   Marcel Juge (regular cuvée)
Guy de Barjac   Jean Lionnet
Jean-Luc Colombo   Robert Michel (regular cuvée)
Courbis   J. L. Thiers
Delas Frères Chante Perdrix   Alain Voge Cuvée Barriques
Paul Jaboulet-Ainé

SOUTHERN RHÔNE

Côtes du Rhône and Côtes du Rhône-Villages—An Overview

Type of wine produced:	Red, white, and rosé wines
Grape varieties planted:	Mostly Grenache, but Syrah, Mourvèdre, and Cinsault can be found. Most white wines are made from Grenache Blanc and Clairette, but great hopes have been raised by Viognier.
Acres currently under vine:	115,000
Quality level:	A vast diversity in quality from poor to splendid
Aging potential:	Most wines must be drunk within 4 years of the vintage. Several, particularly Fonsalette and Coudoulet, can improve and last for 15 years

General characteristics: Tremendous diversity in styles, from light and fruity, to deep, full bodied, tannic, and concentrated
Greatest recent vintages: 1994, 1990, 1989, 1988
Price range: $6–$20

RATING THE CÔTES DU RHÔNE PRODUCERS

* * * * *(OUTSTANDING)

Domaine des Amouriers
Daniel Brusset-Les Hauts de Montmirail
Auguste Clape
Coudoulet de Beaucastel
Domaine Gramenon Ceps Centenaire
Domaine Gramenon Cuvée de Laurentides

Domaine de la Guichard
Jean-Marie Lombard
Domaine de l'Oratoire St.-Martin
Château Rayas Fonsalette
Château Rayas Fonsalette Cuvée Syrah
Château des Tours

* * * *(EXCELLENT)

Domaine de l'Amandier
Domaine de l'Ameillaud
Domaine des Anges
Domaine Les Aussellons
Domaine de la Becassonne
La Borie
Domaine André Brunel
Cabasse
De la Canorgue
Cave Jaume
Clos de la Mure
Domaine de Couroulu
Georges Duboeuf Domaine des Aires
    Vieilles
Georges Duboeuf Domaine des Moulins
Domaine de l'Espigouette
Domaine de Fenouillet
Domaine Gramenon
Du Grand Moulas
Château du Grand Prébois
Domaine des Grands Devers
Guigal
Paul Jaboulet-Ainé Parallel 45

Domaine Mitan
Domaine des Moulins
Domaine Pelaquié
Domaine de Piaugier Les Briguières
Domaine de Piaugier Montmartel
Plan Dei
Domaine de la Présidente
Rabasse-Charavin
Domaine Réméjeanne
Domaine Richard
St.-Estève
Domaine Saint-Gayan
Château Saint-Maurice
Domaine Ste.-Anne
Domaine Ste.-Apollinaire
Domaine Santa Duc
Domaine de la Solitude
Domaine La Soumade
Domaine des Treilles
Le Val des Rois
La Vieille Ferme Gold Label
Vieux Chêne (various cuvées)

* * *(GOOD)

D'Aigueville
Paul Autard
La Berthete
Roman Bouchard
August Clape
Daniel Combe
Domazon
Estagnol
Domaine de Font Sane Côtes du Ventoux
Domaine Les Gouberts

Malijay
Domaine Millières
Domaine Mireille et Vincent
Domaine de Mont-Redon
Domaine de la Mordorée ***/****
Domaines Mousset
Nero-Pinchon Ste.-Agathe
Château Pesquie
Domaine St.-Michel
Domaine St.-Pierre

Château de Trignon
Domaine de Verquière

Vidal-Fleury
La Vieille Ferme (other cuvées)

Châteauneuf du Pape—An Overview

Type of wine produced:	97% Red 3% White
Grape varieties planted:	13 (actually 14 if the white clone of Grenache is included). In practice, Grenache, Syrah, Mourvèdre, and Cinsault dominate for the red wines; Grenache Blanc and Clairette for the whites.
Acres currently under vine:	8,200
Quality level:	The red wines are below average to exceptional; not only the diversity of styles but the range in quality of wines produced in Châteauneuf du Pape is as extreme as in any major appellation in France. With the white wines quality tends to be mediocre.
Aging potential:	Red wine: 5–20 years White wine: 1–2 years, with the white wines of Beaucastel and Rayas being the only major exceptions
General characteristics:	There is significant diversity in styles and quality among the red wines. They range from full bodied, generous, rich, round, alcoholic, and long-lived, to soft, short-lived fruity, and Beaujolais-like. The white wines, at their best, are floral, fruity, and clean; most often they are tart, hollow, and boring.
Greatest recent vintages:	1990, 1989, 1988, 1985, 1981, 1979, 1978, 1970, 1967
Price range:	$16–$25, except for some of the luxury cuvées that can fetch $50–$75 a bottle

RATING THE CHÂTEAUNEUF DU PAPE PRODUCERS

* * * * *(OUTSTANDING)

Beaucastel
Beaucastel Hommage à Jacques Perrin
Domaine de Beaurenard Cuvée Boisrenard
Henri Bonneau Cuvée des Celestins
Les Bosquet des Papes Cuvée Chantemerle
Lucien et André Brunel-Les Cailloux
   Cuvée Centenaire
Chapoutier Barbe Rac

Clos du Mont-Olivet La Cuvée du Papet
Clos des Papes
Château de la Gardine Cuvée des
   Générations
Domaine de Marcoux Cuvée Vieilles
   Vignes
Domaine du Pegau Cuvée Réservée
Château Rayas

* * * *(EXCELLENT)

Pierre André
Max Aubert-La Nonciature
Paul Autard
Paul Autard Cuvée La Côte Ronde
Lucien Barrot
Domaine de Beaurenard
Henri Bonneau Cuvée Marie Beurrier
Les Bosquet des Papes
Lucien et André Brunel-Les Cailloux

Château Cabrières Cuvée Prestige
Domaine Chante Cigale (only their
   unfiltered cuvées)
Domaine de Chante Perdrix
Chapoutier La Bernadine (since 1990)
Domaine Gérard Charvin
Domaine Les Clefs d'Or
Domaine Clos du Caillou
Clos du Mont-Olivet

Cuvée du Belvedere
Cuvée du Vatican
Remy Diffonty
Domaine Durieu Cuvée Lucile Avril
Eddie Féraud
Font de Michelle
Font de Michelle Cuvée Étienne Gonnet
Château de la Gardine
Domaine Grand Jean
Guigal
Domaine Haut des Terres Blanches
Paul Jaboulet-Ainé Les Cèdres (prior to 1970 a 5-star producer)
Pierre Jacumin Cuvée de Boisdauphin
Domaine de la Janasse Chaupoins
Domaine de la Janasse Cuvée Vieilles Vignes

Domaine de Marcoux (regular cuvée)
Domaine de Montpertuis Cuvée Tradition
Moulin-Tacussel
Château de la Nerthe
Château de la Nerthe Cuvée des Cadettes (a 5-star producer if the estate stops filtering)
Domaine Pontifical-François Laget
Château Rayas Pignan
Domaine de la Roquette
Domaine Roger Sabon Cuvée Prestige
Domaine Saint-Benoît
Domaine Saint-Laurent
Domaine de la Solitude (since 1990)
Domaine de la Vieille Julienne
Vieux Donjon
Domaine du Vieux Télégraphe

* * *(GOOD)

Jean Avril
Domaine Avril Juliette
Michel Bernard
Domaine Berthet Rayne
Domaine Bois de Boursan
Domaine de Bois Dauphin
Domaine Bouvachon Bovine
Château Cabrières Cuvée Tradition
Caves Perges
Caves St.-Pierre
Domaine des Chanssaud
Domaine du Chantadu
Domaine Chante Cigale (regular cuvée)
Domaine de la Charbonnière
Clos Bimard
Clos des Calvaire
Clos des Pontifes
Clos du Roi
Clos St.-Jean
Clos St.-Michel
Jean Comte de Lauze
La Crau des Papes
Edmond Duclaux
Domaine Durieu (regular cuvée)
Des Fines Roches
Font du Loup
Château Fortia
Lou Fréjau
Domaine du Galet des Papes
Domaine Les Gallimardes
Domaine du Grand Tinel

Domaine Grand Veneur
Domaine de la Janasse (regular cuvée)
Domaine Mathieu
Domaine de la Millière
Domaine de Mont-Redon
Domaine de Montpertuis Cuvée Classique
Domaine de la Mordorée
Domaine de Nalys
Domaine de Palestor
Domaine Pape Gregoire
Père Anselme
Domaine du Père Caboche
Domaine du Père Pape Clos du Calvaire
Roger Perrin
Domaine de la Pinède
Domaine de la Présidente
Domaine des Relagnes-Cuvée Vigneronne
Domaine Riché
Domaine Roger Sabon (regular cuvée)
Domaine Roger Sabon Cuvée Réservée
Domaine de Saint-Siffrein
Domaine Sénéchaux
Simian
Domaine de la Souco-Papale
Domaine Terre Ferme
Domaine Jean Trintignant
Domaine Raymond Usseglio
Vaudieu
Vidal-Fleury
Domaine du Vieux Lazaret

Gigondas—An Overview

Type of wine produced:	Red wine and a small quantity of rosé
Grape varieties planted:	Primarily Grenache, with some Syrah, Mourvèdre, and Cinsault
Acres currently under vine:	2,925
Quality level:	Average to exceptional
Aging potential:	5–15 years
General characteristics:	Robust, chewy, full-bodied red wines are mouth filling and flavorful. At its best, the rare, underrated rosé is fresh and vibrant.
Greatest recent vintages:	1990, 1989, 1985, 1979, 1978
Price range:	$15–$25

RATING THE GIGONDAS PRODUCERS

* * * * *(OUTSTANDING)

Daniel Brusset-Les Hauts de Montmirail
Domaine de Cayron
Domaine de Font-Sane Cuvée Spéciale Fut
  Neuf

Domaine Saint-Gayan
Domaine Santa Duc Cuvée Prestige des
  Hautes Garrigues

* * * *(EXCELLENT)

Edmond Burle
Domaine Le Clos des Cazeaux
Domaine de Font-Sane (regular cuvée)
Les Gouberts Cuvée Florence
Domaine du Gour de Chaule
Guigal
Paul Jaboulet-Ainé (before 1978 and after
  1989)

Domaine de Longue-Toque
Moulin de la Gardette
Domaine des Pesquiers
Domaine de Piaugier
Domaine Raspail-Dominique Ay
Château Redoitier
Domaine Santa Duc (regular cuvée)

* * *(GOOD)

Pierre Amadieu-Domaine
  Romane-Machotte
Domaine La Bastide St.-Vincent
Domaine des Bosquets
Domaine La Bouissière
Cave Co-op
Clos du Joncuas
Domaine de la Daysse
Domaine des Épiers
Domaine La Fourmone-Roger Combe
Domaine Les Gouberts (regular cuvée)
Domaine Le Grande Romane

Domaine du Grapillon d'Or
Domaine de Joncuas
Domaine de la Mavette
Montmirail Cuvée Beauchamps
Domaine du Moutvac
L'Oustau Fauquet
Domaine Les Pallières
Raspail (Gabriel Meffre)
Domaine du Terme
Domaine Les Teysonnières
Domaine Les Tourelles
Château de Trignon

Muscat de Beaumes de Venise—An Overview

Type of wine produced: A sweet fortified wine—*vin doux naturel*
Grape varieties planted: Muscat
Acres currently under vine: 576
Quality level: Very good to outstanding
Aging potential: 1–4 years
General characteristics: A sweet, decadently rich, intensely perfumed wine
Greatest recent vintages: 1994, 1993, 1991, 1990
Price range: $15–$25

RATING THE MUSCAT BEAUMES DE VENISE PRODUCERS

* * * * *(OUTSTANDING)

Chapoutier
Domaine de Coyeux
Domaine Durban

Paul Jaboulet-Ainé
Vidal-Fleury

* * * *(EXCELLENT)

Domaine Castaud-Maurin

Domaine St.-Sauveur

* * *(GOOD)

Cave Co-op

Vacqueyras—An Overview

Type of wine produced: Primarily red wine, with a small quantity of dry rosé
Grape varieties planted: Primarily Grenache
Acres currently under vine: 4,300
Quality level: Good, and improving
Aging potential: 3–8 years
General characteristics: Virtually identical to Gigondas—peppery, mouthfilling, sometimes rustic, but always full bodied and heady
Greatest recent vintages: 1990, 1989, 1988
Price range: $10–$15

RATING THE VACQUEYRAS PRODUCERS

* * * * *(OUTSTANDING)

Domaine des Amouriers

Château des Tours

* * * *(EXCELLENT)

Domaine Le Clos des Cazaux
Domaine Le Couroulu
Domaine La Fourmone-Roger Combe
Domaine de la Garrique

Montmirail Deux Frères
Domaine Le Sang des Cailloux
Vidal-Fleury

*** *(GOOD)*

Paul Jaboulet-Ainé   Domaine de Montvac
Domaine de la Jaufrette   Château des Roques
Domaine des Lambertins   Le Vieux Clocher
Domaine de la Monardière

1995–1996 BUYING STRATEGY

Given the frightful irregularity of the 1994, 1993, and 1992 vintages, consumers are well advised to taste before buying. To the extent that any great 1991 Côte Rôties or 1990s from just about any Rhône Valley appellation can still be found, they should be gobbled up. My instincts suggest that the growing legion of Rhône wine enthusiasts have already squirreled away the finest wines from the last great vintages, 1990 and 1989, so today the Rhône desperately needs an exceptional vintage.

The 1994 vintage will be the best one in the last three years for both the northern and southern Rhône and 1993 offers a large supply of very good Châteauneuf du Pape, but problematic wines abound in the north.

RECENT VINTAGES

Two years ago when the last *Wine Buyer's Guide* was published, the Rhône Valley was awash in high-quality wines from nearly every appellation. Why? The three high-quality, abundant years of 1988, 1989, and 1990 had Rhône Valley vignerons filled with optimism for the future. Today, it is an entirely different picture, with the four most recent vintages— 1991, 1992, 1993, and 1994—all difficult years. The majority of the growers, producers, and *négociants* are frustrated by the onslaught of troublesome weather during the last three harvests.

Yet readers should resist the temptation to qualitatively pigeon-hole these four vintages. In each vintage there are appellations that enjoyed considerable success, not to mention producers who successfully handled the dreadful weather hurled at them by Mother Nature. 1994—Much like all the Rhône Valley vintages following the great 1990 vintage, 1994 is another complicated year. The torridly hot, sunny summer offered the potential for another 1990 or 1989, but harvest rains caught most northern producers with unharvested grapes. Nevertheless, the better producers who had low crop yields are pleased with the quality, claiming that the 1994s from Côte Rôtie, Hermitage, and Cornas are superior to 1993 and 1992, and possibly as fine as 1991 or 1985.

In the southern Rhône, many producers were able to harvest a significant portion of their vineyards before the heavy rains began. Early assessments of the 1994 vintage suggest that Châteauneuf du Pape, followed by Gigondas and several of the Côtes du Rhône villages, has produced their richest, most complete cuvées since the great 1990 vintage. Quantities, however, are small, so look for prices to rise if the quality turns out to be as fine as believed. 1993—1993 is both a confusing and an irregular year. The vintage's failures are concentrated in the northern Rhône, especially in Côte Rôtie and Hermitage. Rain and high humidity caused serious problems with mildew and rot in the northern Rhône vineyards, thus devastating producers who were on the verge of having a high-quality vintage. It is possible that an event of historical proportions has emerged from the disastrous 1993 vintage in the northern Rhône. Michel Chapoutier, whose faith in the principles of biodynamic organic farming created such a controversy among his peers, produced brilliant wines in this dreadful year, offering, in the brash Chapoutier's view, incontrovertible evidence of the merits of this philosophy of vineyard farming.

In contrast, the southern Rhône fared well in 1993. Why? Approximately 50%–75% of the crop was harvested before any damaging rain. The 1993 vintage poignantly illustrates how different the microclimates are in the northern and southern Rhône, not to mention the *terroirs* and grape varietals. If the northern Rhône's 1993 vintage looks to be the worst that sector of the Rhône has experienced since 1977, 1975, or 1984, the southern Rhône may turn out a vintage that is capable of rivaling 1988, and perhaps even 1985.

As the tasting notes that follow evidence, plenty of fine wines have emerged from the last three vintages. Selection is always critical, but Rhône wines, particularly the reds, remain France's least-known great wines. While the limited-production, great red wines of the northern Rhône, especially Côte Rôtie and Hermitage, are rare and expensive, the southern Rhône red wines, such as Châteauneuf du Pape, Gigondas, Vacqueyras, and the top Côtes du Rhônes, continue to offer fabulous quality/price rapport.

1992—This year is mediocre in quality, with considerable failures in the Côtes du Rhône villages. Additionally, Gigondas is below average in quality, but Châteauneuf du Pape is surprisingly good, although the wines are lighter and significantly less concentrated than such great years as 1989 and 1990.

In the northern Rhône, the vintage has turned out to be of average quality, with the most meticulous producers turning out surprisingly good, ripe, soft wines that will require early consumption. Chapoutier's 1992s are brilliant wines.

1991—Côte Rôtie enjoyed exceptional success in 1991, and other northern Rhône appellations unquestionably produced very good wines in that vintage. For Côte Rôtie, 1991 has proven to be an exceptional vintage, superior to as well as more consistent than 1990. Other northern Rhône appellations that enjoyed success included Cornas, Hermitage, St.-Joseph, and Crozes-Hermitage.

The southern Rhône appellations were devastated by torrential rains in 1991, and the quality of virtually every Gigondas and Châteauneuf du Pape is suspect, although a few worthy wines have emerged.

1990—This is a superlative vintage throughout the Rhône Valley. In the south, the torridly hot, dry summer resulted in superripe grapes packed with sugar. At the top levels the wines are deeply colored and exceptionally powerful, with high levels of soft tannins, and alcohol of 14%–15+%. The wines have a more roasted, extreme style than the more classic 1989s, but they are sumptuous, as well as loaded with concentrated fruit. It is unquestionably a great vintage in Châteauneuf du Pape, an excellent one in Gigondas, and a top-flight year in most of the Côtes du Rhône villages. The red wines from both Gigondas and Châteauneuf du Pape, despite higher alcohol than the 1989s, will probably mature more quickly than the 1989s because their acidity levels are lower and because the wines are so opulent and precocious. Nevertheless, the top cuvées of Châteauneuf du Pape should easily last for 15–20 years.

If you are a lover of Hermitage and Crozes-Hermitage, grab your wallet! In Hermitage, 1990 looks to be even better than the great 1978 vintage. Gérard Chave, Michel Chapoutier, and Gérald Jaboulet all believe it is the finest year for this renowned appellation since 1961. The massive wines are almost black in color, with extraordinary extraction of fruit, high tannins, and a textural sweetness and succulence. Jaboulet's La Chapelle, Chave's Hermitage, and Chapoutier's luxury cuvée, Le Pavillon, are likely candidates for perfection, provided those who can both find and afford them wait the 15 or more years they will need to attain maturity. Even the wines of Crozes-Hermitage are superconcentrated. Those from Alain Graillot and Paul Jaboulet-Aîné are especially exciting. Côte Rôtie is a mixed bag, with the top cuvées of Chapoutier, Guigal, and a handful of others looking excellent, sometimes extraordinary. Other wines are merely above average in quality. St.-Joseph and Cornas are at least good.

1989—This is unquestionably a great vintage for Châteauneuf du Pape and gets my nod as the finest vintage for that appellation since 1978. In fact, it is 1978 that comes to mind when looking for a vintage of similar characteristics. The hot, dry weather produced small grapes with more noticeable tannins than the 1990s. However, when analyzed, most 1990s have the same level of tannins as the 1989s, but the 1989s taste more structured and more classically rendered. Given the stunning ripeness and reasonable yields, the 1989 Châteauneuf du Papes are nearly as powerful as the 1990s. They have low acidity, spectacular levels of fruit extraction, and a full-bodied, potentially long-lived style. It is a matter of personal taste whether one prefers the 1990s or the 1989s, but both are dazzling vintages. One really has to look to the individual domaine as to who fared better in one vintage or the other. The 1989 vintage is a more consistent one in Gigondas, and again, that appellation's best overall year since 1978. For Rhône wine enthusiasts, these two years offer the best opportunities to replenish your cellars since 1978 and 1979.

Less massive, more supple and opulent wines were produced throughout the northern Rhône. The most successful appellations were Hermitage and Côte Rôtie. The least successful was Cornas. While Côte Rôtie producers were ecstatic after the vintage, only the best cuvées of Guigal and a few other wines have the requisite concentration and grip to live up to the initial hyperbole. While the wines are flattering and will make delicious drinking over the next 10–15 years, this is an excellent rather than a great vintage. In Hermitage it would be considered a great vintage except for the fact that 1990 succeeded it. The top cuvées are rich and full bodied, with 20 or more years of longevity. They also have a softness and are less massive on the palate, particularly when tasted next to the 1990s. The vintage is irregular in Cornas. The heat and drought appear to have caused problems for many vineyards in that appellation. As in Hermitage, Crozes-Hermitage enjoyed an excellent year.

1988—While this is a very good vintage throughout the southern Rhône, it has been overshadowed by the thrilling quality of both 1989 and 1990. The 1988s do not possess the size, alcohol levels, or pure weight and drama of the 1989s or 1990s, but they are full-bodied, classically styled wines with slightly greener tannins and higher acidity. The 1988s should age gracefully, but they will rarely achieve the summit of decadence, complexity, and pleasure that the top 1989s and 1990s will attain.

In the northern Rhône, Côte Rôtie enjoyed a superb vintage that equals 1985, 1983, and 1978. In fact, the 1988 Côte Rôties are significantly better than the 1989s, 1990s, and 1991s. The wines are superconcentrated, with great extraction of fruit, firm structure, and promising potential for longevity. Hermitage is at least excellent, and sometimes superb (consider wines such as Sorrel's Le Gréal, Jaboulet's La Chapelle, and Chave's Hermitage). The wines of Cornas are very good, as are those of Crozes-Hermitage and St.-Joseph.

1987—1987 is a poor to mediocre year in the southern Rhône. In the northern Rhône, this is a delicious vintage for Côte Rôtie, which enjoyed more success than any other northern Rhône Valley appellation. The wines are ripe and concentrated, with a velvety richness. Virtually everyone made good wine. The wines are delicious at present and should last another 5–6 years. The wines of Hermitage are smaller-scaled, but clearly made from ripe fruit, with none of the nasty, herbal, vegetal character that comes from cool, wet, mediocre years. Chave, Sorrel, and Guigal all made tasty 1987s that should continue to drink well for another 7–8 years.

1986—This is an extremely irregular vintage, with medium-weight wines being produced. About 20% of the grapes in the Rhône Valley had not been harvested when the area was inundated with heavy rains on October 12, and the weather that followed over the next two weeks was equally miserable. However, the early pickers did exceptionally well, particularly in the southern Rhône where quality is at least good, sometimes outstanding. Production was less than in the bountiful year of 1985, but because of the late-harvest deluge, selection was critical, and one sees a great deal of irregularity in the range of quality. The wines are firmer, more tannic, and less fat and precocious than the 1985s. The top southern Rhônes from Châteauneuf du Pape and Gigondas appear to have outstanding cellaring potential.

Guigal is the star of the northern Rhône, with a number of stunning cuvées. In view of the amount of rain and potential for rot during the humid, wet harvest season, Guigal's achievement is remarkable. Jaboulet's La Chapelle is also surprisingly good, although narrowly constructed. In spite of these successes, 1986 is a vintage to approach with considerable caution.

1985—My tastings continue to confirm that this vintage has produced very good to excellent wines in the northern Rhône, and very good wines in the south. For Côte Rôtie, it is a great vintage. The wines are very deep in color, quite rich, but not particularly tannic. The overall impression is one of wines fully ripe, rich in fruit, very opulent in style, and quite forward. In Côte Rôtie and Châteauneuf du Pape it is better than 1983. Everywhere it is certainly better than 1982, 1981, and 1980. The white wines were very powerful and rich, but should have been drunk.

1984—This was a rather mediocre vintage of light- to medium-bodied wines that will offer straightforward, one-dimensional drinking over the near term. There are many surprisingly good wines from Châteauneuf du Pape and Gigondas, and the white wines of the entire region were quite good.

1983—This is an excellent vintage in the north, but a very good yet irregular vintage in the south. A hot, dry summer resulted in fully mature grapes loaded with sugar, flavor extract, and hard tannins. For Hermitage, Crozes-Hermitage, and St.-Joseph, the wines are clearly the most age-worthy since 1978, but they are not as massive and rich as the 1978s nor as fruity as the 1985s. At 12 years of age, most 1983s from the northern Rhône are still frightfully tannic and austere. The southern Rhônes are largely fully mature.

Past Great Vintages for the Northern Rhône: 1978, 1972 (Hermitage), 1970, 1966, 1961, 1959

Past Great Vintages for the Southern Rhône: 1981, 1979, 1978, 1970, 1967, 1961, 1957

Rhône Déjà Vu

To the extent that readers are able to find any of the extraordinary 1989s, 1990s, or finest 1991s (only from the north) at retail shops or at the numerous wine auctions increasingly being held in California, New York, and Illinois, following are some of the greatest wines from those vintages. I predict these wines will ultimately prove to be among the greatest Rhône wines ever made.

1990 Thierry Allemand Cornas (93)
1990 Pierre André Châteauneuf du Pape (88)
1990 Domaine des Anges Clos de la Tour (89)
1989 Domaine des Anges Clos de la Tour (87)
1990 Paul Autard Châteauneuf du Pape (87)
1990 Paul Autard Châteauneuf du Pape Cuvée La Côte Ronde (91)
1991 Gilles Barges Côte Rôtie (87–89)
1990 Lucien Barrot Châteauneuf du Pape (89)
1990 Bastide St. Vincent Vacqueyras (87)
1990 Beaucastel Châteauneuf du Pape (94)
1990 Beaucastel Châteauneuf du Pape (white) (88)
1990 Beaucastel Châteauneuf du Pape Vieilles Vignes (white) (90)

1990 Beaucastel Coudoulet (88)
1990 Beaucastel Hommage à Jacques Perrin (99+)
1989 Beaucastel Hommage à Jacques Perrin (100)
1990 Domaine de Beaurenard Châteauneuf du Pape (90)
1990 Domaine de Beaurenard Châteauneuf du Pape Boisrenard (96)
1990 Domaine de Beaurenard Côtes du Rhône (87)
1990 Albert Belle Crozes-Hermitage Cuvée Louis Belle (90)
1990 Albert Belle Hermitage (91)
1991 Domaine de Bois-Dauphin Châteauneuf du Pape Clos des Pontifes (white) (87)
1990 Domaine de Bois-Dauphin Châteauneuf du Pape Clos des Pontifes (88)

1990 Henri Bonneau Châteauneuf du Pape Cuvée des Celestins (100)

1989 Henri Bonneau Châteauneuf du Pape Cuvée des Celestins (98)

1988 Henri Bonneau Châteauneuf du Pape Cuvée des Celestins (95)

1989 Henri Bonneau Châteauneuf du Pape Cuvée Marie Beurrier (89)

1990 Bosquet des Papes Châteauneuf du Pape (92)

1990 Bosquet des Papes Châteauneuf du Pape Cuvée Chantemerle (96)

1990 Roman Bouchard Côtes du Rhône-Villages Valreas (87)

1990 Lucien et André Brunel-Les Cailloux Châteauneuf du Pape (91)

1990 Lucien et André Brunel-Les Cailloux Châteauneuf du Pape Cuvée Centenaire (96)

1990 Daniel Brusset Gigondas Les Hauts de Montmirail (93)

1990 Bernard Burgaud Côte Rôtie (89+)

1989 Edmonde Burle Gigondas Les Pallieroudas (93)

1990 Château Cabrières Châteauneuf du Pape Cuvée Prestige (90)

1990 Domaine du Cayron Gigondas (89+)

1989 Domaine du Cayron Gigondas (90)

1990 Chante-Cigale Châteauneuf du Pape (78–90?)

1990 Chapoutier Châteauneuf du Pape Barbe Rac (95)

1990 Chapoutier Châteauneuf du Pape La Bernadine (89)

1990 Chapoutier Condrieu (white) (88)

1990 Chapoutier Cornas (87)

1990 Chapoutier Côte Rôtie Brune et Blonde (89)

1990 Chapoutier Côte Rôtie Cuvée Mordorée (94)

1990 Chapoutier Crozes-Hermitage Les Meysonniers (88)

1991 Chapoutier Hermitage Chante Alouette (white) (90)

1990 Chapoutier Hermitage Le Pavillon (100)

1989 Chapoutier Hermitage Le Pavillon (100)

1990 Charbonnière Châteauneuf du Pape (87)

1990 Gérard Charvin Châteauneuf du Pape (92)

1990 J. L. Chave Hermitage (red) (98+)

1991 J. L. Chave Hermitage (white) (90)

1990 J. L. Chave Hermitage (white) (92)

1990 J. L. Chave Hermitage Red Label Cathelin (99+)

1990 J. L. Chave St.-Joseph (red) (89)

1991 Domaine du Chêne Condrieu (white) (88)

1991 Domaine du Chêne Condrieu Château de Virieu (white) (88)

1990 Domaine du Chêne Condrieu Julien Vendange Tardive (white) (92)

1990 Domaine du Chêne St.-Joseph (87)

1990 Domaine du Chêne St.-Joseph Anais (88)

1990 August Clape Cornas (91)

1990 Les Clefs d'Or Châteauneuf du Pape (88)

1990 Clos du Caillou Châteauneuf du Pape (91)

1990 Clos des Cazaux Gigondas Cuvée de la Tour Sarrazine (87)

1990 Clos des Cazaux Vacqueyras Saint Roche (87)

1990 Clos des Cazaux Vacqueyras Templiers (89)

1990 Clos du Mont-Olivet Châteauneuf du Pape (90)

1990 Clos du Mont-Olivet Châteauneuf du Pape Cuvée du Papet (94)

1989 Clos du Mont-Olivet Châteauneuf du Pape Cuvée du Papet (94)

1990 Clos de la Mure Côtes du Rhône (88)

1990 Clos des Papes Châteauneuf du Pape (92)

1989 Clusel-Roch Côte Rôtie (90)

1988 Clusel-Roch Côte Rôtie (92)

1991 Jean-Luc Colombo Cornas Les Ruchets (88)

1990 Roger Combe Gigondas l'Ousteau Fauquet (87)

1989 Roger Combe Gigondas l'Ousteau Fauquet (88)

1991 Yves Cuilleron Condrieu (white) (89)

1991 Yves Cuilleron Condrieu Vieilles Vignes (white) (92)

1990 Georges Duboeuf Côtes du Rhône Domaine des Moulins (87)

1990 Domaine Durieu Châteauneuf du Pape (87)

1990 Domaine Durieu Châteauneuf du Pape Cuvée Lucile Avril (88+)

1990 Domaine de l'Espigouette Côtes du Rhône Plan de Dieu (87)

1990 Domaine de Fauterie St.-Joseph (87)

1990 Eddie Féraud Châteauneuf du Pape Cuvée Réservée (90)

1990 Fonsalette Côtes du Rhône (92)

1990 Fonsalette Côtes du Rhône Cuvée Syrah (94)

1990 Font du Loup Châteauneuf du Pape (89)

1990 Font de Michelle Châteauneuf du Pape (89+)

1990 Font de Michelle Châteauneuf du Pape Cuvée Étienne Gonnet (92)

1990 Font-Sane Gigondas (87)

1990 Fourmone Vacqueyras Maître du Chai (88)

1990 Lou Fréjau Châteauneuf du Pape (87)

1990 Château de la Gardine Châteauneuf du Pape (88)

1990 Château de la Gardine Châteauneuf du Pape Cuvée des Générations (93+)

1991 Gentaz-Dervieux Côte Rôtie Côte Brune (90)

1990 Gentaz-Dervieux Côte Rôtie Côte Brune (89)

1990 Robert Girard-Cuvée du Belvedere Châteauneuf du Pape (88)

1990 Les Gouberts Gigondas Cuvée Florence (87)

1990 Gour de Chaulé Gigondas (88)

1989 Gour de Chaulé Gigondas (88)

1990 Alain Graillot Crozes-Hermitage (92)

1990 Alain Graillot Crozes-Hermitage La Guiraude (94)

1990 Alain Graillot Hermitage (89)

1990 Alain Graillot St.-Joseph (89)

1990 Gramenon Côtes du Rhône (88)

1990 Gramenon Côtes du Rhône Cuvée de Laurentides (92)

1989 Gramenon Côtes du Rhône Cuvée de Laurentides (92)

1990 Grand Jean Châteauneuf du Pape (90)

1989 Grand Moulas Côtes du Rhône Villages (87)

1990 Grand Romaine Gigondas (89)

1990 Grand Veneur Châteauneuf du Pape (87)

1989 Grands Devers Côtes du Rhône Enclaves des Papes (90)

1989 Grands Devers Syrah (91)

1990 J. L. Grippat Hermitage (88)

1990 J. L. Grippat Hermitage (white) (89)

1990 J. L. Grippat St.-Joseph Vignes de l'Hospices (90)

1990 Guichard Côtes du Rhône Les Genests (90)

1989 Guigal Châteauneuf du Pape (88)

1989 Guigal Côte Rôtie Brune et Blonde (90)

1988 Guigal Côte Rôtie La Landonne (100)

1988 Guigal Côte Rôtie La Mouline (100)

1988 Guigal Côte Rôtie La Turque (100)

1990 Guigal Côtes du Rhône (88)

1989 Guigal Côtes du Rhône (88)

1989 Guigal Hermitage (90)

1990 Guigal Hermitage (white) (89)

1990 Haut des Terres Blanches Châteauneuf du Pape (88)

1990 Paul Jaboulet-Aîné Châteauneuf du Pape (89)

1991 Paul Jaboulet-Aîné Cornas (87)

1990 Paul Jaboulet-Aîné Côtes du Rhône-Villages (87)

1990 Paul Jaboulet-Aîné Crozes-Hermitage Les Jalets (87)

1990 Paul Jaboulet-Aîné Crozes-Hermitage La Mule Blanche (white) (87)

1990 Paul Jaboulet-Aîné Crozes-Hermitage Thalabert (92)

1990 Paul Jaboulet-Aîné Gigondas (90)

1990 Paul Jaboulet-Aîné Hermitage La Chapelle (99+)

1989 Paul Jaboulet-Aîné Hermitage La Chapelle (95)

1991 Paul Jaboulet-Aîné Hermitage Chevalier de Stérimberg (white) (89)

1990 Paul Jaboulet-Aîné Hermitage Chevalier de Stérimberg (white) (93)

1990 Paul Jaboulet-Aîné St.-Joseph Le Grand Pompée (89)

1990 Paul Jaboulet-Aîné Vacqueyras (87)

1990 Pierre Jacumin-Cuvée de Boisdauphin Châteauneuf du Pape (88+)

1990 Joseph Jamet Côte Rôtie Côte Brune (89)

1990 Janasse Châteauneuf du Pape Chaupoins (92)

1990 Janasse Châteauneuf du Pape Vieilles Vignes (92)

1990 Marcoux Châteauneuf du Pape (91)

1990 Marcoux Châteauneuf du Pape Vieilles Vignes (97)

1989 Mas de Rey Caladoc Bouches du Rhône (85)

1989 Mas de Rey Cuvée Camargue (87)

1990 Mathieu Châteauneuf du Pape (87)

1990 Monpertuis Châteauneuf du Pape Cuvée Tradition (88)

1990 Montmirail Gigondas Beauchamp (89)

1989 Montmirail Vacqueyras Deux Frères (87)

1990 Moulin de la Gardette Gigondas (88)

1990 Moulin-Tacussel Châteauneuf du Pape (87)

1991 Nero-Pinchon Condrieu (white) (87)

1990 Nero-Pinchon Côtes du Rhône Ste.-Agathe (87)

1990 La Nerthe Châteauneuf du Pape Cuvée des Cadettes (89)

1990 Michel Ogier Côte Rôtie Côte Blonde (87)

1990 Pavillon-Mercurol Crozes-Hermitage (88)

1990 Pegau Châteauneuf du Pape Cuvée Réservée (96)

1990 Père Pape Châteauneuf du Pape Clos du Calvaire (87)

1991 André Perret Condrieu Coteau du Chery (white) (89)

1990 André Perret Condrieu Vendange Tardive (white) (94)
1990 André Perret St.-Joseph (87)
1990 André Perret St.-Joseph Les Grisières (88)
1990 Pascal Perrier St.-Joseph (88)
1990 Roger Perrin Châteauneuf du Pape (88)
1990 Pesquier Gigondas (90)
1989 Piaugier Côtes du Rhône Les Briguières (87)
1990 Piaugier Gigondas (87)
1990 Pignan Châteauneuf du Pape (94)
1989 Pignan Châteauneuf du Pape (90)
1990 Pinede Châteauneuf du Pape (87)
1990 Domaine Pontifical-François Laget Châteauneuf du Pape (87)
1990 Pourra Gigondas (87+)
1990 Domaine de la Présidente-M. Aubert Cairanne Goutillonnage (88)
1990 Domaine de la Présidente-M. Aubert Châteauneuf du Pape (87)
1990 Domaine Raspail-Dominique Ay Gigondas (90)
1990 Rayas Châteauneuf du Pape (99)
1990 Rayas Châteauneuf du Pape (white) (91)
1990 Rayas Fonsalette Côtes du Rhône (92)
1990 Rayas Fonsalette Côtes du Rhône Cuvée Syrah (94)
1990 Redoitier Gigondas (87)
1990 Roquette Châteauneuf du Pape (88)
1991 René Rostaing Condrieu (white) (92)
1991 René Rostaing Côte Rôtie (87–88)
1990 René Rostaing Côte Rôtie (87)
1990 René Rostaing Côte Rôtie Côte Blonde (93)
1990 René Rostaing Côte Rôtie La Landonne (91)
1991 Rozay Condrieu (white) (88)
1990 Roger Sabon Châteauneuf du Pape Cuvée Prestige (90)
1990 Saint-Benoît Châteauneuf du Pape Grand Garde (91)
1989 Saint-Gayan Gigondas (91)
1988 Saint-Gayan Gigondas (89)
1989 Santa Duc Côtes du Rhône (87)
1990 Santa Duc Gigondas (89)
1990 Santa Duc Gigondas Cuvée Prestige des Hautes Garrigues (92)
1990 Domaine de la Solitude Châteauneuf du Pape (90)

1990 Henri Sorrel Hermitage (88)
1990 Henri Sorrel Hermitage Le Gréal (95+)
1989 Henri Sorrel Hermitage Le Gréal (95+)
1991 Henri Sorrel Hermitage Les Rocoules (white) (88)
1990 Henri Sorrel Hermitage Les Rocoules (white) (90)
1991 J. M. Sorrel Hermitage (87)
1990 J. M. Sorrel Hermitage Le Vignon (87?)
1990 Souco-Papale Châteauneuf du Pape (87+)
1989 Soumade Côtes du Rhône-Villages Rasteau Prestige (89)
1990 Château des Tours Côtes du Rhône (88)
1990 Château des Tours Vacqueyras (90)
1990 Château des Tours Vin de Pays Vaucluse (87)
1990 Raymond Usseglio Châteauneuf du Pape (88)
1990 L. de Vallouit Châteauneuf du Pape (88)
1990 L. de Vallouit Côte Rôtie Les Roziers (92)
1989 L. de Vallouit Côte Rôtie Les Roziers (89)
1988 L. de Vallouit Côte Rôtie Les Roziers (93)
1990 L. de Vallouit Côte Rôtie Vagonier (89)
1991 L. de Vallouit Hermitage (white) (89)
1989 L. de Vallouit Hermitage Les Greffières (90)
1989 L. de Vallouit St.-Joseph Les Anges (87)
1990 Cuvée du Vatican Châteauneuf du Pape (87)
1990 Vaudieu Châteauneuf du Pape (87)
1990 Georges Vernay Condrieu Coteaux du Vernon (white) (88)
1989 Vidal-Fleury Côte Rôtie La Chatillonne Côte Blonde (90)
1989 Vidal-Fleury St.-Joseph (87)
1990 Vieille Julienne Châteauneuf du Pape (89+)
1990 Le Vieux Donjon Châteauneuf du Pape (92)
1990 Vieux Télégraphe Châteauneuf du Pape (89)
1990 Alain Voge Cornas Cuvée Barriques (87)
1989 Alain Voge Cornas Vieilles Vignes (90)
1989 Vollonnières Côtes du Rhône (86)

THIERRY ALLEMAND * * * *

1993 Cornas	C	86
1992 Cornas	C	87

Over recent vintages Allemand has proven he is one of the best producers of this tiny appellation. He made two of the finest wines in the tough, rain-plagued vintages of 1992 and 1993. His 1993 Cornas is one of the deepest, most saturated, dark ruby/purple-colored wines of any of the Cornas offerings I tasted. The fine ripeness and sweetness displayed in the nose are continued in the flavors of excellent black cherry fruit, licorice, and earth. There is a spicy, medium- to full-bodied finish with soft tannin. Although it will be drinkable early, this is one 1993 Cornas with the depth and concentration to merit serious consideration; it should last for a decade. The 1992 Cornas is also among the most concentrated wines of this appellation. Dark ruby/purple, with an herbaceous, licorice- and black currant–scented nose, it exhibits excellent ripeness, medium body, fine length, and an overall sense of balance. It should be drunk in its first 7–10 years of life.

DOMAINE DES AMOURIERS * * * * *

1992 Côtes du Rhône	A	85
1993 Vacqueyras	B	88
1990 Vacqueyras	B	87

This small estate is making terrific Vacqueyras. The 1993 and 1990 (blends of approximately 60% Grenache, 30% Mourvèdre, and 10% Syrah) are both wine bargains, as well as full-bodied, chewy, exuberant, peppery, fruity Rhône wines. The 1993 is fruitier and less alcoholic, whereas the more powerful 1990 exhibits rustic, animal scents and gobs of peppery, black cherry, earthy fruit. Both wines should drink well for 5–6 years.

Made just outside the appellation of Vacqueyras, the 1992 Côtes du Rhône is packed with peppery, spicy, rich black fruit. It exhibits excellent color, and a chewy, fleshy taste. Drink it over the next several years.

DOMAINE DES ANGES * * * *

1990 Clos de la Tour Cuvée Spéciale	C	88
1990 Côtes du Ventoux	A	85

The 1990 Clos de la Tour Cuvée Spéciale, a special cuvée of 100% Syrah aged in small oak casks, is a deeply colored, superrich, expansively flavored, personality-filled wine. Drink this rich, medium- to full-bodied, velvety-textured wine over the next 7–8 years. The 1990 Côtes du Ventoux is what a wine from this region should be. The nose offers up smoky aromas intermingled with scents of black fruits (plums and cassis). The wine is supple and medium bodied, with no hard edges and a tasty finish. Drink it over the next 2–3 years.

RENÉ BALTHAZAR * * *

1993 Cornas	C	84
1992 Cornas	C	86

Balthazar's 1993 Cornas displays an elegant, light-intensity bouquet of berry fruit, herbs, earth, and spice, tasty, medium-bodied, ripe fruit, and a tough, astringent finish. Although a successful wine for the vintage, the 1992 Cornas is less powerful than usual. It exhibits a dark ruby color, a peppery, spicy, overripe nose, fleshy, chewy fruit, and a surprisingly long, supple finish. Drink it over the next 5–7 years.

GUY DE BARJAC * * *

1993 Cornas	C 86
1992 Cornas	C ?

Always the last vigneron in Cornas to harvest, Barjac could not have liked his chances in 1993 after the deluge dumped frightful quantities of rain on the northern Rhône between September 25 and October 1. Nevertheless, his 1993 Cornas has turned out to be a flattering, light-bodied, round, cleanly made wine with lovely fruit, low acidity, and a velvety texture. Drink it over the next 4–5 years. The 1992 Cornas exudes aromas of decaying vegetation and rot. It is a major disappointment. Judgment reserved until a second bottle can be tasted.

LUCIEN BARROT * * * *

1993 Châteauneuf du Pape	C 86
1992 Châteauneuf du Pape	C 86

As a longtime fan of Barrot's bold, sometimes blockbuster style of Châteauneuf du Pape, I am surprised he has made such easy-to-drink, soft, medium-weight wines. Although good, they lack the intensity noticeable in other vintages, particularly years such as 1989, 1988, 1985, 1981, and 1979. The 1993 Châteauneuf du Pape possesses sweet, charcoal, smoked meat aromas accompanied by ripe black cherry fruit. The wine is fat, expansive, and medium bodied, with excellent ripeness, and a soft, heady finish. Drink it over the next 5–6 years. The similarly styled 1992 Châteauneuf du Pape offers cherry fruit, gobs of glycerin, high alcohol, low acidity, and an easygoing, plump personality. Drink it over the next 5 years.

BEAUCASTEL * * * * *

1993 Beaucastel	D 92
1992 Beaucastel	D 90
1991 Beaucastel	D 76
1992 Châteauneuf du Pape Blanc	D 89
1993 Châteauneuf du Pape Roussanne Vieilles Vignes	E 93
1992 Châteauneuf du Pape Roussanne Vieilles Vignes	E 91
1993 Coudoulet de Beaucastel Rouge	C 87
1992 Coudoulet de Beaucastel Rouge	C 86
1993 Coudoulet de Beaucastel Blanc	C 88
1992 Coudoulet de Beaucastel Blanc	C 87

The Perrin brothers continue to augment the quality of Coudoulet's white wines. The current blend consists of approximately 30% Viognier, 30% Marsanne, 30% Bourboulenc, and the remainder Clairette. The 1993 white Coudoulet de Beaucastel is a rich, medium- to full-bodied, fragrant, juicy wine with lovely freshness, purity, and balance. Drink it over the next 1–2 years. Although less aromatic, the 1992 white Coudoulet de Beaucastel reveals excellent richness, and a medium- to full-bodied, chewy, chunky personality. It merits drinking early.

I had the pleasure of tasting the component parts of the 1993 Châteauneuf du Pape Blanc, which looks to be an excellent wine. Since it has not yet been blended, I will hold judgment. Also excellent, the 1992 Châteauneuf du Pape Blanc exhibits a floral, honeyed bouquet and medium-bodied, firm, chewy flavors. It should drink well for 10–15 years.

The 1993 Châteauneuf du Pape Roussanne Vieilles Vignes (only 4,000 bottles produced) exhibits a huge cherry- and rose-scented nose, tropical fruit–like flavors, great richness and concentration, medium to full body, and wonderful, vibrant, zesty acidity. This rarity, produced from a small parcel of vines averaging 50–60 years, is undoubtedly the finest dry white wine made in the southern Rhône. Although similar, the 1992 Châteauneuf du Pape Roussanne Vieilles Vignes possesses more of an exotic, honeyed, roasted nut– and floral-scented nose, intense, full-bodied flavors, superb concentration, and a long, lush, pure finish. These wines tend to drink beautifully for 2–3 years after bottling and then close up. The Perrins believe they can be aged for 15–20+ years.

As for the red wine cuvées, the Perrins compare the 1993s favorably with 1988. For example, the deep ruby-colored 1993 Coudoulet de Beaucastel offers a pure nose of peppery black raspberry fruit, excellent richness, medium to full body, soft tannin, and low acidity. Drink it over the next decade. The 1993 Beaucastel appears to be better than the fine 1988. Rich and spicy, with a beefy component, a wonderful tar, tobacco, and curranty nose, and sweet, expansive, rich, full-bodied flavors, it will be approachable young and last for 15 or more years.

The 1992 Coudoulet de Beaucastel is more austere and tannic than the 1993. It possesses structure, gobs of ripe, leathery black fruit aromas, and a spicy, firm finish. Drink it over the next 7–10 years. I was impressed with the 1992 Beaucastel, which is significantly richer and more complete than the narrowly constructed, herbaceous, compact 1991. The 1992 boasts a smoky, earthy, peppery, cassis-scented nose, rich, full-bodied flavors, excellent depth, moderate tannin, and a sweet, chewy, impressive finish. Its firmness suggests that 3–4 years of cellaring is necessary; it should keep for 20 years.

I have never been impressed with the 1991 Beaucastel. Even though the Perrins sold over 50% of their production to *négociants*, it is an austere, meagerly endowed Beaucastel. While it will keep for a decade or more, it lacks fruit and charm.

DOMAINE DE BEAURENARD * * * */* * * * *

1993 Châteauneuf du Pape	C	88
1992 Châteauneuf du Pape	C	86
1993 Châteauneuf du Pape Cuvée Boisrenard	D	93
1990 Côtes du Rhône	A	87
1993 Rasteau Côtes du Rhône-Villages	A	85

The Coulon family continues to fashion better and better wines. The 1992 and 1993 vintages of Châteauneuf du Pape offer interesting contrasts. The 1992 Châteauneuf du Pape represents a modern style of Châteauneuf in its wonderfully pure, peppery, black cherry– and herb-scented nose, round, soft, expansive, medium- to full-bodied flavors, and moderate finish. Already delicious, it is capable of lasting for 4–6 years. The 1993 Châteauneuf du Pape possesses a more saturated dark ruby color, an intense, ripe bouquet of jammy black and red fruits, herbs, and spices, full body, admirable concentration, and a supple texture. It is ideal for drinking over the next decade. In 1990 Beaurenard launched a luxury cuvée of Châteauneuf du Pape called Boisrenard. The 1990 was spectacular, and I am delighted to report that the second release of this old-vine cuvée that is bottled unfiltered, the 1993 Boisrenard, is a worthy successor to the outstanding 1990. The color of the 1993 is a black/purple, and the wine displays a judicious use of toasty new oak that causes the black fruit character to jump from the glass. A pure, rich, full-bodied wine with layers of flavor, exceptional concentration, superb balance, and a long, voluptuously textured, chewy finish, it will be drinkable when released and will keep for 15 years.

The 1993 Rasteau Côtes du Rhône-Villages exhibits jammy, black cherry– and herb-scented fruit, medium body, a silky texture, and a mouth-filling fruitiness. Drink it over the next 4–5 years. The 1990 Côtes du Rhône is the type of wine that offers immediate gratification but can last for 4–5 years. The color is a healthy dark plum, and the nose is all sweet black fruits, roasted peanuts, and herbs. This expansive, round, exceptionally pure wine displays no hard edges. Drinking it is a delightful, immensely satisfying experience.

ALBERT BELLE * * * *

1992 Crozes-Hermitage Cuvée Louis Belle	C	91
1992 Crozes-Hermitage Les Pierrelles	C	89
1992 Hermitage	D	92
1992 Hermitage Blanc	D	87

In 1992, Albert Belle, a studious, thoughtful man, made the best wines I have tasted from his small estate. The 1992 Hermitage is sensational. Its huge nose of roasted herbs, jammy black fruit, smoked meat, and spice soars from the glass. The wine possesses great fruit extraction, full body, low acidity, and moderate tannin. It is unevolved and grapy, so give it 3–4 years of cellaring; it will keep for 15 years. It may turn out to be one of the two or three best Hermitages in the 1992 vintage. The two cuvées of 1992 Crozes-Hermitage are superb values, as well as outstanding wines. The 1992 Crozes-Hermitage Les Pierrelles has an intense, herbal, peppery, curranty nose, supple, rich, full-bodied, lush flavors, an exuberant fruitiness, and an expansive finish. It should drink well for 5–7 years. The 1992 Crozes-Hermitage Cuvée Louis Belle is partially aged in new oak casks and bottled unfiltered (as are Belle's other red wines). It offers an intense, ripe bouquet, great richness, a saturated color, and a sensationally long, opulent finish. This medium- to full-bodied Crozes is ideal for drinking over the next decade. It is hard to find a Crozes-Hermitage this stunning!

With its bouquet of pine needles, flowers, and pineapples, and its full-bodied, concentrated fruitiness, Belle's 1992 white Hermitage is undeniably excellent. It is an authoritatively flavored, robust, chewy white wine that should drink and evolve well for 10–12 years.

DOMAINE DE BOIS DAUPHIN * * *

1993 Châteauneuf du Pape	C	88
1992 Châteauneuf du Pape	C	84
1993 Châteauneuf du Pape Blanc	C	85

As these three offerings attest, proprietor Jean-Pierre Versino is a fine winemaker. The 1993 Châteauneuf du Pape Blanc is significantly better than most of its peers. It displays an attractive ripe pear–scented nose, a fleshy, honeyed fruitiness, and excellent purity, acidity, and body. It should be drunk up.

The 1993 Châteauneuf du Pape exhibits a deep, ruby/purple color, a big, spicy, herbal, curranty nose, and sweet, round, generous, medium- to full-bodied flavors with moderate tannin in the finish. It will be at its peak of maturity in 2–3 years and last for 10–12 years. Built on a smaller scale, the 1992 Châteauneuf du Pape possesses a spicy, herb and black cherry fruitiness, medium body, a more compact flavor profile than the 1993, and a soft, clean finish. It is a good commercial effort that should be drunk up.

HENRI BONNEAU * * * * *

1991 Châteauneuf du Pape	D	89
1992 Châteauneuf du Pape Cuvée Marie Beurrier (see note)	D	91
1990 Châteauneuf du Pape Cuvée Marie Beurrier	D	94
1990 Châteauneuf du Pape Cuvée des Celestins	E	100
1991 Vin de Table	B	87

For the handful of people who are permitted into the ancient, dark labyrinth that serves as the cellars of Châteauneuf du Pape's resident philosopher/genius winemaker, it is the experience of a lifetime. Henri Bonneau, who is never shy about offering his opinion on any subject, from overcropping to fishing to French politics, produces what I consider to be the greatest wine of the appellation. Long before I met Monsieur Bonneau his wines were so prized by European insiders that there was already a waiting list. He has gradually increased the amount of wine he is willing to sell to America, which now accounts for approximately 100+ cases of his profound Châteauneuf du Pape Cuvée des Celestins, and 100–200 cases of his Châteauneuf du Pape Cuvée Marie Beurrier. Bonneau decided not to make any Marie Beurrier or Celestins in 1991, and will probably not offer a Celestins in 1992. He was optimistic that there would be a Celestins in 1993, and based on the half-dozen *foudres* I tasted from in his cellars, it looks to be a fine vintage, although not as powerful and rich as his extraordinary 1988, 1989, and 1990.

Networking readers with excellent contacts may be able to run down a bottle of the 1990 Châteauneuf du Pape Cuvée des Celestins that was released in May 1994. It was bottled much later than normal because of its extraordinary power and intensity. The purple/black color and huge nose of smoked game, exotic spices, licorice, and massive quantities of jammy black fruit are mind boggling. The wine, which hits the palate with phenomenal concentration and extract, is mammothly constituted. It must be well over 15% alcohol (forget what the label indicates), yet all that power is buried beneath lavish quantities of rich fruit. Now that it is in the bottle, the 1990 looks to be even better than Bonneau's amazing 1989. Good luck in trying to find any! Although it is not ready for prime-time drinking, who can resist it? This monumental Châteauneuf du Pape should last for 30+ years. If you can't find the Celestins, don't despair. The 1990 Châteauneuf du Pape Cuvée Marie Beurrier is nearly as profound. Bonneau feels it is lighter than his Celestins, but in Bonneau's vocabulary, *light* means "massive"! This huge, concentrated wine possesses much of the same character as the 1990 Celestins, but it is slightly less tannic and powerful. However, it is unquestionably a wine of extraordinary size and enormous extract and richness. It should drink well for 20+ years.

In 1991 Bonneau declassified all of his Celestins and Marie Beurrier into a regular bottling of 1991 Châteauneuf du Pape. It is an amazingly good wine, and among the strongest offerings I tasted from this dreadful vintage. It offers an earthy, leathery, meaty, rich nose, dusty tannin, full body, and shockingly intense extract for such an appalling vintage. It admirably demonstrates what late-harvested fruit from old, low-yielding vines can produce under deplorable harvest conditions. Drink it over the next decade. There is also a cuvée of 1991 Vin de Table, which is a rustic, robust, exuberant wine with a huge nose of spicy, peppery, herbs, and leathery fruit, full body, and soft tannin. A delicious, mouth-filling wine, it would embarrass many Châteauneuf du Papes from a top vintage!

Note: There is likely to be a Cuvée Marie Beurrier in 1992, but not a Celestins. I tasted four different cuvées, all of them ranging from 14.2% to 15.2% natural alcohol. All of them exhibited overripe aromas of *sur-maturité,* and bouquets of jammy black cherries, apricots, and peaches. Full bodied, intense, and moderately tannic, it should be an excellent Châteauneuf du Pape. But Bonneau was not sure whether he would call it Cuvée Marie Beurrier, or simply label it as a straight Châteauneuf du Pape. The wine will not be released for at least a year.

PATRICK ET CHRISTOPHE BONNEFOND * * * *
1992 Condrieu Côte Chatillon D 88

I did not taste Bonnefond's 1993, but they unquestionably made one of the finest wines of the vintage in 1992. The wine possesses excellent ripeness, a honeyed, peach/apricot fruitiness, a succulent, fat, chewy texture, and copious amounts of glycerin, alcohol, and fruit in the long finish. Drink it over the next year.

LE BOSQUET DES PAPES * * * *

1993 Châteauneuf du Pape	C	88
1992 Châteauneuf du Pape	C	86
1993 Châteauneuf du Pape Cuvée Chantemerle	D	92
1990 Châteauneuf du Pape Cuvée Chantemerle	D	96

Madam Boiron and her husband produce stylish, complete, complex Châteauneuf du Pape that can be drunk when released, yet my experience suggests they have a track record of maturing gracefully for 10–15 years. The 1993 Châteauneuf du Pape appears to be a very good wine, with a dark ruby color, a sweet, fragrant bouquet of black fruits, herbs, and spices, excellent concentration, full body, fine richness and ripeness, and a supple finish. It should drink well for 7–10 years. The 1992 Châteauneuf du Pape is a round, delicious wine with surprising robustness and power for a Châteauneuf from this medium-weight vintage. The wine exhibits a sweet, jammy fruitiness and medium to full body. Drink it over the next 7–8 years.

In 1990 this estate launched its first luxury cuvée made from old vines and bottled without filtration. There are approximately 400 cases each of the 1990 and 1993 Châteauneuf du Pape Cuvée Chantemerle. The just-released 1990 Cuvée Chantemerle is a spectacular wine with a staggering perfume of black fruits, minerals, pepper, and flowers. Exceptionally rich, with stupendous concentration, and a viscous texture suggesting low yields and old vines, this profound Châteauneuf du Pape is delicious; it should last for two decades or more. An exceptional effort! The 1993 Cuvée Chantemerle looks to be nearly as compelling, although less powerful and alcoholic. It has a saturated, dark purple color and a sweet, perfumed nose of jammy black fruits, roasted herbs, and a chocolatey, earthy character. Superrich and full bodied, with high alcohol and moderate tannin, this chewy, brilliant wine should evolve for 15–20 years.

DOMAINE LA BOUISSIÈRE * * *

1993 Gigondas	C	86
1992 Gigondas	C	79

The dark-colored, backward, spicy, medium- to full-bodied 1993 Gigondas exhibits above-average quality, fine depth, and a spicy, moderately long finish. It should drink well for 7–8 years. The 1992 Gigondas reveals a pruny, herbal, tea-scented nose with hints of raspberry fruit. The wine is attenuated, with a compact flavor profile, and a short finish. Drink it over the next 2–3 years.

LUCIEN ET ANDRÉ BRUNEL-LES CAILLOUX * * * */* * * * *

1993 Domaine de la Becassonne Côtes du Rhône	A	86
1992 Domaine André Brunel Côtes du Rhône	A	90
1991 Domaine André Brunel Côtes du Rhône Cuvée Sommelongue	A	86
1993 Châteauneuf du Pape Les Cailloux	C	92
1992 Châteauneuf du Pape Les Cailloux	C	92
1993 Châteauneuf du Pape Les Cailloux Blanc	C	88

One of Châteauneuf du Pape's most energetic, competent, and talented proprietors, André Brunel has fashioned some beautiful wines from his vineyard holdings outside Châteauneuf du Pape. The 1993 Domaine de la Becassonne Côtes du Rhône, a dry white wine made from Grenache Blanc, Clairette, and Marsanne, reveals an attractive citrusy, floral bouquet, admirable concentration, medium body, and wonderful ripeness and length. I am not a great fan of white Côtes du Rhônes, but this personality-filled wine provides pleasure. Drink it over the next year.

The 1992 Domaine André Brunel Côtes du Rhône, an 80% Grenache/20% Syrah blend, is an awesome example of Côtes du Rhône from a difficult vintage. It exhibits a huge nose of kirsch and cassis, sweet, jammy, ripe, full-bodied flavors with superb concentration, and an expansive, chewy texture. Frankly, I mistook this wine for a high-class Châteauneuf du Pape rather than a Côtes du Rhône! This is a stunning wine, as well as an extraordinary wine bargain! Drink it over the next 5–6 years. The 1991 Domaine André Brunel Côtes du Rhône Cuvée Sommelongue includes 25% of Brunel's Châteauneuf du Pape Les Cailloux in the blend, giving the wine more intensity and richness. Made from 25-year-old vines of Syrah and Grenache, this spicy, peppery, black cherry–scented wine possesses good richness, medium body, and a moderately long finish. It should drink well for 2–3 years.

With respect to André Brunel's three current Châteauneuf du Pape releases, the 1993 Châteauneuf du Pape Les Cailloux Blanc, which has been barrel-fermented and bottled with minimal clarification, is about as good as white Châteauneuf du Pape gets. I am not a great fan of these monolithic, neutral-tasting wines, but this example offers a gorgeously ripe nose of honeyed tropical fruits, butter, and flowers, long, chewy, full-bodied flavors, a subtle touch of wood, and crisp acidity to keep everything fresh, vibrant, and well focused. Drink it over the next year.

The 1993 and 1992 red Châteauneuf du Pape Les Cailloux offerings are among the stars of these two vintages. The 1993 exhibits a dark ruby/purple color, a super nose of pure black raspberry fruit, licorice, herbs, and spice, explosive richness, superb ripeness, an opulent, chewy texture, and a long, full-bodied, intense finish with that wonderfully sweet jamminess that characterizes top-notch Châteauneuf du Pape in a fine vintage. It should drink well young and keep for 15+ years. More surprising is the 1992 Les Cailloux. Keep in mind that the cuvée I am describing is the one sold to importer Robert Kacher. It represents 850 cases of Brunel's oldest vines aged in one-third new oak. The wine is one of the superstars of what is an average- to a slightly above-average-quality vintage. It reveals an impressively saturated dark ruby/purple color, and a profound, sweet, exotic nose of black raspberries, spices, and sweet vanillin. Full bodied, dense, and concentrated, with gobs of glycerin, plenty of extract, and high alcohol, this decadently styled Châteauneuf du Pape should be drunk over the next 12–15 years.

DANIEL BRUSSET-LES HAUTS DE MONTMIRAIL * * * * *

1993	Cairanne Côtes du Rhône	A	87
1991	Cairanne Côtes du Rhône	A	87
1992	Gigondas Les Hauts de Montmirail	C	90
1991	Gigondas Les Hauts de Montmirail	C	89

Daniel Brusset is well known for producing rich, huge, full-bodied Gigondas wines from his Les Hauts de Montmirail estate. With respect to Brusset's 1992 Gigondas Les Hauts de Montmirail, the following notes apply only to the cuvée sold to the American importer. The wine reveals a dark ruby color and a forceful bouquet of sweet vanillin, toasty new oak, black fruits, herbs, and roasted nuts. Ripe and full bodied, with layers of jammy fruit, this supple, generously endowed Gigondas exhibits none of the dilution or vegetal character revealed by many wines of this appellation. An exceptional effort for the vintage, it should be drunk over the next decade. The 1991 vintage was dreadful in the southern Rhône, so one can imagine what severe selection, not to mention winemaking talent, it must have taken to fashion such an impressive wine. Produced from yields of only 18 hectoliters per hectare, Brusset's 1991 Gigondas Les Hauts de Montmirail displays a profound deep black/ruby color, and a huge, chocolatey, black cherry and herb nose that offers up sweet aromas of ripe, undiluted fruit. Full bodied, with layers of fruit and richness, this sumptuously ripe wine should drink well for 7–8 years. This is an amazing achievement given the vintage!

The 1993 Côtes du Rhône Cairanne, aged in 1-year old casks, exhibits a saturated dark ruby color, a big, spicy nose of herb, cedar, and black cherry scents, full body, superripeness, and a wonderful chewy, fat fruitiness that flows across the palate. This is a heady, delicious Côtes du Rhone for drinking over the next 2–3 years. Brusset included 20% of his oak-aged Gigondas in the 1991 Cairanne Côtes du Rhône. The result is a densely colored wine with a super nose of black raspberries, spicy pepper, and truffles. Deep, rich, medium-bodied flavors are loaded with fruit. The finish is all velvet and silk. Drink it over the next 2–3 years.

BERNARD BURGAUD * * * *

1992 Côte Rôtie	D	87
1991 Côte Rôtie	D	90

Bernard Burgaud's 1992 Côte Rôtie reveals an excellent deep garnet color with a purple hue, an evolved bouquet of herbs, black fruits, and damp earth, fine fatness, excellent richness, and medium to full body. The wine's flattering, soft style suggests it should be consumed over the next 7–8 years. It is a fine effort from a vintage that has produced more good wines than I initially believed. Burgaud's outstanding 1991 Côte Rôtie is a dense, opaque black/purple-colored wine with a powerful nose of black fruits, herbs, and flowers. Full bodied with super extraction, it offers a rich, authoritative, well-structured taste, and a whoppingly long, dramatic finish. With moderate tannin and terrific concentration, it should be drinkable now and last for 15 years.

CHÂTEAU CABRIÈRES * * */* * * *

1993 Châteauneuf du Pape Blanc	C	76
1992 Châteauneuf du Pape Cuvée Prestige	D	88

This estate is splendidly situated on the high plateau of Châteauneuf du Pape, adjacent to the appellation's famous estate of Mont-Redon. Both estates, because of the exceptional exposition of their vineyards, have the potential to produce the greatest wines of the appellation. Lamentably, neither appears inclined to exploit this position. Cabrières has made considerable progress since I first visited the estate a decade ago. The Châteauneuf du Pape Blanc still tends to be made in an understated, light style. Although pleasant, the 1993 is an uncritical, quaffing wine.

However, it appears the proprietor has lightened up on the fining and filtration of the red wines, as those cuvées have taken on more richness. The only red wine I tasted on my recent visit was the 1992 Châteauneuf du Pape Cuvée Prestige. It exhibits aromas of black olives, cassis, and Provençal herbs, a spicy, medium- to full-bodied palate, excellent richness, and a chewy texture. Long and succulent, with decent acidity and light tannin, it should be drunk over the next 7–8 years.

DOMAINE DE CAYRON * * * * *

1993 Gigondas	C	88
1992 Gigondas	C	?

This estate tends to produce blockbuster, superconcentrated Gigondas that are favorites of admirers of southern Rhône wines. The 1993 Gigondas should turn out to be nearly outstanding, although I cannot see it equaling the quality of proprietor Faraud's 1988, 1989, and 1990. The 1993 exhibits a saturated black/purple color, a highly extracted, earthy nose of truffle, roasted herb, and black cherry scents, rich, concentrated fruit, super length and ripeness, and a lush texture. On the other hand, the 1992 Gigondas appears to be a disaster in the making, with a singed, raisiny, vegetal nose, sweet, soupy flavors, and a lack of grip and focus. Since the outstanding 1990 has just been released, readers should be beating a path to their merchants to purchase that wine.

DOMAINE DE CHANTE PERDRIX * * * *

1993 Châteauneuf du Pape	C	89

Chante Perdrix's 1993 Châteauneuf du Pape appears to be one of the better wines of the vintage, exhibiting an exotic bouquet of overripe plums, black raspberries, olives, cedar, and floral notes. The wine possesses excellent to outstanding concentration, a lavish, corpulent, chewy texture, and a moderately long, supple finish. It should drink exceptionally well early and last for a decade.

CHAPOUTIER * * * * *

1993 Châteauneuf du Pape Barbe Rac	E	92
1992 Châteauneuf du Pape Barbe Rac	E	92
1991 Châteauneuf du Pape Barbe Rac	E	87
1993 Châteauneuf du Pape La Bernardine	E	91
1992 Châteauneuf du Pape La Bernardine	E	91
1993 Condrieu	D	88
1992 Condrieu	D	89
1992 Cornas	C	89
1993 Côte Rôtie	D	88
1992 Côte Rôtie	D	90
1993 Côte Rôtie Cuvée Mordorée	E	90
1992 Côte Rôtie Cuvée Mordorée	E	92
1991 Côte Rôtie Cuvée Mordorée	E	100
1993 Côtes du Rhône Belle Ruche	C	86
1993 Côtes du Rhône Belle Ruche Blanc	C	85
1992 Côtes du Rhône Belle Ruche Blanc	C	87
1993 Crozes-Hermitage Les Meysonniers	C	87
1992 Crozes-Hermitage Les Meysonniers	C	85
1993 Hermitage Chante Alouette	D	91
1992 Hermitage Chante Alouette	D	94
1993 Hermitage Cuvée de l'Orvée	E	96+
1992 Hermitage Cuvée de l'Orvée	E	98
1991 Hermitage Cuvée de l'Orvée	E	96
1993 Hermitage Le Pavillon	E	93
1992 Hermitage Le Pavillon	E	95

1991	Hermitage Le Pavillon	E	100
1993	Hermitage La Sizeranne	D	90
1992	Hermitage La Sizeranne	D	92
1991	Hermitage La Sizeranne	D	94
1992	Hermitage Vin de Paille	?	96+
1991	Hermitage Vin de Paille	?	98
1993	St.-Joseph Deschants	C	89
1992	St.-Joseph Deschants	C	89
1993	St.-Joseph Deschants Blanc	C	83
1992	St.-Joseph Deschants Blanc	C	87

I can state without hesitation that Michel Chapoutier is one of this planet's bright shining lights. He has taken over a *négociant*/domaine known for producing rustic, coarse, frequently oxidized wines and through his own vision of quality (absolutely no compromises) he has propelled his family's firm to the pinnacle of wine quality. This is especially apparent in the 1993 vintage, a year about which Michel Chapoutier claims, "One could truthfully say it was the worst vintage of the century."

Chapoutier, who reduced his vineyards' yields to frightfully modest levels of 15 to 30 hectoliters per hectare, halted the use of all chemicals, and began to farm organically, has become a true believer in the biodynamic principles of farming. I must admit that I had always thought of biodynamic farming as the extreme of organic farming, appearing to be some sort of sorcery or cult activity. But consider the three most outspoken advocates of biodynamic farming, Lalou Bize-Leroy, Nicolas Joly, and Michel Chapoutier.

In 1993 where mildew and rain destroyed 80%–90% of the grapes in Hermitage, only 10% of Chapoutier's vineyards were damaged by rot. Moreover, Chapoutier's losses were restricted to those vines adjacent to his neighbors, all of whom relied on the use of chemicals. Chapoutier believes that the 1993 vintage will finally make skeptics realize the significance of biodynamics. For readers who want to pursue this subject, the classic treatise on biodynamic farming is *Agriculture* by Rudolph Steiner. It has been translated from its original language, German, to English by the Bio-Dynamic Farming and Garden Association, Inc., P.O. Box 550, Kimberton, PA 19442. Steiner's lectures on the subject, which were made in Germany in 1924, read as if one were listening to the teachings or rantings of some cult leader or wizard. Yet the proof of his beliefs is to be found in Chapoutier's 1993s. These wines stand *alone* in the northern Rhône by virtue of the fact that they are so much more successful than their peers. Chapoutier's 1993s taste as if they came from an excellent to exceptional vintage—impossible to explain except for his viticultural techniques.

Chapoutier's obsession with tiny yields and natural, pure wines that reflect the vineyard's *terroir*, soil, and varietal aromatic and flavor profile are well displayed in his current and up-coming white wine releases. The 1993 Côtes du Rhône Belle Ruche Blanc exhibits a lovely, citrusy, fresh, fruity nose, medium body, crisp acidity, and a tasty finish. The 1992 Côtes du Rhône Belle Ruche Blanc is richer and fuller, with wonderful vibrancy, loads of flavor, fine acidity, and a lively bouquet. Both wines should be consumed over the next 2–3 years.

This firm has begun to produce small quantities of Condrieu. The 1993 Condrieu displays an intense aroma of peaches, honey, and flowers. There is excellent acidity, medium to full body, and admirable concentration welded to a sense of elegance and grace. The richer 1992 Condrieu reveals a honeyed, floral, mineral component, fine acidity, and brilliant delineation and focus to its rich, medium- to full-bodied personality. Both Condrieu offerings will last for 3–4 years.

Chapoutier continues to turn out a Chablis-inspired white wine from his holdings in St.-Joseph. Both the 1992 and 1993 mineral-scented and -flavored St.-Joseph Deschants Blancs are beautifully made northern white Rhônes. The 1993 possesses a floral, fragrant, apricot/peachlike bouquet, medium body, excellent ripeness, chewy, fleshy fruit, and crisp acidity. It displays a natural, pure feel. The 1992 shares a similar peach/floral-scented nose, elegant, crisp, medium-bodied flavors, and beautiful precision and balance. Both wines should drink well for 5–7 years.

This firm makes outstanding white Hermitage. The 1993 Hermitage Chante Alouette is a large-scaled, thick, flowery, mineral, honeyed wine with a pronounced aroma of acacia flowers. Deep and full bodied, with gobs of fruit, it is a superb white Hermitage for drinking over the next 10–20 years. Even richer, the 1992 Hermitage Chante Alouette exhibits an intense, honeyed, vanillin, floral-scented nose. An immense, full-bodied wine loaded with fruit, glycerin, alcohol, and richness, it lingers on the palate for nearly a minute. It has the potential to last for 20–25 years. These wines, which can taste monochromatic and heavy alone, take on amazing vibrancy and life with food.

Readers lucky enough to have access to any of the 300–500 cases of the luxury cuvée called Hermitage Cuvée de l'Orvée should use whatever contact they have to latch on to a bottle or two of the 1993, 1992, or 1991. Made from Chapoutier's oldest vines on the Hermitage Hill (average age of 75 years), these are closed, mineral-dominated, honeyed wines that are completely dry but fabulously rich with an intensity and breadth of flavor that would embarrass many of Burgundy's Le Montrachets. The 1993 Hermitage Cuvée de l'Orvée was closed and reticent when I tasted it last spring. Made from yields of under 15 hectoliters per hectare, it hits the palate with extraordinary precision and richness. The whoppingly long finish lasts for more than 60 seconds. It is a magnificently rich, unevolved, huge, dry white wine that should last for two to three decades. I thought the 1992 Hermitage Cuvée de l'Orvée was virtually perfect. A huge, buttery, honeyed, lychee nut–scented nose is as exotic as it is profound. The wine possesses a richness and intensity that not only expresses the essence of the stony, granite soil found on the steep hillsides of Hermitage, but also extraordinary concentration. Full bodied, fabulously rich, and well delineated, this is the greatest white Hermitage I have tasted. Although the 1991 Hermitage Cuvée de l'Orvée may turn out to be as compelling, at the moment it is not as exotic. The wine is full bodied and stunningly rich, with honeyed, peach blossom, acacia flower, mineral scents, and unctuously textured, thick, rich, chewy flavors. The acidity provides zest and vibrancy. Once again, the finish lasts for up to a minute. It should last for 20–30 years. These are monumental dry white wines!

Chapoutier's 1993 Côtes du Rhône Belle Ruche, made from extremely low yields (25 hectoliters per hectare) of 100% Grenache, possesses a berry-scented nose, medium body, soft, elegant, expansive flavors, and a supple texture. Its perfume and softness are very Pinot-like. Drink it over the next 5–6 years.

Because Michel Chapoutier makes so many outstanding northern Rhône wines, his Châteauneuf du Pape receives less attention than it merits. There are two cuvées of Châteauneuf du Pape, La Bernardine and a luxury cuvée called Barbe Rac. In 1993, the southern Rhône's harvest occurred under primarily ideal conditions, in complete contrast to the north. The 1993 Châteauneuf du Pape La Bernardine exhibits a dark ruby/purple color, a big, peppery, spicy, cassis-scented nose, rich, full-bodied flavors, superb depth and ripeness, and a long, heady, glycerin-imbued, alcoholic finish. It is a potentially outstanding example of Châteauneuf du Pape that should last for 15 or more years. The black/purple-colored 1992 Châteauneuf du Pape La Bernardine offers a gorgeously perfumed bouquet of exotic spices, herbs, pepper, leather, and black fruits. Made from only 15 hectoliters per hectare, this dense, magnificently concentrated wine possesses fabulous ripeness, gobs of rich, chewy fruit, and a long, heady, spectacular finish. Soft enough to be drunk, it should evolve gracefully for two decades.

Both the 1993 and 1992 Châteauneuf du Pape Barbe Rac offerings are awesome. Made from vines planted in 1901 and 1902, there are only 250 cases of each vintage—for the world! The opaque purple/black-colored 1993 Châteauneuf du Pape Barbe Rac reveals a sensational, huge nose of sweet black raspberry jam, roasted herbs, and pepper. It is reminiscent of a great Rayas, only more intense. Full bodied, with 15% natural alcohol, this mammothly constituted wine is one of Châteauneuf's superstars in 1993. The 1992 Châteauneuf du Pape Barbe Rac comes across as possibly more profound, probably because it is lower in acidity as well as a year older. The saturated purple color is followed by a huge, soaring nose of spices, cedar, licorice, black fruits, and smoke. There is great richness, immense body, an unctuous, chewy texture (from microscopic yields), and a blockbuster finish. This is an amazing Châteauneuf du Pape! Both of these wines will drink well young, yet will evolve for 30 years. The 1991 Châteauneuf du Pape Barbe Rac is one of the two or three best wines I tasted in Châteauneuf du Pape from this dreadful vintage. It displays a deep ruby color, a spicy, herbaceous-scented nose, and rich, curranty fruit. Although it possesses a more narrow flavor profile, there is medium to full body, as well as excellent concentration and ripeness. With more noticeable tannin than the 1992 and 1993, it will benefit from 2–3 years of cellaring; it should keep for 15 years.

Chapoutier is a significant vineyard holder in the northern Rhône. His St.-Joseph Deschants has become the firm's most enticing wine bargain, as it resembles a mini-Hermitage in its richness and complexity. The 1993 St.-Joseph Deschants (a horrendous vintage for just about every northern Rhône producer) is a black/purple-colored wine with exceptional intensity, a smoky, licorice-, mineral-, and cassis-scented nose, and medium- to full-bodied, ripe, supple flavors. It should drink well for 10–15 years. The 1992 St.-Joseph Deschants (made from less than 20 hectoliters per hectare) exhibits a fabulous bouquet of powdered flint, black currants, herbs, and smoke. Rich and full bodied, with superb ripeness and density, this is a beautifully pure, delicious wine for drinking over the next 10–15 years.

Chapoutier also excelled with the firm's Crozes-Hermitage Les Meysonniers in 1993. Made from less than one ton per acre, it displays a dark ruby/purple color, a spicy, crisp, subtlely herbaceous and smoky nose, tasty, medium-bodied, ripe flavors, low acidity, and an attractive, fleshy finish. Drink it over the next 7–8 years. The 1992 Crozes-Hermitage Les Meysonniers possesses a wonderful, sweet, peppery, herbaceous-scented nose, expansive, jammy flavors, excellent ripeness, admirable purity, and an attractive chewiness from high glycerin and low yields. Drink it over the next 7–8 years.

This firm makes a tiny quantity of Cornas. A fine effort, the black-colored 1992 Cornas offers a sweet nose of roasted nuts, black cherries, and spice. Medium to full bodied, with moderate tannin, and an alluring suppleness, this is a Cornas for drinking in its first decade of life.

With respect to Côte Rôtie, Chapoutier's aim is to produce an exceptionally perfumed, soft, elegant cuvée of Côte Rôtie, and a luxury cuvée that takes Côte Rôtie's black raspberry, exotic fruitiness and elegance to the limits of intensity, à la Marcel Guigal's La Mouline. The 1993 Côte Rôtie is a dark-colored, light-bodied wine built for finesse and style. With its moderately intense bouquet of spices, black pepper, and olives, this medium-bodied, soft, pretty wine should be drunk over the next 7–8 years. The 1992 Côte Rôtie shares a similar smoky, black olive–scented nose, medium body, wonderful black cherry and black raspberry flavors, and a burgundian-like expansiveness and softness. It should be drunk during its first decade of life.

Chapoutier has fashioned three terrific luxury cuvées of Côte Rôtie Mordorée. The lightest of the trio, the 1993 Côte Rôtie Cuvée Mordorée, exhibits an intense perfume of cassis, Provençal herbs, sweet oak, and black fruits. The wine is voluptuously textured and soft, with a superb sense of elegance and finesse, and more concentration and richness than I found in most 1993 Côte Rôties. The amazingly rich 1992 Côte Rôtie Cuvée Mordorée is a candidate for Côte Rôtie of the vintage. It possesses a fabulous, exotic bouquet of cassis, minerals, olives, coffee, and spicy new oak. Staggeringly rich, with layers of voluptuously textured fruit, this sumptuously styled wine is already complex and delicious; it promises to last for 10–15 years. I thought Chapoutier's 1991 Côte Rôtie Cuvée Mordorée to be in the same class as the great single-vineyard Côte Rôties made by Marcel Guigal (e.g., La Mouline, La Turque, and La Landonne). The Mordorée is more akin to La Mouline in its seductive, otherworldly fragrance and layers of sweet, expansive, velvety-textured fruit. Only 400 cases were made of this saturated purple-colored wine. Its huge bouquet and spectacularly rich, layered personality offer an astonishing example of what low yields from a naturally farmed vineyard and an unfined, unfiltered winemaking philosophy can achieve.

Chapoutier is proud to boast that while he is now the largest vineyard owner in Hermitage (85 acres, or about one-fourth of the entire appellation), he is only third when it comes to wine production! The black-colored 1993 Hermitage La Sizeranne reveals a huge, roasted, smoky, dense nose, superb richness and ripeness, full body, and layers of flavor. This magnificent wine will need to be cellared for 5–6 years; it has the potential to last for three decades. Keep in mind that in 1993, Gérard Jaboulet declassified all of his Hermitage La Chapelle and Gérard Chave was not sure whether he would estate-bottle any Hermitage under his name. Other producers were unsure of what they would do when I visited them several months ago. Chapoutier's Hermitage tastes as if it came from 1990, not 1993—a testament, in his opinion, to the biodynamic farming principles enunciated by Rudolph Steiner seventy years ago. The 1992 Hermitage La Sizeranne displays a smoky, roasted herb–, tar-, and cassis-scented nose, rich, full-bodied, fabulously concentrated flavors, and a blockbuster finish. The amount of tannin in the finish suggests 3–5 years of cellaring is required; it is a candidate for two decades of aging. The 1991 Hermitage La Sizeranne is spectacular. The saturated color and beautifully pure nose of cassis, licorice, and roasted scents are followed by a full-bodied, superconcentrated wine that is every bit as concentrated and intense as the 1990. It will drink well for 25 or more years.

In a short period of time (Michel's first vintage was 1989) Chapoutier's Hermitage Le Pavillon has become a wine of mythical proportions. Produced from extremely old vines, some dating from the mid-nineteenth century, with yields averaging under 15 hectoliters per hectare, this is the richest, most concentrated and profound wine made in Hermitage. There are rarely more than 500 cases. The 1993 Hermitage Le Pavillon exhibits an opaque black color, and a penetrating fragrance of minerals, spices, black fruits, and vanillin. Superconcentrated, full bodied, and dense, with layer upon layer of fruit, this is a nearly perfect wine from an appallingly horrendous vintage. The similarly styled 1992 Hermitage Le Pavillon offers an exotic nose of Asian spice, minerals, licorice, and essence of black currants and black cherries. Amazingly rich and intense, with a finish that lasts for over a minute, this is another monumental effort. It is slightly lower in acidity than the 1993 and 1991, but wow, what intensity and length! The 1991 Hermitage Le Pavillon follows the pattern of the 1989 and 1990—it is another perfect wine. The saturated black/purple color is followed by a compelling bouquet of spices, roasted meats, and black and red fruits. Enormously concentrated yet with brilliant focus and delineation to its awesomely endowed personality, this extraordinary wine should age effortlessly for 30+ years.

Chapoutier's efforts at making sweet Vin de Paille from raisined and dried-out Hermitage grapes have been highly successful. The 1992 Hermitage Vin de Paille exhibits a buttery, honeyed nose, viscous, thick, superrich flavors, and a syrupy finish with enough acidity to give it uplift and vibrancy. The 1991 Hermitage Vin de Paille possesses a more roasted, honeyed marmalade character, awesome concentration and richness, and a blockbuster finish. These wines, which are only available in half-bottles (that should be enough to serve at least 25–30 people), will last for 50+ years.

As a postscript, I am a novice when it comes to old marcs, but Chapoutier is releasing a Cuvée Marc Senior, a rare brandy that has been aging in a barrel for 30 years with no water additions. It is the product of a long process of evaporation and reduction. It smelled absolutely sublime and the flavors were as velvety as any frightfully high-alcohol, after-dinner drink could be. Fans of these fiery beverages should be on the lookout for this rarity.

DOMAINE DE LA CHARBONNIÈRE * * *

1993	Châteauneuf du Pape	C	84
1992	Châteauneuf du Pape	C	86
1993	Châteauneuf du Pape Blanc	C	85
1993	Châteauneuf du Pape Vieilles Vignes	D	87
1992	Châteauneuf du Pape Vieilles Vignes	D	88

Proprietor Michel Maret continues to provide evidence that this is an estate to be taken seriously. The 1993 Châteauneuf du Pape Blanc offers an attractive, fresh, pure bouquet of floral and pear scents, medium to full body, lively fruit, an admirable mid-palate, and an attractive finish. Drink it over the next year.

In both 1992 and 1993, the Domaine de la Charbonnière produced a regular cuvée and a special cuvée of old-vines Châteauneuf. The lightest cuvée, the 1993 Châteauneuf du Pape, is an attractive, supple wine. The richer, fuller 1993 Châteauneuf du Pape Vieilles Vignes exhibits more noticeable tannin. It should drink well for a decade.

The 1992s are both successful wines for the vintage. The 1992 Châteauneuf du Pape reveals a moderately saturated ruby color, and a flattering, perfumed bouquet of jammy red and black fruits, herbs, and spice. Soft, fat, fleshy, and chewy, this is a low-acid, heady wine for drinking over the next 5–6 years. The 1992 Châteauneuf du Pape Vieilles Vignes possesses a dark ruby color, as well as an impressively rich fragrance of black and red fruits, leather, cedar, and herbs, excellent extraction, full body, adequate acidity, and light tannin in the finish. This multidimensional wine is among the more concentrated efforts of the vintage. Drink it over the next 10–12+ years.

DOMAINE GÉRARD CHARVIN * * * *

1993	Châteauneuf du Pape	C	91
1992	Châteauneuf du Pape	C	87
1990	Châteauneuf du Pape	C	93
1992	Côtes du Rhône	B	87

I am happy to see that an American importer has picked up the wines of Laurent Charvin, a producer I was fortunate to run across several years ago in Châteauneuf du Pape. Charvin produces wines from low-yielding old vines and bottles them unfiltered for his American importer. This knockout 1992 Côtes du Rhône possesses a huge, intense bouquet of black raspberries, excellent ripeness, medium to full body, and a chewy, supple texture. It is better than many Châteauneuf du Papes. Since it was bottled without filtration, all of the vineyard's character and the fruit's intensity are alive and well! Drink this beauty over the next 3–4 years.

Charvin has turned in an exemplary performance in 1993. With its intense raspberry-dominated bouquet and flavors, the 1993 Châteauneuf du Pape displays the essence of old-vine, raspberrylike flavor that recalls the great wines from the microscopic Pomerol estate of Lafleur. A deeply saturated dark ruby color is followed by a sweet, expansive, concentrated wine with moderately firm tannin in the long finish. While approachable young, it will reach its plateau of maturity in 4–5 years and last for up to 15 years. The 1992 Châteauneuf du Pape exhibits Charvin's telltale bouquet of ripe, pure, rich, raspberry fruit. Full bodied, with excellent depth, an expansive, supple texture, low acidity, and a velvety finish, it should be drunk over the next 7–8 years.

Charvin's offering was one of the stars of my tastings of 1990 Châteauneuf du Papes. Charvin has made 166 cases from one lot that was bottled completely unfiltered for the American market. The wine found in France has been filtered, so this is another example of a dedicated, small importer getting an appreciably better cuvée of wine exclusively for the American market. Charvin, who owns 23 acres of old vines (the average age is 45, with some nearly 70 years of age), makes Châteauneuf du Pape from 85% Grenache and the balance Mourvèdre and Cinsault. His 1990 is a blockbuster wine. The dark, saturated ruby color is followed by an unevolved, superrich nose of roasted herbs, nuts, black fruits, and Asian spices. Spectacularly rich, with an unctuous, multidimensional flavor profile, and a chewy, robust finish, this big wine (14.5% alcohol) exhibits marvelous balance, as well as the potential to last for 10–15 years. Domaine Charvin's style is close in spirit to that of Château Rayas and Henri Bonneau.

J. L. CHAVE * * * * *

1992	Hermitage	E	89
1991	Hermitage	E	89
1993	Hermitage Blanc	D	85
1992	Hermitage Blanc	D	88
1991	Hermitage Blanc	D	90
1991	Hermitage Cuvée Cathelin Red Artist's Label	EE	96
1990	Hermitage Cuvée Cathelin Red Artist's Label	EE	99+

Gérard Chave is grooming his talented son, Jean-Louis, to ultimately take over the helm of this extraordinary domaine that has been making brilliant wines since the late fifteenth century. Chave was depressed by the horrible weather that battered the 1993 crop, but in tasting through all of his 1993 red cuvées, it appeared to me that enough fine wine was made that he should bottle a Hermitage. When I saw him in the spring he was unsure as to whether or not he would declassify the entire production or make a 1993 Hermitage cuvée from his best lots. Certainly the wine I tasted was as good as his delicious 1987, and to my mind, better than his 1984 and 1981.

There will be an estate-bottled 1993 Hermitage Blanc. Although it is light by Chave's standards, it exhibits some of the flowery, peachlike fragrance achieved by white Hermitage. Medium bodied, with higher than normal acidity, this is Chave's lightest white Hermitage since the 1984. However, it is a tasty, elegant wine that will need to be drunk in its first decade of life. The 1992 Hermitage Blanc is a more powerful, richer wine, with full body, a peach/apricot- and honey-scented nose, admirable concentration, and a long, opulent finish. It should drink well for 10–15 years. The fat, rich 1991 Hermitage Blanc offers a big, juicy nose of acacia flowers and honeyed fruit, medium to full body, and loads of flavor. While it is not as broadly flavored or as powerful as the 1990 and 1989, it is a delicious, well-made, excellent example of white Hermitage that should last for 10–15 years.

Chave's 1992 red Hermitage should turn out to be outstanding. Softer than most vintages, it exhibits a dark ruby color, a big, ripe nose of cassis fruit with peppery, olivelike overtones, and medium- to full-bodied, rich, concentrated flavors. When I tasted it the blend was just completed, and this looks to be an outstanding Hermitage that will mature quickly by Chave's standards. Unlike the 1990, no patience is required; it should drink well during its first 15–20 years of life. The beautifully elegant, stylish 1991 red Hermitage displays an open-knit bouquet of red and black fruits, spices, flowers, and smoke. With excellent richness and medium to full body, this deep, graceful wine should turn out to be slightly richer than the 1987, and perhaps equal to the sumptuous 1982. It should last for 20–25 years.

In 1991, Chave made 2,500 bottles of a Hermitage Cuvée Cathelin that is significantly richer and more profound than the classic cuvée. It offers an opaque dark purple color, and a huge nose of cassis, vanillin, smoke, and flowers. Full bodied, dense, and powerful, this deeply concentrated, rich, magnificent Hermitage will benefit from 3–5 years of cellaring and last for 25–30+ years.

The 1990 Hermitage Cuvée Cathelin is more influenced by new oak than the classic cuvée, but the oak takes a backseat to the wine's superb raw materials. The wine exhibits fabulous concentration, richness, intensity, and length, as well as a mind-boggling finish. I cannot say it is superior to the classic cuvée. The Cuvée Spéciale possesses more of an international new oak signature. The 1990 Cuvée Spéciale should not be drunk for 10–15 years; it has the potential to last for 30–50 years! Only tiny allotments of the 1990 and 1991 Cuvée Spéciales were allocated to the American market, as Chave has a loyal European clientele that have made his wines among the rarest and hardest to find.

DOMAINE DU CHÊNE-M. AND D. ROUVIÈRE * * * *

1992 Condrieu	D	88
1993 Condrieu Cuvée Julien	D	87
1992 St.-Joseph Anais	C	86
1991 St.-Joseph Anais	C	87

Owned by the Rouvière family, this estate produced a fine 1992 Condrieu. It exhibits a lovely, exotic, honeysuckle- and tropical fruit–scented bouquet, admirable richness, medium to full body, a fat, fleshy character, and a lush finish. Drink it over the next year. The sweeter 1993 Condrieu Cuvée Julien represents this domaine's Vendange Tardive style. There is excellent ripeness, a sense of freshness, full body, and copious amounts of heady alcohol and sweetness in the finish.

Rouvière's top cuvée of St.-Joseph, the Anais, is a successful wine in 1992. Aromas of black cherry fruit are accompanied by spicy, vanillin, oaky notes. The wine is round, supple, and medium bodied, with low acidity and a lush, chewy texture. Drink it over the next 6–7 years. The 1991 St.-Joseph Anais is a gorgeously ripe, richly fruity, smoky, medium- to full-bodied, luscious wine. This soft, velvety-textured St.-Joseph offers excellent purity, attractive, toasty vanillin notes, and creamy richness. Drink it over the next 3–5 years.

LOUIS CHEZE * * *

1992 Condrieu	D	88
1991 St.-Joseph Cuvée Caroline	C	88

The 1992 Condrieu is fat, honeyed, soft, low in acidity, and ideal for drinking over the next 6–12 months. The excellent, nearly outstanding, 1991 St.-Joseph Cuvée Caroline reveals superb cherry fruit aromas, with smoky oak in the background. There is wonderful richness, great ripeness, surprising opulence, and a long, luscious finish. Drink this lovely St.-Joseph over the next 7–8 years.

AUGUSTE CLAPE * * * *

1993 Cornas	D	87
1992 Cornas	D	87
1991 Cornas	C	90

An assemblage of grapes from Clape's different vineyard sites, the 1993 Cornas exhibits a dark ruby color, a sweet bouquet of cassis and minerals, moderate tannin, medium body, and excellent depth and richness. Moreover, there is a chocolatey/licorice component to the flavors of this successful wine. It should drink well for 7–10 years. Clape's 1992 Cornas is one of the few successful wines of the vintage. It reveals deep color, a licorice-, mineral-, and cassis-scented nose, medium body, and a touch of overripe blackberries. With its deep, smoky, robust flavors, and moderately long, tannic finish, it will benefit from 1–2 years of cellaring and will keep for 10–12 years. Clape's 1991 Cornas is more elegant and less concentrated than Noël Verset's (his friend and competitor). It exhibits medium to full body, excellent depth, and a spicy, moderately tannic finish. Drinkable now, it should improve and last for 8–10 years.

DOMAINE LES CLEFS D'OR * * * *

1993 Châteauneuf du Pape	C	86
1992 Châteauneuf du Pape	C	84

One of my favorite domaines has made a very good 1993 and an atypically light, understated 1992. The 1993 Châteauneuf du Pape offers an attractive raspberry- and cherry-scented nose, medium to full body, fine depth and ripeness, and a soft, velvety-textured finish. Drink it over the next 5–8 years. The easygoing 1992 Châteauneuf du Pape is a light-bodied wine with adequate concentration and a smooth finish. Drink it over the next 3–4 years.

DOMAINE CLOS DU CAILLOU * * * */* * * * *

1993 Châteauneuf du Pape	?	91
1993 Châteauneuf du Pape Blanc	C	82

Proprietor Claude Pouizin's 1993 Châteauneuf du Pape Blanc is a competently made, solid, crisp, medium-bodied wine with decent fruit. Drink it over the next year. The exotic, jammy, honeyed, apricot- and orange-scented 1993 Châteauneuf du Pape, which displays elements of overripeness, is an exotic, full-bodied, lush, heady wine with wonderful intensity, and a big, rich finish that oozes with glycerin, alcohol, and fruit. It should be drinkable when released and last for 7–8 years. Proprietor Pouizin did not present his 1992 for tasting.

CLOS DU JONCUAS * * *

1993 Gigondas	B	86
1992 Gigondas	B	76

The deeply colored, surprisingly tannic, full-bodied, chewy, one-dimensional but immensely mouth-filling 1993 Gigondas should be a 10- to 15-year wine. With respect to the 1992 Gigondas, a leafy, vegetal component accompanies its coffee, spicy, fruitcake flavors, hard tannin, and pruny, high-alcohol finish. Although awkward and perplexing, it is not unlikable. Drink it over the next 4–5 years.

CLOS DU MONT-OLIVET * * * */* * * * *

1993 Châteauneuf du Pape	C	88
1992 Châteauneuf du Pape	C	85
1993 Châteauneuf du Pape Blanc	C	86

Joseph Sabon and his sons have fashioned a 1993 Châteauneuf du Pape Blanc that is one of the better wines I tasted from a generally undistinguished group of 1993 whites. It reveals a big, honeyed, floral-scented bouquet, full-bodied, rich flavors, good freshness, and a clean finish. Drink it over the next year.

Clos du Mont-Olivet's 1993 Châteauneuf du Pape exhibits a dark ruby color, an enticing bouquet of black olives, Provençal herbs, cherries, and pepper. A seductive, sweet, expansive, unstructured wine with little tannin, but plenty of juicy, succulent fruit, it should be drunk over the next 7–8 years. The 1992 Châteauneuf du Pape possesses a spicy, roasted, cherry-scented nose, surprisingly fine grip and structure for a 1992, medium body, and good depth and ripeness in the moderately long finish. Drink it over the next 7–10 years. None of the estate's special cuvée, Cuvée du Papet (superb in 1989 and 1990), was made in either 1992 or 1993.

CLOS DE LA MURE * * * *

1992 Côtes du Rhône	A	85
1990 Côtes du Rhône	A	87

The attractive, spicy, cherry-scented 1992 Côtes du Rhône offers medium body, a supple texture, and chewy glycerin in the finish. The wine's brightness and vibrancy suggest it should drink well for 1–2 years. By the way, proprietor Michel's vineyard is located in Mondragon, the sleepy village that contains my favorite southern Rhône Valley restaurant —La Beaugravière, owned by proprietor/chef, Jullien, and worth a detour for any Rhône wine enthusiast.

Proprietor Michel has turned out an absolutely luscious Côtes du Rhône in 1990. It possesses a deep color, a huge bouquet of ripe berry fruit, herbs, and black cherries, full-bodied, spicy, supple flavors, and a rich, intense finish. This is a juicy example of just what sensational values still exist in the southern Rhône. Drink it over the next 2–3 years.

CLOS DES PAPES * * * * *

1993 Châteauneuf du Pape	D	91
1992 Châteauneuf du Pape	D	89+
1993 Châteauneuf du Pape Blanc	C	85

The Avril family produce classic, long-lived Châteauneuf du Papes that handsomely repay cellaring. I have been a longtime admirer of this estate and have had many a great bottle, with the 1966, 1970, 1978, 1989, and 1990 (especially the latter) standing out as terrific wines. Because of intelligent winemaking, low yields, and strict selection, Avril has turned out two of the finest wines of these vintages. The 1993 Châteauneuf du Pape is a classically made wine with a sweet, peppery, spicy, herb and black cherry nose, full-bodied, rich, moderately tannic flavors that explode on the back of the palate, and a long, tightly knit, rich finish. As is often the case with Clos des Papes, this wine will benefit from 3–4 years of cellaring and will keep for 15 or more years. One of the most concentrated wines I tasted from the vintage, the 1992 Châteauneuf du Pape exhibits a dark ruby/purple color, a big, spicy, black cherry– and cedary-scented nose, superb richness, a chewy, unctuous texture, and moderate tannin in the long finish. Cellar it for 2–4 years and drink it over the subsequent 15 years. It should merit an outstanding rating in several years.

The 1993 Châteauneuf du Pape Blanc reveals a straightforward nose of ripe pears, medium body, and fine purity and acidity. It should be drunk over the next year.

CLUSEL-ROCH * * * */* * * * *

1992 Côte Rôtie	D	89
1991 Côte Rôtie	D	88

1991 Côte Rôtie Les Grandes Places	D 94+
1990 Côte Rôtie Les Grandes Places	D 94

When I first visited Domaine Clusel-Roch over a decade ago, Gilbert Clusel's father was running the estate, and, to put it mildly, I was disappointed with the quality level I found. However, that was 15 years ago, and recent vintages of Clusel-Roch have convinced me that this is one of the new stars of this small appellation. It was not easy to make a 1992 Côte Rôtie this rich, ripe, and complex. However, Gilbert Clusel decided to use all of the fruit from his best vineyard, Les Grandes Places, in the 1992 regular cuvée, resulting in a rich wine. Aged in small barrels of which about 35% are new, this unfiltered 1992 Côte Rôtie reveals a saturated dark ruby/purple color, a moderately intense nose of cassis, pepper, herbs, and spice, medium to full body, outstanding richness and ripeness, moderate tannin, and admirable purity and length. This fleshy, meaty Côte Rôtie can be drunk now or aged for 10–12 years. The 1991 Côte Rôtie Les Grandes Places is a spectacular Côte Rôtie. The opaque purple color is followed by lavish aromas of sweet, jammy cassis, herbs, Asian spices, and black pepper. The wine possesses extraordinary richness, great density and purity, full body, and an overwhelming sense of proportion and elegance. Copious amounts of tannin are well integrated in the wine's velvety texture. Clusel-Roch made one of the finest 1990 Côte Rôties, and the 1991 appears to be as noteworthy. It will be at its plateau of maturity in 3–5 years and will keep for 15–20. Wow!

The 1991 Côte Rôtie reveals a dark ruby/purple color and a big nose of violets, black raspberries, and sweet, smoky scents. The wine exhibits gorgeous levels of opulent fruit, medium to full body, adequate acidity, and a chewy, rich finish. Drink it over the next 7–10 years. The stupendous 1991 Côte Rôtie Les Grandes Places possesses a saturated purple/black color and a spectacular nose of grilled meats, Asian spices, black fruits, and new oak. Superbly concentrated, with low acidity and layers of ripe, rich fruit, this full-bodied, stunningly rich, pure wine should drink well for 15 years.

JEAN-LUC COLOMBO * * */* * * * *

1992 Cornas	C 86
1993 Cornas Les Ruchets	D 88
1992 Cornas Les Ruchets	D 89
1991 Cornas Les Ruchets	D 92

Colombo has made some minor adjustments in the vinification and upbringing of his wines. In the lighter, more trouble-plagued vintages of 1992 and 1993 the maceration period was extended for nearly a month. In addition, in 1993 Colombo did his malolactic fermentation in barrel. Moreover, he has thrown away his filter and only fines his wines. The results are richer, more complete and interesting wines that are now among the finest of the appellation. Colombo's controversial use of new oak casks (80% new oak and 20% 1-year-old barrels are routinely employed) met with skepticism early in his career. He appears to have now found the best method of integrating the flavors of oak into the wine without undermining the character of Cornas. Colombo's 1992s and 1993 are candidates for the most successful wines of the appellation.

The 1993 Cornas Les Ruchets exhibits a soft, ripe, round, attractive bouquet of peppery black currants and cherries. The wine is medium bodied, with excellent depth, an interesting spicy character, surprising length, and moderate tannin. It will benefit from 2–3 years of cellaring and will keep for 10–12 years.

In 1992 there are two Cornas cuvées. The supple 1992 Cornas offers attractive new oak in its straightforward bouquet of black cherries and roasted nuts, with its low acidity, and a tasty, chunky feel. Drink it over the next 7–8 years. The 1992 Cornas Les Ruchets is one of the best wines I tasted from Cornas. The wine possesses an attractive, spicy, toasty, cassis-scented nose, rich, earthy, concentrated flavors, medium to full body, adequate acidity, and a soft, opulent finish. This is undoubtedly a top-notch success for this year. It should drink well for at least a decade.

The 1991 Cornas Les Ruchets boasts a nearly opaque dark ruby/purple color, a tremendous nose of black fruits (raspberries and plums), Provençal herbs, and subtle, toasty new oak. Rich and full bodied, with layers of fruit, low acidity, and a voluptuous texture, this rich, concentrated Cornas reveals surprising finesse and complexity for a wine from this appellation. Yet, it in no way does it lose what the French call "typicity." It should drink well for 10–12 years.

DANIEL COMBE * * *

1990 Côtes du Rhône Vignoble de la Jasse	A	86

Made just to the north of Châteauneuf du Pape, this is a generously endowed, pure, richly fruity, supple wine bursting with aromas and lavish quantities of red and black fruits. It goes down the gullet oh so easily! Drink this bargain over the next 2–3 years.

COURBIS * * *

1993 Cornas Champelrose	?	84
1992 Cornas Champelrose	?	76
1992 Cornas Sabarotte	?	85

Maurice and Dominique Courbis produced a light- to medium-bodied 1993 Cornas Champelrose with attractive, moderately intense raspberry and cherry fruit. Soft and already evolved, this lightweight Cornas should be drunk over the next 3–4 years. The 1992 Cornas Champelrose reveals more dilution, a mushroomy, earthy quality (rot?), light body, and dusty, hard tannin in the finish. It lacks fruit and depth. The 1992 Cornas Sabarotte is cleaner, with a solid, foursquare personality. It should drink well for 4–6 years.

YVES CUILLERON * * * * *

1993 Condrieu	D	90
1992 Condrieu	D	87
1992 Condrieu Les Chaillets de l'Enfer	D	90
1993 Condrieu Les Chaillets Vieilles Vignes	D	93
1993 Condrieu Les Eguets Vendange Tardive	D	93
1993 St.-Joseph Blanc	C	89
1992 St.-Joseph Cuvée Prestige	C	90
1991 St.-Joseph Cuvée Prestige	C	89

Yves Cuilleron has emerged as one of the stars of the northern Rhône. It is a dead heat as to whether Cuilleron or André Perret makes the most lavishly rich, exotic, and complex Condrieu. Cuilleron offers numerous cuvées, all of which are at least excellent. Even the 1993 Condrieu is a superb wine, with great fruit, a big, honeyed, exotic bouquet, and full-bodied flavors that ooze richness and character. It is a wine to drink during its first 1–2 years of life. The spectacular 1993 Condrieu Les Chaillets Vieilles Vignes is as concentrated and intense as Viognier can get. Still unevolved (a good sign for 3–4 years of evolution), it makes a blockbuster impact on the palate with enormous levels of extract, glycerin, alcohol, and fruit. Don't miss this dry, wonderfully ripe, lavishly rich wine! The immense, sweet 1993 Condrieu Les Eguets Vendange Tardive is also impressive. It is exceptionally rich, with terrific extraction, as well as balance and freshness. What does anyone eat with a wine of such enormous proportions?

Although ripe, tasty, and medium to full bodied, the 1992 Condrieu is less exotic and complete when compared with the 1993. The 1992 Condrieu Les Chaillets de l'Enfer (I did not see this wine in 1993) is a rich, full-bodied, unctuously textured, thick Condrieu with enough acidity to provide focus, and superrich, concentrated flavors. Again, it presents difficulties when matching with food, but who can ignore such a dramatic, ostentatious wine? All of Cuilleron's Condrieus should be consumed over the next 2–4 years.

Cuilleron has also turned in a fine effort with his 1993 St.-Joseph Blanc. Made from a blend of Marsanne and Roussanne, this wine reveals a honeyed, cherry-scented nose, excellent richness and definition, and a creamy texture to accompany the dry, surprisingly long finish. Drink it over the next several years.

The two red wine cuvées are terrific, as well as reasonably priced. The 1992 St.-Joseph Cuvée Prestige is made from Cuilleron's oldest vines. Its healthy, dark ruby/purple color is accompanied by a broad aromatic display of black fruits, herbs, and vanilla. Wonderfully rich, expansive, and concentrated, this full-bodied, velvety-textured wine should drink well for a decade. There is a spicy, peppery, herbal side to the abundant quantities of cassis fruit found in the 1991 St.-Joseph Cuvée Prestige. The wine is finely tuned, with admirable underlying acidity, excellent concentration, and a rich, medium- to full-bodied, long, moderately tannic finish. It will undoubtedly turn out to be as good as the 1992, although it is more structured and firmer.

DOMAINE DE LA DAYSSE * * *

1993 Gigondas	C	86
1992 Gigondas	C	82

In both 1992 and 1993, Domaine de la Daysse produced soft, easygoing, round wines with the 1993 revealing more depth, medium body, and an attractive black raspberry, earthy nose. The soft, straightforward 1992 possesses adequate depth and a decent finish. There is no known American importer for this producer.

REMY DIFFONTY * * * *

1992 Châteauneuf du Pape	C	87

Remy Diffonty has a reputation as Châteauneuf du Pape's leading curmudgeon. I have only met him once, and he did not exhibit a great deal of enthusiasm for roving wine taster/critics seeking information. However, I have always enjoyed his wines and have several vintages in my cellar. The oldest, the 1970, is just beginning to show some fatigue. Diffonty produces a full-bodied, high-alcohol, boldly styled Châteauneuf du Pape. The 1992 is an immensely pleasing wine with a knockout nose of roasted coffee, herbs, and red and black fruits. Powerful and full bodied, with a lush, herb-tinged, black cherry fruitiness, and gobs of glycerin and alcohol, it is not a wine to sip while sitting poolside.

DUMIEN-SERETTE * * * *

1991 Cornas	C	90

This tiny producer owns only 3.2 acres of vines that boast an average age of 35 years. After 12 months in large oak *foudres* the wine is bottled unfiltered. The first vintage I tasted from proprietor Gilbert Serette, the 1991, possesses a saturated purple/black color, a rich nose of truffles, black cherries, and other ripe red and black fruits, full body, exceptional richness, a layered feel on the palate, and a long, surprisingly supple, voluptuous finish. There is plenty of extract, but none of the ferocious tannin frequently seen in Cornas. Drink it over the next 10–12 years.

DOMAINE DE L'ESPIGOUETTE * * * *

1993 Côtes du Rhône Plan de Dieu	A	87
1991 Côtes du Rhône Plan de Dieu	A	86
1990 Côtes du Rhône Plan de Dieu	A	87
1991 Côtes du Rhône Syrah Vieilles Vignes	A	86
1993 Côtes du Rhône Vieilles Vignes	A	87+
1991 Côtes du Rhône Vieilles Vignes	A	85
1990 Côtes du Rhône-Villages	A	83
1991 Vin de Pays	A	85
1990 Vin de Pays	A	85

The excellent domaine of Bernard Latour generally produces immensely satisfying, full-bodied wines that are typical of the highest quality level of the Côtes du Rhône appellation. These two 1993s are the best wines produced at Domaine de l'Espigouette since 1990. The 1993 Côtes du Rhône Plan de Dieu exhibits an intense, saturated dark ruby/purple color, an unevolved but promising nose of earthy, black cherry fruit, medium to full body, a supple texture, excellent concentration, and a long, soft finish. This young wine possesses 4–6 years of aging potential. Although more concentrated, the peppery 1993 Côtes du Rhône Vieilles Vignes is more tannic and less flattering at present. Muscular, rich, and deeply colored, with plenty of extract and promise, it is a candidate for 5–8 years of cellaring.

This estate is one of the most reliable in the Rhône Valley. The fact that they made such competent wines in vintages such as 1991 (an exceptionally difficult year in the southern Rhône) is indicative of their seriousness. Although these 1991 offerings are less powerful and concentrated than their 1989s and 1990s, they are ripe and fruity. For starters, there is the 1991 Vin de Pays, a rich, ripe, dense, peppery, black cherry–scented and –flavored wine that is meant to be consumed over the next several years. As all of these wines do, it offers a gutsy mouthful of wine. The big, spicy 1991 Côtes du Rhône Vieilles Vignes is more rustic, but is well made and ideal for consuming over the next 1–2 years. The excellent 1991 Côtes du Rhône Syrah Vieilles Vignes reveals a bouquet redolent of smoked herbs, hickory, and cassis. Tasty, soft, and supple, with excellent ripeness and a heady finish, it should be drunk over the next 2–3 years. The 1991 Côtes du Rhône Plan de Dieu is the most complete of these wines. There is more intensity to the bouquet, and the flavors are fuller and longer in this medium- to full-bodied, peppery, spicy, pure, well-made wine with copious quantities of red and black fruits, and a soft finish. Drink it over the next 1–2 years.

The 1990 Vin de Pays is a surprisingly deep, big, chunky wine with gobs of flavor, and a chocolatey, roasted, black cherry–scented bouquet. It is hard to believe that for $6 one can find loads of fruit, a full-bodied texture, and plenty of grip and character. This fabulous value should drink well for at least another 3–4 years. I even liked it better than proprietor Bernard Latour's 1990 Côtes du Rhône-Villages. While the latter wine is solid, ripe, peppery, and spicy, it did not have the depth of the Vin de Pays. The 1990 Côtes du Rhône Plan de Dieu is a big, meaty, chocolatey, robust wine, with aromas of roasted cassis and nuts, chewy, intensely concentrated flavors, and a long, robust, heady finish. Drink this beauty over the next 4–5 years.

DOMAINE FARJON * * *

1993 Condrieu	D 84

Domaine Farjon's 1993 Condrieu's citrusy, lemon blossom bouquet suggests young vines. The wine displays fine ripeness, medium body, and a dry, straightforward finish. Drink it over the next year.

DOMAINE DE FENOUILLET * * * *

1993 Côtes du Rhône Beaumes de Venise	A 87
1991 Côtes du Rhône Beaumes de Venise	A 85
1990 Côtes du Rhône Beaumes de Venise	A 87
1992 Côtes du Ventoux	A 86

The Domaine de Fenouillet is a new discovery. With quality this good and prices so low, consumers with access to the wines of the Domaine de Fenouillet should derive a great deal of satisfaction. The 1993 Côtes du Rhône from the small town of Beaumes de Venise is an excellent white Côtes du Rhône, with a floral- and apricot-scented bouquet, dry, rich, medium-bodied flavors, and a crisp, lusty finish. Drink it over the next year.

Among the red wines, there is a delicious, supple, herb- and berry-scented 1992 Côtes du Ventoux that requires drinking over the next 2–3 years, and a richer, more expansive, velvety-textured 1991 Côtes du Rhône Beaumes de Venise made from 80% Grenache, 15% Mourvèdre, and 5% Cinsault. This attractive wine is unquestionably a success for this tough vintage. The 1990 Côtes du Rhône Beaumes de Venise offers a big, spicy, herb and black cherry nose, medium- to full-bodied flavors, impressive ripeness, and a velvety, smooth, alcoholic finish. Drink it over the next 2–3 years.

FERRATON PÈRE ET FILS * * * *

1991 Hermitage Cuvée des Miaux	D 89+
1990 Hermitage Cuvée des Miaux	D 96

I previously rated the 1990 Hermitage Cuvée des Miaux 90 points, indicating that I thought it was the finest Hermitage Ferraton has made. I have recently tasted it twice, once in France and once stateside, and it was markedly superior to my original review. Small quantities are still available. From what is unquestionably the greatest Hermitage vintage since 1961, this wine is black in color, with a huge, developing bouquet of jammy cassis, mineral, spicy, floral, and licorice scents. Massively endowed, with frightfully high levels of glycerin, extract, and tannin, this is an old-style, superconcentrated, beautifully pure, well-delineated Hermitage for drinking between 2005 and 2040.

Although Ferraton's 1991 Hermitage Cuvée des Miaux does not possess the gargantuan size of the 1990, it is a highly successful wine that should merit an outstanding rating with another 4–5 years of cellaring. The densely saturated color is followed by a big, spicy, peppery, cassis-scented nose, full-bodied, tannic flavors, and a tough, tannic finish. Made from immensely impressive raw materials, this wine is oh, so backward. Do not touch a bottle before the end of the century; it should last through the first three decades of the twenty-first century.

FONT DE MICHELLE * * * *

1993 Châteauneuf du Pape	C 87
1992 Châteauneuf du Pape	C 87
1993 Châteauneuf du Pape Blanc	B 86

1993 Châteauneuf du Pape Cuvée Étienne Gonnet	C	91
1992 Châteauneuf du Pape Cuvée Étienne Gonnet	C	89

This consistently excellent domaine is well worth seeking out in all but the worst vintages. They are one of the most successful practitioners of white Châteauneuf du Pape. The 1993 exhibits a perfumed, honeyed, floral bouquet, attractive fruit, medium to full body, and a wonderfully fresh, forceful, alcoholic finish. Drink it over the next year.

In certain vintages the Gonnet brothers produce two cuvées, their Cuvée Classique and a selection from the richest vats and/or the oldest vines; it is called Cuvée Étienne Gonnet. Interestingly, this selection was made in both 1992 and 1993. Most consumers are likely to encounter the regular cuvée. The lovely, round, seductive 1993 Châteauneuf du Pape offers a deep ruby color, an excellent bouquet of herbs, black fruits, and spice, low acidity, and loads of glycerin and alcohol in the corpulent finish. Drink it over the next 5–6 years. The 1993 Châteauneuf du Pape Cuvée Étienne Gonnet exhibits toasty vanillin (from new oak casks), an intense, black cherry–scented bouquet, fat, ripe, opulent flavors, chewy texture, and plenty of heady alcohol and glycerin in the lusty finish. The copious amounts of tannin are buried under lavish quantities of fruit. This looks to be an outstanding Châteauneuf du Pape.

The 1992 Châteauneuf du Pape boasts a wonderfully sweet bouquet of cedar, herbs, coffee, and cherries. Medium to full bodied, with supple texture, this is a generously endowed, concentrated, plump wine for drinking over the next 6–7 years. The 1992 Châteauneuf du Pape Cuvée Étienne Gonnet displays an attractive olive-, black cherry–, and herb-scented nose, excellent ripeness, full body, soft tannin, and a heady finish. Drink it over the next decade. A friend told me that in the state of Minnesota magnums of the outstanding 1990 Cuvée Étienne Gonnet are being sold at $30–$35 a bottle. Subscribers in that state should put that information to good use, as 1990 is a terrific example of this luxury cuvée.

DOMAINE DE FONT-SANE * * * * *

1993 Gigondas	C	88
1992 Gigondas	C	87

One of the finest Gigondas estates, the Domaine de Font-Sane was successful in 1993. To their credit, they also made an excellent wine in the distressingly bad vintage of 1992. The dark ruby/purple-colored 1993 Gigondas offers an excellent nose of cassis, licorice, and flowers, medium- to full-bodied flavors, moderate tannin, and excellent purity and ripeness. It should drink well for 10–12 years. The 1992 Gigondas exhibits a surprising amount of purple in its color (it is one of the darkest wines of the vintage), admirable ripeness, medium body, moderate tannin, and a rich, chewy finish. It requires 1–2 years of cellaring and should keep for 10–12 years. Unquestionably, this is a top success for the vintage.

CHÂTEAU FORTIA * * *

1992 Châteauneuf du Pape	C	77
1993 Châteauneuf du Pape Blanc	C	72

This historic estate, once capable of making some of the most riveting wines of the southern Rhône, is going through tough times. The quality has declined steadily over the last decade or more. The last great wine from Château Fortia was their 1978. There have been above-average-quality efforts since then, especially the 1985, but the 1993 Châteauneuf du Pape Blanc is a barely acceptable wine with a sterile bouquet and nondescript, muted, neutral flavors. The 1992 Châteauneuf du Pape displays earthy, spicy, diluted flavors of dried fruit, tobacco, and herbs, medium body, and a simple, compact finish. What a shame!

DOMAINE LA FOURMONE-ROGER COMBE * * * *

1993 Gigondas	B	86
1992 Gigondas	B	74

The elegant 1993 Gigondas displays fine body and ripeness, and a spicy, clean, berrylike fruitiness. It will have to be drunk in its first 5–7 years of life. The light ruby/rusty-colored 1992 Gigondas reveals a vague bouquet of cedar and earthy fruit. Watery, soft, and light bodied, the wine's quality reflects the torrential rains that nearly destroyed the Gigondas vignerons in 1992.

LOU FRÉJAU * * *

1993 Châteauneuf du Pape	?	87

This property fashions good Châteauneuf du Pape (the 1985 is still delicious at 10 years of age). The 1993, the only sample proprietor Serge Chastan presented, boasts an excellent deep ruby color, a ripe olive– and black cherry–scented nose, medium to full body, admirable ripeness, soft tannin, and low acidity. It should drink well during its first 7–8 years of life.

DOMAINE DE GACHON-PASCAL PERRIER * * * * *

1991 St.-Joseph	C	91

Lovers of 100% Syrah wines from superold vines (40–60 years) should be sure to latch on to a few bottles of this Hermitage look-alike. Aged in 20% new oak casks and bottled unfiltered for the American importer, this magnificently scented (black cherries, herbs, licorice, and Asian spices), full-bodied, superconcentrated wine is one of the greatest St.-Josephs I have tasted. The wine's purity and intensity of flavor are wonderful to behold, and the finish lasts for over a minute. Approachable now, it promises to last for two decades. In 1991, many Rhône Valley appellations enjoyed greater success than they did in 1990 and 1989, especially the appellations of Côte Rôtie, Condrieu, St.-Joseph, and Cornas, all situated on the western bank of the Rhône River.

PIERRE GAILLARD * * *

1993 Condrieu	D	82

This light-bodied, compact, short Condrieu is pleasant in an understated, polite manner, and is elegant and cleanly made. Drink it over the next year.

DOMAINE DU GALET DES PAPES * * */* * * *

1993 Châteauneuf du Pape	C	80
1992 Châteauneuf du Pape	C	86
1993 Châteauneuf du Pape Blanc	C	78
1993 Châteauneuf du Pape Vieilles Vignes	D	86
1992 Châteauneuf du Pape Vieilles Vignes	D	87+

Proprietor Jean-Luc Mayard's wines often taste better out of bottle than they do from cask. Thus, the 1993 Châteauneuf du Pape, which tasted light and diluted, but pleasantly round and ripe, may improve after bottling. Although the 1993 Châteauneuf du Pape Vieilles Vignes exhibits more length and body, it appears straightforward and monolithic for a special cuvée. It offers a peppery, herbal, cherry-scented nose, medium to full body, light tannin in the finish, and the potential for a decade of aging.

The 1992s appear to be better wines. The 1992 Châteauneuf du Pape reveals a sweet, juicy, herb-, black cherry–, and earthy-scented nose, medium- to full-bodied, expansive, round flavors exhibiting glycerin and fatness, and a soft, pleasant finish. The 1992 Châteauneuf du Pape Vieilles Vignes is more backward and structured, with excellent saturated dark ruby color, a spicy, restrained but rich nose, and full-bodied, moderately tannic, concentrated flavors. Cellar it for 2–3 years and drink it over the subsequent 10–15 years.

As for this property's white Châteauneuf du Pape, the 1993 is made in the same style as so many of the neutral, insipid white Châteauneufs. A straightforward, medium-bodied, uninteresting wine, it should be drunk soon. It is puzzling why this appellation, which can produce so many hedonistic, decadent, compelling red wines, produces so few outstanding white wines.

HENRI GALLET * * * */* * * * *

1992 Côte Rôtie	D	90
1991 Côte Rôtie	D	91
1990 Côte Rôtie	D	94

Made exclusively from 40-year-old vines from the Côte Blonde, Gallet's 1990 is a candidate for one of the great Côte Rôties of the good to very good 1990 vintage. Gallet, who used to sell all of his grapes to Marcel Guigal, bottled this wine after aging it in old oak *foudres*. The exceptionally dark color is followed by a sensational nose of jammy black fruits, smoke, licorice, and herbs. The spectacular richness, unctuousness, and viscous texture strongly suggest it is made from old vines and low yields. Layer upon layer of rich, jammy fruit is buttressed by moderate tannins and low acidity. This stunning Côte Rôtie should drink well for the next decade or longer. Wow!

The 1991, aged in both small oak casks (about 30% new) and *foudres,* and bottled unfiltered, represents the elegant, "Musigny" style that Côte Rôtie can sometimes achieve. It boasts a fragrant, intense bouquet of violets, cassis, cedar, herbs, and smoked duck. An exceptionally soft, velvety-textured Côte Rôtie, it may lack the 1990's power and extract, but it more than compensates for that deficiency with its finesse and perfume. I do not mean to imply this is a light-bodied wine lacking depth. It is a rich, complex, complete wine that is already drinking beautifully, yet promises to age gracefully for a decade. This is Côte Rôtie at its most seductive.

It is going to be difficult to find Côte Rôties this rich and complex from the rain-plagued 1992 vintage. Gallet has produced an open-knit, fragrant (aromas of black raspberries, peppers, and truffles) wine that should be drunk over the next 7–8 years. It has more in common with his seductive, compelling 1991 than the blockbuster, dense, concentrated, muscular 1990. Offering copious amounts of jammy, black cherry and raspberry fruit, the 1992 displays an exotic side (Gallet included about 8% Viognier in the blend), and a medium- to full-bodied, smooth-as-silk finish.

CHÂTEAU DE LA GARDINE * * * */* * * * *

1993 Châteauneuf du Pape	C	89
1992 Châteauneuf du Pape	C	89+

The Brunel family did not show me their white Châteauneuf du Pape, probably realizing I have consistently found it too oaky. The red wine cuvées continue to affirm this estate's ascendancy and commitment to making some of the finest wines of the appellation. Château de la Gardine has always made fine Châteauneuf du Pape, but consistency was not a strong characteristic. However, since the mid-eighties it has been one of the most reliable estates in Châteauneuf du Pape. In Châteauneuf du Pape's great years, for example 1989 and 1990, a cuvée aged in small oak casks from the oldest vines of the estate, called Les Générations, is produced. Readers should be aware that the 1990 was released in 1993. It is an extraordinarily rich, profound Châteauneuf du Pape that should age well for 20 years. It is unlikely that there will be a Cuvée Les Générations in 1993 or 1992. In both 1992 and 1993 Gardine has made classic, full-bodied, rich wines with considerable extract and concentration. The 1993 offers a deep, saturated ruby/purple color, and smoky new oak in the nose accompanied by forceful, jammy, black cherry, and peppery scents. Full bodied, with excellent depth and moderate tannin, it will benefit from 2–4 years of cellaring; it should keep for 15 years. The 1992 is one of the most tannic, concentrated, intense wines I tasted from that vintage. In fact, most 1992 Châteauneuf du Papes are ready to drink, but Gardine's will benefit from 2–4 years of cellaring given its ferocious tannin level. A top-flight effort for the vintage, it possesses a saturated, dark ruby color, a fragrant, black cherry, herb, leather, and toasty nose, full body, excellent concentration, and a long, spicy, closed finish.

DOMAINE DE LA GARRIQUE * * * *

1990 Vacqueyras	B 88

This late-released Vacqueyras from the superb 1990 vintage is a knockout. Proprietor Bernard has fashioned a big, rich, unfined and unfiltered wine that is loaded with fruit and finishes with a full-bodied blast of highly extracted fruit, low acidity, and sweet tannin. Drink this terrific Vacqueyras over the next 4–5 years.

VINCENT GASSE * * * */* * * * *

1991 Côte Rôtie Côte Brune	D 95
1990 Côte Rôtie Côte Brune	D 89

The United States has received a whopping 25 cases of this tiny (2.5 acres) estate's production. The vineyard, which abuts the famed La Landonne vineyard, has produced a black/ purple-colored 1991, with a promising, intense bouquet of jammy black currants, herbs, smoky bacon fat, and Asian spices, particularly soy sauce. Full bodied, with exceptional concentration and intensity, this layered wine possesses moderate tannin and a blockbuster, chewy finish. Cellar it for 2–3 years and drink it over the following two decades. Bravo!

The 1990 vintage is not the great vintage in Côte Rôtie that it is in St.-Joseph, Crozes-Hermitage, Cornas, and Hermitage. This excellent unfiltered wine has been aged in 25% new oak casks. Part of the vineyard consists of old vines in the La Landonne vineyard, which Gasse's neighbors, Marcel Guigal and René Rostaing, have exploited so successfully. This organically made wine possesses a huge nose of smoky bacon fat, roasted black fruits, and herbs. Spicy, rich, and fleshy, with low acidity, and a good inner core of ripeness and fruit, medium to full body, and a soft, rich finish, it should be drunk over the next 7–8 years.

J. M. GÉRIN * * */* * * *

1993 Condrieu	D 81
1992 Condrieu	D 86
1991 Côte Rôtie Champin Le Seigneur	D 89
1991 Côte Rôtie Les Grandes Places	D 93

Gérin has been fashioning excellent wines, so it is surprising that his 1993 Condrieu is dominated by toasty new oak. Beneath the heavy cosmetic overlay of wood the wine exhibits light body and some ripeness, but this is not an exciting Condrieu. On the other hand, the 1992 Condrieu reveals more fleshiness, less oak, and plenty of honeysuckle/peach/apricot fragrance. Medium to full bodied, with loads of chunky, fleshy fruit, high alcohol, and low acid, this is a delicious Condrieu for drinking over the next 2–3 years.

These are the two most impressive Côte Rôties Gérin has produced in nearly two decades. The 1991 Côte Rôtie Champin Le Seigneur displays a deep color, a sweet, herb- and black raspberry–scented nose, sweet, soft, ripe flavors, low acidity, and a ripe, round finish.

Although not a blockbuster wine, nor particularly concentrated, it does possess plenty of finesse, a succulent texture, and an affable personality. Drink it over the next 5–6 years. In 1991 Gérin's top cuvée of Côte Rôtie, Les Grandes Places (made from very old vines), boasts an opaque dark ruby/purple color, and a superb nose of jammy black fruits, exotic spices, smoke, and new oak. Rich, with layers of fruit, low acidity, and a spectacularly long finish, this voluptuously textured concentrated wine is a classic example of Côte Rôtie. It should drink well for the next 10–15 years.

DOMAINE DU GOUR DE CHAULE * * * *

1993 Gigondas	B	78

Readers should be looking for the excellent, sometimes outstanding, 1990 or excellent 1989 Gigondas from this top-notch producer. Those two wines are significantly fuller and richer than anything produced since. The medium-weight 1993 is a ripe, well-made wine that lacks the depth, power, and intensity of other efforts from this producer.

ALAIN GRAILLOT * * * */* * * * *

1992 Crozes-Hermitage	C	85
1991 Crozes-Hermitage	B	85
1993 Crozes-Hermitage Blanc	C	82
1992 Crozes-Hermitage Blanc	C	87
1992 Crozes-Hermitage La Guiraude	C	87
1991 Crozes-Hermitage La Guiraude	C	87
1992 Hermitage	D	86+
1992 St.-Joseph	C	85
1991 St.-Joseph	C	87

When I saw him in the spring of 1994, the talented Alain Graillot was depressed about his 1993s, as the mildew and rot resulting from the torrential rains had ruined the prospects for high quality. It remains to be seen what red wines will emerge from his cellars in 1993, as he had not yet decided whether to declassify his 1993 reds. The light 1993 white Crozes-Hermitage is pleasing in a straightforward, simplistic manner. It offers citrusy scents, medium body, and a crisp, short, clean finish. On the other hand, the 1992 white Crozes-Hermitage, from a vintage where most of the grapes were harvested before the damaging rains fell, exhibits an exotic, honeyed, apricot/peachlike aroma, fat, luscious, unctuously textured flavors, and plenty of power, body, glycerin, and alcohol in the finish. It is a big, dense, white Crozes for drinking over the next 3–4 years.

Graillot's 1992 red wine cuvées are not as profound as his 1991s, 1990s, or 1989s. They are soundly made, round, supple wines that will provide good near-term drinking. The 1992 Crozes-Hermitage reveals a spicy, ripe, cassis-scented nose, medium-bodied flavors, and moderate tannin in the finish. Drink it over the next 5–6 years. The 1992 Crozes-Hermitage La Guiraude possesses more toasty new oak, a black cherry– and herb-scented nose, rich fruit, a soft texture, low acidity, and light tannin in the finish. Drink it over the next 7–8 years.

The elegant, light-bodied, stylish 1992 St.-Joseph will offer friendly drinking over the next 5–6 years. I have never been an admirer of Graillot's Hermitage. While peppery, spicy, medium to full bodied, and tannic, the 1992 Hermitage lacks the depth and intensity expected from the finest wines of this hallowed appellation. Cellar this wine for 3–4 years (I hope the fruit doesn't fade) and drink it over the subsequent 6–7 years.

The 1991 Crozes-Hermitage displays a spicy, smoky, ripe, cassis-scented nose, medium body, soft tannin, and a supple, fruity finish. Drink it over the next 4–5 years. The 1991 Crozes-Hermitage La Guiraude exhibits more density and toasty vanillin from being aged in new oak barrels, as well as a medium-bodied, moderately tannic, more concentrated palate. Although soft enough to be drunk now, it possesses the potential to last for 8–10 years. For pure elegance and a satiny smooth texture, check out Graillot's 1991 St.-Joseph. Anyone who closely studies the 1991 northern Rhône vintage will discover that the western bank of the Rhône produced wines that are superior to those from right-bank vineyards. It is one of those anomalies that becomes apparent only after tasting across the field of play. The 1991 St.-Josephs are delicious wines, as are the 1991s from Condrieu and Côte Rôtie. This lush St.-Joseph offers gobs of pure black cherry and cassis fruit, medium body, light tannin, and a heady, opulently textured, long finish. Drink it over the next 4–5 years.

DOMAINE GRAMENON * * * * *

1992	Côtes du Rhône	A	89
1991	Côtes du Rhône	A	87
1990	Côtes du Rhône	A	88
1990	Côtes du Rhône Ceps Centenaire	A	92
1992	Côtes du Rhône Cuvée de Laurentides	A	92
1991	Côtes du Rhône Cuvée de Laurentides	A	89
1991	Côtes du Rhône Cuvée Syrah	A	90
1993	Viognier	B	88

For readers lucky enough to have access to the exquisite wines of Domaine Gramenon, these are sumptuous examples of Côtes du Rhône. They are also amazing bargains, competing with some of France's greatest wines. In 1992 there is no Cuvée Centenaire (from their 100-year-old vines) as it was blended into these two cuvées. The 1992 Côtes du Rhône possesses a decadent nose of melted chocolate, ripe cassis, and smoky, roasted aromas. Expansively flavored, with gorgeous glycerin and extract levels, as well as superb ripeness, this lavishly concentrated, opulently textured wine should drink well for 5–6 years. The spectacular 1992 Côtes du Rhône Cuvée de Laurentides, a blend of mostly Grenache with about 25% Syrah, is aged in 50% new oak barrels. Its huge black cherry– and black raspberry– scented, exotic nose with hints of coffee, hickory, and cedar is marvelous. A wine of exceptional definition, layers of concentrated fruit, and a lusty, wonderfully rich, mouth-filling finish, it is one of the most extraordinary wine bargains in the market. There are only a few hundred cases available for the American market, so move quickly if you want to secure any of this blockbuster Côtes du Rhône. Drink it over the next 7–8 years.

The key to proprietor Laurent's success in 1991 was a superstrict selection. Less than 50% of his production found its way into the different cuvées. The 1991 Côtes du Rhône, made from 80% Grenache, 10% Mourvèdre, and 10% Syrah, reveals a big, deep, ruby/ purple color, a spicy, chocolatey, peppery nose, deep, chewy, berry flavors, excellent rich-ness, and a long, ripe, heady finish. It should drink well for another 3–4 years. The 1991 Côtes du Rhône Cuvée de Laurentides, a 90% Grenache/10% Syrah blend, offers an explosive nose of black fruits, cedar, herbs, and licorice. It exhibits great richness and ripeness, medium to full body, soft tannins, and a long, stunning finish. Drink it over the next 4–5 years. The 1991 Côtes du Rhône Cuvée Syrah can blow away many 1990s (a superb vintage). To achieve this kind of color, flavor concentration, and complexity in a 1991 Syrah from the southern Rhône could not have been easy. The opaque, dark plummy/ purple color is indicative of a wine that has undoubtedly not been fined or filtered. The huge, smoky, black truffle– and cassis-scented nose is a knockout. Even more compelling is the decadent, multilayered richness, the medium- to full-bodied, velvety-textured, rich fruit, and the explosive finish. This sumptuous, ready-to-drink, 100% Syrah should continue to evolve for 6–7 years.

Laurent's late-released 1990 Côtes du Rhône Ceps Centenaire, made from 110-year-old Grenache vines, is a blockbuster Côtes du Rhône. In fact, I would willingly pay $20 for this remarkable wine. About 100 cases came into the United States, so it is sure to fly off retailers' shelves. The color is an opaque, saturated dark ruby/purple, and the nose leaps from the glass, offering up sweet, jammy aromas of kirsch, roasted chocolate-covered peanuts, and hickory. This unctuous, thick, rich wine reminds me of the spectacular Châteauneuf du Pape from Château Rayas. An unbelievable Côtes du Rhône, even considering the age of the vines and the tiny yields. Readers can be sure that if this wine came from the prestigious appellation of Burgundy or Bordeaux, it would be priced at $60–$75 a bottle and no one would blink an eye. Drink it over the next 10–12 years. The 1990 Côtes du Rhône, from vineyards near Valréas, is a rich wine with a huge nose of black fruits, herbs, and dried pit fruits. There are sweet, expansive, full-bodied flavors, wonderful purity and balance, and a gorgeously long, heady finish. Produced from an organically farmed vineyard, the wine was made from 70% Grenache and the rest a field blend of Cinsault, Syrah, and Mourvèdre. All of these wines are bottled unfined and unfiltered, so expect sediment to develop if they are not gulped down over the next year or two.

The 1993 Viognier from Domaine Gramenon is an excellent example of what this grape is capable of producing in the Rhône Valley. The wine has tropical fruit/spring flower garden scents, opulent, rich, full-bodied flavors, a soft texture, and a dry, heady, alcoholic finish. Drink it over the next year.

CHÂTEAU DU GRAND PRÉBOIS * * * *

1993 Côtes du Rhône	A	86

This Côtes du Rhône estate is owned by François and Jean-Pierre Perrin, who are more frequently associated with Château Beaucastel and La Vieille Ferme. Château du Grand Prébois turns out textbook, clean, richly fruity, ripe, medium- to full-bodied Côtes du Rhônes that are meant to be drunk when released, yet are capable of lasting for 3–4 years. The 1993 displays a healthy ruby/purple color, berry, herb, and pepper scents, and sweet strawberry and raspberry fruit flavors, with dusty, light tannin in the finish. Drink it over the next 3–5 years.

DOMAINE DU GRAND TINEL * * *

1993 Châteauneuf du Pape	C	86
1992 Châteauneuf du Pape	C	85

Producer Elie Jeune makes big, flavorful, soft, alcoholic wines that are easy to drink. As with most of the moderate- to large-sized Châteauneuf du Pape estates, Jeune follows the annoying practice of bottling wines as they are sold. The easy-to-drink 1993 Châteauneuf du Pape is a corpulent, fleshy, high-alcohol wine that lacks grip but provides interest. Consumption over the next 5–7 years is required. The plump, full-bodied, fleshy 1992 Châteauneuf du Pape exhibits a distinctive olive, herb, currant nose and plenty of alcohol and glycerin. Drink it over the next 5–6 years.

DOMAINE DU GRAPILLON D'OR * * *

1993 Gigondas	C	84
1992 Gigondas	C	73

The light, pleasant, medium-bodied, soft 1993 Gigondas should be drunk over the next 5–7 years. The 1992 Gigondas displays the light, dusty garnet color of the vintage, raisiny fruit, light body, and an alcoholic finish.

J. L. GRIPPAT * * */* * * *

1992 Hermitage Blanc	D	88
1992 St.-Joseph	C	73
1992 St.-Joseph Blanc	C	86

Grippat's two 1992 whites are both very good wines. Grippat has always demonstrated confidence in his white wine–making, so it is not surprising that the 1992 St.-Joseph exhibits a floral, honeyed, tropical fruit–scented nose, and tasty, medium- to full-bodied flavors revealing depth, low acidity, and admirable ripeness. Drink it over the next 2–3 years. The 1992 Hermitage displays a honeyed, pineapple, and floral note, unctuously textured, thick, fat flavors, low acidity, and an excellent, powerful, alcoholic finish. It is a weighty although fragile wine, so I would opt for drinking it over the next 2–4 years.

The only red wine cuvée I tasted was a vegetal, diluted, straightforward 1992 St.-Joseph. It is too herbaceous for my taste and lacks ripeness and depth. Drink it over the next 3–4 years.

DOMAINE DE LA GUICHARD * * * * *

| 1992 Côtes du Rhône Les Genests | A | 86 |
| 1991 Côtes du Rhône Les Genests | A | 86 |

One of the finest domaines of the Côtes du Rhône, Domaine de la Guichard fashioned an admirable cuvée in what was clearly a difficult year. Made from 60% Grenache and 40% Syrah from yields of only 25 hectoliters per hectare, the 1991 Les Genests reveals a deep ruby/purple color, as well as an excellent bouquet of black raspberries, pepper, and herbs. Medium bodied, with soft tannin, excellent ripeness, and a lush, generous, expansive personality, this gutsy Côtes du Rhône should drink well for 1–2 more years. Although not as concentrated as the 1989 and 1990, the 1992 Les Genests exhibits a ripe, black cherry–scented bouquet, and medium-bodied, moderately concentrated, supple flavors. It is a juicy style of Côtes du Rhône with the emphasis on fruit rather than spice. Arnaud Guichard bottled this 70% Grenache/30% Syrah blend unfiltered—customary practice here. Drink it over the next 2–3 years.

GUIGAL * * * * *

1990 Châteauneuf du Pape	C	90
1989 Châteauneuf du Pape	C	88
1993 Condrieu	D	89
1992 Condrieu	D	88
1991 Côte Rôtie Côtes Blonde et Brune	D	90
1990 Côte Rôtie Côtes Blonde et Brune	D	90
1993 Côte Rôtie La Landonne	EE	87
1992 Côte Rôtie La Landonne	EE	88
1991 Côte Rôtie La Landonne	EE	100
1990 Côte Rôtie La Landonne	EE	100

1993 Côte Rôtie La Mouline	EE	89
1992 Côte Rôtie La Mouline	EE	86
1991 Côte Rôtie La Mouline	EE	100
1990 Côte Rôtie La Mouline	EE	99
1993 Côte Rôtie La Turque	EE	88
1992 Côte Rôtie La Turque	EE	87
1991 Côte Rôtie La Turque	EE	100
1990 Côte Rôtie La Turque	EE	98
1991 Côtes du Rhône	A	82
1990 Côtes du Rhône	A	88
1993 Côtes du Rhône Blanc	A	86
1992 Côtes du Rhône Blanc	A	85
1991 Côtes du Rhône Blanc	A	79
1990 Gigondas	C	87+
1991 Hermitage	D	88
1990 Hermitage	D	94
1989 Hermitage	D	90+
1992 Hermitage Blanc	D	85
1991 Hermitage Blanc	D	87

Marcel Guigal's genius is nothing new to longtime readers, as I have been praising his wines for over 15 years. What is remarkable about Guigal is that despite the enormous empire he has built (both underground and above ground) in the drab, one-horse village of Ampuis, he remains as obsessed with quality as he was in 1978. The more accolades he garners, the harder he pushes himself to prove what heights the wines of the Rhône can achieve— whether it be a $9 bottle of Côtes du Rhône or a $125 bottle of single-vineyard Côte Rôtie. I am happy to report that Guigal has purchased one of the finest vineyards in Condrieu. In the next outstanding vintage for Condrieu, a single-vineyard wine will be released.

Guigal's standard white wine cuvées, especially his Côtes du Rhône, have shown continued improvement, although it was more difficult to turn out a concentrated, ripe wine in 1992 and 1993 than in 1990. The dry 1993 and 1992 Côtes du Rhône Blancs possess ripe, elegant fruit and medium body. Because of the addition of nearly 20% Viognier, they offer honeysuckle-scented bouquets and chewy flavors. Because of its freshness, I preferred the 1993 slightly more than the medium-bodied, tasty 1992.

Guigal's Condrieus are fermented in one-third new oak casks and two-thirds tank and then blended. The 1992 Condrieu is a lovely, medium-bodied wine with a honeyed, flowery-scented perfume. The wine reveals excellent ripeness, adequate acidity, and admirable depth and richness. It should be drunk over the next 2 years. The 1993 Condrieu should turn out to be as good as the 1992, but not up to the level of the 1991. It exhibits an attractive honeyed fatness, medium to full body, good rather than great depth and length, and wonderful freshness and elegance. Drink it over the next 1–2 years.

Both cuvées of white Hermitage I tasted were medium-bodied wines. The 1992 is made in a lighter, more straightforward style than usual, but the vintage has contributed to its character. The 1991 is a softer, riper, richer wine made in a precocious, flattering style. Both wines are best drunk in their first 7–8 years of life. Readers should also look for the 1990 white Hermitage, which I have reviewed in the past. It is the richest, most concentrated white Hermitage Guigal has recently produced.

Among the red wines, the outstanding bargain is the Côtes du Rhône. The just-released 1991 contains a hefty quantity of Syrah to beef it up, as this was a weak vintage in the southern Rhône. Firm, tannic, austere, and compact, the tannin finishes with harshness, suggesting the wine may dry out before it blossoms. While it is a solid, chunky wine, it is not comparable to the 1990 Côtes du Rhône. The latter wine, made from 25% Syrah, 45% Grenache, and the rest Mourvèdre and other Rhône varietals, offers an enticing bouquet of pepper, herbs, and red and black fruits. Soft, round, and medium to full bodied, with a mouth-filling texture and plenty of character, it is one of the best bargains in full-flavored red wines. Drink it over the next 3–5 years.

Guigal's other cuvées from the southern Rhône are consistently very good, and sometimes outstanding. The 1990 Gigondas (made from one-third Mourvèdre and two-thirds Grenache) possesses a deep, dark ruby color, a big, spicy, leathery, black fruit–scented nose, sweet, fat, full-bodied flavors, firm structure, moderate tannin, and an excellent finish. It will benefit from 12 months of aging and has the potential to merit a 90-point score in 2–3 years. It will last for 12–15 years. Guigal made top cuvées of Châteauneuf du Pape in both 1989 and 1990. The 1989 Châteauneuf du Pape would receive more attention if it were not for the blockbuster 1990. The 1989 reveals a dark ruby color, a big, dusty nose scented with black cherries, pepper, and herbs, excellent depth and richness, full body, soft tannin, and a chewy finish. A more complete wine, the 1990 Châteauneuf du Pape possesses richer fruit, more concentration, power, and unctuosity, and a blockbuster finish. As with all his southern Rhône cuvées, Guigal fashioned this wine from purchased juice. With its whopping 14% alcohol and big, spicy style, the 1990 should drink well for 14–15 years, perhaps longer.

Guigal's best recent red Hermitage, probably the best he has ever produced, is the 1990. Marcel Guigal believes it is the finest Hermitage made at this firm since 1955. I have followed the 1990 since I first tasted its component parts. It exhibits a nose of intense peppery, jammy, black raspberry fruit intertwined with scents of smoke, vanillin, and spices. With full body, great depth of fruit and purity, and considerable tannin in the finish, it is already approachable because of its long aging in *foudres* and small barrels. This rich, thick, concentrated wine should drink well for 20–25 years. Readers may still be able to find some of Guigal's 1989 Hermitage in the marketplace. Now that it has been in the bottle several years, the wine has taken on some firmness and the tannin appears more noticeable. Less concentrated than the knockout 1990, the 1989 reveals a tight but promising nose of minerals, black currants, and roasted herbs, great richness, full body, and significant power and tannin. The 1991 Hermitage, made primarily from two vineyards on Hermitage Hill called Méal and Bessards, is lighter than either the 1989 or the 1990. It is a medium-weight, elegant, ripe wine with expansive richness, and a moderately tannic finish. It should drink well for 10–15 years.

While every millionaire wine connoisseur would like to find a bottle or two of Guigal's single-vineyard Côte Rôties, the regular cuvée of Côte Rôtie is typical of the best wines of the vintage, as well as a barometer for the style of Côte Rôtie in a given year. The 1991 Côte Rôtie Côtes Blonde et Brune exhibits the soft, succulent, precocious character of this rich, velvety-textured vintage. Forward, with gobs of sweet, toasty oak intermingled with lavish quantities of cassis, smoke, and pepper, it is a lush, medium- to full-bodied wine with low acidity and ripe tannin. Already delicious, it should drink well for at least a decade. The 1990 Côte Rôtie Côtes Blonde et Brune has turned out to be outstanding. It offers a sweet, expansive, smoky, bacon fat–, cassis-scented nose, and rich, full-bodied, opulent flavors. It is neither as tannic as the 1988 nor as soft as the flattering, up-front 1989. Readers should give the 1989 Côte Rôtie Côtes Blonde et Brune a try, as it is the most developed, accessible, and delicious of the regular cuvées of Guigal's Côte Rôtie.

In previous issues of *The Wine Advocate,* I have gone into great detail on the single-vineyard Côte Rôties. Briefly, La Mouline's blend can vary, but it generally contains 8%–12% Viognier. La Mouline is the wine I find to possess the most intense perfume. It is also the most supple and seductive wine of this trio. While it is the shortest-lived, two decades of aging potential are possible, even in lighter-weight vintages. If La Mouline is the Mozart of the Guigal portfolio, La Landonne is the Brahms. Unlike La Mouline, which comes from the Côte Blonde, La Landonne's vineyard is planted in the heavier soils of the Côte Brune. Made from 100% Syrah, it is a dense, powerful, broodingly backward, chewy wine that only gives up its charm and character after 7–10 years of cellaring, even in light vintages. It has 30–40 years of aging potential and is the least attractive of the single-vineyard wines to consume young, although it is extremely easy to admire. La Turque, the newest of the Guigal single-vineyard Côte Rôties, also comes from a young vineyard in the Côte Brune, where the grapes are grown on an extremely precipitous slope with a 60+-degree gradient. It represents a synthesis in style between La Mouline and La Landonne. From time to time La Turque's blend will include 5%–7% Viognier. While it is not as tannic or muscular as La Landonne, it is usually as concentrated and as compelling as La Mouline. The small production of the three single-vineyard wines makes them nearly impossible to find. There are normally 300–500 cases of La Turque, 800 of La Landonne, and 600–700 of La Mouline.

When I saw Marcel Guigal in late March of 1994, the 1993s were clearly the lightest wines he had made from these three vineyards since 1984 or 1981. They will all turn out to be ripe, soft, medium-bodied wines, with only La Landonne revealing grip and tannin. Both La Mouline and La Turque possess medium ruby colors and sweet, ripe, jammy noses. Although 1993 was a tough vintage (the worst in the last 20 years for many northern Rhône producers), Guigal has turned out very good single-vineyard Côte Rôties that will need to be drunk during their first 5–10 years of life.

The 1992s are not as jammy as the 1993s, but they offer a more noticeable green pepper component. The 1992 La Mouline is reminiscent of the weedy, herbal, peppery, cassis-scented 1984 and 1981. Medium bodied and soft, it will require early drinking. The 1992 La Turque exhibits medium-bodied, soft, peppery, cassis fruit, good ripeness, but not much depth or intensity. The 1992 La Landonne is the most extracted of the single-vineyard wines, with moderate tannin, some sweetness and density, and better color saturation than the other cuvées. Readers should keep in mind that as impressive as these wines are when tasted from cask, they almost always become richer and more interesting after bottling. Ironically, to the north in Burgundy, most finished wines rarely taste as rich as they did prior to bottling. As enthusiastic as my notes are for Guigal's wines from cask, they always taste better out of bottle!

Readers should have already claimed Guigal's 1991 single-vineyard Côte Rôties. In 1991, Côte Rôtie enjoyed the most success of any appellation of France. The harvest was completed before the damaging rains arrived. The 1991 La Mouline appears to be another perfect wine in the making, with a staggering bouquet of violets, bacon fat, sweet cassis fruit, and toasty oak. The wine exhibits superb density. It is tasting even richer and more concentrated than it did during its first several years of life. With 8% Viognier in the blend and made from extremely low yields (only 400 cases produced), it is a phenomenal wine. I find it more seductive than the nearly perfect 1990. The 1991 La Turque behaves as if it wants to be the northern Rhône's answer to Richebourg and Musigny. However, with the exception of Domaine Leroy, you cannot find a Richebourg or Musigny with the richness and complexity of this awesome wine. The saturated dark purple color is followed by a wine that is surprisingly lighter in the mouth than its great flavor intensity and rich extraction would suggest. It is a winemaking tour de force in that Guigal has been able to cram phenomenal levels of fruit, complexity, and richness into this velvety-textured wine without causing it to taste heavy. It will be delicious when released, yet capable of lasting for 15 or more years. The 1991 La Landonne will provide multimillionaires with plenty of pleasure over the next 20 years. They can also debate whether it or the perfect 1990 is the better wine. The 1991's bouquet offers huge, smoky, new saddle leather, licorice, Asian spice, and meaty, cassis scents. Black in color, with layers of richness, huge body, massive extraction, and a phenomenal finish, it is another legend from Marcel Guigal. It will be the least precocious of the 1991s, needing until the turn of the century to open and develop; it should keep for 25–30+ years.

The 1990 single-vineyard Côte Rôties, which were released in the spring of 1994, are the Côte Rôties of the vintage. The year 1990 was not an easy one in this appellation because of the severe drought and heat wave that stressed the vineyards. As I have said previously, 1991 and 1989 are consistently better years for most of the Côte Rôtie producers. However, Guigal has turned in exceptional efforts with these three single-vineyard wines. The super-concentrated 1990 La Mouline is closer in style to the otherworldly 1988 than I would have thought. Extremely rich, with a huge, toasty nose of bacon fat, cassis, and floral scents, as well as phenomenally rich flavors, it is a wine known for its voluptuousness and extraordinary intensity. This amazing wine should drink well for 20+ years. The 1990 La Turque offers an overwhelming perfume of jammy black cherries, cassis, toast, and minerals. With its sweet, generous, incredibly harmonious personality, it is an unforgettable wine. With sweet tannin, low acidity, and one of the most velvety-textured, decadently rich palates I have encountered, this fabulous wine has a finish that lasts more than a minute. The 1990 La Landonne is a perfect wine! Fortunately, over 800 cases were produced. It possesses an opaque black color, and a huge nose scented with truffles, licorice, cassis, and pepper. While it is one of the most concentrated wines I have ever poured across my palate, it is perfectly balanced, with adequate underlying acidity, huge extraction of ripe fruit and tannin, and a phenomenal 70-second or longer finish. This is the essence of Syrah! Give this monumental wine 7–10 years of cellaring; it will last for 40–45+ years.

DOMAINE HAUT DES TERRES BLANCHES * * * *

1993 Châteauneuf du Pape	C 87
1992 Châteauneuf du Pape	C 86

Filicien Diffonty turns out elegant, burgundian-like Châteauneuf du Papes with expansive perfumes of raspberries, cherries, cedar, and herbs. They are medium- to full-bodied wines with soft, rich, fruity flavors, low acidity, and light tannin. Always delicious young, they have the uncanny ability to age well for 15 years. The 1993 displays gobs of raspberry fruit, an elegant personality, medium to full body, and a soft, ripe, round finish. The similarly styled 1992 exhibits sweet, jammy, raspberry flavors well displayed in an easy-to-appreciate format. Drink it over the next decade.

PAUL JABOULET-AINÉ * * * * *

1991 Cornas	C 87
1990 Cornas	C 86
1990 Côtes du Rhône Parallel 45	A 85
1990 Côtes du Ventoux	A 86
1990 Crozes-Hermitage Les Jalets	C 87

1991 Crozes-Hermitage La Mule Blanche	B	86
1990 Crozes-Hermitage La Mule Blanche	C	87
1991 Crozes-Hermitage Thalabert	C	87
1990 Crozes-Hermitage Thalabert	C	92
1991 Hermitage La Chapelle	D	89
1990 Hermitage La Chapelle	D	99+
1991 Hermitage Chevalier de Stérimberg	D	89
1990 Hermitage Chevalier de Stérimberg	D	93
1990 St.-Joseph Le Grand Pompée	C	89
1990 Vacqueyras	A	87

Fans of the Jaboulet firm will be disappointed to hear that Gérard Jaboulet and his family considered 1993 to be such a disastrous vintage for them that no Hermitage La Chapelle or Crozes-Hermitage Thalabert will be produced. Everything was either declassified, or, as Gérard Jaboulet told me, "made into one of the world's most expensive rosés."

It is time for consumers to start taking a closer look at the white wines from Jaboulet. For years they were acceptable as opposed to thrilling, but that has changed. Even Jaboulet's 1991 Crozes-Hermitage La Mule Blanche, a tank-fermented blend of 50% Marsanne and 50% Roussanne, displays gobs of honeyed, lemony fruit, excellent definition, rich, medium to full body, crisp acidity, and a long, lush finish. It is a fine example of a white northern Rhône. The fact that the 1990 Crozes-Hermitage La Mule Blanche is slightly bigger and more honeyed has more to do with the vintage than with Jaboulet's winemaking efforts. The 1990 continues to offer considerable body and richness for a modest price.

The most interesting news is the stunning white Hermitage being produced by Jaboulet. The 1991 Hermitage Chevalier de Stérimberg, a 45% Roussanne/55% Marsanne blend, was not put through malolactic fermentation, as was the 1990. It did, however, spend 2 months in new oak casks. Rich, deep, and full bodied, without the power and authority of the 1990, it possesses excellent richness, a honeyed nose and texture, and deep, long, luscious flavors. These wines can last for decades, so I would not be surprised to see this offering hold up for 20 or more years. No doubt the 1990 Hermitage Chevalier de Stérimberg will last two to three decades. Also made from a blend of 45% Roussanne and 55% Marsanne, it spent 7 months in oak and was put through malolactic fermentation. It is the finest dry white wine I have tasted from Jaboulet. After having had it three times, I wonder why there are so few aficionados of white Hermitage. I know these wines will require patience, but the 1990 should evolve effortlessly for 25–30 years. If you are looking for something other than Chardonnay, check out this full-bodied, brilliantly made wine.

Having gone through Jaboulet's 1990 red wine offerings five times (four for the Hermitage La Chapelle), I must say that this is the firm's best overall year since 1961. The lightest cuvée, the 1990 Crozes-Hermitage Les Jalets exhibits a huge nose of black fruits, herbs, smoke, and damp woodsy aromas. In the mouth, it is dense, rich, and opulent, with gobs of fruit, wonderful extraction, and a long, velvety finish. Drink it over the next 7–8 years. The 1990 St.-Joseph Le Grand Pompée is a thick, rich wine that is about as concentrated as St.-Joseph can be. After several years of cellaring, it may merit an outstanding rating. The opaque, saturated purple color is followed by a huge nose of black currants and minerals, full-bodied, highly extracted flavors, good acidity, a significant lashing of tannin, and a long, authoritative finish. Approachable now, it would benefit from 3–4 years of cellaring and should last for 10–15. The 1990 Cornas is tannic and austere, with a forceful, spicy, peppery, herb- and earth-scented nose. Medium to full bodied, with considerable tannins but excellent concentration, this wine needs 5–6 years of cellaring. It should last for 12–15 years. Buyers looking for a super bargain should squirrel away a case or two of Jaboulet's 1990 Côtes du Ventoux. It is hard to believe that so much flavor and character can be found in a wine that sells for $6 a bottle. The blend of 65% Grenache and 35% Syrah has resulted in a deeply colored wine, with an excellent, big, jammy-scented nose, spicy, medium- to full-bodied flavors, and light tannins in the excellent finish. It may improve for 1–2 years, and is capable of 5–6 years of evolution. The backward 1990 Côtes du Rhône Parallel 45, a 55% Grenache and 45% Syrah blend, could benefit from another year of cellaring. The saturated, deep ruby color, and big, peppery, roasted cassis nose suggest excellent extraction of flavor. The wine is medium to full bodied, with some tough tannins in the finish. I would not be in a rush to consume this impressively endowed wine. Jaboulet's 1990 Vacqueyras is made from nearly 100% Grenache. The huge, sweet nose of jammy fruit and smoke is appealing. The wine is full bodied, with excellent concentration, low acidity, fine depth, and sweet, ripe tannins in the finish. Drinkable now, it should last for up to a decade. The 1990 Crozes-Hermitage Thalabert is an unqualified winner. Moreover, the price makes it a bargain. My instincts suggest it will easily eclipse the 1978. The 1990 exhibits a huge, roasted Syrah nose, and the massive power that was produced by the hot sun and drought of this vintage. It has also benefited from an unbelievably long 40-day maceration. The huge, smoky, superripe nose of herbs, coffee, and cassis is followed by a densely packed, authoritatively rich, nearly massive, surprisingly well-balanced wine. It should evolve gracefully for at least 10–15 years. The 1990 Hermitage La Chapelle is a monumental Hermitage. It is almost black in color. When I saw it again with Jaboulet, it was paired against the 1989, 1988, 1983, and 1978. It will prove to be the finest La Chapelle made since 1961. Remarkably, it is even richer, deeper, and more highly extracted than the perfect 1978. The percentage of new oak was increased to 50% because of the wine's power. The maceration period lasted an amazing 44 days. While Jaboulet experimented with filtration during the mid-eighties, this wine was put in the bottle with no processing. The huge nose of pepper, underbrush, and black fruits displays amazing intensity. In the mouth, the wine has awesome concentration, extraordinary balance and power, and a fabulously long, huge finish that lasts for more than a minute. The tannins are considerable, but the lavish quantities of sweet fruit and multidimensional, layered feel to the wine make it one of the most incredible young red wines I have ever tasted. **A.M.: 2005–2040+.** It is a legend in the making!

In 1991 Jaboulet's Cornas was put in small oak casks for the first time to tame its savage character. The 1991 Cornas offers an attractive perfume of red and black fruits as well as some toasty new oak. It is medium bodied, round, and ideal for drinking over the next 7–8 years. Value seekers always search out Jaboulet's Crozes-Hermitage Thalabert. The 1991 Crozes-Hermitage Thalabert possesses the sweet perfume of spicy black fruits, round, opulent, full-bodied flavors, surprisingly good concentration, low acidity, and soft tannins in the finish. Like the 1985, it will be a Thalabert to drink in its first decade of life. The 1991 Hermitage La Chapelle, which had a 40-day maceration, was harvested terrace by terrace because of the unsettled weather. It is successful, with a personality not far removed from the 1985. Soft and ripe, it reveals an excellent deep purple color, a rich, unformed but intense nose, medium- to full-bodied flavors, excellent concentration, sweet tannins, and low acidity. It should drink well for 15 years.

JEAN-PAUL AND JEAN-LUC JAMET * * * * *
1991 Côte Rôtie   D 94

I have upgraded my opinion of this wine after having had it several times on this side of the Atlantic. It is exhibiting even greater richness and intensity than I indicated when I gave it a whoppingly high score of 92 and profiled it at the end of 1993 in *The Wine Advocate.* Aged in one-third new oak with one-third of the blend coming from Jamet's holdings in the La

Landonne vineyard on the Côte Brune, the wine offers a huge, intense, spicy nose of smoked meats, black raspberries, herbs, and new saddle leather. Masculine, rich, and chewy, with massive flavor extraction and spicy new oak in evidence, as well as a phenomenal finish, this Côte Rôtie needs another 3–4 years of cellaring; it should keep for 15–20 years. Very impressive!

DOMAINE DE LA JANASSE * * * *

1993 Châteauneuf du Pape Blanc	C	87
1993 Châteauneuf du Pape Cuvée Chaupoins	C	92
1992 Châteauneuf du Pape Cuvée Chaupoins	C	85+
1993 Châteauneuf du Pape Cuvée Tradition	C	88
1993 Châteauneuf du Pape Cuvée 20th Anniversaire	C	92
1993 Châteauneuf du Pape Cuvée Vieilles Vignes	C	93

Proprietor Aimé Sabon continues to be one of the bright stars of Châteauneuf du Pape. I was only shown one cuvée of 1992, the Châteauneuf du Pape Cuvée Chaupoins. It exhibits a saturated ruby color, a spicy, pruny, earthy nose, sweet, expansive, generous flavors, medium body, and rustic, coarse tannin in the finish. Although it lacks harmony and balance, it possesses good raw materials. Drink it for its exuberance over the next 7–8 years.

The 1993 offerings are vastly superior to the 1992 cuvée. The 1993 Châteauneuf du Pape Cuvée Chaupoins boasts a saturated dark ruby/purple color, and a terrific nose of sweet cassis fruit, tobacco, herbs, and spice. Highly extracted, intense, and full bodied, with the essence of black cherry and black raspberry fruit, this long, ripe, moderately tannic wine is built to last for 15–20 years, although it will be drinkable in 2–3 years. Even more impressive, the opaque, saturated purple-colored 1993 Châteauneuf du Pape Cuvée 20th Anniversaire reveals an intense, cassis-scented bouquet intertwined with aromas of licorice, Provençal herbs, and subtle, toasty new oak. Rich and concentrated, with a wonderful black fruit character, this full-bodied, expansively flavored, terrific Châteauneuf should drink well between 1998 and 2010. Equally superb, as well as more opulent and decadent in its jammy, rich fruitiness, is the 1993 Châteauneuf du Pape Cuvée Vieilles Vignes. The wine displays a fabulous exotic nose of Asian spices, black fruits, leather, and truffles, and layer upon layer of lavishly rich, unctuously textured fruit. This full-bodied, chewy, fleshy Châteauneuf du Pape will be at its best by the end of the century and will last for 10–15 years into the next.

The 1993 Châteauneuf du Pape Cuvée Tradition, the lightest offering from the Domaine de la Janasse, possesses a dark ruby color, a moderately intense bouquet of black cherries and earth, a dusty, soft, medium- to full-bodied palate, and a sweet (from ripeness, not added sugar), long, ripe, tarry finish. Drink it over the next 7–10 years.

Lastly, for the last 5 or 6 years the Domaine de la Janasse has consistently produced one of the few delicious white Châteauneuf du Papes. The 1993 Châteauneuf du Pape Blanc exhibits a savory, richly fruity, tropical fruit–scented nose, deep, medium- to full-bodied flavors, crisp acidity, and a moderately long finish. It should drink well for 3–4 years.

MARCEL JUGE * * * *

1993 Cornas	C	85

This is a light-bodied, pleasant wine with a supple, clean, black fruit character, soft tannin, and low acidity. It is an attractive effort in what was a tough vintage.

JEAN LIONNET * * *

1993 Cornas Rochepertuis	C	86
1992 Cornas Rochepertuis	C	?

Lionnet's top cuvée of Cornas, Rochepertuis, is aged in small barrels, of which a high percentage are new. The 1993 Cornas Rochepertuis has turned out surprisingly well for the vintage. It exhibits a dark ruby color, a sweet, vanillin, curranty nose, rich, medium-bodied, ripe flavors, and a decent finish. Drink it over the next 6–7 years. The 1992 Cornas Rochepertuis is a problematic wine. It possesses a stale, mushroomy nose (rot?), light body, and a diluted, short finish. Judgment reserved until a second bottle can be tasted.

DOMAINE DE LONGUE-TOQUE * * * *

1990 GIGONDAS	C	89

Proprietor Serge Chapalain, like such recalcitrant southern Rhône Valley mavericks as Henri Bonneau and Jacques Reynaud, has finally begun to sell some of his Gigondas in the United States. The average age of the vines in Chapalain's vineyard is over 50 years. The 1990 Gigondas, a blend of 20% Syrah, 10% Mourvèdre, and 70% Grenache, displays an enticing, fragrant bouquet of plums, black truffles, and herbs. Soft and full bodied, with sweet tannin in the finish, this concentrated, generously endowed wine fills the mouth with a velvety texture. It is ideal for drinking over the next 7–8 years.

DOMAINE DE MARCOUX * * * * *

1993 Châteauneuf du Pape	C	88
1992 Châteauneuf du Pape	C	87
1993 Châteauneuf du Pape Vieilles Vignes	D	91
1992 Châteauneuf du Pape Vieilles Vignes	D	94?

The Armenier family farms this serious estate by the principles of biodynamic agriculture made famous by the German professor, Rudolph Steiner. This property makes excellent Châteauneuf du Pape, with their cuvée Vieilles Vignes one of France's most profound wines. They were successful in both 1992 and 1993.

The 1993 Châteauneuf du Pape exhibits a dark ruby color, a big, jammy, black cherry– and raspberry-scented nose, sweet, medium- to full-bodied flavors, and a heady alcoholic finish. It should be drunk its first 7–8 years of life. The 1993 Châteauneuf du Pape Vieilles Vignes may not be bottled separately. Proprietor Armenier showed me his *foudre* of wine made from his oldest vines, but he was uncertain as to whether it would be blended back into the regular cuvée. While not as exceptional as the Cuvée Vieilles Vignes made in 1992, 1990, and 1989, the wine possesses a saturated dark purple color, a huge nose of black raspberries, violets, and spice, that old-vine sweet essence of fruit, full body, and a glycerin-dominated, chewy, whoppingly long finish. A wonderfully pure wine that will last for two decades, it could bolster Marcoux's standard Châteauneuf du Pape by at least several points.

The exuberant, in-your-face 1992 Châteauneuf du Pape is a jammy, decadently styled wine with a sweet, cedary, Provençal herb– and cherry-scented nose, lush, voluptuously textured flavors, low acidity, and copious amounts of alcohol. It should drink well for the next decade. Except for its high level of alcohol, the 1992 Châteauneuf du Pape Vieilles Vignes could easily be mistaken for the great Pomerol, Lafleur. It boasts a phenomenal black/purple color, a huge nose of jammy black raspberries, flowers, and minerals, amazing concentration and unctuosity, and a staggeringly long finish with so much extraction and depth that the moderate tannin level is hardly noticeable. If there is a deficiency, it is the bouquet of some bottles that have a distinct off-aroma of decay. While it will offer superb drinking young, it will be at its plateau of maturity in 7–8 years and will last for two decades. It is one of the greatest wines of this average- to above-average-quality vintage.

DOMAINE DE MAROTTE * * *

1990	Côtes du Ventoux Cuvée Prestige	B	86
1992	Côtes du Ventoux Cuvée Tradition	A	84

Domaine de Marotte's 1992 Cuvée Tradition reveals a pronounced bouquet of Provençal herbs, pepper, and berry fruit. Light to medium bodied, supple, and quaffable, it is lighter than the 1990 Cuvée Prestige, which is a richer, more complete wine. The 1992 should be served chilled and should be drunk over the next year. The more concentrated, intense, peppery, black cherry– and herb-scented 1990 Cuvée Prestige offers medium body, lovely pure fruit, and a moderately long finish. It should drink well for 2–3 years.

ROBERT MICHEL * * *

1993	Cornas	C	86
1992	Cornas	C	75?

Readers should note that I did not taste (assuming it will be produced) Michel's top cuvée of old vines, the hillside vineyard Cornas called La Geynale. The 1993 Cornas is a soft, moderately colored wine with low acidity, and an absence of tannin and grip. It possesses adequate ripeness, as well as moderate alcohol. Drink it over the next 5–7 years. The thin, compact 1992 Cornas exhibits a funky, earthy, overtly herbal aroma and lacks ripeness. With airing, a touch of mushroomy rot emerges.

DOMAINE MILLIÈRES * * *

1992	Côtes du Rhône	A	85

Proprietor Michel Arnauld has turned out a ripe, jammy, medium- to full-bodied, mouth-filling wine with abundant quantities of fruit, glycerin, and alcohol. Drink it over the next 2–3 years.

DOMAINE MIREILLE ET VINCENT * * *

1990	Côtes du Rhône	A	85

This delicious, peppery- and raspberry-scented and -flavored, soft-as-silk Côtes du Rhône makes for a generous mouthful of wine. Its uncomplicated, lush fruitiness, velvety texture, and heady finish are all that a Côtes du Rhône should be. Drink it over the next year.

DOMAINE DE MONT-REDON * * *

1993	Châteauneuf du Pape	C	86
1992	Châteauneuf du Pape	C	86
1993	Châteauneuf du Pape Blanc	C	86
1992	Côtes du Rhône	A	85

Mont-Redon, which has the most extraordinary vineyard in Châteauneuf du Pape, continues to be satisfied making good to very good, rather than profound, wine. The 1993 Châteauneuf du Pape Blanc reveals delicious, honeyed, floral, fresh, fruit salad aromas, medium to full body, adequate acidity, and a pure, lively finish. Drink it over the next year.

The two red wine cuvées are both medium-bodied, cleanly made, mainstream, commercial wines. The 1993 Châteauneuf du Pape exhibits an attractive, moderately intense, ripe, black fruit personality, accompanied by a weedy, peppery component. With good depth and a soft, straightforward finish, it should drink well for 10–12 years. Although more developed, the 1992 Châteauneuf du Pape is similarly sized, with a likable black cherry, herb, and cedary nose, peppery, ripe, medium-bodied flavors, soft texture, and a juicy finish.

The fact that Mont-Redon's tasty, spicy, fruity, medium- to full-bodied 1992 Côtes du Rhône is nearly as good as their Châteauneuf du Pape speaks highly of the Côtes du Rhône, but it should make readers long for more richness and intensity in the Châteauneuf. The Côtes du Rhône, which is a noteworthy bargain, should drink well for 3–4 years. Oh, how I wish Mont-Redon would return to the blockbuster, unfiltered, highly concentrated style of Châteauneuf du Pape that made this historic estate a reference point for Châteauneuf du Pape! There has not been a truly profound wine from Mont-Redon since the great 1961 Châteauneuf du Pape.

DOMAINE DU MONTEILLET * * * */* * * * *

1992 Condrieu	D	94
1992 St.-Joseph	C	90
1991 St.-Joseph	C	90

I tasted through the 1992 Condrieus of just about every producer and *négociant* and there is not a better example to be found than this 1992 Condrieu from Antoine Montez, one of the up-and-coming stars in the northern Rhône. Half of his tiny production was fermented in wood and the other half in stainless steel. This knockout Condrieu defines the character of the Viognier grape grown on the sun-drenched hillsides of this microscopic appellation. The super nose of honeyed peaches, apricots, and spring flowers jumps from the glass. Super concentration, an unctuously thick, rich texture with enough acidity to give freshness, and full body make for a spectacular glass of Condrieu. As longtime readers know, I am a firm believer in drinking these wines in their first 1–2 years of life for their freshness and aromatic intensity.

The 1991 St.-Joseph from Pascal Perrier's Domaine Gachon and this 1992 St.-Joseph from Domaine du Monteillet are two of the richest, most compelling examples I have tasted from this appellation. Made from yields of 35 hectoliters per hectare, and bottled unfiltered for the American importer, Monteillet's St.-Joseph exhibits a dense, saturated, black/purple color, and a huge nose of black cherries, herbs, and underbrush. Fabulously concentrated, with amazing richness, ripeness, and length, this full-bodied wine is an exquisite bargain. It should drink well for 15 or more years. The 1991 is a candidate for the best 1991 from St.-Joseph. New oak was not employed, so you can imagine the richness of the peppery, black currant–flavored Syrah fruit in this wine. There is a deep, viscous texture, sweet, chewy flavors, and gobs of fruit in the finish. Although it will age for up to a decade, I would opt for drinking this beauty over the next 7–8 years.

DOMAINE DE MONTPERTUIS * * * *

1992 Châteauneuf du Pape Cuvée Classique	C	87
1990 Châteauneuf du Pape Cuvée Tradition	D	92

Proprietor Paul Jeune made no Cuvée Tradition in 1992. That cuvée is made from 60- to 110-year-old, low-yielding vines and is designed to last for 10–20 years. The 1992 Châteauneuf du Pape Cuvée Classique, which includes all of the old-vine production, possesses a deep ruby color, a ripe, sweet, lovely nose, fat, chewy, black cherry– and herb-scented flavors, and a moderately long, spicy, heady finish. Bottled unfiltered, it will be released this fall. Readers may still be able to find some of Jeune's spectacular 1990 Châteauneuf du Pape Cuvée Tradition, which has begun to display even more character than it did when first bottled. The deep ruby/purple color is followed by a big, spicy, peppery nose of herbs, black cherries, and black raspberries, full body, and gobs of glycerin and richness, as well as moderate tannin in the finish. Approachable now, it should continue to age well for 15 years.

DOMAINE DE LA MORDORÉE * * */* * * *

1993 Châteauneuf du Pape	C	88
1992 Châteauneuf du Pape	C	88
1992 Côtes du Rhône	B	84
1992 Lirac	B	88

The Delorme family, known for their full-bodied, rich rosé that has made the village of Tavel world famous, has come on strong lately with their red wine program. Made in a modern style and crammed with rich black fruit, their full-bodied Châteauneuf du Papes are wonderfully pure and rich. It may be tempting to conclude that these wines are too obviously commercial, given their cleanliness and rich fruit, but I was seduced by both the 1992 and 1993 Châteauneuf du Papes. They are deeply colored, full-bodied wines revealing impeccable winemaking and considerable respect for the character of this appellation. They are easy to drink, supple, and lush, and should be immensely pleasing with wine neophytes as well as connoisseurs. Drink both over the next 7–8 years. The 1992 was judged the finest Châteauneuf du Pape of the vintage by other proprietors in the annual wine competition known as the Festival of St.-Marc.

The 1992 Lirac, a blend of equal parts Mourvèdre, Syrah, and Grenache, is as good as the estate's excellent 1992 Châteauneuf (which sells for nearly $15 more a bottle). The Lirac exhibits a saturated dark ruby/purple color, a big, forceful bouquet of herbs, black cherries, pepper, and spice, medium- to full-bodied, supple flavors, and a chewy, long finish. It is a mouth-filling, wonderfully pure wine for drinking over the next 4–5 years.

I also tasted an attractive, fruity, light- to medium-bodied 1992 Côtes du Rhône from Domaine de la Mordorée. Well made, tart, vibrant, and exuberant, it should be drunk over the next 3–4 years.

MOULIN DE LA GARDETTE * * * *

1993 Gigondas	C	86
1992 Gigondas	C	72

The 1993 Gigondas exhibits an earthy, floral-, licorice-, and cherry-scented nose, and medium- to full-bodied, spicy flavors, with fine concentration, glycerin, and moderate tannin. It should be drunk over the next decade. The disappointing 1992 Gigondas displays a stale vegetable, faded rose, weedy, burnt coffee aroma, and thin, harshly tannic flavors.

MOULIN-TACUSSEL * * * *

1993 Châteauneuf du Pape	C	87
1992 Châteauneuf du Pape	C	85

I have always found it fascinating that this estate turns out such minty-scented wines. The dark ruby-colored 1993 Châteauneuf du Pape's nose exhibits an intense minty note, and an attractive spicy, black cherry component. Medium bodied, with fine depth and roundness, this is a solidly made, attractive, adequately endowed Châteauneuf du Pape for drinking over the next 5–6 years. In the 1992 Châteauneuf du Pape the minty characteristic is accompanied by ripe black cherry fruit intertwined with scents of tar. Medium bodied and fruity, with decent glycerin and alcohol, this soft, easy-to-drink, medium-weight Châteauneuf should be consumed over the next 4–5 years.

DOMAINE DE NALYS * * *

1993 Châteauneuf du Pape	C	85
1992 Châteauneuf du Pape	C	87
1993 Châteauneuf du Pape Blanc	C	87

This estate generally produces one of the best white wines of the appellation. The 1993 Châteauneuf du Pape Blanc stood out for its lush, tropical fruit, honeyed bouquet, and pure, medium- to full-bodied, concentrated flavors. This delicious, personality-filled white wine should last for 1–2 years.

Domaine de Nalys has long believed in the practice of carbonic maceration for their red Châteauneuf du Pape. Consequently, they are soft, fruity wines that are engaging when young, but only in the finest vintages do they have the ability to age and improve for more than a decade. Although extremely light, the 1993 Châteauneuf du Pape is pleasing and seductive with its soft, plush, chewy, cherry and raspberry fruit, low acidity, light tannin, and alcoholic finish. Drink it over the next 5–6 years. The 1992 Châteauneuf du Pape is a more interesting wine. It reveals deep, ruby color, and an excellent nose of tobacco, cedar, prunes, and jammy black cherries. Fat and chewy, with copious amounts of alcohol in the finish, it should be drunk over the next 5–6 years.

CHÂTEAU DE LA NERTHE * * * *

1993 Châteauneuf du Pape	C	88
1992 Châteauneuf du Pape	C	87
1991 Châteauneuf du Pape	C	78
1993 Châteauneuf du Pape Blanc	C	87
1992 Châteauneuf du Pape Blanc	C	86
1991 Châteauneuf du Pape Blanc	C	79
1993 Châteauneuf du Pape Blanc Clos de Beauvenir	D	88
1992 Châteauneuf du Pape Blanc Clos de Beauvenir	D	86
1993 Châteauneuf du Pape Cuvée des Cadettes	D	92
1992 Châteauneuf du Pape Cuvée des Cadettes	D	88+

In top vintages Château de la Nerthe produces four Châteauneuf du Pape cuvées—two white and two red, with the Cuvée des Cadettes and Clos de Beauvenir representing their prestige offerings of red and white wine, respectively.

The standard cuvée of white Châteauneuf du Pape is a blend of 25% Grenache, 25% Clairette, 25% Bourboulenc, and 25% Roussanne. The 1993 is a well-made wine with an intriguing bouquet of flowers, pears, and spice. Rich and full bodied, with attractively supple, fleshy flavors, this is a wine to drink over the next year. The soft 1992 Châteauneuf du Pape Blanc offers a spicy-scented, mineral nose and medium body. Revealing evidence of oak, the 1991 Châteauneuf du Pape Blanc may be beginning to dry out, as the fruit's concentration is suspicious.

With respect to the luxury cuvée of white Châteauneuf du Pape, the Clos de Beauvenir is made from 60% Roussanne and 40% Clairette. It is barrel-fermented and bottled without going through a malolactic fermentation. The 1993 Châteauneuf du Pape Clos de Beauvenir exhibits an intense, complex nose of rose petals, honey, and cherries. Deep, rich, and full bodied, displaying a judicious touch of toasty new oak, it should drink well for 1–2 years. The spicy 1992 Châteauneuf du Pape Clos de Beauvenir reveals well-integrated oak notes, an excellent bouquet, and ripe, medium-bodied flavors that, while not complex, are fruity and enjoyable.

With respect to the red wines, Château de la Nerthe has moved away from excessive intervention and has begun to bottle the top cuvée, des Cadettes, without filtration. Made from a blend of 55% Grenache, 15% Syrah, 15% Mourvèdre, 5% Cinsault, and the rest various red grape varietals, the regular cuvée of 1993 Châteauneuf du Pape offers wonderfully sweet, cassis aromas, clean, ripe, medium-bodied flavors, and a long, rich, stylish, well-balanced finish. Drink this well-made wine over the next decade. The 1993 Châteauneuf du Pape Cuvée des Cadettes, made from 60% Mourvèdre and 40% Grenache, is a more highly extracted and structured wine. It also shows more evidence of small-oak-cask aging. The wine's opaque purple color is followed by a superextracted, jammy, cassis nose, intertwined with aromas of toasty new oak. Rich, full bodied, and dense, it boasts phenomenal potential for 15–20 years of evolution. It could turn out to be the best Cuvée des Cadettes made under the new ownership.

The 1992 Châteauneuf du Pape is an elegant, medium- to full-bodied wine with moderate tannin, adequate depth, and spicy, black cherry and raspberry fruit. Drink this stylized yet tasty Châteauneuf du Pape over the next 7–8 years. The 1992 Châteauneuf du Pape Cuvée des Cadettes reveals lavish quantities of sweet, toasty new oak in its nose. Possessing an international style and personality (much more so than the 1993), it is deep, rich, medium to full bodied, and overall an excellent wine. The only complaint may be that it lacks the typicity I seek in a classic Châteauneuf du Pape. It should drink well for 10–15 years.

No Cuvée des Cadettes was made in 1991. The regular 1991 Châteauneuf du Pape is a successful wine in what was a dreadfully difficult vintage. Although more herbaceous and compact than normal, it exhibits adequate ripeness, straightforward, medium-bodied black cherry fruit, and a spicy finish. Drink it over the next 5–6 years.

Château de la Nerthe appears to be moving in the right direction, with less emphasis on sculpturing and interventionist winemaking techniques. It is potentially one of the two or three greatest domaines in the southern Rhône. I remain optimistic that this historic property's full potential will be exploited.

ROBERT NIERO * * * *

1992 Condrieu Coteau de Chery	D	91

Before readers get too excited about this wine, be forewarned that only one barrel (25 cases) was purchased for sale in the United States. Aged in new oak casks, it is a tribute to the wine's concentration and intensity that no noticeable oak can be detected in the bouquet or flavors. The wine boasts a big, exotic, honeyed, apricot-scented bouquet, and full-bodied, unctuously textured flavors. Drink it over the next year.

MICHEL OGIER * * * *

1992 Côte Rôtie	D	87
1991 Côte Rôtie	D	93
1991 La Rosine Syrah VDP	C	89

Looking for a wine that smells and tastes like Côte Rôtie for about half the price of most wines from that tiny appellation? Check out Michel Ogier's 1991 La Rosine made from 100% Syrah from vineyards adjacent to Côte Rôtie. It reveals a huge, bacon fat–, cassis–, and vanillin-scented nose, sweet, chewy flavors, a supple texture, and a beautiful, graceful, seductive finish. Drink it over the next 3–4 years. I highly touted Ogier's brilliant 1991 Côte Rôtie when I tasted it from cask. Now that it has been bottled, it is a sensational Côte Rôtie. Ogier's style is one of exceptional elegance married to a velvety-textured, supple, rich fruitiness. His Côte Rôties are not as masculine or robust as others, relying more on complexity and finesse. The 1991 displays an ethereal bouquet of ripe cassis, bacon, vanilla, and violets. This deep, medium-weight wine with extraordinary finesse, fragrance, and length on the palate would embarrass many a Musigny from Burgundy. Drink it over the next 10–12 years. The 1992 Côte Rôtie is lighter, with a more noticeable herbaceous side to its cassis and smoky flavors. Soft, ripe, and medium bodied, but lacking the concentration achieved in top years, it should be drunk over the next 5–7 years.

DOMAINE DE L'ORATOIRE ST.-MARTIN * * * * *

1993 Côtes du Rhône Cairanne	A	87
1993 Côtes du Rhône Cairanne Prestige	B	89

Run by the Alary Wine Company, this domaine proved to be a discovery. Bottled without filtration, these are wonderfully pure, concentrated, richly fruity wines that are ideal for drinking within their first 5–6 years of life. The 1993 Côtes du Rhône Cairanne reveals a saturated dark ruby/purple color, a big, juicy bouquet of black cherries, herbs, and peppery scents, supple, medium- to full-bodied flavors, and a long, heady finish. Its forwardness and charm are noteworthy. The 1993 Côtes du Rhône Cairanne Prestige is made from 100-year-old vines, of which 60% are Mourvèdre. It is a dead ringer for a top Châteauneuf du Pape. The wine offers a penetrating bouquet of new saddle leather, black fruits, pepper, herbs, and truffles. Deep, full bodied, and supple, with layers of fruit, it should drink well for 7–8 years. Impressive!

DOMAINE PAPE GREGOIRE * * *

1993 Châteauneuf du Pape	C	89?
1992 Châteauneuf du Pape	C	?
1993 Châteauneuf du Pape Blanc	C	70

The 1993 Châteauneuf du Pape Blanc from Pierre Giraud is simple, diluted, and lacking fruit. Both cuvées of the red wine were oxidized; thus I will reserve judgment until the wines can be retasted. I did feel the 1993 Châteauneuf du Pape appeared to be a hugely extracted, big, thick, full-bodied, old-style Châteauneuf, but the reductive/oxidized nose was a problem. The 1992 Châteauneuf du Pape was even more oxidized. Even allowing for that, it was much lighter and not nearly as concentrated as the 1993.

DOMAINE DU PEGAU * * * * *

1993 Châteauneuf du Pape	C	90
1992 Châteauneuf du Pape	C	90
1991 Châteauneuf du Pape	C	77
1993 Châteauneuf du Pape Blanc	C	?

The Feraud father and daughter are protégés of the great Henri Bonneau. Their wines are closest in style to Bonneau's Cuvée des Celestins. While none of these offerings will be as extraordinary as the wine produced in 1990, 1989, 1985, and 1981, their 1992 and 1993 are among the top wines of the vintage. The 1993 Châteauneuf du Pape exhibits a saturated dark ruby/purple color, and a spicy, peppery, jammy bouquet of black fruits, damp earth, and herbs. Rich and full bodied, with excellent, potentially outstanding, concentration, this wine will last for 15+ years. The 1992 Châteauneuf du Pape exhibits a huge, earthy, herbal, black cherry, and chocolatey, exotic nose, superrich, full-bodied flavors, a saturated color (it is one of the darkest 1992s I tasted), low acidity, and a fleshy, alcoholic, intense finish. Already delicious, it will evolve gracefully for 14–15 years. The 1991 Châteauneuf du Pape is a competent, correct wine in what was a dreadful vintage. It is spicy and weedy, with peppery, black cherry fruit, medium body, and a compact, narrowly constructed finish.

Pegau's white wines are controversial, and unquestionably not to my taste. The 1993 Châteauneuf du Pape Blanc possesses an evolved, almost oxidized-looking color, and an odd bouquet that made me think of pears macerated in Cognac. A heavy, tiring style of wine, it lacks freshness and comes across as bizarre.

DOMAINE DU PÈRE CABOCHE * * *

1993 Châteauneuf du Pape	C	85
1992 Châteauneuf du Pape	C	75
1993 Châteauneuf du Pape Blanc	C	72

This estate offers straightforward, easygoing wines that require early consumption. As with most white Châteauneuf du Pape, Père Caboche's 1993 is short on flavor, light, hollow, and neutral.

The two red Châteauneuf du Papes are soft, fruity wines. The 1993 possesses considerably more depth and berry fruit than the lean, high-acid, meagerly constituted 1992.

ANDRÉ PERRET * * * * *

1992 Condrieu Coteau du Chery	D	90
1992 St.-Joseph	C	86
1992 St.-Joseph Les Grisières	C	87

Perret often produces the most complex, rich wine of Condrieu. The fragrant 1992 Condrieu Coteau du Chery, from one of the most highly respected parcels in this tiny appellation, is redolent of spring flowers and peach blossoms. The honeyed, full-bodied, unctuous texture buttressed by adequate acidity makes for a hefty mouthful of dry white wine. Drink this luscious Condrieu over the next year.

The St.-Josephs are both well-made, supple, easy-to-drink wines, suggesting consumption is required over the next 5–6 years. The 1992 St.-Joseph offers a sweet, raspberry aroma, medium body, velvety texture, and ripeness and fruit in the finish. The 1992 St.-Joseph Les Grisières displays evidence of toasty new oak in its vanillin-, black cherry–, and raspberry-scented nose. There is sweet, ripe fruit, medium body, and an overall sense of elegance married to wonderful ripeness. This beautifully made wine could easily be mistaken for a grand cru red burgundy. Drink it over the next 7–8 years.

ROGER PERRIN * * *

1993 Châteauneuf du Pape	C	88
1992 Châteauneuf du Pape	C	87

Perrin has produced good wines in both 1993 and 1992. The 1993 reveals evidence of aging in new oak casks, given the sweet vanillin– and ripe cherry–scented nose. The wine exhibits lovely ripeness, medium to full body, admirable fruit and depth, and a soft, lush finish. It will require drinking in its first 5–7 years of life. The fatter 1992 displays more evidence of extraction and ripeness in its nose of black cherries, pepper, and herbs, and lush, medium- to full-bodied, succulent flavors. Forward and delicious, it is ideal for drinking over the next 6–7 years.

CHÂTEAU PESQUIE * * *

1992 Côtes de Ventoux Cuvée des Terrasses	A	86
1990 Côtes de Ventoux Quintessence	A	88

These are two noteworthy wines from southern France's beautiful Côtes de Ventoux. The 1992 Cuvée des Terrasses is an immensely charming, round, deliciously fruity wine that disarms the taster with its blast of cherry fruit, supple texture, chewy glycerin, and medium-bodied, velvety-textured finish. Everything is in harmony in this easy-to-drink wine. Its joy should continue for 1–2 years. Less charming but more massive, fuller bodied, and fleshier is the 1990 Quintessence. A more concentrated and ambitious wine, with impressive components, it displays full body, plenty of extract, wonderful juicy, peppery, cassis, and black cherry fruit, and a long, lush, heady finish. One of the most concentrated wines I have tasted from the Côtes de Ventoux, it should drink well for 7–8 years.

DOMAINE DES PESQUIERS * * * *

1993 Gigondas	?	85
1992 Gigondas	?	75

A medium-weight, moderately tannic, good Gigondas produced from the forward-tasting 1993 vintage, this wine is lighter than expected, but it exhibits a peppery, black fruit character and a spicy finish. The 1992 Gigondas reveals a meaty, prune- and underbrush-scented nose, disjointed flavors, and a soft, tannic, awkward finish.

DOMAINE DE PIAUGIER * * * *

1990 Côtes du Rhône Sablet Les Briguières	A	86
1990 Côtes du Rhône Sablet Montmartel	A	86

This excellent Gigondas domaine turns out two vineyard-designated wines from Sablet. Both 1990s exhibit deep ruby/purple colors, peppery, spicy, richly fruity noses, medium to full body, soft tannin, and voluptuous, fleshy, chewy textures. Drink them both over the next 2–3 years.

CHRISTOPHE PICHON * * * *

1993 Condrieu	D	89

This excellent, full-bodied Condrieu possesses Viognier's intoxicating perfume, excellent richness, adequate acidity, and a fleshy, heady finish. Drink it over the next year.

PHILIPPE PICHON * * * * *

1993 Condrieu	D	83

This light-bodied, floral, tropical fruit–scented wine begins well, but it finishes without much authority or depth. Drink it over the next year.

DOMAINE DE LA PINÈDE * * *

1992 Châteauneuf de Pape	C	88
1993 Châteauneuf du Pape Blanc	C	85

The Domaine de la Pinède is a reliable, underrated Châteauneuf du Pape producer. The 1993 Châteauneuf du Pape Blanc offers a distinctive nose of ripe pineapples, crisp, medium-bodied, elegant flavors, and a fresh, lively finish. Drink it over the next year. I did not taste a 1993, but the 1992 Châteauneuf du Pape is one of the better wines of the vintage. A smoky, cedary, pine needle, herb, and black cherry nose is followed by a fat, lush wine with full body, low acidity, and soft tannin. It is a delicious Châteauneuf for drinking over the next 6–8 years.

DOMAINE PONTIFICAL-FRANÇOIS LAGET * * * *

1992 Châteauneuf du Pape	C	85

The 1992 Châteauneuf du Pape offers a pruny, peppery, spicy nose, jammy, overripe flavors, and hard tannin in the finish. Its elements are not in harmony and its future may be problematic, given the ferociousness of the tannin.

DOMAINE RASPAIL-DOMINIQUE AY* * * *

1993 Gigondas	C	82
1992 Gigondas	C	73

One of my favorite estates appears to be going through a troublesome period. The 1993 Gigondas is extremely light for this property, with medium body, and soft, fruity flavors exhibiting a peppery, red fruit character. The wine lacks depth, focus, and richness. Drink it over the next 5–6 years. The soft 1992 Gigondas is disappointingly short, light, and diluted. It requires consumption.

CHÂTEAU RAYAS* * * * *

1992 Fonsalette Blanc	C	75
1991 Fonsalette Côtes du Rhône	D	83
1991 Fonsalette Côtes du Rhône Cuvée Syrah	D	92+
1991 Pignan Châteauneuf du Pape	D	89
1990 Pignan Châteauneuf du Pape	D	95
1992 Rayas Blanc	D	78
1993 Rayas Châteauneuf du Pape	D	85
1992 Rayas Châteauneuf du Pape	D	88

While the idiosyncratic proprietor of this estate, Jacques Reynaud, is hardly inspired by the 1992 Rayas Châteauneuf du Pape, it is a fine example of Rayas. It possesses a medium ruby color, a big, peppery nose of herb, and jammy raspberry and cherry scents, spicy, medium-bodied flavors, noticeable alcohol, a dusty component, and an exuberant, rustic, heady finish. It is a typical, albeit light, flavorful Rayas, capable of lasting for up to a decade. The 1993 Rayas is the lightest wine made at this estate since 1986. Drink it over the next 5–6 years.

The 1991 Pignan Châteauneuf du Pape is a better bargain, as it contains all of the declassified Rayas. While it is extremely tannic (unusual for a wine from Reynaud), the opaque ruby/purple color, and big, sweet, leathery, licorice- and black fruit–scented nose are impressive. There is huge fruit and amazing extract, as well as ferocious tannin in this impressive, well-built, large-scaled wine. It will easily merit an outstanding score if the tannin melts away before the fruit fades. Drink it between 1997 and 2010. I thought the loosely knit 1991 Fonsalette Côtes du Rhône to be tasty in a monolithic manner, soft, medium bodied, and pleasant.

The 1991 Fonsalette Côtes du Rhône Cuvée Syrah's amazing opaque, black/purple color is followed by a huge nose of roasted herbs and cassis that roars from the glass. With a natural alcohol of more than 14% (from yields of 20–25 hectoliters per hectare), this massive, phenomenally extracted, gigantic wine needs 10 years of cellaring! It should last for 20–30 years. I purchased and cellared the 1978 Fonsalette Cuvée Syrah and it is not even close to maturity after nearly 16 years of aging! The awesome 1991 tastes as if it came from a top vintage.

The monumental 1990 Rayas is both impossible to find and to afford (it is fetching the equivalent of $75–$90 in France). Proprietor Jacques Reynaud's 1990 Pignan (a separate vineyard, but in practice the second wine of Rayas) is awesome. Black/purple-colored, with a gorgeous, sweet nose of pepper, cassis, and licorice, this superconcentrated, long, expansive, formidably endowed wine is loaded with character. Approachable now, it should mature gracefully for 15–20 years. So rich that it could easily surpass Rayas in many vintages, it is an immensely impressive Châteauneuf du Pape!

The two 1992 white wines are mediocre. Exhibiting an advanced color as well as some oxidation, the 1992 Fonsalette Blanc is watery, foursquare, and simple. The 1992 Rayas Blanc possesses more acidity, medium body, but little depth or character.

CHÂTEAU REDOITIER * * * *

1993 Gigondas	C	87
1992 Gigondas	C	89

This property is one of Gigondas's emerging stars. The 1993 Gigondas offers a saturated color, a big, chunky, fleshy, peppery, black cherry nose with a touch of Provençal herbs, and full-bodied, tasty, concentrated flavors. It should drink well for at least a decade. The big surprise is how well Redoitier's 1992 Gigondas has turned out. An intense, old-vine aroma of overripe black fruits is followed by a clean, pure wine displaying none of the vegetal, pruny, mushroomy character afflicting so many of the 1992s from Gigondas. The wine is powerful, with fine density, dark color, and low acidity. It does appear fragile, suggesting it should be drunk earlier rather than later.

DOMAINE DES RELAGNES-CUVÉE VIGNERONNE * * *

1993 Châteauneuf du Pape	C	87
1992 Châteauneuf du Pape	C	87

I have had mixed emotions about the quality of the Domaine des Relagnes wines over the last 15 years. In some vintages they are immensely seductive, rich, complex Châteauneuf du Pape. In other vintages the wines have appeared to be excessively filtered and incapable of living up to their prebottling concentration and intensity. Let's hope proprietor Boiron goes easy on the filtration, as he has produced excellent raw materials in 1993. The 1993 Châteauneuf du Pape possesses an admirable dark ruby color, a big, plummy, pruny nose of ripe black cherries, herbs, and spice, full body, and gobs of glycerin and fat. This alcoholic, chewy, rich wine should offer a decadent mouthful of Châteauneuf du Pape over the next 7–8 years . . . if it is not stripped at bottling. The medium to dark ruby-colored 1992 Châteauneuf du Pape reveals an expansive, sweet, floral, jammy nose, and broad, chewy flavors. Drink it over the next 7–8 years.

HERVÉ RICHARD * * * *

1991 Condrieu	D	94

A recent discovery, Hervé Richard owns only 5 acres of vines in Condrieu. His yields in 1991 were 25 hectoliters per hectare and the natural alcohol in this 1991 Condrieu is 14%. One of the most concentrated Condrieus I have tasted, this unfiltered wine exhibits a sensational nose of apricots, honey, and spring flowers. Extraordinarily rich yet totally dry, with great focus to its massive components, this is a dramatic Condrieu for drinking with rich fish dishes and creamy fowl and veal courses. I favor drinking Condrieu young, so my advice is to consume it over the next year. Only a few cases of this wine were imported to the United States, so do not expect to find it in every mom-and-pop liquor store.

DOMAINE RICHÉ * * *

1993 Châteauneuf du Pape	C	86
1992 Châteauneuf du Pape	C	77

There is no contest between these two vintages of Domaine Riché Châteauneuf du Pape. The 1993 is a ripe, well-made, commercially oriented Châteauneuf du Pape with wonderful warmth, generosity, and fat, herbal, peppery, cherry flavors. Exhibiting lushness, glycerin, and fatness, it should be drunk over the next 5–6 years. The light, shallow 1992 offers decent fruit, medium body, and an undistinguished, compact finish. Drink it over the next 2–3 years.

DOMAINE DE LA ROQUETTE * * * *

1993 Châteauneuf du Pape	C	88
1992 Châteauneuf du Pape	C	86
1993 Châteauneuf du Pape Blanc	C	75

The Brunier family, synonymous with the renowned Domaine de Vieux Télégraphe, owns this property, which has been producing fine wines over recent vintages. However, I am no fan of Domaine de la Roquette's 1993 Châteauneuf du Pape Blanc. It is monochromatic, vaguely fruity, and medium bodied. Drink it over the next year.

The 1993 Châteauneuf du Pape offers jammy, cassis, pepper, and herb scents in a perfumed style. Medium to full bodied, with excellent concentration, round flavors, and a soft, lush finish, it should be drunk over the next 5–6 years. The medium- to full-bodied 1992 Châteauneuf du Pape displays a bouquet of prunes, overripe black cherries, and herbal/peppery scents, tarry, chewy flavors, low acidity, and plenty of alcohol in the heady finish. Although slightly overripe, it provides a solid, chewy mouthful of wine. Readers may be lucky enough to still find some of Domaine de la Roquette's 1990 Châteauneuf du Pape, which I have rated as high as 90. Powerful and rich, it is the best wine produced under the Brunier regime.

RENÉ ROSTAING * * * * *

1993 Côte Rôtie	D	86
1992 Côte Rôtie	D	86
1993 Côte Rôtie Côte Blonde	D	89
1992 Côte Rôtie Côte Blonde	D	87
1991 Côte Rôtie Côte Blonde	D	92
1993 Côte Rôtie La Landonne	D	90
1991 Côte Rôtie La Landonne	D	94
1993 Côte Rôtie Côte Brune La Viaillère	D	87
1991 Côte Rôtie Côte Brune La Viaillère	D	92

Rostaing was one of the more successful producers in the rain-plagued vintage of 1993. As the scores and following tasting notes attest, Rostaing was able to obtain good levels of concentration, producing soft, seductive, complex, character-filled wines. He pruned 50% of his grapes in August and did a severe triage as the harvested grapes were brought in. His 1993 Côte Rôtie displays a medium ruby color, a smoky bouquet, elegant, adequately concentrated, spicy flavors, and soft tannin. It will require drinking in its first 5–7 years of life. The 1993 Côte Rôtie Côte Brune La Viaillère, which is made and bottled by Rostaing, but still appears under the label of his father-in-law, Albert Dervieux, is a muscular, tannic, rustic wine with excellent color. It may ultimately be overburdened because of its high acidity and tannin. La Viaillère, a potentially great vineyard, generally hits the peaks in years of extraordinary sunshine, heat, and ripeness. Rostaing's portion of this vineyard averages 80 years of age. The 1993 Côte Rôtie La Landonne looks to be outstanding. Made from vines averaging between 25 and 80 years old, it exhibits a black color, a nose of licorice, Asian spices, and smoky, cassis scents, rich, full-bodied, concentrated flavors, adequate acidity, and moderate tannin in the long finish. This outstanding wine is especially admirable in view of the difficult harvest conditions. It will age well for 10–15 years. The most sweet and seductive of all Rostaing's Côte Rôties, the 1993 Côte Rôtie Côte Blonde offers a perfumed, floral-, black cherry–, and cassis-scented nose, smoky, creamy-textured, ripe flavors, and soft tannin. Drink it during its first 10 years of life.

Rostaing produced only two cuvées in 1992, a vintage he terms the hardest, most difficult he has ever encountered. The 1992 Côte Rôtie generic bottling (which includes all of his declassified La Landonne) exhibits a medium ruby color, a soft, cherry, earthy nose, lovely, light- to medium-bodied flavors, low acidity, and an attractive finish. Almost burgundian in its lightness, perfume, and lushness, it should be drunk over the next 5–7 years. The peppery, herbal, and black raspberry–scented nose of the 1992 Côte Rôtie Côte Blonde is followed by a wine with smoky, medium-bodied flavors, some vanillin from oak aging, and a short but pleasing, fruity finish. It should drink well for 7–8 years.

René Rostaing's 1991s offer persuasive evidence of just how impressive this vintage is in Côte Rôtie. The 1991 Côte Rôtie Côte Brune La Viaillère is fabulous. Rostaing aged it in new oak casks (the larger *demi-muids,* rather than the normal 55-gallon *barrique*). Made from 80-year-old vines, this wine exhibits the animal, meaty, earthy side of Côte Rôtie. The nearly black color is followed by huge aromas of soy sauce, smoked game, and black raspberries intertwined with scents of toasty new oak. Full bodied, tannic, and loaded with extract, this voluptuous, exquisite Côte Rôtie should drink well for 15 or more years. The 1991 Côte Rôtie Côte Blonde is a sweeter, fatter, more voluptuously styled wine with soft tannin and none of the rusticity or animal character of the La Viaillère. Sweet and expansive on the palate, it makes for a seductive, generous mouthful of wine. It should drink well for 8–10 years. Perhaps the best of these 1991s is the 1991 Côte Rôtie La Landonne. As you might anticipate, there is considerable rivalry between Rostaing and his neighbor, Guigal. Rostaing is quick to assert that his La Landonne vines are considerably older than those of Guigal. This black-colored wine offers up an exquisite perfume of licorice, violets, black-berries, and toast, staggering concentration, smooth tannin, and low acidity. It is a gorgeous, exceptionally opulent, multidimensional wine with layers of flavor. It should drink well for 10–15 years.

DOMAINE ROGER SABON * * * *

1993 Châteauneuf du Pape Blanc	C	77
1992 Châteauneuf du Pape Cuvée Prestige Unfiltered	D	90
1992 Châteauneuf du Pape Cuvée Réservée	D	86
1993 Châteauneuf du Pape Les Olivets	D	88

Domaine Roger Sabon produces a range of Châteauneuf du Papes. In ascending order of richness, they are Les Olivets (the basic cuvée), Cuvée Réservée (a riper, richer wine), and the Cuvée Prestige (an unfiltered, intense wine representing the estate's richest, most age-worthy wine). The estate also makes a dull, straightforward white Châteauneuf du Pape that lacks character and intensity.

In 1993, proprietor Sabon only presented the 1993 Châteauneuf du Pape Les Olivets, but I feel certain there will be a Cuvée Réservée and Cuvée Prestige. The tastiness of Les Olivets bodes well for the success of this estate in this vintage. The wine exhibits a saturated dark ruby color, a sweet, jammy nose of black cherries, herbs, and pepper, and a voluptuously rich, chewy palate with excellent depth and length. Drink it over the next 7–8 years.

In 1992, I tasted the two top cuvées of red wine, the Cuvée Réservée and Cuvée Prestige Unfiltered. I enjoyed them both, with the lusty 1992 Châteauneuf du Pape Cuvée Réservée exhibiting a generous, roasted nut– and herb-scented, richly fruity nose, copious quantities of chunky fruit, loads of alcohol, and an appealing, mouth-filling personality. Drink it over the next 4–5 years. The outstanding, decadently styled 1992 Châteauneuf du Pape Cuvée Prestige Unfiltered offers lavish quantities of jammy red and black fruits, roasted herbs, smoked nuts, and pepper in the bouquet. Full bodied, rich, fat, and unctuous, this is a lusty, no-holds-barred Châteauneuf for drinking over the next 7–8 years. Sabon, who is president of the syndicate of growers, has made an important statement in bottling his 1992 unfiltered. With so many French wine producers having been brainwashed by foreign importers, European sommeliers, and some of Europe's most brain-dead consumers who fail to realize that sediment in a wine is a healthy sign, it is good to see more and more intelligent growers refusing to strip their wines by such potentially eviscerating and devastating procedures as excessive fining and filtration.

DOMAINE SAINT-BENOÎT * * * *

1993	Châteauneuf du Pape Blanc	C	70
1993	Châteauneuf du Pape Cuvée de Grand Garde	C	88
1992	Châteauneuf du Pape Cuvée de Grand Garde	C	86+
1993	Châteauneuf du Pape Élise	C	87
1992	Châteauneuf du Pape Élise	C	84
1993	Châteauneuf du Pape Soleil et Festins	B	84?
1992	Châteauneuf du Pape Soleil et Festins	B	75–85?

Domaine Saint-Benoît's 1993s look significantly stronger than the 1992s. The 1993 Châteauneuf du Pape Soleil et Festins displays an extremely peppery, perfumed nose, medium body, soft flavors, and an herbal, alcoholic finish. This is likely to be a controversial style of Châteauneuf because of its exaggerated, peppery character. The dark, saturated-colored 1993 Châteauneuf du Pape Élise reveals fine extract, monochromatic flavors, medium body, and light tannin in a compact finish. The 1993 Châteauneuf du Pape Cuvée de Grand Garde exhibits evidence of aging in small oak casks with its toasty vanillin-scented nose backed up by impressive black cherry fruit. The wine is round, with medium to full body, lovely ripeness, and a spicy, moderately tannic finish. It should drink well for 7–8 years.

The 1992 Châteauneuf du Pape Soleil et Festins has demonstrated bottle variation. When I tasted it in France it appeared to be a deep, rich, soft, straightforward wine made in a plump style. It was somewhat commercial, but easy to understand and appreciate. Several bottles I tasted this side of the Atlantic were less concentrated and angular. The 1992 Châteauneuf du Pape Élise offers plummy, straightforward fruit intertwined with scents of leather, pepper, and herbs. Round and medium bodied, with decent ripeness and moderate tannin, it is a straightforward, medium-weight Châteauneuf du Pape. The 1992 Châteauneuf du Pape Cuvée de Grand Garde exhibits more of everything. The aromatics display interesting spicy, peppery, black cherry aromas, and the flavors are medium to full bodied with adequate concentration, and moderate acidity and tannin. Drink it over the next 7–9 years.

The 1993 Châteauneuf du Pape Blanc is insipid.

SAINT-DESIRAT CAVE CO-OP * * *

1990	St.-Joseph Cuvée Côte Diane	B	87
1992	Syrah Vin de Pays	A	86

I rarely see any offerings from this co-op, but based on these two examples they are making attractive, tasty red wines. The purple-colored 1992 Syrah exhibits a big, spicy, peppery, black raspberry–scented nose, excellent varietal character, ripe, tasty, soft, medium-bodied flavors, and a surprisingly long finish. Drink this excellent Syrah over the next 2–3 years. Aged in small oak casks, the 1990 St.-Joseph Cuvée Côte Diane is an impressive example from this underrated appellation on the western flank of the Rhône River. Its deep, opaque, ruby/purple color is followed by a moderately intense bouquet of toasty new oak and black currants, medium to full body, rich, sweet fruit, soft tannin, and a long, concentrated finish. While drinkable now, it will age gracefully for 8–10 years.

DOMAINE SAINT-GAYAN * * * *

1992	Côtes du Rhône	A	85
1992	Gigondas	C	85
1991	Gigondas	C	84
1990	Gigondas	C	90
1989	Rasteau Côtes du Rhône-Villages	B	87

In the tough vintages of 1991 and 1992 Saint-Gayan has fashioned easy-to-drink, round, modestly ripe, soft wines that should be consumed over the next 4–5 years. The 1992 Côtes du Rhône possesses depth for the vintage, as well as a supple texture. It is as good as the herbaceous, peppery, medium-bodied, supple 1992 Gigondas and the surprisingly well-made, round, fruity 1991 Gigondas. Should you be able to find any, the real star is Saint-Gayan's 1990 Gigondas, an opaque purple/garnet-colored wine with a huge bouquet of smoked olives, herbs, black fruits, and gamey scents. Full body, an unctuous texture, thick, rich flavors, and loads of concentration have combined to create a terrific Gigondas for drinking over the next 10–15 years.

This 1989 Rasteau Côtes du Rhône-Villages is a full-bodied, rich, concentrated, powerful wine from a superb vintage. The saturated purple color, big, peppery nose of black cherries, leather, and spices, and deep, full-bodied, superconcentrated flavors make a noteworthy impact on the palate. This mouth-filling, velvety-textured wine is ideal for drinking over the next 5–7 years.

DOMAINE SAINT-LAURENT * * * *

1990	Châteauneuf du Pape	C	89

Robert Senard owns a tiny parcel of 40-year-old vines located on the plateau behind the village of Châteauneuf du Pape, sandwiched between Beaucastel and Rayas. This is his first release in the American market, and I am delighted that this Châteauneuf du Pape has been bottled without any filtration. Its personality is similar to the rich, fleshy, up-front, flashy style of Claude Pouizin's Clos du Caillou estate, about which I have written flattering things since the 1988 vintage. A big nose of pepper, black cherries, and cedary fruit is followed by an opulent, fleshy, rich, fat wine that is oozing with fruit, glycerin, and alcohol. The tannins are nearly obliterated by the cascade of fruit, and the acidity is low, so drink this lavish, chewy Châteauneuf over the next 4–5 years.

CHÂTEAU SAINT-MAURICE * * * *

1990	Côtes du Rhône-Villages	A	87

This deeply colored wine boasts a big, earthy, peppery, cassis-scented nose, long, ripe, glycerin-imbued, rich, medium- to full-bodied flavors, a soft texture, and a spicy, heady, alcoholic finish. Drink it over the next 2–3 years.

DOMAINE LE SANG DES CAILLOUX * * * *

1990	Vacqueyras	B	87

When you look at this deeply colored wine, think about the name of the domaine—the Blood of the Stones. This rich, full-bodied Vacqueyras (a Côte du Rhône village now entitled to its own appellation status) is a broadly flavored, big, deep wine bursting with fruit, glycerin, alcohol, and character. Drink it over the next 3–4 years.

DOMAINE SANTA DUC * * * * *

1991 Côtes du Rhône	A	84
1992 Gigondas	C	88
1991 Gigondas	C	88
1993 Gigondas Cuvée Prestige des Hautes Garrigues	C	92

Since the mid- to late eighties proprietor Yves Gras has become one of the most fashionable and highly sought-after wine producers in Gigondas. Readers may remember I gave exceptional reviews to both his 1990 and 1989 Cuvée Prestige des Hautes Garrigues. The 1993 Cuvée Prestige des Hautes Garrigues is the finest Gigondas I tasted in that vintage. The wine displays a black color, and a superrich nose of raspberries, jammy cherries, and spice. Full bodied, with splendid concentration, moderate tannin, and loads of glycerin, it should prove to be a large-scaled, impressively concentrated Gigondas for drinking during its first 15 years of life.

The 1992 vintage was a much more difficult one in Gigondas than in Châteauneuf du Pape. Most of the 1992s I tasted when I visited the area in March were unimpressive. However, that cannot be said about Santa Duc's 1992 Gigondas. It offers a sweet, jammy nose of roasted nuts, Provençal herbs, and black cherry fruit. Medium to full bodied, with expansive, sweet fruitiness, moderate tannin, and admirable structure, this is a serious, well-endowed Gigondas for drinking over the next decade.

Gras's genius for turning out high-quality wines in dreadful years is even more apparent in 1991. Only one-third of his production was estate-bottled. The dark ruby-colored 1991 Gigondas exhibits an enticing chocolatey, cedary, Provençal herb–scented nose, sweet, jammy, black cherry fruit, fruitcakelike flavors, and a spicy, medium-bodied, soft finish. It is a super effort from this undistinguished vintage. Drink it over the next 5–6 years. Although lighter than usual, the 1991 Côtes du Rhône is a peppery, spicy, berry-scented, supple wine revealing fine ripeness, admirable fruit, and a pronounced peppery component. Drink it over the next 18 months.

LYLIANE SAUGERE * * * *

1991 Côte Rôtie	D	87
1990 Hermitage	D	90

The 1991 Côte Rôtie is soft, fleshy, and forward (even for the vintage), with attractive peppery, herbaceous, bacon-scented aromas, a soft, medium-bodied, plush texture, and plenty of ripe flavor. The finish is all glycerin and alcohol. Drink it over the next 5–6 years. The knockout wine, however, is the 1990 Hermitage. As Rhône wine enthusiasts know, 1990 appears to be the greatest vintage for Hermitage since 1961. This massive wine exhibits an opaque dark ruby/purple color, and a huge bouquet of smoke, pepper, black raspberries, and minerals. Full bodied, superconcentrated, with huge reserves of fruit and glycerin, as well as sweet tannin, this large-scaled, expansively flavored wine should drink well for 15–20 years. Impressive! Readers will be interested to note these wines are made under the auspices of Michel Chapoutier.

DOMAINE SÉNÉCHAUX * * *

1993 Châteauneuf du Pape	C	86
1993 Châteauneuf du Pape Blanc	C	75

Alain Roux of Château Trignon recently purchased this estate. This should result in wines of consistently good quality. I believe 1993 is the first vintage under the Roux ownership. The 1993 Châteauneuf du Pape Blanc is a straightforward, simple, full-bodied, but monolithic wine.

The soft 1993 Châteauneuf du Pape displays attractive, round, supple flavors of Provençal herbs and sweet cherries, light tannin, medium to full body, and a lush personality. It should be drunk over the next 5–6 years. No 1992 red wine was presented for tasting.

DOMAINE DE LA SOLITUDE * * * *

1992 Côtes du Rhône	A	85
1992 Côtes du Rhône Blanc	A	85

These are tasty, ready-to-drink wines from the well-known Châteauneuf du Pape estate of the same name. The 1992 white wine is surprisingly flavorful for a southern white Rhône, with excellent creamy, buttery, pineapplelike fruit, low acidity, and a plump character. Drink it over the next year. The 1992 red Côtes du Rhône is a mouth-filling peppery, plummy, black cherry–scented wine with attractive, medium-bodied, herbaceous, smooth flavors, and admirable power and ripeness. The wine's softness suggests it should be drunk over the next 2–3 years.

HENRI SORREL * * * */* * * * *

1993 Crozes-Hermitage	C	83
1992 Crozes-Hermitage	C	84
1991 Crozes-Hermitage	C	85
1993 Hermitage	D	84
1992 Hermitage	D	87
1991 Hermitage	D	88
1992 Hermitage Le Gréal	D	90
1991 Hermitage Le Gréal	D	93+
1993 Hermitage Les Rocoules	D	87
1992 Hermitage Les Rocoules	D	88
1991 Hermitage Les Rocoules	D	89+

Marc Sorrel produces classic, traditionally styled white and red wines from his small holdings in Hermitage and Crozes-Hermitage. All of the wines, including the whites, go into the bottle without any filtration. There are generally 75–100 cases (3–4 barrels) of white Crozes-Hermitage made from 90% Marsanne and 10% Roussanne. The 1993 Crozes-Hermitage offers light, elegant, lemony, earthy fruit, medium body, decent acidity, and a soft finish. It will require drinking in its first 3–4 years of life. The 1992 Crozes-Hermitage possesses more fatness and an oilier texture, as well as fine ripeness, a honeyed, flowery bouquet, and low acidity. It should drink well for 5–6 years. The best of this trio, the 1991 Crozes-Hermitage exhibits more depth, better focus and delineation, and medium- to full-bodied, chunky, monolithic flavors.

All three vintages of Sorrel's white Hermitage achieved a minimum of 13% natural alcohol. The 1993 Hermitage Les Rocoules, from what Sorrel claims is "the worst vintage I've ever seen," has turned out well. Harvested under appalling weather conditions, the wine has fleshy, earthy, mineral-dominated, spicy fruit, fine ripeness, weight, and depth, and moderate length, as well as the potential to last 5–10 years. The fatter, more luscious

1992 Hermitage Les Rocoules displays honeyed, apricot, peachlike notes, an alluring thickness, earthy, mineral funkiness, and a spicy, long, heady finish. Made in a corpulent yet charming style, it is best drunk during its first decade of life. Not surprisingly, the 1991 Hermitage Les Rocoules is the best wine of this trio (1991 is the best recent vintage in the northern Rhône). It offers a honeyed apple, citrusy, mineral-scented nose, rich, full-bodied flavors that exhibit excellent concentration, and a spicy, chewy finish with fine glycerin, alcohol, and fruit. It should drink well for 10–20 years.

Sorrel's red wines are favorites among connoisseurs. The 1993 Hermitage is reasonably palatable in view of the northern Rhône's disastrous harvest conditions. A medium ruby-colored wine, it has a burgundian-like openness, softness, and herbal, peppery spiciness. Although not very concentrated, it is round, low in acidity, soundly made, and ideal for drinking over the next 5 years. When I saw Sorrel in March 1994, he said there would be no Le Gréal produced in 1993, as it was destined to be blended into his regular Hermitage that he calls Cuvée Classique.

In 1992, both a regular cuvée and Le Gréal were produced. The dark ruby-colored 1992 Hermitage reveals a peppery, herbaceous, sweet, cassis- and tar-scented nose, soft, voluptuously textured flavors, excellent richness, and a ripe, medium-bodied, soft finish. Already drinkable, it should last for a decade. The 1992 Hermitage Le Gréal (from vines planted in 1928) offers an opaque black/purple color, a sweet, exotic nose of licorice, leather, beef, and black currant scents, full-bodied, dense, concentrated flavors, low acidity, moderate tannin, and an intense finish. An outstanding wine for the vintage, it is one of the finest 1992 northern Rhônes.

The 1991 Hermitage is extremely good, with a dark ruby/purple color, a spicy, leathery, herb- and peppery-scented nose, excellent depth, chewy, tannic flavors and texture, and a spicy, tough yet long finish. It will benefit from 3–5 years of cellaring and will keep for 15 or more years. The spectacular, black-colored 1991 Hermitage Le Gréal, made from yields of under 20 hectoliters per hectare (less than in 1990), reveals a huge bouquet of Asian spices, licorice, black fruits, earth, and vanillin. Fabulously concentrated and full bodied, with moderate tannin and layers of thick, juicy Syrah fruit, this terrific Hermitage should be drunk between 2000 and 2020. Sorrel's former importer for much of the United States, Vinstar in northern California, has ceased representing the wines because of their "hand-crafted" nature.

DOMAINE DU TERME * * *

1993 Gigondas	C	87?
1992 Gigondas	C	85

One of two successful wines from this estate, the 1993 Gigondas was still going through malolactic fermentation when I tasted it in late March 1994, making it difficult to fully assess. It unquestionably possesses an opaque saturated purple color, a dense, black cherry–scented nose, and long, rich, medium- to full-bodied flavors with moderate tannin. It should be one of the more concentrated and structured wines of the 1993 vintage. Domaine du Terme also produced a sweet, soft, fruitcake-scented, grapy, alcoholic 1992 Gigondas that has avoided the vegetal, pruny, damp, woodsy quality exhibited by many of the rain-plagued 1992s. A fine effort, it should be consumed over the next 3–4 years.

J. L. THIERS * * *

1993 Cornas	C	85

The young Jean-Louis Thiers is garnering considerable respect from established Cornas growers. His 1993 Cornas (hardly a showcase vintage) is a surprisingly successful wine. An attractive light perfume of ripe cassis, licorice, and herbs is followed by a soft, pure wine with medium body, fine depth, and more fruit than most wines from this appellation. Drink it over the next 5–6 years.

DOMAINE LES TOURELLES * * *

1993 Gigondas	C	85
1992 Gigondas	C	73

The fruity, medium-bodied 1993 Gigondas displays moderate intensity, attractive black cherry and dusty olive notes, and a spicy, soft, medium-bodied finish. It should be drunk over the next 4–5 years. The light-bodied 1992 Gigondas lacks concentration and suffers from excessively high tannin in the meager finish.

CHÂTEAU DES TOURS * * * * *

1992 Côtes du Rhône	B	85
1992 Côtes du Rhône Blanc	B	79
1992 Vacqueyras	C	86
1990 Vin de Pays Vaucluse	A	85

Emanuel Reynaud, the nephew of and possible heir apparent to Jacques Reynaud, the proprietor of Rayas, has made some terrific wines from this southern Rhône Valley estate. Unfortunately, defective corks in some of his 1990s created enormous marketing problems, a tragedy in light of the superb quality of Reynaud's wines. Those problems appear to be behind Reynaud. The 1990 Vin de Pays Vaucluse exhibits an excellent dark ruby color, a spicy, tar- and berry-scented nose, and soft, medium-bodied, easygoing flavors. It should be drunk over the next 2–3 years. Although he is working with less impressive raw materials, his 1992 red wines have turned out well. The 1992 Côtes du Rhône displays a smoky, roasted herb– and black cherry–scented nose, medium-bodied, concentrated flavors, dusty tannin, and a spicy, moderately long finish. It should drink well for 4–5 years. The richest, as well as most powerful and alcoholic of this quartet of wines, is the 1992 Vacqueyras. It offers a saturated deep ruby color, a handsome bouquet of earthy, herb and black cherry scents, medium to full body, a lovely, supple texture, and a heady, lusty finish. Drink it over the next 5–6 years.

The 1992 Côtes du Rhône Blanc is a fat, oily wine with a monolithic character, but plenty of chunky fruit. Typical of most Côtes du Rhône whites, it is big and chewy but lacks charm and finesse.

CHÂTEAU DE TRIGNON * * *

1992 Côtes du Rhône	A	85
1993 Gigondas	B	83
1992 Gigondas	B	81
1993 Sablet	A	85

This well-run estate in the southern Rhône has fashioned a lively, perfumed, medium-bodied, fruity 1993 Sablet. One of the better white Côtes du Rhône villages, it merits consumption over the next year. The medium ruby-colored 1992 Côtes du Rhône offers olive-tinged, cherry-scented fruit in its straightforward bouquet. Medium bodied and supple, with good concentration and a silky finish, this fresh, fruity wine should drink well for 1–2 years.

Trigon made a light-bodied, fruity, straightforward 1993 Gigondas, and one of the better 1992 Gigondas. The latter wine offers a soft, fruity, alcoholic style with no vegetal character or pruny overripeness. Both wines should be drunk over the next 5–6 years.

GEORGES VERNAY* * * *

1993 Condrieu	C	87
1993 Condrieu Coteaux du Vernon	D	90
1992 Condrieu Coteaux du Vernon	D	88
1993 Viognier	C	75

Vernay has long been considered one of the reference points of Condrieu, largely because he produces more wine than just about any other grower. His Viognier from young vines has never impressed me. The 1993 is a light-bodied, straightforward, simple wine of no particular distinction. However, the medium- to full-bodied, tasty, ripe apricot-scented and -flavored 1993 Condrieu is a high-quality wine possessing lavish amounts of fruit. Drink it over the next year.

Vernay's luxury cuvée of Condrieu, the 1993 Condrieu Coteaux du Vernon (from a steep terraced vineyard situated across from the famed Condrieu restaurant/hotel, Beau Rivage) is a full-bodied wine offering a smorgasbord of aromas such as peach blossoms, apricots, honey, and cherries. The wine exhibits excellent depth and richness, outstanding balance, and a long, lusty, unevolved finish. It should drink well between now and 1998. Vernay's excellent 1992 Condrieu Coteaux du Vernon exhibits less of a honeyed, concentrated feel. Nevertheless, it is a big, dense, chewy, full-bodied, ripe wine with all the classic Viognier characteristics. Drink it over the next 1–2 years.

NOËL VERSET* * * * *

1993 Cornas	C	82
1992 Cornas	C	84
1991 Cornas	C	92

The 1993 and 1992 Cornas are two of the lightest and least distinguished efforts Verset has produced since I began visiting him in 1980. Verset owns some of the oldest and best-placed vines in Cornas, so the fact that his wines are lighter and less concentrated than usual should demonstrate to readers just what deplorable conditions producers endured in these 2 years. The medium ruby-colored 1993 Cornas displays a faint perfume of black fruits, minerals, and herbs. Although the attack begins well, the wine is hollow in the middle, with light body, and a spicy, tough finish. It may fill out with additional aging in Verset's ancient *foudres,* but don't count on it. The 1992 Cornas offers a pronounced vegetal nose, ripe cassis fruit, and hard, tough tannin in the finish. It appears more concentrated and complete than the 1993, but it is frightfully tannic for its modest flavor dimensions.

The 1991 Cornas (from an underrated vintage for northern Rhône appellations such as Condrieu, Côte Rôtie, and Cornas) possesses a dense, opaque black/purple color and a huge, sweet perfume of cassis, truffles, and licorice. Exceptionally opulent and superconcentrated with low acidity, this full-bodied wine is ideal for drinking over the next 10–12 years.

VIDAL-FLEURY* * * *

1990 Châteauneuf du Pape	C	89
1989 Châteauneuf du Pape	C	87
1992 Châteauneuf du Pape Blanc	C	85
1992 Condrieu	D	88
1990 Cornas	C	85
1991 Côte Rôtie La Chatillonne Côte Blonde	D	92

1990	Côte Rôtie La Chatillonne Côte Blonde	D	90
1991	Côte Rôtie Côtes Blonde et Brune	D	89
1990	Côte Rôtie Côtes Blonde et Brune	D	88
1991	Côtes du Rhône	A	84
1990	Côtes du Rhône	A	86
1993	Côtes du Rhône Blanc	A	86
1991	Côtes du Ventoux	A	77
1990	Côtes du Ventoux	A	86
1991	Crozes-Hermitage Blanc	B	84
1990	Gigondas	B	87
1989	Gigondas	B	85
1989	Hermitage	D	86
1988	Hermitage	D	82
1992	Muscat de Beaumes de Venise	C	90
1990	St.-Joseph	C	89
1992	St.-Joseph Blanc	C	86
1991	Vacqueyras	A	84
1990	Vacqueyras	A	87

With all the investments made at the historic firm of Vidal-Fleury by its owner, Marcel Guigal, the quality of wines now emerging has improved dramatically, even though the vintages are less exciting than those in the late eighties. This is evident in Vidal-Fleury's white wines, which have a tendency to be muted and neutral. However, the 1993 Côtes du Rhône Blanc is a good choice for retailers, restaurants, and consumers looking for a perfumed, medium-bodied, fresh, vibrant, dry white wine. Generous portions of Viognier in the blend give the wine a honeyed, floral-scented nose. The 1991 Crozes-Hermitage Blanc exhibits surprising intensity and fatness. There is a big, medium-bodied, voluptuous mouth-feel, but not much complexity. Slightly better is the honeyed, floral-scented 1992 St.-Joseph Blanc, a buttery style of wine with surprising character and the intriguing mineral scent that comes from St.-Joseph's steep, hillside vineyards. The austere, backward 1988 Hermitage Blanc lacks depth and plentitude. It will last for 10–15 years, but I do not anticipate its developing into a distinctive wine. The 1992 Châteauneuf du Pape Blanc offers a flowery, straightforward, fruity nose, solid flavors, medium to full body, and a crisp finish. Drink it over the next year. I was impressed with Vidal-Fleury's 1992 Condrieu, a honeyed, exotic, full-bodied wine with excellent ripeness, and that long, lavish, in-your-face fruit that the best Condrieus possess.

The great red wine buys from Vidal-Fleury are generally the wines from the Côtes du Ventoux and Côtes du Rhône, as well as their terrific Vacqueyras and excellent Gigondas. The 1991s are more herbaceous, compact, lighter, and less powerful than the 1990s, which, fortunately, can still be easily found on many retailers' shelves. For example, the 1990 Côtes du Ventoux offers gobs of berry fruit and spice, wonderful richness, and a fleshy, long, alcoholic finish. A mouth-filling wine with considerable character, it is worth buying by the case for consuming over the next 2–4 years. The 1990 Côtes du Rhône exhibits loads of alcohol, a big, sweet, peppery, herb- and black cherry–scented nose, dusty, earthy, rich, full-bodied flavors, and a lot of character and generosity. It will last for 3–4 years. My favorite wine, the 1990 Vacqueyras reveals an intense, spicy, peppery, herb- and cherry/raspberry-scented nose, deep, rich, supple flavors, copious amounts of fat, glycerin, and alcohol, and a lusty finish. Drink this succulent Vacqueyras over the next 5–6 years.

While Vidal-Fleury's 1989 Gigondas offers plenty of cassis fruit, dusty tannin, excellent intensity, and medium to full body, their 1990 Gigondas is even better. With deep ruby/purple color, and a rich nose of licorice, cassis, herbs, and pepper, this long, voluptuous, deep wine is a top-notch Gigondas for drinking over the next decade. The Châteauneuf du Papes range from a hard, tannic but very good to excellent, firmly structured 1989, which should evolve well for at least a decade, to a slightly fuller, more opulent and powerful 1990, which should last for 10–12 years.

With respect to the northern red Rhônes, Vidal-Fleury generally makes a fine Crozes-Hermitage, but the wine that stood out in my tasting was the 1990 St.-Joseph. A huge, bacon fat– and cassis-scented nose is followed by a wine with superb intensity, wonderful purity, vibrant fruit, medium to full body, and a handsome marriage of power and elegance. It should drink well for 7–8 years. It is a knockout wine that is available for a song! Although the 1990 Cornas reveals the rustic, earthy, coarse side of the northern Rhône, it possesses fine cassis fruit, plenty of dusty tannin, and a spicy, medium- to full-bodied finish. For its price and pedigree, the 1989 Hermitage is straightforward, with moderate tannin, and medium to full body.

Vidal-Fleury's finest, as well as most expensive, northern Rhône wines are from their holdings in Côte Rôtie. The regular cuvée of 1990 Côte Rôtie Côtes Blonde et Brune exhibits subtle aromas of bacon fat, roasted nuts, and black raspberries, deep color, excellent ripeness, and a soft, supple finish. Drink it over the next 10–12 years. The 1991 Côte Rôtie Côtes Blonde et Brune is one of the best efforts Vidal-Fleury has produced in recent years. With deeper color, more perfume (bacon fat, smoke, and black raspberries), and a silky, creamy-textured feel, it is Côte Rôtie at its most seductive. Drink it over the next 10 years. Although Vidal-Fleury's famed single-vineyard Côte Rôtie La Chatillonne Côte Blonde is limited in availability (500–700 cases produced), it is potentially a superb wine. The 1990 displays an intoxicating perfume of cloves, pepper, spice, and black fruits. Rich and medium to full bodied, with a shorter finish than the bouquet and attack suggest, it is a complex, multidimensional wine for drinking over the next 10 years. The outstanding 1991 Côte Rôtie La Chatillonne Côte Blonde offers a fragrant personality of big, ripe scents of jammy black and red fruits, toasty oak, herbs, pepper, and the appellation's famous bacon fat aroma. Voluptuously textured, with soft tannin and low acidity, this unctuously rich wine should drink well for 10–15 years.

Lastly, do not miss Vidal-Fleury's top-notch 1992 Muscat de Beaumes de Venise. This is an underpriced, underrated dessert wine with a honeyed apricot-scented nose, and rich, intense flavors. Moderately sweet, with good underlying acidity, and plenty of lush fruit, it should be drunk over the next 2–3 years.

LA VIEILLE FERME * * * *

1993	Côtes du Lubéron	A	85
1990	Côtes du Rhône Gold Label	A	86
1993	Côtes du Rhône Gold Label Reserve	A	85
1992	Côtes du Rhône Reserve	A	87
1990	Côtes du Ventoux	A	86
1992	Côtes du Ventoux Le Mont	A	87

The *négociant* wines of La Vieille Ferme are made by Jean-Pierre Perrin, the coproprietor of the renowned Château Beaucastel. They have become popular in the United States, and justifiably so. Of late, the firm's finest efforts were from the 1989 and 1990 vintages. The disappointing 1991s followed (most of the production was sold in Europe). The newest releases include reassuringly fine 1993 whites and 1992 reds.

The uncomplex 1993 Côtes du Luberon is an easygoing, ripe, soft, fruity wine, with low acidity and plump, tasty, chewy fruit. Drink it over the next year. The 1993 Côtes du Rhône Gold Label Reserve is made in a richer, fuller-bodied, heavier style. The blend of 80% Bourboulenc and 20% Grenache gives the wine a heavier style, but it is really a question of whether readers prefer the light, crisp, floral, citrusy freshness of the Côtes du Luberon, or the fleshier, more chubby and earthy style of the Côtes du Rhône. Both wines should be drunk over the next year.

The red wines are knockout bargains. The 1992 Côtes du Ventoux Le Mont exhibits a saturated dark ruby color, a big, sweet nose of jammy cassis fruit and spices, with a touch of pepper and herbs in the background, medium body, lush, juicy flavors, and an excellent finish. It is a mouth-filling, generous, smooth-as-silk dry red wine for drinking over the next 2–3 years. Bolder, with more black cherries and pepper in the nose, the 1992 Côtes du Rhône Reserve is made from an intriguing blend of 45% Grenache, 15% Mourvèdre, 10% Syrah, and the remainder Counoise, Cinsault, and Carignan. With a dense, chewy palate, as well as some tannin in the finish, it is capable of lasting 4–6 years.

The 1990 Côtes du Ventoux, a blend of 60% Grenache, 20% Syrah, 15% Mourvèdre, and 5% Cinsault, is richly fruity and supple, with great color, an excellent bouquet of cassis and herbs, and a long, tasty, round finish. Perfect for casual sipping, restaurants would be smart to use this as a house wine, given its wide commercial appeal. The 1990 Côtes du Rhône Gold Label, a serious blend of 40% Grenache, 20% Mourvèdre, 10% Syrah, 10% Cinsault, and the rest various other Rhône varietals, is a surprisingly big, bold, dramatically flavored, spicy, berry-scented wine, with admirable intensity, soft tannins, a heady alcohol and glycerin content, and a robust, spicy finish. I would not be surprised to see this wine evolve even more complexity and character over the next 4–5 years. By the way, should you run across any of the 1989s from La Vieille Ferme, they, too, are still drinking well and merit consideration. I should also note that none of the 1991s merit a recommendation.

DOMAINE DE LA VIEILLE JULIENNE * * * *

1993 Châteauneuf du Pape	C	86
1992 Châteauneuf du Pape	C	85
1993 Châteauneuf du Pape Blanc	C	65

Known for its rustic red wines, this estate has lightened its style and begun to produce more civilized, accessible wines. I rarely taste Vieille Julienne's white wines, but the 1993 Châteauneuf du Pape Blanc is made in a heavy, oxidized, dull, flat style. I found it to be below average in quality.

The 1993 and 1992 red Châteauneuf du Papes are both medium to dark ruby-colored wines with elegant, peppery, berry- and herb-scented noses, and round, medium-bodied personalities exhibiting low acidity and light tannin. Both should be drunk over the next 5–7 years. These two vintages are a far cry from the huge, sometimes savage, bold, dense wines of previous years.

VIEUX DONJON * * * *

1992 Châteauneuf du Pape	C	88
1993 Châteauneuf du Pape Blanc	C	82

This is one of my favorite estates, and I have been an admirer as well as a purchaser of Vieux Donjon's 1983, 1985, 1989, and 1990 (the best wine I have tasted from this property). The 1992 Châteauneuf du Pape is excellent for the vintage. One of the deepest-colored 1992s, it possesses a surprisingly saturated color, an attractive, ripe nose of cassis fruit, Provençal herbs, and cedar, sweet, expansive, attractively endowed flavors, full body, low acidity, and light tannin. It should provide seductive drinking for at least a decade.

Vieux Donjon also produced a tiny quantity of white wine in 1993. The one-dimensional 1993 Châteauneuf du Pape Blanc is a straightforward, compact, well-made wine that should be drunk over the next year.

DOMAINE DU VIEUX TÉLÉGRAPHE * * * *

1993 Châteauneuf du Pape	C	90
1992 Châteauneuf du Pape	C	87
1992 Vin de Pays Vaucluse Le Pigeoulet	A	85

Over recent years the Brunier family has fashioned a tasty, light- to medium-bodied, ripe, herb-, berry-, and spice-scented, supple red wine called Le Pigeoulet. The 1992 is round, easy to drink and to understand, and ideal for uncritical quaffing over the next 1–3 years. The 1993 Châteauneuf du Pape displays a big, peppery, licorice-, herb-, and blackberry-scented nose, fat, intense, opulent, full-bodied flavors, an unctuous texture, low acidity, and a smooth-as-silk finish. Reminiscent of a hypothetical blend of 1985 and 1989, it should drink well for 10–12 years. The 1992 Châteauneuf du Pape is an excellent example from this average- to slightly above-average-quality vintage. The wine reveals a medium to dark ruby color, a spicy, herb- and black cherry–scented nose, medium to full-bodied, expansive flavors that possess an attractive sweetness and lushness, low acidity, and a ripe, corpulent, heady finish. Drink it over the next 7–9 years.

FRANÇOIS VILLAND * * * *

1993 Condrieu Coteaux des Poncins	D	90
1992 Condrieu Coteaux des Poncins	D	88

The young, 25-year-old François Villand is an up-and-coming star of Condrieu. His 1993 Condrieu Coteaux des Poncins, harvested largely before any rain fell, offers a big, smoky, cherry/apricot/peachlike nose, dense, concentrated, unctuously textured flavors, and a long, heady, ripe finish. Drink this decadent Condrieu over the next 1–2 years. Although less opulent, the 1992 Condrieu Coteaux des Poncins is a ripe, medium- to full-bodied, tasty, succulent Condrieu displaying the intense fruit and perfume of the Viognier grape. It should be drunk over the next year.

ALAIN VOGE * * * */* * * * *

1991 Cornas	C	90
1993 Cornas Vieilles Vignes	C	87
1992 Cornas Vieilles Vignes	C	86

Voge produces his Cornas from old vines grown on steep hillsides. The 1993 Cornas Vieilles Vignes reveals a fine deep color (it is among the darker-colored wines of this appellation), a spicy, ripe, peppery, black fruit–scented nose, round, ripe, soft, medium-bodied flavors, admirable concentration, some fat and flesh, and a soft finish. Drink it over the next 7–8 years. The 1992 Cornas Vieilles Vignes offers an herbaceous, black cherry–scented nose, sweet, ripe fruit, medium body, and a moderately long, supple finish. Drink it over the next 5–6 years. These are both successful wines for the vintages.

The 1991 regular cuvée is a rich, earthy, black raspberry–scented wine with full body, admirable depth and ripeness, and a long, spicy finish. Although rustic, it is loaded with character, ripe fruit, fine richness, and moderate tannin. This is a Cornas for drinking over the next 7–8 years.

BERGERAC AND THE SOUTHWEST

The Basics

TYPES OF WINE
This remote corner of France, while close to Bordeaux, remains an unexplored territory when it comes to wine. Some appellations have recognizable names such as Madiran, Bergerac, Cahors, and Monbazillac, but how many consumers can name one producer, good or bad, from the Côtes du Frontonnais, Gaillac, Pacherenc du Vic Bilh, Côtes de Duras, or Pécharmant? The best wines are serious, broodingly deep red wines from Madiran, Pécharmant, and Cahors; lighter, effusively fruity reds from Bergerac and the Côtes du Frontonnais; and some fine sweet white wines from Monbazillac and Jurançon. Remarkable dry white wine values are plentiful in the Côtes de Gascogne.

GRAPE VARIETIES
In addition to the well-known varieties such as Cabernet Sauvignon, Merlot, and Syrah, this vast area is home to a number of grape varieties that are little known and mysterious to the average consumer. In Madiran, there is the Tannat; in the Côtes du Frontonnais, the Mauzac and Negrette. For the white wines of Pacherenc du Vic Bilh and Jurançon, rare varieties such as the Gros Manseng, Petit Manseng, Courbu, and Arrufiac are planted.

FLAVORS
The red wines of Bergerac are light and fruity; those of Madiran and Cahors, dense, dark, rich, and often quite tannic. The red wines from the Côtes de Buzet, Côtes de Duras, and Côtes du Frontonnais, often vinified by the carbonic maceration method, are light, soft, and fruity. The best dry white wines are crisp, light, and zesty. Some surprisingly rich, sweet wines that resemble a fine Sauternes can emerge from Monbazillac and Jurançon.

AGING POTENTIAL
Except for the top red wines of Madiran, Pécharmant, and Cahors, all of the wines from France's southwest corner must be drunk within 5 years.

Bergerac: 2–5 years
Cahors: 4–12 years
Côtes de Buzet: 1–5 years
Côtes de Duras: 1–4 years
Gaillac: 1–4 years

Jurançon: 3–8 years
Madiran: 6–15 years
Monbazillac: 3–8 years
Pécharmant: 3–10 years

OVERALL QUALITY LEVEL

The overall quality level is extremely irregular. Improvements have been made, but most wines are sold for very low prices, so many producers have little incentive to increase quality. For the top estates listed below, the quality is good to excellent.

FRANCE'S GREATEST WHITE WINE VALUE?

Just about every shrewd importer has been making a trek to the area of Armagnac in search of crisp, fruity, deliciously light, dry white wines from a region not entitled to either appellation or VDQS status, the Côtes de Gascogne. Grapes such as Ugni Blanc, Colombard, Gros Menseng, and Sauvignon produce dry wines with crisp acidity, fragrant, lemony, fruity bouquets, zesty, lively flavors, and light- to medium-bodied, crisp finishes. Almost all sell for under $6 a bottle. They have proven exceptionally successful in the American market-place. These are wines to buy by the case and drink within 12 months of the vintage. For example, the 1994s (released in spring 1995) should be consumed by spring 1996. If you are not already eagerly gulping these light, fruity wines, you are missing one of the most unlikely success stories in the wine world. The most successful, palate- and purse-pleasing dry white wines are those from Domaine de Pouy, Domaine de Pomès, Domaine de Tariquet, Domaine de Rieux, Domaine de Tuilerie, Domaine Varet, Domaine Lasalle, Domaine de Joy, Domaine de Puits, and Domaine de Puts.

FRANCE'S LEAST-KNOWN AND RAREST SWEET WINE?

Adventurous readers looking for a fascinating sweet wine that is an insider's secret should check out the remarkable offerings of Domaine Cauhaupé, Domaine Guirouilh, Clos Uroulat, and Cru Lamouroux. These sweet white wines age for 15–20 years in top vintages such as 1989 and 1990, with flavors not dissimilar to a top Barsac/Sauternes, only with a more roasted nut character. Prices are moderate for wines of such quality.

MOST IMPORTANT INFORMATION TO KNOW

Learn the top two or three estates for each of the better-known appellations and their styles of wine.

1995–1996 BUYING STRATEGY

These wines are for the shrewd and adventurous consumer who wants to experience different aromas and flavors at a bargain-basement price. For white wines, stick to recent vintages such as 1994 and 1993. The red wines, particularly those of Madiran and Cahors, can easily be drunk back to the early 1980s, as long as the wines have been well stored by retailers. However, the recent top vintages for Madiran and Cahors are 1990 (exceptional), followed by 1989 (very good), 1988 (good), and 1986 (very good). Recent vintages, 1993, 1992, and 1991, are average in quality. The 1994 vintage should be the finest of the last four harvests.

RATING BERGERAC AND THE SOUTHWEST'S BEST PRODUCERS

Dry Red Wines

* * * * *(OUTSTANDING)

Château de la Grezette (Cahors)

Château Montus (Madiran)

Domaine Pichard Cuvée Vigneau
(Madiran)

* * * *(EXCELLENT)

Domaine de l'Antenet (Cahors)

Château d'Aydie-Laplace (Madiran)

Domaine de Barréjat (Madiran)

Domaine Bibian (Madiran)

Domaine Bouscassé (Madiran)

Château Calabre (Bergerac)

Château Champerel (Pécharmant)

Clos La Coutale (Cahors)

Clos de Gamot (Cahors)

Clos de Triguedina Prince Phobus (Cahors)

Domaine Pichard (Madiran)

* * *(GOOD)

Château de Belingard (Bergerac)

Château de Cayrou (Cahors)

Château de Chambert (Cahors)

Clos de Triguedina (Cahors)

Château Court-Les-Mûts (Bergerac)

Domaine Jean Cros (Gaillac)

Domaine de Durand (Côtes de Duras)

Domaine du Haut-Pécharmant
(Pécharmant)

Domaine de Haute-Serre (Cahors)

Château de la Jaubertie (Bergerac)

Château Michel de Montague (Bergerac)

Château de Padère (Buzet)

Château de Panisseau (Bergerac)

Château Le Payssel (Cahors)

Château Pech de Jammes (Cahors)

Château du Perron (Madiran)

Château de Peyros (Cahors)

Château Pineraie (Cahors)

Château Poulvère (Bergerac)

Château St.-Didier Parnac (Cahors)

Domaine des Savarines (Cahors)***/****

Château Thénac (Cahors)

Domaine Theulet et Marsalet (Bergerac)

Château de Tiregand (Pécharmant)

* *(AVERAGE)

Domaine de Boliva (Cahors)

Château La Borderie (Bergerac)

Château Le Caillou (Bergerac)

Domaine Constant (Bergerac)**/***

Les Côtes d'Oit (Cahors)

Duron (Cahors)

Château Le Fagé (Bergerac)

Domaine de Paillas (Cahors)

Château Peyrat (Cahors)

Domaine de Quattre (Cahors)

Dry White Wines

* * * *(EXCELLENT)

Château de Bachen (Tursan)

Château Calabre (Bergerac)

Château Court-Les-Mûts (Bergerac)

Château Grinou (Bergerac)

Domaine de la Jaubertie (Bergerac)

Château de Panisseau (Bergerac)

Château Tiregard-Les Galinux (Bergerac)

* * *(GOOD)

Château Belingard (Bergerac)

Château Haut-Peygonthier (Bergerac)

Domaine de Joy (Côtes de Gascogne)

Domaine Lasalle (Côtes de Gascogne)

Domaine de Pomès (Côtes de Gascogne)

Domaine de Pouy (Côtes de Gascogne)

Domaine de Puits (Côtes de Gascogne)

Domaine de Puts (Côtes de Gascogne)

Domaine de Rieux (Côtes de Gascogne)
Domaine de Saint-Lannes (Côtes de Gascogne)

Domaine Tariquet (Côtes de Gascogne)
Domaine de Tuilerie (Côtes de Gascogne)
Domaine Varet (Côtes de Gascogne)

Sweet White Wines

* * * * *(OUTSTANDING)

Domaine Cauhaupe Cuvée Quintessence
(Jurançon)

* * * *(EXCELLENT)

Domaine Cauhaupe (Jurançon)
Clos Uroulat (Jurançon)
Cru Lamouroux (Jurançon)

Domaine Guirouilh Cuvée Petit Cuyalaa
(Jurançon)

* * *(GOOD)

Domaine Bellegarde Sélection de Petit
Marseng (Jurançon)
Château Le Fage (Monbazillac)

Château du Treuil-de-Nailhac
(Monbazillac)

* *(AVERAGE)

Domaine Bru-Baché (Jurançon)
Henri Burgue (Jurançon)

Clos Lapeyre (Jurançon)
Château Rousse (Jurançon)

2. ITALY

The Basics

TYPES OF WINE

The glories of Piedmont (aside from the scenery and white truffles) are the robust, rich, multidimensional red wines made from the Nebbiolo grape. The top wines made from the Nebbiolo—Barbaresco, Barolo, Gattinara, and Spanna—are at their best between 6 and 15 years of age, but can last up to 25 years. At the opposite extreme are the wines called Dolcetto d'Alba, which are wonderfully supple, rich, and fruity, but are meant to be drunk within their first 4–5 years of life. Then there is Barbera. Historically too acidic for non-Italian palates, a new generation of winemakers has begun to turn out splendid and expensive examples. Lastly, there is Cabernet Sauvignon, and a host of insipid, usually inferior red wines that are less likely to be seen in the international marketplace. I am referring to Freisa, Grignolino, and Brachetto. Piedmont's white wine production is growing, and while most of the wines are overpriced and bland, some potential is evident with the indigenous Arneis grape and Cortese di Gavi. Chardonnay is making its ubiquitous presence felt; Erbaluce di Caluso is underrated; and Moscato, the low-alcohol, fizzy, slightly sweet wine, is perhaps Piedmont's best value in white wine. Lastly, there is the ocean of sweet, industrially produced Asti Spumante.

GRAPE VARIETIES

Nebbiolo, Barbera, and Dolcetto are the top red wine grapes in Piedmont, producing the finest wines. For the white wines, the Muscat, Arneis, Cortese di Gavi, and Erbaluce di Caluso are the most successful. Of course, there are many other grapes, but the wines made from these varietals are generally of little interest.

Flavors

RED WINES

Barolo Barolo is one of the world's most stern, tannic, austere yet full-flavored wines; the aromas of road tar, leather, Bing cherries, tobacco, and dried herbs dominate. It is a massive yet intensely fragrant wine.

Barbaresco   Often better balanced as well as lighter than Barolo (less tannin, more fruit), with the same aromas and flavors, Barbaresco frequently has more intense jammy fruit, and sometimes more cedar and chocolate; it can be sublime.

Dolcetto   Purple in color and not at all sweet, as the name incorrectly implies, this dry, exuberant, effusively fruity and grapy wine tastes of blackberries, almonds, chocolate, and spices, and is very soft and supple. It is a joyful wine.

Barbera   In the old days it was too acidic, harsh, and oxidized—and was dirt cheap. The new-style Barberas, often aged in 100% new French oak, exhibit saturated purple color, great fruit, and superrichness that serve to balance out the naturally high acidity. The best Barberas will set consumers back $25–$50, so their potential market is microscopic. But a taste of the 1989s or 1990s can be addictive.

Gattinara/Spanna   These wines come from Nebbiolo grown in the hills north of Barolo and Barbaresco. Intense tar and earthy aromas dominate, and there is a pronounced Oriental spice-box character to the bouquet. The wines tend to be softer and fruitier than Barolo, but no less age-worthy.

Carema   The lightest of the Nebbiolo-based wines, Carema, made in a marginal mountainous climate near Valle d'Aosta, can be quite smooth, fruity, and elegant, but adequate ripeness is often a problem.

A CLOSER LOOK AT THE BAROLO AND BARBARESCO REGIONS

The Barolo region consists of over 3,000 acres of vineyards, most of them situated on the hillsides surrounding five villages—La Morra, Serralunga d'Alba, Monforte d'Alba, Barolo, and Castiglione Falletto.

Barolo   This old village is located south of La Morra. Barolo is said to combine the velvety, supple, easygoing, more feminine side of Nebbiolo with considerable structure and concentration. The word *classic* is frequently used to describe the wines of Barolo by the local cognoscenti. Barolo ranks fourth in importance among the five most significant winemaking communes of Barolo. Barolo has 375 acres of vineyards shared by 139 growers. By analogy to Bordeaux, Barolo might be considered the Margaux or St.-Julien of this viticultural zone.

Highly Regarded Barolo Vineyards: Bricco delle Viole, Brunate (this vineyard is shared with La Morra), Cannubi (often considered the most historic and among the finest of the Barolo vineyards), Cannubi Boschis, Castellero, Cerequio (also shared with La Morra), Costa di Rose, Sarmassa, and La Villa

Castiglione Falletto   The smallest of the five principal Barolo communes in terms of acreage and growers, Castiglione Falletto is a picture-postcard-perfect hilltop village situated between Barolo and Serralunga d'Alba. The vineyards are all on steep hillsides ringing the village. Allowing for different styles of wines, Castiglione Falletto's reputation is for wines of boldness, richness, full body, power, and concentration—in brief, the Pauillac of Barolo. There are 255 acres of vines owned by 93 growers.

Highly Regarded Castiglione Falletto Vineyards: Bricco Boschis, Fiasc, Monprivato, Montanello, Rocche, and Villero

Monforte d'Alba   The hilltop town of Monforte d'Alba is the third-largest vineyard area in Barolo, consisting of 486 acres farmed by 185 growers. Once again, all the vineyards are situated on steep hillsides. Monforte d'Alba appears to be the St.-Estèphe of Barolo. The locals claim that Barolo's longest-lived, most concentrated, firmest wines are produced from the hillsides of this small town.

Highly Regarded Monforte d'Alba Vineyards: Bussia (there is a bevy of subvineyards within Bussia, such as Bricotto, Cicala, Colonella, Dardi, Gran Bussia, and Soprana) and Ginestra

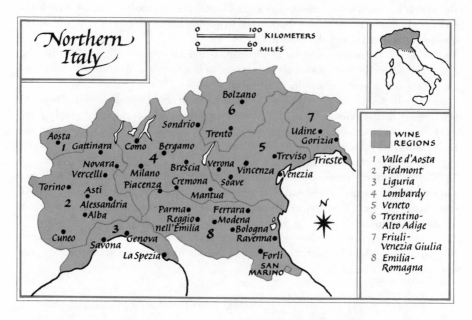

Northern Italy

0   100 KILOMETERS
0   60 MILES

Bolzano
6
Sondrio
Aosta
1   Gattinara   Como   Bergamo
Trento
Udine
7
Gorizia
5
Treviso
Trieste
Novara
Vercelli
Brescia
Verona
Vincenza
Venezia
Milano
4
Torino
Piacenza
Cremona
Soave
Asti
Mantua
2   Alessandria
Alba
Parma
Ferrara
Reggio
Modena
nell'Emilia
8
Bologna
Ravenna
Cuneo
3   Genova
Savona
La Spezia
Forli
SAN
MARINO

N

WINE REGIONS

1 Valle d'Aosta
2 Piedmont
3 Liguria
4 Lombardy
5 Veneto
6 Trentino-Alto Adige
7 Friuli-Venezia Giulia
8 Emilia-Romagna

Southern Italy

San Severo
Manfredonia
Benevento
Foggia
Bari
Napoli
2
Salerno
Rionero
Matera
Ostuni
1
Potenza
Brindisi
Metaponto
Taranto
3
Gallipoli
Cetraro
Ciro
Paola
Cosenza
4
Catanzaro
Caraffa
Palermo
Messina
Reggio di Calabria
Trapani
Marsala
Taormina
5
Catania
Agrigento
Siracusa
Ragusa

TYRRHENIAN SEA

N
W   E
S

WINE REGIONS

1 Campania
2 Puglia
3 Basilicata
4 Calabria
5 Sicily

0   60 MILES
0   100 KILOMETERS

MILES
0   60

KILOMETERS
0   50   100

Central Italy

ADRIATIC

SEA

LIGURIAN

SEA

8

•Pesaro

•Lucca
•Pisa
•Livorno
•Firenze
Arrezo•

•Ancona

•Macerata

Siena•

1

3

2

Perugia•

Ascoli Piceno

CORSICA

Grosseto•

•Spoleto

Terni•

L'Aquila•

•Pescara
•Chieti

Viterbo•

5

4

Roma•

Isernia•

6

•Latina

TYRRHENIAN

SEA

Olbia•

•Sassari
•Alghero

Nuoro
•

•Bosa

7

Tortoli•

Oristano•

Cagliari•

N

W   E

S

WINE REGIONS

1 Tuscany   5 Lazio
2 Marche   6 Molise
3 Umbria   7 Sardinia
4 Abruzzo   8 San Marino

(another vineyard noted for its numerous subplots, such as Casa Mate, Ciabot, La Coste, Mentin, Pernot, Pian della Poldere, Sori Ginestra, and Vigne del Gris)

La Morra   La Morra, another picture-postcard, pretty hilltop village, is believed to produce the most supple, seductive Barolos. Keeping in mind that individual winemaking styles can easily transcend the historic generalities attributed to a particular area, La Morra's Barolos are believed to be the most velvety-textured and easiest to drink when young. La Morra is to Barolo what the appellation of Pomerol is to Bordeaux. Of the five winemaking zones, La Morra is the largest, with 955 acres under vine and 372 registered producers.

Highly Regarded La Morra Vineyards: Arborina, Brunate, Cerequio, Fossati, Giachini, Marcenasco, Monfalletto, Rocche, Rocchette, La Serra, and Tettimorra

Serralunga d'Alba   With just under 500 acres, this is the second-largest zone in the Barolo area. There is more limestone to be found in Serralunga d'Alba's hillside vineyards than elsewhere. Interestingly, it was in this zone that Angelo Gaja purchased a 70-acre parcel to launch his Barolo estate, and it is in this commune that Bruno Giacosa makes his famed Rionda vineyard Barolo, often considered Barolo's most classic wine. The wines of Serralunga d'Alba are among the richest and fullest bodied, with great staying power. Continuing the comparison with appellations of Bordeaux, these wines might well be considered a synthesis in style of Pauillac/St.-Estèphe, but, of course, with a Nebbiolo personality.

Highly Regarded Serralunga d'Alba Vineyards: Arione, Brea, Ceretta, La Delizia, Falletto, Francia, Gabutti, Lazzarito, Ornato, Parafada, Rionda, and Sperss

Barbaresco   There are only three major production zones in the Barbaresco region—Neive (around the village of the same name), Barbaresco (around the picturesque, old village), and Treiso (around the town of the same name). All of Barbaresco's vineyards are on hillsides.

Highly Regarded Barbaresco Vineyards: Barbaresco—Asili, Costa Russi, Montefico, Montestefano, Porra, Rabaja, Rio Sordo, Sori San Lorenzo, and Sori Tilden; Neive—Albesani, Basarin, and Gallina; Treiso—Marcarini and Pajore

SOME THOUGHTS ON THE MODERN VERSUS TRADITIONAL STYLE OF BAROLO AND BARBARESCO

Today it is fashionable among wine journalists to argue about whether Barbaresco and Barolo are made in the so-called modern style, or made by the "traditionalists" with a healthy respect for the customs of the past. The modernists are said to believe in producing supple wines from riper fruit and aging the wines in small new oak casks. Since they are produced from riper fruit, the wines tend to be lower in acidity, and possess a more creamy-textured personality with sweeter tannin. Many of these wines are stunning and have deservedly won plaudits from wine critics throughout the world. The old- or traditional-style wine makers of Barolo usually eschew aging in new oak casks, preferring to age the wines in large old *foudres*. They make little concession to modern-day taste that demands up-front, forward wines. These wines can also be profound. The traditionally made Barolos and Barbarescos often taste more tannic. But when they are rich and concentrated (as many are), wines made by the modern style are compelling, since they rely entirely on the intensity of their fruit to express the personality of the vineyard. Great wines emerge from both schools. In fact, the finest Barolos or Barbarescos, whether they are made by a modernist or traditionalist, share more common characteristics than differences. Both schools of thought believe in harvesting physiologically mature fruit. Both schools adhere to the belief that low yields and nonmanipulative winemaking result in wines that best express their *terroirs*. Both schools avoid the excessive use of clarification techniques such as fining and filtration.

Barolo and Barbaresco are produced in what must be one of the most pure, unspoiled, virgin countrysides of Europe. All of the finest vineyards are situated on steep hillsides. The

locals all possess firmly held opinions as to the quality that emerges from vineyards throughout these two zones.

WHITE WINES

Arneis The ancient wine of Piedmont, Arneis is a rich, gloriously fruity, mouth-filling
wine that is soft, even unctuous. This may seem to imply a certain heaviness, but the best
examples are light and a joy to drink.

Gavi or Cortese di Gavi Often outrageously overpriced and frightfully bland, this supposedly prestigious wine is high in acidity, has a lemony, flinty, stony character, and in the
best examples, has good body.

Moscato d'Alba One of the world's most seductive wines to smell and drink, Moscato
d'Alba when well made, and when drunk within 18 months of the vintage, is a gorgeously
fragrant, apricot- and floral-scented, slightly sweet, crisp, vibrant wine that is ideal as an
aperitif. It should not be confused with the cloyingly sweet Asti Spumanti.

AGING POTENTIAL

Barbera: 5–15 years	Gattinara/Spanna: 8–20 years
Barbaresco: 8–25 years	Arneis: 2–3 years
Barolo: 8–25 years	Gavi: 2–4 years
Carema: 6–12 years	Moscato: 12–18 months
Dolcetto: 3–5 years	

OVERALL QUALITY LEVEL

The best Piedmont wines are impeccably made, brilliant wines. Producers such as Bruno
Giacosa, Angelo Gaja, Elio Altare, and Luciano Sandrone, to name just a few, fashion wines
of great individuality and uncompromising quality. But despite the number of compelling
Barolos, Barbarescos, and some *barrique*-aged Barberas, a considerable quantity of wine
made in Piedmont is still technically defective, with shrill levels of acidity, and a flawed,
musty taste. Some of this is the result of inferior grapes still being utilized, but most of it is
due to indifferent, as well as careless and primitive, winemaking methods. In short, Piedmont offers the best and worst in wine quality. If you are going to shop with confidence, you
must know who are the finest producers.

MOST IMPORTANT INFORMATION TO KNOW

Learning the top producers for Barbaresco, Barolo, Nebbiolo d'Alba, Barbera, and Dolcetto
is of utmost importance. However, since the early eighties, more and more of the best
producers have begun to make single-vineyard wines, so some understanding of the finest
vineyards and who is successfully exploiting them is required. Below is a list of the major
Piedmontese vineyards that consistently stand out in my tastings, and the producers making
the finest wine from these vineyards.

PIEDMONT'S BEST RED WINES

VINEYARD	WINE	BEST PRODUCER(S)
Alfiera	Barbera d'Asti	Marchesi Alfieri
Annunziata	Barolo	Lorenzo Accomasso, Silvio Grasso, the late Renato Ratti
Arborina	Barolo, Nebbiolo	Elio Altare
Arionda or Vigna Rionda	Barolo	Bruno Giacosa

VINEYARD	WINE	BEST PRODUCER(S)
Asili	Barbaresco	Bruno Ceretto, Produttori del Barbaresco, Bruno Giacosa
Baroco	Barbaresco	Roagna
Basarin	Barbaresco	Castello di Neive, Moccagatta
Batasiolo	Barolo	F.lli Dogliani
Bernadotti	Barbaresco	Giuseppe Mascarello
Bianca	Barolo	Fontenafredda
Big	Barolo	Poderi Rocche Manzoni Valentino
Bofini	Barolo	Batasiolo
Boscaretto	Barolo	F.lli Dogliani, Scarpa, Batasiolo
Boschis	Barolo	Cavalotto
Briacca	Barolo	Vietti
Bric Balin	Barbaresco	Moccagatta
Bric del Fiasc	Barolo	Paolo Scavino
Bric in Pugnane	Barolo	Giuseppe Mascarello
Bricco Asili	Barbaresco	Bruno Ceretto
Bricco Asili Faset	Barbaresco	Bruno Ceretto
Bricco Cicala	Barolo	Aldo Conterno
Bricco Colonello	Barolo	Aldo Conterno
Bricco del Drago Vigna Le Mace	Dolcetto	Cascina Drago
Bricco Faset	Barbaresco	La Spinona
Bricco Fiasco	Barolo	Azelia
Bricco della Figotta	Barbera d'Asti	Giacomo Bologna
Bricco Marun	Barbera d'Alba	Matteo-Correggia
Bricco Punta	Barolo	Azelia
Bricco Rocche	Barolo	Bruno Ceretto
Bricco dell'Uccellone	Barbera	Giacomo Bologna
Bricco Viole	Barolo, Barbera d'Alba	G. D. Vajra
Bricco Visette	Barolo	Gian Marco Ghisolfi
Briccolina	Barolo	Batasiolo
Maria de Brun	Barbaresco	Ca Rome
Brunate	Barolo	Giuseppe Rinaldi, Elvio Cogno, Ceretto, Luigi Copo, Robert Voerzio, Vietti, Sebaste, Michele Chiarlo, Marcarini
Bussia	Barolo	Bruno Giacosa, Clerico, Fennochio, Giuseppe Mascarello, Michele Chiarlo, Sebaste, Alfredo Prunotto
Ca' Du Ciuvin	Barbera d'Alba	Cerutti
Camp Gros	Barbaresco	Marchese di Gresy
Campo Quadro	Barbaresco	Punset-Marina Marcarino
Cannubi	Barolo	L. Sandrone, Luciano Rinaldi, Bartolo Mascarello, Marchesi di Barolo, Paolo Scavino, Enrico Scavino, E. Pora, Carretta, Giacomo e Figli Brezza, Alfredo Prunotto
Cannubi-Boschis	Barolo	L. Sandrone, Francesco Rinaldi

VINEYARD	WINE	BEST PRODUCER(S)
Casa Mate	Barolo	Elio Grasso
Cascina Alberta	Barbaresco	Contratto
Cascina Francia	Barolo, Dolcetto, Barbera	Giacomo Conterno
Cascina Nuova	Barolo	Elio Altare
Cascina Palazzo	Barolo	Francesco Rinaldi
Cascina Rocca	Barbaresco	Riccardo Cortese
Castelle	Gattinara	Antoniolo
Castiglione	Barolo	Vietti
Cerequio	Barolo	Michele Chiarlo, Cogno-Marcarini, F. Oddero, Roberto Voerzio, Marengo-Marenda
Ciabot Berton	Barolo	Luigi Oberto
Ciabot Mentin Genestra	Barolo	Clerico
Clara	Barbera d'Alba	Luigi Viberti
Codana	Barolo	Paolo Scavino, Vietti
Cole	Barbaresco	Moccagatta
Collina della Vedova	Barbera d'Asti	Alfiero Boffa
Conca	Barolo	Renato Ratti
Conca Tre Pile	Barbera d'Alba	Aldo Conterno
Costa Russi	Barbaresco	Angelo Gaja
Crichet Paje	Barbaresco	Roagna
Cua Longa	Barbera d'Asti	Alfiero Boffa
Darmagi	Cabernet Sauvignon	Angelo Gaja
Delizia	Barolo	Fontanafredda
DLA Roul	Barolo	Poderi Rocche Manzoni Valentino
Falletto	Barolo	Bruno Giacosa
Faset	Barbaresco	F.lli Oddero, Luigi Bianco, Bruno Ceretto
Francia Serralunga	Barolo	Giacomo Conterno
Gaiun	Barbaresco	Marchese di Gresy
Gallina	Barbaresco	Bruno Giacosa
La Ghiga	Barbaresco	La Spinona
Giachini	Barolo	Renato Corino
Giada	Barbera d'Alba	Andrea Oberto
Ginestra	Barolo	Clerico, Prunotto, Renzo Seghesio, Conterno Fantino
Gramolere	Barolo	Manzone
Gran Bussia	Barolo	Aldo Conterno
Gris	Barolo	Conterno Frantino
Il Crottino	Barbera d'Asti	Giorgio Carnevale
Il Fale	Barbera d'Asti	Viarengo e Figlio
Larigi	Barbera	Elio Altare
Lazzarito	Barolo	Fontanafredda, Vietti
Marcenasco	Barolo	Renato Ratti
Margaria	Barolo	Michele Chiarlo
Margheria	Barolo	Massolino-Vigna Rionda
Mariondino	Barolo	Armando Parusso
Martinenga	Barbaresco	Marchese di Gresy

VINEYARD	WINE	BEST PRODUCER(S)
Masseria	Barbaresco	Vietti
Messoirano	Barbaresco, Barbera, Dolcetto	Castello di Neive
Moccagatta	Barbaresco	Produttori del Barbaresco
Monfalletto	Barolo	Cordero di Montezemolo
Monfortino	Barolo	Giacomo Conterno
Monprivato	Barolo	Giuseppe Mascarello, Brovia
Montanello	Barolo	Tenuta Montanello
Monte Stefano	Barbaresco	Produttori del Barbaresco, Alfredo Prunotto
Montefico	Barbaresco	Produttori del Barbaresco
Montetusa	Barbera	Poderi Bertelli
La Mora	Barolo	Renato Corino
Mugiot	Barbera d'Alba	Piazzo
Ornato	Nebbiolo, Barbera, Barolo	Pio Cesare
Osso San Grato	Gattinara	Antoniolo
Otinasso	Barolo	F.lli Brovia
Ottin Fiorin Collina Gabuti	Barolo	Cappellano
Ovello	Barbaresco	Produttori del Barbaresco
Pajana	Barolo	Clerico
Panirole	Barbera d'Alba	Giuseppe Mascarello
Parussi	Barolo	Terra da Vino
Pian della Polvere	Barolo	R. Fenocchio
Pian Romualdo	Barbera d'Alba	Alfredo Prunotto
Pomorosso	Barbera d'Asti	Coppo
Pora	Barbaresco	Produttori del Barbaresco
Pozzo	Barbera	Renato Corino
Prapo	Barolo	Bruno Ceretto
Rabaja	Barbaresco	Produttori del Barbaresco, Giuseppe Cortese, Bruno Rocca
Rabera	Barolo	G. E. Vagra, Giuseppe Rinaldi
Rapet	Barolo	Ca Rome
Rio Sordo	Barbaresco	Brovia, Produttori del Barbaresco
Rionda (same as Arionda)	Barolo	Bruno Giacosa, Michel Chiarlo, Giuseppe Mascarello, Ca Rome, Massolino-Vigna Rionda
Rocche	Barolo	Brovio, Renato Corino, Andrea Oberto, Armando Parusso, Aurelio Settimo, Vietti
Rocche di Bussia	Barolo	F.lli Oddero, Parusso
Rocche di Castiglione Falletto	Barolo	Bruno Giacosa, Vietti, Parusso
Rocche de la Morra	Barolo, Barbera	Roche di Costamagna
Ronchi	Barbaresco	Albino Rocca
La Rosa	Barolo	Fontanafredda
Rosignolo	Barbera d'Alba	Cantine Sant'Evasio
San Pietro	Barolo	Fontanafredda
San Rocco	Barolo	Erevi Virginia Ferrero

VINEYARD	WINE	BEST PRODUCER(S)
Santo Stefano	Barbaresco	Bruno Giacosa, Castello di Neive
La Serra	Barolo	Cogno-Marcarini, Roberto Voerzio, Marcarini
Serra Boella	Barbaresco	Cigliuti
Sori d'Paytin	Barbaresco	Pasquero-Secondo
Sori San Lorenzo	Barbaresco	Angelo Gaja
Sori Tilden	Barbaresco	Angelo Gaja
Sori Valgrande	Barbaresco	F.lli Grasso Cascina Valgrande
Sperss	Barolo	Angelo Gaja
Terlo Ravera	Barolo	Enrico e Marziano Abbona
Truchet	Barbera d'Asti	Giovine Riconda
Val Preti	Nebbiolo	Matteo-Correggia
Vecchie	Barbera d'Asti	Vinchio e Vaglio
Vignabajla	Dolcetto	Angelo Gaja
Vignarey	Barbera d'Alba	Angelo Gaja
Vignasse	Barbera d'Alba	Roberto Voerzio
Le Vigne	Barolo	Luciano Sandrone
La Villa	Nebbiolo, Barbera	Elio Altare, Aldo & Ricardo Seghesio
Villero	Barolo	Giuseppe Mascarello, Bruno Giacosa, Cordero di Montezemolo
La Volta	Barolo	Bartolomeo di Cabutto
Zonchera	Barolo	Bruno Ceretto

PIEDMONT'S BEST WHITE WINES

Americans have always had a fondness for the slightly sweet, sparkling Asti Spumantes of Italy. While "serious" wine enthusiasts have an attitude problem with Asti drinkers, the fact is that there is Asti Spumante in the market, even from such industrial-sized producers as Cinzano, Martini and Rossi, and on a smaller scale, Fontanafredda, that is fresh, clean, and yes . . . delicious!

However, the real jewel among these slightly sweet, sparkling wines from northern Italy is not Asti Spumante, but rather Moscato d'Asti. While most Asti Spumantes possess an alcohol level similar to most of the world's dry wines (around 12%), Moscato d'Asti rarely has an alcohol level in excess of 5.5%. Although these sparkling wines are usually bottled with a regular cork rather than a champagne-style cork, they are effervescent, bubbly wines. Their low alcohol, combined with their extraordinary, fragrant, perfumed character, makes them the most underrated delicious aperitif or dessert wines produced in Europe. Most Moscato d'Asti is vintage-dated and readers should be purchasing nothing older than 1993. The 1994 vintage, which has just been released and is appearing in the marketplace, is the vintage of choice. These wines are meant to be drunk within 7–8 months of release. They are among the most thrillingly light, exuberant, fresh, perfumed wines in the world. The lack of aggressive bubbles, in addition to the low alcohol, accentuates the freshness and liveliness of these wines. They are the perfect summer wine!

The following Moscato d'Asti producers make wines that have consistently stood out for their freshness, elegance, and wonderfully perfumed peach, apricot, and floral bouquets. Most Moscato d'Asti is attractively priced between $8 and $12 a bottle.

MOSCATO D'ASTI'S BEST PRODUCERS

Note: Buy only the freshest vintage; in 1995, that would be 1994.

Giuseppe Barbero Bricco Riella	Icardi La Rosa Selvatica
Gian Lugi Bera	La Morandina
Giorgio Carnevale	Elio Perrone Clarté
Cascina Fonda	Elio Perrone Sourgal
La Caudrina	G. Rivetti
La Caudrina-La Galeisa	Paolo Saracco
Tenuta del Fant Il Falchetto	Paolo Saracco Moscato d'Autunno
Marchesi di Gresy La Serra	Sator Arepo Tenet-Vigna Senza Nome
Sergis Grimaldi	Gianni Voerzio Vigna Sergente

OTHER FINE WHITE WINES FROM PIEDMONT

For what one gets in the bottle, the top white wines of Piedmont are vastly overpriced (Gavi prices have fallen, but this neutral-tasting wine continues to be a rip-off). The exception is the aforementioned lovely flower blossom— and apricot-scented Moscato, and the dry version of Erbaluce. Arneis, a perfumed dry white wine with loads of character, is my favorite white from Piedmont. However, at prices of $18–$30, it is expensive. Chardonnay and Sauvignon have arrived in Piedmont; Angelo Gaja produces the finest, but also the most expensive.

The best Piedmont white wines are listed below. Readers should look for the 1994s and 1993s—nothing older!

WINE	PRODUCER(S)
Arneis	Bruno Giacosa, Castello di Neive, Bruno Ceretto
Brut Spumante	Bruno Giacosa
Chardonnay Bussiador	Aldo Conterno
Chardonnay Gaia and Rey	Angelo Gaja
Chardonnay Giarone	Poderi Bertelli
Chardonnay Rossi-Bass	Angelo Gaja
Cortesi di Gavi	Pio Cesare, Broglia Fasciola
Erbaluce di Caluso	Carretta, Boratto, Ferrando
Gavi	La Scolca, La Chiara
Roero Arneis	Carretta
Sauvignon Alteni di Brassica	Angelo Gaja
Traminer	Poderi Bertelli

1995–1996 BUYING STRATEGY

Recently there have been two great Piedmontese vintages, 1990 and 1989, and one excellent vintage, 1988. Readers who love Nebbiolo, Barbera, Barbaresco, and Barolo are well advised to take a serious look at the 1990s, 1989s, and 1988s. The top wines are very expensive, as quantities are small, and most of the production is sold in Europe. Avoid vintages such as 1981, 1983 (grossly overrated by the wine press), 1984, 1986, 1991, and 1992. If you can still find any of the superb 1985s or great 1982s, do not hesitate to buy them. The 1982s are just beginning to drink beautifully and the 1985s can be drunk or cellared. Both vintages have the potential to last at least another 10–15 years. When buying Dolcetto, stick to the 1994s and 1993s, unless you are lucky enough to find an excellent 1990 or 1989, both great vintages that produced sumptuous Dolcettos that will age for 7–8 years.

For older vintages of Barolo, Barbaresco, or the less-well-known Gattinara/Spanna, look for the 1979s, which are delicious and fully mature, as well as underrated; the great 1978s (one of the finest long-term vintages); and 1971, a spectacular Piedmont vintage that is just now reaching its full potential.

VINTAGE GUIDE

1994—Despite heavy rains in September, most Piedmontese producers have expressed satisfaction, even delight, with the quality of the red wines produced from Nebbiolo. It appears that the early harvesters had more difficulty than those who waited, and were rewarded with Indian summer–like conditions in October. This could turn out to be a surprisingly good vintage, but it will not come close to equaling the majesty of 1989 and 1990.

1993—1993 was also adversely affected by rain, but all the Piedmontese producers I spoke with expressed far greater satisfaction with their 1993s than with their 1992s or 1991s. Many producers feel the wines will turn out to be as good as the 1987s, and in some cases as fine as the 1988s. Certainly the wines will not possess the opulence, richness, or expansiveness revealed by the 1990s and 1989s. The early-released Dolcettos I have tasted were above average.

1992—Rain hit Piedmont during the harvest, causing sugars to drop, acidity to fall, and ripeness to be uneven. For the second year in a row Piedmont turned out lighter-styled wines. Certainly 1992 was a bigger crop than 1991, but many serious producers reported low-sugar readings, and were hoping 1992 would turn out to be as pleasant and charming as 1987. This may have been optimistic given the fact that the harvest was only a week old when three straight weeks of rain inundated most of the vineyards.

1991—A relatively small crop was harvested of lightweight Barolos, Barbarescos, Dolcettos, and Nebbiolo d'Albas. It is an average-quality vintage, believed to be on a par with 1987 and 1986. The wines will be drinkable early, with a maximum of 10 years of aging potential. In a year such as this, the growers who were more selective produced more interesting wines.

1990—This is a magnificent vintage with aromatic wines of extraordinary richness, high glycerin and alcohol, and spectacular intensity. The colors are deeply saturated ruby/purple. Most producers claim these wines are richer, fuller, and potentially greater than the exceptional 1989s. Producers such as Gaja, Giacosa, and Altare believe that the 1990 Piedmontese wines will have to be considered along with the 1971 and 1947 as one of the three finest vintages for Piedmont following World War II. High praise indeed.

1989—A vintage of abundant quantity, superhigh quality, and great ripeness and richness. The wines possess surprisingly sound acidity given their dizzying level of alcohol and dense, rich, chewy flavors. Wealthy Italian-wine collectors will have fun for decades comparing the merits of their favorite producers in years such as 1989 and 1990.

1988—This overly hyped year has turned out to be very good, but it is not a great vintage. In fact, I do not think it is as good as 1982 or 1985. The wines are austere and lack the great ripeness that was achieved in 1989 and 1990. They exhibit considerable tannin, which is not always balanced out by deep, rich fruit. Given the fact that the 1989s and 1990s are unlikely to be priced any higher than the 1988s, I would skip this vintage and concentrate your resources on its two younger siblings.

1987—*Pessimism* was the word of the day during the growing season of 1987, but the wines have turned out surprisingly well, and comparisons with the underrated vintage of 1980 are not invalid. The wines are lighter than usual but do show excellent fruit, ripeness, and a forward, charming personality. This will be a good commercial vintage to drink early on.

1986—A fair year—no better and no worse, despite some perennial Italian-wine cheerleaders who are calling 1986 another great year. The red wines are well colored and balanced, and have some depth and tannin to shed. They lack drama and boldness, but this is a good, useful vintage, as the quantity of wine produced was high.

1985—Gaja, Ceretto, and their peers call this one of the greatest vintages of the century. I believe they said the same thing about 1990, 1989, 1988, 1982, 1978, and 1971. Nevertheless, broker Neil Empson claims it is better than either 1982 or 1978, which is difficult to imagine given the superlative quality of the latter two years. However, one taste of these wines reveals a flamboyant, rich, intense, velvety fruitiness not very unlike the opulence of 1982. There are many very rich, lush, sensational wines that will drink well over the next 10 years.

1984—Justifiably maligned by the press corps (as was the case everywhere in Europe), this vintage in Piedmont is average to below average in quality, with the wines light and forward, but deficient in fruit.

1983—A vintage of rather tannic, stern wines, the 1983s may turn out to be similar to the unyielding 1974s. Most wines have a hollow, dry, astringent taste and lack fruit.

1982—A very great vintage. The wines are loaded with ripe, rich fruit, and have plenty of tannins, full body, and real alcoholic punch to them. They are tasting surprisingly forward, but given the fact that most great vintages of Barolo and Barbaresco can last for 15–25 years, the 1982s offer an opportunity to enjoy a rich, dense, ripe, full, and fruity Barolo or Barbaresco during its entire life in the bottle. Despite the accessible nature of this vintage, the top wines should keep 25 years. A year to buy, but most of the finest wines disappeared long ago.

1981—Rain during September ruined what could have been a very good year. Many of the best growers declassified their entire crop. My tastings have revealed compact, short wines that are of little interest.

1980—Somewhat of a sleeper vintage, the 1980s are medium-bodied, rather light wines, but the good growers have produced wines with plenty of fruit, soft tannins, and charm. It is a vintage to drink up.

1979—One of the best vintages for current drinking is 1979. Elegant, ripe, fruity wines were produced. They may lack the muscle, power, and great concentration of a vintage such as 1978 or 1982, but they offer plenty of finesse and complexity. Not to be overlooked.

1978—This is a great vintage of very long-lived wines: huge in structure, very tannic, very concentrated, and the best of them still a good 5 years away from maturity. The crop size was small; the style of the wines, aggressive, rich, and tough. They have developed very slowly, causing impatient critics to downgrade them, but this is a great vintage that just needs more time.

1977—A horrendous year of rain and cold weather. Most good growers declassified their entire crop.

1976—Another bad year; the wines lacked ripeness, had excessive tannins, and are now drying out.

1975—The first of a trio of consecutive poor vintages, the 1975s I have tasted have had aromas of tea, light-intensity flavors, and shallow personalities.

1974—This is a highly rated vintage, but one I find overrated. After 18 years the wines remain rather hard and tannic, and continue to reveal a lack of ripeness and richness. Perhaps time will prove me wrong, but most of the Piedmont wines from 1974 lack length, grace, and charm.

1973—Relatively easy-to-drink, soft, pleasant, light wines were produced in 1973. All should have been drunk by now.

1972—As in most of Europe's viticultural regions, rain was the ruination of this vintage.

1971—Until the advent of the remarkably promising 1982s, 1985s, 1989s, and 1990s the

1971s were, and may remain, the reference point for Piedmont. Rich, perfumed, and deeply concentrated, these wines have entered their plateau of maturity. They are all fully mature, so only the best examples should be kept another 10–15 years.

OLDER VINTAGES

The 1970s are very good, eclipsed in stature by the admittedly greater 1971s; the 1969s are average in quality and best drunk up. The 1968s are disastrous; the 1967s very good, but now beginning to slip; the 1966s and 1965s below average to poor; and the 1964 another great vintage. Well-stored bottles of 1964 Piedmontese wines are gloriously rich and scented.

RATING PIEDMONT'S BEST PRODUCERS

*****(OUTSTANDING)*

Elio Altare Barbera Vigna Larigi
Elio Altare Barolo Vigna Arborina
Batasiolo Barolo Cru Bofani
Giacomo Bologna Barbera d'Asti Bricco
   della Figotta
Giacomo Bologna Barbera dell'Uccellone
Brovia Barolo Monprivato
Brovia Barolo Rocche
Bruno Ceretto Barolo Bricco Rocche
Clerico Barolo Bricotto Bussia
Clerico Barolo Ciabot Mentin Ginestra
Clerico Barolo Pajana
Aldo Conterno Barolo Bussia Soprano
Aldo Conterno Barolo Gran Bussia
Aldo Conterno Barolo Gran Bussia Riserva
Aldo Conterno Barolo Vigna Cicala Bussia
Aldo Conterno Barolo Vigna Colonnello
   Bussia
Giacomo Conterno Barolo Cascina Francia
   Riserva
Giacomo Conterno Barolo Monfortino
Renato Corino Barolo La Mora
Renato Corino Barolo Vigna Giachini
Cascina Drago Bricco del Drago Vigna Le
   Mace
Angelo Gaja Barbaresco Costa Russi
Angelo Gaja Barbaresco Sori San Lorenzo
Angelo Gaja Barbaresco Sori Tilden
Angelo Gaja Barolo Sperss
Bruno Giacosa Barbaresco Asili

Bruno Giacosa Barbaresco Santo Stefano
Bruno Giacosa Barolo Falletto
Bruno Giacosa Barolo Rionda
Bruno Giacosa Barolo Le Rocche
Bruno Giacosa Barolo Villero
Marchese di Gresy Barbaresco Martinenga
   Camp Gros
Marchese di Gresy Barbaresco Martinenga
   Gaiun
Bartolo Mascarello Barolo
Giuseppe Mascarello Barbera d'Alba
   Panirole
Giuseppe Mascarello Barolo Monprivato
Alfredo Prunotto Barolo Bussia
Renato Ratti Barolo Marcenasco Conca
Renato Ratti Barolo Marcenasco Rocche
Poderi Rocche Manzoni Valentino Barolo
   Riserva Vigna Big
Luciano Sandrone Barolo Cannubi Boschis
Luciano Sandrone Barolo Le Vigne
Enrico Scavino Barolo Bric del Fiasc
Enrico Scavino Barolo Cannubi
G. D. Vajra Barbera d'Alba Riserva Bricco
   della Viole
G. D. Vajra Barolo Bricco della Viole
Vietti Barolo Brunate
Vietti Barolo Rocche
Roberto Voerzio Barolo Brunate
Roberto Voerzio Barolo Cerequio
Roberto Voerzio Barolo La Serra

****(EXCELLENT)*

Enrico and Marziano Abbona Barbaresco
Enrico and Marziano Abbona Barbera
   d'Alba
Enrico and Marziano Abbona Barolo

Marchesi Alfieri Barbera d'Asti
Elio Altare Barolo
Elio Altare Dolcetto
Elio Altare La Villa****/*****

Antoniolo Gattinara Osso San Grato
Antoniolo Gattinara San Francesco
Antoniolo Gattinara Vigneto Castelle
Azelia Dolcetto d'Alba Bricco dell'Oriolo
Azelia Dolcetto d'Alba Vigneto Azelia
F.lli Barale Barbaresco Rabaja
F.lli Barale Barolo Castellero
Batasiolo Barbaresco
Batasiolo Barolo
Batasiolo Barolo Cru Boscareto
Batasiolo Barolo Cru Briccolina
Batasiolo Dolcetto d'Alba
Batasiolo Moscato d'Asti
Bava Barbera d'Asti Superiore
Bera Moscato d'Asti
Poderi Bertelli Barbera Giarone
Poderi Bertelli Barbera Montetusa
Alfiero Boffa Barbera d'Asti Collina della
    Vedova
Alfiero Boffa Barbera d'Asti Vigna Cua
    Longa
Alfiero Boffa Barbera d'Asti Vigna More
Giacomo e Figli Brezza Barolo Cannubi
Brovia Barbera d'Alba Sori del Drago
Brovia Barolo Garblet Sue
Ca del Baio Barbaresco Asili
Ca Rome Barbaresco Maria di Brun
Ca Rome Barolo Vigna Rionda
Bartolomeo di Cabutto Barolo La Volta
Dott. G. Cappellano Barolo Ottin Fiorin
    Collina Gabuti
Giorgio Carnevale Barbera d'Asti Il
    Crottino
Tenuta Carretta Barbaresco
Tenuta Carretta Barolo Cannubi
Bruno Ceretto Barbaresco Bricco Asili
Bruno Ceretto Barolo Brunate
Bruno Ceretto Barolo Prapo
Bruno Ceretto Barolo Zonchera
Cerutti Barbera d'Alba Ca' Du Ciuvin
Pio Cesare Barbaresco
Pio Cesare Barolo Ornato
Pio Cesare Dolcetto d'Alba
Michele Chiarlo Barbera d'Asti Valle del
    Sole
Michele Chiarlo Barolo Brunate
Michele Chiarlo Barolo Vigna Rionda
Cigliuti Barbaresco
    Serraboella ****/*****
Cigliuti Barbera d'Alba Serraboella
Guasti Clemente Barbera d'Asti

Clerico Arté
Clerico Dolcetto
Aldo Conterno Barbera d'Alba Conca Tre
    Pile
Paolo Conterno Barbera d'Alba Ginestra
Coppo Barbera d'Asti Camp du Rouss
Coppo Barbera d'Asti Pomorosso
Renato Corino Barbera Vigna Pozzo
Renato Corino Dolcetto
Giuseppe Cortese Barbaresco Rabaja
Alessandria Crissante Ruge
Cascina Drago Bricco del Drago
Cascina Drago Dolcetto d'Alba
Cascina Drago Nebbiolo
Luigi Einaudi Barolo ****/*****
Ricardo Fenocchio Barbera d'Alba
    Pianpolvere Soprano
Ricardo Fenocchio Barolo Pianpolvere
    Soprano
F.lli Ferrero Barolo Annunziata
Fontanafredda Barolo Le Delizia
Fontanafredda Barolo Gallaretto
    Serralunga
Fontanafredda Barolo La Rosa
Conterno Frantino Barolo Sori
    Ginestra ****/*****
Conterno Frantino Barolo Vigna del
    Gris ****/*****
Angelo Gaja Barbaresco
Angelo Gaja Barbera d'Alba Vignarey
Gian Marco Ghisolfi Barolo Bricco Visette
Bruno Giacosa Barbaresco Gallina
Elio Grasso Barolo Vigna Casa Mate
Elio Grasso Barolo Vigna Chiniera
F.lli Grasso Cascina Valgrande Barbaresco
    Sori Valgrande
Marchese di Gresy Barbaresco Martinenga
Marchese di Gresy Dolcetto Monte
    Aribaldo
Manzone Barbera d'Alba
Manzone Barolo Le Gramolere ****/*****
Marcarini Barolo Brunate ****/*****
Marcarini Barolo La Serra ****/*****
Marengo-Marenda Barolo Cerequio
Bartolo Mascarello Dolcetto d'Alba
Massolino-Vigna Rionda Barolo Sori Vigna
    Rionda
Massolino-Vigna Rionda Barolo Sori
    Vigneto Margheria
Massolino-Vigna Rionda Barolo Vigna
    Rionda

Matteo-Correggia Barbera d'Alba Bricco Marun ****/*****

Matteo-Correggia Nebbiolo d'Alba Val Preti

Moccagatta Barbaresco Basarin

Moccagatta Barbaresco Bric Balin

Moccagatta Barbaresco Cole

Castello di Neive Barbaresco Santo Stefano

Andrea Oberto Barbera d'Alba Giada

Andrea Oberto Barolo Vigneto Rocche

Luigi Oberto Barolo Ciabot Berton ****/*****

Palladino Barbaresco

Armando Parusso Barolo Bussia Rocche

Armando Parusso Barolo Rocche

Armando Parusso Dolcetto d'Alba Mariondino

Elia Pasquero Barbaresco Sori Paitin

Poggio Petorcino Barolo

Produttori di Barbaresco Barbaresco Asili

Produttori di Barbaresco Barbaresco Moccagatta

Produttori di Barbaresco Barbaresco Monte Stefano

Produttori di Barbaresco Barbaresco Ovello

Produttori di Barbaresco Barbaresco Rabaja

Alfredo Prunotto Barbaresco Monte Stefano

Alfredo Prunotto Barbera d'Alba Pian Romulado

Alfredo Prunotto Barolo Cannubi ****/*****

Renato Ratti Barolo Marcenasco

Giovine Riconda Barbera d'Asti Superiore Vigna del Truchet

Francesco Rinaldi Barolo ****/*****

Giuseppe Rinaldi Barolo

Giuseppe Rinaldi Barolo Brunate Riserva ****/*****

Giuseppe Rivetti La Spinetta Pin Vino da Tavola

Roagna Barbaresco

Roagna Barbaresco Baroco

Albino Rocca Barbaresco Ronchi

Albino Rocca Barbaresco Vigneti Loreto e Brich Ronchi ****/*****

Bruno Rocca Barbaresco Rabaja ****/*****

Rocche di Costamagna Barolo Rocche de la Morra

Rocche di Costamagna Barolo Rocche de la Morra Vigna Francesco

Poderi Rocche Manzoni Valentino Barolo Riserva ****/*****

Poderi Rocche Manzoni Valentino Barolo Riserva DLA Roul

Luciano Sandrone Barolo

Luciano Sandrone Dolcetto ****/*****

Cantine Sant'Evasio Barbera d'Alba Rosignolo

Giancarlo Scaglione Le Grive Vino da Tavola

Enrico Scavino Barbera Carati

Enrico Scavino Barolo

Aldo & Ricardo Seghesio Barolo La Villa ****/*****

Aurelio Settimo Barolo Vigneti Rocche

Tenuta La Tenaglia Emozioni Vino da Tavola

Tenuta La Tenaglia Giorgio Tenaglia Vino da Tavola

Terra da Vino Barbera d'Asti La Luna e I Falò

Viarengo e Figlio Barbera d'Asti Il Fale Superiore

Luigi Viberti Barbera d'Alba Vigna Clara

Luigi Viberti Barolo ****/*****

Vietti Barbaresco Masseria

Vietti Barolo Castiglione

Vietti Barolo Lazzarito

Vietti Barolo Villero

Vinchio e Vaglio Barbera d'Asti Superiore Vigne Vecchie

Roberto Voerzio Barbera d'Alba Vignasse ****/*****

Roberto Voerzio Dolcetto d'Alba Privino

Roberto Voerzio Vignaserra Vino da Tavola

* * *(GOOD)

Cantina Anselma Barolo

Antoniolo Gattinara

Azelia Barolo Bricco Fiasco ***/****

Azelia Barolo Bricco Punta ***/****

Marchesi di Barolo Barbaresco

Marchesi di Barolo Barolo di Barolo

Marchesi di Barolo Barolo Cannubi

Marchesi di Barolo Barolo Sarmassa

Pietro Berruti Barbaresco La Spinona

Bersano Barbera d'Asti Cascina Cremosina

Poderi Bertelli Cabernet I Fossaretti

F.lli Serio & Battista Borgogno Barolo
Cannubi

Giacomo e Figli Brezza Barbera d'Alba
Cannubi ***/****

Giacomo e Figli Brezza Barolo Bricco
Sarmassa ***/****

Ca Dei Gancia Barolo Cannubi

Ca Rome Barbaresco

Ca Rome Barolo Vigna Carpegna

Ca Rome Barolo Vigna Rapet

Bartolomeo di Cabutto Barbera d'Alba
Bricco della Viole

Dott. G. Cappellano Barolo

Tenuta Carretta Barbera Bric Quercia

Tenuta Carretta Nebbiolo d'Alba Bric
Paradiso ***/****

Tenuta Carretta Nebbiolo d'Alba Bric
Tavoleto ***/****

F.lli Casetta Barbaresco Vigna Ausario

F.lli Casetta Barbera d'Alba Vigna
Lazaretto

Cascina Castlet Barbera d'Asti

Cascina Castlet Barbera d'Asti Superiore

Cavallotto Barolo Bricco Boschis

Bruno Ceretto Barbaresco Asij

Bruno Ceretto Barbaresco Bricco Asili
Faset ***/****

Bruno Ceretto Barbera d'Alba Piana

Bruno Ceretto Dolcetto d'Alba Rossana

Bruno Ceretto Nebbiolo d'Alba Lantasco

Pio Cesare Barbera d'Alba

Pio Cesare Barolo

Michele Chiarlo Barbera d'Asti

Michele Chiarlo Barilot

Michele Chiarlo Countacc! Vino da Tavola

Aldo Conterno Il Favot

Giacomo Conterno Barbera d'Alba Cascina
Francia

Cordero di Montezemolo Barbera d'Alba

Cordero di Montezemolo Barolo Enrico VI

Cordero di Montezemolo Barolo Monfalletto

Cordero di Montezemolo Dolcetto
Monfalletto

Giuseppe Cortese Dolcetto d'Alba

Luigi Dessilani Gattinara

Luigi Dessilani Ghemme

Luigi Dessilani Spanna

Az. Agr. Dosio Barolo Vigna Fossati

Luigi Einaudi Dolcetto

Fantino-Conterno Barbera d'Alba Vignato

Tenuta Dei Fiori Barbera d'Asti

Fontanafredda Barbera d'Alba Vigna
Raimondo ***/****

Fontanafredda Barolo

Gianni Gagliardo Barolo La Serra

Angelo Gaja Dolcetto d'Alba Vignaveja

Angelo Gaja Nebbiolo d'Alba
Vignaveja ***/****

F.lli Giacosa Barbaresco Rio Sordo

F.lli Giacosa Barolo Pira

F.lli Grasso Cascina Valgrande Barbaresco
Bricco Spessa

F.lli Grasso Cascina Valgrande Barbaresco
Riserva

Silvio Grasso Barbera d'Alba Fontanile

Icardi Barbera d'Alba Vigna dei Gelsi

Icardi Nebbiolo delle Langhe

Eredi Lodali Barbaresco Rocche dei Sette
Fratelli

Manzone Dolcetto

Manzone Nebbiolo

Marengo-Marenda Barbaresco Le Terre
Forti

Marengo-Marenda Barbera Le Terre Forti

Giuseppe Mascarello Barbera d'Alba
Fasana

Giuseppe Mascarello Barolo
Dardi ***/****

Giuseppe Mascarello Dolcetto Gagliassi

Massolino-Vigna Rionda Barolo Parafada

Moccagatta Barbera Basarin

Guido Molino Barolo Vigna Conca

Castello di Neive Dolcetto d'Alba Basarin

Castello di Neive Dolcetto d'Alba
Messoriano

Luigi Oberto Barbera d'Alba Ciabot Berton

Vittorio Ochetti e Alfonso Pierluigi
Barbera d'Asti Superiore

Armando Parusso Barbera
Pugnane ***/****

Agostino Pavia e Figli Barbera d'Asti
Bricco Blina

Luigi Pellissero Barbaresco Vanotu

Elio Perrone Barbera delle Langhe Vigna
Grivo

Piazzo Barbaresco Riserva

Piazzo Barbaresco Sori Fratin

Piazzo Barbera d'Alba Mugiot

Piazzo Barolo Poderi di Mugiot

Produttori di Barbaresco Barbaresco
Produttori di Barbaresco Barbaresco Pora
Alfredo Prunotto Barbaresco
Alfredo Prunotto Barbera d'Alba
Alfredo Prunotto Barbera d'Alba Fiulot
Punset-Marina Marcarino Barbaresco
  Campo Quadro
Bruno Rocca Nebbiolo d'Alba
Rocche di Costamagna Barbera d'Alba
  Rocche de la Morra
Rocche di Costamagna Rocche della
  Rocche
Gigi Rosso Barbaresco Viglino
Gigi Rosso Barolo Cascina Arione
Il Milin Rovero Barbera d'Asti
Il Milin Rovero Barbera d'Asti Vigneto
  Gustin
Scarpa Barbaresco
Scarpa Barbaresco Payore Barberis di
  Treiso
Scarpa Barolo Boscaretti di Serralunga
  d'Alba ***/****

Scarpa Barolo I Tetti di Neive
Scarpa Rouchet Vino da Tavola
Enrico Scavino Dolcetto d'Alba
Mauro Sebaste Barolo Le Coste
Aldo & Ricardo Seghesio Barbera
Aldo & Ricardo Seghesio Dolcetto d'Alba
Aurelio Settimo Barolo
Sigilla dell'Abate Barolo Riserva
Emiliana Martini Sonvico Barbera d'Asti
  Superiore Vigna dell'Angelo
Sottimano Barbaresco Brichet
Terricci Terricci Vino da Tavola
Azienda Trinchero Barbera d'Asti La
  Barslina
Vaselli Santa Giulia Rosso
Viarengo e Figlio Barbera d'Asti Il Fale
Viarengo e Figlio Barbera d'Asti Morra
Vietti Barbera d'Alba Pian Romualdo
Vietti Barbera d'Alba Scarrone
Villa Monte Rico Vino da Tavola
Villa La Selva Selvamaggio
Gianni Voerzio Barolo La Serra

* *(AVERAGE)

Michele Chiarlo Barbaresco
Tenuta Colue Barolo Colue
Granco Fiorina Barolo
Fontanafredda Barbaresco
Fontanafredda Barbera d'Alba
De Forville Barbaresco
De Forville Barbera d'Alba Ca' Gorssa
Gianni Gagliardo Barbera d'Asti La Matta
Angelo Gaja Cabernet Sauvignon Darmagi
  /*
Attilio Ghisolfi Barbera d'Alba
Bruno Giacosa Dolcetto d'Alba Plinet di
  Trezzo **/***
Bruno Giacosa Nebbiolo d'Alba
  Valmaggiore
F.lli Giacosa Barbera d'Alba Maria Gioana
F.lli Grasso Cascina Valgrande Barbera
  d'Alba
Umberto e Ratti Mentone Barolo
Az. Agr. Luigi Minuto Barbaresco Cascina
  Luisin

F.lli Oddero Barolo Vigna Rionda
Luigi Pellissero Barbera d'Alba Ronchi
Punset-Marina Marcarino Barbaresco
  Punset
Az. Vit. Roche Barbera d'Alba
Gigi Rosso Barbera d'Alba del Buon
  Ricordo
Gigi Rosso Nebbiolo d'Alba
Enrico e Giacomo Saffirio Barolo
Scaglia Barbera d'Asti
Sylla Sebaste Barolo Bussia
Giovanni Viberti Barbera d'Alba Bricco
  Airoli
Giovanni Viberti Barolo Bricco Viotta
Giovanni Viberti Barolo San Pietro
Giovanni Viberti Barolo La Volta
Cantine Vignaioli Barbaresco
Villa Ile Barbera d'Alba Garassino
Villa Montersino Barolo

ENRICO AND MARZIANO ABBONA
Barbaresco * * * *, Barbera d'Alba * * * *, Barolo * * * *

1989 Barbaresco	D	88
1990 Barbera d'Alba Vigneto Ravera Barriques	B	87
1989 Barolo Vigneto Terlo Ravera	D	90

This producer's 1989 Barbaresco offers a medium ruby color with some amber at the edge, and a classic nose of cedar, roses, grilled nuts, spices, and tar. Medium to full bodied, this soft, fleshy wine can be drunk now or aged for 10–12 years.

An outstanding example of the vintage, the 1989 Barolo is softer than many 1989s, but still structured, rich, and full bodied, with a classic Nebbiolo profile of roses, tar, tobacco, cedar, and jammy cherry fruit. Although high in alcohol, it is rich and generous. Drink it over the next 15 or more years.

The beautifully made, stylish 1990 Barbera d'Alba Vigneto Ravera Barriques displays plenty of color, excellent, nearly outstanding, concentration, fresh, vibrant acidity, medium to full body, and gobs of spice and ripe fruit. The new oak from *barrique* aging has been well integrated. Tight and unevolved, it should evolve gracefully for a decade.

MARCHESI ALFIERI
Barbera d'Asti * * * *

1990 Barbera d'Asti Alfiera	C	89
1990 Barbera d'Asti La Tota	C	87

The medium-bodied 1990 Barbera d'Asti Alfiera offers a forceful peppery, herbaceous, leathery nose. Surprisingly soft and round, with good fruit and body, this is a ripe, attractive Barbera for drinking over the next 5–6 years. Alfieri's 1990 Barbera d'Asti La Tota is less concentrated, with a deceptively shallow color. However, the big, nearly gaudy bouquet offers lavish quantities of sweet, smoky new oak combined with gobs of ripe, sweet, jammy fruit. This soft wine is one of the most flattering Barberas of the vintage. It is not likely to make old bones (it should be drunk over the next 2–3 years), but there is no doubting its seductive, voluptuous, medium-bodied personality.

ELIO ALTARE
Barbera Vigna Larigi * * * * *, Barolo * * * *, Barolo Vigna Arborina * * * * *,
Dolcetto * * * *, La Villa * * * */* * * * *

1990 Barolo	D	92
1990 Barolo Vigna Arborina	D	96
1989 Nebbiolo delle Langhe	C	88
1990 Vigna Arborina	D	97
1989 Vigna Arborina	D	90
1991 Vigna Larigi	D	79
1990 Vigna Larigi	D	92
1989 Vigna Larigi	D	93
1991 La Villa	D	87
1990 La Villa	D	89

Altare's superripe, rich, voluptuously textured 1990 Barolo caresses the palate with gobs of sweet fruit, high glycerin, and a creamy richness. Soft and fat in its rich chewiness, the wine possesses marvelous intensity, as well as considerable tannin, most of which is buried beneath lavish quantities of jammy fruit judiciously touched by toasty vanillin new oak. Drink this decadent Barolo over the next 15 years. The highly saturated, opaque color of the 1990 Barolo Arborina suggests an exceptionally concentrated wine. The huge nose of new saddle leather, ripe plum/black cherry fruit, and smoky new oak is a turn-on. Full bodied, with layers of chewy fruit and that elusive Nebbiolo flavor of tar, this seductive wine possesses a huge, expansive, chewy richness and a sweet finish due to the 1990 vintage's great ripeness. Drink it over the next 15 or more years.

Altare generally makes some of the most interesting Piedmontese wines from Nebbiolo and Barbera. However, the 1991 Vigna Larigi demonstrates the vintage's shortcomings. The wine's compactness and high-acid, short finish are in complete contrast to the sumptuous 1989 and 1990. The wine possesses deep color, an excessive amount of new oak, but a relatively good attack. However, once the wine hits the palate there is not much left. Even a genius such as Altare cannot make a silk purse out of a sow's ear.

On the other hand, Altare's 100% Nebbiolo, the 1990 Vigna Arborina, is even more profound than his Barolos. Aged in small oak casks, this awesome wine has a density and extraction of flavor that must be tasted to be believed. The huge nose of black fruits, tar, and spices soars from the glass. Superrich, extraordinarily well balanced, and long and intense, it is the essence of wine. Drinkable now, it should evolve for 12–15 or more years. If you can find any, it is a must-purchase! Altare's 1990 La Villa, a blend of equal parts of Nebbiolo and Barbera, offers a big, smoky, toasty, fruity nose, sweet, ripe, medium- to full-bodied flavors, excellent richness, and a soft, moderately long finish. Drink it over the next 7–8 years. The 1990 Vigna Larigi, made from 100% Barbera, exhibits attractive subtle toasty oaky components married nicely to stunning aromas of sweet black fruits. The wine is deep, full bodied, spicy, and opulent. Drink it over the next decade.

The 1989 Vigna Arborina and 1989 Vigna Larigi, both aged in small oak casks, were made in extremely limited quantities. The 1989 Vigna Arborina reveals an intense opaque ruby/purple color, a big, oaky, intensely fruity nose, great richness, and a full-bodied, luscious, opulent finish. The moderate tannin levels are nearly concealed by the wealth of fruit. The finish lasts for over a minute. This gorgeous, voluptuous wine can be drunk now or held for up to a decade. The 1989 Vigna Larigi is a compelling example of what the Barbera grape can attain. The color is an opaque purple and the nose offers up sweet aromas of vanillin, smoke, and black fruits. There is exceptional richness, and a thrilling mid-palate with considerable expansion and sweetness of fruit, as well as a long finish. This pure, rich, medium- to full-bodied wine should continue to provide dazzling drinking over the next 7–10 years.

The 1989 Nebbiolo delle Langhe is marked by more noticeable new oak. With its sweet, vanillin, spicy, black fruit–scented nose, and long, deep, full-bodied, black cherry flavors, it makes for a succulent, gorgeous mouthful of wine. What is so admirable about Altare's winemaking is the purity, richness, and overall balance he manages to obtain. Furthermore, he has that rare talent of producing wines that are drinkable young, yet give every indication of lasting for extended periods when well cellared.

In what was a difficult vintage in Piedmont, Altare's 1991 La Villa (a proprietary blend) exhibits an impressively saturated dark ruby/purple color, sweet, ripe, berry fruit, gobs of toasty new oak, and a medium-bodied, soft finish. Drink it over the next 5–6 years.

CANTINA ANSELMA
Barolo * * *

1990 Barolo	D	?
1989 Barolo	D	87

Old-style, traditionally made, controversial wines are produced by this small estate. The 1989 Barolo offers an herbal, tarlike, black cherry–scented nose, full-bodied, dense, thick flavors, rustic tannin, and a deep, long finish. Approachable now, it should drink well for 15 years. The 1990 Barolo barrel sample I tasted was oxidized. Judgment reserved.

ANTONIOLO
Gattinara * * *, Gattinara Osso San Grato * * * *, Gattinara San Francesco * * * *,
Gattinara Vigneto Castelle * * * *

1989 Gattinara	C	88
1990 Gattinara Osso San Grato	D	90
1989 Gattinara Osso San Grato	D	89+
1989 Gattinara San Francesco	D	87
1989 Gattinara Vigneto Castelle	D	90

This 62-acre estate (40 acres under vine) has enjoyed a long tradition of making full-bodied, earthy, forceful wines from Gattinara. The current releases are the most impressive wines I have tasted from Antoniolo. The 1989 Gattinara possesses a dark garnet color, a plummy, earthy, leathery nose, big, ripe, roasted, cherry flavors, full body, high acidity, and a fine finish. Approachable now, it should drink well for a decade or more. The 1989 Gattinara Osso San Grato (from a single vineyard) exhibits a pronounced spicy, tree bark–like, black cherry–scented nose, intense, full-bodied flavors with considerable structure, moderate acidity, and a spicy, long finish. Although young and unevolved, it can be drunk now or cellared for 15 years. The 1990 Gattinara Osso San Grato offers more richness and a fat succulence to its chewy, fleshy, black cherry and plumlike flavors. Spicy, with licorice and leathery components, this expansive, full-bodied wine possesses moderate tannin, sound acidity, and a long, powerful finish. It should last for 10–15 years.

The 1989 Gattinara San Francesco (another single vineyard) does not have the concentration or intensity of the other bottlings. It exhibits plenty of charm and earthy/herb/cherry fruit, medium body, and a tannic finish. Drink it over the next 7–8 years. Lastly, the 1989 Gattinara Vigneto Castelle is the most supple and velvety textured of Antoniolo's wines. It reveals a berry, jammy, black cherry, and curranty bouquet, as well as opulent, ripe flavors, low acidity, layers of fruit, plenty of glycerin, and a spicy, alcoholic finish. It should drink well for 10–15 years.

AZELIA
Barolo Bricco Fiasco * * */* * * *, Barolo Bricco Punta * * */* * * *,
Dolcetto d'Alba Bricco dell'Oriolo * * * *, Dolcetto d'Alba Vigneto Azelia * * * *

1990 Barolo Bricco Fiasco	C	90
1989 Barolo Bricco Fiasco	C	91
1990 Barolo Bricco Punta	D	90
1989 Barolo Bricco Punta	D	90
1992 Dolcetto d'Alba	A	87

1990 Dolcetto d'Alba Bricco dell'Oriolo	B	86
1990 Dolcetto d'Alba Vigneto Azelia	B	86

Luigi Scavino, from the same family as Enrico Scavino, has always caught my attention because of his excellent Dolcettos. However, in the two superb vintages of 1989 and 1990, Scavino has turned out some spectacular Barolos from the Bricco Punta and Bricco Fiasco vineyards. The extraordinary quality of these two vintages makes it virtually impossible to pick a favorite. Readers will adore the huge, sweet, chocolatey, black cherry– and herb-scented nose of the 1989 Barolo Bricco Punta. A rich, luscious, supple style of Barolo, it exhibits intense concentration, adequate acidity, and a ripe, round, velvety-textured finish. It is a Barolo for drinking during its first 12–15 years of life. The 1989 Barolo Bricco Fiasco displays a mineral element to its flamboyant, tar- and black cherry–scented nose. Deep, full bodied, and concentrated, it is more structured and tannic than the Bricco Punta. This awesomely rich Barolo is a noteworthy candidate for two decades of cellaring. Approachable now, it will improve gracefully for 10–12 years.

The 1990 Barolo Bricco Punta reveals smoky, toasty, vanillin scents in the nose, causing me to conclude that new small oak barrels were utilized during the wine's upbringing. The oak complements rather than dominates this full-bodied, highly concentrated wine's huge, jammy, black cherry fruitiness, and glycerin-endowed, rich, thick, viscous flavors. Soft and already flattering and seductive, this big-styled, voluptuous Barolo should be drunk over the next 12–15 years. As for the 1990 Barolo Bricco Fiasco, the toasty new oak is apparent in the wine's large-scaled, intensely fragrant nose of black fruits, underbrush, and tar. Full bodied, with a wonderfully sweet, expansive, chewy mid-palate, and generous finish, this terrific Barolo possesses slightly more structure and tannin than the Bricco Punta. It has the capacity to last for 20+ years. Readers should note the modest prices.

Not many Dolcettos from the inconsistent 1992 vintage are this enjoyable. This excellent 1992 Dolcetto reveals a wonderful jammy, cherry nose, ripe, richly fruity, fleshy flavors, and an excellent finish. Drink it over the next several years. The two tasty 1990 Dolcettos differ slightly in style. Both enjoy excellent ruby color, and fragrant, fruity noses, but the Vigneto Azelia is softer and not as high in acidity. Their wonderful purity of flavor, medium body, and crunchy, delicious fruit are delightfully displayed in this ripe vintage. Drink both wines over the next 1–3 years.

F.LLI BARALE

Barbaresco Rabaja * * * *, Barolo Castellero * * * *

1990 Barbaresco Rabaja	C	88
1989 Barbaresco Rabaja	C	87
1989 Barolo Castellero	C	88

Barale's 1989 Barbaresco Rabaja is a solid, medium- to long-term wine. Its deep ruby color and spicy, red fruit–scented bouquet are followed by flavors that exhibit fine ripeness, full body, moderate tannin, and a solid inner core of fruit. The complexity Nebbiolo can achieve should be more evident after 3–4 years of bottle age. The 1990 Barbaresco Rabaja looks to be slightly sweeter and fatter, with high glycerin and elevated alcohol. While fuller bodied and richer than the 1989, it also reveals a positive note of overripeness. It should drink well for 10–12 years. These are both very good to excellent Barbarescos.

The 1989 Barolo Castellero possesses such an overripe, cherry jam, old-vine character that the intensity of the bouquet reminds me of the great Pomerol, Lafleur. Once past the bouquet, it does not exhibit the intensity of Lafleur, but it does offer medium- to full-bodied, supple flavor with admirable purity of black cherry fruit. The sweetness is a result of ripeness, not residual sugar. With a moderately long, round, supple finish, this seductive Barolo should be consumed over the next decade.

MARCHESI DI BAROLO
Barbaresco* * *, Barolo di Barolo* * *, Barolo Cannubi* * *, Barolo Sarmassa* * *

1990 Barbaresco	D	87
1990 Barolo di Barolo	D	85
1990 Barolo Cannubi	D	89
1989 Barolo Cannubi	D	87
1990 Barolo Sarmassa	D	88
1989 Barolo Sarmassa	D	87

The late Sheldon Wasserman probably stated it best in his comprehensive book on the red wines of Italy when he wrote, "Marchesi di Barolo owns 100 acres of vineyards, including some of the best sites in Barolo, a fact unfortunately not evident in their wines." This longtime underachiever has finally begun to turn out rich, complex wines. The 1990 Barbaresco offers a spicy, leathery, cherry-scented nose, tasty, medium-bodied flavors with fine depth, and a moderately tannic finish. It should be at its best in 2–3 years and last for a decade or more.

Both 1989 single-vineyard Barolos, the Sarmassa and Cannubi, reveal toasty new oak, excellent ripeness, medium to full body, and a rich, pure, modern style that offers concentration, complexity, and plenty of sweet, ripe fruit. Both are wines to drink during their first decade of life. They represent a dramatic improvement in the commitment to quality from one of Barolo's most historic estates.

With respect to the 1990 vintage, the Marchesi di Barolo produced two wines that are probably the finest Barolos they have made in 30 or more years. The 1990 Barolo Sarmassa exhibits excellent ripeness in its herbal, spicy, smoky, black cherry–scented nose, deep, rich, full-bodied, concentrated flavors, and a long, supple finish. Drink this hedonistic Barolo over the next 10 years. Slightly more impressive is the multidimensional, complex 1990 Barolo Cannubi, a fuller-bodied, more concentrated and delineated wine with excellent purity and length. Drink it over the next 10–15 years. On the other hand, the lighter 1990 Barolo di Barolo is compact and straightforward, without the flavor depth or dimension of Marchesi di Barolo's other 1990s and 1989s.

BATASIOLO
Barbaresco* * * *, Barolo* * * *, Barolo Cru Bofani* * * * *, Barolo Cru Boscareto* * * *, Barolo Cru Briccolina* * * *, Dolcetto d'Alba* * * *, Moscato d'Asti* * * *

1990 Barbaresco	C	87
1990 Barolo	C	87
1990 Barolo Cru Bofani	D	93
1990 Barolo Cru Boscareto	D	89
1989 Barolo Cru Boscareto	D	87
1990 Barolo Cru Briccolina	D	90?
1993 Dolcetto d'Alba	A	86

Batasiolo is one of the largest vineyard owners in Piedmont, owning over 250 acres, a vast empire in view of the tiny Barolo and Barbaresco estates that tend to resemble the morsellated Burgundy landscape. In the past, I have found Batasiolo wines to be straightforward and monolithic. Whether it's the quality of the vintage or an obvious effort to raise the quality level, Batasiolo's 1990s all performed exceptionally well. The 1990 Barbaresco's medium ruby color reveals some amber, suggesting considerable evolution. The big, spicy, cherry, leathery nose is followed by a sweet, round, soft-textured wine that is ideal for drinking over the next 6–7 years.

I tasted four separate Barolos, including three single-vineyard wines. The 1990 Barolo regular cuvée exhibits an attractive, open-knit, ripe, smoky, dusty, herb- and black cherry–scented nose, ripe, supple, chewy, medium- to full-bodied flavors, a soft texture, and a smooth finish. It is meant to be drunk in its first 7–8 years of life. Among the three single-vineyard Barolos, the most expensive wine, the 1990 Barolo Cru Briccolina, may be controversial, given the lavish quantities of toasty new oak apparent in the wine's spicy, smoky, vanillin-scented bouquet. The wine exhibits immensely impressive extraction of flavor, layers of full-bodied, black cherry fruit, and a long, heady, rich, moderately tannic finish. It will easily last 20 years, but I hope the oak becomes more integrated. The softest, easiest-to-consume wine among the single-vineyard offerings is the 1990 Barolo Cru Boscareto. It offers up a gorgeous nose of sweet, jammy fruit, herbs, and damp earthy, trufflelike aromas. Rich, with full body, and admirable ripeness and length, this generously endowed wine should drink well for 10–15 years. My favorite is the 1990 Barolo Cru Bofani. It possesses a superb, multidimensional bouquet of herbs, tobacco, smoke, black fruits, and licorice. Great richness combined with outstanding delineation among its component parts, full body, and an explosive finish have combined to result in a lusty, decadently styled Barolo. It can be drunk now or cellared for 15 or more years. These are impressive performances from Batasiolo.

I only tasted one single-vineyard 1989 Barolo from Batasiolo, the Cru Boscareto. It is an elegant, lovely wine with plenty of sweet, jammy, cherry fruit and dusty tannin. Overall it is a modern-style Barolo with the emphasis on suppleness, finesse, and up-front, forward fruit. Drink it over the next 7–8 years.

Made in an up-front, modern, flattering style, Batasiolo's intensely fragrant, richly fruity 1993 Dolcetto d'Alba possesses fine purity and ripeness, as well as loads of cherry fruit accompanied by an intriguing herb and roasted nut component. Drink it over the next 2–3 years.

BAVA
Barbera d'Asti Superiore * * * *

1990 Barbera d'Asti Superiore	C	89
1990 Barbera d'Asti Superiore Stradivario	C	87

The full-bodied, opulently styled, rich, supple 1990 Barbera d'Alba Superiore offers loads of fruit, a textured, layered feel in the mouth, and gobs of glycerin, fruit, body, and alcohol. Obviously made from very ripe fruit, it is a hedonistic, smashingly rich, complex Barbera for drinking over the next 7–8 years. The 1990 Barbera d'Asti Superiore Stradivario reveals toasty new oak in its nose intertwined with ripe black cherry and spicy fruit. Medium to full bodied and concentrated, with noticeable glycerin and fleshiness, this mouth-filling, delicious Barbera should be drunk over the next 5–7 years.

PIETRO BERRUTI
Barbaresco La Spinona * * *

1990 Barbaresco La Spinona	C	88
1989 Barbaresco La Spinona	C	88

Both of these Barbarescos are excellent, possibly outstanding, wines made in a traditional, powerful style that offers considerable concentration, extract, chewy tannin, and heady alcohol. The 1989 offers a dark garnet/ruby color, and a subdued, backward, earthy, black cherry–scented nose. Full bodied, with impressive concentration, and a moderately tannic, tightly knit finish, it needs 5–7 years of cellaring and should last for 20 or more years. The similarly styled, dense, concentrated, and ferociously tannic 1990 is impressively endowed. This full-bodied, layered wine will require 5–6 years of cellaring and last for two decades. Both wines are cleanly made, but they are not candidates for early drinking.

BERSANO
Barbera d'Asti Cascina Cremosina* * *

1990 Barbera d'Asti Cascina Cremosina	C	86

This rustic, spicy, medium- to full-bodied Barbera possesses high acidity and chunky fruit. Less civilized than many of its peers, it should drink well for 5–8 years.

PODERI BERTELLI
Barbera Giarone* * * *, Barbera Montetusa* * * *, Cabernet I Fossaretti* * *

1988 Barbera Giarone	D	86
1989 Barbera Montetusa	D	90
1989 Cabernet I Fossaretti	D	85

Bertelli is an interesting winemaker who has gone from strength to strength during the decade of the eighties. His best wines continue to be Barberas. The 1988 Barbera Giarone is a light, herbaceous, meaty wine with pronounced aromas of truffles and damp earth. Soft, oaky, and enticing in its complexity and individuality, it should drink well for 5–6 years. The exceptional 1989 Barbera Montetusa exhibits a saturated deep purple color, and a spectacular nose of sweet, toasty new oak, ripe black fruits, and flowers. Deep, rich, and full bodied, this wine is crammed with fruit and glycerin. Its finish must last nearly a minute. Drink it over the next 10–15 years.

Bertelli was one of the first Italian producers to make a Cabernet. To date, they have been irregular. The 1989 is sweeter and riper than the 1988, with plenty of new oak. However, it is good rather than exciting. Their prices make them frightfully bad values.

ALFIERO BOFFA
Barbera d'Asti Collina della Vedova* * * *, Barbera d'Asti Vigna Cua Longa* * * *,
Barbera d'Asti Vigna More* * * *

1990 Barbera d'Asti Collina della Vedova	C	89
1990 Barbera d'Asti Vigna Cua Longa	C	90
1990 Barbera d'Asti Vigna More	C	87

All three of these expensively packaged (tall, heavy Italian glass bottles) are noteworthy Barberas that are ideal for drinking over the next 5–7 years. The 1990 Vigna More offers an attractive ruby color, a straightforward nose of black fruits, excellent ripeness, medium body, and crisp acidity. As for the 1990 Collina della Vedova, it exhibits a deeper color, and a more enticing bouquet of ripe fruit, floral scents, and new oak notes from aging in barrel. It also tastes riper, with sweeter fruit, and a longer, riper finish. It is a persuasive example of a rich, elegant wine for drinking now and over the next several years. The most backward of this trio is the 1990 Vigna Cua Longa. A saturated purple color, admirable ripeness, medium to full body, sweet, toasty vanillin (from aging in small oak casks), and impressive purity and balance combine to create an authoritatively flavored, complex, and decadent Barbera.

GIACOMO BOLOGNA

Barbera d'Asti Bricco della Figotta* * * * *, Barbera dell'Uccellone* * * * *

1990	Barbera d'Asti Bricco della Figotta	D	96
1989	Barbera d'Asti Bricco della Figotta	D	90
1990	Barbera dell'Uccellone	D	93
1989	Barbera dell'Uccellone	D	92

For many Barbera fanatics, this producer is the varietal's reference point. It is difficult to argue with Bologna's supporters, as these offerings are mind-boggling in their complexity, intensity, mouth-feel, and sensational richness. Where do I begin? The 1990 Barbera dell'Uccellone is aromatically reserved at first, but there is no doubting its healthy dark ruby/purple color. As the wine sits in the glass, ripe fruit and floral scents emerge. Stunningly full bodied, with layers of richness and expansiveness, and a smashingly long finish, this is a profound Barbera. Everything is held together by well-integrated acidity. It should drink well for 10–15 more years. The blockbuster 1990 Barbera d'Asti Bricco della Figotta is the finest Barbera I have tasted. It exhibits an opaque, saturated color, a huge, emerging bouquet of sweet new oak, floral scents, and marvelous quantities of ripe black fruits. The wine's highly extracted richness, excellent balance, adequate acidity, light tannin, and superrich, full-bodied finish are impressive. Like its sibling, it is a masterpiece that exhibits the extraordinary heights Barbera can achieve. If you can afford as well as find them, these wines offer mind-boggling tasting experiences.

The 1989 offerings, also from an opulent, dramatically rich vintage, are examples of what viscosity and depth can be obtained from this grape. Both wines display dark, nearly black/purple colors and huge perfumes of smoke, toast, herbs, and black fruits, as well as evidence of aging in new oak casks. I thought the 1989 Barbera dell'Uccellone possessed slightly more flesh, a longer finish, and more aromatic dimension, but at this level of quality I am splitting hairs. In short, these are terrific Barberas! Delicious to drink now, they should last for at least a decade.

F.LLI SERIO & BATTISTA BORGOGNO

Barolo Cannubi* * *

1990	Barolo Cannubi	C	76
1989	Barolo Cannubi	C	86

This producer turned out a good, sweet, superripe, medium-bodied, soft, spicy 1989 Barolo from the highly regarded Cannubi vineyard. Made in a forward, commercial style, it should be drunk over the next 6–7 years. The 1990 Barolo Cannubi exhibits a shallow color, some spicy fruit in the nose, but a monochromatic personality with flavors that lack concentration, grip, and intensity.

GIACOMO E FIGLI BREZZA

Barbera d'Alba Cannubi* * */* * * *, Barolo Bricco Sarmassa* * */* * * *,
Barolo Cannubi* * * *

1990	Barbera d'Alba Cannubi	D	86?
1989	Barolo Bricco Sarmassa	D	88
1989	Barolo Cannubi	D	90

Although I am not familiar with this producer's track record, I thought highly of both of these Barolo offerings. The 1989 Barolo Bricco Sarmassa possesses a saturated dark ruby color, a big, chocolatey, spicy, black cherry–scented nose, lovely, full-bodied, concentrated flavors with a touch of herbs, and a long, moderately tannic finish. It can be drunk young or cellared for 15 years. The outstanding 1989 Barolo Cannubi offers a persuasive bouquet of jammy black cherries, herbs, tar, and tobacco. It is a powerfully constructed wine with full body, great richness and ripeness, and plenty of tannin. The color saturation suggests high extraction of fruit. This is a Barolo to put away for 4–5 years and to drink over the subsequent 10–15.

The rustic, old-style 1990 Barbera d'Alba Cannubi exhibits an impressive dark ruby color. The mushroomy, earthy, damp cellar–like bouquet unfortunately obscures much of the wine's ripe fruit. Made in a style that was more common 20 or 30 years ago, the wine's high acidity gives it a sharp, angular, shrill personality that is unlikely to be appreciated by many contemporary palates. Once past the acidity, there is no doubting the wine's full body, laudable concentration, and extract levels. It is a candidate for 15–20 years of cellaring.

BROVIA
Barbera d'Alba Sori del Drago * * * *, Barolo Garblet Sue * * * *,
Barolo Monprivato * * * * *, Barolo Rocche * * * * *

1992 Barbera d'Alba Sori del Drago	C	85
1990 Barbera d'Alba Sori del Drago	C	88
1990 Barolo Garblet Sue	D	89
1989 Barolo Garblet Sue	D	88
1990 Barolo Monprivato	D	93
1989 Barolo Monprivato	D	92+
1990 Barolo Rocche	D	92
1989 Barolo Rocche	D	90+

This old-style, traditional producer believes in long macerations, resulting in frightfully tannic, tough, closed wines that are loaded with concentrated fruit. In lighter vintages there can be too much tannin and structure for the wine's extract. In years such as 1989 and 1990 (provided a reader is willing to wait 7–10 years), these wines should prove to be spectacular —classic, old-style, textbook Barolos. The dark-colored 1989 Barolo Garblet Sue reveals a spicy nose and flavors that exhibit excellent depth, as well as mouth-filling tannin. There is a searing ferociousness to the wine's structure and tannin. Give this wine 10 years of cellaring and drink it over the subsequent 15. The 1989 Barolo Monprivato is one of the most massive, backward wines of the vintage, with huge extraction of fruit and enough mouthwatering tannin to render it nearly unapproachable for 7–8 years. The huge, full-bodied, muscular style takes some getting used to, but, wow, what concentration and length! Do not touch a bottle before the turn of the century. Although the 1989 Barolo Rocche starts slowly, it is extremely full bodied, backward, firm, and loaded with tannin. Again, the wine's dusty, cherry aromas of tar, as well as its massive weight, suggest there is more than enough extract to stand the test of time.

The 1990s are similarly styled, with sweeter fruit. The 1990 Barolo Garblet Sue tastes more elegant and forward than the 1989. The 1990 Barolo Monprivato is enormous, powerful, frightfully tannic, yet highly promising. However, if you are over 35 years of age you might want to reconsider buying this powerhouse wine. The 1990 Barolo Rocche exhibits more sweetness than the 1989, as well as a jammy, black cherry, dusty, earthy nose, and huge, full-bodied, massive flavors. It requires 5–7 years of cellaring. All of these offerings are cleanly made, old-style, enormously thick and tannic Barolos that require 5–10 years of cellaring; they are capable of lasting for 30 or more years.

Brovia's 1992 Barbera d'Alba Sori del Drago offers a spicy, herb-, tomato-, and curranty-scented nose, medium body, good ripeness, and a tasty, slightly acidic but vibrant, exuberant finish. It is neither complex nor concentrated, so drink it over the next 2–4 years. The greatness of the 1990 vintage is again evidenced by the 1990 Barbera d'Alba Sori del Drago. It reveals an opaque ruby/purple color, and a forceful, jammy nose of spices, black and red fruits, and wood. Deep, muscular, and powerful, this rich, chewy wine should drink well for 10–15 years.

CA DEL BAIO
Barbaresco Asili * * * *

1990 Barbaresco Asili	D	88

A lovely, rich, tobacco-, cherry-, and rose petal–scented wine, this full-bodied Barbaresco from the renowned Asili vineyard displays oodles of sweet, superripe, jammy fruit. The velvety texture suggests that prospective purchasers can drink or cellar this beauty.

CA DEI GANCIA
Barolo Cannubi * * *

1990 Barolo Cannubi	D	86?
1989 Barolo Cannubi	D	87

The 1989 Barolo Cannubi offers copious quantities of rich, ripe, cherry-, tar-, and rose-scented fruit, medium to full body, excellent depth, and a long, ripe, spicy finish. Easy to drink, it should continue to age well for 10 years. The 1990 Barolo Cannubi is dominated by toasty new oak. Although there is plenty of depth, the oak dominates at present.

CA ROME
Barbaresco * * *, Barbaresco Maria di Brun * * * *, Barolo Vigna Carpegna * * *,
Barolo Vigna Rapet * * *, Barolo Vigna Rionda * * * *

1990 Barbaresco	C	86
1989 Barbaresco	C	87
1990 Barbaresco Maria di Brun	D	90
1989 Barbaresco Maria di Brun	D	89
1989 Barolo Vigna Carpegna	C	87
1990 Barolo Vigna Rapet	C	87
1989 Barolo Vigna Rapet	C	89
1989 Barolo Vigna Rionda	C	90

Ca Rome's penchant for making stylish, elegant, pure, medium-weight Barbarescos is well displayed in the 1989 vintage. The regular cuvée of 1989 Barbaresco offers a beautiful nose, supple flavors, excellent ripeness, and that pervasive cherry/tobacco/leather fruitiness that Nebbiolo routinely obtains. Drink this graceful, stylish wine over the next 7–8 years. The 1989 Barbaresco Maria di Brun (named after the proprietor's mother) is richer, with a sweeter jamminess to its chewy fruit, an opulent, velvety-textured palate, and long, medium- to full-bodied, concentrated flavors that caress the palate. Already seductive, this wine should drink well for 8–10 years.

The 1990 Barbaresco is made in an elegant, ripe, medium-bodied style with gobs of rich cherry fruit presented in a straightforward manner. The spicy, chewy texture and fine length are admirable. Drink it over the next 7–8 years. The 1990 Barbaresco Maria di Brun is a denser, fuller-bodied wine with highly extracted flavors, a sweet, black cherry component to its aromatics and flavors, and a long, moderately tannic finish. Approachable now, it is capable of lasting for 10–12 years.

In the past, I have been unpersuaded by what appeared to be blatantly commercial, excessively soft, user-friendly Barolos. Having said that, the 1989s and 1990s are considerably more serious and concentrated than their predecessors. There are three fine 1989 single-vineyard Barolos. The 1989 Barolo Vigna Carpegna is the most refined and technically correct of the trio, but because it is so subtle, polite, and understated, it lacks the drama and hedonism of its two siblings. Nevertheless, it is a medium- to full-bodied, crisp, oenologically correct, ripe wine that will provide enjoyment over the next 5–6 years. The darker-colored 1989 Barolo Vigna Rapet offers a denser constitution, a spicy, new saddle leather– and cherry-scented nose, and excellent definition and length. It should be drunk over the next 7–8 years. My favorite wine is the 1989 Barolo Vigna Rionda, made from that superb vineyard in the Serralunga area that Bruno Giacosa has made world famous. This wine combines the estate's penchant for turning out impeccably clean, elegantly styled wines with Nebbiolo's meaty, full-bodied, rich personality. There is outstanding depth and richness, notable purity, gobs of lusty, cherry fruit, and a long, spicy, full-bodied finish. Drink it over the next 10–12 years.

Ca Rome's understated 1990 Barolo Vigna Rapet is an attractively spicy, cedary, cherry-scented wine with medium body, soft, nicely concentrated flavors, and an easygoing finish. Although it lacks the power and authority of the 1989, it is a very good, ready-to-drink Barolo.

BARTOLOMEO DI CABUTTO
Barbera d'Alba Bricco della Viole * * *, Barolo La Volta * * * *

1990 Barbera d'Alba Bricco della Viole	C	85?
1989 Barolo La Volta	D	90

This relatively obscure producer has fashioned a fabulously rich, perfumed 1989 Barolo La Volta redolent of sweet black cherries, herbs, earth, and spices. There is great intensity, full body, moderate tannin, and superlative levels of extract and glycerin. The heady alcohol makes for a decadent mouthful of wine. Drink it between now and 2010. Very impressive!

A slight lees note and a touch of leather and smoked meat are sure to make this 1990 Barbera d'Alba Bricco della Viole controversial among the oenologically correct bunch. The wine exhibits a dark ruby color, medium body, above-average concentration, and a spicy, slightly acidic finish. Drink it over the next 5–6 years.

DOTT. G. CAPPELLANO
Barolo * * *, Barolo Ottin Fiorin Collina Gabuti * * * *

1990 Barolo	D	89
1989 Barolo	D	87
1990 Barolo Ottin Fiorin Collina Gabuti	D	92
1989 Barolo Ottin Fiorin Collina Gabuti	D	88+

Cappellano, who has a reputation for not wanting his wines to be compared with others, has been reluctant in the past to show his products in a comparative tasting. The 1989 Barolo offers plenty of purity, a beautifully fragrant tar- and black cherry–scented nose, and deep, medium- to full-bodied, supple flavors that linger on the palate. It should be drunk over the next 10–15 years. The 1989 Barolo Collina Gabuti reveals more tannin, as well as more depth and length. More closed than the regular cuvée, it will benefit from 2–3 years of cellaring and will keep for 15 years.

Both 1990s appear to be smoother, richer, fuller-bodied Barolos. The 1990 Barolo exhibits a darker, more saturated color with a sweet, intense nose of licorice, spices, and black fruits, full-bodied, concentrated flavors, and moderate tannin. It needs 3–4 years of cellaring and will last for 15 years. The 1990 Barolo Collina Gabuti looks to be superb. Although still in cask, it displays fabulous depth and richness. If the sample I tasted was representative, it is a potentially magnificent Barolo with layers of flavor, sweet tannin, and gobs of extract, glycerin, alcohol, and flavor, not to mention personality. It should be drunk in 3–4 years and has the potential to last for two decades.

GIORGIO CARNEVALE
Barbera d'Asti Il Crottino * * * *

1990 Barbera d'Asti Il Crottino	C	89

This impressive 1990 Barbera d'Asti Il Crottino exhibits a youthful yet forceful bouquet of damp earth, spices, and red and black fruits. Full bodied, powerful, and expansive, with high alcohol as well as broad, expansive flavors, this wine is drinkable now, yet it will easily last for a decade.

TENUTA CARRETTA
Barbaresco * * * *, Barbera Bric Quercia * * *, Barolo Cannubi * * * *, Nebbiolo d'Alba Bric Paradiso * * */* * * *, Nebbiolo d'Alba Bric Tavoleto * * */* * * *

1990 Barbaresco	C	91
1989 Barbaresco	C	89
1990 Barbera Bric Quercia	D	88
1990 Barolo Cannubi	D	92
1989 Barolo Cannubi	D	90

These wines are unequivocally from the traditional school of Piedmontese winemaking. Their rustic side, evidenced by huge quantities of ferocious tannin, is accompanied by deep, full-bodied, concentrated wine with layers of pure, ripe fruit. Still revealing plenty of tannin, the 1989 Barbaresco exhibits a sweet, cedary, tobacco, spicy, cherry bouquet and flavors. Full bodied, with excellent density and extraction, but slightly rough-textured, this large-scaled wine can be drunk now or cellared for up to 15–20 years. The 1990 Barbaresco has an element of overripeness, but it is fabulously rich, full bodied, and intense. The leathery, herb- and cherry-scented nose is followed by bold, tannic, powerful flavors. Ideally it needs 2–3 years of cellaring; it will keep for 15–20 years.

The marvelous 1989 and 1990 Barolos are made in a traditional, robust, tannic yet superrich style. Both emanate from the highly regarded Cannubi vineyard. The 1989 Barolo Cannubi is more developed aromatically, with its marvelously sweet, plummy, cherry, spicy nose, and deep, full-bodied, large-scaled flavors oozing with extract and tannin. This wine will benefit from 5–6 years of cellaring and will last for 20 or more years. The 1990 Barolo Cannubi is even larger-scaled (and that's saying something), with explosive levels of extract, tannin, glycerin, body, and alcohol. Although it must have 14.5%–15% alcohol, there is no noticeable hotness, because of the wine's sheer concentration. This extroverted, macho, beefy Barolo should be drunk between 1998 and 2015. Impressive!

With respect to the 1990 Barbera Bric Quercia, toasty, vanillin, smoky new oak and curranty fruit aromas jump from the glass. The wine possesses plenty of body, excellent, nearly outstanding, richness, and a dense, chewy, spicy finish. Although approachable, it promises to last for at least a decade.

F.LLI CASETTA
Barbaresco Vigna Ausario * * *, Barbera d'Alba Vigna Lazaretto * * *

1989 Barbaresco Vigna Ausario	C	87
1990 Barbera d'Alba Vigna Lazaretto	B	86+

Having never previously tasted this producer's wines, I have no sense of their track record. The 1989 Barbaresco Vigna Ausario displays an evolved medium ruby color with garnet and amber hues. The heady, jammy nose of herbs, underbrush, and cherries is followed by a ripe, lush, high-alcohol wine with a soft, chewy texture, and fine depth. While delicious now, the wine's size augurs well for 7–8 years of graceful aging.

The big, old-style, rustic 1990 Barbera d'Alba Vigna Lazaretto offers plenty of chunky, tar-scented and -flavored fruit, a slight earthiness, and considerable alcohol, glycerin, acidity, and depth. Although relatively soft because of the ripeness achieved in 1990, it is an unmistakable example from the old school of Piedmontese winemaking. Drink it over the next 7–8 years.

CASCINA CASTLET
Barbera d'Asti * * *, Barbera d'Asti Superiore * * *

1990 Barbera d'Asti	B	88
1990 Barbera d'Asti Superiore	B	85

It is not supposed to work out this way, but the regular bottling of the Cascina Castlet's 1990 Barbera d'Asti is a more appealing and better balanced wine than the 1990 Superiore. The 1990 regular bottling offers a healthy dark ruby color, a sweet, jammy bouquet, and lush, soft flavors, and comes across as a fleshy Barbera for drinking over the next 4–5 years. The 1990 Barbera d'Asti Superiore is supposed to be a more ambitious and serious wine. It exhibits some toasty oak notes, more tannin, and an unclean leeslike note in the otherwise satisfactory bouquet. It is a more backward, less flattering wine that may be "bigger" than its sibling, but it is obviously not better.

CAVALLOTTO
Barolo Bricco Boschis * * *

1989 Barolo Bricco Boschis	C	87

The 1989 Barolo Bricco Boschis is an old-style, tannic, spicy wine crammed with dusty, herb-tinged, cherry fruit. It offers full body, excellent concentration, and a moderately tannic finish. Cellar it for 4–5 years and drink it over the subsequent 15.

BRUNO CERETTO
Barbaresco Asij * * *, Barbaresco Bricco Asili * * * *, Barbaresco Bricco
Asili Faset * * */* * * *, Barbera d'Alba Piana * * *, Barolo Bricco Rocche * * * * *,
Barolo Brunate * * * *, Barolo Prapo * * * *, Barolo Zonchera * * * *,
Dolcetto d'Alba Rossana * * *, Nebbiolo d'Alba Lantasco * * *

1990 Barbaresco Asij	D	88
1988 Barbaresco Asij	D	86
1990 Barbaresco Bricco Asili	D	95
1989 Barbaresco Bricco Asili	D	91
1988 Barbaresco Bricco Asili	D	87
1987 Barbaresco Bricco Asili	D	86
1990 Barbaresco Bricco Asili Faset	D	92
1989 Barbaresco Bricco Asili Faset	D	89
1988 Barbaresco Bricco Asili Faset	D	87
1991 Barbera d'Alba Piana	C	84

1990 Barbera d'Alba Piana	C	87
1990 Barolo Bricco Rocche	EE	95
1989 Barolo Bricco Rocche	EE	93+
1990 Barolo Brunate	D	93
1989 Barolo Brunate	D	93
1990 Barolo Prapo	D	92
1989 Barolo Prapo	D	87?
1989 Barolo Zonchera	D	90

Ceretto has a propensity to produce easy-to-drink, delicately styled Piedmontese wines. While this is evident in the two blockbuster vintages of 1989 and 1990, the Ceretto brothers have made more concentrated and powerful wines than usual. Ceretto enjoyed superb success in both vintages, producing wines opulent enough to be drunk, but with enough concentration and richness to last for 10–15 years. These are top-class efforts!

Both 1989 Barbarescos from the Bricco Asili vineyard can be drunk now as well as over the next 12–14 years. The 1989 Bricco Asili Faset offers a medium ruby color, a ripe, highly scented nose of cedar and black cherries, an expansive, chewy richness, and a soft opulent texture. Underlying the wine's flattering components is a sweet, moderate tannin level and low acidity. This beautiful wine may merit an even higher rating. The exquisite 1989 Bricco Asili exhibits a smoky, roasted, vanillin element to its fruity character. Rich and full, with an intoxicating cigar box aroma to its personality, this concentrated, lush wine provides stunning drinking.

The immensely impressive 1990s include a seductive, elegant, stylish 1990 Asij. Its aromatics are dominated by a sweet cherry component. It offers lovely medium-bodied flavors in a soft, plush format. Drink it over the next 8–9 years. The 1990 Bricco Asili Faset reveals a superb nose of roasted herbs and black cherries, medium to full body, wonderfully ripe flavors, and a long, expansive, concentrated finish that exhibits no hard edges. It should drink well for 12–15 years. The most stunningly perfumed and richest of Ceretto's 1990 Barbarescos is the 1990 Bricco Asili. Deeper-colored, with an intensely fragrant bouquet of roasted herbs, nuts, oak, and sweet, ripe fruit, this wine possesses great richness, full body, a succulent texture, and a finish that lasts for nearly a minute. Drink this gorgeously proportioned, decadently hedonistic Barbaresco over the next 10–15 years. Bravo!

Ceretto's 1989s and 1990s are unquestionably the finest Barolos I have tasted from this firm. Ceretto's proclivity to produce elegant, graceful, easygoing wines has not been compromised in either vintage, but the wines boast terrific richness and concentration. The result is a bevy of riveting Barolos that can be drunk early, or aged for 15 or more years. The 1989 Barolo Prapo is extremely hard, tannic, tight, and closed. Medium to full bodied and weighty in the mouth, the wine was impenetrable when I tasted it—atypical for Ceretto. Perhaps I caught it at an unflattering stage. The other three single-vineyard offerings from Ceretto performed marvelously. The 1989 Barolo Zonchera is the most forward and easy to appreciate of the 1989s. Supple, with an intensely scented nose of black cherries, herbs, and vanillin, this medium- to full-bodied Barolo displays impeccable harmony among its component parts, and a long, sweet, ripe, luscious finish. It should drink well for at least a decade. The most tannic wine is the 1989 Barolo Bricco Rocche. A large-scaled, superconcentrated, muscular wine for Ceretto, it will require 4–5 years of cellaring and should last for 20 or more years. Rich, with layers of fruit, it exhibits a promising bouquet, as well as superb ripeness and intensity. The finish goes on and on. This may turn out to be one of Ceretto's longest-lived Barolos. The 1989 Barolo Brunate is another dazzling effort. The huge bouquet of tobacco, herbs, sweet black cherry fruit, and roasted nuts is a knockout. Dense, concentrated, and full bodied, with layers of flavor, this stunningly proportioned, large-scaled Barolo retains a sense of grace and elegance. Drink it over the next 15–20 years.

The 1990s are all outstanding, combining fabulous extract levels with aromatic bouquets and opulent, voluptuously rich flavors, textures, and finishes. The 1990 Barolo Prapo is very sweet (not from sugar, but from grape ripeness), with a long, moderately tannic, concentrated finish. More powerful and revealing greater extract levels than its 1989 sibling, it will benefit from 2–3 years of cellaring and last for 20 years. The 1990 Barolo Brunate is the most aromatic and perfumed of the three 1990 Barolos I tasted. Concentrated and full bodied, with sweet tannin, ripe fruit, and a luscious, multidimensional personality, this wine should drink well for 15–20 years. The bouquet of the awesomely concentrated, compelling 1990 Barolo Bricco Rocche soars from the glass, offering aromas of melted road tar, sweet, jammy, cherry fruit, tobacco, and fruitcake. Massive yet graceful flavors cascade over the palate, revealing considerable viscosity, glycerin, and extraction of flavor. The wine is deep, expansive, and chewy. The finish is something to behold. There is undoubtedly plenty of tannin lurking beneath the fruit, so this wine can be drunk now and over the next 15–20 years. Kudos to the Ceretto brothers!

All three 1988 Barbarescos would benefit from more cellaring. Although the Bricco Asili and Bricco Asili Faset were closed, both are elegant wines with bouquets that suggest Bing cherries, cedar, and leather. On the palate, they are medium bodied and tannic. While similar in weight and personality, I thought the Bricco Asili was a more classic Nebbiolo with its sweet, dusty, cherry fruit. The Bricco Asili Faset is jammier, perhaps because it was made from riper grapes. Both wines should evolve gracefully for at least 8–10 years. The Barbaresco Asij is a medium-bodied, stylish Barbaresco that can be drunk now, or cellared for 7–8 years. I should note that all three Barbarescos were tight when they were first opened, and needed a minimum of one hour's breathing. Even the following day the wines were considerably more flattering to taste than immediately after opening. The 1987 Barbaresco Bricco Asili is medium ruby/garnet in color, with an intense bouquet of leather, truffles, spices, and dried fruits. This soft, round, adequately concentrated wine offers delicious drinking at present, and should be given consideration by restaurants and consumers looking for serious Italian wines for immediate consumption. It will last for at least another 3–4 years.

Ceretto's 1991 Barbera d'Alba Piana is an attractive, lighter-bodied wine than the richer, more concentrated 1990. Nevertheless, the 1991 offers plenty of charm. It is an ideal wine for restaurants looking for a food-friendly red wine. It possesses gobs of cherry, strawberry, and curranty fruit, adequate acidity, and some spice. The 1990 Barbera d'Alba Piana exhibits deeper color, and more body, richness, glycerin, alcohol, and impact. It will drink well for 5–7 years.

CERUTTI

Barbera d'Alba Ca' Du Ciuvin * * * *

1990 Barbera d'Alba Ca' Du Ciuvin   C   89

Another beautiful 1990 Barbera, this dark ruby-colored wine reveals loads of toasty scents and a ripe, black fruit character. Rich and supple, with impressive purity and balance, and a gentle, opulent finish, it should drink well for a decade.

PIO CESARE

Barbaresco * * * *, Barbera d'Alba * * *, Barolo * * *, Barolo Ornato * * * *,
Dolcetto d'Alba * * * *

1990 Barbaresco	D 92
1989 Barbaresco	D 90
1990 Barbera d'Alba	C 87
1990 Barolo	D 90
1989 Barolo	D 91
1990 Barolo Ornato	D 92
1989 Barolo Ornato	D 91

These are the two finest Barbarescos I have tasted from this traditional producer. These wines offer sumptuous levels of rich, concentrated fruit, and subtle smoky, vanillin scents (evidence of small *barrique* aging) that harmonize admirably with expansive aromas of black cherries, herbs, tobacco, and spices. The full-bodied 1989 displays great depth and richness, a glycerin-imbued, chewy texture, and loads of extract, glycerin, and alcohol in the blockbuster finish. Approachable now, it should easily last for 15+ years. Pio Cesare's 1990 is built along the same lines, only deeper and less evolved, with splendidly extracted, rich, full-bodied fruit flavors crammed into a large-framed, muscular wine. Although just as approachable in its youth as the 1989, it should keep for two decades or more. It is a candidate for the finest Barbaresco Pio Cesare has made.

It has been 20+ years since this estate has produced Barolos of such stature. Pio Cesare has turned out two full-bodied, concentrated, deeply flavored wines that should age for up to two decades. Because of the abundant sweet fruit and ripe tannin in 1989 and 1990, the wines can be approached when released. The 1989 is a more typical Barolo than the 1989 Barolo Ornato. Displaying no evidence of oak cask aging, the 1989 Barolo exhibits huge, ripe aromas of black fruits intermingled with scents of licorice, spices, tar, and herbs. Full bodied and deep, with moderate tannin, this large-scaled, intensely concentrated, supple wine will age into the first decade of the next century. The 1989 Barolo Ornato reveals hints of toasty vanillin from new oak casks, a huge, ripe bouquet of tar and spicy fruit, generous, full-bodied, highly extracted flavors, adequate acidity, and plenty of tannin in the long, rich finish. Although made in a more international style, it is a superb example of a modern-style Barolo.

The two cuvées of 1990 are made along similar lines. The 1990 Barolo is an intensely flavored, aromatic (tar, roses, black cherries) wine, with full body, a succulent texture, gobs of fruit, and high tannin in the finish. Cellar it for 2–3 years and drink it over the next 20. The big, smoky, toasty, tar- and black cherry–scented nose of the 1990 Barolo Ornato explodes from the glass. Full bodied, with staggering concentration, glycerin, and alcohol, as well as a whoppingly long finish, this big, dense wine should drink well for two decades. How delighted I am to see Pio Cesare turn out Barbarescos and Barolos of such high quality!

The 1990 Barbera d'Alba offers red fruit aromas, medium to full body, fine concentration, a mouth-filling, chewy texture, and decent acidity. It is ideal for drinking over the next 7–8 years.

MICHELE CHIARLO

Barbaresco* *, Barbera d'Asti* * *, Barbera d'Asti Valle del Sole* * * *, Barilot* * *,
Barolo Brunate* * * *, Barolo Vigna Rionda* * * *, Countacc! Vino da Tavola* * *

1993 Barbera d'Asti	B	86
1990 Barbera d'Asti Superiore	C	84
1990 Barbera d'Asti Valle del Sole	C	87
1990 Barilot	D	87
1990 Barolo	D	87
1989 Barolo	D	87
1990 Barolo Brunate	D	88
1989 Barolo Brunate	D	89
1990 Barolo Vigna Rionda	D	89+
1989 Barolo Vigna Rionda	D	90
1990 Countacc! Vino da Tavola	D	86

This winery changed its name from Gran Duca, upgraded its labels, began to put its wines in expensive designer bottles, and since 1990 has been making far more interesting wines than in the past. Chiarlo has made a huge qualitative leap with the 1989 and 1990 Barolos. Previously the wines displayed a degree of blandness that bordered on insipidness. The three 1989s are all excellent to outstanding wines. The straight cuvée of 1989 Barolo exhibits wonderful ripeness and fatness, plenty of depth, and a big, spicy, aromatic bouquet. Drink it over the next decade. Toasty new oak aromas complement copious amounts of ripe, herbaceous, black cherry fruit in the 1989 Barolo Vigna Rionda. Made in a modern, pure, supple style, it possesses fine fruit and length. The 1989 Barolo Brunate reveals a big, sweet, jammy, tobacco- and cherry-scented nose, opulent, rich, full-bodied flavors, and fine length. Both the 1989 Rionda and 1989 Brunate should drink well for 15 years.

The 1990 Barolo displays more structure than the 1989, excellent density and ripeness, and enough tannin to warrant laying it away for 2–3 years; it should last for up to 15 years. Chiarlo's 1990 Barolo Brunate could be the Heitz Martha's Vineyard of Piedmont with its distinctive black cherry-, curranty-, and minty-scented nose, and long, deep, concentrated flavors that reveal considerable body and moderate tannin. It is a different style of Barolo, but it is exceptionally well made. The 1990 Barolo Vigna Rionda is the most tannic and backward of these offerings. It possesses promising extract levels, an excellent black cherry-, tar-, and floral-scented nose, and a spicy, long, full-bodied finish.

The 1990 Barbera d'Asti Superiore is a straightforward, crisp, tart, berry-scented wine with good fruit, medium body, and a decent finish. Drink it over the next 5–6 years. The more serious and ambitious 1990 Barbera d'Asti Valle del Sole exhibits a creamier texture, riper, fuller-bodied fruit, fine richness, and spicy, new barrel notes. It should drink well for 5–8 years.

Chiarlo's 1993 Barbera d'Asti offers a delicious, medium- to full-bodied, round, supple mouthful. Ripe and soft, it is ideal for restaurants or consumers looking for a delicious and satisfying Barbera for drinking over the next 2–3 years.

These beautifully packaged (heavy, tall, designer bottles and labels) wines offer immediate gratification in their up-front, precocious personalities. The 1990 Countacc! is a soft, herbaceous, round, fruity, direct wine with no hard edges. Easy to understand and to drink, it should be consumed over the next 4–5 years. The 1990 Barilot (a Barbera/Nebbiolo blend aged in small oak casks) exhibits none of the Countacc!'s herbaceousness. It possesses more jammy black cherry and curranty fruit, medium to full body, a well-integrated touch of toasty new oak, and a long, lush finish. A charming, flattering Vino da Tavola, it should have broad appeal. Moreover, it will drink well for 5–6 years.

CIGLIUTI

Barbaresco Serraboella* * * */* * * * *, Barbera d'Alba Serraboella* * * *

1990 Barbaresco Serraboella	D	94+
1988 Barbaresco Serraboella	D	88
1990 Barbera d'Alba Serraboella	B	88
1989 Barbera d'Alba Serraboella	B	85

Cigliuti has a well-deserved reputation for turning out some of Piedmont's most stylish and elegant wines. The 1990 Barbera d'Alba Serraboella reveals a saturated deep purple color and a sweet, fragrant nose of spices, ripe tomatoes, and plummy fruit. There is superb density and flavor without the searing, abrasive acidity that can be Barbera's principal defect. This big, rich, lusty Barbera may lack complexity, but it does deliver copious quantities of fruit. Drink it over the next decade. This highly reliable winery has not managed to tame Barbera's frightfully high acidity, but in the case of the 1989, they have counterbalanced the high acidity with superextraction of fruit. Dark ruby/purple-colored, medium bodied and spicy, with its wonderful purity of raspberry fruit and high acidity, it is an ideal accompaniment to any tomato-based sauce. Drink it over the next 5–7 years.

The 1990 Barbaresco Serraboella has nearly unmatched elegance and finesse combined with extraordinary richness of fruit, and stunning, well-delineated black cherry, flowery aromas and flavors. Medium to full bodied, it possesses perfect balance as well as admirable intensity and complexity. Barbaresco is rarely more compelling. Drink it over the next 6–15 years. The 1988 Barbaresco Serraboella offers a complex nose of dried pit fruit, spicy wood, and an earthy herbaceousness. There is excellent ripeness, moderate tannins, medium to full body, and a moderately tannic, spicy finish. Although more evolved than many 1988s, it will benefit from 1–2 years in the cellar, and should last for a decade or more.

GUASTI CLEMENTE

Barbera d'Asti* * * *

1990 Barbera d'Asti	C	88

This big, thick, chewy, sweet, expansive wine reveals a saturated ruby/purple color, gobs of fruit, body, and alcohol, and a lusty, decadent finish. It is an in-your-face, intense Barbera for drinking over the next 10–12 years.

CLERICO

Arté* * * *, Barolo Bricotto Bussia* * * * *, Barolo Ciabot Mentin Ginestra* * * * *,
Barolo Pajana* * * * *, Dolcetto* * * *

1990 Arté	D	90
1990 Barolo Bricotto Bussia	D	96
1989 Barolo Bricotto Bussia	D	93
1988 Barolo Bricotto Bussia	D	88
1990 Barolo Ciabot Mentin Ginestra	D	94+
1989 Barolo Ciabot Mentin Ginestra	D	95
1988 Barolo Ciabot Mentin Ginestra	D	92

1990 Barolo Pajana	E 96+
1990 Dolcetto	C 88

Clerico's performance in 1990 further establishes him as one of Piedmont's superstars. Unfortunately, only microscopic quantities of these wines are available. The splendidly ripe, rich 1990 Barolo Bricotto Bussia reveals great fruit, superb purity, and an intense, exotic, spicy, cherry, perfumed personality. The finish goes on and on in this full-bodied, superintense, velvety-textured, spectacularly concentrated, low-acid wine. Drink this awesome Barolo over the next two decades. The most tannic and closed of this trio of Clerico 1990s is the 1990 Barolo Ciabot Mentin Ginestra. Although the wine obviously has great depth and huge reserves of fruit, it is closed aromatically. Most of its richness and power are noticeable at the back of the mouth—always a good sign. Give it 3–4 years of cellaring; it is a candidate for two decades of drinkability. In 1990 Clerico produced a special cuvée of Barolo called Pajana, from a tiny parcel of vines within the Ginestra vineyard. The wine was aged for 18 months in 100% new oak casks. The only evidence of the new oak is some spicy vanillin and smoke in the nose, which should give readers a good idea of this wine's splendid concentration of black and red fruits. Exceptionally long and sweet (because of the great ripeness and tiny yields), the wine's finish lasts for more than a minute. An intoxicating perfume of black fruits, spices, and smoke, with a touch of hickory and licorice, makes this a totally profound wine. Drink it over the next 20 years.

Clerico's 1989 Barolo Bricotto Bussia has an unrivaled, pure, sweet cherry–like bouquet. The spectacular perfume is followed by an opulent, unctuously textured, thick, rich Barolo that is bursting with fruit and personality. Its low acidity, high alcohol, and glycerin all make for a hedonistic mouthful of wine. Drink it over the next 15–20 years. As impressive as the Barolo Bricotto Bussia is, the 1989 Barolo Ciabot Mentin Ginestra is compelling. It combines magnificent power and massiveness with exceptional elegance and finesse—a rare and difficult combination to achieve. The color is dense dark ruby/purple. Although reticent at first, with airing, the nose offers huge aromas of smoked nuts, flowers, minerals, and black and red fruits. Spectacularly rich and deep, this staggeringly proportioned Barolo should be at its best between 1997 and 2012.

The 1988 Barolo Bricotto Bussia is closed. With airing, aromas of gamelike smoked meat, tar, and dusty fruit emerge. There is excellent richness, a beautiful black cherry fruitiness, and an elegant, pure, stylish finish. This is not blockbuster Barolo, but a medium-weight wine. It should drink well for 12–15 years. Clerico's 1988 Barolo Ciabot Mentin Ginestra is a super wine, with a dense dark ruby color and a big, ripe nose of tar, spices, and earthy red fruit. In the mouth, the wine displays superconcentration, as well as a ripe, full-bodied, glycerin-dominated, tannic finish. The wine has terrific potential and extremely high tannins, but it is still backward and unevolved. Drink it between now and 2007.

Clerico's 1990 proprietary wine, Arté, is the best Arté since the 1985. It reveals a huge, sweet, oaky, curranty nose, long, luscious, voluptuously textured flavors, and a heady, expansive finish. Drink it over the next 7–8 years.

The 1990 Dolcetto reveals a brilliant dark purple color, a big, exuberant nose of ripe fruit and flowers, lusciously rich, fleshy fruit, and a clean, velvety finish with just enough acidity to provide grip.

TENUTA COLUE
Barolo Colue * *

1989 Barolo Colue	C 79

Light, soft, fruity flavors are followed by a spicy, ripe wine with adequate length. Compared with the other 1989s, this wine comes across as diluted and thin, although it is pleasant in a straightforward style.

ALDO CONTERNO

Barbera d'Alba Conca Tre Pile* * * *, Barolo Bussia Soprano* * * * *,
Barolo Gran Bussia* * * * *, Barolo Gran Bussia Riserva* * * * *,
Barolo Vigna Cicala Bussia* * * * *, Barolo Vigna Colonnello Bussia* * * * *,
Il Favot* * *

1990 Barbera d'Alba Conca Tre Pile	C	89
1989 Barbera d'Alba Conca Tre Pile	C	88
1990 Barolo Bussia Soprano	E	95
1989 Barolo Bussia Soprano	D	94
1989 Barolo Bussia Soprano Vigna Cicala	D	92
1989 Barolo Bussia Soprano Vigna Colonnello	D	93
1989 Barolo Gran Bussia	D	95+
1990 Barolo Gran Bussia Riserva	EE	95
1989 Barolo Gran Bussia Riserva	EE	98
1990 Barolo Vigna Cicala Bussia	EE	95
1989 Barolo Vigna Cicala Bussia	E	96
1990 Barolo Vigna Colonnello Bussia	EE	96
1989 Barolo Vigna Colonnello Bussia	E	96
1990 Dolcetto d'Alba Bussia Soprano	C	88
1990 Il Favot	D	87

Every Italian wine authority, from the late Sheldon Wasserman, to Burton Anderson, to Victor Hazan, to Roberto Parkero, considers Aldo Conterno to be one of the great masters of his craft. The staggering array of wines he produced in 1989 and 1990 confirms that no one in Piedmont is making greater Barolo than Aldo Conterno and his sons. If you love great wine, these are must-purchases; if you love Barolo, a pilgrimage to your favorite Italian wine shop is in order! It is virtually impossible to pick a favorite among Conterno's 1989s and 1990s. However, the 1990s appear even more massive, structured, and tannic than the flamboyant, superconcentrated, flashy 1989s.

The superconcentrated 1990s are all outstanding wines. When I tasted them they appeared more structured, tannic, and backward than the 1989s. Perhaps it is just the one year difference in age, but the advantage the 1989s enjoy over the 1990s at present is that their fruit is sweeter and more evolved. Wine enthusiasts throughout the world should be beating a path to their retailers to buy both the 1989s and the 1990s. By the way, Aldo Conterno is one of Piedmont's sweetest people, proving that sometimes nice guys do finish first!

The 1989 Barolos include the 1989 Bussia Soprano, a huge, superconcentrated, powerhouse of a wine that exudes aromas of sweet black cherries, truffles, spices, and some intriguing spring flower blossom scents. Extremely intense, full bodied, and spicy, with oodles of rich, fleshy fruit, this profound wine possesses high tannin that is sweet rather than astringent, and a mind-boggling finish. This awesome Barolo can be drunk at an early age, but it should keep for 25–30 or more years.

The offerings from the Bussia Soprano subvineyards of Vigna Cicala and Vigna Colonnello are both sensational bottles of wine. The more velvety textured, opulent, and voluptuous of this dynamic duo is the 1989 Vigna Colonnello. In addition to its spectacular concentration, there is a huge, sweet, leathery, black fruit–scented nose, as well as layers of chewy, fleshy fruit that nearly conceal considerable tannin. The alcohol is in the mid 14% range. Although seductive at present, this spectacularly rich, voluptuous Barolo should age effortlessly for 25–30 years. The earthy, raspberry, black cherry, and tar aromas of the 1989 Vigna Cicala explode upward from the glass. This is the most massive and structured of the three single-vineyard Barolos. The tannin and fruit extraction are both extremely high. This wine requires minimal cellaring of 3–5 years, after which it will last, and perhaps even improve, for 25–30 years. The 1989 Gran Bussia Riserva is nearly perfection. My notes included such words as *magnificent, awesome, frightening extract levels, decadent,* and *opulent.* Not much more can be said, other than that this wine is even richer, more aromatically compelling, and longer than the other three 1989 Conterno offerings.

The 1989 Barolo Gran Bussia reveals a saturated deep ruby/purple color, and a huge nose of smoky tobacco, black cherries, herbs, and truffles. Although the wine is tannic, it exhibits stellar concentration, fine acidity, and spectacular length. This massive Barolo will require considerable cellaring. **A.M.: 1998–2020.** Conterno's most flattering Barolo is the 1989 Vigna Cicala Bussia. Slightly less saturated in color, with a huge nose of smoke, jammy red berries and blackberries, licorice, herbs, and tobacco, this opulent, voluptuously textured Barolo has significant tannin, but it is nearly buried under lavish quantities of sweet, expansive fruit. This hedonistic Barolo should continue to evolve for 15 or more years. Of these three wines, the Vigna Cicala Bussia is the one to drink first. Although the 1989 Barolo Vigna Colonnello Bussia is deeply colored, tannic, and backward, it displays tremendous potential for future evolution. The wine has an herb and tobacco character, huge body and extract, and considerable glycerin, tannin, and alcohol in the finish. It will not be at its best until the late nineties, but it should evolve gracefully through the first two decades of the next century.

Aldo Conterno has also delivered three tremendous efforts with his less expensive, but no less joyful, 1990 and 1989 Barberas and 1990 Dolcetto. The 1990 Barbera d'Alba Conca Tre Pile offers a performance not unlike Ravel's "Bolero." It begins slowly, then increases speed, intensity, and dimension as it unfolds on the palate. The color is a healthy dark ruby. The nose is somewhat closed but does offer good, clean, ripe black and red fruits. If its aromatic reticence is of concern to any of Conterno's legion of admirers, the flavors are reassuring. It possesses well-focused, sweet, ripe Barbera fruit presented in a medium-bodied format. There is adequate underlying acidity, excellent purity, and a refreshing vibrancy to the wine. While not the biggest, most ostentatious or oaky Barbera, it is a textbook, classic example of the vintage and the varietal. Drink it over the next decade. The 1989 Conca Tre Pile reveals a deep ruby/purple color, a sweet, rich, jammy nose, medium body, superextraction of fruit, and surprisingly low acidity. The result is a voluptuous mouthful of wine. Drink it over the next 4–6 years. Gushing with abundant quantities of fruit, the 1990 Dolcetto d'Alba Bussia Soprano is voluptuous and fat, with a velvety finish.

The dense, rich, spicy, vanillin-scented 1990 Il Favot reveals medium to full body, loads of jammy fruit, evidence of aging in new oak casks (given its smoky, toasty aromas and flavors), and a moderately long, rich finish. Still tight and unevolved, it promises to drink well for 7–10 years.

GIACOMO CONTERNO
Barbera d'Alba Cascina Francia * * *, Barolo Cascina Francia Riserva * * * * *,
Barolo Monfortino * * * * *

1991 Barbera d'Alba Cascina Francia	C	74
1989 Barbera d'Alba Cascina Francia	C	87+
1990 Barolo Cascina Francia Serralunga	D	94

1989 Barolo Cascina Francia Serralunga	D	90+
1988 Barolo Cascina Francia Serralunga	D	92
1985 Barolo Cascina Francia Serralunga	D	94
1987 Barolo Monfortino	E	93
1985 Barolo Monfortino	EE	96

Conterno, whose wines I have followed since the mid-sixties, is unquestionably the quintessential traditionalist when it comes to Barolo. No concessions are made to modern-day tastes. Consequently, his wines are among the most concentrated, as well as the most rustic and tannic. From time to time there have also been levels of volatile acidity that modern-day technocrats would consider obscene, but that actually can add to the wine's complexity and character, up to a point. The current releases include the fabulous 1985 Barolo Cascina Francia Serralunga. It possesses the classic Nebbiolo nose of roses and tar, as well as masses of rich red and black fruits. Unctuous and intense, with spectacular fruit, it offers great fragrance and massive body to go along with its high extract and huge tannin. The 1988 Barolo Cascina Francia Serralunga also offers a rose- and tar-scented nose, deep, full-bodied flavors with aggressive tannin, plenty of ripeness and glycerin, and a heady, spicy, cherry-, leather-, and herb-flavored finish. Drink this huge, large-scaled, full-throttle Barolo over the next 20 years. The same can be said for the 1989, which is slightly more supple because of the nature of the vintage. The 1990 Barolo Cascina Francia Serralunga, which will not be released for several years, is a huge, blockbuster wine that may turn out to be one of the most concentrated wines of that great vintage. One can only imagine what Conterno's Monfortino might taste like in 2025!

As for the 1985 and 1987 Monfortinos, the 1985 Barolo Monfortino possesses a deep ruby color, and a saturated bouquet of saddle leather, spices, smoked meats, herbs, and truffles. This rich, ferociously tannic, massive, backward, nearly impenetrable wine should be cellared for 8–10 years. Drink it between 2001 and 2025. It is a superb Monfortino. While many producers have said the 1987 Barolo vintage was average in quality, Conterno enjoyed great success. The 1987 Monfortino is unquestionably the Barolo of the vintage. Its saturated dark color and huge nose of truffles, tar, and sweet tobacco tinged with black cherry fruit are followed by a wine with gobs of glycerin, amazing power and richness, and a monstrously long, tannic finish. A great wine from a so-so vintage, it should be at its best between 1997 and 2020. Those of you who love wine loaded with lavish new oak, sweet, crunchy fruit, and squeaky-clean, simple flavors should be sure to taste these wines before you decide to buy. Though fabulous wines, they are not for everybody.

The 1991 Barbera d'Alba Cascina Francia is a narrowly constructed, compact wine with sharp edges, barely average fruit extraction, and a spicy, astringent, acidic finish. I do not foresee it improving with time. In complete contrast, the 1989 Barbera d'Alba Cascina Francia offers a curry, herb, and black cherry and black currant aroma, full body, power, structure, muscle, and excellent ripeness. It is youthful and unevolved, with a tightness and plumpness to its personality. A boldly styled, rustic, mouth-filling, satisfying Barbera, drink it over the next 10–12 years.

PAOLO CONTERNO
Barbera d'Alba Ginestra * * * *

1990 Barbera d'Alba Ginestra	C	88+

Although unevolved, this saturated dark ruby/purple-colored wine offers considerable promise. It possesses superb richness and intensity, medium to full body, moderate acidity, and a backward yet rich, earthy, black fruit character. This is one of the few 1990 Barberas that I would recommend laying away for 1–2 years. It should last for 12–15+ years.

COPPO

Barbera d'Asti Camp du Rouss * * * *, Barbera d'Asti Pomorosso * * * *

1990 Barbera d'Asti Camp du Rouss	C	86
1990 Barbera d'Asti Pomorosso	D	90
1989 Barbera d'Asti Pomorosso	D	83?

Coppo's 1990 Barbera d'Asti Camp du Rouss exhibits lovely cherry, spicy, herbal fruit, tasty, medium-bodied flavors, attractive fatness and sweetness, and a round, generous personality. Drink it over the next 4–5 years. The excessive amount of new oak displayed by the 1989 Barbera d'Asti Pomorosso nearly obliterates the wine's fruit. There is some ripeness, but the overall impression is too woody for such a medium-bodied, delicate style of wine. It is good, but a less heavy hand with the oak would have resulted in a more attractive, better balanced wine. On the other hand, in the 1990 Barbera d'Asti Pomorosso the proportions of oak and extraction are in balance. The 1990 is richer, more highly extracted, and fuller bodied, with gobs of glycerin and layers of rich, ripe fruit. The overall impression is one of creamy suppleness enhanced by moderate levels of toasty, smoky, new oak. It is a sumptuous wine that should drink well for 6–7 years.

CORDERO DI MONTEZEMOLO

Barbera d'Alba * * *, Barolo Enrico VI * * *, Barolo Monfalletto * * *, Dolcetto Monfalletto * * *

1990 Barbera d'Alba	C	88
1990 Barolo	D	84
1989 Barolo	D	76
1990 Barolo Enrico VI	D	85
1989 Barolo Enrico VI	D	79
1988 Barolo Enrico VI	D	89
1988 Barolo Monfalletto	D	86+

Cordero di Montezemolo was one of the early advocates of the modern style of Barolo, emphasizing soft tannin and precocious, flattering, ripe fruit. I admired some of this estate's wines from the seventies and eighties, but these 1990 and 1989 offerings were among the lightest and least concentrated wines I tasted. The shallow, medium-bodied 1989 Barolo is made in a soft, commercial style that requires consumption over the next 2–3 years. Also light, the 1989 Barolo Enrico VI exhibits more ripeness, as well as a short finish.

The two 1990s possess more richness and jamminess, but they are essentially one-dimensional, straightforward wines of no real depth or complexity. It is one thing to produce a rich, concentrated wine that can be drunk young, but it is an entirely different thing to produce a wine that *must* be drunk young because of a lack of substance and concentration.

The 1988 Barolo Monfalletto displays a medium ruby color, a sweet, cherry-scented nose, and alcoholic, heady flavors dominated by significant acidity and tannin. It will either dry out before the tannins melt away, or develop more richness. My score may be optimistic. The deep color and persistent classic perfume of roasted nuts, roses, and black truffles make the 1988 Barolo Enrico VI a sure bet. Round, rich, and thick in the mouth with plenty of tannin, this full-bodied wine needs several more years of cellaring. Drink it between 1996 and 2005.

I am pleased to see this producer turn out a fine, rich, ripe, concentrated, lavishly fruity 1990 Barbera d'Alba, as his 1990 Barolos were mediocre. This wine exhibits luscious concentration and a lusty, full-throttle, rich, husky style. Drink it over the next decade.

RENATO CORINO
Barbera Vigna Pozzo* * * *, Barolo La Mora* * * * *, Barolo Vigna Giachini* * * * *,
Dolcetto* * * *

1991	Barbera Vigna Pozzo	C	85
1990	Barbera Vigna Pozzo	D	89
1988	Barolo La Mora	D	93
1990	Barolo Vigna Giachini	D	94
1989	Barolo Vigna Giachini	D	96
1990	Barolo Vigneto Rocche	D	96
1991	Dolcetto	B	86

One of my favorite Barolo producers (his wines have an almost Pomerol-like unctuosity and richness), Corino has again turned in a superlative performance in 1990. Although the 1990 Barolo Vigna Giachini is tighter, more structured, and tannic than its 1989 counterpart, there is no doubting its mind-blowing richness and huge reserves of juicy, succulent black cherry and plum fruit that are so noticeable on the palate and in the fragrant, intense aroma. Drink this full-bodied, superpure Barolo after 2–3 years of cellaring; it should last for two decades. The 1990 Barolo Vigneto Rocche exhibits the vintage's telltale opulence, sweetness of fruit, and spectacular concentration. It possesses a stunning combination of massive power and extract, as well as considerable polish and grace. This authoritative, stunningly seductive Barolo tastes even more forward than the Vigna Giachini. Nevertheless, it will last for 20+ years. Corino's 1989 Barolo Vigna Giachini is a blockbuster. If Pétrus were made from Nebbiolo, would it taste like this? Dark in color, with a huge, sweet, spicy, exotic nose of black fruits and minerals, this young, unevolved wine exhibits spectacular depth, a multilayered feel, and a persistence and richness that last for over a minute. Although soft enough to be drunk now, it has just begun its evolution, which should continue gracefully over the next 15–20 years. Absolutely magnificent!

Corino produces the most saturated-colored Piedmontese wines I have seen. The 1988 Barolo La Mora exhibits a superjammy nose of black fruits, licorice, minerals, and melted road tar. There is spectacular depth, layer upon layer of chewy, thick, glycerin-endowed fruit, and a moderately tannic, robust finish. The wine is immensely impressive, but needs at least 5–6 years to develop more complexity and shed some of its toughness. This powerful, monster-sized 1988 Barolo possesses the requisite extraction of fruit to stand up to its ferocious tannins.

Corino fashioned a gorgeous, perfumed, round, intensely fruity 1991 Dolcetto that should be drunk over the next 3 years. It offers extraordinary purity of fruit. The 1990 Barbera Vigna Pozzo reveals a purple/black color, a huge nose of wild black fruits and spices, a rich, medium- to full-bodied, succulent texture, and an explosively rich finish. If it had more complexity, it would have merited an outstanding score. Nevertheless, it is a superrich Barbera. For the vintage, the 1991 Barbera Vigna Pozzo is very good. The color is a healthy deep ruby/purple, and the wine displays solid, chunky, berry fruit, medium body, and laudable ripeness. More compact and smaller-scaled than the 1990, it should drink well for 2–3 years.

GIUSEPPE CORTESE
Barbaresco Rabaja* * * *, Dolcetto d'Alba* * *

1990	Barbaresco Rabaja	C	90
1989	Barbaresco Rabaja	C	88

1992 Dolcetto d'Alba	A	85
1991 Dolcetto d'Alba	A	87

Cortese's sexy, dramatic, flashy style of Barbaresco is well displayed in both the 1989 and 1990 vintages. Both are forward, evolved wines, with super bouquets of cherries, herbs, cedar, and underbrush. The 1989 offers explosively supple, ripe, rich fruit in a full-bodied format. It is an opulent style of Barbaresco for drinking over the next 7–10 years. The similarly styled 1990 is deeper-colored, richer, and more expansive on the palate, as well as more alcoholic. It merits drinking over the next 10–12 years. These are gorgeously flattering, rich Barbarescos for consumers or restaurants that lack the patience to wait for some of the more muscular, tannic wines from these two vintages to reach maturity.

One of two attractive Dolcettos, the 1991 exhibits more ripeness and a fruitier, more luscious mouth-feel. Loaded with crunchy fruit, it is medium bodied, soft, and charming. Although lighter, the 1992 is round, richly fruity, medium bodied, and attractive. Both wines should be drunk over the next 2–3 years.

ALESSANDRIA CRISSANTE
Ruge * * * *

1989 Ruge	D	90

In style, this wine made with 100% Barbera reminds me of some of the luxury cuvées of Barbera produced at the estate of Giacomo Bologna. There was a lavish use of toasty new oak barrels, but the oak adds an aromatic and flavor dimension that complements rather than dominates the massive, sweet black cherry fruit character. This mouth-filling wine offers full body, significant glycerin, high extract, and heady alcohol. The finish lasts for more than half a minute. This beautifully made, ostentatious Barbera will have heads turning and mouths watering.

LUIGI DESSILANI
Gattinara * * *, Ghemme * * *, Spanna * * *

1990 Spanna	A	86

Although Dessilani can make delicious, inexpensive wine, too many of his wines are flawed by excessive, rancid smells of lees. Of the three new Dessilani releases I tried, the 1990 Barbera reeked of old lees, giving it an intense, disagreeable character. Another wine also was suspect. However, there are no such problems with this 1990 Spanna. It displays a medium ruby color and a rich nose of black raspberries and spices. Medium bodied, with admirable fruit and extraction, as well as attractive glycerin and alcohol levels, this amply endowed wine should drink well for another 2–3 years.

AZ. AGR. DOSIO
Barolo Vigna Fossati * * *

1989 Barolo Vigna Fossati	C	87

An excellent Barolo made in a traditional style, this rustic, large-bodied, expansively flavored wine reveals abundant flavors of cherries, herbs, and a provocative dusty, earthy, spiciness. Admirable concentration, depth, and tannin result in a mouth-filling wine that should be at its best between 1998 and 2010.

CASCINA DRAGO
Bricco del Drago * * * *, Bricco del Drago Vigna Le Mace * * * * *,
Dolcetto d'Alba * * * *, Nebbiolo * * * *

1990 Bricco del Drago	C	87
1989 Bricco del Drago	C	87

1990 Bricco del Drago Vigna Le Mace	C	91
1989 Bricco del Drago Vigna Le Mace	C	90
1990 Dolcetto d'Alba	B	90
1990 Nebbiolo	C	88
1989 Nebbiolo	B	86

Among the masses Cascina Drago is a relatively unknown name, but among Italian wine insiders it is a wine to search out. This small (25 acres) estate has been in the same family, the De Giacomi family, since 1721. The excellent 1989 and 1990 Nebbiolos are fine examples of this noble grape. The 1989 Nebbiolo reveals plenty of tobacco scents, sweet, black cherry fruit, an alluring fatness, and a lush, silky finish. Drink it over the next 5–6 years. Sweeter and more expansive, the 1990 Nebbiolo exhibits a velvety texture, deep, rich, chewy flavors, and gobs of nearly overripe fruit. It should drink well for 6–7 years.

The winery's high reputation is based on their proprietary wines called Bricco del Drago. Cascina Drago was the first Italian estate to utilize small oak casks and to blend Nebbiolo and Dolcetto. They produce stunning wines that can age well for 10 to as long as 20 years. The 1989 Bricco del Drago possesses a wonderfully pure, leathery, herb- and black cherry–scented nose reminiscent of a classic Merlot. There is excellent richness, gobs of spicy, full-bodied fruit, and a soft, lush finish. The similarly styled 1990 Bricco del Drago exhibits a roasted herb and nut character intertwined with lavish quantities of red and black fruits (especially cherries). Drink this long, opulent wine over the next 5–7 years.

The star of this estate is the single-vineyard Bricco del Drago Vigna Le Mace. Both the 1989 and 1990 are outstanding wines with saturated, opaque purple colors. The 1989 Bricco del Drago Vigna Le Mace offers a rich nose of black currants, vanillin, spice, and roasted herbs. Exceptionally rich and full bodied, with stunning concentration and length, it is approachable enough to consume now, yet it should age well for 12–15 years. The 1990 Bricco del Drago Vigna Le Mace promises to be even more of a blockbuster wine with at least two decades of aging potential. The superripe nose of jammy, black currant and black cherry fruit is followed by a wine with sensational concentration, full body, gobs of glycerin, and moderately sweet tannin in the heady finish. It is a terrific wine! Production of the regular cuvée of Bricco del Drago is approximately 4,000 cases per year, and for the Vigna Le Mace, 500 cases. The blend is 85% Dolcetto and 15% Nebbiolo.

The 1990 Dolcetto d'Alba is as delicious, seductive, and satisfying as Dolcetto can be. The color is a vibrant deep ruby and the nose explodes from the glass, offering up intense, jammy, berry aromas. In the mouth, this gorgeously made wine is packed with pure, vibrant fruit, and exhibits medium body, a satiny texture, and enough acidity to give focus and to frame the lavish amounts of fruit this wine possesses. Drink it over the next 2–3 years.

LUIGI EINAUDI
Barolo* * * */* * * * *, Dolcetto* * *

1989 Barolo	D	95

This blockbuster, old-style, opaque purple-colored Barolo has undoubtedly seen little fining or filtering! Extraordinarily extracted, with a huge nose of melted road tar, plums, cherries, Asian spices, and roses, this mammothly constructed, superrich, superb wine is a heavy-weight Barolo, with gobs of glycerin, extract, tannin, and alcohol. It should be civilized with another 5–6 years of cellaring and last for 25 or more years. Enough of this nonsense that traditionally styled Barolo can't be great!

FANTINO-CONTERNO
Barbera d'Alba Vignato * * *

1991 Barbera d'Alba Vignato	C	76
1990 Barbera d'Alba Vignato	C	88

Fantino-Conterno's 1991 Barbera d'Alba Vignato is typical of most wines from this vintage —light bodied, with average concentration, and pleasant but uninspiring depth and ripeness. Its style, softness, and lack of depth suggest it should be consumed over the next 2–3 years. On the other hand, the 1990 Barbera d'Alba Vignato exhibits far more intense fruit, spicy oak, and considerably more ripeness, glycerin, alcohol, and extraction of flavor. It is a generously endowed, well-made and well-balanced wine, with soft acid and a chewy, lush texture. Drink it over the next 7–8 years.

RICARDO FENOCCHIO
Barbera d'Alba Pianpolvere Soprano * * * *, Barolo Pianpolvere Soprano * * * *

1990 Barbera d'Alba Pianpolvere Soprano	C	88
1989 Barolo Pianpolvere Soprano	D	89

Fenocchio fashions seductive, burgundian-like Barolos that are easy to drink young but have a cunning ability to age gracefully. I recently tasted their 1985, a gorgeously opulent wine not dissimilar to the 1989. The sweet, richly fruity 1989 offers copious amounts of spicy oak and cherries in the nose, followed by lush, voluptuously textured, concentrated flavors that linger on the palate. It should drink well for 7–8 years. This is an enticing style of Barolo.

The 1990 Barbera d'Alba Pianpolvere Soprano reveals an enticing openness and expansive personality reminiscent of a high-class red burgundy. The wine's bouquet jumps from the glass, offering up a multitude of scents such as toast, smoke, herbs, and sweet, jammy fruit. The medium ruby/garnet color is followed by a wine with no hard edges—just a plump, plush, velvety texture oozing with fleshy red and black fruit. Soft and delicious, it is ideal for consuming over the next 5–6 years.

F.LLI FERRERO
Barolo Annunziata * * * *

1989 Barolo Annunziata	C	88

This is the type of wine that can get lost in a tasting of so many big, mammoth, blockbuster wines. There is a sense of grace, elegance, and richness in the wonderfully pure black cherry/cedary/tobacco–scented nose. Full-bodied, ripe flavors display good integration of tannin and acidity, as well as excellent depth and length. Drink it over the next 10–15 years.

TENUTA DEI FIORI
Barbera d'Asti * * *

1990 Barbera d'Asti	D	87

This well-made Barbera exhibits a dark ruby/purple color, gobs of rich, tarry, black fruit, spicy scents, full body, excellent richness, purity, and balance, moderate acidity, and a long finish. Drink it over the next 10+ years.

GRANCO FIORINA
Barolo * *

1989 Barolo	C	81

A light, soft, commercially styled Barolo, this 1989 exhibits decent fruit, medium body, and some ripeness, but it lacks complexity and depth.

FONTANAFREDDA

Barbaresco* *, Barbera d'Alba* *, Barbera d'Alba Vigna Raimondo* * */* * * *, Barolo* * *,
Barolo Le Delizia* * * *, Barolo Gallaretto Serralunga* * * *, Barolo La Rosa* * * *

1989 Barbaresco	C	78
1991 Barbera d'Alba	B	76
1990 Barbera d'Alba Vigna Raimondo	B	88
1990 Barolo	C	87
1989 Barolo	C	86
1989 Barolo Le Delizia	D	90
1989 Barolo Gallaretto Serralunga	D	87
1989 Barolo La Rosa	D	91

Fontanafredda is one of Piedmont oldest estates. Interestingly, in my college and law school days the Fontanafredda Barolos were my introduction to the wonders of Piedmontese wines. A few bottles of the 1970 and 1971, bearing price tags of $5.99, remain in my cellar. Both wines are still drinking beautifully, revealing no signs of decline, a testament to just how long these wines can last. In top vintages, Fontanafredda can produce a half dozen or more single-vineyard Barolos. In the tastings I did in Piedmont, the winery presented one bottling of 1990 and four bottlings of 1989, three of which were single-vineyard wines. The quality of the 1989s looks to be very high. The 1989 Barolo reveals medium body, excellent ripeness, tasty, spicy, curranty fruit, a supple texture, and fine length. Already drinking well, it should keep for a decade. The 1989 Barolo Gallaretto Serralunga is the lightest, most easy to taste, with an attractive, supple, lush fruitiness, medium to full body, and a spicy, long finish. It will drink well for 12–15 years. I thought the 1989 Barolo Le Delizia was even more developed, with a wonderfully fragrant, intense bouquet, a sweet, supple, smoky, jammy, cherry fruitiness, full body, and an opulent finish. It can be drunk now or cellared for 10–15 years. The most concentrated 1989 is the Barolo La Rosa. This vineyard, one of the largest of the Fontanafredda crus, produced a wine with great depth, full body, a ripe, cherry-, herb-, cedary-scented nose, and rich, deep, fleshy, moderately tannic flavors. Approachable now, it promises to last for 10–15 years.

The 1990 Barolo offers fine ripeness, a soft, fleshy, chewy texture, excellent definition, and admirable length. It will drink well over the next decade.

While the light-bodied, innocuous, shallow 1989 Barbaresco offers immediate drinkability, it lacks the concentration, character, and complexity found in most Barbarescos from this vintage.

The top-notch 1990 Barbera d'Alba Vigna Raimondo possesses a dark ruby color, a flattering, precocious, sweet nose of spice and red and black fruit, full body, outstanding concentration, excellent purity, sweet, black cherry, curranty flavors, well-integrated acidity, and a long, crisp finish. It should drink well young and age gracefully. It is an impressive Barbera. The light ruby-colored 1991 Barbera d'Alba is diluted, soft, straightforward, and one-dimensional.

DE FORVILLE

Barbaresco* *, Barbera d'Alba Ca' Gorssa* *

1990 Barbaresco	C	82
1993 Barbera d'Alba Ca' Gorssa	B	85

Typical of De Forville's elegant, understated style, this 1990 Barbaresco reveals spicy, cedary-, tobacco-, leather-, and cherry-scented fruit. Although pleasant, this one-dimensional wine lacks concentration and finishes with medium-bodied, ripe fruit. The medium-bodied, ripe berry–scented and –flavored 1993 Barbera d'Alba Ca' Gorssa is a tasty, straightforward Barbera that requires consumption over the next 2–4 years.

CONTERNO FRANTINO
Barolo Sori Ginestra * * * */* * * * *, Barolo Vigna del Gris * * * */* * * * *

1990 Barolo Sori Ginestra	D	90+
1989 Barolo Sori Ginestra	D	91
1990 Barolo Vigna del Gris	D	89+
1989 Barolo Vigna del Gris	D	91

As the following notes so admirably attest, Conterno Frantino is an up-and-coming Piedmontese star. Both 1989s are terrific wines. The 1989 Barolo Vigna del Gris offers copious quantities of sweet, jammy, black cherry fruit intermingled with aromas of herbs, tar, and smoke. The wine is full bodied, with excellent definition, richness, and purity of fruit. The style falls somewhere between the rustic traditionalist one and that of the small *barrique*-aging modernist approach. Drink it over the next 15–16 years. The 1989 Barolo Sori Ginestra is a fuller-bodied, bigger, more tannic and muscular wine than the more elegant Vigna del Gris. It is not nearly as flattering and seductive to drink now, but in 4–5 years it should prove to be exceptional. It will last for 20 years.

Both the 1990 cuvées were closed and more difficult to assess, hence the more conservative scores. With more time in the bottle, these wines will prove to be as persuasive as the 1989s. The 1990 Barolo Vigna del Gris offers a dense, saturated, dark ruby color, a reticent but promising nose of black cherry fruit, damp earth, and minerals, and a spicy, meaty, full-bodied flavor that exhibits considerable tannin, glycerin, and alcohol. Although it is a candidate for two decades worth of aging, I would not touch a bottle for 3–4 years. The intense 1990 Barolo Sori Ginestra reveals more tannin, structure, and body than the Vigna del Gris. The elegance of the Vigna del Gris is complemented nicely by the muscular, fuller-bodied, denser, more structured style of the Sori Ginestra. Again, my instincts suggest sitting on the Sori Ginestra for 4–5 years and drinking it over the next 15–20 years.

GIANNI GAGLIARDO
Barbera d'Asti La Matta * *, Barolo La Serra * * *

1989 Barbera d'Asti La Matta	C	74
1989 Barolo La Serra	D	88?

The 1989 Barolo La Serra's controversial nose of sweaty leather, truffles, tobacco, black fruits, and damp underbrush is followed by a deep, full-bodied, rich, concentrated wine with gobs of glycerin and concentration, as well as a full-bodied, moderately tannic finish. This well-made Barolo is likely to draw fire from technocrats, given the funky aged-beef and roasted-herb scents in the bouquet. Drink it over the next 12–15 years.

Light ruby-colored, with a nondescript, uninteresting nose, this medium-bodied, sharply acidic 1990 Barbera d'Asti La Matta lacks concentration and a finish. It is surprisingly light and malnourished for a wine from this vintage.

ANGELO GAJA
Barbaresco * * * *, Barbaresco Costa Russi * * * * *, Barbaresco Sori San Lorenzo * * * * *, Barbaresco Sori Tilden * * * * *, Barbera d'Alba Vignarey * * * *, Barolo Sperss * * * * *, Cabernet Sauvignon Darmagi * */* * *, Dolcetto d'Alba Vignaveja * * *, Nebbiolo d'Alba Vignaveja * * * */* * * *

1990 Barbaresco	E	93
1989 Barbaresco	E	91

1990 Barbaresco Costa Russi	EE	94
1989 Barbaresco Costa Russi	EE	90
1990 Barbaresco Sori San Lorenzo	EE	95+
1989 Barbaresco Sori San Lorenzo	EE	96+
1990 Barbaresco Sori Tilden	EE	97+
1989 Barbaresco Sori Tilden	EE	96+
1990 Barbera d'Alba Vignarey	D	92
1990 Barolo Sperss	E	95
1989 Barolo Sperss	E	93
1988 Barolo Sperss	E	92
1990 Chardonnay Gaja & Rey	E	93
1991 Chardonnay Rossj Bass	D	88
1991 Dolcetto d'Alba Vignaveja	C	89
1989 Nebbiolo d'Alba Vignaveja	C	87

Consistently one of the reference points for Italian wines, Angelo Gaja has fashioned some spectacular white wines. His 1991 Chardonnay Rossj Bass is a more delicately styled, floral, richly fruity, medium-bodied wine with admirable depth and richness, adequate acidity, and a spicy touch of subtle new oak. It should drink well for 2–3 years. In contrast, the 1990 Chardonnay Gaja & Rey is a blockbuster Chardonnay by any standards. A huge buttery, floral, smoky nose is followed by a viscous, superrich, multilayered Chardonnay that has more in common with a grand cru from Burgundy's Chassagne-Montrachet than an Italian Chardonnay. While delicious now, it should last for another 2–3 years.

The red wine offerings include an excellent 1991 Dolcetto d'Alba Vignaveja, which reveals abundant chocolaty, cherry fruit, light to medium body, and a spicy finish. A staggering Barbera in all respects, the saturated dark ruby/purple-colored 1990 Barbera d'Alba Vignarey offers up a sweet nose of vanillin, red and black fruits, and spices. Full bodied, with layers of concentrated fruit, impressive purity, and a finish that lasts for at least 40 seconds, this great effort should drink well for 10–12 years. Readers who are unwilling to splurge on a $60-$75 bottle of Barbaresco or Barolo should take a look at this stunning Barbera. It offers spectacular quality.

Although Gaja's 1989 Nebbiolo d'Alba Vignaveja is lighter than I would expect, it is attractively fruity, with a moderately intense, spicy aroma, and soft, medium- to full-bodied, supple flavors. It should drink well for another 5–6 years.

The Barbarescos are among the glories of this estate, and the 1989s and 1990s promise to be the best produced since 1985 and 1982. Choosing between these two sensational vintages will not be easy. Gaja's 1989 Barbaresco offers sweet, rich, tobacco, black cherry, spicy fruit touched gently by new oak. It is made in a full-bodied, powerful style, with admirable depth. Approachable now, this wine should only improve over the next 10–12 years; it will last for two decades. The three single-vineyard Barbarescos include the 1989 Costa Russi, the most monolithic and "new world–like" wine of this trio. The deep ruby/ purple color is followed by scents of new oak. There is less of a Nebbiolo character than I would like to see. One has to admire the wine's terrific concentration and overall sense of balance, but I found it interesting that in several tastings, lovers of Nebbiolo (including me) thought it to be the least impressive of these Barbarescos. Those who tend to like a more international style preferred it. Nevertheless, it is a superb wine for drinking between 1997 and 2009. Both the 1989 Sori San Lorenzo and 1989 Sori Tilden are monuments to the Nebbiolo grape, as well as to Barbaresco. The 1989 Sori San Lorenzo is one of the two most concentrated wines I have tasted from this vineyard. There is a sweetness and unctuosity to the fruit that I did not detect in either the great 1985 or the 1982. Still tannic, backward, and unevolved, this huge, rich, spice-, tobacco-, and black cherry–scented wine is massive on the palate. It should be at its best between 1998 and 2015. It is a remarkable winemaking effort! Not surprisingly, the 1989 Sori Tilden is even more massive, as well as the most backward, tannic, muscular, and masculine of these Gaja Barbarescos. With tons of tannin, and a broad, rich, fleshy, expansive personality, it is the least flattering. Do not touch a bottle for at least 6–7 years. It should last until 2020.

Admirers of great wine will no doubt be debating the merits of Gaja's 1989s and 1990s for the next two or three decades. Both are spectacular vintages. When I tasted them side by side, the 1990s possessed a slight edge in terms of concentration and power. That does not mean they will ultimately turn out better, but they are fabulously impressive wines of unprecedented complexity, stature, and richness. I do not think Angelo Gaja has made a better cuvée of his classic Barbaresco (there's nothing "regular" about either the price or the quality!) than the 1990. From its deep, saturated, dark ruby color, to its big, spicy, roasted nose of red and black fruits, nuts, and cedar, this huge, massive, superconcentrated wine exhibits layers of flavors. Although present, the tannin is sweet, giving the wine a precocious, approachable style. It is a blockbuster Barbaresco for drinking over the next 15–20 years.

Among the three single-vineyard Barbarescos, the most compelling is the Sori San Lorenzo. The 1990 is a massive wine with a staggering yet unevolved nose of herbs, hickory, smoked meats, cedar, and red and black fruits. Spectacularly concentrated, with layers of flavor, this dense, blockbuster wine should be cellared for 4–6 years and drunk through the first two or more decades of the next century. The most massive of Gaja's Barbarescos is the huge, thick, smoky 1990 Sori Tilden. This enormously rich, profound wine is full bodied and magnificently concentrated with admirable underlying acidity, and plenty of tannin. The finish lasts for over a minute. Cellar it for 5–6 years and drink it over the next 30. I always find the Costa Russi to be the most new world–like of Gaja's Barbarescos, often resembling a hypothetical blend of a great Zinfandel and a stunning new oak–aged Châteauneuf du Pape. The 1990 Costa Russi displays the telltale Nebbiolo character in its thick, rich, jammy, black cherry–scented nose, complemented by wonderfully fragrant aromas of grilled vegetables and sweet vanillin from new oak. Deep and full bodied, with chewy, unctuous, concentrated flavors, this is another awesome Barbaresco. It will be approachable in 2–3 years and last for 20–25.

Gaja's longtime dream of owning vineyards in Barolo has finally been realized. No one who loves his wines will be disappointed with his first Barolo releases. Moreover, by Gaja's standards, even the price is palatable. The 1988 Barolo Sperss exhibits a deep color, tremendous extraction of fruit, and soft acids and tannins. It is a backward, unevolved, potentially exceptional wine. Tightly packed, full bodied, and muscular, its wonderful tar-, rose-, and black cherry–scented nose is just beginning to emerge. Drink it between now and 2010. The 1989 Barolo Sperss gives the impression of being more evolved, softer, and fatter. Although there appears to be more depth of fruit, and the nose is more expressive, sweeter, and more flamboyant, a thorough examination of the wine reveals considerable tannin. Nevertheless, the rich, ripe, broad, expansive fruit, full-bodied, chewy texture, and soft acids make for a decadently rich, complex, compelling bottle of Barolo. Drink it between now and 2012. Gaja's 1990 Barolo Sperss is even richer, fuller, and deeper than the spectacular 1989 and outstanding 1988. The 1990 exhibits Gaja's signature in its extraordinary purity of flavor and layered richness, full body, and moderately tannic finish. It offers a huge, classic Barolo nose of roses, black fruits, smoke, and a whiff of tar. Dense and large-scaled, as well as stylish and graceful, this immensely impressive wine is supple enough to be drunk, but it is capable of lasting 25–30 years.

For all his success, the admirable Angelo Gaja remains fanatically committed to excellence, and because of that he is Piedmont's reference point, as well as an inspiration to many of the young growers just beginning to estate-bottle their wines.

ATTILIO GHISOLFI
Barbera d'Alba* *

1990 Barbera d'Alba	C	81

This ruby-colored Barbera d'Alba is a pleasant, straightforward, commercial wine. It possesses some ripeness, soft fruit, and a light- to medium-bodied, quick finish. Drink it over the next 2–4 years.

GIAN MARCO GHISOLFI
Barolo Bricco Visette* * * *

1990 Barolo Bricco Visette	C	90

I lament the fact that I do not know anything about this producer, nor could I find any information in my reference library. However, based on the 1990 Barolo Bricco Visette I tasted, I am impressed! The wine exhibits stunning concentration and an opulent style, with a rich, concentrated, black cherry fruitiness complemented by at least partial aging in spicy new oak barrels. With low acidity and a precocious, up-front, quasi-modern style that combines power and finesse, this beautifully made Barolo should drink well for 12–15 years.

BRUNO GIACOSA
Barbaresco Asili* * * * *, Barbaresco Gallina* * * *, Barbaresco Santo Stefano* * * * *,
Barolo Falletto* * * * *, Barolo Rionda* * * * *, Barolo Le Rocche* * * * *,
Barolo Villero* * * * *, Dolcetto d'Alba Plinet di Trezzo* */* * *,
Nebbiolo d'Alba Valmaggiore* *

1990 Barbaresco Asili	E	93
1990 Barbaresco Gallina	E	90+
1990 Barbaresco Santo Stefano Riserva	E	95+
1989 Barbaresco Santo Stefano Riserva	E	90+
1988 Barbaresco Santo Stefano Riserva	E	94
1990 Barolo Falletto di Serralunga Riserva	E	95+
1989 Barolo Falletto di Serralunga Riserva	E	94+
1989 Barolo Rionda Riserva	E	95
1990 Barolo Villero	E	94+
1989 Barolo Villero	E	92+

It is refreshing that Bruno Giacosa, the quiet and dignified winemaking genius of Neive, is the least promotion-conscious winemaker in Italy. Justifiably, he prefers to let his wines do the talking for him. The 1988 Barbaresco Santo Stefano Riserva is a deep ruby-colored, fragrant wine with intense aromas of cedar, cherry jam, tobacco, and herbs. Full bodied and expansive, with layers of sweet fruit, this wine offers immediate appeal, but it promises to evolve gracefully for 10–20 years. The rich, thick fruit nearly obscures the tannin. It is a monument to the heights Nebbiolo can achieve! The 1989 Barbaresco Santo Stefano Riserva (which Giacosa compares with the 1982) is a firm, closed, densely concentrated wine that gives only hints of its potential. With airing, it offers up a sweet, gamey, cherry- and tobacco-scented perfume. However, its richness is most noticeable at the back of the palate. Its full-bodied personality exhibits considerable tannin.

Readers should make every effort to obtain the 1990 Barbarescos from Bruno Giacosa. Giacosa, never given to overstatement, compares his 1990s with the 1971s. His 1971 Barbaresco Santo Stefano is the finest bottle of Nebbiolo I have ever drunk! The 1990 Barbaresco Gallina is a lusciously rich, deeply concentrated, full-bodied, spicy wine. It requires 2–3 years of cellaring and should last for 12–15 years. I recently had a bottle of 1978 Barbaresco Gallina, which is still performing beautifully and is capable of another 5–7 years of cellaring. Giacosa has also produced a microscopic quantity of Barbaresco from a small parcel of the Asili vineyard. Only 2,000 bottles were produced. Is it the Musigny of Barbaresco? The 1990 Barbaresco Asili is a quintessentially elegant, ripe, fragrant wine with wonderfully sweet, harmonious, cherry fruit intertwined with hints of cedar, truffles, and roasted nuts. Full bodied, with layers of opulent fruit supported admirably by fine acidity and tannin, it should drink well for 15 or more years.

The blockbuster 1990 Barbaresco Santo Stefano Riserva (red label) exhibits a profound nose of sweet fruit, smoked meats, spice, and fruitcakelike scents. Exceptionally deep, concentrated, and full bodied, with wonderful richness, as well as a layered, concentrated texture, this moderately tannic wine should be at its best by the late nineties and last through the first two decades of the next century. If Giacosa is correct and this wine turns out to be a modern-day clone of the 1971, expect this wine to merit a three-digit-point score circa 2005!

Giacosa has always produced some of Italy's greatest Barolos. Made in an enlightened traditional style and meant for long-term cellaring, these can be austere and backward early in life. Yet they are sure bets to develop magnificently, usually peaking at age 15 or 20. The 1989s look to be superb Barolos. The most forward and the best candidate for early drinking is the 1989 Barolo Villero. The dark ruby color is followed by a tight but promising nose of roses, tar, and sweet red and black fruit. There is huge richness and density of fruit extraction, tremendous body, and a long, tannic, spicy finish that lasts for at least a minute. The wine will benefit from 4–5 years of cellaring; it can mature for 20 years. The 1989 Barolo Rionda Riserva (red label) from the famous vineyard in Serralunga offers a gorgeously sweet, opulently expansive nose of cedar, black and red fruits, spices, tobacco, tar, and smoke. Magnificently rich, with layers of nearly overripe black cherry fruit, this unctuously thick, full-bodied, tannic wine needs at least 5–6 years of cellaring; it should last for 20–30 years. The 1989 Barolo Falletto di Serralunga Riserva (red label) is the most backward of these wines, with a ferocious tannin level balanced by rich, concentrated, thick, chewy flavors. Full bodied, but massive and nearly impenetrable, this wine of great dignity should be cellared through the turn of the century and should be drunk over the following 30 years!

In 1990, Giacosa's Barolos are full bodied, backward, and concentrated, as well as admirably rich and intense. The two 1990s I tasted included the mammothly constructed, wonderfully pure, aromatic 1990 Barolo Villero and the huge, massively proportioned, thick, muscular 1990 Barolo Falletto di Serralunga Riserva (red label). Readers who adore Bruno Giacosa's faithful adherence to traditionally styled Barolo will be thrilled by these wines.

F.LLI GIACOSA
Barbaresco Rio Sordo * * *, Barbera d'Alba Maria Gioana * *, Barolo Pira * * *

1989 Barbaresco Rio Sordo	C	87
1990 Barbera d'Alba Maria Gioana	C	82
1989 Barolo Pira	D	86

Made for near-term consumption, the 1989 Barbaresco Rio Sordo reveals an elegant, charming, sweet nose of jammy fruit, weeds, and tobacco. Fat, round, and soft, with low acidity, admirable ripeness, and rich fruit, this luscious Barbaresco should be drunk over the next 5–7 years. The 1989 Barolo Pira displays a typical Barolo nose of rose petals, tar, and dusty, herbaceous, cherry fruit, followed by a fat, tasty, easily understood wine with adequate ripeness, medium to full body, and a soft finish. Drink this wine over the next 7–8 years. The dark ruby/purple color of the 1990 Barbera d'Alba Maria Gioana is followed by spicy, herbal scents. This medium-bodied, compact wine is straightforward and pleasant. Drink it over the next 4–5 years.

ELIO GRASSO
Barolo Vigna Casa Mate * * * *, Barolo Vigna Chiniera * * * *

1990 Barolo Vigna Casa Mate	D	91
1989 Barolo Vigna Casa Mate	D	86
1990 Barolo Vigna Chiniera	D	88

The only 1989 I tasted was the Barolo Vigna Casa Mate. It exhibits an herbaceous, rich nose of ripe cherry fruit, a lush, soft, plush palate, low acidity, and a heady, round, alcoholic finish. It should be drunk over the next 5–7 years.

Both of the 1990 Barolos possess burgundian-like perfumes, lusciousness, and expansive, chewy textures. The 1990 Barolo Vigna Chiniera reveals the same herbaceousness I detected in the 1989 (atypical for most Barolos from the 1989 and 1990 vintages), as well as sweet, ripe, juicy flavors, a certain fatness, low acidity, and a plump, decadent style. This sexy, easy-to-drink Barolo should be consumed over the next decade. The 1990 Barolo Vigna Casa Mate shares the same seductive, voluptuously textured style, but it is more concentrated, with fine grip and greater richness and length. I find this impressively put together, hedonistic style of Barolo enjoyable.

F.LLI GRASSO CASCINA VALGRANDE
Barbaresco Bricco Spessa * * *, Barbaresco Riserva * * *, Barbaresco Sori Valgrande * * * *,
Barbera d'Alba * *

1990 Barbaresco Bricco Spessa	B	87
1990 Barbaresco Riserva	D	87
1990 Barbaresco Sori Valgrande	D	88
1989 Barbaresco Sori Valgrande	D	89
1990 Barbera d'Alba	C	83

I admired the hedonistic, velvety-textured, fat, succulent style of the 1989 Sori Valgrande. The wine offers dramatic, extroverted aromas of herbs, cherries, cedar, and spices. Fat, luscious, and ideal for drinking over the next 7–8 years, this full-bodied, flashy style of Barbaresco will have many admirers.

All three 1990s were backward, dense, concentrated, full-bodied, closed wines. They all exhibit deep ruby colors, gobs of extract, medium to full body, a high tannin level, and equally high alcohol. All three were in a closed, difficult-to-assess stage, but the purity, extract, and size of these Barbarescos suggest high quality and 10–20 years of longevity. My scores are intentionally conservative, but these wines merit interest.

Medium dark ruby-colored, with a tight, earthy, spicy nose, and compact, moderately endowed, medium-bodied flavors, the 1990 Barbera d'Alba possesses high acidity (especially for a 1990), giving it the impression of lacking flesh and tasting short.

SILVIO GRASSO
Barbera d'Alba Fontanile * * *

1990 Barbera d'Alba Fontanile	B	87

This robust, mouth-filling, richly fruity Barbera possesses enough acidity to give it focus and balance. The impressive saturated dark purple color is followed by a round, generous, mouth-filling wine with no hard edges. Drink it over the next 5–7 years.

MARCHESE DI GRESY

Barbaresco Martinenga * * * *, Barbaresco Martinenga Camp Gros * * * * *, Barbaresco
Martinenga Gaiun * * * * *, Dolcetto Monte Aribaldo * * * *

1990 Barbaresco Martinenga	D	91
1988 Barbaresco Martinenga	E	86
1990 Barbaresco Martinenga Camp Gros	E	95
1989 Barbaresco Martinenga Camp Gros	E	92
1988 Barbaresco Martinenga Camp Gros	E	87
1990 Barbaresco Martinenga Gaiun	E	93
1989 Barbaresco Martinenga Gaiun	E	90
1988 Barbaresco Martinenga Gaiun	E	88

The Marchese di Gresy's La Martinenga vineyard is highly regarded by everyone in Barbaresco. This producer vinifies and bottles separately two parcels within La Martinenga called Camp Gros and Gaiun. This vineyard, which abuts both the esteemed Rabaja and Asili vineyards, is entirely owned by di Gresy. The style of wine that emerges is one of extraordinary finesse and elegance. In 1989 and 1990 di Gresy's wines are the finest I have tasted from this estate. In the past their emphasis on medium-weight, forward, lighter Barbarescos has tended to compromise this vineyard's full potential. The 1989s and 1990s, while offering the classic, elegant style favored by Marchese di Gresy, possess more richness and concentration than preceding years.

In 1990, di Gresy's Barbarescos possess a deeper richness and higher alcohol. They appear to have been made from even riper, more concentrated fruit than the superb 1989s. The 1990 Martinenga exhibits a stunningly pure nose of black cherries, vanillin, and spices, lovely fruit and ripeness, medium to full body, and a soft, unctuously textured palate. It should drink well for 10–15 years. The 1990 Martinenga Gaiun reveals a deep ruby color (deeper than the 1989), a sweet, cedary-, baked nut–, and red and black fruit–scented nose, an overall sense of elegance and harmony, and lush, medium- to full-bodied flavors with sweet, well-integrated tannin. It is a quintessentially elegant example of Barbaresco with stunning flavor concentration and precision. The 1990 Martinenga Camp Gros is a profound wine, offering a staggering perfume of ripe black cherries, spring flowers, smoky oak, and a cigar box/fruitcake–like component. Dense, concentrated, and rich, the telltale opulence and jamminess of the vintage are well represented. This wine possesses admirable underlying structure, ripe tannin, and a heady yet gorgeously soft and silky-textured finish. Although approachable, it promises to be one of di Gresy's longest-lived Barbarescos, lasting easily through the first decade of the next century.

While I did not see the Martinenga offering in 1989, I did taste the two single-vineyard offerings, the Martinenga Gaiun and the Martinenga Camp Gros. The local cognoscenti claim that the Gaiun section of the Martinenga vineyard, which abuts the famous Asili vineyard, produces smoother, more velvety-textured wines than the Camp Gros section, which abuts the Rabaja vineyard. The 1989 Martinenga Gaiun is as seductive a style of red wine as readers are likely to encounter. Its immense perfume of roses, cherries, smoke, and sweet fruit envelops the taster. The flavors are more intense and concentrated than the wine's medium ruby color would suggest. Drink this soft, explosively fruity, supple, complex wine over the next 10–12 years while waiting for some of the more rustic, fuller-bodied

Barbarescos to mature. The 1989 Martinenga Camp Gros possesses less charm, more dusty tannin, and a fuller-bodied, richer, more concentrated, muscular style than the Gaiun. Nevertheless, it is a more complete Barbaresco because of its great richness and ripeness. Yet its ethereal bouquet is reminiscent of the Gaiun. The Camp Gros should last for 15 or more years.

All three of the 1988s possess the classic Nebbiolo nose of roses, cherries, and tar. All exhibit light to moderate tannins, moderate concentration, and soft, supple finishes. The most expansive and richest on the palate is the Martinenga Gaiun; the lightest and shortest is the Martinenga.

ICARDI

Barbera d'Alba Vigna dei Gelsi * * *, Nebbiolo delle Langhe * * *

1990 Barbera d'Alba Vigna dei Gelsi	C	87?
1990 Nebbiolo delle Langhe	B	85

Save for a slight touch of oxidation in the nose, the 1990 Barbera d'Alba Vigna dei Gelsi is an impressively endowed, jammy Barbera exhibiting the record-setting ripeness and high sugar the grapes achieved in Piedmont's 1990 vintage. The dark ruby/purple color is followed by gobs of rich, sweet, fat, black raspberry and currant fruit. I detected little tannin in this low-acid wine. It should be drunk over the next 4–5 years. Although the ripe, soft, velvety-textured 1990 Nebbiolo delle Langhe is neither complex nor deep, it provides appealing, fruity, soft flavors in a medium-bodied format. Drink it over the next several years.

EREDI LODALI

Barbaresco Rocche dei Sette Fratelli * * *

1990 Barbaresco Rocche dei Sette Fratelli	C	88?
1989 Barbaresco Rocche dei Sette Fratelli	C	89?

Both vintages of Eredi Lodali's Barbarescos are unusual. The 1989 exhibits a distinctive herbaceous, chocolaty aroma. The wine smells and tastes as if someone took an overripe black cherry, immersed it in melted chocolate, and sprinkled Provençal herbs on it. Although this may sound like a strange concoction, the wine possesses exceptional concentration, a rustic, traditional, spicy style, and moderate tannin. It will not appeal to those who admire the newer style of Piedmontese red wine that contains lavish quantities of sweet new oak and red and black fruits. The 1989 Rocche dei Sette Fratelli should age effortlessly for 10–15 years. The 1990 is cut from the same cloth, with a melted road tar aspect accompanying the herbaceous, chocolaty component and abundant quantities of jammy cherry fruit. Full bodied, dense, concentrated, and obviously made from low yields, this is a controversial Barbaresco.

MANZONE

Barbera d'Alba * * * *, Barolo Le Gramolere * * * */* * * * *, Dolcetto * * *

1990 Barbera d'Alba	C	88
1990 Barolo Le Gramolere	D	93
1989 Barolo Le Gramolere	D	92+
1988 Barolo Le Gramolere	D	90?
1990 Barolo Le Gramolere di Grazia Cuvée	D	96
1991 Dolcetto	C	86

In 1990, Manzone offers two cuvées of superripe, opulent, dense, concentrated, full-bodied, sexy Barolo. The more widely available 1990 Barolo Le Gramolere offers an open-knit, dramatic bouquet of herbs, spices, black cherries, and leather. Concentrated, with great purity and overall balance, this lush, sweet, flavorful Barolo is ideal for drinking over the next decade. Marc di Grazia, who represents Manzone's wines, produced 140 cases of a special cuvée made from Manzone's oldest vines. The nearly perfect 1990 Barolo Le Gramolere di Grazia Cuvée offers a huge, opaque dark purple color, and a sweet, fragrant nose of floral scents (roses?), vanillin, and jammy black cherries. Thick, chewy flavors with exceptional purity and delineation linger on the palate. The wine is well structured, but most tasters will only notice the lavish quantities of fruit and richness. Drink it over the next 10–15 years.

The 1989 Barolo Le Gramolere is an intensely spicy, long, thick wine with gobs of glycerin, alcohol, and tannin. A massive 1989, with exceptional extraction of fruit as well as a sensational finish, it should drink well between 1997 and 2015.

The extremely saturated, opaque, dark ruby color of the 1988 Barolo Le Gramolere is atypical for Barolo. The nose offers up funky, kinky, tar, mineral, and sweaty saddle leather aromas intertwined with superripe black fruit notes. There is tremendous ripeness, but this big wine has a disjointed feel. With such impressive extraction of flavor, this Barolo should prove to be outstanding, provided one has the patience to wait 5–7 years. It is a controversial style of Barolo.

Manzone made a gorgeous 1990 Barbera d'Alba. Exhibiting a dark ruby/purple color and a huge nose of mint and black cherry cough syrup, it is rich and full bodied, with superlative ripeness and a long, lusty finish. It should drink well for at least 10 years. Manzone's 1991 Dolcetto is one of the better examples I have tasted from that vintage. It offers a perfumed nose of cherries and roses, and a rich, exuberant, fruity personality with a soft finish. It should be consumed immediately.

MARCARINI

Barolo Brunate * * * */* * * * *, Barolo La Serra * * * */* * * * *

1990	Barolo Brunate	D	90+
1989	Barolo Brunate	D	90
1990	Barolo La Serra	D	90
1989	Barolo La Serra	D	89

The Marcarini estate in La Morra is one of Barolo's most respected producers. Their 1989s and 1990s are tightly knit, closed, but promising wines that require 4–5 years of cellaring. The 1990 Barolo La Serra is a rustic, full-bodied, cherry-, herb-, and tar-scented wine with tremendous body, gobs of tannin, and a closed, hard personality. I am sure this wine will merit an outstanding rating in 5–6 years, but when I tasted it in March, it was nearly impenetrable. Patience is required! The 1990 Barolo Brunate appears to possess greater richness of fruit, a more persuasive personality, and deep, big, full-bodied flavors with considerable tannin. It needs 5–6 years of cellaring and will keep for two decades.

The 1989 Barolo La Serra offers a deep ruby color, a spicy nose of dried cherry, new saddle leather scents, full-bodied flavors, and a long, dense finish with noticeable tannin and alcohol. It should be cellared for 3–4 years and will keep for two decades. The 1989 Barolo Brunate exhibits greater richness, a more expansive, fuller-bodied palate, and a longer finish. It may also be slightly riper. This is a rich yet closed, backward style of Barolo that needs 5–6 years of aging. Drink it between 1999 and 2015.

MARENGO-MARENDA
Barbaresco Le Terre Forti * * *, Barbera Le Terre Forti * * *, Barolo Cerequio * * * *

1990 Barbaresco Le Terre Forti	C	88
1990 Barbera Le Terre Forti	B	84
1990 Barolo Cerequio	C	88
1989 Barolo Cerequio	C	89

Formerly known as the Vinicola Piedmontese, a company owned by four businessmen from Alba, this firm operates largely as a *négociant*, buying grapes for vinification in their modern winery in La Morra. Their 1989s and 1990s are noteworthy values. The 1990 Barbaresco Le Terre Forti offers an attractive, sweet, cherry, cedary, spicy nose, round, generous, succulent flavors, medium to full body, light tannin, and a long, heady, alcoholic finish. It is ideal for drinking over the next 7–10 years.

The 1989 Barolo Cerequio exhibits a textbook nose of tar, black cherries, and herb scents, ripe, full-bodied flavors, superb depth and ripeness, and moderate tannin in the spicy, rich finish. It will benefit from 2–3 years of cellaring and should keep for 15 years. The 1990 Barolo Cerequio may be slightly less concentrated, although that is hard to ascertain given that it is also more tannic. A deep, rich, full-bodied, well-made Barolo, oozing with ripe fruit, glycerin, body, and alcohol, it should be drunk between 1996 and 2010.

With respect to the 1990 Barbera Le Terre Forti, a medium ruby color is followed by a spicy, ripe nose in this straightforward, medium-bodied Barbera. It should be drunk over the next 4–5 years.

BARTOLO MASCARELLO
Barolo * * * * *, Dolcetto d'Alba * * * *

1990 Barolo	D	96
1989 Barolo	D	96

With a production of only about 1,500 cases, Bartolo Mascarello has a well-deserved cult following among admirers of the traditional style of Barolo. His just-bottled 1989 Barolo reveals an opaque dark ruby/purple color, and a huge, classic bouquet representing the essence of rose petals, intermingled with scents of superripe red and black fruits, earth, and a whiff of tar. The wine is powerful, rich, and exceptionally well balanced, with magnificent concentration and a long, spicy, hugely tannic finish that is not out of balance for the wine's exceptional extraction of fruit. Because of the superripeness achieved in the 1989 vintage, this wine can be drunk young, but promises to last for decades to come. A brilliant effort!

Remarkably, the 1990 Barolo may turn out to be slightly superior. Massive, with huge extraction of fruit, and a fabulously fragrant nose of cedar, jammy black cherries, herbs, and roses, this extremely concentrated, well-integrated wine is a monumental example of Barolo. It will provide great drinking for 30 or more years. Like the 1989, the super level of ripeness achieved by most Piedmontese producers in 1990 makes this wine very accessible, even seductive when young.

GIUSEPPE MASCARELLO
Barbera d'Alba Fasana * * *, Barbera d'Alba Panirole * * * * *, Barolo Dardi * * */* * * *,
Barolo Monprivato * * * * *, Dolcetto Gagliassi * * *

1990 Barbera d'Alba Fasana	C	88+?
1990 Barbera d'Alba Panirole	C	92

1990 Barolo Monprivato	D	93
1989 Barolo Monprivato	D	92

For a producer with a long track record for massive, savagely tannic, blockbuster Barolos that need a decade of cellaring, I found Mascarello's 1989 and 1990 Barolo Monprivato to be gloriously up-front, decadent, and hedonistic. Neither wine lacked the explosive richness and massiveness that Mascarello achieves in great years, but they are more seductive, lusher, and softer than his longtime followers might expect. More flattering and supple than usual, these wines will be drinkable at an earlier age, but still are capable of lasting 20–25 years—now that's progress! The 1989 displays the huge, classic Barolo nose of tar, roses, black cherries, herbs, and cedar. Massively full bodied, with layers of concentration, yet surprisingly succulent, this wine offers great extraction of fruit, grip, and a gorgeous finish. Drink it between 1997 and 2020. The opulent 1990 is splendidly concentrated, full bodied, and amazingly mouth filling. It can be drunk when released next year, or held for 20–25 years. It is tempting to say that Giuseppe Mascarello might be moving in the direction of a more modern style. I suspect both of these wines possess frightfully high tannin levels, but because of the sensational ripe fruit of the 1989 and 1990 vintages, these wines are so concentrated that much of the tannin is obscured.

These massive, blockbuster Barberas exhibit dark, saturated, ruby/purple colors. The 1990 Barbera d'Alba Panirole is a wine of enormous richness, ripeness, glycerin, body, and fruit. I had the 1971 Mascarello Barbera recently, and it was still in remarkable condition, so who knows how long these 1990s will last. My guess, in spite of how drinkable the wine may be, is 20+ years. It is a stunning example of the extraordinary ripeness and concentration achieved in this spectacular vintage. I am less confident about Mascarello's 1990 Barbera d'Alba Fasana. Although every bit as full and muscular as its sibling, its aromatic profile contains a funky, wet dog, furry component, as well as a touch of acetone. Once past that, there is no doubting the exceptional ripeness, the big, rich, chewy style, and the stunning length. Perhaps this wine will become more civilized with aging; it certainly will last 20+ years.

MASSOLINO-VIGNA RIONDA

Barolo Parafada* * *, Barolo Sori Vigna Rionda* * * *, Barolo Sori Vigneto Margheria* * * *, Barolo Vigna Rionda* * * *

1990 Barolo Parafada	D	88
1990 Barolo Sori Vigna Rionda	D	90
1989 Barolo Sori Vigna Rionda	D	90
1990 Barolo Sori Vigneto Margheria	D	90
1989 Barolo Sori Vigneto Margheria	D	88
1989 Barolo Vigna Rionda	D	87

This firm owns 11 acres in the highly regarded Rionda vineyard near the village of Serralunga d'Alba. Bruno Giacosa makes one of Italy's greatest Barolos from this vineyard. Massolino has raised the quality of its wines over recent years. I was impressed with the bevy of 1989 and 1990 Barolos I tasted. All were classic, textbook examples of Barolo, ranging from excellent to outstanding quality. The 1989 Barolo Vigna Rionda displays spicy herb and cherry fruit, a traditionally styled, moderately tannic texture, and light tannin in the finish. The overall impression is one of suppleness and a forward, easy-to-drink style. Consume it over the next 10–12 years. The 1989 Barolo Sori Vigna Rionda exhibits greater depth and richness, as well as a more intense perfume of tar, spices, and black cherries. Full bodied, long, concentrated, and ripe, with a moderately tannic finish, it is drinkable now, but will easily keep for 15 or more years. The 1989 Barolo Sori Vigneto Margheria possesses lovely soft, fruity flavors presented in a medium- to full-bodied, elegant format. With soft tannin and low acidity, it is the lightest of the wines I tasted from Massolino; it should be drunk over the next 7–8 years.

Among the three 1990s, I admired the 1990 Barolo Sori Vigna Rionda for its deep, full-bodied, pure richness, spicy, black cherry and earthy aromatics, and rich, rustic, authoritatively flavored finish. It should drink well for 15 or more years. The 1990 Sori Vigneto Margheria reveals more depth, body, and power than the more elegant and lighter 1989. Impressively thick, rich, and deep, it is made in a style that can be drunk now or aged for 15 years. Lastly, the lovely 1990 Barolo Parafada is a medium-bodied, velvety Barolo with fine richness and depth, and a spicy, long finish. Possessing less stuffing and structure than the other offerings, it should be consumed over the next 5–6 years.

MATTEO-CORREGGIA

Barbera d'Alba Bricco Marun * * * */* * * * *, Nebbiolo d'Alba Val Preti * * * *

1991 Barbera d'Alba Bricco Marun	C	78
1990 Barbera d'Alba Bricco Marun	D	94
1990 Nebbiolo d'Alba Val Preti	D	90

Correggia's single-vineyard 1990 Barbera d'Alba Bricco Marun is one of the greatest Barberas I have ever tasted. The dark purple color is followed by an intense bouquet, which screams from the glass, offering aromas of plums, black currants, licorice, and spices. Rich and full bodied, with awesome extract levels, this unbelievably rich, complex wine can be drunk now or cellared for another 10–12 years. Amazing! The 1991 Barbera d'Alba Bricco Marun exhibits a healthy ruby/purple color, a pleasant but simple nose of ripe fruits, and a medium-bodied, short, attenuated flavor profile. Although the wine is serviceable and correct, it does not possess the aromatic and flavor dimensions of its predecessors in 1990 and 1989.

The 1990 Nebbiolo d'Alba Val Preti was made from yields of 2 tons per acre and aged in 100% new oak. The wine's 14% alcohol is buried under a cascade of lavishly rich, sweet-tasting (the wine is totally dry) black cherry and plum fruit. Combined with the sexy aromas of toast and vanillin it makes for an exceptionally well delineated, rich, full-bodied, spectacularly well-endowed wine that should drink well for another 10–15 years.

UMBERTO E RATTI MENTONE

Barolo * *

1989 Barolo	C	72

One of the most disappointing wines in my Piedmont tastings, this short, thin, hard, tough, intensely herbaceous wine lacks ripeness, concentration, and depth.

AZ. AGR. LUIGI MINUTO

Barbaresco Cascina Luisin * *

1989 Barbaresco Cascina Luisin	C	73

The most disappointing offering among the 1989 Barbarescos I tasted, this lean, vegetal, compact wine lacks ripeness, richness, and length.

MOCCAGATTA

Barbaresco Basarin * * * *, Barbaresco Bric Balin * * * *, Barbaresco Cole * * * *,
Barbera Basarin * * *

1990 Barbaresco Basarin	C	90
1990 Barbaresco Bric Balin	D	92+

1990 Barbaresco Cole	D	92+
1990 Barbera Basarin	C	88

The 1989 and 1990 vintages were such great ones that producers who generally make good wines often turned out sensational ones. Moccagatta's 1990s are the best I have tasted from this producer. For starters there is the 1990 Barbera Basarin, a gorgeously assembled, rich, authoritatively flavored, spicy, fruity wine that cuts a deep impression on the palate. Drink it over the next decade.

The three 1990 Barbarescos offer slightly different styles. The most developed and opulent, as well as the best for near-term drinking (over the next 10–12 years), is the 1990 Barbaresco Basarin. It is rich, with a spicy, smoky, black cherry–scented nose, lavish quantities of fruit, full body, and a lovely, velvety-textured finish. The most tannic of this trio, the 1990 Barbaresco Cole is also the biggest and densest. Although rich, superintense, large-scaled, and tannic, it needs at least 3–4 years in the cellar. The wine's purity, size, harmony, and finish are impressive. Drink it between 1997 and 2015. The 1990 Barbaresco Bric Balin will benefit from some cellaring. Although it is voluptuous, flattering, and succulent, this full-bodied, rich wine displays stunning length. It is another great Barbaresco from this exceptional vintage. Drink it between now and 2010.

GUIDO MOLINO
Barolo Vigna Conca * * *

1989 Barolo Vigna Conca	C	86

This straightforward, plump, chewy, commercially styled Barolo is cleanly made, with plenty of ripe fruit, medium to full body, and a soft, supple texture. Drink it over the next 5–7 years.

CASTELLO DI NEIVE
Barbaresco Santo Stefano * * * *, Dolcetto d'Alba Basarin * * *,
Dolcetto d'Alba Messoriano * * *

1989 Barbaresco Santo Stefano	D	89
1985 Barbaresco Santo Stefano	D	88

The 1989 Barbaresco Santo Stefano is clearly the best example of this wine made by the Castello di Neive since 1982. The big, leathery, meaty, herb- and tobacco-scented bouquet is followed by a rich, concentrated, medium- to full-bodied wine. It has already shed some of its tannin, and can be drunk now or over the next 12–15 years. The dark ruby/garnet color of the 1985 Santo Stefano is just beginning to display some amber/orange at the edge, and the explosive bouquet of dried red fruits, mushrooms, and, I believe, white truffles soars from the glass. This full-bodied, concentrated, yet surprisingly forward Barbaresco is beautifully endowed with layer upon layer of sweet, expansive fruit. The finish is long, alcoholic, and impressive. Drinkable now, this excellent Barbaresco should continue to evolve for another 5–10 years.

ANDREA OBERTO
Barbera d'Alba Giada * * * *, Barolo Vigneto Rocche * * * *

1990 Barbera d'Alba Giada	D	91
1990 Barolo Vigneto Rocche	E	89
1989 Barolo Vigneto Rocche	E	87+

From my two tastings, this producer's microscopic quantities of Barolo appear to be excellent, possibly outstanding. Perhaps an American importer should pay a visit to Mr. Oberto's cellars. The 1989 Barolo Vigneto Rocche is backward, tannic, and powerful, offering only a hint of what lies behind the wall of astringency and toughness. The impressive deep color is followed by a big, rich, weighty feel. Although completely closed, this wine is made with a healthy respect for the traditional school. Mouth-searing tannin suggests this wine should be laid away for at least 5–6 years; it is a 20+-year wine. The 1990 Vigneto Rocche offers a classy bouquet of elegant, sweet, black cherry fruit combined with intriguing scents of roses, minerals, and cedar. Full bodied, with exceptional concentration and depth, silky tannin, and a lusty, alcoholic finish, this big, strapping, expansively flavored Barolo is impressive. Drink it over the next 15 years.

The spectacular 1990 Barbera d'Alba Giada exhibits a saturated dark ruby/purple color, and an explosive nose of vanilla, smoke, and sweet black cherry and curranty fruit. Staggeringly rich, with superb balance, this full-bodied, yet fresh, lively, fleshy Barbera is a knockout. It can be drunk now or cellared for a decade. The sweet, creamy vanillin character indicates the wine was aged in small oak casks. It is a marvelous accompaniment to the wine's highly extracted, ripe fruit.

LUIGI OBERTO
Barbera d'Alba Ciabot Berton * * *, Barolo Ciabot Berton * * * */* * * * *

1990 Barbera d'Alba Ciabot Berton	C	86+
1990 Barolo Ciabot Berton	E	91
1989 Barolo Ciabot Berton	E	88+

Two terrific Barolos were produced by Luigi Oberto in 1989 and 1990. The softer, more supple offering is the 1989 Barolo Ciabot Berton. It exhibits great fruit, an intriguing flowery, cherry- and tar-scented nose, thick, juicy, succulent flavors, gobs of glycerin, full body, and a long finish. Drink it over the next 15 years. Made in a silky-textured, forward style, the 1990 Barolo Ciabot Berton reveals awesome richness, great thickness and juiciness on the palate, and plenty of spicy, rich, tobacco, herb, and black cherry fruit flavors that linger and linger. Drink it over the next 10–15 years.

With a dark ruby color and a tight but promising nose of red and black fruits, the full-bodied, closed yet impressively endowed 1990 Barbera d'Alba Ciabot Berton exhibits fine acidity, a berry fruitiness, and a tight but impressive finish. It will benefit from 6–12 more months of cellaring and may ultimately turn out better than my score suggests. It is a candidate for 10 or more years of cellaring.

VITTORIO OCHETTI E ALFONSO PIERLUIGI
Barbera d'Asti Superiore * * *

1990 Barbera d'Asti Superiore	B	87

This producer has turned out an attractive Barbera d'Asti that should have broad popular appeal. It offers a straightforward nose of jammy fruit, and soft, supple, superripe berry flavors. The acidity is surprisingly soft and the finish is long and authoritative. Drink it over the next 3–4 years.

F.LLI ODDERO
Barolo Vigna Rionda * *

1989 Barolo Vigna Rionda	C	82

This solid, one-dimensional, medium- to full-bodied wine displays good fruit and plenty of underlying tannin and spice, but it does not express much personality or complexity. Drink it over the next 10–15 years.

PALLADINO
Barbaresco * * * *

1990 Barbaresco		C 88+

I was impressed by the 1990 Barbaresco. The wine displays a rich, concentrated, fragrant bouquet of dried herbs and rich black cherry fruit. Full bodied, with excellent concentration and a spicy, chewy texture, this dense, impressively endowed, pure wine is a classic example of a Nebbiolo from the Barbaresco region. Drink it over the next 12–15 years.

ARMANDO PARUSSO
Barbera Pugnane * * */* * * *, Barolo Bussia Rocche * * * *, Barolo Rocche * * * *,
Dolcetto d'Alba Mariondino * * * *

1990 Barbera Pugnane	C 85
1990 Barolo	D 91+
1990 Barolo Bussia Rocche	D 95
1989 Barolo Bussia Rocche	D 92
1988 Barolo Bussia Rocche	D 87
1990 Barolo Mariondino	D 93
1989 Barolo Mariondino	D 89
1989 Barolo Mariondino Falletta	D 89
1988 Barolo Mariondino Falletta	D 89

Parusso's 1990 Barolos are spectacular successes. The 1990 Barolo reveals a superripe, tar- and cherry-scented nose, dense, voluptuously textured, massive fruit flavors, and moderate tannin in the finish. The wine can be drunk now, but ideally purchasers should wait 1–3 years and consume it over the subsequent 15 or more. The 1990 Barolo Mariondino offers a huge nose of sweet, dried cherries, tobacco, and saddle leather. With great richness, and huge reserves of fruit, glycerin, and alcohol, this velvety-textured, powerful, moderately tannic wine moves across the palate with conviction and intensity. With 2–3 years of cellaring this wine will be even better; it will last for 20 years. Perhaps even more magnificent is Parusso's 1990 Barolo Bussia Rocche. While it is difficult to articulate, there is an extra dimension to the sweet, fragrant, spicy, richly fruity aromas, as well as more depth and intensity to the wine's flavors and finish. With a dark, saturated color and full body, this is an awesome, modern-style Barolo for drinking between 1998 and 2015.

The 1990 Barbera Pugnane reveals good ripeness and chewiness, a dense texture, plenty of perfume, and a spicy, crisp, zesty finish. It should drink well for another 5–7 years. Parusso's two best wines among his newest releases are the 1989 Barolo Mariondino and 1989 Barolo Bussia Rocche. The 1989 Barolo Mariondino exhibits tons of sweet, spicy new oak in the nose, as well as abundant quantities of ripe red and black fruits, such as cherries. The wine has a deep, velvety texture with a lingering, super finish. Drink it over the next 10–15 years. Parusso's fabulous 1989 Barolo Bussia Rocche displays an opaque deep ruby color, and a sweet, spicy, stunning nose with the telltale Nebbiolo aromas of tar and roses. There is super richness and extraction of fruit, a multidimensional, medium- to full-bodied texture, and moderately high tannins in the long finish. Drink it between 1996 and 2010.

Parusso's style of Barolo is lighter than that of many other producers. His 1988 Barolo Bussia Rocche displays a medium ruby color, a sweet, fruity nose, medium- to full-bodied flavors, moderate tannins, and a spicy, moderately endowed finish. The modern style makes it more approachable and easier to understand. Parusso's 1988 Barolo Mariondino Falletta is more intense, with a pronounced nose of Bing cherries, smoked almonds, and earth, considerable tannin, full body, and excellent concentration. It possesses a supple texture, particularly for a young Barolo. Drink it over the next 10–12 years.

ELIA PASQUERO
Barbaresco Sori Paitin* * * *

1990 Barbaresco Sori Paitin	D	88+
1989 Barbaresco Sori Paitin	D	90

Pasquero has turned in two superlative performances with respect to his single-vineyard Barbaresco. Perhaps because the 1989 has had more time to evolve, it appears more complex and easier to comprehend than the large-scaled, full-bodied, rich, concentrated, but tannic 1990. The 1989 reveals evidence of new oak cask aging in its smoky, vanillin nose complemented by generous aromas of sweet black cherries, cedar, and spices. The wine is full bodied, deep, and rich, with a harmonious integration of moderate tannin, and a long, lusty, expansive richness. While approachable now, it should be at its best by the late nineties and easily last through the first decade of the next century. The concentrated, spicy, massive 1990 is backward, tannic, and in need of at least 5–6 years of cellaring. If the tannin becomes more integrated with the wine's other components, it will be outstanding. It should last for 20 years.

AGOSTINO PAVIA E FIGLI
Barbera d'Asti Bricco Blina* * *

1990 Barbera d'Asti Bricco Blina	B	87

I admired this wine for many reasons. Although it is not the biggest, most dramatic, or most concentrated wine from this stunning vintage, it is deceptively charming, voluptuous, and seductive. The healthy ruby/purple color is followed by attractive aromas of ripe fruit, spices, and earth. Supple and lush, with excellent concentration and ripeness, this precocious, crowd-pleasing wine should be drunk over the next 5–6 years.

LUIGI PELLISSERO
Barbaresco Vanotu* * *, Barbera d'Alba Ronchi* *

1990 Barbaresco Vanotu	D	87+
1989 Barbaresco Vanotu	D	88
1990 Barbera d'Alba Ronchi	B	84

This small estate–bottler has a reputation for turning out spicy, concentrated Barbaresco. The tightly knit 1989 Vanotu is a tannic, full-bodied wine with excellent ripeness, a heady, high-alcohol content, and excellent concentration and richness. The telltale Barbaresco aromas of spicy, jammy cherries, cedar, and cigar box are apparent. This wine will benefit from 2–3 years of cellaring, as the tannin is more astringent than in the other offering; it will last for 12–15 years. The deeply colored 1990 Vanotu is full bodied, with excellent depth and a tannic finish. The wine needs 3–4 years of cellaring and should last for two decades. Neither of these wines exhibits the complexity Nebbiolo can achieve, but I suspect that is because they are more backward than many of their peers.

Pellissero's 1990 is a solid Barbera d'Alba Ronchi with plenty of body, above-average concentration, fine ripeness, high acidity for a 1990, and a spicy finish. Drink it over the next 5–6 years.

ELIO PERRONE
Barbera delle Langhe Vigna Grivo* * *

1990 Barbera delle Langhe Vigna Grivo	B	86

This muscular, powerfully built wine exhibits a dense ruby/purple color, considerable spice, and a tight, backward personality. While it possesses power and depth, it is monolithic. My instincts suggest cellaring it for a year and drinking it over the following 10–12 years.

POGGIO PETORCINO
Barolo * * * *

1989 Barolo	D	88+

Since Elvio Cogno left the Marcarini firm, he has been making wines under this estate name. The 1989, the first vintage I have tasted, is a dense, tannic, powerful, closed wine that was difficult to assess. There is enough viscously thick, cherry fruit and depth to suggest it could merit an outstanding rating in 5–6 years.

PIAZZO
Barbaresco Riserva * * *, Barbaresco Sori Fratin * * *, Barbera d'Alba Mugiot * * *,
Barolo Poderi di Mugiot * * *

1989 Barbaresco Riserva	C	85
1990 Barbaresco Sori Fratin	C	85+
1990 Barbera d'Alba Mugiot	B	89
1990 Barolo Poderi di Mugiot	D	86

In the comparative tastings of 1990 and 1989 Barbarescos I conducted in Piedmont, the wines of Armando Piazzo came across as (1) more herbal and (2) designed for short-term drinking. Both of these offerings reveal attractive, herbaceous, cherry-scented noses, medium-bodied, spicy, soft flavors, and admirable concentration. The 1990 Sori Fratin exhibits more tannin and an enticing, smoky, tarlike element to its flavors. Both wines are best consumed over the next 5–7 years.

Made in a correct, easy-to-drink and -appreciate style, the soft, ripe, attractively made 1990 Barolo Poderi di Mugiot reveals medium body and moderate tannin. Consume it over the next 5–7 years.

This stunning, saturated purple-colored 1990 Barbera d'Alba Mugiot offers an intense fragrance of spice and black fruits. Full bodied, with layers of concentrated fruit and superb ripeness, this lusty, pure, rich, supple Barbera may merit an outstanding rating after 1–2 more years of bottle age. It is impressive in all respects. Drink it over the next 10–12 years.

PRODUTTORI DI BARBARESCO
Barbaresco * * *, Barbaresco Asili * * * *, Barbaresco Moccagatta * * * *,
Barbaresco Monte Stefano * * * *, Barbaresco Ovello * * * *, Barbaresco Pora * * *,
Barbaresco Rabaja * * * *

1990 Barbaresco	C	88
1989 Barbaresco	C	88
1989 Barbaresco Asili	D	92
1989 Barbaresco Moccagatta	D	90+
1989 Barbaresco Monte Fico	D	87?
1990 Barbaresco Monte Stefano	D	90
1989 Barbaresco Monte Stefano	D	90
1990 Barbaresco Ovello	D	92
1989 Barbaresco Ovello	D	90

1990 Barbaresco Pora	D	92
1990 Barbaresco Rabaja	D	92+
1989 Barbaresco Rabaja	D	90
1989 Barbaresco Rio Sordo	D	89

The Produttori di Barbaresco is unquestionably a terrific source for Barbarescos that rival the best made in Piedmont. Although there is a tendency to scoff at wines made by cooperatives, the quality of the wines from this superbly run operation is as high as that from any highly committed, passionate estate-bottler. I have been an enthusiastic admirer, buyer, and drinker of this co-op's wines since the 1978 vintage. Given the superb quality of the 1989s and 1990s, these wines represent the *finest values* from these two great Piedmontese vintages. The cooperative is quick to declassify any Barbaresco to a generic Nebbiolo if it is not of an acceptably high quality level. They harvest and vinify separately as many as ten vineyards, of which I tasted seven in 1989 and four single-vineyard cuvées in 1990. Most Italian-wine experts consider the Rabaja and Asili to be their two best bottlings. As my notes and scores attest, that is akin to splitting hairs at this high level of quality.

The 1990s are similar to the 1989s, although they are higher in alcohol with a more noticeable element of overripeness in their thick, jammy, sweet, corpulent style. All are full bodied and concentrated, with excellent structure to go along with the massive size. The 1990 Barbaresco Pora (I did not taste the 1989) is sensational, as is the 1990 Barbaresco Rabaja. At $15, the 1990 regular Barbaresco is a great introduction to the big, rich, chewy, classic style of the Produttori di Barbaresco's wines. The Produttori di Barbaresco gets my vote as the best-run and most committed cooperative regarding quality, and, most important for prospective purchasers, as a source for exceptional Barbaresco wine values!

The overall quality of Produttori's 1989 vintage is superb. However, the wines all taste different and vary in intensity, texture, and extract levels. For a super bargain in rich, spicy, rose/cherry/tar-scented Barbaresco, readers are well advised to check out the full-bodied, beautifully concentrated, supple, seductive 1989 Barbaresco. Already delicious, it promises to last for a decade. The 1989 Barbaresco Rio Sordo is made in a medium-bodied, elegant, supple style with superb ripeness, richness, and fruit, but less muscle, tannin, and alcohol than some of the fuller styles. It is best drunk over the next 10–12 years. The 1989 Barbaresco Moccagatta is a richer, fuller-bodied wine with splendid aromatics (roasted herbs, jammy Bing cherries, and sweet cedar), moderate tannin, and excellent opulence and length. It will be at its best between now and 2010. Combining extraordinary richness with great purity and finesse, the 1989 Barbaresco Asili is a head-turning, hedonistic example of Barbaresco at its finest. The wine exhibits layers of sweet, opulent, rich fruit, and a decadent bouquet of explosive red and black fruits, herbs, and spices. This impeccably crafted, well-delineated Barbaresco can be drunk now or cellared for 15–20 years. The 1989 Barbaresco Ovello displays a sweet plum/coffee/roasted nut, Pomerol-like component. Supple, with terrific ripeness and opulence, it possesses a degree of viscosity and sweetness that makes it a wine for unabashed hedonists. The acidity is lower and the color, concentration, and overall length make it a sure bet to last for 15 years, although there is no reason to defer your gratification.

My score for the 1989 Barbaresco Monte Fico may turn out to be conservative, as it is the tightest, most backward, and stingiest wine among the Produttori di Barbaresco's 1989s. Although it appears lighter, there is such a heavy overlay of tannins I had a hard time penetrating its austerity and structure to see what is behind them. Cellar this wine for 2–3 years and see if more richness and concentration emerge. The 1989 Barbaresco Rabaja should rival this co-op's Asili vineyard for top marks in 1989. It is a fabulously rich, dense, concentrated wine with a huge cigar box–, cedary-, and black cherry–scented nose, and expansive, full-bodied, viscously textured flavors. The extraction is mind-boggling and the finish lasts for almost a minute. It is a spectacular, high-alcohol Barbaresco that can be drunk now or cellared for up to two decades. The deeply colored 1989 Barbaresco Monte Stefano reveals a sweet bouquet of black cherries and herbs, full-bodied, supple flavors, low acidity, great richness, and a wonderful, chewy, expansive inner core of fruit that suggests old vines and/or low yields. It should drink well for 15 years.

ALFREDO PRUNOTTO

Barbaresco * * *, Barbaresco Monte Stefano * * * *, Barbera d'Alba * * *,
Barbera d'Alba Fiulot * * *, Barbera d'Alba Pian Romulado * * * *, Barolo Bussia * * * * *,
Barolo Cannubi * * * */* * * * *

1990	Barbaresco	C	88
1990	Barbaresco Monte Stefano	D	92+
1989	Barbaresco Monte Stefano	D	93
1988	Barbaresco Monte Stefano	D	90
1989	Barbera d'Alba	C	85
1993	Barbera d'Alba Fiulot	A	86
1990	Barbera d'Alba Pian Romulado	C	89
1988	Barbera d'Alba Pian Romulado	C	87
1990	Barolo	C	90
1990	Barolo Bussia	D	92+
1989	Barolo Bussia	D	94
1988	Barolo Bussia	D	90
1990	Barolo Cannubi	D	94
1989	Barolo Cannubi	D	91
1988	Barolo Cannubi	D	87+

This producer, now owned by the Tuscan firm of Antinori, continues to turn out superlative examples of Piedmontese wines. The 1989 Barbaresco Monte Stefano is a deeply colored, rich, large-scaled, thick, ripe concentrated wine. There is plenty of tannin to this voluptuous, sexy Barbaresco that should drink well for the next 10–15 years.

The 1990s are more tannic and fatter. The 1990 Barbaresco shares with the 1989 Monte Stefano the voluptuous, seductive style, although it is not as concentrated. Full bodied, rich, and intense, it provides a hedonistic glass of Barbaresco. Drink it over the next 7–8 years. The 1990 Barbaresco Monte Stefano reveals a gorgeously scented nose of smoked nuts, black cherries, cedar, and spice. Full bodied with layers of concentrated, highly extracted fruit, this massive wine appears to be more tannic and backward than its 1989 sibling. The finish is immensely long. While approachable now, it will be at its best between 1998 and 2012+.

The 1989 Barolo Cannubi and 1989 Barolo Bussia are deeply colored, with great concentration, as well as rich, expansive, sweet, superconcentrated flavors. The 1989 Cannubi is more elegant and not as powerful as the 1989 Bussia, which is a huge, well-endowed, glycerin-infused, giant Barolo that should drink well for 15 or more years.

Prunotto has followed the gorgeous 1989 Barolos with superlative performances in 1990. The regular 1990 Barolo exhibits evidence of aging in small oak casks in its sweet scents of vanillin combined with abundant quantities of black cherry fruit and tar. Full bodied and densely concentrated, with considerable tannin in the finish, this large-scaled, rich Barolo should be cellared for 3–4 years and drunk over the subsequent 15 years. It is a bargain for the vintage. The 1990 Barolo Cannubi is a titanic example of Barolo, with immense structure, massive richness, tremendous length, and a huge, ripe nose of spicy fruitcake, cedar, and red and black fruits. Its sweet inner core of fruit is something to behold. The wine needs at least 3–4 years of cellaring and should last for 25 years. The 1990 Barolo Bussia is the most closed of this trio of large-scaled, traditionally made wines. Crammed with rich, glycerin-imbued, sweet, jammy fruit, considerable body and extraction, and a monster finish, it needs 4–5 years of cellaring. It is a candidate for 25+ years of aging.

The 1988 Monte Stefano, which is evolving quickly, is delicious to drink. The medium ruby color is already showing some amber at the edge. The nose reveals earthy, sweet berry, spicy aromas that are followed by a smooth, velvety-textured wine with gorgeous fruit and a soft, luscious finish. Drink it over the next 7–8 years.

Both of the 1988 Barolos are more tannic than the Barbarescos, as well as surprisingly forward and developed, with classic aromas of tar, tobacco, and sweet cherry fruit. They can be drunk now or cellared for another 12–15 years.

The Barberas offer ripe, spicy fruit, an enticing perfume of tomatoes and herbs, and excellent fat and glycerin to balance out their naturally high acidity. The 1989 Barbera d'Alba displays the superripeness that was easily attained in this vintage, but it does not yet boast the complexity of the 1988 Barbera d'Alba Pian Romulado. The latter wine is a big, opulent, deep Barbera with surprising length and complexity. Both wines should drink well for the next 4–5 years, possibly longer. Prunotto's Barbera d'Alba Fiulot is among the first-bottled 1993 Barberas. It is a light-bodied, deliciously fruity, supple, velvety-textured wine with loads of character and spicy, berry fruit, and a round finish. It is meant to be drunk over the next 2–3 years.

The more ambitious and complex 1990 Barbera d'Alba Pian Romulado exhibits a stunning nose of vanillin, jammy fruit, and spices. Superripe, medium to full bodied, and made in a lush, decadent style, this low-acid, fleshy Barbera should drink well over the next 7–10 years.

PUNSET-MARINA MARCARINO
Barbaresco Campo Quadro* * *, Barbaresco Punset* *

1989 Barbaresco Campo Quadro	D	89
1990 Barbaresco Punset	C	86
1989 Barbaresco Punset	C	84

The 1989 and 1990 Barbaresco Punsets are both monolithic, straightforward, medium- to full-bodied, one-dimensional wines. However, the 1989 Barbaresco Campo Quadro is nearly exceptional. From the deep ruby color to the fragrant bouquet of jammy black cherries intermingled with scents of herbs and leafy tobacco, this wine offers deep, concentrated, rich fruit in a full-bodied, intensely concentrated style. In addition to a high tannin level, this wine reveals a supple, chewy personality that provides considerable pleasure and complexity. Drink it over the next 10–12 years.

RENATO RATTI
Barolo Marcenasco* * * *, Barolo Marcenasco Conca* * * * *,
Barolo Marcenasco Rocche* * * * *

1990 Barolo Marcenasco	D	92
1989 Barolo Marcenasco	D	90
1990 Barolo Marcenasco Conca	D	93

1989 Barolo Marcenasco Conca	D	90
1990 Barolo Marcenasco Rocche	D	93
1989 Barolo Marcenasco Rocche	D	90

The late Renato Ratti was one of the most influential voices in Piedmont, urging his fellow producers to pursue a strategy aimed at higher quality, knowing full well that the only way Barolo could make a name for itself in the international marketplace was because of the greatness and individuality of its wines. Ratti's Barolos have long been a model for the elegant, graceful, rich, supple style of Barolo that can be drunk when released. While a handful of critics have suggested these are wines that must be drunk up early, while working on this book I retasted bottles of 1978 from my cellar that were marvelous.

Although the aromatic and flavor profile of the Nebbiolo grape is completely different from Pinot Noir, Nebbiolo and Pinot Noir share an intense, sweet fragrance, a textural chewiness, and an expansiveness that contribute to these varietals' seductiveness. This firm boasts a brilliant record of producing a creamy-textured, ripe, fat, round, generous, sexy style of Barolo that is a thrill to drink young or old. The 1989s and 1990s are Ratti's most successful vintages since 1978.

The 1989 Barolo Marcenasco exhibits a sweet, smoky, black cherry–scented nose, and ripe, opulent, supple flavors that exhibit fine concentration, low acidity, and a cascade of generous fruit in the lusty, heady finish. Drink it over the next 10–12 years. The 1989 Marcenasco Conca is similarly smoky, with a touch more herbaceousness in the nose. Fatter and riper, with oodles of seductively rich black cherry fruit wrapped in a smoky, tar-tinged package, this is another wine to drink in its first decade of life. The precociousness of the 1989 Marcenasco Rocche is a turn-on. The huge nose of coffee beans, chocolate, tar, black cherries, and smoke is a knockout. Ripe, rich, full bodied, and supple, this forward wine should easily drink well for up to a decade.

Ratti's 1990s are similar to the 1989s in their opulence, superripe richness of fruit, excellent extraction, sweet, jammy flavors, and heady, alcoholic, lush finishes. Each is slightly more concentrated and deeper than their 1989 counterparts, hence the higher ratings. The 1990s also possess deeper color saturation. The 1990s will be ready to drink when released, but they will age easily for 10–15+ years. These are among Piedmont's most voluptuous Barolos!

GIOVINE RICONDA
Barbera d'Asti Superiore Vigna del Truchet * * * *

1990 Barbera d'Asti Superiore Vigna del Truchet	D	89

This top-notch Barbera exhibits evidence of aging in new oak. The nose of smoke, vanillin, and rich red and black fruits is followed by a supple, full-bodied wine with excellent richness, ripe, jammy fruit, adequate underlying acidity, and a heady, surprisingly silky-textured finish. Drink it over the next 5–7 years. Impressive!

FRANCESCO RINALDI
Barolo * * * */* * * * *

1989 Barolo	D	90

This mammoth, old-style, wonderfully pure, superconcentrated, behemoth of a wine exhibits a saturated color, a huge, classic Barolo nose of melted road tar, roses, and black fruits, and a dense, concentrated, chewy, full-bodied palate with superb extraction of fruit. Well balanced for its size, its softness is a result of the great ripeness achieved in the 1989 vintage. Although it can be drunk early, it is a 25-year wine.

GIUSEPPE RINALDI
Barolo * * * *, Barolo Brunate Riserva * * * */* * * * *

1990 Barolo	D	91
1989 Barolo	D	88+
1988 Barolo Brunate Riserva	D	93

There can be no doubt that Giuseppe Rinaldi stands squarely in the midst of Barolo's traditionalists. These are authoritatively flavored, rich, rustic, savagely tannic, old-style Barolos that often shock modern-day sensitivities with their blasts of tannin, sometimes funky smells, and thick, chewy fruit. Rinaldi's 1989 Barolo is, to the surprise of no one, massively endowed, extremely backward, and almost impossible to evaluate at such a young age. It needs 5–7 years of cellaring and will last for 20–25 years. Given the monstrous tannins, the question of whether it will ever achieve complete harmony should be left to a wizard. Nevertheless, one has to admire its huge, full-bodied richness, purity, and faithfulness to this particular style of Barolo. Do not open a bottle before the turn of the century. Rinaldi's 1990 Barolo is cut from the same mold. As tannic, rustic, and uncivilized as it appears, it possesses greater richness, more aromatic and flavor dimension, and because of its high extraction of fruit, a better chance to reach old age in a relatively balanced state of drinkability with its fruit, tannin, acid, and alcohol in harmony. I am on the side that favors these two controversial, blockbuster style of wines, but readers should be aware that they require considerable patience.

The old-style 1988 Barolo Brunate Riserva will be adored by consumers who love the style of Giacomo Conterno and Bartolo Mascarello. It possesses the huge, truffle-, earthy-, smoked nut–, and black fruit–scented nose that one either adores or finds slightly dirty. A huge, full-bodied wine, it has mouth-filling, glycerin-dominated, rich, chewy, sweet flavors, surprising suppleness, and a massive finish with gobs of fruit and equally impressive tannin levels. It is likely to be a controversial Barolo, but I thought it to be spectacular. Drink it over the next 15–20 years.

GIUSEPPE RIVETTI
La Spinetta Pin Vino da Tavola * * * *

1990 La Spinetta Pin Vino da Tavola	D	91

Giuseppe Rivetti produces one of Piedmont's most sensational Moscatos, so I was delighted to taste this luxury red wine cuvée aged in small oak casks. Tasted twice (to raves from me as well as numerous swoons from several guests), this Vino da Tavola exhibits a saturated dark ruby/purple color, and a huge, roasted nose of vanillin, herbs, spice, and sweet, jammy, black currant and raspberry fruit. Full bodied with low acidity and a luscious, chewy, voluptuous texture, this is a stunning, dramatically styled red wine for drinking over the next 7–10 years. Readers will need a special contact to latch on to a bottle or two.

ROAGNA
Barbaresco * * * *, Barbaresco Baroco * * * *

1989 Barbaresco	D	90
1990 Barbaresco	D	92
1990 Barbaresco Baroco	D	93

Roagna's 1989 Barbaresco offers a fragrant nose of sweet, jammy cherries, herbs, cedar, and tobacco, followed by a wine with superb ripeness, outstanding concentration and richness, a lush, creamy, opulent texture, and excellent length. Already seductive, this chewy Barbaresco should drink well for 10–15 years.

The 1990s look to be richer, potentially profound wines. The 1990 Barbaresco exhibits a superintense, spicy, cedary, fruity nose, deep, full-bodied, thickly concentrated flavors, and a powerful finish. It possesses the suppleness of the 1989 as well as more strength, power, and concentration. Roagna's 1990 Barbaresco from the Baroco vineyard reveals evidence of new oak in its toasty, smoky, vanillin-, and black cherry–scented nose. The wine displays a deep ruby color (more saturated than his other offerings) and a splendidly rich, full-bodied finish with noticeable tannin and high alcohol. Approachable now, it should last for 10–15+ years.

ALBINO ROCCA
Barbaresco Ronchi* * * *, Barbaresco Vigneti Loreto e Brich Ronchi* * * */* * * * *

1990 Barbaresco Ronchi	C	89
1989 Barbaresco Vigneti Loreto e Brich Ronchi	C	89
1988 Barbaresco Vigneti Loreto e Brich Ronchi	C	87

I have had little experience with this producer, but this 1990 Barbaresco Ronchi had a huge nose of sweet saddle leather, black cherry fruit, and herbs. Soft, voluptuous, and rich, as well as elegant and stylish, this full-bodied, suave, velvety-textured Barbaresco can be drunk now and over the next 10 years. The 1989 and 1988 Barbaresco Vigneti Loreto e Brich Ronchi are tasty, round, full-bodied, rustic, generously endowed Barbarescos. Although the 1989 possesses a sweeter fleshiness, both wines offer fine aromatic character, plenty of depth, and enough sweet fruit, softness, and tannin to be drunk now, yet the depth and grip to last for 10 or more years.

BRUNO ROCCA
Barbaresco Rabaja* * * */* * * * *, Nebbiolo d'Alba* * *

1990 Barbaresco Rabaja	D	90
1989 Barbaresco Rabaja	D	91
1990 Nebbiolo d'Alba	C	85

Bruno Rocca is an up-and-coming producer fashioning small quantities of wine from one of Barbaresco's great vineyards. Made in a modern style, 50% of the wine is aged in small French oak barrels, of which one-third is new. Although I have a slight preference for the 1989, with 4–5 years of aging these sentiments may change. The 1989 exhibits a moderately intense, stylish bouquet of new saddle leather, spicy, smoky, vanillin, toasty oak, and deep, rich, cherry fruit. The wine displays exceptional purity, full body, excellent delineation, and a moderately long finish. It is a graceful yet authoritatively flavored Barbaresco for drinking over the next 10–15 years. Although softer and less focused, the 1990 is fat, ripe, and voluptuously textured with oodles of sweet red and black fruit dominating its personality. I would not be surprised to see it merit an outstanding score after it picks up some structure. More approachable and seemingly more evolved than the 1989, it can be drunk over the next 7–10 years.

Made in a traditional style, the rustic 1990 Nebbiolo d'Alba exhibits spicy, curranty fruit, cedar, tobacco, and earthy undertones, and a spicy, medium-bodied finish. Drink it over the next 2–3 years.

ROCCHE DI COSTAMAGNA
Barbera d'Alba Rocche de la Morra* * *, Barolo Rocche de la Morra* * * *,
Barolo Rocche de la Morra Vigna Francesco* * * *, Rocche della Rocche* * *

1990 Barbera d'Alba Rocche de la Morra	B	87–89?
1990 Barolo Rocche de la Morra	C	89
1990 Barolo Rocche de la Morra Vigna Francesco	C	90

1989 Barolo Rocche de la Morra Vigna Francesco	C 87
1990 Rocche della Rocche	C 86

Given how well the wines of this producer performed, I am surprised they are not more readily found in export markets. The 1989 Barolo Vigna Francesco, from a tiny subvineyard of Annunziata in La Morra, exhibits attractive earthy, cherry, and herbal scents in its fragrant bouquet, ripe, rich, full-bodied flavors, soft tannin, and a heady, alcoholic finish. Forward and seductive, it will easily last for 10–15 years.

Both 1990 Barolos reveal deeper color, as well as more concentration and depth. The 1990 Barolo Rocche de la Morra offers an impressive opaque dark ruby color, explosive ripeness, a supple, rich, concentrated style, gobs of fruit, and a long, moderately tannic finish. It will be approachable early in life and will age well for 15 or more years. With respect to the 1990 Barolo Vigna Francesco, the smoky, vanillin component in its otherwise ripe, fragrant nose of black cherries, saddle leather, and rose petals reveals evidence of partial aging in small new oak casks. Succulent and opulent, this superb, rich, full-bodied wine shows impeccable winemaking and considerable personality and style. It should drink well for 15–20 years.

With a more forthcoming bouquet, the 1990 Barbera d'Alba Rocche de la Morra would have been outstanding. The wine's flavors, concentration, ripeness, and overall textural aspects suggest high class. The healthy, saturated dark ruby/purple color is followed by a reticent (or is it just closed?) nose. The uninspiring aromatic profile is deceptive given the explosive richness and ripeness exhibited by this wine. Impressively endowed, with voluptuous, sweet layers of fruit, this is a large-scaled, supple Barbera for drinking over the next 5–7 years. The medium ruby-colored, supple-styled, easy-to-drink 1990 Rocche della Rocche offers fine body, a silky texture, fine depth, adequate acidity, and a heady, alcoholic finish. It is ideal for consuming over the next 4–5 years.

PODERI ROCCHE MANZONI VALENTINO
Barolo Riserva* * * */* * * * *, Barolo Riserva DLA Roul* * * *,
Barolo Riserva Vigna Big* * * * *

1989 Barolo Riserva	D 93
1989 Barolo Riserva DLA Roul	D 90?
1989 Barolo Riserva Vigna Big	D 94

This excellent, sometimes superb, producer rarely receives the publicity he merits. I have long thought that Valentino's 1978 Barolo Riserva is about as classic a Barolo as one could find. The 1982s and 1985s were also excellent. While the 1990s were not presented for tasting, three bottles of 1989s proved to be dramatic, head-turning wines with considerable richness and personality. The 1989 Barolo Riserva Vigna Big merits its name. This is a large-scaled, explosively rich, densely concentrated, broad-flavored, compelling Barolo with evidence of small oak cask aging in its toasty, vanillin scents in its otherwise jammy, black cherry–, herb-, and earthy-scented nose. Full bodied and rich, with gobs of glycerin, tannin, extract, and alcohol, this "big" but approachable Barolo should drink well young and last for 20 or more years. The 1989 Barolo Riserva DLA Roul is dominated by toasty new oak aromas. Once past this, the wine offers spectacular concentration, plenty of intensity and body, and a closed but modern international style. With more time in the bottle the oakiness should be less intrusive. This is clearly an outstanding wine. Drink it between 1997 and 2015. In many respects the 1989 Barolo Riserva may be Valentino's most classic expression of Barolo. It offers up a provocative nose of sweet cherries, tar, floral scents, and truffles. Huge, massive, concentrated fruit is buttressed by equally high levels of tannin. Spicy, thick, and rich, with exceptional structure and delineation, this outstanding Barolo is even richer than the stupendous 1978 that I recently drank. Cellar it for 3–5 years and drink it over the subsequent 20 years.

AZ. VIT. ROCHE
Barbera d'Alba* *

1990 Barbera d'Alba	B	66

A musty note in an otherwise green, herbal nose is followed by sharp, high-acid, shrill flavors that insulted my palate. The finish is short and attenuated.

GIGI ROSSO
Barbaresco Viglino* * *, Barbera d'Alba del Buon Ricordo* *, Barolo Cascina Arione* * *, Nebbiolo d'Alba* *

1990 Barbaresco Viglino	C	85
1989 Barbaresco Viglino	C	87
1990 Barbera d'Alba del Buon Ricordo	B	81
1990 Barolo Cascina Arione	C	87
1989 Barolo Cascina Arione	C	86
1990 Nebbiolo d'Alba	B	85

I had a preference for the richer, more complex and aromatic 1989 Barbaresco Viglino over the soft, elegant yet surprisingly light and easygoing 1990 Barbaresco Viglino. Rosso's style emphasizes up-front, precocious drinking in a low-acid, smooth-as-silk format. The 1989 possesses more concentration and ripeness than the round, straightforward 1990. Both wines should be consumed over the next 5–6 years.

Both vintages of Gigi Rosso's Barolo are made in an up-front, soft, fleshy, medium- to full-bodied style with excellent purity, fine ripeness, and a chewy, seductive fruitiness. Although they are not destined to be long-lived, for drinking in their first 7–8 years of life these are attractive wines.

I found the 1990 Barbera d'Alba del Buon Ricordo to be lean, austere, and high in acidity, without much flesh, fruit, or extraction. Cleanly made, it may blossom with several years in the bottle, but it is less intense than many of its siblings from this great Piedmontese vintage.

Rosso's soft, herb- and berry-scented 1990 Nebbiolo d'Alba possesses ripe fruit, medium body, a round softness, and a spicy finish. Drink it over the next 2–3 years.

IL MILIN ROVERO
Barbera d'Asti* * *, Barbera d'Asti Vigneto Gustin* * *

1990 Barbera d'Asti Rouve	B	86
1990 Barbera d'Asti Vigneto Gustin	B	86?

The 1990 Barbera d'Asti Vigneto Gustin will undoubtedly be controversial given its late harvest and its slightly overripe style that offers up copious quantities of jammy fruit, tar, and spice scents. Medium bodied, with soft fruit, this chunky wine should drink well for 5–6 years. Some readers will find the 1990 Barbera d'Asti Rouve superior to my rating because it is a charming, richly fruity, soft, delicious Barbera for drinking over the next 3–4 years. It is not complex, but if a wine were measured on just a hedonistic scale, it would rate a few points higher. It is pure, exuberant, and lively.

ENRICO E GIACOMO SAFFIRIO
Barolo * *

1990 Barolo	C	87
1989 Barolo	C	78

Although the 1989 Barolo was a healthy bottle, the wine was light and shallow, and finished short—hardly a worthy representative of this terrific vintage. The 1990 Barolo I tasted was traditionally styled with a spicy, tar, cherry, prunelike nose, rich, full-bodied, concentrated flavors, and moderate tannin in the rustic finish. It possesses more strength, intensity, and extract than the 1989.

LUCIANO SANDRONE
Barolo * * * *, Barolo Cannubi Boschis * * * * *, Barolo Le Vigne * * * * *,
Dolcetto * * * */* * * * *

1990 Barolo Cannubi Boschis	D	99
1989 Barolo Cannubi Boschis	D	97
1988 Barolo Cannubi Boschis	D	93
1990 Barolo Le Vigne	D	95

In my tasting circle we refer to Luciano Sandrone, one of the finest Barolo producers, as "Super Sandrone." His performances during the decade of the eighties were mind-boggling. The 1989 Barolo Cannubi Boschis is another treasure to be added to Sandrone's impressive résumé. Backward for a 1989, it exhibits a dense purple color, a blossoming nose of smoky new oak, black fruits, and tar, rich, full-bodied, multilayered flavors, and awesome dimension and persistence in the mouth. **A.M.: 1996–2010.**

Sandrone appears to have topped what he achieved in 1982, 1985, 1988, and 1989 with a nearly perfect 1990 Barolo from the Cannubi Boschis vineyard. There are only 1,600 cases of this blockbuster Barolo for the world, but should you have the requisite contacts to be able to latch on to a few bottles, don't hesitate! It is an amazingly rich, superbly balanced, profound Barolo that is crammed with flavor. It exhibits a hauntingly intense bouquet of roses, black cherries, new leather, and a touch of tar. Great richness and extraordinary precision are its hallmarks. This massive wine is a riveting tasting and drinking experience. Do not be misled by the wine's appearance of immediate drinkability. Many of the 1989 and 1990 Barolos are so sweet and precocious there is a temptation to forget how much tannin is buried beneath the decadent levels of fruit. The 1990 Cannubi Boschis should peak in 7–10 years and last for at least 20 or more. An awesome effort! In 1990 Sandrone also produced 100 cases of a single-vineyard Barolo called Le Vigne. Although more developed and less tannic and muscular than the Cannubi Boschis, it is a spectacularly ripe, rich, unctuously textured wine that is gorgeous to smell and taste.

The 1988 Cannubi Boschis promises to rival his 1985, but will it be as stunning as his 1982? Traditionally styled, the 1988 is unbelievably intense, with a super nose of damp earth and black fruits. There is sensational chewy, ripe, opulent fruit, softer tannins than many producers appear to have obtained, and a massively long, heady finish. Approachable now, this wine should hit its peak of maturity in 3–4 years and last for up to 15.

CANTINE SANT'EVASIO
Barbera d'Alba Rosignolo * * * *

1990 Barbera d'Alba Rosignolo	C	90

This Barbera from the Nizza Monferrato region is stylishly packaged in a 500-milliliter bottle. It is an impressively endowed wine with a saturated dark ruby/purple color, a moderately intense nose of black fruits and spices, full-bodied, ripe, highly extracted flavors, and crisp acidity. This large-scaled Barbera should drink well for at least a decade. Wow!

SCAGLIOLA
Barbera d'Asti* *

1990 Barbera d'Asti	B	76

First, the good news. This wine is cleanly made, with decent color, medium body, and some spicy notes. The bad news is that it lacks concentration and is high in acidity, and that the finish consists mainly of alcohol and acid.

GIANCARLO SCAGLIONE
Le Grive Vino da Tavola* * * *

1990 Le Grive Vino da Tavola	D	91

An immensely impressive, dry red wine, this Vino da Tavola from Piedmont exhibits a saturated dark ruby/purple color, and a spicy, Pomerol/St.-Émilion–like nose of cedar, jammy plums, and black cherries. Full bodied and opulent, with layers of rich, creamy fruit, this pure, well-focused, mouth-filling, surprisingly elegant wine should drink well for 10–12 years.

SCARPA
Barbaresco* * *, Barbaresco Payore Barberis di Treiso* * *, Barolo Boscaretti di Serralunga d'Alba* * */* * * *, Barolo I Tetti di Neive* * *, Rouchet Vino da Tavola* * *

1990 Rouchet Vino da Tavola	C	87

Scarpa usually makes impossibly backward, tough-textured red wines, so what a delight it was to find his 1990 Rouchet so enjoyable. It is bursting with sweet red and black fruits, and has a supple texture, plenty of body, and moderate alcohol levels. This delicious, exuberantly fruity, medium- to full-bodied wine should drink well for 4–6 years.

ENRICO SCAVINO
Barbera Carati* * * *, Barolo* * * *, Barolo Bric del Fiasc* * * * *, Barolo Cannubi* * * * *

1991 Barbera Carati	C	84
1990 Barbera Carati	C	88
1990 Barolo	D	92
1989 Barolo	D	90
1990 Barolo Bric del Fiasc	D	96
1989 Barolo Bric del Fiasc	D	93+
1988 Barolo Bric del Fiasc	D	90
1990 Barolo Cannubi	D	95
1989 Barolo Cannubi	D	96
1988 Barolo Cannubi	D	87

Scavino's single-vineyard 1991 Barbera Carati is a successful wine for this mediocre vintage. The wine reveals evidence of new oak in its smoky, toasty nose, and possesses ripe fruit, medium body, good ripeness, and a spicy, compact finish. It is one of the better Barberas I tasted from the 1991 vintage. The 1990 Barbera Carati exhibits a dense purple color, a fragrant nose of red and black fruits, spices, and herbs, a gorgeously rich, medium- to full-bodied, chewy texture, superlative fruit extraction, and a spicy, rich finish. Drink it over the next 7–8 years.

Scavino's 1990 Barolos are immense, statuesque wines of exceptional richness and complexity. The softest, most fragrant, and the one most ready for prime-time drinking is the 1990 Barolo. The dark ruby/garnet color is followed by a sweet nose of nuts, cedar, fruitcake, and black fruits. This soft, opulent, full-bodied, luscious wine should drink well for at least a decade. The 1990 Barolo Cannubi is a stunningly elegant wine with greater depth and richness than the regular cuvée. It offers a fascinating display of grace allied to considerable power and richness. The fruit's sweetness (from low yields and ripe grapes) is marvelous to behold. This flashy, complex wine is approachable now, yet capable of lasting for 10–15 years. The 1990 Barolo Bric del Fiasc boasts the most saturated color of this impressive trio. The bouquet suggests a flattering, up-front style of wine in its complex nose of Asian spices, smoky new oak, black cherries, and herbs. This wine possesses great density along with considerable structure and plenty of tannin. The formidable finish offers copious quantities of jammy fruit, glycerin, and heady alcohol. Drink this blockbuster Barolo between 1997 and 2010.

Scavino's three 1989 Barolos are spectacular. The 1989 Barolo has an earthy, meaty, gamelike nose with tremendous fruit, long, rich, supple, dense flavors, plenty of alcohol and glycerin, and a lusty yet supple finish. It should drink well for 12–15 years. The 1989 Barolo Cannubi is a legend in the making. Its spectacular nose of sweet black fruits, licorice, grilled meats, and smoky new oak is followed by a wine with immense richness, stunning opulence, a multidimensional personality, and a spectacularly long, well-delineated finish. Approachable now, it promises to drink well and even to improve for another 15–20 years. The 1989 Barolo Bric del Fiasc is also rich and full, but more backward, revealing more tannin than the other two 1989 offerings. After 5–6 years of cellaring, it should rival the 1989 Barolo Cannubi. These are the finest Barolos I have tasted from Scavino.

Scavino's 1988 Barolo Bric del Fiasc exhibits an intense ruby color that is followed by an elegant, spicy, herbal, cherry-scented nose intermingled with aromas of earth and roasted nuts. A full-bodied, extremely tannic feel accompanies ripe, superbly extracted flavors. The wine is tight but promising. Drink it now through 2005. Given its huge overlay of tannin, the 1988 Barolo Cannubi reveals a traditional style of winemaking. It is less flattering and the wine is even tighter and more austere than the Barolo Bric del Fiasc. Nevertheless, aromas of almonds, cherries, and tar are present in this classic Barolo. Drinkable now, it will last through 2005.

MAURO SEBASTE
Barolo Le Coste * * *

1989 Barolo Le Coste   C   87

I was impressed with this wine's deep, fragrant, black cherry–scented nose, supple, medium- to full-bodied flavors, excellent purity, and fine delineation. Drink this modern-style, flavorful, medium-weight Barolo over the next decade.

SYLLA SEBASTE
Barolo Bussia * *

1989 Barolo Bussia   C   85

A soft, spicy, ripe wine with good concentration, medium body, low acidity, and an easygoing finish, this 1989 lacks the profound richness, structure, and concentration of many top Barolos. Nevertheless, it is elegant, attractive, and ideal for drinking over the next 6–7 years.

ALDO & RICARDO SEGHESIO
Barbera* * *, Barolo La Villa* * * */* * * * *, Dolcetto d'Alba* * *

1991 Barbera	C	86
1990 Barolo La Villa	D	96
1989 Barolo La Villa	D	93+
1988 Barolo La Villa	D	92

This tiny producer in Monforte has turned out three deeply colored, magnificent examples of Barolo. The 1988 La Villa exhibits a telltale Barolo nose of jammy Bing cherries, dried pit fruit, almonds, and tar. In the mouth, there is superlative richness, a full-bodied, moderately tannic, chewy texture, and an intense, robust finish. It should be at its best between now and 2008. The 1989 La Villa is a spectacular example of this terrific vintage. With a deep ruby color, and a bouquet that soars from the glass, offering scents of sweet, jammy, cherry fruit, almonds, smoke, and truffles, this wine displays fabulous fruit, full body, and a tremendously powerful, rich, moderately tannic finish. It is impressive now, and will be at its best through 2012. The 1990 Barolo La Villa is another blockbuster Barolo from this incredible vintage. Its massive size and awesome aging potential are typical of many Barolos from Monforte d'Alba. The opaque dark purple color, stunning nose, and sweet black fruits are followed by a full-throttle, large-scaled wine with spectacular concentration. For its immense size the wine is extraordinarily well balanced, with plenty of sweet fruit, as well as high but ripe tannin. Drink it between 1999 and 2025.

Seghesio's 1991 Barbera is a smoky, herb-, almost tomato-scented wine with tasty, rich, soft, supple fruit, and a moderately long finish. Drink it over the next 4–5 years.

AURELIO SETTIMO
Barolo* * *, Barolo Vigneti Rocche* * * *

1989 Barolo	C	87
1989 Barolo Vigneti Rocche	C	89

These are two excellent wines that admirably display the vintage's superripe, rich, opulent qualities, and high alcohol and extract levels. The 1989 Barolo is a soft, smooth-textured wine with excellent ripeness, gobs of fat, juicy, tobacco, coffee, and berry fruitiness, good cleanliness, and plenty of stuffing. Drink it over the next 8–9 years. The 1989 Barolo Vigneti Rocche possesses more structure, a more persuasive inner core of herb-tinged, jammy, black cherry, fruit, excellent depth, full body, and a forceful, aromatic bouquet of tobacco, cedar, and black fruits. Drink it over the next 15 years.

SIGILLA DELL'ABATE
Barolo Riserva* * *

1989 Barolo Riserva	C	87

Jammy, sweet, superripe scents of herb-tinged black cherries and spices tumble out of the glass. Rich, medium to full bodied, with excellent depth, and a spicy, moderately long finish, this wine is soft enough to be drunk now but will keep for 10–15 years.

EMILIANA MARTINI SONVICO
Barbera d'Asti Superiore Vigna dell'Angelo* * *

1990 Barbera d'Asti Superiore Vigna dell'Angelo	B	86

This attractive, supple, well-focused, rich wine offers a dark ruby/purple color and a nose of ripe fruit and spice. Medium to full bodied, with excellent extraction and purity, it should be drunk over the next 5–7 years.

SOTTIMANO
Barbaresco Brichet* * *

1989 Barbaresco Brichet	C 87+?

This eccentric-smelling and -tasting wine stood out in my tastings as being different from its peers. While the wine reveals the sweet, jammy, cherry character of the 1989 vintage, it also possesses pronounced, atypical evergreen forest aromas. The wine exhibits excellent concentration, medium to full body, and moderate tannin in the long finish. Although it should drink well for the next 10–12 years, it will be controversial given its kinky aromatic profile.

TENUTA LA TENAGLIA
Emozioni Vino da Tavola* * * *, Giorgio Tenaglia Vino da Tavola* * * *

1990 Emozioni Vino da Tavola	D 90
1990 Giorgio Tenaglia Vino da Tavola	D 89

Proprietor Paolo Boselli fashioned a rich, concentrated, full-bodied 1990 Giorgio Tenaglia Vino da Tavola. It boasts an impressive ruby/purple color, some spicy, smoky new oak intertwined with scents of black currants and licorice, a smooth texture, moderate tannin, and plenty of alcohol and depth. Drinkable now, this rich wine should continue to evolve for a decade. The appropriately named 1990 Emozioni is an impressive, rich, full-bodied wine bursting with black currant and black cherry fruit. A gentle use of toasty new oak barrels adds to the wine's intense concentration. Pure and full bodied, with stunning precision and admirable fruit extraction, this sweet (from low yields, not residual sugar) wine offers a wonderful, chewy, expansive palate. It is an immensely impressive Piedmontese Vino da Tavola that should drink well for 7–12 years.

TERRA DA VINO
Barbera d'Asti La Luna e I Falò* * * *

1990 Barbera d'Asti La Luna e I Falò	C 88
1989 Barolo Parussi	C 89

I am not sure whether this is the same producer as the Terra da Barolo, which is a co-op. The 1989 Barolo Parussi is a delicious effort, as the wine offers evidence of small oak cask aging with its smoky, vanillin, sweet, jammy, red and black fruit–scented nose. Medium to full bodied, with round, opulent flavors, and a generous finish, this delicious Barolo is ready to drink. It should last for 10 years.

This impressive, well-endowed, dark ruby/purple-colored 1990 Barbera d'Asti La Luna e I Falò displays evidence of aging in new oak casks given the vanillin, smoky notes in its bouquet and flavors. Full bodied, rich, and supple, it is ideal for drinking over the next 7–8 years.

TERRICCI
Terricci Vino da Tavola* * *

1990 Terricci Vino da Tavola	C 85

This slightly hard, spicy, leathery, earthy wine possesses a solid ruby color, medium body, firm tannin, and a structured, concentrated feel. It should blossom over the next 12 months and last for 5–7 years.

AZIENDA TRINCHERO
Barbera d'Asti La Barslina* * *

1990 Barbera d'Asti La Barslina	C	88

This lavishly fruity, medium- to full-bodied Barbera has immense appeal given its purity, lushness, and gorgeously ripe, concentrated fruit. There are no hard edges to this silky-textured wine. Low acidity, excellent ripeness, and overall intensity will provide delicious drinking over the next 5–6 years.

G. D. VAJRA
Barbera d'Alba Riserva Bricco della Viole* * * * *, Barolo Bricco della Viole* * * * *

1990 Barbera d'Alba Riserva Bricco della Viole	C	94+

Twenty years from now, long after this review has been forgotten, somebody will discover a bottle of this wine languishing in the corner of a dark, damp cellar and will be blown away by its quality. This tiny producer has turned out a majestically rich, full-bodied, blockbuster Barbera that requires 5 more years of cellaring. It displays an opaque purple color, and intense, awesomely concentrated flavors that need to be tasted to be believed. Clearly made from what must have been late-harvested grapes, it is remarkably rich, with low acidity, and sensational extract. With spectacular purity, richness, and full-bodied intensity, it should be a profound wine, provided its purchasers have patience.

VASELLI SANTA GIULIA
Rosso* * *

1990 Rosso	C	86

Made from a Sangiovese/Cabernet Sauvignon blend, this 1990 Rosso offers attractive berry fruit in its light-intensity, spicy, subtly herbaceous nose. The wine possesses medium body, a round, easygoing personality, and a fine, slightly alcoholic finish. Drink it over the next 4–5 years.

VIARENGO E FIGLIO
Barbera d'Asti Il Fale* * *, Barbera d'Asti Il Fale Superiore* * * *, Barbera d'Asti Morra* * *

1990 Barbera d'Asti Il Fale	C	86
1990 Barbera d'Asti Il Fale Superiore	C	90
1990 Barbera d'Asti Morra	C	86

The Il Fale exhibits loads of ripe berry fruit, soft, medium to full body, and fine focus, clarity, and purity. It is a delicious, up-front Barbera for drinking over the next 4–5 years. The nearly outstanding Il Fale Superiore possesses a deeper color, and a touch of vanillin to accompany the abundant quantities of sweet, ripe, red and black fruits. Full bodied, surprisingly opulent, rich, and already delicious, it should age effortlessly for a decade. The 1990 Barbera d'Asti Morra is a soft, gentle, lusciously fruity wine with excellent ripeness, and a flattering, up-front appeal. Round and fruity, with low acidity, it should be consumed over the next 4–5 years. These are impressive Barberas!

GIOVANNI VIBERTI
Barbera d'Alba Bricco Airoli* *, Barolo Bricco Viotta* *, Barolo San Pietro* *,
Barolo La Volta* *

1990 Barbera d'Alba Bricco Airoli	B	62?
1989 Barolo Bricco Viotta	D	85?

1989 Barolo San Pietro	D	80
1989 Barolo La Volta	D	77

Given the superlative quality of the 1989 vintage, these Barolos lack concentration. My favorite, which is destined to be controversial, is the 1989 Barolo Bricco Viotta, a sweet, round, generous, soft wine. Although it exhibits excellent fruit, there is an intensely herbaceous, vegetal character. The 1989 Barolo San Pietro also reveals an herbaceous side, less concentration, and enough fruit to give it straightforward appeal. Drink it over the next 5–6 years. The 1989 Barolo La Volta lacks concentration and finishes short, without any complexity or intensity.

The 1990 Barbera d'Alba Bricco Airoli revealed a stinky lees smell, as well as a sharp and acidic character. It was nearly unpalatable. Unfortunately, I was able to taste only one bottle.

LUIGI VIBERTI
Barbera d'Alba Vigna Clara * * * *, Barolo * * * */* * * * *

1990 Barbera d'Alba Vigna Clara	C	90
1990 Barolo	D	90
1989 Barolo	D	90

Both the 1990 and 1989 Barolos are made in the modern style, emphasizing superb purity of fruit, rich sweetness (from physiologically mature grapes), soft tannin, and low acidity. Perhaps because it has a year of bottle age, the 1989 Barolo displays a complex bouquet of smoky, tar-scented black fruits. Full bodied, with layers of flavor, it is a beautifully made, supple Barolo for drinking over the next 10–12 years. The similarly styled 1990 Barolo is less complex, probably because it is younger. Wonderfully rich, and full bodied, with excellent purity and delineation to its generously endowed personality, it should also drink well for 12 or more years.

The sexy, voluptuously textured, concentrated 1990 Barbera d'Alba Vigna Clara is oozing with ripe fruit. It reveals a spicy, black fruit–scented nose, stunning flavor richness, and an extravagant lushness. A thrilling, crowd-pleasing Barbera, it should drink well for 7–8 years.

VIETTI
Barbaresco Masseria * * * *, Barbera d'Alba Pian Romulado * * *, Barbera d'Alba
Scarrone * * *, Barolo Brunate * * * * *, Barolo Castiglione * * * *, Barolo Lazzarito * * * *,
Barolo Rocche * * * * *, Barolo Villero * * * *

1989 Barbaresco Masseria	D	92
1988 Barbaresco Masseria	D	90
1991 Barbera d'Alba Pian Romulado	C	84
1990 Barbera d'Alba Pian Romulado	C	87
1990 Barbera d'Alba Scarrone	C	85
1990 Barolo Brunate	D	93
1989 Barolo Brunate	D	93+
1988 Barolo Brunate	D	90+
1989 Barolo Castiglione	D	92
1990 Barolo Lazzarito	D	89
1989 Barolo Lazzarito	D	89

1990 Barolo Rocche	E	93
1989 Barolo Rocche	E	94
1988 Barolo Rocche	E	92+

Alfredo Currado is one of the great gentlemen of Piedmont, so it is delightful to share with readers the enthusiastic reviews that follow. The 1989 is a superb Barbaresco Masseria. It offers a blockbuster nose of tar, black cherries, and spice, and a fabulously rich, full-bodied, highly extracted palate. This superconcentrated, huge Barbaresco can be drunk now or cellared for 20 years.

Currado (or Vietti, as most people mistakenly call him) has turned out four superb Barolos in 1989 that possess subtle differences in their flavor and aromatic profiles. The softest, most flattering is the 1989 Barolo Lazzarito. Voluptuous, rich, and concentrated, with a textbook Barolo nose of rose petals, tar, and sweet cherry fruit intermingled with scents of smoky tobacco, the wine offers excellent concentration, full body, moderate tannin, and a long, lusty finish. Approachable now, it possesses the most precocious personality of these four wines and is best drunk within the first 15 years of life. The 1989 Barolo Brunate is a huge, massive, tannic powerhouse, with great depth, superb definition, and gobs of earthy, black cherry, and tarlike flavors. There is a sweetness to its inner core of concentrated fruit. The wine's finish lingers for almost a minute. Although it can be drunk now, 3–5 years of cellaring will be beneficial. Readers who have cold cellars will be delighted to hear that this is a 20+-year wine. In comparison, the 1989 Barolo Castiglione is as rich and concentrated, but less structured and sweeter and more succulent. It is a gorgeously proportioned, rich, hedonistic Barolo. While it appears to possess less tannin, the massive amount of fruit may be hiding more tannin than it currently reveals. It is a great full-bodied, wonderfully pure Barolo for drinking over the next two decades. It may be splitting hairs, but the 1989 Barolo Rocche appears to be the richest, and most massive, structured, and backward of these offerings. Huge and thick, with the classic nose of roasted herb, tar, rose petal, and black cherry scents, the wine offers layers of lavishly concentrated, ripe fruit, huge body, significant tannin, and a blockbuster finish. This is one Vietti Barolo that will require 7–8 years of cellaring. It has the potential to last for up to 30 years.

With respect to the three 1990 Barolos I tasted from Vietti, the 1990 Barolo Lazzarito displays an attractive nose of roasted, melted tar, black fruit, and almond scents, excellent richness, medium to full body, and a soft, heady, alcoholic finish. An excellent wine, it may merit an outstanding score, but in my tasting it was significantly less profound than the two other offerings. The 1990 Barolo Brunate is extremely ripe and deep, with layers of glycerin-imbued, rich fruit, full body, gobs of tannin, and a massive finish that lasts for 60 seconds. It possesses the telltale smoky ripeness and jammy richness of the 1990 vintage, as well as plenty of structure. Drink it between 1997 and 2020. Also full bodied and rich, the 1990 Barolo Rocche is more structured and tannic than the Brunate, as well as awesomely concentrated, with huge extract, and a monstrously long, thick, blockbuster finish. It will merit aging until the turn of the century, after which it will last for 20–25 years.

Vietti's 1988s are classic wines from this traditional Piedmontese winemaker. They are big, forceful, tannic wines that are meant to be cellared. The 1988 Barbaresco Masseria exhibits a dusty, dark ruby color, a jammy, black cherry– and roasted nut–scented nose, rich, powerful, full-bodied flavors, and tons of tannin in the relatively hard, tough finish. A.M.: 1997–2012. The 1988 Barolo Rocche has a similar color, as well as a classic Barolo nose of roses, tar, and black cherry fruit. Rich and full bodied, with significant tannins and crisp acidity, this wine finishes with considerable muscle, with most of its exceptional richness perceived at the end of the palate. Do not touch a bottle before 1998;

it should keep for 15–25 years thereafter. The similarly styled 1988 Barolo Brunate is broodingly backward, tannic, dense, full bodied, and loaded with extract. It will need another 5–6 years in the cellar. **A.M.: 1998–2012.**

Vietti's 1991 Barbera d'Alba from the excellent Pian Romulado vineyard is lighter than usual, with an austere personality. I do not anticipate the emergence of more fruit, so drink it up over the next several years. The 1990 Barbera d'Alba Pian Romulado is more typical of what proprietor Alfredo Currado can produce. It exhibits a saturated dark ruby/purple color, a spicy, herb-, vanilla-, and black fruit–scented nose, medium to full body, adequate acidity, and plenty of glycerin and alcohol in the gutsy finish. Still young, it promises to keep for 10–15 years.

The 1990 Barbera d'Alba Scarrone tastes more backward, with more leafy tobacco and herbal scents. It is medium bodied, with fine concentration, but a degree of hardness bordering on astringency lowered my rating.

CANTINE VIGNAIOLI
Barbaresco * *

1990 Barbaresco	C	86
1989 Barbaresco	C	83
1989 Barbaresco Vigneto Castellizzano	C	86

These two 1989s are among the most developed Barbarescos I tasted. Both wines offer medium ruby colors, soft, supple textures, and generous amounts of spicy, tobacco-scented, cherry fruit. The 1989 regular Barbaresco does not possess the stuffing and opulence of the medium- to full-bodied 1989 Vigneto Castellizzano Barbaresco. My instincts suggest both wines should be consumed over the next 5–7 years.

The 1990 Barbaresco exhibits a red and black fruit–scented nose with elements of smoke and herbs. Fat and ripe, this chewy, soft Barbaresco will offer delicious drinking during its first 6–8 years of life.

VILLA ILE
Barbera d'Alba Garassino * *

1990 Barbera d'Alba Garassino	B	78+

This wine tasted atypical for the vintage. Although it possesses good saturation and ripeness, it has high acidity, a backward, impenetrable personality, and little charm or finesse. It is hard to know what will emerge with aging.

VILLA MONTERSINO
Barolo * *

1989 Barolo	C	85

This lighter-styled Barolo offers attractive tarry, spicy, fruity scents, medium body, fine ripeness, and a soft, straightforward finish. In most vintages it would be considered a very good wine, but in the context of what was achieved in 1989 and 1990, it comes across as tasty but compact and one-dimensional.

VINCHIO E VAGLIO
Barbera d'Asti Superiore Vigne Vecchie * * * *

1990 Barbera d'Asti Superiore Vigne Vecchie	C	89

This excellent wine reveals obvious signs of aging in new oak casks. The dense ruby/purple color is followed by a big, spicy, herb- and black fruit–scented nose, rich, full-bodied, multidimensional flavors, wonderful length and opulence, and impressive purity. Drink it over the next 7–10 years.

GIANNI VOERZIO
Barolo La Serra * * *

1990 Barolo La Serra	D 87
1989 Barolo La Serra	D 86

Both vintages of Gianni Voerzio's Barolo La Serra are made in a modern style, emphasizing toasty new oak, ripe, supple black fruit flavors, low acidity, and a fleshy, user-friendly finish. The 1990 exhibits slightly more depth. Both wines should be drunk over the next 7–8 years.

ROBERTO VOERZIO
Barbera d'Alba Vignasse * * * */* * * * *, Barolo Brunate * * * * *, Barolo Cerequio * * * * *,
Barolo La Serra * * * * *, Dolcetto d'Alba Privino * * * *, Vignaserra Vino da Tavola * * * *

1990 Barbera d'Alba Vignasse	C 90
1990 Barolo Brunate	D 93
1989 Barolo Brunate	D 92
1990 Barolo Cerequio	D 95
1989 Barolo Cerequio	D 90
1990 Barolo La Serra	D 92
1989 Barolo La Serra	D 93
1990 Vignaserra Vino da Tavola	D 88

These wines from Roberto Voerzio combine the best of the modern style in their purity and toasty new oak, with the finest components—strength, richness, and power—of the traditional school. They are exceptional in both the 1989 and 1990 vintages. All eight wines share a splendid opulence, purity, superrichness, and lusciousness.

In 1989, the most tannic wine is the Barolo Brunate. Full bodied and spicy, with a pervasive, herb-, cedar-, and black cherry–scented nose, and dense, muscular, massive flavors, it will require 3–4 years of cellaring and will keep for 20. The 1989 Barolo La Serra is explosively ripe and supple, with a smoky, exotic nose, dense, chewy, fleshy, flamboyant flavors, and a succulent, juicy finish. Sexy and appealing now, this wine should continue to drink well for 15 years. Moderately tannic and slightly less concentrated than the Brunate and La Serra is the 1989 Barolo Cerequio. It offers a decadent nose of jammy, sweet black cherry fruit and spice. Ripe, full bodied, and rich, this is a wine to drink over the next 12–15 years.

Among the 1990s, I thought the 1990 Barolo La Serra to be extremely voluptuous in texture and seductive in style with a fragrant, sweet cherry, herb, and coffeelike nose, and spicy, full-bodied, moderately tannic flavors. While the wine can be approached now, it will benefit from 2–3 years of cellaring; it will last for 15 years. The powerful 1990 Barolo Brunate reveals more tannin than the other cuvées, as well as splendid levels of rich, chewy fruit. Cellar it for 3–4 years and consume it over the following 15. Lastly, Roberto Voerzio's 1990 Barolo Cerequio is the darkest-colored 1990, with a profound nose of roses, hickory smoke, and black cherries. Full bodied, with magnificent concentration and great delineation, this awesome Barolo appears to have a slight edge on its two impressive siblings. Kudos to this Piedmont producer's efforts over recent vintages.

The 1990 Barbera d'Alba Vignasse is a knockout example of this underrated and generally overlooked varietal. It exhibits a dense purple color, a big, rich, ripe nose of black fruits, stunning concentration and extract, full body, enough crisp acidity to give focus and vibrance to the wine's flavors, and a long finish. This sensational Barbera should drink well for 10–15 years. Bravo!

The 1990 Nebbiolo/Barbera blend, Vignaserra Vino da Tavola, is a lusciously fruity, medium- to full-bodied, soft wine that is ideal for drinking over the next 5–6 years. Think of it as the Pomerol of Piedmont! It possesses savory jammy, berry fruit buttressed by attractive spice and underlying acidity. With noticeable alcoholic clout, it is immensely satisfying on a hedonistic level, as well as full of personality.

TUSCANY

The Basics

TYPES OF WINE

Beautiful Tuscany is the home of Italy's most famous wine, Chianti, and one of Italy's most celebrated wines, Brunello di Montalcino. Both wines can be either horrendous or splendid. Quality is shockingly irregular. Yet it is in Tuscany that Italy's wine revolution is being fought, with adventurous and innovative producers cavalierly turning their backs on the archaic regulations that govern wine production. They are making wines, often based on Cabernet Sauvignon, Merlot, and Sangiovese, aged in small oak casks, filled with flavor and personality, and put in designer bottles. I disagree completely with those critics who have called them French look-alikes, and though entitled to be called only Vino da Tavola, they represent some of the most exciting red wines made in the world. The same cannot be said for Tuscany's white wines. Except for the light, tasty whites called Vernaccia from the medieval hill fortress of San Gimignano, Tuscan whites are ultraneutral, boring wines. Shame on those producers who package these wines in lavish-looking bottles that are appallingly overpriced.

GRAPE VARIETIES

The principal and greatest red wine grape of Tuscany is Sangiovese. The highest-yielding, most insipid wine from Sangiovese comes from the most widely planted clone called Sangiovese Romano. The better producers are using clones of Sangiovese with names such as Sangioveto, Prugnolo, and Brunello. These all produce a richer, deeper, more complex wine. Of course, Cabernet Sauvignon, Merlot, Cabernet Franc, and even Pinot Noir and Syrah are making their presence felt in Tuscany.

As for the white wines, there is the sharp, uninteresting Trebbiano, produced in ocean-sized quantities. Trebbiano is an inferior grape and the results are distressingly innocuous wines. Vernaccia has potential, and of course there are such international bluebloods as Chardonnay and Sauvignon Blanc. Tuscany, in my mind, means red not white wine, but if you are inclined to try a white wine, then take a look at my list of recommended producers for Vernaccia di San Gimignano.

FLAVORS

Chianti Classico It is virtually impossible to provide specific information given the extraordinary range in quality—from musty, poorly vinified, washed-out wines to ones with soft, supple, raspberry, chestnut, and tobacco flavors, crisp acidity, medium body, and a fine finish. Stick to only the recommended producers that are listed subsequently. Remember, at least 50% of wines called Chianti, despite tighter regulations governing quality, are thin, acidic, and unpleasant.

Brunello di Montalcino It should be rich, powerful, tannic, superbly concentrated, and heady, with a huge, spicy bouquet of smoky tobacco, meat, and dried red fruits. Only a few are. Most close encounters offer an alarming degree of tannin and musty old oak to the detriment of fruit. Selection is critical. Rosso di Montalcino is red wine made from the Brunello clone of Sangiovese that is not aged long enough to qualify as Brunello di Montalcino. It is often much less expensive and considerably fresher.

Carmignano This is an underrated viticultural area wherein the wines show good fruit, balance, and character. The best of them behave like Chiantis with more character and structure. Not surprisingly, Carmignano is made from Sangiovese with 10%–15% Cabernet added.

Vernaccia di San Gimignano Tuscany's best dry white table wine, this nutty, zesty, dry, fruity white is meant to be drunk within 2–3 years of the vintage. It is a satisfying rather than thrilling wine.

Vino Nobile di Montepulciano A neighbor of Chianti with identical characteristics (the grape is the same), Vino Nobile di Montepulciano costs more but rarely provides more flavor or pleasure.

Morellino di Scansano This is an emerging viticultural region south of Siena. I have tasted the wines from only a few estates, but it appears this is an area that requires more attention. Made from Sangiovese, Morellino di Scansano may be the frugal consumer's alternative to Brunello di Montalcino. The wines are rich, expansive, and, for now, undervalued!

Other Tuscan Whites The names Bianco di Pitigliano, Bianco Vergine della Valdichiana, Galestro, Montecarlo, Pomino, and any Tuscan producer's name plus the word *bianco* translate into wines that taste wretchedly neutral and bland, and provide no more flavor than a glass of water. Sadly, most of them cost $12–$25, so the operative words are *caveat emptor!*

Vino da Tavolas The most thrilling red wines of Tuscany are the designer show wines that are being made by Tuscany's most innovative growers. They can be 100% Cabernet Sauvignon, 100% Sangiovese, or a blend of these two grapes plus Cabernet Franc. Even some Merlot, Syrah, and Pinot Noir can now be found. They are usually aged in mostly new French oak casks. Top Tuscan vintages, such as 1982, 1985, 1988, and 1990, can offer sensational aromatic dimension and remarkable flavor breadth. Following are the best-known Vino da Tavolas, their top vintages, and grapes used.

GUIDE TO THE BEST-KNOWN VINO DA TAVOLAS

NAME	PRODUCER	TOP VINTAGES	PRIMARY GRAPE	RATING
Acciaiolo	Fattoria di Albola	1990, 1988	Sangiovese	***
Agricoltori del Geografico	Geografico	1990, 1988	Cabernet/Sangiovese	****
Alte d'Altesi	Altesino	1990, 1988	Sangiovese	****
Altero	Poggio Antico	1988	Sangiovese	****
Anagallis	Lilliano	1990, 1988	Sangiovese	****
Ania	Gabbiano	1990, 1988	Cabernet Sauvignon	***

NAME	PRODUCER	TOP VINTAGES	PRIMARY GRAPE	RATING
Armonia	Querciavalle	1990, 1988	Sangiovese/Canaiolo	***
Balifico	Castello di Volpaia	1990, 1988	Sangiovese	****
Barco Reale	Capezzana	1990, 1988	Cabernet Sauvignon	***
Bel Convento	Del Roseti	1988	Sangiovese	**
Bianchi-V. Scanni	Monsanto	1990, 1988	Sangiovese	***/****
Predicatodi Biturica	Geografico	1990, 1988	Sangiovese	***
Boro Cepparello	Isole e Olena	1990, 1988	Sangiovese	***
Boscarelli	Boscarelli	1990, 1988	Sangiovese	****
Brancaia	Fonterutoli	1990	Sangiovese	***
Bruscone dei Barbi	Barbi	1990, 1988	Sangiovese	**
Buriano	Rocca di Castagnoli	1990	Cabernet Sauvignon	***
Ca' del Pazzo	Caparzo	1990, 1988	Sangiovese	****
Cabernet Sauvignon	Altesino	1990, 1988	Cabernet Sauvignon	****
Cabernet Sauvignon	Avignonesi	1990, 1988	Cabernet Sauvignon	****
Cabreo Il Borgo	Ruffino	1988	Cabernet Sauvignon/ Sangiovese	***
Cabreo Vigneto	Ruffino	1990, 1988	Sangiovese	***
Campaccio Barrique	Terrabianca	1988	Sangiovese	*****
Cancelli	Badia a Coltibuono	1990	Sangiovese	***
Capannelle Barrique	Rossetti	1990, 1988	Sangiovese	***
Capannelle Rosso	Capannelle	1990, 1988	Sangiovese	***
Capannelle Rosso	Rossetti	1990, 1988	Sangiovese	***
Carmartina	Fattoria Querciabella	1990, 1988	Sangiovese	***
Carmerlengo	Pagliarese	1990, 1988	Sangiovese	**/***
Case Via	Fontodi	1990	Syrah	****
Castruccio	Castruccio	1990	Sangiovese	***
Cerviolo	San Fabiano Calcinaia	1988	Sangiovese	***/****
Cetinaia	San Polo	1990, 1988	Sangiovese	**
Cignale	Castello di Querceto	1990, 1988	Cabernet Sauvignon	****/*****
Cipresso	Terrabianco	?	Sangiovese	*****
Colle Picchioni- Vassallo	Paola di Mauro	1990, 1988	Sangiovese	**
Collezione de Marchi l'Ermo	Isole e Olena	1990, 1988	Syrah	****
Coltassala	Castello di Volpaia	1990, 1988	Sangiovese	****
Coltibuono Rosso	Badia a Coltibuono	1990, 1988	Sangiovese	***
I Coltri Rosso	Melini	1990, 1988	Cabernet Sauvignon/ Sangiovese	**

NAME	PRODUCER	TOP VINTAGES	PRIMARY GRAPE	RATING
Colvecchio	Banfi	1990	Syrah	**
Concerto	Fonterutoli	1990, 1988	Sangiovese	***
Coniale di Castellare	Castellare di Castellina	1990, 1988	Cabernet Sauvignon/ Sangiovese	****/****
Cortaccio	Villa Cafaggio	1990, 1988	Cabernet Sauvignon	*****
La Corte	Castello di Querceto	1990, 1988	Sangiovese	****
Donna Marzia	Giuseppe Zecca	1990, 1988	Sangiovese	**
Elegia	Poliziano	1990, 1988	Prugnolo	****
Etrusco	Cannatoio	1990	Sangiovese	**
Farnito	Capineto	1990	Cabernet Sauvignon	****
Flaccianello	Fontodi	1990, 1988	Sangiovese	****
Fontalloro	Felsina Berardenga	1990, 1988	Sangiovese	****
Gerardino	Vignamaggio	1988	Sangiovese	***
Geremia	Castello di Cacchiano	1990, 1988	Sangiovese	***
Geremia	E. Ricasoli-Firidolfi	1988	Sangioveto/Canaiolo	*****
Ghiaie della Furba	Cappezzana	1990, 1988	Cabernet Sauvignon	***/****
La Giola di Riecine	Riecine	1990, 1988	Sangiovese	****
Granchiaia	Le Macie	1990, 1988	Sangiovese	**
Grattamacco	Podere Grattamacco	1990, 1988	Sangiovese	**
Grifi	Avignonesi	1990, 1988	Sangiovese	****
Grosso Senese	Il Palazzino	1990, 1988	Sangiovese	****/*****
Isole e Olena Rosso	Isole e Olena	1990, 1988	Sangiovese	**
Liano	Umberto Cesari	1990, 1988	Sangiovese	**
Logaiolo	Fattoria dell'Aiola	1990, 1988	Sangiovese	**
Maestro Raro	Felsina	1990, 1988	Cabernet Sauvignon	****/*****
Magiolo	Castelli del Grevepesa	1990	Cabernet Sauvignon/ Sangiovese	***
Marzeno di Marzeno	Zerbina	1990, 1988	Sangiovese	**
Masso Tondo	Le Corti	1990, 1988	Sangiovese	****
Merlot	Avignonesi	1990, 1988	Merlot	****
Merlot	Castelgiocondo	1990	Merlot	***/****
Monte Antico	Monte Antico	1990, 1988	Sangiovese	****
Monte Vertine	Monte Vertine	1990, 1988	Sangiovese	***
Mormoreto	Frescobaldi	1990, 1988	Cabernet Sauvignon/ Sangiovese	***
Nemo	Monsanto	1990, 1988	Cabernet Sauvignon	****
Nero del Tondo	Ruffino	1988	Pinot Noir	**
Niccolo da Uzzano	Castello di Uzzano	1990, 1988	Sangiovese	**
Ornellaia	L. Antinori	1990, 1988	Cabernet Sauvignon	*****
Ornellaia Masseto	L. Antinori	1988	Merlot	*****
Palazzo Altesi	Altesino	1990, 1988	Sangiovese	****/*****
Il Pareto	Nozzole	1990, 1988	Cabernet Sauvignon	****/*****
Parrina	DOC	1990, 1988	Sangiovese	**

NAME	PRODUCER	TOP VINTAGES	PRIMARY GRAPE	RATING
Percarlo	San Giusto	1990, 1988	Sangiovese	*****
Le Pergole Torte	Monte Vertine	1990, 1988	Sangiovese	****
Piano del Cipresso	Terrabianca	1988	Sangiovese	****/*****
Poggio Brandi	Fattoria Baggiolino	1990, 1988	Sangioveto	****
Porta della Pietra	John Matta	1988	Sangiovese	****
Prunaio	Viticcio	1990, 1988	Sangiovese	****
Querciagrande	Podere Capaccia	1990	Sangiovese	****
Il Querciolaia	Castello di Querceto	1990, 1988	Cabernet Sauvignon/ Sangiovese	****
RF	Castello di Cacchiano	1990, 1988	Sangiovese	****
R and R	Castello di Gabbiano	1990, 1988	Cabernet Sauvignon/ Sangiovese	****
Ripa della More	Vicchiomaggio	1990, 1988	Cabernet Sauvignon/ Sangiovese	****
Rocca di Montegrossi	Castello di Cacchiano	1990, 1988	Sangiovese	****
Roccato	Rocca delle Macie	1990, 1988	Cabernet Sauvignon/ Sangiovese	****
Rosso di Altesino	Altesino	1990	Cabernet Sauvignon/ Sangiovese	****
Rosso dell'Oca	Fattoria di Petriolo	1990, 1988	Merlot	****
Saffredi	Le Pupille	1990	Sangiovese/Merlot/ Alicante	*****
Sammarco	Castello di Rampolla	1990, 1988	Cabernet Sauvignon	*****
San Felice	Predicato di Biturica	1990, 1988	Sangiovese	**
San Martino	Villa Cafaggio	1990, 1988	Sangiovese	*****
Sangioveto di Coltibuono	Badia a Coltibuono	1990, 1988	Sangiovese	****
Sangioveto Grosso	Monsanto	1990, 1988	Sangiovese	****
Santa Cristina	Antinori	1990, 1988	Sangiovese	**
Santacroce	Castell'In Villa	1990, 1988	Sangiovese	****
Sassello	Castello di Verrazzano	1990, 1988	Sangiovese	**
Sassicaia	San Guido	1990, 1988	Cabernet Sauvignon	*****
Secentenario	P. Antinori	nonvintage	Cabernet Sauvignon/ Sangiovese	****
Ser Gioveto	Rocca delle Macie	1990, 1988	Sangiovese/ Cabernet Sauvignon	***/****
Ser Niccolo	Conti Serristori	1990, 1988	Sangiovese	**
Il Sodaccio	Monte Vertine	1990, 1988	Sangiovese	*****
I Sodi di San Niccolo	Castellare	1990, 1988	Sangiovese	***
Sodole	Guicciardini Strozzi	1990, 1988	Sangiovese	****/*****
Solaia	P. Antinori	1990, 1988	Cabernet Sauvignon	*****

NAME	PRODUCER	TOP VINTAGES	PRIMARY GRAPE	RATING
Solatia Basilica	Villa Cafaggio	1990, 1988	Sangiovese	****/*****
Soldera Intistieri	Soldera	1988	Sangiovese	***/****
Sorbaiano Montescudaio	Geografico	1990	Sangiovese	***
Spargolo	Cecchi	1990	Sangiovese	**
Le Stanze	Poliziano	1990, 1988	Cabernet Sauvignon	****
Stielle	Rocca di Castagnoli	1990	Cabernet Sauvignon/ Sangiovese	***/****
Summus	Banfi	1990	Sangiovese/Pinot Noir/Cabernet Sauvignon	**
Tavernelle	Villa Banfi	1988	Cabernet Sauvignon	**
Tignanello	Antinori	1990, 1988	Sangiovese	*****
Tinscvil	Castello di Monsanto	1990, 1988	Sangiovese	****
Tremalvo	Barone Ricasoli	1988	Cabernet Sauvignon	**
L'Unico	Petroio	1990	Cabernet Sauvignon/ Merlot/Pinot Noir	***
Vigna L'Apparita	Castello di Ama	1990, 1988	Merlot	****/*****
Vigna di Bugialla	Poggerino	1990, 1988	Cabernet Sauvignon/ Sangiovese	****
Vigna Il Chiuso	Fattoria di Ama	1990, 1988	Pinot Noir	***
Vigna di Fontevecchia	Agricola Camigliano	1990, 1988	Sangiovese	**
Vigna Pianacci	Castello di Luiano	1990, 1988	Sangiovese	**
Vigna Il Vallone	Santa Anna	1990, 1988	Cabernet Sauvignon/ Sangiovese	****
Le Vignacce	Villa Cilnia	1990, 1988	Sangiovese	***/****
Vigneto La Gavine	Villa Cerna	1990	Cabernet Sauvignon	****
Vigorello	San Felice	1988	Cabernet Sauvignon/ Sangiovese	***
Villa di Bagnolo	Marchesi Pancrazi	1990	Pinot Noir	***
Vinattieri Rosso II	M. Castelli	1990, 1988	Sangiovese	***
Vocato	Villa Cilnia	1988	Cabernet Sauvignon	***

AGING POTENTIAL

Brunello di Montalcino: 8–25 years
Carmignano: 5–8 years
Chianti Classico: 3–15 years †
Rosso di Montalcino: 5–8 years
Tuscan Whites: 1–2 years
Vino Nobile di Montepulciano: 5–10 years
Vino da Tavolas (red wine blends): 5–20 years

† Only a handful of Chianti producers make wines that age and last this long.

OVERALL QUALITY LEVEL

For one of the world's most famous wine regions, the quality, while on the upswing, is depressingly variable. Some famous estates in Brunello continue to live off their historic reputations while making poor wine, and there is an ocean of mediocre Chianti producers. The exciting new-breed Sangiovese/Cabernet, Cabernet Franc, and Merlot wines can be superb, but they are produced in limited quantities and are expensive. As for the white wines, the situation is intolerable, and the Italians need to wake up to the fact that high-tech, computerized, stainless-steel tanks, centrifuges, sterile bottling, and obsessive reliance on micropore filter machines are a fail-safe policy for making pleasureless wines.

MOST IMPORTANT INFORMATION TO KNOW

Forget the Italian wine regulations that are supposed to promote a better product. There are many disgustingly poor wines that carry the government's highest guarantee of quality, the DOCG, or Denominazione di Origine Controllata e Garantita. Many of the Vino de Tavolas are vastly superior wines, and this title is supposedly left for Italy's lowest level, the generic wines. The operative rule is, who are the top producers? Then and only then will you be able to make your way through the perilous selection process for Italian wines.

BUYING STRATEGY

For Tuscany wines, the buying strategy is simple: Purchase all of the 1990s or late-released 1988 Riservas from Brunello di Montalcino and Chianti that you can. The years 1991, 1992, and 1993 were problematic because of preharvest and harvest rain. Certainly the two best vintages of the last decade have been 1985 and 1990, with 1988 coming in third. It will be slim pickings when the 1991s, 1992s, and 1993s flood the marketplace in 1996 and 1997, but of the three vintages, 1993 is markedly superior to either 1992 or 1991.

VINTAGE GUIDE

1994—While some favorable and overoptimistic reports have emerged from the promotional arms of the Tuscan wine industry, this vintage received too much rain at the wrong time. While some good wines will be made, it is clearly an irregular vintage of, at best, average quality.

1993—Although this is an average vintage on paper, the better producers will undoubtedly turn out better cuvées, with good ripeness, but perhaps excessive tannin and acidity. The best Chianti producers have managed to produce good wine.

1992—First reports were ominous, but growers seemed more enthusiastic after the wines had finished malolactic fermentation in spring 1993. Rain interrupted the harvest, but most of the white wine grapes were in, and many producers were not far from finishing the red wine harvest. Look for the wines to be soft and fruity, with relatively low acidity. Because of the rains there will be frightful irregularity. This is not a vintage that can be summarized in a general fashion, but the successful wines will be drinkable young, and short-lived.

1991—This was a very difficult year throughout Tuscany; it may turn out like 1987. If so, some light, agreeable, correct wines that need to be drunk in the first 3–5 years of the vintage will be made. On paper, it is a below-average-quality vintage.

1990—This is the best year for Tuscany since the fabulous 1985 vintage. The wines exhibit terrific color, superripe aromas, wonderful richness, and surprisingly crisp acidity, something that is difficult to achieve in years of great ripeness. Even the lower-level Chiantis, many of which can be found for under $10 a bottle, are drinking deliciously, and should last until 1995–1996. The bigger Chiantis and Chianti Classico Riservas will last for 10–15 years, and the Cabernet Sauvignon/Sangiovese–based Vino da Tavolas should last for 15 or more years. In Brunello di Montalcino, this is the greatest vintage in three decades!

1989—Tuscany was inundated by rain in 1989. Consequently, the wines exhibit a certain hollowness and lightness. Some competent examples have emerged, but this is a below-average-quality vintage.

1988—Touted as a great year in Tuscany, 1988 is certainly a very good one. The wines display pronounced tannins and considerable structure. In some cases the green, astringent tannins suggest that not all the grapes reached full physiological maturity. Nevertheless, there are enough good wines to rate this vintage as one of the best of the decade, eclipsed in quality by 1985, 1982, and 1990.

1987—Light, agreeable, pleasantly fruity wines were made in 1987, but most are now fading. Avoid.

1986—A good vintage that at present is lost in the hype surrounding 1985. The wines are well balanced and round. The Chianti Classico Riservas are especially recommended.

1985—A smashing, no-holds-barred, incredible year with the wines bursting at the seams with a superripe, velvety, opulent, plummy fruitiness, full body, and a lushness and precociousness not seen since 1971. The wines are seductive, glamorous, voluptuous, and fabulously tasty. The lighter-styled Chiantis should have been drunk up; the serious Chiantis and Vino da Tavolas will drink well until 2000–2005. The Brunellos will keep for another 20 years. The wines from the top producers are not to be missed.

1984—A dreadful year, much worse in Tuscany than in Piedmont to the north. Rain and a paucity of sunshine were the culprits. No doubt the trade will say the wines are light and commercial, but at this point, this looks to be a vintage to pass up.

1983—Quite highly regarded. Tuscany had weather similar to that experienced in Bordeaux hundreds of miles to the west. A drought year of intense heat caused sugars and the consequent alcohol level to skyrocket in the grapes. The wines are ripe, alcoholic, fat, low in acidity, and jammy, with deep layers of fruit. Drink them between now and 1999.

1982—Considered more "classic" than 1983, which I suppose means less powerful and less opulently fruity and rich wines. Certainly it is a good vintage with firm tannins, fine depth, and ripeness. The second-best year between 1975 and 1990, 1982 is a year to be taken seriously. For Brunello di Montalcino, it is the best vintage since 1970.

OLDER VINTAGES

Avoid 1978, 1977, 1976, 1974, 1973, and 1972; 1971 and 1970 are superb years if the wines have been well stored.

RATING TUSCANY'S BEST PRODUCERS

Note: Most producers make both a Chianti Classico and a Chianti Classico Riserva. In the following chart, for purposes of simplification, the star rating shown for each producer's Chianti Classico also pertains to their Chianti Classico Riserva, unless otherwise noted. I have treated Brunello di Montalcino and Brunello di Montalcino Riserva in the same manner. Single-vineyard Chiantis are treated as a separate qualitative item, as are the vast number of vino da tavolas. Production of the single vineyards and vino da tavolas as is often extremely small, often not more than 500–1,000 cases. Thus as with so many great wines of the world, availability is poor outside a handful of the top Italian wine specialist shops.

*****(OUTSTANDING)*

Altesino Brunello di Montalcino Montosoli	L. Antinori Merlot Masseto Vino da Tavolo
Altesino Brunello di Montalcino Vigna Altesino	L. Antinori Ornellaia Vino da Tavola
	P. Antinori Solaia Vino da Tavola
Ambra Carmignano Riserva Vigna Alta	P. Antinori Tignanello Vino da Tavola

Felsina Berardenga Chianti Classico Riserva Rancia

Case Basse Brunello di Montalcino

Costanti Brunello di Montalcino

Monte Vertine Il Sodaccio Vino da Tavola

Ornellaia Merlot Masseto Vino da Tavola

Ornellaia Vino da Tavola

Pertimali Brunello di Montalcino

Ciacci Piccolomini d'Aragona Brunello di Montalcino

Le Pupille Saffredi Vino da Tavola

Castello dei Rampolla Sammarco Vino da Tavola

E. Ricasoli-Firidolfi Rocca di Montegrossi Geremia Vino da Tavola

Ruffino Chianti Classico Riserva Ducale (gold label)

San Giusto a Rententano Percarlo Vino da Tavola

San Guido Sassicaia Vino da Tavola

Terrabianca Campaccio Vino da Tavola

Terrabianca Campaccio Riserva Vino da Tavola

Terrabianca Chianti Riserva Croce

Azienda Agricola La Torre (Luigi Anania) Brunello di Montalcino

Castell'In Villa Chianti Classico Riserva

Villa Cafaggio Cortaccio Vino da Tavola

Villa Cafaggio San Martino Vino da Tavola

* * * *(EXCELLENT)

Altesino Alte d'Altesi Vino da Tavola

Altesino Brunello di Montalcino

Altesino Cabernet Sauvignon Vino da Tavola

Altesino Palazzo Altesi Vino da Tavola ****/*****

Castello di Ama Merlot Vigna L'Apparita Vino da Tavola

Ambra Carmignano

P. Antinori Chianti Classico Peppole

P. Antinori Chianti Classico Riserva Badia a Passignano

P. Antinori Chianti Classico Riserva Marchese

P. Antinori Secentenario Vino da Tavola

Avignonesi Merlot Vino da Tavola

Avignonesi Vino Nobile di Montepulciano

Badia a Coltibuono Chianti Classico

Badia a Coltibuono Sangioveto di Coltibuono Vino da Tavola

Barbi Brunello di Montalcino

Barbi Brunello di Montalcino Riserva

Barbi Brunello di Montalcino Vigna del Fiore

Felsina Berardenga Chianti Classico

Felsina Berardenga Fontalloro Vino da Tavola

Boscarelli Boscarelli Vino da Tavola

Boscarelli Vino Nobile di Montepulciano

La Braccesca Vino Nobile di Montepulciano

Caparzo Brunello di Montalcino La Casa

Caparzo Ca del Pazzo Vino da Tavola

Frederico Carletti Vino Nobile di Montepulciano

Castelgiocondo Brunello di Montalcino Riserva

Cerbaiona Brunello di Montalcino ****/*****

Costanti Rosso di Montalcino

Dei Vino Nobile di Montepulciano

Dei Vino Nobile di Montepulciano Riserva

Fontodi Chianti Classico

Fontodi Chianti Classico Riserva

Fontodi Chianti Classico Riserva Vigna del Sorbo

Fontodi Flaccianello Vino da Tavola

Castello di Gabbiano R and R Vino da Tavola

Geografico Agricoltori del Geografico Vino da Tavola

Gracciano Vino Nobile di Montepulciano

Isole e Olena Collezione de Marchi l'Ermo Vino da Tavola

Lilliano Anagallis Vino da Tavola

Lisini Brunello di Montalcino

Monsanto Chianti Classico Il Poggio ****/*****

Monsanto Nemo Vino da Tavola

Monsanto Sangioveto Grosso Vino da Tavola

Monsanto Tinscvil Vino da Tavola

Monte Antico Rosso

Monte Vertine Le Pergole Torte Vino da Tavola

Monte Vertine Riserva Vino da Tavola

Moris Farms Morellino di Scansano

Nozzole Chianti Classico Riserva

Nozzole Il Pareto Vino da
Tavola****/*****

Podere Il Palazzino Chianti Classico

Podere Il Palazzino Chianti Classico
Riserva

Podere Il Palazzino Grosso Senese Vino da
Tavola****/*****

Pertimali Rosso di Montalcino

Ciacci Piccolomini d'Aragona Rosso di
Montalcino

Poggio Antico Altero Vino da Tavola

Poggio Antico Brunello di
Montalcino****/*****

Poggio Brandi Vino da Tavola

Il Poggione (Roberto Franceschi) Brunello
di Montalcino

Le Pupille Morellino di Scansano
Riserva

Castello di Querceto Chianti Classico

Castello di Querceto Chianti Classico
Riserva

Castello di Querceto Cignale Vino da
Tavola****/*****

Castello di Querceto La Corte Vino da
Tavola

Castello di Querceto Il Querciolaia Vino
da Tavola

Castello dei Rampolla Chianti Classico
Riserva

E. Ricasoli-Firidolfi Chianti Classico

E. Ricasoli-Firidolfi Chianti Classico
Riserva

E. Ricasoli-Firidolfi Chianti Classico
Riserva Rocca di Montegrossi

Ruffino Chianti Classico Riserva Ducale
(tan label)

San Felice Brunello di Montalcino
Campogiovanni

San Giusto a Rententano Chianti Classico

Fattori Santa Anna Vigna Il Vallone Vino
da Tavola

Guicciardini Strozzi Sodole Vino da
Tavola****/*****

Terrabianca Chianti Scassino

Terrabianca Cipresso Vino da Tavola

Azienda Agricola La Torre (Luigi Anania)
Rosso di Montalcino

Val di Suga Brunello di Montalcino

Val di Suga Brunello di Montalcino Vigna
Spuntali

Castell'In Villa Chianti Classico

Castell'In Villa Santacroce Vino da Tavola

Villa Cafaggio Chianti Classico

Villa Cafaggio Solatio Basilica Vino da
Tavola****/*****

Castello di Volpaia Balifico Vino da
Tavola

Castello di Volpaia Chianti Classico
Riserva

Castello di Volpaia Coltassala Vino da
Tavola

* * *(GOOD)

Altesino Rosso di Altesino

Altesino Rosso di Montalcino

Castello di Ama Chianti Classico

Castello di Ama Chianti Classico
single-vineyard cuvées ***/****

Avignonesi Cabernet Sauvignon Vino da
Tavola

Avignonesi Grifi Vino da Tavola

Badia a Coltibuono Chianti Cetamura

Badia a Coltibuono Coltibuono Rosso Vino
da Tavola

Erik Banti Morellino di Scansano

Boscarelli Chianti Colli Senesi

Brolio Chianti Classico Riserva

Caparzo Brunello di Montalcino

Carpineto Chianti Classico Riserva

Case Basse Soldera Intistieri Vino da
Tavola ***/****

Castelgiocondo Merlot Vino da
Tavola ***/****

Castellare Chianti Classico

Castellare I Sodi di San Niccolo Vino da
Tavola

Castruccio Vino da Tavola

Colognole Chianti Ruffina

Dievole Chianti Classico Novecento

Dievole Chianti Classico Riserva

Dievole Chianti Classico Vigna Dieuele

Dievole Chianti Classico Vigna Sessina

Castello di Farnetella Chianti Colli
Senesi

Fonterutoli Brancaia Vino da Tavola

Fonterutoli Chianti Classico ***/****

Fonterutoli Chianti Ser Lapo

Fonterutoli Concerto Vino da Tavola

Fossi Chianti

Frescobaldi Montesodi Chianti Ruffina
Frescobaldi Mormoreto Vino da Tavola
Castello di Gabbiano Ania Vino da Tavola
Castello di Gabbiano Chianti Classico
  Riserva***/****
Cantina Gattavecchi Chianti Colli Senesi
Cantina Gattavecchi Vino Nobile di
  Montepulciano
Geografico Brunello di Montalcino
Geografico Chianti Classico
Geografico Chianti Classico Castello di
  Fagnano
Geografico Chianti Classico Contessa di
  Radda
Geografico Sorbaiano Montescudaio Vino
  da Tavola
Isole e Olena Boro Cepparello Vino da
  Tavola
Isole e Olena Chianti Classico
Lanciola Chianti Fiorentini
Lanciola Chianti Le Masse di Greve
La Leccia Chianti Classico
Lilliano Chianti Classico
Lilliano Chianti Classico Riserva Eleanora
Le Masse di San Leolino Chianti Classico
Le Masse di San Leolino Chianti Classico
  Riserva

Monsanto Chianti Classico
  Riserva***/****
Petroio Chianti Classico Montetondo
Petroio L'Unico Vino da Tavola
Poggio Antico Rosso di Montalcino
Poggio Bonelli Chianti Classico Riserva
Poggio Galiga Chianti Rufina
S. Quirico Chianti
Roccadoro Chianti Classico
Rodano Chianti Classico
Ruffino Cabreo Il Borgo Vino da Tavola
Ruffino Chianti Classico
Ruffino Chianti Classico Aziano
Ruffino Chianti Classico Nozzole
San Felice Vigorello Vino da Tavola
Fattori Santa Anna Rosso di Santa Anna
Talosa Chianti
Talosa Rosso di Montalcino
Talosa Vino Nobile di Montepulciano
Toscolo Chianti Classico
Toscolo Chianti Classico Riserva
Tenuta Trerose Vino Nobile di
  Montepulciano Riserva
Villa di Geggiano Chianti Classico Riserva
Castello di Volpaia Chianti Classico

* *(AVERAGE)

P. Antinori Santa Cristina Vino da Tavola
Costanti Chianti Colli Senesi
Poggio al Sorbo Chianti Classico
Ruffino Nero del Tondo Vino da Tavola

San Felice Chianti Classico
San Felice Chianti Classico Riserva Il
  Grigio
San Felice Vino da Tavola

ALTESINO

Alte d'Altesi Vino da Tavola * * * *, Brunello di Montalcino * * * *, Brunello di Montalcino
Montosoli * * * * *, Brunello di Montalcino Vigna Altesino * * * * *, Cabernet Sauvignon
Vino da Tavola * * * *, Palazzo Altesi Vino da Tavola * * * */* * * * *, Rosso di Altesino * * *,
Rosso di Montalcino * * *

1990	Alte d'Altesi	D	92
1988	Alte d'Altesi	D	90
1988	Brunello di Montalcino	D	90
1988	Brunello di Montalcino Montosoli	D	92+
1985	Brunello di Montalcino Vigna Altesino	E	92
1990	Palazzo Altesi	D	90
1988	Palazzo Altesi	D	90
1990	Rosso di Altesino	B	90
1990	Rosso di Montalcino	C	90

A top-notch producer, Altesino has turned out a bevy of super wines. The 1990 Palazzo Altesi (100% Sangiovese Grosso, of which 25% is vinified by the carbonic maceration method) is a voluptuously styled, fat, fleshy wine offering gobs of sweet, smoky, black cherry and curranty fruit, a decadent personality, and a lush, glycerin-imbued, alcoholic, sumptuously rich finish. Forward and seductive, it should be drunk over the next 5–7 years. The 1990 Alte d'Altesi (a 30% Cabernet Sauvignon/70% Sangiovese Grosso blend) is another terrific wine from this producer. It exhibits an impressive dark ruby/purple color, and a huge, smoky nose with scents of jammy red and black fruit and barbecue sauce. Full bodied, with wonderful suppleness and a layered impression on the palate, this concentrated, rich, delicious wine can be drunk now and over the next 8–9 years.

If you are looking for more tannin, check out Altesino's 1988 Brunello di Montalcino. An outstanding example of Brunello, the color is impressively dark, and the emerging bouquet exhibits licorice, Asian spices, fruitcake, minerals, and plenty of highly extracted fruit. Full bodied, with outstanding concentration, moderate tannin, and an expansive personality, this impressive Brunello should drink well for 10–20 years. The 1988 Brunello di Montalcino Montosoli is also superb. It offers outstanding density and richness, tremendous body, and a massive constitution. There is a copious amount of curranty, tobacco-tinged, rich fruit, as well as considerable glycerin, alcohol, and tannin in the finish. Although approachable, it is far from full maturity. Drink it between 1998 and 2025

The superb 1985 Vigna Altesino has enough opulence and richness to be consumed now, although it would be a shame not to lay away a few bottles for drinking around the turn of the century. Dark ruby/garnet, with a huge bouquet of smoke, black fruit, cocoa, and herb scents, this impressively endowed, full-bodied wine is highly extracted, but has slightly lower acidity than many other 1985 Brunellos. No doubt the wine was made from superripe grapes. Long, opulent, and dramatic, this is a beautifully made Brunello for drinking over the next 15 or more years.

The 1988 Alte d'Altesi (a blend of Sangiovese Grosso and Cabernet Sauvignon aged in new oak casks) is a stunning wine. The huge nose of cedar, tobacco, black fruits, and spices is intensely fragrant. This full-bodied wine is bursting with glycerin, reveals impressive extraction of fruit, moderate tannins, and a spicy, long, rich finish. Drinkable now, this wine should continue to evolve beautifully over the next decade. Altesino's 1988 Palazzo Altesi (made completely from the Sangiovese Grosso grape grown in their Montosoli vineyard) is a more evolved, sweet-scented wine with huge aromas of jammy, earthy, red and black fruits intermingled with herbs and toasty new oak. It is expansive, full bodied, even voluptuous, with soft tannins and an opulent, long finish. It is a seductive red wine. Drink it over the next 7–8 years.

Altesino has scored successfully with both the 1990 Rosso di Montalcino and 1990 Rosso di Altesino. The former wine exhibits great density of fruit, superrichness, a perfumed nose of cassis, spices, and herbs, and a lush finish. Drink it between now and 2002. The softer Rosso di Altesino is equally stunning, with a sweet nose of jammy berry fruit, leather, vanillin, and smoke, as well as a rich, medium- to full-bodied texture. Drink this juicy, exciting Vino da Tavola between now and 2001.

CASTELLO DI AMA

Chianti Classico* * *, Chianti Classico single-vineyard cuvées* * */****,
Merlot Vigna L'Apparita* * * */* * * * *

1990 Chianti Classico	C	87
1988 Chianti Classico Vigneto Bellavista	D	88+
1988 Chianti Classico Vigneto Bertinga	D	89
1988 Chianti Classico Vigneto La Casuccia	D	86

1988 Chianti Classico Vigneto San Lorenzo	D	87

1988 Merlot Vigna L'Apparita	E	93

This producer turns out a relatively austere, tannic, tight-fisted style of Chianti that is not my favorite, but one has to admire the wines' purity and structure. The wines are more architectural than hedonistic. With that in mind, readers would be better off spending the $16 asked for the 1990 Chianti Classico than over twice that amount on the single-vineyard wines, which are only negligibly better. The 1990 Chianti Classico is an elegant wine, with a pure, ripe cherry–scented nose, supple, medium-bodied flavors, fine ripeness, and a tasty, spicy, long finish. Drink it over the next 4–5 years.

My favorite of the single-vineyard Chiantis is the 1988 Vigneto Bertinga. Dark-colored, with an intriguing nose of tar, roasted pine nuts, and cherries, it is firm and tannic, with medium body, and fine extraction of flavor in the long finish. Drink it between now and 2003. The 1988 Chianti Classico San Lorenzo exhibits tougher tannins, and more firmness and tightness. While the color is deep ruby and there is excellent underlying fruit and ripeness, this wine requires 2–3 years of patience. If the tannins do not fully melt away, my rating will look too generous. The 1988 Vigneto Bellavista reveals an impressive deep ruby/purple color, a big, spicy, tobacco-, herb-, and leather-scented nose, spicy, ripe, rich flavors, and plenty of underlying depth to back up the tannins. It appears to be the best candidate for an outstanding score after another 1–2 years of cellaring. It should drink well for 12–15 years. The 1988 La Casuccia has 15% Merlot blended in, but you would never know that by its tightness, hardness, tough tannins, and astringent finish. The color is impressive and there is good underlying fruit, but again, this is a closed, austere style of Chianti that some readers may enjoy more than I did.

I have never had any doubts about Castello di Ama's magnificent Merlot. The 1988 Vigna L'Apparita is a spectacular wine, with black/purple color, and a huge nose of cassis, black cherries, licorice, and vanillin. It offers staggering concentration, great definition, and a medium- to full-bodied, terrific finish. Although there is plenty of tannin, the copious quantities of fruit overwhelm it. While approachable now, this Merlot should age beautifully for 10–15 years. Made in frightfully tiny quantities, it will require "insider" contacts to find a bottle or two.

AMBRA

Carmignano* * * *, Carmignano Riserva Vigna Alta* * * * *

1990 Carmignano	C	92

1990 Carmignano Riserva Vigna Alta	D	91+

Ambra has become my favorite producer of Carmignano. I am a sucker for their superrich, expansive, creamy-textured style of red wine. Ambra's wines are the Pomerols of Tuscan viticulture. The 1990 Carmignano is the best regular cuvée I have tasted from this producer. It reveals sensational richness, a terrific nose of black fruits and spices, low acidity, a luscious, fleshy, chewy texture, and a whoppingly long finish. Although impossible to resist now, it should continue to drink well for at least a decade. The 1990 Riserva Vigna Alta will probably merit an even higher score in 3–4 years. Even more concentrated than the regular cuvée, it is buttressed by more noticeable spicy new oak, has a higher tannin level, and is more structured and backward. It does not sing quite as loudly as the regular cuvée, but it is an impressively endowed, rich, multidimensional wine for drinking between 1996 and 2008.

L. ANTINORI

Merlot Masseto Vino da Tavola* * * * *, Ornellaia Vino da Tavola* * * * *

1990	Merlot Masseto Vino da Tavola	E	95
1988	Merlot Masseto Vino da Tavola	E	93
1990	Ornellaia Vino da Tavola	E	92
1988	Ornellaia Vino da Tavola	E	92

Unfortunately, the availability of this spectacular 1988 single-vineyard Merlot is limited. Made by Marchese Lodovico, it rivals the superb Tuscan Merlots produced by Avignonesi and Castello di Ama. Its rarity and price make it a collector's item. Stunningly rich and densely concentrated, it exhibits saturated color, a big, rich, black cherry– and toasty oak–scented nose, opulent, superconcentrated flavors, adequate acidity, and a blockbuster finish. It should drink well for 10–12 more years.

If readers are unable to find any 1988 Merlot Masseto, run to your favorite wine specialist and secure a bottle of the 1990 Masseto, another blockbuster effort from this small winery. The 1990 exhibits an opaque purple/black color, a huge, exotic nose of chocolate, black plums, cherries, Asian spices, and sweet vanilla. Full bodied, with silky tannin, and gorgeous layers of fleshy, chewy fruit, this highly extracted yet beautifully proportioned Merlot should drink well for 10–15 years.

As for the two outstanding Ornellaia vintages, the 1988 is more evolved and complex, and the 1990 appears more compact and streamlined. The latter wine is bursting with black cherry and curranty fruit, and has some smoky, new oak, and a medium- to full-bodied, long finish with decent acidity and moderate tannin. The 1988 is more developed, displaying no age to its color. Full bodied and concentrated, it is a beautiful example of a wine that brilliantly marries power with finesse. It should drink well for 10–15 years.

P. ANTINORI

Chianti Classico Peppole* * * *, Chianti Classico Riserva Badia a Passignano* * * *, Chianti Classico Riserva Marchese* * * *, Santa Cristina Vino da Tavola* *, Secentenario Vino da Tavola* * * *, Solaia Vino da Tavola* * * * *, Tignanello Vino da Tavola* * * * *

1990	Chianti Classico Riserva Badia a Passignano	C	91
1990	Solaia	EE	94
1990	Tignanello	D	93

Antinori's 1990 Tignanello (a blend of primarily Sangiovese with some Cabernet Sauvignon) is the best example I have tasted of this wine since the marvelously opulent, rich 1985. Rich yet supple, and expansive enough to be consumed with great pleasure, it offers a dark ruby/purple color and a big, smoky, earthy nose of nearly overripe cherry and currantlike fruit. Full bodied, with exceptional concentration and purity, this distinctive, spicy wine should drink well for 10–15 years. The 1990 Solaia is slightly more concentrated, with a saturated purple color, and a classic, international nose of cassis, lead pencil, vanillin, and smoke. It is gorgeously rich, with a fat, unctuous texture, and a long, highly extracted finish. Well balanced and already delicious, it remains unevolved and is potentially a 12- to 20-year wine. In the context of recent Solaias, I would rate it a worthy competitor to the otherworldly 1985. It is certainly much more opulent, with sweeter, jammier, richer fruit than the 1988 (most recently rated 88 points).

The 1990 Badia a Passignano is a terrific single-vineyard Chianti Classico. Made from Sangiovese and aged for 15 months in small oak casks, it is a powerful, rich, intense, medium- to full-bodied Chianti with a healthy dark ruby/purple color, a big, spicy, black cherry– and leather-scented nose, rich, concentrated, moderately tannic flavors, and an authoritative finish. Young and exuberant yet approachable, this large-scaled, superimpressive Chianti should age effortlessly for 10 or more years. Kudos to Piero Antinori.

AVIGNONESI
Cabernet Sauvignon Vino da Tavola * * *, Grifi Vino da Tavola * * *, Merlot Vino da Tavola * * * *, Vino Nobile di Montepulciano * * * *

1988 Grifi	D	87
1988 Merlot	D	90

An impeccably run Tuscan winery, Avignonesi is known for making one of the best Vin Santos in Italy (check out their 1983 if you like this sweet, nutty-flavored, sherrylike style). They also produce excellent red wines. I have been a consistent admirer of their Cabernet Sauvignon–based wine called Grifi, which has been delicious in vintages such as 1982, 1983, and 1985. The 1988 Grifi (a blend of 50% Cabernet Sauvignon and 50% Prugnolo Gentile) offers up a moderately intense bouquet of cherries, oak, and herbs. In the mouth, there is good structure, and a sense of firmness and tightness, as well as excellent ripeness, a medium-bodied, rich palate, and fine length. The wine will benefit from another several years of cellaring and should last for at least a decade. The 1988 Merlot reveals a dark ruby/purple color and a huge nose of jammy plums and cassis intermingled with scents of toast and smoke. It is a beautifully etched, well-delineated, medium- to full-bodied Merlot, bursting with fruit yet with surprising structure and firmness for its ripe aroma and taste. Delicious now, it should continue to drink well for 7–8 years.

BADIA A COLTIBUONO
Chianti Cetamura * * *, Chianti Classico * * * *, Coltibuono Rosso Vino da Tavola * * *, Sangioveto di Coltibuono Vino da Tavola * * * *

1990 Chianti Cetamura	A	87
1990 Chianti Classico	C	89
1988 Chianti Classico Riserva	C	87
1990 Coltibuono Rosso	A	86
1988 Sangioveto di Coltibuono	D	89

This superlative Chianti producer continues to offer one spectacular bargain that consumers would be foolish to ignore. The Chianti Cetamura was delicious in 1988, and is even better in 1990. The wine offers a terrific purity and richness of fruit, a medium- to full-bodied, soft texture, and a fragrant berry-, spice-, tobacco-, and herb-scented nose. Already delicious, it will keep until 1997–1998. What a joy it is to find a wine of this quality level priced at $8 a bottle. The nearly outstanding 1990 Chianti Classico displays a beautifully complex, smoky, berry-scented nose, rich, full-bodied flavors that exhibit excellent concentration and ripeness, low acidity, and an opulent, fleshy, heady finish. Drink it between now and 2002. This renowned producer has fashioned a smoky, earthy, ostentatiously styled 1988 Sangioveto. The wine exhibits a dark ruby color, copious amounts of toasty new oak, and layers of chewy, supple, jammy fruit. It is complex, delicious, and flattering to taste, as well as capable of lasting 8–10 years. In contrast, the 1988 Chianti Classico Riserva is more structured, tannic, and backward, disclosing a classic Chianti aromatic profile of saddle leather, tobacco, herbs, and rich, black cherry fruit. It is medium to full bodied and impressively deep, but young and moderately tannic. Give it 1–2 years of cellaring and drink it over the subsequent 10–12 years.

The 1990 Coltibuono Rosso is made from a blend of Sangiovese and Cabernet Sauvignon. It is meant to be drunk within its first 3–4 years of life. Few readers will find fault with its pure, ripe berry scents, round, expansive, medium-bodied, generous, plump flavors, and satiny smooth finish.

ERIK BANTI
Morellino di Scansano* * *

1992 Morellino di Scansano	A	86

This richly fruity, silky-textured, berry-scented and -flavored wine makes for an opulent mouthful of juicy fruit. It is ideal for drinking over the next 1–2 years.

BARBI
Brunello di Montalcino* * * *, Brunello di Montalcino Riserva* * * *, Brunello di Montalcino Vigna del Fiore* * * *

1988 Brunello di Montalcino	D	88+
1990 Brunello di Montalcino Vigna del Fiore	D	93
1988 Brunello di Montalcino Vigna del Fiore	D	90

Although Barbi fashioned some marvelous Brunellos throughout the sixties and early seventies, it has been a long time since I have tasted a Barbi Brunello as good as these three offerings. The big, tannic, backward 1988 Brunello di Montalcino exhibits a medium to dark ruby color, and a moderately intense bouquet of cedar, herbs, and jammy fruit. Full bodied, powerful, tannic, and long, with excellent concentration and structure, this is a Brunello to lay away for 1–3 years and to drink over the subsequent 15. The 1988 Brunello di Montalcino Vigna del Fiore exhibits a wonderful, attractive, complex nose of new saddle leather, Asian spices, sweet red and black fruits, and cedar. Full bodied, with velvety texture, and intense fruit that is beginning to mellow into a complex format, this rich, powerful Brunello can be drunk now or cellared for another 10–15 years. Impressive!

The 1990 Vigna del Fiore (which will not be released until 1996) is a densely colored, rich, massive Brunello with juicy, succulent fruit, full body, layers of concentration, and a long, spicy, sweet, supple finish. Based on the handful of 1990 Brunello di Montalcinos I have seen, this may be a great vintage for this historic viticultural zone.

FELSINA BERARDENGA
Chianti Classico* * * *, Chianti Classico Riserva Rancia* * * * *, Fontalloro Vino da Tavola* * * *

1990 Chianti Classico	B	88
1990 Chianti Classico Riserva	C	87
1988 Chianti Classico Riserva	C	88
1990 Chianti Classico Riserva Rancia	C	89
1988 Chianti Classico Riserva Rancia	C	90
1990 Fontalloro	D	88

A bright shining star in Tuscany, Felsina produces some of the region's longest-lived Chiantis. The youthful, unevolved 1990 Chianti Classico Riserva requires 1–2 more years of cellaring. It should last for 10–15 years. Rich, muscular, and powerful, it possesses admirable depth and ripeness, and moderate tannin that provides support and focus. The wine gives an impression of bigness and richness. Readers should lay away this wine for 1–2 years and then follow its evolution for a decade or more. Although similar, the 1990 Chianti Classico Riserva Rancia exhibits a more saturated dark ruby/purple color, and the wine is longer and more highly extracted as well as more tannic. This can be one of the most dazzling Chiantis made in Tuscany. Although tight and backward, the 1990 demonstrates the potential to evolve into an exciting wine. My palate suggests at least 2 years of cellaring is required. It should keep for 10–15 years.

Felsina's proprietary red wine, the 1990 Fontalloro, exhibits gobs of sweet, jammy, red and black fruits, spicy new oak aromas, medium body, and a crisp finish that ends more quickly than the wine's intensity suggests. An excellent proprietary red, it should drink well for 5–7 years.

The 1990 Chianti Classico offers sweet, ripe black fruit aromas intermingled with hints of damp earth, wood, and leather. It is elegant and round, with lovely fruit, soft tannins, and adequate acidity. The 1990 will keep 6–10 years. The 1988 Chianti Classico Riserva has a rich, licorice, earthy (truffles?), black cherry–scented nose, rich, full-bodied, expansive flavors, good tannin, adequate acidity, and a long finish. Drink it between now and 2005. The backward 1988 Riserva Rancia exhibits superb richness and tremendous density to go along with its saturated dark ruby color. It is a large-scaled, superrich Chianti that can be drunk now, but should evolve gracefully until 2008.

BOSCARELLI
Boscarelli Vino da Tavola * * * *, Chianti Colli Senesi * * *,
Vino Nobile di Montepulciano * * * *

1988 Boscarelli Vino da Tavola	D	88+?
1990 Vino Nobile di Montepulciano	C	86
1990 Vino Nobile di Montepulciano Riserva	D	87+

The firmly structured, backward 1990 Vino Nobile di Montepulciano Riserva reveals admirable stuffing, plenty of spicy, leathery, black cherry fruit, medium to full body, and good acidity. It is a well-built, muscular wine that requires 1–2 years of cellaring; it should last for 12–15 years. While the regular cuvée of 1990 Vino Nobile di Montepulciano is extremely tannic and backward, it possesses a healthy dark ruby/garnet color, fine concentration, medium to full body, and good depth of fruit. It needs 2–3 years of cellaring. Boscarelli's 1988 Vino da Tavola (100% Sangiovese, aged in small oak casks) is an excruciatingly backward, dense, full-bodied, muscular wine with nearly an excess of tannin. The wine's backwardness and toughness are cause for concern, but there is so much ripe fruit crammed into this wine that it appears to be a potential candidate for a graceful evolution —if the tannin melts away before the fruit. It is a big, chewy, rich wine offering up plenty of tobacco, roasted herbs, leather, and curranty/cherry fruit. Purchase it only if you can give it 3–4 years of cellaring.

LA BRACCESCA
Vino Nobile di Montepulciano * * * *

1990 Vino Nobile di Montepulciano	C	89

A top-notch example from this small wine region, this voluptuously textured, rich, lush style of Vino Nobile offers a big, sweet, curranty, cedary, spicy nose, wonderfully pure, chewy, black cherry and curranty fruit, low acidity, and a lush, glycerin- and alcohol-dominated, lusty finish. Drink it over the next decade.

BROLIO
Chianti Classico Riserva * * *

1988 Chianti Classico Riserva	C	86

This firmly structured, spicy Chianti exhibits good cherry fruit, medium body, noticeable structure, and an austere but pleasingly dry, long finish. It should drink well for 4–5 years.

CAPARZO
Brunello di Montalcino* * *, Brunello di Montalcino La Casa* * * *,
Ca del Pazzo Vino da Tavola* * * *

1988 Brunello di Montalcino	D	86
1988 Brunello di Montalcino La Casa	D	90

Although austere and compact, this 1988 Brunello di Montalcino possesses enough positive attributes to merit a recommendation, although I would have liked to detected more flesh and concentration. It is a muscular, highly structured wine with noticeably hard tannin, plenty of spice, good ripeness, and sweet, attractive fruit in the mid-palate. The wine's bouquet is closed but promising. It may merit a higher score with another 1–2 years of cellaring, and will keep for 10–15 years. The 1988 Brunello di Montalcino La Casa is a richer, fuller-bodied wine, with an intense nose of cedar, new saddle leather, and earthy, black cherry fruit. This powerful wine can be drunk now but promises to age effortlessly for 10–15 years.

FREDERICO CARLETTI
Vino Nobile di Montepulciano* * * *

1990 Vino Nobile di Montepulciano	B	88

This dense ruby-colored, rich, medium- to full-bodied wine displays a spicy, sweet nose of overripe black cherries and spice, excellent ripeness, and a layered impression on the palate. There is light tannin in the substantial finish. It should drink well for 7–8 years. Excellent value.

CARPINETO
Chianti Classico Riserva* * *

1990 Chianti Classico Riserva	B	87

An excellent Chianti, this dark ruby/garnet-colored wine offers a spicy, earthy, black cherry–scented nose, medium to full body, muscular, austere, authoritative flavors, and a spicy, moderately tannic finish. It is just beginning to open and should age well for 7–8 years.

CASE BASSE (SOLDERA)
Brunello di Montalcino* * * * *, Soldera Intistieri Vino da Tavola* * */* * * *

1990 Brunello di Montalcino	EEE	98
1988 Brunello di Montalcino	EEE	93

This large-scaled, intensely fragrant 1988 Brunello offers up a lavishly exotic and decadent bouquet of grilled meats, hickory smoke, and jammy peaches, as well as red and black fruits, coffee, and spices. Full bodied, with authoritatively rich, supple flavors oozing with glycerin and extract, this meaty, multidimensional, velvety-textured wine can be drunk now and over the next 12–15 years. The 1990 Brunello di Montalcino from Case Basse is a modern day classic, as well as one of the greatest Brunellos I have ever tasted. It exhibits a deep-ruby color, and a magnificent, rich, complex nose of roasted herbs, sweet, jammy, red and black fruits, cedar, spice, and oak. The wine is extremely powerful and full bodied, with layers of highly concentrated, ripe fruit. Despite its massive size, it retains a gracefulness and sense of elegance. The velvety texture and layers of fruit conceal the wine's high tannin. It is approachable young, but should age effortlessly for 15–20 years.

CASTELGIOCONDO
Brunello di Montalcino Riserva* * * * , Merlot Vino da Tavola* * */* * * *

1988 Brunello di Montalcino Riserva	E	87
1986 Brunello di Montalcino Riserva	E	88+
1991 Merlot Vino da Tavola	C	88

This dark ruby/garnet-colored 1986 Brunello di Montalcino Riserva offers an intriguing bouquet of new saddle leather, spice, earth, and ripe fruit. Full bodied, with hard tannin, as well as plenty of robust, rich, concentrated fruit, this spicy, backward, firmly structured Brunello requires 2–4 years of cellaring; it should keep for 10–15+ years. The 1988 Brunello di Montalcino Riserva is among the softest Brunellos of the vintage. Medium ruby with some amber, this smooth, fruity wine possesses a leafy tobacco– and jammy cherry–scented bouquet, fine body, light tannin, and a velvety-textured style. Drink it over the next 7–8 years.

The impressively rich, spicy 1991 Merlot (from a mediocre Tuscan vintage) offers further proof of what heights this varietal is capable of reaching in selected Tuscan vineyards. The wine exhibits a complex nose of spicy new oak, mocha, and creamy berry fruit. Medium to full bodied, lush and rich, with enough acidity to provide focus, this generously endowed, concentrated wine should drink well for 7–8 years. Bravo to Castelgiocondo for this impressive effort!

CASTELLARE
Chianti Classico* * *, I Sodi di San Niccolo Vino da Tavola* * *

1990 Chianti Classico Riserva	C	89
1990 I Sodi di San Niccolo Vino da Tavola	D	87
1988 I Sodi di San Niccolo Vino da Tavola	D	86

The 1990 Chianti Classico Riserva exhibits a dark ruby/garnet color, a rich, intense nose of cedar, damp earth, leather, and jammy, black cherry fruit. Medium to full bodied and soft, it is a gorgeously rich, velvety-textured Chianti for drinking over the next 7–8 years.

Both of these Vino da Tavolas are well-made wines, offering plenty of earthy, gamey, leathery scents intertwined with those of ripe black cherries and herbs. The 1990 is slightly more elegant and richer, with better overall balance, whereas the 1988 emphasizes more structure and is higher in tannin, as well as lean and austere in the finish. I prefer the greater fruit extraction and higher level of ripeness in the 1990. Both wines should be drunk over the next 5–6 years.

CASTRUCCIO
Vino da Tavola* * *

1992 Vino da Tavola	A	87

This delicious Tuscan red wine displays a spicy, leathery scent, medium body, crisp acidity, and loads of supple berry fruit. It is a complex wine reminiscent of a high-class Chianti.

COLOGNOLE
Chianti Ruffina* * *

1990 Chianti Ruffina	A	86

A fleshy, opulently styled Chianti, this 1990 offering from Colognole is bursting with gobs of red and black fruits, and displays plenty of glycerin, medium to full body, and a satiny smooth texture. Even though it is undeniably delicious at present, it should continue to evolve for at least 2–3 years.

COSTANTI
Brunello di Montalcino* * * * *, Chianti Colli Senesi* *, Rosso di Montalcino* * * *

1988 Brunello di Montalcino	D	93+
1991 Rosso di Montalcino	C	88

Made by one of the most serious and traditional producers of Brunello di Montalcino, Costanti's 1991 Rosso is a noteworthy success from a mediocre year. It exhibits an attractive garnet/ruby color, sweet, cedary, roasted nut and curranty fruit, some earthy, leathery, spicy notes, medium to full body, low acidity, and a supple, fleshy texture. It should drink well for the next 5–7 years. The outstanding 1988 Brunello di Montalcino is a wine to be laid away for 3–5 years, although masochists who love lavish quantities of tannin might want to take the plunge now. It is a huge, massive Brunello, with a dark garnet/ruby color, and an intense, unevolved fragrance of smoke, roasted meats, herbs, and red and black fruits. Spicy, rich, and full bodied, with layers of extract, glycerin, alcohol, and tannin, this is a reassuringly old-style, yet cleanly made, massively constituted Brunello for drinking between 2000 and 2025.

DEI
Vino Nobile di Montepulciano* * * *, Vino Nobile di Montepulciano Riserva* * * *

1990 Vino Nobile di Montepulciano	C	92
1990 Vino Nobile di Montepulciano Riserva	D	87+

Dei's 1990 Vino Nobile di Montepulciano reveals how terrific this vintage was for Tuscany. Dei always makes good wines, but this offering has a level of richness and a headiness and length that one sees only in the greatest vintages. The stunning nose of sweet, jammy, black cherry fruit, herbs, and spices is followed by an expansive, superconcentrated wine that is full bodied and heady, with relatively high alcohol and a long, satiny, decadent finish. Drink this delicious wine now and over the next 8–10 years.

With a dark ruby color and a spicy, vanillin, berry-scented nose, the backward yet potentially high-class 1990 Vino Nobile di Montepulciano Riserva possesses plenty of depth, ripeness, medium to full body, and a firm underpinning of acidity and tannin. If possible, purchasers should try to give it another year of cellaring; it will evolve gracefully over the next decade.

DIEVOLE
Chianti Classico Novecento* * *, Chianti Classico Riserva* * *,
Chianti Classico Vigna Dieuele* * *, Chianti Classico Vigna Sessina* * *

1990 Chianti Classico Novecento	C	87
1988 Chianti Classico Riserva	C	85

Dievole's 1988 Chianti Classico Riserva is a straightforward, solidly made wine with a spicy, cherry, leathery nose and flavors, medium body, and slight toughness in the finish, which kept my rating down. The 1990 Chianti Classico Novecento is a sweeter, richer, plumper style of Chianti, with greater depth and more complexity. It possesses an excellent briary fruit character accompanied by vague components of cedar, tobacco, and new saddle leather, plenty of ripe fruit, suppleness, and medium to full body. It is ideal for drinking over the next 5–7 years.

CASTELLO DI FARNETELLA
Chianti Colli Senesi* * *

1990 Chianti Colli Senesi	A	86

This firm, earthy, intensely spicy Chianti reveals the superripeness achieved in the 1990 vintage. Deep ruby-colored, full, and spicy, with some tannins to shed, this robust, tasty Chianti can be drunk now or cellared for 4–6 years.

FONTERUTOLI
Brancaia Vino da Tavola* * *, Chianti Classico* * */* * * *, Chianti Ser Lapo* * *,
Concerto Vino da Tavola* * *

1990 Brancaia	C	86
1991 Chianti Classico	B	84
1990 Chianti Classico	B	87
1988 Chianti Ser Lapo	C	87
1990 Concerto	D	88

Fonterutoli is a reliable source of high-class Tuscan wine. The 1991 Chianti Classico exhibits a spicy, more compact personality than found in vintages such as 1990 and 1985, as well as a medium-bodied, straightforward appeal. Drink it over the next 3–4 years. The 1990 Chianti Classico displays the excellent ripeness and sweetness of fruit achieved in this vintage. The dark ruby/purple color is followed by a spicy, leathery, earthy, black fruit–scented nose, and sweet, round, ripe, opulent flavors. Drink it over the next 5–8 years.

I have inconsistent tasting notes on Fonterutoli's 1988 Chianti Ser Lapo. At its best, it is a wine with an impressively saturated dark ruby/purple color, a big, forceful nose of grilled herbs, roasted fruit, vanillin, and earthy/leathery notes. The wine is rich and medium to full bodied, with moderate tannin. The style of the 1988 vintage (less opulent fruit and more structured wines) is in complete contrast to the fleshy richness of the 1990 vintage.

The 1990 Brancaia (Fonterutoli's Vino da Tavola), a blend of Sangiovese and Merlot, is good, although it lacks intensity and complexity. It exhibits fine color, medium body, an herbaceous character, and sweet, round, spicy, earthy fruit. Drink it over the next 5–6 years. This producer's best effort among the current releases is the 1990 Concerto, an 80% Sangiovese/20% Cabernet Sauvignon blend. The wine possesses an impressive, saturated, nearly opaque ruby/purple color, a bold, spicy nose of vanillin, black currants, cherries, licorice, and smoke, great depth, a rich, full-bodied palate, moderate tannin, good acidity, and a powerfully rich, long finish. Drink it between now and 2003.

FONTODI
Chianti Classico* * * *, Chianti Classico Riserva* * * *, Chianti Classico Riserva Vigna del Sorbo* * * *, Flaccianello Vino da Tavola* * * *

1990 Chianti Classico	B	87
1988 Chianti Classico Riserva	C	86
1990 Chianti Classico Riserva Vigna del Sorbo	D	88+
1990 Flaccianello della Pieve	D	87

The 1990 Chianti Classico is an excellent wine, displaying pure, rich, spicy fruit, medium body, soft tannins, and a long, chewy finish. Delicious now, it will last for 5–7 years.

The saturated, dark-colored 1990 Chianti Classico Riserva Vigna del Sorbo, a wine of considerable richness, offers a spicy, leathery, cedary nose and flavors, medium to full body, moderate tannin, and adequate acidity. Although tightly knit, backward, and unevolved, it displays loads of promise. With 1–2 additional years of cellaring it may merit an outstanding rating. It is a rich, harmonious Chianti for drinking over the next 10–12 years. The more obvious and open-knit 1988 Chianti Classico Riserva offers attractive, ripe, earthy fruit, medium body, fine intensity and depth, and a good finish. It is an appealing, medium-weight Chianti with excellent ripeness and richness. Drink it over the next 7–8 years.

Although Fontodi's 1990 proprietary red wine, the Flaccianello della Pieve (100% Sangiovese), is dominated by considerable quantities of new oak, it is undoubtedly made from ripe, lusciously rich, chewy fruit. This could have been an outstanding wine if a lighter hand had been employed with the oak. Nevertheless, it is a lush, well-made, pure wine that is ideal for drinking over the next 7–8 years.

FOSSI
Chianti * * *

1990 Chianti	A 85

Fossi has turned out an attractive, soft, herb-, leather-, and berry-scented 1990 Chianti with medium body, fine acidity, and a crisp, long finish. Drink it over the next 3–4 years.

FRESCOBALDI
Montesodi Chianti Ruffina * * *, Mormoreto Vino da Tavola * * *

1990 Montesodi Chianti Ruffina	D 86
1990 Mormoreto Vino da Tavola	D 87

The dark ruby-colored 1990 Montesodi Chianti Ruffina is an austere wine with plenty of cherry fruit, spice, and tannin. Medium bodied and reserved, it is a classy effort, largely because of its purity and fine balance. It should drink well for at least 7–8 years. Made primarily from Cabernet Sauvignon, the 1990 Mormoreto Vino da Tavola exhibits a rich, deep, saturated ruby/purple color, a ripe, curranty bouquet, and rich, jammy, slightly herbaceous, berrylike flavors. Medium to full bodied and soft, it is ideal for drinking over the next 7–8 years.

CASTELLO DI GABBIANO
Ania Vino da Tavola * * *, Chianti Classico Riserva * * */* * * *,
R and R Vino da Tavola * * * *

1986 R and R Vino da Tavola	D 88

This well-run estate has turned out an interesting 1986 R and R, a Vino da Tavola made from 60% Cabernet Sauvignon and Cabernet Franc, 30% Sangiovese, and 10% Merlot. The wine is rich, with an herbaceous, cassis-scented nose, medium- to full-bodied flavors, soft tannins and acidity, and a spicy, opulent finish. It is reminiscent of a classy St.-Émilion. It should drink well until the beginning of the next century.

CANTINA GATTAVECCHI
Chianti Colli Senesi * * *, Vino Nobile di Montepulciano * * *

1988 Vino Nobile di Montepulciano	B 85

Although made in a lighter style, this is a charming, elegant, medium ruby-colored Vino Nobile offering a bouquet of spicy notes intertwined with herbs, cherries, and wood. Medium bodied and soft, with noticeable acidity, this fragrant, easygoing wine should be drunk over the next 4–5 years.

GEOGRAFICO
Agricoltori del Geografico Vino da Tavola * * * *, Brunello di Montalcino * * *,
Chianti Classico * * *, Chianti Classico Castello di Fagnano * * *, Chianti Classico Contessa di
Radda * * *, Sorbaiano Montescudaio Vino da Tavola * * *

1988 Brunello di Montalcino	D 87
1990 Chianti Classico	A 87

1990 Chianti Classico Castello di Fagnano	A	87

1989 Sorbaiano Montescudaio Vino da Tavola	C	86

This firm deserves more recognition for its delicious wines that sell at reasonable prices. Given their quality, these two 1990 Chianti Classicos will not linger on retailers' shelves. The single-vineyard 1990 from the Castello di Fagnano offers a spicy, earthy, black cherry– and licorice-scented nose, a deep, velvety texture, medium-bodied flavors, excellent ripeness, and a spicy finish. Drink it between now and 1999. The 1990 Chianti Classico also exhibits a deep ruby color, a big, spicy, smoky, roasted nut–like bouquet, ripe, medium-bodied, low-acid flavors, and plenty of glycerin and alcohol in the lusty finish. Drink it before the end of the century.

Geografico has fashioned a soft, smoky, herbaceous, round, gentle 1989 Sorbaiano Montescudaio (an 80% Sangiovese/20% Cabernet Sauvignon blend). An attractive wine for this tough vintage, it should be drunk over the next 4–5 years. The 1988 Brunello di Montalcino reveals plenty of new saddle leather and sweet, cherry, curranty fruit in its earthy, spicy nose. The wine is supple, with low acidity, precociously forward, soft, fruity flavors, and medium to full body. It is ideal for drinking now and over the next 7–8 years.

GRACCIANO
Vino Nobile di Montepulciano* * * *

1990 Vino Nobile di Montepulciano	D	90

This is the finest wine I have tasted from Gracciano, raising hopes that this producer has moved to a new quality level. This 1990 offers a huge fragrance of flowers, roasted nuts, and sweet cherry fruit. Chewy and full bodied, with noticeably high alcohol, this wine possesses loads of fleshy, dramatic, black fruit presented in a forward, plump, opulent style. Consume it between now and 2000.

ISOLE E OLENA
Boro Cepparello Vino da Tavola* * *, Chianti Classico* * *,
Collezione de Marchi l'Ermo Vino da Tavola* * * *

1990 Chianti Classico	B	87

1988 Chianti Classico	B	86

Isole e Olena's juicy, richly fruity, densely colored 1990 Chianti Classico offers additional evidence of how fine this Tuscan vintage has turned out. The color is very deep, and the nose offers up spicy, raspberry, cherrylike flavors. The fruit is crammed into a medium-bodied, tightly knit package with crisp acidity and light tannins in the finish. It is a vibrant, exuberant Chianti that should be drunk between now and 2001. The 1988 Chianti Classico offers a fragrant perfume of black raspberries, oak, and toast. In the mouth, there is a lovely, medium-bodied, supple texture, with excellent fruit, decent acidity, and a velvety smooth, impressively long finish. Neither large-scaled nor wimpishly light, it is a tasty wine for drinking over the next 5–6 years.

LANCIOLA
Chianti Fiorentini* * *, Chianti Le Masse di Greve* * *

1991 Chianti Fiorentini	A	85

1990 Chianti Le Masse di Greve	B	90

I found many of Tuscany's 1991 red wines mediocre or disappointing. This 1991 Chianti Fiorentini from Lanciola exhibits atypically fine fruit, a ripe, cherry, spicy character, perhaps too much tannin for its size and depth, but good purity and a pleasing, medium-bodied personality. Drink it over the next 2–3 years. The 1990 Chianti Le Masse di Greve is a sensational example of the heights Chianti can attain. The saturated, nearly opaque garnet/ purple color is followed by a huge nose of spices, roasted herbs, anise, and jammy black cherries. Ripe, full bodied, and rich, with moderate tannin and a structured, muscular, yet expansively rich, viscous texture, this large-scaled, superconcentrated wine should drink well for 10–15 years. Impressive!

LA LECCIA
Chianti Classico * * *

1990 Chianti Classico	B	87

The enticing nose of roasted nuts, herbs (did I detect a whiff of fresh tomatoes?), and ripe black cherry fruit is abundantly evident in both the aromatic and flavor profiles of this expansive, nearly sweet (from admirable extraction) wine. Made in a precocious, flattering style, it should drink well for 4–5 years.

LILLIANO
Anagallis Vino da Tavola * * * *, Chianti Classico * * *, Chianti Classico Riserva Eleanora * * *

1990 Chianti Classico	B	87
1988 Chianti Classico Riserva	C	89

The 1990 Chianti Classico is the type of Chianti restaurants should be buying by the boatload. It is exuberant, rich, and fruity, with a good Chianti's classic Bing cherry-, leathery-, tobacco-, and herb-scented nose, wonderfully pure, ripe, medium- to full-bodied flavors, soft tannins, and a luscious finish. It was drinking gorgeously in 1993, but there is so much fruit and body it will easily last another 5–8 years. Lilliano's terrific 1988 Chianti Classico Riserva exhibits a smoky, tobacco, curranty bouquet, full-bodied, densely concentrated flavors, impeccable balance, crisp acidity, and moderate tannins in the long finish. Delicious and complex, it promises to evolve gracefully for at least a decade.

LISINI
Brunello di Montalcino * * * *

1988 Brunello di Montalcino	D	90

I remember having some wonderful Lisini Brunellos in the mid-seventies, after which the quality dropped. Since 1983, this firm has been making a comeback. The 1988 Brunello di Montalcino offers a complex nose of roasted nuts, earth, and copious quantities of black fruits. Full bodied yet rich and concentrated, with decent acidity, moderate tannins, and a terrific finish, this precocious yet muscular wine can be drunk now, but it has the requisite depth to last until 2010+.

LE MASSE DI SAN LEOLINO
Chianti Classico * * *, Chianti Classico Riserva * * *

1990 Chianti Classico	B	87
1988 Chianti Classico Riserva	C	89

This tiny estate of approximately 10 acres is known for producing wines of great ripeness from extremely low yields. Moreover, they are bottled unfiltered for the American importer. The 1990 Chianti Classico, made almost entirely from Sangiovese, displays a saturated garnet/dark ruby color, and an excellent bouquet of spicy herbs, new saddle leather, and ripe black cherry fruit touched by vague cedar scents. Full bodied, with excellent purity, richness, and lushness, this big yet structured Chianti should drink well for 7–8 years. The 1988 Chianti Classico Riserva reveals an impressive, saturated garnet color, an enticing, moderately intense, fruitcake/cigar box/licorice/overripe black cherry–scented nose, rich, full-bodied flavors, impressive concentration, and a long finish. Bigger than the 1990 regular cuvée, it has the potential to last for a decade or more.

MONSANTO

Chianti Classico Il Poggio* * * */* * * * *, Chianti Classico Riserva* * */* * * *, Nemo Vino da Tavola* * * *, Sangioveto Grosso Vino da Tavola* * * *, Tinscvil Vino da Tavola* * * *

1985 Chianti Classico Il Poggio   D   94

This single-vineyard Chianti from one of Tuscany's legendary producers is the best wine Monsanto has produced since the glorious duo of 1970 and 1971. A late-released Tuscan 1985, the quality makes the wait worthwhile. It is expensive, but this is exemplary juice! A huge nose of cedar, roasted berries, herbs, and tobacco leaps from the glass with remarkable intensity. The mouth-feel is one of voluptuous, superconcentrated, multidimensional fruit, glycerin, and hefty alcohol. This full-bodied, spectacular Chianti is already drinking magnificently, and based on past vintages, it can be expected to improve for at least another 7–8 years and last through most of the first decade of the next century. An exceptional wine, it serves as a benchmark for what heights Chianti can attain.

MONTE ANTICO
Rosso* * * *

1990 Rosso   A   88

Monte Antico's 1990 exhibits the mouth-filling, medium- to full-bodied, supple style that has made Monte Antico both a delicious red wine and a terrific wine bargain. It possesses a big, smoky, roasted herb– and black cherry–scented nose, chewy, intensely flavorful, robust flavors, decent acidity, light tannin, and a velvety-textured finish. It comes across as a hypothetical blend of a top-notch Chianti Classico and a Brunello di Montalcino. Interestingly, only a 12-foot-wide stream separates the Monte Antico vineyard from the vineyards of Brunello di Montalcino. The 1990 Monte Antico Rosso should drink well for 3–4 years. This wine merits buying by the case. Don't miss it!

MONTE VERTINE
Le Pergole Torte Vino da Tavola* * * *, Riserva Vino da Tavola* * * *,
Il Sodaccio Vino da Tavola* * * * *

1990 Le Pergole Torte Vino da Tavola   D   92

1990 Riserva Vino da Tavola   D   89

1990 Il Sodaccio Vino da Tavola   D   90

The 1990s from proprietor Sergio Manetti are the finest I have tasted from this high-profile Tuscan producer. All three wines exhibit considerable ripeness, as well as wonderfully layered, textured palates with gobs of ripe black cherry fruit intertwined with spicy new oak. The 1990 Le Pergole Torte (100% Sangioveto) reveals a compelling bouquet of roasted herbs, nuts, and sweet, jammy, plumlike fruit. The 1990 Il Sodaccio (100% Sangioveto) adds a chocolatey note to its rich, intense, black cherry–scented, medium- to full-bodied flavors. The 1990 Riserva is the most open and easy to drink of this trio (although all of these wines are flattering and accessible). A blend of Sangioveto and Canaiolo, the Riserva is lighter bodied and less intense than Le Pergole Torte and Il Sodaccio. Monte Vertine does not produce blockbuster wines in the sense of huge body and tannic, muscular personalities. The objective is to turn out polished, balanced yet rich and flavorful wines that are renowned for their harmony and elegance. The Riserva should drink well for 7–8 years, and Le Pergole Torte and Il Sodaccio for 7–12 years.

MORIS FARMS
Morellino di Scansano * * * *

1991 Morellino di Scansano Estate	A	86
1990 Morellino di Scansano Riserva	A	90

The 1991 Morellino di Scansano regular bottling offers a big, earthy, leathery, jammy, black cherry–scented nose, medium to full body, a chewy texture, plenty of fruit, and loads of gutsy character. It is a robust, earthy, full-flavored wine for drinking with equally intense dishes. The terrific 1990 Morellino di Scansano Riserva reveals a wonderfully fragrant, intense bouquet of cedar, red and black fruits, truffles, saddle leather, and a suggestion of toasty new oak. Full bodied, with exceptional richness and layers of ripe fruit, this intense wine is drinking well now, yet it promises to last for 5–6 years.

NOZZOLE
Chianti Classico Riserva * * * *, Il Pareto Vino da Tavola * * * */* * * * *

1990 Chianti Classico Riserva	C	87
1990 Il Pareto Vino da Tavola	D	90
1989 Il Pareto Vino da Tavola	D	87
1988 Il Pareto Vino da Tavola	D	89

Nozzole's impressive Cabernet Sauvignon–based Il Pareto performed admirably in three consecutive vintages. Certainly one would expect the 1988 and 1990 to be high class, but even the 1989 (a tough year for Tuscan wine producers) has turned out to be a fine effort. It exhibits a moderately dark purple color, a moderately intense bouquet of vanillin, black currants, and black cherries, admirable richness, cedary flavors, and a lush, supple finish. It should drink well for 7–8 years. The youthful 1988 may ultimately merit a higher score. It displays a saturated dark ruby/purple color with no signs of age. The wine's nose of explosively ripe, jammy, black fruit is complemented by a judicious use of spicy new oak barrels. Full and rich, with excellent delineation, medium to full body, and a slightly tannic finish, it should drink well for a decade. The 1990 is the best of this trio. It offers a tight but promising bouquet of jammy fruit, smoky, toasty new oak, and a cedary, spice box character. Full bodied, with an opulently rich palate, moderate tannin, and a heady finish dominated by the wine's glycerin, extraction of fruit, and alcohol, it should drink well for 10–15 years.

The classically made 1990 Chianti Classico Riserva exhibits textbook leather and berry scents, a spicy, medium- to full-bodied personality, excellent flavor concentration, tart acidity, and admirable robustness. Drink it over the next 5–7 years.

PODERE IL PALAZZINO
Chianti Classico * * * *, Chianti Classico Riserva * * * *,
Grosso Senese Vino da Tavola * * * */* * * * *

1988 Chianti Classico Riserva	C	90
1990 Grosso Senese Vino da Tavola	D	93+

Il Palazzino's 1988 Chianti Classico Riserva is one of the stars of the vintage. An exquisite nose of raspberries and spices is followed by a deep, rich, generously endowed wine with soft acidity, and huge masses of fruit buttressed by oak and glycerin. Drink this rich, medium- to full-bodied, dramatic Chianti between now and 2002. The 1990 Grosso Senese exhibits more promise than flattering aromas and flavors. It displays an impressively saturated dark ruby/purple color, and a reticent but emerging bouquet of smoky oak, leafy tobacco, and copious quantities of black raspberry fruit. The tannins and surprisingly high acidity give the wine a toughness and backward feel, but this is one case where there is more than enough fruit to carry it for 10–15 years. Impressive—but patience is essential! **A.M.: 1998–2010.**

PERTIMALI
Brunello di Montalcino* * * * *, Rosso di Montalcino* * * *

1990 Brunello di Montalcino	E	94
1988 Brunello di Montalcino	D	95+
1990 Brunello di Montalcino Riserva	EE	94+
1988 Brunello di Montalcino Riserva	E	94+
1990 Rosso di Montalcino	C	87

This tiny estate makes some of the finest red wines in Tuscany. The 1990 Rosso di Montalcino is a rich, full wine, with a huge, earthy, leathery, black cherry–scented nose, round, generous, succulent flavors, plenty of body, and plenty of glycerin and soft tannins in the finish. Drink it between now and 2002.

I am beginning to think that if I had only one Brunello di Montalcino to drink it would have to be Pertimali. This producer has been making spectacular wines since 1982. Unfortunately, quantities are microscopic, making availability a major headache. The awesome and inspirational 1988 Brunello di Montalcino is superextracted, with an opaque, deep ruby/purple color, and a highly promising nose of roasted nuts, black fruits, herbs, and Asian spices. The wine is massively rich yet impeccably well balanced, with fabulous purity, and a multidimensional feel to it. If you can find any, it is a must-purchase. **A.M.: 1996–2010.**

The 1990 Brunello di Montalcino Riserva is a wine of immense proportions and extraordinary complexity. I cannot say it is better than the regular cuvée since, in large measure, it possesses the same exuberance, personality, and depth of fruit. Yet it has an additional dimension of complexity and perfume. Dark ruby-colored, with a spicy, cedary, tobacco- and fruitcake-scented nose, this full-bodied, expansive wine offers a sensational attack. Even more noteworthy is the wine's length, which unfolds and expands impressively. Loads of tannin and alcohol infuse this wine with a joyous potential of 15–20 or more years of longevity. It is a stunning Brunello di Montalcino Riserva that can be drunk now or cellared. As prodigious a wine as it is, it will be extremely hard to find, given the microscopic quantities produced.

PETROIO
Chianti Classico Montetondo* * *, L'Unico Vino da Tavola* * *

1990 Chianti Classico Montetondo	A	85

Petroio's 1990 Chianti Classico Montetondo is an elegant, stylish, fruity wine with soft tannins, an attractive berry fruitiness, and a smooth finish. It should be drunk before the end of 1997.

CIACCI PICCOLOMINI D'ARAGONA
Brunello di Montalcino* * * * *, Rosso di Montalcino* * * *

1988 Brunello di Montalcino Riserva	D	90
1990 Rosso di Montalcino	C	90
1988 Rosso di Montalcino	C	89

I would have rated the 1988 Brunello di Montalcino Riserva even higher if it had not been for a whiff of lees in the wine's otherwise noteworthy bouquet. The modestly saturated ruby/

garnet color is followed by a big, spicy, smoky, herb- and red fruit–scented nose. This full-bodied, superbly balanced, concentrated wine is soft for a Brunello, and high in alcohol, with loads of cedary-, tobacco-, and curranty-flavored fruit. Approachable now, but capable of lasting for 15 more years, this is an impressively rich, spicy, smoky style of Brunello di Montalcino.

Two of the most stunning Rosso di Montalcinos I have ever tasted, these wines sell for one-third to one-fourth the price of the winery's Brunello di Montalcino. The 1990 reveals a dense, highly saturated, deep ruby/purple color. The nose offers up sweet smells of black fruits, minerals, herbs, and spices. In the mouth, there is massive concentration, full body, and moderate tannins in the long finish. Given the ripeness, glycerin, and richness, this wine can be drunk now, but it promises to improve for at least 7–10 years. I should also note that the label indicates this wine was produced from a single vineyard called Vigna della Fonte. Can you imagine how profound this producer's Brunello di Montalcino must be in 1990? The 1988 offering is deeply colored, with an intense nose of jammy black cherries, cedar, and Provençal herbs. In the mouth, there is exceptional richness, a big, full-bodied, brawny texture, and an explosively fruity, luscious, voluptuous finish. Drink this terrific wine over the next 6–7 years.

POGGIO AL SORBO
Chianti Classico* *

| 1990 Chianti Classico | A 85 |

This 1990 Chianti Classico reveals the virtues of the 1990 vintage—superripeness, low acidity, soft tannins, and plenty of fruit. Displaying an excellent medium to dark ruby color, a straightforward, immensely enjoyable berry-scented nose, medium body, and a fleshy, velvety-textured finish, this is a Chianti meant for drinking over the next 3–4 years.

POGGIO ANTICO
Altero Vino da Tavola* * * *, Brunello di Montalcino* * * */* * * * *,
Rosso di Montalcino* * *

1988 Altero	D 91
1988 Brunello di Montalcino	D 94
1991 Rosso di Montalcino	C 85

One of Brunello di Montalcino's emerging stars, Poggio Antico continues to produce some impressive Brunellos. The 1991 Rosso di Montalcino (the lighter, more supple sibling of Brunello) exhibits attractive, curranty, cedary fruit, medium to full body, a sweet, round, supple texture, and a soft, pleasant finish. This straightforward wine is ideal for drinking over the next 2–3 years. The profound 1988 Brunello di Montalcino boasts a huge nose of black cherries and spice box aromas intermingled with scents of wood, smoke, herbs, and cedar, full body, an unctuous, voluptuous texture, great concentration, and surprisingly low acidity. Poggio Antico's 1988 has tamed the vintage's toughness, producing a decadent, hedonistic Brunello that should drink well now and over the next 12–15 years.

This estate's proprietary red wine, or Vino da Tavola, the 1988 Altero, a small cask–aged wine, exhibits a fragrant bouquet of vanillin, herbs, and sweet, jammy, curranty, cassis fruit. Fat, chewy, opulent, and full bodied, it offers a wonderful, expansive, nearly viscous mouth-feel. Low in acidity, lush, and forward, with gobs of fruit intertwined with toasty new oak, it is a head-turning, ostentatious wine for drinking over the next 10–12 years.

POGGIO BONELLI
Chianti Classico Riserva* * *

| 1990 Chianti Classico Riserva | C 88 |

An impressively deep, rich, leathery, spicy, red and black fruit–scented and –flavored wine, Bonelli's 1990 Chianti Classico Riserva offers medium to full body, moderate tannin, and good structure to go along with its depth of fruit. Approachable now, it should age well for a decade.

POGGIO BRANDI
Vino da Tavola * * * *

1990 Vino da Tavola	D	89?

I tasted this wine only once. Made in extremely limited quantities, availability is restricted to some of the nation's finest Italian restaurants and a selected number of top wine shops specializing in Italian wines. The dark garnet color with an amber edge is followed by a decadent, rich wine with jammy, black cherry and peach fruit lavishly layered in a cedary, full-bodied, thick, chewy wine. Surprisingly, there is noticeable volatile acidity. Nevertheless, personality abounds in this opulent, velvety-textured, chewy wine that is sure to be controversial. Drink it over the near term.

POGGIO GALIGA
Chianti Rufina * * *

1990 Chianti Rufina	A	86

A big persuasive nose of tar, licorice, spices, leather, and black fruits is followed by a tasty, chunky, velvety-textured wine with excellent ripeness, and a long, heady finish. Although there is a certain rusticity to this Chianti, it is admirable for its depth and generous fruitiness. Drink it over the next 1–2 years.

IL POGGIONE (ROBERTO FRANCESCHI)
Brunello di Montalcino * * * *

1988 Brunello di Montalcino	C	89?

This impressive, large, full-bodied Brunello di Montalcino reveals some surprising amber at the edge, but it tastes youthful, with all of its potential still to be achieved. The wine exhibits a big, spicy, leathery, earthy, berry-scented nose, considerable body, and high tannin. Although the fruit is sweet, generous, and expansive, this wine may have a tendency to dry out before the tough tannin mellows. Drink it over the next 12–15 years.

LE PUPILLE
Morellino di Scansano Riserva * * * *, Saffredi Vino da Tavola * * * * *

1989 Morellino di Scansano Riserva	C	86
1988 Morellino di Scansano Riserva	B	88
1990 Saffredi Vino da Tavola	D	94

Made from 85% Sangiovese and 15% Alicante, the 1988 Morellino di Scansano Riserva possesses explosive fruit, and a huge, exotic nose of new saddle leather, cedar, spices, and gobs of rich, ripe berries. Thick, complex, and rich, with a full-bodied, velvety-textured feel, this attractive, generously endowed wine should drink well for 4–5 years. In the difficult Tuscan vintage of 1989, Le Pupille turned out a ripe Sangiovese-based wine (with some Alicante added). The 1989 Morellino di Scansano Riserva reveals sweet, expansive, ripe fruit, light tannin, and a medium-bodied, spicy, supple finish. I have found few 1989 Tuscan wines that are so well balanced. Most have a tendency to be astringent and hollow, but this wine is an exception. Drink it over the next 4–5 years.

The spectacular 1990 Saffredi (a blend of Sangiovese, Merlot, and Alicante) is a limited-production gem. Only 200 cases are available, so don't expect to easily find it. The wine boasts an opaque ruby/purple color, a huge, fabulously scented, penetrating bouquet of red and black fruits, smoky new oak, flowers, and spices. The wine is superconcentrated, with great purity and ripeness of fruit, high glycerin, a voluptuous texture, and a long, rich, concentrated finish. It is a beautifully balanced, powerful yet elegant wine that can be drunk now or cellared for 10–15 years. Impressive!

CASTELLO DI QUERCETO
Chianti Classico* * * *, Chianti Classico Riserva* * * *,
Cignale Vino da Tavola* * * */* * * * *, La Corte Vino da Tavola* * * *,
Il Querciolaia Vino da Tavola* * * *

1988 Chianti Classico Riserva Il Picchio	C	88
1988 Cignale Vino da Tavola	D	89+

The 1988 Cignale, a 95% Cabernet Sauvignon/5% Merlot blend, made from a tiny vineyard that yielded only one ton of fruit per acre, is a wine of great richness, power, and fruit. The intense bouquet of herbs and jammy cassis is followed by a full-bodied, structured, tightly knit wine with plenty of tannin, and a long, closed finish. Two to 3 years of cellaring is required; it should keep for 10–15 or more years. It is a potential candidate for an outstanding rating by the turn of the century. Also well endowed and impressive is this estate's 1988 Chianti Classico Riserva Il Picchio. It offers up an enticing perfume of underbrush, red and black fruits, truffles, and spice. Medium bodied with excellent ripeness and concentration, this wine is structured and rich enough to benefit from 1–3 years of cellaring. It will keep for 10–12 years.

S. QUIRICO
Chianti* * *

1990 Chianti	A	87

This is a controversial style of Chianti, with a bouquet that offers rich, earthy, berry scents combined with aromas of grilled sausage. The wine reveals an expansive, soft texture, excellent ripeness and depth, fine length, and an overall round, generous personality. Drink it between now and 1998.

CASTELLO DEI RAMPOLLA
Chianti Classico Riserva* * * *, Sammarco Vino da Tavola* * * * *

1990 Chianti Classico Riserva	C	90
1990 Sammarco Vino da Tavola	D	93

This outstanding Tuscan producer has been exceptionally consistent over the last decade, so it is not surprising that their 1990s performed brilliantly. The 1990 Chianti Classico Riserva exhibits an impressively saturated dark ruby/garnet color, and a spicy nose of ripe black cherries, earth, smoke, and roasted nuts. Very concentrated, medium to full bodied, with some moderate tannin still to be shed, this admirably endowed, rich, black cherry–flavored wine can be drunk now, but it promises to be even better in 2–3 years; it will last for 10–12 years. The 1990 Sammarco may prove to be a worthy rival to the glorious 1985. The saturated ruby/purple/garnet color is followed by an intense yet youthful fragrance of ripe black fruits, vanillin, and minerals. Full bodied, rich, beautifully delineated, and structured, it possesses considerable body, tannin, and extract. Although accessible, it is extremely young and ideally should have another 2–4 years of cellaring. It should age well for 15+ years. As I have said many times, Sammarco always reminds me of a top Graves, because of the tobacco/mineral component it often displays.

As a postscript, I recently had the 1985 Sammarco, largely because a subscriber had written to say it was falling apart. From my cellar, the wine remains remarkably youthful. Revealing no amber color, it offered a sensational nose of lead pencil, cassis, and new oak, as well as a gorgeously rich, powerful palate. Although close to maturity, it is capable of lasting for another 10–15 years.

E. RICASOLI-FIRIDOLFI

Chianti Classico* * * *, Chianti Classico Riserva* * * *, Chianti Classico Riserva Rocca di Montegrossi* * * *, Rocca di Montegrossi Geremia Vino da Tavola* * * * *

1990 Chianti Classico	B	89
1988 Chianti Classico Riserva	C	86
1990 Chianti Classico Riserva Rocca di Montegrossi	C	90
1990 Rocca di Montegrossi Geremia Vino da Tavola	D	92

The 1990 Chianti Classico Riserva Rocca di Montegrossi is a dark ruby-colored, rich, full-bodied Chianti with admirable ripeness, purity, and a spicy, leathery, tobacco, dusty black cherry component in both its aromatic and flavor profiles. While it will benefit from another 1–2 years of cellaring, the wine possesses enough structure to last for 10–12 years. It is an impressively built yet elegant style of Chianti. This producer's Vino da Tavola, the 1990 Geremia (a blend of Sangioveto and Canaiolo), boasts an impressive dark ruby/purple color, and a big, expansive nose of cedar, vanillin, black cherries, and currants. Very sweet (from ripeness, not sugar) with oodles of fruit, this lavishly rich, full-bodied, lush wine is reminiscent of a top-notch Pomerol, given its opulence and velvety texture. It is easy to overlook the moderate tannin level in the wine's finish. The Geremia is also a candidate for 10–12 years of cellaring.

The excellent 1988 Chianti Classico Riserva is crisp and tight, with relatively hard tannins, but fine underlying ripeness, and rich fruit. Its firmness and structure suggest to me that the tannins will probably outlive the fruit. Drink it over the next 7–8 years. On the other hand, the 1990 Chianti Classico exhibits a gorgeously perfumed, sensual nose of black fruits, wonderful purity, a voluptuous texture, medium to full body, and a satiny-textured finish. It is gorgeous for drinking over the next 6–7 years.

ROCCADORO
Chianti Classico* * *

1990 Chianti Classico	A	86

This wine possesses an attractive ruby color, and a nose that consists mostly of cherry fruit, smoke, and earth. Although not the most complex 1990 Chianti Classico, it offers an exuberance and purity to its medium-bodied, ripe, fruity personality.

RODANO
Chianti Classico* * *

1990 Chianti Classico	B	87+

This powerfully built, dense, broodingly backward Chianti reveals loads of fruit and glycerin, as well as moderate tannin. Still unevolved, it requires 1–2 more years of cellaring; it should keep for 10–12 years.

RUFFINO

Cabreo Il Borgo Vino da Tavola* * *, Chianti Classico* * *, Chianti Classico Aziano* * *, Chianti Classico Nozzole* * *, Chianti Classico Riserva Ducale (gold label)* * * * *, Chianti Classico Riserva Ducale (tan label)* * * *, Nero del Tondo Vino da Tavola* *

1990 Chianti Classico Riserva Ducale (Gold Label)	C	92
1988 Chianti Classico Riserva Ducale (Gold Label)	C	90
1988 Chianti Classico Riserva Ducale (Tan Label)	C	87

The 1990 wine exhibits the opulence and abundant richness of this great Tuscan vintage. A saturated plum/garnet color complements a sweet bouquet of cedar, roasted herbs, smoked meats, and jammy, black cherry fruit. This full-bodied, spicy, concentrated wine possesses muscle, power, and moderate tannin. It will benefit from 2–3 years of cellaring and will easily last for 20+ years. It appears to be one of the best Riserva Ducales Ruffino has produced. The 1988 gold label is a great example of a spicy, complex, leathery, richly fruity Chianti full of character and complexity. The saturated garnet/plum color is followed by a wine with loads of herb, smoke, saddle leather, Asian spice, and black fruit scents. Rich and full bodied, with admirable acidity and moderate tannin, this delicious, youthful wine is capable of lasting another two decades.

The spicy, earthy, robust 1988 Chianti Classico Riserva Ducale (tan label) reveals a mushroomy note in its otherwise attractive bouquet. The mushroom character blows off with airing, to be followed by rich, medium- to full-bodied, chewy, cherry and leathery flavors, good spice, plenty of alcohol, and a soft yet firm finish. Drink it over the next 5–6 years. Readers should not confuse the tan label Riserva Ducale with the more expensive and more ambitiously styled and concentrated gold label Riserva Ducale.

SAN FELICE
Brunello di Montalcino Campogiovanni * * * *, Chianti Classico * *, Chianti Classico Riserva Il Grigio * *, San Felice Vino da Tavola * *, Vigorello Vino da Tavola * * *

1988 Brunello di Montalcino Campogiovanni	C	89

San Felice has produced a precocious, already delicious and complex Brunello di Montalcino from their 30-acre Campogiovanni vineyard. The color is a healthy dark ruby, and the nose offers up expressive and intense aromas of sweet red and black fruits, roasted nuts, and cedar. Full bodied, rich, round, and generous, this large-scaled, velvety-textured Brunello di Montalcino can be drunk now and over the next 10–12 years. This is unquestionably one of the most seductive and succulent 1988s I have tasted from Brunello di Montalcino.

SAN GIUSTO A RENTENTANO
Chianti Classico * * * *, Percarlo Vino da Tavola * * * * *

1990 Chianti Classico	C	86
1990 Chianti Classico Riserva	C	88
1988 Chianti Classico Riserva	C	88+
1990 Percarlo	D	93

This producer has released some thrilling wines over the last few years, particularly their 1985 proprietary red table wine called Percarlo. The seductive 1990 Percarlo is a worthy rival to the otherworldly 1985. The deep ruby/purple color is followed by a nose that offers abundant amounts of smoky, toasty new oak and cassis. Voluptuous, medium to full bodied, with exceptional concentration and delineation, this rich Vino da Tavola has consistently been one of the stars of Tuscany. Drink it now through 2010.

The most recent San Giusto releases include their 1990 Chianti Classico, a surprisingly light wine for this producer, made in an up-front, fruity, medium-bodied style with spicy, cherry fruit, soft tannins, and enough richness to carry it until 1998. The 1988 Chianti Classico Riserva is a more complete and complex wine, exhibiting a deep ruby color, and an excellent nose of saddle leather, black fruits, herbs, tobacco, and spice. Rich and dense, with layer upon layer of richly extracted fruit, this youthful, bigger-styled Chianti can be drunk now and will last for 10 years.

San Giusto a Rententano has fashioned a rich, medium- to full-bodied, spicy 1990 Chianti Classico Riserva with gorgeous cherry/raspberry fruit intertwined with aromas and flavors of licorice, earth, leather, and spices. Already delicious, it possesses the structure and extraction level to last for at least a decade.

SAN GUIDO
Sassicaia Vino da Tavola* * * * *

1990 Sassicaia Vino da Tavola	E 94+

The 1990 Sassicaia appears to be the finest wine made at this estate since the nearly perfect 1985. It boasts a saturated purple, almost bluish color, and a sensational yet unevolved and youthful aromatic profile of sweet, nearly overripe black currants, cedar, tobacco, and toasty new oak. Full bodied, with staggering concentration and extract levels, this tannic, superpure, well-defined Cabernet possesses low enough acidity and sweet enough tannin to make it accessible to those readers unable to defer their gratification. But do not expect this wine to attain its plateau of maturity before the end of the century; it will last through 2010.

FATTORI SANTA ANNA
Rosso di Santa Anna* * *, Vigna Il Vallone Vino da Tavola* * * *

1992 Rosso di Santa Anna	A 86
1990 Vigna Il Vallone Vino da Tavola	C 89

This tiny 12-acre Tuscan estate produced an excellent bargain with their 1992 Rosso di Santa Anna. The wine displays round, leathery, meaty flavors, a soft texture, and ripe fruit in a medium-bodied, straightforward manner. Drink it over the next 1–2 years. The proprietary red wine (referred to as Vino da Tavola), the 1990 Vigna Il Vallone, is a blend of Cabernet Sauvignon, Sangiovese, and several Sangiovese clones. It is a rich wine, with a dark ruby color, a spicy, leathery, smoky-scented nose, excellent ripeness, medium to full body, moderate tannin, and a long, spicy finish. There is a touch of vanillin, but less than expected given the fact that it was largely aged in new oak casks.

GUICCIARDINI STROZZI
Sodole Vino da Tavola* * * */* * * * *

1990 Sodole	C 90

This rich, complex, full-bodied wine is just beginning to open up aromatically. The bouquet is reticent and the wine requires coaxing, preferably in a large Riedel Bordeaux glass. The wine's dark color is followed by vague hints of oak, damp earth, black fruits, fennel, and herbs. The wine is rich, with its high extraction hiding what appears to be a moderate tannin level. Chewy, powerful, and spicy, this complex Vino da Tavola made from 100% Sangiovese should drink well for 8–12 years.

TALOSA
Chianti* * *, Rosso di Montalcino* * *, Vino Nobile di Montepulciano* * *

1990 Chianti	A 86

Talosa's bargain-priced 1990 Chianti offers wonderfully ripe fruit, a lovely chewy texture, vivid purity, and a tasty, medium-bodied, heady finish. It is all a Chianti should be— satisfying and a joy to drink. Consume it between now and 1998.

TERRABIANCA
Campaccio Vinoda Tavola* * * * *, Campaccio Riserva Vino da Tavola* * * * *,
Chianti Riserva Croce* * * * *,
Chianti Scassino* * * *, Cipresso Vino da Tavola* * * */* * * * *

1990 Campaccio	C 93
1990 Campaccio Riserva	D 93+

1989 Campaccio Riserva	D	89
1988 Chianti Riserva Croce	C	92
1990 Chianti Scassino	B	88
1990 Cipresso	C	91

The Terrabianca estate has benefited from significant financial investments, and the results are superb wines, which, in my opinion, are underpriced given the exceptional quality level.

The 1990 Chianti Scassino offers a wonderful toasty, roasted nut–, herb–, and black cherry–scented nose, rich, full-bodied flavors, excellent concentration, and a deep, spicy finish. It should drink well for a decade. The 1988 Chianti Riserva Croce reveals a saturated, opaque garnet/purple color, a huge nose of roasted hazelnuts, cedar, cassis, and truffles, and full body. The wine is wonderfully rich, expansive, and almost sweet because of the fruit's richness. With a long, intense finish and moderate tannin, 2–3 years of cellaring will be beneficial. This is a great example of a 1988 Riserva that should age well for two decades.

Terrabianca's 1990 Cipresso, made from 100% Sangiovese, exhibits a fragrant, intense perfume of spicy, new French oak, sweet cassis fruit, chocolate, and herbs. The wine possesses great concentration, a supple, full-bodied, chewy texture, layers of ripe fruit, and a long, velvety-textured finish. It should drink well for 10–15 years. Like most of the Terrabianca wines from great Tuscan vintages, it is underpriced vis-à-vis its quality.

The 1990 Campaccio, a blend of Sangiovese and Cabernet Sauvignon, displays a big, smoky, herb- and black currant–scented nose, superb richness, a huge, chewy, full-bodied palate, admirable purity, and dazzling length. Supple enough to be drunk now, it promises to last for 10–15 years. In the relatively difficult Tuscan vintage of 1989, Terrabianca has turned out a fine 1989 Campaccio Riserva. It offers an herb-, tobacco-, vanillin-, and cassis-scented nose, rich, medium- to full-bodied flavors, adequate acidity, and a smooth, concentrated finish with gobs of ripe fruit. Drink it over the next 7–8 years. The 1990 Campaccio Riserva is a must-purchase for enthusiasts of great Tuscan proprietary red wines. It possesses a stunning nose of lead pencil aromas (a Mouton-Rothschild smell-alike), cassis, tobacco, vanillin, and cedar. The wine's opaque purple color suggests (and the flavors confirm it) great concentration. There are chocolatey, cassis flavors that ooze from the wine's innards. Full, rich, and spectacularly well balanced with adequate acidity and moderate tannin in the blockbuster finish, this is a monumental example of a Tuscan Sangiovese/Cabernet Sauvignon blend. Drink it over the next 15–20 years.

AZIENDA AGRICOLA LA TORRE (LUIGI ANANIA)
Brunello di Montalcino* * * * *, Rosso di Montalcino* * * *

1990 Brunello di Montalcino	D	93+
1988 Brunello di Montalcino	D	93
1991 Rosso di Montalcino	B	86

This estate is a noteworthy discovery. The 1991 vintage for Rosso di Montalcino is not highly regarded, but this producer's 1991 Rosso is an elegant, well-made, ripe, supple wine exhibiting jammy fruit, medium to full body, and that telltale, leathery, tobacco, ripe berry component of a top-notch Brunello. Drink it over the next 3–4 years.

Both the 1988 and 1990 Brunello di Montalcinos are statuesque wines of immense power, richness, body, and alcohol. Brunello enthusiasts will want to take note of the 1990. The wine exhibits a dark ruby/garnet color, and an ostentatious bouquet of Asian spices, jammy black cherries, herbs, cedar, and leather. Dense and concentrated, with adequate acidity, this stunningly proportioned, massive Brunello should drink well young and hit its peak in

7–10 years; it will last for 20+ years. The 1988 displays a similar size, without the decadent overripe characteristics of the 1990. Yet who can ignore its smashingly intense nose of leather, smoked game, meat, and fruitcake scents, gobs of black cherry fruit flavors, super opulence, moderate tannin, and ample glycerin, alcohol, and body? While approachable because of its glorious display of fruit, it will benefit from 4–5 years of cellaring; it is a 20-year wine.

TOSCOLO
Chianti Classico * * *, Chianti Classico Riserva * * *

1990 Chianti Classico	A	85

Toscolo's 1990 Chianti Classico exhibits a straightforward but intense red fruit character, medium body, soft tannins, and a velvety, lusciously fruity finish. Drink it over the next 2–3 years.

TENUTA TREROSE
Vino Nobile di Montepulciano Riserva * * *

1988 Vino Nobile di Montepulciano Riserva	C	87

Some notes of vanillin and lees are intertwined with scents of ripe black and red cherries in this wine's moderately intense bouquet. Sweet, jammy fruit possesses adequate underlying acidity, moderate tannin, and medium to full body. This rich, approachable Vino Nobile di Montepulciano Riserva should age gracefully for 7–10 years.

VAL DI SUGA
Brunello di Montalcino * * * *, Brunello di Montalcino Vigna Spuntali * * * *

1988 Brunello di Montalcino Vigna Spuntali	D	90

This complex Brunello di Montalcino offers an enticing bouquet of new saddle leather, ripe fruit, earth, and spices. Cedary and berry flavors accompany a rich wine with moderate tannin, full body, a fleshy feel, and excellent purity and balance. Although approachable now, it should last for 12–15 years.

CASTELL'IN VILLA
Chianti Classico * * * *, Chianti Classico Riserva * * * * *, Santacroce Vino da Tavola * * * *

1990 Chianti Classico	B	89
1990 Chianti Classico Riserva	C	91
1988 Chianti Classico Riserva	C	90
1988 Santacroce Vino da Tavola	D	87?

This serious estate is dedicated to low-yielding vineyards that produce long-lived Chianti. At a recent tasting I had the 1971, 1975, and 1977 Riservas, rating them, respectively, 88, 90, and 89 points. They shared a vibrant personality that exhibited rich, sweet, ripe fruit that had not yet begun to fade. The 1988 and 1990 Riservas have the potential to easily last as long.

The top-notch 1990 Chianti Classico exhibits an earthy, licorice- and black cherry–scented nose, full body, outstanding ripeness and richness, and a sweet, jammy, leathery, Asian spice character. This delicious Chianti is capable of lasting for 5–7 years. The 1990 Chianti Classico Riserva raises the extraction and tannin levels, and possesses greater ripeness and a longer finish. It reveals a similar cigar box, Asian spice character. With its lavish quantities of black cherry fruit and that wonderful, sweet expansiveness that comes from low yields, not sugar, it is a glorious Chianti that should drink well for 15+ years. The 1988 Chianti Classico Riserva is a dense, full-bodied, rich, concentrated, powerful Chianti with moderate tannin, crisp acidity, and a roasted herb/black cherry/leathery character. It will benefit from several years of cellaring and will last for 15+ years.

Castell'In Villa's proprietary red wine, the *barrique*-aged 1988 Santacroce (a blend containing 90% Sangiovese), is a more controversial wine. Perhaps I tasted it during an evolutionary stage where the oak was more blatantly displayed than usual. Despite the wine's impressive flavor extraction and ripe fruit, the wood component dominated the wine's otherwise impressive components. The vanillin smokiness is apparent in both the nose and flavors. This could turn out to be a knockout wine, but unless the oakiness develops a subtle character and becomes better integrated, this wine will have a tendency to taste out of balance.

VILLA CAFAGGIO
Chianti Classico* * * *, Cortaccio Vino da Tavola* * * * *, San Martino Vino
da Tavola* * * * *, Solatio Basilica Vino da Tavola* * * */* * * * *

1990 Chianti Classico	B	88
1990 Cortaccio Vino da Tavola	C	90
1990 San Martino Vino da Tavola	C	91
1990 Solatio Basilica Vino da Tavola	C	89

An excellent estate, Villa Cafaggio fashioned four impressive wines in 1990. The most flattering, supple, and easily drinkable wine of this quartet is the 1990 Chianti Classico. The medium ruby color does not suggest the intense, jammy, cherry perfume and stylish, lush, supple, medium-bodied flavors that the taster encounters. This decadent, round, velvety-textured Chianti is a real turn-on. It is reminiscent of a lighter-styled Château Lafleur from Pomerol! Drink it over the next 4–5 years. The 1990 Solatio Basilica, from several small vineyards planted with Sangiovese, reveals a deeper color as well as more sweetness and ripeness. Although similar to the Chianti Classico, it is deeper, fuller, and riper. It shares the rich, black cherry fragrance and sweetness of fruit offered by the estate's Chianti, but the Solatio Basilica is higher in alcohol and more influenced by *barrique* aging. It is an example of an exceptionally elegant yet immensely pleasing, seductive wine. Drink it over the next 5–7 years.

The outstanding 1990 Cortaccio is made from 100% Cabernet Sauvignon. It exhibits a saturated deep ruby/purple color, and an intense, forceful, complex nose of sweet, creamy new oak and black currants. Medium to full bodied, with layers of rich, highly extracted fruit, yet supple and elegant, this lush, generously endowed wine can be drunk now, yet possesses the balance to age well for 7–10 years. The 1990 San Martino is made from two-thirds Sangiovese and one-third Sangiovese Grosso. Like its sibling, the Cortaccio, it is aged in small French oak casks. It has more typicity in a Tuscan sense than the Cortaccio, which possesses that international Cabernet Sauvignon/new oak cask personality. Does the San Martino exhibit more character? Perhaps. The wine displays a healthy dark ruby color, an earthy, black cherry– and vanillin-scented nose, full body, more structure than Villa Cafaggio's other wines, moderate tannin, and excellent depth and richness. With another year of cellaring, more richness and complexity will emerge. It is a candidate for 10–15 years of drinkability. These four offerings are impressive!

VILLA DI GEGGIANO
Chianti Classico Riserva* * *

1990 Chianti Classico Riserva	C	87

This delicious, medium ruby-colored Chianti offers a fragrant bouquet of sweet black cherry fruit intertwined with floral scents, a lush, round, generous, supple texture, and medium body. It is a flattering, precocious style of Chianti for drinking over the next 4–5 years.

CASTELLO DI VOLPAIA

Balifico Vino da Tavola* * * *, Chianti Classico* * *, Chianti Classico Riserva* * * *,
Coltassala Vino da Tavola* * * *

1990 Balifico Vino da Tavola	D 87
1990 Coltassala Vino da Tavola	D 88+

I recently tasted through a number of new offerings from this fine Chianti producer, Castello di Volpaia. I found the 1990 Riserva, 1988 Riserva, and 1991 regular bottling to be uninspiring, straightforward wines. However, the two proprietary reds, the 1990 Balifico (65% Sangioveto and 35% Cabernet Sauvignon) and the 1990 Coltassala (95% Sangioveto and 5% Mammolo), are both excellent wines. The nicely concentrated 1990 Balifico is a tightly knit, spicy, medium-bodied wine with an obvious influence from new oak. It requires another 1–2 years of cellaring; it should last for a decade. Potentially more promising, the 1990 Coltassala exhibits a darker color, as well as more tannin. Fortunately, it is also richer, riper, and fuller, with a sweeter, more expansive finish. Although austere and backward, it is extremely well made. Drink it between 1996 and 2005.

OTHER SIGNIFICANT WHITE WINES OF ITALY

Tuscany's White Wines

Improvements are certainly noticeable, but the overall situation with respect to Tuscany's white wines remains unsatisfactory. Although much has been made of the modern style of white winemaking, Tuscany continues to rely on high-tech processing to fashion too many white wines that are bland and fruitless, packaged in designer bottles, and sold at $20 and up a bottle. Wines such as San Quirico's Vernaccia di San Gimignano, Antinori's Bianco Toscaro, Borro della Sala Castello della Sala, and Galestro, Avignonesi's Chardonnay Il Marzocco, Castello Banfi's Sauvignon Serena, Isole E Olena's Chardonnay, Nozzole's Chardonnay, Frescobaldi's Pomino, and the wave of luxury-priced, designer-packaged Chardonnays (such as Castello d'Albola's Le Fagge, Castellare's Canonico, Felsina Berardenga's I Sistri, Castello di Ama's Vigna al Poggio, Caparzo's Les Grance, Banfi's Fontanelle, Montellori's Castelrapiti, and Ruffino's Cabero la Pietra and Libaio, a Chardonnay/Sauvignon blend), are frightfully overpriced and usually too oaky. I find it hard to believe that consumers are gullible enough to buy these slick products.

The only Tuscany white wine that I can recommend consistently is the Vernaccia di San Gimignano from the best producers. Supposedly it was Michelangelo's favorite wine! It is not made from overoaked Chardonnay or from the bland, neutral, tart Trebbiano, but from the Vernaccia grape that comes from the amazing, medieval, fortified hill town of San Gimignano. At its best, it is refreshingly crisp, light, nutty flavored, and dry, and it is a wonderful match with fish or chicken. The best recent vintage is 1994; the 1993s are correct wines.

Vernaccia di San Gimignano Recommended Producers

The finest Vernaccias have come from the following producers.

Falchini	Guiccardini Strozzi
di Pancole	Guiccardini Strozzi San Biagio Riserva
Pietraserena Vigna del Sol	Teruzzi & Puthod
San Quirico	Teruzzi & Puthod Terre di Tufo

Other Tuscan White Wines of Merit

Avignonesi Bianco Vergine Valdichiana
Avignonesi Il Vignola (Sauvignon Blanc)
Badia a Coltibuono Cetamura
Badia a Coltibuono Trappoline

Fontodi Meriggio (Traminer/Pinot Bianco/
   Sauvignon blend)
Poliziano Bianco Vergine Valdichiana
La Stella Lunaia Bianco di Pitgliano

OTHER ITALIAN WHITE WINES

ARGIOLAS (SARDINIA)* * *

1993 Bianco	B	86

This 1993 Bianco is a modern-style, fruity, fresh, medium-bodied wine with surprising concentration and character, as well as a dry, vibrant, pure finish. It should be consumed with fish or fowl over the next year.

FEUDI DI SAN GREGORIO (CAMPANIA)* * *

1993 Fiano di Avellino	C	88
1993 Greco di Tufo	B	89

This producer, whose vineyards are located near Naples, has fashioned an extremely aromatic 1993 Greco di Tufo with lovely fruit, and a delicious, Viognier-like floral fragrance intertwined with the scent of peaches and apricots. The wine offers a pleasing vibrancy, and delicious, dry, crisp flavors. The 1993 Fiano di Avellino is another aromatic, medium-bodied, dry white wine with excellent purity, surprising richness and intensity, and a long, crisp finish. These wines do not reveal any evidence of cask aging, which I believe is to their benefit. They display gorgeously ripe, fragrant bouquets, and loads of fruit. Both of these white wines should be drunk over the next 1–2 years.

REGALEALI (SICILY)* * *

1993 Bianco	B	86
1992 Nozze d'Oro	C	88

The 1993 Bianco displays elegant, crisp, floral fruit, medium body, and admirable freshness and liveliness. It should be drunk over the next year. More enticing is Regaleali's 1992 Nozze d'Oro. Although it may appear expensive, this wine, made from what is thought to be a Sauvignon Blanc clone with a Muscat-like fragrance, exhibits an impressively penetrating nose of honeyed melons and flowers. The lovely fragrance is followed by enough acidity to provide delineation and focus, and a zesty, vibrant, luscious finish. This is one of the best dry white Italian wines I have ever tasted. Don't let its rapture pass you by—drink it over the next year. I also appreciated the old-style label. The black-and-white photograph of a husband and wife was taken at the Regaleali's fiftieth-wedding-anniversary celebration.

OTHER SIGNIFICANT RED WINES OF ITALY

FATTORIA DI ANGELLI (VENETO)* * *

1991 Valpolicella Classico Superiore	A	85

What a relief to find a Valpolicella with a bouquet, lovely flavor, excellent balance, and a soft, light-bodied, spicy, berry and smoked nut–like fruitiness. Drink it over the next 1–2 years.

ARGIOLAS (SARDINIA)* * */* * * *

1992 Costera	B	87
1992 Perdera	A	86
1989 Turriga	C	90

The prospects are good for high-quality wines from Sardinia, which is experiencing a profound winemaking revolution. Not only are the hillside vineyards being resurrected and replanted, but some of Italy's most influential oenologists (for example, Signor Tacchis, the winemaking architect behind Solaia and Sassicaia) are frequent visitors to this island. The following offerings are all impressively made wines, with two notable values and one potentially outstanding effort.

The 1992 Perdera reveals an excellent medium to dark ruby color, a black cherry– and raspberry-scented nose, pure, ripe berry fruit, soft tannin, adequate acidity, and a generous mouth-feel and finish. This soft, well-made wine is ideal for consuming over the next 3–4 years. The 1992 Costera, made from a grape called Cannonau (indigenous to Sardinia and believed to be this island's clone of Grenache), exhibits a thick, smoky, peppery, spicy, black fruit–scented nose, full body, an unctuous, chewy, fleshy texture, and fine purity and length in the heady finish. This boldly flavored, rich, meaty wine should drink well for 5–6 years. The most intriguing Argiolas wine is the 1989 Turriga. A dazzling nose of smoke, black cherries, damp earth, sweet oak, and cedar jumps from the glass. This dark ruby/garnet-colored wine is full bodied, and wonderfully expansive and chewy, with gobs of fruit, excellent purity, and a voluptuously textured finish. Even though it is already delicious, it possesses outstanding concentration and balance, so expect it to drink well for at least a decade. Very impressive!

CORNACCHIA (ABRUZZI)* * * *

1992 Montepulciano d'Abruzzo	A	88

This dark ruby/purple-colored wine offers a big, peppery, spicy, rich, fruity nose, earthy, full-bodied flavors, superb extraction, and a luscious, rich, chewy finish. It is reminiscent of an excellent Châteauneuf du Pape from France's Rhône Valley (but Châteauneuf du Pape of this quality does not sell for a lowly $9.50).

DAL FORMO ROMANO (VENETO)* * * *

1988 Valpolicella Superiore	D	91

My reference point for Valpolicella has always been those produced by Quintarelli, but this wine is unquestionably the greatest Valpolicella I have ever tasted. One does not expect a Valpolicella to be this complex, rich, and potentially age-worthy. The nose offers up huge aromas of ripe plums, spices, and sweet cedary scents. Unctuously textured, with lavish quantities of fruit, this medium- to full-bodied, velvety-textured wine is undeniably seductive, as well as thoroughly delicious. Although the price seems high for a Valpolicella, this is a great red wine! This decadently styled Valpolicella should drink well for at least 5–7 years.

FARNESE (ABRUZZI)* * *

1991 Montepulciano d'Abruzzo	A	86

This medium to dark ruby-colored wine is loaded with round, sweet, black cherry and raspberry fruit. It also boasts a velvety texture and a lush finish. Restaurants should consider serving it by the glass.

FEUDI DI SAN GREGORIO (CAMPANIA)* * *

1993 Albenta	A	86

The 1993 Albenta is a plum- and cherry-scented, spicy, dry red wine with medium body, fine freshness, and a mouth-filling, chewy texture. Although not complex, it is a well-made, satisfying red wine for drinking over the next 3–4 years.

FILOMUSI GUELFI (ABRUZZI)* * *

1991 Montepulciano d'Abruzzo	A	86

Just about every offering from Montepulciano d'Abruzzo that I have tasted from high-quality importers is top notch, as well as bargain priced. This full-bodied, gutsy, robust red wine exhibits gobs of peppery, earthy, chewy fruit, glycerin, and headiness, and an expansive, immensely satisfying mouth-feel in the finish. It should drink well for 2–3 years, but why defer your gratification? As big and rich as they are, most Montepulciano d'Abruzzos are delicious when released.

LIBRANDI (CALABRIA)* * *

1991 Ciro Rosso	A	86
1987 Duca San Felice	B	87
1989 Gravello	C	89+

These three red wine offerings from southern Italy's so-called boot all possess rich, overripe, robust, intense personalities. The 1991 Ciro Rosso is made from the obscure Gaplioppo grape. The wine exhibits a big, spicy, melted road tar, earthy, rustic, peppery nose, chewy, thick, rich flavors of sweet, jammy cherries, and low acidity. This mouth-filling, alcoholic wine is filled with character. Drink it over the next 3–4 years. The 1987 Duca San Felice offers up a spicy, cedary, jammy, cherry-scented nose, with a touch of chocolate and truffles. Stylistically it is reminiscent of a ripe, medium- to full-bodied Grenache-based wine from France's Languedoc-Roussillon, such as a Minervois. This mouth-filling, supple, dense wine is a candidate for 5–6 years of cellaring. The most impressive wine of this trio (also the most expensive) is the 1989 Gravello. Made from 60% Gaplioppo and 40% Cabernet Sauvignon, this is a rich, spicy, smoky, toasty wine (some new oak cask aging has obviously taken place), with great ripeness, wonderful richness, a full-bodied, layered personality, soft tannin, and chewy fruit in the finish. This wine is capable of 5–8 years of cellaring. These are all intriguing, distinctive wines with broad appeal.

LUNGAROTTI (UMBRIA)* * *

1991 Rubesco Rosso di Torgiano	B	84
1985 San Giorgio Vino da Tavola Umbria	C	88

The well-known firm of Lungarotti has turned out a pleasant, medium ruby-colored, soft, earthy 1991 Rubesco that is ideal for uncritical drinking. With a nice spicy note, ripe fruit, and medium body, it should last for 2–3 years. More impressive, as well as more expensive and limited in availability, is the 1985 San Giorgio, a Cabernet Sauvignon–based wine. It reveals a mature ruby color with some lightening at the edges. The cedary, spicy, curranty nose is reminiscent of a very good St.-Julien or Pauillac. The wine exhibits medium to full body, an attractive suppleness, smoky, well-integrated oak, and sweet, round, expansive flavors. It is supple, delicious, complex, and ideal for drinking over the next 4–6 years.

ROBERTO MAZZI (VENETO)* * *

1991 Valpolicella Classico Superiore	B	87

Along with the enviable Quintarelli, Mazzi is one of a handful of superstars toiling in the vineyards of Valpolicella. This 1991 is an extremely delicate wine that requires a degree of introspection. The color is a feeble light ruby, but the nose offers up subtle yet focused scents of roasted herbs, nuts, and sweet red fruits. Extremely well balanced, with a lusciousness and subtlety, this medium-bodied, finesse-style wine should be drunk over the next 2–4 years.

ELIO MONTI (ABRUZZI)* * */* * * *

1992 Montepulciano d'Abruzzo	A	88
1990 Montepulciano d'Abruzzo	A	87

The 1992 Montepulciano d'Abruzzo from Elio Monti is a terrific example of just how much good wine a consumer is capable of finding for under $10. The opaque, dense, purple/black color is followed by a huge but uncomplex nose of ripe cassis fruit, black cherries, and subtle licorice and earthy notes. Gorgeously rich and fruity, as well as deep and full bodied, this huge yet velvety-textured wine can be drunk now or cellared for 5–6 years. Since it was bottled unfiltered, expect this wine to throw a little sediment given its saturated color and dense, chewy, rich style.

A powerhouse, opaque purple-colored wine that has been bottled without fining or filtration, the amazingly rich, hugely extracted, generous, expansive, soft, plushly textured 1990 is oozing with aromas and flavors of herbs, blackberries, and spices. The tannin is soft, the fruit is impressive, and the level of pleasure and mouth-filling satisfaction are remarkable for the wine's price.

REGALEALI (SICILY)* * *
Cabernet Sauvignon* * * *, Rosso* * *, Rosso del Conte* * * *

1990 Cabernet Sauvignon	D	91+
1989 Cabernet Sauvignon	D	87
1989 Regaleali	A	86
1993 Rosé	B	87
1991 Rosso	B	86
1990 Rosso	B	87
1989 Rosso del Conte	C	88
1988 Rosso del Conte	C	88

Since I first tasted this producer's wines there has been extraordinary improvement in quality with the modern-style, distinctive, dry whites as well as the reds. There is even an aromatic, full-bodied, dry rosé that merits accolades!

I am a sucker for a full-bodied, crisp, dry rosé that relies on flavor extraction rather than sugar for its body and personality. Regaleali's 1993 Rosé is a delicate, authoritatively flavored rosé with an attractive, berry-scented nose, and considerable flavor, all presented in a subtle fashion. Drink it over the next year.

The two newest red wines include the 1991 Rosso, a reasonably good value in a plumply styled, chewy, black cherry–scented and –flavored wine. While it may lack complexity, it offers good body and fruit. Drink it over the next 2–3 years. The 1989 Rosso del Conte exhibits plenty of black cherry and cassis fruit in the nose, as well as notes of toasty new oak and herbs. This well-defined, structured wine is deep, long, and crammed with ripe fruit, and has light tannin and decent acidity. Already delicious, this impressive wine should age well for up to a decade. Made from 8-year-old vines, Regaleali's 1990 Cabernet Sauvignon is a massive example of Cabernet. It exhibits a black/purple color, phenomenal extract and richness, and a big, chewy, cassis, cherry, licorice, and chocolatey nose with hints of saddle leather in the background. Full bodied and moderately tannic, this extremely young, unevolved wine should continue to improve for up to a decade and last for 20 years. Bravo!

The 1990 Rosso exhibits an earthy, tar- and black fruit—scented nose, spicy, mouth-filling, chewy flavors, plenty of glycerin, adequate acidity, and a robust finish. It is a rustic, generously endowed wine for drinking over the next 5–6 years. The 1988 Rosso del Conte is made from a selection of Regaleali's best grapes and is fermented longer. The result is a more jammy, concentrated, darker-colored wine that offers a decade or more of aging potential. The wine reveals gobs of earthy, black cherry and curranty fruit, a touch of Asian spice, and a velvety, smooth, heady finish. Drinkable now, it should age well for at least 10 more years.

Regaleali's first Cabernet Sauvignon release, the 1989, augurs well for the potential of this varietal on the sun- and wind-drenched slopes of Sicily. It possesses a dark ruby/purple color, a big, smoky, black plum– and cherry-scented nose, unctuously rich, thick, chewy flavors, moderate tannin, low acidity, and a spicy finish. Drink it over the next 7–8 years. The 1989 Regaleali displays a deep ruby color, a spicy, richly fruity, chocolatey, roasted fruit nose, excellent richness and definition, and a deep, full-bodied, lusty finish. It should drink well between now and 2001.

LE SALETTE (VENETO)* * *

1991 Valpolicella Classico	A	85

So much of the Valpolicella found in American wine shops is from industrial-sized giants that turn out such diluted, soulless wines that few consumers are likely to find any pleasure in them. This is the real thing! At its best, Valpolicella should be an exuberant, richly fruity, velvety-textured wine that is vibrant and lively. This example from Le Salette is all that and more. There is good fruit, it is a delight to drink, and the wine exhibits personality. Consume it over the next year.

SILVIO IMPARATO (CAMPANIA)* * * * *

1993 Montevetrano	D	96
1992 Montevetrano	D	94
1991 Montevetrano	D	90

Perhaps the most thrilling part of my profession is to taste a great wine that I know nothing about, has never been imported to the United States, and is a relatively new creation of a visionary. A wine that meets these criteria is Montevetrano, produced by Silvia Imparto, an Italian photographer who has a south-facing hillside vineyard (average age of the vines is 30 years) planted with 60% Cabernet Sauvignon, 30% Merlot, and 10% Aglianco. After a long maceration, the wine is aged 12 months in new French oak and bottled without filtration. Only 400 cases are produced each year. The wine is remarkable for its complexity, intensity, and richness—sort of a Sassicaia of the southern Naples hillside! I tasted the 1991, 1992, and 1993, and rated them 90, 94, and 96 respectively! They are world class wines by any standard of measurement. All three vintages are capable of 10–15+ years of evolution, although their ripe sweetness of fruit and supple, full-bodied textures make them deliciously approachable. As with so many things of high quality, these impeccably made wines are very limited in availability, but, hey, hey, I have done my job. I urge readers to join me in making Montevetrano a household name!

DR. COSIMO TAURINO (APULIA)* * * *

1986 Notarpanaro	B	90
1985 Notarpanaro	A	89
1983 Notarpanaro	A	90
1988 Patriglione	C	88

1990 Salice Salentino	A	87
1988 Salice Salentino Riserva	A	89
1986 Salice Salentino Riserva	A	87

Taurino's Salice Salentino has long been one of the world's best wine bargains. The newest release, the 1990, continues to offer huge appeal, as well as value. It may be even better than previous examples. Some of the tar/earth notes that are disliked by some consumers have disappeared in favor of a wonderfully pure, smoky, black cherry– and curranty-scented nose. The wine is medium to full bodied, with a multilayered, rich, fleshy texture, gobs of fruit, and a smooth-as-silk finish. A delicious bargain, it will offer a robust, gutsy, chewy glass of dry red wine over the next 5–10 years. It is a wine worth buying by the case. The 1986 Notarpanaro increases the levels of concentration, glycerin, body, and alcohol, and adds an element of rusticity and tannin. The wine is full bodied, chewy, thick, and rich. It is a winter-weight wine that is best consumed with a hearty soup, a cassoulet, or a stew. Despite its fullness and richness, it is extremely easy to drink. Consider it Italy's answer to a blockbuster, heavyweight Châteauneuf du Pape from France, or a California late-harvested Zinfandel, but without any residual sugar. Lastly, sugar addicts should check out the extremely ripe, raisiny, chewy 1988 Patriglione. It provides an almost overwhelming glass of wine and is meant to be served at the end of a meal, with a cheese course or by itself. Its viscous texture and intense, earthy, tar and jammy black cherry aromas and flavors ooze across the palate. This distinctive wine is clearly the most controversial of these three offerings. The Notarpanaro and Patriglione are both such rich, alcoholic wines that they will have no difficulty holding their fruit and aging well for 10 or more years.

Looking for the greatest wine value from Italy? There are no better wine bargains than the full-bodied, robust, black cherry– and tar-scented, richly flavored, exuberant, fleshy 1986 and 1988 Salice Salentino Riservas. These are among the finest red wine values in the world. These big, rich, pure, well-balanced wines are perfect for bistro cooking. If you have not yet discovered the thrills these wines provide, don't hesitate. Virtually any vintage of Salice Salentino will age well for 10–12 years. The Riserva, which is the same wine but has been aged longer at the winery, has a slightly more mellow, softer style.

The 1985 and 1983 Notarpanaros are even richer wines, with darker, more saturated colors, licorice-, truffle-, black curranty-, and black cherry–scented noses, huge masses of fruit and glycerin, full body, and super length and ripeness. The 1983 is slightly more drinkable, but it has at least another decade of life in it. The younger, more backward 1985 should last through the first decade of the next century. Consumer alert—these are dazzling bargains!

VILLA DIANA (ABRUZZI)* * *

1992 Montepulciano d'Abruzzo	A	85

Consumers and retailers are intelligently stockpiling just about any Montepulciano they can find. These big, dense, chewy wines, which are sold for a song, are Italy's potential gold mine. The 1992 Villa Diana is a terrific wine for the price, offering a dark ruby/purple color, tart, crisp, richly fruity flavors, medium body, excellent purity, and a nicely textured mouth-feel. It should drink well for another 3–4 years. A super value!

FATTORIA ZERBINA (MARZENO FANZA)* * * *

1990 Marzeno di Marzeno Vino da Tavola Romagna	C	91
1990 Pietramora Sangiovese di Romagna	C	89

I was very impressed with the high quality of these two offerings from this producer, a new discovery for me. The 1990 Pietramora (100% Sangiovese) is a dark ruby/purple-colored wine with gobs of rich, black currant and black cherry fruit nicely touched by subtle oak. Medium to full bodied, pure, rich, and supple, this delicious, well-knit wine should drink well for 5–6 years. The 1990 Marzeno di Marzeno is a 50% Sangiovese/50% Cabernet Sauvignon blend aged in small oak casks, of which 30% are new. It possesses a nearly opaque ruby/purple color, and a big, spicy nose of vanilla, black currants, and flowers. Medium to full bodied, with considerable flavor, purity, and extraction, as well as exceptional balance, this rich, supple, lightly tannic, impressive wine could easily be mistaken for a top Tuscan Vino da Tavola. The finish lasts for nearly 45 seconds. It should drink well for at least a decade.

3. GERMANY

The Basics

Germany's winedom is controlled by the 1971 law that divided German wines into seven grades, all based on ascending levels of ripeness and sweetness, as well as price. These seven levels are:
1. Tafelwein
2. Qualitätswein (QbA)
3. Kabinett
4. Spätlese
5. Auslese
6. Beerenauslese
7. Trockenbeerenauslese

   In addition to these there are other categories of German wines. The Trocken and Halbtrocken wines are the two generic types of dry German wine. The Trockens tend to be drier, but also boring, thin wines with little body or flavor. Halbtrockens also taste dry but are permitted to have slightly more residual sugar and are marginally more interesting. I rarely recommend either because they are not very good; they are commercial creations made to take advantage of the public's demand for "dry" wine. A third type of wine is called Eiswein, Germany's rarest and most expensive wine. It is made from frozen grapes, generally picked in December or January, or even February. It is quite rare, and a very, very sweet wine, but has remarkably high acidity and can last and improve in the bottle for decades. It does have great character, but one must usually pay unbelievably steep prices to experience it.

   There are also the sparkling wines of Germany called Deutscher Sekt, which should be drunk only by certified masochists, as they are a ghastly lot of overly sulfured wines. Lastly, there is the German wine that everyone knows about, the ubiquitous Liebfraumilch. This sugary, grapy drink is to quality German wine what California wine coolers are to that state's serious producers' wines.

GRAPE VARIETIES
Müller-Thurgau Representing 25% of Germany's vineyards, Müller-Thurgau has become the most widely planted grape because of its predilection to give prolific yields of juice (90–100 hectoliters per hectare is not uncommon). Ignore all of the self-serving

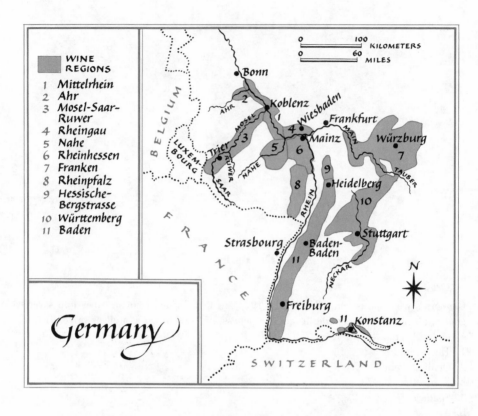

WINE
REGIONS

1 Mittelrhein
2 Ahr
3 Mosel-Saar-
   Ruwer
4 Rheingau
5 Nahe
6 Rheinhessen
7 Franken
8 Rheinpfalz
9 Hessische-
   Bergstrasse
10 Württemberg
11 Baden

Germany

BELGIUM

LUXEMBOURG

FRANCE

SWITZERLAND

Bonn

Koblenz

Wiesbaden

Frankfurt

Mainz

Würzburg

Trier

Heidelberg

Strasbourg

Baden-
Baden

Stuttgart

Freiburg

Konstanz

KILOMETERS
MILES

AHR

MOSEL

RUWER

SAAR

NAHE

RHEIN

MAIN

TAUBER

NECKAR

Rheingau

KILOMETERS
MILES

Bereich
Johannisberg

Dotsheim

Frauenstein

Rauenthal

Kiedrich

Wiesbaden

Wicker

Hochheim

Lorchhausen
Lorch

Schloss Vollrads

Schloss
Johannisberg

Eltville

Erbach

Hattenheim

Oestrich

Mittelheim

Winkel

Geisenheim

Mainz

Bingen

Rüdesheim

Rheinhessen

Nahe

NAHE

RHEIN

MAIN

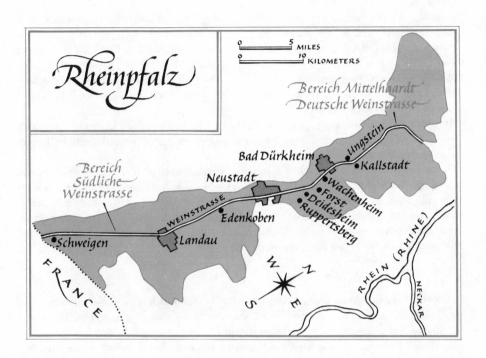

Rheinpfalz

0 — 5 MILES
0 — 10 KILOMETERS

Bereich Mittelhaardt
Deutsche Weinstrasse

Bereich
Südliche
Weinstrasse

Ungstein

Bad Dürkheim

Kallstadt

Neustadt

Wachenheim

Forst

Deidesheim

Ruppertsberg

WEINSTRASSE

Edenkoben

Schweigen

Landau

FRANCE

RHEIN (RHINE)

NECKAR

N W S E

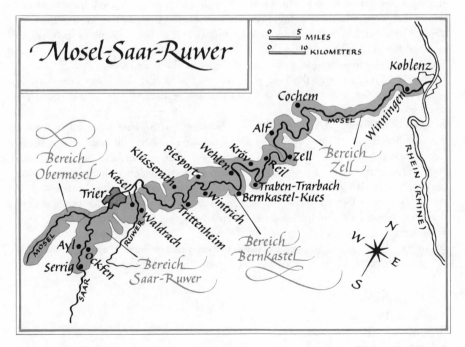

Mosel-Saar-Ruwer

0 — 5 MILES
0 — 10 KILOMETERS

Koblenz

Cochem

Winningen

MOSEL

Alf

Bereich
Obermosel

Piesport

Wehlen

Kröv

Zell

Bereich
Zell

Klüsserath

Reil

Kasel

Traben-Trarbach

Bernkastel-Kues

Trier

Wintrich

Trittenheim

MOSEL

Waldrach

RUWER

Bereich
Bernkastel

Ayl

Ockfen

Serrig

SAAR

Bereich
Saar-Ruwer

RHEIN (RHINE)

N W S E

promotion from German wine importers about Müller-Thurgau, because it is not a great wine grape, and the Germans have planted it for quantity, not quality.

Riesling While Riesling only accounts for 20% of the vineyards in Germany, it produces about 95% of that country's finest wines. If the bottle does not say Riesling on it, then chances are you are not getting Germany's best wine. Riesling achieves its greatest pinnacles of success in Germany, whether it be a dry, crisp, tangy Kabinett or a decadently sweet, nectarlike Trockenbeerenauslese.

Sylvaner This unimpressive grape accounts for 10% of Germany's vineyards and rarely results in anything interesting. Most Sylvaners have either a nasty vegetal streak to them or are simply dull and flat.

Other Grape Varieties Much of Germany's problem today is that a large proportion of its vineyards are planted with mediocre grape varieties. The remaining 45% of the vineyards generally consists of grapes that have little personality and names such as Kerner, Gutedel, Morio-Muskat, Bacchus, Faberrebe, Huxelrebe, Optima, and Ebling. The only other grapes that can do something special are Gewürztraminer, Rulander (Pinot Gris), Scheurebe, and Germany's answer to Pinot Noir, Spatburgunder.

FLAVORS

Müller-Thurgau At its best it resembles a can of fruit salad, obvious but pleasant in an open-knit, uncomplicated manner. At its worst, it tastes washed out, acidic, green, and reminiscent of a watered-down, mediocre Riesling.

Riesling The most exciting flavors in German wines come from Riesling. In the drier and slightly sweet versions there is a lovely concoction of apple, lime, wet stone, and citric flavors and scents. As the Riesling becomes sweeter, the flavors move in the direction of tropical fruits such as mangoes and pineapples, as well as honeyed apples, peaches, and apricots. Behind all the flavor (in the top Rieslings) is a steely, zesty, vibrant natural fruit acidity that gives those wines an exceptional degree of clarity and focus.

Rulander From some of the best vineyards in Baden and the Rheinpfalz this grape produces oily, rich, honeyed, intense wines that are probably the most underrated great white wines of Germany.

Scheurebe Discovered by Dr. G. Scheu, Scheurebe is a clone achieved by crossing Sylvaner and Riesling. Once scoffed at for its neutral character, this varietal has become increasingly popular with consumers. Top producers of Scheurebe, such as Müller-Catoir, H. & R. Lingenfelder, and Kruger-Rumpf, have performed wonders with this grape, producing deeply flavored wines that feature flowery, curranty fruit and rich, complex personalities.

Spatburgunder German Pinot Noir is a grotesque and ghastly wine that tastes akin to a defective, sweet, faded, and diluted red burgundy from an incompetent producer. Need I say more?

Sylvaner On occasion, Sylvaner from selected vineyards in Franken and the Rheinhessen can be a rich, muscular, deep wine, but more often it is vegetal, thin, and dull.

AGING POTENTIAL

Auslese: 3–15 years
Beerenauslese: 10–40+ years
Kabinett: 3–6 years
Liebfraumilch: 8–16 months
Qualitatswein (QbA): 2–4 years
Spätlese: 3–10 years
Tafelwein: 8–16 months
Trockenbeerenauslese: 10–40+ yrs

OVERALL QUALITY LEVEL

The top level of quality is impeccably high, and dominated by small estates that usually produce Riesling. However, the German government has been inexcusably remiss over recent decades in allowing too many high-yielding, low-quality grapes to be planted (the 1987 average yield per hectare was an incredible 97 hectoliters), and has allowed consumers to become increasingly skeptical about the seriousness of German wine quality. For example, in the mediocre year of 1987, 77% of the wine produced was allowed to be called QbA and only 2% was declassified as simple table wine (Tafelwein). That's ridiculous. A campaign to promote the top-quality German estates that are making the finest German wines is long overdue. Until the consumer begins to believe that Germany is serious about quality, sales of these wines will remain difficult.

THE MOST IMPORTANT INFORMATION TO KNOW

For American readers, while a number of importers have small portfolios of German wines, there are three major players who dominate the German wine business in America. From a consumer's perspective, the most important is Terry Theise Selections, whose wines are imported by the Milton S. Kronheim Company in Washington, D.C. In less than a half dozen years Terry Theise has done more for the image of high-quality German wines than anyone in the previous eight decades. By ignoring many of the overrated, more famous German wine names, and by beating the back roads of less-renowned viticultural regions, Theise has put together a portfolio of producers who turn out individualistic wines of astonishing quality, often at modest prices. Theise keeps his profit margins low so the wines can be effectively represented in the marketplace. The result is a bevy of phenomenal wines and extraordinary wine bargains. If you are going to seriously buy German wines, look for the words *Terry Theise Selection* on the label. You are unlikely to be disappointed.

Between the other two major players in the German wine market, the most visible and promotion-conscious is Rudy Weist of ILNA Selections in Santa Barbara, California. Weist has long felt that the reason German wines have not enjoyed widespread popularity is because they are inexpensive. His portfolio is concentrated on the more renowned and prestigious domaines that are all members of an elite association of winemaking estates collectively referred to as the VDP. Each of these estates sports a neck or back label that identifies its members. There are over 200 members. In theory, all of them are dedicated to producing the highest quality wines, usually from Riesling. There are a number of fabulous producers in this group, as well as an appalling number of underachievers who charge exceptionally high prices because their wines are produced from renowned vineyards. Moreover, there is a premium charged for the wines represented by Weist because of his belief that higher prices translate into higher prestige. As my tasting notes often attest, Theise's wines, from the same vineyards but from less well-known producers, often outperform those from Weist.

The third major importer of German wines is Bob Rice of Chapin Cellars in Virginia Beach, Virginia. Rice is a low-profile importer who is content to have most of his German producers represented regionally, so you are not likely to see him promoting his name as much as that of his producers. His reasonably priced portfolio includes numerous excellent wines.

In addition to becoming familiar with these German wine importers, there are other facts to keep in mind when buying German wines:

1. There are 11 major wine-producing zones in Germany. Within these zones there are 3 subdistricts, the most general of which is called a Bereich. This is used to describe a wine from anywhere within the boundaries of that particular Bereich. An analogy that may help facilitate this distinction would be the closest French equivalent, a wine entitled to appellation Bordeaux Contrôlée or Appellation Bourgogne Contrôlée. Within the Bereich there are

more specific boundaries called Grosslagen, to which the closest French equivalent would be the generic Appellation St.-Julien Contrôlée or Appellation Morey St.-Denis Contrôlée. These would be wines that are not from a specific château or specific vineyard, but from a specific region or collection of sites for vineyards. There are 152 different Grosslagen in Germany. The most specific zone in Germany is called an Einzellagen, which is a specific site or vineyard. There are 2,600 of them in Germany, and again, by analogy, the closest French equivalent would be a specific St.-Julien château such as Ducru-Beaucaillou, or a specific premier cru or grand cru burgundy vineyard in Morey St.-Denis such as Clos des Lambrays. Perhaps this will help one to understand the breakdown of the German wine zones. However, few people have the patience to memorize the best Einzellagens or Grosslagens, so it is much more important to try to remember the names of some of the best producers.

2. The majority of the best producers in Germany are located in the following 9 wine zones.

OVERALL CHARACTERISTICS OF THE NINE MAJOR GERMAN WINE ZONES

Middle Mosel   For German wine lovers, as well as tourists to Germany's wine regions, the Middle Mosel is the most beloved and scenic. The frightfully steep, slate-based slopes are so forbidding it seems impossible vineyards could be planted on such dangerously precipitous hills. With its plethora of high-profile producers, such as J. J. Prüm, Willi Haag, Ernest Loosen, and Dr. Thanisch, this region has no shortage of admirers and potential buyers. The fact is that while Riesling grown on these slopes has unlimited potential, this is also an area filled with overpriced, underachieving producers who have long lived off their reputations. Nevertheless, anybody who has tasted a great Wehlener Sonnenuhr, Brauneberger Juffer, Erdener Treppchen, Zeltinger Sonnenuhr, or Graacher Himmelreich knows that this area's soils can produce magical Rieslings. By analogy, the Middle Mosel is to Germany what Puligny-Montrachet is to Burgundy. While there are a number of great producers, prices are high, and the quality is frightfully irregular.

Lower Mosel   This obscure vineyard area with supersteep slopes is located at the junction of the Mosel and the Rhine. The wines from the Lower Mosel are underestimated, a fact that consumers should put to good use. Try some recent vintages from two of this area's most spectacular producers, von Schleinitz and von Heddesdorff, and experience the high quality available at reasonable prices. Although the vineyard sites are not considered to be as ideal as those in the Middle Mosel, top Lower Mosel producers can produce wines equal in quality to those from the Middle Mosel.

Saar   Also referred to as the Upper Mosel, this cool region is able to maintain the steely, razor blade sharpness of the Riesling grape. Many authorities consider the Saar vineyards to be among the greatest in Germany, but as in the Middle Mosel, fame has its price. Some fabulous producers are located in this area. However, some well-known Saar producers have a tendency to overcrop, making relatively hollow, flabby wines that lack definition. Superlative producers include the likes of Egon Müller, Dr. Wagner, von Kesselstatt, and, from time to time, Zilliken.

Ruwer   Trier is the spiritual and commercial center for the Ruwer wines. Textbook, quintessential Rieslings emerge from this area from producers such as Friedrich-Wilhelm-Gymnasium, Geltz Zilliken, Karthäuserhof, von Kesselstatt, Karlsmuhle, and von Schubert's Maximin Grunhaus.

Rheingau   Many of the most famous producers of German wine are located in this highly renowned region. However, it is not unusual for many of the unknown overachievers to outperform their more celebrated neighbors. Three of the most prominent underachievers are Schloss Groenesteyn, Schloss Vollrads, and Schloss Johannisberg. If you want to taste what many consider to be some of the finest Rieslings made in Germany, check out producers such as H. H. Eser, Freiherr zu Knyphausen, Deinhard's Konigin Victoria Berg, Dr. Heinrich Nagler, and the best cuvées of Schloss Schonborn.

Rheinhessen All of the German wine zones offer considerable diversity in quality, but none more than the Rheinhessen, which has Nierstein as its commercial center. Müller-Thurgau and Sylvaner are the two most popular grape varieties of this region. Additionally, such odd grapes as Scheurebe, Huxelrebe, and Kerner have found an enthusiastic reception among this region's producers. This is also the region where most of Germany's Liebfraumilch is produced. Consumers often make major errors in buying wines from this region. Over recent years, some of the best producers have included Freiherr Heyl zu Herrnsheim, J.U.H.A. Strub, and Merz.

Rheinpfalz The Rheinpfalz is the warmest of the major German wine zones. Although Müller-Thurgau is widely planted, it is Riesling, Rulander, and Scheurebe that produce the most stunning wines. If you think German wines are too understated, light, and wimpish, check out the powerful, meaty, fleshy, supergenerous wines from the Rheinpfalz. The quality level appears to be hitting new heights with every vintage. This is the home of the producer Müller-Catoir, who is making the most riveting wines of Germany. It is also the base for supertalented producers such as H. & R. Lingenfelder, Kurt Darting, Klaus Neckerauer, Koehler-Ruprecht, Kimich, Werlé, and perhaps one of the best known Rheinpfalz estates, Dr. Burklin-Wolf.

Nahe This is another underrated source of high-class Riesling, as well as a wine zone with a competitive group of producers who, for now, lack the one superstar needed to draw worldwide attention to this region's virtues. A Nahe wine is considered to possess some of the character of a Saar wine, and the spice, meatiness, and flesh of a Rheingau. The curranty, smoky aromas of a Nahe is reminiscent of that found in a red wine, making it among the most distinctive of all German wines. None of the Nahe producers are well known, so prices tend to be low, except for those producers who are members of the prestigious VDP group (e.g., Hans Crusius). Top producers include von Plettenberg, Hehner-Kiltz, Kruger-Rumpf, Adolph Lotzbeyer, and perhaps the finest, Helmuth Donnhoff and Prince zu Salm.

Franken With the wonderful city of Würzburg as its commercial center, the wines of Franken have developed a considerable cult following. Although these wines fetch high prices and are put in unattractive squat bottles that are impossible to bin, Franken wines can be bold, dramatic, and heady. Moreover, they enjoy remarkable loyalty from their admirers. This is one region where the Sylvaner grape hits heights that exist nowhere else on earth. The two best estates are Burgerspital and Hans Wirsching. I have also been increasingly impressed (especially by the 1990s) with wines from Schloss Sommerhausen. Once past the quality of these superlative producers it is caveat emptor.

3. The best German wines are those produced at the Kabinett, Spätlese, Auslese, Beerenauslese, and Trockenbeerenauslese levels of ripeness and sweetness. Most consumers tasting a Kabinett would not find it particularly sweet, although there is residual sugar in the wine. Because of a high natural acidity found in German wines, a Kabinett generally tastes fresh, fruity, but not sweet to most palates. However, most tasters will detect a small amount of sweetness in a Spätlese, and even more with an Auslese. All three of these types of wines are ideal wines for having as an aperitif or with food, whereas the wines entitled to Beerenauslese and Trockenbeerenauslese designations are clearly dessert wines that are very rich and quite sweet. One should keep in mind that the alcohol level in most German wines averages between 7% and 9%, so one can drink much more of this wine without feeling its effects. One of the naïve criticisms of German wines is that they do not go well with food. However, anyone who has tried a fine Kabinett, Spätlese, or Auslese with Oriental cuisine, with roast pork, or even with certain types of fowl such as pheasant or turkey can tell you that these wines work particularly well, especially Spätlese and Auslese.

4. The best German wines age like a fine Bordeaux. In great vintages, such as 1990 or 1971, one can expect a Kabinett, Spätlese, or Auslese from a top producer to evolve and improve in the bottle for 5–10 years. Beerenauslese and Trockenbeerenauslese have the ability in a great vintage to improve for two or three decades. This is a fact, not a myth, to which those who have recently tasted some of the great Ausleses from 1959 can easily attest. German wines at the top levels, from the top producers, do indeed improve remarkably in the bottle, although the trend among consumers is to drink them when they are young, fresh, and crisp.

VINTAGE GUIDE

1994—The superb weather in October will result in an abundant crop of sweeter-styled wines. Quality is reported to be uneven, but enthusiasm and excitement abound. In complete contrast to the stylish, elegant, high-acid 1993s, the 1994s should be relatively powerful and rich.

1993—Delicate, crisp, light-bodied wines were produced in bountiful quantities. The vintage favors Kabinett, Spätlese, and Auslese producers.

1992—This looks to be a promising vintage with some superlative, drier-style wines coming from the Ruwer and Middle Mosel. Most estates reported it was very difficult to produce sweet wines in these areas. Therefore, this will be a vintage of mostly Kabinetts and Spätleses—a good sign for consumers looking for wines from the drier end of the German wine spectrum. All things considered, 1992 should be a very fine year throughout the Mosel, Saar, Ruwer regions, with less superrich dessert wines than in years such as 1990 and 1989. In the Rheingau, Rheinpfalz, and Rheinhessen, the vintage looks to be excellent, with plenty of rich wines, as well as sweet late-harvest wines, particularly in the Rheinhessen. Many of the top producers are superenthusiastic about the prospects of this vintage given the superb ripeness that was achieved and the relatively small yields. Producers in the Rheinhessen and Rheinpfalz have already begun to compare 1992 with 1990, so this may turn out to be one of the most successful viticultural regions in Europe.

1991—This has turned out to be a surprisingly good vintage, far better than many of the doom and gloom reports suggested. Although not of the level of 1990 or 1989 in terms of rich, intense, sweet Spätlese and Auslese wines, it is a very appealing vintage, particularly for the top estates in the drier Kabinett styles. The downside of the 1991 vintage is that some wines have shrill levels of acidity, raising questions as to whether their fruit will hold up. Most German-wine specialists suggest this was a year of the winemaker rather than of Mother Nature, and those producers who were able to keep yields down and who picked physiologically ripe fruit made wines with crisp acidity and good depth and character. Those who didn't made hollow, high-acid wines that merit little attention.

1990—By all accounts this is an outstanding, perhaps even great vintage. The wines have fabulous ripeness, surprisingly crisp acidity, and an intense perfume and mid-palate. In addition to many outstanding Kabinetts and Spätleses, this is another vintage, much like 1989, where there were spectacular sweet Ausleses and even more decadently rich Beerenauslese and Trockenbeerenauslese wines produced. If you are a German-wine enthusiast, this vintage warrants a serious look.

1989—This is another top-notch vintage that has been compared with 1976, 1971, and 1959. The late harvest and the extraordinary amount of sweet wine made at the Auslese, Beerenauslese, and Trockenbeerenauslese levels garner considerable enthusiasm. Unlike 1990, where every wine zone enjoyed success, or 1991, where it was a question of the winemaker's ability, in 1989 the Saar, Rheinpfalz, Ruwer, and Rheinhessen produced top wines. This was not a rain-free harvest, production yields were high, and acidity levels in many cases remain suspiciously low, suggesting most consumers would be well advised to drink the wines below the Auslese level over the next 3–4 years. One area of good, but somewhat disappointing wines in the context of the vintage is the Middle Mosel, where a number of the most famous domaines overcropped and have produced somewhat fluid, loosely knit, fragile wines.

1988—The strength of this vintage is the Middle Mosel. Based on my tastings, the drier Kabinetts and Spätlese offerings look to be the best wines made. This vintage has now been largely forgotten in all the hype over 1989 and 1990, so bargains can be found.

1987—A mediocre vintage followed an unusual growing season that was characterized by a poor, wet, cold summer but a glorious September and a mixed bag of weather in October. The quality is expected to be better than either 1980 or 1984, and many growers reported harvests close in size to those in 1986. The average production was a whopping 96 hectoliters per hectare, which is excessive. Interestingly, this appears to be a good year for the rare nectarlike Eisweins. Consumers should be drinking their wines that are below the Auslese level over the next several years.

1986—A copious crop of grapes has resulted in pleasant, agreeable, soft, fruity wines that will have broad commercial appeal. Because of the size of the crop, prices dropped after the smaller-than-normal crop in 1985. All in all, this vintage will be regarded by the trade as a useful, practical year of good rather than great wines. Wines below the Auslese level should be drunk up over the next several years.

1985—The German wine trade has touted this year rather highly, but except for a handful of areas, it is not comparable to the outstanding 1983 vintage. Nevertheless, it is a very good year with a moderate production of wines with good acidity and more typical textures and characteristics than the opulent, richly fruity 1983s. Like 1983, the dryness during the summer and fall prevented the formation of *Botrytis cinerea*. The Rieslings in many cases can be very good, but will be firmer and slower to evolve and less open than the more precocious, overt, fruity 1983s. Overall, the 1985s should be at their best between now and 1998. The top successes are in the Middle Mosel, with potentially great wines from villages such as Urzig and Erden. Wines below the Auslese level should be drunk over the next 1–2 years.

1984—Fresh, light, very pleasant, straightforward wines that are neither green nor too acidic were produced in this vintage of average quality and below-average quantity. They will not keep, so drink up the 1984s. The Mosel estate of Dr. F. Weins-Prüm Erben made excellent wines in 1984, as did Monchhof.

1983—This vintage has received the most publicity since the 1976 vintage. Most growers seem to feel that it is certainly the best since the 1976. It was a very large crop throughout all viticultural areas of Germany, but it was especially large and exceptional in quality in the Mosel-Saar-Ruwer region. The wines have excellent concentration, very fine levels of tartaric rather than green malic acidity, and a degree of precocious ripeness and harmonious roundness that gives the wines wonderful appeal now. However, because of their depth and overall balance, they should age well for another 4–5 years. The vintage seemed strongest at the Spätlese level, as there were very little Auslese, Beerenauslese, and Trockenbeerenauslese wines produced. Nineteen eighty-three is also a great year for Eiswein, where, as a result of an early freeze, above-normal quantities of this nectarlike, opulent wine were produced. However, despite larger quantities than normal, the prices are outrageously high for the Eisweins, but very realistic and reasonable for the rest of the wines.

OLDER VINTAGES

The great sweet wine vintage that can still be found in the marketplace is 1976, a vintage that, by German standards, produced incredibly ripe, intense, opulent wines, with a significant amount of wine produced at the Auslese and Beerenauslese levels. The top wines should continue to last for another 5–15 years. Some critics have disputed the greatness of this vintage, saying that the 1976s are low in acidity, but that is a minority point of view. The wines remain reasonably priced at the Auslese level, but the Beerenausleses and Trockenbeerenausleses from this vintage are absurdly expensive. The 1977 vintage should be avoided, and 1978, unlike in France, was not a particularly successful year in Germany. Well-kept 1975s can provide great enjoyment, as can the wines from another great vintage, 1971. I would avoid the wines from 1972, and the once good 1973s are now in serious decline!

RATING GERMANY'S BEST PRODUCERS

* * * * * (OUTSTANDING)

Kurt Darting (Rheinpfalz)

Fritz Haag (Mosel)

Heribert Kerpen (Mosel)

J. F. Kimich (Rheinpfalz)

H. & R. Lingenfelder (Rheinpfalz)

Egon Müller (Saar)

Müller-Catoir (Rheinpfalz)

Klaus Neckerauer (Rheinpfalz)

J. J. Prüm (Mosel)

Willi Schaefer (Mosel)

von Schubert-Maximin Grunhaus (Ruwer)

Selbach-Oster (Mosel)

Werlé (Rheinpfalz)

* * * * (EXCELLENT)

Christian-Wilhelm Bernard (Rheinhessen)

von Bretano (Rheingau)

Burgerspital (Franken)

Dr. Burklin-Wolf (Rheinpfalz)

J. J. Christoffel (Mosel)****/*****

Schlossgut Diel (Nahe)

Hermann Donnhoff (Nahe)

August Eser (Rheingau)

H. H. Eser-Johannishof (Rheingau)

F. W. Gymnasium (Mosel)

Willi Haag (Mosel)

Freiherr von Heddesdorff (Mosel)

Hehner-Kiltz (Nahe)

Weingut-Weinhaus Henninger (Rheinpfalz)

Freiherr Heyl zu Herrensheim (Rheinhessen)

von Hövel (Saar)

Immich-Batterieberg (Mosel)

E. Jakoby-Mathy (Mosel)

Weingut Karlsmuhle (Mosel-Ruwer)

Christian Karp-Schreiber (Mosel)

Karthauserhof (Christophe Tyrell) (Ruwer)

von Kesselstatt (Mosel-Saar)

Freiherr zu Knyphausen (Rheingau)

Koehler-Ruprecht (Rheinpfalz)

Konigin Victoria Berg-Deinhard (Rheingau)

Kruger-Rumpf (Nahe)

Kuhling-Gillot (Rheinhessen)

Franz (Gunter) Kunstler (Rheingau)

Dr. Loosen-St.-Johannishof (Mosel)

Alfred Merkelbach (Mosel)

Meulenhof/Erben Justen/Erlen (Mosel)

Monchhof (Mosel)

Nahe Staatsdomaine (Nahe)

Pfeffingen (Rheinpfalz)

von Plettenberg (Nahe)

Jochen Ratzenberger (Mittelrhein)

Jakob Schneider (Nahe)

von Simmern (Rheingau)****/*****

J.U.H.A. Strub (Rheinhessen)

Dr. Heinz Wagner (Saar)

* * * (GOOD)

Paul Anheuser (Nahe)

Basserman-Jordan (Rheinpfalz)

Erich Bender (Rheinpfalz)

Josef Biffar (Rheinpfalz)

Bischoflisch Weinguter (Mosel)

Bruder Dr. Becker (Rheinhessen)

Christoffel-Berres (Mosel)

Conrad-Bartz (Mosel)

Hans Crusius (Nahe)

Josef Deinhart (Mosel-Saar)

Epenschild (Rheinhessen)

Dr. Fischer (Saar)

Four Seasons Co-op (Rheinpfalz)
Hans Ganz (Nahe)
Gebruder Grimm (Rheingau)
Gernot Gysler (Rheinhessen)
Grans-Fassian (Mosel)
Gunderloch-Usinger (Rheinhessen)
J. Hart (Mosel)
Dr. Heger (Baden)
von Hövel (Mosel)
Toni Jost (Mittelrhein)***/****
Klaus Klemmer (Mittelrhein)
Johann Koch (Mosel)
Gebruder Kramp (Mosel)
Lehnert-Matteus (Mosel)
Josef Leitz (Rheingau)
Licht-Bergweiler (Mosel)
Lieschied-Rollauer (Mittelrhein)
Schloss Lieser (Mosel)
Weingut Benedict Loosen Erben (Mosel)
Adolf Lotzbeyer (Nahe)
Weingut Merz (Rheinhessen)
Herbert Messmer (Rheinpfalz)
Theo Minges (Rheinpfalz)
Eugen Muller (Rheinpfalz)
Dr. Heinrich Nagler (Rheingau)
Peter Nicolay (Mosel)
von Ohler'sches (Rheinhessen)
Dr. Pauly Bergweiler (Mosel)
Petri-Essling (Nahe)
Okonomierat Piedmont
    (Mosel-Saar-Ruwer)

S. A. Prüm (Mosel)
S. A. Prüm-Erben (Mosel)
Erich Wilhelm Rapp (Nahe)
Reuscher-Haart (Mosel)
Max Ferdinand Richter (Mosel)
Salm (Nahe)
Prinz zu Salm (Nahe)
Peter Scherf (Ruwer)
von Schleinitz (Mosel)
Georg Albrecht Schneider (Rheinhessen)
Schloss Schonborn (Rheingau)
Schumann-Nagler (Rheingau)
Wolfgang Schwaab (Mosel)
Seidel-Dudenhofer (Rheinhessen)
Bert Simon (Saar)
Schloss Sommerhausen (Franken)
Sturm (Rheinhessen)
Dr. Thanisch (Mosel)
Unckrich (Rheinpfalz)
Christophe Vereinigte Hospitien (Mosel)
Wegeler-Deinhard (Mosel, Rheinpfalz,
    Rheingau)
Adolf Weingart (Mittlerhein)
Dr. F. Weins-Prüm (Mosel)
Domdechant Werner (Rheingau)
Winzer Vier Jahreszeiten (Pfalz)
Gunter Wittman (Rheinhessen)
Wolff-Metternich (Rheinhessen)
G. Zilliken (Mosel)

* * *(AVERAGE)*

Baumann (Rheinhessen)
Bollig-Lehnert (Mosel)
von Buhl (Rheinpfalz)
Stephan Ehlen (Mosel)
Alexandre Freimuth (Rheingau)
Le Gallais (Mosel)
Siegfried Gerhard (Rheingau)
Martin Gobel (Franken)
Schloss Groenestegn (Rheingau)
Louis Guntrum (Rheinhessen)
Schloss Johannishoff (Rheingau)
Burgermeister Carl Koch (Rheinhessen)
Lucashof (Rheinpfalz)

Milz-Laurentiushof (Mosel)
Claus Odernheimer/Abteihof St.-Nicolaus
    (Rheingau)
Geh. Rat Aschrott'sche (Rheingau)
J. Peter Reinert (Mosel-Saar)
Schloss Reinhartshausen (Rheingau)
Schloss Saarstein (Saar)
Schmidt-Wagner (Mosel)
Henrich Seebrich (Rheinhessen)
Staatsweingüter Eltville (Rheingau)
Studert-Prüm/Maximinhof (Mosel)
Schloss Vollrads (Rheingau)

PAUL ANHEUSER (NAHE)* * *

1992 Kreuznacher Krotenpfuhl Riesling Auslese	C	87
1992 Kreuznacher Krotenpfuhl Riesling Spätlese	C	84?
1992 Niederhauser Pfingstweide Riesling	B	86

I immensely enjoyed the aromas of sweet corn and fruit in the excellent, medium-bodied, dry, crisp 1992 Niederhauser Pfingstweide Riesling. It is not a candidate for long aging, so drink it over the next several years. Although muted, the 1992 Kreuznacher Krotenpfuhl Riesling Spätlese is concentrated, surprisingly dry, and tightly knit. Perhaps I caught it in an awkward stage. The honeyed, tropical fruit–scented nose of the 1992 Kreuznacher Krotenpfuhl Riesling Auslese exhibits some botrytis. The wine reveals thick, rich, moderately sweet flavors and a long finish. It should be drunk over the near term.

BAUMANN (RHEINHESSEN)* *

1992 Oppenheimer Sacktrager Riesling Kabinett	B	82
1992 Oppenheimer Sacktrager Riesling Spätlese	C	72

The 1992 Oppenheimer Sacktrager Riesling Kabinett is straightforward, fruity, and soft, whereas the 1992 Spätlese offering is musty and awkward, with an annoying dirtiness.

ERICH BENDER (RHEINPFALZ)* * *

1992 Bissersheimer Goldberg Scheurebe Spätlese	A	87
1992 Bissersheimer Steig Huxelrebe Beerenauslese	B	90

I do not know this producer well, but based on the two wines I tasted, this is a superb source for value-priced, exotic, flamboyant, rich wines. The 1992 Bissersheimer Goldberg Scheurebe Spätlese offers a stunning nose of honeyed tropical fruit and floral scents. Sweet, ripe, loaded with concentration, and low in acidity, it is a terrific bargain for drinking over the next 1–3 years. Even the 1992 Bissersheimer Steig Huxelrebe Beerenauslese is an exceptional value for a dessert-style wine. Rich, with a sweet, fragrant, black cherry nose, long, unctuously textured, deeply concentrated flavors, and a thick finish, it lacks acidity, but exhibits outstanding richness and complexity. Drink it over the next 5–7 years.

JOSEF BIFFAR (RHEINPFALZ)* * *

1992 Deidesheimer Kalkofen Riesling Auslese	D	91
1991 Deidesheimer Kalkofen Riesling Auslese	C	84
1991 Deidesheimer Kieselberg Riesling Spätlese Halbtrocken	C	91
1991 Deidesheimer Leinhohle Riesling Kabinett	B	88
1992 Deidesheimer Maushohle Riesling Spätlese Trocken	C	87

I tasted an assortment of both 1991s and 1992s from the Rheinpfalz estate of Josef Biffar. The 1992 Deidesheimer Maushohle Riesling Spätlese Trocken offers a fragrant, elegant, spicy, floral-scented nose, lovely fruit flavors, and an excellent dry, crisp finish. It should drink well for 4–5 years. The superb 1991 Deidesheimer Kieselberg Riesling Spätlese Halbtrocken exhibits an intense, stony, cherry, flinty nose, rich, crisp, medium-bodied, dry flavors, and a long, well-balanced finish. It will drink well for 7–8 years. Biffar also turned in an admirable performance with the opulently styled, individualistic 1991 Deidesheimer Leinhohle Riesling Kabinett. This wine reveals a pronounced perfume of incense, currants, and exotic tropical fruits. It will undoubtedly be controversial given its atypically dramatic, forward, rich character. Drink it over the next 5–6 years.

The 1992 Deidesheimer Kalkofen Riesling Auslese possesses a rich, floral, black cherry–scented nose reminiscent of a red wine. Dense, with huge, off-dry flavors, and an explosively long, unctuously textured, superrich finish, this knockout wine suffers only from a slight deficiency in acidity. Drink it over the next 4–5 years. Biffar's green, leafy 1991 Deidesheimer Kalkofen Riesling Auslese exhibits high acidity and a compact, ungenerous personality.

BOLLIG-LEHNERT (MOSEL)* *

1992	Piesporter Goldtropchen Riesling Kabinett	B	76
1992	Trittenheimer Apotheke Riesling Auslese	C	75
1992	Trittenheimer Apotheke Riesling Spätlese	C	75

These drier-style Rieslings are undistinguished efforts lacking ripeness and richness. High yields and the harvesting of physiologically unripe grapes may be the reasons for such green, lean-style Rieslings.

J. J. CHRISTOFFEL (MOSEL)* * * */* * * * *

1992	Erdener Treppchen Riesling Auslese	C	88
1992	Erdener Treppchen Riesling Kabinett	B	90
1992	Erdener Treppchen Riesling Spätlese	C	90
1992	Urziger Wurzgarten Riesling Auslese	C	89
1992	Urziger Wurzgarten Riesling Auslese 1 Star	C	90
1992	Urziger Wurzgarten Riesling Auslese 2 Stars	D	91
1992	Urziger Wurzgarten Riesling Auslese 3 Stars	D	91
1992	Urziger Wurzgarten Riesling Beerenauslese	E	98
1992	Urziger Wurzgarten Riesling Eiswein	E	96
1992	Urziger Wurzgarten Riesling Spätlese	C	90

Christoffel's Mosel estate has turned in one of the strongest performances of any proprietor in the 1992 vintage. These wines stood out for their richness, intensely perfumed personalities, and gloriously long, ripe, well-balanced finishes. This is a producer to seek out in the 1992 vintage.

The 1992 Erdener Treppchen Riesling Kabinett is both a knockout wine and a great value. The gloriously perfumed nose, dry, medium-bodied flavors, and long finish offer considerable excitement. Readers will find it difficult to choose between the two Spätlese offerings: the 1992 Urziger Wurzgarten and the 1992 Erdener Treppchen. Both exhibit tremendous concentration, wonderfully pure, fragrant bouquets, and long, well-balanced, medium-bodied, off-dry personalities. The Urziger Wurzgarten is more flamboyant and captivating—at present—whereas the Erdener Treppchen appears to be holding more in reserve. Both are fine values.

Christoffel produced five Auslese cuvées in 1992. The 1992 Erdener Treppchen Riesling Auslese offers a lovely floral, honeyed fruitiness, an off-dry, medium-bodied personality, and a lush finish. The basic cuvée of 1992 Urziger Wurzgarten Riesling Auslese reveals a well-defined, focused personality, considerable length, excellent ripeness, and an off-dry, medium-bodied character similar to the Erdener Treppchen. Between the three cuvées designated by 1, 2, and 3 stars, it is almost impossible to pick a favorite. The 1992

Urziger Wurzgarten Riesling Auslese 1 Star possesses a penetrating perfume, a medium-dry personality, superb ripeness, and loads of berry and flower scents in its bouquet and flavors. The 1992 Urziger Wurzgarten Riesling Auslese 2 Stars exhibits a pronounced strawberry character, as well as excellent focus. The wine is rich and long, with superb extraction of flavor, wonderful clarity, and a medium sweet finish. The 1992 Urziger Wurzgarten Riesling Auslese 3 Stars boasts a mineral/slatelike personality and lavish, up-front fruit. When tasted side by side with the other cuvées, it does not possess the structure of the 2-star cuvée, or the berry fruitiness of the 1-star. However, it is an outstanding, lavishly rich, decadent, moderately sweet Riesling. All three of these Ausleses should be drunk over the next 5–6 years.

The 1992 Urziger Wurzgarten Riesling Eiswein reveals zesty acidity, fabulous ripeness, a penetrating, minerallike fragrance, and great richness that lingers on the palate. The 1992 Urziger Wurzgarten Riesling Beerenauslese offers a light golden color, and a huge, honeyed, cherry- and tropical fruit–scented nose. It is a lavishly rich, superbly well-balanced wine with crisp acidity and an exuberant, vibrant personality. These are two of the most compelling sweet wines of the vintage; they will last for several decades.

CONRAD-BARTZ (MOSEL)* * *

1992	Trarbacher Schlossberg Riesling Kabinett	B	78
1992	Trarbacher Schlossberg Riesling Spätlese	B	87
1992	Trarbacher Taubenhaus Riesling Auslese	C	85
1992	Wolfer Goldgrube Riesling Spätlese	B	82

Conrad-Bartz's 1992s are an acceptable but uninspiring group of wines. The tightly knit 1992 Trarbacher Schlossberg Riesling Kabinett possesses a tart, crisp, high acidity, light body, a paucity of fruit, and a closed, short, dry finish. Although the 1992 Wolfer Goldgrube Riesling Spätlese is cleanly made and reveals some elegance, it is light bodied and dry for a Spätlese, and it quickly evaporates on the palate, exhibiting little finish or length.

More interesting is the 1992 Trarbacher Schlossberg Riesling Spätlese, a rich, elegant wine with a stony, slatey nose, precision, excellent depth and ripeness, and a dry, spicy finish. This lovely, concentrated Riesling is the finest 1992 Conrad-Bartz offering I tasted. The 1992 Trarbacher Taubenhaus Riesling Auslese displays a ripe, boldly scented nose of honeyed fruit and earth. While the wine exhibits fine richness and medium sweetness, it lacks focus and comes across as being monochromatic. Although a good Auslese for the vintage, it is unexciting.

KURT DARTING (RHEINPFALZ)* * * * *

1992	Durkheimer Feuerberg Portugieser Weissherbst Halbtrocken	A	86
1992	Durkheimer Fronhof Riesling Spätlese	B	88
1990	Durkheimer Fronhof Scheurebe Auslese	B	93
1991	Durkheimer Fronhof Scheurebe Spätlese Halbtrocken	B	89
1992	Durkheimer Hochbenn Riesling Kabinett	A	88
1988	Durkheimer Nonnengarten Rieslaner Auslese	B	92
1992	Durkheimer Nonnengarten Rieslaner Beerenauslese	C	87
1992	Durkheimer Nonnengarten Riesling Kabinett Trocken	B	89
1990	Durkheimer Spielberg Riesling Spätlese Trocken	C	87
1990	Ellerstadter Bubeneck Riesling Spätlese Halbtrocken	B	89

1992 Ellerstadter Bubeneck Riesling Spätlese Trocken	B	89
1991 Riesling Extra Trocken	C	86
1990 Riesling Extra Trocken	C	87
1992 Ungsteiner Bettelhaus Rieslaner Trockenbeerenauslese	D	96
1992 Ungsteiner Bettelhaus Riesling Spätlese	B	90
1992 Ungsteiner Herrenberg Riesling Auslese	B	90
1992 Ungsteiner Herrenberg Scheurebe Beerenauslese	C	?
1991 Weisser Burgunder Brut	C	87

Kurt Darting is one of Germany's most exciting winemakers, as evidenced by his admirable performance in 1992. His two Trocken offerings include a gorgeously ripe, lovely, steely, impressively endowed, dry 1992 Durkheimer Nonnengarten Riesling Kabinett Trocken and an equally compelling, highly extracted, rich, fragrant, medium-bodied, dry 1992 Ellerstadter Bubeneck Riesling Spätlese Trocken. One rarely finds a dry white wine with this much flavor and complexity for $11–$12. Both wines should drink well for 4–5 years. Darting also offers an interesting rosé on the market. The 1992 Durkheimer Feuerberg Portugieser Weissherbst Halbtrocken is an exuberant, fresh, lively rosé with surprising elegance, and admirable flavor length that comes from extract, not sugar. Moreover, it is priced absurdly low. Drink it over the next year.

I tasted one 1991 from Darting, a fine floral, muscat-scented, sparkling wine, the 1991 Riesling Extra Trocken. Its excellent fruit is reminiscent of peaches and minerals. While good, it does not offer the value Darting's other wines provide. Speaking of bargains, the liter bottling of Darting's 1992 Durkheimer Hochbenn Riesling Kabinett is a complex, rich, off-dry Riesling priced at $9 a liter. The wine reveals great intensity, wonderfully pure fruit, superb balance, and a big, ripe nose of tropical fruit and stones. Drink it over the next several years. The fairly priced 1992 Ungsteiner Bettelhaus Riesling Spätlese is an unctuously textured, rich, dense wine with a dry finish. With gobs of bold, exotic fruit in its nose and flavors, this extroverted, flashy Riesling is not for the shy. More powerful, but slightly less provocative and ostentatious, the 1992 Durkheimer Fronhof Riesling Spätlese is well chiseled, with excellent definition, and an off-dry, long finish.

At the sweeter end of the spectrum, Darting's 1992 Ungsteiner Herrenberg Riesling Auslese is a sensationally opulent, buttery style of wine with terrific extract, evolved aromas and flavors, huge quantities of fruit, medium sweetness, and a sensational finish. It should drink well for 5–10 years.

Darting made three supersweet 1992s. The unctuous, deep amber-colored 1992 Ungsteiner Herrenberg Scheurebe Beerenauslese's initial aromas of stinky, fish oil–like scents give way to an herbaceous, floral component, yet this odd component reappears in the wine's flavor and finish. I am unable to evaluate this bizarre wine. More exotic, yet still funky is Darting's 1992 Durkheimer Nonnengarten Rieslaner Beerenauslese. Fat and sweet, without any definition, this thick, unctuously styled wine lacks acidity. Drink it over the next 5–6 years. Darting's most successful supersweet wine from the 1992 vintage is the Ungsteiner Bettelhaus Rieslaner Trockenbeerenauslese. Dark golden-colored, with a huge, honeyed nose of buttered cookies, flowers, and caramelized fruits, this supersweet, thick, viscously textured wine exhibits layers of fruit, and adequate acidity, vibrancy, and focus. Moreover, it is a reasonably good value for a Trockenbeerenauslese. It should drink well for 10 or more years.

Darting's 1990 Riesling Extra Trocken offers up a richly fruity, peach-scented nose and good effervescence. Dry and elegant, it is one of the best sparkling wines I have tasted from

Germany. The 1991 Weisser Burgunder Brut possesses more body, less fruit, and comes across as a tropical fruit–scented, austere sparkling wine with pinpoint bubbles and lingering effervescence. The finish is ripe, dry, and crisp. For the $5 difference in price, I would opt for the 1990 Riesling Extra Trocken, but both are fine examples of German sparkling wines.

Darting's 1990 Durkheimer Spielberg Riesling Spätlese Trocken exhibits a big, spicy, cinnamon- and apple-scented nose, tasty, crisp, generously extracted flavors, rich, gorgeous, baked-apple fruitiness, and a dry, crisp, long finish. Even more dramatic, the 1991 Durkheimer Fronhof Scheurebe Spätlese Halbtrocken reveals a beautiful nose of tropical fruits and flowers. This dry, ripe, intensely perfumed, medium-bodied wine offers richness, precision, and an elegant, ripe, long finish. It should drink well for 5–6 years. The 1990 Ellerstadter Bubeneck Riesling Spätlese Halbtrocken shares a similar apricot/peach-scented nose, off-dry, rich, gorgeously fruity (tropical fruits) flavors, that intense ripeness and precision that Darting routinely obtains, and a long finish. Drink it over the next 5–6 years.

The 1988 Durkheimer Nonnengarten Rieslaner Auslese is a terrific wine, as well as a great bargain. The wine displays a relatively mature medium gold color, a huge honeyed nose, superb freshness on the palate, and an off-dry, lavishly fruity, beautifully structured style. Its stunning richness and near-perfect balance make for a sumptuous glass of Rieslaner (the grape created from crossing Riesling with Sylvaner). Darting's 1990 Durkheimer Fronhof Scheurebe Auslese has a light to medium gold color, an intensely spicy, earthy, perfumed nose, great ripeness, and a surprisingly dry style. It is literally stuffed with fruit. The awesomely long finish is not to be missed. Only 110 cases of this wine are available in the American market, so do not waste any time. It should drink well for 5–8 years.

SCHLOSSGUT DIEL (NAHE)* * * *

1992 **Dorsheimer Goldloch Riesling Auslese**	D	87+
1992 **Dorsheimer Goldloch Riesling Spätlese**	D	89
1992 **Dorsheimer Pittermannchen Riesling Auslese**	D	86?
1992 **Dorsheimer Pittermannchen Riesling Spätlese**	D	88+
1992 **Riesling Eiswein**	EE	99
1992 **Riesling Eiswein Gold Capsule**	EEE	99
1992 **Riesling Gold Capsule**	D	94

Diel is considered to be one of the most serious estates in Germany. He is also one of that country's wine writers. The selection of 1992s I tasted from Diel ranged from impressive to awesome. However, Diel is not shy about pricing; these wines are expensive. From an aromatic standpoint, the 1992 Dorsheimer Pittermannchen Riesling Spätlese is closed and tight, but there is splendid concentration, great ripeness, loads of intensity, and layers of flavor that linger in the off-dry, wonderfully pure finish. This wine will merit an outstanding rating with another 1–2 years of bottle age. It should keep for 7–8 years. Similarly styled, with a backward personality yet stunningly concentrated flavors that are presented in an off-dry, medium- to full-bodied style is the 1992 Dorsheimer Goldloch Riesling Spätlese.

With respect to Diel's two Auslese selections, both are sweet, as well as more muted and monochromatic than his other wines. While they possess impressive concentration, both wines are straightforward, low-acid Rieslings. Although very good, these wines may have been in a dumb stage when I tasted them. I would opt for drinking them over the next 5–6 years.

Diel produced tiny quantities of a 1992 Riesling Gold Capsule. Allegedly containing

25% Eiswein, it is a stupendous, full-bodied wine with great fruit and ripeness, medium sweetness, superb balance, and zesty underlying acidity that pulls everything into brilliant clarity. This spectacular, medium-weight Riesling should drink well for another decade. The 1992 Riesling Eiswein (6.5% alcohol) is a profound effort. It is a light and refreshing sweet wine with high acidity, layers of concentrated fruit, and an awesome finish that lasts for over a minute. This is a 30- to 40-year wine. Equally stunning is the 1992 Riesling Eiswein Gold Capsule, a frightfully priced wine. Not even a soothsayer could accurately predict how long this wine will last, but my guess is 30–40 years.

HERMANN DONNHOFF (NAHE)* * * *

1991	Niederhauser Hermannshohle Riesling	B	87
1992	Niederhauser Hermannshohle Riesling Auslese	C	92
1989	Niederhauser Hermannshohle Riesling Auslese	C	90
1991	Niederhauser Hermannshohle Riesling Kabinett	B	89
1992	Niederhauser Hermannshohle Riesling Spätlese Halbtrocken	C	90
1991	Niederhauser Hermannshohle Riesling Spätlese #31	C	87
1991	Oberhauser Brucke Riesling	B	86
1992	Oberhauser Brucke Riesling Auslese	D	89+
1991	Oberhauser Brucke Riesling Auslese	D	93
1992	Oberhauser Brucke Riesling Eiswein AP #3	EE	96
1992	Oberhauser Brucke Riesling Eiswein AP #10	E	90
1992	Oberhauser Brucke Riesling Spätlese	C	87
1991	Oberhauser Brucke Riesling Spätlese	C	89
1992	Schlossbockelheimer Felsenberg Riesling Spätlese Trocken	C	83
1990	Schlossbockelheimer Felsenberg Riesling Trocken	B	87

Hermann Donnhoff is unquestionably one of the stars of the Nahe. Many of his 1992 offerings displayed brilliant winemaking. The only disappointing wine is Donnhoff's 1992 Schlossbockelheimer Felsenberg Riesling Spätlese Trocken, a light, elegant, superdelicate, dry wine with high acidity, an unripe, grapefruitlike nose and flavors, and short, austere finish. The cassis-scented, big, rich, medium- to full-bodied, dry, ripe, elegant 1992 Niederhauser Hermannshohle Riesling Spätlese Halbtrocken screams for attention. It offers considerable length, as well as outstanding penetration and delineation. Donnhoff's fine 1991 Niederhauser Hermannshohle Riesling Kabinett exhibits an orange/tangerine-scented nose, fruity, light- to medium-bodied, fresh, apricotlike flavors, and crisp acidity in a spicy finish. It may merit an outstanding score after 6–12 months of bottle age. It should drink well for a decade. In contrast, the 1992 Oberhauser Brucke Riesling Spätlese lacks structure and delineation. It offers a decadently intense bouquet of sweet, ripe tangerine fruit and minerals. Rich, round, and off-dry, with gorgeous ripeness, but low acidity, it should be drunk over the next 3–4 years.

Among the two Auslese offerings, I preferred the less-expensive 1992 Niederhauser Hermannshohle Riesling Auslese. Some CO_2 gives the wine spritziness. The big, sweet, cherry- and tropical fruit–scented nose is followed by fabulously rich, medium-bodied flavors that coat the palate with lavish opulence. Bold, rich, and huge, this well-balanced wine should be drunk over the next 5–7 years. By comparison, the 1992 Oberhauser Brucke Riesling Auslese is not as well focused. It exhibits an off-dry, interesting cherry-scented nose, ripe but monolithic flavors, and a chunky finish. Although formidably rich and impressive, it lacks the aromatic and flavor dimension of the Niederhauser Hermannshohle.

The two rare half bottles of Eiswein include a tightly knit, crisp, deep, ripe, outstanding 1992 Oberhauser Brucke Riesling Eiswein AP #10, and a profound 1992 Oberhauser Brucke Riesling Eiswein AP #3. The AP #3 is significantly richer, more complex, and better-balanced, with 20 or more years of aging potential.

The 1990 Schlossbockelheimer Felsenberg Riesling Trocken exhibits a pure bouquet of wet stones and floral fruit. Elegant, with finesse and class, this dry, flavorful wine should continue to drink well for 3–4 years. Both the 1991 Niederhauser Hermannshohle Riesling and the 1991 Oberhauser Brucke Riesling are light-bodied, crisp wines with spicy, fruity noses, fine flavor intensity, delicacy, and crispness. The Oberhauser Brucke is slightly richer, as well as more backward. Both should be drunk over the next 2–5 years. The closed 1991 Niederhauser Hermannshohle Riesling Spätlese #31 is more promising than flattering at present. There is intense extract, a solid underpinning of acidity, and an earthy, cherrylike fruitiness to this off-dry, excellently concentrated wine. The 1991 Oberhauser Brucke Riesling Spätlese reveals a bing cherry component to its spicy, richly fruity nose. It offers deeper fruit than the Niederhauser Hermannshohle, excellent definition, and a dry, tightly knit, closed finish. Both of these Spätlese wines will benefit from another year of cellaring; they should last for 5–7 years.

Donnhoff's 1989 Niederhauser Hermannshohle Riesling Auslese and 1991 Oberhauser Brucke Riesling Auslese are terrific examples of Riesling. The 1989 Niederhauser Hermannshohle offers a super nose of spices, botrytis, and rich fruit. Deep, concentrated, and extracted, this off-dry, well-focused wine should continue to drink well for another 5–7 years. Even richer, the phenomenally extracted 1991 Oberhauser Brucke Riesling Auslese possesses a huge, fragrant nose, followed by a wine made in a medium sweet style. This well-defined Auslese should drink well for 5–7 years.

AUGUST ESER (RHEINGAU)* * * *

1992 Hallgartener Schonhell Riesling Spätlese Trocken	C	85
1992 Rauenthaler Rothenberg Riesling Kabinett	C	87
1992 Rauenthaler Rothenberg Riesling Spätlese	C	88

Eser's 1992 Hallgartener Schonhell Riesling Spätlese Trocken is a crisp, tightly knit, light-bodied wine with fine purity and flavor definition, but a short finish. The 1992 Rauenthaler Rothenberg Riesling Kabinett offers a citrusy, floral, cherry-scented nose, a chewy texture, layered, ripe flavors, admirable density, and a spicy, dry finish. The finest offering I tasted from Eser is the 1992 Rauenthaler Rothenberg Riesling Spätlese. This sexy wine displays a honeyed, floral, fruity nose, full- to medium-bodied flavors, superb richness, spicy, ripe fruit, and a long, off-dry finish. It is a beautifully well-balanced wine capable of lasting 5–6 years.

H. H. ESER-JOHANNISHOF (RHEINGAU)* * * *

1992 Geisenheimer Klauserweg Riesling Halbtrocken	A	88
1992 Johannisberger Goldatzel Riesling Spätlese	B	88
1992 Johannisberger Holle Riesling Auslese	D	92
1990 Johannisberger Riesling Auslese	D	92
1992 Johannishof Riesling Auslese	D	90
1992 Winkeler Hasensprung Riesling Kabinett	B	87

Eser's 1992 Geisenheimer Klauserweg Riesling Halbtrocken is a highly extracted, rich, intense wine with a gorgeous nose of spicy, cherry fruit, dry, crisp, pure flavors, a touch of minerals, and a long finish. There is tremendous exuberance to the fruit in this bold, large-scaled Riesling Halbtrocken. Moreover, it is a great bargain. The dry 1992 Winkeler Hasensprung Riesling Kabinett offers admirable clarity, a pear/peach/mineral/stony-scented nose, medium body, excellent fruit, and a dry, crisp finish. It should drink well for 5–6 years. The terrific cinnamon- and spice-filled nose of the 1992 Johannisberger Goldatzel Riesling Spätlese is followed by an off-dry wine with lovely fruit, fine extraction, and a softer texture than Eser's other offerings. It should be drunk over the next 5–6 years.

The 1992 Johannishof Riesling Auslese displays a sweet, honeyed, richly fruity nose, medium-bodied, luscious flavors with gobs of extract, and a superlong finish. It will require drinking during its first 6–7 years of life. The exceptionally rich, pure, fragrant 1992 Johannisberger Holle Riesling Auslese possesses a knockout bouquet, ripe, splendidly rich, well-defined flavors, and a smashingly long finish. It is moderately sweet, but, wow, what intensity, purity, and balance! It should drink well for 7–8 years.

Among a half-dozen 1990 and 1991 offerings from Eser-Johannishof, the 1990 Johannisberger Riesling Auslese was the undisputed star. A great wine, with fabulous perfume, ripe, dense, rich, off-dry flavors, superb precision, wonderful purity, and great overall balance and class, this is a spectacular expression of Riesling that should age effortlessly for at least a decade.

DR. FISCHER (SAAR)* * *

1992 Ockfener Bockstein Riesling Kabinett	B	87
1992 Ockfener Bockstein Riesling Spätlese	C	87

Two very good examples of the vintage, Dr. Fischer's Kabinett and Spätlese from the Ockfener Bockstein vineyard exhibit attractive, moderately intense, stony/apple/floral-scented noses, admirable concentration, and exuberant finishes. Both wines are dry for their respective levels and should drink well for 4–5 years.

ALEXANDRE FREIMUTH (RHEINGAU)* *

1992 Geisenheimer Klauserweg Riesling Kabinett Trocken	B	77
1992 Geisenheimer Mauserchen Riesling Kabinett Halbtrocken	B	85
1992 Geisenheimer Monchspfad Riesling Auslese	C	?

Freimuth's 1992 offerings range from a vaguely perfumed, resiny, austere, tart, impenetrable 1992 Geisenheimer Klauserweg Riesling Kabinett Trocken, to a user-friendly, tender, perfumed, soft, ripe, richly fruity 1992 Geisenheimer Mauserchen Riesling Kabinett Halbtrocken. The latter wine typifies the soft, fruity style of the 1992 vintage. Freimuth's 1992 Geisenheimer Monchspfad Riesling Auslese was a troubled wine when I tasted it. Excessive SO_2 at bottling has resulted in a dirty, match stick–scented nose. In addition, the earthy, herbal, high-acid flavors are unappealing.

GEBRUDER GRIMM (RHEINGAU)* * *

1990 Cuvée Max Riesling Brut	C	90
1992 Rudesheimer Berg Rottland Riesling Auslese	C	92

These are the finest two wines I have tasted from Grimm. I cannot think of a better German sparkling wine than the 1990 Cuvée Max Riesling Brut I poured across my palate. It possesses pinpoint, tiny, uniform bubbles, a delicate bouquet of fresh oranges and flowers, wonderful precision to its flavor, and a dry, rich, and long finish. This wine was kept on its lees for 2½ years. It is a noteworthy achievement. Grimm also fashioned a blockbuster 1992

Rudesheimer Berg Rottland Riesling Auslese. This medium straw-colored, full-bodied wine is a rich, dry Riesling with masses of fruit, a spectacularly fragrant, flowery, honeyed nose, and a finish that goes on and on. A stunningly built, massive, drier-styled Auslese, it should age well for 7–8 years. Impressive!

GERNOT GYSLER (RHEINHESSEN)* * *

1992 Weinheimer Holle Riesling Spätlese Trocken	B	88
1992 Weinheimer Holle Rulander Eiswein	C	87
1992 Weinheimer Mandelberg Riesling Spätlese	B	79

The 1992 Weinheimer Holle Riesling Spätlese Trocken is a fine bargain. The ripe, steely, floral-scented nose is followed by a wine with showy, ostentatious, exuberant, fruity flavors and a fine finish. A super value, it should drink well for 4–5 years. Because of its compact, compressed personality and lack of concentration, the 1992 Weinheimer Mandelberg Riesling Spätlese is not as impressive. Although it exhibits some ripeness, it tails off quickly. The understated, spicy 1992 Weinheimer Holle Rulander Eiswein is well made, delicate, and subtle, with a good but unexciting finish.

FRITZ HAAG (MOSEL)* * * * *

1992 Brauneberger Juffer Sonnenuhr Riesling Auslese #18	D	89
1992 Brauneberger Juffer Sonnenuhr Riesling Gold Capsule Auslese #17	E	92
1992 Brauneberger Juffer Sonnenuhr Riesling Kabinett #11	C	90
1992 Brauneberger Juffer Sonnenuhr Riesling Long Gold Capsule Auslese #16	EEE	93
1992 Brauneberger Juffer Sonnenuhr Riesling Spätlese #5	C	86
1992 Brauneberger Juffer Sonnenuhr Riesling Spätlese #15	D	91

Fritz Haag has turned in a bevy of lovely 1992s. For starters, there is the 1992 Brauneberger Juffer Sonnenuhr Riesling Kabinett #11. It exhibits a gorgeously earthy, stony, floral-scented nose, and lovely fruit that marries elegance with considerable depth. Drink this dry, rich, zesty wine over the next 5–6 years. I preferred Haag's Kabinett to his 1992 Brauneberger Juffer Sonnenuhr Riesling Spätlese #5, the later wine that is soft and delicious, but less focused than his other offerings. The compelling, mineral, lemon/apple blossom bouquet of the 1992 Brauneberger Juffer Sonnenuhr Spätlese #15 is superb. Off-dry, with great clarity and layers of fruit, this formidably endowed, precocious-tasting wine should drink well for 5–7 years.

Haag's 1992 Brauneberger Juffer Sonnenuhr Riesling Auslese #18 is lighter than the other Auslese wines, with medium sweetness, excellent ripeness, a fragrant mineral/fruity nose, admirable focus, and a long finish. Already drinking well, it can be consumed over the next 6–7 years. The 1992 Brauneberger Juffer Sonnenuhr Riesling Gold Capsule Auslese #17 is outrageously ripe and perfumed, with medium sweetness, staggering extraction of fruit, and a long, honeyed finish. It possesses great delineation for its formidable richness. It should drink well for 7–8 years. Haag's 1992 Long Gold Capsule Auslese #16 (from the same vineyard) is slightly richer, with a cherry, mineral, honeyed-apple component, wonderful density, moderate sweetness, adequate acidity, and a penetrating, well-defined personality. It is a great Auslese, not withstanding the outrageous price that reflects both Haag's reputation and the minuscule quantities available.

WILLI HAAG (MOSEL)* * * *

1992	Brauneberger Juffer Riesling Auslese AP #3	D	92
1992	Brauneberger Juffer Riesling Kabinett #4	B	88
1992	Brauneberger Juffer Riesling Kabinett #7	B	88
1992	Brauneberger Juffer Riesling Kabinett #11	B	90
1992	Brauneberger Juffer Riesling Spätlese	B	90
1992	Brauneberger Juffer Riesling Spätlese #8	B	85
1992	Brauneberger Juffer Sonnenuhr Riesling Auslese #5	D	90
1992	Brauneberger Juffer Sonnenuhr Riesling Auslese AP #10	D	95
1992	Brauneberger Juffer Sonnenuhr Riesling Auslese Long Gold Capsule	EEE	96
1992	Brauneberger Juffer Sonnenuhr Riesling Spätlese	C	90
1992	Brauneberger Juffer Sonnenuhr Riesling Spätlese #1	C	87
1991	Haag's Riesling #1	B	86

In 1992, Willi Haag has fashioned forward, soft, lovely, concentrated Rieslings. Most of the offerings are identified by specific *füder* numbers. Among the three Kabinett offerings, *füder* #7 exhibits an interesting, spearmint and slatelike, crisp nose, tight, closed, high-acid flavors, and considerable class. It does not possess the ripeness of *füder* #11. The latter wine is soft, up front, and fruity, with explosive ripeness and a flamboyant style. It is amazing that both wines come from the same vineyard yet are so different. *Füder* #4 represents a synthesis in style of #7 and #11. It is not as high in acidity nor as green as the mineral-dominated #7, nor as explosively rich and precocious as #11. All three of these Kabinetts should be drunk over the next 5–6 years. Although #7 may last longer, I wonder if it will ever display the charm and character of its siblings.

With respect to the Spätlese offerings, *füder* #8 and *füder* #1 are good to very good, but both lack the aromatic and flavor dimension of Haag's best wines. *Füder* #8 is chunky, crisp, and one-dimensional, whereas *füder* #1 is delicious, tasty, and ready to drink, although lacking acidity. The two unnumbered offerings, the 1992 Brauneberger Juffer Sonnenuhr Riesling Spätlese and the 1992 Brauneberger Juffer Riesling Spätlese are both outstanding wines. The Brauneberger Juffer is soft, with a distinctive mineral earthiness, rich, long, cherry flavors, medium sweetness, and great fruit in the long finish. Even more impressive is the Brauneberger Juffer Sonnenuhr, a highly extracted, dramatic wine with gobs of fruit, an intense perfume, and a medium sweet, long finish. Both wines are best drunk over the next 4–5 years.

There are also four Auslese offerings, three with *füder* numbers and one with the designation Long Gold Capsule, an auction wine that is available at a frightfully high price. All of these are outstanding efforts. The Brauneberger Juffer #3 is a superextracted, rich, unctuously styled, medium sweet wine with great *terroir* character, as well as huge quantities of fruit. The Brauneberger Juffer Sonnenuhr #10 is even more spectacular, with sumptuous levels of fruit, fine underlying acidity, and a smashingly long finish. Although slightly drier, the Brauneberger Juffer Sonnenuhr Riesling #5 displays wonderful ripeness, medium body, great precision, and tremendous length. Lastly, the Long Gold Capsule Brauneberger Juffer Sonnenuhr Riesling is very sweet, with tremendous ripeness, that wonderful cherry/floral fruitiness, and a stunningly long finish. Given its price, it is only negligibly better than the $31 Brauneberger Juffer Sonnenuhr Riesling Auslese #10. All of these wines possess the vintage's forward style and should be drunk over the next 5–6 years.

The steely 1991 Haag's Riesling #1, which is declassified Riesling from the great Brauneberger Juffer vineyard, reveals a tight but subtle nose of flowers, minerals, and steel. A pleasant, tasty, dry wine, it possesses high acidity, as well as underlying fruit and character. Drink it over the next several years.

J. HART (MOSEL)* * *

1992 Piesporter Falkenberg Riesling Trocken	A	86
1992 Piesporter Goldtropfchen Riesling Auslese	C	86
1992 Piesporter Goldtropfchen Riesling Halbtrocken	B	76
1992 Piesporter Goldtropfchen Riesling Kabinett	B	86
1992 Piesporter Goldtropfchen Riesling Spätlese	B	85

Hart has produced pleasant to very good Rieslings in 1992. The only disappointing wine is the 1992 Piesporter Goldtropfchen Riesling Halbtrocken, a diluted, light-bodied wine with no finish.

The other wines range from a peach-scented, dry, ripe, medium-bodied, attractive 1992 Piesporter Falkenberg Riesling Trocken, to a fruity, off-dry, medium-bodied, well-balanced, up-front 1992 Piesporter Goldtropfchen Riesling Kabinett. The 1992 Piesporter Goldtropfchen Riesling Spätlese is a ripe, apricot-scented wine with light to medium body and a straightforward finish. Drink it over the next 1–2 years. The 1992 Piesporter Goldtropfchen Riesling Auslese is much sweeter, with a lovely cherry nose, and soft, round, expansive flavors that lack acidity but exhibit fine ripeness and concentration. As with the other wines, it should be drunk over the near term.

FREIHERR VON HEDDESDORFF (MOSEL)* * * *

1991 Winninger Uhlen Riesling QbA	A	88
1991 Winninger Uhlen Riesling Halbtrocken	A	87

Von Heddesdorff made super 1991s. This Winninger Uhlen Riesling Halbtrocken has a fragrant, stony, mineral, citrusy, and floral-scented nose, dry, richly extracted flavors, and a crisp, flavorful, penetrating finish. Drink it over the next several years. The 1991 Winninger Uhlen Riesling QbA exhibits a more earthy, spicy-scented nose, elegant, dense, boldly rich flavors, and a dry, medium-bodied, impressively long finish. It should drink well for 2–3 years. A super bargain in Riesling!

HEHNER-KILTZ (NAHE)* * * *

1992 Riesling	A	87
1992 Schlossbockelheimer Felsenberg Riesling Kabinett Halbtrocken	B	87
1992 Schlossbockelheimer Felsenberg Riesling Kabinett Trocken	B	87
1991 Schlossbockelheimer Felsenberg Riesling Trocken	B	86
1992 Schlossbockelheimer Kupfergrube Riesling Auslese	B	85
1991 Schlossbockelheimer Kupfergrube Riesling Trocken	B	88

All of Hehner-Kiltz's reasonably priced offerings from the Nahe are well made. For example, the 1992 Schlossbockelheimer Felsenberg Riesling Kabinett Trocken is a stony, dry, elegant, light- to medium-bodied wine that is tightly packed with plenty of fruit and character. Drink it over the next 4–5 years. The same vineyard's Halbtrocken designation exhibits a similar character, as well as gobs of extract, admirable crisp acidity, and wonderful fruit and ripeness. The best value is the 1992 Riesling, an off-dry, flowery, richly fruity, medium-bodied wine exhibiting impressive extract, excellent definition, and a refreshingly zesty finish. Drink it over the next several years. Ironically, the most expensive 1992 I tasted from Hehner-Kiltz, the Schlossbockelheimer Kupfergrube Riesling Auslese, was less impressive. Although well made and relatively dry for an Auslese, it is straightforward and unevolved.

The 1991 Schlossbockelheimer Felsenberg Riesling Trocken exhibits an intense, mineral, floral-scented nose, excellent, crisp, dry, medium-bodied flavors, fine extraction, considerable depth and character, and a zesty, clean finish. Even better is the 1991 Schlossbockelheimer Kupfergrube Riesling Trocken. Its huge nose is followed by a wine with gorgeous fruit, multidimensional flavors, and an enticing texture loaded with fruit and buttressed by crisp acidity. This is a lovely, ripe, extracted wine that should have remarkable flexibility with a wide assortment of food.

WEINGUT-WEINHAUS HENNINGER (RHEINPFALZ)* * * *

1989 Jagersekt Riesling Extra Trocken	B	88
1990 Privatissime Riesling Extra Brut	C	89

Henninger's 1990 Privatissime Riesling Extra Brut is an impressively well-made, high-class German sparkling wine that competes favorably with many champagnes. Its tiny, pinpoint bubbles, dry, frothy freshness, and delicate flavors suggest drinking it over the next several years. The less expensive 1989 Jagersekt Riesling Extra Trocken is nearly as good, with a light- to medium-bodied, yeasty nose, excellent lemon/applelike flavors, fine ripeness, and a soft finish. Drink it over the next year.

FREIHERR HEYL ZU HERRNSHEIM (RHEINHESSEN)* * * *

1992 Niersteiner Hipping Riesling Spätlese Trocken	C	90
1991 Niersteiner Olberg Riesling Auslese	C	89
1990 Niersteiner Olberg Riesling Auslese	C	89
1992 Niersteiner Pettenthal Riesling Spätlese Halbtrocken	C	90
1992 Niersteiner Rosenberg Sylvaner Trocken	B	92
1992 Sylvaner Trocken	A	85

Heyl's two Sylvaners range from an earthy, ripe, fine 1992 Sylvaner Trocken, to a sensational 1992 Niersteiner Rosenberg Sylvaner Trocken. The latter wine ranks among the best German Sylvaners I have tasted. Full bodied, with a sensational nose of spices, minerals, and pears, this rich, spectacularly intense, dry wine is loaded with fruit, exhibits excellent clarity, as well as an amazingly long finish. For $10, it must be one of the great bargains of the vintage. It should drink well for at least 4–5 years. Can Sylvaner really produce such a multidimensional wine?

Another superlative effort, Heyl's 1992 Niersteiner Hipping Spätlese Riesling Trocken offers a smoky, mineral, earthy, fruity nose, dry, long, medium-bodied flavors, excellent depth, and a long, crisp finish. Lastly, Heyl's 1992 Niersteiner Pettenthal Riesling Spätlese is a Halbtrocken, although that word does not appear on the label. It reveals a huge nose of ripe peaches, minerals, and damp earth. Spicy, spectacularly rich, with great fruit and precision, this lusty, superbly well-balanced wine offers considerable finesse and impressive extraction.

It is interesting to compare the 1990 and 1991 Niersteiner Olberg Riesling Ausleses from Heyl zu Herrnsheim. I found them to be qualitative equals, which says something about what this producer achieved in the 1991 vintage. With wonderful ripeness, pure fruit, and a slightly softer style, the 1990 is made in a deep, off-dry, delicate manner. It should drink well for 7–8 years. The more powerful and intense 1991 exhibits a dramatic, rich, deep, slightly off-dry finish. The acidity keeps everything in check. My instincts suggest that yields were significantly lower in the 1991. While the 1991 should last longer than the 1990, I would opt for drinking it in its first 7–8 years of life.

IMMICH-BATTERIEBERG (MOSEL)* * * *

1991 Enkircher Batterieberg Riesling Spätlese	C	90+
1991 Enkircher Batterieberg Riesling Spätlese Halbtrocken	C	88
1991 Enkircher Zeppwingert Riesling Spätlese	C	90

An impressive trio of wines, the dry 1991 Enkircher Batterieberg Riesling Spätlese Halbtrocken offers opulent, rich fruit, a spicy, vanillin, botrytised nose, excellent flavor depth and precision, and a ripe, long, luscious finish. The off-dry 1991 Enkircher Zeppwingert Riesling Spätlese is a powerful, authoritatively flavored, atypically big, ripe, lusty, superfragrant, rich wine. It should be drunk over the next decade. The 1991 Enkircher Batterieberg Riesling Spätlese possesses super depth, exceptional richness and intensity, but remains relatively closed and unevolved. Put this wine away for 2–3 years and drink it over the following 10 years.

E. JAKOBY-MATHY (MOSEL)* * * *

1992 Kinheimer Hubertuslay Riesling Spätlese	B	85
1992 Kinheimer Hubertuslay Riesling Spätlese Halbtrocken	B	85
1992 Kinheimer Rosenberg Riesling Eiswein	E	93

Jakoby-Mathy's Spätlese and Spätlese Halbtrocken offerings from the Kinheimer Hubertuslay vineyard are both light-bodied wines with crisp fruit, freshness, purity, and balance. Although well made, they lack the personality and concentration seen in the vintage's finest efforts. The 1992 Kinheimer Rosenberg Riesling Eiswein lacks neither individuality nor richness. It offers up a spectacularly intense nose of honeyed fruit, flowers, and minerals. Sweet, with great flavor depth, and wonderful length, the zesty acidity keeps the wine's massive richness in harmony. This is a 20- to 30-year wine.

TONI JOST (MITTELRHEIN)* * */* * * *

1992 Bacharacher Hahn Riesling Auslese	D	90
1992 Bacharacher Hahn Riesling Kabinett	C	82
1992 Bacharacher Hahn Riesling Spätlese AP #16	C	90
1992 Bacharacher Hahn Riesling Spätlese AP #22	C	90
1992 Bacharacher Hahn Riesling Spätlese Halbtrocken	C	90

Jost's 1992 Bacharacher Hahn Riesling Kabinett is a shy, understated, light-bodied, off-dry style of Kabinett. The other offerings are all flamboyant to the point of ostentatiousness! For example, the 1992 Bacharacher Hahn Riesling Spätlese Halbtrocken offers an exotic peach/apricot/cherry nose reminiscent of a Rhône Valley Condrieu. The wine is loaded with massive amounts of fruit. Medium bodied, with superb concentration and richness, this wine made me think of Viognier, not Riesling. Drink this terrific wine over the next 2–3 years.

Jost's two Spätlese offerings, AP #16 and AP #22 (*füder* #22 also sports a 1-star indication) are similarly styled. Qualitative equals, they both offer extroverted, perfumed, ripe, flashy bouquets, luscious, rich, medium-bodied, off-dry, concentrated flavors oozing with fruit, and bold, spicy finishes. Readers who admire understated, superrefined Rieslings are forewarned that these are dramatic wines. Both should be consumed over the next 2–3 years.

Jost's 1992 Bacharacher Hahn Riesling Auslese exhibits a penetratingly fragrant, blockbuster bouquet of honeyed fruit, gorgeous richness, and medium body. Slightly sweeter than the two Spätlese offerings, it should be consumed during its first 3–4 years of life.

WEINGUT KARLSMUHLE (MOSEL-RUWER)* * * *

1992 Kaseler Kehrnagel Riesling Spätlese Halbtrocken	B	85
1992 Lorenzhofer Felslay Riesling Spätlese Trocken	C	85
1992 Lorenzhofer Mauerchen Riesling Kabinett	B	87
1992 Lorenzhofer Riesling	B	88
1992 Lorenzhofer Riesling Halbtrocken	B	86

Karlsmuhle turned in a good but uninspiring performance. The well-perfumed 1992 Lorenzhofer Felslay Riesling Spätlese Trocken offers fine acidity and a dry, light-bodied palate. Drink it over the next 1–2 years. The 1992 Lorenzhofer Riesling Halbtrocken exhibits a similar floral, perfumed bouquet, delicate, dry, light-bodied flavors, and a fresh finish. An attractive wine for the price, it should drink well for 1–2 years. The pretty, subtle, exceptionally light-bodied, finesse-filled 1992 Kaseler Kehrnagel Riesling Spätlese Halbtrocken has a decent but short finish. Consume this dry, pleasant wine over the next 1–2 years.

My favorite wine is the 1992 Lorenzhofer Riesling. It exhibits an intense, floral bouquet, very good ripeness, full body, surprising glycerin, and a long, rich, complete finish. A noteworthy value, it should also be drunk over the next 1–2 years. The 1992 Lorenzhofer Mauerchen Riesling Kabinett reveals shockingly high acidity for a 1992, delicate fruit, light body, and excellent depth and focus. Like all of these offerings from Karlsmuhle, it should be drunk over the next several years.

CHRISTIAN KARP-SCHREIBER (MOSEL)* * * *

1991 Karp's Riesling	B	87

A citrusy, stony, floral- and apple-scented nose is followed by a wine with excellent flavor concentration, light to medium body, an elegant personality, and good purity and crispness in a moderately long finish. Drink it over the next several years.

KARTHAUSERHOF (CHRISTOPH TYRELL) (RUWER)* * * *

1992 Eitelsbacher Karthauserhof Riesling Auslese	D	89
1992 Eitelsbacher Karthauserhof Riesling Auslese #10	D	91
1990 Eitelsbacher Karthauserhof Riesling Auslese #23	D	92
1992 Eitelsbacher Karthauserhof Riesling Kabinett Halbtrocken	C	85
1992 Eitelsbacher Karthauserhof Riesling Spätlese	D	90
1992 Eitelsbacher Karthauserhof Riesling Spätlese Trocken	C	82
1992 Eitelsbacher Karthauserhof Riesling QbA	B	76

Karthauserhof's drier 1992s are austere, backward, tightly wound wines that were not easy to assess. However, I believe I am being fair in saying that wines such as the 1992 Eitelsbacher Karthauserhof Riesling Spätlese Trocken and the 1992 Riesling Kabinett Halbtrocken were lacking fruit. Certainly the crisp, dry, apple-scented noses and austere, fresh flavors of these wines were attractive in an understated style. The Halbtrocken evidenced more length. The greenness, austerity, tightness, and lack of depth are also problematic with the 1992 Eitelsbacher Karthauserhof Riesling QbA.

The quality jumps significantly with the 1992 Eitelsbacher Karthauserhof Riesling Spätlese, a wine with a delicate but multidimensional personality. The terrific but subtle bouquet of minerals and fruit is followed by a wine with tremendous firmness, richness, and length. Exceptionally delicate, as well as rich and dry for a Spätlese, it should prove to be an uncommonly long-lived 1992, lasting for at least a decade. The 1992 Eitelsbacher Karthauserhof Riesling Auslese offers an attractive apple/mineral nose, lovely ripeness and elegance, very good concentration, and a persuasive finish. It should last well.

The two finest wines I tasted from this estate included the 1992 Eitelsbacher Karthauserhof Riesling Auslese #10 and the 1990 Eitelsbacher Karthauserhof Riesling Auslese #23. The #10 exhibits a sensational nose of botrytised fruit and minerals, and sweet, rich flavors presented in a light-bodied, crisp, austere format. It lingers on the palate in excess of 30 seconds. The 1990 #23 reveals a similar character, with more of a cherry component to its bouquet, as well as denser, richer fruit and superb length. The 1992 should last for 10 or more years, whereas the 1990 has the potential to last for 2 decades.

HERIBERT KERPEN (MOSEL)* * * * *

1992	Bernkasteler Bratenhofchen Riesling Auslese	C	90
1992	Bernkasteler Bratenhofchen Riesling Spätlese	C	93
1991	Bernkasteler Bratenhofchen Riesling Spätlese	C	86
1991	Kerpen's Riesling	B	87
1992	Wehlener Sonnenuhr Riesling Auslese	C	90
1992	Wehlener Sonnenuhr Riesling Auslese #4	C	91
1992	Wehlener Sonnenuhr Riesling Kabinett	B	87
1991	Wehlener Sonnenuhr Riesling Kabinett	B	86
1992	Wehlener Sonnenuhr Riesling Spätlese Halbtrocken	C	89
1991	Wehlener Sonnenuhr Riesling Spätlese Halbtrocken	C	89

One of the Mosel's new superstars, Heribert Kerpen's soft and flattering 1992s are of high quality. The 1992 Wehlener Sonnenuhr Riesling Spätlese Halbtrocken reveals a lovely, floral, elegant bouquet with whiffs of melon in the background, medium sweet, ripe flavors with hints of minerals and slate, and a round, lovely finish. With more precision, this wine would have been outstanding. Surprisingly soft for a Kerpen offering, the 1992 Wehlener Sonnenuhr Riesling Kabinett exhibits an attractive, steely, ripe nose and excellent flavor extraction, but less focus and delineation. Drink this dry Riesling over the next 4–5 years. The 1992 Bernkasteler Bratenhofchen Riesling Spätlese is a sensational wine. The terrific bouquet of minerals, ripe apple/lemon scents, and spring flowers soars from the glass. The wine offers superb extraction of flavor, a cassislike component to its taste, and a dazzlingly long, crisp, blazingly well-defined finish. It is a superb Spätlese for drinking over the next 5–6 years.

In 1992 there are three Auslese offerings. The 1992 Wehlener Sonnenuhr Riesling Auslese (1 star) reveals a riveting citrusy, slate/mineral-scented nose, deep, lovely, rich flavors that exhibit fabulous ripeness, and a soft finish. This outstanding wine should be drunk over the next 4–5 years because of its precocious personality. In comparison, the 1992 Bernkasteler Bratenhofchen Riesling Auslese is restrained, with better focus, a wonderful core of rich, medium sweet, slatelike, vanillin, cherry fruit, and a long, exuberant finish. It is a terrific Auslese for drinking over the next 5–6 years. Kerpen's 1992 Wehlener Sonnenuhr Riesling Auslese #4 (2 stars) is impressively rich, with excellent acidity for a 1992, a wonderfully ripe, honeyed character, fat, fleshy flavors, and a superb finish. Softer than usual, this bold, beautifully focused, admirably extracted Riesling should be drunk in its youth.

Kerpen's 1991 Wehlener Sonnenuhr Riesling Spätlese Halbtrocken reveals a stunning nose of slate and flowers. Light, but oh, so pure and delicate, yet rich, this gracefully rendered, crisp, dry wine should continue to drink well for another 4–5 years. The generic 1991 Kerpen's Riesling, supposedly made from 100% Wehlener Sonnenuhr grapes, is made in an off-dry, floral, peach-scented style, with excellent ripeness, wonderful purity, and a rich, light-bodied finish. Drink it over the next 2–3 years. The 1991 Wehlener Sonnenuhr Riesling Kabinett is slightly less endowed than Kerpen's Riesling. Nevertheless, it is still a tart, crisp, floral wine that I may have caught in a closed stage. The finish is dry, fruity, and pleasant. Drink it over the next 2–3 years. Kerpen's 1991 Bernkasteler Bratenhofchen Riesling Spätlese is a medium-bodied, soft, almost diffuse style of Riesling that some readers may find unattractive. Although not up to the quality of Kerpen's 1989s and 1990s, I enjoyed the copious quantities of fruit, the purity, and the unreleased CO_2 that gives the wine a spritzy quality. Those familiar with Kerpen's classic style of Riesling will be surprised by the somewhat unstructured nature of this offering. Drink it over the next 1–2 years.

VON KESSELSTATT (MOSEL-SAAR)* * * *

1992 Josephshofer Riesling Auslese	D	91
1992 Piesporter Goldtropfchen Riesling Kabinett	C	89
1992 Scharzhofberger Riesling Spätlese	C	90

Based on the limited sampling I had of von Kesselstatt's 1992s, this looks to be one of the vintage's best performers. These three wines are brilliant expressions of Riesling. The 1992 Piesporter Goldtropfchen Riesling Kabinett exhibits an intense perfume, dry, elegant, stylish, concentrated flavors, and a crisp, tasty, exceptionally long finish. Drink this beauty over the next 4–5 years. Both the 1992 Scharzhofberger Riesling Spätlese and the 1992 Josephshofer Riesling Auslese are dry for the level of ripeness they exhibit. Both are superbly concentrated wines, with extraordinary clarity and admirable balance and length. Two terrific Rieslings, they should drink well for 7–8 years.

J. F. KIMICH (RHEINPFALZ)* * * * *

1992 Deidesheimer Grainhubel Riesling Auslese	C	90
1992 Deidesheimer Herrgottsacker Riesling Auslese	C	89
1992 Deidesheimer Herrgottsacker Riesling Kabinett	B	90
1991 Deidesheimer Herrgottsacker Riesling Kabinett	B	89
1991 Deidesheimer Herrgottsacker Riesling Kabinett Halbtrocken	B	87
1992 Deidesheimer Herrgottsacker Riesling Spätlese	B	86
1992 Deidesheimer Kieselberg Riesling Spätlese Halbtrocken	C	89
1992 Forster Elster Riesling Kabinett	B	90
1992 Forster Stift Gewürztraminer Spätlese	C	86
1992 Forster Stift Gewürztraminer Spätlese Trocken	C	86
1992 Forster Ungeheuer Riesling Spätlese	C	76
1992 Forster Ungeheuer Riesling Spätlese Trocken	C	90
1992 Ruppertsberger Reiterfad Riesling Kabinett Halbtrocken	B	87

One of my favorite German producers, Kimich fashions personality-filled, lavishly fruity, sometimes exotic wines with intense bouquets and flavors. Most of his 1992 offerings are successful. The 1992 Forster Ungeheuer Riesling Spätlese Trocken defines the Kimich style with its up-front, perfumed nose of ripe peaches, minerals, and exotic fruits. The wine reveals crisp acidity, excellent ripeness, medium to full body, and a dry, fleshy, long finish. Drink it over the next 3–4 years. The 1992 Ruppertsberger Reiterfad Riesling Kabinett Halbtrocken exhibits a peach/cherry-scented nose, long, ripe, bold flavors, a floral component, and a moderately long, rich, dry finish. While not as stunningly proportioned as the Forster Ungeheuer, it is a fine wine for drinking over the next 4–5 years. The sexy, exotic, seductive 1992 Deidesheimer Kieselberg Riesling Spätlese Halbtrocken is rich and long, with an opulent, lush, fat fruitiness supported by decent acidity. This up-front, precocious-tasting wine should be drunk over the next several years.

Kimich's two Kabinett offerings, the 1992 Forster Elster and 1992 Deidesheimer Herrgottsacker, are both sensational wines, as well as great bargains. The Forster Elster offers an earthy, cinnamon-scented nose, intense, concentrated, dry flavors with great purity and ripeness, and a long, lusty finish. More exotic, the Deidesheimer Herrgottsacker's personality leans toward tropical fruits such as pineapples. The wine exhibits Kimich's telltale concentration and a layered, deep, ripe, viscously textured palate. It is off-dry, with an impressive finish. Both Kabinetts should be drunk over the next 3–4 years.

For whatever reason, Kimich's two Spätlese offerings were not as impressive. The 1992 Deidesheimer Herrgottsacker Riesling Spätlese is tough, backward, and dry. Although rich, it lacks expressiveness. The 1992 Forster Ungeheuer Riesling Spätlese's light, lean, austere, ungenerous personality is disappointing. In contrast, the 1992 Deidesheimer Herrgottsacker Riesling Auslese offers a smoky, honeyed nose, ripe, luscious flavors, fine acidity, medium body, and a Condrieu-like, unctuously thick, rich finish. The 1992 Deidesheimer Grainhubel Riesling Auslese is extremely dry for an Auslese, with massive proportions, full body, deep, long, concentrated flavors, and a spicy finish. Drink both of these Ausleses over the next 3–5 years.

Kimich normally produces one of Germany's finest Gewürztraminers. While both the 1992 Forster Stift Gewürztraminer Spätlese Trocken and the 1992 Forster Stift Gewürztraminer Spätlese are very good wines, neither possesses the flavor dimension of his 1990s. The Spätlese Trocken exhibits Gewürztraminer's lychee nut/rose petal fragrance, and an attractive pineapplelike fruitiness in its dry, austere personality. The similarly styled Forster Stift Spätlese is dominated by its exotic lychee nut character, and reveals a dry, medium-bodied finish. Both wines should be consumed over the next 2–3 years.

The dry, aromatic, medium-bodied 1991 Deidesheimer Herrgottsacker Riesling Kabinett Halbtrocken offers gorgeous fruit, is zesty and well focused, with a surprisingly long finish. It is hard to believe Riesling at this price could get much better. The 1991 Deidesheimer Herrgottsacker Riesling Kabinett is a terrific wine, with a big, spicy, full, exotic-scented nose, dense cherry, medium-bodied, dry flavors, wonderful focus and crispness, and an uplifting finish. Drink it over the next 2–3 years.

FREIHERR ZU KNYPHAUSEN (RHEINGAU)* * * *

1992	Erbacher Riesling Kabinett	B	83
1991	Erbacher Marcobrunn Riesling Kabinett	C	90
1992	Erbacher Marcobrunn Riesling Spätlese	C	90
1992	Erbacher Michelmark Riesling Trockenbeerenauslese	E	96
1991	Erbacher Steinmorgen Riesling Kabinett	B	88
1992	Hattenheimer Wisselbrunner Riesling Spätlese Trocken	C	88
1992	Kiedricher Riesling Trocken	B	87

Knyphausen's Rheingau estate has turned out some attractive wines in the ripe, fruity, soft, yet delicious 1992 vintage. The 1992 Kiedricher Riesling Trocken is a dry, rich, big, almost Chablis-like Riesling with excellent purity and an austere, dry, stony finish. It is a bargain. The softer, more flattering 1992 Hattenheimer Wisselbrunner Riesling Spätlese Trocken exhibits some botrytis, as well as fat, ripe, medium-bodied flavors displaying considerable alcohol (14.5%!). This decadent, dry Riesling is made in a bold, user-friendly style. It is an impressive wine for drinking over the next 4–5 years. By comparison, the 1992 Erbacher Riesling Kabinett is compact. An earthiness in the nose dominates the wine's understated, floral/fruit component. The wine exhibits fine extract, medium body, and a dry, short finish. Drink it over the near term.

The exotic 1992 Erbacher Marcobrunn Riesling Spätlese is an opulent, superfragrant wine with an off-dry, full-bodied palate, aromas and flavors reminiscent of incense, and a rich, layered, kinky style. A wine of great personality and richness, it should drink well for 7–8 years. The spectacular 1992 Erbacher Michelmark Riesling Trockenbeerenauslese is a decadently rich, honeyed, botrytised, lusciously sweet wine with superb balance, fine underlying acidity, and a finish that lingers for over a minute. It should last for 20–30 years.

These are both brilliant 1991s: The 1991 Erbacher Steinmorgen Riesling Kabinett reveals an inner strength and intensity of flavor, great character, admirable richness, and a dry, medium-bodied, lively style. There is a curranty, spicy richness to its fruit. Drink it over the next 7–8 years. The superb 1991 Erbacher Marcobrunn Riesling Kabinett is dry, with a huge, spicy, cinnamon- and baked apple–scented nose, ripe, medium-bodied, highly concentrated flavors, and a dry, crisp, quintessentially elegant finish. Already delicious, it should improve in the bottle over the next 1–2 years and last for up to a decade.

BURGERMEISTER CARL KOCH (RHEINHESSEN)* *

1990 Oppenheimer Kreuz Riesling Kabinett	B	87

Displaying an exotic, cinnamon, apple-scented nose, ripe, tasty, rich flavors, excellent concentration, and a dramatic personality, this 1990 Riesling Kabinett manages to retain a delicacy and a long, crisp finish. Drink it over the next 2–3 years.

KOEHLER-RUPRECHT (RHEINPFALZ)* * * *

1992 Kallstadter Saumagen Muskateller Auslese	D	90
1992 Kallstadter Steinacker Riesling Kabinett	B	87

I enjoyed Koehler-Ruprecht's 1992 Kallstadter Steinacker Riesling Kabinett, a deep, spicy, off-dry Riesling that tastes surprisingly bold and rich for a Kabinett. Fine underlying acidity and balance suggest that this Kabinett should drink well for 6–7 years. The 1992 Kallstadter Saumagen Muskateller Auslese is a large-scaled, exotic, flamboyant wine with intensely rich fruit, a medium degree of sweetness, and a spicy, long, heady finish. It offers a knockout, kinky, explosively fruity nose, as well as loads of personality. Drink it over the next 3–4 years.

KRUGER-RUMPF (NAHE)* * * *

1992 Munsterer Dautenflanzer Riesling Spätlese	B	87
1992 Munsterer Dautenflanzer Scheurebe Spätlese	B	90
1992 Munsterer Kapellenberg Riesling Kabinett #5	B	88
1992 Munsterer Kapellenberg Sylvaner Kabinett Halbtrocken	B	79
1992 Munsterer Pittersberg Riesling Auslese	B	77

Kruger-Rumpf turned in an irregular performance in 1992, producing three excellent to outstanding wines and two mediocre offerings. The mediocrities include a straightforward, stone-scented, dry, light-bodied, one-dimensional 1992 Munsterer Kapellenberg Sylvaner Kabinett Halbtrocken and a dry, austere, light-bodied, unimpressively extracted 1992 Munsterer Pittersberg Riesling Auslese.

The excellent 1992 Munsterer Kapellenberg Riesling Kabinett #5 possesses an off-dry personality, great ripeness of fruit, a stunning floral character, and a long, rich, ripe, concentrated finish. Already delicious, it should drink well for 5–6 years. The 1992 Munsterer Dautenflanzer Scheurebe Spätlese is not only a noteworthy bargain, but also an intensely perfumed (apricots, peaches, flowers), rich, concentrated, well-focused wine with a long, lusty, intense finish. Its exotic, flamboyant character suggests it should be drunk over the next 3–4 years. The 1992 Munsterer Dautenflanzer Riesling Spätlese is a spicy, rich, light- to medium-bodied wine with excellent concentration, a fine finish, and good delineation to its component parts. Slightly more restrained than the Scheurebe, it should be consumed over the near term.

KUHLING-GILLOT (RHEINHESSEN)* * * *

1992 Bodenheimer Heitersbrunnchen Scheurebe Kabinett	A	87
1992 Bodenheimer Kapelle Riesling Kabinett	A	86
1992 Oppenheimer Kreuzkerner Riesling Auslese	B	88
1992 Oppenheimer Riesling Halbtrocken	A	87
1992 Oppenheimer Sacktrager Riesling Auslese	C	89
1992 Oppenheimer Sacktrager Riesling Trockenbeerenauslese	D	90

Readers should put to good use the fact that this underrated producer tends to sell his wines at relatively low prices. There are not many $9 white wines that offer as much fruit, complexity, and overall grace as the 1992 Oppenheimer Riesling Halbtrocken. This lovely wine should drink well for 1–2 years. Also fairly priced, the 1992 Bodenheimer Kapelle Riesling Kabinett offers a ripe, perfumed nose of juicy fruit and flowers. It is a pretty wine, with considerable elegance, a soft texture, and a dry, moderately long finish. Drink it over the next 1–2 years. The 1992 Bodenheimer Heitersbrunnchen Scheurebe Kabinett reveals the typical exotic, lush Scheurebe perfume. This dry, rich, medium-bodied wine possesses tons of fruit; it should be drunk over the next several years.

The Auslese offerings from Kuhling-Gillot include a fairly priced, sweet, lusciously fruity, medium-bodied, honeyed 1992 Oppenheimer Kreuzkerner Riesling Auslese, and a classically made, moderately sweet, fragrant, light- to medium-bodied, intensely fruity 1992 Oppenheimer Sacktrager Riesling Auslese. Both are precocious wines that should be drunk over the next 2–3 years. Lastly, the 1992 Oppenheimer Sacktrager Riesling Trockenbeerenauslese exhibits a deep, evolved color, a honeyed nose of overripe fruit and smoked beer nuts, rich, full-bodied flavors with gobs of sweetness and glycerin, and a fat, low-acid, nearly cloying finish. This outstanding wine should be drunk during its first 7–8 years of life.

FRANZ (GUNTER) KUNSTLER (RHEINGAU)* * * *

1992 Hochheimer Herrenberg Riesling Spätlese Trocken	C	84
1992 Hochheimer Hofmeister Riesling Halbtrocken	B	77
1992 Hochheimer Holle Riesling Auslese	D	90
1992 Hochheimer Holle Riesling Kabinett Trocken	C	87
1992 Hochheimer Stielweg Riesling Spätlese Trocken	C	90

Among this estate's three Trocken offerings, I found the 1992 Hochheimer Holle Riesling Kabinett Trocken to possess an intriguing nose of peanuts and vegetables, with earthy, crisp, medium-bodied, dry flavors. It is a tightly knit, well-endowed wine that expresses considerable personality. The earthy-style, spicy 1992 Hochheimer Herrenberg Riesling Spätlese Trocken reveals a meaty component, as well as more shortness and austerity than was noticeable in the Hochheimer Holle. The pick of this trio is the 1992 Hochheimer Stielweg Riesling Spätlese Trocken. It exhibits a superb bouquet of tropical fruit and minerals. Rich and well focused, this elegant wine offers plenty of extract, as well as an immensely satisfying, dry, rich, exuberant finish. It should drink well for 5–6 years.

Kunstler's 1992 Hochheimer Hofmeister Riesling Halbtrocken is excessively tart, without enough fruit and flesh to cover its framework. Those masochistic readers who enjoy tart, superaustere, dry German Rieslings will find more joy than I did. Lastly, the 1992 Hochheimer Holle Riesling Auslese was harvested at Beerenauslese sugar levels. The light golden color and the fragrant, exotic nose of sweet, candied, honeyed fruit, cherries, and spices is a knockout. Rich, with superb ripeness, this medium-bodied, concentrated wine should drink well for 7–8 years.

JOSEF LEITZ (RHEINGAU)* * *

1992 Rudesheimer Berg Roseneck Riesling Spätlese	C	74
1992 Rudesheimer Berg Rottland Riesling Kabinett Halbtrocken	B	85
1992 Rudesheimer Berg Rottland Riesling Spätlese Trocken	C	87
1992 Rudesheimer Bischofsberg Riesling Kabinett	B	78
1992 Rudesheimer Bischofsberg Riesling Trocken	B	?
1992 Rudesheimer Kirchenpfad Riesling Spätlese	C	91
1992 Rudesheimer Klosterberg Riesling	B	85?

The unimpressive 1992 Rudesheimer Bischofsberg Riesling Kabinett is light bodied, short, and malnourished. The lifeless Rudesheimer Berg Roseneck Riesling Spätlese exhibits an unusual, leeslike, yeasty nose, crisp, tightly knit, tough flavors, and a frightfully austere finish.

On a more positive note, the 1992 Rudesheimer Berg Rottland Riesling Spätlese Trocken exhibits a big, bold bouquet of tropical fruit and honeyed apples, fine crispness and finesse, and a dry, moderately long finish. Drink it over the next 2–4 years. The 1992 Rudesheimer Berg Rottland Riesling Kabinett Halbtrocken "free run" is a more earthy, mineral-scented wine with freshness and surprising glycerin in its soft, expansive palate, and a moderately long, fleshy finish. It is an uncomplicated, mouth-filling Riesling for drinking over the next several years.

The distinctive, earthy, *terroir* character of the Rudesheimer vineyard is apparent in the 1992 Rudesheimer Klosterberg Riesling. The wine is overwhelmingly earthy, with an interesting cherry component. Medium to full bodied, with admirable richness, and a long, intense finish, this wine is likely to be controversial. The 1992 Rudesheimer Bischofsberg Riesling Trocken will also be perceived as an unusual wine. The intensely earthy, frightfully high-acid level makes for an austere, difficult-to-penetrate and -assess Riesling. Although extremely dry, it displays some underlying extract.

The most interesting wine I tasted from Leitz was the 1992 Rudesheimer Kirchenpfad Riesling Spätlese. It offers great depth of fruit, an exotic, honeyed, cherry, spicy nose, tremendous flavor depth, and a long, off-dry, concentrated finish. It can be drunk now or cellared for 4–5 years.

LIESCHIED-ROLLAUER (MITTELRHEIN)* * *

1991 Bacharacher Wolfshohle Riesling Spätlese	C	89

This wine's bouquet soars from the glass offering up aromas of baked apples, minerals, and flowers. Long, ripe, and off-dry, this broad-flavored, expansive, rich, soft 1991 is seductive and ideal for drinking over the next 3–4 years.

SCHLOSS LIESER (MOSEL)* * *

1992 Lieser Niederberg Helden Riesling Kabinett	B	86
1992 Lieser Sussenberg Riesling Auslese	D	86
1992 Lieser Sussenberg Riesling Kabinett	B	86
1992 Lieser Schlossberg Riesling Spätlese	B	87
1992 Schloss Lieser Riesling Halbtrocken	C	86
1992 Schloss Lieser Riesling Trocken	A	87

This estate, run by Thomas Haag (Willi Haag's son), who apprenticed under the Nahe's Donnhoff, has turned out attractive, soft 1992s that are very good, but limited in their aging ability. Certainly a fine value, the elegant 1992 Schloss Lieser Riesling Trocken offers an attractive apple/floral/mineral-scented nose, lovely ripeness, and crisp, dry fruit. This is an inexpensive, delicious, concentrated Riesling for consuming over the next 3–4 years. The 1992 Schloss Lieser Riesling Halbtrocken exhibits a flowery, vividly pure bouquet, excellent fresh, dry, medium-bodied flavors, and a tasty, crisp finish. It is also a fine bargain.

Among the two Kabinetts from Schloss Lieser, the 1992 Lieser Niederberg Helden Riesling Kabinett reveals a crisp, floral, stony nose, and well-made, dry, light-bodied flavors. The 1992 Lieser Sussenberg Riesling Kabinett offers more of an applelike/flowery nose, slightly more ripeness, as well as more length and richness on the palate. Both are medium-weight, drier-style Kabinetts for drinking early—in their first 3–4 years of life.

The fairly priced, off-dry 1992 Lieser Schlossberg Riesling Spätlese possesses rich fruit, a soft, round style, excellent richness, attractive mineral/tropical fruit elements, and a gentle finish. The 1992 Lieser Sussenberg Riesling Auslese is sweet, fat, muted, and monolithic, but delicious in an obvious, commercial style. Although very good, more finesse and precision would have elevated the score. Both of these wines should be drunk over the next 3–4 years.

H. & R. LINGENFELDER (RHEINPFALZ)* * * * *

1991 Freinsheimer Goldberg Riesling Kabinett	B	88
1992 Freinsheimer Goldberg Riesling Spätlese	C	89
1992 Freinsheimer Goldberg Scheurebe Auslese	D	99
1992 Freinsheimer Musikantenbuckel Scheurebe Beerenauslese	EE	95
1992 Freinsheimer Scheurebe Spätlese Trocken	C	92
1991 Grosskarlbacher Burgweg Scheurebe Kabinett Trocken	B	89
1992 Grosskarlbacher Osterberg Riesling Spätlese Halbtrocken	C	91

One of the stars of the Rheinpfalz, Lingenfelder has turned in a superlative performance in 1992. Not many wines, even those selling for twice the price, can deliver the fragrance and juicy, succulent richness of the 1992 Freinsheimer Scheurebe Spätlese Trocken. An explosively rich, perfumed wine oozing with fruit and character, this dry, fragrant Scheurebe is a turn-on. Drink it over the next 2–4 years. Lingenfelder's 1992 Grosskarlbacher Osterberg Riesling Spätlese Halbtrocken is another rich, dry, full-bodied wine with an explosively fragrant nose, intense flavor, and admirable structure. This large-scaled, dry Riesling will age for 6–8 years.

Similarly styled, the dry, full-bodied 1992 Freinsheimer Goldberg Riesling Spätlese exhibits superb purity of fruit, as well as a long, ripe, cherry-flavored, bold finish. Lingenfelder is not shy about giving consumers remarkable flavor and intensity. The 1992 Freinsheimer Goldberg Scheurebe Auslese is hauntingly close to perfection. A spectacular honeyed, curranty, floral-scented nose is followed by a rich, slightly sweet wine with stunning precision to its massively endowed, concentrated flavors. This huge wine, which was picked at Beerenauslese ripeness and fermented nearly dry, is a blockbuster effort that must be tasted to be believed. Given its sublime quality and spectacular concentration and power, the price of $17 a half-bottle is a steal.

Lastly, Lingenfelder's 1992 Freinsheimer Musikantenbuckel Scheurebe Beerenauslese possesses a huge nose of tropical fruit and flowers, thick, rich flavors exhibiting considerable botrytis, a honeyed, unctuous texture, and a long, moderately sweet finish. The dizzyingly high alcohol level of 13.5% is well concealed by the wine's fruit. This is a knockout, sweet wine for drinking over the next 10–15 years.

I was immensely turned on by the gorgeous, perfumed, elegant style of Lingenfelder's 1991 Grosskarlbacher Burgweg Scheurebe Kabinett Trocken. With its spring flower–like nose, dry, stunningly crisp, rich, fruit flavors, and light-bodied but lengthy feel, this is a gorgeous, dry Scheurebe for drinking over the next several years. The 1991 Freinsheimer Goldberg Riesling Kabinett is also dry, with a spicy, elegant, floral, fruit-scented nose, an inner core of rich, ripe fruit, light to medium body, and a pure, mineral-flavored, long finish. It will drink well for 4–6 years.

DR. LOOSEN-ST.-JOHANNISHOF (MOSEL)* * * *

1992 Erdener Pralat Riesling Auslese	D	?
1992 Erdener Pralat Riesling Spätlese	D	87
1992 Erdener Treppchen Riesling Kabinett	C	88
1992 Erdener Treppchen Riesling Spätlese	C	90
1992 Wehlener Sonnenuhr Riesling Auslese	D	89
1992 Wehlener Sonnenuhr Riesling Beerenauslese	EE	96
1992 Wehlener Sonnenuhr Riesling Kabinett	C	87
1992 Wehlener Sonnenuhr Riesling Spätlese	C	90

In the past, Dr. Loosen's admirable winemaking efforts have been spoiled by a tendency to utilize excessive amounts of SO_2 at bottling. For starters, Loosen's two Kabinetts offer excellent purity, dry, ripe flavors, and vivid richness. The 1992 Wehlener Sonnenuhr reveals more vanillin, mineral, and floral scents, whereas the 1992 Erdener Treppchen displays a stony, nutty quality. It is also fuller on the palate, with a slightly off-dry finish. Both wines are up-front, forward Kabinetts that should be consumed over the next 4–5 years.

Dr. Loosen's three Spätlese offerings range from two stunning examples from the Wehlener Sonnenuhr and Erdener Treppchen vineyards, to a sweet, full, chunky Erdener Pralat. The 1992 Wehlener Sonnenuhr Riesling Spätlese possesses a creamy richness, an impressively fine aromatic profile, and long, deep, rich, off-dry flavors. The 1992 Erdener Treppchen Riesling Spätlese exhibits more of a stony, mineral character in the nose, as well as superbly rich, well-balanced, off-dry, medium-bodied flavors that linger on the palate. The 1992 Erdener Pralat Riesling Spätlese lacks precision and definition compared with the other two Spätlese offerings. The Erdener Pralat is a rich, sweet, fleshy, low-acid Riesling. It will have to be drunk early.

The 1992 Wehlener Sonnenuhr Riesling Auslese is a powerful, clean, rich, deep, full-bodied wine with considerable intensity and fruit. With additional precision, it would have merited an outstanding score. The 1992 Erdener Pralat Riesling Auslese exhibits excessive SO_2, making it impossible to evaluate. Superwealthy readers with a weakness for superrich Rieslings will enjoy Dr. Loosen's 1992 Wehlener Sonnenuhr Riesling Beerenauslese. It displays a medium amber color, a huge, sweet, honeyed nose, and awesomely concentrated, fruit-filled flavors. A high-octane, superrich wine, it could serve as the dessert! It should drink well for 40–50 years.

ADOLF LOTZBEYER (NAHE)* * *

1992 Feilbingerter Konigsgarten Scheurebe Eiswein	EE	92
1992 Feilbingerter Konigsgarten Scheurebe Spätlese	B	85
1992 Niederhauser Stollenberg Riesling Auslese	C	86
1991 Niederhauser Stollenberg Scheurebe Kabinett	B	86

Lotzbeyer's fine 1992 Feilbingerter Konigsgarten Scheurebe Spätlese and 1992 Niederhauser Stollenberg Riesling Auslese are both soft, plump, sugary, sweet wines with excellent ripeness. They falter in terms of focus and crispness. The Feilbingerter Konigsgarten is also slightly herbal, but is attractive in a corpulent sense because of its ripeness and chunky, fleshy fruitiness. Displaying an intriguing cinnamon/curranty component, the soft, rich Niederhauser Stollenberg lacks the acidity necessary for lift and definition.

The knockout 1992 Feilbingerter Konigsgarten Scheurebe Eiswein offers a huge, perfumed, flowery nose, great ripeness and richness, superb balance, fine acidity, and an astonishingly long, crisp finish. There is no deficiency in acidity in this superb effort. It should age easily for 15–20 years.

The 1991 Niederhauser Stollenberg Scheurebe Kabinett offers an intriguing nose of vanilla, almonds, and flowers that is followed by a soft, pretty wine with plenty of fruit, medium body, and a crisp, delicious finish. Bouquet lovers will go bonkers over this fragrant offering.

ALFRED MERKELBACH (MOSEL)* * * *

1992 Erdener Treppchen Riesling Auslese #7	C	90
1992 Erdener Treppchen Riesling Auslese #11	C	89
1992 Erdener Treppchen Riesling Spätlese #6	B	90
1992 Kinheimer Rosenberg Riesling Spätlese	B	88
1992 Urziger Wurzgarten Riesling Auslese #13	C	88
1992 Urziger Wurzgarten Riesling Auslese #16	C	90
1992 Urziger Wurzgarten Riesling Auslese #22	C	87
1992 Urziger Wurzgarten Riesling Auslese #23	C	92
1992 Urziger Wurzgarten Riesling Spätlese #10	B	89

Merkelbach, who has performed at exceptionally high qualitative levels over recent vintages, has succeeded in 1992, producing classic examples of the vintage—rich, plump, ripe, moderately sweet wines that combine heady perfumes with plenty of elegance and purity. Among the three Spätlese offerings, the 1992 Kinheimer Rosenberg Riesling Spätlese exhibits an elegant floral bouquet and moderate sweetness. The 1992 Erdener Treppchen Riesling Spätlese #6 possesses tremendous length and depth, as well as an intense fragrance (it is made from 60-year-old, ungrafted vines). The 1992 Urziger Wurzgarten Riesling

Spätlese #10 reveals copious quantities of steely, mineral scents, although it is more delicate than the other two Spätlese wines. All three Spätlese wines should drink well for 5–7 years.

There is a bevy of Auslese offerings from Merkelbach in 1992. The 1992 Erdener Treppchen Riesling Auslese #11 is a lovely, rich, medium-bodied wine with excellent ripeness and moderate sweetness. The Erdener Treppchen Riesling Auslese #7 offers a pronounced mineral, stony component to its bouquet, as well as superb richness, with slightly more length and ripeness.

Merkelbach has four cuvées of Urziger Wurzgarten Riesling Auslese. All are fine wines, with *füder* #22 possessing a strawberry-scented nose, tightly knit flavors, and a crisp, light-bodied finish. *Füder* #13 is richer, with a curranty, ripe berry fruitiness, combined with elegance, stunning purity and definition, and a long, moderately sweet finish. *Füder* #16 and *füder* #23 won my highest rankings among these four wines. They both exhibit exceptional richness, superb clarity, and fabulous bouquets. The #16 is off-dry, with a powerful penetrating bouquet, a long, crisp finish, and admirable underlying acidity to buttress its ripeness and concentration. Also off-dry, *füder* #23 reveals alluring strawberry/cherry scents, as well as great length, exuberance, and vibrancy. The two latter wines should drink well for 5–6 years.

WEINGUT MERZ (RHEINHESSEN)* * *

1992 Ockenheimer Hockenmuhle Riesling Auslese	C	86+
1991 Ockenheimer Hockenmuhle Riesling Kabinett Halbtrocken	A	85
1992 Ockenheimer Klosterweg Riesling Auslese Halbtrocken	C	90
1992 Ockenheimer Kreuz Riesling Spätlese Halbtrocken	B	87
1991 Ockenheimer Laberstall Riesling Kabinett Trocken	B	85
1992 Ockenheimer Laberstall Riesling Spätlese Trocken	B	87

The fairly priced 1992 Ockenheimer Laberstall Riesling Spätlese Trocken exhibits an intriguing peach/pineapple/cold steel–scented nose, elegant, ripe, medium-bodied, fruity flavors, purity, and a dry, crisp, long finish. Drink it over the next 4–5 years. The 1992 Ockenheimer Kreuz Riesling Spätlese Halbtrocken is another noteworthy buy. In addition to the steely scents, there is an element of smoke to go along with some cherry fruit. The wine is long, pure, rich, and dense, with crisp acidity, and a fruity, dry finish. Drink it over the next 4–5 years.

The 1992 Ockenheimer Klosterweg Riesling Auslese Halbtrocken possesses exceptional intensity, a subtle peach- and floral-scented nose, superb purity and extraction, wonderful ripeness and richness of fruit, layers of flavor, and a dry, impressively well-endowed finish. This large-scaled Riesling should drink well for 7–8 years. The 1992 Ockenheimer Hockenmuhle Riesling Auslese is a surprisingly drier-styled, tightly knit Auslese, with good fruit and a backward, unevolved, compact personality. It was closed when I tasted it.

Merz's 1991 Ockenheimer Laberstall Riesling Kabinett Trocken offers a dried cherry pit– mineral-scented nose, spicy, long, stony flavors, and a clean, lean, zesty finish. Drink it over the next several years. The dry 1991 Ockenheimer Hockenmuhle Riesling Kabinett Halbtrochen reveals a curranty, mineral-scented nose, high acidity, and wet stone, peachlike flavors. Drink it over the next year.

HERBERT MESSMER (RHEINPFALZ)* * *

1992 Burrweiler Schawer Riesling Auslese	D	86
1992 Burrweiler Schawer Riesling Halbtrocken	B	78
1992 Burrweiler Schawer Riesling Trockenbeerenauslese	EE	92

1992 Burrweiler Schlossgarten Riesling Kabinett	B	86
1992 Burrweiler Schlossgarten Weissburgunder Beerenauslese	E	92

While I found Messmer's 1992 Burrweiler Schawer Riesling Halbtrocken to be light, tart, and one-dimensional, the 1992 Burrweiler Schlossgarten Riesling Kabinett is very good, with a spicy richness, medium body, and long, dry flavors. The 1992 Burrweiler Schawer Riesling Auslese exhibits a distinctive floral, fruity, slate-scented nose vaguely reminiscent of a Mosel. It is a well-focused wine with excellent length, terrific acidity, and a sweet, long finish. This Riesling should drink well for 5–7 years.

The 1992 Burrweiler Schlossgarten Weissburgunder Beerenauslese (Pinot Blanc) offers an intriguing honeyed, tangerine- and vanillin-scented nose, fabulously rich, peachy flavors, and tremendous sweetness and unctuosity in the crisp, well-balanced finish. This sweet, dessert-style Pinot Blanc should drink well for 10–15 years. I was equally impressed with the supersweet, honeyed 1992 Burrweiler Schawer Riesling Trockenbeerenauslese. Oozing with thick, rich flavors, the wine is not cloying because of adequate acidity. For its richness and size, it displays an exuberant, zesty finish. It will last for 20 or more years.

WEINGUT MEULENHOF/ERBEN JUSTEN ENLEN (MOSEL)* * * *

1991 Erdener Pralat Riesling Spätlese #16	C	90
1992 Erdener Treppchen Riesling Auslese #18	C	87
1992 Erdener Treppchen Riesling Kabinett #19	B	88
1990 Wehlener Sonnenuhr Riesling Auslese Gold Cap	C	91
1991 Wehlener Sonnenuhr Riesling Kabinett #6	B	88
1992 Wehlener Sonnenuhr Riesling Kabinett #23	B	86

The dry 1992 Erdener Treppchen Riesling Kabinett #19 reveals a lovely, ripe, cassis, curranty, floral-scented nose, fine ripeness, and a long, crisp, ripe, medium-bodied finish. In comparison, the 1992 Wehlener Sonnenuhr Riesling Kabinett #23 is one-dimensional and more compressed, with a slatey, mineral-scented nose, excellent ripeness, and crisp acidity. The 1992 Erdener Treppchen Riesling Auslese #18 offers copious amounts of ripe, medium sweet, rich fruit in a chunky, fleshy format. A tasty, decadently styled, low-acid Riesling, it should be drunk over the next 3–4 years.

Meulenhof's 1991 Wehlener Sonnenuhr Riesling Kabinett #6 offers a huge floral and mineral-scented nose, elegant, medium-bodied flavors that reveal wonderful ripeness, and an open-knit, precocious personality that suggests this wine will make ideal drinking over the next 4–5 years. The 1991 Erdener Pralat Riesling Spätlese #16 exhibits an immensely fragrant bouquet of minerals, citrusy fruits, and apples. There is good crisp acidity, as well as succulent richness, long, off-dry, precise flavors, and zesty acidity. Drink this beautiful wine over the next 3–5 years. Lastly, the 1990 Wehlener Sonnenuhr Riesling Auslese Gold Cap possesses a huge nose of peach, apricot, and floral scents, great depth and richness, some evidence of botrytis, and a slightly sweet, impeccably well-balanced finish. It too should drink well for 4–5 years.

THEO MINGES (RHEINPFALZ)* * *

1992 Flemlinger Bischofskreuz Riesling Halbtrocken	A	74
1992 Flemlinger Vogelsprung Scheurebe Spätlese	B	90
1992 Flemlinger Zechpeter Riesling Kabinett	B	87

The tart, exceptionally lean, hard, thin 1992 Flemlinger Bischofskreuz Riesling Halbtrocken is disappointing. However, the 1992 Flemlinger Zechpeter Riesling Kabinett exhibits high extract, good purity, medium body, and a dry, impressively endowed, crisp finish. It is a bargain for $10. The most intriguing and seductive wine among this trio is the 1992 Flemlinger Vogelsprung Scheurebe Spätlese. The wine offers an exotic, kinky nose of flowers, cherries, and honeyed tropical fruit, tremendous richness, and a long, off-dry, rich finish. Despite its size, the overall impression is one of balance and vivaciousness. An exceptional bargain, it should drink well for 3–4 years.

EUGEN MÜLLER (RHEINPFALZ)* * */* * * *

1992 Forster Jesuitengarten Riesling Spätlese	B	87
1992 Forster Kirchenstuck Riesling Auslese	D	88
1991 Forster Kirchenstuck Riesling Auslese	D	79+
1992 Forster Ungeheuer Scheurebe Trockenbeerenauslese	E	87

Müller's off-dry offerings include a tightly knit, ripe, elegant 1992 Forster Jesuitengarten Riesling Spätlese, a superbly perfumed, austere, frightfully subtle, and understated 1992 Forster Kirchenstuck Riesling Auslese, and a charmless, hard, excessively acidic, tight-fisted 1991 Forster Kirchenstuck Riesling Auslese.

The thick 1992 Forster Ungeheuer Scheurebe Trockenbeerenauslese exhibits a honeyed, cherry component and comes across as cloying and one-dimensional. Although it is impressively endowed and certainly very good, it is not up to the high standards set by other producers' Trockenbeerenauslese wines. All things considered, Eugen Müller has made good but unexciting 1992s.

MÜLLER-CATOIR (RHEINPFALZ)* * * * *

1992 Gimmeldinger Mandelgarten Riesling Spätlese Halbtrocken	D	92
1992 Haardter Burgergarten Gewürztraminer Auslese Trocken	D	92
1991 Haardter Burgergarten Muskateller Kabinett Trocken	C	87
1992 Haardter Burgergarten Riesling Kabinett	C	89
1991 Haardter Burgergarten Riesling Kabinett	C	89
1992 Haardter Burgergarten Riesling Spätlese Trocken	C	87
1991 Haardter Burgergarten Riesling Spätlese Trocken	C	91
1990 Haardter Herrenletten Gewürztraminer Spätlese Trocken	C	93
1992 Haardter Herrenletten Grauburgunder Auslese	D	93
1992 Haardter Herrenletten Riesling Eiswein	EE	99
1992 Haardter Herrenletten Riesling Kabinett Trocken	C	87
1991 Haardter Mandelring Scheurebe Kabinett	C	90
1992 Haardter Mandelring Scheurebe Spätlese	C	91?
1992 Haardter Mandelring Scheurebe Spätlese Trocken	C	90
1992 Mussbacher Eselshaut Rieslaner Auslese	D	96
1991 Mussbacher Eselshaut Rieslaner Spätlese Trocken	D	93
1992 Mussbacher Eselshaut Rieslaner Trockenbeerenauslese	EEE	99
1992 Mussbacher Eselshaut Riesling Auslese	D	93

1992 Mussbacher Eselshaut Riesling Beerenauslese	E	93
1992 Mussbacher Eselshaut Riesling Kabinett Halbtrocken	C	89

Müller-Catoir is Germany's most fashionable winemaker, enjoying a position among connoisseurs much like that of such illustrious French winemakers as Jean-François Coche-Dury, Comte Lafon, Michel Niellon, and Olivier and Leonard Humbrecht. Müller-Catoir's aromatic wines are undoubtedly superripe and multi-dimensional, as well as exceptionally complex. Most important, they are delicious! Not surprisingly, Müller-Catoir excelled in the 1992 vintage, with two of the firm's sweeter cuvées approaching perfection.

Both the 1992 Haardter Herrenletten Riesling Kabinett Trocken and the 1992 Haardter Burgergarten Riesling Spätlese Trocken exhibit excellent potential. At present, both are powerful, backward wines that perform well at the end of one's palate. The Haardter Herrenletten is crisp, full, and dry, with a peach/apricot fruit character, high acidity, impressive extract, and an austere finish. While the wine is exceptionally closed, it should drink well for 7–8 years. The impressive Haardter Burgergarten is also dry, tight-fisted, backward, and unapproachable. Give it a year of cellaring and drink it over the following 7–8 years. The powerful yet elegant 1992 Haardter Mandelring Scheurebe Spätlese Trocken displays an intense perfume of honey and flowers. Full bodied and dry, with layers of deeply extracted flavors, this impeccably balanced, full-bodied Scheurebe should drink well for the next 5–6 years. Müller-Catoir has consistently produced Germany's finest dry Gewürztraminer, and the 1992 Haardter Burgergarten Gewürztraminer Auslese Trocken continues the extraordinary success this producer has enjoyed with this fickle varietal. A spectacularly exotic, lavishly scented nose of cinnamon, cherries, lychees, and roses is followed by a wine with superrich grapefruit and cherrylike flavors, and a decadent, overblown, huge, dry, blockbuster finish. This wine achieved 15.6% alcohol—naturally! Gewürztraminer does not get any bolder or fuller bodied than this monster! Drink it with intensely flavored dishes such as foie gras, or by itself.

While the 1992 Mussbacher Eselshaut Riesling Kabinett Halbtrocken is well knit, rich, long, and dry, with lovely ripeness and length, the wine is overwhelmed when tasted beside the 1992 Gimmeldinger Mandelgarten Riesling Spätlese Halbtrocken. The latter wine reveals a gorgeous perfume of exotic fruits and flowers, long, rich, off-dry, full-bodied flavors, superb purity and definition, and a dazzling finish. It should drink well for 5–6 years.

Müller-Catoir's tendency to produce more structured wines than most others in 1992 is evident with the beautifully poised, perfumed, crisp, well-delineated 1992 Haardter Burgergarten Riesling Kabinett. Dry, with excellent depth and richness, as well as a backward personality, this is a 1992 that should open with 1–2 years of cellaring, and keep for a decade. I thought the 1992 Haardter Mandelring Scheurebe Spätlese to be a stunning success. While it possesses terrific richness and layers of flavor, it will undoubtedly be controversial given its herbal, Sauvignon-like nose that may be too pungent and intense for some tasters. The unusually provocative nose works well with the wine's richness and brilliantly well-focused, full-bodied character.

At first I was shocked by the medium dark golden color of the 1992 Haardter Herrenletten Grauburgunder (Pinot Gris) Auslese. From a color perspective it appears evolved, but the nose offers rich, buttery, waxy, fresh, and lively aromas. Dry and full bodied, with a smoky, creamy richness, an exotic, honeyed, tropical fruit character, and an admirably long finish, this is another flamboyantly styled, broad-shouldered wine for drinking with intensely flavored dishes. The 1992 Mussbacher Eselshaut Riesling Auslese possesses a spectacular nose of flowers, minerals, and honeyed fruits. Firm and dry, with huge richness and an unctuous texture bolstered by fine acidity, this tightly knit, marvelously proportioned wine should drink well for 7–8 years. Even richer and more amazingly perfumed and compelling is Müller-Catoir's 1992 Mussbacher Eselshaut Rieslaner Auslese. It displays layer upon layer of fruit, well-integrated acidity, and a huge, blockbuster, exuberant, crisp finish. Relatively dry for an Auslese, it should drink well for 7–8 years.

Müller-Catoir's sweet wine offerings range from an exceptional 1992 Mussbacher Eselshaut Riesling Beerenauslese (honeyed peach and apricot fruit combined with minerals), to the nearly perfect 1992 Haardter Herrenletten Riesling Eiswein and the 1992 Mussbacher Eselshaut Rieslaner Trockenbeerenauslese. Mere words cannot do justice to the Haardter Herrenletten Eiswein. One of the finest sweet wines I have poured across my palate, this superrich, hauntingly well-balanced, fresh wine is a winemaking tour de force. It should drink well for 25–30 years. The Mussbacher Eselshaut Trockenbeerenauslese (only 50 half-bottles are available for the world) exhibits a Côte Rôtie–like, smoky, bacon fat–scented nose. Lavishly rich, with stunning precision and phenomenally high extract, this gigantically-proportioned wine never tastes heavy or cloying because of its superb natural acidity. It is an awesome, seamless wine that should keep for 25+ years!

To no one's surprise, Müller-Catoir's 1991s are stunning wines. The 1991 Haardter Burgergarten Muskateller Kabinett Trocken is a flowery, full-flavored, richly fruity wine. Although it does not possess the aromatic and flavor dimension that Catoir has obtained in some other wines, the wine has admirable personality and offers considerable pleasure. Drink it over the next 2–3 years. The 1991 Haardter Burgergarten Riesling Spätlese Trocken possesses an exotic, superintense nose, gorgeously rich, highly extracted fruit, fabulous precision, not to mention intensity, and a dry, long, explosive finish. It is a big, flamboyant wine for drinking over the next 4–5 years. I was also knocked out by the 1991 Mussbacher Eselshaut Rieslaner Spätlese Trocken. A potentially staggering wine, it exhibits a huge nose of what Alsatians call petrol (a vague gasolinelike smell), minerals, and peaches/apricots. The wine possesses enormous stature, fabulous richness (the essence of Rieslaner), and a dry, multidimensional, long, full-bodied finish. It has to be tasted to be believed! Drink it over the next 5–6 years.

Catoir fashions a Gewürztraminer that would even impress the Humbrecht family in Alsace. The 1990 Haardter Herrenletten Gewürztraminer Spätlese Trocken is undoubtedly among the best German Gewürztraminers I have tasted. An exotic nose of cherries, roses, lychee nuts, and spice is followed by an unctuous wine with stunning precision to its explosively rich, dry, full-bodied flavors. It admirably reveals what low yields, unmanipulative winemaking, super vineyards, and dedicated winemakers are all about. Drink it over the next 4–5 years.

While less dramatic, Müller-Catoir's two 1991 Kabinetts are still exquisite wines. The 1991 Haardter Burgergarten Riesling Kabinett reveals a spicy, austere bouquet, deep, excellent cherry, mint-like flavors, and a dry, crisp, full-flavored finish. Drink it over the next 5 years. The 1991 Haardter Mandelring Scheurebe Kabinett is more perfumed and seductive because of the Scheurebe grape. Slightly off-dry, but staggeringly rich, and well defined, it is a gloriously seductive mouthful of wine. Drink it over the next 2–3 years.

KLAUS NECKERAUER (RHEINPFALZ)* * * * *

1992	Weisenheimer Altenberg Riesling Auslese Halbtrocken	C	93
1991	Weisenheimer Altenberg Riesling Spätlese Halbtrocken #54	B	90
1992	Weisenheimer Goldberg Riesling Kabinett #33	B	90
1991	Weisenheimer Goldberg Riesling Kabinett	B	86
1990	Weisenheimer Hahnen Huxelrebe Trockenbeerenauslese	EEE	90
1992	Weisenheimer Hahnen Riesling Auslese #97	C	95
1992	Weisenheimer Halde Riesling Spätlese #105	C	87

1991 Weisenheimer Halde Riesling Spätlese #60	B	87
1992 Weisenheimer Halde Scheurebe Auslese #13	C	95
1992 Weisenheimer Hasenzeile Dornfelder Weissherbst Auslese Trocken	C	87
1992 Weisenheimer Hasenzeile Riesling Auslese #92	D	92
1991 Weisenheimer Hasenzeile Riesling Spätlese	B	89

Neckerauer is one of my favorite Rheinpfalz producers, so I was not surprised by the degree of enjoyment provided by the perfumed, strawberry/raspberry-scented rosé, the 1992 Weisenheimer Hasenzeile Dornfelder Weissherbst Auslese Trocken. This delicate yet authoritatively flavored wine is unusual because of its fragrant personality. Delicious, subtle, and long, my only objection is its stiff price. Drink it over the next year. The blockbuster 1992 Weisenheimer Altenberg Riesling Auslese Halbtrocken reveals an explosive nose of gorgeously ripe fruit. Dry, with a rich, full-bodied personality, this big, spicy, intensely flavored wine exhibits fine underlying acidity, and a long, zesty finish. Drink it with richly flavored foods.

The 1992 Weisenheimer Goldberg Riesling Kabinett #33 is a sensational bargain. The intriguing bouquet of mustard, cassis, and flowers jumps from the glass. The wine possesses terrific up-front fruit, medium body, wonderful purity, and a long, dry finish. It should drink well for 4–5 years. The 1992 Weisenheimer Halde Riesling Spätlese #105 is not as expressive as the Kabinett. Its medium gold color is followed by an attractive nose of ripe currants. Medium bodied with concentrated flavors, the wine appears muted and less well-formed.

Neckerauer's 1992 Weisenheimer Hahnen Riesling Auslese #97 and 1992 Weisenheimer Halde Scheurebe Auslese #13 are explosively rich, concentrated, off-dry wines that offer stunning drinking. Yet they could not be more different. The Riesling #97 is the quintessential, classic model of finesse and elegance married to incredibly intense, meticulously well-focused fruit flavors. Although large-scaled, the wine never loses its style. Drink this gorgeous, forward Riesling over the next 5–6 years. The Scheurebe #13 exhibits an overwhelmingly intense, perfumed, blockbuster nose of honeyed fruits and flowers. Rich, with oodles of flavor, adequate acidity, and a pure, rich, intense finish, it is more ostentatious than the Riesling, but just as concentrated. The 1992 Weisenheimer Hasenzeile Riesling Auslese #92 offers an Asian spice, incense-scented bouquet, gobs of unctuously rich, thick fruit, medium body, and moderate sweetness in the finish. It is big, luscious, and typical of the 1992 vintage, offering a glorious mouthful of Riesling for drinking over the next 5–6 years.

While impressive, the frightfully expensive, dark golden-colored 1990 Weisenheimer Hahnen Huxelrebe Trockenbeerenauslese is thick, viscous, supersweet, and nearly syrupy. It supposedly took three years to finish its fermentation! Undoubtedly an outstanding effort, it appears fragile and may not be a candidate for extended cellaring.

Neckerauer's 1991 Weisenheimer Altenberg Riesling Spätlese Halbtrocken is a powerful, rich, dry wine that exhibits an interesting exotic, spicy, bacon fat–scented nose, authoritative flavors, crisp acidity, and a lusty, dry finish. Drink this showboat of a wine over the next 3–4 years. The 1991 Weisenheimer Halde Riesling Spätlese #60 offers up an earthy, spicy, pungent nose, dry, austere, admirably concentrated and well-knit flavors, and a crisp, tight finish. It should be drunk over the next 4–5 years. Somewhat off-dry, the rich 1991 Weisenheimer Hasenzeile Riesling Spätlese displays a cinnamon- and spice-scented, richly fruity nose, medium-bodied, wonderfully extracted flavors, fine balance, and a cherry pit fruit component in the moderately long finish. Drink it over the next 4–5 years.

The spicy, earthy, mineral-scented nose of the 1991 Weisenheimer Goldberg Riesling Kabinett is followed by a wine with delicious fruit, faint smells of cinnamon, and a spicy, long, rich, dry, nearly explosive finish. It should be consumed over the next 2–3 years.

CLAUS ODERNHEIMER/ABTEIHOF ST.-NICOLAUS (RHEINGAU)* *

1992 Johannisberger Erntebringer Riesling	A	84
1992 Johannisberger Erntebringer Riesling Kabinett	B	74
1991 Johannisberger Vogelsang Riesling Kabinett	B	78
1992 Winkeler Jesuitengarten Riesling Spätlese	C	86

The four offerings I tasted from the Claus Odernheimer estate varied considerably in quality. The 1992 Johannisberger Erntebringer Riesling, a reasonably good value for its liter price of $9, offers attractive pineapple fruit, and an off-dry, ripe, crisp finish. The dry, monolithic 1992 Johannisberger Erntebringer Riesling Kabinett exhibits an unusual earthiness. The tightly knit, one-dimensional 1991 Johannisberger Vogelsang Riesling Kabinett lacks fruit, although it is pleasant in a straightforward style. The best of this quartet is the tightly knit, high-acid 1992 Winkeler Jesuitengarten Riesling Spätlese. It displays fine ripeness, crisp acidity, and a moderately long finish.

GEH. RAT ASCHROTT'SCHE (RHEINGAU)* *

1992 Hochheimer Holle Riesling Kabinett	B	78
1992 Hochheimer Holle Riesling Spätlese	C	82

The Kabinett is dull and one-dimensional. Although the Spätlese offering exhibits more fruit and perfume, it is a foursquare, chunky wine.

JOCHEN RATZENBERGER (MITTELRHEIN)* * * *

1989 Bacharacher Kloster Furstental Riesling Spätlese Halbtrocken	B	89
1992 Bacharacher Wolfshohle Riesling Spätlese	C	89
1991 Steeger St.-Jost Riesling	B	89+
1992 Steeger St.-Jost Riesling Spätlese	C	89+

The late-released 1989 Bacharacher Kloster Furstental Riesling Spätlese Halbtrocken is an excellent, dry, medium-bodied wine. The intriguing nose of baked apples and cinnamon makes for a distinctive introduction. The wine is long, well balanced, with good acidity, and plenty of flavor. The 1991 Steeger St.-Jost Riesling possesses impressively high extract, crisp acidity, and a dry, backward, unevolved personality. It may merit an outstanding score after another year of cellaring. An excellent bargain, it will last for a decade.

With respect to the two 1992 offerings, Ratzenberger's 1992 Bacharacher Wolfshohle Riesling Spätlese reveals an interesting bouquet of vanilla custard and honeyed melons. Long, rich, and fleshy, with gobs of fruit, this off-dry, well-made wine is loaded with personality. Drink it over the next 4–5 years. Interestingly, the 1992 Steeger St.-Jost Riesling Spätlese possesses honeyed melon scents intertwined with a walnutlike character. More delineated than the Bacharacher Wolfshohle, with excellent ripeness, medium body, and layers of fruit, this is an impressively endowed, backward Riesling from this estate in the Mittelrhein.

J. PETER REINERT (MOSEL-SAAR)* *

1992 Ayler Kupp Riesling Kabinett	B	77
1992 Wiltinger Schlossberg Riesling Auslese	C	81

I tasted two uninteresting wines from Reinert—a light, diluted 1992 Ayler Kupp Riesling Kabinett, and an apple-scented, fruity, one-dimensional 1992 Wiltinger Schlossberg Riesling Auslese.

REUSCHER-HAART (MOSEL)* * *

1992 Piesporter Goldtropfchen Riesling Auslese	D	82
1990 Piesporter Goldtropfchen Riesling Auslese	D	90
1992 Piesporter Goldtropfchen Riesling Kabinett	B	87
1991 Piesporter Goldtropfchen Riesling Kabinett	B	87
1991 Piesporter Goldtropfchen Riesling Spätlese	C	87
1990 Piesporter Goldtropfchen Riesling Spätlese AP #5	C	89
1990 Piesporter Goldtropfchen Riesling Spätlese AP #6	C	91

For such top-quality Mosels, these impressive wines appear to be underpriced in the marketplace. Reuscher-Haart's 1992 Piesporter Goldtropfchen Riesling Kabinett offers a wonderful, elegant, slate- and floral-scented nose, rich, medium-bodied flavors, fine acidity, and an off-dry, crisp finish. It tastes superior to the 1992 Piesporter Goldtropfchen Riesling Auslese, a light-bodied wine of unimpressive extraction and a one-dimensional personality.

The 1991 Piesporter Goldtropfchen Riesling Kabinett reveals a fragrant nose of tropical fruit and minerals, lovely, rich, dry flavors, loads of fruit, and a crisp, mineral-flavored, long finish. It is a wonderful wine for drinking over the next 3–4 years. The 1991 Piesporter Goldtropfchen Riesling Spätlese possesses a penetrating floral-scented nose, ripe apple, floral, and mineral flavors, an off-dry, ripe, zesty, light-bodied personality, and admirable purity. It should be drunk over the next 3–4 years.

There are two cuvées of 1990 Piesporter Goldtropfchen Riesling Spätlese. The AP #5 boasts wonderfully precise flavors, an intriguing minty, floral-scented nose, long, fat, nearly superb length, and a great inner core of fruit and acidity. Still young and backward, it should drink well for another decade. The off-dry AP #6 exhibits greater aromatic dimension, richer, more layered fruit flavors, light to medium body, and that superpurity and mineral component that makes a top German Riesling so compelling. Both are impressive wines, but I felt the AP #6 to be more complete. It should also last for at least a decade.

Although somewhat backward, Reuscher-Haart's 1990 Piesporter Goldtropfchen Riesling Auslese displays tremendous definition and extraction of flavor. Off-dry and impressively endowed, this Auslese is tightly knit and just now beginning to open. Drink it between now and 2003.

MAX FERDINAND RICHTER (MOSEL)* * *

1992 Brauneberger Juffer Riesling Spätlese	C	86
1992 Brauneberger Juffer Sonnenuhr Riesling Auslese	C	88
1992 Brauneberger Juffer Sonnenuhr Riesling Spätlese	C	87
1992 Graacher Domprobst Riesling Auslese	C	88

All four of Richter's 1992s are made in a rich, medium sweet style that faithfully expresses the ripeness and softness of the 1992 vintage. For that reason, they are wines to drink over the next 3–4 years. That being said, there is a lot of richness and character to these wines. The two Spätlese offerings taste like many other producers' Ausleses. The 1992 Brauneberger Juffer Sonnenuhr reveals more complexity in its flowery, honeyed, mineral-scented nose.

The Auslese offerings are both top-notch, sweet wines exhibiting honeyed apricot/apple fruitiness, and long, fat finishes.

WILLI SCHAEFER (MOSEL)* * * * *

1992 Graacher Domprobst Riesling Auslese #1	D	93
1992 Graacher Domprobst Riesling Beerenauslese	EE	96
1992 Graacher Domprobst Riesling Hochgewachs	B	89
1992 Graacher Domprobst Riesling Kabinett	B	89
1992 Graacher Domprobst Riesling Spätlese	B	87+
1992 Graacher Himmelreich Riesling Auslese	C	92
1992 Wehlener Sonnenuhr Riesling Kabinett	B	89

Willi Schaefer consistently fashions superlative wines at his Mosel estate. Moreover, his prices remain uncommonly fair. Except for the supersweet Beerenauslese, all of these offerings are fine bargains. For example, the 1992 Graacher Domprobst Riesling Hochgewachs is a seductive, classically styled, off-dry Riesling with an alluring perfume of flowers, minerals, and fruit. Light bodied, delicate, tasty, and refreshing, it should be drunk over the next 4–5 years. Schaefer's two Kabinetts, the 1992 Wehlener Sonnenuhr Riesling Kabinett, and the 1992 Graacher Domprobst Riesling Kabinett, should give German-wine enthusiasts fits trying to pick a favorite. Both exhibit lovely perfumed personalities, with great ripeness and purity of fruit, light body, and that understated, graceful, off-dry character that Schaefer balances beautifully with crisp acidity. Although not the most intense wines of the vintage, they are among the most elegant and refined. Both should drink well for 4–5 years.

The 1992 Graacher Domprobst Riesling Spätlese is high in acidity and unevolved. It suffers in comparison with some of the more forward, opulent Rieslings of the vintage, but I am sure it will benefit from 1–2 years of cellaring, after which it may merit an outstanding score. It is the least evolved of Schaefer's 1992s.

Both Auslese offerings are fabulous. The 1992 Graacher Himmelreich Riesling Auslese reveals an intense, mineral and floral fragrance, off-dry, rich, medium-bodied flavors with superb clarity and ripeness, and a long, slatelike finish. Drink this marvelously perfumed, classic Riesling over the next 5–6 years. Slightly richer, with even more focus, the 1992 Graacher Domprobst Riesling Auslese #1 is a tightly knit, remarkably expressive Riesling made in a delicate yet authoritatively flavored, off-dry style. It should drink well for 5–7 years.

Lastly, Schaefer's 1992 Graacher Domprobst Riesling Beerenauslese is sublime. A huge, honeyed, floral, penetrating fragrance jumps from the glass. Medium sweet, with superripeness, the wine tastes vibrant and crisp due to its well-integrated acidity that balances the wine's exceptional richness. It should drink well for 20+ years.

VON SCHLEINITZ (MOSEL)* * *

1991 Koberner Weisenberg Riesling	A	85

This super high-acid wine is loaded with fruit, exhibits a ripe, penetrating nose of apple, floral scents, dry, medium-bodied flavors, and a finish that is loaded with fruit as well as exceptionally high acids. This wine is for acid lovers, although there is plenty of underlying fruit and the wine has impressive extract.

SCHMITT-WAGNER (MOSEL)* *

1992 Longuicher Maximiner Herrenberg Riesling Auslese	C	82
1992 Longuicher Maximiner Herrenberg Riesling Kabinett	B	79

Neither of these wines from the Longuicher Maximiner Herrenberg vineyard offers much interest. The Riesling Kabinett is soft, diffuse, and unstructured. The Riesling Auslese is richer and fruitier, but flabby, one-dimensional, and foursquare.

GEORG ALBRECHT SCHNEIDER (RHEINHESSEN)* * *

1992 Niersteiner Bildstock Riesling Kabinett	A	86
1991 Niersteiner Bildstock Riesling Kabinett	A	86
1992 Niersteiner Hipping Riesling Auslese	C	89
1992 Niersteiner Hipping Riesling Kabinett	B	76
1992 Niersteiner Hipping Riesling Spätlese	B	?
1992 Niersteiner Hipping Riesling Spätlese Halbtrocken	B	89
1991 Niersteiner Oelberg Riesling Kabinett	A	86
1992 Niersteiner Oelberg Riesling Spätlese	B	85
1991 Niersteiner Oelberg Riesling Spätlese	B	86
1992 Niersteiner Pettenthal Riesling Spätlese	B	86

Save for the musty, suspicious bottle of 1992 Niersteiner Hipping Riesling Spätlese and the dull but straightforward, pleasant, and sweet 1992 Niersteiner Hipping Riesling Kabinett, Schneider's other selections are good to excellent. They include a flamboyant, sweet 1992 Niersteiner Hipping Riesling Spätlese Halbtrocken that offers loads of tropical fruit (pineapples) and a long, rich, luscious finish. Soft and forward, it should be drunk over the next several years. The 1992 Niersteiner Bildstock Riesling Kabinett is a light-bodied, elegant, pretty wine with good fruit and an off-dry finish. It requires near-term consumption.

Schneider produced three cuvées of sweet-style Spätlese. The delicious 1992 Niersteiner Pettenthal Riesling Spätlese is a sweet, ripe, forward wine that should be drunk over the next several years. The 1992 Niersteiner Oelberg Riesling Spätlese exhibits a similar sweetness, a fat personality, and loads of glycerin, giving it a plump, husky style. While not classic, its delicious, forward, commercial style will have admirers.

One of the best wines Schneider produced in the 1992 vintage is the 1992 Niersteiner Hipping Riesling Auslese. It possesses a bold personality, a big, rich, tropical fruit–scented nose, medium sweetness, and long, thick flavors that while lacking acidity, offer considerable concentration and intensity. Drink it over the next 3–4 years.

The 1991 Niersteiner Bildstock Riesling Kabinett displays an elegant, classy, mineral, apple blossom–scented nose, ripe, fruity, light-bodied flavors, great purity and penetration, and a dry, crisp finish. It should drink well for 1–2 years. The 1991 Niersteiner Oelberg Riesling Kabinett exhibits an even more flowery-scented nose, and is higher in acidity, with off-dry, rich, fruity flavors. Drink this lovely, crisp, lightweight Riesling over the next 1–2 years. Schneider's 1991 Niersteiner Oelberg Riesling Spätlese is a super bargain for a slightly sweet Riesling. There is evidence of botrytis in the apricot, smoky nose. There is tons of fruit, fine extraction, medium body, and wonderful purity and balance. Drink it over the next 2–3 years.

JAKOB SCHNEIDER (NAHE)* * * *

1992 Niederhauser Kertz Riesling Spätlese Halbtrocken	B	87
1992 Niederhauser Klamm Riesling Auslese	D	88

Schneider's Nahe estate has produced a soft, dry, medium- to full-bodied 1992 Niederhauser Kertz Riesling Spätlese Halbtrocken. This muscular-style, dry Riesling should drink well for 5–6 years. The 1992 Niederhauser Klamm Riesling Auslese exhibits a similarly broad, muscular, rich style, moderate sweetness, powerful, honeyed, ripe flavors, and excellent purity and focus.

SCHLOSS SCHONBORN (RHEINGAU)* * *

1992 Erbacher Marcobrunn Riesling Auslese	D	89
1992 Hattenheimer Pfaffenberg Riesling Spätlese	C	85
1992 Riesling Kabinett	B	73

The sharp, lean, angular 1992 Riesling Kabinett is disappointing. The tasty 1992 Hatten-heimer Pfaffenberg Riesling Spätlese is strikingly sweet and fleshy, without any delineation to its components. The star of this trio is the 1992 Erbacher Marcobrunn Riesling Auslese. Exceptionally sweet and honeyed, with superb ripeness, admirable acidity, and a long, rich finish, this boldly styled Riesling should drink well for 4–5 years.

VON SCHUBERT-MAXIMIN GRUNHAUS (RUWER)* * * * *

1992 Abtsberg Riesling QbA	C	89
1992 Abtsberg Riesling Auslese	D	92+
1992 Abtsberg Riesling Auslese #64	E	93+
1992 Abtsberg Riesling Kabinett	C	91
1991 Abtsberg Riesling Kabinett	C	90+
1992 Abtsberg Riesling Spätlese	D	91
1991 Abtsberg Riesling Spätlese	D	88
1992 Abtsberg Riesling Trocken	C	87
1992 Herrenberg Riesling Auslese	D	90+
1991 Herrenberg Riesling QbA	C	90
1992 Herrenberg Riesling Trocken	D	88
1991 Riesling Valckenberg Edition	C	89

This superb estate can always be counted on to make extremely backward, potentially long-lived, complex wines that are usually among the most classic expressions of German Riesling. For starters, the delicious, crisp 1992 Abtsberg Riesling Trocken reveals a subtle, intense nose of apples and minerals. Long and concentrated, it is also a reasonable value for a wine from this estate. The 1992 Herrenberg Riesling Trocken exhibits some unreleased CO_2. It is a full, boldly styled, rich wine with considerable ripeness, and a deep, spicy, dry finish. It should age well for 10 years. The 1992 Abtsberg Riesling QbA offers a superb nose of minerals (liquid slate?), flowers, and green apples. Delineated, yet oh, so concen-trated and pure, this rich, superbly made wine is already drinking well; it will keep for a decade.

The outstanding 1992 Abtsberg Riesling Kabinett is a typically backward, dense, concen-trated von Schubert wine, with great precision, explosively rich, cherry/mineral flavors, and an amazingly long, dry finish. For a 1992, it is a potentially long-lived wine (10 or more years). Equally impressive because of its tremendous concentration of flavor and outstanding focus and clarity is the 1992 Abtsberg Riesling Spätlese. It exhibits sensational ripeness, with everything buttressed by crisp acidity. It should prove to be an uncommonly long-lived 1992, lasting for 10 or more years.

Von Schubert produced three sensational cuvées of Auslese. Although they are all back-ward, they vary in degrees of ripeness and concentration. The 1992 Herrenberg Riesling Auslese offers a penetrating, fragrant bouquet, and long, rich, deep flavors that are just beginning to reveal some evolution. Even more backward, the dry 1992 Abtsberg Riesling

Auslese is superconcentrated, with superb precision to its flavors. It needs 3–4 years of cellaring and should last for 20–25 years. The most concentrated of this trio is the 1992 Abtsberg Riesling Auslese #64. Exhibiting awesome density and ripeness that is crammed into a light- to medium-bodied format, this terrific wine should last for 2 decades. The only issue open to question is the estate's pricing policy.

This renowned producer did better in 1991 with its drier wines than the Spätlese and Auslese offerings. I enjoyed the 1991 Abtsberg Riesling Spätlese, but felt the 1991 Abtsberg Riesling Auslese was not of high enough quality to be recommended. The Spätlese is the least impressive wine of this quartet. While it possesses excellent fruit, and a stylish, wet stone, crisp, fruity, nicely extracted personality, it is light and undernourished compared with von Schubert's other wines. High among von Schubert's normally expensive offerings (fame has its price) is the 1991 Riesling Valckenberg Edition. Lovers of the high-acid style will enjoy this beautiful Riesling. However, there is more than naturally high acidity to this wine. It displays a classy, mineral, green apple, floral-scented nose, concentrated, ripe, dry, medium-bodied flavors, and a long, uplifting finish. It should drink well for at least 5–8 years. The 1991 Herrenberg Riesling QbA is more flattering and open, with a rich, floral, honeyed apple, stony-scented nose, deep, dry, compressed yet concentrated flavors, fine acidity, and a lovely finish. It should also age well for 5–8 years. The most backward of the von Schubert offerings is the 1991 Abtsberg Riesling Kabinett. Despite its tightness and unevolved style, there is no doubting its profound character and richness. There are unbelievable layers of mineral-scented and -flavored applelike fruit, yet it tastes light, crisp, zesty, and beguiling. The finish is remarkably long in this dry, brilliantly etched wine.

WOLFGANG SCHWAAB (MOSEL)* * *

1991	Erdener Herrenberg Riesling	B	85
1990	Erdener Pralat Riesling Auslese	C	90
1992	Erdener Treppchen Riesling Auslese #31	C	88
1990	Erdener Treppchen Riesling Auslese #3	C	89

Looking for a liter bottle of attractively priced Riesling? Schwaab's 1991 Erdener Herrenberg Riesling is a flowery, crisp, light-bodied, off-dry Riesling offering fine purity and excellent varietal character. Drink it over the next 1–2 years. The 1992 Erdener Treppchen Riesling Auslese #31 exhibits an intoxicating peach/citrusy nose, ripe, superrich, off-dry flavors, admirable definition, and a long, lusty finish. Drink this large-scaled Riesling over the next 5–6 years.

Wolfgang Schwaab's 1990 Erdener Treppchen Riesling Auslese #3 offers a floral, slate-scented nose, tasty, rich, crisp flavors, beautiful balance, and a long, off-dry, convincing finish. Drink it over the next 5–6 years. The 1990 Erdener Pralat Riesling Auslese possesses an intense, beautifully well-defined nose of wet stones, citrusy fruit, apples, and flowers. Wonderfully rich yet well focused, this off-dry, multidimensional, layered style of Riesling displays gorgeous fruit and personality. It makes for a crisp, uplifting, delicious glass of Riesling. Drink it over the next 7–8 years.

HENRICH SEEBRICH (RHEINHESSEN)* *

1992	Niersteiner Bruckchen Sylvaner Kabinett	A	70
1992	Niersteiner Hipping Riesling Auslese	C	80
1992	Niersteiner Hipping Riesling Spätlese	C	72
1991	Niersteiner Oelberg Riesling Spätlese	A	87

1992 Niersteiner Oelberg Scheurebe Kabinett	A	72
1992 Niersteiner Rosenberg Riesling Kabinett	B	78

All the 1992 offerings are mediocre wines. The Kabinetts are cloyingly sweet, flabby, lacking precision, disjointed, and uninteresting. The 1992 Niersteiner Hipping Riesling Spätlese suffers from excessive softness, a lack of precision, and a short finish. It does exhibit plump, fruity aromas and flavors. Lastly, Seebrich's 1992 Niersteiner Hipping Riesling Auslese is sweet, one-dimensional, ripe, and mouth filling. It should be drunk over the next several years.

On the other hand, the intensely perfumed, medium sweet 1991 Niersteiner Oelberg Riesling Spätlese reveals wonderful cherry, apple, and peachlike fruit, good acidity, and a long, lush, soft finish. Drink it over the next 1–2 years.

SELBACH-OSTER (MOSEL)* * * * *

1992 Bernkasteler Badstube Riesling Spätlese	C	90
1991 Bernkasteler Badstube Riesling Spätlese	C	90
1992 Bernkasteler Schlossberg Riesling Spätlese Halbtrocken	C	89
1992 Graacher Domprobst Riesling Auslese	C	92
1991 Graacher Domprobst Riesling Auslese	D	89+
1992 Wehlener Klosterberg Riesling Spätlese	C	87
1992 Zeltinger Himmelreich Riesling Auslese	C	90
1992 Zeltinger Himmelreich Riesling Spätlese AP #1	C	87
1992 Zeltinger Schlossberg Riesling Eiswein	EEE	96
1992 Zeltinger Schlossberg Riesling Kabinett	B	89
1991 Zeltinger Schlossberg Riesling Kabinett	B	87
1992 Zeltinger Schlossberg Riesling Spätlese	C	87
1992 Zeltinger Sonnenuhr Riesling Auslese 2 Stars	D	89
1991 Zeltinger Sonnenuhr Riesling Kabinett	B	86
1992 Zeltinger Sonnenuhr Riesling Spätlese	C	91
1991 Zeltinger Sonnenuhr Riesling Spätlese #49	C	89
1991 Zeltinger Sonnenuhr Riesling Spätlese Gold Cap	C	92
1992 Zeltinger Sonnenuhr Riesling Spätlese Halbtrocken	C	89

This excellent producer continues to excel, regardless of vintage conditions. Although Selbach-Oster's two Halbtrockens, the 1992 Bernkasteler Schlossberg Riesling Spätlese Halbtrocken and 1992 Zeltinger Sonnenuhr Riesling Spätlese, received equal numerical ratings, they are different. The dry Bernkasteler Schlossberg is more perfumed, with lovely rich fruit, and an overwhelming floral character. The Zeltinger Sonnenuhr is more dominated by citrusy, mineral, steely components in its bouquet. More muscular, with wonderful density and excellent ripeness, its finish is dry and long. Both of these Halbtrockens should drink well for 4–5 years. The 1992 Zeltinger Schlossberg Riesling Kabinett is a firm, tightly knit, light-bodied, dry wine with considerable extract, and a crisp, backward finish. It is a good value, but it needs another 6–12 months to open.

Selbach-Oster produced five Spätlese offerings in 1992. All are at least very good, with several outstanding. The 1992 Zeltinger Himmelreich Riesling Spätlese AP #1 is fat, soft, up front, and ideal for drinking over the next 3–4 years. It is the most precocious. Similarly styled is the 1992 Wehlener Klosterberg Riesling Spätlese. It boasts a gloriously ripe, flashy bouquet, big, rich, medium-bodied flavors that reveal significant amounts of up-front fruitiness, low acidity, and an off-dry, rich finish. The classy, character-filled 1992 Zeltinger Schlossberg Riesling Spätlese is the lightest bodied, and tastes less extracted. It reveals admirable mineral ripeness, as well as a slightly diffuse component. Although ripe, off-dry, and impressive, it is not as complete or complex as the 1992 Bernkasteler Badstube Riesling Spätlese or the 1992 Zeltinger Sonnenuhr Riesling Spätlese. The two latter wines are both top-class offerings. The Bernkasteler Badstube exhibits a pronounced, intensely perfumed nose of ripe cherry fruit, minerals, and flowers. Rich and medium to full bodied, with loads of flavor, this well-balanced, crisp, off-dry wine should drink well for 5–6 years. The Zeltinger Sonnenuhr has a dominating mineral/slate bouquet, and a gorgeously ripe, medium-bodied, layered palate with considerable length. It should drink well for 5–6 years.

The 1992 Zeltinger Himmelreich Riesling Auslese is a beautifully poised, soft, fleshy wine with an exuberant personality, an off-dry character, and gobs of fruit and freshness in its long finish. Slightly richer, with an even more perfumed personality, is the 1992 Graacher Domprobst Riesling Auslese. This is a compellingly rich, long, intensely flavored wine that never loses its sense of grace and style. The 1992 Zeltinger Sonnenuhr Riesling Auslese 2 Stars is supposed to taste better. Obviously, Selbach feels it is his best offering, given the star rating and price. A lovely wine, it tastes softer and less delineated than Selbach's other cuvées of Auslese. However, it did not show as well as either the Zeltinger Himmelreich or the Graacher Domprobst.

Lastly, the 1992 Zeltinger Schlossberg Riesling Eiswein is a stupendous effort, with an unctuously rich palate, a spectacular perfume of honeyed tropical fruits and flowers, and great precision and focus. Superb underlying acidity is the key to this terrific Eiswein. It should drink well for 25 years.

These six 1991s are classic examples of Riesling. Consumers will like the steely, slatey, apple, and citrus fruit of Selbach-Oster's 1991 Zeltinger Schlossberg Riesling Kabinett. Dry and crisp, it provides a lovely glass of vividly pure, well-focused Riesling for drinking over the next 4–5 years. The 1991 Zeltinger Sonnenuhr Riesling Kabinett is also stylish, although more closed than the Schlossberg. There are interesting oily, petrollike aromas, and lean, tightly knit, concentrated flavors. It was superclosed when I tasted it, but should drink well for 4–5 years.

The top-notch 1991 Bernkasteler Badstube Riesling Spätlese offers up a fragrant bouquet of lime, minerals, apples, and fruit. This rich, slightly off-dry wine is typical of so many of the Selbach-Oster wines in its commendable purity, sensational definition, and preciseness. Drink it over the next 5–6 years. The 1991 Zeltinger Sonnenuhr Riesling Spätlese #49 exhibits an intense, steely, wet stone, floral-scented nose, zesty, high acidity, and ripe, rich, beautifully extracted flavors all presented in a light-bodied format. It should drink well for the next 6–7 years. The fabulous 1991 Zeltinger Sonnenuhr Riesling Spätlese Gold Cap is also a great bargain. The penetrating nose of slate, apples, citrus, and flowers is followed by a highly extracted, marvelously constructed, seamless style of wine that flows across the palate dispensing multiple nuances and subtleties. It tastes light yet rich. An exceptional Riesling, this Zeltinger Sonnenuhr Gold Cap should drink well over the next 7–8 years.

The 1991 Graacher Domprobst Riesling Auslese may merit an outstanding score after another year or so in the bottle. The wine is tight, but it appears to have terrific potential with its floral- and mineral-scented nose and deep, rich, medium-bodied flavors that reveal wonderful ripeness, elegance, and focus. The authoritative finish is off-dry.

VON SIMMERN (RHEINGAU)* * * */* * * * *

1992 Eltviller Sonnenberg Riesling Kabinett	C	86
1992 Erbacher Marcobrunn Riesling Auslese	D	92
1992 Rauenthaler Baiken Riesling Spätlese	C	90

Von Simmern's renowned Rheingau estate fashioned an earthy, pithy, crisp, dry, concentrated 1992 Eltviller Sonnenberg Riesling Kabinett. Although austere, the wine possesses considerable character and personality. Drink it over the next 4–5 years. The 1992 Rauenthaler Baiken Riesling Spätlese possesses an off-dry personality, and a moderately intense bouquet of spices, minerals, baked apples, and tropical fruit. Deep, rich, and layered, this wine exhibits excellent purity and fine balance. While drinkable now, it should last for another 5–7 years. The sweet 1992 Erbacher Marcobrunn Riesling Auslese displays a honeysuckle-scented bouquet, gobs of rich, ripe fruit, decent acidity, and a superb, long, pure finish. Made in a sweet, concentrated style, this impressive wine should drink well for 5–7 years.

SCHLOSS SOMMERHAUSEN (FRANKEN)* * *

1990 Eibelstadter Kapellenberg Gewürztraminer Spätlese Trocken	C	88
1990 Sommeracher Steinbach Riesling Spätlese Trocken	C	87
1991 Sommerhauser Reifenstein Riesling Kabinett Trocken	B	87
1991 Randersacker Marsberg Sylvaner Kabinett Trocken	B	87

These offerings from Franken are dry, full-flavored wines with a pronounced earthy, cinnamon, gingery scent that may take some readers by surprise. The 1991 Sommerhauser Reifenstein Riesling Kabinett Trocken exhibits a gingery component, dry, deep, rich, medium- to full-bodied flavors, and a spicy, austere, stony finish. Drink it over the next decade. The 1990 Sommeracher Steinbach Riesling Spätlese Trocken displays more cinnamon and ginger, and is more elegant and less forceful. It offers a delicious glassful of austere yet complex Riesling. It too should last for up to a decade. The 1991 Randersacker Marsberg Sylvaner Kabinett Trocken reveals surprising personality for a Sylvaner. It offers plenty of spice, good richness, and a tasty, medium-bodied, elegant, crisp, dry finish. Drink it over the next 5–6 years. I was also impressed by this producer's rose, cherry, intensely spicy-scented 1990 Eibelstadter Kapellenberg Gewürztraminer Spätlese Trocken. Medium bodied, with a bold personality, dense, ripe flavors, and a big, dry, flamboyant finish, it should drink well for another 4–5 years.

STAATSWEINGÜTER ELTVILLE (RHEINGAU)* *

1992 Rauenthaler Baiken Riesling Kabinett	C	76
1992 Steinberger Riesling Kabinett	C	78

This state-run winery has produced two disappointing efforts. The 1992 Steinberger Riesling Kabinett is austere, lean, and lacking fruit. The 1992 Rauenthaler Baiken Riesling Kabinett is thin, diluted, and short.

J.U.H.A. STRUB (RHEINHESSEN)* * * *

1992 Niersteiner Bruckchen Riesling Spätlese #7	B	88
1991 Niersteiner Hipping Riesling Kabinett	B	86
1992 Niersteiner Hipping Riesling Auslese #19B	C	88
1992 Niersteiner Paterberg Riesling Eiswein	E	89
1991 Niersteiner Paterberg Riesling Kabinett	B	86

1992 Niersteiner Paterberg Riesling Spätlese	B	81
1991 Niersteiner Rehbach Riesling Kabinett Trocken	B	87
1992 Niersteiner Riesling Kabinett Halbtrocken #14	B	87

Strub's 1992 Niersteiner Riesling Kabinett Halbtrocken #14 is a notable bargain. The wine possesses admirable depth and purity of fruit, floral and cherry scents in the nose, and a honeyed, peachlike fruitiness in its full-bodied, crisp, dry finish. Drink it over the next several years. The 1992 Niersteiner Paterberg Riesling Spätlese is muted and chunky compared with the less expensive Halbtrocken. Although pleasant, it is one-dimensional. I was more impressed with the 1992 Niersteiner Bruckchen Riesling Spätlese #7. It offers a distinctive personality and dry, medium-bodied, bold flavors. A big, earthy/peach-scented nose is followed by a wine with excellent depth and ripeness in addition to a graceful personality. This dry Riesling offers considerable flexibility with food.

Strub's 1992 Niersteiner Hipping Riesling Auslese #19B is a full-styled, slightly sweet, powerful, alcoholic Auslese with a muscular personality. It is a large-scaled, beefy Riesling for drinking over the next 5–6 years. Lastly, the 1992 Niersteiner Paterberg Riesling Eiswein displays good ripeness, high acidity, and luscious fatness, but it lacks the extra dimension I tasted in many other 1992 Eisweins. It is reasonably priced.

The 1991 Niersteiner Rehbach Riesling Kabinett Trocken displays a perfumed, floral nose, elegant, ripe, tasty fruit flavors, admirable intensity, a lovely purity of flavor, and a dry, smoked peachy flavor in the long finish. It should drink well for 2–3 years. Strub's delicate 1991 Niersteiner Paterberg Riesling Kabinett exhibits good structure and extraction of flavor, as well as crisp acidity. Stylish, aromatic, and wonderfully fresh and lively, it should be consumed over the next several years. The 1991 Niersteiner Hipping Riesling Kabinett is richer and higher in acidity, with that uncompromising purity and flavor that are the hallmarks of a top-notch German Riesling. There is beautiful precision to its flavors, and an understated yet authoritative personality to this light-bodied, refreshing wine. Drink it over the next 2–3 years.

STUDERT-PRÜM/MAXIMINHOF (MOSEL)* *

1992 Graacher Himmelreich Riesling Kabinett	B	86
1992 Wehlener Sonnenuhr Riesling Kabinett	B	87
1992 Wehlener Sonnenuhr Riesling Spätlese	C	86

The excellent floral-scented, dry, crisp 1992 Graacher Himmelreich Riesling Kabinett will provide a light-bodied, tasty glass of Riesling for consuming over the next 3–4 years. Richer and more aromatic is the floral- and mineral-scented 1992 Wehlener Sonnenuhr Riesling Kabinett. Dry, with admirable depth and ripeness, this is a lovely, classically styled Riesling for drinking over the next 4–5 years. Interestingly, the 1992 Wehlener Sonnenuhr Riesling Spätlese, although solidly made, is muted and lacking the finesse and complexity of the Kabinett offering.

UNCKRICH (RHEINPFALZ)* * *

1992 Kallstader Annaberg Scheurebe Auslese	B	85
1991 Kallstader Saumagen Riesling Auslese	B	88
1992 Kallstader Saumagen Riesling Kabinett	A	87
1992 Kallstader Saumagen Riesling Spätlese	B	87

The 1992 Kallstader Saumagen Riesling Kabinett is a noteworthy value. Made in a sweet, soft, expansive style with excellent ripeness, low acidity, and a fine finish, it is an excellent, fruity Kabinett for drinking over the near term. Unckrich's tendency to turn out fleshy, low-acid, chewy wines is also evidenced by the 1992 Kallstader Saumagen Riesling Spät-lese. Although slightly heavier, it is still rich, with medium sweetness, low acidity, and an attractive honeyed, cherry fruitiness. It should be drunk over the next several years. The 1992 Kallstader Annaberg Scheurebe Auslese exhibits considerable sweetness and ripe-ness, but it is heavy and monolithic. It is a pleasant wine for drinking over the near term.

The 1991 Kallstader Saumagen Riesling Auslese is a sensational bargain, offering a wine with medium sweetness, an intense perfume of honeyed apples and apricots, decent acidity, and a wonderfully long, light- to medium-bodied finish that lingers for half a minute. It is hard to believe a Riesling Auslese of this quality can be found for $10. Drink it over the next 1–3 years.

DR. HEINZ WAGNER (SAAR)* * * *

1992 Ockfener Bockstein Riesling Kabinett	B	87
1992 Ockfener Bockstein Riesling QbA	B	87
1991 Ockfener Bockstein Riesling QbA	A	87
1992 Ockfener Bockstein Riesling Spätlese	C	86
1992 Saarburger Rausch Riesling Kabinett	B	90
1992 Saarburger Rausch Riesling QbA	B	88
1991 Saarburger Rausch Riesling QbA	A	87
1992 Saarburger Rausch Riesling Spätlese	C	86

If you are looking for a source of great values as well as textbook mineral/floral-scented Riesling, check out Heinz Wagner. His two QbA Rieslings from the Ockfener Bockstein and Saarburger Rausch vineyards are splendid bargains in dry, intense, impeccably well-made Riesling. The 1992 Ockfener Bockstein Riesling QbA exhibits fine ripeness, superb clarity, gobs of mineral scents, and a lovely, long, crisp finish. Drink it over the next several years. The 1992 Saarburger Rausch Riesling QbA is more complex, with a liquid stone/mineral/floral-scented nose, rich, medium-bodied, deep flavors, a wonderful intense inner core of fruit, and a dry, crisp finish. It should drink well for 3–4 years.

I was equally impressed with Wagner's 1992 Ockfener Bockstein Riesling Kabinett and 1992 Saarburger Rausch Riesling Kabinett. The Ockfener Bockstein Kabinett is sweeter than the QbA, offering a combination of applelike fruit and mineral notes in a medium-bodied, off-dry format. The superb acidity of the Saarburger Rausch Kabinett gives it enviable definition. This is the most concentrated and complete of the Wagner wines, with an intense bouquet and layers of rich, ripe fruit. The wine's acidity makes it taste surpris-ingly fresh, exuberant, and zesty. Drink it over the next 3–4 years.

Wagner's two Spätlese offerings are very good. The 1992 Saarburger Rausch Riesling Spätlese exhibits a liquid slate/citrusy, applelike bouquet, an off-dry palate with average focus, and a soft, round finish. Its lack of acidity is apparent. While the crisp, steely/minerallike character in the 1992 Ockfener Bockstein Riesling Spätlese is impressive, this is the most backward and unevolved wine from Wagner. There is plenty of length (most of the wine's personality shows up at the back of the palate), so I suggest cellaring it for at least a year. It should keep for 4–5 years.

The excellent 1991 Saarburger Rausch Riesling QbA offers a moderately intense stony, mineral, apple-scented nose, and lovely rich, dry, medium-bodied flavors, as well as good extraction, and a crisp, fresh finish. It should drink well for another 1–2 years. The 1991 Ockfener Bockstein Riesling QbA is slightly fatter, bigger, and richer, without as much delineation as the Saarburger Rausch. This dry, crisp, well-delineated wine should drink well over the next several years.

ADOLF WEINGART (MITTELRHEIN)* * *

1992 Bopparder Hamm Feuerlay Riesling Auslese AP #10	C	90
1992 Bopparder Hamm Feuerlay Riesling Auslese AP #12	C	89
1992 Bopparder Hamm Feuerlay Riesling Hochgewachs	B	87
1992 Bopparder Hamm Ohlenberg Riesling Auslese Trocken	C	83
1992 Bopparder Hamm Ohlenberg Riesling Kabinett Halbtrocken	B	90
1992 Bopparder Hamm Ohlenberg Riesling Spätlese	B	86

Weingart's 1992 Bopparder Hamm Ohlenberg Riesling Auslese Trocken is compact, closed, yet dry, elegant, and pleasant. On the other hand, the 1992 Bopparder Hamm Ohlenberg Riesling Kabinett Halbtrocken is superb. It offers an exuberant, vibrant nose of wet stones, flowers, and fruit, lovely, light- to medium-bodied, dry flavors, and surprisingly intense extract and richness in the crisp, lingering finish. This is an outstanding dry Riesling for drinking over the next 4–5 years. Another intensely fruity, exuberant, fleshy, dry wine is the 1992 Bopparder Hamm Feuerlay Riesling Hochgewachs. For $10 this is a good bargain. It is a fresh, lively, pure style of Riesling that should be drunk over the next 3–4 years.

The only Spätlese I tasted was a fruity, soft, attractive, medium-bodied 1992 Bopparder Hamm Ohlenberg Riesling Spätlese. A good wine, it is not of the high quality of several other offerings. Weingart turned in fine performances with two cuvées of Bopparder Hamm Feuerlay Riesling Auslese. *Füder* #12 is an off-dry, medium-bodied wine with excellent extract, and a fresh, graceful nose of flowers and ripe fruit. This layered, concentrated, impressively endowed 1992 will drink well for 5–6 years. In complete contrast, *füder* #10 reveals an exotic bouquet of cherry, cinnamon, mineral, and lychee nut scents reminiscent of a varietal other than Riesling. The spiciness continues in the medium-bodied flavors that exhibit excellent fatness, depth, and richness. This will be a controversial, but to my mind, an immensely tasty, decadently styled Riesling for drinking over the next 3–4 years.

WERLÉ (RHEINPFALZ)* * * * *

1990 Deidesheimer Leinhohle Riesling Kabinett	B	91
1989 Deidesheimer Leinhohle Riesling Kabinett	C	90
1991 Forster Jesuitengarten Riesling Spätlese	C	88
1992 Forster Kirchenstuck Riesling Spätlese	D	90
1990 Forster Kirchenstuck Riesling Spätlese	D	93
1991 Forster Kirchenstuck Riesling Spätlese	D	90
1990 Forster Pechstein Riesling Kabinett Trocken	B	90
1990 Forster Ungeheuer Riesling Spätlese	C	89+
1992 Ruppertsberger Nussbien Riesling Spätlese	C	93
1991 Ruppertsberger Nussbien Riesling Spätlese	D	90+

One of my favorite German wine producers, Werlé's Rieslings are filled with personality. He consistently obtains superb flavor extraction in his tightly packed, dry wines that also age well. The 1990 Deidesheimer Leinhohle Riesling Kabinett exhibits a knockout nose of sweet corn, vanillin, and ripe, honeyed fruit. This rich, full-bodied, dry wine coats the palate with layers of fruit superbly balanced by underlying acidity. The finish is powerful and long. This wine should drink well for at least a decade. The two 1991 Spätlese offerings include a super dry, austere, rich, pithy, backward, tart 1991 Forster Jesuitengarten Spätlese and the intense, pungent, herb- and superripe fruit–scented 1991 Forster Kirchenstuck Spätlese. The former wine needs 3–4 years of aging because of its difficult-to-penetrate style, but there is great length and extraction. On the other hand, the Forster Kirchenstuck is more fragrant, flattering, and exhibits considerable power, ripeness, and richness. It is reminiscent of the style of wine produced by Müller-Catoir.

The two 1992s I tasted from Werlé included an opulent, highly extracted, full-bodied, off-dry Forster Kirchenstuck Riesling Spätlese. Its honeyed, floral nose is super. Even more impressive is the wine's precision, richness, balance, and elegance. Like most 1992s it is already drinking well; unlike most 1992s it has the potential to last for up to 10 years. Werlé's best wine among his current releases is the spectacular, outrageously rich, full-bodied, dry 1992 Ruppertsberger Nussbien Riesling Spätlese. It possesses an exotic, flamboyant bouquet, spicy, rich, highly extracted flavors, admirable precision and balance, and an immensely impressive finish. Approachable now, it should drink well for a decade.

The exceptionally dry 1990 Forster Pechstein Riesling Kabinett Trocken offers up a superb peach- and mineral-scented nose, excellent ripe fruit, medium body, and long, authoritative, crisp flavors. It should drink well for another decade. The 1989 Deidesheimer Leinhohle Riesling Kabinett exhibits a superripe cherry, spicy nose, great fruit and length, and an amazing combination of power and delicacy. Another dry, full-flavored, intense Riesling, it too should age for up to a decade.

The 1990 Forster Ungeheuer Riesling Spätlese displays a floral, spicy nose, lovely, broad, dry, rich flavors, and a tight yet concentrated, zesty finish. This Spätlese needs another 1–2 years in the bottle to reveal its best; it should last 10–15 years. Undoubtedly picked at Auslese-level ripeness, the 1990 Forster Kirchenstuck Riesling Spätlese boasts a huge perfume of spices, flowers, minerals, and wet stones. This fabulously concentrated, off-dry, full-bodied wine possesses awesome flavor extraction, brilliant focus, moderate acidity for buttressing the rich fruit, and a finish that lasts for over 30 seconds. Only available in 500-milliliter bottles, it should be drunk over the next 10–12 years. Werlé's tightly knit 1991 Ruppertsberger Nussbien Riesling Spätlese offers a pungent, mineral, stony nose, and layers of dry, crisp fruit flavors that exhibit high acidity as well as admirable ripeness. This big, backward wine needs 1–2 years in the cellar; it should last for at least a decade. Werlé's wines remain reasonably priced, largely because he is so underrated.

WINZER VIER JAHRESZEITEN (PFALZ)* * *

1992 Durkheimer Feuerberg Gewürztraminer Spätlese	A	88
1992 Durkheimer Feuerberg Rulander Spätlese	A	88
1992 Durkheimer Feuerberg Scheurebe Kabinett	A	87

Three excellent bargains in German wine, the 1992 Scheurebe Kabinett exhibits an exotic, intense, fragrant perfume of cherries and flowers, gobs of tropical fruit, wonderful purity, and a dry, crisp finish. Drink it over the next 1–2 years. The 1992 Rulander Spätlese possesses a creamy, buttery, honeyed nose, rich, full-bodied, chewy flavors, and copious quantities of alcohol in its heady, lush finish. It is a big, voluptuous, off-dry Rulander (Pinot Gris) for drinking over the next several years. Not surprisingly, this producer's off-dry 1992 Gewürztraminer Spätlese exhibits a honeyed grapefruit, intensely spicy nose with a rose-scented component, rich, medium- to full-bodied, expressive flavors, and excellent ripeness.

GUNTER WITTMANN (RHEINHESSEN)* * *

1992 Westhofener Auelerde Bacchus Kabinett	B	90
1992 Westhofener Morstein Riesling Auslese	D	92
1992 Westhofener Steingrube Albalonga Auslese	D	89

1992 Westhofener Steingrube Albalonga Trockenbeerenauslese	EE	95
1992 Westhofener Steingrube Riesling Spätlese	C	86

I continue to be impressed with the idiosyncratic, but undeniably seductive and perfumed wines produced at Gunter Wittmann's Rheinhessen estate. I adored the 1992 Westhofener Auelerde Bacchus Kabinett. This $10 wine, made from a grape created by the cloning of Sylvaner and Pinot Blanc, is a dramatic, flamboyant Kabinett with loads of honeyed cherry, orange, and apple scents, gorgeous ripeness, and a long, fruity, off-dry finish. This in-your-face wine should be drunk over the next several years. Wittmann's 1992 Westhofener Steingrube Riesling Spätlese is an off-dry, medium-bodied, tightly knit wine with crisp acidity, lovely fruit, and a long finish.

The slightly sweet 1992 Westhofener Steingrube Albalonga Auslese falls just short of an outstanding rating because of its overwhelmingly, unctuously textured, thick, fruity flavors that lack the acidity needed to give the wine more uplift and precision. This tremendously exotic, deep, rich, off-dry wine is sure to be controversial. There is no doubting the classic aromatic and flavor profile of the sweet 1992 Westhofener Morstein Riesling Auslese, which reveals a huge perfume of honeyed cherries and flowers. Medium to full bodied, with superb extraction of flavor, and a long, zesty finish, this beautiful Auslese should be drunk over the next 3–4 years.

Lastly, Wittmann's 1992 Westhofener Steingrube Albalonga Trockenbeerenauslese possesses a medium gold color, a nectarlike, intense bouquet of honeyed tropical fruits that soars from the glass, and a thick, unctuous texture with outstanding underlying acidity. This large-scaled, decadently rich wine should drink well for 10–20 years. As a postscript, all of Gunter Wittmann's vineyards are farmed organically.

4. PORTUGAL

PORT

Americans have finally begun to realize the great pleasures of a mature vintage port after a meal. For years, this sumptuous and mellow fortified red wine was seriously undervalued, as most of it was drunk in the private homes and clubs of the United Kingdom. Prices, which soared in the early and mid-eighties, collapsed in the early nineties. Although there is not much vintage port produced (there are rarely more than four declared vintages a decade), the international recession and bloated marketplace have resulted in stable prices.

WHAT TO BUY

1. There is no question that the last few years have seen a significant decline in prices for 1985 (a super year) and 1983 (another fine year). However, prices have begun to firm up for these two vintages, although good deals can still be found. There has been little appreciation of price for these two top vintages. Certainly the decision by a number of port houses to declare a vintage in 1991 and 1992 suggests that the saturated marketplace is no longer as serious an impediment to port sales. Readers should check out wine auctions where numerous top ports can be obtained at modest prices.
2. I have always felt that an investment of at least 10 years of patience is necessary when purchasing the newest vintage port, but I have friends who enjoy drinking these wines in their exuberant, grapy youth. Nevertheless, it appears to be a waste of money to invest $30 or more in a young vintage port and not give it the chance to age and reveal all of its subtlety and complexity.
3. Readers can expect considerable controversy to emerge regarding the two most recently declared vintage port years, 1991 and 1992. There have been some excellent to outstanding single quinta ports from 1987 and 1990, but no broadly declared vintage year until 1991, and to a lesser extent, 1992. Even these two "vintage port" years provide evidence that there is little agreement among the principal port lodges as to the superiority of one over the other. A year ago I tasted through all of the bottled 1991s, and I concluded it was a very good to excellent vintage. But my opinion was in the minority. Most observers claimed 1991 was of the same caliber as 1970, an outstanding vintage. While there was a plethora of impressive 1991 ports, the vintage is more reminiscent of such very good to excellent years as 1966 or 1980, rather than such unequivocally great years as 1963, 1970, or 1977. I also believed (and still do) that readers are better served by purchasing

the outstanding, still available 1983s and 1985s, which have not moved up in price, rather than by investing in the similarly priced 1991s. After having retasted the 1991s, I continue to prefer the 1983 and 1985 vintages.

In contrast, 1992 appears to be a sensational vintage. Ironically, the famed port lodges of Graham's, Dow, Croft, Cockburn, Warre, and Quinta do Noval all declared 1991 a vintage, thus precluding the possibility of 1992 being a vintage year for these firms. Two of Portugal's greatest port lodges, Fonseca and Taylor, declared 1992 rather than 1991 a vintage year. And, yes, Fonseca and Taylor have produced two of the most profound young ports I have ever tasted! In addition, houses such as Dow and Churchill have fashioned 1992 single quinta ports that are richer and more stunning than their 1991 vintage ports. In short, 1992 is a fabulous year. Stylistically, the 1992s tend to resemble the 1985s, more than the sterner, more closed and backward 1977s. The 1992 vintage appears to be the richest, most impressive one since 1977, although I have noticed my tasting notes and point scores continue to edge up for the 1985 ports.

4. There has been an explosion of single quinta offerings, many of them as superb as the top vintage port. Extremely strong efforts were produced by a number of port houses in 1987, 1990, and 1991. There should also be some top-notch 1992 single quinta ports from those houses that declared vintages in 1991.

VARIOUS PORT STYLES

Crusted Port   Rarely seen today, crusted port is usually a blend of several vintages that is bottled early and handled in the same manner as a vintage port. Significant sediment will form in the bottle and a crusted port will have to be decanted prior to drinking.

Tawny Port   One of the least expensive ways of securing a mature port is to buy the best shippers' tawny ports. Tawny ports are aged in wood by the top houses for 10, 20, 30, 40, or even 50 years. Tawny port represents a blend of vintages. Tawnys can have exceptional complexity and refinement. I highly recommend some of the best tawnys from firms such as Taylor Fladgate, Fonseca, and Graham's.

Ruby and Branded Ports   Ruby ports are relatively straightforward, deeply colored, young ports that are cherished for their sweet, grapy aromas and supple, exuberant, yet monolithic taste. Most of these ports are meant to be drunk when released. Each house has its own style. Four of the most popular include Fonseca's Bin No. 27, Taylor's 4XX, Cockburn's Special Reserve, and Graham's Six Grapes. Stylistically, all four of these ruby or branded ports are different. The richest and fullest is the Fonseca Bin No. 27; the most complex is usually the Taylor 4XX; the sweetest and fruitiest is the Graham Six Grapes; and the most mature and evolved, as well as least distinguished, the Cockburn Special Reserve.

White Port   I have never understood the purpose of white port, but the French find it appealing. However, the market for these eccentricities is dead.

Late Bottled Vintage Port (L.B.V.P.)   Certain vintages are held back in cask longer than 2 years (the time required for vintage port) and bottled 5–7 years following the vintage. These ports tend to throw less sediment, as much of it has been already deposited in cask. In general, late bottled ports are ready to drink when released. I often find them less interesting and complex than the best tawnys and vintage ports.

Single Quinta Vintage Port   This has become an increasingly important area, especially since the late eighties, when a number of vintages, particularly 1987, 1990, 1991, and 1992, could have been declared vintage years but were not because of the saturated marketplace. Many of the best single quintas, or vineyards, have been offered as vintage-dated single quinta ports. These are vintage ports from a single vineyard. Most port authorities feel it is the blending from various vineyards that gives vintage port its greatest character. Others will argue that in a top year, the finest single quinta ports can be as good as a top vintage port. I tend to believe that a great vintage port is superior to a single quinta port, yet the finest single quintas from 1987, 1990, 1991, and 1992 are stunning. Star ratings of the different single quinta port producers are provided where I have had sufficient tasting experience (more than two vintages) to offer a qualitative ranking.

SINGLE QUINTA VINTAGE PORTS

Quinta Agua Alta (Churchill)

Quinta Boa Vista (Offley)

Quinta do Bomfim (Dow)

Quinta do Cachao (Messias)

Quinta da Cavadinha (Warre)

Quinta do Confradeiro (Sandeman)

Quinta da Corte (Delaforce)

Quinta do Crasto (a consortium)

Quinta da Eira Velha (R. Newan)

Quinta Fojo (Churchill)

Quinta do Forte (Delaforee)

Quinta da Foz (Calem)

Quinta Guimaraens† (Fonseca)

Quinta do Infantado (Roseira)

Quinta Malvedos† (Graham's)

Quinta da Roeda (Croft)

Quinta de la Rosa (Bergquist)

Quinta do Seixo (Ferreira)

Quinta do Tua (Cockburn)

Quinta de Val da Figueria (Calem)

Quinta de Vargellas (Taylor Fladgate)

Quinta do Vau (Sandeman)

Quinta do Vesuvio (Symington)

Vintage Port   Potentially the finest and most complex, and the subject of most of this chapter, are the vintage ports. Vintage ports are declared by the port shippers the second spring after the harvest. Nineteen ninety-one was declared a vintage year by most of the top port shippers. For example, Graham's, Dow, Quinta do Noval, and Warre had declared it a vintage, but Fonseca and Taylor did not, preferring to declare 1992 instead. Vintage port, which is a blend of the very best cuvées from various vineyards, is bottled unfiltered 2 years after the harvest. It can improve and last for 50 or more years. To be a vintage port there must be exceptional ripeness, a great deal of tannin, and plenty of rich fruit and body. In fact, the quality of a shipper's vintage port is the benchmark by which a shipper is evaluated in the international marketplace. Each top house has a distinctive style, which I have tried to capture in the tasting notes.

VINTAGE GUIDE

The greatest port vintages in this century have been 1912, 1927, 1931, 1935, 1945, 1948, 1955, 1963, 1970, 1977, 1983, 1985, and 1992.

VINTAGE YEARS FOR MAJOR FIRMS

Cockburn   1947, 1950, 1955, 1960, 1963, 1967, 1970, 1975, 1983, 1985, 1991

Croft   1945, 1950, 1955, 1960, 1963, 1966, 1970, 1975, 1977, 1982, 1985, 1991

Dow   1945, 1947, 1950, 1955, 1960, 1963, 1966, 1970, 1972, 1975, 1977, 1980, 1983, 1985, 1991

Fonseca   1945, 1948, 1955, 1960, 1963, 1966, 1970, 1975, 1977, 1980, 1983, 1985, 1992

Graham's   1945, 1948, 1955, 1960, 1963, 1966, 1970, 1975, 1977, 1980, 1983, 1985, 1991

Quinta do Noval   1945, 1947, 1950, 1955, 1958, 1960, 1963, 1966, 1967, 1970, 1975, 1978, 1982, 1985, 1991

† These ports tend to be blends made from various vineyards rather than products of a single vineyard.

Quinta do Noval Nacional 1931, 1950, 1960, 1962, 1963, 1964, 1966, 1967, 1970, 1975, 1978, 1980, 1982, 1985, 1987
Sandeman 1945, 1947, 1950, 1955, 1957, 1958, 1960, 1962, 1963, 1966, 1967, 1970, 1975, 1977, 1980, 1982, 1985
Taylor Fladgate 1945, 1948, 1955, 1960, 1963, 1966, 1970, 1975, 1977, 1980, 1983, 1985, 1992
Warre 1945, 1947, 1950, 1955, 1958, 1960, 1963, 1966, 1970, 1975, 1977, 1980, 1983, 1985, 1991

RATING PORTUGAL'S BEST PRODUCERS OF PORT

* * * * * (OUTSTANDING)

Dow   Quinta do Noval Nacional
Fonseca   Taylor Fladgate
Graham's

* * * * (EXCELLENT)

Churchill   Graham's Malvedos
Churchill Quinta Agua Alta   Quinta do Infantado Touriga Nacional
Cockburn   Quinta do Noval
Croft   Symington Quinta do Vesuvio
Dow Quinta do Bomfim   Taylor Quinta de Vargellas
Ferreira Quinta do Seixo   Warre
Fonseca Guimaraens

* * * (GOOD)

Calem Quinta da Foz   Offley Forrester
Croft Quinta do Roed   Poças Junior
Delaforce   Quinta do Passadouro ***/****
Delaforce Quinta do Forte   Quinta de la Rosa ***/****
Ferreira   Ramos-Pinto
Gould Campbell   Sandeman
Quarles Harris   Sandeman Quinta do Vau
Martinez   Smith-Woodhouse
Niepoort   Warre Quinta da Cavadinha

* * (AVERAGE)

Almeida Barros   Messias
Borges & Irmao   Osborne
J. W. Burmester   Pintos dos Santos
C. da Silva   Quinta do Crasto
Calem   Quinta do Panascal
H. & C. J. Feist   Quinta do Romaneira
Feuerheerd   Vasconcellos
Hooper   Wiese & Krohn
C. N. Kopke   Van Zellers

CALEM* * */* * * *

Shipper's Special Reserve Port	C	84
Twenty-Year-Old Tawny Port	D	82

Both of these wines exhibited light orange/ruby/brown colors, with the Special Reserve Port possessing slightly more fruit, medium weight, and a sweet finish. The brown/amber-colored Twenty-Year-Old Tawny Port is drying out. While still pleasant and complex, with nutty/raisiny flavors, it is in decline and should be drunk up.

CHURCHILL* * * *

1992 Agua Alta Single Quinta Vintage	D	93
1990 Agua Alta Single Quinta Vintage	D	92
1991	D	89

Churchill's 1991 Vintage Port is a milder-mannered, less-concentrated, and less-impressive port than their single-vineyard 1992 Agua Alta offering. The 1991 Vintage is a medium-weight, dry, streamlined port with an excellent black fruit character, as well as fine purity and richness. It will be drinkable young and have 15–20 years of aging potential. In the context of the vintage and this port lodge, it is marginally uninspiring. The opaque black/purple-colored 1990 Agua Alta exhibits an intense fragrance of black fruits and chocolate, full body, admirable power and richness, and is significantly more concentrated than the 1991 Vintage. It is also less evolved and in need of 5–10 years of cellaring. It is a 25- to 30-year port. Very impressive!

As for Churchill's 1992 Agua Alta, it is a big, thick, chocolatey, blockbuster-style vintage port, with considerable tannin, superb flavor extraction, massive body, and huge length. It will require 5–6 years of aging, but patience will be rewarded; this wine will prove to be a stunning example of the 1992 vintage and will last for 25–30 years.

Past Glories: Agua Alta—1987 (93)

COCKBURN* * * *

1991	D	88

Ripe, moderately intense, tasty aromas of damp earth, tar, and black fruits are followed by a full-bodied wine with excellent richness, and a firmly delineated personality with good tannin, moderate sweetness, and a long finish. Although very good, it is unexciting in the context of other ports of the vintage.

Past Glories: Quinta do Tua—1987 (94); Vintage Port—1985 (90), 1983 (95), 1955 (92)

CROFT* * * *

1991	D	93

This impressive vintage port, from a firm that has not been numbered among the great port houses of the last century, may turn out to be the most impressive wine from Croft in decades. The healthy purple/black color is followed by copious aromas of licorice, chocolate, and overripe black fruits. Full bodied and unctuously textured, with layers of juicy, succulent, full-throttle fruit, glycerin, high alcohol, and powerful tannin, this large-scaled, youthful vintage port will benefit from 7–10 years of cellaring. It should drink well for 30 + years.

Past Glories: 1963 (90)

DOW* * * * *

1992 Quinta do Bomfim Vintage Port	D	93
1991	D	90

Dow's 1992 Quinta do Bomfim is an expressive, fragrant, up-front style of port with a pungent, peppery, floral, cassis-scented nose, full-bodied, rich, chewy, ripe flavors, light tannin, and sensational extract and length. The wine explodes on the back of the palate, announcing its considerable richness and intensity. This port should drink well young, and last for 30 years. The firmly structured, moderately tannic, impressively colored and concentrated 1991 Vintage Port is less precocious and more reserved. It may develop along the lines of the stern but powerful 1977. The wine offers a classic display of black fruits, licorice, and chocolate aromas and flavors, as well as a full-bodied, muscular style with considerable tannin and firmness. Give it 10–12 years of cellaring and drink it over the following 30+.

Past Glories: Quinta do Bomfim—1990 (95); Vintage Port—1983 (93), 1977 (95), 1970 (90), 1966 (91), 1963 (93), 1945 (93)

FONSECA* * * * *

1992	D	97
1991 Guimaraens Vintage Port	D	93
1988 Late-Bottled Vintage Port	C	88
Twenty-Year-Old Tawny Port	D	86
Thirty-Year-Old Tawny Port	EE	91

Fonseca has scored in both the 1991 and 1992 vintages, with the 1992 a majestic young port that should ultimately rival, perhaps even surpass this house's most recent great efforts (1985, 1977, 1970, and 1963). This colossal vintage port reveals a nearly opaque black/ purple color, and an explosive nose of jammy black fruits, licorice, chocolate, and spices. Extremely full bodied and unctuously textured, this multilayered, enormously endowed port reveals a finish that lasts for over a minute. It is a magnificent port that will age well for 30– 40 years. The 1991 Guimaraens is the most impressive bottle I have tasted of this offering. The opaque purple color, and sweet, copious aromas of cassis, licorice, and flowers, are followed by a supple, rich, full-bodied, precocious-tasting port that is already easy to drink. While it will be quick to develop, it still requires another 4–5 years of aging. It is extremely impressive because of its sumptuous texture and rich, pure fruit.

The Twenty-Year-Old Tawny is a dry, medium-weight port, with an amber/brown color, some fruit, and an austere personality. The Thirty-Year-Old Tawny is far superior, with excellent richness, as well as a complex, jammy, roasted nut, spicy, cedary nose. It exhibits more fruit, body, concentration, and length. Lastly, Fonseca's 1988 Late-Bottled Vintage Port is an excellent, sweet, intense, full-bodied port that is more monolithic than their best tawny and vintage ports. The attractive, spicy, chocolatey, blackberry, and cherry flavors make this an appealing, supple port for drinking now and over the next 15 or so years.

Past Glories: 1985 (96), 1983 (92), 1977 (94), 1970 (97), 1966 (92), 1963 (97), 1955 (96), 1948 (100), 1945 (92)

GOULD CAMPBELL * * *

1991	D	90+

This big, rich, firmly structured, full-bodied port exhibits a dense purple color, a tight but promising nose with elements of flowers, jammy black raspberries, earth, and spice. Vaguely reminiscent of a Dow or Warre in its emphasis on restraint and dryness, this beautiful, well-delineated, cleanly made port will be at its prime by the turn of the century, and easily last for 2 decades thereafter.

Past Glories: 1983 (90), 1977 (90)

GRAHAM'S * * * * *

1992 Malvedos Vintage Port	D	92
1991	D	94

Typically sweet, plump, fleshy, and fat, the opaque purple-colored 1992 Malvedos Vintage Port reveals copious aromas of flowers, licorice, and black fruits, gorgeously seductive, voluptuously textured flavors, light tannin, and a long, alcoholic finish. It should drink well in 2–3 years and last for up to 20. Graham's 1991 Vintage Port gets my nod as the port of the vintage. While keeping in mind that Graham's aims for a sweeter-styled port, there is no doubting the opaque purple/black color, or the explosive nose of black fruits, licorice, spring flowers, and tar. Thick and full bodied, with a satiny texture and a blockbuster, alcoholic finish, this is a top-notch vintage port.

Past Glories: Malvedos Centenary—1990 (92), 1987 (92), 1986 (92), 1976 (90), 1958 (90); Vintage Port—1985 (97), 1983 (94), 1980 (90), 1977 (95), 1970 (95), 1966 (92), 1963 (96), 1955 (95), 1948 (99), 1945 (96)

NIEPOORT * * *

1991	D	89
1992 Jubilée	D	92

While both of these moderately sweet ports are flattering and precocious for their respective vintages, I had a definite preference for the denser, richer, more aromatic and concentrated 1992 Jubilée. This forward 1992 is deeply colored, rich, and exhibits admirable structure and length. Drink it between 1998 and 2025. The 1991 Vintage Port offers generous levels of sweet black fruits, full body, a velvety, supple texture, and a fine finish. Drink it over the next 20 years.

QUINTA DO INFANTADO * * * *

1992	D	95+
1991	D	92
Vintage Character Organic Port	C	90

The massive, chocolatey, black fruit–scented and –flavored 1991 Vintage Port is extremely full bodied, slightly sweet, impressively rich, pure, and long, with a thick, unctuous texture. It requires 7–10 years of cellaring. It is an impressive showing from this small port lodge. There were only 1,000 cases produced of the 1992 Vintage Port, and they are not likely to languish on retailers' shelves. A saturated, black/purple color is followed by a huge, ripe, pure nose of jammy blackberry and cassis fruit that is vaguely reminiscent of such great 1990 Hermitages as Chapoutier's Le Pavillon, Jaboulet's La Chapelle, or Chave's red label Cuvée Cathelin. Awesome concentration, massive body, an unctuous texture oozing with fruit, glycerin, and extract, and a blockbuster finish all suggest this will be a monumental port. Drink it between 2000 and 2030.

The Vintage Character Organic Port is extremely rich and dense, with gobs of black raspberry fruit, a thick, chewy texture, and a full-bodied, slightly sweet, long finish. It should drink well for 15+ years. This appears to be a port lodge on the ascent!

QUINTA DO NOVAL * * * *

1991	C	89
1987 Nacional	E	92
1985 Nacional	E	96

A lighter-styled 1991, Quinta do Noval's offering exhibits attractive blackberry and black raspberry, floral scents in its perfumed nose. Slightly sweet and rich, but lighter than most ports of the vintage, this stylish, restrained, understated wine should age well for 20–25 years. I do not see it ever developing into a great port.

The Quinta do Noval Nacional is a legendary (due mainly to the fame of the 1931) vintage port made only in selected vintages from vines that have never been grafted to American rootstock. Traditionally, for every purchase of 50 cases of vintage port, 6 bottles of Nacional are available. The 1987 exhibits an opaque purple color, and a closed but promising nose of rich, black raspberry fruit, pepper, and earth. Full bodied, tannic, and extremely backward, this is a port that consumers should not touch before 2005. It should keep for 20–40 years. The 1985 Nacional is more opulent and rich, as well as structured and dense. The wine's opaque purple color is followed by a huge, flamboyant bouquet of black fruits, flowers, and spices. This large-scaled, massively endowed vintage port should be at its plateau of maturity by 2005 and last for 30 or more years thereafter.

Past Glories: Nacional—1970 (94), 1966 (92), 1963 (99), 1931 (100)

QUINTA DO PASSADOURO * * */* * * *

1992	D 92+

Produced and bottled by Niepoort, this opaque purple-colored port is more backward and tannic than Niepoort's vintage wines. Impressively endowed, with a reticent but promising nose of chocolate, blackberry fruit, truffles, and licorice, this full-bodied, massive, moderately sweet port should be cellared until 2000. It will age well for 20–30 years. Impressive!

QUINTA DE LA ROSA * * */* * * *

Finest Reserve Port	B 92
1992	C 93

Quinta de la Rosa's Finest Reserve Port is a stunning example of what can be achieved and found in nonvintage port blends. This small port lodge has turned out a terrific, full-bodied, garnet/ruby-colored wine with a big, chocolatey, black cherry, cedary nose, full-bodied, unctuously textured flavors, and gobs of fruit and richness, as well as an off-dry, impressive finish. Drink it over the next decade or more. The powerhouse 1992 Vintage Port exhibits a huge, highly extracted, chocolate- and black raspberry–scented nose, full body, unctuously textured flavors, moderate tannin, and a chewy, long finish. It requires 7–8 years of cellaring, as it is revealing more structure than other 1992s. It should keep for 25–30 years.

SANDEMAN * * *

1988 Quinta do Vau	D 93

I have not seen any vintage ports from Sandeman since 1985, but this 1988 single quinta is a spectacularly rich, concentrated, impressive port. It offers an opaque purple color and a bouquet that displays ostentatious aromas of jammy red and black fruits, licorice, spices, and spring flowers. Extremely full-bodied, yet velvety-textured, unctuous, and layered with concentrated fruit, there is enough complexity and smoothness to this moderately sweet, expansively flavored port to be drunk now, as well as over the next 15–20 years. Very impressive!

SMITH-WOODHOUSE * * *

1992	D 87
1991	D 88

Among all of the 1992 vintage ports, this wine is significantly less concentrated than such massively fruity, opulent, and colossal wines as Fonseca and Taylor. The wine is rich and medium bodied, with plenty of ripe fruit, but it does not possess the extra dimension of complexity and character found in many 1992s. It should drink well for 20+ years. The 1991 is a supple, rich, forward-styled vintage port with moderately deep color, plenty of red and black fruits, a thick, chewy texture, light tannin, and an overall sense of suppleness without significant weight or muscle. It will be drinkable young and last for 20+ years.

SYMINGTON * * * *

1992 Quinta do Vesuvio	D	90
1991	D	89+

A supple, charming, dark ruby/purple-colored wine, Quinta do Vesuvio's 1992 Vintage Port offers excellent concentration, a velvety texture, not much weight or tannin, a precocious, penetrating fragrance, sweet fruit, medium to full body, and a gentle finish. It will drink well young and last for 20 years. The 1991's impressive color and flashy nose of pepper, spice, earth, black truffles, and black fruits, suggest a developed, forward character. Medium to full bodied, with significant tannin and moderate sweetness, this 1991, although impressive, was almost overwhelmed in a blind, peer-group tasting by some of the more rich and concentrated examples. Already approachable, give the 1991 5–7 years of cellaring and drink it over the next 20–25.

Past Glories: Quinta do Vesuvio—1990 (93)

TAYLOR FLADGATE * * * * *

1988 Late-Bottled Vintage Port	C	89
1991 Quinta de Vargellas Vintage Port	D	95
1992	D	100
Ten-Year-Old Tawny Port	C	93
Twenty-Year-Old Tawny Port	D	92
Thirty-Year-Old Tawny Port	EE	87

Taylor's 1992 Vintage Port is unquestionably the greatest young port I have ever tasted. It represents the essence of what vintage port can achieve. The color is an opaque black/purple, and the nose offers up fabulously intense aromas of minerals, cassis, blackberries, licorice, and spices, as well as extraordinary purity and penetration. Yet this is still an unformed and infantile wine. If Château Latour made a late-harvest Cabernet Sauvignon, I suspect it might smell like this. In the mouth, the wine is out of this world, displaying layer upon layer of concentrated black fruits backed by well-integrated tannin and structure. This is a massive, magnificently rich, full-bodied port that will be far more flattering in its youth than were such Taylors as the 1983, 1977, or 1970. It possesses awesome fruit, marvelous intensity, and lavish opulence, all brilliantly well delineated by the wine's formidable structure. This monumental 30- to 50-year port is a must-purchase for port aficionados! Also noteworthy is the fact that the 1992 Taylor commemorates the 300th anniversary of this firm, as evidenced by the special bottle Taylor used for this port.

The exciting news does not stop with Taylor's historic 1992. Taylor Fladgate's 1991 Quinta de Vargellas is the finest Vargellas I have tasted. The opaque purple color is followed by aromatics that are more closed than most 1991s. In the mouth, it is a wine of extraordinary richness and brilliantly delineated components. This exceptionally rich, backward port possesses layer upon layer of fruit, a thick, chewy, unctuous texture, firm structure and tannin, and a finish that lasts for more than a minute. It is an exquisite port that will age for 25–30 years.

It is my opinion that Taylor's tawny ports are the best of their type. When tasted against other tawnys, they all exhibit more aromatic personalities, greater fruit and ripeness, and a wonderful sweetness and length. The Ten-Year-Old Tawny is a personal favorite, as well as the best bargain among these ports. The Thirty-Year-Old Tawny is drier than the Twenty-Year, revealing more orange and brown color, more raisiny notes in its aromatics and flavors, and higher alcohol in the finish. Although I find it admirable, I prefer the richer, more vibrant Twenty-Year-Old Tawny.

Lastly, Taylor's 1988 Late-Bottled Vintage is a dark, opaque-colored wine with rich, sweet, chocolatey, black cherry flavors, and excellent ripeness and richness. Although it does not reveal the complexity of top vintage ports, it is well made and approachable. Drink it over the next 20+ years.

Past Glories: Vintage Ports—1985 (90), 1983 (94), 1980 (90), 1977 (96), 1970 (96), 1966 (91), 1963 (96), 1955 (96), 1948 (100), 1945 (96); Quinta de Vargellas—1987 (90)

WARRE * * * *

1992 Quinta da Cavadinha	D	91
1991	D	90

Closed and reticent to the point of shyness, Warre's 1992 Quinta da Cavadinha opens impressively after 15–20 minutes of airing. The color is a dark ruby/purple, and the nose emerges to reveal licorice, tar, and jammy black fruit scents. It is a full-bodied, well-structured, beautifully focused, classically rendered vintage port that is capable of 20–25 years of cellaring. It should be close to full maturity after 7–10 years of cellaring. Warre's dark-colored 1991 Vintage Port is a stylish, elegant, medium-weight, rich port with floral and berry scents, high tannin, noticeable structure, and a reserved personality that opens with airing. Do not touch a bottle for 5–7 years; drink it over the following 20–25 years.

Past Glories: Vintage Port—1985 (90), 1983 (90), 1977 (92), 1963 (90)

TABLE WINES

Except for the unctuous, rich, almost decadent joys of vintage port and Madeira, one of the greatest nectars of all is Muscatel de Setubal. The Setubal from J. M. da Fonseca is legendary. The 1966 (rated 91) and 1962 Roxo (rated 98) are sensational wines with which to conclude a meal. The potential for fine wine from Portugal has yet to be discovered by most wine enthusiasts. Of course, the ubiquitous, spritzy, rather sweet Portuguese rosés are known the world over and are what many consumers first drink when they deem themselves too old or too sophisticated for soda pop. But Portugal produces some good red wines (that could even be superb if winemaking were not still adhering to nineteenth-century practices), as well as a few lively, crisp, tart white wines, the best of which are the *vinho verdes.* The best of the dry red wines are from such regions as Dão, Bairrada, and the Douro; the most reliable whites are from Palacio de Brejoeira, Antonio de Pires da Silva, and Casal Mendes.

VINTAGE GUIDE

Vintages in Portugal seem to have relevance only to the port trade. For the dry red table wines, none of the wineries seem to think vintages matter, but the Fonseca family, irrefutably Portugal's leading producer of dry red table wine, claims the finest recent years include 1992, 1991, 1990, 1988, 1986, and 1980.

RATING PORTUGAL'S BEST PRODUCERS OF TABLE WINES

* * * * (EXCELLENT)

Quinta do Carmo (Alentejo)	J. M. da Fonseca (Morgado do
Casal de Valle Pradinhos (Douro)	Reguengo-Portalegre)
Quinta do Cotto (Grande Escolha)	J. M. da Fonseca (Quinta da Camarate)
Ferreira (Barca Velha)	J. M. da Fonseca (Rosado Fernandes)
J. M. da Fonseca (Dão Terras Altas)	Vimompor Quinta du Pedro (Vinho Verde)
J. M. da Fonseca (Garrafeira TE)	

*** (GOOD)

Carvalho, Ribeiro, Ferreira (Garrafeira)
Carvalho, Ribeiro, Ferreira (Serradayres)
Caves do Barrocas (Garrafeira)
Caves Dom Teodosio (Garrafeira)
Caves San João (Bairrada)
Caves Velhas
Quinta da Cismeira (Douro)
Conde de Santar (Dão)
Quinta do Confradeiro (Douro)
Falcoaria
J. M. da Fonseca (Pasmados)
J. M. da Fonseca (Periquita)

J. M. da Fonseca (Periquita Reserva)
Luis Pato (Bairrada)
João Pires (Quinta da Bacalhoa)
João Pires (Tinta de Anfora)
Porta dos Cavalheiros (Dão)
Quinta da Lagoalva de Cima
Quinta de la Rosa
Sogrape (Grao Vasco)
Sogrape Vila Real (Douro)
Tuella (Douro)
Vasconcellos

** (AVERAGE)

Arruda Cooperative
Borges
Caves Alianca (Dão)
Caves Alianca (Vinho Verde)
Caves St.-Jao (Garrafeira)
Caves Vaie do Rodo (Douro)

Quinta da Aveleda (Vinho Verde)
Quinta da Pacheca
Reguengos (Garrafeira)
Santa Marta Penaguiao (Doura)
J. Serra (Serra Vidigueira)
Vercoope (Vinho Verde)

5. SPAIN

The Basics

Aside from the glories of sherry, which is synonymous with Spain, this beautiful sun-drenched country is best known as a treasure trove for red wine values. The majority of white wines, which once tasted musty and oxidized, are, thanks to high technology, usually innocuous, with sterile personalities and no real flavor. There are a few exceptions, such as the fragrant, crisp, tasty whites made from the Albarino grape, especially those from the Bodegas de Vilarino. Other refreshing, inexpensive white wines have emerged from Albet I Noya Sat, Angel Lorenzo's Martivilli, Sat Godeval, Vitivinicola Del Ribeiro, and the Sauvignon Blanc of the Marquis de Grinon. And while the booming Spanish sparkling wine business stays in the headlines, few makers of sparkling wine actually produce exceptional wine; most of it is reliably pleasant, relatively innocuous, and very cheap—under $10.00 —hence the appeal.

Red wine is king in Spain, but regrettably this country is still one of unrealized potential rather than of existing achievement. The best red wines all come from northern Spain. The areas that stand out for quality are the famous Rioja region, the generally well-known Penedès viticultural area in Catalonia near the Mediterranean coast, the Ribera del Duero region, and several emerging areas such as Navarra and Toro. To understand Spanish red wines one must first realize that the Spanish want their red wines supple, with an aged taste of maturity, as well as a healthy (many would say excessive) dosage of oak. Once you realize this, you will understand why many Spanish wineries, called *bodegas,* age their wines in huge oak or concrete vats for 7 or 8 years before they are released. The Spanish are not fond of grapy, tannic, young wines, so expect the wineries to mature the wines for the Spanish consumer. Consequently, most Spanish wines have a more advanced color, and are smooth and supple with the sweet vanillin taste of strong oak (usually American) well displayed. Many wineries actually hold back their best lots for a decade or more before releasing them, enabling the consumer to purchase a mature, fully drinkable wine.

GRAPE VARIETIES

RED WINES

Cabernet Sauvignon   An important part of Spain's most expensive and prestigious red wine, the Vega Sicilia, Cabernet Sauvignon has flourished where it has been planted in Spain.

Carinena In English this is the Carignan grape, and in Spain this workhorse grape offers the muscle of Arnold Schwarzenegger. Big and brawny, the tannic, densely colored wine made from this grape varietal is frequently used as a blending agent, particularly with Grenache.

Fogoneu This varietal is believed to be related to the French Gamay. It produces light, fruity wines that are meant to be drunk young. Most Fogoneu is planted on the island of Majorca.

Garnacha The Spanish spelling of Grenache, Garnacha is widely planted in Spain. There are three types of Garnacha utilized. The Garnacha Blanc, which produces white wines, is relatively limited, although it is especially noticeable in Tarragona. The Garnacha Tinto, which is similar to the Grenache known in France, is one of the most widely planted red wine grapes in Spain. There is also the Garnacha Tintorera, which is actually Alicante, the grape that produces black-colored, tannic, dense wines. It is primarily used for blending.

Merlot This relatively new varietal for Spain has performed well. It is planted primarily in the Ribera del Duero.

Monastrell This varietal produces sweet, alcoholic wines. Although widely planted, it is most frequently found in hotter microclimates.

Tempranillo The finest indigenous red wine grape of Spain, Tempranillo travels under a number of names. In Penedès it is called Ull de Llebre and in the Ribera del Duero, Tinto. It provides rich, well-structured wines with good acidity, and plenty of tannin and color. The bouquet often exhibits an intense black raspberry character. It makes an ideal blending mate with Garnacha, but is complex enough to stand on its own.

WHITE WINES

The white wine grapes parade under names such as Albarino, Chardonnay, Macallo, Malvasia, Palomina (utilized for sherry), Parellada (the principle component of most sparkling wine cuvées), Pedro-Ximenez, Riesling, Sauvignon, Torrontes, Verdejo, Xarello, and Moscatel. Few of these varietals have proven to be capable of making anything more than neutral-tasting wines, but in the mid-nineties, several appear to have potential, as yields have been kept low and the wines have been impeccably vinified, not eviscerated by food-processor techniques. Perhaps the best is the Albarino, which, when produced by a top winery in Galicia, has a stunning perfume similar to that of a French Condrieu. However, in the mouth the wine is much lighter, with less body and intensity. At its best, it is light, refreshing, and fragrant.

Other white wines that have shown potential include some of the Chardonnays, and Torrontes, which, when made in Galicia, has a perfumed personality, lovely fruit salad–like flavors, and a pleasant finish.

FLAVORS

Penedès The dominant winery here is Torres, which produces a bevy of excellent red wines from the typical Spanish varietals. Yet the top wine is the 100% Cabernet Sauvignon Black Label Gran Coronas that has a rich, open-knit bouquet of plums, sweet oak, and often licorice and violets. Its chief rival is the Cabernet Sauvignon from Jean León, another concentrated, blackberry-scented and -flavored, full-throttle wine with a whopping influence from sweet, toasty oak. The best vintages are 1990, 1989, 1987, 1984, 1981, and 1978.

Ribera del Duero Two of Spain's greatest red wines are produced in this broad river valley: Pesquera, which comes primarily from the Tempranillo grape, and Vega Sicilia, primarily a Cabernet Sauvignon/Merlot/Malbec wine. What is noticeable about these wines is the remarkable purity of berry fruit that can be found in the top vintages. Take superripe

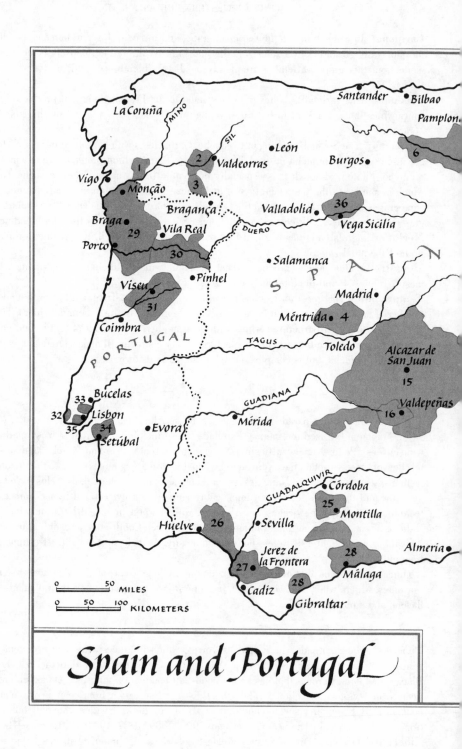

Spain and Portugal

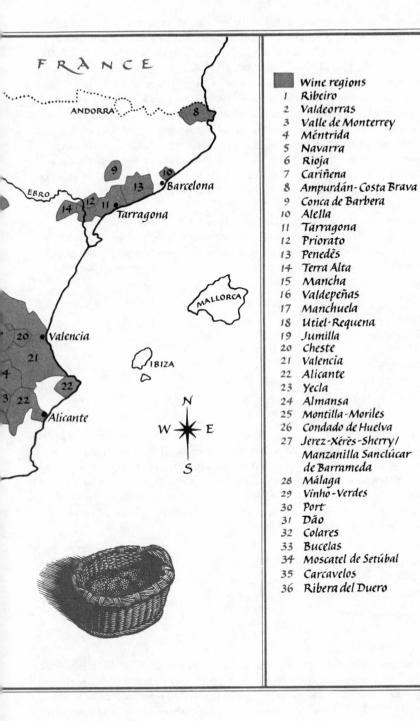

FRANCE

ANDORRA

EBRO

8

9

13 •Barcelona

14 12 11
Tarragona

10

MALLORCA

20 •Valencia

21

4

22

3 22

•Alicante

IBIZA

N
W ✳ E
S

Wine regions
1 Ribeiro
2 Valdeorras
3 Valle de Monterrey
4 Méntrida
5 Navarra
6 Rioja
7 Cariñena
8 Ampurdán-Costa Brava
9 Conca de Barbera
10 Alella
11 Tarragona
12 Priorato
13 Penedès
14 Terra Alta
15 Mancha
16 Valdepeñas
17 Manchuela
18 Utiel-Requena
19 Jumilla
20 Cheste
21 Valencia
22 Alicante
23 Yecla
24 Almansa
25 Montilla-Moriles
26 Condado de Huelva
27 Jerez-Xérès-Sherry/
   Manzanilla Sanclúcar
   de Barrameda
28 Málaga
29 Vinho-Verdes
30 Port
31 Dão
32 Colares
33 Bucelas
34 Moscatel de Setúbal
35 Carcavelos
36 Ribera del Duero

fruit and combine it with a minimum of 3 years (in the case of Vega Sicilia, 8–12 years) in oak casks, and you have powerfully heady, supple, explosively rich wines that offer a great deal of spicy, sweet, toasty, vanillin-scented oak. The best vintages have been 1994, 1991, 1990, 1989, 1986, 1983, 1982, 1976, 1975, 1968, and 1962.

Rioja   When made by the best producers, such as La Rioja Alta or Muga, Rioja will be a mature wine having a medium-ruby color often with a touch of orange or brown (normal for an older wine), and a huge, fragrant bouquet of tobacco, cedar, smoky oak, and sweet, ripe fruit. On the palate, there will be no coarseness or astringence because of the long aging of the wine in cask and/or tank prior to bottling. Despite its suppleness, the wine will keep for 5–10 years after its release. Even a young Rioja, released after just 3–4 years, such as a Marqués de Cáceres, will show a ripe, fat, rich, supple fruitiness, and a soft, sweet, oaky character. The best vintages include 1994, 1991, 1990, 1989, 1987, 1982, 1981, 1978, 1973, 1970, 1968, 1964, and 1958.

Toro   Once known for overwhelmingly alcoholic, heavy wines, Toro has adopted modern technology, and the results have been some rich, full-bodied, deeply flavored, southern Rhône–like wines from wineries such as Farina. They taste similar to the big, lush, peppery wines of France's Châteauneuf du Pape and Gigondas, and they represent astonishing values. The best vintages are 1990 and 1989.

AGING POTENTIAL
Navarra: 5–7 years
Penedès: 6–15 years
Ribera del Duero: 6–30 years †
Rioja: 6–25 years ††
Sparkling White Wines: 3–6 years

OVERALL QUALITY LEVEL
While it may be fashionable to tout the quality and value of all Spanish wines, the only wines with serious merit are the red wines, and sadly, only a small percentage can hold up to the best international competition. Most of the whites are still atrociously boring, and while the sparkling wines are inexpensive, only a few offer value. Despite the fabulous climate and high percentage of old vines, most of Spain's winemakers have not yet realized their potential, which is formidable.

MOST IMPORTANT INFORMATION TO KNOW
Knowing the names of the best producers, and a few top recent vintages (1982, 1985, 1986, 1987, 1990, 1991, and 1994) will get you a long way if you avoid the white wines from this country.

1995–1996 BUYING STRATEGY
In practice, vintages are less important in Spain than in France or Italy. As in many hot areas, ripeness is not usually a problem. But Spain's most famous viticultural region, Rioja, can experience heavy rains at an inopportune time, as they did in years such as 1992, 1984, 1979, 1977, and 1972. Most of the best Riojas have become pricey and no longer represent the values they once did. The best recent vintages include 1994, 1991, 1990, 1989, 1988, 1986, and 1985. For the luxury-priced Gran Reservas, the 1982s and 1981s from the best

† Only the wines of Pesquera and Vega Sicilia will keep 25–30 and 40–50 years, respectively.
†† Only a handful of Rioja wines, principally the Gran Reservas from La Rioja Alta, Marqués de Murrieta, and CVNE, can age this long.

bodegas can be stunning. For the inexpensive red wines, my buying strategy is to stay within 5–7 years of the vintage, although there are exceptions.

Most of Spain's great bargains in red wine emerge, not from Rioja or the Duero, but from such backwater viticultural regions as Priorato, Jumilla, Navarra, Toro, and Valdepeñas.

While I buy and taste Spanish white wine, I rarely drink it. I have not found any reason to change this practice, although some of the tasty Arborinas from Galicia offer persuasive evidence that improvements have been made. Yet these wines are priced at $15–$20, which is far too expensive for what is in the bottle.

VINTAGE GUIDE

1994—Spanish wine producers are beating their breasts with considerable enthusiasm, claiming 1994 is Spain's vintage of the century. It was one of the hottest years on record, and unlike France, Spain was not troubled by September rain. Reports from such great wine regions as Rioja and Ribera del Duero are nothing short of spectacular. Such lesser known regions as Toro, Priorato, Navarra, and Penedès are also raving about their wines' quality.

1993—A more homogenous and successful vintage in Spain than in other Western European wine regions, 1993 is a very good vintage that will undoubtedly be overshadowed by the greatness of 1994.

1992—This is a mixed vintage because of the heavy rains that hit most of northern Spain. In Rioja, producers talked about a great vintage until the harvest was picked in a soaking downpour. Good- rather than outstanding-quality wines have emerged. At least one great wine was produced: the 1992 Cabernet Sauvignon of Marqués de Griñon from his Dominio de Valdepusa.

1991—1991 was a better vintage for most of Spain than it was in France. Many top viticultural areas, such as Ribera del Duero and Rioja, have produced high-quality wines. Spain is one of Europe's surprising success stories in this vintage.

1990—Overall an abundant, high-quality crop was produced throughout Spain, but the quality is less consistent than in France or Italy.

1989—Another generous, abundant crop of good-quality wine was produced.

1988—A cooler but certainly good year for Spain, with most areas reporting good rather than excellent or outstanding quality.

1987—Rioja is considered to be of very high quality and not far off the mark of wines produced in Rioja's two best vintages of the decade of the eighties, 1981 and 1982. Elsewhere, the vintage is mixed, although it is generally considered to be above average in quality.

1986—Considered to be spectacular in the Duero, the crop size was down from 1985. In Rioja it is a good year.

1985—Virtually every wine-producing region of Spain reported 1985 to be a very successful, high-quality vintage. In Rioja it was a record-setting crop in size.

1984—This vintage has a terrible reputation because of a poor, cool European summer, but the better red wines of Spain have turned out to be among the best made in Europe.

1983—A hot, dry year caused some problems, but the wines range from good to very good.

1982—For Rioja and Ribera del Duero, this was the finest vintage since 1970 and largely regarded as a great year, superior to 1985, and equal to 1986 in the Duero.

1981—Spain enjoyed a very good vintage in 1981, but as time has passed it has become apparent that Rioja had an exceptional year, in many cases equal to 1982.

1980—An average-quality year.

1979—A good year in the Penedès area, but only average in Rioja.

1978—For Rioja, Penedès, and the Ribera del Duero, the best overall vintage between 1970 and 1981.

OLDER VINTAGES

For most of northern Spain, 1970 was a great vintage. Prior to that, 1964 was another superb vintage. Well-kept bottles of 1970 and 1964 red wines from Rioja and the Ribera del Duero are still excellent.

RATING SPAIN'S BEST PRODUCERS OF DRY RED TABLE WINES

* * * * * (OUTSTANDING)

Costers del Siurdana—Clos de l'Obac (Priorato)
CVNE Contino (Rioja)
Marqués de Griñon Cabernet Sauvignon (Dominio de Valdepusa)
Muga Prado Enea Reserva (Rioja)
Marqués de Murrieta Castillo Ygay Gran Reserva (Rioja)

Pesquera Ribera del Duero (Castilla-León)
La Rioja Alta Reserva 890 (Rioja)
La Rioja Alta Reserva 904 (Rioja)
Vega Sicilia N.V. Gran Reserva Especial (Ribera del Duero)
Vega Sicila Unico Reserva (Castilla-León)

* * * * (EXCELLENT)

Albet I Noya Sat (Penedès)***/****
René Barbier (Cataluna)
Can Rafols dels Caus Penedès (Cataluna)
Bodegas Julian Chivite 125 Anniversario Reserva (Navarra)
CVNE Imperial (Rioja)
CVNE Viña Real (Rioja)
Domecq-Marqués de Arienzo Reserva (Rioja)
Faustino Martinez Faustino I (Rioja)
Marqués de Griñon (Ribera del Duero)
Marqués de Griñon (Rioja)
Jean Léon Penedès (Cataluna)
Martinez Bujanda Conde de Valdemar (Rioja)
Martinez Bujanda Conde de Valdemar Gran Reserva (Rioja)
Bodegas Muga (Rioja)****/*****

Marqués de Murrieta Reserva (Rioja)
Bodegas La Granja Remelluri (Rioja)
La Rioja Alta Viña Alberdi (Rioja)
La Rioja Alta Arana (Rioja)
La Rioja Alta Ardanza (Rioja)
Marqués de Riscal Baron de Chirel (Rioja)
Scala dei Priorato Cartoixa Priorat (Cataluna)
Scala dei Priorato Clos Mogador (Cataluna)
Sierra Cantabria (Rioja)
Torres Gran Sangre de Toro Penedès (Cataluna)
Vega Sicilia Valbuena Ribera del Duero (Castilla-León)
Bodegas de Vilarino-Cambados (Rias Baixas)
Vinicola del Priorat (Priorato)

* * * (GOOD)

Agricola de Borja (Campo de Borja)
Señorío de Almansa (Castillo-La Mancha)
Amezola de la Mora (Rioja)
Arboles de Castillejo (La Mancha)
Palacio de Arganza Bierzo (Castilla-León)
Bodegas Ismael Arroyo (Ribera del Duero)***/****
Pablo Barrigon Tovar (Castilla-León)
Pablo Barrigon Tovar San Pablo (Castilla-León)
Pablo Barrigon Tovar Viña Cigalena Reserva (Castilla-León)

Pablo Barrigon Tovar Viña Solona (Castilla-León)
Masia Barril Priorato (Cataluna)
Bilbainas Viña Pomal (Rioja)
Marqués de Cáceres (Rioja)
Marqués de Cáceres Reserva (Rioja)
Campo Viejo (Rioja)
Julian Chivite Gran Feudo (Navarra)
Martin Codax Albarino white wine (Galicia)
CVNE Cune (Rioja)
Estola (Castillo-La Mancha)

Farina Colegiata Toro (Castilla-León)
Farina Gran Colegiata Toro (Castilla-León)
Faustino Martinez Faustino V (Rioja)
Faustino Martinez Faustino VII
   (Rioja)
Franco Españolas Bordon (Rioja)
Inviosa Lar de Barros (Extremadura)
Baron de Ley El Coto (Rioja)
Lan Viña Lanciano Reserva (Rioja)
Los Llanos Valdepeñas (Castillo-La
   Mancha)
Lopez de Heredia Bosconia Reserva
   (Rioja)
Lopez de Heredia Tondonia Reserva
   (Rioja)
Bodegas Magana (Navarra)
Martinez Bujanda Conde Valdemar Viño
   Tinto (Rioja)
Mauro Ribera del Duero (Castilla-León)
Montecillo Viña Monty Reserva (Rioja)
Bodegas Hermanos Morales (La Mancha)
De Muller Tarragona (Cataluna)
Ochoa Reserva (Navarra)
Parxet Alella white wine (Cataluna)
Perez Pascuas Viña Pedrosa Ribera del
   Duero (Castilla-León)
Pazo de Señorans Rias Baixas white wine
   (Galicia)
Piqueras Castilla de Almansa (Castillo-La
   Mancha)

Salvador Poveda (Alicante)
Raimat Costers del Segre (Cataluna)
Rioja Santiago Gran Condal (Rioja)
Riojanas Monte Real Reserva (Rioja)
Santiago Ruiz Rias Baixas Albarino white
   wine (Galicia)
Bodegas de Sarria Gran Viño del Señorío
   Reserva (Navarra)
Bodegas de Sarria Viña del Perdon
   (Navarra)
Scala dei Priorato Negre (Cataluna)
Taja proprietary red wine (Monastrel)
Miguel Torres Coronas Penedès (Cataluna)
Miguel Torres Gran Coronas Penedès
   (Cataluna)
Miguel Torres Gran Coronas Black Label
   Penedès (Cataluna); since 1981, for
   vintages prior to and including
   1981 *****
Migues Torres Gran Viña Sol Green Label
   Penedès (Cataluna)
Miguel Torres Viña Sol Penedès (Cataluna)
Viñas del Vero Compania Somontano
   (Aragon)
Castilla de Vinicole Grand Verdad
   (Castillo-La Mancha)
Castilla de Vinicole Señorío de Duadianeja
   (Castillo-La Mancha)

* * (AVERAGE)

Alavesas Solar de Samaniego (Rioja)
Los Arcos Bierzo (Castilla-León)
Masia Bach Penedès (Cataluna)
Berberana Berberana Reserva (Rioja)
Berberana Carta de Plata (Rioja)
Berceo (Rioja)
Beronia (Rioja)
Bilbainas Viña Paceta (Rioja)
Bilbainas Viña Zaco (Rioja)
Bleda Jumilla (Murcia)
Bordejé (Aragon)
Borruel (Aragon)
Campo Viejo (Rioja)
Carricas (Navarra)
Casa de la Viña (Castillo-La
   Mancha)
Castano Yecla (Murcia)
Corral Don Jacobo (Rioja)
Cueva del Granero (Castillo-La Mancha)

Augusto Egli (Valencia)
Eval (Alicante)
Freixenet Penedès (Cataluna)
Frutos Villar Cigales (Castilla-León)
Poveda Garcia (Alicante)
Irache Gran Irache (Navarra)
Lagunilla Viña Herminia (Rioja)
Lan Lander (Rioja)
Lopez de Heredia Cubillo (Rioja)
Louis Megia Duque de Estrada
   (Castillo-La Mancha)
Marqués de Monistrol Penedès
   (Cataluna)
Montecillo Cumbrero (Rioja)
Olarra Anares (Rioja)
Olarra Anares Gran Reserva (Rioja)
Olarra Cerro Añon Gran Reserva (Rioja)
Olarra Cerro Añon Reserva (Rioja)
Frederico Paternina Banda Azul (Rioja)

Frederico Paternina Conde de los Andes
  Gran Reserva (Rioja)
Frederico Paternina Viña Vial (Rioja)
Penalba Lopez Ribera del Duero
  (Castilla-León)
Pulido Romero (Medellin)
Raimat (Costers del Segre)
Castell del Remei (Cataluna)
Ribero Duero Ribera del Duero
  (Castilla-León)

Marqués de Riscal Gran Reserva (Rioja)
Marqués de Riscal Reserva (Rioja)
Ruiz (Canamero)
Miguel Torres Pinot Noir Penedès
  (Cataluna)
Unidas Age Marqués de Romeral (Rioja)
Unidas Age Siglo (Rioja)
Viños de León (Castilla-León)

RATING SPAIN'S BEST PRODUCERS OF SPARKLING WINE

* * * * * (OUTSTANDING)

None

* * * * (EXCELLENT)

None

* * * (GOOD)

Bilbainas
Cadiz
Cavas Ferret
Chandon
Gran Cordornieu Brut
Freixenet Cuvée DS
Freixenet Reserva Real
Juvé y Champs Gran Cru

Juvé y Champs Gran Reserva
Juvé y Champs Reserva de la Familia
Mont Marcal Brut
Josep-Maria Raventos Blanc Brut
Segura Viudas Aria
Segura Viudas Brut Vintage
Segura Viudas Reserva Heredad

* * (AVERAGE)

Castellblanch
Conde de Caralt
Paul Cheneau
Cordornieu Extra Dry
Cordornieu Non-Plus-Ultra
Cordornieu Rosé Brut
Freixenet Brut Nature
Freixenet Carta Nevada

Freixenet Cordon Negro
Lembey
Marqués de Monistrol
Muga Conde de Haro
Castello de Perelada
Segura Viudas Brut
Segura Viudas Rosé

SPAIN'S GREATEST RED WINE BARGAINS

Agricola de Borja (Campo de Borja)
Albet I Noya Sat (Penedès)
Señorío de Almansa (Castillo-La Mancha)
Arboles de Castillejo (La Mancha)
Ismael Arroyo (Ribera del Duero)
Berberana d'Avalos Tempranillo (Rioja)
Berberana d'Avalos Tempranillo Tinto
  (Rioja)
Farina Colegiata Toro (Castilla-León)

Farina Gran Colegiata Toro (Castilla-León)
Marqués de Griñon (Rioja)
Marqués de Griñon Durius (Rioja)
Jean León Penedès (Cataluna)
Los Llanos Valdepeñas (Castillo-La
  Mancha)
Bodegas Magana (Navarra)
Martinez Bujanda Conde Valdemar Viño
  Tinto (Rioja)

Bodegas Hermanos Morales (La Mancha)
Marqués de Murrieta Tinto Crianza (Rioja)
La Rioja Alta Viña Arana (Rioja)
La Rioja Alta Viña Ardanza (Rioja)

Bodegas de Sarria Gran Viño del Señoría
Reserva (Navarra)
Bodegas Sierra Cantabria (Rioja)
Vinicola del Priorato (Priorato)

ALBET I NOYA SAT (PENEDÈS)* * * *

1993 Albet I Noya (Barrel Fermented)	B	87
1991 Cabernet Sauvignon	B	86
1990 Tempranillo	B	88

A good value from the Mediterranean coastal area of Penedès, the 1991 Cabernet Sauvignon exhibits a dark, saturated ruby/purple color and sweet, jammy fruit in the nose intertwined with scents of tobacco, aggressive herbal overtones (from young vines?), and obvious new oak. Despite the noticeable herbaceousness and wood, this wine possesses plenty of sweet, ripe, black currant fruit in a medium- to full-bodied, exuberant and forceful style. Although not complex, it is mouth filling, as well as a sound value in Cabernet Sauvignon. I have a preference for the more seductive, charming, voluptuously textured 1990 Tempranillo. It displays loads of black raspberry, black cherry, and curranty fruit in its dramatic nose. Full bodied and velvety textured, with plenty of glycerin and alcohol that give a wine that mouth-filling, chewy character, this well-made, pure wine is ideal for consuming over the next 5–7 years.

Unlike the other white wine offerings from Jorge Ordonez, the 1993 Albet I Noya is barrel fermented. It admirably combines a toasty vanillin oak character with plenty of ripe tropical fruit intertwined with intriguing cherry scents. Bold and big, with a dramatic, new world style, this chewy, low-acid wine is ideal for drinking over the next year.

ARBOLES DE CASTILLEJO (LA MANCHA)* * *

1990	A	87+

Made by the Bodegas Torres Filoso, this deeply flavored, concentrated, closed wine reveals fine potential, and the price makes it a steal. The saturated ruby/purple color is followed by cassis, black cherry, and earthy scents. The wine displays superrichness, medium to full body, moderate tannin, and a concentrated, chewy, youthful finish. It should improve for 1–2 years and last for 8–10.

BODEGAS ISMAEL ARROYO (RIBERA DEL DUERO)* * */* * * *

1992 Mesoneros de Castilla	A	85
1990 Mesoneros de Castilla Crianza	B	87
1989 Valsotillo Reserva	C	87

The 1992 Mesoneros de Castilla, made from 100% Tinta del Pais, is a top-notch bargain offering soft, flattering, grapy, currant, and cherry fruit in an easy-to-understand, medium-bodied format. There is good depth and plenty of tasty fruit. Drink it over the next 1–2 years. The 1990 Mesoneros de Castilla Crianza is an unevolved, dark ruby/purple-colored wine with black cherry and cassis fruit, medium to full body, moderate tannin, and a fresh, lively, youthful, tart finish. It requires another 1–2 years of cellaring and should last for a decade or more.

Made from a barrel selection of the winery's best lots, the 1989 Valsotillo Reserva is a more powerful wine, with a dark ruby color, a big, earthy, herb- and black cherry–scented nose, full-bodied flavors with excellent flavor extraction, and a rich, tannic, concentrated, fruity finish. Drink it over the next 5–6 years.

RENÉ BARBIER (CATALUNA)* * *

1991 Clos Mogador Priorat	D	92

This luxury cuvée, made from old Grenache vines, aged in small French oak casks, and bottled unfiltered, is a magnificent example of what Spain can produce at the top quality level. The wine reveals an opaque purple color, a huge bouquet of spicy, smoky-scented oak, combined with lavish quantities of jammy black currants and kirsch. Superripe, full bodied, with layers of rich, explosively ripe, concentrated fruit, this voluptuously textured wine will provide thrilling drinking for 10–15 years. The yields for this 1991 were 20 hectoliters per hectare, or about 1½ tons from tightly spaced vines.

AGRICOLA DE BORJA (CAMPO DE BORJA)* * *

1993 Borsao	A	85

A sensational value, this 1993 dry red wine is made from 80% Garnacha and 20% Tempranillo. A supple, richly fruity (raspberries and cherries) wine, it possesses good purity, balance, and a user-friendly personality. Drink it over the next 2–3 years.

CLOS DE L'OBAC (PRIORATO)* * * * *

1992	D	88+
1991	D	90
1990	D	91
1989	D	90

These impressive wines are all made from a blend of approximately 48% Garnacha, 46% Cabernet Sauvignon, and the remainder small quantities of Syrah, Merlot, and Mazuelo. The wines are aged in small French oak casks for 15–18 months and bottled without filtration. They are opaquely colored, full-bodied, powerful wines with excellent richness and a personality akin to a top-class Bordeaux, so much so that it would be interesting to insert a Clos de l'Obac in a blind tasting with first- or second-growth Bordeaux. Even a superb palate would have trouble ferreting out the Spanish wine.

The youthful 1992 exhibits a dark ruby/purple color, a tight but promising nose of toasty new oak, black cherries, and cedar, full body, excellent ripeness and extraction, and moderate tannin in the finish. Although approachable, it will not be fully mature for 3–4 years. Also deep ruby/purple colored, the 1991 offers an attractive, youthful nose of cassis and smoky new oak, full body, admirable extraction, a layered feel, and moderate tannin in the finish. The 1990 reveals the same opaque ruby/purple color, and a wonderfully sweet, smoky nose that combines a judicious amount of new wood with copious amounts of black cherry and currantly aromas. The wine possesses a layered feel, an impressive degree of opulence, highly extracted, sweet, rich fruit, and a finish that lasts for half a minute. It is an impressive, large-scaled wine that should age well for 10–15 years. The similarly styled 1989 displays more complexity (a floral note has emerged), full body, sweet, jammy fruit, excellent purity, harmony, and balance, and a long finish. It is a knockout, new-style Spanish red wine that should have many admirers.

BODEGAS FARINA (TORO)* * *

1990 Collegiata Tinto	A	87
1987 Gran Collegiata Tinto Reserva	A	88
1989 Gran Peromato	A	83
1991 Peromato Tinto	A	85

The wines of this *bodega* in Spain's Toro region have consistently been good buys. Although the 1989 Gran Peromato is aggressively oaky, it is a round, ripe, toasty wine with fine fruit, soft tannins, and low acidity. It should drink well for 3–4 more years. The deeper-colored 1990 Collegiata Tinto offers a complex nose of spicy, robust, peppery, black cherry, and earthy scents. It is a full-bodied, chunky wine loaded with gutsy levels of fruit, glycerin, and soft tannin. Drink this lusty, mouth-filling, uncomplicated wine over the next 4–5 years.

The light-bodied 1991 Peromato Tinto is a straightforward, richly fruity, berry-scented and -flavored wine with good body, chewy glycerin and heady alcohol in its silky smooth finish. It is meant to be drunk within 5–6 years of the vintage. The 1987 Gran Collegiata Tinto Reserva is a knockout bargain. It possesses a dark ruby color, a big, spicy, meaty, roasted herb– and black cherry–scented nose, full body, rich, satiny-smooth flavors, and noticeable alcohol in the gutsy, lusty finish. A voluptuously textured, chewy wine reminiscent of a mouth-filling, supple, heady southern Rhône Valley wine, it is worth buying by the case. Drink it over the next 4–5 years.

I tasted the 1986 Black Label Gran Reserva, but I cannot recommend it because of the excessive oak that dominates the wine's personality.

MARQUÉS DE GRIÑON (RIOJA)* * * */* * * * *

1992 Cabernet Sauvignon Dominio de Valdepusa	C	92
1992 Rioja	A	87
1988 Rioja Reserva Coleccion Personal	C	89
1994 Sauvignon Blanc Durius	A	86
1992 Tinto Durius	A	87

Carlos Falcon, the Marqués de Griñon, produces high-quality wines in three viticultural areas. The least expensive wines, the Durius offerings, include a 1994 Sauvignon Blanc and a 1992 Tinto. Both are well-made wines from the Valladoib region. The crisp, aromatic, herb- and fig-scented Sauvignon is a delicious, light- to medium-bodied, dry, crisp wine that is a breakthrough for Spain with respect to this varietal. It should be drunk during its first several years of life. Another outstanding bargain is the 1992 Tinto Durius, a blend composed primarily of Grenache. Although not complex, the wine is rich and mouth filling, with a Côtes du Rhône–like, peppery, spicy, black cherry–scented nose, excellent, pure, rich, chewy flavors, and plenty of glycerin, alcohol, and fruit. Drink it over the next 4–5 years.

The Marqués de Griñon produces 40,000 cases of a modestly priced, delicious Rioja. The 1992 Rioja exhibits a medium dark ruby color, and a soft, spicy, sweet American oak–scented nose intertwined with scents of black and red fruits. Supple and velvety-textured, it possesses excellent purity, gobs of fruit, and a long, silky finish. Drink it over the next 4–5 years. There are only 6,000 cases of the 1988 Rioja Reserva Coleccion Personal. This is a broader, more complex, tobacco-, mineral-, vanillin-, and curranty-scented and -flavored wine with layers of rich, opulently textured fruit, medium to full body, a wonderful, expansive sweetness from ripe grapes (not sugar), and a lush finish. It should drink well for 5–7 years.

While the Marqués de Griñon has always made very good wines, his finest offering to date is the 1992 Cabernet Sauvignon Dominio de Valdepusa from his vineyards in La Mancha. There are 6,000 cases of this 100% French oak–aged wine, whose vinification and upbringing are overseen by none other than the omnipresent, world-class oenologist, Pomerol's Michel Rolland. The wine is splendidly rich, with an opaque ruby/purple color, a huge nose of black currants, lead pencil, and sweet yet subtle oak, layers of flavor, great extraction and richness, sweet tannin, and a long, complex finish that is bursting with jammy black currant fruit. This terrific Cabernet Sauvignon is unquestionably the finest the Marqués de Griñon has ever produced. Approachable already, it promises to last for 15–20 years.

The Marqués de Griñon is not content to rest on his laurels. Barrel samples of the 1994 Syrah suggest this is going to be a blockbuster that should make some of the Rhône Valley's top producers nervous. Approximately 4,000 cases will be made. The outstanding barrel samples were smoky and rich, with that wonderful bacon fat and cassis character. Readers should also be on the lookout for a new offering from the Marqués de Griñon produced from a vineyard in the Ribera del Duero, not far from Pesquera. The 1994, which is being aged in new oak casks, was spectacular when tasted from barrel. It will be released in 1996.

BODEGAS MAGANA (NAVARRA)* * *

1990 EVENTUM	A	86

Bodegas Magana's 1990 Eventum, a blend of 70% Merlot and 30% Tempranillo, exhibits a healthy dark purple color, a plummy, curranty-scented nose with a whiff of caramel and spice, admirable richness, a supple, fleshy character, and a heady finish. Although not complex, it is a tasty, straightforward Merlot-based wine for drinking over the next 3–4 years. It is bottled unfiltered and made from the oldest Merlot vineyard in Spain—planted in 1974.

BODEGAS HERMANOS MORALES (LA MANCHA)* * *

1991 Gran Créacion	A	89
N.V. Viña Estil	A	85

A terrific value, the 1991 Gran Créacion, a blend of 40% Cabernet Sauvignon and 60% Tempranillo, must be tasted to be believed. It is hard to find a wine this rich, complex, and age worthy for $6.50 a bottle. Bottled unfiltered, this wine exhibits a dark saturated ruby/purple color, a big, spicy, black currant, and oaky nose, wonderfully rich, full-bodied, black currant and black cherry flavors, layers of deep, juicy fruit, excellent purity, light tannin, and a lusty, heady finish. This knockout wine should drink well for 4–5 years. How I would love to run across wines of this quality and price more frequently! Also a delicious bargain, the N.V. Viña Estil, made from a clone of Tempranillo called Cencibel, displays attractive, ripe, curranty fruit offered in a straightforward manner, a grapy, round, fruity taste, and a spicy, surprisingly long finish. It is ideal for drinking over the next 1–2 years.

BODEGAS MUGA (RIOJA)* * * */* * * * *

1990 Muga Rioja Reserva (Unfiltered)	B	89
1989 Muga Rioja Reserva (Unfiltered)	B	90
1993 Muga Rosado (Barrel Fermented)	A	88
1985 Prado Enea Rioja Gran Reserva	D	89+
1981 Prado Enea Rioja Gran Reserva	D	92

One of Rioja's finest wineries, the Bodegas Muga fashions traditionally styled, rich, age-worthy, complex Rioja wines. To their credit, all of their red wines are bottled unfiltered. The current releases include the sensational 1989 Muga Rioja Reserva. For $12, this is a terrific wine bargain. Made from 70% Tempranillo, 20% Garnacha, and 10% Graciano, this rich, complex wine exhibits a Graves-like nose of minerals, caramel, vanilla, and superrich blackcurrant and cherry fruit. This sweet (from the high extraction of ripe fruit), full-bodied wine reveals that elusive lead pencil character found in some Bordeaux wines (especially in Pauillac), deep, chewy, concentrated flavors, a sense of elegance, a supple personality, and a long finish. Already delicious and complex, it promises to age effortlessly for at least a decade. The 1990 Muga Rioja Reserva does not appear to be quite as rich as the 1989. It is more structured and backward, so perhaps 1–2 more years of cellaring will prove beneficial. Nevertheless, it is an impressively endowed, dark ruby-colored wine with an excellent bouquet of cedar, spicy oak, smoke, and red and black fruits. With medium to full body, harmonious yet powerful flavors, and moderate tannin in the finish, this rich wine should be drunk over the next decade.

The 1985 Prado Enea Rioja Gran Reserva is one of the most expensive wines in the Ordonez portfolio. Yet readers should keep in mind it is just being released after aging for a decade at the winery. (Spain's top producers age their wines until they approach maturity and then release them into the marketplace. They are among a small number of producers worldwide who follow this philosophy.) The 1985 Prado Enea Rioja Gran Reserva exhibits an amber/dark garnet color, copious amounts of red and black fruit aromas and flavors, and an underlying mineral, tobacco, and lead pencil–like character. There is plenty of tannin in the excellent finish. It is a tightly knit, amazingly youthful Rioja that will benefit from another 2–3 years of cellaring. It will drink well for 20+ years and is a strong candidate for an outstanding rating. The exceptional 1981 Prado Enea Rioja Gran Reserva also exhibits a Bordeaux-like aromatic character (scents of tobacco, black currants, and cedar are reminiscent of a great Graves). It offers gorgeously rich, opulent fruit in addition to a knockout bouquet that soars from the glass. Deep, rich curranty fruit is intertwined with flavors of spice, fruitcake and tobacco. Dense, concentrated, well balanced, delicious, and complex, this decadent wine promises to evolve for 10–15 more years. Impressive!

Muga's 1993 Muga Rosado is reminiscent of a dry, full-bodied, raspberry- and strawberry-scented and boldly flavored Tavel from France's southern Rhône Valley. It is a brash, full-bodied, dramatic rosé that is loaded with flavor. It should age well for several years. Made from 60% Garnacha, 30% Tempranillo, and 10% Viura, it admirably demonstrates just how much flavor can be crammed into a Spanish rosé. Do not miss it!

MARQUÉS DE MURRIETA (RIOJA)* * * */* * * * *

1992	Pazo de Barrantes Albarino	C	87
1987	Rioja Castillo Ygay	D	88
1985	Rioja Castillo Ygay	D	90
1978	Rioja Castillo Ygay	D	93
1968	Rioja Castillo Ygay	EEE	93
1964	Rioja Castillo Ygay	EEE	83
1959	Rioja Castillo Ygay	EEE	92
1982	Rioja Gran Reserva	D	93
1990	Rioja Reserva	C	88+
1988	Rioja Reserva	C	88
1991	Tinto Crianza	B	84
1990	Tinto Crianza	B	88

The Bodegas Marqués de Murrieta is considered to be one of the finest producers of Rioja. Some authorities claim their top Reserva wines and special luxury cuvée, the Castillo Ygay (produced in only the finest vintages), are among the greatest expressions of Rioja. According to the renowned Dutch wine writer, Hubrecht Duijker, in his classic book, *The Wines of Rioja* (Mitchell Beazley, 1985), Murrieta may be the oldest continuously functioning *bodega* in Rioja, having been founded in approximately 1860.

The offerings I tasted include their Albarino white wine, the 1992 Pazo de Barrantes. A crisp, aromatic, peach-scented wine with medium body and lovely flowery fruit, it is Spain's answer to France's Condrieu, although it is lighter bodied and less unctuous.

The true glories of Marqués de Murrieta are the red wines. The still young and unevolved 1990 Rioja Reserva is dominated by American oak. It offers a healthy dark ruby color as well as a tremendous amount of fruit and purity. Unless you enjoy copious quantities of wood, I recommend cellaring it for another 2–3 years. Like all of these wines, it possesses an ageless quality and will undoubtedly last for 20 years. Because it is a few years older, the 1988 Rioja Reserva's oak is more integrated with the wine's black cherry–scented, rich fruit. There is plenty of suppleness and alcohol, as well as character. The 1982 Rioja Gran Reserva is the first wine from Murrieta's current releases to exhibit complexity. Nineteen eighty-two is a great Rioja vintage. Unfortunately, most of the finest *bodegas'* wines never made it out of Spain. This wine reveals a huge, sweet, nose of black cherry, cedar, spice, and vanillin scents, rich, opulent, full-bodied flavors, stunning concentration, and great length and richness.

The limited bottling Castillo Ygays can be aged in wood for phenomenally long periods. According to Hubrecht Duijker, the 1934 was released into the market after it had been aged 1 year in tank, 35 years in wood, and 5 years in bottle! This is obviously not a *bodega* that believes in rushing its wine to the market! The current releases include the 1987 Castillo Ygay. It is a deep ruby/purple-colored, ripe, dense, concentrated, tannic wine with plenty of spicy notes. The superior 1985 Castillo Ygay is still young, with great fruit, body, and ripeness, as well as a stunning finish. Closer to full maturity, the 1978 Castillo Ygay is a wine of exceptional sweetness, jammy, ripe, black cherry and curranty fruit, gobs of sweet oak, a supple, gorgeously rich, opulent texture, and a chewy, long finish. Another sensational Castillo Ygay is the 1968. It is an extremely dense, concentrated, full-bodied wine with loads of flavor. Less attractive, the 1964 Castillo Ygay exhibits a leafy, high-acid, lean, tart style. While I was shocked by its young color and youthfulness, this vintage lacks the ampleness and generosity of the other Castillo Ygays. A small quantity of 1959 Castillo Ygay has also been released. An outstanding wine, it exhibits a dark ruby/purple color with no amber at the edge, a huge, sweet, oaky, jammy, black cherry– and vanillin-scented nose, voluptuously textured, full-bodied flavors, and super extraction and length.

The moderately priced 1991 Tinto Crianza is a lighter-weight wine than the 1990. Although dominated by toasty, vanillin, spicy oak, it displays rich berry fruit as well as excellent purity and concentration. The 1990 Tinto Crianza displays a dark ruby color, and a fragrant, spicy nose of new oak and gobs of red and black fruits. Full bodied, with copious quantities of jammy black cherry and cassis fruit, with a smooth-as-silk, velvety texture, this seductive wine can be drunk now, although it will mature gracefully for a decade. It has been a long time since I tasted a Rioja this sumptuous for under $20.

BODEGAS LA GRANJA REMELLURI (RIOJA)* * * *

1990 Rioja Reserva	B	89+
1989 Rioja Reserva	B	90

This producer's reputation for high-quality wine is well deserved. Readers who taste the 1989 Rioja Reserva will be turned on by its allegiance to Bordeaux, with its small *barrique*-aged character and opaque purple color, as well as to Rioja, with its wonderful sweetness of fruit. It is an authoritatively flavored, powerful wine that combines high fruit extraction with admirable purity and elegance. It possesses full body, an opaque purple color, a big, impressive bouquet of black cherries and cassis, excellent delineation, and a beefy, rich finish. The wine is accessible because of its superripe fruit, but there is plenty of tannin underlying the layers of extract. This rich, concentrated, impressive wine competes favorably with wines selling for two to three times the price. It should age well for 10–12 years. The

1990 Rioja Reserva has recently been bottled. Largely because of that, it appears more structured, less forthcoming, and more difficult to fully assess. The impressive dark ruby/purple color is followed by a reticent bouquet. With coaxing, the wine displays hints of jammy black currants, smoky new oak, and new saddle leather. There is lovely sweetness from ripe fruit, full body, and considerable tannin, the latter component revealing some toughness in the finish. Cellaring of 1–2 years is clearly required. Given the wine's concentration, it is a candidate for 10+ years of aging. At present, the 1989 is far more flattering and open knit.

LA RIOJA ALTA (RIOJA)* * * */* * * * *

1986 Arana Reserva	C	86
1986 Ardanza Reserva	C	89
1983 Gran Reserva 904	D	90
1978 Gran Reserva 890	D	92
1989 Viña Alberdi Reserva	C	87

Eschewing the modern style of Rioja that is bottled after several years of aging in American oak casks, Rioja Alta remains one of the few Spanish *bodegas* dedicated to making traditionally styled Riojas. While I do not want to denigrate the modern style, there is a lot to be said for wines such as these. They are released when fully mature, yet they hold for a considerable amount of time. These five offerings all demonstrate impeccable winemaking. They possess plenty of sweet, vanillin, smoky new oak, as well as wonderfully ripe, succulent textures.

The 1989 Viña Alberdi Reserva reveals elegant, vanillin, berry scents, lovely, rich, medium-bodied flavors, and a soft, plush finish that lingers on the palate. It is one of the softest, most finesse-filled wines in the Rioja Alta portfolio. The 1986 Arana Reserva offers a complex, cigar box–scented nose, soft, ripe, medium-bodied flavors, a lovely sense of balance, and a sweet finish. Both of these wines should be drunk over the next 5–7 years.

The best bargain in terms of dollars for quality is the Ardanza Reserva. The 1986 exhibits a knockout nose of grilled nuts, smoke, vanillin, and red and black fruits. Concentrated and decadently rich, with a hedonistic suppleness and a heady spiciness to accompany the high glycerin and lusty alcohol in the finish, this is a generous, complex Rioja for drinking over the next decade.

Rioja's Gran Reservas are rare and expensive. The demand for them by the best Spanish restaurants ensures that only tiny quantities leave the country. The 1983 Gran Reserva 904 possesses a Graves-like nose of tobacco, cedar, smoke, and ripe red fruits. Flavorful and rich, yet managing to taste light and elegant, this ripe, concentrated, beautifully made, smooth-as-silk wine is capable of lasting 10 more years. The 1978 Gran Reserva 890 reveals a medium ruby color with considerable amber at the edge. The huge nose of cedar, jam, tobacco, minerals, and smoke is compelling. Sweet, fleshy, and rich, with wonderful harmony among its component parts, this fully mature, rich, chewy wine should drink well for another decade.

SCALA DEI PRIORATO (CATALUNA)* * */* * * *

1989 Negre	A	86

This wine, made from 100% Grenache, has a character not unlike a southern Rhône wine. Reminiscent of a Châteauneuf du Pape, this 1989 Negre possesses a roasted, herb- and berry-scented nose, rich, glycerin-infused, deep, full-bodied flavors, and a lusciously intense, heady, alcoholic finish. Drinkable now, it should age nicely for 5–7 more years.

BODEGAS SIERRA CANTABRIA (RIOJA)* * * *

1991 Codice Rioja	A	86
1989 Codice Rioja	A	87
1990 Sierra Cantabria Crianza	A	87
1987 Sierra Cantabria Crianza Rioja	A	86
1987 Sierra Cantabria Reserva Rioja	A	88
1990 Sierra Cantabria Tinto Joven Rioja	A	85
1993 Sierra Cantabria Tinto Rioja	A	85

The strong point of this *bodega* is its young wines. Older vintages are available, and while they can be good, I have found the more recent vintages to represent the most enticing price/quality rapport. For example, it is hard to beat the 1993 Tinto Rioja for quality and value. It is a dark ruby-colored, spicy wine, with attractive leafy, curranty aromas and flavors, excellent ripeness, medium body, and a moderately long finish. It should drink well for 3–4 years. The richer, more hedonistic 1991 Codice Rioja exhibits a more intense bouquet of smoky vanillin, black cherries, and herbs, more fat, glycerin, and alcohol, as well as a red and black fruit character. This supple, spicy, surprisingly complex and concentrated wine is a steal at $6. Drink it over the next 4–5 years.

The 1990 Crianza (aged for 2 years prior to release) is a terrific bargain. It reveals nicely integrated spicy new oak, an elegant bouquet of tobacco and ripe, curranty and cherrylike fruit, round, spicy, medium-bodied flavors, and a lush, heady finish. Although fully mature, it is capable of lasting for 4–5 years. Slightly more expensive, but still an outstanding value, is Sierra Cantabria's 1987 Reserva Rioja. Made from 90% Tempranillo and 10% Garnacha, this succulently styled Rioja possesses moderately intense new oak in the nose as well as a whiff of lead pencil, loads of ripe red and black fruits, a tasty, medium- to full-bodied, velvety-textured palate, excellent concentration, and a clean, well-defined finish. It should drink well for 4–5 years.

The 1989 Codice Rioja possesses the richest flavors of this trio, as well as excellent ripeness, good purity and complexity, a big, spicy, oaky, richly fruity nose, and a luscious finish. Drink it over the next 2–3 years. The price is unbelievably fair. The 1990 Tinto Joven Rioja has an almost Beaujolais-like nose of bananas and bubble gum. In the mouth, there is good ripeness, a rich, round, generous palate, and a tasty, fruity finish. Drink it over the near term. Lastly, the 1987 Crianza Rioja exhibits more oak than the above two wines, an attractively ripe, berry-scented nose, sweet, velvety-textured flavors, purity and cleanliness, and a spicy, long finish. It should be consumed over the next 3–4 years.

VEGA SICILIA (RIBERA DEL DUERO)* * * * *

1991 Alion Ribera del Duero	EEE	89
N.V. Reserva Especial	EEE	93
1989 Valbuena (Pink Label)	EEE	93

The 1991 Alion Ribera del Duero is the first wine released by this winery since its purchase by Vega Sicilia. Made from 100% Tempranillo and aged in small French oak casks, this is an impressive debut. It offers a rich, sweet, ripe, toasty, black fruit–scented nose, opulent, lush, concentrated, full-bodied flavors, wonderful fatness as a result of high glycerin, and a silky smooth, heady finish. Approachable now, it should age beautifully for 10–12 years.

The 1989 Valbuena is unquestionably the finest Valbuena I have tasted. If this is a forerunner of what we can expect from the 1989 Unico Reserva (not yet released), I can imagine how thrilling that wine must be. The Valbuena displays an opaque dark ruby/purple color, a staggeringly intense nose of sweet, toasty new oak, black cherries, cassis, and fragrant spicy scents. It possesses superb intensity, wonderful opulence, and a full-bodied, luscious finish. As with the other Vega Sicilia offerings, it has immediate appeal, but its extract levels and power suggest it will last for 10–15 years.

From time to time Vega Sicilia releases a superexpensive Riserva Especial, which is a blend of old vintages. The current release is a blend of the 1959, 1960, and 1961 vintages. It is a superb, still youthful wine with a big, smoky, vanillin-currant-scented nose, and rich, full bodied, velvety-textured flavors that linger on the palate. Very impressive, full-bodied, with great purity and richness, this is a staggering yet remarkably youthful wine that should age well for another 20 years.

BODEGAS DE VILARINO-CAMBADOS (RIAS BAIXAS)* * * *

1994 Martin Codax	B 87

This may be the most popular Spanish white wine. Made from the fragrant, exotically perfumed Albarino grape, it is Spain's answer to France's Condrieu. While it does not possess Condrieu's body, glycerin, or fatness, it offers an intense floral perfume with scents of ripe peaches and apricots, fine underlying acidity, medium body, and loads of fruit buttressed by acidity and presented in a pure, clean, well-focused style. Drink it over the next year.

VINICOLA DEL PRIORAT (PRIORATO)* * * *

1993 Onix	A 87
1992 Onix	A 87
1991 Onix Reserva	B 88

All three of these wines, made from Garnacha, Mazuelo, and a tiny quantity of Cabernet Sauvignon, are from the appellation of Priorato. They are full, rich wines made in a style similar to a forceful, beefy, peppery, full-bodied wine from one of the better southern Rhône villages. All are husky, mouth-filling, expansively flavored wines. For example, the 1992 Onix displays an excellent color, a big, sweet, pepper, grapy nose, chewy, rich, lush flavors, and a spicy, velvety-textured finish. The 1993 Onix exhibits more alcohol, as well as jammy cherry notes to accompany its full-bodied, unctuous texture. Not surprisingly, its color is a more saturated ruby/purple. The full-bodied, rich, intense 1991 Onix Reserva boasts layers of attractive black currant and cherry fruit, excellent purity, a touch of spicy wood, and a long, alcoholic, slightly tannic finish. All three of these wines should drink well for 4–5 years.

A VERTICAL TASTING OF SPAIN'S, AND ONE OF THE WORLD'S, GREATEST RED WINES—VEGA SICILIA

Vega Sicilia is Spain's most renowned and expensive red wine. Its top cuvée, called Unico Reserva, is often held for 20 years or more before being released. For example, the 1970, considered to be one of the greatest Vega Sicilias of the century, was just released in 1995. Older vintages of Vega Sicilia are virtually impossible to find outside of a few Spanish wine cellars.

1983 Vega Sicilia Unico Reserva	93

The huge, opaque-colored 1983 Unico Reserva still tastes like a barrel sample. It is fat and grapy, with massive flavor concentration, an expansive, sweet, jammy, black currant fruitiness, spicy oak, and a long, robust, spicy finish. My rating is slightly lower than it was when I tasted this wine last year, but there is no doubting the wine's awesome levels of extract.

Still tasting extremely undeveloped and unevolved, it requires a decade more of cellaring, although its sweetness and great ripeness of fruit make it accessible now.

1982 Vega Sicilia Unico Reserva   94

In contrast to the opaque, dense purple color of the 1983, the 1982 possesses a healthy, medium to dark ruby color. Far more evolved aromatically, the 1982 offers complex, intense scents of new oak, smoke, black and red fruits, and vanilla. Once again, the impression on the palate is one of gorgeously succulent fruit, and a sweet, expansive, ripe wine with an unctuous texture and an explosively rich, generous finish. It can be drunk now or cellared for 20–25 years.

1980 Vega Sicilia Unico Reserva   91

A youthful, healthy, dark ruby/purple color is followed by a less ostentatious and evolved bouquet than is revealed by the 1982. The 1980 displays Unico's telltale lavish, toasty new oak, vanillin, and smoke aromas, as well as earthy, red and black fruit scents. Spicy, dense, and medium to full bodied, with tough tannin in the background, this remains a young, more narrowly constructed and structured wine than either the 1982 or 1983. Cellar it for an additional 3–4 years, and drink it over the subsequent 15–25 years.

1979 Vega Sicilia Unico Reserva   89

This wine has scored higher in previous tastings. In the company of other Unicos, it appears leaner, more backward, and austere. Hard tannin dominates this medium-bodied wine, which exhibits a dark ruby color with a touch of amber at the edge. Closed and spicy, this wine requires 4–5 more years of cellaring. Based on this tasting, the 1979 does not appear to be a candidate for greatness, although this bottle may have been less representative.

1976 Vega Sicilia Unico Reserva   93

The 1976 Unico Reserva offers a smoky, roasted nose indicative of a hot, dry growing season. There are copious quantities of jammy black cherries and sweet, toasty, vanillin oak in the wine's multifaceted, intriguing bouquet. Sweet, lush, opulent fruit cascades across the palate, exhibiting low acidity, generous amounts of glycerin and alcohol, and layers of richness. This full-bodied, large-scaled wine is within 2–3 years of full maturity; it should keep for 20+ years.

1975 Vega Sicilia Unico Reserva   96+

The 1975 vintage has always been one of Vega Sicilia's greatest ones, and this tasting confirmed that the 1975 Unico Reserva has the potential to be one of this historic winery's finest offerings. The wine's beautiful, saturated, dense ruby/purple color is followed by a tight but rich nose of black and red fruits, spices, and toasty oak. Deep, with huge body and massive flavor extraction, this wine combines awesome power and richness with considerable structure and delineation. It appears to be a legendary Vega Sicilia in the making. Although enjoyable to drink now, it will not reach its plateau of maturity for 10–15 years; it will last for 30 or more years.

1974 Vega Sicilia Unico Reserva   90+?

A perplexing wine, the extremely youthful, dark ruby/purple-colored 1974 Unico exhibits a shy, albeit promising nose of smoky, cedary, black cherry fruit, tart, medium- to full-bodied flavors, little tannin, and a more monolithic personality than most Vega Sicilia wines. It remains extremely young. If I had had this wine in a blind tasting, I would have guessed it to be 5–6 years old, not 20. Whether or not it will expand and develop complexity remains my only reservation. Otherwise, it is a rich, pure, well-made, big wine that has not begun to open.

1973 Vega Sicilia Unico Reserva   85

The 1973 displays a mature ruby color with considerable amber at the edge. Soft, ripe flavors are accompanied by annoyingly high acidity, giving the wine a tough, lean, compact feel. Spicy, with ripe fruit and a one-dimensional personality, this wine will keep for 10–15 years, although it did not exhibit a great deal of strength or personality at this tasting.

1972 Vega Sicilia Unico Reserva   87

A spicy, melted-road-tar, earthy, black cherry, and toasty nose is followed by a medium-bodied Vega Sicilia with fine ripeness, attractive sweetness, underlying acidity, and a round, generous finish. The wine's ruby color exhibits slight amber at the edge. Close to full maturity, the 1972 is unlikely to develop into a profound example of Unico.

1970 Vega Sicilia Unico Reserva   96

I have always believed the 1968 (which has just been released in magnum) is the most concentrated and potentially profound Vega Sicilia yet produced. The 1970 falls just a notch below the 1968 in terms of pure extraction. It surpasses the 1968 in its exceptional perfume and seductive, gorgeously textured, voluptuous, and sexy style. The color is a healthy dark ruby. The nose offers up smashingly intense aromas of lavishly oaked, but gorgeously pure black cherries and currants. The wine is full bodied, and nearly sweet tasting because of the fruit's exceptional ripeness. Expansive and deep, with the wood, tannin, and acidity nearly masked by the sheer quantity of fruit, the 1970 Vega Sicilia Unico is a velvety-textured, seamless, rich, profound wine that is more approachable than the 1968, yet along with that legendary wine, remarkably fresh and youthful. It is astonishing that a 25-year-old wine could look, smell, and taste so young, yet also be so complex. No one knows how Vega Sicilia achieves such brilliance, but the proof is in the bottle. This wine is frightfully expensive ($135–$150 per bottle), as well as absurdly rare (most of it is gobbled up by millionaires in Spain and Western Europe), but it is a winemaking tour de force and one of the world's greatest red wines. The 1970 Vega Sicilia Unico should drink well for 15–25 more years.

1969 Vega Sicilia Unico Reserva   85

One of the lightest-bodied wines in this tasting, the 1969 offers a medium ruby/garnet/rust color, followed by sweet, earthy, cedar, and black cherry aromas and flavors. Good concentration, light body, underlying acidity, and a short, compact finish result in a straightforward wine.

1968 Vega Sicilia Unico Reserva   98+

An awesome wine! Judged only by the unevolved, saturated, dense ruby/purple color, this 27-year-old wine could easily be mistaken for a 2-year-old claret. The nose offers up copious aromas of sweet, jammy, black plums, black cherries, and cassis, as well as gorgeous, smoky, vanillin, floral, and licorice scents that tease the olfactory senses with the promise of considerable thrills. Extremely full bodied, massively rich, and unctuous, with layers of jammy fruit, adequate acidity, and moderate tannin, this huge wine's well-focused, structural component keeps everything in balance. There is a freshness, youthfulness, and extraordinary degree of promise in this amazingly young, fabulously concentrated Unico Reserva. It should take its place in wine history beside the greatest clarets of the decade of the sixties. Look for the 1968 Unico to age effortlessly for another 30+ years. An amazing wine!

1966 Vega Sicilia Unico Reserva   95

The most burgundian (that's *great* burgundy, by the way) wine of the tasting, the 1966 Unico Reserva exhibits a huge, fragrant, penetrating bouquet of sweet, jammy, black cherry fruit, cedar, smoke, and earth. The saturated, dark ruby color reveals a hint of amber at the edge. Full bodied, succulent, and velvety, this gorgeously proportioned, decadently styled Vega Sicilia is fully mature, yet its balance, freshness, and thrilling level of flavor extraction suggest it should easily glide through 15–20 more years. If readers have the financial means to drink one fully mature vintage of Vega Sicilia's Unico Reserva, it should be the 1966 or 1953.

1965 Vega Sicilia Unico Reserva   86

A healthy dark ruby color suggested a youthful wine. The tight, uncomplicated nose of wood and ripe fruit left me searching for more nuances and complexity. This lean, medium-bodied, admirably concentrated, foursquare-style Vega Sicilia can be drunk now or cellared for another 10 years. I do not see it evolving into anything more than an above-average-quality wine.

1964 Vega Sicilia Unico Reserva   94

This wine's graceful, spicy, cedary, black currant–scented nose is reminiscent of a classic St.-Julien/Pauillac. Any evidence of new oak has been well concealed by the wine's evolution. Medium to full bodied, with an opulent texture, an attractive, sweet inner core of ripe fruit, and a soft, lightly tannic finish, this fully mature, beautifully made Vega Sicilia admirably balances power and finesse. Drink it over the next 10–15 years.

1962 Vega Sicilia Unico Reserva   95

The 1962 has been a consistently gorgeous wine. In this vertical tasting, the 1962, while fabulously complex, succulent, and rich, tasted less mature and more backward than either the 1964 or the 1966. The wine has lost little of its deep, saturated, dark ruby color. A huge, fragrant bouquet combining jammy red and black fruits, herbs, vanillin, smoke, and cedar is followed by a full-bodied wine with sweet, generous flavors, light tannin, and a finish that lasts for 30–40 seconds. This knockout Unico is fully mature, yet remains fresh, vibrant, and lively. It will last for at least 15–20 more years.

1960 Vega Sicilia Unico Reserva   78?

This is the lowest rating I have ever bestowed on this wine, so perhaps this bottle was not the finest. Certainly the 1960 has never been one of the great Vega Sicilias, but at this tasting, the wine appeared to lack fruit, displayed an earthy, musty-scented nose, and lean, dry, hard, herb-tinged flavors. It was a low-key, straightforward wine without enough fruit or flesh.

1957 Vega Sicilia Unico Reserva   89?

Other tasters were more excited by this wine than I. While it was unquestionably excellent, I thought the lavish quantities of toasty new oak still dominated the wine—even after 38 years! It revealed a solid, medium ruby color, a cedary, vanillin, smoky, frightfully oaky nose, delicate, medium-bodied flavors, and a sweet, ripe finish. The wine appeared to gain strength in the glass and broaden on the palate. Although it was very good, the 1957 was not one of the stars of the tasting.

1955 Vega Sicilia Unico Reserva   78?

Oxidized notes and an absence of fresh fruit suggest this wine has one foot in the grave. Some attractive sweet, toasty, vanillin oak notes remain, but this fragile wine is drying out.

1953 Vega Sicilia Unico Reserva   94

An ethereal bouquet of sweet red and black fruits, flowers, cedar, smoke, and wood soars from the glass. This silky smooth, opulently rich, expansive, generous Vega Sicilia coats the palate with gorgeously ripe fruit, complemented by generous amounts of glycerin and alcohol. The wood has all been absorbed, leaving a complex, elegant, rich wine that is at its apogee. Never having had the 1953 before, it is hard to know what it tasted like 10 years ago, but it remains totally intact and is capable of lasting 10–15 more years.

1948 Vega Sicilia Unico Reserva   86?

My score may be more generous than this wine merits. My tasting notes do not support a rating this high, as I thought the wine to be coarse and tannic, with hot alcohol in the finish. However, it displays a gorgeously complex, fragrant nose of spices and red and black fruits. As the wine sat in the glass, some oxidized notes emerged. High acid and an absence of tannin give the wine a hard, tough, rustic personality. It is a wine with more value at auction than in a consumption sense.

1942 Vega Sicilia Unico Reserva   90

Sweet, rich, wonderfully vibrant, pure red and black fruits combined with smoke and spice result in an enticing wine. Still medium bodied with lively acidity, this fragrant, fully mature yet fresh, well-focused Vega Sicilia has unquestionably stood the test of time.

1939 Vega Sicilia Unico Reserva   55

Disgusting dirty cellar aromas combined with a Madeira-like quality make this wine undrinkable. Was it the bottle, or are all 1939 Unico Reservas this bad?

THE WINES OF NORTH AMERICA

California
Oregon
Washington State

6. CALIFORNIA

The Basics

Virtually every type of wine seen elsewhere in the wine world is made in California. Fortified port-style wines, decadently sweet, late-harvest Rieslings, sparkling wines, and major red and white dry table wines from such super grapes as Chardonnay and Cabernet Sauvignon —all are to be found in California.

GRAPE VARIETIES
The fine wines of California are dominated by Cabernet Sauvignon and Chardonnay, as much of the attention of that state's winemakers is directed at these two grapes. However, California makes wonderful red Zinfandel and increasing amounts of world-class Merlot and Syrah, plus some Petite Sirah. Despite improved quality, Pinot Noir is still a questionable wine in the hands of all but several dozen or so California wine producers. Two notable trends in the late eighties have proven popular with consumers. These include the proliferation of proprietary red wine blends (usually Cabernet Sauvignon–dominated and superexpensive), and the development of authoritatively flavored, robust, supple red wines made from blends of Syrah, Carignane, Grenache, Mourvèdre, and Alicante, collectively referred to as the "Rhône Rangers." As for the white wines, Sauvignon Blanc and Semillon, and blends thereof, can be wonderfully complex and fragrant, but the great majority remain nondescript wines. It is a shame that Chenin Blanc has so little sex appeal among consumers, because it can be a very inexpensive, delicious drink. Colombard and Muscat suffer from the same image problems as Chenin Blanc, but shrewd consumers know the good ones and seek them out. Gewürztraminer and dry Rieslings have been dismal wines, although a handful of wineries have broken through the wall of mediocrity. For years California has made it simple for the consumer, naming its wines after the varietal from which it is made. By law a Chardonnay or Cabernet Sauvignon must contain 75% of that grape in the wine. The recent trend, accompanied by very high prices, has been to produce luxury-priced proprietary wines with awe-inspiring, often silly names such as Dominus, Opus, Rubicon, Trilogy, and Insignia. These wines are supposed to be the winery's very best lots of wine blended together for harmony. Some of them are marvelous. But remember: All of them are expensive and most of them are overpriced.

CLEAR
LAKE

Sacramento

33
34
35

31
32

MONO
LAKE

Stockton

Oakland
San
Francisco
San Mateo
San Jose

13

14 15

Santa Cruz

Monterey

16

Fresno

17
20 19 18

21

Tulare

San Miguel
Paso Robles
22 23

KERN

San Luis Obispo
24
25

Bakersfield

Santa Maria 26

Lompoc 27

PACIFIC

OCEAN

SAN JOAQUIN

Los
Angeles
Santa Ana

N
W E
S

KILOMETERS 0   50   100   150   200
MILES 0   50   100

California

NORTH COAST

1 Anderson Valley
2 Potter Valley
3 McDowell Valley
4 Clear Lake
5 Guenoc Valley
6 Dry Creek Valley
7 Alexander Valley
8 Knights Valley
9 Russian River Valley
10 Sonoma Valley
11 Napa Valley
12 Los Carneros

CENTRAL COAST

13 Livermore Valley
14 Santa Cruz Mountains
15 Santa Clara Valley
16 Mount Harlan
17 Chalone
18 Arroyo Seco
19 Santa Lucia Highlands
20 Carmel Valley
21 San Lucas
22 York Mountain
23 Paso Robles
24 Edna Valley
25 Arroyo Grande
26 Santa Maria Valley
27 Santa Ynez Valley
28 Temecula

INTERIOR

29 Solano County Green Valley
30 Suisun Valley
31 Clarksburg
32 Lodi
33 El Dorado
34 Shenandoah Valley
35 Fiddletown

NEVADA

Death Valley
Junction

MOJAVE

●Barstow

DESERT

San
Bernardino

Palm Springs

28

SALTON
SEA

San
Diego

Flavors

RED WINE VARIETALS

Cabernet Franc   Now being used by more and more wineries to give complexity to a wine's bouquet, Cabernet Franc is a cedary, herbaceous-scented wine that is usually lighter in color and body than either Cabernet Sauvignon or Merlot. It rarely can stand by itself, but used judiciously in a blend, it can provide an extra dimension. Reference-point California wines with significant proportions of Cabernet Franc that have stood the test of time include the 1971 Robert Mondavi Reserve Cabernet, 1977 Joseph Phelps Insignia red wine, La Jota's 1986, 1990, 1991, 1992, and 1993 Cabernet Franc, Dalla Valle's 1990, 1992, 1993, and 1994 Maya (an exquisite wine with nearly 50% Cabernet Franc in the blend), and the Havens Bourriquot (two-thirds Cabernet Franc).

Cabernet Sauvignon   The king of California's red wine grapes, Cabernet Sauvignon, produces densely colored wine with aromas that can include black currants, chocolate, cedar, leather, ground meat, minerals, herbs, tobacco, and tar. Cabernet Sauvignon reaches its pinnacle of success in Napa, Sonoma, and the Santa Cruz Mountains, although a few excellent examples have emanated, infrequently, from Paso Robles, Santa Ynez, and Monterey. The more vegetal side of Cabernet Sauvignon, with intense smells of asparagus and green beans, is found in wines from Monterey or Santa Barbara, two areas that have generally proven too cool for this varietal.

Merlot   If Cabernet Sauvignon provides the power, tannin, and structure, Merlot provides opulence, fatness, higher alcohol, and a lush, chewy texture when crop yields are not too high. It has grown in importance in California. One strong trend is an increased number of wines that are made predominantly from the Merlot grape. Telltale aromas of a top Merlot include scents of plums, black cherries, toffee, tea, herbs, sometimes tomatoes, and a touch of orange. Merlot wines will never have the color density of a Cabernet Sauvignon because the Merlot grape's skin is thinner, but they are lower in acidity and less tannic. The higher alcohol and ripeness result in a fleshy, chewy wine that makes wonderful early drinking. Wines made primarily from Merlot are here to stay. The best examples can challenge the best of France, but far too many remain hollow, frightfully acidified, as well as too tannic and vegetal.

Petite Sirah   Unfortunately, this varietal has fallen from grace. Petite Sirah, in actuality the Duriff grape, is unrelated to the true Syrah, yet it produces almost purple-colored, very tannic, intense wines with peppery, cassis-scented bouquets. The wines age surprisingly well, as 15- to 20-year-old examples have shown a consistent ability to hold their fruit. The complexity and bouquet will rarely be that of a Cabernet or Merlot, but these are important wines. The Petite Sirah grape has adapted well to the warmer microclimates of California.

Pinot Noir   The thin-skinned, fickle Pinot Noir is a troublesome grape for everybody. While California continues to produce too many mediocre, washed-out, pruny, vegetal wines from this varietal, no American region has demonstrated more progress with Pinot Noir than California. Major breakthroughs have been made. While good Pinot Noirs are increasingly noticeable from the North Coast areas of Mendocino, Napa, and Sonoma, fine Pinot Noirs also emanate from further south—the Santa Cruz Mountains, the Monterey area, and Santa Barbara. A good Pinot Noir will exhibit medium to dark ruby color, an intense explosion of aromatics, including red and black fruits, herbs, earth, and floral aromas. Pinot Noir tends to drop what tannin it possesses quickly, so some acidity is important to give it focus and depth. Most Pinot Noirs are drinkable when released. Few evolve and improve beyond 7–8 years in the bottle. Consumers should be particularly apprehensive of any Pinot Noir that tastes too tannic.

Sangiovese   The Italian ancestry of many northern California grape growers and producers is increasingly evident with the number of wineries making Sangiovese. There are significant new plantations of this varietal, which is the most important red wine grape in the pastoral countryside of Tuscany, Italy. It is the predominant grape of most Chiantis and Vino da Tavolas. In California's fertile soils it achieves mind-boggling crop levels—8–12 tons of fruit per acre. Without effective pruning practices or severe crop thinnings, the wines produced are diluted, thin, acidic, and of little interest. However, when the vines are crop-thinned by 40%–50%, the result can be fruity, strawberry/cherry/leather-scented and -flavored wines with medium body and penetrating acidity that is ideal for cutting through tomato-based sauces and working with the fusion Mediterranean/Pacific Rim cuisines found in California and elsewhere. To date, impressive Sangiovese has emerged from such wineries as Staglin Family Vineyards, Swanson, and Ferrari-Carano. The largest plantations are found in the Atlas Peak Vineyard, whose wines have been disappointing to date. Many producers are beginning to add some Cabernet Sauvignon to the blend in order to give the wine more color, body, and depth, as the higher crop yields tend to produce a lighter wine than desired.

Syrah   Syrah is the great red grape varietal of France's Rhône Valley. An increasing number of California wineries have begun to bottle 100% Syrah wines, and some have been exquisite. The style ranges from light, fruity, almost Beaujolais-like wines, to black/ purple-colored, thick, rich, age-worthy, highly extracted wines bursting with potential. A great Syrah will possess a hickory, smoky, tar, and cassis-scented nose, rich, full-bodied, occasionally massive flavors, and considerable tannin. Like Cabernet Sauvignon, a Syrah-based wine is a thoroughbred when it comes to aging, easily lasting for 10–20 or more years. Swanson, Edmunds St. John, Dehlinger, Truchard, Havens and Thackrey have made the most compelling examples.

Zinfandel   Seemingly against all odds, Zinfandel, the red, full-bodied type, is making a fashion comeback. Its reasonable price, combined with its gorgeous, up-front, peppery, berry (cherries, blackberries, and raspberries) nose, spicy fruit, and lush, supple texture have helped to boost its image. Additionally, Zinfandel's burgeoning popularity might be explained by a growing, and may I say healthy trend away from excessively priced glamour wines, particularly the chocolate and vanilla flavors of California's Chardonnay and Cabernet Sauvignon. Zinfandel is grown throughout California, but the best clearly comes from relatively old vines grown on hillside vineyards. Selected vineyards (especially head-pruned old vines) from Napa, the Dry Creek Valley, Sonoma, Sierra Foothills, Paso Robles, and Amador have consistently produced the most interesting Zinfandels. While soil certainly plays an important role (gravelly loam is probably the best), low yields, old vines, and harvesting fully mature, physiologically rather than analytically ripe fruit are even more important. Today, most Zinfandels are made in a medium- to full-bodied, spicy, richly fruity style, somewhat in the image of Cabernet Sauvignon. While there is some backbone and structure, it is usually a wine that consumers can take immediate advantage of for its luscious, rich fruit, and can drink during the first decade of its life. While many Zinfandels can last longer, my experience suggests the wines rarely improve after 7–8 years and are best drunk within that time.

Carignane   A somewhat lowly regarded grape that deserves more attention, some of California's oldest vineyards are planted with Carignane. As wineries such as Trentadue and Cline have proven, where there are old vines, low yields, and full ripeness, the wines can have surprising intensity and richness in a Rhône-like style. There is a dusty earthiness to most Carignane-based wines that goes along with its big, rich, black fruit and spicy flavors.

Alicante Bouchet   Another grape that has fallen out of favor because of its low prestige, its standing remains revered by those who know it well. It yields a black/purple-colored wine with considerable body and richness. It needs time in the bottle to shed its hardness, but when treated respectfully, as the two Sonoma wineries, Trentadue and Topolos, do, this can be an overachieving grape that handsomely repays cellaring. When mature, the wine offers a Châteauneuf du Pape–like array of spicy, earthy flavors, and significant body and alcohol. Coturri has made some monster wines from this grape.

Mourvèdre/Mataro   This variety is making a comeback. Some wineries, such as Edmunds St. John, Cline Cellars, and Sean Thackrey, have turned out fascinating wines from this varietal. Mataro produces a moderately dark-colored wine with a mushroomy-, earthy-, raspberry-scented nose, surprising acidity and tannin, and considerable aging potential.

Flavors

WHITE WINE VARIETALS

Chardonnay   The great superstar of the white wines, Chardonnay at its best can produce majestically rich, buttery wines with seemingly layers of flavors suggesting tropical fruits (pineapples and tangerines), apples, peaches, and even buttered popcorn when the wine has been barrel-fermented. It flourishes in all of California's viticultural districts, with no area having superiority over another. Great examples can be found from Mendocino, Sonoma, Napa, Carneros, Monterey, Santa Cruz, and Santa Barbara. The problem is that of the 600+ California wineries producing Chardonnay, less than 100 make an interesting wine. Crop yields are too high, the wines are manufactured rather than made, and are excessively acidified, making them technically flawless, but lacking bouquet, flavor intensity, and character. The results are tart, vapid wines of no interest. Moreover, the wines have to be drunk within 12 months of the vintage. Another popular trend has been to intentionally leave sizable amounts of residual sugar in the wine while trying to hide part of it with additions of acidity. This cosmetically gives the wine a superficial feel of more richness and roundness, but these wines also crack up within a year of the vintage. Most Chardonnays are mediocre and overpriced, with very dubious aging potentials. Yet they remain the most popular "dry" white wine produced in California.

Chenin Blanc   This maligned, generally misunderstood grape can produce lovely aperitif wines that are both dry and slightly sweet. Most wineries lean toward a fruity, delicate, perfumed, light- to medium-bodied style that pleases increasing numbers of consumers who are looking for delicious wines at reasonable prices. This varietal deserves more attention from consumers.

French Colombard   Like Chenin Blanc, Colombard is a varietal that is rarely accorded much respect. Its charm is its aromatic character and crisp, light-bodied style.

Gewürztraminer   Anyone who has tasted a fine French Gewürztraminer must be appalled by what is sold under this name in California. A handful of wineries, such as Navarro, Z. Moore, and Babcock, have produced some attractive, although subdued Gewürztraminers. The bald truth remains that most California Gewürztraminers are made in a slightly sweet, watery, shallow, washed-out style.

Muscat   There are several Muscat grapes used in California. This is an underrated and underappreciated varietal that produces remarkably fragrant and perfumed wines that are loaded with tropical fruit flavors. They are ideal as an aperitif wine or with desserts.

Pinot Blanc   Pinot Blanc is a more steely, crisper, firmer wine than Chardonnay. In the hands of the best producers it can have considerable richness and intensity. Because it often receives less exposure to aging in new oak casks, the wine possesses more vibrancy and fruit than most Chardonnays.

Pinot Blanc   This grape, a staple of Alsace, France, where it is used to produce richly fruity, but generally straightforward, satisfying wines, has had mixed success in California. Some producers have barrel-fermented it, attempting to produce a large-scale, Chardonnay-style wine, with little success. Chalone is one of the few wineries to have succeeded with this style. In my opinion, Pinot Blanc is best vinified in a manner that emphasizes its intense fruity characteristics, which range from honeyed tangerines and oranges, to a more floral, applelike fruitiness. Pinot Blancs do not typically age well, but they provide immediate appeal and satisfaction in an exuberant yet uncomplicated manner. The finest Pinot Blancs have emerged from Arrowood, Murphy-Goode, Wild Horse, Benziger, and Beringer. Most Pinot Blancs should be drunk within 2–3 years of the vintage, the only exception being those made in a full-bodied, structured style such as Chalone.

Sauvignon Blanc California winemaking has failed miserably to take advantage of this grape. Overcropping, excessive acidification, and a philosophy of manufacturing the wines have resulted in hundreds of neutral, bland, empty wines with no bouquet or flavor. This is unfortunate, because Sauvignon is one of the most food-friendly and flexible wines produced in the world. It can also adapt itself to many different styles of fermentation and upbringing. At its best, the nonoaked examples of this wine possess vivid, perfumed noses of figs, melons, herbs, and minerals, crisp fruit, wonderful zesty flavors, and a dry finish. More ambitious barrel-fermented styles that often have some Semillon added can have a honeyed, melony character, and rich, medium- to full-bodied, grassy, melon and figlike flavors that offer considerable authority. Unfortunately, too few examples of either type are found in California. No viticultural region can claim a monopoly on either the successes or the failures.

Semillon One of the up-and-coming California varietals, on its own, Semillon produces wines with considerable body and creamy richness. It can often be left on the vine, and has a tendency to develop botrytis, which lends itself to making sweet, honeyed, dessert wines. But Semillon's best use is when it is added to Sauvignon, where the two make the perfect marriage, producing wines with considerable richness and complexity.

White Riesling or Johannisberg Riesling Occasionally some great late-harvest Rieslings have been made in California, but attempts at making a dry Kabinett- or Trocken-style Riesling as produced in Germany most frequently result in dull, lifeless, empty wines with no personality or flavor. Most Riesling is planted in soils that are too rich and in climates that are too hot. This is a shame. Riesling is another varietal that could prove immensely popular to the masses.

AGING POTENTIAL

Cabernet Franc: 5–15 years
Cabernet Sauvignon: 5–25 years
Chardonnay: 1–3 years
Chenin Blanc: 1–2 years
Colombard: 1–2 years
Gamay: 2–4 years
Merlot: 5–10 years
Muscat: 1–3 years
Petite Sirah: 5–15 years

Pinot Blanc: 1–3 years
Pinot Noir: 4–7 years
Riesling (dry): 1–2 years
Riesling (sweet): 2–8 years
Sauvignon Blanc: 1–2 years
Semillon: 1–4 years
Sparkling Wines: 2–7 years
Syrah: 5–20 years
Zinfandel: 3–10 years

OVERALL QUALITY LEVEL

The top 3 or 4 dozen producers of Cabernet Sauvignon, Merlot, or proprietary red wines, as well as the 3 dozen or so who produce Chardonnay, make wines that are as fine and as multidimensional as anywhere in the world. However, for well over 17 years my tastings have consistently revealed far too many California wines that are not made, but manufactured. Excessively acidified by cautious oenologists, and sterile-filtered to the point where there is no perceptible aroma, many wines possess little flavor except for the textural abrasiveness caused by shrill levels of acidity and high alcohol, and in the case of the red wines, excessive levels of green, astringent tannins. Producers have tried to hide their excessive crop yields by leaving residual sugar in the finished wine hoping to give the impression of more body. This practice is only a quick fix, as the white wines tend to fall apart 6–9 months after bottling and the red wines taste cloying.

The time-honored philosophy of California winemaking, which includes the obsession with the vineyard as a manufacturing plant; the industrial winemaking in the cellars; and the preoccupation with monolithic, simplistic, squeaky-clean wines that suffer from such strictly controlled technical parameters, is weakening. It is no secret that the principal objective of most California wineries has been to produce sediment-free, spit-polished, stable wines. The means used to attain this goal too frequently eviscerate the wines of their flavor, aromas, personality, and pleasure-giving qualities. But significant changes (especially noticeable in vintages of the nineties) are underfoot.

Only a fool could ignore the fact that California is now producing many of the greatest wines in the world. While most retailers legitimately carp about the microscopic allocations they receive of the limited-production gems from the most fashionable wineries, it is obvious that California wine quality is surging to greater and greater heights.

Why am I so bullish on California wines? Consider the following:

1. California has had 5 consecutive vintages of largely dazzling quality. Starting with 1990, every vintage has provided that state's growers with enough high-quality fruit to turn out numerous sensational wines. The 1991 vintage is unquestionably a great one for red wines, less so for the whites. The 1992 vintage produced rich, opulently styled red and white wines. The most perplexingly irregular of the last five vintages is 1993. However, the top red and white 1993s can be sensational in a more restrained and classic fashion than 1992, 1991, and 1990. And now readers can add 1994, the fifth straight great year for California.

What does a reasonably intelligent person make of this? California is in a position to dominate the American fine wine scene for the next 3–4 years. The 1994 vintage looks to be an especially exceptional one, with some Cabernet producers, borrowing a little hyperbole from the French, calling it the vintage of the century. The 1994 output is likely to be more mixed for Chardonnay and Pinot Noir producers in Carneros, and especially in Santa Barbara, areas most negatively impacted by the heavy rains that fell in early October.

2. Even more important than the 5 consecutive vintages of outstanding quality is the shift in mind-set of many top wine producers. I have had little help from my colleagues in attempting to change the industrial/food-processor mentality espoused by the University of California at Davis. For as long as I can remember, this school of thought resulted in sterile, frightfully acidic, nearly undrinkable harsh and hollow wines that, amazingly, garnered raves from segments of the West Coast wine press. Large, highly influential wineries such as Robert Mondavi, Beringer, Newton, and now Sterling are fully cognizant of how much damage was wrought by such an antiwine philosophy, designed largely for the standardization of bulk wine production. Handcrafted wines that reflected the *terroir*, vintage, and varietal, in addition to providing immense pleasure, have had an enormous influence on others. A decade ago it was distressing to see the number of wineries that automatically, without any thought whatsoever, compromised and in many cases destroyed a wine by blind faith in the following techniques: (a) by harvesting grapes based on analytical rather than physiological ripeness; (b) by adding frightfully high levels of tartaric acid to the fermenting juice because it was the "risk-free" thing to do; (c) by processing the youthful grape juice utilizing centrifuges and filters that eviscerated and purified the wine before it had a chance to develop any personality; (d) by prefiltering wine intensely before it was allowed to go to barrel; and (e) by fining and sterile-filtering everything as a rule of thumb so that a wine had no aromatics and nothing but a monolithic personality. The adoption of a less-traumatic

and less-interventionalistic wine philosophy, emphasizing the importance of the vineyard's fruit and preserving its characteristics, is increasingly widespread. The results are increasing quantities of compellingly rich, natural-tasting, unprocessed wines that should be causing French wine producers to shudder. And while many wineries continue to fight this trend toward higher-quality, more-natural wines, often with considerable support from a gullible wine press, the fact is that you, the wine consumer, are the beneficiary!

3. As financially devastating as the phylloxera epidemic has been for California viticulture, the silver lining is that the replanting of vineyards over the last decade has addressed important issues that key industry personnel refused to acknowledge as being important prior to this epidemic. Many new vineyards have been planted with tighter spacing, thus making the vines struggle. The result is deeper root systems and vines that produce lower quantities of higher-quality grapes. Additionally, the problem of varietals planted in the wrong soils and/or microclimates can be rectified by these new plantations. Superior rootstocks and less productive clones that produce smaller crops with more individual character are other positive results of the phylloxera epidemic. As time passes, it will become evident that the mistakes made in the forties, fifties, and sixties have been largely corrected, ironically because of phylloxera. If the grapes from these new vineyards are markedly superior, as they should be, it takes no genius to realize that wine quality will also improve.

4. The influence of the French, combined with a new generation of well-traveled, open-minded, revisionist California winemakers, must also be given credit for the remarkable progress in quality. California wines are as rich as they have ever been, but they no longer possess the heaviness of those great vintages of the sixties and seventies. Do readers realize why the finest French cuisine and French wines are cherished throughout the world as standards of reference? Because France, in both her cooking and her wines, achieves, at the highest level of quality, extraordinary intensity of flavor without weight or heaviness. Call this elegance, harmony, finesse, or whatever, but it is what I now detect in increasing numbers of California's finest wines.

1995–1996 BUYING STRATEGY

After erratic, so-so years in 1988 and 1989, California is on a roll, with terrific vintages in 1990, 1991, 1992, 1993, and 1994. There are an unprecedented 5 years in a row where most of the state's producers have turned out wines that were made from ripe fruit. Only the top producers who keep crop yields to a minimum and refuse to excessively manipulate and process their wines will turn out the best wines, but it is clearly a time to be buying California wines. The pipeline is filled with 5 top vintages!

The best California buys continue to be the Rhône Ranger blends and Zinfandels for red wines, and when you can find them, the good Chenin Blancs, Sauvignon Blancs, and Colombards for white wines.

VINTAGE GUIDE

1994—Many Cabernet Sauvignon, Zinfandel, and Syrah producers are calling this the vintage of the century. September rains caused a few problems in Santa Barbara, the Central Coast, and Carneros, but the cool, extremely long growing season was ideal for all red wine varietals. This should be an exceptional year, especially in Napa, Sonoma, and Mendocino. My early tastings confirmed a high promise, especially for the north coast Cabernets.

1993—If the 1993s are not as dramatic as the finest 1994s, 1992s, 1991s, and 1990s, they are by no means inferior. This is another rich, velvety-textured vintage for red wines, and a beautifully balanced year for whites. This vintage has been criticized for reasons I am unable to understand, but there are many great wines.

1992—An abundant crop was harvested that ranged from very good to superb in quality. When Mother Nature is as generous as she was in most viticultural regions in 1992, the potential high quality can be diluted by excessive crop yields and harvesting grapes that are not physiologically mature. However, the top producers have turned out fat, rich, opulent, low-acid, dramatic wines. The white wines need to be drunk up. The finest reds are flattering and richly fruity, and will keep for 10–20 years.

1991—A cool, surprisingly long growing season resulted in potentially excessive crop yields. However, those producers who had the patience to wait out the cool weather and harvest fully mature fruit, as well as to keep their yields down, made some superb red wines that will compete with the finest 1994s, 1993s, 1992s, 1990s, 1987s, 1986s, 1985s, and 1984s. For all the red wine varietals it is a splendid year, with many producers expressing a preference for their 1991s because of the incredibly long hang-time on the vine. The 1991 vintage produced an enormous crop of good white wines that should be consumed by the end of 1995.

1990—For Cabernet Sauvignon, Zinfandel, and other major red wine varietals, 1990 was a mild growing season. The crop was moderate in size, particularly when compared with 1991 and 1992. The wines are concentrated, rich, and well made. It was a banner year for California's top red wines. For Chardonnay, it was a super year, but most of these wines should have been consumed by mid-1994.

1989—What started off as a promising vintage was spoiled by significant September rains that arrived before most producers were able to harvest. There is no question that the better drained hillside vineyards suffered less dilution than the vineyards on the valley floors. In addition, those producers who had the foresight to wait out the bad weather were awarded with some beautifully hot, Indian summer weather that lasted through much of October. Virtually everything, both white and red, was harvested during or immediately after the rains, resulting in diluted and problematic wines. Those wines (1) from well-drained hillside vineyards; (2) from producers who waited for the rains to stop; (3) from producers who gave their vineyards a chance to throw off the excess moisture; and (4) from those who waited sufficient time for the grapes to replenish their acids and sugars, made fine wines that will suffer only because of the general mediocre reputation of this vintage. Certainly all of the white wines from 1989 should have been consumed by now. Some excellent to outstanding red wines were produced, but selection is critical.

1988—A cooler-than-normal summer had an impact on the concentration levels of most of the red wines. However, the top Cabernet Sauvignons and Zinfandels, as well as other red wine varietals, were not without some charm and pleasure. They are soft, up-front, consistent wines that lack depth and aging potential. Most California 1988 red wines should be drunk by 1998. The 1988 vintage was a better one for Chardonnay and Sauvignon, but if you have any stocks languishing in your wine cellar, their time may already have passed.

1987—This has turned out to be more mixed than I initially believed, but there is no question that even at the bottom level of the quality hierarchy the wines are at least good. At the top level, there are many outstanding red wines, particularly Zinfandel and Cabernet-based wines that show superb color, wonderful richness, and considerable aromatic dimension. While some wines resemble the soft, forward, precocious 1984s, others have the structure and depth of the finest 1985s. The best producers have made wines with considerable richness and the potential for 10–15 more years of aging. Along with 1990 and 1991, 1987 is one of the finest Zinfandel vintages in the last 2 decades.

1986—Overshadowed by the resounding acclaim for 1985, 1986 has produced rich, buttery, opulent Chardonnays that have lower acidities than the 1985s, but frequently more fruit and plumpness. The best examples should have been drunk up (Mount Eden, Chalone, and Stony Hill being three exceptions). The red wines follow a similar pattern, exhibiting a rich, ripe, full-bodied character with generally lower acids than the nearly perfect 1985s, but also more tannins and body. It appears to be an excellent year for red wines that should age quite well.

1985—On balance, this should still turn out to be the finest vintage for California Cabernet Sauvignon between 1974 and 1990. An ideal growing season preceded near-perfect conditions for harvesting, especially in Napa and Sonoma, followed by Santa Cruz and Mendocino. The Cabernets are both rich and long-lived. While less extroverted and opulent in their youth than the 1984s, they are certainly longer-lived. Revisionists have begun to question the relatively high acidity and lean, compact, evolutionary stage many of the wines are going through in 1995/1996, but this should be temporary. The finest wines are superrich, but less showy and dramatic than most people expect from California Cabernet. It is a slow-developing year for sure!

1984—An excellent year, somewhat overshadowed by 1985, 1984 was one of the hottest years on record, with temperatures frequently soaring over 100 degrees Fahrenheit during the summer. An early flowering and early harvest did create problems, as many grape varietals ripened at the same time. The style of the Chardonnays and Cabernets is one of very good to excellent concentration, an engaging, opulent, forward fruitiness that gives the wines appeal in their infancy, but good overall balance. Mendocino is less successful than elsewhere, but the ripe, rich, forward character of the wines of this vintage gives them undeniable charm and character. The majority of winemakers call 1985 a more classic year, 1984 a more hedonistic and obvious year. Recent tastings of the top 1984 Cabernets have shown wines that are all drinking splendidly now and should continue to hold their fruit for at least another decade. The top red wines are splendidly rich and dramatic, and more impressive in 1995 than the more ballyhooed 1985s. Only a handful of the white wines still retain their fruit.

1983—An average year for most of California's viticultural regions, although the Chardonnays from Napa were very good—but most are now too old. The Cabernets are medium bodied, rather austere, and lack the flesh and richness found in top years. Nevertheless, some stars are to be found (i.e., Hess Collection Reserve, Opus One, Château Montelena, and Dunn). The red wines will keep for at least another 2–4 years.

1982—The growing season was plagued by heavy rains, then high temperatures. The press seemed to take a cautionary approach to the vintage, and as it turns out, justifiably so. Sonoma is more consistent than Napa, and Santa Cruz is surprisingly weak in 1982. The Sonoma red wines are ripe, rich, very forward, and much more interesting than those of Napa, which range in quality from outstanding to out of balance. The Chardonnays were mediocre, diluted, and lacking depth and acidity.

1981—Like 1984, it was a torridly hot growing season that had all varietals ripening at once. The harvest commenced early. Many fine, ripe, rich, dramatic Chardonnays were produced, but they should have been drunk up by 1987. The Cabernets are good rather than exciting, with the best of them having another 2–4 years of life. Most 1981 Cabernets, because of their forward character, should be drunk before 1997.

1980—A relatively long, cool growing season had wineries predicting a classic, great vintage. The Cabernets are very good, but hardly great. The Cabernets do, however, have good acidity levels and seem by California standards to be evolving rather slowly. This is a vintage that has a top-notch reputation, but in reality appears to be a very fine rather than a monumental year.

OLDER VINTAGES

Since I fervently believe California's Chardonnays and Sauvignon Blancs rarely hold their fruit or improve after 3 years, older vintages are of interest only with respect to California red wines, principally Cabernet Sauvignon.

1979—This year produced a good vintage of tannic, well-endowed wines that are now fully mature.

1978—An outstanding vintage (and a very hot year) that produced concentrated, rich, plummy, dense wines that have aged well. The best examples should continue to offer splendid drinking for at least another 10–15 years. This has turned out to be a great year for California Cabernet.

1977—An above-average vintage that rendered elegant, fruity, supple wines that are now just beginning to tire a bit.

1976—A hot, drought year in which production yields per acre were very small. The wines are very concentrated and tannic, sometimes out of balance. Nevertheless, the great examples from this vintage (where the level of fruit extract matches the ferocity of the tannins) should prove to be among the longest-lived Cabernets of this generation. Despite irregularity here, there are some truly splendid Cabernets.

1975—A cool year, most authorities consider the wines rather hollow and short-lived. However, some magnificent examples have emerged from this vintage that should last for another 10–15 years. As a general rule, most 1975 California Cabernets should be consumed over the next 4–5 years.

1974—One of the great blockbuster years for California Cabernet, as well as a year that introduced many American consumers to the potential for full-bodied, rich, complex wines from the best wineries. While many have criticized the wines for aging erratically and quickly, the best 1974s exhibit a richness, voluptuousness, and intensity that recalls such vintages as 1984, 1987, and 1990. Some of the top 1974s are not yet ready for prime-time drinking. However, this is a vintage that must be approached with caution on the auction market because of the potential for badly stored, abused bottles. Additionally, there are some major disappointments from big names.

1973—A large crop was harvested after a moderately warm, but not hot summer. The quality is uneven, but the wines are well balanced, with many having the potential for long aging.

1972—A rain-plagued vintage, much like 1989, it is almost impossible to find any successes that have survived 20 years of cellaring.

1970, 1969, 1968, 1958, 1951—All great vintages.

Where to Find California's Best Wine Values

(Wineries That Can Be Counted On for Value)

Alderbrook (Sauvignon Blanc, Chardonnay)

Amador Foothill Winery (white Zinfandel)

Arrowood Domaine du Grand Archer (Chardonnay, Cabernet Sauvignon)

Bel Arbors—Fetzer (Zinfandel, Sauvignon Blanc, Merlot)

Belvedere (Chardonnay cuvées)

Beringer (Knights Valley Chardonnay, Sauvignon Blanc, Meritage white, Gamay Beaujolais)

Bonny Doon (Clos de Gilroy, Ca' Del Solo cuvées, Pacific Rim Riesling)

Buehler (Zinfandel)

Carmenet (Colombard)

Cline (Côtes d'Oakley)

Duxoup (Gamay, Charbono)

Edmunds St.-John (New World and Port o'Call reds, Pinot Grigio and El Niño whites)

Estancia (Chardonnay cuvées, Meritage red)

Fetzer (Sundial Chardonnay)

Franciscan (Merlot, Chardonnay)

Guenoc (Petite Sirah, Zinfandel)

Hacienda (Chenin Blanc)

Hess Collection (Hess Select Chardonnay, Cabernet Sauvignon)

Husch Vineyard (Chenin Blanc, Gewürztraminer, La Ribera Red)

Kendall-Jackson (Vintner's Reserve Chardonnay, Fumé Blanc, Vintner's Reserve Zinfandel)

Kenwood (Sauvignon Blanc)

Konocti (Fumé Blanc)

Laurel Glen (Counterpoint and Terra Rosa proprietary red wines)

Liberty School—Caymus (Cabernet Sauvignon, Sauvignon Blanc, Chardonnay)

J. Lohr (Gamay, Cypress Chardonnay)

Marietta Cellars (Old Vine Red, Zinfandel, Cabernet Sauvignon)

Mirassou (white burgundy—Pinot Blanc)

Robert Mondavi (the Woodbridge wines are fine bargains)

Monterey Vineyard (Classic cuvées of Merlot, Cabernet Sauvignon, Chardonnay, Sauvignon Blanc, and Zinfandel, generic Classic White and Classic Red)

Moro Bay Vineyards (Chardonnay)

Mountain View Winery (Sauvignon Blanc, Chardonnay, Pinot Noir, Zinfandel)

Murphy-Goode (Fumé Blanc)

Napa Ridge—Beringer (Chardonnay, Sauvignon Blanc)

Newton (Claret Proprietary Red Wine)

Parducci (Sauvignon Blanc)

Robert Pecota (Gamay)

J. Pedroncelli (Sauvignon Blanc, Zinfandel, Cabernet Sauvignon)

Joseph Phelps (Vins du Mistral cuvées)

R. H. Phillips (Night Harvest cuvées of Chardonnay and Sauvignon Blanc)

Preston (Cuvée du Fumé)

Ravenswood (Zinfandel and Merlot Vintner's blends)

Château Souverain (Chardonnay, Merlot, Cabernet Sauvignon, Sauvignon Blanc)

Stratford (the Chardonnay and Canterbury line of wines, particularly Chardonnay and Sauvignon Blanc)

Ivan Tamas (Trebbiano, Fumé Blanc, and Chardonnay)

Topolos (Grand Noir Proprietary Red Wine, Zinfandel, Alicante Bouschet)

Trentadue (Old Patch Red, Zinfandel, Carignane, Sangiovese, Petite Sirah, Merlot, N.V. Alexander Valley red, Salute Proprietary Red Wine)

Westwood (Barbera)

RATING CALIFORNIA'S BEST PRODUCERS OF CABERNET SAUVIGNON, MERLOT, OR BLENDS THEREOF

* * * * * (OUTSTANDING)

Araujo Estate Cabernet Sauvignon Eisele Vineyard (Napa)

Beringer Chabot Vineyard (Napa)

Beringer Merlot Bancroft Vineyard (Napa)

Beringer Private Reserve (Napa)

Don Bryant (Napa)

Caymus Special Selection (Napa)

Colgin-Schrader Lamb Vineyard (Napa)

Conn Valley Vineyard (Napa)

Dalla Valle (Napa)

Dalla Valle Maya Proprietary Red Wine (Napa)

John Daniel Society (Napa)

Dunn (Napa)

Dunn Howell Mountain (Napa)

Ferrari-Carano Reserve Red Proprietary Wine (Sonoma)

Fisher Coach Insignia (Sonoma) (since 1991)

Fisher Lamb Vineyard (Napa) (since 1992)

Fisher Merlot RCF Vineyard (Napa) (since 1992)

Fisher Wedding Vineyard (Sonoma) (since 1992)

Grace Family Vineyard (Napa)

Harlan Estate Proprietary Red Wine (Napa)

Hartwell Stag's Leap (Napa)

Hess Collection Reserve (Napa)

La Jota Anniversary Cuvée (Napa)

Laurel Glen (Sonoma)

Matanzas Creek Merlot (Sonoma)

Peter Michael Les Pavots Proprietary Red Wine (California)

Robert Mondavi Reserve (Napa) (since
  1987)
Château Montelena Estate (Napa)
Newton Merlot (Napa)
Joseph Phelps Insignia Proprietary Red
  Wine (Napa)
Ravenswood Pickberry Proprietary Red
  Wine (Sonoma)

Ridge Monte Bello (Santa Cruz Mountain)
Shafer Hillside Select (Napa) (since 1991)
Silver Oak (Alexander Valley)
Silver Oak (Napa)
Simi Reserve (Sonoma) (since 1986)
Stag's Leap Cask 23 Proprietary Red Wine
  (Napa)
Philip Togni (Napa)

* * * * (EXCELLENT)

Arrowood (Sonoma)
Bellerose Merlot (Sonoma)
Black and Blue Proprietary Red Wine
  (Napa)****/*****
Clos Pegase Hommage Proprietary Red
  Wine (Napa)
B. R. Cohn Olive Hill Vineyard (Sonoma)
Coturri Jessandre Vineyard (Sonoma)
Coturri Merlot Feingold Vineyard
  (Sonoma)
Coturri Remick Ridge Vineyard (Sonoma)
Coturri View's Land Vineyard (Sonoma)
Dehlinger Bordeaux Blend (Sonoma)
Durney Reserve (Monterey)****/*****
Elyse Morisoli Vineyard (Napa)
Étude (Napa)
Far Niente (Napa)
Gary Farrell Ladi's Vineyard (Sonoma)
Gary Farrell Merlot Ladi's Vineyard
  (Sonoma)
Ferrari-Carano (Sonoma) (since 1991)
Ferrari-Carano Merlot (Sonoma) (since
  1991)
Flora Springs Reserve (Napa) (since 1991)
Flora Springs Trilogy Proprietary Red
  Wine (Napa) (since 1991)
Forman (Napa)
Foxen (Santa Barbara)
Franciscan Meritage Oakville Estate
  (Napa)
Gainey Cabernet Franc Limited Selection
  (Santa Ynez)
Geyser Peak Estate Reserve (Sonoma)
Geyser Peak Reserve Alexandre
  Proprietary Red Wine (Sonoma)
Girard (Napa)
Girard Reserve (Napa)
Harrison Winery (Napa)
Havens Bourriquot (Napa)
Havens Merlot Reserve (Napa)
Heitz Bella Oaks (Napa)

Heitz Martha's Vineyard (Napa) (prior to
  1986 a 5-star wine)
Hess Collection (Napa)
Paul Hobbs Hyde Vineyard (Sonoma)
Jaeger-Inglewood Merlot Inglewood
  Vineyard (Napa)
Justin Cabernet Franc (Paso Robles)
Justin Cabernet Sauvignon (Paso Robles)
Justin Isosceles Proprietary Red Wine
  (Paso Robles)
Justin Merlot (Paso Robles)
Kendall-Jackson Cardinale Meritage
  Proprietary Red Wine (California) (since
  1991)
Kendall-Jackson Grand Reserve
  (California) (since 1991)
Kenwood Artists Series (Sonoma)
Kenwood Jack London Vineyard (Sonoma)
La Jota (Napa)****/*****
La Jota Cabernet Franc (Napa)****/*****
Laurel Glen Terra Rosa (Sonoma)
Marietta (Sonoma)
Merryvale Profile Proprietary Red Wine
  (Napa)
Robert Mondavi Oakville Unfiltered (Napa)
Monticello Corley Reserve (Napa)
Newton (Napa)****/*****
Opus One (Napa)****/*****
Page Mill Volker Eisele Vineyard (Napa)
Pahlmeyer Jayson Proprietary Red Wine
  (Napa)
Peachy Canyon (Paso Robles)
Joseph Phelps Backus Vineyard (Napa)
Pride Mountain Vineyards (Napa)
Rancho Sisquoc Cellar Select Red Estate
  (Santa Maria)
Ravenswood Merlot Sangiacomo (Sonoma)
Rochioli Reserve Neona's Vineyard
  (Sonoma)
Rockland (Napa)****/*****
Rubicon Proprietary Red Wine (Napa)

St. Francis Reserve (Sonoma)
St. Francis Merlot Reserve (Sonoma)
Santa Cruz Mountain Merlot (Santa Ynez)
Seavey (Napa)****/*****
Selene Merlot (Napa)
Shafer Merlot (Napa)
Signorello Founder's Reserve (Napa)
Silver Oak Bonny's Vineyard (Napa)
   (discontinued after 1992)****/*****
Silverado Limited Reserve (Napa)
Château Souverain Winemaker's Reserve
   (Sonoma)
Spotteswoode (Napa)
Spring Mountain Estate Chevalier
   Vineyard (Napa)
Stag's Leap Fay Vineyard
   (Napa)****/*****
Stag's Leap Wine Cellars Stag's Leap
   Vineyard (Napa)

Staglin (Napa)
Sterling Diamond Mountain Ranch (Napa)
   (since 1992)
Stonestreet Legacy Proprietary Red Wine
   (Alexander Valley)
Swanson (Napa)
Swanson Merlot (Napa)****/*****
Tudal (Napa)
Tulocay (Napa)
Viader Proprietary Red Wine (Napa)
Villa Mt. Eden Signature Series
   (Mendocino)
Vine Cliff Cellars (Napa)
Von Strasser (Napa)
White Rock Claret Proprietary Red Wine
   (Napa)
Whitehall Lane Morisoli (Napa)
ZD Estate (Napa)

* * * (GOOD)

Ahlgren Bates Ranch (Santa Cruz)
Ahlgren Besson Vineyard (Santa Cruz)
Alexander Valley (Sonoma)
Amizetta Vineyards (Napa)
S. Anderson (Napa)
Arrowood Merlot (Sonoma)
Barnett Spring Mountain (Napa)***/****
Barnett Spring Mountain Rattlesnake Hill
   (Napa)***/****
Beaulieu Cabernet Sauvignon Private
   Reserve (Napa)***/****
Bellerose Cuvée Bellerose (Sonoma)
Benziger (Glen Ellen)
Benziger Tribute (Glen Ellen)
Beringer Knight's Valley (Napa)
Boeger (El Dorado)
Boeger Merlot (El Dorado)
Brutocao Albert Vineyard (Mendocino)
Brutocao Merlot (Mendocino)
Buehler (Napa)***/****
Burgess Cellars Vintage Selection (Napa)
Cain Cellars Cain Five Proprietary Red
   Wine (Napa)
Cain Cellars Merlot (Napa)
Carmenet Proprietary Red Wines (Sonoma)
Caymus (Napa)***/****
Chalk Hill (Sonoma)***/**** (since 1990)
Château Chèvre Merlot (Napa)
Cinnabar (Santa Cruz)***/****
Clos du Bois (Sonoma)

Clos du Bois Briarcrest (Sonoma)
Clos du Bois Marlstone (Sonoma)
Clos du Bois Merlot (Sonoma)
Clos Pegase (Napa) (since 1992)
Clos Pegase Merlot (Napa) (since 1992)
Clos du Val Merlot (Napa)
Clos du Val Reserve (Napa)
Cloverdale Ranch Estate (Alexander
   Valley)***/****
Cooper-Garrod Cabernet Franc (Santa
   Cruz)
Cooper-Garrod Cabernet Sauvignon (Santa
   Cruz)
Corison (Napa)
Cosentino (Napa)
Cuvaison (Napa)
Cuvaison Merlot (Napa)
Dehlinger (Sonoma)
Dehlinger Merlot (Sonoma)
Dry Creek Meritage (Sonoma)
Duckhorn (Napa)
Duckhorn Merlot (Napa)
Duckhorn Merlot 3 Palms Vineyard (Napa)
Durney (Monterey)
Eberle (Paso Robles)
Estancia (Alexander Valley)
Estancia Meritage Proprietary Red Wine
   (Alexander Valley)
Estancia Merlot (Alexander Valley)
Far Niente (Napa)

Gary Farrell (Sonoma)
Fetzer Barrel Select (California)
Field Stone Alexander Valley (Sonoma)
Field Stone Reserve (Sonoma)
Firestone (Santa Ynez)
Firestone Reserve (Santa Ynez)
Firestone Vintage Reserve Proprietary Red
  Wine (Santa Ynez)
Louis Foppiano Fox Mountain Reserve
  (Sonoma)
Franciscan Oakville Estate (Napa)
Franciscan Merlot (Napa)
Frog's Leap (Napa)
Frog's Leap Merlot (Napa)
Gainey Cabernet Franc (Santa Barbara)
Gainey Merlot Limited Selection (Santa
  Barbara)***/****
E. & J. Gallo Estate (Sonoma)
E. & J. Gallo Private Reserve (Sonoma)
Grgich Hills Merlot (Napa)
Groth Merlot (Napa)
Groth Reserve (Napa) (*****before 1987)
Gundlach-Bundschu Cabernet Franc
  (Sonoma)
Gundlach-Bundschu Rhinefarm Vineyard
  (Sonoma)
Hanna (Sonoma)
Harbor Winery (Sacramento)
Havens Wine Cellar Merlot (Napa)
Heitz (Napa)
Homewood (Alexander Valley)
Husch (Mendocino)
Husch Estate La Ribera (Mendocino)
Iron Horse Cabernets Proprietary Red
  Wine (Sonoma)
Johnson-Turnbull (Napa)
Johnson-Turnbull Vineyard
  Selection 67***/****
Jordan (Sonoma)
Judd's Hill (Napa)***/****
Kalin Cellars Reserve (Marin)
Robert Keenan (Napa)
Robert Keenan Merlot (Napa)
Kathryn Kennedy (Santa Clara)
Kenwood (Sonoma)
Klein Vineyards (Santa Cruz)
La Jota Little J (Napa)
Laurel Glen Counterpoint (Sonoma)
Liberty School (California)
Livingston Moffett Vineyard
  (Napa)***/****

J. Lohr VS-1 (Paso Robles)
Long (Napa)
Longoria (Santa Ynez)
Longoria Cabernet Franc (Santa Ynez)
Longoria Merlot (Santa Ynez)
Maacama Creek Melim Vineyard (Sonoma)
Madrone (El Dorado)
Madrone Cabernet Franc (El Dorado)
Madrone Quintet Reserve Red Table Wine
  (El Dorado)
Michel-Schlumberger (Dry Creek)
Robert Mondavi Napa (Napa)
Château Montelena Calistoga Cuvée
  (Napa)
Monterey Vineyards Classic Cabernet
  Sauvignon (California)
Monterey Vineyards Classic Merlot
  (California)
Monterey Vineyards Classic Red
  (California)
Monticello Cellars Jefferson Cuvée (Napa)
Monticello Cellars Merlot (Napa)
Mount Eden (Santa Clara)***/****
Murphy-Goode Merlot (Sonoma)
Murrieta's Well Vendimia Proprietary Red
  Wine (Livermore)
Napa Ridge (Napa)
Nelson Estate Cabernet Franc (Napa)
Newton Claret (Napa)
Niebaum-Coppola Estates Rubicon (Napa)
Oakville Ranch (Napa)
Peachy Canyon Merlot (Paso Robles)
J. Pedroncelli Reserve
  (Sonoma)***/****
Robert Pepi Vine Hill Ranch (Napa)
Joseph Phelps (Napa)***/****
Joseph Phelps Eisele Vineyard (Napa)
  (between 1987 and 1990) (*****before
  1987)
Joseph Phelps Merlot (Napa)
Pine Ridge Andrus Reserve
  (Napa)***/****
Pine Ridge Diamond Mountain
  (Napa)***/****
Pine Ridge Merlot (Napa)***/****
Pine Ridge Rutherford Cuvée
  (Napa)***/****
Pine Ridge Stag's Leap District
  (Napa)***/****
Rabbit Ridge Proprietary Red
  Wine***/****

A. Rafanelli (Sonoma)

Rancho Sisquoc Cabernet Franc (Santa Barbara)

Rancho Sisquoc Estate (Santa Barbara)

Rancho Sisquoc Merlot Estate (Santa Barbara)

Ravenswood (Sonoma)

Ravenswood Merlot Vintner's Blend (North Coast)

Raymond Private Reserve (Napa)

Renaissance (Yuba)

Ridge Santa Cruz (Santa Clara)

Ritchie Creek (Napa)

J. Rochioli (Sonoma)***/****

Rocking Horse (Napa)

St. Clement (Napa) (since 1991)

St. Clement Oroppas (Napa)***/****

St. Francis Merlot (Sonoma)

Santa Cruz Mountain Bates Ranch (Santa Cruz)***/****

Sebastiani single-vineyard cuvées (Sonoma)

Shafer Stag's Leap (Napa)

Signorello Unfined/Unfiltered (Napa)***/****

Silverado (Napa)

Silverado Merlot (Napa)

Simi (Sonoma)

Château Souverain (Sonoma) (since 1990)

Château Souverain Merlot (Sonoma)

Spring Mountain Estate Miravalle Vineyard (Napa)

Stag's Leap Wine Cellars (Napa)

Stonestreet (Alexander Valley)

Stonestreet Merlot (Alexander Valley)

Stratford Merlot (Napa)

Tantalus (Sonoma)

The Terraces (Napa)

Trefethen Reserve (Napa)

Trentadue (Sonoma)

Trentadue Merlot (Sonoma)***/****

Truchard Merlot (Napa)

Vichon (Napa)

Vichon Merlot (Napa)

Vichon Stag's Leap District (Napa)

Vita Nova Cabernet Franc (Santa Barbara)

Whitehall Lane (Napa)

Whitehall Lane Merlot Summer's Ranch (Alexander Valley)

Whitehall Lane Reserve (Napa)***/****

* * (AVERAGE)

Alexander Valley Vineyard Merlot (Sonoma)**/***

Austin Cellars (Santa Barbara)

Bargetto (Santa Cruz)

Beaulieu Beau Tour (Napa)**/***

Beaulieu Rutherford (Napa)**/***

Bel Arbors (California)

Bel Arbors Merlot (California)

Belvedere Wine Co. (Sonoma)

Belvedere Wine Co. Merlot (Sonoma)

Benziger Merlot (Glen Ellen)

Brander Bouchet Proprietary Red Wine (Santa Ynez)**/***

Buena Vista Carneros (Sonoma)

Buena Vista Private Reserve (Sonoma)

Buttonwood Farm Merlot (Santa Ynez)

Cafaro (Napa)

Cafaro Merlot (Napa)

Cakebread Cellars (Napa)

Carey Arabesque Proprietary Red Wine (Santa Ynez)

Chappellet (Napa)

Chappellet Merlot (Napa)

Chimney Rock (Napa)

Clos Pegase Merlot (Napa)

Clos du Val (Napa)

B. R. Cohn Merlot (Sonoma)

Congress Springs Noblesse Proprietary Red Wine (Santa Clara)

Conn Creek (Napa)

Creston Manor (San Luis Obispo)

Cronin (Santa Cruz)

Cutler Cellar (Sonoma)

De Loach (Sonoma)

De Moor (Napa)

Diamond Creek Gravelly Meadow (Napa)**/***, *****before 1987

Diamond Creek Lake (Napa)**/***, *****before 1987

Diamond Creek Red Rock Terrace (Napa)**/***, *****before 1987

Diamond Creek Volcanic Hill (Napa)**/***, *****before 1987

Dry Creek (Sonoma)**/***

Firestone Merlot (Santa Barbara)

Folie à Deux (Napa)

Louis Foppiano (Sonoma)

Freemark Abbey Bosché (Napa)

Freemark Abbey Sycamore (Napa)
Gainey Merlot (Santa Ynez)
Gan Eden (Sonoma)
Georis (Monterey)**/***
Glen Ellen (Sonoma)
Grand Cru Vineyards (Sonoma)
Greenwood Ridge (Sonoma)
Groth (Napa)
Guenoc Beckstoffer Vineyard (Carneros)
Gundlach-Bundschu (Sonoma)**/***
Hacienda (Sonoma)
Hacienda Antares Proprietary Red Wine
   (Sonoma)
Hagafen (Napa)
Hallcrest (Santa Cruz)
Hanzell (Sonoma)**/***
Haywood (Sonoma)
William Hill Gold Label Reserve (Napa)
William Hill Silver Label (Napa)
Indian Springs Merlot (Sierra Foothills)
Inglenook (Napa)
Inglenook Reserve Cask (Napa)**/***
Inglenook Reunion Proprietary Red Wine
   (Napa)
Jekel Home Vineyard (Monterey)
Jekel Symmetry Proprietary Red Wine
   (Monterey)
Château Julien (Monterey)
Château Julien Merlot (Monterey)
Kendall-Jackson Vintner's Reserve
   (California)
Konocti (Lake)**/***
Konocti Merlot (Lake)
Charles Krug Vintage Selection (Napa)
Lakespring (Napa)
Lakespring Reserve (Napa)
Leeward (Ventura)
J. Lohr Reserve (Santa Clara)
Markham (Napa)
Markham Merlot (Napa)
Louis Martini (Sonoma)
Louis Martini Monte Rosso
   (Sonoma)**/***
Mayacamas (Napa) (*****before 1976)
McDowell Valley Vineyards (California)
Meridian Vineyards (San Luis Obispo)
Mirassou (Santa Clara)
Montevina (Amador)
Morgan Winery (Monterey)
J. W. Morris Fat Cat (Sonoma)
Mount Veeder (Napa)

Mount Veeder Meritage Proprietary Red
   Wine (Napa)
Mountain View Winery (Santa Clara)
Murphy-Goode (Sonoma)**/***
Nalle (Sonoma)
Domaine Napa (Napa)
Nevada City (Nevada County)
Newlan (Napa)
Neyers (Napa)
Gustave Niebaum Collection (Napa)**/***
Parducci (Mendocino)
Parducci Merlot (Mendocino)
Fess Parker Merlot (Santa Barbara)
Robert Pecota (Napa)
J. Pedroncelli (Sonoma)
Peju Province (Napa)
R. H. Phillips (Yolo)
Château Potelle (Napa)
Preston Vineyards (Sonoma)
Quail Ridge (Napa)
Rabbit Ridge (Sonoma)
Raymond Napa (Napa)
Raymond Private Reserve**/***
Rocking Horse Claret (Napa)
Rombauer (Napa)
Roudon-Smith (Santa Cruz)
Round Hill (Napa)
Round Hill Reserve (Napa)**/***
Rubissow-Sargent (Napa)
Rubissow-Sargent Merlot (Napa)
Rutherford Hill (Napa)
Rutherford Hill Merlot (Napa)
   (****before 1985)
St. Andrews (Napa)
Château St. Jean (Sonoma)
St. Supery (Napa)
Santa Barbara Winery (Santa Barbara)
Santa Ynez Cabernet Sauvignon Port
   (Santa Ynez)
Sarah's Vineyard Innocence (Santa
   Clara)
Sarah's Vineyard Merlot (Santa Clara)
V. Sattui (Napa)
Sebastiani regular cuvées (Sonoma)
Seghesio (Sonoma)
Sequoia Grove (Napa)
Sequoia Grove Estate (Napa)
Shenandoah Vineyards Amador
   (Amador)**/***
Sierra Vista (El Dorado)
Silverado (Napa)

Robert Sinsky Claret (Sonoma)
Smith and Hook Merlot (Santa Lucia)
Stag's Leap Winery Napa (Napa)
Steltzner (Napa)
Steltzner Merlot (Napa)
Sterling Merlot (Napa)
Sterling Napa (Napa)
Sterling Reserve Proprietary Red Wine
  (Napa)**/***
Stevenot (Calaveras)
Stone Creek (Napa)
Stonegate (Napa)
Stonegate Merlot (Napa)
Stratford (California)
Straus Merlot (Napa)
Rodney Strong Alexander's Crown
  (Sonoma)**/***
Rodney Strong Reserve (Sonoma)**/***
Rodney Strong Sonoma (Sonoma)

Rombauer Merlot (Napa)
Sullivan (Napa)**/*****
Sullivan Merlot (Napa)**/*****
Sutter Home (Napa)
Ivan Tamas (Livermore)
Tobin James (Paso Robles)
Trefethen Eshcol Red (Napa)
Vichon Coastal Selection (Napa)
Villa Mt. Eden California (Napa)
Villa Mt. Eden Cellar Select (Napa)
Villa Zapu (Napa)
Vita Nova Reservatum (Santa
  Barbara)**/***
Weinstock Cellars (Sonoma)
Wellington Vineyards (Sonoma)
Whitehall Lane Merlot Knight's Valley
  (Napa)**/***
Wild Horse (San Luis Obispo)**/***
J. Wile and Sons (California)

RATING CALIFORNIA'S BEST PRODUCERS OF CHARDONNAY

* * * * * (OUTSTANDING)

Arrowood Cuvée Michel Berthoud
  (Sonoma)
Beringer Private Reserve (Napa)
Beringer Sbragia Select (Napa)
Ferrari-Carano Reserve (Sonoma)
Fisher Whitney's Vineyard (Sonoma)
Foxen (Santa Barbara)
Gainey Limited Selection (Santa Ynez)
Hanzell Vineyards (Sonoma)
Kalin Cellars Cuvée LD (Sonoma)
Kalin Cellars Cuvée W (Livermore)
Kistler Vineyards Cuvée Kathleen
  (Sonoma)
Kistler Vineyards Durell Vineyard
  (Sonoma)
Kistler Vineyards Dutton Ranch (Sonoma)
Kistler Vineyards Hudson Vineyard
  (Sonoma)
Kistler Vineyards Kistler Estate (Sonoma)
Kistler Vineyards McCrea Vineyard
  (Sonoma)
Marcassin Hudson Vineyard
  (Carneros)
Marcassin Lorenzo Vineyard (Sonoma)

Marcassin Upper Barn Gauer Vineyard
  (Sonoma)
Merryvale Silhouette (Napa)
Peter Michael Clos du Ciel (Sonoma)
Peter Michael Cuvée Indigene (Napa)
Peter Michael Monplaisir (Sonoma)
Peter Michael Pointe Rouge (Sonoma)
Robert Mondavi Reserve (Napa)
Mount Eden Vineyards Santa Cruz Estate
  (Santa Clara)
Newton Unfiltered (Napa)
Pahlmeyer Unfiltered (Napa)
Joseph Phelps Ovation (Napa)
Sanford Barrel Select (Santa Barbara)
Sanford Sanford & Benedict Vineyard
  (Santa Barbara)
Silverado Limited Reserve (Napa)
Steele Lolonis Vineyard (Mendocino)
Steele Du Pratt Vineyard (Mendocino)
Steele Sangiacomo Vineyard (Carneros)
Robert Talbott Estate (Monterey)
Robert Talbott Diamond T Estate
  (Monterey)
Williams-Selyem Allen Vineyard (Sonoma)

* * * * (EXCELLENT)

Alderbrook Reserve (Sonoma)
Arrowood (Sonoma)

Au Bon Climat Bien Nacido (Santa
  Barbara)

Au Bon Climat Sanford & Benedict Vineyard (Santa Barbara)
Au Bon Climat Talley Vineyard (Santa Barbara)
Bancroft (Napa)
Byron Reserve (Santa Barbara)
Cain Cellars (Napa)
Calera Mt. Harlan (San Benito)
Cambria cuvées (Santa Maria)
Chalone Estate (Monterey)
Chalone Estate Reserve (Monterey)
Chimère (Santa Barbara)
Cinnabar (Santa Clara)
Crichton Hall (Napa)
Cronin cuvées (San Mateo)
De Loach O.F.S. (Sonoma)
Dehlinger (Russian River)
Dehlinger Montrachet Cuvée (Russian River)
Durney Estate (Monterey)
Edna Valley (San Luis Obispo)
El Molino (Napa)
Ferrari-Carano (Sonoma)
Flora Springs Barrel Fermented (Napa)
Forest Hill (Sonoma)
Forman (Napa)
Franciscan (Napa)
Girard (Napa)
Girard Reserve (Napa)
Green and Red Catacula Vineyard (Napa)
Harrison (Napa)
Hess Collection (Napa)
Paul Hobbs Dinner Vineyard (Sonoma)
Kalin Cellars Cuvée CH (Sonoma)
Kalin Cellars Cuvée DD (Marin)
Kendall-Jackson Camelot Vineyard (Lake)
Kistler Vineyards Vine Hill Road (Sonoma)****/*****
La Jota Vineyard (Napa)
Long Vineyards (Napa)
Longoria (Santa Barbara)
Matanzas Creek (Sonoma)****/*****
Peter McCoy Clos des Pierres Vineyard (Sonoma)****/*****
Merryvale Reserve (Napa)

Château Montelena (Napa)****/*****
Mount Eden MacGregor Vineyard (Edna Valley)
Napa Ridge Frisinger Vineyard (Napa)
Napa Ridge Reserve (North Coast)
Newton (Napa)
Patz and Hall (Napa)****/*****
Pine Ridge Vieilles Vignes (Napa)****/*****
Pinnacles (Franciscan Winery) (Monterey)
Château Potelle VGS Mount Veeder (Napa)
Rabbit Ridge (Sonoma)
Rabbit Ridge Russian River Valley (Sonoma)
Rancho Sisquoc Estate (Santa Barbara)
Kent Rasmussen (Carneros)
Ravenswood Sangiacomo (Sonoma)
Ridge Howell Mountain (Napa)
Ridge Santa Cruz Mountain (Santa Cruz)
J. Rochioli (Sonoma)
St. Francis Reserve (Sonoma)
Salmon Creek (Napa)
Sanford (Santa Barbara)
Shafer (Napa)
Signorello Vineyards (Napa)
Signorello Vineyards Founder's Reserve (Napa)****/*****
Sonoma-Loeb Private Reserve (Sonoma)
Château Souverain single-vineyard cuvées (Sonoma)****/*****
Steele California (Sonoma)
Steele Durell Vineyard (Sonoma)
Stonestreet (Sonoma)
Stony Hill (Napa)****/*****
Swanson (Napa)****/*****
Robert Talbott Logan (Monterey)
Talley Vineyards (Arroyo Grande)
Marimar Torres (Sonoma)
Trefethen (Napa)
Château Woltner St. Thomas Vineyard (Napa)
Château Woltner Titus Vineyard (Napa)
ZD (Napa)

* * * *(GOOD)*

Acacia (Napa)
Acacia Marina Vineyard (Napa)
Adler Fels (Sonoma)
Alderbrook (Sonoma)

S. Anderson (Napa)
Arrowood (Sonoma)
Arrowood Domaine de Grand Archer (Sonoma)

Au Bon Climat (Santa Barbara)

Babcock (Santa Barbara)

Bargetto Cyprus (Central Coast)

Belvedere Wine Company (Sonoma)

Benziger (Sonoma)

Beringer (Napa)

Beringer Proprietor Grown
   (Napa)***/****

Bernardus (Monterey)

Brander Tête de Cuvée (Santa Ynez)

Brutocao (Mendocino)

Burgess Cellars Triere Vineyard (Napa)

Byron Estate (Santa Barbara)

Calera Central Coast (California)

Canepa (Alexander Valley)***/****

Chalk Hill (Sonoma)***/**** (since 1991)

Christophe (Napa)

Domaine de Clarck (Monterey)

Clos du Bois Barrel-Fermented (Sonoma)

Clos du Bois Calcaire (Sonoma)***/****

Clos du Bois Flintwood (Sonoma)***/****

Clos Pegase (Napa)

B. R. Cohn Olive Hill Vineyard (Sonoma)

Cooper-Garrod (Santa Cruz)

De Loach (Sonoma)

Edmeades Estate (Mendocino)

Elliston (Central Coast)

Estancia (Franciscan Vineyards) (Napa)

Far Niente (Napa)***/****

Gary Farrell (Sonoma)

Fetzer Barrel Select (Mendocino)

Fetzer Sundial (California)

Flora Springs (Napa)

Thomas Fogarty (Monterey)

Folie à Deux (Napa)

Frog's Leap (Napa)

Gainey (Santa Barbara)

E. & J. Gallo Estate***/****

Gan Eden (Sonoma)

Gan Eden Reserve (Sonoma)

Gauer Estate (Sonoma)

Geyser Peak (Sonoma)

Grgich Hills (Napa)

Guenoc Estate (Lake County)

Guenoc Genevieve Magoon Vineyard
   (Guenoc Valley)

Guenoc Reserve (Lake County)***/****

Hacienda Clair de Lune
   (Sonoma)***/****

Handley (Dry Creek)***/****

Hanna (Sonoma)

Harbor (Napa)

Hess Collection Hess Select (Napa)

Hidden Cellars (Mendocino)

Husch Vineyards (Mendocino)

Iron Horse Vineyards (Sonoma)

Jekel Vineyard (Monterey)

Château Julien Sur Lie (Monterey)

Kendall-Jackson Proprietor's Grand
   Reserve (California)

Kendall-Jackson Vintner's Reserve
   (California)

Kenwood Vineyards Beltane Ranch
   (Sonoma)

Kistler (Sonoma)

Konocti (Lake)

Charles Krug Carneros Reserve (Napa)
   (since 1990)

Kunde Estate Reserve (Sonoma)

La Crema (California)***/****

La Crema Reserve (California)***/****

Landmark cuvées (Sonoma)

Liparita Cellars (Napa)***/****

J. Lohr Riverstone (Monterey)

Lolonis (Mendocino)

MacRostie (Carneros)

Meridian Vineyards (San Luis Obispo)

Michel-Schlumberger (Dry Creek)

Robert Mondavi (Napa)

Monterey Vineyards Classic Chardonnay
   (Monterey)

Monticello Cellars Corley Reserve (Napa)

Monticello Cellars Jefferson Cuvée (Napa)

Morgan (Monterey)

Morro Bay (Central Coast)***/****

Mount Eden Santa Barbara (Santa
   Barbara)***/****

Murphy-Goode (Sonoma)

Murphy-Goode Reserve (Sonoma)

Napa Ridge (Napa)

Navarro Vineyards (Mendocino)

Fess Parker (Santa Barbara)

Philippe-Lorraine (Napa)

R. H. Phillips Vineyard (Yolo)

Pine Ridge Knollside Cuvée (Napa)

Pine Ridge Stag's Leap District (Napa)

Rombauer (Napa)

Rutherford Hill XVS Reserve (Napa)

St. Francis (Sonoma)

Saintsbury (Napa)

Saintsbury Reserve (Napa)

Santa Barbara (Santa Ynez)

Santa Barbara Winery Lafond Vineyard
(Santa Ynez)***/****
Sarah's Estate (Santa Clara)
Sarah's Ventana Vineyard (Santa Clara)
Sausal Winery (Sonoma)
Seavey (Napa)
Sebastiani single-vineyard cuvées
(Sonoma)
Silverado Vineyards (Napa)
Simi Winery (Sonoma)
Simi Winery Reserve (Sonoma)***/****
Robert Sinsky (Sonoma)
Sonoma-Cutrer Cutrer (Sonoma)***/****
Sonoma-Cutrer Les Pierres
(Sonoma)***/****
Sonoma-Cutrer Russian River Ranches
(Sonoma)
Sonoma-Loeb (Sonoma)
Château Souverain (Sonoma) (since 1990)
Stag's Leap Wine Cellars Reserve (Napa)
Sterling Diamond Mountain Ranch (Napa)
Sterling Winery Lake (Napa)

Storrs (Santa Cruz)
Stratford (Napa)
Stratford Partner's Reserve (Napa)
Rodney Strong Chalk Hill (Sonoma)
Ivan Tamas (Livermore)
Thomas-Hsi (Napa)***/****
Tiffany Hill (San Luis Obispo)***/****
Truchard (Carneros/Napa)***/****
Vichon (Napa)***/****
Vine Cliff Cellars Proprietress Reserve
(Napa)
Vita Nova (Santa Barbara)
Wente Brothers Reserve (Alameda) (since
1988)
Wente Brothers Wente Vineyard
(Alameda) (since 1988)
William Wheeler (Sonoma)
Whitehall Lane Reserve (Napa)
Wild Horse (Central Coast)
Château Woltner Estate Reserve (Napa)
Château Woltner Frederique Vineyard
(Napa)

* * *(AVERAGE)*

Alexander Valley (Sonoma)
David Arthur (Napa)
Austin Cellars (Santa Barbara)
Beaulieu Carneros Reserve (Napa)**/***
Beaulieu Napa Beaufort (Napa)**/***
Bel Arbors (California)
Boeger (El Dorado)
Bon Marché (Napa)
Bonny Doon (Santa Cruz)
Bouchaine (Los Carneros)
Bouchaine (Napa)
David Bruce (Santa Cruz)
Buena Vista Carneros (Sonoma)
Buena Vista Private Reserve (Sonoma)
Davis Bynum (Sonoma)
Cakebread Cellars (Napa)
Calloway Calla-Lees (Temecula)
Carey Cellars Barrel Select (Santa
Barbara)
Chalone Gavilan (Monterey)**/***
Chamisal (San Luis Obispo)
Chappellet (Napa)
Chimney Rock (Napa)
Clos du Val (Napa)
Congress Springs (Santa Clara)
Conn Creek (Napa)
Cosentino (Napa)

Cottonwood Canyon (San Luis Obispo)
Creston Manor (San Luis Obispo)
Cuvaison (Napa)
De Moor (Napa)
Dry Creek (Sonoma)
Eberle (Paso Robles)
Fetzer Bonterra
Firestone (Santa Barbara)
Louis Foppiano (Sonoma)
Fox Mountain Reserve (Sonoma)
Freemark Abbey (Napa)
Freemont Creek (California)
Glass Mountain (Napa)
Glen Ellen (Sonoma)
Grand Cru (Sonoma)
Groth Vineyards (Napa)
Gundlach-Bundschu (Sonoma)
Hagafen (Napa)**/***
Hagafen Reserve (Napa)
Havens (Napa)
Haywood Winery (Sonoma)
William Hill Gold Label Reserve (Napa)
William Hill Silver Label (Napa)
Indian Springs (Sierra Foothills)
Inglenook (Napa)
Inglenook Reserve (Napa)
Jordan Vineyard (Sonoma)

Château Julien Barrel Fermented
(Monterey)**/***

Karly (Amador)

Robert Keenan (Napa)

Lakespring (Napa)

Leeward (Central Coast)**/***

J. Lohr Cypress (Santa Clara)**/***

Markham Vineyards (Napa)

Louis Martini (Napa)**/***

Mayacamas (Napa)

McDowell Valley Vineyards (Mendocino)

The Meeker Vineyard (Sonoma)

Meridian (San Luis Obispo)**/***

Merry Vintners (Sonoma)**/***

Merryvale Vineyards (Napa)

Mirassou (Monterey)

Morgan Reserve (Monterey)**/***

J. W. Morris Douglass Hill
(Sonoma)**/***

J. W. Morris Gravel Bar (Sonoma)**/***

Mount Veeder (Napa)

Mountain View Winery (Santa Clara)

Napa Creek Winery (Napa)

Newlan (Napa)

Gustave Niebaum Collection Bayview
Vineyard (Napa)**/***

Gustave Niebaum Collection Laird
Vineyard (Napa)**/***

Noble Hill Vineyards (Santa Cruz)**/***

Obester Winery Barrel Fermented
(Mendocino)**/***

Ojai (Ventura County)

Page Mill (Santa Clara)

Parducci (Mendocino)

J. Pedroncelli (Sonoma)**/***

Robert Pepi (Napa)

Joseph Phelps (Napa)

Joseph Phelps Sangiacomo (Napa)

Château Potelle (Napa)

Quail Ridge (Napa)

Qupé (Santa Barbara)**/***

Raymond (Napa)

Raymond Private Reserve (Napa)**/***

Richardson (Sonoma)

Round Hill (Napa)

Rutherford Hill Jaeger Vineyard (Napa)

St. Andrews (Napa)

St. Clement (Napa)

Château St. Jean (all cuvées) (Sonoma)

St. Supery (Napa)

Santa Barbara Winery Reserve (Santa
Ynez)**/***

Schug Cellars Beckstoffer Vineyard
(Carneros)

Sea Ridge (Sonoma)

Sebastiani regular cuvées (Sonoma)

Seghesio Winery (Sonoma)

Sequoia Grove Carneros (Napa)

Sequoia Grove Estate (Napa)

Sierra Vista (El Dorado)

Spring Mountain (Napa)

Stag's Leap Wine Cellars (Napa)

Stearns Wharf (Santa Barbara)

Sterling (Napa)

Stevenot (Calaveras)

Stone Creek (all cuvées) (Napa)

Taft Street Winery (Sonoma)

Tulocay (Napa)

Vichon Coastal Selection (California)

Villa Mt. Eden Grand Reserve (Napa)

Villa Zapu (Napa)

Weinstock Cellars (Sonoma)**/***

Mark West Vineyards (Sonoma)

Westwood (El Dorado)

William Wheeler (Sonoma)

White Oak (Sonoma)

White Oak Limited Reserve (Sonoma)

Whitehall Lane Le Petit (Napa)

Windemere (Sonoma)

Zaca Mesa (Santa Barbara)

RATING CALIFORNIA'S BEST PRODUCERS OF PINOT NOIR

***** (OUTSTANDING)

Au Bon Climat La Bauge Au Dessus Bien
Nacido Vineyard (Santa Barbara)

Au Bon Climat Sanford & Benedict
Vineyard (Santa Barbara)

Calera Jensen Vineyard (San Benito)

Calera Mills Vineyard (San Benito)

Calera Reed Vineyard (San Benito)

Calera Selleck Vineyard (San Benito)

Kistler Cuvée Catherine (Sonoma)

Kistler Hirsch Vineyard (Sonoma)

Kistler Vine Hill Vineyard (Sonoma)

Robert Mondavi Reserve (Napa)

J. Rochioli Reserve Vintage Selection East
Block (Sonoma)

J. Rochioli Reserve Estate Three Corner
Vineyard (Sonoma)
J. Rochioli Reserve Estate West Block
(Sonoma)
Sanford Barrel Select (Santa Barbara)

Sanford Sanford & Benedict Vineyard
(Santa Barbara)
Williams-Selyem Allen Vineyard (Sonoma)
Williams-Selyem Rochioli Vineyard
(Sonoma)

* * * * *(EXCELLENT)*

Au Bon Climat (Santa Barbara)
David Bruce Reserve (Santa Cruz)
Cambria Julia's Vineyard (Santa Maria)
(since 1991)
Chimère (Santa Maria)
Conn Valley Vineyards Valhalla Vineyard
(Napa)
Coturri Freiberg Vineyard (Sonoma)
Dehlinger Reserve (Sonoma)
El Molino (Napa)
Gary Farrell Bien Nacido Vineyard (Santa
Barbara)
Gary Farrell Howard Allen Vineyard
(Sonoma)
Foxen Sanford & Benedict Vineyard (Santa
Barbara)
Gainey Sanford & Benedict Vineyard
(Santa Barbara)
Kalin Cellars Cuvée DD (Sonoma)
Kalin Cellars Cuvée JL (Sonoma)

Kistler Camp Meeting Ridge (Sonoma)
Longoria (Santa Ynez)
Martinelli (Sonoma)
Mount Eden Vineyards Estate (Santa Cruz)
Kent Rasmussen (Carneros)
J. Rochioli Estate (Sonoma)
Saintsbury Carneros (Napa)
Saintsbury Reserve (Napa)
Sanford (Santa Barbara)
Siduri Rose Vineyard (Anderson
Valley)****/*****
Signorello (Napa)
Solitude Sangiacomo Vineyard (Napa)
Stonestreet (Sonoma)
Talley Vineyards (San Luis Obispo)
Lane Tanner Sanford & Benedict Vineyard
(Santa Barbara)
Williams-Selyem Cohn Vineyard (Sonoma)
Williams-Selyem Olivet Lane Vineyard
(Russian River)

* * * *(GOOD)*

Au Bon Climat Talley Vineyard (Arroyo
Grande)
Bernardus (Santa Barbara)
Big Horn Reserve (Santa Barbara)
Byron (Santa Barbara)
Byron Reserve (Santa Barbara)
Carneros Creek (Napa)
Château de Baun (Sonoma)
Coturri Horn Vineyard (Sonoma)
Domaine de Clarck (Monterey)
Dehlinger (Sonoma)
Edna Valley Vineyards (San Luis Obispo)
Étude (Napa)***/****
Ferrari-Carano (Napa)
Foxen (Santa Maria)
The Hitching Post (Santa Maria)***/****
The Hitching Post Sanford & Benedict
Vineyard (Santa Barbara)***/****
Kendall-Jackson Grand Reserve
(California)
La Jota cuvées (Sonoma)
Meridian Reserve (Santa Barbara)

Robert Mondavi (Napa)
Monticello Estate (Napa)
Morgan (Monterey)
Navarro (Mendocino)***/****
Page Mill Bien Nacido Vineyard (Santa
Barbara)
Saintsbury Garnet (Napa)
Santa Barbara (Santa Barbara) (since
1989)
Santa Barbara Reserve (Santa
Barbara)***/**** (since 1989)
Santa Cruz Mountain (Santa Cruz)
Robert Sinsky (Sonoma)
Steele Carneros (Sonoma)
Steele Sangiacomo Vineyard
(Sonoma)***/****
Robert Stemmler (Sonoma)
Stonestreet (Sonoma)***/****
Lane Tanner (Santa Barbara)
Westwood (El Dorado)
Wild Horse Cheval Sauvage (Santa
Barbara)

* * (AVERAGE)

Acacia Iund Vineyard (Napa)**/***
Acacia St. Clair (Napa)**/***
Adler Fels (Sonoma)
Alexander Valley (Sonoma)
Austin Cellars (Santa Barbara)
Austin Cellars Reserve (Santa Barbara)
Beaulieu Carneros Reserve (Napa)
Bon Marché (Napa)
Bouchaine (Napa)
David Bruce (Santa Cruz)**/***
Buena Vista (Sonoma)
Davis Bynum (Sonoma)
Calera (Central Coast)**/***
Cambria (Santa Maria)
Caymus (Napa)
Chalone Estate (Monterey)**/***
Clos du Val (Napa)
Cottonwood Canyon (Santa Barbara)
Cronin (Santa Cruz)
De Loach (Sonoma)
Thomas Fogarty (Santa Cruz)
Gainey (Santa Barbara)
Girard (Napa)
Gundlach-Bundschu (Sonoma)
Hacienda (Sonoma)
Hanzell Vineyards (Sonoma)
Husch (Mendocino)
Charles Krug Carneros Reserve (Napa)

Meridian (Santa Barbara)
Mountain View Winery
  (California)**/***
Parducci (Mendocino)
Fess Parker (Santa Barbara)
Pepperwood Springs (Mendocino)
Richardson (Sonoma)**/***
Roudon-Smith (Santa Cruz)
Santa Ynez Rancho Vineda Vineyard
  (Santa Maria)
Schug Cellars Beckstoffer Vineyard
  (Carneros)
Schug Cellars Heinemann Vineyard (Napa)
Sea Ridge (Sonoma)
Sterling (Napa)
Rodney Strong River East Vineyard
  (Sonoma)
Joseph Swan (Sonoma)
Truchard (Napa)
Tulocay (Napa)
Tulocay Haynes Vineyard (Napa)
Mark West (Sonoma)
Whitcraft Bien Nacido Vineyard (Santa
  Barbara)**/***
Whitcraft Olivet Lane Vineyard (Russian
  River)**/***
Whitehall Lane (Napa)
ZD (Napa)

RATING CALIFORNIA'S RHÔNE RANGERS

* * * * * (OUTSTANDING)

Araujo Estate Syrah Eisele Vineyard
Beringer Viognier Hudson Ranch
Black and Blue (Havens Wine Cellar)
Calera Viognier
Edmunds St. John Syrah Durell Vineyard
Edmunds St. John Syrah Grand Heritage
La Jota Petite Sirah
Qupé Syrah Bien Nacido Vineyard
Ravenswood Icon (Blend)

Ridge York Creek Petite Sirah
Rockland Petite Sirah
Swanson Syrah
Sean Thackrey Orion (Syrah)
Sean Thackrey Sirius (Petite Sirah)
Sean Thackrey Taurus (Mourvèdre)
Turley Cellars Petite Sirah Aida Vineyard
Turley Cellars Petite Sirah Hayne
  Vineyard

* * * * (EXCELLENT)

Arrowood Syrah
Bonny Doon Clos de Gilroy (Grenache)
Bonny Doon Le Sophiste (Blend)
Bonny Doon Vin Gris de Cigare Rosé
Cambria Syrah Tepusquet Vineyard
Cline Cellars Côtes d'Oakley (Blend)

Cline Cellars Mourvèdre
Coturri Alicante Bouchet Ubaldi Vineyard
Coturri Petite Sirah Ubaldi Vineyard
Dehlinger Syrah
Edmunds St. John Les Côtes Sauvage
Edmunds St. John El Niño

Edmunds St. John Mourvèdre
Edmunds St. John Port o' Call (Blend)
Ferrari-Carano Syrah
Field Stone Petite Sirah
Forman La Grande Roche (Grenache)
Frey (Syrah)
Havens Syrah
Jade Mountain Les Jumeaux (Blend)
Jade Mountain Marsanne
Jade Mountain Mourvèdre
Jade Mountain La Provençale (Blend)
Jade Mountain Syrah
Kendall-Jackson Syrah Durell Vineyard
Marietta Old Vine Red

Marietta Petite Sirah
Fess Parker Syrah
Preston Syrah
Qupé Marsanne
Qupé Viognier
Ridge Mataro Evangelo Vineyard
Trentadue Old Patch Red (Blend)
Trentadue Petite Sirah
Trentadue Salute
Truchard Syrah
Wellington Vineyards Côtes de Sonoma
   Old Vines
Wellington Vineyards Syrah Alegrai
   Vineyards

* * * (GOOD)

Arrowood Viognier
Benziger
Bonny Doon Le Cigare Volant (blend)
Bonny Doon Cinsault
Bonny Doon Old Telegram (Mourvèdre)
Bonny Doon Pinot Meunier
Bonny Doon Syrah
David Bruce Petite Sirah
Edmunds St. John Viognier
Elyse Coeur de Val
Elyse Nero Misto Proprietary Red
   Wine ***/****
Fetzer Petite Sirah Reserve
Field Stone Petite Sirah
Field Stone Viogner Staten Family Reserve
Guenoc Petite Sirah
Hop Kiln Petite Sirah
Marietta Cellars Petite Sirah
McDowell Valley Vineyards Les Vieux
   Cépages
Ojai Syrah
Joseph Phelps Vin du Mistral cuvées

R. H. Phillips Mourvèdre EXP
R. H. Phillips Viognier EXP
Preston Faux Proprietary Red Wine
Preston Marsanne
Qupé Bien Nacido Cuvée ***/****
Qupé Los Olivos Cuvée ***/****
Qupé Syrah
Ritchie Creek Viognier
Santino Satyricon (Blend)
Shenandoah Serene (Blend)
Sierra Vista Fleur de Montagne (blend)
Sierra Vista Lynelle (blend)
Stag's Leap Winery Petite Sirah
Joseph Swan Côtes du Rosa Unfiltered
Joseph Swan Vin du Mystère
Topolos Alicante Bouschet ***/****
Topolos Grand Noir
Topolos Petite Sirah ***/****
Trentadue Carignane
William Wheeler RS Reserve (Blend)
Zaca Mesa Syrah/Malbec

* * (AVERAGE)

Alban Viognier
Alderbrook Syrah Shiloh Hill Vineyard
Christopher Creek Petite Sirah
Christopher Creek Syrah
Duxoup Syrah
Louis Foppiano Petite Sirah
Jory (various cuvées)
Karly Petite Sirah
La Jota Viognier

Meridian Syrah
J. W. Morris Petite Sirah Bosun Crest
Parducci Bono Syrah **/***
Parducci Petite Sirah **/***
Joseph Phelps Syrah
Preston Viognier
Roudon-Smith Petite Sirah
Sierra-Vista Syrah
Domaine de la Terre Rouge **/***

William Wheeler Quintet (Blend)
Zaca Mesa Alamo Cuvée (Blend)
Zaca Mesa Malbec

Zaca Mesa Mourvèdre
Zaca Mesa Syrah

RATING CALIFORNIA'S BEST PRODUCERS OF ITALIAN-INSPIRED VARIETALS—SANGIOVESE, BARBERA, NEBBIOLO

***** (OUTSTANDING)

Coturri Jessandre Vineyard
   (Sangiovese/Cabernet)

Wild Horse Malvasia Bianca Barrel
   Fermented

**** (EXCELLENT)

Au Bon Climat Barbera
Coturri Sangiovese Jessandre Vineyard
Edmunds St. John Pinot Grigio
Edmunds St. John Pallini Rosso
Ferrari-Carano Siena
Robert Mondavi Barbera
Kent Rasmussen Dolcetto

Kent Rasmussen Sangiovese
Shafer Firebreak (Sangiovese/Cabernet)
Staglin Family Vineyard Stagliano
   Sangiovese
Swanson Sangiovese
Ivan Tamas Trebbiano
Wildhorse Tocai Fruilano

*** (GOOD)

Bonny Doon Ca do Solo Il Fiasco
Brindiamo Gioveto
Brindiamo Nebbiolo
Brindiamo Rosso Vecchio
Dalla Valle Pietre Rosso
Flora Springs Sangiovese
Konrad Barbera
Robert Mondavi Sangiovese
Robert Mondavi Malvasia

Mosby Moscato di Fior
Mosby Primativo ***/****
Preston Barbera ***/****
Sterling Pinot Grigio
Sterling Sangiovese
Sean Thackrey Pleiades
Trentadue Sangiovese ***/****
Westwood Barbera

** (AVERAGE)

Atlas Peak Sangiovese
Il Podere Dell'Olivos Ariosa
Il Podere Dell'Olivos Barbera
Il Podere Dell'Olivos Nebbiolo

Mosby Brunello di Santa Barbara Carrari
   Vineyard
Sebastiani Barbera**/***

RATING CALIFORNIA'S BEST PRODUCERS OF SAUVIGNON BLANC AND SEMILLON AND BLENDS THEREOF

***** (OUTSTANDING)

Ferrari-Carano Fumé Blanc Reserve
   (Sonoma)
Gainey Sauvignon Blanc Limited Selection
   (Santa Ynez)
Kalin Cellars Sauvignon Blanc Reserve
   (Potter Valley)
Matanzas Creek Sauvignon Blanc (Sonoma)

Peter Michael Sauvignon Blanc
   l'Apres-Midi (California)
Robert Mondavi Fumé Blanc Reserve
   (Napa)
Simi Sendal Proprietary White Wine
   (Sonoma)

* * * * *(EXCELLENT)*

Araujo Estate Sauvignon Blanc Eisele
  Vineyard (Napa)
Babcock Sauvignon Blanc (Santa
  Barbara)
Babcock Sauvignon Blanc 11 Oaks Ranch
  (Santa Barbara)
Byron Sauvignon Blanc (Santa Barbara)
Caymus Conundrum Proprietary White
  Wine (Napa)
Chalk Hill Sauvignon Blanc (Sonoma)
  (since 1991)
Clos du Bois Sauvignon Blanc (Alexander
  Valley)
Cronin Sauvignon Blanc (Napa)
Dry Creek Fumé Blanc (Sonoma)
Gary Farrell Sauvignon Blanc Rochioli
  Vineyard (Russian River)
Flora Springs Soliloquy Proprietary White
  Wine (Napa)
Handley Cellars Sauvignon Blanc (Dry
  Creek)
Hidden Cellars Alchemy Proprietary
  White Wine (Mendocino)
Hidden Cellars Sauvignon Blanc
  (Mendocino)

Kalin Cellars Sauvignon Blanc (Potter
  Valley)
Kalin Cellars Semillon (Livermore)
Karly Sauvignon Blanc (Amador)
Kenwood Vineyards Sauvignon Blanc
  (Sonoma)
Robert Mondavi Fumé Blanc (Napa)
Murphy-Goode Fumé Blanc Reserve
  (Sonoma)
Navarro Sauvignon Blanc (Mendocino)
Preston Cuvée de Fumé (Sonoma)
Rancho Sisquoc Sauvignon Blanc (Santa
  Barbara)
J. Rochioli Sauvignon Blanc (Sonoma)
J. Rochioli Sauvignon Blanc Reserve
  (Sonoma)****/*****
Sanford Sauvignon Blanc (Santa Barbara)
Selene Sauvignon Blanc (Napa)
Signorello Sauvignon Blanc (Napa)
Signorello Semillon Barrel Fermented
  (Napa)
Spottswoode Sauvignon Blanc (Napa)
Rodney Strong Sauvignon Blanc
  Charlotte's Home Vineyard (Sonoma)
Philip Togni Sauvignon Blanc (Napa)

* * * *(GOOD)*

Ahlgren Semillon (Santa Cruz)
Alderbrook Sauvignon Blanc (Sonoma)
Babcock Fathom Proprietary White Wine
  (Santa Barbara)
Beaulieu Fumé Blanc (Napa)
Bel Arbors Sauvignon Blanc (California)
Bellerose Sauvignon Blanc (Sonoma)
Benziger Fumé Blanc (Sonoma)
Beringer Meritage (Napa)
Beringer Sauvignon Blanc (Napa)
Bernadus Sauvignon Blanc (Monterey)
Brander (Santa Ynez)
Brutocao Sauvignon Blanc (Mendocino)
Buena Vista Fumé Blanc (Lake)
Buttonwood Farm Sauvignon Blanc (Santa
  Ynez)
Cain Cellars Sauvignon Musqué
  (Napa)***/****
Carmenet Meritage Proprietary White
  Wine (Sonoma)
Caymus Sauvignon Blanc (Napa)
De Loach Fumé Blanc (Sonoma)

De Lorimer Spectrum Estate (Alexander
  Valley)
Duckhorn Sauvignon Blanc (Napa)
Ferrari-Carano Fumé Blanc
  (Sonoma) ***/****
Fetzer Fumé Blanc (Mendocino)
Fetzer Sauvignon Blanc Barrel Select
  (Mendocino)
Field Stone Sauvignon Blanc (Sonoma)
Gabrielli Ascenza White Table Wine
  (Mendocino)
Gainey Sauvignon Blanc (Santa Ynez)
Geyser Peak Sauvignon Blanc (Sonoma)
Geyser Peak Semchard
Grgich Hills Fumé Blanc (Napa)
Guenoc Winery Langtry Meritage (Lake
  County)
Louis Honig Cellars Sauvignon Blanc
  (Napa)
Husch Vineyards Sauvignon Blanc
  (Mendocino)
Iron Horse Fumé Blanc (Sonoma)

Karly Sauvignon Blanc (Amador)
Konocti Fumé Blanc (Lake County)
Lakewood Sauvignon Blanc (Clear Lake)
Lakewood Semillon (Clear Lake)
Liberty School California White Wine
  (Caymus—Napa)
Lolonis Fumé Blanc (Mendocino)
Monterey Vineyards Classic Sauvignon
  Blanc (California)
Morgan Sauvignon Blanc (Monterey)
Mt. Konocti Semillon/Chardonnay (Lake
  County)
Murphy-Goode Fumé Blanc (Sonoma)
Napa Ridge Sauvignon Blanc (Napa)
Ojai Cuvée Speciale Ste. Helene
  (California)***/****
Ojai Sauvignon Blanc (California)

Page Mill Sauvignon Blanc (San Luis
  Obispo)
R. H. Phillips Sauvignon Blanc (Yolo)
Preston Vineyards Cuvée de Fumé (Dry
  Creek)
Rabbit Ridge Proprietary White Wine
  (Sonoma)***/****
Rabbit Ridge Sauvignon Blanc (Sonoma)
Stag's Leap Sauvignon Blanc Rancho
  Chimiles (Napa)
Rodney Strong Sauvignon Blanc
  Charlotte's Home Vineyard
  (Sonoma)***/****
Ivan Tamas Fumé Blanc
  (Livermore)***/****
William Wheeler Fumé Blanc (Sonoma)

* * (AVERAGE)

Adler Fels Fumé Blanc (Sonoma)
Austin Sauvignon Blanc (Santa Barbara)
Austin Sauvignon Blanc Reserve (Santa
  Barbara)
Davis Bynum Fumé Blanc (Sonoma)
Calloway Fumé Blanc/Sauvignon Blanc
  (Temecula)
Christophe Sauvignon Blanc (Napa)
Clos Pegase Sauvignon Blanc (Napa)
Clos du Val Semillon (Napa)
Louis Foppiano Sauvignon Blanc (Sonoma)
E. & J. Gallo Sauvignon Blanc (California)
Glen Ellen Sauvignon Blanc (Sonoma)
Grand Cru Sauvignon Blanc (Sonoma)
Groth Sauvignon Blanc (Napa)
Hanna Sauvignon Blanc (Sonoma)
Inglenook Gravion Proprietary White Wine
  (Napa)
Innisfree Sauvignon Blanc (Napa)
Jekel Scepter Proprietary White Wine
  (Monterey)
Château Julien Sauvignon Blanc
  (Monterey)

Lakespring Sauvignon Blanc (Napa)
Liberty School Sauvignon Blanc
  (California)
Louis Martini Sauvignon Blanc (Napa)
Mayacamas Sauvignon Blanc (Napa)
Obester Sauvignon Blanc (Mendocino)
J. Pedroncelli Primavera Mista Proprietary
  White Wine (California)
Joseph Phelps Sauvignon Blanc (Napa)
Château Potelle Sauvignon Blanc (Napa)
St. Clement Sauvignon Blanc (Napa)
Château St. Jean Fumé Blanc (all cuvées)
  (Sonoma)
St. Supery Sauvignon Blanc (Napa)
Santa Ynez Semillon (Santa Ynez)
Seghesio Sauvignon Blanc (Sonoma)
Shenandoah Sauvignon Blanc (Amador)
Silverado Sauvignon Blanc (Napa)
Simi Semillon (Napa)
Steltzner Sauvignon Blanc (Napa)
Sterling Sauvignon Blanc (Napa)
Stratford Sauvignon Blanc (California)
Weinstock Sauvignon Blanc (Sonoma)

RATING CALIFORNIA'S BEST PRODUCERS OF ZINFANDEL

* * * * * (OUTSTANDING)

Au Bon Climat Sauret Vineyard (Paso
  Robles)
De Loach O.F.S. (Russian River)
Franus Brandlin Ranch (Napa)

Franus George Hendry Vineyard (Napa)
Lytton Springs Reserve (Sonoma)
Martinelli Jackass Hill (Sonoma)
Peachy Canyon West Side (Paso Robles)

Ravenswood Belloni Vineyard (Sonoma)
Ravenswood Cooke Vineyard (Sonoma)
Ravenswood Dickerson Vineyard (Napa)
Ravenswood Old Hill Vineyard (Sonoma)
Ravenswood Monte Rosso Vineyard (Sonoma)
Ridge Geyserville Proprietary Red Wine (primarily Zinfandel) (Sonoma)
Ridge Lytton Springs (Sonoma)
Ridge Pagani Ranch (Sonoma)

Rosenblum Cellars Michael Marston Vineyard (Napa)
Rosenblum Cellars Samsel Vineyard (Sonoma)
Storybook Mountain Reserve (Napa)
Topolos Rossi Ranch (Sonoma)
Turley Cellars Aida Vineyard (Napa)
Turley Cellars Hayne Vineyard (Napa)
Turley Cellars Whitney Vineyard (Napa)

* * * * (EXCELLENT)

Bialé Aldo's Vineyard (Napa)
Cline (Contra Costa)
Cline Reserve (Contra Costa)
Coturri Chauvet Vineyard (Sonoma)
Coturri Philip Coturri Estate (Sonoma)
De Loach single-vineyard cuvées (Sonoma)
Dry Creek Old Vines (Sonoma)****/*****
Eberle (Paso Robles)
Edmunds St. John (Napa)
Elyse Howell Mountain (Napa)
Elyse Morisoli Vineyard (Napa)
Gary Farrell (Russian River)
Ferrari-Carano (Dry Creek)****/*****
Franciscan (Napa)
Frey (Mendocino)
E. & J. Gallo Frei Ranch Vineyard (Sonoma)
Green and Red Chiles Mill Vineyard (Napa)
Hidden Cellars (Mendocino)
Hop Kiln Winery Primativo (Sonoma)
Kendall-Jackson Ciapusci Vineyard (Mendocino)
Kendall-Jackson Dupratt Vineyard (Lake)
Kendall-Jackson Proprietor's Grand Reserve (Lake County)
Lamborn Family Vineyard (Napa)
Limerick Lane Cellars (Sonoma)
Marietta Cellars (Sonoma)
Martinelli Jackass Vineyard (Sonoma)****/*****
Meeker Vineyard (Sonoma)
Robert Mondavi (Napa)
Château Montelena (Napa)
Monterey Peninsula Ferrero Ranch (Amador)
Norman (Paso Robles)
Peachy Canyon Reserve (Paso Robles)
Château Potelle Mount Veeder (Napa)

Preston (Sonoma)
Rabbit Ridge (Sonoma)
A. Rafanelli (Sonoma)****/*****
Ravenswood Old Vines (Sonoma)
Renwood (Amador)
Ridge (Paso Robles)
Ridge Dusi Ranch (Paso Robles)
Rosenblum Cellars (Contra Costa)
Rosenblum Cellars (Paso Robles)
Rosenblum Cellars (Sonoma)
Rosenblum Cellars Richard Sauret Vineyard (Paso Robles)
Rosenblum Cellars George Hendry Vineyard (Napa)
Rosenblum Cellars Brandlin Ranch (Napa)
Ross Valley (Sonoma)
St. Francis Old Vines (Sonoma)****/*****
Saddleback Cellar (Napa)
Saucelito Canyon Vineyard (Arroyo Grande)
Sausal Winery (Sonoma)
Sausal Winery Private Reserve (Sonoma)****/*****
Scherrer Old Vines (Alexander Valley)
Schuetz-Oles-Korte Ranch (Napa)
Storybook Mountain Eastern Exposure (Napa)
Storybook Mountain Estate (Napa)
Storybook Mountain Howell Mountain (Napa)
Joseph Swan cuvées (Sonoma)
The Terraces (Napa)
Topolos Ultimo (Sonoma)****/*****
Turley Cellars Sears Vineyard (Napa)
Wellington Old Vine (Sonoma)
Whaler Vineyard Estate Flagship (Mendocino)

* * * (GOOD)

Amador Foothill Grand Père Vineyard (Amador)

Benziger (Sonoma)

Beringer (Napa)

Boeger (El Dorado)

David Bruce (Santa Cruz)

Brutocao Cellars (Mendocino)

Buehler (Napa)

Cakebread Cellars (Napa)

Caymus (Napa)

Clos du Bois (Sonoma)

Clos du Val (Napa)

Cosentino The Poet (Napa)

Cosentino The Zin (Sonoma)

D'Annco Old Vines***/****

Deer Park (Napa)

Deux Amis (Sonoma)

De Loach Estate (Sonoma)

De Moor (Napa)

Dry Creek (Sonoma)

Edizione Pennino (Niebaum-Coppola— Napa)

Edmeades Estate (Mendocino)

Fetzer Barrel Select (Mendocino)

Fetzer Reserve (Mendocino)

Frick (Santa Cruz)

Fritz (Sonoma) (since 1988)

Frog's Leap Winery (Napa)

Greenwood Ridge Vineyards (Sonoma)

Grgich Hills (Sonoma)

Guenoc (Lake County)

Gundlach-Bundschu (Sonoma)

Gundlach-Bundschu Rhinefarm Vineyard (Sonoma)***/****

Hop Kiln (Sonoma)

Kendall Jackson Vintner's Reserve (California)

Kenwood Jack London Vineyard (Sonoma)***/****

Lake Sonoma Old Vine Reserve (Dry Creek)***/****

Mara (Alexander Valley)

Mariah Vineyards (Mendocino)***/****

Z. Moore Danato Proprietary Red Wine ***/****

Mountain View Winery (Amador)

Nalle (Sonoma)

J. Pedroncelli (Sonoma)

Joseph Phelps (Alexander Valley)

Quivira (Sonoma)***/****

Ravenswood Vintner's Blend (Sonoma)

Ridge Howell Mountain (Napa)

Ridge Sonoma (Santa Clara)

Rocking Horse Lamborn Vineyard (Napa)

Seghesio Winery (Sonoma)

Seghesio Winery Reserve (Sonoma)

Shenandoah Sobon Estate (Amador)

Sierra Vista (El Dorado)

Signorello (Napa)

Sky Vineyards (Napa)

Sonora TC Vineyard (Amador)

Château Souverain (Dry Creek)

Steele ***/****

Sterling (Napa)

Rodney Strong Old Vines River West Vineyard (Russian River)

Summit Lake (Napa)***/****

Sutter Home Reserve (Amador)

Tobin James (Paso Robles)

Topolos Russian River Valley (Russian River)

Trentadue (Sonoma)***/****

Turley Cellars Moore Vineyard (Napa)

Wellington Vineyards Old Vines (Sonoma)***/*****

Mark West Robert Rue Vineyard (Sonoma)

Whaler Vineyard Estate (Mendocino)

Wild Horse (San Luis Obispo)

* * (AVERAGE)

Bel Arbors (California)

Burgess Cellars (Napa)

Duxoup Wineworks (Sonoma)

Eagle Ridge Fiddletown (Amador)

Louis Foppiano Reserve (Sonoma)

Harbor Winery (Sacramento)**/****

Haywood Winery (Sonoma)

Karly (Amador)

Charles Krug (Napa)

Lolonis (Mendocino)

Louis Martini (Sonoma)

Mazzocco (Sonoma)

Montevina (Amador) (****/*****before 1979)

J. Morris Kramer Ridge (Sonoma)

Obester (San Mateo)

Parducci (Mendocino)

Roudon-Smith (Santa Cruz)

Round Hill (Napa)
St. Supery Vineyards (Napa)
Santa Barbara Beaujour (Santa Ynez)
Santino Wines (Amador)
V. Sattui Suzanne's Vineyard (Napa)
Sebastiani (Sonoma)
Shenandoah Special Reserve (Amador)

Stevenot (Calaveras)**/***
Sutter Home (California)
Teldeschi (Sonoma)**/*****
Twin Hills Ranch (Paso Robles)
Villa Mt. Eden Cellar Select
    (California)**/***
White Oak (Sonoma)

RATING CALIFORNIA'S BEST SPARKLING WINE PRODUCERS

* * * * * (OUTSTANDING)

None

* * * * (EXCELLENT)

Domaine Chandon Reserve Brut (Napa)
Maison Deutz Blanc de Noir (San Luis
    Obispo)
Iron Horse cuvées (Sonoma)

Mumm Blanc de Noir Rosé (Napa)
Roederer L'Ermitage (Anderson Valley)
Roederer Estate (Anderson Valley)

* * * (GOOD)

Domaine Carneros (Napa)
Domaine Chandon Blanc de Noir (Napa)
Domaine Chandon Brut (Napa)
Domaine Chandon Etoile (Napa)
Maison Deutz (San Luis Obispo)
Handley (Mendocino)
Robert Mondavi Brut (Napa)
Monticello Domaine Montreaux (Napa)

Domaine Mumm Brut Prestige Cuvée
    (Napa)***/****
Domaine Mumm Brut Winery Lake Cuvée
    (Napa)***/****
Schramsberg J. Schram (Napa)
Tribault Brut (Monterey)
Tribault Brut Rosé (Monterey)

* * (AVERAGE)

S. Anderson cuvées (Napa)**/***
Beaulieu Brut (Napa)
Domaine Carneros (Napa)
Culbertson Blanc de Noir (Riverside)
Culbertson Brut (Riverside)
Culbertson Brut Rosé (Riverside)
Richard Cuneo (Sonoma)
Gloria Ferrer cuvées (Sonoma)**/***
Jordan J Cuvée (Sonoma)

Mirassou (Monterey)
Piper Sonoma (Sonoma)**/***
Santa Ynez Brut (Santa Ynez)
Scharffenberger Cellars cuvées
    (Mendocino)
Schramsberg Vineyards cuvées (Napa)
Shadow Creek Champagne Cellars Brut
    (San Luis Obispo)

ACACIA (NAPA)
Chardonnay * * *, Chardonnay Marina Vineyard * * *, Pinot Noir Cuvées * */* * *

1991 Chardonnay Marina Vineyard	Napa	C	89
1991 Pinot Noir Iund Vineyard	Napa	C	86

Acacia's 1991 Chardonnay from the Marina Vineyard is their best Chardonnay in the last
4–5 years. It offers a smoky, richly fruity, stylish, complex bouquet, medium- to full-bodied,
well-defined flavors, adequate acidity, and a lot of personality. The finish exhibits fine

concentration and overall balance. Drink it over the next several years. The medium ruby-colored 1991 Pinot Noir Iund Vineyard displays a fragrant, spicy, black cherry–, vanillin-scented bouquet, soft, gentle, satiny-textured flavors, and a moderately long finish with no hard edges. This fully mature, stylish Pinot Noir should continue to drink well for at least 3–4 years.

ADLER FELS (SONOMA)

Chardonnay* * *, Fumé Blanc * *, Gewürztraminer * *, Pinot Noir * *

1991 Chardonnay Coleman Reserve	Sonoma	C	88

I have been a frequent critic of many of this winery's offerings, but this 1991 is an impressive Chardonnay. Hopefully, it signals a new direction in Adler Fels's winemaking. It exhibits wonderfully rich, crisp, mineral/floral/buttery fruit aromas, excellent depth, a deep, spicy, honeyed richness, fine underlying acidity, and a long finish. This is a top-notch California Chardonnay for drinking over the next 1–2 years. Bravo!

ALDERBROOK (SONOMA)

Chardonnay* * *, Chardonnay Reserve* * *, Sauvignon Blanc* * *

1993 Sauvignon Blanc	Dry Creek	A	83

This 1993 is a melony, subtly styled Sauvignon Blanc with good body, fruit, and freshness.

ALEXANDER VALLEY VINEYARD (SONOMA)

Cabernet Sauvignon* * *, Chardonnay * *, Chenin Blanc* * *, Merlot* */* * *, Pinot Noir* *

1992 Dry Chenin Blanc	Alexander Valley	A	86

A delightful, light-bodied, cleanly made, aromatic wine, this tasty, dry Chenin Blanc is ideal for drinking as an aperitif wine. It should be consumed over the next year.

AMADOR FOOTHILL WINERY (AMADOR)

White Zinfandel * * *, Zinfandel * * *

1992 Zinfandel	Amador	B	85
1991 Zinfandel Eschen Vineyard Fiddletown	Amador	B	77
1991 Zinfandel Ferrero Vineyard	Amador	B	86
1991 Zinfandel Grand Père Vineyard	Amador	B	87

Typically light ruby colored, this jammy, medium- to full-bodied, lovely textured 1992 Zinfandel displays plenty of strawberry and cherry fruit. With a lush, straightforward personality, this Zinfandel will make fine drinking over the next 5 years. Sixty-one percent of the grapes used in the blend came from the Biagi Vineyard and 39% from the Ferrero Vineyard.

The 1991 Zinfandels have exceptionally high alcohol contents, with all of them well over 14%. The Grand Père is 15%. Despite these high percentages, the alcohol is never that noticeable in the mouth. Loaded with glycerin and fruit, the wines are made in a soft, round style. The lightest of this trio, the 1991 Eschen Vineyard, offers an attractive peppery nose, not a great deal of depth, and a short, lean finish. It is a competent, but unexciting Zinfandel. Although the 1991 Ferraro Vineyard is the deepest colored, it is surprisingly light colored when compared with most 1991 Zinfandels. The wine is medium bodied, with uncomplex sweet, jammy, ripe fruit that adequately conceals the high alcohol. Given its softness, it should be drunk over the next 3–4 years. The most interesting wine of these three offerings is the medium ruby-colored 1991 Grand Père. Given the fact that its alcohol is over 15%, the wine's fiery side is largely unnoticeable. There is attractive jammy, raspberry fruit in the nose, medium body, fine glycerin, and a lusty finish. It should be drunk over the next 5–6 years.

S. ANDERSON (NAPA)

Cabernet Sauvignon * * *, Chardonnay * * *, Sparkling Wines * */* * *

1991 Cabernet Sauvignon Richard Chambers Vineyard	Stag's Leap	D	88
1990 Cabernet Sauvignon Richard Chambers Vineyard	Stag's Leap	D	89

The 1991 Cabernet Sauvignon Richard Chambers Vineyard's spicy, olive- and black currant–scented nose is followed by a medium- to full-bodied, cedary, chocolatey, cassis-flavored wine with a velvety texture, admirable depth, and a smooth finish. This wine represents the more herbal style of Cabernet Sauvignon, but this component is well integrated with the wine's other components. Drink it over the next 7–8 years. The dramatic, rich, sweet, smoky, cassis-scented nose of the 1990 Cabernet Sauvignon Richard Chambers Vineyard is followed by a wine with tremendous richness, an unctuous texture, and a long, glycerin, tannin, and alcohol-endowed finish. Drink this impressive, full-bodied wine over the next 10–12 years.

ARAUJO ESTATE WINES (NAPA)

Cabernet Sauvignon Eisele Vineyard * * * * *, Sauvignon Blanc Eisele Vineyard * * * *, Syrah Eisele Vineyard * * * * *

1993 Cabernet Sauvignon Eisele Vineyard	Napa	D	96
1992 Cabernet Sauvignon Eisele Vineyard	Napa	D	95
1991 Cabernet Sauvignon Eisele Vineyard	Napa	D	96
1993 Sauvignon Blanc Eisele Vineyard	Napa	C	88
1993 Syrah Eisele Vineyard	Napa	D	93

I have long been an admirer of this vineyard situated at the base of the mountains in northern Napa Valley just to the south of Calistoga. Longtime readers may remember the ecstatic reviews of the 1974 Conn Creek Eisele Vineyard Cabernet Sauvignon, the great 1975 Joseph Phelps Eisele Vineyard Cabernet Sauvignon, and its successors. The new owners, Bart and Daphne Araujo, who purchased the vineyard from the Eisele family, are intent on pushing the level of quality to new heights. There will only be about 3,000 cases of the Eisele Estate Cabernet Sauvignon, so connoisseurs will undoubtedly be fighting over the limited quantities available. There is also a small amount of Sauvignon Blanc, which will be sold only to the winery's mailing-list clients. Future plans include the production of a Syrah as well as a Viognier.

The barrel-fermented 1993 Sauvignon Blanc was made from ripe fruit and tiny yields. It reveals its concentration and personality in the intensely melony, stylish bouquet, rich, delicious, concentrated flavors, and undeniable sense of elegance and balance. It is a dry, exceptionally well-made Sauvignon with considerable personality and character. Drink it over the next 1–2 years.

The impressive 1993 Syrah Estate, which may not be released commercially because of the frightfully small quantities, exhibits an opaque purple color, and a moderately fragrant, smoky, intense, cassis-scented nose. The wine's massive feel in the mouth, as well as its huge, chocolatey, roasted flavors, suggests considerable promise for 20+ years of aging.

The saturated dark purple-colored 1991 Cabernet Sauvignon Eisele Vineyard boasts a sensational bouquet of minerals and jammy cassis intertwined with subtle aromas of toasty oak and flowers. The wine possesses great extraction, superb balance and harmony, layers of flavor, and significant tannin in the long finish. It is an immensely impressive, beautifully balanced, large-scaled Cabernet that can be drunk with pleasure despite its high tannin and extract level. It will age effortlessly for 20+ years. The 1992 Cabernet Sauvignon Eisele Vineyard is another fabulous wine from this superb vineyard. It displays a sweet, pure nose of black currants, minerals, and spices. Full bodied, tannic, and powerful, as well as undeveloped, it exhibits the potential for 20–25 years of aging. A splendidly rich Cabernet Sauvignon, with outstanding balance and purity, it will not be mature before the turn of the century. Even more stunning, the 1993 Cabernet Sauvignon Eisele Vineyard may eclipse the great 1991. It offers a huge nose of black cherries, black currants, minerals, and vanillin, a stunning display of superconcentrated fruit, full body, and power allied with grace and harmony. The finish continues for nearly a minute. This terrific California Cabernet Sauvignon beautifully presents additional evidence that this is one of the greatest single vineyards in Napa.

ARROWOOD (SONOMA)

Cabernet Sauvignon * * * *, Chardonnay * * *, Chardonnay Cuvée Michel Berthoud * * * * *, Chardonnay Domaine de Grand Archer * * *, Chardonnay Reserve Special * * * *, Malbec * * * *, Merlot * * *, Pinot Blanc Sara Lee's Vineyard * * * *, Special Select Late Harvest Riesling * * * * *, Syrah * * * *, Viognier * * *

1992	Cabernet Sauvignon	Sonoma	C	89
1991	Cabernet Sauvignon	Sonoma	C	90
1990	Cabernet Sauvignon	Sonoma	C	87
1993	Cabernet Sauvignon Domaine de Grand Archer	Sonoma	A	87
1992	Cabernet Sauvignon Reserve Speciale	Sonoma	C	90+
1990	Cabernet Sauvignon Reserve Speciale	Sonoma	D	90
1994	Chardonnay	Sonoma	D	90
1993	Chardonnay	Sonoma	D	90
1993	Chardonnay Cuvée Michel Berthoud	Sonoma	C	92
1994	Chardonnay Domaine de Grand Archer	Sonoma	A	87
1993	Malbec	Sonoma	C	89
1992	Malbec	Sonoma	C	87
1992	Merlot	Sonoma	C	88
1991	Merlot	Sonoma	C	89
1994	Pinot Blanc Sara Lee's Vineyard	Russian River	C	90
1994	Viognier	Russian River	C	89

These are unquestionably the finest wines Dick Arrowood has yet produced. His secondary label, Domaine de Grand Archer, is a noteworthy bargain. The delicious, light- to medium-bodied, fruity 1994 Chardonnay Domaine de Grand Archer goes down the gullet easily and pleasantly. There are copious amounts of tropical fruit in the nose and flavors. This medium-bodied wine is clean, tasty, and ideal for drinking over the next 12 months.

The other Chardonnays include a limited bottling of 1993 Chardonnay Cuvée Michel Berthoud, the second Arrowood Chardonnay to undergo full malolactic fermentation. Its fragrant nose of honeyed fruit and rich, full-bodied, complex flavors provide ample joy and pleasure. This big, bold, yet graceful Chardonnay should be drunk over the next 2–4 years. The 1994 Chardonnay, which will be released in late 1995, possesses a decadent nose of honeyed tropical fruits well integrated with subtle new oak. It is opulently textured, with superb ripeness, a sweet inner core of fruit (from concentration, not sugar), and a long, full-bodied finish.

I was also turned on by Arrowood's 1994 Pinot Blanc from the Sara Lee Vineyard in the

Russian River. It exhibits a textbook Pinot Blanc nose of tangerines and floral scents. Medium to full bodied, with crisp, zesty, underlying acidity, this wine admirably marries finesse and richness. It is loaded with flavor and one of the finest examples of Pinot Blanc I have tasted from California and should drink well for 2–3 years.

As for the 1994 Viognier, Dick Arrowood continues to demonstrate more confidence when working with this fickle varietal. He now ferments half in the tank and half in the barrel. The 1994, which went through 100% malolactic fermentation, is his finest example yet. It offers great ripeness, a honeyed, apricot, and peachlike fragrance, full body, loads of flavor, and a soft, lush finish. Drink it before the end of 1996.

All the Arrowood red wines from the 1990 vintage forward display a more natural texture and have largely been bottled unfined and unfiltered when possible. This departure in philosophy for Arrowood has resulted in wines with more complex aromatic profiles and wonderfully rich, full-flavored personalities. Other enticing wines from Arrowood include the 1992 Merlot, which displays a spicy-, herb-, roasted coffee–, and chocolate-scented nose, deep color, plenty of rich, ripe fruit, and a long, velvety finish. It should drink well for at least a decade. The knockout 1991 Merlot exhibits fragrant aromas of coffee and chocolate, and deep black cherry and black currant fruit. Medium to full bodied, with a satiny texture and admirable length, this Merlot should drink well for a decade.

Like all of Arrowood's red wines, the 1992 Cabernet Sauvignon is bottled without fining or filtration. It exhibits a deep ruby/purple color, an excellent nose of cassis and spicy wood, as well as a medium- to full-bodied finish with gobs of supple, ripe fruit. It should drink well for 12–15 years. The superb 1992 Cabernet Sauvignon Reserve Speciale is the finest Cabernet I have tasted from Dick Arrowood. The opaque purple color is followed by a fragrant nose of cassis and spice, full-bodied, beautifully delineated, concentrated flavors with ripe, sweet tannin. The wine needs 2–3 years of cellaring; it should keep for 20+ years. Bravo!

Readers should also look for the 1993 Domaine de Grand Archer Cabernet Sauvignon, a sweet, ripe, supple Cabernet for drinking over the next 4–5 years. Unfortunately, there are only 1,100 cases, but it is a terrific bargain in user-friendly Cabernet Sauvignon.

The 1991 Cabernet Sauvignon may turn out to be Arrowood's finest regular bottling of Cabernet Sauvignon. Made from a blend of 80% Cabernet Sauvignon, 7% Merlot, 5% Cabernet Franc, and the rest Malbec, this deeply colored wine possesses a rich, fragrant nose of cassis, herbs, and subtle oak. Sweet, ripe, and medium to full bodied, with well-delineated acidity and moderate tannin, this beautifully made, authoritatively flavored, elegant wine should drink well for 15 or more years. Made from a similar blend, the 1990 Cabernet Sauvignon reveals spicy, cedary, cassis-scented aromas, medium-bodied flavors possessing layers of richness, adequate acidity, and a spicy, round, generous finish with noticeably soft tannin. Arrowood's emphasis on combining high-quality fruit with an elegant style and excellent flavor depth is well displayed in this offering. The 1990 Cabernet Sauvignon Reserve Speciale (only 240 cases of magnums were produced) is an outstanding wine. It possesses a bold, aromatic profile of cassis, herbs, sweet oak, licorice and minerals, full body, excellent density, beautiful balance and purity, and a long, moderately tannic finish. Like the other Arrowood offerings, it demonstrates impeccable flavor purity and excellent balance.

As for some of the newest red wine releases, Arrowood is doing super things with the Malbec grape. A barrel sample of the terrific 1994 Malbec was reminiscent of a hypothetical blend of the two Pomerol estates of Château L'Évangile and La Conseillante. The 1993 Malbec exhibits a deep ruby/purple color, gobs of black currant fruit intertwined with scents of truffles, medium body, and loads of flavor, but not the power and tannin found in Cabernet Sauvignon.

Another Arrowood red wine offering worth following is the 1994 Syrah, of which there will be 400 cases, all from the Sara Lee's Vineyard. The wine reveals gobs of licorice and cassis fruit, full body, wonderful sweetness and expansiveness on the palate, and a supple, velvety texture. It will be a Syrah to drink early in life, although it possesses the depth to last for a decade.

How impressive it is to see Dick Arrowood, one of California's most influential winemakers, move in the direction of less manipulation and lower processed wines. Bravo!

AU BON CLIMAT (SANTA BARBARA)

Barbera* * * *, Chardonnay* * *, Chardonnay Bien Nacido* * * *, Chardonnay Sanford & Benedict Vineyard* * * *, Chardonnay Talley Vineyard* * * *, Pinot Noir* * * *, Pinot Noir La Bauge Au Dessus Bien Nacido Vineyard* * * * *, Pinot Noir Sanford & Benedict Vineyard* * * * *, Pinot Noir Talley Vineyard* * *, Zinfandel Sauret Vineyard* * * * *

1993	Chardonnay Estate Le Bouge d'à Côté	Santa Barbara	D	89+
1993	Chardonnay Reserve Sanford & Benedict Vineyard	Santa Ynez	D	91
1993	Chardonnay Reserve Talley Vineyard	Arroyo Grande	D	88
1992	Pinot Noir Estate La Bauge au Dessus	Santa Barbara	D	88
1993	Pinot Noir Sanford & Benedict Vineyard	Santa Ynez	D	89
1993	Pinot Noir Talley Vineyard Rosemary's	Arroyo Grande	D	93
1992	Pinot Noir Talley Vineyard Rosemary's	Arroyo Grande	D	90

Jim Clendenen, who now labels his wines "mind behind," has turned out an exquisite 1993 Talley Vineyard Rosemary's Pinot Noir that should send chills up the spines of even the most quality conscious Burgundians. The color is a healthy dark ruby, with a smashingly intense aromatic profile that blasts from the glass. Jammy, sweet red and black fruits, spice, and smoke saturate the olfactory senses. In the mouth, the wine is all satiny smooth, velvety textured, voluptuous richness with layers of sweet, expansive, ripe fruit, full body, beautifully integrated acidity, and no hard edges. The finish lasts for at least 30–45 seconds. This is a gorgeous Pinot Noir for drinking over the next 5–7 years. Bravo! If the 1993 Talley Vineyard Rosemary's was not so remarkable, most of the accolades would go to the 1992. The latter wine exhibits less color saturation, but wonderfully sweet, expansive fruit, fine aromatics, with a touch more spice and less of a jammy, red-fruit character. It is medium to full bodied, velvety, soft, and long, with plenty of alcohol, glycerin, and fruit in the finish. Drink it over the next 4–5 years.

The 1993 Pinot Noir La Bauge au Dessus is more compact and structured, offering a good ruby/garnet color, a spicy, animal, herb, smoky, gamelike element in the nose, juicy red fruit, and a medium- to full-bodied personality. Although fully mature, the wine's structure indicates it will age for another 4–6 years. Having just had the 1990 at a tasting in Oregon (the wine performed spectacularly), I do not believe the 1993 equals the quality of the 1990 or 1991. Nevertheless, the 1993 is a fine wine that most Pinot powermongers would be pleased to own and drink. Lastly, the 1993 Pinot Noir Sanford & Benedict Vineyard displays a medium- to dark-ruby color, a vivid, herbal, sweet, berry-scented nose, a good attack with plenty of soft, ripe, velvety fruit, and a narrow finish with moderate tannin and noticeable acidity. It is an excellent Pinot Noir that should be consumed over the next 4–5 years.

Au Bon Climat's 1993 Chardonnays are all structured, tightly knit but promising, concentrated wines that can be drunk now, although they will blossom further with another 4–6 months of bottle age. The 1993 Chardonnay Reserve Talley exhibits a clean, intriguing nose of minerals, spice, ripe fruit, and oak. Medium to full bodied, with admirable concentration, plenty of acidity, and a well-delineated style, this mouthfilling, restrained Chardonnay should drink well for 3–4 years. Also nicely proportioned, the 1993 Chardonnay Estate Le

Bouge d'à Côté reveals more honeyed fruit in the nose, full body, good integrated acidity and new oak, and a long, rich finish. There is a layered feel to this youthful, unevolved Chardonnay, which appears to have 4–5 years of aging potential. The 1993 Chardonnay Reserve Sanford & Benedict Vineyard is tightly structured, as well as exceptionally rich and mouthfilling, with a layered palate, full body, and rich, mineral, honeyed, citrusy fruit flavors nicely complemented by smoky oak. Long, intense, and pure, this is an impressively large-scaled Chardonnay that is just beginning to blossom. Look for it to age gracefully for 4–5 years.

If you are lucky enough to come across a few bottles of ABC's 1991 Zinfandel Sauret Vineyard, don't hesitate to latch on to them. I lament the fact that only 25 cases (1 barrel) of this great Zinfandel were produced. The combination of black raspberry and jammy black cherry fruit along with smoky, toasty new oak gives the wine a Côte Rôtie–like bouquet. The thrills do not stop with the bouquet. This Zinfandel possesses unctuous, full-bodied richness, low acidity, and enough tannin to provide support. Drink it over the next decade.

Lastly, readers should be on the lookout for Au Bon Climat's 1992 Barbera, a superrich, flamboyant wine that must be Jim Clendenen's homage to the great Piedmontese Barbera winemaker, Elio Altare. It has the potential to be the best Barbera ever made in America!

Great wine is meant to be both thrilling and joyous. That is what Au Bon Climat's objectives must certainly be. Bravo!

AUSTIN CELLARS (SANTA BARBARA)

Cabernet Sauvignon**, Chardonnay**, Pinot Noir**, Pinot Noir Reserve**, Sauvignon Blanc**, Sauvignon Blanc Reserve**

1991 Cabernet Sauvignon Mille Delices	Santa Barbara	C	80
1991 Cabernet Sauvignon Perry's Reserve	Santa Barbara	C	84
1991 Chardonnay	Santa Barbara	C	72
1991 Pinot Noir Reserve	Santa Barbara	C	78
1991 Sauvignon Blanc Lucas Vineyard	Santa Ynez	B	85
1991 Sauvignon Blanc Reserve	Santa Ynez	B	68

This proved to be an uninspiring group of wines. I should note, however, that barrel samples of the 1992s revealed more character, so perhaps Austin Cellars is turning over a new leaf. I found the 1991 Sauvignon Blanc Reserve to be oxidized, with entirely too much oak obliterating what little fruit remained. Completely out of balance, it can only get worse. The 1991 Sauvignon Blanc Lucas Vineyard is far better, with an intense, grassy, melony, pungent nose, lush, honeyed, melony, fruity flavors, and a crisp, long finish. It is the most interesting wine in this portfolio, but some readers may find the grassiness overblown. The 1991 Chardonnay's fruit is also obliterated by the wood.

The red wines range from a correct, spicy, jammy 1991 Pinot Noir Reserve to an even more jammy, cassis-scented, ripe, unctuous, thick, one-dimensional 1991 Cabernet Sauvignon Perry's Reserve. The 1991 Cabernet Sauvignon Mille Delices offers more chocolate notes in its bouquet, as well as intense vegetal elements to go along with its spicy, black cherry fruitiness. Both Cabernets are made in a fat, unstructured, overripe style that I found clumsy.

BABCOCK VINEYARDS (SANTA BARBARA)

Chardonnay***, Fathom Proprietary White Wine***, Gewürztraminer**, Johannisberg Riesling****, Sauvignon Blanc****, Sauvignon Blanc 11 Oaks Ranch****

1993 Chardonnay Mount Carmel Vineyard	Santa Ynez	D	87
1993 Chardonnay Talley Vineyard	San Luis Obispo	D	86

1991	Gewürztraminer	Santa Barbara	B	84
1992	Johannisberg Riesling Late Harvest Barrel Fermented	Santa Barbara	C	89
1992	Pinot Noir Estate	Santa Ynez	D	90
1992	Pinot Noir Sanford & Benedict Vineyard	Santa Ynez	D	86
1993	Riesling Estate	Santa Ynez	C	86

Babcock has been garnering considerable praise. These wines are impressive more for their subtlety and restraint than for any bold precociousness. I admire the delicate style of Babcock's 1993 Dry Riesling Estate. Initially it appears almost too understated for its own good, but in the mouth lovely floral, apple, and mineral components emerge. It will be superflexible with an assortment of cuisines if drunk over the next year. The 1993 Chardonnay from the Talley Vineyard offers a restrained bouquet of honeyed lemons, apples, and a touch of wood, high acidity, medium to full body, and excellent concentration. The wine's personality is more similar to a top-class Chablis than a fatter, unctuously textured, husky white burgundy from the Côte d'Or. The hallmarks of the 1993 Chardonnay Mount Carmel Vineyard are its understated and measured personality. This wine creeps up on the taster, offering more richness than the tight, unforthcoming bouquet suggests. The more I tasted it as it sat in the glass, the more I admired it. Both of these Chardonnays should keep for 4–5 years.

The two offerings of 1992 Pinot Noir include a stylish, supple, light ruby-colored 1992 Pinot Noir from the Sanford & Benedict Vineyard. It is soft, with adequate acidity, not a great deal of depth, but undeniable charm, and a flattering personality. Drink it over the next 1–2 years. In contrast, the 1992 Pinot Noir Estate exhibits a deeper color, more concentrated, highly extracted fruit, medium body, and a stylish, elegant, Volnay-like character. It is not too far-fetched to suggest that one could easily be tasting a wine from the likes of the Marquis d'Angerville when sniffing and swallowing Babcock's 1992 Estate Pinot Noir. More firmly structured than the Sanford & Benedict Pinot Noir, the Estate should age well for 4–5 years.

Unfortunately, the winery chose not to show me their 1991 Estate Pinot Noir or 1991 Pinot Noir from the superb Sanford & Benedict Vineyard. I did taste a soft, spicy, good 1991 Gewürztraminer, and an even more enjoyable full-bodied, medium-sweet, lychee nut– and rose petal–scented, 100% barrel-fermented, late-harvest 1992 Johannisberg Riesling. In a blind tasting, Babcock's 1992 Johannisberg Riesling could easily be mistaken for a Riesling Vendange Tardive from Alsace. Its fine acidity made the wine taste zesty and alive.

BANCROFT (NAPA)
Chardonnay * * * *

1992	Chardonnay Howell Mountain	Napa	C	87
1991	Chardonnay Howell Mountain	Napa	C	90
1990	Chardonnay Howell Mountain	Napa	C	89

Some readers will be familiar with the Bancroft winery because of the superb Merlot the Beringer winery produces from grapes they purchase from this vineyard. There is also a small amount of estate-bottled wine, including some excellent Chardonnay. The tightly knit, restrained 1992 Chardonnay Howell Mountain begins slowly, offering up subtle hints of lemons, oranges, and apples, as well as stony scents. It hits the palate with medium to full body, and then grows in the mouth, finishing with considerable flavor authority, intensity, and well-integrated acidity. This youthfully elegant offering is an intriguing, mineral-dominated Chardonnay that should improve over the next year and last for 4–5. The ripe, well-balanced 1990 offers plenty of buttery, pineapple fruit in the nose, spicy, subtly oaky, rich flavors, medium to full body, and fine underlying acidity. Surprisingly, it is more backward than the flattering and evolved 1991. The latter wine is quite seductive, with gobs of rich fruit, full body, and a deep, long, lusty finish. The 1990 should drink well for another 2–3 years, and the 1991 will require consumption over the next several years.

BARNETT VINEYARDS (NAPA)

Cabernet Sauvignon Spring Mountain* * */* * * *, Cabernet Sauvignon Spring Mountain Rattlesnake Hill* * */* * * *

1993 Cabernet Sauvignon Spring Mountain	Napa	D	88
1992 Cabernet Sauvignon Spring Mountain	Napa	D	90
1991 Cabernet Sauvignon Spring Mountain	Napa	D	92
1993 Cabernet Sauvignon Spring Mountain Rattlesnake Hill	Napa	D	89
1991 Cabernet Sauvignon Spring Mountain Rattlesnake Hill	Napa	D	96

I was blown away by the excellent 1991 and 1992 Cabernet Sauvignon cuvées from Barnett Vineyards. These people understand great winemaking and their wine demonstrates what heights Napa Valley Cabernet Sauvignon can potentially obtain. The 1992 Cabernet Sauvignon Spring Mountain is among the most distinctive Cabernets I have tasted from California. It offers up an intense fragrance of violets, black raspberries, and herbs gently touched by toasty oak. This medium- to full-bodied wine is powerful, rich, and elegant, with sweet tannin, an expansive mouth-feel, and a Margaux-like stylishness and grace. Drink it over the next 15+ years. The 1991 Cabernet Sauvignon Spring Mountain displays a saturated dark purple color, and a complex, rich, intense bouquet of black currants intertwined with aromas of sweet licorice, subtle herbs, and faint notes of toasty oak. Medium to full bodied, with exquisite purity and flavor richness, this beautifully-balanced, concentrated wine admirably marries authoritative power with considerable grace and elegance. The wine is soft enough to be consumed, yet possesses the overall balance and depth to last for 10–15 years. Superb! It will be frustrating trying to find any of the 25-case production of the 1991 Cabernet Sauvignon Spring Mountain Rattlesnake Hill. This wine is an intensified version of the Spring Mountain regular cuvée. A profound bottle of Napa Valley Cabernet Sauvignon, it should last for 20–25 years. Readers should make every effort to track down these two remarkable wines.

As for Barnett's 1993s, the Cabernet Sauvignon Spring Mountain reveals the intense fragrance and perfume this vineyard routinely achieves. Copious aromas of raspberries, violets, and cranberries leap from the glass. The wine is medium bodied, pure, and elegant with less concentration than the terrific wines made in 1991 and 1992; drink it over the next 10–15 years. The 1993 Cabernet Sauvignon Spring Mountain Rattlesnake Hill offers a sweet, currant nose, an exquisite elegance, and wonderfully rich, ripe fruit with moderate tannin in the finish. Neither as intense nor as muscular as the 1991s or 1992s, it is a stylish, complex Cabernet Sauvignon that should drink well during its first 10–15 years of life.

BEAULIEU (NAPA)

Brut* *, Cabernet Sauvignon Beau Tour* */* * *, Cabernet Sauvignon Private Reserve* * */
* * * *, Cabernet Sauvignon Rutherford* */* * *, Chardonnay Carneros Reserve* */* * *,
Chardonnay Napa Beaufort* */* * *, Fumé Blanc* * *, Pinot Noir Carneros Reserve* *,
Special Burgundy* * *

1993 Sauvignon Blanc	Napa	A	86
1990 Special Burgundy	California	C	87

Beaulieu's 1990 Special Burgundy (a blend of 50% Petite Sirah, 40% Charbono, 5% Early Burgundy, and 5% Napa Gamay) is a delicious, full-bodied, chunky wine loaded with spicy, peppery, herb-tinged red and black fruits. With full body and excellent depth, it is ideal for drinking now and over the next decade.

A delicious, dry, melony, herb-tinged Sauvignon, this fresh, fruity, zesty, light-bodied 1993 can be drunk as an aperitif or served with an assortment of foods. Drink it over the next year.

BELLEROSE VINEYARD (SONOMA)

Cabernet Sauvignon Cuvée Bellerose * * *, Merlot * * * *, Sauvignon Blanc * * *

1988 Merlot Reserve	Dry Creek	C	88

Bellerose's 1988 red wines were among the stars of the vintage, with the 1988 Merlot Reserve offering an explosively rich, coffee-, cassis-, and mocha-scented nose, medium to full body, excellent depth and richness, and a long, gutsy finish. It can be drunk now, but should last and improve for up to a decade.

BELVEDERE WINE COMPANY (SONOMA)

Cabernet Sauvignon * *, Chardonnay * * *, Merlot * *

1993 Chardonnay	Sonoma	A	87
1992 Chardonnay	Alexander Valley	A	87
1992 Chardonnay Preferred Stock	Sonoma	C	89

Belvedere continues to fashion deliciously fruity, medium to full-bodied wines with considerable personality. Their best buy is the 1992 Alexander Valley Chardonnay, which will undoubtedly be discounted for even less than $9. It possesses an attractive, honeyed apple character, medium to full body, good purity, enough acidity for freshness, and a heady, satisfying, mouth-filling finish. Drink it over the next year. The 1992 Chardonnay Preferred Stock, while not twice the wine, is a slightly richer, more obvious wine with new oak and higher acidity. A rich, boldly styled wine, it offers a buttery, honeyed-apple style of fruit. It should last for 1–2 years.

The 1993 Chardonnay from Sonoma is a clean, citrusy, honeyed-apple–, buttery-flavored and -scented wine with a nice touch of oak. It is medium to full bodied and cleanly made, with enough acidity to provide balance and zest. Drink it over the next 1–2 years.

BENZIGER (SONOMA)

Cabernet Sauvignon * * *, Cabernet Sauvignon Tribute * * *, Chardonnay * * *, Fumé Blanc * * *, Merlot * *, Pinot Blanc * * *, Proprietary White Wine * * */* * * *, White Burgundy * * *, Viognier * * *, Zinfandel * * *

1993 Fumé Blanc	Sonoma	A	86
1992 Fumé Blanc	Sonoma	A	86
1991 Malbec Imagery Series	Alexander Valley	C	87
1992 Pinot Blanc	Sonoma	B	87
1993 Viognier Imagery Series	Sonoma	C	87
1992 White Burgundy Imagery Series	Yountville	C	89
1992 Zinfandel	Sonoma	A	87
1991 Zinfandel	Sonoma	A	86

This winery continues to turn out attractive wines that are made to be drunk within a few years of release. The 1992 Pinot Blanc, which offers honeyed, cherry, and orange marmalade–like flavors, excellent richness, and a lusty personality, is sure to garner many friends. The 1993 Viognier Imagery Series exhibits Viognier's telltale, honeysuckle, peach, and apricot scents, medium to full body, supple, chewy richness, and a fine finish. It should be drunk within the next year.

Although not the biggest, most tannic or powerful Zinfandel, Benziger's 1992 Zinfandel is enjoyable for its juicy, succulent, richly fruity style that dances across the palate with considerable suppleness and ripeness. Soft and round, as well as elegant, this wine should be drunk over the next 2–3 years. Benziger's 1991 Zinfandel is a supple, richly fruity, easy-to-understand, briary, spicy Zinfandel with no hard edges. It possesses a chewy, soft texture, and a heady, alcoholic finish. It is ideal for restaurants and consumers desiring a plush style of Zinfandel.

More complex and intriguing is Benziger's 1991 Malbec Imagery Series. Outside of Argentina, it is rare today to find Malbec standing on its own. Certainly no one produces it any more in Bordeaux, and the best Malbecs today emanate from some of Argentina's old vineyards in the Mendoza Valley. Benziger's Malbec exhibits the elegant, floral, curranty, penetrating fragrance of this underrated varietal. In the mouth it is all finesse, with its soft, supple, medium-bodied, creamy texture, and rich fruit flavors. There is nothing heavy, tannic, or overbearing about this stylish, fragrant, persuasive example of Malbec. Drink it over the next 5–6 years.

Benziger has fashioned an elegant, spicy, richly fruity 1993 Fumé Blanc displaying subtle notes of honey, melon, and herbs. There is fine flavor concentration and enough acidity to provide vibrancy. Drink it over the next year. The attractive, well-made 1992 Fumé Blanc exhibits the soft, ripe, fat character of the vintage. The wine possesses oodles of opulent fruit and a lovely honeyed, melon-flavored finish. Drink it over the next year.

The 1992 White Burgundy Imagery Series, an interesting blend of 52% Chardonnay, 24% Pinot Blanc, and 24% Pinot Meunier, exhibits a lavishly rich, opulent personality, a gorgeous bouquet of honeyed fruit, full-bodied, concentrated, vividly pure, fresh flavors touched gently by the judicious use of toasty new oak, and a deep, chewy finish. Drink it over the next year.

BERINGER (NAPA)

Cabernet Sauvignon Chabot Vineyard* * * * *, Cabernet Sauvignon Knight's Valley* * *, Cabernet Sauvignon Private Reserve* * * * *, Chardonnay* * *, Chardonnay Private Reserve* * * */* * * * *, Chardonnay Proprietor Grown* * */* * * *, Chardonnay Sbragia Select* * * * *, Chenin Blanc* * *, Gamay* * *, Meritage White* * *, Merlot Bancroft Vineyard* * * * *, Sauvignon Blanc* * *, Viognier* * *, Zinfandel* * *

1993	Cabernet Sauvignon	Knight's Valley	B	91
1992	Cabernet Sauvignon	Knight's Valley	B	90
1991	Cabernet Sauvignon	Knight's Valley	C	89
1992	Cabernet Sauvignon Chabot Vineyard	Napa	D	99+
1991	Cabernet Sauvignon Chabot Vineyard	Napa	D	97+
1990	Cabernet Sauvignon Chabot Vineyard	Napa	D	95
1989	Cabernet Sauvignon Chabot Vineyard	Napa	D	90
1993	Cabernet Sauvignon Private Reserve	Napa	D	96
1992	Cabernet Sauvignon Private Reserve	Napa	D	96+
1991	Cabernet Sauvignon Private Reserve	Napa	D	95

1990 Cabernet Sauvignon Private Reserve	Napa	D	93
1989 Cabernet Sauvignon Private Reserve	Napa	D	90
1993 Chardonnay	Napa	B	87
1993 Chardonnay Private Reserve	Napa	C	92
1992 Chardonnay Private Reserve	Napa	C	93
1992 Chardonnay Proprietor Grown	Napa	B	89
1993 Chardonnay Sbragia Select	Napa	C	94
1992 Chardonnay Sbragia Select	Napa	C	96
1993 Merlot Bancroft Vineyard	Howell Mountain	D	95
1992 Merlot Bancroft Vineyard	Howell Mountain	D	95
1991 Merlot Bancroft Vineyard	Howell Mountain	D	93
1990 Merlot Bancroft Vineyard	Howell Mountain	D	89
1989 Merlot Bancroft Vineyard	Howell Mountain	D	89
1993 Meritage Red	Napa	B	92
1992 Meritage Red	Napa	B	90
1993 Meritage White	Knight's Valley	A	89
1994 Nouveau	Napa	A	86
1992 Sauvignon Blanc	Napa	A	86
1993 Viognier	Napa	C	90
1992 Viognier Hudson Ranch	Napa	C	94
1992 Zinfandel	Napa	B	87

It is especially admirable when a winery the size, stature, and importance of Beringer continues to push the quality of its offerings to greater and greater heights. Given how successful this property has become, it would be easy to rest on its already sterling reputation, but no one at this historic winery appears satisfied with maintaining the status quo. Beringer has been on an amazing hot streak. Even more remarkable, given the huge diversity of high quality wines that emerge from this winery, consumers will find that upcoming releases are even more compelling than previous Beringer offerings—high praise indeed! Additionally, small experimental lots of dazzling wines such as Pinot Blanc, Pinot Auxerrois, Pinot Gris, Viognier, and Melon, sold only at the winery, prove that Beringer intends to produce more than world-class Merlot-, Chardonnay-, and Cabernet Sauvignon–based wines.

Given the tiny quantities (under 50 cases) of 1992 Pinot Gris, 1992 Pinot Blanc, 1992 Pinot Auxerrois, and 1992 Melon made, it is sufficient to say that if you ever visit Beringer and notice any of these wines for sale, do not hesitate to buy a few bottles. The blockbuster, rich, honeyed, orange, concentrated 1992 Pinot Blanc and the more mineral-scented, enticing, rich 1992 Pinot Auxerrois are terrific efforts. There are 200 cases of the 1993 Viognier. It possesses an exotic, honeysuckle-scented, intensely fruity nose, full body, excellent richness, and a long, dry, unctuously textured finish. Given the fragility of Viognier's intense perfume, it is a wine to drink during the first 18 months after bottling. Beringer's 1993 Meritage White from Knight's Valley (made from 56% Sauvignon Blanc and 44% Semillon) is nearly outstanding. It displays a forceful, boldly stated nose of waxy, lusciously ripe fruit, full body, excellent purity and vibrance, and an exuberant, dry, lengthy finish. It should drink well for several years.

Beringer now produces three separate cuvées of Chardonnay. The least expensive (and a bargain) is the tasty 1993 Chardonnay Napa. It emphasizes copious quantities of fleshy, buttery, apple, and honeyed fruit. Round, with good underlying acidity and excellent purity and balance, it is ideal for drinking over the next year. Beringer's 1992 Proprietor Grown Chardonnay emphasizes rich, ripe, honeyed-apple, buttery fruit, and is meant to be consumed within several years of the vintage. The 1992 is softer and more unctuously textured than the 1991.

At the next quality level is Beringer's Private Reserve Chardonnay. The 1993 Private Reserve Chardonnay offers a bold, buttery, richly fruity nose, full-bodied, creamy, fleshy flavors, decent acidity, and a whoppingly long finish. If you are looking for more oak, as well as richer fruit, Beringer's 1992 Private Reserve Chardonnay is another example of the rich, full-bodied, fat style that California's 1992 white wines possess. It is a massively rich, thick Chardonnay, with loads of fruit, an attractive toasty, vanillin nose, and a long, lush finish. It should drink well for at least 2–3 years.

The top cuvée of Beringer Chardonnay is the Sbragia Select, a luxury cuvée (although it is certainly not priced as such) named after the prodigiously talented Beringer winemaker, Ed Sbragia. The 1992 Chardonnay Sbragia Select is an amazing, smoky, buttery, full-bodied wine oozing with personality and decadence because of its extraordinary richness. It could not have been easy to produce such a well-balanced wine. The 1993 Sbragia Select Chardonnay may be a trifle restrained, but who can complain when a wine is this rich, pure, complex, full bodied, and impeccably well balanced? The light gold color is followed by aromas of overripe apples, honeyed oranges, mangoes, and subtle oak. Full bodied, yet sensationally well balanced with adequate acidity, this wine is seamless as well as profound. This is about as rich a mouthful of Chardonnay as you are likely to encounter. Drink it over the next 3–4 years.

With respect to Beringer's red wines, if you like your reds light, exuberant, perfumed, and fruity, don't miss Beringer's 1994 Nouveau. One of the best examples made in the new world, it offers a blast of strawberry, cherry, and raspberry fruit, a tangy, vibrant personality, and light to medium body. It is meant to be drunk within its first 4–6 months of life, although it will last for more than a year.

Beringer's Cabernet Sauvignons and Merlots continue to move from strength to strength. There are now five cuvées, starting with the Cabernet Sauvignon from Knight's Valley, and more recently a Meritage red wine, followed by the three flagship reds of the Beringer empire —the Merlot from the Bancroft Vineyard on Howell Mountain, the Cabernet Sauvignon from the Chabot Vineyard, and the Private Reserve Cabernet Sauvignon.

The Knight's Valley Cabernet Sauvignon has been a terrific bargain over recent years. The 1991 Knights Valley Cabernet Sauvignon is excellent. The wine displays an impressively saturated, deep ruby/purple color, and an easy-to-admire, rich bouquet of cassis and spice. Full-bodied and loaded with concentration, this big, supple wine is a noteworthy value in high-class Cabernet Sauvignon. Drinkable now, it should age well for 10–15 years. The 1992 may merit an outstanding rating after another year or two of age. It offers an impressively saturated dark ruby/purple color, and wonderfully ripe cassis fruit intermingled with scents of jammy cherries, spices, and herbs. Rich, deep, and supple, it is ideal for drinking over the next 7–10 years. The 1993 Cabernet Sauvignon Knight's Valley is the best Knight's Valley Cabernet Beringer has yet made. The wine is outstanding in its display of superrich, black currant, herb, mocha, and spicy fruit, a sweet, full-bodied, concentrated palate, and a long, generous finish. It should drink well for at least 10–12 years.

Beringer's Private Reserve Cabernet Sauvignon has always been a deceptively supple, soft, easy-to-drink wine when released. Recent vintages, while taking on additional power and concentration, appear to be made in a similar flattering, velvety-textured style. If you have given up on the 1989 vintage for California Cabernet, think again. Beringer's 1989 Private Reserve is one of the stars of the vintage. Unlike many of the hollow, aggressively tannic 1989s, this dark-colored wine is loaded with rich, chocolatey, black currant fruit, and spicy, toasty oak. Although it reveals harder tannin than is found in the 1990 and 1991, the tannin is not out of balance. This long, rich, full-bodied, impressively endowed Cabernet Sauvignon will benefit from 2–3 more years of cellaring; it will keep for 15 more years. The generously endowed, dark purple-colored 1990 Private Reserve is a rich, opulent, full-bodied wine loaded with layers of flavor, copious amounts of juicy fruit, sweet tannin, and moderate amounts of lavish oak. Less muscular and concentrated than the 1991, it is a superb expression of a Napa Valley Cabernet Sauvignon. It should drink well for at least 12–15 years. The 1991 Cabernet Sauvignon Private Reserve possesses even more concentration, a smashing bouquet of smoky, unctuously textured black and red fruits, sweet, generous, decadently rich flavors, low acidity, and a voluptuously long, juicy finish. This fabulous Cabernet Sauvignon should drink well for 15 or more years. The 1992 and 1993 Private Reserve Cabernet Sauvignons are the two most promising Beringer Cabernet Sauvignons made under the Reserve designation. Both possess extraordinary aromas and flavors, as well as saturated black/purple colors, huge, rich noses of spring flowers, black fruits, and spicy oak, followed by fabulously rich, multidimensional flavors presented in a full-bodied style. The 1992 is more flamboyant, largely because it has an additional year of age. The 1993 exhibits the same sweetness of fruit and spectacular length and intensity. I would not be surprised to see all of these wines, which I have rated conservatively, come close to perfection!

One of the hardest wines to find among Beringer's superstars is their Chabot Vineyard (from the Napa Valley) Cabernet Sauvignon. The production of approximately 300 cases is aged in 100% new oak and is made from frightfully small yields. As with Beringer's other successful Cabernets in 1989, the 1989 Cabernet Sauvignon Chabot Vineyard reveals an impressively saturated dark ruby/purple color, a rich bouquet, and dense, chewy, full-bodied flavors with more noticeable tannin than in the 1990 and 1991. Already approachable, it should last for 12–14 years. The 1990 Cabernet Sauvignon Chabot Vineyard is a gorgeously rich, velvety-textured, opulent wine with layers of chocolatey, cassis fruit. Rich and full bodied, it is a more tannic wine than the Bancroft Merlot, but, wow, what personality! The 1991 Cabernet Sauvignon Chabot Vineyard appears to have gained additional weight since I tasted it last. It is a legend in the making (as is the 1992). The 1991 is nearly off the quality-level charts. The black/purple color and huge nose of roasted black fruits, herbs, earth, and vanilla are followed by an awesomely concentrated wine with a richness and intensity that must be tasted to be believed. The elevated tannin is nearly masked by the wine's other components, such as fruit, glycerin, and hefty alcohol. This extraordinary Cabernet Sauvignon should age well for 25+ years. The 1992 Cabernet Sauvignon Chabot Vineyard may merit a perfect score in time. It is as spectacular and riveting a Cabernet as I have ever tasted from California. Its seamless personality offers extraordinarily rich, black fruit scents intertwined with aromas of spices, flowers, herbs, licorice, and chocolate. The wine fills the mouth but never tastes heavy or overdone, rather amazing given its intensity. This superbly rendered, potentially legendary Cabernet Sauvignon is sure to have Cabernet enthusiasts scrambling over the tiny quantities.

The 1992 and 1993 Meritage Red are primarily Cabernet-based wines, with some Petite Verdot and Merlot in the blend. Both are impressive wines, as well as exceptional bargains. The 1992 Meritage Red offers an impressive color, big, spicy, jammy, black and red fruit scents, and a supple, velvety-textured, medium- to full-bodied, long finish. It is ideal for drinking over the next 7–8 years. While the 1993 Meritage Red is a year or two away from release, it should prove to be even better than the 1992, as the cask sample I tasted was even richer and more aromatically complex.

Beringer has made significant investments in Howell Mountain vineyards, where they produce a superb Merlot from their Bancroft Vineyard. Consumers can expect larger quantities of Beringer's Howell Mountain wines, as they have planted a large vineyard directly across the driveway leading to Randy Dunn's winery. As for recent Bancroft Vineyard Merlots, the dark ruby-colored 1990 Merlot Bancroft Vineyard displays attractive spicy oak intermingled with scents of ripe red and black fruits, medium to full body, and a rich, sweet, long finish. It is less muscular than the nearly outstanding 1989 Merlot Bancroft Vineyard. It is a big, rich, chocolatey, toffee-scented wine that displays considerable evidence of aging in toasty new oak. A full-bodied, fleshy wine, it is a terrific example from this irregular vintage. It matches the intensity of the 1990. The 1991 boasts a huge nose of chocolate and nearly overripe black cherries, with some oak and herbs adding to the bouquet's complexity. The wine is full bodied, with a layered, opulent personality, superripeness, and a heady, chocolatey finish. It should drink well for 10–15 years. The 1992 Merlot Bancroft Vineyard is a massive example of Merlot. The saturated ruby/purple color and huge, intense bouquet of melted chocolate, prunes, jammy black cherries and black currants are followed by incredibly rich, unctuously textured, layered flavors that go on and on. It is an extremely impressive, large-scaled Merlot that should drink well for 15 or more years. The 1993 Merlot Bancroft Vineyard is cut from the same cloth as the massive 1992. It is a blockbuster, thick, chocolatey, black and red fruit–scented and –flavored wine with full body, gobs of glycerin and extract, and a huge finish. These Merlots appear to be able to handle 2 decades of cellaring.

This fine winery fashioned a velvety-textured, aromatic, spicy 1992 Zinfandel with gobs of black cherry fruit intertwined with aromas of smoke and toast. Ripe, deliciously fleshy and supple, this medium-bodied, satiny-smooth wine should be drunk over the next 4–5 years.

The 1992 Sauvignon Blanc appears to be California's answer to Château Margaux's Pavillon Blanc. It is a wonderfully well-focused, concentrated wine with gobs of honeyed-herb and smoky-scented fruit, fine body, and an overall sense of elegance and crispness. This impressive, dry white wine is unbelievably flexible with an assortment of cuisines. Drink it over the next 1–2 years.

Ratings for Older Vintages of Beringer's Cabernet Sauvignon Private Reserve: 1988 (85), 1987 (93), 1986 (92), 1985 (91), 1984 (89), 1982 (87), 1981 (86), 1978 (90)

Ratings for Older Vintages of Beringer's Merlot Bancroft Vineyard: 1988 (85), 1987 (90)

BERNARDUS (MONTEREY)
Chardonnay * * *, Pinot Noir * * *, Sauvignon Blanc * * *

1992 Chardonnay	Monterey	B	86
1992 Pinot Noir Bien Nacido Vineyard	Santa Barbara	C	87
1993 Sauvignon Blanc	Monterey	A	87

The medium ruby-colored 1992 Pinot Noir Bien Nacido Vineyard represents the hedonistic side of Pinot. Lavishly oaked, with gobs of rich black cherry fruit, it is lush, velvety textured, and heady in the mouth. In short, it is a beautifully pure, richly fruity crowd-pleasing wine that is unmistakably Pinot. Drink it over the next 3–4 years.

The 1993 Sauvignon Blanc produced by Bernardus is cut from the same cloth as their sumptuous, velvety-textured Pinot Noir. A flowery, melony, gloriously ripe and fruity Sauvignon, its bouquet leaps from the glass and the wine is full of fruit. Dry and medium bodied, with excellent definition and purity, it is another crowd pleaser. Drink it over the next 12 months. The tasty 1992 Chardonnay offers copious quantities of buttered apple– and pineapple-flavored fruit, fine acidity, and a spicy, medium- to full-bodied finish. Drink it over the next year.

BIALÉ VINEYARDS (NAPA)
Zinfandel Aldo's Vineyard * * * *

1993 Zinfandel Aldo's Vineyard	Napa	C	89

Made from a vineyard planted in 1937, the dark ruby-colored, spicy, toasty, oaky-scented 1993 Zinfandel Aldo's Vineyard appears to have had the benefit of abundant quantities of new oak barrels. The dark color is accompanied by wonderfully ripe, opulent raspberry fruit, medium to full body, and a deep, long, toasty, slightly tannic finish. Drink it over the next 7–8 years.

BLACK AND BLUE (NAPA)
Proprietary Red Wine * * * */* * * * *

1992 Proprietary Red Wine	Napa	D	91

This special cuvée, made for the proprietor of the Campanile Restaurant in southern California at Michael Havens Wine Cellars in Napa, offers both a smashing package (a heavy, expensive bottle and a poster-quality, artsy label) and terrific wine. Nearly opaque purple-colored, it possesses gobs of pure, persuasive, and intense blackberry and cassis fruit. Full bodied, with a voluptuously textured, rich, layered feel in the mouth, this large-scale, impressively endowed tribute to such French Syrah/Cabernet blends as the renowned Domaine Trevallon in Provence, can be drunk now or cellared for 10–12 years. Very limited in availability (272 cases).

BOEGER WINERY (EL DORADO)
Cabernet Sauvignon * * *, Chardonnay * *, Merlot * * *, Zinfandel * * *

1990 Zinfandel Joseph and Nichellini Vineyards	Napa	B	76

A lean, austere, high-acid Zinfandel without enough flesh or fruit, this 1990 should be consumed over the near term.

BONNY DOON VINEYARD (SANTA CRUZ)
Ca' del Solo Cuvées * * *, Chardonnay * *, Chenin Blanc * * *, Cigare Volant * * *, Cinsault * * *, Clos de Gilroy Grenache * * * *, Old Telegram Mourvèdre * * *, Pinot Meunier * * *, Riesling * * *, Le Sophiste * * * *, Syrah * * *, Vin Gris de Cigare (Rosé)* * * *

1993 Ca' del Solo Big House Red	California	A	85
1993 Ca' del Solo Big House White	California	A	86
1992 Ca' del Solo Il Fiasco	California	A	87
1993 Chenin Blanc Pacific Rim	Monterey	A	84
1992 Cinsault	Sonoma	B	88
1994 Clos de Gilroy	California	A	87
1992 Le Sophiste (Roussanne/Marsanne)	California	C	88
1991 Old Telegram	California	C	90
1991 Pinot Meunier (Blanc de Noir)	California	C	87
1993 Riesling Pacific Rim	Monterey	A	86
1992 Syrah Estate	Santa Cruz	D	92
1994 Vin Gris de Cigare Rosé	California	A	87

Randall Grahm's newest releases appear to be the most impressive wines he has produced in years. One never knows what to expect from Bonny Doon Vineyard, but that's what makes it fun. For bargain hunters, there is a bevy of top selections that please both the palate and the purse. The offerings of 1993 Ca' del Solo Big House Red and Big House White are attractively made, tasty wines. The 1993 Ca' del Solo Big House Red (a blend of Mourvèdre, Grenache, Syrah, Barbera, Sangiovese, Nebbiolo, Pinot Meunier, Cinsault, and Charbono— wow!) exhibits straightforward, ripe fruit, medium body, and a soft texture. The 1993 Ca' del Solo Big House White offers an appealing, exotic bouquet of flowery, berry scents. Medium bodied, soft, and delicious fruity, this is a tasty white wine value.

Randall Grahm has turned out two cuvées of Pacific Rim wines—a 1993 Chenin Blanc and a 1993 Riesling. Although flabby, the off-dry 1993 Pacific Rim Chenin Blanc is enjoyable for its fresh fruit and fragrance. It is ideal for drinking over the next year. The orange/apple-scented 1993 Pacific Rim Riesling reveals an enticing fragrance, more delineation and focus, and a medium-bodied, dry finish. Drink this delicious Riesling over the next year.

The larger-scaled white wines include the 1991 Pinot Meunier, an interesting, butter- and tangerine-scented wine with a honeyed-fruit character, medium to full body, and a luscious finish. Only 100 cases were produced. This dry, complex wine should drink well for 2–3 years. The 1992 Le Sophiste (Roussanne and Marsanne) is my pick for the most intriguing wine bottle and capsule treatment (a top hat) in the business. The wine possesses copious amounts of honeyed fruit intermingled with apple blossom scents, considerable richness and extract, full body, and an enticing, glycerin-imbued, natural feel. Dry and boldly decadent, it is ideal for drinking over the next year with such rich fish dishes as salmon.

I was superimpressed with the gorgeously fruity, medium-bodied, concentrated, velvety-textured 1992 Ca' del Solo Il Fiasco. A knockout, everyday, dry red wine with considerable character and gobs of fruit, it should drink well for 2–3 years. I have always been a fan of Randall Grahm's Clos de Gilroy. Like its predecessors, the 1994 Clos de Gilroy is a lovely, perfumed, intensely fruity (strawberries and cherries), dry, medium-bodied wine. It should be served chilled and drunk over the next 12 months.

The intense dry red wines from Bonny Doon's portfolio include an excellent 1992 Cinsault made from an old vineyard in the Dry Creek area. Only 100 cases were produced. This wine boasts gorgeous, raspberry and black cherry fruit, medium to full body, superb purity, and a chewy finish with light tannin and adequate acidity. It should drink well for 5–6 years. I thought the 1991 Old Telegram to be the finest Grahm has made since his debut release of this wine. Made from 100% Mourvèdre, and, according to Grahm, picked at riper sugar levels and with more bleeding of the tanks to increase the concentration, this opaque ruby/purple-colored wine exhibits a superb nose of red and black fruits, leather, spice, and subtle wood. Full bodied and superconcentrated yet supple, expansive, and chewy, I was turned on by its sumptuousness, as well as by its potential to age gracefully for 7–8 years. Bonny Doon's 1992 Syrah Estate from the Santa Cruz Mountains is an exceptional example of this varietal. It reveals an opaque purple color, a huge, smoky, cassis-scented bouquet, and layers of rich, thick, chewy fruit presented in a full-bodied format. There is plenty of tannin lurking beneath the wine's stunning concentration, so do not be concerned about this wine cracking up. It is an explosively rich, complex Syrah that should drink well for 15–20 years.

Lastly, I have always been a fan of Grahm's Vin Gris de Cigare, although recent vintages have been somewhat monochromatic. The 1994 displays fine body, layers of juicy, straw-berry and cherry fruit, and a spicy, full finish. It is a terrific rosé for drinking over the summer, either with food or by itself.

BRANDER (SANTA YNEZ)
Bouchet Proprietary Red Wine* */* * *, Chardonnay Tête de Cuvée* * *

1990 Bouchet Proprietary Red Wine	Santa Ynez	C	82
1989 Bouchet Proprietary Red Wine	Santa Ynez	C	84
1992 Chardonnay Tête de Cuvée	Santa Ynez	C	88

I am delighted to see Brander moving to a more concentrated and interesting style of Chardonnay. This lusty, vanillin-, ripe apple-, and butter-scented 1992 Tête de Cuvée exhibits great fruit, medium to full body, and a rich, heady finish. Drink it over the next 1–2 years.

The Bouchet Proprietary Red Wine is a blend of Cabernet Sauvignon, Cabernet Franc, and Merlot. The 1989 Bouchet, which has more Cabernet Franc in the blend, is similar to a light- to medium-weight St.-Émilion with its herbaceous, spicy, chocolatey, fruity nose. Austere and compact, more length, depth, and flesh could have elevated its rating. The 1990 Bouchet is herbaceous, but pleasant in a monochromatic style. Those who like their red wines weedy will rate it higher than I.

BRINDIAMO (SOUTHERN CALIFORNIA)
Gioveto * * *, Nebbiolo * * *, Rosso Vecchio * * *

1993 Gioveto	California South Coast	B	85
1993 Nebbiolo	California South Coast	B	85
1993 Rosso Vecchio	California South Coast	B	86

Although these offerings may appear to have been made in Italy, they are produced by the Dorton Winery (Culbertson Sparkling Wines) in southern California. My favorite wine of this trio is the least expensive, the 1993 Rosso Vecchio. Made from 44% Mourvèdre, 30% Grenache, 21% Petite Sirah, and 5% Negrette, it offers a healthy dark ruby color, a big, spicy, sweet, berry- and jammy-scented nose, supple, rich flavors with fine extract, and a velvety texture. An excellent bargain, it should drink well for 2–4 years.

The 1993 Nebbiolo is also a respectable effort from this varietal grown in vineyards in the Temecula Valley. The wine reveals an attractive, berry/floral-scented nose, medium body, clean, ripe fruit, admirable suppleness, and vibrant acidity that gives focus and zest. This delicious Nebbiolo will offer ideal drinking over the next 2–3 years.

The 1993 Gioveto, a blend of 70% Sangiovese/15% Cabernet Sauvignon/15% Merlot, is a more earthy-style wine, with a leathery, berry quality, peppery, spicy fruit, medium body, good intensity, and a more structured, fuller feel than the Nebbiolo.

This winery also released a 1993 Pinot Noir, which I would rate in the mid- to upper-seventies. Although not nearly as good as the other three offerings, it was correct, cleanly made, and not as vegetal as might be expected from such southern vineyards.

DAVID BRUCE WINERY (SANTA CRUZ)
Chardonnay * *, Petite Sirah * * *, Pinot Noir* */* * * *, Zinfandel * * *

1991 Zinfandel	San Luis Obispo	B	76
1991 Zinfandel Vintner's Select	San Luis Obispo	B	72

Made from 80% Zinfandel and 20% Petite Sirah, the 1991 Zinfandel (regular cuvée) offers an attractive, peppery, spicy, earthy nose, and lean, austere, hard-edged flavors that possess too much tannin and not enough fruit. Its future is dubious. Extremely tart, lean, and acidic, with a hollow, compact finish, the 1991 Zinfandel Vintner's Select lacks concentration, depth, and charm. I wish David Bruce would return to the individualistic style of winemaking that brought him fame and controversy 2 decades ago.

BRUTOCAO CELLARS (MENDOCINO)
Cabernet Sauvignon Albert Vineyard * * *, Chardonnay * * *, Merlot * * *, Sauvignon
Blanc * * *, Zinfandel * * *

1992 Cabernet Sauvignon Albert Vineyard	Mendocino	B	86
1992 Chardonnay	Anderson Valley	B	87
1993 Chardonnay Bliss Vineyard	Mendocino	B	87
1992 Chardonnay Bliss Vineyard	Mendocino	B	86
1992 Merlot Unfined/Unfiltered	Mendocino	C	86
1993 Sauvignon Blanc Estate	Mendocino	B	85
1993 Zinfandel Hopland Ranch	Mendocino	B	87
1992 Zinfandel Unfined/Unfiltered	Mendocino	B	86

Brutocao continues to offer attractive wines (in both quality and price) with admirable levels of up-front, precocious, ripe fruit, soft textures, and friendly personalities. The medium-bodied, deliciously fruity 1993 Chardonnay Bliss Vineyard possesses gobs of ripeness, fine underlying acidity, and copious quantities of apple, pear, buttery fruit that are presented in a soft, nicely concentrated, fresh style. Drink it over the next year. The 1992 Chardonnay Bliss Vineyard offers toast and vanillin in a ripe, zesty bouquet. Medium bodied, fresh, lively, and tasty, this attractive wine should be drunk over the next year. The 1992 Chardonnay from Anderson Valley exhibits a more honeyed character to its ripe, citrusy flavors. The wine displays excellent depth, medium body, good delineation, and a vibrant, exuberant finish. Drink it over the next year.

The attractive herb-, fig-, melony-scented and -flavored 1993 Sauvignon Blanc Estate is medium bodied, lively, and exuberant with adequate body and a pleasant finish. Drink it over the next 10–12 months.

The 1992 Cabernet Sauvignon Albert Vineyard exhibits attractive, peppery, ripe black currant– and herb-scented fruit, medium body, and a supple, round texture. While there is not a great deal of complexity, the wine offers plenty of mouth-filling Cabernet fruit that is not burdened by excessive wood, acidity, or tannin. Drink it over the next 4–5 years.

The 1993 Zinfandel Hopland Ranch is a gorgeously delicious, hedonistic, round, satiny-textured, fleshy Zinfandel loaded with raspberry and black cherry fruit. The wine lacks total brilliance because all of this property's red wines (from their organically farmed vineyards) are bottled unfined and unfiltered. This lush Zinfandel should drink well for 3–4 years. Brutocao's dark ruby-colored 1992 Unfined and Unfiltered Zinfandel is an up-front, spicy, perfumed wine with excellent ripeness, a rich, medium-bodied, creamy texture, fine flavors, and gobs of berry fruit in the heady, alcoholic, velvety finish. Drink it over the next 2–3 years.

I enjoyed the 1992 Merlot from Mendocino. Neither complex, nor a behemoth that will assault the palate, it reveals a deep ruby/purple color, a big, black cherry and spicy nose, chunky, fleshy flavors, and a soft, easy-to-understand and -appreciate finish. Drink it over the next 3–4 years.

DON BRYANT (NAPA)
Cabernet Sauvignon * * * * *

1993 Cabernet Sauvignon	Napa	D	95
1992 Cabernet Sauvignon	Napa	D	91

Over the next year readers should be on the lookout for some of the 1,000-case production of Don Bryant's Cabernet Sauvignon from an old vineyard on Pritchard Hill near the

Chappellet Vineyard. Bryant's 1992 Cabernet Sauvignon offers an impressive black/purple color, dusty tannin, immense concentration, full body, and enormous richness in the finish. Even more exciting is the extraordinary 1993 Cabernet Sauvignon. It possesses an opaque black/purple color, and a huge bouquet of black raspberries, cassis, vanillin, licorice, and spices. The wine is superrich, with sweet tannin, an expansive mouth-feel, and an awesome finish. It will be approachable when released, but it will not hit its stride until the turn of the century; it will last for 10–15 years thereafter.

BUEHLER VINEYARDS (NAPA)
Cabernet Sauvignon* * */* * * *, Pinot Blanc* *, White Zinfandel* * *, Zinfandel* * *

1990 Cabernet Sauvignon	Napa	C	88
1992 Zinfandel	Napa	A	87

Although not a blockbuster Cabernet such as those wines Buehler produced between 1978 and 1984, the 1990 is still a huge, massive, rich, full-bodied wine with an opaque ruby/purple color, a spicy, earthy, black cherry–scented nose, excellent richness, full body, and plenty of sweet, jammy fruit in the moderately tannic finish. Drink it over the next 12–15 years.

Buehler's 1992 Zinfandel is a terrific bargain in user-friendly, easy-to-drink, ripe, concentrated, fat Zinfandel. A big, peppery, black raspberry–scented nose and supple, chewy flavors are well displayed and delightfully accessible. Drink this dry, delicious Zinfandel over the next 3–5 years.

BURGESS CELLARS (NAPA)
Cabernet Sauvignon Vintage Selection* * *, Chardonnay Triere Vineyard* * *, Zinfandel* * *

1991 Chardonnay Triere Vineyard	Napa	C	89

The 1991 Chardonnay Triere Vineyard is a reassuringly fine wine from Burgess, a winery that has played it too safe over recent vintages, offering relatively straightforward red and white wines. The wine is a boldly flavored, deep, complex wine with attractive lemony, buttery, applelike fruit touched subtly by the judicious use of new oak. Full bodied, with excellent concentration, an enticing nutty, buttery element to its flavors, crisp acidity, and a long finish, it can be drunk over the next 1–2 years.

BUTTONWOOD FARM (SANTA BARBARA)
Merlot* *, Sauvignon Blanc* * *

1991 Merlot	Santa Ynez	C	78
1990 Merlot	Santa Ynez	C	85
1991 Sauvignon Blanc	Santa Ynez	B	86

Although a small amount of their production is estate-bottled, Buttonwood Farm is a large vineyard that is primarily known as a major source of grapes for other wineries. With respect to their estate-bottled wines, the 1991 Sauvignon Blanc (12% Semillon is utilized in the blend) exhibits an herb, floral, and melony nose, crisp, medium-bodied flavors that reveal fine ripeness, and an excellent, moderately long finish. Stylish and flavorful, it should be drunk over the next year. The 1990 Merlot displays attractive sweet fruit, deep color, an overall sense of balance, and adequate quantities of the flesh that makes Merlot so seductive. In contrast, the 1991 Merlot possesses high acidity, and a lean, compact, austere personality. Although it reveals good depth and cleanliness, from a pleasure perspective it offers less appeal than the 1990 because of its excessively high acidity.

BYRON (SANTA BARBARA)

Chardonnay Estate* * *, Chardonnay Reserve* * * *, Pinot Blanc* * *, Pinot Noir* * *, Pinot Noir Reserve* * *, Sauvignon Blanc* * * *

1992 Chardonnay Estate	Santa Maria	C	85
1991 Chardonnay Estate	Santa Barbara	B	87
1992 Chardonnay Reserve	Santa Barbara	C	90
1991 Chardonnay Reserve	Santa Barbara	C	88
1993 Pinot Blanc	Santa Barbara	B	86
1991 Pinot Noir	Santa Barbara	B	74
1992 Pinot Noir Reserve	Santa Barbara	B	81
1992 Sauvignon Blanc Reserve	Santa Barbara	C	87

The Byron winery, which was acquired by Robert Mondavi in 1990, continues to turn out attractive Sauvignon Blanc and Chardonnay. Improvements are warranted with respect to the Pinot Noir program. The Chardonnay offerings are rich, lavishly oaked wines with copious quantities of buttery, honeyed-apple, and pineapple-like fruit. Fans of smoky, roasted, buttery, salty beer nuts and unctuously textured, thick Chardonnay should love the flashy, chewy, large-scale 1992 Chardonnay Reserve. There is no doubting its immense appeal. Most California Chardonnays this precocious and oaky tend to quickly drop their fruit. Nevertheless, this wine will offer irresistible drinking over the next year.

The spicy 1992 Chardonnay Estate is neither as rich nor as thick as the 1991 Reserve. Both wines are best drunk over the next several years. Made in a medium- to full-bodied style, the 1991 Chardonnay Estate is a rich, full, mouth-filling wine with plenty of honeyed tropical fruits and a judicious use of toasty new oak. Tasty, plump, medium to full bodied, with a lot of flavor and subtle oak, it should be drunk within its first 3–4 years of life.

The tasty, ripe, orange- and honey-scented 1993 Pinot Blanc is fruity, round, and ideal for drinking over the next 8–12 months. Byron's 1992 Sauvignon Blanc Reserve is also a meritorious wine. Mineral, spicy, and herb components add complexity to its generously fruity, medium-bodied, pure character. It should be consumed over the next year.

Byron's Pinot Noirs lack aromatic and flavor dimension. The 1992 Pinot Noir Reserve, which has not yet been released, displays some elegance and a spicy, red fruit character, but comes across on the palate as simple, light, short, and compact. The 1991 Pinot Noir reveals some earthy, funky lees aromas that dissipate with airing. However, the wine offers little excitement, with medium-bodied, straightforward, cherry fruitiness and crisp acidity.

CAIN CELLARS (NAPA)

Cain Five Proprietary Red Wine* * * *, Chardonnay* * * *, Merlot* * * *, Sauvignon Musqué* * */* * * *

1992 Cain Five Proprietary Red Wine	Napa	D	91
1990 Cain Five Proprietary Red Wine	Napa	D	89

The 1992 Cain Five, a blend of 54% Cabernet Sauvignon, 35% Merlot, 2% Cabernet Franc, 1% Petit Verdot, and 8% Malbec, exhibits a dark purple/black color, and an intense black cherry nose with hints of smoke, roasted nuts, and herbs. There is a heady degree of alcohol in this spicy, dense, richly concentrated wine, a seductive, opulent texture, low acidity, and a lush, decadent finish. It should provide delicious early drinking and easily keep for 12–15 years. The 1990 Cain Five's dense ruby/purple color, and big, seductive nose of jammy cassis, olives, and subtle vanillin are followed by an opulently rich wine with smooth tannin, low acidity, and long, luscious, decadently ripe flavors. Drink it over the next 10–12 years.

CAKEBREAD CELLARS (NAPA)

Cabernet Sauvignon* *, Chardonnay* *, Zinfandel* * *

1992 Zinfandel Howell Mountain Unfiltered	Napa	B	88

The 1992 Zinfandel is one of the best efforts I have tasted from Cakebread Cellars for more than a decade. Their Zinfandel reveals a dark ruby/purple color, and an excellent bouquet of black cherries, minerals, spice, and smoke. Medium to full bodied, with considerable depth, admirable density, and moderate tannin, this tightly knit, powerful wine from Howell Mountain will benefit from 2–3 years of cellaring. It should keep for a decade or more.

CALERA WINE COMPANY (SAN BENITO)

Chardonnay Central Coast* * *, Chardonnay Mount Harlan* * * *, Pinot Noir Single-Vineyard Cuvées* * * * *, Viognier* * * * *

1993 Pinot Noir	Central Coast	C	87
1992 Pinot Noir	Central Coast	C	83
1992 Pinot Noir Jensen Vineyard	Mount Harlan	D	90
1992 Pinot Noir Mills Vineyard	Mount Harlan	D	89
1992 Pinot Noir Reed Vineyard	Mount Harlan	D	87
1992 Pinot Noir Selleck Vineyard	Mount Harlan	D	89
1993 Viognier	Mount Harlan	D	93

The 1993 Viognier is a powermonger, oozing with juicy, honeyed, apricot/peachlike aromas and flavors. Full bodied, rich, and loaded with concentration, Calera's Viognier remains the reference point for this varietal in California. Recent vintages of Chardonnay, particularly the 1993, were barely average in quality.

Calera was among the first California wineries to capture the expressive fragrance, elusive complexity, sweet ripeness, and expansive texture of the fickle Pinot Noir grape. Since the mid-eighties, their track record for producing consistently delicious and distinctive wines has been impeccable. While proprietor Josh Jensen's obsession with vineyard-designating all of his Pinot Noirs is well documented, I continue to wonder if there are enough differences between the wines to justify the separate identities.

There is always a generic offering from the Central Coast. Both 1992 and 1993 Central Coast Pinot Noirs offer sweet, ripe palates, but the 1993 exhibits more color saturations, an aromatic, lingering, spicy bouquet, as well as riper, richer, more complete flavors. It offers a seductive glass of fully mature Pinot Noir for drinking over the next 2–3 years. When tasted beside the 1993, the 1992 comes across as lighter, but still a user-friendly, delicious, herb- and berry-scented and flavored wine.

As the numerical scores indicate, there are subtle differences between the four vineyard-designated wines. All are medium to full bodied, with sound, medium to dark ruby/garnet colors, and various degrees of Pinot's vegetal quality evident in the aromatics. The 1992 Reed Vineyard Pinot Noir reveals a sweet, cherry, curranty nose with plenty of spice and earth, as well as a subtle leafy character. The wine's attack is excellent, but it finishes abruptly. Nevertheless, it is a well-made structured Pinot Noir that should be drunk over the next 6–7 years. The 1992 Selleck Vineyard Pinot Noir displays a darker hue to its color, a less flattering bouquet, and rich, ripe herb and cherrylike flavors that are medium to full bodied, concentrated, and well balanced. It should drink well for the next 5–7 years.

My favorite of the single-vineyard offerings is the 1992 Jensen Vineyard Pinot Noir. The least herbal and deepest colored of this quartet, this sweet, full-bodied, velvety-textured wine boasts excellent ripeness and intense fruit, an attractive layered quality, an inner core of succulent fruit, and a heady, lush finish. This is an opulent, delicious, mouthfilling Pinot

Noir to be drunk over the next 6–7 years. The 1992 Mills Vineyard Pinot Noir is a rich, fragrant, spicy, jammy, berry-scented wine with medium to full body, gobs of fruit, and a sweet (from concentration, not sugar), glycerin-imbued, alcoholic finish. It is a rich, luscious style of Pinot Noir for drinking over the next 5–7 years. Although Calera has significantly more competition, their wines remain reference points for just how good Pinot Noir can be.

CAMBRIA WINERY AND VINEYARD (SANTA MARIA)
Chardonnay Cuvées* * * *, Pinot Noir Julia's Vineyard * * * * (since 1991), Syrah Tepusquet
Vineyard* * * *

1993 Chardonnay Katherine's Vineyard	Santa Maria	C	89
1992 Chardonnay Katherine's Vineyard	Santa Maria	C	88
1993 Chardonnay Reserve	Santa Maria	C	88
1992 Chardonnay Reserve	Santa Maria	C	88
1993 Pinot Noir Julia's Vineyard	Santa Maria	C	86
1992 Pinot Noir Julia's Vineyard	Santa Maria	C	87
1991 Pinot Noir Julia's Vineyard	Santa Maria	C	87
1992 Syrah Tepusquet Vineyard	Santa Maria	D	89

This winery, which is owned by Kendall-Jackson, has established a good track record for lavishly oaked, lusty, rich Chardonnays. Their Pinot Noir program began with some difficulty, but appears to have improved significantly over the last few vintages.

The 1993 Chardonnay Reserve exhibits good structure and well-integrated acidity, as well as copious amounts of tropical fruit nicely complemented by toasty French oak. It offers a spicy, vanilla-, orange-, and honeyed-apple–scented nose, and good citrusy, medium-bodied flavors. Drink it over the next 1–2 years. The 1993 Chardonnay Katherine's Vineyard is oozing with honeyed tropical fruit accompanied by a touch of oak. There is crisp acidity, full body, and a bold, dramatically flavored personality. Drink it over the next 1–2 years. The 1992 Chardonnay Katherine's Vineyard and 1992 Chardonnay Reserve are rich, toasty, honeyed, buttery Chardonnays with admirable intensity and up-front appeal. They will need to be consumed in their first 2–3 years of life.

The 1993 Pinot Noir from Julia's Vineyard exhibits a medium ruby/garnet color, a sweet, spicy, herb- and berry-scented nose, elegant, attractive flavors, a velvety texture, and a soft, easygoing, charmingly seductive finish. Drink it over the next 2–3 years. An attractive, hedonistic Pinot Noir, with medium ruby color, a big, spicy, plum- and raspberry-scented nose, round, generous, ripe flavors, full body, excellent definition, and a lusty finish, Cambria's 1992 Julia's Vineyard is all a thick, juicy Pinot Noir should be. Consume it over the next 2–3 years. Cambria's 1991 Pinot Noir Julia's Vineyard offers a medium to dark ruby color, and aromas of nearly overripe plums, underbrush, and flowers. It has a succulence bordering on fatness, a fleshy, voluptuous texture, and a lusty, heady finish. Drink this decadent Pinot Noir over the next 2–4 years.

Another impressive Syrah from California's south central coast, Cambria's dark ruby/purple-colored 1992 displays a forceful nose of spicy, peppery black cherries and black currants, opulently rich, full-bodied flavors, considerable extract, and a moderate tannin level. The wine is loaded with rich, concentrated fruit and is easy to drink considering its girth and intensity. It has not yet developed much complexity, but there are layers of fruit in this impressively endowed wine. Drink it over the next 10–12 years.

CANEPA (ALEXANDER VALLEY)
Chardonnay* * */* * * *

1992 Chardonnay Canepa Vineyard	Alexander Valley	C	88

With a pleasing bouquet of citrus and honey notes, well-integrated, toasty new oak, and a fresh finish, this attractively made, ripe, medium- to full-bodied 1992 Chardonnay should be drunk over the next 12–18 months.

CARARI (SANTA BARBARA)
Chenin Blanc* * *, Dago Red* * *, Rosé* *

N.V. Chenin Blanc	Santa Ynez	A	84
N.V. Dago Red	Santa Ynez	A	84
N.V. Rosé	Santa Ynez	A	81

One of the largest growers in Santa Barbara, Carari produces three inexpensive nonvintage blends for everyday drinking. They are surprisingly good and . . . cheap! Discounters can even price these wines at $3 a bottle. The two best wines are the floral, aromatic Chenin Blanc, which is made from 1991 and 1992 grapes, and the Dago Red, a substantial, rich, straightforward, husky wine with plenty of body, fruit, and character. There is also a straightforward, clean, fruity Rosé. No one will be disappointed with the quality one gets for these low prices.

CAREY CELLARS (SANTA BARBARA)
Arabesque Proprietary Red Wine* *, Chardonnay Barrel Select* *

1990 Arabesque Proprietary Red Wine	Santa Ynez	C	74
1989 Arabesque Proprietary Red Wine	Santa Ynez	C	72
1991 Chardonnay Barrel Select	Santa Ynez	C	84

Carey's 1991 Chardonnay Barrel Select offers good fruit integrated with some spicy, vanillin-scented new oak, a plump personality, as well as adequate flesh and length. The proprietary red wine, Arabesque, is unimpressive in both 1989 and 1990. The 1989 Arabesque, a 40% Cabernet Sauvignon/40% Merlot/20% Cabernet Franc blend, reveals a strong vegetal element in the nose. The wine is soft, diffuse, and short. The 1990 Arabesque, a 70% Cabernet Sauvignon/15% Merlot/15% Cabernet Franc blend, offers a leafy-scented nose, tannic, compact flavors, and an annoying vegetal personality that I found unappealing.

CARMENET VINEYARD (SONOMA)
Colombard Old Vines* * * *, Proprietary Red Wines* * *, Meritage Proprietary White Wine* * *

1992 Cabernet Franc Moon Mountain Vineyard	Sonoma	C	84
1991 Colombard Old Vines	Napa	A	86
1992 Meritage Moon Mountain Estate	Sonoma	C	86

Even allowing for the delicate, understated, light-bodied style of the 1992 Cabernet Franc from the Moon Mountain Vineyard, this is a reasonably fruity, but one-dimensional wine. The 1992 Meritage Moon Mountain Estate, while elegant and light to medium bodied, exhibits more classy fruit, as well as an attractive, supple texture. Both wines should drink well for 10–12 years.

I doubt there is a dry white table wine from California that I enjoy more than the Colombard Old Vines offerings from Carmenet. They undeniably demonstrate that if the vines are old enough, the yields low enough, and the wine treated as if it were from a more renowned varietal than the lowly Colombard, many consumers could be drinking rich, tasty, personality-filled white table wines for under $10. The 1991 is a beauty, with gorgeous levels of fruit, an attractive perfume, medium body, crisp acidity, and plenty of mid-palate fruit, as well as length. It is a fun wine—never tiring or boring to drink.

CAYMUS VINEYARD (NAPA)

Cabernet Sauvignon * * */* * * *, Cabernet Sauvignon Special Selection * * * * *, Conundrum Proprietary White Wine * * * *, Pinot Noir * *, Sauvignon Blanc * * *, Zinfandel * * *

1991 Cabernet Sauvignon	Napa	C	87
1991 Cabernet Sauvignon Special Selection	Napa	EE	90
1990 Cabernet Sauvignon Special Selection	Napa	D	94
1993 Conundrum Proprietary White Wine	California	C	90
1992 Sauvignon Blanc	Napa	A	89

Few wineries in the world can boast such an enviable record of consistent excellence as that of Caymus. The 1993 Conundrum Proprietary White Wine possesses a gorgeously fragrant nose of tropical fruits with a subtle touch of toasty oak. In the mouth, there is voluptuous fruit, a dry, succulent, juicy texture, and a long, crisp finish. A delightful wine, usually made from an innovative blend of Chardonnay, Muscat, Semillon, and Sauvignon Blanc, it can be drunk either as an aperitif or with seafood or chicken. Be sure to consume it over the next 1–2 years.

While Caymus's Conundrum is an exotic wine, readers should not overlook their excellent Sauvignon Blanc. The 1992 Sauvignon Blanc, which has been barrel-fermented, will keep its gorgeous richness, perfume, and intensity for another 12–20 months. Consumers are well advised to buy this wine by the case and serve it with chicken or fish dishes. It is the best Sauvignon Caymus has yet made. The wine is kept on its lees for 7 months, which imparts richness and intensity.

The Cabernet Sauvignon Special Selection, which spends significant time in oak, can be one of California's most riveting wines. First made in 1975, there have been some exceptionally concentrated, powerful wines that are still young and evolving (i.e., the 1978, 1976, and 1975). The decade of the eighties produced less profound Cabernet Sauvignon Special Selections, with the exception of the 1984 and 1985. Since then, the wine has moved to less of a blockbuster style, with the emphasis on more elegance, without sacrificing the wine's richness and intensity. The 1990 Cabernet Sauvignon Special Selection appears to be the best Caymus has produced since 1986 and 1985. In February 1994, 2,000 six-bottle cases were released. The wine offers a saturated, dark purple color and a rich, spicy, oaky nose backed up by generous quantities of jammy black currants. Ripe, highly extracted, and full bodied, with copious amounts of sweet tannin and layers of fruit, this is a knockout, flamboyantly styled Cabernet for drinking over the next 15 or more years. The 1991 Special Selection is a very soft, oaky, medium-bodied wine to drink over the next 10–15 years.

Dark ruby/purple-colored, with an intriguing nose of spicy new oak, black currants, and a pronounced herbaceousness, the 1991 Cabernet Sauvignon exhibits lush, medium- to full-bodied flavors, moderate tannin, fine ripeness, and the lavish oak Caymus Cabernets routinely display. This is a delicious, robust, herbaceous example of Cabernet Sauvignon that will drink well for over a decade.

Ratings for Older Vintages of Caymus's Cabernet Sauvignon: 1989 (85), 1988 (83), 1987 (90)

Ratings for Older Vintages of Caymus's Cabernet Sauvignon Special Selection: 1988 (85), 1987 (89), 1986 (94), 1985 (92), 1984 (96), 1983 (89), 1982 (88), 1981 (91), 1980 (93), 1979 (92), 1978 (98), 1976 (99), 1975 (98)

CHALK HILL WINERY (SONOMA)
Cabernet Sauvignon * * */* * * * (since 1990), Chardonnay Estate * * */* * * * (since 1991),
Sauvignon Blanc * * * * (since 1991)

1991 Cabernet Sauvignon	Sonoma	C	87+
1990 Cabernet Sauvignon	Sonoma	C	88
1992 Chardonnay Estate	Sonoma	C	90
1991 Chardonnay Estate	Sonoma	C	88
1993 Sauvignon Blanc	Sonoma	B	87

A winery worth noting, Chalk Hill has dramatically improved the quality of its wines. Matanzas Creek's former winemaker, David Ramey, is now entrenched at Chalk Hill, and the first efforts under his helmsmanship are impressive. The 1992 Chardonnay Estate is a full-blown, buttery, smoky rich wine with gobs of flavor, a voluptuous texture, and a flattering, up-front style that begs for consumption over the next year.

The complex 1993 Sauvignon Blanc offers surprising richness, a bold, dramatic bouquet of melons, spicy oak, herbs, and rich fruit, medium to full body, and layers of concentration. Drink this rich, dry, impressive Sauvignon over the next 2–3 years. The powerful 1991 Chardonnay Estate is admirably endowed, with a lusty nose of toasty oak, honeyed fruit, and butter. Rich, full bodied, and heady, this impressive Chardonnay should drink well for several more years.

The 1991 Cabernet Sauvignon exhibits a dark opaque ruby/purple color and a reticent but promising bouquet of cassis, black cherries, and spicy oak. It is moderately tannic, with medium to full body, excellent depth, and crisp, underlying acidity, suggesting the wine is unevolved and youthful. Give it 2–3 years in the cellar and drink it over the following 15 years. The 1990 Cabernet Sauvignon may turn out to be one of the sleepers of this exceptional vintage. It is densely colored, with a rich, black currant–scented nose, spicy, full-bodied, concentrated flavors, decent acidity, admirable soft tannins, and a rich, authoritative finish. The wine is relatively unevolved, but its copious quantities of sweet fruit make it accessible now. Drink it over the next 10–12 or more years.

CHALONE VINEYARDS (MONTEREY)
Chardonnay Estate * * * *, Chardonnay Gavilan * */* * *, Chardonnay Reserve Estate * * * *,
Chenin Blanc Estate Reserve * * * *, Pinot Blanc * * * *, Pinot Noir Estate * */* * *

1992 Chardonnay Estate	California	C	90
1991 Chardonnay Estate	Monterey	C	90
1992 Chardonnay Estate Reserve	California	C	90+
1991 Chardonnay Estate Reserve	California	C	91+
1992 Chenin Blanc Estate Reserve	California	C	90
1992 Pinot Blanc Estate	California	C	88
1991 Pinot Blanc Estate	Monterey	C	91
1990 Pinot Blanc Estate Reserve	California	D	91+

Tucked away in the foothills of Salinas, not far from Soledad, Chalone can produce California's longest-lived Pinot Blanc and Chardonnay, and in some vintages, its most compelling. Although I am not a fan of the meaty, heavy, coarse, age-worthy Pinot Noir, the greatest new world Chardonnays I have tasted are Chalone's 1980 and 1981. When I last tasted them, in spring 1993, they were still in terrific condition. For whatever reason, Chalone has never returned to the style of those blockbuster wines. Despite a troublesome period (too many moldy-smelling bottles between 1982 and 1984), the winery still turns out some of the most lavishly rich, intense Chardonnays and Pinot Blancs.

The 1992 Chardonnay regular bottling (the only offering available to consumers, as the Reserve wines are sold only to stockholders; I purchased them from a stockholding friend) offers a subtle bouquet, considerable body and acidity, and attractive oak, earthy, smoky, buttery popcorn–like flavors. My instincts suggest it will benefit from another 6–12 months of cellaring; it should keep for 5–6 years. Chalone's 1991 Chardonnay should turn out slightly better than the 1989 and 1990. It appears to be a return to the more forceful, rich style of the Chalone Chardonnays produced before 1982. Unquestionably, a lightening of style occurred between 1983 and 1988 (some of which was attributable to the so-so vintages of 1987 and 1988), but the 1991 is an authoritatively rich, buttery, full-bodied wine with loads of extract, deep, layered flavors that cut considerable depth on the palate, and a spicy, rich, fresh, unevolved finish. It appears to be a synthesis in style of the blockbuster 1981 and the more elegant 1982; it should drink well for 10–12 years.

Both the 1992 and 1991 Reserve Chardonnays are backward, Burgundian-style wines with well-integrated acidity, full body, and outstanding depth, richness, and length. These backward, closed Chardonnays are in need of 1–3 years of cellaring. Both promise to age gracefully for 6–10 years. The 1991 has slightly more extract and body. Stockholders should consider themselves lucky if they get any bottles of Chalone's 1990 Chardonnay Reserve. It is clearly the best Reserve Chardonnay made at Chalone since the spectacular 1980 and 1981. As they say, it's loaded! Crammed with buttery apple/pineapple, nutty fruit, this viscous, rich, well-balanced Chardonnay has all of its massive intensity well defined by crisp natural acids. Approachable now, it is a candidate for long-term cellaring.

The 1991 Pinot Blanc is a super effort, revealing a subtle oaky, orange, lemony, buttery nose, and lovely rich, ripe flavors allied to considerable elegance. The acidity is admirable. Based on how well some of Chalone's older Pinot Blancs, such as 1982, 1981 (absolutely awesome), and 1980 (another blockbuster), have aged, this wine should easily make it through the next decade.

Although unevolved, the 1990 Pinot Blanc Estate Reserve (available only to stockholders) possesses gorgeously rich fruit, tremendous depth, a mineral/orangelike fruitiness, and stunning length. Based on previous vintages, it should drink well for a decade or more.

Unfortunately, only small quantities of the 1992 Chenin Blanc Estate Reserve were made. It is a dead ringer for a great dry Loire Valley Chenin Blanc, given its huge, rich, concentrated fruit, gentle touch of oak, and full-bodied, spicy, blockbuster finish. Texturally similar to a big, chewy Chardonnay, this dry Chenin Blanc has always been one of Chalone's specialties and is worth a special effort to find. It should drink well for 4–5 years.

Ratings for Older Vintages of Chalone's Chardonnay Estate: 1990 (91), 1989 (87), 1988 (82), 1987 (87), 1986 (86), 1985 (86), 1984 (87), 1983 (85), 1982 (88), 1981 (93), 1980 (96), 1979 (86)

Ratings for Older Vintages of Chalone's Chardonnay Reserve Estate: 1990 (93), 1988 (84), 1986 (90), 1984 (78), 1983 (90), 1981 (92), 1980 (96)

Ratings for Older Vintages of Chalone's Pinot Blanc Estate: 1990 (90), 1988 (88), 1987 (87), 1986 (86), 1985 (86), 1984 (87), 1983 (87), 1982 (88), 1981 (90), 1980 (91), 1979 (86)

Ratings for Older Vintages of Chalone's Pinot Blanc Estate Reserve: 1988 (87), 1986 (84), 1983 (90), 1981 (91), 1980 (93)

CHIMÈRE (SANTA BARBARA)
Chardonnay* * * *, Pinot Noir* * * *

1993 Chardonnay	Santa Barbara	C	87
1991 Pinot Noir	Edna Valley	C	88+
1991 Pinot Noir Unfined/Unfiltered	Santa Maria	C	90

Chimère's winemaker formerly crafted the wines at the Chalone-owned Edna Valley Vineyard. The limited-production 1991 Unfined/Unfiltered Pinot Noir (230 cases) reveals a big, beefy, meaty, cinnamon, spice, and black fruit–scented nose reminiscent of a good Côte de Nuits. There is superrichness, full body, plenty of ripe, delicious fruit, and a lusty, satiny-smooth finish. It should drink well for 5–6 years.

The intriguing, concentrated, powerful 1991 Pinot Noir from Edna Valley possesses excellent varietal character, a smoky, gamey, animal-like note, wonderfully ripe fruit, medium to full body, and moderate tannin in the long finish. All its component parts are impressive, but my instincts suggest 1–2 years of cellaring should result in less tannin and more richness. I admire the individualistic, personality-filled style this winery has achieved.

The 1993 Chardonnay's medium straw color suggests some skin contact during winemaking. This big, mouth-filling, dry Chardonnay displays sweet, ripe, honeyed, orange/apricot/applelike fruit, full body, and plenty of power and extract. A slight rusticity kept my score from going higher. Drink it over the next 1–2 years.

CHRISTOPHE VINEYARDS (NAPA)
Cabernet Sauvignon*, Chardonnay* * *, Sauvignon Blanc* *

1992 Chardonnay	Napa	A	86

A terrific bargain in Chardonnay, this soft, plump, generously endowed wine is not complex, but it offers rich, chewy, buttery, apple fruit in a straightforward, mouth-filling, concentrated style. Drink it over the next 1–2 years.

CINNABAR VINEYARD AND WINERY (SANTA CLARA)
Cabernet Sauvignon* * */* * * *, Chardonnay* * * *

1991 Chardonnay	Santa Cruz	C	89+

This highly structured, tightly knit, full-bodied Chardonnay exhibits superb length, concentration, and flavor intensity. I generally have no faith in the aging potential of most California Chardonnays, but there are certain wineries in specific areas (for example, Santa Cruz) that can produce Chardonnays that can evolve and improve for 4–5 years. This wine is a strong bet to do just that.

CLINE CELLARS (SONOMA)
Côtes d'Oakley* * * *, Mourvèdre* * * *, Zinfandel* * * *

1993 Côtes d'Oakley	Contra Costa	A	87
1993 Zinfandel	Contra Costa	B	89
1992 Zinfandel	Contra Costa	B	87
1991 Zinfandel	Contra Costa	B	88
1993 Zinfandel Big Break	Contra Costa	C	91
1993 Zinfandel Bridgehead Vineyard	Contra Costa	C	90+
1993 Zinfandel Reserve	Contra Costa	C	91
1992 Zinfandel Reserve	Contra Costa	B	91
1991 Zinfandel Reserve	Contra Costa	B	89

The 1993s may be the most impressive group of wines Cline Cellars has yet produced. The 1993 Zinfandel Contra Costa exhibits a healthy dark ruby/purple color, a big, berry- and loamy earth–scented nose, full body, adequate tannin, and an abundance of wild berry fruit. Drink it over the next 5–8 years. The opaque purple-colored 1993 Zinfandel Big Break reveals a huge nose of sweet berry fruit and earth. Massive, rich, and totally dry, this high-alcohol, seriously concentrated wine can be drunk now or cellared for 10–15 years. It is a rich, mouth-filling wine crammed with black cherry and black raspberry fruit. The 1993 Zinfandel Bridgehead Vineyard displays considerable structure and tannin, but there is no doubting the excellent concentration of ripe berry fruit. It is spicy and intense, but more closed than the other offerings. Lastly, the 1993 Zinfandel Reserve is the best-balanced of these large, full-throttle wines. It offers an opaque ruby/purple color, a big, spicy, berry-scented nose, full body, light to moderate tannin, adequate acidity, and superb purity and richness. The regular cuvée should last for a decade, and the Bridgehead, Reserve, and Big Break for 20 years.

The 1992 Zinfandel displays a dark, opaque purple color, a dusty, rich, black fruit–scented nose, highly extracted, dry, full-bodied flavors, and moderate tannin in the finish. There is plenty of stuffing and character, so 1–2 years of cellaring may reveal an even higher-rated wine. It should keep for up to a decade. Even more opaque, the 1992 Zinfandel Reserve offers a stunningly rich, concentrated perfume of black fruits, minerals, and spice. With great breadth and expansiveness, this super-concentrated, immensely impressive, full-bodied Zinfandel possesses superb harmony and balance for its generous size. Although approachable now, 2–3 years of cellaring will be beneficial; it should last for 15 years.

Both 1991 cuvées are excellent wines. The 1991 regular bottling displays a deep ruby color with a slightly purple edge, a penetrating, fragrant, smoky, peppery, earthy nose, excellent richness and fruit, fine underlying acidity and tannin for support, and a long, lusty finish. It should drink well for 7–8 years. The 1991 Reserve offers a slightly more opaque purple color, some noticeable vanillin in the bouquet that suggests new oak was employed, a black cherry–, raspberry–, peppery-scented nose, wonderful purity and richness, full body, and a heady, intensely spicy, immensely satisfying, opulent finish. It too should continue to drink well for another 7–8 years.

One of California's most successful "Rhône Rangers," Cline has consistently produced attractive wines. The 1993 Côtes d'Oakley succeeds in emulating a Côtes du Rhone. With juicy, succulent, robust, peppery fruitiness, attractive weight and balance on the palate, and a soft, fleshy finish, it should be consumed over the next 3–4 years.

CLOS DU BOIS WINERY (SONOMA)

Briarcrest * * *, Cabernet Sauvignon * * *, Chardonnay Barrel-Fermented * * *, Chardonnay Calcaire * * */* * * *, Chardonnay Flintwood * * */* * * *, Malbec L'Etranger * * *, Marlstone * * *, Merlot * * *, Sauvignon Blanc * * * *, Zinfandel * * *

1991 Chardonnay Calcaire	Alexander Valley	C	90
1991 Chardonnay Flintwood	Dry Creek	C	90
1991 Malbec L'Etranger	Alexander Valley	B	85
1991 Merlot	Sonoma	B	86
1990 Merlot	Sonoma	B	86
1991 Zinfandel	Sonoma	B	87

Clos du Bois has consistently produced one of California's reasonably priced, user-friendly Merlots. The 1991 exhibits a ripe, herbaceous, coffee-, mocha-, and berry-scented nose, soft, plush, medium-bodied flavors, low acidity, and a fleshy finish. It is all Merlot should be—delicious, up front, and a joy to drink. Consume it over the next 5–6 years. The 1990 is a delicious, somewhat commercial yet richly fruity, fleshy, in-your-face Merlot. Twenty percent Cabernet Sauvignon in the blend gives the wine more definition. This juicy, succulent, fruity Merlot should be consumed over the next 2–3 years.

Malbec has fallen out of favor in Bordeaux, although a handful of châteaux still have tiny parcels planted with it (i.e., Cheval Blanc and La Conseillante). Today this varietal reaches its greatest heights in Argentina, where wineries such as Bodega Weinert produce extraordinary wines from 70- to 90-year-old, low-yielding Malbec vines. In California it is just getting a foothold, but Clos du Bois's 1991 Malbec L'Etranger displays just what Malbec can offer. It possesses the softness of Merlot and the complexity of Cabernet Sauvignon. It is never going to be heavy or exceptionally tannic. What it does offer is a penetrating bouquet, good ripe cassis fruit, surprising richness, with a Burgundian-like tendency to reveal more on the palate than its modest color suggests. This is a lightweight, attractive wine with a seductive suppleness.

Tasty, full flavored, and charming, Clos du Bois's 1991 Zin possesses soft acids, light tannins, and a generous, mouth-filling appeal. The spicy, herbaceous nose is loaded with black fruits. Drink this excellent, satiny-smooth Zinfandel over the next 4–5 years.

After some indifferent performances in the late eighties, it is good to see this Sonoma winery get back on track with these excellent vineyard-designated Chardonnays. The 1991 Flintwood cuvée possesses excellent focus, a rich, toasty, smoky, mineral, applelike fruitiness, medium to full body, and admirable ripeness and length. It should be drunk within 4 years of the vintage. In contrast, the 1991 Calcaire Chardonnay is a bigger, more obvious, tropical fruit-dominated wine. It combines richness with elegance, but the toasty, tropical fruit character is quite evident. Drink it over the next 2 years.

CLOS PEGASE (NAPA)

Cabernet Sauvignon * * * (since 1992), Chardonnay * * *, Hommage Proprietary
Red Wine * * * * (since 1992), Merlot * * *, Sauvignon Blanc * *

1992	Cabernet Sauvignon	Napa	C	89+
1993	Chardonnay	Napa/Carneros	B	89
1992	Hommage Proprietary Red Wine	Napa	C	92
1992	Merlot	Napa	C	89

Clos Pegase has begun to use only grapes from their own vineyards. That, plus what certainly must be a less interventionist winemaking approach, has resulted in the finest wines they have yet produced. I enjoyed all three of their 1992 offerings. The 1992 Merlot Napa Estate possesses gobs of attractive curranty, vanillin, smoky aromas, excellent density and ripeness, and a medium- to full-bodied, supple finish. It should drink well young and last for a decade. The 1992 Cabernet Sauvignon Napa Estate shares a similar opulence, with even greater depth, and the vintage's superb ripeness. Well-displayed, deeply concentrated, full-bodied flavors reveal fine balance and length. My instincts suggest the wine will be drinkable early and last for 15 or more years. The outstanding proprietary red wine, the 1992 Hommage, exhibits a superb nose of cassis, licorice, herbs, and fruitcakelike aromas. Full bodied, with exceptional depth, low acidity, fabulous richness, and a medium- to full-bodied, lush feel that nearly obscures the sweet tannin, this appears to be Clos Pegase's first stunning wine. It should have 15 or more years of longevity.

Clos Pegase's 1993 Chardonnay is the first authoritatively rich, powerful example of just how good this winery's offerings have become. Rich and full bodied, with excellent fruit extraction and purity, it offers long, lush, honeyed tropical fruit and a nice touch of oak in a balanced format. Drink it before the end of 1996.

CLOVERDALE RANCH (ALEXANDER VALLEY)
Cabernet Sauvignon Estate * * */* * * *

1991 Cabernet Sauvignon Estate	Alexander Valley	C	87

This is a soft, forward, round, generous Cabernet Sauvignon for the vintage. It exhibits graceful, sweet cassis fruit, medium body, a sense of balance, and soft tannin in the moderately long finish. Drink it over the next 5–7 years.

COLGIN-SCHRADER CELLARS (NAPA)
Cabernet Sauvignon Lamb Vineyard * * * * *

1993 Cabernet Sauvignon Lamb Vineyard	Napa	C	95
1992 Cabernet Sauvignon Lamb Vineyard	Napa	E	92

This up-and-coming producer is making 100% Cabernet Sauvignon from the Lamb Vineyard on Howell Mountain. The 1993 is a wine to seek out, although the tiny production means quantities are limited. The wine boasts an opaque black color and a huge, sweet, jammy nose of cassis fruit, minerals, flowers, and new oak. Powerfully authoritative flavors that ooze glycerin and fruit extraction are also elegant and harmonious. The tannin is buried beneath an amazing amount of concentration. The wine finishes with great focus and delineation. It is a spectacular, promising Cabernet Sauvignon that has me drooling in anticipation of its release. It should drink well for at least 20 years. The 1992 is nearly as impressive, but is more supple and not quite as complex or as concentrated.

CONGRESS SPRINGS WINERY (SANTA CLARA)
Chardonnay * *, Noblesse Proprietary Red Wine * *

1992 Chardonnay San Ysidro	California	A	85
1990 Noblesse Proprietary Red Wine	California	A	85

The crisp, ripe, flavorful, fresh 1992 Chardonnay displays an attractive buttery, apple blossom–scented nose, medium body, good depth, commendable structure and focus, and a zesty, dry, fruity finish. Drink it over the next year. The 1990 Noblesse, a blend of 60% Merlot, 35% Cabernet Sauvignon, and 5% Cabernet Franc, offers a medium to dark ruby color, an herbaceous, cedar-, and curranty-scented nose, ripe cherry and roasted nut–like flavors, fine ripeness, medium body, and a soft finish. It is a tasty red wine for drinking over the next 2–3 years.

CONN VALLEY VINEYARD (NAPA)
Cabernet Sauvignon * * * * *, Pinot Noir Valhalla Vineyard * * * *

1993 Cabernet Sauvignon	Napa	D	93
1992 Cabernet Sauvignon	Napa	D	92
1991 Cabernet Sauvignon	Napa	D	93
1990 Cabernet Sauvignon	Napa	D	92
1994 Pinot Noir Valhalla Vineyard	Napa	D	92
1993 Pinot Noir Valhalla Vineyard	Napa	D	91

A source for impressive Cabernet Sauvignon, Conn Valley Vineyard rarely receives the publicity the wines merit. The Anderson family owns 25 acres of vineyard producing approximately 5,000 cases of Cabernet Sauvignon, as well as a small quantity of fine Pinot Noir. The vineyard, situated in the Conn Valley about 5 miles west of St. Helena, turns out beautifully rich, black currant–flavored wines that have demonstrated an impressive purity of flavor and aging potential. The saturated black/purple-colored 1993 Cabernet Sauvignon offers an unevolved but juicy, succulent nose of black currants, violets, and spices. Rich and full bodied, this wine may turn out to resemble the opulently styled 1990. The 1992 Cabernet Sauvignon was exhibiting an atypically backward, tannic personality when I last tasted it. It displays the Conn Valley hallmark of gorgeously sweet, rich black currant fruit and full body, as well as a European-like, natural texture and multidimensional palate. After its release in the fall of 1995 it should prove to be one of the top wines of the vintage. The 1991 Cabernet Sauvignon is one of the most forward, velvety-textured wines made by the Andersons. The wine exhibits a beautifully saturated, dark purple color, and a nose of sweet cassis fruit, oak, flowers, and spices. This medium- to full-bodied, smoothly textured wine can be drunk now or cellared for 20 years. All Conn Valley's Cabernet Sauvignons are aged for nearly 2 years and bottled unfiltered. The 1990 is a synthesis in style between the 1992 and 1991. It possesses the 1992's opulence and precocious, rich, forward fleshiness and sweetness of black currant fruit as well as the lovely floral perfume and brilliant harmony so evident in the 1991. The tannin is soft, the acidity is decent, and the concentration levels are impressive. Drink this rich, impressively endowed wine over the next 12–15 years. Winemakers Gus and Todd Anderson are quickly propelling Conn Valley into the elite grouping of superstar Cabernet Sauvignon producers.

Perhaps the best-kept secret of the Anderson family's Conn Valley Vineyard is the microscopic quantities they make of Pinot Noir (approximately 150 cases). Since they began utilizing new oak barrels from one of Burgundy's finest coopers, the wines have soared in quality. The 1993 is one of the few California Pinot Noirs to possess that black fruit, almost Côte de Nuits character that is reminiscent of a top grand cru from Vosne-Romanée. The 1993 exhibits a dark ruby color, a gorgeously sweet nose of red and black fruits, a spicy, ripe, expansive mid-palate, and loads of black cherry and raspberry fruit in the finish. There is plenty of glycerin, high alcohol, and a lusty personality. This is a gorgeous Pinot for drinking before the end of the century. The 1994 appears to be even better and could easily be mistaken for a top-notch Echèzeaux from Burgundy. It exhibits a dark ruby color with purple hints, followed by a sweet, jammy nose of smoky oak, bacon fat, chocolate, black cherry, and raspberry fruit, a lush, sweet texture from ripeness and low yields rather than sugar, and a heady, full-bodied finish. This gloriously decadent, lusty Pinot Noir should send shudders up the spines of many Burgundians.

Ratings for Older Vintages of Conn Valley Cabernet Sauvignon: 1989 (87), 1988 (89), 1987 (88)

COOPER-GARROD (SANTA CRUZ)

Cabernet Franc * * *, Cabernet Sauvignon * * *, Chardonnay * * *

1993 Chardonnay	Santa Cruz	C	85

This citrusy, earthy Chardonnay exhibits attractive apple and pineapplelike fruit, medium to full body, not much complexity, but a natural-tasting palate with well-integrated acidity. Drink it over the next 2–3 years.

COSENTINO WINE COMPANY (NAPA)

Cabernet Sauvignon * * *, Chardonnay * *, The Poet * * *, The Zin * * *

1992 The Zin	Sonoma	B	86
1991 The Zin	Russian River	B	87

The delicious, straightforward 1992 Zinfandel offers a medium ruby color, excellent ripeness, a soft, sweet, round, supple texture, and spicy, tarry, oaky flavors in the moderately long finish. Drink it over the next 3–4 years. The 1991 Zinfandel exhibits deeply saturated color, a big, spicy, oaky nose combined with rich, berry fruit, and medium to full body. The finish is soft, with low acidity and admirable fruit. Drink it over the next 4–5 years. Quite a seductive style!

H. COTURRI AND SONS (SONOMA)

Alicante Bouchet Ubaldi Vineyard* * *, Cabernet Sauvignon Jessandre Vineyard* * * *,
Cabernet Sauvignon Remick Vineyard* * * *, Merlot Feingold Vineyard * * * *, Pinot Noir
Horn Vineyard* * *, Sangiovese Jessandre Vineyard* * * * *, Zinfandel Chauvet
Vineyard* * * *, Zinfandel Philip Coturri Estate* * * *, Zinfandel Sonoma Mountain* * * *

1993 Alicante Bouchet Ubaldi Vineyard	Sonoma	B	88
1992 Alicante Bouchet Ubaldi Vineyard	Sonoma	B	87
1992 Cabernet Sauvignon Jessandre Vineyard	Sonoma	C	91
1991 Cabernet Sauvignon Remick Ridge Vineyard	Sonoma	C	89
1990 Cabernet Sauvignon Remick Ridge Vineyard	Sonoma	C	90
1993 Merlot Feingold Vineyard	Sonoma	C	90
1992 Pinot Noir Horn Vineyard	Sonoma	B	87
1993 Sangiovese Jessandre Vineyard	Sonoma	C	92
1993 Zinfandel Estate	Sonoma	C	90
1992 Zinfandel Chauvet Vineyard	Sonoma	B	91
1991 Zinfandel Chauvet Vineyard	Sonoma	B	90
1993 Zinfandel Philip Coturri Estate Vineyard	Sonoma	C	92
1992 Zinfandel Sonoma Mountain	Sonoma	B	93

None of my reviews provoke more controversy than those of Coturri. For every reader who writes to thank me for turning them on to these organically made, unfined, unfiltered, unsulfured wines, there are others who have accused me of consuming excessive amounts of illegal substances before tasting Coturri's wines, or, even worse, just incompetence. The debate over Coturri's wines is due to the fact that some Coturri wines (which I have not recommended) are flawed by excessive amounts of volatile acidity, off aromas, etc. Of the winery's current releases, the first bottles tasted of the 1992 Sonoma Valley Cabernet Sauvignons from the Horn Vineyard and Blue Mountain Vineyard possessed frightfully high levels of volatile acidity and could not be recommended. Additional tastings from other bottles revealed potentially outstanding wines. Perhaps Coturri's adherence to a puristic approach to bottling barrel by barrel, thus refusing to assemble all of the barrels into a master blend, should be discontinued. This practice, also used by numerous Burgundians, results in notoriously frustrating bottle variation. Nevertheless, the following wines were superrich, pure examples of their varietals. They are too interesting and provocative not to recommend. However, readers who prefer wines that fall within strictly defined parameters are forewarned. Those who possess adventurous spirits and are interested in different winemaking styles should try one of Coturri's offerings before investing in a case. These are some of the most intriguing, albeit controversial wines I have ever tasted.

The 1993 Merlot from the Feingold Vineyard is Coturri's debut Merlot release. I did not find anything controversial about this superconcentrated, rich wine. Because Coturri utilizes no SO$_2$, my instincts suggest the wine may evolve quickly, although I have not found that to be the case with several older bottlings I have in my cellar. The 1993 Merlot offers a saturated black/purple color and a huge, rich nose of spices, earth, and black cherry fruit. Amazingly full bodied and unctuous, with low acidity and magnificent fruit and richness, this thick, chewy Merlot should drink well for 5–7 years, possibly longer.

The 1992 Coturri Cabernet Sauvignon is not marred by excessive volatile acidity. Let's hope all the barrels are consistent, as the wine I tasted came from one specific barrel. This is another huge, massive (14.4% alcohol) Cabernet with gobs of peppery cassis fruit and lavish flavor extraction. The wine is rich, spicy, and amazingly long, with its huge density and concentration concealing moderate tannin. Approachable now, this wine should drink well for 7–8 years, possibly longer.

The 1991 Cabernet Sauvignon Remick Ridge Vineyard is almost as idiosyncratic as the Pinot Noir. Its bouquet of jammy cassis, prunes, melted road tar, and spice leaps from the glass. The wine possesses a late harvest–like style with its massive, concentrated, jammy fruit, full body, unctuous texture, and glycerin-dominated, long finish. This superripe, blockbuster Cabernet Sauvignon will last for 15+ years. Wines such as this take on more structure and focus as they mature. Coturri's 1990 Cabernet Sauvignon Remick Ridge Vineyard is closer to the modern-day image of California Cabernet than their other wines. It reveals an opaque, thick, plum/purple color, a spicy, black cherry, earthy-scented nose, and unctuous, viscous, rich flavors that offer spicy clove, truffle, and cherry/black raspberry fruit. There is superb density, fine balance, and a long finish covering what appears to be high but ripe tannin. This wine will need to be decanted as it will no doubt deposit considerable sediment. If you do not like an intense perfume of earthy, olive, cedary scents in Cabernet Sauvignon, try another producer's more straightforward, politically correct example. Coturri's Cabernet should last for 10–15 years.

Less controversial is Coturri's 1993 Alicante Bouchet from the Ubaldi Vineyard. It is black colored, with an earthy nose of black cherry, licorice, and mineral scents that is followed by a dense, extraordinarily concentrated, full-bodied wine with massive flavor extraction. This dry, ripe wine is best served with barbecued food and winter-weight stews or cassoulets. The 1992 Alicante Bouchet Ubaldi Vineyard is one of the most concentrated red wines I have ever tasted. Although not particularly complex, it boasts an opulent texture, and enormous richness of fruit and depth. It is not so much unusual as just overwhelmingly rich, thick, and big. This wine will make a great complement to a winter-weight stew, soup, or aromatic cheeses.

Coturri's Zinfandels, which are among California's most exotic and distinctive, are organically produced, unfined and unfiltered, and made from wild yeasts. In personality, they fall somewhere between an Italian Amarone and the massive, late-harvest Zinfandels that were popular in the mid-seventies. The 1992s are unqualified successes. For example, the Chauvet Vineyard cuvée reveals an opaque purple color, a huge nose of sweet black fruits, Asian spices, cedar, and herbs. Dense, ripe, and full bodied, with exceptional concentration, this voluptuously textured, thick, chewy Zinfandel requires significantly flavored food. It should drink well for 10–15 years. The saturated, black/purple-colored Sonoma Mountain Zinfandel offers a huge nose of jammy black cherries, licorice, herbs, and spices. This superconcentrated, unctuously textured, blockbuster wine possesses layers of flavor and surprisingly fine balance for its gargantuan framework. The finish lasts for nearly a minute. It will evolve for 2 decades.

As one would expect, the Amarone-style 1991 Zinfandel from the Chauvet Vineyard has its own distinctive personality. There is some volatile acidity, but the wine is fabulously concentrated, and the nose offers up everything from funky, earthy smells to huge aromas of black raspberries and Asian spices. There is sensational extraction, a thick, chewy texture, and a blockbuster finish. For those readers willing to overlook a small amount of volatile acidity and to drink this Zin with some heavy-duty bistro cooking or cheese, it will make an immensely favorable impression, and should drink well for another 7–10 years.

Zinfandel fanatics should try a bottle of Coturri's 1993 Zinfandel Estate and 1993 Zinfandel Philip Coturri Estate Vineyard. Although the 1993 Zinfandel Estate possesses some residual sugar, it is extremely rich, with a huge, black fruit, spice, and roasted herb–scented nose, gigantic body, glycerin, and flavor extraction, and a low-acid, off-dry finish. It should drink well for 5–6 years. Even more impressive is the exceptionally rich 1993

Zinfandel Philip Coturri Estate. One of the richest, most intense, well-balanced Zinfandels I have ever tasted, this 15.3% alcohol wine does not taste alcoholic, because of its tremendous amounts of fruit and concentration. It should drink well for 5–7 years or longer. The aging curve suggested for these wines is conservative in view of the fact that no SO_2 is used, so Coturri must rely on the wine's high alcohol content for ageability. Intriguing, controversial, but frequently riveting wines are the rule of thumb from this idiosyncratic producer.

The 1992 Pinot Noir Horn Vineyard's dark garnet/purple color is followed by a bouquet of sweet, jammy black fruits, aromas of fresh cow manure (my grandfather was a dairy farmer, so I am familiar with the odor), and herb, truffle, and spice scents. There is remarkable richness (it is almost too concentrated for Pinot Noir), and a chewy, full-bodied texture, with the fruit nearly obscuring some light tannin. It is a fascinating wine, but tasters should be prepared for a walk on the wild side with this Pinot. Age will undoubtedly make it more civilized; it should last for 10 years.

These wines are not for everybody, nor are they intended to be. They are limited-production, eccentric wines that I find fascinating to taste and to drink.

CRONIN VINEYARDS (SAN MATEO)
Cabernet Sauvignon * *, Chardonnay Cuvées * * * *, Pinot Noir * *, Sauvignon Blanc * * * *

1992 Chardonnay	Alexander Valley	C	87
1992 Chardonnay	Napa	C	89

I have enjoyed many opulent, concentrated, personality-filled Chardonnays from Cronin. The 1992 Alexander Valley Chardonnay exhibits spicy vanillin and ripe, honeyed fruit in the nose, medium body, admirable ripeness and richness, and a long, soft finish. The 1992 Napa Chardonnay is slightly more oily, with a more noticeably unctuous texture that shares a similarly opulent, fleshy palate, and a moderately intense, citrusy, buttery bouquet. This is an excellent, nearly outstanding Chardonnay for drinking over the next year.

CUVAISON (NAPA)
Cabernet Sauvignon * * *, Chardonnay * *, Merlot * * *

1990 Cabernet Sauvignon	Napa	C	88
1992 Merlot	Napa	C	89

This winery continues to exhibit signs of improvement. The dark ruby/purple color and moderately intense nose of herbs, chocolate-covered black cherries, and flowerlike, underbrush scents are admirable. Medium to full bodied, with light tannin that gives the wine a slight toughness, this rich, smoky, mocha-, chocolate-, and berry-flavored wine should drink well for 5–6 years.

The most impressive Cabernet Sauvignon Cuvaison has recently produced, the dark-colored 1990 offers an attractive, moderately intense bouquet of olives, cassis, and vanillin. Rich and chewy, with medium to full body, excellent depth, adequate acidity, and a long finish, this wine is delicious; it will keep for 12–15 years.

DALLA VALLE VINEYARDS (NAPA)
Cabernet Sauvignon * * * * *, Maya Proprietary Red Wine * * * * *, Pietre Rosso * * *

1993 Cabernet Sauvignon Estate	Napa	D	95
1992 Cabernet Sauvignon Estate	Napa	D	96
1991 Cabernet Sauvignon Estate	Napa	D	94
1990 Cabernet Sauvignon Estate	Napa	D	93
1989 Cabernet Sauvignon Estate	Napa	D	88

1993 Maya Proprietary Red Wine	Napa	EE	99
1992 Maya Proprietary Red Wine	Napa	EE	100
1991 Maya Proprietary Red Wine	Napa	EE	99
1990 Maya Proprietary Red Wine	Napa	EE	96
N.V. Pietre Rosso	Italy/Napa	D	88

Dalla Valle has propelled itself into the top echelon of California Cabernet Sauvignon and proprietary red wines. The owners, Gustave and Naoko Dalla Valle, are admirably supported by winemaker Heidi Barrett (the wife of winemaker/proprietor Bo Barrett of Château Montelena). This team is producing awesomely concentrated wines from their 25-acre hillside vineyard overlooking the Napa Valley floor. There is no secret to their success. The wines are made from fully ripened fruit and are neither excessively processed nor handled. There are only 2,000 cases of the Cabernet Sauvignon. The microscopic production of Dalla Valle's proprietary red wine, Maya (named after the proprietors' daughter), usually contains between 45% and 55% Cabernet Franc. I am not overstating the case by saying that the finest Cabernet Franc I have tasted in the new world is from Dalla Valle's vineyard.

The 1993 Cabernet Sauvignon Estate looks to be another full-bodied, highly extracted, rich, pure Cabernet with 15–20 years of aging potential. The copious quantities of pure cassis fruit and intense fragrance of this wine will make it a sure winner. The 1992 Cabernet Sauvignon Estate is a worthy successor to the blockbuster 1990 and 1991. Huge, sweet aromas of black fruits, spices, and oak are followed by a wine with great fruit extraction, full body, layers of richness, and that multidimensional, layered feel that this producer routinely obtains. The flattering personality of the 1992 has turned out a more unctuous and voluptuous wine than even the 1991 or 1990. Moreover, it will have 15+ years of aging potential. The 1991 Cabernet Sauvignon Estate (88% Cabernet Sauvignon and the rest Cabernet Franc and Merlot) is an opaque, deeply saturated, purple-colored wine with a supersweet, pure nose of black cherries, cassis, minerals, and vanilla. The wine possesses exceptional richness, full body, ripe tannin, and a blockbuster finish. Approachable now, it promises to evolve for 2 decades. The 1990 Cabernet Sauvignon Estate (88% Cabernet Sauvignon, 10% Cabernet Franc, 2% Merlot) reveals an astonishingly deep color, as well as a huge aroma of smoky cassis, chocolate, and licorice. In the mouth, it is a powerful wine, with great stuffing, wonderful structure, enough acid and tannin to frame the wine's immense size, and a formidable finish. I was told the yields were a minuscule 2 tons per acre. While it should not be drunk before the mid to late nineties, it has the potential to easily last for 20 years.

The 1993 Maya is a sensational, blockbuster wine of exceptional richness and personality. An opaque purple, with a sweet, cassis aroma, this awesomely concentrated wine reveals well-integrated tannin, acid, and wood. A monument in the making, the 1993 Maya should reach full maturity in a decade and last for 25–30 years. Amazing!

The awesome 1992 Maya is performing better than the 1991 did at a similar stage. The more flattering 1992 reveals a saturated purple color and an intense fragrance of black raspberries, cassis, flowers, and minerals. The wine possesses great fruit, superb density, wonderful purity and balance, and a compelling extra dimension both aromatically and texturally. It is destined to be one of California's legendary wines. If the 1992 improves as much as the 1991, it will also be a strong candidate for a perfect rating. The 1991 Maya (made from equal proportions of Cabernet Franc and Cabernet Sauvignon) has developed incredibly since I tasted it nearly a year ago and rated it 94. The wine is black/purple colored and offers up a compelling bouquet of flowers, minerals, black fruits, vanilla, and spices. There is huge extraction of fruit, full body, outstanding purity and balance, moderate tannin, and a tremendous layered feel on the palate. All of this intensity and richness is brilliantly pulled off without any sense of heaviness. I can understand wanting to drink this wine immediately, as it is an extraordinarily impressive young wine, but it should be given another 4–6 years of cellaring; it is a candidate for 25 years of aging. It is also a strong candidate for a 3-digit score in a few years. This is a winemaking tour de force! The 1990 Maya is a monster in the making. Its supersaturated, opaque black/ruby color is followed by a tight but promising nose of earth, cassis, smoke, and gobs of sweet fruit. It is even richer and more tannic than the regular Cabernet. The finish is long, sweet, and compelling.

One of Dalla Valle's more intriguing projects is the European/American blend of Sangiovese (purchased from a Chianti estate in Tuscany) and Cabernet Sauvignon and Cabernet Franc from the estate's vineyards. I usually deplore these efforts as crude marketing gimmicks, but the Dalla Valley N.V. Pietre Rosso is so good I have to give the proprietor credit for putting together a lovely, full-bodied, spicy, enticing wine with plenty of Sangiovese character buttressed by the sweet black-fruit character of Napa Cabernet Sauvignon. This wonderfully pure wine is reminiscent of a luxury-priced Italian Vino da Tavola. Although soft and delicious, it possesses the backbone and stuffing necessary to last for 5–6 years.

Ratings for Older Vintages of Dalla Valle's Cabernet Sauvignon Estate: 1988 (90), 1987 (89)

Ratings for Older Vintages of Dalla Valle's Maya Proprietary Red Table Wine: 1989 (89+), 1988 (93)

THE JOHN DANIEL SOCIETY (NAPA)
Dominus Proprietary Red Wine * * * * *

1994 Dominus	Napa	D	99
1992 Dominus	Napa	D	97
1991 Dominus	Napa	D	99
1990 Dominus	Napa	D	98

The John Daniel Society, owned by the renowned Bordelais Christian Moueix, was founded in 1982. Their wine, called Dominus, is produced from a famous 120-acre Napa Valley vineyard called Napanook, just to the west of Yountville. Christian Moueix, who purchased the estate from his partners, Robin Lail and Marci Smith, in 1994, and also oversees the winemaking of such Bordeaux superstars as Pétrus, Trotanoy, Latour à Pomerol, and Magdelaine, has utilized traditional Bordeaux techniques to produce a world-class Cabernet-based wine. Moueix's minimal interventionist winemaking philosophy, which follows such traditional practices as (1) severe crop thinning to guarantee conservative yields; (2) a late harvest in order to obtain physiologically ripe grapes; (3) minimum or no acid adjustments; (4) the avoidance of sterile filtration that eviscerates and denudes a wine; and (5) the refusal to rely on a heavy cosmetic overlay of toasty new oak to flatter wine writers, is resulting in some of the most profound wines made in the new world.

Christian Moueix surprised many people by selling off the production from the 1993 vintage, as he was unhappy with the wine's overall balance. Although there will not be a 1993 Dominus, they have certainly made up for it with an extraordinary effort in 1994, which promises to rival the otherworldly 1991. The 1994, which had a significantly long hang time for the grapes (nearly 130 days, contrasted with the normal 100–105), is a wine of great intensity, massive richness, yet no heaviness or harsh tannin. The blend of 72% Cabernet Sauvignon/12% Merlot/11% Cabernet Franc/5% Petit Verdot resulted in a wine with extraordinary aromas of red and black fruits, magnificent layers of jammy fruit buttressed by low acidity, and formidable albeit ripe, sweet, friendly tannin. There are 8,000 cases of this exceptional wine that should drink well when released and age effortlessly for 25+ years.

The 1992 Dominus, of which there are 7,000 cases made from a blend of 52% Cabernet Sauvignon, 22% Cabernet Franc, 22% Merlot, and the remainder Petit Verdot, is an opulent, opaquely concentrated wine with great ripeness of fruit, and a huge nose of earth, black cherries, mocha, and herbs. Full-bodied, with a layered, multidimensional personality, adequate acidity, and a super finish, this should prove to be another fabulous Dominus for drinking over the next 20–25 years. It is more forward than the 1991 or 1990.

As for the 1991, 6,500 cases were produced of this potentially perfect wine. While this vintage of Dominus contains no Merlot in the blend, every time I taste it I am reminded of a great vintage of Pétrus such as 1982, 1989, or 1990. Although different, the 1991 Dominus possesses extraordinary intensity, remarkable opulence, and amazing fruit extraction, all welded to a full-bodied structure. The wine's sensational purity and inner core of depth must be tasted to be believed. The 1991 will be approachable young, yet it exhibits the potential to last for 25 years. It is unquestionably the greatest Dominus made to date and is a potential legend in the making.

The spectacularly complex, rich 1990 Dominus magically combines the finest elements of Napa Valley (strength, ripeness, and full body) with those of Bordeaux (finesse, elegance, and complexity). The opaque dark ruby/purple color suggests considerable intensity, low yields, and great richness. A huge, soaring bouquet offers aromas of cassis, black cherries, subtle herbs, vanillin, and spices. This full-bodied, voluptuously textured, superconcentrated, multidimensional wine is more flattering and opulent than previous Dominus vintages, which tended to be tannic as well as rich. Although approachable and already complex (I have already consumed 3 bottles), the magnificent 1990 Dominus should evolve gracefully for 20–30 years.

Ratings for Older Vintages of Dominus: 1989 (92), 1988 (91), 1987 (96), 1986 (91), 1985 (93), 1984 (90), 1983 (90)

D'ANNCO (NAPA)
Zinfandel Old Vines * * */* * * *

1991 Zinfandel Old Vines	Napa	C	87

D'Annco's exotic 1991 Zinfandel exhibits aromas of incense intermingled with a spicy, wild raspberry character. Rich and full bodied, with copious amounts of fruit and no evidence of new oak, this intriguing, rustic Zin is loaded. If more complexity emerges, my rating will look conservative. Drink it over the next 8–10 years.

DE LOACH VINEYARDS (SONOMA)
Cabernet Sauvignon * *, Chardonnay * * *, Chardonnay O.F.S. * * * *, Fumé Blanc * * *,
Gewürztraminer * *, Pinot Noir * *, Zinfandel Estate * * *, Zinfandel O.F.S. * * * * *, Zinfandel
Single-Vineyard Cuvées * * * *

1993 Chardonnay	Russian River	D	90
1992 Chardonnay	Russian River	B	87
1993 Chardonnay O.F.S.	Russian River	C	90
1993 Fumé Blanc	Russian River	A	86
1992 Zinfandel	Russian River	B	90
1992 Zinfandel Barbieri Ranch	Russian River	C	88
1991 Zinfandel Barbieri Ranch	Russian River	B	86
1992 Zinfandel Gambogi Ranch	Russian River	C	90
1992 Zinfandel O.F.S.	Russian River	C	90
1992 Zinfandel Papera Ranch	Russian River	C	87
1991 Zinfandel Papera Ranch	Russian River	B	87

| 1992 Zinfandel Peletti Ranch | Russian River | C | 88 |
| 1991 Zinfandel Peletti Ranch | Russian River | B | 85 |

Consistently one of California's finest Chardonnays, De Loach's 1993 O.F.S. (Our Finest Selection) displays gobs of buttery, honeyed, tropical fruit, full body, more structure and delineation than is generally found in this offering, and an exuberant, zesty, mouth-filling, alcoholic finish. A terrific example of bigness and boldness allied to freshness and liveliness, it should be drunk over the next year.

The 1993 is the finest Fumé Blanc this winery has yet produced. It exhibits a full-throttle bouquet of herbs, smoke, and lavishly ripe, honeyed fruit. Mouth filling, rich, and medium bodied, with loads of fruit, vibrancy, and a heady finish, it will provide plenty of pleasure over the next 12 months.

De Loach has produced a bevy of delicious 1992 Zinfandels that surpass even the wonderful array of Zinfandels this winery produced in 1990 and 1991. All of the single-vineyard Zins come from old vines. For example, the Barbieri Ranch is from a vineyard planted in 1905; the Gambogi Ranch is from a vineyard planted in 1909; the Papera Ranch is from an 18-acre vineyard planted in 1934; and the Peletti Ranch is from a vineyard planted in 1928. The O.F.S. is a blend of the best barrels. No one will be disappointed with any of these offerings.

Even De Loach's 1992 Zinfandel regular cuvée is an outstanding wine. Although it is often overlooked by consumers rushing to purchase the O.F.S. and single-vineyard offerings, it is a blockbuster, rich, supple, voluptuously textured wine with tremendous concentration and a heady, spicy finish. It is a textbook Zinfandel that should not be missed. Drink it over the next 3–4 years. The 1992 Zinfandel Barbieri Ranch is a soft, ripe, fat wine with aromas and flavors suggestive of black cherries and raspberries. Deep, richly fruity, and velvety textured, it is ideal for consuming over the next 5–6 years. The 1992 Zinfandel Gambogi Ranch is a richer, fuller-bodied, deeper wine with a darker color, a peppery, black rasp-berry–scented nose, enviable richness and ripeness, and a long, deep, full-bodied finish. Although approachable now, it has the potential to last for a decade. The 1992 Papera Ranch Zinfandel exhibits a spicy, peppery, black cherry nose, tasty, medium-bodied flavors, and excellent depth and ripeness. It is slightly shorter and lighter than the other offerings. The deep ruby-colored 1992 Zinfandel Peletti Ranch offers a big, spicy, dense, medium- to full-bodied, concentrated palate, and a spicy, moderately tannic finish. It will benefit from 6–12 months of cellaring and should last for 8–10 years. The 1992 Zinfandel O.F.S. is a powerful, superbly concentrated, rich, full-bodied Zinfandel with huge, massive flavors, plenty of alcohol (15.7%), and a long, dry, lusty finish. Pure and rich, it can be drunk now or held for 10–12+ years. This is an impressive group of Zinfandels!

De Loach's three single-vineyard 1991 Zinfandels are slightly less intense and more acidic than the 1990 offerings. The 1991 Pelletti Ranch is ripe and tasty, but straightforward and one-dimensional. The quality of the fruit is attractive, and the wine is ideal for drinking over the next 3–5 years. The 1991 Barbieri Ranch exhibits a spicy, raspberry-scented nose, ripe, supple, medium-bodied flavors, fine extraction, and a tasty, moderately long finish. Drink it over the next 5 years. The best of this trio is the 1991 Papera Ranch, a deeper, more aromatic and expansively flavored wine with medium to full body, a rich, peppery, raspberry-scented nose, more glycerin and flesh than the other two Zinfandels, as well as a longer, richer finish. It should drink well for 5–7 years.

DE LORIMER (ALEXANDER VALLEY)
Spectrum Estate * * *

| 1992 Spectrum Estate | Alexander Valley | B | 86 |

The 1992 Spectrum Estate, a Semillon/Sauvignon Blanc blend, reveals a fleshy, oily, herb, waxy nose, flavorful, ripe, medium-bodied flavors, and an attractively long finish. A beefy-style wine, it should work well with grilled fish.

DEER PARK WINERY (NAPA)
Zinfandel * * *

1991 Zinfandel	Howell Mountain	C	86+
1992 Zinfandel Reserve Beatty Ranch	Howell Mountain	C	88

The 1992 Zinfandel Reserve Beatty Ranch from the underrated Deer Park Winery reveals a saturated dark ruby color, a reticent but ripe, dusty, black cherry–scented nose, and excellent spicy, concentrated flavors with a backward, unevolved character. Moderately tannic, with considerable power, this Zinfandel will benefit from 2–3 years of cellaring; it should keep for 10–12 years. A typical Howell Mountain wine—deeply colored, broodingly backward, austere, and tannic, yet endowed with considerable depth of fruit—the dense, medium- to full-bodied, very good to excellent 1991 Zinfandel requires buyers to defer their gratification for at least 2–3 years. Given past examples, it should shed much of its tannin and evolve into a graceful, complex, spicy, peppery wine that will last for a decade.

DEHLINGER WINERY (SONOMA)
Bordeaux Blend Proprietary Red Wine * * * *, Cabernet Sauvignon * * *, Chardonnay * * * *, Chardonnay Montrachet Cuvée * * * *, Merlot * * *, Pinot Noir * * */* * * *, Syrah * * * *

1993 Bordeaux Blend Proprietary Red Wine	Russian River	C	91
1992 Bordeaux Blend Proprietary Red Wine	Russian River	C	89
1992 Cabernet Sauvignon	Russian River	C	88
1991 Cabernet Sauvignon	Russian River	C	85
1993 Chardonnay Estate	Russian River	C	87
1992 Chardonnay Montrachet Cuvée	Russian River	C	91
1993 Pinot Noir Goldridge Vineyard	Russian River	C	89
1993 Pinot Noir Estate	Russian River	C	89
1992 Pinot Noir Estate	Russian River	C	88
1992 Pinot Noir Reserve	Russian River	D	90
1993 Syrah Estate	Russian River	C	92
1992 Syrah Estate	Russian River	C	89+

Dehlinger's Pinot Noirs go from strength to strength, with a rich, smoky, ripe plum/cherry, supple 1992 Estate and a more reserved, richer, more structured and concentrated 1992 Pinot Noir Reserve. In 1993 there is a vineyard designated Pinot, the Goldridge Pinot Noir, that exhibits a smoky-, herbal-, sweet black cherry–scented nose and unctuously textured, rich, medium- to full-bodied flavors with low acidity and plenty of charm and flesh. The 1993 Estate Pinot Noir reveals deep, earthy Pinot fruit, an herbal tinge, and plenty of gamy, overripe cherry notes. All of these Pinot Noirs are drinkable upon release and capable of lasting 5–7 years.

Dehlinger has experimented with Cabernet Franc, which I have found to be of average quality. The herbaceous 1992 will be their last vintage of that varietal. On the other hand, the winery is doing an increasingly fine job with Cabernet Sauvignon. The 1992 offers up a sweet, black currant nose, full body, obvious, ripe, juicy fruit, a succulent texture, and plenty of spice in the long, heady finish. It should drink well for 10–15 years. The leaner 1991 Cabernet Sauvignon possesses higher acidity, as well as more herbal characteristics.

Dehlinger's proprietary red wine, Bordeaux Blend, deserves a more impressive name. Both the 1992 and 1993 are blends of 55% Cabernet Sauvignon and 45% Merlot. Both are rich, full-bodied, concentrated wines with considerable intensity and sweet, black currant fruit intermingled with hints of chocolate, vanilla, smoke, and black cherries. Opulent, rich, and mouth filling, they are ideal for drinking over the next 10–15 years. For whatever reason, they tend to be overlooked in the Dehlinger portfolio.

Dehlinger's 1993 Syrah will eclipse the fine 1992. Its powerful nose of jammy cassis fruit is followed by a large-scale, muscular, rich, concentrated wine with soft, ripe tannin. It should drink well for 10–15 years.

The 1992 Syrah's healthy, saturated purple color and tight, spicy nose with a hint of jammy black fruits are followed by a full-bodied, moderately tannic wine. Although closed yet formidably concentrated, powerful, and rich, it requires 1–3 more years of cellaring. It should age effortlessly for 10–15 years. Impressive!

Dehlinger's 1993 Chardonnay Estate is a cross between a steely, mineral-dominated Chablis premier cru and a fuller, fleshier Chardonnay from the Côte d'Or. Cleanly made, with a steely, orange/applelike fruitiness, well-integrated acidity, medium to full body, and a long, zesty finish, it is a delightful, flexible Chardonnay to drink with an assortment of food. The excellent 1992 Chardonnay Montrachet Cuvée possesses superb intensity and length, as well as that distinctive mineral character found in certain Burgundian vineyards, particularly the Perrières vineyard in Meursault and the Montrachet vineyard shared by the villages of Puligny-Montrachet and Chassagne-Montrachet. This wine exhibits full body, splendid concentration, vibrant acidity, and a well-delineated, large-scale finish. A knock-out Chardonnay, it should be drunk over the next 1–2 years.

DEUX AMIS (SONOMA)
Zinfandel * * *

1992 Zinfandel	Sonoma	B	89
1991 Zinfandel	Sonoma	B	89

A textbook Zinfandel, Deux Amis's 1992 displays a spicy, peppery, black raspberry–scented nose, medium to full body, excellent definition and richness, and a well-focused, ripe, moderately long, lightly tannic finish. Drinkable now, it should last for a decade. The admirable saturation of the 1991 Zinfandel's deep ruby/purple color is undoubtedly caused by the addition of a small amount of Petite Sirah. An excellent nose of peppery spices and black raspberries is followed by a rich, full-bodied, concentrated wine that is loaded with fruit. The alcohol is 14.2%, giving this Zinfandel plenty of glycerin and texture. Drink it over the next 5–7 years.

DIAMOND CREEK VINEYARDS (NAPA)
Single-Vineyard Cabernet Sauvignons produced before 1987 * * * * *, Single-Vineyard Cabernet Sauvignons produced after 1987 * */* * *

1992 Cabernet Sauvignon Gravelly Meadow	Napa	D	88
1992 Cabernet Sauvignon Red Rock Terrace	Napa	D	88
1992 Cabernet Sauvignon Volcanic Hill	Napa	D	89

After the less than inspirational efforts Diamond Creek has produced since 1984, these three cuvées of 1992 Cabernet Sauvignon exhibit better richness, excellent purity, and deep ruby/purple colors. Nevertheless, for longtime fans of Diamond Creek Cabernet, weaned on the blockbuster, rich, occasionally rustic, but always individualistic and distinctive as well as supercomplex and concentrated wines of the seventies and early eighties, there has clearly been a radical change in style. Although these wines may be more elegant and consistent, they are also less interesting. That is not to say they are not good. But anyone who has tasted Diamond Creek Cabernet Sauvignon from 1974, 1975, 1976, 1977, or 1978, as well as vintages through the early eighties, knows that, when mature, these wines are riveting examples of California Cabernet Sauvignon. There now appears to be an emphasis on a more sculptured, elegant style.

The most flattering of this trio at present is the 1992 Gravelly Meadow Cabernet Sauvignon. It offers attractive, juicy fruit, an austere structure reminiscent of a barrel sample of young Bordeaux, and a medium-bodied, moderately tannic finish. It is a well-made, polite style of Cabernet that proponents would say is filled with finesse and style. I like it, but I would have enjoyed seeing a bit more forceful richness and concentration, à la the old Diamond Creeks. Although richer, the 1992 Cabernet Sauvignon Volcanic Hill is also extremely tannic and backward. It should easily merit a score in the upper 80s when fully mature in 10–12 years. There is impressive, pure cassis fruit, medium body, and gobs of tannin in the finish. Do not touch a bottle for at least 7–8 years, as it is one of the most backward 1992s. The same can be said for the 1992 Red Rock Terrace Cabernet Sauvignon. More similar in style to the Volcanic Hill than the Gravelly Meadow, this medium-bodied wine is dense and rich, with considerable tannin in the finish. Give it at least 7–8 years of cellaring.

All of these offerings should turn out to be very fine Cabernet Sauvignons with at least 2 decades of aging potential. However, the move toward a more stylish, elegant, and refined Cabernet Sauvignon appears to have condemned Diamond Creek to following the pack. While they are very good, well-made wines, I lament the fact that they have so little in common with the Diamond Creek Cabernet Sauvignons made between 1974 and 1984.

DRY CREEK VINEYARD (SONOMA)

Cabernet Sauvignon * */* * *, Chardonnay * *, Fumé Blanc * * * *, Meritage * * *, Zinfandel Old Vines * * * */* * * * *

1992 Dry Chenin Blanc	California	A	85
1992 Fumé Blanc	Sonoma	A	85
1992 Zinfandel Old Vines	Sonoma	B	90
1991 Zinfandel Old Vines	Dry Creek	B	92

Another excellent Zinfandel from this consistent producer, the dark ruby/purple-colored 1992 offers a beautiful, ripe, pure nose of red and black fruits, medium body, a soft, voluptuous texture, and gobs of flavor interwoven with sweet vanillin, oaky notes. Ripe, long, moderately powerful yet with a sense of elegance, this supple wine should be drunk over the next 5–7 years. The 1991 Zinfandel Old Vines is the most stunning Dry Creek Zinfandel since their superb 1987 Old Vines cuvée. A saturated dark ruby/purple color is followed by a huge, sweet, explosive nose of black fruits and minerals. There is dazzling richness, full body, tremendous density, glycerin, and opulence to its compelling flavor extraction, and a satiny-smooth finish. Don't miss it! Buy it by the case and drink it over the next 7–8 years.

The 1992 Dry Chenin Blanc's refreshing, light-intensity, floral-scented bouquet is followed by a light- to medium-bodied, dry wine that is ideal as an aperitif. The 1992 Fumé Blanc offers a moderately herbaceous-scented nose and medium-bodied, crisp, herbal, and melon-scented flavors. It is a stylish, refreshing Sauvignon for drinking over the next year.

DUNN VINEYARDS (NAPA)

Cabernet Sauvignon Howell Mountain * * * * *, Cabernet Sauvignon Napa * * * * *

1993 Cabernet Sauvignon	Napa	D	90
1992 Cabernet Sauvignon	Napa	D	94
1991 Cabernet Sauvignon	Napa	D	91+
1990 Cabernet Sauvignon	Napa	D	93
1993 Cabernet Sauvignon Howell Mountain	Napa	D	96+
1992 Cabernet Sauvignon Howell Mountain	Napa	D	97
1991 Cabernet Sauvignon Howell Mountain	Napa	D	93+
1990 Cabernet Sauvignon Howell Mountain	Napa	D	96

Having closely followed Dunn's Cabernet Sauvignons since the debut 1979 vintage, I think it is remarkable how consistent these wines have been. Dunn's great early successes, especially the 1982s, were followed by a succession of rich, tannic wines in 1984, 1985, 1986, and 1987, two tough years in 1988 and 1989, and, as with most northern California wineries, an unprecedented run of great years starting in 1990. The wines are always impressive for their strength, massive body, and highly extracted black currant fruit. Dunn, who believes in filtering but not fining, tends to use the former technique as a way of bringing a measure of refinement to the brute strength and power his wines possess. It is too early to say, but if there is any weakness to Dunn's Cabernets it would be the surprising lack of bottle bouquet. Dunn vehemently believes that filtration has nothing to do with this, and that it is only a matter of time before his Cabernets exhibit more aromatic evolution.

Despite his success, Dunn has kept his operation modest in size. Approximately 5,000 cases are produced, and this is generally evenly split between the Napa and Howell Mountain bottlings. The two cuvées are similar in personality and quality, with the Napa sometimes revealing less astringent tannin. However, blind tastings reveal both wines to have similar aromatic and flavor profiles. Of these four vintages, the 1992 appears to be the greatest recent vintage for Dunn, rivaling what he achieved in 1990, 1984, and 1982. The 1991s are backward and tannic, but frightfully powerful and highly extracted. The 1993s appear slightly lighter by Dunn's standards. That is not to say they will be wimpish wines, as they are rich and concentrated.

As for Dunn's 1993s, I find my adjectives somewhat restricted in describing these wines. They are remarkably similar in style, with opaque purple colors. The scents that emerge are not so much complex as they are intense and promising. There are ripe, rich, pure notes of black raspberries, cassis, minerals, and oak. Both 1993 cuvées are extremely full bodied and tannic.

What makes the 1992s so incredible is that one of the vintage's hallmarks is the voluptuous, opulent, and succulent nature of the fruit. In Dunn's offerings, that translates into wines that are huge, massive, and rich, but with a sweeter, more expansive, chewy middle palate. Both of these Cabernets are 20- to 30-year wines, but I suspect the softer Napa cuvée will be drinkable in 5–7 years.

The most tannic and backward wines of these vintages are the 1991s. Consumers may be shocked by how tough, tannic, and backward the Napa Cabernet tastes. It possesses Dunn's wonderfully pure, rich, black currant flavors, as well as length, intensity, and full body. Yet the tannin levels in this tight wine are formidable. The 1991 vintage is one where the Howell Mountain Cabernet is noticeably thicker and more highly extracted. It is a huge, rich, powerful wine with great depth, as well as a boatload of tannin. Do not touch a bottle of either of these 1991s for at least 5–6 years.

While Dunn's Cabernets slumped in quality in the difficult vintages of 1988 and 1989, the 1990s exhibit exceptional richness, depth, power, and ferocious tannins. The 1990 Cabernet Sauvignon Napa is an opaque, awesomely concentrated, tannic wine with little aromatic development. **A.M.: 1996–2008.** The massive 1990 Howell Mountain exhibits huge tannin, but immense concentration. The richest Dunn Cabernet since the 1984s? **A.M.: 1999–2020.** They are not as superconcentrated as Dunn's wines from the early and mid-eighties. The Howell Mountain is slightly more tannic, and the Napa more open. Both possess a telltale mineral, cassis, flowery nose, and rich, full-bodied, dense, highly extracted, tannic personalities.

Ratings for Older Vintages of Dunn's Cabernet Sauvignon: 1989 (87), 1988 (84), 1987 (91), 1986 (92), 1985 (92), 1984 (94), 1983 (88), 1982 (92), 1980 (92)

Ratings for Older Vintages of Dunn's Cabernet Sauvignon Howell Mountain: 1989 (86), 1988 (84), 1987 (94), 1986 (94), 1985 (95), 1984 (95), 1983 (88), 1982 (95), 1981 (90), 1979 (90)

DURNEY VINEYARD (MONTEREY)
Cabernet Sauvignon * * *, Cabernet Sauvignon Reserve * * * */* * * * *, Chardonnay
Estate * * * *

1985 Cabernet Sauvignon Reserve	Carmel Valley	D	92
1990 Chardonnay Estate	Carmel Valley	C	90

There is no doubt that Monterey is a top-notch source for Chardonnay. Durney continues to produce full-throttle, rich, exceptionally age-worthy Chardonnays that can easily last for 5–7 years, an uncommonly long time for California Chardonnay. The 1990 Chardonnay may not hit its stride for another year, but it is a dramatic, blockbuster wine. Even more significant, in an area known for exceptionally vegetal Cabernet Sauvignons, Durney has frequently produced terrific Cabernets that can last for 12–20 years. The 1985 Cabernet Sauvignon Reserve is Durney's finest Cabernet since the great 1978. It clearly exhibits what heights this winery can achieve in an area not known for this varietal. Nearly black in color, this massive wine is still youthful and in need of cellaring. The earthy, cassis nose opens with airing. Exceptionally rich, full bodied, and multidimensional, this tightly knit wine will last for another 20 or more years.

DUXOUP WINEWORKS (SONOMA)
Charbono * * *, Gamay * * *, Syrah * *, Zinfandel * *

1990 Charbono	Napa	A	87
1990 Gamay	Napa	A	85

This winery excels with its inexpensive, exuberantly fruity, rich wines made from Charbono and Gamay. Both wines are loaded with a huge, grapy, black fruit character, as well as admirable intensity and concentration. They are wines to drink within their first 5–6 years of life.

EAGLE RIDGE WINERY (AMADOR)
Zinfandel Fiddletown * *

1991 Zinfandel Fiddletown	Amador	B	80

An attractive, straightforward, spicy nose is followed by a decently concentrated, ripe, light- to medium-bodied Zinfandel with noticeable alcohol in the finish. Drink it over the next 1–2 years.

EBERLE WINERY (PASO ROBLES)
Cabernet Sauvignon* * *, Chardonnay* */* * *, Zinfandel* * * *

1993 Zinfandel Sauret Vineyard	Paso Robles	B	90
1992 Zinfandel Sauret Vineyard	Paso Robles	B	87

Eberle's full throttle 1993 Zinfandel Sauret Vineyard exhibits an opaque purple color and a huge lavishly oaked, berry-scented nose. Thick, full-bodied, massively endowned flavors contain considerable alcohol (14.8%) and the wine's mouthfilling, glycerin-imbued superb finish lasts for nearly a minute. This extroverted, muscular, well-balanced Zinfandel should drink well for a decade. Readers are forewarned—this is not a wimpy wine!

The excellent, medium- to full-bodied 1992 Zinfandel Sauret Vineyard exhibits a dark ruby color, a dusty, raspberry-, loamy-scented nose, dense, concentrated flavors, excellent purity, and light to moderate tannin. An engaging suppleness suggests this wine should be drunk over the next 7–8 years.

EDIZIONE PENNINO (NIEBAUM-COPPOLA) (NAPA)
Zinfandel* * *

1992 Zinfandel	Napa	B	87
1991 Zinfandel	Napa	B	87

Made at the Niebaum-Coppola winery under the guidance of the well-known California winemaking consultant, Tony Soter, both the 1992 and 1991 Zinfandels exhibit saturated deep ruby colors, spicy, black cherry–scented noses, excellent structure, and medium- to full-bodied personalities. Both are cleanly made, with plenty of spice and ripeness. I could not decide whether I preferred the 1991 or the 1992. The 1992 tastes slightly softer, and the 1991 possesses more structure and noticeable tannin. Both wines should drink well for the next 5–6 years.

EDMEADES ESTATE (Mendocino)
Chardonnay* * *, Zinfandel* * *

1993 Zinfandel Ciapusci Vineyard	Mendocino	C	86
1993 Zinfandel Zeni Vineyard	Mendocino	C	89

If you can find any of the Zinfandel offerings from the Kendall-Jackson-owned Edmeades Estate, the 1993 Zinfandel Ciapusci Vineyard exhibits a nearly opaque dark ruby color, and a moderately intense nose of berry fruit and earth. Closed, with moderate tannin, this is a structured, tightly knit wine that will benefit from 1–2 years of cellaring. The tannin level is cause for worry, but there is good ripeness and richness. Drink it between 1997 and 2007. The 1993 Zinfandel Zeni Vineyard (from 70-year-old vines) reveals a similar dark ruby color, as well as a more promising and open nose of red and black fruits and spice, highly extracted black-raspberry and cherry flavors, full body, and light tannin in the structured finish. The wine is young, exuberant, fresh, and pure. Drink it over the next decade.

EDMUNDS ST. JOHN (ALAMEDA)
Les Côtes Sauvages* * * *, El Niño* * * *, Mourvèdre* * * *, Pallini Rosso* * * *, Pinot Grigio* * * *, Port o' Call* * * *, Syrah Cuvées* * * * *, Viognier* * *, Zinfandel* * * *

1992 El Niño	California	B	87
1992 Les Côtes Sauvages	California	B	89
1991 Les Côtes Sauvages	California	B	90
N.V. Les Côtes Sauvages Cuvée Wahluke	California	B	88

1993	Pallini Rosso	California	B	89
1993	Pinot Grigio	El Dorado	B	87
1989	Port o' Call	California	B	87
N.V.	Port o' Call Lot 90	California	B	87
1993	Syrah	California	B	88+
1992	Syrah Durell Vineyard	Sonoma/Carneros	C	93
1991	Syrah Durell Vineyard	Sonoma	C	91+
1990	Syrah Durell Vineyard	Sonoma	C	93
1992	Syrah Grand Heritage	California	C	92
1993	Viognier	Knight's Valley	C	89
1991	Zinfandel	California	C	90
1992	Zinfandel Howell Mountain	Napa	B	92

Steve Edmunds is one of those rare winemakers who seems to have the touch no matter what he does in the world of wine. If you are looking for a succulent, gorgeously opulent, smooth-as-silk wine made from 79% Zinfandel and 21% Grenache, the 1993 Pallini Rosso should meet your needs. It is a medium to dark ruby-colored wine bursting with ripe berry, peppery, spicy fruit. Medium to full bodied, soft, and crammed with berry fruit, this wine will offer ideal drinking over the next 3–4 years. What a shame there are not more wines of this quality that provide immediate gratification.

The 1992 El Niño, an innovative blend of 30% Charbono, 30% Grenache, 28% Barbera, and 12% Syrah, is all that a robust, exuberant, mouth-filling, dry red wine should be. It possesses a spicy, peppery nose, fine richness, medium to full body, soft tannin, and adequate acidity. Drink it over the next 2–3 years. The 1992 Syrah Grand Heritage sounds to me like a play on the southern hemisphere's greatest dry red wine, the Grange Hermitage from Australia's Penfolds winery. The Grand Heritage offers a huge, smoky, bacon fat– and cassis-scented nose, massively rich, superconcentrated flavors, commendable purity, and an unctuous texture. It can give the Grange Hermitage, as well as a great Hermitage from the Rhône Valley, plenty of competition. This immensely impressive, superrich wine is accessible enough to be drunk now, but concentrated and balanced enough to last for 15+ years.

The 1993 Syrah is a dark ruby/purple-colored wine with a tight but promising nose of smoke, black currants, and earth. Although full bodied, moderately tannic, rich, and full, it is not a blockbuster Syrah such as Edmunds St. John produced in 1992 and 1991. Nevertheless, it is a 10- to 15-year wine that should reach its apogee in 4–5 years. The blockbuster 1992 Syrah Durell Vineyard is a must-purchase for Syrah fanatics or wine enthusiasts who cannot get enough Hermitage. One of the greatest Syrahs this property has produced, the purple/black color is followed by a huge, fragrant nose of smoked meats, toast, chocolate, and jammy black currants. The wine displays exceptional flavor concentration, great structure and richness, beautifully integrated acidity, and ripe tannin. This full-bodied, massive, exquisitely balanced Syrah is capable of 20–25 years of evolution. A prodigious effort!

The 1991 Syrah from the Durrell Vineyard is a dead ringer for a great Hermitage. The huge, smoky, bacon fat–scented nose delivers aromas of ground beef, leather, and massive black fruit. Extraordinarily concentrated, with soft tannin, high extract and acidity levels, as well as impeccable balance, it will age well for 10–15 years.

The 1992 is another superb Zinfandel from Edmunds St. John. The suggestion of superconcentration in the huge, opaque, dark ruby/purple color is easily confirmed with one sniff and sip. The enormous bouquet of black raspberries, chocolate, cherries, herbs, and coffee is as exotic as it is multidimensional. The wine exhibits opulently rich, expansive, full-bodied flavors oozing with extraction. This is a terrific, full-bodied yet supple, voluptuously textured Zinfandel for drinking over the next decade. Made from a blend of 82% Zinfandel (52% from El Dorado and 30% from Amador) and the remainder Grenache and Mourvèdre, the 1991 Zinfandel's dense purple color is followed by aromas of sweet, jammy black fruits, licorice, pepper, and minerals. Deep, rich, and full bodied, this impressively extracted wine exhibits moderate tannins, adequate acidity, and an impressive finish. Approachable now, it should evolve gracefully for another 7–10 years.

The 1993 Pinot Grigio is a fun wine. Its wonderfully honeyed, richly fruity nose is followed by a wine with medium body, admirable depth, excellent purity, and heady alcohol. Although it is unlikely to win many first-place awards, it offers a level of pleasure that cannot be measured by a score. Drink it over the next year. If winemaker/proprietor Steve Edmunds had obtained more perfume in his 1993 Viognier, it would compete with Calera for first place in California's Viognier sweepstakes. There are enticing, subdued, floral, honeysuckle and peachlike notes, but the real hedonistic blast is delivered on the palate. It is explosively rich and viscous, with gorgeous layers of fruit, glycerin, and alcohol. The younger generation would call it yummy! Drink it over the next year.

The N.V. Les Côtes Sauvages Cuvée Wahluke (a 1990 with Washington State Grenache in the blend, hence the official "nonvintage" status) is a rich, exuberant, full-bodied wine loaded with ripe fruit. It will make delicious drinking over the next 1–3 years. One of America's most underrated great Rhône Ranger wines is Les Côtes Sauvages. A blend of grapes such as Syrah, Mourvèdre, and Grenache, it is the California version of a French Châteauneuf du Pape. The Rhône Ranger 1992 Côtes Sauvage exhibits copious quantities of ripe black fruits, pepper, and spice, full body, and a silky-smooth, hedonistic finish. Already delicious, it possesses the requisite depth and balance to age gracefully for 5–8 years. The 1991 exhibits a big, peppery, spicy, black fruit–scented bouquet, chewy, deep, concentrated flavors, full body, and excellent purity and focus. Drink it over the next decade.

The grapy nonvintage Port o' Call Lot 90 offers a big, fleshy, chewy mouthful of wine. The 1989 Port o' Call is a knockout, chunky, robust, fleshy wine oozing with scents of herbs and black cherry and black raspberry fruit. Full bodied, opulent, and providing a mouthful of delicious red wine, it is the perfect foil for the substantial, hearty fare served at your local bistro.

EL MOLINO (NAPA)
Chardonnay* * * *, Pinot Noir* * * *

| 1992 Chardonnay | Napa | C | 88 |
| 1992 Pinot Noir | Napa | D | 90 |

This winery produces supple, full-bodied, heady, rich Pinot Noirs that are about as seductive as this varietal can be. The 1992's brilliant, polished, dark-ruby color is followed by a restrained nose that, with coaxing, offers up sweet berry scents. The real treat is the decadently rich, fat, jammy flavors that cascade over the palate as if this wine were liquid velvet. It is not going to be an ager (but how many Pinot Noirs or red burgundies actually improve beyond 5–7 years?), so drink it over the near term. This was one of the most seductive wines of my tastings!

I like the complex aromatics this winery routinely achieves in its Chardonnay. The 1992 Chardonnay appears more closed than previous offerings, but there is still plenty to enjoy. It exhibits a Meursault-like, smoky, buttery, nutty, honeyed character, excellent richness, medium to full body, and a long finish. With more extraction, this would have been an exceptional effort. Drink it over the next 1–3 years.

ELLISTON VINEYARDS (ALAMEDA)
Chardonnay * * *, Pinot Blanc * *, Pinot Gris * * *

1993 Pinot Gris Sunol Vineyard	California	B	86

This excellent Pinot Gris has a bouquet that exhibits ripe fruit flavors. The wine is lush to the point of fatness, medium bodied, and chewy textured and offers a lovely fresh finish. It will provide an excellent accompaniment with fish or poultry dishes over the next year.

ELYSE (NAPA)
Cabernet Sauvignon Morisoli Vineyard * * * *, Coeur de Val * * *, Nero Misto Proprietary Red Wine * * */* * * *, Zinfandel Howell Mountain * * * *, Zinfandel Morisoli Vineyard * * * *

1992 Cabernet Sauvignon Morisoli Vineyard	Napa	C	93
1992 Coeur de Val	Napa	C	87
1992 Nero Misto Proprietary Red Wine	Napa	C	88
N.V. Nero Misto Proprietary Red Wine	Napa	C	89
1992 Zinfandel Howell Mountain	Napa	C	87+
1991 Zinfandel Howell Mountain	Napa	C	91+
1992 Zinfandel Morisoli Vineyard	Napa	C	87
1991 Zinfandel Morisoli Vineyard	Napa	C	88

This excellent winery (actually a warehouse/garage) continues to carve out a well-deserved reputation for its interesting red wine portfolio. The innovative 1992 Nero Misto, a blend of approximately 50% Petite Sirah, 25% Zinfandel, and the rest "wonderful lesser-known black grapes," according to the label, offers an earthy, chewy, full-bodied wine with excellent fruit and ripeness and a supple, fleshy texture. Some damp, earthy smells blow off with swirling, making the wine even more appealing. The more alcoholic 1992 Coeur de Val possesses huge quantities of fruit, lighter body, and a smoother, more supple texture than the Nero Misto. Its delicious, up-front, fleshy fruitiness is both charming and user-friendly. Both the Nero Misto and Coeur de Val should be drunk over the next 2–4 years. This winery has turned out an exceptional 1992 Cabernet Sauvignon. This black/purple-colored wine displays a terrific bouquet of jammy black currant fruit intertwined with scents of licorice and vanillin. Deep and full bodied, with impressive balance to its large framework, this moderately tannic, superbly concentrated Cabernet Sauvignon should drink well for 15 years.

The nonvintage Nero Misto is worth purchasing by the case. It is an interesting blend of 46% Petite Sirah, 28% Zinfandel, and 26% unfashionable red wine varietals—whatever that means. This black/purple-colored wine offers a super nose of pepper, black fruits, licorice, and minerals, tremendous depth of fruit, ripe, medium- to full-bodied, rich flavors, a chewy texture, and a long finish. It reveals this winery's predilection to produce pure, well-delineated wines.

Elyse's two 1992 Zinfandels are slightly less impressive than their 1991 counterparts. The dark ruby/purple-colored 1992 Zinfandel Howell Mountain is a backward, highly structured, tannic wine with a reticent but promising bouquet of minerals and black fruits and medium-bodied, tart, crisp flavors that reveal fine concentration. It will benefit from 2–3 years of cellaring; it should last for a decade. The 1992 Zinfandel Morisoli Vineyard displays copious amounts of pure, black raspberry fruit, medium to full body, excellent richness, and a long, spicy finish. In comparison with the Howell Mountain cuvée, it is more accessible, less structured and tart, and more flattering to drink. It should be consumed over the next 5–7 years.

Elyse has produced 350 cases of a 1991 Zinfandel from Howell Mountain that might have been crafted by Randy Dunn if he were making Zinfandel. It is a blockbuster, broodingly backward, dense wine with a saturated black/purple color and a closed but promising nose of minerals and black raspberries. Deep and full bodied, with tremendous extraction of fruit, as well as high tannins, this should prove to be an uncommonly long-lived Zinfandel. It needs at least 2–3 years of cellaring. Zinfandel has a tendency to drop its tannins more quickly than Cabernet Sauvignon, so it may come around even sooner. This massive, large-scale Zinfandel that has such terrific focus and wonderful richness should be drunk between 1996 and 2005+. Although the 1991 Zinfandel Morisoli Vineyard does not enjoy the saturated black/purple color of the Howell Mountain offering, it is still a deep ruby/purple-colored wine. The nose offers an elegant concoction of red and black fruits, pepper, and spices. Long, rich, and medium to full bodied, with fine balance and harmony, this stylish wine is about as graceful as Zinfandel can be. Drink it over the next decade.

ESTANCIA (FRANCISCAN VINEYARDS) (NAPA)
Cabernet Sauvignon * * *, Chardonnay * * *, Meritage Proprietary Red Wine * * *,
Merlot * * *

1993 Chardonnay	Monterey	A	86
1992 Chardonnay	Monterey	A	85
1991 Meritage Proprietary Red Wine	Alexander Valley	A	85

Estancia, part of the Franciscan group, continues to turn out reasonably priced, well-made wine. The 1993 Chardonnay from Monterey exhibits surprising flavor authority for an $8.50 Chardonnay. There is an attractive buttery, honeyed fruitiness, fine purity, some toasty notes in the bouquet, as well as plenty of guts and heady alcohol in the finish. As the fruit begins to fade the oak will become more noticeable. Drink it over the next year. The 1992 Chardonnay offers creamy, orange- and apple-scented aromas and flavors, medium body, adequate underlying acidity, and a crisp, steely finish. Drink it over the next year.

The 1991 Meritage, a stylish blend of 65% Cabernet Sauvignon, 25% Cabernet Franc, and 10% Merlot, is a medium-bodied, supple, curranty-scented and -flavored wine that should be drunk over the next 5–6 years.

ÉTUDE (NAPA)
Cabernet Sauvignon * * * *, Pinot Noir * * */* * * *

1992 Cabernet Sauvignon	Napa	D	91

The well-known California oenologist, Tony Soter, produces this wine. Not surprisingly, it is a graceful, polished, stylish Cabernet with an impressive color, excellent ripeness, medium body, and a moderately tannic finish. Soter's handprint is clearly evident in this elegant, understated, and well-knit, tightly strung wine that should age well for 10–15 years.

FAR NIENTE (NAPA)
Cabernet Sauvignon * * */* * * *, Chardonnay * * */* * * *

1991 Cabernet Sauvignon Estate	Napa	D	89+
1990 Cabernet Sauvignon Estate	Napa	D	90

A top-notch effort from Far Niente, the 1991 Cabernet Sauvignon requires several more years of cellaring, as it remains closed and forbiddingly backward and tight. From its opaque ruby/purple color, to its impressively pure, rich nose of cassis, herbs, and oak, this full-bodied, powerful, highly extracted, moderately tannic Cabernet is a candidate for 10–

15 more years of cellaring. Don't be surprised to see this wine merit an outstanding score in 6–7 years. The 1990 exhibits wonderful black raspberry, vanillin smokiness in its bouquet. Full-bodied and loaded with flavor, it displays fine length, balance, and purity. Approachable now, it promises to be at its best in 4–5 years and last for 15 or more. Bravo!

GARY FARRELL (SONOMA)

Cabernet Sauvignon * * *, Cabernet Sauvignon Ladi's Vineyard * * * *, Chardonnay * * *,
Merlot Ladi's Vineyard * * * *, Pinot Noir Cuvées * * * *, Sauvignon Blanc * * * *,
Zinfandel * * * *

1991 Cabernet Sauvignon Ladi's Vineyard	Sonoma	C	87+
1990 Cabernet Sauvignon Ladi's Vineyard	Sonoma	C	88
1992 Chardonnay Howard Allen Vineyard	Russian River	C	89
1991 Merlot Ladi's Vineyard	Sonoma	C	89+
1990 Merlot Ladi's Vineyard	Sonoma	C	88
1991 Pinot Noir Howard Allen Vineyard	Sonoma	D	88
1991 Zinfandel	Russian River	C	87

This is one of California's most popular wineries. And why not? Farrell has also turned in a fine effort with the 1992 Howard Allen Vineyard Chardonnay, a full-bodied, concentrated wine with a honeyed, apple, citrusy, floral-scented nose, well-integrated oak, and a rich, full-bodied, long finish. It should drink well for 1–2 years.

For the second year in a row, Gary Farrell has turned out a knockout, superconcentrated, powerful, densely extracted, full-bodied Merlot from the Ladi's Vineyard. The 1991 is more structured and tighter than the 1990, but the saturated, dark ruby/purple color, big, smoky, black cherry, chocolatey nose, and rich, concentrated flavors with moderate tannin should serve this wine well over the next 7–10 years. The 1991 Cabernet Sauvignon Ladi's Vineyard exhibits a saturated dark ruby/purple color, a tight, spicy, ripe, cassis-, herb-, and vanillin-scented nose, medium body, and high acidity that gives the wine a degree of tart leanness. Impressively long, rich, and well balanced, it is capable of extended cellaring. Drink it between 1997 and 2010.

Produced mostly from the highly reputed Collins Vineyard, the 1991 Zinfandel exhibits a dark ruby color, a moderately intense, spicy, black cherry nose, excellent definition, medium body, tart acidity, and a flavorful, spicy finish. It should drink well for 5–8 years.

The superexpensive 1991 Pinot Noir from the excellent Howard Allen Vineyard exhibits a deep ruby color, a big, spicy, minty, berry-scented nose, lovely rich, full-bodied flavors, outstanding flavor extract, and a spicy, long finish. The mint component is unusually pronounced for Pinot Noir, but overall this is a rich, complex Pinot for drinking over the next 7–8 years. The 1990 Merlot Ladi's Vineyard is a deep ruby-colored, richly extracted, black cherry–, chocolate-, herb-, vanillin-scented and -flavored wine with fine ripe fruit. It is also well structured for a Merlot, with slightly higher acidity than usually found in this varietal. Drink this appealing wine over the next 5–7 years. Farrell's 1990 Cabernet Sauvignon Ladi's Vineyard displays a moderately intense, wonderfully pure, rich, cassis-scented nose intertwined with aromas of new oak and herbs. Deep and rich, with a pronounced spiciness, this medium- to full-bodied, generously endowed wine possesses moderate tannins and crisp acidity. Drink it over the next 10–12 years.

FERRARI-CARANO WINERY (SONOMA)

Cabernet Sauvignon * * * *, Chardonnay * * * *, Chardonnay Reserve * * * * *, Fumé
Blanc * * * *, Fumé Blanc Reserve * * * * *, Merlot * * * *, Pinot Noir * * *, Reserve Red
Proprietary * * * * *, Siena * * * *, Syrah * * * *, Zinfandel * * * */* * * * *

1992 Cabernet Sauvignon	Sonoma	C	91
1991 Cabernet Sauvignon	Sonoma	C	90
1993 Chardonnay	Alexander Valley	C	89
1993 Chardonnay Reserve	Napa/Sonoma	D	92
1992 Chardonnay Reserve	Napa/Sonoma	D	92
1991 Chardonnay Reserve	Napa/Sonoma	D	90
1994 Fumé Blanc	Sonoma	A	88
1993 Merlot	Sonoma	C	90
1992 Merlot	Sonoma	C	89
1992 Reserve Red Proprietary Wine	Sonoma	E	96
1991 Reserve Red Proprietary Wine	Sonoma	E	93
1990 Reserve Red Proprietary Wine	Sonoma	E	91
1989 Reserve Red Proprietary Wine	Sonoma	E	89
1993 Siena (Sangiovese/Cabernet Sauvignon/Merlot)	California	D	90
1992 Siena (Sangiovese/Cabernet Sauvignon/Merlot)	California	D	87
1991 Siena (Sangiovese/Cabernet Sauvignon/Merlot)	California	D	82
1994 Syrah	Sonoma	D	92
1993 Syrah	Sonoma	D	87
1993 Zinfandel	Sonoma	C	90

While Ferrari-Carano has long been known for its strikingly perfumed, rich, fruity, honeyed Fumé Blancs and Chardonnays, the red wines produced during the nineties have soared in quality. Current and up-coming releases suggest Ferrari-Carano is about to strike gold with its bevy of red wines, including Zinfandel, Merlot, a Sangiovese/Cabernet Sauvignon/Merlot blend called Siena, Cabernet Sauvignon, and their spectacular proprietary wine called Reserve Red (the name does not do justice to this wine's extraordinary quality). This winery has barely scratched its potential, as their 14 different vineyards encompass 500 acres. Production is currently 100,000 cases, but it will rise as newer vineyards come into production. The winemaking is directed by George Bursick, one of the most talented members of his profession.

Ferrari-Carano's 1994 Fumé Blanc offers further evidence that this winery makes one of the most concentrated, sexy Sauvignons. A blend of 60% tank-fermented juice and 40% barrel-fermented juice, this wine's honeyed, melony character, wonderfully ripe, fresh fruit, and medium body are loaded with flavors.

There are two cuvées of Chardonnay. The 1993 regular cuvée from Alexander Valley exhibits plenty of the up-front, precocious, fleshy tropical fruit this winery achieves with great regularity. The emphasis is on purity, opulence, and an easy-to-understand, rich style. The Reserve Chardonnays (about 3,500 cases per year) are 100% barrel-fermented and aged in 100% new oak. They are usually a blend of fruit from Napa and Sonoma. They are richer, fuller-bodied, more ambitiously styled Chardonnays that need to be drunk in their first 2–3 years of life. Recent vintages have all been immensely impressive. The 1991 Reserve Chardonnay exhibits gobs of fresh fruit, well-integrated, toasty oak, and a creamy, full-bodied, opulent texture. The 1992 Chardonnay Reserve is a knockout, flamboyant Chardonnay with smoky oak, masses of sweet, rich, honeyed fruit, and a glycerin-imbued, viscous texture. It is a terrific, decadently styled Chardonnay for drinking before the end of 1997. The 1993 Chardonnay Reserve is equally impressive. It is full bodied and dense, with layers of flavor, and a long, lusty finish.

The proprietary wine called Siena (usually a blend of Sangiovese, Cabernet Sauvignon, and Merlot) has evolved from a two-thirds Cabernet Sauvignon–based wine in 1991 to a 70% Sangiovese wine in 1994 (the finest Siena to date). The 1991 is a good beginning effort; the 1992 builds on it with attractive cherry fruit, good ripeness, medium body, and a spicy finish. The 1993 Siena jumps significantly in quality, with more of a cedary, cherry nose, excellent flavor richness and definition, and a spicy, easygoing finish with just enough acidity to provide focus. The Siena to gobble up as soon as it hits the marketplace is the 1994. With the highest percentage of Sangiovese, it is the fruitiest, most sumptuous Siena to date. It is meant to be drunk in its first 5–7 years of life. It is a vibrant, lively, medium-bodied red wine with excellent richness and plenty of personality.

Recent Ferrari-Carano Merlots have not exhibited the herbal, vegetal character that plagued this winery's first Merlot releases. The 1992 Merlot (80% Merlot, 7% Petit Verdot, 5% Cabernet Sauvignon, and 4% Cabernet Franc) exhibits loads of chocolaty, black cherries, a sweet, expansive, vibrant mid-palate, full body, excellent ripeness, and a velvety texture. It should drink well for 5–6 years. The 1993 Merlot is a larger-scale wine made from 89% Merlot and the rest Malbec, Cabernet Sauvignon, and Cabernet Franc. The wine offers a purple-ruby color, great fruit and intensity, plenty of alcohol and glycerin, full body, and a decadent, lavishly rich, seductive style that is hard to ignore. It should drink well for at least a decade.

The herbaceousness that also plagued the Cabernet Sauvignons is no longer present, as Ferrari-Carano has begun to manage its vineyards in a manner that minimizes the vegetal aromas and flavors. For example, the outstanding 1991 Cabernet Sauvignon reveals an opaque purple color, a spicy, rich, cassis-scented nose, full body, tremendous density, that chewy unctuosity that winemaker George Bursick obtains in so many wines, and a soft, moderately tannic finish. It should drink well for 10–15 years. Possessing even greater fruit, the 1992 Cabernet Sauvignon is extremely full bodied, with a big, smoky, chocolaty, black currant–scented nose, plenty of muscle and intensity, and a long, chewy finish. It should drink well for 15 + years.

Perhaps the best-kept secret from Ferrari-Carano is their Reserve Reds, which are expensive, but bottled in very tall, heavy Italian glass bottles. The debut release was the 1989, which was a very good wine. That has been followed by superb efforts in 1990, 1991, and 1992. The blends have been relatively consistent, utilizing between 65% and 70% Cabernet Sauvignon, 4%–10% Petit Verdot, a small percentage of Merlot, ranging from nearly 9% in 1990 to 23% in 1993, and an intriguing amount of Malbec (11.5% in 1990, 4% in 1991, and 16% in 1992). The only wine to exhibit any herbaceousness is the 1990 Reserve Red. It offers a black currant–, olive-, and Provençal herb–scented nose, layers of rich, sweet, jammy fruit, full body, and gobs of glycerin and alcohol that nearly conceal the substantial tannin in the finish. It is a big, rich, lusty wine that because of its low acidity and sweet tannin can be drunk now or cellared for 15+ years. The 1991 Reserve Red is even deeper, with a more classical profile of black fruits, toasty oak, minerals, and spices. Extremely full bodied and concentrated, with exceptional balance and extraction, it should drink well from its release and last for 20+ years. The greatest Reserve Red to date appears to be the 1992, which, interestingly, contains the smallest percentage of Cabernet Sauvignon (54%), and the highest percentage of Malbec (16%) and Cabernet Franc (11%). It displays a fabulous fragrance of black currants, violets, minerals, licorice, and smoky oak. Splendidly full bodied, with huge flavor extraction, but no sense of heaviness or overbearing tannin, this large-scale, massively endowed, profound example of proprietary red should peak by the middle of the first decade of the next century and drink well for 20–25 years thereafter. It is a knockout!

This winery has always turned out small quantities of stunningly full-bodied, rich, heady Zinfandel, and the 1993, which tips the scales at 14.4% alcohol, is another big, peppery, richly fruity, unctuously textured wine. Time spent in American oak gives it a flamboyant, smoky spiciness.

Lastly, there will be tiny quantities of Syrah released from Ferrari-Carano's 20-acre Syrah vineyard. The 1993 Syrah (150 cases) is certainly a good first effort, although it lacks the depth and intensity I noticed in the barrel sample of the stunningly rich, full-bodied 1994 Syrah.

Ferrari-Carano is one of the bright shining success stories of California, and it has a brilliant future ahead of it.

FETZER VINEYARD (MENDOCINO)
Cabernet Sauvignon Barrel Select * * *, Chardonnay Barrel Select * * *, Chardonnay Bonterra * */* * *, Chardonnay Sundial * * *, Chenin Blanc * *, Fumé Blanc * * *, Gewürztraminer *, Petite Sirah Reserve * * *, Riesling *, Sauvignon Blanc Barrel Select * * *, Zinfandel Barrel Select * * *, Zinfandel Reserve * * *

1992 Chardonnay Bonterra	Mendocino	A	83
1994 Chardonnay Sundial	California	A	85
1994 Fumé Blanc	Mendocino	A	84
1993 Sauvignon Blanc Barrel Select	Mendocino	A	86
1990 Zinfandel Barrel Select	Mendocino	B	82

The oaky 1992 Chardonnay Bonterra exhibits good fruit and body. Enjoy it over the next 8–12 months for its simplistic, straightforward style. The three 1993 cuvées all emphasize freshness, lively fruit, and medium body. All require consumption over the next year. In fact, the earlier you buy them and drink them, the better they will taste. The 1994 Sundial Chardonnay offers generous quantities of honeyed, apple fruit, excellent freshness, medium body, enough acidity for clarity and zest, and a fleshy, citrusy mouthful of fruit. It appears slightly bolder and more plump, but every bit as fresh as previous bottlings. Drink it over the next year. The 1993 Sauvignon Blanc Barrel Select reveals a subtle touch of oak, as well as attractive, melony, fig, and herb aromas and flavors in a medium-bodied format. The herbaceous, Loire Valley–style 1994 Fumé Blanc is softer than the dry Sauvignon.

Surprisingly one-dimensional and oaky, the 1990 Zinfandel lacks intensity and complexity. Fetzer generally does a better job with its Barrel Select offerings. With this wine, what one gets is a slightly above-average, pleasant wine that should be consumed over the next 2–3 years.

FIELD STONE (SONOMA)
Cabernet Sauvignon Alexander Valley * * *, Cabernet Sauvignon Reserve * * *, Petite Sirah * * * *, Sauvignon Blanc * * *, Viognier Staten Family Reserve * * *

1992 Viognier Staten Family Reserve	Alexander Valley	C	88

It is hard to get an idea of just how great California Viognier may become as most of the vineyards are extremely young. Many Viogniers are extremely light and herbal, the exceptions generally being those made by Calera, Qupé, and Edmunds St. John. In 1992, Field Stone's Staten family has fashioned a wonderfully rich, textbook Viognier offering a big, honeysuckle/peach/apricot-scented nose, thick, unctuously textured flavors, and a spicy finish with flavors of new oak. Drink this big, bold Viognier within 3–4 years of the vintage.

FIRESTONE VINEYARDS (SANTA BARBARA)

Cabernet Sauvignon* * *, Cabernet Sauvignon Reserve* * *, Chardonnay* *, Gewürztraminer* * *, Merlot* *, Johannisberg Riesling* * *, Vintage Reserve Proprietary Red Wine* * *

1990 Cabernet Sauvignon	Santa Ynez	B	85
1990 Cabernet Sauvignon Reserve	Santa Ynez	C	87
1993 Gewürztraminer	Santa Barbara	A	85
1991 Vintage Reserve Proprietary Red Wine	Santa Ynez	C	89

For 20 years, this beautifully designed winery, perched on a mesa in the Santa Ynez Valley north of Los Olivos, has been producing wines with mixed results. Recent vintages suggest that the quality of the Chardonnays and Cabernets is moving upward. The most striking characteristics of the subtly herbaceous 1990 Cabernet Sauvignon are its attractive, spicy, chocolaty, berry-scented nose, fleshy, supple, medium- to full-bodied flavors, and its round, generous, satiny finish. Drink this delicious Cabernet over the next 6–7 years. Restaurants would be smart to consider it as a house wine. More serious, and unquestionably the best Cabernet Sauvignon Firestone has yet produced, is the 1990 Cabernet Sauvignon Reserve. It offers all the suppleness of the 1990 regular bottling, as well as more generous quantities of cassis, vanillin, and spice in the bouquet. The wine has excellent depth, a chewy, layered texture, and a long, rich, well-balanced finish. The moderate tannins are nearly submerged beneath the considerable extraction of fruit. This Cabernet can be drunk now or cellared for a decade or more. The 1991 Vintage Reserve Proprietary Red Wine may turn out to be Firestone's finest red wine to date. Still in barrel, there will be 675 cases of this 60% Cabernet Franc/28% Merlot/12% Cabernet Sauvignon blend. It reveals a huge, seductive nose of black cherries, herbs, and spices. Rich, deep, and full bodied, with superb color saturation and purity, this is unquestionably the best red wine I have tasted from Firestone. Let's hope it does not get overly processed at bottling, because it is an enticing wine with considerable style and personality. It will drink well for 10–12 years.

The 1993 Gewürztraminer is a dry, spicy wine with moderate varietal character and a full-bodied, powerful, alcoholic finish. Try it with Asian dishes. It is a good effort.

FISHER VINEYARDS (SONOMA)

Cabernet Sauvignon Coach Insignia* * * * *, Cabernet Sauvignon Lamb Vineyard* * * * *, Cabernet Sauvignon Wedding Vineyard* * * * *, Chardonnay Coach Insignia* * *, Chardonnay Whitney's Vineyard * * * * *, Merlot RCF* * * * *

1993 Cabernet Sauvignon Coach Insignia	Napa	C	92
1992 Cabernet Sauvignon Coach Insignia	Sonoma/Napa	C	92
1991 Cabernet Sauvignon Coach Insignia	Napa	C	92
1990 Cabernet Sauvignon Coach Insignia	Sonoma/Napa	C	89
1993 Cabernet Sauvignon Lamb Vineyard	Napa	D	96
1993 Cabernet Sauvignon Wedding Vineyard	Sonoma	D	92
1992 Cabernet Sauvignon Wedding Vineyard	Sonoma	D	95
1991 Cabernet Sauvignon Wedding Vineyard	Sonoma	D	93+
1994 Chardonnay Coach Insignia	Sonoma	C	89

1993 Chardonnay Coach Insignia	Sonoma	C	89
1992 Chardonnay Coach Insignia	California	C	91
1994 Chardonnay Whitney's Vineyard	Sonoma	D	93
1993 Chardonnay Whitney's Vineyard	Sonoma	D	92
1992 Chardonnay Whitney's Vineyard	Sonoma	C	93
1993 Merlot RCF Vineyard	Napa	D	89
1992 Merlot RCF Vineyard	Sonoma/Napa	C	90
1991 Merlot RCF Vineyard	Napa	C	88

Fisher Vineyards, perched high in the mountains not far from the Sonoma/Napa county line, is making a bevy of profound wines that merit considerable interest. The rise in quality, complexity, and potential of Fisher's wines is one of the bright shining stories in recent California wine history. Proprietor Fred Fisher deserves considerable praise for moving his wines away from the tart, lean, highly acidified and processed, oenologically correct style to wines bursting with personality, flavor, and high quality.

The Chardonnays emanating from this estate are some of the finest now being made in California. Readers should also look for the 1994 and 1993 Chardonnays from Whitney's Vineyard. Since there are only 400–500 cases of Chardonnay produced from this 20-year-old vineyard on the hillside next to the winery, it is a good idea to get your order in quickly. The 1994 promises to be a stunning Chardonnary with plenty of rich fruit, full body, great purity and depth on the palate, and a long, lusty finish. It may be even better than the spectacular 1993 Chardonnay Whitney's Vineyard, which displays a telltale, honeyed tangerine/orange peel nose, well-integrated toasty oak (50% new oak is utilized), and full-bodied, layered, concentrated finish. These Chardonnays are best drunk in their first 2–4 years of life. Both the 1994 and 1993 Chardonnay Coach Insignia exhibit noses of honeyed tangerines and other tropical fruits, layered, rich, gutsy mouth-feels, adequate acidity, and lusty, rich finishes. Both wines should drink well for 1–2 years. For those readers unable to wait, the 1992 Chardonnay Coach Insignia is even better, with its beautiful, intense bouquet of honeysuckle, tropical fruit, butter, and spice. The wine displays superb richness, a layered, opulent texture, and admirable purity and balance. It is a gorgeously rich, mouth-filling Chardonnay for drinking over the next several years. The 1992 Chardonnay Whitney's Vineyard (only 300 six-bottle cases of this surefire superstar were produced) is another spectacularly concentrated Chardonnay. With a honeyed, tangerine/orange and buttery fruit-iness, great ripeness, medium to full body, gorgeously integrated acidity, as well as a judicious dose of smoky new oak, this flavorful, complex, multidimensional Chardonnay should drink well for another 2–3 years.

The 1993 Merlot RCF Vineyard exhibits a dark purple color, a forceful, intense nose of chocolaty black cherries, sweet, full-bodied flavors, excellent concentration, and a firm, moderately tannic finish. It will benefit from 1–2 years of cellaring and should drink well for 12+ years. The 1992 Merlot RCF Vineyard (a vineyard situated near the famed Eisele Vineyard in northern Napa Valley) is a superintense, chocolaty, black cherry–scented Merlot that is bursting with flavor, glycerin, and alcohol. This rich, chewy, sumptuous Merlot is even better from bottle than a cask sample I sampled earlier. Expansive and round, it offers an up-front, flattering style. Drink it over the next 10–12 years. The impressively dark ruby/purple color of the 1991 Merlot RCF is followed by a spicy, ripe nose of black cherries, herbs, and chocolate. This rich, medium- to full-bodied, long wine is loaded with fruit and fine, crisp acidity. A beautifully made, rich Merlot, it should drink well for 5–8 years.

The 1993 Cabernet Sauvignon Coach Insignia is another terrific effort from Fred Fisher. It possesses the hallmarks of recent Fisher releases—spectacular ripeness and richness, as well as massive, chocolaty, ripe black currant fruit presented in a full-bodied, expansive, wonderfully pure and concentrated style. The wine's high extraction, the judicious use of toasty oak, and gorgeous ripeness and length suggest it should be drinkable when released and last for 15+ years. The 1992 Coach Insignia is a sumptuously rich, superconcentrated, gorgeously proportioned Cabernet Sauvignon that tasted less tannic than the Merlot. I suspect if analyzed the tannin level in the Cabernet would be higher, but the wine is so concentrated it comes across as precocious and flattering. This densely colored, chewy, exquisitely pure example of California Cabernet should drink surprisingly well at 5–6 years of age and last for 15–20 years. Very impressive! The opaque ruby/purple-colored 1991 Cabernet Sauvignon Coach Insignia offers a powerful, pungent nose of cassis, black fruits, chocolate, vanillin, and licorice. The wine oozes with superrichness, full body, glycerin, and nicely hidden alcohol and moderate tannin in the finish. While the quantity produced (1,600 cases) will not make it the most widely available Cabernet Sauvignon, shrewd readers should be able to find a few bottles before it is scarfed up by Cabernet lovers. Approachable now, it has the potential to last for 15+ years.

If this isn't enough good news, consider the Cabernet Sauvignons from the Wedding Vineyard. The 1993 Cabernet Sauvignon Wedding Vineyard offers an opaque purple color, a sweet nose of jammy black currant fruit intertwined with scents of herbs, licorice, minerals, and smoky oak. Sweet, expansive, and ripe, with considerable power, flavor authority, and extraction, this sensational Cabernet Sauvignon should drink well young and keep for 20 years. The 1992 Cabernet Sauvignon Wedding Vineyard is an awesome example of California Cabernet. It is opulent as well as tannic, with huge, chocolaty, roasted herb, cassis aromas, magnificent flavor concentration, a big, graceful richness on the palate, and stunningly focused components that coat the palate with viscous flavors and superlative purity of character. This is a staggering Cabernet for drinking over the next 20+ years. More backward, as well as strikingly rich and unequivocally superb is Fisher's 1991 Cabernet Sauvignon Wedding Vineyard. There are only 100 six-bottle cases of this Sonoma Cabernet. The wine exhibits a black/purple color, and a tight but promising nose of cassis, underbrush, vanillin, and chocolate-covered black raspberries. Full bodied, with superb definition, structure, and tannin, this wine possesses immense concentration and a wonderfully natural mouth-feel. It should open up with 2–4 more years of cellaring and keep for at least 20 years. The 1990 Cabernet Sauvignon Coach Insignia exhibits a moderately intense bouquet of vanillin, smoke, and cassis, excellent richness, a medium- to full-bodied, supple style, and a long, pure yet authoritative finish. This elegant yet boldly flavored wine should drink well for 12–14 years.

It will not be released until 1996, but readers should be aware of Fisher's 1993 Cabernet Sauvignon from the Lamb Vineyard. It promises to be Fred Fisher's finest Cabernet to date. The wine's black color is followed by an extraordinary amount of sweetness and expansiveness that could only come from extremely ripe fruit and tiny yields. The finish lasts for nearly a minute. This spectacular Cabernet Sauvignon provides additional evidence of just what peaks of quality Fred Fisher's winemaking team has achieved over the last several years.

FLORA SPRINGS (NAPA)

Cabernet Sauvignon Reserve * * * * (since 1991), Chardonnay * * * *, Sangiovese * * *, Soliloquy Proprietary White Wine * * * *, Trilogy Proprietary Red Wine * * * * (since 1991)

1993 Cabernet Sauvignon Reserve	Napa	E	91
1992 Cabernet Sauvignon Reserve	Napa	E	90

1991 Cabernet Sauvignon Reserve	Napa	E	91+
1994 Chardonnay	Carneros	C	91
1993 Chardonnay	Carneros	C	88
1994 Sangiovese	Napa	C	88
1993 Sangiovese	Napa	C	85
1994 Soliloquy Proprietary White Wine	Napa	C	90
1993 Trilogy Proprietary Red Wine	Napa	E	92
1992 Trilogy Proprietary Red Wine	Napa	E	92+
1991 Trilogy Proprietary Red Wine	Napa	E	89

While Flora Springs owns over 500 acres of vineyards, only 20–25% of the vineyard's production is used for the 30,000 cases of estate-bottled wines. There has been a highly laudable move toward more natural winemaking techniques, with less processing and acidification since the beginning of the nineties. The results are wines that rank with the finest being produced in northern California. This winery has always fashioned good Chardonnay, but the new small lots of unfined and unfiltered Chardonnay from Carneros (200–400 cases) are outstanding wines. The 1993 exhibits loads of ripe fruit, full body, good spice, and a creamy finish. It should be drunk before the end of 1996. Even better is the gorgeous 1994, which offers a honeyed pear/peach– and oak-scented nose, with rich, full-bodied flavors, enough acidity for focus, and a heady, concentrated finish.

This winery has long been known for its 1,000–1,500 cases of barrel-fermented Sauvignon Blanc. A recent vertical tasting held at the winery confirmed that it is a wine that requires drinking in its first 1–2 years of life, but as good as it is, who cares? It is 100% Sauvignon Blanc that comes from a 30-year-old vineyard that is thought to be one of California's oldest Sauvignon vineyards. The 1993 is fresh and lively, with plenty of honeyed, herbal, mineral, and figlike fruit. There is good ripeness, medium body, and a crisp, long finish. It needs to be drunk up, as these wines have a life span of 2–4 years. The 1994 exhibits greater purity and liveliness, a vivacious personality with plenty of ripeness, medium to full body, and a crisp, long finish.

No one was more critical of Flora Springs' proprietary red wine, Trilogy, than I during the eighties. Things have unquestionably changed, as this wine, usually a blend of approximately 40% Cabernet Sauvignon, 40% Merlot, and the rest Cabernet Franc, has become a serious entry into the high-quality proprietary red wine sweepstakes. It is aged in 50% new French oak, and since 1991 does not appear to have been processed. Consequently, it is far more lively, with a more natural texture, greater aromatics, and a creamier, more pleasing flavor profile. The 1991 offers a cassis-, smoky-, black currant–scented nose, elegant, soft, medium-bodied flavors, moderate tannin, and a complex, cedary, black fruit profile. Drink it over the next 10–12 years. The 1992 Trilogy reveals spicy oak in the nose, sweet red and black fruits, and a stylish yet authoritatively flavored palate with plenty of black cherry and black currant fruit nicely infused with toasty oak and spice. The acidity and tannin are both well integrated. This suave yet flavorful red wine should drink well for the next 15+ years. The finest Trilogys to date are the 1993 and 1994. The 1993 reveals toasty oak in the nose, as well as aromas of sweet black fruits intertwined with complex scents of lead pencil and spice. Deep and rich, with medium to full body, great ripeness of fruit, and purity, this seductive, multidimensional proprietary red wine is supple enough to be drunk when released, but capable of lasting 20+ years. Barrel samples of the 1994 reveal another stunning wine that may prove to be even better than the 1993.

Since 1989, this winery has been producing 700 cases of Cabernet Sauvignon Reserve.

The slightly closed and tannic 1990 is more reminiscent of the red wines made at Flora Springs during the decade of the eighties than what has been achieved in the nineties. The 1991 exhibits a real jump in quality. It reveals outstanding sweet cassis fruit, full body, layers of concentrated flavor, well-integrated acidity, ripe tannin, and an expansive, long, young, but highly promising future. The wine requires 3–4 years of cellaring and should age well for 15–20 years. The 1992 Cabernet Sauvignon Reserve boasts a dark, opaque ruby/purple color, a big, smoky, black cherry, cassis, and chocolaty nose, full body, plenty of tannin, and a ripe, rich finish. It also needs several years of cellaring and should age for 15–20 years. The 1993 Cabernet Sauvignon Reserve displays a dense, plum/purple color, and huge, overripe aromas of sweet black currants and smoky oak. The wine is extremely rich and concentrated, wtih low acidity, a mouth-filling, full-bodied personality, and impressive length. All of these wines are bottled unfined and unfiltered.

Flora Springs' Sangiovese have been good examples of this varietal. They are wines made to be drunk in their first 4–5 years of life. The 1993 (2,800 cases) exhibits ripe curranty fruit, medium body, crisp acidity, light tannin, and a fresh, lively finish. Drink it over the next 3–4 years. The finest Sangiovese I have yet tasted from Flora Springs is the 1994. It offers greater sweetness of fruit, more expansiveness, well-measured acidity, and a rich, curranty, cherry, and leathery finish.

FOREST HILL (SONOMA)
Chardonnay* * * *

1991 Chardonnay Private Reserve	Sonoma	C	90

Forest Hill has burst on the California wine scene with an excellent 1991 Chardonnay. The tightly knit 1991 is rich, beautifully pure, and well balanced, with aromas and flavors of vanillin, ripe apples, and honey. It is capable of aging for 3–4 years.

FORMAN WINERY (NAPA)
Cabernet Sauvignon* * * *, Chardonnay* * * *

1991 Cabernet Sauvignon	Napa	D	94
1990 Cabernet Sauvignon	Napa	D	92
1992 Chardonnay	Napa	C	88

Rick Forman continues to be one of the best practitioners of nonmalolactic-fermented Chardonnay. The 1992 Chardonnay possesses excellent purity, ripe fruit, medium body, and a crisp, tart, tasty finish. It is a delicious, lively Chardonnay for drinking over the next 1–2 years. For readers' information, a vertical tasting of the Forman Chardonnays from the mid-eighties through recent releases poignantly revealed that (1) they survive as they get older, (2) they become greener and more Sauvignon-like with each additional year of cellaring, and (3) because of the green, tart acidity that develops, they are far less enjoyable after 2–3 years of cellaring than when they are young. For these reasons, I recommend drinking them within their first several years of life.

Forman's 1991 Cabernet Sauvignon (packaged in a heavy, broad-shouldered bottle) may be the most impressive Cabernet he has made. The wine's softer, fleshier palate suggests a lighter hand in acidification. The saturated black/ruby/purple color is followed by copious aromas of wonderfully rich and ripe cassis intertwined with vague mineral and vanilla scents. Full bodied, with terrific richness, layers of fruit, and a multidimensional personality, this gorgeously made, opulent Cabernet Sauvignon can be drunk now or cellared for 15–20 years. Forman's 1990 Cabernet Sauvignon is a deep purple-colored wine displaying a superexpressive nose of black currants, licorice, and vanillin. With a beautifully etched, medium- to full-bodied feel, exquisite concentration, decent acidity, and firm but soft, sweet tannins, this is a graceful, authoritatively flavored Cabernet for drinking over the next 12–15 years.

FOXEN VINEYARD (SANTA BARBARA)

Cabernet Sauvignon* * * *, Chardonnay* * * * *, Chenin Blanc* * * *, Pinot Noir* * *, Pinot Noir Sanford & Benedict Vineyard* * * *

1990 Cabernet Sauvignon	Santa Barbara	C	89+
1993 Chardonnay	Santa Maria	C	91
1992 Chardonnay	Santa Maria	C	90
1991 Chardonnay	Santa Maria	C	91
1992 Chardonnay Tinaquaic Vineyard	Santa Maria	D	91
1993 Chenin Blanc Barrel-Fermented	Santa Barbara	B	90
1992 Chenin Blanc Barrel-Fermented	Santa Barbara	B	87
1991 Chenin Blanc Barrel-Fermented	Santa Barbara	B	86
1992 Pinot Noir	Santa Maria	C	86
1991 Pinot Noir	Santa Maria	C	86
1992 Pinot Noir Sanford & Benedict Vineyard	Santa Barbara	D	88+
1991 Pinot Noir Sanford & Benedict Vineyard	Santa Barbara	D	90

Foxen is another idiosyncratic Santa Barbara winery marching to a different beat. This small winery offers distinctive, original, and frequently outstanding wines that possess a character completely different from anything you are likely to taste from north coast viticultural regions such as Napa, Mendocino, and Sonoma.

Foxen is fashioning some noteworthy barrel-fermented dry Chenin Blanc. If you like light, floral, crisp, delicate Chenin Blanc, Foxen's Chenin will require some adjustment. It is likely to be controversial because it is so rich and dry. It offers lovely honeyed, floral, tropical fruit, wonderful precision, and a surprisingly well-integrated, subtle oakiness. Foxen's 1993 Chenin Blanc is a terrific effort for this varietal. Superrich yet vibrant and lively, Chenin's floral, orange, and honeyed components are beautifully presented. I was knocked out by this wine. Consume it over the next 1–2 years. The 1992 displays slightly deeper fruit flavors, but both the 1991 and 1992 are large-scale Chenin Blancs that should drink nicely for 2–3 years.

Foxen has always made powerful, unctuously textured, multidimensional Chardonnay, and the 1993 is another noteworthy effort. It offers a huge, tropical fruit– and toasty new oak–scented nose. Fine underlying acidity buttresses this thick, rich, flavorful wine that avoids being heavy and overbearing, yet is authoritatively flavored. Because of its superb balance, this wine should drink well for 2–4 years. The lavishly rich, decadent 1992 Chardonnay offers bountiful aromas of smoky oak, buttery tropical fruit, and spice. Rich, with layers of expansive, chewy varietal fruit, and fine acidity, this lusty, intense, full-bodied Chardonnay should drink well for 1–2 years. Impressive! The super 1991 Chardonnay is light to medium straw-colored, with a flamboyant, even audacious nose of butter, honey, oak, and ripe oranges and apples. This superrich, densely packed, full-bodied Chardonnay possesses excellent underlying acidity to support its considerable weight and intensity. Drink it over the next 2–3 years. The bold, ostentatious, complex, superconcentrated, multidimensional 1992 Chardonnay Tinaquaic Vineyard is a knockout example of this varietal. Exhibiting well-integrated, crisp acidity and toasty new oak, this rich, forceful, mouth-filling Chardonnay should drink well for 1–2 years.

The 1992 Pinot Noir from Santa Maria offers up an aromatic, peppery nose of herb, black cherry, and spicy new oak scents, underlying tannin, and a compact finish. It is a good example of Pinot Noir that should drink well for 4–5 years. The 1992 Pinot Noir Sanford & Benedict Vineyard is a candidate for 5–7 years of cellaring. It boasts a saturated color, an exuberant, peppery, herb-, and berry-scented nose with well-integrated oak, moderate tannin, surprisingly tart acidity, and loads of rich, concentrated flavor. It is an impressive, large-scale Pinot, but with less acidity it would have merited a score in the 90s.

Readers fortunate enough to have access to the outstanding 1991 Pinot Noir Sanford & Benedict Vineyard should not hesitate to buy it. One of the deepest-colored Pinot Noirs I saw, this undeveloped Pinot offers a beautiful nose of black fruits (plums and raspberries), vanillin, and earth. Rich, with plenty of glycerin and sweet, ripe fruit, this deep, profound, full-bodied, heady Pinot Noir exhibits intense black raspberry and black cherry flavors that are well knit and offer considerable length in the explosive finish. The overall impression is one of a young, but voluptuous, luxuriously rich Pinot Noir for drinking over the next 6–7 years. The 1991 Pinot Noir from the Santa Maria Valley displays a deep ruby color, a spicy, herbal, black cherry–scented nose, tasty, round, generous flavors, but not the complexity, definition, or mind-boggling depth of the 1991 Sanford & Benedict Vineyard.

Foxen makes Santa Barbara's finest Cabernet Sauvignon. Impressively colored and tightly knit, it suffers from none of the vegetal character that plagued Santa Barbara Cabernets and Merlots until the late eighties. The 1990 Cabernet Sauvignon may merit an outstanding score in 2–3 years. It possesses a black/purple, saturated color, a tight yet blossoming bouquet of cassis, herbs, and spices, big, rich, full-bodied flavors buttressed by considerable acidity, moderate tannin, and a long, crisp, powerful finish. Drink it between now and 2003.

FRANCISCAN VINEYARDS (NAPA)

Cabernet Sauvignon Oakville Estate * * *, Chardonnay * * * *, Meritage Oakville Estate * * * *, Merlot * * *, Zinfandel * * * *

1990 Cabernet Sauvignon Oakville Estate	Napa	C	88
1992 Chardonnay Cuvée Sauvage Unfiltered	Napa	C	87?
1991 Merlot Oakville Estate	Napa	B	88
1991 Zinfandel Oakville Estate	Napa	B	87

The opaque dark garnet/purple color of the 1991 Merlot Oakville Estate suggests considerable intensity and richness. A big, black cherry– and chocolate-scented, lavishly oaky nose soars from the glass in an unrestrained manner. Thick and intense, with an unctuous texture and exotic richness, this lusty Merlot provides an impressive, flamboyant mouthful. Drink it over the next 6–7 years. The 1990 Cabernet Sauvignon Oakville Estate is more refined and less boldly scented. Deeply colored, ripe, and opulent, with stylish, harmonious flavors, well-integrated tannin, and a soft finish, it should drink well for 7–10 years.

The 1991 Zinfandel Oakville Estate resembles a top-notch Chianti Classico or a Brunello di Montalcino. The color leans toward garnet rather than purple. The nose offers big, earthy, tar, peppery, plum, and raspberry scents. The wine is lush, medium to full bodied, rich, and expansive with soft tannins and a spicy finish. Delicious now, it should continue to offer tasty drinking for another 5–6 years.

With its lavishly smoky, bold, toasty, oaky nose, the 1992 Chardonnay Cuvée Sauvage Unfiltered is clearly a controversial style of Chardonnay. Thick, lusty, and chewy, with copious fruit as well as plenty of pungent oak, it reminds me of the aggressively woody Meursaults made by Michelot-Buisson. Although this wine will never be accused of having finesse, it is sure to have its admirers. Drink it over the next year.

FRANUS (NAPA)

Cabernet Sauvignon George Hendry Vineyard* * * *, Zinfandel Brandlin Ranch* * * * *,
Zinfandel George Hendry Vineyard* * * * *

1993 Cabernet Sauvignon George Hendry Vineyard	Napa	C	91
1992 Cabernet Sauvignon George Hendry Vineyard	Napa	C	89
1993 Zinfandel Brandlin Ranch	Napa	C	90
1992 Zinfandel Brandlin Ranch	Napa	C	92
1993 Zinfandel George Hendry Vineyard	Napa	C	90
1992 Zinfandel George Hendry Vineyard	Napa	C	89

Peter Franus, a young, energetic producer who is smitten by the grape, has sought out some of the finest hillside vineyard sources for Zinfandel and Cabernet Sauvignon. He has built his production of Zinfandel to 1,800 cases and Cabernet Sauvignon to 120 cases. His wines, which are bottled unfined and unfiltered, are aged in one-third new French oak for 18–20 months. Zinfandel lovers are advised to compare the Franus Zinfandels (they are smartly packaged in a designer bottle) with those of Dr. Rosenblum, since they purchase fruit from two of the same sources.

The Franus 1993 Zinfandel George Hendry Vineyard (850 cases) offers an attractive, complex nose of smoky vanillin and red and black raspberry scents. The wine is dense, powerful, and rich, with great fruit and purity, and a nicely structured, highly extracted, full-bodied finish. This is an impressive, large-scale yet graceful Zinfandel for drinking over the next 7–8 years. The 1993 Zinfandel Brandlin Ranch (900 cases from a head-pruned, 70-year-old vineyard on Mt. Veeder) exhibits an opaque ruby/purple color, wonderfully sweet, oaky- and vanillin-scented, rich, concentrated, cherry and raspberry fruit in the nose, an expansive, full-bodied, deeply etched, flavorful personality, good spice and purity, and a heady, long finish.

The 1992 Zinfandel George Hendry Vineyard exhibits a big, peppery-, curranty-, prune-, and raspberry-scented nose with a sweet oak component, a creamy texture, full-bodied, moderately tannic flavors, and a long, spicy finish. It is less sweet and more structured than the juicy 1993. The terrific 1992 Zinfandel Brandlin Ranch boasts gobs of sweet black cherry fruit and pepper, a big, spicy, full-bodied, tannic personality, and a long, heady, blockbuster finish. Both of these Zinfandels possess the potential to last for 10 years, although they are best consumed in their first 7–8 years.

Peter Franus also produced a 1992 and 1993 Cabernet Sauvignon from the George Hendry Vineyard, but in 1994 he lost access to this fruit. The 1993 Cabernet Sauvignon George Hendry Vineyard is a wine of considerable richness, with classic cassis aromatic and flavor profiles, full body, moderate tannin, wonderful purity, and that layered feel in the mouth. It should drink well for 15–20 years. The 1992 Cabernet Sauvignon George Hendry Vineyard offers sweet, jammy, black currant aromas with attractive oak, cedar, and herbs in the background. It is full bodied, with excellent purity, high extraction, well-integrated tannin and acidity, as well as a natural mouth-feel. I have not had much experience with Peter Franus's wines, but he appears to have the Midas touch when it comes to Zinfandel and Cabernet Sauvignon.

FRITZ CELLARS (SONOMA)

Zinfandel* * * (since 1988)

1992 Zinfandel 80-Year-Old Vines	Sonoma	B	76
1991 Zinfandel 80-Year-Old Vines	Sonoma	B	85

Medium ruby colored, with a reticent but spicy bouquet, the 1992 Zinfandel 80-Year-Old Vines comes across as narrowly constructed given its high acidity and tart, lean personality. My guess is that it was either excessively acidified or the grapes were harvested too early, as none of the sweet, voluptuous red and black fruit so common in this vintage was apparent when I tasted it. The 1991 Fritz Zinfandel exhibits a pungent roasted oak bouquet and briary, lean, austere flavors that seem unusually streamlined and compact. Although good, my instincts suggest it is a bit too sculptured and acidified. There should be more flesh, suppleness, and richness given what appear to be fine raw materials.

GABRIELLI (MENDOCINI)
Ascenza White Table Wine * * *

1991	Ascenza White Table Wine	Mendocino	A	87
1990	Ascenza White Table Wine	Mendocino	A	86

These two efforts are full-bodied, rich, fruity, impressively intense wines that are mouth-filling and full of character.

GAINEY VINEYARDS (SANTA BARBARA)
Cabernet Franc Limited Selection * * * *, Chardonnay * * *, Merlot * *, Merlot Limited Selection * * */* * * *, Pinot Noir * *, Pinot Noir Sanford & Benedict Vineyard * * * *, Sauvignon Blanc * * *, Sauvignon Blanc Limited Selection * * * * *

1992	Cabernet Franc Limited Selection	Santa Ynez	C	88+
1990	Cabernet Franc Limited Selection	Santa Ynez	C	87
1992	Chardonnay Limited Selection Unfiltered	Santa Ynez	D	92
1992	Chardonnay	Santa Barbara	B	88
1991	Chardonnay	Santa Barbara	B	82
1990	Merlot	Santa Ynez	B	83
1990	Merlot Limited Selection	Santa Ynez	C	86
1991	Pinot Noir	Santa Maria	B	86
1990	Pinot Noir	Santa Barbara	B	82
1992	Pinot Noir Bien Nacido Vineyard	Santa Maria	C	76
1992	Pinot Noir Sanford & Benedict Vineyard	Santa Ynez	D	85
1991	Pinot Noir Sanford & Benedict Vineyard	Santa Barbara	C	89
1991	Sauvignon Blanc	Santa Ynez	A	87
1993	Sauvignon Blanc Limited Selection	Santa Ynez	C	90
1992	Sauvignon Blanc Limited Selection	Santa Ynez	C	91
1991	Sauvignon Blanc Limited Selection	Santa Ynez	C	90

Located in the Santa Ynez Valley, this attractive winery has had a mixed track record since its debut vintage in the mid-eighties. However, under the increasingly inspired winemaking helm of Rick Longoria, Gainey has begun to exploit its considerable potential. Vintages in the nineties should make Gainey Vineyard a more noteworthy competitor at the top end of the fine wine market.

Significant improvement is noticeable with the winery's Sauvignon Blanc. There are now two offerings. Eight hundred ninety cases of the 1993 Sauvignon Blanc Limited Selection were produced. Following its explosive nose of figs, melons, honey, and subtle, toasty new oak, this rich, medium- to full-bodied wine reveals a multidimensional personality, with exquisite flavor definition and dazzling depth and length. It is a beautifully made, high-class, barrel-fermented Sauvignon that compares favorably with the world's finest. Moreover, it should last for several years. There are only 895 cases of the superb 1992 Sauvignon Blanc Limited Selection, which I find comparable to some of the great French Sauvignons. It reveals a judicious use of toasty new oak, a big, honeyed, melon, and flinty nose, rich, unctuously textured, chewy flavors, superb delineation and focus, and an intense finish. Dry and superconcentrated, yet not heavy in the mouth, this is a brilliant effort. The 1991 Sauvignon Blanc (regular bottling) displays a moderately intense melon- and fruit-scented nose, and ripe, tasty flavors with crisp acidity and excellent length and definition. The 1991 Sauvignon Blanc Limited Selection, which has been 100% barrel-fermented, is superb. A spicy, vanillin-, mineral-, and herb-scented nose is followed by deep, rich, beautifully ripe, well-focused flavors, medium body, excellent depth, and a crisp, luscious finish. It is a dead ringer for a top white Graves. Both Sauvignons should be drunk over the next several years.

Gainey also produces two cuvées of Chardonnay. Gainey's 1992 Chardonnay Limited Selection Unfiltered has a microscopic production of only 310 cases. I suspect Gainey fanatics in Santa Barbara will prevent this wine from reaching the rest of the country, and who can blame them? The 1992 possesses a huge, fragrant nose of honeyed tropical fruits and subtle wood. Full bodied, with spectacular concentration and wonderful purity and crispness, this broadly flavored, expansive, succulent Chardonnay should drink well for 1–3 years. The 1992 Chardonnay from Santa Barbara exhibits a Meursault-like, nutty, smoky, richly fruity aroma. Pure, rich, concentrated flavors with well-integrated, crisp acidity give the wine an elegant, vibrant personality. This fresh, well-made Chardonnay will drink well for another 2 years.

Gainey did not produce a Limited Selection Chardonnay in 1991. The 1991 Chardonnay (regular bottling) is closed, although it does reveal some toasty, spicy oak in the nose. Lean, with medium body and an austere personality, this is a straightforward Chardonnay for drinking over the next several years.

I remember well the vegetal red wines produced by Gainey in the eighties, but this problem has been rectified. Although their 1990 Merlot is austere, lean, and herbaceous, the 1990 Merlot Limited Selection offers plenty of black cherry fruit, a subtle, herbaceous component, rich, spicy, medium-bodied flavors, and more opulence and chewiness than the regular cuvée. Both Merlots should be consumed over the next 4–5 years.

Although I have been generally unimpressed with the Cabernet Sauvignon, Merlot, and Cabernet Franc from southern California, a few wineries have enjoyed success with these varietals. Certainly Gainey's 1992 Cabernet Franc Limited Selection (220 cases) is a text-book Cabernet Franc, exhibiting the varietal's penetrating perfume of cassis and herbs, as well as a rich display of ripe cassis and fruit, all presented in a medium-weight, elegant format gently infused with toasty new oak. At its finest, Cabernet Franc is a wine of sheer finesse and elegance, intensely flavorful, yet never heavy or flabby. Gainey has fashioned just such a wine with this effort. Approachable and delicious now, this wine should age well for at least a decade. The 1990 Cabernet Franc Limited Selection is even more enticing, with a spicy, black fruit– and vanillin-scented bouquet, excellent richness and definition, as well as a long, silky finish. Deliciously forward, it promises to last for 5–7 years.

Gainey has made its best Pinot Noirs to date with the 1991s and 1992s. The only unexciting Pinot I tasted is the 1990 Pinot Noir Santa Barbara, a straightforward, ripe, tasty, spicy wine with good fruit, but not much aromatic or flavor complexity. It is ideal for uncritical quaffing over the next several years. The two cuvées of 1991 Pinot Noir are more serious wines, and I am delighted to report that they were bottled unfiltered—a first for this winery. The 1991 Pinot Noir Santa Maria exhibits a moderately intense, spicy, herb- and berry-scented nose, round, fleshy flavors, a sense of elegance, and a succulent, soft finish. It should be consumed over the next 4–5 years. The 1991 Pinot Noir from Santa Barbara's superb Sanford & Benedict vineyard displays a deeper color, and a rich, spicy, vanillin-, plum-, and raspberry-scented nose. There is gorgeous richness, a multidimensional flavor profile, plenty of power, yet a wonderful velvety texture and layered feel. Drink this sumptuous Pinot Noir over the next 5–6 years.

I found the 1992 Pinot Noir Bien Nacido Vineyard to be pungently peppery, vegetal, and lighter in flavor extraction than expected. Overall, it is a pleasant, straightforward Pinot with an annoying herbaceousness to its modest flavor dimension. In contrast, the 1992 Pinot Noir Sanford & Benedict Vineyard exhibits a deeper color, a bigger red-and-black-fruit character, a more subtle herbaceous component, medium to full body, and a lavish, spicy, smoky new oak note. It should be drunk over the next 2–3 years.

E. & J. GALLO WINERY (MODESTO)

Cabernet Sauvignon */* *, Cabernet Sauvignon Estate * * *, Cabernet Sauvignon Private Reserve * * *, Chardonnay */* *, Chardonnay Estate * * */* * * *, Sauvignon Blanc * *, Zinfandel Frei Ranch Vineyard * * */* * * *, Other Wines * *

1986	Cabernet Sauvignon	Sonoma	A	85
1987	Zinfandel	Sonoma	A	85
1991	Zinfandel Frei Ranch Vineyard	Dry Creek	B	89
1990	Zinfandel Frei Ranch Vineyard	Dry Creek	B	87

I have followed with great interest Gallo's serious commitment to making high-class wines. Their luxury-priced Chardonnay ($30) was a noteworthy wine, although too expensive. On the other hand, their luxury-priced Cabernet Sauvignon ($60) tasted as if it had been made within strict technical parameters by a nonrisk-taking oenologist. It possessed excellent raw materials, but it was too tart. However, Gallo perhaps has recognized that excessive acidity does interfere with the wine's pleasure. The 1991 Zinfandel Frei Ranch Vineyard exhibits a chewy, creamy texture, opulent, raspberry and cherry fruit, attractive sweet vanillin from new oak, and medium to full body. It is an excellent, possibly outstanding Zinfandel that should drink well for 5–8 years. While the 1990 Zinfandel Frei Ranch Vineyard is also tasty, it is more obviously tart and does not possess the breadth and expansiveness of the 1991. Nevertheless, it is a well-made Zinfandel with plenty of peppery, spicy, berry fruit and medium to full body. These are noteworthy efforts that consumers will enjoy. Kudos to Gallo.

Gallo has the vineyards, as well as resources, to do whatever they wish. If the 1986 Cabernet Sauvignon and 1987 Zinfandel had possessed more personality and bouquet, they would have easily merited scores 2 to 3 points higher, which tells you how much flavor and pleasure are to be found. The noses are similar, with some spicy, earthy characteristics. The Cabernet has slightly more herbaceousness. What is especially notable about these two inexpensive wines is their flavor. The 1987 Zinfandel exhibits medium to full body, plenty of berry fruitiness, good purity, and a round, generous, surprisingly long finish. The 1986 Cabernet Sauvignon is rich and medium to full bodied, with an underlying subtle herbaceousness in both its aromatic profile and flavors. Fleshy, with soft tannins, it is ideal for drinking now and over the next 3–4 years. There is one caveat. Wineries the size of Gallo may well have different lots of wine that are sold under the same varietal name and vintage. Let's hope there was only one bottling of the 1986 Cabernet Sauvignon and 1987 Zinfandel, and that what I tasted is identical to what readers will taste. If not, I would appreciate readers advising me. These are two wines worth buying, particularly when you consider that many of the big retail discount operations will probably sell them at $4.50.

GEYSER PEAK WINERY (SONOMA)

Cabernet Sauvignon Estate Reserve* * * *, Chardonnay* * *, Reserve Alexandre Proprietary
Red Wine* * * *, Sauvignon Blanc* * *, Semchard* * *, Soft Johannisberg Riesling* * *

1993 Chardonnay	Sonoma	A	87
1993 Semchard	California	A	88
1993 Soft Johannisberg Riesling	North Coast	A	86

Geyser Peak has turned in an off-dry, deliciously fruity, excellent 1993 Soft Johannisberg
Riesling with loads of tropical fruit and apple scents in the nose, a vivacious personality,
and a crisp, lively finish. It is meant to be drunk as an aperitif over the next 8–12 months.
Geyser Peak's terrific blend of 75% Semillon and 25% Chardonnay must be one of the
finest dry white wine values in America. The 1993 Semchard is crammed with fruit and
waxy, buttery aromas. Full bodied, with deep, concentrated flavors that cascade across the
palate offering wonderful ripeness and enough acidity to provide lift and vibrancy, it is a
wine to drink over the next year. This is a white wine worth buying by the case. The 1993
Chardonnay offers an intense bouquet of tropical fruits and oak, medium to full body,
excellent flavor definition, low acidity, and a heady finish. It should also be drunk over the
next year.

GIRARD WINERY (NAPA)

Cabernet Sauvignon* * * *, Cabernet Sauvignon Reserve* * * *, Chardonnay* * * *,
Chardonnay Reserve* * * *, Chenin Blanc* * */* * * *, Pinot Noir* *

1992 Cabernet Sauvignon	Napa	C	89
1991 Cabernet Sauvignon	Napa	C	89+
1990 Cabernet Sauvignon	Napa	C	89+
1992 Cabernet Sauvignon Reserve	Napa	D	94
1991 Cabernet Sauvignon Reserve	Napa	D	90+
1990 Cabernet Sauvignon Reserve	Napa	D	93+
1992 Chardonnay	Napa	C	85
1992 Chardonnay Reserve	Napa	C	87

Girard continues to rank among the most consistent producers of top-flight Napa Cabernet
Sauvignon. The major difference between the regular bottling and the Reserve is that the
latter exhibits a more obvious use of oak and it is more concentrated and tannic. While the
1992 Reserve is considerably deeper, no one can accuse the regular bottling of being
malnourished. In fact, from its dark purple color to its ripely scented nose of red and black
fruits and spicy oak, this sweet, concentrated, full-bodied wine displays great fruit extraction, excellent purity of flavor, and a soft, opulent, unctuously textured finish. It is very
forward (unusual for a Girard Cabernet), so I would not be surprised to see this wine close
up after bottling. The 1992 Reserve offers a blast of sweet cassis fruit. Smoky, subtly
herbaceous, vanillin, and cassis flavors are presented in an intense, full-bodied, richly
concentrated style. Gobs of tannin are balanced by copious quantities of rich, succulent
fruit. This large-scale, tannic, massive Cabernet Sauvignon will be one of the slower-
developing wines of the vintage. It is a likely candidate for 20 or more years of evolution.

Girard's regular bottling of 1991 Cabernet Sauvignon is a fine bargain given its high
quality and 10–15 years of aging potential. It reveals a saturated dark ruby/purple color,
and a promising nose of cassis and black cherries intermixed with scents of oak and
earth. Full bodied and concentrated, with moderate tannin and a powerful finish, it offers
considerable richness and aging potential. Some readers may prefer it to the 1991 Cabernet

Sauvignon Reserve, a backward, more elegantly styled wine displaying intensity, medium body, excellent richness, and a structured personality. Five to six years of cellaring is mandatory given its elevated tannin level. The wine is extremely young and unevolved, yet it promises to last for 15–20 years.

The 1990 Cabernet Sauvignon Estate exhibits a saturated, opaque, dark ruby/purple color, an unevolved, but gloriously ripe, rich nose of cassis fruit and vanillin, and rich, full-bodied, tannic, backward flavors that reveal superb concentration and firm tannin. Put this wine away for 4–5 years and drink it over the next 2 decades. The 1990 Cabernet Sauvignon Reserve is all of the above, but even more powerful, tannic, richer, and fuller. It is a huge wine, with fabulous sweetness of fruit and a blockbuster finish. Do not touch it before 1998; expect it to last for 20 or more years.

Girard's 1992 Chardonnay displays an attractive, orange blossom– and pineapple-scented nose, round, fleshy, soft flavors, fine richness, and a clean finish. Drink it over the next year. The 1992 Chardonnay Reserve is a fatter, more buttery and concentrated wine with more noticeable glycerin and alcohol levels, as well as toasty, smoky oak. A big, rich wine that borders on heaviness, it is mouth-filling and immensely satisfying. Drink it over the next 12–18 months.

GLASS MOUNTAIN (NAPA)
Chardonnay * *

1992 Chardonnay	California	A	86

This excellent value in Chardonnay appears under the second label of the Markham Winery. It reveals attractive fruit, medium body, and fine purity and ripeness.

GRACE FAMILY VINEYARDS (NAPA)
Cabernet Sauvignon * * * * *

1991 Cabernet Sauvignon	Napa	E	89

A soft, elegant, medium-bodied Cabernet Sauvignon, the Grace Family Vineyards' 1991 lacks the concentration and intensity of the winery's marvelous past efforts. Nevertheless, there are generous amounts of rich, black cherry, and cassis fruit, a gentle touch of toasty new oak, and a velvety finish. It is a Cabernet Sauvignon to drink over the next decade.

GREEN AND RED VINEYARD (NAPA)
Chardonnay Catacula Vineyard * * * *, Zinfandel Chiles Mill Vineyard * * * *

1991 Chardonnay Catacula Vineyard	Napa	C	87
1992 Zinfandel Chiles Mill Vineyard Unfiltered	Napa	B	88+
1991 Zinfandel Chiles Mill Vineyard	Napa	B	88

Although the deep ruby-colored 1992 Zinfandel from the Chiles Mill vineyard exhibits a complex, sweet, herb- and berry-scented nose, as well as excellent ripeness and fragrance, it tastes far less evolved than the bouquet suggests. Full bodied and concentrated, with admirable structure and depth, this immensely impressive Zinfandel combines power and elegance in a harmonious format. Drink it over the next 10–12 years. Deep ruby/purple colored, with a spicy, briary, berry-scented nose, the 1991 Chiles Mill Zinfandel possesses crisp acids, medium body, and an overall sense of elegance and balance. One of the more stylish, graceful Zinfandels produced, it should age well for up to a decade.

This low-profile producer has fashioned a 1991 Chardonnay with excellent ripeness, a spicy, subtle, oaky, mineral-scented nose, buttery fruit presented in a medium- to full-bodied format, and fine underlying acidity. Drink it over the next 1–2 years.

GREENWOOD RIDGE VINEYARDS (SONOMA)
Cabernet Sauvignon* *, Zinfandel* * *

1992 Zinfandel Scherrer Vineyard	Sonoma	B	88
1991 Zinfandel Scherrer Vineyard	Sonoma	B	88

The impressive, dark ruby/purple-colored 1992 Zinfandel exhibits loads of rich black raspberries and spice in its moderately intense bouquet. Deep, full bodied and rich, with moderate tannin and plenty of depth, this large-scale Zinfandel should be drunk over the next decade. The deep ruby/purple-colored 1991 Zinfandel Scherrer Vineyard offers sweet scents of jammy fruit and spices, excellent richness, and a plush, voluptuous texture that nearly conceals a moderate tannin level. Large-scale and robust yet well balanced, it should be drunk over the next 7–8 years.

GRGICH HILLS CELLARS (NAPA)
Cabernet Sauvignon* * *, Chardonnay* * *, Fumé Blanc* * *, Zinfandel* * *

1992 Zinfandel	Sonoma	B	82
1991 Zinfandel	Sonoma	B	89

Grgich Hills' 1992 Zinfandel exhibits high acidity, an unevolved, backward personality, and short, lean, cherrylike flavors presented in a medium-bodied format. Perhaps further clarification will soften this austere, tough-textured wine. Grgich Hills' 1991 Zinfandel is one of the better Zinfandels Grgich Hills has made. The color is a brilliant, saturated purple. The nose offers plenty of black fruit scents in its fragrant aroma. Rich, full bodied, and deep, with admirable concentration, this wine offers excellent fruit, glycerin, and alcohol. It should drink well for 10 years.

GROTH VINEYARDS AND WINERY (NAPA)
Cabernet Sauvignon* *, Cabernet Sauvignon Reserve* * * (before 1987* * * * *), Merlot* * *, Sauvignon Blanc* *

1990 Merlot	Napa	C	86

This soft, coffee-, chocolate-, herb-, and berry-scented wine reveals medium body, fine richness, a chunky, corpulent feel in the mouth, and a spicy, ripe finish. Drink it over the next 3–4 years.

GUENOC WINERY (LAKE COUNTY)
Cabernet Sauvignon Beckstoffer Vineyard* *, Chardonnay Estate* * *, Chardonnay Genevieve Magoon Vineyard* * *, Chardonnay Reserve* * */* * * *, Langtry Meritage White Wine* * *, Petite Sirah* * *

1993 Chardonnay	Guenoc Valley	B	86
1993 Chardonnay Genevieve Magoon Vineyard	Guenoc Valley	C	86
1991 Langtry Meritage	Lake	D	86

I suspect readers who enjoy lavish quantities of new oak on the palate will rate these wines higher. I enjoyed the quality of fruit and the wines' generous, open-knit, flattering personality, but readers are forewarned that they border on being too toasty, smoky, and woody—to the detriment of the fruit's quality. The soft, buttery 1993 Chardonnay Genevieve Magoon Vineyard is a forceful, smoky, old-style California Chardonnay. Its only drawback is too much oak. Drink it over the next 4–8 months before the fruit begins to fade. From a less weighty, more refined drinking perspective, I prefer Guenoc's 1993 Chardonnay. It is far less oaky and easier to consume than the heavy, smoky Magoon Vineyard and is richly fruity and cleanly made. Drink it over the next year.

The 1991 Langtry Meritage is a darkly-colored, oaky, rich, medium- to full-bodied wine with fine purity and a supple, fleshy texture. Drink it over the next 5–8 years. Although appealing, less wood would do wonders for this winery's top offerings.

GUNDLACH-BUNDSCHU WINERY (SONOMA)

Cabernet Franc* * *, Cabernet Sauvignon* */* * *, Cabernet Sauvignon Rhinefarm Vineyard* * *, Chardonnay* *, Gewürztraminer*, Pinot Noir* *, Zinfandel* * *, Zinfandel Rhinefarm Vineyard* * */* * * *

1991 Cabernet Sauvignon Rhinefarm Vineyard	Sonoma	C	86
1991 Zinfandel	Sonoma	B	82
1991 Zinfandel Rhinefarm Vineyard	Sonoma	B	86

Medium bodied, pleasant, and straightforward, the 1991 Zinfandel displays a peppery, black fruit character, soft tannins, and a short finish. Drink it over the next 2–3 years. Both the 1992 Zinfandel Rhinefarm Vineyard and the 1991 Cabernet Sauvignon Rhinefarm Vineyard are crowd-pleasing, medium-weight, spicy, fruity, well-made wines. The 1991 Zinfandel Rhinefarm Vineyard exhibits spicy, peppery, berry fruit, medium body, fine depth, and a chunky finish. Drink it over the next 2–4 years. The 1991 Cabernet Sauvignon Rhinefarm Vineyard displays an intriguing hickory-, cedar-, and herb-scented nose, ripe, curranty fruit, and an overall spicy personality. This supple Cabernet is ideal for drinking over the next 5–6 years.

HAGAFEN WINERY (NAPA)

Cabernet Sauvignon* *, Chardonnay* */* * *, Chardonnay Reserve* *, Pinot Noir*

1992 Cabernet Sauvignon Reserve	Napa	C	87

The impressive saturated dark color of Hagafen's 1992 Cabernet Sauvignon Reserve is followed by a closed nose that opens with swirling to reveal roasted black cherry, cassis, and underbrush scents. The wine possesses excellent concentration, the telltale sweetness and fleshiness of the 1992 vintage, as well as a spicy, long finish. Although it reveals more obvious tannin, this big, brawny wine should last for 15 or more years.

HANNA WINERY (SONOMA)

Cabernet Sauvignon* * *, Chardonnay * * *, Sauvignon Blanc* *

1993 Sauvignon Blanc	Sonoma	A	87

This 1993 Sauvignon Blanc stands out for its admirable ripeness, wonderfully aromatic, perfumed, herb, honey, and melony nose, fine texture, excellent purity, crisp acidity, and vibrancy. Drink it over the next year.

HARLAN ESTATE (NAPA)

Proprietary Red Wine* * * * *

1993 Proprietary Red Wine	Napa	EE	93
1992 Proprietary Red Wine	Napa	EE	96
1991 Proprietary Red Wine	Napa	EE	94

Harlan Estate, owned by Bill Harlan, is a luxury, world-class, Cabernet Sauvignon–based wine produced from a steep, terraced vineyard on the western side of Napa Valley, high above Napa's famous Martha's Vineyard. Approximately 24 acres are in vine, and the yields to date have been very low. Bill Harlan, better known as one of the principals of Merryvale Vineyards and Napa's exquisite Meadowood Country Club and Resort, has only one objective: to produce one of the greatest red wines of California. Based on these three vintages, Harlan Estate will create quite a frenzy among wine enthusiasts. The 1991, to be released in September 1995, is limited in quantity, as fewer than 1,000 cases were produced.

The wines are a blend of approximately two-thirds Cabernet Sauvignon and the remainder Cabernet Franc and Merlot. Bob Levy, Merryvale's winemaker, and Michel Rolland, the well-known Bordeaux oenologist, are the architects behind these exceptional efforts. Stylistically the wines are the Napa Valley equivalent of a hypothetical La Mission-Haut-Brion/ Cheval-Blanc blend. They are rich, powerful wines with unmistakable elegance, complexity, and purity. The 1993 exhibits a saturated, opaque ruby/purple color, and a superb bouquet of vanillin, cassis, licorice, and minerals. Rich, with superbly extracted, ripe, flavorful fruit, this impeccably balanced classic wine will have 20–25 years of aging potential after its release in 1997. The 1992 is a prodigious wine. It reveals a Mouton-Rothschild–like bouquet of jammy cassis, toasty oak, and lead pencil aromas. It is a ripe, rich, layered, highly concentrated, full-bodied wine with impressive definition. Its hallmark is great intensity without heaviness—a difficult marriage to attain. It is a splendid example of the quality of fruit that can be achieved from well-tended vineyards producing tiny yields. The emerging bouquet of the dark ruby/purple-colored 1991 jumps from the glass, offering up scents of ripe cassis fruit, toasty new oak, olive and herb notes, as well as whiffs of chocolate and licorice. Once again the wine possesses great fruit, full body, well-integrated tannin, enough acidity to provide delineation to its component parts, and a seamless, rich finish. Readers should be on the lookout for the 1991, as it will be one of the great wines of Napa.

HARRISON WINERY (NAPA)
Cabernet Sauvignon * * * *, Chardonnay * * * *

1992 Cabernet Sauvignon	Napa	C	89?

Harrison's 1992 Cabernet Sauvignon appears to possess fabulous raw materials. It is made in a huge, massive, blockbuster style with an opaque dark purple color and chewy, ripe flavors. However, its nose is totally subdued and unexpressive. Despite considerable coaxing as the wine sat in the glass, it refused to open aromatically. My instincts suggest it has outstanding potential, although it will require patience. It will not shed its tannin until the mid to late nineties, and it should last through the first 2 decades of the next century.

HARTWELL (NAPA)
Cabernet Sauvignon Stag's Leap * * * * *

1991 Cabernet Sauvignon Stag's Leap	Napa	E	90
1990 Cabernet Sauvignon Stag's Leap	Napa	E	92

Elegant, lighter, and more restrained than the blockbuster 1990, Hartwell's 1991 Cabernet Sauvignon Stag's Leap is an explosively rich, deep ruby/purple-colored wine with an attractive bouquet of vanillin, spice, cassis, and herbs. Medium to full bodied and rich, it is an excellent example of Cabernet Sauvignon that admirably marries power and intensity with a sense of style and grace. Although drinkable now, it will last 15+ years.

With respect to the 1990 Cabernet Sauvignon, readers will have to have the right contacts to secure a bottle or two of the 100 cases (4 barrels) of this wine made from a 1-acre, hillside vineyard in the Stag's Leap area. The vineyard was planted with vine cuttings from the famous Grace Family vineyard in Napa. The wine is outstanding. Dark ruby/purple color exhibits considerable saturation and suggests admirable richness. The bouquet jumps from the glass, offering up jammy aromas of black currants, minerals, spice, and subtle new oak. This impressively built wine possesses great richness, full body, adequate acidity, and layers of concentrated fruit. Although soft enough to be consumed, its exceptional concentration, balance, and intensity suggest it will last for a minimum of 2 decades.

HAVENS WINERY (NAPA)

Bourriquot Proprietary Red Wine * * * *, Merlot * * *, Merlot Reserve * * * *, Sauvignon Blanc
Clock Vineyard * * *, Syrah * * * *

1993 Bourriquot Proprietary Red Wine	Napa	C	89
1992 Bourriquot Proprietary Red Wine	Napa	C	90
1993 Merlot	Napa	B	86
1992 Merlot	Napa	B	86
1993 Merlot Reserve	Napa	C	90
1992 Merlot Reserve	Napa	C	91
1991 Merlot Reserve	Napa	C	87
1994 Sauvignon Blanc Clock Vineyard	Napa	A	82
1993 Syrah	Carneros	C	91
1992 Syrah	Carneros	C	87

Mike Havens, working out of a warehouse in the city of Napa, appears to have settled into an admirable pattern, producing richer and richer Merlots, complemented by a fine Syrah, and a Cheval Blanc–inspired proprietary red wine called Bourriquot. There is also a small quantity of Sauvignon Blanc. Havens supplements his Carneros vineyard with purchased grapes. The 40% barrel-fermented and 60% tank-fermented 1994 Sauvignon Blanc Clock Vineyard is a light-bodied, crisp, refreshing, pleasant, but essentially one-dimensional Sauvignon for drinking within a year of its release.

There are two cuvées of Merlot, a softer cuvée designed for early consumption and a more concentrated, larger-scaled Reserve offering. Recent vintages have moved toward less acidification and riper fruit, resulting in wines with significantly more charm, flesh, and succulence. The 1993 Merlot exhibits a deep ruby color, a spicy-, coffee-, smoky-, black cherry–scented nose, medium body, good suppleness, and a fine finish. Drink it before the end of the century. The 1992 Merlot possesses some tart acids, medium body, good fruit, a compact style, and a pH of 3.4. Although a trifle underripe, it is a good wine; just don't expect to be knocked over by it. In contrast, the 1992 Merlot Reserve (which includes 22% Cabernet Franc) exhibits greater richness, a wonderful nose of spicy, earthy black cherries, an opulent, full-bodied constitution, and a lush, velvety-textured finish. Its flesh and opulence are a big step up from the very good, but tannic and acidic 1990 and 1991 Merlot Reserves. The similarly styled 1993 Reserve Merlot exhibits fat, curranty, cherry fruit, medium to full body, excellent purity, and a succulent texture. Both the 1992 and 1993 Reserves should drink well for at least a decade. The 1994 Merlot Reserve, which will be a breakthrough Merlot for Havens, is clearly the finest Merlot this energetic young producer has yet made.

Havens's proprietary red wine, which is an intriguing blend of two-thirds Cabernet Franc and one-third Merlot (virtually identical to Cheval Blanc's blend), is very limited in availability (only 300 cases produced each year). The 1992 Bourriquot offers spicy, menthol/cassis/mineral and black cherry aromas and flavors. It is full bodied, with excellent concentration, a soft, velvety texture, and a long finish with some tannin lurking in the background. Although accessible, it is capable of lasting for 10–15 years. The 1993 Bourriquot reveals loads of sweet black currant fruit gently touched by toasty oak and herbs, as well as a juicy, voluptous texture, moderately sweet tannin, an expansive mid-palate, and a fine finish. It should drink well for 15+ years. The top Bourriquot is the 1994, which will not hit retailers' shelves until winter 1997.

Lastly, Havens is turning out fine Syrahs from Carneros. The 1992 (from 4-year-old vines) exhibits good color, some weediness, but true varietal character. Medium bodied, with fine density, and some hard tannin in the finish, it is a noteworthy effort for such a young vineyard. The 1993 Syrah offers up a big, smoky-, bacon fat-, and cassis-scented nose with Hermitage-like aromas and texture. Its sweet, overripe jammy fruit and excellent density and full body must conceal the wine's tannin, although not much is evident when tasting the wine. This will be a forward, flattering, mouth-filling Syrah for drinking during its first 10–12 years of life. Once again, the 1994 Syrah, which was still in barrel when I tasted it, will be a knockout effort.

HAYWOOD WINERY (SONOMA)
Cabernet Sauvignon Sonoma* *, Cabernet Sauvignon California*, Chardonnay* *,
Zinfandel* *

1991 Zinfandel	Sonoma	B	83
1992 Zinfandel Rocky Terrace Unfined/Unfiltered	Sonoma	B	79?

Smoky new oak dominates the 1992 Zinfandel Rocky Terrace's meager bouquet. On the palate, the wine exhibits a frightful hardness, tough, lean personality, high acidity, and a lack of flesh, ripeness, and fruit. Spice, mineral, and woodsy aromas combine with moderate fruit to offer a straightforward, solidly knit, tightly strung 1991 Zinfandel that errs on the side of being too shy and austere. Nevertheless, this Zin is attractive, albeit lightweight. Drink it over the next 5 years.

HESS COLLECTION WINERY (NAPA)
Cabernet Sauvignon* * * *, Cabernet Sauvignon Reserve* * * * *, Chardonnay* * * *,
Hess Select Chardonnay* * *

1990 Cabernet Sauvignon	Napa	B	90
1992 Cabernet Sauvignon Hess Select	California	A	86
1990 Cabernet Sauvignon Reserve	Napa	D	93+
1989 Cabernet Sauvignon Reserve	Napa	D	90
1991 Chardonnay	Mount Veeder	C	89
1993 Chardonnay Hess Select	California	A	86

Hess Collection's 1991 Mount Veeder Chardonnay is a wonderfully elegant, classic expression of Chardonnay emphasizing finesse over power and concentration. I immensely enjoyed its crisp, buttery, floral, apple-scented and -flavored fruit, and the medium- to full-bodied, long finish. Drink it over the next 2–3 years.

The Hess Select wines are consistently noteworthy bargains. The 1993 Chardonnay offers attractive tropical fruit scents, crisp acidity, medium weight, and an overall sense of balance. It is a tasty Chardonnay for drinking over the next year. It is not easy to find high-quality Cabernet Sauvignon for under $10 a bottle, but Hess Select has managed to turn out a 1992 with plenty of up-front, tasty black currant fruit, excellent concentration, an expansive, surprisingly generous mouth feel, and a spicy, currant, fruity finish. It is a Cabernet made in a generous, user-friendly style. Drink it over the next 4–5 years.

The three earlier Cabernet Sauvignon releases include a super bargain—the 1990 Napa Valley Cabernet Sauvignon. Its dark saturated color is followed by a big, aromatic nose of ripe cassis fruit and subtle toasty vanillin new oak. The wine possesses outstanding concentration, a wonderful, rich, velvety-textured feel, and a concentrated, long finish. Delicious now, it promises to keep for 12–15 years. I have seen this wine discounted to about $15 a bottle, making it an outstanding bargain. The 1990 Cabernet Sauvignon Reserve is another exceptional Reserve offering from Hess Collection. This is always a more tannic wine, exhibiting an elevated use of new oak, as well as huge, concentrated flavors, full body, and wonderful density and concentration. It does not possess the flattering, up-front appeal of the 1990 regular cuvée. However, it is a more complete, richer wine with the potential for more complexity. It needs to be cellared for 4–5 years and drunk over the subsequent 20–25.

The 1989 Hess Collection Cabernet Sauvignon Reserve, from a vintage that has been beaten up badly by the wine press, is an outstanding success for the year. In 1989, many of the hillside vineyards were not as negatively impacted by the heavy rains as were the valley vineyards. This dark ruby/purple-colored wine reveals excellent purity, and gobs of cassis fruit intermingled with scents of minerals, licorice, and herbs. Full bodied, with deep layers of concentration and moderate tannin, this immensely impressive wine should be cellared for several years and drunk over the following 12–15 years.

HIDDEN CELLARS (MENDOCINO)
Alchemy Proprietary White Wine* * * *, Chardonnay* * *, Sauvignon Blanc* * * *,
Zinfandel* * * *

1991	Alchemy	Mendocino	B	90
1992	Zinfandel	Mendocino	B	86

Hidden Cellars is a California winery that continues to turn out interesting, delicious wines that do not get as much publicity as they deserve. The superb 1991 Alchemy could easily pass for a white Graves. It offers rich aromas of melons, figs, and toast, an unctuous, deep, chewy texture, a gorgeous inner core of ripe fruit, and a long, nicely extracted, well-balanced, rich, dry finish. It should last 3–4 years. The tasty, ripe, medium-bodied 1992 Zinfandel is loaded with fruit, purity, and a spicy, peppery, berry-flavored finish. Drink it over the next 3–4 years.

THE HITCHING POST (SANTA BARBARA)
Pinot Noir* * */* * * *, Pinot Noir Sanford & Benedict Vineyard* * */* * * *

1993	Pinot Noir	Santa Maria	C	84
1993	Pinot Noir Bien Nacido Vineyard	Santa Maria	C	87
1993	Pinot Noir Sanford & Benedict Vineyard	Santa Ynez	C	87

These three Pinot Noirs, available from the Hitching Post Restaurant, are fragrant, spicy, meaty wines with good depth and richness. The straightforward 1993 Pinot Noir Santa Maria exhibits an herb, earth, and berry-scented nose, a good attack, but high acidity in the finish. It is a pleasant, yet tart medium-bodied Pinot for drinking over the next several years. The 1993 Pinot Noir Bien Nacido Vineyard reveals a deeper color, a lovely texture with a layered, rich berry fruit and spice personality, lush glycerin, and heady alcohol in the finish. Drink it over the next 4–5 years. The 1993 Pinot Noir Sanford & Benedict Vineyard offers a sweet nose, wonderfully expansive, ripe, earthy flavors, medium to full body, and a supple texture. It should drink well for 4–5 years.

PAUL HOBBS (SONOMA)
Cabernet Sauvignon Hyde Vineyard* * * *, Chardonnay Dinner Vineyard* * * *

1991	Cabernet Sauvignon Hyde Vineyard	Carneros/Napa	C	87
1992	Chardonnay Dinner Vineyard	Sonoma	C	89
1991	Chardonnay Dinner Vineyard	Sonoma	C	90

I tasted several interesting Pinot Noirs from Hobbs, but the wine that knocked me out was the superb 1991 Chardonnay. It offers splendid purity of flavor, great opulence, abundant fruit, a sweet, ripe, honeyed nose, and long, rich, layered, lingering flavors. Consume this terrific, lusty Chardonnay over the next 1–2 years. The light gold-colored 1992 Chardonnay Dinner Vineyard is a beautifully made, mouth-filling wine with lavish quantities of toasty new oak and buttery tropical fruit and popcornlike flavors. In addition to its crisp acidity, this full-bodied wine has an impressive finish. Drink it over the next 1–2 years.

The 1991 Cabernet Sauvignon Hyde Vineyard exhibits a saturated dark ruby/purple color, a jammy, herb- and black cherry–scented nose, medium body, admirable flavor definition and purity, and a fine finish. Unevolved and tight, it will benefit from 1–3 years of cellaring and last for 10–12 years.

HOP KILN WINERY (SONOMA)
Petite Sirah* * *, Zinfandel Primativo* * * *, Zinfandel Sonoma* * *

1992 Zinfandel	Sonoma	B	86
1991 Zinfandel	Sonoma	B	89
1992 Zinfandel Primitivo	Sonoma	C	90

The 1992 Zinfandel displays a lovely bouquet of moderately intense berry fruit, an attractive, medium- to full-bodied personality, and supple, fleshy flavors that linger on the palate. It should last for 5–7 years. In comparison, the 1992 Zinfandel Primitivo exhibits a deeper color, more intense black raspberry and black cherry scents, full body, a seductive, voluptuous texture, and a sweet (from glycerin and alcohol, not sugar), long, concentrated, ripe finish. It will be seductive young and should evolve gracefully for 10–12 years.

The sweet, ripe, wonderfully pure black raspberry and peppery nose of the 1991 Zinfandel is a lovely prelude to a sumptuously styled, full-bodied wine with loads of extract, and a satiny-textured personality. Long, ripe, and opulent, it should be drunk over the next 5–6 years.

HUSCH VINEYARDS (MENDOCINO)
Cabernet Sauvignon* * *, Chardonnay* * *, Chenin Blanc * * * *, Estate La Ribera Red* * *,
Gewürztraminer* *, Pinot Noir* *, Sauvignon Blanc* * *

1993 Chenin Blanc	Anderson Valley	A	86
1992 Estate La Ribera Red	Mendocino	A	86
1993 Gewürztraminer	Anderson Valley	A	84
1992 Gewürztraminer	Anderson Valley	A	86
1993 Sauvignon Blanc	Mendocino	A	86

I am rarely disappointed by an offering from Husch, as they consistently turn out remarkably tasty, fairly priced, unpretentious wines. Although their 1993 Chenin Blanc is not quite as good as their knockout 1992, it is to be admired for its floral-scented nose, delicate fruit, lovely, ripe, off-dry, light- to medium-bodied flavors, and crisp, clean, and zesty fruit. It also possesses some unreleased CO_2 that gives it a spritzy exuberance. Husch's 1993 Sauvignon Blanc exhibits the attractive flinty, melony side of this varietal, accompanied by a subtle touch of herbs. Light to medium bodied, crisp, and fruity, it will provide refreshing drinking over the next year.

I am not a fan of most California Gewürztraminer, but Husch's reasonably priced 1992 is faithful to Gewürztraminer's varietal character. It offers a big, spicy, floral, and apricot/ lychee nut–scented nose, dry, medium-bodied, lovely fruit, and a crisp, surprisingly long finish. Although the 1993 Gewürztraminer is not high on intense varietal character, it is a tasty, medium-bodied, spicy wine with fine grapefruit/peach/herbaceouslike fruit, an enchanting crispness and freshness, and considerable flexibility with food. It should be drunk over the next year.

I have enjoyed past examples of Husch's La Ribera Red, and the 1992 reveals a straight-forward black and red fruit–scented nose, excellent flavor concentration and suppleness, medium body, surprising acidity, and a smooth, silky finish. Even though it is made from 100% Cabernet Sauvignon, it is reminiscent of a fine, modern-styled Sangiovese or Chianti. Drink it over the next 2–3 years

IRON HORSE RANCH AND VINEYARDS (SONOMA)

Cabernets Proprietary Red Wine* * *, Chardonnay* * *, Fumé Blanc* * *, Sparkling Wine Cuvées* * * *

1993 Chardonnay Estate Cuvée Joy	Green Valley	C	88

First impressions suggest an understated, delicate Chardonnay that might easily get lost in a blind tasting. However, it does not take long to recognize that this is a Chardonnay of considerable richness, with a layered palate, and an intriguing, underlying mineral compo-nent. The subtly perfumed nose of citrusy, ripe fruit is followed by authoritative, restrained flavors. There is a Chablis-like character to this wine, which has beautifully integrated wood and acidity. The wine's length also suggests high quality. Do not be surprised to see this Chardonnay open and perform even more impressively with 4–6 more months of bottle age. It should last for 3–4 years.

JADE MOUNTAIN (NAPA)

Marsanne* * * *, Mourvèdre* * * *, Rhône Ranger Blended Cuvées* * * *, Syrah* * * *

1991 Les Jumeaux	California	B	90
1990 Les Jumeaux	California	B	89
1993 Marsanne/Viognier	California	B	90
1991 Mourvèdre	California	C	92
1990 Mourvèdre	California	C	86
1991 La Provençale	California	B	90
1990 La Provençale	California	B	87
1991 Syrah	Sonoma	C	91
1990 Syrah	Sonoma	C	89

Jade Mountain, which only began producing wines in 1988, has quickly emerged as one of the elite California wineries dedicated to complex, rich wines made from grapes more associated with France's Rhône Valley than northern California. Jade Mountain's first releases were impressive, but the winery's latest offerings are superb. The vineyard, located 1,200 feet above the valley floor on Mount Veeder, is largely planted with Syrah, Mourvèdre, Grenache, and Viognier. A small amount of Cabernet Sauvignon is also grown and used for blending. Readers will find Jade Mountain's wines to be rich and full bodied, with superb purity. Their cassis flavors and subtle, herbal influence are unmistakably Rhône in charac-ter. The grape's fruit and personality stand out.

The wines include an outstanding 1993 Marsanne/Viognier. The Marsanne provides muscle, fleshiness, and body, and the Viognier contributes a combination of honeysuckle, tropical fruit, and apricot scents and juicy fruit, resulting in an excellent wine. Moreover, the price is uncommonly fair. This wine should drink well for 12–18 months. The 1991 Les Jumeaux is made from 50% Mourvèdre, 33% Cabernet Sauvignon, and 17% Syrah. Not only is it a sensational value, it is a terrific wine, displaying an opaque purple color, and a big, rich nose of cassis, licorice, herbs, and spices. Full bodied, supple, and chewy, with gobs of luscious fruit, the tannin is dominated by the purity and quality of the fruit. It should drink well for at least a decade. More peppery, with notes of olives and black fruits, the 1991

Provençal is made from 55% Mourvèdre, 33% Syrah, and 12% Grenache. It is a more obvious, direct wine with superb color, layers of rich red and black fruit, and a stunningly opulent, rich finish. Already flattering and delicious, it is capable of lasting for a decade. I was knocked over by the complexity and personality of the 1991 Mourvèdre—made from 100% Mourvèdre—from vines averaging 70 years of age. It possesses a tree bark– and trufflelike scent combined with vibrant, formidable scents of ripe black fruits and herbs. Rich and full bodied, with the most structure of the Jade Mountain offerings (as well as the most concentration), this dazzling example of Mourvèdre is among the finest 100% Mourvè-dre wine I have tasted from the new world. With its obvious tannin, 2–3 years of cellaring would be beneficial. The wine can be drunk now, but it promises to last for 15 or more years. Lastly, the impressive 1991 Syrah exhibits a saturated purple color, a pure, sweet, ripe bouquet of black currants, and unevolved yet full-bodied, concentrated flavors oozing extraction, glycerin, and personality. Although this young wine does not yet reveal the complexity and aromatic dimensions of the other Jade Mountain wines, it is loaded with potential. It is soft because of its excellent ripeness and rich, concentrated character. Drink it over the next 15+ years.

The 1990s are an impressive portfolio of Rhône Valley–inspired wines. They all exhibit wonderfully ripe fruit, fine richness, and a great deal of personality. Made in a forward style, the 1990 Mourvedre is the only wine that does not express its varietal character as strongly as it might have. Nevertheless, it possesses a deep ruby/purple color, a spicy, earthy-scented nose, rich, intense, black fruit flavors, good viscosity and glycerin, and a spicy, lush finish. Drink it over the next 4–5 years. The 1990 La Provençale, a Mourvèdre/Syrah blend, reveals a big, dramatic nose of black pepper and spices. It is voluptuous, with gobs of black cherry and raspberry fruit, plenty of glycerin, and a heady, rich, medium- to full-bodied finish. It should drink well for 5–7 years. Jade Mountain's 1990 Les Jumeaux (the twins), a Cabernet Sauvignon/Mourvèdre blend, tastes akin to a California rendition of a top-notch Bandol. It offers an excellent saturated deep ruby/purple color, a spicy, peppery nose of cassis, earth, and herb-scents, layer upon layer of velvety-textured, jammy black fruit flavors, an unctuous texture, and a rich, long, satisfying finish. It will last for at least 7–8 years. Lastly, the 1990 Syrah reveals more evidence of toasty, smoky, vanillin new oak in the nose, as well as rich, bacon fat, meaty, cassis flavors, massive quantities of fruit, and a full-bodied, moderately tannic finish. This should prove to be the longest-lived wine of this quartet, yet it can be drunk now given its superb ripeness and relatively low acidity.

These are immensely impressive wines that combine the rare virtues of superb quality and modest price.

JUDD'S HILL (NAPA)
Cabernet Sauvignon * * */* * * *

| 1992 Cabernet Sauvignon | Napa | C | 92 |
| 1991 Cabernet Sauvignon | Napa | C | 89 |

All of this fledgling Napa Valley winery's first releases have been impressive. Their glorious 1992 Cabernet Sauvignon possesses an opaque dark purple color and a huge nose of sweet cassis fruit, herbs, vanillin, and spice. This plump, corpulent wine is loaded with ripe fruit, has enough underlying acidity to hold its ample component parts together, and finishes with richness, authority, and definition. As with many 1992s, it will drink well early, but it should last for at least 15 years. Impressive! The 1991 is a harmonious, elegant yet rich Cabernet Sauvignon with a deep purple color, medium body, a supple texture, impressive richness, and a sense of grace and balance. The velvety finish possesses moderate tannin that is largely concealed by the wine's rich fruit. Drink it over the next 12–15 years.

JUSTIN WINERY AND VINEYARD (SAN LUIS OBISPO)

Cabernet Franc* * * *, Cabernet Sauvignon* * * *, Isosceles Proprietary Red Wine* * * *,
Merlot* * * *

1991 Cabernet Franc	Paso Robles	C	89
1989 Cabernet Franc	Paso Robles	C	87
1989 Cabernet Sauvignon	Paso Robles	C	89
1991 Cabernet Sauvignon Society Reserve	Paso Robles	C	92
1991 Isosceles Reserve Proprietary Red Wine	Paso Robles	C	94
1989 Isosceles Reserve Proprietary Red Wine	Paso Robles	C	90
1988 Isosceles Reserve Proprietary Red Wine	Paso Robles	C	90
1987 Isosceles Reserve Proprietary Red Wine	Paso Robles	C	86
1991 Merlot	Paso Robles	C	87
1989 Merlot	Paso Robles	C	89
1988 Merlot	Paso Robles	C	88

Justin Winery and Vineyard is quickly taking its place among the top producers of California red wines. Owner Justin Baldwin owns a 65-acre vineyard west of the town of Paso Robles dedicated largely to Cabernet Sauvignon, Merlot, Cabernet Franc, and Chardonnay. While I have not tasted the Chardonnay, the high quality of Justin's wines was first brought to my attention when I tasted their 1989s. The current releases, the 1991s, are showstopping wines of considerable stature, richness, and complexity.

Recent releases bear the San Luis Obispo/Paso Robles geographic origin. The 1991 Merlot exhibits a medium dark ruby color, a flattering, oaky, smoky, cherry nose, rich, medium- to full-bodied flavors with dusty tannin, and an overall supple personality. Although not yet in the league of Merlot superstars such as Newton and Matanzas Creek, Justin's Merlot is unquestionably head and shoulders above the ocean of vegetal, hollow, tart Merlots being produced in California and elsewhere. It should drink well for 7–8 years. Justin's 1991 Cabernet Franc is a more complex wine, displaying gobs of sweet red and black fruit in its fragrant bouquet. Medium to full bodied, with a luscious, savory, expansive palate loaded with fruit, this complex, supple, mouth-filling wine exhibits the complexity of this varietal. It is a fleshy wine that maintains elegance and finesse. Although noticeable, the tannin is well integrated and the acidity is not intrusive. It should drink well for 12–15 years.

Justin's 1991 Cabernet Sauvignon Society Reserve is exceptional. The opaque purple color is followed by a nose of wonderfully ripe black currant and cherry scents intertwined with aromas of smoke, herbs, vanillin, and minerals. It is full bodied, and stunningly proportioned with loads of richness, a chewy, concentrated feel, and a superb finish. The wine's richness masks a moderate tannin level. Accessible now, it will be fully mature by the end of the century and will last for 15–20 years thereafter. Readers lucky enough to run across a bottle of the 1991 Isosceles, a proprietary red wine made from 57% Cabernet Sauvignon, 22% Cabernet Franc, and 21% Merlot, will have no problem believing that Justin kept their best lots for this outstanding wine. It reveals a dazzling bouquet of smoky, jammy, black and red fruit complemented by spicy oak. This superbly concentrated, young, marvelously extracted and large-scale wine cuts a deep swath across the palate. The tannin is sweet and ripe, and the wine's acidity provides focus to its generous components. This dazzling proprietary red wine should age effortlessly for up to 2 decades.

The 1989 Cabernet Franc reminds me of a classic St.-Émilion, with its suave graceful style, rich mid-palate, and elegant, soft finish. There is a touch of herbs, but the overwhelming aromas are those of red and black fruits and spicy oak. It should drink well over the next 5–7 years. The 1989 Cabernet Sauvignon exhibits a spicy, cedary, black fruit–scented nose, rich, medium- to full-bodied flavors, and fine elegance, depth, and length.

The 1989 Merlot is a terrific example of this varietal. Chocolaty, black cherry, and mocha aromas and flavors dominate this full-bodied, opulent wine that makes for quite a mouthful of succulent fruit. Delicious, complex, and exceptionally well balanced, it should be drunk over the next 7–8 years. The 1988 Merlot, which can stand up to the best wines of that vintage, possesses a huge bouquet of chocolate and cassis fruit that is followed by jammy, rich, opulent, even sumptuous flavors exhibiting low acidity but plenty of intensity. This is a gorgeously decadent Merlot for drinking over the next 5–7 years.

The 1989 proprietary Isosceles, a blend of 59% Cabernet Sauvignon, 24% Merlot, and 17% Cabernet Franc, is a dead ringer for a top-class Bordeaux. It displays wonderful richness and opulence, a complex nose, and rich, multidimensional flavors. It too should drink well for the next decade. The 1988 Isosceles, made from a blend of 58% Cabernet Sauvignon, 30% Merlot, and 12% Cabernet Franc, is an outstanding wine, with superconcentration, a big, herbaceous, black currant–, coffee-, and smoky-scented bouquet, lush, full-bodied, highly extracted flavors that display soft tannins, and just enough acidity to provide balance and delineation. Approachable now, this impressively constituted wine should easily last for 10–15 years. The 1987 Isosceles, made from 59% Cabernet Sauvignon, 30% Merlot, and 11% Cabernet Franc, is lighter and less well endowed, but it is round, with a velvety texture and rich, green pepper, black raspberry, and oaky flavors. It should be drunk over the next 4–5 years.

Paso Robles remains an obscure California viticultural region, but if this region's other wineries begin to produce wines of this quality, it will undoubtedly become one of California's hot spots.

KALIN CELLARS (MARIN)

Cabernet Sauvignon Reserve * * *, Chardonnay Cuvée CH * * * *, Chardonnay Cuvée DD * * * *, Chardonnay Cuvée LD * * * * *, Chardonnay Cuvée W * * * * *, Cuvée d'Or Sweet Dessert Wine * * * */* * * * *, Pinot Noir Cuvée DD * * * *, Pinot Noir Cuvée JL * * * *, Sauvignon Blanc * * * *, Sauvignon Blanc Reserve * * * * *, Semillon * * * *

1990	Chardonnay Cuvée CH	Sonoma	D	91
1990	Chardonnay Cuvée DD	Sonoma	D	90
1981	Chardonnay Cuvée L	Sonoma	D	90
1990	Chardonnay Cuvée LD	Sonoma	D	92
1991	Chardonnay Cuvée LR	Sonoma	D	90
1990	Chardonnay Cuvée W	Livermore	D	94
1989	Pinot Noir	Sonoma	D	87
1990	Pinot Noir Cuvée DD	Sonoma	D	94
1980	Pinot Noir Cuvée JL	Sonoma	D	90
1990	Sauvignon Blanc	Potter Valley	C	90

Most California Chardonnays drop their fruit by the time they are 3 years of age. Kalin's Chardonnays do not begin to open until they are 4 or 5. For example, at 14 years of age the 1981 Chardonnay Cuvée L is as fresh as a 6-month-old barrel sample. The crisp, mineral, apple blossom, buttery nose is followed by rich, vibrant, well-focused flavors that offer medium to full body and excellent underlying acidity. Given the fact that this wine has evolved at a glacial pace, I would not be surprised to see it last for at least another decade.

By the standards of Kalin's other Chardonnays, which often are forbiddingly tight and restrained when released, the 1991 Chardonnay Cuvée LR is quite soft. The nose offers ripe, citrusy scents intertwined with those of tangerines and subtle oak. Beautifully integrated acidity, full body, superb concentration, and a well-knit, well-balanced personality make for a generous mouthful of complex, even compelling Chardonnay. I am shocked by how flattering this wine is showing, given the bottle aging most Kalin wines require. If complexity in its simplest definition is the attraction that keeps the taster reaching for another glass, then this wine may merit an even higher score, as I could not resist it. Drink it over the next 4–5 years. The 1990 Chardonnay Cuvée LD may be one of the most concentrated Chardonnays I have tasted from proprietors Frances and Terry Leighton. The wine exhibits a mineral/citrusy, subtly honeyed nose, superrich, intense, concentrated flavors with a wonderful underpinning of natural acidity, and a long, intense finish. It tends to start off slowly in the attack, but an explosive finish suggests incredible aging ability. Kalin's Chardonnays actually improve with cellaring, so do not be surprised to see this wine age and evolve for 10–15 years. The 1990 Chardonnay Cuvée W from Livermore possesses a surprisingly evolved medium gold color. An exotic, incenselike, gravelly nose soars from the glass. It is followed by a wine with phenomenal extract, a honeyed, intense richness, layers of flavor, and an extremely dry, full-bodied finish. This is one of the most distinctive Chardonnays I have tasted from Kalin. Although the color suggests maturity, the impression in the mouth is of a wine that will last for a decade or more. The 1990 Cuvée CH Chardonnay possesses massive flavor extraction, wonderful underlying crisp acidity, and a tight, unforthcoming nose that, with airing, gives up floral, mineral scents combined with ripe fruit. There is explosive richness in the mouth, and the finish must last for nearly a minute. This is an unevolved, young but impressive Chardonnay, which, given Kalin Cellars' track record, should age effortlessly for at least a decade. The 1990 Chardonnay Cuvée DD is a rich, well-knit wine with reserves of fruit and body and an unevolved yet promising bouquet of lemony/apple blossoms. Subtle nutty fruit is followed by a wine with considerable richness and definition. As with so many of Kalin's Chardonnays, it can be expected to last for up to a decade. These Chardonnays are unlike any other from California, so if you are looking for tooty-fruity, bubble gum aromas and lavish quantities of new oak you will be disappointed with the distinctive, compelling styles of Chardonnay produced by Kalin.

I do not believe I have ever tasted a more complex and profound Pinot Noir than Kalin's 1990 Pinot Noir Cuvée DD from Sonoma. Anyone who is familiar with the Domaine de la Romanée-Conti's magnificent 1980 La Tâche might want to try a bottle of Kalin's Cuvée DD for comparison. It possesses a huge fragrance of macerated prunes/plums, smoked meats, jammy raspberries and cherries, and loads of smoke and herb notes. The flavors are reminiscent of tea and smoked duck. The wine is full bodied, with huge richness, great precision, and freshness, as well as a heady, spicy, lightly tannic finish. It should drink well for 10–15 years. Years ago I remember tasting Kalin's 1979 Pinot Noir Cuvée DD, which was a dead ringer for one of great grand crus of the Domaine de la Romanée-Conti. Whatever the Leightons are doing with Pinot Noir, the 1990 is a mind-boggling, possibly historic effort.

Although the 1989 Pinot Noir from Sonoma is light by this producer's standards, it reveals attractive, meaty, berry flavors, a wonderful spicy earthiness, and excellent freshness and length. It is not likely to be as long lived as the 1988 and 1987 Cuvée DD's, but it will last for 5–6 years.

A recent library release, Kalin's compelling 1980 Pinot Noir Cuvée JL exhibits a bouquet reminiscent of a great grand cru from Morey St.-Denis. An exotic Asian spice component, rich, black fruit, and earthy, herbal scents offer extraordinary interest, not to mention intense perfume. Medium to full bodied, with excellent concentration and remarkable freshness, this sensational Pinot Noir possesses one of the most complex aromatic and flavor profiles I have experienced from American Pinot Noir. If the finish were less austere, this wine would have received a rating in the upper 90s, a remarkable achievement and an example of the genius of Frances and Terry Leighton. There is considerable sediment, so tasters may want to decant it.

The 1990 Sauvignon Blanc is made from an old Potter Valley vineyard that yielded only 2.5 tons of grapes per acre. Compare that with the average production of 5–8 tons per acre of other Sauvignon vineyards and you will appreciate why this wine possesses so much concentration and personality.

Ratings for Older Vintages of Kalin's Chardonnay Cuvée LD: 1989 (88), 1988 (87)
Ratings for Older Vintages of Kalin's Chardonnay Cuvée W: 1989 (90)
Ratings for Older Vintages of Kalin's Pinot Noir Cuvée DD: 1988 (90), 1987 (92)
Ratings for Older Vintages of Kalin's Sauvignon Blanc Reserve: 1990 (92)
Ratings for Older Vintages of Kalin's Semillon: 1989 (90)

KARLY WINERY (AMADOR)
Chardonnay * *, Sauvignon Blanc * * * *, Zinfandel * *

1991 Zinfandel	Amador	B	84

I generally like Karly's Zinfandels more than I did the spicy, straightforward, light- to medium-bodied, pleasant, but essentially one-dimensional 1991. Drink it over the next 3–4 years.

KENDALL-JACKSON VINEYARD (LAKE)
Cabernet Sauvignon Grand Reserve * * * * (since 1991), Cabernet Sauvignon Vintner's Reserve * *, Cardinale Meritage Proprietary Red Wine * * * * (since 1991), Chardonnay Camelot Vineyard * * * *, Chardonnay Proprietor's Grand Reserve * * *, Chardonnay Vintner's Reserve * * *, Johannisberg Riesling Vintner's Reserve * * *, Merlot * *, Syrah Durell Vineyard * * * *, Zinfandel Ciapusci Vineyard * * * *, Zinfandel Dupratt Vineyard * * * *, Zinfandel Proprietor's Grand Reserve * * * *, Zinfandel Vintner's Reserve * * *

1992 Cabernet Sauvignon Grand Reserve	California	C	92
1991 Cabernet Sauvignon Grand Reserve	California	C	90
1992 Cardinale Meritage Proprietary Red Wine	California	E	92
1991 Cardinale Meritage Proprietary Red Wine	California	E	89+
1992 Chardonnay Camelot Vineyard	Santa Maria	B	88
1992 Chardonnay Proprietor's Grand Reserve	California	C	90
1992 Chardonnay Vintner's Reserve	California	B	86
1993 Johannisberg Riesling Vintner's Reserve	California	A	85
1991 Merlot Proprietor's Grand Reserve	California	C	88
1993 Pinot Noir Grand Reserve	California	D	87
1993 Sauvignon Blanc Vintner's Reserve	California	A	86
1992 Zinfandel Edmeades-Zeni Vineyard	Mendocino	C	93
1992 Zinfandel Grand Reserve	California	C	86
1990 Zinfandel Proprietor's Grand Reserve	California	C	90
1992 Zinfandel Vintner's Reserve	California	B	86
1990 Zinfandel Vintner's Reserve	California	A	86

I do not know of anyone who has ever complained about the quality of Kendall-Jackson's white wines. In contrast, the red wines, until the 1991 vintage, tasted shrill (too much added acidity), sterile, devoid of aromatic profiles, sharp, compact, and ungenerous. This has all changed under the new winemaker, John Hawley, who has drastically reduced the acidification. Moreover, he is bottling the top red wines naturally, aiming for no filtration if possible.

Consumers can already taste the results with the 1991 Merlot Proprietor's Grand Reserve. A rich wine with a bouquet of coffee, black fruits, herbs, and velvety-textured, ripe fruit, medium to full body, and admirable extraction, it will drink well for 7–8 years. Even the 1993 Pinot Noir Grand Reserve exhibits all the seductive, voluptuous qualities of Pinot Noir. It possesses a lovely, sweet, black cherry–scented nose with a whiff of herbs and oak. It is fat, juicy, and succulent, with low acidity and a generous finish. Drink it over the next 2–3 years.

The turnaround in quality of this winery's red wines is profoundly obvious when tasting the new vintages of the Cabernet Sauvignon Grand Reserve and the proprietary wine called Cardinale. The Cabernet Sauvignon Grand Reserve is more typically Californian in proportions, as it is a bigger, more blockbuster-style wine than the Cardinale. Previous vintages were pleasant, but often too tart and sterile. The new-look 1991 exhibits a deep ruby/purple color, and a moderately intense bouquet of toast, black cherries, and cassis. Flamboyantly rich, full-bodied, with fabulously juicy, succulent fruit, this hedonistic Cabernet should drink well for at least a decade. A terrific example of the varietal, the 1992 Cabernet Sauvignon Grand Reserve is the best Cabernet Kendall-Jackson has yet produced. The wine possesses a black/purple color, a huge, knockout nose of jammy black fruits, herbs, smoke, and vanillin. Full bodied, with an opulent texture, this wine will be a crowd pleaser when released in 1996.

The luxury-priced Cardinale has been disappointing—until 1991. Yes, I know the wine has received rave reviews from the West Coast wine press, but all readers need do is go back and taste it in vintages such as 1987, 1988, 1989, and 1990. They offer an objective lesson in California's oenologically correct winemaking. Today, all of these wines taste too acidic, are devoid of any aromatic development, and texturally are compact and attenuated. Beginning in 1991, the wines reveal far less acidity, a more natural, layered taste, and elegance allied to considerable richness. The Cardinale is not meant to have the block-buster, juicy, succulent fruitiness of the Grand Reserve, so readers should not expect it to be as ostentatious. The 1991 Cardinale should drink well for 15 or more years. Even more impressive is the 1992 Cardinale. It reveals a dense, opaque, black/purple color, and a sensational nose of Asian spices, toasty new oak, cassis, and herbs. Full bodied and intense, with underlying gracefulness and style, this is the first vintage where Cardinale has merited its lofty price.

The Chardonnay Vintner's Reserve is one of the better values in the marketplace. While the 1992 is less obviously sweet than its predecessors, it is an opulent, fruity, medium-bodied Chardonnay with excellent fruit and a rich, zesty finish. It is meant to be drunk over the next 8–12 months. The fuller, richer, more oak-influenced 1992 Chardonnay Camelot Vineyard is full bodied, rich, and layered, with crisp acidity. It should be drunk over the next year. More ambitiously styled as well as fuller bodied, with gobs of fat, viscously textured fruit, the 1992 Chardonnay Proprietor's Grand Reserve offers a knockout bouquet of tropical fruits (oranges and pineapples) and spicy new oak. This is a full-bodied, decadent style of Chardonnay for drinking over the next year.

Kudos to Kendall-Jackson for turning out an elegant, medium dry, floral-scented, re-freshing 1993 Johannisberg Riesling Vintner's Reserve. It reveals lovely floral and applelike fruit, light body, and wonderful freshness. Drink it over the next year as an aperitif. Another excellent offering from Kendall-Jackson's inexpensive Vintner's Reserve program, the melony, subtly herbaceous, medium-bodied 1993 Sauvignon Blanc Vintner's Reserve is fresh and lively, with good fruit and a crisp, dry finish. Drink it over the next 8–12 months.

I am sure there must be more to the 1992 Zinfandel Grand Reserve than the 1992 Zinfandel Vintner's Reserve. Although they are clearly different, I liked them equally as much. The more supple 1992 Zinfandel Vintner's Reserve offers gobs of spicy, ripe, tasty berry fruit, medium body, light tannin, and a fleshy, vibrant finish. It will not make old bones, but it is a well-made, juicy Zinfandel for drinking over the next 2–3 years. The 1992 Zinfandel Grand Reserve exhibits more spice, tannin, and body, but I did not enjoy it any more than the lower-priced Vintner's Reserve. Well made, with plenty of cherry fruit, a saturated color, and fine depth, it should be drunk over the next 4–5 years. The stunning 1992 Zinfandel Edmeades-Zeni Vineyard possesses an opaque ruby/purple color, and a sensational bouquet of spices, black and red fruits, and pepper. Rich and concentrated, with great balance for its size, this well-endowed, chewy, deliciously pure, vibrant Zinfandel will drink well for 8–12+ years. Readers who do not want to experience any tannic roughness should give it 2–3 years in the cellar, permitting some of its moderate tannin to melt away.

Bursting with peppery berry fruit, the soft, medium-bodied 1990 Zinfandel Vintner's Reserve exhibits excellent purity and a ripe, generous finish. Drink it over the next several years. The 1990 Zinfandel Proprietor's Grand Reserve is a stunningly proportioned, opulent wine that is bursting with black fruit aromas. Full bodied and luscious, it will provide exciting drinking for another 5–6 years.

KENWOOD VINEYARDS (SONOMA)

Cabernet Sauvignon Artist Series Vineyard* * * *, Cabernet Sauvignon Jack London Vineyard* * * *, Chardonnay Beltane Ranch* * *, Sauvignon Blanc* * * *, Zinfandel Jack London Vineyard* * */* * * *

1990 Cabernet Sauvignon Jack London Vineyard	Sonoma	C	90
1992 Chardonnay Reserve	Sonoma	C	87
1993 Sauvignon Blanc	Sonoma	A	87
1992 Sauvignon Blanc	Sonoma	A	86

Black/purple in color, the 1990 Cabernet Sauvignon Jack London Vineyard possesses a controversial nose of loamy, earthy scents, black truffles, and rich cassis. Phenomenally extracted and rich, as well as loaded with tannin, this full-bodied, mammothly constituted wine is long, rich, and in need of 5–7 years of cellaring. A huge Cabernet Sauvignon, it should keep for at least 20 or more years.

I also tasted Kenwood's 1990 Cabernet Sauvignon Artist's Series. It may turn out to be an outstanding wine after 10–15 years of cellaring, but it was impossible to evaluate because of the massive tannin level.

The 1992 Chardonnay Reserve offers up an apple blossom, honeyed nose that is followed by a rich, deep, concentrated wine with spicy oak, adequate acidity, and generous amounts of alcohol, glycerin, and fruit in the finish. Drink it over the next year.

Kenwood is a sure winner when it comes to turning out aromatic, crisp, dry, light- to medium-bodied Sauvignons. The 1993 is another tasty, herb-, fig-, melon-scented and -flavored wine that once again proves the remarkable flexibility of this varietal with many foods. Drink it over the next year. The 1992 Sauvignon Blanc exhibits a pronounced melony/herb-scented nose, followed by a light- to medium-bodied wine loaded with rich fruit presented in a medium-bodied format. This attractively styled Sauvignon should have broad appeal if drunk over the next year.

KISTLER VINEYARDS (SONOMA)

Chardonnay * * *, Chardonnay Cuvée Kathleen * * * * *, Chardonnay Durell Vineyard * * * * *, Chardonnay Dutton Ranch * * * * *, Chardonnay Hudson Vineyard * * * * *, Chardonnay Kistler Estate * * * * *, Chardonnay McCrea Vineyard * * * */* * * * *, Chardonnay Vine Hill Road Vineyard * * * */* * * * *, Pinot Noir Camp Meeting Ridge * * * *, Pinot Noir Cuvée Catherine * * * * *, Pinot Noir Hirsh Vineyard * * * * *, Pinot Noir Vine Hill * * * * *

1992 Chardonnay	Sonoma	C	87
1992 Chardonnay Cuvée Kathleen	Sonoma	E	96
1993 Chardonnay Durell–Sand Hill Vineyard	Sonoma	D	95
1992 Chardonnay Durell–Sand Hill Vineyard	Sonoma	D	90
1991 Chardonnay Durell–Sand Hill Vineyard	Sonoma	D	90
1993 Chardonnay Dutton Ranch	Sonoma	D	95
1992 Chardonnay Dutton Ranch	Sonoma	D	93
1993 Chardonnay Kistler Estate	Sonoma	D	96
1992 Chardonnay Kistler Estate	Sonoma	D	95
1991 Chardonnay Kistler Estate	Sonoma	D	94
1993 Chardonnay McCrea Vineyard	Sonoma	D	93
1992 Chardonnay McCrea Vineyard	Sonoma	D	95
1991 Chardonnay McCrea Vineyard	Sonoma	D	90
1993 Chardonnay Vine Hill Road Vineyard	Sonoma	D	93
1992 Chardonnay Vine Hill Road Vineyard	Sonoma	D	92+
1991 Chardonnay Vine Hill Road Vineyard	Sonoma	D	87
1993 Pinot Noir Cuvée Catherine	Sonoma	D	94
1992 Pinot Noir Cuvée Catherine	Sonoma	D	92
1991 Pinot Noir Cuvée Catherine	Sonoma	D	92

At their new installation on Vine Hill Road in Sonoma County, Mark Bixler and Steve Kistler have produced the best wines in their distinguished careers. When Kistler's 1993 Chardonnays are released, readers will have to move quickly if they want to purchase a few bottles. They are the best Chardonnays Kistler has made—and that's saying something, particularly after the great success of this winery's 1992s. These wines, which are made in a Burgundian style, with significant lees contact, a healthy percentage of new oak (all from the Burgundy cooper François Frères), are usually bottled without filtration. They are beautiful examples of Chardonnay that easily compare with Burgundy's fine premiers and grands crus.

The 1993s possess even more texture, richness, and concentration than the 1992s. The 1993 Chardonnay McCrea Vineyard boasts plenty of fatness, ripe, buttery, apple, and toasty scents and flavors, as well as a full-bodied personality and a tremendous finish. Unlike most California Chardonnays, it will drink well for 3–4 years. The 1993 Chardonnay Dutton Ranch offers a more roasted, hazelnut, honeyed ripeness, great concentration, full body, and a character not unlike a hypothetical blend of Bâtard-Montrachets from the two stellar Burgundian producers, Niellon and Ramonet. This rich wine should age and improve for another 4–5 years. Speaking of comparisons with Burgundy, the 1993 Vine Hill Road Chardonnay has a Corton-Charlemagne–like mineral component, and a structured, backward, broodingly rich, firm personality. Everything is present, but the wine is less forthcoming and flattering than Kistler's other 1993 cuvées. Another backward but fabulously rich, nearly perfect Chardonnay is the 1993 Chardonnay Kistler Estate. As one might expect from a wine made from yields of under 2 tons per acre (frightfully low for Chardonnay), this rich wine possesses a compelling bouquet of buttery, honeyed fruit, roasted nuts and vanilla, layers of concentration, and a full-bodied, crisp, powerful finish. It is a brilliant blend of awesome concentration and unbelievable elegance. The 1993 Chardonnay Durell–Sand Hill Vineyard reveals a mineral-dominated, tropical fruit–scented nose, fine underlying acidity, fabulous richness and presence on the palate, and an amazingly long finish. A candidate for the best Durell–Sand Hill Vineyard Chardonnay Kistler has yet made, it unfolds in the mouth to reveal extraordinary richness and intensity.

The 1992 Chardonnay Sonoma, a blend of lots deemed lacking sufficient intensity, thus excluded from the final blend of the single-vineyard wines, is a tasty, very good to excellent Chardonnay revealing a complex bouquet of vanillin, roasted nuts, and buttery fruit scents. Spicy and medium bodied, with admirable depth and an attractive freshness and purity, it should be drunk over the next 2–3 years. The 1992 Chardonnay Durell–Sand Hill Vineyard offers a wonderful honeyed, citrusy nose, an elegant, intensely flavorful, full-bodied personality, and a long, crisp, zesty finish. It is a large-framed, expansively flavored Chardonnay that should drink well for 4–6 years. The 1992 Chardonnay Dutton Ranch exhibits a superb bouquet of smoked nuts, vanillin, rich, buttery apples, and flowers. Full bodied, with terrific depth, adequate underlying acidity, and broad, rich, refreshing flavors, this juicy, intense, complex Chardonnay should drink well for 5–6 years.

Consumers will adore the 1992 Chardonnay McCrea Vineyard. It reveals a mineral-dominated bouquet that is reminiscent of a grand cru Chablis. A rich, full-bodied wine, it offers a lovely combination of honeyed tropical fruits, graceful acidity, and an exceptionally long finish. The wine is even more impressive at the back of the palate than in its attack. Drink this profound California Chardonnay over the next 5–7 years. The 1992 Chardonnay Vine Hill Road is a tightly structured, more acidic, closed Chardonnay. There is no question concerning its outstanding quality, as it is full bodied, with layers of fruit. It offers a touch of oak and a long finish. The big, powerful, rich 1992 Chardonnay Kistler Vineyard displays stunning breadth and length. It could easily be confused with a grand cru Chassagne-Montrachet. With a spicy, honeyed, grilled nut element, spectacular layers of fruit, and an unctuous texture, this blockbuster, impeccably well-balanced Chardonnay should be drunk over the next 5–6 years. Lastly, there are 500 cases of Kistler's 1992 Chardonnay Cuvée Kathleen. It is what the French would call a *tête de cuvée*, or a selection of the finest barrels, and is meant to represent the essence of Kistler's style in the richest, most concentrated wine. As excellent as the other Kistler cuvées are, readers can imagine what opulence and intensity this wine possesses. It is a fabulously concentrated, honeyed style of Chardonnay with great balance and purity.

Kistler's 1991 Chardonnays are not as opulent and explosively rich as their 1990s. Nevertheless, they are delicious, multidimensional Chardonnays. One of the stars is the 1991 McCrea Vineyard, a light golden-colored, tightly knit, rich wine, with a spicy, vanillin, honey, buttery, apple-scented nose, and flavors that display impressive acid, integration, and balance. This wine should blossom with several more months of bottle age and last for 2–3 years.

The 1991 Kistler Durell–Sand Hill Vineyard is more elegant, with more mineral scents, and leaner, more austere flavors, as well as plenty of underlying depth to merit its lofty score. Ripe and rich, with a spicy finish, this wine needs several more months of bottle age and should last for 3–4 years.

The slightly deeper-colored 1991 Vine Hill Road Vineyard exhibits more alcohol and plenty of richness. Slightly chunkier, it offers a big, fleshy mouthful of interesting Chardonnay fruit. Drink it over the next several years.

The 1991 Kistler Estate Chardonnay exhibits the same smoky, buttery, hazelnut-scented nose as a great Chassagne-Montrachet or Meursault. Magnificently rich and unctuous, with full body and layers of fruit, this spectacular Chardonnay offers celestial pleasure. It should drink well for at least 4–5 years.

This winery is to be admired for its bevy of superb Chardonnays, but they are also Pinot Noir fanatics. Kistler continues to exhibit remarkable improvement with their Pinot Noir program. Both the 1992 and 1993 should propel this property's reputation for Pinot into the upper echelons of new world producers. The sensational 1993 Cuvée Catherine possesses a smoky, sweet, earthy, black fruit character reminiscent of a top premier or grand cru from Vosne-Romanée. In the mouth the wine displays exquisite richness and ripeness, a fleshy, voluptuous texture, and a stunning finish. It should drink well for 7–8 years. It is clearly one of the finest Pinot Noirs I have tasted from California. The 1992 Cuvée Catherine offers a super burgundianlike nose of red and black fruits, herbs, spices, and toast. Expansive, full, and rich, without any heaviness, this is a beautifully proportioned, seductive Pinot for drinking over the next 5–6 years. Just under 200 cases of this exquisite 1991 Pinot Noir were produced. A beautifully made Pinot Noir, it captures all of the elegant, ethereal elements of this fickle grape. The color is deep ruby and the nose offers up floral, berry, herb, and spice notes. In the mouth the secret of Pinot Noir is admirably revealed—the wine is rich and expansive, with hefty alcohol, but the impression is one of subtleness and lightness. The type of Pinot Noir that must send chills up the spines of top burgundy estates, it displays what extraordinary progress many California wineries have made with this difficult grape. As with any top-notch Pinot Noir, it can be drunk now or cellared for 7–10 years.

After tasting through the 1994 Chardonnays still in barrel (they are scheduled for release in spring 1997), it is obvious that this is another stunning vintage for Kistler. All the Chardonnays, which spend time in small French oak barrels of which 50% are new and 50% are 1 year old, are bottled with minimal clarification, in many cases with no fining or filtration. In 1994, Kistler produced 300 cases of a new Chardonnay from the highly renowned Carneros vineyard called Hudson, which is planted with an old Wente clone of Chardonnay. Look for another spectacular, age-worthy, rich, powerful Chardonnay.

There are also several new Pinot Noirs from this winery that has finally abandoned its Cabernet Sauvignon in favor of Pinot. Vine Hill is the home vineyard, the Camp Meeting Ridge is on the Sonoma Coast, and the Hirsch Vineyard is a cooler climate coastal vineyard that has produced a powerful, rich Pinot Noir. These wines appear to be among the finest Pinot Noirs being produced in California. They are worthy rivals to just about anything produced in Burgundy.

All things considered, this winery is in that special "zone," producing exceptionally high-quality wines in a low-profile, humble manner. Kudos to Kistler!

Ratings for Older Vintages of Kistler's Chardonnay Durell–Sand Hill Vineyard: 1990 (92)
Ratings for Older Vintages of Kistler's Chardonnay Dutton Ranch: 1991 (87), 1990 (90)
Ratings for Older Vintages of Kistler's Chardonnay Kistler Estate: 1990 (95)
Ratings for Older Vintages of Kistler's Chardonnay McCrea Vineyard: 1990 (91)
Ratings for Older Vintages of Kistler's Chardonnay Vine Hill Road Vineyard: 1990 (91)

KONRAD (AMADOR)
Barbera * * *

1992 Barbera   Amador   B   87

This excellent, deeply colored Barbera offers a straightforward nose of jammy ripe fruit, medium to full body, excellent concentration and purity, and a spicy, clean finish. Drink it over the next 5–6 years.

LA CREMA (SONOMA)

Chardonnay * * */* * * *, Chardonnay Reserve * * */* * * *

1992 Chardonnay	California	B	87
1992 Chardonnay Reserve	California	C	88

Two full-throttle, toasty, buttery, honeyed Chardonnays were produced by La Crema in 1992. The regular cuvée emphasizes the fruit aspects of this varietal, whereas the Reserve offers more toasty new oak and concentration. Both are full-bodied, excellent Chardonnays with lovely purity and overall balance. Readers should consume them over the next 8–12 months.

LA JOTA VINEYARD (NAPA)

Cabernet Franc * * * */* * * * *, Cabernet Sauvignon * * * */* * * * *, Cabernet Sauvignon Anniversary Cuvée * * * * *, Chardonnay * * * *, Little J* * *, Petite Sirah* * * * *, Pinot Noir* * *, Viognier* *

1993 Cabernet Franc	Howell Mountain	D	92
1992 Cabernet Franc	Howell Mountain	D	93
1991 Cabernet Franc	Howell Mountain	D	90
1990 Cabernet Franc	Howell Mountain	D	88+
1993 Cabernet Sauvignon	Howell Mountain	D	93
1992 Cabernet Sauvignon	Howell Mountain	D	93
1991 Cabernet Sauvignon	Howell Mountain	D	93
1990 Cabernet Sauvignon	Howell Mountain	D	92
1993 Cabernet Sauvignon 12th Anniversary	Howell Mountain	D	94
1992 Cabernet Sauvignon 11th Anniversary	Howell Mountain	D	98
1991 Cabernet Sauvignon 10th Anniversary	Howell Mountain	D	94+
1991 Chardonnay	Howell Mountain	D	93
N.V. Little J	Howell Mountain	B	86
1993 Petite Sirah	Napa	C	93
1992 Petite Sirah	Napa	C	90
1991 Petite Sirah	Howell Mountain	C	93
1993 Pinot Noir Hellenthal Vineyard	Sonoma	C	88
1993 Pinot Noir Quail Hill Vineyard	Russian River	C	86
1993 Viognier Barrel-Fermented	Howell Mountain	C	87
1993 Viognier Cold-Fermented	Howell Mountain	C	88

La Jota's 20 acres of vineyards situated high up on Howell Mountain behind the small village of Angwin have consistently proven to be a superb source for red wines, particularly Cabernet Sauvignon and Cabernet Franc. That production has been recently supplemented by a good Viognier, a frequently superb Petite Sirah (made from purchased grapes from

Dunn's Park-Muscatine Vineyard), and most recently an impressively rich Chardonnay and two Pinot Noirs from Sonoma.

Like a number of California's wineries, La Jota has had four great vintages in a row, not including 1994, a year that many are calling the vintage of the century for Napa Cabernet. The 1993s (which will not be released until early 1996) include a super 1993 Cabernet Franc. It reveals the fragrant, perfumed, menthol/cassis character of this varietal, supple, elegant, savory flavors, medium body, a gentle, gracious, layered, richly fruity taste, and a long, firm, well-delineated personality. It should drink well for 10–15 years. The 1993 Cabernet Sauvignon Howell Mountain Selection may prove to be superior to the excellent 1992 and 1991. It exhibits an opaque black/purple color and a huge nose of spicy oak, licorice, black raspberries, and black cherries. The wine possesses great density, richness, and ripeness, as well as a full-bodied, moderately tannic finish. The blockbuster 1993 Cabernet Sauvignon 12th Anniversary Release (of which there are only 1,500 cases produced) exhibits an opaque purple color, a promising bouquet of spring flowers, black fruits, earth, and vanillin, great intensity, full body, layers of rich, dense, highly extracted fruit, a supple, velvety texture, and a long, moderately tannic finish.

The just-released 1992s are stunning. The 1992 Cabernet Franc boasts a penetrating bouquet of jammy black cherries, flowers, and subtle notes of mint, and a soft, voluptuously textured, medium- to full-bodied palate. The wine is deliciously forward, already exhibiting surprising complexity, and is ideal for drinking now and over the next 12–15 years. It is one of the finest Cabernet Francs I have yet to taste from California. The 1992 Cabernet Sauvignon Howell Mountain Selection is a broad-shouldered, intensely flavored, full-bodied wine with gobs of black currant fruit gently infused with subtle new oak. It possesses the opulence and density of the 1992 vintage and can be drunk now or over the next 20 years. The 1992 Cabernet Sauvignon 11th Anniversary Release (the only Cabernet aged in 100% new oak) is a spectacular wine, among the greatest Cabernet Sauvignons I have recently tasted. The superb nose explodes from the glass, offering a decadent level of sweet black fruits, flowers, vanilla, and spice. Full bodied, sweeter, and more expansive and chewy than the other cuvées, this lavishly rich, beautifully balanced, pure Cabernet Sauvignon can be drunk early in its life, but it promises to last for 20–25 years. It is a tour de force in winemaking! Frugal shoppers wanting a super bargain should check out Little J, a nonvintage blend of Cabernet Sauvignon from the 1992 and 1993 harvests. About 1,200 cases are made of this wonderfully ripe, exuberant, fleshy, full-bodied Cabernet. Although it lacks complexity, it compensates for that deficiency with its juicy, succulent fruitiness. It should drink well for 5–8 years and is certainly one of the best values in the Cabernet Sauvignon marketplace.

As I already stated, La Jota is buying grapes from the Park-Muscatine Vineyard on Howell Mountain that is now owned by Randy Dunn. From these purchased grapes La Jota fashions an intensely flavored Petite Sirah. The 1991 was one of the finest California Petite Sirahs I have tasted, and the 1992, while slightly less prodigious, is still an impressively endowed, black/purple-colored wine with a sweet nose of jammy black fruits and earth. It is full bodied and velvety textured, with tremendous fruit extraction and depth. Drinkable now, the wine's aging potential is 20+ years. The 1993 Petite Sirah may rival the spectacular 1991. The 1993 exhibits a black/purple color and a promising nose of black raspberries, plums, spice, and oak. Dense, full bodied, and chewy, with moderate tannin and a sweetness and expansiveness that suggest very old vines and low yields, it is a wine to search out when it is released next year.

In 1993 La Jota produced 100 cases of two single-vineyard Pinot Noirs. They are competent first efforts. Given the fact that the well-known Helen Turley of Marcassin and Turley Cellars has been consulting at La Jota, I expect more interesting Pinots to emerge. The 1993 Pinot Noir Quail Hill Vineyard, from the Russian River, exhibits medium ruby color, an attractive sweet, herbal, minty nose, tasty, medium-bodied flavors with good ripeness, fleshy fruit, and a spicy finish. This forward wine should be drunk over the next 2–3 years. More complex and enticing is the 1993 Pinot Noir from the Hellenthal Vineyard on the cool, windswept Sonoma coast. The wine displays an attractive earthy, black fruit–scented nose, wonderfully sweet, expansive, full-bodied flavors, delicious notes of black cherries, spices, and herbs, and a long finish. It is close to being outstanding. Drink it over the next 3–4 years.

La Jota's three 1991 red wine offerings are all noteworthy. This winery has established a reliable track record for high-quality Cabernet Franc. Based on past vintages, I would not be surprised to see the 1991 Cabernet Franc put on weight and merit an outstanding score with another 2–4 years of bottle age. It exhibits an attractive cedary-, plum-, cassis-, and herb-scented nose, dense, ripe, medium- to full-bodied flavors, soft tannin, an easygoing acidity level, and a long, lush, opulent finish. Although appealing to drink now, it will last 15–20 years. The two 1991 Cabernet Sauvignons are 4–6 years away from enjoyable drinking. The 1991 Howell Mountain Cabernet Sauvignon is a dense, full-bodied bruiser of a wine, with an opaque color, and a promising but restrained bouquet of minerals, smoke, and black currants. Full bodied, rich, and intense, as well as tannic and backward, it is a wine made for the long term rather than for immediate drinkability. The 1991 Cabernet Sauvignon 10th Anniversary Release reveals a similar character, with richer fruit, and more sweetness and intensity on the palate. However, the tannin level is frightfully high, making this wine a candidate for drinking between 2000 and 2025. Both of these are immensely impressive Cabernet Sauvignons.

La Jota fashioned a magnificent 1991 Petite Sirah from old vines on Howell Mountain. A spectacular wine, it is the equivalent of the dazzling Petite Sirahs made by Ridge from their York Creek and Devil's Hill vineyards. An opaque black/purple color is followed by a spectacular nose of jammy cassis and minerals. The wine exhibits layers of sweet black raspberry fruit, huge body, soft tannin, and a finish that must last for over a minute. There is remarkable purity and balance for a wine of this stature. Although young and unevolved, it makes for an impressive mouthful of Petite Sirah. It should keep for at least 2 decades. Only 200 cases were made.

The 1990 Cabernet Sauvignon Howell Mountain is typically backward, tannic, full bodied, and concentrated, but 6–7 years away from accessible drinkability. The color is opaque garnet/purple, and the nose is tight but promising, with scents of minerals, cassis, and spices. Rich and concentrated, as well as ferociously tannic (the tannin is ripe rather than astringent), this promising wine should reach its apogee by the turn of the century and last 20 or more years. The 1990 Cabernet Franc Howell Mountain reveals an intense dark ruby/purple color, a spicy, menthol/cassis-scented nose, medium- to full-bodied, tannic flavors, and impressive concentration and length. It needs 4–5 years of cellaring.

La Jota has been experimenting with different methods of vinifying Viognier. These wines have not been as impressive as the property's red wines, but readers who come across any of the limited quantities of these wines (only 300 cases of each are produced) may find it interesting to compare the 1993 Viognier Cold-Fermented with the 1993 Barrel-Fermented. Although similar, I prefer the Cold-Fermented since the exotic honeysuckle, intensely perfumed quality of Viognier is more well defined. Both wines are medium to full bodied, with good ripeness, concentration, and fruit. The 1993 Viognier Barrel-Fermented exhibits some noticeable oak and comes across as slightly more structured and less dramatic than the Cold-Fermented. Both wines should be drunk over the next 1–2 years.

I am delighted to see that La Jota has added a Chardonnay to its impressive portfolio of wines. The 1991 Chardonnay offers an intense bouquet of spicy oak combined with rich, honeyed, floral, fruity aromas, superb depth, full body, fine acidity, a sense of balance, and a long, rich, concentrated finish. It should drink well for 1–3 years.

LAKE SONOMA (SONOMA)
Zinfandel Old Vine Reserve * * */* * * *

1992 Zinfandel Old Vine Reserve	Dry Creek	B	88

The muscular, dark ruby/purple-colored 1992 Zinfandel Old Vine Reserve exhibits excellent ripeness and depth of fruit. Rich, expansive, and chewy, the peppery, black cherry and black raspberry side of Zinfandel is well displayed. There is excellent purity and an overall sense of balance to this big, full-bodied wine. Drink it over the next 10–12 years.

LAKEWOOD (CLEAR LAKE)
Sauvignon Blanc * * *, Semillon * * *

1993 Sauvignon Blanc	Clear Lake	A	85
1993 Semillon	Clear Lake	A	86

Lakewood's light-bodied, pungently aromatic 1993 Sauvignon Blanc is a fresh, lively wine with good varietal character and a crisp finish. Drink it over the next 8–12 months. The fuller, more honeyed, boldly styled, dry 1993 Semillon possesses chewy fruit and finishes with enough acidity to provide focus and crispness. Both of these offerings are excellent values. For the record, Lakewood's other current release, the 1992 Chevriot (a 50/50 Sauvignon/Semillon blend), tastes too overtly woody.

LAMBORN FAMILY VINEYARD (NAPA)
Zinfandel * * * *

1991 Zinfandel Phoenix Vintage Howell Mountain	Napa	C	86+
1992 Zinfandel Pre-Nuptial Howell Mountain	Napa	C	86

Lamborn Family's Zinfandel is a tough-textured, tannic, backward style of wine, making early assessment potentially scurrilous. A touch of elegance accompanies the medium ruby color and hints of rich, tasty fruit in the 1992 Zinfandel Pre-Nuptial cuvée. Medium bodied, with high acidity and ferociously high tannin, this wine needs 3–4 years of cellaring. Will it dry out before the fruit emerges? Cut from the same mold, the 1991 Phoenix Vintage is an unevolved, tannic, compact wine that needs 4–5 years of cellaring. There is attractive ripe, pure, black cherry and black raspberry fruit lurking beneath the acidity and tannin, and the finish is longer and more persuasive than in the 1992. If it blossoms after cellaring, my rating will look stingy.

LANDMARK VINEYARDS (SONOMA)
Chardonnay Cuvées * * *

1993 Chardonnay Damaris Reserve	Alexander Valley	C	88
1992 Chardonnay Damaris Reserve	Alexander Valley	C	87
1993 Chardonnay Overlook	Sonoma	B	88
1992 Chardonnay Overlook	Sonoma	B	86

The 1993 Chardonnays are both full bodied, powerful, richly flavored wines exhibiting layers of fruit, a judicious use of oak, and heady, rich finishes. The 1993 Chardonnay Damaris Reserve is fatter and more unctuous than the Overlook cuvée, but both are impressive examples of their varietal. Drink them over the next year.

The two lovely 1992 Chardonnays exhibit a judicious use of spicy oak, fine ripeness, full body, and tasty personalities. The 1992 Chardonnay Overlook is lighter, whereas the 1992 Chardonnay Damaris Reserve offers more fat and intensity. Drink both wines over the next 12 months. A third 1992 Chardonnay from the Two Williams Vineyard in Sonoma was forbiddingly tough, hard, and much less charming than the above two offerings.

LAUREL GLEN (SONOMA)
Cabernet Sauvignon* * * * *, Counterpoint* * *, Terra Rosa* * * *

1992 Cabernet Sauvignon	Sonoma	D	95
1991 Cabernet Sauvignon	Sonoma	D	93
1990 Cabernet Sauvignon	Sonoma	D	95
1991 Counterpoint	Sonoma	C	88
1991 Terra Rosa	Sonoma	A	88
1990 Terra Rosa	Sonoma	A	88

Another dazzling effort from Patrick Campbell, the gorgeously opulent, voluptuously tex-tured, superconcentrated 1992 Cabernet Sauvignon exhibits an enticingly complex bouquet of chocolate, cedar, herbs, cassis, and damp, woodsy aromas. Full bodied, with the sweet, juicy, succulent fruit that is the vintage's trademark, this wine possesses low enough acidity and sweet enough tannin to be approachable young, but it should keep for 2 decades. The 1991 Cabernet Sauvignon reveals an opaque dark ruby color as well as a huge nose with aromas reminiscent of leg of lamb cooked over a wood fire and doused with Provençal herbs. The gorgeous, big, meaty, herbaceous, sweet black fruit aromas and flavors are followed by superripe, rich, luxurious flavors. There is plenty of tannin to provide the framework, and the result is one of the most impressive wines I have yet to taste from this superb estate. The 1990 Cabernet Sauvignon exhibits a spectacular nose of smoky cassis, herbs, and sweet leathery, meaty aromas. Unctuous and flattering, this full-bodied, multidimensional, gorgeously put together wine should be approachable young but will last for 15–20 years.

Shrewd buyers have been searching out Laurel Glen's Terra Rosa for the last several years. And why not? The winery's Cabernet Sauvignon is on strict allocation and costs $30 or more a bottle. At $10 a bottle, the 1991 Terra Rosa is one of the best buys in the marketplace. Its terrific nose of Provençal herbs, black cherries, and cassis is followed by a deep, concentrated, supple wine that is all a dry, rich, complex red wine should be. Quality such as this normally costs $25–$50 a bottle. Buy it by the case and enjoy it over the next 4–6 years. Laurel Glen's 1991 Counterpoint exhibits a dark, opaque color, a big, herbaceous, chocolaty, cassis-scented nose, thick, rich, medium- to full-bodied flavors, and a long, lusty finish. It should drink well for up to a decade.

The 1990 Terra Rosa offers a huge nose of cedar, olives, and dusty black currant fruit, a rich, sweet, expansive palate, and a long, lush finish. It should drink well for the next 5–6 years.

Ratings for Older Vintages of Laurel Glen's Cabernet Sauvignon: 1988 (90), 1987 (91), 1986 (90), 1985 (92), 1984 (90), 1982 (73), 1981 (90)

LIBERTY SCHOOL (CAYMUS-NAPA)
Cabernet Sauvignon* * *, California White Wine* * *, Sauvignon Blanc* *

1991 Cabernet Sauvignon	Paso Robles	A	87

A terrific bargain among current Cabernet Sauvignon releases, this dark ruby/purple-colored wine possesses loads of cassis fruit in the bouquet, a rich, lush, silky-textured feel, and copious amounts of ripe, lusty fruit. Drink it over the next 4–5 years.

LIMERICK LANE CELLARS (SONOMA)
Zinfandel* * * *

1991 Zinfandel	Russian River	B	90
1992 Zinfandel Collin's Vineyard	Russian River	B	90

Limerick Lane's Zinfandel Collin's Vineyard is one of the stars of the 1992 Zinfandel vintage. From its terrific nose of jammy black cherries, herbs, spices, and pepper to its explosively rich flavors of black raspberries and black cherries, this succulent, full-bodied wine is a knockout. Layers of supple, chewy fruit, full body, and that wonderful sweet expansiveness that comes from glycerin and high alcohol make this creamy-textured, decadently styled, dry Zinfandel a star. It should drink well for 8–10 years. Although limited in availability, it is a must-purchase for Zinfandel fanatics!

The exceptional 1991 Zinfandel is loaded with spicy, peppery, black cherry and raspberry fruit. Medium to full bodied, with excellent depth as well as brilliant focus to its flavors, this sumptuously styled, focused, delicious Zinfandel has the potential to last for 7–8 years.

J. LOHR WINERY (SANTA CLARA)

Cabernet Sauvignon Cypress*, Cabernet Sauvignon Reserve* * *, Cabernet Sauvignon VS-1 * * *, Chardonnay Cypress* */* * *, Chardonnay Riverstone* * *, Gamay* * *, Johannisberg Riesling* * *, Merlot Cypress*

1990 Cabernet Sauvignon VS-1	Paso Robles	C	86
1992 Chardonnay Riverstone	Monterey	B	86
1993 Johannisberg Riesling Bay Mist	Monterey	A	86

The 1990 Cabernet Sauvignon VS-1 is a straightforward, well-made, medium-bodied Cabernet with enough cassis fruit and character to merit a recommendation. The wine borders on being too lean, but some sweet fruit comes through on the palate. Drink it over the next 5–6 years.

The fleshy, full-bodied, mouth-filling 1992 Chardonnay Riverstone offers lovely freshness, an exuberant personality, and a spicy finish. Woodsy notes are present, but they are not overwhelming. Drink it over the next year. The Kabinett-style, off-dry 1993 Johannisberg Riesling Bay Mist is loaded with fruit and displays an excellent penetrating fragrance of flowers, apples, and underripe peaches. Fruity, with the necessary acidity to balance out the small amount of residual sugar, as well as a long, crisp, authoritative finish, this is a delectable Riesling for drinking over the next year.

LONG VINEYARDS (NAPA)

Cabernet Sauvignon* * *, Chardonnay* * * *

1992 Cabernet Sauvignon	Napa	D	87

The 1992 Cabernet Sauvignon exhibits excellent color, a ripe, fat personality with plenty of chewy cassis fruit, a touch of herbs, and noticeable tannin in the finish. At present, it lacks delineation, but that will undoubtedly develop with bottle age. Very good, it should have 15 years of life ahead of it.

LONGORIA (SANTA BARBARA)

Cabernet Franc* * *, Cabernet Sauvignon* * *, Chardonnay* * * *, Merlot* * *, Pinot Noir* * * *

1990 Cabernet Franc	Santa Ynez	C	85
1990 Cabernet Sauvignon	Santa Ynez	C	87
1992 Chardonnay	Santa Barbara	C	91
1990 Merlot	Santa Ynez	C	87
1989 Pinot Noir Benedict Vineyard	Santa Ynez	D	88

Rick Longoria, the winemaker for Gainey Vineyards, has been turning out many admirable wines under his own label. There are 85 cases of the 1990 Cabernet Franc, 440 cases of the

1990 Merlot, and 105 cases of the 1990 Cabernet Sauvignon. All are well-made wines. The 1990 Cabernet Franc is the lightest of this trio, with a clean, classy, herbaceous, berry-scented nose, medium-bodied, crisp flavors, and a pleasant aromatic dimension. Drink it over the next 4–5 years. The soft, seductive 1990 Merlot offers an attractive berry-scented nose, spicy, peppery, cherry, and herblike fruit flavors, a soft, supple texture, and a moderately long, smooth, silky finish. It too should be drunk over the next 4–5 years. Although supple, the 1990 Cabernet Sauvignon is not as evolved or as immediately flattering as the Merlot, but it is well made, with medium body, moderate tannins, and an adequate finish. The powerful, dense, backward 1989 Pinot Noir Benedict Vineyard will benefit from another 1–2 years of bottle age. It offers a dense, deep, plum/ruby/purple color, and a tight yet promising bouquet of spices, earth, and black cherries. Rich and full bodied, with its tannins concealing the rich fruit, this should be an uncommonly long-lived Pinot Noir. Unfortunately, only 160 cases were produced, so this wine is available only in the California marketplace.

The 1992 is a superb example of Santa Barbara Chardonnay. It exhibits a honeyed, tropical fruit–scented nose with well-integrated, toasty oak. Full bodied, crisp, and pure, with layers of flavor, this intense, brilliantly made wine should drink well for 2–3 years. Bravo!

MAACAMA CREEK (SONOMA)
Cabernet Sauvignon Melim Vineyard * * *

1991 Cabernet Sauvignon Melim Vineyard Reserve	Alexander Valley	B	87

Looking for a 1991 Cabernet Sauvignon that can be drunk now or aged for 7–8 years? This supple, richly fruity, excellent Cabernet from the low-profile producer, Maacama Creek, is a noteworthy offering. The wine reveals good ripeness, fine roundness, and plenty of length. Drink it over the next 7–8 years.

MADRONE (EL DORADO)
Cabernet Franc * * *, Cabernet Sauvignon * * *, Quintet Reserve Red Table Wine * * *,
Shiraz/Cabernet * * *

1992 Cabernet Franc	El Dorado	B	85
1991 Cabernet Sauvignon	El Dorado	B	86
1992 Quintet Reserve Red Table Wine	El Dorado	B	87
1993 Shiraz/Cabernet	El Dorado	A	86

These fairly priced wines are attractive, well-made bargains. The 1992 Cabernet Franc will not compete with the likes of La Jota, but it is a medium ruby-colored, spicy, fragrant wine with medium body, pure fruit, and an easygoing finish. Drink it over the next 4–5 years. The dark ruby-colored 1993 Shiraz/Cabernet (70% Shiraz/30% Cabernet Franc) offers attractive, supple fruit, a spicy, berry-scented nose, fine ripeness, medium body, and a smooth finish. It is ideal for drinking over the next 3–4 years. It is a noteworthy value.

The dark ruby-colored 1991 Cabernet Sauvignon possesses a straightforward, ripe cassis nose, medium to full body, light tannin, and a rich, harmonious palate. Drink it over the next 5–7 years. The finest of these offerings is the 1992 Quintet (a 53% Cabernet Sauvignon, 22% Merlot, 20% Cabernet Franc, 4% Petite Verdot, and 1% Malbec blend). It exhibits ripe, curranty fruit, a St.-Émilion–like personality in its elegance and medium-bodied style, fresh acidity, rich, spicy fruit, a nice touch of oak, and an authoritative finish. It should drink well for 7–8 years.

MARA (SONOMA)
Zinfandel * * *

1992 Zinfandel Unfined/Unfiltered	Alexander Valley	B	86

A straightforward, chunky Zinfandel, with loads of spicy, peppery, black cherry fruit, medium body, fine concentration, and a soft finish, this 1992 should be drunk over the next 4–5 years.

MARCASSIN (SONOMA)
Chardonnay Hudson Vineyard * * * * *, Chardonnay Lorenzo Vineyard * * * * *, Chardonnay Upper Barn Gauer Vineyard * * * * *

1994 Chardonnay Hudson Vineyard	Carneros	D	96
1993 Chardonnay Hudson Vineyard	Carneros	D	96
1993 Chardonnay Lorenzo Vineyard	Sonoma	D	94
1992 Chardonnay Lorenzo Vineyard	Sonoma	D	93
1994 Chardonnay Upper Barn Gauer Vineyard	Sonoma	D	97
1993 Chardonnay Upper Barn Gauer Vineyard	Sonoma	D	97
1992 Chardonnay Upper Barn Gauer Vineyard	Sonoma	D	97

Fortunately for wine consumers and for the stature of California wines, there has been increasing focus on the philosophy of winemaker/proprietor Helen Turley and her husband, John Wetlaufer. Ms. Turley, a strong-minded, immensely talented woman who began her career at Robert Mondavi, is a leading consultant for some of the finest wineries in California. Her noninterventionist winemaking philosophy, which eschews any type of processing in favor of wild yeasts, no acidification, and no fining or filtration, has produced prodigious wines. She also deserves credit for her positive influence on a younger generation of winemakers who are increasingly dedicated to capturing the full character of the vineyard and the grape varietal. She is the antithesis of the industrial, food-processor mentality embraced by technicians at the University of California at Davis that has dominated California winemaking. With Ms. Turley and her husband, as well as the growing number of similarly minded peers, rests the hope for what I see as a splendid golden age for California wine.

Turley's production of Marcassin's three Chardonnays soars to a whopping 500 cases in 1993! However, do not expect to see one bottle on a retailer's shelf. All of it is sold via a private mailing list. Readers who want to latch on to a few bottles of some of the world's greatest Chardonnay should get on this list. Furthermore, your check should be in the mail within 10 minutes of receipt of their offer, preferably by Federal Express. All of the following wines were scheduled to be released in April 1995.

After what Helen Turley and John Wetlaufer achieved with their Chardonnays in 1991 and 1992, it is hard to believe their 1993s could be any more profound. But they are. The 1993 Chardonnay Upper Barn Gauer Vineyard reveals an extraordinary bouquet of honeyed fruit, floral (acacia?) notes, and well-integrated, toasty oak. The wine is layered with enormous richness, yet there is no heaviness or dullness. It offers sharply focused, full-bodied, powerful, yet compellingly complex flavors. The wine's finish is marvelous. A product of a wild yeast fermentation, minimal racking, and natural bottling without filtration, this is an extraordinary expression of Chardonnay that should drink well for at least 5–7 years. The 1993 Chardonnay Lorenzo Vineyard from the Sonoma Coast is a more mineral-dominated wine with a tightly focused personality. Although immensely concentrated and rich, it is not as forthcoming and ostentatious as the Gauer Vineyard. With the wine's layers of flavor, purity, extraordinary natural mouth-feel, and sumptuous finish, it also belongs in the same class as a handful of the world's greatest Chardonnays. It should age well for up to a decade. The 1993 Chardonnay from the Hudson Vineyard (Marcassin's smallest production) may ultimately turn out to be this property's finest wine. Although backward, it exhibits an amazingly textured, chewy, honey and buttery fruit character, extraordinary purity, a promising yet unevolved aromatic profile, and an inner core of concentration. Drinking this wine is akin to biting into a cream puff crammed with heavenly goodies. All of these wines are put through complete malolactic fermentation, are totally dry, and are bottled unfiltered.

With respect to the 1992s, the 1992 Chardonnay Upper Barn Gauer Vineyard exhibits a spectacular bouquet of honeyed fruit, roasted hazelnuts, full-bodied, opulently rich, chewy flavors, fabulous purity and delineation, and a finish that lasts for almost a full minute. The new oak is brilliantly integrated, and the overall impression is one of extraordinary richness and expansiveness, without any heaviness. This profound Chardonnay should drink well for 5 years. The 1992 Chardonnay Lorenzo Vineyard offers more crisp, mineral, and tropical fruit scents, as well as rich, voluptuously textured flavors, admirable underlying acidity, and layers of fruit—all attributable to low yields and natural winemaking. These wines spend nearly a year on their lees and are then bottled with minimal racking, no filtration, and little or no fining.

Marcassin also produced a microscopic quantity of 1992 Chardonnay from the Hudson Vineyard. It may be the richest of all the 1992 Marcassins, with an exceptional aromatic and flavor profile. I only tasted it once, rating it a show-stopping 97.

The two cuvées of 1994 Marcassin Chardonnay I tasted reveal further evidence of what a genius and legacy Helen Turley and her husband John Wetlaufer have achieved. The 1994 Upper Barn Gauer Vineyard Chardonnay reveals a sweet, leeslike, honeyed richness, an exceptional texture, thick fruit, and a full-bodied, concentrated finish with good integrated acidity and subtle oak. This exquisite Chardonnay should drink well for 5–6 years. The 1994 Hudson Vineyard Chardonnay appears to be another legend in the making. A fabulously concentrated, complex, multidimensional, layered wine oozing with flavor, it will embarrass many a Burgundy grand cru. It is concentrated, complex, and compelling. In blind tastings where I have placed Marcassin against the very best Burgundy produces, the Marcassin wines have exhibited aromatic and flavor superiority. The sweetness of fruit, complexity, and ability of these wines to express extraordinary richness without heaviness are mind-boggling. The Hudson Vineyard should drink well for 5–8 years.

Those readers who continue to believe that only the Côte d'Or can produce world-class Chardonnays should consider the following. In a recent blind tasting that included Marcassin's 1992 Upper Barn Chardonnay, and several great vintages of Montrachet, Chevalier-Montrachet, and Bâtard-Montrachet from Domaine Leflaive, Michel Niellon, and Louis Latour, France's finest taster, Michel Bettane, confirmed what I had already come to believe: Marcassin is producing wines that are superior to France's grands crus. Hard to believe, but true!

Ratings for Older Vintages of Marcassin's Chardonnay Upper Barn Gauer Vineyard: 1991 (95)

Ratings for Older Vintages of Marcassin's Chardonnay Lorenzo Vineyard: 1990 (94)

MARIAH VINEYARDS (MENDOCINO)
Zinfandel * * */* * * *

1992 Zinfandel   Mendocino C 88

This full-bodied, muscular, alcoholic Zinfandel is loaded with cherry and raspberry fruit, has gorgeous purity and balance and a silky-smooth texture. It will make many friends among Zinfandel advocates. Drink it over the next 4–5 years.

MARIETTA CELLARS (SONOMA)

Cabernet Sauvignon* * * *, Old Vine Red* * * *, Petite Sirah* * *, Zinfandel* * * *

1992	Cabernet Sauvignon	Sonoma	B	89+
1991	Cabernet Sauvignon	Sonoma	B	89
1990	Cabernet Sauvignon	Sonoma	B	92
N.V.	Old Vine Lot 14	Sonoma	A	90
N.V.	Old Vine Lot 13	Sonoma	A	87
N.V.	Old Vine Lot 12	Sonoma	A	88
1990	Petite Sirah	Sonoma	B	89
1992	Zinfandel	Sonoma	B	90
1991	Zinfandel	Sonoma	A	88
1990	Zinfandel	Sonoma	A	90

Marietta Cellars' N.V. Old Vine red wine is unquestionably one of the finest bargains in the red wine marketplace. It is generally made from two-thirds Zinfandel and the rest a blend of Petite Sirah, Carignane, Grenache, and who knows what. There are abundant quantities (12,000 cases) of Lot 14, composed of 58% Zinfandel, 34% Petite Sirah, and the remainder Gamay and Carignane, but this wine jumps off retailers' shelves as quickly as it arrives. And why shouldn't it? This dark ruby/purple-colored wine possesses a stunning nose of black fruits (plums, cassis, and cherries), medium to full body, terrific richness, a supple, chewy, fleshy texture, and a long, ripe, heady finish. A mouth-filling, gutsy, exceptionally well-made red wine, it is an *amazing value!* Moreover, this satiny smooth wine is capable of lasting for 7–8 years. The Lot 13 is a sumptuously rich, spicy, peppery, berry-scented wine with full body, a wonderful, succulent texture, and copious amounts of juicy fruit. While supple, it should drink well for 4–5 years. The Lot 12 is a robust, mouth-filling, bargain-priced, husky red wine.

The 1992 Cabernet Sauvignon (a 92% Cabernet Sauvignon, 5% Merlot, 3% Cabernet Franc blend, of which there are 1,200 cases) requires 1–3 years to shed its tannin. It reveals a dense, saturated, ruby/purple color, and a tight but promising nose of pure, sweet, jammy black currants, oak, and spices. Full-bodied, high-quality, pure, beautifully extracted, layered fruit is balanced by hefty tannin and low acidity. Made in a style similar to the tight, structured 1991, this husky, rich Cabernet is not as open as the opulent 1990. It should keep for 12–15+ years. Kudos to Marietta Cellars for offering reasonably priced thrills to wine consumers! The 1991 Cabernet Sauvignon is nearly opaque in color. More backward and less flattering than the 1990, it is loaded with ripe cassis fruit. This is a full-bodied wine that offers superb value as well as 10–15 years of aging potential. Marietta's 1990 Cabernet Sauvignon from Sonoma exhibits a saturated black/purple color, as well as a huge nose of jammy cassis, flowers, and spices. Full bodied, with nearly viscous, superpure, gorgeously rich flavors that are well endowed with glycerin and a lusty, impressive finish, this great California Cabernet Sauvignon merits buying by the case. It should drink well for another 10–15 years. Unfortunately, just under 1,400 cases were produced, so availability is limited. An exceptional value!

The black/purple color of the 1990 Petite Sirah suggests a massively extracted wine. The nose reluctantly offers up aromas of earth, licorice, and black fruits. Ripe and full bodied, with moderate tannin and low acidity, this big, chewy, robust wine should drink well for 10–15+ years.

Marietta Cellars' 1992 Zinfandel (approximately 1,600 cases produced) is a superb example of the vintage. A decadently styled Zinfandel, it boasts a huge, ostentatious nose of pepper and black fruits, with a touch of flowers and earth for complexity. A mouth-filling wine with high levels of extract, glycerin, alcohol, and wonderfully lush fruit, this dense yet well-balanced Zinfandel should drink well for 6–8 years. Ooooeee! The 1991 Zinfandel is all juicy, peppery, black raspberry fruit. Full bodied, soft, and rich, this velvety-textured wine is ideal for drinking over the next 5–7 years. Marietta has produced an uncommonly rich, flamboyant 1990 Zinfandel. There are plenty of good values in Zinfandel, but it is still hard to find a spectacularly rich, fragrant, black raspberry–scented, full-bodied, unctuously textured Zinfandel of this quality for $10. It should drink well for 6–7 years.

MARKHAM WINERY (NAPA)
Cabernet Sauvignon* *, Chardonnay* *, Merlot* *

1990 Cabernet Sauvignon	Napa	C	87

The 1990 is the best Cabernet Sauvignon Markham has produced. Fine deep ruby/purple color is followed by a wine with an attractive spicy, cassis, herbal, tasty nose, medium- to full-bodied, elegant flavors, admirable depth, unobtrusive tannin and acidity, and a spicy finish. Drink it over the next 10–12 years.

MARTINELLI (SONOMA)
Pinot Noir* * * *, Zinfandel Jackass Hill* * * * *, Zinfandel Jackass Vineyard* * * *

1994 Pinot Noir	Russian River	B	89
1993 Pinot Noir	Russian River	B	87
1994 Zinfandel Jackass Hill	Russian River	C	95
1993 Zinfandel Jackass Hill	Russian River	C	94
1994 Zinfandel Jackass Vineyard	Russian River	C	91
1993 Zinfandel Jackass Vineyard	Russian River	C	89

The Martinelli family has been growing grapes in Sonoma's Russian River valley for nearly 100 years. Since the late eighties, small quantities of wine, particularly Zinfandel, Chardonnay, Pinot Noir, and occasionally Gewürztraminer, have been produced. Some of their fruit has become famous in the hands of other producers, particularly their Jackass Hill Zinfandel, which the small, high-quality Somona winery of Williams-Selyem purchased. Additionally, Martinelli's Gewürztraminer has been translated into the finest Gewürztraminers in America by their nearby neighbor, Z. Moore. Since 1993, under the guidance of consultant Helen Turley and winemaker Steve Martinelli, quality has soared, and grapes that used to be sold to other wineries are going into Martinelli's own estate-bottled wines—something that should thrill most consumers.

Martinelli's Zinfandel include wines from the Jackass vineyard and the famed Jackass Hill vineyard, which is a 3-acre, nonterraced vineyard that is supposedly the steepest head-pruned Zinfandel vineyard in California. The vines, planted in 1905, produce extraordinarily intense Zinfandel flavors that are captured perfectly in this limited-production Zinfandel bottling that achieves nearly 15% alcohol, and is completely dry! The two 1993 Zinfandels, of which there are 400 cases of the Jackass Vineyard and 375 cases of the Jackass Hill, are sensational wines by any standard of measurement. The 1993 Zinfandel Jackass Vineyard displays an opaque ruby/purple color, a huge, dramatic, fragrant nose of Asian spices, black and red fruits, minerals, and oak. It possesses great richness, full body, a velvety-textured, rich, inner core of fruit, and a long, heady finish that lasts more than a minute. This is not a light, innocuous Zinfandel (the alcohol is 15.3%). It is dry, pure, and amazingly well balanced. Drink it over the next 8–10 years. Remarkably, the 1993 Zinfandel Jackass Hill is a leading candidate for Zinfandel of the vintage. The opaque black/purple color is followed by a sensational nose of raspberry ice cream/candy that envelops the taster. The wine hits the palate with a glorious cascade of red and black fruits, an unctuous texture, and layer upon layer of rich, well-balanced, ripe fruit. This full-bodied, astonishingly concentrated Zinfandel should drink well for 10–12 years.

The 1994 Jackass Vineyard Zinfandel is even richer, with full body, gorgeous levels of sweet Zinfandel fruit, a real opulence to its voluptous texture, and remarkable intensity. The 1994 Jackass Hill Zinfandel is a huge, massive, well-balanced wine that is one of the most thrilling Zinfandels I have ever tasted. It should drink well for 10–12 years. These are some of the greatest Zinfandels made in California!

The two Pinot Noir offerings are fermented with wild yeasts and aged in small French oak barrels, of which 66% are new. Both wines exhibit a Domaine Dujac–like roundness, perfume, and up-front, precocious, evolved complexity. While less intense than the more expansive, more opulent, 1994, the 1993 Pinot Noir is a delicious, richly fruity, sweet-tasting wine with gobs of berry, herb, and spicy aromas and flavors, a chewy mid-palate, and a soft, velvety finish. Unfortunately, only 175 cases were produced. The 1994 Pinot Noir reveals more fruit intensity, as well as a more voluptous, layered texture. The wine offers beautiful, herb, smoke, and cherry fruit, medium to full body, and a satiny smooth finish. It should drink well for 3–4 years. Both wines are bottled without fining and filtration. There are approximately 400 cases of this lovely Pinot Noir.

LOUIS M. MARTINI (NAPA)

Cabernet Sauvignon * *, Cabernet Sauvignon Monte Rosso * */* * *, Chardonnay * */* * *,
Pinot Noir *, Sauvignon Blanc * *, Zinfandel * *

1990 Cabernet Sauvignon Monte Rosso Vineyard	Sonoma	C	86

Louis Martini, a perennial underachiever, has fashioned an attractive 1990 Cabernet Sauvignon from its Monte Rosso vineyard. The fact that the wine actually has a bouquet (herbs, smoke, red and black fruits) is encouraging. The wine is soft and supple, with good ripeness, medium body, and a plump, smooth-as-silk finish. Drink it over the next 5–6 years.

MATANZAS CREEK WINERY (SONOMA)

Chardonnay * * */* * * *, Merlot * * * * *, Sauvignon Blanc * * * * *

1992 Chardonnay	Sonoma	C	91
1991 Chardonnay	Sonoma	C	90
1990 Chardonnay Journey	Sonoma	E	93
1992 Merlot	Sonoma	C	95
1991 Merlot	Sonoma	C	92
1990 Merlot	Sonoma	C	93
1993 Sauvignon Blanc	Sonoma	C	90

Matanzas Creek is a laudable winery in every respect. While everything that emerges is of the highest quality, Matanzas Creek has established itself as a reference-point winery for Sauvignon Blanc, Chardonnay, and Merlot.

The 1993 Sauvignon Blanc may have reached a new dimension of complexity and deliciousness. It is a beautifully made wine with both finesse and intense flavor. From its glorious honey, melon, and herb-scented nose, to its medium-bodied, crisp yet intense flavors, this harmonious, personality-filled Sauvignon is a knockout. It should prove remarkably flexible. Drink it over the next 12 months.

The 1992 Chardonnay's exotic nose of rich tropical fruit, vanillin, and flowers is followed by a full-bodied wine with well-balanced flavors that are gently touched by oak. It is a full-flavored yet elegant Chardonnay for drinking over the next 1–2 years. The crisp, subtle, medium-bodied, elegant 1991 Chardonnay is loaded with fruit, personality, and character. Matanzas Creek has also released 300 cases of the 1990 Chardonnay Journey. From a qualitative perspective, it is a complex, hazelnut- and buttery-scented wine with enormous richness, superb purity, full body, and a long finish. My instincts suggest it should drink well for 1–2 years. However, the going rate for Chardonnays of this quality and rarity is $30–$40 a bottle—not $70. A top-quality wine is unquestionably expensive to make, but the price asked for this wine is indefensible.

Matanzas Creek's 1992 Merlot may be the finest Merlot made in the new world. The color is a dark saturated ruby/purple. While the nose is more closed than when I tasted the barrel sample, it offers huge, rich scents of black cherries, cassis, and vanillin. Full bodied, with exceptional concentration and depth, this fabulously rich Merlot should last for 12–15 years. A winemaking tour de force!

The 1991 Merlot reveals that telltale smoky, coffee, mocha nose that reminds me of one of my favorite flavors of ice cream from Baskin-Robbins—Jamoca Almond Fudge. In the mouth, the creamy texture, sweet, ripe fruit, and lusciousness make for a delicious glass of wine. The 1990 Merlot offers up to a decade's worth of hedonistic drinking. It exhibits wonderfully rich, toffee, coffee, berry fruit flavors married brilliantly with sweet, toasty new oak. The creamy texture, sweet, ripe fruit, and lusciousness make for a delicious glass of wine. The finish is explosively rich.

MAZZOCCO (SONOMA)
Zinfandel * *

1992 Zinfandel	Sonoma	B	84
1990 Zinfandel	Sonoma	B	79

The light- to medium-bodied, pleasant 1992 Zinfandel offers spicy, berry fruit in the nose, tasty, light-bodied flavors, no tannin, an attractive, supple, easygoing fruitiness, and a short finish. This cleanly made wine is ideal for uncritical quaffing over the next 1–2 years. If it were not for a charred, smoky, excessively oaky nose, the 1990 Zinfandel would merit a higher score. There is admirable deep fruit, and on the palate, I can sense full body and good raw materials, but they are dominated by wood. As a result, the oak enjoys the upper hand in this out-of-balance, late-released 1990 Zinfandel.

PETER MCCOY (SONOMA)
Chardonnay Clos des Pierres Vineyard * * * */* * * * *

1992 Chardonnay Clos des Pierres Vineyard	Knight's Valley	C	88
1991 Chardonnay Clos des Pierres Vineyard	Knight's Valley	C	90

I enjoy this mineral- and stony-scented Chardonnay that behaves like a top-class French Chablis. The 1992 Chardonnay Clos des Pierres makes a persuasive argument for followers of *terroir*. There is medium to full body, a tightly knit structure, and wonderful purity and delineation to its personality. Drink it over the next several years. The 1991 was made from what must be extremely low yields, given its layers of rich Chardonnay fruit nicely integrated with crisp acidity and subtle oak. This is a complex, elegant, persuasively flavored Chardonnay for drinking over the next 4–5 years.

MEEKER VINEYARD (SONOMA)
Zinfandel * * * *

1992 Zinfandel Gold Leaf Cuvée	Dry Creek	B	89+
1991 Zinfandel Gold Leaf Cuvée	Dry Creek	B	87+
1992 Zinfandel Sonoma Cuvée	Sonoma	B	86+

Both the 1992 Zinfandels are firmly structured, tannic, large-scale wines with austere, backward personalities. Although rich, full-bodied, concentrated, and powerful, the 1992 Sonoma Cuvée is forbiddingly tough and backward. Unless you are a masochist, I would not touch a bottle until the tannin has melted away in 2–3 years. The 1992 Gold Leaf Cuvée exhibits a deeper, more saturated, dark purple color, and an earthy, cassis, peppery, spicy nose with attractive mineral scents. Layers of concentrated fruit are buttressed by considerable body and tannin. This large-scale, alcoholic, blockbuster style of Zinfandel should age well for 10–15 years. If it sheds its tannin without losing any fruit this will be an outstanding wine in 3–4 years.

Meeker Vineyard has produced one of the most tannic, backward 1991 Zinfandels. The color is excellent, and the nose is tight and unforthcoming. This deep, full-bodied, rich, impressively endowed wine needs 1–3 years of cellaring; it should keep for 10–12 more years.

MERIDIAN (SAN LUIS OBISPO)
Chardonnay* */* * *, Pinot Noir Reserve* * *

1991 Pinot Noir Reserve	Santa Barbara	B	86

Meridian is in San Luis Obispo and most of its wines emanate from the Paso Robles viticultural area. However, Meridian's winemaker, Chuck Ortman, does venture south to buy Chardonnay and Pinot Noir. The 1991 Meridian Pinot Noir Reserve from Santa Barbara County is an attractive, easy-to-understand, richly fruity wine with a soft texture, a spicy, herb- and berry-scented fragrance, and lush, round, generous, silky-textured flavors. It should flow easily down the gullet over the next 3–4 years.

MERRYVALE VINEYARDS (NAPA)
Chardonnay Reserve* * * *, Chardonnay Silhouette* * * * *, Profile Proprietary Red Wine* * * *

1993 Chardonnay Reserve	Napa	D	90
1992 Chardonnay Reserve	Napa	D	86
1993 Chardonnay Silhouette	Napa	D	94
1991 Profile Proprietary Red Wine	Napa	D	92
1990 Profile Proprietary Red Wine	Napa	D	90+

This property has recently shown significant progress in the quality and complexity of its wines. Winemaker Bob Levy and consulting French oenologist Michel Rolland have moved to a more natural winemaking style, with full malolactic fermentation for the whites. In addition, the reds are now bottled with little or no fining or filtration. There is also significantly less acidification. The results are more texturally enticing and complete wines.

The 1993 Chardonnay Silhouette (only 800+ cases were produced) is a wine of extraordinary richness and character. Aged 15 months in new Louis Latour barrels, with significant lees contact, and put through complete malolactic fermentation, this Chardonnay is similar to a great Burgundy grand cru such as Bâtard or Chevalier-Montrachet. It offers a gorgeously seductive, rich, honeyed, apple-, spring flower blossom–scented nose that exhibits a judicious touch of sweet oak. Full bodied, with formidable intensity and outstanding ripeness, this wine brilliantly marries power and concentration with a sense of elegance and grace. It is an outstanding Chardonnay that will put Merryvale in the spotlight. The full-bodied 1993 Chardonnay reveals lovely, honeyed, buttery popcorn, and applelike fruit, adequate acidity, excellent purity, and a mouth-filling, long, vibrant finish. It should drink well for several more years. Less impressive, but still very good is the 1992 Chardonnay. More restrained and monolithic, it is a pleasing wine, although it is nowhere near the level of the 1993 cuvées.

Merryvale's top red wine is their proprietary red wine called Profile. It is a Cabernet Sauvignon–based wine that contains as much as 20%–35% Merlot in vintages such as 1992 and 1993. Aged in small oak casks, of which 50% are new, it is bottled without fining or filtration. The 1991 Profile offers an exceptional glass of wine. The opaque dark/ruby/purple color and subtle, minty, toast-, and mineral-scented nose are followed by a full-bodied wine with great definition, outstanding ripeness and richness, and a European sense of elegance and grace. The ripe tannin and new oak are well integrated. Approachable now, this wine promises to evolve and improve for at least a decade. It will keep for 15–20 years. The recently released 1990 Profile exhibits loads of rich cassis fruit combined with scents of minerals and spice. The tannin is more aggressive than in the 1991, but there is no doubting the wine's rich, concentrated, full-bodied style that is both stylish and intense. Unlike the more approachable 1991, this atypically backward 1990 warrants 2–3 years of cellaring; it should age for 2 decades. Barrel tastings of the 1992 were less impressive, but the 1993 looks to be an outstanding, stylish, elegant wine with the emphasis on complexity, ripe fruit, and measured use of wood.

PETER MICHAEL WINERY (SONOMA)
Chardonnay Cuvées* * * * *, Les Pavots Proprietary Red Wine* * * * *, Sauvignon Blanc
l'Après-Midi* * * * *

1993 Chardonnay Clos du Ciel	Sonoma	D	91
1992 Chardonnay Clos du Ciel	California	D	92
1993 Chardonnay Cuvée Indigène	Sonoma	D	93
1992 Chardonnay Cuvée Indigène	California	D	94
1993 Chardonnay Cuvée Pointe Rouge	Sonoma	D	95
1992 Chardonnay Cuvée Pointe Rouge	California	D	96
1993 Chardonnay Monplaisir	Sonoma	D	92
1992 Chardonnay Monplaisir	California	D	94
1993 Les Pavots Proprietary Red Wine	California	D	91
1992 Les Pavots Proprietary Red Wine	California	D	94
1991 Les Pavots Proprietary Red Wine	California	D	91+
1990 Les Pavots Proprietary Red Wine	California	D	90+
1993 Sauvignon Blanc l'Après-Midi	Howell Mountain	C	92
1992 Sauvignon Blanc l'Après-Midi	California	C	90

Under the direction of the enormously talented winemaker, Mark Aubert, a protégé of Helen Turley, this winery has moved to the top hierarchy of quality in California Chardonnay, Sauvignon Blanc, and Cabernet Sauvignon. Utilizing Burgundian winemaking techniques, the gorgeously ripe, pure fruit of several of California's finest vineyards is transformed into rich wines that go through complete malolactic fermentation and are not filtered at bottling. Peter Michael also produces one of the finest and most complex California Sauvignon Blancs. Lastly, lest readers think of this winery as only a white wine specialist, their Cabernet Sauvignon called Les Pavots is a remarkably elegant, Bordeaux-style red wine with considerable character and aging potential. The following wines were all released in 1995, save for the 1993 Les Pavots, which will be released in September 1996. Readers who may have missed the glorious 1992s are forewarned about the buying frenzy that is likely to ensue when these 1993s hit the marketplace.

The winery's excellent Sauvignon Blanc (approximately 450 cases are produced) is fashioned from grapes grown in a vineyard on Howell Mountain. It is 100% Sauvignon, put through a complete malolactic fermentation, and then barrel-fermented. Recent vintages have also been bottled unfiltered. The 1993 Sauvignon Blanc is a worthy successor to the terrific 1992. It possesses a honeyed, melony bouquet with a subtle influence of wood. With great fruit vibrancy, medium body, and a long, dry, refreshing aftertaste, this rich wine is in an elite class shared by only a handful of other California Sauvignon Blancs.

The Chardonnays are all noteworthy wines. The 1993 Chardonnay Clos du Ciel represents the winery's largest single cuvée, as nearly 2,000 cases are produced. The wine exhibits delicious oak beautifully integrated with gobs of ripe, honeyed apple fruit. There is a natural mouth-feel, as well as enough acidity to provide focus and a dry, crisp, elegant, authoritatively flavored finish. Drink it over the next 5–6 years. There are 1,500 cases of the 1993 Chardonnay Monplaisir, made from Gauer Ranch grapes. This wine reveals a mineral component, along with tremendous quantities of rich fruit, plenty of intensity, full body, a beautiful, well-knit personality, and a long, dry finish. It will drink well for 3–5 years.

The top Chardonnay cuvées (that's relative given the superb level of quality of all Peter Michael's wines) include the 1993 Chardonnay Cuvée Indigène, a wine completely fermented with wild yeasts and aged in 100% new French oak casks made by Burgundy *négociant* Louis Latour. There are only 400 cases of this wine, which has an uncommon resemblance to a great Burgundy grand cru. There is almost a red fruit character accompanying the honeyed-apple/pineapple, lavishly rich personality. Full bodied, dry, and rich, with a natural texture, this super Chardonnay should drink well for 5–6 years. Even smaller quantities (100 cases) were made of the 1993 Chardonnay Cuvée Pointe Rouge. The winery's luxury cuvée, it is fashioned from a blend of the finest barrels. The wine displays an extra dimension of richness, extraordinary concentration and length, wonderful purity, and a spectacular bouquet filled with aromas of ripe fruit, toast, and honey.

The red wine is a blend of Cabernet Sauvignon with small quantities of Merlot, Cabernet Franc, and occasionally Malbec. The 1993 Les Pavots (80% Cabernet Sauvignon, 10% Cabernet Franc, and 10% Malbec) was made from yields of 1–1.5 tons per acre. It exhibits a stylish, Bordeaux-like nose of red and black fruits, minerals, and spices. The wine is elegant, flavorful, medium bodied, stylish yet intense, as well as well balanced. It should drink well for 15+ years. The 1992 Les Pavots (92% Cabernet Sauvignon, 5% Merlot, and 3% Cabernet Franc) reveals a saturated dark ruby/purple color, and a wonderfully sweet, smoky nose offering up scents of meat and black currants. The integration of new oak is impeccable in this full-bodied, expansively flavored, sumptuously styled wine that is obviously made in more of a California style than the more polished 1993 and 1991. The wine was aged for 24 months in small oak casks, of which 50% were new, and bottled unfiltered. It should evolve beautifully for 20–25 years.

Peter Michael's 1992 Sauvignon Blanc l'Après-Midi is a light straw-colored wine, with a wonderfully fragrant, perfumed nose of melons, honey, figs, and floral scents, and intense flavors, but no heaviness. Medium bodied, with great fruit, purity, and balance, this superb Sauvignon can be drunk now or cellared for 3–4 years.

The 1992 Chardonnay Clos du Ciel from Howell Mountain reveals a rich, lemony, buttery, subtle vanillin-scented nose, full-bodied, concentrated flavors with a classical Chardonnay profile, and a vibrant, concentrated finish. Bottled unfiltered and without acidification, this wine offers a natural, pure impression on the palate. It should drink well for 3–5 years. The 1992 Chardonnay Monplaisir is a more exotic, buttery, honeyed style of wine bursting with concentrated fruit. Enormously rich and full bodied, yet never thick or clumsy on the palate, it exhibits marvelous balance and a fabulously long finish. The 1992 Chardonnay Cuvée Indigène is a beautifully made wine with a smoky, hazelnut-scented nose followed by voluptuously textured, rich, full-bodied flavors. The superb balance, noteworthy purity, and delineation are commendable. Drink it over the next 3–4 years. The limited-production 1992 Chardonnay Cuvée Pointe Rouge is this producer's *tête de cuvée*, as it is made from the finest barrels. This concentrated wine displays a huge, heavenly perfume of honeyed tropical fruits, smoky nuts, vanillin and spice, great richness, full body, adequate acidity, and a smashingly long, intense finish. It should drink well for 3–4 years.

The 1990 Les Pavots is a beautifully made, black currant–scented wine with medium body, wonderful integrated acidity, and a rich, concentrated finish. It could easily be confused with a top-class Médoc given its structure and finesse allied to intense flavors. The Bordeaux-like 1991 Les Pavots offers a fragrant, pure, black currant–scented nose, rich, medium- to full-bodied flavors, and a fine underpinning of acidity and moderate tannin. Its long finish admirably combines power and intensity with finesse. Neither wine is close to maturity. While they are accessible, I recommend 3–5 years of cellaring; each is capable of lasting for 2 decades.

MICHEL-SCHLUMBERGER (SONOMA)
Cabernet Sauvignon * * *, Chardonnay * * *

1992 Cabernet Sauvignon Reserve	Dry Creek	C	86
1992 Chardonnay Benchland Estate	Dry Creek	C	86

Formerly known as Domaine Michel, Michel-Schlumberger has fashioned a 1992 Cabernet Sauvignon that displays a strong vanillin (from new oak barrels) spicy component to its moderately intense, curranty aromas. It offers admirable ripeness and richness, medium body, and a subtle, understated, elegant style. It should drink well for a decade.

The citrusy medium-weight 1992 Chardonnay Benchland Estate reveals crisp acidity, a finesse-style personality, an intriguing mineral/lemon component, and lively fruit on the palate. It can easily be utilized as an aperitif.

ROBERT MONDAVI WINERY (NAPA)
Barbera* * * *, Cabernet Sauvignon* * *, Cabernet Sauvignon Oakville Unfiltered* * * *, Cabernet Sauvignon Reserve* * * * * (since 1987) (between 1975 and 1985* * *) (between 1971 and 1974* * * * *), Chardonnay* * *, Chardonnay Reserve* * * * *, Chenin Blanc* * * *, Fumé Blanc* * *, Fumé Blanc Reserve* * * */* * * * *, Pinot Noir* * *, Pinot Noir Reserve* * * * *, Zinfandel* * * *

1993 Barbera	Sonoma	C	91
1992 Cabernet Sauvignon Oakville Unfiltered	Napa	C	92
1993 Cabernet Sauvignon Reserve	Napa	D	93
1992 Cabernet Sauvignon Reserve	Napa	D	95
1991 Cabernet Sauvignon Reserve	Napa	D	96+
1990 Cabernet Sauvignon Reserve	Napa	D	96
1991 Cabernet Sauvignon Unfiltered	Napa	C	90
1990 Cabernet Sauvignon Unfiltered	Napa	C	87
1993 Chardonnay	Carneros	C	89
1993 Chardonnay	Napa	C	90
1992 Chardonnay	Napa	C	86
1993 Chardonnay Reserve	Napa	D	93
1992 Chardonnay Reserve	Napa	D	91
1991 Chardonnay Reserve	Napa	D	89

1992	Fumé Blanc	Napa	B	87
1993	Fumé Blanc Reserve	Napa	C	92
1992	Fumé Blanc Reserve	Napa	C	91
1991	Fumé Blanc Reserve	Napa	C	89
1991	Merlot	Napa	C	88
1992	Pinot Noir	Carneros	C	88
1992	Pinot Noir	Napa	C	88
1993	Pinot Noir Reserve	Napa	D	91
1992	Pinot Noir Reserve	Napa	D	92
1993	Sauvignon Blanc Stag's Leap District	Napa	B	87
1993	Zinfandel	Napa	C	93
1992	Zinfandel	Napa	C	88
1991	Zinfandel	Napa	B	82
1992	Zinfandel Unfiltered	Napa	B	87

This venerable Napa winery, which, justifiably, has enormous influence on the quality and direction of California winemaking, continues to perform admirably, pushing quality at both the vineyard and winery to greater heights. Readers who mistakenly believe size is not synonymous with quality must be surprised by the bevy of extraordinary wines turned out by the Mondavis. This winery's movement away from California's tendency to produce wines with excessive amounts of added acidity that are tart, often eviscerated (because of too much fining and filtering), began in 1987 with their Reserve reds. It has been vigorously continued, with the Mondavis now bottling virtually all their top white wines without filtration—a tribute to this family's commitment and dedication to excellence. Mondavi's new and upcoming releases reinforce Mondavi's position as the spiritual and qualitative leader of that segment of the California wine industry dedicated to producing world-class, compelling wines.

The partially barrel-fermented 1993 Sauvignon Blanc from the Stag's Leap District is a richly fruity, honey-, melon-, and herb-scented wine displaying wonderful ripeness, gorgeous intensity of flavor, and a fresh, lively, medium-bodied, crisp palate. It should drink well for several years. The 1992 Fumé Blanc possesses loads of sweet, herbal fruit, a touch of honey, noticeable toasty oak, and a creamier, fuller, chewier texture than the more delicate Sauvignon Blanc from Stag's Leap. The Fumé Blanc should drink well for 1–2 years.

Both the 1992 and the 1993 Fumé Blanc Reserves are terrific wines that are among the finest wines from this varietal made in California. Mondavi's Reserve Fumé is produced from some of Napa's oldest Sauvignon vines, some of which were planted in 1945. The 1992 Fumé Blanc Reserve's rich, exotic nose of herbs, honeyed fruit, and spice is followed by rich, full-bodied, impressively extracted flavors buttressed by crisp acidity. It is a head-turning, attention-getting wine. As good as the 1992 is, the 1993 Fumé Blanc Reserve is even better, with greater richness, more precision, and a sensationally intense, multidimensional bouquet. It was bottled unfiltered. The 1992 Fumé Blanc Reserve should last for 1–2 years, and the 1993 Reserve a year or two longer.

Mondavi's Chardonnays continue to go from strength to strength. The 1993 Chardonnay Carneros offers tasty, ripe fruit, wonderful freshness, medium to full body, and a buttery, baked apple, lemony note. The wine possesses excellent depth and freshness. It should drink well for several years. The unfiltered 1993 Chardonnay Napa reveals outstanding fruit extraction, admirable purity, medium to full body, adequate underlying acidity, and a long, fresh, elegant finish. The big, buttery, toasty, lavishly oaked and honeyed, fully mature 1992 Chardonnay Reserve needs to be drunk over the next 1–2 years. It possesses unctuously rich, full-bodied flavors, as well as a nutty, Meursault-like personality. The enormous progress being made in Mondavi's Chardonnay program is especially evident in the 1993 Chardonnay Reserve. It is a wine that could easily pass for a Bâtard-Montrachet from Louis Latour. Mondavi's Chardonnay possesses all the power and spectacular richness and concentration of the 1992, but offers more focus with a sense of elegance and finesse. Powerful, rich, dense, and mouth filling, but never heavy, this wine's oak is extremely well integrated. It may be the finest Reserve Chardonnay Mondavi has yet made. I would not be surprised to see this wine last for 4–6 years, possibly longer.

The 1992 Chardonnay is one of the best regular cuvées Mondavi has made to date. It possesses gobs of ripe, concentrated, creamy fruit, an attractive apple/floral component, and a medium-bodied, lively, fresh finish. It should drink well for 2–3 years.

The big 1991 Chardonnay Reserve is typically ripe, toasty, honeyed, and richly oaky. This medium- to full-bodied wine should last for 2–3 years. While expensive, it is one of the best California Chardonnays produced. The oaky, honeyed, lavishly rich 1991 Fumé Blanc Reserve offers copious quantities of herb- and fig-flavored fruit. It is superflexible with food. Drink it before the end of 1994.

No one in California has made as much progress with the temperamental Pinot Noir grape as Robert Mondavi. The non-Reserve bottlings, which must give burgundy producers nightmares, are excellent wines. For example, the 1992 Pinot Noir Napa possesses a dark ruby color, a lovely, ripe, black cherry–, herb-, and spice-scented nose, and a sweet, expansive palate. This excellent Pinot Noir should drink well for 3–4 years. The 1992 Pinot Noir Carneros reveals an even more burgundylike nose in its spice, cherry, and vanilla aromas. The wine displays a beautiful aromatic and flavor profile, medium body, excellent ripeness, and a soft, velvety-textured feel. It should drink well for 3–4 years.

The Pinot Noir Reserve bottlings offer an extra dimension aromatically, as well as more fat and flavor extraction. Readers will love the seductive, voluptuously textured 1992 Pinot Noir Reserve. This dark ruby-colored wine boasts a sweet, sexy nose, wonderfully opulent flavors, full body, and a lusciously rich, heady finish. Drink this knockout Pinot Noir over the next 5–6 years. The 1993 Pinot Noir Reserve does not reveal the decadently opulent style of the 1992. Nevertheless, it is an outstanding Pinot Noir that could easily eclipse most Burgundy grands crus in a blind tasting. The wine exhibits gobs of rich black cherry and vanillin flavors, full body, outstanding concentration, and a velvety texture. It too should last for 5–6 years.

Mondavi has jumped into the Zinfandel sweepstakes. The debut release was an atypically mediocre 1991. The 1992 Zinfandel is a big improvement over the uninspiring 1991. With a deep ruby color and a ripe, spicy, raspberry-scented nose, this lush, velvety-textured, medium- to full-bodied wine reveals no hard edges. It is soft, supple, and altogether delicious for drinking over the next 3–4 years. The 1993 Zinfandel is a knockout! A decadent, ripe, full-bodied, blockbuster Zinfandel (14.7% alcohol), this dry wine is loaded with spicy, peppery, earthy, berry aromas and unctuously rich, full-bodied, crunchy flavors. It will drink well for at least a decade. I predict this effort will propel Mondavi into the upper echelon of Zinfandel competition.

After producing a number of unexciting Cabernet Sauvignons in the early eighties, Mondavi has gotten this program back on track. Even the non-Reserve cuvées, which are now bottled unfiltered, go from strength to strength. The 1990 Cabernet Sauvignon may be the best regular offering Mondavi has produced in over 15 years. It possesses a dark ruby/ purple color, an enticing nose of vanilla, cassis, herbs, and spices, excellent concentration, a supple, medium- to full-bodied personality, adequate acidity, and a fine finish. It should drink well for 8–10 years. Readers should beat a path to their wine merchant and stock up on the 1991 Cabernet Sauvignon Unfiltered. This is the finest regular Cabernet Sauvignon Mondavi has made. It offers an opaque dark ruby/purple color, a superb nose of black currants, vanillin, mint, and toast, outstanding richness, great purity, medium to full body, an attractive suppleness, and a long, rich finish. Although it can be drunk now, it should age effortlessly for 10–15 years.

In 1992 Mondavi produced the first unfiltered Cabernet Sauvignon with an Oakville designation. This wine could easily pass for a Reserve bottling. Much like the unfiltered 1991 cuvée, it is a wine superior to many of the Reserves made between 1976 and 1985. The 1992 Oakville possesses a big, forceful, intense bouquet of smoky, toasty oak, sweet cassis fruit, chocolate, and a dash of herbs and vanilla. There is outstanding concentration, full body, moderate tannin, and a sweet, expansive, layered feel. This terrific Cabernet should drink well for 15 or more years.

To no one's surprise, Mondavi's greatest wines are the Reserve Cabernet Sauvignons, which compete favorably with the finest first-growth Bordeaux. Mondavi's 1990 Cabernet Sauvignon Reserve appears to be a worthy rival of the great 1987 Mondavi Reserve. Although marginally less powerful than that magnificent wine, the 1990 exhibits an opaque dark ruby/purple color, and a huge nose that offers up abundant aromas of sweet, toasty, new oak, jammy cassis, and roasted nuts. This full-bodied wine reveals a gorgeous concentration of cassis fruit welded to sweet, soft tannins. There is a wonderful inner core of richness and concentration, as well as a finish that is disarmingly velvety until some tannins emerge as the wine sits in the glass. This superconcentrated, beautifully made wine should age magnificently for 15–20 years. A spectacular effort! Over the last decade, the top Mondavi Reserves have been the 1987 and 1990, but every time I return to the 1991 Reserve I realize that the exceptional rating I bestowed on it was too low! Although it is not as showy or opulent as the 1990, I am now convinced there is more to it as it continues to reveal greater and greater extraction and more length. It appears to be a candidate for 20–25 years of stunningly delicious longevity. More open than when I tasted it a year ago, it exhibits an opaque purple color, and a blossoming bouquet of subtle mint, jammy cassis, smoky oak, and spice. The wine possesses great balance, sensational concentration, a multidimensional, layered feel, and firm tannin in the long finish.

If you miss the 1991 Reserve, try to find a few bottles of the sumptuously rich, decadent, showy 1992 Cabernet Sauvignon Reserve that is about to be released. It is a sweeter, riper, more unctuously styled Cabernet. While it may lack some of the classicism of the 1991 Reserve, it is a superrich, full-bodied, flamboyant, unctuously textured wine that should drink well for 20+ years. The 1993 Cabernet Sauvignon Reserve is another outstanding effort from Mondavi. The wine displays loads of cassis fruit, licorice, herbs, and well-integrated toasty new oak, full body, an understated, elegant personality, and outstanding length, ripeness, and extraction. It will drink well for 2 decades. Given the fact that there are now 15,000–18,000 cases of the Cabernet Sauvignon Reserve, Mondavi clearly is able to produce extraordinary wines in surprisingly high quantities.

Mondavi's 1991 Merlot exhibits spicy, cherry fruit, a healthy dark ruby color, fine suppleness, and a chewy, round, generous texture. It does not possess the complexity or length of the Cabernet, but it remains a fine effort that should provide delicious drinking for 7–8 years.

Mondavi has shown an experimental and innovative side. The 1993 Barbera, which, surprisingly, comes from Sonoma rather than Napa, is outstanding. Made from extremely old vines, this wine reveals a saturated, dark ruby/purple color, a huge, intense nose of roasted herbs, jammy black cherry fruit, deep, concentrated, superrich flavors, and a knock-out finish. It is one of the best Barberas I have tasted from California.

Ratings for Older Vintages of Robert Mondavi's Cabernet Sauvignon Reserve: 1989 (81), 1988 (84), 1987 (98), 1986 (88), 1985 (81), 1984 (80), 1983 (75), 1982 (78), 1981 (76), 1980 (79), 1979 (72), 1978 (89), 1977 (76), 1976 (84), 1975 (87), 1974 (95), 1973 (87), 1971 (94), 1970 (not a Reserve, but the unfiltered wine) (88)
Ratings for Older Vintages of Robert Mondavi's Chardonnay Reserve: 1990 (90)
Ratings for Older Vintages of Robert Mondavi's Pinot Noir Reserve: 1991 (89), 1990 (88)

MONTEREY PENINSULA (AMADOR)
Zinfandel Ferrero Ranch * * * *

1991 Zinfandel Ferrero Ranch		Amador	C 88

I have had some stunning wines, as well as some funky examples from this winery, so I am never quite sure what to expect. However, Monterey Peninsula always offers a distinctive, personality-filled wine that is usually made outside mainstream notions of varietal reference points. The 1991 Zinfandel Ferrero Ranch possesses a jammy, black cherry–scented nose with some spicy, earthy notes, and ripe, opulent, sweet, jammy flavors that go on and on. Full bodied, and loaded with glycerin and fruit, this robust, easily accessible style of Zinfandel may merit an outstanding score in another 1–2 years if more complexity develops.

CHÂTEAU MONTELENA (NAPA)
Cabernet Sauvignon Calistoga Cuvée * * *, Cabernet Sauvignon Estate * * * * *,
Chardonnay * * * */* * * * *, Johannisberg Riesling * * *, Zinfandel * * * *

1992 Cabernet Sauvignon Calistoga Cuvée	Napa	C	86
1992 Cabernet Sauvignon Estate	Napa	D	93
1991 Cabernet Sauvignon Estate	Napa	D	95+
1990 Cabernet Sauvignon Estate	Napa	D	93+
1989 Cabernet Sauvignon Estate	Napa	D	89+
1993 Chardonnay	Napa	C	90
1992 Chardonnay	Napa	C	91
1991 Chardonnay	Alexander Valley	C	90
1991 Chardonnay	Napa	C	90
1992 Chardonnay 20th Anniversary	Napa	D	91
1993 Johannisberg Riesling	Potter Valley	A	88
1992 Zinfandel Estate	Napa	C	89

Every time I participate in a blind tasting of a specific vintage of California Cabernets, whether it be 1974, 1975, 1976, 1977, 1978, 1980, 1981, 1982, etc., Château Montelena's wines consistently come out near or at the top. The style of their Cabernet Sauvignon Estate has remained an uncompromising blend of superripe fruit, power, concentration, and tannin. The only refinement has been that the type of tannin achieved in vintages in the nineties is softer, giving the wines earlier accessibility. That has been obtained without sacrificing any of the splendid richness and purity that are the hallmarks of Montelena's Cabernets.

The 1992 Cabernet Sauvignon Estate exhibits an opaque purple color, the vintage's telltale, sweet, jammy, roasted fruit character, wonderful ripeness, an expansive, chewy, moderately tannic palate, and a whoppingly long finish. It is cut from the same mold as the luscious 1984 and 1982 Montelena Cabernets. The incredible 1991 Cabernet Sauvignon Estate is an exceptional Cabernet. It may be the most promising wine among the bevy of

Montelena Cabernets produced over the last 2 decades, rivaling their profound 1987. The 1991 is extremely closed and backward, and in need of 5–6 years of cellaring. The color is a dense, opaque purple. The nose offers up Château Montelena's telltale, pure aromas of cassis, minerals, and spicy oak. Full bodied, spectacularly rich, and highly extracted, with moderate to high tannin, this is a youthful, exuberent, stunning example of Napa Cabernet Sauvignon. Its inner core of cassis fruit is something to behold! It should hit its peak around the turn of the century and last for 20 years thereafter. Don't miss it! The 1990 Cabernet Sauvignon Estate is a backward, but splendidly concentrated, broad, expansively flavored, full-bodied Cabernet with a high level of tannin. Its stunning display of highly extracted, black currant fruit judiciously wrapped in toasty oak is impressive. It is a 20- to 30-year wine. The 1989 Cabernet Sauvignon Estate is one of the stars of the vintage. The nearly opaque black/purple color suggests terrific concentration. The wine possesses a full-bodied, layered richness, without the hollowness and harsh tannin that plagued many 1989s. Although there is noticeable tannin, it is in balance, and drier than in vintages such as 1990, 1991, and 1992. This wine needs 3–4 years in the cellar; it should keep through the first decade of the next century.

Montelena has introduced a less expensive Cabernet Sauvignon they call Calistoga Cuvée. It is a more supple wine, yet it still manages to offer some of the rich cassis fruit and power and depth of the exquisite Estate Cabernet. The 1992 Calistoga Cuvée exhibits an excellent opaque ruby/purple color, rich black cherry and cassis fruit, medium to full body, fine ripeness and depth, and a supple, round texture. It should drink well for 5–7 years.

Winemaker/proprietor Bo Barrett is thrilled with what looks to be another great California Cabernet Sauvignon vintage in 1994. Wine enthusiasts looking for the best money can buy should be thrilled that this property, like many of the better California north coast wineries, has had an unprecedented five consecutive terrific vintages.

Montelena also produces one of the few classic, nonmalolactic-fermented, relatively long-lived California Chardonnays. It is the antithesis of the modern trend toward Burgundian-styled Chardonnay winemaking (which I adore), in its crisp, tart, exuberantly rich, vibrant fruit character. The 1993 Napa Chardonnay (the Alexander Valley cuvée of Chardonnay is no longer being produced) exhibits loads of ripe apple fruit, a citrusy, tight but promising nose, rich, full-bodied, brilliantly well-delineated flavors, and a crisp finish. It should drink well for at least 4–5 years.

Château Montelena celebrated its twentieth anniversary with the release of the eponymous 1992 Chardonnay. It offers abundant quantities of wonderful lemony/applelike fruit, no noticeable oak, beautiful balance, superb concentration, and a mineral character, all of which are delineated by the wine's acidity. It is the antithesis of the bold, opulent, oaky, unctuously textured style of Chardonnay. Some vintages of Montelena Chardonnay age remarkably well, and the 1992 will last for 5–8 years.

The 1992 Napa Chardonnay exhibits the sweet, full-bodied, opulent, ripe style of this vintage. More forward and flattering than most Montelena Chardonnays, this wine can undoubtedly be consumed within its first 4–5 years of life. The 1991 Alexander Valley Chardonnay displays fine up-front fruit. Neither sweet nor soft (as many California Chardonnays can be), it is rounder and juicier than the Napa Valley bottling. An excellent citrusy, tropical fruit–scented nose is followed by fine acidity, crispness, and a vibrant, long, medium- to full-bodied finish. It should drink well for at least 4–5 years. The 1991 Chardonnay Napa cuvée reveals a textbook Montelena lemony/apple bouquet, a vague scent of buttery popcorn, crisp acidity, and rich, multidimensional, layered flavors. Typical of many Château Montelena Chardonnays, it offers wonderful purity and richness presented in an understated, subtle manner. It should drink well for at least 4–5 years.

Readers looking for a super bargain should check out Montelena's 1993 Johannisberg

Riesling from Potter Valley. This dry, Alsatian-styled Riesling is an exuberant, medium- to full-bodied wine with gobs of peach/apricot fruit, long, well-extracted flavors, and a crisp, dry finish. Drink it over the next several years.

Montelena's 1992 Zinfandel Estate is made in a succulent, generous style with loads of peppery, nearly overripe, jammy cherry and raspberry fruit, full body, plenty of glycerin and alcohol, and a heady, lush finish. It is best drunk over the next 3–4 years.

Ratings for Older Vintages of Château Montelena's Cabernet Sauvignon Estate: 1988 (86), 1987 (98), 1986 (92), 1985 (94), 1984 (93), 1983 (89), 1982 (92), 1981 (82), 1980 (91), 1979 (91), 1978 (93), 1977 (92), 1976 (91), 1975 (84), 1974 (Sonoma) (90)

MONTEREY VINEYARDS (MONTEREY)

Classic Cabernet Sauvignon * * *, Classic Chardonnay * * *, Classic Merlot * * *, Classic Red * * *, Classic Sauvignon Blanc * * *, Classic White * * *

1991 Classic Cabernet Sauvignon	California	A	85
1993 Classic Chardonnay	California	A	85
1991 Classic Gamay Beaujolais	California	A	85
1990 Classic Merlot	California	A	85
1990 Classic Red	California	A	85
1993 Classic Sauvignon Blanc	California	A	84
1993 Classic White	California	A	85

Most consumers looking for easy-to-drink quality wines probably bypass this prolific producer, since their products are often stacked in unattractive piles at liquor stores. That is a shame, because the quality of these Monterey Vineyards wines is appealing. The offerings from Monterey Vineyards are more than merely competently made, inexpensive wines. They are delicious, and should have broad appeal to both neophytes and more finicky connoisseurs. Given the overwhelming number of vapid California-produced Sauvignon Blancs, I was surprised by the amount of personality and character present in this estate's 1993 Classic Sauvignon Blanc. There are melon and herbs to be found in its moderately intense bouquet. It is crisp, pure, and fresh, as well as a delight to drink. Rather than challenge its aging potential, I would recommend consumption over the next year. I was even fond of the 1993 Classic Chardonnay. It displays elegant, floral, applelike fruit flavors, good, crisp acidity, a stylish, graceful personality, and true varietal character. Drink it over the next year. Amazingly, the 1993 Classic White, a generic blend, is even better. It gets my nod as one of the finest white wine values in the world.

The 1990 Classic Red offers a Côtes du Rhône–like, peppery, berry fruitiness, a chunky, medium-bodied, soft texture, and a spicy, ripe, nearly fat finish. It makes for a tasty mouthful of dry red wine. The 1991 Classic Cabernet Sauvignon displays a spicy, herbaceous, berry-scented nose, medium-bodied flavors, good structure, some tannin, and a clean, surprisingly long finish. It should drink well for at least 2–3 years. The 1990 Classic Merlot is rounder, tastes sweeter and more expansive, with low acidity, and a ripe, coffee, chocolaty, berry-scented personality. Like the Cabernet and Classic Red, it is ideal for drinking over the next 2–3 years. If you are tired of tasting too many tannic, overly oaked, processed, acidified "boutique" wines at $15–$30 or more a bottle, try one of these modestly priced gems from Monterey Vineyards. Restaurants looking for an exuberantly fruity, crunchy, fresh, delicious tasting red wine should make the 1991 Classic Gamay Beaujolais their house wine. Clean and vibrant with depth and balance, this wine also provides joy to go along with its remarkable value. It should be drunk over the next year.

MONTICELLO CELLARS (NAPA)
Cabernet Sauvignon Corley Reserve * * * *, Cabernet Sauvignon Jefferson Cuvée * * */* * * *, Chardonnay Corley Reserve * * *, Chardonnay Jefferson Cuvée * * *, Domaine Montreaux Sparkling Wine * * *, Merlot * * *, Pinot Noir Estate * * *

1992 Cabernet Sauvignon Corley Reserve	Napa	C	88
1990 Cabernet Sauvignon Corley Reserve	Napa	C	93
1992 Chardonnay Corley Reserve	Napa	C	89
1990 Merlot Estate	Napa	C	88

Monticello's tannic, backward style of Cabernet Sauvignon makes tasting their wines at a young age difficult. Although the 1992 Corley Reserve is extremely tannic, it reveals wonderfully pure cassis fruit, medium to full body, excellent concentration, and a long, unevolved finish. One of the most backward 1992 California Cabernets I tasted, it needs 7–8 years of cellaring and should last for 2 decades. The sensational 1990 Cabernet Sauvignon Corley Reserve reveals a saturated purple color, a huge, smoky, chocolaty, cassis-scented nose, and massive, superbly extracted black cherry flavors nicely touched by new oak and presented in a full-bodied, multidimensional format. The blockbuster finish goes on and on. Drink it between 1996 and 2012.

Monticello's 1990 Merlot Estate is likely to be controversial given its exotic spicy, meaty, jammy, black cherry–scented nose. This fat, luscious wine admirably demonstrates what Merlot is all about—sumptuous pleasure!

The 1992 Chardonnay Corley Reserve is a buttery, toasty, rich, chewy, unctuously textured Chardonnay for drinking over the next year.

Z. MOORE WINERY (SONOMA)
Gewürztraminer * * * *, Danato Proprietary Red Wine * * */* * * *

1990 Danato Proprietary Red Wine	California	C	88
1992 Gewürztraminer Barrel-Fermented Dry	Russian River	A	88
1992 Gewürztraminer Martinelli Vineyard New Barrel	Russian River	C	90

This winery continues to provide positive proof that it is a benchmark producer for Gewürztraminer in the new world. The 1992 Gewürztraminer Barrel-Fermented Dry displays a big, intense, pungent bouquet of spicy fruit, excellent richness, medium to full body, and a long, dry finish. Drink this delicious, textbook Gewürztraminer over the next 2–3 years. Even better is the 1992 Gewürztraminer Martinelli Vineyard New Barrel. The finest Gewürztraminer I have ever tasted from the new world, it offers a terrific nose of lychee nuts, roses, and honeyed pineapples. Intense, concentrated, full bodied, dry, and long, this is a stunning example of this varietal. Drink it over the next several years.

Z. Moore also produces a proprietary red wine. Sporting a fashionable black label, the 1990 Danato is made from 50% Zinfandel, 40% Syrah, and 10% Cabernet Sauvignon grown in both Sonoma and Mendocino counties. An impressive, full-flavored, gutsy, dry red wine, it exhibits a big, spicy, black cherry–scented nose and chewy, concentrated flavors. With a bit more complexity it would have merited an outstanding rating. An ideal accompaniment to full-flavored, barbecued foods, it will drink well for 4–8 years.

MORRO BAY VINEYARDS (CENTRAL COAST)
Chardonnay * * */* * * *

1993 Chardonnay Central Coast	California	A	87

Morro Bay's excellent 1993 Chardonnay Central Coast, made at the Edna Valley winery under the supervision of the staff at Chalone, is a terrific bargain. Full bodied and rich, it exhibits a moderately intense, oaky, apple blossom/honeyed-peach–scented nose, and medium- to full-bodied, concentrated flavors. Drink this clean, well-made Chardonnay over the next 1–2 years.

MOSBY (SANTA BARBARA)

Brunello di Santa Barbara Carrari Vineyard * *, Gewürztraminer * *, Moscato di Fior * * *, Primativo * * */* * * *

1991 Brunello di Santa Barbara Carrari Vineyard	Santa Barbara	B	76
1991 Gewürztraminer Dry Barrel-Fermented	Santa Barbara	A	84
1992 Moscato di Fior (Dry)	Santa Barbara	B	86
1992 Primativo	Santa Barbara	B	88
1991 Primativo	Santa Barbara	B	86

One has to admire the interesting group of wines offered by Bill Mosby. Where else in America can you find a dry wine made from the orange Muscat grape? It is one of the most interesting and distinctive wines I tasted in Santa Barbara. The totally dry 1992 Moscato di Fior offers up huge aromas of tangerines and oranges, ripe, tasty, velvety fruit, and a crisp, long, dry finish. It would marry beautifully with various Asian dishes. Mosby also produces a Brunello di Santa Barbara from Carrari Vineyard, one of the largest vineyards in Los Alamos. The 1991 was the most disappointing wine I tasted from this winery. Light, straight-forward, and spicy, it is diluted and short.

One cannot make the same accusation against the two Primativo offerings. Both are big, chunky, husky wines with tremendous reserves of fruit, unctuous, dense textures, fine body, and peppery, spicy, ripe fruit. Although they are short on complexity, they are attractive, full-bodied, rustic wines for drinking with your favorite Italian dishes. They have the requisite concentration to last for 4–5 years. Longtime readers know I am not a great fan of California Gewürztraminer, so I was pleasantly surprised by this 1991 Gewürztraminer's pungent nose, which reminded me of a lighter-weight Gewürztraminer from Alsace. It is straightforward, with decent fruit, a spicy personality, and a crisp finish. There is enough character to suggest that Gewürztraminer may have potential in Santa Barbara.

MT. EDEN VINEYARDS (SANTA CLARA)

Cabernet Sauvignon * * */* * * *, Chardonnay MacGregor Vineyard * * * *, Chardonnay Santa Barbara * * */* * * *, Chardonnay Santa Cruz Estate * * * * *

1992 Cabernet Sauvignon Old Vine Reserve	Santa Cruz	C	92
1990 Cabernet Sauvignon Old Vine Reserve	Santa Cruz	D	93
1993 Chardonnay MacGregor Vineyard	Edna Valley	C	91
1992 Chardonnay MacGregor Vineyard	Edna Valley	C	88
1993 Chardonnay Estate	Santa Cruz	D	88
1992 Chardonnay Estate	Santa Cruz	D	96
1991 Chardonnay Estate	Santa Cruz	D	92
1990 Chardonnay Estate	Santa Cruz	D	90

The 1992 Cabernet Sauvignon Old Vine Reserve's flavors possess a haunting intensity reminiscent of some of the wines made by the microscopic Pomerol estate of Lafleur. The wine exhibits a sweet, jammy intensity that comes from unbelievably small yields and old vines. This wine is made in a different style than California's north coast Cabernets. The color is opaque, the concentration level is phenomenal, and the wine possesses spectacular length. However, there appears to be a stronger mineral character underlying the wine's distinctive black raspberry and cherry flavors. While the wine's extraction and depth are noteworthy, this full-bodied, tannic wine will require considerable patience. Could this be a replay of the beautiful and stunning, but still unevolved 1973 Mount Eden? **A.M.: 2002–2030.**

The 1990 is the finest Cabernet Sauvignon made at this highly respected estate since the 1973 and 1974. The broodingly opaque purple color is followed by a promising bouquet of cassis, smoke, and minerals. Exquisite purity of fruit, immense extraction, and excellent balance make this full-bodied, superrich Cabernet a sure bet for 20–30 years of cellaring. The well-integrated tannin and whoppingly long finish are impressive. It was kept open for 3 days without showing a trace of oxidation. **A.M.: 1998–2025.**

The 1993 Chardonnay from Edna Valley's MacGregor Vineyard is the best example Mt. Eden has yet produced from this source. This rich wine offers an ostentatious display of tropical fruits, honey, and vanilla, full body, superb purity, layers of Chardonnay fruit, enough acidity to provide brilliance and focus, and a blockbuster finish. This hedonistic Chardonnay should drink well for 2 years. The big, forceful 1992 Chardonnay from the MacGregor Vineyard offers considerable tropical fruit, butter, honey, and toasty oak aromas. With admirable body, a lush texture, and a heady, ripe, alcoholic finish, it is meant for near-term consumption, so do not buy more than you can reasonably consume over the next 9–12 months.

The Montrachet of California? If the 1993 is only very good, the 1992 Chardonnay Estate is a spectacular bottle of full-throttle, decadently rich Chardonnay. Buttery notes accompanied by scents of toast, nuts, and honeyed fruit jump from the glass. The wine swells on the palate, offering layers of unctuously textured, succulent fruit. The wine's tendency to be overblown is avoided by its nicely integrated acidity. This blockbuster, rich, superb Chardonnay is a dead ringer for a great grand cru from Burgundy's Côte d'Or. The only question is how long will it last—I say 4–8 years. Don't dare serve this wine chilled; treat it like a red wine and consume it at room temperature to permit a display of all its amazing richness and complexity. A tour de force!

The 1991 and 1990 Chardonnay Estates offer bouquets of toasty new oak, earthy, buttery fruit, and minerals. They are tightly knit, rich, full-bodied, concentrated wines that are dead ringers for a top premier cru or grand cru white burgundy. Based on past efforts, these wines should last for 4–8 years.

MT. KONOCTI (LAKE)
Semillon/Chardonnay * * *

1993 Semillon/Chardonnay	Lake County A	86

The blending of Semillon and Chardonnay, first practiced by Australian winemakers, is a good idea. This 60% Semillon/40% Chardonnay blend from Mt. Konocti exhibits gobs of citrusy, herb, melony, and figlike fruit, medium body, a fleshy, fresh feel in the mouth, and a crisp, dry, long finish. It will provide considerable flexibility with food. Drink it over the next year.

MT. VEEDER WINERY (NAPA)
Cabernet Sauvignon * *, Chardonnay * *, Meritage Proprietary Red Wine * *

1990 Cabernet Sauvignon	Napa C	87+

How good it is to see this estate again turn out fine wines. The 1990 Cabernet Sauvignon would have been exceptional if it had not been so tart and high in acidity. Although stern, it is an opaque-colored, intense, medium- to full-bodied wine, with copious amounts of spicy, earthy, black cherry fruit, excellent richness and density, and a long, moderately tannic finish. Drink it between 1996 and 2008.

MOUNTAIN VIEW WINERY (SANTA CLARA)

Cabernet Sauvignon * *, Chardonnay * *, Pinot Noir * */* * *, Zinfandel * * *

1991	Cabernet Sauvignon	North Coast	A	85
1992	Chardonnay	Monterey	A	86
1992	Pinot Noir	Napa/Monterey	A	84
1992	Sauvignon Blanc	North Coast	A	85
N.V.	Zinfandel Lot 91	Amador	A	86

Long known for their excellent value, I find it amazing that Mountain View can make a $7 Pinot Noir that is better than 70% of California's Pinot Noirs selling for $15 or more a bottle. This 1992 Pinot Noir stood out in my tasting of three dozen California Pinots as being among the most correct, fruity, clean, and natural tasting. The wine's straightforward cherry and berry fruit is presented in a supple, medium-bodied, spicy style that I find amazingly well done. It possesses adequate varietal character and wonderful softness. Restaurants looking for an inexpensive Pinot Noir to serve by the glass will make a lot of friends with this wine. The same can be said for the nonvintage Zinfandel Lot 91 from Amador. It is hard to find this much flavor, varietal character, spice, pepper, and cherry fruit in such a bargain-priced, medium- to full-bodied, deliciously pure, ripe Zinfandel. It will provide lovely drinking now and over the next 2–3 years. I also enjoyed Mountain View's supple 1991 Cabernet Sauvignon, a dark ruby-colored wine with a straightforward cassis, herb-tinged bouquet. With fine extraction, chewy glycerin, good cleanliness, and a lively red and black fruit character, this medium-bodied Cabernet should be drunk over the next 3–4 years.

The 1992 Sauvignon Blanc reveals textbook varietal character in its herb-, flint-, and melony-scented nose. Medium bodied and dry, with good fruit and crispness, this is a lively, fresh Sauvignon for drinking over the next 8–12 months. The 1992 Chardonnay (which contains 9% Pinot Blanc) is also an attractive, creamy-textured wine with buttery, Wheat Thin–like flavors, admirable body and purity, adequate acidity, and a satisfying mouth-feel in the finish. Drink it over the next year. I am delighted to report that there are 72,000 cases of the 1992 Chardonnay, which should bring a smile to thousands of wine enthusiasts.

Mountain View Winery has always made high quality/low priced wines, but these are among the best I have tasted.

P.S. Just so I am not inundated with phone calls, I did taste the 1990 Merlot, which is the only current offering I cannot recommend. The wine is too vegetal and herbal for my taste, but readers who like that style of Merlot may rate it higher than the 76 points I bestowed upon it.

MURPHY-GOODE (SONOMA)

Cabernet Sauvignon * */* * *, Chardonnay * * *, Chardonnay Reserve * * *, Fumé Blanc * * *, Fumé Blanc Reserve * * * *, Merlot * * *, Pinot Blanc * * */* * * *

1992	Cabernet Sauvignon Estate	Alexander Valley	C	87
1993	Chardonnay Barrel-Fermented	Alexander Valley	C	87
1992	Chardonnay Reserve	Alexander Valley	C	92
1993	Fumé Blanc	Alexander Valley	A	87
1992	Merlot Estate	Alexander Valley	C	86
1993	Pinot Blanc Estate Barrel-Fermented	Alexander Valley	C	87

This underpublicized winery consistently turns out delicious, elegantly styled wines that are meant to be consumed in their youth. Although the 1992 Merlot Estate and the 1992 Cabernet Sauvignon are not cut from the blockbuster, full-bodied mold of many wines of this vintage, they are to be admired for their delicate, suave style emphasizing medium body, crisp, ripe, pure fruit, adequate acidity, and a soft, round finish. The Merlot should be drunk over the next 7–8 years and the stylish, attractive Cabernet Sauvignon over the next 7–10 years.

Another excellent wine from Murphy-Goode, the melony-, herb-, and spicy-scented 1993 Fumé Blanc exhibits medium body, a suggestion of honey, and a lush finish. Drink it over the next year. The terrific, decadently styled 1993 Pinot Blanc Estate Barrel-Fermented offers loads of honeyed tangerine and buttery apple fruit, medium to full body, a vague notion of vanillin, and considerable suppleness and flesh. It is not a wine designed for intellectual introspection, but rather for delivering a burst of pleasure. Drink it over the next 8–12 months.

The blazingly well-delineated 1993 Chardonnay Barrel-Fermented offers generous quantities of honeyed pineapples and other tropical fruits. Rich and medium to full bodied, it exhibits a subtle use of oak to complement the wine's exuberant, fruity personality. It is refreshing, pure, and will offer delightful drinking over the next 12–18 months. It expands and grows on the palate—a positive characteristic. The decadent 1992 Chardonnay Reserve offers lavish quantities of oak and huge masses of sumptuous tropical fruits such as honeyed pineapples, oranges, and tangerines. This full-bodied, voluptuously textured Chardonnay should be drunk over the next year.

MURRIETA'S WELL (LIVERMORE)
Vendimia Proprietary Red Wine * * *

1992 Vendimia Proprietary Red Wine	Livermore	D	87

This medium-bodied, lighter-styled 1992 is made from an intriguing blend of 55% Cabernet Sauvignon, 13% Cabernet Franc, 15% Merlot, and 17% Zinfandel. Different from the north coast Cabernets in its cranberry, herbal-scented nose, graceful, light-bodied, flavorful and concentrated personality, and soft, low acid, supple flavors, it is a 1992 to drink over the next 5–7 years.

NALLE (SONOMA)
Cabernet Sauvignon * *, Zinfandel * * *

1991 Zinfandel	Dry Creek	B	89

If someone wanted to try a wine that represented the classic, full-bodied, full-blooded style of California Zinfandel, Nalle's 1991 Zinfandel would be among my top choices. Not as flamboyant, exotic, or complex as some, or as heady, alcoholic, or sumptuous as others, Nalle's 1991 is just a terrific Zinfandel. The dark ruby/purple color, classic Zinfandel nose of black raspberries and spices, graceful, medium- to full-bodied texture, and amply-endowed flavors bursting with ripe fruit make for a gorgeously seductive wine. It is not likely to make old bones, but 7–8 years of life are within reach.

NAPA RIDGE (NAPA)
Cabernet Sauvignon * * *, Chardonnay * * *, Chardonnay Frisinger Vineyard * * * *,
Chardonnay Reserve * * * *, Chenin Blanc * *, Gewürztraminer * *, Sauvignon Blanc * * *,
White Zinfandel * *

1991 Cabernet Sauvignon Oak Barrel	Central Coast	B	86
1993 Chardonnay	Central Coast	A	88
1993 Chardonnay Frisinger Vineyard	Napa	B	89

1992 Chardonnay Reserve	North Coast	B	88
1993 Gewürztraminer	Central Coast	A	86
1993 Sauvignon Blanc	North Coast	A	86

This winery is on a hot streak, turning out numerous well-made, bargain-priced wines. The 1993 Sauvignon Blanc North Coast reveals a delicate, floral, fig, herb, melony nose, clean, light- to medium-bodied flavors with gobs of fruit, and a surprisingly long, dry finish. Drink it over the next year.

Another good value and fine wine from this consistent producer of delicious wines, Napa Ridge's 1993 Gewürztraminer reveals a textbook, spicy nose, exotic, ripe flavors, medium body, and a long, tasty, off-dry finish. This surprisingly delicious Gewürztraminer should drink well for the next 12 months. A knockout value in Chardonnay, the stunningly rich, ripe, opulent 1993 Central Coast cuvée is bursting with tropical fruit scents intermingled with subtle oak. It possesses the finish of a wine costing twice as much. This is a delicious, mouth-filling Chardonnay to buy by the case, as long as readers intend to consume it over the next year. The 1993 Chardonnay Frisinger Vineyard offers intense scents of vanilla, spice, smoke, honey, and ripe apple fruit. Medium to full bodied, chewy, and fleshy, with superb purity and remarkable concentration (particularly for a Chardonnay priced under $25 a bottle), this big, rich Chardonnay is being sold for a song. Drink it over the next 1–2 years.

The opulent, oaky yet bold, dramatic 1992 Chardonnay Reserve exhibits gobs of toasty vanillin-scented, buttery fruit and rich, unctuously textured, thick, full-bodied flavors. Drink it over the next year.

The delicious, supple 1991 Cabernet Sauvignon Oak Barrel offers attractive cherry, herb, and spicy scents, medium-bodied, round flavors with soft tannin, and adequate acidity. It is a juicy style of Cabernet Sauvignon meant to be enjoyed by the masses. Drink it over the next 3–4 years.

NAVARRO VINEYARDS (MENDOCINO)
Chardonnay * * *, Pinot Noir * * */* * * *, Sauvignon Blanc * * * *

1992 Chardonnay	Anderson Valley	A	85

I have consistently enjoyed the well-made, fruity wines from Navarro. The 1992 Chardonnay possesses an attractive spicy, vanillin, apple-scented nose, medium body, fine flavor extraction, adequate acidity, and a vibrant, fresh, exuberant finish. It should be drunk over the next year.

NEWTON VINEYARDS (NAPA)
Cabernet Sauvignon * * * */* * * * *, Chardonnay * * * *, Chardonnay Unfiltered * * * * *,
Claret * * * *, Merlot * * * * *

1993 Cabernet Sauvignon	Napa	D	92
1992 Cabernet Sauvignon	Napa	D	92+
1991 Cabernet Sauvignon	Napa	D	94
1990 Cabernet Sauvignon	Napa	D	94
1992 Chardonnay	Napa	C	87
1993 Chardonnay Unfiltered	Napa	D	94+
1992 Chardonnay Unfiltered	Napa	D	93
1993 Claret	Napa	B	86
1992 Claret	Napa	B	86

1993 Merlot	Napa	D	91
1992 Merlot	Napa	D	90
1991 Merlot	Napa	D	94
1990 Merlot	Napa	D	93

After a decade of changes in direction, the spectacular hillsides that are collectively called the Newton Vineyards began to produce wines of extraordinary complexity and intensity. Proprietors Peter Newton and his wife, Su Hua, along with their talented winemaker, John Konigsgaard, and famed Bordeaux oenologist, Michel Rolland, are making no compromises in what are some of the most celestial wines being produced in California. Since 1990, the quality of their wines has soared to the top of the California hierarchy.

The 1993 Merlot, which is bottled without fining or filtration, incldues 5% Cabernet Sauvignon and 15% Cabernet Franc. It reveals a more saturated color than the 1992 Merlot, intense, black cherry, earth, and oak aromas, rich, full-bodied, concentrated flavors, and moderate tannin. The wine will benefit from 2–3 years of cellaring and keep for 15+ years.

The Newton Merlots are the finest now being made in California. The 1992 Merlot is a worthy successor to their exceptionally fine 1991. The thick, dark ruby/purple color is followed by aromas of sweet, jammy black cherries, earth, spice, and wood. Round and generous, with gobs of intensity and moderate tannin, this large-scale, rich, concentrated Merlot will benefit from 1–2 years of cellaring; it will age well for 10–15 years. The 1991 Merlot possesses an exotic, Asian-spice, chocolate, mocha, sweet black cherry–scented bouquet, thick, succulent, voluptuous flavors, admirable fruit, glycerin, and body, and a whoppingly long finish. This is a superrich, intense, spectacular, exotic, flamboyant Merlot that should last for 8–15 years. The 1990 Merlot rivals the best wines of Pomerol and is more flamboyant than the terrific 1990 Matanzas Creek. It should also prove to be long-lived. Drink it over the next 10–14 years.

The 1992 and 1993 Claret are cuvées created from wines deemed not sufficiently rich or structured enough to go into the estate-bottled Merlot and Cabernet Sauvignon. Newton's Claret, of which there are approximately 3,000 cases, is a good value. The 1992 exhibits straightforward, ripe, red and black currant fruit, medium body, and light tannin. It can be drunk now or held for 7–8 years. The 1993 Claret also displays plenty of red and black currant fruit, more structure and tannin, as well as medium body and a spicy finish.

The extraordinary, blockbuster 1991 Cabernet Sauvignon offers a spectacular nose of black currants, truffles, vanillin, mineral, floral, and menthol scents. Massive, with huge extraction, beautiful balance, and a finish that lasts for over a minute, this majestic Cabernet should prove a worthy rival to Newton's 1990. It will keep for 15–20 years. For wonderful structure, massiveness, and chocolaty cassis, check out Newton's 1990 Cabernet Sauvignon. With a huge nose of chocolate, cedar, and cassis, this rich, full-bodied, spectacular wine offers unbelievably concentrated flavors, firm, sweet tannins, and enough acidity to give it grip and delineation. All of these Newton offerings were bottled unfiltered. The 1992 Cabernet Sauvignon (only 1,600 cases) is a powerful, backward, cassis-scented and -flavored wine with an opaque ruby/purple color, and youthful, unevolved aromas and flavors. It cuts a deep swath on the palate, but it requires 4–5 years of cellaring. Look for this wine to be more user-friendly by 2000 and last for 15–20 years thereafter. In contrast, the 1993 Cabernet Sauvignon (once again unfined and unfiltered) is more precocious and flattering with seemingly lower acidity, a more velvety texture, wonderful richness, and an opulent, forward, cassis fruitiness that is easy to understand. Highly extracted, rich, and full, with no hard edges, unlike the more structured and tannic 1992, the 1993 will be drinkable upon release and will age effortlessly for 20–25 years.

Newton continues to offer two Chardonnay cuvées—a regular wine and an unfiltered offering sold in a designer bottle. Newton's newest releases include the 1993 Unfiltered Chardonnay. Happily, there are 2,000 cases of this remarkably rich, concentrated wine. What places the Newton Unfiltered Chardonnay in Chardonnay's top league is its extraordinary intensity, multidimensional, layered texture that is reminiscent of a great white burgundy from Coche-Dury, and its honeyed, orange peel aromas and flavors that are wrapped gently with subtle oak. The 1993 is perhaps the best Chardonnay Newton has yet made—which is saying something! The 1992 Chardonnay displays a moderately intense, candylike nose of sweet, tropical fruit. Soft, rich, and pure, with medium to full body, this plump, one-dimensional Chardonnay should drink well for another year. Far more compelling, the limited-production 1992 Unfiltered Chardonnay is more restrained than its 1991 sibling. Nevertheless, it is a blockbuster Chardonnay, with a huge, decadent nose of honeyed, buttery fruit and smoky, toasty, new oak. Full bodied, wonderfully pure and rich, with admirable buttressing and well-integrated acidity, this wine possesses exquisite concentration and balance, as well as a long finish. It is among the best Chardonnays being produced in California.

Fans of Newton should recognize that the winery is beginning to produce some Viognier from a 5-acre vineyard. The first crop yielded just one barrel, but the wine was striking in its richness, intensity, and faithful varietal character. While the 1994 will not be released commercially, hopefully the 1995 will be of similar merit.

NORMAN VINEYARD (PASO ROBLES)
Zinfandel * * * *

1992 Zinfandel	Paso Robles	B	90

Although I have no previous experience with this producer, I was knocked out by this opaque-colored Zinfandel. The wine offers a superb, fragrant nose of black cherries, raspberries, and minerals. Gobs of flavor extraction and richness make this full-bodied, multidimensional Zinfandel a terrific example of the fuller-bodied style of this varietal. The wine possesses wonderful purity and has achieved its flavor extraction and concentration without being burdened by harsh tannin. Drink this luscious, decadently styled Zinfandel over the next decade.

OAKVILLE RANCH (NAPA)
Cabernet Sauvignon * * * *

1990 Cabernet Sauvignon	Napa	C	92
1991 Cabernet Sauvignon Reserve	Napa	D	90

This up-and-coming producer has fashioned an explosively rich, opulent, full-bodied 1990 Cabernet Sauvignon loaded with rich cassis fruit and spicy oak. Superbly concentrated and well balanced, with wonderful sweetness and ripeness, this admirably extracted, full-bodied wine remains young and unevolved, but oh, so promising! It will develop well over the next 15 years. Impressive! Although frightfully backward and tannic, the 1991 Cabernet Sauvignon Reserve is crammed with juicy, succulent, black currant fruit. An opaquely colored wine, it is muscular and concentrated and made for collectors/connoisseurs who have the patience to wait 4–5 years for the wine to mesh together. Massive, extracted, and impressively built for the long haul, it should be a Cabernet Sauvignon that lasts 20+ years.

OBESTER WINERY (SAN MATEO)
Chardonnay * */* * *, Sauvignon Blanc * *, Zinfandel * * *

1991 Zinfandel	Mendocino	B	86

This attractive 1991 Zinfandel exhibits excellent ripeness, a round, generous, spicy, fruity personality, medium body, and a soft, lush finish. Drink it over the next 1–2 years.

OJAI VINEYARD (VENTURA COUNTY)
Chardonnay * *, Cuvée Spéciale Ste. Helene * * */* * * *, Sauvignon Blanc * * *, Syrah * * *

1991 Chardonnay	Arroyo Grande	C	84
1991 Sainte Helene Reserve	Arroyo Grande	B	87
1993 Sauvignon Blanc/Semillon	California	C	87
1991 Syrah	California	C	87
1990 Syrah	California	C	86

Adam Tolmach, one of the winemaking pioneers of Santa Barbara and coproprietor of Au Bon Climat, operates this small vineyard that is increasingly dedicated to the "Rhône Ranger" philosophy. One of Ojai's best wines is their Sauvignon Blanc/Semillon blended proprietary white wine called Sainte Helene Reserve. The 1991 is composed of 67% Sauvignon and 33% Semillon. With an excellent nose of melons, herbs, and spice, and rich, medium to full body, this persuasively flavored wine possesses both power and grace. Drink it over the next 1–2 years with chicken or fish dishes. The full-bodied, ambitiously styled 1993 Sauvignon (75%)/Semillon (25%) reveals a touch of oak, considerable body and flavor extraction, and a firm, closed, and unevolved personality. An underlying mineral component in the fruit flavors should emerge after several months of bottle age. The wine is a candidate for 2–3 years of aging, an atypically long period for this varietal in California. Because it is a full-throttle wine, intensely flavored dishes are advised.

The 1991 Chardonnay from the Arroyo Grande Valley is well made, but essentially one-dimensional. I liked it, but I was not excited by it.

More interesting are the two red wine cuvées. The soft 1990 Syrah offers a jammy nose of cassis, intertwined with aromas of pepper and spicy oak. Medium bodied and round, it is meant to be consumed over the next 5–6 years. The 1991 Syrah is slightly more concentrated and fuller, with more grip and structure. It exhibits a peppery, cassis-scented nose, unctuous, soft flavors, and a mouth-filling finish. It has the potential to last for 7–8 years.

OPUS ONE (NAPA)
Proprietary Red Wine * * * */* * * * *

1992 Proprietary Red Wine	Napa	E	92
1991 Proprietary Red Wine	Napa	E	93
1990 Proprietary Red Wine	Napa	E	91

The 1992 Opus One, a blend of 89% Cabernet Sauvignon, 8% Cabernet Franc, and 3% Merlot, offers a beautiful dark ruby/purple color, a big, spicy nose of cassis, lead pencil, and smoky oak, round, full-bodied, broad, fat flavors crammed with black fruits, soft tannin, low acidity, and a fleshy, full-bodied finish. This rich wine confirms just how fine these wines have become since the 1990 vintage.

Opus One's 1991 (91% Cabernet Sauvignon, 8% Cabernet Franc, 1% Merlot) is a gorgeously rich, opaque ruby/purple-colored wine with a knockout nose of smoke, cassis, vanilla, and a whiff of herbs and licorice. Full-bodied, with surprisingly supple, concentrated, chocolaty, cassis, and black currant flavors that ooze across the palate, this voluptuously textured example of Opus One is atypical in a vintage that produced so many backward wines. There is no question the wine possesses plenty of tannin, but it is admirably concealed by the copious quantities of concentrated fruit. This Opus can be drunk now as well as over the next 15+ years.

The 1990 (87% Cabernet Sauvignon, 10% Cabernet Franc, 3% Merlot) is a terrific Opus, with a broader, deeper palate and less of the overly sculptured, structured feel that past examples have revealed. It exhibits a dark ruby/purple color, and a spicy, rich, sweet nose of cassis, vanillin, lead pencil, herbs, and minerals. Medium to full bodied, with low acidity, sweet tannin, and wonderful layers of ripe, pure, rich fruit, the wine is in complete harmony, without being excessively acidified or brutally tannic. This is a gorgeous Opus for drinking over the next 16–18 years. My instincts suggest it is the most promising Opus One made to date.

PAGE MILL (SANTA CLARA)
Cabernet Sauvignon Volker Eisele Vineyard * * * *, Chardonnay * *, Pinot Noir * * *, Sauvignon Blanc * * *

1992 Chardonnay Bien Nacido Vineyard	Santa Maria	C	87
1991 Pinot Noir Bien Nacido Vineyard	Santa Maria	C	87
1992 Sauvignon Blanc French Camp Vineyard	San Luis Obispo	A	86

Page Mill is an underrated winery that merits more attention. The ambitiously styled, serious, austere, dry, medium-bodied, spicy, herb and flinty 1992 Sauvignon Blanc French Camp Vineyard will be forbidding if not drunk with seafood or poultry. Drink this wine over the next 1–2 years. Page Mill's 1992 Chardonnay from the highly respected Bien Nacido Vineyard reveals copious quantities of tropical fruit in its moderately intense bouquet, rich, long, medium- to full-bodied flavors with good underlying acidity, and a fresh, vibrant, tart finish. It should drink well for another year.

Page Mill produces a good, albeit herbaceous, richly fruity Pinot Noir from the same Bien Nacido Vineyard. The 1991 exhibits a medium ruby color, a spicy, herbal, cherry/strawberry-scented nose, creamy texture, and fine length. Forward and ready to drink, the finish suggests there may be greater depth lurking under the wine's moderate acidity. Drink it over the next 1–3 years.

PAHLMEYER (NAPA)
Caldwell Vineyard Proprietary Red Wine * * * *, Chardonnay * * * * * (since 1993), Jayson Proprietary Red Wine * * * *

1992 Caldwell Vineyard Proprietary Red Wine	Napa	D	91
1991 Caldwell Vineyard Proprietary Red Wine	Napa	D	87+
1990 Caldwell Vineyard Proprietary Red Wine	Napa	D	89
1991 Caldwell Vineyard Minty Cuvée Proprietary Red Wine	Napa	D	89
1993 Chardonnay Not Filtered	Napa	D	93
1992 Chardonnay Unfiltered	Napa	C	88
1991 Chardonnay Unfiltered	Napa	C	92
1992 Jayson Proprietary Red Wine	Napa	C	90

Recent efforts from Pahlmeyer have suggested that some of the hard, tough tannins that were part of the rich style Pahlmeyer achieved with earlier releases have been tamed. There has been no loss of richness, but the smoother, riper tannin is a noteworthy achievement. This is good news, as effective tannin management is often ignored by many Cabernet producers. The densely, ruby/purple-colored 1992 Jayson Proprietary Red Wine possesses an intense, complex fragrance of black currants, smoke, spices, and vague underbrush notes. Full bodied and ripe, with a velvety texture and gobs of black cherry and black currant fruit, this silky, opulently styled Proprietary Red Wine is already drinking well, yet it is capable of lasting for 10–15 years.

The 1992 Caldwell Vineyard Proprietary Red Wine, a blend of Cabernet Sauvignon, Cabernet Franc, Merlot, and Petit Verdot, is a powerful, big, rich, concentrated, massive, muscular wine that requires 5–8 years of cellaring. Although it offers superb concentration, there is more tannin present in the finish than is evident in many 1992s. Although extremely tannic, but not at the expense of the wine's balance, this offering appears to possess the requisite concentration of ripe fruit to balance out the tannin. This richly scented (charcoal, cassis, vanillin) wine should last for 2 decades.

The 1991 Caldwell Vineyard Minty Cuvée Proprietary Red Wine is a wine that surely merits its name. The opaque purple color is followed by a huge nose of cassis and—no doubt about it—mint. The wine is full bodied, supple, and round, with good depth, and at least 7–12 years of evolution. In contrast, the 1991 Proprietary Red Wine Caldwell Vineyard is muscular, tannic, and concentrated, as well as backward and closed to the extent that it is nearly impenetrable. The color, mouth-feel, ripeness, and extraction are present, but the high level of astringent tannin may be cause for concern if it does not sufficiently melt away. This wine needs another 3–4 years of cellaring.

The 1990 Caldwell Vineyard Proprietary Red Wine's deep ruby/purple color and bouquet that offers pure, moderately intense aromas of smoke, cassis, and spicy oak, are followed by a wine with deep, ripe, rich, curranty flavors, firm, elevated tannins, and high acidity. Noticeable tartness from the acidity kept the score low. This wine should age well for 12–15 years.

The 1993 Chardonnay Not Filtered is a sensational effort from Jason Pahlmeyer. It appears unquestionable that more and more California wineries are taking the risks necessary to turn out Chardonnays that are better than all but a dozen or so white burgundies. Pahlmeyer, like several other California producers, has done this in 1993, fashioning a Chardonnay that could easily pass for a great burgundy grand cru. It does not possess the most polished color, but who cares, given the aromatic and flavor intensity and dimensions? Gorgeous aromas, from honey to acacia flowers to ripe apples and oranges, soar from the glass. Full bodied, and extremely lively and rich with stunning layers of pure fruit, subtle oak, and decent acidity, this is a winemaking tour de force. If I did not know better, I would think I was drinking a 1990 Corton-Charlemagne from the likes of Jean-François Coche-Dury. This California Chardonnay should last for 3–4 years.

Pahlmeyer's 1992 Chardonnay Unfiltered was exhibiting too much oak when I tasted it. Better integration of the wood would have resulted in an outstanding score, as the wine is not lacking personality, richness, or character. Loaded with opulent, chewy Chardonnay fruit, it is pure, well balanced, and delicious and satisfying despite the wood's aggressiveness. Drink it over the next 1–2 years. The rich, creamy-textured 1991 unfiltered Chardonnay is oozing with nutty, buttery, baked-apple fruit, as well as the multilayered feel one finds in minimally processed wines, wonderful purity, and a soft, rich, well-focused finish. This is Pahlmeyer's finest Chardonnay to date. Drink it over the next 1–3 years. Accolades to Pahlmeyer for taking the risk and bottling this Chardonnay unfined and unfiltered, giving the consumer all the flavor inherent in the grapes!

PARDUCCI WINE CELLARS (MENDOCINO)

Bono Syrah * */* * *, Cabernet Sauvignon * *, Chardonnay * *, French Colombard * * *, Merlot * *, Petite Sirah * */* * *, Pinot Noir * *, Zinfandel * *

1990	Cabernet Sauvignon	Mendocino	A	84
1993	Chardonnay	Mendocino	A	86
1991	Petite Sirah	Mendocino	A	86
1993	Sauvignon Blanc	North Coast	A	86

Parducci can be relied on to turn out fine values, as evidenced by this quartet of bargains. The two white wine offerings include an excellent herb-scented, fruity, medium-bodied 1993 Sauvignon Blanc, and a fuller, chunkier, more fleshy but no less charming 1993 Chardonnay. Both wines should be consumed over the next year.

The very good 1991 Petite Sirah exhibits a saturated dark purple color, a peppery-, damp earth-, and black fruit-scented nose, medium to full body, surprisingly soft flavors, good extraction, and an uncomplicated, robust, chewy personality. It should drink well for 5–6 years. The 1990 Cabernet Sauvignon offers aromas and flavors of hickory smoke, cedar, and red currants, medium body, decent flavor concentration, and an uncomplicated, straightforward character. It should drink well for 3–4 years.

FESS PARKER (SANTA BARBARA)
Chardonnay* * *, Pinot Noir* *, Merlot* *, Riesling* * * *, Syrah* * * *

1992 Chardonnay	Santa Barbara	B	86
1992 Chardonnay Reserve	Santa Barbara	C	86
1992 Chardonnay Reserve American Tradition	Santa Barbara	C	87
1993 Johannisberg Riesling	Santa Barbara	A	86
1990 Merlot	Santa Barbara	B	75
1992 Syrah	Santa Barbara	B	90

Fess Parker has approached all things in his life with considerable passion, and success has followed. With his son Eli established as winemaker, and the well-known and talented Jed Steele as consultant, this Santa Barbara winery has gone from strength to strength. I have never been a fan of California Riesling, but Parker has been able to extract its subtle floral components and funnel them into a light-bodied, wonderfully vibrant, fresh, pure wine. Most tasters would consider the 1993 Johannisberg Riesling to be dry, although technically it is off-dry. It is a delicious aperitif wine that is light but flavorful. Drink it over the next year.

The Santa Barbara Chardonnays are medium- to full-bodied wines offering attractive quantities of fresh, lively, tropical fruit married with gentle amounts of toasty oak. The less expensive 1992 Chardonnay is more direct and obviously fruity, whereas the 1992 Chardonnay Reserve American Tradition is a more ambitiously styled, fuller, more noticeably oaky wine. With admirable structure and fruit, it is best consumed over the next 1–2 years. The tasty, fleshy 1992 Chardonnay Reserve reveals copious quantities of tropical fruit judiciously touched by subtle oak. Soft, medium to full bodied, with excellent purity and ripeness, as well as a heady finish, it should drink well for 1–2 years.

Fess Parker's 1992 Syrah is a terrific bargain for such a fabulously concentrated, rich, multidimensional red wine. It leads me to believe that Santa Barbara's microclimate is well adapted to the production of high-quality Syrah. This nearly opaque purple-colored Syrah exhibits a big, smoky, cassis-scented nose. Expansive, rich, full-bodied flavors reveal super-concentration, commendable purity, lovely harmony, admirable ripeness, sweet tannin, and a finish that lasts for nearly 40 seconds. Supple for a young Syrah, this beautifully made wine should drink well for 10–15 years.

Although spicy, the 1990 Merlot is short and compact, without enough flesh or texture.

PATZ AND HALL (NAPA)
Chardonnay* * * * */* * * * *

1992 Chardonnay	Napa	C	89

This property's dazzling 1990 Chardonnay was followed by a good but slightly woody 1991. The 1992 reveals a tight, subtle bouquet of intense honeyed, buttery aromas, expansive, rich, dramatic flavors exhibiting outstanding ripeness and concentration, and admirable balance. This big, heady, alcoholic wine should be consumed over the next 1–2 years.

PEACHY CANYON WINERY (PASO ROBLES)

Cabernet Sauvignon* * * *, Merlot* * *, Zinfandel Dusi Ranch* * * *, Zinfandel
Reserve* * * *, Zinfandel West Side* * * *

1993 Zinfandel Dusi Ranch	Paso Robles	C	93
1992 Zinfandel Dusi Ranch	Paso Robles	C	89
1993 Zinfandel East Side	Paso Robles	C	90
1991 Zinfandel Especiale	Paso Robles	C	90
1993 Zinfandel West Side	Paso Robles	C	90+
1992 Zinfandel West Side	Paso Robles	C	88+
1991 Zinfandel West Side	Paso Robles	C	88

Wow! These are impressive Zinfandels with three totally different personalities. Readers who are familiar with the decadent, overripe cherry fruitiness of a great Pomerol, such as Lafleur, will see a resemblance in Peachy Canyon's 1993 Zinfandels from their East Side and West Side vineyards. The 1993 Zinfandel East Side (13.8% alcohol) exhibits an old-vine, intense, cherry-scented nose that borders on overripeness. It is full bodied, wonderfully expansive and chewy, with light tannin, low acidity, and a gorgeously layered, unctuously textured finish. This is a terrific Zinfandel for drinking over the next 7–8 years. The 1993 Zinfandel West Side adds exotic spices to the essence of cherry fruit. The wine is extremely full bodied and rich, with gobs of alcohol, exceptional concentration, and a late-harvest, dry, full-bodied, heady finish. This is a superb Zinfandel for drinking over the next decade. Amazingly, the extroverted 1993 Zinfandel Dusi Ranch is even richer. Sensationally ripe and rich, it offers awesome flavor intensity, amazing balance for its size, and a viscous, rich, full-bodied finish that lasts 45+ seconds. It does not possess the intense cherriness of the other wines given its massive composition, but it is a huge, winter-weight Zinfandel to cuddle alongside during a cold, damp day. Its alcohol is listed as a dizzyingly high 15.1%.

For pure opulence and decadently rich, full-bodied, luscious Zinfandel fruit, readers should check out Peachy Canyon's heady, thrilling 1992 Zinfandel Dusi Ranch. Its alcohol is close to 15%, but who can deny its sweet, ripe, black cherry–, and black raspberry–scented nose and flavors, and the juicy, full-bodied, glycerin-imbued, heady finish? This forceful, up-front, seductive Zinfandel is unlikely to languish on retailers' shelves. It should drink well for another decade. The 1992 Zinfandel West Side, another offering from Paso Robles that possesses 14.5% alcohol, reveals more tannin, as well as a noticeably peppery, herb, and black fruit–scented nose. Although as rich as the Dusi Ranch, it is less flattering and seductive at present. As there is more structure, body, and tannin, this wine will benefit from 1–2 years of cellaring. Both wines may merit outstanding ratings in another year or two. Once again Peachy Canyon has demonstrated a sure touch with this varietal.

Peachy Canyon has fashioned impressive Zinfandels in 1991. The dark ruby-colored 1991 Zinfandel West Side possesses a spicy, peppery, ripe fruit–scented nose, and tasty, rich, seductive flavors that reveal fine concentration as well as a sense of elegance and style. This excellent, rich, velvety-textured Zin will make delicious drinking over the next 5–6 years. The 1991 Zinfandel Especiale reveals a denser, more saturated dark ruby/purple color. The bouquet explodes from the glass, offering intensely ripe aromas of raspberries, spicy black pepper, and minerals. There is superb extraction of fruit, a deep, chewy, unctuous texture, and a long, spicy, rich, briery finish. Drink this classic, large-scale wine over the next decade.

The full-bodied, rich 1992 Merlot is more pleasing from its mouth-filling richness, textural suppleness, and layered feel than from a complexity perspective. Perhaps more will develop with aging, but for now, this big, dark ruby-colored Merlot displays gobs of fruit, plenty of body, high alcohol (14.3%), and excellent purity. It offers an unformed but generous mouthful of big, chewy, ripe Merlot. Drink it over the next 7–8 years.

J. PEDRONCELLI WINERY (SONOMA)

Cabernet Sauvignon* *, Cabernet Sauvignon Reserve* * */* * * *, Chardonnay* */* * *,
Chenin Blanc* *, Gamay Beaujolais* *, Pinot Noir*, Primavera Mista Proprietary White
Wine* *, Zinfandel* * *, Zinfandel Rosé* * *

1992 Primavera Mista Proprietary White Wine	California	A	85
1992 Zinfandel	Sonoma	A	85
1991 Zinfandel	Dry Creek	A	82

Pedroncelli has turned out a fairly priced, tasty, flattering, easygoing 1992 Zinfandel with good varietal character, fine purity, medium body, and a soft, user-friendly finish. Drink this attractive wine over the next 5–6 years. A blend of Chardonnay, Sauvignon Blanc, Chenin Blanc, and Riesling, the fresh, lively 1992 Primavera Mista should be drunk over the next year.

A reticent, nearly nonexistent nose makes me wonder if the 1991 Zinfandel was sterile filtered. Otherwise, the wine displays deep color, ripe, tasty raspberry fruit, medium body, and a crisp, stylish nose. A bit more bouquet and this wine would have merited a score in the mid-eighties.

JOSEPH PHELPS VINEYARDS (NAPA)

Cabernet Sauvignon Napa* *, Cabernet Sauvignon Backus Vineyard* * * *, Cabernet
Sauvignon Eisele Vineyard* * * (between 1987 and 1990) (before 1987* * * * *),
Chardonnay* *, Chardonnay Sangiacomo* *, Gewürztraminer* *, Insignia Proprietary Red
Wine* * * * *, Merlot* * *, Sauvignon Blanc* *, Syrah* * *, Vin du Mistral Selections* * *,
Zinfandel* * *

1993 Cabernet Sauvignon	Napa	C	90
1991 Cabernet Sauvignon	Napa	C	87
1993 Cabernet Sauvignon Backus Vineyard	Napa	D	92
1992 Cabernet Sauvignon Backus Vineyard	Napa	D	92
1991 Cabernet Sauvignon Backus Vineyard	Napa	D	90
1991 Cabernet Sauvignon Eisele Vineyard	Napa	D	92
1993 Chardonnay Ovation	Napa	D	92
1993 Insignia Proprietary Red Wine	Napa	E	95
1992 Insignia Proprietary Red Wine	Napa	E	95
1991 Insignia Proprietary Red Wine	Napa	E	92+
1991 Merlot	Napa	C	86
1993 Le Mistral	Napa	A	88
1994 Vin du Mistral Grenache Rosé	California	A	89
1992 Vin du Mistral Syrah	Napa	A	90
1994 Viognier	Napa	A	88

This winery has exhibited a mysterious track record since the mid-eighties. When I looked back at my tasting notes of California's greatest Cabernets, the name Joseph Phelps is one of the most frequent entries, particularly for such wines as the 1974 Insignia, 1975 Cabernet Sauvignon, 1975 Eisele Vineyard, 1976 Insignia, and 1978 Eisele Vineyard. All of these wines remain extraordinary examples of the monumental heights California Cabernet Sauvignon can attain. Since the mid-eighties, the wines in the Phelps portfolio—including their flagship offerings, the Backus Vineyard Cabernet Sauvignon, the proprietary red Insignia, and the Eisele Vineyard Cabernet (which they no longer produce, as the vineyard has been sold)—have been compact, lean, and nearly devoid of bouquets. Even the 1990s, so phenomenal from cask, taste significantly less impressive from bottle.

If my instincts are correct, this short-term flirtation with risk-free winemaking has changed. All the vintages since 1990 reveal more intense bouquets, texturally taste more natural, with less acidification, and possess flavors that have not been stripped by an overzealous use of fining agents and filters.

The Joseph Phelps winery, a reference point until the mid-eighties, has indeed returned to form with the thrilling wines of 1991, 1992, 1993, and 1994.

Joseph Phelps's newest releases include a stunning rosé, the 1994 Vin du Mistral Grenache Rosé. One of the finest California rosés, this crisp, lively wine offers gobs of berry fruit, medium to full body, a surprisingly extracted personality, fragrant aromas, and excellent richness and length. Several more up-and-coming wines from the Vin du Mistral series include the 1994 Viognier, a two-thirds barrel-fermented/one-third tank-fermented wine of which there are 2,000 cases available. It is the right stuff, with plenty of apricot, peach, and honey in both the aromas and flavors, medium body, crisp acidity, and gobs of freshness and zestiness. Another top-notch, reasonably priced Vin du Mistral is the 1993 Le Mistral, mostly Grenache, but with some Petite Sirah, Mourvèdre, Syrah, and Carignane in the blend. California's answer to a big, rich, fleshy Rhône wine, it exhibits a deep ruby color, a lot of pepper, black cherry, and raspberry fruitiness, full body, some fatness and chewiness, and a lusty, heady finish. It is a mouth-filling, rich wine for drinking over the next 4–5 years. The 1992 Syrah Vin du Mistral is the finest Syrah Phelps has yet made. It reveals a dark purple color, a smoky, sweet cassis, spicy nose, deep, luxuriously rich, opulent flavors, medium to full body, and a long, expansive finish without the aggressive tannin sometimes provided by Syrah. It should drink well young and last for 10–12 years.

The stunning 1992 Cabernet Sauvignon releases include the less minty, but opulent, rich, full-bodied, highly concentrated, creamy-textured 1992 Cabernet Sauvignon Backus Vineyard. Long known for its minty, chocolate-scented nose, the 1992 displays plenty of cassis and chocolate, but less mint than usual. It can be drunk young and cellared for 15–20 years. The 1992 Insignia, the flagship proprietary wine of the Joseph Phelps portfolio, is a 67% Cabernet Sauvignon/33% Merlot blend. The wine is extraordinary, with an opaque purple color, a big, spicy-, licorice-, vanillin-, smoky-, cassis-scented nose, sweet, ripe, massive flavor concentration, and well-integrated acidity and tannin, which make for an unctuous texture and a juicy mouthful of wine. It should drink well for 20+ years. It may be the most opulent and hedonistic Insignia since the debut release in 1974.

Among the 1993s, the regular cuvée of Cabernet Sauvignon may turn out to be the finest Phelps has made since their gorgeous 1985. Rich and full bodied, with loads of fruit and soft, sweet tannin, and a strong black currant character, it should drink well for 15 years. The 1993 Cabernet Sauvignon Backus Vineyard exhibits a chocolaty, minty, cassis-scented nose, and huge, unctuously textured, black fruit flavors wrapped nicely with smoky oak. The wine is full bodied, with low acidity, nicely integrated wood, and high tannin. It should drink well for 20+ years. The 1993 Insignia (80% Cabernet Sauvignon/20% Merlot) is another spectacular effort. Aged in 100% new oak casks, this wine will not be ready to drink before 2000, but it is a candidate for 20–25 years of delicious drinking. It boasts an opaque black/purple color, a fabulous nose of violets, black currants, spice, and subtle oak, full body, rich, sweet tannin, low acidity, and a long, heady, highly extracted finish. It's a beauty! The 1991 Cabernet Sauvignon Eisele Vineyard (the last Eisele produced at Phelps) is full bodied, with powerful mineral and black currant flavors, considerable tannin, and a dense, chewy finish. The wine will not reach full maturity until the turn of the century, but it should last for 20+ years.

The 1993 Ovation Chardonnay is unequivocally the finest Chardonnay ever made by Joseph Phelps. Bottled unfined and unfiltered, it possesses the massiveness, richness, and intensity of a Puligny- or Chassagne-Montrachet grand cru. There is well-integrated, toasty, smoky oak, an unctuous texture, great purity and thickness of fruit, and a long, heady finish. Drink it over the next 1–2 years.

The standard cuvées of 1991 Cabernet Sauvignon and 1991 Merlot display more aromatics and intense flavors than any red wine offering from Joseph Phelps since the mid-eighties. The dark purple-colored 1991 Merlot reveals an attractive, black cherry–scented nose, medium body, fine ripe fruit, some tartness, and a fresh, zesty finish. Drink it over the next 5–7 years. The 1991 Cabernet Sauvignon displays an opaque purple color, a big, spicy, cassis-scented nose, rich, medium- to full-bodied flavors, moderate tannin, good but not excessive acidity, and a compact, impressive finish. Accessible now, it promises to last for 14–15 years. This could turn out to be one of the best standard Cabernet Sauvignon cuvées Joseph Phelps has made since the sensational 1975.

The 1991 Cabernet Sauvignon Backus Vineyard exhibits an opaque purple color, and a huge nose of cassis, mint, licorice, and toasty oak. Full bodied, with great flavor extraction, this wine possesses an inner core of fruit, lovely suppleness from the sweetness of the tannin, and a long, rich, authoritative finish. It can be drunk now as well as over the next 10–15 years. The 1991 Insignia is a powerful, backward, full-bodied wine with considerable aging potential. A saturated black/purple color suggests high extraction of flavor as well as youthfulness. The restrained, spicy, herb-, cassis-, and vanilla-scented nose is followed by rich, intense, tannic, lingering flavors that coat the palate. Give this broodingly large-scaled wine 5–7 years of cellaring and drink it between 2000 and 2020.

R. H. PHILLIPS VINEYARD (YOLO)

Cabernet Sauvignon * *, Chardonnay * * *, Mourvèdre * * *, Sauvignon Blanc * * *,
Viognier * * *

1993 Chardonnay Barrel Cuvée	Yolo	A	87
1993 Sauvignon Blanc Night Harvest Cuvée	California	A	86
1993 Viognier Estate	Dunnigan Hills	A	88

R. H. Phillips has made thousands, even hundreds of thousands of wine drinkers happy with these inexpensive, delicious dry white wines. This winery follows the intelligent policy of preserving the freshness and liveliness of the fruit, getting the wine into the bottle quickly, and selling it at prices that must make the competition shudder. The 1993 Night Harvest Sauvignon Blanc is a textbook herb, melony, crisp, flinty Sauvignon with an attractive bouquet, lively, medium-bodied flavors, and gobs of fruit in the finish. It should drink well for another year.

I have always enjoyed R. H. Phillips's Chardonnay, but they have outdone themselves with the 1993 Barrel Cuvée. It offers as much flavor, character, and joy as can be packed into a Chardonnay for such a low price. Enormous quantities are made of this honeyed, orange-, and apple-scented wine with crisp, fresh, lush flavors, medium to full body, loads of fruit, and enough acidity to provide balance. Drink it over the next year. Consumers should be stocking up on these wines by the caseload given the superb value they represent.

R. H. Phillips's 1993 is a terrific buy in Viognier, as most wines from this flashy varietal sell for $20–$40. A honeysuckle, peach/apricot-scented wine, it is made in a fresh, medium-bodied, fruity style with loads of flavor and personality. Drink this exotic, delicious Viognier over the next year. Readers may want to consider case purchases.

PINE RIDGE WINERY (NAPA)

Cabernet Sauvignon Andrus Reserve* * * */* * * *, Cabernet Sauvignon Diamond Mountain* * * */* * * *, Cabernet Sauvignon Rutherford Cuvée* * * */* * * *, Cabernet Sauvignon Stag's Leap* * * */* * * *, Chardonnay Knollside Cuvée* * *, Chardonnay Stag's Leap* * *, Chardonnay Vieilles Vignes* * * */* * * * *, Chenin Blanc* * *, Merlot* * * */* * * *

1993 Cabernet Sauvignon Howell Mountain	Napa	C	92
1992 Cabernet Sauvignon Rutherford Cuvée	Napa	C	87
1993 Cabernet Sauvignon Stag's Leap District	Napa	C	90
1992 Cabernet Sauvignon Stag's Leap	Napa	C	90
1991 Cabernet Sauvignon Stag's Leap	Napa	C	88
1992 Chardonnay Knollside Cuvée	Napa	C	87
1991 Chardonnay Knollside Cuvée	Napa	C	87
1993 Chardonnay Stag's Leap District	Napa	C	88
1992 Chardonnay Vieilles Vignes	Napa	D	90
1993 Chenin Blanc Yountville Cuvée	Napa	A	85
1993 Merlot	Carneros	C	91
1992 Merlot	Carneros	C	88
1993 Merlot Selected Cuvée	Napa	C	89
1992 Merlot Selected Cuvée	Napa	C	86
1991 Merlot Selected Cuvée	Napa	C	87

Winemaker/proprietor Gary Andrus is frequently hitting the bull's-eye. If readers have not followed Pine Ridge's recent releases, they should give these wines a try, as just about everything has increased significantly in quality, as recent wines have been bottled without fining or filtration.

The dense, black/ruby-colored 1993 Merlot offers up spicy, toasty, black cherry and mocha/coffeelike flavors, as well as attractive, plump, juicy, chocolaty/cherry fruit, and admirable body, glycerin, and length. The wine is soft enough to be drunk when released, but it should age well for 10–12 years. The 1993 Cabernet Sauvignon Stag's Leap District displays black olive, spice, herb, and cherry/cassis fruit,wonderful richness allied to considerable elegance, outstanding intensity, and overall grace and balance. It is an attractive wine for drinking over the next 15+ years. For those with considerable patience, the 1993 Cabernet Sauvignon Howell Mountain is the most backward, structured, formidably tannic wine of this trio. It exhibits an opaque ruby/purple color, a tight but promising nose of minerals and black fruits, dense, full-bodied flavors, and significant tannic clout in the finish. It requires cellaring until the turn of the century and should last for 20 years thereafter.

The 1993 Merlot Selected Cuvée is a raspberry, cherry-scented and -flavored, medium-bodied wine with excellent depth, and a satiny-smooth texture. Drink it over the next 5–7 years. The dark-colored 1992 Merlot Selected Cuvée is a round, fruity wine with hints of herbs, mocha, and wood. It is ideal for drinking over the next 4–5 years. The 1992 Merlot

Carneros reveals a dark ruby color, a spicy, black cherry–, smoky–, chocolate-scented nose, sweet black cherry and cassis flavors, admirable richness and density, and an overall sense of elegance to go along with its concentration. It will drink well for 7–8 years. The fruity, fresh 1991 Merlot Selected Cuvée is an elegant, lighter-styled Merlot with excellent cherry, mocha fruitiness, medium body, and a soft, lush finish. Drink it over the next 5–7 years.

The 1992 Cabernet Sauvignon Stag's Leap admirably reveals the vintage's telltale characteristics such as (1) a superb saturated color, (2) a forceful, aromatic profile of roasted, rich, cassis scents, and (3) a sweet, expansive, unctuously textured palate. With low acid, this forward, gorgeously concentrated Cabernet will offer considerable pleasure in its youth, but will last for 15 or more years. The 1992 Cabernet Sauvignon Rutherford Cuvée displays an intriguing, moderately intense nose of cassis, coffee, and cherries gently infused with spicy wood. Medium to full bodied, soft, and already delicious, it should drink well for 8–10 years.

Dark ruby, with an open-knit bouquet of cassis, spice, toast, and herbs, the round, gracefully built, medium- to full-bodied 1991 Cabernet Sauvignon Stag's Leap exhibits excellent richness, a sense of harmony among its component parts, and a long, supple finish with sweet tannin. Although not made in a blockbuster style, there is plenty of depth and richness, as well as a sense of finesse and balance. Drink it over the next decade.

The 1993 Chardonnay Stag's Leap District offers layers of ripe apple/pineapplelike fruit, crisp, underlying acidity, a dash of toasty oak, and a medium- to full-bodied, brilliantly focused personality. This elegant, flavorful wine is best consumed over the next 1–2 years. The citrusy, flavorful, medium-bodied 1992 Chardonnay Knollside Cuvée exhibits a Chablis-like crispness, admirable flavor intensity, a honeyed, floral aspect, and a fine finish. Drink it over the next 1–2 years. The profound 1992 Chardonnay Vieilles Vignes (from vines planted in 1964) is the finest Chardonnay yet produced by Pine Ridge. It possesses an inner core of rich, full-bodied, concentrated, honeyed, tropical fruit notes intertwined with a mineral-like character. The gorgeous bouquet is followed by a full, rich, concentrated wine buttressed by fine acidity and the judicious use of toasty new wood. Drink it over the next 1–2 years. The elegant, understated yet authoritatively rich 1991 Chardonnay Knollside Cuvée displays an attractive nose of spice, pineapple, and floral scents. Medium bodied, with admirable richness, focus, and crispness, as well as an excellent finish, this is a stylish, flavorful wine for drinking over the next 1–2 years. Tasting 1994 cuvées of Chardonnay, Cabernet Sauvignon, and Merlot at Pine Ridge's magnificent underground caves made me think that this will be the vintage that pushes this well-run winery into Napa Valley's top echelon.

The light-bodied, fragrant, crisp, fruity 1993 Yountville Cuvée represents a delicious aperitif-style, dry Chenin Blanc. Drink it over the next year.

PINNACLES (FRANCISCAN-MONTEREY)
Chardonnay * * * *

1992 Chardonnay		Monterey	C	87

This full-bodied, buttery, round, generous Chardonnay possesses adequate acidity, a touch of smoky oak, and plenty of flesh and richness. Drink it over the next 8–12 months.

CHÂTEAU POTELLE (NAPA)
Chardonnay VGS Mount Veeder * * * *

1991 Chardonnay VGS Mount Veeder		Napa	C	88

A late-released 1991, Château Potelle's VGS Mount Veeder Chardonnay is a full-bodied wine that admirably balances power and elegance. The restrained, closed, spearminty-, spicy-, mineral-, and honey-scented nose is followed by medium- to full-bodied flavors, and well-integrated oak and acidity. It should drink well for 1–2 years.

PRESTON VINEYARDS (SONOMA)

Barbera* * */* * * *, Cabernet Sauvignon* *, Chenin Blanc* * *, Cuvée de Fumé* * *, Faux
Proprietary Red Wine* * *, Marsanne* * *, Syrah* * * *, Viognier* *, Zinfandel* * * *

1992 Barbera Estate	Dry Creek	B	87
1993 Cuvée de Fumé	Dry Creek	A	87
1993 Faux Proprietary Red Wine	Dry Creek	B	87
1994 Gamay Beaujolais	Dry Creek	B	86
1992 Zinfandel	Dry Creek	B	87

It is refreshing to see a winery that believes wine is synonymous with fun. From the colorful labels and capsules to the wines themselves, there is an obvious conviction at Preston Vineyards that wine is a beverage of pleasure. These wines from Preston will deliver some inexpensive thrills. The dark-colored 1994 Gamay Beaujolais is loaded with rich, strawberry and cherry fruit. Medium-bodied, crisp, and fresh, it will offer delightful drinking over the next year with anything from pizza and hamburgers to steak au poivre. The 1993 Faux is a Rhône Valley–inspired, fleshy, smooth-as-silk, smoky, berry-, herb-, and peppery-scented red wine with gobs of fruit, medium body, and a satiny-textured finish. It is best drunk over the next 12 months. Don't hesitate to serve either of these wines slightly chilled. The excellent 1992 Barbera possesses a deep ruby/purple color, a straightforward but enticing nose of red and black fruits, medium body, crisp acidity, and excellent purity and freshness. It should work wonders with a variety of food—from grilled hamburgers to more complicated courses such as tomato-based pastas. Drink it over the next 4–6 years.

Preston's style of Zinfandel emphasizes elegance and gracefulness without sacrificing this varietal's ripe, spicy character. The 1992 exhibits a deep ruby color, a stylish, spicy, berry-scented nose, suave, tangy, medium-bodied flavors exhibiting fine ripeness and extraction, and a spicy, well-defined, vibrant finish. Drink it over the next 4–5 years for its understated, attractive qualities.

The 1993 Cuvée de Fumé is a blend of 76% Sauvignon and 24% Semillon, the latter providing more fatness and length. Consumers will love its crisp, pure, herbal/honeyed, melon-scented nose and spicy, rich, medium-bodied, intense, fresh flavors. Drink this bargain-priced wine over the next year.

PRIDE MOUNTAIN VINEYARDS (NAPA)
Cabernet Sauvignon* * * *

1992 Cabernet Sauvignon	Napa	D	88

This dense, backward, rich Cabernet remains unevolved and almost like a barrel sample. The dark, murky, ruby/purple color suggests there has not been a lot of processing. The nose offers copious amounts of ripe, berry aromas lavishly touched by spicy new oak. This full-bodied, concentrated wine exhibits a touch of herbs in its abundant cassis flavors. The moderate tannin is neither astringent nor hard. Drink it between 1998 and 2015. Statisticians should note that it is 85% Cabernet Sauvignon and 15% Cabernet Franc; only 1,000 cases were produced.

QUIVIRA (SONOMA)
Zinfandel* * */* * * *

1992 Zinfandel	Dry Creek	B	85
1991 Zinfandel	Dry Creek	B	89

Something that always stands out in Quivira's Zinfandels is their beautiful purity of flavor. Gobs of sweet, toasty new oak and pure black cherries are readily apparent in the 1992

Zinfandel's moderately fragrant bouquet. Medium bodied, with fine fruit and purity, as well as a sense of style, this suave, elegant Zinfandel should drink well for 3–5 years. The 1991 is an unequivocal success, combining the ripe raspberry, lush Zinfandel fruit with toasty, smoky new oak. This lush, medium- to full-bodied wine exhibits layers of fruit, fine definition, and heady alcohol in the lusty finish. Drink it over the next 5–7 years.

QUPÉ WINERY (SANTA BARBARA)

Bien Nacido Cuvée* * */* * * *, Chardonnay* */* * *, Los Olivos Cuvée* * */* * * *,
Marsanne* * * *, Syrah* * *, Syrah Bien Nacido* * * * *, Viognier* * * *

1992 Bien Nacido Cuvée	Santa Barbara	C	90
1991 Chardonnay Sierra Madre Reserve	Santa Barbara	C	78?
1991 Los Olivos Cuvée	Santa Barbara	C	90
1992 Marsanne Los Olivos Vineyard	Santa Barbara	B	87
1991 Syrah	Central Coast	B	88
1991 Syrah Bien Nacido Reserve	Santa Barbara	C	90
1992 Viognier Los Olivos Vineyard	Santa Barbara	C	89

The wines of Bob Lindquist, the owner/winemaker of Qupé, continue to go from strength to strength. His current offerings are the best he has yet produced. This is a winery dedicated to the rich, bold personalities of Rhône Valley varietals. In fact, other than Calera, no other California winery makes a better Viognier. The 1992 Viognier Los Olivos Vineyard displays a huge, honeysuckle, apricot/peach-scented nose, superabundant, unctuous fruit flavors, and a dry, rich finish. Only 120 cases of this luscious Viognier were produced. If you are lucky enough to find any, serve it with crab cakes or grilled salmon. Qupé's 1992 Bien Nacido Cuvée, an innovative blend of 50% Viognier and 50% Chardonnay, is similarly styled, although slightly more defined, as well as richer and longer on the palate. It shares with the 1992 Viognier a compelling fragrance of spring flowers, peaches, and apricots, but there is more definition and body because of the Chardonnay's influence. It is a great dry white wine that may last for up to 2 years. Wonderful juice! I preferred the 1992 Marsanne Los Olivos Vineyard to the winery's 1991 Chardonnay Sierra Madre Reserve. The latter wine comes across as aggressively oaky, with the wood dominating the fruit. Additionally, I detected some greenness to the wood. Readers who have an insatiable thirst for vanillin oak will enjoy it more than I did. The Marsanne, one of the finest I have tasted from California, has more fruit, charm, and personality than many produced in the Rhône Valley. There is excellent depth, an attractive bouquet, and lovely, long, rich, medium-bodied flavors. It should drink well for another 2 years.

The three red wine cuvées I tasted all possess saturated deep ruby/purple colors. Velvety-textured, rich, full-bodied wines, they reveal exceptional winemaking. The 1991 Syrah Central Coast exhibits a dark ruby/purple color, a sweet nose of cassis, herbs, and pepper, a rich, gorgeously fruity, viscous mid-palate, and a soft finish. Delicious now, it should continue to evolve nicely for another 6–8 years. The 1991 Los Olivos Cuvée, a 60% Syrah/ 40% Mourvèdre blend, offers more aromatic complexity in its spicy, earthy, black raspberry–, and cherry-scented nose. With marvelous concentration, and a gamy, meaty side to its long, full-bodied, superconcentrated flavors, it is reminiscent of a top Bandol, and a stunning example of what can be produced from Rhône varietals planted in this area of California. Drink it over the next 6–7 years. Another explosively rich, superconcentrated, black/purple-colored wine is the 1991 Syrah Bien Nacido Reserve. A huge nose of tobacco, pepper, cassis, and herbs is followed by a wine with surprisingly soft tannins, penetrating richness, and a long, tannic, spicy finish. It is a terrific Syrah for drinking over the next decade.

RABBIT RIDGE VINEYARDS WINERY (SONOMA)

Cabernet Sauvignon* *, Chardonnay Sonoma* * * *, Chardonnay Russian River Valley* * * *,
Proprietary Red and White Wines* * */* * * *, Sauvignon Blanc* * *, Zinfandel* * * *

1989 Allure Proprietary Red Wine	Sonoma	A	85

This winery continues to impress me with its rich, pure, tasty wines that admirably express their varietal characteristics. Moreover, they offer considerable pleasure. Their delicious, inexpensive 1989 Allure, a Rhône Ranger blend, offers fleshy, rich, peppery, berry fruit in a medium-bodied, velvety-textured format.

A. RAFANELLI WINERY (SONOMA)

Cabernet Sauvignon* * *, Zinfandel* * * */* * * * *

1992 Zinfandel Unfiltered	Dry Creek	B	89
1991 Zinfandel Unfiltered	Sonoma	B	90

Dark ruby/purple colored, with an intense, gorgeously ripe nose of black raspberries, spice, and pepper, the long, medium- to full-bodied, expansively flavored, velvety-textured 1992 Zinfandel possesses loads of rich, concentrated fruit and light tannin in the heady finish. Drink it over the next 7–8 years. The deep purple-colored 1991 Zinfandel offers a blossoming bouquet of black fruits, minerals, and licorice. Superbly concentrated and full bodied, this powerful wine manages to retain an overall sense of grace and balance. The high yet soft tannins suggest the best is yet to emerge. I would recommend drinking this wine between now and 2002.

RANCHO SISQUOC WINERY (SANTA BARBARA)

Cabernet Franc* * *, Cabernet Sauvignon Estate* * *, Cellar Select Red Estate* * * *,
Chardonnay Estate* * * *, Franken Riesling (Sylvaner)* * * *, Merlot Estate* * *, Sauvignon
Blanc* * * *

1991 Cabernet Franc	Santa Maria	B	86
1989 Cabernet Sauvignon Estate	Santa Maria	B	87
1989 Cellar Select Red Estate	Santa Maria	C	88
1991 Chardonnay Estate	Santa Maria	B	88
1993 Franken Riesling (Sylvaner)	Santa Maria	A	86
1991 Johannisberg Riesling Estate	Santa Maria	A	87
1990 Merlot Estate	Santa Maria	B	86
1993 Sauvignon Blanc	Santa Maria	A	88

Virtually all of the 4,000+ cases of Rancho Sisquoc's wines are sold via a mailing list or directly from the winery, so subscribers are not likely to see much of this producer's wines on retailers' shelves. Such is the case with many of Santa Barbara's highest-quality wineries. This vast ranch includes over 200 acres, but most of the grapes are sold to wineries such as Robert Mondavi, Foxen, and Gainey. The wines that are bottled under the Rancho Sisquoc label are a distinctive group that includes a Sylvaner made from exceptionally old vines— a rarity in California. The 1993 Franken Riesling (Sylvaner) possesses more character, fruit, and charm than most Sylvaners from Alsace. Its delicately presented fruit has excellent definition and crispness. Consume this tasty wine as an aperitif or with dishes ranging from Asian to Mexican. The 1991 Johannisberg Riesling is one of the best dry American Rieslings I have tasted. Floral scented, with considerable body and length, as well as an inner core of mineral, applelike fruit, and broad, expansive flavors, this classy, complex, impeccably made wine is delicious. The 1993 Sauvignon Blanc reminds me of the white Graves made at Château Fieuzal. A big nose of toasty, smoky new oak, honeyed melon, and sweet figs is followed by a wine that is loaded with rich fruit, medium body, crisp acidity, and a long, opulent finish. It is an herb-tinged Sauvignon. Rancho Sisquoc's 1991 Chardonnay Estate offers a medium golden color, a big, buttery, honeyed-apple, tangerine-scented nose, opulent, deep fruit, fine acidity, and a luscious, long finish. Like the Sauvignon, it should be consumed over the next 2–3 years.

Rancho Sisquoc's Cabernet Sauvignon and Cabernet Franc vineyards are considered to be among the best in Santa Barbara. All their red wines possess crisp, high natural acidity, dense, almost purple saturated colors, and leafy, black fruit characters. The acidity makes them taste austere and crisp, but there is fine underlying flesh and richness. The dense purple-colored 1991 Cabernet Franc exhibits wonderful purity. The 1990 Merlot Estate is a lush, fleshy, densely concentrated wine with plenty of cherry fruit. Drink it over the next 6–7 years. Even better is the 1989 Cellar Select Red Estate wine, a blend of Cabernet Sauvignon, Cabernet Franc, and Merlot. It exhibits that full, natural, unmanipulated, unprocessed taste that so many Santa Barbara wines share. The acidity is all natural, and the wine possesses a wonderful color, a great mouth-feel, a chewy texture, and copious quantities of red and black fruits nicely touched by subtle new oak. Drink this long, attractive wine over the next 6–7 years. The 1989 Cabernet Sauvignon Estate offers a huge, herbaceous, black cherry, chocolaty, vanillin-scented nose, full-bodied, concentrated flavors that offer power allied with surprising elegance and finesse, crisp acidity, and impressive length. It can be drunk now or cellared for up to a decade.

RAVENSWOOD WINERY (SONOMA)

Cabernet Sauvignon * * *, Chardonnay Sangiacomo * * * *, Icon Proprietary Red Wine * * * * *, Merlot Sangiacomo * * * *, Merlot Vintner's Blend * * *, Pickberry Proprietary Red Wine * * * * *, Zinfandel Belloni * * * * *, Zinfandel Cooke Vineyard * * * * *, Zinfandel Dickerson Vineyard * * * * *, Zinfandel Old Hill Vineyard * * * * *, Zinfandel Old Vines * * * *, Zinfandel Monte Rosso * * * * *, Zinfandel Vintner's Blend * * *

1991 Cabernet Sauvignon	Sonoma	C	87
1993 Merlot Sangiacomo	Sonoma	C	90
1992 Merlot Sangiacomo	Sonoma	C	91
1992 Merlot Vintner's Blend	North Coast	A	86
1993 Pickberry Proprietary Red Wine	Sonoma	C	93
1992 Pickberry Proprietary Red Wine	Sonoma	C	95
1991 Pickberry Proprietary Red Wine	Sonoma	D	92+
1993 Zinfandel Belloni/Wood Lane Vineyard	Sonoma	C	92+
1992 Zinfandel Belloni Vineyard	Sonoma	C	95
1991 Zinfandel Belloni Vineyard	Sonoma	C	92+
1993 Zinfandel Cooke Vineyard	Sonoma	C	90
1992 Zinfandel Cooke Vineyard	Sonoma	C	92
1991 Zinfandel Cooke Vineyard	Sonoma	C	93
1993 Zinfandel Dickerson Vineyard	Napa	C	87
1992 Zinfandel Dickerson Vineyard	Napa	C	87
1991 Zinfandel Dickerson Vineyard	Napa	C	92+
1993 Zinfandel Monte Rosso Vineyard	Sonoma	C	91

1993	Zinfandel Old Hill Ranch	Sonoma	C	90+
1992	Zinfandel Old Hill	Sonoma	C	90+
1991	Zinfandel Old Hill	Sonoma	C	95
1993	Zinfandel Old Vines	Sonoma	C	87
1992	Zinfandel Old Vines	Sonoma	B	89
1991	Zinfandel Old Vines	Sonoma	B	89

With Ravenswood's production soaring to nearly 100,000 cases (60% is their budget-priced Vintner's Blend Zinfandel and Merlot), it is amazing that proprietor/winemaker, Joel Peterson, continues to turn out such intense wines, particularly in view of the cramped cellars in which he must work. The small quantities of single-vineyard Zinfandel he produces, usually only 500–600 cases, with the potential of significantly more of the Belloni/Wood cuvée, continue to be among the most enticing, flavorful, and distinctive California Zinfandels. The 1993s are all excellent to outstanding wines, with only the Dickerson Vineyard not living up to previous vintages' standards.

Readers are most likely to come across a bottle of the 1993 Old Vines Zinfandel, as there is much more of it than the other cuvées. It exhibits dark ruby/purple color, a sweet, black cherry–, earth-, and spicy-scented nose, layered, opulent flavors, full body, adequate acidity, and a gutsy, robust finish. It can be drunk now or cellared for 5–6 years. I continue to admire the wines that emerge from the Cooke Vineyard. The 1993 reveals a saturated, plummy/purple color, rich, black raspberry aromas with hints of licorice, truffle, and earth scents, gobs of chewy, unctuously textured fruit that suggests old vines, and a full-bodied, expansive, highly extracted finish. This complex Zinfandel can be drunk over the next 10–12 years. The 1993 Zinfandel Dickerson Vineyard (apparently being replanted) has less color saturation, and less concentration and extract than is found in the 1990 and 1991 Dickerson. Typical for this vineyard, the nose offers up a touch of mint, along with other, more Cabernet-oriented aromatics. Delicate and classy, with medium body and good concentration, this is a stylish, compact wine by Ravenswood's standards. Drink it over the next decade.

It must be a sign of the difficult times that the Louis Martini winery is selling Zinfandel grapes from their renowned Monte Rosso vineyard, but it is a bonus for consumers. Ravenswood's 1993 Zinfandel Monte Rosso is a knockout example of what this vineyard can produce when not overcropped or overprocessed. The wine exhibits an opaque purple color, sweet, mineral and black fruit aromas, and adequate acidity. It is a rich, classically structured, powerful, authoritatively flavored wine with layers of fruit, and a moderately tannic, spicy finish. Although delicious, it only hints at what will emerge with 12–18 additional months of cellaring.This silky, structured, well-focused Zinfandel will have many admirers. Drink it over the next 10–12 years. The opaque/black/purple-colored 1993 Zinfandel Belloni/Wood Lane is the quintessential California Zinfandel with its full-bodied, opulent richness, layers of highly extracted black cherry, black raspberry, and peppery fruit, and noticeably high alcohol accompanying the wine's deep, thick, richness. Because of the vintage's low acidity it is forward, yet enormously rich and intense. Zinfandel does not get much better than this! Drink it over the next decade. Lastly, the 1993 Zinfandel Old Hill offers up a dusty, earthy, spicy nose, followed by rustic, full-bodied, broad-shouldered flavors, a massive, heady, slightly tannic finish, and an uncivilized personality. This rich wine possesses an intriguing texture, but the earthy components, combined with more tannin than other offerings, make this wine less flattering to drink at present. Give it 8–12 months of cellaring and drink it over the following 12+ years.

Ravenswood's wines are not for those tasters seeking subtle, lighter-styled offerings. The

1993 Merlot Sangiacomo exhibits an opaque purple color, a big, smoky-, herb-, coffee-, and black cherry–scented nose, dense, medium- to full-bodied flavors, crisp, underlying acidity, attractive sweetness and succulence to its flavors and texture, and moderate tannin in the finish. This wine will benefit from 1–3 years of cellaring and will last for 12–15 years. The impressively built, opaque purple-colored 1993 Pickberry is an extremely powerful, chewy wine with considerable fruit extraction, huge body, high tannin, and superb purity and richness. It requires 5–6 years of cellaring and will drink well for 20+ years. It may turn out to be as good as the glorious 1992. For now, I would give the 1992 a slight edge because its fruit quality and texture provide more fat and intensity. However, that is splitting straws.

Readers should look for Joel Peterson's first Rhône Ranger blend, the 1994 Icon. It is a Sonoma blend of 50% Syrah, 25% Grenache, and 25% Mourvèdre. I was immensely impressed with the wine when I tasted it prior to bottling.

Of all the Ravenswood Zinfandels produced, the one readers are most likely to encounter is the Sonoma Old Vines (6,350 cases). The 1992 Old Vines Zinfandel is a terrific, full-bodied, extroverted Zinfandel with a dark ruby/purple color, a richly oaky, black cherry–, and hickory-scented nose, concentrated flavors, a supple personality, and a spicy, long, heady finish. Drink it over the next 7–8 years. The stunning 1992 Zinfandel Cooke Vineyard exhibits a fabulously intense, vanillin-, coffee-, herb-, and black raspberry–scented nose. Opaque purple colored, rich, and full-bodied, with loads of juicy black fruit (raspberries and cherries) in its flavors, this admirably concentrated wine reveals moderate tannin in the finish. It will benefit from 1–2 years of cellaring and should keep for 10–15 or more years.

The pick of the 1992 Ravenswood Zins is the opaque, saturated, black-colored 1992 Zinfandel Belloni Vineyard. Exhibiting a huge nose of roasted, smoky, peppery, berry fruit, full-bodied, superconcentrated flavors, moderate tannin, and a long, unctuously textured, chewy finish, it is approachable (I thought it already delicious), but 2–3 years of cellaring will prove beneficial for this blockbuster, decadently styled Zinfandel.

In the past I have remarked that the black currant and minty-scented nose of the Zinfandel from Napa's Dickerson Vineyard had more than a vague similarity to Bordeaux's famed Pauillac, Château Mouton-Rothschild. The dark ruby-colored 1992 Zinfandel Dickerson Vineyard possesses the telltale mint and cassis, but in more modest amounts than usual. The wine exhibits considerably less concentration and depth than such recent vintages as 1990 and 1991. In fact, both the Belloni Vineyard and Cooke Vineyard blew away the Dickerson. Although the latter wine is expansive and excellent, it is more narrowly constructed than previous efforts. Drink it between 1996 and 2005. Lastly, the 1992 Zinfandel Old Hill is rich, tannic, and alcoholic, with a spicy, overt, toasty, black cherry nose, full-bodied, dense, concentrated flavors, and loads of spice, alcohol, and glycerin in the finish. It needs 2–3 years of cellaring to shed its considerable tannin.

The 1991 Sonoma Old Vines Zinfandel is a big, expansive wine bursting with smoky, peppery, berry fruit. There is significant tannin (which is more noticeable in the 1991 than in the 1990), as well as a big, spicy, sweet nose, and broad, audacious flavors. The purity of fruit is super, and the finish long, lusty, and heady. This wine will benefit from another 6–12 months of bottle age and should last for 7–9 years. As in 1990, the most sexy and flattering wine is the 1991 Cooke Vineyard Zinfandel. The deep ruby/purple color is followed by a smoky, earthy, plummy nose. There is a Pomerol-like velvety texture and lushness to this heady wine with tremendous quantities of succulent, rich fruit. Fragrant, lusty, and voluptuous—altogether a real turn-on—it is presently the most complex and satisfying of the Ravenswood Zins. Drink it over the next decade.

The 1991 Zinfandel Belloni Vineyard displays an opaque, saturated black/purple color, and an unevolved nose of soaring scents of black raspberries, earth, and pepper. There is exceptional density of fruit, spectacular intensity and structure, as well as a full-bodied, moderately tannic, well-delineated finish. Along with the 1991 Zinfandel Old Hill, the

Belloni Vineyard offerings get my nod as potentially one of the two finest Zinfandels Ravenswood has produced. But be forewarned, the Belloni needs at least 3–4 years of cellaring. It should last through most of the first decade of the next century. The 1991 Zinfandel Old Hill is the quintessential Zinfandel. It exhibits an opaque purple color, and a huge, peppery, black raspberry–scented nose with subtle oak in the background. In the mouth it is pure decadence—rich, fabulously concentrated, expressive, and chewy. Layer upon layer of black raspberry fruit coat the palate with glycerin and alcohol. This is a fabulous Zinfandel for drinking now and over the next 12–15 years. True to form, the 1991 Zinfandel from the Dickerson Vineyard in Napa reveals a Mouton-Rothschild–like minty- and cassis-scented nose. Although deeply colored, it is not as saturated as either the Old Hill or the Belloni Vineyard Zinfandels. The Dickerson Vineyard cuvée is a classic Zinfandel marked by its Napa heritage. There is not quite the richness of the Belloni, nor the seductive powers of the Cooke or Old Hill offerings. Nevertheless, it is a blockbuster, full-bodied, superconcentrated, well-structured Zinfandel that needs another 1–2 years of cellaring. It will keep for 10–12 or more years.

The 1992 Pickberry appears to be the finest proprietary red wine winemaker Joel Peterson has yet produced. It exhibits a fabulously saturated color and an explosive nose of smoke, cassis, herbs, and vanillin. There is great extraction of fruit, excellent purity, fine underlying acidity, and abundant tannin. The latter two components are essential to buttress this full-throttle, massively constituted wine. If my notes suggest too much of a good thing, don't be misled. This is a classically rendered wine that should glide through the next 2 decades.

The 1992 Merlot Sangiacomo Vineyard possesses more noticeable high acidity than the 1992 Pickberry, as well as a saturated deep ruby/purple color, a ripe, perfumed nose of red and black fruits and herbs, a medium- to full-bodied, chewy texture, excellent density, and outstanding length. If it develops more complexity and the acidity becomes less noticeable, this should turn out to be an exceptional Merlot with 10–15 years of aging potential. The deeply colored 1992 Merlot Vintner's Blend offers a straightforward, enticing nose of spices, black cherries, and underbrush, followed by excellent richness, chewy, glycerin-imbued fatness, and a tasty, fleshy finish. It is a delightful, surprisingly intense Merlot for drinking over the next 4–5 years.

The 1991 Cabernet Sauvignon exhibits spicy, vanillin new oak, excellent herb-tinged, cedar, and cassis fruit, medium to full body, moderate tannin, and a long finish. Approachable now, it will benefit from 2–3 years of cellaring and will last for 10–15 years. The 1991 Pickberry Proprietary Red Wine (a blend of approximately two-thirds Merlot and the remainder mostly Cabernet Sauvignon with a tiny touch of Cabernet Franc) is another great success for this luxury-priced proprietary wine. The opaque ruby/purple color is followed by intense aromas of chocolate, cassis, herbs, and meaty scents. Deep and full bodied, with high tannin, fine acidity, and superb richness, this wine will benefit from 2–4 years of cellaring; it will last for 20 years.

Ratings for Older Vintages of Ravenswood Pickberry Proprietary Red Wine: 1990 (92), 1987 (91+), 1986 (92)

Ratings for Older Vintages of Ravenswood Zinfandel Sonoma: 1990 (88), 1989 (81), 1988 (78), 1987 (90), 1986 (89), 1985 (89)

Ratings for Older Vintages of Ravenswood Zinfandel Cooke: 1990 (94)

Ratings for Older Vintages of Ravenswood Zinfandel Dickerson: 1990 (95), 1989 (83), 1988 (83), 1987 (94), 1986 (92), 1985 (92)

Ratings for Older Vintages of Ravenswood Zinfandel Old Hill: 1990 (92), 1989 (84), 1988 (82), 1987 (93), 1986 (94), 1985 (90)

RAYMOND VINEYARD AND CELLAR (NAPA)
Cabernet Sauvignon Napa* *, Cabernet Sauvignon Private Reserve* */* * *,
Chardonnay* */* * *, Chardonnay Private Reserve* */* * *

1992 Chardonnay	Napa	B	85
1992 Chardonnay Private Reserve	Napa	C	88

Two solid Chardonnays from Raymond, the 1992 regular bottling is a pleasing, fruity, slightly woody, medium- to full-bodied, cleanly made Chardonnay that should be drunk over the next year. The 1992 Private Reserve is a rich, fat, ripe, opulent, full-bodied Chardonnay with moderate wood, plenty of alcohol (it tastes higher than the 12.5% shown on the label), and a thick, chewy, glycerin-imbued, gutsy finish. It should drink well for 1–2 years.

RENWOOD (AMADOR)
Zinfandel Cuvées* * * *

1993 Zinfandel Grand Père Vineyard	Amador	C	90
1993 Zinfandel Old Vine	Amador	C	90
1993 Zinfandel Old Vine Eschen Vineyard Fiddletown	Amador	C	92

Winemaker Scott Harvey turns out limited-production, exceptionally high quality Zinfandels from some of Amador's most renowned vineyards. The Old Vine cuvée comes from a 54-year-old plot, a youngster when compared to the 83-year-old Eschen Vineyard and 125-year-old Grand Père Vineyard. The 1993 Zinfandel Old Vine reveals a saturated black/ruby color, a late-harvest nose of prunes, overripe black cherries, spices, and earth. Full bodied, with sweet, expansive, opulently textured fruit, this wine finishes dry despite what appears to be a late-harvest style. Massive and rich, it is reminiscent of a pre-1978 Montevina Zinfandel from the same region. Drink it over the next 8–10 years as its high alcohol will unquestionably hold it together. The 1993 Zinfandel Old Vine Eschen Vineyard Fiddletown exhibits the most saturated black/purple color of this trio, and an enormously promising black-cherry and raspberry-scented nose that soars from the glass. This highly extracted, full-bodied, velvety-textured, mouthfilling, in-your-face, alcoholic, dry Zinfandel is remarkably well balanced given its size. Drink it over the next 10–15 years. Most readers will enjoy this wine more if they do not take notice of the alcohol content listed on the label.

Lastly, the 1993 Zinfandel Grand Père Vineyard offers a dark garnet/ruby purple color, decadent, sweet, earthy, cherry scents, a heavyweight, huge, full-bodied impact on the palate, an unctuous texture, and thick, viscous flavors that flow slowly across the palate. It is a dead-ringer for the 1975 Montevina Late Bottled, an Amador Zinfandel that remains remarkably fresh, fruity, and delicious at age twenty. I would opt for drinking the Grand Père over the next 12–15 years. By the way, the 125-year-old Grand Père Vineyard is reputed to be the oldest vineyard in California. These are impressive wines!

RIDGE VINEYARDS (SANTA CLARA)
Cabernet Sauvignon Monte Bello* * * * *, Cabernet Sauvignon Santa Cruz* * *, Chardonnay
Howell Mountain* * * *, Chardonnay Santa Cruz Mountains* * * *, Geyserville Proprietary
Red Wine* * * * *, Mataro Evangelo* * * *, Petite Sirah York Creek* * * * *, Zinfandel Dusi
Ranch* * * *, Zinfandel Howell Mountain* * *, Zinfandel Lytton Springs* * * * *, Zinfandel
Pagani Ranch* * * * *, Zinfandel Paso Robles* * * *, Zinfandel Sonoma* * *

1992 Cabernet Sauvignon	Santa Cruz	C	89
1991 Cabernet Sauvignon	York Creek	C	87
1990 Cabernet Sauvignon	Santa Cruz	C	89

1992 Cabernet Sauvignon Monte Bello	Santa Cruz	D	96
1991 Cabernet Sauvignon Monte Bello	Santa Cruz	D	92+
1991 Chardonnay	Santa Cruz	C	89
1992 Geyserville Proprietary Red Wine	Sonoma	C	92
1991 Geyserville Proprietary Red Wine	Sonoma	C	90
1992 Mataro Evangelo Vineyard	Contra Costa	C	89
1990 Petite Sirah	York Creek	C	90
1991 Zinfandel	Paso Robles	C	90
1992 Zinfandel Dusi Ranch	Paso Robles	C	90
1992 Zinfandel Lytton Springs	Sonoma	C	94
1991 Zinfandel Lytton Springs	Sonoma	C	92
1992 Zinfandel Pagani Ranch	Sonoma	C	92

The third straight superlative vintage for Ridge, the 1992 Zinfandels are big, rich, decadent wines with higher alcohol levels than the 1991s or 1990s, and possibly more voluptuous and opulent textures. The large-scale, dry 1992 Zinfandel Dusi Ranch (14.9% alcohol) displays a deep ruby/purple color, and a forceful, expansive nose of crushed, jammy black cherries and loamy, earthy scents. Full bodied, with an unctuous texture, and plenty of glycerin and fatness, this chewy, decadent Zinfandel can be drunk over the next 7–8 years.

The 1992 Geyserville Proprietary Red Wine (65% Zinfandel, 20% Carignane, and 15% Petite Sirah) offers an opaque dark ruby/purple color, and a huge, roasted meat, smoky, spicy, black raspberry–scented nose. With gobs of rich, chewy fruit, low acidity, and admirable power and richness, this thick, juicy, succulently styled, decadent wine should drink well for 10–15 years. Lastly, the 1992 Zinfandel Lytton Springs looks to be an awesome example from this great Zinfandel vineyard. The color is an opaque dark purple, and the nose soars from the glass, offering wonderfully ripe, pure aromas of black raspberries, cherries, spice, and sweet vanillin scents. Full bodied, with great intensity, layers of deep, chewy fruit, low acidity, and wonderful purity and definition, this blockbuster Zinfandel (14.9% alcohol) should drink well for a decade or more.

Dark ruby colored, with an intensely fragrant bouquet of black and red fruits, pepper, and spicy wood, the supple 1992 Mataro Evangelo Vineyard is medium to full bodied, with loads of delicious glycerin-imbued, chewy fruit. A joy to drink, Ridge's 1992 Mataro (Mourvèdre) should continue to drink well for 6–7 years. My instincts suggest this would be a flexible wine to serve with a multitude of dishes.

The 1992 Cabernet Sauvignon from the Santa Cruz Mountains is a boldly styled, opulent, richly fruity, fat Cabernet bursting with superripe fruit. Loaded with glycerin, spice, and extract, it should be drunk over the next decade.

The 1992 Cabernet Sauvignon Monte Bello looks to be one of the greatest examples of Monte Bello Cabernet Sauvignon Ridge has produced. Only 40% of the crop made it into the final blend, which consists of 75% Cabernet Sauvignon, 11% Merlot, 10% Petit Verdot, and 4% Cabernet Franc. The wine offers a black/purple color, a profound nose of minerals, cassis, licorice, and spices, spectacular richness, and a great mid-palate that boasts layers of fruit. Admirable purity, fine underlying acidity, and considerable sweet, ripe tannin make this another compelling effort. Given the stunning 1990 Ridge Monte Bello and the exceptional promise of both the 1991 Monte Bello and the 1993 Monte Bello, Ridge has a quartet of stunning Cabernets that rival, and possibly eclipse, what this winery achieved in 1968, 1969, 1970, and 1971. Assuming good cellar conditions, the 1992 Monte Bello should have 30–35 years of longevity. The 1991 Monte Bello tastes similar to a classic Bordeaux in the sense that the lead pencil–, cassis-, licorice-scented nose is reminiscent of a high-class Pauillac. One would never guess it was aged in American oak, because the wood character is so subtle and well balanced. A rich yet restrained wine, it exhibits a formidable inner core of intensity as well as great balance and superb style. Given the glacial pace at which the Monte Bello Cabernets evolve, I suspect owners will still be extolling this wine's virtues in 25–30 years. I would not touch a bottle before the turn of the century. The 1991 should prove to be a classic Monte Bello and among the best wines produced by Ridge.

The 1991 Chardonnay is a big, muscular, oaky, buttery wine that should not be consumed by anybody looking for wimpish, understated Chardonnay. With excellent richness and balance, as well as a big, spicy, forceful character, it should drink well for 1–3 years.

Among the 1991 red wine offerings is a superb single-vineyard offering, the 1991 Pagani Ranch Zinfandel. I adored this 84% Zinfandel, 10% Petite Sirah, and 6% Alicante blend. It must be from super-old vines given its massive concentration of fruit and intensity. The spicy, peppery, earthy, black raspberry–scented nose is followed by a rich, full-bodied wine with layers of fruit, and a finish that nearly lasts a minute. This wine represents the essence of the Zinfandel grape. Drink it over the next 7–10 years. The 1991 Cabernet Sauvignon York Creek Vineyard is not yet ready for drinking, unless you have a masochistic urge to be slammed by its considerable tannin. The dark ruby/purple color is followed by a promising nose of cassis, damp earth, and minerals. Muscular and full-bodied, with excellent density, admirable ripeness, and a moderately tannic finish, this is a wine to cellar for 2–3 years and drink through the first decade of the next century. The 1991 Zinfandel Lytton Springs (80% Zinfandel, 12% Petite Sirah, 6% Grenache, 2% Carignane) also has over 14% alcohol, and like its sibling, its superconcentration of fruit covers any alcoholic heat. The deep ruby/purple color is followed by gobs of jammy black currant and black raspberry fruit. This big, heady, spicy, chewy, fleshy wine is soft and succulent, with a velvety finish. Drink it over the next 7–8 years. I thought Ridge's 1991 Zinfandel from Paso Robles was the best I have tasted from this impeccably run winery. Gushing with black cherry and black raspberry fruit, it is a soft, corpulent wine because of its lush, chewy, fleshy style, with superb ripeness and richness, as well as a long, unctuous, rich finish. Because it is one of the most seductive 1991 Zinfandels, readers should not buy more than they will drink over the next 5–6 years.

The big 1991 Geyserville proprietary red wine (50% Zinfandel, 30% Carignane, and 20% Petite Sirah) has 14.3% alcohol, but there is so much fruit that the wine's power and alcohol are masked. The color is deep ruby/purple, and the nose offers up fragrant ripe aromas of black fruits, minerals, and oak. Surprising elegance is allied with superconcentrated, rich fruit. The finish is all fruit, glycerin, and lushness. This seductive, spicy, mouth-filling wine should drink well for 8–10 years.

Petite Sirah lovers will be delighted to hear that Ridge's 1990 York Creek Petite Sirah is another winner. Although backward and closed, it is hard to ignore its opaque purple color, and big, flashy nose of licorice, cassis, and spicy oak. Full bodied, with massively concentrated flavors, this behemoth should be laid away for 4–5 years. As vertical tastings of Ridge York Creek Petite Sirah have proven, top vintages of this wine last for 18–25 years.

The 1990 Cabernet Sauvignon Santa Cruz cuvée is one of the best Santa Cruz offerings Ridge has made in years. Fashioned from vineyards below the famed Monte Bello vineyard, this deep ruby/purple-colored wine reveals a fragrant nose of underbrush and black fruits. Full bodied and fleshy, with rich, jammy, black raspberry, smoky, earthy flavors, as well as a succulent personality, this fleshy, reasonably priced Cabernet offers a husky mouthful of wine. It should continue to drink well for 10–12 years.

Ratings for Older Vintages of Ridge Vineyards Cabernet Sauvignon Monte Bello: 1990 (93+),

1989 (75), 1988 (77), 1987 (90), 1986 (85), 1985 (92), 1984 (94), 1982 (74), 1981 (90), 1980 (78), 1978 (92), 1977 (92), 1976 (69), 1975 (85), 1974 (90), 1973 (83), 1972 (90), 1971 (93) (There is also a 1971 Ridge Eisele Vineyard Cabernet Sauvignon that I have rated as high as 94), 1970 (94), 1964 (90)

Ratings for Older Vintages of Ridge Vineyards York Creek Petite Sirah: 1988 (88), 1987 (90), 1986 (90), 1985 (92), 1984 (86), 1982 (90), 1979 (93), 1976 (91), 1975 (89), 1974 (82), 1973 (83), 1972 (83), 1971 (92)

Note: Under their advance tasting program, Ridge also bottled tiny lots of a mammoth-sized, stupendous Petite Sirah from the very old vines of the Devil's Hill vineyard.

J. ROCHIOLI (SONOMA)

Cabernet Sauvignon * * *, Chardonnay * * * *, Chardonnay Reserve * * * */* * * * *, Gewürztraminer *, Pinot Noir East Block * * * * *, Pinot Noir Estate * * * *, Pinot Noir Three Corner Vineyard * * * * *, Pinot Noir West Block * * * * *, Sauvignon Blanc * * *, Sauvignon Blanc Reserve * * * */* * * * *

1993 Cabernet Sauvignon Reserve Neona's Vineyard	Russian River	D	91
1993 Chardonnay	Russian River	C	88
1993 Chardonnay Reserve	Russian River	D	92
1993 Pinot Noir Estate	Russian River	D	88
1993 Pinot Noir Reserve Estate Three Corner Vineyard	Russian River	D	90
1992 Pinot Noir Reserve Estate Three Corner Vineyard	Russian River	D	90
1993 Pinot Noir Reserve Estate West Block	Russian River	D	92
1992 Pinot Noir Reserve Estate West Block	Russian River	D	92
1992 Pinot Noir Reserve Vintage Selection East Block	Russian River	E	90+
1994 Sauvignon Blanc	Russian River	B	87
1994 Sauvignon Blanc Reserve	Russian River	C	90

Rochioli's 1993 Pinot Noirs are very impressive. This family, which planted their vineyard in 1938 and continues to sell nearly 70% of the crop to other growers, seems intent on estate-bottling more of their wines. Pinot Noir fanatics can be grateful, as they have three beautiful Pinot Noirs in 1993 and 1992 that were all bottled without fining or filtration. Unfortunately, quantities are small, ranging from 75 cases to a mere 200 cases. The 1993 Pinot Noir Estate exhibits a framboise-scented nose, sweet, ripe, raspberry and cherry flavors, full body, and a soft, silky finish. The 1993 Pinot Noir Three Corner Vineyard reveals a similar raspberry-scented nose, more expansive, richer flavors, good structure lurking behind the lavish fruit, smoky oak, and a spicy, opulent, full-bodied finish. I have had the sensational 1993 Pinot Noir West Block on two different occasions—at the winery and in a blind tasting of some of the top American Pinot Noirs. It stands out for its gloriously perfumed, black cherry— and raspberry-scented nose with hints of toasty oak and floral aromas. It is full-bodied, with gobs of concentration and glycerin, an unctuous texture, and a whoppingly long, luxurious, satiny finish. It should drink well for 7–8 years.

From time to time Rochioli also produces a terrific Pinot Noir with an East Block designation. The 1994 barrel sample was stunning.

The dark ruby-colored 1992 Three Corner Vineyard cuvée offers sweet fruit, light tannin, full body, and a long, lush finish. It should drink well for 5–6 years. My favorite of this trio is the 1992 West Block. Its knockout bouquet of black fruits, toasty new oak, and flowers is followed by gorgeously ripe, sweet, fleshy flavors with enough acidity to provide delineation and grip. This stunning Pinot Noir is among the best I have tasted from the new world. Consume it over the next 7–8 years. The most expensive wine is the backward and tannic 1992 Vintage Selection East Block. It is not as flattering or seductive as the West Block or Three Corner Vineyard Pinots. While it is unquestionably a fine wine, the price is hard to comprehend vis-à-vis the others.

Rochioli also turns out fine Chardonnays. The 1993 offers a sweet, creamy texture, excellent ripeness, tropical fruit, a nice infusion of wood, and a crisp finish. Unfortunately, there are only 200 cases of the 1993 Chardonnay Reserve, a powerful, rich, opulently styled wine with gobs of fruit, a pure, honeyed fruitness, dizzyingly high alcohol in the finish, and enough acidity to provide freshness and intensity.

Perhaps the most underappreciated wine in the Rochioli portfolio is their Sauvignon Blanc. Made from old vines, the 1994 Sauvignon Blanc from the Russian River displays a crisp, melony, fragrant nose, medium-bodied, lively flavors, and a dry finish, Even better is the 1994 Sauvignon Blanc Reserve, a 100% barrel-fermented Sauvignon from what is believed to be Sonoma's oldest Sauvignon vineyard, which was planted in 1959. The wine offers a melony, fig, and subtly herbaceous nose, wonderfully rich, honeyed flavors, medium to full body, and amazing concentration and intensity. It is aged in 50% new French oak barrels. Sadly, only 100 cases were produced.

Lastly, Rochioli produces about 150 cases of Cabernet Sauvignon. The current release is the 1992 Cabernet Sauvignon Reserve Neona's Vineyard, an opaque black/purple-colored wine with a terrific nose of cassis, smoke, and minerals, full body, layers of concentration, and a voluptuously textured, long finish with light tannin.

Given the quality of the wines being produced at Rochioli, it is a shame so little of the production (only 8,500 cases) is estate-bottled.

ROCKING HORSE (NAPA)
Cabernet Sauvignon * * *, Claret * *, Zinfandel * * *

1990 Zinfandel Lamborn Vineyard	Howell Mountain	B	86

The dark, plum-colored 1990 Zinfandel Lamborn Vineyard displays a spicy, vanillin-scented nose, and rustic, full-bodied flavors dominated by tough tannins. The excellent underlying extraction of fruit is accompanied by a certain astringence and firmness that suggest cellaring may be beneficial. On the other hand, the tannins may turn out to be too excessive for the wine's fruit. Time will tell. I would wait at least 2 years before pulling the cork on what appears to be a good wine. It should last for up to a decade.

ROCKLAND (NAPA)
Cabernet Sauvignon * * * */* * * * *, Petite-Sirah * * * * *

1992 Cabernet Sauvignon	Napa	D	90
1992 Petite Sirah	Napa	D	92

The 1992 Petite Sirah is from the family-owned vineyard of Peter Michael Winery's highly talented winemaker, Mark Aubert. Made from 45-year-old vines situated outside Calistoga, near Château Montelena, the wine was aged for 24 months in 25% new oak casks and bottled unfiltered. It is a tremendously impressive Petite Sirah, with more Syrah characteristics than Petite Sirah. The color is an opaque purple. Although initially closed, the nose opens to reveal aromas of smoke, black currants, and black raspberries. Full bodied, rich, and beautifully balanced, with unobtrusive, but noticeable tannin, as well as adequate acidity and a sensational finish, the wine coats the mouth with a viscous feel. While accessible, it is not yet ready for prime-time drinking. This superb effort should hit its peak in 3–4 years and last for 20. Equally impressive is the 1992 Cabernet Sauvignon made from a vineyard situated just above the renowned Grace Family Vineyard. A blend of 76% Cabernet Sauvignon, 12% Merlot, and 12% Cabernet Franc, the wine is aged 30 months in oak casks (of which 45% are new), and is bottled without filtration. The wine exhibits a healthy, deep ruby/purple color, and a promising and emerging nose of gorgeously sweet black currant fruit nicely touched by new wood. Tannic, backward, and rich, as well as pure and promising, this full-bodied, muscular Cabernet Sauvignon should drink well from the late nineties through the first decade of the next century.

ROMBAUER VINEYARDS (NAPA)
Cabernet Sauvignon * *, Chardonnay * * *, Merlot * *

| 1993 Chardonnay | Carneros | B | 87 |

It has been ages since I have been able to recommend a Rombauer wine, so I was delighted to see the strong performance of this 1993 Chardonnay. It exhibits a lovely nose of spring flowers, honey, and buttery fruit, a multitextured feel, freshness and ripeness, and medium to full body. It is a delicious, generously endowed Chardonnay for drinking over the next year.

ROSENBLUM CELLARS (ALAMEDA)
Zinfandel Michael Marston Vineyard * * * * *, Zinfandel Other Cuvées * * * *, Zinfandel Samsel Vineyard * * * * *

1992 Zinfandel	Contra Costa	B	88
1991 Zinfandel	Contra Costa	B	87
1992 Zinfandel Brandlin Ranch Mount Veeder	Napa	C	90
1991 Zinfandel Brandlin Ranch Mount Veeder	Napa	C	90
1992 Zinfandel George Hendry Vineyard	Napa	C	89
1992 Zinfandel George Hendry Vineyard Reserve	Napa	C	92
1991 Zinfandel George Hendry Vineyard Reserve	Napa	C	88
1991 Zinfandel Michael Marston Vineyard	Napa	C	90
1992 Zinfandel Old Vines	Sonoma	B	88
1992 Zinfandel Samsel Vineyard Maggie's Reserve	Sonoma	C	87
1991 Zinfandel Samsel Vineyard Maggie's Reserve	Sonoma	C	90
1992 Zinfandel Richard Sauret Vineyard	Paso Robles	C	89
1991 Zinfandel Richard Sauret Vineyard	Paso Robles	C	87
N.V. Zinfandel Vintner's Cuvée VIII	California	A	87
N.V. Zinfandel Vintner's Cuvée VI	California	A	87

Rosenblum Cellars continues to rank among California's leading Zinfandel producers. Their N.V. Zinfandel Vintner's Cuvée VIII is one of the most exceptional buys in the marketplace. It exhibits a dark ruby color, an excellent ripe berry-scented nose, round, lush, velvety-textured flavors, and a spicy, fleshy finish. Readers would be hard-pressed to find a more generous mouthful of wine for the price. Drink it over the next several years. The 1992 Zinfandel Contra Costa is also an attractively priced, well-made wine. Its dark ruby color is followed by a big, sweet, black raspberry–scented nose, a velvety texture, heady alcohol, and juicy, chewy glycerin in the finish. Drink it over the next 5–6 years. The 1992 Zinfandel Richard Sauret Vineyard from Paso Robles offers intense black and red fruit scents in its spicy, dusty, earthy nose. A black cherry component dominates this full-bodied, tannic, dense, impressive but somewhat monolithic wine. It will provide a big, chunky, rustic mouthful over the next 7–8 years. Hopefully, more finesse and charm will emerge. The saturated, dark-colored 1992 Zinfandel Old Vines from Sonoma is a plump, ripe, full-bodied wine with gobs of jammy black cherry fruit, a plush texture, and a low-acid, round finish. Delicious now, it should drink well for another 7–8 years.

The outstanding 1992 Zinfandel from Mount Veeder's Brandlin Ranch reveals a saturated dark purple color, a wonderfully pure, intense, mineral-, cassis-, and black cherry–scented nose, great richness and ripeness, medium to full body, and layers of concentrated fruit buttressed by spicy oak and adequate acidity. This large-scale, rich, harmonious wine should drink well for a decade. Rosenblum's 1992 Zinfandel Samsel Vineyard Maggie's Reserve is leaner and less intense than the 1991 and 1990. It displays a dark ruby/purple color, a spicy, moderately intense bouquet, a compact, medium-bodied format, and a ripe, moderately tannic, spicy finish. Drink it over the next decade.

In 1992 there are both regular cuvée and reserve offerings from Napa's George Hendry Vineyard. The 1992 Zinfandel George Hendry regular cuvée is dark ruby/purple colored, with a smoky, meaty, black fruit–scented nose, rich, full-bodied flavors, gobs of concentration, and a moderately long, spicy, tannic finish. It will benefit from 1–2 years of cellaring and keep for 12–15 years. The 1992 Zinfandel George Hendry Reserve exhibits a more saturated ruby/purple color, a huge cassis-, cherry-, and raspberry-scented nose with vague notes of oak and minerals. Deep and full bodied with loads of concentration, this stunningly rich, broad-shouldered, blockbuster Zinfandel is amazingly well balanced for its size and intensity. Drink it over the next 10–15 years.

The 1991 offerings are all marvelous wines. Readers should especially take note of the nonvintage Vintner's Cuvée VI, which is a super bargain. Its soft, fleshy, peppery-, raspberry scented nose and flavors offer wonderful ripeness in a lush, opulent, heady style. It should drink well for 3–4 years. The spicy, rich, medium- to full-bodied, soft, chewy 1991 Zinfandel Richard Sauret Vineyard in Paso Robles should be drunk over the next 5–6 years. Rosenblum's 1991 Zinfandel Samsel Vineyard Maggie's Reserve from Sonoma Valley is a more backward, age-worthy Zin. The saturated purple color, spicy, peppery, black fruit–scented nose, and rich, intense, medium- to full-bodied flavors are buttressed by surprisingly crisp acidity and moderate tannins. The finish is long and persuasive. Drink this wine over the next decade. The 1991 Zinfandel from the George Hendry Vineyard on Napa's Mount Veeder is made in a completely different style. A flowery, fragrant, penetrating, evolved bouquet is followed by a wine with crisp, rich, wonderfully pure fruit, excellent definition, medium body, and a spicy, well-endowed style. Drinkable now, this wine promises to last for up to a decade.

Rosenblum Cellar's 1991 Zinfandel from the Michael Marston Vineyard exhibits a sensational nose of black cherries, black raspberries, minerals, and vague scents of chocolate and pepper. It is a blockbuster wine, with massive quantities of fruit, glycerin, and alcohol. This large-scale, full-throttle Zin is the biggest of the Rosenblum offerings. Drink it over the next 10–12 years. The 1991 Zinfandel from Contra Costa reveals a plummy color, a big, spicy, cinnamon- and pepper-scented nose, dense, chewy, full-bodied flavors, and plenty of extract and glycerin. With its husky mouth-feel, it is ideal for drinking over the next 5–6 years. Lastly, the 1991 Zinfandel Brandlin Ranch (from a vineyard on Mount Veeder) possesses fabulous purity and richness to its black raspberry fruitiness. Full bodied, with spicy, moderate tannins, and a multilayered feel, this big yet gracefully made, well-balanced Zinfandel should last for 7–10 years.

Rosenblum Cellars appears intent on challenging Ravenswood and Ridge as one of California's leading Zinfandel producers.

ROSS VALLEY (SONOMA)
Zinfandel * * * *

1990 Zinfandel Tom and Kelly Parsons Vineyard	Sonoma	B	88?

I immensely enjoyed the 1987 Ross Valley Zinfandels, but the 1989s were hard, hollow wines. One bottle of the 1990 Zinfandel hit the palate with excessive acidity and green, harsh tannins. Another bottle was gorgeous—rich, deep, generously endowed, and full bodied. It was loaded with fruit, had excellent structure, and a long finish. Should I assume the better bottle is a more valid example of this wine's quality?

ROUND HILL (NAPA)
Cabernet Sauvignon * *, Cabernet Sauvignon Reserve * */* * *, Chardonnay * *, Zinfandel * *

1990 Zinfandel	Napa	B	78
1992 Zinfandel R.H.	Napa	B	72
1992 Zinfandel Reserve	Napa	B	74

I do not find excessively acidified wines to be attractive or pleasingly palatable. Although the two 1992 offerings exhibit fine color, high, tart, green acidity gives them a sharp, thin, angular feel. They are totally charmless. The 1990 offers plenty of ripeness, but light body and a short finish. Drink it up.

ST. CLEMENT VINEYARDS (NAPA)
Cabernet Sauvignon * * *, Chardonnay * *, Oroppas Proprietary Red Wine * * */* * * *,
Sauvignon Blanc * *

1990 Cabernet Sauvignon	Napa	C	88
1991 Merlot	Napa	C	86
1991 Oroppas Proprietary Red Wine	Napa	C	87

It has been a long time since I recommended three wines from St. Clement. The new Japanese owner, Sapporo, has gotten serious about upgrading the quality. The 1990 Cabernet Sauvignon displays a dense purple color, a ripe, vanillin-scented nose, and rich, medium- to full-bodied flavors that reveal admirable glycerin and extract, as well as a sense of balance. The bouquet and flavors demonstrate that the wine has not been excessively processed or acidified. I also enjoyed the 1991 Merlot. The impressive opaque ruby/purple color is followed by big, rich, black cherry aromas intermingled with scents of olives. Smooth, rich, and robust, this is a chunky, delicious Merlot for drinking over the next 4–5 years. St. Clement's proprietary red wine, the 1991 Oroppas (Sapporo spelled backward), offers a deep ruby/purple color and a sweet jammy nose of black fruits and toasty new oak. The wine has yet to develop complexity. It is a rich, full-bodied, concentrated, low-acid wine with pure flavors. Drink it over the next 12–15 years.

ST. FRANCIS VINEYARD (SONOMA)
Cabernet Sauvignon Reserve * * * *, Chardonnay * * *, Chardonnay Reserve * * * *,
Merlot * * *, Merlot Reserve * * * *, Muscat Canelli * * * *,
Zinfandel Old Vines * * * */* * * * *

1990 Cabernet Sauvignon Reserve	Sonoma	C	90
1993 Chardonnay	Sonoma	A	86
1992 Chardonnay Reserve Estate	Sonoma	C	93
1990 Merlot Estate	Sonoma	C	87
1990 Merlot Reserve	Sonoma	C	88
1992 Zinfandel Old Vines Unfined/Unfiltered	Sonoma	B	92

This fabulous Zinfandel is made from a blend of grapes from Sonoma's 68-year-old vines of the Francesco Vineyard and the 100-year-old vines of the Pagani Vineyard. Its dark, saturated, ruby/purple color is followed by a huge nose of Asian spices, American oak, and black cherries. Bursting with concentrated fruit, this full-bodied wine reveals an unctuous texture, gobs of glycerin, and head-spinning alcohol in the finish. Drink this rich, opulently styled Zinfandel over the next 5–7 years. It is one of the stars of the vintage!

Rich and buttery, with copious quantities of tropical fruit, this clean, delicious 1993 Chardonnay is ideal for drinking over the next year. The gorgeously rich 1992 Chardonnay Reserve Estate is a knockout! From its soaring bouquet of grilled nuts, honey, butter, and ripe apples, to its lush, full-bodied, graceful flavors that exhibit layers of fruit, wonderful complexity, and fine underlying acidity, this may be the finest Chardonnay St. Francis has yet made! Drink it over the next 1–2 years.

The flamboyant 1990 Merlot Reserve exhibits a huge nose of rich, chocolaty, herb, and plumlike fruit, followed by coffee, berrylike flavors, a viscous texture, low acidity, and a lusty, heady finish. It will not last long, but for drinking over the next 5–6 years it will make for a delicious, exotic glassful of Merlot. The 1990 Merlot Estate possesses a deep ruby/purple color, an excellent nose of herbs and cassis, a supple, richly fruity, lush texture, and a heady, alcoholic, rich finish. It should drink well for 4–5 years.

The dark, opaque, purple-colored 1990 Cabernet Sauvignon Reserve reveals an intense nose of ripe cassis, Asian spices, herbs, and earth. Full bodied, with spectacular concentration, a fat, chewy fruitiness, and a long, moderately tannic, authoritatively rich finish, it should drink well for 10–15 years.

SADDLEBACK CELLAR (NAPA)
Zinfandel * * * *

1993 Zinfandel	Napa	C	91
1992 Zinfandel	Napa	C	91

Saddleback Cellar is owned by Nils Venge, the former winemaker at both Villa Mt. Eden and Groth. If you are considering serving roasted boar at your next dinner party, this monstrous, yet immensely impressive, black/purple-colored, portlike 1993 Zinfandel is the wine to drink. It possesses an element of *sur-maturité*, offering up a huge, jammy, black-cherry, licorice, peppery, and herb-scented nose. Exceptionally rich and full bodied, with no residual sugar, but a very ripe, blockbuster, chewy style, this enormous Zinfandel must carry at least 14+% alcohol. Fortunately, the wine has balance. Drink this Zinfandel over the next decade. The 1992 Zinfandel admirably displays Venge's talent for turning out blockbuster, opulent, concentrated, seductive, decadent wines. The impressive deep, opaque, dark ruby color is followed by a huge bouquet of jammy black cherries, leather, chocolate, and spice. Full bodied and dense, with copious amounts of glycerin, this heady, chewy, succulently textured Zinfandel should drink superbly for 7–8 years. Don't miss it!

SAINTSBURY WINERY (NAPA)
Chardonnay * * *, Chardonnay Reserve * * *, Pinot Noir Carneros * * * *, Pinot Noir
Garnet * * *, Pinot Noir Reserve * * * *

1990 Pinot Noir	Carneros	C	87
1991 Pinot Noir Garnet	Carneros	B	86
1990 Pinot Noir Reserve	Carneros	D	91

Proprietors David Graves and Dick Ward have produced a light, delicate 1991 Pinot Noir Garnet that is reminiscent of a good Côte de Beaune from France. Soft, expansive, and perfumed, it is a wine that offers immediate appeal. It should have been a huge success with restaurants wanting to offer their clients tasty Pinot Noir at a reasonable price. Along with the Garnet cuvée, they also make a more ambitious, richer Carneros bottling. It emphasizes more black fruits, body, glycerin, and slightly higher alcohol. It is also framed by more noticeable use of oak. It has always been a very good wine, with its personality defined by its rich, juicy, succulent black cherry fruitiness. In 1990 Saintsbury offered a limited-production Pinot Noir Reserve. It is unquestionably one of the finest Pinot Noirs I have tasted from California. A stunning wine, it offers a huge perfume of toasty new oak and red and black fruits. Opulent and voluptuous, with copious quantities of sweet, expansive Pinot fruit, this wine is impossible to resist, but gives promise of lasting another 4–6 years.

SALMON CREEK VINEYARDS (NAPA)
Chardonnay * * * *

1992 Chardonnay Bad Dog Ranch	Napa	C	88
1991 Chardonnay Bad Dog Ranch	Napa	C	87

These Chardonnays, made by the former vineyard manager for Dominus, Daniel Baron, possess a high-toned, intense, mineral-scented character reminiscent of a top-class Chablis. Stylistically they are a world apart from most California Chardonnays. While the 1992 is more alcoholic, richer, and fatter, it possesses a pervasive, stony, mineral character and zesty, crisp, well-integrated, natural-tasting acidity. Although lighter, the 1991 is medium bodied, concentrated, elegant, and graceful. Both wines should drink well for 2–4 years.

SANFORD WINERY (SANTA BARBARA)
Chardonnay * * * *, Chardonnay Barrel Select * * * * *, Chardonnay Sanford & Benedict Vineyard * * * * *, Pinot Noir * * * *, Pinot Noir Barrel Select * * * * *, Pinot Noir Sanford & Benedict Vineyard * * * * *, Sauvignon Blanc * * * *

1992 Chardonnay	Santa Barbara	C	90
1991 Chardonnay	Santa Barbara	C	89
1992 Chardonnay Barrel Select Unfiltered	Santa Barbara	D	92
1991 Chardonnay Barrel Select Unfiltered	Santa Barbara	D	90
1992 Chardonnay Sanford & Benedict Vineyard	Santa Barbara	D	90
1992 Pinot Noir Barrel Select Sanford & Benedict Vineyard	Santa Barbara	D	87
1991 Pinot Noir Barrel Select Sanford & Benedict Vineyard	Santa Barbara	D	91
1990 Pinot Noir Barrel Select Sanford & Benedict Vineyard	Santa Barbara	D	93
1991 Pinot Noir	Santa Barbara	C	90
1993 Pinot Noir Vin Gris	Santa Barbara	A	87

As the scores attest, Sanford is one of California's most fashionable wineries. Consumers are demanding more flavor and complexity, and Sanford's wines deliver the goods. While these wines may be criticized for lacking subtlety, they are exciting wines that can dazzle the palate.

My enthusiasm for the 1993 Pinot Noir Vin Gris is based on consuming it over the next 6 months. It is a fun wine that will be adored by most readers. It is the color of a slab of smoked salmon, with a gorgeously ripe, perfumed nose of berry fruit and a dash of herbs, and a medium-bodied, deliciously fruity taste. It is vibrant, juicy, and oh, so satisfying to drink—provided it is drunk soon!

Long known for its brilliant, dramatic, oaky Chardonnays, lovers of that lusty, no-holds-barred style of Chardonnay will be thrilled with Sanford's current releases. Sanford's full-bodied, compelling 1992 Chardonnay Barrel Select Unfiltered hits the palate with the power of a full-force gale, remains there for a lengthy period, and finishes with a wallop of juicy, buttery fruit buttressed by decent acidity. It is an extroverted, rich, boldly styled Chardonnay with all its components in balance. The oak is barely noticeable because of the superb extraction of fruit. The bouquet has yet to fully emerge, but there is no doubting that Sanford has produced another winner. It was made to be drunk with lobster! Drink it over the next several years. The 1991 Chardonnay Santa Barbara possesses a big, expressive nose of honeyed tropical fruits and toasty oak. Fleshy, rich, and concentrated, it is all a Chardonnay should be. Moreover, it is nicely held together with crisp acidity, essential in a wine of these proportions. The 1991 Chardonnay Barrel Select Unfiltered makes for a huge mouthful of buttery tropical fruit. Full bodied and loaded, this full-throttle Chardonnay's richness and fruit nearly buries the abundant quantities of toasty new oak. The crisp acidity puts everything in focus in this blockbuster Chardonnay. My experience with the aging of California Chardonnay has been one disappointment after another, so don't tempt fate! Drink this beauty over the next 12–18 months. Sanford's 1992 Chardonnay is an exotic, flamboyant, in-your-face style of wine, offering coconut, buttery, orange blossom, and honeyed aromas that jump from the glass. The wine possesses exceptional balance for its excellent depth, richness, and full-bodied, juicy, chewy style. Drink it over the next year. The 1992 Chardonnay from the Sanford & Benedict Vineyard is a compelling example of its type. Although not as fleshy and powerful as the 1991 Barrel Select, it is persuasively rich and full bodied, with a multilayered personality, a subtle use of toasty new oak, and gobs of flavor, all buttressed by excellent acidity. It may actually improve over the next 2–3 years.

Sanford's Pinot Noirs have become increasingly exquisite and are now among the four or five best made American Pinot Noirs. The 1991 Pinot Noir Santa Barbara is a superrich wine with a ravishing nose of raspberries, plums, pepper, and spicy new oak. There is a silky, voluptuous texture, gobs of rich fruit, soft tannins, and wonderful length. A superb example of the heights Pinot Noir can reach in Santa Barbara, it should drink well for another 4–5 years. Remarkably, the 1990 Pinot Noir Sanford & Benedict Vineyard Barrel Select is richer and more profound. In fact, it is one of the greatest American Pinot Noirs I have ever tasted. The dense, deep color is followed by dazzling aromas of oriental spices, black cherries, toast, and flowers. There is stunning concentration, full body, magnificent richness, and a chewy, succulent, heady finish. This is Pinot Noir at its most decadent and sumptuous! Drink it over the next 7–8 years.

The 1992 Pinot Noir Barrel Select Sanford & Benedict Vineyard is once again a seductive, spicy Pinot that is drinking well now and should last for 3–4 years. The light ruby color is followed by a fragrant nose offering scents of well-integrated spicy oak, herbs, and sweet berry fruit. Medium to full bodied, supple, and expansive, with lovely purity, delineation, and fruit, this is a soft, well-balanced, user-friendly Pinot Noir.

SANTA BARBARA WINERY (SANTA BARBARA)

Cabernet Sauvignon * *, Chardonnay * * *, Chardonnay Lafond Vineyard * * */* * * *,
Chardonnay Reserve * */* * *, Pinot Noir* * * (since 1989), Pinot Noir Reserve * * */* * * *
(since 1989), Zinfandel Beaujour* * *

1992 Beaujour Zinfandel	Santa Ynez	A	85
1992 Chardonnay	Santa Ynez	B	88
1991 Chardonnay Lafond Vineyard Unfiltered	Santa Ynez	D	90

1990 Chardonnay Lafond Vineyard	Santa Ynez	D	87
1992 Chardonnay Reserve	Santa Ynez	C	90
1991 Chardonnay Reserve	Santa Ynez	C	78
1990 Dry Chenin Blanc	Santa Ynez	A	76
1990 Pinot Noir Reserve	Santa Ynez	C	86
1991 Sauvignon Blanc Reserve Musque	Santa Ynez	B	87

Another California winery that has continued to improve the quality of its wines, Santa Barbara's three new Chardonnay releases are noteworthy. It is hard to argue with the quality/ value ratio of the 1992 Santa Ynez Chardonnay. It is a big, rich, fleshy wine with excellent purity, gobs of fruit, great balance, fresh acidity, and lovely length. Drink it over the next 12–18 months. With the 1992 Chardonnay Reserve there is more oak in evidence, giving the wine a more honeyed, vanillin, and spice-scented nose, as well as excellent, creamy-textured, full-bodied flavors. The wine's hazelnut quality is reminiscent of a top-notch Meursault. It should drink well for 2 years. The 1991 Chardonnay Lafond Vineyard reveals substantial mineral scents in the bouquet, as well as buttery pineapples and toasty, vanillin notes from new oak casks. Ripe and full bodied, with densely extracted flavors, fine purity, and well-integrated acidity, it should be drunk over the next 2–3 years.

I found the 1990 Dry Chenin Blanc, which has been barrel-fermented, to be oaky and unusual, without the charm and finesse one would expect from this varietal. On the other hand, the 1991 Sauvignon Blanc Reserve Musque offers a big, floral-, herb-, and fruit-scented nose, and delicious, ripe, zesty flavors buttressed nicely by crisp acidity. This personality-filled Sauvignon will work well with a variety of dishes. Drink it over the next year. The flabby 1991 Chardonnay Reserve lacks grip, and excessive oak hides most of the wine's fruit. However, the excellent 1990 Chardonnay Lafond Vineyard exhibits a complex, Meursault-like nuttiness, excellent acidity, a generous yet judicious use of toasty new oak, and plenty of rich, buttery, hazelnut fruitiness. This single-vineyard offering from Santa Barbara is consistently the winery's best Chardonnay.

The red wines include a 1992 Beaujour Zinfandel, a deeply colored, richly fruity, plump, satisfying wine for uncritical quaffing at your favorite bistro or trattoria. It is a shame California does not produce more wines such as this; it is easy to understand, delicious to drink, and fairly priced. Drink it chilled over the next year. The soft, herbaceous, cherry-scented nose of the 1990 Pinot Noir Reserve is followed by round, smooth, slightly oaky, easygoing flavors, and a velvety finish. It should be drunk over the next 2–3 years.

SANTA CRUZ MOUNTAIN VINEYARD (SANTA CRUZ)
Cabernet Sauvignon Bates Ranch * * */* * * *, Merlot Santa Ynez * * * *,
Pinot Noir * * */* * * *

1991 Merlot	California	C	90+

Is this the most powerful and concentrated Merlot ever made in California? I am not sure, as some of the idiosyncratic, sometimes superb Merlots from Napa's tiny Sullivan winery, as well as Coturri's 1993 Feingold Vineyard Merlot appear to be this concentrated. However, Ken Burnap has hit the bull's eye with this monstrous 1991 Merlot, which, despite its massiveness, has kept its component parts in balance. Made from 91% Merlot, 8% Cabernet Sauvignon, and 1% Cabernet Franc, all from the Bates Ranch Vineyard, this opaque purple-colored wine offers an enticing nose of melted chocolate, jammy black cherries, roasted nuts, and herbs. Extremely rich, with huge, oozing, black cherry and chocolaty flavors, this amazingly concentrated, low acid, velvety-textured wine exhibits a level of fruit extraction that must be tasted to be believed. Approachable now because of its sheer quantity of unctuously textured, fleshy Merlot fruit, I would not be surprised to see this wine improve and age well for 15+ years. After tasting so many diluted, vegetal, and frightfully acidic California Merlots, what a thrill it is to find a Merlot of this quality!

SANTA YNEZ WINERY (SANTA BARBARA)

Brut Sparkling Wine* *, Cabernet Sauvignon Port* *, Pinot Noir Rancho Vineda Vineyard* *, Semillon* *

1987	Brut Sparkling Wine	Santa Ynez	B	82
1984	Brut Sparkling Wine	Santa Ynez	C	78?
1991	Cabernet Sauvignon Port	Santa Ynez	C	78
1990	Pinot Noir Rancho Vineda Vineyard	Santa Maria	C	67
1990	Semillon	Santa Ynez	A	74

These offerings are of average quality. The 1990 Semillon exhibits a cheesy sort of nose, decent flavor concentration, and high acidity. The two Sparkling Wines were more interesting, although unusual in their styles. The 1987 Brut is soft and fruity, with an intensely perfumed, Muscat-like nose, as well as fruity, ripe, slightly sweet flavors. The 1984 Brut is dry, with some oxidized, onion-skin aromas, yet surprisingly full, bold flavors. It is a controversial style to say the least.

In keeping with this winery's unusual line-up of wines, there is a 1991 Cabernet Sauvignon Port, a thick, unctuous, monolithic wine with plenty of concentration but no sense of complexity or direction. Lastly, the 1990 Pinot Noir Rancho Vineda Vineyard reveals a musty, pruny, overripe nose, and raisiny, thick, disjointed, flabby flavors.

SANTINO WINES (AMADOR)

Zinfandel* * *, Zinfandel Fiddletown Vineyard* * *, Zinfandel Grand-Père Vineyard* * *

1991	Zinfandel	Amador	A	75
1991	Zinfandel Grand Père Vineyard	Amador	B	90

While the 1991 regular cuvée of Zinfandel is spicy and fruity, but monolithic, simple, and short, the 1991 Zinfandel Grand Père (from a 125-year-old vineyard) is superb. The huge, spicy, peppery, tar-, and black cherry–scented nose is followed by a wine with copious quantities of fruit, huge amounts of glycerin, and noticeably high alcohol in the heady finish. It is a big, chewy, succulently textured Zinfandel for drinking over the next 5–6 years.

V. SATTUI WINERY (NAPA)

Cabernet Franc Rosenbrand Vineyard*, Cabernet Sauvignon Cuvées* *, Zinfandel Suzanne's Vineyard* * *

1991	Zinfandel Suzanne's Vineyard	Napa	B	74

This excessively acidified, tart, lean, hard 1992 Zinfandel Suzanne's Vineyard shows neither Zinfandel's varietal character, nor the charm and pleasure consumers expect and deserve. With more and more of California's finest wineries repudiating the philosophy of excessive additions of acidity, it is time that Sattui addresses this issue.

SAUCELITO CANYON VINEYARD (ARROYO GRANDE)

Zinfandel* * * *

1992	Zinfandel	San Luis Obispo	B	89
1991	Zinfandel	Arroyo Grande	B	89
1993	Zinfandel Arroyo Grande Valley Estate	Arroyo Grande	C	90
1992	Zinfandel Arroyo Grande Valley Estate	Arroyo Grande	B	90

This excellent Zinfandel producer continues to turn out fine wines. I have enjoyed many Zinfandels from Saucelito Canyon over recent years and, not surprisingly, the 1993 should prove to be as delicious and complete as any of its predecessors. It is a whoppingly big, rich Zinfandel (14.5% alcohol), with a deep ruby/purple color, supersweet, ripe, briary, black-cherry and currant scents added to its flamboyant aromatic profile, great ripeness and richness, medium to full body, a velvety, voluptuous texture, and layers of jammy red and black fruits. Pure and seductive, this wine is ideal for drinking over the nest 7–8 years. The 1992 Zinfandel from San Luis Obispo displays an intriguing nose of black fruits, roasted peanuts, and herbs. Well focused, with gorgeous levels of chewy, concentrated fruit, this up-front, precocious, flattering style of Zinfandel is meant to be drunk now and over the next 5–6 years. The 1992 Arroyo Grande Valley Estate Zinfandel exhibits a dark ruby/purple color, a big, jammy, black cherry–, herb-, and smoky-scented nose, and thick, rich flavors with enough acidity to give focus and delineation to this full-bodied, concentrated wine. With low acidity and a luscious style, it should be drunk over the next 5–7 years.

A classic Zinfandel, the 1991 Saucelito Canyon's aromas of pepper, raspberries, and black cherries jump from the glass. Deep, broad, and expansive, this velvety-textured, full-bodied wine is already delicious. Drink it over the next 4–6 years.

SAUSAL (SONOMA)
Chardonnay * * *, Zinfandel * * * *, Zinfandel Private Reserve * * * */* * * * *

1993 Zinfandel	Alexander Valley	C	90
1992 Zinfandel	Alexander Valley	B	89
1991 Zinfandel	Alexander Valley	B	89
1991 Zinfandel Private Reserve	Alexander Valley	C	90

This winery consistently fashions high-class, powerful Zinfandels. Sausal's 1993 carries 14% alcohol in a full-bodied format. The wine offers a saturated dark ruby/purple color, and a fragrant, intense nose of black cherries, underbrush, pepper, and spice. Full bodied, well balanced, and admirably concentrated, it possesses just enough oak and acidity to give the wine structure and definition. It will offer delicious drinking over the next decade. The 1992 Zinfandel is a textbook example of the winery's penchant for full-bodied, deeply concentrated, earthy, peppery, spicy wines. Rich and concentrated, with superb fruit extraction, it exhibits a licorice and black cherry–scented nose, loads of glycerin, body, and alcohol, and a long, lightly tannic finish. This slightly rustic, personality-filled Zinfandel should last for 10–15 years.

The husky, deep ruby-colored 1991 Zinfandel Private Reserve exhibits a spicy, herb-, peppery-, and black fruit–scented nose, thick, rich, full-bodied flavors, excellent concentration, and a chewy, gutsy, heady finish. Despite its size and overall richness, this wine will benefit from 1–3 years of cellaring and keep for 10–15 years. This 1991 Zinfandel is a big, thick, dark, saturated, broodingly backward wine with superb extraction of flavor, a thick, chewy texture, and gobs of extract, glycerin, and fruit. It should offer a splendid mouthful of Zinfandel for at least 10 years.

SCHERRER WINES (ALEXANDER VALLEY)
Zinfandel * * * *

1993 Zinfandel Old and Mature Vines	Alexander Valley	C	89+
1992 Zinfandel Old Vines Unfiltered	Alexander Valley	C	90
1991 Zinfandel Old Vines Scherrer Vineyard	Alexander Valley	C	90

The 1993 Zinfandel Old and Mature Vines exhibits a healthy, dark ruby/purple color, a big, undeveloped but promising nose of peppery, black-raspberry and cherry fruit, full body, excellent to outstanding concentration, decent acidity, and light tannin. Bottled without fining or filtration, this is a pure, young, immensely impressive Zinfandel that should drink well for a decade. The beautifully made 1992 Zinfandel Old Vines Unfiltered reveals a dark ruby/purple color, and a tight but promising bouquet of spice and red and black fruits. Concentrated, with layers of flavor, this full-bodied, moderately tannic, intense wine will benefit from 1–2 years of cellaring and will last for 10–15 years. It is to be admired for its stunning concentration combined with superb purity of flavor and outstanding focus. While it will be hard to find, the 1991 Zinfandel Old Vines Scherrer Vineyard is worth trying to track down. A powerhouse Zinfandel, with 14.3% alcohol, its thick, unctuous appearance suggests high extraction of fruit and old vines. The deep ruby/purple color is followed by a powerful, unformed bouquet of black fruits, pepper, and earth. Full bodied, with spectacular richness, low acidity, and plenty of alcohol and glycerin in the long finish, this is a Zinfandel for consuming over the next 10–12 years.

SEAVEY (NAPA)
Cabernet Sauvignon* * * */* * * * *, Chardonnay* * *

1991	Cabernet Sauvignon	Napa	D	93+
1992	Chardonnay	Napa	C	87

These wines, made by the former winemaker at Grace Family vineyards, emanate from an old hillside vineyard in Conn Valley. The 1992 Chardonnay exhibits too much oak for my taste, but I admired its rich concentration, full body, and smoky, hazelnut, honeyed, apple, and tropical fruit flavors. The oak appears to have muted some of the wine's vibrancy, so drink it over the next 1–2 years. Unfortunately, only 750 cases of the spectacular 1991 Cabernet Sauvignon were produced. It boasts an opaque purple color, and a promising but extremely youthful, unevolved nose of black currants, licorice, herbs, and spicy oak. Very rich, with great ripeness, intensity, and a layered feel on the palate, this powerful, grapy, youthful Cabernet Sauvignon possesses well-integrated tannin and acidity. Approachable because of its opulent personality, it will improve over the next 10+ years and drink well for a decade or more. It is a remarkably concentrated, impressive Cabernet Sauvignon that collectors with patience should gobble up.

SEBASTIANI WINERY (SONOMA)
Barbera* */* * *, Cabernet Sauvignon Regular Cuvée* *, Cabernet Sauvignon Single-Vineyard Cuvées* * *, Chardonnay Regular Cuvée* *, Chardonnay Single-Vineyard Cuvées* * *, Other Wines* *

1990	Barbera	Sonoma	A	84
1989	Cabernet Franc	Sonoma	A	85
1990	Cabernet Sauvignon	Sonoma	A	86
1992	Chardonnay	Sonoma	A	86
1993	Chardonnay Dutton Ranch	Russian River	C	87
1991	Zinfandel	Sonoma	A	86

It is good to see a large operation such as Sebastiani offering wines of such quality at reasonable prices. Sebastiani's 1993 Dutton Ranch Chardonnay offers a subtle, vanilla, Wheat Thin, buttery, fruity nose, medium- to full-bodied, classy flavors, excellent purity and richness, and a moderately long finish. It should drink well for 1–2 years. The excellent 1992 Chardonnay reveals a wonderful aroma of ripe, honeyed pears, medium to full body, fine richness and depth, and a sense of balance and purity. A noteworthy value, it should be consumed over the next 12 months.

The dark ruby-colored 1990 Barbera exhibits that varietal's noticeable acidity, but it is not excessive. This monolithic, uncomplicated, spicy wine is attractive for its fresh fruitiness and tart, clean mouth-feel. Satisfying in a straightforward manner, it will work well with tomato-based pasta dishes. The best value of this group of wines is the excellent, full-bodied, spicy, black cherry– and raspberry-scented and -flavored 1991 Zinfandel. Also a super value, it should drink well for 4–5 years. Don't miss it! The attractive, complex, elegant 1989 Cabernet Franc (from a maligned vintage) displays a dark ruby/garnet color, an herbaceous, earthy, cassis-scented nose, medium body, lovely ripeness, and a St.-Émilion-like personality. Revealing none of 1989's harshness or hollowness, it should drink well for 4–5 years. The very good 1990 Cabernet Sauvignon possesses the darkest, most saturated color, as well as a spicy, earthy, cassis-scented nose, medium body, above-average concentration, and a moderately long finish. Although there is some underlying tannin and structure, this is an accessible Cabernet for drinking over the next 5–6 years.

SEGHESIO WINERY (SONOMA)

Cabernet Sauvignon * *, Chardonnay * *, Pinot Noir *, Sauvignon Blanc * *, Zinfandel * * *, Zinfandel Reserve * * *

1992 Zinfandel	Sonoma	A	75
1991 Zinfandel	Sonoma	A	83
1991 Zinfandel Old Vines	Alexander Valley	B	86

While the straightforward, light-bodied 1992 Zinfandel is acceptable in a bland, commercial sense, it offers little concentration, simple, fruity flavors, and a short finish. Drink it over the next 2–3 years. Seghesio's 1991 regular offering of Zinfandel is a correct, tasty, medium-bodied, pleasant wine for uncritical quaffing. It should be consumed over the next 2–3 years. The 1991 Old Vines reveals a sweeter note to its spicy, raspberry, earthy-scented nose, as well as more alcohol, plenty of berry fruit, and a succulent texture. Drink it over the next 4–5 years.

SELENE (NAPA)

Merlot * * * *, Sauvignon Blanc * * * *

1992 Merlot	Napa	C	90
1993 Sauvignon Blanc Hyde Vineyard	Napa	C	88

I need to find out more about this winery given the impressive credentials of these two offerings. The 1993 Sauvignon Blanc is bursting with honeyed melon, figs, and herb-scented and -flavored fruit. Medium-bodied, crisp, beautifully delineated, and oh, so pure, it will offer lovely drinking over the next year. Terrific California Merlots are few and far between. Selene's 1992 Merlot is the real thing! My only quibble is that the toasty new oak is a trifle high, but even so, I cannot resist the copious quantities of gorgeously rich, chocolaty, coffee, black cherry fruitiness. The wine reveals a velvety texture, superb purity, and wonderful presence and balance in the mouth. This is a knockout Merlot for drinking over the next 5–7 years.

SHAFER VINEYARDS (NAPA)

Cabernet Sauvignon Hillside Select * * * * * (since 1991), Cabernet Sauvignon Stag's Leap * * *, Chardonnay * * * *, Merlot * * * *

1994 Cabernet Sauvignon Hillside Select	Napa	D	96
1993 Cabernet Sauvignon Hillside Select	Napa	D	93
1992 Cabernet Sauvignon Hillside Select	Napa	D	95
1991 Cabernet Sauvignon Hillside Select	Napa	D	94

1990 Cabernet Sauvignon Hillside Select	Napa	D	92
1993 Cabernet Sauvignon Stag's Leap	Napa	C	90
1992 Cabernet Sauvignon Stag's Leap	Napa	C	90
1991 Cabernet Sauvignon Stag's Leap	Napa	C	87
1994 Chardonnay Barrel Red Shoulder Ranch	Carneros	C	91
1993 Chardonnay Barrel Select	Napa	C	88
1994 Firebreak (Sangiovese)	Napa	C	88
1993 Firebreak (Sangiovese)	Napa	C	87
1992 Firebreak (Sangiovese)	Napa	C	88
1994 Merlot	Carneros	C	90
1993 Merlot Stag's Leap	Napa	C	88
1992 Merlot Stag's Leap	Napa	C	87

This winery continues to build on its fine reputation, pushing the quality to higher and higher levels. Shafer's 50-acre estate vineyard, located in the heart of the Stag's Leap District, is supplemented by an additional 70 acres in Carneros. The winery continues to be innovative, offering a very good Sangiovese called Firebreak that has a small percentage (usually less than 20%) of Cabernet Sauvignon included in the blend for color and bulk. Shafer's Chardonnays have also jumped significantly in quality, as evidenced by the 1994 debut vineyard-designated Red Shoulder Ranch. It is a superrich, expansive, multidimensional Chardonnay aged in 50% new oak casks and put through a wild yeast fermentation with no malolactic fermentation. There is 100% barrel fermentation and plenty of *sur lees* contact. It sets the standard as the finest Shafer Chardonnay to date, and gives an idea of what will be forthcoming in future vintages. Two major reasons for Shafer's dramatic improvement in quality have been (1) the winery's movement away from sterile filtration and (2) their decision to practice little or no acidification, both of which have occurred since 1991. The results are far more aromatics and richness in the Shafer wines.

Shafer's Merlots have generally been good to very good, but rarely outstanding, although they have been above the rank and file of California Merlots. Of the three newest vintages, the 1992 Merlot exhibits a rich, black cherry and chocolaty nose, medium body, good purity, fine suppleness, and some tannin in the finish. The 1993 Merlot reveals more fatness and a velvety texture, as well as an intense, black cherry, chocolate, herb, coffee character. The sweetness and less aggressive tannin give it a slight edge over the 1992. The best Merlot Shafer has yet made is the 1994, which offers layers of sweet, creamy black fruits wrapped with smoky oak in what has turned out to be a medium- to full-bodied, layered wine with wonderful purity and expansiveness. Most of the Shafer Merlots contain between 82% and 85% Merlot with small additions of Cabernet Sauvignon and Cabernet Franc.

The Cabernet Sauvignon Stag's Leap District has also jumped in quality, as John Shafer's son, Doug Shafer, abandoned sterile filters in favor of no fining and only a polishing, coarse filtration at bottling. That, plus less acidification, giving the wines a higher pH, has resulted in a more revealing and beautiful expression of the gorgeous fruit obtained from the Stag's Leap District vineyards. The 1992 Cabernet Sauvignon Stag's Leap includes 7% Cabernet Franc and 4% Merlot. It offers a wonderfully pure cassis nose, a velvety texture, plenty of ripeness, and some structure and tannin in the medium- to full-bodied finish. It should drink well for 10–15 years. The 1993 Cabernet Sauvignon Stag's Leap does not reveal the 1992's tannin and structure, displaying a sweeter, more jammy mid-palate, and wonderful layered black currant flavors intertwined with subtle scents of herbs, smoky oak, and spice. It is a deep, rich, user-friendly Carbernet that should drink well for 12–15 years. I like its balance more than the muscular 1992s. The most beautiful Stag's Leap Cabernet Sauvignon yet produced is the 1994. The long growing season resulted in an opaque purple-colored wine, with fabulously rich, ripe scents of black currants and cassis. It is an elegant yet authoritatively flavored, full-bodied wine with soft, sweet tannin, and no toughenss or heaviness. It should drink well for 15–20 years.

The excellent 1992 Firebreak reveals a sweet, cherry-, leathery-, spicy-scented nose, medium body, a soft belly of fruit, and a clean, crisp finish. It should be drunk before the end of the century. The 1993 Firebreak exhibits a similar style, perhaps slightly lighter in body with more emphasis on elegance. The finest Firebreak appears to be the 1994, which possesses greater dimension, a more layered feel, and sweet, long, rich fruit. All of these wines, given the forwardness of the Sangiovese, require consumption in their first 4–5 years of life.

As for the upcoming releases of Shafer's luxury cuvée, the Hillside Select Cabernet Sauvignon, the 1993 is a superb example of Cabernet. The opaque purple color is followed by abundant aromas of black currants, sweet oak, smoke, and minerals, great richness, and some tannin. Although it is a candidate for 20–25 years of aging, it will undoubtedly be gobbled up by Cabernet Sauvignon enthusiasts before it ever reaches full maturity. The exquisite quality of the fruit is hard to resist, despite the wine's youthful exuberance. The finest Hillside Select Cabernet Sauvignon may turn out to be the 1994, a stupendous effort that is truly great stuff! Crammed with black currant fruit, gorgeous purity and ripeness, as well as massive concentration, without any heaviness, high alcohol, or astringency, this is a seamless, velvety-textured, magnificent Cabernet that should hit its peak around the turn of the century and last for 20 years thereafter.

After tasting over six dozen 1994 California Cabernets, it appears safe to say that this vintage has extremely high potential. It would be foolish to say more great wines were made in 1994 than in 1993, 1992, 1991, and 1990, but given the extraordinary progress and movement toward less interventionistic winemaking by so many top producers, the quality of wine from the vintage with the longest "hang time" (the days between fruit set and harvest, usually 100–110, amounted to 125–140 in 1994 for many North Coast Cabernet producers) does indeed offer exciting possibilities. Shafer's opaque purple-colored 1994 Hillside Select looks to be a profound wine. The supersweet black fruit aromas have already absorbed the new oak—an indication of just how much richness and sweet fruit are present! The wine reveals sweet tannin, low but adequate acidity, full body, great precision and purity, and a marvelously long finish that lasts for almost a minute. This should prove to be one of the all time great wines from Shafer. It will have an aging curve of at least 30+ years.

The 1993 Hillside Select is an outstanding Cabernet Sauvignon offering up a wonderfully sweet, fragrant nose of *pain grillée,* blackcurrants, licorice, and herbs. Rich and full bodied, with an expansive, fleshy palate possessing gobs of blackcurrant fruit, the wine gives a sweet impression, but the sweetness is from ripe fruit, not residual sugar. The wine's low acidity and high pH of 3.68 (reminiscent of such great Bordeaux vintages as 1982, 1961, and 1959) have resulted in a voluptuous, user-friendly, complex, ripe Cabernet. After its release in fall 1997, this should be a precocious wine that will drink well for 20–25 years.

The 1992 Cabernet Sauvignon Hillside Select is a great wine. The dark purple/black opaque color is accompanied by a smoky, roasted nut-, licorice-, and cassis-scented nose that soars from the glass. This decadently styled, spectacularly rich Cabernet reveals a sweet inner core of fruit, terrific concentration, layers of flavor, adequate acidity, and considerable tannin lurking beneath its opulent texture. Shafer's Cabernets always display considerable grace and elegance, so expect this beefy wine to take on more finesse as it evolves. The 1990 Shafer Cabernet Sauvignon Hillside Select is a soft, restrained wine, with a healthy, dark ruby color, ripe tannin, medium body, a gentle, rich, graceful fruitiness, and excellent purity. Deceptively easy to drink now, it promises to age well for 10–15 years.

I found Shafer's 1991 Cabernet Sauvignon Stag's Leap District to be an elegant, polished, richly fruity wine similar to a fine Margaux, with riper fruit and more body and weight. It should drink well for 7–8 years.

The 1993 Barrel Select is one of the finest Shafer Chardonnays I have recently tasted. It exhibits a light golden color, and a subtle yet rich nose of roasted nuts, buttery fruit, and a smoky, earthy character. Full-bodied and rich, with a generous mouth-feel but no sense of heaviness or flabbiness, this well-proportioned, generously endowed Chardonnay is reminiscent of a top premier cru from Chassagne-Montrachet. Its seamless style speaks highly of its winemaking. Drink it over the next 1–2 years.

Ratings for Older Vintages of Shafer Cabernet Sauvignon Hillside Select: 1989 (90), 1988 (87), 1987 (90), 1986 (93), 1985 (90), 1984 (87), 1983 (87), 1982 (87), 1979 (94), 1978 (95)

SHENANDOAH VINEYARDS (AMADOR)

Cabernet Sauvignon Amador* */* * *, Sauvignon Blanc* *, Zinfandel Special Reserve* *, Zinfandel Sobon Estate* * *

1991 Zinfandel	Amador	A	60
1991 Zinfandel Special Reserve	Amador	B	74

Two disappointing Zinfandels, the 1991 regular cuvée is abrasively tannic, hard, and charmless. The 1991 Special Reserve offers negligibly more fruit, but the spicy nose leaves little to get excited about. The wine is short, hard, tannic, and lacking fruit and flesh.

SIERRA VISTA (EL DORADO)

Cabernet Sauvignon* *, Chardonnay* *, Fleur de Montagne* * *, Lynelle* * *, Syrah* *, Zinfandel* * *

1991 Fleur de Montagne	El Dorado	A	86
N.V. Lynelle	El Dorado	A	85
1992 Zinfandel Estate	El Dorado	B	89

This impressive 1992 Zinfandel Estate exhibited a saturated black/purple color, and an intense bouquet of floral scents, black fruit, and spice. Dense and rich, with massive concentration and full body, this highly extracted, impressive Zinfandel should turn out to be one of the best red wines produced by Sierra Vista—if it is not overly processed at bottling. I will keep my fingers crossed.

Sierra Vista's recent releases offer good, gutsy, clean fruit, medium body, soft textures, and plenty of personality and style. The 1991 Fleur de Montagne (a blend of Grenache, Syrah, Cinsault, and Zinfandel) is the more generous wine, with a longer finish. It possesses a peppery, black cherry, herb-scented bouquet, and admirably concentrated flavors. Drink it over the next 2–3 years. The nonvintage Lynelle (the same blend) is a lighter version of the Fleur de Montagne. A hearty, mouth-filling, velvety-textured wine, as well as a super bargain, it should be drunk over the next 1–2 years.

SIGNORELLO VINEYARDS (NAPA)

Cabernet Sauvignon Founder's Reserve* * * *, Cabernet Sauvignon Unfined/Unfiltered* * */
* * * *, Chardonnay* * * *, Chardonnay Founder's Reserve* * * */* * * * *, Pinot
Noir* * * *, Sauvignon Blanc* * * *, Semillon Barrel Fermented* * * *, Zinfandel* * *

1991 Cabernet Sauvignon Unfined/Unfiltered	Napa	D	89
1993 Chardonnay	Napa	C	85

1992 Chardonnay Founder's Reserve Unfiltered	Napa	D	92
1993 Sauvignon Blanc Barrel Fermented	Napa	C	87
1992 Semillon Barrel Fermented	Napa	C	88

I recently had the opportunity to visit the small Signorello winery and get a firsthand look at what Ray Signorello, Jr., is doing to produce such delicious, albeit expensive, wines. As with many highly committed California wine producers, he believes in utilizing wild yeasts, doing extensive *sur lees* aging for the whites, little racking, and, where appropriate, no fining or filtration, even for the white wines. The results have been impressive. Moreover, after tasting barrel samples of 1993 wines, I can unequivocally state that there has been no drop in quality.

Signorello's two basic cuvées of 1993 Sauvignon and Chardonnay placed well in several peer group tastings. The 1993 Chardonnay possesses plenty of fruit, fine body, a sense of elegance, and a tasty, clean, exuberant style. It should be drunk over the next year. The 1993 barrel-fermented Sauvignon Blanc exhibits a fuller style, with loads of smoky, toasty, honeyed fruit, excellent ripeness, a rich chewiness, and good body and length. A bolder, more dramatically styled Sauvignon than generally found in California, it should drink well for another year.

Signorello produces one of the half-dozen finest Semillons made in California. The 1992 Barrel Fermented Semillon, which spends nearly 12 months on its lees, exhibits an exotic, waxy, honeysucklelike nose, long, rich, dense flavors, full body, and a dry, crisp, long finish. It should be drunk with grilled fish and poultry, as it is an intensely flavored wine. The 1992 Chardonnay Founder's Reserve Unfiltered reveals a dramatic bouquet of honeyed tropical fruits and smoky oak. Made from low yields, this expansively flavored, opulently textured, chewy, medium- to full-bodied Chardonnay possesses considerable intensity accompanied by a fresh, vibrant feel. I am not a great believer in the aging potential of these wines, so drink both offerings over the next year.

Signorello also produced a rich, black currant– and spice-scented, full-bodied 1991 Cabernet Sauvignon that marries the finesse-filled, elegant style of Cabernet with considerable flavor authority. Medium bodied, with layers of fruit, fine underlying acidity, and moderate tannin in the finish, this tightly knit wine should be cellared for 1–2 years and drunk over the subsequent 12–15 years.

SILVER OAK CELLARS (NAPA)

Cabernet Sauvignon Alexander Valley * * * * *, Cabernet Sauvignon Napa * * * * *, Cabernet Sauvignon Bonny's Vineyard * * * */* * * * *

1993 Cabernet Sauvignon	Alexander Valley	D	95
1992 Cabernet Sauvignon	Alexander Valley	D	95
1991 Cabernet Sauvignon	Alexander Valley	D	92
1990 Cabernet Sauvignon	Alexander Valley	D	91
1989 Cabernet Sauvignon	Alexander Valley	D	89
1993 Cabernet Sauvignon	Napa	D	96
1992 Cabernet Sauvignon	Napa	D	96
1991 Cabernet Sauvignon	Napa	D	95
1990 Cabernet Sauvignon	Napa	D	93
1989 Cabernet Sauvignon	Napa	D	90
1992 Cabernet Sauvignon Bonny's Vineyard	Napa	E	93

1991 Cabernet Sauvignon Bonny's Vineyard	Napa	E	90
1990 Cabernet Sauvignon Bonny's Vineyard	Napa	E	94
1989 Cabernet Sauvignon Bonny's Vineyard	Napa	E	87?
1988 Cabernet Sauvignon Bonny's Vineyard	Napa	E	90

Silver Oak's Cabernet Sauvignons are among the most popular wines of California. I have heard mind-boggling stories about the huge throng of people, ranging from lawyers in three-piece suits, to showgirls and Hell's Angels on motorcycles, that show up at the winery on the day Silver Oak releases its newest vintage. What a testament to the immensely popular style of these wines! Production has increased to approximately 10,000 cases of the Napa Valley cuvée and 30,000 cases of the Alexander Valley Cabernet. However, 65% of the production is sold within California and 60% of the total production goes directly to restaurants. Following the release of the 1992, the Bonny's Vineyard Cabernet Sauvignon, a sometimes great, sometimes controversial wine because of its overt herbaceous character, will be blended with the Napa Valley wine, thus ending the nightmarish distribution problems created by the tiny production of this single-vineyard Cabernet Sauvignon.

I have often pondered why Silver Oak's Cabernets are so popular. Certainly Justin Meyer has always believed in harvesting very ripe, physiologically mature fruit. Moreover, he has never spared any expense in utilizing a high percentage of new oak. For example, the Napa Valley Cabernet Sauvignon is aged for 30 months in 100% new oak and the Alexander Valley wine is aged for 30 months in 50% new oak and 50% used barrels. It seems to me the reason for the success of these wines is that Meyer has always recognized (1) that wine is a beverage of pleasure, (2) that the wine's texture is of considerable significance, and (3) that excessive acidification of his Cabernets would compromise their character as well as their hedonistic value. This philosophy has ensured a voluptuous, rich, chewy style of Cabernet, without the shrill, tart, high-acid, compact, lean, unpleasant character of many other California Cabernets. Justin Meyer's winemaking decisions have resulted in lavishly rich, exotic, crowd-pleasing Cabernets that can drink fabulously well young but have the cunning ability to age well for 12–15 or more years.

As for the recent vintages, the stunning 1990s will be followed by equally profound 1991s, 1992s, and 1993s.

The 1993 Cabernet Sauvignon Alexander Valley exhibits a dark black/ruby/purple color, a big, sweet nose of jammy black currants, fruitcake, cherries, and vanillin, full-bodied, chocolaty, black raspberry, currancy flavors with a slight touch of herbs, an unctuous palate, and a whoppingly lush, chewy finish. It should last for 10–15 years after its release. The 1993 Cabernet Sauvignon Napa Valley reveals even greater extract as well as superb focus and definition, great ripeness, a lavishly rich, decadently thick, juicy palate, superb concentration, and plenty of sweet tannin in the long, chewy finish. Slightly deeper and better-focused than the Alexander Valley, it is a candidate for 15+ years of aging.

The 1992 Alexander Valley Cabernet Sauvignon offers a huge mouthful of highly extracted, black currancy, full-bodied, expansively rich wine. It is California's answer to Pauillac's famed Lynch-Bages, only richer and thicker. A knockout, opulent wine for the vintage, it will be a head-turning, flamboyant effort when released in 1996. The 1992 Napa Valley Cabernet Sauvignon is awesome in its glorious display of spice, black fruits, vanilla, and phenomenally rich fruit. It is full bodied, with layer upon layer of richness, massive concentration, an inner core of depth, and an amazing finish. I can hardly wait for its release! Like the Alexander Valley, it will drink sumptuously well young, yet last for 10–15 years after its release. The Bonny's Vineyard Cabernet Sauvignon 1992 possesses huge extract, massive fruit and body, and a noticeable herbaceous component. Nevertheless, it is hard to resist this wine's sweet, chewy, fleshy fruit.

As for the 1991s, the 1991 Alexander Valley Cabernet Sauvignon boasts a dark ruby color, a sweet vanillin, herb, and black currant–scented nose, gobs of rich, herb-tinged, juicy fruit, the opulent texture that Silver Oak routinely obtains, and plenty of fat, glycerin, and alcohol in the long finish. The 1991 Cabernet Sauvignon Napa Valley cuvée exhibits more classic cassis notes without the subtle herbaceousness of the Alexander Valley wine. It is a multilayered, fabulously rich, intense wine with full body, a velvety texture, and oodles of fruit, glycerin, and soft tannin in the finish. The 1991 Bonny's Vineyard Cabernet Sauvignon (the last release from this single vineyard) reveals a telltale bell pepper aroma, rich, chocolaty, black cherry flavors, a supple texture, outstanding fruit extraction, and a long, lusty finish. I prefer the 1990 Bonny's Vineyard, which possesses more of a cigar box character, with considerable black cassis in its flavors. Dense and full bodied, it exhibits exceptional extraction, plenty of glycerin, and a finish that lasts nearly a minute.

The 1990 Alexander Valley Cabernet offers aromas of fruitcake, black cherries, cassis, and spice. Dense, rich, opulent, and supple, this is a wine to drink in its first 10–12 years of life. The 1990 Napa Cabernet exhibits a Graves-like bouquet of tobacco, cassis, minerals, and spice. Chewy and full bodied, with stunning extraction of fruit, this velvety wine should drink well for 12–15 years.

The 1989 Cabernet Sauvignon Alexander Valley exhibits a spicy, vanillin, and black olive–scented nose, rich, velvety, medium- to full-bodied flavors, low acidity, and a long, lush, jammy fruit-filled finish. It does not possess any of the hard tannin or hollowness that plague many 1989s. Drink it over the next 7–8 years. The 1989 Napa Cabernet Sauvignon offers beautifully pure aromas of black currants, smoky, toasty, new oak, and licorice. Opulent and full bodied, with excellent concentration of fruit, this rich, impressively endowed Cabernet should drink well for at least a decade. I am convinced the 1989 Bonny's Vineyard Cabernet will be a "love it or hate it" wine. The herbaceousness has the upper hand in the strong vegetal aromas that dominate the bouquet. Once past that, it is a well-endowed, rich, full-bodied, impressively constructed and extracted wine with copious amounts of cassis fruit. The herbaceous character is at the limit of acceptability.

The most successful wine for this property in 1988 is the 1988 Bonny's Vineyard Cabernet Sauvignon. It is a subtly herbaceous, cassis- and sweet oak–scented wine, with medium to full body, lush, round, generous fruit, and a soft finish. Drink it over the next 5–7 years.

Ratings for Older Vintages of Silver Oak Cellars Cabernet Sauvignon Alexander Valley: 1988 (82), 1987 (89), 1986 (90), 1985 (92), 1984 (92), 1983 (85), 1981 (87), 1975 (89)

Ratings for Older Vintages of Silver Oak Cellars Cabernet Sauvignon Napa: 1988 (84), 1987 (90), 1986 (91), 1985 (96), 1984 (95), 1983 (78), 1982 (88)

Ratings for Older Vintages of Silver Oak Cellars Cabernet Sauvignon Bonny's Vineyard: 1987 (86), 1986 (92), 1985 (96), 1984 (97), 1983 (87), 1982 (83), 1981 (86), 1980 (87)

Ratings for Older Vintages of Silver Oak Cellars Cabernet Sauvignon North Coast: 1974 (87), 1973 (89)

SILVERADO VINEYARDS (NAPA)

Cabernet Sauvignon * * *, Cabernet Sauvignon Limited Reserve * * * *, Chardonnay * * *,
Chardonnay Limited Reserve * * * * *, Merlot Estate * * *, Sauvignon Blanc * *

1991	Cabernet Sauvignon Limited Reserve	Napa	D	93
1990	Cabernet Sauvignon Limited Release	Napa	D	89
1991	Cabernet Sauvignon Stag's Leap	Napa	C	87
1992	Chardonnay Limited Reserve	Napa	D	93
1992	Merlot Estate	Napa	C	87

This vineyard produces expensive but superb Limited Reserve wines from the Chardonnay and Cabernet Sauvignon grapes. The 1992 Chardonnay Limited Reserve is a spectacularly concentrated, honeyed wine bursting with tropical fruit and moderate sweet, toasty new oak aromas and flavors as well as gobs of glycerin and alcohol. With spectacular length, the wine still tastes unevolved, an indication that it may age and perhaps even improve for another 3–5 years.

The first Limited Reserve Cabernet Sauvignon, the 1991, is a knockout effort. Although Silverado has a tendency to take great raw materials and add excessive acidity in the winemaking process, that did not happen with this marvelously rich, natural-tasting Cabernet. The wine possesses an opaque purple color, a big, sweet nose of cassis and new oak, and full-bodied, concentrated, well-balanced flavors with a harmonious integration of wood, acidity, alcohol, and tannin. Although still young and unevolved, this wine promises to last and improve for 12–15+ years.

A step lower in quality is the smoky, black cherry, toasty 1992 Merlot Estate. With fine purity and an attractive mouth-feel, it is ideal for drinking over the next 5–6 years.

The 1991 Cabernet Sauvignon Stag's Leap offers an impressively saturated dark ruby/purple color, a spicy, weedy, cassis-scented nose, and medium-bodied, crisp, pure, concentrated, long flavors. It is a stylish, restrained Cabernet Sauvignon for drinking over the next decade. Dark ruby/purple-colored, with a tight, clean, polished bouquet of cassis, minerals, and toasty new oak, the medium-bodied 1990 Cabernet Sauvignon Limited Release possesses excellent ripeness and elegance. Well knit and attractively proportioned, it exhibits fine depth, and moderate tannins in the finish. The wine should improve for 5–7 years and last for 15–20. Only the price is lamentable.

SIMI WINERY (SONOMA)

Cabernet Sauvignon * * *, Cabernet Sauvignon Reserve * * * * * (since 1986),
Chardonnay * * *, Chardonnay Reserve * * */* * * *, Chenin Blanc * *, Rosé of Cabernet
Sauvignon * * *, Semillon * *, Sendal Proprietary White Wine * * * * *

1991 Cabernet Sauvignon Reserve	Alexander Valley	D	94
1990 Chardonnay Reserve	Sonoma	D	91
1993 Rosé of Cabernet Sauvignon	Sonoma	A	86
1991 Sendal Proprietary White Wine	Sonoma	C	88

Simi's 1991 Cabernet Sauvignon Reserve (actually a blend that includes 6% Merlot and 2% Cabernet Franc) is an impressive, complex, authoritatively flavored yet elegant Cabernet that combines the elegance of Bordeaux with the rich, ripe fruit of California. The deep, dense, ruby/purple color is followed by an unformed but promising nose of black currants, vanilla, and spice. Rich and full bodied, as well as exceptionally well balanced and supple, with moderate tannin and impressive extraction, this rich, multilayered Cabernet Sauvignon is accessible enough to be drunk now, but should age for 2 decades.

When a reader puts his or her nose in a glass of Simi's intensely fragrant 1993 Rosé of Cabernet, it is akin to walking into a perfume factory. It is a gloriously aromatic (berries and herbs), medium-bodied, sweet wine that is pure, exuberant, and fruity. Keep in mind that it is a wine to be consumed very young.

Simi's 1990 Chardonnay Reserve from Sonoma County is among the most impressive Reserve Chardonnays this property has yet produced. It boasts a complex, smoky, roasted nut, and buttery nose, and rich, full-bodied, concentrated flavors that exhibit enough acidity for delineation and balance. The finish is all opulent, rich fruit. Reminiscent of a big, fleshy Meursault-Charmes or premier cru from Chassagne-Montrachet, it should be drunk over the next 3–5 years. Simi's 1991 Sendal displays a French Graves–like melony, rich, discreet nose, medium-bodied, lovely flavors, and an authoritative, fruity, dry finish. Impressive!

SKY VINEYARDS (NAPA)
Zinfandel * * *

1991 Zinfandel Mount Veeder	Napa B	87

A dark ruby/purple color and a vibrant nose of pure black cherries offer considerable excitement. The wine is concentrated, spicy, and long, with excellent structure and a tightly knit personality. As delicious as it already is, this wine will benefit from 2–3 years of cellaring and will keep for a decade.

SONOMA-CUTRER (SONOMA)
Chardonnay Cutrer Vineyard * * */* * * *, Chardonnay Les Pierres * * */* * * *, Chardonnay Russian River Ranches * * *

1992 Chardonnay	Russian River C	87
1992 Cutrer Vineyard	Sonoma C	89

It is encouraging to see this large Chardonnay producer reducing yields and obtaining more flavor and character in their Chardonnay cuvées. The 1992 Cutrer Vineyard (note the vineyard name, rather than the varietal, is emphasized on the sporty new label) is an attractive, medium- to full-bodied wine with ripe fruit, fine underlying acidity, an attractive texture, and nice length. It exhibits a Chablis-like character, but with more intensity and ripeness. Drink it over the next 1–2 years.

The 1992 Chardonnay is a spicy, vanillin, richly fruity wine offering medium to full body, gobs of tasty fruit, fine acidity, and a clean, long finish. Drink it over the next 1–2 years.

SONOMA-LOEB (SONOMA)
Chardonnay * * *, Chardonnay Private Reserve * * * *

1992 Chardonnay	Sonoma C	87
1993 Chardonnay Private Reserve	Sonoma D	89
1992 Chardonnay Private Reserve	Sonoma D	90

These no-holds-barred Chardonnays are made in a style that emphasizes copious quantities of buttery fruit. The rich, fleshy, full-bodied 1993 Chardonnay Private Reserve is bursting with copious quantities of buttered tropical fruit gently infused with spicy, smoky oak. Bold, delicious, and mouth filling, it should drink well for 1–2 years. The 1992 Sonoma Chardonnay possesses an excellent nose of ripe Chardonnay fruit, full body, low acid, a fleshy palate, and a rich finish. Drink it over the next year. The 1992 Chardonnay Private Reserve reveals more smoky, toasty new oak accompanied by lavish, honeyed, buttery, apple, and tangerinelike flavors. A rich, stunningly concentrated Chardonnay, it should be matched with intensely flavored foods. Drink it over the next year.

SONORA WINERY AND PORT WORKS (AMADOR)
Zinfandel TC Vineyard * * *

1991 Zinfandel TC Vineyard	Amador B	87?

Although this chunky, rustic, old-style 1991 Zinfandel oozes with personality and flavor, its rough-and-tumble style, high tannins, fiery alcohol, and thick fruit may not be admired by everyone. There is plenty of intensity and chewiness, not much complexity, and a leathery, meaty character. Given its size and overall structure, it should last for at least a decade.

CHÂTEAU SOUVERAIN (SONOMA)

Cabernet Sauvignon * * * (since 1990), Cabernet Sauvignon Winemaker's Reserve * * * *,
Chardonnay Sonoma * * * (since 1990), Chardonnay Single Vineyard Cuvées * * * */* * * * *,
Merlot * * *, Zinfandel * * *

1991 Cabernet Sauvignon	Alexander Valley	B	88
1990 Cabernet Sauvignon	Alexander Valley	B	88
1991 Cabernet Sauvignon Winemaker's Reserve	Alexander Valley	C	90
1992 Chardonnay Allen Vineyard Reserve	Russian River	B	90
1992 Chardonnay Barrel Fermented	Sonoma	B	88
1993 Chardonnay Rochioli Vineyard Unfined	Russian River	B	93
1992 Merlot	Alexander Valley	B	85
1991 Merlot	Alexander Valley	B	87
1992 Zinfandel	Dry Creek	B	86

Recent releases of virtually every wine in the Château Souverain portfolio have demonstrated a sensational quality/price rapport. The 1992 Merlot from Alexander Valley is an attractively oaky, spicy, berry-scented wine with herbaceous, mocha-tinged, black cherry–like flavors, medium body, a velvety texture, and a fleshy, fat finish. It is a delicious Merlot for drinking over the next 4–5 years. The 1991 Merlot reveals smoky, olive-tinged, toasty new oak, chocolaty, cherry components, soft, round, lush flavors, a sweet, chewy texture, and heady alcohol. It is an excellent, bargain-priced Merlot for drinking over the next 4–5 years.

Readers looking for a sensational bargain in high-quality Cabernet Sauvignons should get their orders in for Château Souverain's 1991 Cabernet Sauvignon Winemaker's Reserve. It should prove to be a worthy successor to the 1990. The wine's opaque ruby/purple color is followed by an attractive cassis-, black cherry–, herb-, and smoky-scented nose, concentrated, rich, full-bodied flavors exhibiting suppleness and toasty oak, adequate acidity, and moderate tannin in the long finish. This knockout Cabernet Sauvignon should drink well for 10–15 years.

The 1991 Cabernet Sauvignon is unquestionably one of Souverain's finest Cabernets since those two brilliant 1974 offerings. It exhibits a saturated dark ruby/purple color, a blossoming nose of cassis, herbs, and spicy new oak, medium to full body, excellent concentration, soft enough tannin to make it accessible and delicious now, but enough structure and concentration to last for 10–12 years. The low price makes this beautiful wine a super bargain! The 1990 Cabernet Sauvignon (33,000 cases produced, so no complaints about not finding it) offers a big, bold, chocolaty, vanillin, spicy, sweet, black currant–scented nose, soft, attractive, fleshy flavors, medium to full body, and a seductively rich, lush finish. A fine bargain, it is ideal for drinking over the next 10–12 years.

The 1992 Zinfandel exhibits aromas of toasty new oak in its black cherry– and herb-scented nose. Soft, with medium body and low acidity, this fleshy, flattering wine should be drunk over the next 2–3 years.

The 1993 Chardonnay Rochioli Vineyard Unfined is a spectacular Chardonnay! No matter how many times I tasted it, it reminded me of a big, rich, Bâtard-Montrachet from the likes of Michel Niellon or Louis Latour. Extremely rich and full bodied, as well as fresh and lively with beautifully integrated acidity, and a stunning perfume of oranges, honey, butter, and subtle oak, this full-bodied, opulently styled wine is never heavy or tiring to drink given its well-integrated, crisp acidity. This is a dazzling effort from Château Souverain. Run, don't walk, to your specialty wine merchant to latch on to as many bottles as you can manage! Drink it over the next 2–3 years.

The excellent honeyed, tropical fruit–scented nose of the 1992 Barrel Fermented Chardonnay is followed by a wine with soft, fleshy, medium- to full-bodied flavors, wonderful purity, delicious fruit, and a long finish. This beautiful wine should drink well for 1–2 years. Château Souverain's 1992 Chardonnay Reserve from the highly acclaimed Allen Vineyard was bottled unfiltered and sells for the unbelievably low price of $15.50. There are only 450 cases of this superb Chardonnay displaying a hazelnut, buttery, apple-scented nose, complex, rich, full-bodied flavors, wonderful viscosity and depth, and a long, crisp, chewy finish. It should drink well for 1–2 years.

SPOTTSWOODE VINEYARD AND WINERY (NAPA)
Cabernet Sauvignon * * * *, Sauvignon Blanc * * *

1992 Cabernet Sauvignon	Napa	D	92
1990 Cabernet Sauvignon	Napa	D	87
1993 Sauvignon Blanc	Napa	B	89

What makes Spottswoode's 1992 Cabernet Sauvignon so impressive is its classically rich and pure black currant–, vanillin-, and herb-scented nose, medium- to full-bodied, deeply etched flavors, excellent balance, and authoritative power welded to a sense of finesse and grace. Older vintages of Spottswoode Cabernet Sauvignon have not developed the aromatic dimensions I would have predicted, but my optimism has been renewed by this terrific effort.

The 1990 Cabernet Sauvignon offers an elegant bouquet of subtle cassis, followed by ripe, long, attractive flavors that possess admirable concentration. A restrained style of wine, it exhibits fine overall balance and a moderately long finish. As with most Spottswoode Cabernets, it displays an attractive purity of flavor. Drink it over the next decade.

Unquestionably, the 1993 is the finest Sauvignon Spottswoode has produced. It exhibits an intense fragrance of fresh herbs, honey, vanilla, and ripe fruit. This zesty, exuberant, concentrated, medium-bodied Sauvignon possesses excellent freshness and focus. If more wineries begin to turn out Sauvignons such as this, look for a rebound in popularity for this varietal. Drink it over the next year.

SPRING MOUNTAIN VINEYARDS (NAPA)
Cabernet Sauvignon Estate * * * *, Cabernet Sauvignon Estate Chevalier Vineyard * * * *,
Cabernet Sauvignon Estate Miravalle Vineyard * * * *

1993 Cabernet Sauvignon Estate	Napa	D	89
1993 Cabernet Sauvignon Estate Chevalier Vineyard	Napa	D	91
1992 Cabernet Sauvignon Estate Miravalle Vineyard	Napa	D	89

This estate, which includes all the Spring Mountain vineyards, the old Château Chevalier vineyards, and some of the Draper vineyards that are under lease, is being resurrected by an ambitious group led by Tom Ferrell that is determined to produce impressive wines from these well-established vineyards. The debut vintage of Cabernet Sauvignon is 1992. Given the significant investment and commitment to quality, this should be an operation to keep a close eye on as the production moves up.

The first releases include the 1992 Cabernet Sauvignon Miravalle Vineyard (700 cases), which reveals a dark ruby/purple color, an elegant, spicy nose of red and black currants, good concentration, a sense of balance and style, and a crisp, long, pure finish. It should drink well for 10–15+ years. The 1993 Spring Mountain Estate Cabernet Sauvignon (7,000 cases) exhibits the same elegance and the subtle use of toasty new oak, excellent cassis fruit, a touch of minerals, and fine purity and length. There is also a tiny quantity (300 cases) of the 1993 Spring Mountain Estate Cabernet Sauvignon Chevalier Vineyard, which is the richest, most concentrated wine of this trio. This wine exhibits great purity of black currant fruit, a spicy-, licorice-, mineral-scented bouquet, full body, and a sense of balance and grace without astringent tannin or high alcohol/heaviness. It is a classic, concentrated Cabernet Sauvignon that should drink well for 15+ years.

Barrel samples of the 1994s, which will probably include the winery's first proprietary red wine (yet to be named), looked to be of even higher quality. This should be a big-time player in the Cabernet Sauvignon sweepstakes.

STAGLIN FAMILY VINEYARDS (NAPA)
Cabernet Sauvignon * * * *, Sangiovese * * * *

1994 Cabernet Sauvignon	Napa	D	91
1993 Cabernet Sauvignon	Napa	D	88
1992 Cabernet Sauvignon	Napa	D	89+
1991 Cabernet Sauvignon	Napa	D	88
1990 Cabernet Sauvignon	Napa	D	90
1994 Stagliano Sangiovese Staglin Family Vineyard	Napa	EE	90
1993 Stagliano Sangiovese Staglin Family Vineyard	Napa	EE	90

Readers should be on the lookout for any of the quantity (150 cases) of Stagliano Sangiovese. While extremely expensive, the 1994 is one of the more faithful and promising examples of Sangiovese from Napa. It reveals a spicy-, cherry-, new saddle leather–scented nose, good, tasty, round, soft fruit with enough acidity to provide crispness, and a medium-bodied, soft finish. It should be drunk during its first 5–7 years of life. My only criticism is the lofty price.

To date, the best California Sangiovese I have tasted has been Staglin's gorgeously opulent, rich 1992. Despite a price tag that is 30%–40% higher than most of Italy's finest Chiantis, the 1993 Stagliano Sangiovese is a terrific effort. The wine displays a healthy dark ruby/purple color, and a sweet, expansive nose of jammy black cherries, new saddle leather, and spices. An opulent, superripe wine with low acidity, luscious, layered, succulent fruit, and a smooth, satiny finish, this is unequivocally a hedonistic, seductive, outstanding Sangiovese for consuming over the next 4–5 years.

Staglin's 1992 Cabernet Sauvignon is at least excellent, possibly outstanding. This dark ruby/purple-colored, medium-bodied, finesse-style Cabernet appears reticent and extremely tight and backward, but with airing it reveals a subtle yet attractive nose of cedar, spice, herbs, and cassis, excellent richness, an impressive sense of balance, and a beautifully knit, stylish finish. In a blind tasting, I would easily mistake it for a Left Bank Bordeaux. Give it 2–3 more years of cellaring and drink it over the subsequent 12–15 years.

Stylish, slightly sculptured, and impressively made, the 1991 Cabernet Sauvignon displays a judicious use of toasty new oak, a deep, herb-, and black currant–scented bouquet, elegant, medium- to full-bodied flavors, and fine length. There is a sense of restraint and politeness to go along with the wine's undeniable richness. Approachable now, it should last for 12–15 or more years. An exceptionally elegant, stylistic Cabernet Sauvignon, the 1990 appears to be trying to imitate a graceful Bordeaux. Its purity, sense of style, and deep, rich, spicy, cassis flavors, intertwined with well-integrated new oak, make for an impressive performance. There is good underlying acidity as well as an impeccable sense of balance. This restrained yet successful wine brilliantly juxtaposes richness and finesse. It should last for at least a decade.

The 1993 Cabernet Sauvignon is a cranberry- and red currant–scented and –flavored wine with an elegant, medium-bodied personality, good spice and crispness, and less intensity and complexity than the 1992 or 1991. The 1994 Cabernet Sauvignon (4,000) cases) is potentially the finest Cabernet this small, high-quality winery has produced. It exhibits great sweetness of fruit, a smoky, black curranty nose with just enough oak, medium to full body, wonderful intensity and purity, and a spicy, long finish. It should drink well early in life and last for 15+ years.

STAG'S LEAP WINE CELLARS (NAPA)

Cabernet Sauvignon Fay Vineyard* * * */* * * * *, Cabernet Sauvignon Napa* * *, Cabernet Sauvignon Stag's Leap Vineyard* * */* * * *, Cask 23 Proprietary Red Wine* * * * *, Chardonnay Napa* *, Chardonnay Reserve* * *, Sauvignon Blanc* * *

1992	Cabernet Sauvignon	Napa	C	87
1991	Cabernet Sauvignon	Napa	C	87
1992	Cabernet Sauvignon Fay Vineyard	Napa	D	93
1991	Cabernet Sauvignon Fay Vineyard	Napa	D	90+
1990	Cabernet Sauvignon Fay Vineyard	Napa	D	90
1992	Cabernet Sauvignon Stag's Leap Vineyard	Napa	D	90
1990	Cabernet Sauvignon Stag's Leap Vineyard	Napa	D	89
1992	Cask 23 Proprietary Red Wine	Napa	E	94+
1991	Cask 23 Proprietary Red Wine	Napa	E	96
1990	Cask 23 Proprietary Red Wine	Napa	E	91
1993	Chardonnay	Napa	C	87
1992	Chardonnay	Napa	C	83
1993	Chardonnay Reserve	Napa	D	90
1992	Chardonnay Reserve	Napa	D	87
1992	Hawk Crest Cabernet Sauvignon	California	A	86
1993	Hawk Crest Chardonnay	California	A	85
1992	Merlot	Napa	C	87
1993	Sauvignon Blanc Rancho Chimiles	Napa	B	86

This winery enjoys a much deserved fine reputation for its bevy of complex, elegant, authoritatively flavorful red wines, particularly the Fay Vineyard Cabernet Sauvignon and the Cask 23 Proprietary Red Wine, the latter one of California's benchmark wines. The white wine program has been less impressive, although progress is evident with each new vintage.

Consumers will find the understated, delicate, light- to medium-bodied 1993 Sauvignon Blanc Rancho Chimiles to be a fresh, lively, crisp wine that relies on subtlety for much of its appeal. Drink it over the next year. Among the Chardonnays, there is no doubting the value to be found in the 1993 Hawk Crest Chardonnay, a blend of grapes purchased from Mendocino and Sonoma. Fruity, ripe, and medium bodied, this tasty Chardonnay is ideal for drinking over the next year. While the 1992 Napa Valley Chardonnay is good, the 1993 is even better, revealing more richness and texture, as well as finesse and flavor. The understated, crisp, elegant 1992 exhibits a monolithic personality.

The differences between the two Reserve Chardonnays are interesting to note. The 1992

Chardonnay Reserve, which was 100% barrel-fermented in new oak, is made in a delicate, Chablis-like style. It offers crisp acidity, medium body, and an unobtrusive personality. On the other hand, the 1993 Chardonnay Reserve possesses more character in its ripe, tropical fruit and honeyed nose, greater flavor depth, more interesting texture, and a lusher, riper finish. This is the finest Chardonnay yet produced by owner Warren Winiarski.

It is no secret that the red wines remain the raison d'être for most admirers of Stag's Leap Wine Cellars. For thrifty, smart readers, the 1992 Hawk Crest Cabernet Sauvignon is one of the most attractive Cabernet bargains in the marketplace. It possesses lively, ripe, jammy, berry, cassis fruit, a round texture, generous flavors, and a soft, straightforward, delicious finish. Drink it over the next 3–4 years.

With respect to red wines that appear under the Stag's Leap Wine Cellars label, consumers will love the heady, velvety-textured, chocolate- and black cherry–scented and –flavored, tasty 1992 Merlot. The wine is soft, spicy, not especially rich, but extremely well balanced and seductive in a charming, open-knit, moderately intense style. It should drink well for 4–5 years. The 1992 Cabernet Sauvignon Napa exhibits a dark ruby/garnet color, a heady nose of herbs, spices, smoke, and curranty fruit, excellent richness, medium to full body, a supple texture, and a fine finish. Drink it over the next 7–8 years. It was almost as good as the 1992 Cabernet Sauvignon Stag's Leap Vineyard. The latter wine displays more complexity, a deeper ruby/purple color, a jammy-, plum-, and curranty-scented nose, a velvety texture, and a medium- to full-bodied personality with well-integrated spicy notes. It should drink well for at least a decade. More profound is the outstanding 1992 Cabernet Sauvignon Fay Vineyard. It possesses a sweet, alluring bouquet, a deeper, more saturated color, and a seductive fragrance matched by flattering, rich, opulent flavors that cascade over the palate. The acidity is sound. The wine exhibits wonderful concentration, as well as loads of rich fruit. Approachable now, it should last for 10–15 years after its release in 1995. The 1992 Cask 23 Proprietary Red Wine boasts a huge bouquet that jumps from the glass offering up scents of vanilla, Asian spices, black cherries, cassis, smoke, and anise. It is wonderfully opulent, with a voluptuous texture, nicely integrated yet largely hidden tannin, gobs of pure, rich, ripe fruit, and superb harmony. While already impressively endowed and well balanced, this wine should evolve gracefully for at least 15 years.

As for the 1991s, the 1991 Cabernet Sauvignon Fay Vineyard reveals the gorgeously perfumed, complex bouquet that this winery routinely obtains. This wine possesses more structure and firmer tannin than the outstanding 1990 Fay Vineyard Cabernet, but no less richness. There is super fruit, ripeness, medium to full body, and plenty of intensity, but unlike most of this producer's red wines, it needs 1–2 more years of cellaring. It should drink well for 15+ years. The superb 1991 Cask 23 Proprietary Red Wine appears to be one of the truly outstanding examples of this expensive proprietary red wine. The wine's saturated dark purple color is followed by a huge, unevolved but sexy nose of toasty new oak, dense, black cherry and jammy cassis fruit, and vague scents of underbrush and spice. Extremely rich and concentrated, it offers intriguing black currant and coffee flavors, full body, remarkable harmony, and a finish that lasts for nearly a minute. Still young, unevolved, and less flattering at present than the more open-knit 1990, it merits cellaring of 2–4 years. Readers who have followed Stag's Leap Wine Cellars' Cask 23 since the debut vintage of 1974 realize these wines are often deceptively easy to drink when young, yet age amazingly well despite what appears to be their forward, flattering, precocious personalities.

Stag's Leap's telltale aromatic profile of weedy, black curranty, coffee, and spicy aromas is well displayed in the medium-bodied, opulently textured, soft, rich, already delicious 1991 Cabernet Sauvignon. It reveals excellent purity of fruit, low acidity, and a velvety-textured, rich finish. Drink it over the next 7–8 years.

The 1990 Stag's Leap Cabernet possesses a stylish, elegant bouquet of subtle, toasty vanillin from new oak, black cherries, anise, and herbs. The wine offers complex, rich, multidimensional flavors, with excellent extraction, low acidity, ripe fruit, and a medium- to full-bodied finish. There is wonderful richness allied to an overall sense of elegance. Drink it over the next 10–12 years. The 1990 Cabernet Sauvignon Fay Vineyard exhibits a rich, chocolaty, berry-scented nose intermingled with aromas of toasty new oak. Graceful, velvety textured, soft and supple, this medium- to full-bodied, rich, pure, admirably concentrated Cabernet reveals no hard edges. Drink it over the next 10–12 years.

No Cask 23 was produced in 1988 or 1989, but the 1990 is gorgeous. The 1990 Cask 23 exhibits a telltale bouquet of sweet, jammy cassis, herbs, coffee, olives, cedar, and chocolate. The Cask 23 always offers one of the most complex and enticing Cabernet-based bouquets in California. Soft, medium- to full-bodied, harmonious flavors, with well-integrated tannin and low acidity make for a generous, velvety-textured mouthful of classically proportioned, compelling Cabernet. Like most of the finest vintages of Cask 23, it is delicious young, but possesses the cunning ability to age effortlessly for 12–15 or more years.

Ratings for Older Vintages of Stag's Leap Wine Cellars Cask 23: 1987 (91), 1986 (91), 1985 (97), 1984 (93), 1983 (79), 1978 (93), 1977 (87), 1974 (90)

STEARNS WHARF (SANTA BARBARA)
Chardonnay* *, Chenin Blanc* * *

1992 Chenin Blanc La Presta Vineyard	Santa Ynez	A	86

The floral aromas and crisp, ripe, tasty fruit in the medium-bodied, excellent 1992 Chenin Blanc result in a delicious wine with considerable flexibility. I would opt for drinking it as an aperitif.

STEELE (LAKE COUNTY)
Chardonnay* * * *, Chardonnay Durell Vineyard* * * *, Chardonnay Lolonis Vineyard* * * * *, Chardonnay Du Pratt Vineyard* * * * *, Chardonnay Sangiacomo Vineyard* * * * *, Pinot Noir* * *, Pinot Noir Sangiacomo Vineyard* * */* * * *, Zinfandel Cuvées* * */* * * *

1992 Chardonnay	California	C	90
1991 Chardonnay	California	C	89
1992 Chardonnay Bien Nacido Vineyard	Santa Barbara	C	91
1992 Chardonnay Dennison Vineyard	Mendocino	C	90
1992 Chardonnay Du Pratt Vineyard	Mendocino	C	87
1991 Chardonnay Du Pratt Vineyard	Mendocino	C	90
1992 Chardonnay Durell Vineyard	Sonoma	C	89+
1991 Chardonnay Durell Vineyard	Sonoma	C	88
1992 Chardonnay Lolonis Vineyard	Mendocino	D	92
1991 Chardonnay Lolonis Vineyard	Mendocino	D	90
1992 Chardonnay Sangiacomo Vineyard	Carneros	C	87
1991 Chardonnay Sangiacomo Vineyard	Carneros	C	91
1992 Zinfandel Catfish Vineyard	Clear Lake	C	88
1992 Zinfandel Pacini Vineyard	Mendocino	C	88

Jed Steele's new enterprise located in Kelseyville, California, is giving every indication of being a bright new star. The supertalented Steele appears to have the touch regardless of whether the wine is Zinfandel, Chardonnay, or Syrah. The 1992 Zinfandels offer classic examples of Zinfandel's wonderful fruit. Eschewing the blockbuster, thick, tannic, heavy-weight style, Steele has chosen to emphasize the wonderfully zesty, vibrant, juicy Zinfandel fruit. Both wines are medium to full bodied, with admirable purity, lovely, supple textures, and plenty of vibrancy and character. The lighter 1992 Zinfandel Catfish Vineyard is an immensely seductive, charming wine that goes down the gullet all too easily. Drink it over the next 5–7 years. The 1992 Zinfandel Pacini Vineyard is more structured and concentrated, but its emphasis too is on up-front, deliciously fresh berry fruit presented in a medium- to full-bodied, supple format. These delicious Zinfandels should please both the neophyte and the connoisseur.

The 1992s, the second vintage of Chardonnays I have tasted from this property, are as impressive as the 1991s. The outstanding California Chardonnay is the most widely available (4,000 cases), but the single-vineyard Chardonnays range from a microscopic quantity of 75 cases of Durell and Dennison, to 300 cases of Lolonis and Du Pratt. All of these Chardonnays are characterized by layers of rich, crisp, pure, up-front fruit, medium to full body, excellent balance, a generous yet subtle use of toasty oak, and ripe, long, luscious finishes.

The 1992 Chardonnay California is a top-flight Chardonnay. The wine has not been excessively acidified, offering a rich, buttery, toasty, fruity nose, medium- to full-bodied, well-balanced flavors, decent acidity, and a lusty finish. Among the single-vineyard offerings, the most mineral scented, closed, and delicate is the 1992 Chardonnay Du Pratt Vineyard. It exhibits admirable ripeness and a Chablis-like crispness and stony character. The buttery, ripe, medium-bodied 1992 Chardonnay Sangiacomo Vineyard possesses good fruit extraction, a compact personality, and a shorter finish.

The other single-vineyard Chardonnays include a tightly knit, closed, full-bodied, impressively endowed 1992 Durell Vineyard Chardonnay, which will benefit from 4–6 months of cellaring, an exceptional, fat, juicy, unctuously textured, full-bodied 1992 Chardonnay Dennison Vineyard, a richly fruity, aromatic, densely packed, vividly pure 1992 Chardonnay Bien Nacido Vineyard, and perhaps my preference, the exceptionally concentrated, authoritatively rich yet subtle and graceful 1992 Lolonis Vineyard Chardonnay. The latter wine appears to possess even more length than the other Chardonnays. All of these wines, which exhibit impeccable winemaking skills, should drink well for another 1–2 years.

All of the 1991 Chardonnays possess great fruit, excellent to outstanding richness, and superb purity and focus. The California offering is rich and opulent, with gobs of fruit as well as just enough acidity for balance. The elegant Durell Vineyard Chardonnay exhibits higher acidity and is more restrained. Attractive peachlike aromas add to the overall complexity and character of the wine. Yet this is the most tightly knit and highest in acidity. It may even improve over the next 6–12 months. The Du Pratt Vineyard Chardonnay also reveals high, crisp acidity, as well as wonderful levels of fruit, a medium- to full-bodied texture, and that enticing orange, ripe apple, tangerinelike character that is often found in top white burgundies. The oak also appears more restrained, although none of these wines is excessively woody.

For my palate, the two best 1991s include the Lolonis Vineyard Chardonnay—a full-throttle, rich, smoky, buttery wine, with superextraction of flavor, less acidity than the Du Pratt and Durrell, a chewy, fleshy texture, and stunning length. The other blockbuster is the deep, rich Sangiacomo Vineyard Chardonnay. It is an exquisite wine with huge reserves of fruit, an intense, floral, buttery, apple, and spicy bouquet, rich, medium- to full-bodied flavors, and an admirably long finish. I doubt that any of these wines are meant to make old bones, but they should continue to drink well for the next 2 years. Don't miss them!

STELTZNER VINEYARDS (NAPA)
Cabernet Sauvignon* *, Merlot* *, Sauvignon Blanc* *

1992 Sauvignon Blanc Estate Oak Knoll Ranch	Napa	A	86

A refreshing, lively, herb-, melon-, and subtly oaky-scented, medium-bodied wine with fine fruit and freshness, Steltzner's 1992 Sauvignon Blanc from the Oak Knoll Ranch should be drunk over the next year.

STERLING VINEYARDS (NAPA)
Cabernet Sauvignon Diamond Mountain Ranch* * */* * * * (since 1992), Cabernet Sauvignon Napa* *, Chardonnay Diamond Mountain Ranch* * *, Chardonnay Napa* *, Chardonnay Winery Lake* * *, Merlot* *, Pinot Noir* *, Reserve Proprietary Red Wine* */* * *, Sauvignon Blanc* *, Zinfandel* * *

1993 Cabernet Sauvignon Diamond Mountain Ranch	Napa	C	91
1992 Cabernet Sauvignon Diamond Mountain Ranch	Napa	C	90
1993 Chardonnay Estate	Napa	B	88
1992 Reserve Proprietary Red Wine	Napa	D	90
1991 Reserve Proprietary Red Wine	Napa	D	88+
1993 Merlot Three Palms Vineyard	Napa	C	88
1992 Merlot Three Palms Vineyard	Napa	C	89
1993 Zinfandel	Napa	B	86

Significant winemaking changes are underway at the beautiful Sterling winery perched on a hilltop south of Calistoga. For some time I have been an outspoken critic of this winery, as it was one of California's leading underachievers. Despite huge financial resources and great vineyards at Sterling, many of the wines tasted processed, excessively acidified, and devoid of aromatics and flavor after bottling. Winemaker Bill Dyer, an accomplished, talented man, appears to have gotten the attention of the corporate owners, because top red wine cuvées from the 1992 and 1993 vintages are destined, according to Dyer, to go into the bottle naturally. One can also detect less acidification and a more natural texture and taste. All of this will immensely benefit the consumer, for if this winery has awakened as much as my instincts suggest, such a development can only have a positive influence on California winemaking.

The 1992 and 1993 Merlots from the Three Palms Vineyard were bottled without fining or filtration. They exhibit deeper, more saturated colors, and more expressive bouquets of chocolate, black cherries, mocha, and wood. The 1992 is more expansive, without losing its sense of elegance, whereas the 1993 is less evolved and more structured.

Progress is also noticeable with the Diamond Mountain Cabernet Sauvignons. The 1992 exhibits a saturated black/ruby color, a big, cassis-, herbal-, licorice-, vanillin-scented nose, full body, and plenty of flavor depth and concentration. It is a candidate for 2 decades of aging. The 1993 is sweeter, with even greater fruit and intensity, and a long, chocolaty, cassis finish.

The Reserve Proprietary Red Wine is also benefitting from Sterling's new noninterventionist winemaking philosophy. The 1992 offers gobs of cassis fruit, full body, fine richness, a touch of toasty new oak, and a long, chewy, rich finish. I hope the tart, hollow, aromatically sterile character of the Reserves made in the eighties is a thing of the past. The rich, multidimensional, concentrated 1991 Reserve (a blend of 64% Cabernet Sauvignon, 18% Merlot, 10% Cabernet Franc, and 8% Petite Verdot) displays a saturated dark ruby/purple color, and a promising nose of black cherries, cassis, minerals, and spicy oak. It is medium bodied, with admirable complexity, some sweetness from ripe fruit, and a rich, moderately tannic finish. It will improve for 3–4 years and will last for well over a decade.

Sterling has also recognized the surging popularity of Zinfandel. The 1993 Zinfandel, from a vineyard near St. Helena, is a tasty, medium-bodied, richly fruity wine that is ideal for drinking in its first 5–6 years of life.

California readers should consider getting their name on Sterling's mailing list, as they are also making small quantities of high-quality Pinot Grigio, Sangiovese, and limited-production cuvées of Chardonnay and Pinot Noir that are only sold at the winery. There is a delicious, wonderfully vibrant, rich, fruity 1993 Pinot Grigio that was bottled without filtration. It is one of the best I have tasted from California. There is also a 1993 Chardonnay made from a clone with a Muscat-like fragrance.

STONESTREET (SONOMA)
Cabernet Sauvignon* * *, Chardonnay* * * *, Legacy Proprietary Red Wine* * * *,
Merlot* * *, Pinot Noir* * */* * * *

1990 Cabernet Sauvignon	Alexander Valley	C	86
1993 Chardonnay	Sonoma	C	88
1991 Legacy Proprietary Red Wine	Alexander Valley	D	88
1991 Merlot	Alexander Valley	C	85
1992 Pinot Noir	Sonoma	D	87

I have had little tasting experience from this winery, which is under the same ownership as Kendall-Jackson. The 1991 Merlot is a soft, herbaceous, ripe, plump wine that has not been excessively acidified. It displays plenty of fleshy fruit in a straightforward, medium-bodied format. Drink it over the next 3–4 years. The similarly styled 1990 Cabernet Sauvignon offers up curranty, olivelike notes intertwined with those of toasty oak. This dark ruby-colored wine exhibits fine ripeness, a round, plush texture, and a smooth finish. Drink it over the next 5–6 years. More intriguing, as well as more complex and concentrated, is Stonestreet's 1991 Legacy, a proprietary red wine made from 41% Cabernet Sauvignon, 34% Cabernet Franc, and 25% Merlot. The wine possesses a dark ruby color, a sweet nose of black cherries, cassis, smoke, and vanilla, medium to full body, and an attractive marriage of power and finesse. This velvety-textured, ripe, pleasure-filled red wine can be drunk now or cellared for 10 years.

I tasted two 1992 Pinots from Stonestreet. One, a limited-production unfiltered Reserve, was rated 85, but I thought the regular bottling was better. The 1992 Pinot Noir regular bottling revealed less oak, yet more sweet, rich, supple-textured fruit, a lovely bouquet of berry, earth, and spice, and a silky-smooth, seductive finish. It should drink well for 4–5 years.

The 1993 Chardonnay is a bold, ostentatiously styled, Meursault-like wine offering forceful, enticing aromas of smoke, honeyed peaches, apples, and buttery notes. Rich, chewy, full bodied, and admirably concentrated, this is a large-scale, delicious Chardonnay for consuming by mid-1996.

STORYBOOK MOUNTAIN VINEYARDS (NAPA)
Zinfandel* * * *, Zinfandel Eastern Exposures* * * *, Zinfandel Estate* * * *, Zinfandel
Howell Mountain* * * *, Zinfandel Reserve* * * * *

1991 Zinfandel	Napa	B	90
1992 Zinfandel Eastern Exposures	Napa	B	89

1992 Zinfandel Estate	Napa	B	88+
1992 Zinfandel Howell Mountain	Napa	C	89+
1991 Zinfandel Howell Mountain	Napa	C	88+
1992 Zinfandel Reserve	Napa	C	90+
1991 Zinfandel Reserve	Napa	C	90+

Storybook Mountain produces what many observers believe to be California's longest-lived Zinfandels. Even their Estate cuvée can last for 15+ years, with the Reserve a potential candidate for a quarter of a century of longevity. Proprietor Jerry Seps believes in making long-lived, serious Zinfandels that possess enough suppleness to be appreciated young. In 1992 there are two cuvées meant to be consumed early, although both should last and perhaps improve over a long span of years. The first 1992 Zinfandel to be released is the 1992 Eastern Exposures Zinfandel, a blend of lots that were deemed both complex and supple. It is the most velvety-textured and easily drunk of the 1992 Storybook Mountain Zinfandels. It displays an impressively saturated, dark ruby/purple color, a ripe, black cherry– and cassis-scented nose, opulent, medium- to full-bodied flavors, excellent purity and ripeness, and an accessible, rich, lush finish. Drinkable now, it should last for 12–15 years. The 1992 Napa Estate exhibits a dark, saturated, purple color, a spicy, ripe, scented nose of black raspberry fruit and minerals, excellent richness and concentration, loads of tannin, and mineral flavors in the background. The wine will benefit from 2–3 years of cellaring and last for 15–20 years.

The 1992 Zinfandel Howell Mountain is the most ferociously tannic and backward of the Storybook Mountain Zinfandels. It reveals a stony/mineral component to its spicy, ripe, black currant fruitiness. While the wine is medium to full bodied, admirably concentrated, and brilliantly well focused, it needs 4–5 years of cellaring; it will keep for 15–20 years. The stunning 1992 Zinfandel Reserve is a highly extracted, firm, austere, full-bodied wine loaded with concentrated fruit. It is also highly structured with considerable tannin and good underlying acidity. Rich, powerful, elegant, and complex, this wine needs 5–8 years of cellaring; it should keep for 25 or more years. These impressive Zinfandels behave brilliantly in the bottle!

The 1991 Napa Zinfandel is the easiest to drink and most flattering of this trio of 1991s. It boasts a deep ruby/purple color, a big, sweet, peppery, raspberry-scented nose, rich, medium- to full-bodied flavors, fine underlying acidity to bring everything into focus, and a lovely, rich, long finish. Storybook Mountain's Zinfandels generally need considerable bottle age to strut their stuff, but this 1991 Zinfandel is among the more precocious wines that I have tasted from this winery. Drinkable now, it will easily last for 10–12 years. The 1991 Howell Mountain is an age-worthy, tannic, backward, spicy Zinfandel that is completely closed yet loaded with potential. It needs at least 4–5 years in the cellar and should last for 12–15 more. Big, brawny, and concentrated, patience is most definitely required. Storybook Mountain's 1991 Zinfandel Reserve promises to rival the quality of the wonderful 1990 and 1987. It reveals a deep ruby/purple color, a broodingly backward, intriguing nose of minerals, black fruits, spices, and pepper, superlative extraction of fruit, full body, high tannin levels, and crisp acidity. There is a layered, multidimensional feel to the wine. As with the Howell Mountain, patience is essential. **A.M.: 1997–2010.**

STRATFORD (NAPA)

Cabernet Sauvignon * *, Chardonnay Napa * * *, Chardonnay Partner's Reserve * * *,
Merlot * * *, Sauvignon Blanc * *

1991 Zinfandel	California	A	86

The 1991 Zinfandel exhibits a classic peppery, raspberry-scented nose, medium to full body, excellent color, admirable purity, and a long, zesty finish. While not complex, it is satisfying and mouth filling. Drink it over the next 2–3 years.

RODNEY STRONG (SONOMA)

Cabernet Sauvignon Alexander's Crown* */* * *, Cabernet Sauvignon Reserve* */* * *, Cabernet Sauvignon Sonoma* *, Chardonnay Chalk Hill Vineyard* * *, Pinot Noir River East Vineyard* *, Sauvignon Blanc Charlotte's Home Vineyard* * */* * * *, Zinfandel Old Vines River West Vineyard* * *

1992	Cabernet Sauvignon	Sonoma	B	86
1994	Sauvignon Blanc Charlotte's Home Vineyard	Northern Sonoma	B	87
1992	Zinfandel Old Vines River West Vineyard	Russian River	B	87
1991	Zinfandel Old Vines River West Vineyard	Russian River	B	76?
1990	Zinfandel Old Vines River West Vineyard	Russian River	B	76

How nice it is to see so many fine Sauvignons finally emerging from California. These inexpensive wines are remarkably flexible with food and offer delicious drinking during their first 1–2 years of life. Rodney Strong's 1994 displays an excellent bouquet of floral, honey, and melon scents. Medium bodied, round, and generous, with a spicy, clean finish, it should be drunk over the next year.

The 1992 Zinfandel Old Vines River West displays a healthy dark ruby color, a spicy, vanilla-, smoky-, peppery-, and berry-scented nose, and medium- to full-bodied, expansive, rich, ripe flavors with well-integrated oak. Soft and round, it is ideal for drinking over the next 5–6 years. It is a very seductive Zinfandel. The 1991 Zinfandel Old Vines River West's medium ruby color is followed by a wine with vague scents of fruit and dusty, peppery spice. The attack begins well with some ripeness, but the frightfully high tannin dominates the meager fruit. The overall impression is one of hardness, astringency, and lack of fruit. An exceptionally lean, hard-edged, tough style of Zinfandel, the 1990 appears to have been stripped at bottling. The high acid and deficient fruit have resulted in a hollow, emaciated wine with little charm or personality.

Strong's 1992 Cabernet Sauvignon is a fine value, offering a minty-, herb-, black curranty–scented nose, medium body, attractive fruit, velvety texture, and admirable purity, ripeness, and length. Drink this delicious, bargain-priced Cabernet over the next 4–5 years.

SUMMIT LAKE VINEYARDS AND WINERY (NAPA)
Zinfandel* * */* * * *

1992	Zinfandel Howell Mountain	Napa	B	87+
1991	Zinfandel Howell Mountain	Napa	B	87+

The dense, highly extracted, tannic 1992 Zinfandel should be purchased by those who either (1) have a fondness for tough-textured wines, or (2) have the patience to wait 3–4 years for the wine to soften. Summit Lake's black/purple-colored 1992 Zinfandel Howell Mountain is loaded with spice, minerals, and black raspberry fruit, as well as a forbiddingly tannic, tough finish. All the component parts appear to be in balance, so it is just a matter of outwaiting the tannin.

With respect to the 1991 Zinfandel, an exceptionally saturated, opaque purple color is followed by a wine with a tight, closed bouquet. Even with coaxing, little aroma emerges, save for some vague, sweet smells of black fruits, minerals, and pepper. The impression of an impenetrable, backward style of Zinfandel is confirmed by the taste. The wine is massive to the point of being huge, with tremendous extraction of fruit as well as mouth-searing, hard, tough tannins. While this wine needs at least 4–5 years of cellaring, it possesses the requisite depth and overall balance to age for 12–15 years, making it an uncommonly long-lived Zinfandel.

SUTTER HOME WINERY (NAPA)

Cabernet Sauvignon* *, White Zinfandel* *, Zinfandel* *, Zinfandel Reserve* * *

1991 Zinfandel	Amador	A	85

One might quibble that the 1991 Zinfandel is made in a soft, fruity, commercial style, but there is no doubting that it is generously endowed with ripe, peppery, raspberry fruit, with good body, and a clean, rich, satisfying finish. Drink it over the next 3–4 years.

JOSEPH SWAN VINEYARDS (SONOMA)

Côtes du Rosa* * *, Pinot Noir cuvées* *, Vin du Mystère* * *, Zinfandel cuvées* * * *

1993 Côtes du Rosa Unfiltered	Russian River	B	87
1991 Vin du Mystère	Sonoma	B	88
1992 Zinfandel Frati Ranch	Russian River	C	90
1991 Zinfandel Frati Ranch	Russian River	C	90+
1992 Zinfandel Stellwagen Vineyard	Sonoma	C	?
1991 Zinfandel Stellwagen Vineyard	Sonoma	C	92
1992 Zinfandel V.H.S.R. Vineyard	Russian River	C	90?
1991 Zinfandel Zeigler Vineyard	Russian River	C	90+

Warning: These controversial wines fall far outside the mainstream of Zinfandel winemaking! The opaque, dark purple/garnet-colored 1992 Zinfandel V.H.S.R. exhibits a huge, earthy, black fruit–scented nose with noticeable volatile acidity. Yes, the volatile acidity is a flaw, but there are numerous other elements that outweigh this defect. The wine is dry, fat, and chewy, with gobs of fruit and spectacular density and concentration. This controversial, mammoth-sized Zinfandel should be drunk with hefty, winter-weight stews, or by itself after the main course. It should evolve for 10–20 or more years and become more civilized with aging. The 1992 Zinfandel Stellwagen displays a more evolved garnet color. The bizarre bouquet of melted road tar, damp, leafy vegetation, smoked game, and wet dog fur goes beyond even my definition of kinky. The wine reveals fine ripeness, but the unusual aromas are followed by an equally eccentrically flavored wine. Although soft and concentrated, it is extremely weird. Swan's 1992 Zinfandel Frati Ranch is a personality-filled, exceptionally powerful, superconcentrated, heavy, thick wine. It exhibits extraordinary fruit extraction without the excessively eccentric style of the Stellwagen or the volatile acidity of the V.H.S.R. The opaque purple color and huge, black cherry–, herb-, spicy-, and earthy-scented nose are followed by a full-bodied wine with an unctuous texture and a massive finish. It is so enormous it merits drinking by itself.

The 1993 unfiltered Côtes du Rosa reveals an impressively saturated color, loads of black cherry fruit and fragrant spices, medium to full body, and an expansive chewiness that makes for a satisfying glass of dry, supple red wine. It will drink well for 3–4 years. The 1991 Vin du Mystère, made from 100-year-old vines, offers a peppery, black raspberry–scented nose, medium to full body, a juicy fatness and textural suppleness, and a long, heady, rich finish. A joy to drink, it will age well for 5–7 years.

The 1991 Zinfandels are the most reassuringly rich, complex wines I have tasted in years from this historic winery. Made for cellaring, they are enormously endowed, tannic, backward wines with considerable body and concentration. All three promise to be thrilling wines, provided buyers exercise some patience. If you do not mind some tannic bite, they can be enjoyed now. The 1991 Zinfandel Frati Ranch exhibits a Barolo-like nose of melted road tar and black fruits. Exceptionally tannic in the mouth, it boasts impressive extraction of flavor, full body, and a deep, long, superrich finish. Most of the depth can be sensed at the back of the mouth. **A.M.: 1996–2005.** The 1991 Zinfandel Zeigler Vineyard reveals an earthy-, licorice-, black truffle–scented nose intertwined with aromas of peppery black raspberries. The color is nearly opaque. The wine possesses wonderful richness, tremendous extraction of sweet Zinfandel fruit, and a layered, spicy but forbiddingly tannic, blockbuster finish. This dark-purple-colored Zin should be at its best between 1996 and 2006. With its garnet color, the 1991 Zinfandel Stellwagen Vineyard even looks different. More developed, it is the easiest of this trio to drink. The big, smoky, cedary, black fruit–scented nose soars from the glass. This spectacularly rich, unctuous, remarkably concentrated Zinfandel offers admirable body and glycerin, as well as softer tannins than its two siblings. Drink this gloriously rich, full-throttle wine over the next decade. How delighted I am to see such quality reemerge from Joseph Swan!

SWANSON VINEYARDS AND WINERY (NAPA)
Cabernet Sauvignon * * * *, Chardonnay * * * */* * * * *, Late Harvest Semillon * * * * *,
Merlot * * * */* * * * *, Sangiovese * * * *, Syrah * * * * *

1992	Cabernet Sauvignon	Napa	C	89+
1991	Cabernet Sauvignon	Napa	C	88+
1993	Chardonnay	Carneros	C	90
1991	Late Harvest Semillon	Napa	C	93+
1993	Merlot	Napa	C	86
1993	Sangiovese	Napa	C	91
1992	Sangiovese	Napa	C	90
1993	Syrah	Napa	D	92

This winery is doing plenty of things right, which is good news for consumers. The 1993 Chardonnay Carneros is the finest Chardonnay Swanson has yet produced. Fortunately, there are 2,400 cases. The wine exhibits a wonderful, honeyed pear–, orange peel–, and apple-scented nose, creamy, full-bodied flavors revealing high-quality smoky oak, and excellent purity and richness. The wine was put through a slight fining, but was bottled without filtration. It should drink well for 2–3 years.

Swanson is one of a handful of wineries turning out outstanding Sangiovese. The 1992 is a gorgeous Chianti look-alike with loads of sweet cherry fruit, a soft, spicy, rich palate, and a heady finish. The 1993 is even better, and a terrific example of how fine Sangiovese can be. Swanson takes the potential yields of 12 tons per acre and cuts over half the grapes off in an attempt to produce 5 tons per acre, which is still a high yield. The 1993 possesses a classic Sangiovese nose of cherries, earth, new saddle leather, and spice, medium body, great fruit intensity, good underlying acidity (to cut through all those tomato-based sauces), and a clean, vibrant, rich finish. Drink this delicious wine within 3–5 years of its release.

Although the 1993 Merlot is tightly knit and lean, with higher acidity than expected, it reveals good color, abundant black cherry fruit, and medium body. Drink it over the next 5–6 years. What this winery has done with Syrah is well-evidenced by the spectacular 1992. That wine has been followed by 400 cases of stunning 1993 Syrah. It exhibits a smoky-, bacon fat–, cassis-scented nose, and rich, full-bodied, dense, powerful flavors with moderate tannin. Give it 4–5 years of cellaring and drink it over the subsequent 15–20.

Like the other wines, Swanson's Cabernet Sauvignons continue to improve. Both the 1991 and 1992 are tannic, backward Cabernets with good depth, medium to full body, excellent flavor extraction, and spicy, earthy, sweet cassis characters. The 1991 will be the longer lived, although the 1992 will be more flattering and precocious. Both wines need 4–5 years of cellaring and should keep for 15–20. Lastly, in some vintages tiny quantities (about 150 cases of half bottles) are produced of Late Harvest Semillon. It is a beautifully made wine that could easily be mistaken for a great Barsac such as Château Climens. Swanson's 1991 Late Harvest Semillon, a blend of 83% Semillon and 17% Sauvignon Blanc that is fermented and aged in 100% new oak, is a stunningly proportioned, elegant yet authoritatively rich wine that should drink well for 10–15 years. If you don't think California wineries can produce decadently rich, honeyed, sweet wines with finesse and balance, check out this wine.

The 1992 Syrah (from the same vineyard Sean Thackrey utilized to produce his exquisite Orion) is a dead ringer for a great northern Rhône. The opaque black/purple color is followed by a spectacular nose of bacon fat, smoked herbs, and cassis that roars from the glass. Rich, with sensational concentration, sweet tannin, an expansive, mouth-filling, chewy texture, and magnificent purity and delineation, this profound wine is approachable yet should age effortlessly for 15–20+ years. Readers may wish to make a mental note that barrel samples of the 1993 Syrah suggest an equal level of quality! Bravo!

ROBERT TALBOTT VINEYARDS (MONTEREY)
Chardonnay Diamond T Estate * * * * *, Chardonnay Estate * * * * *, Logan
Chardonnay * * * *

1992 Chardonnay	Monterey	D	91
1991 Chardonnay	Monterey	D	91
1990 Chardonnay	Monterey	D	93
1991 Chardonnay Diamond T Estate	Monterey	D	92
1990 Chardonnay Diamond T Estate	Monterey	D	91+

This superb producer has turned out an intense, mineral-scented wine that comes as close as anything I have tasted in California to resembling a great grand cru from the renowned Chablis producer, Jean-Marie Raveneau. Talbott's 1991 Chardonnay from the Diamond T Estate possesses great fruit, full body, a superbly well-delineated personality, and excellent underlying acidity. A rich, multidimensional Chardonnay with considerable finesse and force, it should be drunk over the next 2–4 years.

The 1992 Chardonnay Estate is similarly styled, rich, full, superbly well focused and balanced, with layers of fruit, yet considerable elegance. The 1991 regular cuvée of Chardonnay offers great depth and grip as well as a delineated, structured feel and superb purity. A large-scale, rich wine, it should drink well for 4–5 years.

The 1990 Diamond T Estate cuvée is a closed, tightly knit wine that could easily benefit from another 6–12 months of bottle age. The honeyed, pineapple-, mineral-, floral-scented nose emerges reluctantly. Full bodied, rich, tightly knit, and closed, this broodingly deep, graceful, multidimensional Chardonnay should drink well for 4–5 years. The 1990 Chardonnay reveals a huge bouquet filled with aromas of oranges, butter, minerals, and spicy oak. The wine is full bodied yet brilliantly well balanced by crisp acidity. Rich and deep, this compelling example of California Chardonnay is capable of lasting 3–4 more years, although its charms are impossible to resist now.

TALLEY VINEYARDS (SAN LUIS OBISPO)
Chardonnay * * * *, Pinot Noir * * * *

1993 Chardonnay	Arroyo Grande Valley	C	88

Although tight and unevolved, this Chardonnay is very promising. The nose hints at ripe fruit, subtle oak, spice, vanillin, oranges, and honey. Medium to full bodied, with excellent acidity, fine concentration, and an overall sense of purity and balance, this tightly knit, crisp, authoritatively flavored Chardonnay should benefit from 6 more months of cellaring. It will last for 2–4 years.

IVAN TAMAS (SANTA CLARA)
Cabernet Sauvignon* *, Chardonnay* * *, Fumé Blanc* * */* * * *, Trebbiano* * * *

1992 Chardonnay Haynes Ranch	Livermore	A	86
1992 Chardonnay Reserve	Livermore	B	87
1992 Fumé Blanc Figoni Ranch	Livermore	A	87
1993 Trebbiano	Livermore	A	86

This winery continues to turn out flavorful, personality-filled wines that sell at bargain prices. The delicious 1993 Trebbiano is richer, more honeyed, and bigger than any Italian Trebbiano I know. It offers a floral, ripe nose, solidly built, fresh, medium- to full-bodied flavors, and considerable richness and exuberance. Drink it over the next 12 months with full-flavored fish and poultry dishes.

The 1992 Chardonnay Reserve emphasizes gorgeously rich, ripe fruit, full body, and a lusty, decadent personality. Drink it over the next year. While far from complex, the 1992 Chardonnay Haynes Ranch is unequivocally a rich, full-bodied, mouth-filling, generously endowed Chardonnay for drinking over the next year.

The 1992 Fumé Blanc is a rich, full-bodied, concentrated wine with a pronounced melon and herb character, as well as fine length and concentration.

LANE TANNER (SANTA BARBARA)
Pinot Noir* * *, Pinot Noir Sanford & Benedict Vineyard* * * *

1991 Pinot Noir	Santa Barbara	C	86
1991 Pinot Noir Sanford & Benedict Vineyard	Santa Barbara	D	89+

This small operation specializes in uncommonly bold, dark-colored, spicy Pinot Noir. The 1991 Pinot Noir Santa Barbara offers deep color, a ripe, herbal, black cherry–scented nose, medium-bodied, nicely extracted flavors, and admirable spice and flesh in the crisp finish. Drink it over the next 5–6 years. The deeper-colored 1991 Pinot Noir Sanford & Benedict Vineyard exhibits an herbaceous, black cherry, mineral, spicy nose, superrich, medium- to full-bodied flavors, a multidimensional, layered texture, and plenty of sweet, ripe fruit in the well-delineated, long finish. It will benefit from another 1–2 years of cellaring and should last for 10 years. Do not be surprised to see it merit an outstanding score after another 6–12 months in the bottle.

TANTALUS (SONOMA)
Cabernet Sauvignon* * *

1992 Cabernet Sauvignon	Sonoma	C	86

Tantalus's 1992 Cabernet Sauvignon exhibits a deep, saturated color, a muted, shy, aromatic profile, and rich, medium- to full-bodied, rustic flavors, as well as a blast of tannin in the finish. Although there is excellent fruit, the wine tastes withdrawn, particularly when tasted beside the more explosive examples of the 1992 vintage. It should easily keep for 12–16 years.

TELDESCHI (SONOMA)
Zinfandel* * */* * * * *

1990 Zinfandel	Dry Creek	C	67
1987 Zinfandel	Dry Creek	C	90

1986 Zinfandel	Dry Creek	C	90
1985 Zinfandel	Dry Creek	C	92

Another spectacular Zinfandel from a little-known Sonoma producer, the opaque black/ purple color of Teldeschi's 1985 Zinfandel is followed by a nose that offers up sensationally rich aromas of black raspberries, licorice, and minerals. There is exceptional concentration, and this rich, full-bodied wine is bursting with fruit and character. Drink this profound Zinfandel over the next 10–15 years. The 1986 is another blockbuster Zinfandel, with an opaque purple color, and an intense, heady perfume of chocolate, cedar, and black raspberry. There is great richness, voluptuous texture, plenty of tannin, and a lingering finish. Drinkable now, it should continue to age well for another 7–8 years. The 1987 is super Zinfandel selling at a terrific price. From its opaque dark ruby/purple color, to its huge nose of black raspberry fruit and spice, this intense, rich, full-bodied wine exhibits velvety tannins, plenty of glycerin and concentration, as well as a long finish. While drinkable now, this wine should easily last for 10–15 years. This is a dazzling Zinfandel from what must be the best vintage for that varietal in the last 20 years. Amazingly, this Zinfandel held up 6 days in an open bottle without showing a trace of oxidation! Only 600 cases of the 1987 were produced from 75-year-old vines. All of these wines were bottled unfined and unfiltered.

Teldeschi may be California's best-kept secret when it comes to great Zinfandel, but the wines can be inconsistent, as evidenced by the poor 1990.

SEAN THACKREY & CO. (MARIN)
Orion Syrah * * * * *, Pleiades * * * *, Sirius Petite Sirah * * * * *, Taurus Mourvèdre * * * * *

1992 Orion Old Vines	California	D	92
1992 Pleiades Old Vines	California	C	86
1991 Sirius Petite Sirah Marston Vineyard	Napa	D	93

The 1992 Pleiades is a medium-bodied, spicy, minty, fruity wine with a distinctive character, soft, supple flavors, and a spicy finish. Unlike Sean Thackrey's other wines, it is a wine to drink over the next 3–5 years. Another top success from this boutique-sized producer, the 1992 Orion (100% Syrah) exhibits an opaque black/purple color, and a telltale cassis and minty aroma intertwined with scents of sweet oak, spice, and licorice. Full bodied with impressive ripeness and richness of fruit, this is another terrific wine from Sean Thackrey. It should age gracefully for 10–15+ years.

The 1991 Sirius, made from the old vines of Napa's Marston Vineyard, is another blockbuster, massively concentrated, chocolaty, meaty, cassis-flavored, spicy wine with exceptional body, superb richness, a supple texture, and a long, concentrated finish. Once again the color is nearly saturated purple. It appears more precocious and flattering than prior vintages. Reminiscent of the great 1991 Petite Sirah made by La Jota, Sean Thackrey's exquisite 1991 Sirius can be drunk now or cellared for 20+ years.

Ratings for Older Vintages of Sean Thackrey Orion: 1990 (92), 1989 (91), 1988 (93)
Ratings for Older Vintages of Sean Thackrey Sirius: 1990 (93), 1989 (90)
Ratings for Older Vintages of Sean Thackrey Taurus: 1990 (90), 1989 (90), 1988 (90)

TOBIN JAMES (PASO ROBLES)
Zinfandel Cuvées * * *

1990 Zinfandel Big Shot	Paso Robles	C	83
1990 Zinfandel Blue Moon Reserve	Paso Robles	C	80
1991 Zinfandel Solar Flair	Paso Robles	C	86

Both the 1990 Big Shot and Blue Moon Reserve Zinfandels are dry, solidly made wines with straightforward peppery, spicy fruit. A bit more breadth of flavor and length, not to mention flavor extraction, would have elevated their scores. The 1991 Solar Flair Zinfandel is a late-harvest, medium-sweet monster (15.4% alcohol) Zinfandel, the likes of which I have not tasted since some of Montevina's superlative releases back in the mid-seventies. A monolithic wine loaded with richness and sweet, jammy (and I mean *jammy*) black raspberry fruit, it is a well-made curiosity. If served with the right cheeses, it will offer an interesting glassful of Zinfandel.

PHILIP TOGNI VINEYARDS (NAPA)
Cabernet Sauvignon * * * * *, Sauvignon Blanc * * * *

1993 Cabernet Sauvignon	Napa	D	90
1992 Cabernet Sauvignon	Napa	D	95
1991 Cabernet Sauvignon	Napa	D	95
1990 Cabernet Sauvignon	Napa	D	96
1993 Sauvignon Blanc	Napa	?	87

This small 10-acre estate situated high on Spring Mountain produces some of the most distinctive Napa Valley wines. The 1993 Sauvignon Blanc, made in a vivacious, crisp, melony style, is clearly California's rendition of a Pouilly-Fumé as interpreted by Mr. Togni. It is bone dry, never acidified, and is uninfluenced by wood aging. Delicious!

Togni's Cabernet Sauvignon, generally made from a Bordeaux-like blend of 82% Cabernet Sauvignon, 15% Merlot, and 3% Cabernet Franc, and aged 22 months in small French oak casks of which 25%–40% are new, is one of the richest, most complex Cabernets made in California. Every time I have the opportunity to go back and taste an older vintage I am impressed with the complex aromatics the wine develops. How reassuring it is to see these Cabernets become even more impressive with bottle age. The first Philip Togni Cabernet Sauvignon vintage was 1983, a wine that remains not only young, but one of the top wines from this unimpressive vintage for most other Napa wineries. The upcoming releases look to be sensational, with the 1992 now being released, and the 1993 in a year.

The 1993 Cabernet Sauvignon exhibits a healthy, nearly opaque dark ruby/purple color, a spicy nose of herb, jammy cassis, licorice, and toast scents, peppery, full-bodied, supple flavors, superripeness, a chewy texture, and outstanding length. It is more forward than vintages such as the 1990 and 1991. Since bottling, the 1992 Cabernet Sauvignon continues to display the remarkable richness and opulence it possessed from cask. The wine offers a saturated dark purple color, a jammy, plum-, black cherry–, herb-, and spice-scented nose, expansive, chewy, full-bodied flavors, superb depth, moderate tannin, low acidity, and a blockbuster finish. It should drink well for more than 2 decades. The 1991 Cabernet Sauvignon has never tasted better. Continuing to fill out and lengthen, the wine reveals wonderfully sweet, black cherry, and spicy fruit, cassis flavors, full body, an unctuous texture, and lavish quantities of fruit obscuring the wine's moderate tannin. Although delicious, it is a decade away from its plateau of maturity, where it should remain for another decade or more. Togni's ability to harvest ripe, sweet fruit is also evident in the 1990 Cabernet Sauvignon, a wine with awesome intensity. It may be the most opulent of these 4 vintages. According to Togni, 1990 produced his smallest crop, which may account for the wine's extraordinary concentration and intensity. It exhibits ripe fruit buttressed by sweet toasty oak, and jammy black cherry and black currant flavors. The wine is just beginning to open up and strut its stuff.

Togni has been a longtime believer in not acidifying, and his wines are never filtered at bottling.

Ratings for Older Vintages of Philip Togni Cabernet Sauvignon: 1989 (87), 1988 (90), 1988 (Tan Bark Hill cuvée) (87), 1987 (89), 1986 (91), 1985 (90), 1984 (92)

TOPOLOS AT RUSSIAN RIVER (SONOMA)

Alicante Bouschet* * */* * * *, Grand Noir* * *, Old Vineyard Reserve* * */* * * *, Petite Sirah* * */* * * *, Zinfandel Rossi Ranch* * * * *, Zinfandel Russian River Valley* * *, Zinfandel Ultimo* * * */* * * *

1990	Alicante Bouschet	Russian River Valley	B	86+
1989	Alicante Bouschet	Russian River Valley	B	86+
1988	Grand Noir	Sonoma	A	86
1992	Old Vineyard Reserve	Sonoma	B	90
1987	Petite Sirah Rossi Ranch	Russian River Valley	B	88+
1991	Zinfandel	Sonoma	B	85
1992	Zinfandel Rossi Ranch	Sonoma	C	92+
1991	Zinfandel Rossi Ranch	Sonoma	C	89
1991	Zinfandel Rossi Ranch Old Vines	Russian River	B	90
1989	Zinfandel Rossi Ranch Old Vines	Russian River	B	87
1992	Zinfandel Russian River Valley	Sonoma	B	87
1992	Zinfandel Ultimo	Sonoma	C	?
1991	Zinfandel Ultimo	Sonoma	C	88?
1988	Zinfandel Ultimo	Sonoma	B	88

Topolos, a winery dedicated to organic farming and the use of old vines, produced 534 cases of a blended red wine from the 80-year-old vines grown on Sonoma's Papani Ranch. The 1992 Old Vineyard Reserve is a terrific value as well as a mouth-filling, rich, concentrated wine. The dense, saturated, black/purple color is followed by a big, peppery, curranty, earthy nose. The wine offers stunning richness, a smooth, supple texture, moderate tannin, and a full-bodied, exceptionally long finish. This unevolved, young, powerful wine should provide heady drinking for 10–15 years. Is this California's answer to Châteauneuf du Pape?

Topolos has produced a medium-bodied, spicy, peppery, richly fruity 1992 Zinfandel Russian River Valley. Soft, with fine flavor extraction and a chunky, mouth-filling feel, it should be drunk over the next 3–4 years. The spectacular 1992 Zinfandel Rossi Ranch (from 80-year-old vines) represents the essence of black raspberry fruit intermingled with spicy, peppery notes. It is not as controversial as the 1990 Rossi Ranch, and is richer and more extracted than the 1991. The 1992 reveals an opaque purple color, huge density and concentration of fruit, and moderate tannin in the finish. Although approachable now, 2–3 years of cellaring will be beneficial. This wine should age effortlessly for 12–15 years. The 1992 Zinfandel Ultimo Old Vines is a perplexing wine. The moderate ruby color is followed by light, spicy, candied fruit aromas. This medium-bodied, tannic, astringent wine displays a hollow mid-range as well as a lack of sweetness and depth. Perhaps it is going through an unflattering stage, but I did not detect enough concentration (rarely a problem with this winery) to stand up to the ferocious tannin level. Judgment reserved.

Topolos's 1991 Zins are not as powerful and concentrated as the 1990s. The 1991 Zinfandel Sonoma is actually soft and medium bodied, with light tannins, plenty of ripe fruit, and a forward, supple texture. It should be drunk over the next 4–5 years. The 1991 Rossi Ranch Zinfandel displays a style not dissimilar from the Ravenswood Dickerson

Vineyard. Minty, camphorlike aromas are intertwined with sweet scents of black raspberries. There is a densely saturated purple color, but not the thickness or extraordinary concentration of the blockbuster 1990. It is also not as tannic or backward as the 1990. Nevertheless, this is a rich, full-bodied, tightly knit Zinfandel with exceptionally high extraction of flavor and crisp acidity. It requires 2–3 years of cellaring and should keep for up to a decade. Topolos's 1991 Zinfandel Ultimo is likely to be a controversial wine. From its meaty-, garlicky-, sausage-, and peppery black raspberry–scented nose, to its spicy, rich, exotic flavors, it has that unmistakable animal character found in certain burgundies and Rhône Valley wines. Concentrated, and with softer tannins than the Rossi Ranch, readers are advised that this will undoubtedly be a "love it or leave it" wine. Those who adore it will be delighted to know that it should keep for at least 7–10 years.

Topolos's Alicante Bouschets are undoubtedly controversial wines. They exhibit saturated black/purple colors, and a thickness and richness that I have never experienced in a young, dry red wine. Alicante Bouchet does not have a reputation for developing into the most complex of wines, but the 1990 and 1989 vintages produced superconcentrated wines with none of the late-harvest, pruny, raisiny character that one would expect from such rich wines. It appears to me that Topolos might be better off blending some Grenache, Syrah, or even Zinfandel with their Alicante Bouchet, which is what the French do to tame the rustic, savage qualities of this varietal. However, should you want to experience one of the richest wines made in the world, take a look at these Alicante Bouchets. Their prices make them a steal, even if they never turn into harmonious wines.

The 1988 Grand Noir is slightly more civilized, offering peppery, earthy aromas and flavors, as well as smoky, rich fruit. Medium to full bodied, spicy and deep, it should be drunk over the next 3–4 years.

The 1991 Zinfandel from Rossi Ranch (an 80-year-old vineyard) is almost black colored, with a huge, pure nose of black currants, mint, raspberries, and minerals. Spectacularly rich and full bodied, it will benefit from 5–6 years of cellaring; it should drink well from 1997 to 2010+. The softer, more approachable 1989 Zinfandel Rossi Ranch is not as superconcentrated. Big and deep for the vintage, it should drink well over the next 8–10 years. Topolos's Ultimo is another superlative cuvée of Zinfandel that appears to be more approachable than the Zinfandel Rossi Ranch. The 1988 Ultimo offers fragrant, earthy, black fruit, a spicy, peppery, raspberry-scented nose, fine body and glycerin, an expansive, rich texture, and a long, intense finish. It is the most supple of these three Zinfandels. Drink it over the next 5–7 years.

This winery also produces a blockbuster, dense, purple-colored Petite Sirah. The 1987 exhibits aromas of pepper, cassis, and damp earth. You are going to have to brush your teeth after drinking this wine given its saturation and intensity. It needs a decade to reach its apogee. **A.M.: 2002–2010+.**

TRENTADUE WINERY (SONOMA)
Cabernet Sauvignon * * *, Carignane * * * *, Merlot * * */* * * *, Old Patch Red
Proprietary Red Wine * * * *, Petite Sirah * * * *, Salute * * * *, Sangiovese * * */* * * *,
Zinfandel * * */* * * *

1987 Cabernet Sauvignon	Sonoma	B	86
1991 Carignane	Alexander Valley	B	87
1988 Carignane	Alexander Valley	A	87
1987 Merlot	Sonoma	A	87
1991 Old Patch Red	Alexander Valley	B	89

1988	Old Patch Red	Alexander Valley	A	90
1985	Old Patch Red	Alexander Valley	A	90
1990	Old Patch Red Lot 1	Alexander Valley	B	87
1991	Petite Sirah	Sonoma	B	90
1987	Petite Sirah	Alexander Valley	B	90
N.V.	Red Table Wine	California	A	87
1991	Salute	California	A	88
1992	Zinfandel	Sonoma	B	86
1991	Zinfandel	Sonoma	B	88
1990	Zinfandel	Sonoma	B	87

Trentadue has changed its label, and perhaps the style of its wines as well. It is too soon to know for sure, but every one of this winery's 1992s appeared lighter and more accessibly fruity, with less body, power, and concentration than such previous vintages as 1991 and 1990. Nevertheless, the 1992 Zinfandel is still an attractive, medium- to full-bodied, round, supple wine with juicy blackberry fruit, underlying, vague scents of earth, spice, and pepper, and a medium-bodied, moderately long finish. Drink it over the next 4–6 years.

Trentadue's husky 1991 Zinfandel displays a nearly opaque black/ruby color, a huge, full-bodied, velvety-textured taste, and rich, heady, spicy, long flavors. It should be drunk over the next 7–8 years. The smooth-as-silk 1990 Zinfandel exhibits generous black cherry aromas and flavors. It is full bodied, supple, and ideal for drinking over the next 5–6 years.

Few California wineries produce good Carignane, but Trentadue does. The 1991 exhibits a big, black cherry, spicy nose, rich, elegant, medium- to full-bodied flavors, and a lush finish. Drinkable now, it should mature gracefully for another 7–8 years. The 1988 Carignane is reminiscent of both an Italian Amarone and a California late-harvest Zinfandel. While it is not a sweet wine, this hefty, robust effort is oozing with peppery, spicy, chunky fruit, with gobs of body, and a lusty, nearly thick finish. If served with full-flavored cuisine, or with powerful cheeses, this personality-filled wine will make a favorable impression. It should easily drink well for another decade.

Perhaps the most amazing red wine made in California is Trentadue's proprietary red wine called Old Patch Red. It is a field blend of Carignane, Petite Sirah, Zinfandel, and Alicante from vines planted in the nineteenth century. In 1995, the average age of these vines was 109 years. The 1988, 1990, and 1991 Old Patch Reds all possess a superb southern Rhône-like nose of oriental spices, superripe red and black fruits, pepper, and new saddle leather. There is gorgeous richness, an expansive, full-bodied, chewy lusciousness, as well as considerable depth, focus, and length. It is hard to pick a favorite, as they are relatively similar. The 1991 is slightly richer and deeper. Only the 1985 Old Patch Red stands out as different. Displaying a late-harvest Zinfandel character, in a blind tasting it could be mistaken for a huge, chewy Amarone. It should continue to drink well for another 5–6 years. These are amazing wines for the price. Unfortunately, less than 2,000 cases are produced, so move quickly.

Looking for a smoky, chocolaty, black cherry–scented and –flavored Merlot at a reasonable price? Trentadue's 1987 Merlot offers the superripeness, admirable concentration, and chewy texture expected from a top vintage. It also possesses lavish amounts of fruit and flavor. Deep, yet already impressive and evolved, this is a full-flavored, personality-filled Merlot. Drink it over the next 5–7 years. What about Trentadue's Petite Sirah? As one might expect, given the house style of this winery, both the 1987 and 1991 display an impenetrable, black/purple, broodingly deep color. The noses offer up aromas of superripe black raspberries, peppery spices, and loads of fruit. In the mouth, it is an enormously concentrated, rich, chewy wine, with soft tannins, and layers of fruit and extract. The tannins are undoubtedly higher than one might suspect, but there is so much richness the structure of these wines is nearly obscured. These bargain-priced, blockbuster Petite Sirahs are for drinking over the next 10–15 years.

Trentadue's 1987 Cabernet Sauvignon conjures up memories of old-style California Cabernets that were heavily extracted, chunky, and coarse, but wow, what fruit and intensity. While this wine will never win any awards for finesse or elegance, I would not be surprised to see it embarrass many of its more prestigious siblings in a blind tasting in 10 or so years. Rich, with a nose of black fruits, smoke, and herbs, this full-bodied wine displays soft tannins, and an unmistakable voluptuous, intense style.

Trentadue has begun to offer another proprietary red wine called Salute. It is the winery's least expensive wine, selling for around $7 a bottle. The 1991 should be snapped up by any consumer looking for an authoritatively flavored, graceful red wine with smooth tannins, a huge bouquet of red and black fruits, deep, cherry and raspberrylike flavors, and a ripe, luscious, long finish. Drink it over the next 5–6 years. Another inexpensive wine, a blend of Carignane and Zinfandel, is Trentadue's nonvintage Red Table Wine. The wine's overall impression is one of raspberries. They appear in the bouquet and flavors of this soft, superbly fruity, full-bodied wine. It too should be consumed over the next 3–5 years.

TRUCHARD VINEYARDS (NAPA)
Chardonnay * * */* * * *, Merlot * * *, Pinot Noir * *, Syrah * * * *

1992	Chardonnay	Carneros/Napa	C	88
1990	Merlot	Carneros/Napa	C	87
1993	Syrah	Carneros/Napa	C	90
1992	Syrah	Napa	C	87

This excellent 1992 Chardonnay exhibits a judicious touch of toasty new oak that is well integrated with the wine's deep, rich, full-bodied, honeyed, tropical fruit flavors. There is a broad, husky feel on the palate, but enough acidity to give the wine delineation. Drink it over the next year.

The textbook 1993 Syrah exhibits a classic nose of smoky bacon fat and cassis. The dark ruby/purple color is accompanied by a flattering, up-front nose that jumps from the glass. There is no astringent tannin to be found in this velvety-textured, rich, full-bodied, gorgeously opulent Syrah. Deep and soft, this is a top-class effort from this Napa winery. Drink it over the next 10–12 years. The 1992 Syrah offers a lovely peppery, black fruit–scented nose, excellent ripeness, fine concentration, medium to full body, a soft, easily accessible texture, and a smooth, velvety finish. Drink it over the next 5–8 years.

Truchard's plump, deep ruby–colored 1990 Merlot exhibits a spicy, mocha-, herb-, and black cherry–scented nose, round, ripe, rich, medium- to full-bodied flavors, a satiny texture, and a lush, chewy finish. It is all that a Merlot should be. Drink it over the next 5–7 years.

TURLEY CELLARS (NAPA)
Petite Syrah Aida Vineyard * * * * *, Petite Sirah Hayne Vineyard * * * * *, Zinfandel Aida Vineyard * * * * *, Zinfandel Hayne Vineyard * * * * *, Zinfandel Moore Vineyard * * *, Zinfandel Sears Vineyard * * * *, Zinfandel Whitney Vineyard * * * * *

| 1994 | Petite Syrah Aida Vineyard | Napa | C | 92+ |
| 1993 | Petite Syrah Aida Vineyard | Napa | C | 95 |

1994 Petite Syrah Hayne Vineyard	Napa	C	92+
1993 Petite Syrah Hayne Vineyard	Napa	C	91
1994 Zinfandel Aida Vineyard	Napa	C	89
1993 Zinfandel Aida Vineyard	Napa	C	91
1994 Zinfandel Hayne Vineyard	Napa	C	93
1993 Zinfandel Hayne Vineyard	Napa	C	95
1994 Zinfandel Moore Vineyard	Napa	C	91
1993 Zinfandel Moore Vineyard	Napa	C	88
1994 Zinfandel Sears Vineyard	Napa	C	89
1994 Zinfandel Whitney Vineyard	Napa	C	91

Under the collaborative talents of Larry Turley and his sister, Helen Turley, this new winery, with its bevy of spectacular releases which hit the marketplace in April 1995, is sure to create rabid consumer reaction. These are boldly styled, dramatic Zinfandels and Petite Sirahs. Quantities are limited, but the quality is spectacular.

The 1993 Zinfandel Moore Vineyard (an ancient vineyard planted in the early 1900s just west of the town of Napa) exhibits an impressive dark ruby/purple color, a big, peppery, spicy, black and red fruit–scented nose, dense, full-bodied flavors with nicely integrated tannin, and a long, heady finish. It should be drinkable upon release and age well for at least a decade. The 1993 Zinfandel from the Hayne Vineyard near the town of St. Helena is a colossal effort. Black/purple-colored, with a huge, multidimensional nose of black fruits, Asian spices, wood, and pepper, this wine reveals great richness and concentration, a remarkable velvety texture, supple, nearly unctuously rich, thick flavors, and enough acidity and tannin to provide structure and focus. It is an incredible Zinfandel that should drink well for 15+ years. The 1993 Zinfandel Aida Vineyard is an exotic, herb-tinged, fabulously spicy, rich wine with gobs of chewy fruit. Full-bodied, with excellent purity and plenty of power at the back of the palate, this wine should drink well during its first 10–12 years of life.

Petite Sirah lovers will go bonkers over Turley Cellars' 1993 Petite Syrah (Turley Cellars has decided to spell Syrah with a y rather than an i) from the Hayne Vineyard and the even more impressive 1993 Petite Syrah Aida Vineyard. The former wine offers a saturated color, a big, black cherry, earthy, peppery nose, full-bodied, superrich, layered flavors, and surprisingly sweet tannin in the long, heady finish. The awesomely made 1993 Petite Syrah Aida Vineyard (from vines planted in 1911) may be a wine that lasts and improves for 25–30+ years. It boasts an opaque black/purple color, a tight, backward, immensely promising nose of licorice, pepper, black fruits, truffles, and wood, and huge flavor extraction. It is a quintessential expression of Petite Sirah—pure, rich, and amazingly well balanced with extraordinary length.

Turley Cellars' 1994s are further evidence of just what a terrific new producer this winery is. They have added two new offerings from old head-pruned Zinfandel vineyards in Napa Valley: the Whitney Vineyard near Calistoga, which was planted in 1895 (only 150 cases), and the Sears Vineyard in Napa Valley. The 1994 Zinfandel Aida Vineyard reveals excellent peppery, berry, spicy fruit, sweetness and softness, and a rich, medium- to full-bodied finish. It should drink well for the next decade. The 1994 Zinfandel Whitney Vineyard exhibits even greater fruit, more sweetness, better color saturation, and a spicy, sweet berry finish. The hallmark of all these Zinfandels is purity, definition, and intensity of flavor, without any heaviness or harshness. The 1994 Zinfandel Sears Vineyard offers a big, peppery, black and red fruit–scented nose, plenty of spice, a chewy texture, and a long, heady, full-bodied finish. The 1994 Zinfandel Moore Vineyard is more fleshy, with less acidity than its younger sibling, the 1993 Moore Vineyard. Made from a vineyard planted in 1906, this wine exhibits gobs of black fruits, full body, a saturated color, and a big, spicy, rich finish. The 1994 Zinfandel Hayne Vineyard is the superstar of these high-quality Zinfandels. It is a huge, rich, full-bodied, massive style of Zinfandel that manages to avoid being too thick and unwieldy. It boasts great intensity, gobs of rich, peppery, spicy, black cherry fruit, a wonderful sweet inner core of concentration, and a finish that lasts for 30–45 seconds.

The two 1994 Petite Syrahs from the Aida and Hayne vineyards are monster wines. Both exhibit black/purple colors, huge, concentrated fruit, mouth-searing tannin levels, frightening intensity and flavor extraction, and good balance. If purchasers are willing to wait a decade, something magical will develop in the bottle. Consumers are forewarned— these two wines are not likely to provide much pleasure for another decade.

TWIN HILLS RANCH (PASO ROBLES)
Zinfandel * * *

1991 Zinfandel Estate	Paso Robles	B	87

The debut release from this winery, the 1991 Twin Hills Ranch is an excellent Zinfandel. The deep ruby/purple color is followed by a nose of black fruits intermingled with scents of spicy oak and minerals. Medium to full bodied, with 13.9% alcohol, and admirable extraction of flavor and purity, this impressive, powerful, well-endowed Zin should be drunk over the next 6–7 years.

VIADER (NAPA)
Proprietary Red Wine * * * *

1993 Proprietary Red Wine	Napa	D	90
1992 Proprietary Red Wine	Napa	D	90
1991 Proprietary Red Wine	Napa	D	90
1990 Proprietary Red Wine	Napa	D	89

Viader is one of the most magnificently situated California vineyards I have ever visited. Located on a steeply terraced slope on Howell Mountain, the vineyard consists of 18 acres planted with 60% Cabernet Sauvignon and 40% Cabernet Franc. With nearly 2,000 vines per acre, this is a more tightly spaced vineyard than most conventional California planta- tions. Crop sizes have been minuscule—1¼ tons per acre on average! The result is a wine the proprietor claims is Napa's answer to Cheval Blanc. A high percentage of Cabernet Franc gives the wine elegance, and the Cabernet Sauvignon provides structure, tannin, and backbone. The wines' interesting aromatic profiles offer intensely perfumed bouquets of black and red fruits, spices, menthol, and floral scents. They are medium to full bodied, with a Bordeaux-like mouth-feel. The emphasis is on finesse as opposed to power. The 1993 possesses gobs of sweet fruit, with the Cabernet Franc dominating the wine's personality at present. Although it will not be released for 2 years, it has the potential to develop into an extremely complex, aromatic wine of considerable stature. In a blind tasting, it would be extremely difficult to pick this wine out as a California Cabernet Sauvignon. Although rounder and more supple, the 1992 displays telltale curranty, menthol, and floral notes in the nose, spicy, rich, medium- to full-bodied flavors, and outstanding elegance and finesse. The 1991, a blend of 54% Cabernet Sauvignon and 46% Cabernet Franc, is a backward wine that exhibits considerable promise. The dark opaque ruby/purple color is accompanied by a bouquet that reluctantly offers up scents of cassis, herbs, and damp earth. The wine is rich, structured, and full bodied, with copious amounts of cassis flavors, density without heaviness, and an overall sense of balance, moderate tannin, and crisp acidity. Give it 1–2 years of cellaring; it should drink well for 10–15 years.

A blend of 68% Cabernet Sauvignon and 32% Cabernet Franc, the elegant 1990 Proprietary Red Wine offers a complex, fragrant bouquet of spices, herbs, black fruits, and spring flowers. The wine is medium bodied, with admirable definition, excellent richness, crisp underlying acidity, no obvious new oak, but a subtle, cassis, vanillin component to its flavors, and a stylish, medium-bodied finish. Several additional years in the bottle should result in more aromatic development. If the flavors broaden, this will clearly be an outstanding effort. It is already an impressive wine in a delicate, restrained style.

This beautifully packaged product (a heavy glass bottle with broad shoulders and a designer label) is filled with a wine that is as distinctive as the packaging. All the Viader wines offer compelling evidence that they should last and evolve, hopefully improve, for at least 12–15+ years.

VICTORIA (NAPA)
Gewürztraminer * * * *

1993 Gewürztraminer	Napa	B	87

California winemakers are changing my previous impressions with the bevy of high-quality Gewürztraminers that are emerging. Except for a handful of efforts from the likes of Z. Moore, I have never been convinced that interesting Gewürztraminer could be produced in California. However, Victoria's 1993 Gewürztraminer reveals the varietal's telltale aromas of rose petal, grapefruit, and spices. It possesses excellent concentration, medium body, and a dry, long finish. This delicious, fresh, lively Gewürztraminer should drink well for 1–2 years.

VILLA MT. EDEN WINERY (NAPA)
Cabernet Sauvignon California * *, Cabernet Sauvignon Cellar Select * *, Cabernet Sauvignon Signature Series * * * *, Chardonnay Grand Reserve * *, Pinot Blanc * * * *, Pinot Noir *, Zinfandel Cellar Select * */* * *

1992 Cabernet Sauvignon Signature Series	Mendocino	D	92
1992 Chardonnay Cellar Select	Napa	B	87
1993 Chardonnay Grand Reserve	Carneros	B	87
1992 Chardonnay Grand Reserve	Napa	B	90
1993 Pinot Blanc Grand Reserve Bien Nacido Vineyard	Santa Barbara	B	87
1992 Zinfandel Cellar Select	California	B	85
1990 Zinfandel Cellar Select	California	B	72

It has been nearly a decade since Villa Mt. Eden merited such enthusiastic reviews. These are wonderfully rich, lusty Chardonnays revealing excellent varietal character, medium to full body, fine concentration, and an intelligent use of oak. The 1993 Chardonnay Grand Reserve's big, smoky, oaky, buttery nose is followed by a medium- to full-bodied, richly fruity wine that should be drunk over the next year. It is too easygoing and too delicious not to be drunk up over the near term. The 1992 Chardonnay Cellar Select should be drunk over the next year, whereas the 1992 Chardonnay Grand Reserve, because of its additional richness and explosively long finish, will last for 2–3 years. Bravo to Villa Mt. Eden's owners, Château Ste. Michelle, for putting this winery back on the path of excellence.

With a bouquet of honeydew melons, ripe apples, and a touch of oranges, the plump, medium- to full-bodied, supple, fleshy 1993 Pinot Blanc Grand Reserve Bien Nacido Vineyard is ideal for drinking over the next year. How encouraging it is to see so many delicious Pinot Blancs that have not been excessively acidified and/or overoaked emerging from California.

This limited-production (300 cases), luxury-priced Cabernet Sauvignon Signature Series is made jointly by Jed Steele and Michael McGrath for the Stimson Lane–owned Villa Mt. Eden Vineyard. Made from the finest lots of the vintage, it is aged in small French oak casks (of which 50% are new), and bottled unfiltered. The 1992's impressive opaque purple color is followed by a bouquet of jammy cassis fruit and subtle toasty new oak. The wine is medium to full bodied, expansive, rich, and velvety textured, with layers of concentrated fruit, superb purity, and a long, supple finish. Although approachable now, it possesses the requisite depth, balance, and intensity to age gracefully for 10–15 years. Impressive! Note: This wine opened significantly with breathing and continued to improve and develop further nuances and flavors.

A pleasant, soft, fruity, round wine, Villa Mt. Eden's 1992 Zinfandel Cellar Select offers good, clean berry fruit, low acidity, and spicy, toasty oak in the background. Drink it over the next 2–3 years. The washed-out, hollow, appallingly stylized and sterile 1990 Zinfandel possesses no bouquet, and little fruit or flavor. Acid, tannin, and wood are its principal components. This obviously stripped, sterile-filtered wine takes the fun out of Zinfandel.

VINE CLIFF CELLARS (NAPA)
Cabernet Sauvignon * * * *, Chardonnay Proprietress Reserve * * *

1993 Cabernet Sauvignon Estate	Napa	D	91
1992 Cabernet Sauvignon Estate	Napa	D	90
1991 Cabernet Sauvignon Estate	Napa	D	88
1990 Cabernet Sauvignon Estate	Napa	D	89+
1993 Chardonnay Proprietress Reserve	Napa	E	91
1992 Chardonnay Proprietress Reserve	Napa	E	89

This high-quality newcomer burst on the scene with an excellent 1990 Cabernet Sauvignon. This impressively rich yet elegant wine combines an understated finesse with richness, balance, and length. It offers a saturated dark ruby/purple color, a polite nose of black cherries, new oak, and spices, and sweet, ripe, rich fruit buttressed nicely by moderate tannin and adequate acidity. It may merit an outstanding score after 1–2 more years in the bottle; it will last for 12–15 more years.

The 1993 Chardonnay Proprietress Reserve appears to be the finest Chardonnay this young, promising winery has yet made. It exhibits high-quality smoky, toasty oak that adds attractiveness and personality to the wine's rich, sweet, buttery, tropical fruit. Full bodied and pure, with enough underlying acidity to provide crispness and delineation, this full-scale Chardonnay should be drunk before the end of 1996.

Although quantities of the elegant, authoritatively rich 1992 Chardonnay Proprietress Reserve are small, California readers should be able to locate a bottle or two. Full bodied, with an attractive nose of spice, vanillin, and ripe applelike fruit, it is a stylish, concentrated wine with plenty of depth and well-integrated acidity. The newest Cabernet Sauvignon releases include the 1991, which reveals plenty of cassis fruit, excellent purity, medium body, more tart acidity than necessary, fine balance, good raw materials, and a more restrained, low-pH style than more recent vintages. The 1992 exhibits deep, rich cassis fruit, full body, noticeably less high acidity, and a fresher, more user-friendly style. With the low acidity, the wine's beautiful fruit intensity and fleshy texture are more accessible, resulting in a complex, rich, impressively endowed wine that should drink well young but last for 15+ years.

The finest Vine Cliff Cabernet Sauvignon to date appears to be the 1993. It displays a big, smoky, black currant–scented nose intertwined with scents of toasty oak. Sweet, ripe, and expansive, with layers of concentration, adequate acidity, and a long, rich finish, it should drink well for 15+ years.

VITA NOVA (SANTA BARBARA)
Cabernet Franc * * *, Chardonnay * * *, Reservatum * */* * *

1990 Cabernet Franc	Santa Barbara	B	88
1991 Chardonnay	Santa Barbara	C	79
1989 Reservatum	Santa Barbara	C	79
1988 Reservatum	Arroyo Grande	C	87
1991 Reservatum Semillon	Santa Barbara	C	87

Vita Nova is the creation of Au Bon Climat's Jim Clendenen and Qupé's Bob Lindquist. The wines are made from grapes purchased from different sources. The quality is generally high, although I was struck by the fact that the 1991 Chardonnay went over the edge in terms of excessive use of oak. It exhibits a light golden color, and the fruit is already taking a backseat to the wood component. More interesting is the 1991 Reservatum Semillon, made from grapes purchased from Santa Barbara's excellent Buttonwood Farm. It offers a waxy, melony, perfumed nose, ripe, gorgeous, richly textured flavors that display considerable body and glycerin, and a crisp, husky finish. This big, dry white wine requires intensely flavored fish or fowl dishes to be at its best.

The red wine offerings include a lean, tart, austere, high-acid 1989 Reservatum. Although well made, it is far too compact and malnourished to merit high marks. More interesting is the 1990 Cabernet Franc, which has 25% Cabernet Sauvignon in the blend. It offers a sweet, spicy, herbaceous, cherry-scented nose, opulent, richly fruity, velvety-textured flavors, and a lush, heady finish. Drink it over the next 5–6 years for its exuberant richness and chewy flavors. The 1988 Reservatum, made from grapes grown in the Arroyo Grande Valley, reveals a dark ruby color, an herbaceous, black fruit–scented nose, rich, medium-bodied flavors, and a generous finish. It lacks the complexity and length of the 1990 Cabernet Franc, but it is an attractive wine for drinking over the next 5–6 years.

VON STRASSER (NAPA)
Cabernet Sauvignon * * * *

1992 Cabernet Sauvignon Diamond Mountain	Napa	C	90

An impressively colored, rich, full-bodied Cabernet Sauvignon, this wine may merit a higher score if it develops additional complexity. Certainly there is no deficiency in richness or extract. The wine displays a pungent black cherry, herb, and smoky nose, top-notch, chewy, pure, ripe, black currant flavors, adequate acidity, and a soft, tannic finish. Approachable now, it promises to be at its best in 2–4 years and keep for 15 or more.

VOSS VINEYARDS (SONOMA)
Zinfandel * * * *

1991 Zinfandel	Alexander Valley	C	89

This powerful Zinfandel from Alexander Valley reveals a forceful nose of peppery, black raspberry fruit, full body, excellent depth, an intriguing earthy/black fruit character, and a deep, full-bodied, voluptuously textured finish. Drink it over the next 7–8 years.

WELLINGTON VINEYARDS (SONOMA)
Cabernet Franc*, Cabernet Sauvignon* *, Côte de Sonoma* * *, Proprietary Red Wine* * *, Zinfandel* * */* * * *

1991 Côte de Sonoma Old Vines	Sonoma	A	86
1992 Merlot	Sonoma	B	86
1992 Zinfandel 100-Year-Old Vines	Sonoma	B	93
1990 Zinfandel Old Vines	Sonoma	B	87

I have enjoyed a number of this winery's offerings. If the 1992 Merlot had been a bit more intense and forthcoming, it would have merited a higher score. It offers a healthy, impressive dark ruby/purple color, and a reticent but clean nose of berry fruit and spice. The straightforward nose hardly does justice to the wine's flavors, which are rich and full bodied, with an excellent, chewy texture, a nice touch of new oak, and a long, supple finish. If the bouquet improves (and there is a good chance of that happening), this wine will merit a score several points higher. Drink this chunky, fleshy, impressively rich Merlot over the next 7–8 years.

Wellington's blockbuster, full-throttle, old vine 1992 Zinfandel is a huge, rich, superconcentrated, velvety-textured, high-alcohol (15%) Zinfandel that is neither raisiny, overripe, nor clumsy. Everything is held together by good structure. The wine's most impressive component is the rush of gorgeously pure, black cherry and raspberry fruit intertwined with scents of spice and pepper. This "big ole boy" should age effortlessly for 7–8 years, but who will have the patience to wait that long given the wine's current decadence and thrills?

The attractive, rich, complex 1990 Zinfandel Old Vines displays an earthy, peppery, black fruit–scented nose, full-bodied, soft, chewy flavors, and good length. Drink it over the next 5–6 years. The 1991 Côte de Sonoma is a big, bold, hearty, husky red wine with chunky flavors, excellent ripeness, and a mouth-filling, luscious texture. Succulent and velvety enough to be drunk now, it promises to last for 5–6 years.

WHALER VINEYARD WINERY (MENDOCINO)
Pinot Noir*, Zinfandel Estate* * *, Zinfandel Estate Flagship* * * *

1992 Zinfandel Estate	Mendocino	B	86
1991 Zinfandel Estate	Mendocino	B	82
1992 Zinfandel Estate Flagship	Mendocino	C	87
1991 Zinfandel Estate Flagship	Mendocino	C	86

The silky, stylish, elegant, berry-scented and -flavored, medium-bodied, soft 1992 Zinfandel is ideal for drinking over the next 4–5 years. The supple 1992 Zinfandel Flagship exhibits sweeter, riper, concentrated fruit, higher alcohol, and more body, glycerin, and length. It should drink well young and last for a decade or more.

Whaler's light- to medium-ruby-colored 1991 regular Zinfandel displays a vague notion of ripe fruit in a nondescript bouquet. Round, attractive, soft flavors salvage the uninspirational first impression. This supple Zin is ideal for drinking over the next 3–4 years. The 1991 Zinfandel Flagship is a richer, deeper, spicier wine that makes a broader and deeper impact on the palate. Rich and pure, with heady alcohol in the finish, it should be drunk over the next 5–6 years. Neither wine is as complete and delicious as Whaler's excellent 1990s.

WHITCRAFT WINERY (SANTA BARBARA)
Pinot Noir Bien Nacido Vineyard* */* * *, Pinot Noir Olivet Lane Vineyard* */* * *

1993 Pinot Noir "N" Bien Nacido Vineyard	Santa Maria	D	83
1993 Pinot Noir "Q" Bien Nacido Vineyard	Santa Maria	E	?

The 1993 Pinot Noir "Q" is an intriguing, although controversial wine. The color is an evolved garnet with some amber at the edge. Herbaceous, with a sweet, chocolaty, overripe cherry component, this medium- to full-bodied wine does not lack extract or richness, but the underlying vegetal character is noticeable in both the aromatics and the flavors. Spicy and rich, with a plush texture, it appears to be a "love it or leave it" Pinot Noir. As the numerical evaluation suggests, I am on the fence, unable to make up my mind about this one. It should drink well for 4–5 years. The darkly colored 1993 Pinot Noir "N" Bien Nacido Vineyard offers up a spicy, intensely herbaceous, chocolate-covered cherries-scented nose. This wine is beefy and rich, with excellent concentration and medium to full body, but an underlying vegetal streak permeates the wine's aromatics and flavors. It should drink well for 5–6 years.

WHITE OAK VINEYARDS (SONOMA)
Chardonnay Meyers Limited Reserve * *, Chardonnay Sonoma * *, Zinfandel * *

1992 Zinfandel	Sonoma	B	74
1992 Zinfandel Church Vineyard	Alexander Valley	B	77
1992 Zinfandel Limited Reserve	Sonoma	B	78
1992 Zinfandel Unfined/Unfiltered	Dry Creek	B	77

The light- to medium-bodied 1992 Zinfandel reveals simple, straightforward, soft, mono-lithic, fruity flavors. Drink it over the next 1–2 years. The austere, compact 1992 Zinfandel Church Vineyard possesses surprisingly high acidity and a lean, understated personality. It lacks concentration and is too tart. The 1992 Limited Reserve Zinfandel exhibits more aromatic intensity, but the high acidity gives it a tart, short, compact, hard feel in the mouth. The tannins are astringent and green. Although there are good underlying raw materials, they are overwhelmed by the high acidity. The 1992 Unfined/Unfiltered Zinfandel suffers from the same characteristics; it is a narrowly focused, high-acid, tart wine with an absence of flesh, flavor concentration, and personality.

WHITE ROCK VINEYARDS (NAPA)
Claret Proprietary Red Wine * * * *

| 1991 Claret Proprietary Red Wine | Napa | C | 88+ |
| 1990 Claret Proprietary Red Wine | Napa | C | 90 |

These are very interesting wines, combining Bordeaux-like structural profiles with the sweet, chewy, ripe fruit of California. Both offerings require 2–4 years of cellaring. The 1991 Claret exhibits an impressively saturated ruby/purple color, followed by a promising nose of coffee, cedar, black currants, cherries, and spices. It is a classically structured wine with moderate tannin, good purity, and a medium-bodied, long finish. Tight but rich, it is best drunk between 2000 and 2010. The 1990 Claret reveals a sweeter, more opulent, black currant and cherry fruitiness, a medium- to full-bodied format, outstanding ripeness, bal-ance, and length, and moderate tannin. Although more approachable than the 1991, it still requires 2–3 years of cellaring; it should keep for 15+ years. These are stylish, authorita-tively flavored wines that clearly merit their "Claret" name.

WHITEHALL LANE WINERY (NAPA)
Cabernet Sauvignon Morisoli Vineyard * * * *, Cabernet Sauvignon Napa * * *, Cabernet Sauvignon Reserve * * */* * * *, Chardonnay Le Petit * *, Chardonnay Reserve * * *, Merlot Knight's Valley * */* * *, Merlot Summer's Ranch * * *, Pinot Noir* *

| 1990 Cabernet Franc | Napa | C | 87 |
| 1991 Cabernet Sauvignon Morisoli Vineyard | Napa | D | 87 |

1990 Cabernet Sauvignon Morisoli Vineyard	Napa	D	91
1990 Cabernet Sauvignon Reserve	Napa	D	88
1989 Cabernet Sauvignon Reserve	Napa	D	87
1992 Merlot Knight's Valley	Napa	C	85
1991 Merlot Knight's Valley	Napa	C	88
1990 Merlot Summer's Ranch	Alexander Valley	C	90

Whitehall Lane's 1992 Merlot Knight's Valley is a good, compact, ripe, medium-bodied wine with attractive spice, chocolate, and berry fruitiness, adequate structure and cleanliness, and a medium-bodied, spicy finish. Drink it over the next 4–5 years. Consumers wanting an up-front, hedonistic Merlot should take note of this 1991 Merlot from Knight's Valley. It offers a big, kinky, exotic nose of chocolate, coffee, smoke, and jammy berry fruit. Rich, medium to full bodied, and lush, with plenty of alcohol, it is ideal for drinking now and over the next 5–7 years. The sumptuous, superconcentrated 1990 Merlot Summer's Ranch offers a big, chocolaty, black cherry–scented nose, spicy, deep, fleshy, authoritatively rich flavors, and a finish that goes on and on. With good underlying acidity and some tannin, this is a flamboyant, rich Merlot for drinking over the next 7–8 years.

High-quality California Cabernet Francs are few and far between, although more wineries appear to be obtaining the elusive fragrance and finesse that top-notch Cabernet Franc can provide. Whitehall Lane's 1990 Cabernet Franc exhibits a delicious, spice-, menthol-, herb-, and cherry-scented nose, and ripe, luscious, expansive, rich flavors that avoid any sense of heaviness. In fact, the wine tastes elegant, medium bodied, and stylish. This is a wonderfully supple, complex Cabernet Franc for drinking over the next 6–7 years.

The 1992 Cabernet Sauvignon Morisoli Vineyard is tighter and more restrained and backward than the 1990 offering. It reveals a healthy deep ruby/purple color, a tight, reticent bouquet, and rich, medium- to full-bodied, moderately tannic flavors. While it will never develop the richness, opulence, and seductiveness of the 1990, it is certainly very good. The 1990 Cabernet Sauvignon Morisoli Vineyard is stunning. The saturated, nearly opaque purple color and huge nose of jammy cassis, vanillin, spices, and licorice are accompanied by deeply etched, full-bodied, yet opulently textured flavors that are mouth filling, concentrated, and elegant. Long, with tremendous reserves of fruit, glycerin, and sweet, yet noticeable tannins, this is another sensational 1990 California Cabernet Sauvignon that adds further strength to the argument that 1990 is a terrific vintage. The 1990 Cabernet Sauvignon Reserve could have been outstanding if the property had cut back on acid adjustments. The spicy, oaky, vanillin- and cassis-scented nose reveals the use of new oak. The wine possesses a tart, acid edge (I will never understand why so many wineries permit this much acidification), medium to full body, excellent ripe, rich, black currant fruit, vague whiffs of tobacco and herbs, and a medium-bodied, moderately tannic finish. It should drink well for 10–15 years.

The 1989 Cabernet Sauvignon Reserve is one of the better efforts from this irregular vintage. The saturated deep ruby/purple color is followed by moderately intense aromas of mint and cassis. Medium bodied, with admirable richness, firm tannins, adequate acidity, and a graceful personality, this stylish Cabernet will drink well for another decade.

Not recommended, but worth noting, is the 1991 Cabernet Sauvignon Reserve. This acidic, austere wine is excruciatingly tannic, slightly hollow in the middle, and dominated by new oak. It does possess some positive traits (I rated it 84+), but it does not compare with the winery's 1990.

WILD HORSE WINERY (SAN LUIS OBISPO)

Cabernet Sauvignon* */* * *, Chardonnay* * *, Malvasia Bianca Barrel Fermented* * * * *,
Pinot Blanc* * * *, Pinot Noir* * *, Tocai Fruilano* * * *, Zinfandel* * *

1993 Chardonnay	Central Coast	B	88
1994 Malvasia Bianca Barrel Fermented	Monterey	B	90
1994 Pinot Blanc	Monterey	B	88
1994 Tocai Fruilano	Central Coast	B	87

Winemaker Ken Volk continues to turn out reasonably priced, well-made wines with broad crowd appeal. In 1994, the winery added a crisp, tasty, dry, richly fruity and enticing Tocai Fruilano. This wine nicely complements the exquisite Malvasia Bianca pioneered by Wild Horse, a winery that turns out gorgeous white wine and solidly made, but more straightforward red wines. The 1994 Pinot Blanc is a delicious, fun wine with gobs of fruit, a lovely honeyed orange/lime character, terrific purity (a characteristic of all Wild Horse's white wines), medium to full body, and a soft, generous finish. Drink it over the next 12 months with a wide variety of foods. I was turned on by the 1994 Malvasia Bianca, a dry, fragrant, perfumed wine with aromas of fruit cocktail, backed up by heavenly floral scents. The wine is light to medium bodied, dry, crisp, and delectable. It will make a delicious aperitif wine, or can be sipped without food over the next year before its gorgeous bouquet begins to fade. The 1993 Chardonnay is a rich, full-bodied, buttery, orange- and apple-scented and -flavored wine with well-integrated, crisp acidity, a fresh, lively personality, and a long finish. It should drink well for 1–2 years.

WILLIAMS-SELYEM (SONOMA)

Chardonnay Allen Vineyard* * * * *, Pinot Noir* * * *, Pinot Noir Allen Vineyard* * * * *,
Pinot Noir Olivet Lane Vineyard* * * *, Pinot Noir Rochioli Vineyard* * * * *, Zinfandel
Martinelli Vineyard* * * * *

1992 Chardonnay Allen Vineyard	Russian River	D	92
1990 Chardonnay Allen Vineyard	Russian River	D	90
1993 Pinot Noir	Sonoma	D	85
1993 Pinot Noir Cohn Vineyard	Sonoma	D	86
1993 Pinot Noir Olivet Lane	Russian River	D	87

This small winery sells its entire production via a mailing list. They have carved out an outstanding reputation for lavishly oaked, expansively flavored, decadent Pinot Noir. But these offerings demonstrate that Williams-Selyem also has a fine touch with other varietals. They are certainly not afraid of producing high-alcohol wines. The 1992 Chardonnay Allen Vineyard's label suggests the alcohol content is a whopping 15.4%. If that shocks readers' sensitivity, keep in mind that many grand cru white burgundies, particularly from years such as 1992 and 1989, often contain 15% alcohol. Alcohol not only preserves a wine, it adds a sweet, creamy texture to it. Many winemakers are so frightened by the possibility of producing a wine high in alcohol that they harvest their vineyard before the grapes are physiologically ripe. The results are predictable—tart, lean, compact, green wines. What is amazing about this 1992 Chardonnay is that the alcohol is barely perceptible on the palate. I am sure anyone who gulped down a whole bottle would realize its power, but the point is that the wine's merit is its remarkable concentration and intensity. At first I thought the aromatics were muted, but after leaving the bottle open for a day, wonderful honeyed, citrusy, floral blossom, and vanilla aromas emerged. As readers may imagine, the wine is superconcentrated and intense. It will age magnificently for 4–6 years.

The 1990 Chardonnay is controversial in high-tech circles. Made in a burgundian, full-bodied, rich, lavishly oaked, buttery style, it first appears closed and woody, but after 10 minutes in the glass a multitude of honeyed, buttery, apple, and floral aromas emerge, and the oak begins to take a backseat to the wine's other characteristics. Deep, unctuous, thick, and chewy, it will prove to be a superrich, complex, nearly decadent style of Chardonnay for drinking over the next 3–5 years.

The Williams-Selyem winery has long been a reference point for complex, sumptuous Pinot Noir. That being said, I thought the 1993s possessed a degree of herbaceousness and higher acidity than previous releases. The 1993 Olivet Lane Pinot Noir displays an evolved, medium ruby color with garnet and amber at the edge. It offers a fragrant, smoked-game, spicy, berry, and herb-scented nose, medium body, good rather than excellent/outstanding concentration, and surprisingly high, tart acidity in the finish. The wine will age well for 3–4 years, but it is not as concentrated or layered as most Williams-Selyem Pinots. The 1993 Sonoma Coast Pinot Noir is made in a cool-climate style with a light to medium ruby color already revealing some lightening at the edge. The nose is spicy and herbaceous, with sweet oak but not as much fruit as one expects from this winery. The wine is medium bodied, slightly tart, with earthy, herb, and cherry flavors presented in a restrained, elegant format. Drink it over the next 3–5 years. Lastly, the 1993 Cohn Vineyard Pinot Noir reveals a similar medium ruby color with some lightening at the edge. The nose offers up moderately intense aromas of earth, herbs, berry fruit, and new oak. With an attractive supple texture, good concentration, adequate acidity, and noticeable alcohol and oak in the finish, this round Pinot should drink well for 3–4 years. As an unabashed fan of this winery's Pinot Noir, I must admit to being uninspired by the 1993s.

CHÂTEAU WOLTNER (NAPA)

Chardonnay Estate Reserve * * *, Chardonnay Frederique Vineyard * * *, Chardonnay St. Thomas Vineyard * * * *, Chardonnay Titus Vineyard * * * *

1993	Chardonnay	Howell Mountain	B	87
1992	Chardonnay	Howell Mountain	B	88
1992	Chardonnay Frederique Vineyard	Howell Mountain	D	88
1992	Chardonnay St. Thomas Vineyard	Howell Mountain	D	88
1992	Chardonnay Titus Vineyard	Howell Mountain	D	90

The least expensive Chardonnay in Château Woltner's portfolio, the 1993 Howell Mountain cuvée offers an attractive, richly fruity nose, excellent concentration, and a medium- to full-bodied, round, supple personality. This well-made, reasonably priced wine will provide mouth-filling pleasure over the next 12 months.

This Howell Mountain estate has turned out structured, rich, complex 1992 Chardonnays. The regular cuvée, the 1992 Howell Mountain Chardonnay, is nearly as good as the top cuvées, as well as significantly less expensive. It displays an opulent, buttery-, vanillin-, and mineral-scented nose, rich, medium- to full-bodied flavors, structure, and an overall sense of balance. It should drink well for 2–3 years. The 1992 Chardonnay Frederique Vineyard exhibits an intense bouquet that hits the palate with a compactness, then picks up and finishes with convincing fruit, richness, and glycerin. It is impressive for its intensity and elegance. The 1992 Chardonnay St. Thomas Vineyard is richer than both the Howell Mountain and Frederique Vineyard Chardonnays. It possesses a mineral/wet stone component in its orange blossom/lemon/ripe apple–scented nose, and has medium to full body, crisp acidity, and a long finish. It should drink well for 3–4 years. The most concentrated of the estate-bottled single-vineyard Chardonnays is the 1992 Chardonnay Titus Vineyard. Although it reveals tightness and high acidity in the finish, there is outstanding depth and loads of potential in this full-bodied, burgundian-style Chardonnay. Drink it over the next 2–3 years.

ZACA MESA (SANTA BARBARA)

Alamo Cuvée* *, Chardonnay* *, Malbec* *, Mourvèdre* *, Syrah/Malbec* * *, Syrah* *

1992 Alamo Cuvée	Santa Barbara	B	78
1991 Chardonnay	Santa Barbara	B	85
1990 Chardonnay Reserve	Santa Barbara	C	74
1991 Malbec	Santa Barbara	B	82
1991 Mourvèdre	Santa Barbara	B	73
1991 Syrah	Santa Barbara	B	76
1991 Syrah/Malbec	Santa Barbara	D	86
1993 Z Cuvée	Santa Barbara	B	86

It is ironic that Zaca Mesa, which produced some of Santa Barbara's finest winemakers (Ken Brown of Byron, Jim Clendenen and Adam Tolmach of Au Bon Climat, and Bob Lindquist of Qupé), has had such an irregular quality record. As the following tasting notes demonstrate, there is not much to get excited about. However, there is good news. The highly talented Daniel Gehrs, who has fashioned some marvelous white wines under his own label, has been hired as the full-time winemaker at Zaca Mesa. If he is given the independence he deserves, I predict the quality of Zaca Mesa's wines will soar. Gehrs's first true vintage will be 1993, as he arrived following the 1992 harvest.

The finest wines at present include the 1991 Chardonnay, which offers good fruit in a straightforward, medium- to full-bodied style, and the 1991 Syrah/Malbec. This 70% Syrah/ 30% Malbec blend, the only wine I have tasted made from this combination of grapes, is a delicious wine. The dark ruby color is followed by a spicy, floral, cassis-scented nose, fleshy, ripe, opulent flavors, excellent richness, and good depth. Drink it over the next 4–5 years.

The 1993 Z Cuvée, a Rhône Ranger blend of 49% Grenache, 43% Mourvèdre, and the rest Syrah, exhibits a healthy dark ruby color, an attractive nose of pepper and red and black fruits, round, ripe, medium-bodied flavors, and a pure, gentle, velvety finish. It will offer ideal drinking over the next 3–4 years.

The other wines include a lean, excessively acidic and oaky 1990 Chardonnay Reserve, and a soft, light, one-dimensional 1992 Alamo Cuvée, a red wine made from 50% Grenache, 35% Mourvèdre, and 15% Syrah. I like the idea behind the blend, but this offering is one-dimensional and simple. Good but not exciting, the 1991 Malbec possesses straightforward flavors, and little complexity or personality. The disappointing 1991 Mourvèdre is light colored, with musty, tree bark–like flavors, and a thin, hollow personality. Similar, but slightly fruity, the 1991 Syrah is a light example of this varietal, with little depth or personality.

Although most of these wines are indifferent examples, look for things to dramatically improve under Daniel Gehrs.

ZD WINERY (NAPA)

Cabernet Sauvignon* * *, Cabernet Sauvignon Estate* * * *, Chardonnay* * * *,
Pinot Noir* *

1992 Cabernet Sauvignon	Napa	C	91
1992 Chardonnay	California	C	89
1993 Chardonnay Anniversary Vintage	California	C	90

ZD produces two cuvées of Cabernet Sauvignon in some years—a wine from purchased grapes (this offering), and an estate-bottled Cabernet Sauvignon. ZD's style offers full-blown, intense, nearly overripe fruit in a large-framed, superconcentrated format. If the wine were to be criticized, it would be for a lack of restraint. This meaty, thick, peppery, spicy, chewy wine is long on flavor, big on muscle, and offers a hefty mouthful of Cabernet fruit. It possesses the tannin and structure necessary to last for 15–20 years.

While I continue to disagree with readers who claim that ZD Chardonnays last and improve for more than 4–5 years, I remain a big fan of this winery. The 1992 Chardonnay displays ZD's no-holds-barred, big, toasty, vanillin, honeyed tropical fruit nose, fat, juicy flavors, and a succulent texture. Drink it over the next 1–2 years. The 1993 Chardonnay Anniversary Vintage increases the intensity level with a forceful dosage of intense tropical fruit, honey, and toasty oak. The wine offers copious amounts of fruit, glycerin, alcohol, and wood, resulting in a mouth-filling glass of decadent, luscious Chardonnay. Drink it over the next 1–2 years.

7. OREGON

The Basics

Oregon makes wine from most of the same grapes as California, although the cooler, more marginal climate in Oregon's best viticultural area, the Willamette Valley, has meant more success with cool-climate varietals such as Pinot Noir, than with hotter-climate varietals such as Cabernet Sauvignon, Merlot, Syrah, and Grenache. Chardonnay, Riesling, and Sauvignon Blanc have done well in Oregon, but the great white hope here is Pinot Gris, which has shown fine potential and a knack for being the perfect partner for the salmon of the Pacific Northwest. There is also believed to be good potential for high-quality sparkling wine in Oregon, but the efforts to date have been insipid. Oregon's wines are distinctive, with a kinship to European wines. The higher natural acidities, lower alcohol content, and more subtle nature of Oregon's wines bode well for this area's future.

GRAPE VARIETIES
Chardonnay I don't doubt for a minute that Oregon can make some wonderful Chardonnay, but far too many winemakers have let it spend too much time in oak, and have not chosen the best clones for their vineyards. The Chardonnay grape is naturally high in acidity in Oregon, and therein lies the principal difference between Chardonnay grown in Oregon and that grown in California. In California, the majority of Chardonnays must have tartaric acid added to them for balance. In Oregon, the wines must be put through a secondary or malolactic fermentation, à la Burgundy, in order to lower their acids.
Pinot Gris This is the hardest wine to find, as virtually all of it is sold and drunk before it has a chance to leave Oregon. However, winery owners, knowing a hot item, are planting as much of it as they can get their hands on. Fruitier and creamier than Chardonnay, Pinot Gris, from the world's most underrated great white wine grape, can be a delicious, opulent, smoky wine with every bit as much character and even more aging potential than Chardonnay. While it is a specialty of Oregon, much of it is mediocre and diluted. To date, Eyrie and Ponzi have led the way with this grape.
Pinot Noir As in Burgundy, the soil, yield per acre, choice of fermentation yeasts, competence of the winemaker, and type of oak barrel in which this wine is aged profoundly

Note: I have a one-third interest in an Oregon vineyard that was commercially bonded in 1992 and began selling wine in 1993. Because of an obvious conflict of interest, this wine will never be mentioned or reviewed in anything written by me.

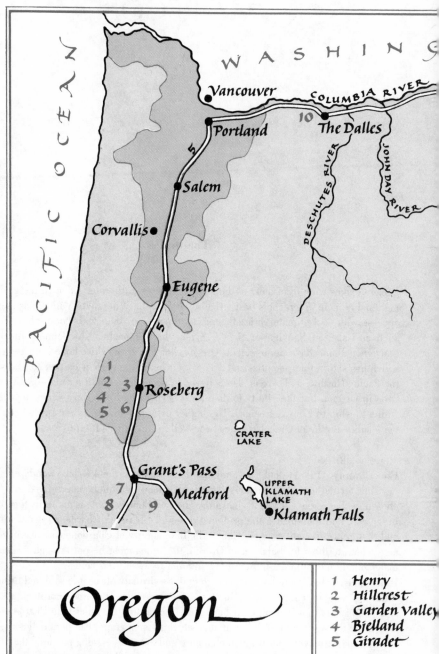

WASHING

Vancouver

COLUMBIA RIVER

10

The Dalles

Portland

DESCHUTES RIVER

JOHN DAY RIVER

Salem

Corvallis

Eugene

1
2   3   Roseberg
4
5   6

CRATER
LAKE

Grant's Pass

7
8   9   Medford

UPPER
KLAMATH
LAKE

Klamath Falls

Oregon

1   Henry
2   Hillcrest
3   Garden Valley
4   Bjelland
5   Giradet

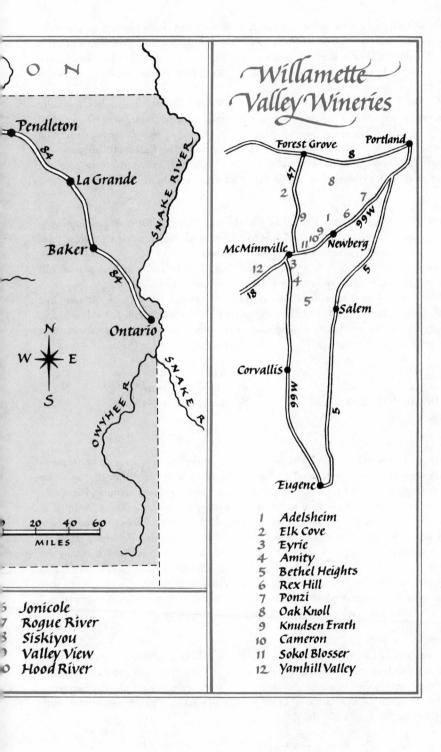

Willamette Valley Wineries

Pendleton

La Grande

Baker

Ontario

Forest Grove

Portland

McMinnville

Newberg

Salem

Corvallis

Eugene

1 Adelsheim
2 Elk Cove
3 Eyrie
4 Amity
5 Bethel Heights
6 Rex Hill
7 Ponzi
8 Oak Knoll
9 Knudsen Erath
10 Cameron
11 Sokol Blosser
12 Yamhill Valley

6 Jonicole
7 Rogue River
8 Siskiyou
9 Valley View
0 Hood River

MILES

20 40 60

N
W   E
S

influences its taste, style, and character. The top Oregon Pinot Noirs can have a wonderful purity of cherry, loganberry, and raspberry fruit, and can reveal an expansive, seductive, broad, lush palate, and crisp acids for balance. Yet far too many are washed out and hollow because of the tendency to harvest less than fully mature fruit and to permit crop yields to exceed 3 tons per acre.

Other Grape Varieties   With respect to white wines, Gewürztraminer has generally proven no more successful in Oregon than in California. However, Oregon can make good Riesling, especially in the drier Alsace style. I have yet to see a good example of Sauvignon Blanc or Semillon, or for that matter decent sparkling wine. The Cabernet Sauvignon and Merlot have not been special to date, although some made from vineyards in the southern part of the state have resulted in several good, rather than exciting wines.

FLAVORS

Chardonnay   Compared with California Chardonnay, those of Oregon are noticeably higher in acidity, more oaky, and have less of a processed, manipulated taste than their siblings from California. In many cases the oak is excessive.

Pinot Gris   A whiff of smoke, the creamy taste of baked apples and nuts, and gobs of fruit characterize this white wine that has shown outstanding potential in Oregon.

Pinot Noir   Red berry fruits dominate the taste of Oregon Pinot Noirs. Aromas and flavors of cherries, loganberries, blackberries, and sometimes plums with a streak of spicy, herbaceous scents characterize these medium-ruby-colored wines. Pinot Noir should never be astringent, harsh, or opaque purple in color, and it rarely ever is in Oregon.

AGING POTENTIAL

Chardonnay: 2–5 years   Pinot Noir: 3–8 years
Dry/Off-Dry Rieslings: 2–4 years   Sparkling Wines: 1–4 years
Pinot Gris: 1–3 years

OVERALL QUALITY LEVEL

Bearing in mind that most Oregon wineries started as underfinanced, backyard operations where the owner/winemakers learned as they went along, it is surprising that so many interesting wines have emerged from winemakers who had no textbook training, but plenty of hands-on experience. Although this pioneering approach to winemaking has resulted in some stunning, individualistic wines, it has also resulted in poor choices of grape clones, poorly planted vineyards, as well as some questionable winemaking decisions. In short, Oregon as a viticultural region is where California was in the late sixties. While they are just beginning to realize the potential for Pinot Noir and Pinot Gris, they must be wondering why they planted Riesling, Sauvignon Blanc, and Chardonnay in many of the places they did. This, plus the amazing number of new, meagerly capitalized winery operations, has resulted in a pattern of quality that ranges from poor to excellent.

MOST IMPORTANT INFORMATION TO KNOW

To purchase good wine, know the best wineries and their best wines. However, some additional information worth knowing is that the finest Pinot Noirs generally come from a stretch of vineyards in the Willamette Valley southwest of Portland. For Cabernet Sauvignon and Merlot, the warmer Umpqua Valley to the south, and the Grant's Pass area further south are better regions for those varietals.

VINTAGE GUIDE

1994—Early signs indicate this will be a highly concentrated, tannic Pinot Noir crop, and an irregular vintage for Pinot Gris and Chardonnay. The crop size was small, with most vineyards claiming production to be off by 20%–60% due to poor weather during the flowering season. Early cask tastings revealed rich Pinot Noirs with more structure and tannin than normal. It will be a question of balance, with the finest wines possessing the requisite fruit to stand up to the ferocious tannin. The white wines will range from excellent to mediocre, depending on the harvest date.

1993—A cool summer followed by warm weather in September and October resulted in a vintage that appears to have eclipsed 1992. The top Pinot Noirs reveal voluptuous textures, fragrant personalities, and a suppleness and richness that suggest this may be a break-through vintage for Oregon Pinot Noir. The limited quantities produced by the finest produc-ers will make the top wines hard to find.

1992—This could have been the finest vintage for Oregon Pinot Noirs in decades. The weather was almost too hot and dry. However, beneficial rains arrived toward the end of the growing season and alleviated what was considerable stress in many of the hillside vine-yards. Unfortunately, too many producers, worried about low acidity, used a heavy hand when adding acidity, resulting in many wines with incongruous personalities—very ripe flavors and tart, lean-textured personalities. Nevertheless, some terrific Pinot Noirs and big, dramatic, ostentatious Chardonnays have emerged. The Chardonnays must be drunk up, but the finest Pinot Noirs will keep for a decade.

1991—This is a very good, potentially excellent vintage of wines that does not have the power or drama of the 1992s, or the intensity of the 1990s. Nevertheless, rain at the end of the harvest caught those growers who had excessive crop yields and were waiting for further maturity. For that reason, this is a tricky vintage to handicap, but certainly the Pinot Noirs look richly fruity, although softer and less structured than the 1992s and less tannic than the 1990s. It has good potential for high-quality wine—both red and white.

1990—A top vintage if yields were kept to a minimum, 1990 had plenty of heat and adequate rain, and the harvest occurred under ideal conditions. In fact, if it were not for 1992, this would be the best Oregon vintage in several decades. From the top producers, the Pinot Noirs are rich and full, as are some of the Chardonnays. If there is a disappointment, it is that many of the Pinot Gris wines lack concentration because yields were too high.

1989—This is a good vintage for Pinot Noir, Chardonnay, and Pinot Gris. The wines may not have the intensity of the 1990s, but they are generally rich, soft, elegant wines. In many respects it is a more typical, classic vintage for Oregon's best producers than 1990 or 1992.

1988—The first of an amazing succession of good years for the Oregon wine business. Fine weather, an abundant crop, and a trouble-free harvest have resulted in a number of excellent Pinot Noirs and Chardonnays.

1987—An excessively hot year resulted in most growers' harvesting too soon because they were afraid of losing acidity in their grapes. However, the stress of the summer's heat caused many vineyards not to reach physiological maturity. As a consequence, many 1987s are lean, too acidic, and disappointing. Six years after the vintage the best wines still have a hard edge. It is unlikely they will ever fully blossom. If only the growers had waited!

OLDER VINTAGES

As a general rule, most Oregon Pinot Noirs must be consumed within 7–8 years of the vintage. There are always a few exceptions, as anyone who has tasted the 1975 Eyrie or 1975 Knudsen Erath Pinot Noirs can attest. But in general, aging Oregon Pinot Noir for longer than 7–8 years is a dangerous gamble.

Oregon's white wines should be drunk within several years of the vintage, even though they tend to have better natural acidity than their California counterparts. Yields are frequently too high, and the extract levels questionable, so whether it is Pinot Gris, Chardonnay, or dry Riesling, if you are not drinking these wines within 3–4 years of the vintage you are more likely to be disappointed than pleasantly surprised.

Note: I have a one-third interest in an Oregon vineyard that was commercially bonded in 1992 and began selling wine in 1993. Because of an obvious conflict of interest, this wine has not been reviewed.

RATING OREGON'S BEST PRODUCERS OF PINOT NOIR

* * * * * (OUTSTANDING)

Adelsheim Elizabeth's Reserve
Archery Summit Red Hills Estate
Bethel Heights Flat Block Reserve

Domaine Drouhin Reserve
Evesham Wood Cuvée J
Ponzi Reserve

* * * * (EXCELLENT)

Adelsheim Seven Springs Vineyard
Amity Winemaker's Reserve
Arterberry Winemaker's Reserve
Bethel Heights Southeast Block
Bethel Heights Wadenswil
Christom
Christom Reserve
Domaine Drouhin
Edgefield
Elk Cove La Bohème
Elk Cove Estate Reserve
Elk Cove Wind Hill Vineyard

Evesham Wood (regular cuvée)
Oak Knoll Vintage Select
Panther Creek Late Release Reserve
Ponzi (regular cuvée)
Redhawk Reserve
Redhawk Stangeland Reserve
St. Innocent O'Connor Vineyard
St. Innocent Seven Springs Vineyard
Domaine Serene Reserve
Domaine Serene Evenstad Reserve
Sokol Blosser Redland Vineyard
Willamette Valley Vineyard (all cuvées)

* * * (GOOD)

Acme Wineworks (John Thomas)
Adams Reserve
Adelsheim Eola Hills Vineyard
Amity Estate
Bethel Heights Estate
Bridgeview Winemaker's Reserve
Cameron Reserve
Chehalem Ridge Crest
Eyrie Reserve
Knudsen Erath
Lange

Laurel Ridge Vineyard
McKinley
Oak Knoll
Panther Creek
Panther Creek First Release
Redhawk
Rex Hill Archibald Vineyard
Rex Hill Dundee Hills Vineyard
Sokol Blosser
Witness Tree Vineyard

* * (AVERAGE)

Alpine
Alpine Reserve
Ashland
Autumn Wind
Château Benoit
Château Benoit Reserve
Bridgeview
Broadley
Cooper Mountain

Davidson Winery
Duck Pond Cellars
Elk Cove (regular cuvée)
Eola Hills
Eyrie (regular cuvée)
Flynn Vineyards
Forgeron Vineyard
Foris Vineyards
Girardet Cellars

Henry Estate Winery
Hinman Vineyards
Hood River Vineyards
Rex Hill Vineyards (regular cuvée)
Rex Hill Medici Vineyard
Shafer Vineyard Cellars
Springhill Cellars

Stangeland
Tualatin Vineyards
Tyee Cellars
Van Duzer
Veritas Vineyard
Yamhill Valley Vineyards

RATING OREGON'S BEST PRODUCERS OF PINOT GRIS

* * * * * (OUTSTANDING)

None

* * * * (EXCELLENT)

Chehalem Ridge Crest
Evesham Wood

Eyrie
Ponzi Vineyards

* * *(GOOD)

Adelsheim

Lange Reserve

RATING OREGON'S BEST PRODUCERS OF CHARDONNAY

* * * * * (OUTSTANDING)

None

* * * * (EXCELLENT)

Evesham Wood (unfiltered)
Eyrie Reserve
Montinore Winemaker's Reserve

Panther Creek
Redhawk Reserve
Redhawk Stangeland Vineyard

* * * (GOOD)

Acme Wineworks (John Thomas)
Adams
Adams Reserve
Adelsheim Reserve
Argyle
Bridgeview Vineyard
Cameron Reserve
Elk Cove La Bohème
Evesham Wood
Eyrie
Girardet Cellars
Kramer Vineyards
Lange

Lange Reserve
McKinley Special Selection
Montinore
Ponzi Reserve
St. Innocent Seven Springs Vineyard
Shafer Vineyard Cellars
Sokol Blosser Redland
Sokol Blosser Yamhill
Tualatin Vineyards
Valley View Anna Maria Reserve
Veritas Vineyard
Witness Tree Vineyard

* * (AVERAGE)

Adelsheim (regular cuvée)
Alpine
Amity
Autumn Wind

Château Benoit
Bethel Heights
Cameron Vineyard
Cooper Mountain

Davidson Winery
Duck Pond Cellars
Flynn Vineyards
Henry Estate Winery
Hinman
King's Ridge
Marquam Hill
Oak Knoll
Ponzi Vineyards

Rex Hill Vineyards
Springhill Cellars
Stangeland Winery
Tyee Cellars
Valley View Vineyard
Van Duzer
Willamette Valley
Witness Tree
Yamhill Valley Vineyards

ADAMS VINEYARD WINERY

Chardonnay * */* * *, Pinot Noir * */* * *, Sauvignon Blanc * *

1990 Chardonnay	B	86
1991 Chardonnay	B	87
1991 Chardonnay Reserve	B	88
1991 Pinot Noir	B	84
1990 Pinot Noir	B	84
1990 Pinot Noir Reserve	B	85

The 1990 Chardonnay exhibits a nutty bouquet, good richness, medium body, crisp acidity, and the potential to last another 2–3 years. The slightly sweeter 1991 Chardonnay displays more ripeness, good definition, and a spicy, buttery, oak- and apple-scented nose and flavors. It should last for 1–2 years. The best of this trio is the 1991 Chardonnay Reserve, which boasts more intensity and spicy new oak, a thicker viscosity, a chewy texture, and a deep, long, excellent finish. Drink this attractive Chardonnay over the next 3–4 years.

The three Pinot Noir offerings were less impressive than other vintages of Adams. The 1991 Pinot Noir displays a soft, berry-scented nose, pleasant, round, elegant, but insubstantial flavors, and a short, narrow finish. Drink it over the next several years. The grapy 1990 Pinot Noir is tasty, with good ripeness and a spicy finish, but it is essentially simple, one-dimensional, and destined to be short-lived. Consume it over the next 3–5 years. While the 1990 Pinot Noir Reserve is less flattering than either of the regular bottlings, it offers more depth and tannin, and finishes with power and spice. But I wonder if the tannins will outlive the wine's fruit. If not, my rating may look conservative. Drink it up.

ADELSHEIM

Chardonnay * *, Chardonnay Reserve * * *, Pinot Blanc * * *, Pinot Gris * * *, Pinot
Noir * * *, Pinot Noir Elizabeth's Reserve * * * * *, Pinot Noir Ridge Crest
Vineyard * * * */* * * * *, Pinot Noir Seven Springs Vineyard * * * */* * * * *

1992 Chardonnay	B	85
1992 Chardonnay Reserve	C	86
1991 Chardonnay Reserve	C	87
1993 Pinot Noir	C	87
1991 Pinot Noir	C	85
1992 Pinot Noir Elizabeth's Reserve	D	90
1991 Pinot Noir Elizabeth's Reserve	C	87+

1993 Pinot Noir Ridge Crest Vineyard	C	90
1992 Pinot Noir Seven Springs Vineyard	C	90
1991 Pinot Noir Seven Springs Vineyard	C	88

Adelsheim's 1991 Pinot Noir reveals an attractive, light, herbaceous, cherry-scented nose, spicy, round, supple flavors, medium body, and a smooth finish. Drink it over the next several years. Although the 1991 Pinot Noir Elizabeth's Reserve possesses gobs of sweet fruit, it is tight, with high acid and moderate tannin in the long finish. While there is plenty of depth, this backward wine is in need of 6–12 months of bottle age. There is no need to be patient with respect to the 1991 Pinot Noir from the Seven Springs Vineyard. A big, smoky, and ripe cherry-scented nose jumps from the glass. Rich, with fine acidity and definition, this medium-bodied wine possesses excellent concentration and a lovely, harmonious finish. Drink it over the next 6–7 years.

Among the Chardonnays is a straightforward, fresh, tasty, elegant, well-endowed 1992 Chardonnay with an Oregon appellation, a more ambitious, oaked, nutty, rich 1992 Chardonnay Reserve from Yamhill, and a complex, rich, well-structured 1991 Chardonnay Reserve from Yamhill. The Oregon bottling should be drunk over the next year. The 1992 Reserve Chardonnay should also be consumed early. Its oak is not as prominent, but there is good underlying richness and depth. The best wine of this trio is the grilled nut- and buttery-scented 1991 Chardonnay Reserve. It admirably marries elegance and richness in a medium-bodied format. Drink it over the next 1–2 years.

There are some exciting new Pinot Noirs emerging from Adelsheim. The 1993 Pinot Noir Ridge Crest Vineyard looks to be a knockout example from this vineyard located on the Ribbon Ridge not far from the Adelsheim winery. The wine exhibits a saturated dark ruby/purple color, a super nose of black fruits, smoke, earth, and vanillin, wonderfully textured, multidimensional flavors, deep, ripe, black cherry, and black raspberry fruit, and a long, harmonious, silky finish. This should be an early candidate for one of the top 1993 Oregon Pinot Noirs. If you are not willing to pay $25, check out Adelsheim's 1993 Pinot Noir bearing the Oregon appellation. This is a delicious, crowd-pleasing, soft, velvety-textured wine with gobs of ripe cherry fruit, fine purity, and a savory character. It should drink well for the next 2–3 years.

The outstanding 1992 Pinot Noir offerings are among the top wines of that vintage. The 1992 Pinot Noir Seven Springs Vineyard offers a dark ruby color, and a superb nose of black cherry fruit intertwined with scents of wood, earth, spice, and smoked meats. Deep, medium to full bodied, with excellent purity, balance, and nicely integrated acidity and tannin, this is a beautifully made Pinot that should drink well young but should age well for 7–9 years. The 1992 Pinot Noir Elizabeth's Reserve could turn out to be the best Pinot of all, although it is more restrained aromatically and comes across as slightly more structured and tannic. Shy and reticent at first, this dark ruby-colored, rich wine opens in the glass to reveal impressive levels of black cherry fruit buttressed by decent acidity and wood. Exhibiting more tannin than the other Adelsheim offerings, it is a candidate for a decade of cellaring. With Pinots this delicious, Burgundians had better wake up! Bravo to owner David Adelsheim and winemaker Don Kautezner!

AMITY VINEYARDS
Chardonnay * *, Dry Gewürztraminer * * * *, Dry Riesling * *, Gamay Noir * * * *,
Pinot Noir * * *, Pinot Noir Winemaker's Reserve * * * *

1989 Pinot Noir	B	85
1988 Pinot Noir	B	86
1988 Pinot Noir Winemaker's Reserve	C	88

Amity has a policy of releasing their Pinot Noirs after they have had sufficient bottle age. Sometimes this works, while other times the fruit is muted and faded by the time the wines arrive on the market. The 1989 Pinot Noir reveals an attractive herbal, earthy, smoky aroma, round, deep flavors, medium body, and a long, soft finish. It is an attractive, smoky, earthy style of Pinot Noir that should drink nicely for another 3–4 years. The 1988 Pinot Noir offers a smoked game–like aroma, tasty, elegant flavors, fine definition and depth, and a moderately tannic finish. Drink it over the next 2–3 years. The 1988 Pinot Noir Winemaker's Reserve represents Amity's finest cuvée of Pinot Noir. This offering often has enormous potential, but I sometimes wonder if it is not released too late, after some of its exuberance has begun to fade. The excellent 1988 boasts a deep garnet color, a big, smoky, gamy, Pinot nose with aromas of leafy fruit and earth. Dense, spicy, and rich, with medium to full body and firm, ripe tannins in the finish, this Pinot Noir should continue to drink well for 3–5 years. It has a resemblance to a rustic wine from Burgundy's Côte de Nuits.

ARCHERY SUMMIT
Pinot Noir Red Hills Estate * * * * *

1993 Pinot Noir	D	89
1993 Pinot Noir Red Hills Estate	D	92

These are the debut releases from this promising vineyard owned by Napa Valley's Pine Ridge Winery. Gary Andrus, the winemaker/partner at Pine Ridge, is in full control of the winemaking here and these releases attest to the lofty goals he has set. The 1993 Pinot Noir, made from grapes purchased from the Weber Vineyard and blended with grapes from the Red Hills Estate Vineyard (owned by Archery Summit), is a beautifully made Pinot with a fragrant, black cherry, raspberry, and smoky-scented nose, a voluptuous texture, rich, sweet, expansive flavors, and a soft, round, generous finish. This seductive Pinot Noir could easily be mistaken for a premier cru from Méo-Camuzet. Drink it over the next 4–5 years. The limited-production 1993 Pinot Noir Red Hills Estate is splendid. It offers a deep color, followed by a knock-out nose of jammy black fruits, flowers, and toasty vanillin oak. It is gloriously rich, velvety-textured, opulent, and loaded with flavor and intensity. This terrific wine is one of the finest Oregon Pinot Noirs I have tasted. Drink it over the next 5–6 years.

There is even more good news. Barrel samples of Archery Summit's 1994s struck me as some of the finest Pinot Noirs I have tasted. Archery Summit, whose winery T-shirt logo is "Ba-Ba-Ba-Ba Bad to the Beaune," is for real!

CHÂTEAU BENOIT WINERY
Chardonnay * *, Pinot Noir * *, Pinot Noir Reserve * *, Sauvignon Blanc * *

1991 Pinot Noir	B	82
1991 Pinot Noir Reserve	B	86

The 1991 Pinot Noir reveals a light ruby color, a spicy nose of cherry fruit and herbs, and tasty, soft, fruity flavors that fall off in the finish. Drink it over the next 1–2 years. The deeper-colored 1991 Pinot Noir Reserve exhibits an excellent nose of earthy, smoky, red fruits, and herbs. Supple and fat, with excellent ripeness of fruit, this medium-bodied, velvety-textured wine will make ideal drinking over the next 2–3 years.

BETHEL HEIGHTS
Chardonnay Estate * * *, Pinot Gris * * *, Pinot Noir Estate * * *, Pinot Noir Flat Block * * * *, Pinot Noir Southeast Block Reserve * * * *, Pinot Noir Wadenswil Block * * * *

1990 Chardonnay Estate	B	74
1993 Chardonnay Estate Reserve	C	88

1993 Pinot Gris	B	85
1992 Pinot Noir Estate	C	87
1991 Pinot Noir Estate	C	87
1990 Pinot Noir Estate	C	87
1991 Pinot Noir Estate First Release	C	82
1991 Pinot Noir Estate Flat Block	D	90
1992 Pinot Noir Estate Flat Block Reserve	D	89
1992 Pinot Noir Estate Southeast Block Reserve	C	88
1991 Pinot Noir Estate Southeast Block Reserve	D	89
1990 Pinot Noir Reserve	C	88
1992 Pinot Noir Estate Wadenswil Block	C	88

The 1991 Pinot Noir Estate reveals toasty new oak, excellent ripeness, a sweet, round, medium-bodied, supple texture, and loads of ripe fruit in the finish. Drink it over the next 3–5 years. The 1991 Pinot Noir Estate Southeast Block Reserve offers a knockout bouquet of superripe, jammy cherries, smoke, and vanillin. With ripe, full-bodied, deep, concentrated flavors, excellent purity, and a smooth texture, this luscious Pinot Noir should also be drunk over the next 3–5 years. Similarly styled, but more expansive and richer is the 1991 Pinot Noir Estate Flat Block. Its nose of black and red fruit is followed by rich, full-bodied, layered flavors, low acidity, and gobs of fruit, glycerin, and heady alcohol in the finish. It is a decadent Pinot Noir for drinking over the next 4–5 years. These are impressive 1991s. The 1991 Pinot Noir Estate First Release succeeds in its effort to be a round, supple, fruity Pinot for drinking over the near term. Medium ruby colored, with an attractive berry-scented nose, succulent fruit flavors, soft tannins, and low acidity, it makes for a delicious and inexpensive glass of Pinot Noir.

The 1990 Pinot Noir Estate offers up a cherry, earthy, herblike nose reminiscent of a good premier cru from France's Côte de Beaune. With admirable elegance, ripeness, medium body, and a rich, crisp finish, it should be drunk over the next 3–4 years. Although the 1990 Pinot Noir Reserve is slightly better, it costs $10 more. The additional sweetness of fruit, increased flavor dimension, and spicy new oak do not justify the price differential. Nevertheless, it is a generously endowed, seductive Pinot Noir for drinking over the next 3–4 years.

The 1990 Chardonnay Estate is light, fruity, and soft, lacking grip, character, and interest.

Bethel Heights has fashioned an attractive, elegant, tasty, light straw–colored 1993 Pinot Gris. This dry, fruity wine is best consumed over the next year. I also enjoyed the 1993 Chardonnay Estate Reserve. Unlike the blatantly oaky, nearly fruitless 1992 Estate Reserve Chardonnay, the 1993 is loaded with attractive buttery, apple/orange, roasted nutlike fruit flavors. It is medium to full bodied, with fine purity, and an excellent finish. Drink it over the next year.

This winery excels at making stylish, seductive, richly fruity Pinot Noirs that resemble high-class premiers crus from the Côte de Beaune. These four fine offerings from the 1992 vintage exhibit little difference in quality, although I expect the Reserve wines to gain additional weight in the bottle. All of these wines are best consumed in their first 6–7 years of life. The most obvious value is the 1992 Estate Pinot Noir. An attractive black cherry/floral-scented nose is followed by supple, medium-bodied flavors exhibiting fine ripeness, chewy glycerin, and an expansive palate. This delicate, elegant Pinot Noir should be drunk over the next 3–4 years. Readers may be unaware that the two most commonly planted

Pinot Noir clones in Oregon are Pommard, which tends to result in darkly colored, powerful, tannic wines, and Wadenswil, which emphasizes the more seductive, velvety-textured, elegant side of Pinot Noir. The 1992 Estate Pinot Noir Wadenswil Block is a medium ruby, voluptuously textured, delicious, opulently styled, silky-smooth wine that is ideal for drinking over the next 4–5 years. The wine reveals impressive purity, wonderful black cherry and strawberry fruit flavors, fine glycerin, medium body, and a layered impression in the mouth. The similarly styled 1992 Pinot Noir Estate Flat Block Reserve reveals a deeper color, and a sweeter, jammier, black cherry–scented nose with a more evident influence of toasty new barrels. The wine is broad, expansive, rich, smooth, full bodied, and long in the mouth. My rating may be conservative, as this wine is capable of meriting 90 points with a little more bottle development. It should drink well for 5–6 years. The 1992 Pinot Noir Estate Southeast Block Reserve exhibits lavish quantities of black cherry fruit and sweet oak in its bouquet, wonderful purity, medium to full body, fine depth, and a soft finish. If this wine had been slightly more concentrated it would have received an outstanding score. All four of these Bethel Heights Pinot Noirs are made in a seductive style that clearly demonstrates Pinot Noir's hedonistic appeal.

BRIDGEVIEW VINEYARDS
Chardonnay * * *, Chardonnay Barrel Select * * *, Dry Gewürztraminer Vintage Select * * * *, Pinot Gris * *, Pinot Noir Winemaker's Reserve * * *, Riesling Vintage Select * * *

1990 Pinot Noir Winemaker's Reserve	B	74
1989 Pinot Noir Winemaker's Reserve	B	73

I have reservations about both of Bridgeview's Pinot Noirs. The 1989 Pinot Noir Winemaker's Reserve is malnourished, excessively acidic, and short in the finish. While pleasantly scented, it appears to already be losing its fruit and drying out. On the other hand, the 1990 Pinot Noir Winemaker's Reserve is at the limit of being too pruny and raisiny. The overripe fruitiness has some attractive jammy fruit flavors, but the overall impression is one of diffuseness and a muddled character. It should be consumed over the next 1–3 years.

CAMERON WINERY
Chardonnay * * *, Pinot Noir Unfiltered * * *

1990 Pinot Noir Unfiltered	B	86
1989 Pinot Noir Unfiltered Abbey Ridge	C	88

Cameron's two unfiltered Pinot Noirs include a 1990 regular cuvée that exhibits plenty of oak as well as gobs of spicy, earthy, leafy Pinot fruit with a meaty, smoky quality. Deep, round, and attractive, it is ideal for consuming over the next 1–2 years. The 1989 Pinot Noir from Oregon's excellent Abbey Ridge Vineyard displays light color, but an intensely aromatic bouquet of smoked meats, black and red fruits, leafy vegetables, and spicy oak. Medium bodied and round, with considerable fatness and glycerin, this wine improved with airing. While drinkable, it should last for another 1–3 years.

CHEHALEM
Chardonnay Ridge Crest Vineyard * * * *, Pinot Gris Ridge Crest Vineyard * * * *, Pinot Noir Ridge Crest Vineyard * * *

1993 Pinot Noir Ridge Crest Vineyard	C	83+?
1992 Pinot Noir Ridge Crest Vineyard	C	86?
1993 Pinot Noir Ridge Crest Vineyard Wadenswil Selection	D	85+?

The 1992 Pinot Noir Ridge Crest Vineyard would have received a higher score, but it gives off a slight cardboard scent that I often associate with filter pads. That's a shame, because the wine possesses an impressively saturated dark ruby/purple color, a mouth-filling, chunky personality with gobs of earthy, black cherry fruit, fine glycerin, and a moderately tannic, smoky, rich finish. The wine was unquestionably made from high-quality raw materials, but I am perplexed by the cardboard component in what is an otherwise impressive bouquet. Let's hope it dissipates, as this wine is capable of lasting another 6–8 years.

The 1993 Pinot Noir Ridge Crest Vineyard reveals a polished, bright ruby color, a reticent, closed set of aromatics, tart, medium-bodied, clean, strawberry-and-cherry fruit flavors with a whiff of chocolate and oak, and a crisp, acidic finish. My instincts suggest excellent raw materials were excessively acidified, giving the wine a narrow, compact personality. Hopefully, it will open, but a lighter touch with added acidity would have resulted in a more user-friendly, complex, and complete wine. The 1993 Pinot Noir Wadenswil Selection (from the Ridge Crest Vineyard) possesses a similar personality. This Pinot Noir clone's greater aromatics are expressed in the subtle nose of cherries and strawberries. The color is a highly polished medium to dark ruby. The tart acidity—much of it added, I'm sure—gives the wine an artificial narrowness, which is sad given what are obviously fine raw materials. There is good ripe, cherry and strawberry fruit presented in a medium- to full-bodied format, as well as fine extraction, midpalate, and length. Unfortunately, the tart acidity is a throwback to the way technocrats from the University of California at Davis have been suggesting wines should be made for decades. Because of their high acidities, both of these wines should last for 5–7 years, but I am not sure either will ever fully blossom.

CHRISTOM

Chardonnay * * * *, Pinot Gris * * *, Pinot Noir * * * *, Pinot Noir Reserve * * * *

1993	Pinot Noir	C	86
1993	Pinot Gris	B	86
1992	Chardonnay	C	89
1992	Pinot Noir	C	86
1993	Pinot Noir Reserve	D	87
1992	Pinot Noir Reserve	C	87
1992	Pinot Noir Reserve Canary Hill	D	90

This winery has been relying on purchased fruit until its own vineyards come into production in 1995. The owner, Paul Gerrie, a Burgundy aficionado, and winemaker, Steve Doerner, made splendid 1994s, but readers will have to wait another year for those wines to hit the marketplace. For drinking now, the 1993s are good wines made in a forward, ripe style. The 1993 Pinot Noir exhibits a medium ruby color, and subtle aromatics displaying earth, wood, and red fruits. The wine is far more open and attractive on the palate, offering up sweet red and black-cherry flavors, medium body, a silky texture, and a fleshy, moderately long finish. Drink it over the next 3–4 years. As for Christom's 1993 Pinot Noir Reserve (600 cases produced), the color is a trifle more saturated than the regular offering, and the nose offers up more expressive, perfumed scents of red and black fruits intertwined with herb and new-oak aromas. The characteristic velvety texture Christom routinely achieves is present in this seductive, sumptuously ripe, rich wine. Slightly richer extract would have pushed my score up a few notches. This is a beautifully made, elegant, perfumed, intense, supple Pinot Noir that should drink well for 4–5 years. Guzzle these beauties while waiting for the spectacular 1994s.

The 1992 Pinot Noir reveals a complex bouquet of smoke, ripe black cherries, and herbs, medium ruby color, a sweet, round, supple texture, and attractive flavors that exhibit fine depth, as well as soft acid and tannin. The finish is long and smooth. Drink this elegant, rich Pinot Noir over the next 4–5 years.

There is a microscopic quantity of the 1992 Pinot Noir Reserve Canary Hill produced, so this wine is unlikely to be found except by consumers who purchase their wine directly from the winery. It offers a terrific Domaine de la Romanée-Conti-like nose of smoked meats, jammy red and black fruits, and Asian spices. Although the color is only medium ruby, the wine is lusciously ripe, generous, and seductive. It is not going to be an ager, so drink it over the next 3–4 years. Readers are more likely to find Christom's 1992 Pinot Noir Reserve, a light ruby-colored wine that exemplifies the finesse-styled Pinot Noir. It reveals a gorgeously fresh, pure bouquet of cherries, spice, and new oak. Medium bodied, with some acidity lurking in the background, this round, delicious Pinot should drink well for the next 3–4 years.

DOMAINE DROUHIN
Pinot Noir* * * *, Pinot Noir Reserve* * * * *

1993	Pinot Noir	D	88
1991	Pinot Noir	D	90
1990	Pinot Noir	D	87
1992	Pinot Noir Laurène	D	90

Domaine Drouhin's 1990 Pinot Noir is a soft, elegant wine with an attractive black cherry- and toasty new oak–scented nose. Well-structured flavors exhibit fine ripeness and texture as well as moderate length and noticeable tannins. Drink it over the next 2–3 years. It has more than a casual resemblance to a top Côte de Beaune. The 1991 Pinot Noir, the first wine made from Drouhin's own vineyard and completely vinified by his daughter, Veronique, is a major breakthrough for Drouhin's Oregon operation. I would boldly suggest that this wine is better than most of Drouhin's French Pinot Noir offerings. The color is nearly opaque dark ruby. The nose offers up splendidly ripe scents of black fruits, smoke, toasty oak, and minerals. Rich and medium to full bodied, with layer upon layer of sweet fruit, this volup-tuous, rich wine possesses the component parts to drink well young, but will last for 5–6 years. Impressive!

The medium dark ruby-colored, sexy 1992 Pinot Noir Laurène offers a flashy bouquet of ripe strawberries, cherries, and toasty, smoky vanillin from new oak casks. The wine reveals fat, chewy, ripe flavors, velvety texture, wonderful purity, and a long, lush, heady finish. It is a deceptively charming yet concentrated Pinot Noir that appears too delicious to make "old bones," but it will age well for 5–6 years. The designation "Laurène" is in honor of Veronique Drouhin's daughter, who was born in 1992. This is the only time this designation will be used, and this offering is equivalent to the estate's Reserve bottling.

The classically styled, wonderfully opulent, round, supple 1993 Pinot Noir reveals a medium ruby color, and sweet, seductive aromas of ripe black cherries intertwined with scents of oak and spice. Medium bodied, silky, concentrated, and voluptuous, this layered wine oozes with cherry flavors. Already delicious, it is capable of lasting for 5–7 years. I suspect it is no coincidence that this wine tastes like a fine premier cru from the hillside vineyards behind the town of Beaune.

ELK COVE VINEYARDS
Chardonnay* * *, Dry Riesling* *, Pinot Noir* * *, Pinot Noir Dundee Hills* * *, Pinot Noir La Bohème* * * *, Pinot Noir Wind Hill* * * *

1993	Pinot Noir	B	85
1992	Pinot Noir	B	87

1991 Pinot Noir Dundee Hills	C	87+
1990 Pinot Noir Dundee Hills	C	86
1990 Pinot Noir Elk Cove Vineyard	C	84
1992 Pinot Noir Estate Reserve	C	88
1990 Pinot Noir Estate Reserve	C	87
1992 Pinot Noir La Bohème	C	88
1991 Pinot Noir La Bohème	C	88
1990 Pinot Noir La Bohème	C	88
1990 Pinot Noir Wind Hill	C	88

This winery continues to turn out distinctive wines, emphasizing the elegant, complex, finesse side of Pinot Noir. Most Elk Cove Pinots possess deceptively light to medium ruby colors. The 1993 Pinot Noir even reveals some amber at the edge. Readers weaned on intensely saturated Cabernet Sauvignons and Syrah-based wines should be aware that color is not nearly as important for Pinot Noir as it is for other varietals. For example, Elk Cove Pinots possess much more intensity and flavor than their light-ruby colors would suggest. The soft, round 1993 Pinot Noir is all elegance in its charming strawberry- and floral-scented nose. A stylish wine reminiscent of a fine Côte de Beaune, it is ideal for drinking over the next 3–4 years.

The 1992 Pinot Noir reveals the vintage's richer, sweeter, more extracted and riper personality. Aromatically, it offers wonderfully sweet, jammy strawberries and cherries, a judicious touch of toasty vanillin, and a long, ripe, attractive, supple texture. It displays fine purity and a burgundian palate. Drink it over the next 5–6 years. The 1992 Pinot Noir Estate Reserve displays a light to medium ruby color, a big, forceful nose of red and black fruits, toasty oak, and spices. Rich and velvety textured, with lusciously ripe fruit, an overall sense of grace and balance, and a soft, silky finish, it should drink well for 5–7 years. The stylish 1992 Pinot Noir La Bohème Vineyard is the most burgundian of these offerings. It tastes like a hypothetical blend of a Corton and premier cru from one of the hillsides behind the town of Beaune. It offers up a beautifully rich, black cherry-, earthy-, and vanillin-scented nose, firm, medium- to full-bodied flavors exhibiting fine ripeness, a nice touch of wood, and a well-structured, tannic finish. While La Bohème will have the most aging potential, these Pinot Noirs are all wines to be consumed over the near term.

I found the 1991 Pinot Noir La Bohème especially appealing, with its spicy, cinnamon-, and vanillin-scented nose, ripe, open-knit, generous flavors, its sense of balance and grace, and spicy, berry fruit in the finish. It will not make old bones, but it should drink well for 4–5 years. Although the 1991 Pinot Noir Dundee Hills is a bigger, more muscular and tannic wine, it possesses both charm and elegance. Deeply colored, it offers wonderful rich fruit and spicy, herb, clove, red and black fruit scents and flavors. Drink it over the next 5–6 years.

With the exception of the Elk Cove Vineyard offering, the 1990 Pinot Noirs are very good to excellent. The pleasant, spicy 1990 Pinot Noir Elk Cove Vineyard is a one-dimensional, straightforward wine that should be consumed over the next several years. I like the big, up-front, gamy, smoked meat-, cinnamon-, and berry-scented nose of the 1990 Pinot Noir Dundee Hills. Since it is already revealing considerable evolution in the nose as well as some amber at the edge, I would drink this medium-bodied, lush Pinot over the next 1–2 years. It is full of charm and character. The 1990 Pinot Noir Estate Reserve offers a similar gamy, clove-, and cinnamon-scented nose, but richer, riper flavors with more tannin, glycerin, and body. Already delicious, my instincts suggest it will last 3–5 years.

The two best Pinot Noirs from Elk Cove in 1990 are the La Bohème Vineyard and the Wind Hill Vineyard. The 1990 La Bohème Pinot Noir is less spicy, with more cherry, herb, and floral components in its bouquet. Elegant, succulent, and juicy, this luscious Pinot exhibits soft tannins, low acidity, and copious amounts of fruit. It should continue to offer seductive drinking for 2–3 years. The deep ruby-colored 1990 Pinot Noir Wind Hill reveals a sweet, fragrant nose of black fruits, herbs, and smoke. Fat and delicious, it possesses a succulent texture, gobs of glycerin, soft tannins, and a heady finish. It is all that an up-front, lusty Pinot Noir should be. Drink it over the next 2–3 years.

EVESHAM WOOD

Chardonnay * * *, Chardonnay Tête de Cuvée * * * *, Pinot Gris * * * *, Pinot Noir* * * *, Pinot Noir Cuvée J* * * * *

1992 Pinot Noir Estate Unfiltered	C	89
1993 Pinot Noir Unfiltered	C	89
1991 Pinot Noir Unfiltered	C	88
1993 Pinot Noir Unfiltered Cuvée J	D	91
1992 Pinot Noir Unfiltered Cuvée J	D	90
1991 Pinot Noir Unfiltered Cuvée J	D	93
1990 Pinot Noir Unfiltered Cuvée J	C	90

Winemaker/proprietor Russ Raney continues to exhibit considerable talent with Pinot Noir. Virtually all of his wines go in the bottle unfiltered, which explains in part the rich, chewy texture and length Raney achieves.

Somewhat closed, the 1991 Pinot Noir Unfiltered exhibits a deep ruby color and a promising nose of spicy oak, jammy red and black fruits, and meat. It has a chewy texture, a deep, concentrated feel, medium to full body, and firm tannins. This impressively endowed Pinot Noir may garner a higher score when some of the tannins melt away. The 1990 Pinot Noir Cuvée J (made from a yeast cultured from the sediment in a bottle of Henri Jayer's red burgundy; hence the name) is another stunning wine. At present it is not as dramatic or flamboyant as the great 1989 Cuvée J, but it may turn out to be just as compelling. It reveals a deep color, and a tight but intense bouquet of sweet red and black fruits, spicy oak, and minerals as well as a floral component. The wine is dense, rich, and full bodied, with good acidity, soft, abundant tannins, and a lusty, rich finish. I cannot help wondering if the Henri Jayer yeast is the cause for the extra aromatic and flavor dimensions in this impressive Pinot Noir.

Evesham Wood's exceptional 1991 Pinot Noir Cuvée J is even more perfumed and richer than the 1990. The nose soars from the glass with scents of smoky new oak, and jammy black cherries and raspberries. Velvety textured and rich, with layers of fruit, this gorgeous wine should be drunk over the next 6–8 years. The expansive, intense, richly aromatic 1991 Pinot Noir Seven Hills Vineyard is nearly as compelling as the Cuvée J.

The 1993 Unfiltered Pinot Noir possesses an impressive, murky (clearly unfiltered), medium-to-dark ruby color. The nose offers up ripe scents of black and red fruits, earth, oak, and spice. Medium to full bodied, with a beautifully concentrated, voluptuous palate, this cleanly made, rich, authoritative-tasting wine exhibits plenty of heady alcohol, good glycerin, and a long, supple finish. Drink it over the next 5–7 years.

The intense, full-bodied, gorgeously rich, opulent, lavishly oaked 1993 Unfiltered Cuvée J is Pinot Noir at its most exotic and flamboyant. Some vintages have indeed been unbelievably similar to a great Henri Jayer Echézeaux or Richebourg. The 1993 remains unformed and youthful, but wow, what concentration and excitement it provides. Both the new oak and exhilarating level of ripe, highly concentrated red and black fruits make their presence known. The wine offers a dense, saturated color, exquisite richness, full body, and a velvety textured, long finish. A tour de force in Oregon Pinot Noir, it is the type of wine that demonstrates the extraordinary potential for this varietal in the cool Oregon climate. Unfortunately, this wine is so limited in availability that only a handful of readers will be able to purchase it. Hopefully, more wines of this caliber will emerge from Oregon. Drink it over the next 7–8 years.

The wood plays a supporting and helpful role in the 1992 Pinot Noir Estate Unfiltered. This wine exhibits gobs of black raspberry and cherry fruit in its fragrant, moderately intense bouquet. It is medium to full bodied, with the chewy, velvety suppleness expected from a top-notch Pinot Noir, and fine richness, alcohol, and fruit extraction. What tannin that can be detected is buried beneath the wine's richness and ripeness. Drink this beauty over the next 5–7 years. Evesham Wood's Pinot Noir Cuvée J is usually one of the top three or four Pinots produced in Oregon. The 1992 has more competition because of the terrific quality of the 1992 Oregon Pinot vintage, but it is still one of that state's most ostentatious Pinots. Lamentably, the limited quantities produced mean the wine rarely gets beyond the grasp of Pinot enthusiasts in the Pacific Northwest. The wine exhibits a healthy dark ruby color, a beautiful, sweet bouquet of jammy red and black fruits gently touched by sweet, toasty, smoky new oak, layers of ripe fruit, medium body, and outstanding richness that never becomes heavy or ponderous. This is an authoritatively flavored yet elegant wine that has just begun to open up and develop. It should drink well for at least 6–7 years.

THE EYRIE VINEYARDS
Chardonnay * * * *, Pinot Gris * * * *, Pinot Noir * */* * *

1990 Chardonnay	C	87
1990 Pinot Noir	C	78

David Lett, grandfather of the Oregon wine industry, is capable of producing fine Pinot Gris and rich, opulent Chardonnay. The 1990 Chardonnay is tightly knit, with good depth, an attractive apple/butter/lemony bouquet, crisp acidity, and a medium-bodied finish. It should evolve nicely for at least 2–3 years.

Lett's Pinot Noirs continue to be among the lightest colored in Oregon. It is hardly a secret that he has been surpassed in quality by a number of other Oregon producers, most notably Ponzi, Panther Creek, Domaine Drouhin, Evesham Wood, and Domaine Serene. Lett's reaction to his critics has been to question the competence of anyone who claims his Pinot Noirs too frequently lack richness, elegance, character, and charm. His 1990 Pinot Noir, which I tasted twice, reveals an unimpressive light ruby color, a vague yet pleasant diluted cherry- and herb-scented nose, light to medium body, excessive acidity, and a dry, austere, herbaceous finish. While the wine's shrill levels of acidity will keep it alive for years to come, its hollowness and lack of fruit are troublesome.

FIRESTEED CELLARS
Pinot Noir * */* * *

1993 Pinot Noir	A	84

It would be nice to see more Pinots of this quality and price range emerge from Oregon. The wine is soft and fruity, with a jammy, cherry character intertwined with a touch of herbs. It goes down the gullet very easily and is ideal for drinking over the next year. This is a *négociant* brand with the wines being produced at Knudsen Erath.

FORIS VINEYARDS

Cabernet Sauvignon Reserve* * *, Chardonnay Reserve* * * *, Gewürztraminer* * *, Pinot Gris Rogue Valley* * *, Pinot Noir* * *

1990 Cabernet Sauvignon Reserve	B	85
1991 Pinot Noir	A	85
1989 Pinot Noir	A	70

The light-bodied 1991 Pinot Noir is a soft, round, graceful wine that exhibits no hard edges, low acidity, and plenty of ripe berry fruit. Drink it over the next 1–2 years. The disappointing 1989 Pinot Noir is light bodied and shallow, with a short, watery finish.

Foris's 1990 Cabernet Sauvignon Reserve is a thick, rich, medium-bodied wine with good color and fruit, but not excessive tannin or acidity. Drink it over the next 7–8 years.

KNUDSEN ERATH

Chardonnay* *, Pinot Gris* *, Pinot Noir* * *, Pinot Noir Niederberger Vineyard* * */* * * *, Pinot Noir Reserve Leland Vineyard* * * *

1991 Pinot Noir	B	85
1990 Pinot Noir	B	84
1992 Pinot Noir Niederberger Vineyard	C	86+
1991 Pinot Noir Reserve	C	86
1990 Pinot Noir Reserve	C	86
1992 Pinot Noir Reserve Leland Vineyard	C	87+
1992 Pinot Noir Vintage Select	C	86
1991 Pinot Noir Vintage Select	B	86

An underrated producer of Oregon Pinot Noir, Knudsen Erath offers a bevy of different styles, ranging from low-priced, generic Pinot Noirs to top-of-the-line wines from vineyards such as Leland and Niederberger. Since 1987 proprietor Dick Erath and his son have increased the concentration level in many of their Pinots, making them worthy candidates for up to a decade of cellaring. Occasionally a Knudsen Erath wine will provide superb drinking for as long as 12–15 years after the vintage (e.g., 1975).

With respect to the 1991s, the uncomplex 1991 Pinot Noir is soft, ripe, and tasty, with gobs of fruit, and round, generous flavors presented in a velvety-textured, supple style. Restaurants looking for a good Oregon Pinot Noir to serve by the glass should take note of this user-friendly, easygoing wine. It should drink well for 3–5 years. The 1991 Pinot Noir Vintage Select exhibits a more complex nose of coffee, berry fruit, vanillin, and herbs. Soft, with a moderately concentrated, medium-bodied feel, this attractive, elegantly wrought Pinot Noir should drink well for another 5–7 years. The 1991 Pinot Noir Reserve is slightly expansive on the palate, with a big, gamy, spicy, berry- and herb-scented nose, excellent richness, and a softer, lusher, but shorter finish. It should be consumed over the next 3–4 years.

The 1990 Pinot Noir exhibits a soft, herb- and berry-scented nose, ripe, round, medium-bodied flavors, and a smooth finish. Drink it over the next year. The 1990 Pinot Noir Reserve is a medium-bodied wine, with a leafy, raspberry-, cherry-scented nose, firm, moderately tannic flavors, good body and cleanliness, and a compact finish. While it is not likely to improve, it should hold at its present quality level for another 1–2 years.

The 1992 Pinot Noir cuvées are backward, tannic, and oaky. The 1992 Pinot Noir Reserve Leland Vineyard reveals lavish quantities of oak and plenty of hard tannin, as well as excellent concentration and a medium- to full-bodied personality. The wine requires 2–

3 years of cellaring and will keep for up to 10 years. For example, the 1987 Leland Vineyard Reserve is just beginning to blossom. The 1992 Pinot Noir Niederberger Vineyard is also tannic and closed, but the wine's oak is intrusive to the point of dominating its personality. I may have just caught the wine at a bad stage, but I would have liked to have seen less oak and more fruit. Nevertheless, it is a dark ruby-colored, highly structured, austere Pinot Noir that requires 3–4 years of cellaring. Lastly, the lighter-styled 1992 Pinot Noir Vintage Select is made in a soft, supple, richly fruity style. The Vintage Select is supposedly more complex, but for now my money is on the least expensive Pinots in the Knudsen Erath line-up.

KRAMER VINEYARDS
Chardonnay * * *, Pinot Gris * * *, Pinot Noir * * *, Riesling * * *

1991 Pinot Noir Estate	B	87
1990 Pinot Noir Estate	B	86
1991 Pinot Noir Reserve	C	85

The regular cuvée of 1991 Pinot Noir is ripe, round, and generous, with fine balance, attractive fruit, adequate acidity, and a smooth finish. The 1991 Reserve Pinot Noir reveals more evidence of toasty new oak, but less fruit. It is meant to be more structured, and perhaps deeper, but it comes across as less exuberant than the regular cuvée. Both wines should be drunk over the next 3–4 years.

The 1990 Pinot Noir Estate is as concentrated as the 1991, but tastes slightly less complex and multidimensional. It exhibits a deep ruby color, a spicy, cherry-scented nose, and an elegant use of toasty oak. Delicious, round, and supple, it is ideal for drinking over the next 1–2 years.

MONTINORE VINEYARDS
Chardonnay Winemaker's Reserve * * * *, Pinot Gris * * *, Pinot Noir Estate * *, Pinot Noir Winemaker's Reserve * * *

1990 Pinot Noir Estate	B	78
1992 Pinot Noir Winemaker's Reserve	C	86
1990 Pinot Noir Winemaker's Reserve	C	86
1989 Pinot Noir Winemaker's Reserve	C	83

Although the light ruby-colored 1990 Pinot Noir Estate does not possess much body, it does offer pleasant, spicy, herbal, fruity notes and a soft texture. Drink it over the next several years. Far superior is the 1990 Pinot Noir Winemaker's Reserve. It boasts a medium ruby color, a big, spicy, herb- and cherry-scented nose, fine body, excellent ripeness, and soft tannins in the moderately long finish. It can be drunk now and over the next 2–3 years. The 1989 Pinot Noir Winemaker's Reserve exhibits more oak and tartness, as well as excellent richness, admirable cleanliness, and an overall sense of balance. While it has shed much of its tannin, given its high acidity, it should last for 2–3 years.

The 1992 Pinot Noir Winemaker's Reserve offers lush, ripe, black cherry fruit, wood, and earthy aromas, a supple, smooth-as-silk texture, and a round, attractive finish. It should be drunk over the next 3–4 years.

OAK KNOLL
Chardonnay * *, Pinot Noir * * *, Pinot Noir Vintage Select * * */* * * *

1992 Pinot Noir	B	86
1990 Pinot Noir	C	84

1990 Pinot Noir Vintage Select	C	87
1991 Pinot Noir Winemaker's Reserve	C	86+

Tightly knit for a 1991, Oak Knoll's top Pinot Noir cuvée, the Winemaker's Reserve, exhibits a healthy, medium-to-dark ruby color, a sweet raspberry- and cherry-scented nose, medium body, firm tannin, fine ripeness, and a tightly knit, compact finish. It would benefit from another 6–12 months of cellaring.

The 1990 Pinot Noir regular cuvée exhibits deep color, excellent jammy ripeness, some tough tannins in the finish, but good fruit, medium body, and low acidity. Drink this straightforward, richly fruity Pinot over the next 2–3 years. The 1990 Pinot Noir Vintage Select is a more serious wine, with tight but toasty, ripe, gamy, raspberry scents, medium body, good concentration, decent acidity, and hard tannins in the heady finish. Drink it now and over the next decade.

The seductive, soft, lush 1992 Pinot Noir displays gobs of black cherry fruit, vague notes of damp earth, and a medium-bodied, round, tasty finish. Drink it over the next 3–4 years.

PONZI

Chardonnay Reserve * *, Dry Riesling * * * *, Pinot Gris * * * *, Pinot Noir * * * *, Pinot Noir Reserve * * * * *

1994 Pinot Gris	B	87
1993 Pinot Noir	C	86
1992 Pinot Noir	C	88
1993 Pinot Noir Reserve	D	87+
1992 Pinot Noir Reserve	D	92
1991 Pinot Noir Reserve	D	92
1990 Pinot Noir Reserve	D	91

Dick Ponzi continues to produce wines that are frequently reference points for Oregon's wine industry. Ponzi always makes a good Pinot Gris. Their 1994 is an aromatic, fruity, creamy-textured, lovely wine with excellent ripeness, medium to full body, and a spicy, creamy-textured finish. It should be drunk before Summer 1996. Ponzi produced no regular cuvée of Pinot Noir in 1990, but fortunately there are 700 cases of the 1990 Pinot Noir Reserve. Once again it is a super wine, as well as the most likely candidate for the Pinot Noir of the vintage in Oregon. It displays a deep, saturated, dark ruby color, and a dramatic nose of black fruits, herbs, smoked game, and toasty oak. The wine is rich, medium to full bodied, with super purity of flavor, and a long, opulent finish. For fans of Ponzi who have followed the bevy of superlative Pinot Noirs he has produced, the 1990 is closer in style to the 1988 than the 1989. However, it is more tannic and structured than either of those vintages, and needs 3–6 years of cellaring. Quite impressive!

Ponzi's Pinot Noirs are always distinctive wines that drink well young yet have the cunning ability to age well. I recently attended a blind tasting where Ponzi's superb 1988 Pinot Noir Reserve was included with some $100+ bottles of Burgundy grands crus. Not one of the tasters (all French wine enthusiasts) recognized the Ponzi Pinot as a non-French wine. Moreover, it was placed first by a majority of the participants, dominating some very renowned and prestigious French burgundies. Ponzi has been on a hot streak since the mid-eighties, with a bevy of top-notch Pinot Noirs. The 1992 Pinot Noir is a soft, accessible wine with an attractive nose of black fruits and earth, soft, velvety-textured flavors, medium body, and a luscious finish. Although it is drinking extremely well, it should age gracefully for at least 7–8 years. The knockout bouquet of the 1992 Pinot Noir Reserve soars from the glass, offering aromas of black raspberries, cherries, spices, smoked meats, and vague scents of oak and herbs. The saturated dark ruby color and sweet, rich, expansive palate suggest low yields and outstanding winemaking. The wine possesses enough structure to last and evolve for a decade or more, but it is already a rich, velvety-textured wine. Tasters will have untold joy comparing it with Ponzi's earlier Reserves.

Ponzi's 1993s are several notches below the exquisite Pinot Noirs made here in 1992, 1991, 1990, 1989, and 1988, as well as what look to be sensational 1994s. They are very good examples of Ponzi Pinots, although slightly more advanced in their evolutions. The 1993 Pinot Noir is closed aromatically, but it does reveal a medium-to-dark ruby color with some amber at the edge. Once past the tight and restrained bouquet (it had just recently been bottled), the wine exhibits a chewy, supple texture, an earthy, smoked-meat character, rich berry fruit, and a good finish. It should be drunk over the next 4–5 years. Also closed, the 1993 Pinot Noir Reserve reveals a more evolved garnet color. The wine's high acidity surprised me, but it is accompanied by some attractive, sweet, gamey, smoky, berry fruit, medium body, and a structured, long finish. This restrained wine requires 6–12 more months of aging to fully open.

REX HILL VINEYARDS
Pinot Gris * *, Pinot Noir * *, Pinot Noir single-vineyard cuvées * * *

1989 Pinot Noir	C	86
1990 Pinot Noir Archibald Vineyard	C	87
1989 Pinot Noir Dundee Hills Vineyard	C	86
1989 Pinot Noir Maresh Vineyard	C	72
1988 Pinot Noir Medici Vineyard	C	78
1992 Pinot Noir Reserve	D	86

Rex Hill has a marketing policy of holding back their wines for several years. I am not sure this is a good idea, as their late-released wines frequently taste dried out and excessively oaky. Because of this policy, I only tasted one 1990 Pinot Noir, the Archibald Vineyard. It possesses a fine color, a big, spicy, gamy, oaky nose, rich, medium-bodied flavors, and a spicy, moderately tannic finish. It should be consumed over the next 4–5 years. The 1989 Pinot Noir regular cuvée reveals good depth, a chunky, medium-bodied, corpulent style as well as spicy wood, herbs, and black fruit notes in its flavor and finish. The 1989 Pinot Noir Dundee Hills offers up a fragrant nose of chocolate candy, herbs, and black cherries. It displays fine richness, plenty of oak, medium body, and a crisp finish. More structured than the regular cuvée, it is a worthy candidate for 4–5 years of cellaring. The 1989 Pinot Noir Maresh Vineyard is disappointing. Although the medium color is fine, there is an absence of ripeness in the nose, and on the palate the wine is harsh, astringent, short, completely out of balance, and dominated by acidity, tannin, and wood. The 1988 Pinot Noir Medici, which I rated 83 several years ago, continues to display a berry, smoky, earthy nose, but the fruit has faded and astringent tannins have now taken control, giving the wine a narrow, nasty finish. Clearly losing its fruit, this wine will become more attenuated with further cellaring.

Recently I also tried two wines I had liked considerably more when tasted a few years ago. The 1985 Pinot Noir Dundee Hills and 1985 Pinot Noir Maresh Vineyard have both lost much of their fruit and taken on a hard, tannic, malnourished character as they continue to dry out, with the acids and tannins the principal components left in the wine's composition.

More concentration and less reliance on new oak, in addition to lowering the tannin levels, plus earlier bottling and earlier release dates might solve some of these problems.

Rex Hill's 1992 Pinot Noir Reserve offers a medium ruby color followed by a jammy bouquet of red and black fruits and spicy oak. The wine has a good attack and plenty of charm in a straightforward, lush, supple style. Drink it over the next 4–5 years.

ST. INNOCENT WINERY
Chardonnay Freedom Hill Vineyard * * * *, Chardonnay Seven Springs Vineyard * * *, Pinot Noir O'Connor Vineyard * * * *, Pinot Noir Seven Springs Vineyard * * * *

1992 Pinot Noir O'Connor Vineyard	C	90
1990 Pinot Noir O'Connor Vineyard	B	87
1992 Pinot Noir Seven Springs Vineyard	C	90+
1991 Pinot Noir Seven Springs Vineyard	C	86
1990 Pinot Noir Seven Springs Vineyard	C	87

I prefer the two 1990 Pinot Noirs, both of which exhibit complexity and a fine touch. The softer 1990 Pinot Noir O'Connor Vineyard is reminiscent of the style of the Domaine Drouhin Pinot Noirs in 1988 and 1989. It offers a Côte de Beaune–like nose of spicy oak, cherries, and floral scents. Ripe and tasty, with a soft, velvety texture, smooth tannins, and a well-balanced, elegant personality, it is a delicious Pinot Noir for drinking over the next 2–3 years. The 1990 Pinot Noir Seven Springs Vineyard is richer, fuller, and more obviously oaky, with a slightly deeper color. While the wine reaches the limit of too much wood, there appear to be adequate reserves of fruit to support the wine's structure. The nose offers aromas of blackberries, herbs, and spices. The wine is medium bodied, with moderate tannins, and excellent concentration. If the oak becomes more subdued and the fruit pushes to the forefront, this wine may deserve an even higher rating.

Medium ruby colored, with an attractive nose of bing cherries, herbs, and oak, the spicy, soft, moderately concentrated 1991 Pinot Noir Seven Springs Vineyard should be drunk over the next 4–5 years.

St. Innocent's two outstanding Pinot Noirs are worth a special effort to find. The saturated, dark ruby/purple color of the 1992 Pinot Noir O'Connor Vineyard is followed by a super Pinot nose of black raspberries and cherries intertwined with spicy wood and loamy/earthy aromas. The wine is superconcentrated and full bodied, with ripe tannin, an expansive, chewy, mouth-feel, excellent purity, and a long, lusty finish. Drink it over the next 6–7 years. The 1992 Pinot Noir Seven Springs Vineyard also exhibits an impressively saturated dark ruby/purple color. It is more tightly knit and backward aromatically, but airing reveals scents of peppery black cherries and spicy oak. Full bodied, with noticeable tannin, this is a rich, generously endowed, concentrated wine that should age well for 7–8 years. Kudos to winemaker Mark Vlossak.

DOMAINE SERENE
Pinot Noir Evenstad Reserve * * * *, Pinot Noir Reserve * * * *

1993 Pinot Noir Carter Vineyard	D	89+
1992 Pinot Noir Evenstad Reserve	C	88
1993 Pinot Noir Evenstad Reserve	D	87+
1991 Pinot Noir Evenstad Reserve	C	87+
1990 Pinot Noir Evenstad Reserve	D	90
1993 Pinot Noir Reserve	D	87
1992 Pinot Noir Reserve	C	86
1991 Pinot Noir Reserve	C	87

Domaine Serene has been a welcome newcomer to the Oregon wine scene. The 1993 Evenstad Reserve reveals a medium ruby color and a burgundian-like, earthy-, spicy-, herb-, and black cherry–scented nose that jumps from the glass. The wine offers plenty of sweet, ripe fruit, good acidity, and moderate tannin in the finish. Although it is 6–12 months away from prime-time drinking, this beautifully pure Pinot Noir is already aromatically complex, long, and rich. Inserted in a blind tasting of top burgundies, it would be hard to pick it out as an Oregon Pinot Noir. Cellar it until early 1996 and drink it over the following 4–5 years. Made in a more precocious style, the 1993 Reserve offers a medium ruby color, attractive, burgundian-like, sweet, jammy, cherry, smoked-meat, herb, and earthy scents, medium to full body, softer, more user-friendly tannin and acid levels, and a sweet, ripe finish with good delineation and crispness. It will provide delicious drinking over the next 3–4 years.

The limited-production 1993 Carter Vineyard boasts the darkest, most saturated color of this trio of fine Pinot Noirs. Initially, the toasty vanillin oak suppresses the wine's fruit character, but within five minutes the wine opens to reveal gobs of black cherry fruit. Full bodied, with more noticeable tannin and structure, as well as greater depth of fruit, this young, promising, backward Pinot Noir should hit its peak in 12–18 months and last for 5–7 years. These are all impressive, well-made, burgundian-smelling and -tasting examples of Oregon Pinot Noir. The 1992s are charming, lighter-styled wines bearing a remarkable resemblance to a Beaune premier cru. The light ruby-colored 1992 Pinot Noir Reserve offers a clean, cherry- and vanillin-scented nose, supple, velvety-textured, medium-bodied fruit flavors, and a soft finish. It should be drunk over the next 4–5 years. The 1992 Pinot Noir Evenstad Reserve is also light ruby colored, with more noticeable new oak in the nose, more tannin and structure, as well as more extract, and a long, graceful, strawberry/cherry/spicy note to its finish. It should drink well for 5–6 years.

The deep ruby-colored 1991 Pinot Noir Reserve displays a moderately intense nose of sweet black cherries, damp earth, and vanillin. Ripe, rich, open, and supple, this delicious, concentrated Pinot Noir should be drunk over the next 5–7 years. The 1991 Pinot Noir Evenstad Reserve may turn out to be longer lived. If it develops a more expansive palate, it will be a better wine as well. There is more evidence of new oak in its toasty-, smoky-, vanillin-scented nose. Deep ruby/purple colored, the wine exhibits fine richness, medium body, excellent ripeness, and a long, spicy, more structured finish. It will benefit from another 6–12 months of bottle age and should keep for 7–8 years.

The deeply colored 1990 Pinot Noir Reserve Evenstad offers excellent richness and definition, great flavor dimension, and a complex nose of black cherry scents intermingled with aromas of spices and sweet new oak. Rich and full bodied, it exhibits a silky texture and a long, lush finish. Admirably, the Domaine Serene did not filter this wine. It should drink well for 3–4 years.

SEVEN HILLS WINERY

Cabernet Sauvignon Seven Hills Vineyard * * *, Merlot Seven Hills Vineyard * * *

1989 Cabernet Sauvignon Seven Hills Vineyard	C	87
1990 Merlot Seven Hills Vineyard	C	88

Seven Hills has consistently done fine work with its Merlot and Cabernet Sauvignon produced from the Seven Hills Vineyard. The 1990 Merlot is close to being a blockbuster. It possesses considerable tannin for a Merlot. The thick, dark ruby/purple color, the rich, cherry, chocolaty, toffee-scented nose, and deep, chewy flavors are a result of modest yields and considerable extraction of fruit. The wine is in a burly stage of evolution, but sweetness and richness of fruit are clearly present. Don't be surprised to see it turn out to be an outstanding wine. Drink it between now and 2003. The 1989 Cabernet Sauvignon Seven

Hills Vineyard reveals a saturated, purple/black color, and an unevolved but promising bouquet of ripe, jammy, cassis fruit, herbs, and licorice. Dense and rich, with a full-bodied, tannic personality, this big, brawny Cabernet Sauvignon needs at least 1–2 years of cellaring. **A.M.: 1996–2005.**

SOKOL BLOSSER

Chardonnay Redland Vineyard * * *, Pinot Noir * * *, Pinot Noir Redland Vineyard * * * *

1992 Pinot Noir	C	86
1991 Pinot Noir	B	86
1990 Pinot Noir	B	86
1992 Pinot Noir Redland Vineyard	C	87
1991 Pinot Noir Redland Vineyard	C	86
1990 Pinot Noir Redland Vineyard	C	90

I found the 1992 Pinot Noir to be a charming, well-focused, medium ruby-colored wine with lovely cherry fruit, noticeable toasty oak, spice, medium body, and grip. It is ideal for drinking over the next 2–4 years. The 1992 Pinot Noir Redland Vineyard, essentially a reserve selection usually made from the oldest parcels in the Durant and Highland vineyards, exhibits more ripeness, a touch of herbaceousness, and a fuller-bodied, firmer structure. The wine possesses good red and black fruit character, an attractive, forthcoming bouquet, but more backward flavors. It should drink well for 5–6 years.

Although Sokol Blosser's 1991 red wines are good, they are not as complex or rich as their 1990s. The 1991 Pinot Noir offers spicy, herbaceous black cherry fruit, medium weight, fine ripeness, and a tasty, soft, compact finish. The 1991 Pinot Noir Redland Vineyard exhibits even more herbaceousness in the nose, as well as higher acidity, fine purity and ripeness, and a medium-bodied, spicy finish. While I enjoyed these wines, I would have liked to have seen more depth. Drink both offerings over the next 3–4 years.

I have enjoyed Sokol Blosser's 1990 Pinot Noir. It offers a medium ruby color, and a big, berry- and cherry-scented nose intertwined with aromas of oak, earth, and herbs. Medium to full bodied, with fine richness, a supple texture, and a long finish, this delicious Pinot Noir should be consumed over the next 2–3 years. The 1990 Pinot Noir Redland Vineyard is a beautiful example of this varietal. Deep ruby colored, with an explosive nose of sweet, toasty oak, berry fruit, smoked herbs and meats, and a subtle touch of vanillin, this rich, full-bodied wine has exquisite balance, elegance combined with power, and superb depth of fruit in the long, lush finish. Drink it over the next 5–6 years. Bravo!

TUALATIN VINEYARDS

Chardonnay Estate * * *, Pinot Noir Estate * *

1990 Pinot Noir Estate	A	82
1988 Pinot Noir Estate	A	82
1993 Pinot Noir Estate Barrel Aged	B	85
1993 Pinot Noir Estate Private Reserve	C	86
1992 Pinot Noir Estate Private Reserve	C	85

Tualatin has generally made better Chardonnays than Pinot Noirs, but I was unimpressed with such offerings as their 1992 Barrel Aged and 1992 Private Reserve Chardonnays. On the other hand, the Pinot Noirs have shown some improvement. Although they are not among the leaders of Oregon Pinot, they are pleasant, straightforward, herbaceous, cherry-scented wines with soft textures and plenty of delicious fruit. The supple 1993 Pinot Noir Estate

Barrel Aged displays straightforward, vanillin- and berry-scented fruit. It is ideal for drinking over the next 2 years. The 1993 Pinot Noir Estate Private Reserve Barrel Select exhibits more ripeness, body, and concentration. It should drink well for 3–4 years. Although the 1992 Pinot Noir Estate Private Reserve has been acidified more than necessary, it is a cherry-scented, ripe, medium-bodied, pleasant Pinot for consuming over the next 2–4 years.

The reasonably priced 1990 and 1988 Pinot Noirs should elicit some consumer attention. Their extremely light colors are deceptive, as they are both fruity, round, tasty wines that only lack depth and complexity. Given how fresh the 1988 is, it should last longer than one might suspect. Clearly of the understated, lighter school of Pinot Noir winemaking, they make for a pleasant drinking experience.

WILLAMETTE VALLEY VINEYARD

Chardonnay Canary Hill Vineyard * * * *, Chardonnay Elton Vineyard * * *, Chardonnay Founder's Reserve * * *, Pinot Gris * * * *, Pinot Noir * * * *, Pinot Noir Founder's Reserve * * * *, Pinot Noir O.V.D. * * * *, Pinot Noir Whole Berry Fermentation * * * *

1993 Pinot Noir	B	86
1992 Pinot Noir	B	87
1993 Pinot Noir Founder's Reserve	C	88+
1992 Pinot Noir Founder's Reserve	C	88+
1992 Pinot Noir Oregon Trail Commemorative Release	C	86
1992 Pinot Noir O.V.D.	C	89
1994 Pinot Noir Whole Berry Fermented	B	87
1993 Pinot Noir Whole Berry Fermentation	B	88
1992 Pinot Noir Whole Berry Fermentation	B	88

Willamette Valley Vineyards has quickly risen to the top echelon of quality producers in Oregon. Their secret is producing richly fruity, supple, cleanly made, delicious wines that are filled with varietal character. Winemaker Dean Cox's Whole Berry Fermented Pinot Noir may be the world's most delicious and accessible Pinot. It has been a knock-out wine in some vintages. Meant to be drunk within 1–2 years of its release, it is a delicious, reasonably priced Pinot Noir—how many times do you find that combination! The 1994 exhibits a healthy, deep ruby color, an intensely fragrant nose of crushed cherry and raspberry fruit, soft, opulent flavors, and a silky smooth finish. If you want to see just how seductive Pinot Noir made in an easy-to-drink style can be, don't miss this delicious, beautifully made wine. The 1993 Pinot Noir (packaged in an attractive, decanterlike bottle) reveals a dark ruby/purple color, a moderately intense, berry, earthy bouquet, medium body, attractive spice, good depth, and firm tannin in the finish. It should drink well for 5–6 years. The 1993 Pinot Noir Founder's Reserve reveals a saturated, polished, dark-ruby color, wonderfully sweet, jammy, berry fruit, medium to full body, well-integrated tannin, and a long, ripe, heady finish. Cellar this wine for 6–12 months and drink it over the next 5–6 years.

The beautiful fruit quality of the 1994s and 1993s is also seen in the 1992 Pinot Noir O.V.D. and in the 1992 Pinot Noir Founder's Reserve. The O.V.D. exhibits a dark saturated ruby/purple color, rich, ripe, black cherry and raspberry scents, a touch of toasty oak, a creamy, rich, expansive, voluptuously textured palate, and a supple finish. It is a gorgeously made, well-endowed Pinot for drinking over the next 5–7 years. The 1992 Founder's Reserve Pinot Noir is the most ambitious wine in Willamette Valley Vineyard's portfolio, as well as the most backward, oaky, and structured. It requires 1–2 years of cellaring to allow some of the tannin to melt away. This tannic wine is admirably endowed, rich, and full. It should last for a decade. The fat 1992 Pinot Noir Willamette Valley is loaded with black cherry fruit, and offers plenty of glycerin and alcohol in its velvety-textured finish. The nose of the 1992 Pinot Noir Whole Berry Fermentation soars from the glass, offering scents of flowers, jammy black cherries, and spice. Rich and medium to full bodied, with wonderful sweet ripe fruit, this luscious wine is impressive and delicious. The 1992 Pinot Noir Oregon Trail Commemorative Release is similarly styled, with slightly more structure. Again, the emphasis is on immediate gratification. These are delicious wines for drinking in their first 3–4 years of life.

8. WASHINGTON STATE

A number of emerging trends may finally focus attention on the rapidly improving wines of Washington. First, escalating European wine prices, the weak dollar, and increasing international competition for wines of limited availability may force all but the most wealthy wine consumers to look elsewhere for quality wines at reasonable prices. Washington wines could prove to be a significant alternative. Second, Washington has a bevy of quality wines, including Cabernets, Merlots, Chardonnays, and Sauvignon Blancs, priced to compete in the $8–$12 range occupied primarily by budget imports, and Australian and Chilean wines. This segment of the marketplace is ignored by most of California's finest producers. This presents an opportunity for Washington's producers to become more widely known as consumers taste and compare. Third, the giant Château Ste.-Michelle winery has dominated the Washington wine scene in years past. Together with its sister winery Columbia Crest, these wineries account for 50% of the state's production. With a bevy of excellent vintages in the pipeline (1994, 1993, 1992, 1991, 1990, and 1989), optimism is the rule of the day among Washington State's long-ignored winemakers.

The Basics

TYPES OF WINE
Virtually all the varietals seen in California are grown in Washington. The most notable exception is Zinfandel. However, Washington's answer to this is Lemberger, a fruity, red vinifera grape that is capable of being made into a Beaujolais-style, nonoak-aged wine, or more infrequently into a serious, cellar-worthy wine. A few producers are dabbling with Pinot Noir, and not surprisingly, have failed. Experiments with Syrah, Nebbiolo, and Cabernet Franc have begun, and the results to date have been mediocre.

Washington's wineries are banking on Chardonnay, Cabernet Sauvignon, and especially Merlot to bring them to prominence. There is also some hope for Sauvignon Blanc and Semillon. Approximately one-quarter of the state's vineyards are planted with Riesling, but this will diminish in time, because newly planted vineyards rarely include this varietal. Fortunately, Washington's consumers appear to enjoy Riesling, which is usually bargain priced ($6–$8), and producers continue to crank it out because it is easy and inexpensive to make—the perfect cash-flow wine. For Riesling aficionados, these wines represent fine values. Washington also produces this country's best Chenin Blancs and Muscats. Their

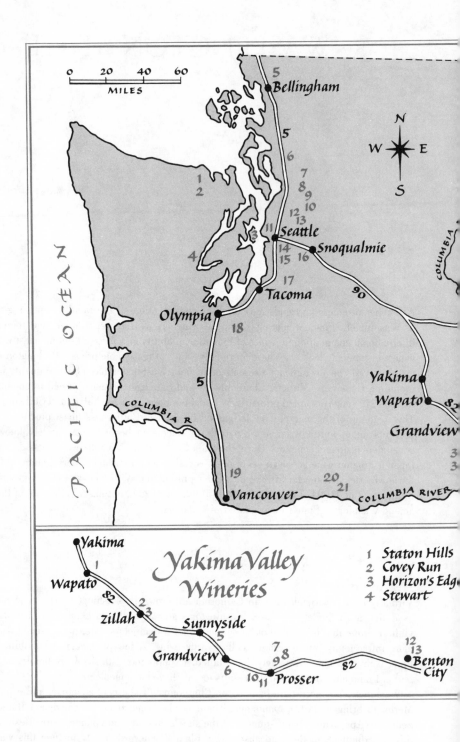

MILES

Bellingham

Seattle
Snoqualmie

Tacoma

Olympia

Yakima
Wapato
Grandview

Vancouver
COLUMBIA RIVER

PACIFIC OCEAN

COLUMBIA R.

Yakima

Wapato

Zillah

Sunnyside

Grandview

Prosser

Benton City

Yakima Valley Wineries

1 Staton Hills
2 Covey Run
3 Horizon's Edge
4 Stewart

Washington

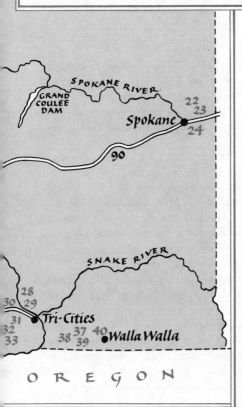

crisp natural acidity, easily obtained due to Washington's northern latitude, makes these wines, finished in an off-dry to slightly sweet style, the ideal summer sipping and picnic wines. Sadly, the market for these wines is limited. For better or worse, the state's future rests with the superstar grapes—Cabernet Sauvignon, Merlot, and Chardonnay. The good news is that these are the wines the marketing people claim consumers desire. The bad news is that Washington State must compete with California in the already congested marketplace.

RED WINE VARIETALS

Cabernet Sauvignon   This is Washington's most successful grape variety. In capable hands, it renders an almost opaque purple wine. Cabernet Sauvignon usually ripens fully in eastern Washington, resulting in wines with curranty, plummy, cedary aromas, excellent extract, medium to full body, and good depth and concentration. Overwhelming aromas and flavors of herbs and vegetables are rarely as intrusive in Washington Cabernet Sauvignons as they can be in California.

Merlot   Washington producers are hoping that Merlot will bring the state fame. Because of the young age of the vineyards and the inexperience of the winemakers, the quality of Washington's Cabernet Sauvignon is clearly superior to its Merlot.

To no one's surprise, Washington Merlot yields a wine that is more supple than Cabernet. The acids are lower and the tannins less aggressive. However, a number of Merlots continue to exhibit an herbaceous character, and frequently lack the depth of flavor and concentration of the state's best Cabernets. As a group they are pleasant, but rarely exciting, except, of course, for Leonetti Cellars' and Château Ste.-Michelle's brilliant Merlots.

Pinot Noir   This fickle grape variety is no easier to tame in Washington than in California. Nothing tasted to date remotely resembles what Pinot Noir can achieve in Burgundy, or selected California and Oregon vineyards.

Lemberger   Originally grown in Germany, this grape, like Zinfandel, is highly adaptable and can be successfully made in a variety of styles. Just a handful of wineries make Lemberger (vineyard acreage is less than 1% of the total in the state). This is lamentable, because the wine can be tasty, fruity, and quite quaffable when not oak aged and when served lightly chilled. Sadly, much of the Lemberger produced is dull and overcropped.

WHITE WINE VARIETALS

Chardonnay   Washington Chardonnay occupies 15% of vineyard acreage and can ripen fully while retaining excellent natural acidity. This has caused increasing numbers of producers to barrel-ferment it, and to encourage their Chardonnay to complete malolactic fermentation. Extended lees contact, in vogue in California, is also favored by many Washington producers. A number of wineries have invested heavily in new French oak barrels and are trying to make a wine in the Côte de Beaune style. Others are going after a fruitier style (à la Fetzer's Sundial), while others are aiming for something in between. In short, there is a wide range of styles, but the potential for making excellent Washington State Chardonnay exists, although much of it remains unrealized.

Chenin Blanc   Washington is capable of making wonderful Chenin Blanc in a slightly sweet style due to the naturally crisp acidity. Yet most wineries seemed surprised that anyone would be interested in tasting this ignored, often maligned varietal. However, at $8 a bottle from producers such as Hogue or Snoqualmie, Chenin Blanc can be a true delight, especially on a hot summer day.

Gewürztraminer   Fortunately, plantings of this varietal are rapidly decreasing in Washington. It has proven no more successful in Washington than in California.

Muscat Like Chenin Blanc, Muscat grown in Washington can render delicious, crisp, aromatic, perfumed wines that are incredibly refreshing on hot summer days. Latah Creek, Covey Run, Stewart, and Snoqualmie are particularly successful with Muscat. In addition, the price is right.

Sauvignon Blanc When vinified in Washington, the potentially extroverted, herbal, grassy qualities of this grape are held in check. Many wineries also give the wines some exposure to oak barrels. As in California, most wineries strive for a safe, middle-of-the-road style that too often results in bland, insipid wines. Washington State Sauvignons are, however, priced to sell in the $6–$10 range, which makes them attractive to consumers.

Semillon This is a grape with excellent potential in Washington. It yields a wine with plenty of body and richness combined with the lively acidity typically found in Washington grapes. Only two wineries seem to be fully exploiting Semillon's potential. L'Ecole No. 41's offerings of Semillon compete with California's Kalin Cellars for America's best Semillon. Woodward Canyon's Charbonneau White, a Graves-style blend of Semillon and Sauvignon Blanc, is another skillfully rendered wine that prominently displays the glories of Semillon.

White (Johannisberg) Riesling Washington's Rieslings are good, but often simple and one-dimensional when compared to the slaty, mineral-scented, aromatic complexity and incredible lightness and zestiness attainable in the best German Rieslings. However, Washington's abundant quantities of Rieslings are practically given away, usually selling for less than $6.

Several producers make superb late harvest Rieslings. Blackwood Canyon, Yakima River Winery, and Stewart have been particularly successful, and prices are, again, remarkably modest.

RECENT VINTAGES

1994—A small crop of highly concentrated wines had producers excited about the quality, but disappointed in the quantity. This should turn out to be a top-notch year for red wines, and a very good one for whites. Look for prices to rise given the small crop.

1993—This is certainly a very good vintage, but look for more irregularity given the fact that it was a cooler year than either 1994 or 1992. The white wines should be aromatic and ideal for drinking early in their lives. At their finest, the red wines will be intense and rich, but less consistent than either 1992 or 1994.

1992—A hot, dry year resulted in fine overall ripeness and considerable optimism. This will be a year for opulent, fruity white wines and rich, powerful Cabernet Sauvignons.

1991—This should turn out to be a good to very good, somewhat irregular year because of the relatively high crop yields and irregular growing season. For producers who kept yields moderate and picked physiologically ripe fruit, it should turn out to be a high-quality year.

1990—Initially believed to be less successful than either 1988 or 1989, producers are now exhibiting far greater enthusiasm for their red wines. Generalizations concerning such a vast, diverse viticultural region are fraught with the potential for error. With that caveat in mind, the 1990 red wines tend to be supple, rich, and forward. The hot summer and ideal harvest conditions produced fully ripe fruit for producers who harvested at the last moment. The red wines should exceed the quality of the whites. In many cases the red wines should prove to be as good as the highly acclaimed 1988s and 1989s.

1989—Moderate temperatures allowed full ripening of the grapes. The red varietals were deeply colored, perfumed, and richly flavored. The white varietals had full fruit and good sugar levels balanced by excellent acidity. Washington producers appear unanimous that this is a potentially great vintage.

1988—An excellent vintage for both reds and whites, but without the depth and concentration of 1989. The reds should, however, be long-lived and stylish. The white wines should have been consumed several years ago.

OLDER VINTAGES

(Red Wines)

1987—This is a vintage of correct, attractive wines without the flesh of 1988 and 1989.

1986—1986 has turned out to be a mediocre vintage. Most of the reds lack concentration.

1985—This is a tannic vintage in which only the most skilled winemakers made balanced wines. The finest wines are muscular, big, and long-lived.

1984—This was a poor vintage for Washington and is best ignored.

1983—The top red-wine producers consider 1983 to be a superb vintage, and, along with 1989 and 1994, one of the best years in memory. The finest wines are only now beginning to open up and will need another 5 to 10 years to reach their apogee. The wines have depth, flavor, flesh, balance, and excellent structure. The 1983 Château Ste.-Michelle Cold Creek Reserve Cabernet Sauvignon is a dazzling example from this vintage.

RATING WASHINGTON'S BEST PRODUCERS OF CABERNET SAUVIGNON, MERLOT, OR BLENDS THEREOF

* * * * * (OUTSTANDING)

De Lille Proprietary Red Wine
Leonetti Cellars Cabernet
  Sauvignon
Leonetti Cellars Cabernet Sauvignon
  Reserve

Leonetti Cellars Cabernet Sauvignon Seven
  Springs Reserve
Quilceda Creek Cabernet Sauvignon
Quilceda Creek Cabernet Sauvignon
  Reserve

* * * * (EXCELLENT)

Leonetti Cellars Merlot
Château Ste.-Michelle Château Reserve
  Proprietary Red Wine
Château Ste.-Michelle Merlot Indian Wells
  Vineyard
Andrew Will Cabernet Sauvignon
Andrew Will Cabernet Sauvignon Reserve

Andrew Will Merlot Ciel du Cheval
Andrew Will Merlot Sunshine
Woodward Canyon Cabernet Sauvignon
Woodward Canyon Cabernet Sauvignon
  Canoe Ridge Vineyard
Woodward Canyon
  Charbonneau * * * */* * * * *

* * * (GOOD)

Chinook Merlot
Columbia Crest Cabernet Sauvignon
Columbia Crest Merlot
Columbia Winery Cabernet Franc Red
  Willow Vineyard
Columbia Winery Cabernet Sauvignon Otis
  Vineyard
Columbia Winery Cabernet Sauvignon
  Sagemoor Vineyard
Columbia Winery Merlot Red Willow
  Vineyard
L'Ecole No. 41 Merlot

Hogue Cabernet Sauvignon
Hogue Cabernet Sauvignon Reserve
Hogue Merlot
Hogue Merlot Reserve
Kiona Cabernet Sauvignon
Kiona Merlot
Latah Creek Cabernet Sauvignon Reserve
Latah Creek Merlot
Preston Cabernet Sauvignon
Château Ste.-Michelle Cabernet Sauvignon
Château Ste.-Michelle Cabernet Sauvignon
  Estate

Château Ste.-Michelle Cabernet Sauvignon Cold Creek Vineyard
Château Ste.-Michelle Cabernet Sauvignon River Ridge Vineyard

Château Ste.-Michelle Merlot Cold Creek Vineyard
Seven Hills Cabernet Sauvignon
Seven Hills Merlot

* * (AVERAGE)

Arbor Crest Cabernet Sauvignon
Arbor Crest Merlot
Blackwood Canyon Cabernet Sauvignon
Blackwood Canyon Merlot
Bookwalter Cabernet Sauvignon
Canoe Ridge Cabernet Sauvignon
Cascade Estates Cabernet Sauvignon
Coventry Vale Cabernet Sauvignon
Covey Run Cabernet Sauvignon
Facelli Cabernet Sauvignon
French Creek Cabernet Sauvignon
Gordon Brothers Cabernet Sauvignon
Barnard Griffin Cabernet Sauvignon

Hinzerling Cabernet Sauvignon
Hyatt Merlot
Latah Creek Cabernet Sauvignon
Mercer Ranch Cabernet Sauvignon
Quarry Lake Cabernet Sauvignon
Redford Cabernet Sauvignon
Silver Lake Cabernet Sauvignon
Snoqualmie Cabernet Sauvignon
Staton Hills Cabernet Sauvignon
Stewart Cabernet Sauvignon
Paul Thomas Cabernet Sauvignon
Tucker Cabernet Sauvignon

RATING WASHINGTON'S BEST PRODUCERS OF CHARDONNAY

* * * * * (OUTSTANDING)

Woodward Canyon Estate Reserve

Woodward Canyon Roza Berge Vineyard

* * * * (EXCELLENT)

Hogue
Hogue Reserve
McCrea
Château Ste.-Michelle Cold Creek Vineyard

Château Ste.-Michelle River Ridge Vineyard
Woodward Canyon Columbia Valley

* * * (GOOD)

Chinook
Columbia Crest
Gordon Brothers
Barnard Griffin
Hyatt
Latah Creek

Château Ste.-Michelle Chardonnay
Château Ste.-Michelle Chardonnay Cold Creek Vineyard
Stewart
Paul Thomas Reserve

* * (AVERAGE)

Arbor Crest * */* * *
Blackwood Canyon
Bookwalter
Canoe Ridge
Carroway
Cascade Estates
Champs de Brionne
Columbia Winery * */* * *
Covey Run

French Creek
Barnard Griffin
Hinzerling
Hoodsport
Horizon's Edge
Kiona
Mount Baker
Preston
Silver Lake

Snoqualmie
Staton Hills
Paul Thomas

Tucker
Waterbrook
Zillah Oaks

RATING WASHINGTON'S BEST PRODUCERS OF OTHER WINES

* * * * * (OUTSTANDING)

L'Ecole No. 41 Semillon
Yakima River Ice Wine

Yakima River Late Harvest Riesling

* * * * (EXCELLENT)

Columbia Crest Sauvignon Blanc/Semillon
Hogue Chenin Blanc
Hogue Dry Riesling
Hogue Fumé Blanc
Hogue Semillon
Hogue Semillon/Chardonnay

Thurston Wolfe Black Muscat
Thurston Wolfe Late Harvest Semillon
Washington Hills Chenin Blanc
Woodward Canyon Charbonneau White
   (Semillon/Sauvignon Blanc)

* * * (GOOD)

Arbor Crest Muscat
Arbor Crest Riesling
Arbor Crest Sauvignon Blanc
Bainbridge Island Müller-Thurgau
Blackwood Canyon Chenin Blanc
Blackwood Canyon Gewürztraminer
Blackwood Canyon Late Harvest Riesling
Cavatappi Winery Nebbiolo
Columbia Crest Winery Sauvignon Blanc
Columbia Winery Johannisberg Riesling

Kiona White Riesling
Latah Creek Riesling
Latah Creek Sauvignon Blanc
McCrea Tierra del Sol
Quarry Lake Sauvignon Blanc
Domaine Ste.-Michelle Sparkling Wine
   cuvées
Stewart Late Harvest Riesling
Andrew Will Chenin Blanc * * */* * * *

ARBOR CREST
Cabernet Sauvignon * *, Chardonnay * */* * *, Merlot * *, Muscat * * *, Riesling * * *,
Sauvignon Blanc * * *

1993 Chardonnay Cameo Reserve	A	85
1993 Dry Riesling Dionysus Vineyard	A	82
1993 Johannisberg Riesling	A	85
1993 Muscat Canelli	A	85
1993 Sauvignon Blanc Bacchus Vineyard	A	86

Arbor Crest continues to turn out very good, budget-priced white wines led by their crisp, flinty, melony Sauvignon, flowery Muscat, and a bevy of tasty Rieslings ranging from dry to slightly sweet. The Chardonnay cuvées merit mixed reviews, although they are generally at least average in quality, often far better. The red wines have been less consistent, revealing near-vegetal flavors and not enough intensity. Recent releases of Cabernet Franc, Merlot, and Cabernet Sauvignon indicate improvements are warranted.

The white wines all need to be drunk within several years of release. They are to be prized for their vibrancy, purity, and freshness.

COLUMBIA CREST WINERY
Cabernet Sauvignon * * *, Chardonnay * * *, Merlot * * *, Sauvignon Blanc * * *

1989	Cabernet Sauvignon Barrel Select	B	86
1989	Merlot Barrel Select	B	87
1988	Reserve Red Proprietary Wine	B	85
1993	Sauvignon Blanc	A	86
1993	Sauvignon Blanc/Semillon	A	85

This winery continues to turn out well-made, attractive red wines meant to be drunk in their first 4–5 years of life. The 1989 Cabernet Sauvignon Barrel Select exhibits an impressively deep ruby/purple color, an excellent spicy, vanillin-, and cassis-scented nose, medium-bodied, concentrated flavors with tart acids, and moderate tannins. Drinkable now, it should age well for 5–6 years. I preferred the 1989 Merlot Barrel Select as it is more opulent and less tart. Deeply colored, with a mocha-, spicy-, berry-, and herb-scented nose, it offers rich, medium-bodied flavors and a long, soft, yet well-balanced finish. Drink it over the next 5–6 years. The 1988 Reserve Red possesses a hardness that kept my score low. It exhibits fine spicy, ripe cassis fruit, and plenty of depth and richness, but the acidity level is too high for my taste. Nevertheless, I like the general character of the wine. Drink it over the next 5–6 years.

Columbia Crest's white wine offerings are generally well-made, crisp, fruity wines with medium body, and fine ripeness, length, and purity. The 1993 Sauvignon Blanc/Semillon is a light, delicate, and subtle wine with crisp fruit, a zesty, light-bodied dryness, and a tangy, citrusy finish. It should be drunk over the next year. The 1993 Sauvignon is also filled with fruit, and is dry, medium bodied, and ideal to consume with fish or poultry.

COLUMBIA WINERY
Cabernet Franc Red Willow Vineyard * * *, Cabernet Sauvignon Otis Vineyard * * *, Cabernet Sauvignon Sagemoor Vineyard * * *, Chardonnay * */* * *, Johannisberg Riesling * * *, Merlot Red Willow Vineyard * * *, Sauvignon Blanc * *, Semillon * *

1991	Cabernet Franc	C	85
1992	Cabernet Franc Red Willow Vineyard	B	85
1991	Cabernet Sauvignon	B	78
1989	Cabernet Sauvignon Otis Vineyard	C	87
1989	Cabernet Sauvignon Sagemoor Vineyard	C	87+
1993	Chardonnay Wyckoff Vineyard	B	84
1993	Chevrier	A	81
1993	Gewürztraminer	A	75
1993	Johannisberg Riesling	A	86
1993	Johannisberg Riesling Cellarmaster's Reserve	A	87
1991	Merlot Milestone Red Willow Vineyard	C	87
1992	Merlot Red Willow Vineyard	C	87
1993	Sauvignon Blanc	A	78
1993	Semillon/Chardonnay	A	78

My tasting notes reveal significant inconsistency and variability with Columbia Winery, but recent releases appear to indicate that this winery is on a more even path of quality. I do not remember enjoying this winery's previous Riesling offerings as much as I did the two 1993s, which are delicate and flavorful, with good acidity, and plenty of stony, applelike, citrusy, Riesling fruit. Both wines are deliciously fresh and vibrant, with a drinkability window of 2–3 years.

I thought the 1993 Sauvignon Blanc, 1993 Chevrier, and 1993 Semillon/Chardonnay were all acidic, tart wines, without the requisite fruit necessary to stand up to the structure and acid. Although the Chardonnays are too oaky for my tastes, they are pleasant, straightforward, well-made wines.

This winery's red wines are usually far more interesting. The 1992 Cabernet Franc Red Willow Vineyard exhibits an attractive herb-, black cherry-, and earthy-scented nose, soft, intense flavors, moderate tannin, and a fine finish. It should improve for several more years and last for 10–15. The 1992 Merlot Red Willow Vineyard displays textbook black cherry notes that nicely complement the toasty, vanillin, spicy oak. The wine possesses moderate tannin, medium body, and an especially long finish. This young, exuberant Merlot should only get better over the next 2–3 years; it will last for 10–12 years.

The 1991 Cabernet Sauvignon is a simple, straightforward wine with excessive tannin and noticeable deficiencies in extraction and flavor.

Other Cabernet Sauvignon, Cabernet Franc, and Merlot wines that consumers may still come across in the marketplace include the following wines. The 1989 Cabernet Sauvignon from the renowned Otis Vineyard exhibits a saturated, deep ruby/purple color, and a big, spicy nose filled with moderately ripe aromas of black currants, herbs, and toasty new oak. The wine exhibits excellent richness, crisp acidity, plenty of spice, and copious quantities of tannin. Although it could use an additional year of cellaring, this excellent Cabernet promises to last for 10–15 years. The 1989 Cabernet Sauvignon Sagemoor Vineyard possesses less noticeable tannin and better integrated new oak. It is deeply-colored, well-balanced, full-bodied wine with a cedary, spicy, currant-scented nose, and tight but promising, rich, deep flavors. **A.M.: now–2005.**

Columbia Winery's 1991 Cabernet Franc is an elegant example of this varietal that is rarely seen in Washington. Medium bodied, with an herb-, mineral-, and black currant-scented nose, soft flavors, and a pleasant, short finish, it should drink well for 5 or more years. If the wine fills out, it will merit a higher rating. I also enjoyed the 1991 Merlot Milestone from the Red Willow Vineyard. Lavishly oaky, with ripe, curranty fruit, spicy, medium-to full-bodied flavors, and admirable acidity, this attractive, chunky Merlot should drink well for 6–7 years.

Columbia Winery also produces a small quantity of Syrah from the Red Willow Vineyard. At its finest it is a 3-star wine.

DE LILLE CELLARS
Proprietary Red Wine * * * * *

1992 Chaleur Estate Proprietary Red Wine	D	91+
1992 D 2 Proprietary Red Wine	B	89

This new Washington State winery is dedicated to producing world-class proprietary red wines based on a Bordeaux-like blend of Cabernet Sauvignon, Merlot, and Cabernet Franc. The debut release, the 1992 Chaleur Estate, offers an impressively saturated, nearly opaque ruby/purple color, a spicy, vanillin, sweet, red and black fruit-scented nose, rich, full-bodied, gorgeously proportioned flavors that nearly conceal the moderate tannin level, and a long, intense finish. This is an immensely impressive, large-scale, beautifully balanced wine that is approachable now but promises to hit its stride by the turn of the century and last for 10–15 years thereafter.

The second label, D 2, possesses less color saturation, a slightly more evolved nose of black fruits, smoke, and vanilla, round, generous, concentrated, supple flavors, and a fine finish. If this is the producer's second wine, this property's selection process may be too severe! These are impressive debut performances from what looks to be a very serious entry into Washington State's fine wine marketplace.

BARNARD GRIFFIN

Cabernet Sauvignon* *, Chardonnay* * *, Fumé Blanc* *, Merlot* *, Semillon* *

1992	Cabernet/Merlot	A	87
1993	Chardonnay Barrel Fermented	B	82
1993	Fumé Blanc	A	86
1992	Merlot	B	85
1993	Semillon Barrel Fermented	A	79

The dry 1993 Fumé Blanc exhibits gobs of melony, herb scents and flavors, fine concentration, a sense of freshness and balance, and a zesty finish. Drink it over the next year. The 1993 Semillon Barrel Fermented is aggressively woody and blatantly herbaceous, without sufficient fruit. The 1993 Barrel Fermented Chardonnay exhibits plenty of oak, but not enough fruit for balance.

The 1992 Cabernet/Merlot offers a saturated dark ruby color, a moderately intense, attractive nose of cassis, mocha, and herbs, medium-to full-bodied, concentrated flavors, a supple texture, and a long finish. This is a generously endowed, supple wine that can be drunk now or cellared for 5–6 years. The 1992 Merlot exhibits adequate color, attractive red and black fruit notes, medium body, hard tannin, and high acidity.

HOGUE CELLARS

Cabernet Sauvignon* * *, Cabernet Sauvignon Reserve* * *, Chardonnay* * * *, Chardonnay Reserve* * * *, Chenin Blanc* * * *, Riesling* * * *, Fumé Blanc* * * *, Merlot* * *, Merlot Reserve* * *, Semillon* * * *, Semillon/Chardonnay* * * *

1990	Cabernet Sauvignon	B	83
1989	Cabernet Sauvignon	B	85
1990	Cabernet Sauvignon Reserve	B	88
1989	Cabernet Sauvignon Reserve	B	87
1993	Chardonnay	A	86
1993	Chardonnay Reserve	B	86
1993	Chenin Blanc	A	87
1993	Dry Johannisberg Riesling	A	86
1990	Dry Riesling Reserve Schwartzman Vineyard	B	86
1993	Fumé Blanc	A	86
1992	Merlot	B	82
1992	Merlot Reserve	B	87
1993	Semillon	A	87
1992	Semillon	A	86
1993	Semillon/Chardonnay	A	86
1992	Semillon/Chardonnay	A	87

The Hogue family knows what it takes to be successful. They have a brilliant track record for turning out delicious, bargain-priced wines. The bulk of the production is in excellent white wines, but the red wines are also consistently well made. Bottled early to preserve their freshness and fruit, Hogue's white wines are among the most delicious made in Washington State. The 1993 Johannisberg Riesling is a light-bodied, dry, crisp, delicious, and fruity wine that should make many friends. The same can be said of the floral-scented, off-dry, richly fruity 1993 Chenin Blanc. It possesses some trapped CO_2 that gives it even more vivaciousness. This winery makes some of Washington State's most interesting Fumé Blanc and Semillon. The 1993 Fumé Blanc exhibits a melony, honey-scented nose, pleasing, ripe, fruity flavors, medium body, and a dry finish. The 1993 Semillon is more pungent, displaying Semillon's herb, waxy component, medium body, and a fat, chewy richness balanced by the right amount of acidity. Hogue also does a fine job with Semillon/Chardonnay. Again, the emphasis is on bright, crisp, lively fruit flavors, as well as purity and depth. The 1993 reveals good depth, ripe fruit, and adequate acidity. The 1993 Chardonnay Reserve displays a spicy component, as well as medium to full body, good ripeness, and a crisp finish.

The 1993 Dry Johannisberg Riesling offers an attractive floral, citrusy nose, tasty, light-bodied flavors, lovely fruit, and a long, crisp, dry finish. It is an ideal lighter-styled aperitif wine. The 1990 Dry Riesling Reserve Schwartzman Vineyard displays a green apple character to its bouquet, excellent richness, admirable depth in the finish, and a dry, minerallike quality to its fruit. Although austere, it is an impressively well-endowed, complex Riesling that should drink well for 3–4 years. Hogue always does a fine job with Semillon and Sauvignon, so it is not surprising that the 1992 Semillon reveals a big, perfumed nose, excellent ripeness, and a rich, fleshy, chewy texture with gobs of fruit. It is the ideal soulmate for some of the Pacific Northwest's wonderful salmon. Neither would I have any difficulty drinking Hogue's 1992 Fumé Blanc with the region's salmon. Crisper and lighter bodied than the Semillon, it offers an attractive, herb-and melon-scented nose, lovely ripe fruit, fine purity, and a crisp finish. Their 1992 Semillon/Chardonnay displays a big, spicy, waxy, fruity nose, rich, medium-bodied, flavors, lovely freshness, and a long aftertaste. This forceful, rich, dry wine would work well with intensely flavored fish and poultry dishes. All of these white wines should be drunk over the next 12–18 months.

As for current red wine releases, the 1992 Merlot is a fruity, exuberant, straightforward Merlot without much intensity. It offers attractive, herb, berry, and mochalike aromas and flavors. Drink it over the next 2–3 years. The medium ruby-colored 1990 Cabernet Sauvignon exhibits a straightforward, cassis-scented nose backed up by spicy wood and herbs, moderate tannin, and adequate depth. The 1990 Cabernet Sauvignon Reserve possesses more interesting aromatics, riper fruit, more richness, and slightly more tannin in the finish. It is an attractive wine that is accessible now, but promises to age well for up to a decade. The 1992 Merlot Reserve is made in a richly fruity, herb-and berry-scented style, with gobs of lush fruit, adequate acidity, and a chocolate, chewy, meaty finish. Drink it over the next 7–8 years.

Although not profound, the 1989 Cabernet Sauvignon is an up-front, ripe, tasty, round, generously endowed Cabernet for drinking over the next 3–4 years. There is fine fruit, softness, a supple texture, and an easygoing, pure finish. The 1989 Cabernet Sauvignon Reserve admirably combines elegance, power, and concentration. More deeply extracted than the regular bottling, it displays an herbal-, cassis-scented nose with attractive, subtle smoky oak notes, and a round, velvety-textured finish. Drink it over the next 5–6 years.

KIONA VINEYARDS
Cabernet Sauvignon * * *, Merlot * * *, White Riesling * * *

1990	Cabernet Sauvignon	B	85
1989	Cabernet Sauvignon	B	87
1990	Merlot	B	86
1993	White Riesling	A	86

This fine producer has turned out four attractive wines. Between the two Cabernets, the 1989 Yakima Valley Cabernet Sauvignon is more concentrated than the lighter, softer, ready-for-prime-time-drinking 1990 Washington State Cabernet. The 1989 cuvée offers a classic Cabernet nose of spicy new oak, cassis, and a subtle touch of herbs. It is long, rich, and expansive, with wonderful sweet fruit and a supple, luscious finish. Drink it over the next 7–8 years. The light-to medium-bodied, low-acid 1990 Cabernet Sauvignon exhibits excellent fruit. While delicious as well as user-friendly, it is not as concentrated or long as the 1989. The 1990 Merlot displays a lovely chocolaty, cherry-scented nose, ripe, medium-bodied flavors, low acidity, and a chewy, heady finish. Drink it over the next 4–5 years.

Kiona's 1993 White Riesling is a crisp, delicate wine with excellent fruit intensity, fine underlying acidity, and a light yet penetrating perfume that will provide broad appeal. Drink it over the next year.

LATAH CREEK WINE CELLARS
Cabernet Sauvignon * *, Cabernet Sauvignon Reserve * * *, Riesling * * *,
Sauvignon Blanc * * *

1991	Cabernet Sauvignon	C	85
1991	Cabernet Sauvignon Reserve	C	86
1993	Dry Johannisberg Riesling	A	85
1993	Sauvignon Blanc	A	85

Latah Creek's Cabernets are both big, muscular, tough wines with admirable concentration as well as plenty of cassis and herbal aromas and flavors. The 1991 regular bottling is not complex, but for the price, it is loaded with flavor, chewy fruit, and a plump, robust finish. Drink it over the next 5–7 years. The rich 1991 Cabernet Sauvignon Reserve exhibits a licorice, weedy, cassis character. This deeply colored wine is backward and tannic, but there appears to be adequate fruit behind the wall of tannin. Cellar it for 1–2 years and drink it between 1996 and 2004.

The 1993 Dry Johannisberg Riesling tastes slightly off-dry rather than totally dry. Nevertheless, it possesses a lovely floral, honeyed bouquet, rich, ripe, sweet fruit, medium body, and admirable depth and purity. Drink it over the next year. The 1993 Sauvignon Blanc displays an herbal, gunflintlike bouquet that is reminiscent of some of the lighter cuvées from Sancerre or Pouilly-Fumé. Light bodied, with crisp fruit, attractive ripeness, and a tart, zesty finish, it should be drunk over the next year.

L'ECOLE NO. 41
Cabernet Sauvignon * * *, Merlot * * *, Semillon * * * * *

1991	Cabernet Sauvignon	C	88
1990	Cabernet Sauvignon	C	87
1992	Chardonnay	C	87
1992	Merlot	C	87

1992 Semillon	B	88

1991 Semillon	B	88

If you are looking for full-throttle, intensely flavored red wines that may lack elegance and finesse, but will never cheat the consumer in terms of richness and mouth-filling levels of extract, glycerin, and alcohol, check out L'Ecole No. 41's fairly priced offerings. The 1991 Cabernet Sauvignon's lavish use of sweet oak has nicely buttressed the deep, unctuously textured, thick, full-bodied flavors that flow generously from this wine. There is admirable purity, wonderful black currant fruit, and a concentrated, fleshy style. Drink it over the next 7–8 years. The 1990 Cabernet Sauvignon is also a big, thick wine with superconcentration and superb fruit. It borders on being almost too ripe. If the wine develops more delineation and more of a structured feel, it will merit an outstanding rating. These lavishly rich, mouth-filling Cabernet Sauvignons should drink well for 7–10 years. Not surprisingly, L'Ecole No. 41's 1992 Merlot is a big, in-your-face style of wine, with lavish quantities of toasty new oak, excellent chocolaty, mocha, and black cherry flavors, a succulent texture, and a long, slightly tart finish. Drink it over the next 4–5 years for its uncomplicated, gutsy style.

Kalin Cellars in California and L'Ecole No. 41 in Washington State produce America's finest Semillons. L'Ecole No. 41's 1991 and 1992 Semillons are rich, full-bodied, lavishly endowed wines with loads of fruit and personality. The 1992 is more solidly built and tighter, but both wines display a honeyed, waxy fruitiness, fleshy, chewy textures, and loads of depth and richness. They would be superb accompaniments with rich fish dishes or poultry, but they would not make good aperitif wines given their bold personalities. Both should last for 4–5 years. This winery has also turned in a fine effort with its 1992 Chardonnay. It is an opulent, lusty-style wine with plenty of buttery fruit, a thick, juicy texture, and heady alcohol in the finish. Drink it over the next 1–2 years.

LEONETTI CELLAR
Cabernet Sauvignon* * * * *, Cabernet Sauvignon Seven Hills Vineyard* * * * *,
Merlot* * * *

1991 Cabernet Sauvignon	D	91

1990 Cabernet Sauvignon	C	92

1989 Cabernet Sauvignon Seven Hills Vineyard Reserve	D	95

1992 Merlot	C	88

1991 Merlot	C	87

1990 Select Red Table Wine	D	89

A classic, chocolaty, smoky, spicy, berry-scented Merlot, Leonetti's 1992 offers plush, rich, concentrated fruit, medium to full body, soft, sweet tannin, and a smooth, silky finish. Drink it over the next 5–7 years. Leonetti Cellars' 1991 Merlot displays more of a chocolaty, berry, smoky character than the herbaceousness it exhibited when first released. The wine is powerful and rich, with superripeness and sweetness. While not of the stature of some previous Leonetti Merlots, it is a fine wine for drinking over the next 5–6 years.

Along with Quilceda Creek and Woodward Canyon, Leonetti Cellar produces Washington State's finest Cabernet Sauvignon. Readers should try and find the 1990 Select Red Table Wine, an opaque, densely colored wine with a huge bouquet of coffee, black currants, smoke, and herbs. Rich and full bodied, it offers super concentrated, jammy fruit flavors, generous levels of supporting tannin and acidity, and a clean, robust, mouth-filling finish. While supple enough to be drunk now, it should last for 7–8 years. The 1991 Cabernet Sauvignon exhibits a bold, flamboyant bouquet of herbs, cassis, chocolate, and spicy new oak. The wine is fat, with layers of flavor, gobs of glycerin, a wonderful chewy richness that is the result of low yields, and a lush, concentrated finish. The tannin levels are unaggressive, meaning this wine can be drunk now and over the next 10–15 years. Leonetti's blockbuster 1990 Cabernet Sauvignon will benefit from 2–3 years of cellaring. It exhibits a black/purple color, and a fabulous fragrant nose of toasty new oak, cassis, and spices. Full bodied, magnificently concentrated, gracefully balanced by good acidity and ripe, gentle tannins, this expansive, brilliantly defined Cabernet is another terrific effort from this producer. Lastly, the 1989 Cabernet Sauvignon Seven Hills Vineyard may turn out to be one of the greatest Washington State Cabernet Sauvignons ever made. It should rival some of the sensational Quilceda Creek Cabernets. Leonetti Cellars' 1989 Seven Hills Vineyard Cabernet possesses an opaque purple color, and a huge nose of cassis fruit, licorice, herbs, and spicy wood. This full-bodied wine exhibits extraordinary richness and intensity, moderate tannin, and a blockbuster finish. What is so remarkable is the inner core of sweet, expansive, chewy fruit that is crammed in this wine. This lavishly rich Cabernet Sauvignon is approachable now and promises to drink well for at least 2 decades.

QUILCEDA CREEK VINTNERS
Cabernet Sauvignon * * * * *, Cabernet Sauvignon Reserve * * * * *

1990	Cabernet Sauvignon	C	90
1989	Cabernet Sauvignon	C	88+
1990	Cabernet Sauvignon Reserve	D	96
1989	Cabernet Sauvignon Reserve	D	96
1988	Cabernet Sauvignon Reserve	D	94

Make no mistake about the Quilceda Creek Cabernet Sauvignons: They are world-class Cabernets that compete with the finest wines from Bordeaux, Napa Valley, Sonoma, and the Santa Cruz Mountains. Unfortunately, there are only 1,000 cases of their regular bottling and 200 or so of their Reserve, which was inaugurated with the 1988 vintage. The wines spend 2 1/2 years in small oak casks, of which 33%–50% are new. Most of the fruit comes from the Red Mountain Vineyard.

The regular bottlings in both 1989 and 1990 are deep, rich, full-bodied wines with saturated colors and copious amounts of sweet cassis fruit intelligently married with toasty new oak. They are ripe, concentrated, graceful, and harmonious. The acid, tannin, and alcohol are well integrated in both offerings. The 1990 is slightly more open, whereas the 1989 appears more backward and in need of at least 4–5 years of cellaring. Both wines should last for 15 or more years.

The Reserves are outrageously rich, complex wines. Lamentably, with only 200 cases available (much of it gobbled up by locals), most readers will never have a chance to taste this wine. The 1988 Reserve Cabernet offers a huge nose of spicy, cedary cassis fruit, and dense, superrich, concentrated flavors with gorgeous texture, huge body, and an impeccable sense of balance. A superb Cabernet Sauvignon from start to finish, it should drink well for 20 or more years. If you get your name on the winery's mailing list you may end up with a bottle or two of either the 1989 or 1990 Reserve. The 1989 Cabernet Sauvignon Reserve is an awesome bottle of wine, with a huge nose of cedar, cassis, minerals, and vanillin. It reveals spectacular purity, great extraction of flavor, full body, and layers of fruit that come across as phenomenally well delineated and well balanced. This is a winemaking tour de force! It should last for up to 20 years. The least evolved wine of this trio, the 1990 Reserve Cabernet exhibits a huge, chocolaty-, cassis-, herb-, and mineral-scented nose and rich, full-bodied flavors judiciously touched by sweet, toasty new oak. With exceptionally well-integrated acid, elevated but sweet and ripe tannin, and a finish that lasts for almost a minute, this is another stunning example of what heights Cabernet Sauvignon can reach in Washington State.

At a tasting several years ago in Seattle, I had a chance to take another look at the 1987, 1986, and 1985 regular bottlings (the Reserve designation was not employed in those vintages). I rated the 1987 (93), the 1986 (92), and the 1985 (94). These wines, made by the Golitzin family, with, no doubt, some inspiration provided by proprietor/winemaker Alex Golitzin's late uncle, André Tchelistcheff, are extraordinary!

CHÂTEAU STE.-MICHELLE

Cabernet Sauvignon* * *, Cabernet Sauvignon Estate* * *, Chardonnay* * *, Chardonnay Cold Creek Vineyard* * *, Château Reserve Proprietary Red Wine* * * *, Merlot* * *, Merlot Indian Wells Vineyard* * * *, Riesling* *, Sauvignon Blanc* *

1992	Cabernet Sauvignon	B	86
1991	Cabernet Sauvignon	C	85
1990	Cabernet Sauvignon	C	85
1989	Cabernet Sauvignon	C	85
1991	Cabernet Sauvignon Estate	C	87+
1993	Chardonnay Barrel Fermented	B	82
1992	Château Reserve Proprietary Red Wine	C	85
1990	Château Reserve Proprietary Red Wine	D	89
1993	Chenin Blanc	A	85
1993	Gewürztraminer	A	80
1993	Johannisberg Riesling	A	85
1992	Merlot	B	86
1990	Merlot	C	85
1989	Merlot	C	86
1992	Merlot Indian Wells Vineyard	C	90
1991	Merlot Indian Wells Vineyard	C	89
1993	Sauvignon Blanc	A	86
1993	Semillon	A	85

Château Ste.-Michelle has three levels of wine quality. The least expensive offerings (often the best bargains) are their bevy of white wines made from such grapes as Johannisberg Riesling, Sauvignon, Semillon, Gewürztraminer, and Chenin Blanc. Among the newest releases, the 1993 Johannisberg Riesling is a dry, crisp, refreshing wine that will work as an aperitif wine or as an accompaniment with light dishes. The 1993 Sauvignon Blanc exhibits a flinty-, spicy-, herb-scented nose, light to medium body, and fine fruit and freshness. It is capable of lasting several years. The 1993 Semillon is a clean, waxy/lemony example of this varietal. This vintage reveals a touch of oak as well as more fruit than usual.

Château Ste.-Michelle's Gewürztraminers have been largely mediocre, but from time to time this property does a fine job with Chenin Blanc. The 1993 displays a flowery-scented nose, off-dry flavors, and a crisp finish. Drink it over the next 1–2 years.

Château Ste.-Michelle's second level of wines include their Chardonnays, Merlots, and Cabernet Sauvignons. These wines are generally made from purchased fruit and tend to be priced in the $12–$15 range. Although they never hit the highest notes, they are competent, correct wines with good varietal character and easygoing personalities. Of the current examples, the pleasant, charming, fruity 1993 Chardonnay Barrel Fermented is easy to understand and consume. It should be drunk over the next several years. The 1992 Merlot exhibits straightforward, berry fruit, a subtle personality, and a crisp finish. The 1992 Cabernet Sauvignon is deeper, with more noticeable tannin, and has an attractive nose of red currants and spicy oak. Both the 1992 Merlot and 1992 Cabernet Sauvignon should drink well for 4–6 years.

At the third level are Château Ste.-Michelle Reserve offerings. These include the Château Reserve Proprietary Red Wine, the single-vineyard Chardonnay from the Cold Creek Vineyard, and the Indian Wells Vineyard Merlot. The property's flagship wines, they have become so popular that they are difficult to find, even though most of them sell for over $20 a bottle. The most recent red wine releases include the deep, rich, generous 1991 Merlot Indian Wells Vineyard, a structured, but intensely concentrated wine that should drink well for 10–15 years. The 1992 Indian Wells Merlot is even more impressive, with greater depth, as well as plenty of structure to accompany its rich, meaty, mocha/black cherry/chocolaty flavors. This beautifully made wine admirably demonstrates what heights Merlot can reach in Washington State. The 1991 Cabernet Sauvignon Estate is an impressively rich, medium- to full-bodied wine with plenty of oak, good acidity, and moderate tannin in the finish. It will benefit from another 1–2 years of cellaring.

Older releases that remain in the marketplace include the following wines. The 1991, 1990, and 1989 Cabernet Sauvignons are all competently made, correct, above-average-quality wines. All three vintages exhibit fine color and ripeness, medium body, crisp, tart acidity, and compact personalities. If this winery could get their acidity level lower, the wines would possess more interesting textures and an even broader appeal. Nevertheless, they are cleanly made Cabernet Sauvignons for drinking in their first 5–6 years of life. Where well stored, they may last even longer.

The soft 1990 Merlot offers chocolaty, berry, herbaceous fruit, a velvety texture, and a spicy finish. Drink it over the next 4–6 years. I found the 1990 Château Reserve to be a dead ringer for a classic Médoc. It reveals an elegant, understated, complex, cedary-, cassis-, and vanillin-scented bouquet, admirable depth of fruit, an attractive layered texture, and a wonderful marriage of richness and finesse. It should drink well for at least 10–12 years. The 1989 Merlot offers a moderately scented, black cherry, spicy, oaky nose, and rich, ripe, medium- to full-bodied, expansive, velvety-textured, long flavors. Drink it over the next 5–7 years.

DOMAINE STE.-MICHELLE
Sparkling Wines * * *

N.V. **Blanc de Blancs Brut Sparkling**	A	85
N.V. **Brut Sparkling**	A	86
N.V. **Champagne Brut**	A	85

The huge Washington State winery of Château Ste.-Michelle produces their sparkling wines under the Domaine Ste.-Michelle label. These three sparklers are fine bargains. The wines are clean, with crisp, zesty fruit, good effervescence, and light-bodied, fruity finishes. The Blanc de Blancs tastes more delicate than the slightly fuller Champagne Brut. The Brut Sparkling displays attractive small uniform bubbles, good effervescence, a clean, apple-and-Wheat Thin-scented nose, light-bodied flavors, and fine freshness and fruit. It should drink well for 1–2 years.

SNOQUALMIE WINERY
Cabernet Sauvignon * *

1992 Cabernet Sauvignon	B	87

This impressive wine exhibits a fine deep ruby/purple color, a ripe, spicy, attractive bouquet, long, rich, medium-to full-bodied flavors, and a tart but attractive finish. Drink it over the next 5–7 years.

ANDREW WILL CELLARS
Cabernet Sauvignon * * * *, Chenin Blanc * * */* * * *, Merlot * * * *

1992 Cabernet Sauvignon	C	86?
1991 Cabernet Sauvignon	C	88
1990 Cabernet Sauvignon	C	89
1991 Cabernet Sauvignon Reserve	C	90
1993 Chenin Blanc Lulu	B	89
1992 Merlot	C	89
1990 Merlot Ciel du Cheval	C	88
1989 Merlot Ciel du Cheval	C	88
1991 Merlot Sunshine	C	87

Andrew Will is an up-and-coming Washington State star, and these wines deserve to be discovered by all who appreciate complex, rich, exceptionally well-made wine. There is a bevy of top choices from this quality producer. The 1993 Chenin Blanc Lulu is a citrusy, slightly austere, mineral-flavored wine with excellent acidity, a wonderful inner core of fruit and freshness, and a dry, crisp, vibrant finish. It should drink well for several years.

The Merlots all exhibit deep colors and concentrated, supple styles, with fine depth and richness. The 1992 Merlot offers a deep ruby color, good acidity, a chocolaty-, mocha-, berry-scented nose and flavors, and an intense, medium- to full-bodied finish. The 1991 Merlot Sunshine is spicy, round, long, and generous. While drinkable, it will last for another 7–8 years. The 1990 Merlot Ciel du Cheval reveals a stemmy, herbaceous note in its bouquet that complements rather than interferes with the copious quantities of black cherry and plumlike fruit. This dense, rich, medium- to full-bodied, impressive wine possesses loads of depth and a long finish. Drink it over the next decade. The 1989 Merlot Ciel du Cheval is also top notch. Big, rich, full bodied, dense, and chewy, it is the most muscular and concentrated of these three Merlots. Although it still has some tannin to resolve, it is exhibiting a chocolaty, coffee, black fruit character. It should drink well for at least a decade.

Will generally does not miss a step with his Cabernet Sauvignons. The 1992 Cabernet Sauvignon is an oaky, rich wine, although somewhat coarse and disjointed, with plenty of depth, but not much balance or harmony at present. Hopefully, several years of cellaring will bring its component parts into better focus. The 1991 Cabernet Sauvignon displays a big, spicy, herbaceous, cassis-scented nose, excellent purity, rich, medium- to full-bodied flavors, a sense of grace and elegance, and moderate tannin in the long finish. Approachable now, this wine will be even better in 2–3 years; it will last for 10 or more years. The outstanding 1991 Cabernet Sauvignon Reserve is richer and fuller, with more fruit and more noticeable new oak, as well as additional structure. An impressive, full-bodied, concentrated wine, it possesses well-integrated acidity, gobs of cassis fruit, and a long finish. Drink it between now and 2005. The dense, rich 1990 Cabernet Sauvignon offers aromas of cedar, chocolate, and black currants, concentrated, full-bodied flavors, and a long finish with well-integrated acidity and sweet tannin. Drink it over the next 10–12 years. These are impressive wines from a winery that has not yet been discovered.

WOODWARD CANYON

Cabernet Sauvignon* * * *, Cabernet Sauvignon Canoe Ridge Vineyard* * * *, Charbonneau Proprietary Red Wine* * * */* * * * *, Charbonneau Proprietary White Wine* * * *, Chardonnay Columbia Valley* * * *, Chardonnay Reserve* * * * *, Chardonnay Roza Berge Vineyard* * * * *

1992 Cabernet Sauvignon Canoe Ridge Vineyard	C	89
1992 Cabernet Sauvignon Columbia Valley	D	84
1993 Chardonnay Columbia Valley	C	90
1992 Chardonnay Columbia Valley	C	87
1993 Chardonnay Reserve	D	91
1992 Chardonnay Reserve	C	89+
1992 Chardonnay Roza Berge Vineyard	C	89

This superb Washington State winery continues to turn out fine Chardonnays. The 1993 Chardonnay Columbia Valley exhibits a burgundian-like nose of honeyed fruit and lees, rich, expansive, chewy flavors, wonderful definition, and an opulent, richly fruity, full-bodied finish. It is a gorgeous Chardonnay for drinking over the next several years. The 1993 Chardonnay Reserve reveals a spicier nose, as well as additional evidence of toasty new oak. With good integrated acidity, this full-bodied wine appears less ostentatious and less delicious than the regular offering. Perhaps its additional structure and wood element have given it more restraint.

The 1992 Columbia Valley Chardonnay offers a lovely concoction of butterscotch, apples, and subtle oak in its bouquet and flavors. This tasty, medium-bodied wine exhibits admirable acidity and a moderately long finish. Drink it over the next year. Although the 1992 Chardonnay Roza Berge Vineyard is initially closed, it blossoms in the glass. Rich and dense, with highly extracted flavors, well-integrated acidity, and excellent length, this buttery, ripe, elegant Chardonnay should drink well for 2–3 years. The most tightly knit wine, as well as potentially the best, is the 1992 Chardonnay Reserve. It possesses higher acidity and is more restrained in both its aromatic and flavor profile, but there is no doubting its authoritative richness and depth. Given its expansive, full-bodied, lingering flavors, it will benefit from 4–5 months of cellaring and keep for 4–5 years.

Woodward Canyon's red wines have become lighter over recent years, as if proprietor Rick Small is searching for greater elegance and accessibility. In the past there have been some exceptionally rich Cabernets, along with proprietary white and red wines called Charbonneau. The two newest Cabernet Sauvignon releases include a medium ruby-colored 1992 Columbia Valley Cabernet Sauvignon that possesses over 20% Merlot in the blend. It is a velvety, elegant, herbaceous, woody wine that does not reveal the intensity or purity of fruit necessary to merit a higher score. It is also acidic in the finish and appeared less interesting each time I tasted it. The 1992 Cabernet Sauvignon Canoe Ridge exhibits a medium to dark ruby color, an attractive, oaky, black cherry– and raspberry-scented nose, silky, round, generous flavors, and a smoky, spicy finish. Already delicious, it is a surprisingly accessible, easygoing Cabernet for drinking over the next 5–6 years.

THE BEST OF THE REST

Australia
New Zealand
Argentina
Chile
Greece
Hungary
Israel
Lebanon
Switzerland

9. AUSTRALIA

You name it and the Australians no doubt grow it, make it into wine, blend it with something else, and give it an odd bin number. Australian wines have been hot for 3 years, and not just in America. The combination of quality and value that many of them offer is the hottest thing in town from London to New York. Australia, like California in America, and Alsace in France, labels its wine after the grape (or grapes) that it is made from. All the major grape varietals are used here, and amazingly, great wines are turned out from all the varietals. The major viticultural districts (listed alphabetically) are:

Adelaide Hills (South Australia)   Located in southern Australia, this is a high-altitude, cooler-climate region. Petaluma is its most famous winery. Mountadam makes Australia's finest Chardonnay from vineyards in the Adelaide Hills.

Barossa Valley (South Australia)   In southern Australia, this huge, well-known viticultural area north of Adelaide is the home of some of the titans of Australia's wine industry (i.e., Penfolds, Henschke, Tollana, Seppelt, Wolf Blass, Orlando, and Hill Smith).

Bendigo (Victoria)   Bendigo is an up-and-coming area, although it has a long history as a wine-producing region. Balgownie is the finest winery there.

Central Victoria (Victoria)   The traditionally styled wines of Château Tahbilk are the best that come from Central Victoria and the Goulburn Valley. The wines are powerful, full bodied, and fruity from this area.

Clare Valley (South Australia)   Located north of Adelaide and the Barossa Valley, this area is known for its white rather than red wines.

Coonawarra (South Australia)   Coonawarra is perhaps the most famous, and according to some, the best red-wine-growing area of Australia. Situated in south Australia, west of the Goulburn Valley, top wineries such as Lindemans (their Limestone Ridge and St. George Vineyards are there), Petaluma, Penfolds, Rosemount, Orlando, Reynella, and Mildara pull their grapes from Coonawarra. The two best wineries actually located in Coonawarra are the Bowen Estate and Hollick.

Geelong (Victoria)   Southwest of Melbourne near the coast is the small area of Geelong. The most renowned wineries are Anakie and Bannockburn, but everyone is talking about the potential of Hickinbotham's Anakie, a winery of high quality.

Glenrowan (Victoria)   Located in northeastern Victoria, this hot area is famous for its inky, rich, chewy red wines, especially the full-throttle Shiraz from one of Australia's historic producers, Bailey's. A more commercial Cabernet and Shiraz is made by Wynns. At nearby Milawa, Brown Brothers, one of the most successful high-quality Australian wineries, makes its home.

SOUTH
AUSTRALIA

NEW

DARLING

•Lilydale

Clare
Watervale
Auburn
Waikerie   •Renmark
BAROSSA VALLEY   •Nuriootpa   •Berri
Angaston
Tanunda
Adelaide
McLaren   SOUTHERN
Vale   VALES
Langhorne
Creek

•Buronga
Mildura

MURRAY

V   I

C

T

Echuca•

Bendigo•
GOULBURN
VALLEY

•Coonawarra   •Great Western

HOPKINS

Melbourn

Geelong•

Australia

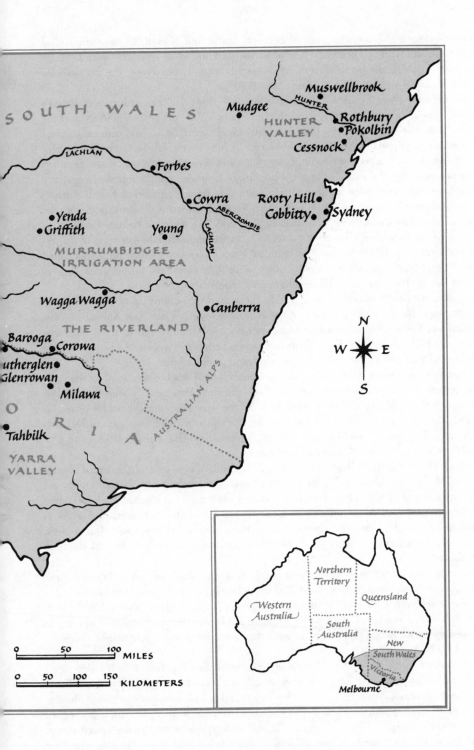

SOUTH WALES

Muswellbrook
Mudgee
HUNTER
HUNTER VALLEY
Rothbury
Pokolbin
Cessnock

LACHLAN
Forbes

Cowra
Rooty Hill
ABERCROMBIE
Cobbitty
Sydney

Yenda
Griffith
Young
LACHLAN
MURRUMBIDGEE IRRIGATION AREA

Wagga Wagga
Canberra

THE RIVERLAND

Barooga
Corowa
utherglen
Glenrowan
AUSTRALIAN ALPS
Milawa

O
R
I
A

Tahbilk

YARRA VALLEY

N
W   E
S

0   50   100   MILES

0   50   100   150   KILOMETERS

Western Australia

Northern Territory

Queensland

South Australia

New South Wales

Victoria

Melbourne

Great Western (Victoria) Situated between Ararat and Stawell, to the northwest of Melbourne and Geelong, is an area known for its sparkling wines (primarily from the huge producer Seppelt), and for its smooth, fat, low-acid, but tasty red wines. The top red-wine producers are Mount Langi Ghiran and Cathcart Ridge.

Hunter Valley (New South Wales) Less than a 3-hour drive from Sydney is Australia's famed Hunter Valley. It is to Sydney what the Napa Valley is to San Francisco and the Médoc is to Bordeaux—a major tourist attraction and source for some of Australia's most desired wines. Originally this area was known for its rich, exotic, full-bodied red wines from the Shiraz and Cabernet Sauvignon grapes, but more recently Chardonnay and Semillon have proven successful as well. No doubt because of their size and the intense competitive spirit here, this area's wineries are well represented in the export market. Familiar names from the Hunter Valley include Tyrell, Rothbury Estate, Lindemans, Rosemount, Saxonvale, Lake's Folly, Arrowfield, Hungerford Hill, Brokenwood, Evans, and Wyndham Estate.

Lower Great Southern (Western Australia) In the remote southwestern tip of Australia, approximately 150 miles south of Perth, is a vast, burgeoning viticultural area called Lower Great Southern. Apple orchards thrive more than vineyards, but wineries such as Mount Barker, Redmond, and Alkoomi have good reputations.

Margaret River (Western Australia) In the very southwestern tip of this country is the Margaret River viticultural zone. Australian wine experts claim that Australia's most French-like Cabernet Sauvignons and Chardonnays come from this area, which produces wines with higher natural acidities. There are some superb producers located here, including the likes of Vasse Felix, Moss Wood, Leeuwin Estate, and Cullens.

McLaren Vale (South Australia) The traditional fare of this hot area south of Adelaide was high-alcohol Grenache wines that were thick and rich. This has all changed in the last 10 years with the advent of cold fermentations and the perception that the public yearns for lighter, fruitier wines. Some of the greats of the Australian wine business are in McLaren Vale, including Hardy's and its higher-quality sibling, Reynella. Smaller wineries of note are Wirra Wirra, Woodstock, and Kay Brothers.

Mudgee (New South Wales) Located in New South Wales west of the famed Hunter Valley, Mudgee (an aboriginal name meaning "nest in the hills") with its cool nights and hot days has proven not only to be a top-notch red wine area, but also an excellent source for tropical fruit-scented, luxuriously rich Chardonnays. For whatever reason, the wines of Mudgee also tend to be less expensive than those from other top areas. One winery, Montrose, dominates the quality scene; two other fine producers are Miramar and Huntington Estate.

Murrumbridge Irrigation Area (New South Wales) This area, which has to be irrigated, is in New South Wales about 250 miles due west of Sydney. The region has a mediocre reputation for quality wines that appears justified given what I have tasted, although several producers, such as McWilliams and De Bortoli, have managed to turn out interesting wines. When the wines are good they are a bargain, as prices from this area, called the MIA, are inexpensive.

Padthaway (South Australia) This southern Australian viticultural area has developed a strong following for its white wines, especially the Chardonnay and Sauvignon Blanc. Padthaway is one of Australia's newest "hot" areas and two of Australia's largest producers, Lindemans and Seppelt, have shown just how tasty the white wines can be from this region.

Pyrenees (Victoria) The attractive, rolling-hill countryside of the Pyrenees, northwest of Melbourne, forms a triangle between Redbank, Moonambel, and Avoca. The top wines are the reds from the Cabernet Sauvignon and Shiraz grapes. The best white wines are from the Sauvignon grape. Wineries of note include Redbank, Taltarni, Mount Avoca, and Château Remy.

Riverland (South Australia) Located in South Australia, Riverland is to Australia what the San Joaquin Valley is to California. This vast source of grapes of mediocre quality is dominated by huge cooperatives and producers who turn out Australia's jug wines and bag-in-the-box generic wines. Some big enterprises have their jug wine business centered here, including Penfolds, Kaiserstuhl, Angove, Berri, and Renmano. While most of the wines from this area are decidedly insipid, some good-value, fresh whites at bargain-basement prices can be found.

Rutherglen (Victoria)   Rutherglen is synonymous with Australia's fortified sweet wines, many of which are extraordinary. The famous sweet, nectarlike, ageless Ports and fortified Muscats and Tokays of William Chambers, Campbells, and Seppelt are made from Rutherglen grapes.

Swan Valley (Western Australia)   This hot, arid area in Western Australia, just north-east of the coastal city of Perth, produces large-framed, muscular red wines and increasingly better white wines. Houghton is the area's most famous winery, but good wines are made by Evans and Tate, as well as Moondah Brook.

Yarra Valley (Victoria)   This is the viticultural area most in fashion in Australia, and its proponents argue that the climate and resulting wines come closest in spirit to those of Bordeaux and Burgundy in France. I am not convinced. Located in Victoria, this is a cool-climate area outside Melbourne, and every major red and white glamour varietal is planted, from Cabernet Sauvignon, Merlot, and Pinot Noir to Chardonnay, Riesling, and Gewürztraminer. The best wineries are Lillydale, Yarra Yering, Coldstream Hills, and St. Huberts.

GRAPE VARIETIES

Red Wines

Cabernet Sauvignon   This varietal excels in Australia and generally produces a very fruity, often jammy, intensely curranty, fat wine, sometimes low in acidity, but round, generous, and surprisingly age-worthy in spite of an acid deficiency.

Pinot Noir   There are those who claim to have made successful wines from this infinitely fickle varietal, but the great majority of Australian Pinot Noirs to date have either been raisiny, unusual, often repugnant, or watery, pale, and innocuous. Two wineries that are likely candidates to produce fine Pinot Noir are Tarra Warra and Coldstream Hills. Except for these two producers, anyone who suggests Australia is making good Pinot Noir does not have the consumer's best interests at heart.

Shiraz   Despite the Aussies' present-day infatuation with Cabernet Sauvignon, Merlot, and Pinot Noir, this is the grape that makes their greatest wines. The problem is that there is an enormous amount of it, and only a handful of producers treat Shiraz (Syrah) with the respect and care that is accorded Cabernet. It can produce Australia's greatest red wine when left to stand on its own, as Penfolds Grange Hermitage convincingly proves, or it can offer more dimension and character to a red wine when blended with Cabernet Sauvignon, as Penfolds and Petaluma have proven time and time again.

White Wines

Chardonnay   The shrewd Aussies, taking full advantage of the wine consumer's thirst for Chardonnay wines, have consistently offered plump, fat wines filled with the flavors of apples, pears, oranges, and ripe melons. Although the wines still tend to be overoaked, or worse, artificially oaked, more and more Australian Chardonnays are fresh and exuberant, and bottled early to preserve their youthful grapy qualities. With the advent of centrifuges and micropore filters, many Chardonnays have no bouquet or flavor. The one major disap-

PARKER'S WINE BUYER'S GUIDE

pointment is the aging potential of these naturally low-acid wines, but most consumers are drinking them within several months of purchase, so this is probably a moot issue.

Gewürztraminer   Contrary to the local salespeople, who hype the quality of Gewürztraminer, this grape produces insipid, pale, watery wines that are a far cry from what Gewürztraminer does in France.

Marsanne   Château Tahbilk and Michelton are proponents of this grape, which tends to turn out one-dimensional, bland wines.

Muscat   This hot-climate grape excels in Australia and is at its best in the decadently rich, sweet, fortified Muscats that can age for decades. It is also made into a medium-sweet table wine with which Brown Brothers does a particularly admirable job.

Riesling   Australia has proven to be the new world's best alternative to German-made Rieslings. This grape has done extremely well with Kabinett and Spatlese-style drier Rieslings in the Barossa Valley and Adelaide Hills. Wineries such as Petaluma, Pewsey Vale, Rosemount, and Hill Smith have turned out some spectacular Beerenauslese and Trockenbeerenauslese-style sweet wines. Overall, this grape gets good marks from me in Australia.

Sauvignon Blanc   The results have been mixed, as the hot climate causes this grape to overripen and to take on a grotesque, vegetal, oily, thick fruitiness. There are some fresh, tasty, dry Sauvignons coming from Australia, but for now, New Zealand consistently beats Australia when it comes to quality Sauvignon-based wines.

Semillon   Semillon can be delicious, whether it is blended with Chardonnay or Sauvignon, or allowed to stand by itself. It produces big, creamy, rich wines loaded with flavor. Wineries such as Rothbury, Rosemount, Montrose, Peter Lehmann, Henschke, and Evans and Tate have done better with Semillon than anyone. Some great sweet wines have been made from Semillon affected by the botrytis fungus. Look for those from Rothbury, Rosemount, and Peter Lehmann, which are world class.

FLAVORS

Red Wines

Cabernet Sauvignon   These wines can be very ripe, often overripe, with sweet, intense black currant flavors, supple, fat textures, and oodles of fruit. When poorly made or overly acidified, the wines are musty, dirty, and tart.

Pinot Noir   Raisiny, pruny fruit flavors with no finesse or complexity represent appallingly bad examples of Pinot Noir.

Shiraz   Intense aromas of cassis, leather, licorice, cedar, tar, and pepper are found in wines that have a healthy dosage of Shiraz. Quite full bodied and rich, with softer tannins than Cabernet Sauvignon, these wines are drinkable young, but frequently age better than the more glamorous Cabernet Sauvignons.

White Wines

Chardonnay   Tropical fruit flavors predominate in this creamy-textured, voluptuous wine. Oak is sometimes too noticeable, but better-balanced wines with the fruit in the forefront have been the rule in recent vintages.

Gewürztraminer   Where's the spice and exotic lychee nut character found in the great Gewürztraminers of Alsace? These are generally watery, thin wines that are usually disappointing.

Marsanne   Marsanne can be described as usually neutral, or as Jancis Robinson says, "reminiscent of glue." It usually tastes much better old than young, but because it tastes so uninteresting young, no one ages it.

Muscat   Huge aromas of brown sugar, fruitcake, crème brûlée, buttered and baked apricots, and oranges with honey and nuts give this varietal its appeal.

Riesling   The classic Riesling aromas of spring flowers, green apples, and wet stones are present in the drier versions of this wine. As the wines get sweeter, aromas and flavors of oranges, peaches, apricots, butter, baked apples, and honeyed nuts arise.

Sauvignon Blanc   Unfortunately, these wines seem to either be feeble, bland, and tasteless, or oily, vegetal, and grotesque.

Semillon   In the drier versions, lemon-lime aromas intertwined with honey and toasty oak are often the most interesting. With the sweet versions, buttery nuts and honey-coated raisin flavors take over.

AGING POTENTIAL

Cabernet Sauvignon:
   5–10 years
Pinot Noir: 4–6 years
Shiraz: 5–20 years
Chardonnay: 1–2 years
Gewürztraminer: 1–2 years
Marsanne: 4–12 years

Muscat (Dry): 1–3 years
   (Fortified): 5–50+ years
Riesling (Dry): 1–4 years
   (Sweet): 4–10 years
Sauvignon Blanc: 1–3 years
Semillon (Dry): 2–8 years
   (Sweet): 4–12 years

OVERALL QUALITY LEVEL

At the top level, wines such as the Penfolds Grange Hermitage or Bin 707 Cabernet Sauvignon are as fine as any red wine made in the world. Unfortunately, there are too few of them in Australia. Australia's overall wine quality is barely average, with oceans of mediocre and poorly made wines. There are, however, plenty of good, agreeable wines at attractive prices, and therein lies the reason for the success of Australia's wines. Australia is among the leaders in offering tasty, user-friendly wines at low prices. In that area, Australian wines have very little competition.

MOST IMPORTANT INFORMATION TO KNOW

Given the remarkable diversity, the best thing for a consumer to do is to memorize the names of some of the better producers, and restrict your initial purchases to the surefire successes from that particular winery—usually Chardonnay, Cabernet, and Shiraz. Use the producers' chart for each varietal as a guideline until you have decided which wines and producers you prefer.

1995–1996 BUYING STRATEGY

For 99% of Australia's wines, buy only what you intend to drink over the next year. Except for a few red wines, the open-knit, plump, overtly fruity, low-acid style of Australian wines is ideal for consuming immediately, but their aging potential is nonexistent. For white wines, restrict your buying to 1995 and 1994. For inexpensive red wines, you can safely buy any vintage back to 1986 without worrying about the wine's senility. Furthermore, keep in mind that Australia does indeed produce sensational, world-class, late-harvest and fortified wines at a fraction of the price one has to pay for a German Beerenauslese or Trockenbeerenauslese, a French Sauternes, or vintage or tawny port. These wines, often absurdly low-priced, are well worth seeking out.

VINTAGE GUIDE

As in California, constant sunny weather virtually guarantees at least good-quality wines in Australia, but each year is different as a result of drought, heat or cold waves, and hail. However, the extremes in quality that one often sees in Europe do not exist in Australia.

1994—A very fine vintage has been reported throughout Australia. The red wines in particular are reputed to be rich and powerful.

1993—A good to very good vintage with high quality possible, but an abundant crop size in most regions will contribute to irregularity.

1992—A cooler than normal year in most of Australia's wine-producing regions has resulted in a significant range in quality. Overall, 1992 should turn out to be an above-average-quality year.

1991—An irregular yet promising vintage, particularly for the red wine.

1990—This year has all the characteristics of a top-flight vintage, possibly the finest for Australia's red wines since 1986.

1989—A large, high-quality crop was reported throughout Australia.

1988—Early reports indicate a terrific year for red wines. It was a mixed bag for the whites, which should have been drunk up years ago.

1987—An exceptionally cool and late year all over Australia, the crop size was down, but the quality is considered to be very good to exceptional.

1986—The crop size varied from average to well above average, but the quality is very good to excellent in all major districts. Many producers rate 1986 and 1987 the two best back-to-back years of the decade for red wines.

1985—The second of four straight cool years, the 1985 vintage is highly regarded for its Cabernet Sauvignons. Overall, a good red wine vintage, particularly in New South Wales, but it is far from a great vintage, as most producers prefer 1987, 1986, and 1983 to 1985, although in the Great Southern region growers felt it was a top-notch vintage. It was a cool, very dry year.

1984—A huge crop everywhere translated into lighter, less concentrated wines. In particular, the Hunter Valley suffered because of excessive rainfall.

1983—An exceptionally hot, dry year resulted in some full-blown, now senile, white wines, and some rich, intense, outstanding red wines, especially in the Hunter Valley, But overall this vintage looks to be the worst of this decade for quality.

1982—A large crop of good wines was produced. No one has called it great, and the successes would appear to be mostly in Southern Australia.

RATING AUSTRALIA'S BEST PRODUCERS OF
CABERNET SAUVIGNON AND SHIRAZ

* * * * * (OUTSTANDING)

Henschke Shiraz Hill of Grace (Barossa)

Henschke Shiraz Mount Edelstone (Barossa)

Peter Lehmann Stonewell Shiraz (Barossa)

Parker Estate Cabernet Sauvignon Terra Rossa First Growth (Coonawarra)

Penfolds Cabernet Sauvignon Bin 707 (South Australia)

Penfolds Shiraz Grange Hermitage (South Australia)

* * * * (EXCELLENT)

Bowen Estate Cabernet Sauvignon (South Australia)

Coriole Redstone Cabernet Sauvignon (McLaren Vale)

Huntington Estate Cabernet Sauvignon Bin FB (Mudgee)

Lillydale Cabernet Sauvignon (Yarra Valley)

Lindemans Shiraz/Cabernet Limestone Ridge (New South Wales)

Lindemans Pyrus Proprietary Red Wine (New South Wales)

Lindemans Cabernet Sauvignon St. George (New South Wales)

Oak Ridge Estate Cabernet Sauvignon (Yarra Valley)

Orlando Cabernet Sauvignon Jacaranda Ridge Coonawarra (South Australia)

Penfolds Shiraz Bin 128 (South Australia)

Penfolds Shiraz/Cabernet Koonunga Hill (South Australia)

Penfolds Shiraz Magill Estate (South Australia)

Penley Estate Cabernet Sauvignon

Petaluma Cabernet Sauvignon Coonawarra (South Australia)

Redbank Cabernet Sauvignon Long Paddock (Victoria)

Redbank Sally's Paddock (Victoria)

Rothbury Estate Shiraz (Hunter Valley)

St. Hurbert's Cabernet Sauvignon (Yarra Valley)

Château Tahbilk Cabernet Sauvignon (Goulburn)

Château Tahbilk Shiraz (Goulburn)

Thistle Hill Cabernet Sauvignon (Goulburn)

Château Tahbilk Shiraz (Goulburn)

Thistle Hill Cabernet Sauvignon (Mudgee)

Virgin Hills Cabernet Sauvignon (Victoria)

Wolf Blass Cabernet Sauvignon President's Selection Black Label (Victoria)

Wolf Blass Cabernet Sauvignon Yellow Label (Victoria)

Wynns Cabernet Sauvignon John Riddoch (Coonawarra)

Yarra Yering Cabernet Sauvignon Dry Red #1 (Yarra Valley)

Yarra Yering Shiraz Dry Red #2 (Yarra Valley)

* * * (GOOD)

Alkoomie Cabernet Sauvignon (Western Australia)

Ashbrook Estate Cabernet Sauvignon (Western Australia)

Bailey's Cabernet Sauvignon (Glenrowan)

Balgownie Cabernet Sauvignon (Bendigo)

Brand's Laira Cabernet Sauvignon (Coonawarra)

Brokenwood Cabernet Sauvignon (New South Wales)

Brown Bros. Cabernet Sauvignon (Victoria)

Capel Vale Cabernet Sauvignon (Western Australia)

Cullens Cabernet Sauvignon (Margaret River)

Fern Hill Cabernet Sauvignon (McLaren)

Hickinbotham Cabernet Sauvignon (Geelong)

Hungerford Hill Cabernet Sauvignon (Hunter Valley)

Tim Knappstein Cabernet Sauvignon (Clare Valley)

Peter Lehmann Cabernet Sauvignon (Barossa)

Peter Lehmann Shiraz (Barossa)

Leeuwin Estate Cabernet Sauvignon (Margaret River)

Lindemans Cabernet Sauvignon (Coonawarra)

Goeff Merrill Cabernet Sauvignon (South Australia)

Mildara Cabernet Sauvignon (Coonawarra)

Montrose Cabernet Sauvignon (Mudgee)

Moss Wood Cabernet Sauvignon (Margaret River)

Mount Langi Ghiran Shiraz (Victoria)

Orlando RF Cabernet Sauvignon (South Australia)

Redman Cabernet Sauvignon (Coonawarra)

Rosemount Cabernet Sauvignon Show Reserve (Coonawarra)

Saxonvale Cabernet Sauvignon (Hunter Valley)

Seppelt Cabernet Sauvignon (Barossa)

Seville Estate Cabernet Sauvignon (Victoria)

Taltarni Cabernet Sauvignon (Victoria)

Taltarni Shiraz (Victoria)

Vasse Felix Cabernet Sauvignon (Western Australia)

Wright's Cabernet Sauvignon (Western Australia)

Wyndham Estates Cabernet Sauvignon (South Australia)

Wyndham Estates Shiraz (South Australia)

RATING AUSTRALIA'S BEST PRODUCERS OF CHARDONNAY

*****(OUTSTANDING)*

None

****(EXCELLENT)*

Bannockburn (Geelong)
Clyde Park (Geelong)
Leeuwin Artists Series (Margaret River)
Mooroodug Estate (Mornington Peninsula)
Mountadam (Adelaide Hills)

Rosemount Roxburgh (Hunter Valley)
Rosemount Show Reserve (Coonawarra)
Rothbury Estate Broken Back Vineyard (Hunter Valley)

*** (GOOD)*

Cassegrain (New South Wales)
Cold Stream Hills (Yarra Valley)
Craigmoor (Mudgee)
Cullens (Margaret River)
Hungerford Hill (Hunter Valley)
Katnook Estate (Coonawarra)
Krondorf (Barossa)
Lake's Folly (New South Wales)
Lindemans Bin 65 (New South Wales)
Michelton (Goulburn)
Miramar (Mudgee)
Moss Wood (Western Australia)
Orlando RF (South Australia)

Penley Estate (Coonawarra)
Petaluma (South Australia)
Reynella (Southern Vales)
Rothbury Estate Broken Back Vineyard Reserve (Hunter Valley)
Seppelt (Barossa)
Mark Swann (South Australia)
Tarra Warra (Victoria)
Tyrells Vat 47 (New South Wales)
Wynn's (Coonawarra)
Yarra Yering (Yarra Valley)
Yeringsberg (Yarra Valley)

** (AVERAGE)*

Balgownie (Victoria)
Brown Brothers (Victoria)
Capel Vale (Western Australia)
Cold Stream Hills Four Vineyards (Yarra Valley)

Cold Stream Hills Lillydale (Yarra Valley)
Mildara (Coonawarra)
Orlando (South Australia)

RATING AUSTRALIA'S BEST PRODUCERS OF DRY SAUVIGNON BLANC AND SEMILLON

*****(OUTSTANDING)*

None

****(EXCELLENT)*

Henschke (Barossa)

Rothbury Estate (Hunter Valley)

*** (GOOD)

Berri Estates (South Australia)   Peter Lehmann (Barossa)
Evans and Tate (Margaret River)   Lindemans (Padthaway)
Tim Knappstein (Clare Valley)   Mildara (Coonawarra)
Krondorf (Barossa)   Rosemount (Hunter Valley)

RATING AUSTRALIA'S BEST PRODUCERS OF SWEET SAUVIGNON BLANC AND SEMILLON

***** (OUTSTANDING)

Peter Lehmann (Barossa)   Rothbury Estate (Hunter Valley)
Rosemount (Hunter Valley)

RATING AUSTRALIA'S BEST PRODUCERS OF FORTIFIED WINES

***** (OUTSTANDING)

Wm. Chambers Rosewood Tokay and   Seppelt Para Port
    Muscat   Seppelt Show Wines
Morris Muscat and Tokay Liquor   Yalumba Port

AUSTRALIA'S GREATEST WINE BARGAINS FOR LESS THAN $10

Berry Estates Semillon
Brown Brothers Cabernet Sauvignon
Brown Brothers Chardonnay King Valley
Brown Brothers Muscat Lexia
Coldridge Chardonnay
Coldridge Semillon/Chardonnay
Peter Lehmann Cabernet Sauvignon
Peter Lehmann Shiraz
Lindemans Chardonnay Bin 65
Michelton Semillon/Chardonnay
Montrose Cabernet Sauvignon
Montrose Chardonnay
Montrose Shiraz
Orlando Cabernet Sauvignon Jacob's Creek
Orlando Chardonnay Jacob's Creek
Orlando Sauvignon Blanc Jacob's Creek
Oxford Landing Cabernet Sauvignon
Oxford Landing Chardonnay
Penfolds Cabernet/Shiraz Koonunga Hill
Penfolds Chardonnay
Roo's Leap Chardonnay
Roo's Leap Fumé Blanc
Rosemount Cabernet Sauvignon/Shiraz
    Diamond Reserve
Rosemount Diamond Reserve Red
Rosemount Diamond Reserve White
Rosemount Semillon/Chardonnay Diamond
    Reserve
Rosemount Shiraz Diamond Reserve
Rothbury Estate Chardonnay Broken Back
    Vineyard
Rothbury Estate Shiraz
Seppelt Cabernet Sauvignon Black Label
Seppelt Cabernet Sauvignon Reserve Bin
Seppelt Chardonnay Black Label
Seppelt Chardonnay Reserve Bin
Seppelt Semillon/Chardonnay
Seppelt Shiraz Black Label
Seppelt Shiraz Reserve Bin
Seppelt Tawny Strafford Port
Tyrells Long Flat Red
Wolf Blass Cabernet Sauvignon Yellow
    Label
Wolf Blass Shiraz President's Selection
Wyndham Estates Cabernet Sauvignon Bin
    444
Wyndham Estates Chardonnay Bin 222
Yalumba Clocktower Port

10. NEW ZEALAND, ARGENTINA, CHILE, GREECE, HUNGARY, ISRAEL, LEBANON, SWITZERLAND

NEW ZEALAND

Mention the words *cool climate* and many a wine writer will be searching for the next free junket to discover the undiscovered great wines of country XYZ. New Zealand is a case in point. Has anyone noticed the lavish press this country receives from the English wine media? I may be one of the few wine writers left in the world who has not taken a free business trip to New Zealand (or anywhere for that matter) to taste these "remarkable" new wines from this hot new "cool climate" viticultural paradise. However, I have done my homework, tasting as many of these wines as I can get my lips on. After wading through all the hype, the only potential I can determine is that Sauvignon Blanc and Chardonnay seem to merit some of the enthusiasm generated by the media.

The Sauvignon Blancs elicit the most excitement. They are surprisingly rich, varying from mildly herbaceous to overwhelmingly green. What makes them stand out is that the well-integrated acidity tastes natural, and the best examples possess a stunning mid-palate and length. All you have to do is taste the likes of a Sauvignon Blanc from Cloudy Bay, followed by Stoneleigh, Kumeu River, Morton Estate, Montana, and Selaks, to see that special wines can emerge from this varietal. However, once past these six wineries, the Sauvignons are often ferociously vegetal and washed out.

As for Chardonnay, New Zealanders have learned to handle the cool-climate acidity by putting their wines through full malolactic fermentation, giving them *lees* contact, and plenty of exposure to French oak. However, when yields are not kept low, the Chardonnays taste like a two-by-four, with enough oak to turn off a wine-loving lumberjack. The finest Chardonnays, showing balance between oak and fruit, have emerged from my pick as New Zealand's finest winery, Cloudy Bay, followed by Kumeu River, Te Mata, Matua Valley, Corbins, Villa Maria (*barrique*-fermented), Babich's Irongate, Delegats, Morton Estate Hawke's Bay, Selaks, and the Vidal Reserve.

New Zealand's attempts with Cabernet Sauvignon, Merlot, and Pinot Noir continue to be annoyingly herbaceous and/or atrociously vegetal. It is appalling that anyone can find something to praise in these offerings. If you like wines that taste like liquified asparagus made by the Jolly Green Giant, you will find some merit in them. Although recent vintages suggest New Zealand's wineries are coming closer to purging some of this grotesque character, these wines still possess a nasty vegetal streak. The best red wines to date have come from Te Mata on New Zealand's North Island where some surprisingly plummy, black currant, herbaceous reds made from Cabernet Sauvignon and Merlot have emerged. For the other red wines, there are only two words to keep fixed in your mind—*caveat emptor!*

While there remains considerable enthusiasm for New Zealand's Müller-Thurgau and Gewürztraminer, the only Gewürztraminer that tasted remotely close in quality to those Alsace, France, produces came from another North Island near Gisbourn, Matawhero, which appears to have an uncanny ability to produce wines with that elusive, rose petal, lychee nut scent.

Is all the excitement generated by the enormous press coverage New Zealand's wines receive warranted? No. However, this country does produce some very fine Sauvignons.

RATING NEW ZEALAND'S BEST PRODUCERS OF CHARDONNAY

* * * * * (OUTSTANDING)

None

* * * * (EXCELLENT)

Cloudy Bay   Villa Maria Reserve Bin

* * * (GOOD)

Babich's Irongate	Selaks
Delegats	Te Mata
Kumeu River	Vidal Reserve
Morton Estate Hawke's Bay	

RATING NEW ZEALAND'S BEST PRODUCERS OF SAUVIGNON

* * * * * (OUTSTANDING)

Cloudy Bay

* * * * (EXCELLENT)

Delegats Proprietor's Reserve	Nautilus
Henderson	Selaks
Kumeu River	Stoneleigh
Matua Valley	Te Mata
Montana Marlborough	Villa Maria Reserve Bin

ARGENTINA

I suspect few people realize that the population of Argentina ranks among the world leaders in per capita consumption of wine. Not only do these fun-loving people consume wine, but the country is the world's fifth leading producer of wine, making 275 million cases of wine from 750,000 acres of vineyards. While Argentina has lagged behind Chile in promoting its wines, it is beginning to become more export conscious.

Are the wines of interest? The white wines from well-known grapes such as Sauvignon, Semillon, and Chardonnay are either uninteresting (sterile and fruitless), or clumsy (oxidized and dirty). On the other hand, the red wines from Argentina's top *bodegas* can possess considerable flavor dimension as well as complex aromatic profiles. In fact, the Bodega Weinert is producing South America's greatest red wines. Their wines are the qualitative equals of the finest reds in the world! Two other wineries that merit significant international attention are Catena and Etchart. Interestingly, Etchart hired the famed Libourne oenologist, Michel Rolland, to advise them on winemaking and viticultural practices, and Catena employs the highly regarded California oenologist, Paul Hobbs.

Two other wineries for top red wines are Pascual Toso, making solid Cabernet Sauvignons, and Trapiche, producing fine red wines at bargain prices and representing the top-quality wines of the Bodega Navarro Correas. Another world-class producer whose Cabernet Sauvignons rank just behind those of Bodega Weinert and Etchart is Flichman's Caballero de la Cepa.

Argentina's immense potential has not been fully exploited by the American wine trade. Given the high quality of their red wines, this situation will undoubtedly change. Prices for their best wines will certainly escalate once the world begins to recognize the exceptional quality produced at Argentina's top wineries.

RATING ARGENTINA'S BEST PRODUCERS

* * * * * (OUTSTANDING)

Catena Cabernet Sauvignon Agrelo
   Vineyard
Bodega Weinert Cabernet Sauvignon

Bodega Weinert Cavas de Weinert
Bodega Weinert Malbec

* * * * (EXCELLENT)

Luigi Bosca Malbec
Caballero de la Cepa Cabernet Sauvignon
Catena Chardonnay Agrelo Vineyard
Etchart Cabernet Sauvignon (since 1991)
Etchart Malbec (since 1991)
Nicolas Fazio Malbec

Navarro Correas Colección Privada
   Cabernet Sauvignon * * * */* * * * *
San Telmo Malbec
Pascual Toso Cabernet Sauvignon
Bodega Weinert Carrascal
Bodega Weinert Merlot

Bianchi Cabernet Sauvignon Particular

Bianchi Chenin Blanc (a white wine)

Bianchi Malbec

Humberto Canale Cabernet Sauvignon
  Reserva

Humberto Canale Merlot Reserva

Etchart Torrontes (a white wine)

Flichman Cabernet Sauvignon

Nicolas Fazio Cabernet Sauvignon

Château Mendoza Cabernet Sauvignon

Château Mendoza Merlot

Mendoza Peaks Cabernet Sauvignon

San Telmo Cuesta del Madero (Cabernet
  Sauvignon/Malbec)

Trapiche Cabernet Sauvignon Oak Aged

Leon Unzue Malbec

* * (AVERAGE)

Andean Cabernet Sauvignon

Clos du Moulin Cabernet
  Sauvignon

Goyenechea (Aberdeen Angus) Cabernet
  Sauvignon

Comte de Valmont Cabernet Sauvignon

VALENTIN BIANCHI * * *

1994 Dry Chenin Blanc Elsa's Vineyard	A	85
1990 Malbec Elsa's Vineyard	A	86

Bianchi's floral-scented, dry, crisp, richly fruity, well-made 1994 Chenin Blanc boasts a fruit cocktail/spring flower garden-scented nose and plenty of fresh, lively fruit flavors. Drink it over the next 8–12 months. The 1990 Malbec offers admirable complexity and richness, a big, spicy, black cherry-scented nose, rich, full-bodied flavors, soft tannins, and excellent definition and balance. It is amazing for the price! Drink it over the next 2–3 years.

CABALLERO DE LA CEPA * * * *

1989 Cabernet Sauvignon Estate	A	87
1987 Cabernet Sauvignon Estate	A	87

Along with the Bodega Weinert and Etchart, Caballero de la Cepa is one of my three favorite Argentine bodegas. This 1989 exhibits a wonderfully rich, overripe, black cherry-scented nose and flavors. Medium bodied, satiny smooth, and loaded with fruit, it possesses the same intense essence of cherry flavor found in some Pomerols from ripe vintages. This Cabernet should drink well for 5–7 years. Caballero de la Cepa's 1987 lovely offering displays a deep ruby color, a rich, cedary, black currant, earthy-scented nose, medium to full body, admirable extract and glycerin, soft tannins, and a velvety-textured finish. Drink it over the next 3–4 years.

CATENA * * * */* * * * *

1993 Chardonnay Agrelo Vineyard	C	88
1992 Cabernet Sauvignon Agrelo Vineyard	C	89

Catena is making South America's finest Chardonnay, with some helpful guidance from Californian Paul Hobbs. The 1993 Catena Chardonnay Agrelo Vineyard (100% barrel-fermented) exhibits an attractive, ripe, vanilla- and apple/honey-scented nose, pure, rich, medium- to full-bodied flavors, and a lusty finish. Drink it over the next year. The dark ruby-colored 1992 Catena Cabernet Sauvignon Agrelo Vineyard offers a fragrant bouquet of cassis and sweet oak, deep, rich, velvety-textured flavors, and light tannin in the finish. Bottled without filtration, it should drink well for 6–8 years.

ETCHART * * * *

1990 Tinto Fino	A	89
1989 Tinto Fino	A	87

At the time of writing, the distribution of Etchart wines in the United States remains an enigma. Several sources told me that Austin Nichols is the new American importer, but calls to the wine department brought a bewildering array of noncommittal responses. Let's hope somebody recognizes that this emerging Argentina *bodega* is challenging Bodega Weinert as South America's most promising wine producer. The famed Libourne oenologist, Michel Rolland, is a consultant to Etchart, and his stylistic signature is recognizable in these two top offerings. Blends of Cabernet and Malbec both possess saturated dark ruby/purple colors, forceful, fragrant, cassis-scented bouquets, medium- to full-bodied, ripe, concentrated as well as expansive flavors, excellent purity and balance, and moderate tannin. The 1989 is slightly less powerful than the nearly outstanding 1990. Wines of such quality/price rapport are rare, so why is the American importer dragging its feet regarding the availability of these wines in the marketplace?

FLICHMAN * * *

1990 Cabernet Sauvignon Private Reserve	A	86
1989 Cabernet Sauvignon Private Reserve	A	86

This is a nicely concentrated, spicy, black currant–scented and –flavored, supple Cabernet Sauvignon. Some tannin is present in the finish, and the wine has more astringence than found in most South American wines, but it is a spicy, cleanly made Cabernet that is ideal for drinking over the next 5–7 years. The excellent 1989 Cabernet Sauvignon possesses a deep ruby color, a rich, raspberry-scented nose, soft, medium- to full-bodied flavors, light tannin, and a smooth finish. Drink it over the next 2–3 years.

CHÂTEAU MENDOZA * * *

1987 Cabernet Sauvignon	A	86
1987 Merlot	A	85

These excellent wines are delicious for drinking over the next 2–3 years. The 1987 Merlot is not as expressive in its bouquet as in its flavors, which are fleshy, rich, and filled with ripe, opulent berry fruit. The finish is long and lusty. The 1987 Cabernet Sauvignon is more serious. A cassis-, herb-, and spicy-scented wine, with medium to full body, light tannins, and a long, well-endowed finish, it should last for 4–5 years.

MENDOZA PEAKS * * *

1988 Cabernet Sauvignon	A	85

Fully mature, spicy, soft, and medium bodied, this 1988 Cabernet Sauvignon exhibits cedar, jammy, berry fruit, velvety texture, and a smooth finish. Drink it over the next year.

NAVARRO CORREAS * * * */* * * * *

1988 Cabernet Sauvignon Colección Privada	A	88
1987 Cabernet Sauvignon Colección Privada	A	87

Navarro Correas' Cabernet Sauvignon Colección is usually a top-notch wine selling at a bargain price. The 1988 reveals a garnet color with a touch of amber at the edge. The well-developed bouquet offers up scents of chocolate, cedar, black cherries, cassis, and smoke. The wine possesses excellent concentration, a medium- to full-bodied palate, and a spicy, expansive, fat, luscious finish. It should drink well for 4–5 years. This is a top-class, fully mature Cabernet Sauvignon from Argentina. Another top-notch effort, the chocolate-, coffee-, herb-, and berry-scented 1987 exhibits an intense bouquet, rich, velvety-textured, medium-bodied flavors, and a soft, smooth finish that is loaded with fruit, glycerin, and moderate alcohol. A blend of 80% Cabernet Sauvignon and 20% Merlot that has been aged in oak for 18 months prior to bottling, this wine should drink well for another 3–4 years or longer.

TRAPICHE * * *

| 1990 Malbec | A | 85 |

This spicy, oak-tinged, black cherry–scented wine possesses attractive, elegant flavors, medium body, fine depth, and an alluring softness. Drink it over the next 2–3 years.

LEON UNZUE * * *

| 1987 Malbec | A | 86 |

This complex wine offers up aromas of cassis and chocolate intertwined with herbs and earth. A rich, chunky, medium-bodied Malbec with excellent fruit, glycerin, and length, it promises to keep for another 3–4 years.

BODEGA WEINERT * * * */* * * * *

1985 Cabernet Sauvignon	B	90
1983 Cabernet Sauvignon	B	89
1988 Carrascal	A	87
1985 Carrascal	A	88
1983 Carrascal	A	88
1985 Cavas de Weinert	B	90
1983 Cavas de Weinert	B	89
1990 Merlot	B	90
1988 Merlot	B	87

I have made no secret of my belief that Bodega Weinert is indisputably South America's finest wine producer. Because these wines are produced from old vines and low yields (about one-fourth to one-third the yields of most Argentinean and Chilean wineries) prices tend to be slightly higher. That may have discouraged some retailers from taking a position on these wines, on the theory that Chilean and Argentinean wines should not be priced over $6-$7 a bottle. The point to remember is that if you get a great wine for $10, $12, or $15, it is a bargain; if you get garbage for $5, there is no value.

Weinert's 1990 Merlot is one of the finest Merlots I have tasted from the new world. It comes close to competing with the likes of Matanzas Creek and Ravenswood in Sonoma, or Leonetti in Washington State. The wine possesses a deep, saturated purple color, and a thick, rich nose of black cherries, mocha fudge, and a touch of coffee. Displaying none of the vegetal, herbaceous components that plague so many new world Merlots, it is full bodied, with an unctuous texture, wonderfully concentrated, rich fruit, and a long, rich, finish. Velvety textured, concentrated, and delicious, it should drink well for 7–8 years. The 1988 Carrascal, a blend of Malbec, Merlot, and Cabernet Sauvignon, exhibits a cedary, spicy, curranty nose, medium body, wonderful elegance, and a Bordeaux-like personality reminiscent of a hypothetical blend of a St.-Émilion and a Graves. Drinkable now, it is capable of lasting for 7–8 years.

I continue to enjoy Weinert's 1985 and 1983 Cabernet Sauvignon, and 1985 and 1983 Cavas de Weinert proprietary reds. Their Cabernet Sauvignon is unquestionably the most concentrated, fullest, most age-worthy Cabernet in South America. It, along with their luxury cuvée, the Cavas de Weinert, sells in the $12-$15 range. They are comparable to wines selling for two to three times that price, but for South American wines they are expensive. Readers who have access to quality-oriented merchants should demand the chance to try these remarkable wines.

The 1988 Merlot exhibits a rich, saturated color, and a big, flamboyant nose of black cherries, cocoa, and spices. It is medium to full bodied, opulent, voluptuously textured, juicy, succulent, and a joy to drink. It will last nicely for at least 5–6 years. Both the 1985 and 1983 Cabernet Sauvignons reveal big, chocolaty, hickory, cassis-scented noses, considerable body, a multidimensional, layered texture to their flavors, and long, richly extracted, impressive finishes. The 1983, which is showing some amber at the edge, offers more spice and coffee, cedary scents than the younger, less-evolved 1985. Both wines are capable of at least a decade of aging. They should be compared with wines costing $20–$25, not $10.

Although the 1983 and 1985 Carrascals are lighter than the Cabernets, they are not wimpish wines. Rich, with big, expressive bouquets, medium to full body, soft tannins, and fleshy, rich, chocolate, berry, herb, and coffee flavors, these two offerings should be drunk over the next 5–8 years. As for the Cavas de Weinert offerings, these wines represent the winery's top cuvées of Malbec, Cabernet Sauvignon, and Merlot. They share much of the same character as the other Weinert wines, with super depth of fruit, excellent ripeness, and a natural, rich, aromatic dimension to accompany their bold, classic flavor profiles. These wines should continue to drink well for 8–10 years. Both have considerable proportions of Malbec in their blends.

CHILE

I began covering Chile's wines in the early 1980s and was probably the first wine writer to praise the values emerging from this country. However, a decade and a half later there is both good and bad news.

The good news is that the wines of Chile are still low priced. The bad news is that quality has slipped—badly. Every time I do a tasting of new releases from Chile my disappointment grows, along with a disturbing feeling that quality is being increasingly compromised. Consider some of the Chilean wineries to first be successful in the American market nearly a decade ago. It is appalling to taste what they are now putting in the bottle. Wineries such as Saint Morillion, Santa Rita, Canepa, Miguel Torres, Carta Vieja, and Valdivieso are turning out Chardonnays, Sauvignons, Merlots, and Cabernets that are unquestionably produced from yields of well over 100–120 hectoliters per hectare. These washed-out wines possess no flavor, and even at $5–$6 a bottle, represent poor values. Worldwide demand and greed are the culprits. In short, too many Chilean wines are washed-out, insipid, thin, and fruitless. Sadly, they reflect the dangers that can be caused by phenomenal press coverage and appalling overproduction. Because they are inexpensive, retailers consider them hot items and stack cases of these wines next to their cash registers. However, the quality of most Chilean wine is no longer what it once was. Many Chilean producers need a wake-up call!

There are some positive signs that Chile may be bouncing back—an influx of French money from Bordeaux (i.e., the Rothschild family of Lafite-Rothschild, and Cos d'Estournel's Bruno Prats and Château Margaux's director, Paul Pontallier). However, consumers should remember that just because the wines are inexpensive, it does not mean they are good. The following chart puts things into perspective.

RATING CHILE'S BEST PRODUCERS

* * * * * (OUTSTANDING)

Cousino Macul Cabernet/Merlot Finis
   Terrae

* * * * (EXCELLENT)

Casa Lapostelle Sauvignon Blanc
Concho y Toro Cabernet Sauvignon Don
   Melchor
Concho y Toro Cabernet Sauvignon
   Marques de Casa Concho

Cousino Macul Cabernet Sauvignon
   Antiguas Reserva
Bruno Paul
Los Vascos Cabernet Sauvignon Reserva

* * * (GOOD)

Concho y Toro Cabernet Sauvignon
   Castillero del Diablo
Concho y Toro Chardonnay Castillero del
   Diablo
Cousino Macul Cabernet Sauvignon

Errazuriz Panquehue Cabernet Sauvignon
   Don Maximiano
Santa Monica Cabernet Sauvignon
Los Vascos Cabernet Sauvignon
Los Vascos Sauvignon Blanc

* * (AVERAGE)

Caliterra Cabernet Sauvignon
Caliterra Chardonnay
Canepa Sauvignon Blanc
Carta Vieja (all cuvées)
Cousino Macul Chardonnay
Cousino Macul Sauvignon Blanc
Sage Estate (all cuvées)
Saint Morillon Cabernet Sauvignon
Santa Carolina Cabernet Sauvignon
Santa Carolina Chardonnay
Santa Carolina Merlot
Santa Rita Cabernet Sauvignon 120 Estate

Santa Rita Cabernet Sauvignon Medalla
   Real
Santa Rita Sauvignon Blanc 120 Estate
Tolva Cabernet Sauvignon
Tolva Sauvignon Blanc
Miguel Torres (all cuvées)
Traverso Cabernet Sauvignon
Traverso Merlot
Undurraga Cabernet Sauvignon
Undurraga Sauvignon Blanc
Valdivieso Sparkling N.V. Brut

GREECE

The overall quality of Greece's wines has been improving over the last few years. Nevertheless, there are still too many oxidized, poorly made, bizarre wines that are not likely to enjoy a following outside of transplanted Greek nationals, or restaurants specializing in food from this beautiful country. If you want to sample a true Greek wine, check out the Metaxas Retsina, Greece's only legitimate contribution to viticulture. While most non-Greeks find it akin to chewing on a pine tree, it is considered a national treasure in Greece.

If you want to try a more conventional wine from Greece, consider the following producers. The largest and best-known Greek winery is Achaia-Clauss. Their Patias white wine is enjoyable. Another producer with somewhat higher standards is Boutari, whose top wines are called Naoussa, a relatively forceful, dry red wine, and Santorini, made from vineyards on the extraordinary volcanic island of the same name. Their dry wine is called Thira, and their reds are called Santino and Atlantis. There is often a roasted character to the fruit, but I have had examples with surprising intensity and personality.

Greece's finest red-wine producer is Château Carras. Their Limnio and regular cuvée, both from the Côtes de Meliton, are excellent wines by any standard of measurement. Another medium-weight red wine that is now being aged in oak is Boutari's Goumenissa. If you want to try one of the sweet, superconcentrated Greek red wines, the top wine emanates from an area called Mavrodaphne. There are numerous producers of this kinky, thick wine, which is something of an acquired taste.

A Greek wine I have been drinking since my hippie days of traveling through the Greek Islands is the supercheap dry rosé called Roditys. Still enjoyable today, the best is made by Cambas. Another inexpensive, competent producer of both white and red wines is Kuros, who makes Patias and Nemea that generally sell for well under $7 a bottle.

HUNGARY

With the fall of communism and the beginning movements of capitalistic society, Hungary's potential for high-quality wine could be enormous. This country has plenty of ancient vineyards as well as a historic tradition of wine appreciation.

The greatest Hungarian wine, as well as one of the finest in the world, is Tokaji (Tokay), the famous sweet wine served at the finest European tables prior to the communist takeover. It lives up to its reputation, resembling a mature Sauternes. The wine has different levels of sweetness, designated by something the Hungarians call *puttonyos*. The maximum is 6, a phenomenally rich, sweet wine that makes for a decadent experience. Most Tokays range between 3 and 4 *puttonyos*, making them relatively sweet. They can age for 40–50 years.

Some innovative American importers, such as New England Wine and Spirits, Co. in North Branford, Connecticut, have been tapping into this unrealized market. One can expect others to soon follow. The French, including several of Bordeaux's most dynamic and respected businessmen, Jean-Michel Cazes, Michel Rolland, and Jean-Michel Arcaute, have invested heavily in vineyards and wineries for making great Tokay.

Hungary is also an undiscovered source for a number of relatively rich, full red wines. Historically, the best-known is the Bull's Blood red wine, known in Hungary as Bikaver. Today the wine is diluted and far lighter than consumers would expect.

Given the stability of Hungary's government and the blossoming economy, look for some growers to find foreign investors willing to help them break away from the huge regional cooperatives that have long-dominated Hungarian wine production. Other growers will undoubtedly sell out to foreigners. Over the next decade, small estates, producing wines with the name of the varietal and the village on their labels, will undoubtedly begin to emerge. Michel Rolland and Jean-Michel Arcaute's estate is Château Pajzos. Presently, it is impossible to know what other producers' names might be.

The following grapes enjoy the highest reputation in Hungary. European authorities have long known that these varietals have the potential to make wines of surprisingly high quality. Consumers should keep an eye out for these Hungarian varietals:

Ezerjo   A grape that produces perfumed, fleshy white wine.

Furmint   The classic grape of Tokaji, it can also be vinified totally dry.

Keknyelu   This varietal produces relatively full-bodied, fleshy, dry white wines.

Leanyka   It turns out intensely fragrant, perfumed white wines that have immense potential if vinified in a modern style.

Szurkebarat   The Hungarian equivalent of Pinot Gris, this grape results in superrich, full-bodied dry and sweet whites.

Nagyvurgundi   A grape thought to be a clone of Pinot Noir that is indigenous to Hungary, it makes rich, full, expansively flavored wines, particularly from the villages of Szekszard and Villany.

Medoc Noir   A red wine varietal, this grape produces fleshy, supple, richly fruity wines that can be drunk young.

ISRAEL

Wine production in Israel has moved away from the sweet wines that were so prevalent 20 years ago, to drier styles that offer more international appeal. Although the workmanlike grapes, such as Alicante, Grenache, Muscat, and Carignane, are still in existence, many of the newest vineyards are planted with internationally renowned varietals such as Cabernet Sauvignon, Chardonnay, Sauvignon Blanc, and French Colombard. The three most widely represented brand names in the United States are Carmel, Gamla, and Yarden.

The Carmel wines include sticky, sweet offerings with names such as Concord King David and Sacramental Grape King David. They also make some drier-styled wines, the best of which is their Shiraz Carmel Vineyards, Cabernet Sauvignon Carmel Vineyards, Sauvignon Blanc Carmel Vineyards, and Chardonnay Rothschild.

Yarden produces an excellent rosé, called Cabernet Blanc, a fine Sauvignon Blanc, an adequate Chardonnay, and from time to time decent Merlot and Cabernet Sauvignon. Yarden's wines tend to be more expensive than other Israeli wines, so expect to spend $15–$18 for a bottle of Yarden Vineyards wine. They may be the best wines produced in Israel, but the price differential is not justified.

LEBANON

The top wine of the Middle East is an amazing story. Thirty kilometers (18 miles) from the savage and senseless civil war that once tore apart Beirut is Château Musar, a winemaking estate founded in the thirties and one that makes superlative wines from a blend of Cabernet Sauvignon, Syrah, and Cinsault. Owner/winemaker Serge Hochar had vintages wiped out because no harvesters would risk their lives to pick the grapes, but still he continues. His wine training came from his father and from a stint in Bordeaux, but the wines remind me of the best and most complex Châteauneuf du Papes. They are full bodied, very fragrant, rich and supple enough to drink young, but if the very good 1966 and exquisite 1970 are any indication, they will last 10, even 20 years. The vintages now on the market are the 1975, 1977, 1978, 1979, 1980, 1981, 1982, and 1983. Retailing for approximately $15–$25 a bottle, the wines are undeniable bargains given the quality.

SWITZERLAND

The only bargain I have ever discovered in Switzerland was to fly to Geneva, rent my car there, then drop my car off in Paris at the conclusion of my trip. By originating my rental in Switzerland, I avoided France's 33% tax on car rentals. One does not visit Switzerland on a budget. Like everything else in the country, its wines are frightfully expensive—always have been, always will be. Although one might quibble over the price, the quality of many Swiss wines is very good, especially the fragrant, richly fruity wines made from a grape called Chasselas, which does better in Switzerland than anywhere else. The Chasselas white wines appear not only under the grape's own name, but also under the names Fendant, Dezaley, and Neuchatel. Switzerland's top vineyards are centered either on the steep slopes above Lake Geneva in an area called Vaud, or further east around the town of Sion in an area called Valais. The Chasselas grape, or Fendant as it is called in Valais, produces an aromatic white wine that at its best suggests a Condrieu in bouquet, and a medium-bodied, stainless steel–fermented, yet fleshy Chardonnay in texture and weight. If it were not so expensive (usually $20 and up a bottle), it would be quite popular. It is Switzerland's best white wine. Red wine, the best of which is called Dole and is a blend of Pinot Noir and Gamay, is an adequate, serviceable red, though never worth its stiff price tag.

APPENDIXES

Producers Who Routinely Make Delicious Wine for Under $10 a Bottle

Abbaye de Tholomies Réserve Minervois (France)

J. B. Adam Pinot Blanc (Alsace)

Agricola de Borja Borsao Tinto (Spain)

Agricola de Borja Viña Borgia Tinto (Spain)

Alderbrook Sauvignon Blanc Dry Creek Valley (California)

Gilbert Alquier (France)

Domaine de Alysses Coteaux du Varois (France)

Domaine de l'Ameillaud Vins du Pays Vaucluse (France)

Domaine des Amouriers Vacqueyras (Rhône Valley)

Fattoria di Angelli Soave Classico (Italy)

Fattoria di Angelli Valpolicella Classico Superior (Italy)

Arboles de Castillejo La Mancha (Spain)

Arbor Crest Sauvignon Blanc (Washington)

Argiolas Perdera (Italy)

Domaine de L'Arjolle Cabernet (France)

Domaine de L'Arjolle Cuvée de L'Arjolle (France)

Domaine de L'Arjolle Sauvignon (France)

Arrowood Chardonnay Domaine du Grand Archer Sonoma (California)

Pierre d'Aspres (France)

Domaine d'Aula Côtes de Gascogne (France)

Azelia Dolcetto d'Alba (Italy)

Badia a Coltibuono Chianti Cetamura (Italy)

Badia a Coltibuono Coltibuono Rosso (Italy)

Dona Baissas (France)

Erik Banti Morellino di Scansano (Italy)

Domaine Bargemone Côtes de Provence Rosé (France)

Domaine Bargemone Côtes de Provence Rouge (France)

Barrier Reef Cabernet Sauvignon (Australia)

Barrier Reef Sauvignon Blanc (Australia)

Domaine de Bassac Vins du Pays d'Oc (France)

Batasiolo Dolcetto d'Alba (Italy)

Beaulieu Sauvignon Blanc Napa (California)

Château Beauregard Corbières (France)

Domaine de Beaurenard Côtes du Rhône Villages Rasteau (France)

Domaine de la Becasonne Côtes du Rhône (France)

Bel Arbors Zinfandel (California)

Château Bel Eveque Corbières (France)

Château Belingard Bergerac (France)

Belvedere Chardonnay Russian River Valley (California)

Domaine du Belvezet Vins du Pays l'Ardèche (France)

Erich Bender Bissersheimer Goldberg Scheurebe Spatlese (Germany)

Benton Lane Pinot Noir (Oregon)

Benziger Fumé Blanc Sonoma (California)

Beringer Zinfandel Napa (California)

Château Bertinerie Côtes de Blaye Blanc Sec (France)

Valentin Bianchi Dry Chenin Blanc Elsa's Vineyard (Argentina)

Domaine Bibian Madiran (France)

Domaine du Bois Monsieur Monts de la Grage VDP Blanc (France)

Domaine du Bois Monsieur Monts de la Grage VDP Rouge (France)

Pierre Boniface Aprémont (France)

Bonny Doon Vineyard Ca' Del Solo Big House Red (California)

Bonny Doon Vineyard Ca' Del Solo Big House White (California)

Bonny Doon Vineyard Ca' Del Solo Il Fiasco (California)

Bonny Doon Vineyard Chenin Blanc Pacific Rim Monterey (California)

Bonny Doon Vineyard Clos de Gilroy (California)

Bonny Doon Vineyard Riesling Pacific Rim Monterey (California)

Bonny Doon Vineyard Vin Gris de Cigare (California)

Domaine de la Borne Muscadet de Sevre et Maine (France)

Brown Brothers Lexia Late Harvest Muscat (Australia)

Brown Brothers Sauvignon Blanc King Valley (Australia)

Domaine André Brunel Côtes du Rhône (France)

Daniel Brusset Cairanne Côtes du Rhône (France)

Buehler Zinfandel Napa (California)

Caballero de la Cepa Cabernet Sauvignon Estate (Argentina)

Cabert Pinot Grigo Grave del Friuli (Italy)

Château Calabre Bergerac Merlot (France)

Château Calabre Bergerac Rosé (France)

Château Calabre Sauvignon Montravel (France)

Château de Calce Côtes de Roussillon (France)

Château de Campuget Costières de Nimes (red) (France)

Château de Campuget Costières de Nimes (white) (France)

Domaine de Capion Merlot Vins du Pays d'Oc (France)

Domaine de Capion Syrah Vins du Pays d'Oc (France)

Domaine de Capion Vins du Pays Futs de Chene (France)

Carmenet Colombard Old Vines (California)

Castruccio Vino da Tavola (Italy)

Cave Mont Bazin Grenache (France)

Caves Coop d'Aléria Réserve du Président (France)

Domaine Challon Bordeaux Blanc (France)

Domaine de Champagna (France)

Domaine de la Charmoise Sauvignon (France)

Gérard Charvin Côtes du Rhône (France)

Les Chemins de Bassac Vins du Pays d'Oc (France)

Les Chemins de Bassac Vins du Pays d'Oc Cap de l'Homme (France)

Les Chemins de Bassac Vins du Pays d'Oc Pierre Elie (France)

Guy Chevalier Cabernet/Syrah Vins du Pays l'Aude (France)

Guy Chevalier La Coste Corbières (France)

Guy Chevalier l'Église Corbières (France)

Guy Chevalier Le Texas Syrah Vins du Pays l'Aude (France)

Domaine de Clairfont Vins du Pays Vaucluse (France)

Cline Côtes d'Oakley (California)

Clos du Bois Merlot Sonoma (California)

Clos de la Mure Côtes du Rhône (France)

Clos Resseguier Cahors (France)

Clos Rosiers de Muscadet de Sevre et Maine (France)

Clos Villemajou de Corbières Blanc (France)

Clos Villemajou de Corbières Rouge (France)

Codice Sierra Cantabria (Spain)

Coldridge Semillon/Chardonnay (Australia)

Coldridge Shiraz/Cabernet (Australia)

Château la Colombière Côtes du Frontonnais (France)

Columbia Crest Sauvignon Blanc (Washington)

Columbia Crest Sauvignon Blanc/Semillon (Washington)

Columbia Crest Semillon/Chardonnay Columbia Valley (Washington)

Commanderie de la Bargemone (France)

Concha y Toro Marques de Casa Concha Cabernet/Sauvignon Puente Alto (Chile)

Congress Springs Chardonnay San Ysidro (California)

Congress Springs Noblesse Proprietary Red Wine (California)

Cornacchia Montelpulciano d'Abruzzo (Italy)

Cortese Dolcetto d'Alba (Italy)

Coturri Alicante Bouchet Ubaldi Vineyard Sonoma (California)

Château Coucheroy White Graves (France)

Domaine Courberce Cabernet Sauvignon Vins du Pays d'Oc (France)

Domaine de Couroulu (France)

Château Courrière Rongieras Lussac St.-Émilion (France)

Cousino Macul (Chile)

Château Coussergues Baronnie Blanc VDP Côtes de Thongue (France)

Thomas Coyne Zinfandel Sonoma (California)

Cuvée des Messes Basses Côtes du Ventoux (France)

Domaine Dalicieux Beaujolais Blanc (France)

Kurt Darting Durkheimer Feuerberg Portugieser Weissherbst Halbtrocken (Germany)

Kurt Darting Durkheimer Fronhof Riesling Spatlese (Germany)

Kurt Darting Durkheimer Hochbenn Riesling Kabinett (Germany)

Kurt Darting Durkheimer Nonnengarten Riesling Kabinett Trocken (Germany)

Kurt Darting Ellerstadter Bubeneck Riesling Spatlese Trocken (Germany)

Kurt Darting Ungsteiner Bettelhaus Riesling Spatlese (Germany)

Marcel Deiss Pinot Blanc Bergheim (France)

Domaine Deletang Sauvignon de Touraine (France)

Château Derbos Graves Blanc (France)

Marc Deschamps Pouilly sur Loire (France)

Deux Rives Corbières Blanc (France)

Deux Rives Corbières Rouge (France)

Deux Roches St. Véran Vieilles Vignes (France)

Daniel Domergue N.V. Assemblage (France)

Château Dona Baissas Côtes de Roussillon (France)

Château Dona Baissas Côtes de Roussillon Vieilles Vignes (France)

Dry Creek Dry Chenin Blanc (California)

Dry Creek Fumé Blanc Sonoma (California)

Georges Duboeuf Beaujolais-Villages Domaine Granit Bleu (Beaujolais)

Georges Duboeuf Beaujolais-Villages Flower Label (Beaujolais)

Georges Duboeuf Brouilly Château Nervers (Beaujolais)

Georges Duboeuf Brouilly Flower Label (Beaujolais)

Georges Duboeuf Domaine Baron de Bruny (Côtes de Luberon)

Georges Duboeuf Chénas Flower Label (Beaujolais)

Georges Duboeuf Chiroubles Domaine Desmures (Beaujolais)

Georges Duboeuf Côtes du Rhône Domaine des Moulin (Rhone)

Georges Duboeuf Fleurie Château de Grand Pré (Beaujolais)

Georges Duboeuf Fleurie Château Deduits (Beaujolais)

Georges Duboeuf Fleurie Clos des Quatre Vents (Beaujolais)

Georges Duboeuf Fleurie Domaine des Quatre Vents (Beaujolais)

Georges Duboeuf Fleurie Flower Label (Beaujolais)

Georges Duboeuf Julienas Château des Poupets (Beaujolais)

Georges Duboeuf Julienas Domaine de la Seigneurie (Beaujolais)

Georges Duboeuf Julienas Flower Label (Beaujolais)

Georges Duboeuf Morgon Jean Descombes (Beaujolais)

Georges Duboeuf Moulin à Vent Domaine des Rosiers (Beaujolais)

Georges Duboeuf Moulin à Vent Flower Label (Beaujolais)

Georges Duboeuf Régnié Domaine du Potet (Beaujolais)

Georges Duboeuf Régnié Flower Label (Beaujolais)

Georges Duboeuf Saint Amour Domaine de la Pirolette (Beaujolais)

Georges Duboeuf Domaine St. Lucie Pic St. Loup (Côteaux Languedoc)

Georges Duboeuf Viognier l'Ardèche (Rhone)

Laurent Dumas Beaujolais-Villages (Beaujolais)

Domaine de L'Ecu Muscadet Sur Lie (France)

Edmunds St. John El Nino (California)

Edmunds St. John Pinot Grigio El Dorado (California)

Edmunds St. John Port o' Call (California)

Eser-Johannishof Geisenheimer Klauserweg Ries. Halbt. (Germany)

Eser-Johannishof Winkeler Hasensprung Riesling Kabinett (Germany)

Château L'Espigne Fitou (France)

Domaine de L'Espigouette Côtes du Rhône Vieilles Vignes (France)

Domaine de L'Espigouette Côtes du Rhône Villages Plan de Dieu (France)

Estancia Chardonnay Monterey (California)

Estancia Meritage Alexander Valley (California)

Château Etang des Colombes Corbières Cuvée du Bicentenaire (France)

Etchart Tinto Fino (Argentina)

Bodegas Farina Collegiata Tinto (Toro) (Spain)

Bodegas Farina Gran Collegiata Tinto Reserva (Spain)

Bodegas Farina Gran Peromato (Spain)

Bodegas Farina Peromato Tinto (Spain)

Gary Farrell Sauvignon Blanc Rochioli Vineyard (California)

Château Fauchey Premières Côtes de Bordeaux (France)

Domaine de Fenouillet Côtes du Rhône Beaumes-de-Venise (France)

Domaine de Fenouillet Côtes du Rhône Beaumes-de-Venise Blanc (France)

Domaine de Fenouillet Côtes du Rhône Ventoux (France)

Domaine des Feraud Côtes de Provence (France)

Domaine des Feraud Côtes de Provence Blanc (France)

Charles de Fere Blanc de Blancs Brut Sparkling Wine (France)

Charles de Fere Chardonnay Tradition Brut Sparkling Wine (France)

Domaine de la Ferrandière Chardonnay Vins du Pays d'Oc (France)

Domaine de la Ferrandière Merlot Vins du Pays d'Oc (France)

Domaine de la Ferrandière Sauvignon Vins du Pays d'Oc (France)

Fetzer Chardonnay Bonterra Mendocino (California)

Fetzer Chardonnay Sundial (California)

Fetzer Fumé Blanc Mendocino (California)

Fetzer Sauvignon Blanc Barrel Select Mendocino (California)

Feudi di San Gregorio Albente (Italy)

Fiegl Pinot Grigio Collio (Italy)

Fiegl Sauvignon Collio (Italy)

Pierre Fil Minervois (France)

Pierre Fil Minervois Oak Aged (France)

Filomusi Guelfi Montepulciano d'Abruzzo (Italy)

Firestone Vineyard Gewürztraminer Santa Barbara (California)

Flichman Cabernet Sauvignon Private Reserve (Argentina)

Fonseca (Portugal)

Château les Fontaines Côtes de Roussillon (France)

Domaine de Fontsainte Corbières (France)

Domaine de Fontsainte Gris de Gris Corbières (France)

Fortant de France Cabernet Sauvignon Collection VDP d'Oc (France)

Fortant de France Chardonnay Collection VDP d'Oc (France)

Fortant de France Merlot Collection VDP d'Oc (France)

Fortant de France Sauvignon Blanc Collection VDP d'Oc (France)

Gabrielli Ascenza White Table Wine Mendocino (California)

Poggio Galiga Chianti Rufina (Italy)

Domaine la Garrigue Vacqueyras (France)

Château Gassies Premières Côtes de Bordeaux (France)

Domaine Gauby Côtes du Roussillon (France)

Gautier Vouvray Sec (France)

Domaine de la Gautière (France)

Geyser Peak Semchard (California)

Geyser Peak Soft Johannisberg Riesling North Coast (California)

Domaine de Gournier Chardonnay Vins du Pays (France)

Domaine de Gournier Merlot Vins du Pays (France)

Domaine de Gournier Sauvignon Blanc Vins du Pays (France)

Domaine Gramenon Côtes du Rhône (France)

Domaine Gramenon Côtes du Rhône Cuvée Laurentides (France)

Château Grand Moulin Corbières (France)

La Grande Vignolle Saumur Champigny (France)

Château des Grandes Noelles Muscadet (France)

Domaine des Grands Devers (France)

Château la Grave Minervois (France)

Château Graville Lacoste Graves (France)

Château de la Greffière Mâcon La Roche Vineuse Vieilles Vignes (France)

Barnard Griffin Cabernet/Merlot Columbia Valley (Washington)

Barnard Griffin Fumé Blanc Columbia Valley (Washington)

Marques de Grinon Sauvignon Blanc Durius (Spain)

Marques de Grinon Tinto Durius (Spain)

Domaine Grinou Bergerac (France)

Guenoc Petite Sirah North Coast (California)

Domaine de la Guichard Côtes du Rhône Les Genests (France)

Guigal Côtes du Rhône (France)

Guigal Côtes du Rhône Blanc (France)

Gernot Gysler Weinheimer Holle Riesling Spatlese Trocken (Germany)

Hanna Sauvignon Blanc Sonoma (California)

J. Hart Piesporter Falkenberg Riesling Trocken (Germany)

Château Haut-Fabregues Faugères (France)

Hehner-Kiltz Riesling (Germany)

Hehner-Kiltz Schlossbockelheimer Felsenberg Riesling Kabinett Halbtrocken (Germany)

Hehner-Kiltz Schlossbockelheimer Felsenberg Riesling Kabinett Trocken (Germany)

Hess Select Chardonnay (California)

Freiheer Heyl Niersteiner Rosenberg Silvaner Trocken (Germany)

Freiherr Heyl Silvaner Trocken (Germany)

Hogue Cellars Dry Johannisberg Riesling Yakima Valley (Washington)

Hogue Cellars Fumé Blanc Columbia Valley (Washington)

Hogue Cellars Semillon/Chardonnay Columbia Valley (Washington)

Hogue Cellars Semillon Columbia Valley (Washington)

Château de L'Horte Corbières (France)

Château Hostens-Picant Cuvée des Demoiselles (France)

Husch Vineyard Chenin Blanc Anderson Valley (California)

Husch Vineyard Gewürztraminer Anderson Valley (California)

Husch Vineyard La Ribera Red Mendocino (California)

Husch Vineyard Sauvignon Blanc Mendocino (California)

Ile de Beauté Merlot Vins du Pays (Corsica)

Paul Jaboulet Ainé (France)

La Jaja de Jau Vins du Pays d'Oc Blanc (France)

Le Jaja de Jau Vins du Pays Rouge Côtes Catalan (France)

Les Jamelles Chardonnay Vins du Pays d'Oc (France)

Les Jamelles Cinsault Vins du Pays d'Oc (France)

Les Jamelles Merlot Vins du Pays d'Oc (France)

Château de Jau Côtes du Roussillon Blanc (France)

Château de Jau Côtes du Roussillon Villages (France)

Domaine de Jau Les Clos de Paulilles Rosé Collioure (France)

Château de Jonquières Corbières (France)

Domaine de Jougla (France)

Domaine de Joy Côtes de Gascogne (France)

Weingut Karlsmuhle Lorenzhofer Riesling (Germany)

Kendall-Jackson Chardonnay Vintner's Reserve (California)

Kendall-Jackson Johannisberg Riesling Vintner's Reserve (California)

Kendall-Jackson Zinfandel Vintner's Reserve (California)

Kenwood Sauvignon Blanc Sonoma (California)

J. F. Kimich Deidesheimer Herrgottsacker Riesling Kabinett (Germany)

J. F. Kimich Forster Elster Riesling Kabinett (Germany)

J. F. Kimich Ruppertsberger Reiterfad Riesling Kabinett Halbtrocken (Germany)

Freiherr Zu Knyphausen Kiedricher Riesling Trocken (Germany)

Kruger-Rumpf Munsterer Kapellenberg Riesling Kabinett #5 (Germany)

Kuhling-Gillot Bodenheimer Heitersbrunnchen Scheurebe Kabinett (Germany)

Kuhling-Gillot Bodenheimer Kapelle Riesling Kabinett (Germany)

Kuhling-Gillot Oppenheimer Kreuzkerner Riesling Auslese (Germany)

Kuhling-Gillot Oppenheimer Riesling Halbtrocken (Germany)

La Crema Chardonnay (California)

Domaine Lafarge Macon Bray (France)

Domaine Lalande Sauvignon Côtes de Gascogne (France)

Maison de Lamartine Beaujolais-Villages (France)

Landmark Chardonnay Overlook Sonoma (California)

Pierre Laplace N.V. Bearn Lisere d'Or Madiran (France)

Château Lastours Gaillac Blanc (France)

Château Lastours Gaillac Rosé (France)

Domaine Latour-Boisée Cuvée Marie Claude (France)

Domaine Latour-Boisée Minervois Unfiltered (France)

Louis Latour Chardonnay Ardèche (France)

Louis Latour Macon Lugny Les Genièvres (France)

Laurel Glen Terra Rosa Sonoma (California)

Peter Lehmann Riesling (Australia)

Peter Lehmann Semillon (Australia)

Peter Lehmann Shiraz (Australia)

Liberty School (California)

Librandi Ciro Rosso (Italy)

Lindemans Chardonnay Bin #65 (Australia)

Lindemans Semillon/Chardonnay Bin #77 (Australia)

J. Lohr Chardonnay Estate Riverstone Monterey (California)

Bodegas Angel Lorenzo Martivilli (Spain)

Los Vascos Cabernet Sauvignon (Chile)

Los Vascos Cabernet Sauvignon Reserve (Chile)

Los Vascos Chardonnay (Chile)

Los Vascos Sauvignon Blanc (Chile)

Bodegas Magana Eventum Crianza (Spain)

Maître d'Estournel (France)

Jean Manciat Mâcon Villages Franlieu (France)

Albert Mann Pinot Auxerrois Vieilles Vignes (France)

Marietta Cellars Old Vine Lot 14, 15, etc. Sonoma (California)

Domaine Maris Minervois Carte Noir (France)

Domaine de Marotte Côtes du Ventoux Cuvée Prestige (France)

Domaine de Marotte Côtes du Ventoux Cuvée Tradition (France)

Marques de Murrieta Tinto Crianza Rioja (Spain)

Mas de Bressades Cabernet Sauvignon/ Syrah (France)

Mas de Bressades Syrah (France)

Mas Champart Saint Chinian (France)

Mas de Gourgonnier Côteaux d'Aix en Provence Les Baux (France)

Mas de Rey (France)

Domaine Matibat Cabernet Sauvignon Vins du Pays (France)

Domaine Matibat Merlot Vins du Pays (France)

Domaine de la Metairie des Perdreaux Corbières (France)

Château les Miaudoux Bergerac Sec (France)

Michel Frères Cremant de Bourgogne Sparkling Rosé (France)

Michel Frères Cremant de Bourgogne Sparkling White (France)

Château Milhau-Lacugue Saint Chinian (France)

Domaine Millières Côtes du Rhône (France)

Theo Minges Fleminger Vogelsprung Scheurebe Spatlese (Germany)

Theo Minges Fleminger Zechpeter Riesling Kabinett (Germany)

Mirassou White Burgundy (California)

Domaine Mireille et Vincent Côtes du Rhône (France)

Mitchelton Cab/Mac (Australia)

Mitchelton Chardonnay (Australia)

Mitchelton Marsanne (Australia)

Mitchelton Riesling (Australia)

Mitchelton Semillon/Chardonnay (Australia)

Robert Mondavi Zinfandel Unfiltered Napa (California)

Domaine de Mont Redon Côtes du Rhône (France)

Elio Monte Montepulciano d'Abruzzo (Italy)

Monte Antico Rosso (Italy)

Monterey Vineyards Classic Cabernet Sauvignon (California)

Monterey Vineyards Classic Chardonnay (California)

Monterey Vineyards Classic Gamay Beaujolais (California)

Monterey Vineyards Classic Merlot (California)

Monterey Vineyards Classic Red (California)

Monterey Vineyards Classic Sauvignon Blanc (California)

Monterey Vineyards Classic White (California)

Montrose (Australia)

Monzio Compagnoni Valcalepio Bianco (Italy)

Z. Moore Gewürztraminer Barrel Fermented Dry (California)

Bodegas Hermanos Morales Gran Creación (Spain)

Domaine de la Mordorée Côtes du Rhône (France)

Domaine de la Mordorée Lirac (France)

Moris Farms Morellino di Scansano Estate (Italy)

Moris Farms Morellino di Scansano Riserva (Italy)

Morro Bay Vineyards Chardonnay Central Coast (California)

Mount Konocti Semillon/Chardonnay Lake County (California)

Mountain View Vintners Cabernet Sauvignon North Coast (California)

Mountain View Vintners Chardonnay Monterey (California)

Mountain View Vintners Pinot Noir Napa/Monterey (California)

Mountain View Vintners Sauvignon Blanc North Coast (California)

Mountain View Vintners Zinfandel Lot 91 Amador (California)

Bodegas Muga Rosado (Spain)

Murphy-Goode Fumé Blanc Alexander Valley (California)

Napa Ridge Cabernet Sauvignon Oak Barrel Central Coast (California)

Napa Ridge Chardonnay Central Coast (California)

Napa Ridge Gewürztraminer Central Coast (California)

Napa Ridge Sauvignon Blanc (California)

Navarro Chardonnay Anderson Valley (California)

Navarro Correas Cabernet Sauvignon Colección (Argentina)

Bodegas Nekeas Cabernet/Tempranillo Vega Sindoa (Spain)

Bodegas Nekeas Chardonnay Vega Sindoa (Spain)

Domaine La Noble Chardonnay (France)

Domaine La Noble Merlot (France)

Domaine La Noble Sauvignon Blanc (France)

Château D'Oupia Minervois (France)

Château Palais Cahors (France)

Château de Paraza-Cuvée Spéciale Minervois (France)

Parducci Cabernet Sauvignon Mendocino (California)

Parducci Chardonnay Mendocino (California)

Parducci Petite Sirah Mendocino (California)

Parducci Sauvignon Blanc North Coast (California)

Fess Parker Johannisberg Riesling Santa Barbara (California)

Luis Pato Quinta do Riberirnho (Portugal)

Le Payssel Gaillac (France)

Château Peconnet Premières Côtes de
Bordeaux (France)

Pedroncelli Primavera Mista Proprietary
White Wine (California)

Pedroncelli Zinfandel Sonoma (California)

Château de Pena Côtes de
Roussillon-Villages (France)

Château de Pena Cuvée de Pena Vin de
Table Lot 93 (France)

Penfolds (Australia)

Château Pesquie Côtes de Ventoux Cuvée
des Terrasses (France)

Château Pesquie Côtes de Ventoux
Quintessence (France)

Le Petit Chambord Cheverny (France)

Château de la Peyrade Muscat Sec Cuvée
des Lilas VDP d'Oc (France)

Joseph Phelps Le Mistral Napa (California)

Joseph Phelps Vin du Mistral (California)

Joseph Phelps Vin du Mistral Grenache
(California)

Joseph Phelps Vin du Mistral Grenache
Rosé (California)

Joseph Phelps Vin du Mistral Syrah
(California)

R. H. Phillips Chardonnay Barrel Cuvée
(California)

R. H. Phillips Sauvignon Blanc Night
Harvest Cuvée (California)

Domaine Piccinini Minervois (France)

Domaine de Pierrefeu Costières de Nimes
(France)

Pine Ridge Chenin Blanc Yountville
Cuvée Napa (California)

Domaine Piquemal Cuvée Pierre Audonnet
(France)

Château Pique-Segue Montravel (France)

Château Plaisance Côtes du Frontonnais
(France)

Henri Poiron Muscadet (France)

Domaine de Pouy Côtes de Gascogne Ugni
Blanc (France)

Preston Vineyards Chenin Blanc
(California)

Preston Vineyards Cuvée de Fumé Dry
Creek Valley (California)

Jacky Preys Sauvignon de Touraine Clos
des Pillotières (France)

Jacky Preys Sauvignon de Touraine
Vieilles Vignes Fie Gris (France)

Le Prieuré des Mourgues Saint Chinian
(France)

Domaine Provenquière Chardonnay Vins
du Pays d'Oc (France)

Quenard Chignin (France)

Domaine de Quilla Muscadet Sur Lie
(France)

Domaine de Quilla Muscadet Vieilles
Vignes (France)

J. Ratzenberger Bacharacher Kloster
Furstental Riesling Spatlese
Halbtrocken (Germany)

J. Ratzenberger Steeger St. Jost Riesling
(Germany)

Château Rauzan-Despagne Bordeaux
Blanc Sec (France)

Ravenswood Merlot Vintner's Blend North
Coast (California)

Château Reyssac Bergerac (France)

Château Richard Bergerac Rouge (France)

Château Richard Bergerac Sec (France)

Domaine de Roally Macon Viré (France)

Château de Rochemorin Graves (France)

Telmo Rodriguez Alma (Spain)

Domaine La Roque Chasan Vins du Pays
(France)

Domaine La Roque Sur Lie Vins du Pays
(France)

Roquette Sur Mer La Clape Coteaux du
Languedoc Blanc (France)

Roquette Sur Mer La Clape Coteaux du
Languedoc Rouge (France)

Rosemount Estates Cabernet Sauvignon
Hunter Valley (Australia)

Rosemount Estates Chardonnay Hunter
Valley (Australia)

Rosemount Estates Semillon/Chardonnay
(Australia)

Rosemount Estates Shiraz/Cabernet
(Australia)

Rosemount Estates Shiraz Hunter Valley
(Australia)

Rosenblum Cellars Zinfandel Vintner's
Cuvée VIII (California)

Domaine du Sacre-Coeur Saint Chinian
(France)

Château Saint-Auriol Corbières Blanc
(France)

Château Saint-Auriol Corbières Rouge
(France)

St. Estève (France)

St. Francis Chardonnay Sonoma
(California)
Domaine Saint-Gayan Côtes du Rhône
(France)
Domaine Saint-Gayan Rasteau (France)
Domaine de Saint-Lannes Côtes de
Gascogne Blanc (France)
Château Saint-Maurice Côtes du
Rhône-Villages (France)
Sainte-Eulalie Minervois (France)
Château Ste. Michelle Chenin Blanc
(Washington)
Château Ste. Michelle Dry Riesling River
Ridge Vineyard (Washington)
Château Ste. Michelle Sauvignon Blanc
(Washington)
Château Ste. Michelle Sauvignon Blanc
Barrel Fermented (Washington)
Domaine Ste. Michelle Brut Sparkling
(Washington)
Domaine la Salle (France)
Domaine Salvat Côtes du Roussillon Blanc
(France)
Domaine Salvat Fenouille VDP Coteaux
des Fenouilledes (France)
Domaine Salvat Muscat Sec VDP Coteaux
des Fenouilledes (France)
Domaine Sancet Côtes de Gascogne
(France)
Santa Monica (Chile)
Willi Schaefer Graacher Domprobst
Riesling Hochgewachs (Germany)
G. A. Schneider Niersteiner Bildstock
Riesling Kabinett (Germany)
G. A. Schneider Niersteiner Hipping
Riesling Spatlese Halbtrocken
(Germany)
G. A. Schneider Niersteiner Oelberg
Riesling Spatlese (Germany)
G. A. Schneider Niersteiner Pettenthal
Riesling Spatlese (Germany)
Bernard Schoffit Pinot Blanc (Auxerrois)
Cuvée Caroline (France)
Sebastiani Barbera Sonoma (California)
Sebastiani Cabernet Franc Sonoma
(California)
Sebastiani Cabernet Sauvignon Sonoma
(California)
Sebastiani Chardonnay Sonoma
(California)
Sebastiani Zinfandel Sonoma (California)

Selbach-Oster Zeltinger Schlossberg
Riesling Kabinett (Germany)
Seppelt (Australia)
Domaines de Serres-Mazard Corbières
(Oak Aged) (France)
Shooting Star Chardonnay Mendocino
(California)
Bodegas Sierra Cantabria Codice Rioja
(Spain)
Bodegas Sierra Cantabria Crianza Rioja
(Spain)
Bodegas Sierra Cantabria Rosé Rioja
(Spain)
Bodegas Sierra Cantabria Tinto Rioja
(Spain)
Sierra Vista Fleur de Montagne El Dorado
(California)
Sierra Vista Lynelle El Dorado (California)
Simi Sauvignon Blanc Sonoma (California)
Domaine de la Solitude Côtes du Rhône
Blanc (France)
Domaine de la Solitude Côtes du Rhône
Rouge (France)
Château Souverain Cabernet Sauvignon
Alexander Valley (California)
Château Souverain Chardonnay Barrel
Fermented Sonoma (California)
Château Souverain Merlot Alexander
Valley (California)
Château Souverain Zinfandel Dry Creek
(California)
Pierre Sparr Chasselas Vieilles Vignes
(France)
Pierre Sparr Gewürztraminer Carte d'Or
(France)
Pierre Sparr Pinot Blanc Reserve (France)
Pierre Sparr Pinot Gris Carte d'Or
(France)
Pierre Sparr Riesling Carte d'Or (France)
Steltzner Sauvignon Blanc Estate Oak
Knoll Ranch Napa (California)
Stoneleigh Sauvignon (New Zealand)
J.U.H.A. Strub Niersteiner Riesling
Kabinett Halbtrocken #14 (Germany)
Joseph Swan Vin du Mystère Sonoma
(California)
Taja Monastrell (Spain)
Domaine Talmard Mâcon Chardonnay
(France)
Ivan Tamas Chardonnay Haynes Ranch
Livermore (California)

Ivan Tamas Fumé Blanc Figoni Ranch Livermore (California)

Ivan Tamas Trebbiano Livermore (California)

Domaine du Tariquet Côtes de Gascogne (France)

Dr. Cosimo Taurino Notarpanaro (Italy)

Dr. Cosimo Taurino Salice Salentino Riserva (Italy)

Château Tayac (France)

Domaine des Terres Dorées Chardonnay Beaujolais (France)

Château Thieuley Bordeaux Blanc (France)

Pierre-Yves Tijou Anjou Sec (France)

Topolos Old Vineyard Reserve Sonoma (California)

Pascual Toso (Argentina)

Château Tour des Gendres Bergerac Blanc (France)

Château Tour des Gendres Bergerac Rosé (France)

Château Tour des Gendres Bergerac Rouge (France)

Trapiche Malbec (Argentina)

Tre Monti Albana di Romagna (Italy)

Tre Monti Sangiovese di Romagna (Italy)

Trentadue Carignane (California)

Trentadue Old Patch Red (California)

Domaine de Triennes Les Aureliens Vins du Pays du Bar (France)

Château du Trignon Côtes du Rhône (France)

Château du Trignon Sablet (France)

Domaine Trois Frères Chardonnay (France)

Antonin Truffer Chardonnay Brut Tradition (France)

Château de la Tuilerie Carte Noir (Black Label) Costières de Nimes (France)

Tyrrell's Wines Dry Red Vat 9 (Australia)

Tyrrell's Wines Long Flat Red (Australia)

Tyrrell's Wines Long Flat White (Chardonnay/Semillon) (Australia)

Unckrich Kallstader Saumagen Riesling Kabinett (Germany)

Undurraga Chardonnay Estate Santa Ana (Chile)

Undurraga Chardonnay Sauvignon Reserve (Chile)

Undurraga Sauvignon Blanc (Chile)

Val d'Orbieu Réserve St. Martin Cabernet Sauvignon VDP d'Oc (France)

Val d'Orbieu Réserve St. Martin Chardonnay Gold Cuvée VDP d'Oc (France)

Val d'Orbieu Réserve St. Martin Chardonnay VDP d'Oc (France)

Val d'Orbieu Réserve St. Martin Marsanne VDP d'Oc (France)

Val d'Orbieu Réserve St. Martin Mourvèdre VDP d'Oc (France)

Val d'Orbieu Réserve St. Martin Muscat Petits Grains VDP d'Oc (France)

Val d'Orbieu Réserve St. Martin Rosé de Syrah VDP d'Oc (France)

Val d'Orbieu Réserve St. Martin Sélection Blanc VDP d'Oc (France)

Val d'Orbieu Réserve St. Martin Sélection Rouge VDP d'Oc (France)

Val d'Orbieu Réserve St. Martin Syrah VDP d'Oc (France)

Val d'Orbieu Réserve St. Martin Viognier VDP d'Oc (France)

Château Val-Joanis (France)

Domaine Valette Mâcon Chaintré Vieilles Vignes (France)

Domaine de la Vallongue Coteaux d'Aix Les Baux (France)

Domaine de la Vallongue Coteaux d'Aix Les Baux Cuvée Murielle (France)

Abbaye de Valmagne (France)

Domaine Valmalle Syrah (France)

Victoria Gewürztraminer Napa (California)

Vidal-Fleury Côtes du Rhône (France)

Vidal-Fleury Côtes du Rhône Blanc (France)

Vidal-Fleury Côtes du Ventoux (France)

Vidal-Fleury Vacqueyras (France)

La Vieille Ferme (France)

Domaine des Vieilles Pierres Mâcon Vergisson (France)

Domaine du Vieux Télégraphe Le Pigeoulet VDP Vaucluse (France)

Villa Diana Montepulciano d'Abruzzo (Italy)

Villa Majnoni Valcalepio Rosso (Italy)

Villa Monte di Chianti (Italy)

Villa Mt. Eden Chardonnay Cellar Select Napa (California)

Villa Volpe Sauvignon (Italy)

Domainde de Villemajou Corbières Gold
  Label (New Oak Barrel) (France)
Château La Voulte Gasperets Corbières
  Cuvée Réservée (France)
Dr. Heinz Wagner Ockfener Bockstein
  Riesling QbA (Germany)
Dr. Heinz Wagner Saarburger Rausch
  Riesling QbA (Germany)
Bodega Weinert Carrascal (Argentina)
Bodega Weinert Merlot (Argentina)
A. Weingart Bopparder Hamm Feuerlay
  Riesling Hochgewachs (Germany)
A. Weingart Bopparder Hamm Ohlenberg
  Riesling Spatlese (Germany)

Winzer. Vier Jahreszeiten Durkheimer
  Feuerberg Gewürztraminer Spatlese
  (Germany)
Winzer. Vier Jahreszeiten Durkheimer
  Feuerberg Rulander Spatlese (Germany)
Winzer. Vier Jahreszeiten Durkheimer
  Feuerberg Scheurebe Kabinett
  (Germany)
G. Wittmann Westhofener Auelerde
  Bacchus Kabinett (Germany)
David Wynn Chardonnay (Australia)
David Wynn Semillon/Chardonnay
  (Australia)

Barrel Tasting Reports

1994 RED BORDEAUX

SUMMARY OF 1994 RED BORDEAUX

EXTRAORDINARY POTENTIAL (96–100)

None

EXCEPTIONAL POTENTIAL (90–95)

L'Angélus (St.-Émilion)*
L'Arrosée (St.-Émilion)
Beau Séjour Bécot (St.-Émilion)
Clinet (Pomerol)*
La Dominique (St.-Émilion)
Ducru-Beaucaillou (St.-Julien)
L'Église-Clinet (Pomerol)
L'Évangile (Pomerol)*
La Fleur de Gay (Pomerol)
Gazin (Pomerol)
Grand Mayne (St.-Émilion)
Haut-Brion (Pessac-Léognan)
Lafleur (Pomerol)
Latour (Pauillac)*
Léoville-Barton (St.-Julien)

Léoville Las Cases (St.-Julien)
Château Margaux (Margaux)
La Mission Haut-Brion (Pessac-Léognan)
Montrose (St.-Estèphe)
Mouton-Rothschild (Pauillac)
Pavie-Macquin (St.-Émilion)
Pétrus (Pomerol)
Pichon-Lalande (Pauillac)
Le Pin (Pomerol)
Pontet-Canet (Pauillac)
Rausan-Ségla (Margaux)
Le Tertre-Roteboeuf (St.-Émilion)
Troplong-Mondot (St.-Émilion)*
Valandraud (St.-Émilion)

EXCELLENT POTENTIAL (88–89)

Ausone (St.-Émilion)*
Beaurégard (Pomerol)*
Beauséjour Duffau (St.-Émilion)*
Bon Pasteur (Pomerol)*
Branaire (St.-Julien)

Cadet Piola (St.-Émilion)
Canon La Gaffelière (St.-Émilion)*
Chauvin (St.-Émilion)
Cheval Blanc (St.-Émilion)
Domaine de Chevalier (St.-Émilion)

* These wines possess the potential to move up to the next category.

Clerc-Milon (Pauillac)
Clos du Clocher (Pomerol)
Clos Fourtet (St.-Émilion)
Clos du Marquis (St.-Julien)
Clos de L'Oratoire (St.-Émilion)
Clos René (Pomerol)*
La Conseillante (Pomerol)
Cos d'Estournel (St.-Estèphe)*
Cos Labory (St.-Estèphe)
La Couspade (St.-Émilion)
Couvent des Jacobins (St.-Émilion)
La Croix du Casse (Pomerol)
Ferrand-Lartigue (St.-Émilion)*
De Fieuzal (Pessac-Léognan)
Figeac (St.-Émilion)
Fontenil (Fronsac)
Forts de Latour (Pauillac)
La Gaffelière (St.-Émilion)
Giscours (Margaux)
Grand Pontet (St.-Émilion)
Grand-Puy-Ducasse (Pauillac)
Grand-Puy-Lacoste (Pauillac)*
Haut-Bailly (Pessac-Léognan)
Lafite-Rothschild (Pauillac)
Lafon Rochet (St.-Estèphe)

Lagrange (St.-Julien)
Larmande (St.-Émilion)
Lascombes (Margaux)
Latour à Pomerol (Pomerol)
La Louvière (Graves)
Lynch-Bages (Pauillac)
Monbousquet (St.-Émilion)*
Nenin (Pomerol)
Palmer (Margaux)
Pape-Clément (Pessac-Léognan)*
Parenchère-Raphael Gazaniol (Bordeaux
    Supérior)
Pensées de Lafleur (Pomerol)
Petit Village (Pomerol)
Phélan-Ségur (St.-Estèphe)
Pichon Longueville Baron (Pauillac)
Potensac (Médoc)
Prieuré-Lichine (Margaux)
Rochemorin (Graves)
St.-Pierre (St.-Julien)*
Smith-Haut-Lafitte (Graves)
Soutard (St.-Émilion)
Trotanoy (Pomerol)
Trotte Vieille (St.-Émilion)
Vieux Château Certan (Pomerol)

SLEEPERS OF THE VINTAGE

Chauvin (St.-Émilion)
Clerc-Milon (Pauillac)
Clos du Clocher (Pomerol)
Clos de L'Oratoire (St.-Émilion)
Clos René (Pomerol)
Corbin (St.-Émilion)
La Couspade (St.-Émilion)
La Croix du Casse (Pomerol)
La Dominique (St.-Émilion)
Ferrand-Lartigue (St.-Émilion)
Fontenil (Fronsac)
Grand Mayne (St.-Émilion)

Larmande (St.-Émilion)
Léoville-Barton (St.-Julien)
La Louvière (Graves)
Monbousquet (St.-Émilion)
Nenin (Pomerol)
Pavie-Macquin (St.-Émilion)
Phélan-Ségur (St.-Estèphe)
Pontet-Canet (Pauillac)
Prieuré-Lichine (Margaux)
Le Tertre-Roteboeuf (St.-Émilion)
Troplong-Mondot (St.-Émilion)
Valandraud (St.-Émilion)

Note: The following wines were tasted from the barrel, hence the approximate range in ratings as indicated by the parentheses. This is for readers of this guide interested in purchasing wines from this excellent Bordeaux vintage.

1994 L'Angélus (St.-Émilion)   (93–96)

What hasn't this estate done right since the 1988 vintage? St.-Émilion's most consistent wine since 1988, and Bordeaux's most concentrated wine since 1990, L'Angélus has turned in a monumental performance in 1994. Is it St.-Émilion's answer to the 1990 Montrose? Proprietor Bouard feels the 1994 L'Angélus is more classic than the 1990, and just a notch

* These wines possess the potential to move up to the next category.

below it in quality. It contains more Cabernet Franc (55%) than usual, with the balance Merlot. Unquestionably a great wine, as well as one of the potential wines of the vintage, it will require considerable cellaring, so those who lack patience are advised to search out the more forward 1992 or 1993 L'Angélus. The color is an inky, opaque black/purple, and the nose offers up intense aromas of cassis, roasted nuts, herbs, vanillin, licorice, and spices. It is magnificently concentrated, with gobs of sweet tannin, unbelievable extraction of flavor, decent acidity, and a knockout, mind-bogglingly long finish. Do not expect this wine to be ready to drink before the turn of the century. It is potentially a wine that will last 50+ years. If you have not yet discovered how great the wines of L'Angélus have been since 1988, isn't it about time?

1994 D'Angludet (Margaux) (85–87)

Proprietor Peter Sichel has turned in a pleasingly proportioned, sweet, supple 1994 with admirable ripeness, medium body, and firm tannin in the attractively long finish. It should be drinkable early, and keep for 12–15 years.

1994 D'Armailhac (Pauillac) (86–87)

This wine stands out among the tannic, forceful, backward 1994s as a more approachable and user-friendly claret. The 30% Merlot/25% Cabernet Franc/45% Cabernet Sauvignon blend has resulted in a medium to dark ruby/purple-colored wine with an attractive, appealing bouquet of sweet cherries, currants, and spicy new oak. The wine is medium bodied, with very good concentration, a plush, round, generous fruitiness, and a slightly tannic finish. Although deceptively forward, this wine will require 2–3 years of cellaring; it will last for 15 years.

1994 L'Arrosée (St.-Émilion) (88–91)

Although closed, this promising 1994 is crammed with rich, unctuously textured ripe fruit bound together by formidable tannin. A marvelously saturated purple color is followed by a full, dense, beautifully delineated, long, and complete wine. It will require 6–8 years of cellaring and should age well for 25+ years. This impressive L'Arrosée may turn out to be the modern-day equivalent of the long-lived, complex 1961.

1994 Ausone (St.-Émilion) (89–92)

Ausone is frightfully difficult to comprehend, whether it is 6 months or 25 years of age. The 1994 is a ripe, surprisingly rich, flattering style of Ausone that is vaguely reminiscent of the wonderful 1983. The color is a healthy ruby/purple and the nose jumps from the glass, offering up gobs of floral, sweet cassis, and mineral scents. Medium bodied, this wine relies on finesse, elegance, and delicacy rather than on power and body. This stylish, concentrated, well-balanced, harmonious wine should age gracefully for 30 years.

1994 Bahans Haut-Brion (Pessac-Léognan) (85–87)

With an easygoing, telltale Graves nose of spice, minerals, tobacco, and black currants, a supple texture, and ripe fruit, this elegant, medium-bodied, attractive Bahans should drink well during its first 7–8 years of life.

1994 Balestard La Tonnelle (St.-Émilion) (86–88)

The 1994 is the finest Balestard La Tonnelle produced in many years. Reminiscent of the 1982, it is a darkly colored, powerful, muscular, intense wine. It compensates for its lack of finesse with a blustery display of rich, concentrated, herb-tinged, black cherry fruit, an unctuous texture, and moderate tannin in the forceful finish. It will benefit from several years of cellaring and should last for 15 years.

1994 Beau Séjour Bécot (St.-Émilion)   (90–92)

This is unquestionably the finest wine I have yet tasted from the Bécot family. An opaque black/purple color suggests considerable concentration and intensity. The huge nose of sweet, toasty, smoky new oak and copious quantities of black and red fruits intertwined with Asian spices is followed by a sweet, outstanding wine of huge concentration, full body, and moderately high tannin. This powerful, authoritatively flavored, intense wine requires 5–6 years of cellaring; it should last for 15+ years. Impressive!

1994 Beaurégard (Pomerol)   (88–90+)

The 1994 may be the finest wine Beaurégard has ever produced. This estate is another Bordeaux château that has been making better and better wines, especially since the early nineties. The dense purple color and sweet nose of smoke, minerals, and black raspberries are enthralling. Full bodied, with layers of unctuously textured fruit, low acidity, moderately high tannin, and outstanding potential, it should drink well between 1998 and 2010+.

1994 Beauséjour Duffau (St.-Émilion)   (87–88+?)

The proprietor did not want his 1994 shown, as it had just been racked and he felt it needed time to rebound. I did taste a week-old sample of the 1994 Beauséjour-Duffau at a *négoci-ant's* office. Of all the St.-Émilion premier grands crus classés, this wine reveals the most opaque, dense, purple color. There was a muted nose (undoubtedly due to the age of the barrel sample), medium to full body, high flavor extraction, and formidable tannin in the finish. This property made a monumental wine in 1990, and very good wines in 1992 and 1993. The 1994 may be superior to either the 1992 or 1993, so this evaluation could look conservative once I have had a chance to see a fresher sample of the wine. There is no doubting that the 1994 is the most concentrated wine among the lackluster premier grands crus classés of St.-Émilion.

1994 Belair (St.-Émilion)   (86–87)

Belair normally produces a tannic, hard wine, so how do I explain the fact that in the tannic 1994 vintage, this estate has turned out a soft, open-knit, forward, sweet, creamy-styled claret? It exhibits a dark ruby color, plenty of sweet black raspberry and black cherry fruit, medium body, Belair's telltale mineral, stony component, and moderate tannin. The 1994 may be the most flattering Belair I have tasted out of barrel since the 1983. It should drink well for 10–15+ years.

1994 Bellegrave (Pomerol)   (83–85)

This elegant, understated, richly fruity wine displays medium body, low acidity, and an attractive, smooth, supple finish. It should drink well for 7–8 years.

1994 Beychevelle (St.-Julien)   (82–85)

Tasted three times with similar notes, Beychevelle's 1994 is an elegant, light-bodied wine revealing herbal, red cherry scents, and firm, earthy, spicy flavors that are presently domi-nated by harsh, underripe tannin. Although it should turn out to merit the above rating, the wine's lack of personality and slight, hard style are worrisome.

1994 Bon Pasteur (Pomerol)   (88–90)

The "good pastor" has turned out a rich, well-structured, concentrated Pomerol whose style resembles a hypothetical blend of the 1988 and 1990. It will require 4–5 years of cellaring, but it will last for 15–18 years. The color is an impressive dark purple, and the nose offers up an array of scents, ranging from mocha/coffee to black cherries, herbs, and smoky wood. Medium to full bodied, with excellent depth, it is a fine, well-focused example of the vintage.

1994 Bonalgue (Pomerol)   (86–87)

One of the most underrated Pomerol estates (and still available at a reasonable price), this medium- to full-bodied wine exhibits a healthy, saturated ruby/purple color, and sweet aromas of coffee and black cherries intertwined with scents of herbs. The wine possesses excellent concentration, fine purity, and a light to moderately tannic finish. It will need 1–2 years of cellaring and should drink well for 12–15.

1994 Bourgneuf (Pomerol)   (84–85?)

I detected musty, unusual woodsy aromas in this wine that tended to dissipate within several minutes. Once past the funky smells, this chunky, rustic Pomerol exhibited rough tannin, medium body, rich fruit, and a husky, burly style that should offer reasonably pleasant drinking over the next 10–15 years.

1994 Branaire (St.-Julien)   (87–89+?)

Branaire declassified 50% of their 1994 harvest and increased the percentage of Merlot in the blend. Their yields were also down by 30% over 1993. The result is a highly successful 1994 exhibiting a moderately dark ruby/purple color, ripe fruit offering attractive toasty oak aromas combined with scents of black currants, a fat, seductive, moderately fleshy texture, and an overall sense of elegance, despite moderate tannin in the finish. Although Branaire will never make a blockbuster St.-Julien, this should turn out to be an excellent wine that will be able to be drunk early on, but will keep for 12–16 years.

1994 La Cabanne (Pomerol)   (87–88)

I have never been impressed with La Cabanne, but the 1994 barrel sample was so rich, powerful, and concentrated that it made me wonder what took place at this estate in 1994. Unfortunately, La Cabanne's proprietor was unavailable so I could not question him. This is an extremely rich, concentrated, impressively endowed wine that is far superior to anything I have previously tasted from La Cabanne. Readers will no doubt understand my desire to try this wine several more times in order to confirm my initial tasting impressions. If subsequent tastings are as convincing, La Cabanne is unquestionably a sleeper of the vintage, as well as a noteworthy achievement. The wine should drink well for 10–15 years.

1994 Cadet Bon (St.-Émilion)   (85–87+)

A dark ruby/purple color is followed by an herb-, cassis-, and black cherry–scented wine with hints of vanilla in the background. The wine possesses medium body, above-average to very good richness, some sweetness, and moderately high tannin in the austere finish. A bit more flesh (which may come from cask aging) will help this wine score in the mid to upper-eighties. It is a candidate for 12–15 years of cellaring.

1994 Cadet Piola (St.-Émilion)   (87–88+)

Although I have always enjoyed this estate's wines, they have a tendency to make frightfully tannic, hard wines that require time to open. While the opaque black/purple-colored 1994's aromatics are backward, the tannin is sweet and ripe and there is plenty of black cherry fruit to balance out the wine's structural components. There are loads of power and intensity in this rustic yet promising wine. It will need 5–6 years of cellaring and should keep for 20.

1994 Calon-Ségur (St.-Estèphe)   (83–87?)

An earthy nose of underbrush and ripe fruit offers a dichotomy of scents. This dark ruby/garnet-colored wine exhibits better than average extraction and ripe fruit, but the 1994 Calon-Ségur finishes with a boatload of tough tannin. Calon-Ségur is not an easy wine to taste young, but the 1994 appeared skimpy in a flight of its peers (i.e., Cos d'Estournel, Lafon Rochet, Phélan-Ségur, and Montrose).

1994 Canon (Canon-Fronsac)   (77–81)

The 1994 Canon exhibits meager body and a lean, angular style. It is deficient in fruit, ripeness, and extraction. The moderate tannin only exaggerates the wine's fragile balance.

1994 Canon (St.-Émilion)   (83–85?)

One of my favorite estates has produced a light-bodied, herbal, earthy, woody wine that tastes closed, tannic, and austere. Unless more fruit and charm emerge, this will be a disappointment.

1994 Canon de Brem (Canon-Fronsac)   (83–85)

After considerable coaxing, attractive, sweet, berry, and curranty fruit emerge. The wine exhibits a medium to dark ruby color, straightforward, soft flavors, and light to moderate tannin in the finish. This is a well-made but one-dimensional wine lacking the depth this fine vineyard usually achieves.

1994 Canon La Gaffelière (St.-Émilion)   (88–90)

It will be interesting to see if Canon La Gaffelière is promoted in the new 1995 classification of the wines of St.-Émilion. Certainly the efforts produced by Count Stephan Neipperg have been impressive, especially since 1988. The 1994 (85% of the harvest was included in the top wine) is a 58% Merlot/42% Cabernet Franc blend that admirably exhibits the style that has emerged from Canon La Gaffelière since the late eighties. This dense wine possesses an opaque dark purple color, a big, smoky, lavishly oaked, sweet nose of black fruits, licorice, and vanilla, plenty of fat, potentially outstanding richness, and a smooth, moderately tannic finish. It should reach full maturity in 3–4 years and last for 15 or more.

1994 Canon Moueix (Canon-Fronsac)   (82–84)

Medium dark ruby colored, with a spicy, mineral-, black cherry-, and currant-scented nose, this pleasant wine offers good fruit, medium body, and light tannin in the finish. It is an elegant Canon-Fronsac that should drink well during its first 7–8 years of life.

1994 Cantenac-Brown (Margaux)   (84–86?)

Some wines from the 1994 vintage appear to have been made in a style that sought the highest extraction and longest maceration possible, perhaps in an effort to extract more flavor under the assumption that several weeks of cold, rainy weather had diluted the grapes. Those wines, of which Cantenac-Brown is one, are tough, hard, and slightly hollow in the middle, with an abundance of abrasive sharpness and astringency. This wine was tasted on three separate occasions, and while it appeared to have some soft fruit behind its structural skeleton, it was not sufficient to give the wine balance. Another year of cellaring should reveal whether it possesses the equilibrium necessary to merit readers' interest.

1994 Canuet (Margaux)   (68–72)

The second wine of Cantenac-Brown is extremely herbaceous, tannic, and lacking depth of fruit in the middle palate and finish.

1994 Cap de Mourlin (St.-Émilion)   (86–87)

An impressively endowed, seductive, rich, velvety-textured wine with extremely high Merlot in evidence (coffee, herbs, berry fruit), this fleshy, corpulently styled wine exhibits fine concentration and a long, alcoholic finish. It should drink well during its first 10–12 years of life.

1994 Carbonnieux (Pessac-Léognan) (86–88)

This textbook, lighter-styled Graves offers wonderfully complex tobacco and black currant aromas presented in a light- to medium-bodied, finesse style. It is an immensely satisfying, richly fruity wine that should drink well young and keep for 15+ years.

1994 De Carles (Fronsac) (78–83)

This light-bodied, delicate, currant-scented and -flavored wine will offer pleasant, straightforward drinking during its first 5–7 years of life.

1994 Certan-Giraud (Pomerol) (85–87)

Always a corpulent wine, Certan-Giraud's 1994 displays fine color, admirable quantities of sweet, jammy fruit, and a short finish (particularly in view of the impressive attack). This medium- to full-bodied wine appears to have a slight hole in the middle. Nevertheless, it is a very good wine for drinking over the next 6–9 years.

1994 Certan de May (Pomerol) (88–90?)

Recent cask samples of Certan de May have displayed an annoying, musty, damp wood component in the bouquet that detracts from what is otherwise a powerful, rich, highly concentrated, well-made wine. Last year I had similar complaints about the 1993, whose flavors were flawed by a damp, cardboard aroma. Although it is reminiscent of a badly corked bottle, it is not the result of a moldy cork. The 1994 reveals a subtle mustiness that is less objectionable than the aggressively moldy smells in the 1993, but the problem is cause for grave concern. This is very sad, because what Madame Barreau and her son have achieved is impressive. Certan de May is a potentially outstanding wine, with a superb, opaque purple color, a rich, concentrated, full-bodied style, and a highly extracted, long, tannic finish. This could be a 20-year wine with impressive credentials, but the musty woodiness must be considered.

1994 Chauvin (St.-Émilion) (87–89+?)

The Chauvin samples I tasted were potentially outstanding. The question mark has been inserted only because I thought the wine was exhibiting a considerable amount of oak, and my recollection is that only about 30%–40% of the harvest is aged in new oak casks. The black/purple-colored 1994 Chauvin displays gobs of superjammy black cherries and sweet, toasty oak. Fat, opulent, full-bodied flavors are low in acidity, but moderately tannic. This could turn out to be a sleeper of the vintage if the wine's quality holds up after its *élevage* and bottling. This estate should be one to watch closely.

1994 Cheval Blanc (St.-Émilion) (87–89+)

Although this 50% Cabernet Franc/50% Merlot blend is richer than the lightweight wine produced in 1992, as well as the 1993 (which, by the way, is tasting far better; I would now rate it 87–88 points), it is not the most concentrated Cheval Blanc. The color is an attractive dark ruby with purple tints. The wine reveals the classic Cheval Blanc aromatic profile with sweet oak, menthol, black currant, and spicy scents. Medium bodied and delicate, with admirable richness and a soft, seductive, satiny-smooth style, this wine was so velvety textured, I could have consumed it from the cask. If the 1994 Cheval Blanc puts on more weight (it often has a tendency to improve greatly after 3–5 years of age), this will be an outstanding wine, but it is not of the quality Cheval Blanc achieved in 1990, 1989, 1985, 1983, and 1982. This is not a 1994 with a high tannin level, so it will unquestionably drink well young.

1994 Domaine de Chevalier (Pessac-Léognan) (87–88)

A dark ruby/purple color is followed by a fragrant nose of overripe black cherries. Surprisingly sweet and less oaky than usual, this classically styled Graves possesses medium body and firm, powerful tannin. It will require 8–10 years of cellaring and should last for 20 years.

1994 Clerc-Milon (Pauillac) (87–90)

Is Clerc-Milon the Pomerol of Pauillac? Recent vintages have been silky smooth, with abundant ripeness and round, opulent textures. Made from a blend of 40% Merlot, 45% Cabernet Sauvignon, and 15% Cabernet Franc, the 1994 exhibits a fine dark ruby/purple color, and a forthright, intense nose of smoked nuts, jammy black currants, and lavish wood. Sweet and succulent, with excellent concentration, this medium-bodied wine offers fat and fleshiness, as well as elegance and complexity. It should drink well when released and should last for 12–15+ years.

1994 Clinet (Pomerol) (94–96)

Black magic! I don't think any fountain pen ink could be darker than the 1994 Clinet. A legend in the making, the 1994 Clinet may rival the virtually perfect 1989. Along with the 1994 L'Angélus and 1994 Troplong-Mondot, it is one of the three most concentrated wines of the vintage, with layer upon layer of extraordinarily pure, amazingly rich, astonishingly extracted black fruits. This full-bodied, explosive, blockbuster 1994 should drink well by the end of the century, and should last for at least 30 years. It is superior to the 1990 and 1988 Clinet—no small accomplishment. A winemaking tour de force!

1994 Clos du Clocher (Pomerol) (88–90)

A powerful, dark-colored wine with high tannin as well as impressive fruit extraction and considerable body (loads of glycerin), this wine offers an overripe, forceful, massive mouthful of delicious Pomerol. In most vintages Clos du Clocher is a loosely built wine, but the 1994 exhibited great ripeness of fruit, surprising size and intensity, and more focus and delineation than this estate normally achieves. The 1994 Clos du Clocher should be one of the sleepers of the vintage. Drink it between 1999 and 2015.

1994 Clos L'Église (Pomerol) (72–74)

This sinewy, hard, compact wine does not possess enough fruit to balance out the harsh tannin level. Its compressed style makes for an angular, attenuated wine that offers no charm.

1994 Clos Fourtet (St.-Émilion) (87–89+)

Given Clos Fourtet's strong effort in 1990, as well as this 1994 that will ultimately eclipse the 1990, I believe readers should recognize the reemergence of this estate as a serious provider of high-quality wine. The 1994's saturated purple color is accompanied by extremely rich, sweet Merlot scents (jammy black cherries and herbs). This full-bodied, tannic wine, with an unctuous, sweet mid-palate, requires 3–4 years of cellaring; it should age well for 15+ years.

1994 Clos du Marquis (St.-Julien) (87–89)

Along with Bahans Haut-Brion and Forts de Latour, Clos du Marquis is one of Bordeaux's three finest second wines. The 1994 appears to be another noteworthy effort. It exhibits much of the same character as Léoville Las Cases, but it is not as concentrated or as potentially long-lived. The saturated dark ruby/purple color is followed by a sweet, jammy nose of herbs and black currants, medium body, excellent ripeness, and a multilayered, fleshy finish that delivers considerable fruit buttressed by moderate tannin. This wine should drink well during its first 15 years of life.

1994 Clos de L'Oratoire (St.-Émilion) (87–88)

Stephan Neipperg, the proprietor of Canon La Gaffelière, acquired this estate several years ago. He feels the 1994 is the first wine that expresses the style he desires. It is a large-scale, powerful, muscular St.-Émilion with an opaque ruby/purple color, plenty of red and black fruits in the spicy-, oaky-, olive-scented nose, medium to full body, excellent concentration, and loads of tannin in the finish. The low acidity and sweet fruit suggest this wine will drink well early, but will last for 15 years.

1994 Clos René (Pomerol) (88–91)

I cannot recall tasting a young Clos René as impressive as the 1994. Hopefully, the proprietor will not excessively manipulate and process the wine at bottling, stripping it of its wonderfully succulent, rich fruitiness. The wine reveals an opaque purple color followed by an overripe nose of cassis, plums, prunes, and herbs. Unctuously textured, with terrific extract, low acidity, and plenty of tannin lurking behind the fruit, this jammy, thick, right-bank claret should age well for 15+ years.

1994 Clos St. Martin (St.-Émilion) (77–82)

One of a handful of 1994s with a cool-climate, low-pH style, tart acidity, and light to medium body, the predominant characteristic of this wine's bouquet is red rather than black currants. While elegant and finesse filled, it does not possess enough concentration or ripe fruit. Drink it over the next 7–8 years.

1994 La Clotte (St.-Émilion) (86–87)

La Clotte generally displays a forward, plump, low-acid, richly fruity style. The 1994 exhibits more jammy black cherries than seen in recent vintages, as well as an enthralling sweetness. Forward, with low acidity, plenty of fruit, medium to full body, and a plump, heady, user-friendly personality, it should drink well during its first decade of life. If more complexity develops, it will merit a higher score.

1994 La Clusière (St.-Émilion) (72–76)

Light ruby with a watery rim, this wine reveals mostly herb and oak notes in the nose. High acidity dominates the palate, and the finish is too brief. It is a disappointing effort.

1994 La Conseillante (Pomerol) (89–91)

Although the 1994 is a classic La Conseillante, it is not as concentrated as the 1990 or 1989. The 1994 exhibits a deep, dark ruby/purple color, this estate's telltale floral-, black raspberry–, vanillin-scented nose, a velvety-textured, rich, medium-bodied palate, and considerable finesse, ripeness, and delicacy, in addition to a silky-smooth finish. Tasted three times, La Conseillante's 1994 was nearly impossible to spit out because of its seductive, fragrant personality. This wine will be drinkable when released, and should age well for 15 or more years.

1994 Corbin (St.-Émilion) (86–89)

Corbin has a tendency to make excessively fruity, loosely constructed wines that require drinking in their first 10–12 years of life. The rich, intense 1994 possesses more tannin than usual, as well as plenty of baby fat, corpulent black cherry and curranty fruit, high glycerin levels, and plenty of alcohol and tannin. This fleshy St.-Émilion should age well for 10–15 years.

1994 Cordeillan-Bages (Pauillac)   (83–86)

The annoying herbaceousness often present in this wine cannot be found in the barrel sample of 1994 Cordeillan-Bages. The color is a healthy deep purple. The wine exhibits light to medium body, round, soft, fruity, up-front aromas and flavors, good purity and balance, and a tannic but clean finish. Drink it over the next 10–12 years.

1994 Cos d'Estournel (St.-Estèphe)   (89–91)

Only 50% of the harvest went into the 1994 Cos d'Estournel, a 60% Cabernet Sauvignon/ 40% Merlot blend. The deep, saturated, dark ruby/purple color is followed by gobs of toasty vanillin scents from new oak, a rich, sweet, pure nose of cassis, medium body, potentially outstanding concentration and definition, and a ripe, moderately tannic finish. This elegant, authoritatively flavored wine should be at its best between 2000 and 2020.

1994 Cos Labory (St.-Estèphe)   (86–88?)

The only reservation I have about the 1994 Cos Labory is its formidable tannin level. This black/purple-colored wine is strong, muscular, and well built, and readers who have the patience to wait a minimum of 10–12 years for it to soften may be well rewarded. If the wine fleshes out and exhibits more ripeness and richness in the mid-palate and finish, it may merit an outstanding rating. However, this backward wine will test most Bordeaux lovers' patience. It has the potential to last for 30 or more years.

1994 La Couspade (St.-Émilion)   (87–89)

This microestate (18 acres) is lowering yields, practicing a partial malolactic fermentation in new oak, and trying hard to raise the quality level of the wine. The results are opulent, rich, fat, well-endowed wines that exhibit plenty of ripeness, considerable new oak, a lush texture, and 10–12 years of aging potential. The 1994 is the most promising La Couspade the proprietors, the Aubert brothers, have yet made.

1994 Couvent de Jacobins (St.-Émilion)   (87–89)

This property has turned out a rich, chocolaty-, herb-, and berry-scented wine with medium to full body, a succulent texture, and gobs of glycerin and sweet fruit in the finish. This attractive, plump St.-Émilion should drink well for 7–8 years.

1994 La Croix du Casse (Pomerol)   (88–89+)

The saturated, nearly opaque black/purple color makes this wine a candidate for one of the darkest-colored wines of the vintage. The nose offers up enthralling scents of black raspberries, licorice, and sweet, smoky oak. Rich, powerful, and deep, with medium to full body, and noticeably high tannin in the finish, this generously endowed wine will require 2–4 years of cellaring; it should keep for 15 or more years.

1994 Croizet-Bages (Pauillac)   (82–85)

The owners of Croizet-Bages appear to be responding to greater consumer awareness of the quality levels of specific Bordeaux châteaux. This may be the finest Croizet-Bages made in more than 20 years. Although light bodied, there is good ripeness, an attractive nose of cassis fruit, herbs, and vanilla, and a clean, pure, slightly tannic, but overall soft and pleasing finish. It should drink well young and keep for 12–15 years.

1994 Cruzeau (Pessac-Léognan)   (86–87)

One of the estates in the André Lurton empire, Cruzeau has turned out a lovely, elegant, ripe 1994 with telltale tobacco scents, a richly fruity character, medium body, excellent purity, and light tannin in the finish. It should drink well for 7–8 years.

1994 Curé Bon (St.-Émilion) (85–86)

The wines of this estate, which has an impressive strategic position near Belair on the village of St.-Émilion's hillsides, are made from 80% Merlot and 20% Cabernet Franc. The wine comes from grapes grown on a small 15-acre vineyard, and tends to be elegant, with moderate flavor extraction and an up-front, forward appeal. The 1994 displays good rather than exceptional color saturation, light to medium body, fine ripeness, a touch of dilution, and spicy, moderately hard tannin in the finish. It requires several years of cellaring and should keep well for 10–15.

1994 Dassault (St.-Émilion) (84–86)

Dassault makes a popular, but essentially straightforward, soft, fruity wine that is meant to be drunk in its first 6–7 years of life. No one will find anything objectionable about the 1994, a smooth-as-silk, medium-bodied wine with an attractive purple color, and sweet red and black fruit gently infused with smoky, toasty oak. Clean, pure, and satisfying, this wine should be a good bargain, even with the collapse of the dollar.

1994 La Dauphine (Fronsac) (77–81)

Although this medium-bodied wine reveals some soft fruit, it is diluted and hollow. It will require drinking during its first decade of life.

1994 Dauzac (Margaux) (85–86+?)

Each time I tasted this wine the saturated purple color was impressive. The aromatics include spice, new wood, and black fruits. Ferociously tannic, hard, and tough, with good weight and a sense of ripeness, the tannin appears to be out of balance for the wine's ripeness and richness. However, it is too early to write off this muscular, beefy Margaux. First impressions indicate 10 years of cellaring may be required. Moreover, it is capable of 25–30 years of evolution. If they have not already done so, readers should note that Dauzac, now under the administration of André Lurton, appears to have rebounded after an extended period of mediocrity. Dauzac has produced more promising and interesting wines in both 1993 and 1994.

1994 Destieux (St.-Émilion) (85–86)

Well colored, dense, spicy, and full, this stern, tannic, beefy wine should age well for 8–15 years.

1994 La Dominique (St.-Émilion) (91–93)

Could the 1994 La Dominique be even better than the spectacular 1990, 1989, and 1982? An opaque purple color is followed by a sensational, pure, intense nose of overripe black raspberries, cherries, and plums. Extremely full bodied, with layers of fruit extraction, this opulently textured wine possesses a huge, chewy midsection, and a blockbuster finish that nearly conceals significant tannin. This is a superb wine, and one of the stars of the vintage. It should drink well after 2–3 years of cellaring, and should last for 20 years.

1994 Ducru-Beaucaillou (St.-Julien) (91–93+)

An exceptional Ducru-Beaucaillou, the 1994 reveals an opaque dark purple color, and the classic Ducru nose of sweet cassis fruit intertwined with subtle notes of minerals, herbs, vanillin, and spring flowers. Sweet and rich, with medium body, high tannin, and a long, explosive finish, this wine possesses the requisite depth, flesh, and fruit extraction to stand up to the wine's formidable structure. My instincts suggest it may rival the 1990, 1989, and 1985, perhaps even the 1982. Like many 1994 Bordeaux, it requires 8–10 years of cellaring, and it should last for 30 years.

1994 Duhart-Milon-Rothschild (Pauillac)   (83–85)

The Rothschild estate has been attempting to upgrade Duhart-Milon, so I was surprised this wine did not perform better. It is light bodied, crisp, and tart, with a cool-climate, low-pH taste that resembles Cabernet Sauvignons from Carneros or New Zealand rather than from Bordeaux. Although elegant and graceful, good fruit extraction, ripeness, and a long finish were not in evidence. The wine will require patience, as there is abundant tannin in the finish.

1994 L'Église-Clinet (Pomerol)   (91–93)

This is the finest L'Église-Clinet made since the estate's exceptional 1985. The wine possesses an impressive saturated purple color, super aromatics in the cassis-scented nose, wonderfully succulent, full-bodied, unctuously textured, expansive, jammy flavors that coat the palate, and a full-bodied, terrific finish. As the wine sits in the glass some tannin emerges from behind the cascade of fruit. Look for this large-scale, immensely impressive, beautifully balanced L'Église-Clinet to drink well in 3–5 years and to last for 20 or more.

1994 L'Évangile (Pomerol)   (94–96)

L'Évangile's 1994 is an awesome effort that may rival, perhaps eclipse the 1990. The only other L'Évangile it appears to resemble is the 1975—a great wine in an irregular vintage. The 1994 displays a saturated purple color, and a huge nose of violets, cassis, licorice, and minerals, with no evidence of new oak. Massive on the palate, with extraordinary concentration, high tannin, low acidity, and a dazzlingly long finish that lasts for nearly a minute, this is a wine of outstanding richness and impressive structure. I do not believe it will be flattering to drink young. It will require 10–12 years of cellaring and will keep for 30+ years. A tour de force in winemaking!

1994 Faurie de Souchard (St.-Émilion)   (81–85)

Medium ruby/purple, with an open-knit nose suggesting the herbaceous side of Cabernet Franc, this round, soft, light- to medium-bodied wine is all finesse. It lacks the concentration and length necessary to merit higher marks. Drink it during its first 10 years of life.

1994 Ferrand-Lartigue (St.-Émilion)   (88–91)

This tiny, 5-acre property is aiming to produce one of the top luxury wines of Bordeaux's right bank, competing with the lavishly priced Pomerol, Le Pin, and the up-and-coming St.-Émilion estate, Valandraud. Ferrand-Lartigue produced 40 hectoliters per hectare in 1994 from a vineyard that was picked grape by grape rather than bunch by bunch! Twenty harvesters were brought in to harvest the 5 acres of old vines (with an average age of 40 years) in a single day. The result is a wine that is slightly less concentrated than the superb 1993, but equally exotic and flashy. Ostentatiously rich, smoky, and oaky, this wine has a similarity to Le Pin and Le Tertre-Roteboeuf. There is an intoxicating nose, nearly unctuously rich, fat, velvety-textured flavors with copious quantities of jammy black cherry fruit, and a smooth-as-silk, heady finish. This should turn out to be one of the most dramatic and sexy wines of the vintage. Drink it during its first 10 years of life.

1994 Feytit Clinet (Pomerol)   (81–83)

Medium ruby colored with a tight but earthy, cherry-scented nose, this slightly tannic wine exhibits moderate concentration, good cleanliness, and a simple, straightforward style. Drink it during its first 7–8 years of life.

1994 De Fieuzal (Pessac-Léognan)   (88–90+)

I am more optimistic about the 1994 De Fieuzal than I have been about other recent vintages. That's saying something given the number of good wines this estate has produced.

The 1994 is the most concentrated Graves I tasted save for La Mission Haut-Brion. It reveals an opaque purple/garnet color as well as forceful, expansive, fragrant scents of tobacco, tar, and sweet red and black fruits. Full bodied, tannic, and powerful, this massive, large-scale Fieuzal will need 5–8 years of cellaring; it will age well for 20–25 years. Very impressive—but definitely a wine that will require patience.

1994 Figeac (St.-Émilion)   (87–89)

After disappointing efforts in both 1992 and 1993, Figeac has rebounded with a strong effort in 1994 that is not far off the standard set by the estate's dazzling 1990. A high percentage of Cabernet Sauvignon in a St.-Émilion often translates into lighter-bodied wines. Figeac's 1994 exhibits excellent depth and concentration, as well as some of the subtle herbaceousness that can accompany Cabernet's olive-tinged, cassis fruit. At its best, Figeac combines noteworthy suppleness, elegance, finesse, and fine intensity. The latter component is often compromised in lighter vintages. That is not the case in 1994, as this seductive, complex, fragrant, stylish wine should drink well young and age gracefully for 12–15 years. This attractive effort may merit an exceptional score if it gains more weight.

1994 La Fleur (St.-Émilion)   (83–86)

La Fleur has produced good wines in recent vintages, and the 1994 is another richly fruity, ripe, medium-bodied wine with moderate tannin, slight dilution in the mid-palate, and a clean, fresh, lively finish. Drink it during its first decade of life.

1994 La Fleur de Gay (Pomerol)   (91–94)

An opaque, black/purple color makes the 1994 La Fleur de Gay a candidate for one of the most saturated wines of the vintage. The awesome nose of licorice, cassis, new oak, and spices is followed by a massively rich yet remarkably elegant wine with highly extracted fruit, marvelous balance, and a muscular, tannic finish. Although large scale, it is never heavy or out of balance. It will require 4–5 years of cellaring and should drink well for 20+ years.

1994 La Fleur Gazin (Pomerol)   (83–85)

Although light bodied and moderately concentrated, this wine displays attractive elegance, sweet cherry fruit with a touch of earth and wood, as well as a round, easygoing finish. It will offer pleasant drinking over the next decade.

1994 La Fleur Pétrus (Pomerol)   (86–87)

For whatever reason, the 1994 La Fleur Pétrus does not possess the richness, sweetness, and intensity of this estate's 1993 (unusual, as the 1994s are generally richer, riper, and more unctuous than the 1993s). This 1994 exhibits a soft, ripe, coffee- and sweet berry–scented nose with subtle new oak aromas in the background. The wine offers plenty of tannic clout in the finish, but the mid-palate displays barely above-average concentration and extract. After 4–5 years of cellaring, it should turn out to be a firm, elegant wine for drinking over the following 15 years.

1994 La Fleur Pourret (St.-Émilion)   (83–86)

An attractive, deep ruby color and a subtle but spicy, herb-, and black cherry–scented nose are followed by a medium-bodied wine with above-average fruit concentration and hard tannin in the finish. This should turn out to be a well-balanced effort.

1994 Fonplégade (St.-Émilion)   (86–88)

Fonplégade has produced an attractive wine combining some of the finest elements of the 1994 vintage—superb color, excellent ripeness and maturity, and good structure and purity.

Also admirable are the medium-bodied, sweet, expansive mid-palate and rich fruit in the long finish. It will require several years of cellaring and should keep for 12–15 years.

1994 Fonroque (St.-Émilion)   (74–76?)

Tasted twice, this wine was hard, vegetal, tannic, and lacking ripeness and fruit. The excessive tannin only exacerbates the undernourished style. The 1994 Fonroque is a strong candidate to dry out after 5–6 years of cellaring.

1994 Forts de Latour (Pauillac)   (87–88)

Latour's second wine contains more Cabernet Sauvignon (70%) than the grand vin. It is a very impressive second wine with a dense purple color, a rich, moderately intense nose of sweet cassis, minerals, and vanilla, medium to full body, and a moderately tannic, long finish. It requires 5–7 years of cellaring and should last for 15+ years.

1994 Franc-Mayne (St.-Émilion)   (83–86)

Franc-Mayne's tendency to possess a pronounced herbaceous component is apparent in the 1994. The wine exhibits an impressive ruby/purple color and a spicy, medium-bodied format with adequate concentration, low acidity, and firm tannin in the finish. It will require 2–3 years of cellaring and will last for 15 years.

1994 La Gaffelière (St.-Émilion)   (87–88)

This elegant St.-Émilion exhibits a healthy, medium to dark ruby color, attractive, sweet fruit in its aromatic profile, medium body, moderate tannin, and a crisp, spicy, well-knit finish. It should open in 5–6 years and should keep for 15 or more.

1994 La Garde Réserve du Château (Pessac-Léognan)   (85–87)

This up-and-coming estate is turning out very good white and red wines. The medium-bodied 1994 is elegant, subtle, ripe, with admirable fruit and depth. It is a wine of charm and finesse that should last for 10–12 years.

1994 Le Gay (Pomerol)   (78–80?)

Le Gay is known for its rustic, backward, powerful wines, which, in top vintages, possess an old-vine fruit intensity that compensates for the aggressive tannin levels. In 1994, there is little fruit in evidence. The wine tastes extremely hard and astringent, exhibiting a glaring deficiency in fruit extraction. I cannot see it ever turning around, but perhaps miracles will occur in cask.

1994 Gazin (Pomerol)   (90–92)

Gazin has been fashioning top-flight wines lately, producing very fine wines in both 1992 and 1993. The 1994 is the best Gazin made in the last 35 years. The dark, nearly opaque plum/purple color is followed by scents of vanilla, roasted herbs, coffee, and lavish quantities of jammy black fruits (cherries). Rich, medium to full bodied, with enough acidity for definition, this is a voluptuously styled, graceful Pomerol that will drink well young and will last for 15 or more years.

1994 Giscours (Margaux)   (87–89)

A strong effort from Giscours, this dark purple-colored 1994 possesses a sweet, nearly overripe nose of plums intertwined with scents of herbs, pine trees, cassis, and spices. Full bodied and powerful, with moderate tannin and excellent concentration, this full-flavored, broad-shouldered wine will need 2–5 years of cellaring; it should keep for 15.

1994 Gloria (St.-Julien)   (86–87)

The precocious, flattering style is textbook Gloria. Dark ruby/purple, with plenty of fat, ripe, cassis fruit intermingled with scents of Provençal herbs, this medium-bodied, moderately tannic wine emphasizes up-front, in-your-face, juicy fruit. Drink it over the next decade.

1994 Grand Corbin (St.-Émilion)   (85–87)

Overripe Merlot notes are presented in a straightforward, monolithic style. The low-acid, chunky, husky 1994 Grand Corbin exhibits plenty of body and tannin, but not much finesse or delineation.

1994 Grand Mayne (St.-Émilion)   (90–92)

Grand Mayne has been coming on strong since the late eighties. In 1994, the highly competent Nonys, a husband-and-wife team, have turned in one of the vintage's top performances. The wine's color is black/purple and the nose offers up wonderfully sweet scents of red and black fruits, violets, minerals, vanilla, and a subtle herbaceous note. With full body, outstanding concentration, low acidity, and a riveting, astringently tannic finish, this well-proportioned, rich yet elegant wine should be ready to drink in 5–6 years; it will keep for 20 years. For the statisticians among my readership, this is a 75% Merlot/25% Cabernet Franc blend.

1994 Grand Pontet (St.-Émilion)   (87–88)

This opaque, plum-colored, chewy, lavishly oaked wine reveals gobs of jammy red and black fruits, as well as noticeably high glycerin, tannin, and concentration. Although not complex, it offers considerable strength and richness. Give it 2–3 years to shed its tannin and consume it over the following 15 years.

1994 Grand-Puy-Ducasse (Pauillac)   (87–88)

Another reasonably priced Pauillac, the 1994 Grand-Puy-Ducasse exhibits a saturated, dense purple color, wonderfully sweet, pure, cassis aromas, medium to full body, sweet, chewy, glycerin-imbued, fleshy flavors, and moderate tannin in the long finish. There is adequate fruit to balance out the wine's structure. One of the most forward, precocious 1994 Pauillacs, it will be drinkable in 3–5 years and will age well for 2 decades.

1994 Grand-Puy-Lacoste (Pauillac)   (88–90+)

Only 55% of Grand-Puy-Lacoste's harvest was utilized in 1994. The wine exhibits this property's propensity to turn out thick, black/purple-colored clarets. Although the sweet, rich, concentrated cassis fruit is not yet exhibiting any complexity, the wine is concentrated and full bodied, with considerable tannin in the finish. It does not resemble such opulent, voluptuously textured vintages as 1990 or 1982. My instincts suggest it will be a modern-day version of the 1966 or 1970 Grand-Puy-Lacostes. Patience is required, as this wine needs a decade of cellaring; it is capable of lasting for a quarter of a century. If more fat and ripeness emerge and the tannin softens, this wine will easily merit an outstanding score.

1994 La Grave (Pomerol)   (85–86)

Usually one of the most elegantly styled Pomerols, the 1994 La Grave exhibits a clever blend of new oak and red currant/black cherry fruit. It is medium bodied, fresh, and lively, with a soft texture, round, gentle fruitiness, and just enough tannin to give it focus and delineation. The finish is sweet and seductive. Drink this pleasant claret during its first decade of life.

1994 Gruaud Larose (St.-Julien)   (86–87)

Gruaud's 1994 offers an excellent, saturated ruby/purple color, and a tight, but sweet nose of ripe berry and cassis fruit and underbrush. It is medium bodied, with admirable concentration and massive tannin. But the question must be asked—will the tannin become more integrated as it ages in the barrel? If not, it will be an austerely styled, mid-80-point wine that will age well for 2 decades.

1994 Guillot (Pomerol)   (85–87)

Made in a yummy, sweet, plush style, the 1994 Guillot exhibits a deep ruby/purple color, gobs of chunky Merlot fruit, and a fleshy, low-acid, tannic finish. It should drink well during its first decade of life.

1994 Guillot Clauzel (Pomerol)   (86–87)

This dense, ruby/purple-colored wine offers plenty of jammy black fruit aromas, abundant sweet, fat, glycerin-imbued fleshiness and a velvety texture. Fleshy, expansive, and seductive, this should be an opulently styled Pomerol when released.

1994 Haut-Bages-Libéral (Pauillac)   (78–83)

Tasted three times, this wine consistently revealed light body, a soft center with evidence of dilution, moderately high tannin, and herbal, curranty flavors. It is an understated, undernourished wine that should last for 10–12 years.

1994 Haut-Bailly (Pessac-Léognan)   (88–90)

Another wine of considerable elegance and finesse, Haut-Bailly can often be overlooked when young. The 1994 confirms once again how consistent this property has been over recent years. It displays a sweet, jammy, cherry-scented nose intertwined with scents of minerals and toasty, vanillin oak, medium body, light to moderate tannin, wonderful depth and precision, and a silky, graceful finish. Although the tannin is noticeable, it is overshadowed by the wine's excellent harmony. Drink it during its first 15 years of life.

1994 Haut-Batailley (Pauillac)   (85–86)

Haut-Batailley is always an elegant and velvety-textured wine. The 1994 exhibits some rough tannin in the finish, which detracts from an otherwise pretty, ripe wine that has more in common with a St.-Julien than with a Pauillac. The color saturation and initially pure aromatics are excellent, but following the fine attack, the tannin takes over, giving the wine a classic austere Bordeaux style. It requires 4–5 years of cellaring and should keep for 10–15+ years.

1994 Haut-Brion (Pessac-Léognan)   (92–94)

No first-growth administrator has been on a hotter streak in terms of consistency and quality than Haut-Brion's Jean Delmas, where nearly everything since the late seventies has been meritorious. Haut-Brion's terrific 1994 does not possess either the thick, unctuous texture or the weight of La Mission. Like La Mission, it contains more Merlot than normal, but the result is an elegant wine with medium to full body, exceptional concentration and purity, great balance and harmony, a dazzling aromatic profile consisting of sweet, mineral, cassis, and white chocolate scents, similar flavors, an enthralling texture, and a long, highly concentrated finish. This is a gorgeously supple and precocious Haut-Brion that avoids tasting heavy or out of balance, rather amazing for such a young wine. The 1994 reminds me of the 1985, but with more plumpness and fat. Only 66% of Haut-Brion's harvest (which ended on September 24) made it into the grand vin.

1994 Haut-Maillet (Pomerol)   (84–86)

This well-made, moderately tannic, fat, nicely concentrated, well-balanced wine should offer good near-term drinking. It is capable of lasting 8–10 years.

1994 D'Issan (Margaux) (85–87)

D'Issan's delicate, understated, finesse style is well represented in the 1994 vintage. The wine reveals a healthy, medium ruby color, an attractive, moderately intense nose of red and black fruits, with a faint floral note, light to medium body, fine ripeness, moderate intensity, some sweetness, clean, subtle flavors, and a pleasant, slightly tannic finish. This wine should be drinkable early and last for 15 years.

1994 Kirwan (Margaux) (85–87)

Kirwan has been producing better wines recently. The 1994 offers an intense, moderately dark purple color, and a tight but pleasant, subdued aromatic profile (black fruits and new oak). With above-average concentration, this ripe, well-structured, medium-bodied, tannic wine requires 5–7 years of cellaring; it will keep for 15–20.

1994 Lafite-Rothschild (Pauillac) (86–90?)

Lafite-Rothschild's harvest began on September 20 and finished surprisingly late (especially in the Médoc), on October 7. Only 55% of the harvest was deemed of high-enough quality to be put in the final wine. The 1994 Lafite may contain the highest percentage of Cabernet Sauvignon of any Lafite produced this century. The final blend includes 96% Cabernet Sauvignon, 2% Petit-Verdot, and 2% Merlot. I found it difficult to understand the 1994 Lafite. Certainly the color is about as dense as one would want from a top-class, 6-month-old Bordeaux, but the nose is tight, and the wine compressed, compact, and brutally tannic and impenetrable. I kept searching for an inner core of fruit on the mid-palate, without any luck. While sweet fruit is present, the wine is frightfully backward and tannic; thus Lafite's famed subtleness, finesse, and elegance are buried behind a wall of tannin. This should turn out to be an outstanding wine, but it will need 15+ years of cellaring. A more accurate assessment will only be possible after another year of cask aging. For now, I prefer the 1993 Lafite-Rothschild to the 1994.

1994 Lafleur (Pomerol) (91–93+)

Once again this property has turned out an extremely backward, pure, highly structured, superbly concentrated wine that will require a decade of patience. The wine reveals a dark ruby/purple color, and wonderfully pure scents of jammy black cherries, plums, and truffles. Sweet and long, with formidably high tannin, this massive, full-bodied wine is a candidate for 25–35 years of cellaring. This is another opulent, superconcentrated Lafleur, but it possesses a more austere side than other vintages such as 1990, 1989, 1985, 1983, and 1982.

1994 Lafon Rochet (St.-Estèphe) (87–88+)

The Tesseron family struck pay dirt in 1994 with their other Médoc property, Pontet-Canet, so it was not surprising to see how well the 1994 Lafon Rochet turned out. It is a saturated purple-colored, tannic, backward, classic (in the sense of being made in an austere, medium- to full-bodied, ripe, backward style) wine. Although it smells and tastes ripe, there is a ton of tannin in the finish. It requires 8–10 years of cellaring, and it should keep well for 25 or more years. Could this turn out to be a modern-day version of the 1970, which was so promising in its first 10–15 years of life, but is now drying out and becoming more austere without ever fully blossoming?

1994 Lagrange (Pomerol) (82–85+)

My rating may turn out to be conservative in view of how closed, tannic, and backward Lagrange's 1994 appeared. The color is a healthy ruby/purple. The wine tasted rich with good extract, but the tannin obliterated much of the fruit, leaving only an impenetrable, backward Pomerol. Give it 2–4 years of cellaring and drink it over the next 12–15.

1994 Lagrange (St.-Julien) (87–89+)

This opaque purple-colored wine offers up a sweet, smoky, oaky nose, followed by thick, rich, chewy black currant flavors, full body, high tannin, and low acidity. An intense, powerful wine that has been lavishly oaked, the 1994 Lagrange should age well for 15–25 years.

1994 La Lagune (Ludon) (84–86)

Often one of my favorite properties, La Lagune has turned out a medium-bodied wine with light-intensity flavor. Some noticeable herbaceousness and aggressively astringent tannin give me cause for concern. Although this wine may become better balanced, it could be an attenuated, angular 1994 that did not escape the effect of the September rains.

1994 Lalande Borie (St.-Julien) (85–87)

This wine reveals fine color saturation and black cherry fruitiness, medium body, attractive fleshiness (there is 35% Merlot in the blend), and a sweet, round, precocious style. It is ideal for drinking during its first decade of life.

1994 Langoa-Barton (St.-Julien) (86–87)

An attractive dark ruby/purple color is followed by a tight but sweet nose of cassis fruit, medium body, moderate tannin, good concentration, and a fine finish. Well balanced, with low acidity and above-average extract, this should turn out to be an elegant example of St.-Julien for drinking between 2000 and 2015.

1994 Larcis Ducasse (St.-Émilion) (86–87+)

This property has a tendency to turn out tannic, tough, impenetrable wines that require better fruit extraction to balance out the hardness. However, that does not appear to be a problem with the husky, broad-shouldered 1994. The moderately dark ruby/purple color is followed by aromas of sweet, spicy, black fruits, oak, herbs, and damp earth. With medium to full body, a high tannin level, plenty of concentration, low acidity, and a backward style, this St.-Émilion will require 4–6 years of cellaring. It should admirably repay those with patience.

1994 Larmande (St.-Émilion) (88–89)

Black/purple colored, with plenty of toasty new oak and ripe fruit in the nose, this full-bodied, large-proportioned wine exhibits high tannin, impressive extraction, low acidity, and a fleshy, tough finish. Big and rich, it should drink well for 10–15 years. A sleeper!

1994 Laroze (St.-Émilion) (85–87)

This impressive barrel sample revealed more oak than the property routinely utilizes. A forward, low-acid, plump wine, it reveals plenty of sweet, fat fruit, a healthy dark ruby color, light to moderate tannin, and a heady, alcoholic finish. It should drink well during its first 10 years of life.

1994 Lascombes (Margaux) (88–89)

Readers who have been following my Bordeaux reports for the last 16 years know that Margaux has traditionally been the most disappointing Bordeaux appellation, with far too many underachievers. However, I am delighted to report that several properties are emerging as serious producers of top-class Bordeaux wine. Over recent vintages, Lascombes has given evidence of doing something special. The 1994 appears to be the finest wine Lascombes has made since 1970 and 1966. Their production of 37 hectoliters per hectare is one of the lowest in the Médoc. The final blend of 48% Merlot, 50% Cabernet Sauvignon, and 2% Petit-Verdot has resulted in an exotic, rich, sweet, fleshy wine with a supple texture, excellent color, and admirable purity and depth. Interestingly, Lascombes is now doing a malolactic fermentation for all its Merlot in new oak casks, influenced no doubt by the huge success of Le Pin and L'Angélus. The result is a wine with more richness, fatness, and better integration of wood. I would not be surprised to see Lascombes's 1994 turn out to be an outstanding wine. It is an exotic, forward, fleshy claret with exceptional depth, fine ripeness, and a long, medium- to full-bodied finish. It should drink well early and should last for 15+ years. Kudos!

1994 Latour (Pauillac) (93–95+)

Latour's 1994 is clearly the top first-growth among the Médocs, in addition to being an early candidate for the wine of the vintage. Only 52% of the harvest was utilized, and the blend may shock those readers used to the high percentage of Cabernet Sauvignon Latour routinely employs. The 1994 is composed of 68% Cabernet Sauvignon, a whopping 27% Merlot (the highest quantity used this century), 4% Cabernet Franc, and 1% Petit-Verdot. The superb maturity of the Merlot and the difficulties experienced with some of the cuvées of underripe Cabernet Sauvignon were the reasons behind the selection process. It was a daring but brilliant move. The 1994 Latour is an opaque purple-colored, remarkably powerful, rich, old-style wine that, despite the high Merlot content, is one of the most backward and richest wines of the vintage. Latour appears to have everything together in this wine, which possesses gorgeously well-delineated, sweet, highly extracted, concentrated fruit, noticeably ripe tannin, and an explosively long, authoritative finish. It will unquestionably develop into one of the larger-scaled, more massive wines of the vintage, but 10–15 years of cellaring will be required, as it is a 40- to 50-year wine. Administrator Christian Le Sommer and new proprietor François Pinault were thrilled with what they achieved in 1994. Chills go up my spine at the thought of what the 1994 Latour would have tasted like had it not rained in September. Bravo!

1994 Latour à Pomerol (Pomerol) (87–88)

The excellent 1994 Latour à Pomerol exhibits a healthy dark ruby/purple color, wonderfully sweet aromas of roasted coffee and sweet, jammy black cherry fruit, medium to full body, expansive chewiness, and considerable tannin in the long finish. If it continues to fill out and gain more depth, it may turn out to be as fine as the 1970. Despite its abundance of ripe fruit, it will need 5–6 years of cellaring; it is a candidate for 15 years of aging.

1994 Léoville-Barton (St.-Julien) (92–95)

After tasting this wine on four separate occasions, it is apparent that Léoville-Barton is one of the great successes of the vintage. Given proprietor Anthony Barton's reasonable pricing policy, this should be one of the knockout values to consider buying as a wine future. The color is a saturated black/purple to the rim. The wine exhibits an unformed but gloriously sweet nose of black fruits, minerals, lead pencil, licorice, and vanilla. Terrific concentration is immediately evident in this rich, full-bodied, multidimensional wine. Although there is loads of tannin, the overall impression is one of purity, intensity, and stunning richness, all buttressed and defined by adequate acidity and ripe but noticeable tannin. This should turn out to be not only a classic St.-Julien, but one of the great Léoville-Bartons, possibly surpassing what this property achieved in 1990, 1986, 1985, and 1982. It is a must-purchase for Bordeaux enthusiasts! **A.M.: 2005–2030.**

1994 Léoville Las Cases (St.-Julien) (92–95)

Michel Délon, the proprietor of this renowned second-growth (first-growth in quality, however) stated that if the rain had not arrived when it did, he was, "convinced 1994 would have been the greatest vintage of the century." Léoville Las Cases produced a modest 45 hectoliters per hectare, with the older vines producing an average of 20 hectoliters per hectare. Only *40%* of the harvest was utilized in the grand vin. The 1994 is a classic Las Cases, with the sweetness, fleshiness, and richness of such great Las Cases as 1990, 1985, and 1982, as well as the structure, power, and tannic definition of the classic backward *vin de garde* 1986. The wine displays a nearly opaque dark ruby/purple color, and the telltale Las Cases nose of vividly pure black currants, minerals, and subtle new oak. There is great flavor extraction, superb balance and purity, and moderate to high tannin in the finish. It is a wine of exceptional intensity and texture, which is remarkable given its medium body. Because of the low acidity, it should be approachable by age 5 and last for 25–30 years.

1994 La Louvière (Graves)   (88–90)

Black/purple colored, with a promising nose of ripe currants, plums, and raspberries, this powerful, highly extracted, thick wine possesses full body, a boatload of tannin, and a huge finish. It will require 7–8 years of cellaring, and it will keep for 20 years.

1994 Lynch-Bages (Pauillac)   (88–90)

Tasted three times, with each sample revealing high tannin and a tough, muscular style, the 1994 Lynch-Bages possesses sufficient depth and ripe fruit to stand up to the tannin. There is serious weight and fat to this full-bodied, large-scale wine, but it is the most backward, tannic Lynch-Bages made in the last 20 years. If it develops more sweetness and expansiveness on the palate, it may merit a low 90s score. It is better balanced than its stablemate, Pichon Longueville Baron (both estates share the same winemaking team). Lynch-Bages will require 7–10 years of cellaring and will last for 20–25 years.

1994 Lynch-Moussas (Pauillac)   (85–86)

I do not think I have ever seen a Lynch-Moussas with so much color, ripeness, and richness of fruit. Although monolithic, it is far more concentrated and balanced than other recent efforts. It should be drinkable early and last for 15 years.

1994 Magdelaine (St.-Émilion)   (85–87)

Tasted twice, Magdelaine's 1994 exhibits light to medium body, ripe cherry fruit, surprisingly high acidity, and a crisp, narrowly focused personality. There is plenty of tannin, but I am not sure there is sufficient depth of ripeness or fruit extraction to carry this wine beyond 10–12 years of age.

1994 Malartic-Lagravière (Pessac-Léognan)   (85–87)

This is the finest wine I have tasted from Malartic-Lagravière in years. The property is now being run by the Laurent-Perrier champagne house, and a stricter selection in addition to significant investment in the *chai* and vineyard are beginning to pay off. The wine exhibits a healthy dark ruby color, an attractive olive-, black cherry–, and spicy, new oak–scented bouquet, medium body, elegant, ripe flavors, and a crisp finish. It should drink well for 10–12 years.

1994 Malescot St.-Exupéry (Margaux)   (84–86)

A healthy-colored 1994 with plenty of purple nuances as well as attractive thickness, the 1994 Malescot St.-Exupéry is lighter bodied than most wines, with an herbaceous/green tea component to its aromas and flavors. Following a good initial attack with attractive, sweet fruit, the tannin takes over, and the lack of body, flavor extraction, and balance raises doubts. It will need 4–5 years of cellaring and should last for 10–15.

1994 Marbuzet (St.-Estèphe)   (85–86)

Beginning with 1994, Marbuzet is no longer the second wine of Cos d'Estournel. It is now produced from the château's own vineyards. The new second wine of Cos d'Estournel is appropriately called Les Pagodes de Cos. The 1994 Marbuzet reveals medium body, a round, fruity personality, fine purity, a sense of elegance, and light to moderate tannin in the finish. It should drink well during its first decade of life.

1994 Château Margaux (Margaux) (90–92)

Forty-seven percent of the harvest made it into the 1994 Château Margaux. The wine is reminiscent of their 1985, with more structure and tannin. It exhibits a deep, opaque ruby/purple color, and an attractive, sweet nose of black currants, spice, toast, and floral scents. Good fatness, layered richness, impressive extraction of fruit, and fine purity are noticeable in this medium-bodied, elegant yet concentrated wine. The finish exhibits sweet but noticeable tannin. The wine will firm up in the barrel. This outstanding Margaux should drink well during its first decade of life and keep for 20–35 years. By the way, the 1993 Margaux, which was just about to be bottled, continues to taste like one of the stars of that vintage.

1994 Marquis de Terme (Margaux) (86–87+)

The 1994 Marquis de Terme is a dark-colored, hulking, large-scale tannic wine. I am not fully convinced there is sufficient fruit behind the big structure to fill out the wine and make it more charming and fat. Backward, tannic, and closed, it is one of those wines that could go either way—continue to exhibit more fruit and flesh, or develop more astringent tannin. It is too soon to know for sure, but this 1994 should turn out to be at least a very good, albeit an angular, hard style of wine. It possesses 2 decades of aging potential.

1994 Mazeris (Canon-Fronsac) (79–84)

A medium ruby color and ripe, cherry, curranty fruit are followed by a light-bodied wine with a short finish displaying well-integrated tannin and acidity. Drink it during its first 7–8 years of life.

1994 Mazeyres (Pomerol) (87–88)

This estate has emerged from the throes of mediocrity to produce a lovely, elegantly styled wine with plenty of rich, black cherry–, mocha-flavored fruit presented in a medium-bodied format. There is light tannin, as well as good extraction, and an overall sense of grace and elegance. It will require 1–3 years of cellaring and will keep for 12–15.

1994 La Mission Haut-Brion (Pessac-Léognan) (92–94)

Over half of La Mission Haut-Brion's 1994 blend is Merlot, resulting in a dense, black/ruby/purple-colored wine with considerable flesh and muscle, as well as a chewy, unctuously textured palate. This beautifully concentrated, powerful, sweet, creamy, and precocious wine is already flattering. A full-bodied, impressive Graves, it may firm up after bottling, but at present it appears to be a wine to drink after 3–4 years of aging. It should last for 20–25 years.

1994 Monbousquet (St.-Émilion) (89–92)

Is this the sleeper of the vintage? A new proprietor who is relentlessly pursuing all the best this vineyard can produce has completely resurrected this well-known St.-Émilion. The 1994 Monbousquet has more in common, stylistically, with the 1990 or 1982 vintages. An opaque purple color is followed by a huge, lavishly rich wine with full body, an unctuous texture, and layers of sweet, chewy Merlot fruit. The final blend includes more than 80% Merlot, resulting in a thrillingly rich, sumptuously textured wine that should be a reasonably priced (even allowing for the pathetically weak dollar) crowd-pleaser. Drink it over the next 10–15 years. A sleeper!

1994 Monbrison (Margaux)   (74–77)

Darkly colored, with a spicy, herbaceous, earthy, red and black fruit–scented nose, this medium-bodied, harshly tannic wine tastes short and diluted. Moreover, it lacks the ripeness, flesh, and extract necessary to stand up to the structure. It will undoubtedly dry out after 7–15 years of cellaring.

1994 Montrose (St.-Estèphe)   (91–94)

Readers must realize that Montrose, often referred to as the poor person's Latour, has been at the top of the Bordeaux heap since the 1989 vintage. They turned out a profound 1989, an exceptionally classic wine in 1990, one of the finest 1991s, and a pleasant, if soft, 1992 and 1993. The 1994 (65% of the crop was kept for the Montrose label) is a 65% Cabernet Sauvignon/25% Merlot/10% Cabernet Franc blend. More similar to the 1990 than the 1989, the 1994 exhibits an opaque purple color. The nose offers intense, overripe cassis aromas mixed with minerals, vanilla, and floral scents. Extremely powerful and remarkably concentrated, this unctuously textured, massive wine is crammed with highly extracted fruit that nearly masks a tannin level equal to that achieved in 1990. One of the most promising wines of the vintage, the 1994 Montrose is a candidate for 30–40 years of cellaring. It will not be drinkable before the age of 10. This is another brilliant effort from the Charmolue family!

1994 Montviel (Pomerol)   (85–86+)

A strong effort from Montviel, the deep, saturated ruby/purple color and sweet nose of cherries, oak, and earth are followed by a medium-bodied wine with sweet, fat, ripe fruit, light tannin, and a fine finish. It should drink well during its first decade of life.

1994 Moulin du Cadet (St.-Émilion)   (85–86)

The 1994 Moulin du Cadet exhibits attractive ripe fruit, a supple, velvety texture, a moderate level of well-integrated tannin, fine purity, and interesting aromas of black fruits, stones, and spice. Drink it during its first decade of life.

1994 Moulinet (Pomerol)   (85–86)

A good showing for an estate that often turns out light-bodied, loosely knit wines, this graceful 1994 offers ripe fruit, good balance, and the right amount of tannin for its delicate style. Drink it over the next 7–8 years.

1994 Mouton-Rothschild (Pauillac)   (90–92)

Mouton-Rothschild's 1994 is undoubtedly a success. Made from 80% Cabernet Sauvignon, 10% Merlot, and 10% Cabernet Franc, most of the harvest was completed between September 22 and 25, with a small percentage of the grapes picked as late as October 2. The wine possesses a healthy dark purple color, and Mouton's telltale, sexy nose of coffee, fruitcake, cassis, and spices. Rich, with medium to full body and undeniable power, this is a concentrated, structured wine with enough fat, flesh, and extraction to balance out the wine's formidable tannin level. It possesses better integration of new oak, as well as richer, riper fruit than I found in the 1990, 1989, or 1988. The 1994, which follows a strong effort from Mouton in 1993, was made in smaller quantities, as Mouton produced 20% less wine in 1994 than 1993. A riper, more tannic, fatter, more complete and complex wine than the 1993, it should be cellared for 10 years and will last for 30+ years.

1994 Nenin (Pomerol)   (87–89+)

This is clearly the finest Nenin since the powerful, still tannic 1975. For many years Nenin has not produced a wine that was as good as the *terroir* permitted, so it is a pleasure to see this opaque, ruby/purple-colored wine with considerable tannin, ripeness, and fruit extraction. It appears to be Pomerol's answer to Montrose. Made from a blend of 70% Merlot, 20% Cabernet Franc, and 10% Cabernet Sauvignon, and aged in a high percentage of new oak casks, it is extremely full bodied and backward, with enough power and structure to see it through the next 2 decades. Proprietor Despujol has renovated his cellar with state-of-the-art stainless-steel tanks, has lowered yields, and has increased the percentage of new oak— and the wines show it!

1994 Olivier (Pessac-Léognan) (80–84)

Once again there is an objectionable level of raw oak in Olivier's barrel samples. The 1994 does possess medium body, good ripeness, and some elegance, but everything is masked by the blatant use of new wood.

1994 Les Ormes de Pez (St.-Estèphe) (79–84)

Tasted three times, this wine possesses some ripe fruit, but the tannin level is higher than the wine's ripeness and concentration can support. Perhaps it will flesh out with more barrel aging. It displays impressive color and aging potential, but not enough richness or mid-palate.

1994 Les Ormes Sorbet (Médoc) (86–87)

A fragrant nose of sweet, jammy fruit is followed by a medium-bodied, concentrated, serious wine with well-integrated new oak. This classic overachieving property merits consideration.

1994 Palmer (Margaux) (87–89+)

A moderately dense purple color is followed by an intense, enveloping, sweet, blackberry-, plum-, and floral-scented nose. Typically fleshy, with ripe, soft, medium- to full-bodied flavors, Palmer's 1994 appears to be a less concentrated version of the stunning 1989. There is light tannin in the finish, but this wine's overall impression is one of fleshy, ripe, seductive fruit. If it puts on more weight and fills out (a strong possibility given Palmer's tendency to flesh out), this wine could merit an outstanding rating. It should drink well early and last for 15 or more years.

1994 Pape-Clément (Pessac-Léognan) (89–90+)

This property continues to build on a decade of ripe, elegant, flavorful wines. The 1994 harvest produced just under 40 hectoliters per hectare. Pape-Clément is practicing a malolactic fermentation for part of the Merlot crop, and has begun to bottle its red wines without any filtration. While the 1994 may not be as powerful as either the 1990 or 1986, it boasts a complex, spicy, black currant– and tobacco-scented nose, medium body, a sweet, rich mid-palate, and firm tannin in the long finish. Give it 4–6 years of cellaring, and enjoy it over the subsequent 15–20 years.

1994 Pavie (St.-Émilion) (85–87)

Pavie's 1994 is a low-key, restrained, elegant wine with medium body, adequate concentration, moderately hard tannin, and a pleasant finish. Drink it between 1997 and 2008.

1994 Pavie-Decesse (St.-Émilion) (82–86)

Where's the fruit? Typically backward and tannic, Pavie-Decesse's 1994 reveals spice and moderate ripeness in the nose, an abundance of astringent, hard tannin, medium body, and fine depth. If the tannin becomes sufficiently integrated, this will be a good effort. It should last for 20 years.

1994 Pavie-Macquin (St.-Émilion)   (90–91+?)

This biodynamically farmed vineyard has the lowest yields in Bordeaux, old vines, and a winemaking style that produces very rich, dark-colored, black raspberry– and truffle-scented wines that are highly extracted, tannic, and promising. One of the most concentrated wines of the vintage, the black/purple-colored 1994 is filled with promise, but do not expect the tannin to melt away for at least a decade. **A.M.: 2004–2020.**

1994 Pensées de Lafleur (Pomerol)   (88–89)

Lafleur's second wine, the 1994 Pensées de Lafleur possesses a dark ruby color, more forward, black cherry, and cassis scents, medium to full body, less tannin than its sibling, and a sweet, pure, well-focused finish. I would opt for drinking it in 5–6 years; it should keep for 15+ years.

1994 Petit Figeac (St.-Émilion)   (83–86)

Although this wine exhibits little complexity, it possesses attractive, rich, ripe fruit, a dense ruby/purple color, a toasty new oak component, and a compact but good finish. The tannin is buried beneath a cascade of fruit. Drink it over the next decade.

1994 Petit Village (Pomerol)   (88–91)

Exhibiting outstanding potential, the 1994 Petit Village is among the most gloriously decadent and exotic wines made by this estate in the past 15 years. The thick, dark ruby/purple color is followed by aromas of sweet, jammy black cherries intertwined with scents of new oak, spice, and underbrush. Chewy, fleshy, and corpulent, with enough acidity and tannin to buttress its big, thick style, this wine should drink well during its first 15 years of life.

1994 Pétrus (Pomerol)   (91–93+)

Although the 1994 Pétrus is slightly less concentrated than the exceptional 1993 (one of the top candidates for wine of the vintage), it is unquestionably a powerful, tannic, backward wine that surpasses what this estate produced in such very good vintages as 1985 and 1986. The color is a deep, dark ruby/purple. With coaxing, the closed nose offers up scents of coffee, herb-tinged, jammy black cherries, and toasty new oak. The wine is superbly concentrated, with a high tannin level, and a long, structured, backward finish. Do not touch a bottle before 2005; it will last for 25–40 years.

1994 Phélan-Ségur (St.-Estèphe)   (86–88)

This is probably the finest overachieving, unclassified St.-Estèphe château. The property made excellent, close to outstanding wines in both 1989 and 1990, a good wine in 1991, and competent wines in 1992 and 1993. The 1994 is a potentially long-lived wine, with an impressive saturated purple color, sweet, jammy cassis aromas, medium body, moderate tannin, and fine ripeness and chewiness in the mouth and finish. It will require 4–5 years of cellaring and should keep for 2 decades.

1994 Pibran (Pauillac)   (78–82)

This wine reveals a fine, ripe color, a low pH, and a tart, high-acid style that is at odds with most other wines of the vintage. If the lean, narrowly focused 1994 Pibran gains weight it could merit a score in the low 80s. If not, it will be a hard, angular Pauillac that will age well but will never provide much charm.

1994 Pichon Longueville Baron (Pauillac)   (87–88+?)

Tasted on four occasions, this wine displayed its telltale saturated purple color, but it is questionable whether there is enough depth, extraction of fruit, and ripeness to stand up to the wine's structured, tannic profile, which is reminiscent of a 1975-style wine. The 1994 Pichon Baron offers a good attack with plenty of pure black currant fruit and spicy, smoky new oak, but the mid-palate falls off, and there is no fatness to be found. Although the finish is long, it consists of intense as well as painful tannin. If this wine fills out it will merit a score in the upper eighties. There is no doubt that it will last for 30 years, but will it blossom and provide pleasure and sweet, creamy fruit?

1994 Pichon Longueville Comtesse de Lalande (Pauillac)   (91–94)

Pichon-Lalande has fashioned one of the great successes of the vintage. Only 50% of the harvest was utilized in the final blend, which consists of 35% Merlot, 45% Cabernet Sauvignon, 12% Cabernet Franc, and 8% Petit-Verdot. On the three occasions I tasted the 1994 it was consistently glorious, exhibiting a saturated purple color, and a stunningly pure, rich nose of black raspberries and cassis intermingled with scents of smoke, licorice, and minerals. Medium to full bodied, with a wonderful sweet mid-palate, this powerful, authoritatively flavored, elegant, complex wine possesses sweet tannin, gorgeous delineation to its component parts, and a finish that lasts nearly 45 seconds. It is hard to compare the 1994 with other recent Pichon-Lalande vintages. It does not possess the weight or softness of the 1982 or 1983, but it is more concentrated and rich than the 1985 or 1990, more approachable and flattering than the 1986, and more structured than the 1989. For Pichon-Lalande fans, 1994 will be a must-purchase. Proprietor Madame de Lencquesaing informed me there is now a third label being produced, so the second wine, Comtesse de Lalande, will not contain every cuvée deemed unacceptable for the grand vin. The 1994 Pichon-Lalande should drink well in 4–5 years and will last for 20–25.

1994 Le Pin (Pomerol)   (92–94)

After several uninspiring efforts, Le Pin has performed beautifully in the 1994 vintage, fashioning a wine that may ultimately be better than the 1989 and 1990. It is rare that I bestow Le Pin such a high score at this stage, as it is a wine that fattens up and becomes more complex during the first 5–6 years of its aging curve. To date, most vintages have tasted significantly better in bottle than in cask, à la Cheval Blanc and a handful of other Bordeaux wines. The 1994 exhibits Le Pin's sexy, telltale, exotic, *pain grillé* nose intertwined with lavish quantities of overripe, jammy black cherries and cassis. It possesses an addictive sweetness and thick, juicy fruit presented in a fleshy, medium- to full-bodied style with no hard edges. This wine is about as sexy and opulent as a 1994 can be. Given this thrilling showing, it should be drinkable when released and should be capable of lasting for 15–20 years.

1994 Pitray (Côtes de Castillon)   (86–87)

This excellent estate has turned in a fine performance, producing a ripe, juicy, clean, fat, supple, Merlot-dominated wine. It should drink well for 7–8 years.

1994 Plince (Pomerol)   (84–86)

This attractive, chunky, medium-bodied Pomerol displays plenty of ripe fruit, a monolithic personality, fine depth, and a chewy, moderately tannic finish. Drink it over its first 10–12 years of life.

1994 Pontet-Canet (Pauillac)   (91–93)

I had this wine on three occasions with identical tasting notes. When I tasted it at the château, I told the proprietor, Alfred Tesseron, I thought it was the finest Pontet-Canet made under his administration, and possibly the greatest wine from this estate since 1961. Tesseron agreed, indicating this was the most severe selection he had ever authorized, permitting only 50% of the harvest to be included in Pontet-Canet, and utilizing a whopping

41% Merlot in the final blend, which also includes 53% Cabernet Sauvignon and 6% Cabernet Franc. In a subsequent tasting of Pauillacs, this wine stood out as one of the densest, richest, sweetest wines of the vintage, with a massive style, high, firm tannin, extraordinary opulence and richness, and more than enough fruit to hold up to the wine's powerful tannic structure. Deeply colored, full bodied, and rich, it is destined to become one of the great Pontet-Canets, of which there have been too few, especially in view of the vineyard's potential. The 1994 will need 5–7 years of cellaring and will keep for 25–30 years. A winner! Readers interested in buying Bordeaux futures should take note, as Pontet-Canet is often one of the lowest-priced Pauillacs.

1994 Potensac (Médoc)   (86–88)

This knockout effort from the cru bourgeois estate owned by Michel Délon exhibits a healthy, dark, saturated ruby/purple color, an intense nose of cassis, medium body, sweet, ripe fruit, and a low-acid, tannic finish. It should drink well young and last for 12+ years. Moreover, it will be an excellent value.

1994 Prieuré-Lichine (Margaux)   (88–90)

With the assistance of Libourne oenologist Michel Rolland, owner Sacha Lichine is fashioning more highly extracted, richer, fuller-bodied wines than produced by his father, the late Alexis Lichine. The successful 1994 exhibits an intense, dark purple color, sweet, spicy, cedary, jammy aromas, classic, medium- to full-bodied, tannic, backward flavors, and excellent length and overall purity. This may be the largest-framed, most concentrated Prieuré-Lichine made in the past 30 years. Unlike most Prieurés (which tend to be light and early-maturing), the 1994 will require 5–6 years of cellaring; it will last for 2 decades.

1994 Prieurs de la Commanderie (Pomerol)   (85–87)

A strong effort from this small estate, this opaque, ruby/purple-colored 1994 possesses sweet, jammy fruit, toasty new oak, fine concentration, moderate tannin, and a dense, chewy personality. It should open in 2–3 years and should drink well for a decade.

1994 Puy Blanquet (St.-Émilion)   (80–83?)

This wine displays a good ruby color, but a lightweight, moderately concentrated style with tough tannin in the finish. I don't see it ever pulling itself together and offering much charm or character.

1994 Rahoul (Graves)   (85–86)

Made in an attractive, medium-bodied, seductive, silky style, Rahoul's 1994 is elegant, fruity, soft, and well made. Drink it over the next 5–8 years.

1994 Rausan-Ségla (Margaux)   (90–92)

Most Bordeaux enthusiasts recognize that Rausan-Ségla's return to fine-wine production began with a stunning 1983. With the acquisition of this estate by Chanel, it is poised to become the second finest wine of the appellation (following only Margaux). In 1994 a brutal selection process resulted in only 45% of the production going into the first wine, which is a blend of 80% Cabernet Sauvignon and 20% Merlot. The high percentage of Cabernet Sauvignon is due to the fact that most of Rausan-Ségla's Merlot vineyards are young and not well drained—a deadly combination in such a wet year as 1994. This powerful 1994 will require patience. The color is an opaque, dense purple/black. The nose offers toasty new oak aromas (60% new oak barrels are utilized each year), along with those of subtle, ripe cassis fruit. Full bodied, with a 1986-ish feel, high tannin, considerable power and thickness, and potentially higher ripeness and intensity than the 1986 possessed, the 1994 will require 10 years of cellaring; it should last for 25 or more years. It is unquestionably the most powerful and concentrated 1994 of the Margaux appellation.

1994 Rauzan-Gassies (Margaux)   (82–85)

Rauzan-Gassies can be terribly inconsistent—often too tannic and not as pure and well delineated as its peers. The 1994 reveals a softer, more user-friendly style, with a healthy deep ruby color, a moderately intense bouquet of ripe red and black fruits, medium body, surprisingly soft tannin for a 1994, some evidence of dilution, and a vague herbaceousness. It appears to be a midweight, slightly above-average effort that should drink well for 12–15 years.

1994 Roc des Cambes (Côtes de Bourg)   (85–88)

Run by François Mitjavile, Roc de Cambes is undoubtedly the finest wine in the Côtes de Bourg. The 1994 is a round, generous, precociously styled wine with abundant quantities of sweet black cherry fruit, intertwined with subtle scents of earth and vanilla. This ripe, velvety-textured offering is ideal for drinking over the next 5–7 years. A crowd pleaser!

1994 Rochemorin (Graves)   (87–88)

This unheralded, underrated wine, made by André Lurton, is clearly undervalued. The 1994 exhibits a textbook Graves personality with its mineral, tobacco, and curranty nose. Medium to full bodied, with excellent concentration, light to moderate tannin, and low acidity, this easy-to-understand wine should drink well for a decade.

1994 St.-Pierre (St.-Julien)   (88–91)

For some reason I rarely taste this wine before it is bottled, but if the 1994 continues to perform as strongly as it did in March 1995, it will create quite a buzz in Bordeaux wine circles. Full bodied and concentrated, with a sweet, chewy mid-palate, excellent color saturation, and a long, well-balanced, moderately tannic finish that lasts for more than 30 seconds, this powerful, impressively endowed wine will be approachable young and will last for 20 years.

1994 De Sales (Pomerol)   (?)

Usually one of my favorite Pomerol values, the 1994 De Sales is a light-bodied, vegetal wine with insufficient fruit. It comes across as musty, weedy, and short. Judgment reserved.

1994 La Serre (St.-Émilion)   (85–87)

An impressively colored wine, the 1994 La Serre reveals cherry fruit intermingled with loamy, earthy scents (the smell of *terroir?*). This medium-bodied wine does not possess the hard tannin of the vintage. Offering a new-oak component, medium to full body, and admirable ripeness, it should merit a score in the mid to upper 80s if it is not overly processed at bottling. Drink it between 1998 and 2010.

1994 Siran (Margaux)   (?)

This opaque purple-colored wine possesses no bouquet other than vague earthy, black fruit scents. It was tough, hard, tannic, and closed, and I was unsuccessful in my attempts to penetrate the tannin and structure to see what quality of fruit was actually obtained. Judgment reserved.

1994 Smith-Haut-Lafitte (Graves)   (88–90)

After visiting this estate several times, in addition to meeting the new proprietors, the Cathiards, I have been impressed with their wines, despite the fact that the new owners have not yet enjoyed a harvest free of rain. Nevertheless, how many other châteaux made better wines in 1991, 1992, 1993, and 1994 than in 1990? This is one of the most seriously run Graves estates (for both white and red wines). The finest wine yet produced by Smith-Haut-Lafitte, the 1994 has the potential to merit an outstanding rating. While it represents 75% of the total harvest, keep in mind that yields at this estate are modest given the severe crop-thinning procedures employed. Made from a blend of 50% Merlot, 45% Cabernet Sauvignon, and 5% Cabernet Franc, the 1994 exhibits a healthy, moderately opaque ruby/purple color, and a gorgeous, up-front nose of black raspberries, spice, and toast. It is one of the most charming, poised, and perfectly balanced 1994s I tasted. Although not a blockbuster in the style of L'Angélus or Pontet-Canet, it is a ripe, beautifully proportioned, silky-textured wine with enough concentration and tannin to last for 15–20 years. Bravo!

1994 Soutard (St.-Émilion)   (87–90)

This black-colored wine possesses an intense nose of Asian spices, earth, smoke, and jammy black fruits. Full bodied, with high tannin and low acidity, this unctuously styled, chewy, flamboyant, and potentially long-lived Soutard is reminiscent of this estate's 1982 at the same stage of development.

1994 Talbot (St.-Julien)   (85–87)

Longtime Talbot enthusiasts will find this offering to be unusually elegant and finesse-styled, with less body and a sweeter, more up-front appeal. Although the color is a dark ruby, it is not as opaque or saturated as many wines of the vintage. The nose of fresh, vibrant, cassis fruit is followed by a medium-bodied wine with a moderate to high tannin level, and a crisp, new world–like, tart, clean, vibrant finish. If more complexity and flesh develop, the wine will merit a score in the upper eighties, but this solidly made Talbot will probably remain austere. It should drink well for 15–18 years.

1994 Tertre-Daugay (St.-Émilion)   (78–82)

This straightforward, round, supple, light-bodied St.-Émilion lacks concentration. Although pleasant and cleanly made, it is unexciting.

1994 Le Tertre-Roteboeuf (St.-Émilion)   (90–92)

Le Tertre-Roteboeuf's obsessive/compulsive, as well as loquacious proprietor, François Mitjavile, has turned out a rich, powerful 1994 that equals in strength and extraction his outstanding 1993. One of the last to harvest (finishing October 10, 12 days after most other châteaux), Mitjavile's wine exhibits an opaque purple color, and a heady nose containing celestial quantities of black cherries, spices, and new oak. This voluptuously sweet-textured, jammy, nearly decadent St.-Émilion is the type of wine that should send shivers up the spines of some of the more highly renowned St.-Émilion premiers grands crus classés estates that are seemingly content to live off their reputations. Like most Le Tertre-Roteboeufs, the 1994 will be drinkable upon release and will last 15 or more years.

1994 La Tour Figeac (St.-Émilion)   (86–89)

This wine could turn out to be nearly outstanding. It possesses an intense as well as sexy black plum– and black cherry–scented nose, voluptuously textured, sweet, jammy flavors, and enough new wood to pull things together. It is a plump, amply endowed wine that although low in acidity, reveals enough integrated tannin to offer a dozen years of delicious drinking.

1994 La Tour Haut-Brion (Graves)   (85–87)

La Tour Haut-Brion's high percentage of Cabernet Sauvignon is evident in the weedy, olive, and black currant–scented nose. Although it is perfumed and intense, it may be too herbaceous for some tasters. Sweet fruit, admirable purity, and a moderately long finish can be found in this medium-bodied wine that should drink well for 10–12 years.

1994 La Tour Martillac (Graves)   (85–86)

Lavish oak, ripe cherries, plums, and other sweet red and black fruits are presented in a medium-bodied, easy-to-understand, user-friendly style. The 1994 La Tour Martillac should drink well young and last for a decade.

1994 Les Tourelles de Longueville (Pauillac)   (74–76)

The impressive color is deceptive, as this is a light-bodied, diluted wine lacking fruit, richness, and flesh.

1994 Troplong-Mondot (St.-Émilion)   (92–95+)

It is hard to believe that Troplong-Mondot's 1994 might turn out to be greater than the estate's profound 1990 and 1989. The 1994 represents the essence of wine, with a superconcentrated style and extraordinary purity and grace despite its awesome richness and size. It is interesting that women (in this case Christine Valette) often produce some of the most concentrated and massive wines of France. The color is an opaque black/purple, and the nose offers up sensationally promising scents of black fruits, licorice, vanillin, and spices. Awesomely concentrated, with layers of fruit, this wine is tannic, pure, and harmonious. It will require 5–6 years of cellaring and will keep for 20–25. If Troplong-Mondot is not elevated in the new 1995 classification of St.-Émilion wines, along with L'Angélus and Le Tertre-Roteboeuf, possibly Canon La Gaffelière, Grand Mayne, and La Dominique as well, there is little justice.

1994 Trotanoy (Pomerol)   (87–89+)

Trotanoy's dark ruby-colored 1994 offers a sweet nose of roasted coffee, white chocolate, and black cherries. A large-scale wine with considerable power, medium body, excellent concentration, and rustic tannin in the finish, this firm, austerely styled Trotanoy will require 5–6 years of cellaring. It is a candidate for 2 decades of aging. At this stage of development, I cannot see it equalling the outstanding 1993, or, for that matter, the softer 1992.

1994 Trotte Vieille (St.-Émilion)   (86–88)

Trotte Vieille's 1994 possesses one of the most saturated colors of all the St.-Émilion premiers grands crus, which in general exhibit far less color extraction and ripeness than the better grands crus classés. This wine reveals significant new oak, medium body, ripe fruit, low acidity, and high tannin in the finish. If the component parts come together over the next few years, this may turn out to be an exceptional wine. It will require 4–5 years of cellaring and will last for 15 or more.

1994 Valandraud (St.-Émilion)   (90–93)

This explosively rich wine is the product of an intensely dedicated young man, Jean-Luc Thunevin, who is intent on making compelling wines. The first vintages have all been promising, and the 1994 appears to be the finest yet produced. Made primarily from tiny yields (mostly Merlot), vinified in cask (100% are new), and bottled naturally with no filtration, Valandraud is the Le Pin of St.-Émilion. Lavishly rich, oaky, and perfumed, this voluptuously textured, full-bodied wine is loaded with ripe, jammy fruit. Who would not be seduced or impressed by this up-and-coming star of Bordeaux? Drink it over the next 10–15 years.

1994 Vieux Château Certan (Pomerol)   (89–92)

Three tastings of this wine suggested that, along with the 1990 and 1986, the 1994 is one of this property's strongest efforts over the past 35 years. It is a dark, dense, purple-colored wine with a moderately intense, complex nose of spices, herbs, olives, black fruits, and subtle new oak. The wine possesses outstanding extraction of flavor, medium to full body, a sense of grace and overall balance, and moderate tannin in the long, chewy finish. Cellar it for 4–5 years to shed some of its tannin; it will keep for 20 years.

1994 Villemaurine (St.-Émilion) (74–78)

Once again, this property has fashioned a one-dimensional, tannic, hard wine with an austere personality that exhibits little fruit or intensity. Only the color is impressive.

1994 Yon Figeac (St.-Émilion) (75–78)

Light to medium dark ruby, with a spicy, herbal nose, light body, an element of dilution, and a short, tannic finish, Yon Figeac's 1994 does not exhibit much character.

1994 DRY WHITE BORDEAUX

Note: The following wines were tasted from barrel, hence the approximate range in ratings as indicated by the parentheses. This is for readers of this guide interested in purchasing wines from this excellent Bordeaux vintage.

1994 L'Arrivet Haut-Brion (Pessac-Léognan) (82–85)

This light- to medium-bodied, smoky-, herb-, and honey-scented wine offers above-average concentration, forward-tasting fruit, and a short, compact finish. Drink it over the next 5–6 years.

BAUDUC
1994 Les Trois Hectares (86–87)

An explosion of honeyed, melony fruit bursts from this straightforward, ripe, delicious wine that is meant to be drunk in its first 1–2 years of life. It is medium bodied, pure, and loaded.

1994 Blanc de Lynch-Bages (Bordeaux) (87–89)

Production is up to 42,000 bottles of this Semillon/Sauvignon/Muscadelle blend. The wine offers citrusy, perfumed, floral scents intertwined with those of new oak and ripe melony and tropical fruit. Light to medium bodied, this fresh, lively wine will provide delightful drinking over the next 2–3 years.

1994 Bonnet (Entre-Deux-Mers) 85

Already bottled, this richly fruity, crisp, lively white wine is made at the home estate of the well-known André Lurton. With gobs of fruit and a crisp, fresh style, it is ideal for drinking over the next year.

1994 Carbonnieux (Pessac-Léognan) (87–88)

Strong scents of spicy vanillin from new oak casks have the upper hand in the otherwise herb-scented, moderately intense bouquet. The wine exhibits lovely fruit, crisp acidity, high evidence of new oak barrels, and a crisp, medium-bodied finish. It should drink well for at least a decade.

1994 Carsin (Bordeaux) (86–87)

1993 Carsin Cuvée Prestige (Bordeaux) 87

The 1994 Carsin, made primarily of Sauvignon, exhibits a smoky, waxy character, good intensity, medium body, and an attractive, ripe finish. Drink it over the next year. The recently bottled 1993 Cuvée Prestige is a well-endowed, rich, fruity wine with fine body, a sense of gracefulness, and a tasty finish.

1994 Chantegrive Cuvée Caroline (Graves)   (87–88)

Chantegrive's luxury cuvée of white Graves is aged in new oak casks, resulting in a buttery, honeyed, oaky wine with gobs of ripe fruit, a heady, alcoholic finish, a good mid-palate, and a plump, succulent personality. This will not be a long-lived wine, so drink it over the next 4–5 years.

1994 Domaine de Chevalier (Pessac-Léognan)   (91–92+)

This could turn out to be the finest Domaine de Chevalier since the 1983 and 1985. Displaying less oak than normal, the big, honeyed cherry–, smoky-, and melon-scented nose is followed by a full-bodied, powerful, dense, highly concentrated wine that lingers on the palate for nearly 45 seconds. Domaine de Chevalier's white wine is often more advanced and forward out of barrel than from bottle, but this should be one of the bigger, more concentrated and powerful Domaine de Chevaliers made in the last 20 years. Given the performance of past top vintages, expect this wine to close up for 10–15 years after bottling. It will age well for 25–30+ years.

1994 La Coudraie (Entre-Deux-Mers)   85

This bottled, ripe, fruity, low-acid, pure, tasty wine is an ideal accompaniment to seafood and poultry dishes. Drink it over the next year.

1994 Couhins-Lurton (Pessac-Léognan)   (89–91)

This is one of my favorite dry white Graves, although it is virtually impossible to find. Made by André Lurton, it is 100% Sauvignon and aged in 40% new oak barrels. Although it begins life slowly, it blossoms beautifully after 4–5 years of cellaring. The delicate 1994 exhibits the pure, rich aromatics usually possessed by this wine. Scents of licorice, smoke, melon, and figs are followed by a medium-bodied wine with wonderful intensity, a great mid-palate of ripe fruit, and an elegant, dry, crisp finish. By the way, the 1993 is even better, undoubtedly because it has a year of bottle age. This is a true thoroughbred in terms of both quality and aging potential.

1994 Cruzeau (Pessac-Léognan)   (87–88)

Deliciously honeyed, melony fruit intertwined with scents of mineral and oak are presented in a medium-bodied, elegant, fresh, vibrant style. Dry and crisp, with plenty of length, the 1994 Cruzeau should be drunk over the next 3–4 years.

1994 De Fieuzal (Pessac-Léognan)   (91–93)

A terrific example from this estate that usually makes one of the best white wines of Graves, the citrusy, honeyed, smoky nose soars from the glass. Medium to full bodied, with exquisite concentration, superb focus, and a fresh, long, rich, structured finish, this terrific Fieuzal should age well for 15+ years.

1994 Fontenil (Entre-Deux-Mers)   (85–86)

This is another fruity, well-made wine with admirable richness and a straightforward, easygoing style.

1994 De Frances (Graves)   (72–75)

I found this dry white Graves to be extremely vegetal, with too much of a green tea/asparagus aromatic/flavor component. It is light to medium bodied, with good acidity and no oak showing.

1994 Le Gay (Bordeaux)   83

Already bottled, this crisp, fruity, Semillon-based wine is soft, round, and ideal for consuming over the next year.

1994 Haut-Bergey (Graves)   (80–83)

Apple/lemonlike notes are followed by a crisp, light-bodied wine that displays some of the effects of September's heavy rains. Drink this pleasant but unexciting wine over the next 5–6 years.

1994 Haut-Brion (Pessac-Léognan)   (94–96)

This spectacular dry white Graves is a likely candidate to rival the 1989 produced at Haut-Brion. The harvest began at the end of August. The wine possesses the texture of a great Burgundy grand cru given its thick unctuosity. The superb nose of honeyed fruits and smoky oak is far more developed and ostentatious than its sister, the more subtle and backward Laville-Haut-Brion. Awesomely rich, with a chewy texture and great purity and definition, this is a ravishingly intense, full-bodied, dry white wine that should age well for 30+ years.

1994 Laville-Haut-Brion (Pessac-Léognan)   (90–93)

This tightly knit, medium-bodied wine exhibits an intense, sweet nose of toast, minerals, honey, and spices. There is ripe fruit and intensity on the palate, but the overall impression is one of a backward, undeveloped wine. It has 20–25 years of aging potential.

1994 La Louvière (Pessac-Léognan)   (88–90)

Pungent *terroir* scents of earth, minerals, and smoke combine with ripe fruit in this medium-bodied, soft, supple, concentrated wine. The finish is long and persuasive. It appears less structured than some of the other 1994s, so I would opt for drinking it during its first decade of life.

1994 Magneau (Graves)   (86–88)

1994 Magneau Cuvée Julien (Graves)   (87–89)

This underrated estate deserves more attention. The 1994 regular cuvée reveals excellent intensity, an elegant, crisp, herb-, smoke-, and mineral-scented nose, with excellent fruit and focus on the palate. The 1994 Cuvée Julien, a blend of equal parts Semillon and Sauvignon, exhibits more buttery, smoky, vanillin oak, nearly outstanding concentration, plenty of fruit, and a fresh, lively style. Both wines should drink well over the next 3–4 years.

1994 Malartic-Lagravière (Pessac-Léognan)   (88–90)

The finest white wine made at this estate in years, the new owners, the Laurent Perrier group, have added Semillon to what used to be a 100% Sauvignon wine. The result is a richer, more intense, compelling example of white Graves. There is a honeyed melon, spicy, pungent, subtle herbaceousness, freshness, sweet fruit, and wonderful delineation to this medium-bodied wine. It should drink well for 15–20 years.

1994 Olivier (Pessac-Léognan)   (85–87)

This intensely fruity white Graves offers honeyed citrus aromas, medium body, a sense of elegance, and gobs of ripe fruit presented in a user-friendly style. Drink it over the next 5–6 years.

1994 Pape-Clément (Pessac-Léognan) (90–92)

In addition to the resurgent quality of Pape-Clément's red wine, this estate is making one of the most enticing dry white Graves of the region. A 10% Muscadelle, 35% Sauvignon, and 55% Semillon blend, the 1994 is outstanding. The nose jumps from the glass offering up copious scents of tropical fruits, honeyed figs, and smoke. Rich, with superb purity and intensity, this medium-bodied, deliciously fruity, stylish white wine is hard to resist. Although flattering, it will keep for 10–15 years. Impressive!

1993 Pavillon Blanc de Margaux (Bordeaux) 90

Although I did not have a chance to taste the 1994, the bottled 1993 Pavillon Blanc (100% Sauvignon) is one of the finest wines I have recently seen from this property. It is a textbook Sauvignon, with purity, richness of fruit, and a honeyed, melony, fig, smoky, citrusy nose, super delineation and vibrancy, excellent concentration, and a crisp, dry, zesty finish. More accessible, as well as more richly fruity than most Pavillon Blancs, this fine white Bordeaux should drink well for 10–15 years.

1994 Rahoul (Graves) (87–89)

The finest Rahoul I have yet tasted, the sweet aromas of overripe honeydew melons and herbs are followed by a soft, concentrated white Graves with medium body, low acidity, and an up-front, precocious personality. Consume it over the next 5–7 years.

1994 Rochemorin (Pessac-Léognan) (88–89)

Wonderfully concentrated and intense, this soft, medium- to full-bodied, delectable white wine offers attractive smoky oak scents, as well as excellent purity and delineation. Drink this textbook white Graves over the next 4–5 years.

1994 Smith-Haut-Lafitte (Pessac-Léognan) (90–91)

The Cathiard family continues to push the quality level of Smith-Haut-Lafitte to higher and higher levels. This 100% barrel-fermented Sauvignon offers gorgeous portions of rich, honeyed fig and melony fruit, great purity, and well-integrated new oak. Neither heavy nor excessively alcoholic, this charming, complex, beautifully made white Graves should drink well for 15 years.

1994 Talbot Caillou Blanc (Bordeaux) (86–87)

Significantly better than the vegetal 1993, this crisp, aromatic, delicate, richly fruity wine exhibits good ripeness, light to medium body, and a fresh, lively finish. It is a wine to consume over the next 1–3 years.

1994 Thieuley (Bordeaux) (85–86)

1994 Thieuley Cuvée Francis Courselle (Bordeaux) (87–88)

Some of Bordeaux's best-kept secrets are the dry white wines from Thieuley. The 1994 is aromatic, crisp, and fresh, with plenty of melony fruit, light to medium body, good acidity, and a clean, fresh, lively finish. In complete contrast is the 1994 Cuvée Francis Courselle, a barrel-fermented, rich, honeyed, heavy, oaky wine with plenty of fruit, more intensity, and less flexibility with food.

1994 La Tour Martillac (Pessac-Léognan) (88–90)

This low-acid, plump, rich, well-endowed wine offers a generous and intense nose of smoky new oak, ripe fruit, and figs. Rich, with low acidity and an unctuous texture, this wine offers considerable concentration in a slightly heavier style than many of its peers. It is medium to full bodied and can handle 8–12 years of aging.

1994 La Vieille France Cuvée Marie (Graves)   (90–92)

Only 200 cases were made of this special cuvée that is aged and vinified in small oak casks. It is a superb dry white Graves with a honeyed, rich, smoky, fruity nose, medium to full body, admirable purity, and an intense, lively style with well-integrated wood. It should drink well for 3–4 years. An impressive discovery!

1993 CALIFORNIA CABERNET SAUVIGNONS

Note: The following wines were tasted from the barrel, hence the approximate range in ratings as indicated by the parentheses. This is provided for readers of this guide interested in purchasing wines from this excellent California vintage.

ARAUJO ESTATE WINES

1993 Cabernet Sauvignon Eisele Vineyard   Napa   (95–97)

Araujo Estate's 1993 Cabernet Sauvignon Eisele Vineyard may eclipse the great 1991. It offers a huge nose of black cherries, black currants, minerals, and vanillin, a stunning display of superconcentrated fruit, full body, and power allied with grace and harmony. The finish continues for nearly a minute. This terrific California Cabernet Sauvignon beautifully presents additional evidence that this is one of the greatest single vineyards in Napa.

BERINGER

1993 Cabernet Sauvignon   Knight's Valley   (90–92)

1993 Cabernet Sauvignon Private Reserve   Napa   (95–98)

1993 Merlot Bancroft Vineyard   Howell Mountain   (94–96)

Beringer's 1993 Cabernet Sauvignon Knight's Valley will not be released for another year, but readers should be prepared for the best Knight's Valley Cabernet Beringer has yet made. The wine is outstanding in its display of superrich, black currant, herb, mocha, and spicy fruit, its sweet, full-bodied, concentrated palate, and long, generous finish. It should drink well for at least 10–12 years. Along with the 1992 Private Reserve, the 1993 Private Reserve Cabernet Sauvignon is one of the most promising Beringer Cabernets made under the Reserve designation. The 1993 possesses extraordinary aromas and flavors, as well as a saturated black/purple color, a huge, rich nose of spring flowers, black fruits, and spicy oak, followed by fabulously rich, multidimensional flavors presented in a full-bodied style. Additionally, this wine offers sweet fruit and spectacular length and intensity.

The 1993 Merlot Bancroft Vineyard is cut from the same cloth as the massive 1992. It is a blockbuster, thick, chocolaty-, black and red fruit–scented and –flavored wine with full body, gobs of glycerin and extract, and a huge finish. It should age well for 2 decades.

DON BRYANT

1993 Cabernet Sauvignon   Napa   (94–96)

Don Bryant's extraordinary 1993 Cabernet Sauvignon possesses an opaque black/purple color, and a huge bouquet of black raspberries, cassis, vanillin, licorice, and spices. The wine is superrich, with sweet tannin, an expansive mouth-feel, and an awesome finish. It will be approachable when released, but it will not hit its stride until the turn of the century; it will last for 10–15 years thereafter.

CAIN CELLARS

1993 Cain Five Proprietary Red Wine   Napa   (85–86?)

Although this wine possesses attractive ripe, dense, black cherry and curranty fruit, it is extremely herbaceous, with strong scents of herbs, accompanied by aromas of black olives, toasty new oak, and moderate fruit. Its vegetal character is more powerful than I prefer. Otherwise, it is medium bodied, with light tannin, and an adequate finish. It should be drinkable when released and should last for a decade.

CARMENET

1993 Cabernet Franc Moon Mountain Estate	Sonoma	(87–90)
1993 Meritage Moon Mountain Estate	Sonoma	(87–90)
1993 Vin de Garde Moon Mountain Estate	Sonoma	(88–90+?)

In the past, I have given Carmenet's barrel samples very good reviews, only to be less impressed with the wines as they age in the bottle. The 1985s certainly did not live up to the accolades I bestowed upon them from barrel. Let's hope the 1993s, which show excellent potential, perform as well out of bottle. Although the 1993 Cabernet Franc will not make anyone forget La Jota's Cabernet Franc, it is an attractive, complex, rich wine with a smoky, black currant, herbal nose, surprisingly fat, sweet, ripe, expansive fruit, and a medium-bodied, soft, silky finish. It should drink well for a decade. The supple 1993 Meritage (83% Cabernet Sauvignon/17% Cabernet Franc) possesses a smoky, spicy, oaky, black cherry– and currant-scented nose, medium body, fine ripeness and purity, and an overall sense of grace and balance. It should be drinkable early in its life and should last for 10–15 years. The 1993 Vin de Garde (76% Cabernet Sauvignon/24% Cabernet Franc) is (presumably because of its name) meant to be Carmenet's longest-lived red wine. It reveals gobs of intensity, concentration, and richness, as well as velvety sweet tannin, medium to full body, and excellent to outstanding ripeness, extraction, and potential. Its spicy, herbal side is less pronounced than in the other two offerings. It should drink well for 15+ years after its release.

CLOS PEGASE

1993 Cabernet Sauvignon Estate	Napa	(87–89)
1993 Hommage Proprietary Red Wine	Napa	(88–90)

Known more for the architectural style of the winery and its art collection, Clos Pegase is becoming more serious about its wine. Improvements have been noticeable since 1991. I am delighted to report that the 1993s look to be at least very good, possibly exceptional. The 1993 Cabernet Sauvignon Estate exhibits a smoky, sweet, cassis-scented nose, expansive, rich, chewy flavors with fine ripeness and density, and a husky, fleshy mouth-feel. There is good underlying tannin, but the fruit dominates—always a good sign. Look for this wine to firm up and drink well young; it will last for 10–15 years. The 1993 Hommage Proprietary Red Wine is an opulent, spicy, full-bodied wine with terrific fruit, purity, and richness. There is adequate acidity, an expansive, enticing, chewy texture, and fine length. It should drink well young and should last for 10–15 years.

COLGIN-SCHRADER

1993 Cabernet Sauvignon Herb Lamb Vineyard	Napa	(94–96)

This up-and-coming producer is making 100% Cabernet Sauvignon from the Lamb Vineyard. The 1993 is a wine to seek out, although the tiny production means quantities are limited. The wine boasts an opaque black color, and a huge, sweet, jammy nose of cassis fruit, minerals, flowers, and new oak. Powerfully authoritative flavors that ooze glycerin and fruit extraction are also elegant and harmonious. The tannin is buried beneath an amazing amount of concentration. The wine finishes with great focus and delineation. It is a spectacular, promising Cabernet Sauvignon that has me drooling in anticipation of its release. It should drink well for at least 20 years.

CONN VALLEY VINEYARD

| 1993 Cabernet Sauvignon | Napa (92–94) |

This saturated black/purple-colored 1993 Cabernet Sauvignon offers an unevolved but juicy, succulent nose of black currants, violets, and spices. Rich and full bodied, this authoritatively flavored, yet elegant wine may turn out to resemble the opulently styled 1990.

CORISON

| 1993 Cabernet Sauvignon | Napa (90–91) |

A very impressive effort from Corison, the 1993 Cabernet's dark ruby/purple color is followed by a smoky, sweet, jammy, black currant–scented nose, beautiful, ripe, cassis flavors, attractive suppleness, and a medium- to full-bodied, lush finish. It should drink well for 15 years.

CUVAISON

| 1993 Cabernet Sauvignon | Napa (84–86) |
| 1993 Merlot | Napa (86–89) |

The opaque ruby/purple-colored 1993 Merlot exhibits more richness, intensity, and character than the surprisingly soft, medium-bodied, moderately concentrated Cabernet Sauvignon. The Merlot offers terrific fruit, plenty of chocolaty, mocha, herb, and black cherry flavors, an expansive, round, generous palate, and a medium-bodied, velvety finish. It should drink well for 10–12 years. The pleasant, above-average-quality 1993 Cabernet Sauvignon is soft, with pleasing cassis aromas framed by subtle oak. Spicy, round, and low in acidity, it is a wine to drink during its first 5–7 years of life.

DALLA VALLE

| 1993 Cabernet Sauvignon Estate | Napa (94–96) |
| 1993 Maya Proprietary Red Wine | Napa (96–100) |

Dalla Valle's 1993 Cabernet Sauvignon Estate looks to be another full-bodied, highly extracted, rich, pure Cabernet with 15–20 years of aging potential. The copious quantities of pure cassis fruit and intense fragrance of this wine will make it a sure winner. The 1993 Maya is a sensational, blockbuster wine of exceptional richness and personality. Opaque purple, with a sweet, cassis aroma, this awesomely concentrated wine reveals well-integrated tannin, acid, and wood. A monument in the making, the 1993 Maya should reach full maturity in a decade, and last for 25–30 years. Amazing!

DIAMOND CREEK

| 1993 Cabernet Sauvignon Gravelly Meadow | Napa (86–88) |
| 1993 Cabernet Sauvignon Volcanic Hill | Napa (89–91) |

I have had serious reservations about the quality of Diamond Creek's wines and the dramatic change in style following the 1984 vintage. These two 1993s appear to be very good, but they are not made in the style of the great Diamond Creek Cabernets made in 1978, 1977, 1976, and 1974. Devotees of those wines would not recognize the still tannic but far less concentrated, tough, austere style of wine now being produced. The 1993 Gravelly Meadow possesses good fruit, extremely high tannin (excessive?), and a medium-bodied, spicy finish. It needs 5–6 years of cellaring, as it is atypically backward for a 1993. The 1993 Volcanic Hill exhibits smoky, black cherry fruit, is medium to full bodied, and excruciatingly tannic. Is there enough fat, flesh, and flavor extraction to stand up to the tannin? Does anyone know why a winery that became legendary among California Cabernet Sauvignon enthusiasts would completely change the style of its wines after having enjoyed such remarkable success and loyalty from its fans?

DUNN VINEYARDS

1993 Cabernet Sauvignon	Napa	(92–95)
1993 Cabernet Sauvignon Howell Mountain	Napa	(96–100)

When I tasted these two wines last year at the winery I found them to be closed and tight, particularly when tasted next to the more opulent, voluptuous, open 1992s. In a recent tasting these immensely impressive wines were more open, displaying greater richness and breadth of flavor than previously. The 1993 Napa Cabernet Sauvignon reveals Dunn's typical opaque black/purple color, and a sweet, ripe, pure nose of black currants and minerals complemented by subtle oak. It is a rich, full-bodied, terrifically endowed Cabernet that seems more accessible than some of Dunn's tougher, harder, more backward vintages such as 1991 and 1985. It will require 3–4 years of cellaring and should have no difficulty attaining 20 years of age without losing any fruit. The 1993 Cabernet Sauvignon Howell Mountain may be even richer than the exquisite 1992. It offers the essence of Cabernet Sauvignon in its thick, rich, pure, black currant flavors that ooze across the palate. The wine is not heavy, but it is so phenomenally concentrated and extracted that it leaves the taster speechless. Most Dunn Howell Mountain Cabernets require a minimum of 10–15 years of cellaring. My instincts suggest the 1993 possesses sweeter, riper tannin than usual. Both of these wines are colossal efforts that were performing gorgeously when tasted in March 1995. Is the Dunn Howell Mountain a wine that will last 50+ years?

ÉTUDE

1993 Cabernet Sauvignon	Napa	(91–93)

With a stunning black/purple color and an intense, pure fragrance of black fruits and subtle new oak, this medium- to full-bodied, multilayered wine combines California's lavishly rich, intense fruit with an underlying sense of elegance and style, à la a top-notch Château Margaux. The finish builds in the mouth, and the overall sense is one of exceptional richness, balance, and purity. It should drink well young because of its forward personality, and should last for 20 years. Very impressive!

FISHER

1993 Cabernet Sauvignon Coach Insignia	Napa	(90–93)
1993 Cabernet Sauvignon Lamb Vineyard	Napa	(95–98)

Fisher's 1993 Cabernet Sauvignon from the Lamb Vineyard promises to be Fred Fisher's finest Cabernet to date. The wine's black color is followed by an extraordinary amount of sweetness and expansiveness that could only come from extremely ripe fruit and tiny yields. The finish lasts for nearly a minute. This spectacular Cabernet Sauvignon provides additional evidence of just what peaks of quality Fred Fisher's winemaking team has achieved over the last several years. The 1993 Cabernet Sauvignon Coach Insignia is another terrific effort. It possesses the hallmarks of recent Fisher releases, namely spectacular ripeness and richness, as well as massive, chocolaty, ripe, black currant fruit presented in a full-bodied, expansive, wonderfully pure and concentrated style. It reveals admirable extraction, a nice touch of oak, and gorgeous ripeness and length. Given its supple style, it should be drinkable when released and last for 15+ years.

FLORA SPRINGS

1993 Cabernet Sauvignon Reserve	Napa	(90–93)
1993 Trilogy Proprietary Red Wine	Napa	(91–93)

The 1993 Cabernet Sauvignon Reserve exhibits a dense, plum/purple color, and huge, almost overripe aromas of sweet black currants and smoky oak. The wine is extremely rich and concentrated, with a mouth-filling, full-bodied personality and impressive length. There is no hint of excessive acidity. Let's hope the wine goes into the bottle with little intervention, as the raw materials are clearly dazzling. It should drink well for 15–20+ years. The 1993 Trilogy reveals more toasty new oak in the nose, as well as aromas of sweet black fruits intertwined with complex scents of lead pencil and spice. Deep and rich, with medium to full body, great ripeness of fruit, and purity, this seductive, multidimensional, proprietary red wine is beautifully made, supple enough to be drunk when released, but capable of lasting 20 years. It has no resemblance to the one-dimensional, vapid group of wines Flora Springs produced in the decade of the eighties. Bravo!

GIRARD

1993 Cabernet Sauvignon Estate	Napa	(87–89)
1993 Cabernet Sauvignon Reserve	Napa	(90–92?)

I admire this winery, but it has a tendency to produce excessively structured, frightfully tannic wines that require years to open up. It's often questionable whether the fruit will last as long as the tannin. Certainly Girard's 1993 Cabernet Sauvignon Estate is made in a more user-friendly style with its soft, generous, fleshy, supple, cassis flavors complemented by subtle herb and toasty new oak notes. The wine is medium to full bodied, chewy, and mouth filling. It should drink well young and last for 10–15 years. The 1993 Cabernet Sauvignon Reserve is a classic Girard offering—formidably tannic, very intense, marvelously concentrated, but, oh so backward and almost excruciatingly painful to taste. There is tremendous purity, full body, a ton of extract, and a boatload of hard, tough tannin. Lay this wine away for a minimum of 10–12 years; it will last for 25–30. Whether or not it will achieve greatness depends on the fruit outlasting the tannin. Impressive, but potential buyers should recognize the risk inherent in stashing away this wine for at least a decade.

HARLAN ESTATE

1993 Proprietary Red Wine	Napa	(92–95)

Made from a blend of approximately two-thirds Cabernet Sauvignon and the remainder Cabernet Franc and Merlot, Harlan Estate's 1993 exhibits a saturated, opaque ruby/purple color, and a superb bouquet of vanillin, cassis, licorice, and minerals. With superbly extracted, ripe, flavorful fruit, this rich, impeccably balanced, classic wine will have 20–25 years of aging potential after its release in 1997.

HARRISON

1993 Cabernet Sauvignon	Napa	(88–90)

Made from a vineyard on Pritchard Hill, Harrison's 1993 Cabernet Sauvignon reveals some aggressive oak that borders on being excessive. Otherwise, it possesses impressively extracted, rich, black cherry and cassis flavors intertwined with hints of Provençal herbs. The wine is medium to full bodied, spicy, rich, moderately tannic, and well made. If it develops more complexity and the oak becomes better integrated, it may merit an outstanding rating.

HESS COLLECTION

1993 Cabernet Sauvignon	Napa	(87–89)

There may be a Reserve bottling as well, but I only tasted the regular cuvée of 1993 Hess Collection Cabernet. It offers an impressive black/ruby/purple color, followed by pure, moderately intense aromas of cassis, minerals, licorice, and toasty oak. Medium to full bodied and ripe, with chewy fruit, adequate acidity, and light to moderate tannin in the long finish, this wine may merit an outstanding score after bottling. Given the reasonable price, it may represent a noteworthy bargain.

LA JOTA

1993 Cabernet Franc	Howell Mountain	(91–93)
1993 Cabernet Sauvignon	Howell Mountain	(92–95)
1993 Cabernet Sauvignon 12th Anniversary Release	Howell Mountain	(96–98)

La Jota, whose 1992s and 1991s were among the greatest wines of those fine vintages, appears to have struck pay dirt once more with an exhilarating, profound, 1993 Cabernet Sauvignon 12th Anniversary Release. It possesses a huge, intense, provocative nose of ripe cassis fruit, smoke, Asian spices, toasty oak, and assorted black fruits. Although full bodied, huge, and concentrated, the wine avoids being heavy or overbearing. There is a marvelous inner core of fruit extraction, fine structure, moderate tannin, and a mind-boggling, long finish. This wine is a worthy rival to the spectacular 1992 11th Anniversary Release. The super 1993 Cabernet Franc reveals the fragrant, perfumed, menthol/cassis character of this varietal, supple, elegant, savory flavors, medium body, a gentle, gracious, layered, richly fruity taste, and a long, firm, well-delineated personality. It should drink well for 10–15 years. The 1993 Cabernet Sauvignon Howell Mountain selection may prove to be superior to the excellent 1992 and 1991. It exhibits an opaque black/purple color, and a huge nose of spicy oak, licorice, black raspberries, and black cherries. The wine possesses great density, richness, and ripeness, as well as a full-bodied, moderately tannic finish.

I also tasted a barrel sample of the 1994 13th Anniversary Release. A number of North Coast Cabernet Sauvignon producers are calling 1994 the vintage of the century. While La Jota's 1994 is indeed a mind-boggling example of Cabernet Sauvignon, it is impossible to say it is superior to the 1993 or 1992. But, wow! If this is typical of what top producers have done in 1994, readers will be in for another smashingly exciting vintage.

LAUREL GLEN

1993 Cabernet Sauvignon	Sonoma	(94–96)

Laurel Glen has been producing one dazzling effort after another, especially since 1990. The wines are agonizingly difficult to find in the marketplace. This blockbuster, backward 1993 Cabernet Sauvignon rivals Girard's Reserve as one of the most powerful, tannic wines of the vintage. But there is more sweetness and a higher level of concentration and ripe fruit in the Laurel Glen offering, making its aging potential less risky. This is a huge, massive, herb, black currant/black cherry, smoky, chocolaty wine with gobs of fruit, eye-popping extract levels, and mouth-searing tannin. Based on this barrel sample, my best guess for the wine's anticipated maturity is between 2002 and 2025. Impressive! But patience is definitely required.

LONG VINEYARDS

1993 Cabernet Sauvignon	Napa	(82–85?)

Although it exhibits an impressively saturated color, this lean, compact Cabernet Sauvignon reveals an excess of tannin, a slight deficiency in ripeness, and an overall sense of toughness and rusticity without enough fat, fruit, or charm. At present, the tannin dominates what appears to be a meager expression of Cabernet Sauvignon fruit.

MATANZAS CREEK

1993 Merlot	Sonoma	(92–94)

This is a close rival to Matanzas Creek's sumptuous, extremely rich, profoundly concentrated 1992 Merlot. It reveals a saturated, dense purple color, a huge, smoky, chocolaty-, jammy black cherry–scented nose, dense, chewy flavors, full body, great purity and balance, and sweet, ripe tannin in the long, blockbuster finish. It is a gorgeously built Merlot that should drink well for the next 10–15+ years. Matanzas Creek is hot!

PETER MICHAEL

1993 Les Pavots Proprietary Red Wine	California	(93–94)

This wine appears to have put on weight and richness since I tasted it at the winery late last year. Made from a blend of Cabernet Sauvignon, Cabernet Franc, and Malbec, it displays an impressive, opaque ruby/purple color, followed by a superb nose of sweet, jammy black fruits, minerals, herbs, and spices. The wine is full bodied and rich, with exceptional length and balance, as well as gorgeously extracted, pure flavors. It seems sweeter, more expansive, and deeper than when tasted in 1994. One of the top efforts of the vintage, it is another compelling Cabernet Sauvignon from this winery that remains better known for their exquisite Chardonnays and Sauvignon Blancs. Although accessible, Les Pavots possesses enough tannin and extract to merit 4–5 years of cellaring; it will last for 20–25 years. Once again, Les Pavots combines the best of the rich, ripe California fruit with a Bordeaux-like elegance and complexity.

MICHEL-SCHLUMBERGER

1993 Cabernet Sauvignon Reserve Estate	Sonoma	(86–89)
1993 Merlot Estate	Sonoma	(85–88)

Winemaker Fred Payne has turned out a supple, round, smoky-, herbal-, curranty-, and cherry-scented and -flavored 1993 Merlot. Easygoing, with good concentration, it will be ready to drink when released. It should last for 5–8 years. The 1993 Cabernet Sauvignon Reserve reveals generous (excessive?) aromas of aggressive new oak, medium ruby color, fine density, ripeness, and richness, and moderate tannin in the long finish. It will be approachable and easy to drink and to understand when released. It should last for a decade.

ROBERT MONDAVI

1993 Cabernet Sauvignon Reserve	Napa	(92–94)

The 1993 Cabernet Sauvignon Reserve is another outstanding effort from Mondavi. The wine displays loads of cassis fruit, licorice, herbs, and well-integrated, toasty new oak, full body, an understated, elegant personality, and outstanding length, ripeness, and extraction. It will drink well for 2 decades.

PAHLMEYER

1993 Proprietary Red Wine	Napa	(88–91)

Pahlmeyer's 1993 has an unbelievable resemblance to a fine vintage of Bordeaux's renowned Château Léoville Las Cases. The saturated dark ruby/purple color is followed by a wonderfully pure, vivid nose of black currants, minerals, and spicy, high-quality oak. Medium to full bodied, rich and elegant, this well-endowed, beautifully concentrated, graceful Cabernet Sauvignon will need 5–7 years of cellaring; it will keep for 20+ years. This fascinating wine could easily be confused with a top-class Médoc if tasted blind.

PINE RIDGE

1993 Cabernet Sauvignon Howell Mountain	Napa	(90–92)
1993 Cabernet Sauvignon Stag's Leap District	Napa	(90–93)
1993 Merlot	Carneros	(89–91)

Winemaker/proprietor Gary Andrus is frequently hitting the bull's-eye. If readers have not followed Pine Ridge's recent releases, they should give these wines a try, as just about everything has increased significantly in quality, pushing Pine Ridge to the upper echelon of California's finest wine producers. All of the following wines will be bottled without fining or filtration.

The dense, black/ruby-colored 1993 Merlot offers up spicy, toasty, black cherry and mocha/coffeelike flavors, as well as attractive, plump, juicy, chocolaty/cherry fruit, and admirable body, glycerin, and length. The wine is soft enough to be drunk when released, but it should age well for 10–12 years. The 1993 Cabernet Sauvignon Stag's Leap District displays black olive, spice, herb, and cherry/cassis fruit, wonderful richness allied to considerable elegance, outstanding intensity, and overall grace and balance. It is an attractive wine for drinking over the next 15+ years. For those with considerable patience, the 1993 Cabernet Sauvignon Howell Mountain is the most backward, structured, formidably tannic wine of this trio. It exhibits an opaque ruby/purple color, a tight but promising nose of minerals and black fruits, dense, full-bodied flavors, and significant tannic clout in the finish. It requires cellaring until the turn of the century and should last for 20 years thereafter.

RAVENSWOOD

1993 Merlot Sangiacomo	Sonoma	(88–91)
1993 Pickberry Proprietary Red Wine	Sonoma	(91–94)

Ravenswood's wines are not for those tasters seeking subtle, lighter-styled offerings. The 1993 Merlot Sangiacomo exhibits an opaque purple color, a big, smoky-, herb-, coffee-, and black cherry–scented nose, dense, medium- to full-bodied flavors, crisp, underlying acidity, attractive sweetness and succulence to its flavors and texture, and moderate tannin in the finish. This wine will benefit from 1–3 years of cellaring and will last for 12–15. The impressively built, opaque purple-colored 1993 Pickberry is an extremely powerful, chewy wine with considerable fruit extraction, huge body, high tannin, and superb purity and richness. It requires 5–6 years of cellaring and will drink well for 20+ years. It may turn out to be as good as the glorious 1992. For now, I would give the 1992 a slight edge because its fruit quality and texture provide more fat and intensity. However, that is splitting hairs.

RIDGE

1993 Cabernet Sauvignon Monte Bello	Santa Cruz	(92–94+)

Ridge has enjoyed an astonishing track record for over 30 years. Vintages since 1990 have all produced exquisite Cabernet Sauvignon. In my opinion, Ridge produces the Château Latour of California. It is unquestionably the longest-lived Cabernet Sauvignon made in that beautiful state, and it generally needs 10–15 years of cellaring before it begins to open. Yet there never seems to be a problem with the fruit holding in the top vintages, something that cannot be said for many other wines—from either the new world or Europe. Ridge's 1993 Cabernet Sauvignon displays stunningly rich, concentrated fruit, a mineral-, toasty-, and cassis-scented nose with plenty of sweetness and ripeness, extremely full body, sensational extract, moderately high tannin, and decent underlying acidity. This generous, powerful, full-bodied wine requires 5–10 years of cellaring. Many 1993s are forward, soft, and easy to understand, but this offering will require considerable patience. However, I have no doubts about the fruit balancing out the wine's tannin. This is a wine to buy for your children. Drink it between 2008 and 2035.

SHAFER

1993 Cabernet Sauvignon Hillside Selection	Stag's Leap	(92–95)

This is an impressive Cabernet Sauvignon. It exhibits superb richness and intensity yet manages to avoid a heavy-handed feel and an excess of tannin and power. There is a sense of wonderful richness, an inner core of sweet cassis fruit nicely complemented by high-quality, toasty vanillin from new oak casks, a long, rich finish, and a superb sense of elegance and harmony. As the wine sits in the glass, aromas of black cherries, flowers, and spices emerge. Shafer's Cabernets tend to be understated and subtle when young, but they can blossom beautifully after 5–6 years of cellaring. It is surprising how developed and complex this wine already is. A terrific effort in this top-notch vintage, Shafer's 1993 Hillside Selection should drink well young and should keep for 15–20 years.

SILVER OAK CELLARS

1993 Cabernet Sauvignon	Alexander Valley	(94–96)
1993 Cabernet Sauvignon	Napa Valley	(96–97)

The 1993 Cabernet Sauvignon Alexander Valley exhibits a dark black/ruby/purple color, a big, sweet nose of jammy black currants, fruitcake, cherries, and vanillin, full-bodied, chocolaty, black raspberry, curranty flavors with a slight touch of herbs, an unctuous palate, and a whoppingly lush, chewy finish. It should last for 10–15 years after its release. The 1993 Cabernet Sauvignon Napa Valley reveals even greater extract as well as superb focus and definition, great ripeness, a lavishly rich, decadently thick, juicy palate, superb concentration, and plenty of sweet tannin in the long, chewy finish. Slightly deeper and better focused than the Alexander Valley, it is a candidate for 15+ years of aging.

SIMI WINERY

1993 Cabernet Sauvignon Reserve	Sonoma	(88–90)

Based on this single tasting, Simi's 1993 Cabernet Sauvignon does not appear to equal what the winery achieved in both 1990 and 1991. (I have not tasted the 1992 Reserve.) Nevertheless, it remains a fine, potentially outstanding Cabernet Sauvignon with a stronger herbaceous component than in recent vintages such as 1986, 1990, and 1991. The wine exhibits an impressive ruby/purple color, and a sweet, ripe nose of cassis fruit, herbs, and smoky new oak. Medium to full bodied, well balanced, with adequate acidity, sweet tannin, and a long finish, this is a stylish, rich Cabernet Sauvignon that should drink well young, and last for 12–15 years.

SPOTTSWOODE

1993 Cabernet Sauvignon	Napa	(90–92)

This saturated purple-colored wine's reticent but promising bouquet emerges after considerable coaxing. On the palate, the wine reveals a tight structure, powerfully rich, concentrated fruit, a sense of finesse and elegance, and a long, moderately tannic finish. The wine is tight, but exceptionally well made with fine concentration, admirable harmony among its various components, and noteworthy purity. It should drink well between 2000 and 2015.

STELTZNER

1993 Cabernet Sauvignon	Napa	(83–85)

I recognize that this winery prefers a light- to medium-bodied, polished, subtle style of Cabernet Sauvignon, but I would like to see more intensity, ripeness, and most of all, character. Steltzner's 1993 Cabernet Sauvignon is a straightforward, attractive, easygoing Cabernet that will be drinkable upon release, and will last for a decade.

STERLING VINEYARDS

1993 Cabernet Sauvignon Diamond Mountain Ranch	Napa	(91–92)
1993 Merlot Three Palms Vineyard	Napa	(87–89)

The laudable winemaking changes being implemented at Sterling Vineyards are evident in both their Cabernet Sauvignon and Merlot cuvées. The 1993 Diamond Mountain Ranch Cabernet Sauvignon is even better than the 1992. It is sweeter, with greater fruit and intensity, as well as a long, chocolaty, cassis finish. The well-structured 1993 Merlot Three Palms Vineyard, bottled without fining or filtration, exhibits a deep, saturated color, and an expressive bouquet of chocolate, black cherries, mocha, and wood.

PHILIP TOGNI

1993 Cabernet Sauvignon	Napa	(90–92)

Togni's thick, chewy, juicy, succulent style of Cabernet Sauvignon is well displayed. The saturated purple color is followed by aromas of black olives, cassis, and subtle toasty oak. Full bodied and rich, with great intensity and flavor, this is another dazzling effort from Philip Togni. It does not appear to be as dramatic or as spectacularly rich as the 1992, 1991, and 1990. Kudos to Togni for producing four distinctive and magnificent Cabernet Sauvignons to start the decade of the nineties. The 1993 should be more flattering and drinkable at an earlier age than either the 1992 or 1991.

VIADER

1993 Estate Proprietary Red Wine	Napa	(88–92)

Made with a high percentage of Cabernet Franc in the blend, Viader's proprietary red wine is Napa Valley's answer to Cheval Blanc. The interesting aromatic profile offers an intensely perfumed bouquet of black and red fruits, spices, menthol, and floral scents. Medium to full bodied, with a Bordeaux-like mouth-feel, the emphasis is on finesse as opposed to power. The 1993 Estate possesses gobs of sweet fruit, with the Cabernet Franc dominating the wine's personality at present. Scheduled for release in 1996 it has the potential to develop into an extremely complex, aromatic wine of considerable stature. In a blind tasting, it would be difficult to pick this wine out as a California Cabernet Sauvignon.

VINE CLIFF CELLARS

1993 Cabernet Sauvignon	Napa	(90–92)

This looks to be the finest Cabernet Sauvignon Vine Cliff has yet produced. An impressively rich, dark purple-colored wine, it reveals admirable purity, medium to full body, and a long, concentrated finish filled with black fruit flavors gently touched by spicy oak. As with most 1993s, Vine Cliff's offering will be drinkable upon release and capable of lasting for 15–20 years.

VON STRASSER

1993 Cabernet Sauvignon Diamond Mountain	Napa	(90–92)

Von Strasser has fashioned an impressively made, well-balanced 1993 Cabernet Sauvignon that is a noteworthy successor to the outstanding 1992. It exhibits a black/purple color, and an attractive nose of sweet cassis fruit complemented by vanillin and herbs. It is medium to full bodied, and oozing with extract and ripeness, buttressed by adequate acidity and firm, moderately intense tannin. Put it away for 3–4 years and drink it over the following 15+.

WHITEHALL LANE WINERY

1994 Cabernet Sauvignon Morisoli Vineyard	Napa	(90–93)
1993 Cabernet Sauvignon Morisoli Vineyard	Napa	(88–91)
1994 Merlot Leonardini Vineyard	Napa	(90–92)
1993 Merlot Leonardini Vineyard	Napa	(86–88)

The 1993 Cabernet Sauvignon Morisoli Vineyard reveals an impressive saturated purple color, excellent purity, ripe cassis fruit, medium to full body, good tannin, adequate acidity, and a long, rich finish. It should be drinkable upon release and should age well for 10–15 years. The terrific 1994 Morisoli Vineyard Cabernet Sauvignon exhibits a black/purple color, fabulous sweetness and ripeness of fruit, full body, layers of extract and richness, and a stunning finish. The tannin is sweet and long. This gorgeous Cabernet appears to be a terrific effort from what looks to be a sensational vintage for north coast Cabernet Sauvignon.

These are both impressive Merlots. Although the 1993 is lighter, it remains a rich, medium- to full-bodied, spicy, ready-to-drink Merlot with plenty of berry fruit and nicely integrated oak. It should drink well for 5–7 years. The blockbuster 1994 exhibits a black/purple color, fabulously ripe, rich, concentrated fruit, full body, and great purity and balance. This is an immensely impressive Merlot that should age well for a decade or more.

ZD WINES

1993 Cabernet Sauvignon	Napa (87–89+?)

This is a muscular, heavyweight style of Cabernet Sauvignon. It possesses a dense, black/purple color, lavish quantities of toasty oak, plenty of glycerin and alcohol, and a chewy, thick texture. Although somewhat monolithic, it is so impressively endowed that it deserves enthusiastic notes. While it will never be the most complex, fragrant, or suave Cabernet, it should age effortlessly for 2 decades.

Estimated Maturity Charts

EXPLANATION OF THE CHARTS

Given the number of inquiries I receive about when a particular wine has reached a point in its evolution that it is said to be ready to drink, I have provided an estimated range of years over which specific vintages of the following wines should be consumed. Before one takes this guide too literally, let me share with you the following points.

1. If you like the way a wine tastes when young, don't hesitate to enjoy it in spite of what the chart may say.
2. I have had to make several assumptions. First, readers have purchased the wine in a healthy state. Second, readers are cellaring their wines in a cool, humid, odor- and vibration-free environment that does not exceed 68° F in the summer.
3. The estimates are an educated guess (made in June 1995) based on how the wine last tasted, normally ages, and its quality, balance, and depth for the vintage in question.
4. The estimates are conservative in the sense that good storage conditions are essential. I have assumed a maturity based on my own palate, which tends to prefer a younger wine that has more freshness and exuberance over one that has begun to fade, but that may still be quite delicious and complex. I do not have an English palate.

Consequently, if you have cool, ideal cellars, the beginning year in the estimated range of maturity may tilt in favor of drinking the wine on the young side. I presume most readers would prefer, given a choice, to open a bottle too early rather than too late, and this philosophy has governed my projected maturity period for each wine.

HOW TO READ THE CHARTS

N/M   = This wine was not produced or declared in this vintage.

N/T   = No recent and/or no tasting experience.

Now   = Totally mature, and not likely to improve; this wine should be drunk over the next 2–4 years.

Now ↓   = Probably in decline.

Now–2005 = The wine has begun to enter its plateau of maturity where it should be expected to remain, possibly even improve, until 2005, at which time it may begin to slowly decline.

1998–2010 = This is the estimated range of years in which I believe the wine will be in its plateau period—the years over which it will be at its best for drinking. Please keep in mind that Bordeaux wines from top vintages tend to decline slowly (just the opposite of Burgundy) and a top wine from an excellent vintage may take 10–15 years to lose its fruit and freshness after the last year in the stated plateau period.

General Vintage

A vintage chart should be regarded as a very general overall rating of a particular viticultural region. Such charts are filled with exceptions to the rule ... astonishingly good wines from skillful or lucky vintners in years rated mediocre, and thin, diluted characterless wines from incompetent or greedy producers in great years.

	REGIONS	1970	1971	1972	1973	1974	1975	1976	1977	1978	1979	1980	
Bordeaux	St. Julien/Pauillac St.-Estèphe	87R	82R	67C	65C	68C	**89T**	84R	73C	87R	85R	78R	
	Margaux	85R	83R	71C	65C	74C	78E	77R	71C	87R	87R	79C	
	Graves	87R	86R	75C	76C	76C	**89T**	71C	75C	**90R**	**88R**	78C	
	Pomerol	**90R**	87R	65C	70C	75R	**94R**	82R	72C	84R	86R	79C	
	St.-Émilion	85R	83R	65C	67C	62C	85R	82R	60C	84R	84R	72R	
	Barsac/Sauternes	84R	86R	55C	65C	50C	**90T**	87R	50C	75R	75R	85R	
Burgundy	Côte de Nuits (Red)	82C	87C	86R	58C	64C	50C	86C	60C	**88C**	77C	84C	
	Côte de Beaune (Red)	82C	87C	83C	60C	62C	50C	86C	55C	86R	77C	78C	
	White	83C	**88C**	84C	87C	75C	65C	86C	80C	**88R**	**88R**	75C	
Rhône	North: Côte Rôtie Hermitage	**90R**	84R	86R	72R	70C	73C	82R	72R	**98E**	87R	83R	
	South: Châteauneuf du Pape	**88R**	82C	86C	74C	70C	60C	75C	70C	**97R**	**88R**	77C	
	Beaujolais	—	—	—	—	—	—	86C	50C	84C	80C	60C	
	Alsace	80C	**90R**	55C	75C	74C	82C	**90R**	70C	80C	84R	80C	
	Loire Valley	—	—	—	—	—	—	86C	70C	85C	83C	72C	
	Champagne	85C	**90C**	N.V.	82C	N.V.	**90R**	**90R**	N.V.	N.V.	**88R**	N.V.	
Italy	Piedmont	84R	**90R**	50C	70R	85T	65C	67C	67C	**95T**	86R	70R	
	Chianti	84C	**88C**	50C	68C	80R	84R	60C	72R	**85C**	75C	70C	
	Germany	80C	**90R**	50C	67C	60C	85R	**90R**	70C	72C	84R	65R	
	Vintage Port	**90R**	N.V.	78C	N.V.	N.V.	82R	N.V.	**95T**	83E	N.V.	84T	
Spain	Roija	**90R**	74C	67C	86R	65C	84R	86R	70C	**84R**	79R	75R	
	Penedes	—	—	—	—	—	—	—	—	—	—	85R	
Aust.	New So. Wales & Victoria	—	—	—	—	—	—	—	—	—	—	**88C**	
California-N. Coast	Cabernet Sauvignon	**92R**	70C	65C	**88R**	**90R**	85R	**90T**	84R	**92R**	80R	87R	
	Chardonay	83C	82C	84C	85C	75C	86C	80C	83C	86C	83C	**88C**	
	Zinfandel	**96C**	60C	50C	86C	**88C**	80C	87C	85R	86R	83R	82R	
	Pinot Noir	—	—	—	—	—	—	—	—	84R	80C	85R	
Ore.	Pinot Noir	—	—	—	—	—	—	—	—	—	—	86C	
Wash.	Cabernet Sauvignon	—	—	—	—	—	—	—	—	—	—	—	

Guide 1970–1994

Key: 90–100 = The Finest; 80–89 = Above Average to Excellent; 70–79 = Average; 60–69 = Below Average; Below 60 = Poor

Explanation of Symbols: C = Caution, may now be too old or irregular; E = Early maturing; T = Still Tannic and Youthful; R = Ready to drink; N.V. = Nonvintage; **Bold Print = The Top Vintages**

1981	1982	1983	1984	1985	1986	1987	1988	1989	1990	1991	1992	1993	1994
85R	**98R**	86R	72C	**92R**	**94T**	82R	87T	**97E**	**98T**	75R	79E	86T	**90T**
82R	86R	**95R**	68C	86R	**90T**	76R	85E	85E	**90E**	74R	75E	86T	85T
84R	**88R**	**89R**	79R	**90R**	89E	84R	**89E**	**89E**	**90R**	74R	75E	87T	**88T**
86R	**96R**	**90R**	65C	**88R**	87T	85C	**89T**	**95E**	**95E**	60C	82R	**88T**	**92T**
82R	**94R**	**89R**	69C	87R	**88E**	74C	**88E**	**88E**	**98T**	65C	75R	84C	87T
85R	75R	**88T**	70C	85R	**94T**	70R	**98T**	**90E**	**96T**	70C	70C	70C	78E
72C	82C	85C	78R	87R	74C	85R	86E	87R	**92R**	86T	78R	87T	79E
74C	80C	78C	70C	87R	72C	79C	86R	**88R**	**90R**	72E	82R	86T	78E
86C	**88C**	85C	80C	**89R**	**90R**	79R	82R	**92R**	87R	70C	**92R**	72C	**89E**
75C	85R	**89T**	75E	**90E**	84T	86E	**92E**	**96E**	**92T**	**92E**	78E	65C	**88E**
88R	70C	87R	72C	**88R**	78C	60C	**88R**	**96T**	**95E**	70C	78R	**89E**	**88E**
83C	75C	86C	75C	87C	84C	85C	86C	**92C**	86C	**90R**	77C	86R	87R
86C	82C	**93R**	75C	**88R**	82R	83R	86R	**93R**	**93R**	75E	85E	87R	**93E**
82C	84C	84C	68C	**88R**	87R	82R	**88R**	**92R**	**90R**	75R	80R	86R	87R
84R	**90R**	84R	N.V.	**95R**	**89R**	N.V.	**88E**	**90R**	**93E**	N.V.	N.V.	N.V.	N.V.
80R	**92E**	75C	65C	**92E**	78R	85E	**90T**	**96E**	**96E**	76E	74C	86E	85E
82C	86R	80R	60C	**93R**	84R	73R	**89T**	72C	**90E**	73E	72C	84R	86R
82R	80R	**90R**	70R	85R	80R	82R	**89R**	**90E**	**92E**	85E	**90R**	87R	**90R**
N.V.	86T	**92E**	N.V.	**95E**	N.V.	N.V.	N.V.	N.V.	N.V.	**90E**	**95E**	N.V.	?
87R	92R	74R	78R	82R	82E	82E	87E	**90E**	87E	76E	85E	87E	**90E**
84R	87R	85R	86R	85R	77R	**88E**	87E	**88E**	87E	74E	82E	87E	**90E**
85C	83C	76R	84R	86R	**90E**	87E	85E	**88E**	**88E**	**89E**	87R	87R	88E
85R	86R	76C	**92R**	**92T**	**90E**	**90E**	75E	84T	**94E**	**94T**	**93E**	**91E**	**95T**
86C	85C	85C	**88C**	84C	**90C**	75C	**89C**	76C	**90R**	85R	**92R**	**90R**	88R
82R	80R	78R	**88R**	**88E**	87E	**90R**	82R	83R	**91R**	**91R**	**90R**	**90E**	**90T**
83C	84C	85C	85R	86E	84R	86E	87R	85R	86E	86R	**88R**	**88E**	86R
86C	84C	**90C**	65C	87R	85R	72R	**88R**	86R	**90R**	87R	**88R**	**89R**	**92E**
—	78C	**92E**	72C	86T	78R	85E	**88E**	**92E**	87E	85C	**89E**	87E	**90T**

BORDEAUX	1994	1993	1992	1991	1990	1989	1988	1987
L'Angélus	2000–2050	1998–2012	Now–2004	Now–2000	Now–2015	Now–2015	Now–2010	N/T
d'Armaihac	2000–2015	1996–2006	Now–2000	Now–1994	Now–2003	Now–2000	Now–1998	Now
L'Arrosée	2002–2023	1996–2008	Now–2002	N/M	Now–2020	Now–1999	Now–2000	Now
Ausone	1997–2025	2010–2030	2000–2009	N/M	2010–2040	2015–2035	2008–2040	Now–2020
Batailley	N/T	N/T	Now–2004	Now–2001	1998–2010	2000–2018	1997–2008	Now
Belair	1997–2012	2000–2015	1997–2002	N/M	1997–2012	1995–2010	1998–2010	Now–1998
Beychevelle	1999–2012	1998–2010	Noq–2000	Now–2001	Now–2002	Now–2008	Now–2002	Now ↓
Bon Pasteur	2002–2020	1996–2010	Now–2002	N/M	Now–2005	Now–2003	Now–2008	Now
Branaire-Ducru	1997–2012	1998–2015	Now–2001	Now–1999	Now–2005	Now–2005	Now–1998	Now
Brane-Cantenac	N/T	N/T	Now–2000	Now	Now–2004	Now–2004	Now–1996	Now ↓
Calon-Ségur	2000–2015	N/T	Now–2000	1996–2005	1996–2010	1996–2010	1998–2020	Now
Canon	2000–2015	2002–2017	Now–2004	N/M	2000–2025	1996–2010	1996–2012	Now
Canon-la-Gaffelière	2000–2015	1996–2010	Now–2003	N/M	1997–2010	Now–2002	Now–2004	Now
Cantemerle	N/T	2000–2010	Now–2001	Now	Now–1999	1996–2010	Now–2005	Now ↓
Canenac-Brown	2000–2015	2000–2020	Now–2000	Now–2002	Now–2003	Now–2001	Now–2000	Now
Certan de May	2000–2020	2000–2018	1996–2006	N/M	1998–2015	Now–2010	1996–2015	Now
Chasse-Spleen	N/T	1998–2010	Now–2003	Now	Now–2003	1996–2015	Now–2006	Now
Chevel Blanc	2000–2020	1999–2015	Now–2001	N/M	1997–2015	Now–2010	Now–2008	Now
Domaine de Chevalier	2005–2025	2000–2015	Now–2004	1996–2005	1997–2008	1996–2015	Now–2008	Now–1998
Clerc-Milon	1997–2012	1996–2006	Now–2003	Now–2005	Now–2008	Now–2010	Now–2001	Now
Clinet	2000–2030	2000–2020	1997–2008	Now–2004	1997–2010	1997–2015	Now–2010	Now–2000
La Conseillante	1997–2012	1996–2003	Now–1999	Now	Now–2012	1996–2010	Now–1999	Now
Cos d'Estournel	2000–2020	2000–2020	Now–2005	Now–2004	1996–2012	Now–2009	2000–2020	Now–1997
La Dominique	2000–2020	1997–2008	Now–2000	N/M	Now–2005	1996–2008	Now–2001	Now ↓
Ducru-Beaucaillou	2005–2025	2002–2027	1998–2010	1998–2009	1999–2015	1999–2020	1996–2008	Now–1999
Duhart-Milon-Rothschild	2003–2005	1997–2012	Now–2002	1996–2004	1999–2007	Now–2008	Now–2010	Now
L'Église-Clinet	2000–2020	1997–2010	Now–2001	Now	Now–2007	Now–2000	Now–2002	Now
L'Enclos	1996–2005	Now–2005	Now	Now	Now–2006	Now–2002	Now	Now
L'Evangile	2008–2040	2000–2015	Now–2001	N/M	2000–2020	Now–2008	Now–2002	Now–2002
Figeac	1998–2012	Now–2008	Now	N/M	Now–2010	Now–2002	Now	Now
La Fleur de Gay	2002–2022	2000–2012	1998–2009	Now–1999	1998–2008	1998–2010	1996–2010	Now–2005
La Fleur Pétrus	2002–2017	2000–2015	Now–2005	N/M	Now–2005	1996–2009	Now–2000	Now–1996
Les Forts de Latour	2003–2018	1996–2012	Now–2003	Now–2002	Now–2005	Now–2004	Now–2002	Now–1997
La Gaffelière	2002–2017	2000–2010	Now–2002	Now–2000	Now–2008	1996–2010	Now–2000	Now ↓
Le Gay	2005–2015	2002–2017	Now–2000	N/M	1996–2010	2005–2030	1997–2020	—
Giscours	2000–2015	1996–2006	Now–2003	Now–2003	Now–2005	Now–2005	Noq–1996	Now
Gloria	1997–2007	1997–2008	Now–2001	Now	Now–1999	Now–2000	Now–1997	Now
Grand Mayne	2002–2022	1997–2010	Now–2002	N/T	Now–2010	1998–2008	Now–2002	Now
Grand-Puy-Ducasse	2000–2020	N/T	Now–2002	Now	Now–1999	Now–2002	Now–1996	Now
Grand-Puy-Lacoste	2007–2032	2000–2015	Now–2002	Now–2008	1997–2010	1996–2010	Now–2005	N/T
La Grave à Pomerol	1997–2007	1996–2006	Now–2000	N/M	Now–2002	Now–2002	Now–2001	Now
Gruaud-Larose	1997–2007	2005–2030	Now–2005	Now–2005	1997–2015	2000–2025	2000–2025	Now–2000
Haut-Bages-Libéral	1997–2007	1998–2010	Now–2001	Now–2001	Now–2005	Now–2000	Now–1998	Now
Haut-Bailly	1997–2012	1996–2014	Now–2005	N/M	Now–2010	Now–2012	Now–2005	Now
Haut-Batailley	2002–2017	1996–2006	Now–2000	Now–2002	Now–2005	Now–2006	Now–1998	Now
Haut-Brion	1998–2025	1996–2021	1998–2010	1997–2008	1998–2010	1998–2020	1997–2015	Now
Haut-Marbuzet	Now–2008	Now–2006	Now–2000	N/M	Now–2005	Now–2002	Now–2003	Now
D'Issan	1998–2013	Now–2008	Now	Now	Now–2004	Now–1997	Now	Now

1986	1985	1983	1982	1981	1979	1978	1976	1975
Now–1998	Now	Now	Now ↓	—	—	—	—	—
Now–2002	Now–2000	Now–2000	Now–2000	Now–1996	Now	Now	Now ↓	Now ↓
1998–2010	Now–2004	Now–2003	Now–2005	Now–1996	Now	Now	Now ↓	Now ↓
1997–2020	Now–2010	Now–2020	2000–2030	1996–2010	1996–2010	1998–2015	Now–2025	Now–2005
1998–2010	Now–2005	Now–2000	Now–2010	Now	Now–2000	Now–2000	Now	Now–2000
Now–2000	Now–1999	Now–2005	1996–2008	Now	Now–2007	Now–1995	Now	Now
1998–2010	Now–2000	Now–2000	Now–2010	Now	Now	Now	Now	Now–2005
Now–2005	Now	Now	Now–2005	Now	Now	Now	Now ↓	Now
Now–1999	Now	Now	Now–2007	Now–1996	Now	Now	Now	Now–2005
Now–2005	Now	Now–2005	Now–2005	Now ↓	Now ↓	Now ↓	Now ↓	Now
1997–2015	Now–2000	Now–1997	1998–2020	Now	Now	Now	Now	Now–2005
1998–2010	Now–2007	Now–2015	Now–2020	Now–2000	Now–2005	Now–2005	Now	Now–2010
Now–2005	Now	Now	Now	—	—	—	—	—
Now–1998	Now–1997	Now–2010	Now–2000	Now	Now ↓	Now	Now ↓	Now–2003
1996–2008	Now–2000	Now–2000	Now–2005	Now–2004	Now	Now	Now ↓	Now–2003
1997–2015	Now–2007	Now–2000	2000–2020	Now–2008	Now–2008	Now	Now	Now–2000
1997–2010	Now–2005	Now	Now–2000	Now–1996	Now–1996	Now–2005	Now	Now–2005
Now–2010	Now–2010	Now–2010	1997–2015	Now–2000	Now	Now–2005	Now	Now–2004
1998–2015	Now–2005	Now–2005	Now	Now–2000	Now	Now–2005	Now	Now
Now–2006	Now–2000	Now	Now–1998	Now	Now	Now	Now	Now
Now–2000	Now ↓	Now ↓	Now ↓	Now ↓	Now ↓	Now ↓	Now ↓	Now ↓
Now–2005	Now–2005	Now	Now–2006	Now–2003	Now ↓	Now	Now ↓	Now–1999
1998–2015	Now–2010	Now–2000	1996–2010	Now	Now	Now–2000	Now	Now–2000
Now–2005	Now–1996	Now–2000	Now–2007	Now	Now	Now–2000	Now ↓	Now
1999–2015	Now–2010	Now–2005	2000–2020	Now–2010	Now	Now–2005	Now	Now–2015
1996–2008	Now–2000	Now–2000	1997–2010	Now–2003	Now	Now	Now ↓	Now
Now–2005	1997–2010	Now	Now–2000	Now	Now	Now	Now ↓	Now
Now–1998	Now–2000	Now–1997	Now–2000	Now	Now	Now	Now	Now–2002
Now–2002	1997–2015	Now–2003	Now–2010	Now ↓	Now	Now	Now ↓	Now–2010
Now–2005	Now–2002	Now	Now–2010	Now ↓	Now ↓	Now	Now ↓	Now–2000
Now–2003	Now–1998	Now	Now ↓	N/M	N/M	N/M	N/M	N/M
Now–1998	Now–1997	Now–1997	1996–2008	Now	Now	Now	Now ↓	1996–2010
Now–2003	Now–1998	Now–1996	Now–2008	Now–2000	Now–1996	Now–2000	Now	Now
Now–2006	Now–1997	Now	Now–2000	Now	Now ↓	Now ↓	Now ↓	Now–2008
1998–2010	Now–2008	Now–2005	2000–2020	Now ↓	Now–2004	Now–1999	Now ↓	1998–2010
Now	Now	Now	Now	Now	Now–2003	Now–2006	Now	1997–2010
Now–2002	Now–1997	Now	Now–2005	Now	Now	Now	Now ↓	Now–2005
—	—	—	—	—	—	—	—	—
Now–2000	Now–1997	Now	Now	Now	Now	Now	Now ↓	Now
1997–2015	Now–2005	Now–2005	1996–2015	Now	Now	Now–2001	Now	Now–2000
Now–1997	Now	Now	Now–2005	Now	Now	Now	Now	Now
2000–2025	Now–2008	Now–2008	1996–2020	Now–2000	Now–2003	Now–2008	Now	2000–2020
Now–2010	Now–2005	Now	Now–2006	Now–2000	Now	Now	Now	Now–2003
Now–2000	Now–2000	Now–1997	Now–2000	Now	Now–2000	Now–1998	Now ↓	Now
Now–2002	Now	Now	Now–2005	Now	Now	Now	Now	Now
1998–2015	Now–2010	Now–2005	1997–2015	Now–2003	Now–2005	Now–2000	Now	Now–2015
Now–2003	Now–1997	Now–2000	Now–2005	Now	Now	Now	Now	Now
Now–2003	Now–1997	Now–2003	Now–1997	Now	Now	Now–1996	Now ↓	Now ↓

BORDEAUX (cont.)	1994	1993	1992	1991	1990	1989	1988	1987
Lafite-Rothschild	2012–2030	2000–2020	1998–2010	Now–2004	2000–2030	1997–2020	2000–2035	Now–1997
Lafleur	2007–2040	2010–2040	2000–2015	N/M	2000–2030	2000–2030	2000–2030	N/M
Lafon-Rochet	2005–2030	2000–2010	1998–2008	1997–2005	1998–2022	1996–2015	1996–2003	Now
Lagrange St.-Julien	2001–2020	1996–2012	Now–2015	Now–2002	1996–2010	Now–2010	1997–2008	Now–1996
La Lagune	1998–2006	1996–2008	Now–2002	Now–2005	Now–2006	Now–2008	Now–2005	Now
Lanessan	1998–2009	1996–2008	Now–1999	Now	Now–2006	Now–2004	Now–2008	Now
Larmande	1998–2010	1996–2008	Now–2002	N/M	1996–2003	Now–2001	Now–2002	—
Lascombes	1998–2013	1997–2008	Now–2000	Now–2001	Now–2003	Now–2002	Now–2002	—
Latour	2010–2050	2006–2026	1997–2010	2000–2012	2005–2040	1997–2015	2000–2025	Now–2001
Latour à Pomerol	2003–2018	2000–2015	Now–2002	2000–2012	Now–2004	Now–2010	Now–1999	Now
Léoville-Barton	2005–2030	2002–2022	Now–2006	Now–2007	1998–2020	1996–2010	1996–2012	Now
Léoville Las Cases	2002–2030	2002–2027	Now–2010	1996–2008	2000–2025	1998–2020	1996–2020	Now–2000
Léoville-Poyferré	N/T	1997–2010	Now	1998–2006	1998–2025	1997–2015	1996–2006	Now
La Louvière	2005–2025	1996–2010	Now–2005	N/M	Now–2006	Now–1998	Now–2002	Now
Lynch-Bages	2007–2030	2002–2017	Now–2004	Now–2004	1996–2010	2000–2020	Now–2010	Now
Magdelaine	1998–2010	1998–2008	1998–2005	N/M	1998–2008	2000–2025	1998–2005	Now
Malescot St.-Exupéry	2002–2017	N/T	Now–2002	Now–2001	Now–2009	Now–2003	Now–2005	Now
Château Margaux	1997–2030	1998–2022	Now–2009	1996–2002	1997–2030	1996–2015	2000–2015	Now–2000
Maucaillou	N/T	N/T	Now	Now	Now–2002	Now–2001	Now–1998	Now
Mayney	N/T	1998–2009	Now–2000	Now–2000	1996–2010	1996–2020	1996–2015	Now
La Mission Haut-Brion	2000–2025	1996–2016	Now–2010	Now–2005	1998–2015	1997–2020	1996–2012	Now–2000
Montrose	2007–2040	2004–2030	1998–2009	2000–2015	2000–2045	2000–2025	Now–2005	Now
Mouton-Rothschild	2007–2037	1996–2016	Now–2008	1998–2009	1999–2020	1998–2020	1999–2020	1998–2010
Les-Ormes-de-Pez	1999–2008	1996–2006	Now–2002	Now–2001	Now–2008	Now–2000	Now–1999	Now
Palmer	1997–2012	1996–2010	Now–2000	Now–2004	Now–2006	Now–2012	Now–2006	Now–1999
Pape-Clément	2002–2022	2000–2020	Now–2000	Now–2002	1998–2010	Now–2005	Now–2008	Now
Pavie	1997–2008	2004–2012	Now–2006	1997–2003	1999–2015	1996–2010	1996–2006	N/T
Petit-Village	1997–2012	1996–2006	Now	Now	Now–2005	Now–2000	Now–2000	Now
Pétrus	2005–2045	2005–2040	2000–2015	N/M	2000–2025	2000–2035	2002–2030	1997–2010
Pichon-Longueville Baron	2004–2025	2002–2022	1996–2009	1997–2010	1996–2020	2000–2020	1996–2008	Now–1998
Pichon Lalande	2002–2027	1998–2012	Now	Now–2009	Now–2000	Now–2012	Now–2008	Now
Le Pin	1997–2017	Now–2015	Now–2002	N/M	Now–2007	Now–2004	Now–2003	Now–1997
Pontet-Canet	2003–2030	2000–2020	Now–2004	Now–2000	1997–2020	2000–2015	1996–2005	Now
Potensac	1997–2010	1996–2008	Now	Now	Now–2003	Now–1999	Now	Now
Poujeaux	1998–2009	1996–2002	Now	Now	Now–2005	Now–2003	Now–2005	Now
Prieuré-Lichine	2003–2023	1996–2010	Now–2003	Now–2001	1996–2005	Now–2005	Now–2003	Now ↓
Rausan-Ségla	2007–2035	2002–2022	Now–2005	1996–2010	1997–2020	Now–2012	1997–2012	N/M
St.-Pierre	1997–2017	N/T	Now–2004	Now–2001	1996–2007	Now–2010	Now–2000	Now
de Sales	2002–2025	1999–2015	Now	N/M	Now–2005	Now–2003	Now–1997	Now ↓
Sociando-Mallet	2000–2018	2005–2020	1999–2010	1996–2006	2000–2020	1997–2010	1996–2008	Now
Soutard	1998–2015	2000–2015	Now–2001	Now	1996–2020	2000–2020	1998–2020	—
Talbot	1997–2015	1996–2006	Now–2003	Now	Now–2008	Now–2008	1996–2010	Now–1998
du Tertre	N/T	N/T	Now–2002	Now–2002	1996–2008	Now–1998	Now–2003	Now
Le Tertre-Roteboeuf	1997–2012	1996–2010	Now	Now	Now–2010	Now–2010	Now–2010	Now
La Tour Haut-Brion	1997–2008	1996–2010	Now–2002	Now–2000	Now–2003	Now–2000	Now–2002	Now
Troplong-Mondot	2003–2028	2000–2020	1998–2010	Now–2002	1996–2015	1996–2012	Now–2007	Now
Trotanoy	2003–2023	2005–2020	1998–2010	N/M	Noq–2008	Now–2010	Now–2005	Now
Vieux Château Certan	2002–2022	1996–2010	Now–2002	N/M	1996–2010	1996–2005	Now–2010	Now–1997

1986	1985	1983	1982	1981	1979	1978	1976	1975
2000–2030	1997–2010	1998–2025	2000–2040	Now–2008	1996–2005	Now–2005	Now–2005	1997–2015
2000–2025	2000–2020	Now–2010	Now–2015	Now ↓	2000–2030	Now–2018	Now ↓	2000–2035
1996–2008	Now–1999	Now–2005	Now–2008	Now	Now–1998	Now	Now	Now–2000
2000–2020	Now–2008	Now–1998	Now–2000	Now	Now	Now	Now	Now
1997–2010	Now–2004	Now–2003	Now–2010	Now–1998	Now	Now–2003	Now	Now–2003
Now–2006	Now–1996	Now–2000	Now–2003	Now	Now	Now	Now	Now–2003
Now–2005	Now–2000	Now–1997	Now–2000	Now	—	Now	—	—
Now–2000	Now–2000	Now–2003	Now–2001	Now	Now	Now	Now	Now–2003
2000–2015	Now–2008	Now–2005	1998–2040	Now–2006	Now–2000	Now–2010	Now–2005	1998–2030
Now–2005	Now–2005	Now–2000	Now–2005	Noq–1997	Now	Now	Now	Now
1997–2020	Now–2007	Now–2002	1998–2015	Now	Now	Now–1996	Now	Now–2005
2000–2035	Now–2010	Now–2010	1996–2030	Now–2005	Now–1998	Now–2015	Now	1996–2010
1997–2020	Now–1998	Now–2005	1999–2020	Now	Now	Now	Now ↓	Now–2006
Now–2000	Now–2000	Now–2000	Now–2002	Now	Now	Now	N/T	Now
1998–2020	Now–2005	Now–2000	Now–2010	Now	Now ↓	Now ↓	Now ↓	Now
Now–1998	Now–2003	Now–2003	1996–2010	Now–2000	Now	Now	Now	Now–2005
Now–2001	Now–1997	Now–2000	Now–2000	Now	Now	Now	Now ↓	Now
2000–2050	Now–2025	2000–2030	1997–2030	Now–2010	Now–2010	Now–2010	Now ↓	Now ↓
Now–1998	Now–1998	Now	Now–1996	Now	Now	Now	Now	Now
1997–2010	Now–2005	Now–2003	Now–2010	Now–1997	Now	Now–2000	Now	Now–2005
1996–2012	Now–2015	Now–2005	Now–2015	Now–2006	Now–2005	Now–2010	Now	Now–2025
1996–2015	Now–2000	Now–1997	Now–2004	Now–1997	Now–1999	Now–2000	Now–2002	2000–2030
2000–2040	Now–2010	Now–2010	2000–2040	Now–2000	Now–2000	Now–2000	Now	2000–2015
Now–2000	Now	Now	Now	Now	Now	Now	Now	Now
Now–2010	Now–2005	1997–2015	Now–2005	Now–1997	Now–2005	Now–2005	Now	Now–2000
1996–2015	Now–2000	Now ↓	Now ↓	Now ↓	Now ↓	Now ↓	Now ↓	Now–2003
1996–2010	Now–2005	Now–2005	1997–2010	Now	Now–2000	Now	Now	Now
Now–2000	Now–1997	Now–1998	Now–2000	Now	Now	Now ↓	Now ↓	Now ↓
1998–2010	2000–2020	Now–2015	2000–2030	1998–2008	1997–2010	Now–2005	Now	2000–2050
Now–2005	Now–1998	Now–1996	Now–2002	Now	Now	Now	Now	Now
1996–2015	Now–2005	Now–2015	Now–2010	Now–1997	Now–1996	Now–1996	Now	Now–1998
1996–2005	Now–2005	Now–2005	Now–2005	Now	Now	N/M	N/M	N/M
1996–2015	Now–2005	Now–2002	Now–2005	Now	Now	Now	Now	Now–2000
Now–1998	Now–1996	Now	Now–2000	Now	Now	Now	Now	Now
Now–2010	Now–1998	Now–2000	Now–2005	Now	Now	Now	Now	Now
Now–2006	Now	Now–2003	Now–2005	Now	Now ↓	Now	Now ↓	Now
2000–2020	Now–2000	Now–2005	Now–1997	Now ↓	Now ↓	Now ↓	Now ↓	Now ↓
1996–2012	Now–1998	Now–1998	Now–2002	Now–2000	Now–1996	Now–1996	Now ↓	Now–2000
Now	Now	Now	Now–1998	Now	Now	Now	Now ↓	Now
2000–2035	Now–2015	Now–2001	1998–2015	Now–2000	Now–1998	Now–2005	Now–2000	Now–2010
1997–2015	1996–2010	Now–2003	Now–2005	Now–1996	Now	Now	Now	Now–2005
Now–2015	Now–2005	Now–2005	Now–2015	Now–2000	Now	Now–2000	Now	Now–2000
Now–2005	Now–1998	Now–2001	Now–1998	Now	Now–2005	Now–2000	Now ↓	Now ↓
Now–2002	Now–2000	Now–1999	Now–1998	N/T	N/T	N/T	N/T	N/T
Now–2000	Now–1997	Now–2000	1996–2010	Now–2004	Now–2000	Now–2010	Now	Now–2030
Now–2005	Now–1998	Now	Now	Now	Now	Now	Now	Now
Now–2005	Now–2000	Now–2001	Now–2010	Now–2002	Now	Now	Now	Now–2007
1996–2010	Now–2000	Now–2000	Now–2005	Now–2003	Now	Now	Now	Now–2000

RED BURGUNDY	1993	1992	1991	1990	1989	1988
Bertrand Ambroise Nuits St.-Georges Les Vaucrains	2000–2025	1998–2010	1998–2009	1998–2020	Now–2010	Now–2000
Domaine de L'Arlot Nuits St.-Georges Clos de Forêts	Now–2006	Now–2001	Now–2002	Now	Now	Now
Comte Armand Pommard Clos des Epeneaux	N/T	Now	N/T	2004–2034	Now–2002	Now–2002
Robert Arnoux Vosne-Romanée Les Suchots	Now	Now	Now–2004	Now–2000	Now–1998	Now–2002
Bichot-Clos Frantin Vosne-Romanée Les Malconsorts	N/T	N/T	N/T	Now	Now	Now–2005
Bourée Père et Fils Charmes-Chambertin	N/T	N/T	N/T	1997–2008	1996–2004	1998–2008
Bourée Père et Fils Clos de la Roche	N/T	1998–2002	N/T	1999–2010	Now–1997	Now–2002
R. Chevillon Nuits St.-Georges Les St.-Georges	2000–2005	1997–2001	1997–2012	Now–2003	Now–2002	Now–2002
R. Chevillon Nuits St.-Georges Les Vaucrains	2000–2005	1997–2001	1996–2006	Now–2002	Now–2001	1996–2003
Chopin-Groffier Clos Vougeot	1998–2004	Now–2004	Now–2004	Now–2012	Now–2003	Now–2000
J. Confuron-Cotetidot Clos Vougeot	2000–2005	1998–2005	Now–2005	Now–2004	Now–2003	Now–2010
J. Confuron-Cotetidot Vosne-Romanée Les Suchots	2000–2015	1997–2005	N/T	Now–2000	Now–2001	Now–2010
Courcel Pommard Rugiens	1997–2005	Now	N/T	Now–2000	Now–1998	Now–2000
J. Drouhin Charmes-Chambertin	N/T	Now	N/T	Now–2002	Now–1998	Now–2002
Drouhin-Larose Bonnes Mares	N/T	N/T	N/T	N/T	N/T	N/T
Drouhin-Larose Chambertin Clos de Bèze	N/T	N/T	N/T	N/T	N/T	N/T
Claude & Maurice Dugat Charmes-Chambertin	1998–2008	Now–2004	Now–2004	1996–2005	Now–1999	1996–2006
Claude & Maurice Dugat Griottes-Chambertin	1998–2010	Now–2005	Now–2004	1996–2008	Now–2001	1996–2006
Dujac Bonnes Mares	1998–2006	Now–2000	1996–2004	Now–2002	Now	Now–1998
Dujac Charmes-Chambertin	Now–2004	Now–2000	1996–2003	Now–2000	Now	Now
Dujac Clos de la Roche	1998–2006	Now–2000	1998–2013	Now–2004	Now	Now–2000
Dujac Clos St.-Denis	1997–2004	Now–2000	1998–2010	Now–2005	Now	Now–2000
René Engel Grands Echézeaux	1999–2009	Now–2000	Now–2004	Now–2000	Now–1998	Now–1997
Michel Esmonin Gevrey-Chambertin Clos St.-Jacques	1998–2009	Now–2000	N/T	Now–2010	Now–2010	Now–1998
A. Girardin Pommard Les Epenots	2005–2010	1997–2000	N/T	2002–2030	1996–2016	Now–2006
A. Girardin Pommard Les Rugiens	2005–2010	1997–2000	N/T	2002–2035+	1998–2028	Now–2005
Machard de Gramont Nuits St.-Georges Les Damodes	2000–2006	1998–2001	Now–1999	1996–2004	Now–2007	Now–2000
Jean Gros Clos Vougeot	N/T	N/T	N/T	Now–2002	N/T	N/T
Jean Gros Richebourg	1998–2008	Now–2000	Now–2002	Now–2000	Now–2000	Now–1998
Haegelen-Jayer Clos Vougeot	2000–2015	Now–2002	N/T	Now–2010	Now–2002	1998–2006
Haegelen-Jayer Echézeaux	2000–2012	Now–2002	N/T	Now–2006	Now–2002	1996–2006
Louis Jadot Beaune Clos des Ursules	2000–2015	Now	N/T	1996–2010	Now–2002	1996–2008
Louis Jadot Bonnes Mares	2002–2012	Now–2001	1998–2006	1998–2015	Now–2010	1997–2010
Louis Jadot Chambertin-Clos de Bèze	2001–2010	1996–2003	1996–2005	1998–2025	Now–2008	1998–2015
Louis Jadot Chambolle-Musigny Les Amoureuses	1999–2012	1996–2002	Now–2004	Now–2010	Now–2003	1996–2007
Louis Jadot Chapelle-Chambertin	1997–2009	Now–2001	Now–2005	2000–2010	Now–1998	Now–1997
Louis Jadot Clos Vougeot	2000–2012	1997–2004	Now–2008	2000–2020	Now–2010	Now
Louis Jadot Gevrey-Chambertin-Clos St.-Jacques	2002–2010	Now–2004	N/T	1997–2009	Now–2006	Now–2005
Henri Jayer Echézeaux	2001–2012	N/T	N/T	1996–2009	Now–2005	1997–2009
Henri Jayer Nuits St.-Georges Meurgers	N/T	N/T	N/T	N/T	N/T	N/T
Henri Jayer Richebourg	N/T	N/T	N/T	N/T	N/T	N/T
Henri Jayer Vosne-Romanée Les Brûlées	N/T	N/T	N/T	N/T	N/T	N/T
Henri Jayer Vosne-Romanée Cros Parantoux	N/T	N/T	N/T	Now–2008	Now–2002	1996–2007
Jayer-Gilles Echézeaux	2000–2010	Now–2000	Now–2004	Now–2007	Now–2006	Now–2005
Michel Lafarge Volnay-Clos des Chênes	N/T	Now–2000	N/T	1996–2008	Now–2000	1996–2005
Michel Lafarge Volnay-Clos du Château des Ducs	N/T	Now–2000	N/T	Now–2005	Now–1999	Now–2006
P. Leclerc Gevrey-Chambertin Les Cazetiers	Now–2003	Now–2000	1998–2015	Now–2010	Now–2002	1997–2008
P. Leclerc Gevrey-Chambertin Combe aux Moines	Now–2003	Now–2000	1998–2015	1997–2015	1996–2007	1997–2010
R. Leclerc Gevrey-Chambertin Combe aux Moines	Now–2008	Now–2000	Now–2005	Now–2004	Now–2000	1996–2005

1987	1986	1985	1983	1982	1980	1979	1978	1976
Now–1997	—	—	—	—	—	—	—	—
Now	—	—	—	—	—	—	—	—
Now	Now	Now–2005	Now–1997	Now	Now	Now	Now	Now–1998
Now	Now	Now	Now	Now	Now	Now	Now	N/T
Now	Now	Now–2003	Now–1998	Now	Now	Now	Now	N/T
Now	Now	Now–2003	Now–2000	Now	Now	Now	Now–1998	N/T
Now	Now	Now–2005	Now–2003	Now	Now	Now	Now	N/T
Now	Now	Now–2000	Now–2000	Now	Now	Now	Now	N/T
Now	Now	Now–2003	Now–2002	Now	Now	Now	Now	N/T
Now	Now	—	—	—	—	—	—	—
Now–2000	Now–1998	—	—	—	—	—	—	—
Now–1999	Now–1997	—	—	—	—	—	—	—
Now–1996	Now	Now–2000	Now	Now	Now	Now	Now	Now–1998
Now	Now	Now–2000	Now	Now	Now	—	—	—
Now	Now	Now–1998	Now	Now	Now	Now	Now	Now
Now	Now	Now–2000	Now	Now	Now	Now	Now	Now–1996
—	—	—	—	—	—	—	—	—
—	—	—	—	—	—	—	—	—
Now	Now	Now–2000	Now	Now	Now	Now	Now–2000	Now–2000
Now	Now	Now–2000	Now	Now	Now	Now	Now–1996	Now
Now	Now	Now–2000	Now	Now	Now	Now	Now–2000	Now–2003
Now	Now	Now–2000	Now	Now	Now	Now	Now–2000	Now–2003
Now	Now	Now–2003	Now	Now	N/T	N/T	N/T	N/T
Now–1997	—	—	—	—	—	—	—	—
1996–2001	Now	—	—	—	—	—	—	—
1996–2001	Now	—	—	—	—	—	—	—
Now	Now	Now	Now	Now	Now	Now	Now	N/T
—	—	—	Now	Now	Now	Now	Now–2000	N/T
Now	Now	Now–2000	Now	Now	Now	Now	Now–2000	N/T
Now	Now–1998	—	—	—	—	—	—	—
Now	Now–1996	—	—	—	—	—	—	—
Now–1996	Now	Now–2000	Now–2000	Now	N/T	Now	Now–2000	N/T
Now	Now–1996	Now–2002	N/T	N/T	N/T	N/T	N/T	N/T
Now–2002	Now–1998	Now–2008	Now–2003	N/T	N/T	N/T	N/T	N/T
Now–2001	Now–1996	Now–2001	N/T	N/T	N/T	N/T	N/T	N/T
Now–1996	Now–1996	Now–2000	N/T	N/T	N/T	N/T	N/T	N/T
Now–2002	Now	Now–2002	Now–2005	N/T	N/T	N/T	Now–1998	Now
Now–1998	Now	Now–1999	N/T	Now	N/T	N/T	N/T	N/T
Now–2000	Now–2000	Now–2003	Now–1997	Now	Now	Now	Now–1998	N/T
Now–2000	Now–1996	Now–2000	Now–1998	Now	Now	Now–1997	Now–1996	N/T
Now–2005	Now–2000	Now–2005	Now–2005	Now	Now–2000	Now	Now–2001	N/T
Now–2002	Now–1997	Now–2002	Now–1996	Now	Now	Now	Now–1998	N/T
Now–2000	Now–1997	Now–2002	Now–1996	Now	Now–1996	Now	Now–1996	N/T
Now–2000	Now	Now–1996	Now–1996	Now	N/T	N/T	N/T	N/T
Now–1998	Now	Now	Now	Now	—	—	—	—
Now–1999	Now	—	—	—	—	—	—	—
Now–2000	Now	Now–2005	Now–2000	Now	Now–1998	Now–1998	N/T	N/T
Now–2000	Now	Now–2008	Now–2000	Now	Now–2000	Now–1996	N/T	N/T
Now	Now	Now–2000	Now–1997	Now	Now	Now	N/T	N/T

RED BURGUNDY (continued)	1993	1992	1991	1990	1989	1988
Lejeune Pommard Les Rugiens	N/T	Now	1997–2005	Now–2010	Now–2002	Now–2007
Leroy Chambertin	2005–2025	1998–2010	2001–2030	2000–2040	2000–2030	Now–2015
Leroy Clos de la Roche	2000–2020	1997–2010	2000–2020	1996–2030	Now–2025	—
Leroy Clos Vougeot	1998–2010	Now–2010	1998–2010	2002–2030	Now–2010	Now–2010
Leroy Mazis-Chambertin	N/T	N/T	2000–2015	—	—	—
Leroy Richebourg	2000–2020	1997–2010	Now–2013	2002–2035	Now–2030	Now–2020
Leroy Romanée St.-Vivant	2000–2020	1997–2012	Now–2013	1998–2028	1998–2015	Now–2020
Leroy Vosne-Romanée Les Brûlées	2001–2020	Now–2006	Now–2012	1996–2010	Now–2010	1996–2007
H. Lignier Clos de la Roche	2000–2018	Now–2006	1996–2012	1996–2010	Now–2000	1996–2005
Maume Mazis-Chambertin	N/T	1998–2002	2002–2008	2005–2025	1998–2008	1998–2010
Méo-Camuzet Clos Vougeot	2000–2005	Now–2003	Now–2002	Now–2000	Now–2000	Now–2000
Méo-Camuzet Richebourg	2002–2015	Now–2002	Now–2002	Now–2000	Now–2000	Now–2000
Méo-Camuzet Vosne-Romanée aux Brûlées	1999–2014	Now–2000	Now–2003	Now–2000	Now–1999	Now–1998
Mongeard-Mugneret Clos Vougeot	1999–2005	Now–2000	Now–2010	Now–2004	Now–1999	Now–2000
Mongeard-Mugneret Grands Echézeaux	1997–2007	Now–2002	Now–2005	Now–2004	Now	Now–1998
Mongeard-Mugneret Richebourg	1999–2010	Now–2002	Now–2005	Now–2004	Now	Now–2000
H. de Montille Pommard Les Pézerolles	N/T	1998–2002	N/T	2000–2030	1999–2010	2000–2015
H. de Montille Pommard Les Rugiens	N/T	2000–2005	N/T	2000–2035	1999–2015	2000–2015
H. de Montille Volnay Taillepieds	N/T	2000–2005	N/T	2006–2030	1998–2010	2000–2015
A. Morot Beaune Les Bressandes	2001–2012	Now–2005	N/T	Now–2008	Now–2010	Now–2010
A. Morot Beaune Les Teurons	2002–2015	1998–2010	N/T	1998–2018	1996–2010	Now–2010
Mugneret-Gibourg Clos Vougeot	2000–2005	Now–2000	Now–2007	2000–2010	Now–2000	Now–2010
Mugneret-Gibourg Echézeaux	2000–2005	Now–2000	1996–2006	1996–2008	Now–1996	Now–2000
Mugneret-Gibourg Ruchottes-Chambertin	2000–2005	1998–2004	1996–2004	1996–2008	Now–1999	Now–2005
A. Mussy Pommard Les Epenots	Now–2007	Now	1996–2004	Now–2005	Now	Now–2005
Ponsot Chambertin	2004–2012	Now–2006	Now–2007	1997–2010	Now–2003	Now–2005
Ponsot Clos de la Roche Vieilles Vignes	2001–2020	1998–2008	Now–2013	1996–2012	Now–2002	Now–2005
Ponsot Clos St.-Denis Vieilles Vignes	2000–2015	1998–2006	Now–2010	1997–2010	Now–2002	Now–2005
Pothier-Rieusset Pommard Les Rugiens	N/T	Now–2002	N/T	2000–2010	1998–2010	1998–2009
Pousse d'Or Volnay Clos de la Bousse d'Or	N/T	Now	1996–2003	1997–2007	Now–2000	Now–2005
Domaine de la Romanée-Conti Grands Echézeaux	1999–2005	Now–2003	1998–2010	Now–2008	Now–2005	Now–2007
Domaine de la Romanée-Conti Richebourg	2002–2007	Now–2003	1998–2010	1996–2010	Now–2008	1998–2010
Domaine de la Romanée-Conti Romanée-Conti	2005–2015	1996–2004	1998–2010	Now–2020	1996–2010	1998–2018
Domaine de la Romanée-Conti Romanée St.-Vivant	2004–2009	Now–2003	Now–2005	Now–2010	Now–2008	1996–2010
Domaine de la Romanée-Conti La Tâche	2003–2010	1996–2004	1998–2018	1997–2020	1998–2010	Now–2015
J. Roty Charmes-Chambertin	1998–2008	1996–2004	N/T	1998–2010	Now–2005	1996–2012
J. Roty Mazis-Chambertin	2000–2012	1997–2005	N/T	1998–2015	Now–2006	1996–2012
Georges et Christophe Roumier Bonnes Mares	2000–2010	1997–2005	1998–2010	Now–2008	Now–1999	Now–2010
Georges et Christophe Roumier Clos Vougeot	N/T	1996–2002	Now–2003	1998–2018	Now–2000	1996–2010
Georges et Christophe Roumier Musigny	N/T	1996–2004	1997–2008	Now–2008	Now–2000	Now–2010
Georges et Christophe Roumier Ruchottes-Chambertin	N/T	N/T	Now–2010	Now–2003	Now–2010	Now–2003
A. Rousseau Chambertin	1997–2010	1998–2006	2000–2020	1997–2010	Now–2005	1998–2010
A. Rousseau Chambertin Clos de Bèze	1999–2015	1998–2006	1997–2015	Now–2010	Now–2010	1998–2010
A. Rousseau Gevrey-Chambertin Clos St.-Jacques	1999–2010	Now–2005	2000–2015	Now–2006	Now–2000	1996–2008
C. Serafin Gevrey-Chambertin Les Cazetiers	2001–2005	1998–2008	1997–2005	1996–2010	Now–2010	Now–2002
Tollot-Beaut Corton-Bressandes	2000–2010	Now	N/T	Now–2005	Now–2000	Now
Château de la Tour Clos Vougeot	1997–2004	Now	Now–2003	Now–2002	Now–1999	Now–2000
Comte de Vogüé Bonnes Mares	2001–2008	Now	2000–2015	1997–2010	Now–2003	Now
Comte de Vogüé Musigny Vieilles Vignes	2002–2012	Now	2000–2020	1999–2020	1996–2005	Now

1987	1986	1985	1983	1982	1980	1979	1978	1976
Now–2002	Now	—	—	—	—	—	—	—
N/T	N/T	1998–2010	N/T	N/T	N/T	N/T	Now–2010	Now–2010
—	—	—	—	—	—	—	—	—
N/T	N/T	1998–2007	N/T	N/T	N/T	N/T	Now–2005	Now–2005
N/T	N/T	Now–2008	N/T	N/T	N/T	N/T	N/T	N/T
—	—	—	—	—	—	—	—	—
—	—	—	—	—	—	—	—	—
—	—	—	—	—	—	—	—	—
Now–1997	Now–1996	1996–2005	Now–1998	Now	Now	Now	Now–1998	N/T
Now–2002	Now–2002	Now–2010	Now–2010	Now	Now	Now	N/T	N/T
Now	Now	N/T	N/T	N/T	N/T	N/T	N/T	N/T
Now–2001	Now	Now	N/T	N/T	N/T	N/T	N/T	N/T
Now–1997	Now	Now	N/T	N/T	N/T	N/T	N/T	N/T
Now	Now	Now–2001	Now–2005	Now	Now	Now	Now	Now
Now	Now	Now–2003	Now–2005	Now	Now	Now	Now	Now
Now–1998	Now	Now–1998	N/T	N/T	N/T	N/T	N/T	N/T
—	—	—	—	—	1996–2010	—	1999–2015	—
Now–2008	Now–1997	Now–2009	Now–2005	Now–2000	Now–2010	N/T	Now–2010	N/T
—	—	—	—	—	—	—	—	—
Now–2001	Now	Now–2003	Now	Now	Now	Now	Now	Now
Now–2003	Now	Now–2003	Now	Now	Now	Now–1997	Now	Now
Now	Now	1996–2010	1996–2001	Now	Now–1996	Now	Now–2000	N/T
Now	Now	Now–2005	Now–2006	Now	Now–1996	Now	Now–2000	N/T
Now	Now	Now–2008	1996–2003	Now	Now–1998	Now	Now–2010	N/T
Now–1998	Now	Now–2000	Now	Now	Now	Now	Now	N/T
Now	Now	Now–2005	Now–2008	Now	N/T	N/T	N/T	N/T
Now	Now	Now–2005	Now–2007	Now	Now–2010	Now–1999	Now–2003	Now–2001
Now–1997	Now	Now–2005	Now–2007	Now	Now–2005	Now–1999	Now–2000	Now–2000
Now	Now	Now–2003	Now	Now	Now	Now–2000	Now–2003	Now–2000
Now–1996	Now	Now–2001	Now–1998	Now	Now	Now	Now	Now–2005
Now	Now	Now–2008	Now–2000	Now	Now	Now	Now–2000	Now
Now	Now	Now–2008	Now–2000	Now	Now	Now	Now	Now
1997–2008	Now	1998–2010	Now–2004	Now	Now	Now	Now–2000	Now
Now	Now	Now–2004	Now	Now	Now	Now	Now	Now
Now–2002	Now	Now–2012	Now–2010	Now	Now	Now	Now	Now
Now–2000	Now	1998–2010	Now	Now	Now–2000	Now	Now–1998	N/T
Now–2003	Now–1997	1997–2012	Now	Now	Now–2001	Now	Now–1998	N/T
Now	Now	Now	Now–2005	Now	Now	Now	Now	Now
Now	Now	Now	Now–2008	Now	Now	N/T	Now–2000	N/T
Now	Now	Now	Now–2003	Now	Now	Now	Now	Now
Now–2004	Now–2003	Now–2005	Now	Now	N/T	Now–2000	N/T	
Now–2003	Now–1998	Now–2005	1996–2008	Now	Now	Now	—	Now
Now–2002	Now–1998	Now–2006	1996–2010	Now	Now	Now	—	Now
Now	Now	Now–2000	Now–2006	Now	Now	Now	—	Now
Now	Now	N/T	N/T	N/T	N/T	N/T	N/T	N/T
Now	Now	Now	Now	Now	Now	Now	Now	Now
Now–1998	Now	Now	N/T	N/T	N/T	Now	Now	Now
Now–2000	Now	Now	Now	Now	Now	Now	Now	Now
Now	Now	Now	Now	Now	Now	Now	Now	Now

RHÔNE VALLEY	1993	1992	1991
Beaucastel Châteauneuf du Pape	Now–2008	Now–1999	Now–1999
Beaucastel Cuvée Jacques Perrin	N/M	N/M	N/M
H. Bonneau Châteauneuf du Pape Cuvée des Celestins	?	Now–2004	N/M
Les Bosquet des Papes Châteauneuf du Pape	Now–2002	Now	Now
Bosquet des Papes-Chantemerle	1999–2010	N/M	N/M
Lucien et André Brunel-Les Cailloux Châteauneuf du Pape	Now–2005	Now–2005	Now–2000
Lucien et André Brunel-Les Cailloux Centenaire	N/M	N/M	N/M
Chapoutier Châteauneuf du Pape Barbe Rac	1997–2009	Now–2000	1997–2008
Chapoutier Hermitage Chante-Alouette (white)	Now–2008	Now–2010	Now–2000
Chapoutier Hermitage Le Pavillon	2000–2020	1998–2015	2000–2030
Chapoutier Hermitage Le Sizeranne	1998–2015	1997–2010	Now–2010
J. L. Chave Hermitage	Now–2005	Now–2007	Now–2001
J. L. Chave Hermitage Blanc	Now–2005	Now–2010	Now–2002
J. L. Chave Red Label Cathelin	N/M	N/M	1998–2030
A. Clape Cornas	Now–2004	1996–2003	Now–2010
Les Clefs d'Or Châteauneuf du Pape	Now–2000	Now–2000	Now
Clos du Mont-Olivet Châteauneuf du Pape	Now–2005	Now–2005	Now
Clos du Mont Olivet Cuvée du Papet	N/M	N/M	N/M
Clos des Papes Châteauneuf du Pape	1997–2006	Now–2002	Now
Coudoulet Côtes du Rhône	Now–2001	Now	Now
Fonsalette Côtes du Rhône	Now–2002	Now–2000	Now
Fonsalette Côtes du Rhône Syrah	N/T	N/T	2003–2015
Guigal Côte Rôtie (regular cuvée)	N/T	N/T	Now–2002
Guigal Côte Rôtie La Landonne	1997–2005	1996–2008	2000–2025
Guigal Côte Rôtie La Mouline	1997–2005	1996–2006	Now–2020
Guigal Côte Rôtie La Turque	1997–2005	1996–2006	Now–2010
Guigal Hermitage	N/T	N/T	1997–2010
Paul Jaboulet Crozes-Hermitage Thalabert	N/T	N/T	Now–2004
Paul Jaboulet Hermitage La Chapelle	N/T	N/T	1998–2006
Jamet Côte Rôtie	N/T	N/T	1997–2010
Marcoux Vieilles Vignes	1998–2010	Now–2005	N/M
Montmirail Gigondas (Brusset)	Now–2005	Now–2004	Now
Pegau Châteauneuf du Pape	Now–2008	Now–2010	Now
Rayas Châteauneuf du Pape	Now–2004	Now–2004	N/M
René Rostaing Côte Rôtie Côte Blonde	Now–2006	Now–2003	Now–2009
René Rostaing Côte La Landonne	1996–2010	N/M	Now–2012
Saint-Gayan Gigondas	Now–2000	Now–1998	Now
Santa Duc Gigondas Cuvée Prestige	1996–2010	N/M	N/M
Henri Sorrel Hermitage Le Gréal	N/M	Now–2007	2000–2020
Henri Sorrel Hermitage Les Rocoules (white)	Now–2002	Now–2000	Now–2010
de Vallouit Côte Rôtie Les Roziers	N/T	N/T	N/T
de Vallouit Hermitage Greffières	N/T	N/T	N/T
N. Verset Cornas	Now	Now	Now–2004
Vieux Donjon Châteauneuf du Pape	N/T	Now–2002	Now
Vieux Télégraphe Châteauneuf du Pape	Now–2002	Now–1999	Now
Voge Cornas Cuvée Vieilles Vignes	Now–2002	Now–2000	Now–2007

1990	1989	1988	1985	1983	1982	1978
1996–2020	Now–2028	Now–2005	Now–2005	Now–2000	Now	1998–2020
2002–2040	2005–2040	N/M	N/M	N/M	N/M	N/M
1996–2020	1998–2020	Now–2010	Now–2008	Now–2005	N/T	Now–2015
1996–2010	Now–2005	Now–2000	Now–2000	Now	Now	Now–1997
1998–2015	N/M	N/M	N/M	N/M	N/M	N/M
Now–2005	1996–2010	Now–2002	Now–2000	Now–1996	Now	Now–2000
Now–2008	Now–2008	N/M	N/M	N/M	N/M	N/M
Now–2025	Now–2017	N/M	N/M	N/M	N/M	N/M
Now–2010	Now–2010	Now–2005	Now–2000	Now–2005	Now	Now–2000
2000–2040	2000–2030	N/M	N/M	N/M	N/M	N/M
1998–2025	1997–2015	Now–2005	Now–1998	Now–1997	Now	Now
2005–2040 +	1998–2030	1996–2015	1996–2010	2000–2025	Now–2005	Now–2030
Now–2010	Now–2002	Now–2010	Now–2005	Now–2008	Now–2000	Now–2005
2005–2040	N/M	N/M	N/M	N/M	N/M	N/M
1997–2012	1996–2010	Now–2002	Now–2005	1996–2008	Now–1997	Now–2008
Now–2010	1996–2013	Now–2005	Now–2000	Now	Now	Now–2003
Now–2010	1996–2015	Now–2005	Now–2008	Now	Now	Now–2008
1998–2015	1997–2012	N/M	N/M	N/M	N/M	N/M
1997–2017	1998–2010	Now–2004	Now–1999	Now–1998	Now	Now–2002
Now–2000	Now–2004	Now–2000	Now	Now	Now	Now–1998
Now–2007	Now–2007	Now–2000	Now–2000	Now	Now–2000	Now–2005
2002–2025	2002–2027	1998–2015	1998–2015	2000–2015	N/T	1998–2015
Now–2003	Now–2005	Now–2012	Now–2006	1996–2006	Now–1997	Now–2000
2000–2020	1996–2025	2000–2040	1998–2025	1998–2035	Now–2008	Now–2023
Now–2015	Now–2010	Now–2020	1996–2015	1998–2015	Now–2005	Now–2020
Now–2008	Now–2007	Now–2025	Now–2010	N/M	N/M	N/M
Now–2010	Now–2007	1996–2025	Now–2005	Now–2010	Now–2005	Now–2003
Now–2007	Now–2007	Now–2000	Now–2000	Now–2005	Now	Now–2000
2005–2040 +	2000–2035	2004–2020	1996–2008	2000–2030	Now–2008	1998–2020
1996–2007	1996–2014	1998–2016	Now–2010	Now–2005	Now	N/T
1999–2025	1998–2025	N/M	N/M	N/M	N/M	N/M
Now–2012	Now–2006	Now–2002	Now	Now	N/T	N/T
Now–2018	Now–2007	Now–2006	Now–2005	Now–2000	N/T	Now–1999
Now–2012	1997–2010	Now–2005	Now–2005	Now	N/M	Now–2003
Now–2002	Now–2002	Now–2002	Now–2003	1996–2008	—	—
Now–2004	Now–2004	Now–2005	1996–2005	1998–2009	—	—
Now–2006	Now–2006	Now–2003	Now–1999	N/T	N/T	N/T
Now–2008	Now–2006	N/T	—	—	—	—
2005–2040	2000–2035	1998–2005	1996–2008	1998–2008	—	1998–2030
1998–2020	Now–2010 +	Now–2010 +	Now–2001	Now–2000	—	Now–2009
Now–2004	Now–2000	1996–2010	Now–2004	—	—	—
2000–2020	Now–2012	2000–2025	1996–2005	Now–2008	—	—
Now–2008	Now–2000	1998–2008	Now–2010	1998–2008	Now	Now–2005
Now–2012	Now–2008	Now–1998	Now–2000	Now–1999	Now	Now–2006
Now–2005	Now–2005	Now–2000	Now–2000	Now	Now	Now–2005
Now–2008	Now–2007	N/T	N/T	N/T	N/T	N/T

CALIFORNIA CABERNET SAUVIGNON	1993	1992	1991	1990	1989	1988	1987	1986
Araujo Estate-Eisele Vyd.	2005–2025	1999–2020	2000–2025	N/M	N/M	N/M	N/M	N/M
Beaulieu Private Reserve	N/T	N/T	N/T	Now–2001	Now–2002	Now–2002	Now–2005	1996–2010
Beringer Chabot Vyd.	N/T	1997–2015	1998–2015	1996–2012	N/T	N/T	Now–2010	Now–2009
Beringer Merlot Bancroft Vyd.	1996–2016	1996–2012	Now–2005	—	—	N/T	N/T	N/T
Beringer Private Reserve	2000–2020	1996–2012	Now–2009	Now	Now–2003	Now–1999	Now–2007	Now–2003
Buehler	N/T	Now–2006	Now–2005	1996–2005	Now–2005	Now–1998	Now–2004	Now
Burgess Vintage Selection	N/T	N/T	N/T	Now–2000	Now–2000	Now–1999	Now–2004	Now–2000
Carmenet Reserve	N/T	N/T	1997–2010	1996–2008	N/T	Now–2002	Now–2006	Now–2005
Caymus	N/T	Now–2005	Now–2005	Now–2007	Now–2000	Now–1998	Now–2002	Now–2002
Caymus Special Selection	N/T	N/T	1996–2009	Now–2010	Now–2000	Now–2001	Now–2003	Now–2005
Conn Valley	1998–2015	1997–2010	Now–2012	Now–2010	Now–2004	Now–2000	Now–2004	N/M
Dalla Valle	2000–2015	Now–2012	1997–2012	1997–2010	1998–2008	N/T	N/M	N/M
Dalla Valle Maya	2006–2036	1998–2030	1998–2015	1997–2010	Now–2008	Now–2000	N/M	N/M
Diamond Creek (all 3 Vyds.)	2002–2015	1996–2005	1996–2006	Now–2006	Now–2004	Now–2005	Now–2000	Now
Dominus	N/M	1996–2015	Now–2018	1996–2010	Now–2010	Now–2008	1998–2010	Now–2008
Duckhorn Merlot	N/T	N/T	Now–2002	Now–2003	Now–1997	Now	Now	Now–1998
Dunn Howell Mountain	2007–2050	2002–2025	2000–2008	1998–2012	1996–2008	1996–2005	2000–2015	1996–2010
Dunn Napa	2000–2020	2000–2020	2000–2008	1998–2012	1996–2008	1996–2005	1998–2010	1996–2008
Fisher Coach Insignia	1996–2012	Now–2008	1997–2014	1997–2012	Now–2002	Now–2002	Now–2007	Now–2008
Forman	N/T	Now–2008	1996–2008	1996–2010	Now–2002	Now–2000	Now–2002	Now–2000
Grgich Hills	N/T	N/T	N/T	1996–2006	Now–2004	Now–2004	Now–2008	Now–2007
Groth Reserve	N/T	N/T	Now–2004	Now–2002	Now	Now–2000	Now–2001	Now–2010
Heitz Bella Oaks	N/T	N/T	N/T	Now–2008	Now–2005	1996–2005	Now–2008	1996–2005
Heitz Martha's Vineyard	N/T	N/T	N/T	1996–2010	Now–2008	Now–2003	1997–2010	1997–2010
Jordan	N/T	N/T	Now–2006	Now–2005	Now–2000	Now–1999	Now–2002	Now–2000
La Jota Anniversary	2002–2030	1997–2015	1997–2015	1998–2010	Now–2006	Now–2005	1996–2007	Now–2008
La Jota Cabernet Franc	1996–2010	Now–2007	Now–2010	N/T	N/T	N/T	Now–2005	N/M
Laurel Glen	2002–2025	1996–2015	1998–2010	1996–2010	Now–2002	Now–2002	Now–2003	Now–2000
Matanzas Creek Merlot	1996–2010	Now–2010	Now–2005	Now–2002	Now	Now	Now	Now
Peter Michael Les Pavots	2000–2025	1997–2010	1996–2015	Now–2009	N/M	N/M	N/M	N/M
Robert Mondavi Reserve	1996–2016	Now–2010	Now–2015	Now–2012	Now–1998	Now–2003	1998–2015	Now–2003
Château Montelena	N/T	1996–2012	2000–2020	1998–2015	Now–2008	1996–2008	1999–2025	Now–2010
Monticello Corley Reserve	N/T	2000–2014	1998–2009	1997–2010	Now–2004	Now	Now–2005	Now–2005
Mt. Eden	N/T	2002–2030	2000–2015	1998–2015	1996–2005	1997–2005	1997–2007	1996–2005
Newton Merlot	N/T	Now–2006	Now–2005	Now–2005	Now–1997	Now–1998	Now–1997	Now
Opus One	N/T	N/T	Now–2010	Now–2008	Now–2001	Now–2001	Now–2001	Now–2009
Joseph Phelps Eisele Vyd.	N/T	N/M	1997–2008	1996–2008	1997–2007	Now–2002	1996–2006	Now–2005
Joseph Phelps Insignia	N/T	1998–2012	Now–2008	Now–2007	Now–2003	Now–2000	Now–2003	Now–2005
Ridge Monte Bello	2008–2035	2000–2030	2000–2025	1999–2015	1996–2004	Now–2005	1997–2020	Now–2005
Shafer Hillside	1997–2017	1996–2008	Now–2008	Now–2008	Now–2005	Now–1999	Now–2001	Now–1999
Silver Oak (Alex. Valley & Napa)	1998–2013	Now–2008	Now–2008	Now–2006	Now–2005	Now–1999	Now–2002	Now–2005
Simi Reserve	1996–2010	N/T	Now–2010	Now–2012	Now–2006	Now–2003	2000–2015	Now–2005
Spottswoode	2000–2015	Now–2006	Now–2005	Now–2005	Now–2000	Now–2002	Now–2003	Now–2003
Stag's Leap Cask 23	1997–2010	1996–2008	1997–2010	Now–2007	N/M	N/M	Now–2008	Now–2000
Philip Togni	Now–2015	1996–2012	2000–2015	1996–2018	Now–2003	Now–2010	Now–2005	Now–2008
Tudal	N/T	N/T	1996–2008	1998–2008	N/T	Now–2003	Now–2005	Now–2002
Viader	1998–2012	1997–2007	1996–2006	N/T	N/T	N/M	N/M	N/M

1985	1984	1983	1982	1981	1980	1979	1978	1977	1976
N/M	N/M	N/M	N/M	N/M	N/M	N/M	N/M	N/M	N/M
1996–2010	Now–2000	Now–2000	Now–2005	Now–1998	Now–2005	Now–2005	Now	Now	1996–2020
Now–2009	Now–2009	N/T	N/T	N/T	N/T	N/T	N/T	N/T	N/T
N/T	N/T	N/T	N/T	N/T	N/T	N/T	N/T	N/T	N/T
Now–2005	Now–2000	Now–1996	Now–2000	Now	Now	Now	Now	Now	N/T
Now	Now–1997	Now–1996	Now–1996	Now	Now–1997	Now–1996	Now–2002	Now	N/T
Now–2003	Now–2000	Now	Now	Now	Now	Now	Now–2000	Now	Now–2000
Now–2005	Now–2003	Now–2000	Now–1998	N/T	N/T	N/T	N/T	N/T	N/T
Now–2005	Now–1998	Now	Now	Now	Now–1998	Now–1998	Now–1996	Now	Now–2002
Now–2010	Now–2010	Now	Now–2000	Now–1997	Now–2005	Now–2000	Now–2010	Now	Now–2010
N/M	N/M	N/M	N/M	N/M	N/M	N/M	N/M	N/M	N/M
N/M	N/M	N/M	N/M	N/M	N/M	N/M	N/M	N/M	N/M
N/M	N/M	N/M	N/M	N/M	N/M	N/M	N/M	N/M	N/M
Now	Now–2008	Now–1996	Now–2002	Now–1998	Now–2001	Now–2008	Now–2010	Now–2000	1998–2015
1996–2015	Now–2005	1998–2010	N/M	N/M	N/M	N/M	N/M	N/M	N/M
Now–2005	Now–2000	Now	Now	Now	Now	Now	Now	—	—
2005–2025	1996–2010	Now–2010	Now–2020	Now–2009	Now–2005	Now–2005	N/M	N/M	N/M
1999–2010	Now–2000	Now–2001	Now–2015	N/T	N/T	N/T	N/M	N/M	N/M
N/T	N/T	N/T	N/T	N/T	N/T	N/T	N/T	N/T	N/T
Now–2000	Now–2000	Now–2000	N/M	N/M	N/M	N/M	N/M	N/M	N/M
Now–2003	Now–2000	Now–1997	Now–2000	N/T	N/T	N/T	N/T	N/T	N/T
Now–2010	Now–1996	Now	N/M	N/M	N/M	N/M	N/M	N/M	N/M
Now–2005	Now–2002	Now–1998	Now–1997	Now	Now	N/T	N/T	N/T	N/T
1998–2012	Now–2010	Now–2005	Now–2003	Now–1997	Now–2004	Now–2003	Now	Now	1998–2015
Now–2002	Now–2000	Now	Now	Now	Now	Now	Now	Now	Now
Now–2010	Now–2005	Now–2000	Now–1997	N/M	N/M	N/M	N/M	N/M	N/M
N/M	N/M	N/M	N/M	N/M	N/M	N/M	N/M	N/M	N/M
Now–2002	Now–1998	Now	Now	Now–1998	N/T	N/T	N/T	N/T	N/T
Now	Now	N/T	N/T	N/T	N/T	N/T	N/T	N/T	N/T
N/M	N/M	N/M	N/M	N/M	N/M	N/M	N/M	N/M	N/M
Now	Now–1996	1996–2005	Now–2010	Now–2005	Now–2010	Now–2000	Now–2000	Now–2000	Now–2005
1998–2017	Now–2010	Now	Now	Now	Now	Now–1996	Now–2002	Now	Now
Now–2004	Now–2005	Now–2000	Now–2005	Now–2004	Now–2005	Now–2000	Now–2010	Now–2000	Now–2001
1998–2010	Now–2000	Now	Now	N/T	N/T	N/T	N/T	N/T	N/T
Now	Now	N/T	N/T	Now–1996	Now	Now–1998	Now–1998	N/T	Now
Now–2000	Now–2000	Now–2000	Now	Now–1998	Now	Now	Now	—	—
Now–2010	Now–2002	1996–2003	Now–1996	Now	Now–2005	Now–2001	Now–2000	Now–1998	1996–2010
Now–2008	Now–2005	Now–1999	Now–1997	Now–2002	—	Now–1998	Now–2008	Now–1996	—
1998–2020	Now–2020	Now–2006	Now	Now–2010	Now–2009	N/M	Now–2008	Now–2015	Now–2000
Now–2000	Now	Now	N/M	N/M	N/M	N/M	N/M	N/M	N/M
Now–2003	Now–2000	Now–1996	Now–1998	Now	Now	Now	N/T	N/T	N/T
Now–2005	Now–2002	N/T	Now–2000	N/T	N/T	N/T	N/T	N/T	N/T
1998–2010	Now–2002	Now–1998	Now–1999	N/M	N/M	N/M	N/M	N/M	N/M
1997–2010	Now–2000	Now–1996	N/M	N/M	M/M	Now	Now–2002	Now–2000	N/M
1996–2008	Now–2005	1996–2009	N/M	N/M	N/M	N/M	N/M	N/M	N/M
Now–2003	Now–2000	Now	Now–1996	N/T	N/T	N/M	N/M	N/M	N/M
N/M	N/M	N/M	N/M	N/M	N/M	N/M	N/M	N/M	N/M

INDEX

ROBERT PARKER gave up a career in law to devote himself full time to evaluating and writing about wine. In 1978, he founded *The Wine Advocate*. He lives with his wife, Pat, daughter, Maia, and various basset hounds in the countryside of northern Maryland.

MUCH OF THE MATERIAL in this book is based upon tastings and research done in conjunction with the publishing of *The Wine Advocate*, an independent consumer's guide to fine wines, which is issued six times a year. A one-year subscription to *The Wine Advocate* costs $40.00 for delivery in the continental United States, $50.00 for Canada, and $70.00 for air-mail delivery anywhere in the world. Subscriptions or a sample copy may be obtained by writing to *The Wine Advocate*, P.O. Box 311, Monkton, MD 21111, or by sending a fax to 410-357-4504.